BUSINESS STATISTICS OF THE UNITED STATES

BUSINESS STATISTICS OF THE UNITED STATES

Patterns of Economic Change

22nd Edition

2017

Edited by Susan Ockert

Lanham, MD

Published in the United States of America
by Bernan Press, a wholly owned subsidiary of
The Rowman & Littlefield Publishing Group, Inc.
4501 Forbes Boulevard, Suite 200
Lanham, Maryland 20706

Bernan Press
800-462-6420
www.rowman.com

ISBN-13:   978-1-59888-948-2
eISBN-13: 978-1-59888-949-9

ISSN: 1086-8488

∞™ The paper used in this publication meets the minimum requirements of
American National Standard for Information Sciences—Permanence of
Paper for Printed Library Materials, ANSI/NISO Z39.48-1992.

Manufactured in the United States of America.

CONTENTS

PREFACE

Business Statistics of the United States: Patterns of Economic Change, 22nd Edition, 2017 is a basic desk reference for anyone requiring statistics on the U.S. economy. It contains more than 3,000 economic time series portraying the period from World War II to December 2016 in industry, product, and demographic detail. In the case of about 200 key series, the period from 1929 through 1948 is depicted as well.

Additionally, for three important statistical series that have been compiled monthly on a continuous basis, monthly and annual data are included going back to 1919 for industrial production and 1913 for consumer and producer prices. Annual data for money and credit have also been taken back before 1929, including money supply figures back to 1892 and some interest rates back to 1919.

The National Income and Product Accounts (NIPAs) were comprehensively revised in July 2013, changing some measurement concepts, changing base periods for price indexes and real output, and as a result altering all the data back to 1929. *Business Statistics* incorporates fully revised data for over 700 series from this data set and productivity and costs series that are based on the revised NIPAs, all extended and updated through 2016. The important new concepts introduced in the NIPA revision are explained in the Notes and Definitions to Chapters 1, 4, 5, and 6. In all, this edition provides, in one volume, unparalleled, up-to-date background information on the course of the U.S. economy.

The data are predominantly from federal government sources. Of equal importance are the extensive background notes for each chapter, which help users to understand the data, use them appropriately, and, if desired, seek additional information from the source agencies.

Chapters are organized according to subject matter. For most time series, users will find an initial page displaying the latest two years of monthly data, or three years of quarterly data, for the most recent completed years, along with annual averages for the last completed 40, 50, or even 60 years.

For the most important series for which we have long-term historical data, this initial page will be labeled with "A" after the table number, and identified in the title by the additional words "Recent Data." It will be immediately followed by pages labeled with "B" after the table number and identified by the words "Historical Data," which will show all available historical data annually back as far as possible, and monthly or quarterly back to the earliest available postwar year. In some cases, additional tables of historical data will be included.

The monthly index of industrial production is shown back to 1919, and monthly indexes of consumer and producer prices back to 1913. In both cases, these are the earliest dates for which the originating agencies (respectively, the Federal Reserve Board and the Bureau of Labor Statistics [BLS] have compiled a continuous series).

The leading article "Cycle and Growth Perspectives" provides other information and techniques to assist in using and interpreting the data. A new section has been added, titled "The Great Recession," which provides data from 2007–2009 and the recovery from 2010–2016.

THE PLAN OF THE BOOK

The history of the U.S. economy is told in major U.S. government sets of statistical data: the national income and product accounts compiled by the Bureau of Economic Analysis (BEA); the data on labor force, employment, hours, earnings, and productivity compiled by the Bureau of Labor Statistics (BLS); the price indexes collected by BLS; and the financial market and industrial production data compiled primarily by the Board of Governors of the Federal Reserve System (FRB). All of these sets exist in annual and either monthly or quarterly form beginning in 1946, 1947, or 1948; many are available, at least annually, as far back as 1929, and a few even farther back; and three are available monthly back to the teens of the 20th century.

In Part A, *Business Statistics* presents the aggregate United States economy in a number of important dimensions. The presentations begin with the national income and product accounts, or NIPAs. The NIPAs comprise a comprehensive, thorough, and internally consistent body of data. They measure the value of the total output of the U.S. economy (the gross domestic product, or GDP) and they allocate that value between its quantity, or "real," and price components. They show how the value of aggregate demand is generated by consumers, business investors, government, and foreign customers; how much of aggregate demand is supplied by imports and how much by domestic production; and how the income generated in domestic production is distributed between labor and capital.

Production estimates covering only the sectors of the economy traditionally labeled "industrial"—manufacturing, mining, and utilities—are shown in Chapter 2, after the presentation of the overall NIPAs in Chapter 1.

Median income—the best measure of the economic well-being of the typical American—income distribution, and poverty statistics from a Census household survey are presented in Chapter 3.

Then, more detail from the NIPAs is presented for the demand components of economic activity. GDP, by its product-side definition, consists of the sum of consumption expenditures, business investment in fixed capital and inventories, government purchases of goods and services, and exports minus imports—as in the elementary economics blackboard identity "GDP = C + I + G + X – M)." Chapters on each of these components—consumption, investment, government, and foreign trade—are presented in Part A.

Following these chapters, there are a chapter on prices, two chapters on the compensation of labor and capital inputs and the amount and productivity of labor input, one chapter on energy inputs into production and consumption, and one chapter on money, interest, assets, and debt.

At the end of Part A, comparisons of output, prices, and labor markets among major industrial countries are presented, along with statistics on the value of the dollar against other currencies.

While GDP is initially defined and measured by adding up its demand categories and subtracting imports, this output is produced in industries—some in the old-line heavy industries such as manufacturing, mining, and utilities, but an increasing share in the huge and heterogeneous group known as "service-providing" industries. Part A gives a number of measures of activity classified by industry or industrial sector: industrial production, profits, and employment-related data. Further industry information is provided in Part B, including new quarterly indicators of GDP by industry.

Industry data collection is important because demands for goods and services are channeled into demands for labor and capital through the industries responsible for producing the requested goods and services. These data are reported using the North American Industry Classification System (NAICS). This system, introduced in 1997 to replace the older Standard Industrial Classification System (SIC), delineates industries that are better defined in relation to today's demands and more closely related to each other by technology. Notable examples include more detailed data available on service industries, a more rational grouping of the computer and electronic product manufacturing subsector, and the creation of the Information sector. See the References at the end of this Preface.

NAICS industries are groupings of producing units—not of products as such—and are grouped according to similarity of production processes. This is done in order to collect consistent data on inputs and outputs, which are then used to measure important concepts, such as productivity and input-output parameters. Emphasis on the production process helps to explain a number of ways in which the NAICS differs from the SIC.

- Manufacturing activities at retail locations, such as bakeries, have been classified separately from retail activity and put into the Food manufacturing industry.

- Central administrative offices of companies have a new sector of their own, Management of companies and enterprises (sector 55). For example, the headquarters office of a food-producing corporation is considered part of the new sector instead of part of the food manufacturing industry.

- Reproduction of packaged software, which was classified as a business service in the SIC, is now classified in sector 334, Computer and electronic product manufacturing, as a manufacturing process.

- Electronic markets and agents and brokers, formerly undifferentiated components of wholesale trade industries, have a sector of their own (425).

- Retail trade in NAICS (sectors 44 and 45) now includes establishments such as office supply stores, computer and software stores, building materials dealers, plumbing supply stores, and electrical supply stores, that display merchandise and use mass-media advertising to sell to individuals as well as to businesses, which were formerly classified in wholesale trade.

In Part B, *Business Statistics* shows GDP, income, employment, hours, and earnings by industry, followed by statistics for key sectors such as petroleum, housing, manufacturing, retail trade, and services.

Notes and definitions. Productive use of economic data requires accurate knowledge about the sources and meaning of the data. The notes and definitions for each chapter, shown immediately after that chapter's tables, contain definitions, descriptions of recent data revisions, and references to sources of additional technical information. They also include information about data availability and revision and release schedules, which helps users to readily access the latest current values if they need to keep up with the data month by month or quarter by quarter.

A NOTE ON THE IMPORTANCE OF ECONOMIC STATISTICS

To retrieve money and credit data for earlier years, the editor of *Business Statistics* had to consult old printed volumes, where she encountered some inspiring prefatory words in the Federal Reserve Board volume *Banking and Monetary Statistics* (1943). These words were written by the Fed's longtime statistics chief, E. A. Goldenweiser, in the stately cadences of an earlier era, about the financial statistics collected in that volume. But they well express the hope and expectation of statisticians and economists that their work can lead to better economic decisions:

These serried ranks of organized statistics on banking and finance, even though they may inspire awe, should also inspire confidence. They are an augury that credit policy can be based in the future, as in the past, on fact rather than on fancy.

THE HISTORY OF *BUSINESS STATISTICS*

The history of *Business Statistics* began with the publication, many years ago, of the first edition of a volume with the same name by the U.S. Department of Commerce's Bureau of Economic Analysis (BEA). After 27 periodic editions, the last of which appeared in 1992, BEA found it necessary, for budgetary and other reasons, to discontinue both the publication and the maintenance of the database from which the publication was derived.

The individual statistical series gathered together here are all publicly available. However, the task of gathering them from the numerous different sources within the government and assembling them into one coherent database is impractical for most data users. Even when current data are readily available, obtaining the full historical time series is often time-consuming and difficult. Definitions and other documentation can also be inconvenient to find. Believing that a *Business Statistics* compilation was too valuable to be lost to the public, Bernan Press published the first edition of the present publication, edited by Dr. Courtenay M. Slater, in 1995. The first edition received a warm welcome from users of economic data. Dr. Slater, formerly chief economist of the Department of Commerce, continued to develop *Business Statistics* through four subsequent annual editions. The previous editor worked with Dr. Slater on the fourth and fifth editions. In subsequent editions, she has continued in the tradition established by Dr. Slater of ensuring high-quality data, while revising and expanding the book's scope to include significant new aspects of the U.S. economy and longer historical background.

Nearly all of the statistical data in this book are from federal government sources and all are available in the public domain. Sources are given in the applicable notes and definitions.

The data in this volume meet the publication standards of the federal statistical agencies from which they were obtained. Every effort has been made to select data that are accurate, meaningful, and useful. All statistical data are subject to error arising from sampling variability, reporting errors, incomplete coverage, imputation, and other causes. The responsibility of the editor and publisher of this volume is limited to reasonable care in the reproduction and presentation of data obtained from established sources.

The 2017 edition has been edited by Susan Ockert.

Susan Ockert has worked as an economist in the military, for the federal government, and at regional and state levels. She earned her Masters of Economics at George Mason University in Fairfax, Virginia as well as her Masters of International Management at the Thunderbird University in Glendale, Arizona. She also taught macro- and micro economics in three states, several community colleges, and at the collegiate level.

REFERENCES

The NAICS is explained and laid out in *North American Industry Classification System: United States, 2017*, from the Executive Office of the President, Office of Management and Budget. Changes introduced in these updatings have been relatively minor and have not affected the definitions of the industry divisions presented in *Business Statistics*.

Information on differences between NAICS and SIC can be found in *North American Industry Classification System: United States, 1997*, from the Executive Office of the President, Office of Management and Budget (which contains matches between the 1997 NAICS and the 1987 SIC), and *North American Industry Classification System: United States, 2002* (which contains matches that show the relatively few changes from the 1997 NAICS to the 2002 NAICS).

All three of these volumes are available from Bernan Press. These volumes fully describe the development and application of the new classification system and are the sources for the material presented in this volume. Information is also available on the NAICS Web site at <http://www.census.gov/naics>. Additional background information can also be found in Bernan Press's *Business Statistics of the United States: 2002* (8th edition), pp. xxiv–xxviii.

CYCLE AND GROWTH PERSPECTIVES

This 22nd edition of *Business Statistics of the United States* presents comprehensive and detailed data on U.S. economic performance through December 2016, going back to the end of World War II. These numbers show changes in many dimensions—prices and quantities, to take the two most obvious. There are patterns of fluctuation and, simultaneously, patterns of enduring change. This article will present some ways of looking at these movements and trying to make sense of them.

We begin with a general discussion of business cycles in the United States economy, including a chronology of the cycles occurring in the years covered by this volume.

- Following this is an example of the use of monthly and quarterly data, such as those provided in this book, to track recession and recovery.

- Then, other examples are provided of important analytical techniques for extracting key information from statistical series, particularly for focusing on growth issues.

- The last section of this article concerns measuring the economic well-being of the typical American.

BUSINESS CYCLES IN THE U.S. ECONOMY: RECESSIONS AND EXPANSIONS

The study of economic fluctuations in the United States was pioneered by Wesley C. Mitchell and Arthur F. Burns early in the twentieth century, and was carried on subsequently by other researchers affiliated with the National Bureau of Economic Research (NBER), an independent, nonpartisan research organization. These analysts observed that indicators of the general state of business activity tended to move up and down over periods that were longer than a year and were therefore not accounted for by seasonal variation. Although these periods of expansion and contraction were not uniform in length, and thus not "cycles" in any strict mathematical sense, their recurrent nature and certain generic similarities caused them to be called "business cycles." NBER has identified 32 complete peak-to-peak business cycles over the period beginning with December 1854.

The first NBER-established business cycle dates, identifying the months in which peaks and troughs in general economic activity occurred, were published in 1929. The dates of current cycles are established, typically within a year or so of their occurrence, by the NBER Business Cycle Dating Committee. This group, first formed in 1978, consists of eight economists who are university professors, associated with research organizations, or both.

Business cycle dates are based on monthly data, and have been identified for periods long before the availability of quarterly data on real gross national product (GDP). It is important to understand that even in the period since 1947 for which quarterly real GDP exists, the NBER identification of a recession does not always coincide with the frequently cited definition, "two consecutive quarters of decline in real GDP."

The NBER monthly and quarterly dates of the cycles from 1891 to the latest announced turning point—the June 2009 trough ending the recession that began in December 2007—are shown in Table A-1 below. The quarterly turning points are identified by Roman numerals. NBER considers that the trough month is both the end of the decline and the beginning of the expansion, based on the concept that the actual turning point was some particular day within that month. Thus, the latest recession ended in June 2009, and the current expansion also began in June 2009.

May 1891 (II)	January 1893 (I)
June 1894 (II)	December 1895 (IV)
June 1897 (II)	June 1899 (III)
December 1900 (IV)	September 1902 (IV)
August 1904 (III)	May 1907 (II)
June 1908 (II)	January 1910 (I)
January 1912 (IV)	January 1913 (I)
December 1914 (IV)	August 1918 (III)
March 1919 (I)	January 1920 (I)
July 1921 (III)	May 1923 (II)
July 1924 (III)	October 1926 (III)

TABLE A-1. BUSINESS CYCLE REFERENCE DATES

1891–2009

TROUGH	PEAK
November 1927 (IV)	August 1929 (III)
March 1933 (I)	May 1937 (II)
June 1938 (II)	February 1945 (I)
October 1945 (IV)	November 1948 (IV)
October 1949 (IV)	July 1953 (II)
May 1954 (II)	August 1957 (III)
April 1958 (II)	April 1960 (II)
February 1961 (I)	December 1969 (IV)
November 1970 (IV)	November 1973 (IV)
March 1975 (I)	January 1980 (I)
July 1980 (III)	July 1981 (III)
November 1982 (IV)	July 1990 (III)
March 1991 (I)	March 2001 (I)
November 2001 (IV)	December 2007 (IV)
June 2009 (II)	

SOURCE: National Bureau of Economic Research, http://www.nber.org/cycles.
For additional information on NBER and its business cycle studies, see the NBER Web site at <http://www.nber.org/cycles>.

THE U.S. ECONOMY 1929–1948

While there has been much discussion in recent years of the "Great Depression," there is surprisingly little familiarity with the basic statistical record of the period between 1929 and the end of World War II. Reproducing material from Chapter 18 of the 15th edition of *Business Statistics,* we present here an explanation of that period from the NBER business cycle perspective, along with a graphic overview and narration of its economic developments as recorded in the statistics now presented in Part A of this volume.

The NBER chronology, presented in Table A-1 in the preceding article "Cycle and Growth Perspectives," may surprise readers who are looking for "The Great Depression" and are not familiar with the NBER approach to business cycles. As NBER perceives it, a downtrend in economic activity began in August 1929 (<u>before</u> the stock market crash) and lasted until March 1933. This 43-month period has been called the "Great Contraction": it was the longest period of economic decline since the 1870s, and more than double the length of the longest recession identified and completed since that time (the one from December 2007 to June 2009, which lasted 18 months). For the rest of the 1930s—excepting a 13-month recession in 1937–1938—the economy is viewed by the NBER as having been in an expansion phase. The NBER chronology does not use the term "depression."

However, the term "Great Depression" is often colloquially used for the entire 1929–1939 period, even though the economy was expanding for most of the period following March 1933. This is because economic activity during that time, though increasing, remained below the likely capacity of the economy, as is indicated in Figures A-1 and A-2 below.

It should also be noted that NBER construes the entire period from June 1938 through February 1945 as a business cycle expansion. The recovery from the 1937–1938 recession merged into a further, continued rise in activity that reflected the outbreak of war in Europe in September 1939, a consequent preparedness effort in the United States, and an increase in demand from abroad for U.S. output. The United States entered the war after being attacked by Japan in December 1941, launching an all-out war production effort at that time.

The February 1945 end of the "wartime expansion" (as NBER terms the period June 1938–February 1945) preceded the end of the war (the European war ended in May 1945 and the Pacific war concluded in August 1945). A brief recession associated with demobilization occurred from February to October 1945, followed by the first postwar expansion, which lasted from October 1945 to November 1948.

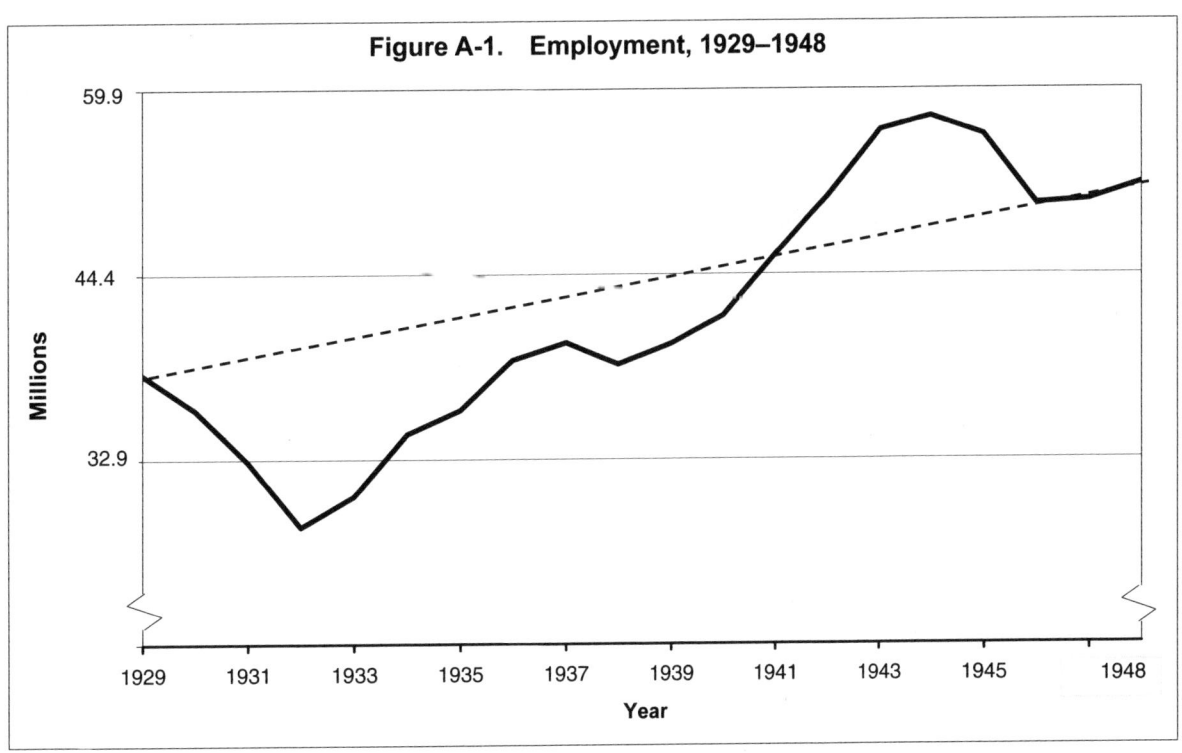

Figure A-1. Employment, 1929–1948

In the graphs that follow, summary annual statistics for the years 1929 through 1948 are presented, depicting the economy during two of its most tumultuous decades. This period encompasses the "great contraction," the economic collapse that began in August 1929 and lasted until March 1933; a subsequent period of recovery, which failed to return many important economic indicators to their expected trend levels and was interrupted by a new, though less severe, recession; apprehension of coming war, then the outbreak of war in Europe in September 1939, leading to increased war-related production; United States participation in all-out war, beginning with the Japanese attack on Pearl Harbor on December 7, 1941, and ending in 1945, with supercharged production and employment rates; then, rapid demobilization, and return to a high peacetime rate of economic activity by 1948.

For a first overall view of the economy during these decades, Figure A-1 shows total U.S. employment as calculated by the Bureau of Economic Analysis, including all private and government jobs, both civilian and military. In this graph a trend line is shown connecting the two peacetime high employment levels of 1929 and 1948.

- More than one-fifth of all the jobs held in the U.S. economy in 1929 were gone by 1932. In the subsequent recovery, total employment was back at the 1929 level by 1936, but only because of government employment, including over 3 ½ million work relief jobs; private industry employment would not recover to its 1929 level until 1941. (Table 10-21)

- Because the recovery was incomplete and economic activity did not recover to a trend level until after the decade's end, the entire decade of the 1930s is often described as "The Great Depression."

- During the war, men were drafted into the armed forces, practically all of the unemployed were put back to work, and women were drawn into the labor force, resulting in a period of what might be called "super-employment." After the war, employment fell back to a more normal trend level. (Tables 10-1C and 10-21)

- The unemployment rates for the prewar period calculated by the Bureau of Labor Statistics, unlike the employment data used in Figure A-1, count people on government work relief programs as unemployed. By this reckoning, unemployment rose from 3.2 percent of the civilian labor force in 1929 to a peak of 24.9 percent in 1933, and got no lower than 14.3 percent for the rest of the 1930s, as shown in Figure A-2. (Table 10-1C)

- State and local governments started hiring people for work relief in 1930. The federal government's programs began in 1933, and in 1936 and 1938 agencies such as the WPA and the CCC employed over 3 ½ million people. When workers in these programs are counted as employed rather than unemployed, the high point for unemployment was 22.5 percent in 1932, and it was reduced to 9.1 percent in 1937, as shown by the dashed line in Figure A-2. (Tables 10-1C and

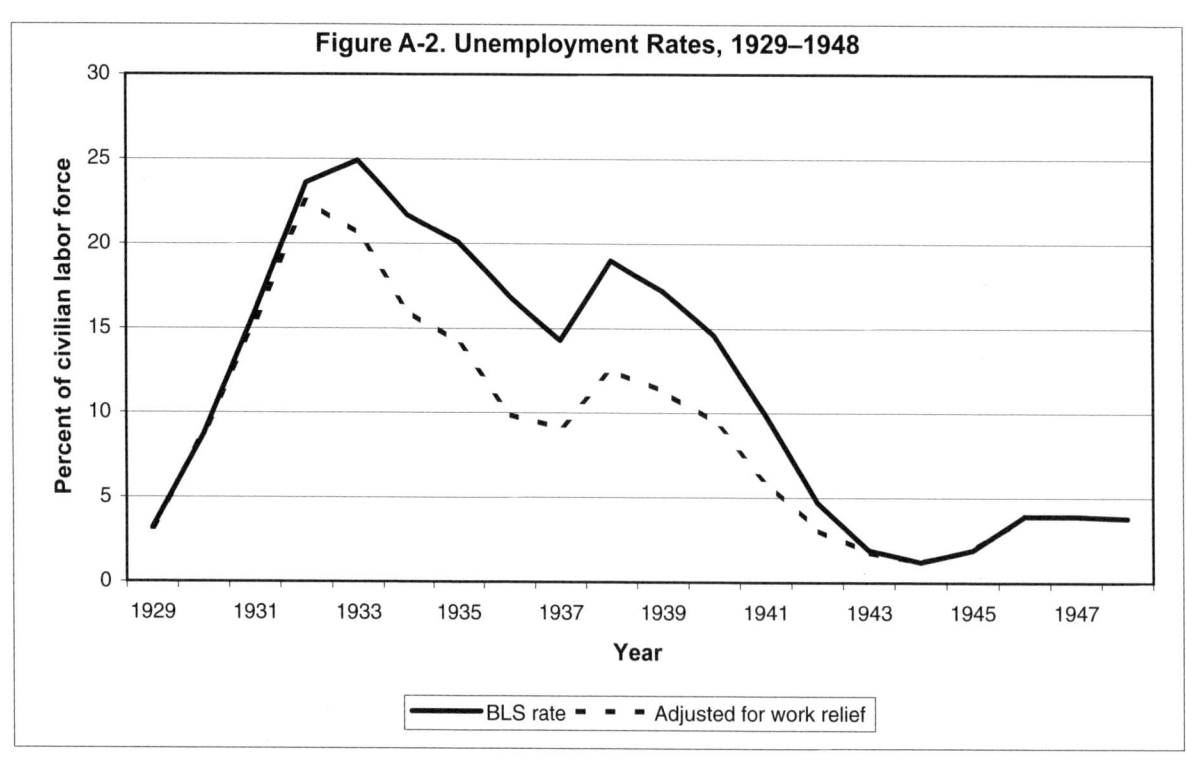

Figure A-2. Unemployment Rates, 1929–1948

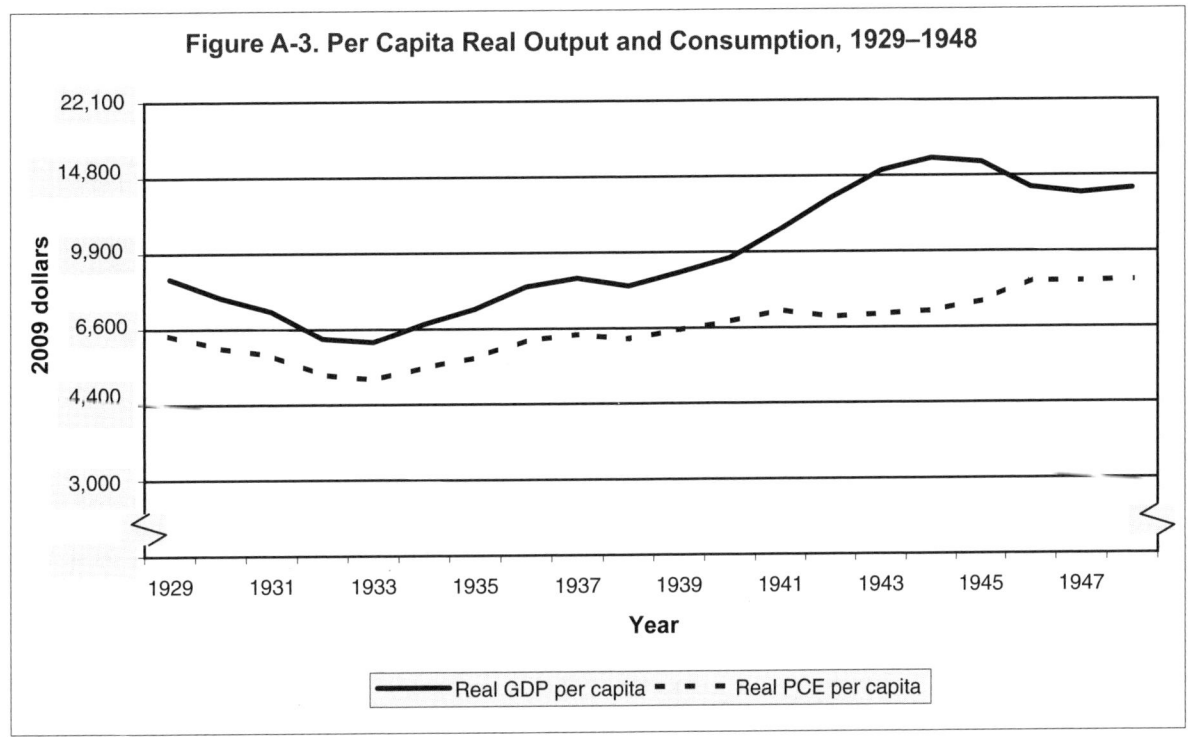

Figure A-3. Per Capita Real Output and Consumption, 1929–1948

10-21; see Notes and Definitions to Chapter 10 for further explanation.)

- By 1943, the economy reached a state of over-full employment, which would have been associated with runaway inflation if not for comprehensive price, wage, and production controls; the years of full wartime production, 1943 through 1945, all saw unemployment rates below 2 percent. After demobilization, the unemployment rate returned to just under 4 percent. (Table 10-1C)

- Real GDP declined 26.7 percent from 1929 to 1933—28.9 percent on a per capita basis. Per capita output recovered almost to the 1929 level in 1937 but fell back 4.1 percent in the 1938 recession. Output then nearly doubled from 1939 to the peak war production year, 1944; the per capita annual growth rate was 12.4 percent. Output fell back during the demobilization, but in 1948 was still at a per capita level representing a 5.0 percent per year growth rate since 1939. (Tables 1-3B and 4-1B)

- Per capita personal consumption expenditures fell 20.9 percent from 1929 to 1933. The decline would have been greater if consumers had not dipped into their assets to keep their living standards from declining as steeply as their incomes; the personal saving rate was negative in 1932 and 1933. Real per capita consumption recovered to the 1929 level by 1937. Despite rationing and shortages, real per capita consumption

spending declined little during the war years. In 1948, it was 29.3 percent above the 1939 level. (Table 1-3B)

- Why was the 1929–1933 contraction so deep and long-lasting? By some, blame is placed on U.S. government tax increases and imposition of new trade barriers (the Smoot-Hawley Tariff), which undoubtedly made their contribution. A substantial number of well-regarded economists, however, point primarily to deflation and its interaction with debt. The price index for personal consumption expenditures, whose rate of change is shown in Figure A-4, declined 27.2 percent from 1929 to 1933, for an annual average <u>deflation</u> rate of 7.6 percent. Current and prospective price declines make debt more burdensome and debtors more likely to default, as interest payments remain fixed while incomes and asset values decline. (Table 1-6B)

- Current and prospective price declines also make borrowing prohibitively expensive; a low nominal interest rate becomes high in real terms (since the real rate is the nominal rate <u>minus</u> the inflation rate, and subtraction means changing the sign and adding). A dollar in the hands of a prospective lender will be worth more in terms of purchasing power if he simply holds on to it than if he invests it in some real economic asset or activity whose price will be lower at the end of the year. There is no feasible way for a central bank to lower interest rates below zero in order to reduce real rates in the presence of deflation. As Figure A-4 shows, real rates

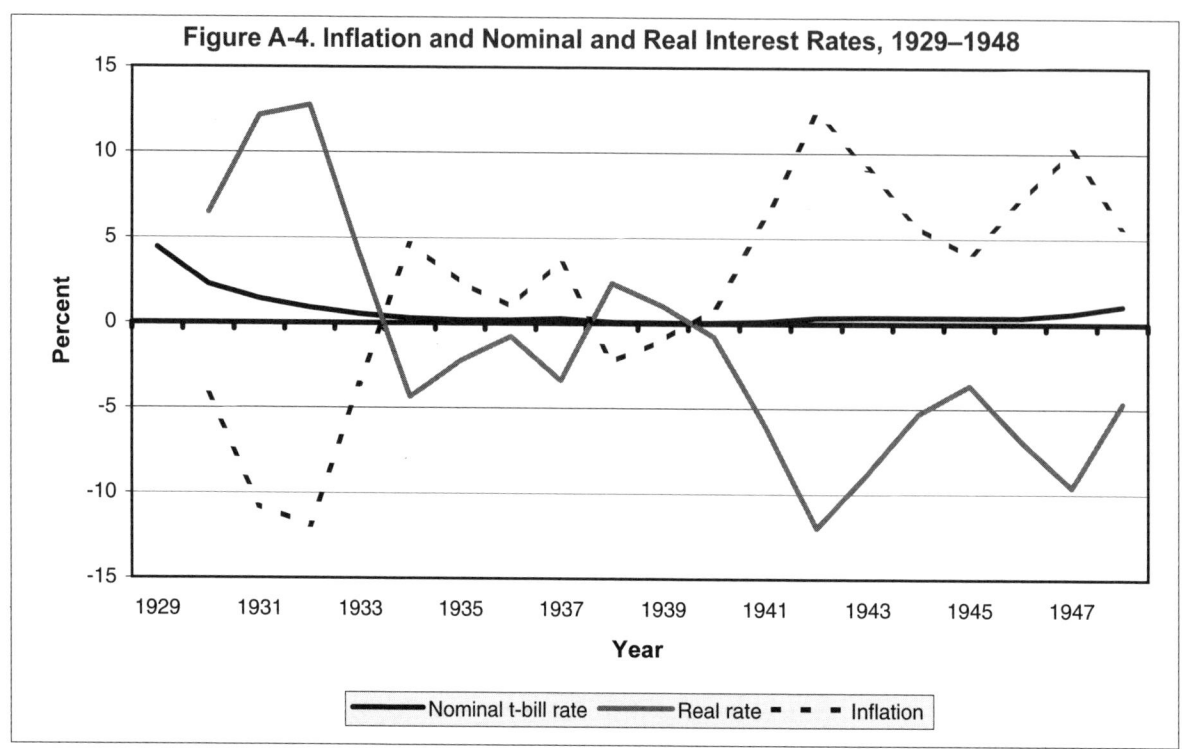

Figure A-4. Inflation and Nominal and Real Interest Rates, 1929–1948

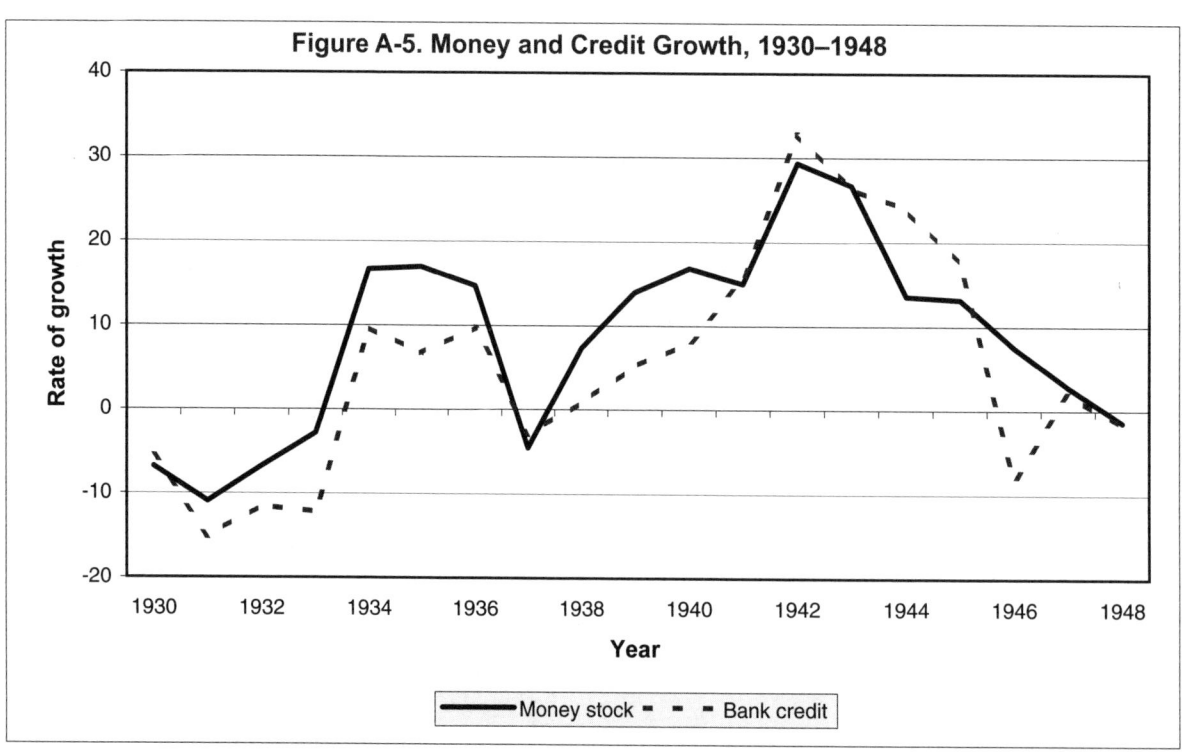

Figure A-5. Money and Credit Growth, 1930–1948

were high from 1930 through 1933 despite near-zero market nominal rates on Treasury bills. (Tables 12-9B and 1-6B)

- Deflation was rooted in deep and sustained declines in the dollar volumes of money and credit, as shown in Tables 12-1B and 12-4B and illustrated in Figure A-5. The money

stock (currency and demand deposits) declined 27 percent from June 30, 1929, to June 30, 1933. Loans and investments at all commercial banks declined 29 percent over the same period. Commercial paper outstanding plunged 76 percent between December 1929 and December 1932, and bankers' acceptances were down 59 percent.

- Positive money and credit growth after 1933 was reflected in moderate rates of price increase and moderately negative—which means stimulative—real interest rates. As can be seen in Figures A-5 and A-6, there was a monetary component to the 1937-38 recession. There was also a premature federal budget retrenchment at that time. (Table 6-14B)

- During the war, monetary policy was pre-empted by wartime needs. Interest rates were held low to facilitate the financing of huge federal deficits. (Tables 6-14B and 12-9B)

- Worker incomes increased during the wartime boom as employment, average hours, and hourly wages all rose. But inflation and consumer spending were held down by price and production controls and rationing. Personal saving rates soared when there was little to buy and the government emphasized the sale of "war bonds"; the saving rate reached 26 percent in 1943 and 1944, then fell back to 4.2 percent in 1947, almost equal to its 1929 level. (Tables 1-6B, 4-1B, 8-1C, and 10-9)

THE GREAT RECESSION 2007–2009 AND RECOVERY 2010–2016

The Great Recession began in December 2007 and ended in June 2009, which makes it the longest recession since World War II. A recession, as defined by the National Bureau of Economic Research (NBER), is a "period of falling economy spread across the economy, lasting more than a few months, normally visible in real GDP, real income, industrial production and wholesale-retail sales."

During the most current recession, housing starts fell, millions of jobs vanished, real GDP shrank, and the net worth of households declined significantly. The unemployment rate increased from 4.7 percent in November 2007 to 10.0 percent in October 2009. The last time unemployment was in double digits was December 1982.

Even though the Great Recession officially ended in June 2009, the return to a "normal" U.S. economy has been sluggish. Employment numbers finally recuperated in May 2014, almost five years after the end of the recession. The unemployment was down to 4.7 percent at the end of 2016, equaling the rate just before the recession started.

All 7.7 million job losses between December 2007 and February 2010 were recaptured and employment surpassed 152 million by 2016. However, different industries, like construction, are still struggling to recover their workforce. Employment in the construction industry in 2016 was still 12 percent below its high in 2007. Chapter 15 describes employment by sector and industry.

Housing data is presented in Chapter 16 and includes information on new construction, building permits and new house prices. New housing starts declined drastically between 2005 and 2009. By 2016, housing starts were still 43 percent below the high in of 2.1 million in 2005.

As unemployment grew and wages lowered, real income has not fully recovered to its high of $57,843 in 1999. In 2016, median household income grew to $56,516—the first increase in eight years. As income has risen, poverty has decreased. In 2015, 13.7 percent of the U.S. population was in poverty. Additionally, over 90 percent of the U.S. population now are covered by health insurance.

International trade, imports and exports, and current account balance information is depicted in Chapter 7 while foreign exchange data is found in Chapter 13. The United States has been a debtor nation since the 1980s meaning it must borrow from the world to pay its current account deficit.

For consumers, two trends have been beneficial. First, inflation, as measured by the Consumer Price Index, slowed considerably. In addition, crude oil prices, which is used to manufacture gasoline, have plummeted in recent years.

GENERAL NOTES

These notes provide general information about the data in Tables 1-1 through 16-14. Specific notes with information about data sources, definitions, methodology, revisions, and sources of additional information follow the tables in each chapter.

MAIN DIVISIONS OF THE BOOK

The tables are presented in two parts:

Part A (Tables 1-1 through 13-2) pertains principally to the U.S. economy as a whole. Generally, each table presents, on its initial page, annual averages as far back as data availability and space permit, and quarterly or monthly values for the most recent year or years. For many important series, this initial page is followed by full annual and quarterly or monthly histories as far back as they are available on a continuous, consistent basis. Some chapters present data for the United States only in aggregate, while others—such as the chapters concerning industrial production and capacity utilization (chapter 2), capital expenditures (chapter 5), profits (chapter 9), and employment, hours, and earnings (chapter 10)—also have detail for industry groups.

Data by industry are classified using the North American Industry Classification System (NAICS), as far back as such data are made available by the source agencies.

Part B focuses on the individual industries that together produce the gross domestic product (GDP).

- Chapter 14 contains data on the value of GDP, quantity production trends, and factor income by NAICS industry group.

- Chapter 15 provides further detail on payroll employment, hours, and earnings classified according to NAICS.

- Chapter 16 presents various data sets for key economic sectors. Some of the tables are based on definitions of products, rather than of producing establishments, and are valid for either classification system. This is the case for Tables 16-1, New Construction; 16-2, Housing Starts and Building Permits, New House Sales, and Prices; and 16-7, Motor Vehicle Sales and Inventories. Tables 16-3 through 16-6 and 16-8, 16-10, and 16-11, which cover manufacturing and retail and wholesale trade, show data classified according to NAICS. Table 16-14 presents data for services industries classified according to NAICS.

Characteristics of the Tables and the Data

The subtitles or column headings for the data tables normally indicate whether the data are *seasonally adjusted, not seasonally adjusted,* or *at a seasonally adjusted annual rate.* These descriptions refer to the monthly or quarterly data, rather than the annual data; annual data by definition require no seasonal adjustment. Annual values are normally calculated as totals or averages, as appropriate, of unadjusted data. Such annual values are shown in either or both adjusted or unadjusted data columns.

Seasonal adjustment removes from a monthly or quarterly time series the average impact of variations that normally occur at about the same time each year, due to occurrences such as weather, holidays, and tax payment dates.

A simplified example of the process of seasonal adjustment, or deseasonalizing, can indicate its importance in the interpretation of economic time series. Statisticians compare actual monthly data for a number of years with "moving average" trends of the monthly data for the 12 months centered on each month's data. For example, they may find that in November, sales values are usually about 95 percent of the moving average, while in December, usual sales values are 110 percent of the average. Suppose that actual November sales in the current year are $100 and December sales are $105. The seasonally adjusted value for November will be $105 ($100/0.95) while the value for December will be $95 ($105/1.10). Thus, an apparent increase in the unadjusted data turns out to be a decrease when adjusted for the usual seasonal pattern.

The statistical method used to achieve the seasonal adjustment may vary from one data set to another. Many of the data are adjusted by a computer method known as X-12-ARIMA, developed by the Census Bureau. A description of the method is found in "New Capabilities and Methods of the X-12-ARIMA Seasonal Adjustment Program," by David F. Findley, Brian C. Monsell, William R. Bell, Mark C. Otto and Bor-Chung Chen (*Journal of Business and Economic Statistics*, April 1998). This article can be downloaded from the Bureau of the Census Web site at <http://www.census.gov>.

Production and sales data presented at *annual rates*—such as NIPA data in dollars, or motor vehicle data in number of units—show values at their annual equivalents: the values that would be registered if the seasonally adjusted rate of activity measured during a particular month or quarter were maintained for a full year. Specifically, seasonally adjusted monthly values are multiplied by 12 and quarterly values by 4 to yield seasonally adjusted annual rates.

Percent changes at seasonally adjusted annual rates for quarterly time periods are calculated using a compound interest formula, by raising the quarter-to-quarter percent change in a seasonally adjusted series to the fourth power. See the article

"Cycle and Growth Perspectives" for an explanation of compound annual growth rates.

Indexes. In many of the most important data sets presented in this volume, aggregate measures of prices and quantities are expressed in the form of indexes. The most basic and familiar form of index, the original Consumer Price Index, begins with a "market basket" of goods and services purchased in a base period, with each product category valued at its dollar prices—the amount spent on that category by the average consumer. The value weight ascribed to each component of the market basket is moved forward by the observed change in the price of the item selected to represent that component. These weighted component prices—which constitute the quantities in the base period repriced in the prices of subsequent periods—are aggregated, divided by the base period aggregate, and multiplied by 100 to provide an index number. An index calculated in this way is known as a *Laspeyres index*. In general, economists believe that Laspeyres price indexes have an upward bias, showing more price increase than they would if account were taken of consumers' ability to change spending patterns and maintain the same level of satisfaction in response to changing relative prices.

A *Paasche index* is one that uses the weights of the current period. Since the weights in the Paasche index change in each period, Paasche indexes only provide acceptable indications of change relative to the base period. Paasche indexes for two periods neither of which is the base period cannot be correctly compared: for example, a Paasche price index for a recent period might increase from the period just preceding even if no prices changed between those two periods, if there was a change in the composition of output toward prices that had previously increased more from the base period. When the national income and product account (NIPA) measures of real output were Laspeyres measures, using the weights of a single base year, the implicit deflators (current-dollar values divided by constant-dollar values) were Paasche indexes. Just as Laspeyres price indexes are upward-biased, Paasche price indexes are downward-biased because they overestimate consumers' ability to maintain the same level of satisfaction by changing spending patterns.

In recent years, government statisticians—with the aid of complex computer programs—have developed measures of real output and prices that minimize bias by using the weights of both periods and updating the weights for each period-to-period comparison. Such measures are described as chained indexes and are used in the NIPAs, the index of industrial production, and an experimental consumer price index. Chained measures are discussed more fully in the notes and definitions for Chapter 1, Chapter 2, and Chapter 8. The "Fisher Ideal" index, the "superlative" index, and the "Tornqvist formula" are all types of chained indexes that use weights for both periods under comparison.

Detail may not sum to totals due to rounding. Since annual data are typically calculated by source agencies as the annual totals or averages of not-seasonally-adjusted data, they therefore will not be precisely equal to the annual totals or averages of monthly seasonally-adjusted data. Also, seasonal adjustment procedures are typically multiplicative rather than additive, which may also prevent seasonally adjusted data from adding or averaging to the annual figure. Percent changes and growth rates may have been calculated using unrounded data and therefore differ from those using the published figures.

The data in this volume are from federal government sources and may be reproduced freely. A list of data sources is shown below.

The tables in this volume incorporate data revisions and corrections released by the source agencies through mid-2014, including the July annual revision of the NIPAs and the resulting August revision of productivity and costs.

DATA SOURCES

The source agencies for the data in this volume are listed below. The specific source or sources for each particular data set are identified at the beginning of the notes and definitions for the relevant data pages.

Board of Governors of the Federal Reserve System

20th Street & Constitution Avenue NW
Washington, DC 20551

Data Inquiries and Publication Sales:
Publications Services
Mail Stop 127
Board of Governors of the Federal Reserve System
Washington, DC 20551
Phone: (202) 452-3245

Quarterly Publication:
As of 2006, the *Federal Reserve Bulletin* is available free of charge and only on the Federal Reserve Web site.
URL:
http://www.federalreserve.gov

Census Bureau
U.S. Department of Commerce
4700 Silver Hill Road
Washington, DC 20233

URL:
http://www.census.gov

Ordering Data Products:
Call Center: (301) 763-INFO (4636)
E-mail Questions:
webmaster@census.gov

E-sales:
http://www.census.gov/mp/www/censtore.html

Bureau of Economic Analysis
U.S. Department of Commerce
Washington, DC 20230

Data Inquiries:
Public Information Office
Phone: (202) 606-9900

Monthly Publication:
Survey of Current Business
Available online.
URL:
http://www.bea.gov

Bureau of Labor Statistics
U.S. Department of Labor
2 Massachusetts Avenue NE
Washington, DC 20212-0001
(202) 691-5200

URL:
http://www.bls.gov

Data Inquiries:
Blsdata_staff@bls.gov

Monthly Publications available online:
Monthly Labor Review
Employment and Earnings
Compensation and Working Conditions
Producer Price Indexes
CPI Detailed Report

Employment and Training Administration
U.S. Department of Labor
200 Constitution Avenue NW
Washington, DC 20210
(877) US2-JOBS

URL:
http://www.doleta.gov

http://www.itsc.state.md.us

Energy Information Administration
U.S. Department of Energy
1000 Independence Avenue SW
Washington, DC 20585
Data Inquiries and Publications:
National Energy Information Center
Phone: (202) 586-8800
E-mail: infoctr@eia.doe.gov

Monthly Publication:
Monthly Energy Review, as of 2007 available only on the EIA
Web site, free of charge.

URL:
http://www.eia.doe.gov

Federal Housing Finance Agency
FHFAinfo@FHFA.gov
(202) 414-6921,6922
(202) 414-6376

URL:
http://www.fhfa.gov/hpi

U.S. Department of the Treasury
Office of International Affairs
Treasury International Capital System

URL:
http://www.treas.gov/tic

To order government publications
Superintendent of Documents
Government Printing Office
Washington, DC 20402
(202) 512-1800

URL:
http://bookstore.gpo.gov

PART A: THE U.S. ECONOMY

CHAPTER 1: NATIONAL INCOME AND PRODUCT

SECTION 1A: GROSS DOMESTIC PRODUCT: VALUES, QUANTITIES, AND PRICES

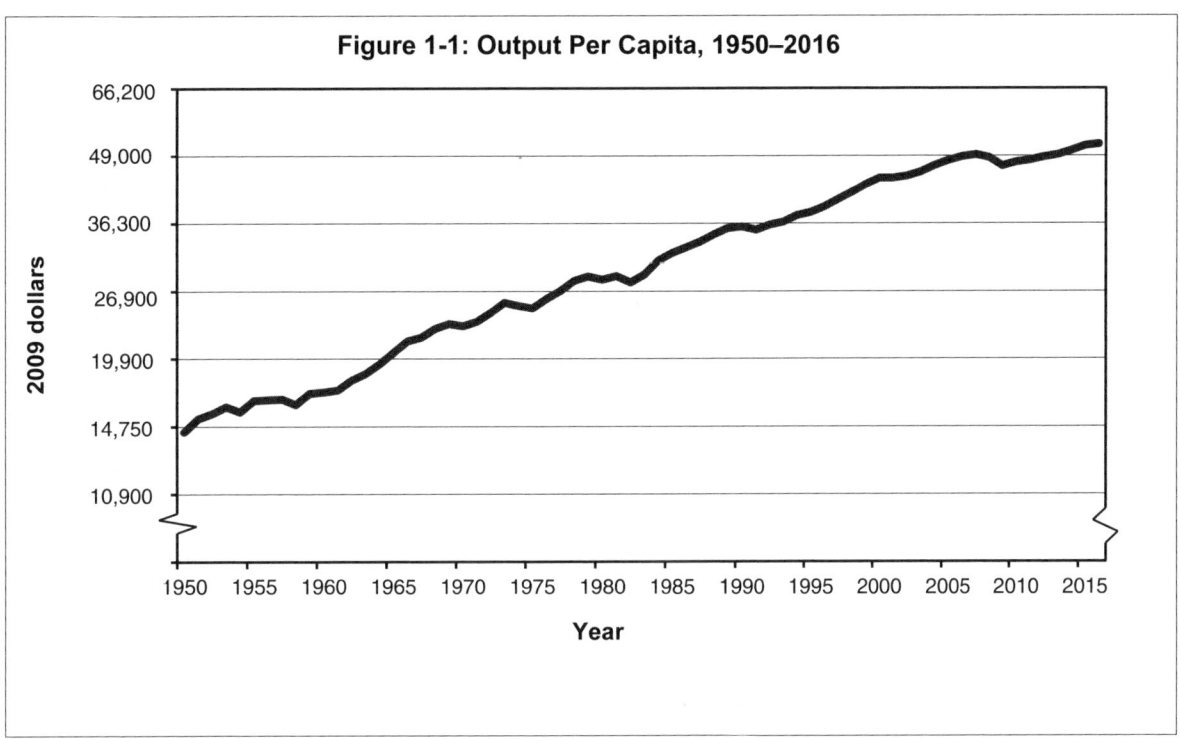

Figure 1-1: Output Per Capita, 1950–2016

- As presented in the preface, the output approach to GDP consists of four components: consumption, business investment, government taxes and spending and the foreign trade balance (exports – imports). GDP is one of the most comprehensive and closely watched economic statistics in not only the United States but also globally. Both current and real (without inflation) GDP is calculated along with its growth rate. For more details of GDP, see the Notes and Definitions at the end of this chapter.

- Historically, U.S. GDP growth rates have hovered around 3 percent since the National Income and Product Accounts (NIPA) were developed during the Great Depression. In fact, the four years of the Great Depression (1930–1933) was the longest stretch of time with economic growth rates of less than 3 percent until the Great Recession hit in 2009. For the seven-year period between 2010 and 2016, GDP annual growth rates have been between 2.8 and 4.4 percent. The longest stretch of years with growth greater than 3 percent was from the 1983 to 1989. In 2015, the growth rate was 4.0 percent, however in 2016 this had shrunk to 2.8 percent. (Table 1-1A)

- Real GDP per capita—the constant-dollar average value of production for each man, woman, and child in the population—rose from $14,398 (2009 dollars) in 1950 to $49,300 in 2007, a growth rate of 2.2 percent per year. Reflecting the recession that began in December 2007, it declined 4.8 percent from 2007 to 2009. Over the seven years since then, per capita GDP recovered 10.1 percent and surpassed its 2007 peak. The history of per capita GDP is charted in Figure 1-1, graphed on a "ratio scale," with equal vertical distances signifying equal percent changes. (Table 1-3A)

Table 1-1A. Gross Domestic Product: Recent Data

(Billions of dollars, quarterly data are at seasonally adjusted annual rates.)   **NIPA Tables 1.1.5, 1.2.5**

Year and quarter	Gross domestic product	Personal consumption expenditures	Gross private domestic investment					Exports and imports of goods and services			Government consumption expenditures and gross investment			Addendum: final sales of domestic product
			Total	Fixed investment			Change in private inventories	Net exports	Exports	Imports	Total	Federal	State and local	
				Nonresidential	Residential									
1950	300.2	192.2	56.5	30.0	20.7	5.8	0.7	12.4	11.6	50.7	29.5	21.3	294.4
1951	347.3	208.5	62.8	34.2	18.7	9.9	2.5	17.1	14.6	73.5	50.0	23.6	337.4
1952	367.7	219.5	57.3	34.9	18.9	3.5	1.2	16.5	15.3	89.8	64.8	25.0	364.2
1953	389.7	233.0	60.4	38.8	19.7	1.9	-0.7	15.3	16.0	97.0	70.3	26.7	387.8
1954	391.1	239.9	58.1	38.6	21.4	-1.9	0.4	15.8	15.4	92.8	63.3	29.5	393.1
1955	426.2	258.7	73.8	43.4	25.4	5.0	0.5	17.7	17.2	93.3	61.0	32.2	421.2
1956	450.1	271.6	77.7	49.7	24.0	4.0	2.4	21.3	18.9	98.5	63.1	35.4	446.2
1957	474.9	286.7	76.5	53.1	22.6	0.8	4.1	24.0	19.9	107.5	68.4	39.1	474.1
1958	482.0	296.0	70.9	48.5	22.8	-0.4	0.5	20.6	20.0	114.5	71.5	43.0	482.4
1959	522.5	317.5	85.7	53.1	28.6	3.9	0.4	22.7	22.3	118.9	73.5	45.3	518.5
1960	543.3	331.6	86.5	56.4	26.9	3.2	4.2	27.0	22.8	121.0	72.8	48.2	540.1
1961	563.3	342.0	86.6	56.6	27.0	3.0	4.9	27.6	22.7	129.8	77.4	52.5	560.3
1962	605.1	363.1	97.0	61.2	29.6	6.1	4.1	29.1	25.0	140.9	85.5	55.4	599.0
1963	638.6	382.5	103.3	64.8	32.9	5.6	4.9	31.1	26.1	147.9	87.8	60.0	633.0
1964	685.8	411.2	112.2	72.2	35.1	4.8	6.9	35.0	28.1	155.5	90.2	65.3	681.0
1965	743.7	443.6	129.6	85.2	35.2	9.2	5.6	37.1	31.5	164.9	93.1	71.7	734.5
1966	815.0	480.6	144.2	97.2	33.4	13.6	3.9	40.9	37.1	186.4	106.5	79.8	801.4
1967	861.7	507.4	142.7	99.2	33.6	9.9	3.6	43.5	39.9	208.1	120.0	88.1	851.9
1968	942.5	557.4	156.9	107.7	40.2	9.1	1.4	47.9	46.6	226.8	127.9	98.8	933.4
1969	1 019.9	604.5	173.6	120.0	44.4	9.2	1.4	51.9	50.5	240.4	131.1	109.3	1 010.7
1970	1 075.9	647.7	170.1	124.6	43.4	2.0	4.0	59.7	55.8	254.2	132.7	121.4	1 073.9
1971	1 167.8	701.0	196.8	130.4	58.2	8.3	0.6	63.0	62.3	269.3	134.4	134.9	1 159.5
1972	1 282.4	769.4	228.1	146.6	72.4	9.1	-3.4	70.8	74.2	288.2	141.5	146.7	1 273.3
1973	1 428.5	851.1	266.9	172.7	78.3	15.9	4.1	95.3	91.2	306.4	145.6	160.8	1 412.7
1974	1 548.8	932.0	274.5	191.1	69.5	14.0	-0.8	126.7	127.5	343.1	158.1	185.0	1 534.8
1975	1 688.9	1 032.8	257.3	196.8	66.7	-6.3	16.0	138.7	122.7	382.9	172.8	210.2	1 695.2
1976	1 877.6	1 150.2	323.2	219.3	86.8	17.1	-1.6	149.5	151.1	405.8	183.8	222.1	1 860.5
1977	2 086.0	1 276.7	396.6	259.1	115.2	22.3	-23.1	159.4	182.4	435.8	198.8	237.0	2 063.6
1978	2 356.6	1 426.2	478.4	314.6	138.0	25.8	-25.4	186.9	212.3	477.4	216.7	260.7	2 330.8
1979	2 632.1	1 589.5	539.7	373.8	147.8	18.0	-22.5	230.1	252.7	525.5	237.7	287.8	2 614.2
1980	2 862.5	1 754.6	530.1	406.9	129.5	-6.3	-13.1	280.8	293.8	590.8	272.4	318.5	2 868.8
1981	3 211.0	1 937.5	631.2	472.9	128.5	29.8	-12.5	305.2	317.8	654.7	311.7	343.0	3 181.1
1982	3 345.0	2 073.9	581.0	485.1	110.8	-14.9	-20.0	283.2	303.2	710.0	345.6	364.4	3 359.9
1983	3 638.1	2 286.5	637.5	482.2	161.1	-5.8	-51.6	277.0	328.6	765.7	380.2	385.6	3 643.9
1984	4 040.7	2 498.2	820.1	564.3	190.4	65.4	-102.7	302.4	405.1	825.2	407.6	417.5	3 975.3
1985	4 346.7	2 722.7	829.6	607.7	200.1	21.8	-114.0	303.2	417.2	908.4	449.3	459.2	4 324.9
1986	4 590.2	2 898.4	849.1	607.8	234.8	6.6	-131.9	321.0	452.9	974.5	478.4	496.1	4 583.6
1987	4 870.2	3 092.1	892.2	615.2	249.8	27.1	-144.8	363.9	508.7	1 030.8	500.2	530.5	4 843.1
1988	5 252.6	3 346.9	937.0	662.3	256.2	18.5	-109.4	444.6	554.0	1 078.2	508.8	569.3	5 234.1
1989	5 657.7	3 592.8	999.7	716.0	256.0	27.7	-86.7	504.3	591.0	1 151.9	531.4	620.5	5 630.0
1990	5 979.6	3 825.6	993.5	739.2	239.7	14.5	-77.9	551.9	629.7	1 238.4	560.0	678.3	5 965.0
1991	6 174.0	3 960.2	944.3	723.6	221.2	-0.4	-28.6	594.9	623.5	1 298.2	580.7	717.4	6 174.4
1992	6 539.3	4 215.7	1 013.0	741.9	254.7	16.3	-34.7	633.1	667.8	1 345.4	586.6	758.8	6 523.0
1993	6 878.7	4 471.0	1 106.8	799.2	286.8	20.8	-65.2	654.8	720.0	1 366.1	578.4	787.7	6 857.9
1994	7 308.8	4 741.0	1 256.5	868.9	323.8	63.8	-92.5	720.9	813.4	1 403.7	572.7	831.1	7 245.0
1995	7 664.1	4 984.2	1 317.5	962.2	324.1	31.2	-89.8	812.8	902.6	1 452.2	575.4	876.8	7 632.9
1996	8 100.2	5 268.1	1 432.1	1 043.2	358.1	30.8	-96.4	867.6	964.0	1 496.4	578.2	918.2	8 069.4
1997	8 608.5	5 560.7	1 595.6	1 149.1	375.6	70.9	-102.0	953.8	1 055.8	1 554.2	582.4	971.8	8 537.6
1998	9 089.2	5 903.0	1 735.3	1 252.8	418.8	63.7	-162.7	953.0	1 115.7	1 613.5	584.1	1 029.4	9 025.4
1999	9 660.6	6 307.0	1 884.2	1 361.6	461.8	60.8	-256.6	992.0	1 248.6	1 726.0	610.4	1 115.6	9 599.8
2000	10 284.8	6 792.4	2 033.8	1 493.8	485.4	54.5	-375.8	1 096.8	1 472.6	1 834.4	632.4	1 202.0	10 230.2
2001	10 621.8	7 103.1	1 928.6	1 453.9	513.0	-38.3	-368.7	1 026.7	1 395.4	1 958.8	669.2	1 289.5	10 660.1
2002	10 977.5	7 384.1	1 925.0	1 348.9	557.6	18.5	-426.5	1 002.5	1 429.0	2 094.9	740.6	1 354.3	10 959.0
2003	11 510.7	7 765.5	2 027.9	1 371.7	636.9	19.3	-503.7	1 040.3	1 543.9	2 220.8	824.8	1 396.0	11 491.4
2004	12 274.9	8 260.0	2 276.7	1 463.1	749.7	63.9	-619.2	1 181.5	1 800.7	2 357.4	892.4	1 465.0	12 211.1
2005	13 093.7	8 794.1	2 527.1	1 611.5	856.1	59.6	-721.2	1 308.9	2 030.1	2 493.7	946.3	1 547.4	13 034.1
2006	13 855.9	9 304.0	2 680.6	1 776.3	837.4	67.0	-770.9	1 476.3	2 247.3	2 642.2	1 002.0	1 640.2	13 788.9
2007	14 477.6	9 750.5	2 643.7	1 920.6	688.7	34.5	-718.5	1 664.6	2 383.2	2 801.9	1 049.8	1 752.2	14 443.2
2008	14 718.6	10 013.6	2 424.8	1 941.0	515.9	-32.0	-723.1	1 841.9	2 565.0	3 003.2	1 155.6	1 847.6	14 750.6
2009	14 418.7	9 847.0	1 878.1	1 633.4	392.2	-147.6	-395.4	1 587.7	1 983.2	3 089.1	1 217.7	1 871.4	14 566.3
2010	14 964.4	10 202.2	2 100.8	1 658.2	381.1	61.5	-512.7	1 852.3	2 365.0	3 174.0	1 303.9	1 870.2	14 902.8
2011	15 517.9	10 689.3	2 239.9	1 812.1	386.0	41.8	-580.0	2 106.4	2 686.4	3 168.7	1 303.5	1 865.3	15 476.2
2012	16 155.3	11 050.6	2 511.7	2 007.7	442.2	61.8	-565.7	2 198.2	2 763.8	3 158.6	1 292.5	1 866.1	16 093.5
2013	16 691.5	11 361.2	2 706.3	2 094.4	519.5	92.4	-492.0	2 276.6	2 768.6	3 116.1	1 229.5	1 886.6	16 599.1
2014	17 427.6	11 863.7	2 916.4	2 268.3	570.2	78.0	-509.5	2 373.6	2 883.2	3 157.0	1 218.1	1 938.9	17 349.6
2015	18 120.7	12 332.3	3 093.6	2 336.2	645.4	111.9	-524.0	2 264.9	2 789.0	3 218.9	1 224.0	1 994.9	18 008.8
2016	18 624.5	12 820.7	3 057.2	2 316.3	705.9	35.1	-521.2	2 214.6	2 735.8	3 267.8	1 231.5	2 036.3	18 589.4
2014													
1st quarter	17 031.3	11 640.2	2 780.7	2 194.7	542.2	43.8	-516.4	2 340.0	2 856.4	3 126.9	1 216.6	1 910.3	16 987.5
2nd quarter	17 320.9	11 791.9	2 895.0	2 251.5	560.8	82.7	-512.7	2 391.3	2 903.9	3 146.6	1 215.5	1 931.2	17 238.2
3rd quarter	17 622.3	11 941.1	2 992.0	2 316.0	577.4	98.6	-489.1	2 389.0	2 878.1	3 178.2	1 228.3	1 949.9	17 523.7
4th quarter	17 735.9	12 081.4	2 997.9	2 310.9	600.2	86.8	-519.8	2 374.4	2 894.2	3 176.5	1 212.2	1 964.2	17 649.1
2015													
1st quarter	17 874.7	12 142.2	3 094.6	2 328.6	617.4	148.6	-538.2	2 289.0	2 827.3	3 176.2	1 218.7	1 957.5	17 726.1
2nd quarter	18 093.2	12 284.2	3 096.3	2 343.2	635.0	118.1	-507.1	2 303.9	2 811.0	3 219.8	1 224.9	1 994.8	17 975.1
3rd quarter	18 227.7	12 407.8	3 115.7	2 353.5	656.5	105.7	-530.8	2 256.6	2 787.4	3 235.0	1 222.6	2 012.5	18 122.0
4th quarter	18 287.2	12 494.9	3 067.7	2 319.7	672.6	75.4	-520.1	2 210.1	2 730.2	3 244.7	1 229.9	2 014.8	18 211.8
2016													
1st quarter	18 325.2	12 571.5	3 031.6	2 291.2	698.3	42.2	-526.2	2 166.5	2 692.8	3 248.3	1 227.9	2 020.4	18 283.0
2nd quarter	18 538.0	12 755.0	3 023.1	2 311.2	699.7	12.2	-501.6	2 201.8	2 703.4	3 261.5	1 228.2	2 033.3	18 525.9
3rd quarter	18 729.1	12 899.4	3 048.0	2 329.1	702.4	16.5	-492.8	2 248.4	2 741.3	3 274.6	1 234.6	2 040.0	18 712.7
4th quarter	18 905.5	13 056.9	3 126.2	2 333.7	723.0	69.5	-564.3	2 241.5	2 805.8	3 286.8	1 235.4	2 051.4	18 836.1

Table 1-1B. Gross Domestic Product: Historical Data

(Billions of dollars, quarterly data are at seasonally adjusted annual rates.)   **NIPA Tables 1.1.5, 1.2.5**

Year and quarter	Gross domestic product	Personal consump-tion expen-ditures	Gross private domestic investment				Exports and imports of goods and services			Government consumption expenditures and gross investment			Addendum: Final sales of domestic product
			Total	Fixed investment		Change in private inventories	Net exports	Exports	Imports	Total	Federal	State and local	
				Nonresi-dential	Residential								
1929	104.6	77.4	17.2	11.6	4.1	1.5	0.4	5.9	5.6	9.6	1.9	7.7	103.0
1930	92.2	70.1	11.4	9.2	2.5	-0.2	0.3	4.4	4.1	10.3	2.0	8.3	92.4
1931	77.4	60.7	6.5	5.8	1.9	-1.1	0.0	2.9	2.9	10.2	2.0	8.1	78.5
1932	59.5	48.7	1.8	3.3	0.9	-2.4	0.0	2.0	1.9	9.0	2.0	7.0	61.9
1933	57.2	45.9	2.3	3.0	0.7	-1.4	0.1	2.0	1.9	8.9	2.4	6.5	58.6
1934	66.8	51.5	4.3	3.8	1.0	-0.6	0.3	2.6	2.2	10.7	3.4	7.3	67.4
1935	74.3	55.9	7.4	4.8	1.4	1.1	-0.2	2.8	3.0	11.2	3.6	7.6	73.1
1936	84.9	62.2	9.4	6.4	1.8	1.2	-0.1	3.0	3.2	13.4	5.8	7.7	83.7
1937	93.0	66.8	13.0	8.2	2.2	2.6	0.1	4.0	4.0	13.1	5.3	7.9	90.4
1938	87.4	64.3	7.9	6.3	2.2	-0.6	1.0	3.8	2.8	14.2	5.9	8.3	88.0
1939	93.5	67.2	10.2	6.9	3.2	0.2	0.8	4.0	3.1	15.2	6.2	9.0	93.3
1940	102.9	71.3	14.6	8.5	3.6	2.4	1.5	4.9	3.4	15.6	6.8	8.8	100.6
1941	129.4	81.1	19.4	10.8	4.2	4.3	1.0	5.5	4.4	27.9	19.1	8.8	125.0
1942	166.0	89.0	11.8	7.5	2.4	1.9	-0.3	4.4	4.6	65.5	56.7	8.8	164.1
1943	203.1	99.9	7.4	6.6	1.6	-0.7	-2.2	4.0	6.3	98.1	89.5	8.6	203.9
1944	224.6	108.6	9.2	8.6	1.5	-0.9	-2.0	4.9	6.9	108.7	100.1	8.6	225.5
1945	228.2	120.0	12.4	12.1	1.8	-1.5	-0.8	6.8	7.5	96.6	87.3	9.3	229.6
1946	227.8	144.3	33.1	19.2	8.0	6.0	7.2	14.2	7.0	43.2	32.1	11.1	221.8
1947	249.9	162.0	37.1	25.5	12.2	-0.6	10.8	18.7	7.9	40.0	25.8	14.2	250.5
1948	274.8	175.0	50.3	28.9	15.8	5.7	5.5	15.5	10.1	44.0	27.1	16.9	269.1
1949	272.8	178.5	39.1	26.9	14.8	-2.7	5.2	14.5	9.2	50.0	30.5	19.6	275.5
1947													
1st quarter	243.1	156.3	35.9	24.8	10.5	0.5	10.9	18.4	7.5	40.1	26.6	13.4	242.6
2nd quarter	246.3	160.2	34.5	25.2	10.6	-1.2	11.3	19.5	8.2	40.3	26.5	13.8	247.5
3rd quarter	250.1	163.7	34.9	25.4	12.5	-2.9	11.8	19.4	7.7	39.8	25.3	14.5	253.0
4th quarter	260.3	167.8	43.2	26.5	15.3	1.5	9.3	17.6	8.3	40.0	24.8	15.2	258.9
1948													
1st quarter	266.2	170.5	47.2	28.2	15.3	3.6	7.3	16.9	9.6	41.2	25.5	15.7	262.5
2nd quarter	272.9	174.3	50.3	28.0	16.4	5.9	5.2	15.2	10.0	43.1	26.7	16.4	267.0
3rd quarter	279.5	177.2	52.5	29.1	16.3	7.2	4.9	15.4	10.5	44.8	27.5	17.3	272.3
4th quarter	280.7	178.1	51.3	30.2	15.2	6.0	4.5	14.6	10.1	46.8	28.7	18.0	274.7
1949													
1st quarter	275.4	177.0	43.1	28.6	14.2	0.4	6.5	16.1	9.6	48.8	30.2	18.6	275.0
2nd quarter	271.7	178.6	36.2	27.5	13.9	-5.1	6.3	15.6	9.4	50.6	31.3	19.3	276.8
3rd quarter	273.3	177.9	39.5	26.1	14.7	-1.3	5.2	14.1	8.9	50.6	30.5	20.1	274.6
4th quarter	271.0	180.4	37.5	25.6	16.5	-4.7	3.0	12.1	9.1	50.1	29.8	20.3	275.7
1950													
1st quarter	281.2	183.1	46.7	26.4	18.3	2.0	2.2	11.7	9.5	49.2	28.6	20.6	279.2
2nd quarter	290.7	187.0	52.3	28.9	20.6	2.8	1.6	11.9	10.2	49.9	29.0	20.9	287.9
3rd quarter	308.5	200.7	58.6	31.9	22.6	4.2	-0.7	12.3	13.0	50.0	28.4	21.5	304.3
4th quarter	320.3	198.1	68.4	32.9	21.5	14.0	-0.2	13.5	13.7	53.9	31.8	22.1	306.3
1951													
1st quarter	336.4	209.4	64.6	33.1	21.1	10.4	0.2	15.0	14.9	62.3	39.6	22.7	326.0
2nd quarter	344.5	205.1	67.4	34.1	18.5	14.8	1.9	17.1	15.2	70.0	46.6	23.4	329.7
3rd quarter	351.8	207.8	62.0	34.8	17.4	9.7	3.7	18.1	14.3	78.3	54.3	24.0	342.0
4th quarter	356.6	211.7	57.1	34.6	17.7	4.7	4.2	18.2	14.0	83.6	59.3	24.2	351.9
1952													
1st quarter	360.2	213.1	58.1	35.1	18.3	4.7	3.7	18.7	15.0	85.3	60.9	24.3	355.5
2nd quarter	361.4	217.2	53.0	35.8	18.8	-1.5	2.0	16.6	14.6	89.2	64.1	25.1	362.9
3rd quarter	368.1	219.7	57.2	32.9	18.8	5.6	0.0	15.2	15.3	91.2	66.2	25.0	362.5
4th quarter	381.2	227.9	60.7	35.8	19.6	5.3	-1.0	15.3	16.3	93.7	68.1	25.6	376.0
1953													
1st quarter	388.5	231.5	61.7	37.8	20.0	3.9	-0.7	15.1	15.8	96.0	69.7	26.4	384.6
2nd quarter	392.3	233.2	62.1	38.5	20.1	3.6	-1.3	15.2	16.4	98.2	71.9	26.2	388.7
3rd quarter	391.7	233.9	61.4	39.6	19.5	2.3	-0.0	16.0	16.3	96.9	70.0	26.9	389.4
4th quarter	386.5	233.4	56.4	39.2	19.3	-2.0	-0.3	15.2	15.5	97.0	69.5	27.5	388.5
1954													
1st quarter	385.9	235.4	55.7	38.3	19.4	-2.0	-0.4	14.4	14.8	95.1	66.8	28.4	387.9
2nd quarter	386.7	238.2	55.4	38.2	20.7	-3.4	0.3	16.4	16.2	92.8	63.7	29.1	390.1
3rd quarter	391.6	240.6	59.0	38.9	22.2	-2.1	0.6	15.9	15.3	91.4	61.3	30.1	393.7
4th quarter	400.3	245.4	62.1	38.9	23.6	-0.3	1.1	16.6	15.5	91.6	61.2	30.4	400.7
1955													
1st quarter	413.8	251.8	68.7	39.5	25.4	3.8	1.1	17.3	16.2	92.2	60.7	31.5	409.9
2nd quarter	422.2	256.8	72.7	42.1	26.0	4.6	-0.2	16.9	17.1	92.8	60.9	32.0	417.6
3rd quarter	430.9	261.0	74.7	44.8	25.6	4.3	0.7	18.1	17.4	94.4	61.9	32.5	426.6
4th quarter	437.8	265.1	78.9	47.1	24.6	7.2	0.2	18.3	18.1	93.6	60.5	33.1	430.6
1956													
1st quarter	440.5	266.6	78.3	47.8	24.1	6.4	0.4	19.4	18.9	95.2	61.0	34.2	434.1
2nd quarter	446.8	269.3	77.0	49.1	24.4	3.6	1.9	20.9	19.0	98.6	63.5	35.1	443.2
3rd quarter	452.0	272.5	78.3	50.7	24.0	3.6	2.6	21.8	19.3	98.6	62.8	35.8	448.4
4th quarter	461.3	277.9	77.1	51.4	23.5	2.2	4.5	23.1	18.5	101.7	65.2	36.5	459.0
1957													
1st quarter	470.6	282.3	77.7	52.5	23.1	2.2	4.8	24.9	20.1	105.7	67.9	37.8	468.4
2nd quarter	472.8	284.6	77.9	52.6	22.6	2.7	4.1	24.4	20.3	106.2	67.5	38.7	470.2
3rd quarter	480.3	289.2	79.3	54.1	22.5	2.8	4.0	23.8	19.8	107.8	68.4	39.4	477.5
4th quarter	475.7	290.8	71.0	53.2	22.3	-4.5	3.4	23.0	19.6	110.4	70.0	40.4	480.2
1958													
1st quarter	468.4	290.3	66.7	49.4	21.4	-4.0	1.1	20.5	19.5	110.2	68.7	41.5	472.4
2nd quarter	472.8	293.2	65.1	47.8	21.5	-4.2	0.5	20.5	20.1	114.0	71.5	42.5	477.0
3rd quarter	486.7	298.3	72.0	47.4	23.0	1.5	0.9	20.6	19.7	115.5	71.9	43.6	485.1
4th quarter	500.4	302.2	80.0	49.3	25.4	5.2	-0.3	20.6	20.8	118.4	73.9	44.5	495.1

Table 1-1B. Gross Domestic Product: Historical Data—*Continued*

(Billions of dollars, quarterly data are at seasonally adjusted annual rates.)   NIPA Tables 1.1.5, 1.2.5

| Year and quarter | Gross domestic product | Personal consumption expenditures | Gross private domestic investment | | | | Exports and imports of goods and services | | | Government consumption expenditures and gross investment | | | Addendum: Final sales of domestic product |
| | | | Total | Fixed investment | | Change in private inventories | Net exports | Exports | Imports | Total | Federal | State and local | |
				Nonresidential	Residential								
1959													
1st quarter	511.1	309.9	83.2	50.9	28.3	3.9	0.4	21.8	21.4	117.6	72.3	45.3	507.2
2nd quarter	524.2	315.9	89.4	52.7	29.4	7.3	0.0	22.6	22.5	119.0	73.6	45.4	517.0
3rd quarter	525.2	321.1	83.6	54.4	28.8	0.4	0.6	23.5	22.9	119.9	74.5	45.4	524.8
4th quarter	529.3	323.2	86.5	54.4	28.0	4.1	0.6	23.1	22.5	119.0	73.8	45.2	525.2
1960													
1st quarter	543.3	326.7	96.5	56.3	29.0	11.2	2.7	26.0	23.3	117.4	70.9	46.5	532.1
2nd quarter	542.7	332.6	87.1	57.2	26.7	3.2	4.2	27.6	23.5	118.9	71.0	47.8	539.5
3rd quarter	546.0	332.5	86.4	56.2	25.9	4.3	4.2	27.0	22.9	122.9	74.1	48.8	541.7
4th quarter	541.1	334.5	76.0	55.9	25.9	-5.8	5.8	27.5	21.7	124.9	75.3	49.6	546.9
1961													
1st quarter	545.9	335.0	78.4	55.0	25.9	-2.5	5.8	27.5	21.7	126.8	75.3	51.5	548.5
2nd quarter	557.4	339.9	84.1	56.2	26.1	1.8	5.5	27.4	21.9	127.9	76.2	51.7	555.6
3rd quarter	568.2	342.8	90.9	56.7	27.6	6.7	3.9	27.2	23.3	130.6	78.1	52.5	561.6
4th quarter	581.6	350.1	92.9	58.5	28.5	6.0	4.4	28.3	23.9	134.2	79.9	54.3	575.6
1962													
1st quarter	595.2	355.4	98.1	59.7	29.0	9.4	4.0	28.3	24.3	137.8	83.3	54.5	585.8
2nd quarter	602.6	361.0	96.7	61.4	29.9	5.4	5.8	30.7	24.9	139.1	84.1	55.0	597.1
3rd quarter	609.6	364.9	98.2	62.1	29.9	6.2	3.8	29.0	25.1	142.7	87.0	55.7	603.4
4th quarter	613.1	371.1	95.0	61.8	29.8	3.4	2.8	28.4	25.6	144.2	87.6	56.6	609.8
1963													
1st quarter	622.7	374.7	99.7	62.0	30.8	6.9	3.9	29.1	25.2	144.4	86.2	58.2	615.8
2nd quarter	631.8	378.9	101.6	63.9	32.9	4.8	6.5	32.4	25.9	144.8	85.7	59.1	627.0
3rd quarter	645.0	385.8	104.6	65.7	33.2	5.7	3.9	30.6	26.7	150.6	89.8	60.8	639.2
4th quarter	654.8	390.5	107.2	67.7	34.5	5.1	5.4	32.2	26.8	151.7	89.6	62.1	649.8
1964													
1st quarter	671.1	400.1	110.5	69.1	36.2	5.1	7.3	34.2	27.0	153.3	90.0	63.2	666.0
2nd quarter	680.8	408.1	110.5	71.1	35.0	4.5	7.1	34.8	27.7	155.1	90.1	65.0	676.3
3rd quarter	692.8	417.0	112.6	73.4	34.5	4.7	6.4	34.8	28.4	156.8	90.8	66.0	688.1
4th quarter	698.4	419.6	115.0	75.3	34.6	5.0	6.9	36.2	29.3	156.9	89.9	67.0	693.4
1965													
1st quarter	719.2	430.3	126.5	80.2	34.8	11.5	4.6	33.1	28.5	157.8	89.4	68.4	707.7
2nd quarter	732.4	437.2	127.0	83.4	35.1	8.6	7.5	39.1	31.7	160.6	90.1	70.6	723.8
3rd quarter	750.2	446.4	131.2	86.7	35.3	9.3	4.9	36.9	32.0	167.6	94.4	73.2	740.9
4th quarter	773.1	460.4	133.8	90.6	35.5	7.6	5.5	39.5	33.9	173.5	98.7	74.8	765.5
1966													
1st quarter	797.3	470.8	144.2	94.4	35.9	13.9	4.4	39.4	35.0	177.9	101.2	76.8	783.5
2nd quarter	807.2	475.9	143.5	96.8	34.4	12.3	5.2	41.5	36.2	182.6	104.0	78.6	794.8
3rd quarter	820.8	485.0	143.2	98.3	33.0	11.9	2.2	40.4	38.2	190.4	109.9	80.5	808.9
4th quarter	834.9	490.8	145.9	99.2	30.2	16.5	3.6	42.4	38.8	194.7	111.1	83.5	818.4
1967													
1st quarter	846.0	495.1	142.8	98.0	29.4	15.4	4.6	44.0	39.4	203.6	117.9	85.7	830.6
2nd quarter	851.1	504.2	137.5	98.3	32.9	6.3	4.5	43.5	39.0	204.8	117.9	87.0	844.7
3rd quarter	866.6	511.4	142.8	98.8	34.8	9.3	2.9	42.4	39.5	209.4	120.9	88.5	857.4
4th quarter	883.2	518.9	147.7	101.7	37.5	8.4	2.2	43.9	41.7	214.4	123.1	91.2	874.8
1968													
1st quarter	911.1	536.9	152.3	105.6	38.3	8.4	1.1	45.5	44.4	220.9	126.3	94.5	902.7
2nd quarter	936.3	550.6	158.9	105.3	39.6	14.1	1.9	47.4	45.4	224.8	127.1	97.7	922.2
3rd quarter	952.3	566.7	155.7	107.6	40.4	7.7	1.3	49.5	48.2	228.6	128.5	100.1	944.7
4th quarter	970.1	575.6	160.8	112.2	42.6	6.0	1.1	49.2	48.2	232.7	129.7	103.0	964.1
1969													
1st quarter	995.4	587.8	172.4	116.0	44.9	11.5	0.2	44.0	43.8	235.0	129.6	105.5	983.9
2nd quarter	1 011.4	599.2	172.7	118.4	45.1	9.2	1.2	53.9	52.7	238.2	129.7	108.5	1 002.1
3rd quarter	1 032.0	609.5	177.6	122.4	45.0	10.2	1.0	53.3	52.4	244.0	133.3	110.6	1 021.8
4th quarter	1 040.7	621.5	171.6	123.3	42.5	5.8	3.3	56.5	53.1	244.3	131.9	112.4	1 035.0
1970													
1st quarter	1 053.5	632.6	168.1	123.8	42.5	1.8	3.4	56.9	53.5	249.4	133.5	115.9	1 051.7
2nd quarter	1 070.1	642.5	171.5	125.0	41.4	5.1	5.4	60.6	55.2	250.7	131.7	119.0	1 065.0
3rd quarter	1 088.5	654.5	173.9	126.3	42.6	5.1	3.8	60.3	56.4	256.2	132.3	123.9	1 083.4
4th quarter	1 091.5	661.2	166.8	123.5	47.2	-4.0	3.2	61.1	57.9	260.4	133.5	126.9	1 095.4
1971													
1st quarter	1 137.8	680.2	189.5	126.3	51.0	12.3	4.4	63.1	58.7	263.7	133.3	130.4	1 125.6
2nd quarter	1 159.4	694.3	197.3	129.5	57.0	10.9	-0.2	63.1	63.3	268.0	134.2	133.8	1 148.5
3rd quarter	1 180.3	706.7	202.1	131.2	60.7	10.2	-0.1	65.4	65.5	271.7	135.5	136.2	1 170.1
4th quarter	1 193.6	722.9	198.4	134.7	64.0	-0.3	-1.7	60.3	61.9	274.0	134.7	139.3	1 193.9
1972													
1st quarter	1 233.8	740.1	213.0	140.6	69.2	3.2	-3.5	68.6	72.2	284.3	141.4	142.9	1 230.6
2nd quarter	1 270.1	758.6	226.8	144.0	70.8	12.0	-4.3	67.2	71.4	289.0	144.6	144.4	1 258.1
3rd quarter	1 293.8	777.1	233.1	147.0	72.4	13.7	-2.6	71.5	74.1	286.3	138.5	147.8	1 280.1
4th quarter	1 332.0	801.9	239.7	155.0	77.3	7.5	-3.1	76.1	79.2	293.5	141.7	151.8	1 324.5
1973													
1st quarter	1 380.7	826.5	254.3	162.8	80.9	10.6	-1.4	84.0	85.4	301.3	145.9	155.4	1 370.1
2nd quarter	1 417.6	842.0	268.2	171.3	78.7	18.2	2.5	91.9	89.5	304.9	146.5	158.4	1 399.4
3rd quarter	1 436.8	860.5	264.3	176.6	77.9	9.8	6.4	97.6	91.1	305.6	143.4	162.2	1 427.1
4th quarter	1 479.1	875.6	280.9	180.1	75.7	25.0	9.0	107.6	98.7	313.7	146.5	167.2	1 454.1
1974													
1st quarter	1 494.7	893.8	268.4	183.4	72.4	12.5	6.4	116.7	110.3	326.1	151.9	174.3	1 482.1
2nd quarter	1 534.2	922.3	277.4	188.8	71.2	17.4	-2.7	126.7	129.4	337.3	154.7	182.5	1 516.8
3rd quarter	1 563.4	951.1	271.0	194.5	70.9	5.6	-7.0	126.6	133.6	348.3	159.5	188.8	1 557.8
4th quarter	1 603.0	960.9	281.3	197.6	63.3	20.4	0.0	136.6	136.6	360.8	166.4	194.4	1 582.6

Table 1-1B. Gross Domestic Product: Historical Data—*Continued*

(Billions of dollars, quarterly data are at seasonally adjusted annual rates.) **NIPA Tables 1.1.5, 1.2.5**

Year and quarter	Gross domestic product	Personal consumption expenditures	Gross private domestic investment				Exports and imports of goods and services			Government consumption expenditures and gross investment			Addendum: Final sales of domestic product
			Total	Fixed investment		Change in private inventories	Net exports	Exports	Imports	Total	Federal	State and local	
				Nonresidential	Residential								
1975													
1st quarter	1 619.6	987.1	244.3	193.1	61.2	-10.0	16.5	141.4	124.9	371.7	167.6	204.1	1 629.6
2nd quarter	1 656.4	1 015.8	243.3	193.3	64.0	-14.0	21.6	136.8	115.2	375.8	169.0	206.8	1 670.4
3rd quarter	1 713.8	1 049.6	265.2	197.8	68.8	-1.4	12.0	134.1	122.1	387.0	174.9	212.1	1 715.2
4th quarter	1 765.9	1 078.5	276.2	202.9	73.0	0.3	13.8	142.5	128.7	397.3	179.7	217.6	1 765.5
1976													
1st quarter	1 824.5	1 112.3	304.6	209.5	80.4	14.7	4.7	143.6	138.9	402.9	180.5	222.4	1 809.8
2nd quarter	1 856.9	1 132.0	322.3	215.0	84.8	22.4	-0.5	146.6	147.1	403.2	182.0	221.2	1 834.5
3rd quarter	1 890.5	1 161.3	328.3	222.6	84.9	20.8	-4.1	151.8	155.8	404.9	183.6	221.3	1 869.7
4th quarter	1 938.4	1 195.1	337.6	230.2	96.9	10.5	-6.6	156.1	162.7	412.3	189.0	223.3	1 927.9
1977													
1st quarter	1 992.5	1 230.6	360.3	243.3	102.2	14.8	-21.1	155.4	176.4	422.7	192.9	229.8	1 977.7
2nd quarter	2 060.2	1 258.5	389.7	253.7	116.5	19.5	-21.1	161.9	183.0	433.1	197.7	235.3	2 040.7
3rd quarter	2 122.4	1 289.7	414.1	263.3	120.0	30.9	-20.6	162.3	182.9	439.1	200.0	239.1	2 091.5
4th quarter	2 168.7	1 327.9	422.3	275.9	122.2	24.1	-29.6	157.8	187.4	448.1	204.5	243.6	2 144.6
1978													
1st quarter	2 208.7	1 357.8	434.8	282.4	126.9	25.5	-38.7	164.6	203.3	454.8	207.7	247.1	2 183.2
2nd quarter	2 336.6	1 415.3	470.6	309.3	137.0	24.3	-22.6	186.2	208.8	473.3	214.8	258.5	2 312.3
3rd quarter	2 398.9	1 446.2	492.4	325.1	142.3	25.0	-23.8	191.3	215.1	484.0	218.6	265.4	2 373.9
4th quarter	2 482.2	1 485.4	515.8	341.4	145.8	28.5	-16.4	205.4	221.8	497.4	225.8	271.7	2 453.7
1979													
1st quarter	2 531.6	1 521.0	525.8	356.7	145.3	23.9	-18.2	211.7	229.8	502.9	229.1	273.8	2 507.7
2nd quarter	2 595.9	1 561.5	539.3	364.3	147.6	27.4	-22.2	220.9	243.1	517.3	234.9	282.4	2 568.5
3rd quarter	2 670.4	1 616.0	545.6	383.0	150.5	12.1	-23.0	234.3	257.3	531.8	238.6	293.0	2 658.3
4th quarter	2 730.7	1 659.5	547.9	391.3	148.0	8.6	-26.8	253.7	280.5	550.2	248.1	302.1	2 722.2
1980													
1st quarter	2 796.5	1 706.5	554.6	404.5	140.2	9.9	-35.8	268.5	304.3	571.2	259.7	311.6	2 786.6
2nd quarter	2 799.9	1 708.9	519.3	394.7	116.9	7.8	-15.2	277.4	292.6	586.9	271.0	315.9	2 792.2
3rd quarter	2 860.0	1 767.7	495.1	405.7	123.2	-33.9	5.5	284.7	279.2	591.8	272.0	319.8	2 893.9
4th quarter	2 993.5	1 835.4	551.5	422.8	137.8	-9.1	-6.7	292.5	299.2	613.4	286.8	326.6	3 002.6
1981													
1st quarter	3 131.8	1 890.7	619.4	443.0	137.6	38.8	-14.3	305.5	319.7	636.0	296.5	339.4	3 093.0
2nd quarter	3 167.3	1 921.9	609.8	462.9	135.3	11.7	-13.5	308.5	322.0	649.0	309.4	339.6	3 155.5
3rd quarter	3 261.2	1 961.2	652.3	482.1	126.2	44.0	-7.6	302.3	309.9	655.2	312.5	342.7	3 217.2
4th quarter	3 283.5	1 976.1	643.4	503.8	114.8	24.8	-14.8	304.7	319.4	678.8	328.5	350.3	3 258.7
1982													
1st quarter	3 273.8	2 014.4	588.3	500.1	109.7	-21.5	-16.3	293.2	309.5	687.4	332.5	354.9	3 295.3
2nd quarter	3 331.3	2 041.1	593.6	490.1	107.7	-4.2	-4.4	294.7	299.1	701.0	339.5	361.5	3 335.4
3rd quarter	3 367.1	2 089.2	593.0	478.7	108.4	5.8	-29.6	279.6	309.3	714.5	347.6	366.9	3 361.3
4th quarter	3 407.8	2 150.9	549.2	471.5	117.5	-39.8	-29.6	265.3	294.9	737.2	362.9	374.4	3 447.6
1983													
1st quarter	3 480.3	2 190.6	565.5	462.1	138.5	-35.1	-24.5	270.7	295.3	748.8	370.1	378.7	3 515.4
2nd quarter	3 583.8	2 254.5	613.8	466.4	155.0	-7.7	-45.4	272.5	318.0	761.0	378.8	382.2	3 591.5
3rd quarter	3 692.3	2 324.3	652.3	485.4	171.1	-4.2	-65.2	278.2	343.4	780.9	391.7	389.2	3 696.5
4th quarter	3 796.1	2 376.7	718.5	514.7	179.9	23.9	-71.4	286.6	358.0	772.3	380.1	392.2	3 772.2
1984													
1st quarter	3 912.8	2 422.8	790.9	531.5	186.4	73.0	-95.0	293.0	388.0	794.2	391.1	403.0	3 839.8
2nd quarter	4 015.0	2 481.2	818.9	558.3	191.3	69.3	-104.3	302.2	406.5	819.2	406.9	412.2	3 945.7
3rd quarter	4 087.4	2 519.7	838.9	576.6	190.9	71.3	-103.8	305.7	409.6	832.7	409.5	423.2	4 016.0
4th quarter	4 147.6	2 568.9	831.7	590.9	192.9	48.0	-107.8	308.6	416.4	854.7	423.0	431.7	4 099.6
1985													
1st quarter	4 237.0	2 643.9	809.9	599.4	194.2	16.2	-91.3	306.0	397.3	874.5	432.2	442.3	4 220.8
2nd quarter	4 302.3	2 691.2	827.0	609.1	196.3	21.6	-114.4	304.1	418.6	898.5	443.8	454.7	4 280.7
3rd quarter	4 394.6	2 764.7	822.2	604.4	201.4	16.3	-116.9	297.3	414.2	924.6	458.7	465.9	4 378.3
4th quarter	4 453.1	2 700.0	859.5	618.1	208.4	33.1	-133.4	305.4	438.9	936.1	462.4	473.7	4 420.0
1986													
1st quarter	4 516.3	2 834.7	863.5	613.5	219.5	30.4	-126.0	313.4	439.4	944.2	459.7	484.4	4 485.9
2nd quarter	4 555.2	2 863.0	855.2	605.0	234.6	15.7	-128.9	315.1	444.0	965.8	474.5	491.3	4 539.6
3rd quarter	4 619.6	2 929.7	835.8	602.0	240.9	-7.0	-139.0	320.5	459.4	993.0	492.9	500.2	4 626.6
4th quarter	4 669.4	2 966.1	842.1	610.6	244.3	-12.8	-133.6	335.0	468.6	994.8	486.4	508.4	4 682.2
1987													
1st quarter	4 736.2	2 998.3	871.2	596.6	246.7	28.0	-141.2	336.5	477.7	1 008.0	489.6	518.4	4 708.3
2nd quarter	4 821.5	3 068.8	874.6	608.4	249.7	16.5	-147.0	355.4	502.3	1 025.0	499.2	525.9	4 804.9
3rd quarter	4 900.5	3 133.5	876.5	625.5	250.0	1.0	-145.5	371.9	517.3	1 036.0	502.2	533.7	4 899.5
4th quarter	5 022.7	3 167.6	946.5	630.5	252.8	63.1	-145.4	392.1	537.5	1 054.0	509.8	544.2	4 959.6
1988													
1st quarter	5 090.6	3 249.0	908.6	641.5	250.1	17.0	-124.0	418.7	542.7	1 057.0	504.0	553.0	5 073.7
2nd quarter	5 207.7	3 309.0	934.5	659.4	255.5	19.6	-106.6	439.5	546.1	1 070.8	505.4	565.4	5 188.1
3rd quarter	5 299.5	3 378.3	942.0	666.3	257.5	18.2	-99.3	453.6	552.8	1 078.4	505.8	572.6	5 281.3
4th quarter	5 412.7	3 451.3	962.8	681.9	261.7	19.1	-107.7	466.6	574.3	1 106.4	520.0	586.4	5 393.6
1989													
1st quarter	5 527.4	3 506.1	1 005.4	696.3	260.9	48.1	-101.0	485.2	586.2	1 116.9	517.5	599.3	5 479.2
2nd quarter	5 628.4	3 569.5	1 001.0	708.9	255.8	36.3	-88.2	507.2	595.4	1 146.1	531.8	614.3	5 592.2
3rd quarter	5 711.6	3 625.6	996.5	731.2	255.5	9.8	-75.1	509.4	584.4	1 164.6	538.5	626.1	5 701.7
4th quarter	5 763.4	3 670.1	995.9	727.5	251.9	16.6	-82.8	515.4	598.2	1 180.2	537.7	642.5	5 746.9
1990													
1st quarter	5 890.8	3 754.5	1 010.8	740.9	256.0	14.0	-88.5	538.2	626.8	1 214.0	552.6	661.4	5 876.9
2nd quarter	5 974.7	3 800.2	1 014.8	734.2	246.9	33.7	-68.8	545.9	614.8	1 228.6	559.5	669.1	5 941.0
3rd quarter	6 029.5	3 863.4	1 000.7	744.3	234.5	21.9	-75.0	555.1	630.1	1 240.4	558.0	682.4	6 007.6
4th quarter	6 023.3	3 884.4	947.6	737.6	221.3	-11.3	-79.1	568.2	647.3	1 270.4	570.0	700.5	6 034.7

Table 1-1B. Gross Domestic Product: Historical Data—*Continued*

(Billions of dollars, quarterly data are at seasonally adjusted annual rates.)   **NIPA Tables 1.1.5, 1.2.5**

Year and quarter	Gross domestic product	Personal consumption expenditures	Gross private domestic investment				Exports and imports of goods and services			Government consumption expenditures and gross investment			Addendum: Final sales of domestic product
			Total	Fixed investment		Change in private inventories	Net exports	Exports	Imports	Total	Federal	State and local	
				Nonresidential	Residential								
1991													
1st quarter	6 054.9	3 890.2	924.6	729.8	210.3	-15.5	-47.1	573.2	620.3	1 287.2	582.9	704.3	6 070.4
2nd quarter	6 143.6	3 943.7	926.6	726.8	217.8	-18.0	-23.2	590.7	613.9	1 296.6	585.5	711.1	6 161.6
3rd quarter	6 218.4	3 989.6	947.5	720.1	226.5	0.8	-21.1	600.6	621.7	1 302.4	580.9	721.5	6 217.6
4th quarter	6 279.3	4 017.1	978.8	717.6	230.1	31.1	-23.1	615.2	638.3	1 306.5	573.7	732.9	6 248.2
1992													
1st quarter	6 380.8	4 117.7	956.8	714.2	242.4	0.2	-20.5	625.3	645.8	1 326.9	578.6	748.3	6 380.6
2nd quarter	6 492.3	4 173.4	1 013.1	736.7	253.2	23.2	-32.8	626.2	659.0	1 338.7	582.2	756.5	6 469.1
3rd quarter	6 586.5	4 245.4	1 024.2	748.6	255.1	20.5	-38.5	639.4	677.9	1 355.4	592.7	762.8	6 566.0
4th quarter	6 697.6	4 326.2	1 058.0	768.3	268.3	21.3	-47.1	641.4	688.5	1 360.5	593.0	767.5	6 676.2
1993													
1st quarter	6 748.2	4 368.5	1 083.9	776.6	271.4	35.9	-55.7	643.6	699.3	1 351.5	577.0	774.5	6 712.2
2nd quarter	6 829.6	4 437.5	1 094.5	792.4	278.0	24.1	-63.2	653.1	716.3	1 360.9	575.6	785.3	6 805.5
3rd quarter	6 904.2	4 506.0	1 095.9	798.4	290.9	6.6	-68.4	650.9	719.3	1 370.6	578.9	791.7	6 897.6
4th quarter	7 032.8	4 572.0	1 153.0	829.5	306.9	16.6	-73.4	671.6	745.0	1 381.3	582.0	799.3	7 016.2
1994													
1st quarter	7 136.3	4 640.9	1 202.1	841.1	315.6	45.4	-80.6	681.2	761.8	1 373.9	564.4	809.5	7 090.9
2nd quarter	7 269.8	4 702.9	1 265.1	855.7	327.9	81.4	-90.6	707.0	797.6	1 392.4	569.0	823.4	7 188.4
3rd quarter	7 352.3	4 773.1	1 251.6	871.9	326.4	53.2	-96.9	736.9	833.8	1 424.4	584.0	840.5	7 299.0
4th quarter	7 476.7	4 847.2	1 307.2	906.6	325.4	75.1	-101.9	758.6	860.6	1 424.2	573.4	850.8	7 401.5
1995													
1st quarter	7 545.3	4 883.3	1 327.3	944.3	321.8	61.2	-105.3	781.6	886.9	1 440.0	577.6	862.4	7 484.1
2nd quarter	7 604.9	4 955.0	1 303.8	956.6	313.5	33.8	-109.5	798.9	908.3	1 455.6	579.7	875.9	7 571.2
3rd quarter	7 706.5	5 020.5	1 303.2	965.5	326.4	11.3	-74.4	831.4	905.8	1 457.3	576.9	880.4	7 695.2
4th quarter	7 799.5	5 077.9	1 335.6	982.5	334.6	18.4	-69.8	839.4	909.2	1 455.7	567.3	888.5	7 781.1
1996													
1st quarter	7 893.1	5 153.8	1 355.2	1 003.6	344.7	6.9	-88.8	847.9	936.7	1 472.9	577.2	895.8	7 886.3
2nd quarter	8 061.5	5 244.1	1 418.6	1 026.6	361.4	30.5	-93.7	859.0	952.8	1 492.5	582.5	910.0	8 031.0
3rd quarter	8 159.0	5 298.3	1 474.4	1 059.1	364.3	51.1	-114.2	859.6	973.8	1 500.5	576.9	923.6	8 108.0
4th quarter	8 287.1	5 376.1	1 480.0	1 083.5	361.8	34.7	-88.8	903.8	992.6	1 519.8	576.3	943.6	8 252.4
1997													
1st quarter	8 402.1	5 456.7	1 522.0	1 106.8	365.4	49.8	-108.8	918.4	1 027.2	1 532.2	572.1	960.1	8 352.3
2nd quarter	8 551.9	5 495.1	1 589.9	1 129.2	372.3	88.4	-85.2	954.5	1 039.7	1 552.2	585.7	966.5	8 463.6
3rd quarter	8 691.8	5 603.5	1 625.3	1 178.4	379.0	67.9	-96.8	974.1	1 070.9	1 559.8	585.4	974.4	8 623.8
4th quarter	8 788.3	5 687.6	1 645.3	1 181.9	385.8	77.7	-117.0	968.3	1 085.3	1 572.4	586.5	985.9	8 710.7
1998													
1st quarter	8 889.7	5 745.9	1 712.3	1 212.4	394.8	105.1	-135.2	963.0	1 098.2	1 566.7	571.5	995.3	8 784.6
2nd quarter	8 994.7	5 857.8	1 694.8	1 246.1	411.3	37.3	-162.3	947.3	1 109.6	1 604.4	586.6	1 017.8	8 957.4
3rd quarter	9 146.5	5 952.8	1 739.8	1 259.8	427.6	52.4	-174.6	935.3	1 109.9	1 628.6	584.7	1 043.8	9 094.1
4th quarter	9 325.7	6 055.5	1 794.4	1 292.9	441.5	60.0	-178.7	966.3	1 145.0	1 654.3	593.6	1 060.8	9 265.6
1999													
1st quarter	9 447.1	6 129.0	1 850.6	1 319.9	447.4	83.4	-208.5	961.6	1 170.1	1 676.0	594.5	1 081.5	9 363.7
2nd quarter	9 557.0	6 253.0	1 845.8	1 351.4	459.3	35.1	-245.4	972.8	1 218.2	1 703.7	601.1	1 102.6	9 521.9
3rd quarter	9 712.3	6 357.2	1 890.9	1 383.8	466.6	40.5	-276.1	1 002.4	1 278.5	1 740.2	614.6	1 125.6	9 671.8
4th quarter	9 926.1	6 488.9	1 949.4	1 391.4	473.8	84.2	-296.5	1 031.2	1 327.7	1 784.2	631.6	1 152.7	9 841.9
2000													
1st quarter	10 031.0	6 642.7	1 945.9	1 445.5	484.2	16.2	-352.8	1 054.0	1 406.8	1 795.1	618.1	1 177.0	10 014.9
2nd quarter	10 278.3	6 737.3	2 071.8	1 494.7	486.6	90.4	-359.6	1 092.7	1 452.3	1 828.9	639.3	1 189.6	10 187.9
3rd quarter	10 357.4	6 845.1	2 055.8	1 515.5	483.1	57.2	-388.5	1 125.2	1 513.7	1 845.0	636.2	1 208.9	10 300.2
4th quarter	10 472.3	6 944.4	2 061.6	1 519.4	487.8	54.3	-402.4	1 115.4	1 517.8	1 868.7	636.1	1 232.6	10 417.9
2001													
1st quarter	10 508.1	7 020.4	1 967.5	1 501.5	496.7	-30.6	-391.7	1 096.7	1 488.4	1 911.9	652.5	1 259.4	10 538.8
2nd quarter	10 638.4	7 072.1	1 967.0	1 467.6	511.0	-11.6	-359.3	1 054.6	1 413.9	1 958.6	666.4	1 292.3	10 649.9
3rd quarter	10 639.5	7 103.4	1 937.3	1 445.0	522.4	-30.1	-366.7	998.5	1 365.2	1 965.5	674.9	1 290.6	10 669.6
4th quarter	10 701.3	7 216.6	1 842.7	1 401.5	522.1	-80.8	-357.0	957.1	1 314.1	1 999.1	683.3	1 315.8	10 782.1
2002													
1st quarter	10 834.4	7 251.4	1 910.0	1 371.9	538.3	-0.2	-375.3	973.3	1 348.6	2 048.3	714.4	1 333.9	10 834.7
2nd quarter	10 934.8	7 344.5	1 925.6	1 351.6	554.8	19.1	-416.0	1 007.5	1 423.5	2 080.6	733.1	1 347.6	10 915.6
3rd quarter	11 037.1	7 433.1	1 927.9	1 343.7	558.9	25.3	-431.6	1 021.6	1 453.2	2 107.7	746.2	1 361.6	11 011.8
4th quarter	11 103.8	7 507.2	1 936.5	1 328.4	578.3	29.8	-483.0	1 007.6	1 490.6	2 143.1	768.8	1 374.2	11 074.0
2003													
1st quarter	11 230.1	7 593.5	1 960.2	1 327.8	601.4	31.0	-501.6	1 011.5	1 513.1	2 178.0	789.3	1 388.7	11 199.1
2nd quarter	11 370.7	7 684.6	1 970.5	1 359.1	611.9	-0.4	-501.4	1 012.3	1 513.7	2 216.9	831.4	1 385.5	11 371.0
3rd quarter	11 625.1	7 845.5	2 048.3	1 388.5	651.6	8.1	-499.9	1 042.5	1 542.4	2 231.2	830.5	1 400.8	11 617.0
4th quarter	11 816.8	7 938.5	2 132.8	1 411.5	682.9	38.4	-511.7	1 094.8	1 606.5	2 257.3	848.1	1 409.3	11 778.4
2004													
1st quarter	11 988.4	8 076.8	2 155.2	1 400.3	706.0	48.9	-546.6	1 141.3	1 687.9	2 303.1	872.5	1 430.6	11 939.5
2nd quarter	12 181.4	8 186.3	2 259.5	1 440.2	743.1	76.2	-608.0	1 172.3	1 780.3	2 343.6	886.7	1 456.8	12 105.2
3rd quarter	12 367.7	8 312.7	2 311.3	1 485.6	763.4	62.3	-638.0	1 186.0	1 824.0	2 381.8	906.9	1 474.9	12 305.5
4th quarter	12 562.2	8 464.3	2 380.8	1 526.5	786.2	68.0	-684.0	1 226.4	1 910.5	2 401.2	903.3	1 497.9	12 494.1
2005													
1st quarter	12 813.7	8 573.1	2 475.2	1 560.5	815.1	99.5	-676.8	1 268.2	1 945.0	2 442.2	931.2	1 511.0	12 714.2
2nd quarter	12 974.1	8 723.9	2 469.5	1 595.2	843.7	30.6	-689.1	1 300.1	1 989.2	2 469.7	938.2	1 531.5	12 943.5
3rd quarter	13 205.4	8 888.1	2 527.2	1 633.8	875.5	17.9	-731.4	1 310.9	2 042.3	2 521.6	963.1	1 558.4	13 187.5
4th quarter	13 381.6	8 991.3	2 636.5	1 656.4	889.9	90.2	-787.5	1 356.4	2 143.9	2 541.3	952.8	1 588.5	13 291.4
2006													
1st quarter	13 648.9	9 134.3	2 699.7	1 729.4	895.9	74.4	-777.2	1 417.2	2 194.4	2 592.2	995.3	1 596.9	13 574.5
2nd quarter	13 799.8	9 253.7	2 697.0	1 761.0	858.7	77.3	-781.6	1 463.4	2 245.0	2 630.7	998.7	1 631.9	13 722.5
3rd quarter	13 908.5	9 374.3	2 684.4	1 793.6	813.7	77.1	-805.6	1 480.1	2 285.7	2 655.4	1 000.4	1 655.0	13 831.4
4th quarter	14 066.4	9 453.6	2 641.6	1 821.2	781.3	39.1	-719.4	1 544.5	2 263.9	2 690.6	1 013.5	1 677.0	14 027.3

Table 1-1B. Gross Domestic Product: Historical Data—*Continued*

(Billions of dollars, quarterly data are at seasonally adjusted annual rates.)
NIPA Tables 1.1.5, 1.2.5

Year and quarter	Gross domestic product	Personal consumption expenditures	Gross private domestic investment				Exports and imports of goods and services			Government consumption expenditures and gross investment			Addendum: Final sales of domestic product
			Total	Fixed investment		Change in private inventories	Net exports	Exports	Imports	Total	Federal	State and local	
				Nonresidential	Residential								
2007													
1st quarter	14 233.2	9 591.9	2 634.2	1 864.7	749.3	20.2	-728.5	1 580.5	2 308.9	2 735.6	1 018.3	1 717.3	14 213.1
2nd quarter	14 422.3	9 700.9	2 671.9	1 907.5	717.3	47.1	-733.0	1 625.1	2 358.0	2 782.5	1 040.8	1 741.7	14 375.2
3rd quarter	14 569.7	9 799.2	2 658.2	1 937.9	671.7	48.6	-712.1	1 687.5	2 399.6	2 824.3	1 063.9	1 760.5	14 521.0
4th quarter	14 685.3	9 910.0	2 610.6	1 972.3	616.4	21.9	-700.6	1 765.4	2 466.0	2 865.3	1 076.1	1 789.1	14 663.4
2008													
1st quarter	14 668.4	9 974.4	2 527.0	1 981.6	565.5	-20.1	-756.8	1 814.6	2 571.4	2 923.8	1 110.7	1 813.1	14 688.6
2nd quarter	14 813.0	10 095.8	2 493.3	1 978.7	538.4	-23.9	-759.4	1 920.5	2 679.9	2 983.4	1 140.5	1 842.9	14 836.9
3rd quarter	14 843.0	10 124.9	2 435.9	1 947.3	507.4	-18.8	-773.6	1 923.6	2 697.2	3 055.9	1 180.0	1 875.9	14 861.8
4th quarter	14 549.9	9 859.6	2 243.1	1 856.2	452.1	-65.1	-602.4	1 709.1	2 311.6	3 049.7	1 191.2	1 858.5	14 615.1
2009													
1st quarter	14 383.9	9 770.2	1 972.1	1 712.3	405.5	-145.6	-393.9	1 519.5	1 913.4	3 035.4	1 182.2	1 853.1	14 529.5
2nd quarter	14 340.4	9 769.8	1 825.9	1 637.5	376.3	-187.9	-341.7	1 522.7	1 864.5	3 086.5	1 214.6	1 871.9	14 528.3
3rd quarter	14 384.1	9 890.8	1 786.4	1 600.3	392.0	-205.9	-405.6	1 596.4	2 002.0	3 112.5	1 233.2	1 879.3	14 590.1
4th quarter	14 566.5	9 957.1	1 928.0	1 583.6	395.2	-50.8	-440.6	1 712.3	2 152.9	3 122.0	1 240.7	1 881.3	14 617.3
2010													
1st quarter	14 681.1	10 044.5	1 989.5	1 594.4	383.1	12.1	-488.7	1 753.2	2 241.9	3 135.7	1 269.2	1 866.5	14 669.0
2nd quarter	14 888.6	10 137.7	2 092.7	1 641.8	400.8	50.1	-523.2	1 814.0	2 337.3	3 181.5	1 304.6	1 876.9	14 838.5
3rd quarter	15 057.7	10 233.4	2 164.6	1 677.4	365.6	121.5	-535.0	1 869.8	2 404.9	3 194.7	1 321.6	1 873.1	14 936.1
4th quarter	15 230.2	10 393.2	2 156.5	1 719.3	374.7	62.4	-503.7	1 972.2	2 475.9	3 184.2	1 320.1	1 864.2	15 167.8
2011													
1st quarter	15 238.4	10 523.5	2 123.5	1 722.4	374.8	26.3	-562.5	2 033.3	2 595.8	3 153.8	1 298.1	1 855.8	15 212.1
2nd quarter	15 460.9	10 651.4	2 212.7	1 768.5	381.1	63.0	-586.9	2 108.3	2 695.3	3 183.8	1 314.9	1 869.0	15 397.9
3rd quarter	15 587.1	10 754.5	2 228.2	1 854.5	388.6	-14.9	-572.4	2 142.9	2 715.3	3 176.8	1 305.9	1 870.9	15 602.0
4th quarter	15 785.3	10 827.9	2 395.2	1 902.9	399.6	92.6	-598.1	2 141.0	2 739.1	3 160.4	1 294.9	1 865.5	15 692.7
2012													
1st quarter	15 973.9	10 956.2	2 460.8	1 971.5	423.8	65.4	-614.7	2 169.6	2 784.3	3 171.6	1 300.5	1 871.0	15 908.4
2nd quarter	16 121.9	11 008.3	2 534.8	2 016.2	429.4	89.3	-580.9	2 199.8	2 780.7	3 159.6	1 293.7	1 865.9	16 032.6
3rd quarter	16 227.9	11 073.6	2 529.9	2 011.7	444.1	74.1	-535.2	2 209.4	2 744.5	3 159.6	1 297.0	1 862.6	16 153.9
4th quarter	16 297.3	11 164.3	2 521.3	2 031.2	471.7	18.4	-531.8	2 214.0	2 745.8	3 143.5	1 278.9	1 864.6	16 278.9
2013													
1st quarter	16 475.4	11 256.7	2 617.6	2 058.3	495.7	63.6	-519.5	2 242.2	2 761.7	3 120.7	1 245.3	1 875.4	16 411.8
2nd quarter	16 541.4	11 284.5	2 658.1	2 077.1	516.5	64.5	-514.7	2 253.1	2 767.8	3 113.4	1 231.4	1 882.0	16 476.8
3rd quarter	16 749.3	11 379.1	2 750.8	2 094.2	531.1	125.5	-492.9	2 274.1	2 767.0	3 112.3	1 220.2	1 892.1	16 623.8
4th quarter	16 999.9	11 524.4	2 798.6	2 147.9	534.8	115.9	-440.9	2 337.1	2 777.9	3 117.7	1 220.9	1 896.8	16 883.9
2014													
1st quarter	17 031.3	11 640.2	2 780.7	2 194.7	542.2	43.8	-516.4	2 340.0	2 856.4	3 126.9	1 216.6	1 910.3	16 987.5
2nd quarter	17 320.9	11 791.9	2 895.0	2 251.5	560.8	82.7	-512.7	2 391.3	2 903.9	3 146.6	1 215.5	1 931.2	17 238.2
3rd quarter	17 622.3	11 941.1	2 992.0	2 316.0	577.4	98.6	-489.1	2 389.0	2 878.1	3 178.2	1 228.3	1 949.9	17 523.7
4th quarter	17 735.9	12 081.4	2 997.9	2 310.9	600.2	86.8	-519.8	2 374.4	2 894.2	3 176.5	1 212.2	1 964.2	17 649.1
2015													
1st quarter	17 874.7	12 142.2	3 094.6	2 328.6	617.4	148.6	-538.2	2 289.0	2 827.3	3 176.2	1 218.7	1 957.5	17 726.1
2nd quarter	18 093.2	12 284.2	3 096.3	2 343.2	635.0	118.1	-507.1	2 303.9	2 811.0	3 219.8	1 224.9	1 994.8	17 975.1
3rd quarter	18 227.7	12 407.8	3 115.7	2 353.5	656.5	105.7	-530.8	2 256.6	2 787.4	3 235.0	1 222.6	2 012.5	18 122.0
4th quarter	18 287.2	12 494.9	3 067.7	2 319.7	672.6	75.4	-520.1	2 210.1	2 730.2	3 244.7	1 229.9	2 014.8	18 211.8
2016													
1st quarter	18 325.2	12 571.5	3 031.6	2 291.2	698.3	42.2	-526.2	2 166.5	2 692.8	3 248.3	1 227.9	2 020.4	18 283.0
2nd quarter	18 538.0	12 755.0	3 023.1	2 311.2	699.7	12.2	-501.6	2 201.8	2 703.4	3 261.5	1 228.2	2 033.3	18 525.9
3rd quarter	18 729.1	12 899.4	3 048.0	2 329.1	702.4	16.5	-492.8	2 248.4	2 741.3	3 274.6	1 234.6	2 040.0	18 712.7
4th quarter	18 905.5	13 056.9	3 126.2	2 333.7	723.0	69.5	-564.3	2 241.5	2 805.8	3 286.8	1 235.4	2 051.4	18 836.1

Table 1-2A. Real Gross Domestic Product: Recent Data

(Billions of chained [2009] dollars, quarterly data are at seasonally adjusted annual rates.)   **NIPA Tables 1.1.6, 1.2.6**

Year and quarter	Gross domestic product	Personal consumption expenditures	Gross private domestic investment				Exports and imports of goods and services			Government consumption expenditures and gross investment			Residual	Addendum: final sales of domestic product
			Total	Fixed investment		Change in private inventories	Net exports	Exports	Imports	Total	Federal	State and local		
				Nonresidential	Residential									
1955	2 739.0	1 637.3	337.7	. . .	. . .	. . .	. . .	74.1	92.9	901.0	. . .	. . .	-118.2	2 733.9
1956	2 797.4	1 685.1	336.8	. . .	. . .	. . .	. . .	86.3	100.4	903.2	. . .	. . .	-113.6	2 800.5
1957	2 856.3	1 726.8	324.2	. . .	. . .	. . .	. . .	93.9	104.7	944.8	. . .	. . .	-128.7	2 874.7
1958	2 835.3	1 741.7	300.6	. . .	. . .	. . .	. . .	81.2	109.6	976.7	. . .	. . .	-155.3	2 858.6
1959	3 031.0	1 840.5	358.4	. . .	. . .	. . .	. . .	89.5	121.2	1 000.9	. . .	. . .	-137.1	3 031.9
1960	3 108.7	1 891.0	359.7	. . .	. . .	. . .	. . .	105.1	122.8	1 007.0	. . .	. . .	-131.3	3 114.1
1961	3 188.1	1 929.9	360.9	. . .	. . .	. . .	. . .	105.6	122.0	1 060.6	. . .	. . .	-146.9	3 195.7
1962	3 383.1	2 025.4	403.8	. . .	. . .	. . .	. . .	111.0	135.8	1 129.5	. . .	. . .	-150.8	3 374.4
1963	3 530.4	2 108.8	431.2	. . .	. . .	. . .	. . .	118.9	139.5	1 157.1	. . .	. . .	-146.1	3 525.3
1964	3 734.0	2 234.4	465.2	. . .	. . .	. . .	. . .	132.9	146.9	1 185.9	. . .	. . .	-137.5	3 734.8
1965	3 976.7	2 376.0	529.6	. . .	. . .	. . .	. . .	136.6	162.5	1 224.2	. . .	. . .	-127.2	3 955.2
1966	4 238.9	2 510.6	577.1	. . .	. . .	. . .	. . .	146.0	186.7	1 331.0	. . .	. . .	-139.1	4 196.9
1967	4 355.2	2 585.6	556.9	. . .	. . .	. . .	. . .	149.4	200.3	1 436.4	. . .	. . .	-172.8	4 334.1
1968	4 569.0	2 734.0	590.2	. . .	. . .	. . .	. . .	161.2	230.1	1 485.7	. . .	. . .	-172.0	4 553.4
1969	4 712.5	2 836.2	623.1	. . .	. . .	. . .	. . .	169.0	243.2	1 488.0	. . .	. . .	-160.6	4 697.7
1970	4 722.0	2 903.0	585.2	. . .	. . .	. . .	. . .	187.0	253.6	1 457.7	. . .	. . .	-157.3	4 740.5
1971	4 877.6	3 013.8	645.5	. . .	. . .	. . .	. . .	190.3	267.1	1 431.0	. . .	. . .	-135.9	4 870.6
1972	5 134.3	3 198.7	718.2	. . .	. . .	. . .	. . .	205.1	297.2	1 424.2	. . .	. . .	-114.7	5 126.0
1973	5 424.1	3 357.2	796.8	. . .	. . .	. . .	. . .	243.8	311.0	1 419.6	. . .	. . .	-82.3	5 392.4
1974	5 396.0	3 329.5	744.0	. . .	. . .	. . .	. . .	263.0	303.9	1 451.8	. . .	. . .	-88.4	5 378.4
1975	5 385.4	3 405.1	623.5	. . .	. . .	. . .	. . .	261.4	270.1	1 483.8	. . .	. . .	-118.3	5 434.6
1976	5 675.4	3 595.0	742.5	. . .	. . .	. . .	. . .	272.8	323.0	1 491.6	. . .	. . .	-103.5	5 651.9
1977	5 937.0	3 746.5	848.4	. . .	. . .	. . .	. . .	279.4	358.3	1 509.2	. . .	. . .	-88.2	5 900.9
1978	6 267.2	3 911.2	946.6	. . .	. . .	. . .	. . .	308.8	389.3	1 553.7	. . .	. . .	-63.8	6 225.5
1979	6 466.2	4 004.1	979.8	. . .	. . .	. . .	. . .	339.4	395.8	1 582.6	. . .	. . .	-43.9	6 450.3
1980	6 450.4	3 991.5	881.2	. . .	. . .	. . .	. . .	376.0	369.5	1 612.5	. . .	. . .	-41.3	6 492.1
1981	6 617.7	4 050.8	958.7	. . .	. . .	. . .	. . .	380.6	379.3	1 628.0	. . .	. . .	-21.1	6 587.0
1982	6 491.3	4 108.4	833.7	. . .	. . .	. . .	. . .	351.5	374.5	1 658.0	. . .	. . .	-85.8	6 546.7
1983	6 792.0	4 342.6	911.5	. . .	. . .	. . .	. . .	342.5	421.7	1 721.6	. . .	. . .	-104.5	6 830.6
1984	7 285.0	4 571.6	1 160.3	. . .	. . .	. . .	. . .	370.4	524.4	1 783.2	. . .	. . .	-76.1	7 196.3
1985	7 593.8	4 811.9	1 159.5	. . .	. . .	. . .	. . .	382.8	558.4	1 904.0	. . .	. . .	-106.0	7 581.7
1986	7 860.5	5 014.0	1 161.3	. . .	. . .	. . .	. . .	412.2	606.1	2 007.7	. . .	. . .	-128.6	7 872.6
1987	8 132.6	5 183.6	1 194.4	. . .	. . .	. . .	. . .	457.1	642.0	2 066.9	. . .	. . .	-127.4	8 113.1
1988	8 474.5	5 400.5	1 223.8	. . .	. . .	. . .	. . .	531.2	667.2	2 094.8	. . .	. . .	-108.6	8 466.9
1989	8 786.4	5 558.1	1 273.4	. . .	. . .	. . .	. . .	592.7	696.6	2 155.1	. . .	. . .	-96.3	8 765.5
1990	8 955.0	5 672.6	1 240.6	. . .	. . .	. . .	. . .	645.0	721.5	2 224.3	. . .	. . .	-106.0	8 952.7
1991	8 948.4	5 685.6	1 158.8	. . .	. . .	. . .	. . .	687.6	720.4	2 250.9	. . .	. . .	-114.1	8 968.6
1992	9 266.6	5 896.5	1 243.7	. . .	. . .	. . .	. . .	735.3	771.0	2 262.1	. . .	. . .	-100.0	9 262.5
1993	9 521.0	6 101.4	1 343.1	. . .	. . .	. . .	. . .	759.4	837.6	2 243.3	. . .	. . .	-88.6	9 511.0
1994	9 905.4	6 338.0	1 502.3	. . .	. . .	. . .	. . .	826.5	937.5	2 245.5	. . .	. . .	-69.4	9 837.7
1995	10 174.8	6 527.6	1 550.8	. . .	. . .	. . .	. . .	911.5	1 012.5	2 257.5	. . .	. . .	-60.1	10 151.3
1996	10 561.0	6 755.6	1 686.7	. . .	. . .	. . .	. . .	986.0	1 100.6	2 279.2	. . .	. . .	-45.9	10 536.6
1997	11 034.9	7 009.9	1 879.0	. . .	. . .	. . .	. . .	1 103.5	1 248.8	2 322.0	. . .	. . .	-30.7	10 956.0
1998	11 525.9	7 384.7	2 058.3	. . .	. . .	. . .	. . .	1 129.3	1 394.8	2 370.5	. . .	. . .	-22.1	11 452.3
1999	12 065.9	7 775.9	2 231.4	1 510.1	633.8	75.5	-377.1	1 159.1	1 536.2	2 451.7	815.3	1 643.6	-112.4	11 994.9
2000	12 559.7	8 170.7	2 375.5	1 647.7	637.9	66.2	-477.8	1 258.4	1 736.2	2 498.2	817.7	1 689.1	-83.6	12 494.9
2001	12 682.2	8 382.6	2 231.4	1 608.4	643.7	-46.2	-502.1	1 184.9	1 687.0	2 592.4	849.8	1 751.5	-90.9	12 729.6
2002	12 908.8	8 598.8	2 218.2	1 498.0	682.7	22.5	-584.3	1 164.5	1 748.8	2 705.8	910.8	1 802.4	-70.5	12 888.9
2003	13 271.1	8 867.6	2 308.7	1 526.1	744.5	22.6	-641.9	1 185.0	1 826.9	2 764.3	973.0	1 795.3	-45.5	13 249.0
2004	13 773.5	9 208.2	2 511.3	1 605.4	818.9	71.4	-734.8	1 300.6	2 035.3	2 808.2	1 017.1	1 792.8	-19.6	13 702.2
2005	14 234.2	9 531.8	2 672.6	1 717.4	872.6	64.3	-782.3	1 381.9	2 164.2	2 826.2	1 034.8	1 792.3	-2.2	14 168.8
2006	14 613.8	9 821.7	2 730.0	1 839.6	806.6	71.6	-794.3	1 506.8	2 301.0	2 869.3	1 060.9	1 808.8	-3.8	14 542.3
2007	14 873.7	10 041.6	2 644.1	1 948.4	654.8	35.5	-712.6	1 646.4	2 359.0	2 914.4	1 078.7	1 836.1	-9.7	14 836.2
2008	14 830.4	10 007.2	2 396.0	1 934.4	497.7	-33.7	-557.8	1 740.8	2 298.6	2 994.8	1 152.3	1 842.4	-13.6	14 865.7
2009	14 418.7	9 847.0	1 878.1	1 633.4	392.2	-147.6	-395.4	1 587.7	1 983.2	3 089.1	1 217.7	1 871.4	0.2	14 566.3
2010	14 783.8	10 036.3	2 120.4	1 673.8	382.4	58.2	-458.8	1 776.6	2 235.4	3 091.4	1 270.7	1 820.8	-1.1	14 722.2
2011	15 020.6	10 263.5	2 230.4	1 802.3	384.5	37.6	-459.4	1 898.3	2 357.7	2 997.4	1 236.4	1 761.0	-10.8	14 979.0
2012	15 354.6	10 413.2	2 465.7	1 964.1	436.5	54.7	-447.1	1 963.2	2 410.2	2 941.6	1 213.5	1 728.1	-19.7	15 292.3
2013	15 612.2	10 565.4	2 616.5	2 032.9	488.3	78.7	-404.9	2 031.5	2 436.4	2 857.6	1 142.8	1 714.1	-23.7	15 521.1
2014	16 013.3	10 868.4	2 761.7	2 172.7	505.2	67.8	-427.7	2 118.4	2 546.1	2 839.1	1 115.0	1 723.0	-37.5	15 932.9
2015	16 471.5	11 264.3	2 905.4	2 223.5	556.9	100.5	-545.3	2 127.1	2 672.4	2 878.5	1 114.1	1 762.8	-44.8	16 354.3
2016	16 716.2	11 572.1	2 858.3	2 210.4	587.4	33.4	-586.3	2 120.1	2 706.3	2 900.2	1 114.6	1 783.6	-49.8	16 664.1
2014														
1st quarter	15 757.6	10 713.4	2 652.5	2 112.6	487.6	38.7	-411.0	2 075.8	2 486.8	2 827.2	1 118.1	1 708.2	-30.3	15 707.4
2nd quarter	15 935.8	10 805.1	2 750.6	2 160.6	503.0	69.9	-426.2	2 121.8	2 548.0	2 834.7	1 113.7	1 719.9	-35.7	15 852.3
3rd quarter	16 139.5	10 909.9	2 826.4	2 215.1	508.5	85.6	-416.7	2 125.1	2 541.8	2 849.5	1 122.1	1 726.4	-41.3	16 040.3
4th quarter	16 220.2	11 045.2	2 817.3	2 202.4	521.8	76.9	-456.9	2 150.8	2 607.7	2 845.0	1 106.1	1 737.4	-42.8	16 131.6
2015														
1st quarter	16 350.0	11 145.3	2 905.4	2 214.7	536.1	132.2	-524.1	2 126.4	2 650.5	2 855.7	1 110.3	1 743.9	-41.8	16 202.3
2nd quarter	16 460.9	11 227.9	2 911.3	2 230.7	551.1	105.6	-526.2	2 145.8	2 672.0	2 879.9	1 115.1	1 763.1	-43.7	16 338.6
3rd quarter	16 527.6	11 304.6	2 925.5	2 238.8	565.2	96.2	-559.3	2 124.1	2 683.4	2 888.3	1 112.0	1 774.4	-46.5	16 414.1
4th quarter	16 547.6	11 379.3	2 879.2	2 209.9	575.3	68.2	-571.5	2 111.9	2 683.5	2 890.2	1 118.9	1 769.7	-47.1	16 462.1
2016														
1st quarter	16 571.6	11 430.5	2 849.8	2 187.5	593.7	40.6	-584.2	2 098.1	2 682.3	2 903.2	1 114.6	1 786.6	-41.4	16 512.7
2nd quarter	16 663.5	11 537.7	2 830.2	2 205.3	586.5	12.2	-572.4	2 112.5	2 684.9	2 896.3	1 112.1	1 782.3	-48.2	16 632.6
3rd quarter	16 778.1	11 618.1	2 847.2	2 224.0	579.8	17.6	-557.3	2 145.3	2 702.6	2 899.9	1 116.5	1 781.6	-54.2	16 741.1
4th quarter	16 851.4	11 702.1	2 905.7	2 224.9	589.8	63.1	-631.1	2 124.4	2 755.5	2 901.2	1 115.2	1 784.1	-55.2	16 770.0

Note: Chained (2009) dollar series are calculated as the product of the chain-type quantity index and the 2009 current-dollar value of the corresponding series, divided by 100. Because the formula for the chain-type quantity indexes uses weights from more than one period, the corresponding chained-dollar estimates are usually not additive. The residual column is the difference between the total and the sum of the most detailed components shown in the Bureau of Economic Analysis (BEA) published data.

. . . = Not available.

Table 1-2B. Real Gross Domestic Product: Historical Data

(Billions of chained [2009] dollars, quarterly data are at seasonally adjusted annual rates.)   **NIPA Tables 1.1.6, 1.2.6**

Year and quarter	Gross domestic product	Personal consumption expenditures	Gross private domestic investment				Exports and imports of goods and services			Government consumption expenditures and gross investment			Residual	Adden-dum: Final sales of domestic product
			Total	Fixed investment		Change in private inventories	Net exports	Exports	Imports	Total	Federal	State and local		
				Nonresidential	Residential									
1929	1 056.6	781.0	123.6	0.0	0.0	0.0	0.0	40.5	52.7	165.7	0.0	0.0	-1.5	1 067.5
1930	966.7	739.1	84.2	0.0	0.0	0.0	0.0	33.5	45.8	182.5	0.0	0.0	-26.8	995.4
1931	904.8	716.1	54.7	0.0	0.0	0.0	0.0	27.8	40.0	190.1	0.0	0.0	-43.9	937.7
1932	788.2	651.9	20.2	0.0	0.0	0.0	0.0	21.8	33.1	184.2	0.0	0.0	-56.8	832.3
1933	778.3	637.6	27.3	0.0	0.0	0.0	0.0	21.9	34.5	178.0	0.0	0.0	-52.0	807.4
1934	862.2	683.1	45.2	0.0	0.0	0.0	0.0	24.4	35.3	199.7	0.0	0.0	-54.9	883.7
1935	939.0	724.6	78.6	0.0	0.0	0.0	0.0	25.7	46.2	206.0	0.0	0.0	-49.7	939.0
1936	1 060.5	798.3	99.3	0.0	0.0	0.0	0.0	27.0	45.7	239.1	0.0	0.0	-57.5	1 062.1
1937	1 114.6	827.8	122.3	0.0	0.0	0.0	0.0	34.0	51.4	229.4	0.0	0.0	-47.5	1 106.3
1938	1 077.7	814.6	84.2	0.0	0.0	0.0	0.0	33.6	40.0	246.8	0.0	0.0	-61.5	1 091.6
1939	1 163.6	860.1	105.6	0.0	0.0	0.0	0.0	35.5	42.0	268.3	0.0	0.0	-63.9	1 171.4
1940	1 266.1	904.7	143.8	0.0	0.0	0.0	0.0	40.4	43.0	277.9	0.0	0.0	-57.7	1 251.6
1941	1 490.3	968.6	176.0	0.0	0.0	0.0	0.0	41.4	52.9	467.1	0.0	0.0	-109.9	1 460.8
1942	1 771.8	945.7	98.0	0.0	0.0	0.0	0.0	27.3	48.0	1 084.2	0.0	0.0	-335.4	1 771.1
1943	2 073.7	972.0	61.1	0.0	0.0	0.0	0.0	23.0	60.5	1 626.0	0.0	0.0	-547.9	2 100.6
1944	2 239.4	999.7	73.0	0.0	0.0	0.0	0.0	24.8	63.3	1 826.3	0.0	0.0	-621.1	2 268.9
1945	2 217.8	1 061.5	93.9	0.0	0.0	0.0	0.0	34.7	67.3	1 604.5	0.0	0.0	-509.5	2 253.7
1946	1 960.9	1 193.6	225.0	0.0	0.0	0.0	0.0	74.9	55.8	566.8	0.0	0.0	-43.6	1 932.7
1947	1 939.4	1 216.4	216.5	0.0	0.0	0.0	0.0	85.4	53.0	482.5	0.0	0.0	-8.4	1 967.7
1948	2 020.0	1 243.9	272.9	0.0	0.0	0.0	0.0	67.3	61.8	510.6	0.0	0.0	-12.9	2 001.2
1949	2 008.9	1 278.5	210.9	0.0	0.0	0.0	0.0	66.7	59.6	566.1	0.0	0.0	-53.7	2 046.9
1947														
1st quarter	1 934.5	1 199.4	222.7	. . .	. . .	. . .	. . .	91.0	54.7	478.7	. . .	. . .	-2.6	1 949.8
2nd quarter	1 932.3	1 219.3	205.6	. . .	. . .	. . .	. . .	89.8	55.7	482.8	. . .	. . .	-9.5	1 962.9
3rd quarter	1 930.3	1 223.3	199.6	. . .	. . .	. . .	. . .	85.3	49.4	485.9	. . .	. . .	-14.4	1 977.9
4th quarter	1 960.7	1 223.6	238.2	. . .	. . .	. . .	. . .	75.6	52.1	482.5	. . .	. . .	-7.1	1 980.4
1948														
1st quarter	1 989.5	1 229.8	262.6	. . .	. . .	. . .	. . .	72.2	58.8	488.6	. . .	. . .	-4.9	1 987.1
2nd quarter	2 021.9	1 244.1	278.9	. . .	. . .	. . .	. . .	65.4	61.1	505.0	. . .	. . .	-10.4	1 997.8
3rd quarter	2 033.2	1 245.9	281.7	. . .	. . .	. . .	. . .	67.0	64.3	515.0	. . .	. . .	-12.1	2 001.8
4th quarter	2 035.3	1 255.8	268.3	. . .	. . .	. . .	. . .	64.6	63.2	533.8	. . .	. . .	-24.0	2 017.8
1949														
1st quarter	2 007.5	1 257.9	228.0	. . .	. . .	. . .	. . .	72.3	61.3	548.6	. . .	. . .	-38.0	2 025.8
2nd quarter	2 000.8	1 277.1	197.7	. . .	. . .	. . .	. . .	71.7	60.4	572.5	. . .	. . .	-57.8	2 051.9
3rd quarter	2 022.8	1 280.0	214.1	. . .	. . .	. . .	. . .	65.7	58.0	577.6	. . .	. . .	-56.6	2 051.0
4th quarter	2 004.7	1 298.8	203.6	. . .	. . .	. . .	. . .	56.9	58.8	565.8	. . .	. . .	-61.6	2 058.8
1950														
1st quarter	2 084.6	1 320.4	251.9	. . .	. . .	. . .	. . .	56.0	60.5	557.1	. . .	. . .	-40.3	2 091.8
2nd quarter	2 147.6	1 342.1	278.9	. . .	. . .	. . .	. . .	56.6	63.8	566.6	. . .	. . .	-32.8	2 147.7
3rd quarter	2 230.4	1 411.0	302.9	. . .	. . .	. . .	. . .	58.1	78.8	557.3	. . .	. . .	-20.1	2 224.0
4th quarter	2 273.4	1 368.4	341.3	. . .	. . .	. . .	. . .	62.8	78.9	597.2	. . .	. . .	-17.4	2 204.9
1951														
1st quarter	2 304.5	1 401.5	306.5	. . .	. . .	. . .	. . .	66.0	78.9	660.9	. . .	. . .	-51.5	2 271.6
2nd quarter	2 344.5	1 361.9	313.6	. . .	. . .	. . .	. . .	72.4	76.3	748.8	. . .	. . .	-75.9	2 284.7
3rd quarter	2 392.8	1 377.7	290.5	. . .	. . .	. . .	. . .	74.2	69.8	830.9	. . .	. . .	-110.7	2 361.2
4th quarter	2 398.1	1 385.8	267.3	. . .	. . .	. . .	. . .	73.5	68.0	874.8	. . .	. . .	-135.3	2 396.7
1952														
1st quarter	2 423.5	1 388.9	274.3	. . .	. . .	. . .	. . .	77.4	75.9	900.5	. . .	. . .	-141.7	2 417.7
2nd quarter	2 428.5	1 416.1	253.6	. . .	. . .	. . .	. . .	68.9	75.5	930.7	. . .	. . .	-165.3	2 458.4
3rd quarter	2 446.1	1 423.0	267.2	. . .	. . .	. . .	. . .	63.5	80.1	940.0	. . .	. . .	-167.5	2 436.7
4th quarter	2 526.4	1 473.3	286.5	. . .	. . .	. . .	. . .	63.9	87.3	955.6	. . .	. . .	-165.6	2 517.0
1953														
1st quarter	2 573.4	1 490.8	292.6	. . .	. . .	. . .	. . .	62.8	85.2	985.5	. . .	. . .	-173.1	2 570.9
2nd quarter	2 593.5	1 499.8	294.3	. . .	. . .	. . .	. . .	63.2	89.6	1 005.9	. . .	. . .	-180.1	2 591.8
3rd quarter	2 578.9	1 496.3	288.1	. . .	. . .	. . .	. . .	65.8	89.2	1 006.2	. . .	. . .	-177.3	2 586.5
4th quarter	2 539.8	1 486.4	267.3	. . .	. . .	. . .	. . .	63.6	84.9	992.4	. . .	. . .	-185.0	2 572.0
1954														
1st quarter	2 528.0	1 491.8	265.4	. . .	. . .	. . .	. . .	60.7	80.0	967.3	. . .	. . .	-177.2	2 558.3
2nd quarter	2 530.7	1 511.3	264.8	. . .	. . .	. . .	. . .	69.5	87.1	934.3	. . .	. . .	-162.1	2 567.9
3rd quarter	2 559.4	1 531.8	277.6	. . .	. . .	. . .	. . .	67.2	81.9	914.3	. . .	. . .	-149.6	2 593.7
4th quarter	2 609.3	1 564.0	289.7	. . .	. . .	. . .	. . .	70.3	82.7	908.6	. . .	. . .	-140.6	2 635.7
1955														
1st quarter	2 683.8	1 599.1	318.7	. . .	. . .	. . .	. . .	73.0	87.5	909.2	. . .	. . .	-128.7	2 686.1
2nd quarter	2 727.5	1 629.7	337.9	. . .	. . .	. . .	. . .	71.2	92.5	900.5	. . .	. . .	-119.3	2 720.9
3rd quarter	2 764.1	1 649.8	343.1	. . .	. . .	. . .	. . .	75.9	94.1	906.1	. . .	. . .	-116.7	2 760.7
4th quarter	2 780.8	1 670.5	351.1	. . .	. . .	. . .	. . .	76.3	97.5	888.3	. . .	. . .	-107.9	2 768.1
1956														
1st quarter	2 770.0	1 673.2	341.1	. . .	. . .	. . .	. . .	79.9	101.6	888.1	. . .	. . .	-110.7	2 763.7
2nd quarter	2 792.9	1 678.8	338.4	. . .	. . .	. . .	. . .	85.3	101.0	905.9	. . .	. . .	-114.5	2 795.2
3rd quarter	2 790.6	1 682.6	335.4	. . .	. . .	. . .	. . .	88.1	101.9	898.3	. . .	. . .	-111.9	2 797.4
4th quarter	2 836.2	1 705.8	332.2	. . .	. . .	. . .	. . .	92.1	97.2	920.7	. . .	. . .	-117.4	2 845.7
1957														
1st quarter	2 854.5	1 717.5	327.1	. . .	. . .	. . .	. . .	98.1	105.0	940.7	. . .	. . .	-123.9	2 871.3
2nd quarter	2 848.2	1 720.5	326.8	. . .	. . .	. . .	. . .	95.2	105.8	935.7	. . .	. . .	-124.2	2 861.4
3rd quarter	2 875.9	1 734.1	334.2	. . .	. . .	. . .	. . .	92.5	103.8	943.5	. . .	. . .	-124.6	2 883.4
4th quarter	2 846.4	1 734.9	308.5	. . .	. . .	. . .	. . .	89.7	104.1	959.3	. . .	. . .	-141.9	2 882.6

Note: Chained (2009) dollar series are calculated as the product of the chain-type quantity index and the 2009 current-dollar value of the corresponding series, divided by 100. Because the formula for the chain-type quantity indexes uses weights from more than one period, the corresponding chained-dollar estimates are usually not additive. The residual column is the difference between the total and the sum of the most detailed components shown in the Bureau of Economic Analysis (BEA) published data.

. . . = Not available.

Table 1-2B. Real Gross Domestic Product: Historical Data—*Continued*

(Billions of chained [2009] dollars, quarterly data are at seasonally adjusted annual rates.)   **NIPA Tables 1.1.6, 1.2.6**

Year and quarter	Gross domestic product	Personal consumption expenditures	Gross private domestic investment				Exports and imports of goods and services			Government consumption expenditures and gross investment			Residual	Addendum: Final sales of domestic product
			Total	Fixed investment		Change in private inventories	Net exports	Exports	Imports	Total	Federal	State and local		
				Nonresidential	Residential									
1958														
1st quarter	2 772.7	1 711.1	287.7	...	...	...	...	80.8	105.7	950.8	...	...	-152.0	2 812.0
2nd quarter	2 790.9	1 725.1	281.9	...	...	...	...	81.2	110.2	974.7	...	...	-161.8	2 828.0
3rd quarter	2 855.5	1 753.5	303.5	...	...	...	...	81.5	108.5	980.6	...	...	-155.1	2 869.1
4th quarter	2 922.3	1 777.1	329.4	...	...	...	...	81.2	114.2	1 000.7	...	...	-151.9	2 925.1
1959														
1st quarter	2 976.6	1 809.4	347.4	...	...	...	...	86.6	117.1	989.4	...	...	-139.1	2 980.6
2nd quarter	3 049.0	1 837.3	374.4	...	...	...	...	89.5	122.8	1 001.7	...	...	-131.1	3 029.9
3rd quarter	3 043.1	1 856.5	350.2	...	...	...	...	92.3	124.0	1 010.3	...	...	-142.2	3 063.3
4th quarter	3 055.1	1 858.6	361.6	...	...	...	...	89.8	120.8	1 002.1	...	...	-136.2	3 053.8
1960														
1st quarter	3 123.2	1 876.3	398.0	...	...	...	...	101.1	125.4	985.2	...	...	-112.0	3 087.7
2nd quarter	3 111.3	1 900.1	360.9	...	...	...	...	107.5	126.3	995.8	...	...	-126.7	3 118.6
3rd quarter	3 119.1	1 892.5	360.0	...	...	...	...	104.8	122.6	1 020.0	...	...	-135.6	3 117.2
4th quarter	3 081.3	1 894.9	320.1	...	...	...	...	106.9	116.8	1 026.8	...	...	-150.6	3 132.9
1961														
1st quarter	3 102.3	1 894.4	328.4	...	...	...	...	106.2	116.3	1 042.0	...	...	-152.4	3 138.6
2nd quarter	3 159.9	1 922.6	351.4	...	...	...	...	104.7	117.7	1 044.4	...	...	-145.5	3 172.7
3rd quarter	3 212.6	1 932.0	378.7	...	...	...	...	104.2	125.5	1 066.4	...	...	-143.2	3 199.7
4th quarter	3 277.7	1 970.7	385.0	...	...	...	...	107.4	128.4	1 089.7	...	...	-146.7	3 271.9
1962														
1st quarter	3 336.8	1 991.7	405.7	...	...	...	...	107.1	132.4	1 110.7	...	...	-146.0	3 312.7
2nd quarter	3 372.7	2 016.1	402.5	...	...	...	...	117.4	135.2	1 116.0	...	...	-144.1	3 367.5
3rd quarter	3 404.8	2 032.5	409.4	...	...	...	...	110.8	137.0	1 141.7	...	...	-152.6	3 394.8
4th quarter	3 418.0	2 061.3	397.4	...	...	...	...	108.4	138.6	1 149.6	...	...	-160.1	3 422.7
1963														
1st quarter	3 456.1	2 075.2	418.3	...	...	...	...	111.0	135.4	1 134.1	...	...	-147.1	3 439.6
2nd quarter	3 501.1	2 095.1	425.0	...	...	...	...	124.0	138.6	1 135.1	...	...	-139.5	3 499.1
3rd quarter	3 569.5	2 123.7	438.0	...	...	...	...	117.3	142.1	1 185.4	...	...	-152.8	3 563.8
4th quarter	3 595.0	2 141.4	443.4	...	...	...	...	123.2	141.7	1 173.7	...	...	-145.0	3 598.8
1964														
1st quarter	3 672.7	2 183.6	460.0	...	...	...	...	130.8	141.5	1 177.3	...	...	-137.5	3 674.7
2nd quarter	3 716.4	2 222.0	458.3	...	...	...	...	133.0	144.7	1 187.9	...	...	-140.1	3 719.8
3rd quarter	3 766.9	2 262.8	469.0	...	...	...	...	131.9	148.6	1 189.4	...	...	-137.6	3 766.0
4th quarter	3 780.2	2 269.2	473.5	...	...	...	...	135.9	152.6	1 189.0	...	...	-134.8	3 778.7
1965														
1st quarter	3 873.5	2 319.0	518.6	...	...	...	...	121.2	147.1	1 187.7	...	...	-126.7	3 839.9
2nd quarter	3 926.4	2 345.5	520.0	...	...	...	...	144.0	164.5	1 202.0	...	...	-120.6	3 909.2
3rd quarter	4 006.2	2 385.9	538.1	...	...	...	...	135.7	165.2	1 241.7	...	...	-130.0	3 983.0
4th quarter	4 100.6	2 452.9	541.6	...	...	...	...	145.5	173.2	1 265.4	...	...	-131.6	4 088.6
1966														
1st quarter	4 201.9	2 489.1	584.9	...	...	...	...	143.0	177.7	1 289.0	...	...	-126.4	4 158.7
2nd quarter	4 219.1	2 495.4	576.2	...	...	...	...	149.2	182.1	1 313.4	...	...	-133.0	4 180.5
3rd quarter	4 249.2	2 523.8	572.0	...	...	...	...	143.6	192.3	1 349.1	...	...	-147.0	4 217.1
4th quarter	4 285.6	2 534.2	575.3	...	...	...	...	148.3	194.5	1 372.4	...	...	-150.1	4 231.3
1967														
1st quarter	4 324.9	2 548.9	561.2	...	...	...	...	151.2	197.5	1 429.8	...	...	-168.7	4 276.7
2nd quarter	4 328.7	2 583.7	540.9	...	...	...	...	149.8	196.0	1 424.2	...	...	-173.9	4 323.1
3rd quarter	4 366.1	2 596.9	556.8	...	...	...	...	146.2	198.5	1 440.2	...	...	-175.5	4 348.2
4th quarter	4 401.2	2 612.7	568.8	...	...	...	...	150.4	209.0	1 451.4	...	...	-173.1	4 388.3
1968														
1st quarter	4 490.6	2 674.8	580.2	...	...	...	...	154.7	221.3	1 477.2	...	...	-175.0	4 479.0
2nd quarter	4 566.4	2 715.6	602.4	...	...	...	...	157.8	224.7	1 485.0	...	...	-169.7	4 524.8
3rd quarter	4 599.3	2 766.6	586.0	...	...	...	...	167.1	238.2	1 489.7	...	...	-171.9	4 590.2
4th quarter	4 619.8	2 779.1	592.3	...	...	...	...	165.0	236.2	1 491.0	...	...	-171.4	4 619.6
1969														
1st quarter	4 691.6	2 810.2	627.2	...	...	...	...	145.2	213.9	1 494.7	...	...	-171.8	4 667.2
2nd quarter	4 706.7	2 828.2	623.5	...	...	...	...	177.8	256.1	1 490.0	...	...	-156.7	4 691.2
3rd quarter	4 736.1	2 841.9	636.2	...	...	...	...	173.6	252.8	1 493.5	...	...	-156.3	4 715.4
4th quarter	4 715.5	2 864.6	605.5	...	...	...	...	179.5	250.0	1 473.9	...	...	-158.0	4 717.0
1970														
1st quarter	4 707.1	2 882.3	587.4	...	...	...	...	180.9	249.2	1 466.9	...	...	-161.2	4 728.1
2nd quarter	4 715.4	2 895.6	588.7	...	...	...	...	188.9	254.1	1 450.2	...	...	-153.9	4 719.5
3rd quarter	4 757.2	2 921.1	598.3	...	...	...	...	188.3	253.5	1 456.5	...	...	-153.5	4 761.5
4th quarter	4 708.3	2 913.1	566.5	...	...	...	...	190.1	257.5	1 457.2	...	...	-161.1	4 752.8
1971														
1st quarter	4 834.3	2 968.9	632.5	...	...	...	...	190.8	254.4	1 436.1	...	...	-139.6	4 810.3
2nd quarter	4 861.9	2 996.1	650.5	...	...	...	...	190.4	273.6	1 432.8	...	...	-134.3	4 843.6
3rd quarter	4 900.0	3 020.0	658.4	...	...	...	...	198.3	279.7	1 432.4	...	...	-129.4	4 885.2
4th quarter	4 914.3	3 070.2	640.6	...	...	...	...	181.7	260.7	1 422.6	...	...	-140.1	4 943.3
1972														
1st quarter ...	5 002.4	3 110.8	682.9	...	...	...	...	201.4	298.8	1 429.3	...	...	-123.2	5 012.9
2nd quarter ...	5 118.3	3 170.2	721.6	...	...	...	...	195.5	288.2	1 438.0	...	...	-118.8	5 094.5
3rd quarter ...	5 165.4	3 219.1	731.9	...	...	...	...	207.4	294.2	1 409.3	...	...	-108.1	5 138.7
4th quarter	5 251.2	3 294.6	736.5	...	...	...	...	216.1	307.5	1 420.1	...	...	-108.6	5 257.8

Note: Chained (2009) dollar series are calculated as the product of the chain-type quantity index and the 2009 current-dollar value of the corresponding series, divided by 100. Because the formula for the chain-type quantity indexes uses weights from more than one period, the corresponding chained-dollar estimates are usually not additive. The residual column is the difference between the total and the sum of the most detailed components shown in the Bureau of Economic Analysis (BEA) published data.

. . . = Not available.

Table 1-2B. Real Gross Domestic Product: Historical Data—*Continued*

(Billions of chained [2009] dollars, quarterly data are at seasonally adjusted annual rates.) **NIPA Tables 1.1.6, 1.2.6**

Year and quarter	Gross domestic product	Personal consumption expenditures	Gross private domestic investment Total	Fixed investment Nonresidential	Fixed investment Residential	Change in private inventories	Net exports	Exports	Imports	Government Total	Federal	State and local	Residual	Addendum: Final sales of domestic product
1973														
1st quarter	5 380.5	3 354.8	779.6	. . .	. . .	. . .	. . .	232.0	321.7	1 431.6	. . .	. . .	-95.8	5 368.7
2nd quarter	5 441.5	3 353.4	812.9	. . .	. . .	. . .	. . .	243.2	312.4	1 424.5	. . .	. . .	-80.1	5 394.8
3rd quarter	5 411.9	3 365.3	783.4	. . .	. . .	. . .	. . .	244.0	303.8	1 406.4	. . .	. . .	-83.4	5 399.9
4th quarter	5 462.4	3 355.5	811.3	. . .	. . .	. . .	. . .	256.0	306.0	1 415.8	. . .	. . .	-70.2	5 406.4
1974														
1st quarter	5 417.0	3 326.2	765.0	. . .	. . .	. . .	. . .	259.2	295.7	1 442.4	. . .	. . .	-80.1	5 401.0
2nd quarter	5 431.3	3 337.9	761.9	. . .	. . .	. . .	. . .	271.8	311.3	1 451.6	. . .	. . .	-80.6	5 407.5
3rd quarter	5 378.7	3 351.6	722.4	. . .	. . .	. . .	. . .	257.2	305.9	1 453.5	. . .	. . .	-100.1	5 390.8
4th quarter	5 357.2	3 302.5	726.8	. . .	. . .	. . .	. . .	263.9	302.8	1 459.9	. . .	. . .	-93.1	5 314.1
1975														
1st quarter	5 292.4	3 330.1	609.7	. . .	. . .	. . .	. . .	265.8	272.4	1 476.1	. . .	. . .	-116.9	5 352.6
2nd quarter	5 333.2	3 385.7	591.6	. . .	. . .	. . .	. . .	258.0	250.6	1 466.2	. . .	. . .	-117.7	5 407.4
3rd quarter	5 421.4	3 434.1	637.5	. . .	. . .	. . .	. . .	253.7	271.5	1 489.5	. . .	. . .	-121.9	5 455.7
4th quarter	5 494.4	3 470.5	655.2	. . .	. . .	. . .	. . .	268.0	286.0	1 503.4	. . .	. . .	-116.7	5 522.6
1976														
1st quarter	5 618.5	3 539.9	718.5	. . .	. . .	. . .	. . .	266.2	303.9	1 506.5	. . .	. . .	-108.7	5 599.5
2nd quarter	5 661.0	3 572.4	746.9	. . .	. . .	. . .	. . .	268.9	317.1	1 491.4	. . .	. . .	-101.5	5 619.2
3rd quarter	5 689.8	3 610.3	749.5	. . .	. . .	. . .	. . .	276.7	330.0	1 483.9	. . .	. . .	-100.6	5 654.8
4th quarter	5 732.5	3 657.5	755.1	. . .	. . .	. . .	. . .	279.5	340.9	1 484.4	. . .	. . .	-103.1	5 734.2
1977														
1st quarter	5 799.2	3 699.3	790.1	. . .	. . .	. . .	. . .	275.0	357.1	1 497.3	. . .	. . .	-105.4	5 788.5
2nd quarter	5 913.0	3 719.7	846.8	. . .	. . .	. . .	. . .	282.4	360.3	1 512.0	. . .	. . .	-87.6	5 880.7
3rd quarter	6 017.6	3 755.2	889.6	. . .	. . .	. . .	. . .	284.6	355.3	1 515.4	. . .	. . .	-71.9	5 942.6
4th quarter	6 018.2	3 811.8	867.3	. . .	. . .	. . .	. . .	275.5	360.4	1 512.1	. . .	. . .	-88.1	5 991.7
1978														
1st quarter	6 039.2	3 833.8	884.2	. . .	. . .	. . .	. . .	281.9	384.5	1 513.9	. . .	. . .	-90.1	5 999.9
2nd quarter	6 274.0	3 915.6	941.6	. . .	. . .	. . .	. . .	311.3	385.8	1 554.1	. . .	. . .	-62.8	6 235.2
3rd quarter	6 335.3	3 932.0	969.1	. . .	. . .	. . .	. . .	314.7	390.8	1 566.4	. . .	. . .	-56.1	6 292.4
4th quarter	6 420.3	3 963.5	991.5	. . .	. . .	. . .	. . .	327.2	396.2	1 580.6	. . .	. . .	-46.3	6 374.5
1979														
1st quarter	6 433.0	3 983.6	993.1	. . .	. . .	. . .	. . .	327.5	395.1	1 566.9	. . .	. . .	-43.0	6 396.4
2nd quarter	6 440.8	3 981.3	992.2	. . .	. . .	. . .	. . .	328.4	397.2	1 583.0	. . .	. . .	-46.9	6 398.0
3rd quarter	6 487.1	4 020.4	975.5	. . .	. . .	. . .	. . .	340.2	391.1	1 585.1	. . .	. . .	-43.0	6 489.4
4th quarter	6 503.9	4 031.2	958.2	. . .	. . .	. . .	. . .	361.6	399.7	1 595.4	. . .	. . .	-42.8	6 517.7
1980														
1st quarter	6 524.9	4 025.0	951.6	. . .	. . .	. . .	. . .	371.7	400.0	1 620.2	. . .	. . .	-43.6	6 530.6
2nd quarter	6 392.6	3 934.5	870.7	. . .	. . .	. . .	. . .	378.7	371.0	1 625.9	. . .	. . .	-46.2	6 403.9
3rd quarter	6 382.9	3 976.9	813.3	. . .	. . .	. . .	. . .	377.9	344.3	1 601.9	. . .	. . .	-42.8	6 487.1
4th quarter	6 501.2	4 029.6	889.2	. . .	. . .	. . .	. . .	375.6	362.8	1 601.8	. . .	. . .	-32.2	6 546.9
1981														
1st quarter	6 635.7	4 050.8	971.7	. . .	. . .	. . .	. . .	382.7	378.3	1 622.8	. . .	. . .	-14.0	6 581.1
2nd quarter	6 587.3	4 050.1	931.3	. . .	. . .	. . .	. . .	384.8	378.9	1 627.9	. . .	. . .	-27.9	6 597.1
3rd quarter	6 662.9	4 066.4	983.5	. . .	. . .	. . .	. . .	376.6	374.6	1 621.6	. . .	. . .	-10.6	6 602.2
4th quarter	6 585.1	4 035.9	948.4	. . .	. . .	. . .	. . .	378.4	385.3	1 639.9	. . .	. . .	-32.2	6 567.5
1982														
1st quarter	6 475.0	4 062.6	854.9	. . .	. . .	. . .	. . .	362.0	374.3	1 638.2	. . .	. . .	-68.4	6 544.5
2nd quarter	6 510.2	4 077.6	853.8	. . .	. . .	. . .	. . .	364.1	368.2	1 648.9	. . .	. . .	-66.0	6 542.9
3rd quarter	6 486.8	4 109.1	845.7	. . .	. . .	. . .	. . .	348.0	385.3	1 659.3	. . .	. . .	-90.0	6 502.1
4th quarter	6 493.1	4 184.1	780.3	. . .	. . .	. . .	. . .	332.1	370.2	1 685.8	. . .	. . .	-119.0	6 597.2
1983														
1st quarter ...	6 578.2	4 224.8	807.5	. . .	. . .	. . .	. . .	337.4	378.6	1 701.9	. . .	. . .	-114.8	6 671.5
2nd quarter ...	6 728.3	4 308.4	879.1	. . .	. . .	. . .	. . .	338.4	407.7	1 719.1	. . .	. . .	-109.0	6 769.8
3rd quarter ...	6 860.0	4 384.0	934.2	. . .	. . .	. . .	. . .	343.5	439.5	1 747.3	. . .	. . .	-109.5	6 894.7
4th quarter	7 001.5	4 463.1	1 025.1	. . .	. . .	. . .	. . .	350.5	461.1	1 718.0	. . .	. . .	-84.1	6 986.3
1984														
1st quarter	7 140.6	4 490.9	1 124.2	. . .	. . .	. . .	. . .	357.8	498.1	1 738.1	. . .	. . .	-72.3	7 000.0
2nd quarter	7 266.0	4 554.9	1 160.7	. . .	. . .	. . .	. . .	366.7	519.0	1 777.1	. . .	. . .	-74.4	7 169.7
3rd quarter	7 337.5	4 589.9	1 185.8	. . .	. . .	. . .	. . .	374.8	532.4	1 791.8	. . .	. . .	-72.4	7 236.8
4th quarter	7 396.0	4 650.6	1 170.4	. . .	. . .	. . .	. . .	382.4	548.0	1 826.0	. . .	. . .	-85.4	7 339.8
1985														
1st quarter	7 469.5	4 729.7	1 138.3	. . .	. . .	. . .	. . .	383.4	535.9	1 848.0	. . .	. . .	-94.0	7 466.4
2nd quarter ...	7 537.9	4 774.1	1 157.7	. . .	. . .	. . .	. . .	382.5	562.3	1 891.0	. . .	. . .	-105.1	7 528.6
3rd quarter	7 655.2	4 865.8	1 149.8	. . .	. . .	. . .	. . .	377.0	556.8	1 935.4	. . .	. . .	-116.0	7 650.2
4th quarter	7 712.6	4 878.3	1 192.2	. . .	. . .	. . .	. . .	388.3	578.7	1 941.8	. . .	. . .	-109.3	7 681.6
1986														
1st quarter	7 784.1	4 919.6	1 191.9	. . .	. . .	. . .	. . .	400.5	578.1	1 958.0	. . .	. . .	-107.8	7 757.8
2nd quarter	7 819.8	4 974.6	1 171.0	. . .	. . .	. . .	. . .	404.8	602.7	1 997.8	. . .	. . .	-125.7	7 820.1
3rd quarter	7 898.6	5 064.7	1 139.5	. . .	. . .	. . .	. . .	414.1	619.4	2 043.4	. . .	. . .	-143.7	7 932.3
4th quarter	7 939.5	5 097.1	1 143.0	. . .	. . .	. . .	. . .	429.5	624.2	2 031.5	. . .	. . .	-137.4	7 980.2
1987														
1st quarter	7 995.0	5 097.9	1 173.8	. . .	. . .	. . .	. . .	429.8	620.5	2 044.3	. . .	. . .	-130.3	7 972.0
2nd quarter ...	8 084.7	5 168.6	1 174.4	. . .	. . .	. . .	. . .	447.5	636.0	2 062.9	. . .	. . .	-132.7	8 083.1
3rd quarter ...	8 158.0	5 228.5	1 174.6	. . .	. . .	. . .	. . .	466.9	648.3	2 067.7	. . .	. . .	-131.4	8 181.3
4th quarter	8 292.7	5 239.5	1 254.6	. . .	. . .	. . .	. . .	484.3	663.2	2 092.8	. . .	. . .	-115.3	8 216.0

Note: Chained (2009) dollar series are calculated as the product of the chain-type quantity index and the 2009 current-dollar value of the corresponding series, divided by 100. Because the formula for the chain-type quantity indexes uses weights from more than one period, the corresponding chained-dollar estimates are usually not additive. The residual column is the difference between the total and the sum of the most detailed components shown in the Bureau of Economic Analysis (BEA) published data.

. . . = Not available.

Table 1-2B. Real Gross Domestic Product: Historical Data—*Continued*

(Billions of chained [2009] dollars, quarterly data are at seasonally adjusted annual rates.)   **NIPA Tables 1.1.6, 1.2.6**

Year and quarter	Gross domestic product	Personal consumption expenditures	Gross private domestic investment				Exports and imports of goods and services			Government consumption expenditures and gross investment			Residual	Addendum: Final sales of domestic product
			Total	Fixed investment		Change in private inventories	Net exports	Exports	Imports	Total	Federal	State and local		
				Nonresidential	Residential									
1988														
1st quarter	8 339.3	5 332.7	1 194.4	...	...	...	...	511.2	660.1	2 078.6	...	...	-117.5	8 338.6
2nd quarter ...	8 449.5	5 371.8	1 222.9	...	...	...	...	525.5	652.5	2 086.1	...	...	-104.3	8 442.3
3rd quarter	8 498.3	5 417.7	1 229.7	...	...	...	...	535.9	667.9	2 087.5	...	...	-104.6	8 489.7
4th quarter	8 610.9	5 479.7	1 248.4	...	...	...	...	552.2	688.3	2 126.8	...	...	-107.9	8 597.0
1989														
1st quarter	8 697.7	5 505.0	1 290.7	...	...	...	...	568.7	691.5	2 117.2	...	...	-92.4	8 645.4
2nd quarter ...	8 766.1	5 530.9	1 278.3	...	...	...	...	593.6	694.8	2 151.8	...	...	-93.7	8 731.3
3rd quarter	8 831.5	5 585.9	1 266.9	...	...	...	...	599.7	693.8	2 169.8	...	...	-97.0	8 837.3
4th quarter	8 850.2	5 610.5	1 257.7	...	...	...	...	608.7	706.4	2 181.5	...	...	-101.8	8 847.7
1990														
1st quarter	8 947.1	5 658.7	1 270.0	...	...	...	...	635.2	728.8	2 215.8	...	...	-103.8	8 947.5
2nd quarter ...	8 981.7	5 676.4	1 270.4	...	...	...	...	643.1	727.6	2 221.2	...	...	-101.8	8 951.7
3rd quarter	8 983.9	5 699.3	1 245.6	...	...	...	...	648.0	724.6	2 219.9	...	...	-104.3	8 971.2
4th quarter	8 907.4	5 656.2	1 176.3	...	...	...	...	653.7	705.2	2 240.2	...	...	-113.8	8 940.1
1991														
1st quarter	8 865.6	5 636.7	1 137.1	...	...	...	...	657.7	697.1	2 251.2	...	...	-120.0	8 905.8
2nd quarter ...	8 934.4	5 684.0	1 137.2	...	...	...	...	681.6	709.5	2 259.2	...	...	-118.1	8 978.7
3rd quarter	8 977.3	5 711.6	1 159.8	...	...	...	...	697.8	729.5	2 250.8	...	...	-113.2	8 996.6
4th quarter	9 016.4	5 710.1	1 201.0	...	...	...	...	713.5	745.6	2 242.3	...	...	-104.9	8 993.4
1992														
1st quarter	9 123.0	5 817.3	1 178.9	...	...	...	...	726.4	751.0	2 259.7	...	...	-108.3	9 141.1
2nd quarter ...	9 223.5	5 857.2	1 245.7	...	...	...	...	726.7	763.4	2 256.8	...	...	-99.5	9 209.5
3rd quarter	9 313.2	5 920.6	1 255.8	...	...	...	...	742.1	775.4	2 268.4	...	...	-98.3	9 304.2
4th quarter	9 406.5	5 991.1	1 294.2	...	...	...	...	745.9	794.0	2 263.5	...	...	-94.2	9 395.1
1993														
1st quarter	9 424.1	6 013.8	1 324.6	...	...	...	...	747.6	811.2	2 237.8	...	...	-88.5	9 388.5
2nd quarter ...	9 480.1	6 067.8	1 332.1	...	...	...	...	756.5	827.9	2 240.3	...	...	-88.7	9 462.3
3rd quarter	9 526.3	6 134.8	1 323.1	...	...	...	...	754.5	838.8	2 245.1	...	...	-92.4	9 542.3
4th quarter	9 653.5	6 189.1	1 392.5	...	...	...	...	778.9	872.5	2 250.0	...	...	-84.5	9 651.0
1994														
1st quarter	9 748.2	6 260.1	1 446.2	...	...	...	...	786.5	892.9	2 222.1	...	...	-73.8	9 703.9
2nd quarter ...	9 881.4	6 308.6	1 517.1	...	...	...	...	813.1	926.1	2 235.1	...	...	-66.4	9 788.3
3rd quarter	9 939.7	6 357.5	1 492.2	...	...	...	...	843.5	952.2	2 272.7	...	...	-74.0	9 888.1
4th quarter	10 052.5	6 425.9	1 553.5	...	...	...	...	863.0	979.0	2 252.2	...	...	-63.1	9 970.6
1995														
1st quarter	10 086.9	6 442.9	1 570.3	...	...	...	...	879.6	1 000.4	2 256.8	...	...	-62.3	10 021.6
2nd quarter ...	10 122.1	6 500.7	1 537.7	...	...	...	...	891.9	1 009.9	2 268.6	...	...	-66.9	10 092.8
3rd quarter	10 208.8	6 560.3	1 528.6	...	...	...	...	930.5	1 013.4	2 262.4	...	...	-59.6	10 213.8
4th quarter	10 281.2	6 606.4	1 566.7	...	...	...	...	943.8	1 026.4	2 242.1	...	...	-51.4	10 277.2
1996														
1st quarter	10 348.7	6 667.7	1 590.6	...	...	...	...	955.2	1 059.7	2 246.8	...	...	-51.9	10 361.5
2nd quarter ...	10 529.4	6 740.1	1 667.7	...	...	...	...	970.7	1 083.4	2 282.8	...	...	-48.5	10 511.9
3rd quarter	10 626.8	6 780.7	1 744.5	...	...	...	...	978.6	1 118.6	2 285.2	...	...	-43.6	10 565.3
4th quarter	10 739.1	6 834.0	1 743.9	...	...	...	...	1 039.6	1 140.6	2 301.9	...	...	-39.7	10 707.5
1997														
1st quarter	10 820.9	6 906.1	1 781.6	...	...	...	...	1 059.4	1 189.3	2 301.3	...	...	-38.2	10 782.4
2nd quarter ...	10 984.2	6 937.4	1 880.0	...	...	...	...	1 101.7	1 229.3	2 325.3	...	...	-30.9	10 874.8
3rd quarter	11 124.0	7 056.1	1 913.6	...	...	...	...	1 127.2	1 274.6	2 329.0	...	...	-27.3	11 047.2
4th quarter	11 210.3	7 139.9	1 940.7	...	...	...	...	1 125.7	1 302.1	2 332.5	...	...	-26.4	11 119.7
1998														
1st quarter	11 321.2	7 213.6	2 027.1	...	...	...	...	1 130.9	1 351.0	2 319.0	...	...	-18.4	11 195.3
2nd quarter ...	11 431.0	7 341.0	2 013.4	...	...	...	...	1 118.5	1 381.9	2 366.0	...	...	-26.0	11 388.3
3rd quarter	11 580.6	7 437.5	2 067.2	...	...	...	...	1 113.3	1 400.5	2 387.6	...	...	-24.5	11 519.6
4th quarter	11 770.7	7 546.8	2 125.5	...	...	...	...	1 154.5	1 445.7	2 409.4	...	...	-19.8	11 706.1
1999														
1st quarter	11 864.7	7 618.7	2 186.1	1 459.0	623.0	97.5	-340.4	1 126.4	1 466.9	2 418.1	801.2	1 624.5	-137.3	11 773.6
2nd quarter ...	11 962.5	7 731.5	2 188.0	1 497.3	632.7	45.3	-371.1	1 137.9	1 509.0	2 431.7	805.2	1 634.0	-112.1	11 921.8
3rd quarter	12 113.1	7 819.3	2 242.8	1 539.3	637.4	51.5	-393.9	1 171.3	1 565.2	2 460.3	819.4	1 648.0	-99.0	12 066.3
4th quarter	12 323.3	7 934.1	2 308.6	1 544.9	642.1	107.5	-402.9	1 200.9	1 603.8	2 496.7	835.6	1 668.1	-101.1	12 218.0
2000														
1st quarter	12 359.1	8 054.9	2 287.8	1 599.9	645.3	23.6	-449.0	1 219.2	1 668.1	2 476.2	804.6	1 680.8	-80.1	12 340.0
2nd quarter ...	12 592.5	8 132.2	2 424.5	1 650.5	641.9	108.7	-464.9	1 254.7	1 719.6	2 506.4	832.8	1 681.2	-83.1	12 483.4
3rd quarter	12 607.7	8 211.3	2 394.1	1 667.9	632.0	68.7	-493.5	1 285.5	1 779.0	2 501.2	818.9	1 691.0	-84.8	12 540.3
4th quarter	12 679.3	8 284.4	2 395.6	1 672.3	632.6	63.9	-503.8	1 274.3	1 778.1	2 509.0	814.6	1 703.6	-87.0	12 615.8
2001														
1st quarter	12 643.3	8 319.4	2 285.3	1 658.8	635.3	-37.9	-494.0	1 254.5	1 748.5	2 546.3	832.3	1 722.9	-83.3	12 681.9
2nd quarter ...	12 710.3	8 340.8	2 277.1	1 621.2	645.2	-12.8	-483.8	1 213.0	1 696.8	2 596.4	848.7	1 756.8	-101.0	12 725.7
3rd quarter	12 670.1	8 371.2	2 236.6	1 600.0	649.2	-36.9	-508.7	1 154.1	1 662.8	2 594.6	855.9	1 747.3	-104.5	12 708.2
4th quarter	12 705.3	8 499.1	2 126.9	1 553.6	645.0	-97.4	-521.8	1 118.0	1 639.8	2 632.4	862.6	1 778.9	-73.4	12 802.6
2002														
1st quarter	12 822.3	8 524.6	2 202.8	1 522.1	666.2	-3.8	-546.0	1 140.9	1 686.9	2 671.3	884.0	1 795.9	-80.0	12 828.1
2nd quarter ...	12 893.0	8 568.1	2 224.9	1 501.9	682.7	26.5	-567.7	1 172.1	1 739.8	2 696.9	904.7	1 799.8	-74.5	12 870.4
3rd quarter	12 955.8	8 628.0	2 224.6	1 493.0	684.7	32.4	-585.1	1 180.5	1 765.6	2 717.8	919.0	1 805.9	-60.5	12 926.0
4th quarter	12 964.0	8 674.4	2 220.7	1 475.1	697.1	35.1	-638.4	1 164.5	1 802.9	2 737.1	935.7	1 807.9	-67.1	12 931.2

Note: Chained (2009) dollar series are calculated as the product of the chain-type quantity index and the 2009 current-dollar value of the corresponding series, divided by 100. Because the formula for the chain-type quantity indexes uses weights from more than one period, the corresponding chained-dollar estimates are usually not additive. The residual column is the difference between the total and the sum of the most detailed components shown in the Bureau of Economic Analysis (BEA) published data.

. . . = Not available.

Table 1-2B. Real Gross Domestic Product: Historical Data—*Continued*

(Billions of chained [2009] dollars, quarterly data are at seasonally adjusted annual rates.)

NIPA Tables 1.1.6, 1.2.6

Year and quarter	Gross domestic product	Personal consumption expenditures	Gross private domestic investment				Exports and imports of goods and services			Government consumption expenditures and gross investment			Residual	Addendum: Final sales of domestic product
			Total	Fixed investment		Change in private inventories	Net exports	Exports	Imports	Total	Federal	State and local		
				Nonresidential	Residential									
2003														
1st quarter	13 031.2	8 712.5	2 239.5	1 478.6	709.8	36.3	-620.3	1 157.6	1 777.9	2 728.3	935.9	1 798.5	-63.0	12 995.4
2nd quarter ...	13 152.1	8 809.5	2 251.3	1 514.3	721.0	-0.2	-649.7	1 156.2	1 805.9	2 771.2	982.8	1 791.7	-50.7	13 152.6
3rd quarter ...	13 372.4	8 939.4	2 330.9	1 544.7	762.3	7.6	-642.1	1 187.0	1 829.1	2 771.2	977.1	1 798.0	-37.3	13 364.6
4th quarter	13 528.7	9 008.8	2 413.1	1 566.8	785.0	46.6	-655.4	1 239.2	1 894.6	2 786.3	996.0	1 793.0	-32.1	13 483.2
2004														
1st quarter	13 606.5	9 096.4	2 414.5	1 549.4	794.2	56.4	-676.1	1 276.6	1 952.7	2 793.9	1 003.0	1 793.3	-28.2	13 551.1
2nd quarter ...	13 706.2	9 155.5	2 500.9	1 583.8	819.5	81.9	-740.0	1 293.1	2 033.0	2 809.9	1 013.0	1 799.0	-22.2	13 624.3
3rd quarter ...	13 830.8	9 243.0	2 539.4	1 626.9	825.3	71.1	-753.0	1 300.6	2 053.6	2 820.7	1 030.7	1 791.0	-16.3	13 759.6
4th quarter	13 950.4	9 337.8	2 590.6	1 661.4	836.7	76.2	-769.9	1 332.1	2 102.0	2 808.2	1 021.8	1 787.7	-11.0	13 873.9
2005														
1st quarter	14 099.1	9 409.2	2 664.4	1 681.9	856.4	111.3	-774.1	1 352.6	2 126.8	2 814.1	1 027.6	1 787.6	-10.1	13 988.8
2nd quarter ...	14 172.7	9 511.5	2 630.5	1 706.1	872.3	33.0	-773.5	1 377.6	2 151.2	2 818.9	1 029.8	1 790.2	-0.4	14 138.5
3rd quarter ...	14 291.8	9 585.2	2 657.9	1 737.4	881.9	18.2	-777.7	1 379.2	2 156.9	2 841.0	1 048.6	1 792.9	3.7	14 271.7
4th quarter	14 373.4	9 621.3	2 737.6	1 744.3	879.9	94.8	-803.9	1 418.1	2 222.0	2 830.7	1 033.2	1 798.6	-2.3	14 276.4
2006														
1st quarter	14 546.1	9 729.2	2 773.8	1 808.7	871.7	78.6	-799.0	1 471.0	2 269.9	2 853.5	1 058.9	1 794.9	1.1	14 468.8
2nd quarter ...	14 589.6	9 781.0	2 755.7	1 831.3	827.8	84.4	-799.1	1 498.5	2 297.6	2 864.1	1 057.7	1 806.9	-4.6	14 506.3
3rd quarter ...	14 602.6	9 838.1	2 727.6	1 853.1	781.6	81.9	-819.7	1 495.5	2 315.2	2 870.4	1 058.0	1 813.0	-6.7	14 520.3
4th quarter	14 716.9	9 938.4	2 663.0	1 865.2	745.2	41.4	-759.3	1 562.1	2 321.4	2 889.1	1 069.0	1 820.6	-5.5	14 673.7
2007														
1st quarter	14 726.0	9 990.7	2 638.5	1 897.2	711.2	19.6	-771.0	1 587.7	2 358.7	2 882.7	1 054.5	1 829.0	-6.7	14 703.3
2nd quarter ...	14 838.7	10 024.6	2 674.7	1 934.4	682.7	49.4	-753.7	1 615.7	2 369.4	2 907.0	1 071.2	1 836.4	-7.1	14 785.5
3rd quarter ...	14 938.5	10 069.2	2 658.1	1 964.4	639.2	50.2	-703.2	1 665.6	2 368.7	2 928.0	1 091.6	1 836.7	-10.3	14 885.9
4th quarter	14 991.8	10 081.8	2 605.2	1 997.6	586.1	23.0	-622.6	1 716.7	2 339.3	2 939.8	1 097.5	1 842.5	-15.3	14 970.1
2008														
1st quarter	14 889.5	10 061.0	2 517.5	1 998.1	540.0	-20.2	-623.7	1 737.9	2 361.6	2 952.0	1 115.2	1 836.9	-20.1	14 909.4
2nd quarter ...	14 963.4	10 077.9	2 472.6	1 986.6	516.3	-26.4	-550.4	1 790.0	2 340.4	2 975.0	1 135.7	1 839.3	-17.6	14 992.9
3rd quarter ...	14 891.6	10 005.1	2 403.8	1 933.0	490.9	-20.7	-526.9	1 766.1	2 293.0	3 016.2	1 169.1	1 847.1	-7.2	14 910.7
4th quarter	14 577.0	9 884.7	2 190.0	1 820.1	443.6	-67.4	-530.3	1 669.2	2 199.5	3 035.9	1 189.3	1 846.6	-10.1	14 650.0
2009														
1st quarter	14 375.0	9 850.8	1 937.7	1 688.3	401.0	-144.5	-451.3	1 535.3	1 986.7	3 040.5	1 180.1	1 860.4	-9.8	14 527.4
2nd quarter ...	14 355.6	9 806.4	1 820.5	1 634.0	377.0	-190.1	-366.3	1 539.4	1 905.7	3 096.0	1 218.9	1 877.1	-1.9	14 545.8
3rd quarter ...	14 402.5	9 865.9	1 804.7	1 613.1	395.4	-206.1	-383.6	1 593.3	1 977.0	3 113.0	1 235.6	1 877.4	4.6	14 605.1
4th quarter	14 541.9	9 864.8	1 949.6	1 598.4	395.7	-49.6	-380.4	1 682.9	2 063.4	3 106.8	1 236.2	1 870.6	6.8	14 586.9
2010														
1st quarter	14 604.8	9 917.7	2 012.9	1 615.0	383.0	9.8	-408.8	1 708.2	2 116.9	3 084.3	1 247.8	1 836.5	4.0	14 591.5
2nd quarter ...	14 745.9	9 998.4	2 116.9	1 659.3	403.5	48.8	-469.7	1 748.1	2 217.8	3 106.2	1 273.4	1 832.8	-1.8	14 694.3
3rd quarter ...	14 845.5	10 063.1	2 185.7	1 692.8	368.1	116.2	-498.4	1 797.5	2 296.0	3 103.5	1 285.0	1 818.5	-1.8	14 724.5
4th quarter	14 939.0	10 166.1	2 166.1	1 728.1	375.1	58.1	-458.1	1 852.6	2 310.7	3 071.5	1 276.4	1 795.2	-5.0	14 878.3
2011														
1st quarter	14 881.3	10 217.1	2 125.9	1 724.1	374.4	25.1	-466.2	1 862.3	2 328.5	3 012.2	1 241.2	1 771.1	-10.4	14 855.3
2nd quarter ...	14 989.6	10 237.7	2 208.0	1 761.0	379.3	57.5	-455.2	1 890.7	2 345.9	3 009.0	1 246.0	1 763.0	-3.4	14 924.5
3rd quarter ...	15 021.1	10 282.2	2 214.0	1 840.8	386.8	-13.0	-454.3	1 910.6	2 364.9	2 990.0	1 233.3	1 756.8	-17.0	15 035.1
4th quarter	15 190.3	10 316.8	2 373.7	1 883.1	397.6	80.8	-461.7	1 929.7	2 391.3	2 978.3	1 225.2	1 753.1	-12.0	15 101.0
2012														
1st quarter	15 291.0	10 379.0	2 429.6	1 938.1	422.5	56.0	-462.7	1 942.6	2 405.3	2 963.7	1 223.9	1 739.8	-15.1	15 225.0
2nd quarter ...	15 362.4	10 396.6	2 489.1	1 973.7	426.3	76.6	-452.7	1 964.4	2 417.0	2 949.4	1 214.8	1 734.5	-17.4	15 276.9
3rd quarter ...	15 380.8	10 424.1	2 482.0	1 963.4	437.3	70.6	-446.8	1 974.1	2 420.9	2 940.9	1 216.2	1 724.7	-19.9	15 302.7
4th quarter	15 384.3	10 453.2	2 462.2	1 981.4	459.8	15.5	-426.0	1 971.7	2 397.8	2 912.3	1 199.0	1 713.3	-26.5	15 364.6
2013														
1st quarter	15 491.9	10 502.3	2 543.0	2 006.7	475.9	49.6	-414.4	1 991.1	2 405.5	2 880.6	1 166.1	1 714.1	-26.5	15 434.3
2nd quarter ...	15 521.6	10 523.9	2 574.3	2 019.0	489.5	52.6	-421.1	2 015.5	2 436.6	2 866.2	1 150.5	1 715.2	-26.4	15 459.1
3rd quarter ...	15 641.0	10 573.1	2 656.8	2 029.6	496.8	109.0	-416.1	2 031.0	2 447.1	2 852.0	1 135.5	1 715.7	-20.2	15 516.6
4th quarter	15 793.9	10 662.2	2 692.0	2 076.3	491.1	103.6	-368.1	2 088.6	2 456.6	2 831.5	1 119.1	1 711.5	-21.6	15 674.3
2014														
1st quarter	15 757.6	10 713.4	2 652.5	2 112.6	487.6	38.7	-411.0	2 075.8	2 486.8	2 827.2	1 118.1	1 708.2	-30.3	15 707.4
2nd quarter ...	15 935.8	10 805.1	2 750.6	2 160.6	503.0	69.9	-426.2	2 121.8	2 548.0	2 834.7	1 113.7	1 719.9	-35.7	15 852.3
3rd quarter ...	16 139.5	10 909.9	2 826.4	2 215.1	508.5	85.6	-416.7	2 125.1	2 541.8	2 849.5	1 122.1	1 726.4	-41.3	16 040.3
4th quarter	16 220.2	11 045.2	2 817.3	2 202.4	521.8	76.9	-456.9	2 150.8	2 607.7	2 845.0	1 106.1	1 737.4	-42.8	16 131.6
2015														
1st quarter	16 350.0	11 145.3	2 905.4	2 214.7	536.1	132.2	-524.1	2 126.4	2 650.5	2 855.7	1 110.3	1 743.9	-41.8	16 202.3
2nd quarter ...	16 460.9	11 227.9	2 911.3	2 230.7	551.1	105.6	-526.2	2 145.8	2 672.0	2 879.9	1 115.1	1 763.1	-43.7	16 338.6
3rd quarter ...	16 527.6	11 304.6	2 925.5	2 238.8	565.2	96.2	-559.3	2 124.1	2 683.4	2 888.3	1 112.0	1 774.4	-46.5	16 414.1
4th quarter	16 547.6	11 379.3	2 879.2	2 209.9	575.3	68.2	-571.5	2 111.9	2 683.5	2 890.2	1 118.9	1 769.7	-47.1	16 462.1
2016														
1st quarter	16 571.6	11 430.5	2 849.8	2 187.5	593.7	40.6	-584.2	2 098.1	2 682.3	2 903.2	1 114.6	1 786.6	-41.4	16 512.7
2nd quarter ...	16 663.5	11 537.7	2 830.2	2 205.3	586.5	12.2	-572.4	2 112.5	2 684.9	2 896.3	1 112.1	1 782.3	-48.2	16 632.6
3rd quarter ...	16 778.1	11 618.1	2 847.2	2 224.0	579.8	17.6	-557.3	2 145.3	2 702.6	2 899.9	1 116.5	1 781.6	-54.2	16 741.1
4th quarter	16 851.4	11 702.1	2 905.7	2 224.9	589.8	63.1	-631.1	2 124.4	2 755.5	2 901.2	1 115.2	1 784.1	-55.2	16 770.0

Note: Chained (2009) dollar series are calculated as the product of the chain-type quantity index and the 2009 current-dollar value of the corresponding series, divided by 100. Because the formula for the chain-type quantity indexes uses weights from more than one period, the corresponding chained-dollar estimates are usually not additive. The residual column is the difference between the total and the sum of the most detailed components shown in the Bureau of Economic Analysis (BEA) published data.

Table 1-3A. U.S. Population and Per Capita Product and Income: Recent Data

(Dollars, except as noted; quarterly data are at seasonally adjusted annual rates.)   **NIPA Table 7.1**

Year and quarter	Population (mid-period, thousands)	Current dollars							Chained (2009) dollars					
		Gross domestic product	Personal income	Dispos-able personal income	Personal consumption expenditures				Gross domestic product	Dispos-able personal income	Personal consumption expenditures			
					Total	Durable goods	Nondur-able goods	Services			Total	Durable goods	Nondur-able goods	Services
1950	151 684	1 979	1 542	1 417	1 267	214	556	497	14 398	10 033	8 969	446	3 254	5 281
1951	154 287	2 251	1 714	1 539	1 351	206	603	543	15 296	10 197	8 955	402	3 248	5 498
1952	156 954	2 343	1 801	1 597	1 398	199	621	578	15 649	10 371	9 081	387	3 313	5 647
1953	159 565	2 443	1 877	1 669	1 460	217	628	615	16 115	10 697	9 359	425	3 360	5 788
1954	162 391	2 409	1 863	1 678	1 477	208	628	641	15 745	10 661	9 389	416	3 354	5 886
1955	165 275	2 579	1 964	1 765	1 565	247	645	673	16 573	11 172	9 906	496	3 466	6 074
1956	168 221	2 676	2 071	1 854	1 614	239	666	710	16 630	11 502	10 017	469	3 525	6 253
1957	171 274	2 772	2 151	1 924	1 674	245	686	742	16 677	11 589	10 082	465	3 532	6 353
1958	174 141	2 768	2 179	1 958	1 700	227	701	772	16 282	11 519	10 002	422	3 520	6 451
1959	177 130	2 950	2 276	2 038	1 793	253	721	818	17 112	11 811	10 390	464	3 616	6 655
1960	180 760	3 006	2 338	2 083	1 834	252	727	855	17 198	11 877	10 461	464	3 602	6 776
1961	183 742	3 066	2 401	2 143	1 861	241	733	888	17 351	12 097	10 504	441	3 615	6 912
1962	186 590	3 243	2 514	2 238	1 946	265	748	933	18 131	12 482	10 855	484	3 670	7 128
1963	189 300	3 373	2 603	2 315	2 021	286	760	974	18 650	12 766	11 140	521	3 695	7 325
1964	191 927	3 573	2 753	2 482	2 142	310	796	1 037	19 456	13 485	11 642	562	3 816	7 654
1965	194 347	3 827	2 937	2 641	2 282	342	840	1 101	20 462	14 144	12 226	624	3 958	7 978
1966	196 599	4 146	3 157	2 819	2 445	365	905	1 175	21 561	14 726	12 770	668	4 130	8 276
1967	198 752	4 336	3 350	2 983	2 553	372	931	1 250	21 913	15 198	13 009	670	4 173	8 521
1968	200 745	4 695	3 640	3 207	2 777	423	995	1 359	22 760	15 728	13 619	737	4 307	8 882
1969	202 736	5 031	3 947	3 432	2 982	446	1 057	1 479	23 244	16 102	13 990	757	4 382	9 186
1970	205 089	5 246	4 216	3 713	3 158	439	1 116	1 604	23 024	16 643	14 155	729	4 428	9 438
1971	207 692	5 623	4 488	3 998	3 375	493	1 154	1 728	23 485	17 191	14 511	792	4 455	9 642
1972	209 924	6 109	4 876	4 287	3 665	555	1 226	1 885	24 458	17 821	15 237	881	4 586	10 088
1973	211 939	6 740	5 372	4 747	4 016	616	1 350	2 050	25 593	18 725	15 841	964	4 673	10 466
1974	213 898	7 241	5 841	5 135	4 357	609	1 502	2 246	25 227	18 343	15 566	894	4 517	10 571
1975	215 981	7 820	6 329	5 645	4 782	658	1 617	2 507	24 934	18 613	15 766	887	4 512	10 863
1976	218 086	8 609	6 871	6 079	5 274	773	1 732	2 769	26 024	19 002	16 484	988	4 681	11 221
1977	220 289	9 469	7 511	6 613	5 795	871	1 854	3 070	26 951	19 406	17 007	1 065	4 740	11 569
1978	222 629	10 585	8 353	7 322	6 406	958	2 022	3 425	28 151	20 080	17 568	1 109	4 859	11 977
1979	225 106	11 693	9 232	8 037	7 061	1 005	2 273	3 783	28 725	20 248	17 788	1 091	4 930	12 207
1980	227 726	12 570	10 177	8 861	7 705	994	2 518	4 193	28 325	20 158	17 528	993	4 865	12 261
1981	230 008	13 960	11 289	9 785	8 424	1 061	2 719	4 644	28 772	20 458	17 611	993	4 877	12 351
1982	232 218	14 405	11 969	10 442	8 931	1 090	2 783	5 058	27 953	20 685	17 692	982	4 881	12 477
1983	234 333	15 526	12 675	11 170	9 758	1 259	2 897	5 602	28 984	21 214	18 532	1 112	4 994	13 008
1984	236 394	17 093	13 883	12 284	10 568	1 447	3 052	6 068	30 817	22 480	19 339	1 259	5 155	13 393
1985	238 506	18 225	14 743	12 991	11 416	1 506	3 175	6 646	31 839	22 960	20 175	1 373	5 264	13 972
1986	240 683	19 071	15 480	13 661	12 042	1 751	3 217	7 075	32 659	23 632	20 832	1 491	5 402	14 292
1987	242 843	20 055	16 290	14 274	12 733	1 820	3 353	7 559	33 489	23 929	21 346	1 507	5 446	14 801
1988	245 061	21 434	17 450	15 386	13 657	1 939	3 519	8 200	34 581	24 826	22 037	1 578	5 539	15 327
1989	247 387	22 870	18 675	16 380	14 523	1 998	3 757	8 768	35 517	25 340	22 467	1 598	5 635	15 666
1990	250 181	23 901	19 611	17 235	15 291	1 987	3 974	9 331	35 794	25 555	22 674	1 573	5 637	15 957
1991	253 530	24 352	20 011	17 688	15 620	1 882	4 024	9 714	35 295	25 395	22 426	1 469	5 546	16 003
1992	256 922	25 452	21 069	18 684	16 408	1 978	4 107	10 324	36 068	26 133	22 951	1 533	5 579	16 431
1993	260 282	26 428	21 703	19 211	17 178	2 119	4 191	10 868	36 580	26 216	23 441	1 626	5 647	16 718
1994	263 455	27 742	22 536	19 906	17 996	2 305	4 325	11 366	37 598	26 611	24 057	1 735	5 797	17 025
1995	266 588	28 749	23 561	20 753	18 696	2 385	4 426	11 886	38 167	27 180	24 486	1 782	5 870	17 328
1996	269 714	30 033	24 719	21 615	19 532	2 507	4 603	12 422	39 156	27 719	25 047	1 893	5 970	17 629
1997	272 958	31 538	25 941	22 527	20 372	2 621	4 731	13 020	40 427	28 397	25 681	2 023	6 073	17 977
1998	276 154	32 913	27 498	23 759	21 376	2 822	4 814	13 740	41 737	29 723	26 741	2 241	6 226	18 587
1999	279 328	34 585	28 599	24 617	22 579	3 063	5 124	14 393	43 196	30 350	27 838	2 500	6 465	19 087
2000	282 398	36 419	30 585	26 206	24 053	3 232	5 454	15 367	44 475	31 524	28 933	2 685	6 599	19 828
2001	285 225	37 240	31 525	27 179	24 904	3 301	5 553	16 050	44 464	32 075	29 390	2 798	6 647	20 093
2002	287 955	38 122	31 789	28 127	25 643	3 422	5 602	16 619	44 829	32 754	29 862	2 975	6 706	20 275
2003	290 626	39 606	32 657	29 198	26 720	3 501	5 863	17 356	45 664	33 342	30 512	3 157	6 877	20 531
2004	293 262	41 857	34 280	30 697	28 166	3 682	6 208	18 276	46 967	34 221	31 399	3 386	7 037	20 993
2005	295 993	44 237	35 859	31 760	29 711	3 808	6 598	19 304	48 090	34 424	32 203	3 537	7 204	21 465
2006	298 818	46 369	38 130	33 589	31 136	3 869	6 960	20 307	48 905	35 458	32 868	3 653	7 370	21 841
2007	301 696	47 987	39 776	34 826	32 319	3 927	7 216	21 177	49 300	35 866	33 284	3 784	7 422	22 063
2008	304 543	48 330	41 052	36 101	32 881	3 619	7 465	21 796	48 697	36 078	32 860	3 557	7 272	22 028
2009	307 240	46 930	39 366	35 616	32 050	3 331	7 080	21 640	46 930	35 616	32 050	3 331	7 080	21 640
2010	309 801	48 303	40 275	36 274	32 931	3 456	7 399	22 077	47 720	35 685	32 396	3 504	7 177	21 716
2011	312 114	49 719	42 467	37 811	34 248	3 605	7 917	22 725	48 125	36 305	32 884	3 689	7 251	21 952
2012	314 377	51 388	44 263	39 455	35 151	3 791	8 102	23 257	48 841	37 179	33 123	3 932	7 245	21 974
2013	316 569	52 726	44 457	39 157	35 888	3 922	8 190	23 776	49 317	36 414	33 375	4 147	7 316	21 958
2014	318 887	54 651	46 469	40 869	37 203	4 065	8 386	24 752	50 216	37 441	34 082	4 400	7 441	22 314
2015	321 173	56 420	48 426	42 392	38 398	4 257	8 301	25 840	51 286	38 720	35 072	4 707	7 618	22 854
2016	323 391	57 591	49 255	43 194	39 645	4 363	8 381	26 900	51 690	38 988	35 784	4 932	7 775	23 214
2014														
1st quarter	318 003	53 557	45 553	40 045	36 604	3 959	8 318	24 327	49 552	36 856	33 690	4 248	7 374	22 123
2nd quarter	318 543	54 375	46 190	40 672	37 018	4 055	8 389	24 575	50 027	37 268	33 920	4 375	7 415	22 202
3rd quarter	319 183	55 211	46 760	41 134	37 412	4 103	8 431	24 878	50 565	37 581	34 181	4 448	7 455	22 357
4th quarter	319 817	55 456	47 367	41 621	37 776	4 144	8 404	25 228	50 717	38 052	34 536	4 528	7 522	22 571
2015														
1st quarter	320 328	55 801	47 767	41 825	37 905	4 189	8 221	25 496	51 041	38 391	34 793	4 606	7 555	22 726
2nd quarter	320 846	56 392	48 360	42 332	38 287	4 260	8 299	25 728	51 305	38 692	34 995	4 695	7 590	22 816
3rd quarter	321 458	56 703	48 608	42 580	38 598	4 282	8 370	25 946	51 414	38 794	35 167	4 744	7 650	22 885
4th quarter	322 058	56 782	48 964	42 827	38 797	4 296	8 313	26 188	51 381	39 003	35 333	4 783	7 677	22 989
2016														
1st quarter	322 549	56 814	48 833	42 853	38 975	4 286	8 260	26 429	51 377	38 964	35 438	4 788	7 715	23 050
2nd quarter	323 064	57 382	49 248	43 209	39 481	4 337	8 380	26 764	51 580	39 086	35 713	4 879	7 793	23 171
3rd quarter	323 675	57 864	49 519	43 390	39 853	4 388	8 386	27 080	51 836	39 080	35 894	4 980	7 779	23 279
4th quarter	324 275	58 301	49 420	43 323	40 265	4 441	8 498	27 326	51 966	38 828	36 087	5 082	7 812	23 356

Table 1-3B. U.S. Population and Per Capita Product and Income: Historical Data

(Dollars, except as noted; quarterly data are at seasonally adjusted annual rates.)   **NIPA Table 7.1**

Year and quarter	Population (mid-period, thousands)	Current dollars							Chained (2009) dollars					
		Gross domestic product	Personal income	Disposable personal income	Personal consumption expenditures				Gross domestic product	Disposable personal income	Personal consumption expenditures			
					Total	Durable goods	Nondurable goods	Services			Total	Durable goods	Nondurable goods	Services
1929	121 878	858	700	685	635	81	278	276	8 669	6 917	6 408	263	2 479	3 812
1930	123 188	748	621	608	569	62	248	260	7 847	6 411	6 000	215	2 325	3 693
1931	124 149	623	529	521	489	48	208	233	7 288	6 145	5 768	185	2 282	3 571
1932	124 949	476	402	396	390	32	161	197	6 308	5 306	5 218	140	2 068	3 334
1933	125 690	455	376	369	366	30	159	177	6 192	5 122	5 073	135	2 048	3 191
1934	126 485	528	427	420	407	36	189	182	6 817	5 579	5 401	154	2 201	3 327
1935	127 362	583	478	469	439	43	205	191	7 373	6 080	5 689	185	2 311	3 419
1936	128 181	662	540	530	485	53	228	205	8 273	6 802	6 228	224	2 559	3 607
1937	128 961	721	579	564	518	57	240	221	8 643	6 990	6 419	234	2 606	3 753
1938	129 969	672	532	517	494	47	230	217	8 292	6 556	6 268	193	2 623	3 694
1939	131 028	713	562	551	513	55	235	224	8 881	7 046	6 565	227	2 721	3 807
1940	132 122	779	601	588	540	63	245	232	9 583	7 464	6 847	257	2 813	3 921
1941	133 402	970	734	716	608	77	279	252	11 171	8 558	7 261	294	2 954	4 113
1942	134 860	1 231	940	903	660	57	322	282	13 138	9 598	7 012	185	2 929	4 293
1943	136 739	1 485	1 142	1 020	731	55	357	319	15 166	9 922	7 109	163	2 907	4 572
1944	138 397	1 623	1 226	1 099	785	56	381	348	16 181	10 109	7 223	149	2 933	4 769
1945	139 928	1 631	1 256	1 117	857	65	418	374	15 850	9 885	7 586	164	3 080	4 970
1946	141 389	1 611	1 292	1 170	1 021	121	489	411	13 869	9 679	8 442	292	3 324	5 142
1947	144 126	1 734	1 350	1 213	1 124	151	538	434	13 457	9 109	8 440	336	3 241	5 066
1948	146 631	1 874	1 457	1 326	1 194	167	566	461	13 776	9 425	8 483	352	3 210	5 111
1949	149 188	1 829	1 416	1 304	1 196	178	546	472	13 466	9 340	8 569	374	3 202	5 144
1947														
1st quarter	143 156	1 698	1 328	1 194	1 092	145	523	424	13 513	9 167	8 378	326	3 225	5 057
2nd quarter	143 803	1 713	1 320	1 185	1 114	148	535	431	13 437	9 022	8 479	331	3 266	5 107
3rd quarter	144 462	1 731	1 369	1 232	1 133	151	544	438	13 362	9 211	8 468	334	3 266	5 073
4th quarter	145 135	1 794	1 382	1 239	1 156	162	551	443	13 510	9 036	8 431	354	3 208	5 023
1948														
1st quarter	145 761	1 826	1 418	1 272	1 170	162	559	449	13 649	9 175	8 437	351	3 205	5 055
2nd quarter	146 341	1 865	1 450	1 320	1 191	164	568	458	13 816	9 424	8 501	352	3 223	5 114
3rd quarter	146 973	1 902	1 481	1 356	1 206	172	568	466	13 834	9 537	8 477	356	3 190	5 119
4th quarter	147 659	1 901	1 478	1 353	1 206	169	567	470	13 784	9 546	8 505	350	3 217	5 146
1949														
1st quarter	148 298	1 857	1 431	1 311	1 193	165	558	471	13 537	9 318	8 482	342	3 215	5 157
2nd quarter	148 891	1 825	1 418	1 304	1 199	177	550	472	13 438	9 326	8 578	370	3 211	5 162
3rd quarter	149 529	1 827	1 408	1 299	1 190	183	537	471	13 528	9 346	8 560	386	3 170	5 129
4th quarter	150 211	1 804	1 405	1 299	1 201	189	539	473	13 346	9 356	8 646	399	3 207	5 121
1950														
1st quarter	150 852	1 864	1 501	1 391	1 214	194	540	479	13 819	10 035	8 753	413	3 234	5 162
2nd quarter	151 385	1 921	1 505	1 389	1 235	197	547	491	14 186	9 969	8 866	415	3 260	5 274
3rd quarter	152 039	2 029	1 554	1 429	1 320	246	570	504	14 670	10 051	9 280	511	3 302	5 333
4th quarter	152 724	2 097	1 605	1 457	1 297	218	567	512	14 886	10 067	8 960	446	3 214	5 342
1951														
1st quarter	153 336	2 194	1 659	1 500	1 365	232	600	533	15 029	10 038	9 140	458	3 260	5 466
2nd quarter	153 947	2 237	1 711	1 539	1 332	200	594	539	15 229	10 221	8 846	391	3 200	5 481
3rd quarter	154 655	2 275	1 731	1 552	1 343	195	602	546	15 472	10 290	8 908	382	3 252	5 524
4th quarter	155 389	2 295	1 753	1 562	1 363	196	614	553	15 433	10 223	8 918	379	3 275	5 512
1952														
1st quarter	156 033	2 308	1 759	1 561	1 366	197	607	561	15 532	10 176	8 901	380	3 234	5 557
2nd quarter	156 644	2 307	1 778	1 574	1 387	198	617	572	15 503	10 264	9 040	385	3 297	5 622
3rd quarter	157 324	2 340	1 815	1 610	1 397	187	626	583	15 548	10 425	9 045	361	3 340	5 672
4th quarter	158 043	2 412	1 849	1 640	1 442	210	635	594	15 985	10 601	9 322	421	3 374	5 726
1953														
1st quarter	158 648	2 449	1 870	1 660	1 459	222	634	604	16 221	10 689	9 397	434	3 382	5 763
2nd quarter	159 234	2 463	1 888	1 678	1 465	220	631	613	16 287	10 788	9 419	430	3 385	5 810
3rd quarter	159 963	2 449	1 879	1 671	1 463	216	624	622	16 122	10 688	9 354	425	3 338	5 819
4th quarter	160 713	2 405	1 870	1 665	1 452	210	622	621	15 803	10 602	9 249	411	3 328	5 749
1954														
1st quarter	161 389	2 391	1 862	1 675	1 459	204	627	628	15 664	10 612	9 244	397	3 346	5 778
2nd quarter	162 044	2 386	1 852	1 667	1 470	208	625	637	15 617	10 579	9 326	414	3 323	5 854
3rd quarter	162 792	2 405	1 856	1 672	1 478	204	628	646	15 722	10 642	9 410	414	3 350	5 929
4th quarter	163 585	2 447	1 880	1 694	1 500	214	632	654	15 951	10 794	9 560	438	3 390	5 971
1955														
1st quarter	164 266	2 519	1 911	1 720	1 533	234	636	662	16 338	10 924	9 735	475	3 411	6 016
2nd quarter	164 926	2 560	1 949	1 753	1 557	247	643	667	16 537	11 120	9 881	499	3 460	6 036
3rd quarter	165 674	2 601	1 985	1 784	1 576	256	645	674	16 684	11 273	9 958	512	3 467	6 071
4th quarter	166 481	2 630	2 006	1 801	1 592	249	655	688	16 703	11 350	10 034	497	3 521	6 161
1956														
1st quarter	167 190	2 635	2 031	1 819	1 594	237	661	696	16 568	11 418	10 008	472	3 545	6 194
2nd quarter	167 869	2 661	2 057	1 841	1 604	237	663	704	16 637	11 479	10 001	471	3 522	6 228
3rd quarter	168 654	2 680	2 079	1 860	1 616	235	667	714	16 546	11 484	9 977	460	3 508	6 264
4th quarter	169 497	2 721	2 113	1 890	1 640	245	671	724	16 733	11 601	10 064	473	3 519	6 314
1957														
1st quarter	170 218	2 765	2 131	1 904	1 659	250	678	730	16 770	11 586	10 090	479	3 525	6 312
2nd quarter	170 915	2 766	2 150	1 922	1 665	247	682	737	16 664	11 620	10 067	466	3 524	6 340
3rd quarter	171 684	2 798	2 168	1 940	1 684	244	695	745	16 751	11 631	10 101	461	3 557	6 357
4th quarter	172 463	2 758	2 154	1 929	1 686	240	690	755	16 505	11 509	10 059	453	3 517	6 397

Table 1-3B. U.S. Population and Per Capita Product and Income: Historical Data—*Continued*

(Dollars, except as noted; quarterly data are at seasonally adjusted annual rates.)   NIPA Table 7.1

Year and quarter	Population (mid-period, thousands)	Current dollars							Chained (2009) dollars					
		Gross domestic product	Personal income	Disposable personal income	Personal consumption expenditures				Gross domestic product	Disposable personal income	Personal consumption expenditures			
					Total	Durable goods	Nondurable goods	Services			Total	Durable goods	Nondurable goods	Services
1958														
1st quarter	173 116	2 705	2 151	1 931	1 677	228	692	757	16 016	11 379	9 884	421	3 473	6 365
2nd quarter	173 781	2 721	2 157	1 940	1 687	222	697	768	16 060	11 411	9 927	413	3 491	6 433
3rd quarter	174 535	2 788	2 195	1 972	1 709	226	705	779	16 360	11 590	10 047	420	3 539	6 492
4th quarter	175 340	2 854	2 211	1 986	1 724	232	708	784	16 666	11 678	10 135	434	3 571	6 504
1959														
1st quarter	176 045	2 903	2 240	2 009	1 760	248	716	796	16 908	11 730	10 278	455	3 603	6 557
2nd quarter	176 727	2 966	2 279	2 041	1 787	257	719	811	17 253	11 871	10 396	471	3 619	6 629
3rd quarter	177 481	2 959	2 282	2 042	1 809	261	722	826	17 146	11 805	10 460	478	3 618	6 690
4th quarter	178 268	2 969	2 304	2 058	1 813	247	726	839	17 138	11 837	10 426	453	3 624	6 741
1960														
1st quarter	179 694	3 024	2 321	2 069	1 818	253	721	844	17 380	11 883	10 442	464	3 604	6 748
2nd quarter	180 335	3 009	2 341	2 086	1 844	257	732	855	17 253	11 915	10 536	473	3 631	6 798
3rd quarter	181 094	3 015	2 345	2 088	1 836	254	727	856	17 223	11 885	10 450	467	3 594	6 761
4th quarter	181 915	2 974	2 343	2 087	1 839	246	728	865	16 938	11 827	10 417	453	3 580	6 796
1961														
1st quarter	182 634	2 989	2 358	2 103	1 834	231	730	872	16 986	11 895	10 373	426	3 587	6 837
2nd quarter	183 337	3 040	2 383	2 127	1 854	236	732	886	17 236	12 030	10 487	434	3 622	6 911
3rd quarter	184 103	3 086	2 412	2 154	1 862	242	731	889	17 450	12 139	10 494	442	3 609	6 903
4th quarter	184 894	3 146	2 449	2 189	1 894	252	736	905	17 728	12 320	10 659	462	3 643	6 995
1962														
1st quarter	185 553	3 208	2 478	2 211	1 915	257	743	915	17 983	12 394	10 734	470	3 660	7 036
2nd quarter	186 203	3 236	2 508	2 235	1 939	263	745	930	18 113	12 480	10 828	481	3 662	7 116
3rd quarter	186 926	3 261	2 523	2 243	1 952	265	749	938	18 215	12 497	10 873	483	3 676	7 149
4th quarter	187 680	3 267	2 546	2 261	1 978	275	754	949	18 212	12 556	10 983	502	3 682	7 210
1963														
1st quarter	188 299	3 307	2 567	2 279	1 990	279	757	954	18 354	12 622	11 021	510	3 690	7 215
2nd quarter	188 906	3 345	2 584	2 296	2 006	285	756	964	18 534	12 699	11 091	520	3 690	7 271
3rd quarter	189 631	3 401	2 612	2 324	2 035	288	766	981	18 823	12 790	11 199	524	3 710	7 370
4th quarter	190 362	3 440	2 651	2 361	2 051	293	763	995	18 885	12 949	11 249	530	3 691	7 442
1964														
1st quarter	190 954	3 515	2 693	2 412	2 095	304	778	1 013	19 233	13 162	11 435	549	3 742	7 538
2nd quarter	191 560	3 554	2 734	2 474	2 130	310	791	1 029	19 401	13 473	11 529	562	3 802	7 619
3rd quarter	192 256	3 604	2 774	2 506	2 169	319	000	1 044	19 593	13 598	11 770	578	3 862	7 691
4th quarter	192 938	3 620	2 810	2 534	2 175	308	808	1 059	19 593	13 703	11 761	558	3 856	7 769
1965														
1st quarter	193 467	3 718	2 859	2 565	2 224	336	815	1 073	20 021	13 826	11 991	609	3 882	7 836
2nd quarter	193 994	3 775	2 901	2 600	2 254	334	829	1 091	20 240	13 945	12 091	608	3 908	7 934
3rd quarter	194 647	3 854	2 965	2 672	2 293	343	843	1 108	20 582	14 279	12 257	627	3 954	8 016
4th quarter	195 279	3 959	3 024	2 725	2 358	354	873	1 130	20 999	14 520	12 561	651	4 087	8 126
1966														
1st quarter	195 763	4 073	3 081	2 767	2 405	369	889	1 146	21 464	14 628	12 715	680	4 107	8 189
2nd quarter	196 277	4 112	3 123	2 789	2 424	355	903	1 166	21 496	14 627	12 713	651	4 135	8 256
3rd quarter	196 877	4 169	3 181	2 836	2 463	367	913	1 183	21 583	14 760	12 819	671	4 152	8 298
4th quarter	197 481	4 228	3 240	2 883	2 485	368	913	1 204	21 701	14 885	12 833	668	4 127	8 362
1967														
1st quarter	197 967	4 274	3 287	2 927	2 501	359	921	1 220	21 847	15 070	12 876	654	4 164	8 419
2nd quarter	198 455	4 288	3 314	2 957	2 541	375	927	1 238	21 812	15 151	13 019	681	4 184	8 479
3rd quarter	199 012	4 355	3 374	3 003	2 570	375	933	1 261	21 939	15 251	13 049	673	4 169	8 570
4th quarter	199 572	4 425	3 423	3 042	2 600	379	941	1 280	22 053	15 318	13 092	673	4 176	8 617
1968														
1st quarter	199 995	4 556	3 513	3 120	2 684	404	968	1 312	22 454	15 547	13 374	713	4 249	8 732
2nd quarter	200 452	4 671	3 605	3 197	2 747	414	987	1 346	22 781	15 770	13 547	727	4 291	8 848
3rd quarter	200 997	4 738	3 687	3 230	2 820	436	1 009	1 375	22 883	15 766	13 764	758	4 348	8 937
4th quarter	201 538	4 814	3 755	3 279	2 856	436	1 017	1 403	22 923	15 831	13 790	751	4 337	9 011
1969														
1st quarter	201 955	4 929	3 819	3 311	2 911	446	1 034	1 431	23 231	15 830	13 915	764	4 376	9 072
2nd quarter	202 419	4 996	3 905	3 383	2 960	447	1 048	1 465	23 252	15 968	13 972	760	4 376	9 163
3rd quarter	202 986	5 084	4 000	3 487	3 003	446	1 064	1 492	23 332	16 260	14 001	756	4 380	9 210
4th quarter	203 584	5 112	4 064	3 545	3 053	446	1 079	1 527	23 162	16 339	14 071	750	4 396	9 297
1970														
1st quarter	204 086	5 162	4 125	3 612	3 100	439	1 100	1 561	23 064	16 459	14 123	737	4 423	9 374
2nd quarter	204 721	5 227	4 199	3 684	3 139	445	1 107	1 587	23 033	16 601	14 144	743	4 407	9 404
3rd quarter	205 419	5 299	4 255	3 765	3 186	448	1 118	1 620	23 159	16 803	14 220	744	4 423	9 479
4th quarter	206 130	5 295	4 283	3 791	3 208	424	1 138	1 646	22 841	16 703	14 132	692	4 460	9 494
1971														
1st quarter	206 763	5 503	4 367	3 892	3 290	474	1 141	1 675	23 381	16 986	14 359	764	4 464	9 530
2nd quarter	207 362	5 591	4 467	3 982	3 348	487	1 152	1 709	23 447	17 184	14 449	779	4 461	9 598
3rd quarter	208 000	5 675	4 522	4 030	3 397	497	1 156	1 744	23 557	17 222	14 519	797	4 439	9 659
4th quarter	208 642	5 721	4 595	4 089	3 465	514	1 168	1 783	23 554	17 369	14 715	828	4 455	9 780
1972														
1st quarter	209 142	5 899	4 714	4 142	3 539	529	1 181	1 828	23 919	17 407	14 874	845	4 459	9 922
2nd quarter	209 637	6 059	4 787	4 198	3 619	544	1 213	1 862	24 415	17 543	15 122	865	4 569	10 019
3rd quarter	210 181	6 156	4 897	4 305	3 697	559	1 237	1 900	24 576	17 835	15 316	885	4 620	10 128
4th quarter	210 737	6 321	5 104	4 501	3 805	586	1 272	1 947	24 918	18 493	15 634	929	4 695	10 282

Table 1-3B. U.S. Population and Per Capita Product and Income: Historical Data—*Continued*

(Dollars, except as noted; quarterly data are at seasonally adjusted annual rates.)   NIPA Table 7.1

| Year and quarter | Population (mid-period, thousands) | Current dollars | | | | | | | Chained (2009) dollars | | | | | |
| | | Gross domestic product | Personal income | Disposable personal income | Personal consumption expenditures | | | | Gross domestic product | Disposable personal income | Personal consumption expenditures | | | |
					Total	Durable goods	Nondurable goods	Services			Total	Durable goods	Nondurable goods	Services
1973														
1st quarter	211 192	6 538	5 177	4 578	3 913	624	1 304	1 985	25 477	18 585	15 885	986	4 713	10 392
2nd quarter	211 663	6 697	5 304	4 693	3 978	620	1 329	2 029	25 708	18 691	15 843	972	4 662	10 457
3rd quarter	212 191	6 771	5 420	4 788	4 055	616	1 366	2 072	25 505	18 726	15 860	961	4 673	10 501
4th quarter	212 708	6 954	5 586	4 928	4 116	603	1 399	2 114	25 680	18 885	15 775	936	4 643	10 515
1974														
1st quarter	213 144	7 012	5 651	4 981	4 193	594	1 449	2 150	25 415	18 536	15 605	913	4 571	10 478
2nd quarter	213 602	7 183	5 760	5 063	4 318	611	1 489	2 218	25 427	18 324	15 627	915	4 531	10 559
3rd quarter	214 147	7 301	5 915	5 191	4 441	637	1 530	2 274	25 117	18 295	15 651	918	4 529	10 584
4th quarter	214 700	7 466	6 037	5 303	4 475	592	1 541	2 342	24 952	18 225	15 382	829	4 437	10 663
1975														
1st quarter	215 135	7 528	6 117	5 382	4 588	613	1 563	2 413	24 601	18 158	15 479	845	4 437	10 740
2nd quarter	215 652	7 681	6 249	5 687	4 710	634	1 599	2 478	24 731	18 956	15 700	859	4 524	10 848
3rd quarter	216 289	7 924	6 399	5 693	4 853	679	1 646	2 528	25 065	18 625	15 877	910	4 555	10 869
4th quarter	216 848	8 143	6 548	5 817	4 974	707	1 659	2 608	25 338	18 719	16 004	934	4 532	10 993
1976														
1st quarter	217 314	8 396	6 686	5 938	5 118	751	1 691	2 676	25 854	18 898	16 289	979	4 614	11 098
2nd quarter	217 776	8 527	6 784	6 006	5 198	762	1 713	2 723	25 994	18 956	16 404	981	4 675	11 148
3rd quarter	218 338	8 659	6 933	6 127	5 319	778	1 743	2 798	26 059	19 047	16 536	990	4 699	11 255
4th quarter	218 917	8 855	7 079	6 244	5 459	801	1 780	2 878	26 186	19 109	16 707	1 003	4 735	11 381
1977														
1st quarter	219 427	9 081	7 200	6 340	5 608	838	1 807	2 963	26 429	19 059	16 859	1 037	4 721	11 491
2nd quarter	219 956	9 366	7 403	6 513	5 722	860	1 835	3 026	26 883	19 250	16 911	1 059	4 710	11 507
3rd quarter	220 573	9 622	7 594	6 694	5 847	879	1 858	3 109	27 282	19 490	17 025	1 072	4 720	11 599
4th quarter	221 201	9 804	7 844	6 901	6 003	907	1 915	3 181	27 207	19 810	17 232	1 091	4 807	11 677
1978														
1st quarter	221 719	9 962	8 005	7 049	6 124	894	1 944	3 286	27 238	19 904	17 291	1 060	4 817	11 835
2nd quarter	222 281	10 512	8 251	7 247	6 367	973	2 001	3 393	28 225	20 050	17 616	1 136	4 842	11 982
3rd quarter	222 933	10 760	8 466	7 406	6 487	972	2 044	3 471	28 418	20 135	17 638	1 117	4 865	12 032
4th quarter	223 583	11 102	8 689	7 583	6 644	994	2 099	3 550	28 715	20 235	17 727	1 123	4 913	12 059
1979														
1st quarter	224 152	11 294	8 920	7 788	6 785	996	2 162	3 628	28 699	20 398	17 772	1 107	4 922	12 151
2nd quarter	224 737	11 551	9 077	7 911	6 948	988	2 225	3 735	28 659	20 169	17 715	1 079	4 900	12 195
3rd quarter	225 418	11 846	9 340	8 121	7 169	1 024	2 317	3 827	28 778	20 204	17 836	1 105	4 942	12 207
4th quarter	226 117	12 077	9 589	8 328	7 339	1 013	2 385	3 941	28 763	20 230	17 828	1 074	4 953	12 275
1980														
1st quarter	226 754	12 333	9 838	8 582	7 526	1 023	2 469	4 033	28 775	20 241	17 751	1 054	4 937	12 259
2nd quarter	227 389	12 313	9 925	8 640	7 515	932	2 489	4 095	28 113	19 892	17 303	938	4 856	12 147
3rd quarter	228 070	12 540	10 248	8 923	7 751	988	2 528	4 235	27 987	20 074	17 437	976	4 830	12 246
4th quarter	228 689	13 090	10 692	9 297	8 026	1 033	2 585	4 407	28 428	20 413	17 620	1 003	4 836	12 394
1981														
1st quarter	229 155	13 667	10 927	9 483	8 251	1 074	2 680	4 497	28 957	20 316	17 677	1 030	4 869	12 341
2nd quarter	229 674	13 790	11 109	9 617	8 368	1 049	2 712	4 607	28 681	20 266	17 634	987	4 879	12 391
3rd quarter	230 301	14 161	11 497	9 947	8 516	1 094	2 732	4 690	28 931	20 624	17 657	1 015	4 877	12 346
4th quarter	230 903	14 220	11 619	10 092	8 558	1 026	2 753	4 779	28 519	20 611	17 479	939	4 883	12 325
1982														
1st quarter	231 395	14 148	11 734	10 210	8 705	1 065	2 765	4 875	27 982	20 592	17 557	967	4 881	12 347
2nd quarter	231 906	14 365	11 895	10 344	8 801	1 075	2 754	4 972	28 073	20 665	17 583	969	4 862	12 403
3rd quarter	232 498	14 482	12 042	10 536	8 986	1 084	2 795	5 107	27 900	20 723	17 674	974	4 870	12 490
4th quarter	233 074	14 621	12 204	10 674	9 229	1 134	2 818	5 277	27 859	20 765	17 952	1 016	4 908	12 667
1983														
1st quarter	233 546	14 902	12 339	10 837	9 380	1 151	2 813	5 415	28 107	20 901	18 090	1 024	4 914	12 806
2nd quarter	234 028	15 314	12 528	10 992	9 634	1 237	2 876	5 520	28 750	21 006	18 410	1 096	4 902	12 942
3rd quarter	234 603	15 738	12 749	11 277	9 907	1 289	2 934	5 684	29 241	21 270	18 687	1 136	5 025	13 092
4th quarter	235 153	16 143	13 082	11 570	10 107	1 358	2 962	5 787	29 774	21 678	18 937	1 189	5 074	13 193
1984														
1st quarter	235 605	16 607	13 444	11 911	10 283	1 407	2 998	5 878	30 307	22 078	19 061	1 232	5 077	13 230
2nd quarter	236 082	17 007	13 771	12 202	10 510	1 446	3 060	6 005	30 777	22 400	19 294	1 258	5 178	13 313
3rd quarter	236 657	17 271	14 058	12 435	10 647	1 445	3 062	6 140	31 005	22 652	19 395	1 255	5 169	13 453
4th quarter	237 232	17 483	14 254	12 585	10 829	1 492	3 089	6 248	31 176	22 783	19 604	1 293	5 196	13 575
1985														
1st quarter	237 673	17 827	14 501	12 682	11 124	1 548	3 124	6 452	31 428	22 687	19 900	1 335	5 218	13 795
2nd quarter	238 176	18 064	14 639	13 007	11 299	1 567	3 161	6 572	31 649	23 075	20 044	1 348	5 248	13 898
3rd quarter	238 789	18 404	14 799	13 033	11 578	1 660	3 185	6 733	32 058	22 938	20 377	1 431	5 278	14 054
4th quarter	239 387	18 602	15 032	13 241	11 658	1 603	3 231	6 825	32 218	23 144	20 378	1 378	5 311	14 140
1986														
1st quarter	239 861	18 829	15 252	13 475	11 818	1 633	3 249	6 937	32 453	23 386	20 510	1 403	5 368	14 165
2nd quarter	240 368	18 951	15 396	13 609	11 911	1 694	3 193	7 024	32 533	23 647	20 696	1 450	5 404	14 228
3rd quarter	240 962	19 172	15 565	13 741	12 158	1 850	3 200	7 109	32 779	23 755	21 019	1 570	5 402	14 322
4th quarter	241 539	19 332	15 703	13 815	12 280	1 826	3 225	7 229	32 870	23 741	21 103	1 541	5 433	14 451
1987														
1st quarter	242 009	19 570	15 913	14 051	12 389	1 729	3 295	7 365	33 036	23 890	21 065	1 447	5 430	14 635
2nd quarter	242 520	19 881	16 127	14 017	12 654	1 811	3 349	7 494	33 336	23 609	21 312	1 503	5 460	14 754
3rd quarter	243 120	20 157	16 382	14 370	12 889	1 894	3 376	7 619	33 556	23 978	21 506	1 561	5 451	14 854
4th quarter	243 721	20 608	16 734	14 654	12 997	1 846	3 392	7 758	34 025	24 239	21 498	1 515	5 444	14 961

Table 1-3B. U.S. Population and Per Capita Product and Income: Historical Data—*Continued*

(Dollars, except as noted; quarterly data are at seasonally adjusted annual rates.)   NIPA Table 7.1

Year and quarter	Population (mid-period, thousands)	Current dollars							Chained (2009) dollars					
		Gross domestic product	Personal income	Disposable personal income	Personal consumption expenditures				Gross domestic product	Disposable personal income	Personal consumption expenditures			
					Total	Durable goods	Nondurable goods	Services			Total	Durable goods	Nondurable goods	Services
1988														
1st quarter	244 208	20 845	17 009	14 953	13 304	1 926	3 433	7 945	34 148	24 543	21 837	1 584	5 492	15 138
2nd quarter	244 716	21 281	17 276	15 242	13 522	1 934	3 488	8 100	34 528	24 744	21 951	1 581	5 524	15 240
3rd quarter	245 354	21 599	17 603	15 538	13 769	1 917	3 549	8 303	34 637	24 917	22 081	1 556	5 547	15 418
4th quarter	245 966	22 006	17 909	15 806	14 031	1 977	3 603	8 452	35 008	25 095	22 278	1 593	5 591	15 512
1989														
1st quarter	246 460	22 427	18 391	16 148	14 226	1 974	3 662	8 590	35 291	25 354	22 336	1 582	5 605	15 585
2nd quarter	247 017	22 786	18 572	16 278	14 450	1 997	3 756	8 697	35 488	25 222	22 391	1 600	5 601	15 614
3rd quarter	247 698	23 059	18 745	16 437	14 637	2 041	3 780	8 816	35 654	25 325	22 551	1 632	5 642	15 680
4th quarter	248 374	23 205	18 988	16 654	14 777	1 980	3 830	8 966	35 633	25 459	22 589	1 578	5 690	15 786
1990														
1st quarter	248 936	23 664	19 335	16 995	15 082	2 070	3 913	9 098	35 941	25 615	22 731	1 641	5 670	15 836
2nd quarter	249 711	23 926	19 578	17 197	15 218	1 996	3 928	9 294	35 968	25 688	22 732	1 581	5 659	15 980
3rd quarter	250 595	24 061	19 756	17 358	15 417	1 970	4 003	9 444	35 850	25 607	22 743	1 560	5 648	16 053
4th quarter	251 482	23 951	19 774	17 385	15 446	1 912	4 051	9 483	35 419	25 315	22 491	1 512	5 571	15 958
1991														
1st quarter	252 258	24 003	19 757	17 454	15 422	1 870	4 020	9 531	35 145	25 290	22 345	1 465	5 557	15 905
2nd quarter	253 063	24 277	19 928	17 612	15 584	1 878	4 038	9 668	35 305	25 384	22 461	1 468	5 572	16 015
3rd quarter	253 965	24 485	20 057	17 733	15 709	1 907	4 034	9 769	35 348	25 386	22 490	1 485	5 561	16 024
4th quarter	254 835	24 641	20 300	17 951	15 763	1 874	4 005	9 884	35 381	25 516	22 407	1 456	5 495	16 069
1992														
1st quarter	255 585	24 965	20 698	18 394	16 111	1 941	4 060	10 109	35 694	25 987	22 761	1 509	5 560	16 286
2nd quarter	256 439	25 317	21 015	18 648	16 274	1 954	4 084	10 237	35 968	26 171	22 840	1 514	5 565	16 360
3rd quarter	257 386	25 590	21 173	18 779	16 494	1 990	4 122	10 382	36 184	26 189	23 003	1 541	5 577	16 475
4th quarter	258 277	25 932	21 385	18 911	16 750	2 025	4 161	10 564	36 420	26 188	23 196	1 566	5 614	16 601
1993														
1st quarter	259 039	26 051	21 455	19 074	16 864	2 038	4 166	10 661	36 381	26 258	23 216	1 577	5 603	16 614
2nd quarter	259 826	26 285	21 655	19 178	17 079	2 109	4 181	10 789	36 486	26 224	23 353	1 623	5 630	16 644
3rd quarter	260 714	26 482	21 736	19 208	17 283	2 135	4 191	10 958	36 539	26 150	23 531	1 635	5 667	16 778
4th quarter	261 547	26 889	21 965	19 383	17 481	2 194	4 226	11 061	36 909	26 238	23 663	1 669	5 688	16 835
1994														
1st quarter	262 250	27 212	22 104	19 535	17 696	2 245	4 259	11 192	37 171	26 351	23 871	1 705	5 749	16 929
2nd quarter	263 020	27 640	22 447	19 794	17 880	2 276	4 289	11 315	37 569	26 552	23 985	1 718	5 777	16 999
3rd quarter	263 870	27 863	22 624	19 989	18 089	2 309	4 357	11 423	37 669	26 624	24 093	1 730	5 808	17 060
4th quarter	264 678	28 248	22 065	20 300	18 314	2 387	4 394	11 532	37 980	26 912	24 278	1 786	5 852	17 109
1995														
1st quarter	265 388	28 431	23 267	20 537	18 401	2 341	4 397	11 663	38 008	27 096	24 277	1 744	5 857	17 185
2nd quarter	266 142	28 575	23 447	20 641	18 618	2 356	4 422	11 840	38 033	27 080	24 426	1 757	5 869	17 311
3rd quarter	267 000	28 863	23 659	20 842	18 803	2 407	4 433	11 963	38 235	27 235	24 571	1 801	5 871	17 385
4th quarter	267 820	29 122	23 866	20 990	18 960	2 435	4 449	12 075	38 389	27 308	24 667	1 826	5 884	17 430
1996														
1st quarter	268 487	29 399	24 243	21 257	19 196	2 458	4 511	12 227	38 544	27 501	24 834	1 842	5 907	17 560
2nd quarter	269 251	29 941	24 659	21 541	19 477	2 512	4 604	12 361	39 106	27 685	25 033	1 895	5 966	17 614
3rd quarter	270 128	30 204	24 857	21 734	19 614	2 515	4 614	12 484	39 340	27 815	25 102	1 902	5 989	17 652
4th quarter	270 991	30 581	25 112	21 926	19 839	2 545	4 680	12 613	39 629	27 871	25 218	1 933	6 018	17 691
1997														
1st quarter	271 709	30 923	25 505	22 185	20 083	2 597	4 715	12 771	39 825	28 077	25 417	1 980	6 039	17 801
2nd quarter	272 487	31 385	25 728	22 365	20 166	2 556	4 690	12 920	40 311	28 236	25 460	1 968	6 025	17 884
3rd quarter	273 391	31 792	26 057	22 615	20 496	2 644	4 747	13 106	40 689	28 477	25 810	2 049	6 101	18 040
4th quarter	274 246	32 045	26 467	22 938	20 739	2 688	4 770	13 281	40 877	28 796	26 035	2 095	6 125	18 179
1998														
1st quarter	274 950	32 332	26 989	23 366	20 898	2 683	4 754	13 461	41 176	29 334	26 236	2 106	6 153	18 347
2nd quarter	275 703	32 625	27 378	23 669	21 247	2 790	4 789	13 668	41 461	29 662	26 626	2 207	6 211	18 536
3rd quarter	276 564	33 072	27 680	23 908	21 524	2 839	4 827	13 858	41 873	29 871	26 893	2 262	6 236	18 703
4th quarter	277 400	33 618	27 941	24 091	21 830	2 975	4 886	13 969	42 432	30 023	27 206	2 389	6 301	18 759
1999														
1st quarter	278 103	33 970	28 184	24 308	22 039	2 948	4 980	14 111	42 663	30 216	27 395	2 388	6 401	18 861
2nd quarter	278 864	34 271	28 359	24 431	22 423	3 065	5 085	14 273	42 897	30 208	27 725	2 495	6 443	18 997
3rd quarter	279 751	34 718	28 652	24 646	22 725	3 114	5 146	14 464	43 299	30 314	27 951	2 547	6 452	19 146
4th quarter	280 592	35 376	29 195	25 081	23 126	3 123	5 283	14 720	43 919	30 668	28 276	2 570	6 564	19 343
2000														
1st quarter	281 304	35 659	30 022	25 724	23 614	3 274	5 303	15 037	43 935	31 192	28 634	2 706	6 490	19 590
2nd quarter	282 002	36 448	30 409	26 046	23 891	3 198	5 443	15 250	44 654	31 438	28 837	2 649	6 603	19 777
3rd quarter	282 769	36 629	30 855	26 442	24 208	3 224	5 507	15 477	44 586	31 719	29 039	2 687	6 628	19 908
4th quarter	283 518	36 937	31 048	26 608	24 494	3 230	5 563	15 700	44 721	31 742	29 220	2 699	6 674	20 034
2001														
1st quarter	284 169	36 978	31 535	26 952	24 705	3 261	5 532	15 911	44 492	31 940	29 276	2 737	6 619	20 092
2nd quarter	284 838	37 349	31 590	26 994	24 829	3 228	5 583	16 018	44 623	31 836	29 282	2 728	6 635	20 095
3rd quarter	285 584	37 255	31 482	27 581	24 873	3 235	5 571	16 067	44 366	32 504	29 313	2 752	6 648	20 077
4th quarter	286 311	37 377	31 492	27 189	25 205	3 478	5 524	16 203	44 376	32 020	29 685	2 974	6 687	20 107
2002														
1st quarter	286 935	37 759	31 567	27 840	25 272	3 398	5 523	16 351	44 687	32 728	29 709	2 931	6 697	20 186
2nd quarter	287 574	38 024	31 783	28 134	25 539	3 407	5 592	16 541	44 834	32 821	29 795	2 953	6 686	20 256
3rd quarter	288 303	38 283	31 820	28 168	25 782	3 481	5 607	16 694	44 938	32 696	29 927	3 032	6 685	20 285
4th quarter	289 007	38 421	31 985	28 363	25 976	3 402	5 687	16 887	44 857	32 773	30 014	2 983	6 756	20 371

Table 1-3B. U.S. Population and Per Capita Product and Income: Historical Data—*Continued*

(Dollars, except as noted; quarterly data are at seasonally adjusted annual rates.)   NIPA Table 7.1

Year and quarter	Population (mid-period, thousands)	Current dollars							Chained (2009) dollars					
		Gross domestic product	Personal income	Disposable personal income	Personal consumption expenditures				Gross domestic product	Disposable personal income	Personal consumption expenditures			
					Total	Durable goods	Nondurable goods	Services			Total	Durable goods	Nondurable goods	Services
2003														
1st quarter	289 609	38 777	32 114	28 584	26 220	3 363	5 810	17 047	44 996	32 796	30 084	2 986	6 788	20 405
2nd quarter	290 253	39 175	32 469	28 958	26 475	3 472	5 748	17 255	45 312	33 197	30 351	3 116	6 823	20 473
3rd quarter	290 974	39 952	32 822	29 539	26 963	3 582	5 921	17 460	45 957	33 657	30 722	3 247	6 932	20 575
4th quarter	291 669	40 515	33 220	29 708	27 217	3 586	5 973	17 658	46 384	33 713	30 887	3 280	6 963	20 671
2004														
1st quarter	292 237	41 023	33 560	30 094	27 638	3 635	6 088	17 915	46 560	33 893	31 127	3 328	7 002	20 819
2nd quarter	292 875	41 592	34 047	30 537	27 952	3 659	6 151	18 141	46 799	34 152	31 261	3 354	7 009	20 919
3rd quarter	293 603	42 124	34 436	30 800	28 313	3 693	6 219	18 401	47 107	34 247	31 481	3 411	7 045	21 039
4th quarter	294 334	42 680	35 070	31 353	28 757	3 741	6 370	18 646	47 396	34 589	31 725	3 450	7 091	21 195
2005														
1st quarter	294 957	43 443	35 121	31 145	29 066	3 765	6 428	18 873	47 800	34 183	31 900	3 479	7 167	21 262
2nd quarter	295 588	43 892	35 585	31 533	29 514	3 859	6 485	19 170	47 947	34 380	32 178	3 570	7 183	21 421
3rd quarter	296 340	44 562	36 101	31 961	29 993	3 865	6 682	19 446	48 228	34 469	32 345	3 602	7 181	21 558
4th quarter	297 086	45 043	36 624	32 396	30 265	3 744	6 798	19 723	48 381	34 666	32 386	3 497	7 285	21 616
2006														
1st quarter	297 736	45 842	37 652	33 217	30 679	3 874	6 847	19 958	48 856	35 380	32 677	3 632	7 329	21 712
2nd quarter	298 408	46 245	37 969	33 448	31 010	3 844	6 955	20 212	48 891	35 354	32 777	3 620	7 337	21 820
3rd quarter	299 180	46 489	38 238	33 696	31 333	3 870	7 051	20 412	48 809	35 363	32 884	3 660	7 354	21 864
4th quarter	299 946	46 896	38 657	33 991	31 518	3 888	6 986	20 644	49 065	35 734	33 134	3 699	7 458	21 969
2007														
1st quarter	300 609	47 348	39 322	34 457	31 908	3 903	7 081	20 923	48 987	35 889	33 235	3 733	7 457	22 035
2nd quarter	301 284	47 869	39 659	34 720	32 199	3 933	7 190	21 076	49 251	35 878	33 273	3 778	7 425	22 055
3rd quarter	302 062	48 234	39 884	34 918	32 441	3 940	7 231	21 270	49 455	35 880	33 335	3 810	7 416	22 093
4th quarter	302 829	48 494	40 235	35 209	32 725	3 930	7 359	21 436	49 506	35 819	33 292	3 816	7 392	22 070
2008														
1st quarter	303 494	48 332	40 749	35 688	32 865	3 797	7 427	21 642	49 060	35 998	33 150	3 699	7 335	22 111
2nd quarter	304 160	48 701	41 821	36 742	33 192	3 748	7 624	21 821	49 196	36 677	33 134	3 679	7 370	22 079
3rd quarter	304 902	48 681	41 113	36 175	33 207	3 614	7 702	21 891	48 841	35 747	32 814	3 558	7 255	22 001
4th quarter	305 616	47 609	40 528	35 801	32 261	3 322	7 108	21 832	47 697	35 892	32 344	3 294	7 128	21 924
2009														
1st quarter	306 237	46 970	39 387	35 459	31 904	3 305	6 939	21 661	46 941	35 752	32 167	3 294	7 119	21 756
2nd quarter	306 866	46 732	39 489	35 798	31 837	3 274	6 986	21 577	46 781	35 932	31 957	3 267	7 053	21 636
3rd quarter	307 573	46 767	39 232	35 546	32 158	3 400	7 150	21 608	46 826	35 456	32 076	3 416	7 063	21 597
4th quarter	308 285	47 250	39 356	35 658	32 298	3 343	7 243	21 712	47 170	35 328	31 999	3 346	7 083	21 569
2010														
1st quarter	308 901	47 527	39 608	35 744	32 517	3 367	7 331	21 818	47 280	35 293	32 106	3 383	7 127	21 595
2nd quarter	309 472	48 110	40 111	36 183	32 758	3 440	7 306	22 012	47 649	35 686	32 308	3 478	7 148	21 683
3rd quarter	310 105	48 557	40 450	36 396	33 000	3 467	7 376	22 157	47 872	35 790	32 451	3 527	7 178	21 747
4th quarter	310 752	49 011	40 921	36 768	33 445	3 549	7 580	22 316	48 074	35 965	32 715	3 628	7 255	21 836
2011														
1st quarter	311 253	48 958	42 016	37 436	33 810	3 583	7 771	22 456	47 811	36 346	32 826	3 668	7 277	21 886
2nd quarter	311 781	49 589	42 321	37 692	34 163	3 568	7 940	22 655	48 077	36 228	32 836	3 638	7 267	21 936
3rd quarter	312 407	49 894	42 724	38 017	34 425	3 597	7 968	22 859	48 082	36 347	32 913	3 677	7 233	22 012
4th quarter	313 016	50 430	42 804	38 097	34 592	3 673	7 990	22 928	48 529	36 299	32 959	3 775	7 228	21 972
2012														
1st quarter	313 530	50 948	43 576	38 880	34 945	3 760	8 087	23 098	48 771	36 832	33 104	3 872	7 252	22 001
2nd quarter	314 048	51 336	43 987	39 234	35 053	3 762	8 074	23 217	48 917	37 054	33 105	3 891	7 247	21 990
3rd quarter	314 661	51 573	44 070	39 266	35 192	3 795	8 106	23 291	48 881	36 963	33 128	3 948	7 249	21 959
4th quarter	315 269	51 693	45 412	40 436	35 412	3 847	8 143	23 422	48 797	37 860	33 156	4 018	7 230	21 946
2013														
1st quarter	315 734	52 181	44 038	38 828	35 652	3 922	8 201	23 529	49 000	36 226	33 263	4 108	7 286	21 913
2nd quarter	316 225	52 309	44 327	39 010	35 685	3 912	8 116	23 657	49 084	36 380	33 280	4 123	7 290	21 911
3rd quarter	316 843	52 863	44 613	39 306	35 914	3 918	8 185	23 811	49 366	36 522	33 370	4 156	7 320	21 942
4th quarter	317 474	53 547	44 848	39 481	36 300	3 937	8 260	24 103	49 749	36 528	33 585	4 198	7 369	22 067
2014														
1st quarter	318 003	53 557	45 553	40 045	36 604	3 959	8 318	24 327	49 552	36 856	33 690	4 248	7 374	22 123
2nd quarter	318 543	54 375	46 190	40 672	37 018	4 055	8 389	24 575	50 027	37 268	33 920	4 375	7 415	22 202
3rd quarter	319 183	55 211	46 760	41 134	37 412	4 103	8 431	24 878	50 565	37 581	34 181	4 448	7 455	22 357
4th quarter	319 817	55 456	47 367	41 621	37 776	4 144	8 404	25 228	50 717	38 052	34 536	4 528	7 522	22 571
2015														
1st quarter	320 328	55 801	47 767	41 825	37 905	4 189	8 221	25 496	51 041	38 391	34 793	4 606	7 555	22 726
2nd quarter	320 846	56 392	48 360	42 332	38 287	4 260	8 299	25 728	51 305	38 692	34 995	4 695	7 590	22 816
3rd quarter	321 458	56 703	48 608	42 580	38 598	4 282	8 370	25 946	51 414	38 794	35 167	4 744	7 650	22 885
4th quarter	322 058	56 782	48 964	42 827	38 797	4 296	8 313	26 188	51 381	39 003	35 333	4 783	7 677	22 989
2016														
1st quarter	322 549	56 814	48 833	42 853	38 975	4 286	8 260	26 429	51 377	38 964	35 438	4 788	7 715	23 050
2nd quarter	323 064	57 382	49 248	43 209	39 481	4 337	8 380	26 764	51 580	39 086	35 713	4 879	7 793	23 171
3rd quarter	323 675	57 864	49 519	43 390	39 853	4 388	8 386	27 080	51 836	39 080	35 894	4 980	7 779	23 279
4th quarter	324 275	58 301	49 420	43 323	40 265	4 441	8 498	27 326	51 966	38 828	36 087	5 082	7 812	23 356

Table 1-4A. Contributions to Percent Change in Real Gross Domestic Product: Recent Data

(Percent, percentage points.)　　　　　　　　　　　　　　　　　　　　　　　　　　　　　　　　　NIPA Table 1.1.2

Year and quarter	Percent change at seasonally adjusted annual rate, real GDP	Personal consumption expenditures	Gross private domestic investment				Exports and imports of goods and services			Government consumption expenditures and gross investment		
			Total	Fixed investment		Change in private inventories	Net exports	Exports	Imports	Total	Federal	State and local
				Nonresidential	Residential							
1950	8.7	4.20	5.68	0.91	1.99	2.78	-1.28	-0.65	-0.63	0.11	-0.47	0.58
1951	8.1	1.00	0.05	0.42	-1.11	0.74	0.79	0.96	-0.16	6.22	6.16	0.06
1952	4.1	1.90	-1.44	-0.01	-0.09	-1.34	-0.57	-0.21	-0.36	4.18	4.07	0.11
1953	4.7	2.85	0.87	0.95	0.19	-0.27	-0.68	-0.30	-0.38	1.65	1.32	0.33
1954	-0.6	1.25	-0.61	-0.14	0.42	-0.89	0.39	0.19	0.20	-1.60	-2.20	0.59
1955	7.1	4.50	3.44	1.06	0.88	1.50	-0.04	0.43	-0.47	-0.78	-1.31	0.54
1956	2.1	1.77	-0.05	0.70	-0.47	-0.28	0.36	0.69	-0.33	0.05	-0.20	0.25
1957	2.1	1.49	-0.64	0.20	-0.31	-0.53	0.24	0.41	-0.17	1.01	0.55	0.47
1958	-0.7	0.52	-1.16	-1.04	0.05	-0.17	-0.87	-0.67	-0.19	0.77	0.07	0.69
1959	6.9	3.49	2.82	0.81	1.18	0.83	0.00	0.44	-0.44	0.59	0.29	0.30
1960	2.6	1.67	0.06	0.56	-0.37	-0.13	0.70	0.75	-0.06	0.14	-0.24	0.38
1961	2.6	1.26	0.05	0.08	0.02	-0.05	0.05	0.03	0.03	1.19	0.65	0.54
1962	6.1	3.00	1.82	0.81	0.46	0.55	-0.21	0.25	-0.45	1.50	1.23	0.28
1963	4.4	2.47	1.08	0.59	0.57	-0.07	0.23	0.34	-0.11	0.57	0.03	0.54
1964	5.8	3.56	1.27	1.08	0.31	-0.12	0.35	0.57	-0.22	0.58	-0.05	0.63
1965	6.5	3.79	2.26	1.75	-0.13	0.64	-0.29	0.14	-0.44	0.74	0.10	0.63
1966	6.6	3.37	1.56	1.40	-0.40	0.56	-0.28	0.35	-0.63	1.94	1.34	0.61
1967	2.7	1.76	-0.62	-0.04	-0.11	-0.47	-0.21	0.12	-0.33	1.82	1.32	0.50
1968	4.9	3.38	0.99	0.55	0.53	-0.09	-0.29	0.39	-0.68	0.83	0.22	0.62
1969	3.1	2.21	0.93	0.79	0.14	0.00	-0.03	0.25	-0.28	0.04	-0.33	0.37
1970	0.2	1.39	-1.03	-0.10	-0.22	-0.70	0.33	0.54	-0.21	-0.49	-0.80	0.31
1971	3.3	2.29	1.63	-0.01	1.08	0.56	-0.18	0.10	-0.28	-0.44	-0.80	0.36
1972	5.2	3.67	1.90	0.97	0.87	0.06	-0.19	0.42	-0.61	-0.11	-0.37	0.26
1973	5.6	2.97	1.95	1.50	-0.04	0.48	0.79	1.08	-0.28	-0.07	-0.40	0.32
1974	-0.5	-0.50	-1.24	0.10	-1.08	-0.26	0.73	0.56	0.17	0.49	0.07	0.42
1975	-0.2	1.36	-2.90	-1.13	-0.54	-1.23	0.86	-0.05	0.91	0.49	0.05	0.43
1976	5.4	3.41	2.91	0.66	0.88	1.37	-1.05	0.36	-1.40	0.12	0.02	0.10
1977	4.6	2.59	2.47	1.26	0.97	0.24	-0.70	0.19	-0.89	0.26	0.21	0.04
1978	5.6	2.69	2.21	1.72	0.38	0.12	0.04	0.80	-0.76	0.61	0.24	0.37
1979	3.2	1.44	0.71	1.33	-0.22	-0.40	0.64	0.80	-0.16	0.38	0.21	0.16
1980	-0.2	-0.19	-2.07	0.00	-1.18	-0.89	1.64	0.95	0.69	0.38	0.40	-0.02
1981	2.6	0.91	1.63	0.87	-0.37	1.13	-0.15	0.12	-0.27	0.20	0.43	-0.23
1982	-1.9	0.86	-2.55	-0.53	-0.72	-1.30	-0.59	-0.71	0.12	0.38	0.36	0.01
1983	4.6	3.54	1.60	-0.06	1.38	0.28	-1.32	-0.21	-1.10	0.81	0.67	0.14
1984	7.3	3.32	4.73	2.18	0.65	1.90	-1.54	0.61	-2.15	0.76	0.35	0.41
1985	4.2	3.25	-0.01	0.91	0.11	-1.03	-0.39	0.24	-0.63	1.38	0.80	0.59
1986	3.5	2.63	0.03	-0.24	0.58	-0.31	-0.29	0.53	-0.82	1.14	0.61	0.53
1987	3.5	2.14	0.53	0.01	0.10	0.41	0.17	0.76	-0.59	0.63	0.39	0.24
1988	4.2	2.66	0.45	0.63	-0.05	-0.13	0.81	1.22	-0.41	0.28	-0.13	0.42
1989	3.7	1.86	0.72	0.71	-0.16	0.17	0.51	0.97	-0.46	0.59	0.16	0.43
1990	1.9	1.31	-0.45	0.14	-0.38	-0.21	0.40	0.78	-0.37	0.66	0.20	0.46
1991	-0.1	0.15	-1.09	-0.48	-0.35	-0.25	0.62	0.60	0.01	0.25	0.00	0.25
1992	3.6	2.38	1.11	0.34	0.49	0.28	-0.04	0.66	-0.70	0.11	-0.14	0.24
1993	2.7	2.24	1.23	0.84	0.32	0.07	-0.56	0.31	-0.87	-0.17	-0.31	0.14
1994	4.0	2.52	1.90	0.91	0.38	0.61	-0.40	0.84	-1.24	0.02	-0.30	0.32
1995	2.7	1.94	0.55	1.15	-0.15	-0.44	0.12	1.02	-0.89	0.10	-0.21	0.31
1996	3.8	2.28	1.49	1.13	0.35	0.02	-0.15	0.86	-1.01	0.18	-0.09	0.27
1997	4.5	2.45	2.00	1.37	0.11	0.52	-0.31	1.26	-1.57	0.35	-0.06	0.40
1998	4.5	3.45	1.76	1.42	0.38	-0.04	-1.13	0.25	-1.39	0.38	-0.06	0.44
1999	4.7	3.44	1.60	1.32	0.29	-0.02	-0.97	0.27	-1.24	0.61	0.13	0.49
2000	4.1	3.32	1.25	1.27	0.03	-0.05	-0.82	0.88	-1.70	0.34	0.02	0.32
2001	1.0	1.71	-1.19	-0.34	0.04	-0.89	-0.22	-0.61	0.40	0.67	0.24	0.43
2002	1.8	1.72	-0.11	-0.93	0.29	0.53	-0.64	-0.16	-0.47	0.81	0.46	0.35
2003	2.8	2.10	0.71	0.23	0.47	0.02	-0.42	0.16	-0.59	0.42	0.47	-0.05
2004	3.8	2.59	1.55	0.62	0.56	0.37	-0.66	0.89	-1.55	0.31	0.33	-0.02
2005	3.3	2.36	1.20	0.83	0.41	-0.04	-0.34	0.61	-0.94	0.12	0.13	0.00
2006	2.7	2.04	0.42	0.87	-0.50	0.04	-0.08	0.90	-0.99	0.29	0.18	0.11
2007	1.8	1.50	-0.61	0.76	-1.13	-0.23	0.58	0.99	-0.41	0.30	0.12	0.18
2008	-0.3	-0.23	-1.71	-0.09	-1.12	-0.49	1.11	0.67	0.44	0.54	0.50	0.04
2009	-2.8	-1.08	-3.52	-2.04	-0.73	-0.76	1.19	-1.07	2.26	0.64	0.44	0.20
2010	2.5	1.32	1.66	0.28	-0.07	1.45	-0.46	1.33	-1.79	0.02	0.37	-0.35
2011	1.6	1.55	0.73	0.85	0.01	-0.14	-0.02	0.87	-0.89	-0.65	-0.24	-0.41
2012	2.2	1.01	1.52	1.05	0.33	0.14	0.08	0.46	-0.38	-0.38	-0.15	-0.22
2013	1.7	1.00	0.95	0.43	0.33	0.19	0.29	0.47	-0.18	-0.56	-0.46	-0.09
2014	2.6	1.95	0.90	0.86	0.11	-0.07	-0.16	0.58	-0.74	-0.12	-0.18	0.06
2015	2.9	2.47	0.87	0.30	0.34	0.23	-0.73	0.05	-0.78	0.25	-0.01	0.26
2016	1.5	1.86	-0.28	-0.08	0.20	-0.40	-0.23	-0.04	-0.19	0.13	0.00	0.13
2014												
1st quarter	-0.9	1.27	-0.93	0.85	-0.09	-1.69	-1.14	-0.35	-0.79	-0.11	-0.03	-0.09
2nd quarter	4.6	2.33	2.47	1.16	0.40	0.91	-0.40	1.22	-1.62	0.20	-0.11	0.31
3rd quarter	5.2	2.65	1.90	1.31	0.14	0.44	0.28	0.09	0.18	0.39	0.22	0.17
4th quarter	2.0	3.36	-0.21	-0.30	0.35	-0.26	-1.02	0.65	-1.67	-0.11	-0.40	0.28
2015												
1st quarter	3.2	2.48	2.12	0.30	0.37	1.45	-1.64	-0.59	-1.05	0.27	0.11	0.17
2nd quarter	2.7	2.03	0.14	0.38	0.39	-0.63	-0.03	0.47	-0.50	0.60	0.12	0.48
3rd quarter	1.6	1.86	0.33	0.19	0.36	-0.22	-0.77	-0.51	-0.25	0.21	-0.07	0.28
4th quarter	0.5	1.80	-1.08	-0.67	0.26	-0.68	-0.28	-0.29	0.01	0.05	0.17	-0.12
2016												
1st quarter	0.6	1.23	-0.68	-0.52	0.47	-0.64	-0.28	-0.33	0.04	0.32	-0.10	0.42
2nd quarter	2.2	2.57	-0.45	0.41	-0.18	-0.67	0.28	0.32	-0.04	-0.16	-0.06	-0.11
3rd quarter	2.8	1.92	0.40	0.42	-0.18	0.16	0.36	0.74	-0.37	0.09	0.11	-0.02
4th quarter	1.8	1.99	1.34	0.02	0.26	1.06	-1.61	-0.47	-1.14	0.03	-0.03	0.06

Table 1-4B. Contributions to Percent Change in Real Gross Domestic Product: Historical Data

(Percent; percentage points.)

NIPA Table 1.1.2

Year and quarter	Percent change at seasonally adjusted annual rate, real GDP	Personal consumption expenditures	Gross private domestic investment				Exports and imports of goods and services			Government consumption expenditures and gross investment		
			Total	Fixed investment		Change in private inventories	Net exports	Exports	Imports	Total	Federal	State and local
				Nonresidential	Residential							
1930	-8.5	-3.96	-5.18	-1.84	-1.50	-1.84	-0.30	-0.96	0.65	0.94	0.19	0.74
1931	-6.4	-2.37	-4.28	-3.32	-0.40	-0.56	-0.22	-0.77	0.54	0.48	0.08	0.40
1932	-12.9	-7.00	-5.28	-2.78	-1.02	-1.48	-0.19	-0.80	0.61	-0.42	0.05	-0.47
1933	-1.3	-1.79	1.16	-0.44	-0.24	1.84	-0.11	0.02	-0.13	-0.52	0.76	-1.28
1934	10.8	5.71	2.84	1.31	0.38	1.14	0.33	0.41	-0.08	1.91	1.37	0.54
1935	8.9	4.69	4.54	1.41	0.56	2.58	-0.83	0.21	-1.04	0.50	0.14	0.36
1936	12.9	7.68	2.58	2.10	0.47	0.01	0.24	0.19	0.05	2.44	2.43	0.01
1937	5.1	2.72	2.57	1.42	0.17	0.98	0.45	0.93	-0.48	-0.64	-0.65	0.02
1938	-3.3	-1.15	-4.13	-2.13	0.01	-2.01	0.88	-0.05	0.93	1.09	0.60	0.49
1939	8.0	4.11	2.39	0.71	1.03	0.65	0.07	0.24	-0.17	1.41	0.49	0.92
1940	8.8	3.72	3.99	1.60	0.42	1.97	0.52	0.61	-0.08	0.57	0.87	-0.30
1941	17.7	4.90	3.13	1.58	0.21	1.34	-0.64	0.12	-0.76	10.31	10.83	-0.52
1942	18.9	-1.50	-6.45	-3.16	-1.55	-1.74	-1.19	-1.51	0.32	28.03	28.64	-0.61
1943	17.0	1.52	-2.63	-0.72	-0.55	-1.36	-1.16	-0.42	-0.73	19.31	19.75	-0.44
1944	8.0	1.42	0.72	0.88	-0.10	-0.05	0.01	0.15	-0.15	5.84	5.98	-0.14
1945	-1.0	3.01	1.20	1.40	0.10	-0.30	0.66	0.86	-0.19	-5.84	-5.97	0.14
1946	-11.6	6.29	7.36	2.30	2.30	2.76	3.72	3.16	0.56	-28.95	-29.34	0.39
1947	-1.1	1.21	-0.56	1.28	1.02	-2.86	1.05	0.89	0.16	-2.80	-3.46	0.66
1948	4.1	1.47	3.89	0.48	0.96	2.45	-2.13	-1.59	-0.54	0.93	0.57	0.35
1949	-0.5	1.77	-4.15	-0.94	-0.43	-2.79	0.08	-0.05	0.13	1.77	0.85	0.92
1947												
1st quarter	. . .	. . .	. . .	. . .	. . .	. . .	. . .	. . .	. . .	. . .	. . .	. . .
2nd quarter	-0.4	4.30	-4.71	-0.59	-0.88	-3.25	-0.68	-0.42	-0.26	0.65	0.34	0.31
3rd quarter	-0.4	0.93	-1.83	-0.66	2.67	-3.84	-0.16	-1.68	1.52	0.65	0.12	0.52
4th quarter	6.4	0.24	10.67	1.33	3.97	5.37	-4.22	-3.52	-0.70	-0.24	-0.62	0.38
1948												
1st quarter	6.0	1.50	6.26	2.62	-0.31	3.95	-2.98	-1.31	-1.67	1.23	1.23	0.00
2nd quarter	6.7	3.11	4.31	-1.26	1.38	4.18	-3.00	-2.37	-0.63	2.24	1.57	0.67
3rd quarter	2.3	0.37	0.91	0.21	-0.75	1.46	-0.32	0.49	-0.81	1.30	0.88	0.42
4th quarter	0.4	1.83	-3.04	1.00	-1.74	-2.30	-0.60	-0.79	0.20	2.24	1.66	0.57
1949												
1st quarter	-5.4	0.17	-9.95	-2.06	-1.63	-6.26	2.84	2.44	0.40	1.58	0.59	0.99
2nd quarter	-1.3	3.56	-7.86	-1.55	-0.33	-5.98	0.02	-0.16	0.18	2.94	1.48	1.45
3rd quarter	4.5	0.15	4.98	-1.77	1.74	5.00	-1.31	-1.87	0.55	0.66	-0.50	1.16
4th quarter	-3.5	3.27	-2.51	-0.36	2.67	-4.82	-2.86	-2.66	-0.19	-1.44	-2.01	0.57
1950												
1st quarter	16.9	4.04	14.11	1.36	2.88	9.87	-0.56	-0.21	-0.36	-0.66	-1.46	0.80
2nd quarter	12.7	4.01	7.60	3.32	2.62	1.66	-0.49	0.23	-0.72	1.53	1.26	0.27
3rd quarter	16.3	13.39	6.42	3.45	1.60	1.37	-2.77	0.44	-3.21	-0.71	-0.75	0.04
4th quarter	8.0	-7.71	9.62	-0.07	-1.35	11.04	1.25	1.29	-0.04	4.79	4.78	0.02
1951												
1st quarter	5.6	6.32	-8.87	-1.16	-1.40	-6.32	0.80	0.82	-0.02	7.34	7.61	-0.27
2nd quarter	7.1	-6.88	1.66	0.47	-3.37	4.56	2.33	1.78	0.55	10.01	9.55	0.46
3rd quarter	8.5	2.88	-5.57	0.52	-1.36	-4.73	1.96	0.50	1.46	9.23	9.09	0.14
4th quarter	0.9	1.31	-5.40	-0.54	0.18	-5.03	0.15	-0.17	0.32	4.83	4.86	-0.03
1952												
1st quarter	4.3	0.32	1.72	0.54	0.51	0.66	-0.76	1.14	-1.90	3.02	2.91	0.10
2nd quarter	0.8	4.48	-4.71	0.75	0.37	-5.82	-2.22	-2.19	-0.03	3.29	2.71	0.58
3rd quarter	2.9	1.07	3.26	-2.95	-0.21	6.42	-2.41	-1.36	-1.05	1.00	1.72	-0.72
4th quarter	13.8	8.60	4.66	3.34	1.13	0.19	-1.28	0.20	-1.48	1.81	1.15	0.65
1953												
1st quarter	7.7	2.86	1.35	2.06	0.34	-1.05	0.24	-0.18	0.42	3.20	2.62	0.58
2nd quarter	3.2	1.33	0.40	0.41	0.07	-0.08	-0.70	0.15	-0.85	2.13	2.16	-0.03
3rd quarter	-2.2	-0.71	-1.20	0.92	-0.76	-1.36	0.67	0.65	0.03	-0.99	-1.70	0.71
4th quarter	-5.9	-1.76	-4.24	-0.28	-0.16	-3.80	0.24	-0.53	0.77	-0.17	-0.85	0.67
1954												
1st quarter	-1.8	0.65	-0.16	-0.97	0.22	0.58	0.13	-0.73	0.86	-2.45	-3.47	1.01
2nd quarter	0.4	2.97	0.07	-0.27	1.32	-0.98	0.67	2.11	-1.44	-3.28	-3.41	0.12
3rd quarter	4.6	3.19	3.02	1.09	1.32	0.61	0.36	-0.58	0.94	-1.94	-2.79	0.84
4th quarter	8.0	5.10	2.89	0.04	1.43	1.42	0.48	0.70	-0.22	-0.44	-0.60	0.16
1955												
1st quarter	11.9	5.56	6.40	0.77	1.76	3.87	-0.39	0.57	-0.95	0.34	-0.95	1.29
2nd quarter	6.7	4.64	4.05	2.31	0.33	1.41	-1.37	-0.43	-0.94	-0.64	-1.05	0.41
3rd quarter	5.5	2.96	1.06	2.00	-0.55	-0.39	0.70	1.03	-0.33	0.77	0.79	-0.02
4th quarter	2.4	3.07	1.54	1.22	-1.01	1.33	-0.56	0.05	-0.61	-1.62	-1.82	0.20
1956												
1st quarter	-1.5	0.38	-2.11	-0.61	-0.60	-0.90	0.07	0.80	-0.73	0.13	-0.21	0.34
2nd quarter	3.4	0.79	-0.58	0.73	-0.15	-1.17	1.25	1.20	0.05	1.88	1.47	0.41
3rd quarter	-0.3	0.51	-0.61	0.39	-0.43	-0.57	0.42	0.62	-0.20	-0.66	-0.82	0.17
4th quarter	6.7	3.34	-0.54	0.00	-0.33	-0.21	1.63	0.88	0.75	2.27	1.93	0.34
1957												
1st quarter	2.6	1.64	-0.95	0.23	-0.29	-0.90	-0.01	1.31	-1.32	1.93	1.15	0.79
2nd quarter	-0.9	0.41	-0.06	-0.08	-0.47	0.49	-0.80	-0.62	-0.18	-0.43	-0.71	0.28
3rd quarter	4.0	1.93	1.43	0.93	-0.25	0.75	-0.26	-0.55	0.30	0.85	0.38	0.47
4th quarter	-4.0	0.12	-5.17	-0.99	-0.02	-4.16	-0.61	-0.55	-0.06	1.63	0.81	0.82

. . . = Not available.

Table 1-4B. Contributions to Percent Change in Real Gross Domestic Product: Historical Data—*Continued*

(Percent; percentage points.)   NIPA Table 1.1.2

Year and quarter	Percent change at seasonally adjusted annual rate, real GDP	Personal consumption expenditures	Gross private domestic investment				Exports and imports of goods and services			Government consumption expenditures and gross investment		
			Total	Fixed investment		Change in private inventories	Net exports	Exports	Imports	Total	Federal	State and local
				Nonresidential	Residential							
1958												
1st quarter	-10.0	-3.24	-4.12	-2.69	-0.71	-0.72	-2.05	-1.83	-0.22	-0.57	-1.54	0.97
2nd quarter	2.6	2.11	-1.23	-1.53	0.07	0.23	-0.63	0.12	-0.74	2.41	1.89	0.52
3rd quarter	9.6	4.25	4.41	-0.41	1.31	3.50	0.28	0.10	0.18	0.63	-0.16	0.79
4th quarter	9.7	3.49	5.26	1.45	1.96	1.84	-0.97	-0.01	-0.96	1.91	1.25	0.66
1959												
1st quarter	7.7	4.59	3.82	1.18	2.27	0.36	0.52	1.12	-0.59	-1.27	-1.40	0.13
2nd quarter	10.1	3.95	5.37	1.14	0.77	3.46	-0.31	0.61	-0.92	1.08	0.97	0.11
3rd quarter	-0.8	2.61	-4.41	1.07	-0.42	-5.06	0.34	0.56	-0.22	0.69	0.66	0.04
4th quarter	1.6	0.32	2.05	-0.11	-0.62	2.77	-0.03	-0.47	0.44	-0.77	-0.59	-0.17
1960												
1st quarter	9.2	2.37	6.61	1.48	0.67	4.46	1.65	2.23	-0.58	-1.42	-2.02	0.59
2nd quarter	-1.5	3.05	-6.61	0.63	-1.73	-5.51	1.13	1.22	-0.09	0.93	0.09	0.84
3rd quarter	1.0	-0.97	-0.19	-0.72	-0.58	1.11	0.02	-0.51	0.53	2.14	1.61	0.52
4th quarter	-4.8	0.34	-6.92	-0.07	-0.02	-6.83	1.21	0.41	0.80	0.61	0.21	0.40
1961												
1st quarter	2.7	-0.05	1.52	-0.57	0.08	2.02	-0.07	-0.14	0.07	1.35	0.17	1.18
2nd quarter	7.6	3.70	4.17	0.92	0.08	3.18	-0.47	-0.27	-0.19	0.24	0.48	-0.25
3rd quarter	6.8	1.22	4.81	0.40	1.02	3.39	-1.14	-0.10	-1.04	1.94	1.62	0.32
4th quarter	8.3	4.89	1.22	1.22	0.67	-0.67	0.21	0.60	-0.39	2.03	1.02	1.01
1962												
1st quarter	7.4	2.59	3.56	0.79	0.35	2.42	-0.54	-0.05	-0.49	1.80	2.07	-0.27
2nd quarter	4.4	2.95	-0.46	1.07	0.61	-2.14	1.46	1.81	-0.36	0.44	0.19	0.25
3rd quarter	3.9	1.95	1.12	0.50	-0.01	0.64	-1.34	-1.14	-0.21	2.13	1.68	0.45
4th quarter	1.6	3.40	-1.89	-0.16	-0.03	-1.71	-0.61	-0.41	-0.20	0.66	0.28	0.38
1963												
1st quarter	4.5	1.65	3.28	0.10	0.69	2.49	0.83	0.44	0.39	-1.23	-1.92	0.69
2nd quarter	5.3	2.33	1.07	1.24	1.42	-1.60	1.82	2.19	-0.37	0.11	-0.23	0.33
3rd quarter	8.0	3.32	2.11	1.12	0.40	0.58	-1.48	-1.08	-0.41	4.10	3.10	1.00
4th quarter	2.9	1.99	0.83	1.18	0.65	-0.99	1.01	0.95	0.06	-0.95	-1.46	0.51
1964												
1st quarter	8.9	4.77	2.60	0.88	1.30	0.43	1.25	1.22	0.03	0.31	-0.26	0.58
2nd quarter	4.8	4.21	-0.18	0.97	-1.08	-0.06	-0.01	0.34	-0.35	0.82	-0.04	0.85
3rd quarter	5.5	4.44	1.56	1.35	-0.33	0.53	-0.58	-0.15	-0.43	0.13	-0.29	0.41
4th quarter	1.4	0.69	0.59	0.92	-0.35	0.03	0.16	0.60	-0.44	-0.02	-0.43	0.41
1965												
1st quarter	10.2	5.47	6.38	2.81	0.10	3.46	-1.59	-2.22	0.63	-0.02	-0.38	0.36
2nd quarter	5.6	2.70	0.17	1.66	0.17	-1.66	1.62	3.46	-1.85	1.10	0.12	0.98
3rd quarter	8.4	4.19	2.49	1.68	0.10	0.72	-1.27	-1.21	-0.06	2.97	1.87	1.10
4th quarter	9.8	6.79	0.61	1.89	-0.37	-0.91	0.62	1.44	-0.82	1.76	1.17	0.59
1966												
1st quarter	10.2	3.58	5.71	1.96	0.46	3.29	-0.80	-0.36	-0.44	1.75	1.27	0.48
2nd quarter	1.6	0.60	-1.05	0.75	-1.42	-0.38	0.43	0.86	-0.43	1.67	1.38	0.30
3rd quarter	2.9	2.69	-0.51	0.62	-0.56	-0.57	-1.76	-0.78	-0.99	2.47	2.01	0.46
4th quarter	3.5	0.98	0.42	0.01	-1.69	2.11	0.46	0.65	-0.19	1.61	0.60	1.00
1967												
1st quarter	3.7	1.38	-1.72	-0.75	-0.40	-0.58	0.13	0.39	-0.26	3.93	3.44	0.49
2nd quarter	0.3	3.20	-2.45	-0.10	1.60	-3.95	-0.02	-0.19	0.17	-0.38	-0.60	0.23
3rd quarter	3.5	1.22	1.90	-0.08	0.83	1.15	-0.72	-0.49	-0.23	1.09	0.93	0.16
4th quarter	3.2	1.46	1.42	0.92	0.93	-0.43	-0.40	0.56	-0.95	0.78	0.06	0.72
1968												
1st quarter	8.4	5.66	1.43	1.37	0.06	0.00	-0.52	0.58	-1.10	1.80	1.03	0.77
2nd quarter	6.9	3.64	2.62	-0.57	0.42	2.77	0.11	0.41	-0.30	0.56	-0.26	0.82
3rd quarter	2.9	4.42	-1.84	0.60	0.34	-2.79	0.02	1.18	-1.16	0.32	-0.28	0.60
4th quarter	1.8	1.07	0.71	1.21	0.24	-0.74	-0.09	-0.26	0.17	0.10	-0.25	0.35
1969												
1st quarter	6.4	2.67	3.97	1.17	0.60	2.20	-0.55	-2.43	1.88	0.28	-0.12	0.40
2nd quarter	1.3	1.50	-0.40	0.49	-0.17	-0.72	0.48	3.94	-3.46	-0.30	-0.66	0.36
3rd quarter	2.5	1.14	1.41	1.06	-0.14	0.49	-0.24	-0.51	0.27	0.21	0.10	0.11
4th quarter	-1.7	1.88	-3.30	-0.24	-1.20	-1.86	0.94	0.71	0.23	-1.25	-1.17	-0.08
1970												
1st quarter	-0.7	1.46	-1.93	-0.32	0.01	-1.62	0.23	0.16	0.07	-0.47	-0.88	0.41
2nd quarter	0.7	1.11	0.14	-0.31	-1.00	1.45	0.55	0.95	-0.40	-1.10	-1.34	0.24
3rd quarter	3.6	2.15	1.04	0.15	0.88	0.01	-0.01	-0.06	0.05	0.42	-0.60	1.01
4th quarter	-4.0	-0.59	-3.41	-1.62	1.58	-3.37	-0.11	0.21	-0.32	0.06	-0.18	0.24
1971												
1st quarter	11.1	4.79	7.28	0.36	0.92	6.00	0.37	0.11	0.26	-1.30	-1.52	0.22
2nd quarter	2.3	2.24	1.85	0.58	1.73	-0.46	-1.58	-0.04	-1.54	-0.21	-0.55	0.34
3rd quarter	3.2	1.94	0.83	0.22	0.91	-0.29	0.42	0.90	-0.48	-0.03	-0.19	0.16
4th quarter	1.2	3.98	-1.81	0.96	0.79	-3.57	-0.35	-1.86	1.52	-0.65	-1.23	0.59
1972												
1st quarter	7.4	3.21	4.52	1.55	1.40	1.57	-0.80	2.21	-3.01	0.45	0.31	0.13
2nd quarter	9.6	4.62	4.14	0.83	0.43	2.88	0.22	-0.64	0.87	0.60	0.67	-0.07
3rd quarter	3.7	3.67	1.09	0.70	0.10	0.29	0.79	1.26	-0.46	-1.82	-2.18	0.36
4th quarter	6.8	5.63	0.57	2.19	0.80	-2.43	-0.10	0.92	-1.03	0.71	0.08	0.63
1973												
1st quarter	10.2	4.46	4.38	1.96	0.79	1.63	0.58	1.68	-1.10	0.79	0.57	0.22
2nd quarter	4.6	-0.10	3.23	1.74	-1.22	2.72	1.89	1.16	0.73	-0.41	-0.48	0.07
3rd quarter	-2.2	0.84	-2.67	0.73	-0.96	-2.43	0.75	0.06	0.69	-1.09	-1.56	0.47
4th quarter	3.8	-0.69	2.78	0.36	-0.98	3.41	1.12	1.33	-0.21	0.57	0.01	0.56

Table 1-4B. Contributions to Percent Change in Real Gross Domestic Product: Historical Data—*Continued*

(Percent; percentage points.)   NIPA Table 1.1.2

Year and quarter	Percent change at seasonally adjusted annual rate, real GDP	Personal consump-tion expen-ditures	Gross private domestic investment				Exports and imports of goods and services			Government consumption expenditures and gross investment		
			Total	Fixed investment		Change in private inventories	Net exports	Exports	Imports	Total	Federal	State and local
				Nonresi-dential	Residential							
1974												
1st quarter	-3.3	-2.06	-4.15	-0.06	-1.34	-2.76	1.34	0.36	0.98	1.59	1.01	0.58
2nd quarter	1.1	0.87	-0.24	-0.09	-0.78	0.63	-0.14	1.51	-1.65	0.57	-0.02	0.58
3rd quarter	-3.8	1.04	-3.78	-0.48	-0.61	-2.69	-1.22	-1.81	0.59	0.15	0.21	-0.06
4th quarter	-1.6	-3.49	0.29	-1.28	-2.34	3.91	1.19	0.85	0.35	0.42	0.39	0.04
1975												
1st quarter	-4.7	2.06	-11.55	-2.77	-0.88	-7.90	3.69	0.24	3.45	1.06	-0.38	1.44
2nd quarter	3.1	4.11	-1.89	-1.14	0.44	-1.19	1.47	-1.01	2.48	-0.57	-0.21	-0.36
3rd quarter	6.8	3.56	4.52	0.50	1.02	2.99	-2.80	-0.55	-2.25	1.50	0.86	0.63
4th quarter	5.5	2.61	1.78	0.53	0.69	0.56	0.25	1.76	-1.51	0.87	0.21	0.65
1976												
1st quarter	9.3	4.91	6.25	0.96	1.57	3.72	-2.05	-0.22	-1.83	0.23	-0.33	0.56
2nd quarter	3.1	2.23	2.73	0.58	0.43	1.72	-1.02	0.31	-1.33	-0.88	-0.04	-0.84
3rd quarter	2.1	2.59	0.26	1.00	-0.29	-0.45	-0.38	0.91	-1.29	-0.42	-0.10	-0.31
4th quarter	3.0	3.23	0.49	0.91	2.18	-2.61	-0.75	0.33	-1.08	0.06	0.20	-0.14
1977												
1st quarter	4.7	2.90	3.14	1.77	0.61	0.76	-2.08	-0.51	-1.57	0.78	0.34	0.44
2nd quarter	8.1	1.45	5.22	1.40	2.29	1.53	0.55	0.85	-0.30	0.87	0.59	0.28
3rd quarter	7.3	2.37	3.94	1.05	-0.07	2.96	0.75	0.24	0.51	0.20	0.25	-0.05
4th quarter	0.0	3.62	-1.88	1.56	-0.28	-3.17	-1.49	-1.00	-0.49	-0.21	-0.27	0.06
1978												
1st quarter	1.4	1.36	1.69	0.52	0.20	0.97	-1.70	0.66	-2.35	0.05	0.06	-0.01
2nd quarter	16.5	5.44	5.67	4.12	1.13	0.41	3.11	3.18	-0.07	2.26	0.90	1.36
3rd quarter	4.0	1.00	2.48	1.81	0.27	0.40	-0.13	0.34	-0.47	0.63	0.12	0.51
4th quarter	5.5	1.93	2.02	1.74	-0.04	0.32	0.79	1.28	-0.49	0.73	0.31	0.42
1979												
1st quarter	0.8	1.21	0.15	1.21	-0.57	-0.49	0.13	0.03	0.10	-0.69	0.04	-0.73
2nd quarter	0.5	-0.16	-0.07	-0.10	-0.41	0.44	-0.10	0.09	-0.18	0.81	0.41	0.40
3rd quarter	2.9	2.35	-1.39	1.61	-0.28	-2.72	1.84	1.22	0.62	0.11	-0.04	0.14
4th quarter	1.0	0.61	-1.46	0.11	-0.91	-0.66	1.38	2.18	-0.81	0.51	0.03	0.48
1980												
1st quarter	1.3	-0.42	-0.56	0.59	-1.69	0.54	1.04	1.00	0.04	1.24	1.05	0.20
2nd quarter	-7.9	-5.48	-6.68	-2.67	-3.71	-0.30	3.98	0.73	3.25	0.31	0.89	-0.58
3rd quarter	-0.6	2.62	-4.94	0.35	0.51	-5.80	2.96	-0.07	3.03	-1.24	-0.55	-0.70
4th quarter	7.6	3.32	6.53	1.19	1.62	3.73	-2.25	-0.19	-2.06	0.02	0.23	-0.21
1981												
1st quarter	8.5	1.36	6.97	1.18	-0.43	6.22	-0.89	0.82	-1.71	1.09	0.74	0.36
2nd quarter	-2.9	-0.02	-3.31	1.17	-0.55	-3.93	0.18	0.25	-0.07	0.26	1.08	-0.82
3rd quarter	4.7	0.99	4.32	1.39	-1.32	4.24	-0.34	-0.80	0.45	-0.30	-0.18	-0.12
4th quarter	-4.6	-1.80	-2.82	1.44	-1.61	-2.65	-0.90	0.17	-1.08	0.93	0.60	0.33
1982												
1st quarter	-6.5	1.61	-7.59	-1.45	-0.81	-5.33	-0.49	-1.62	1.12	-0.05	0.07	-0.11
2nd quarter	2.2	0.89	-0.06	-1.89	-0.44	2.26	0.81	0.19	0.61	0.56	0.41	0.15
3rd quarter	-1.4	1.88	-0.62	-1.72	-0.02	1.11	-3.22	-1.57	-1.65	0.53	0.53	-0.01
4th quarter	0.4	4.51	-5.37	-1.05	1.01	-5.33	-0.10	-1.52	1.43	1.35	1.03	0.32
1983												
1st quarter	5.3	2.45	2.36	-0.92	2.36	0.92	-0.29	0.50	-0.78	0.82	0.67	0.15
2nd quarter	9.4	5.06	5.96	0.67	1.86	3.43	-2.46	0.11	-2.57	0.89	0.98	-0.08
3rd quarter	8.1	4.50	4.40	2.13	1.70	0.57	-2.25	0.47	-2.72	1.42	1.05	0.37
4th quarter	8.5	4.06	6.94	3.14	0.79	3.01	-1.14	0.63	-1.76	-1.36	-1.39	0.03
1984												
1st quarter	8.2	2.26	7.23	1.71	0.58	4.94	-2.31	0.65	-2.96	1.01	0.47	0.54
2nd quarter	7.2	3.64	2.67	2.52	0.34	-0.29	-0.87	0.76	-1.63	1.87	1.31	0.56
3rd quarter	4.0	1.95	1.69	1.70	-0.22	0.21	0.36	0.66	-1.02	0.70	0.00	0.71
4th quarter	3.2	3.29	-1.08	1.34	0.02	-2.44	-0.56	0.60	-1.16	1.58	1.16	0.42
1985												
1st quarter	4.0	4.23	-2.14	0.67	0.05	-2.86	0.94	0.07	0.87	1.01	0.48	0.52
2nd quarter	3.7	2.35	1.34	0.83	0.16	0.35	-1.90	-0.08	-1.83	1.93	1.18	0.76
3rd quarter	6.4	4.82	-0.43	-0.62	0.34	-0.15	-0.01	-0.42	0.41	1.98	1.31	0.68
4th quarter	3.0	0.62	2.80	1.00	0.40	1.40	-0.66	0.78	-1.44	0.27	-0.05	0.32
1986												
1st quarter	3.8	2.10	0.04	-0.55	0.76	-0.17	0.92	0.82	0.10	0.70	-0.09	0.78
2nd quarter	1.9	2.77	-1.30	-1.12	1.12	-1.30	-1.33	0.27	-1.60	1.70	1.28	0.42
3rd quarter	4.1	4.55	-1.97	-0.63	0.28	-1.62	-0.45	0.62	-1.07	1.95	1.55	0.40
4th quarter	2.1	1.62	0.24	0.48	0.05	-0.29	0.71	1.03	-0.32	-0.48	-0.63	0.15
1987												
1st quarter	2.8	0.05	1.98	-1.26	-0.04	3.28	0.23	0.03	0.20	0.57	0.35	0.23
2nd quarter	4.6	3.54	0.08	1.00	0.07	-0.99	0.14	1.18	-1.05	0.81	0.71	0.10
3rd quarter	3.7	2.97	0.03	1.39	-0.17	-1.19	0.45	1.28	-0.83	0.23	0.08	0.15
4th quarter	6.8	0.57	4.94	-0.05	0.04	4.95	0.18	1.15	-0.97	1.08	0.49	0.59
1988												
1st quarter	2.3	4.49	-3.62	0.41	-0.36	-3.68	1.94	1.74	0.20	-0.54	-1.00	0.47
2nd quarter	5.4	1.89	1.72	1.14	0.25	0.33	1.44	0.94	0.50	0.34	-0.21	0.55
3rd quarter	2.3	2.17	0.38	0.32	0.01	0.05	-0.31	0.66	-0.97	0.08	-0.12	0.20
4th quarter	5.4	2.93	1.11	0.71	0.13	0.27	-0.21	1.04	-1.25	1.56	1.04	0.53
1989												
1st quarter	4.1	1.18	2.41	0.80	-0.19	1.80	0.85	1.03	-0.17	-0.35	-0.70	0.35
2nd quarter	3.2	1.20	-0.70	0.68	-0.59	-0.79	1.35	1.53	-0.18	1.34	0.86	0.48
3rd quarter	3.0	2.52	-0.64	1.29	-0.08	-1.84	0.44	0.37	0.07	0.70	0.28	0.42
4th quarter	0.9	1.13	-0.53	-0.52	-0.38	0.37	-0.20	0.54	-0.73	0.45	-0.15	0.59

Table 1-4B. Contributions to Percent Change in Real Gross Domestic Product: Historical Data—*Continued*

(Percent; percentage points.)   NIPA Table 1.1.2

Year and quarter	Percent change at seasonally adjusted annual rate, real GDP	Personal consump-tion expen-ditures	Gross private domestic investment				Exports and imports of goods and services			Government consumption expenditures and gross investment		
			Total	Fixed investment		Change in private inventories	Net exports	Exports	Imports	Total	Federal	State and local
				Nonresi-dential	Residential							
1990												
1st quarter	4.5	2.21	0.69	0.63	0.16	-0.10	0.25	1.56	-1.31	1.30	0.61	0.69
2nd quarter	1.6	0.80	0.03	-0.66	-0.68	1.38	0.52	0.46	0.07	0.20	0.11	0.09
3rd quarter	0.1	1.02	-1.30	0.32	-0.89	-0.73	0.44	0.28	0.16	-0.05	-0.36	0.31
4th quarter	-3.4	-1.96	-3.64	-0.78	-0.90	-1.96	1.47	0.33	1.13	0.76	0.24	0.52
1991												
1st quarter	-1.9	-0.92	-2.04	-1.00	-0.78	-0.26	0.69	0.24	0.45	0.41	0.34	0.07
2nd quarter	3.1	2.14	0.05	-0.26	0.42	-0.12	0.65	1.38	-0.73	0.30	0.11	0.19
3rd quarter	1.9	1.24	1.21	-0.42	0.48	1.16	-0.21	0.91	-1.12	-0.30	-0.58	0.28
4th quarter	1.8	-0.07	2.15	-0.05	0.29	1.91	-0.02	0.87	-0.89	-0.31	-0.63	0.33
1992												
1st quarter	4.8	4.85	-1.15	-0.19	0.84	-1.80	0.44	0.72	-0.28	0.67	0.07	0.60
2nd quarter	4.5	1.79	3.40	1.44	0.53	1.43	-0.63	0.03	-0.66	-0.08	-0.02	-0.07
3rd quarter	3.9	2.80	0.51	0.69	0.01	-0.19	0.19	0.82	-0.64	0.45	0.43	0.02
4th quarter	4.1	3.08	1.92	1.19	0.60	0.13	-0.77	0.20	-0.97	-0.16	-0.13	-0.03
1993												
1st quarter	0.8	0.97	1.48	0.44	0.01	1.03	-0.79	0.09	-0.88	-0.92	-1.06	0.14
2nd quarter	2.4	2.32	0.38	0.88	0.22	-0.72	-0.40	0.46	-0.85	0.09	-0.28	0.37
3rd quarter	2.0	2.86	-0.41	0.36	0.61	-1.38	-0.66	-0.10	-0.55	0.17	-0.07	0.24
4th quarter	5.4	2.33	3.38	1.65	0.87	0.87	-0.45	1.22	-1.67	0.18	-0.04	0.22
1994												
1st quarter	4.0	2.99	2.58	0.50	0.26	1.82	-0.62	0.38	-1.00	-0.97	-1.15	0.18
2nd quarter	5.6	2.04	3.37	0.70	0.57	2.09	-0.30	1.29	-1.59	0.46	-0.06	0.52
3rd quarter	2.4	2.02	-1.15	0.77	-0.27	-1.65	0.22	1.45	-1.23	1.29	0.76	0.53
4th quarter	4.6	2.83	2.79	1.83	-0.27	1.24	-0.32	0.93	-1.25	-0.68	-0.86	0.18
1995												
1st quarter	1.4	0.71	0.70	1.80	-0.39	-0.70	-0.20	0.78	-0.98	0.16	-0.19	0.36
2nd quarter	1.4	2.33	-1.49	0.47	-0.52	-1.43	0.15	0.58	-0.43	0.41	0.05	0.36
3rd quarter	3.5	2.40	-0.41	0.31	0.61	-1.33	1.66	1.82	-0.15	-0.19	-0.24	0.05
4th quarter	2.9	1.83	1.69	0.97	0.33	0.40	0.01	0.62	-0.61	-0.66	-0.90	0.24
1996												
1st quarter	2.7	2.41	1.07	1.22	0.45	-0.59	-1.01	0.53	-1.54	0.17	0.25	-0.08
2nd quarter	7.2	2.88	3.39	1.36	0.77	1.26	-0.33	0.73	-1.05	1.22	0.56	0.66
3rd quarter	3.7	1.59	3.23	1.59	-0.04	1.68	-1.15	0.36	-1.51	0.08	-0.32	0.39
4th quarter	4.3	2.08	-0.05	1.30	-0.20	-1.14	1.73	2.64	-0.91	0.53	-0.12	0.65
1997												
1st quarter	3.1	2.78	1.47	1.20	0.09	0.18	-1.13	0.85	-1.98	-0.04	-0.46	0.42
2nd quarter	6.2	1.23	3.98	1.11	0.25	2.62	0.20	1.78	-1.57	0.76	0.59	0.17
3rd quarter	5.2	4.44	1.33	2.33	0.17	-1.17	-0.70	1.05	-1.75	0.12	-0.05	0.17
4th quarter	3.1	3.07	1.06	0.33	0.19	0.55	-1.10	-0.05	-1.05	0.11	-0.07	0.18
1998												
1st quarter	4.0	2.67	3.36	1.65	0.37	1.35	-1.62	0.21	-1.83	-0.40	-0.75	0.35
2nd quarter	3.9	4.58	-0.49	1.74	0.62	-2.86	-1.59	-0.47	-1.12	1.45	0.63	0.81
3rd quarter	5.3	3.46	2.04	0.79	0.54	0.71	-0.83	-0.18	-0.65	0.67	-0.15	0.82
4th quarter	6.7	3.88	2.18	1.55	0.44	0.18	-0.01	1.53	-1.54	0.68	0.32	0.37
1999												
1st quarter	3.2	2.49	2.16	1.17	0.07	0.91	-1.69	-0.99	-0.69	0.27	-0.23	0.50
2nd quarter	3.3	3.88	0.05	1.44	0.30	-1.68	-1.00	0.42	-1.42	0.41	0.13	0.27
3rd quarter	5.1	3.02	1.94	1.57	0.15	0.22	-0.69	1.21	-1.90	0.86	0.45	0.40
4th quarter	7.1	3.93	2.33	0.22	0.15	1.97	-0.23	1.06	-1.29	1.09	0.52	0.57
2000												
1st quarter	1.2	4.01	-0.71	2.00	0.10	-2.81	-1.54	0.64	-2.18	-0.59	-0.95	0.36
2nd quarter	7.8	2.62	4.72	1.85	-0.10	2.97	-0.47	1.25	-1.72	0.90	0.88	0.02
3rd quarter	0.5	2.55	-1.01	0.60	-0.29	-1.31	-0.92	1.05	-1.97	-0.15	-0.42	0.27
4th quarter	2.3	2.35	0.06	0.13	0.02	-0.08	-0.34	-0.37	0.02	0.23	-0.13	0.35
2001												
1st quarter	-1.1	1.09	-3.60	-0.51	0.08	-3.17	0.31	-0.65	0.96	1.07	0.53	0.54
2nd quarter	2.1	0.67	-0.24	-1.31	0.29	0.77	0.28	-1.37	1.64	1.43	0.49	0.95
3rd quarter	-1.3	0.96	-1.29	-0.72	0.12	-0.69	-0.88	-1.92	1.05	-0.05	0.21	-0.26
4th quarter	1.1	4.06	-3.54	-1.55	-0.13	-1.86	-0.48	-1.17	0.69	1.07	0.20	0.88
2002												
1st quarter	3.7	0.82	2.50	-1.02	0.64	2.89	-0.69	0.72	-1.42	1.11	0.64	0.47
2nd quarter	2.2	1.37	0.73	-0.66	0.49	0.90	-0.60	0.98	-1.58	0.73	0.62	0.11
3rd quarter	2.0	1.88	0.00	-0.31	0.06	0.25	-0.51	0.26	-0.77	0.59	0.42	0.17
4th quarter	0.3	1.44	-0.14	-0.64	0.37	0.13	-1.60	-0.50	-1.10	0.55	0.50	0.05
2003												
1st quarter	2.1	1.19	0.57	0.04	0.39	0.15	0.57	-0.21	0.78	-0.24	0.02	-0.26
2nd quarter	3.8	3.02	0.37	1.09	0.34	-1.06	-0.86	-0.04	-0.83	1.23	1.42	-0.19
3rd quarter	6.9	4.04	2.51	0.95	1.25	0.31	0.30	0.96	-0.66	0.02	-0.16	0.18
4th quarter	4.8	2.12	2.53	0.69	0.67	1.16	-0.31	1.58	-1.90	0.43	0.56	-0.13
2004												
1st quarter	2.3	2.62	0.07	-0.50	0.27	0.30	-0.58	1.11	-1.70	0.21	0.20	0.01
2nd quarter	3.0	1.76	2.60	1.06	0.75	0.79	-1.84	0.49	-2.33	0.44	0.29	0.15
3rd quarter	3.7	2.59	1.17	1.30	0.17	-0.31	-0.37	0.22	-0.60	0.30	0.51	-0.21
4th quarter	3.5	2.78	1.52	1.03	0.34	0.15	-0.47	0.93	-1.40	-0.33	-0.25	-0.08
2005												
1st quarter	4.3	2.09	2.17	0.60	0.60	0.97	-0.10	0.61	-0.71	0.18	0.17	0.00
2nd quarter	2.1	2.92	-0.99	0.69	0.48	-2.16	0.04	0.73	-0.69	0.14	0.06	0.07
3rd quarter	3.4	2.09	0.81	0.90	0.29	-0.38	-0.10	0.05	-0.14	0.60	0.53	0.07
4th quarter	2.3	1.00	2.32	0.20	-0.06	2.18	-0.73	1.12	-1.85	-0.29	-0.43	0.15

Table 1-4B. Contributions to Percent Change in Real Gross Domestic Product: Historical Data—*Continued*

(Percent; percentage points.)

NIPA Table 1.1.2

Year and quarter	Percent change at seasonally adjusted annual rate, real GDP	Personal consump-tion expen-ditures	Gross private domestic investment				Exports and imports of goods and services			Government consumption expenditures and gross investment		
			Total	Fixed investment		Change in private inventories	Net exports	Exports	Imports	Total	Federal	State and local
				Nonresi-dential	Residential							
2006												
1st quarter	4.9	3.01	1.10	1.84	-0.25	-0.49	0.18	1.52	-1.34	0.61	0.71	-0.11
2nd quarter	1.2	1.41	-0.51	0.63	-1.33	0.19	0.02	0.78	-0.76	0.27	-0.04	0.31
3rd quarter	0.4	1.56	-0.80	0.61	-1.39	-0.02	-0.57	-0.08	-0.48	0.16	0.01	0.16
4th quarter	3.2	2.75	-1.83	0.34	-1.09	-1.07	1.74	1.90	-0.16	0.51	0.30	0.20
2007												
1st quarter	0.2	1.43	-0.71	0.89	-1.01	-0.58	-0.31	0.72	-1.03	-0.16	-0.39	0.23
2nd quarter	3.1	0.93	1.02	1.03	-0.84	0.83	0.48	0.78	-0.30	0.66	0.46	0.20
3rd quarter	2.7	1.21	-0.44	0.81	-1.26	0.01	1.39	1.38	0.01	0.56	0.55	0.01
4th quarter	1.4	0.34	-1.44	0.88	-1.53	-0.79	2.22	1.41	0.81	0.31	0.16	0.15
2008												
1st quarter	-2.7	-0.56	-2.36	0.00	-1.31	-1.05	-0.11	0.57	-0.67	0.32	0.47	-0.15
2nd quarter	2.0	0.48	-1.21	-0.31	-0.67	-0.24	2.11	1.49	0.62	0.62	0.56	0.07
3rd quarter	-1.9	-1.94	-1.86	-1.42	-0.71	0.26	0.77	-0.69	1.46	1.13	0.91	0.22
4th quarter	-8.2	-3.16	-5.74	-3.00	-1.29	-1.45	0.15	-2.68	2.83	0.56	0.56	0.00
2009												
1st quarter	-5.4	-0.86	-7.02	-3.58	-1.17	-2.26	2.30	-3.62	5.92	0.15	-0.24	0.39
2nd quarter	-0.5	-1.19	-3.25	-1.46	-0.66	-1.12	2.34	0.14	2.20	1.56	1.09	0.47
3rd quarter	1.3	1.68	-0.40	-0.54	0.52	-0.38	-0.45	1.53	-1.98	0.48	0.47	0.01
4th quarter	3.9	-0.01	4.05	-0.37	0.01	4.40	0.06	2.53	-2.47	-0.17	0.02	-0.19
2010												
1st quarter	1.7	1.46	1.77	0.46	-0.35	1.66	-0.85	0.71	-1.55	-0.63	0.32	-0.95
2nd quarter	3.9	2.23	2.86	1.21	0.56	1.09	-1.77	1.12	-2.90	0.61	0.71	-0.10
3rd quarter	2.7	1.77	1.86	0.90	-0.94	1.90	-0.83	1.38	-2.20	-0.07	0.32	-0.39
4th quarter	2.5	2.79	-0.51	0.94	0.19	-1.63	1.12	1.53	-0.41	-0.87	-0.23	-0.63
2011												
1st quarter	-1.5	1.38	-1.07	-0.09	-0.02	-0.96	-0.24	0.27	-0.51	-1.60	-0.95	-0.65
2nd quarter	2.9	0.57	2.14	0.97	0.13	1.04	0.31	0.82	-0.51	-0.08	0.14	-0.22
3rd quarter	0.8	1.20	0.15	2.06	0.19	-2.10	0.01	0.57	-0.56	-0.52	-0.35	-0.17
4th quarter	4.6	0.94	4.16	1.08	0.28	2.80	-0.21	0.56	-0.76	-0.31	-0.21	-0.10
2012												
1st quarter	2.7	1.63	1.47	1.37	0.63	-0.53	-0.02	0.37	-0.40	-0.40	-0.03	-0.36
2nd quarter	1.9	0.45	1.53	0.88	0.10	0.56	0.28	0.61	-0.33	-0.39	-0.24	-0.14
3rd quarter	0.5	0.72	-0.18	-0.27	0.27	-0.18	0.16	0.27	-0.10	-0.22	0.04	-0.26
4th quarter	0.1	0.78	-0.51	0.46	0.57	-1.54	0.58	-0.07	0.65	-0.75	-0.45	-0.30
2013												
1st quarter	2.8	1.32	2.04	0.72	0.41	0.92	0.30	0.52	-0.22	-0.83	-0.86	0.02
2nd quarter	0.8	0.58	0.78	0.35	0.35	0.08	-0.21	0.65	-0.86	-0.37	-0.41	0.03
3rd quarter	3.1	1.28	2.08	0.29	0.18	1.60	0.13	0.41	-0.28	-0.37	-0.39	0.01
4th quarter	4.0	2.29	0.91	1.16	-0.15	-0.11	1.29	1.54	-0.24	-0.53	-0.42	-0.11
2014												
1st quarter	-0.9	1.27	-0.93	0.85	-0.09	-1.69	-1.14	-0.35	-0.79	-0.11	-0.03	-0.09
2nd quarter	4.6	2.33	2.47	1.16	0.40	0.91	-0.40	1.22	-1.62	0.20	-0.11	0.31
3rd quarter	5.2	2.65	1.90	1.31	0.14	0.44	0.28	0.09	0.18	0.39	0.22	0.17
4th quarter	2.0	3.36	-0.21	-0.30	0.35	-0.26	-1.02	0.65	-1.67	-0.11	-0.40	0.28
2015												
1st quarter	3.2	2.48	2.12	0.30	0.37	1.45	-1.64	-0.59	-1.05	0.27	0.11	0.17
2nd quarter	2.7	2.03	0.14	0.38	0.39	-0.63	-0.03	0.47	-0.50	0.60	0.12	0.48
3rd quarter	1.6	1.86	0.33	0.19	0.36	-0.22	-0.77	-0.51	-0.25	0.21	-0.07	0.28
4th quarter	0.5	1.80	-1.08	-0.67	0.26	-0.68	-0.28	-0.29	0.01	0.05	0.17	-0.12
2016												
1st quarter	0.6	1.23	-0.68	-0.52	0.47	-0.64	-0.28	-0.33	0.04	0.32	-0.10	0.42
2nd quarter	2.2	2.57	-0.45	0.41	-0.18	-0.67	0.28	0.32	-0.04	-0.16	-0.06	-0.11
3rd quarter	2.8	1.92	0.40	0.42	-0.18	0.16	0.36	0.74	-0.37	0.09	0.11	-0.02
4th quarter	1.8	1.99	1.34	0.02	0.26	1.06	-1.61	-0.47	-1.14	0.03	-0.03	0.06

Table 1-5A. Chain-Type Quantity Indexes for Gross Domestic Product and Domestic Purchases: Recent Data

(Index numbers, 2009 = 100.) NIPA Tables 1.1.3, 1.4.3, 2.3.3

Year and quarter	Gross domestic product, total	Personal consumption expenditures		Private fixed investment			Exports and imports of goods and services		Government consumption expenditures and gross investment			Gross domestic purchases
		Total	Excluding food and energy	Total	Nonresidential	Residential	Exports	Imports	Total	Federal	State and local	
1950	15.1	13.8	11.3	13.9	8.3	49.3	3.7	3.6	18.4	21.5	16.0	15.0
1951	16.4	14.0	11.5	13.3	8.7	41.4	4.5	3.7	25.2	35.1	16.1	16.1
1952	17.0	14.5	11.8	13.2	8.7	40.7	4.3	4.0	30.2	45.0	16.4	16.8
1953	17.8	15.2	12.4	14.3	9.5	42.2	4.0	4.4	32.2	48.4	17.2	17.7
1954	17.7	15.5	12.6	14.5	9.4	45.7	4.2	4.2	30.1	42.5	18.7	17.6
1955	19.0	16.6	13.6	16.4	10.4	53.1	4.7	4.7	29.2	39.1	20.0	18.8
1956	19.4	17.1	14.0	16.6	11.1	48.9	5.4	5.1	29.2	38.6	20.7	19.1
1957	19.8	17.5	14.3	16.5	11.3	46.0	5.9	5.3	30.6	40.1	21.9	19.5
1958	19.7	17.7	14.4	15.5	10.3	46.5	5.1	5.5	31.6	40.3	23.7	19.5
1959	21.0	18.7	15.3	17.6	11.1	58.1	5.6	6.1	32.4	41.1	24.5	20.9
1960	21.6	19.2	15.8	17.8	11.7	54.2	6.6	6.2	32.6	40.4	25.6	21.3
1961	22.1	19.6	16.2	17.9	11.8	54.4	6.7	6.2	34.3	42.3	27.1	21.8
1962	23.5	20.6	17.1	19.4	12.7	59.6	7.0	6.8	36.6	46.1	27.9	23.2
1963	24.5	21.4	18.0	20.9	13.5	66.6	7.5	7.0	37.5	46.2	29.6	24.2
1964	25.9	22.7	19.2	22.8	14.9	70.6	8.4	7.4	38.4	46.1	31.6	25.5
1965	27.6	24.1	20.5	25.2	17.4	68.8	8.6	8.2	39.6	46.4	33.7	27.2
1966	29.4	25.5	21.7	26.8	19.6	63.0	9.2	9.4	43.1	51.4	35.8	29.1
1967	30.2	26.3	22.4	26.5	19.5	61.4	9.4	10.1	46.5	56.6	37.5	30.0
1968	31.7	27.8	23.7	28.4	20.4	69.7	10.2	11.6	48.1	57.4	39.8	31.5
1969	32.7	28.8	24.7	30.0	21.8	71.9	10.6	12.3	48.2	56.0	41.2	32.5
1970	32.7	29.5	25.2	29.4	21.7	68.1	11.8	12.8	47.2	52.6	42.4	32.5
1971	33.8	30.6	26.3	31.4	21.6	86.2	12.0	13.5	46.3	49.2	43.7	33.6
1972	35.6	32.5	28.1	35.0	23.5	101.2	12.9	15.0	46.1	47.7	44.7	35.5
1973	37.6	34.1	29.9	38.0	26.6	100.6	15.4	15.7	46.0	46.0	45.9	37.2
1974	37.4	33.8	29.9	35.9	26.9	80.8	16.6	15.3	47.0	46.3	47.6	36.7
1975	37.4	34.6	30.5	32.4	24.4	71.1	16.5	13.6	48.0	46.6	49.3	36.3
1976	39.4	36.5	32.3	35.6	25.8	86.8	17.2	16.3	48.3	46.6	49.7	38.7
1977	41.2	38.0	33.9	40.4	28.6	104.6	17.6	18.1	48.9	47.7	49.9	40.7
1978	43.5	39.7	36.7	45.1	32.6	111.6	10.5	10.6	50.3	48.9	51.6	43.0
1979	44.8	40.7	36.7	47.7	35.8	107.4	21.4	20.0	51.2	50.0	52.3	44.0
1980	44.7	40.5	36.7	44.9	35.8	84.9	23.7	18.6	52.2	52.2	52.2	43.2
1981	45.9	41.1	37.5	46.1	38.0	77.9	24.0	19.1	52.7	54.5	51.2	44.4
1982	45.0	41.7	38.1	43.0	36.6	63.8	22.1	18.9	53.7	56.6	51.2	43.8
1983	47.1	44.1	40.6	46.2	36.5	90.6	21.6	21.3	55.7	60.2	51.9	46.4
1984	50.5	46.4	43.0	53.7	42.6	104.0	23.3	26.4	57.7	62.2	53.9	50.5
1985	52.7	48.9	45.6	56.6	45.4	106.4	24.1	28.2	61.6	67.2	56.9	52.7
1986	54.5	50.9	47.7	57.7	44.6	119.6	26.0	30.6	65.0	71.1	59.8	54.7
1987	56.4	52.6	49.6	58.0	44.6	121.9	28.8	32.4	66.9	73.8	61.1	56.4
1988	58.8	54.8	51.8	59.9	46.9	120.8	33.5	33.6	67.8	72.8	63.4	58.3
1989	60.9	56.4	53.4	61.8	49.5	116.9	37.3	35.1	69.8	74.1	66.0	60.1
1990	62.1	57.6	54.7	61.0	50.1	107.0	40.6	36.4	72.0	75.6	68.7	61.0
1991	62.1	57.7	54.8	57.8	48.1	97.5	43.3	36.3	72.9	75.6	70.2	60.6
1992	64.3	59.9	57.2	61.0	49.5	110.9	46.3	38.9	73.2	74.5	71.6	62.7
1993	66.0	62.0	59.3	65.7	53.2	120.0	47.8	42.2	72.6	71.9	72.5	64.8
1994	68.7	64.4	61.8	71.0	57.4	130.7	52.1	47.3	72.7	69.4	74.5	67.7
1995	70.6	66.3	63.8	75.4	63.0	126.3	57.4	51.1	73.1	67.6	76.5	69.4
1996	73.2	68.6	66.3	82.1	68.7	136.6	62.1	55.5	73.8	66.8	78.3	72.1
1997	76.5	71.2	69.1	89.1	76.1	139.9	69.5	63.0	75.2	66.2	81.1	75.5
1998	79.9	75.0	73.2	98.2	84.3	152.0	71.1	70.3	76.7	65.7	84.3	79.7
1999	83.7	79.0	77.3	106.9	92.4	161.6	73.0	77.5	79.4	67.0	87.8	84.1
2000	87.1	83.0	81.6	114.3	100.9	162.6	79.3	87.5	80.9	67.2	90.3	88.1
2001	88.0	85.1	83.9	112.6	98.5	164.1	74.6	85.1	83.9	69.8	93.6	89.2
2002	89.5	87.3	86.3	108.7	91.7	174.0	73.3	88.2	87.6	74.8	96.3	91.3
2003	92.0	90.1	89.2	113.0	93.4	189.8	74.6	92.1	89.5	79.9	95.9	94.1
2004	95.5	93.5	92.8	120.6	98.3	208.8	81.9	102.6	90.9	83.5	95.8	98.1
2005	98.7	96.8	96.2	128.9	105.1	222.5	87.0	109.1	91.5	85.0	95.8	101.5
2006	101.4	99.7	99.4	131.4	112.6	205.6	94.9	116.0	92.9	87.1	96.7	104.2
2007	103.2	102.0	101.8	128.8	119.3	166.9	103.7	119.0	94.3	88.6	98.1	105.4
2008	102.9	101.6	101.8	120.1	118.4	126.9	109.6	115.9	96.9	94.6	98.5	104.0
2009	100.0	100.0	100.0	100.0	100.0	100.0	100.0	100.0	100.0	100.0	100.0	100.0
2010	102.5	101.9	102.0	101.5	102.5	97.5	111.9	112.7	100.1	104.4	97.3	102.9
2011	104.2	104.2	104.7	107.9	110.3	98.0	119.6	118.9	97.0	101.5	94.1	104.5
2012	106.5	105.8	106.6	118.5	120.2	111.3	123.6	121.5	95.2	99.7	92.3	106.7
2013	108.3	107.3	108.2	124.5	124.5	124.5	128.0	122.9	92.5	93.9	91.6	108.1
2014	111.1	110.4	111.7	132.2	133.0	128.8	133.4	128.4	91.9	91.6	92.1	111.0
2015	114.2	114.4	116.1	137.4	136.1	142.0	134.0	134.8	93.2	91.5	94.2	114.9
2016	115.9	117.5	119.4	138.4	135.3	149.8	133.5	136.5	93.9	91.5	95.3	116.8
2014												
1st quarter	109.3	108.8	109.7	128.3	129.3	124.3	130.7	125.4	91.5	91.8	91.3	109.1
2nd quarter	110.5	109.7	111.0	131.5	132.3	128.2	133.6	128.5	91.8	91.5	91.9	110.5
3rd quarter	111.9	110.8	112.4	134.4	135.6	129.6	133.8	128.2	92.2	92.1	92.3	111.8
4th quarter	112.5	112.2	113.7	134.5	134.8	133.0	135.5	131.5	92.1	90.8	92.8	112.6
2015												
1st quarter	113.4	113.2	114.7	135.8	135.6	136.7	133.9	133.7	92.4	91.2	93.2	113.9
2nd quarter	114.2	114.0	115.8	137.4	136.6	140.5	135.1	134.7	93.2	91.6	94.2	114.7
3rd quarter	114.6	114.8	116.6	138.6	137.1	144.1	133.8	135.3	93.5	91.3	94.8	115.3
4th quarter	114.8	115.6	117.5	137.7	135.3	146.7	133.0	135.3	93.6	91.9	94.6	115.6
2016												
1st quarter	114.9	116.1	118.0	137.6	133.9	151.4	132.1	135.3	94.0	91.5	95.5	115.8
2nd quarter	115.6	117.2	119.0	138.1	135.0	149.5	133.1	135.4	93.8	91.3	95.2	116.3
3rd quarter	116.4	118.0	119.9	138.6	136.2	147.8	135.1	136.3	93.9	91.7	95.2	117.0
4th quarter	116.9	118.8	120.9	139.2	136.2	150.4	133.8	138.9	93.9	91.6	95.3	118.0

Table 1-5B. Chain-Type Quantity Indexes for Gross Domestic Product and Domestic Purchases: Historical Data

(Index numbers, 2009 = 100.)   NIPA Tables 1.1.3, 1.4.3, 2.3.3

Year and quarter	Gross domestic product											Gross domestic purchases
	Gross domestic product, total	Personal consumption expenditures		Private fixed investment			Exports and imports of goods and services		Government consumption expenditures and gross investment			
		Total	Excluding food and energy	Total	Nonresi-dential	Residential	Exports	Imports	Total	Federal	State and local	
1929	7.3	7.9	6.5	7.6	5.5	20.4	2.6	2.7	5.4	2.1	10.4	7.3
1930	6.7	7.5	6.1	5.9	4.5	12.6	2.1	2.3	5.9	2.4	11.5	6.7
1931	6.3	7.3	5.9	4.2	3.1	10.7	1.8	2.0	6.2	2.4	12.0	6.3
1932	5.5	6.6	5.3	2.6	1.9	6.1	1.4	1.7	6.0	2.5	11.4	5.5
1933	5.4	6.5	5.1	2.3	1.8	5.1	1.4	1.7	5.8	3.0	10.2	5.4
1934	6.0	6.9	5.4	3.0	2.2	6.6	1.5	1.8	6.5	4.0	10.7	6.0
1935	6.5	7.4	5.7	3.7	2.8	9.0	1.6	2.3	6.7	4.1	11.1	6.5
1936	7.4	8.1	6.3	4.9	3.7	11.2	1.7	2.3	7.7	6.2	11.1	7.4
1937	7.7	8.4	6.5	5.7	4.4	12.1	2.1	2.6	7.4	5.6	11.1	7.7
1938	7.5	8.3	6.3	4.6	3.3	12.1	2.1	2.0	8.0	6.1	11.7	7.4
1939	8.1	8.7	6.8	5.4	3.7	17.0	2.2	2.1	8.7	6.6	12.9	8.0
1940	8.8	9.2	7.1	6.5	4.4	19.0	2.5	2.2	9.0	7.5	12.5	8.7
1941	10.3	9.8	7.7	7.4	5.3	20.2	2.6	2.7	15.1	19.8	11.7	10.3
1942	12.3	9.6	7.5	4.4	3.3	10.5	1.7	2.4	35.1	59.1	10.7	12.3
1943	14.4	9.9	8.0	3.5	2.8	6.5	1.5	3.1	52.6	94.1	9.8	14.6
1944	15.5	10.2	8.2	4.2	3.5	5.6	1.6	3.2	59.1	107.2	9.4	15.7
1945	15.4	10.8	8.7	5.5	4.8	6.4	2.2	3.4	51.9	92.7	9.8	15.5
1946	13.6	12.1	9.6	9.8	7.0	25.5	4.7	2.8	18.3	26.0	10.7	13.1
1947	13.5	12.4	9.8	11.6	8.0	32.6	5.4	2.7	15.6	19.5	12.2	12.8
1948	14.0	12.6	10.1	12.7	8.4	39.0	4.2	3.1	16.5	20.7	12.9	13.7
1949	13.9	13.0	10.5	11.7	7.6	36.1	4.2	3.0	18.3	22.4	14.8	13.6
1947												
1st quarter	13.4	12.2	. . .	11.5	8.1	30.0	5.7	2.8	15.5	19.6	11.9	12.8
2nd quarter	13.4	12.4	. . .	11.2	8.0	28.5	5.7	2.8	15.6	19.7	12.0	12.8
3rd quarter	13.4	12.4	. . .	11.5	7.8	32.9	5.4	2.5	15.7	19.7	12.3	12.7
4th quarter	13.6	12.4	. . .	12.5	8.1	39.2	4.8	2.6	15.6	19.3	12.5	13.1
1948												
1st quarter	13.8	12.5	. . .	12.9	8.5	38.7	4.5	3.0	15.8	19.7	12.5	13.4
2nd quarter	14.0	12.6	. . .	12.8	8.2	40.9	4.1	3.1	16.3	20.4	12.8	13.7
3rd quarter	14.1	12.7	. . .	12.7	8.3	39.6	4.2	3.2	16.7	20.8	13.0	13.8
4th quarter	14.1	12.8	. . .	12.6	8.5	36.7	4.1	3.2	17.3	21.8	13.3	13.8
1949												
1st quarter	13.9	12.8	. . .	11.9	8.1	34.0	4.6	3.1	17.8	22.2	13.9	13.5
2nd quarter	13.9	13.0	. . .	11.5	7.8	33.4	4.5	3.0	18.5	23.0	14.6	13.5
3rd quarter	14.0	13.0	. . .	11.5	7.4	36.3	4.1	2.9	18.7	22.7	15.2	13.7
4th quarter	13.9	13.2	. . .	11.9	7.3	40.7	3.6	3.0	18.3	21.7	15.5	13.7
1950												
1st quarter	14.5	13.4	. . .	12.6	7.5	45.3	3.5	3.1	18.0	20.8	15.9	14.2
2nd quarter	14.9	13.6	. . .	13.7	8.2	49.6	3.6	3.2	18.3	21.3	16.0	14.7
3rd quarter	15.5	14.3	. . .	14.7	8.8	52.3	3.7	4.0	18.0	20.6	16.0	15.4
4th quarter	15.8	13.9	. . .	14.4	8.8	49.9	4.0	4.0	19.3	23.2	16.1	15.6
1951												
1st quarter	16.0	14.2	. . .	13.9	8.6	47.3	4.2	4.0	21.4	27.6	15.9	15.8
2nd quarter	16.3	13.8	. . .	13.3	8.7	41.0	4.6	3.8	24.2	33.1	16.2	16.0
3rd quarter	16.6	14.0	. . .	13.1	8.8	38.4	4.7	3.5	26.9	38.4	16.2	16.2
4th quarter	16.6	14.1	. . .	13.0	8.6	38.8	4.6	3.4	28.3	41.4	16.2	16.3
1952												
1st quarter	16.8	14.1	. . .	13.2	8.7	39.8	4.9	3.8	29.2	43.0	16.3	16.5
2nd quarter	16.8	14.4	. . .	13.4	8.9	40.5	4.3	3.8	30.1	44.7	16.6	16.6
3rd quarter	17.0	14.5	. . .	12.7	8.2	40.1	4.0	4.0	30.4	45.8	16.2	16.8
4th quarter	17.5	15.0	. . .	13.7	8.9	42.3	4.0	4.4	30.9	46.5	16.5	17.4
1953												
1st quarter	17.8	15.1	. . .	14.2	9.4	43.0	4.0	4.3	31.9	48.1	16.9	17.7
2nd quarter	18.0	15.2	. . .	14.3	9.5	43.1	4.0	4.5	32.6	49.5	16.9	17.9
3rd quarter	17.9	15.2	. . .	14.3	9.7	41.5	4.1	4.5	32.2	48.3	17.3	17.8
4th quarter	17.6	15.1	. . .	14.2	9.6	41.2	4.0	4.3	32.1	47.7	17.7	17.5
1954												
1st quarter	17.5	15.2	. . .	14.0	9.4	41.6	3.8	4.0	31.3	45.3	18.4	17.4
2nd quarter	17.6	15.3	. . .	14.2	9.3	44.3	4.4	4.4	30.2	43.0	18.4	17.4
3rd quarter	17.8	15.6	. . .	14.8	9.5	47.0	4.2	4.1	29.6	41.1	18.9	17.6
4th quarter	18.1	15.9	. . .	15.1	9.5	50.0	4.4	4.2	29.4	40.7	19.0	17.9
1955												
1st quarter	18.6	16.2	. . .	15.7	9.7	53.6	4.6	4.4	29.4	39.9	19.8	18.4
2nd quarter	18.9	16.6	. . .	16.3	10.2	54.4	4.5	4.7	29.2	39.1	20.1	18.8
3rd quarter	19.2	16.8	. . .	16.7	10.7	53.2	4.8	4.7	29.3	39.5	20.0	19.0
4th quarter	19.3	17.0	. . .	16.8	11.0	51.0	4.8	4.9	28.8	38.1	20.2	19.1

. . . = Not available.

Table 1-5B. Chain-Type Quantity Indexes for Gross Domestic Product and Domestic Purchases: Historical Data—*Continued*

(Index numbers, 2009 = 100.)   NIPA Tables 1.1.3, 1.4.3, 2.3.3

Year and quarter	Gross domestic product, total	Personal consumption expenditures		Private fixed investment			Exports and imports of goods and services		Government consumption expenditures and gross investment			Gross domestic purchases
		Total	Excluding food and energy	Total	Nonresi-dential	Residential	Exports	Imports	Total	Federal	State and local	
1956												
1st quarter	19.2	17.0	. . .	16.5	10.9	49.7	5.0	5.1	28.7	37.9	20.4	19.0
2nd quarter	19.4	17.0	. . .	16.7	11.1	49.5	5.4	5.1	29.3	38.8	20.6	19.1
3rd quarter	19.4	17.1	. . .	16.7	11.2	48.5	5.5	5.1	29.1	38.2	20.7	19.1
4th quarter	19.7	17.3	. . .	16.6	11.2	47.8	5.8	4.9	29.8	39.5	20.9	19.3
1957												
1st quarter	19.8	17.4	. . .	16.6	11.3	47.1	6.2	5.3	30.5	40.3	21.5	19.5
2nd quarter	19.8	17.5	. . .	16.4	11.3	46.0	6.0	5.3	30.3	39.8	21.6	19.4
3rd quarter	19.9	17.6	. . .	16.6	11.5	45.4	5.8	5.2	30.5	39.9	21.9	19.7
4th quarter	19.7	17.6	. . .	16.3	11.2	45.4	5.7	5.3	31.1	40.4	22.5	19.5
1958												
1st quarter	19.2	17.4	. . .	15.4	10.5	43.6	5.1	5.3	30.8	39.2	23.1	19.1
2nd quarter	19.4	17.5	. . .	15.0	10.1	43.7	5.1	5.6	31.6	40.5	23.5	19.2
3rd quarter	19.8	17.8	. . .	15.3	10.0	46.9	5.1	5.5	31.7	40.3	24.0	19.7
4th quarter	20.3	18.0	. . .	16.2	10.4	51.8	5.1	5.8	32.4	41.2	24.4	20.2
1959												
1st quarter	20.6	18.4	15.0	17.1	10.7	57.6	5.5	5.9	32.0	40.4	24.5	20.5
2nd quarter	21.1	18.7	15.3	17.6	11.0	59.6	5.6	6.2	32.4	41.1	24.6	21.0
3rd quarter	21.1	18.9	15.5	17.8	11.3	58.5	5.8	6.3	32.7	41.7	24.6	21.0
4th quarter	21.2	18.9	15.5	17.6	11.3	56.8	5.7	6.1	32.4	41.2	24.5	21.0
1960												
1st quarter	21.7	19.1	15.7	18.2	11.7	58.6	6.4	6.3	31.9	39.7	24.9	21.4
2nd quarter	21.6	19.3	15.9	17.9	11.8	53.8	6.8	6.4	32.2	39.8	25.5	21.3
3rd quarter	21.6	19.2	15.8	17.5	11.6	52.2	6.6	6.2	33.0	41.0	25.9	21.3
4th quarter	21.4	19.2	15.8	17.5	11.6	52.1	6.7	5.9	33.2	41.1	26.2	21.0
1961												
1st quarter	21.5	19.2	15.8	17.3	11.4	52.3	6.7	5.9	33.7	41.3	27.0	21.2
2nd quarter	21.9	19.5	16.0	17.6	11.7	52.6	6.6	5.9	33.8	41.6	26.8	21.6
3rd quarter	22.3	19.6	16.2	18.0	11.8	55.4	6.6	6.3	34.5	42.8	27.0	22.0
4th quarter	22.7	20.0	16.6	18.6	12.2	57.3	6.8	6.5	35.3	43.6	27.8	22.5
1962												
1st quarter	23.1	20.2	16.8	18.9	12.4	58.3	6.7	6.7	36.0	45.3	27.6	22.9
2nd quarter	23.4	20.5	17.1	19.5	12.8	60.1	7.4	6.8	36.1	45.4	27.7	23.1
3rd quarter	23.6	20.6	17.2	19.6	12.9	60.1	7.0	6.9	37.0	46.8	28.1	23.4
4th quarter	23.7	20.9	17.5	19.6	12.9	60.0	6.8	7.0	37.2	47.0	28.4	23.5
1963												
1st quarter	24.0	21.1	17.6	19.8	12.9	62.1	7.0	6.8	36.7	45.4	28.9	23.7
2nd quarter	24.3	21.3	17.9	20.7	13.3	66.5	7.8	7.0	36.7	45.2	29.2	23.9
3rd quarter	24.8	21.6	18.1	21.2	13.7	67.8	7.4	7.2	38.4	47.8	29.9	24.5
4th quarter	24.9	21.7	18.3	21.9	14.1	69.9	7.8	7.1	38.0	46.5	30.3	24.6
1964												
1st quarter	25.5	22.2	18.7	22.6	14.4	74.2	8.2	7.1	38.1	46.3	30.8	25.0
2nd quarter	25.8	22.6	19.1	22.6	14.7	70.5	8.4	7.3	38.5	46.3	31.5	25.3
3rd quarter	26.1	23.0	19.4	22.9	15.2	69.4	8.3	7.5	38.5	46.0	31.8	25.7
4th quarter	26.2	23.0	19.5	23.1	15.5	68.2	8.6	7.7	38.5	45.6	32.2	25.8
1965												
1st quarter	26.9	23.6	20.0	24.2	16.5	68.5	7.6	7.4	38.4	45.2	32.4	26.6
2nd quarter	27.2	23.8	20.2	24.9	17.1	69.1	9.1	8.3	38.9	45.3	33.3	26.8
3rd quarter	27.8	24.2	20.6	25.5	17.7	69.4	8.5	8.3	40.2	47.0	34.2	27.5
4th quarter	28.4	24.9	21.1	26.1	18.4	68.1	9.2	8.7	41.0	48.1	34.7	28.1
1966												
1st quarter	29.1	25.3	21.5	27.1	19.2	69.8	9.0	9.0	41.7	49.2	35.1	28.8
2nd quarter	29.3	25.3	21.5	26.9	19.5	64.4	9.4	9.2	42.5	50.6	35.4	28.9
3rd quarter	29.5	25.6	21.8	26.9	19.8	62.2	9.0	9.7	43.7	52.5	35.8	29.3
4th quarter	29.7	25.7	22.0	26.2	19.8	55.7	9.3	9.8	44.4	53.1	36.7	29.5
1967												
1st quarter	30.0	25.9	22.0	25.7	19.4	54.2	9.5	10.0	46.3	56.5	37.1	29.7
2nd quarter	30.0	26.2	22.4	26.3	19.4	60.4	9.4	9.9	46.1	55.9	37.4	29.8
3rd quarter	30.3	26.4	22.5	26.6	19.4	63.6	9.2	10.0	46.6	56.9	37.5	30.1
4th quarter	30.5	26.5	22.6	27.4	19.8	67.3	9.5	10.5	47.0	56.9	38.2	30.4
1968												
1st quarter	31.1	27.2	23.2	28.0	20.3	67.5	9.7	11.2	47.8	57.9	38.9	31.0
2nd quarter	31.7	27.6	23.6	28.0	20.1	69.1	9.9	11.3	48.1	57.6	39.6	31.5
3rd quarter	31.9	28.1	24.0	28.4	20.4	70.5	10.5	12.0	48.2	57.3	40.2	31.8
4th quarter	32.0	28.2	24.2	29.1	20.9	71.5	10.4	11.9	48.3	57.0	40.5	31.9

. . . = Not available.

Table 1-5B. Chain-Type Quantity Indexes for Gross Domestic Product and Domestic Purchases: Historical Data—*Continued*

(Index numbers, 2009 = 100.)

NIPA Tables 1.1.3, 1.4.3, 2.3.3

Year and quarter	Gross domestic product, total	Personal consumption expenditures		Private fixed investment			Exports and imports of goods and services		Government consumption expenditures and gross investment			Gross domestic purchases
		Total	Excluding food and energy	Total	Nonresidential	Residential	Exports	Imports	Total	Federal	State and local	
1969												
1st quarter	32.5	28.5	24.4	29.9	21.5	73.9	9.1	10.8	48.4	56.8	40.9	32.4
2nd quarter	32.6	28.7	24.6	30.0	21.7	73.2	11.2	12.9	48.2	56.1	41.2	32.5
3rd quarter	32.8	28.9	24.7	30.5	22.2	72.6	10.9	12.7	48.3	56.2	41.3	32.7
4th quarter	32.7	29.1	24.9	29.8	22.1	67.7	11.3	12.6	47.7	55.0	41.3	32.5
1970												
1st quarter	32.6	29.3	25.0	29.6	21.9	67.7	11.4	12.6	47.5	54.0	41.7	32.4
2nd quarter	32.7	29.4	25.2	29.0	21.8	63.5	11.9	12.8	46.9	52.0	41.9	32.4
3rd quarter	33.0	29.7	25.4	29.5	21.8	67.2	11.9	12.8	47.1	52.0	42.8	32.7
4th quarter	32.7	29.6	25.2	29.5	21.1	74.0	12.0	13.0	47.2	51.8	43.1	32.4
1971												
1st quarter	33.5	30.2	25.8	30.1	21.3	77.8	12.0	12.8	46.5	50.1	43.2	33.3
2nd quarter	33.7	30.4	26.1	31.3	21.6	85.3	12.0	13.8	46.4	49.5	43.6	33.6
3rd quarter	34.0	30.7	26.4	31.8	21.7	89.2	12.5	14.1	46.4	49.3	43.7	33.8
4th quarter	34.1	31.2	26.9	32.6	22.1	92.7	11.4	13.1	46.1	48.0	44.3	33.9
1972												
1st quarter	34.7	31.6	27.4	34.0	22.8	98.7	12.7	15.1	46.3	48.4	44.4	34.6
2nd quarter	35.5	32.2	27.8	34.6	23.2	100.6	12.3	14.5	46.5	49.0	44.3	35.4
3rd quarter	35.8	32.7	28.3	35.0	23.5	101.0	13.1	14.8	45.6	46.7	44.7	35.6
4th quarter	36.4	33.5	29.0	36.5	24.6	104.6	13.6	15.5	46.0	46.7	45.3	36.2
1973												
1st quarter	37.3	34.1	29.8	38.0	25.7	108.1	14.6	16.2	46.3	47.3	45.5	37.1
2nd quarter	37.7	34.1	29.9	38.2	26.6	102.5	15.3	15.8	46.1	46.7	45.6	37.3
3rd quarter	37.5	34.2	30.0	38.1	27.0	98.1	15.4	15.3	45.5	45.0	46.0	37.1
4th quarter	37.9	34.1	30.0	37.8	27.2	93.6	16.1	15.4	45.8	45.0	46.6	37.3
1974												
1st quarter	37.6	33.8	29.9	37.1	27.2	87.5	16.3	14.9	46.7	46.1	47.2	36.8
2nd quarter	37.7	33.9	30.0	36.6	27.2	84.0	17.1	15.7	47.0	46.1	47.8	36.9
3rd quarter	37.3	34.0	30.0	36.0	26.9	81.2	16.2	15.4	47.1	46.3	47.7	36.7
4th quarter	37.2	33.5	29.5	34.1	26.2	70.6	16.6	15.3	47.3	46.7	47.7	36.4
1975												
1st quarter	36.7	33.8	29.8	32.1	24.7	66.6	16.7	13.7	47.8	46.2	49.1	35.7
2nd quarter	37.0	34.4	30.2	31.8	24.1	68.5	16.3	12.6	47.5	46.0	48.8	35.8
3rd quarter	37.6	34.9	30.8	32.5	24.3	73.0	16.0	13.7	48.2	46.9	49.4	36.7
4th quarter	38.1	35.2	31.3	33.2	24.6	76.2	16.9	14.4	48.7	47.1	50.0	37.2
1976												
1st quarter	39.0	35.9	31.9	34.5	25.2	83.4	16.8	15.3	48.8	46.7	50.6	38.2
2nd quarter	39.3	36.3	32.1	35.1	25.5	85.4	16.9	16.0	48.3	46.7	49.7	38.6
3rd quarter	39.5	36.7	32.4	35.5	26.1	84.1	17.4	16.6	48.0	46.5	49.4	38.8
4th quarter	39.8	37.1	32.8	37.2	26.6	94.3	17.6	17.2	48.1	46.7	49.2	39.2
1977												
1st quarter	40.2	37.6	33.3	38.5	27.5	97.1	17.3	18.0	48.5	47.1	49.7	39.8
2nd quarter	41.0	37.8	33.6	40.5	28.3	107.7	17.8	18.2	48.9	47.8	50.0	40.6
3rd quarter	41.7	38.1	34.0	41.0	28.9	107.4	17.9	17.9	49.1	48.1	49.9	41.2
4th quarter	41.7	38.7	34.5	41.7	29.7	106.2	17.3	18.2	49.0	47.7	50.0	41.4
1978												
1st quarter	41.9	38.9	34.7	42.1	30.0	107.1	17.8	19.4	49.0	47.8	50.0	41.7
2nd quarter	43.5	39.8	35.8	44.9	32.3	112.3	19.6	19.5	50.3	48.9	51.5	43.0
3rd quarter	43.9	39.9	36.0	46.2	33.4	113.6	19.8	19.7	50.7	49.1	52.1	43.4
4th quarter	44.5	40.3	36.3	47.2	34.5	113.4	20.6	20.0	51.2	49.5	52.6	43.9
1979												
1st quarter	44.6	40.5	36.4	47.6	35.3	110.6	20.6	19.9	50.7	49.6	51.7	43.9
2nd quarter	44.7	40.4	36.5	47.3	35.3	108.6	20.7	20.0	51.2	50.2	52.2	44.0
3rd quarter	45.0	40.8	37.0	48.1	36.3	107.3	21.4	19.7	51.3	50.1	52.4	44.1
4th quarter	45.1	40.9	37.1	47.7	36.4	103.0	22.8	20.2	51.6	50.1	53.0	44.1
1980												
1st quarter	45.3	40.9	37.0	47.1	36.8	95.1	23.4	20.2	52.4	51.6	53.2	44.1
2nd quarter	44.3	40.0	36.0	43.2	35.1	77.5	23.9	18.7	52.6	52.8	52.5	42.8
3rd quarter	44.3	40.4	36.6	43.7	35.3	79.8	23.8	17.4	51.9	52.0	51.7	42.5
4th quarter	45.1	40.9	37.3	45.4	36.1	87.3	23.7	18.3	51.9	52.3	51.5	43.5
1981												
1st quarter	46.0	41.1	37.6	45.8	36.8	85.2	24.1	19.1	52.5	53.3	51.9	44.5
2nd quarter	45.7	41.1	37.5	46.2	37.6	82.4	24.2	19.1	52.7	54.8	50.9	44.2
3rd quarter	46.2	41.3	37.7	46.2	38.4	76.0	23.7	18.9	52.5	54.6	50.7	44.7
4th quarter	45.7	41.0	37.3	46.0	39.3	68.1	23.8	19.4	53.1	55.4	51.1	44.3

Table 1-5B. Chain-Type Quantity Indexes for Gross Domestic Product and Domestic Purchases: Historical Data—*Continued*

(Index numbers, 2009 = 100.)   NIPA Tables 1.1.3, 1.4.3, 2.3.3

Year and quarter	Gross domestic product, total	Personal consumption expenditures		Private fixed investment			Exports and imports of goods and services		Government consumption expenditures and gross investment			Gross domestic purchases
		Total	Excluding food and energy	Total	Nonresidential	Residential	Exports	Imports	Total	Federal	State and local	
1982												
1st quarter	44.9	41.3	37.5	44.6	38.3	64.2	22.8	18.9	53.0	55.4	51.0	43.6
2nd quarter	45.2	41.4	37.7	43.1	37.0	62.1	22.9	18.6	53.4	56.0	51.2	43.7
3rd quarter	45.0	41.7	38.1	42.1	36.0	62.0	21.9	19.4	53.7	56.7	51.2	43.9
4th quarter	45.0	42.5	38.9	42.1	35.3	67.0	20.9	18.7	54.6	58.1	51.6	44.0
1983												
1st quarter	45.6	42.9	39.4	43.1	34.8	78.5	21.3	19.1	55.1	59.0	51.7	44.6
2nd quarter	46.7	43.8	40.2	44.7	35.3	87.6	21.3	20.6	55.7	60.4	51.6	45.9
3rd quarter	47.6	44.5	40.9	47.2	36.8	96.2	21.6	22.2	56.6	61.8	52.1	47.0
4th quarter	48.6	45.2	41.7	49.9	39.0	100.2	22.1	23.2	55.6	59.7	52.1	48.1
1984												
1st quarter	49.5	45.6	42.3	51.4	40.3	103.2	22.5	25.1	56.3	60.4	52.8	49.4
2nd quarter	50.4	46.3	42.8	53.4	42.1	105.0	23.1	26.2	57.5	62.3	53.5	50.3
3rd quarter	50.9	46.6	43.2	54.5	43.4	103.8	23.6	26.8	58.0	62.3	54.4	50.8
4th quarter	51.3	47.2	43.9	55.5	44.4	103.9	24.1	27.6	59.1	64.0	54.9	51.3
1985												
1st quarter	51.8	48.0	44.7	56.0	44.9	104.1	24.1	27.0	59.8	64.8	55.6	51.7
2nd quarter	52.3	48.5	45.2	56.7	45.6	105.0	24.1	28.4	61.2	66.6	56.6	52.4
3rd quarter	53.1	49.4	46.2	56.4	45.1	107.0	23.7	28.1	62.7	68.7	57.5	53.2
4th quarter	53.5	49.5	46.2	57.5	45.9	109.3	24.5	29.2	62.9	68.6	58.0	53.7
1986												
1st quarter	54.0	50.0	46.7	57.7	45.4	113.8	25.2	29.2	63.4	68.5	59.0	54.0
2nd quarter	54.2	50.5	47.2	57.7	44.5	120.3	25.5	30.4	64.7	70.7	59.6	54.4
3rd quarter	54.8	51.4	48.3	57.4	44.0	121.9	26.1	31.2	66.1	73.3	60.2	55.0
4th quarter	55.1	51.8	48.6	57.9	44.4	122.3	27.1	31.5	65.8	72.1	60.4	55.2
1987												
1st quarter	55.4	51.8	48.7	56.9	43.4	122.1	27.1	31.3	66.2	72.7	60.7	55.6
2nd quarter	56.1	52.5	49.4	57.8	44.3	122.5	28.2	32.1	66.8	73.9	60.8	56.1
3rd quarter	56.6	53.1	50.1	58.8	45.5	121.5	29.4	32.7	66.9	74.0	61.0	56.6
4th quarter	57.5	53.2	50.2	58.7	45.4	121.7	30.5	33.4	67.7	74.7	61.8	57.5
1988												
1st quarter	57.8	54.2	51.1	58.8	45.8	119.5	32.2	33.3	67.3	72.9	62.5	57.5
2nd quarter	58.6	54.6	51.4	59.9	46.8	121.0	33.1	32.9	67.5	72.4	63.3	58.0
3rd quarter	58.9	55.0	51.9	60.2	47.1	121.1	33.8	33.7	67.6	72.1	63.6	58.4
4th quarter	59.7	55.6	52.6	60.9	47.8	121.8	34.8	34.7	68.8	74.0	64.4	59.2
1989												
1st quarter	60.3	55.9	52.8	61.4	48.5	120.7	35.8	34.9	68.5	72.6	64.9	59.7
2nd quarter	60.8	56.2	53.2	61.5	49.2	116.9	37.4	35.0	69.7	74.3	65.6	59.9
3rd quarter	61.3	56.7	53.8	62.6	50.4	116.3	37.8	35.0	70.2	74.8	66.2	60.3
4th quarter	61.4	57.0	53.8	61.8	49.9	113.9	38.3	35.6	70.6	74.5	67.1	60.5
1990												
1st quarter	62.1	57.5	54.6	62.5	50.6	114.9	40.0	36.7	71.7	75.7	68.1	61.1
2nd quarter	62.3	57.6	54.7	61.3	49.9	110.3	40.5	36.7	71.9	75.9	68.3	61.2
3rd quarter	62.3	57.9	54.9	60.8	50.3	104.4	40.8	36.5	71.9	75.2	68.7	61.2
4th quarter	61.8	57.4	54.5	59.2	49.5	98.4	41.2	35.6	72.5	75.7	69.5	60.5
1991												
1st quarter	61.5	57.2	54.3	57.6	48.5	93.2	41.4	35.2	72.9	76.4	69.6	60.1
2nd quarter	62.0	57.7	54.7	57.8	48.2	96.1	42.9	35.8	73.1	76.6	69.9	60.4
3rd quarter	62.3	58.0	55.0	57.8	47.8	99.3	43.9	36.8	72.9	75.4	70.3	60.8
4th quarter	62.5	58.0	55.1	58.1	47.8	101.3	44.9	37.6	72.6	74.1	70.8	61.0
1992												
1st quarter	63.3	59.1	56.3	58.7	47.6	107.1	45.7	37.9	73.2	74.2	71.7	61.7
2nd quarter	64.0	59.5	56.7	60.7	49.2	110.7	45.8	38.5	73.1	74.2	71.6	62.5
3rd quarter	64.6	60.1	57.4	61.4	49.9	110.8	46.7	39.1	73.4	75.0	71.6	63.0
4th quarter	65.2	60.8	58.1	63.2	51.2	115.0	47.0	40.0	73.3	74.7	71.6	63.8
1993												
1st quarter	65.4	61.1	58.4	63.6	51.8	115.1	47.1	40.9	72.4	72.5	71.8	64.0
2nd quarter	65.7	61.6	59.0	64.8	52.8	116.6	47.6	41.7	72.5	71.9	72.4	64.5
3rd quarter	66.1	62.3	59.6	65.8	53.2	121.0	47.5	42.3	72.7	71.7	72.8	64.9
4th quarter	67.0	62.9	60.2	68.4	55.1	127.2	49.1	44.0	72.8	71.6	73.1	65.8
1994												
1st quarter	67.6	63.6	60.9	69.3	55.7	129.1	49.5	45.0	71.9	69.1	73.4	66.6
2nd quarter	68.5	64.1	61.4	70.7	56.6	133.3	51.2	46.7	72.4	69.0	74.2	67.5
3rd quarter	68.9	64.6	62.0	71.2	57.5	131.3	53.1	48.0	73.6	70.7	75.1	67.9
4th quarter	69.7	65.3	62.8	73.0	59.8	129.3	54.4	49.4	72.9	68.7	75.4	68.7
1995												
1st quarter	70.0	65.4	62.9	74.5	62.0	126.4	55.4	50.4	73.1	68.3	76.0	69.0
2nd quarter	70.2	66.0	63.5	74.5	62.6	122.5	56.2	50.9	73.4	68.4	76.6	69.2
3rd quarter	70.8	66.6	64.2	75.5	63.0	127.0	58.6	51.1	73.2	67.8	76.6	69.5
4th quarter	71.3	67.1	64.7	77.0	64.3	129.5	59.4	51.8	72.6	65.8	77.0	70.0

Table 1-5B. Chain-Type Quantity Indexes for Gross Domestic Product and Domestic Purchases: Historical Data—*Continued*

(Index numbers, 2009 = 100.)

NIPA Tables 1.1.3, 1.4.3, 2.3.3

Year and quarter	Gross domestic product											Gross domestic purchases
	Gross domestic product, total	Personal consumption expenditures		Private fixed investment			Exports and imports of goods and services		Government consumption expenditures and gross investment			
		Total	Excluding food and energy	Total	Nonresi-dential	Residential	Exports	Imports	Total	Federal	State and local	
1996												
1st quarter	71.8	67.7	65.3	79.0	65.9	132.8	60.2	53.4	72.7	66.3	76.9	70.6
2nd quarter	73.0	68.4	66.1	81.4	67.6	138.6	61.1	54.6	73.9	67.5	78.0	71.9
3rd quarter	73.7	68.9	66.6	83.3	69.8	138.3	61.6	56.4	74.0	66.8	78.7	72.7
4th quarter	74.5	69.4	67.2	84.6	71.5	136.8	65.5	57.5	74.5	66.4	79.9	73.2
1997												
1st quarter	75.0	70.1	68.0	86.1	73.1	137.5	66.7	60.0	74.5	65.3	80.7	74.0
2nd quarter	76.2	70.5	68.3	87.8	74.7	139.4	69.4	62.0	75.3	66.7	81.0	75.1
3rd quarter	77.2	71.7	69.6	90.9	78.0	140.7	71.0	64.3	75.4	66.5	81.3	76.1
4th quarter	77.7	72.5	70.5	91.6	78.5	142.2	70.9	65.7	75.5	66.4	81.6	76.9
1998												
1st quarter	78.5	73.3	71.4	94.3	81.0	145.2	71.2	68.1	75.1	64.5	82.2	78.0
2nd quarter	79.3	74.6	72.6	97.4	83.7	150.2	70.4	69.7	76.6	66.1	83.7	79.0
3rd quarter	80.3	75.5	73.7	99.3	85.0	154.6	70.1	70.6	77.3	65.7	85.2	80.2
4th quarter	81.6	76.6	75.0	102.0	87.4	158.2	72.7	72.9	78.0	66.4	85.9	81.5
1999												
1st quarter	82.3	77.4	75.6	103.7	89.3	158.8	70.9	74.0	78.3	65.8	86.8	82.5
2nd quarter	83.0	78.5	76.8	106.2	91.7	161.3	71.7	76.1	78.7	66.1	87.3	83.4
3rd quarter	84.0	79.4	77.7	108.6	94.2	162.5	73.8	78.9	79.6	67.3	88.1	84.6
4th quarter	85.5	80.6	79.0	109.1	94.6	163.7	75.6	80.9	80.8	68.6	89.1	86.0
2000												
1st quarter	85.7	81.8	80.5	112.2	97.9	164.5	76.8	84.1	80.2	66.1	89.8	86.6
2nd quarter	87.3	82.6	81.1	114.7	101.0	163.7	79.0	86.7	81.1	68.4	89.8	88.3
3rd quarter	87.4	83.4	82.0	115.1	102.1	161.1	81.0	89.7	81.0	67.3	90.4	88.6
4th quarter	87.9	84.1	82.7	115.4	102.4	161.3	80.3	89.7	81.2	66.9	91.0	89.1
2001												
1st quarter	87.7	84.5	83.1	114.8	101.6	162.0	79.0	88.2	82.4	68.4	92.1	88.8
2nd quarter	88.2	84.7	83.5	113.3	99.2	164.5	76.4	85.6	84.1	69.7	93.9	89.2
3rd quarter	87.9	85.0	83.8	112.4	98.0	165.5	72.7	83.8	84.0	70.3	93.4	89.1
4th quarter	88.1	86.3	85.3	109.8	95.1	164.4	70.4	82.7	85.2	70.8	95.1	89.5
2002												
1st quarter	88.9	86.6	85.6	109.1	93.2	169.8	71.9	85.1	86.5	72.6	96.0	90.4
2nd quarter	89.4	87.0	86.0	108.9	91.9	174.1	73.8	87.7	87.3	74.3	96.2	91.0
3rd quarter	89.9	87.6	86.6	108.5	91.4	174.6	74.3	89.0	88.0	75.5	96.5	91.6
4th quarter	89.9	88.1	87.0	108.2	90.3	177.7	73.3	90.9	88.6	76.8	96.6	92.0
2003												
1st quarter	90.4	88.5	87.4	108.9	90.5	181.0	72.9	89.6	88.3	76.9	96.1	92.3
2nd quarter	91.2	89.5	88.6	111.3	92.7	183.8	72.8	91.1	89.7	80.7	95.7	93.3
3rd quarter	92.7	90.8	89.9	114.8	94.6	194.4	74.8	92.2	89.7	80.2	96.1	94.8
4th quarter	93.8	91.5	90.7	117.0	95.9	200.1	78.1	95.5	90.2	81.8	95.8	95.9
2004												
1st quarter	94.4	92.4	91.6	116.6	94.9	202.5	80.4	98.5	90.4	82.4	95.8	96.6
2nd quarter	95.1	93.0	92.3	119.6	97.0	208.9	81.4	102.5	91.0	83.2	96.1	97.7
3rd quarter	95.9	93.9	93.3	122.0	99.6	210.4	81.9	103.6	91.3	84.6	95.7	98.6
4th quarter	96.8	94.8	94.2	124.3	101.7	213.3	83.9	106.0	90.9	83.9	95.5	99.5
2005												
1st quarter	97.8	95.6	94.9	126.3	103.0	218.3	85.2	107.2	91.1	84.4	95.5	100.6
2nd quarter	98.3	96.6	96.1	128.3	104.4	222.4	86.8	108.5	91.3	84.6	95.7	101.0
3rd quarter	99.1	97.3	96.8	130.3	106.4	224.8	86.9	108.8	92.0	86.1	95.8	101.9
4th quarter	99.7	97.7	97.2	130.6	106.8	224.3	89.3	112.0	91.6	84.8	96.1	102.6
2006												
1st quarter	100.9	98.8	98.6	133.3	110.7	222.2	92.6	114.5	92.4	87.0	95.9	103.7
2nd quarter	101.2	99.3	99.0	132.1	112.1	211.1	94.4	115.9	92.7	86.9	96.6	104.0
3rd quarter	101.3	99.9	99.5	130.8	113.4	199.3	94.2	116.7	92.9	86.9	96.9	104.3
4th quarter	102.1	100.9	100.6	129.5	114.2	190.0	98.4	117.1	93.5	87.8	97.3	104.6
2007												
1st quarter	102.1	101.5	101.1	129.3	116.1	181.3	100.0	118.9	93.3	86.6	97.7	104.8
2nd quarter	102.9	101.8	101.6	129.6	118.4	174.0	101.8	119.5	94.1	88.0	98.1	105.4
3rd quarter	103.6	102.3	102.1	128.8	120.3	163.0	104.9	119.4	94.8	89.6	98.1	105.7
4th quarter	104.0	102.4	102.4	127.7	122.3	149.4	108.1	118.0	95.2	90.1	98.5	105.5
2008												
1st quarter	103.3	102.2	102.2	125.3	122.3	137.7	109.5	119.1	95.6	91.6	98.2	104.9
2nd quarter	103.8	102.3	102.4	123.6	121.6	131.6	112.7	118.0	96.3	93.3	98.3	104.8
3rd quarter	103.3	101.6	102.0	119.7	118.3	125.2	111.2	115.6	97.6	96.0	98.7	104.1
4th quarter	101.1	100.4	100.6	111.8	111.4	113.1	105.1	110.9	98.3	97.7	98.7	102.0
2009												
1st quarter	99.7	100.0	100.1	103.1	103.4	102.2	96.7	100.2	98.4	96.9	99.4	100.1
2nd quarter	99.6	99.6	99.6	99.3	100.0	96.1	97.0	96.1	100.2	100.1	100.3	99.4
3rd quarter	99.9	100.2	100.2	99.1	98.8	100.8	100.4	99.7	100.8	101.5	100.3	99.8
4th quarter	100.9	100.2	100.1	98.4	97.9	100.9	106.0	104.0	100.6	101.5	100.0	100.7

Table 1-5B. Chain-Type Quantity Indexes for Gross Domestic Product and Domestic Purchases: Historical Data—*Continued*

(Index numbers, 2009 = 100.)　　　　　　　　　　　　　　　　　　　　　　　　　NIPA Tables 1.1.3, 1.4.3, 2.3.3

Year and quarter	Gross domestic product												Gross domestic purchases
	Gross domestic product, total	Personal consumption expenditures		Private fixed investment			Exports and imports of goods and services		Government consumption expenditures and gross investment			
		Total	Excluding food and energy	Total	Nonresi-dential	Residential	Exports	Imports	Total	Federal	State and local	
2010												
1st quarter	101.3	100.7	100.6	98.6	98.9	97.6	107.6	106.7	99.8	102.5	98.1	101.3
2nd quarter	102.3	101.5	101.6	101.8	101.6	102.9	110.1	111.8	100.6	104.6	97.9	102.7
3rd quarter	103.0	102.2	102.3	101.7	103.6	93.8	113.2	115.8	100.5	105.5	97.2	103.6
4th quarter	103.6	103.2	103.3	103.8	105.8	95.6	116.7	116.5	99.4	104.8	95.9	104.0
2011												
1st quarter	103.2	103.8	104.0	103.6	105.6	95.4	117.3	117.4	97.5	101.9	94.6	103.6
2nd quarter	104.0	104.0	104.4	105.7	107.8	96.7	119.1	118.3	97.4	102.3	94.2	104.3
3rd quarter	104.2	104.4	104.9	110.0	112.7	98.6	120.3	119.2	96.8	101.3	93.9	104.5
4th quarter	105.4	104.8	105.5	112.6	115.3	101.4	121.5	120.6	96.4	100.6	93.7	105.7
2012												
1st quarter	106.1	105.4	106.4	116.5	118.7	107.7	122.4	121.3	95.9	100.5	93.0	106.4
2nd quarter	106.5	105.6	106.3	118.5	120.8	108.7	123.7	121.9	95.5	99.8	92.7	106.8
3rd quarter	106.7	105.9	106.6	118.5	120.2	111.5	124.3	122.1	95.2	99.9	92.2	106.9
4th quarter	106.7	106.2	107.1	120.5	121.3	117.2	124.2	120.9	94.3	98.5	91.6	106.7
2013												
1st quarter	107.4	106.7	107.5	122.6	122.9	121.3	125.4	121.3	93.3	95.8	91.6	107.4
2nd quarter	107.6	106.9	107.8	123.8	123.6	124.8	126.9	122.9	92.8	94.5	91.7	107.6
3rd quarter	108.5	107.4	108.4	124.7	124.3	126.6	127.9	123.4	92.3	93.3	91.7	108.4
4th quarter	109.5	108.3	109.2	126.7	127.1	125.2	131.5	123.9	91.7	91.9	91.5	109.1
2014												
1st quarter	109.3	108.8	109.7	128.3	129.3	124.3	130.7	125.4	91.5	91.8	91.3	109.1
2nd quarter	110.5	109.7	111.0	131.5	132.3	128.2	133.6	128.5	91.8	91.5	91.9	110.5
3rd quarter	111.9	110.8	112.4	134.4	135.6	129.6	133.8	128.2	92.2	92.1	92.3	111.8
4th quarter	112.5	112.2	113.7	134.5	134.8	133.0	135.5	131.5	92.1	90.0	92.8	112.6
2015												
1st quarter	113.4	113.2	114.7	135.8	135.6	136.7	133.9	133.7	92.4	91.2	93.2	113.9
2nd quarter	114.2	114.0	115.8	137.4	136.6	140.5	135.1	134.7	93.2	91.6	94.2	114.7
3rd quarter	114.6	114.8	116.6	138.6	137.1	144.1	133.8	135.3	93.5	91.3	94.8	115.3
4th quarter	114.8	115.6	117.5	137.7	135.3	146.7	133.0	135.3	93.6	91.9	94.6	115.6
2016												
1st quarter	114.9	116.1	118.0	137.6	133.9	151.4	132.1	135.3	94.0	91.5	95.5	115.8
2nd quarter	115.6	117.2	119.0	138.1	135.0	149.5	133.1	135.4	93.8	91.3	95.2	116.3
3rd quarter	116.4	118.0	119.9	138.6	136.2	147.8	135.1	136.3	93.9	91.7	95.2	117.0
4th quarter	116.9	118.8	120.9	139.2	136.2	150.4	133.8	138.9	93.9	91.6	95.3	118.0

Table 1-6A. Chain-Type Price Indexes for Gross Domestic Product and Domestic Purchases: Recent Data

(Index numbers, 2009 = 100.)   NIPA Tables 1.1.4, 1.6.4, 2.3.4

| Year and quarter | Gross domestic product, total | Personal consumption expenditures | | Private fixed investment | | | Exports and imports of goods and services | | Government consumption expenditures and gross investment | | | Gross domestic purchases |
		Total	Excluding food and energy	Total	Nonresidential	Residential	Exports	Imports	Total	Federal	State and local	
1955	15.6	15.8	16.1	20.8	25.7	12.2	24.4	18.7	10.4	12.8	8.6	15.3
1956	16.1	16.1	16.5	22.0	27.6	12.5	25.2	19.0	10.9	13.4	9.2	15.8
1957	16.7	16.6	17.0	22.8	28.9	12.5	26.2	19.2	11.4	14.0	9.5	16.3
1958	17.1	17.0	17.4	22.9	29.1	12.5	25.9	18.4	11.7	14.6	9.7	16.7
1959	17.3	17.3	17.8	23.1	29.5	12.6	25.9	18.6	11.9	14.7	9.9	16.9
1960	17.5	17.5	18.1	23.3	29.7	12.6	26.3	18.8	12.0	14.8	10.1	17.1
1961	17.7	17.7	18.3	23.2	29.6	12.7	26.7	18.8	12.2	15.0	10.3	17.3
1962	17.9	17.9	18.6	23.2	29.6	12.7	26.8	18.6	12.5	15.2	10.6	17.5
1963	18.1	18.1	18.8	23.2	29.6	12.6	26.7	18.9	12.8	15.6	10.8	17.7
1964	18.4	18.4	19.1	23.3	29.8	12.7	26.9	19.3	13.1	16.1	11.1	18.0
1965	18.7	18.7	19.3	23.7	30.2	13.0	27.8	19.6	13.5	16.5	11.4	18.3
1966	19.3	19.2	19.8	24.2	30.6	13.5	28.6	20.0	14.0	17.0	11.9	18.8
1967	19.8	19.6	20.4	24.9	31.4	14.0	29.7	20.1	14.5	17.4	12.5	19.3
1968	20.7	20.4	21.2	25.9	32.5	14.7	30.4	20.4	15.3	18.3	13.3	20.2
1969	21.7	21.3	22.2	27.2	33.9	15.7	31.4	21.0	16.2	19.2	14.2	21.1
1970	22.8	22.3	23.3	28.3	35.5	16.2	32.6	22.2	17.4	20.7	15.3	22.3
1971	24.0	23.3	24.4	29.8	37.1	17.2	33.8	23.6	18.8	22.4	16.5	23.5
1972	25.0	24.1	25.2	31.0	38.4	18.2	35.3	25.2	20.2	24.4	17.6	24.5
1973	26.4	25.4	26.1	32.8	40.0	19.9	39.9	29.6	21.6	26.0	18.7	25.9
1974	28.8	28.0	28.2	36.0	43.8	21.9	49.2	42.3	23.6	28.0	20.8	28.5
1975	31.4	30.3	30.6	40.4	49.6	23.9	54.2	45.9	25.8	30.5	22.8	31.1
1976	33.2	32.0	32.4	42.7	52.3	25.5	56.0	47.3	27.2	32.4	23.9	32.8
1977	35.2	34.1	34.5	46.0	55.8	28.1	58.3	51.4	28.9	34.3	25.4	35.0
1978	37.7	36.5	36.8	49.8	59.5	31.5	61.8	55.0	30.7	36.4	27.0	37.5
1979	40.8	39.7	39.5	54.3	64.3	35.1	69.3	64.5	33.2	39.0	29.4	40.7
1980	44.5	44.0	43.1	59.4	70.0	38.9	76.3	80.3	36.6	42.9	32.6	45.0
1981	48.7	47.9	46.9	64.8	76.7	42.0	82.0	84.6	40.2	46.9	35.8	49.1
1982	51.6	50.6	49.9	68.5	81.0	44.3	82.3	81.8	42.8	50.2	38.0	51.9
1983	53.7	52.7	52.5	68.7	80.9	45.3	82.7	78.7	44.5	51.8	39.7	53.7
1984	55.6	54.7	54.6	69.4	81.2	46.7	83.4	78.0	46.3	53.8	41.4	55.5
1985	57.3	56.7	56.9	70.4	82.0	48.0	81.0	75.5	47.7	54.9	43.1	57.2
1986	58.5	57.9	58.9	72.1	83.4	50.1	79.6	75.5	48.5	55.2	44.3	58.3
1987	59.9	59.7	60.7	73.6	84.4	52.2	81.4	80.0	49.9	55.7	46.4	60.0
1988	62.0	62.0	63.3	75.6	86.5	54.1	85.6	83.8	51.5	57.4	48.0	62.1
1989	64.4	64.6	65.9	77.6	88.5	55.8	87.0	85.7	53.5	58.9	50.3	64.5
1990	66.8	67.4	68.5	79.3	90.4	57.1	87.5	88.1	55.7	60.8	52.8	67.0
1991	69.1	69.7	70.9	80.7	92.1	57.8	88.4	87.4	57.7	63.1	54.6	69.1
1992	70.6	71.5	73.0	80.7	91.8	58.6	88.0	87.5	59.5	64.6	56.6	70.7
1993	72.3	73.3	75.0	81.6	92.0	60.9	88.1	86.8	60.9	66.0	58.0	72.3
1994	73.9	74.8	76.7	82.9	92.7	63.2	89.2	87.6	62.5	67.8	59.6	73.8
1995	75.4	76.4	78.3	84.2	93.6	65.4	91.2	90.0	64.3	69.9	61.2	75.4
1996	76.8	78.0	79.8	84.3	93.0	66.8	89.9	88.5	65.7	71.1	62.6	76.7
1997	78.1	79.3	81.2	84.4	92.5	68.4	88.3	85.4	66.9	72.2	64.0	77.9
1998	78.9	79.9	82.2	84.0	91.0	70.2	86.3	80.8	68.1	73.1	65.3	78.4
1999	80.1	81.1	83.3	84.2	90.2	72.9	85.6	81.3	70.4	74.9	67.9	79.6
2000	81.9	83.1	84.7	85.5	90.7	76.1	87.2	84.8	73.4	77.3	71.2	81.6
2001	83.8	84.7	86.3	86.3	90.4	79.7	86.6	82.7	75.6	78.7	73.6	83.2
2002	85.0	85.9	87.8	86.6	90.0	81.7	86.1	81.7	77.4	81.3	75.1	84.4
2003	86.7	87.6	89.0	87.7	89.9	85.5	87.8	84.5	80.3	84.8	77.8	86.2
2004	89.1	89.7	90.8	90.5	91.1	91.5	90.8	88.5	83.9	87.7	81.7	88.7
2005	92.0	92.3	92.7	94.5	93.8	98.1	94.7	93.8	88.2	91.4	86.3	91.9
2006	94.8	94.7	94.8	98.2	96.6	103.8	98.0	97.7	92.1	94.4	90.7	94.8
2007	97.3	97.1	96.8	100.0	98.6	105.2	101.1	101.0	96.1	97.3	95.4	97.4
2008	99.2	100.1	98.8	101.0	100.3	103.6	105.8	111.6	100.3	100.3	100.3	100.2
2009	100.0	100.0	100.0	100.0	100.0	100.0	100.0	100.0	100.0	100.0	100.0	100.0
2010	101.2	101.7	101.3	99.2	99.1	99.6	104.3	105.8	102.7	102.6	102.7	101.5
2011	103.3	104.1	102.8	100.5	100.5	100.4	111.0	113.9	105.7	105.4	105.9	104.0
2012	105.2	106.1	104.7	102.1	102.2	101.3	112.0	114.7	107.4	106.5	108.0	105.8
2013	106.9	107.5	106.3	103.7	103.0	106.4	112.1	113.6	109.0	107.6	110.1	107.3
2014	108.8	109.2	108.0	106.0	104.4	112.9	112.1	113.2	111.2	109.3	112.5	109.1
2015	110.0	109.5	109.5	107.1	105.1	115.9	106.5	104.4	111.8	109.9	113.2	109.6
2016	111.4	110.8	111.4	107.8	104.8	120.2	104.5	101.1	112.7	110.5	114.2	110.7
2014												
1st quarter	108.1	108.7	107.3	105.3	103.9	111.2	112.7	114.8	110.6	108.8	111.8	108.5
2nd quarter	108.7	109.1	107.9	105.6	104.2	111.5	112.7	113.9	111.0	109.1	112.3	109.0
3rd quarter	109.2	109.5	108.3	106.3	104.6	113.6	112.4	113.2	111.5	109.5	113.0	109.4
4th quarter	109.4	109.4	108.6	106.9	104.9	115.1	110.4	111.0	111.7	109.6	113.1	109.5
2015												
1st quarter	109.3	108.9	108.8	107.1	105.1	115.2	107.7	106.7	111.2	109.8	112.3	109.1
2nd quarter	109.9	109.4	109.3	107.0	105.0	115.2	107.4	105.2	111.8	109.8	113.1	109.5
3rd quarter	110.3	109.8	109.7	107.2	105.1	116.2	106.2	103.9	112.0	109.9	113.4	109.8
4th quarter	110.5	109.8	110.0	107.3	105.0	116.9	104.7	101.7	112.3	109.9	113.9	109.9
2016												
1st quarter	110.6	110.0	110.6	107.2	104.7	117.6	103.3	100.4	111.9	110.2	113.1	109.9
2nd quarter	111.3	110.6	111.2	107.6	104.8	119.3	104.2	100.7	112.6	110.4	114.1	110.5
3rd quarter	111.6	111.0	111.7	108.0	104.7	121.1	104.8	101.4	112.9	110.6	114.5	110.9
4th quarter	112.2	111.6	112.1	108.4	104.9	122.6	105.5	101.8	113.3	110.8	115.0	111.4

Table 1-6B. Chain-Type Price Indexes for Gross Domestic Product and Domestic Purchases: Historical Data

(Index numbers, 2009 = 100.)   NIPA Tables 1.1.4, 1.6.4, 2.3.4

| Year and quarter | Gross domestic product | | | | | | | | | | | Gross domestic purchases |
| | Gross domestic product, total | Personal consumption expenditures | | Private fixed investment | | | Exports and imports of goods and services | | Government consumption expenditures and gross investment | | | |
		Total	Excluding food and energy	Total	Nonresi-dential	Residential	Exports	Imports	Total	Federal	State and local	
1929	9.9	9.9	10.1	10.3	13.2	5.1	15.0	10.7	5.8	7.3	4.0	9.7
1930	9.5	9.5	9.7	9.9	12.5	5.0	13.6	9.1	5.6	6.9	3.9	9.3
1931	8.6	8.5	8.9	9.1	11.7	4.6	10.7	7.3	5.4	6.9	3.6	8.4
1932	7.6	7.5	7.9	8.1	10.6	3.7	9.3	5.9	4.9	6.6	3.3	7.4
1933	7.4	7.2	7.5	7.9	10.3	3.7	9.3	5.6	5.0	6.6	3.4	7.2
1934	7.8	7.5	7.7	8.3	10.7	4.1	10.7	6.4	5.4	7.0	3.6	7.5
1935	7.9	7.7	7.8	8.3	10.8	4.0	11.0	6.5	5.4	7.1	3.7	7.7
1936	8.0	7.8	7.9	8.4	10.8	4.2	11.4	7.0	5.6	7.7	3.7	7.8
1937	8.3	8.1	8.2	9.1	11.6	4.6	12.1	7.8	5.7	7.8	3.8	8.1
1938	8.2	7.9	8.2	9.2	11.7	4.8	11.6	7.2	5.8	7.9	3.8	7.9
1939	8.0	7.8	8.1	9.2	11.6	4.8	11.4	7.5	5.7	7.8	3.7	7.8
1940	8.1	7.9	8.2	9.4	11.9	4.9	12.4	8.0	5.6	7.5	3.8	7.9
1941	8.7	8.4	8.6	10.1	12.6	5.4	13.5	8.5	6.0	7.9	4.0	8.4
1942	9.4	9.4	9.6	11.1	14.0	5.8	16.4	9.7	6.0	7.9	4.4	9.1
1943	9.8	10.3	10.3	11.7	14.6	6.3	17.9	10.5	6.0	7.8	4.7	9.5
1944	10.1	10.9	11.1	12.1	15.0	6.9	20.1	11.0	6.0	7.7	4.9	9.7
1945	10.3	11.3	11.6	12.5	15.4	7.3	20.0	11.3	6.0	7.7	5.1	10.0
1946	11.6	12.1	12.3	13.7	17.0	8.0	19.3	12.6	7.6	10.1	5.6	11.3
1947	12.9	13.3	13.3	16.1	19.7	9.5	22.4	15.1	8.3	10.9	6.2	12.6
1948	13.6	14.1	14.1	17.4	21.3	10.3	23.6	16.4	8.6	10.8	7.0	13.3
1949	13.6	14.0	14.1	17.8	21.8	10.5	22.2	15.7	8.8	11.2	7.1	13.3
1947												
1st quarter	12.6	13.0	. . .	15.4	18.9	9.0	20.6	13.9	8.4	11.2	6.1	12.3
2nd quarter	12.8	13.1	. . .	15.9	19.4	9.5	22.1	14.8	8.4	11.0	6.2	12.5
3rd quarter	13.0	13.4	. . .	16.3	20.0	9.7	23.2	15.6	8.2	10.6	6.3	12.6
4th quarter	13.2	13.7	. . .	16.7	20.3	9.9	23.8	16.2	8.3	10.6	6.5	12.9
1948												
1st quarter	13.4	13.9	. . .	16.8	20.4	10.1	23.9	16.5	8.4	10.7	6.7	13.1
2nd quarter	13.6	14.0	. . .	17.2	21.0	10.2	23.8	16.6	8.5	10.7	6.9	13.2
3rd quarter	13.8	14.2	. . .	17.7	21.7	10.5	23.5	16.4	8.7	10.8	7.1	13.5
4th quarter	13.8	14.2	. . .	17.9	22.0	10.5	23.2	16.2	8.8	10.9	7.2	13.5
1949												
1st quarter	13.7	14.1	. . .	17.9	21.9	10.6	22.8	15.8	8.9	11.2	7.2	13.4
2nd quarter	13.7	14.0	. . .	17.9	21.8	10.6	22.3	15.6	8.8	11.2	7.0	13.3
3rd quarter	13.5	13.9	. . .	17.7	21.7	10.3	22.0	15.6	8.8	11.0	7.0	13.2
4th quarter	13.6	13.9	. . .	17.6	21.6	10.4	21.7	15.6	8.9	11.3	7.0	13.3
1950												
1st quarter	13.5	13.9	. . .	17.6	21.6	10.3	21.4	15.9	8.8	11.3	6.9	13.2
2nd quarter	13.6	13.9	. . .	17.9	21.9	10.6	21.4	16.3	8.8	11.2	7.0	13.3
3rd quarter	13.8	14.2	. . .	18.4	22.3	11.0	21.6	16.8	9.0	11.3	7.2	13.6
4th quarter	14.1	14.5	. . .	18.7	23.1	11.0	22.0	17.6	9.0	11.3	7.4	13.8
1951												
1st quarter	14.5	14.9	. . .	19.4	23.8	11.3	23.3	19.0	9.4	11.8	7.6	14.3
2nd quarter	14.6	15.1	. . .	19.6	24.2	11.5	24.2	20.0	9.4	11.6	7.7	14.4
3rd quarter	14.7	15.1	. . .	19.8	24.4	11.5	24.9	20.6	9.4	11.6	7.9	14.4
4th quarter	14.9	15.3	. . .	20.0	24.7	11.6	25.3	20.7	9.6	11.8	8.0	14.6
1952												
1st quarter	14.9	15.4	. . .	20.1	24.8	11.7	24.7	19.9	9.5	11.6	8.0	14.6
2nd quarter	14.9	15.4	. . .	20.2	24.9	11.8	24.6	19.5	9.6	11.8	8.1	14.7
3rd quarter	15.1	15.5	. . .	20.2	24.8	11.9	24.5	19.2	9.7	11.9	8.3	14.8
4th quarter	15.1	15.5	. . .	20.2	24.8	11.8	24.5	18.9	9.8	12.1	8.3	14.8
1953												
1st quarter	15.1	15.5	. . .	20.2	24.8	11.9	24.6	18.7	9.7	11.9	8.3	14.8
2nd quarter	15.2	15.6	. . .	20.3	25.0	11.9	24.6	18.5	9.8	11.9	8.3	14.9
3rd quarter	15.2	15.6	. . .	20.5	25.2	12.0	24.5	18.5	9.7	11.9	8.3	14.9
4th quarter	15.3	15.7	. . .	20.4	25.2	11.9	24.4	18.5	9.8	12.0	8.3	15.0
1954												
1st quarter	15.3	15.8	. . .	20.4	25.3	11.9	24.3	18.7	9.8	12.1	8.3	15.0
2nd quarter	15.4	15.8	. . .	20.5	25.4	11.9	24.2	18.8	9.9	12.2	8.4	15.1
3rd quarter	15.3	15.7	. . .	20.5	25.2	12.0	24.1	18.9	10.0	12.2	8.5	15.1
4th quarter	15.4	15.7	. . .	20.5	25.3	12.0	24.1	18.9	10.1	12.4	8.5	15.1
1955												
1st quarter	15.4	15.8	. . .	20.6	25.2	12.1	24.2	18.7	10.1	12.5	8.5	15.1
2nd quarter	15.5	15.8	. . .	20.7	25.4	12.2	24.3	18.7	10.3	12.8	8.5	15.2
3rd quarter	15.6	15.8	. . .	20.9	25.8	12.3	24.4	18.7	10.4	12.9	8.7	15.3
4th quarter	15.7	15.9	. . .	21.2	26.3	12.3	24.6	18.8	10.5	13.0	8.8	15.4
1956												
1st quarter	15.9	15.9	. . .	21.6	27.0	12.4	24.8	18.8	10.7	13.2	9.0	15.6
2nd quarter	16.0	16.1	. . .	21.9	27.2	12.6	25.0	19.0	10.9	13.4	9.1	15.7
3rd quarter	16.2	16.2	. . .	22.2	27.9	12.6	25.3	19.1	11.0	13.5	9.2	15.9
4th quarter	16.3	16.3	. . .	22.4	28.2	12.5	25.6	19.3	11.1	13.6	9.3	16.0
1957												
1st quarter	16.5	16.5	. . .	22.6	28.7	12.5	26.0	19.3	11.2	13.9	9.4	16.1
2nd quarter	16.6	16.6	. . .	22.7	28.8	12.5	26.2	19.3	11.4	14.0	9.6	16.3
3rd quarter	16.7	16.7	. . .	22.9	29.0	12.6	26.2	19.2	11.4	14.1	9.6	16.4
4th quarter	16.8	16.8	. . .	23.0	29.2	12.6	26.2	19.0	11.5	14.2	9.6	16.5

. . . = Not available.

Table 1-6B. Chain-Type Price Indexes for Gross Domestic Product and Domestic Purchases: Historical Data—*Continued*

(Index numbers, 2009 = 100.)   NIPA Tables 1.1.4, 1.6.4, 2.3.4

Year and quarter	Gross domestic product, total	Personal consumption expenditures		Private fixed investment			Exports and imports of goods and services		Government consumption expenditures and gross investment			Gross domestic purchases
		Total	Excluding food and energy	Total	Nonresi-dential	Residential	Exports	Imports	Total	Federal	State and local	
1958												
1st quarter	17.0	17.0	. . .	22.8	29.0	12.5	26.0	18.6	11.6	14.4	9.6	16.6
2nd quarter	17.0	17.0	. . .	22.9	29.1	12.5	25.9	18.4	11.7	14.5	9.7	16.7
3rd quarter	17.1	17.0	. . .	22.9	29.2	12.5	25.8	18.4	11.8	14.6	9.7	16.7
4th quarter	17.1	17.0	. . .	23.0	29.3	12.5	25.9	18.4	11.8	14.7	9.8	16.7
1959												
1st quarter	17.2	17.1	17.6	23.0	29.3	12.5	25.7	18.4	11.9	14.7	9.9	16.8
2nd quarter	17.2	17.2	17.7	23.1	29.5	12.6	25.8	18.5	11.9	14.7	9.9	16.9
3rd quarter	17.3	17.3	17.8	23.2	29.6	12.6	26.0	18.6	11.9	14.7	9.9	16.9
4th quarter	17.4	17.4	17.0	23.2	20.7	12.6	26.3	18.8	11.9	14.7	9.9	17.0
1960												
1st quarter	17.4	17.4	18.0	23.2	29.7	12.6	26.3	18.8	11.9	14.7	10.0	17.0
2nd quarter	17.5	17.5	18.0	23.3	29.7	12.6	26.3	18.7	11.9	14.7	10.0	17.1
3rd quarter	17.6	17.6	18.1	23.3	29.7	12.6	26.4	18.8	12.1	14.9	10.1	17.2
4th quarter	17.6	17.7	18.2	23.2	29.7	12.7	26.3	18.8	12.2	15.0	10.1	17.2
1961												
1st quarter	17.7	17.7	18.2	23.2	29.6	12.6	26.4	18.8	12.2	15.0	10.2	17.3
2nd quarter	17.7	17.7	18.3	23.2	29.6	12.7	26.8	18.8	12.2	15.0	10.3	17.3
3rd quarter	17.7	17.8	18.4	23.2	29.6	12.7	26.7	18.8	12.2	15.0	10.4	17.3
4th quarter	17.8	17.8	18.4	23.2	29.6	12.7	26.9	18.8	12.3	15.0	10.4	17.4
1962												
1st quarter	17.9	17.9	18.5	23.2	29.6	12.7	27.0	18.5	12.4	15.1	10.6	17.4
2nd quarter	17.9	17.9	18.5	23.2	29.6	12.7	26.7	18.6	12.5	15.2	10.6	17.5
3rd quarter	18.0	18.0	18.6	23.2	29.6	12.7	26.7	18.5	12.5	15.3	10.6	17.5
4th quarter	18.0	18.0	18.6	23.2	29.6	12.7	26.7	18.6	12.5	15.3	10.7	17.6
1963												
1st quarter	18.1	18.1	18.7	23.2	29.6	12.7	26.8	18.8	12.7	15.6	10.8	17.7
2nd quarter	18.1	18.1	18.8	23.2	29.6	12.6	26.7	18.9	12.8	15.6	10.8	17.7
3rd quarter	18.1	18.2	18.8	23.1	29.6	12.5	26.7	19.0	12.7	15.4	10.9	17.7
4th quarter	18.2	18.2	18.9	23.2	29.7	12.6	26.7	19.1	12.9	15.8	10.9	17.8
1964												
1st quarter	18.3	18.3	19.0	23.1	29.7	12.4	26.8	19.2	13.0	16.0	11.0	17.9
2nd quarter	18.4	18.4	19.1	23.3	29.8	12.6	26.8	19.3	13.1	16.0	11.0	18.0
3rd quarter	18.4	18.4	19.1	23.3	29.8	12.7	27.0	19.3	13.2	16.2	11.1	18.0
4th quarter	18.5	18.5	19.2	23.6	30.0	13.0	27.3	19.4	13.2	16.2	11.1	18.1
1965												
1st quarter	18.6	18.6	19.2	23.6	30.0	12.9	27.9	19.5	13.3	16.2	11.3	18.2
2nd quarter	18.7	18.7	19.3	23.6	30.1	13.0	27.8	19.5	13.4	16.3	11.3	18.3
3rd quarter	18.8	18.7	19.4	23.7	30.2	12.9	27.8	19.6	13.5	16.5	11.4	18.4
4th quarter	18.9	18.8	19.4	24.0	30.3	13.3	27.7	19.8	13.7	16.9	11.5	18.5
1966												
1st quarter	19.0	18.9	19.5	23.9	30.3	13.1	28.2	19.9	13.8	16.9	11.7	18.6
2nd quarter	19.2	19.1	19.7	24.2	30.6	13.6	28.4	20.1	13.9	16.9	11.9	18.8
3rd quarter	19.4	19.2	19.8	24.2	30.7	13.5	28.7	20.0	14.1	17.2	12.0	18.9
4th quarter	19.5	19.4	20.0	24.5	30.9	13.8	29.2	20.2	14.2	17.2	12.2	19.1
1967												
1st quarter	19.6	19.4	20.1	24.6	31.1	13.8	29.7	20.2	14.2	17.1	12.3	19.1
2nd quarter	19.7	19.5	20.3	24.7	31.2	13.9	29.7	20.1	14.4	17.3	12.4	19.2
3rd quarter	19.9	19.7	20.4	24.9	31.4	14.0	29.7	20.1	14.5	17.5	12.6	19.4
4th quarter	20.1	19.9	20.6	25.2	31.7	14.2	29.8	20.1	14.8	17.8	12.8	19.6
1968												
1st quarter	20.3	20.1	20.9	25.5	32.0	14.5	30.0	20.3	15.0	17.9	13.0	19.8
2nd quarter	20.6	20.3	21.1	25.7	32.3	14.6	30.7	20.4	15.1	18.1	13.2	20.0
3rd quarter	20.8	20.5	21.4	25.9	32.6	14.6	30.3	20.5	15.4	18.4	13.3	20.2
4th quarter	21.0	20.7	21.6	26.4	33.1	15.2	30.5	20.6	15.6	18.7	13.6	20.5
1969												
1st quarter	21.3	20.9	21.8	26.7	33.3	15.5	31.0	20.7	15.7	18.7	13.8	20.7
2nd quarter	21.5	21.2	22.1	27.0	33.6	15.7	31.0	20.8	16.0	19.0	14.1	21.0
3rd quarter	21.8	21.5	22.4	27.3	34.0	15.8	31.4	20.9	16.3	19.5	14.3	21.3
4th quarter	22.1	21.7	22.6	27.6	34.4	16.0	32.2	21.5	16.6	19.7	14.6	21.6
1970												
1st quarter	22.4	22.0	22.9	27.8	34.8	16.0	32.2	21.7	17.0	20.3	14.9	21.9
2nd quarter	22.7	22.2	23.1	28.4	35.4	16.6	32.8	21.9	17.3	20.6	15.2	22.2
3rd quarter	22.9	22.4	23.4	28.4	35.6	16.1	32.7	22.5	17.6	20.9	15.5	22.4
4th quarter	23.2	22.7	23.7	28.7	36.1	16.3	32.8	22.7	17.9	21.2	15.8	22.7
1971												
1st quarter	23.6	22.9	24.0	29.2	36.6	16.7	33.8	23.3	18.4	21.8	16.1	23.0
2nd quarter	23.9	23.2	24.3	29.6	37.0	17.1	33.9	23.4	18.7	22.2	16.4	23.3
3rd quarter	24.1	23.4	24.5	30.0	37.3	17.4	33.7	23.6	19.0	22.6	16.7	23.6
4th quarter	24.3	23.6	24.7	30.2	37.6	17.6	33.9	24.0	19.3	23.0	16.8	23.8
1972												
1st quarter	24.7	23.8	24.9	30.6	38.0	17.9	34.8	24.4	19.9	24.0	17.2	24.2
2nd quarter	24.9	24.0	25.1	30.8	38.3	18.0	35.1	25.0	20.1	24.2	17.4	24.4
3rd quarter	25.1	24.2	25.3	31.1	38.5	18.3	35.2	25.4	20.3	24.4	17.7	24.6
4th quarter	25.4	24.4	25.4	31.6	38.8	18.8	36.0	26.0	20.7	24.9	17.9	24.9

. . . = Not available.

Table 1-6B. Chain-Type Price Indexes for Gross Domestic Product and Domestic Purchases: Historical Data—*Continued*

(Index numbers, 2009 = 100.)   NIPA Tables 1.1.4, 1.6.4, 2.3.4

Year and quarter	Gross domestic product, total	Personal consumption expenditures		Private fixed investment			Exports and imports of goods and services		Government consumption expenditures and gross investment			Gross domestic purchases
		Total	Excluding food and energy	Total	Nonresi-dential	Residential	Exports	Imports	Total	Federal	State and local	
1973												
1st quarter	25.7	24.7	25.6	31.9	39.1	19.1	37.1	26.8	21.0	25.3	18.3	25.2
2nd quarter	26.1	25.1	25.9	32.4	39.7	19.6	38.7	28.9	21.4	25.7	18.6	25.7
3rd quarter	26.6	25.6	26.3	33.1	40.3	20.2	41.0	30.2	21.7	26.2	18.8	26.1
4th quarter	27.1	26.1	26.7	33.6	40.8	20.6	43.0	32.5	22.2	26.7	19.2	26.6
1974												
1st quarter	27.6	26.9	27.1	34.2	41.5	21.0	46.0	37.7	22.6	27.0	19.7	27.3
2nd quarter	28.3	27.6	27.8	35.2	42.8	21.5	47.6	42.0	23.2	27.6	20.4	28.1
3rd quarter	29.1	28.4	28.6	36.6	44.5	22.2	50.3	44.2	24.0	28.3	21.1	28.9
4th quarter	30.0	29.1	29.3	38.0	46.5	22.8	52.9	45.6	24.7	29.3	21.8	29.8
1975												
1st quarter	30.7	29.7	29.9	39.3	48.2	23.4	54.3	46.3	25.2	29.8	22.2	30.4
2nd quarter	31.1	30.0	30.3	40.2	49.4	23.8	54.2	46.4	25.6	30.2	22.7	30.8
3rd quarter	31.7	30.6	30.8	40.7	50.1	24.0	54.0	45.4	26.0	30.6	23.0	31.4
4th quarter	32.2	31.1	31.3	41.3	50.8	24.5	54.4	45.4	26.4	31.3	23.2	31.9
1976												
1st quarter	32.6	31.4	31.8	41.7	51.3	24.6	55.1	46.2	26.7	31.7	23.5	32.2
2nd quarter	32.9	31.7	32.1	42.4	52.0	25.3	55.8	46.9	27.0	32.0	23.8	32.5
3rd quarter	33.3	32.2	32.6	43.0	52.7	25.7	56.1	47.7	27.3	32.4	24.0	33.0
4th quarter	33.9	32.7	33.1	43.7	53.4	26.2	57.1	48.2	27.8	33.2	24.2	33.5
1977												
1st quarter	34.4	33.3	33.7	44.6	54.5	26.9	57.7	49.9	28.2	33.7	24.7	34.1
2nd quarter	35.0	33.9	34.2	45.4	55.3	27.6	58.6	51.3	28.6	34.0	25.2	34.7
3rd quarter	35.4	34.4	34.8	46.4	56.3	28.5	58.3	52.0	29.0	34.2	25.6	35.2
4th quarter	36.0	34.9	35.3	47.4	57.2	29.4	58.6	52.5	29.6	35.2	26.0	35.8
1978												
1st quarter	36.6	35.4	35.9	48.3	58.1	30.2	59.7	53.4	30.0	35.7	26.4	36.4
2nd quarter	37.3	36.2	36.5	49.3	59.0	31.1	61.2	54.7	30.5	36.0	26.8	37.1
3rd quarter	38.0	36.8	37.1	50.3	60.0	32.0	62.2	55.6	30.9	36.6	27.2	37.8
4th quarter	38.8	37.5	37.8	51.3	61.0	32.8	64.3	56.6	31.5	37.4	27.6	38.5
1979												
1st quarter	39.5	38.2	38.3	52.4	62.3	33.5	66.1	58.8	32.1	37.9	28.3	39.2
2nd quarter	40.4	39.2	39.1	53.7	63.7	34.6	68.8	61.8	32.7	38.5	28.9	40.2
3rd quarter	41.2	40.2	39.8	55.0	65.0	35.7	70.4	66.4	33.6	39.1	29.9	41.2
4th quarter	42.0	41.2	40.7	56.1	66.3	36.6	71.7	70.8	34.5	40.6	30.5	42.2
1980												
1st quarter	43.0	42.4	41.7	57.4	67.7	37.6	73.9	76.7	35.3	41.3	31.3	43.4
2nd quarter	43.9	43.5	42.6	58.7	69.3	38.4	74.9	79.5	36.1	42.2	32.1	44.4
3rd quarter	44.9	44.5	43.5	60.0	70.8	39.3	77.0	81.7	36.9	42.9	33.0	45.4
4th quarter	46.2	45.6	44.6	61.3	72.2	40.2	79.6	83.2	38.3	45.0	33.9	46.6
1981												
1st quarter	47.4	46.7	45.6	62.9	74.2	41.1	81.6	85.3	39.2	45.7	35.0	47.8
2nd quarter	48.2	47.5	46.4	64.3	76.0	41.8	81.9	85.8	39.9	46.3	35.7	48.7
3rd quarter	49.1	48.3	47.3	65.4	77.4	42.3	82.1	83.6	40.4	47.1	36.1	49.5
4th quarter	50.0	49.0	48.1	66.7	79.1	42.9	82.3	83.8	41.4	48.7	36.6	50.3
1982												
1st quarter	50.7	49.7	48.8	67.5	80.0	43.6	82.8	83.5	42.0	49.3	37.2	51.0
2nd quarter	51.3	50.1	49.5	68.4	81.0	44.2	82.8	82.0	42.5	49.8	37.7	51.5
3rd quarter	52.0	50.9	50.3	68.8	81.5	44.6	82.2	81.1	43.1	50.4	38.3	52.2
4th quarter	52.6	51.5	51.0	69.0	81.7	44.8	81.7	80.4	43.7	51.3	38.8	52.8
1983												
1st quarter	53.0	51.9	51.7	68.8	81.2	45.0	82.0	78.7	44.0	51.5	39.1	53.1
2nd quarter	53.4	52.4	52.1	68.6	80.9	45.1	82.3	78.7	44.3	51.5	39.5	53.4
3rd quarter	53.9	53.1	52.9	68.6	80.8	45.4	82.8	78.9	44.7	52.0	39.9	54.0
4th quarter	54.3	53.5	53.3	68.8	80.7	45.8	83.6	78.4	45.0	52.3	40.2	54.3
1984												
1st quarter	54.9	54.0	53.8	68.9	80.8	46.1	83.7	78.6	45.7	53.2	40.8	54.9
2nd quarter	55.4	54.6	54.4	69.3	81.1	46.4	84.2	79.1	46.1	53.6	41.2	55.3
3rd quarter	55.8	55.0	55.0	69.6	81.3	46.9	83.4	77.7	46.5	54.0	41.6	55.7
4th quarter	56.2	55.3	55.4	69.8	81.4	47.3	82.5	76.7	46.8	54.3	42.0	56.0
1985												
1st quarter	56.8	56.0	56.1	70.0	81.6	47.5	81.6	74.9	47.3	54.8	42.5	56.6
2nd quarter	57.2	56.5	56.6	70.2	81.8	47.7	81.3	75.2	47.5	54.7	42.9	56.9
3rd quarter	57.5	56.9	57.2	70.5	82.1	48.0	80.6	75.1	47.8	54.8	43.3	57.3
4th quarter	57.8	57.3	57.6	70.9	82.5	48.6	80.4	76.6	48.2	55.3	43.7	57.7
1986												
1st quarter	58.1	57.7	58.2	71.3	82.7	49.2	80.0	76.7	48.2	55.1	43.9	58.0
2nd quarter	58.3	57.6	58.6	71.8	83.2	49.7	79.6	74.4	48.3	55.2	44.1	58.1
3rd quarter	58.6	57.9	59.0	72.4	83.7	50.4	79.1	74.9	48.6	55.3	44.4	58.4
4th quarter	59.0	58.3	59.5	72.9	84.1	50.9	79.7	75.8	49.0	55.4	45.0	58.8
1987												
1st quarter	59.3	58.8	59.9	73.2	84.2	51.5	80.0	77.8	49.3	55.3	45.7	59.3
2nd quarter	59.7	59.4	60.4	73.3	84.2	52.0	81.2	79.8	49.7	55.5	46.2	59.7
3rd quarter	60.1	59.9	61.0	73.6	84.2	52.5	81.5	80.6	50.1	55.8	46.7	60.2
4th quarter	60.6	60.5	61.6	74.3	85.0	53.0	82.8	81.9	50.4	56.0	47.0	60.7

Table 1-6B. Chain-Type Price Indexes for Gross Domestic Product and Domestic Purchases: Historical Data—*Continued*

(Index numbers, 2009 = 100.)   **NIPA Tables 1.1.4, 1.6.4, 2.3.4**

| Year and quarter | Gross domestic product, total | Gross domestic product | | | | | | | | | | Gross domestic purchases |
| | | Personal consumption expenditures | | Private fixed investment | | | Exports and imports of goods and services | | Government consumption expenditures and gross investment | | | |
		Total	Excluding food and energy	Total	Nonresi-dential	Residential	Exports	Imports	Total	Federal	State and local	
1988												
1st quarter	61.1	60.9	62.2	74.9	85.8	53.4	83.8	83.0	50.9	56.8	47.3	61.2
2nd quarter	61.7	61.6	62.9	75.4	86.2	53.9	85.5	84.5	51.3	57.3	47.7	61.8
3rd quarter	62.4	62.4	63.7	75.8	86.6	54.2	86.5	83.6	51.7	57.6	48.1	62.4
4th quarter	63.0	63.0	64.4	76.5	87.4	54.8	86.4	84.3	52.0	57.7	48.7	63.0
1989												
1st quarter	63.6	63.7	65.0	76.9	87.9	55.1	87.2	85.6	52.8	58.5	49.4	63.7
2nd quarter	64.3	64.5	65.6	77.4	88.3	55.8	87.3	86.5	53.3	58.8	50.0	64.4
3rd quarter	64.7	64.9	66.1	77.8	88.8	56.0	86.8	85.1	53.7	59.1	50.5	64.8
4th quarter	65.2	65.4	66.7	78.2	89.2	56.4	86.6	85.5	54.1	59.3	51.2	65.2
1990												
1st quarter	65.9	66.4	67.5	78.7	89.7	56.8	86.6	86.8	54.8	60.0	51.9	66.1
2nd quarter	66.6	66.9	68.2	79.0	90.0	57.0	86.8	85.3	55.3	60.5	52.4	66.6
3rd quarter	67.2	67.8	68.9	79.5	90.7	57.3	87.6	87.8	55.9	60.9	53.0	67.3
4th quarter	67.7	68.7	69.4	79.9	91.3	57.3	88.9	92.6	56.7	61.8	53.8	68.1
1991												
1st quarter	68.4	69.0	70.0	80.6	92.2	57.5	89.1	89.8	57.2	62.7	54.0	68.6
2nd quarter	68.8	69.4	70.6	80.7	92.2	57.8	88.6	87.3	57.4	62.8	54.3	68.9
3rd quarter	69.3	69.9	71.2	80.8	92.2	58.1	88.0	86.0	57.9	63.3	54.8	69.3
4th quarter	69.7	70.4	71.7	80.5	91.9	57.9	88.1	86.4	58.3	63.6	55.3	69.7
1992												
1st quarter	70.0	70.8	72.3	80.4	91.8	57.7	88.0	86.8	58.7	64.0	55.8	70.1
2nd quarter	70.5	71.3	72.8	80.6	91.7	58.3	88.1	87.2	59.3	64.5	56.4	70.5
3rd quarter	70.8	71.7	73.2	80.7	91.8	58.7	88.1	88.3	59.8	64.9	56.9	70.9
4th quarter	71.3	72.2	73.8	81.0	91.8	59.5	87.9	87.6	60.1	65.2	57.3	71.4
1993												
1st quarter	71.7	72.6	74.3	81.3	91.9	60.1	88.0	87.1	60.4	65.4	57.6	71.8
2nd quarter	72.1	73.1	74.8	81.6	91.9	60.8	88.2	87.4	60.7	65.8	58.0	72.2
3rd quarter	72.5	73.5	75.3	81.7	91.9	61.3	88.2	86.6	61.0	66.3	58.1	72.5
4th quarter	72.9	73.9	75.6	82.0	92.2	61.5	88.1	86.2	61.4	66.7	58.4	72.9
1994												
1st quarter	73.3	74.1	76.0	82.4	92.4	62.3	88.5	86.2	61.8	67.0	58.9	73.2
2nd quarter	73.7	74.6	76.5	82.7	92.6	62.7	88.9	87.0	62.3	67.7	59.3	73.6
3rd quarter	74.0	75.1	76.9	83.0	92.8	63.4	89.3	88.5	62.7	67.9	59.8	74.1
4th quarter	74.4	75.4	77.3	83.4	92.9	64.2	89.9	88.8	63.2	68.5	60.3	74.5
1995												
1st quarter	74.9	75.8	77.7	83.9	93.3	64.9	90.8	89.5	63.8	69.5	60.7	74.9
2nd quarter	75.2	76.2	78.2	84.2	93.6	65.3	91.6	90.8	64.2	69.6	61.1	75.3
3rd quarter	75.5	76.5	78.5	84.5	93.8	65.5	91.3	90.3	64.4	69.9	61.4	75.6
4th quarter	75.9	76.9	78.9	84.4	93.6	65.9	90.9	89.4	64.9	70.8	61.6	75.9
1996												
1st quarter	76.3	77.3	79.2	84.3	93.3	66.2	90.7	89.3	65.5	71.5	62.2	76.3
2nd quarter	76.6	77.8	79.6	84.2	92.9	66.5	90.4	88.8	65.4	70.8	62.3	76.5
3rd quarter	76.9	78.1	80.0	84.4	92.9	67.2	89.8	87.9	65.7	71.0	62.7	76.9
4th quarter	77.3	78.7	80.4	84.3	92.7	67.5	88.8	87.9	66.1	71.2	63.2	77.3
1997												
1st quarter	77.6	79.0	80.7	84.4	92.6	67.8	88.6	87.2	66.6	71.9	63.6	77.6
2nd quarter	78.0	79.2	81.1	84.4	92.6	68.1	88.5	85.4	66.8	72.1	63.8	77.7
3rd quarter	78.2	79.4	81.3	84.5	92.5	68.7	88.3	84.8	67.0	72.2	64.1	77.9
4th quarter	78.5	79.7	81.6	84.5	92.1	69.2	87.9	84.1	67.4	72.6	64.6	78.2
1998												
1st quarter	78.6	79.7	81.8	84.1	91.6	69.4	87.0	82.1	67.6	72.8	64.7	78.1
2nd quarter	78.8	79.8	82.1	84.0	91.1	69.8	86.6	81.1	67.8	72.9	65.0	78.2
3rd quarter	79.1	80.0	82.3	83.9	90.8	70.5	85.9	80.0	68.2	73.1	65.5	78.4
4th quarter	79.3	80.2	82.6	84.0	90.5	71.2	85.6	80.0	68.7	73.4	66.0	78.7
1999												
1st quarter	79.6	80.5	82.9	84.1	90.5	71.8	85.4	79.8	69.3	74.2	66.6	78.9
2nd quarter	79.9	80.9	83.1	84.2	90.3	72.6	85.5	80.8	70.1	74.7	67.5	79.4
3rd quarter	80.2	81.3	83.4	84.1	89.9	73.2	85.6	81.7	70.7	75.0	68.3	79.8
4th quarter	80.6	81.8	83.8	84.4	90.1	73.8	85.9	82.8	71.5	75.6	69.1	80.2
2000												
1st quarter	81.2	82.5	84.2	84.9	90.4	75.0	86.5	84.4	72.5	76.8	70.0	81.0
2nd quarter	81.6	82.9	84.5	85.3	90.6	75.8	87.1	84.5	73.0	76.8	70.8	81.4
3rd quarter	82.2	83.4	84.9	85.7	90.9	76.4	87.5	85.1	73.8	77.7	71.5	81.9
4th quarter	82.6	83.8	85.3	85.9	90.9	77.1	87.5	85.4	74.5	78.1	72.4	82.4
2001												
1st quarter	83.1	84.4	85.8	85.9	90.5	78.2	87.4	85.2	75.1	78.4	73.1	82.8
2nd quarter	83.7	84.8	86.1	86.2	90.5	79.2	87.0	83.4	75.4	78.5	73.6	83.2
3rd quarter	84.0	84.9	86.4	86.4	90.3	80.5	86.6	82.2	75.8	78.9	73.9	83.4
4th quarter	84.2	84.9	86.8	86.5	90.2	80.9	85.6	80.2	75.9	79.2	74.0	83.4
2002												
1st quarter	84.5	85.1	87.1	86.4	90.1	80.8	85.3	80.0	76.7	80.8	74.3	83.7
2nd quarter	84.8	85.7	87.6	86.5	90.0	81.3	86.0	81.8	77.2	81.0	74.9	84.2
3rd quarter	85.2	86.2	88.0	86.6	90.0	81.6	86.5	82.3	77.6	81.2	75.4	84.6
4th quarter	85.6	86.6	88.3	87.0	90.1	83.0	86.5	82.7	78.3	82.2	76.0	85.0

Table 1-6B. Chain-Type Price Indexes for Gross Domestic Product and Domestic Purchases: Historical Data—*Continued*

(Index numbers, 2009 = 100.)   **NIPA Tables 1.1.4, 1.6.4, 2.3.4**

Year and quarter	Gross domestic product, total	Personal consumption expenditures		Private fixed investment			Exports and imports of goods and services		Government consumption expenditures and gross investment			Gross domestic purchases
		Total	Excluding food and energy	Total	Nonresidential	Residential	Exports	Imports	Total	Federal	State and local	
2003												
1st quarter	86.2	87.2	88.5	87.4	89.8	84.8	87.4	85.1	79.8	84.3	77.2	85.8
2nd quarter	86.5	87.2	88.9	87.4	89.7	84.9	87.6	83.8	80.0	84.6	77.3	85.9
3rd quarter	86.9	87.8	89.2	87.7	89.9	85.5	87.8	84.3	80.5	85.0	77.9	86.4
4th quarter	87.4	88.1	89.5	88.4	90.1	87.0	88.4	84.8	81.0	85.1	78.6	86.8
2004												
1st quarter	88.1	88.8	90.0	89.2	90.4	88.9	89.4	86.5	82.4	87.0	79.8	87.6
2nd quarter	88.9	89.4	90.6	90.1	90.9	90.7	90.7	87.6	83.4	87.5	81.0	88.4
3rd quarter	89.4	89.9	91.0	91.0	91.3	92.5	91.2	88.9	84.4	88.0	82.3	89.1
4th quarter	90.1	90.7	91.4	91.9	91.9	94.0	92.1	90.9	85.5	88.4	83.8	89.9
2005												
1st quarter	90.9	91.1	92.0	92.9	92.8	95.2	93.8	91.5	86.8	90.6	84.5	90.6
2nd quarter	91.5	91.7	92.5	93.9	93.5	96.8	94.4	92.5	87.6	91.1	85.6	91.3
3rd quarter	92.4	92.7	92.9	95.1	94.0	99.3	95.1	94.7	88.8	91.8	86.9	92.3
4th quarter	93.1	93.5	93.5	96.3	95.0	101.1	95.7	96.5	89.8	92.2	88.3	93.2
2006												
1st quarter	93.8	93.9	94.0	97.2	95.6	102.7	96.4	96.7	90.8	94.0	89.0	93.9
2nd quarter	94.6	94.6	94.6	97.9	96.2	103.7	97.7	97.7	91.9	94.4	90.3	94.6
3rd quarter	95.3	95.3	95.1	98.4	96.8	104.1	99.0	98.7	92.5	94.6	91.3	95.3
4th quarter	95.6	95.1	95.5	99.2	97.7	104.8	98.9	97.5	93.1	94.8	92.1	95.4
2007												
1st quarter	96.7	96.0	96.2	99.8	98.3	105.3	99.6	97.9	94.9	96.6	93.9	96.4
2nd quarter	97.2	96.8	96.5	100.0	98.6	105.1	100.6	99.5	95.7	97.2	94.8	97.1
3rd quarter	97.5	97.3	97.0	100.0	98.6	105.1	101.4	101.3	96.5	97.5	95.9	97.6
4th quarter	97.9	98.3	97.6	100.1	98.7	105.2	102.9	105.4	97.5	98.1	97.1	98.4
2008												
1st quarter	98.5	99.1	98.2	100.3	99.1	104.8	104.5	108.9	99.1	99.6	98.7	99.3
2nd quarter	98.9	100.2	98.7	100.5	99.6	104.4	107.3	114.6	100.3	100.4	100.2	100.2
3rd quarter	99.6	101.2	99.1	101.2	100.7	103.4	109.0	117.7	101.3	100.9	101.6	101.2
4th quarter	99.8	99.7	99.2	101.9	102.0	102.0	102.4	105.2	100.5	100.2	100.6	100.3
2009												
1st quarter	100.0	99.2	99.4	101.4	101.4	101.2	99.0	96.4	99.8	100.2	99.6	99.6
2nd quarter	99.9	99.6	99.9	100.2	100.2	99.8	99.0	97.9	99.7	99.7	99.7	99.7
3rd quarter	99.9	100.3	100.1	99.2	99.2	99.1	100.2	101.3	100.0	99.8	100.1	100.0
4th quarter	100.2	100.9	100.7	99.3	99.1	99.9	101.8	104.4	100.5	100.4	100.6	100.6
2010												
1st quarter	100.5	101.3	100.9	99.0	98.7	100.0	102.7	105.9	101.7	101.7	101.6	101.0
2nd quarter	101.0	101.4	101.2	99.0	99.0	99.3	103.8	105.4	102.4	102.5	102.4	101.3
3rd quarter	101.4	101.7	101.4	99.1	99.1	99.3	104.1	104.7	102.9	102.9	103.0	101.6
4th quarter	102.0	102.2	101.6	99.6	99.5	99.9	106.5	107.1	103.7	103.4	103.8	102.2
2011												
1st quarter	102.4	103.0	102.0	100.0	99.9	100.1	109.2	111.5	104.7	104.6	104.8	102.9
2nd quarter	103.2	104.0	102.6	100.5	100.4	100.5	111.5	114.9	105.8	105.5	106.0	103.9
3rd quarter	103.8	104.6	103.1	100.7	100.8	100.5	112.2	114.8	106.2	105.9	106.5	104.4
4th quarter	103.9	105.0	103.5	101.0	101.1	100.5	111.0	114.6	106.1	105.7	106.4	104.6
2012												
1st quarter	104.5	105.6	104.1	101.5	101.7	100.3	111.7	115.8	107.0	106.3	107.5	105.3
2nd quarter	104.9	105.9	104.6	101.9	102.2	100.7	112.0	115.0	107.1	106.5	107.6	105.6
3rd quarter	105.5	106.2	104.9	102.3	102.5	101.6	111.9	113.4	107.4	106.6	108.0	105.9
4th quarter	105.9	106.8	105.4	102.5	102.5	102.6	112.3	114.5	107.9	106.7	108.8	106.4
2013												
1st quarter	106.3	107.2	105.8	102.9	102.6	104.2	112.6	114.8	108.3	106.8	109.4	106.8
2nd quarter	106.6	107.2	106.1	103.4	102.9	105.5	111.8	113.6	108.6	107.0	109.7	107.0
3rd quarter	107.1	107.6	106.5	103.9	103.2	106.9	112.0	113.1	109.1	107.4	110.3	107.4
4th quarter	107.7	108.1	106.9	104.5	103.5	108.9	111.9	113.1	110.1	109.1	110.8	108.0
2014												
1st quarter	108.1	108.7	107.3	105.3	103.9	111.2	112.7	114.8	110.6	108.8	111.8	108.5
2nd quarter	108.7	109.1	107.9	105.6	104.2	111.5	112.7	113.9	111.0	109.1	112.3	109.0
3rd quarter	109.2	109.5	108.3	106.3	104.6	113.6	112.4	113.2	111.5	109.5	113.0	109.4
4th quarter	109.4	109.4	108.6	106.9	104.9	115.1	110.4	111.0	111.7	109.6	113.1	109.5
2015												
1st quarter	109.3	108.9	108.8	107.1	105.1	115.2	107.7	106.7	111.2	109.8	112.3	109.1
2nd quarter	109.9	109.4	109.3	107.0	105.0	115.2	107.4	105.2	111.8	109.8	113.1	109.5
3rd quarter	110.3	109.8	109.7	107.2	105.1	116.2	106.2	103.9	112.0	109.9	113.4	109.8
4th quarter	110.5	109.8	110.0	107.3	105.0	116.9	104.7	101.7	112.3	109.9	113.9	109.9
2016												
1st quarter	110.6	110.0	110.6	107.2	104.7	117.6	103.3	100.4	111.9	110.2	113.1	109.9
2nd quarter	111.3	110.6	111.2	107.6	104.8	119.3	104.2	100.7	112.6	110.4	114.1	110.5
3rd quarter	111.6	111.0	111.7	108.0	104.7	121.1	104.8	101.4	112.9	110.6	114.5	110.9
4th quarter	112.2	111.6	112.1	108.4	104.9	122.6	105.5	101.8	113.3	110.8	115.0	111.4

Table 1-7. Final Sales

(Quarterly dollar data are at seasonally adjusted annual rates.)

NIPA Tables 1.4.4, 1.4.5, 1.4.6

Year and quarter	Final sales of domestic product			Final sales to domestic purchasers		
	Billions of dollars	Billions of chained (2009) dollars	Chain-type price index, 2009 = 100	Billions of dollars	Billions of chained (2009) dollars	Chain-type price index, 2009 = 100
1950	294.4	2 167.1	13.6	293.7	2 201.6	13.4
1951	337.4	2 328.5	14.5	334.9	2 348.0	14.3
1952	364.2	2 457.5	14.9	363.1	2 493.0	14.6
1953	387.8	2 580.5	15.1	388.5	2 635.5	14.8
1954	393.1	2 588.9	15.2	392.7	2 633.7	14.9
1955	421.2	2 733.9	15.4	420.7	2 782.4	15.1
1956	446.2	2 800.5	16.0	443.8	2 840.1	15.7
1957	474.1	2 874.7	16.5	470.0	2 908.9	16.2
1958	482.4	2 858.6	16.9	481.9	2 917.9	16.5
1959	518.5	3 031.9	17.1	518.1	3 095.0	16.8
1960	540.1	3 114.1	17.4	535.8	3 157.2	17.0
1961	560.3	3 195.7	17.6	555.4	3 238.9	17.2
1962	599.0	3 374.4	17.8	594.9	3 428.4	17.4
1063	633.0	3 525.3	18.0	628.0	3 574.7	17.6
1964	681.0	3 734.8	18.3	674.1	3 775.0	17.9
1965	734.5	3 955.2	18.6	728.9	4 012.3	18.2
1966	801.4	4 196.9	19.1	797.5	4 271.0	18.7
1967	851.9	4 334.1	19.7	848.3	4 420.6	19.2
1968	933.4	4 553.4	20.5	932.1	4 658.1	20.0
1969	1 010.7	4 697.7	21.6	1 009.3	4 807.5	21.0
1970	1 073.9	4 740.5	22.7	1 069.9	4 835.5	22.2
1971	1 159.5	4 870.6	23.9	1 158.9	4 977.5	23.3
1972	1 273.3	5 126.0	24.9	1 276.7	5 247.9	24.4
1973	1 412.7	5 392.4	26.3	1 408.6	5 477.7	25.7
1974	1 534.8	5 378.4	28.6	1 535.6	5 423.1	28.4
1975	1 695.2	5 434.6	31.3	1 679.2	5 432.8	31.0
1976	1 860.5	5 651.9	33.0	1 862.1	5 709.5	32.7
1977	2 063.6	5 900.9	35.0	2 086.7	6 000.6	34.8
1978	2 330.8	6 225.5	37.5	2 356.1	6 324.3	37.3
1979	2 614.2	6 450.3	40.6	2 636.7	6 509.1	40.6
1980	2 868.8	6 492.1	44.3	2 881.9	6 444.9	44.8
1981	3 181.1	6 587.0	48.4	3 193.7	6 548.1	48.9
1982	3 359.9	6 546.7	51.4	3 379.9	6 547.0	51.7
1983	3 643.9	6 830.6	53.4	3 695.5	6 915.2	53.5
1984	3 975.3	7 196.3	55.3	4 078.0	7 385.6	55.3
1985	4 324.9	7 581.7	57.2	4 438.9	7 799.9	57.0
1986	4 583.6	7 872.6	58.3	4 715.5	8 113.3	58.2
1987	4 843.1	8 113.1	59.8	4 987.8	8 340.6	59.8
1988	5 234.1	8 466.9	61.9	5 343.5	8 627.9	61.9
1989	5 630.0	8 765.5	64.3	5 716.7	8 882.8	64.4
1990	5 965.0	8 952.7	66.7	6 042.9	9 034.1	66.9
1991	6 174.4	8 968.6	68.9	6 203.1	8 994.5	69.0
1992	6 523.0	9 262.5	70.5	6 557.7	9 291.5	70.6
1993	6 857.9	9 511.0	72.2	6 923.1	9 591.2	72.2
1994	7 245.0	9 837.7	73.7	7 337.5	9 956.0	73.7
1995	7 632.9	10 151.3	75.3	7 722.6	10 257.3	75.3
1996	8 069.4	10 536.6	76.7	8 165.8	10 657.7	76.6
1997	8 537.6	10 956.0	78.0	8 639.5	11 110.3	77.8
1998	9 025.4	11 452.3	78.9	9 188.2	11 734.2	78.3
1999	9 599.8	11 994.9	80.0	9 856.4	12 391.9	79.5
2000	10 230.2	12 494.9	81.9	10 606.0	12 994.0	81.6
2001	10 660.1	12 729.6	83.7	11 028.8	13 257.3	83.2
2002	10 959.0	12 888.9	85.0	11 385.5	13 499.6	84.3
2003	11 491.4	13 249.0	86.7	11 995.0	13 917.4	86.2
2004	12 211.1	13 702.2	89.1	12 830.2	14 461.3	88.7
2005	13 034.1	14 168.8	92.0	13 755.3	14 975.0	91.9
2006	13 788.9	14 542.3	94.8	14 559.9	15 361.0	94.8
2007	14 443.2	14 836.2	97.4	15 161.7	15 570.2	97.4
2008	14 750.6	14 865.7	99.2	15 473.6	15 435.8	100.2
2009	14 566.3	14 566.3	100.0	14 961.7	14 961.7	100.0
2010	14 902.8	14 722.2	101.2	15 415.5	15 183.6	101.5
2011	15 476.2	14 979.0	103.3	16 056.2	15 442.5	104.0
2012	16 093.5	15 292.3	105.2	16 659.1	15 742.4	105.8
2013	16 599.1	15 521.1	106.9	17 091.1	15 926.3	107.3
2014	17 349.6	15 932.9	108.9	17 859.1	16 361.9	109.2
2015	18 008.8	16 354.3	110.1	18 532.8	16 900.4	109.7
2016	18 589.4	16 664.1	111.6	19 110.6	17 250.3	110.8
2014						
1st quarter	16 987.5	15 707.4	108.2	17 503.9	16 119.2	108.6
2nd quarter	17 238.2	15 852.3	108.7	17 750.9	16 280.3	109.0
3rd quarter	17 523.7	16 040.3	109.3	18 012.8	16 457.9	109.5
4th quarter	17 649.1	16 131.6	109.4	18 168.9	16 590.3	109.5
2015						
1st quarter	17 726.1	16 202.3	109.4	18 264.3	16 727.8	109.2
2nd quarter	17 975.1	16 338.6	110.0	18 482.2	16 866.2	109.6
3rd quarter	18 122.0	16 414.1	110.4	18 652.8	16 973.9	109.9
4th quarter	18 211.8	16 462.1	110.6	18 731.9	17 033.8	110.0
2016						
1st quarter	18 283.0	16 512.7	110.7	18 809.2	17 096.6	110.0
2nd quarter	18 525.9	16 632.6	111.4	19 027.4	17 206.1	110.6
3rd quarter	18 712.7	16 741.1	111.8	19 205.5	17 300.6	111.0
4th quarter	18 836.1	16 770.0	112.3	19 400.4	17 397.7	111.5

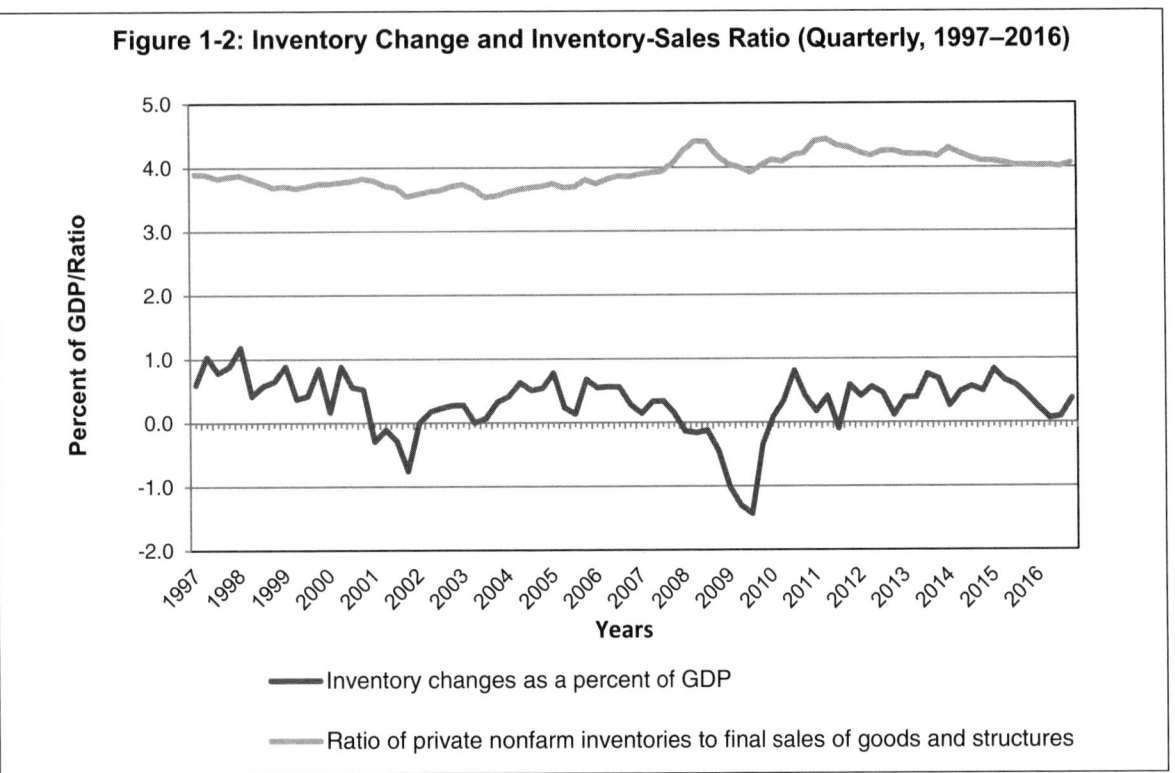

Figure 1-2: Inventory Change and Inventory-Sales Ratio (Quarterly, 1997–2016)

- The change in inventories is part of business investment component that, although small, can be volatile and even negative, reflecting the fact that production is frequently more variable than sales. When inventory change is positive, the economy is producing more than is sold. This is the normal condition, as inventories grow to accommodate a growing level of sales. When inventory change is negative, production is below the rate of sales—which could be because sales rose faster than anticipated, causing involuntary inventory reduction, or on the other hand because production was deliberately cut back in order to get rid of unwanted stocks. Furthermore, it is the <u>change</u> in inventory —the change in an already volatile number—that drives the GDP's <u>growth rate</u>.

- In 2009, following a rapid and unwanted rise in inventories, stocks were reduced at a record rate of $148 billion (2009 dollars), contributing 0.76 percentage points to the 2.8 percent decline in GDP. In 2010, the resumption of inventory-building contributed 1.45 percentage points, more than half of the 2.5 percent GDP increase. This was the largest positive contribution from inventories since 1984. (Tables 1-2A, 1-8A and 1-4A)

- Inventory-sales ratios, such as the version shown in Figure 1-2, show stocks in recent periods to be below 2008 numbers but still relatively high. Inventory investment has been moderate and variable during the recovery. (Tables 1-8A and B)

Table 1-8A. Inventory Change and Inventory-Sales Ratios: Recent Data

(Quarterly dollar data are at seasonally adjusted annual rates.)   **NIPA Tables 5.7.5B, 5.7.6B, 5.8.5B, 5.8.6B**

Year and quarter	Change in private inventories				Ratio, inventories at end of quarter to monthly rate of sales during the quarter					
	Billions of current dollars		Billions of chained dollars ¹		Total private inventories to final sales of domestic business		Nonfarm inventories to final sales of domestic business		Nonfarm inventories to final sales of goods and structures	
	Farm	Nonfarm	Farm	Nonfarm	Current dollars	Chained dollars¹	Current dollars	Chained dollars¹	Current dollars	Chained dollars¹
OLD BASIS										
1960	0.6	2.7	1.7	9.9	4.22	3.37	2.89	2.34	3.93	4.10
1961	0.9	2.1	2.5	7.8	4.12	3.30	2.81	2.29	3.84	4.03
1962	0.6	5.5	1.7	20.4	4.14	3.32	2.82	2.34	3.87	4.11
1963	0.5	5.1	1.4	19.0	3.95	3.25	2.78	2.32	3.81	4.07
1964	-1.2	6.0	-3.8	21.8	3.79	3.17	2.75	2.31	3.79	4.07
1965	0.8	8.4	2.5	30.5	3.77	3.09	2.72	2.29	3.71	3.99
1966	-0.5	14.1	-1.4	50.2	3.92	3.26	2.92	2.50	4.01	4.38
1967	0.9	9.0	2.5	31.5	3.90	3.35	2.99	2.59	4.14	4.57
1968	1.4	7.7	4.1	26.5	3.79	3.33	2.90	2.58	4.03	4.56
1969	0.0	9.2	0.0	30.9	3.88	3.40	2.98	2.68	4.18	4.76
1970	-0.8	2.8	-2.4	8.6	3.81	3.39	2.96	2.68	4.23	4.83
1971	1.7	6.6	4.1	20.6	3.76	3.33	2.88	2.64	4.12	4.75
1972	0.3	8.8	0.4	26.7	3.74	3.18	2.77	2.55	3.94	4.53
1973	1.5	14.4	1.8	40.5	4.20	3.22	2.98	2.62	4.22	4.67
1974	-2.8	16.8	-4.4	39.0	4.52	3.46	3.54	2.88	5.11	5.26
1975	3.4	-9.6	5.8	-21.4	4.04	3.26	3.16	2.66	4.59	4.88
1976	-0.8	18.0	-1.6	37.6	3.95	3.23	3.19	2.68	4.68	4.92
1977	4.5	17.8	7.2	35.7	3.89	3.22	3.16	2.67	4.63	4.87
1978	1.4	24.4	2.1	44.9	3.98	3.14	3.15	2.63	4.54	4.73
1979	3.6	14.4	4.2	23.8	4.19	3.16	3.34	2.64	4.85	4.75
1980	-6.1	-0.2	-7.2	-0.4	4.24	3.13	3.44	2.65	5.08	4.82
1981	8.8	21.0	10.1	28.2	4.17	3.28	3.49	2.75	5.20	5.03
1982	5.8	-20.7	7.5	-27.4	3.97	3.23	3.30	2.68	5.10	4.99
1983	-15.4	9.6	-17.4	10.7	3.69	2.98	3.08	2.52	4.77	4.64
1984	5.7	59.7	6.3	72.3	3.72	3.05	3.16	2.60	4.89	4.72
1985	5.8	16.1	7.0	18.4	3.51	2.98	3.01	2.53	4.74	4.65
1986	-1.5	8.0	-2.3	10.4	3.25	2.90	2.82	2.47	4.49	4.53
1987	-6.4	33.6	-9.1	41.1	3.33	2.90	2.90	2.50	4.65	4.62
1988	-11.9	30.4	-13.1	35.4	3.29	2.81	2.86	2.47	4.63	4.55
1989	0.0	27.7	0.0	30.8	3.23	2.80	2.83	2.47	4.63	4.56
1990	2.4	12.2	2.5	14.0	3.22	2.83	2.82	2.49	4.71	4.66
1991	-1.3	0.9	-1.8	0.4	3.06	2.83	2.70	2.50	4.62	4.74
1992	6.3	10.1	7.1	11.0	2.92	2.73	2.56	2.39	4.41	4.53
1993	-6.2	27.0	-7.5	29.8	2.85	2.68	2.51	2.38	4.33	4.47
1994	12.0	51.8	13.7	55.9	2.89	2.72	2.56	2.40	4.39	4.47
1995	-11.1	42.2	-13.0	44.3	2.88	2.69	2.58	2.40	4.45	4.46
1996	8.6	22.1	8.3	23.2	2.76	2.62	2.47	2.33	4.24	4.28
1997	3.3	67.7	3.7	73.6	2.70	2.65	2.42	2.37	4.17	4.32
NEW BASIS										
1997	3.3	67.7	4.1	80.5	2.60	2.63	2.33	2.35	3.86	4.16
1998	1.3	62.5	1.9	76.4	2.46	2.60	2.24	2.32	3.69	4.07
1999	-2.7	63.5	-4.2	77.7	2.48	2.59	2.27	2.33	3.75	4.08
2000	-1.4	55.9	-2.0	67.1	2.50	2.59	2.28	2.34	3.83	4.12
2001	0.0	-38.3	0.1	-45.8	2.32	2.51	2.12	2.26	3.55	3.97
2002	-2.5	21.0	-3.5	25.5	2.37	2.53	2.16	2.29	3.71	4.09
2003	0.1	19.2	0.1	22.4	2.31	2.43	2.09	2.20	3.56	3.86
2004	8.8	55.1	9.0	62.4	2.38	2.44	2.16	2.21	3.71	3.89
2005	0.2	59.4	0.3	63.9	2.42	2.44	2.21	2.21	3.81	3.89
2006	-3.6	70.5	-4.2	75.4	2.43	2.44	2.23	2.23	3.86	3.93
2007	-0.7	35.2	-0.9	36.5	2.53	2.43	2.30	2.22	4.07	3.93
2008	1.6	-33.6	1.1	-35.0	2.52	2.49	2.29	2.27	4.18	4.13
2009	-1.6	-146.0	-1.6	-146.0	2.40	2.35	2.19	2.13	4.03	3.89
2010	-7.3	68.9	-7.0	65.9	2.53	2.35	2.28	2.14	4.22	3.92
2011	2.1	39.7	1.4	36.6	2.62	2.33	2.33	2.13	4.31	3.86
2012	-19.5	81.3	-12.6	72.7	2.60	2.33	2.34	2.16	4.26	3.86
2013	10.2	82.2	6.0	73.0	2.54	2.34	2.29	2.17	4.17	3.83
2014	-4.8	82.8	-3.3	74.0	2.48	2.33	2.24	2.17	4.10	3.83
2015	0.5	111.5	0.2	102.8	2.38	2.38	2.18	2.23	4.03	3.96
2016	-0.6	35.7	-0.6	34.5	2.35	2.36	2.17	2.21	4.06	3.93
2014										
1st quarter	-6.8	50.7	-4.8	45.8	2.61	2.35	2.35	2.17	4.30	3.86
2nd quarter	-3.3	86.0	-3.5	76.5	2.57	2.34	2.32	2.17	4.22	3.83
3rd quarter	-3.8	102.3	-2.0	90.6	2.53	2.33	2.28	2.16	4.15	3.80
4th quarter	-5.4	92.2	-2.8	82.9	2.48	2.33	2.24	2.17	4.10	3.83
2015										
1st quarter	3.5	145.1	2.3	133.0	2.46	2.35	2.22	2.19	4.10	3.90
2nd quarter	0.2	117.9	0.5	107.8	2.44	2.36	2.22	2.20	4.07	3.90
3rd quarter	0.9	104.8	0.6	97.7	2.40	2.37	2.19	2.21	4.03	3.92
4th quarter	-2.7	78.1	-2.6	72.5	2.38	2.38	2.18	2.23	4.03	3.96
2016										
1st quarter	-2.9	45.1	-2.6	44.6	2.37	2.39	2.17	2.23	4.02	3.96
2nd quarter	3.3	8.9	2.6	9.4	2.36	2.37	2.17	2.21	4.03	3.92
3rd quarter	0.6	15.9	0.8	17.1	2.32	2.35	2.15	2.20	4.01	3.90
4th quarter	-3.5	73.0	-2.9	66.8	2.35	2.36	2.17	2.21	4.06	3.93

¹Before 1997, 2005 dollars; 1997 forward, 2009 dollars.

Table 1-8B. Inventory Change and Inventory-Sales Ratios: Historical Data

(Quarterly dollar data are at seasonally adjusted annual rates.)   **NIPA Tables 5.7.5B, 5.7.6B, 5.8.5B, 5.8.6B**

Year and quarter	Change in private inventories				Ratio, inventories at end of quarter to monthly rate of sales during the quarter					
	Billions of current dollars		Billions of chained dollars [1]		Total private inventories to final sales of domestic business		Nonfarm inventories to final sales of domestic business		Nonfarm inventories to final sales of goods and structures	
	Farm	Nonfarm	Farm	Nonfarm	Current dollars	Chained dollars[1]	Current dollars	Chained dollars[1]	Current dollars	Chained dollars[1]
OLD BASIS										
1929	-0.1	1.7	-0.6	10.6	...	...	...	...	...	...
1930	-0.3	0.0	-1.7	-2.4	...	...	...	...	...	...
1931	0.5	-1.6	3.1	-13.4	...	...	...	...	...	...
1932	0.1	-2.5	0.8	-21.2	...	...	...	...	...	...
1933	-0.1	-1.3	-1.1	-9.4	...	...	...	...	...	...
1934	-0.8	0.2	-5.7	1.0	...	...	...	...	...	...
1935	0.7	0.4	4.0	2.5	...	...	...	...	...	...
1936	-0.9	2.0	-5.4	15.5	...	...	...	...	...	...
1937	0.9	1.7	4.1	7.9	...	...	...	...	...	...
1938	0.4	-1.0	2.8	-6.0	...	...	...	...	...	...
1939	-0.1	0.3	-1.1	2.7	...	...	...	...	...	...
1940	0.5	1.9	2.8	12.4	...	...	...	...	...	...
1941	0.4	3.9	1.9	24.3	...	...	...	...	...	...
1942	1.3	0.6	5.6	3.0	...	...	...	...	...	...
1943	-0.2	-0.5	-1.1	-2.3	...	...	...	...	...	...
1944	-0.3	-0.6	-1.5	-2.5	...	...	...	...	...	...
1945	-0.9	-0.6	-3.3	-3.8	...	...	...	...	...	...
1946	-0.2	6.2	-1.0	31.8	...	...	...	...	...	...
1947	-1.8	1.2	-4.5	4.4	...	...	...	...	...	...
1948	2.7	3.0	6.1	12.4	...	...	...	...	...	...
1949	-0.6	-2.1	-1.9	-8.6	...	...	...	...	...	...
1950	-0.1	5.9	-0.3	22.8	5.81	3.67	3.04	2.30	3.94	3.97
1951	1.0	8.9	2.1	28.4	5.85	3.76	3.15	2.46	4.07	4.24
1952	1.4	2.1	3.1	7.4	5.24	3.74	3.06	2.45	3.98	4.23
1953	0.7	1.2	2.0	4.5	5.04	3.74	3.08	2.45	4.04	4.22
1954	0.2	-2.1	0.5	-7.5	4.74	3.52	2.88	2.28	3.81	3.94
1947										
1st quarter	-1.1	1.6	0.4	6.6	5.90	3.88	2.82	2.27	3.71	3.99
2nd quarter	-2.7	1.5	-4.5	4.2	5.89	3.84	2.82	2.27	3.69	4.00
3rd quarter	-2.5	-0.4	-6.8	-3.7	6.02	3.76	2.76	2.23	3.61	3.93
4th quarter	-0.8	2.3	-6.3	10.5	6.30	3.74	2.81	2.25	3.65	3.93
1948										
1st quarter	1.3	2.4	1.6	11.7	6.00	3.76	2.87	2.27	3.71	3.96
2nd quarter	2.8	3.0	7.7	11.9	6.02	3.81	2.89	2.30	3.76	4.03
3rd quarter	3.4	3.7	8.3	15.0	5.88	3.88	2.97	2.34	3.85	4.10
4th quarter	3.1	2.9	6.6	11.1	5.74	3.91	3.00	2.36	3.90	4.13
1949										
1st quarter	-0.2	0.6	-1.2	-0.4	5.66	3.90	2.97	2.36	3.88	4.14
2nd quarter	-1.2	-4.0	-3.0	-15.1	5.38	3.82	2.83	2.30	3.70	4.02
3rd quarter	-0.9	-0.4	-2.3	-0.6	5.39	3.81	2.82	2.29	3.69	4.00
4th quarter	-0.2	-4.5	-0.9	-18.4	5.23	3.73	2.77	2.23	3.61	3.87
1950										
1st quarter	-0.1	2.2	-1.0	9.7	5.26	3.69	2.76	2.22	3.61	3.84
2nd quarter	-1.3	4.2	-2.5	16.2	5.27	3.62	2.75	2.20	3.57	3.79
3rd quarter	0.5	3.7	0.6	15.2	5.21	3.47	2.72	2.12	3.50	3.63
4th quarter	0.7	13.4	1.5	50.2	5.81	3.67	3.04	2.30	3.94	3.97
1951										
1st quarter	1.2	9.2	2.6	29.0	5.94	3.68	3.12	2.33	4.01	4.01
2nd quarter	0.9	13.8	2.5	44.3	5.99	3.81	3.25	2.45	4.23	4.28
3rd quarter	0.8	9.0	1.6	29.3	5.89	3.79	3.20	2.47	4.16	4.29
4th quarter	1.1	3.6	1.7	11.0	5.85	3.76	3.15	2.46	4.07	4.24
1952										
1st quarter	1.0	3.8	2.7	12.8	5.77	3.79	3.16	2.49	4.11	4.31
2nd quarter	1.9	-3.4	3.6	-10.5	5.63	3.75	3.08	2.44	4.01	4.24
3rd quarter	2.2	3.4	4.5	11.2	5.63	3.85	3.15	2.51	4.13	4.38
4th quarter	0.5	4.8	1.5	16.2	5.24	3.74	3.06	2.45	3.98	4.23
1953										
1st quarter	0.8	3.1	2.5	10.6	5.06	3.69	3.02	2.42	3.93	4.17
2nd quarter	-0.7	4.3	-0.2	14.1	5.00	3.69	3.06	2.43	3.99	4.20
3rd quarter	0.7	1.6	1.8	5.8	4.99	3.72	3.09	2.45	4.05	4.23
4th quarter	2.1	-4.1	3.8	-12.3	5.04	3.74	3.08	2.45	4.04	4.22
1954										
1st quarter	0.8	-2.8	2.1	-9.2	5.02	3.72	3.04	2.42	4.01	4.20
2nd quarter	-0.2	-3.2	0.5	-10.8	4.91	3.66	2.98	2.38	3.93	4.11
3rd quarter	0.7	-2.8	0.8	-9.1	4.85	3.59	2.93	2.32	3.89	4.04
4th quarter	-0.5	0.2	-1.5	-0.9	4.74	3.52	2.88	2.28	3.81	3.94
1955										
1st quarter	-0.1	3.9	-1.7	14.0	4.68	3.46	2.86	2.25	3.77	3.88
2nd quarter	-1.1	5.7	-2.1	20.0	4.57	3.44	2.87	2.26	3.73	3.83
3rd quarter	-1.3	5.6	-2.0	17.9	4.47	3.42	2.89	2.26	3.77	3.85
4th quarter	0.3	6.9	-1.6	22.7	4.43	3.44	2.95	2.29	3.87	3.94
1956										
1st quarter	0.0	6.4	-2.9	20.8	4.50	3.48	3.00	2.33	3.96	4.02
2nd quarter	-1.5	5.0	-3.4	16.2	4.57	3.48	3.03	2.35	3.99	4.04
3rd quarter	-0.8	4.3	-3.2	13.2	4.50	3.48	3.02	2.36	3.98	4.07
4th quarter	-1.6	3.9	-3.3	12.1	4.47	3.45	3.03	2.35	4.00	4.07

[1]Before 1997, 2005 dollars; 1997 forward, 2009 dollars.
. . . = Not available.

Table 1-8B. Inventory Change and Inventory-Sales Ratios: Historical Data—*Continued*

(Quarterly dollar data are at seasonally adjusted annual rates.)   **NIPA Tables 5.7.5B, 5.7.6B, 5.8.5B, 5.8.6B**

Year and quarter	Change in private inventories				Ratio, inventories at end of quarter to monthly rate of sales during the quarter					
	Billions of current dollars		Billions of chained dollars [1]		Total private inventories to final sales of domestic business		Nonfarm inventories to final sales of domestic business		Nonfarm inventories to final sales of goods and structures	
	Farm	Nonfarm	Farm	Nonfarm	Current dollars	Chained dollars[1]	Current dollars	Chained dollars[1]	Current dollars	Chained dollars[1]
1957										
1st quarter	0.3	1.9	-0.9	5.7	4.44	3.44	3.02	2.35	3.97	4.05
2nd quarter	0.7	2.0	-0.2	6.8	4.48	3.48	3.04	2.38	4.00	4.11
3rd quarter	0.5	2.3	1.8	7.5	4.46	3.47	3.03	2.38	3.99	4.10
4th quarter	-1.0	-3.5	1.1	-10.2	4.46	3.48	3.01	2.37	4.01	4.14
1958										
1st quarter	2.2	-6.3	7.6	-20.4	4.67	3.56	3.04	2.41	4.06	4.20
2nd quarter	1.6	-5.8	6.9	-18.6	4.65	3.56	3.00	2.38	4.00	4.17
3rd quarter	2.2	-0.7	6.2	-2.5	4.58	3.48	2.92	2.32	3.92	4.07
4th quarter	1.8	3.4	2.5	10.6	4.50	3.44	2.90	2.30	3.88	4.00
1959										
1st quarter	-0.3	4.2	-3.5	14.9	4.37	3.05	2.83	2.25	3.79	3.93
2nd quarter	-1.9	9.2	-5.3	33.8	4.33	3.34	2.86	2.27	3.85	3.98
3rd quarter	-2.3	2.6	-5.4	9.6	4.25	3.31	2.84	2.27	3.82	3.96
4th quarter	-1.8	5.9	-4.6	21.1	4.26	3.37	2.90	2.32	3.94	4.08
1960										
1st quarter	0.6	10.6	0.4	39.0	4.29	3.37	2.93	2.35	3.96	4.10
2nd quarter	0.9	2.4	1.9	9.0	4.21	3.36	2.91	2.34	3.95	4.11
3rd quarter	1.0	3.3	3.1	12.1	4.27	3.41	2.95	2.38	3.99	4.15
4th quarter	-0.2	-5.6	1.5	-20.2	4.22	3.37	2.89	2.34	3.93	4.10
1961										
1st quarter	0.6	-3.1	2.5	-11.3	4.19	3.35	2.86	2.32	3.90	4.07
2nd quarter	0.6	1.2	2.2	4.7	4.12	3.33	2.83	2.30	3.89	4.07
3rd quarter	0.9	5.7	2.6	21.0	4.17	3.35	2.85	2.32	3.89	4.08
4th quarter	1.4	4.6	2.8	16.8	4.12	3.30	2.81	2.29	3.84	4.03
1962										
1st quarter	1.5	7.9	2.5	29.0	4.15	3.32	2.82	2.32	3.85	4.07
2nd quarter	0.2	5.2	0.8	19.2	4.09	3.29	2.80	2.31	3.84	4.06
3rd quarter	0.2	5.9	1.4	22.0	4.17	3.32	2.83	2.33	3.87	4.09
4th quarter	0.4	3.0	2.2	11.3	4.14	3.32	2.82	2.34	3.87	4.11
1963										
1st quarter	1.9	4.9	7.5	18.2	4.12	3.34	2.83	2.35	3.87	4.12
2nd quarter	0.1	4.8	0.7	17.4	4.04	3.29	2.79	2.32	3.83	4.08
3rd quarter	-0.6	6.4	-1.7	23.6	4.00	3.27	2.79	2.33	3.81	4.07
4th quarter	0.6	4.5	-0.8	16.7	3.95	3.25	2.78	2.32	3.81	4.07
1964										
1st quarter	-0.6	5.8	-3.9	21.1	3.85	3.19	2.74	2.29	3.75	4.01
2nd quarter	-1.2	5.7	-4.3	20.7	3.79	3.17	2.73	2.29	3.75	4.02
3rd quarter	-1.8	6.5	-4.2	23.8	3.78	3.15	2.73	2.29	3.74	4.00
4th quarter	-1.1	6.1	-3.1	21.7	3.79	3.17	2.75	2.31	3.79	4.07
1965										
1st quarter	0.3	11.2	0.9	40.8	3.81	3.17	2.76	2.33	3.79	4.08
2nd quarter	1.1	7.4	2.9	26.9	3.82	3.15	2.75	2.32	3.79	4.08
3rd quarter	0.8	8.5	3.1	30.5	3.78	3.14	2.76	2.32	3.78	4.06
4th quarter	1.0	6.6	3.2	23.7	3.77	3.09	2.72	2.29	3.71	3.99
1966										
1st quarter	0.6	13.2	1.1	46.8	3.80	3.09	2.73	2.31	3.71	4.00
2nd quarter	-1.7	14.0	-2.7	50.2	3.86	3.16	2.80	2.38	3.83	4.16
3rd quarter	-0.6	12.4	-1.7	43.7	3.91	3.19	2.84	2.42	3.88	4.22
4th quarter	-0.4	16.9	-2.3	59.9	3.92	3.26	2.92	2.50	4.01	4.38
1967										
1st quarter	1.7	13.7	3.4	48.6	3.94	3.32	2.98	2.55	4.11	4.50
2nd quarter	2.1	4.2	7.6	14.7	3.92	3.31	2.95	2.54	4.07	4.46
3rd quarter	0.5	8.7	1.4	29.7	3.92	3.34	2.97	2.57	4.10	4.52
4th quarter	-0.9	9.3	-2.2	33.1	3.90	3.35	2.99	2.59	4.14	4.57
1968										
1st quarter	3.0	5.4	7.3	19.1	3.87	3.32	2.94	2.57	4.08	4.51
2nd quarter	4.3	9.8	13.4	33.9	3.87	3.34	2.93	2.58	4.07	4.55
3rd quarter	0.2	7.5	1.2	25.1	3.81	3.32	2.90	2.56	4.03	4.51
4th quarter	-2.0	8.0	-5.5	27.8	3.79	3.33	2.90	2.58	4.03	4.56
1969										
1st quarter	1.8	9.7	3.9	33.0	3.79	3.32	2.90	2.59	4.02	4.54
2nd quarter	1.4	7.8	4.4	26.6	3.83	3.35	2.91	2.61	4.06	4.61
3rd quarter	-1.2	11.4	-2.5	38.6	3.83	3.38	2.94	2.64	4.10	4.67
4th quarter	-1.9	7.7	-5.8	25.5	3.88	3.40	2.98	2.68	4.18	4.76
1970										
1st quarter	1.6	0.2	3.4	0.0	3.86	3.38	2.96	2.66	4.18	4.74
2nd quarter	0.4	4.7	1.9	14.9	3.85	3.40	2.96	2.68	4.20	4.80
3rd quarter	-1.8	6.9	-4.4	21.9	3.84	3.39	2.97	2.67	4.22	4.79
4th quarter	-3.5	-0.5	-10.3	-2.2	3.81	3.39	2.96	2.68	4.23	4.83
1971										
1st quarter	2.5	9.7	6.6	31.3	3.83	3.38	2.95	2.68	4.21	4.81
2nd quarter	4.2	6.7	10.7	20.6	3.81	3.39	2.94	2.68	4.20	4.81
3rd quarter	2.3	7.9	5.8	25.2	3.80	3.38	2.93	2.68	4.18	4.80
4th quarter	-2.3	2.0	-6.8	5.4	3.76	3.33	2.88	2.64	4.12	4.75

[1] Before 1997, 2005 dollars; 1997 forward, 2009 dollars.

Table 1-8B. Inventory Change and Inventory-Sales Ratios: Historical Data—*Continued*

(Quarterly dollar data are at seasonally adjusted annual rates.)

NIPA Tables 5.7.5B, 5.7.6B, 5.8.5B, 5.8.6B

Year and quarter	Change in private inventories				Ratio, inventories at end of quarter to monthly rate of sales during the quarter					
	Billions of current dollars		Billions of chained dollars [1]		Total private inventories to final sales of domestic business		Nonfarm inventories to final sales of domestic business		Nonfarm inventories to final sales of goods and structures	
	Farm	Nonfarm	Farm	Nonfarm	Current dollars	Chained dollars[1]	Current dollars	Chained dollars[1]	Current dollars	Chained dollars[1]
1972										
1st quarter	-0.5	3.7	0.1	11.1	3.72	3.30	2.84	2.62	4.06	4.69
2nd quarter	2.0	10.0	6.8	30.6	3.75	3.27	2.83	2.60	4.03	4.64
3rd quarter	1.0	12.7	1.9	38.5	3.77	3.26	2.83	2.60	4.05	4.66
4th quarter	-1.4	8.9	-7.1	26.5	3.74	3.18	2.77	2.55	3.94	4.53
1973										
1st quarter	-4.2	14.8	-10.7	42.9	3.86	3.11	2.79	2.52	3.92	4.45
2nd quarter	5.0	13.2	12.0	38.3	4.03	3.15	2.86	2.54	4.02	4.51
3rd quarter	2.6	7.2	3.5	20.0	4.11	3.16	2.87	2.56	4.05	4.55
4th quarter	2.8	22.2	2.3	60.9	4.20	3.22	2.98	2.62	4.22	4.67
1974										
1st quarter	-3.3	15.9	-5.2	39.7	4.26	3.27	3.13	2.68	4.42	4.76
2nd quarter	1.0	16.4	0.9	39.6	4.29	3.31	3.28	2.72	4.67	4.86
3rd quarter	-0.1	5.7	1.7	11.7	4.45	3.34	3.40	2.75	4.84	4.93
4th quarter	-8.7	29.2	-15.0	64.9	4.52	3.46	3.54	2.88	5.11	5.26
1975										
1st quarter	7.1	-17.1	16.4	-38.3	4.32	3.42	3.41	2.82	4.94	5.16
2nd quarter	3.1	-17.1	5.4	-38.6	4.26	3.35	3.30	2.75	4.81	5.06
3rd quarter	0.8	-2.2	-1.0	-5.0	4.18	3.31	3.24	2.71	4.69	4.95
4th quarter	2.5	-2.1	2.3	-3.7	4.04	3.26	3.16	2.66	4.59	4.88
1976										
1st quarter	-0.5	15.2	0.1	33.2	4.00	3.22	3.14	2.64	4.56	4.83
2nd quarter	-1.8	24.3	-1.9	51.8	4.07	3.26	3.21	2.69	4.67	4.91
3rd quarter	2.0	18.8	5.4	38.9	4.04	3.28	3.23	2.70	4.74	4.96
4th quarter	-3.0	13.6	-9.8	26.5	3.95	3.23	3.19	2.68	4.68	4.92
1977										
1st quarter	-1.3	16.1	-7.0	33.0	3.96	3.22	3.21	2.68	4.72	4.92
2nd quarter	5.3	14.2	11.3	27.8	3.88	3.19	3.16	2.65	4.62	4.84
3rd quarter	4.4	26.5	16.3	53.8	3.86	3.22	3.16	2.67	4.63	4.88
4th quarter	9.8	14.4	8.4	28.1	3.89	3.22	3.16	2.67	4.63	4.87
1078										
1st quarter	-0.6	26.1	-3.6	48.9	4.02	3.26	3.21	2.72	4.78	5.00
2nd quarter	0.4	23.9	0.2	44.2	3.92	3.14	3.12	2.62	4.55	4.75
3rd quarter	7.2	17.8	11.1	32.3	3.95	3.15	3.13	2.62	4.54	4.74
4th quarter	-1.5	30.0	0.5	54.1	3.98	3.14	3.15	2.63	4.54	4.73
1979										
1st quarter	4.2	19.6	6.6	33.0	4.15	3.17	3.22	2.65	4.66	4.78
2nd quarter	3.1	24.3	5.3	40.4	4.19	3.21	3.29	2.69	4.78	4.87
3rd quarter	6.6	5.5	7.0	8.2	4.16	3.16	3.28	2.64	4.74	4.73
4th quarter	0.3	8.3	-1.9	13.4	4.19	3.16	3.34	2.64	4.85	4.75
1980										
1st quarter	-0.6	10.5	-2.6	17.4	4.25	3.17	3.45	2.66	5.02	4.78
2nd quarter	-5.2	13.0	-5.9	19.3	4.40	3.28	3.57	2.76	5.26	5.02
3rd quarter	-12.5	-21.4	-14.2	-32.6	4.34	3.18	3.50	2.68	5.15	4.88
4th quarter	-6.1	-3.0	-6.0	-5.8	4.24	3.13	3.44	2.65	5.08	4.82
1981										
1st quarter	6.8	31.9	10.3	44.6	4.26	3.17	3.48	2.67	5.13	4.84
2nd quarter	9.9	1.8	10.9	1.7	4.24	3.18	3.47	2.67	5.15	4.87
3rd quarter	11.8	32.1	14.5	42.6	4.20	3.22	3.48	2.71	5.16	4.93
4th quarter	6.5	18.3	4.5	23.8	4.17	3.28	3.49	2.75	5.20	5.03
1982										
1st quarter	5.1	-26.5	6.7	-34.3	4.19	3.28	3.46	2.74	5.20	5.03
2nd quarter	4.3	-8.5	6.4	-12.2	4.15	3.28	3.42	2.74	5.17	5.04
3rd quarter	9.0	-3.2	12.0	-5.5	4.12	3.33	3.43	2.77	5.26	5.15
4th quarter	4.6	-44.4	4.9	-57.5	3.97	3.23	3.30	2.68	5.10	4.99
1983										
1st quarter	-7.3	-27.8	-10.4	-37.3	3.89	3.15	3.19	2.62	4.98	4.89
2nd quarter	-13.0	5.3	-12.6	6.5	3.81	3.09	3.14	2.58	4.89	4.80
3rd quarter	-32.4	28.2	-37.7	34.3	3.73	3.03	3.12	2.55	4.86	4.73
4th quarter	-8.8	32.7	-9.0	39.4	3.69	2.98	3.08	2.52	4.77	4.64
1984										
1st quarter	5.5	67.5	7.4	81.9	3.78	3.02	3.15	2.56	4.87	4.71
2nd quarter	5.6	63.7	6.4	77.2	3.76	3.03	3.16	2.57	4.88	4.69
3rd quarter	6.8	64.5	8.1	78.9	3.75	3.06	3.18	2.60	4.93	4.75
4th quarter	5.0	43.0	3.3	51.0	3.72	3.05	3.16	2.60	4.89	4.72
1985										
1st quarter	7.9	8.3	8.4	8.8	3.60	3.00	3.06	2.55	4.77	4.65
2nd quarter	4.2	17.4	4.8	20.3	3.55	2.99	3.04	2.55	4.76	4.66
3rd quarter	6.6	9.7	9.1	12.0	3.47	2.96	2.98	2.51	4.67	4.60
4th quarter	4.3	28.8	5.9	32.7	3.51	2.98	3.01	2.53	4.74	4.65
1986										
1st quarter	2.5	27.8	1.7	33.3	3.42	2.97	2.94	2.52	4.65	4.63
2nd quarter	-3.5	19.1	-5.9	22.3	3.37	2.97	2.92	2.53	4.63	4.65
3rd quarter	-3.1	-3.9	-4.3	-5.5	3.29	2.92	2.85	2.49	4.52	4.55
4th quarter	-1.8	-11.0	-0.6	-8.5	3.25	2.90	2.82	2.47	4.49	4.53

[1]Before 1997, 2005 dollars; 1997 forward, 2009 dollars.

Table 1-8B. Inventory Change and Inventory-Sales Ratios: Historical Data—*Continued*

(Quarterly dollar data are at seasonally adjusted annual rates.)

NIPA Tables 5.7.5B, 5.7.6B, 5.8.5B, 5.8.6B

Year and quarter	Change in private inventories				Ratio, inventories at end of quarter to monthly rate of sales during the quarter					
	Billions of current dollars		Billions of chained dollars 1		Total private inventories to final sales of domestic business		Nonfarm inventories to final sales of domestic business		Nonfarm inventories to final sales of goods and structures	
	Farm	Nonfarm	Farm	Nonfarm	Current dollars	Chained dollars1	Current dollars	Chained dollars1	Current dollars	Chained dollars1
1987										
1st quarter	-7.7	35.6	-9.7	44.5	3.31	2.94	2.86	2.51	4.62	4.66
2nd quarter	-10.7	27.2	-14.5	33.1	3.30	2.90	2.86	2.49	4.60	4.60
3rd quarter	-4.0	5.0	-5.2	4.1	3.25	2.85	2.82	2.45	4.52	4.51
4th quarter	-3.3	66.4	-7.0	82.5	3.33	2.90	2.90	2.50	4.65	4.62
1988										
1st quarter	-4.4	21.4	-7.6	25.1	3.30	2.86	2.86	2.47	4.61	4.56
2nd quarter	-12.2	31.9	-15.2	38.0	3.29	2.83	2.85	2.46	4.60	4.52
3rd quarter	-11.2	29.4	-11.4	32.6	3.30	2.83	2.85	2.47	4.63	4.57
4th quarter	-19.7	38.8	-18.3	45.9	3.29	2.81	2.86	2.47	4.63	4.55
1989										
1st quarter	7.2	41.0	7.8	46.6	3.32	2.83	2.89	2.48	4.70	4.59
2nd quarter	2.9	33.2	3.6	37.6	3.28	2.83	2.87	2.48	4.65	4.56
3rd quarter	-5.5	15.5	-5.8	16.9	3.21	2.79	2.82	2.45	4.55	4.49
4th quarter	-4.6	21.2	-5.6	22.3	3.23	2.80	2.83	2.47	4.63	4.56
1990										
1st quarter	1.8	12.1	1.7	13.3	3.18	2.78	2.78	2.45	4.53	4.50
2nd quarter	-1.5	35.3	-2.6	39.9	3.17	2.81	2.78	2.47	4.58	4.60
3rd quarter	4.0	17.9	4.4	20.3	3.20	2.82	2.82	2.48	4.67	4.63
4th quarter	5.2	-16.6	6.7	-17.7	3.22	2.83	2.82	2.49	4.71	4.66
1991										
1st quarter	0.0	-15.6	0.7	-18.1	3.18	2.85	2.78	2.51	4.65	4.71
2nd quarter	-0.7	-17.3	-0.5	-20.6	3.08	2.81	2.70	2.47	4.55	4.66
3rd quarter	-10.9	11.7	-13.8	13.1	3.04	2.81	2.69	2.48	4.54	4.67
4th quarter	6.4	24.7	6.1	27.1	3.06	2.83	2.70	2.50	4.62	4.74
1992										
1st quarter	8.0	-7.8	10.5	-7.5	3.00	2.78	2.63	2.44	4.52	4.64
2nd quarter	9.4	13.8	10.9	13.2	2.99	2.77	2.62	2.43	4.50	4.61
3rd quarter	5.1	15.4	4.7	16.6	2.96	2.75	2.60	2.41	4.47	4.57
4th quarter	2.5	18.9	2.4	21.6	2.92	2.73	2.56	2.39	4.41	4.53
1993										
1st quarter	-5.6	41.6	-6.2	46.5	2.95	2.75	2.58	2.42	4.47	4.60
2nd quarter	-4.9	29.0	-5.3	32.3	2.92	2.74	2.57	2.41	4.44	4.56
3rd quarter	-12.5	19.1	-14.2	20.6	2.89	2.72	2.54	2.40	4.42	4.55
4th quarter	-1.7	18.3	-4.1	19.9	2.85	2.68	2.51	2.38	4.33	4.47
1994										
1st quarter	16.5	28.8	19.4	31.1	2.87	2.69	2.51	2.38	4.33	4.48
2nd quarter	17.1	64.3	21.0	70.0	2.86	2.71	2.53	2.39	4.37	4.49
3rd quarter	10.7	42.5	10.6	46.1	2.86	2.71	2.53	2.39	4.36	4.48
4th quarter	3.7	71.5	3.7	76.3	2.89	2.72	2.56	2.40	4.39	4.47
1995										
1st quarter	-5.8	67.0	-5.9	71.2	2.93	2.75	2.62	2.43	4.49	4.52
2nd quarter	-13.7	47.4	-13.6	50.1	2.94	2.75	2.64	2.44	4.55	4.55
3rd quarter	-20.4	31.7	-26.4	32.8	2.90	2.71	2.60	2.41	4.49	4.50
4th quarter	-4.4	22.8	-6.2	22.9	2.88	2.69	2.58	2.40	4.45	4.46
1996										
1st quarter	1.1	5.8	-2.9	6.2	2.84	2.66	2.55	2.38	4.39	4.42
2nd quarter	11.8	18.6	7.4	19.8	2.81	2.63	2.51	2.35	4.30	4.35
3rd quarter	17.1	34.0	27.4	35.0	2.81	2.65	2.50	2.35	4.29	4.34
4th quarter	4.5	30.2	1.3	31.7	2.76	2.62	2.47	2.33	4.24	4.28
1997										
1st quarter	-0.5	50.3	-10.8	53.3	2.74	2.62	2.45	2.33	4.21	4.28
2nd quarter	0.8	87.6	8.2	95.7	2.73	2.65	2.44	2.36	4.21	4.33
3rd quarter	8.3	59.6	10.1	65.5	2.69	2.63	2.41	2.34	4.14	4.27
4th quarter	4.7	73.1	7.2	79.8	2.70	2.65	2.42	2.37	4.17	4.32
NEW BASIS										
1997										
1st quarter	-0.6	50.3	-9.0	59.3	2.64	2.60	2.36	2.31	3.90	4.12
2nd quarter	0.8	87.6	8.7	104.2	2.63	2.63	2.35	2.34	3.89	4.16
3rd quarter	8.3	59.6	10.0	71.1	2.59	2.61	2.32	2.32	3.83	4.11
4th quarter	4.6	73.1	6.6	87.3	2.60	2.63	2.33	2.35	3.86	4.16
1998										
1st quarter	5.6	99.5	6.2	121.1	2.59	2.66	2.33	2.38	3.88	4.21
2nd quarter	-4.9	42.2	-2.6	51.4	2.54	2.63	2.30	2.35	3.82	4.16
3rd quarter	0.5	51.9	3.0	63.9	2.50	2.63	2.27	2.35	3.76	4.14
4th quarter	3.8	56.2	0.9	69.1	2.46	2.60	2.24	2.32	3.69	4.07
1999										
1st quarter	4.1	79.3	-1.9	97.5	2.47	2.62	2.25	2.35	3.71	4.12
2nd quarter	-0.2	35.3	1.1	43.6	2.45	2.60	2.23	2.33	3.68	4.07
3rd quarter	-9.1	49.6	-12.0	60.6	2.46	2.58	2.24	2.32	3.71	4.06
4th quarter	-5.7	90.0	-3.9	109.1	2.48	2.59	2.27	2.33	3.75	4.08
2000										
1st quarter	-17.7	33.9	-20.5	41.0	2.47	2.56	2.26	2.31	3.75	4.05
2nd quarter	5.9	84.5	6.9	101.4	2.47	2.57	2.26	2.32	3.77	4.08
3rd quarter	-1.1	58.4	-2.3	69.7	2.47	2.58	2.27	2.34	3.79	4.10
4th quarter	7.3	47.0	7.9	56.3	2.50	2.59	2.28	2.34	3.83	4.12

1Before 1997, 2005 dollars; 1997 forward, 2009 dollars.

Table 1-8B. Inventory Change and Inventory-Sales Ratios: Historical Data—*Continued*

(Quarterly dollar data are at seasonally adjusted annual rates.)

NIPA Tables 5.7.5B, 5.7.6B, 5.8.5B, 5.8.6B

Year and quarter	Change in private inventories				Ratio, inventories at end of quarter to monthly rate of sales during the quarter					
	Billions of current dollars		Billions of chained dollars [1]		Total private inventories to final sales of domestic business		Nonfarm inventories to final sales of domestic business		Nonfarm inventories to final sales of goods and structures	
	Farm	Nonfarm	Farm	Nonfarm	Current dollars	Chained dollars[1]	Current dollars	Chained dollars[1]	Current dollars	Chained dollars[1]
2001										
1st quarter	5.6	-36.2	6.7	-43.5	2.48	2.57	2.25	2.32	3.80	4.09
2nd quarter	-3.0	-8.6	-3.3	-9.7	2.43	2.56	2.22	2.31	3.72	4.07
3rd quarter	1.8	-31.9	1.7	-38.0	2.40	2.56	2.19	2.31	3.69	4.07
4th quarter	-4.3	-76.6	-4.6	-92.2	2.32	2.51	2.12	2.26	3.55	3.97
2002										
1st quarter	4.1	-4.3	2.7	-6.1	2.33	2.51	2.12	2.26	3.59	3.99
2nd quarter	-10.3	29.5	-10.9	35.8	2.33	2.51	2.13	2.27	3.63	4.03
3rd quarter	-2.9	28.2	-3.7	35.5	2.34	2.51	2.14	2.27	3.65	4.04
4th quarter	-0.8	30.6	-2.0	36.8	2.37	2.53	2.16	2.29	3.71	4.09
2003										
1st quarter	2.8	28.2	3.3	33.0	2.39	2.53	2.17	2.28	3.74	4.07
2nd quarter	-1.4	1.0	-1.0	0.7	2.34	2.49	2.13	2.26	3.67	4.00
3rd quarter	0.9	7.3	0.2	7.4	2.30	2.44	2.08	2.21	3.54	3.87
4th quarter	-2.1	40.5	-1.9	48.6	2.31	2.43	2.09	2.20	3.56	3.86
2004										
1st quarter	4.4	44.4	5.7	50.7	2.34	2.43	2.11	2.20	3.62	3.89
2nd quarter	18.4	57.8	15.7	65.9	2.37	2.45	2.13	2.21	3.66	3.90
3rd quarter	7.7	54.6	8.4	62.8	2.38	2.44	2.15	2.21	3.69	3.89
4th quarter	4.7	63.4	6.0	70.3	2.38	2.44	2.16	2.21	3.71	3.89
2005										
1st quarter	-6.7	106.2	-5.0	115.8	2.40	2.45	2.18	2.22	3.75	3.91
2nd quarter	0.9	29.7	0.8	32.1	2.36	2.43	2.15	2.20	3.69	3.85
3rd quarter	4.3	13.6	3.3	14.9	2.37	2.41	2.16	2.19	3.70	3.82
4th quarter	2.3	87.9	1.9	92.6	2.42	2.44	2.21	2.21	3.81	3.89
2006										
1st quarter	3.7	70.7	1.7	76.9	2.39	2.42	2.19	2.20	3.75	3.83
2nd quarter	-8.1	85.4	-7.3	90.8	2.42	2.44	2.22	2.22	3.82	3.89
3rd quarter	-6.3	83.4	-6.3	87.7	2.45	2.47	2.24	2.25	3.87	3.96
4th quarter	-3.6	42.7	-4.7	46.2	2.43	2.44	2.23	2.23	3.86	3.93
2007										
1st quarter	5.3	14.9	3.2	16.4	2.45	2.44	2.23	2.23	3.90	3.94
2nd quarter	-5.0	52.0	-3.8	53.2	2.46	2.44	2.24	2.23	3.92	3.94
3rd quarter	-2.3	51.0	-2.0	52.3	2.47	2.44	2.25	2.23	3.94	3.95
4th quarter	-0.8	22.8	-1.1	24.1	2.53	2.43	2.30	2.22	4.07	3.93
2008										
1st quarter	-6.9	-13.3	-4.9	-15.0	2.63	2.44	2.40	2.23	4.27	3.98
2nd quarter	3.9	-27.8	2.2	-28.8	2.72	2.42	2.47	2.21	4.41	3.92
3rd quarter	6.6	-25.4	4.6	-25.7	2.70	2.44	2.45	2.23	4.40	3.97
4th quarter	2.8	-67.9	2.7	-70.4	2.52	2.49	2.29	2.27	4.18	4.13
2009										
1st quarter	-0.3	-145.3	-0.7	-144.2	2.45	2.48	2.22	2.26	4.05	4.13
2nd quarter	-1.0	-186.9	-1.0	-189.3	2.42	2.43	2.20	2.21	4.00	4.04
3rd quarter	-5.0	-200.9	-4.2	-201.6	2.37	2.36	2.15	2.14	3.92	3.89
4th quarter	0.0	-50.8	-0.5	-48.8	2.40	2.35	2.19	2.13	4.03	3.89
2010										
1st quarter	-1.3	13.3	-3.0	12.9	2.45	2.35	2.23	2.13	4.12	3.90
2nd quarter	-5.9	56.1	-5.8	54.6	2.43	2.34	2.21	2.13	4.09	3.89
3rd quarter	-11.6	133.2	-9.9	126.8	2.49	2.37	2.25	2.16	4.19	3.97
4th quarter	-10.5	72.8	-9.5	69.1	2.53	2.35	2.28	2.14	4.22	3.92
2011										
1st quarter	0.5	25.7	0.2	25.2	2.64	2.35	2.37	2.15	4.41	3.95
2nd quarter	-1.3	64.3	-0.2	58.9	2.66	2.35	2.39	2.15	4.44	3.95
3rd quarter	3.8	-18.7	2.1	-15.9	2.62	2.32	2.34	2.12	4.34	3.88
4th quarter	5.3	87.4	3.4	78.3	2.62	2.33	2.33	2.13	4.31	3.86
2012										
1st quarter	-8.6	74.0	-6.6	65.8	2.59	2.32	2.31	2.12	4.23	3.83
2nd quarter	-15.3	104.6	-10.3	92.0	2.56	2.33	2.29	2.14	4.18	3.84
3rd quarter	-31.5	105.5	-19.0	97.7	2.60	2.34	2.33	2.16	4.25	3.88
4th quarter	-22.6	41.0	-14.5	35.3	2.60	2.33	2.34	2.16	4.26	3.86
2013										
1st quarter	5.6	58.0	0.2	50.7	2.57	2.33	2.32	2.15	4.21	3.83
2nd quarter	9.1	55.4	5.0	47.3	2.56	2.33	2.31	2.16	4.20	3.84
3rd quarter	14.1	111.4	8.8	100.4	2.55	2.35	2.31	2.17	4.20	3.86
4th quarter	11.8	104.1	9.9	93.4	2.54	2.34	2.29	2.17	4.17	3.83
2014										
1st quarter	-6.8	50.7	-4.8	45.8	2.61	2.35	2.35	2.17	4.30	3.86
2nd quarter	-3.3	86.0	-3.5	76.5	2.57	2.34	2.32	2.17	4.22	3.83
3rd quarter	-3.8	102.3	-2.0	90.6	2.53	2.33	2.28	2.16	4.15	3.80
4th quarter	-5.4	92.2	-2.8	82.9	2.48	2.33	2.24	2.17	4.10	3.83
2015										
1st quarter	3.5	145.1	2.3	133.0	2.46	2.35	2.22	2.19	4.10	3.90
2nd quarter	0.2	117.9	0.5	107.8	2.44	2.36	2.22	2.20	4.07	3.90
3rd quarter	0.9	104.8	0.6	97.7	2.40	2.37	2.19	2.21	4.03	3.92
4th quarter	-2.7	78.1	-2.6	72.5	2.38	2.38	2.18	2.23	4.03	3.96
2016										
1st quarter	-2.9	45.1	-2.6	44.6	2.37	2.39	2.17	2.23	4.02	3.96
2nd quarter	3.3	8.9	2.6	9.4	2.36	2.37	2.17	2.21	4.03	3.92
3rd quarter	0.6	15.9	0.8	17.1	2.32	2.35	2.15	2.20	4.01	3.90
4th quarter	-3.5	73.0	-2.9	66.8	2.35	2.36	2.17	2.21	4.06	3.93

[1]Before 1997, 2005 dollars; 1997 forward, 2009 dollars.

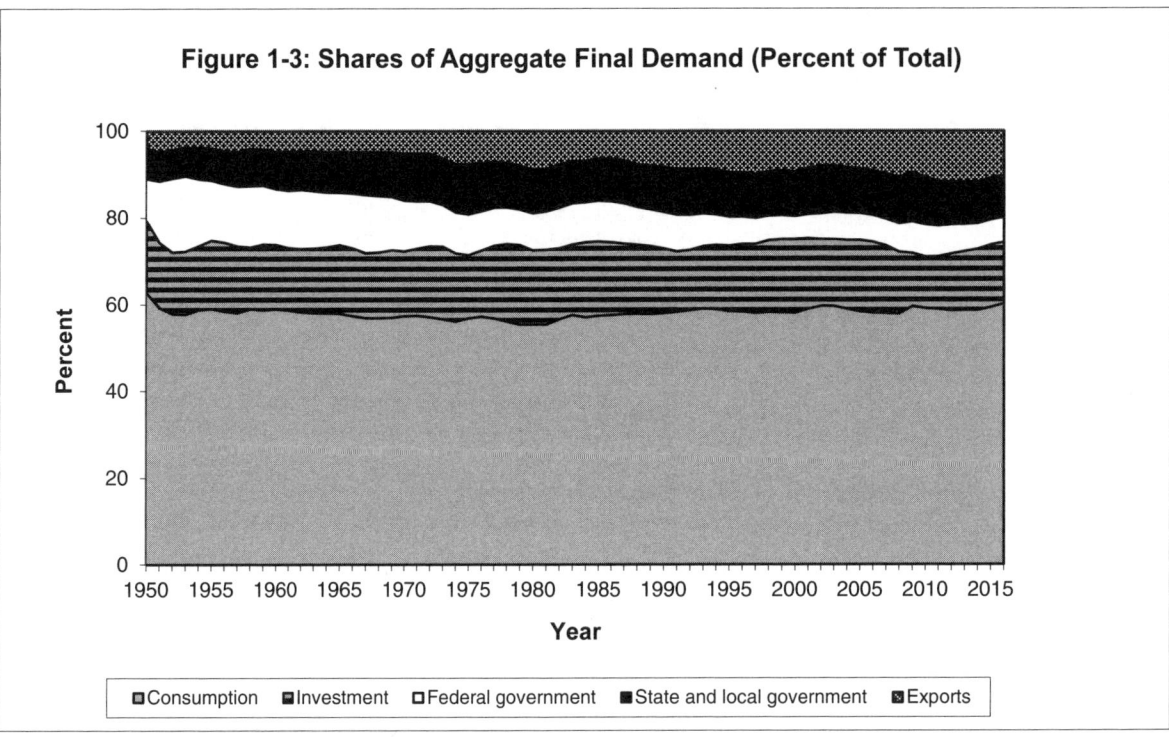

Figure 1-3: Shares of Aggregate Final Demand (Percent of Total)

- People often want to know how various sources of demand, especially consumption spending, affect GDP. Often, it is said that consumption "accounts for" about 70 percent, or sometimes two-thirds, of GDP. That is based on a NIPA table showing the components of GDP as a percent of total GDP. In such a calculation, personal consumption expenditures (PCE) amounted to 68.8 percent of total GDP in 2016, up from a range of 60 to 65 percent earlier in the postwar period. (Table 1-1A)

- Is "amounted to" the same as "accounted for"? No, because the value of PCE includes imported goods and services—coffee, cocoa, and bananas; crude oil from the Middle East, transformed into gasoline; clothing, cars, and toys manufactured overseas—even the money that U.S. consumers spend when they travel. These imports included in PCE don't account for demand for U.S. GDP, which excludes imports; instead, they account for demand for GDP in China and other countries that export to us.

- It is not possible with NIPA data to precisely estimate and subtract out the import content of PCE, and so there is no way to precisely estimate PCE's contribution to GDP. What we can do is calculate PCE and the other sources of aggregate final demand for U.S. output as shares of total final demand; this is shown in Table 1-10 and Figure 1-3. These shares also approximate their contributions to GDP (excluding inventory change) if each final demand source has, in aggregate, about the same percentage import content as total GDP.

- Consumption spending has remained under 60 percent of final demand ever since 1951. (It was greater in 1946 through 1950, as consumers made up for wartime deprivations.) It was near 59 percent in each of the past five years; it has been less in years when investment shares were high. The share of exports has nearly tripled, while the federal government direct spending share remains at less than half of its Korean War highs. (This measure of federal spending does not include government financing of medical care and other consumption spending through transfer payment programs such as Social Security and Medicare.) State and local governments increased their share through the early 1970s. Residential investment was 5.7 percent in 2005, the highest since 1950. By 2016, the ratio had fallen to 3.3 percent but was recovering from low of 2.1 percent in 2011. (Table 1-10)

- The share of imports in the total supply of goods and services in the U.S. market rose from around 4 percent in the 1950s to a high of 14.8 percent in 2011. By 2016, the import share had decreased to 12.8 percent. Only in 2009, the year of maximum inventory liquidation, did the import share temporarily dip back to 12.1 percent. (Table 1-9)

Table 1-9. Shares of Aggregate Supply

(Billions of dollars, quarterly dollar data are at seasonally adjusted rates, percents.) **NIPA Table 1.1.5**

Year and quarter	Aggregate supply (billions of dollars)			Shares of aggregate supply (percent)	
	Total	GDP	Imports	Domestic production (GDP)	Imports
1950	311.8	300.2	11.6	96.3	3.7
1951	361.9	347.3	14.6	96.0	4.0
1952	383.0	367.7	15.3	96.0	4.0
1953	405.7	389.7	16.0	96.1	3.9
1954	406.5	391.1	15.4	96.2	3.8
1955	443.4	426.2	17.2	96.1	3.9
1956	469.0	450.1	18.9	96.0	4.0
1957	494.8	474.9	19.9	96.0	4.0
1958	502.0	482.0	20.0	96.0	4.0
1959	544.8	522.5	22.3	95.9	4.1
1960	566.1	543.3	22.8	96.0	4.0
1961	586.0	563.3	22.7	96.1	3.9
1962	630.1	605.1	25.0	96.0	4.0
1963	664.7	638.6	26.1	96.1	3.9
1964	713.9	685.8	28.1	96.1	3.9
1965	775.2	743.7	31.5	95.9	4.1
1966	852.1	815.0	37.1	95.6	4.4
1967	901.6	861.7	39.9	95.6	4.4
1968	989.1	942.5	46.6	95.3	4.7
1969	1 070.4	1 019.9	50.5	95.3	4.7
1970	1 131.7	1 075.9	55.8	95.1	4.9
1971	1 230.1	1 167.8	62.3	94.9	5.1
1972	1 356.6	1 282.4	74.2	94.5	5.5
1973	1 519.7	1 428.5	91.2	94.0	6.0
1974	1 676.3	1 548.8	127.5	92.4	7.6
1975	1 811.6	1 688.9	122.7	93.2	6.8
1976	2 028.7	1 877.6	151.1	92.6	7.4
1977	2 268.4	2 086.0	182.4	92.0	8.0
1978	2 568.9	2 356.6	212.3	91.7	8.3
1979	2 884.8	2 632.1	252.7	91.2	8.8
1980	3 156.3	2 862.5	293.8	90.7	9.3
1981	3 528.8	3 211.0	317.8	91.0	9.0
1982	3 648.2	3 345.0	303.2	91.7	8.3
1983	3 966.7	3 638.1	328.6	91.7	8.3
1984	4 445.8	4 040.7	405.1	90.9	9.1
1985	4 763.9	4 346.7	417.2	91.2	8.8
1986	5 043.1	4 590.2	452.9	91.0	9.0
1987	5 378.9	4 870.2	508.7	90.5	9.5
1988	5 806.6	5 252.6	554.0	90.5	9.5
1989	6 248.7	5 657.7	591.0	90.5	9.5
1990	6 609.3	5 979.6	629.7	90.5	9.5
1991	6 797.5	6 174.0	623.5	90.8	9.2
1992	7 207.1	6 539.3	667.8	90.7	9.3
1993	7 598.7	6 878.7	720.0	90.5	9.5
1994	8 122.2	7 308.8	813.4	90.0	10.0
1995	8 566.7	7 664.1	902.6	89.5	10.5
1996	9 064.2	8 100.2	964.0	89.4	10.6
1997	9 664.3	8 608.5	1 055.8	89.1	10.9
1998	10 204.9	9 089.2	1 115.7	89.1	10.9
1999	10 909.2	9 660.6	1 248.6	88.6	11.4
2000	11 757.4	10 284.8	1 472.6	87.5	12.5
2001	12 017.2	10 621.8	1 395.4	88.4	11.6
2002	12 406.5	10 977.5	1 429.0	88.5	11.5
2003	13 054.6	11 510.7	1 543.9	88.2	11.8
2004	14 075.6	12 274.9	1 800.7	87.2	12.8
2005	15 123.8	13 093.7	2 030.1	86.6	13.4
2006	16 103.2	13 855.9	2 247.3	86.0	14.0
2007	16 860.8	14 477.6	2 383.2	85.9	14.1
2008	17 283.6	14 718.6	2 565.0	85.2	14.8
2009	16 401.9	14 418.7	1 983.2	87.9	12.1
2010	17 329.4	14 964.4	2 365.0	86.4	13.6
2011	18 204.3	15 517.9	2 686.4	85.2	14.8
2012	18 919.1	16 155.3	2 763.8	85.4	14.6
2013	19 460.1	16 691.5	2 768.6	85.8	14.2
2014	20 310.8	17 427.6	2 883.2	85.8	14.2
2015	20 909.7	18 120.7	2 789.0	86.7	13.3
2016	21 360.3	18 624.5	2 735.8	87.2	12.8
2014					
1st quarter	19 887.7	17 031.3	2 856.4	85.6	14.4
2nd quarter	20 224.8	17 320.9	2 903.9	85.6	14.4
3rd quarter	20 500.4	17 622.3	2 878.1	86.0	14.0
4th quarter	20 630.1	17 735.9	2 894.2	86.0	14.0
2015					
1st quarter	20 702.0	17 874.7	2 827.3	86.3	13.7
2nd quarter	20 904.2	18 093.2	2 811.0	86.6	13.4
3rd quarter	21 015.1	18 227.7	2 787.4	86.7	13.3
4th quarter	21 017.4	18 287.2	2 730.2	87.0	13.0
2016					
1st quarter	21 018.0	18 325.2	2 692.8	87.2	12.8
2nd quarter	21 241.4	18 538.0	2 703.4	87.3	12.7
3rd quarter	21 470.4	18 729.1	2 741.3	87.2	12.8
4th quarter	21 711.3	18 905.5	2 805.8	87.1	12.9

Table 1-10. Shares of Aggregate Final Demand

(Billions of dollars, quarterly dollar data are at seasonally adjusted rates, percents.)

NIPA Table 1.1.5

Year and quarter	Aggregate final demand (billions of dollars)							Shares of aggregate final demand (percent)					
	Total	Consumption (PCE)	Nonresidential fixed investment	Residential investment	Exports	Government consumption and gross investment		PCE	Nonresidential investment	Residential investment	Exports	Federal government	State and local government
						Federal	State and local						
1950	306.1	192.2	30.0	20.7	12.4	29.5	21.3	62.8	9.8	6.8	4.1	9.6	7.0
1951	352.1	208.5	34.2	18.7	17.1	50.0	23.6	59.2	9.7	5.3	4.9	14.2	6.7
1952	379.6	219.5	34.9	18.9	16.5	64.8	25.0	57.8	9.2	5.0	4.3	17.1	6.6
1953	403.8	233.0	38.8	19.7	15.3	70.3	26.7	57.7	9.6	4.9	3.8	17.4	6.6
1954	408.5	239.9	38.6	21.4	15.8	63.3	29.5	58.7	9.4	5.2	3.9	15.5	7.2
1955	438.4	258.7	43.4	25.4	17.7	61.0	32.2	59.0	9.9	5.8	4.0	13.9	7.3
1956	465.1	271.6	49.7	24.0	21.3	63.1	35.4	58.4	10.7	5.2	4.6	13.6	7.6
1957	493.9	286.7	53.1	22.6	24.0	68.4	39.1	58.0	10.8	4.6	4.9	13.8	7.9
1958	502.4	296.0	48.5	22.8	20.6	71.5	43.0	58.9	9.7	4.5	4.1	14.2	8.6
1959	540.7	317.5	53.1	28.6	22.7	73.5	45.3	58.7	9.8	5.3	4.2	13.6	8.4
1960	562.9	331.6	56.4	26.9	27.0	72.8	48.2	58.9	10.0	4.8	4.8	12.9	8.6
1961	583.1	342.0	56.6	27.0	27.0	77.4	52.5	58.7	9.7	4.6	4.7	13.3	9.0
1962	623.9	363.1	61.2	29.6	29.1	85.5	55.4	58.2	9.8	4.7	4.7	13.7	8.9
1963	659.1	382.5	64.8	32.9	31.1	87.8	60.0	58.0	9.8	5.0	4.7	13.3	9.1
1964	709.0	411.2	72.2	35.1	35.0	90.2	65.3	58.0	10.2	5.0	4.9	12.7	9.2
1965	765.9	443.6	85.2	35.2	37.1	93.1	71.7	57.9	11.1	4.6	4.8	12.2	9.4
1966	838.4	480.6	97.2	33.4	40.9	106.5	79.8	57.3	11.6	4.0	4.9	12.7	9.5
1967	891.8	507.4	99.2	33.6	43.5	120.0	88.1	56.9	11.1	3.8	4.9	13.5	9.9
1968	979.9	557.4	107.7	40.2	47.9	127.9	98.8	56.9	11.0	4.1	4.9	13.1	10.1
1969	1 061.2	604.5	120.0	44.4	51.9	131.1	109.3	57.0	11.3	4.2	4.9	12.4	10.3
1970	1 129.5	647.7	124.6	43.4	59.7	132.7	121.4	57.3	11.0	3.8	5.3	11.7	10.7
1971	1 221.9	701.0	130.4	58.2	63.0	134.4	134.9	57.4	10.7	4.8	5.2	11.0	11.0
1972	1 347.4	769.4	146.6	72.4	70.8	141.5	146.7	57.1	10.9	5.4	5.3	10.5	10.9
1973	1 503.8	851.1	172.7	78.3	95.3	145.6	160.8	56.6	11.5	5.2	6.3	9.7	10.7
1974	1 662.4	932.0	191.1	69.5	126.7	158.1	185.0	56.1	11.5	4.2	7.6	9.5	11.1
1975	1 818.0	1 032.8	196.8	66.7	138.7	172.8	210.2	56.8	10.8	3.7	7.6	9.5	11.6
1976	2 011.7	1 150.2	219.3	86.8	149.5	183.8	222.1	57.2	10.9	4.3	7.4	9.1	11.0
1977	2 246.2	1 276.7	259.1	115.2	159.4	198.8	237.0	56.8	11.5	5.1	7.1	8.9	10.6
1978	2 543.1	1 426.2	314.6	138.0	186.9	216.7	260.7	56.1	12.4	5.4	7.3	8.5	10.3
1979	2 866.7	1 589.5	373.8	147.8	230.1	237.7	287.8	55.4	13.0	5.2	8.0	8.3	10.0
1980	3 162.7	1 754.6	406.9	129.5	280.8	272.4	318.5	55.5	12.9	4.1	8.9	8.6	10.1
1981	3 498.8	1 937.5	472.9	128.5	305.2	311.7	343.0	55.4	13.5	3.7	8.7	8.9	9.8
1982	3 663.0	2 073.9	485.1	110.8	283.2	345.6	364.4	56.6	13.2	3.0	7.7	9.4	9.9
1983	3 972.6	2 286.5	482.2	161.1	277.0	380.2	385.6	57.6	12.1	4.1	7.0	9.6	9.7
1984	4 380.4	2 498.2	564.3	190.4	302.4	407.6	417.5	57.0	12.9	4.3	6.9	9.3	9.5
1985	4 742.2	2 722.7	607.7	200.1	303.2	449.3	459.2	57.4	12.8	4.2	6.4	9.5	9.7
1986	5 036.5	2 898.4	607.8	234.8	321.0	478.4	496.1	57.5	12.1	4.7	6.4	9.5	9.9
1987	5 351.7	3 092.1	615.2	249.8	363.9	500.2	530.5	57.8	11.5	4.7	6.8	9.3	9.9
1988	5 788.1	3 346.9	662.3	256.2	444.6	508.8	569.3	57.8	11.4	4.4	7.7	8.8	9.8
1989	6 221.0	3 592.8	716.0	256.0	504.3	531.4	620.5	57.8	11.5	4.1	8.1	8.5	10.0
1990	6 594.7	3 825.6	739.2	239.7	551.9	560.0	678.3	58.0	11.2	3.6	8.4	8.5	10.3
1991	6 798.0	3 960.2	723.6	221.2	594.9	580.7	717.4	58.3	10.6	3.3	8.8	8.5	10.6
1992	7 190.8	4 215.7	741.9	254.7	633.1	586.6	758.8	58.6	10.3	3.5	8.8	8.2	10.6
1993	7 577.9	4 471.0	799.2	286.6	654.8	578.4	787.7	59.0	10.5	3.8	8.6	7.6	10.4
1994	8 058.4	4 741.0	868.9	323.8	720.9	572.7	831.1	58.8	10.8	4.0	8.9	7.1	10.3
1995	8 535.5	4 984.2	962.2	324.1	812.8	575.4	876.8	58.4	11.3	3.8	9.5	6.7	10.3
1996	9 033.4	5 268.1	1 043.2	358.1	867.6	578.2	918.2	58.3	11.5	4.0	9.6	6.4	10.2
1997	9 593.4	5 560.7	1 149.1	375.6	953.8	582.4	971.8	58.0	12.0	3.9	9.9	6.1	10.1
1998	10 141.1	5 903.0	1 252.8	418.8	953.0	584.1	1 029.4	58.2	12.4	4.1	9.4	5.8	10.2
1999	10 848.4	6 307.0	1 361.6	461.8	992.0	610.4	1 115.6	58.1	12.6	4.3	9.1	5.6	10.3
2000	11 702.8	6 792.4	1 493.8	485.4	1 096.8	632.4	1 202.0	58.0	12.8	4.1	9.4	5.4	10.3
2001	12 055.4	7 103.1	1 453.9	513.0	1 026.7	669.2	1 289.5	58.9	12.1	4.3	8.5	5.6	10.7
2002	12 388.0	7 384.1	1 348.9	557.6	1 002.5	740.6	1 354.3	59.6	10.9	4.5	8.1	6.0	10.9
2003	13 035.2	7 765.5	1 371.7	636.9	1 040.3	824.8	1 396.0	59.6	10.5	4.9	8.0	6.3	10.7
2004	14 011.7	8 260.0	1 463.1	749.7	1 181.5	892.4	1 465.0	59.0	10.4	5.4	8.4	6.4	10.5
2005	15 064.3	8 794.1	1 611.5	856.1	1 308.9	946.3	1 547.4	58.4	10.7	5.7	8.7	6.3	10.3
2006	16 036.2	9 304.0	1 776.3	837.4	1 476.3	1 002.0	1 640.2	58.0	11.1	5.2	9.2	6.2	10.2
2007	16 826.4	9 750.5	1 920.6	688.7	1 664.6	1 049.8	1 752.2	57.9	11.4	4.1	9.9	6.2	10.4
2008	17 315.6	10 013.6	1 941.0	515.9	1 841.9	1 155.6	1 847.6	57.8	11.2	3.0	10.6	6.7	10.7
2009	16 549.4	9 847.0	1 633.4	392.2	1 587.7	1 217.7	1 871.4	59.5	9.9	2.4	9.6	7.4	11.3
2010	17 267.9	10 202.2	1 658.2	381.1	1 852.3	1 303.9	1 870.2	59.1	9.6	2.2	10.7	7.6	10.8
2011	18 162.6	10 689.3	1 812.1	386.0	2 106.4	1 303.5	1 865.3	58.9	10.0	2.1	11.6	7.2	10.3
2012	18 857.3	11 050.6	2 007.7	442.2	2 198.2	1 292.5	1 866.1	58.6	10.6	2.3	11.7	6.9	9.9
2013	19 367.8	11 361.2	2 094.4	519.5	2 276.6	1 229.5	1 886.6	58.7	10.8	2.7	11.8	6.3	9.7
2014	20 232.8	11 863.7	2 268.3	570.2	2 373.6	1 218.1	1 938.9	58.6	11.2	2.8	11.7	6.0	9.6
2015	20 797.7	12 332.3	2 336.2	645.4	2 264.9	1 224.0	1 994.9	59.3	11.2	3.1	10.9	5.9	9.6
2016	21 325.3	12 820.7	2 316.3	705.9	2 214.6	1 231.5	2 036.3	60.1	10.9	3.3	10.4	5.8	9.5
2014													
1st quarter	19 844.0	11 640.2	2 194.7	542.2	2 340.0	1 216.6	1 910.3	58.7	11.1	2.7	11.8	6.1	9.6
2nd quarter	20 142.2	11 791.9	2 251.5	560.8	2 391.3	1 215.5	1 931.2	58.5	11.2	2.8	11.9	6.0	9.6
3rd quarter	20 401.7	11 941.1	2 316.0	577.4	2 389.0	1 228.3	1 949.9	58.5	11.4	2.8	11.7	6.0	9.6
4th quarter	20 543.3	12 081.4	2 310.9	600.2	2 374.4	1 212.2	1 964.2	58.8	11.2	2.9	11.6	5.9	9.6
2015													
1st quarter	20 553.4	12 142.2	2 328.6	617.4	2 289.0	1 218.7	1 957.5	59.1	11.3	3.0	11.1	5.9	9.5
2nd quarter	20 786.0	12 284.2	2 343.2	635.0	2 303.9	1 224.9	1 994.8	59.1	11.3	3.1	11.1	5.9	9.6
3rd quarter	20 909.5	12 407.8	2 353.5	656.5	2 256.6	1 222.6	2 012.5	59.3	11.3	3.1	10.8	5.8	9.6
4th quarter	20 942.0	12 494.9	2 319.7	672.6	2 210.1	1 229.9	2 014.8	59.7	11.1	3.2	10.6	5.9	9.6
2016													
1st quarter	20 975.8	12 571.5	2 291.2	698.3	2 166.5	1 227.9	2 020.4	59.9	10.9	3.3	10.3	5.9	9.6
2nd quarter	21 229.2	12 755.0	2 311.2	699.7	2 201.8	1 228.2	2 033.3	60.1	10.9	3.3	10.4	5.8	9.6
3rd quarter	21 453.9	12 899.4	2 329.1	702.4	2 248.4	1 234.6	2 040.0	60.1	10.9	3.3	10.5	5.8	9.5
4th quarter	21 641.9	13 056.9	2 333.7	723.0	2 241.5	1 235.4	2 051.4	60.3	10.8	3.3	10.4	5.7	9.5

SECTION 1B: INCOME AND VALUE ADDED

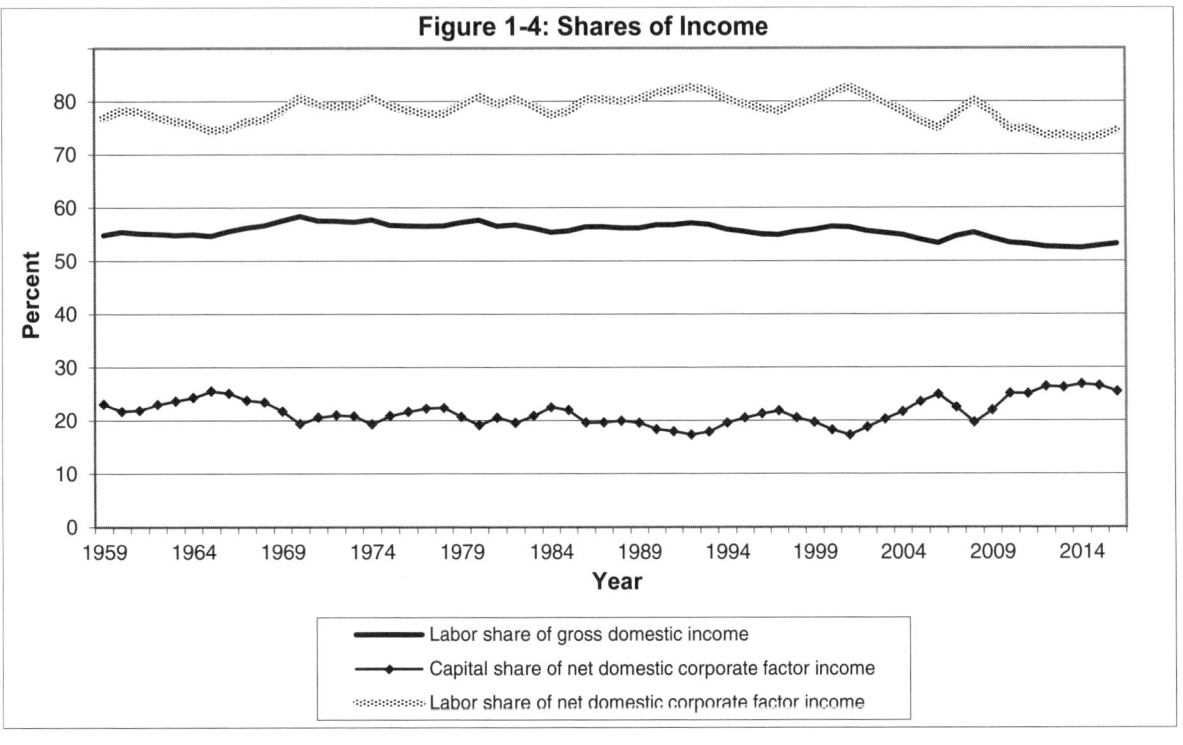

Figure 1-4: Shares of Income

- Recent years have seen a decline in the share of national income paid to workers—not just the share paid out as worker wages, but in total compensation, including all health and other benefits. One indicator of this can be seen in a later chapter, in Tables 9-3A and B, where Bureau of Labor Statistics calculations (based on BEA data) document a declining labor share in the value of output of private nonfarm business. In the tables in Section 1b immediately following this page, BEA compilations show the composition of domestic income, national income, and corporate value added. Table 1-16 shows income share percentages calculated by the editors based on these data. Labor shares rise temporarily in recession years (when the "pie" is smaller) but aside from that effect they have declined over much of the period, and the decline has accelerated in recent years.

- Employee compensation has fallen since the early 1970s to a record low of 52.5 percent in 2014, as shown in the middle line in Figure 1-4. In 2016, the share grew to 53.2 percent. One factor in this decline has been a rising share of output required to replace used-up capital ("consumption of fixed capital"), reflecting increased use of capital per unit of production. In addition, the "net operating surplus," which is largely profits, interest, and proprietor's income, reached a new peak in 2014 at 26.9. (Tables 1-12 and 1-16)

- Narrowing the focus to the corporate business sector, net income shares become clearer. (Proprietor's, i.e. unincorporated business; income includes a labor compensation component of uncertain size.) Total net factor income (that is, net of capital consumption) can be completely attributed to either labor or capital. These shares are also charted in Figure 1-4. Between 1959 and 2004, the shares vary cyclically but seem stable over time, averaging 78.4 percent for labor and 21.6 percent for capital. Since then, they have broken out of that range. The capital share did dip in 2008 to 19.7, to a level higher than in any previous recession, and it reached a new high of 26.9 percent in 2014. Labor's share rose to 74.5 percent in 2016. (Tables 1-14 and 1-16)

Table 1-11. Relation of Gross Domestic Product, Gross and Net National Product, National Income, and Personal Income

(Billions of dollars, quarterly data are at seasonally adjusted annual rates.)   **NIPA Table 1.7.5**

Year and quarter	Gross domestic product	Plus: Income receipts from the rest of the world	Less: Income payments to the rest of the world	Equals: Gross national product	Less: Consumption of fixed capital										Equals: Net national product
					Total	Private					Government				
						Total	Domestic business			House-holds and institutions	Total	General govern-ment	Govern-ment enter-prises		
							Total	Capital consump-tion allow-ances	Less: Capital consump-tion ad-justment						
1955	426.2	3.5	1.1	428.6	48.9	35.0	28.9	28.3	-0.6	6.1	13.9	13.1	0.8	379.7
1956	450.1	3.9	1.1	452.9	54.1	38.8	32.2	30.8	-1.3	6.6	15.3	14.5	0.9	398.8
1957	474.9	4.3	1.2	477.9	58.9	42.3	35.2	33.5	-1.7	7.1	16.7	15.7	0.9	410.0
1958	482.0	3.9	1.2	484.7	62.4	44.9	37.5	35.3	-2.3	7.4	17.5	16.5	1.0	422.2
1959	522.5	4.3	1.5	525.2	65.4	46.8	39.0	37.5	-1.5	7.8	18.6	17.6	1.0	459.8
1960	543.3	4.9	1.8	546.4	67.9	48.2	40.0	39.7	-0.3	8.2	19.7	18.6	1.1	478.5
1961	563.3	5.3	1.8	566.8	70.6	49.8	41.3	41.7	0.4	8.5	20.8	19.7	1.2	496.2
1962	605.1	5.9	1.8	609.2	74.1	51.8	42.9	46.6	3.6	8.8	22.3	21.1	1.2	535.1
1963	638.6	6.5	2.1	643.1	78.0	54.2	44.9	49.9	5.0	9.3	23.8	22.5	1.3	565.1
1964	685.8	7.2	2.3	690.7	82.4	57.3	47.4	53.2	5.8	9.9	25.1	23.7	1.4	608.3
1965	743.7	7.9	2.6	749.0	88.0	61.6	50.9	57.0	6.1	10.7	26.4	24.9	1.5	661.0
1966	815.0	8.1	3.0	820.1	95.3	67.2	55.6	61.9	6.2	11.5	28.1	26.5	1.6	724.8
1967	861.7	8.7	3.3	867.1	103.5	73.3	60.9	66.9	6.0	12.4	30.2	28.4	1.8	763.6
1968	942.5	10.1	4.0	948.6	113.3	80.6	67.0	72.5	5.6	13.6	32.7	30.8	2.0	835.2
1969	1 019.9	11.8	5.7	1 026.0	124.9	89.4	74.2	79.7	5.5	15.2	35.4	33.2	2.2	901.1
1970	1 075.9	12.8	6.4	1 082.3	136.8	98.3	81.8	85.9	4.1	16.5	38.5	36.1	2.5	945.5
1971	1 167.8	14.0	6.4	1 175.4	148.9	107.6	89.4	92.3	2.9	18.2	41.2	38.4	2.8	1 026.5
1972	1 282.4	16.3	7.7	1 291.0	160.9	117.5	97.2	102.3	5.2	20.3	43.4	40.3	3.1	1 130.1
1973	1 428.5	23.5	10.9	1 441.2	178.1	131.5	108.2	111.9	3.7	23.3	46.6	43.1	3.5	1 263.1
1974	1 548.8	29.8	14.3	1 564.3	206.2	153.2	126.1	123.9	-2.2	27.0	53.0	48.7	4.3	1 358.2
1975	1 688.9	28.0	15.0	1 701.9	237.5	178.8	147.9	135.9	-12.0	30.9	58.7	53.7	5.1	1 464.4
1976	1 877.6	32.4	15.5	1 894.4	259.2	196.5	162.2	147.4	-14.8	34.3	62.7	57.2	5.5	1 635.2
1977	2 086.0	37.2	16.9	2 106.2	288.3	221.1	181.5	167.0	-14.5	39.6	67.2	61.2	6.0	1 817.9
1978	2 356.6	46.3	24.7	2 378.2	325.1	252.1	205.5	189.4	-16.2	46.6	72.9	66.3	6.7	2 053.1
1979	2 632.1	68.3	36.4	2 664.1	371.1	290.7	236.4	216.1	-20.2	54.4	80.4	72.8	7.6	2 292.9
1980	2 862.5	79.1	44.9	2 896.7	426.0	335.0	272.8	245.8	-26.9	62.2	91.0	82.3	8.8	2 470.7
1981	3 211.0	92.0	59.1	3 243.9	485.0	381.9	313.5	301.2	-12.3	68.5	103.1	93.1	10.0	2 758.8
1982	3 345.0	101.0	64.5	3 381.5	534.3	420.4	347.5	343.1	-4.4	72.9	113.9	103.1	10.9	2 847.2
1983	3 638.1	101.9	64.8	3 675.2	560.5	438.8	362.8	385.6	22.8	76.0	121.8	110.3	11.5	3 114.7
1984	4 040.7	121.9	85.6	4 077.0	594.3	463.5	382.7	435.6	52.9	80.9	130.8	118.7	12.2	3 482.6
1985	4 346.7	112.7	87.3	4 372.1	636.7	496.4	410.3	493.5	83.2	86.2	140.2	127.3	12.9	3 735.4
1986	4 590.2	111.3	94.4	4 607.1	682.2	531.6	438.1	512.0	73.9	93.4	150.6	136.8	13.8	3 924.9
1987	4 870.2	123.3	105.8	4 887.7	728.0	566.3	464.5	533.1	68.6	101.8	161.6	147.0	14.6	4 159.8
1988	5 252.6	152.1	129.5	5 275.3	782.4	608.3	498.4	563.7	65.3	109.9	174.1	158.5	15.6	4 492.9
1989	5 657.7	177.7	152.9	5 682.5	836.1	650.1	531.8	589.5	57.7	118.2	186.0	169.3	16.7	4 846.4
1990	5 979.6	188.8	154.2	6 014.3	886.8	689.0	563.9	596.0	32.1	125.1	197.8	180.0	17.9	5 127.5
1991	6 174.0	168.4	136.8	6 205.6	931.1	722.4	591.8	611.6	19.8	130.6	208.8	189.9	18.8	5 274.5
1992	6 539.3	152.1	121.0	6 570.4	959.7	744.2	607.9	628.4	20.5	136.3	215.6	195.8	19.8	5 610.7
1993	6 878.7	155.6	123.6	6 910.7	1 003.6	780.0	634.2	658.9	24.7	145.7	223.6	202.5	21.1	5 907.1
1994	7 308.8	184.5	160.7	7 332.6	1 055.6	824.3	669.0	701.6	32.6	155.3	231.2	208.9	22.4	6 277.0
1995	7 664.1	229.8	201.1	7 692.8	1 122.8	882.6	717.8	753.9	36.2	164.8	240.2	216.6	23.6	6 570.0
1996	8 100.2	246.4	214.6	8 132.0	1 176.0	931.0	758.4	808.3	50.0	172.7	245.0	220.4	24.6	6 956.0
1997	8 608.5	280.1	256.0	8 632.6	1 240.0	990.1	807.9	877.0	69.1	182.1	249.9	224.6	25.3	7 392.7
1998	9 089.2	286.8	268.5	9 107.4	1 310.3	1 054.9	860.4	941.4	81.0	194.5	255.3	228.9	26.4	7 797.1
1999	9 660.6	321.4	294.3	9 687.8	1 400.9	1 135.9	925.0	1 023.8	98.9	210.9	264.9	236.9	28.0	8 286.9
2000	10 284.8	382.7	345.7	10 321.8	1 514.2	1 236.6	1 006.5	1 096.1	89.5	230.1	277.7	247.7	30.0	8 807.5
2001	10 621.8	325.3	273.5	10 673.6	1 604.0	1 317.7	1 067.5	1 180.1	112.6	250.2	286.3	254.9	31.4	9 069.6
2002	10 977.5	315.8	267.2	11 026.1	1 662.1	1 368.0	1 101.4	1 284.9	183.5	266.6	294.1	261.2	32.9	9 364.0
2003	11 510.7	356.1	289.0	11 577.8	1 727.2	1 422.4	1 131.6	1 305.4	173.9	290.8	304.9	270.3	34.6	9 850.6
2004	12 274.9	451.4	362.3	12 364.1	1 831.7	1 509.3	1 185.9	1 335.4	149.4	323.4	322.4	284.9	37.5	10 532.4
2005	13 093.7	575.8	483.2	13 186.3	1 982.0	1 635.3	1 273.2	1 174.2	-99.0	362.1	346.7	305.6	41.0	11 204.3
2006	13 855.9	724.2	656.6	13 923.5	2 136.0	1 765.0	1 368.8	1 250.0	-118.8	396.2	371.0	326.6	44.4	11 787.5
2007	14 477.6	875.7	750.1	14 603.2	2 264.4	1 865.0	1 451.2	1 330.0	-121.2	413.7	399.4	351.4	48.0	12 338.9
2008	14 718.6	856.9	684.9	14 890.6	2 363.4	1 936.9	1 522.3	1 584.7	62.4	414.6	426.5	375.5	51.0	12 527.2
2009	14 418.7	648.9	497.8	14 569.8	2 368.4	1 925.7	1 522.4	1 558.6	36.2	403.3	442.7	390.3	52.5	12 201.4
2010	14 964.4	720.0	514.1	15 170.3	2 381.6	1 923.5	1 523.0	1 599.9	76.9	400.5	458.1	403.8	54.3	12 788.8
2011	15 517.9	792.6	546.0	15 764.6	2 450.6	1 971.1	1 572.8	1 823.4	250.6	398.2	479.6	422.1	57.5	13 313.9
2012	16 155.3	801.5	563.9	16 392.8	2 534.2	2 038.0	1 633.4	1 652.2	18.8	404.6	496.2	436.1	60.1	13 858.6
2013	16 691.5	825.5	581.3	16 935.8	2 628.9	2 122.4	1 694.7	1 731.7	37.0	427.7	506.5	444.5	62.0	14 306.9
2014	17 427.6	847.2	612.6	17 662.1	2 748.0	2 231.2	1 775.0	1 837.1	62.1	456.1	516.9	453.0	63.9	14 914.1
2015	18 120.7	812.9	608.4	18 325.2	2 841.5	2 319.6	1 846.9	1 946.9	100.0	472.7	521.9	456.7	65.2	15 483.7
2016	18 624.5	844.3	647.2	18 821.6	2 916.7	2 390.5	1 895.3	2 005.6	110.3	495.3	526.2	459.8	66.4	15 904.8

Table 1-11. Relation of Gross Domestic Product, Gross and Net National Product, National Income, and Personal Income—*Continued*

(Billions of dollars, quarterly data are at seasonally adjusted annual rates.)   NIPA Table 1.7.5

Year and quarter	Net national product	Less: Statistical discrepancy	Equals: National income	Corporate profits with IVA and CCAdj	Taxes on production and imports less subsidies	Contributions for government social insurance, domestic	Net interest and miscellaneous payments on assets	Business current transfer payments, net	Current surplus of government enterprises	Personal income receipts on assets	Personal current transfer receipts	Equals: Personal income	Addendum: Gross national income
						Less:					Plus:		
1955	379.7	2.1	377.6	50.2	31.3	9.1	6.3	1.3	. . .	29.4	15.7	324.6	426.5
1956	398.8	-2.1	400.9	49.6	33.5	10.0	6.9	1.7	. . .	32.4	16.8	348.4	455.0
1957	419.0	-0.4	419.4	49.1	35.5	11.4	8.1	1.8	. . .	35.6	19.5	368.5	478.3
1958	422.2	0.6	421.6	43.9	36.4	11.4	9.6	1.7	. . .	37.3	23.5	379.5	484.1
1959	459.8	0.1	459.6	55.5	40.0	13.8	9.7	1.7	0.5	40.6	24.2	403.2	525.1
1960	478.5	-1.4	479.9	54.7	43.4	16.4	10.7	1.7	0.5	44.3	25.7	422.5	547.8
1961	496.2	-1.0	497.2	55.9	45.0	17.0	12.6	1.9	0.3	47.2	29.5	441.1	567.8
1962	535.1	-0.1	535.2	64.0	48.1	19.1	14.3	2.1	0.4	51.6	30.4	469.1	609.3
1963	565.1	-1.5	566.6	70.5	51.2	21.7	15.3	2.5	0.8	56.0	32.2	492.8	644.6
1964	608.3	0.0	608.3	77.7	54.5	22.4	17.5	3.0	0.8	62.5	33.5	528.4	690.7
1965	661.0	0.8	660.3	89.3	57.7	23.4	19.8	3.5	0.7	68.7	36.2	570.8	748.2
1966	724.8	5.1	719.7	96.1	59.3	31.3	22.5	3.4	0.3	74.2	39.6	620.6	815.0
1967	763.6	3.4	760.2	93.9	64.1	34.9	25.7	3.6	0.2	79.8	48.0	665.7	863.7
1968	835.2	3.2	832.1	101.7	72.2	38.7	27.6	4.2	0.3	87.3	56.1	730.7	945.4
1969	901.1	1.6	899.5	98.4	79.3	44.1	33.6	4.8	0.0	98.7	62.3	800.3	1 024.4
1970	945.5	5.3	940.1	86.2	86.6	46.4	40.5	4.4	-1.2	112.7	74.7	864.6	1 076.9
1971	1 026.5	9.5	1 017.0	100.6	95.8	51.2	45.2	4.2	-1.7	122.3	88.1	932.1	1 165.9
1972	1 130.1	7.1	1 123.0	117.2	101.3	59.2	49.3	4.8	-1.2	133.3	97.9	1 023.6	1 283.9
1973	1 263.1	6.1	1 257.0	133.4	112.0	75.5	57.2	5.7	-2.2	150.6	112.6	1 138.5	1 435.1
1974	1 358.2	7.4	1 350.8	125.7	121.6	85.2	73.5	6.8	-2.7	175.4	133.3	1 249.3	1 550.9
1975	1 464.4	13.2	1 451.1	138.9	130.8	89.3	85.9	9.0	-4.4	195.3	170.0	1 366.9	1 688.7
1976	1 635.2	20.5	1 614.8	174.3	141.3	101.3	89.9	9.1	-2.7	212.6	184.3	1 498.5	1 874.0
1977	1 817.9	19.3	1 798.7	205.8	152.6	113.1	105.9	8.1	-3.3	243.4	194.6	1 654.6	2 087.0
1978	2 053.1	23.2	2 029.9	238.6	162.0	131.3	118.8	10.4	-2.8	278.0	209.9	1 859.7	2 355.0
1979	2 292.9	44.8	2 248.2	249.0	171.6	152.7	141.0	12.8	-3.2	318.3	235.6	2 078.2	2 619.3
1980	2 470.7	43.9	2 426.8	223.6	190.5	166.2	186.2	14.0	-5.1	386.0	280.1	2 317.5	2 852.8
1981	2 758.8	36.7	2 722.1	247.5	224.2	195.7	238.4	16.9	-5.2	472.9	319.0	2 596.5	3 207.2
1982	2 847.2	6.8	2 840.4	229.9	225.9	208.9	277.5	19.3	-3.8	541.3	355.5	2 779.5	3 374.7
1983	3 114.7	54.2	3 060.5	279.8	242.0	226.0	291.8	21.7	-2.3	584.3	384.3	2 970.3	3 621.1
1984	3 482.6	38.7	3 444.0	337.9	268.7	257.5	336.1	29.2	-1.4	665.1	400.6	3 281.8	4 038.3
1985	3 735.4	51.3	3 684.2	354.5	286.8	281.4	348.0	34.1	1.3	712.8	425.4	3 516.3	4 320.8
1986	3 924.9	76.7	3 848.2	324.4	298.5	303.4	365.2	36.0	2.0	755.3	451.6	3 725.7	4 530.4
1987	4 159.8	40.6	4 119.2	366.0	317.3	323.1	369.5	33.3	2.2	779.9	468.1	3 955.9	4 847.2
1988	4 492.9	-0.5	4 493.4	414.9	345.0	361.5	394.7	32.8	5.0	839.4	497.5	4 276.3	5 275.8
1989	4 846.4	64.2	4 782.2	414.2	371.4	385.2	442.7	38.3	6.7	951.9	544.2	4 619.9	5 618.3
1990	5 127.5	91.4	5 036.1	417.2	398.0	410.1	450.1	39.2	3.2	991.2	596.9	4 906.4	5 922.9
1991	5 274.5	88.4	5 186.1	451.3	429.6	430.2	408.5	38.9	7.8	985.5	668.1	5 073.4	6 117.3
1992	5 610.7	110.9	5 499.7	475.3	453.3	455.0	383.7	39.7	9.9	982.1	748.0	5 413.0	6 459.5
1993	5 907.1	152.3	5 754.8	522.0	466.4	477.4	371.4	39.4	10.8	983.6	793.0	5 649.0	6 758.4
1994	6 277.0	136.8	6 140.2	621.9	512.7	508.2	365.9	40.7	11.8	1 029.4	829.0	5 937.3	7 195.8
1995	6 570.0	90.6	6 479.5	703.0	523.1	532.8	376.5	45.0	15.6	1 114.0	883.5	6 281.0	7 602.3
1996	6 956.0	56.6	6 899.4	786.1	545.5	555.1	381.9	52.6	16.9	1 176.5	929.2	6 667.0	8 075.4
1997	7 392.7	12.3	7 380.4	865.8	577.8	587.2	414.7	50.1	17.5	1 258.5	954.9	7 080.7	8 620.3
1998	7 797.1	-60.1	7 857.3	804.1	603.1	624.7	477.8	64.1	16.3	1 342.5	983.9	7 593.7	9 167.6
1999	8 286.9	-37.5	8 324.4	830.2	628.4	661.3	488.0	67.8	16.2	1 329.7	1 026.2	7 988.4	9 725.3
2000	8 807.5	-99.5	8 907.0	781.2	662.7	705.8	565.0	85.3	10.7	1 453.5	1 087.3	8 637.1	10 421.3
2001	9 069.6	-115.0	9 184.6	754.0	669.0	733.2	566.4	99.1	5.2	1 441.3	1 192.6	8 991.6	10 788.6
2002	9 364.0	-72.8	9 436.8	907.2	721.2	751.5	490.5	80.7	7.0	1 390.4	1 284.7	9 153.9	11 098.9
2003	9 850.6	-13.6	9 864.2	1 056.4	758.9	779.3	466.2	76.3	3.9	1 420.5	1 347.3	9 491.1	11 591.4
2004	10 532.4	-8.6	10 540.9	1 283.3	817.6	829.2	403.5	81.4	-1.8	1 503.7	1 421.3	10 052.9	12 372.6
2005	11 204.3	-35.5	11 239.8	1 477.7	873.6	873.3	496.8	93.9	-6.4	1 666.5	1 516.7	10 614.0	13 221.8
2006	11 787.5	-217.3	12 004.8	1 646.5	940.5	922.6	580.9	82.6	-9.3	1 938.4	1 614.6	11 393.9	14 140.8
2007	12 338.9	17.5	12 321.4	1 529.0	980.0	961.4	663.4	98.6	-16.4	2 166.6	1 728.1	12 000.2	14 585.7
2008	12 527.2	99.4	12 427.8	1 285.1	989.4	988.2	693.4	114.4	-21.2	2 167.1	1 956.6	12 502.2	14 791.2
2009	12 201.4	75.3	12 126.1	1 397.0	967.8	964.4	563.4	124.9	-20.6	1 818.0	2 147.5	12 094.8	14 494.5
2010	12 788.8	49.2	12 739.5	1 746.4	1 001.2	984.1	489.4	128.5	-22.9	1 739.6	2 324.7	12 477.1	15 121.1
2011	13 313.9	-38.3	13 352.3	1 816.6	1 042.6	917.8	488.1	131.5	-24.5	1 913.9	2 360.5	13 254.5	15 802.9
2012	13 858.6	-203.3	14 061.9	1 998.2	1 074.0	951.6	527.7	104.7	-19.3	2 123.8	2 366.3	13 915.1	16 596.1
2013	14 306.9	-137.9	14 444.8	2 032.9	1 115.6	1 104.6	504.6	118.4	-20.9	2 056.1	2 428.0	14 073.7	17 073.7
2014	14 914.1	-229.9	15 144.0	2 140.6	1 163.6	1 155.3	535.0	138.9	-17.9	2 245.1	2 544.4	14 818.2	17 892.1
2015	15 483.7	-255.9	15 739.6	2 117.5	1 198.5	1 208.0	583.4	165.0	-14.3	2 387.1	2 684.4	15 553.0	18 581.1
2016	15 904.8	-147.2	16 052.0	2 073.5	1 226.2	1 245.3	570.6	164.0	-10.1	2 377.8	2 768.4	15 928.7	18 968.7

. . . = Not available.

Table 1-11. Relation of Gross Domestic Product, Gross and Net National Product, National Income, and Personal Income—*Continued*

(Billions of dollars, quarterly data are at seasonally adjusted annual rates.) **NIPA Table 1.7.5**

Year and quarter	Gross domestic product	Plus: Income receipts from the rest of the world	Less: Income payments to the rest of the world	Equals: Gross national product	Less: Consumption of fixed capital									Equals: Net national product
					Total	Private					Government			
						Total	Domestic business			Households and institutions	Total	General government	Government enterprises	
							Total	Capital consumption allowances	Less: Capital consumption adjustment					
2014														
1st quarter	17 031.3	840.4	599.2	17 272.5	2 706.1	2 191.8	1 742.8	1 792.2	49.4	449.0	514.3	451.1	63.2	14 566.4
2nd quarter	17 320.9	843.0	612.6	17 551.3	2 731.9	2 216.0	1 764.1	1 822.7	58.6	451.9	515.9	452.4	63.6	14 819.4
3rd quarter	17 622.3	858.1	612.6	17 867.7	2 762.6	2 244.7	1 785.7	1 852.7	67.0	458.9	517.9	453.8	64.1	15 105.1
4th quarter	17 735.9	847.2	626.1	17 957.0	2 791.5	2 272.1	1 807.4	1 881.0	73.6	464.7	519.4	454.8	64.6	15 165.5
2015														
1st quarter	17 874.7	814.6	597.6	18 091.6	2 811.7	2 291.6	1 824.5	1 913.5	89.0	467.2	520.1	455.3	64.8	15 279.9
2nd quarter	18 093.2	823.1	630.4	18 285.9	2 829.6	2 308.2	1 839.2	1 936.3	97.1	469.1	521.4	456.2	65.2	15 456.3
3rd quarter	18 227.7	822.0	630.4	18 419.3	2 854.4	2 331.3	1 856.6	1 958.4	101.8	474.7	523.0	457.6	65.4	15 564.9
4th quarter	18 287.2	791.9	575.1	18 504.1	2 870.5	2 347.2	1 867.3	1 979.3	112.0	479.9	523.2	457.8	65.4	15 633.6
2016														
1st quarter	18 325.2	802.8	626.7	18 501.3	2 880.9	2 358.1	1 875.1	1 979.4	104.3	482.9	522.9	457.4	65.5	15 620.3
2nd quarter	18 538.0	843.8	648.8	18 733.0	2 908.3	2 382.3	1 890.8	1 997.4	106.7	491.5	526.1	460.0	66.1	15 824.7
3rd quarter	18 729.1	848.4	660.1	18 917.5	2 927.6	2 400.7	1 900.9	2 014.6	113.7	499.8	526.9	460.3	66.6	15 989.9
4th quarter	18 905.5	882.1	653.1	19 134.5	2 950.0	2 421.2	1 914.3	2 030.9	116.6	506.9	528.8	461.6	67.2	16 184.5

(Billions of dollars, quarterly data are at seasonally adjusted annual rates.) **NIPA Table 1.7.5**

Year and quarter	Net national product	Less: Statistical discrepancy	Equals: National income	Less:						Plus:		Equals: Personal income	Addendum: Gross national income
				Corporate profits with IVA and CCAdj	Taxes on production and imports less subsidies	Contributions for government social insurance, domestic	Net interest and miscellaneous payments on assets	Business current transfer payments, net	Current surplus of government enterprises	Personal income receipts on assets	Personal current transfer receipts		
2014													
1st quarter	14 566.4	-167.7	14 734.1	1 984.6	1 141.8	1 141.5	503.8	116.2	-18.6	2 142.0	2 479.0	14 485.9	17 199.1
2nd quarter	14 819.4	-217.6	15 037.0	2 149.0	1 160.5	1 145.9	522.9	121.6	-18.1	2 227.9	2 530.4	14 713.5	17 538.6
3rd quarter	15 105.1	-205.7	15 310.8	2 196.6	1 171.1	1 157.8	554.3	181.4	-17.5	2 286.9	2 570.8	14 924.8	17 827.9
4th quarter	15 165.5	-328.7	15 494.2	2 232.0	1 180.8	1 175.9	558.8	136.3	-17.5	2 323.7	2 597.3	15 148.7	18 064.6
2015													
1st quarter	15 279.9	-273.0	15 552.9	2 175.5	1 185.6	1 188.3	576.1	137.5	-15.6	2 350.2	2 645.4	15 301.0	18 147.7
2nd quarter	15 456.3	-263.5	15 719.8	2 175.1	1 196.5	1 201.7	587.7	147.4	-15.1	2 406.9	2 682.7	15 516.1	18 356.7
3rd quarter	15 564.9	-219.6	15 784.5	2 135.9	1 200.4	1 210.3	591.8	146.4	-14.1	2 413.8	2 698.0	15 625.5	18 447.2
4th quarter	15 633.6	-267.6	15 901.3	1 983.3	1 211.6	1 231.9	578.0	228.6	-12.4	2 377.5	2 711.4	15 769.2	18 554.9
2016													
1st quarter	15 620.3	-226.1	15 846.5	2 040.8	1 214.4	1 227.5	574.1	163.2	-9.7	2 374.9	2 739.9	15 751.0	18 551.3
2nd quarter	15 824.7	-132.9	15 957.6	1 996.6	1 214.3	1 245.4	568.0	165.0	-10.3	2 371.4	2 760.2	15 910.1	18 670.9
3rd quarter	15 989.9	-195.2	16 185.1	2 101.2	1 233.5	1 258.2	573.7	151.2	-10.1	2 373.2	2 777.4	16 028.0	18 924.4
4th quarter	16 184.5	-34.4	16 218.9	2 155.2	1 242.5	1 250.2	566.5	176.6	-10.2	2 391.6	2 795.9	16 025.7	18 939.9

Table 1-12. Gross Domestic Income by Type of Income

(Billions of dollars, quarterly data are at seasonally adjusted annual rates.)   **NIPA Tables 1.1.5, 1.10**

Year and quarter	Gross domestic income	Compensation of employees			Taxes on production and imports	Less: Subsidies	Net operating surplus					
								Private enterprises				
		Total	Wages and salaries	Supple-ments to wages and salaries			Total	Total	Net interest and miscel-laneous payments, domestic industries	Business current transfer payments, net	Proprietors' income with IVA and CCAdj	Rental income of persons with CCAdj
1955	424.1	231.0	212.2	18.7	31.5	0.2	. . .	112.9	6.1	1.3	44.3	13.4
1956	452.2	249.7	229.1	20.6	34.2	0.7	. . .	114.9	6.9	1.7	45.8	13.7
1957	475.2	263.1	240.0	23.0	36.6	1.1	. . .	117.8	8.1	1.8	47.8	14.1
1958	481.4	265.2	241.4	23.8	37.7	1.4	. . .	117.5	9.5	1.7	50.2	14.8
1959	522.3	286.4	259.9	26.5	41.1	1.1	130.5	129.9	9.6	1.7	50.3	15.6
1960	544.6	302.0	273.0	29.0	44.5	1.1	131.3	130.9	10.5	1.7	50.6	16.5
1961	564.3	311.2	280.7	30.6	47.0	2.0	137.5	137.2	12.2	1.9	53.2	17.2
1962	605.2	333.0	299.5	33.6	50.4	2.3	150.0	149.6	13.9	2.1	55.2	18.0
1963	640.1	351.2	314.9	36.3	53.4	2.2	159.7	158.9	14.8	2.5	56.4	18.7
1964	685.8	376.9	337.8	39.0	57.3	2.7	172.0	171.2	17.0	3.0	59.1	18.8
1965	743.0	406.3	363.8	42.6	60.7	3.0	190.9	190.2	19.2	3.5	63.7	19.3
1966	809.9	450.3	400.3	50.0	63.2	3.9	205.1	204.8	22.0	3.4	67.9	19.9
1967	858.3	482.9	429.0	53.9	67.9	3.8	207.8	207.6	25.1	3.6	69.5	20.3
1968	939.3	532.1	472.0	60.1	76.4	4.2	221.7	221.4	27.1	4.2	73.8	20.1
1969	1 018.3	586.0	518.3	67.7	83.9	4.5	228.1	228.1	34.1	4.8	77.0	20.4
1970	1 070.5	625.1	551.5	73.6	91.4	4.8	222.0	223.2	41.2	4.4	77.8	20.7
1971	1 158.3	667.0	584.5	82.5	100.5	4.7	246.6	248.3	45.5	4.2	83.9	21.9
1972	1 275.3	733.6	638.8	94.9	107.9	6.6	279.5	280.6	50.3	4.8	95.1	22.8
1973	1 422.4	815.1	708.8	106.3	117.2	5.2	317.3	319.5	59.5	5.7	112.5	23.3
1974	1 541.4	890.3	772.3	118.0	124.9	3.3	323.3	326.0	75.4	6.8	112.2	23.3
1975	1 675.7	950.2	814.9	135.3	135.3	4.5	357.1	361.5	87.5	9.0	118.2	22.5
1976	1 857.1	1 051.3	899.8	151.5	146.4	5.1	405.4	408.1	89.6	9.1	131.0	20.6
1977	2 066.7	1 169.0	994.2	174.8	159.7	7.1	456.8	460.1	104.6	8.1	144.5	16.2
1978	2 333.4	1 320.3	1 120.7	199.7	170.9	8.9	526.1	528.9	120.0	10.4	166.0	16.9
1979	2 587.4	1 481.1	1 253.4	227.7	180.1	8.5	563.6	566.8	143.6	12.8	179.4	16.6
1980	2 818.6	1 626.3	1 373.5	252.8	200.3	9.8	575.7	580.8	187.4	14.0	171.6	19.7
1981	3 174.2	1 795.4	1 511.5	283.9	235.6	11.5	669.6	674.8	235.0	16.9	179.7	25.4
1982	3 338.2	1 894.5	1 587.7	306.8	240.9	15.0	683.5	687.3	273.4	19.3	171.2	26.1
1983	3 584.0	2 014.1	1 677.7	336.4	263.3	21.3	767.4	769.7	289.6	21.7	186.3	27.5
1984	4 002.0	2 217.6	1 845.1	372.5	289.8	21.1	921.4	922.8	336.2	29.2	228.2	27.9
1985	4 295.5	2 389.2	1 982.8	406.4	308.1	21.4	982.9	981.6	360.6	34.1	241.1	29.5
1986	4 513.4	2 545.6	2 104.1	441.5	323.4	24.9	987.1	985.2	385.9	36.0	256.5	21.9
1987	4 829.7	2 725.7	2 257.6	468.0	347.5	30.3	1 058.8	1 056.6	398.7	33.3	286.5	20.2
1988	5 253.1	2 950.9	2 440.6	510.3	374.5	29.5	1 174.8	1 169.8	428.2	32.8	325.8	25.1
1989	5 593.5	3 143.9	2 584.3	559.5	398.9	27.4	1 242.1	1 235.4	483.7	38.3	341.9	24.4
1990	5 888.2	3 345.0	2 743.5	601.5	425.0	27.0	1 258.4	1 255.2	489.1	39.2	354.4	31.4
1991	6 085.7	3 454.7	2 817.2	637.5	457.1	27.5	1 270.2	1 262.3	450.6	38.9	356.0	42.0
1992	6 428.4	3 674.1	2 968.5	705.6	483.4	30.1	1 341.3	1 331.4	422.8	39.7	402.4	64.3
1993	6 726.4	3 824.0	3 082.6	741.3	503.1	36.7	1 432.4	1 421.6	413.0	39.4	430.5	93.6
1994	7 171.9	4 014.1	3 240.6	773.5	545.2	32.5	1 589.5	1 577.7	416.0	40.7	459.5	117.5
1995	7 573.5	4 206.7	3 422.1	784.6	557.9	34.8	1 720.9	1 705.3	436.6	45.0	484.5	129.2
1996	8 043.6	4 426.2	3 620.6	805.6	580.8	35.2	1 895.9	1 879.0	447.9	52.6	547.4	147.0
1997	8 596.2	4 719.1	3 881.2	837.8	611.6	33.8	2 059.4	2 041.9	493.7	50.1	587.9	152.0
1998	9 149.3	5 082.4	4 186.2	896.2	639.5	36.4	2 153.6	2 137.3	557.8	64.1	644.2	169.9
1999	9 698.1	5 417.5	4 465.2	952.3	673.6	45.2	2 251.4	2 235.2	575.7	67.8	700.4	183.1
2000	10 384.3	5 863.1	4 832.4	1 030.7	708.6	45.8	2 344.2	2 333.4	667.6	85.3	757.8	187.7
2001	10 736.8	6 053.8	4 961.6	1 092.1	727.7	58.7	2 410.1	2 404.9	677.8	99.1	836.8	207.5
2002	11 050.3	6 149.7	5 004.2	1 145.5	762.6	41.4	2 517.3	2 510.3	592.9	80.7	871.0	217.3
2003	11 524.3	6 372.7	5 146.1	1 226.6	808.0	49.1	2 665.4	2 661.5	557.4	76.3	900.1	238.0
2004	12 283.5	6 748.8	5 431.2	1 317.6	863.9	46.4	2 885.5	2 887.3	510.1	81.4	962.1	255.4
2005	13 129.2	7 097.9	5 703.1	1 394.8	934.5	60.9	3 175.7	3 182.1	632.2	93.9	979.0	238.4
2006	14 073.2	7 513.7	6 068.8	1 444.9	991.9	51.5	3 483.0	3 492.3	758.1	82.6	1 053.7	207.5
2007	14 460.1	7 908.8	6 405.7	1 503.1	1 034.6	54.6	3 307.0	3 323.5	880.7	98.6	979.2	189.4
2008	14 619.2	8 090.0	6 543.6	1 546.4	1 041.9	52.6	3 176.5	3 197.7	916.4	114.4	1 026.5	262.1
2009	14 343.4	7 795.7	6 260.1	1 535.6	1 026.1	58.3	3 211.6	3 232.2	760.9	124.9	973.0	333.7
2010	14 915.2	7 969.5	6 385.6	1 583.9	1 057.1	55.9	3 562.8	3 585.7	670.6	128.5	1 032.7	402.8
2011	15 556.3	8 277.1	6 641.2	1 635.9	1 102.6	60.1	3 785.9	3 810.5	655.2	131.5	1 143.7	485.3
2012	16 358.5	8 618.5	6 938.9	1 679.6	1 132.1	58.0	4 131.7	4 151.0	691.9	104.7	1 241.4	525.3
2013	16 829.5	8 851.9	7 126.1	1 725.8	1 174.9	59.3	4 233.1	4 254.0	662.8	118.4	1 284.7	567.1
2014	17 657.5	9 267.0	7 487.4	1 779.7	1 221.6	58.1	4 478.9	4 496.9	687.4	138.9	1 315.8	611.7
2015	18 376.6	9 720.0	7 870.6	1 849.4	1 255.8	57.3	4 616.6	4 630.9	752.1	165.0	1 318.8	662.5
2016	18 771.6	9 992.2	8 098.8	1 893.4	1 288.0	61.8	4 636.5	4 646.6	754.6	164.0	1 341.9	707.3
2014												
1st quarter	17 199.1	9 129.4	7 370.9	1 758.5	1 200.2	58.4	4 221.7	4 240.4	655.7	116.2	1 292.7	594.3
2nd quarter	17 538.6	9 185.6	7 417.0	1 768.6	1 218.9	58.4	4 460.5	4 478.6	670.9	121.6	1 319.3	606.7
3rd quarter	17 827.9	9 297.8	7 512.9	1 785.0	1 229.4	58.3	4 596.4	4 613.9	705.1	181.4	1 320.0	618.0
4th quarter	18 064.6	9 455.2	7 648.7	1 806.6	1 238.0	57.2	4 637.1	4 654.5	717.9	136.3	1 331.2	627.9
2015												
1st quarter	18 147.7	9 552.7	7 729.4	1 823.3	1 241.8	56.2	4 597.7	4 613.3	737.2	137.5	1 312.8	639.3
2nd quarter	18 356.7	9 667.3	7 825.1	1 842.2	1 253.0	56.5	4 663.3	4 678.4	756.3	147.4	1 313.9	658.4
3rd quarter	18 447.2	9 742.0	7 885.5	1 856.5	1 258.2	57.7	4 650.4	4 664.5	764.7	146.4	1 323.2	670.9
4th quarter	18 554.9	9 918.0	8 042.5	1 875.5	1 270.2	58.6	4 554.8	4 567.3	750.2	228.6	1 325.4	681.4
2016												
1st quarter	18 551.3	9 851.7	7 978.0	1 873.7	1 274.9	60.4	4 604.2	4 614.0	750.8	163.2	1 327.6	697.6
2nd quarter	18 670.9	9 993.1	8 103.7	1 889.4	1 276.4	62.1	4 555.1	4 565.4	748.6	165.0	1 339.5	704.8
3rd quarter	18 924.4	10 095.1	8 191.8	1 903.4	1 296.6	63.0	4 668.1	4 678.2	760.0	151.2	1 346.1	708.1
4th quarter	18 939.9	10 029.0	8 121.9	1 907.1	1 304.1	61.6	4 718.5	4 728.7	759.1	176.6	1 354.6	718.9

. . . = Not available.

Table 1-12. Gross Domestic Income by Type of Income—*Continued*

(Billions of dollars, quarterly data are at seasonally adjusted annual rates.) **NIPA Tables 1.1.5, 1.10**

Year and quarter	Net operating surplus—Continued						Consumption of fixed capital			Statistical discrepancy	Gross domestic product
	Private enterprises—Continued					Current surplus of government enterprises					
	Corporate profits with IVA and CCAdj, domestic industries						Total	Private	Government		
	Total	Taxes on corporate income	Profits after tax								
			Total	Net dividends	Undistributed corporate profits						
1955	47.8	22.0	25.8	8.9	16.9	. . .	48.9	35.0	13.9	2.1	426.2
1956	46.8	22.0	24.8	9.5	15.4	. . .	54.1	38.8	15.3	-2.1	450.1
1957	46.0	21.4	24.6	9.9	14.8	. . .	58.9	42.3	16.7	-0.4	474.9
1958	41.3	19.0	22.4	9.8	12.5	. . .	62.4	44.9	17.5	0.6	482.0
1959	52.8	23.7	29.1	10.7	18.4	0.5	65.4	46.8	18.6	0.1	522.5
1960	51.5	22.8	28.8	11.4	17.4	0.5	67.9	48.2	19.7	-1.4	543.3
1961	52.6	22.9	29.7	11.5	18.2	0.3	70.6	49.8	20.8	-1.0	563.3
1962	60.3	24.1	36.2	12.4	23.8	0.4	74.1	51.8	22.3	-0.1	605.1
1963	66.4	26.4	40.1	13.0	26.5	0.8	78.0	54.2	23.8	-1.5	638.6
1964	73.2	28.2	45.1	15.0	30.1	0.8	82.4	57.3	25.1	0.0	685.8
1965	84.6	31.1	53.5	16.9	36.6	0.7	88.0	61.6	26.4	0.8	743.7
1966	91.6	33.9	57.7	17.8	39.9	0.3	95.3	67.2	28.1	5.1	815.0
1967	89.1	32.9	56.2	18.3	37.9	0.2	103.5	73.3	30.2	3.4	861.7
1968	96.1	39.6	56.5	20.2	36.3	0.3	113.3	80.6	32.7	3.2	942.5
1969	91.8	40.0	51.8	20.4	31.4	0.0	124.9	89.4	35.4	1.6	1 019.9
1970	79.1	34.8	44.4	20.4	24.0	-1.2	136.8	98.3	38.5	5.3	1 075.9
1971	92.8	38.2	54.6	20.3	34.3	-1.7	148.9	107.6	41.2	9.5	1 167.8
1972	107.7	42.3	65.3	21.9	43.4	-1.2	160.9	117.5	43.4	7.1	1 282.4
1973	118.5	50.0	68.5	23.1	45.4	-2.2	178.1	131.5	46.6	6.1	1 428.5
1974	108.2	52.8	55.5	23.5	32.0	-2.7	206.2	153.2	53.0	7.4	1 548.8
1975	124.2	51.6	72.6	26.4	46.2	-4.4	237.5	178.8	58.7	13.2	1 688.9
1976	157.8	65.3	92.5	30.1	62.4	-2.7	259.2	196.5	62.7	20.5	1 877.6
1977	186.7	74.4	112.2	33.7	78.5	-3.3	288.3	221.1	67.2	19.3	2 086.0
1978	215.7	84.9	130.8	39.6	91.2	-2.8	325.1	252.1	72.9	23.2	2 356.6
1979	214.4	90.0	124.4	41.5	82.9	-3.2	371.1	290.7	80.4	44.8	2 632.1
1980	188.1	87.2	100.9	47.3	53.6	-5.1	426.0	335.0	91.0	43.9	2 862.5
1981	217.8	84.3	133.5	58.3	75.2	-5.2	485.0	381.9	103.1	36.7	3 211.0
1982	197.3	66.5	130.8	61.3	69.4	-3.8	534.3	420.4	113.9	6.8	3 345.0
1983	244.7	80.6	164.1	71.3	92.7	-2.3	560.5	438.8	121.8	54.2	3 638.1
1984	301.3	97.5	203.8	78.5	125.3	-1.4	594.3	463.5	130.8	38.7	4 040.7
1985	316.4	99.4	217.0	85.7	131.3	1.3	636.7	496.4	140.2	51.3	4 346.7
1986	284.9	109.7	175.2	88.3	86.9	2.0	682.2	531.6	150.6	76.7	4 590.2
1987	318.0	130.4	187.5	95.6	91.9	2.2	728.0	566.3	161.6	40.6	4 870.2
1988	357.9	141.6	216.3	98.0	118.2	5.0	782.4	608.3	174.1	-0.5	5 252.6
1989	347.1	146.1	201.0	126.4	74.7	6.7	836.1	650.1	186.0	64.2	5 657.7
1990	341.1	145.4	195.6	144.1	51.6	3.2	886.8	689.0	197.8	91.4	5 979.6
1991	374.9	138.6	236.3	156.2	80.1	7.8	931.1	722.4	208.8	88.4	6 174.0
1992	402.2	148.7	253.5	161.5	92.0	9.9	959.7	744.2	215.6	110.9	6 539.3
1993	445.1	171.0	274.0	184.7	89.3	10.8	1 003.6	780.0	223.6	152.3	6 878.7
1994	543.9	193.1	350.8	197.8	153.0	11.8	1 055.6	824.3	231.2	136.8	7 308.8
1995	610.1	217.8	392.2	226.2	166.1	15.6	1 122.8	882.6	240.2	90.6	7 664.1
1996	684.1	231.5	452.6	263.1	189.5	16.9	1 176.0	931.0	245.0	56.6	8 100.2
1997	758.2	245.4	512.8	292.2	220.6	17.5	1 240.0	990.1	249.9	12.3	8 608.5
1998	701.3	248.4	453.0	314.8	138.2	16.3	1 310.3	1 054.9	255.3	-60.1	9 089.2
1999	708.2	258.8	449.4	306.4	143.1	16.2	1 400.9	1 135.9	264.9	-37.5	9 660.6
2000	635.0	265.1	369.9	355.4	14.5	10.7	1 514.2	1 236.6	277.7	-99.5	10 284.8
2001	583.6	203.3	380.3	329.9	50.4	5.2	1 604.0	1 317.7	286.3	-115.0	10 621.8
2002	748.4	192.3	556.1	352.3	203.8	7.0	1 662.1	1 368.0	294.1	-72.8	10 977.5
2003	889.7	243.8	646.0	401.9	244.1	3.9	1 727.2	1 422.4	304.9	-13.6	11 510.7
2004	1 078.3	306.1	772.2	501.8	270.4	-1.8	1 831.7	1 509.3	322.4	-8.6	12 274.9
2005	1 238.7	412.4	826.3	319.7	506.6	-6.4	1 982.0	1 635.3	346.7	-35.5	13 093.7
2006	1 390.3	473.4	917.0	648.1	268.9	-9.3	2 136.0	1 765.0	371.0	-217.3	13 855.9
2007	1 175.6	445.5	730.1	678.5	51.6	-16.4	2 264.4	1 865.0	399.4	17.5	14 477.6
2008	878.4	309.1	569.3	628.1	-58.8	-21.2	2 363.4	1 936.9	426.5	99.4	14 718.6
2009	1 039.8	269.4	770.3	456.5	313.8	-20.6	2 368.4	1 925.7	442.7	75.3	14 418.7
2010	1 351.2	370.6	980.7	442.5	538.1	-22.9	2 381.6	1 923.5	458.1	49.2	14 964.4
2011	1 394.7	379.1	1 015.6	548.8	466.9	-24.5	2 450.6	1 971.1	479.6	-38.3	15 517.9
2012	1 587.8	447.6	1 140.2	680.1	460.1	-19.3	2 534.2	2 038.0	496.2	-203.3	16 155.3
2013	1 621.0	467.7	1 153.3	790.9	362.4	-20.9	2 628.9	2 122.4	506.5	-137.9	16 691.5
2014	1 743.0	505.3	1 237.7	838.5	399.2	-17.9	2 748.0	2 231.2	516.9	-229.9	17 427.6
2015	1 732.5	507.4	1 225.1	898.6	326.4	-14.3	2 841.5	2 319.6	521.9	-255.9	18 120.7
2016	1 678.7	471.0	1 207.7	822.2	385.5	-10.1	2 916.7	2 390.5	526.2	-147.2	18 624.5
2014											
1st quarter	1 581.4	505.1	1 076.3	814.5	261.8	-18.6	2 706.1	2 191.8	514.3	-167.7	17 031.3
2nd quarter	1 760.1	527.0	1 233.2	837.1	396.1	-18.1	2 731.9	2 216.0	515.9	-217.6	17 320.9
3rd quarter	1 789.5	498.6	1 290.9	836.1	454.8	-17.5	2 762.6	2 244.7	517.9	-205.7	17 622.3
4th quarter	1 841.2	490.6	1 350.5	866.3	484.2	-17.5	2 791.5	2 272.1	519.4	-328.7	17 735.9
2015											
1st quarter	1 786.4	521.9	1 264.6	930.8	333.7	-15.6	2 811.7	2 291.6	520.1	-273.0	17 874.7
2nd quarter	1 802.5	516.7	1 285.8	891.7	394.1	-15.1	2 829.6	2 308.2	521.4	-263.5	18 093.2
3rd quarter	1 759.3	485.6	1 273.8	897.4	376.4	-14.1	2 854.4	2 331.3	523.0	-219.6	18 227.7
4th quarter	1 581.7	505.6	1 076.1	874.6	201.5	-12.4	2 870.5	2 347.2	523.2	-267.6	18 287.2
2016											
1st quarter	1 674.9	455.9	1 219.0	853.0	366.0	-9.7	2 880.9	2 358.1	522.9	-226.1	18 325.2
2nd quarter	1 607.6	471.5	1 136.1	808.4	327.7	-10.3	2 908.3	2 382.3	526.1	-132.9	18 538.0
3rd quarter	1 712.9	487.2	1 225.7	803.3	422.3	-10.1	2 927.6	2 400.7	526.9	-195.2	18 729.1
4th quarter	1 719.6	469.5	1 250.1	824.2	425.9	-10.2	2 950.0	2 421.2	528.8	-34.4	18 905.5

. . . = Not available.

Table 1-13A. National Income by Type of Income: Recent Data

(Billions of dollars, quarterly data are at seasonally adjusted annual rates.)   **NIPA Tables 1.7.5, 1.12**

Year and quarter	National income, total	Compensation of employees							Proprietors' income with IVA and CCAdj			Rental income of persons with CCAdj
		Total	Wages and salaries			Supplements to wages and salaries			Total	Farm	Nonfarm	
			Total	Government	Other	Total	Employer contributions for:					
							Employee pension and insurance funds	Government social insurance				
1955	377.6	230.9	212.2	36.6	175.6	18.7	13.6	5.2	44.3	10.7	33.6	13.4
1956	400.9	249.6	229.0	38.8	190.2	20.6	14.9	5.7	45.8	10.6	35.2	13.7
1957	419.4	263.0	240.0	41.0	198.9	23.0	16.7	6.4	47.8	10.6	37.2	14.1
1958	421.6	265.1	241.3	44.1	197.2	23.8	17.5	6.3	50.2	12.4	37.7	14.8
1959	459.6	286.3	259.8	46.1	213.8	26.5	18.6	7.9	50.3	10.0	40.3	15.6
1960	479.9	301.9	272.9	49.2	223.7	29.0	19.7	9.3	50.6	10.6	39.9	16.5
1961	497.2	311.1	280.5	52.5	228.0	30.6	21.0	9.6	53.2	11.2	42.0	17.2
1962	535.2	332.9	299.4	56.3	243.0	33.6	22.4	11.2	55.2	11.2	44.0	18.0
1963	566.6	351.2	314.9	60.0	254.8	36.3	23.9	12.4	56.4	11.0	45.4	18.7
1964	608.3	376.8	337.8	64.9	272.9	39.0	26.4	12.6	59.1	9.8	49.4	18.8
1965	660.3	406.3	363.8	69.9	293.8	42.6	29.5	13.1	63.7	12.0	51.6	19.3
1966	719.7	450.3	400.3	78.4	321.9	50.0	33.1	16.8	67.9	13.0	54.9	19.9
1967	760.2	482.9	429.0	86.5	342.5	53.9	35.9	18.0	69.5	11.6	57.8	20.3
1968	832.1	532.1	472.0	96.7	375.3	60.1	40.2	20.0	73.8	11.7	62.2	20.1
1969	899.5	586.0	518.3	105.6	412.7	67.7	44.9	22.8	77.0	12.8	64.2	20.4
1970	940.1	625.1	551.6	117.2	434.3	73.6	49.7	23.8	77.8	12.9	64.9	20.7
1971	1 017.0	667.0	584.5	126.8	457.8	82.5	56.0	26.4	83.9	13.4	70.5	21.9
1972	1 123.0	733.6	638.8	137.9	500.9	94.9	63.7	31.2	95.1	17.0	78.1	22.8
1973	1 257.0	815.0	708.8	148.8	560.0	106.3	66.5	39.8	112.5	29.1	83.4	23.3
1974	1 350.8	890.3	772.3	160.5	611.8	118.0	73.3	44.7	112.2	23.5	88.7	23.3
1975	1 451.1	950.2	814.8	176.2	638.6	135.3	88.6	46.7	118.2	22.0	96.2	22.5
1976	1 614.8	1 051.2	899.7	188.9	710.8	151.5	97.1	54.4	131.0	17.2	113.8	20.6
1977	1 798.7	1 169.0	994.2	202.6	791.6	174.8	113.7	61.1	144.5	16.0	128.5	16.2
1978	2 029.9	1 320.2	1 120.6	220.0	900.6	199.7	128.1	71.5	166.0	19.9	146.1	16.9
1979	2 248.2	1 481.0	1 253.3	237.1	1 016.2	227.7	145.1	82.6	179.4	22.2	157.3	16.6
1980	2 426.8	1 626.2	1 373.4	261.5	1 112.0	252.8	163.9	88.9	171.6	11.7	159.9	19.7
1981	2 722.1	1 795.3	1 511.4	285.8	1 225.5	283.0	180.3	103.0	179.7	19.0	160.7	25.4
1982	2 840.4	1 894.3	1 587.5	307.5	1 280.0	306.8	197.0	109.8	171.2	13.3	157.9	26.1
1983	3 060.5	2 013.9	1 677.5	324.8	1 352.7	336.4	216.5	119.9	186.3	6.2	180.1	27.5
1984	3 444.0	2 217.4	1 844.9	348.1	1 496.8	372.5	233.5	139.0	228.2	20.9	207.3	27.9
1985	3 684.2	2 389.0	1 982.6	373.9	1 608.7	406.4	258.7	147.7	241.1	21.0	220.1	29.5
1986	3 848.2	2 543.8	2 102.3	397.2	1 705.1	441.5	283.6	157.9	256.5	22.8	233.7	21.9
1987	4 119.2	2 724.3	2 256.3	423.1	1 833.2	468.0	301.8	166.3	286.5	28.9	257.6	20.2
1988	4 493.4	2 950.0	2 439.8	452.0	1 987.7	510.3	325.6	184.6	325.8	26.8	299.1	25.1
1989	4 782.2	3 142.6	2 583.1	481.1	2 101.9	559.5	365.8	193.7	341.9	33.0	308.9	24.4
1990	5 036.1	3 342.7	2 741.2	519.0	2 222.2	601.5	395.0	206.5	354.4	32.2	322.3	31.4
1991	5 186.1	3 452.0	2 814.5	548.8	2 265.7	637.5	422.4	215.1	356.0	26.8	329.2	42.0
1992	5 499.7	3 671.1	2 965.5	572.0	2 393.5	705.6	477.2	228.4	402.4	34.8	367.6	64.3
1993	5 754.8	3 820.7	3 079.3	589.0	2 490.3	741.3	501.7	239.7	430.5	31.4	399.2	93.6
1994	6 140.2	4 010.1	3 236.6	609.5	2 627.1	773.5	519.4	254.1	459.5	34.7	424.8	117.5
1995	6 479.5	4 202.6	3 418.0	629.0	2 789.0	784.6	520.5	264.1	484.5	22.0	462.4	129.2
1996	6 899.4	4 422.1	3 616.5	648.1	2 968.4	805.6	530.8	274.8	547.4	37.3	510.1	147.0
1997	7 380.4	4 714.7	3 876.8	671.9	3 205.0	837.8	548.3	289.6	587.9	32.4	555.5	152.0
1998	7 857.3	5 077.8	4 181.6	701.3	3 480.3	896.2	589.0	307.2	644.2	28.4	615.7	169.9
1999	8 324.4	5 410.3	4 458.0	733.8	3 724.2	952.3	629.0	323.3	700.4	28.1	672.3	183.1
2000	8 907.0	5 856.6	4 825.9	779.8	4 046.1	1 030.7	685.5	345.2	757.8	31.5	726.3	187.7
2001	9 184.6	6 046.5	4 954.4	822.0	4 132.4	1 092.1	734.1	358.0	836.8	32.1	804.7	207.5
2002	9 436.8	6 141.9	4 996.4	873.2	4 123.3	1 145.5	779.5	366.0	871.0	19.9	851.1	217.3
2003	9 864.2	6 364.5	5 137.8	913.3	4 224.5	1 226.6	844.1	382.5	900.1	38.0	862.0	238.0
2004	10 540.9	6 739.5	5 421.9	952.7	4 469.3	1 317.6	908.9	408.7	962.1	50.4	911.6	255.4
2005	11 239.8	7 086.8	5 692.0	991.5	4 700.4	1 394.8	966.8	428.1	979.0	46.4	932.6	238.4
2006	12 004.8	7 502.3	6 057.4	1 035.0	5 022.4	1 444.9	997.6	447.4	1 053.7	36.0	1 017.7	207.5
2007	12 321.4	7 898.3	6 395.2	1 088.8	5 306.3	1 503.1	1 041.4	461.7	979.2	38.1	941.1	189.4
2008	12 427.8	8 078.3	6 531.9	1 144.1	5 387.8	1 546.4	1 075.1	471.3	1 026.5	47.0	979.5	262.1
2009	12 126.1	7 787.0	6 251.4	1 175.1	5 076.3	1 535.6	1 077.5	458.1	973.0	35.5	937.5	333.7
2010	12 739.5	7 961.4	6 377.5	1 191.1	5 186.4	1 583.9	1 114.6	469.4	1 032.7	46.0	986.7	402.8
2011	13 352.3	8 269.0	6 633.2	1 194.8	5 438.4	1 635.9	1 142.0	493.9	1 143.7	75.5	1 068.1	485.3
2012	14 061.9	8 609.9	6 930.3	1 198.2	5 732.0	1 679.6	1 165.3	514.3	1 241.4	61.6	1 179.8	525.3
2013	14 444.8	8 842.4	7 116.7	1 208.0	5 908.7	1 725.8	1 199.0	526.8	1 284.7	87.8	1 197.0	567.1
2014	15 144.0	9 256.5	7 476.8	1 236.9	6 239.9	1 779.7	1 231.7	548.0	1 315.8	68.1	1 247.7	611.7
2015	15 739.6	9 708.3	7 858.9	1 275.6	6 583.3	1 849.4	1 278.0	571.4	1 318.8	53.7	1 265.1	662.5
2016	16 052.0	9 978.6	8 085.2	1 307.5	6 777.8	1 893.4	1 309.8	583.6	1 341.9	43.2	1 298.7	707.3
2014												
1st quarter	14 734.1	9 119.4	7 360.9	1 223.6	6 137.3	1 758.5	1 217.5	541.0	1 292.7	66.4	1 226.3	594.3
2nd quarter	15 037.0	9 175.0	7 406.4	1 231.8	6 174.7	1 768.6	1 225.5	543.1	1 319.3	76.7	1 242.6	606.7
3rd quarter	15 310.8	9 286.9	7 501.9	1 241.1	6 260.8	1 785.0	1 235.8	549.2	1 320.0	64.2	1 255.8	618.0
4th quarter	15 494.2	9 444.5	7 638.0	1 251.1	6 386.9	1 806.6	1 248.0	558.5	1 331.2	65.3	1 265.9	627.9
2015												
1st quarter	15 552.9	9 541.6	7 718.4	1 258.6	6 459.8	1 823.3	1 261.7	561.6	1 312.8	52.0	1 260.7	639.3
2nd quarter	15 719.8	9 655.9	7 813.7	1 270.4	6 543.3	1 842.2	1 273.9	568.3	1 313.9	53.0	1 260.9	658.4
3rd quarter	15 784.5	9 730.0	7 873.5	1 279.6	6 593.9	1 856.5	1 284.1	572.4	1 323.2	58.7	1 264.5	670.9
4th quarter	15 901.3	9 905.5	8 030.0	1 293.9	6 736.1	1 875.5	1 292.2	583.3	1 325.4	51.0	1 274.3	681.4
2016												
1st quarter	15 846.5	9 838.6	7 964.9	1 295.1	6 669.7	1 873.7	1 298.6	575.1	1 327.6	46.8	1 280.8	697.6
2nd quarter	15 957.6	9 979.6	8 090.2	1 305.0	6 785.2	1 889.4	1 305.5	583.9	1 339.5	46.7	1 292.8	704.8
3rd quarter	16 185.1	10 081.4	8 178.1	1 314.6	6 863.4	1 903.4	1 313.3	590.1	1 346.1	41.4	1 304.6	708.1
4th quarter	16 218.9	10 014.9	8 107.8	1 315.2	6 792.7	1 907.1	1 321.7	585.4	1 354.6	37.8	1 316.7	718.9

Table 1-13A. National Income by Type of Income: Recent Data—*Continued*

(Billions of dollars, quarterly data are at seasonally adjusted annual rates.)   **NIPA Tables 1.7.5, 1.12**

| Year and quarter | Corporate profits with IVA and CCAdj | | | | | Net interest and miscellaneous payments | Taxes on production and imports | Less: Subsidies | Business current transfer payments, net | | | Current surplus of government enterprises | Addendum: Net national factor income |
| | Total | Taxes on corporate income | Profits after tax | | | | | | | | | | |
			Total	Net dividends	Undistributed corporate profits				Total [1]	To persons	To government		
1955	50.2	22.0	28.1	10.5	17.6	6.3	31.5	0.2	1.3	0.9	0.4	. . .	345.1
1956	49.6	22.0	27.7	11.3	16.4	6.9	34.2	0.7	1.7	1.2	0.4	. . .	365.7
1957	49.1	21.4	27.7	11.7	16.0	8.1	36.6	1.1	1.8	1.4	0.4	. . .	382.1
1958	43.9	19.0	24.9	11.6	13.3	9.6	37.7	1.4	1.7	1.2	0.5	. . .	383.6
1959	55.5	23.7	31.8	12.6	19.2	9.7	41.1	1.1	1.7	1.3	0.3	. . .	417.4
1960	54.7	22.8	31.9	13.4	18.5	10.7	44.5	1.1	1.7	1.3	0.4	. . .	434.3
1961	55.9	22.9	33.1	13.9	19.2	12.6	47.0	2.0	1.9	1.4	0.5	. . .	450.0
1962	64.0	24.1	39.9	15.0	24.9	14.3	50.4	2.3	2.1	1.5	0.6	. . .	484.6
1963	70.5	26.4	44.1	16.2	27.9	15.3	53.4	2.2	2.6	1.9	0.7	. . .	512.1
1964	77.7	28.2	49.6	18.2	31.4	17.5	57.3	2.7	3.0	2.2	0.8	. . .	550.0
1965	89.3	31.1	58.2	20.2	38.0	19.8	60.7	3.0	3.5	2.3	1.2	. . .	598.4
1966	96.1	33.9	62.2	20.7	41.6	22.5	63.2	3.9	3.4	2.1	1.3	. . .	656.8
1967	93.9	32.9	61.0	21.5	39.5	25.7	67.9	3.8	3.6	2.3	1.4	. . .	692.3
1968	101.7	39.6	62.1	23.5	38.6	27.6	76.4	4.2	4.2	2.8	1.4	. . .	755.3
1969	98.4	40.0	58.4	24.2	34.2	33.6	83.9	4.5	4.8	3.3	1.5	. . .	815.4
1970	86.2	34.8	51.5	24.3	27.2	40.5	91.4	4.8	4.4	2.9	1.4	. . .	850.4
1971	100.6	38.2	62.5	25.0	37.5	45.2	100.5	4.7	4.2	2.7	1.5	. . .	918.7
1972	117.2	42.3	74.9	26.8	48.0	49.3	107.9	6.6	4.8	3.1	1.7	. . .	1 018.1
1973	133.4	50.0	83.4	29.9	53.5	57.2	117.2	5.2	5.7	3.9	1.8	. . .	1 141.5
1974	125.7	52.8	72.9	33.2	39.7	73.5	124.9	3.3	6.8	4.7	2.1	. . .	1 225.1
1975	138.9	51.6	87.2	33.0	54.3	85.9	135.3	4.5	9.0	6.8	2.2	. . .	1 315.7
1976	174.3	65.3	109.1	39.0	70.0	89.9	146.4	5.1	9.1	6.7	2.4	. . .	1 467.1
1977	205.8	74.4	131.3	44.8	86.6	105.9	159.7	7.1	8.1	5.1	3.0	. . .	1 641.3
1978	238.6	84.9	153.7	50.8	102.9	118.8	170.9	8.9	10.4	6.5	3.9	. . .	1 860.5
1979	249.0	90.0	159.0	57.5	101.4	141.0	180.1	8.5	12.8	8.2	4.5	. . .	2 067.0
1980	223.6	87.2	136.4	64.1	72.3	186.2	200.3	9.8	14.0	8.6	5.4	. . .	2 227.3
1981	247.5	84.3	163.2	73.8	89.4	238.4	235.6	11.5	16.9	11.2	5.7	. . .	2 486.2
1982	229.9	66.5	163.4	77.7	85.6	277.5	240.9	15.0	19.3	12.4	6.9	. . .	2 599.0
1983	279.8	80.6	199.1	83.5	115.7	291.8	263.3	21.3	21.7	13.8	7.9	. . .	2 799.2
1984	337.9	97.5	240.4	90.8	149.5	336.1	289.8	21.1	29.2	19.7	9.4	. . .	3 147.5
1985	354.5	99.4	255.1	97.5	157.5	348.0	308.1	21.4	34.1	22.3	11.8	. . .	3 362.0
1986	324.4	109.7	214.7	106.2	108.5	365.2	323.4	24.9	36.0	22.9	13.0	. . .	3 511.8
1987	366.0	130.4	235.5	112.3	123.2	369.5	347.5	30.3	33.3	20.2	13.1	. . .	3 766.5
1988	414.9	141.6	273.2	129.9	143.3	394.7	374.5	29.5	32.8	20.6	12.2	. . .	4 110.6
1989	414.2	146.1	268.2	158.0	110.2	442.7	398.9	27.4	38.3	23.2	15.1	. . .	4 365.8
1990	417.2	145.4	271.7	169.1	102.7	450.1	425.0	27.0	39.2	22.2	17.0	. . .	4 595.7
1991	451.3	138.6	312.7	180.5	132.2	408.5	457.1	27.5	38.9	17.6	21.3	. . .	4 709.8
1992	475.3	148.7	326.6	189.5	137.1	383.7	483.4	30.1	39.7	16.3	23.6	-0.1	4 996.8
1993	522.0	171.0	351.0	205.3	145.6	371.4	503.1	36.7	39.4	14.1	25.6	-0.3	5 238.2
1994	621.9	193.1	428.8	236.0	192.8	365.9	545.2	32.5	40.7	13.3	27.9	-0.4	5 575.0
1995	703.0	217.8	485.2	259.0	226.2	376.5	557.9	34.8	45.0	18.7	24.9	1.4	5 895.8
1996	786.1	231.5	554.6	303.5	251.1	381.9	580.8	35.2	52.6	22.9	30.7	-1.0	6 284.3
1997	865.8	245.4	620.3	339.5	280.9	414.7	611.6	33.8	50.1	19.4	29.8	0.8	6 735.1
1998	804.1	248.4	555.7	357.1	198.7	477.8	639.5	36.4	64.1	26.0	34.3	3.8	7 173.8
1999	830.2	258.8	571.4	347.9	223.5	488.0	673.6	45.2	67.8	34.0	36.5	-2.6	7 612.0
2000	781.2	265.1	516.1	384.7	131.4	565.0	708.6	45.8	85.3	42.4	41.9	1.0	8 148.3
2001	754.0	203.3	550.7	370.6	180.2	566.4	727.7	58.7	99.1	46.8	43.9	8.5	8 411.4
2002	907.2	192.3	714.8	400.2	314.7	490.5	762.6	41.4	80.7	34.2	46.2	0.2	8 628.0
2003	1 056.4	243.8	812.6	434.0	378.6	466.2	808.0	49.1	76.3	26.3	48.3	1.7	9 025.1
2004	1 283.3	306.1	977.3	564.1	413.2	403.5	863.9	46.4	81.4	16.8	52.4	12.2	9 643.8
2005	1 477.7	412.4	1 065.3	580.5	484.8	496.8	934.5	60.9	93.9	25.7	53.4	14.8	10 278.7
2006	1 646.5	473.4	1 173.1	726.0	447.1	580.9	991.9	51.5	82.6	21.5	58.3	2.8	10 991.0
2007	1 529.0	445.5	1 083.5	818.9	264.6	663.4	1 034.6	54.6	98.6	30.6	62.0	6.0	11 259.3
2008	1 285.1	309.1	976.0	808.6	167.3	693.4	1 041.9	52.6	114.4	36.6	70.6	7.2	11 345.3
2009	1 397.0	269.4	1 127.5	574.6	552.9	563.4	1 026.1	58.3	124.9	38.7	88.5	-2.3	11 054.0
2010	1 746.4	370.6	1 375.9	564.0	811.9	489.4	1 057.1	55.9	128.5	43.0	87.2	-1.7	11 632.7
2011	1 816.6	379.1	1 437.5	703.7	733.9	488.1	1 102.6	60.1	131.5	50.2	89.2	-7.9	12 202.7
2012	1 998.2	447.6	1 550.5	859.4	691.2	527.7	1 132.1	58.0	104.7	42.7	72.6	-10.6	12 902.5
2013	2 032.9	467.7	1 565.2	929.4	635.8	504.6	1 174.9	59.3	118.4	41.1	90.8	-13.5	13 231.7
2014	2 140.6	505.3	1 635.3	986.4	648.9	535.0	1 221.6	58.1	138.9	45.6	102.2	-9.0	13 859.5
2015	2 117.5	507.4	1 610.0	1 039.9	570.1	583.4	1 255.8	57.3	165.0	53.1	112.4	-0.6	14 390.4
2016	2 073.5	471.0	1 602.4	981.9	620.6	570.6	1 288.0	61.8	164.0	57.4	105.9	0.7	14 671.9
2014													
1st quarter	1 984.6	505.1	1 479.5	938.9	540.6	503.8	1 200.2	58.4	116.2	43.2	86.4	-13.3	13 494.7
2nd quarter	2 149.0	527.0	1 622.1	975.9	646.2	522.9	1 218.9	58.4	121.6	44.6	86.5	-9.5	13 773.0
3rd quarter	2 196.6	498.6	1 698.1	998.5	699.6	554.3	1 229.4	58.3	181.4	46.3	141.9	-6.9	13 975.9
4th quarter	2 232.0	490.6	1 741.4	1 032.1	709.2	558.8	1 238.0	57.2	136.3	48.3	94.1	-6.1	14 194.5
2015													
1st quarter	2 175.5	521.9	1 653.7	1 062.0	591.7	576.1	1 241.8	56.2	137.5	50.5	89.5	-2.5	14 245.3
2nd quarter	2 175.1	516.7	1 658.5	1 036.3	622.2	587.7	1 253.0	56.5	147.4	52.4	95.5	-0.6	14 391.0
3rd quarter	2 135.9	485.6	1 650.3	1 048.1	602.2	591.8	1 258.2	57.7	146.4	54.1	90.3	2.0	14 451.8
4th quarter	1 983.3	505.6	1 477.7	1 013.3	464.4	578.0	1 270.2	58.6	228.6	55.4	174.4	-1.3	14 473.5
2016													
1st quarter	2 040.8	455.9	1 584.8	1 000.7	584.1	574.1	1 274.9	60.4	163.2	56.5	106.8	-0.2	14 478.6
2nd quarter	1 996.4	471.5	1 525.1	971.3	553.9	568.0	1 276.4	62.1	165.0	57.3	110.4	-2.7	14 588.5
3rd quarter	2 101.2	487.2	1 614.1	976.3	637.7	573.7	1 296.6	63.0	151.2	57.8	92.4	0.9	14 810.5
4th quarter	2 155.2	469.5	1 685.7	979.1	706.6	566.5	1 304.1	61.6	176.6	58.0	113.8	4.8	14 810.1

[1] Includes net transfer payments to the rest of the world, not shown separately.
. . . = Not available.

Table 1-13B. National Income by Type of Income: Historical Data

(Billions of dollars, quarterly data are at seasonally adjusted annual rates.)   **NIPA Tables 1.7.5, 1.12**

Year and quarter	National income, total	Compensation of employees Total	Wages and salaries Total	Government	Other	Supplements to wages and salaries Total	Employee pension and insurance funds	Government social insurance	Proprietors' income with IVA and CCAdj Total	Farm	Nonfarm	Rental income of persons with CCAdj
1929	94.2	51.4	50.5	5.0	45.5	1.0	1.0	0.0	14.0	5.7	8.4	6.1
1930	83.1	47.2	46.2	5.2	41.0	1.0	1.0	0.0	10.9	3.9	7.0	5.4
1931	67.7	40.1	39.2	5.3	33.9	1.0	1.0	0.0	8.3	3.0	5.3	4.4
1932	51.3	31.4	30.5	5.0	25.5	0.9	0.9	0.0	5.0	1.8	3.3	3.6
1933	49.0	29.8	29.0	5.2	23.9	0.8	0.8	0.0	5.3	2.2	3.0	2.9
1934	58.3	34.6	33.7	6.1	27.6	0.9	0.8	0.0	7.0	2.6	4.4	2.5
1935	66.4	37.7	36.7	6.5	30.2	1.0	1.0	0.0	10.1	4.9	5.2	2.6
1936	75.2	43.3	42.0	7.9	34.1	1.4	1.1	0.2	10.4	3.9	6.4	2.7
1937	83.7	48.4	46.1	7.5	38.6	2.2	1.2	1.0	12.5	5.6	6.9	3.0
1938	77.1	45.5	43.0	8.3	34.8	2.5	1.3	1.2	10.6	4.0	6.6	3.5
1939	82.5	48.6	46.0	8.2	37.7	2.6	1.3	1.3	11.1	4.0	7.1	3.7
1940	91.6	52.8	49.9	8.5	41.4	2.9	1.6	1.4	12.2	4.1	8.2	3.8
1941	117.4	66.2	62.1	10.2	51.9	4.2	2.4	1.7	16.7	6.0	10.6	4.4
1942	152.4	88.1	82.1	16.0	66.1	6.0	4.0	2.0	23.3	9.7	13.7	5.5
1943	187.3	112.8	105.8	26.6	79.2	7.0	4.7	2.3	28.2	11.5	16.7	6.0
1944	201.0	124.4	116.7	33.0	83.8	7.7	5.1	2.5	29.3	11.4	17.9	6.3
1945	201.4	126.4	117.5	34.9	82.6	8.9	5.4	3.5	30.8	11.8	19.0	6.6
1946	201.5	122.6	112.0	20.7	91.3	10.6	5.5	5.1	35.7	14.2	21.5	6.9
1947	219.0	132.5	123.1	17.5	105.6	9.4	5.5	3.9	34.6	14.3	20.2	6.9
1948	245.1	144.5	135.6	19.0	116.5	8.9	5.9	3.0	39.3	16.7	22.6	7.5
1949	240.0	144.5	134.7	20.8	113.9	9.8	6.4	3.3	34.7	12.0	22.7	7.8
1947												
1st quarter	213.6	129.1	118.9	17.1	101.7	10.3	5.6	4.7	36.2	16.0	20.2	6.7
2nd quarter	215.9	130.9	121.3	17.3	103.9	9.7	5.4	4.3	33.3	12.4	20.9	6.8
3rd quarter	219.3	132.9	124.0	17.6	106.4	8.9	5.4	3.5	33.9	14.1	19.8	7.0
4th quarter	227.2	137.0	128.3	18.0	110.3	8.7	5.5	3.2	35.0	14.9	20.0	7.2
1948												
1st quarter	236.1	140.6	131.7	18.3	113.4	8.9	5.7	3.2	36.4	14.5	21.9	7.3
2nd quarter	244.3	142.2	133.4	18.6	114.7	8.9	5.9	3.0	40.2	18.0	22.3	7.5
3rd quarter	249.1	147.0	138.1	19.3	118.8	8.9	6.0	2.9	40.6	17.9	22.7	7.5
4th quarter	251.0	148.1	139.1	19.9	119.2	9.0	6.1	2.9	39.9	16.4	23.5	7.6
1949												
1st quarter	243.6	146.4	136.7	20.4	116.4	9.7	6.2	3.5	35.4	12.7	22.7	7.5
2nd quarter	240.1	144.9	135.0	20.7	114.3	9.9	6.3	3.5	34.9	12.1	22.8	7.7
3rd quarter	240.2	143.8	134.0	21.1	112.9	9.8	6.5	3.3	34.2	11.6	22.6	7.9
4th quarter	236.3	143.0	133.2	21.2	112.0	9.8	6.7	3.0	34.2	11.5	22.7	8.1
1950												
1st quarter	246.7	147.2	136.9	21.2	115.6	10.3	7.1	3.3	36.2	12.2	24.0	8.5
2nd quarter	258.8	153.8	143.0	21.8	121.2	10.8	7.5	3.3	36.8	12.2	24.6	8.7
3rd quarter	275.9	162.5	151.0	23.0	128.1	11.5	8.1	3.4	38.5	13.1	25.4	8.8
4th quarter	286.4	170.3	158.1	24.5	133.5	12.3	8.7	3.6	38.5	13.9	24.6	9.1
1951												
1st quarter	298.2	178.8	165.3	26.7	138.6	13.5	9.4	4.0	40.9	15.0	25.9	9.3
2nd quarter	305.6	185.1	171.0	28.5	142.5	14.1	10.0	4.1	42.5	15.4	27.1	9.6
3rd quarter	310.9	188.1	173.5	30.2	143.3	14.6	10.5	4.1	43.2	15.1	28.1	9.9
4th quarter	317.4	191.7	176.6	31.5	145.1	15.1	11.0	4.1	43.7	15.7	28.0	10.1
1952												
1st quarter	318.9	196.4	181.0	32.4	148.6	15.3	11.2	4.1	41.7	13.7	28.0	10.4
2nd quarter	320.9	197.7	182.1	33.1	149.0	15.6	11.5	4.1	43.0	14.5	28.4	10.7
3rd quarter	327.4	201.8	186.0	33.8	152.2	15.8	11.7	4.1	44.7	16.0	28.8	10.9
4th quarter	338.9	209.6	193.5	34.2	159.3	16.1	11.9	4.2	42.8	13.0	29.7	11.3
1953												
1st quarter	345.0	213.4	197.1	34.3	162.7	16.3	12.1	4.2	43.0	13.0	29.9	11.6
2nd quarter	347.8	216.5	200.0	34.4	165.7	16.5	12.3	4.2	42.3	12.4	29.9	11.9
3rd quarter	346.2	216.8	200.1	34.3	165.9	16.7	12.4	4.3	41.2	11.7	29.5	12.2
4th quarter	338.6	215.4	198.7	34.4	164.3	16.7	12.5	4.2	41.6	11.5	30.0	12.5
1954												
1st quarter	340.2	213.4	196.4	34.4	162.0	17.0	12.4	4.6	42.7	12.9	29.8	12.8
2nd quarter	340.5	213.0	196.0	34.7	161.2	17.0	12.4	4.6	42.1	11.7	30.4	13.0
3rd quarter	343.9	213.5	196.3	35.1	161.2	17.2	12.6	4.6	42.2	11.8	30.5	13.1
4th quarter	352.9	217.8	200.4	35.4	165.0	17.5	12.8	4.6	42.0	10.7	31.3	13.3
1955												
1st quarter	365.3	222.2	204.1	35.5	168.6	18.2	13.1	5.0	43.7	10.9	32.7	13.3
2nd quarter	374.7	228.4	209.9	36.2	173.6	18.6	13.4	5.1	44.3	11.3	33.0	13.4
3rd quarter	382.1	234.2	215.2	37.4	177.8	19.0	13.7	5.2	44.6	10.7	33.9	13.4
4th quarter	388.4	238.7	219.5	37.3	182.2	19.3	14.0	5.3	44.5	10.0	34.5	13.5
1956												
1st quarter	392.1	243.2	223.3	37.8	185.4	19.9	14.3	5.6	44.9	10.2	34.7	13.6
2nd quarter	397.9	247.9	227.5	38.5	189.0	20.4	14.7	5.7	45.3	10.4	34.9	13.6
3rd quarter	402.7	250.8	230.0	39.2	190.8	20.8	15.2	5.7	46.4	10.9	35.5	13.7
4th quarter	410.9	256.7	235.4	39.7	195.7	21.4	15.6	5.8	46.8	10.9	35.8	13.8
1957												
1st quarter	417.6	260.6	238.3	40.2	198.0	22.4	16.0	6.4	46.9	9.9	37.0	13.9
2nd quarter	419.7	262.5	239.6	40.7	198.9	22.8	16.4	6.4	47.7	10.5	37.2	14.0
3rd quarter	423.4	265.1	241.8	41.5	200.3	23.3	16.9	6.4	48.8	11.0	37.8	14.1
4th quarter	416.9	263.7	240.1	41.6	198.5	23.6	17.3	6.3	47.7	10.7	37.0	14.3

Table 1-13B. National Income by Type of Income: Historical Data—*Continued*

(Billions of dollars, quarterly data are at seasonally adjusted annual rates.)   **NIPA Tables 1.7.5, 1.12**

| Year and quarter | Corporate profits with IVA and CCAdj | | | | | Net interest and miscellaneous payments | Taxes on production and imports | Less: Subsidies | Business current transfer payments, net | | | Current surplus of government enterprises | Addendum: Net national factor income |
| | Total | Taxes on corporate income | Profits after tax | | | | | | Total [1] | To persons | To government | | |
			Total	Net dividends	Undistributed corporate profits								
1929	10.8	1.4	9.5	5.8	3.7	4.6	6.8	0.0	0.5	0.4	0.1	0.0	86.9
1930	7.5	0.8	6.7	5.5	1.2	4.8	7.0	0.1	0.5	0.4	0.1	0.0	75.8
1931	3.0	0.5	2.5	4.1	-1.6	4.8	6.7	0.1	0.5	0.4	0.1	0.0	60.6
1932	-0.2	0.4	-0.6	2.5	-3.1	4.5	6.6	0.1	0.6	0.5	0.1	0.0	44.3
1933	-0.2	0.5	-0.7	2.0	-2.7	4.0	6.9	0.2	0.5	0.4	0.1	0.0	41.7
1934	2.5	0.7	1.8	2.6	-0.8	4.0	7.6	0.5	0.5	0.4	0.1	0.0	50.7
1935	4.0	1.0	3.1	2.8	0.2	4.1	8.0	0.6	0.5	0.4	0.1	0.0	58.5
1936	6.2	1.4	4.8	4.5	0.3	3.8	8.5	0.3	0.5	0.4	0.1	0.0	66.4
1937	7.1	1.5	5.6	4.7	0.9	3.7	8.9	0.3	0.5	0.4	0.1	0.0	74.0
1938	5.0	1.0	4.0	3.2	0.8	3.6	8.9	0.5	0.4	0.3	0.2	0.0	68.2
1939	6.6	1.4	5.2	3.8	1.4	3.6	9.1	0.8	0.4	0.3	0.2	0.0	73.7
1940	9.9	2.8	7.0	4.0	3.0	3.3	9.8	0.8	0.5	0.3	0.2	0.0	82.1
1941	15.7	7.6	8.1	4.4	3.7	3.3	11.1	0.5	0.5	0.4	0.2	0.0	106.3
1942	20.8	11.4	9.4	4.3	5.1	3.2	11.5	0.5	0.5	0.3	0.2	0.0	140.9
1943	24.9	14.1	10.8	4.4	6.4	2.9	12.4	0.6	0.6	0.4	0.3	0.0	174.8
1944	25.0	12.9	12.0	4.6	7.4	2.4	13.7	1.0	0.8	0.4	0.4	0.0	187.5
1945	20.5	10.7	9.8	4.6	5.2	2.3	15.1	1.1	0.9	0.5	0.4	0.0	186.6
1946	18.2	9.1	9.1	5.6	3.6	1.9	16.8	1.4	0.7	0.4	0.3	0.0	185.3
1947	24.2	11.3	12.9	6.3	6.6	2.5	18.1	0.4	0.7	0.4	0.3	0.0	200.6
1948	31.4	12.4	19.0	7.0	11.9	2.6	19.7	0.5	0.7	0.4	0.3	0.0	225.2
1949	29.1	10.2	18.9	7.2	11.6	2.9	20.9	0.5	0.7	0.4	0.3	0.0	219.0
1947													
1st quarter	21.5	11.6	9.9	6.0	3.9	2.3	17.7	0.5	0.7	0.4	0.3	...	195.7
2nd quarter	24.5	10.9	13.5	6.3	7.2	2.4	17.7	0.4	0.7	0.4	0.3	...	197.9
3rd quarter	24.6	10.8	13.8	6.5	7.3	2.6	18.0	0.4	0.7	0.4	0.3	...	200.9
4th quarter	26.1	11.8	14.3	6.4	7.9	2.6	19.0	0.3	0.7	0.4	0.3	...	207.8
1948													
1st quarter	30.0	12.1	17.8	7.0	10.8	2.5	19.0	0.4	0.7	0.4	0.4	...	216.8
2nd quarter	31.8	12.8	19.0	6.7	12.3	2.6	19.7	0.3	0.7	0.4	0.3	...	224.3
3rd quarter	31.2	12.6	18.6	7.1	11.5	2.7	20.0	0.6	0.7	0.4	0.3	...	229.0
4th quarter	32.7	12.2	20.5	7.4	13.2	2.7	20.3	0.9	0.7	0.4	0.3	...	230.9
1949													
1st quarter	31.0	11.0	20.0	7.2	12.7	2.8	20.4	0.6	0.7	0.3	0.3	...	223.2
2nd quarter	28.7	9.7	18.9	7.2	11.7	2.9	20.8	0.4	0.7	0.3	0.3	...	219.0
3rd quarter	29.9	10.1	19.8	7.1	12.7	2.9	21.3	0.5	0.7	0.4	0.3	...	218.8
4th quarter	26.6	9.9	16.7	7.4	9.3	3.0	21.2	0.5	0.7	0.4	0.3	...	214.9
1950													
1st quarter	30.1	13.6	16.4	8.3	8.1	3.1	21.6	0.7	0.7	0.4	0.3	...	225.1
2nd quarter	33.9	16.3	17.6	8.4	9.2	3.2	22.5	0.8	0.8	0.5	0.3	...	236.4
3rd quarter	38.4	19.9	18.5	9.2	9.4	3.2	24.4	0.8	0.9	0.6	0.3	...	251.4
4th quarter	41.8	21.8	20.0	9.5	10.5	3.3	23.4	1.1	0.9	0.7	0.3	...	263.2
1951													
1st quarter	40.7	26.3	14.4	8.4	6.1	3.4	25.1	1.2	1.1	0.8	0.3	...	273.2
2nd quarter	40.6	22.3	18.3	8.6	9.7	3.7	24.1	1.1	1.2	0.9	0.3	...	281.5
3rd quarter	41.1	20.1	21.0	8.6	12.4	3.8	24.5	0.9	1.2	0.9	0.3	...	286.1
4th quarter	42.4	21.5	20.8	8.7	12.2	3.9	25.3	1.0	1.2	0.9	0.3	...	291.8
1952													
1st quarter	40.0	19.8	20.2	8.2	12.1	3.9	26.1	0.8	1.2	0.9	0.3	...	292.4
2nd quarter	38.1	18.7	19.5	8.7	10.8	4.1	26.9	0.8	1.2	0.9	0.3	...	293.5
3rd quarter	38.1	18.6	19.5	8.6	10.9	4.2	27.3	0.8	1.2	0.9	0.3	...	299.7
4th quarter	42.4	20.5	21.9	8.8	13.1	4.3	28.1	0.7	1.2	0.9	0.3	...	310.3
1953													
1st quarter	43.3	21.6	21.7	8.4	13.3	4.5	28.7	0.7	1.2	0.9	0.3	...	315.8
2nd quarter	42.5	21.7	20.8	9.2	11.6	4.7	29.2	0.4	1.2	0.9	0.3	...	317.9
3rd quarter	41.3	21.2	20.1	9.0	11.0	4.9	29.3	0.7	1.2	0.8	0.3	...	316.4
4th quarter	34.0	16.6	17.4	8.9	8.5	5.1	29.2	0.2	1.1	0.8	0.3	...	308.5
1954													
1st quarter	36.5	16.4	20.1	9.4	10.7	5.3	28.7	0.1	1.0	0.6	0.3	...	310.7
2nd quarter	37.8	16.9	20.9	8.9	12.1	5.6	28.8	0.7	0.9	0.5	0.3	...	311.5
3rd quarter	39.9	17.9	22.0	9.3	12.7	5.8	28.7	0.3	0.9	0.5	0.4	...	314.6
4th quarter	43.6	19.3	24.3	9.5	14.8	6.0	29.3	0.2	0.9	0.6	0.4	...	322.7
1955													
1st quarter	48.8	21.3	27.5	10.0	17.4	6.2	30.2	0.3	1.1	0.7	0.4	...	334.2
2nd quarter	50.1	21.6	28.5	10.2	18.3	6.3	31.2	0.3	1.2	0.9	0.4	...	342.5
3rd quarter	50.2	22.2	28.0	10.8	17.2	6.3	31.9	0.0	1.4	1.0	0.4	...	348.8
4th quarter	51.6	23.1	28.5	10.9	17.6	6.4	32.5	0.2	1.5	1.1	0.4	...	354.7
1956													
1st quarter	49.4	22.0	27.4	11.2	16.2	6.7	33.0	0.3	1.6	1.2	0.4	...	357.7
2nd quarter	49.6	22.5	27.2	11.2	16.0	6.8	33.6	0.5	1.6	1.2	0.4	...	363.2
3rd quarter	49.3	21.1	28.2	11.2	17.0	7.1	34.6	0.9	1.7	1.3	0.4	...	367.3
4th quarter	50.2	22.3	27.9	11.6	16.3	7.1	35.7	1.2	1.7	1.3	0.4	...	374.6
1957													
1st quarter	51.7	22.8	28.8	11.6	17.2	7.8	36.1	1.3	1.8	1.4	0.4	...	380.9
2nd quarter	50.3	21.9	28.4	11.8	16.6	8.0	36.6	1.2	1.8	1.4	0.4	...	382.5
3rd quarter	49.3	21.4	27.9	11.9	16.0	8.3	37.0	1.1	1.8	1.4	0.4	...	385.6
4th quarter	45.3	19.6	25.7	11.7	14.0	8.3	36.7	1.0	1.8	1.4	0.4	...	379.3

[1] Includes net transfer payments to the rest of the world, not shown separately.
. . . = Not available.

Table 1-13B. National Income by Type of Income: Historical Data—Continued

(Billions of dollars, quarterly data are at seasonally adjusted annual rates.) **NIPA Tables 1.7.5, 1.12**

Year and quarter	National income, total	Compensation of employees							Proprietors' income with IVA and CCAdj			Rental income of persons with CCAdj
		Total	Wages and salaries			Supplements to wages and salaries			Total	Farm	Nonfarm	
			Total	Government	Other	Total	Employer contributions for:					
							Employee pension and insurance funds	Government social insurance				
1958												
1st quarter	411.1	260.2	236.7	42.0	194.7	23.5	17.2	6.3	50.3	13.3	36.9	14.6
2nd quarter	413.0	259.9	236.3	43.1	193.2	23.6	17.3	6.3	50.3	13.0	37.3	14.8
3rd quarter	425.3	267.7	243.8	46.1	197.7	23.8	17.5	6.4	50.1	12.1	38.0	14.9
4th quarter	437.1	272.7	248.4	45.3	203.2	24.3	17.8	6.4	49.9	11.2	38.7	15.0
1959												
1st quarter	449.2	280.2	254.0	45.5	208.6	26.2	18.5	7.8	50.1	10.9	39.2	15.0
2nd quarter	463.2	286.9	260.6	45.8	214.7	26.4	18.5	7.9	50.3	9.9	40.5	15.4
3rd quarter	460.5	287.4	260.9	46.2	214.7	26.5	18.6	7.9	50.4	9.4	41.0	15.8
4th quarter	465.7	290.7	263.9	46.7	217.2	26.8	18.9	7.9	50.6	10.1	40.5	16.0
1960												
1st quarter	479.1	299.3	270.7	47.7	223.0	28.5	19.3	9.3	49.7	9.6	40.1	16.2
2nd quarter	479.8	302.3	273.4	48.6	224.8	28.9	19.6	9.3	50.7	10.6	40.1	16.4
3rd quarter	481.2	303.2	274.0	49.9	224.1	29.2	19.9	9.3	50.9	11.0	39.9	16.5
4th quarter	479.4	302.7	273.3	50.5	222.8	29.4	20.2	9.2	51.0	11.3	39.7	16.7
1961												
1st quarter	481.4	303.7	273.8	51.1	222.7	30.0	20.5	9.5	52.3	11.5	40.8	16.9
2nd quarter	491.1	308.0	277.6	51.8	225.8	30.3	20.8	9.6	52.6	10.9	41.8	17.1
3rd quarter	500.9	313.0	282.3	52.8	229.5	30.8	21.1	9.6	53.3	11.0	42.3	17.3
4th quarter	515.5	319.7	288.4	54.2	234.2	31.2	21.5	9.8	54.5	11.5	43.0	17.5
1962												
1st quarter	524.6	326.2	293.3	55.3	238.0	32.9	21.9	11.0	55.3	11.9	43.5	17.7
2nd quarter	531.8	332.1	298.7	56.0	242.8	33.4	22.2	11.2	55.0	11.1	43.9	18.0
3rd quarter	538.2	334.9	301.2	56.5	244.7	33.8	22.5	11.2	54.9	10.7	44.2	18.2
4th quarter	546.2	338.4	304.2	57.6	246.6	34.1	22.9	11.3	55.8	11.3	44.5	18.3
1963												
1st quarter	553.0	343.4	308.0	58.6	249.3	35.4	23.2	12.2	50.0	11.4	44.6	18.5
2nd quarter	562.1	348.3	312.4	59.4	253.0	36.0	23.6	12.3	55.8	10.8	45.0	18.7
3rd quarter	570.6	353.4	316.8	60.2	256.7	36.6	24.1	12.5	56.2	10.7	45.5	18.8
4th quarter	580.6	359.6	322.2	61.9	260.3	37.3	24.7	12.6	57.6	11.1	46.5	18.8
1964												
1st quarter	593.0	366.0	328.2	63.1	265.1	37.8	25.3	12.4	57.9	9.9	48.0	18.8
2nd quarter	603.1	373.5	334.8	64.2	270.7	38.6	26.1	12.6	58.8	9.5	49.3	18.8
3rd quarter	614.5	380.9	341.4	65.7	275.7	39.5	26.7	12.7	59.3	9.3	50.0	18.9
4th quarter	622.7	387.0	346.7	66.8	279.9	40.3	27.5	12.8	60.5	10.4	50.1	18.8
1965												
1st quarter	641.3	393.8	352.8	67.5	285.4	41.0	28.2	12.8	61.9	11.4	50.5	19.1
2nd quarter	652.6	400.8	358.9	68.5	290.3	42.0	29.0	13.0	63.2	12.0	51.2	19.3
3rd quarter	663.8	409.3	366.2	70.5	295.7	43.1	29.9	13.2	64.0	12.2	51.8	19.5
4th quarter	683.2	421.4	377.1	73.2	304.0	44.3	30.9	13.4	65.6	12.5	53.0	19.5
1966												
1st quarter	703.5	434.1	385.8	74.9	310.8	48.3	31.9	16.5	69.2	14.9	54.4	19.8
2nd quarter	713.4	445.4	395.9	76.9	319.0	49.5	32.8	16.7	67.2	12.7	54.5	19.8
3rd quarter	724.7	456.7	406.1	79.8	326.3	50.6	33.6	17.0	67.2	12.3	54.9	20.0
4th quarter	737.2	464.9	413.5	82.0	331.5	51.4	34.3	17.2	68.1	12.2	55.9	20.0
1967												
1st quarter	743.5	471.1	418.8	83.5	335.4	52.3	34.7	17.6	68.9	11.9	57.0	20.3
2nd quarter	750.2	476.8	423.6	85.0	338.6	53.2	35.4	17.8	68.5	11.1	57.4	20.4
3rd quarter	765.6	486.4	432.0	87.1	344.9	54.4	36.3	18.2	70.5	12.0	58.6	20.4
4th quarter	781.5	497.4	441.6	90.4	351.2	55.8	37.3	18.6	70.0	11.5	58.4	20.3
1968												
1st quarter	802.5	512.2	454.2	92.8	361.5	57.9	38.5	19.4	71.7	11.6	60.1	20.1
2nd quarter	823.7	525.3	465.9	95.2	370.7	59.4	39.6	19.8	73.2	11.2	61.9	20.1
3rd quarter	842.8	539.2	478.3	98.7	379.6	60.9	40.7	20.1	75.0	11.8	63.2	20.2
4th quarter	859.3	551.7	489.4	100.1	389.4	62.3	41.9	20.5	75.5	12.0	63.5	20.0
1969												
1st quarter	875.7	564.2	499.1	101.3	397.8	65.2	43.1	22.1	75.6	11.6	64.1	20.2
2nd quarter	892.1	578.2	511.4	103.1	408.3	66.9	44.3	22.5	77.1	12.5	64.6	20.3
3rd quarter	910.8	595.0	526.4	108.2	418.3	68.6	45.6	23.0	78.0	13.1	64.8	20.5
4th quarter	919.4	606.6	536.5	109.8	426.6	70.1	46.7	23.4	77.3	14.1	63.2	20.5
1970												
1st quarter	923.9	616.7	545.1	114.4	430.7	71.6	47.9	23.7	77.1	13.5	63.5	20.5
2nd quarter	935.8	622.0	549.1	116.5	432.6	72.9	49.1	23.9	76.7	12.4	64.3	20.3
3rd quarter	950.3	630.0	555.7	118.3	437.4	74.3	50.3	23.9	78.5	13.2	65.3	20.9
4th quarter	950.6	631.8	556.4	119.7	436.6	75.5	51.6	23.9	78.9	12.5	66.4	21.2
1971												
1st quarter	987.4	649.9	570.5	123.9	446.6	79.4	53.3	26.1	80.3	13.1	67.2	21.2
2nd quarter	1 007.3	661.8	580.4	125.6	454.8	81.4	55.0	26.4	82.8	13.3	69.6	21.8
3rd quarter	1 025.5	672.2	588.8	128.0	460.8	83.4	56.9	26.5	84.6	13.0	71.6	22.2
4th quarter	1 047.9	684.2	598.4	129.6	468.8	85.8	59.0	26.8	87.9	14.2	73.6	22.6
1972												
1st quarter	1 081.2	710.6	618.5	134.2	484.3	92.1	61.5	30.6	87.9	13.1	74.8	23.2
2nd quarter	1 101.7	724.7	630.4	135.7	494.7	94.4	63.3	31.0	91.3	15.4	75.9	20.3
3rd quarter	1 131.4	738.1	642.3	138.4	503.9	95.8	64.6	31.2	95.5	17.2	78.4	24.0
4th quarter	1 177.6	761.2	664.0	143.3	520.7	97.2	65.4	31.8	105.6	22.4	83.3	23.9

Table 1-13B. National Income by Type of Income: Historical Data—*Continued*

(Billions of dollars, quarterly data are at seasonally adjusted annual rates.)

NIPA Tables 1.7.5, 1.12

Year and quarter	Corporate profits with IVA and CCAdj					Net interest and miscellaneous payments	Taxes on production and imports	Less: Subsidies	Business current transfer payments, net			Current surplus of government enterprises	Addendum: Net national factor income
	Total	Taxes on corporate income	Profits after tax						Total ¹	To persons	To government		
			Total	Net dividends	Undistributed corporate profits								
1958													
1st quarter	39.5	16.9	22.5	11.6	11.0	9.1	36.8	1.1	1.8	1.3	0.5	...	373.6
2nd quarter	40.6	17.2	23.4	11.7	11.7	9.6	37.3	1.3	1.7	1.3	0.5	...	375.2
3rd quarter	44.8	19.4	25.4	11.7	13.7	9.9	37.8	1.5	1.7	1.2	0.5	...	387.3
4th quarter	50.6	22.3	28.3	11.4	16.9	10.0	38.9	1.6	1.6	1.2	0.4	...	398.2
1959													
1st quarter	54.3	23.5	30.8	12.1	18.7	8.9	39.8	1.1	1.6	1.3	0.3	0.5	408.4
2nd quarter	59.1	25.7	33.3	12.5	20.9	9.9	40.3	0.9	1.7	1.3	0.3	0.5	421.6
3rd quarter	54.2	20.1	31.1	12.8	18.3	9.9	41.7	1.1	1.7	1.3	0.3	0.5	417.6
4th quarter	54.5	22.6	32.0	13.0	19.0	10.2	42.4	1.1	1.7	1.4	0.3	0.6	422.1
1960													
1st quarter	58.6	25.1	33.5	13.2	20.3	10.3	43.7	1.0	1.7	1.3	0.4	0.5	434.1
2nd quarter	54.8	23.1	31.7	13.2	18.5	10.3	44.3	1.3	1.7	1.3	0.4	0.6	434.4
3rd quarter	53.8	22.0	31.8	13.5	18.2	10.9	44.9	1.0	1.7	1.3	0.4	0.4	435.2
4th quarter	51.5	20.9	30.6	13.5	17.1	11.3	45.3	1.2	1.8	1.3	0.5	0.4	433.2
1961													
1st quarter	50.2	20.7	29.6	13.6	16.0	11.8	45.8	1.6	1.9	1.3	0.5	0.3	435.0
2nd quarter	54.5	22.1	32.4	13.6	18.7	12.3	46.5	2.0	1.9	1.3	0.5	0.3	444.5
3rd quarter	57.2	23.4	33.9	13.9	19.9	12.7	47.3	2.2	1.9	1.4	0.5	0.3	453.6
4th quarter	61.8	25.4	36.4	14.5	21.9	13.5	48.4	2.3	2.0	1.4	0.6	0.5	466.9
1962													
1st quarter	62.6	23.9	38.6	14.6	24.1	13.3	49.4	2.3	2.0	1.5	0.6	0.4	475.1
2nd quarter	62.5	23.7	38.9	15.0	23.9	14.3	49.9	2.4	2.1	1.5	0.6	0.3	481.8
3rd quarter	64.2	24.4	39.9	15.2	24.7	14.7	50.9	2.2	2.1	1.6	0.6	0.4	486.9
4th quarter	66.9	24.5	42.4	15.4	27.0	15.1	51.3	2.2	2.2	1.6	0.6	0.4	494.5
1963													
1st quarter	67.2	24.6	42.6	15.8	26.9	14.8	52.0	2.0	2.4	1.8	0.6	0.7	499.9
2nd quarter	70.2	26.3	44.0	16.1	27.9	15.0	52.9	2.2	2.5	1.8	0.7	0.8	508.0
3rd quarter	71.7	27.0	44.7	16.3	28.3	15.5	53.9	2.3	2.5	1.9	0.7	0.8	515.6
4th quarter	73.0	27.7	45.3	16.8	28.5	15.9	54.7	2.4	2.6	2.0	0.7	0.9	524.9
1964													
1st quarter	77.1	27.9	49.1	17.5	31.7	16.7	55.7	2.7	2.7	2.1	0.6	0.9	536.5
2nd quarter	77.3	28.0	49.4	18.0	31.3	17.3	56.7	2.9	2.8	2.2	0.6	0.8	545.6
3rd quarter	78.4	28.6	49.9	18.4	31.4	18.0	57.9	2.6	3.2	2.2	1.0	0.6	555.5
4th quarter	78.0	28.2	49.9	18.9	31.0	18.2	58.8	2.7	3.3	2.3	1.0	0.8	562.5
1965													
1st quarter	85.8	29.6	56.3	19.2	37.1	19.1	60.2	2.9	3.5	2.3	1.2	0.7	579.8
2nd quarter	88.0	30.5	57.5	19.9	37.7	19.6	60.3	3.0	3.5	2.3	1.2	0.8	590.9
3rd quarter	89.3	31.1	58.2	20.5	37.6	20.1	60.5	3.0	3.5	2.2	1.2	0.7	602.2
4th quarter	94.0	33.1	60.9	21.2	39.7	20.1	61.8	3.1	3.4	2.2	1.3	0.5	620.6
1966													
1st quarter	97.4	34.2	63.2	21.3	41.9	21.3	61.4	3.6	3.4	2.2	1.3	0.5	641.8
2nd quarter	96.4	34.2	62.2	20.9	41.3	22.0	62.8	3.9	3.4	2.1	1.3	0.3	650.7
3rd quarter	94.8	33.9	61.0	20.5	40.4	22.8	63.7	4.1	3.4	2.1	1.3	0.1	661.6
4th quarter	95.9	33.3	62.6	20.0	42.6	23.9	64.9	4.2	3.4	2.1	1.3	0.2	672.9
1967													
1st quarter	93.3	32.5	60.8	21.1	39.8	24.7	65.6	4.0	3.5	2.2	1.3	0.1	678.3
2nd quarter	92.2	32.2	60.0	21.7	38.3	25.6	66.8	3.9	3.6	2.2	1.4	0.2	683.4
3rd quarter	93.2	32.5	60.7	22.1	38.7	26.0	68.7	3.7	3.7	2.3	1.4	0.3	696.6
4th quarter	96.7	34.4	62.3	21.2	41.1	26.4	70.6	3.7	3.8	2.4	1.4	0.0	710.8
1968													
1st quarter	98.1	38.7	59.4	22.6	36.8	26.8	73.4	4.0	3.9	2.5	1.4	0.3	728.9
2nd quarter	102.1	39.5	62.6	23.4	39.2	27.3	75.4	4.2	4.1	2.7	1.4	0.3	748.0
3rd quarter	102.6	39.7	63.0	24.0	39.0	27.7	77.7	4.2	4.3	2.9	1.4	0.3	764.7
4th quarter	104.1	40.6	63.5	24.2	39.3	28.4	79.1	4.2	4.4	3.0	1.4	0.2	779.8
1969													
1st quarter	103.5	41.5	62.0	24.0	38.1	31.2	80.6	4.3	4.7	3.3	1.5	0.0	794.7
2nd quarter	100.3	40.4	59.9	24.1	35.8	32.9	82.9	4.5	4.8	3.4	1.5	0.0	808.9
3rd quarter	97.4	39.1	58.3	24.3	34.0	34.6	85.2	4.7	4.8	3.4	1.5	0.0	825.5
4th quarter	92.4	38.9	53.6	24.6	29.0	35.7	86.7	4.7	4.8	3.3	1.5	0.0	832.5
1970													
1st quarter	84.7	34.5	50.2	24.5	25.7	37.4	88.5	4.7	4.6	3.1	1.5	-0.7	836.3
2nd quarter	88.5	34.7	53.8	24.3	29.6	39.5	90.5	4.8	4.5	3.0	1.5	-1.3	846.9
3rd quarter	88.4	35.7	52.7	24.2	28.4	41.8	92.5	4.7	4.2	2.8	1.4	-1.3	859.5
4th quarter	83.5	34.2	49.3	24.2	25.1	43.2	94.1	4.8	4.1	2.8	1.4	-1.5	858.7
1971													
1st quarter	96.6	37.8	58.8	25.0	33.8	44.3	97.7	4.8	4.1	2.7	1.5	-1.9	892.3
2nd quarter	98.7	38.6	60.2	25.0	35.2	45.3	98.9	4.8	4.1	2.7	1.4	-1.4	910.5
3rd quarter	101.4	37.9	63.5	25.2	38.4	45.5	101.7	4.5	4.2	2.7	1.5	-1.8	925.9
4th quarter	105.8	38.4	67.4	24.9	42.5	45.8	103.7	4.6	4.2	2.8	1.5	-1.7	946.3
1972													
1st quarter	111.5	40.4	71.2	26.1	45.0	46.6	104.6	6.1	4.5	2.9	1.6	-1.6	979.8
2nd quarter	113.4	40.7	72.8	26.4	46.3	47.9	106.8	6.2	4.7	3.0	1.7	-1.3	997.6
3rd quarter	118.2	42.0	76.2	27.1	49.1	50.2	108.9	7.2	4.9	3.2	1.7	-1.1	1 026.0
4th quarter	125.7	46.4	79.4	27.7	51.7	52.4	111.5	7.1	5.0	3.3	1.7	-0.7	1 068.8

¹Includes net transfer payments to the rest of the world, not shown separately.
. . . = Not available.

Table 1-13B. National Income by Type of Income: Historical Data—*Continued*

(Billions of dollars, quarterly data are at seasonally adjusted annual rates.)　　　　　　　　　　　　　　**NIPA Tables 1.7.5, 1.12**

Year and quarter	National income, total	Compensation of employees								Proprietors' income with IVA and CCAdj			Rental income of persons with CCAdj
		Total	Wages and salaries			Supplements to wages and salaries				Total	Farm	Nonfarm	
			Total	Government	Other	Total	Employer contributions for:						
							Employee pension and insurance funds	Government social insurance					
1973													
1st quarter	1 214.7	787.8	683.4	145.0	538.3	104.4	65.7	38.7		104.1	21.8	82.4	23.6
2nd quarter	1 239.4	805.6	700.2	147.2	553.0	105.4	66.0	39.3		109.9	27.6	82.4	23.5
3rd quarter	1 267.8	822.8	716.2	149.6	566.6	106.6	66.6	39.9		113.8	29.5	84.3	22.5
4th quarter	1 306.0	844.1	735.3	153.4	582.0	108.7	67.6	41.1		122.2	37.5	84.7	23.4
1974													
1st quarter	1 318.2	860.9	748.2	155.6	592.5	112.7	69.1	43.6		115.7	28.6	87.1	23.7
2nd quarter	1 338.9	881.1	765.3	158.2	607.1	115.8	71.3	44.5		108.6	20.1	88.5	23.1
3rd quarter	1 364.9	902.8	783.1	161.3	621.8	119.7	74.4	45.3		111.0	21.5	89.5	23.4
4th quarter	1 381.1	916.5	792.5	166.9	625.6	124.0	78.6	45.4		113.5	23.7	89.8	23.2
1975													
1st quarter	1 388.0	921.2	791.9	170.5	621.4	129.3	83.5	45.7		112.7	19.7	93.0	22.9
2nd quarter	1 418.8	934.1	800.4	174.5	625.9	133.8	87.8	46.0		114.3	20.1	94.2	22.6
3rd quarter	1 477.0	959.0	821.3	177.8	643.5	137.7	90.7	47.0		120.7	23.8	96.9	22.5
4th quarter	1 520.8	986.4	845.8	182.2	663.6	140.6	92.4	48.2		125.2	24.3	100.8	22.1
1976													
1st quarter	1 571.3	1 017.6	871.2	184.8	686.4	146.4	93.3	53.1		126.4	19.4	107.0	21.9
2nd quarter	1 596.9	1 038.4	889.4	187.3	702.1	149.0	95.1	53.9		128.6	17.0	111.6	20.8
3rd quarter	1 628.9	1 061.2	908.5	189.5	719.0	152.8	97.9	54.9		132.7	16.1	116.6	20.3
4th quarter	1 661.9	1 087.7	929.9	194.1	735.8	157.7	102.1	55.7		136.2	16.3	119.9	19.4
1977													
1st quarter	1 705.6	1 116.3	950.0	196.7	753.3	166.2	107.2	59.1		138.6	16.0	122.6	17.1
2nd quarter	1 776.0	1 153.4	980.9	199.7	781.2	172.5	111.9	60.6		140.5	14.1	126.4	16.6
3rd quarter	1 832.8	1 185.3	1 007.5	203.7	803.8	177.8	116.1	61.7		142.4	11.8	130.6	15.8
4th quarter	1 880.3	1 221.0	1 038.2	210.3	827.9	182.8	119.8	63.0		156.5	22.0	134.5	15.3
1978													
1st quarter	1 920.3	1 255.8	1 064.2	214.0	850.3	191.6	122.8	68.8		158.5	18.5	140.0	16.5
2nd quarter	2 014.3	1 302.9	1 106.0	217.2	888.8	197.0	126.0	71.0		166.1	20.9	145.2	16.2
3rd quarter	2 060.3	1 339.2	1 137.1	221.5	915.6	202.0	129.8	72.3		168.3	20.8	147.6	17.4
4th quarter	2 124.8	1 383.0	1 175.0	227.4	947.6	208.0	133.9	74.1		170.9	19.5	151.4	17.6
1979													
1st quarter	2 181.1	1 427.3	1 208.4	231.1	977.2	219.0	138.5	80.5		180.1	23.8	156.3	17.8
2nd quarter	2 219.6	1 458.3	1 234.0	233.1	1 000.9	224.2	142.6	81.6		179.2	21.8	157.3	15.6
3rd quarter	2 270.7	1 498.8	1 268.2	238.2	1 030.0	230.6	147.3	83.3		180.7	22.3	158.5	15.4
4th quarter	2 321.2	1 539.7	1 302.7	246.1	1 056.6	237.0	152.1	84.9		177.8	20.8	157.0	17.6
1980													
1st quarter	2 366.6	1 579.2	1 334.9	251.3	1 083.6	244.4	157.0	87.3		167.6	13.3	154.3	20.0
2nd quarter	2 358.0	1 600.5	1 351.0	257.7	1 093.3	249.5	161.7	87.7		160.3	3.1	157.2	14.1
3rd quarter	2 425.7	1 631.2	1 376.1	263.0	1 113.1	255.1	166.2	89.0		173.4	11.7	161.7	17.0
4th quarter	2 556.8	1 694.0	1 431.7	273.8	1 157.9	262.3	170.5	91.7		185.0	18.7	166.3	27.8
1981													
1st quarter	2 642.6	1 745.2	1 469.1	278.7	1 190.3	276.2	174.5	101.7		188.2	17.6	170.6	26.2
2nd quarter	2 684.2	1 777.5	1 496.2	282.1	1 214.1	281.3	178.3	102.9		176.4	18.2	158.2	24.4
3rd quarter	2 773.6	1 815.4	1 528.7	286.8	1 241.9	286.7	182.1	104.5		182.3	23.3	158.9	24.1
4th quarter	2 788.1	1 843.0	1 551.5	295.7	1 255.8	291.5	186.2	105.3		171.8	17.0	154.9	27.0
1982													
1st quarter	2 791.9	1 866.4	1 567.2	300.4	1 266.8	299.2	190.2	109.0		165.2	14.4	150.8	27.6
2nd quarter	2 838.1	1 885.1	1 580.9	304.6	1 276.3	304.1	194.5	109.6		169.4	12.8	156.6	24.0
3rd quarter	2 858.0	1 905.3	1 596.1	309.2	1 286.9	309.3	199.1	110.1		170.7	11.9	158.8	25.9
4th quarter	2 873.7	1 920.4	1 605.9	316.0	1 289.9	314.6	204.3	110.3		179.5	14.2	165.3	27.0
1983													
1st quarter	2 934.4	1 949.9	1 623.1	319.3	1 303.7	326.9	209.8	117.1		183.3	12.9	170.4	27.4
2nd quarter	3 014.3	1 988.6	1 655.1	323.0	1 332.1	333.5	214.7	118.7		182.6	7.9	174.8	27.4
3rd quarter	3 094.5	2 031.2	1 691.8	327.1	1 364.7	339.5	219.0	120.5		183.8	0.2	183.6	27.4
4th quarter	3 198.8	2 085.9	1 740.1	329.7	1 410.4	345.8	222.6	123.2		195.3	3.8	191.5	27.7
1984													
1st quarter	3 331.3	2 147.1	1 785.2	339.0	1 446.2	361.9	226.3	135.6		221.9	19.5	202.4	26.9
2nd quarter	3 418.3	2 196.8	1 828.2	344.8	1 483.4	368.6	230.4	138.2		231.8	21.3	210.5	25.2
3rd quarter	3 484.7	2 242.6	1 866.7	351.6	1 515.2	375.9	235.6	140.3		232.4	20.4	211.9	27.6
4th quarter	3 541.8	2 283.1	1 899.5	357.2	1 542.4	383.5	241.5	142.0		226.9	22.5	204.4	31.9
1985													
1st quarter	3 607.4	2 327.0	1 933.8	365.6	1 568.2	393.3	248.6	144.7		240.7	22.8	217.8	30.2
2nd quarter	3 655.4	2 365.0	1 963.2	370.0	1 593.2	401.8	255.3	146.4		238.5	20.4	218.0	29.2
3rd quarter	3 716.2	2 406.7	1 996.1	376.8	1 619.3	410.6	262.1	148.5		240.7	19.3	221.5	30.3
4th quarter	3 757.7	2 457.1	2 037.1	383.0	1 654.0	420.0	268.7	151.4		244.3	21.4	223.0	28.4
1986													
1st quarter	3 809.1	2 493.3	2 063.5	387.9	1 675.6	429.8	274.7	155.0		245.6	18.3	227.4	24.8
2nd quarter	3 820.4	2 519.1	2 081.8	393.6	1 688.3	437.2	280.8	156.4		251.6	19.6	232.0	24.2
3rd quarter	3 859.9	2 557.1	2 111.7	399.7	1 712.0	445.3	286.6	158.7		264.4	26.6	237.8	20.5
4th quarter	3 903.4	2 605.9	2 152.2	407.6	1 744.6	453.7	292.4	161.3		264.2	26.6	237.6	18.1
1987													
1st quarter	3 975.2	2 651.0	2 193.7	414.6	1 779.1	457.3	294.4	162.9		275.4	27.3	248.2	18.8
2nd quarter	4 073.4	2 694.2	2 230.1	420.1	1 810.0	464.2	299.4	164.7		282.3	29.0	253.3	17.4
3rd quarter	4 167.3	2 741.8	2 270.6	424.9	1 845.7	471.2	304.2	167.0		289.5	28.8	260.7	21.0
4th quarter	4 260.9	2 810.3	2 330.7	432.8	1 897.8	479.6	309.2	170.4		298.6	30.4	268.2	23.7

Table 1-13B. National Income by Type of Income: Historical Data—*Continued*

(Billions of dollars, quarterly data are at seasonally adjusted annual rates.)   **NIPA Tables 1.7.5, 1.12**

| Year and quarter | Corporate profits with IVA and CCAdj | | | | | Net interest and miscellaneous payments | Taxes on production and imports | Less: Subsidies | Business current transfer payments, net | | | Current surplus of government enterprises | Addendum: Net national factor income |
| | Total | Taxes on corporate income | Profits after tax | | | | | | Total 1 | To persons | To government | | |
			Total	Net dividends	Undistributed corporate profits								
1973													
1st quarter	133.5	49.7	83.8	28.4	55.4	53.0	114.6	5.9	5.6	3.6	1.9	-1.6	1 102.1
2nd quarter	131.3	50.2	81.0	29.3	51.7	54.8	116.2	5.7	5.9	3.9	2.0	-2.0	1 125.0
3rd quarter	133.0	48.6	84.4	30.4	54.0	58.9	118.4	4.7	5.6	4.1	1.6	-2.4	1 150.9
4th quarter	135.8	51.4	84.4	31.5	52.9	62.3	119.7	4.6	5.8	4.2	1.6	-2.8	1 187.8
1974													
1st quarter	130.3	49.7	80.6	32.5	48.0	66.8	120.8	3.6	6.3	4.3	2.0	-2.7	1 197.3
2nd quarter	128.9	52.2	76.8	33.3	43.5	71.6	124.1	2.9	6.6	4.5	2.1	-2.1	1 213.3
3rd quarter	124.3	57.3	67.0	33.6	33.4	75.2	127.1	3.2	7.0	4.9	2.1	2.7	1 236.0
4th quarter	119.3	51.9	67.4	33.5	33.9	80.4	127.7	3.6	7.3	5.2	2.1	-3.2	1 252.9
1975													
1st quarter	117.8	43.8	74.0	32.9	41.0	84.4	128.8	4.2	8.4	6.1	2.2	-4.0	1 259.0
2nd quarter	128.9	46.8	82.2	32.7	49.5	85.1	133.0	4.3	9.1	6.9	2.2	-4.2	1 285.1
3rd quarter	149.8	57.2	92.6	32.9	59.7	86.7	138.2	4.6	9.3	7.1	2.2	-4.6	1 338.7
4th quarter	159.0	58.8	100.2	33.4	66.8	87.3	141.1	4.9	9.4	7.2	2.2	-4.7	1 380.0
1976													
1st quarter	175.1	66.6	108.5	36.2	72.3	86.8	141.7	5.1	9.5	7.0	2.5	-2.7	1 427.9
2nd quarter	173.2	65.2	108.0	38.1	69.9	89.3	144.9	4.8	9.4	7.0	2.4	-2.7	1 450.3
3rd quarter	174.7	64.9	109.9	39.9	69.9	90.9	147.7	5.1	9.1	6.7	2.4	-2.6	1 479.9
4th quarter	174.3	64.5	109.9	41.9	68.0	92.6	151.3	5.5	8.6	6.1	2.5	-2.7	1 510.2
1977													
1st quarter	184.1	68.8	115.3	42.7	72.6	95.2	154.8	5.8	8.2	5.5	2.7	-3.0	1 551.4
2nd quarter	204.9	74.4	130.5	43.9	86.6	103.6	158.0	5.9	7.8	5.0	2.8	-3.1	1 619.0
3rd quarter	219.6	76.7	142.9	45.6	97.3	110.1	161.5	6.4	8.0	4.9	3.2	-3.6	1 673.3
4th quarter	214.5	77.8	136.6	46.8	89.8	114.5	164.3	10.3	8.3	5.0	3.3	-3.7	1 721.7
1978													
1st quarter	209.9	72.5	137.4	48.3	89.2	115.7	166.9	8.7	9.4	5.6	3.7	-3.6	1 756.4
2nd quarter	239.7	86.6	153.1	49.5	103.7	117.8	173.1	8.4	10.0	6.2	3.9	-3.2	1 842.8
3rd quarter	246.2	87.4	158.8	51.8	107.0	118.9	169.7	8.3	10.7	6.7	4.0	-1.9	1 890.0
4th quarter	258.4	92.9	165.5	53.7	111.8	122.7	173.9	10.4	11.4	7.3	4.1	-2.7	1 952.6
1979													
1st quarter	249.7	90.1	159.6	55.4	104.2	128.7	176.4	8.4	12.3	7.9	4.4	-2.8	2 003.6
2nd quarter	252.1	90.9	161.2	56.9	104.3	134.9	178.5	8.8	12.7	8.2	4.5	-2.9	2 040.1
3rd quarter	250.1	90.6	159.5	58.0	101.4	143.2	180.9	8.1	13.0	8.4	4.6	-3.1	2 088.1
4th quarter	244.0	88.4	155.6	59.7	95.9	157.3	184.6	8.9	13.1	8.5	4.6	-4.0	2 136.4
1980													
1st quarter	237.5	97.0	140.5	61.8	78.7	173.0	189.5	9.2	13.2	8.2	5.0	-4.1	2 177.2
2nd quarter	207.0	77.2	129.8	64.3	65.5	180.1	196.9	9.6	13.4	8.3	5.1	-4.8	2 162.1
3rd quarter	214.6	83.2	131.5	64.7	66.8	186.6	204.3	10.1	13.7	8.7	5.0	-5.1	2 222.8
4th quarter	235.1	91.4	143.8	65.6	78.2	205.0	210.6	10.3	15.7	9.3	6.4	-6.2	2 347.0
1981													
1st quarter	244.4	91.1	153.2	68.7	84.5	208.6	230.8	10.6	16.4	10.4	6.1	-6.6	2 412.5
2nd quarter	240.8	82.6	158.2	72.7	85.5	228.4	235.5	10.7	16.6	11.0	5.6	-4.6	2 447.5
3rd quarter	257.8	86.2	171.7	75.9	95.8	255.6	237.5	11.1	17.1	11.5	5.6	-5.1	2 535.2
4th quarter	246.9	77.4	169.5	77.7	91.8	260.9	238.8	13.5	17.5	11.9	5.7	-4.4	2 549.6
1982													
1st quarter	221.8	65.7	156.1	77.7	78.4	272.7	237.4	14.0	18.6	12.0	6.6	-3.8	2 553.7
2nd quarter	236.2	68.4	167.8	76.5	91.2	283.2	238.3	13.6	19.2	12.3	6.9	-3.7	2 598.0
3rd quarter	233.7	68.6	165.1	77.1	87.9	278.0	241.8	13.0	19.5	12.5	7.0	-3.9	2 613.6
4th quarter	227.7	63.2	164.5	79.5	85.0	276.1	246.3	19.4	20.0	12.7	7.2	-3.8	2 630.6
1983													
1st quarter	244.6	64.2	180.4	81.0	99.4	281.1	250.7	19.9	20.3	12.8	7.5	-3.0	2 686.3
2nd quarter	274.7	79.2	195.5	82.1	113.4	282.9	261.2	21.6	20.9	13.2	7.7	-2.5	2 756.2
3rd quarter	291.2	88.3	203.0	84.3	118.6	295.8	267.5	22.2	21.9	14.0	7.9	-2.1	2 829.5
4th quarter	308.6	90.9	217.6	86.4	131.3	307.2	273.7	21.5	23.6	15.3	8.4	-1.6	2 924.6
1984													
1st quarter	336.6	103.9	232.7	88.6	144.1	313.8	281.6	21.2	26.7	17.6	9.1	-2.1	3 046.4
2nd quarter	338.2	102.9	235.3	90.9	144.5	332.6	287.7	21.0	28.6	19.2	9.4	-1.6	3 124.5
3rd quarter	333.6	91.1	242.5	91.1	151.5	348.3	292.2	20.9	30.1	20.6	9.6	-1.3	3 184.5
4th quarter	343.1	92.3	250.8	92.7	158.1	349.7	297.5	21.2	31.2	21.5	9.7	-0.5	3 234.7
1985													
1st quarter	347.9	98.7	249.2	95.4	153.8	349.3	301.0	21.1	32.2	21.9	10.3	0.2	3 295.1
2nd quarter	351.5	97.0	254.6	97.0	157.6	346.9	305.7	21.0	38.1	22.1	16.0	1.5	3 331.0
3rd quarter	368.9	102.3	266.6	98.3	168.3	344.5	311.9	21.3	32.8	22.3	10.5	1.8	3 391.1
4th quarter	349.7	99.7	250.0	99.5	150.5	351.5	313.9	22.0	33.1	22.6	10.5	1.6	3 431.0
1986													
1st quarter	340.7	106.6	234.1	103.2	130.9	366.4	317.5	23.1	42.1	23.3	18.7	1.9	3 470.8
2nd quarter	326.6	106.3	220.2	106.4	113.9	367.2	319.5	24.2	34.5	23.5	11.1	2.0	3 488.7
3rd quarter	315.6	107.3	208.2	107.5	100.8	366.4	326.2	25.5	33.2	23.0	10.2	2.0	3 524.0
4th quarter	314.7	118.5	196.2	107.6	88.6	360.8	330.4	26.8	34.0	22.0	12.0	2.1	3 563.8
1987													
1st quarter	325.9	118.7	207.1	108.8	98.3	359.9	336.0	28.3	34.0	21.3	12.7	2.5	3 630.9
2nd quarter	362.9	132.8	230.1	109.8	120.2	366.1	344.4	30.4	34.4	20.6	13.8	2.2	3 722.9
3rd quarter	386.4	137.9	248.5	113.3	135.2	373.1	352.4	31.3	32.5	19.7	12.8	2.0	3 811.7
4th quarter	388.8	132.4	256.4	117.2	139.2	378.9	357.4	31.1	32.3	19.3	13.0	2.0	3 900.3

1Includes net transfer payments to the rest of the world, not shown separately.

Table 1-13B. National Income by Type of Income: Historical Data—*Continued*

(Billions of dollars, quarterly data are at seasonally adjusted annual rates.)   **NIPA Tables 1.7.5, 1.12**

Year and quarter	National income, total	Compensation of employees							Proprietors' income with IVA and CCAdj			Rental income of persons with CCAdj
		Total	Wages and salaries			Supplements to wages and salaries			Total	Farm	Nonfarm	
			Total	Government	Other	Total	Employer contributions for:					
							Employee pension and insurance funds	Government social insurance				
1988												
1st quarter	4 351.7	2 861.0	2 367.3	442.8	1 924.4	493.8	314.1	179.6	319.3	33.3	286.0	23.0
2nd quarter	4 444.5	2 926.1	2 422.1	449.0	1 973.0	504.0	320.6	183.4	322.8	27.4	295.3	22.6
3rd quarter	4 536.1	2 978.0	2 463.0	454.7	2 008.3	514.9	328.7	186.2	334.0	28.8	305.2	23.9
4th quarter	4 641.2	3 035.1	2 506.8	461.6	2 045.2	528.3	339.0	189.3	327.3	17.7	309.7	30.9
1989												
1st quarter	4 723.2	3 084.0	2 542.2	470.8	2 071.3	541.8	351.0	190.9	348.7	36.7	312.0	26.8
2nd quarter	4 755.2	3 117.5	2 563.4	476.8	2 086.6	554.1	361.7	192.4	340.3	32.6	307.7	24.7
3rd quarter	4 806.5	3 157.6	2 592.0	484.9	2 107.1	565.6	371.3	194.3	338.0	30.3	307.7	22.7
4th quarter	4 843.8	3 211.2	2 634.6	491.9	2 142.7	576.6	379.4	197.2	340.7	32.5	308.2	23.4
1990												
1st quarter	4 952.2	3 278.8	2 686.8	505.9	2 180.9	592.0	389.0	203.0	346.7	34.5	312.2	25.9
2nd quarter	5 034.8	3 334.8	2 735.9	515.8	2 220.1	598.9	392.6	206.2	352.3	32.7	319.6	30.2
3rd quarter	5 064.7	3 373.9	2 768.7	523.2	2 245.5	605.2	396.9	208.3	360.3	31.8	328.5	34.8
4th quarter	5 092.6	3 383.2	2 773.4	531.3	2 242.1	609.8	401.6	208.2	358.4	29.7	328.8	34.6
1991												
1st quarter	5 120.9	3 395.1	2 776.0	543.9	2 232.1	619.1	407.1	212.0	349.1	26.2	322.9	36.2
2nd quarter	5 156.4	3 430.2	2 801.2	547.1	2 254.1	629.0	415.2	213.8	354.8	27.8	326.9	38.6
3rd quarter	5 204.7	3 469.2	2 826.5	550.0	2 276.5	642.7	426.3	216.4	355.5	24.5	331.0	43.0
4th quarter	5 262.5	3 513.5	2 854.2	554.0	2 300.2	659.3	441.0	218.3	364.5	28.6	335.9	50.2
1992												
1st quarter	5 392.4	3 597.6	2 913.5	564.8	2 348.7	684.2	459.1	225.1	380.8	32.9	347.9	53.9
2nd quarter	5 476.6	3 654.4	2 952.8	570.6	2 382.2	701.6	473.8	227.8	397.4	35.4	362.0	61.1
3rd quarter	5 516.2	3 690.7	2 976.1	574.7	2 401.4	714.6	484.6	230.0	410.1	36.7	373.4	68.0
4th quarter	5 613.8	3 741.9	3 019.9	577.9	2 442.0	722.0	491.3	230.7	421.2	34.0	387.1	74.3
1993												
1st quarter	5 619.9	3 747.9	3 018.5	585.4	2 433.1	729.4	494.7	234.7	421.3	28.6	392.8	83.2
2nd quarter	5 722.7	3 803.3	3 065.5	585.7	2 479.8	737.8	498.9	238.9	432.0	34.9	397.1	91.9
3rd quarter	5 768.5	3 838.0	3 093.3	591.5	2 501.9	744.7	503.7	241.0	426.0	26.1	399.9	96.3
4th quarter	5 908.1	3 893.5	3 140.1	593.5	2 546.5	753.4	509.3	244.1	442.6	35.8	406.8	103.2
1994												
1st quarter	5 974.2	3 917.2	3 152.8	601.2	2 551.6	764.4	515.0	249.4	452.9	41.8	411.2	112.7
2nd quarter	6 101.4	3 997.2	3 224.6	608.4	2 616.2	772.6	519.2	253.3	456.9	36.7	420.3	117.4
3rd quarter	6 190.2	4 035.1	3 258.0	611.8	2 646.2	777.0	521.8	255.3	459.7	32.1	427.5	120.7
4th quarter	6 295.2	4 091.0	3 310.9	616.5	2 694.4	780.1	521.6	258.6	468.5	28.0	440.4	119.0
1995												
1st quarter	6 362.0	4 141.3	3 360.6	624.9	2 735.7	780.8	519.9	260.8	470.5	20.3	450.2	122.2
2nd quarter	6 424.1	4 177.6	3 395.3	627.6	2 767.7	782.3	519.5	262.9	475.2	18.4	456.8	126.1
3rd quarter	6 523.3	4 223.7	3 438.2	630.2	2 808.0	785.4	520.1	265.3	487.8	21.4	466.4	130.2
4th quarter	6 608.4	4 268.0	3 478.0	633.4	2 844.6	790.0	522.5	267.5	504.4	28.0	476.3	138.3
1996												
1st quarter	6 729.8	4 321.4	3 525.9	641.5	2 884.4	795.5	525.9	269.6	526.8	36.9	489.9	143.9
2nd quarter	6 857.6	4 393.5	3 590.6	646.3	2 944.3	802.8	529.4	273.4	551.0	44.2	506.9	146.0
3rd quarter	6 938.5	4 455.7	3 646.7	650.1	2 996.5	809.0	532.5	276.5	551.1	33.5	517.6	148.0
4th quarter	7 071.6	4 517.9	3 702.7	654.5	3 048.2	815.2	535.5	279.7	560.6	34.7	525.8	149.9
1997												
1st quarter	7 192.4	4 599.5	3 777.3	663.2	3 114.1	822.2	538.4	283.8	579.4	37.8	541.6	149.0
2nd quarter	7 304.3	4 665.8	3 835.5	667.8	3 167.7	830.2	543.2	287.1	579.0	28.1	550.9	149.9
3rd quarter	7 453.0	4 745.4	3 903.7	674.8	3 228.9	841.7	550.7	291.0	592.5	32.4	560.0	152.6
4th quarter	7 571.8	4 848.1	3 990.9	681.6	3 309.2	857.2	560.8	296.5	600.6	31.2	569.4	156.8
1998												
1st quarter	7 673.1	4 950.4	4 076.3	691.2	3 385.1	874.1	573.0	301.1	621.4	27.9	593.5	161.5
2nd quarter	7 799.0	5 035.9	4 146.2	698.1	3 448.1	889.7	584.5	305.2	633.7	26.4	607.2	167.2
3rd quarter	7 930.2	5 120.9	4 216.8	705.0	3 511.8	904.1	594.7	309.3	649.0	26.6	622.5	172.6
4th quarter	8 026.8	5 204.2	4 287.1	710.9	3 576.2	917.0	603.7	313.3	672.7	32.9	639.7	178.1
1999												
1st quarter	8 178.6	5 298.8	4 368.9	721.3	3 647.6	929.9	610.7	319.3	686.0	33.6	652.3	180.8
2nd quarter	8 250.1	5 352.5	4 410.7	728.1	3 682.7	941.7	620.7	321.0	694.1	28.1	665.9	184.1
3rd quarter	8 343.6	5 429.7	4 472.0	737.6	3 734.5	957.7	634.0	323.6	703.8	26.2	677.6	183.9
4th quarter	8 525.4	5 560.2	4 580.3	748.1	3 832.3	979.9	650.4	329.4	717.9	24.5	693.4	183.6
2000												
1st quarter	8 766.2	5 759.9	4 752.9	765.9	3 987.1	1 006.9	665.8	341.2	724.9	27.0	697.8	184.2
2nd quarter	8 856.3	5 800.8	4 780.1	778.6	4 001.4	1 020.7	679.1	341.6	755.2	33.4	721.9	184.3
3rd quarter	8 976.8	5 914.0	4 872.6	784.2	4 088.4	1 041.4	693.5	347.9	764.7	31.8	732.8	186.9
4th quarter	9 028.7	5 951.7	4 897.8	790.4	4 107.4	1 053.8	703.7	350.2	786.3	33.7	752.6	195.4
2001												
1st quarter	9 171.5	6 059.4	4 982.8	804.5	4 178.2	1 076.7	717.4	359.3	816.2	34.0	782.1	201.7
2nd quarter	9 208.8	6 050.2	4 963.8	815.5	4 148.3	1 086.3	727.9	358.4	835.0	32.5	802.5	207.5
3rd quarter	9 165.5	6 033.7	4 936.6	828.6	4 108.0	1 097.1	740.1	357.0	851.5	32.6	819.0	210.1
4th quarter	9 192.7	6 042.9	4 934.6	839.4	4 095.2	1 108.3	751.1	357.2	844.4	29.2	815.2	210.8
2002												
1st quarter	9 317.6	6 074.8	4 952.5	861.6	4 090.9	1 122.3	759.7	362.6	861.1	17.9	843.3	215.2
2nd quarter	9 394.5	6 137.7	5 000.7	870.4	4 130.3	1 137.0	770.7	366.3	864.8	12.8	852.0	217.4
3rd quarter	9 455.5	6 161.4	5 010.9	877.8	4 133.1	1 150.6	783.4	367.1	873.9	21.3	852.6	216.8
4th quarter	9 579.7	6 193.7	5 021.5	882.7	4 138.8	1 172.1	804.0	368.1	884.3	27.7	856.6	219.8

Table 1-13B. National Income by Type of Income: Historical Data—*Continued*

(Billions of dollars, quarterly data are at seasonally adjusted annual rates.)

NIPA Tables 1.7.5, 1.12

| Year and quarter | Corporate profits with IVA and CCAdj | | | | | Net interest and miscellaneous payments | Taxes on production and imports | Less: Subsidies | Business current transfer payments, net | | | Current surplus of government enterprises | Addendum: Net national factor income |
| | Total | Taxes on corporate income | Profits after tax | | | | | | Total [1] | To persons | To government | | |
			Total	Net dividends	Undistributed corporate profits								
1988													
1st quarter	394.5	129.3	265.2	121.7	143.4	386.3	365.1	30.4	31.1	19.6	11.5	1.7	3 984.1
2nd quarter	409.1	136.6	272.4	126.4	146.0	383.6	372.6	29.8	31.7	20.1	11.6	5.9	4 064.2
3rd quarter	415.7	146.7	269.1	132.8	136.3	396.9	377.6	29.2	33.2	20.8	12.4	6.0	4 148.5
4th quarter	440.2	153.9	286.3	138.7	147.6	412.1	382.5	28.6	35.1	21.9	13.2	6.5	4 245.7
1989													
1st quarter	423.9	158.4	265.5	148.0	117.5	432.9	391.1	28.0	37.2	23.3	14.0	6.5	4 316.3
2nd quarter	415.9	145.0	270.8	155.7	115.1	442.5	397.4	27.4	37.7	23.1	14.5	6.7	4 340.9
3rd quarter	416.5	140.4	276.1	161.1	115.0	449.2	403.8	27.1	39.1	23.2	15.9	0.0	4 304.0
4th quarter	400.7	140.5	260.3	167.1	93.1	446.0	403.2	27.3	39.0	23.1	16.0	6.8	4 422.1
1990													
1st quarter	413.5	139.3	274.2	170.2	104.0	451.0	419.4	27.1	39.4	23.3	16.1	4.6	4 516.0
2nd quarter	433.4	144.9	288.5	169.9	118.6	449.3	419.5	26.9	39.0	22.9	16.0	3.3	4 600.0
3rd quarter	407.1	149.8	257.3	170.0	87.3	447.0	426.9	26.9	38.9	21.9	17.0	2.8	4 623.1
4th quarter	414.6	147.7	266.9	166.2	100.8	452.9	434.2	27.0	39.5	20.7	18.8	2.2	4 643.7
1991													
1st quarter	454.0	141.6	312.3	175.2	137.1	424.2	444.3	27.1	39.8	19.2	20.6	5.5	4 658.5
2nd quarter	451.5	136.8	314.7	180.2	134.6	410.3	451.6	27.2	38.7	17.9	20.7	8.0	4 685.3
3rd quarter	449.4	137.4	311.9	183.1	128.8	407.3	461.2	27.5	38.5	17.0	21.5	8.2	4 724.3
4th quarter	450.5	138.5	312.0	183.6	128.4	392.3	471.3	28.1	38.7	16.4	22.2	9.6	4 771.0
1992													
1st quarter	476.5	148.2	328.3	185.2	143.2	387.8	476.2	28.6	38.6	16.5	22.4	9.4	4 896.7
2nd quarter	477.8	149.8	328.1	188.2	139.9	385.6	481.1	29.2	38.4	16.5	22.0	10.2	4 976.2
3rd quarter	463.2	144.0	319.2	191.0	128.2	379.1	485.9	30.4	38.9	16.3	22.7	10.7	5 011.1
4th quarter	483.5	152.8	330.7	193.7	137.0	382.4	490.3	32.2	43.0	15.9	27.1	9.4	5 103.3
1993													
1st quarter	481.3	158.1	323.1	196.6	126.6	382.5	489.8	35.5	40.2	15.1	25.1	9.1	5 116.2
2nd quarter	509.4	170.1	339.3	201.1	138.2	375.1	497.9	37.6	39.3	14.4	25.1	11.3	5 211.7
3rd quarter	523.6	162.1	361.5	207.6	153.9	367.5	505.0	37.7	38.7	13.7	25.4	11.1	5 251.4
4th quarter	573.7	193.8	379.9	216.0	163.9	360.4	519.8	36.0	39.3	13.1	26.9	11.6	5 373.4
1994													
1st quarter	581.6	174.5	407.0	225.6	181.4	358.5	531.9	33.6	40.7	12.8	28.7	12.2	5 422.9
2nd quarter	604.5	183.6	420.9	233.8	187.1	361.8	544.2	32.4	39.7	12.8	27.7	12.1	5 537.8
3rd quarter	638.5	201.1	437.4	240.0	197.4	364.9	550.2	31.9	41.3	13.2	28.4	11.7	5 619.0
4th quarter	663.1	213.3	449.8	244.5	205.3	378.6	554.7	32.2	41.2	14.2	26.8	11.3	5 720.2
1995													
1st quarter	664.7	217.6	447.1	247.8	199.3	383.1	554.9	34.0	43.6	16.0	25.9	15.7	5 781.8
2nd quarter	689.2	214.8	474.5	253.2	221.2	376.6	553.7	34.6	44.9	17.8	25.1	15.4	5 844.7
3rd quarter	723.2	221.7	501.5	261.8	239.7	373.1	559.2	35.1	45.8	19.6	24.6	15.6	5 937.9
4th quarter	735.0	217.3	517.7	273.0	244.6	373.1	563.9	35.5	45.5	21.4	23.9	15.8	6 018.8
1996													
1st quarter	768.9	221.6	547.4	286.3	261.1	370.3	570.8	35.5	46.8	22.8	24.7	16.5	6 131.3
2nd quarter	781.4	233.4	548.0	298.8	249.3	378.5	577.7	35.4	48.2	23.5	25.8	16.7	6 250.4
3rd quarter	786.6	233.8	552.8	309.8	243.0	384.7	581.6	35.2	48.9	23.2	26.8	17.2	6 326.0
4th quarter	807.3	237.1	570.2	319.3	250.9	394.0	592.9	34.8	66.7	21.9	45.5	17.3	6 429.6
1997													
1st quarter	835.3	238.2	597.0	327.7	269.4	403.8	595.6	34.4	46.9	19.7	27.8	17.4	6 566.9
2nd quarter	857.7	242.9	614.8	335.7	279.0	409.9	610.3	33.6	47.4	18.7	28.5	18.1	6 662.2
3rd quarter	892.6	255.1	637.5	343.5	294.0	416.0	616.6	33.4	53.5	19.0	33.4	17.3	6 799.0
4th quarter	877.5	245.5	632.0	350.9	281.1	429.1	624.0	33.8	52.5	20.4	29.6	17.1	6 912.0
1998													
1st quarter	808.5	248.5	560.0	357.1	202.8	460.7	629.1	33.8	58.9	22.8	31.1	16.4	7 002.5
2nd quarter	805.2	245.5	559.7	359.9	199.8	479.6	635.5	35.0	60.4	25.1	30.4	16.7	7 121.4
3rd quarter	813.2	252.2	561.0	358.5	202.6	489.0	643.0	36.8	62.6	27.1	31.8	16.6	7 244.8
4th quarter	789.6	247.2	542.3	352.8	189.5	482.1	650.3	39.9	74.3	28.9	43.9	15.4	7 326.6
1999													
1st quarter	842.2	256.2	586.0	344.5	241.4	473.2	657.5	42.4	65.2	31.2	35.6	17.3	7 481.0
2nd quarter	835.6	254.1	581.5	341.8	239.7	478.7	667.1	45.0	66.4	32.8	36.2	16.7	7 545.0
3rd quarter	819.2	259.2	560.0	346.6	213.5	490.3	679.0	46.4	67.9	34.8	36.2	16.2	7 627.0
4th quarter	823.9	265.7	558.3	358.7	199.6	509.6	690.8	46.9	71.8	37.1	37.8	14.5	7 795.2
2000													
1st quarter	803.3	274.3	529.0	375.7	153.2	547.1	698.6	45.1	79.1	39.8	41.0	14.2	8 019.4
2nd quarter	792.8	273.1	519.6	386.9	132.8	565.3	707.3	45.5	83.3	41.5	41.8	12.8	8 098.4
3rd quarter	775.8	254.7	521.1	390.2	130.9	573.3	711.3	45.8	87.2	43.3	42.0	9.4	8 214.8
4th quarter	753.0	258.3	494.7	386.0	108.8	574.1	717.1	47.0	91.7	45.2	42.8	6.5	8 260.4
2001													
1st quarter	743.6	224.5	519.1	374.2	144.9	577.4	724.1	55.2	98.5	47.9	42.8	5.8	8 398.4
2nd quarter	774.0	216.6	557.4	368.3	189.1	575.5	724.1	62.0	100.5	48.3	43.2	4.0	8 442.3
3rd quarter	742.3	195.0	547.3	367.1	180.2	564.8	725.4	71.2	100.1	47.0	44.2	8.8	8 402.4
4th quarter	756.2	177.0	579.2	372.7	206.5	548.0	737.2	46.4	97.5	43.9	45.2	2.2	8 402.4
2002													
1st quarter	850.7	179.3	671.5	386.8	284.6	521.3	745.0	42.6	87.8	39.1	46.6	4.3	8 523.2
2nd quarter	881.0	186.0	695.1	398.8	296.2	490.5	756.6	39.8	81.4	35.2	45.9	4.8	8 591.5
3rd quarter	910.1	193.7	716.4	403.7	312.7	475.5	771.8	41.4	77.5	32.3	45.9	9.8	8 637.7
4th quarter	986.8	210.4	776.4	411.4	365.0	474.8	777.0	41.7	76.0	30.2	46.6	9.1	8 759.4

[1] Includes net transfer payments to the rest of the world, not shown separately.

Table 1-13B. National Income by Type of Income: Historical Data—*Continued*

(Billions of dollars, quarterly data are at seasonally adjusted annual rates.)   **NIPA Tables 1.7.5, 1.12**

Year and quarter	National income, total	Compensation of employees Total	Wages and salaries Total	Government	Other	Supplements to wages and salaries Total	Employee pension and insurance funds	Government social insurance	Proprietors' income with IVA and CCAdj Total	Farm	Nonfarm	Rental income of persons with CCAdj
2003												
1st quarter	9 637.2	6 226.6	5 030.9	904.8	4 126.1	1 195.6	821.2	374.4	880.2	31.1	849.1	226.8
2nd quarter	9 778.1	6 318.7	5 102.0	912.4	4 189.6	1 216.7	836.8	379.9	894.1	38.9	855.3	234.0
3rd quarter	9 933.0	6 403.8	5 166.9	915.6	4 251.3	1 237.0	852.1	384.9	907.2	39.8	867.4	239.9
4th quarter	10 108.5	6 508.7	5 251.6	920.4	4 331.2	1 257.1	866.2	390.9	918.7	42.4	876.3	251.3
2004												
1st quarter	10 292.3	6 565.7	5 281.3	941.8	4 339.5	1 284.4	885.0	399.4	947.2	55.3	891.9	254.6
2nd quarter	10 466.5	6 690.3	5 383.6	950.6	4 433.0	1 306.6	900.4	406.2	961.9	53.0	908.9	258.7
3rd quarter	10 659.3	6 823.3	5 492.1	955.7	4 536.5	1 331.2	917.6	413.6	962.1	44.9	917.2	254.6
4th quarter	10 745.7	6 878.9	5 530.6	962.6	4 568.1	1 348.2	932.6	415.6	977.1	48.7	928.4	253.8
2005												
1st quarter	10 981.6	6 952.6	5 579.9	982.5	4 597.4	1 372.7	950.8	421.9	953.3	45.4	907.9	246.1
2nd quarter	11 118.5	7 027.4	5 639.7	987.6	4 652.0	1 387.7	962.6	425.0	960.5	49.0	911.6	242.9
3rd quarter	11 324.4	7 142.2	5 737.3	994.5	4 742.8	1 405.0	974.2	430.8	991.7	48.4	943.3	231.6
4th quarter	11 534.7	7 225.0	5 811.0	1 001.4	4 809.5	1 414.1	979.5	434.5	1 010.3	42.7	967.7	233.1
2006												
1st quarter	11 864.2	7 406.9	5 976.1	1 018.9	4 957.3	1 430.7	986.2	444.6	1 058.7	36.9	1 021.8	223.2
2nd quarter	11 955.0	7 453.0	6 015.2	1 028.1	4 987.1	1 437.7	992.1	445.6	1 062.2	35.9	1 026.3	211.9
3rd quarter	12 061.5	7 508.5	6 060.9	1 040.8	5 020.1	1 447.7	1 000.9	446.7	1 051.1	35.0	1 016.1	204.3
4th quarter	12 138.2	7 641.0	6 177.4	1 052.1	5 125.3	1 463.6	1 011.1	452.5	1 042.7	36.1	1 006.7	190.7
2007												
1st quarter	12 225.8	7 832.1	6 347.9	1 076.2	5 271.8	1 484.2	1 023.5	460.7	992.3	39.2	953.2	177.9
2nd quarter	12 322.8	7 866.8	6 370.9	1 082.5	5 288.5	1 495.9	1 035.8	460.1	972.8	34.3	938.5	189.6
3rd quarter	12 328.1	7 902.1	6 393.9	1 092.4	5 301.5	1 508.2	1 047.7	460.5	966.0	35.2	930.9	192.9
4th quarter	12 408.8	7 992.0	6 467.9	1 104.4	5 363.6	1 524.1	1 058.7	465.4	985.5	43.8	941.8	197.2
2008												
1st quarter	12 474.5	0 077.9	6 539.0	1 127.6	5 411.4	1 538.9	1 068.0	470.9	1 017.7	55.6	962.2	225.3
2nd quarter	12 514.9	8 077.3	6 531.6	1 137.9	5 393.7	1 545.7	1 074.9	470.8	1 045.9	50.0	995.9	250.0
3rd quarter	12 541.2	8 094.9	6 543.9	1 151.0	5 392.9	1 551.0	1 078.6	472.4	1 040.9	42.8	998.1	273.4
4th quarter	12 180.7	8 062.8	6 512.9	1 160.0	5 353.0	1 549.9	1 078.8	471.1	1 001.3	39.6	961.7	299.8
2009												
1st quarter	12 009.4	7 762.4	6 230.6	1 166.9	5 063.7	1 531.8	1 075.3	456.5	944.2	30.2	914.0	310.8
2nd quarter	12 002.0	7 790.5	6 256.3	1 176.0	5 080.3	1 534.2	1 074.9	459.3	944.6	31.9	912.8	325.0
3rd quarter	12 134.2	7 774.0	6 238.9	1 177.7	5 061.3	1 535.0	1 077.4	457.7	976.9	35.7	941.2	344.4
4th quarter	12 358.8	7 821.0	6 279.8	1 180.0	5 099.7	1 541.3	1 082.3	458.9	1 026.3	44.1	982.2	354.6
2010												
1st quarter	12 457.0	7 801.7	6 239.6	1 187.4	5 052.1	1 562.1	1 097.6	464.4	1 017.6	39.2	978.5	380.5
2nd quarter	12 620.8	7 947.1	6 365.5	1 196.8	5 168.7	1 581.6	1 111.8	469.8	1 024.7	43.2	981.5	397.3
3rd quarter	12 868.8	8 019.1	6 426.4	1 190.3	5 236.1	1 592.8	1 121.6	471.2	1 029.2	48.4	980.8	408.3
4th quarter	13 011.5	8 077.9	6 478.6	1 189.8	5 288.8	1 599.3	1 127.3	472.0	1 059.3	53.2	1 006.0	425.0
2011												
1st quarter	13 091.2	8 209.7	6 583.6	1 191.7	5 392.0	1 626.1	1 133.8	492.3	1 103.2	75.6	1 027.6	460.1
2nd quarter	13 255.9	8 248.9	6 615.5	1 198.8	5 416.8	1 633.4	1 140.2	493.2	1 125.2	72.3	1 052.9	478.0
3rd quarter	13 454.8	8 332.0	6 689.6	1 198.4	5 491.2	1 642.4	1 145.1	497.3	1 161.8	77.9	1 083.8	491.6
4th quarter	13 607.2	8 285.4	6 643.9	1 190.2	5 453.6	1 641.6	1 148.8	492.7	1 184.5	76.4	1 108.1	511.6
2012												
1st quarter	13 942.5	8 504.0	6 841.1	1 200.0	5 641.1	1 662.9	1 153.6	509.3	1 213.6	62.4	1 151.1	517.0
2nd quarter	13 997.2	8 550.0	6 878.5	1 196.1	5 682.4	1 671.5	1 160.7	510.8	1 240.2	59.5	1 180.7	523.0
3rd quarter	14 062.3	8 587.6	6 906.8	1 196.2	5 710.7	1 680.8	1 168.9	511.9	1 245.8	59.4	1 186.3	527.3
4th quarter	14 245.5	8 798.0	7 094.6	1 200.7	5 893.9	1 703.4	1 178.0	525.4	1 266.0	64.9	1 201.1	534.0
2013												
1st quarter	14 276.1	8 705.1	6 999.7	1 206.1	5 793.6	1 705.4	1 186.1	519.3	1 291.5	98.0	1 193.5	550.6
2nd quarter	14 382.3	8 823.7	7 102.1	1 207.0	5 895.1	1 721.6	1 195.3	526.3	1 283.0	91.0	1 192.1	561.9
3rd quarter	14 479.4	8 880.6	7 148.2	1 205.0	5 943.2	1 732.4	1 203.6	528.8	1 286.7	91.2	1 195.4	574.4
4th quarter	14 641.5	8 960.4	7 216.7	1 213.8	6 003.0	1 743.7	1 211.0	532.6	1 277.8	70.9	1 206.9	581.3
2014												
1st quarter	14 734.1	9 119.4	7 360.9	1 223.6	6 137.3	1 758.5	1 217.5	541.0	1 292.7	66.4	1 226.3	594.3
2nd quarter	15 037.0	9 175.0	7 406.4	1 231.8	6 174.7	1 768.6	1 225.5	543.1	1 319.3	76.7	1 242.6	606.7
3rd quarter	15 310.8	9 286.9	7 501.9	1 241.1	6 260.8	1 785.0	1 235.8	549.2	1 320.0	64.2	1 255.8	618.0
4th quarter	15 494.2	9 444.5	7 638.0	1 251.1	6 386.9	1 806.6	1 248.0	558.5	1 331.2	65.3	1 265.9	627.9
2015												
1st quarter	15 552.9	9 541.6	7 718.4	1 258.6	6 459.8	1 823.3	1 261.7	561.6	1 312.8	52.0	1 260.7	639.3
2nd quarter	15 719.8	9 655.9	7 813.7	1 270.4	6 543.3	1 842.2	1 273.9	568.3	1 313.9	53.0	1 260.9	658.4
3rd quarter	15 784.5	9 730.0	7 873.5	1 279.6	6 593.9	1 856.5	1 284.1	572.4	1 323.2	58.7	1 264.5	670.9
4th quarter	15 901.3	9 905.5	8 030.0	1 293.9	6 736.1	1 875.5	1 292.2	583.3	1 325.4	51.0	1 274.3	681.4
2016												
1st quarter	15 846.5	9 838.6	7 964.9	1 295.1	6 669.7	1 873.7	1 298.6	575.1	1 327.6	46.8	1 280.8	697.6
2nd quarter	15 957.6	9 979.6	8 090.2	1 305.0	6 785.2	1 889.4	1 305.5	583.9	1 339.5	46.7	1 292.8	704.8
3rd quarter	16 185.1	10 081.4	8 178.1	1 314.6	6 863.4	1 903.4	1 313.3	590.1	1 346.1	41.4	1 304.6	708.1
4th quarter	16 218.9	10 014.9	8 107.8	1 315.2	6 792.7	1 907.1	1 321.7	585.4	1 354.6	37.8	1 316.7	718.9

Table 1-13B. National Income by Type of Income: Historical Data—*Continued*

(Billions of dollars, quarterly data are at seasonally adjusted annual rates.)

NIPA Tables 1.7.5, 1.12

| Year and quarter | Corporate profits with IVA and CCAdj | | | | | Net interest and miscellaneous payments | Taxes on production and imports | Less: Subsidies | Business current transfer payments, net | | | Current surplus of government enterprises | Addendum: Net national factor income |
| | Total | Taxes on corporate income | Profits after tax | | | | | | Total [1] | To persons | To government | | |
			Total	Net dividends	Undistributed corporate profits								
2003													
1st quarter	988.2	231.5	756.6	411.5	345.2	488.0	788.6	45.0	77.7	29.6	47.2	6.1	8 809.8
2nd quarter	1 028.9	227.0	801.9	412.8	389.1	477.9	800.7	57.1	76.4	28.0	47.6	4.5	8 953.6
3rd quarter	1 076.4	247.2	829.1	436.4	392.8	458.9	814.8	47.0	75.9	25.5	48.6	3.0	9 086.2
4th quarter	1 132.1	269.3	862.8	475.3	387.5	439.9	828.0	47.2	75.0	22.0	49.7	2.0	9 250.8
2004													
1st quarter	1 238.7	277.6	961.1	515.5	445.6	409.6	843.4	44.7	77.8	17.5	51.5	0.1	9 415.7
2nd quarter	1 266.8	298.2	968.2	543.1	425.5	398.5	855.5	43.7	79.5	15.4	52.5	-0.9	9 576.2
3rd quarter	1 325.7	320.4	1 005.3	549.0	456.2	394.4	868.6	45.1	78.5	15.7	53.0	-2.7	9 760.0
4th quarter	1 302.2	328.1	974.1	648.7	325.4	411.5	888.4	52.0	89.6	18.4	52.5	-3.7	9 823.4
2005													
1st quarter	1 427.8	405.1	1 022.7	556.6	466.0	460.4	908.4	56.5	94.5	23.5	52.2	-4.9	10 040.2
2nd quarter	1 446.0	395.6	1 050.4	571.4	478.9	481.3	929.5	60.7	97.4	26.4	53.1	-5.7	10 158.1
3rd quarter	1 474.3	403.1	1 071.2	576.8	494.4	516.5	944.7	62.1	93.0	27.2	53.4	-7.3	10 356.2
4th quarter	1 562.9	445.7	1 117.2	617.3	499.9	528.9	955.6	64.3	90.7	25.8	54.9	-7.6	10 560.3
2006													
1st quarter	1 627.4	460.7	1 166.7	687.4	479.3	553.1	975.7	55.7	80.8	22.2	56.7	-5.9	10 869.4
2nd quarter	1 649.2	475.2	1 174.0	718.3	455.7	571.1	988.3	51.5	79.1	20.5	57.7	-8.1	10 947.3
3rd quarter	1 693.5	496.7	1 196.8	734.9	461.9	583.5	996.9	49.9	84.0	20.6	58.8	-10.4	11 040.9
4th quarter	1 615.9	460.8	1 155.0	763.4	391.6	616.1	1 007.0	48.7	86.4	22.6	59.9	-12.8	11 106.3
2007													
1st quarter	1 530.9	474.2	1 056.8	781.9	274.8	634.2	1 022.0	49.5	101.5	26.5	60.9	-15.7	11 167.5
2nd quarter	1 596.9	468.1	1 128.8	822.6	306.2	639.9	1 032.0	58.2	98.8	29.7	60.9	-15.7	11 266.0
3rd quarter	1 518.1	431.1	1 087.1	833.6	253.5	682.1	1 038.8	55.9	99.6	32.2	61.6	-15.6	11 261.2
4th quarter	1 470.0	408.8	1 061.2	837.6	223.7	697.6	1 045.5	54.7	94.3	34.1	64.5	-18.8	11 342.4
2008													
1st quarter	1 383.4	355.3	1 028.1	867.8	160.3	691.7	1 038.1	51.9	112.3	35.3	67.1	-20.2	11 396.1
2nd quarter	1 367.6	344.1	1 023.5	829.8	193.7	689.2	1 047.9	51.6	109.8	36.3	67.2	-21.2	11 430.0
3rd quarter	1 371.3	312.6	1 058.7	800.2	258.6	676.8	1 049.2	52.1	108.1	37.1	66.0	-21.5	11 457.4
4th quarter	1 017.9	224.4	793.5	736.7	56.8	715.9	1 032.4	54.7	127.3	37.8	82.0	-21.9	11 097.7
2009													
1st quarter	1 259.0	215.0	1 044.0	681.3	362.7	671.1	1 014.1	55.2	125.0	37.9	85.8	-21.8	10 947.3
2nd quarter	1 301.0	240.4	1 060.6	585.2	475.4	562.0	1 019.4	55.4	135.2	38.3	100.3	-20.4	10 923.2
3rd quarter	1 463.3	285.0	1 178.3	526.7	651.6	514.4	1 030.1	67.1	117.7	38.9	82.9	-19.5	11 072.9
4th quarter	1 564.7	337.4	1 227.3	505.4	721.9	506.1	1 041.0	55.7	121.5	39.7	84.9	-20.7	11 272.7
2010													
1st quarter	1 658.5	344.8	1 313.7	521.8	791.8	503.3	1 042.2	54.9	129.3	40.6	85.4	-21.2	11 361.5
2nd quarter	1 666.4	351.7	1 314.8	542.8	772.0	482.7	1 054.2	55.5	126.5	41.9	84.5	-22.6	11 518.2
3rd quarter	1 814.0	387.5	1 426.6	576.0	850.5	483.6	1 063.1	56.2	131.1	43.3	89.2	-23.5	11 754.3
4th quarter	1 846.7	398.3	1 448.4	615.2	833.3	488.0	1 069.0	56.9	127.0	46.1	89.7	-24.3	11 896.8
2011													
1st quarter	1 677.4	397.5	1 279.9	658.0	621.9	493.5	1 087.6	58.6	142.6	49.4	91.8	-24.5	11 943.9
2nd quarter	1 790.0	383.4	1 406.6	681.8	724.8	465.6	1 104.2	59.9	127.9	51.1	89.6	-24.1	12 107.8
3rd quarter	1 826.6	351.0	1 475.6	719.1	756.6	493.4	1 104.0	61.0	131.0	51.1	90.0	-24.6	12 305.4
4th quarter	1 972.5	384.5	1 588.0	755.9	832.1	499.6	1 114.6	60.8	124.6	49.4	85.5	-24.9	12 453.6
2012													
1st quarter	2 016.0	442.7	1 573.3	779.7	793.6	525.0	1 129.1	58.4	117.6	45.7	80.5	-21.3	12 775.5
2nd quarter	1 993.6	449.9	1 543.7	811.0	732.7	530.7	1 129.3	58.1	107.9	43.1	73.5	-19.4	12 837.5
3rd quarter	1 999.0	451.0	1 548.1	820.8	727.3	553.1	1 126.8	56.3	97.2	41.4	66.6	-18.2	12 912.8
4th quarter	1 984.0	446.9	1 537.1	1 026.1	511.0	502.2	1 142.9	59.4	96.0	40.7	69.6	-18.3	13 084.2
2013													
1st quarter	1 999.9	452.8	1 547.1	804.5	742.6	532.3	1 166.8	59.3	108.3	40.5	85.2	-17.4	13 079.4
2nd quarter	2 018.7	460.9	1 557.8	1 054.2	503.6	491.5	1 169.8	59.8	114.3	40.7	86.9	-13.3	13 178.8
3rd quarter	2 034.6	473.1	1 561.5	874.8	686.7	490.3	1 179.4	59.5	114.3	41.2	83.5	-10.3	13 266.6
4th quarter	2 078.2	483.9	1 594.2	983.9	610.3	504.5	1 183.7	58.5	136.7	42.0	107.8	-13.2	13 402.1
2014													
1st quarter	1 984.6	505.1	1 479.5	938.9	540.6	503.8	1 200.2	58.4	116.2	43.2	86.4	-13.3	13 494.7
2nd quarter	2 149.0	527.0	1 622.1	975.9	646.2	522.9	1 218.9	58.4	121.6	44.6	86.5	-9.5	13 773.0
3rd quarter	2 196.6	498.6	1 698.1	998.5	699.6	554.3	1 229.4	58.3	181.4	46.3	141.9	-6.9	13 975.9
4th quarter	2 232.0	490.6	1 741.4	1 032.1	709.2	558.8	1 238.0	57.2	136.3	48.3	94.1	-6.1	14 194.5
2015													
1st quarter	2 175.5	521.9	1 653.7	1 062.0	591.7	576.1	1 241.8	56.2	137.5	50.5	89.5	-2.5	14 245.3
2nd quarter	2 175.1	516.7	1 658.5	1 036.3	622.2	587.7	1 253.0	56.5	147.4	52.4	95.5	-0.6	14 391.0
3rd quarter	2 135.9	485.6	1 650.3	1 048.1	602.2	591.8	1 258.2	57.7	146.4	54.1	90.3	2.0	14 451.8
4th quarter	1 983.3	505.6	1 477.7	1 013.3	464.4	578.0	1 270.2	58.6	228.6	55.4	174.4	-1.3	14 473.5
2016													
1st quarter	2 040.8	455.9	1 584.8	1 000.7	584.1	574.1	1 274.9	60.4	163.2	56.5	106.8	-0.2	14 478.6
2nd quarter	1 996.6	471.5	1 525.1	971.3	553.9	568.0	1 276.4	62.1	165.0	57.3	110.4	-2.7	14 588.5
3rd quarter	2 101.2	487.2	1 614.1	976.3	637.7	573.7	1 296.6	63.0	151.2	57.8	92.4	0.9	14 810.5
4th quarter	2 155.2	469.5	1 685.7	979.1	706.6	566.5	1 304.1	61.6	176.6	58.0	113.8	4.8	14 810.1

[1] Includes net transfer payments to the rest of the world, not shown separately.

Table 1-14. Gross and Net Value Added of Domestic Corporate Business

(Billions of dollars, quarterly data are at seasonally adjusted annual rates.)   **NIPA Table 1.14**

Year and quarter	Gross value added of corporate business, total	Consumption of fixed capital	Net value added											Gross value added of financial corporate business
						Net operating surplus								
			Total	Compensation of employees	Taxes on production and imports less subsidies	Total	Net interest and miscellaneous payments	Business current transfer payments	Corporate profits with IVA and CCAdj					
									Total	Taxes on corporate income	Profits after tax			
											Total	Net dividends	Undistributed	
1955	233.1	19.6	213.6	144.6	19.8	49.1	0.2	1.1	47.8	22.0	25.8	8.9	16.9	11.8
1956	250.2	22.1	228.1	158.2	21.5	48.4	0.1	1.4	46.8	22.0	24.8	9.5	15.4	12.9
1957	261.8	24.6	237.2	166.5	22.8	47.9	0.3	1.6	46.0	21.4	24.6	9.9	14.8	13.8
1958	256.9	26.4	230.5	164.0	23.1	43.4	0.7	1.4	41.3	19.0	22.4	9.8	12.5	14.7
1959	287.5	27.6	259.9	180.3	25.6	54.1	-0.1	1.4	52.8	23.7	29.1	10.7	18.4	15.9
1960	300.0	28.5	271.5	190.7	27.8	52.9	-0.1	1.5	51.5	22.8	28.8	11.4	17.4	17.5
1961	308.8	29.5	279.3	195.6	28.9	54.8	0.5	1.7	52.6	22.9	29.7	11.5	18.2	18.4
1962	336.0	30.8	305.2	211.0	31.2	63.0	0.9	1.9	60.3	24.1	36.2	12.4	23.8	19.3
1963	357.5	32.4	325.0	222.7	33.2	69.2	0.5	2.3	66.4	26.4	40.1	13.6	26.5	19.6
1964	386.1	34.4	351.7	239.2	35.6	76.9	0.9	2.7	73.2	28.2	45.1	15.0	30.1	21.6
1965	423.9	37.1	386.7	259.9	37.8	89.1	1.3	3.1	84.6	31.1	53.5	16.9	36.6	23.2
1966	465.2	40.9	424.3	288.5	38.9	96.9	2.4	2.9	91.6	33.9	57.7	17.8	39.9	25.1
1967	491.3	45.1	446.2	308.4	41.4	96.4	4.2	3.1	89.1	32.9	56.2	18.3	37.9	28.1
1968	542.2	50.0	492.2	340.2	47.8	104.2	4.4	3.7	96.1	39.6	56.5	20.2	36.3	31.3
1969	590.8	55.7	535.1	377.5	52.9	104.7	8.6	4.3	91.8	40.0	51.8	20.4	31.4	36.2
1970	612.3	61.8	550.5	398.0	57.0	95.5	12.6	3.7	79.1	34.8	44.4	20.4	24.0	39.4
1971	661.1	67.6	593.5	421.7	62.8	109.0	12.8	3.4	92.8	38.2	54.6	20.3	34.3	43.1
1972	733.2	73.4	659.7	468.2	67.3	124.3	12.7	3.9	107.7	42.3	65.3	21.9	43.4	47.2
1973	820.5	82.0	738.5	526.1	74.1	138.4	15.1	4.8	118.5	50.0	68.5	23.1	45.4	51.7
1974	889.9	96.0	793.9	577.3	78.6	138.0	23.4	6.3	108.2	52.8	55.5	23.5	32.0	59.9
1975	966.0	113.5	852.4	607.8	84.5	160.1	27.7	8.2	124.2	51.6	72.6	26.4	46.2	67.6
1976	1 087.8	125.0	962.7	682.8	91.4	188.5	23.2	7.6	157.8	65.3	92.5	30.1	62.4	73.0
1977	1 233.0	140.5	1 092.5	771.7	100.0	220.8	28.1	6.0	186.7	74.4	112.2	33.7	78.5	85.5
1978	1 407.5	159.3	1 248.3	884.7	108.7	254.9	31.3	7.9	215.7	84.9	130.8	39.6	91.2	103.4
1979	1 565.0	183.4	1 381.7	1 004.4	115.0	262.2	37.0	10.8	214.4	90.0	124.4	41.5	82.9	114.6
1980	1 702.7	212.1	1 490.7	1 102.0	128.6	260.1	59.9	12.0	188.1	87.2	100.9	47.3	53.6	128.5
1981	1 935.2	244.9	1 690.3	1 220.6	154.4	315.3	03.0	14.3	217.8	84.3	133.5	58.3	75.2	146.8
1982	2 018.8	272.5	1 746.2	1 275.1	161.3	309.8	95.9	16.6	197.3	66.5	130.8	61.3	69.4	164.5
1983	2 172.9	285.9	1 887.1	1 353.0	177.4	356.6	92.4	19.5	244.7	80.6	164.1	71.3	92.7	187.4
1984	2 435.3	303.2	2 132.1	1 501.1	195.6	435.4	107.2	26.9	301.3	97.5	203.8	78.5	125.3	209.7
1985	2 605.8	326.9	2 279.0	1 615.9	209.0	454.0	106.7	30.9	316.4	99.4	217.0	85.7	131.3	236.3
1986	2 712.5	349.9	2 362.6	1 723.4	219.6	419.6	105.4	29.3	284.9	109.7	175.2	88.3	86.9	247.1
1987	2 902.9	371.3	2 531.6	1 847.6	233.4	450.6	107.7	24.9	318.0	130.4	187.5	95.6	91.9	260.4
1988	3 151.3	399.4	2 751.9	2 002.3	252.0	497.6	113.3	26.4	357.9	141.6	216.3	98.0	118.2	276.8
1989	3 329.0	427.2	2 901.8	2 119.3	267.5	514.9	134.2	33.6	347.1	146.1	201.0	126.4	74.7	308.2
1990	3 477.3	455.3	3 022.0	2 234.9	284.5	502.6	127.6	34.0	341.1	145.4	195.6	144.1	51.6	316.0
1991	3 564.1	480.9	3 083.2	2 277.8	307.9	497.5	89.0	33.7	374.9	138.6	236.3	156.2	80.1	332.3
1992	3 750.6	496.2	3 254.3	2 420.5	325.9	507.9	71.8	34.0	402.2	148.7	253.5	161.5	92.0	373.4
1993	3 926.9	519.8	3 407.1	2 515.7	343.8	547.6	70.8	31.8	445.1	171.0	274.0	184.7	89.3	391.6
1994	4 219.3	550.4	3 668.9	2 649.0	376.1	643.8	67.6	32.2	543.9	193.1	350.8	197.8	153.0	402.8
1995	4 483.9	593.6	3 890.3	2 787.9	384.8	717.6	70.7	36.9	610.1	217.8	392.2	226.2	166.1	442.5
1996	4 780.2	629.8	4 150.4	2 953.7	398.4	798.3	70.4	43.7	684.1	231.5	452.6	263.1	189.5	484.0
1997	5 153.6	674.0	4 479.6	3 176.6	416.9	886.1	93.5	34.4	758.2	245.4	512.8	292.2	220.6	545.2
1998	5 485.8	719.3	4 766.5	3 447.5	430.8	888.3	134.1	52.8	701.3	248.4	453.0	314.8	138.2	612.1
1999	5 815.5	774.6	5 040.9	3 684.3	454.0	902.6	140.5	53.9	708.2	258.8	449.4	306.4	143.1	645.6
2000	6 227.3	844.5	5 382.8	4 008.9	479.8	894.1	186.6	72.4	635.0	265.1	369.9	355.4	14.5	714.3
2001	6 226.0	894.9	5 331.1	4 015.6	476.3	839.2	170.4	85.1	583.6	203.3	380.3	329.9	50.4	754.8
2002	6 318.8	920.5	5 398.3	3 973.9	506.3	918.1	107.7	61.9	748.4	192.3	556.1	352.3	203.8	779.9
2003	6 544.3	941.5	5 602.8	4 042.0	532.6	1 028.1	87.3	51.0	889.7	243.8	646.0	401.9	244.1	819.8
2004	6 967.7	982.7	5 985.0	4 241.5	571.5	1 172.0	39.2	54.5	1 078.3	306.1	772.2	501.8	270.4	859.8
2005	7 484.0	1 051.6	6 432.4	4 444.5	616.5	1 371.4	72.9	59.8	1 238.7	412.4	826.3	319.7	506.6	951.9
2006	8 026.3	1 128.6	6 897.7	4 683.2	655.8	1 558.7	120.1	48.2	1 390.3	473.4	917.0	648.1	268.9	1 038.3
2007	8 189.1	1 197.5	6 991.6	4 893.0	681.2	1 417.4	172.9	68.9	1 175.6	445.5	730.1	678.5	51.6	985.2
2008	8 092.4	1 259.2	6 833.2	4 939.7	685.0	1 208.5	234.5	95.7	878.4	309.1	569.3	628.1	-58.8	835.7
2009	7 823.9	1 260.6	6 563.3	4 610.0	659.3	1 294.1	157.5	96.7	1 039.8	269.4	770.3	456.5	313.8	964.1
2010	8 235.5	1 262.5	6 973.0	4 706.9	685.9	1 580.2	129.1	99.8	1 351.2	370.6	980.7	442.5	538.1	996.7
2011	8 611.8	1 298.8	7 313.0	4 937.9	721.9	1 653.2	149.1	109.3	1 394.7	379.1	1 015.6	548.8	466.9	1 019.5
2012	9 148.8	1 351.0	7 797.8	5 191.8	742.0	1 863.9	209.3	66.8	1 587.8	447.6	1 140.2	680.1	460.1	1 136.9
2013	9 442.1	1 400.5	8 041.6	5 357.7	775.3	1 908.6	212.9	74.7	1 621.0	467.7	1 153.3	790.9	362.4	1 136.9
2014	10 000.2	1 465.7	8 534.5	5 648.7	811.3	2 074.5	231.0	100.4	1 743.0	505.3	1 237.7	838.5	399.2	1 283.3
2015	10 458.6	1 525.1	8 933.5	5 945.3	835.5	2 152.8	287.4	132.9	1 732.5	507.4	1 225.1	898.6	326.4	1 399.2
2016	10 611.1	1 563.2	9 047.9	6 101.1	857.5	2 089.4	274.4	136.3	1 678.7	471.0	1 207.7	822.2	385.5	1 445.7
2014														
1st quarter	9 664.1	1 438.9	8 225.2	5 555.5	796.8	1 872.9	216.3	75.1	1 581.4	505.1	1 076.3	814.5	261.8	1 199.1
2nd quarter	9 921.3	1 457.1	8 464.2	5 589.8	809.4	2 065.0	222.2	82.7	1 760.1	527.0	1 233.2	837.1	396.1	1 271.5
3rd quarter	10 126.8	1 474.5	8 652.3	5 667.9	816.5	2 167.9	234.5	144.0	1 789.5	498.6	1 290.9	836.1	454.8	1 305.7
4th quarter	10 288.5	1 492.2	8 796.3	5 781.7	822.3	2 192.3	251.1	100.0	1 841.2	490.6	1 350.5	866.3	484.2	1 356.7
2015														
1st quarter	10 329.3	1 506.6	8 822.7	5 833.4	826.3	2 163.1	272.9	103.7	1 786.4	521.9	1 264.6	930.8	333.7	1 354.3
2nd quarter	10 466.5	1 519.0	8 947.5	5 908.9	833.7	2 204.9	287.9	114.5	1 802.5	516.7	1 285.8	891.7	394.1	1 430.4
3rd quarter	10 494.8	1 533.2	8 961.6	5 955.1	836.9	2 169.6	295.4	114.8	1 759.3	485.6	1 273.8	897.4	376.4	1 388.7
4th quarter	10 543.7	1 541.5	9 002.2	6 083.8	844.9	2 073.5	293.2	198.5	1 581.7	505.6	1 076.1	874.6	201.5	1 423.6
2016														
1st quarter	10 491.4	1 547.6	8 943.8	6 003.6	849.0	2 091.2	282.3	134.0	1 674.9	455.9	1 219.0	853.0	366.0	1 346.2
2nd quarter	10 538.1	1 559.8	8 978.3	6 107.7	849.8	2 020.8	275.7	137.5	1 607.6	471.5	1 136.1	808.4	327.7	1 425.7
3rd quarter	10 715.9	1 567.4	9 148.5	6 178.1	862.8	2 107.5	270.8	123.9	1 712.9	487.2	1 225.7	803.3	422.3	1 498.6
4th quarter	10 698.8	1 577.9	9 120.9	6 114.9	868.2	2 137.9	268.6	149.8	1 719.6	469.5	1 250.1	824.2	425.9	1 512.1

Table 1-15. Gross Value Added of Nonfinancial Domestic Corporate Business in Current and Chained Dollars

(Billions of dollars, quarterly data are at seasonally adjusted annual rates.)   NIPA Table 1.14

Year and quarter	Current-dollar gross value added													Gross value added in billions of chained (2009) dollars
	Total	Consumption of fixed capital	Net value added											
			Total	Compensation of employees	Taxes on production and imports less subsidies	Net operating surplus								
						Total	Net interest and miscellaneous payments	Business current transfer payments	Corporate profits with IVA and CCAdj					
									Total	Taxes on corporate income	Profits after tax			
											Total	Net dividends	Undistributed	
1960	282.5	27.6	254.9	180.4	26.6	47.9	3.3	1.3	43.3	19.1	24.2	10.5	13.7	1 219.6
1961	290.4	28.6	261.9	184.5	27.6	49.7	3.8	1.4	44.5	19.4	25.1	10.6	14.5	1 248.6
1962	316.8	29.8	287.0	199.3	29.9	57.8	4.5	1.6	51.8	20.6	31.2	11.6	19.6	1 354.4
1963	337.8	31.3	306.5	210.1	31.7	64.7	4.8	1.6	58.3	22.8	35.5	12.4	23.1	1 437.9
1964	364.5	33.3	331.3	225.7	33.9	71.7	5.3	1.9	64.6	23.9	40.7	14.0	26.7	1 538.8
1965	400.7	35.8	364.9	245.4	36.0	83.5	6.0	2.1	75.4	27.1	48.3	16.2	32.1	1 668.2
1966	440.1	39.4	400.7	272.9	37.0	90.9	7.2	2.6	81.1	29.5	51.6	16.8	34.8	1 791.5
1967	463.2	43.5	419.7	291.1	39.3	89.3	8.6	2.7	78.1	27.8	50.2	17.3	33.0	1 842.9
1968	510.9	48.1	462.8	320.9	45.5	96.4	10.1	2.9	83.4	33.5	49.8	19.0	30.8	1 962.4
1969	554.6	53.5	501.1	356.1	50.2	94.9	13.5	3.0	78.3	33.3	45.0	19.0	25.9	2 040.9
1970	572.8	59.3	513.6	374.5	54.2	84.8	17.8	3.2	63.9	27.3	36.6	18.3	18.3	2 023.2
1971	618.0	64.7	553.3	396.2	59.5	97.6	18.8	3.6	75.2	30.0	45.2	18.1	27.0	2 102.9
1972	685.9	70.2	615.8	439.9	63.7	112.2	20.0	3.9	88.3	33.8	54.5	19.7	34.8	2 262.3
1973	768.8	78.2	690.7	495.1	70.1	125.5	23.7	4.5	97.2	40.4	56.8	20.8	36.1	2 400.0
1974	830.1	91.4	738.7	542.9	74.4	121.3	30.2	3.7	87.4	42.8	44.6	21.5	23.0	2 364.0
1975	898.3	107.7	790.6	569.0	80.2	141.4	32.4	4.7	104.3	41.9	62.4	24.6	37.8	2 330.9
1976	1 014.8	118.3	896.5	640.0	86.7	169.8	30.1	6.7	133.0	53.5	79.6	27.8	51.8	2 521.3
1977	1 147.5	132.6	1 015.0	723.3	94.6	197.0	33.2	8.7	155.1	60.6	94.6	30.9	63.6	2 706.9
1978	1 304.1	150.2	1 154.0	829.5	102.7	221.7	36.8	9.2	175.8	67.6	108.2	35.9	72.3	2 882.7
1979	1 450.4	172.4	1 278.0	942.4	108.8	226.8	43.8	9.0	174.0	70.6	103.4	37.6	65.8	2 975.2
1980	1 574.2	198.9	1 375.4	1 030.7	121.5	223.1	57.8	9.6	155.7	68.2	87.5	44.7	42.8	2 946.0
1981	1 788.4	229.1	1 559.3	1 139.9	146.7	272.8	72.2	10.7	189.9	66.0	123.9	52.5	71.4	3 065.6
1982	1 854.3	253.9	1 600.4	1 183.3	152.9	264.2	82.8	8.1	173.3	48.8	124.5	54.1	70.5	2 998.7
1983	1 985.5	264.6	1 720.9	1 250.1	168.0	302.8	82.3	10.0	210.5	61.7	148.8	63.2	85.6	3 145.4
1984	2 225.5	279.0	1 946.6	1 388.2	185.0	373.4	93.5	10.9	268.9	75.9	193.0	67.2	125.8	3 425.6
1985	2 369.5	299.0	2 070.6	1 490.1	196.6	383.9	97.5	15.4	271.1	71.1	200.0	72.0	128.0	3 584.4
1986	2 465.3	317.9	2 147.5	1 578.2	204.6	364.7	107.6	26.9	230.2	76.2	154.0	72.9	81.1	3 677.9
1987	2 642.5	334.7	2 307.8	1 685.5	216.8	405.5	116.5	29.7	259.4	94.2	165.1	76.3	88.9	3 872.9
1988	2 874.5	357.7	2 516.8	1 825.3	233.8	457.7	136.2	27.0	294.5	104.0	190.5	82.2	108.4	4 110.9
1989	3 020.8	380.1	2 640.7	1 934.8	248.2	457.8	160.1	23.5	274.1	101.2	172.9	105.4	67.6	4 189.0
1990	3 161.2	403.0	2 758.3	2 037.5	263.5	457.2	170.2	24.9	262.1	98.5	163.7	118.3	45.4	4 249.6
1991	3 231.8	424.5	2 807.3	2 071.1	285.7	450.5	157.2	26.1	267.2	88.6	178.6	125.5	53.1	4 227.7
1992	3 377.1	437.8	2 939.4	2 188.7	302.5	448.2	132.0	30.7	285.6	94.4	191.1	134.3	56.9	4 356.5
1993	3 535.3	457.9	3 077.3	2 271.0	319.3	487.0	117.9	29.5	339.6	108.0	231.6	149.2	82.4	4 463.9
1994	3 816.5	484.8	3 331.8	2 398.7	350.7	582.3	116.9	34.7	430.8	132.4	298.4	158.0	140.4	4 738.6
1995	4 041.4	523.7	3 517.7	2 524.6	358.7	634.4	126.3	30.2	477.9	140.3	337.6	178.0	159.6	4 967.4
1996	4 296.1	557.4	3 738.8	2 667.7	371.7	699.4	119.7	37.3	542.3	152.9	389.4	197.6	191.8	5 258.5
1997	4 608.4	598.4	4 010.0	2 862.6	388.9	758.6	127.0	38.5	593.1	161.4	431.7	215.9	215.8	5 609.5
1998	4 873.7	638.2	4 235.5	3 093.8	402.9	738.7	146.8	34.1	557.8	158.7	399.2	241.0	158.1	5 914.8
1999	5 169.9	683.4	4 486.5	3 310.0	424.6	751.9	159.9	45.6	546.4	171.4	375.0	224.7	150.4	6 216.6
2000	5 513.0	741.9	4 771.1	3 597.3	449.9	723.9	198.4	45.5	480.1	170.2	309.9	251.3	58.6	6 515.9
2001	5 471.2	785.3	4 685.9	3 584.6	445.0	656.3	219.1	55.3	382.0	111.2	270.7	245.4	25.3	6 358.4
2002	5 538.9	804.7	4 734.2	3 542.0	472.9	719.3	198.6	52.3	468.4	97.1	371.3	254.8	116.5	6 417.1
2003	5 724.4	818.0	4 906.5	3 595.7	495.8	815.0	169.8	61.8	583.4	132.9	450.5	293.4	157.2	6 558.0
2004	6 107.9	850.2	5 257.7	3 762.8	530.9	964.1	159.9	62.0	742.2	187.0	555.2	364.5	190.7	6 864.7
2005	6 532.1	909.9	5 622.2	3 930.3	573.2	1 118.7	173.6	74.2	870.9	271.9	599.1	170.8	428.3	7 101.3
2006	6 988.0	979.4	6 008.7	4 129.3	610.1	1 269.3	183.9	70.4	1 015.0	307.7	707.3	471.1	236.2	7 389.2
2007	7 203.9	1 040.3	6 163.6	4 305.3	632.5	1 225.8	249.0	62.2	914.6	293.8	620.8	484.6	136.2	7 454.8
2008	7 256.8	1 093.9	6 162.8	4 358.0	632.7	1 172.2	307.5	50.3	814.3	227.4	586.9	474.2	112.7	7 358.5
2009	6 859.8	1 092.0	5 767.8	4 088.4	605.9	1 073.5	283.7	71.8	718.1	177.8	540.2	351.4	188.9	6 859.8
2010	7 238.7	1 094.6	6 144.2	4 158.7	633.0	1 352.5	286.2	83.3	983.0	220.6	762.4	375.5	387.0	7 156.3
2011	7 592.3	1 139.2	6 453.1	4 363.4	670.6	1 419.1	289.7	90.4	1 039.0	228.8	810.2	441.0	369.2	7 333.4
2012	8 011.9	1 186.2	6 825.7	4 593.3	690.4	1 542.0	298.5	93.9	1 149.7	266.7	883.0	517.9	365.0	7 580.6
2013	8 305.2	1 228.2	7 077.0	4 749.7	721.5	1 605.8	281.6	94.7	1 229.6	283.6	946.0	531.9	414.1	7 752.5
2014	8 716.9	1 285.7	7 431.2	5 004.2	746.6	1 680.4	291.6	92.1	1 296.7	291.8	1 005.0	598.3	406.6	8 064.8
2015	9 059.3	1 336.1	7 723.3	5 269.3	764.6	1 689.4	308.9	104.6	1 275.8	281.1	994.7	651.8	343.0	8 358.1
2016	9 165.4	1 364.9	7 800.5	5 406.9	783.0	1 610.6	300.9	85.6	1 224.1	274.1	950.0	685.2	264.8	8 471.7
2014														
1st quarter	8 464.9	1 262.4	7 202.6	4 943.2	733.3	1 526.1	283.8	94.0	1 148.3	285.4	862.9	606.5	256.4	7 869.4
2nd quarter	8 649.7	1 278.0	7 371.7	4 965.6	744.9	1 661.2	288.4	92.8	1 280.1	297.6	982.4	604.6	377.8	8 005.4
3rd quarter	8 821.1	1 293.3	7 527.7	5 016.8	751.4	1 759.5	294.4	91.6	1 373.6	298.2	1 075.4	572.0	503.3	8 139.6
4th quarter	8 931.8	1 309.1	7 622.7	5 091.2	756.7	1 774.8	299.7	90.0	1 385.0	285.8	1 099.2	610.1	489.1	8 245.0
2015														
1st quarter	8 975.1	1 322.2	7 652.8	5 196.3	756.3	1 700.2	305.3	85.7	1 309.2	297.5	1 011.6	636.2	375.4	8 338.2
2nd quarter	9 036.1	1 331.9	7 704.1	5 245.6	763.0	1 695.5	309.4	84.1	1 302.0	310.6	991.5	638.3	353.2	8 319.5
3rd quarter	9 106.2	1 342.8	7 763.3	5 275.7	765.9	1 721.7	311.6	83.1	1 327.1	283.6	1 043.4	660.6	382.8	8 371.3
4th quarter	9 120.1	1 347.3	7 772.8	5 359.6	773.2	1 640.0	309.4	165.6	1 165.0	232.6	932.4	671.9	260.6	8 403.3
2016														
1st quarter	9 145.2	1 353.9	7 791.3	5 343.4	775.3	1 672.7	304.1	80.6	1 288.0	263.1	1 025.0	675.6	349.4	8 426.8
2nd quarter	9 112.4	1 362.6	7 749.9	5 411.2	776.0	1 562.7	301.6	79.9	1 181.2	272.6	908.6	678.8	229.9	8 413.3
3rd quarter	9 217.3	1 367.7	7 849.7	5 457.1	788.0	1 604.6	299.4	81.4	1 223.8	277.5	946.3	680.6	265.7	8 565.5
4th quarter	9 186.7	1 375.6	7 811.0	5 415.9	792.8	1 602.3	298.6	100.4	1 203.4	283.5	919.9	705.9	214.0	8 481.3

Table 1-16. Shares of Income

(Billions of dollars, percent, quarterly data are at seasonally adjusted annual rates.)   **NIPA Tables 1.10, 1.14**

Year and quarter	Gross domestic income, total economy									Net factor income, domestic corporate business				
	Billions of dollars					Percent of total				Billions of dollars			Percent of total	
	Total	Compensation of employees	Taxes on production and imports less subsidies	Net operating surplus	Consumption of fixed capital	Compensation of employees	Taxes on production and imports less subsidies	Net operating surplus	Consumption of fixed capital	Total	Compensation of employees	Net operating surplus	Compensation	Net operating surplus
1959	522.3	286.4	40.0	130.5	65.4	54.8	7.7	25.0	12.5	234.4	180.3	54.1	76.9	23.1
1960	544.6	302.0	43.4	131.3	67.9	55.5	8.0	24.1	12.5	243.6	190.7	52.9	78.3	21.7
1961	564.3	311.2	45.0	137.5	70.6	55.1	8.0	24.4	12.5	250.4	195.6	54.8	78.1	21.9
1962	605.2	333.0	48.1	150.0	74.1	55.0	7.9	24.8	12.2	274.0	211.0	63.0	77.0	23.0
1963	640.1	351.2	51.2	159.7	78.0	54.9	8.0	24.9	12.2	291.9	222.7	69.2	76.3	23.7
1964	685.8	376.9	54.6	172.0	82.4	55.0	8.0	25.1	12.0	316.1	239.2	76.9	75.7	24.3
1965	743.0	406.3	57.7	190.9	88.0	54.7	7.8	25.7	11.8	349.0	259.9	89.1	74.5	25.5
1966	809.9	450.3	59.3	205.1	95.3	55.6	7.3	25.3	11.8	385.4	288.5	96.9	74.9	25.1
1967	858.5	482.9	64.1	207.8	103.5	56.3	7.5	24.2	12.1	404.8	308.4	96.4	76.2	23.8
1968	939.3	532.1	72.2	221.7	113.3	56.6	7.7	23.6	12.1	444.4	340.2	104.2	76.6	23.4
1969	1 018.3	586.0	79.4	228.1	124.9	57.5	7.8	22.4	12.3	482.2	377.5	104.7	78.3	21.7
1970	1 070.5	625.1	86.6	222.0	136.8	58.4	8.1	20.7	12.8	493.5	398.0	95.5	80.6	19.4
1971	1 158.3	667.0	95.8	246.6	148.9	57.6	8.3	21.3	12.9	530.7	421.7	109.0	79.5	20.5
1972	1 275.3	733.6	101.3	279.5	160.9	57.5	7.9	21.9	12.6	592.5	468.2	124.3	79.0	21.0
1973	1 422.4	815.1	112.0	317.3	178.1	57.3	7.9	22.3	12.5	664.5	526.1	138.4	79.2	20.8
1974	1 541.4	890.3	121.6	323.3	206.2	57.8	7.9	21.0	13.4	715.3	577.3	138.0	80.7	19.3
1975	1 675.7	950.2	130.8	357.1	237.5	56.7	7.8	21.3	14.2	767.9	607.8	160.1	79.2	20.8
1976	1 857.1	1 051.3	141.3	405.4	259.2	56.6	7.6	21.8	14.0	871.3	682.8	188.5	78.4	21.6
1977	2 066.7	1 169.0	152.6	456.8	288.3	56.6	7.4	22.1	13.9	992.5	771.7	220.8	77.8	22.2
1978	2 333.4	1 320.3	162.0	526.1	325.1	56.6	6.9	22.5	13.9	1 139.6	884.7	254.9	77.6	22.4
1979	2 587.4	1 481.1	171.6	563.6	371.1	57.2	6.6	21.8	14.3	1 266.6	1 004.4	262.2	79.3	20.7
1980	2 818.6	1 626.3	190.5	575.7	426.0	57.7	6.8	20.4	15.1	1 362.1	1 102.0	260.1	80.9	19.1
1981	3 174.2	1 795.4	224.1	669.6	485.0	56.6	7.1	21.1	15.3	1 535.9	1 220.6	315.3	79.5	20.5
1982	3 338.2	1 894.5	225.9	683.5	534.3	56.8	6.8	20.5	16.0	1 584.9	1 275.1	309.8	80.5	19.5
1983	3 584.0	2 014.1	242.0	767.4	560.5	56.2	6.8	21.4	15.6	1 709.6	1 353.0	356.6	79.1	20.9
1984	4 002.0	2 217.6	268.7	921.4	594.3	55.4	6.7	23.0	14.9	1 936.5	1 501.1	435.4	77.5	22.5
1985	4 295.5	2 389.2	286.7	982.9	636.7	55.6	6.7	22.9	14.8	2 069.9	1 615.9	454.0	78.1	21.9
1986	4 513.4	2 545.6	298.5	987.1	682.2	56.4	6.6	21.9	15.1	2 143.0	1 723.4	419.6	80.4	19.6
1987	4 829.7	2 725.7	317.2	1 058.8	728.0	56.4	6.6	21.9	15.1	2 298.2	1 847.6	450.6	80.4	19.6
1988	5 253.1	2 950.9	345.0	1 174.8	782.4	56.2	6.6	22.4	14.9	2 499.9	2 002.3	497.6	80.1	19.9
1989	5 593.5	3 143.9	371.5	1 242.1	836.1	56.2	6.6	22.2	14.9	2 634.2	2 119.3	514.9	80.5	19.5
1990	5 888.2	3 345.0	398.0	1 258.4	886.8	56.8	6.8	21.4	15.1	2 737.5	2 234.9	502.6	81.6	18.4
1991	6 085.7	3 454.7	429.6	1 270.2	931.1	56.8	7.1	20.9	15.3	2 775.3	2 277.8	497.5	82.1	17.9
1992	6 428.4	3 674.1	453.3	1 341.3	959.7	57.2	7.1	20.9	14.9	2 928.4	2 420.5	507.9	82.7	17.3
1993	6 726.4	3 824.0	466.4	1 432.4	1 003.6	56.9	6.9	21.3	14.9	3 063.3	2 515.7	547.6	82.1	17.9
1994	7 171.9	4 014.1	512.7	1 589.5	1 055.6	56.0	7.1	22.2	14.7	3 292.8	2 649.0	643.8	80.4	19.6
1995	7 573.5	4 206.7	523.1	1 720.9	1 122.8	55.5	6.9	22.7	14.8	3 505.5	2 787.9	717.6	79.5	20.5
1996	8 043.6	4 426.2	545.6	1 895.9	1 176.0	55.0	6.8	23.6	14.6	3 752.0	2 953.7	798.3	78.7	21.3
1997	8 596.2	4 719.1	577.8	2 059.4	1 240.0	54.9	6.7	24.0	14.4	4 062.7	3 176.6	886.1	78.2	21.8
1998	9 149.3	5 082.4	603.1	2 153.6	1 310.3	55.5	6.6	23.5	14.3	4 335.8	3 447.5	888.3	79.5	20.5
1999	9 698.1	5 417.5	628.4	2 251.4	1 400.9	55.9	6.5	23.2	14.4	4 586.9	3 684.3	902.6	80.3	19.7
2000	10 384.3	5 863.1	662.8	2 344.2	1 514.2	56.5	6.4	22.6	14.6	4 903.0	4 008.9	894.1	81.8	18.2
2001	10 736.8	6 053.8	669.0	2 410.1	1 604.0	56.4	6.2	22.4	14.9	4 854.8	4 015.6	839.2	82.7	17.3
2002	11 050.3	6 149.7	721.2	2 517.3	1 662.1	55.7	6.5	22.8	15.0	4 892.0	3 973.9	918.1	81.2	18.8
2003	11 524.3	6 372.7	758.9	2 665.4	1 727.2	55.3	6.6	23.1	15.0	5 070.1	4 042.0	1 028.1	79.7	20.3
2004	12 283.5	6 748.8	817.5	2 885.5	1 831.7	54.9	6.7	23.5	14.9	5 413.5	4 241.5	1 172.0	78.4	21.6
2005	13 129.2	7 097.9	873.6	3 175.7	1 982.0	54.1	6.7	24.2	15.1	5 815.9	4 444.5	1 371.4	76.4	23.6
2006	14 073.2	7 513.7	940.4	3 483.0	2 136.0	53.4	6.7	24.7	15.2	6 241.9	4 683.2	1 558.7	75.0	25.0
2007	14 460.1	7 908.8	980.0	3 307.0	2 264.4	54.7	6.8	22.9	15.7	6 310.4	4 893.0	1 417.4	77.5	22.5
2008	14 619.2	8 090.0	989.3	3 176.5	2 363.4	55.3	6.8	21.7	16.2	6 148.2	4 939.7	1 208.5	80.3	19.7
2009	14 343.4	7 795.7	967.8	3 211.6	2 368.4	54.4	6.7	22.4	16.5	5 904.1	4 610.0	1 294.1	78.1	21.9
2010	14 915.2	7 969.5	1 001.2	3 562.8	2 381.6	53.4	6.7	23.9	16.0	6 287.1	4 706.9	1 580.2	74.9	25.1
2011	15 556.3	8 277.1	1 042.5	3 785.9	2 450.6	53.2	6.7	24.3	15.8	6 591.1	4 937.9	1 653.2	74.9	25.1
2012	16 358.5	8 618.5	1 074.1	4 131.7	2 534.2	52.7	6.6	25.3	15.5	7 055.7	5 191.8	1 863.9	73.6	26.4
2013	16 829.5	8 851.9	1 115.6	4 233.1	2 628.9	52.6	6.6	25.2	15.6	7 266.3	5 357.7	1 908.6	73.7	26.3
2014	17 657.5	9 267.0	1 163.5	4 478.9	2 748.0	52.5	6.6	25.4	15.6	7 723.2	5 648.7	2 074.5	73.1	26.9
2015	18 376.6	9 720.0	1 198.5	4 616.6	2 841.5	52.9	6.5	25.1	15.5	8 098.1	5 945.3	2 152.8	73.4	26.6
2016	18 771.6	9 992.2	1 226.2	4 636.5	2 916.7	53.2	6.5	24.7	15.5	8 190.5	6 101.1	2 089.4	74.5	25.5
2014														
1st quarter	17 199.1	9 129.4	1 141.8	4 221.7	2 706.1	53.1	6.6	24.5	15.7	7 428.4	5 555.5	1 872.9	74.8	25.2
2nd quarter	17 538.6	9 185.6	1 160.5	4 460.5	2 731.9	52.4	6.6	25.4	15.6	7 654.8	5 589.8	2 065.0	73.0	27.0
3rd quarter	17 827.9	9 297.8	1 171.1	4 596.4	2 762.6	52.2	6.6	25.8	15.5	7 835.8	5 667.9	2 167.9	72.3	27.7
4th quarter	18 064.6	9 455.2	1 180.8	4 637.1	2 791.5	52.3	6.5	25.7	15.5	7 974.0	5 781.7	2 192.3	72.5	27.5
2015														
1st quarter	18 147.7	9 552.7	1 185.6	4 597.7	2 811.7	52.6	6.5	25.3	15.5	7 996.5	5 833.4	2 163.1	72.9	27.1
2nd quarter	18 356.7	9 667.3	1 196.5	4 663.3	2 829.6	52.7	6.5	25.4	15.4	8 113.8	5 908.9	2 204.9	72.8	27.2
3rd quarter	18 447.2	9 742.0	1 200.5	4 650.4	2 854.4	52.8	6.5	25.2	15.5	8 124.7	5 955.1	2 169.6	73.3	26.7
4th quarter	18 554.9	9 918.0	1 211.6	4 554.8	2 870.5	53.5	6.5	24.5	15.5	8 157.3	6 083.8	2 073.5	74.6	25.4
2016														
1st quarter	18 551.3	9 851.7	1 214.5	4 604.2	2 880.9	53.1	6.5	24.8	15.5	8 094.8	6 003.6	2 091.2	74.2	25.8
2nd quarter	18 670.9	9 993.1	1 214.3	4 555.1	2 908.3	53.5	6.5	24.4	15.6	8 128.5	6 107.7	2 020.8	75.1	24.9
3rd quarter	18 924.4	10 095.1	1 233.6	4 668.1	2 927.6	53.3	6.5	24.7	15.5	8 285.6	6 178.1	2 107.5	74.6	25.4
4th quarter	18 939.9	10 029.0	1 242.5	4 718.5	2 950.0	53.0	6.6	24.9	15.6	8 252.8	6 114.9	2 137.9	74.1	25.9

NOTES AND DEFINITIONS, CHAPTER 1

TABLES 1-1 THROUGH 1-16

National Income and Product

SOURCE: U.S. DEPARTMENT OF COMMERCE, BUREAU OF ECONOMIC ANALYSIS (BEA)

The Bureau of Economic Analysis (BEA) within the U.S. Department of Commerce, quarterly and annually collect and produce data on how the U.S. economy is functioning. The National Income and Product Accounts (NIPA) are a set of economic accounts that provide information on the value and composition of output produced in the United States during a given period and on the types and uses of the income generated by that production. Featured in the NIPAs is gross domestic product (GDP), which measures the value of the goods and services produced by the U.S. economy in a given time period. GDP is one of the most comprehensive and closely watched economic statistics.

These tables, and others in the chapters that follow, incorporate the results of the 2017 updating of the National Income and Product Accounts (NIPAs) of the United States. Less comprehensive than the 2013 revision, revisions were generally limited to 2013 through 2016.

The 2013 comprehensive benchmark revision, first incorporated in the 18th edition, *Business Statistics 18 (2013)*, altered concepts and numbers all the way back to 1929. BEA adopted an expansion of the basic concept of production embodied in the accounts and changed the method of accounting for an important category of pension plans. Also, the constant-dollar or "real" estimates were restated to 2009 dollars, so that the levels shown are different even if the indicated rates of change are the same.

Fixed investment, one of the basic building blocks of the estimation of gross domestic product, was expanded in this revision by recognizing expenditures for research and development by business, government, and nonprofit institutions serving households (NPISHs) as investment.

The workers and capital that produce this R&D have always been reported in the labor and capital tabulations, but were treated as if they were costs of producing this year's output only. In the national income accounting as in conventional business accounting, the full costs of the R&D were subtracted from current-year business receipts in calculating business profit.

Now, in the NIPAs, the estimated value of the research over the whole life of the product—for example, from the estimated future sales of a new drug—is added to the value produced this year. However, this R&D will lose value over time and, as with a piece of machinery, its use and obsolescence, called consumption of fixed capital (CFC), is estimated and charged against GDP in each year that this capital is in use. For that reason, this change adds more to gross national product than to net national product and income.

The basic concept of the NIPAs requires equivalence (except for measurement error) between the value of output and the income and other charges against that value. The higher values of production are balanced on the income side of the accounts by the higher capital consumption allowances and by addition, to profits and other operating surplus (nonlabor income) components, of the net R&D investment—the difference between gross investment value and current year's CFC. (This does not change the tax accounting treatment. The firm still gets to charge off the entire expenditure in the year it is made, which is the most favorable treatment possible.)

Similarly, BEA is now capitalizing private spending for certain entertainment, literary, and other artistic originals as fixed investment. This includes movies, books, music, and long-lived TV programs such as situation comedies and drama (but not news, sports, games, or reality shows).

In a third expansion of the GDP investment definition, all ownership transfer costs for residential and nonresidential structures are capitalized (instead of only broker's commissions as in the previous treatment).

The other important conceptual change introduced in this revision was the adoption of accrual instead of cash accounting for defined benefit pension plans. This does not increase income and saving (or dis-saving) overall, but relocates it. Pension benefits are credited to the labor income and saving of employees when earned instead of when paid—matched by an equal and opposite change in the surplus or deficit of the employing government or business.

All the quarterly NIPA data published here, including indexes of quantity and price, are seasonally adjusted; this is not specifically noted on each table. All of the quarterly level values in current and constant dollars are also expressed at annual rates, which means that seasonally adjusted quarterly levels have been multiplied by 4 so that their scale will be comparable with the annual values shown, and this is noted on the pertinent *Business Statistics* tables. Where quarterly percent changes are shown, they are expressed as seasonally adjusted annual rates, which means that the quarter-to-quarter change in the level of GDP is calculated and then raised to the 4th power in order to express what that rate of change would be if continued over an entire year; this is noted in the column headings. For further information on these concepts see "General Notes" at the front of this volume.

Each table is notated, just above the table at the right-hand side, with the numbers of the NIPA tables from which the data are drawn.

All data and references are available on the BEA website, <http://www.bea.gov>.

DEFINITIONS AND NOTES ON THE DATA

Basic concepts of total output and income (Tables 1-1, 1-11, 1-12, and 1-13)

The NIPAs depict the U.S. economy in several different dimensions. The basic concept, and the measure that is now most frequently cited, is gross domestic product (GDP), which is the market value of all goods and services produced by labor and property located in the United States.

In principle, GDP can be measured by summing the values created by each industry in the economy. However, it can also, and more readily, be measured by summing all the final demands for the economy's output. This final-demand approach also has the advantage of depicting the origins of demand for economic production, whether from consumers, businesses, or government.

Since production for the market necessarily generates incomes equal to its value, there is also an income total that corresponds to the production value total. This income can be measured and its distribution among labor, capital, and other income recipients can be depicted.

The relationships of several of these major concepts are illustrated in Table 1-11. The definitions of these concepts are as follows:

Gross domestic product (GDP), the featured measure of the value of U.S. output, is the market value of the goods and services produced by labor and property located in the United States. Market values represent output valued at the prices paid by the final customer, and therefore include taxes on production and imports, such as sales taxes, customs duties, and taxes on property.

The term "gross" in gross domestic product and gross national product is used to indicate that capital consumption allowances (economic depreciation) have not been deducted.

GDP is primarily measured by summing the values of all of the final demands in the economy, net of the demands met by imports; this is shown in Table 1-1. Specifically, GDP is the sum of personal consumption expenditures (PCE), gross private domestic investment (including change in private inventories and before deduction of charges for consumption of fixed capital), net exports of goods and services, and government consumption expenditures and gross investment. GDP measured in this way excludes duplication involving "intermediate" purchases of goods and services (goods and services purchased by industries and used in production), the value of which is already included in the value of the final products. Production of any intermediate goods that are not used in further production in the current period is captured in the measurement of inventory change.

In concept, GDP is equal to the sum of the economic value added by (also referred to as "gross product originating in") all industries in the United States. This, in turn, also makes it the conceptual equivalent of *gross domestic income (GDI)*, a new concept introduced in the 2003 revision. GDI is the sum of the incomes earned in each domestic industry, plus the taxes on production and imports and less the subsidies that account for the difference between output value and factor input value. This derivation is shown in Table 1-12. Since the incomes and taxes can be measured directly, they can be summed to a total that is equivalent to GDP in concept but differs due to imperfections in measurement. The difference between the two is known as the *statistical discrepancy*. It is defined as GDP minus GDI, and is shown in Tables 1-11 and 1-12.

Gross national product (GNP) refers to all goods and services produced by labor and property supplied by U.S. residents—whether located in the United States or abroad—expressed at market prices. It is equal to GDP, plus *income receipts from the rest of the world*, less *income payments to the rest of the world*. *Domestic* production and income refer to the location of the factors of production, with only factors located in the United States included; *national* production and income refer to the ownership of the factors of production, with only factors owned by United States residents included.

Before the comprehensive NIPA revisions that were made in 1991, GNP was the commonly used measure of U.S. production. However, GDP is clearly preferable to GNP when used in conjunction with indicators such as employment, hours worked, and capital utilized—for example, in the calculation of labor and capital productivity—because it is confined to production taking place within the borders of the United States.

The income-side aggregate corresponding to GNP is *gross national income (GNI)*, shown as an addendum to Table 1-11. It consists of gross domestic income plus income receipts from the rest of the world, less income payments to the rest of the world. It is used as the denominator for a national saving-income ratio, presented in Chapter 5. National income is the preferred measure for calculating and comparing saving, since it is the income aggregate from which that saving arises. As with GDP and gross domestic income, the statistical discrepancy indicates the difference between the product-side and income-side measurement of the same concept.

Net national product is the market value, net of depreciation, of goods and services attributable to the labor and property supplied by U.S. residents. It is equal to GNP minus the *consumption of fixed capital (CFC)*. CFC relates only to fixed capital located in the United States. (Investment in that capital is measured by private fixed investment and government gross investment.) As of the 2009 comprehensive revision, CFC represents only the normal using-up of capital in the process of production, and no longer includes extraordinary disaster losses such as those caused by Hurricane Katrina and the 9/11 attacks. These losses are still estimated and used to write down the estimates of the capital stock, but they no longer have negative effects on our calculation of current income from production.

National income has been redefined and now includes all net incomes (net of the consumption of fixed capital) earned by U.S. residents, and also includes not only "factor incomes"—net incomes received by labor and capital as a result of their participation in the production process, but also "nonfactor charges"—taxes on production and imports, business transfer payments, and the current surplus of government enterprises, less subsidies. This change has been made to conform with the international guidelines for national accounts, *System of National Accounts (SNA) 1993.* According to *SNA 1993,* these charges cannot be eliminated from the input and output prices.

Since national income now includes the nonfactor charges, it is conceptually equivalent to *net national product* and differs only by the amount of the statistical discrepancy.

The concept formerly known as "national income," which excludes the nonfactor charges, is still included in the accounts as an addendum item, now called "net national factor income." It is shown in Table 1-13. *Net national factor income* consists of compensation of employees, proprietors' income with inventory valuation and capital consumption adjustments (IVA and CCadj, respectively), rental income of persons with capital consumption adjustment, corporate profits with inventory valuation and capital consumption adjustments, and net interest.

By definition, national income and its components exclude all income from capital gains (increases in the value of owned assets). Such increases have no counterpart on the production side of the accounts. This exclusion is partly accomplished by means of the inventory valuation and capital consumption adjustments, which will be described in the definitions of the components of product and income.

DEFINITIONS AND NOTES ON THE DATA

Imputation

The term *imputation* will appear from time to time in the definitions of product and income components. Imputed values are values estimated by BEA statisticians for certain important product and income components that are not explicitly valued in the source data, usually because a market transaction in money terms is not involved. Imputed values appear on both the product and income side of the accounts; they add equal amounts to income and spending, so that no imputed saving is created.

One important example is the imputed rent on owner-occupied housing. The building of such housing is counted as investment,

yet in the monetary accounts of the household sector, there is no income from that investment nor any rental paid for it. In the NIPAs, the rent that each such dwelling would earn if rented is estimated and added to both national and personal income (as part of rental income receipts) and to personal consumption expenditures (as part of expenditures on housing services).

Another important example is imputed interest. For example, many individuals keep monetary balances in a bank or other financial institution, receiving either no interest or below-market interest, but receiving the institution's services, such as clearing checks and otherwise facilitating payments, with little or no charge. In this case, where is the product generated by the institution's workers and capital? In the NIPAs, the depositor is imputed a market-rate-based interest return on his or her balance, which is then imputed as a service charge received by the institution, and therefore included in the value of the institution's output.

DEFINITIONS AND NOTES ON THE DATA

Components of product (Tables 1-1 through 1-6)

Personal consumption expenditures (PCE) is goods and services purchased by persons residing in the United States. PCE consists mainly of purchases of new goods and services by individuals from businesses. It includes purchases that are financed by insurance, such as government-provided and private medical insurance. In addition, PCE includes purchases of new goods and services by nonprofit institutions, net purchases of used goods ("net" here indicates purchases of used goods from business less sales of used goods to business) by individuals and nonprofit institutions, and purchases abroad of goods and services by U.S. residents traveling or working in foreign countries. PCE also includes purchases for certain goods and services provided by government agencies. (See the notes and definitions for Chapter 4 for additional information.) In the 2009 revision, new detail was provided on the allocation of PCE between the household and nonprofit sectors.

Gross private domestic investment consists of gross private fixed investment and change in private inventories.

Private fixed investment consists of both nonresidential and residential fixed investment. The term "residential" refers to the construction and equipping of living quarters for permanent occupancy. Hotels and motels are included in *nonresidential fixed investment*, as described subsequently in this section.

Private fixed investment consists of purchases of fixed assets, which are commodities that will be used in a production process for more than one year, including replacements and additions to the capital stock, and now also including research and development and other intellectual property. It is measured "gross," before a deduction for consumption of existing fixed capital. It covers all investment by private businesses and nonprofit institutions in the United States, regardless of whether the investment is owned by U.S. residents. The residential component includes investment in owner-occupied housing; the homeowner is treated equivalently to a business in these investment accounts. (However, when GDP by sector is calculated, owner-occupied housing is no longer included in the business sector. It is allocated to the households and institutions sector.) Private fixed investment does not include purchases of the same types of equipment and structures by government agencies, which are included in government gross investment, nor does it include investment by U.S. residents in other countries.

Nonresidential fixed investment is the total of nonresidential structures, nonresidential equipment, and intellectual property.

Nonresidential structures consists of new construction, brokers' commissions and other ownership transfer costs on sales of structures, and net purchases of used structures by private business and by nonprofit institutions from government agencies (that is, purchases of used structures from government minus sales of used structures to government). New construction also includes hotels and motels and mining exploration, shafts, and wells.

Nonresidential equipment consists of private business purchases on capital account of new machinery, equipment, and vehicles; dealers' margins on sales of used equipment; and net purchases of used equipment from government agencies, persons, and the rest of the world (that is, purchases of such equipment minus sales of such equipment). It does not include the estimated personal-use portion of equipment purchased for both business and personal use, which is allocated to PCE.

Intellectual property consists of purchases and in-house production of software; research and development; and private expenditures for specified entertainment, literary, and artistic originals. (See above for further description.)

Residential private fixed investment consists of both residential structures and residential producers' durable equipment (including such equipment as appliances owned by landlords and rented to tenants). Investment in structures consists of new units, improvements to existing units, purchases of manufactured homes, brokers' commissions and other ownership transfer costs on the sale of residential property, and net purchases of used residential structures from government agencies (that is, purchases of such structures from government minus sales of such structures to government). As noted above, it includes investment in owner-occupied housing.

Change in private inventories is the change in the physical volume of inventories held by businesses, with that change being valued at the average price of the period. It differs from the change in the book value of inventories reported by most businesses; an *inventory valuation adjustment (IVA)* converts book value change using historical cost valuations to the change in physical volume, valued at average replacement cost.

Net exports of goods and services is *exports of goods and services* less *imports of goods and services*. It does not include income payments or receipts or transfer payments to and from the rest of the world.

Government consumption expenditures is the estimated value of the services produced by governments (federal, state, and local) for current consumption. Since these are generally not sold, there is no market valuation and they are priced at the cost of inputs. The input costs consist of the compensation of general government employees; the estimated consumption of general government fixed capital including software and R&D (CFC, or economic depreciation); and the cost of goods and services purchased by government less the value of sales to other sectors. The value of investment in equipment and structures produced by government workers and capital is also subtracted, and is instead included in government investment. Government sales to other sectors consist primarily of receipts of tuition payments for higher education and receipts of charges for medical care.

This definition of government consumption expenditures differs in concept—but not in the amount contributed to GDP—from the treatment in existence before the 2003 revision of the NIPAs. In the current definition, goods and services purchased by government are considered to be intermediate output. In the previous definition, they were considered to be final sales. Since their value is added to the other components to yield total government consumption expenditures, the dollar total contributed to GDP is the same. The only practical difference is that the goods purchased disappear from the goods account and appear in the services account instead. In the industry sector accounts, the value added by government is also unchanged. It continues to be measured as the sum of compensation and CFC, or equivalently as gross government output less the value of goods and services purchased.

Gross government investment consists of general government and government enterprise expenditures for fixed assets (structures, equipment, software, and R&D). Government inventory investment is included in government consumption expenditures.

DEFINITIONS AND NOTES ON THE DATA

Real values, quantity and price indexes (Tables 1-2 through 1-7)

Real, or chained (2009) dollar, estimates are estimates from which the effect of price change has been removed. Prior to the 1996 comprehensive revision, constant-dollar measures were obtained by combining real output measures for different goods and services using the relative prices of a single year as weights for the entire time span of the series. In the recent environment of rapid technological change, which has caused the prices of computers and electronic components to decline rapidly relative to other prices, this method distorts the measurement of economic growth and causes excessive revisions of growth rates at each benchmark revision. The current, chained-dollar measure changes the relative price weights each year, as relative prices shift over time. As a result, recent changes in relative prices do not change historical growth rates.

Chained-dollar estimates, although expressed for continuity's sake as if they had occurred according to the prices of a single year (currently 2009), are usually not additive. This means that because of the changes in price weights each year, the chained (2009) dollar components in any given table for any year other than 2009 usually do not add to the chained (2009) dollar total. The amount of the difference for the major components of GDP is called the *residual* and is shown in Table 1-2. It is specific to each individual BEA tabulation, corresponding to the sum of the lowest level of aggregation on that tabulation. In time periods close to the base year, residuals are usually quite small; over longer periods, the differences become much larger. For this reason, BEA no longer publishes chained-dollar estimates prior to 1999, except for selected aggregate series. For the more detailed components of GDP, historical trends and fluctuations in real volumes are represented by *chain-type quantity indexes,* which are presented in Tables 1-5, 4-3, 5-4, 5-6, 6-6, 6-7, 6-11, 6-16, 7-2, 7-5, and 14-2.

Chain-weighting leads to complexity in estimating the contribution of economic sectors to an overall change in output: it becomes difficult, for someone without access to the complicated statistical methods that BEA uses, to find the correct answers to questions such as "How much are government spending cuts contributing to the drag on GDP growth?" Because of this, BEA is now calculating and publishing estimates of the arithmetic contribution of each major component to the total change in real GDP. *Business Statistics* reproduces these calculations in Table 1-4. (As will be explained later, users of these calculations should, however, bear in mind that imports are treated as a negative contribution to GDP instead of being subtracted from the demand components that give rise to them.) For further information, see J. Steven Landefeld, Brent R. Moulton, and Cindy M. Vojtech, "Chained-Dollar Indexes: Issues, Tips on Their Use, and Upcoming Changes," *Survey of Current Business* (November 2003); and J. Steven Landefeld and Robert P. Parker, "BEA's Chain Indexes, Time Series, and Measures of Long-Term Economic Growth," *Survey of Current Business* (May 1997).

GDP price indexes measure price changes between any two adjacent years (or quarters) for a fixed "market basket" of goods and services consisting of the average quantities purchased in those two years (or quarters). The annual measures are chained together to form an index with prices in 2009 set to equal 100. Using average quantities as weights while changing weights each period eliminates the substitution bias that arises in more conventional indexes, in which weights are taken from a single base period that usually takes place early in the period under measurement. Generally, using a single, early base period leads to an overstatement of price increase. The CPI-U and the CPI-W are examples of such conventional indexes, technically known as "Laspeyres" indexes. See the "General Notes" at the beginning of this volume and the notes and definitions for Chapter 8 for further explanation.

The chain-type formula guarantees that a GDP price index change will differ only trivially from the change in the implicit deflator (ratio of current-dollar to real value, expressed as a percent). Therefore, *Business Statistics* is no longer publishing a separate table of implicit deflators.

DEFINITIONS AND NOTES ON THE DATA

BEA Aggregates of sales and purchases (Tables 1-1 and 1-5 through 1-7)

Final sales of domestic product is GDP minus change in private inventories. It is the sum of personal consumption expenditures, gross private domestic fixed investment, government consumption expenditures and gross investment, and net exports of goods and services.

Gross domestic purchases is the market value of goods and services purchased by U.S. residents, regardless of where those goods and services were produced. It is GDP minus net exports (that is, minus exports plus imports) of goods and services; equivalently, it is the sum of personal consumption expenditures, gross private domestic investment, and government consumption expenditures and gross investment. The price index for gross domestic purchases is therefore a measure of price change for goods and services purchased by (rather than produced by) U.S. residents.

Final sales to domestic purchasers is gross domestic purchases minus change in private inventories.

DEFINITIONS AND NOTES ON THE DATA

U.S. Population and per capita product and income estimates (Table 1-3)

In Table 1-3, annual and quarterly measures of product, income, and consumption spending are expressed in per capita terms—the aggregate dollar amount divided by the U.S. population. Population data from 1991 forward reflect the results of the 2000 and 2010 Censuses.

DEFINITIONS AND NOTES ON THE DATA

Inventory-sales ratios (Table 1-8)

Inventories to sales ratios. The ratios shown in Table 1-8 are based on the inventory estimates underlying the measurement of inventory change in the NIPAs. They include data and estimates for not only the inventories held in manufacturing and trade (which are shown in Chapter 16), but also stocks held by all other businesses in the U.S. economy.

For the current-dollar ratios, inventories at the end of each quarter are valued in the prices that prevailed at the end of that quarter. For the constant-dollar ratios, they are valued in chained (2009) dollars. In both cases, the inventory-sales ratio is the value of the inventories at the end of the quarter divided by quarterly total sales at <u>monthly</u> rates (quarterly totals divided by 3). In other words, they represent how many months' supply businesses had on hand at the end of the period. This makes them comparable in concept and order of magnitude to the ratios shown in Chapter 16. Annual ratios are those for the fourth quarter.

Inventory data consistent with the 2013 revision are only available from 1997 to date. Tables 1-8A and B show the old estimates for earlier years with an overlap period.

DEFINITIONS AND NOTES ON THE DATA

Shares of aggregate supply and demand (Tables 1-9 and 1-10)

These tables, developed by the editor of *Business Statistics*, are not official NIPA calculations. They are components of current-dollar GDP rearranged in order to highlight relationships that are not always apparent in the official presentation of the NIPAs.

Aggregate supply combines domestic production (GDP) and imports, the two sources that, between them, supply the goods and services demanded by consumers, businesses, and governments in the U.S. economy. In this table the user can observe the growing share of imports that satisfy demands in the U.S. marketplace.

Aggregate final demand is the sum of all final (that is, excluding inventory change) demands for goods and services in the U.S. market—consumption spending, fixed investment, exports, and government consumption and investment. It is different from *final sales of domestic product* (Tables 1-1 and 1-7) because imports are not subtracted; in this table, imports are considered a source of supply, not a negative element of demand. It is different from *gross domestic purchases* (Tables 1-5 and 1-6) because it includes exports, since they are a source of demand for U.S. output, but excludes inventory change. It is like *final sales to*

domestic purchasers (Table 1-7) in excluding inventory change, but different because it also includes exports.

Table 1-10 provides alternative data on the question of the relative importance of consumption spending and other final demands to the U.S. economy. NIPA statistics on PCE as a percent of GDP are frequently cited, but there is a problem with this, since PCE includes the value of imports while GDP does not.

DEFINITIONS AND NOTES ON THE DATA

Components of income (Tables 1-11, 1-12 and 1-13)

There are now two different presentations of aggregate income for the United States: *gross domestic income* (Table 1-12) and *national income* (Table 1-13). As noted above, domestic income refers to income generated from production within the United States, while national income refers to income received by residents of the United States. This means that some of the income components differ between the two tables. Domestic income payments include payments to the rest of the world from domestic industries. National income payments exclude payments to the rest of the world but include payments received by U.S. residents from the rest of the world. These differences are seen in employee compensation, interest, and corporate profits. Taxes on production and imports, taxes on corporate income, business transfer payments, subsidies, proprietors' income, rental income, and the current surplus of government enterprises are the same in both accounts.

All income entries are now calculated on an accrual basis, associating the income with the period in which it was earned rather than when it was paid.

A third important income aggregate is *personal income.* The derivation of this well-known statistic from national income is shown in Table 1-11. See Chapter 4 and its notes and definitions for data and more information.

Compensation of employees is the income accruing to employees as remuneration for their work. It is the sum of wage and salary accruals and supplements to wages and salaries. In the domestic income account, it refers to all payments generated by domestic production, including those to workers residing in the "rest of the world." In the national and personal income accounts, there is a slightly different "compensation of employees," including that received by U.S. residents from the rest of the world but excluding that paid from the domestic production account to workers residing elsewhere.

Wages and salaries consists of the monetary remuneration of employees, including the compensation of corporate officers; corporate directors' fees paid to directors who are also employees of the corporation; commissions, tips, and bonuses; voluntary employee contributions to certain deferred compensation plans, such as 401(k) plans; and receipts-in-kind that represent income. As of the 2003 revision, it also includes judicial fees to jurors and witnesses, compensation of prison inmates, and marriage fees to justices of the peace, all of which were formerly included in "other labor income."

In concept, wages and salaries include the value of the exercise by employees of "nonqualified stock options," in which an employee is allowed to buy stock for less than its current market price. (Actual measurement of these values involves a number of problems, particularly in the short run. Such stock options are not included in the monthly wage data from the Bureau of Labor Statistics, which are the main source for current extrapolations of wages and salaries, and are not consistently reported in corporate financial statements. They are, however, generally included in the unemployment insurance wage data that are used to correct the preliminary wage and salary estimates.) Another form of stock option, the "incentive stock option," leads to a capital gain only and is thus not included in the definition of wages and salaries.

Supplements to wages and salaries consists of *employer contributions for employee pension and insurance funds* and *employer contributions for government social insurance.*

Employer contributions for employee pension and insurance funds consists of employer payments (including payments-in-kind) to private pension and profit-sharing plans, private group health and life insurance plans, privately administered workers' compensation plans, government employee retirement plans, and supplemental unemployment benefit plans. They are now measured in the period in which the employee earns the obligation rather than when the employer makes the cash payment into the fund. This includes the major part of what was once called "other labor income." The remainder of "other labor income" has been reclassified as wages and salaries, as noted above.

Employer contributions for government social insurance consists of employer payments under the following federal, state, and local government programs: old-age, survivors, and disability insurance (Social Security); hospital insurance (Medicare); unemployment insurance; railroad retirement; pension benefit guaranty; veterans' life insurance; publicly administered workers' compensation; military medical insurance; and temporary disability insurance.

Taxes on production and imports is included in the gross domestic income account to make it comparable in concept to gross domestic product. It consists of federal excise taxes and customs duties and of state and local sales taxes, property taxes (including residential real estate taxes), motor vehicle license taxes, severance taxes, special assessments, and other taxes. It is equal to the former "indirect business taxes and nontax liabilities" less most of the nontax liabilities, which have now been reclassified as "business transfer payments."

Subsidies (payments by government to business other than purchases of goods and services) are now presented separately from the current surplus of government enterprises, which is presented as a component of net operating surplus. However, for data representing the years before 1959, subsidies continue to be presented as net of the current surplus of government enterprises, since detailed data to separate the series for this period are not available.

Net operating surplus is a new aggregate introduced in the 2003 NIPA revision—a grouping of the business income components of the gross domestic income account. It represents the net income accruing to business capital. It is equal to gross domestic income minus compensation of employees, taxes on production and imports less subsidies (that is, the taxes are taken out of income and the subsidies are put in), and consumption of fixed capital (CFC). Net operating surplus consists of the surplus for private enterprises and the current surplus of government enterprises. The net operating surplus of private enterprises comprises net interest and miscellaneous payments, business current transfer payments, proprietors' income, rental income of persons, and corporate profits.

Net interest and miscellaneous payments, domestic industries consists of interest paid by domestic private enterprises and of rents and royalties paid by private enterprises to government, less interest received by domestic private enterprises. Interest received does not include interest received by noninsured pension plans, which are recorded as being directly received by persons in personal income. Both interest categories include monetary and imputed interest. In the *national* account, interest paid to the rest of the world is subtracted from the interest paid by domestic industries and interest received from the rest of the world is added. Interest payments on mortgage and home improvement loans and on home equity loans are included as net interest in the private enterprises account.

It should be noted that net interest does not include interest paid by federal, state, or local governments. In fact, government interest does not enter into the national and domestic income accounts, though it does appear as a component of personal income. The NIPAs draw a distinction between interest paid by government and that paid by business.

The reasoning behind this distinction is that interest paid by business is one of the income counterparts of the production side of the account. The value of business production (as measured by its output of goods and services) includes the value added by business capital, and interest paid by business to its lenders is part of the total return to business capital.

However, there is no product flow in the accounts that is a counterpart to the payment of interest by government. The output of government does not have a market value. For purposes of GDP measurement, BEA estimates the government contribution to

GDP as the sum of government's compensation of employees, purchases of goods and services, and consumption of government fixed capital. (See above, and also the notes and definitions to Chapter 6.) This implies an estimate (described as "conservative" by BEA) that the net return to government capital is zero—that is, that the gross return is just sufficient to pay down the depreciation. Consequently, this assumption generates no income, imputed or actual, that might correspond to the government's interest payment.

Supporting the distinction between business and government interest payments, it may be noted that most federal government debt was not incurred to finance investment, but rather to finance wars, to avoid tax increases and spending cuts during recessions, or to stimulate the economy. Furthermore, some of the largest and most productive government investments—highways—are typically financed by taxes on a pay-as-you-go basis and not by borrowing.

Business current transfer payments, net consists of payments to persons, government, and the rest of the world by private business for which no current services are performed. Net insurance settlements—actual insured losses (or claims payable) less a normal level of losses—are treated as transfer payments. Payments to government consist of federal deposit insurance premiums, fines, regulatory and inspection fees, tobacco settlements, and other miscellaneous payments previously classified as "nontaxes." Taxes paid by domestic corporations to foreign governments, formerly classified as transfer payments, are now counted as taxes on corporate income.

In the NIPAs, capital income other than interest—corporate profits, proprietors' income, and rental income—is converted from the basis usually shown in the books of business, and reported to the Internal Revenue Service, to a basis that more closely represents income from current production. In the business accounts that provide the source data, depreciation of structures and equipment typically reflects a historical cost basis and a possibly arbitrary service life allowed by law to be used for tax purposes. BEA adjusts these values to reflect the average actual life of the capital goods and the cost of replacing them in the current period's prices. This conversion is done for all three forms of capital income. In addition, corporate and proprietors' incomes also require an adjustment for inventory valuation to exclude any profits or losses that might appear in the books, should the cost of inventory acquisition not be valued in the current period's prices. These two adjustments are called the *capital consumption adjustment (CCAdj)* and the *inventory valuation adjustment (IVA)*. They are described in more detail below.

Proprietors' income with inventory valuation and capital consumption adjustments is the current-production income (including income-in-kind) of sole proprietorships and partnerships and of tax-exempt cooperatives. The imputed net rental income of owner-occupants of farm dwellings is included, but the imputed net rental income of owner-occupants of nonfarm dwellings is

included in rental income of persons. Fees paid to outside directors of corporations are included. Proprietors' income excludes dividends and monetary interest received by nonfinancial business and rental incomes received by persons not primarily engaged in the real estate business; these incomes are included in dividends, net interest, and rental income of persons, respectively.

Rental income of persons with capital consumption adjustment is the net current-production income of persons from the rental of real property (except for the income of persons primarily engaged in the real estate business), the imputed net rental income of owner-occupants of nonfarm dwellings, and the royalties received by persons from patents, copyrights, and rights to natural resources. Consistent with the classification of investment in owner-occupied housing as business investment, the homeowner is considered to be paying himself or herself the rental value of the house (classified as PCE for services) and receiving as net income the amount of the rental that remains after paying interest and other costs.

Corporate profits with inventory valuation and capital consumption adjustments, often referred to as "economic profits," is the current-production income, net of economic depreciation, of organizations treated as corporations in the NIPAs. These organizations consist of all entities required to file federal corporate tax returns, including mutual financial institutions and cooperatives subject to federal income tax; private noninsured pension funds; nonprofit institutions that primarily serve business; Federal Reserve Banks, which accrue income stemming from the conduct of monetary policy; and federally sponsored credit agencies. This income is measured as receipts less expenses as defined in federal tax law, except for the following differences: receipts exclude capital gains and dividends received; expenses exclude depletion and capital losses and losses resulting from bad debts; inventory withdrawals are valued at replacement cost; and depreciation is on a consistent accounting basis and is valued at replacement cost.

Since *national* income is defined as the income of U.S. residents, its profits component includes income earned abroad by U.S. corporations and excludes income earned by the rest of the world within the United States.

Taxes on corporate income consists of taxes on corporate income paid to government and to the rest of the world.

Taxes on corporate income paid to government is the sum of federal, state, and local income taxes on all income subject to taxes. This income includes capital gains and other income excluded from profits before tax. These taxes are measured on an accrual basis, net of applicable tax credits.

Taxes on corporate income paid to the rest of the world consists of nonresident taxes, which are those paid by domestic corporations to foreign governments. These taxes were formerly classified as "business transfer payments to the rest of the world."

Profits after tax is total corporate profits with IVA and CCAdj less taxes on corporate income. It consists of dividends and undistributed corporate profits.

Dividends is payments in cash or other assets, excluding those made using corporations' own stock, that are made by corporations to stockholders. In the domestic account, these are payments by domestic industries to stockholders in the United States and abroad; in the national account, these are dividends received by U.S. residents from domestic and foreign industries. The payments are measured net of dividends received by U.S. corporations. Dividends paid to state and local government social insurance funds and general government are included.

Undistributed profits is corporate profits after tax with IVA and CCAdj less dividends.

The *inventory valuation adjustment (IVA)* is the difference between the cost of inventory withdrawals valued at replacement cost and the cost as valued in the source data used to determine profits before tax, which in many cases charge inventories at acquisition cost. It is calculated separately for corporate profits and for nonfarm proprietors' income. Its behavior is determined by price changes, especially for materials. When prices are rising, which has been typical of much of the postwar period, the business-reported value of inventory change will include a capital gains component, which needs to be removed from reported inventory change on the product side in order to correctly measure the change in the volume of inventories, and from reported profits on the income side of the accounts in order to remove the capital gains element. At such times, the IVA will be a negative figure, which is added to reported profits to yield economic profits. Occasionally, falling prices—especially for petroleum and products—will result in a positive IVA. No adjustment is needed for farm proprietors' income, as farm inventories are measured on a current-market-cost basis.

Consumption of fixed capital (CFC) is a charge for the using-up of private and government fixed capital located in the United States. It is not based on the depreciation schedules allowed in tax law, but instead on studies of prices of used equipment and structures in resale markets and other service life information.

For general government and for nonprofit institutions that primarily serve individuals, CFC on their capital assets is recorded in government consumption expenditures and in personal consumption expenditures, respectively. It is considered to be the value of the current services of the fixed capital assets owned and used by these entities.

Private capital consumption allowances consists of tax-return-based depreciation charges for corporations and nonfarm proprietorships; BEA estimates for R&D and other intellectual property; and historical cost depreciation (calculated by BEA using a geometric pattern of price declines) for farm proprietorships, rental income of persons, and nonprofit institutions.

The *private capital consumption adjustment (CCAdj)* is the difference between private capital consumption allowances and private consumption of fixed capital. The CCAdj has two parts:

- The first component of CCAdj converts tax-return-based depreciation to consistent historical cost accounting based on actual service lives of capital. In the postwar period, this has usually been a large positive number, that is, a net addition to profits and subtraction from reported depreciation. This is the case because U.S. tax law typically allows depreciation periods shorter than actual service lives. Tax depreciation was accelerated even further for 2001 through 2004. This component is a reallocation of gross business saving from depreciation to profits; gross saving is unchanged, with exactly offsetting changes in capital consumption and net saving.

- The second component is analogous to the IVA: it converts reported business capital consumption allowances from the historical cost basis to a replacement cost basis. It is determined by the price behavior of capital goods. These prices have had an upward drift in the postwar period, which has been much more stable than the changes in materials prices. Hence, this component is consistently negative (serving to reduce economic profits relative to the reported data) but less volatile than the IVA.

In 1982 through 2004, positive values for the first component outweighed negative values for the second, resulting in a net positive CCAdj, an addition to profits. However, when the accelerated depreciation expired in 2005, there was a sharp decline in the consistent-accounting adjustment and it was outweighed by the price adjustment. This led to negative CCAdjs in 2005 through 2007, reducing profits from the reported numbers.

DEFINITIONS AND NOTES ON THE DATA

Gross value added of domestic corporate business (Tables 1-14 and 1-15)

Gross value added is the term now used for what was formerly called "gross domestic product originating." It represents the share of the GDP that is produced in the specified sector or industry. Tables 1-14 and 1-15 show the current-dollar value of gross value added for all domestic corporate business and its financial and nonfinancial components. For the total and for nonfinancial corporations, consumption of fixed capital and net value added are shown, as is the allocation of net value added among employee compensation, taxes and transfer payments, and capital income. Constant-dollar values are also shown for nonfinancial corporations.

The data for nonfinancial corporations are often considered to be somewhat sturdier than data for the other sectors of the economy, since they exclude sectors whose outputs are difficult to evaluate—households, institutions, general government, and financial business—as well as excluding all noncorporate business, in which the separate contributions of labor and capital are not readily measured.

Data availability and revisions

Annual data are available beginning with 1929. Quarterly data begin with 1946 for current-dollar values and 1947 for quantity and price measures such as real GDP and the GDP price index. Not all data are available for all time periods.

New data are normally released toward the end of each month. The "advance" estimate of GDP for each calendar quarter is released at the end of the month after the quarter's end. The "second" estimate, including more complete product data and the first estimates of corporate profits, is released at the end of the second month after the quarter's end, and a "third" estimate including still more complete data at the end of the third month. Wage and salary and related income-side components may be revised for previous quarters as well.

At the end of each July, there is an "annual" revision, incorporating more complete data and other improvements, affecting at least the previous 3 years. Every five years, there is a "comprehensive" revision, such as the 2013 revision incorporated in this volume, corresponding with updated statistics from the quinquennial benchmark input-output accounts and incorporating a revision of the base year for constant-price and index numbers.

The most recent data are published each month in the *Survey of Current Business*. Current and historical data may be obtained from the BEA Web site at <http://www.bea.gov> and the STAT-USA subscription Web site at <http://www.stat-usa.gov>.

REFERENCES

The 2017 annual revision of the NIPAs is presented and described in a July 28, 2017 release on the BEA Web site, and in more detail in the August 2015 *Survey of Current Business*. The 2013 changes in definitions and presentations are described in "Preview of the 2013 Comprehensive Revision of the National Income and Product Accounts," *Survey of Current Business (SCB)*, March 2013, and a subsequent article in the September 2013 *SCB*. Earlier revisions are described in annual *SCB* articles in September or August issues.

Other documentation available on the BEA Web site at <http://www.bea.gov> includes the following: "NIPA Handbook: Concepts and Methods of the U.S. National Income and Product Accounts, October 2009"; separate chapters from the Handbook on Personal Consumption Expenditures, Private Fixed Investment, and Change in Private Inventories; "Measuring the Economy: A Primer on GDP and the National Income and Product Accounts"; "An Introduction to the National Income and Product Accounts"; and "Taking the Pulse of the Economy: Measuring GDP," *Journal of Economic Perspectives*, Spring 2008.

The treatment of employee stock options is discussed in Carol Moylan, "Treatment of Employee Stock Options in the U.S. National Economic Accounts," available on the BEA Web site at <http://www.bea.gov>.

The data for 1929 through 1946 published here have been calculated after the fact and differ from the national income data that were currently available during the 1930s and 1940s. For an article on what was available at that time and the history of the NIPAs during that period, see Rosemary D. Marcuss and Richard E. Kane, "U.S. National Income and Product Statistics: Born of the Great Depression and World War II," *Survey of Current Business*, February 2007, pp. 32-46.

CHAPTER 2: INDUSTRIAL PRODUCTION AND CAPACITY UTILIZATION

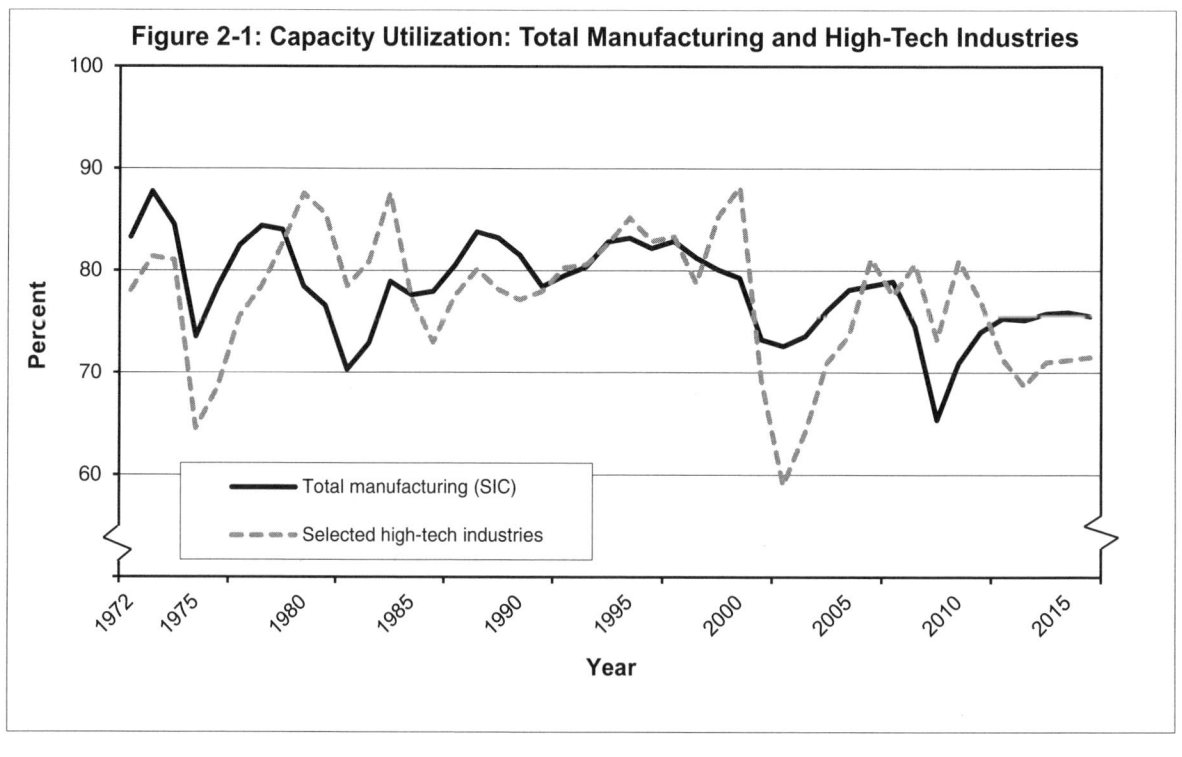

Figure 2-1: Capacity Utilization: Total Manufacturing and High-Tech Industries

- Manufacturing capacity utilization is a key statistic for the U.S. economy, despite being limited to a sector that by some measures has diminished in importance. The Federal Reserve also provides measures of capacity utilization for "total industry"— manufacturing, mining, and utilities. However, mining and utilities are less significant in the context of business cycle analysis, and much of the variation in capacity use by utilities is a result of transitory weather variations, not economic factors. Manufacturing utilization is an important indicator of inflationary pressure and also measures an important element in the demand for new capital goods. (Tables 2-3 and 2-4A)

- Industrial production peaked at 105.3 percent of its 2007 average in November before falling to a low of 87.1 percent in June 2009, a decline of 17.3 percent. In late 2014, the index reached 106.6, an all time high. However, in December 2016, industrial production fell to 103.8. (Table 2-4A)

- Capacity utilization in the high-tech industries (computers and office equipment, communications equipment, and semiconductors and related electronic components) peaked in 2000, before the tech bubble, at 88.2 but declined steeply by 2002. Capacity utilization has recovered but not to its 2000 level as seen in Figure 2-1. (Tables 2-3 and 2-4A)

Table 2-1. Industrial Production Indexes by Market Groups

(Seasonally adjusted, 2012 = 100.)

Year and month	Total industrial production	Final products and nonindustrial supplies	Consumer goods	Durable consumer goods					Nondurable consumer goods
		Total	Total	Total	Automotive products	Home electronics	Appliances, furniture, and carpeting	Miscellaneous durable goods	Total
1970	38.8	39.9	52.9	39.8	35.3	1.0	76.1	60.9	59.4
1971	39.3	40.5	55.9	45.1	45.1	1.1	80.3	64.2	61.1
1972	43.1	44.2	60.4	50.4	48.6	1.3	94.3	72.1	65.0
1973	46.6	47.6	63.1	54.3	52.8	1.5	101.9	75.4	66.9
1974	46.5	47.4	61.3	49.4	45.7	1.4	92.9	72.7	67.0
1975	42.3	44.1	58.8	44.8	44.0	1.2	79.9	64.1	65.8
1976	45.7	47.2	63.6	50.6	50.1	1.4	90.1	71.5	69.9
1977	49.2	51.1	67.6	56.9	56.7	1.7	101.2	79.3	72.4
1978	51.9	54.1	69.7	58.3	56.3	1.9	106.6	82.1	75.0
1979	53.4	55.9	68.6	56.2	50.7	1.9	107.5	82.8	74.5
1980	52.0	55.2	66.0	48.9	39.0	1.9	99.8	76.0	74.5
1981	52.7	56.3	66.4	49.6	40.2	2.0	98.5	77.0	74.8
1982	50.0	54.8	66.3	46.7	39.1	1.8	89.0	72.6	76.1
1983	51.3	56.3	68.7	51.8	45.3	2.6	98.3	74.7	77.0
1984	55.9	61.1	71.9	58.0	50.7	3.2	109.3	82.8	78.5
1985	56.6	62.6	72.6	58.1	50.6	3.4	108.8	83.0	79.5
1986	57.2	63.8	75.0	61.7	54.4	4.2	114.1	85.7	81.3
1987	60.2	67.1	78.2	65.5	58.3	4.2	120.3	91.0	84.2
1988	63.3	70.3	81.1	68.7	61.0	5.3	122.3	95.0	87.0
1989	63.9	71.1	81.5	70.3	63.1	6.0	123.7	95.6	86.7
1990	64.5	71.9	81.8	68.2	59.4	6.5	120.7	94.6	88.3
1991	63.5	70.8	81.7	65.2	55.8	7.6	112.4	91.2	89.5
1992	65.4	72.6	84.3	71.5	64.7	8.7	118.8	94.3	90.4
1993	67.5	75.0	86.9	77.3	71.0	11.0	125.6	98.4	91.5
1994	71.0	78.3	90.5	84.2	78.0	14.4	134.5	104.1	93.7
1995	74.3	81.5	93.0	87.4	79.5	21.0	133.7	107.2	96.0
1996	77.7	84.7	94.7	90.1	80.9	25.6	135.0	110.9	97.2
1997	83.3	90.3	98.2	96.3	87.3	36.0	141.3	113.0	99.6
1998	88.1	95.6	101.8	103.3	93.7	47.2	150.5	117.0	101.9
1999	92.1	98.5	104.0	111.5	104.2	60.3	155.4	120.0	101.8
2000	95.6	101.6	105.9	114.8	105.9	69.8	159.7	123.5	103.3
2001	92.7	99.1	104.9	109.4	101.7	71.6	152.8	114.6	103.8
2002	93.0	98.6	107.0	116.5	112.5	73.5	156.2	118.0	104.2
2003	94.1	99.9	108.4	120.0	118.0	81.4	156.4	118.1	104.9
2004	96.6	101.9	109.6	121.7	117.2	94.6	161.3	120.4	105.9
2005	99.8	106.0	112.5	122.2	113.7	107.1	164.4	124.0	109.5
2006	102.0	108.7	113.2	121.5	109.7	129.4	159.4	126.1	110.5
2007	104.6	110.6	113.2	121.0	112.8	138.5	149.6	122.1	110.7
2008	100.9	105.7	107.2	106.7	93.4	153.5	130.6	112.9	107.2
2009	89.3	93.2	99.2	86.0	75.1	132.4	98.9	93.0	102.9
2010	94.2	96.3	100.3	94.2	90.2	87.5	97.7	99.5	101.9
2011	97.1	98.3	101.4	97.7	96.4	91.6	97.1	100.4	102.3
2012	100.0	100.0	100.0	100.0	100.0	100.0	100.0	100.0	100.0
2013	102.0	100.6	100.7	105.5	108.9	104.9	102.3	102.4	99.5
2014	105.1	101.8	101.5	110.8	118.8	101.8	103.9	103.7	99.2
2015	104.4	101.7	103.9	115.3	126.9	105.5	108.3	103.8	101.0
2016	103.1	101.4	104.5	118.5	132.7	107.4	110.7	104.0	101.0
2015									
January	105.6	102.3	103.2	112.9	122.6	103.7	106.3	103.6	100.7
February	105.4	101.9	103.1	111.0	119.1	102.4	106.6	102.9	101.1
March	105.1	102.0	104.1	113.5	124.5	102.6	105.4	103.3	101.7
April	104.7	101.5	103.5	114.7	126.6	105.1	106.8	103.2	100.7
May	104.3	101.4	103.4	116.5	130.0	106.3	107.4	103.4	100.0
June	104.0	101.3	103.4	114.0	124.0	106.5	107.9	104.0	100.7
July	104.5	102.0	104.9	118.8	134.0	107.1	109.2	103.7	101.4
August	104.5	102.2	104.9	116.6	128.9	106.7	109.1	104.2	102.0
September	104.2	101.7	104.5	116.6	128.5	108.7	110.4	104.1	101.5
October	104.0	101.7	104.4	116.7	129.0	109.4	110.6	103.7	101.2
November	103.4	101.3	103.9	116.2	128.1	103.7	109.6	104.3	100.8
December	102.9	100.8	103.3	116.6	127.8	103.9	110.7	105.2	99.9
2016									
January	103.5	101.6	104.4	117.6	130.5	107.8	111.1	104.2	101.1
February	103.3	101.5	104.5	117.9	131.9	107.4	110.4	103.5	101.1
March	102.5	100.6	103.3	116.6	129.0	108.3	111.2	103.2	100.0
April	102.9	101.3	104.5	117.8	131.4	106.6	110.0	104.1	101.1
May	102.8	101.1	104.2	115.8	127.5	105.5	110.1	103.6	101.2
June	103.1	101.5	104.9	118.3	132.5	105.2	111.2	103.7	101.5
July	103.2	101.5	104.9	118.6	132.9	106.8	110.7	104.0	101.4
August	103.1	101.4	105.1	118.7	133.9	105.4	109.3	103.8	101.6
September	103.0	101.4	104.9	119.8	135.3	104.4	110.4	104.7	101.1
October	103.2	101.4	104.7	120.7	136.7	110.4	111.2	104.6	100.7
November	102.9	101.0	103.6	119.7	134.3	110.5	111.6	104.5	99.6
December	103.8	102.0	105.1	120.7	136.5	110.9	111.3	104.6	101.2

Table 2-1. Industrial Production Indexes by Market Groups—Continued

(Seasonally adjusted, 2012 = 100.)

Year and month	Final products and nonindustrial supplies—Continued												
	Consumer goods—Continued						Business equipment				Defense and space equipment	Construction supplies	Business supplies
	Nondurable consumer goods—Continued												
	Nondurable non-energy consumer goods					Consumer energy products	Total	Transit	Information processing	Industrial and other			
	Total	Foods and tobacco	Clothing	Chemical products	Paper products								
1970	62.1	60.8	498.0	31.8	78.9	48.9	16.2	50.1	1.1	47.9	48.1	62.9	38.8
1971	63.7	62.6	495.1	33.6	80.5	51.2	15.4	48.5	1.0	45.8	43.2	64.9	40.0
1972	67.9	66.1	538.8	36.7	81.2	54.0	17.5	52.9	1.2	52.1	42.0	73.6	44.0
1973	70.1	67.8	549.1	39.5	83.9	54.7	20.3	63.1	1.4	59.2	46.0	79.9	46.7
1974	69.8	68.3	514.9	41.7	82.5	56.3	21.5	61.6	1.7	61.7	47.6	78.1	46.6
1975	68.0	67.0	501.2	40.1	77.8	57.5	19.1	54.2	1.7	54.0	48.0	66.0	42.8
1976	72.4	71.4	527.7	43.7	80.9	60.6	20.4	56.0	2.0	56.2	46.5	71.1	45.6
1977	75.0	72.7	553.6	45.5	88.4	62.9	23.6	66.5	2.6	61.2	41.7	77.3	49.5
1978	77.9	75.5	566.8	48.3	92.8	63.9	26.6	77.1	3.3	65.5	42.4	81.6	52.2
1979	78.0	74.0	505.1	40.4	00.0	65.6	20.0	00.0	4.1	60.6	45.4	83.8	54.0
1980	77.7	76.0	544.3	48.3	94.9	62.7	30.6	84.9	5.2	67.3	54.0	77.6	52.7
1981	78.2	76.2	544.4	49.0	97.2	62.2	31.5	79.5	6.2	67.1	58.4	76.3	53.9
1982	79.8	78.8	542.9	49.1	99.8	62.6	28.8	60.9	7.0	58.1	69.8	69.2	53.2
1983	80.8	78.9	558.4	49.7	104.2	63.0	29.0	59.9	8.1	53.8	70.3	74.0	55.8
1984	82.2	79.8	560.5	50.8	109.5	64.9	33.3	61.8	9.9	61.3	80.5	80.5	60.7
1985	83.5	82.2	537.0	51.3	115.1	64.7	34.6	63.9	10.7	62.1	90.1	82.4	62.2
1986	85.6	83.5	537.1	55.3	116.7	65.8	34.1	58.5	10.8	61.8	95.7	85.1	64.2
1987	88.6	85.4	542.4	59.6	123.3	68.2	36.4	59.3	12.3	64.0	97.7	90.6	68.0
1988	91.2	87.9	534.5	63.2	126.6	71.8	40.2	66.2	14.0	69.5	98.7	92.7	70.6
1989	90.7	87.3	510.4	64.5	127.1	72.2	41.6	69.6	14.3	71.8	98.8	92.3	71.5
1990	92.9	89.8	501.4	66.9	129.6	71.5	43.2	74.5	15.6	71.3	95.3	91.6	73.2
1991	93.9	90.3	499.8	69.3	130.2	73.5	42.6	77.4	15.8	67.5	88.3	86.7	72.1
1992	95.2	91.7	511.5	69.1	131.8	72.7	44.3	75.6	17.8	68.7	81.9	90.4	73.8
1993	95.9	91.0	521.0	71.0	134.9	75.8	46.4	70.8	19.5	73.3	77.4	94.3	76.1
1994	98.4	94.5	530.5	72.5	133.4	76.7	49.5	68.5	22.0	78.2	72.6	101.1	79.1
1995	100.7	96.9	528.0	75.6	134.3	78.6	54.3	67.9	26.6	83.1	70.1	103.5	82.3
1996	101.4	96.6	514.0	79.3	133.7	82.1	59.7	71.7	32.7	86.1	68.3	108.1	85.6
1997	104.6	98.2	512.7	83.8	145.5	81.5	68.6	84.2	41.5	91.4	67.3	113.3	91.6
1998	107.5	100.9	487.1	88.0	152.4	81.2	76.6	98.9	49.8	94.3	70.3	119.3	96.8
1999	106.7	98.9	466.9	89.5	155.4	84.1	80.9	96.8	60.9	92.1	68.2	122.2	100.9
2000	108.2	100.3	451.6	92.9	154.8	85.8	87.2	85.9	74.1	97.6	60.6	124.9	104.8
2001	108.5	100.4	403.1	98.0	150.4	86.8	81.9	82.8	72.2	88.3	66.6	119.1	100.9
2002	108.2	98.6	309.0	106.2	148.2	90.6	76.4	75.0	63.2	86.8	67.3	119.1	101.0
2003	108.9	99.6	291.1	108.7	142.8	91.1	76.4	70.6	66.3	86.4	71.6	118.8	102.9
2004	109.7	100.9	246.2	111.5	143.6	92.7	80.4	74.6	72.5	88.7	70.3	121.6	105.3
2005	113.4	104.3	236.4	117.3	142.1	96.1	86.1	81.7	78.6	93.6	76.9	127.4	109.2
2006	114.7	104.6	229.3	121.5	141.6	96.4	94.0	94.9	89.4	97.3	76.5	130.5	110.9
2007	113.5	104.4	184.2	122.4	135.6	100.5	99.5	98.1	99.5	101.2	91.1	129.4	112.1
2008	109.1	100.9	148.8	118.1	126.9	100.0	97.0	88.1	102.2	99.1	98.3	117.4	107.2
2009	103.5	99.5	108.8	108.9	112.3	100.4	80.2	70.9	91.6	79.1	94.0	90.3	95.0
2010	101.8	99.8	107.6	103.9	106.8	102.3	86.2	80.2	93.2	85.6	101.0	93.6	98.0
2011	102.0	99.7	105.2	105.7	103.9	103.1	91.2	82.9	93.2	93.8	98.1	95.8	99.0
2012	100.0	100.0	100.0	100.0	100.0	100.0	100.0	100.0	100.0	100.0	100.0	100.0	100.0
2013	97.6	101.5	92.2	90.9	95.6	105.3	99.9	105.8	100.2	97.3	97.2	103.0	101.8
2014	97.3	101.2	88.2	91.5	94.2	104.9	101.8	115.5	98.2	97.6	94.0	106.5	102.8
2015	100.2	103.6	86.8	96.8	92.3	102.8	100.9	122.1	99.9	92.6	91.0	107.0	102.0
2016	99.9	104.5	78.0	96.3	85.3	103.6	99.1	118.0	101.6	90.5	89.7	108.4	102.3
2015													
January	99.6	102.3	92.3	96.9	92.4	103.6	102.0	119.4	99.9	95.7	91.3	107.6	102.5
February	99.3	101.9	88.0	97.1	91.6	106.9	101.4	119.4	99.8	94.6	92.6	106.7	102.3
March	100.0	103.4	87.5	96.8	92.0	106.9	101.6	122.2	99.6	93.9	92.0	105.7	101.8
April	99.9	103.3	88.1	96.5	92.3	102.6	101.1	122.3	99.8	92.9	91.1	106.4	102.2
May	99.3	103.1	87.3	95.0	92.8	101.7	101.5	124.0	99.9	92.9	90.5	106.7	102.0
June	100.0	103.0	86.9	96.6	94.1	102.3	101.2	121.5	100.9	93.0	90.7	106.9	101.8
July	100.7	103.8	87.7	97.2	95.7	102.7	101.2	125.4	100.4	91.6	90.6	106.7	101.3
August	101.3	105.1	87.5	97.1	93.7	103.5	101.5	124.3	100.6	92.6	91.1	107.3	101.7
September	100.6	104.3	86.3	97.0	91.8	103.4	100.9	123.5	99.9	92.0	90.4	106.1	101.9
October	100.3	103.8	83.7	97.3	91.0	103.2	100.4	122.8	99.3	91.7	90.2	107.8	102.5
November	100.8	104.6	83.1	97.5	90.7	99.5	99.5	120.7	99.3	91.0	90.4	107.8	102.6
December	100.2	104.2	82.7	96.8	89.3	97.3	98.8	119.8	99.8	89.9	91.0	108.4	102.0
2016													
January	101.0	105.3	80.1	97.5	88.1	100.0	99.4	120.6	100.4	90.4	90.4	109.2	102.7
February	100.7	105.2	80.3	97.0	87.6	101.0	99.3	120.4	100.5	90.2	89.7	109.6	102.3
March	100.5	104.4	79.6	97.7	86.6	96.6	98.8	118.6	100.9	89.9	89.5	108.8	101.5
April	100.3	104.5	77.3	97.5	85.9	102.8	99.4	118.8	100.9	90.8	89.4	108.9	101.8
May	100.2	104.4	76.6	97.2	85.7	103.8	99.0	117.6	101.3	90.5	90.4	108.1	102.0
June	99.9	104.6	76.8	96.4	84.4	106.5	99.3	118.3	100.7	91.1	90.0	107.5	102.2
July	99.6	104.6	76.9	95.6	83.7	107.1	99.1	116.9	100.3	91.4	89.5	108.2	102.6
August	99.4	104.8	76.8	94.8	83.9	108.9	98.6	117.1	101.6	90.0	89.8	107.1	102.4
September	99.5	104.5	78.0	94.9	85.5	106.1	98.7	116.7	101.8	90.2	89.4	107.5	102.5
October	99.5	104.3	78.3	95.5	84.5	104.1	99.0	117.1	103.2	90.0	88.9	108.2	102.3
November	99.2	103.9	77.8	95.5	84.2	99.9	98.9	116.6	103.4	89.9	89.9	109.2	102.3
December	99.3	103.9	77.6	96.3	83.2	107.0	99.7	117.0	103.7	91.1	89.6	109.1	102.9

Table 2-1. Industrial Production Indexes by Market Groups—*Continued*

(Seasonally adjusted, 2012 = 100.)

Year and month	Materials Total	Non-energy materials Total	Durable Total	Consumer parts	Equipment parts	Other	Nondurable Total	Textile	Paper	Chemicals	Energy materials
1970	36.9	29.3	21.8	56.1	4.5	56.9	49.3	114.5	52.8	33.1	70.6
1971	39.1	31.2	22.9	56.5	4.8	60.6	53.4	117.6	57.3	36.8	74.2
1972	37.8	29.3	20.8	47.4	4.4	56.6	53.7	113.3	56.8	37.6	77.8
1973	38.3	29.9	20.9	52.5	4.4	54.5	56.0	118.6	59.4	39.9	78.5
1974	42.2	33.5	23.6	58.4	5.1	61.6	61.7	124.9	63.3	46.4	81.5
1975	46.0	37.1	27.0	67.8	6.0	68.3	64.8	121.6	68.3	51.2	83.5
1976	45.9	37.0	26.7	60.0	6.3	68.1	65.7	113.7	71.7	52.6	83.1
1977	40.8	31.7	22.3	48.4	5.4	56.9	58.8	111.3	62.4	44.1	82.4
1978	44.4	35.3	24.9	61.8	5.8	61.1	65.2	123.9	68.6	50.5	84.2
1979	47.5	38.3	27.1	67.6	6.6	64.7	69.9	132.0	71.7	56.1	86.9
1980	49.9	40.7	29.3	71.5	7.4	69.0	72.5	130.6	75.2	59.6	87.9
1981	51.2	41.9	30.3	67.6	8.2	70.7	73.9	129.4	78.2	62.0	90.3
1982	49.3	39.4	28.0	52.1	8.4	65.5	71.5	126.5	78.8	57.4	91.0
1983	49.6	39.5	28.1	49.6	8.6	65.6	72.0	123.7	80.3	57.9	91.9
1984	45.8	35.6	24.5	42.1	7.9	55.4	68.3	113.1	81.0	51.9	88.0
1985	47.0	38.0	26.1	51.2	8.0	57.9	73.1	126.7	86.1	57.4	85.2
1986	51.5	42.4	30.3	60.9	9.7	64.1	76.3	126.3	91.5	61.0	90.6
1987	51.4	42.4	30.5	63.4	9.6	63.7	75.7	119.4	91.0	59.9	90.0
1988	51.3	43.2	30.9	62.8	9.8	64.9	78.1	124.3	94.9	62.8	86.5
1989	54.0	46.1	33.0	64.4	10.8	69.4	82.7	139.2	99.5	68.3	88.6
1990	57.1	49.0	35.7	69.7	11.7	74.4	85.8	137.8	102.8	72.4	91.6
1991	57.5	49.3	35.9	66.2	12.1	74.7	86.5	140.7	102.8	73.4	92.5
1992	57.8	49.4	35.9	61.6	12.5	75.0	86.8	133.6	103.1	74.2	94.4
1993	57.0	48.4	34.9	58.2	12.5	71.8	85.8	133.5	100.9	73.1	94.5
1994	58.8	50.7	37.2	65.4	13.2	75.6	87.9	141.2	103.4	74.9	93.6
1995	60.8	53.0	39.6	74.0	14.1	78.5	88.9	146.9	103.4	75.4	93.8
1996	64.7	57.2	44.1	85.4	16.0	84.4	91.6	155.8	107.3	77.7	95.3
1997	68.4	61.2	48.7	88.7	19.5	87.5	92.5	153.2	110.1	78.3	96.8
1998	71.9	65.0	53.8	91.0	24.0	90.1	91.6	148.9	106.6	78.7	98.3
1999	77.7	71.8	61.3	98.0	30.4	94.7	95.9	155.5	107.7	84.4	98.2
2000	82.3	77.2	68.0	101.3	37.5	97.2	97.2	154.1	108.8	84.6	98.4
2001	87.3	83.2	75.7	111.5	45.9	98.8	98.4	151.0	110.4	87.0	97.9
2002	91.8	88.3	83.1	111.5	57.2	99.7	97.8	144.5	108.6	87.2	99.6
2003	87.7	83.4	78.8	98.6	57.0	92.9	91.4	127.8	103.0	80.8	98.3
2004	88.6	84.7	80.0	103.5	57.7	92.9	93.1	129.6	103.3	83.6	97.9
2005	89.8	86.2	82.7	102.4	64.3	92.1	92.3	122.9	99.9	84.1	97.9
2006	92.4	89.8	87.2	102.5	71.1	95.8	94.1	117.5	101.1	88.5	97.9
2007	94.6	93.4	92.2	103.6	80.4	97.9	95.2	120.4	100.7	89.3	96.8
2008	96.5	95.7	95.7	100.8	88.0	100.1	95.6	109.3	99.9	91.2	98.0
2009	100.0	100.0	100.0	100.0	100.0	100.0	100.0	100.0	100.0	100.0	100.0
2010	97.6	95.6	97.4	84.3	106.6	95.3	92.7	86.9	95.5	89.1	100.8
2011	86.6	79.7	76.7	56.4	89.6	74.6	84.0	71.4	83.8	79.4	98.4
2012	94.2	89.0	89.4	74.4	105.9	82.9	88.4	79.4	85.3	87.3	102.5
2013	98.6	93.7	98.0	81.3	122.2	87.3	87.7	78.1	85.2	86.2	106.3
2014	103.1	98.1	104.9	89.2	135.0	90.6	88.6	78.7	83.2	87.9	110.9
2015	106.4	100.8	108.9	94.1	140.5	93.3	89.9	77.3	82.8	90.5	115.3
2016	111.8	104.5	115.0	100.6	149.2	97.7	90.4	78.8	81.2	91.7	123.6
2015											
January	104.8	100.1	107.4	94.1	137.4	92.4	90.0	77.8	82.9	90.1	112.0
February	105.1	100.2	107.8	93.6	138.3	92.8	89.9	77.5	83.2	90.5	112.7
March	105.5	100.1	107.6	92.6	137.9	92.9	89.8	78.1	82.9	90.0	114.1
April	105.4	99.9	107.7	92.5	139.0	92.5	89.3	76.4	82.6	89.6	114.1
May	105.9	100.5	107.9	93.1	139.8	92.3	90.3	76.1	83.5	91.2	114.4
June	106.0	100.6	108.1	92.6	140.3	92.5	90.2	77.4	83.4	91.1	114.6
July	106.3	100.5	108.1	91.5	140.2	92.9	90.1	76.6	83.2	90.7	115.6
August	106.9	101.3	109.3	94.5	142.2	93.2	90.2	77.2	83.3	91.2	115.8
September	107.4	101.2	109.8	95.1	142.4	93.7	89.4	77.1	81.9	90.3	117.6
October	107.3	101.6	110.5	95.4	143.0	94.5	89.5	77.7	82.7	90.0	116.3
November	108.2	102.0	111.4	97.3	143.6	95.3	89.3	78.5	81.6	89.8	118.1
December	108.1	102.1	110.8	97.1	142.3	95.0	90.3	77.6	82.2	91.2	117.8
2016											
January	108.3	101.1	110.0	94.9	142.6	94.0	89.1	76.3	81.7	89.8	119.8
February	108.7	102.5	112.1	96.9	145.8	95.6	89.4	73.3	80.3	90.3	118.9
March	109.9	103.1	112.9	97.8	146.5	96.2	89.8	78.8	80.6	90.6	121.0
April	110.4	103.4	113.3	97.8	146.6	96.9	90.0	78.9	82.2	90.5	121.8
May	111.3	104.1	114.8	99.6	149.3	97.7	89.7	76.4	81.0	90.6	123.1
June	112.4	104.9	116.1	100.9	149.5	99.6	89.8	77.7	81.5	90.8	124.6
July	112.4	105.5	116.9	105.3	149.7	99.5	90.1	79.5	80.7	91.7	123.7
August	112.9	105.4	116.4	102.1	150.5	99.2	90.7	78.9	81.1	92.5	124.9
September	113.7	105.7	116.7	102.3	152.2	98.8	90.9	80.2	81.2	92.8	126.8
October	113.5	105.8	116.7	103.3	152.9	98.2	91.1	80.8	80.7	93.0	126.0
November	114.1	106.7	117.6	105.3	154.4	98.5	91.9	82.5	81.2	93.7	126.2
December	114.7	106.9	118.0	104.7	152.6	100.2	91.9	82.9	81.8	93.9	127.3

Table 2-1. Industrial Production Indexes by Market Groups—*Continued*

(Seasonally adjusted, 2012 = 100.)

Year and month	Special aggregates											
	Energy						Non-energy					Total non-energy, excluding high-tech
									Selected high-tech			
	Total	Consumer energy products	Commercial energy products	Oil and gas well drilling	Converted fuels	Primary energy	Total	Total	Computers and peripheral equipment	Communications equipment	Semiconductors and related components	
1970	57.3	42.1	29.0	. . .	55.7	82.7	33.3	0.1	. . .	. . .	. . .	51.3
1971	60.4	45.0	30.5	. . .	59.6	85.6	34.8	0.1	. . .	. . .	. . .	53.4
1972	63.3	47.6	32.8	. . .	62.7	89.7	33.3	0.1	. . .	. . .	. . .	50.9
1973	64.5	49.9	34.5	. . .	64.4	89.0	33.8	0.1	. . .	. . .	. . .	51.8
1974	67.4	52.6	36.4	57.1	68.4	90.4	37.3	0.1	0.0	3.3	0.1	57.0
1975	69.2	53.6	38.4	53.7	71.1	91.5	40.7	0.2	0.1	3.6	0.1	61.9
1976	69.5	55.0	38.4	62.4	70.1	91.9	40.5	0.2	0.1	3.9	0.1	61.2
1977	69.7	56.2	39.8	70.4	67.6	92.7	36.2	0.2	0.1	3.8	0.1	54.6
1978	72.0	59.1	41.9	79.3	71.3	92.7	39.4	0.3	0.1	4.0	0.1	59.1
1979	71.8	61.4	43.3	100.7	74.0	95.4	42.7	0.3	0.2	4.8	0.2	63.6
1980	76.1	62.6	44.6	112.2	73.4	97.7	45.5	0.4	0.3	5.3	0.2	67.1
1981	78.3	64.2	46.7	119.6	76.1	99.9	46.8	0.5	0.4	6.3	0.2	68.4
1982	78.6	61.8	45.9	141.5	74.6	102.0	45.3	0.7	0.6	7.6	0.3	65.2
1983	79.8	61.4	47.1	170.0	73.6	104.0	45.8	0.8	0.8	8.1	0.3	65.3
1984	76.9	61.8	47.7	149.6	67.7	101.0	43.2	0.9	1.0	8.6	0.3	60.9
1985	74.7	62.3	48.7	115.9	67.6	96.6	45.3	1.1	1.4	9.1	0.4	63.1
1986	79.0	64.2	51.3	126.2	71.8	102.8	49.8	1.5	2.0	9.7	0.5	68.6
1987	78.8	64.2	53.2	115.6	71.5	102.1	50.7	1.5	2.4	9.4	0.5	69.6
1988	76.1	65.5	54.7	56.3	68.9	97.9	51.8	1.6	2.5	8.9	0.6	71.2
1989	78.3	67.9	57.6	54.3	72.4	98.7	54.8	1.9	3.3	10.0	0.7	74.5
1990	81.4	71.4	59.5	65.2	75.8	101.4	57.8	2.3	4.0	11.9	0.8	77.8
1991	82.2	71.9	61.7	56.8	78.6	100.7	58.3	2.4	4.2	12.3	0.9	78.2
1992	83.6	71.4	63.5	60.1	79.2	103.4	58.7	2.7	4.5	14.6	1.0	78.2
1993	84.0	73.6	64.4	46.8	79.3	103.5	57.6	2.9	4.7	15.2	1.1	76.2
1994	82.9	72.6	64.0	32.7	80.8	101.0	59.7	3.5	5.9	17.4	1.3	78.2
1995	84.4	75.8	65.9	45.5	82.3	100.1	61.9	4.1	7.3	20.0	1.5	80.3
1996	86.1	76.7	68.5	54.0	83.6	101.8	65.5	5.3	9.1	24.0	2.0	83.8
1997	87.8	78.8	70.9	52.6	84.8	103.4	69.0	7.4	12.6	29.4	3.0	86.0
1998	90.0	82.3	73.2	56.4	86.3	104.8	72.3	10.6	17.9	36.9	4.6	87.3
1999	90.5	81.6	76.2	64.7	87.6	103.8	78.5	15.6	25.4	50.4	7.2	91.6
2000	90.7	81.7	77.5	60.5	88.7	103.4	83.8	21.8	34.9	59.8	10.9	94.9
2001	91.3	84.5	80.5	47.4	90.3	101.4	87.9	31.3	45.9	76.3	17.3	96.1
2002	93.6	86.3	83.7	67.2	92.4	102.7	91.6	43.8	53.5	102.9	26.7	96.8
2003	93.6	87.3	85.1	81.4	89.2	102.4	87.9	44.8	54.1	95.5	28.9	92.1
2004	94.0	91.1	86.9	58.7	91.2	100.7	88.0	44.5	53.3	71.4	33.5	92.3
2005	95.0	91.6	91.2	68.2	91.8	100.4	89.1	53.4	57.8	73.8	44.9	92.3
2006	95.7	92.9	94.1	74.5	94.0	99.3	91.6	60.6	58.4	81.9	54.0	94.2
2007	96.3	96.1	96.7	83.7	95.3	97.3	95.2	71.1	69.6	80.8	67.5	97.1
2008	97.4	95.8	97.3	96.6	95.2	98.9	97.6	84.9	86.5	98.0	78.7	98.5
2009	100.0	100.0	100.0	100.0	100.0	100.0	100.0	100.0	100.0	100.0	100.0	100.0
2010	100.7	99.7	100.2	104.4	98.2	101.7	95.2	115.5	118.9	96.0	123.4	94.1
2011	97.7	99.8	98.5	61.4	93.0	100.1	81.8	103.0	104.1	81.2	113.3	80.6
2012	101.5	102.0	99.9	82.3	98.9	103.5	86.9	127.6	85.0	81.5	172.0	84.9
2013	104.7	102.4	100.8	99.2	98.2	108.9	89.9	146.4	68.8	88.7	213.6	87.3
2014	107.2	100.0	100.9	103.9	98.7	114.9	93.8	164.7	63.8	90.5	252.5	90.7
2015	110.9	104.0	103.2	97.2	97.2	121.2	96.3	180.5	69.9	90.4	282.3	92.8
2016	117.5	107.0	105.6	102.4	99.2	131.6	99.6	191.3	70.7	90.1	305.0	95.9
2015												
January	108.1	101.3	101.9	96.5	95.3	117.5	95.2	175.3	65.3	89.6	274.5	91.8
February	108.8	102.2	102.1	97.1	97.9	117.6	95.8	174.3	66.0	89.4	272.2	92.5
March	110.6	106.0	102.9	97.0	102.3	117.9	95.8	175.2	66.4	89.4	273.8	92.5
April	110.6	106.0	103.1	96.4	97.6	119.6	95.6	178.3	66.9	89.5	280.1	92.2
May	110.2	103.7	102.6	96.3	96.2	120.5	95.8	180.9	67.9	89.6	284.9	92.4
June	109.8	101.6	101.5	96.8	95.1	121.0	96.2	180.4	68.9	89.7	283.2	92.8
July	110.5	101.5	102.2	97.3	94.2	122.7	95.8	182.2	71.4	89.8	285.4	92.3
August	110.5	100.7	102.3	98.1	94.3	122.9	96.5	183.9	73.0	90.1	288.0	93.0
September	112.6	104.1	104.1	98.4	97.2	124.3	96.8	183.1	74.0	90.8	285.3	93.3
October	112.2	106.4	104.3	97.2	97.2	122.6	97.0	184.2	73.0	91.5	287.8	93.5
November	113.7	107.0	105.9	97.5	99.0	124.5	97.3	184.5	73.5	92.2	287.6	93.7
December	113.8	108.2	106.0	98.1	99.6	123.8	97.5	183.2	72.2	93.2	285.0	94.0
2016												
January	115.9	110.7	108.4	97.9	102.7	125.5	96.5	182.9	68.0	90.3	288.7	93.0
February	115.7	113.6	107.1	97.7	101.3	124.7	97.8	185.6	69.3	88.6	294.6	94.3
March	116.8	112.9	105.3	99.6	102.8	127.0	98.6	186.9	70.2	87.5	297.6	95.0
April	116.3	108.3	104.4	100.9	98.0	129.6	98.8	189.7	67.4	89.2	304.1	95.2
May	116.9	107.1	104.2	101.9	98.7	131.1	99.3	194.1	68.7	90.4	311.7	95.5
June	117.1	103.2	103.0	102.3	98.3	133.2	99.8	194.4	70.8	90.8	311.0	96.1
July	116.3	102.0	103.0	102.8	95.0	133.0	100.6	193.5	70.2	90.5	309.5	96.9
August	117.1	101.3	103.6	104.6	97.4	133.9	100.3	192.8	73.0	88.0	308.1	96.6
September	119.4	105.1	106.9	106.6	99.5	135.7	100.4	193.9	72.0	88.6	310.6	96.7
October	118.8	105.0	106.5	105.8	99.8	134.5	100.6	195.7	72.1	91.9	312.3	96.8
November	119.9	108.5	108.7	105.3	101.1	134.4	101.8	195.8	73.8	93.1	310.6	98.0
December	119.7	105.4	106.2	103.3	97.3	137.0	101.8	194.7	71.3	93.0	309.9	98.0

. . . = Not available.

Table 2-2. Industrial Production Indexes by NAICS Industry Groups

(Seasonally adjusted, 2012 = 100.)

Year and month	Total industrial production	Manu-facturing (SIC)	Manufacturing (NAICS) Total	Durable goods manufacturing Total	Wood products	Nonmetallic mineral products	Primary metals	Fabricated metal products	Machinery	Computer and electronic products	Electrical equipment, appliances, and components	Motor vehicles and parts	Aerospace and miscellaneous transport equipment
1970	38.8	36.1	. . .	. . .	. . .	. . .	. . .	. . .	. . .	. . .	. . .	. . .	. . .
1971	39.3	36.7	. . .	. . .	. . .	. . .	. . .	. . .	. . .	. . .	. . .	. . .	. . .
1972	43.1	40.5	38.4	25.8	100.0	94.8	115.3	69.1	54.9	0.6	80.7	45.9	53.5
1973	46.6	44.1	41.9	29.0	96.8	101.8	134.2	76.3	63.4	0.7	90.9	52.4	60.9
1974	46.5	44.0	41.8	28.8	87.9	100.6	137.4	75.0	66.5	0.7	88.7	45.1	62.0
1975	42.3	39.4	37.3	25.0	81.0	90.1	106.6	64.8	57.9	0.7	71.2	39.3	58.8
1976	45.7	43.0	40.8	27.4	91.3	95.1	113.1	69.4	60.4	0.8	80.4	50.2	55.1
1977	49.2	46.6	44.2	30.1	98.4	101.3	114.5	75.3	65.9	1.0	88.6	57.1	55.5
1978	51.9	49.5	47.0	32.4	99.7	108.0	121.8	79.0	70.9	1.2	94.0	59.5	61.2
1979	53.4	51.0	48.4	34.0	96.1	107.8	124.6	82.5	74.9	1.5	97.9	54.4	71.3
1980	52.0	49.2	46.6	32.5	89.0	97.2	109.2	77.8	71.2	1.8	92.1	40.1	76.7
1981	52.7	49.7	47.0	32.9	87.0	93.1	109.3	77.3	70.5	2.1	90.9	39.0	73.0
1982	50.0	47.0	44.3	30.0	78.2	82.4	76.7	69.2	58.9	2.4	81.9	35.2	68.3
1983	51.3	49.2	46.5	31.5	90.5	88.6	79.0	69.7	53.2	2.7	84.7	44.9	65.3
1984	55.9	54.0	51.2	36.0	97.0	95.6	86.8	75.9	62.0	3.4	95.3	53.8	69.6
1985	56.6	54.9	51.9	36.8	98.0	97.3	79.9	76.9	62.2	3.6	93.8	55.8	74.4
1986	57.2	56.1	53.1	37.4	106.5	101.3	78.2	76.4	61.2	3.7	95.6	55.8	78.3
1987	60.2	59.3	56.1	39.6	115.9	106.9	84.5	77.9	62.5	4.2	96.8	57.9	81.2
1988	63.3	62.5	59.3	42.6	115.7	109.1	94.4	81.8	68.8	4.7	101.5	61.9	85.4
1989	63.9	63.0	59.8	43.0	113.8	108.2	92.2	81.2	71.4	4.8	100.0	61.2	90.6
1990	64.5	63.5	60.4	43.2	112.5	106.6	91.2	80.3	69.6	5.3	97.4	57.6	90.9
1991	63.5	62.3	59.3	41.9	105.2	98.1	85.6	76.6	65.3	5.5	92.4	55.0	87.7
1992	65.4	64.6	61.6	44.1	111.1	102.4	88.1	79.0	65.2	6.2	97.9	62.7	81.1
1993	67.5	66.8	63.9	46.5	112.4	104.6	92.3	82.0	70.0	6.8	104.0	69.2	75.6
1994	71.0	70.7	67.9	50.4	119.1	110.5	99.3	89.1	76.7	8.0	111.6	79.5	67.9
1995	74.3	74.3	71.5	54.6	122.1	113.7	100.4	94.6	82.1	10.3	114.2	81.9	64.5
1996	77.7	78.0	75.2	59.6	126.0	121.1	102.7	98.0	84.9	13.4	117.6	82.5	67.0
1997	83.3	84.6	81.6	66.7	129.4	125.2	107.0	102.4	89.6	17.9	122.0	89.0	74.8
1998	88.1	90.2	87.0	73.7	135.1	131.5	108.8	105.7	92.0	23.0	126.4	93.7	86.7
1999	92.1	94.0	91.6	80.1	140.1	132.7	108.7	106.5	90.1	30.4	128.4	103.8	83.5
2000	95.6	98.7	95.6	85.8	138.3	132.8	104.9	110.7	94.8	39.5	134.9	103.3	73.2
2001	92.7	95.0	92.2	82.3	129.6	127.8	95.4	102.7	83.9	40.9	121.5	94.4	77.9
2002	93.0	95.4	92.8	82.5	135.1	127.9	95.5	100.5	80.8	40.4	111.9	103.8	73.7
2003	94.1	96.7	94.2	84.7	134.9	129.1	93.7	99.4	80.4	46.1	109.1	107.6	70.4
2004	96.6	99.7	97.3	88.6	138.4	133.0	101.8	99.8	83.7	54.0	111.0	108.1	69.4
2005	99.8	103.7	101.4	93.8	147.6	138.6	99.0	104.4	88.9	61.0	112.9	108.7	77.3
2006	102.0	106.3	104.2	98.1	148.8	141.2	101.8	110.2	93.1	69.3	113.6	107.1	82.0
2007	104.6	109.2	107.5	103.0	139.2	139.7	103.9	114.9	97.1	79.6	118.4	106.2	96.3
2008	100.9	103.9	102.5	99.4	118.9	123.4	104.1	110.7	94.5	85.7	113.9	85.0	98.2
2009	89.3	89.6	88.5	80.7	90.9	93.0	77.5	85.2	73.5	76.2	89.5	62.3	89.4
2010	94.2	94.8	94.2	89.3	94.1	95.9	95.0	90.7	82.1	86.0	93.1	82.7	90.6
2011	97.1	97.5	97.2	94.8	94.3	97.4	102.0	97.1	92.5	92.8	97.6	90.4	90.5
2012	100.0	100.0	100.0	100.0	100.0	100.0	100.0	100.0	100.0	100.0	100.0	100.0	100.0
2013	102.0	100.9	101.1	102.2	105.8	105.2	103.3	101.8	95.4	103.2	100.0	107.3	102.9
2014	105.1	102.1	102.4	105.1	108.4	109.1	104.1	103.6	96.7	107.8	101.7	117.2	106.8
2015	104.4	102.2	102.6	104.3	112.1	109.6	96.8	100.6	90.6	109.0	101.8	123.3	107.0
2016	103.1	102.2	102.8	104.1	116.5	112.3	93.7	97.6	87.7	110.5	104.0	128.4	104.9
2015													
January	105.6	102.4	102.8	105.2	109.7	110.0	101.1	102.9	94.2	109.5	101.1	119.7	106.8
February	105.4	101.9	102.3	104.3	110.1	108.2	99.0	102.2	93.6	109.3	100.6	116.6	108.3
March	105.1	102.2	102.6	104.5	109.4	107.1	96.7	102.1	92.0	108.9	102.0	121.6	108.4
April	104.7	102.2	102.6	104.4	110.1	108.2	96.6	101.7	91.6	108.8	102.3	122.7	107.5
May	104.3	102.2	102.5	104.6	110.0	108.2	96.1	101.4	91.7	108.5	101.5	125.9	107.2
June	104.0	101.9	102.2	104.1	110.2	108.6	98.5	101.2	90.1	109.3	101.4	120.3	106.7
July	104.5	102.5	102.9	104.8	112.3	109.3	98.0	100.6	89.3	108.9	100.9	129.7	106.7
August	104.5	102.4	102.8	104.5	113.4	110.4	96.2	99.6	90.4	109.2	101.8	124.7	107.2
September	104.2	102.1	102.6	104.1	113.8	109.0	95.0	99.4	89.9	109.0	100.4	125.1	106.6
October	104.0	102.3	102.7	104.2	114.4	111.5	96.2	98.7	89.3	108.6	103.1	125.8	106.1
November	103.4	102.2	102.6	103.7	114.5	111.9	94.9	98.5	87.9	108.5	102.3	124.2	105.9
December	102.9	101.9	102.4	103.6	116.8	113.0	92.8	98.8	86.7	109.2	103.9	123.6	106.4
2016													
January	103.5	102.5	103.0	104.1	117.1	113.3	94.4	98.7	86.5	109.2	104.8	126.7	105.5
February	103.3	102.3	102.9	104.0	116.3	114.0	94.9	98.1	85.7	109.3	105.2	127.6	105.4
March	102.5	102.1	102.7	103.5	116.1	113.4	95.1	97.0	85.9	109.6	103.3	125.5	105.1
April	102.9	102.1	102.7	103.9	115.9	112.8	94.8	97.3	87.5	109.5	102.8	127.7	104.9
May	102.8	101.9	102.5	103.5	114.9	112.0	95.7	97.2	86.8	109.9	103.7	123.6	106.0
June	103.1	102.1	102.7	104.2	115.6	111.8	94.5	97.0	88.8	109.5	104.5	128.4	105.3
July	103.2	102.1	102.8	104.4	114.5	111.5	92.4	97.3	89.5	109.7	104.5	129.4	105.0
August	103.1	101.8	102.5	104.0	114.7	110.4	92.5	97.0	88.3	110.5	103.7	129.6	105.0
September	103.0	102.0	102.7	104.1	114.7	111.1	91.6	97.6	87.8	110.8	103.7	130.2	104.0
October	103.2	102.2	102.9	104.4	116.6	111.4	90.9	98.2	88.0	112.3	103.7	131.2	103.7
November	102.9	102.4	103.1	104.5	121.3	112.4	93.0	97.7	87.8	112.7	103.9	129.4	104.3
December	103.8	102.6	103.3	105.1	120.9	113.0	94.5	97.8	89.4	113.0	103.7	131.0	104.1

. . . = Not available.

Table 2-2. Industrial Production Indexes by NAICS Industry Groups—*Continued*

(Seasonally adjusted, 2012 = 100.)

	Manufacturing (NAICS)—*Continued*											Other manufacturing (non-NAICS)
	Durable goods manufacturing—*Continued*		Nondurable goods manufacturing									
Year and month	Furniture and related products	Miscellaneous manufacturing	Total	Food, beverage, and tobacco products	Textile and product mills	Apparel and leather	Paper	Printing and support	Petroleum and coal products	Chemicals	Plastics and rubber products	
1970	. . .	. . .	. . .	. . .	. . .	. . .	. . .	. . .	. . .	. . .	. . .	. . .
1971	. . .	. . .	. . .	. . .	. . .	. . .	. . .	. . .	. . .	. . .	. . .	. . .
1972	77.6	39.6	64.2	64.0	158.5	499.6	76.4	66.3	68.7	48.3	39.6	119.3
1973	81.3	40.8	67.2	64.6	157.2	507.7	82.6	69.7	67.5	52.9	44.7	123.1
1974	75.1	39.9	67.5	65.8	144.5	477.7	86.2	67.6	72.8	54.9	43.1	123.7
1975	64.5	37.1	62.6	64.4	139.7	466.3	74.6	63.1	71.8	48.3	36.4	117.7
1976	71.9	40.5	68.3	68.8	155.7	490.3	82.4	67.7	79.5	54.0	40.2	121.4
1977	82.4	44.1	73.0	70.3	170.1	514.0	86.0	73.3	85.1	58.8	47.5	133.0
1978	88.8	45.1	75.6	72.8	169.6	525.3	89.8	77.6	85.9	61.8	49.6	137.6
1979	88.6	45.3	76.1	72.3	169.3	492.9	91.2	80.0	91.8	63.2	48.9	140.5
1980	85.5	43.0	73.7	73.5	162.4	502.3	91.0	80.6	81.4	59.7	43.8	145.4
1981	84.8	44.6	74.4	74.2	158.9	502.2	92.2	82.6	77.6	60.7	46.3	148.8
1982	79.9	45.1	73.3	76.5	147.6	499.2	90.7	88.9	74.2	56.8	45.6	150.6
1983	87.6	45.1	76.7	76.5	165.9	513.4	96.5	95.5	75.4	60.7	49.6	154.9
1984	98.1	48.8	80.2	77.6	169.9	512.9	101.3	104.0	77.0	64.3	57.3	162.0
1985	99.2	49.4	80.7	80.1	163.9	490.9	99.2	108.2	75.9	63.8	59.5	168.4
1986	103.6	50.7	83.0	81.1	170.2	489.4	103.1	113.6	75.5	66.7	62.0	171.8
1987	111.1	54.5	87.4	82.7	186.8	495.3	106.4	122.0	79.1	71.8	68.7	181.7
1988	109.9	59.6	90.4	85.0	185.1	487.0	110.5	125.9	81.5	76.0	71.7	180.9
1989	109.5	60.4	90.9	84.6	187.9	465.9	111.7	126.4	80.7	77.4	74.2	178.3
1990	107.3	63.3	92.4	87.0	180.3	456.4	111.7	131.2	80.8	79.2	76.3	176.2
1991	99.2	64.5	92.1	87.7	177.8	453.6	111.9	127.1	79.6	79.0	75.4	169.0
1992	107.0	67.3	94.5	89.0	187.7	466.6	114.7	134.0	79.2	80.2	81.2	165.6
1993	111.5	71.2	95.9	88.8	194.9	475.9	116.0	134.4	79.8	81.1	86.9	166.7
1994	115.2	71.6	99.2	91.6	205.3	481.7	121.0	135.9	82.0	83.2	94.2	165.3
1995	117.1	74.4	100.9	94.2	203.0	478.2	122.7	137.9	83.5	84.6	96.6	165.2
1996	118.1	78.0	101.2	93.5	198.2	467.2	118.9	138.9	85.4	86.3	99.8	163.7
1997	130.8	80.2	105.0	95.6	209.2	466.8	121.4	141.7	88.3	91.4	105.9	177.5
1998	140.1	84.9	106.7	98.6	207.6	444.3	122.3	143.5	86.6	92.9	109.7	188.0
1999	144.7	86.8	107.3	96.8	208.4	423.2	123.3	142.9	90.0	94.8	115.5	193.5
2000	147.2	91.6	107.8	98.1	204.2	408.0	120.0	144.2	89.2	96.2	116.7	192.9
2001	138.0	90.7	104.7	98.0	182.8	358.6	113.2	139.4	88.7	94.5	110.0	180.4
2002	142.7	95.9	106.0	97.0	183.7	282.4	114.6	136.2	93.5	99.9	113.9	174.3
2003	140.5	98.8	106.2	98.7	176.4	262.9	111.9	130.8	92.1	101.6	114.0	169.2
2004	144.5	98.8	107.8	99.1	174.2	230.8	112.8	131.2	97.5	105.7	115.4	170.6
2005	149.8	105.3	110.5	102.7	176.7	225.7	112.4	131.0	100.1	109.3	116.6	169.9
2006	147.7	108.6	111.2	102.9	160.2	220.6	111.2	129.5	101.9	111.9	117.4	168.0
2007	142.1	105.9	112.5	103.1	141.7	179.8	111.7	132.2	104.7	117.5	114.1	158.3
2008	128.3	107.7	105.8	100.2	124.6	144.9	106.9	123.7	100.1	108.6	103.4	144.3
2009	93.1	99.8	97.7	99.5	98.8	106.9	95.4	103.6	98.8	98.1	86.4	120.6
2010	91.9	103.4	99.8	99.8	105.4	107.8	97.3	103.5	97.9	101.3	94.2	111.4
2011	95.0	102.8	99.9	99.6	103.1	106.0	97.3	101.8	100.2	101.4	95.5	106.1
2012	100.0	100.0	100.0	100.0	100.0	100.0	100.0	100.0	100.0	100.0	100.0	100.0
2013	100.8	103.2	100.0	101.7	103.7	92.7	100.2	100.3	104.0	96.6	101.2	95.0
2014	101.3	100.0	99.3	101.6	105.8	88.8	99.3	98.5	100.2	95.6	103.9	94.0
2015	105.9	99.8	100.7	104.3	105.0	87.6	98.3	99.6	98.0	97.3	105.6	90.3
2016	105.8	100.5	101.3	105.6	105.4	79.0	95.8	98.6	100.9	98.0	106.1	84.2
2015												
January	104.2	101.0	100.2	102.9	104.9	93.0	99.6	97.8	97.0	97.2	105.8	90.3
February	105.0	99.1	100.1	102.5	105.9	88.7	98.9	97.8	97.9	97.3	105.1	90.1
March	104.3	99.6	100.4	104.1	105.8	88.3	99.8	99.1	97.0	96.9	104.6	90.9
April	103.7	98.9	100.7	104.1	106.1	89.0	99.9	99.3	98.0	97.3	104.9	91.1
May	104.4	98.3	100.3	103.8	105.9	88.4	99.7	98.8	97.8	96.6	105.1	91.1
June	105.2	101.4	100.2	103.6	105.3	87.8	98.3	99.0	96.7	97.2	104.9	91.1
July	105.8	99.2	100.7	104.6	104.2	88.7	97.9	99.6	97.6	97.3	105.5	91.9
August	106.6	100.4	101.0	105.8	104.2	88.4	97.4	100.7	97.8	96.6	106.7	90.7
September	107.8	99.6	100.9	105.0	103.9	87.2	97.8	100.4	98.3	97.0	106.3	89.6
October	108.4	99.5	101.1	104.6	104.7	84.6	97.4	100.7	100.2	97.6	106.2	89.6
November	108.9	100.2	101.5	105.4	104.4	83.7	96.5	101.1	99.5	98.4	106.1	89.1
December	106.3	100.3	101.1	105.1	104.9	83.6	96.3	100.7	98.4	97.7	106.4	87.8
2016												
January	108.4	100.9	101.8	106.1	107.1	81.1	96.4	100.8	98.5	98.9	106.5	87.1
February	106.6	100.8	101.6	105.9	105.3	81.4	96.2	100.3	99.9	98.2	106.5	87.0
March	106.7	100.7	101.8	105.4	105.2	80.6	95.8	99.2	101.6	99.2	105.7	85.6
April	106.3	101.0	101.2	105.3	104.5	78.3	94.9	98.6	100.3	98.2	106.2	85.3
May	105.6	101.5	101.3	105.5	104.9	77.5	95.6	97.2	100.4	98.3	105.9	84.9
June	105.2	100.7	101.1	105.7	104.9	77.7	95.5	97.8	101.9	97.3	105.7	83.7
July	104.8	101.6	101.1	105.7	105.7	77.9	94.9	97.5	101.5	97.3	107.0	83.3
August	104.3	99.9	100.8	105.8	104.8	77.8	94.6	96.9	101.3	96.7	105.7	82.9
September	104.4	101.6	101.1	105.7	105.9	79.0	95.4	97.8	101.4	97.3	106.4	83.3
October	104.9	100.1	101.2	105.5	106.4	79.3	96.2	98.0	101.2	97.4	106.7	82.8
November	106.4	98.7	101.6	105.1	106.6	78.8	97.3	99.0	102.2	98.4	105.5	82.4
December	106.2	98.7	101.3	105.2	103.8	78.6	96.4	99.6	100.9	98.4	105.0	81.9

. . . = Not available.

Table 2-3. Capacity Utilization by NAICS Industry Groups

(Output as a percent of capacity, seasonally adjusted.)

Year and month	Total industry	Total manufac-turing (SIC)	Manufacturing (NAICS)										
			Total	Durable goods manufacturing									
				Total	Wood products	Nonmetallic mineral products	Primary metals	Fabricated metal products	Machinery	Computer and electronic products	Electrical equipment, appliances, and compo-nents	Motor vehicles and parts	Aerospace and miscel-laneous transpor-tation equipment
1970	81.2	79.4	. . .	77.7	. . .	73.4	79.4	78.4	79.7	. . .	. . .	66.3	75.2
1971	79.6	77.9	. . .	75.4	. . .	74.9	73.0	78.4	73.8	. . .	. . .	79.1	66.8
1972	84.6	83.4	83.3	82.0	92.2	78.9	82.9	85.0	83.1	80.7	89.8	84.3	65.6
1973	88.3	87.7	87.8	88.6	87.8	83.9	94.7	90.9	92.5	85.2	97.7	91.8	73.5
1974	85.1	84.5	84.5	84.7	77.9	81.4	96.5	86.2	91.9	83.2	91.6	76.7	74.4
1975	75.8	73.7	73.6	71.8	70.0	72.6	75.2	72.3	77.7	68.7	70.7	66.1	70.9
1976	79.8	78.3	78.4	76.4	79.4	77.4	78.6	75.9	79.9	72.1	78.7	81.8	66.2
1977	83.4	82.5	82.5	81.2	86.0	82.5	79.3	80.0	85.5	77.9	85.4	89.9	66.2
1978	85.1	84.4	84.4	83.8	84.8	86.4	84.2	80.7	88.6	80.4	87.7	90.7	72.4
1979	85.1	84.1	84.0	84.1	79.8	84.4	86.1	81.7	90.1	83.7	88.8	80.9	81.9
1980	80.8	78.7	78.4	77.6	72.3	75.0	76.0	75.2	83.5	87.0	81.8	59.7	84.6
1981	79.6	76.9	76.6	75.1	70.6	72.2	77.8	72.9	80.5	84.6	78.9	57.2	76.9
1982	73.6	70.9	70.3	66.5	63.8	64.7	57.1	64.8	66.6	81.0	69.7	50.6	69.8
1983	74.9	73.5	72.9	68.7	75.2	70.2	59.9	66.7	60.5	81.9	72.9	67.2	66.4
1984	80.4	79.3	78.9	76.9	81.1	75.5	69.3	73.6	70.9	87.5	82.5	81.6	69.8
1985	79.2	78.1	77.6	75.7	79.7	75.7	67.5	74.1	70.5	80.2	79.1	83.4	72.4
1986	78.6	78.4	78.0	75.4	83.7	78.2	69.6	73.7	70.1	77.4	80.2	79.1	73.9
1987	81.2	81.0	80.5	77.6	85.7	80.7	78.3	75.3	71.9	79.9	82.5	78.2	75.4
1988	84.3	84.0	83.8	82.1	84.2	81.7	88.9	80.0	80.3	81.5	87.3	83.1	79.7
1989	83.8	83.3	83.2	81.8	82.2	80.9	86.3	79.6	83.9	78.9	86.3	81.4	85.3
1990	82.5	81.6	81.5	79.5	80.3	79.4	85.4	77.6	81.5	78.7	84.0	72.4	84.9
1991	79.9	78.6	78.4	75.4	76.1	73.3	80.1	73.9	76.3	78.3	79.1	64.3	83.1
1992	80.5	79.5	79.5	77.0	78.7	77.0	81.3	76.0	75.0	78.9	82.2	72.7	77.7
1993	81.4	80.4	80.4	78.6	78.8	78.7	85.1	76.9	78.4	78.2	86.6	79.0	73.4
1994	83.5	82.7	82.8	81.5	82.8	81.5	90.8	81.3	83.1	79.9	91.9	86.3	67.5
1995	83.9	83.1	83.2	82.1	80.9	81.6	89.0	83.3	85.2	83.2	91.4	83.5	65.1
1996	83.3	82.1	82.2	81.5	81.2	84.8	88.8	82.0	84.4	81.2	90.0	80.4	67.6
1997	84.0	83.0	82.9	82.2	80.9	83.4	90.0	82.0	84.7	81.3	88.6	81.5	73.3
1998	82.7	81.5	81.2	80.5	81.0	83.7	86.2	80.3	81.7	77.3	86.1	78.8	81.1
1999	81.7	80.4	80.1	80.0	81.4	81.5	84.4	78.2	76.1	81.0	83.6	83.1	75.3
2000	81.4	79.7	79.3	79.5	78.1	78.5	82.2	79.3	77.4	83.8	86.2	81.4	65.2
2001	76.1	73.8	73.3	71.4	72.3	73.7	73.8	73.2	68.1	69.4	77.2	72.8	69.6
2002	75.0	73.1	72.6	70.1	75.0	73.2	75.6	72.2	66.9	60.9	73.5	78.8	66.4
2003	76.0	74.0	73.6	71.1	76.0	73.3	74.0	73.4	68.5	64.5	74.6	78.4	63.8
2004	78.1	76.4	76.1	74.0	79.0	73.9	81.8	75.5	72.3	71.4	77.2	77.2	63.4
2005	80.0	78.3	78.1	76.3	80.6	74.8	79.4	79.2	76.0	73.0	80.9	77.4	70.3
2006	80.4	78.6	78.5	77.5	78.0	73.4	79.1	84.0	79.1	77.3	82.9	72.2	73.7
2007	80.7	78.8	78.9	78.6	73.4	69.0	80.3	86.5	82.1	76.8	87.7	71.8	85.7
2008	77.7	74.7	74.6	74.7	63.5	60.0	77.2	81.8	79.7	77.6	85.7	58.0	84.9
2009	68.5	65.5	65.4	61.4	50.5	46.6	55.2	64.5	62.3	70.9	68.8	43.7	74.7
2010	73.6	70.7	70.9	68.7	56.0	50.7	69.0	71.6	69.8	76.8	74.1	59.1	74.2
2011	76.3	73.7	74.0	72.5	60.5	54.2	74.7	77.5	76.7	76.2	79.5	64.3	72.2
2012	77.2	74.8	75.3	75.2	67.4	56.9	75.9	78.3	81.2	75.4	81.0	70.2	78.1
2013	77.3	74.7	75.2	75.1	71.8	60.9	76.2	79.0	76.7	72.8	80.6	72.1	79.0
2014	78.6	75.4	75.8	76.6	71.0	63.7	75.8	81.0	76.5	72.6	82.0	76.8	82.9
2015	76.8	75.5	75.9	75.6	72.0	64.0	71.7	79.5	71.3	71.3	80.1	80.2	82.2
2016	75.7	75.1	75.5	74.6	75.1	65.0	67.7	77.9	68.6	69.8	80.7	82.0	79.4
2015													
January	78.1	75.7	76.1	76.5	70.4	64.2	75.1	80.7	74.5	72.6	80.7	78.3	82.9
February	77.9	75.3	75.8	75.9	70.5	63.2	73.6	80.3	73.9	72.3	80.2	76.2	83.9
March	77.5	75.6	76.0	75.9	70.1	62.6	71.9	80.3	72.7	71.9	81.0	79.4	83.9
April	77.1	75.6	76.0	75.8	70.5	63.2	71.8	80.1	72.2	71.7	81.0	80.1	82.9
May	76.8	75.6	75.9	75.9	70.5	63.2	71.5	79.9	72.3	71.3	80.2	82.1	82.6
June	76.5	75.3	75.7	75.4	70.6	63.4	73.2	79.9	71.0	71.6	79.9	78.3	82.0
July	76.8	75.8	76.1	75.9	72.1	63.8	72.7	79.6	70.3	71.2	79.2	84.4	81.8
August	76.8	75.7	76.1	75.6	72.9	64.5	71.2	78.8	71.1	71.3	79.7	81.0	82.1
September	76.5	75.5	75.9	75.2	73.2	63.6	70.2	78.8	70.6	70.9	78.5	81.1	81.4
October	76.4	75.6	75.9	75.3	73.7	65.1	70.9	78.3	70.1	70.5	80.4	81.4	80.9
November	76.0	75.5	75.8	74.8	73.8	65.2	69.8	78.3	69.0	70.2	79.7	80.3	80.6
December	75.6	75.2	75.6	74.7	75.3	65.8	68.1	78.6	68.0	70.5	80.8	79.7	80.9
2016													
January	76.1	75.6	76.0	75.0	75.5	66.0	69.1	78.6	67.7	70.3	81.4	81.6	80.1
February	75.9	75.4	75.8	74.8	75.0	66.3	69.3	78.2	67.1	70.1	81.6	82.1	80.0
March	75.4	75.2	75.6	74.4	74.9	65.9	69.2	77.4	67.2	70.1	80.1	80.6	79.7
April	75.6	75.1	75.6	74.7	74.7	65.5	68.8	77.6	68.5	69.8	79.7	81.8	79.5
May	75.6	75.0	75.4	74.3	74.1	65.0	69.3	77.6	67.9	69.8	80.4	79.1	80.3
June	75.8	75.1	75.5	74.7	74.5	64.8	68.3	77.4	69.5	69.3	81.0	82.1	79.8
July	75.9	75.1	75.5	74.7	73.7	64.6	66.6	77.7	70.0	69.1	81.1	82.6	79.5
August	75.8	74.7	75.2	74.4	73.8	63.9	66.6	77.5	69.0	69.4	80.5	82.6	79.4
September	75.6	74.9	75.3	74.4	73.8	64.2	65.8	78.0	68.6	69.3	80.6	82.9	78.6
October	75.7	75.0	75.4	74.6	74.9	64.3	65.3	78.5	68.8	70.0	80.6	83.5	78.3
November	75.5	75.1	75.5	74.6	77.9	64.8	66.6	78.2	68.6	70.0	80.8	82.2	78.7
December	76.0	75.2	75.6	74.9	77.7	65.1	67.7	78.2	69.9	69.9	80.7	83.2	78.4

. . . = Not available.

Table 2-3. Capacity Utilization by NAICS Industry Groups—*Continued*

(Output as a percent of capacity, seasonally adjusted.)

Year and month	Durable goods manufacturing—Continued		Nondurable goods manufacturing									Other manufacturing (non-NAICS)
	Furniture and related products	Miscellaneous manufacturing	Total	Food, beverage, and tobacco products	Textile and product mills	Apparel and leather	Paper	Printing and support	Petroleum and coal products	Chemicals	Plastics and rubber products	
1970	83.7	. . .	82.1	84.1	. . .	. . .	86.2	. . .	96.0	76.1	79.2	. . .
1971	84.4	. . .	81.7	84.1	. . .	. . .	86.9	. . .	94.7	75.3	79.8	. . .
1972	93.6	80.4	85.2	85.2	88.9	81.6	91.4	92.3	93.1	80.0	88.5	85.6
1973	94.6	79.5	86.6	84.7	86.3	82.2	94.9	94.0	90.4	83.6	92.5	84.7
1974	83.4	74.6	84.2	83.9	76.3	76.3	95.1	88.0	92.5	84.1	84.2	82.7
1975	69.7	67.6	76.1	80.1	72.6	74.5	80.7	79.6	83.7	71.8	70.1	77.3
1976	76.4	72.4	81.2	83.3	81.5	78.2	87.7	82.3	86.0	77.8	77.3	77.6
1977	84.7	77.6	84.4	82.9	89.1	81.7	90.2	86.0	87.7	81.4	88.4	83.2
1978	86.1	78.7	85.3	83.0	88.4	84.2	92.2	87.4	86.4	82.6	88.6	85.1
1979	83.9	78.4	83.9	81.2	87.9	79.2	90.8	86.0	80.0	83.0	83.7	85.6
1980	75.0	73.3	79.7	80.9	83.9	80.0	88.2	83.7	76.2	76.7	74.1	86.7
1981	71.8	75.6	78.8	80.3	81.0	78.8	86.8	81.2	72.8	76.1	77.6	87.5
1982	66.4	73.6	76.4	81.3	74.6	77.9	83.9	82.4	71.2	69.3	74.5	87.4
1983	72.1	70.8	79.4	80.8	84.2	81.1	88.9	84.4	74.4	72.9	81.5	87.9
1984	78.9	75.9	82.1	81.3	86.0	81.2	91.1	87.2	78.4	76.0	91.2	89.4
1985	77.1	74.1	80.5	82.6	81.7	77.9	87.7	84.9	80.0	73.4	87.0	90.3
1986	78.9	74.0	81.8	82.8	84.3	79.8	90.1	85.7	81.8	75.9	85.3	88.7
1987	82.8	77.3	84.7	83.8	91.3	82.1	90.2	89.3	82.3	81.0	89.5	90.4
1988	80.5	81.9	86.2	85.3	88.8	82.2	91.3	90.5	83.2	84.3	89.1	88.5
1989	79.0	79.9	85.0	83.8	88.4	80.3	90.4	89.2	84.2	83.3	87.1	85.4
1990	76.1	79.6	84.2	83.9	83.5	79.1	89.2	89.0	84.7	83.0	83.8	83.7
1991	70.6	78.2	82.3	83.0	81.7	80.3	87.5	84.2	82.7	81.2	78.6	80.8
1992	76.6	76.9	82.7	82.5	85.6	82.8	88.3	86.1	85.3	79.8	81.9	80.1
1993	79.1	77.0	82.7	81.1	88.0	83.7	88.9	84.4	89.0	79.2	86.6	81.3
1994	80.5	76.9	84.6	83.3	90.2	84.9	90.7	83.6	88.9	80.6	91.4	81.4
1995	79.8	79.6	84.5	84.4	86.2	84.5	89.5	82.8	89.5	80.8	89.8	82.2
1996	78.5	81.3	83.2	82.5	82.2	83.2	85.5	82.6	91.7	80.4	88.7	80.6
1997	83.0	79.7	83.8	82.6	84.3	83.0	87.4	81.0	95.2	81.3	89.5	85.5
1998	82.5	80.1	82.3	83.1	81.7	77.4	87.3	79.5	92.7	78.7	88.2	86.7
1999	80.0	77.9	80.2	78.8	81.5	76.1	86.5	77.7	90.5	77.2	86.9	87.1
2000	76.8	77.6	79.0	77.7	79.3	78.9	84.3	77.1	89.2	76.3	82.7	87.4
2001	70.1	74.0	75.8	76.7	71.4	75.2	80.0	74.9	88.3	72.1	76.7	82.8
2002	71.8	74.6	76.0	75.9	73.5	66.9	81.9	75.0	88.6	73.7	78.7	81.5
2003	70.7	75.2	76.9	77.7	72.6	69.5	81.7	75.3	89.5	73.8	78.9	81.4
2004	76.1	75.5	78.7	77.7	74.6	70.1	83.2	77.1	92.6	76.4	82.7	82.7
2005	79.6	77.9	80.2	79.4	77.9	75.3	83.7	77.2	91.9	77.0	83.4	82.0
2006	78.8	77.4	79.8	79.0	75.0	75.3	83.6	76.8	89.3	77.3	81.6	80.0
2007	75.4	73.6	79.4	78.5	72.1	76.2	83.8	76.3	87.6	78.2	78.6	76.4
2008	71.1	74.5	74.4	76.2	67.8	75.5	82.1	69.4	81.8	71.9	70.5	77.3
2009	57.2	70.1	70.1	75.8	56.5	60.0	77.1	60.2	78.7	67.1	61.1	69.2
2010	60.7	75.1	73.6	76.5	63.8	66.2	81.5	63.8	80.6	71.1	70.3	65.8
2011	66.3	77.1	75.7	78.4	65.6	69.5	81.0	63.8	84.7	73.0	72.3	65.3
2012	71.5	75.4	75.5	78.6	65.9	69.1	82.8	62.9	83.1	71.4	77.3	63.3
2013	72.9	77.3	75.2	79.1	69.3	66.2	82.8	64.0	84.4	68.9	80.2	62.7
2014	74.9	76.5	75.0	77.5	71.2	67.1	83.7	63.6	82.3	69.9	81.9	64.8
2015	78.9	77.6	76.3	77.3	71.3	70.4	85.3	65.6	82.1	72.8	82.3	65.1
2016	79.0	78.4	76.6	77.3	71.6	66.4	85.6	66.5	80.8	74.1	81.7	63.3
2015												
January	77.6	78.3	75.7	77.0	71.0	73.2	85.5	63.7	81.6	71.9	82.8	63.8
February	78.2	76.9	75.7	76.6	71.8	70.1	85.0	63.8	82.5	72.1	82.2	63.9
March	77.7	77.3	76.0	77.6	71.8	70.1	85.9	64.8	81.9	72.0	81.7	64.7
April	77.3	76.9	76.2	77.4	72.0	70.9	86.3	65.1	82.7	72.4	81.9	65.1
May	77.8	76.4	76.0	77.0	71.9	70.7	86.3	64.9	82.5	72.1	82.0	65.4
June	78.4	78.9	76.0	76.8	71.5	70.6	85.2	65.2	81.5	72.7	81.8	65.6
July	78.8	77.1	76.4	77.4	70.8	71.5	85.1	65.7	82.0	72.9	82.2	66.4
August	79.4	78.1	76.6	78.2	70.8	71.5	84.8	66.6	81.9	72.5	83.1	65.8
September	80.3	77.4	76.5	77.6	70.6	70.8	85.4	66.5	82.0	73.0	82.7	65.2
October	80.7	77.4	76.7	77.2	71.2	68.9	85.2	66.9	83.2	73.5	82.6	65.5
November	81.1	78.0	77.0	77.6	71.0	68.4	84.7	67.3	82.2	74.2	82.4	65.3
December	79.2	78.0	76.7	77.4	71.3	68.5	84.7	67.1	80.9	73.8	82.6	64.6
2016												
January	80.8	78.5	77.2	78.0	72.8	66.7	85.0	67.4	80.6	74.8	82.6	64.2
February	79.5	78.5	77.0	77.8	71.6	67.2	85.0	67.2	81.3	74.3	82.5	64.4
March	79.6	78.4	77.1	77.4	71.5	66.8	85.0	66.5	82.3	75.1	81.8	63.5
April	79.3	78.6	76.6	77.3	71.0	65.2	84.4	66.3	80.9	74.4	82.1	63.6
May	78.8	79.1	76.6	77.3	71.3	64.8	85.2	65.4	80.6	74.4	81.8	63.5
June	78.5	78.5	76.4	77.4	71.3	65.2	85.3	65.9	81.5	73.7	81.4	62.8
July	78.2	79.2	76.4	77.4	71.8	65.6	85.0	65.9	80.9	73.6	82.3	62.7
August	77.9	77.9	76.1	77.4	71.1	65.8	84.9	65.6	80.5	73.2	81.2	62.6
September	78.0	79.3	76.3	77.2	71.9	67.1	85.8	66.3	80.4	73.5	81.7	63.2
October	78.5	78.1	76.4	77.0	72.1	67.6	86.7	66.5	80.1	73.6	81.7	63.0
November	79.6	77.1	76.6	76.7	72.3	67.5	87.8	67.2	80.7	74.3	80.7	62.9
December	79.4	77.1	76.4	76.7	70.3	67.6	87.1	67.7	79.6	74.3	80.2	62.8

. . . = Not available.

Table 2-3. Capacity Utilization by NAICS Industry Groups—*Continued*

(Output as a percent of capacity, seasonally adjusted.)

Year and month	Mining	Utilities	Selected high-tech industries				Measures excluding selected high-tech industries		Stage-of-process groups		
			Total	Computers and peripheral equipment	Communications equipment	Semiconductors and related electronic components	Total industry	Manufacturing	Crude	Primary and semi-finished	Finished
1970	89.5	96.4	82.9	. . .	. . .	. . .	81.0	79.2	84.6	81.4	78.2
1971	88.1	95.0	73.7	. . .	. . .	. . .	80.0	78.3	83.5	81.6	75.7
1972	90.8	95.4	78.1	81.5	73.3	81.4	84.9	83.6	88.3	88.1	79.6
1973	91.6	93.0	81.4	82.0	75.1	88.5	88.5	87.9	90.0	92.0	83.2
1974	91.1	86.6	81.0	88.3	73.3	83.5	85.3	84.6	91.0	87.3	80.4
1975	89.5	85.0	64.5	69.0	62.1	63.3	76.2	74.1	84.0	75.2	73.8
1976	89.6	85.6	68.5	76.8	62.0	68.6	80.2	78.8	87.0	80.1	76.9
1977	89.5	86.8	75.5	77.7	72.5	76.7	83.8	82.8	89.1	84.6	79.9
1978	89.7	87.0	78.5	77.7	77.4	80.4	85.4	84.7	88.7	86.3	82.2
1979	91.2	87.1	82.7	78.2	85.6	85.1	85.1	84.1	90.0	85.9	81.8
1980	91.3	85.5	87.6	86.9	91.7	84.6	80.5	78.2	89.4	78.8	79.5
1981	90.9	84.3	85.6	85.3	89.2	83.1	79.3	76.5	89.3	77.2	77.5
1982	84.1	79.9	78.5	70.3	87.2	82.0	73.4	70.4	82.4	70.5	73.1
1983	79.9	79.2	80.9	75.7	85.9	82.7	74.6	73.0	80.0	74.4	73.0
1984	85.9	81.8	87.6	85.4	85.4	91.3	80.0	78.7	85.8	81.1	77.2
1985	84.4	81.7	77.3	76.3	78.7	77.2	79.3	78.2	83.8	79.8	76.6
1986	77.6	80.9	73.0	72.8	75.4	71.5	78.9	78.8	79.1	79.7	77.0
1987	80.2	83.4	77.6	73.8	79.3	80.2	81.4	81.2	82.8	82.8	78.7
1988	84.1	86.7	80.1	76.2	84.1	81.6	84.6	84.3	86.2	85.9	81.8
1989	84.9	86.8	78.1	74.9	79.8	79.9	84.1	83.7	86.6	84.7	81.7
1990	86.6	86.5	77.2	71.4	82.1	79.5	82.8	82.0	87.7	82.7	80.6
1991	85.0	87.8	78.0	73.6	78.3	80.8	80.0	78.6	85.4	80.0	78.2
1992	84.6	86.3	80.3	78.3	79.4	81.8	80.5	79.5	85.6	81.5	78.1
1993	85.3	88.2	80.6	79.7	81.9	80.2	81.5	80.4	85.6	83.3	78.2
1994	86.8	88.3	82.6	75.8	82.9	85.6	83.5	82.7	88.0	86.3	79.1
1995	87.6	89.3	85.2	80.4	79.1	90.2	83.8	82.9	89.1	86.3	79.7
1996	90.4	90.7	82.9	86.2	76.4	84.4	83.4	82.1	89.1	85.5	79.3
1997	91.6	90.1	83.3	81.4	80.3	85.6	84.1	82.9	90.4	85.9	80.2
1998	89.1	92.6	78.8	78.0	84.8	76.2	83.1	81.8	87.1	84.1	80.1
1999	85.9	94.1	85.3	83.2	88.5	84.5	81.4	79.9	85.9	84.2	77.9
2000	90.7	94.3	88.2	80.7	91.2	89.7	80.8	78.8	88.5	83.9	76.8
2001	90.3	90.1	69.2	70.7	69.8	68.3	76.7	74.2	85.7	77.3	72.5
2002	86.2	87.7	59.0	68.9	44.8	63.8	76.2	74.3	83.3	77.4	70.6
2003	87.9	85.8	64.1	73.5	45.9	72.0	76.8	74.8	85.0	78.1	71.5
2004	88.3	84.6	71.0	78.2	53.4	78.6	78.5	76.8	86.6	80.1	73.4
2005	88.6	85.3	73.6	76.1	56.6	82.0	80.4	78.6	86.7	81.7	75.5
2006	90.3	83.9	81.2	78.3	74.7	86.2	80.3	78.4	88.2	81.3	76.2
2007	89.5	85.9	77.6	75.7	76.0	78.2	80.8	78.9	88.7	81.0	77.2
2008	89.7	84.2	80.6	78.4	81.4	81.5	77.6	74.3	87.3	76.7	74.1
2009	80.2	80.5	73.2	90.0	81.6	64.5	68.3	65.2	77.8	65.7	68.3
2010	83.8	82.8	81.0	89.6	81.9	77.1	73.3	70.3	83.3	71.8	71.4
2011	86.0	81.2	77.0	78.1	81.3	75.8	76.3	73.5	84.8	74.3	74.1
2012	87.6	78.2	71.4	70.4	75.7	70.4	77.4	75.0	86.0	74.6	75.3
2013	87.0	79.7	68.7	62.7	81.1	65.9	77.6	74.9	85.9	75.5	74.3
2014	90.4	80.5	71.1	66.8	72.3	71.6	78.9	75.6	88.3	76.7	74.8
2015	82.7	79.4	71.2	71.2	70.3	71.6	77.0	75.7	81.8	76.2	75.4
2016	78.4	77.7	71.6	74.0	72.1	70.7	75.9	75.2	78.7	75.4	75.0
2015											
January	88.2	80.1	71.7	71.0	69.7	72.7	78.3	75.8	86.0	76.6	75.6
February	86.5	83.7	71.6	72.0	69.4	72.4	78.1	75.5	84.7	77.1	75.2
March	84.9	81.5	71.5	71.9	70.2	72.0	77.7	75.7	83.3	76.6	75.7
April	83.6	79.6	71.8	73.9	71.4	71.5	77.3	75.8	82.6	76.4	75.4
May	82.1	79.2	71.5	73.4	72.1	70.6	76.9	75.7	81.5	76.2	75.3
June	81.3	79.7	71.4	73.5	71.6	70.8	76.6	75.5	80.6	76.1	75.2
July	82.1	79.2	71.0	74.6	70.4	70.4	77.0	76.0	81.0	76.3	75.8
August	82.3	79.5	70.9	73.2	69.3	71.1	76.9	75.9	81.1	76.1	76.0
September	81.8	79.9	70.9	71.4	69.2	71.6	76.7	75.6	81.0	76.1	75.6
October	80.8	79.0	71.4	72.3	69.6	71.9	76.5	75.7	80.4	76.2	75.3
November	80.0	76.4	70.2	63.4	70.2	72.0	76.1	75.6	79.9	75.4	75.3
December	79.4	75.5	70.9	64.4	70.7	72.7	75.7	75.4	79.2	75.2	75.0
2016											
January	79.2	76.8	71.4	72.1	70.9	71.4	76.2	75.7	79.2	75.6	75.5
February	79.4	76.4	71.1	70.4	71.1	71.3	76.0	75.6	78.9	75.5	75.3
March	78.4	73.7	71.2	71.6	71.2	71.1	75.5	75.4	78.6	74.6	75.1
April	77.0	78.0	71.0	71.5	71.1	70.8	75.8	75.3	77.4	75.5	75.2
May	77.7	77.7	71.1	73.7	70.7	70.6	75.7	75.1	78.1	75.2	75.0
June	77.7	79.3	71.0	73.9	70.1	70.5	76.0	75.2	78.1	75.7	75.1
July	77.8	79.6	71.2	74.1	69.7	71.1	76.0	75.2	78.3	75.9	74.9
August	77.9	81.1	71.1	74.8	70.3	70.5	75.9	74.9	78.2	75.9	74.6
September	77.8	78.7	71.7	76.0	72.2	70.4	75.7	75.0	78.3	75.5	74.7
October	79.4	77.1	72.5	77.3	74.8	70.2	75.8	75.1	79.4	75.2	74.8
November	79.3	74.5	72.6	75.8	76.2	70.2	75.6	75.2	80.0	74.8	74.6
December	79.0	79.5	72.6	76.4	76.7	69.8	76.1	75.3	79.6	75.9	74.9

. . . = Not available.

Table 2-4A. Industrial Production and Capacity Utilization, Historical Data, 1948–2016

(Seasonally adjusted.)

Year and month	Production indexes, 2007 = 100										Capacity utilization (output as percent of capacity)	
	Total industry	Manufac-turing (SIC)	Market groups								Total industry	Manufac-turing (SIC)
			Consumer goods			Business equipment	Defense and space equipment	Construction supplies	Business supplies	Materials		
			Total	Durable	Nondurable							
1949	14.1	13.3	21.2	14.8	24.5	5.2	7.5	27.2	13.4	12.7	. . .	74.2
1950	16.3	15.5	24.2	19.8	26.5	5.6	8.8	32.7	14.9	15.2	. . .	82.8
1951	17.7	16.7	23.9	17.2	27.4	6.8	21.7	34.0	15.8	16.8	. . .	85.8
1952	18.4	17.4	24.5	16.7	28.5	7.8	30.5	33.8	15.7	17.0	. . .	85.4
1953	19.9	19.0	26.0	19.5	29.3	8.1	36.5	36.3	16.7	18.9	. . .	89.3
1954	18.9	17.7	25.8	18.1	29.7	7.1	32.1	35.7	16.9	17.5	. . .	80.1
1955	21.3	20.0	28.8	22.3	32.0	7.7	29.4	41.1	19.0	20.7	. . .	87.0
1956	22.2	20.8	29.8	21.6	34.0	8.9	28.7	42.3	20.1	21.2	. . .	86.1
1957	22.5	21.0	30.6	21.6	35.1	9.2	30.0	41.7	20.4	21.2	. . .	83.6
1958	21.1	19.6	30.3	19.2	36.1	7.8	30.1	40.2	20.2	19.1	. . .	75.0
1959	23.6	22.0	33.2	22.7	38.7	8.8	31.8	45.1	21.9	22.0	. . .	81.6
1960	24.1	22.5	04.5	23.9	39.9	9.0	32.6	44.0	22.7	22.3	. . .	80.1
1961	24.2	22.6	35.2	23.6	41.2	8.7	33.2	44.4	23.4	22.0	. . .	77.3
1962	26.3	24.6	37.6	26.7	43.1	9.5	38.4	47.1	24.9	24.3	. . .	81.4
1963	27.8	26.0	39.7	29.0	45.1	10.0	41.4	49.3	26.5	25.9	. . .	83.5
1964	29.7	27.8	41.9	31.1	47.3	11.2	40.1	52.3	28.4	28.0	. . .	85.6
1965	32.7	30.8	45.2	36.5	49.3	12.8	44.4	55.5	30.2	31.2	. . .	89.5
1966	35.5	33.6	47.5	38.6	51.7	14.8	52.1	57.9	32.6	34.0	. . .	91.1
1967	36.3	34.3	48.6	37.1	54.4	15.1	59.5	59.4	34.3	33.7	87.0	87.2
1968	38.3	36.2	51.6	41.4	56.5	15.8	59.6	62.5	36.4	35.9	87.3	87.1
1969	40.1	37.8	53.5	43.1	58.4	16.8	56.7	65.2	38.7	38.0	87.4	86.6
1970	38.8	36.1	52.9	39.8	59.4	16.2	48.1	62.9	38.8	36.7	81.2	79.4
1971	39.3	36.7	55.9	45.1	61.1	15.4	43.2	64.9	40.0	37.2	79.6	77.9
1972	43.1	40.5	60.4	50.4	65.0	17.5	42.0	73.6	44.0	41.0	84.6	83.4
1973	46.6	44.1	63.1	54.3	66.9	20.3	46.0	79.9	46.7	44.7	88.3	87.7
1974	46.5	44.0	61.3	49.4	67.0	21.5	47.6	78.1	46.6	44.6	85.1	84.5
1975	42.3	39.4	58.8	44.8	65.8	19.1	48.0	66.0	42.8	39.7	75.8	73.7
1976	45.7	43.0	63.6	50.6	69.9	20.4	46.5	71.1	45.6	43.2	79.8	78.3
1977	49.2	46.6	67.6	56.9	72.4	23.6	41.7	77.3	49.5	46.2	83.4	82.5
1978	51.9	49.5	69.7	58.3	75.0	26.6	42.4	81.6	52.2	48.6	85.1	84.4
1979	53.4	51.0	68.6	56.2	74.5	29.9	45.4	83.8	54.0	49.8	85.1	84.1
1980	52.0	49.2	66.0	48.9	74.5	30.6	54.0	77.6	52.7	48.0	80.8	78.7
1981	52.7	49.7	66.4	49.6	74.8	31.5	58.4	76.3	53.9	48.3	79.6	76.9
1982	50.0	47.0	66.3	46.7	76.1	28.8	69.8	69.2	53.2	44.6	73.6	70.9
1983	51.3	49.2	68.7	51.8	77.0	29.0	70.3	74.0	55.8	45.7	74.9	73.5
1984	55.9	54.0	71.9	58.0	78.5	33.3	80.5	80.5	60.7	50.0	80.4	79.3
1985	56.6	54.9	72.6	58.1	79.5	34.6	90.1	82.4	62.2	50.0	79.2	78.1
1986	57.2	56.1	75.0	61.7	81.3	34.1	95.7	85.1	64.2	50.0	78.6	78.4
1987	60.2	59.3	78.2	65.5	84.2	36.4	97.7	90.6	68.0	52.7	81.2	81.0
1988	63.3	62.5	81.1	68.7	87.0	40.2	98.7	92.7	70.6	55.6	84.3	84.0
1989	63.9	63.0	81.5	70.3	86.7	41.6	98.8	92.3	71.5	56.0	83.8	83.3
1990	64.5	63.5	81.8	68.2	88.3	43.2	95.3	91.6	73.2	56.4	82.5	81.6
1991	63.5	62.3	81.7	65.2	89.5	42.6	88.3	86.7	72.1	55.6	79.9	78.6
1992	65.4	64.6	84.3	71.5	90.4	44.3	81.9	90.4	73.8	57.4	80.5	79.5
1993	67.5	66.8	86.9	77.3	91.5	46.4	77.4	94.3	76.1	59.3	81.4	80.4
1994	71.0	70.7	90.5	84.2	93.7	49.5	72.6	101.1	79.1	63.1	83.5	82.7
1995	74.3	74.3	93.0	87.4	96.0	54.3	70.1	103.5	82.3	66.5	83.9	83.1
1996	77.7	78.0	94.7	90.1	97.2	59.7	68.3	108.1	85.6	70.0	83.3	82.1
1997	83.3	84.6	98.2	96.3	99.6	68.6	67.3	113.3	91.6	75.5	84.0	83.0
1998	88.1	90.2	101.8	103.3	101.9	76.6	70.3	119.3	96.8	79.9	82.7	81.5
1999	92.1	94.8	104.0	111.5	101.8	80.9	68.2	122.2	100.9	84.9	81.7	80.4
2000	95.6	98.7	105.9	114.8	103.3	87.2	60.6	124.9	104.8	89.0	81.4	79.7
2001	92.7	95.0	104.9	109.4	103.8	81.9	66.6	119.1	100.9	85.5	76.1	73.8
2002	93.0	95.4	107.0	116.5	104.2	76.4	67.3	119.1	101.0	86.7	75.0	73.1
2003	94.1	96.7	108.4	120.0	104.9	76.4	71.6	118.8	102.9	87.0	76.0	74.0
2004	96.6	99.7	109.6	121.7	105.9	80.4	70.3	121.6	105.3	90.8	78.1	76.4
2005	99.8	103.7	112.5	122.2	109.5	86.1	76.9	127.4	109.2	92.9	80.0	78.3
2006	102.0	106.3	113.2	121.5	110.5	94.0	76.5	130.5	110.9	94.7	80.4	78.6
2007	104.6	109.2	113.2	121.0	110.7	99.5	91.1	129.4	112.1	98.0	80.7	78.8
2008	100.9	103.9	107.2	106.7	107.2	97.0	98.3	117.4	107.2	95.6	77.7	74.7
2009	89.3	89.6	99.2	86.0	102.9	80.2	94.0	90.3	95.0	84.9	68.5	65.5
2010	94.2	94.8	100.3	94.2	101.9	86.2	101.0	93.6	98.0	91.9	73.6	70.7
2011	97.1	97.5	101.4	97.7	102.3	91.2	98.1	95.8	99.0	95.9	76.3	73.7
2012	100.0	100.0	100.0	100.0	100.0	100.0	100.0	100.0	100.0	100.0	77.2	74.8
2013	102.0	100.9	100.7	105.5	99.5	99.9	97.2	103.0	101.8	103.4	77.3	74.7
2014	105.1	102.1	101.5	110.8	99.2	101.8	94.0	106.5	102.8	108.7	78.6	75.4
2015	104.4	102.2	103.9	115.3	101.0	100.9	91.0	107.0	102.0	107.2	76.8	75.5
2016	103.1	102.2	104.5	118.5	101.0	99.1	89.7	108.4	102.3	104.7	75.7	75.1
1950												
January	14.5	13.7	22.1	16.6	25.1	4.8	7.0	28.2	13.8	13.1	. . .	74.9
February	14.5	13.9	22.2	16.6	25.1	5.0	7.0	29.3	14.2	12.9	. . .	75.4
March	15.0	14.1	22.6	17.3	25.4	5.0	7.1	30.0	14.2	13.8	. . .	76.4
April	15.5	14.7	23.3	18.5	25.8	5.2	7.3	31.6	14.5	14.4	. . .	79.2
May	15.9	15.1	23.8	19.5	26.0	5.4	7.5	31.9	14.6	14.8	. . .	81.0
June	16.4	15.5	24.4	21.1	26.2	5.6	7.8	33.0	14.7	15.3	. . .	83.1
July	16.9	16.0	25.2	22.0	26.8	5.8	8.2	33.9	15.1	15.8	. . .	85.5
August	17.4	16.6	26.0	22.6	27.8	6.1	9.0	34.5	15.4	16.2	. . .	88.4
September	17.3	16.4	25.3	21.6	27.4	6.0	9.9	34.6	15.3	16.4	. . .	87.2
October	17.4	16.5	25.1	21.2	27.2	6.1	10.7	34.9	15.5	16.6	. . .	87.5
November	17.4	16.5	25.0	20.7	27.2	6.1	11.5	34.9	15.6	16.4	. . .	87.0
December	17.7	16.8	25.4	20.5	28.0	6.2	12.4	35.0	15.8	16.7	. . .	88.1

. . . = Not available.

Table 2-4A. Industrial Production and Capacity Utilization, Historical Data, 1948–2016—*Continued*

(Seasonally adjusted.)

Year and month	Production indexes, 2007 = 100										Capacity utilization (output as percent of capacity)	
			Market groups									
	Total industry	Manufac- turing (SIC)	Consumer goods			Business equipment	Defense and space equipment	Construction supplies	Business supplies	Materials	Total industry	Manufac- turing (SIC)
			Total	Durable	Nondurable							
1951												
January	17.7	16.9	25.6	20.1	28.4	6.3	13.8	35.3	16.0	16.5	. . .	88.3
February	17.9	16.9	25.5	20.2	28.4	6.4	15.9	34.9	15.8	16.6	. . .	88.3
March	17.9	17.0	25.2	20.1	27.8	6.5	18.1	35.1	16.1	17.0	. . .	88.4
April	18.0	17.0	24.7	19.2	27.7	6.6	19.8	34.9	16.4	17.1	. . .	88.2
May	17.9	16.9	24.3	18.2	27.4	6.7	20.5	34.7	16.3	17.2	. . .	87.4
June	17.8	16.9	24.0	17.3	27.4	6.8	21.6	34.5	16.0	17.3	. . .	86.6
July	17.6	16.6	23.2	15.5	27.1	6.8	22.8	33.6	15.8	17.0	. . .	84.9
August	17.4	16.4	22.6	14.5	26.9	6.9	23.6	33.5	15.6	16.7	. . .	83.6
September	17.5	16.5	22.9	15.1	26.9	7.1	24.3	33.4	15.5	16.8	. . .	83.7
October	17.5	16.4	22.7	15.0	26.8	7.2	25.3	33.1	15.2	16.6	. . .	83.1
November	17.6	16.5	23.1	15.3	27.2	7.3	26.8	32.8	15.3	16.6	. . .	83.6
December	17.7	16.7	23.3	15.4	27.4	7.4	27.4	32.9	15.3	16.6	. . .	83.9
1952												
January	17.9	16.8	23.5	15.4	27.6	7.6	27.8	33.4	15.4	17.0	. . .	84.4
February	18.0	16.9	23.6	15.3	28.0	7.7	28.1	33.6	15.4	16.9	. . .	84.6
March	18.1	17.0	23.8	15.7	28.0	7.8	28.2	33.4	15.4	16.9	. . .	84.7
April	17.9	16.9	23.8	15.5	28.0	7.7	28.5	32.9	15.3	16.6	. . .	83.6
May	17.7	16.8	23.7	16.0	27.7	7.8	29.4	32.4	15.2	16.3	. . .	83.1
June	17.6	16.6	24.4	16.1	28.7	7.8	30.4	32.2	15.5	15.4	. . .	81.9
July	17.3	16.3	24.0	14.6	28.8	7.5	30.5	32.1	15.7	15.1	. . .	79.8
August	18.4	17.4	24.4	16.0	28.9	7.6	31.0	34.3	15.8	17.0	. . .	85.1
September	19.1	18.0	25.1	17.7	28.9	7.8	31.5	34.6	16.0	18.1	. . .	87.7
October	19.3	18.3	25.5	18.3	29.1	7.8	32.6	35.1	16.3	18.0	. . .	88.8
November	19.7	18.7	26.0	19.4	29.4	7.9	33.2	35.7	16.4	18.5	. . .	90.2
December	19.8	18.8	26.0	19.5	29.4	8.0	34.3	35.9	16.3	18.6	. . .	90.5
1953												
January	19.8	18.9	26.2	20.3	29.4	8.1	34.7	36.5	16.1	18.5	. . .	90.5
February	19.9	19.1	26.4	20.5	29.5	8.1	35.5	37.0	16.4	18.9	. . .	91.1
March	20.1	19.2	26.5	20.7	29.4	8.2	36.2	37.1	16.8	19.2	. . .	91.4
April	20.2	19.3	26.4	20.5	29.5	8.2	36.7	37.3	16.8	19.3	. . .	91.5
May	20.3	19.4	26.5	20.6	29.6	8.1	37.3	36.5	16.9	19.7	. . .	91.7
June	20.2	19.2	26.1	19.8	29.5	8.1	37.5	36.2	16.9	19.7	. . .	90.7
July	20.5	19.4	26.1	19.7	29.4	8.2	37.8	36.7	17.0	20.0	. . .	91.0
August	20.4	19.3	26.0	19.5	29.4	8.2	37.6	36.6	17.0	19.4	. . .	90.6
September	19.9	18.9	25.6	18.7	29.2	8.1	37.5	35.9	16.9	18.9	. . .	88.3
October	19.8	18.7	25.6	18.6	29.3	8.1	37.2	36.0	16.7	18.4	. . .	87.2
November	19.3	18.3	25.2	17.9	29.1	7.8	34.7	35.4	16.7	17.9	. . .	84.7
December	18.8	17.8	24.8	17.2	28.8	7.7	35.0	34.5	16.4	17.5	. . .	82.3
1954												
January	18.7	17.6	24.9	17.0	29.1	7.4	34.3	35.2	16.4	17.3	. . .	81.3
February	18.7	17.6	25.2	17.4	29.3	7.4	34.1	35.3	16.6	17.2	. . .	80.8
March	18.6	17.5	25.3	17.4	29.4	7.2	33.6	35.0	16.6	17.1	. . .	80.2
April	18.5	17.4	25.3	17.6	29.2	7.1	33.1	35.0	16.7	17.0	. . .	79.4
May	18.6	17.5	25.4	17.9	29.2	7.1	32.6	35.5	16.6	17.3	. . .	79.8
June	18.7	17.6	25.6	18.1	29.4	7.0	32.1	34.6	16.8	17.5	. . .	79.9
July	18.7	17.5	25.7	17.9	29.6	7.0	31.9	34.6	16.6	17.5	. . .	79.4
August	18.7	17.5	25.7	18.0	29.6	7.0	31.3	34.4	16.7	17.4	. . .	78.8
September	18.7	17.6	25.9	18.1	29.9	6.9	30.9	36.1	17.2	17.3	. . .	79.2
October	18.9	17.8	26.0	18.4	30.0	6.9	30.6	37.3	17.4	17.7	. . .	79.7
November	19.2	18.1	26.6	18.9	30.5	7.0	30.5	37.7	17.6	18.0	. . .	80.9
December	19.5	18.3	27.0	19.6	30.8	7.0	30.0	38.0	17.8	18.3	. . .	81.8
1955												
January	19.9	18.8	27.6	21.0	30.9	7.1	29.8	38.5	18.0	19.0	. . .	83.5
February	20.2	19.0	27.8	21.2	30.9	7.2	29.8	39.1	18.2	19.4	. . .	84.1
March	20.7	19.4	28.3	21.8	31.4	7.2	29.7	40.4	18.7	20.0	. . .	85.8
April	20.9	19.7	28.5	22.2	31.6	7.5	29.6	40.7	18.6	20.3	. . .	86.7
May	21.3	20.1	28.9	22.7	31.9	7.6	29.6	40.8	18.9	20.7	. . .	87.9
June	21.3	20.1	28.6	22.3	31.8	7.7	29.3	41.6	19.1	20.8	. . .	87.6
July	21.4	20.2	28.7	22.6	31.7	7.7	29.3	41.6	19.0	21.0	. . .	87.7
August	21.4	20.2	28.8	22.6	31.8	7.8	29.1	41.6	18.9	21.0	. . .	87.3
September	21.6	20.3	29.0	22.7	32.1	7.8	29.2	41.9	19.3	21.3	. . .	87.5
October	21.9	20.6	29.5	22.8	32.9	8.2	29.0	41.9	19.5	21.5	. . .	88.4
November	22.0	20.6	29.6	22.6	33.1	8.2	29.0	42.3	19.8	21.4	. . .	88.3
December	22.1	20.9	29.7	22.5	33.4	8.3	29.1	42.6	19.6	21.5	. . .	89.0
1956												
January	22.2	20.8	29.8	22.3	33.6	8.4	28.7	43.3	19.8	21.6	. . .	88.2
February	22.0	20.7	29.7	21.9	33.7	8.5	28.5	43.1	19.8	21.2	. . .	87.4
March	22.0	20.6	29.7	21.9	33.7	8.6	27.9	43.0	20.0	21.1	. . .	87.0
April	22.2	20.9	29.8	22.2	33.7	8.9	28.0	42.8	20.2	21.3	. . .	87.8
May	22.0	20.7	29.6	21.7	33.8	8.8	28.1	42.2	20.0	20.9	. . .	86.3
June	21.8	20.5	29.5	21.2	33.9	8.9	28.1	41.8	20.0	20.6	. . .	85.3
July	21.1	19.7	29.6	21.2	34.0	8.9	28.1	39.6	20.1	19.0	. . .	81.5
August	22.0	20.6	29.8	21.2	34.2	9.0	28.5	41.6	20.1	20.7	. . .	84.9
September	22.5	20.9	29.7	20.9	34.3	9.0	28.7	42.7	20.1	21.8	. . .	86.0
October	22.7	21.1	30.0	21.2	34.5	9.1	29.5	42.4	20.3	22.2	. . .	86.5
November	22.5	21.1	29.8	20.9	34.4	9.2	29.9	42.1	20.3	21.7	. . .	85.8
December	22.8	21.4	30.1	21.7	34.3	9.4	30.6	42.8	20.4	22.1	. . .	86.8

. . . = Not available.

Table 2-4A. Industrial Production and Capacity Utilization, Historical Data, 1948–2016—*Continued*

(Seasonally adjusted.)

Year and month	Production indexes, 2007 = 100										Capacity utilization (output as percent of capacity)	
	Total industry	Manufac-turing (SIC)	Market groups								Total industry	Manufac-turing (SIC)
			Consumer goods			Business equipment	Defense and space equipment	Construction supplies	Business supplies	Materials		
			Total	Durable	Nondurable							
1957												
January	22.7	21.3	30.3	21.8	34.5	9.5	30.7	42.2	20.4	21.6	. . .	86.2
February	22.9	21.6	30.6	22.2	34.9	9.7	30.9	43.5	20.5	21.8	. . .	87.0
March	22.9	21.5	30.7	22.1	35.1	9.6	30.9	42.8	20.4	21.7	. . .	86.4
April	22.6	21.2	30.4	21.4	34.9	9.5	30.9	41.9	20.4	21.4	. . .	85.0
May	22.5	21.1	30.5	21.3	35.0	9.3	30.5	41.7	20.6	21.3	. . .	84.2
June	22.6	21.2	30.6	21.7	35.1	9.3	30.6	42.0	20.4	21.4	. . .	84.6
July	22.7	21.2	30.7	21.5	35.4	9.4	30.3	42.1	20.5	21.5	. . .	84.3
August	22.7	21.3	30.9	22.1	35.4	9.3	30.4	41.7	20.5	21.6	. . .	84.2
September	22.5	21.1	30.9	22.0	35.4	9.2	29.7	41.5	20.5	21.3	. . .	83.2
October	22.2	20.7	30.4	21.2	35.1	9.0	29.0	41.0	20.2	21.0	. . .	81.4
November	21.7	20.2	30.3	21.1	34.9	8.7	28.0	40.5	20.0	20.2	. . .	79.4
December	21.3	19.8	30.1	20.2	35.3	8.5	27.8	39.8	20.0	19.5	. . .	77.5
1958												
January	20.9	19.4	29.7	19.4	35.2	8.3	28.2	39.3	19.9	19.0	. . .	75.7
February	20.4	19.0	29.5	18.7	35.2	8.0	28.4	38.1	19.8	18.4	. . .	73.8
March	20.2	18.8	29.3	18.1	35.2	7.8	29.0	37.9	19.9	17.9	. . .	72.7
April	19.8	18.4	29.0	17.4	35.2	7.7	29.4	37.4	19.7	17.4	. . .	71.3
May	20.0	18.7	29.4	18.0	35.5	7.5	29.7	38.6	19.7	17.7	. . .	71.9
June	20.6	19.2	30.0	18.5	36.1	7.5	30.6	40.2	19.9	18.4	. . .	73.9
July	20.9	19.4	30.4	18.8	36.5	7.5	30.6	39.9	19.9	18.9	. . .	74.3
August	21.3	19.8	30.5	19.1	36.6	7.7	30.9	41.7	20.2	19.5	. . .	75.7
September	21.5	20.0	30.2	17.8	36.8	7.7	31.1	41.8	20.4	19.9	. . .	76.2
October	21.7	20.1	30.5	18.7	36.8	7.8	31.1	41.8	20.8	20.3	. . .	76.4
November	22.4	20.8	31.9	21.9	37.2	8.0	31.3	43.4	20.9	20.8	. . .	79.1
December	22.4	20.9	32.1	22.0	37.2	8.0	31.4	42.8	20.8	20.9	. . .	79.0
1959												
January	22.7	21.3	32.4	22.1	37.7	8.2	31.5	43.7	21.3	21.3	. . .	80.2
February	23.2	21.7	32.7	22.2	38.1	8.3	31.2	44.9	21.5	21.9	. . .	81.4
March	23.5	22.0	32.7	22.6	37.9	8.4	31.3	46.0	21.7	22.5	. . .	82.5
April	24.0	22.5	33.2	22.7	38.6	8.6	31.5	47.3	21.7	23.1	. . .	84.0
May	24.4	22.8	33.4	23.2	38.6	8.9	31.8	47.7	21.7	23.7	. . .	84.9
June	24.4	22.8	33.2	23.4	38.3	9.1	31.8	47.5	22.0	23.6	. . .	84.8
July	23.8	22.4	33.6	23.8	38.6	9.1	32.0	45.7	22.2	22.2	. . .	83.0
August	23.0	21.5	33.7	23.2	39.0	9.0	31.8	42.8	22.1	20.5	. . .	79.5
September	23.0	21.4	33.6	22.5	39.3	9.0	32.0	42.3	22.3	20.4	. . .	79.0
October	22.8	21.3	33.4	23.0	38.8	8.9	31.9	42.4	22.2	20.2	. . .	78.2
November	22.9	21.4	32.7	20.2	39.3	8.8	31.9	43.9	22.2	21.0	. . .	78.5
December	24.4	22.9	33.7	22.7	39.5	8.9	32.1	47.3	22.4	23.3	. . .	83.6
1960												
January	25.0	23.5	34.8	25.2	39.6	9.2	32.4	47.0	22.7	24.0	. . .	85.6
February	24.8	23.3	34.4	24.9	39.2	9.3	32.6	46.5	22.7	23.7	. . .	84.6
March	24.6	23.0	34.5	24.4	39.6	9.3	32.7	45.1	22.6	23.3	. . .	83.2
April	24.4	22.9	34.7	24.4	40.0	9.2	32.5	45.1	23.0	22.7	. . .	82.3
May	24.3	22.7	34.9	24.6	40.1	9.2	32.9	44.6	23.1	22.5	. . .	81.5
June	24.0	22.5	34.7	24.3	39.9	9.1	32.1	43.8	22.9	22.2	. . .	80.2
July	23.9	22.4	34.3	23.4	40.0	9.0	32.8	44.2	22.9	22.2	. . .	79.7
August	23.9	22.3	34.4	23.7	40.0	8.9	33.0	43.1	22.7	22.1	. . .	79.1
September	23.7	22.1	34.3	23.4	39.9	8.8	32.9	42.7	22.6	21.7	. . .	77.9
October	23.6	22.0	34.6	23.6	40.3	8.7	32.6	42.8	22.7	21.6	. . .	77.5
November	23.3	21.6	34.0	22.9	39.9	8.7	32.7	42.3	22.7	21.1	. . .	75.8
December	22.9	21.3	33.7	22.1	39.8	8.5	32.2	41.8	22.3	20.5	. . .	74.3
1961												
January	22.9	21.3	33.5	21.3	40.0	8.6	32.6	41.4	22.6	20.7	. . .	74.1
February	22.9	21.2	33.7	21.2	40.2	8.5	32.3	41.4	22.7	20.5	. . .	73.5
March	23.0	21.3	33.7	21.2	40.2	8.5	32.3	42.3	22.9	20.7	. . .	73.9
April	23.5	21.8	34.5	22.7	40.6	8.6	32.3	43.4	23.0	21.3	. . .	75.4
May	23.8	22.2	34.9	23.4	40.9	8.6	32.3	43.5	23.1	22.0	. . .	76.4
June	24.2	22.5	35.3	24.2	41.0	8.7	32.3	44.5	23.3	22.3	. . .	77.3
July	24.4	22.8	35.6	24.6	41.2	8.7	32.6	45.2	23.5	22.6	. . .	78.1
August	24.7	23.1	35.8	24.7	41.6	8.7	32.7	45.7	23.7	23.1	. . .	79.0
September	24.6	22.9	35.2	23.3	41.3	8.9	33.4	46.1	23.6	23.1	. . .	78.2
October	25.1	23.4	36.2	24.6	42.1	8.9	34.2	46.4	23.9	23.5	. . .	79.6
November	25.5	23.8	36.8	25.7	42.5	9.1	35.0	46.1	24.1	23.8	. . .	80.8
December	25.7	24.1	36.9	26.2	42.5	9.1	35.6	46.4	24.4	24.2	. . .	81.6
1962												
January	25.5	23.8	36.6	25.6	42.3	9.1	36.0	44.3	24.4	24.0	. . .	80.2
February	25.9	24.2	36.8	25.7	42.6	9.2	36.7	46.8	24.6	24.4	. . .	81.4
March	26.1	24.4	37.1	26.1	42.8	9.4	37.2	47.4	24.5	24.4	. . .	81.9
April	26.1	24.4	37.4	26.7	42.9	9.4	37.5	46.8	24.5	24.4	. . .	81.7
May	26.1	24.4	37.6	26.9	43.2	9.4	37.7	46.7	24.9	24.0	. . .	81.3
June	26.0	24.3	37.4	26.5	43.0	9.5	38.1	47.1	24.9	24.0	. . .	80.9
July	26.3	24.6	38.0	27.0	43.6	9.6	38.8	46.9	24.8	24.2	. . .	81.5
August	26.3	24.6	37.6	26.7	43.2	9.7	39.4	47.7	25.0	24.2	. . .	81.4
September	26.5	24.8	37.8	27.0	43.4	9.7	39.5	48.3	25.2	24.4	. . .	81.8
October	26.5	24.8	37.8	27.1	43.2	9.7	39.6	47.5	25.2	24.4	. . .	81.4
November	26.6	25.0	38.0	27.1	43.4	9.7	40.0	47.7	25.3	24.6	. . .	81.8
December	26.6	25.0	38.2	27.4	43.6	9.7	40.2	48.1	25.2	24.5	. . .	81.7

. . . = Not available.

Table 2-4A. Industrial Production and Capacity Utilization, Historical Data, 1948–2016—*Continued*

(Seasonally adjusted.)

Year and month	Production indexes, 2007 = 100										Capacity utilization (output as percent of capacity)	
	Total industry	Manufac-turing (SIC)	Market groups								Total industry	Manufac-turing (SIC)
			Consumer goods			Business equipment	Defense and space equipment	Construction supplies	Business supplies	Materials		
			Total	Durable	Nondurable							
1963												
January	26.8	25.1	38.6	27.6	44.2	9.6	42.0	46.9	25.4	24.6	. . .	81.9
February	27.1	25.4	39.1	27.9	44.7	9.8	41.7	47.0	25.6	25.0	. . .	82.4
March	27.3	25.5	39.2	28.0	45.0	9.7	41.5	47.5	25.4	25.3	. . .	82.6
April	27.5	25.8	39.4	28.2	45.1	9.8	41.5	49.2	26.2	25.6	. . .	83.5
May	27.9	26.1	39.5	28.7	45.0	9.8	41.5	50.2	26.5	26.2	. . .	84.0
June	28.0	26.2	39.7	29.2	45.0	9.8	41.4	50.0	26.4	26.3	. . .	83.9
July	27.8	26.1	39.6	29.1	44.8	9.9	41.0	49.8	26.5	26.0	. . .	83.3
August	27.9	26.2	39.9	29.2	45.3	10.2	41.2	50.0	26.7	25.8	. . .	83.5
September	28.2	26.4	40.0	29.7	45.2	10.1	41.3	49.7	27.0	26.3	. . .	83.8
October	28.4	26.6	40.3	29.8	45.5	10.3	41.3	50.4	27.2	26.5	. . .	84.3
November	28.5	26.7	40.3	30.0	45.5	10.4	41.2	51.0	27.5	26.6	. . .	84.3
December	28.5	26.7	40.6	30.1	45.9	10.4	41.3	50.2	27.3	26.5	. . .	84.0
1964												
January	28.7	26.9	41.0	30.2	46.4	10.6	40.9	50.5	27.6	26.7	. . .	84.5
February	28.9	27.1	40.9	30.4	46.2	10.6	40.5	51.9	27.7	27.1	. . .	84.7
March	28.9	27.1	40.7	30.1	46.0	10.7	40.4	52.0	27.9	27.1	. . .	84.4
April	29.4	27.6	41.7	30.9	47.1	11.0	40.3	52.2	28.3	27.4	. . .	85.6
May	29.5	27.7	42.0	31.1	47.6	11.1	39.6	52.5	28.5	27.6	. . .	85.6
June	29.6	27.7	42.0	31.4	47.3	11.1	39.4	52.1	28.6	27.8	. . .	85.4
July	29.8	28.0	42.6	32.0	47.9	11.3	39.3	53.1	28.6	27.9	. . .	85.9
August	30.0	28.1	42.5	32.2	47.6	11.3	39.5	52.6	28.4	28.4	. . .	86.1
September	30.1	28.3	42.0	31.4	47.3	11.4	39.8	52.2	28.5	28.9	. . .	86.2
October	29.7	27.9	41.2	28.2	47.9	11.3	40.0	52.4	28.5	28.3	. . .	84.6
November	30.6	28.7	42.7	32.0	48.1	11.7	40.5	53.6	28.7	29.2	. . .	86.8
December	31.0	29.2	43.6	33.9	48.3	11.9	40.8	52.9	29.0	29.6	. . .	88.0
1965												
January	31.3	29.5	44.2	34.5	49.0	11.9	41.2	53.3	29.3	29.9	. . .	88.6
February	31.5	29.7	44.3	34.9	48.9	12.1	41.7	54.7	29.4	30.0	. . .	88.7
March	31.9	30.1	44.7	35.9	49.0	12.2	42.4	55.1	29.7	30.5	. . .	89.3
April	32.1	30.3	44.6	35.8	48.8	12.3	42.9	54.3	29.7	30.8	. . .	89.3
May	32.3	30.5	44.9	36.1	49.1	12.5	43.9	54.9	30.0	30.9	. . .	89.4
June	32.6	30.7	45.0	36.4	49.2	12.7	44.4	54.9	30.2	31.3	. . .	89.5
July	32.9	31.2	45.0	36.7	49.0	12.9	45.1	56.5	30.2	31.6	. . .	90.3
August	33.0	31.2	45.0	36.3	49.2	12.9	45.5	55.9	30.4	31.9	. . .	89.9
September	33.1	31.3	45.6	37.0	49.8	13.1	45.6	55.4	30.5	31.6	. . .	89.6
October	33.4	31.5	45.9	37.3	49.9	13.3	46.1	56.3	30.8	31.9	. . .	89.8
November	33.6	31.7	46.1	37.6	50.2	13.6	46.6	57.1	31.0	31.8	. . .	89.6
December	34.0	32.2	46.4	38.3	50.2	13.9	47.0	58.3	31.5	32.2	. . .	90.5
1966												
January	34.3	32.5	46.6	38.5	50.5	14.2	48.0	58.2	31.4	32.6	. . .	90.9
February	34.5	32.7	46.8	38.4	50.7	14.1	48.7	57.6	31.8	33.0	. . .	90.9
March	35.0	33.1	47.1	38.7	51.1	14.4	49.2	58.8	32.1	33.6	. . .	91.6
April	35.1	33.3	47.3	39.4	51.0	14.5	50.2	58.8	31.8	33.5	. . .	91.5
May	35.4	33.5	47.3	38.8	51.3	14.7	51.1	59.1	32.3	33.9	. . .	91.6
June	35.6	33.7	47.5	38.8	51.6	14.8	51.9	58.2	32.7	34.1	. . .	91.5
July	35.8	33.8	47.4	38.1	51.9	15.1	52.6	58.8	33.1	34.2	. . .	91.4
August	35.8	33.9	47.2	37.5	52.0	15.1	53.3	57.1	32.9	34.5	. . .	91.1
September	36.1	34.2	47.4	37.7	52.1	15.3	54.0	57.1	33.1	34.8	. . .	91.2
October	36.4	34.5	48.4	39.6	52.5	15.3	54.8	57.1	33.1	34.9	. . .	91.6
November	36.1	34.2	48.1	38.4	52.8	15.0	55.8	57.2	33.2	34.4	. . .	90.1
December	36.2	34.3	48.0	38.0	52.9	15.2	56.4	57.1	33.3	34.4	. . .	90.0
1967												
January	36.4	34.4	48.5	37.1	54.1	15.1	57.3	58.6	34.0	34.3	89.4	89.8
February	36.0	34.0	47.8	36.1	53.7	15.2	58.0	58.1	33.7	33.6	88.0	88.4
March	35.8	33.9	48.0	36.4	53.7	15.1	58.6	58.2	33.8	33.0	87.1	87.5
April	36.1	34.1	48.8	36.7	54.8	15.1	59.2	58.0	34.1	33.3	87.5	87.7
May	35.8	33.8	47.8	36.2	53.6	15.2	59.6	58.9	33.5	33.0	86.4	86.6
June	35.8	33.8	48.0	35.8	54.1	15.1	59.5	59.2	33.7	32.9	86.0	86.1
July	35.7	33.7	47.9	36.2	53.7	14.8	59.8	59.5	33.8	32.9	85.4	85.3
August	36.4	34.3	48.4	36.7	54.2	15.1	59.9	60.1	34.7	33.9	86.6	86.5
September	36.3	34.3	48.5	36.5	54.4	15.0	60.1	60.6	34.8	33.6	86.1	86.1
October	36.6	34.6	49.1	37.2	55.1	14.9	60.6	60.3	35.1	34.1	86.4	86.4
November	37.2	35.2	50.2	39.3	55.5	15.3	60.7	60.7	35.1	34.4	87.3	87.5
December	37.6	35.6	51.0	40.9	55.9	15.4	60.6	60.7	35.1	34.9	87.8	88.0
1968												
January	37.5	35.5	50.3	39.7	55.5	15.5	60.4	61.1	35.2	35.0	87.4	87.4
February	37.6	35.6	50.6	40.3	55.6	15.5	61.1	61.7	35.5	35.0	87.3	87.4
March	37.8	35.7	50.9	40.2	56.1	15.6	59.9	61.8	35.5	35.2	87.3	87.2
April	37.8	35.7	50.8	40.2	56.0	15.5	58.7	62.2	35.8	35.4	87.1	86.9
May	38.2	36.2	51.1	40.8	56.1	15.8	59.5	62.4	36.2	36.0	87.7	87.6
June	38.4	36.2	51.4	41.1	56.4	15.7	59.8	62.4	36.3	36.1	87.7	87.4
July	38.3	36.1	51.2	40.8	56.4	15.6	59.8	62.5	36.3	36.2	87.2	86.7
August	38.4	36.3	51.9	41.3	57.0	15.7	60.0	62.8	36.7	35.9	87.1	86.8
September	38.6	36.3	52.1	41.8	57.1	15.9	59.9	62.3	36.8	36.0	87.1	86.5
October	38.7	36.6	52.4	42.3	57.3	16.0	58.4	62.2	37.0	36.1	86.9	86.6
November	39.2	37.1	53.1	43.3	57.7	16.0	59.0	63.7	37.4	36.7	87.7	87.5
December	39.3	37.1	52.8	43.7	57.0	16.2	58.7	64.9	37.7	36.9	87.6	87.1

. . . = Not available.

Table 2-4A. Industrial Production and Capacity Utilization, Historical Data, 1948–2016—*Continued*

(Seasonally adjusted.)

Year and month	Production indexes, 2007 = 100										Capacity utilization (output as percent of capacity)	
	Total industry	Manufac- turing (SIC)	Market groups								Total industry	Manufac- turing (SIC)
			Consumer goods			Business equipment	Defense and space equipment	Construction supplies	Business supplies	Materials		
			Total	Durable	Nondurable							
1969												
January	39.5	37.3	53.1	43.6	57.5	16.4	58.7	65.3	37.8	37.0	87.8	87.3
February	39.8	37.6	53.5	43.5	58.2	16.4	58.3	65.9	37.7	37.4	88.1	87.7
March	40.1	37.9	53.9	43.8	58.7	16.6	58.5	66.2	38.9	37.6	88.5	88.0
April	39.9	37.7	53.1	42.6	58.1	16.8	58.1	65.5	38.4	37.7	87.8	87.3
May	39.8	37.6	52.7	42.1	57.8	16.7	58.0	65.1	38.7	37.6	87.2	86.6
June	40.2	37.8	53.3	43.5	57.9	16.8	57.2	65.5	39.0	38.1	87.7	86.8
July	40.4	38.1	54.2	43.5	59.3	17.0	57.0	64.9	38.8	38.2	87.9	87.1
August	40.5	38.1	54.1	43.9	58.9	16.9	56.1	64.8	39.0	38.5	87.8	86.9
September	40.5	38.1	53.7	43.5	58.5	17.1	55.8	64.8	38.9	38.6	87.4	86.4
October	40.5	38.1	53.7	43.7	58.4	17.1	55.3	65.1	39.0	38.6	87.1	86.2
November	40.1	37.7	53.3	41.9	58.4	16.7	54.3	64.7	38.8	38.4	86.0	85.0
December	40.0	07.5	53.3	41.7	59.0	16.7	53.6	64.3	39.3	38.2	85.5	84.2
1970												
January	39.2	36.7	52.4	39.5	58.9	16.5	52.9	62.3	39.2	37.3	83.6	82.1
February	39.2	36.7	53.0	40.1	59.4	16.5	52.0	62.1	38.9	37.1	83.3	81.9
March	39.2	36.6	52.9	40.5	59.0	16.6	50.8	62.6	39.1	37.0	82.9	81.4
April	39.1	36.5	53.1	40.4	59.4	16.5	49.7	63.3	38.9	36.8	82.5	80.9
May	39.0	36.4	53.4	40.5	59.8	16.5	48.6	63.3	38.8	36.7	82.1	80.4
June	38.9	36.3	53.5	41.3	59.5	16.4	47.8	63.0	38.8	36.5	81.6	79.9
July	39.0	36.4	53.7	41.3	59.7	16.4	47.0	63.8	38.9	36.7	81.5	79.9
August	38.9	36.2	52.8	40.1	59.0	16.3	46.6	63.5	38.6	37.1	81.1	79.1
September	38.7	35.9	52.6	39.0	59.3	16.0	46.1	63.4	38.9	36.9	80.3	78.2
October	37.9	35.1	51.9	36.7	59.7	15.5	45.5	62.7	38.7	35.9	78.5	76.2
November	37.7	34.9	51.6	36.8	59.1	15.4	45.1	61.9	38.8	35.7	77.8	75.5
December	38.5	35.8	53.8	41.1	60.1	15.6	44.6	62.6	38.8	36.5	79.3	77.3
1971												
January	38.8	36.1	54.6	42.7	60.4	15.2	45.0	62.7	39.0	37.0	79.7	77.7
February	38.7	36.1	54.6	43.7	59.8	15.3	43.9	63.1	39.4	36.8	79.4	77.6
March	38.7	36.0	54.7	43.7	60.0	15.2	43.5	62.8	39.1	36.8	79.1	77.2
April	38.9	36.2	55.2	44.0	60.5	15.1	43.6	63.4	39.5	37.1	79.3	77.4
May	39.1	36.5	55.2	44.7	60.2	15.0	44.1	63.7	39.5	37.5	79.5	77.7
June	39.3	36.5	55.6	45.1	60.6	15.1	43.4	64.4	39.4	37.7	79.6	77.7
July	39.2	36.6	56.5	45.9	61.5	15.1	43.1	65.0	40.4	36.8	79.2	77.7
August	38.9	36.2	55.8	45.4	60.7	15.3	43.1	63.9	39.9	36.6	78.5	76.5
September	39.6	36.9	56.3	45.4	61.6	15.7	42.7	66.3	40.6	37.3	79.6	77.9
October	39.9	37.5	57.1	46.2	62.3	15.8	42.4	67.2	40.8	37.4	80.0	78.9
November	40.0	37.6	57.6	46.7	62.7	15.9	42.0	67.4	41.3	37.4	80.2	79.0
December	40.5	37.9	57.9	46.9	63.2	16.0	41.4	68.5	41.4	38.2	80.9	79.5
1972												
January	41.5	38.9	58.8	48.3	63.8	16.5	41.4	70.4	42.2	39.4	82.6	81.3
February	41.9	39.2	59.1	48.5	64.2	16.7	41.5	70.7	42.9	39.8	83.2	81.7
March	42.2	39.5	59.1	48.1	64.4	16.9	41.9	71.2	43.3	40.2	83.6	82.1
April	42.6	40.0	59.9	49.5	64.7	17.3	42.1	72.0	43.3	40.6	84.3	82.8
May	42.6	40.0	59.6	49.1	64.5	17.2	41.6	72.4	43.5	40.7	84.0	82.7
June	42.7	40.1	59.6	49.1	64.5	17.3	41.6	73.0	44.0	40.7	84.1	82.8
July	42.7	40.2	60.1	50.2	64.6	17.3	41.6	74.1	44.0	40.5	83.8	82.6
August	43.3	40.7	60.7	50.6	65.3	17.7	41.6	74.6	44.6	41.1	84.7	83.4
September	43.6	41.0	61.0	51.1	65.5	17.8	41.9	75.2	44.5	41.5	85.1	83.9
October	44.2	41.6	61.9	52.3	66.2	18.2	41.9	76.4	45.2	41.9	86.0	84.9
November	44.7	42.1	62.4	53.5	66.2	18.5	43.1	76.9	45.4	42.5	86.7	85.7
December	45.2	42.7	62.9	54.6	66.3	18.7	43.8	76.7	45.5	43.2	87.5	86.6
1973												
January	45.5	43.0	62.7	54.4	66.2	19.0	44.4	77.5	45.8	43.6	87.8	86.9
February	46.2	43.7	63.5	55.4	66.9	19.4	45.3	79.0	46.3	44.2	88.8	88.0
March	46.2	43.8	63.7	55.5	67.0	19.6	45.1	79.5	46.3	44.1	88.5	87.9
April	46.1	43.7	63.1	54.7	66.6	19.8	44.9	79.3	46.3	44.2	88.1	87.5
May	46.4	44.0	63.4	54.5	67.2	20.0	45.2	79.7	46.6	44.4	88.3	87.7
June	46.5	43.9	62.9	54.4	66.6	20.1	45.6	79.8	46.7	44.5	88.1	87.4
July	46.6	44.1	62.8	54.4	66.4	20.4	46.6	80.5	46.9	44.7	88.2	87.5
August	46.6	44.0	62.2	52.7	66.4	20.4	46.6	80.6	46.9	44.8	87.7	87.0
September	47.0	44.4	63.2	54.5	67.0	20.8	46.6	80.5	47.0	45.0	88.2	87.5
October	47.3	44.8	63.4	54.1	67.5	21.1	47.6	80.4	47.4	45.3	88.5	87.9
November	47.5	45.1	63.7	54.1	67.9	21.3	47.3	80.9	47.4	45.6	88.7	88.3
December	47.4	45.2	62.6	52.9	66.9	21.3	46.9	81.6	47.1	45.8	88.3	88.1
1974												
January	47.1	44.8	61.7	50.2	67.2	21.3	46.7	81.8	47.2	45.4	87.4	87.1
February	47.0	44.6	61.5	50.1	66.9	21.2	47.2	80.8	46.9	45.4	86.9	86.5
March	47.0	44.6	61.6	50.1	67.0	21.4	47.2	81.0	47.0	45.2	86.7	86.2
April	46.8	44.4	61.4	49.8	66.9	21.2	47.0	80.3	47.0	45.1	86.2	85.6
May	47.2	44.7	62.0	50.0	67.7	21.5	47.3	80.6	47.3	45.4	86.6	86.0
June	47.1	44.7	62.2	50.6	67.7	21.6	46.5	80.2	47.4	45.2	86.4	85.8
July	47.2	44.7	62.1	50.5	67.6	21.6	47.1	78.6	47.1	45.4	86.2	85.5
August	46.7	44.3	62.1	50.5	67.6	21.5	48.0	77.7	46.9	44.6	85.2	84.6
September	46.7	44.3	61.6	50.4	66.9	21.9	48.1	77.1	46.6	44.8	85.1	84.4
October	46.5	44.0	61.6	49.7	67.2	21.9	48.8	75.7	46.4	44.5	84.6	83.6
November	45.0	42.7	59.8	47.3	65.9	21.6	48.6	73.3	45.3	42.6	81.7	80.9
December	43.4	40.8	57.9	43.4	65.2	20.7	48.0	69.9	44.3	41.0	78.6	77.2

Table 2-4A. Industrial Production and Capacity Utilization, Historical Data, 1948–2016—*Continued*

(Seasonally adjusted.)

Year and month	Total industry	Manufac- turing (SIC)	Consumer goods			Business equipment	Defense and space equipment	Construction supplies	Business supplies	Materials	Total industry	Manufac- turing (SIC)
			Total	Durable	Nondurable							
1975												
January	42.8	39.9	56.6	41.6	64.1	20.2	48.4	69.6	43.6	40.6	77.4	75.5
February	41.8	38.8	55.8	40.4	63.6	19.6	45.9	67.4	42.7	39.7	75.5	73.2
March	41.4	38.3	56.0	40.9	63.6	19.3	46.4	64.9	42.1	39.1	74.6	72.1
April	41.4	38.3	57.1	42.5	64.5	19.1	46.1	64.3	42.2	38.9	74.5	71.9
May	41.3	38.2	57.4	43.6	64.3	18.9	48.4	64.4	42.0	38.6	74.2	71.8
June	41.6	38.6	58.2	44.0	65.3	18.7	49.0	64.0	42.1	38.9	74.6	72.2
July	42.0	39.1	59.7	46.2	66.3	18.8	48.2	64.9	42.5	39.0	75.2	73.1
August	42.4	39.5	60.1	46.9	66.5	18.7	48.1	65.7	42.9	39.7	75.8	73.7
September	43.0	40.2	60.9	47.8	67.3	19.0	49.5	66.4	43.0	40.2	76.6	74.8
October	43.2	40.4	61.0	47.6	67.6	19.1	49.5	66.8	43.3	40.4	76.8	75.0
November	43.3	40.5	61.2	47.7	67.9	19.1	47.4	67.1	43.4	40.6	76.8	75.1
December	43.8	41.0	61.8	48.5	68.2	19.4	48.8	67.1	43.8	41.2	77.6	75.9
1976												
January	44.4	41.5	62.6	49.3	69.0	19.6	48.8	68.8	44.3	41.8	78.6	76.7
February	44.9	42.1	62.8	50.0	69.1	19.7	48.8	69.9	44.4	42.4	79.2	77.7
March	44.9	42.2	62.7	49.9	68.9	19.8	48.8	68.8	44.6	42.6	79.1	77.6
April	45.2	42.5	62.9	49.9	69.1	20.0	47.8	69.7	44.8	42.9	79.4	78.0
May	45.4	42.7	63.4	50.0	69.9	20.1	47.3	70.5	45.1	42.9	79.6	78.2
June	45.4	42.7	63.1	49.7	69.7	20.2	46.8	71.0	44.8	43.1	79.4	78.0
July	45.6	43.1	63.6	50.0	70.2	20.4	45.5	72.6	45.5	43.2	79.7	78.5
August	46.0	43.3	63.6	50.7	69.9	20.7	45.5	71.8	45.6	43.7	80.1	78.8
September	46.1	43.4	63.7	50.4	70.1	20.7	45.1	72.3	46.6	43.7	80.1	78.8
October	46.1	43.4	64.2	51.0	70.5	20.7	45.0	72.2	46.9	43.5	80.0	78.6
November	46.8	44.0	65.3	52.7	71.2	21.4	44.8	72.5	47.1	44.1	80.9	79.3
December	47.3	44.4	65.9	54.0	71.6	21.7	44.0	73.0	47.5	44.6	81.6	80.0
1977												
January	47.0	44.3	65.8	53.8	71.4	21.8	43.4	71.8	47.3	44.2	81.0	79.6
February	47.7	45.1	66.6	54.4	72.3	22.3	43.3	73.4	47.9	44.8	82.0	80.8
March	48.3	45.8	66.7	55.9	71.6	22.7	42.3	75.0	48.2	45.7	82.8	81.7
April	48.8	46.2	67.1	56.3	72.0	23.0	42.6	76.7	48.8	46.1	83.4	82.4
May	49.2	46.6	67.2	56.6	71.9	23.5	42.5	77.8	49.3	46.5	83.9	82.9
June	49.6	47.0	67.7	57.7	72.0	24.0	42.5	78.4	49.8	46.6	84.3	83.3
July	49.6	47.1	67.8	57.7	72.2	24.1	42.4	78.5	49.9	46.7	84.2	83.1
August	49.7	47.3	67.9	57.8	72.4	24.2	42.1	79.1	50.2	46.6	84.0	83.3
September	49.9	47.3	68.0	58.0	72.4	24.3	42.2	78.8	50.4	46.9	84.1	83.1
October	50.0	47.4	68.6	58.0	73.3	24.2	38.4	78.8	50.4	47.1	84.1	83.1
November	50.0	47.5	68.6	58.0	73.4	24.2	38.0	79.2	50.5	47.1	83.9	83.0
December	50.1	48.0	69.3	58.4	74.1	24.5	40.6	80.0	50.9	46.7	83.8	83.6
1978												
January	49.4	47.4	67.5	55.3	73.2	24.0	41.1	78.4	50.7	46.3	82.4	82.2
February	49.7	47.5	68.6	56.7	74.1	24.6	38.9	78.2	50.9	46.2	82.6	82.2
March	50.6	48.4	69.9	58.4	75.2	25.3	42.5	79.6	51.6	46.9	83.9	83.4
April	51.7	49.1	70.4	59.5	75.3	25.9	42.3	81.5	51.8	48.3	85.4	84.5
May	51.8	49.3	69.9	58.6	75.1	26.0	42.5	81.3	52.1	48.7	85.4	84.5
June	52.2	49.7	70.4	58.9	75.5	26.5	43.0	82.1	52.5	49.0	85.8	84.9
July	52.2	49.6	70.0	59.0	74.9	26.7	43.0	82.0	52.4	49.0	85.5	84.6
August	52.4	49.9	69.9	58.7	74.9	27.2	43.4	82.1	52.5	49.1	85.6	84.7
September	52.5	50.1	70.0	58.3	75.3	27.4	43.5	82.4	52.6	49.2	85.6	84.8
October	52.9	50.5	69.9	58.6	75.1	28.0	43.0	83.2	52.9	49.7	86.1	85.2
November	53.3	50.9	70.1	58.7	75.3	28.5	42.8	83.7	53.2	50.1	86.5	85.7
December	53.6	51.3	70.3	58.9	75.5	28.8	43.4	85.1	53.5	50.3	86.7	86.2
1979												
January	53.3	50.9	70.1	59.3	74.9	29.1	43.6	83.0	53.5	49.7	85.9	85.2
February	53.6	51.1	69.6	58.7	74.6	29.4	44.5	83.5	54.0	50.1	86.2	85.3
March	53.7	51.4	69.9	58.5	75.1	29.7	44.2	84.6	54.3	50.1	86.2	85.5
April	53.2	50.6	68.6	55.6	74.8	29.1	43.1	83.3	54.0	49.8	85.1	83.9
May	53.6	51.2	69.1	57.3	74.5	29.9	43.8	83.8	54.2	50.1	85.5	84.7
June	53.6	51.2	68.8	56.6	74.5	30.0	44.2	84.1	53.9	50.1	85.3	84.6
July	53.5	51.3	68.3	55.9	74.1	30.3	45.0	84.1	54.0	50.0	85.0	84.5
August	53.1	50.7	67.5	53.5	74.2	29.9	45.6	83.4	54.2	49.7	84.3	83.2
September	53.2	50.8	67.9	55.4	73.8	30.7	45.9	83.5	53.5	49.4	84.2	83.2
October	53.5	50.9	68.1	55.1	74.2	30.3	47.4	84.1	54.0	49.8	84.5	83.2
November	53.4	50.8	67.9	54.2	74.4	30.3	48.5	83.9	54.3	49.7	84.2	82.9
December	53.5	51.0	67.9	53.9	74.6	30.6	49.5	84.3	54.3	49.6	84.1	82.9
1980												
January	53.7	51.2	67.7	52.9	74.8	31.0	50.0	84.0	53.9	50.0	84.3	83.1
February	53.7	51.1	67.9	52.6	75.3	31.2	52.0	82.7	54.0	49.9	84.2	82.8
March	53.5	50.8	67.4	51.7	75.1	31.0	52.6	81.7	53.8	49.9	83.8	82.0
April	52.5	49.7	66.3	49.5	74.6	30.6	53.2	78.0	52.9	48.7	81.9	80.1
May	51.2	48.2	64.9	46.4	74.2	30.2	53.5	74.8	51.9	47.3	79.8	77.6
June	50.6	47.5	64.6	45.6	74.2	29.8	54.0	73.3	51.2	46.5	78.6	76.2
July	50.2	47.0	64.6	45.5	74.1	29.8	54.3	72.7	51.4	45.7	77.8	75.2
August	50.4	47.4	64.8	45.9	74.3	29.8	54.7	73.7	51.6	45.9	78.0	75.6
September	51.2	48.1	65.4	48.0	74.0	30.4	54.7	75.6	52.3	46.8	79.1	76.6
October	51.8	49.0	65.9	48.9	74.4	30.9	55.6	77.2	52.5	47.4	79.9	77.7
November	52.7	49.9	66.2	50.1	74.2	31.5	56.3	78.8	53.1	48.5	81.1	79.0
December	53.0	50.1	66.2	49.4	74.5	31.5	56.4	78.7	53.7	49.0	81.3	79.0

Table 2-4A. Industrial Production and Capacity Utilization, Historical Data, 1948–2016—*Continued*

(Seasonally adjusted.)

Year and month	Production indexes, 2007 = 100										Capacity utilization (output as percent of capacity)	
	Total industry	Manufac-turing (SIC)	Market groups								Total industry	Manufac-turing (SIC)
			Consumer goods			Business equipment	Defense and space equipment	Construction supplies	Business supplies	Materials		
			Total	Durable	Nondurable							
1981												
January	52.7	49.9	66.2	49.2	74.7	31.6	56.2	78.5	53.7	48.4	80.7	78.5
February	52.5	49.6	66.1	49.0	74.5	31.2	56.1	77.7	53.2	48.3	80.1	77.8
March	52.8	49.8	66.1	49.7	74.1	31.5	56.2	78.0	53.2	48.6	80.3	77.8
April	52.5	50.0	66.2	50.3	74.0	31.9	56.1	78.0	53.5	47.9	79.8	78.0
May	52.8	50.3	66.9	51.1	74.6	31.9	56.6	78.0	54.1	48.2	80.0	78.2
June	53.1	50.0	66.4	50.6	74.1	31.7	57.0	76.8	54.3	48.8	80.2	77.5
July	53.4	50.1	66.9	50.9	74.7	31.7	57.7	77.0	54.6	49.2	80.5	77.5
August	53.4	50.1	66.9	50.6	74.9	31.8	58.5	76.8	54.3	49.1	80.3	77.3
September	53.1	49.9	66.3	49.4	74.7	31.7	59.6	76.3	54.4	48.7	79.6	76.8
October	52.7	49.4	66.7	49.2	75.4	31.7	60.9	74.0	54.0	48.1	78.9	75.9
November	52.1	48.8	66.6	48.4	75.8	31.2	62.4	72.8	53.7	47.2	77.8	74.8
December	51.5	48.0	65.9	46.3	75.8	30.7	64.0	71.5	53.6	46.6	76.7	73.3
1982												
January	50.5	46.9	64.7	45.0	74.7	29.5	63.5	69.0	52.8	45.8	75.0	71.4
February	51.5	48.2	66.5	46.7	76.6	30.5	66.9	71.5	53.9	46.3	76.4	73.2
March	51.1	47.8	66.1	46.5	76.0	30.1	68.0	70.0	53.6	46.0	75.7	72.5
April	50.7	47.4	66.1	47.4	75.5	29.7	68.8	69.5	53.4	45.4	74.8	71.8
May	50.4	47.4	66.2	47.4	75.6	29.5	70.1	69.9	53.1	44.9	74.2	71.6
June	50.2	47.3	66.6	47.7	76.1	29.0	70.4	69.3	53.1	44.8	73.9	71.4
July	50.0	47.3	66.8	48.0	76.2	28.9	71.5	69.2	53.1	44.5	73.6	71.2
August	49.6	46.9	66.6	47.3	76.4	28.2	71.3	69.2	53.1	44.0	72.8	70.5
September	49.5	46.8	66.6	46.6	76.7	28.1	72.1	69.4	53.3	43.8	72.5	70.3
October	49.0	46.2	66.6	46.0	77.1	27.5	71.7	68.4	53.0	43.3	71.8	69.4
November	48.8	45.9	66.5	45.9	76.9	27.3	72.0	68.0	53.0	43.1	71.5	68.9
December	48.5	45.8	65.6	45.9	75.6	27.6	71.5	67.4	52.7	42.7	70.9	68.6
1983												
January	49.4	46.9	67.1	47.8	76.7	27.7	71.0	69.9	53.5	43.7	72.2	70.2
February	49.1	46.8	66.2	47.7	75.4	27.6	69.9	69.5	53.4	43.5	71.7	70.1
March	49.5	47.2	66.5	48.4	75.5	27.8	69.9	70.3	54.2	43.9	72.3	70.7
April	50.1	47.8	67.7	49.4	76.8	27.9	69.3	71.2	54.8	44.4	73.1	71.4
May	50.4	48.4	68.0	50.4	76.8	28.2	69.1	72.6	54.9	44.8	73.6	72.3
June	50.7	48.8	68.3	51.3	76.7	28.5	68.6	73.9	55.2	45.1	74.0	72.8
July	51.5	49.5	69.2	52.4	77.4	29.0	69.4	75.4	55.9	45.8	75.1	73.8
August	52.1	49.8	69.7	53.4	77.7	29.3	69.8	75.7	56.5	46.5	75.9	74.4
September	52.8	50.8	70.6	54.4	78.5	30.1	70.7	76.7	57.4	47.1	77.0	75.7
October	53.3	51.4	70.3	55.1	77.6	30.5	71.4	77.9	57.7	47.7	77.6	76.5
November	53.5	51.6	70.3	55.1	77.6	30.8	71.8	77.7	57.9	48.0	77.8	76.7
December	53.8	51.7	70.4	56.4	77.1	31.1	72.6	77.9	58.0	48.2	78.1	76.9
1984												
January	54.8	52.6	71.9	57.8	78.6	31.7	74.6	78.4	59.1	49.2	79.6	78.2
February	55.1	53.2	71.7	57.9	78.2	32.0	76.1	80.2	59.3	49.4	79.8	78.9
March	55.3	53.4	72.0	58.1	78.6	32.3	76.6	79.7	59.8	49.7	80.1	79.1
April	55.7	53.7	72.2	58.0	79.0	32.6	78.6	80.2	59.8	50.0	80.5	79.4
May	56.0	53.9	71.9	57.5	78.8	32.7	79.3	80.4	60.6	50.4	80.7	79.4
June	56.2	54.1	71.8	57.7	78.6	33.1	80.4	81.0	61.0	50.5	80.9	79.6
July	56.3	54.4	71.9	58.3	78.3	33.6	79.6	80.7	61.2	50.6	81.0	79.8
August	56.4	54.4	71.5	58.7	77.6	33.9	82.2	81.0	61.3	50.6	80.9	79.7
September	56.3	54.3	71.3	57.9	77.7	34.1	84.1	81.3	61.2	50.3	80.5	79.3
October	56.2	54.5	71.9	57.4	78.8	34.2	84.7	81.0	61.5	49.9	80.2	79.4
November	56.4	54.7	72.1	58.3	78.7	34.6	84.1	80.8	61.8	50.1	80.3	79.5
December	56.5	54.9	72.5	59.0	78.9	34.8	85.7	81.6	61.4	49.9	80.2	79.5
1985												
January	56.4	54.7	72.0	58.2	78.6	34.7	86.0	80.2	61.4	50.0	79.9	79.0
February	56.6	54.5	72.5	57.7	79.5	34.4	86.8	80.3	62.0	50.2	80.0	78.5
March	56.7	55.0	72.4	58.4	79.1	34.8	88.2	82.5	61.9	50.1	79.9	78.9
April	56.5	54.7	72.0	57.5	78.9	34.5	88.4	82.4	62.2	50.1	79.5	78.3
May	56.6	54.8	72.1	57.6	79.1	34.6	89.0	82.7	62.4	50.1	79.4	78.2
June	56.6	54.9	72.4	57.5	79.6	34.7	90.2	83.2	62.0	50.0	79.3	78.2
July	56.3	54.6	72.1	57.5	79.1	34.4	89.4	82.8	61.6	49.7	78.6	77.5
August	56.5	54.9	72.5	58.1	79.4	34.5	90.9	83.0	62.2	49.8	78.7	77.8
September	56.7	55.0	72.9	58.1	79.9	34.5	91.5	82.9	62.6	50.0	78.9	77.7
October	56.5	54.8	72.7	57.8	79.9	34.4	92.4	83.0	62.1	49.7	78.5	77.4
November	56.7	55.2	73.1	59.2	79.8	34.7	93.6	83.0	62.3	49.8	78.6	77.8
December	57.3	55.4	73.9	59.3	80.9	34.6	94.5	82.7	63.2	50.5	79.3	78.0
1986												
January	57.6	56.0	74.7	60.7	81.4	34.7	95.1	84.5	63.6	50.6	79.6	78.8
February	57.2	55.7	74.1	60.3	80.6	34.3	93.8	83.7	63.1	50.4	78.9	78.2
March	56.8	55.6	73.8	60.3	80.2	34.3	94.7	83.9	62.8	49.8	78.3	77.9
April	56.8	55.8	74.3	60.2	81.0	34.0	94.8	84.7	63.4	49.7	78.3	78.2
May	56.9	55.9	74.7	60.4	81.5	34.0	95.3	85.2	63.9	49.7	78.4	78.2
June	56.7	55.7	74.7	61.1	81.2	33.7	95.6	84.4	64.3	49.5	78.1	77.9
July	57.1	55.9	75.1	61.8	81.5	33.9	96.1	84.8	64.3	49.8	78.4	78.2
August	57.0	56.1	75.1	62.1	81.3	33.9	96.4	85.7	64.4	49.6	78.2	78.3
September	57.1	56.2	75.2	62.7	81.1	33.9	96.1	85.8	64.5	49.8	78.3	78.4
October	57.4	56.4	75.5	62.7	81.6	33.9	96.4	85.7	64.9	50.1	78.5	78.6
November	57.6	56.7	76.1	63.6	82.0	34.0	96.9	86.0	65.0	50.3	78.8	78.8
December	58.1	57.2	76.8	64.7	82.4	34.2	97.0	86.5	65.9	50.7	79.3	79.3

Table 2-4A. Industrial Production and Capacity Utilization, Historical Data, 1948–2016—*Continued*

(Seasonally adjusted.)

Year and month	Production indexes, 2007 = 100									Capacity utilization (output as percent of capacity)	
	Total industry	Manufac-turing (SIC)	Market groups							Total industry	Manufac-turing (SIC)
			Consumer goods			Business equipment	Defense and space equipment	Construction supplies	Business supplies	Materials		
			Total	Durable	Nondurable							
1987												
January	57.9	57.0	76.0	64.3	81.5	34.3	97.4	87.5	65.4	50.6	79.0	78.9
February	58.7	57.9	77.0	65.4	82.4	35.1	97.9	89.1	65.9	51.2	79.8	79.9
March	58.8	57.9	77.2	65.1	82.9	35.0	97.7	88.7	66.3	51.3	79.8	79.7
April	59.1	58.2	77.1	64.7	83.0	35.3	97.8	89.2	67.0	51.8	80.2	80.0
May	59.5	58.7	77.7	65.0	83.6	35.6	97.5	89.9	67.8	52.0	80.5	80.4
June	59.8	58.9	77.8	64.4	84.2	35.8	97.1	90.1	68.1	52.4	80.7	80.4
July	60.2	59.3	78.4	64.3	85.0	36.1	96.8	90.5	68.6	52.7	81.1	80.9
August	60.7	59.7	78.8	64.9	85.4	36.7	97.8	91.2	68.9	53.2	81.7	81.2
September	60.9	60.0	78.5	65.4	84.6	37.2	98.1	91.6	69.1	53.4	81.7	81.5
October	61.8	61.0	79.9	67.6	85.8	38.0	97.8	92.9	69.6	54.1	82.8	82.6
November	62.1	61.3	80.0	67.5	85.9	38.3	98.1	92.9	69.6	54.6	83.1	82.9
December	62.4	61.7	80.1	66.9	86.3	38.7	99.0	93.7	69.8	54.9	83.4	83.3
1988												
January	62.4	61.6	80.4	66.6	87.0	38.8	101.1	92.1	70.1	54.7	83.4	83.1
February	62.7	61.7	80.8	66.6	87.5	39.1	99.7	92.9	70.6	54.9	83.7	83.2
March	62.8	61.9	80.7	67.2	87.1	39.5	98.9	93.3	70.5	55.1	83.8	83.4
April	63.2	62.4	81.3	68.7	87.2	40.0	98.0	92.9	70.5	55.5	84.3	84.1
May	63.1	62.3	80.9	68.7	86.7	40.2	98.0	93.1	70.0	55.5	84.1	83.9
June	63.3	62.4	80.9	69.0	86.6	40.5	97.3	92.5	70.2	55.7	84.3	84.0
July	63.3	62.4	80.9	67.4	87.2	40.2	98.4	92.5	70.5	55.8	84.3	84.0
August	63.6	62.5	81.4	68.0	87.7	40.3	98.1	91.8	71.0	56.1	84.7	84.0
September	63.4	62.7	80.9	69.3	86.4	40.7	98.5	92.2	70.6	55.8	84.4	84.2
October	63.7	63.0	81.6	70.0	87.1	41.1	98.6	92.5	70.9	55.9	84.7	84.6
November	63.8	63.2	81.7	70.8	86.8	41.1	98.4	92.9	70.9	56.1	84.8	84.7
December	64.1	63.5	82.1	71.6	87.0	41.2	99.0	93.2	71.1	56.4	85.1	85.0
1989												
January	64.3	64.0	82.2	73.3	86.4	41.6	98.9	94.7	71.1	56.5	85.2	85.6
February	64.0	63.4	82.2	72.5	86.7	41.4	98.9	92.4	71.4	56.1	84.7	84.6
March	64.2	63.3	82.3	71.4	87.4	41.2	98.2	92.6	72.0	56.3	84.8	84.4
April	64.2	63.4	82.2	72.0	87.0	41.9	99.6	92.7	71.5	56.3	84.7	84.4
May	63.8	62.9	81.3	70.4	86.5	41.2	100.0	91.8	71.2	56.1	84.0	83.5
June	63.8	63.0	81.4	09.0	87.0	41.8	99.8	92.1	71.5	55.8	83.8	83.5
July	63.2	62.3	79.7	67.4	85.5	41.4	100.3	92.1	70.9	55.6	82.9	82.3
August	63.8	62.8	81.0	69.9	86.2	41.9	100.7	92.1	71.3	56.0	83.5	82.8
September	63.6	62.6	80.7	69.8	85.8	41.7	100.1	91.8	71.5	55.7	83.0	82.4
October	63.5	62.5	80.9	68.5	86.8	41.2	96.4	92.2	71.5	55.8	82.7	82.1
November	63.7	62.7	81.3	69.0	87.0	41.5	95.0	92.2	71.9	56.0	82.8	82.0
December	64.1	62.7	82.5	69.7	88.6	42.1	97.2	91.2	72.2	56.0	83.1	81.9
1990												
January	63.7	62.6	80.7	65.8	87.8	41.6	97.6	93.0	72.8	55.8	82.4	81.5
February	64.4	63.5	81.8	69.9	87.4	42.4	97.4	93.5	72.7	56.3	83.0	82.5
March	64.7	63.8	82.3	71.2	87.6	43.1	96.9	93.3	73.1	56.5	83.2	82.7
April	64.6	63.7	82.1	69.7	87.9	43.0	96.3	92.5	73.1	56.5	83.0	82.3
May	64.7	63.8	81.9	70.2	87.5	43.5	95.5	91.9	73.4	56.6	82.9	82.2
June	64.9	64.0	82.8	71.2	88.2	43.6	95.2	92.2	73.3	56.7	83.0	82.3
July	64.8	63.9	82.1	69.2	88.2	43.8	95.8	91.4	73.6	56.7	82.8	82.0
August	65.0	64.1	82.3	69.0	88.6	44.0	94.4	91.4	73.5	57.0	82.9	82.0
September	65.1	64.0	83.0	69.4	89.4	44.1	94.0	91.1	73.5	56.9	82.9	81.9
October	64.6	63.5	81.7	67.0	88.6	43.9	94.3	90.0	73.4	56.6	82.1	81.1
November	63.9	62.8	80.9	63.5	89.1	42.8	92.7	90.0	73.1	56.0	81.1	80.0
December	63.5	62.3	80.3	62.4	88.7	42.6	93.9	89.4	72.6	55.6	80.4	79.3
1991												
January	63.2	61.9	80.7	62.5	89.2	42.3	92.7	86.1	72.4	55.2	80.0	78.6
February	62.8	61.5	79.9	61.1	88.8	42.0	91.8	85.8	71.8	55.0	79.3	78.0
March	62.4	61.0	80.0	61.4	88.7	42.0	91.2	84.8	70.8	54.5	78.8	77.3
April	62.6	61.2	80.0	62.8	88.1	41.9	88.8	85.4	71.3	54.8	78.9	77.5
May	63.2	61.7	81.4	63.9	89.6	42.2	87.2	85.5	71.9	55.3	79.6	78.0
June	63.7	62.3	82.5	65.6	90.4	42.7	87.5	87.1	72.3	55.6	80.2	78.7
July	63.8	62.5	82.1	66.6	89.4	42.8	86.8	86.7	71.9	56.0	80.2	78.8
August	63.9	62.6	82.2	65.7	89.9	42.7	87.3	87.7	72.3	56.0	80.2	78.9
September	64.4	63.3	83.4	68.5	90.4	43.3	87.0	88.0	72.7	56.3	80.8	79.6
October	64.3	63.2	83.2	68.1	90.2	43.0	87.2	87.1	72.5	56.4	80.5	79.3
November	64.2	63.1	83.3	68.3	90.3	42.9	86.6	87.9	72.6	56.2	80.3	79.1
December	64.0	63.0	82.3	67.7	89.1	42.9	86.0	87.8	72.5	56.2	79.8	78.8
1992												
January	63.6	62.6	81.4	64.8	89.2	42.1	84.8	88.0	72.4	56.1	79.2	78.1
February	64.0	63.1	82.3	67.6	89.2	43.0	84.3	88.7	72.5	56.3	79.6	78.6
March	64.6	63.8	83.1	69.0	89.7	43.5	83.8	89.3	73.0	56.8	80.2	79.3
April	65.1	64.1	83.8	70.3	90.2	44.0	82.3	90.0	73.5	57.2	80.6	79.5
May	65.3	64.5	84.4	72.4	90.1	44.3	82.0	90.8	73.7	57.3	80.7	79.7
June	65.3	64.7	83.9	71.4	89.9	44.4	81.8	90.4	73.7	57.5	80.5	79.8
July	65.9	65.3	85.0	73.3	90.6	44.8	81.0	91.1	74.2	57.9	81.0	80.3
August	65.6	65.0	85.1	72.7	91.0	44.7	80.8	91.3	74.1	57.3	80.5	79.7
September	65.7	65.0	84.6	72.4	90.4	44.8	80.7	91.2	74.3	57.8	80.5	79.6
October	66.2	65.4	85.9	74.0	91.5	45.0	80.5	91.3	74.5	58.1	80.9	79.9
November	66.5	65.7	86.1	74.7	91.5	45.3	80.5	91.0	74.8	58.4	81.1	80.1
December	66.5	65.6	86.0	75.5	91.1	45.7	80.4	91.3	75.1	58.3	81.1	79.8

Table 2-4A. Industrial Production and Capacity Utilization, Historical Data, 1948–2016—*Continued*

(Seasonally adjusted.)

Year and month	Production indexes, 2007 = 100										Capacity utilization (output as percent of capacity)	
	Total industry	Manufac-turing (SIC)	Market groups								Total industry	Manufac-turing (SIC)
			Consumer goods			Business equipment	Defense and space equipment	Construction supplies	Business supplies	Materials		
			Total	Durable	Nondurable							
1993												
January	66.8	66.3	86.5	76.6	91.3	45.9	79.9	91.6	75.2	58.6	81.3	80.4
February	67.1	66.4	86.6	76.3	91.6	45.9	79.3	93.2	75.6	59.0	81.5	80.5
March	67.0	66.3	86.6	76.7	91.4	46.0	78.4	92.4	76.1	58.8	81.3	80.2
April	67.2	66.6	86.7	77.1	91.4	46.3	78.5	92.7	76.1	59.1	81.4	80.5
May	67.0	66.6	86.1	77.2	90.5	46.4	77.6	93.8	75.8	58.9	81.1	80.3
June	67.2	66.5	86.2	76.4	91.0	46.0	77.0	93.7	75.9	59.2	81.1	80.0
July	67.4	66.6	86.9	76.3	92.1	46.0	77.9	94.3	76.0	59.2	81.2	80.1
August	67.3	66.5	86.8	75.5	92.2	45.6	76.4	94.5	76.1	59.2	81.0	79.8
September	67.6	66.9	87.1	77.0	92.0	46.4	76.7	95.0	76.4	59.4	81.3	80.2
October	68.1	67.5	87.6	79.0	91.8	47.4	76.0	95.9	76.5	59.9	81.8	80.8
November	68.4	67.8	87.6	79.7	91.6	47.6	75.9	96.7	76.6	60.3	82.0	80.9
December	68.8	68.2	87.8	80.0	91.7	47.0	76.3	97.8	77.1	60.7	82.3	81.2
1994												
January	69.0	68.3	88.5	81.3	92.1	48.2	74.4	97.5	77.5	60.8	82.4	81.2
February	69.0	68.3	88.6	81.2	92.3	47.7	73.2	96.8	77.7	61.0	82.2	81.1
March	69.8	69.2	89.4	81.9	93.1	48.2	74.0	98.6	78.2	61.7	82.9	81.9
April	70.1	69.8	89.5	82.9	92.9	48.5	74.2	100.1	78.5	62.1	83.1	82.4
May	70.5	70.3	90.1	83.2	93.7	48.7	73.2	100.9	78.6	62.5	83.3	82.6
June	70.9	70.4	90.8	83.9	94.3	48.9	72.3	101.0	79.3	63.0	83.6	82.6
July	71.1	70.7	90.3	84.0	93.6	49.5	71.9	102.0	79.0	63.2	83.4	82.7
August	71.5	71.3	91.4	85.5	94.5	49.6	70.8	101.9	79.2	63.6	83.7	83.0
September	71.7	71.6	90.9	85.8	93.7	50.1	71.5	102.9	79.6	64.0	83.7	83.1
October	72.3	72.3	91.8	86.9	94.6	51.1	71.2	103.3	80.2	64.4	84.2	83.7
November	72.8	72.9	91.9	86.7	94.7	51.7	72.1	103.5	80.4	65.0	84.4	84.0
December	73.6	73.7	92.6	87.6	95.3	52.2	72.3	104.6	81.0	65.9	85.0	84.6
1995												
January	73.7	73.8	92.5	88.0	95.0	52.5	72.2	104.6	81.2	66.0	84.9	84.4
February	73.6	73.6	92.7	87.5	95.5	52.5	71.0	103.3	81.3	65.9	84.5	83.9
March	73.7	73.8	92.6	87.3	95.4	53.0	71.1	103.3	81.5	65.9	84.3	83.8
April	73.7	73.7	92.3	87.1	95.1	53.1	70.7	102.7	81.4	66.1	84.0	83.3
May	73.9	73.8	92.4	86.3	95.6	53.6	70.7	102.0	81.7	66.2	83.9	83.1
June	74.1	74.2	92.9	86.9	96.0	54.3	71.1	102.2	82.1	66.2	83.9	83.2
July	73.8	73.7	92.4	85.0	96.1	54.1	70.4	102.0	82.1	66.0	83.3	82.3
August	74.8	74.5	93.8	87.8	96.9	55.1	70.2	102.9	83.0	66.7	84.0	82.8
September	75.1	75.2	93.9	88.7	96.7	55.6	69.8	104.5	83.0	67.0	84.0	83.2
October	75.0	75.1	93.1	87.7	96.1	55.5	68.9	104.4	83.2	67.2	83.6	82.7
November	75.2	75.2	93.5	87.8	96.5	55.7	67.5	104.5	83.6	67.3	83.4	82.4
December	75.5	75.5	93.8	88.4	96.7	56.2	67.5	105.0	83.5	67.6	83.4	82.3
1996												
January	75.0	74.9	92.6	86.0	96.0	55.5	66.7	103.4	83.2	67.5	82.5	81.2
February	76.2	76.1	94.2	88.4	97.2	56.9	68.6	104.6	84.1	68.4	83.4	82.1
March	76.1	75.9	93.6	85.6	97.5	56.8	68.9	105.8	84.3	68.5	82.9	81.5
April	76.8	76.8	94.4	89.6	97.1	58.2	68.7	106.4	84.2	69.0	83.3	82.0
May	77.3	77.4	94.6	90.1	97.1	59.0	68.8	107.5	85.0	69.6	83.5	82.2
June	78.0	78.2	95.3	91.9	97.4	59.9	68.2	109.3	85.3	70.2	83.8	82.6
July	77.8	78.4	94.5	92.1	96.2	60.5	68.7	108.6	85.3	70.1	83.3	82.3
August	78.3	78.8	94.4	91.2	96.4	60.9	68.6	109.7	86.2	70.7	83.4	82.3
September	78.8	79.5	95.4	92.2	97.5	61.6	68.6	110.0	86.6	71.0	83.6	82.5
October	78.8	79.3	94.8	90.1	97.5	61.4	68.2	110.2	86.8	71.2	83.1	82.0
November	79.5	80.0	95.9	91.4	98.5	62.3	67.7	111.0	87.6	71.7	83.5	82.2
December	80.0	80.7	96.2	92.8	98.3	63.4	67.8	110.4	88.1	72.2	83.6	82.5
1997												
January	80.1	80.8	95.9	92.2	98.1	63.7	66.8	109.4	88.7	72.4	83.3	82.1
February	81.0	81.9	96.4	93.7	98.2	64.8	67.3	111.6	89.6	73.4	83.9	82.8
March	81.6	82.8	97.2	94.9	98.8	65.9	67.1	112.6	89.8	73.8	84.0	83.2
April	81.6	82.7	96.2	92.5	98.4	66.3	67.1	112.3	90.1	74.1	83.6	82.5
May	82.1	83.3	96.9	93.5	99.0	67.1	67.1	113.0	90.7	74.4	83.7	82.7
June	82.5	83.9	96.9	95.3	98.3	68.2	67.0	112.8	91.0	74.8	83.6	82.7
July	83.2	84.4	97.7	95.3	99.4	68.6	67.2	112.9	91.6	75.5	83.8	82.7
August	84.0	85.5	98.6	97.4	99.8	70.2	67.6	113.7	91.9	76.3	84.2	83.2
September	84.8	86.2	99.3	98.2	100.5	70.7	67.5	114.2	93.0	77.1	84.4	83.4
October	85.5	87.0	100.9	99.4	102.2	71.7	67.7	114.9	94.0	77.3	84.6	83.5
November	86.3	87.9	101.2	101.9	101.7	73.1	67.3	115.4	94.4	78.2	84.8	83.8
December	86.5	88.3	100.7	101.6	101.1	73.4	68.3	116.7	94.6	78.7	84.5	83.5
1998												
January	87.0	89.0	101.2	102.1	101.6	74.4	68.9	117.5	94.6	78.9	84.4	83.5
February	87.1	89.1	101.1	101.9	101.5	74.7	69.2	118.1	94.9	79.0	83.9	83.0
March	87.1	89.0	101.2	102.2	101.6	75.1	68.8	117.3	95.4	78.9	83.5	82.3
April	87.4	89.4	101.9	102.6	102.3	75.4	68.8	117.8	95.7	79.1	83.2	82.1
May	88.0	89.9	102.3	103.3	102.6	75.8	69.6	119.2	96.4	79.7	83.2	81.9
June	87.5	89.2	101.1	98.4	102.8	75.8	69.8	118.7	96.5	79.1	82.2	80.7
July	87.1	88.8	100.2	94.4	103.1	75.4	70.8	119.4	97.1	78.8	81.4	79.9
August	88.9	91.0	103.1	105.6	102.9	77.8	71.1	119.8	97.8	80.3	82.7	81.4
September	88.8	90.8	102.2	105.6	101.6	77.8	70.7	119.4	97.8	80.4	82.1	80.7
October	89.5	91.7	102.7	107.6	101.6	78.7	72.2	120.7	98.1	81.1	82.3	81.0
November	89.4	91.9	102.1	107.3	100.8	78.8	72.0	120.9	98.4	81.3	81.9	80.7
December	89.8	92.4	102.1	108.2	100.4	78.9	71.5	122.3	98.4	81.9	81.8	80.8

Table 2-4A. Industrial Production and Capacity Utilization, Historical Data, 1948–2016—*Continued*

(Seasonally adjusted.)

Year and month	Production indexes, 2007 = 100											Capacity utilization (output as percent of capacity)	
	Total industry	Manufac-turing (SIC)	Market groups									Total industry	Manufac-turing (SIC)
			Consumer goods			Business equipment	Defense and space equipment	Construction supplies	Business supplies	Materials			
			Total	Durable	Nondurable								
1999													
January	90.2	92.7	103.1	108.2	101.9	79.0	71.4	121.6	99.2	82.1		81.8	80.6
February	90.7	93.4	103.5	109.1	102.1	79.5	72.0	121.7	99.4	82.7		81.9	80.9
March	90.8	93.4	103.3	108.8	101.8	79.5	71.7	120.4	99.8	83.3		81.7	80.4
April	91.1	93.7	103.2	110.1	101.3	79.9	70.9	120.8	100.0	83.6		81.6	80.4
May	91.7	94.6	104.2	111.1	102.3	80.9	70.0	121.2	100.6	84.1		81.8	80.7
June	91.6	94.3	103.1	110.5	101.0	80.6	69.0	121.3	100.5	84.5		81.4	80.1
July	92.2	94.7	102.7	110.8	100.3	81.3	68.6	122.2	101.2	85.6		81.6	80.1
August	92.5	95.3	104.1	113.4	101.3	81.8	68.0	122.0	101.2	85.6		81.7	80.3
September	92.2	94.9	103.3	111.7	100.9	81.5	65.7	122.1	101.2	85.4		81.0	79.6
October	93.4	96.3	105.4	115.3	102.3	82.2	65.1	123.6	102.1	86.4		81.8	80.5
November	93.8	96.9	105.2	114.5	102.5	82.2	63.6	124.3	102.6	87.3		81.9	80.7
December	94.5	97.6	106.4	114.5	104.0	82.8	62.6	125.6	103.3	87.9		82.2	80.9
2000													
January	94.5	97.7	105.1	116.6	101.5	84.2	62.6	126.0	103.6	88.1		82.0	80.6
February	94.8	97.8	105.7	116.3	102.5	84.7	61.2	126.3	103.7	88.2		81.9	80.4
March	95.2	98.5	105.4	115.8	102.2	85.8	60.8	126.4	104.4	88.7		82.0	80.6
April	95.9	99.2	106.4	117.4	103.0	86.9	59.8	127.0	105.6	89.1		82.3	80.9
May	96.1	99.1	106.4	116.9	103.2	87.5	59.3	125.0	105.5	89.5		82.2	80.4
June	96.2	99.3	106.5	116.4	103.5	87.6	60.1	124.5	105.4	89.6		82.0	80.3
July	96.0	99.4	106.1	114.7	103.6	88.2	61.4	125.1	105.5	89.3		81.6	80.1
August	95.7	98.7	105.5	114.4	102.9	87.8	59.9	124.2	105.1	89.2		81.1	79.2
September	96.1	99.1	106.5	114.7	104.1	88.6	57.3	124.4	105.0	89.5		81.1	79.2
October	95.8	98.8	105.5	113.4	103.2	88.7	60.1	123.9	104.7	89.3		80.6	78.7
November	95.8	98.6	105.9	111.1	104.5	88.4	62.0	123.5	104.9	89.1		80.4	78.2
December	95.6	98.0	106.4	109.4	105.8	87.8	62.5	122.0	104.5	88.6		79.9	77.5
2001													
January	94.9	97.5	105.5	107.4	105.3	87.7	64.2	122.3	104.4	87.7		79.1	76.8
February	94.4	96.9	104.9	107.1	104.5	87.2	63.8	121.1	102.9	87.3		78.4	76.0
March	94.1	96.6	104.8	109.7	103.5	86.6	65.6	121.2	102.3	87.0		78.0	75.6
April	93.9	96.4	105.3	109.9	104.1	84.8	66.2	121.0	101.7	86.9		77.6	75.2
May	93.3	95.6	105.2	110.7	103.7	83.2	66.4	120.2	101.0	86.2		76.8	74.4
June	92.7	95.0	105.1	110.0	103.8	82.3	67.5	119.2	100.6	85.4		76.2	73.7
July	92.2	94.6	104.5	110.3	103.0	81.5	68.4	119.3	100.5	84.7		75.5	73.2
August	92.0	94.1	104.8	109.6	103.5	79.9	67.4	117.9	100.0	84.9		75.2	72.7
September	91.7	93.9	104.3	108.7	103.2	78.8	67.8	117.9	100.1	84.8		74.8	72.4
October	91.3	93.3	104.7	107.6	104.1	77.6	67.6	116.4	99.5	84.3		74.3	71.9
November	90.8	93.1	104.7	109.5	103.4	76.9	66.9	116.1	98.8	83.7		73.8	71.6
December	90.8	93.3	105.3	112.1	103.4	76.3	67.0	117.1	99.0	83.5		73.7	71.7
2002													
January	91.3	93.8	106.4	112.4	104.8	76.0	66.4	116.8	98.7	84.3		74.0	72.0
February	91.4	93.8	106.6	112.7	103.6	75.9	65.9	117.2	98.8	84.8		73.9	71.9
March	92.1	94.6	106.5	113.9	104.4	76.3	65.9	119.0	99.8	85.5		74.4	72.4
April	92.5	94.8	106.3	115.5	103.6	75.8	65.9	118.9	100.4	86.5		74.6	72.5
May	92.9	95.3	106.7	116.1	103.9	76.2	66.0	119.5	100.9	86.8		74.9	72.9
June	93.8	96.3	108.0	117.5	105.1	76.8	66.7	120.4	101.5	87.6		75.6	73.7
July	93.5	96.0	107.8	118.7	104.4	76.4	66.9	118.7	101.5	87.5		75.4	73.4
August	93.6	96.2	107.3	117.8	104.0	76.8	67.2	119.3	101.5	87.7		75.4	73.6
September	93.7	96.3	107.4	117.8	104.3	76.9	68.4	120.3	102.1	87.6		75.5	73.7
October	93.4	96.0	107.2	117.2	104.2	76.5	68.9	119.9	102.6	87.0		75.3	73.4
November	93.9	96.4	108.1	119.9	104.3	76.8	68.5	119.8	102.3	87.7		75.6	73.7
December	93.4	95.9	107.1	118.1	103.7	76.0	71.2	118.9	102.2	87.4		75.3	73.3
2003													
January	94.0	96.4	107.8	119.9	104.0	76.1	71.2	119.3	103.2	87.9		75.8	73.7
February	94.3	96.5	108.8	118.1	106.1	76.1	72.0	118.4	103.3	87.9		76.0	73.8
March	94.0	96.6	108.9	118.4	106.0	76.3	72.0	117.9	103.3	87.4		75.9	73.9
April	93.4	95.8	107.9	117.2	105.2	75.5	71.5	116.7	102.2	87.0		75.3	73.3
May	93.4	95.9	107.6	117.3	104.7	75.5	72.1	118.3	102.6	87.0		75.4	73.4
June	93.5	96.4	107.9	118.4	104.7	75.8	72.2	118.6	102.2	87.1		75.5	73.7
July	93.9	96.6	108.8	121.3	104.9	76.0	71.5	118.0	102.7	87.3		75.8	73.9
August	93.7	96.1	108.0	119.0	104.6	76.1	71.9	118.9	102.4	87.3		75.7	73.6
September	94.3	96.9	108.9	122.1	104.7	76.9	72.0	118.6	102.5	87.9		76.2	74.2
October	94.4	97.0	108.2	121.3	104.0	76.7	71.9	119.2	103.0	88.5		76.3	74.3
November	95.2	98.0	109.2	123.5	104.7	78.2	71.4	120.7	103.5	89.0		76.9	75.1
December	95.2	97.8	109.2	123.5	104.7	77.9	69.6	120.4	103.2	89.1		76.9	75.0
2004													
January	95.3	97.8	109.5	124.1	104.9	78.1	67.7	120.5	103.8	89.3		77.1	74.9
February	95.9	98.5	110.0	123.9	105.7	79.1	69.1	120.4	104.6	89.7		77.5	75.5
March	95.5	98.4	108.9	122.8	104.5	78.9	69.3	120.4	103.8	89.6		77.2	75.4
April	95.9	98.8	109.6	122.9	105.4	79.1	69.2	120.2	104.4	89.9		77.5	75.8
May	96.6	99.6	110.1	121.9	106.4	80.0	69.9	121.6	105.2	90.8		78.2	76.4
June	95.9	98.8	108.5	119.2	105.2	79.8	69.0	120.8	105.1	90.1		77.5	75.8
July	96.6	99.7	108.8	119.7	105.4	81.5	70.1	122.3	105.7	90.8		78.1	76.5
August	96.7	100.2	109.4	120.7	105.8	81.1	70.6	122.3	105.7	90.7		78.2	76.9
September	96.7	100.2	109.3	119.9	106.0	81.3	71.5	121.3	105.5	90.9		78.2	76.8
October	97.7	101.2	110.4	122.6	106.7	82.0	71.6	123.3	106.1	91.8		79.0	77.5
November	97.8	101.1	110.2	120.9	106.9	81.6	72.2	122.9	106.5	92.3		79.1	77.4
December	98.5	101.8	110.9	122.0	107.5	82.3	73.0	122.8	107.3	93.1		79.6	77.8

Table 2-4A. Industrial Production and Capacity Utilization, Historical Data, 1948–2016—*Continued*

(Seasonally adjusted.)

Year and month	Production indexes, 2007 = 100										Capacity utilization (output as percent of capacity)	
	Total industry	Manufac-turing (SIC)	Market groups								Total industry	Manufac-turing (SIC)
			Consumer goods			Business equipment	Defense and space equipment	Construction supplies	Business supplies	Materials		
			Total	Durable	Nondurable							
2005												
January	99.0	102.6	111.4	121.0	108.4	83.7	72.9	124.4	108.2	93.1	79.9	78.3
February	99.7	103.4	112.0	123.8	108.3	84.6	75.6	125.2	108.3	93.8	80.4	78.8
March	99.5	102.9	111.5	121.4	108.4	84.5	77.0	124.0	108.3	93.8	80.2	78.3
April	99.7	103.2	111.3	120.2	108.5	85.4	78.3	126.1	108.9	93.6	80.2	78.4
May	99.8	103.6	112.0	120.4	109.4	86.2	78.0	126.4	109.0	93.4	80.2	78.5
June	100.2	103.8	113.0	121.1	110.4	86.0	78.6	125.4	109.3	93.7	80.4	78.5
July	99.9	103.4	112.5	118.6	110.5	85.5	78.1	126.2	108.9	93.4	80.1	78.0
August	100.1	103.8	113.0	122.1	110.1	86.2	78.8	126.7	109.1	93.3	80.1	78.1
September	98.3	102.8	113.2	124.7	109.7	84.0	75.8	128.5	109.3	89.7	78.5	77.2
October	99.5	104.3	113.2	125.9	109.3	88.6	76.3	131.1	109.8	90.8	79.4	78.2
November	100.5	105.1	113.1	124.2	109.6	89.7	76.6	131.8	110.2	92.7	80.1	78.7
December	101.1	105.3	113.8	122.9	111.0	89.0	76.8	132.8	110.6	93.5	80.5	78.7
2006												
January	101.2	106.1	113.0	124.4	109.5	90.6	75.1	133.7	110.8	93.8	80.5	79.2
February	101.3	105.8	112.4	122.2	109.4	91.0	75.7	132.7	110.8	94.2	80.4	78.8
March	101.5	105.8	113.1	123.2	109.9	91.7	74.0	132.3	111.1	94.1	80.4	78.7
April	101.9	106.3	113.4	123.2	110.4	93.5	74.5	131.8	111.2	94.4	80.7	79.0
May	101.8	105.8	113.1	122.2	110.3	93.1	73.9	130.6	110.9	94.5	80.4	78.5
June	102.1	106.2	113.6	123.1	110.7	93.9	74.8	130.0	111.0	94.8	80.6	78.6
July	102.1	105.9	112.6	118.7	110.6	94.6	76.2	130.4	111.0	95.0	80.4	78.3
August	102.5	106.5	113.6	122.0	111.0	95.1	76.2	129.5	110.7	95.3	80.6	78.6
September	102.3	106.6	113.1	119.9	110.8	95.4	77.1	129.2	110.6	95.1	80.3	78.5
October	102.2	106.2	113.0	118.3	111.3	95.6	78.5	127.8	110.8	95.0	80.1	78.1
November	102.1	106.3	113.1	118.9	111.2	96.0	80.0	127.4	110.3	94.8	79.8	78.0
December	103.2	107.8	113.6	121.7	111.1	97.6	81.8	131.1	111.1	95.8	80.5	79.0
2007												
January	102.7	107.3	112.9	118.5	111.1	95.6	83.8	128.8	111.0	95.7	79.9	78.4
February	103.8	107.7	114.3	120.1	112.3	96.6	84.5	129.2	112.0	96.7	80.6	78.5
March	104.0	108.6	113.3	120.7	110.9	98.4	83.7	130.7	112.4	97.0	80.5	79.0
April	104.7	109.4	114.0	122.9	111.1	99.5	86.1	130.4	113.4	97.7	81.0	79.4
May	104.8	109.3	113.6	122.1	110.9	99.5	87.9	130.2	112.9	98.1	80.8	79.1
June	104.8	109.6	113.7	123.5	110.7	99.5	90.9	130.8	112.2	97.9	80.7	79.2
July	104.7	109.7	113.6	122.2	110.8	99.6	92.3	130.3	111.5	98.1	80.6	79.0
August	104.9	109.4	113.3	121.7	110.7	99.7	93.9	129.5	111.6	98.6	80.7	78.6
September	105.3	109.8	113.3	120.2	111.1	101.3	96.3	129.4	112.3	98.7	80.9	78.8
October	104.8	109.4	112.1	119.7	109.7	100.7	96.3	128.1	111.9	98.7	80.5	78.4
November	105.3	109.9	111.9	120.2	109.3	101.5	98.5	127.8	112.4	99.6	80.9	78.7
December	105.3	110.0	111.7	120.2	109.0	102.5	99.1	128.0	112.0	99.5	81.0	78.7
2008												
January	105.0	109.5	111.3	117.3	109.4	102.6	99.6	127.9	111.7	99.1	80.8	78.4
February	104.7	108.9	111.1	116.6	109.3	102.6	99.3	125.7	111.5	98.7	80.6	77.9
March	104.4	108.5	109.7	113.6	108.3	103.3	99.7	124.2	111.1	98.9	80.4	77.7
April	103.6	107.3	109.0	111.0	108.1	101.1	99.4	122.1	110.0	98.5	79.9	76.9
May	103.1	106.8	108.4	109.9	107.7	101.6	99.0	121.0	109.3	97.9	79.5	76.6
June	102.9	106.2	108.2	110.5	107.3	101.1	100.3	119.7	108.5	97.9	79.4	76.2
July	102.4	105.0	107.4	107.7	107.0	99.3	98.9	119.3	107.6	97.8	79.0	75.4
August	100.9	103.7	105.5	103.3	106.0	97.5	99.0	116.9	106.9	96.3	77.8	74.7
September	96.5	100.2	104.8	102.5	105.2	89.9	96.7	113.7	105.4	90.1	74.4	72.2
October	97.5	99.6	105.1	100.0	106.3	87.3	96.8	111.9	104.4	92.7	75.0	71.9
November	96.3	97.3	104.3	96.2	106.4	88.7	96.2	106.4	102.1	91.4	74.1	70.3
December	93.4	93.9	102.1	91.9	104.8	89.4	95.3	100.4	98.5	87.9	71.8	68.0
2009												
January	91.2	91.1	99.8	82.2	104.8	84.2	94.9	96.3	97.1	86.4	70.0	66.1
February	90.6	90.9	99.9	83.8	104.4	83.9	94.2	94.6	95.9	85.8	69.5	66.1
March	89.2	89.2	99.3	83.5	103.8	82.2	92.7	91.3	94.9	84.2	68.4	64.9
April	88.4	88.5	99.0	83.6	103.3	80.1	92.1	89.7	94.4	83.5	67.7	64.5
May	87.4	87.5	97.7	80.2	102.7	77.7	92.2	89.2	93.8	82.9	67.0	63.9
June	87.1	87.2	97.2	79.4	102.2	76.9	92.6	89.2	93.9	82.6	66.7	63.7
July	88.0	88.4	98.3	86.9	101.5	77.9	93.9	89.4	93.7	83.6	67.4	64.7
August	89.0	89.4	99.3	88.0	102.4	79.0	94.6	89.8	94.3	84.7	68.2	65.6
September	89.6	90.1	100.0	91.6	102.2	79.4	95.4	89.4	94.5	85.6	68.8	66.2
October	89.9	90.3	100.4	90.2	103.2	80.0	94.8	88.1	95.4	85.8	69.1	66.4
November	90.3	91.2	99.8	91.7	102.0	79.7	95.3	89.6	95.5	86.8	69.5	67.2
December	90.5	91.0	99.7	91.0	102.0	81.1	95.2	87.5	96.6	87.0	69.8	67.1
2010												
January	91.6	91.9	100.3	92.2	102.5	82.4	97.5	89.3	96.9	88.1	70.8	68.0
February	91.9	91.9	99.4	90.6	101.8	81.8	98.3	89.3	96.9	89.3	71.2	68.1
March	92.5	93.0	99.7	91.8	101.8	83.3	100.8	90.9	96.7	89.9	71.8	69.0
April	92.9	93.8	98.9	92.2	100.7	84.5	102.0	93.8	97.4	90.4	72.3	69.7
May	94.3	95.2	100.8	95.5	102.1	86.2	102.1	94.4	98.4	91.7	73.5	70.8
June	94.5	95.1	100.5	94.6	102.0	86.5	102.0	94.6	98.3	92.2	73.8	70.9
July	94.9	95.7	101.1	97.9	101.8	87.5	103.6	94.5	98.4	92.5	74.3	71.5
August	95.3	95.9	101.0	95.6	102.4	87.8	103.9	95.1	98.4	93.2	74.7	71.7
September	95.6	95.9	100.6	95.6	101.9	88.2	101.8	95.2	98.4	93.9	75.0	71.9
October	95.4	96.1	100.6	96.0	101.8	88.7	100.5	95.4	97.9	93.5	74.9	72.1
November	95.4	96.1	100.0	94.6	101.4	88.3	100.2	96.0	98.9	93.7	75.0	72.3
December	96.2	96.5	101.1	94.1	102.9	88.9	99.5	94.7	99.4	94.8	75.7	72.6

Table 2-4A. Industrial Production and Capacity Utilization, Historical Data, 1948–2016—*Continued*

(Seasonally adjusted.)

Year and month	Production indexes, 2007 = 100										Capacity utilization (output as percent of capacity)	
	Total industry	Manufac-turing (SIC)	Consumer goods			Business equipment	Defense and space equipment	Construction supplies	Business supplies	Materials	Total industry	Manufac-turing (SIC)
			Total	Durable	Nondurable							
2011												
January	96.1	96.7	101.3	95.8	102.7	89.9	99.2	94.2	99.0	94.4	75.7	72.9
February	95.7	96.7	101.0	97.9	101.8	89.9	98.5	93.7	98.9	93.7	75.4	73.0
March	96.6	97.3	101.2	99.5	101.6	89.7	97.8	94.5	99.2	95.5	76.1	73.5
April	96.3	96.7	101.1	95.7	102.5	88.8	97.3	94.5	98.9	95.0	75.8	73.1
May	96.5	96.8	101.4	96.9	102.5	89.5	97.3	95.6	99.0	95.0	75.9	73.2
June	96.7	96.9	101.2	96.1	102.5	89.5	96.4	95.9	98.8	95.6	76.1	73.3
July	97.1	97.4	101.9	97.2	103.0	90.4	97.0	96.8	99.0	95.7	76.3	73.7
August	97.7	97.7	102.4	98.4	103.4	91.4	97.6	96.5	99.3	96.4	76.7	73.9
September	97.6	98.0	101.7	98.3	102.6	92.1	97.4	96.6	99.6	96.3	76.5	74.1
October	98.3	98.6	101.9	99.9	102.5	93.8	98.5	96.8	99.2	97.2	77.0	74.5
November	98.2	98.3	100.8	98.3	101.4	94.1	100.2	96.7	98.2	97.6	76.8	74.2
December	98.7	98.9	100.7	98.9	101.1	95.5	99.7	98.2	98.8	98.2	77.0	74.6
2012												
January	99.3	99.8	100.6	101.4	100.4	97.4	100.2	99.0	99.1	99.0	77.4	75.2
February	99.6	100.2	100.5	100.9	100.5	97.9	101.1	100.3	99.6	99.3	77.5	75.4
March	99.1	99.6	99.0	99.9	98.7	98.7	101.2	100.0	99.0	98.9	76.9	74.9
April	99.9	100.3	99.9	100.7	99.7	99.7	100.1	101.4	100.1	99.6	77.4	75.3
May	100.0	99.9	100.4	99.9	100.6	100.1	98.7	100.4	100.4	99.7	77.4	74.9
June	100.1	100.1	100.1	100.0	100.2	101.4	97.9	99.6	100.5	99.7	77.3	74.9
July	100.3	99.9	100.3	99.8	100.4	100.2	100.2	99.1	100.4	100.4	77.3	74.7
August	99.9	99.8	99.9	99.2	100.0	100.5	100.3	99.6	100.0	99.8	76.9	74.5
September	99.9	99.7	99.7	98.2	100.1	100.5	99.9	99.4	100.0	100.0	76.8	74.4
October	100.2	99.5	99.5	98.3	99.8	100.2	99.9	99.2	100.1	100.8	76.9	74.2
November	100.7	100.3	100.0	99.8	100.1	101.4	100.3	100.6	100.3	101.2	77.1	74.6
December	101.0	101.0	100.1	102.0	99.6	102.1	100.1	101.2	100.5	101.5	77.2	75.1
2013												
January	100.9	100.7	100.1	101.3	99.7	100.1	99.2	101.7	100.8	101.7	77.0	74.8
February	101.5	101.2	100.6	103.6	99.9	100.9	99.1	103.5	100.8	102.2	77.3	75.1
March	101.8	101.0	101.0	104.6	100.1	101.4	98.6	102.9	101.1	102.6	77.5	74.9
April	101.7	100.6	100.8	104.3	99.9	100.5	98.1	102.4	101.3	102.7	77.3	74.5
May	101.7	100.8	100.6	104.7	99.5	99.9	97.1	102.1	101.7	103.0	77.2	74.7
June	101.9	101.0	100.9	106.0	99.6	99.9	97.4	102.7	101.9	103.1	77.2	74.8
July	101.3	100.0	99.6	102.7	98.8	97.7	96.2	102.3	101.5	103.1	76.7	73.9
August	102.1	101.0	100.3	106.4	98.8	99.5	96.9	102.9	102.1	103.8	77.3	74.6
September	102.6	101.1	100.7	107.3	99.0	100.4	96.7	103.8	102.3	104.4	77.6	74.7
October	102.5	101.2	101.1	107.6	99.4	99.9	96.6	103.9	102.5	104.1	77.4	74.8
November	102.8	101.2	100.9	108.9	99.0	99.6	95.3	104.7	102.4	105.0	77.6	74.7
December	103.1	101.1	101.8	109.1	100.0	98.8	94.7	103.2	103.0	105.3	77.8	74.7
2014												
January	102.6	100.1	100.1	105.4	98.7	99.1	93.8	103.1	102.4	105.3	77.3	73.9
February	103.6	101.2	101.3	109.2	99.3	100.5	94.0	104.1	103.0	106.2	78.0	74.7
March	104.6	101.9	101.7	109.9	99.7	101.7	95.0	105.4	103.2	107.4	78.6	75.3
April	104.8	101.9	101.4	109.2	99.5	101.5	94.6	104.8	102.8	108.1	78.7	75.2
May	105.1	102.1	101.3	110.7	98.9	102.1	94.4	106.4	103.0	108.5	78.8	75.4
June	105.5	102.4	101.3	111.1	98.8	101.9	94.5	106.9	103.0	109.3	79.0	75.6
July	105.5	102.7	101.2	112.7	98.2	102.7	94.7	107.8	102.6	109.2	78.9	75.8
August	105.4	102.3	100.9	111.0	98.3	102.0	93.7	107.6	102.4	109.5	78.7	75.6
September	105.7	102.3	101.3	111.0	98.9	101.5	93.9	107.9	102.7	109.9	78.8	75.6
October	105.8	102.3	101.3	110.7	98.9	102.6	93.7	107.7	102.6	109.9	78.7	75.6
November	106.6	103.2	103.3	114.4	100.5	103.8	93.2	107.7	103.2	110.3	79.2	76.2
December	106.4	102.8	103.0	113.8	100.3	102.3	92.8	108.3	102.3	110.4	78.8	76.0
2015												
January	105.6	102.4	103.2	112.9	100.7	102.0	91.3	107.6	102.5	109.2	78.1	75.7
February	105.4	101.9	103.1	111.0	101.1	101.4	92.6	106.7	102.3	109.2	77.9	75.3
March	105.1	102.2	104.1	113.5	101.7	101.6	92.0	105.7	101.8	108.4	77.5	75.6
April	104.7	102.2	103.5	114.7	100.7	101.1	91.1	106.4	102.2	108.0	77.1	75.6
May	104.3	102.2	103.4	116.5	100.0	101.5	90.5	106.7	102.0	107.3	76.8	75.6
June	104.0	101.9	103.4	114.0	100.7	101.2	90.7	106.9	101.8	106.7	76.5	75.3
July	104.5	102.5	104.9	118.8	101.4	101.2	90.6	106.7	101.3	107.1	76.8	75.8
August	104.5	102.4	104.9	116.6	102.0	101.5	91.1	107.3	101.7	106.8	76.8	75.7
September	104.2	102.1	104.5	116.6	101.5	100.9	90.4	106.1	101.9	106.8	76.5	75.5
October	104.0	102.3	104.4	116.7	101.2	100.4	90.2	107.8	102.5	106.3	76.4	75.6
November	103.4	102.2	103.9	116.2	100.8	99.5	90.4	107.8	102.6	105.4	76.0	75.5
December	102.9	101.9	103.3	116.6	99.9	98.8	91.0	108.4	102.0	104.9	75.6	75.2
2016												
January	103.5	102.5	104.4	117.6	101.1	99.4	90.4	109.2	102.7	105.2	76.1	75.6
February	103.3	102.3	104.5	117.9	101.1	99.3	89.7	109.6	102.3	104.9	75.9	75.4
March	102.5	102.1	103.3	116.6	100.0	98.8	89.5	108.8	101.5	104.3	75.4	75.2
April	102.9	102.1	104.5	117.8	101.1	99.4	89.4	108.9	101.8	104.2	75.6	75.1
May	102.8	101.9	104.2	115.8	101.2	99.0	90.4	108.1	102.0	104.2	75.6	75.0
June	103.1	102.1	104.9	118.3	101.5	99.3	90.0	107.5	102.2	104.6	75.8	75.1
July	103.2	102.1	104.9	118.6	101.4	99.1	89.5	108.2	102.6	104.7	75.9	75.1
August	103.1	101.8	105.1	118.7	101.6	98.6	89.8	107.1	102.4	104.7	75.8	74.7
September	103.0	102.0	104.9	119.8	101.1	98.7	89.4	107.5	102.5	104.3	75.6	74.9
October	103.2	102.2	104.7	120.7	100.7	99.0	88.9	108.2	102.3	104.8	75.7	75.0
November	102.9	102.4	103.6	119.7	99.6	98.9	89.9	109.2	102.3	104.8	75.5	75.1
December	103.8	102.6	105.1	120.7	101.2	99.7	89.6	109.1	102.9	105.3	76.0	75.2

Table 2-4B. Industrial Production: Historical Data, 1919–1947

(Seasonally adjusted, 2007 = 100.)

Year and month	January	February	March	April	May	June	July	August	September	October	November	December	Annual averages
1919													
Industrial production, total ...	5.00	4.80	4.70	4.80	4.80	5.10	5.40	5.50	5.40	5.30	5.20	5.30	5.10
Manufacturing	5.00	4.90	4.70	4.80	4.80	5.10	5.40	5.50	5.30	5.20	5.40	5.30	5.10
1920													
Industrial production, total ..	5.80	5.80	5.70	5.40	5.50	5.60	5.50	5.50	5.30	5.10	4.60	4.40	5.30
Manufacturing	5.80	5.80	5.70	5.40	5.50	5.50	5.30	5.40	5.20	5.00	4.40	4.10	5.30
1921													
Industrial production, total ..	4.10	4.00	3.90	3.90	4.00	4.00	4.00	4.10	4.10	4.40	4.30	4.30	4.10
Manufacturing	3.90	3.90	3.80	3.80	3.90	3.90	3.90	4.10	4.10	4.30	4.40	4.30	4.00
1922													
Industrial production, total ..	4.50	4.70	4.90	4.80	5.00	5.30	5.30	5.10	5.40	5.70	6.00	6.10	5.20
Manufacturing	4.40	4.50	4.70	4.90	5.20	5.40	5.50	5.30	5.40	5.70	5.90	6.00	5.20
1923													
Industrial production, total ..	6.00	6.10	6.30	6.40	6.50	6.50	6.40	6.30	6.10	6.10	6.10	6.00	6.20
Manufacturing	5.90	6.00	6.30	6.30	6.50	6.40	6.30	6.10	6.10	6.00	6.00	5.90	6.10
1924													
Industrial production, total ...	6.10	6.20	6.10	5.90	5.70	5.40	5.30	5.50	5.70	5.90	6.00	6.10	5.80
Manufacturing	6.00	6.10	6.00	5.90	5.60	5.30	5.20	5.40	5.60	5.80	5.90	6.10	5.80
1925													
Industrial production, total ..	6.30	6.30	6.30	6.40	6.40	6.30	6.50	6.40	6.30	6.50	6.70	6.80	6.40
Manufacturing	6.30	6.30	6.40	6.40	6.30	6.30	6.40	6.30	6.30	6.60	6.80	6.90	6.40
1926													
Industrial production, total ..	6.60	6.60	6.70	6.70	6.70	6.80	6.80	6.90	7.00	7.00	7.00	6.90	6.80
Manufacturing	6.80	6.70	6.70	6.70	6.60	6.70	6.70	6.80	6.90	6.90	6.80	6.80	6.80
1927													
Industrial production, total ..	6.90	7.00	7.00	6.90	6.90	6.90	6.80	6.80	6.70	6.60	6.60	6.60	6.80
Manufacturing	6.70	6.80	6.90	6.80	6.90	6.90	6.80	6.70	6.60	6.50	6.50	6.60	6.70
1928													
Industrial production, total ..	6.70	6.80	6.80	6.80	6.90	7.00	7.00	7.20	7.20	7.40	7.50	7.60	7.10
Manufacturing	6.70	6.80	6.80	6.80	6.90	7.00	7.10	7.20	7.30	7.40	7.60	7.70	7.10
1929													
Industrial production, total ..	7.80	7.70	7.80	7.90	8.00	8.10	8.20	8.10	8.10	7.90	7.50	7.20	7.90
Manufacturing	7.70	7.70	7.80	7.90	8.10	8.20	8.20	8.20	8.00	7.90	7.50	7.10	7.90
1930													
Industrial production, total ..	7.20	7.20	7.10	7.00	6.90	6.70	6.40	6.30	6.10	6.00	5.80	5.70	6.50
Manufacturing	7.10	7.10	6.90	7.00	6.80	6.60	6.30	6.10	6.00	5.80	5.70	5.50	6.40
1931													
Industrial production, total ..	5.70	5.70	5.80	5.80	5.80	5.60	5.50	5.30	5.10	4.90	4.80	4.80	5.40
Manufacturing	5.50	5.60	5.70	5.70	5.70	5.40	5.40	5.20	5.00	4.70	4.60	4.60	5.30
1932													
Industrial production, total ..	4.70	4.60	4.50	4.20	4.10	3.90	3.80	3.90	4.20	4.30	4.30	4.20	4.20
Manufacturing	4.60	4.40	4.30	4.00	3.90	3.80	3.60	3.80	4.00	4.10	4.10	4.10	4.10
1933													
Industrial production, total ..	4.10	4.20	3.90	4.20	4.90	5.60	6.20	5.90	5.60	5.30	5.00	5.00	5.00
Manufacturing	4.00	3.90	3.70	4.10	4.80	5.50	6.10	5.80	5.50	5.20	4.80	4.90	4.80
1934													
Industrial production, total ..	5.20	5.50	5.70	5.70	5.80	5.70	5.30	5.30	5.00	5.20	5.20	5.60	5.40
Manufacturing	5.00	5.30	5.50	5.60	5.70	5.60	5.10	5.10	4.80	5.00	5.10	5.40	5.30
1935													
Industrial production, total ..	6.00	6.10	6.10	6.00	6.00	6.10	6.10	6.30	6.50	6.60	6.80	6.90	6.30
Manufacturing	5.90	6.00	6.00	5.90	5.90	5.90	6.00	6.30	6.40	6.60	6.80	6.90	6.20
1936													
Industrial production, total ..	6.80	6.60	6.70	7.10	7.20	7.40	7.50	7.60	7.80	7.90	8.10	8.30	7.40
Manufacturing	6.70	6.50	6.60	7.10	7.20	7.40	7.50	7.70	7.80	7.90	8.10	8.40	7.40
1937													
Industrial production, total ..	8.30	8.40	8.60	8.60	8.70	8.50	8.60	8.50	8.30	7.60	6.90	6.30	8.10
Manufacturing	8.40	8.50	8.60	8.70	8.80	8.60	8.70	8.50	8.20	7.60	6.70	6.00	8.10
1938													
Industrial production, total ..	6.10	6.10	6.10	6.00	5.80	5.90	6.20	6.60	6.80	6.90	7.20	7.30	6.40
Manufacturing	5.90	5.80	5.90	5.70	5.70	5.70	6.00	6.40	6.60	6.80	7.10	7.20	6.20

Table 2-4B. Industrial Production: Historical Data, 1919–1947—*Continued*

(Seasonally adjusted, 2007 = 100.)

Year and month	January	February	March	April	May	June	July	August	September	October	November	December	Annual averages
1939													
Industrial production, total	7.30	7.30	7.40	7.30	7.30	7.50	7.70	7.80	8.30	8.70	8.90	8.90	7.90
Products	6.80	6.90	6.90	6.80	6.80	7.00	7.20	7.40	7.80	8.20	8.40	8.50	7.40
Consumer goods	12.10	12.10	12.30	12.30	12.30	12.50	12.60	12.70	12.80	13.00	13.10	13.10	12.60
Materials	6.50	6.60	6.60	6.40	6.40	6.70	7.00	7.10	7.90	8.60	8.80	8.80	7.28
Manufacturing	6.80	6.90	6.90	6.80	6.80	7.00	7.20	7.40	7.80	8.20	8.40	8.50	7.40
1940													
Industrial production, total	8.80	8.50	8.30	8.50	8.80	9.00	9.20	9.20	9.40	9.50	9.80	10.10	9.10
Products	8.40	8.10	7.90	8.00	8.30	8.70	8.80	8.90	9.10	9.20	9.40	9.70	8.70
Consumer goods	13.10	13.00	12.90	13.00	13.00	13.20	13.10	13.10	13.50	13.70	14.00	14.40	13.30
Materials	8.50	8.10	7.80	8.00	8.40	8.80	9.00	9.10	9.20	9.30	9.50	9.80	8.80
Manufacturing	8.40	8.10	7.90	8.00	8.30	8.70	8.80	8.90	9.10	9.20	9.40	9.70	8.70
1941													
Industrial production, total	10.30	10.70	11.00	11.00	11.50	11.60	11.70	11.90	11.90	12.00	12.00	12.20	11.50
Products	9.90	10.30	10.60	10.80	11.20	11.30	11.50	11.50	11.50	11.60	11.60	11.80	11.10
Consumer goods	14.70	15.10	15.50	15.80	16.30	16.30	16.30	16.40	16.30	16.30	16.30	16.30	16.00
Materials	10.00	10.20	10.60	10.40	11.00	11.20	11.30	11.40	11.40	11.50	11.50	11.80	11.00
Manufacturing	9.90	10.30	10.60	10.80	11.20	11.30	11.50	11.50	11.50	11.60	11.60	11.80	11.10
1942													
Industrial production, total	12.50	12.70	12.90	12.50	12.50	12.50	12.90	13.20	13.50	14.00	14.30	14.70	13.20
Products	12.10	12.40	12.50	12.20	12.20	12.30	12.70	13.10	13.50	14.00	14.40	14.80	13.00
Consumer goods	16.70	16.50	16.50	14.20	14.00	13.80	14.00	14.10	14.20	14.40	14.50	14.80	14.80
Materials	11.80	12.00	12.10	12.40	12.40	12.40	12.60	13.00	13.10	13.50	13.70	13.90	12.70
Manufacturing	12.10	12.40	12.50	12.20	12.20	12.30	12.70	13.10	13.50	14.00	14.40	14.80	13.00
1943													
Industrial production, total	14.80	15.20	15.30	15.50	15.60	15.50	16.00	16.30	16.70	17.00	17.20	17.00	16.00
Products	15.00	15.30	15.40	15.60	15.70	15.80	16.10	16.50	16.90	17.30	17.50	17.20	16.20
Consumer goods	14.40	14.50	14.50	14.70	14.90	15.10	15.40	15.50	15.60	15.50	15.40	15.10	15.00
Materials	14.10	14.40	14.60	14.70	14.70	14.30	14.90	15.20	15.60	15.80	15.90	15.90	15.00
Manufacturing	15.00	15.30	15.40	15.60	15.70	15.80	16.10	16.50	16.90	17.30	17.50	17.20	16.20
1944													
Industrial production, total	17.20	17.30	17.30	17.30	17.20	17.10	17.10	17.30	17.20	17.30	17.10	17.10	17.20
Products	17.50	17.60	17.60	17.60	17.40	17.40	17.40	17.60	17.50	17.60	17.40	17.40	17.50
Consumer goods	15.30	15.30	15.50	15.60	15.70	15.80	15.90	16.30	15.90	15.90	15.90	15.90	15.80
Materials	16.10	16.20	16.20	16.10	15.90	15.60	15.40	15.60	15.60	15.60	15.60	15.70	15.80
Manufacturing	17.50	17.60	17.60	17.60	17.40	17.40	17.40	17.60	17.50	17.60	17.40	17.40	17.50
1945													
Industrial production, total	16.90	16.90	16.70	16.40	16.00	15.60	15.30	13.70	12.50	12.00	12.40	12.50	14.70
Products	17.20	17.10	16.90	16.60	16.10	15.60	15.20	13.40	11.90	11.40	11.80	11.90	14.60
Consumer goods	16.10	16.00	16.00	16.10	16.10	16.30	16.20	16.50	16.30	16.50	17.00	17.20	16.30
Materials	15.50	15.70	15.70	15.50	15.10	14.70	14.10	12.80	11.90	11.20	12.00	12.10	13.90
Manufacturing	17.20	17.10	16.90	16.60	16.10	15.60	15.20	13.40	11.90	11.40	11.80	11.90	14.60
1946													
Industrial production, total	11.80	11.20	12.40	12.10	11.70	12.40	12.80	13.30	13.50	13.80	13.90	14.00	12.70
Products	11.10	10.40	11.70	11.70	11.20	11.80	12.20	12.70	13.00	13.30	13.40	13.50	12.10
Consumer goods	17.90	18.60	18.50	18.70	18.80	18.80	19.30	19.90	20.30	20.50	20.80	20.90	19.40
Materials	10.60	9.30	11.80	11.00	10.10	11.60	12.20	12.70	12.80	13.10	13.00	13.10	11.80
Manufacturing	11.10	10.40	11.70	11.70	11.20	11.80	12.20	12.70	13.00	13.30	13.40	13.50	12.10
1947													
Industrial production, total	14.10	14.20	14.30	14.20	14.20	14.20	14.20	14.20	14.40	14.50	14.70	14.70	14.30
Products	13.40	13.50	13.50	13.50	13.40	13.40	13.40	13.40	13.50	13.70	13.90	13.90	13.60
Consumer goods	20.50	20.40	20.50	20.40	20.30	20.30	20.40	20.50	20.70	21.10	21.40	21.40	20.70
Materials	13.10	13.20	13.70	13.30	13.40	13.30	13.10	13.10	13.30	13.40	13.70	13.50	13.30
Manufacturing	13.40	13.50	13.50	13.50	13.40	13.40	13.40	13.40	13.50	13.70	13.90	13.90	13.60

NOTES AND DEFINITIONS, CHAPTER 2

TABLES 2-1 THROUGH 2-4

Industrial Production and Capacity Utilization

SOURCE: BOARD OF GOVERNORS OF THE FEDERAL RESERVE SYSTEM

The *industrial production index* measures changes in the physical volume or quantity of output of manufacturing, mining, and electric and gas utilities. *Capacity utilization* is calculated by dividing a seasonally adjusted industrial production index for an industry or group of industries by a related index of productive capacity.

The index of industrial production is one of the oldest continuous statistical series maintained by the federal government, and one of the few economic indicators for which monthly data are available before the post-World-War-II period. This edition of *Business Statistics* reprints monthly and annual values for total industrial production and its manufacturing component beginning with January 1919.

In 2015 a revision of the entire industrial production data system included rebasing all of the indexes from the previous comparison base, 2007 = 100 to 2102 = 100. This affected the levels of all current and historical production indexes, though not necessarily the changes that they record over time. All the data shown here reflect the 2011 and all subsequent revisions through March 31, 2017.

Around the 15th day of each month, the Federal Reserve issues estimates of industrial production and capacity utilization for the previous month. The production estimates are in the form of index numbers (2012 = 100) that reflect the monthly levels of total output of the nation's factories, mines, and gas and electric utilities expressed as a percent of the monthly average in the 2012 base year. Capacity estimates are expressed as index numbers, 2012 <u>output</u> (not 2012 <u>capacity</u>) = 100, and capacity utilization is measured by the production index as a percent of the capacity index. Since, for each component industry, the bases of those two indexes are the same, this procedure yields production as a percent of capacity. Monthly estimates are subject to revision in subsequent months, as well as to annual and comprehensive revisions in subsequent years.

Definitions and notes on the data

The *index of industrial production* measures a large portion of the goods output of the national economy on a monthly basis. This portion, together with construction, has also accounted for the bulk of the variation in output over the course of many historical business cycles. The substantial industrial detail included in the index illuminates structural developments in the economy.

The total industrial production index and the indexes for its major components are constructed from individual industry series (312 series for data from 1997 forward) based on the 2007 North American Industry Classification System (NAICS). See the Preface to this volume for information on NAICS.

The Federal Reserve has been able to provide a longer continuous historical series on the NAICS basis than some other government agencies. In a major research effort, the Fed and the Census Bureau's Center for Economic Studies re-coded data from seven Censuses of Manufactures, beginning in 1963, to establish benchmark NAICS data for output, value added, and capacity utilization. The resulting indexes are shown annually for the last 42 years (47 years for aggregate levels) in Tables 2-1 through 2-3.

The Fed's featured indexes for total industry and total manufacturing are on the Standard Industrial Classification (SIC) basis and do <u>not</u> observe the reclassifications under NAICS of the logging industry to the Agriculture sector and the publishing industry to the Information sector. (The reason cited by the Fed was to avoid "changing the scope or historical continuity of these statistics.") One advantage of the SIC index for capacity utilization is that it is a continuous series back to 1948 (shown in Table 2-4A). On the new NAICS basis, production and capacity utilization are shown back to 1972 in Tables 2-2 and 2-3.

The individual series components of the indexes are grouped in two ways: market groups and industry groups.

Market groups. For analyzing market trends and product flows, the individual series are grouped into two major divisions: *final products and nonindustrial supplies* and *materials. Final products* consists of products purchased by consumers, businesses, or government for final use. *Nonindustrial supplies* are expected to become inputs in nonindustrial sectors: the two major subgroups are *construction supplies* and *business supplies*. *Materials* comprises industrial output that requires further processing within the industrial sector. This twofold division distinguishes between products that are ready to ship outside the industrial sector and those that will stay within the sector for further processing.

Final products are divided into *consumer goods* and *equipment*, and *equipment* is divided into *business equipment* and *defense and space equipment*. Further subdivisions of each market group are based on type of product and the market destination for the product.

Industry groups are typically groupings by 3-digit NAICS industries and major aggregates of these industries—for example, *durable goods* and *nondurable goods manufacturing, mining,* and *utilities*. Indexes are also calculated for *stage-of-process* industry groups—*crude*, *primary and semifinished*, and *finished* processing. The stage-of-process grouping was a new feature in the 2002 revision, replacing the two narrower and less well-defined "primary processing manufacturing" and "advanced processing manufacturing" groups that were previously published. *Crude processing* consists of logging, much of mining, and certain basic manufacturing activities in the chemical, paper, and metals industries. *Primary and semifinished processing* represents industries that produce materials and parts used as inputs by other industries. *Finished processing* includes industries that produce goods in their finished form for use by consumers, business investment, or government.

The indexes of industrial production are constructed using data from a variety of sources. Current monthly estimates of production are based on measures of physical output where possible and appropriate. For a few high-tech industries, the estimated value of nominal output is deflated by a corresponding price index. For industries in which such direct measurement is not possible on a monthly basis, output is inferred from production-worker hours, adjusted for trends in worker productivity derived from annual and benchmark revisions. (Between the 1960s and 1997, electric power consumption was used as a monthly output indicator for some industries instead of hours. However, the coverage of the electric power consumption survey deteriorated, and in the 2005 revision, the decision was made to resume the use of hours in those industries, beginning with the data for 1997.)

In annual and benchmark revisions, the individual indexes are revised using data from the quinquennial Censuses of Manufactures and Mineral Industries, the Annual Survey of Manufactures, and the quarterly Survey of Plant Capacity, prepared by the Census Bureau; deflators from the Producer Price Indexes and other sources; the *Minerals Yearbook*, prepared by the Department of the Interior; publications from the Department of Energy; and other sources.

The weights used in compiling the indexes are based on Census value added—the difference between the value of production and the cost of materials and supplies consumed. Census value added differs in some respects from the economic concept of industry value added used in the national income and product accounts (NIPAs). Industry value added as defined in the NIPAs is not available in sufficient detail for the industrial production indexes. See Chapter 14 for data and a description of NIPA value added (equivalently, gross domestic product) by major industry group.

Before 1972, a linked-Laspeyres formula (base period prices) is used to compute the weighted individual indexes. Beginning with 1972, the index uses a version of the Fisher-ideal index formula—a chain-weighting (continually updated average price) system similar to that in the NIPAs. See the "General Notes" article at the front of this book and the notes and definitions for Chapter 1 for more information. Chain-weighting keeps the index from being distorted by the use of obsolete relative prices.

For the purpose of these value-added weights, value added per unit of output is based on data from the Censuses of Manufacturing and Mineral Industries, the Census Bureau's Annual Survey of Manufactures, and revenue and expense data reported by the Department of Energy and the American Gas Association, which are projected into recent years by using changes in relevant Producer Price Indexes.

To separate seasonal movements from cyclical patterns and underlying trends, each component of the index is seasonally adjusted by the Census X-12-ARIMA method.

The index does not cover production on farms, in the construction industry, in transportation, or in various trade and service industries. A number of groups and subgroups include data for individual series not published separately.

Capacity utilization is calculated for the manufacturing, mining, and electric and gas utilities industries. Output is measured by seasonally adjusted indexes of industrial production. The capacity indexes attempt to capture the concept of sustainable maximum output, which is defined as the greatest level of output that a plant can maintain within the framework of a realistic work schedule, taking account of normal downtime and assuming sufficient availability of inputs to operate the machinery and equipment in place. The 89 individual industry capacity indexes are based on a variety of data, including capacity data measured in physical units compiled by government agencies and trade associations, Census Bureau surveys of utilization rates and investment, and estimates of growth of the capital stock.

In the "Explanatory Note" to its monthly release, the statistics cover output, capacity, and capacity utilization in the U.S. industrial sector, which is defined by the Federal Reserve to comprise manufacturing, mining, and electric and gas utilities. Mining is defined as all industries in sector 21 of the North American Industry Classification System (NAICS); electric and gas utilities are those in NAICS sectors 2211 and 2212. Manufacturing comprises NAICS manufacturing industries (sector 31-33) plus the logging industry and the newspaper, periodical, book, and directory publishing industries. Logging and publishing are classified elsewhere in NAICS (under agriculture and information respectively), but historically they were considered to be manufacturing and were included in the industrial sector under the Standard Industrial Classification (SIC) system. In December 2002 the Federal Reserve reclassified all its industrial output data from the SIC system to NAICS.

Revisions

Revisions normally occur annual with the newest release on March 31, 2017. New annual data have been incorporated in addition to the data from the Annual Survey of Manufacturing. The IP indexes for publishing reflect new data for 2014 and revised data for 2013 from the Census Bureau's Service Annual Survey. The Census Bureau recently benchmarked the Service Annual

Survey to the 2012 Economic Census, which resulted in updated estimates for 2008 through 2012. For logging, the IP indexes were updated with 2015 data from the U.S. Forest Service. In addition, the indexes for metallic and nonmetallic minerals were updated with revised annual data for 2015 from the Department of the Interior's U.S. Geological Survey (USGS). Data on prices from the Bureau of Labor Statistics (BLS) were also incorporated into most of the manufacturing indexes.

Data availability

Data are available monthly in Federal Reserve release G.17. Current and historical data and background information are available on the Federal Reserve Web site at <http://www.federalreserve.gov>.

Chain-weighting makes it difficult for the user to analyze in detail the sources of aggregate output change. An "Explanatory Note," included in each month's index release, provides some assistance for the user, including a reference to a an Internet location with the exact contribution of a monthly change in a component index to the monthly change in the total index.

REFERENCES

The G.17 release each month contains extensive explanatory material, as well as references for further detail.

An earlier detailed description of the industrial production index, together with a history of the index, a glossary of terms, and a bibliography is presented in *Industrial Production—1986 Edition*, available from Publication Services, Mail Stop 127, Board of Governors of the Federal Reserve System, Washington, DC 20551.

CHAPTER 3: INCOME DISTRIBUTION AND POVERTY

SECTION 3A: HOUSEHOLD AND FAMILY INCOME

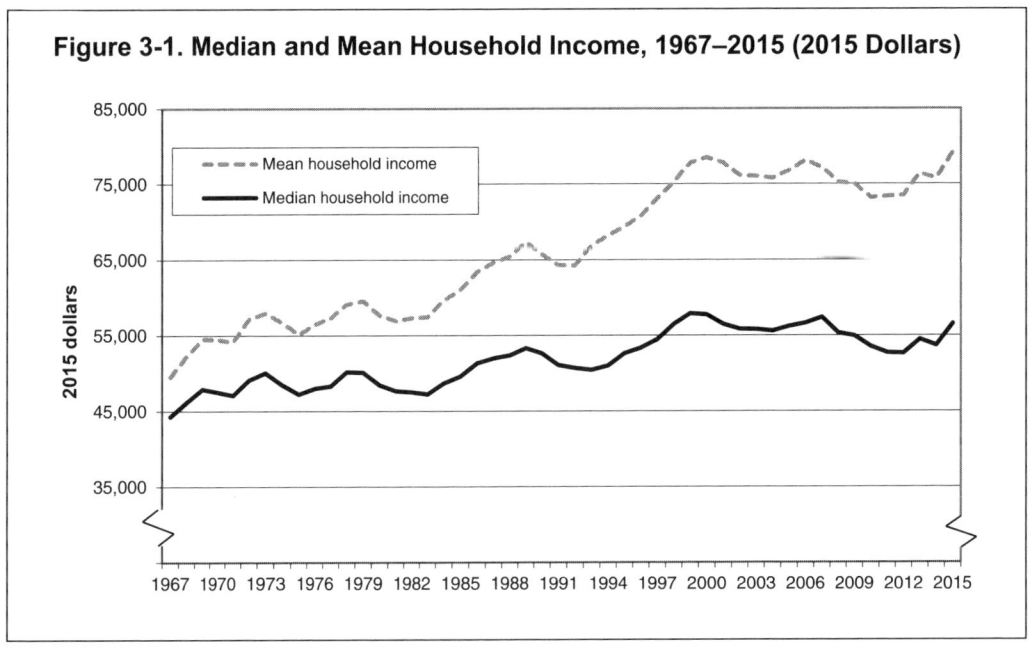

Figure 3-1. Median and Mean Household Income, 1967–2015 (2015 Dollars)

- Measured as cash income before taxes, median household income in 2015 was $56,516, an increase of 5.3 percent from 2014. Income was 2.3 percent below the all-time peak in 1999. From 1999 to 2007, real median household income declined 0.8 percent. In contrast, between 1978, before stagflation, and 1999 income <u>rose</u> an average 0.7 percent <u>per year</u>. Median income is the income of the household at the middle of the income distribution. (Table 3-1)

- Hispanic-origin households experienced the largest increase in median household income at 6.3 percent between 2014 and 2015 followed by non-Hispanic Whites at 4.5 percent and Blacks at 4.2 percent. Asian households experienced a 3.9 percent increase in median household incomes. (Table 3-1)

- For family households, married couple households had the highest median income in 2015 ($84,324), followed by households maintained by men with no wife present ($49,772). Those maintained by women with no husband present had the lowest median household income ($20,168). In 2015, the median earnings of men were still substantially higher than the median earnings of women. In 2015, women earned approximately 80 percent of what men earned. (Table 3-1 and 3-2)

Table 3-1. Median and Mean Household Income and Median Earnings

(2015 dollars, except as noted.)

Year	Number of households (thousands)	Average size of household (number of people)	Median household income — All races	White Total	White Not Hispanic	Black	Asian [1]	Hispanic (any race)	Mean household income, all races	Median earnings of year-round, full-time workers — Male workers	Female workers	Ratio, female to male
1965	...	...	...	...	...	...	...	...	...	43 380	25 089	0.578
1966	...	...	...	...	...	...	...	...	...	44 466	25 740	0.579
1967	60 813	...	44 284	46 181	...	26 813	...	...	49 529	45 189	26 026	0.576
1968	62 214	...	46 192	48 095	...	28 361	...	...	52 259	46 616	27 251	0.585
1969	63 401	...	47 910	50 000	...	30 223	...	...	54 506	49 503	28 995	0.586
1970	64 778	...	47 538	49 514	...	30 137	...	...	54 434	49 987	29 609	0.592
1971	66 676	...	47 076	49 240	...	29 086	...	...	54 141	50 220	29 727	0.592
1972	68 251	...	49 092	51 502	52 236	30 062	...	38 866	57 136	53 350	30 644	0.574
1973	69 859	...	50 083	52 489	52 951	30 897	...	38 801	57 921	54 638	30 911	0.566
1974	71 163	...	48 497	50 719	51 152	30 163	...	38 574	56 713	52 677	31 072	0.590
1975	72 867	2.89	47 227	49 388	49 761	29 649	...	35 480	55 148	51 766	30 894	0.597
1976	74 142	2.86	48 011	50 293	51 318	29 906	...	36 214	56 473	52 450	31 457	0.600
1977	76 030	2.81	48 315	50 807	51 814	29 981	...	37 902	57 314	53 647	31 377	0.585
1978	77 330	2.78	50 184	52 170	53 153	31 352	...	39 321	59 066	53 509	32 118	0.600
1979	80 776	2.76	50 089	52 517	53 256	30 833	...	39 685	59 500	53 186	32 044	0.602
1980	82 368	2.73	48 462	51 127	52 033	29 455	...	37 355	57 637	52 466	31 718	0.605
1981	83 527	2.72	47 658	50 354	51 081	28 256	...	38 228	56 935	51 700	31 125	0.602
1982	83 918	2.73	47 530	49 759	50 594	28 201	...	35 765	57 281	51 027	32 195	0.631
1983	85 407	2.71	47 229	49 529	...	28 107	...	35 969	57 441	50 899	32 742	0.643
1984	86 789	2.69	48 664	51 338	52 404	29 246	...	36 890	59 625	52 114	33 482	0.642
1985	88 458	2.67	49 574	52 281	53 457	31 105	...	36 659	61 009	52 472	34 113	0.650
1986	89 479	2.66	51 329	53 964	55 190	31 090	...	37 835	63 414	53 384	34 724	0.650
1987	91 124	2.64	51 973	54 759	56 264	31 254	64 267	38 561	64 634	53 209	35 027	0.658
1988	92 830	2.62	52 372	55 365	56 891	31 562	62 071	39 164	65 438	52 597	35 675	0.678
1989	93 347	2.63	53 306	56 072	57 278	33 347	66 576	40 425	67 347	52 408	36 215	0.691
1990	94 312	2.63	52 623	54 887	56 142	32 822	67 574	39 244	65 734	50 929	36 188	0.711
1991	95 669	2.62	51 086	53 533	54 812	31 892	61 809	38 478	64 307	51 434	36 026	0.700
1992	96 426	2.66	50 667	53 268	55 056	31 018	62 516	37 372	64 235	50 991	36 538	0.717
1993	97 107	2.67	50 421	53 195	55 153	31 525	61 889	36 936	66 862	50 156	36 263	0.723
1994	98 990	2.65	51 006	53 795	55 531	33 242	63 998	37 026	68 189	49 976	36 780	0.736
1995	99 627	2.65	52 604	55 213	57 392	34 569	62 697	35 289	69 372	49 706	36 705	0.738
1996	101 018	2.64	53 345	55 854	58 298	35 294	65 045	37 434	70 827	50 408	37 478	0.743
1997	102 528	2.62	54 443	57 337	59 698	36 854	66 572	39 176	73 109	51 858	38 295	0.738
1998	103 874	2.61	56 445	59 387	61 604	36 799	67 698	41 123	75 272	52 623	38 982	0.741
1999	106 434	2.60	57 843	60 158	62 762	39 669	72 431	43 700	77 799	53 229	38 896	0.731
2000	108 209	2.58	57 724	60 371	62 718	40 783	76 649	45 596	78 544	53 464	40 035	0.749
2001	109 297	2.58	56 466	59 527	61 918	39 407	71 720	44 882	77 834	53 669	40 677	0.758
2002	111 278	2.57	55 807	...	...	...	...	43 561	76 129	53 304	40 754	0.765
2003	112 000	2.57	55 759	...	...	...	...	42 474	76 031	53 422	40 744	0.763
2004	113 343	2.57	55 565	...	...	...	...	42 953	75 784	52 223	40 252	0.771
2005	114 384	2.57	56 160	...	...	...	...	43 602	76 790	51 143	40 315	0.788
2006	116 011	2.56	56 598	...	...	...	...	44 363	78 167	52 790	41 084	0.778
2007	116 783	2.56	57 357	...	...	...	...	44 165	77 198	52 780	41 296	0.782
2008	117 181	2.57	55 313	...	...	...	...	41 689	75 238	52 537	40 342	0.768
2009	117 538	2.59	54 925	...	...	...	...	41 973	75 007	54 249	41 085	0.757
2010	119 927	2.56	53 507	...	...	...	...	40 862	73 178	54 457	41 739	0.766
2011	121 084	2.55	52 690	...	...	...	...	40 658	73 346	52 966	40 722	0.769
2012	122 459	2.54	52 605	...	...	...	...	40 219	73 493	52 261	41 265	0.790
2013	123 931	2.53	54 462	...	...	...	...	40 336	76 426	52 259	41 365	0.792
2014	124 587	2.54	53 657	...	...	...	...	42 491	75 738	51 456	40 797	0.793
2015	125 819	2.53	56 516	...	...	...	...	45 148	79 263	51 212	40 742	0.796
By race												
Race alone												
2002	...	...	...	59 330	61 717	38 196	69 252	...	...	...	...	...
2003	...	...	...	58 736	61 498	38 159	71 695	...	...	...	...	...
2004	...	...	...	58 478	61 301	37 719	72 072	...	...	...	...	...
2005	...	...	...	58 861	61 564	37 408	74 062	...	...	...	...	...
2006	...	...	...	59 501	61 555	37 538	75 429	...	...	...	...	...
2007	...	...	...	59 506	62 709	38 726	75 478	...	...	...	...	...
2008	...	...	...	57 522	61 060	37 626	72 174	...	...	...	...	...
2009	...	...	...	57 225	60 094	35 954	72 240	...	...	...	...	...
2010	...	...	...	56 149	59 136	34 882	69 776	...	...	...	...	...
2011	...	...	...	54 964	58 330	33 926	68 559	...	...	...	...	...
2012	...	...	...	55 378	58 784	34 358	70 773	...	...	...	...	...
2013	...	...	...	57 674	61 316	35 902	73 568	...	...	...	...	...
2014	...	...	...	56 866	60 256	35 398	74 297	...	...	...	...	...
2015	...	...	...	60 109	62 950	36 898	77 166	...	...	...	...	...
Race alone or in combination												
2002	...	...	...	...	...	38 395	68 803	...	...	...	...	...
2003	...	...	...	...	...	38 216	71 133	...	...	...	...	...
2004	...	...	...	...	...	37 895	72 003	...	...	...	...	...
2005	...	...	...	...	...	37 525	74 007	...	...	...	...	...
2006	...	...	...	...	...	37 730	75 032	...	...	...	...	...
2007	...	...	...	...	...	38 926	75 219	...	...	...	...	...
2008	...	...	...	...	...	37 765	72 097	...	...	...	...	...
2009	...	...	...	...	...	36 137	71 803	...	...	...	...	...
2010	...	...	...	...	...	34 917	68 981	...	...	...	...	...
2011	...	...	...	...	...	34 071	68 418	...	...	...	...	...
2012	...	...	...	...	...	34 768	70 304	...	...	...	...	...
2013	...	...	...	...	...	36 349	73 658	...	...	...	...	...
2014	...	...	...	...	...	35 653	74 829	...	...	...	...	...
2015	...	...	...	...	...	37 211	76 761	...	...	...	...	...

[1] For 1987 through 2001, Asian and Pacific Islander.
. . . = Not available.

Table 3-2. Median Family Income by Type of Family

(2015 dollars, except as noted.)

Year	All families	Married couples			Male householder [1]	Female householder [1]	4-person families	Average size of family (number of people)
		Total	Wife in paid labor force	Wife not in paid labor force				
1947	28 144	28 868	. . .	. . .	27 262	34 126	30 567	3.64
1948	27 400	28 131	. . .	. . .	28 329	31 807	29 816	3.58
1949	27 046	27 812	33 575	26 620	24 557	31 677	29 405	3.54
1950	28 535	29 627	34 416	28 501	26 781	31 959	31 596	3.54
1951	29 553	30 573	36 900	28 956	27 505	31 678	32 844	3.54
1952	30 438	31 776	38 341	29 828	28 286	31 889	34 217	3.53
1953	32 970	33 973	42 009	31 999	31 968	31 695	. . .	3.59
1954	32 101	33 379	41 106	31 207	30 922	32 887	. . .	3.59
1955	34 186	35 586	43 502	33 474	32 421	33 168	38 062	3.58
1956	36 420	37 891	45 388	35 391	31 749	34 633	40 527	3.60
1957	36 635	38 044	45 303	35 654	33 795	33 890	40 486	3.64
1958	36 522	38 158	44 613	35 775	30 584	33 065	40 815	3.65
1959	00 573	40 317	47 744	37 861	32 848	33 840	43 222	3.67
1960	39 374	41 146	48 342	38 673	34 049	34 214	44 103	3.70
1961	39 779	41 874	49 858	38 788	35 160	34 811	44 649	3.67
1962	40 905	43 013	51 241	39 586	39 222	34 465	46 399	3.68
1963	42 333	44 663	52 765	40 910	38 681	35 393	48 355	3.70
1964	43 903	46 329	54 603	42 359	38 710	33 813	50 045	3.70
1965	45 793	47 820	56 587	43 390	40 468	32 209	51 341	3.69
1966	48 210	50 169	59 181	45 624	41 170	30 965	53 389	3.67
1967	49 238	52 391	61 795	47 240	42 293	29 961	55 824	3.63
1968	51 555	54 613	63 823	49 065	43 725	30 432	58 734	3.60
1969	53 934	57 181	66 490	50 766	47 685	28 863	60 738	3.58
1970	53 767	57 303	66 894	50 699	49 108	28 184	60 851	3.57
1971	53 692	57 372	67 098	50 867	45 532	28 189	60 692	3.53
1972	56 340	60 329	70 436	53 502	52 230	28 338	64 916	3.48
1973	57 482	62 142	72 678	54 462	51 238	29 791	65 395	3.44
1974	55 946	60 373	70 338	53 037	50 552	30 356	64 909	3.42
1975	54 971	59 571	69 067	51 096	52 070	29 555	63 501	3.39
1976	56 674	61 392	70 970	52 783	48 725	29 315	65 605	3.37
1977	57 056	62 783	72 235	53 684	51 742	28 168	66 728	3.33
1978	58 834	64 504	73 739	53 884	53 251	28 705	68 132	3.31
1979	59 669	65 281	75 736	53 939	51 203	27 828	68 580	3.29
1980	57 594	63 397	73 637	51 975	47 995	26 690	66 659	3.27
1981	56 002	62 699	73 160	50 842	49 751	27 092	65 723	3.25
1982	55 280	61 381	71 579	50 246	47 512	27 416	65 155	3.26
1983	55 649	61 775	72 690	49 559	49 457	28 513	66 072	3.24
1984	57 453	64 363	75 352	51 256	50 698	30 098	67 590	3.23
1985	58 282	65 353	76 556	51 602	47 538	28 473	68 877	3.21
1986	60 802	67 710	79 147	53 258	51 522	27 674	71 654	3.19
1987	61 833	69 638	81 362	53 188	50 329	27 322	74 044	3.17
1988	61 996	70 081	82 253	52 423	51 666	27 423	75 208	3.16
1989	63 165	71 167	83 572	53 074	51 412	28 134	75 258	3.17
1990	62 203	70 194	82 303	53 250	51 106	27 651	72 932	3.18
1991	61 014	69 598	81 777	51 059	48 132	27 075	73 097	3.17
1992	60 555	69 359	82 414	49 960	45 658	26 697	73 268	3.19
1993	59 718	69 487	82 734	48 826	42 765	27 752	72 970	3.20
1994	61 381	71 158	84 374	49 343	43 922	27 570	74 407	3.19
1995	62 764	72 734	86 274	50 035	46 918	26 739	76 791	3.20
1996	63 651	74 797	87 849	50 782	47 550	26 652	77 522	3.19
1997	65 645	75 990	89 361	53 065	48 548	25 667	78 581	3.18
1998	67 921	78 737	92 646	54 004	51 854	23 248	81 471	3.18
1999	69 485	80 399	94 596	54 756	53 132	23 111	85 029	3.15
2000	69 822	81 337	95 287	55 027	51 923	21 752	86 252	3.14
2001	68 819	80 771	94 827	54 596	48 984	21 503	84 711	3.15
2002	68 085	80 535	95 918	52 832	49 719	20 760	82 646	3.13
2003	67 887	80 260	96 870	52 993	49 011	20 794	83 884	3.13
2004	67 834	79 836	96 434	52 970	50 644	19 681	82 844	3.13
2005	68 201	79 988	95 582	53 956	49 895	19 679	85 335	3.13
2006	68 661	81 588	97 322	53 790	49 190	20 383	86 304	3.13
2007	70 137	82 979	98 807	54 104	50 707	20 983	86 507	3.15
2008	67 726	80 079	95 357	53 394	47 965	19 120	84 182	3.15
2009	66 379	79 126	94 946	52 638	45 846	17 672	82 196	3.16
2010	65 483	78 534	95 010	52 978	46 969	19 081	81 261	3.14
2011	64 259	77 765	93 813	53 130	45 389	17 488	79 641	3.13
2012	64 252	77 976	94 745	52 525	43 727	17 689	82 273	3.12
2013	66 619	79 992	100 098	55 182	48 018	16 524	83 036	3.11
2014	66 709	80 907	97 746	54 842	47 652	17 745	83 509	3.14
2015	70 697	84 324	95 952	56 010	49 772	20 168	88 142	3.14

[1]No spouse present.
. . . = Not available.

Table 3-3. Shares of Aggregate Income Received by Each Fifth and Top 5 Percent of Households

Year	Money income							Equivalence-adjusted income						
	Share of aggregate income (percent)						Gini coefficient	Share of aggregate income (percent)						Gini coefficient
	Lowest fifth	Second fifth	Third fifth	Fourth fifth	Highest fifth	Top 5 percent		Lowest fifth	Second fifth	Third fifth	Fourth fifth	Highest fifth	Top 5 percent	
1967	4.0	10.8	17.3	24.2	43.6	17.2	0.397	5.6	12.0	17.1	23.2	42.1	. . .	0.362
1968	4.2	11.1	17.6	24.5	42.6	16.3	0.386	5.8	12.3	17.4	23.4	41.1	. . .	0.351
1969	4.1	10.9	17.5	24.5	43.0	16.6	0.391	5.8	12.2	17.3	23.4	41.3	. . .	0.353
1970	4.1	10.8	17.4	24.5	43.3	16.6	0.394	5.7	12.1	17.3	23.4	41.5	. . .	0.357
1971	4.1	10.6	17.3	24.5	43.5	16.7	0.396	5.7	12.0	17.2	23.4	41.7	. . .	0.359
1972	4.1	10.4	17.0	24.5	43.9	17.0	0.401	5.6	11.9	17.2	23.4	41.9	. . .	0.362
1973	4.2	10.4	17.0	24.5	43.9	16.9	0.400	5.6	12.0	17.2	23.5	41.7	. . .	0.360
1974	4.3	10.6	17.0	24.6	43.5	16.5	0.395	5.8	12.1	17.3	23.6	41.2	. . .	0.354
1975	4.3	10.4	17.0	24.7	43.6	16.5	0.397	5.6	11.9	17.3	23.6	41.6	. . .	0.359
1976	4.3	10.3	17.0	24.7	43.7	16.6	0.398	5.6	11.8	17.4	23.8	41.5	. . .	0.359
1977	4.2	10.2	16.9	24.7	44.0	16.8	0.402	5.5	11.7	17.3	23.7	41.7	. . .	0.362
1978	4.2	10.2	16.8	24.7	44.1	16.8	0.402	5.4	11.8	17.3	23.7	41.8	. . .	0.363
1979	4.1	10.2	16.8	24.6	44.2	16.9	0.404	5.3	11.7	17.2	23.8	41.9	. . .	0.366
1980	4.2	10.2	16.8	24.7	44.1	16.5	0.403	5.2	11.6	17.3	24.0	41.9	. . .	0.367
1981	4.1	10.1	16.7	24.8	44.3	16.5	0.406	5.0	11.4	17.2	24.0	42.4	. . .	0.373
1982	4.0	10.0	16.5	24.5	45.0	17.0	0.412	4.7	11.1	17.0	23.9	43.2	. . .	0.384
1983	4.0	9.9	16.4	24.6	45.1	17.0	0.414	4.6	11.0	16.9	24.0	43.5	. . .	0.389
1984	4.0	9.9	16.3	24.6	45.2	17.1	0.415	4.6	11.0	16.8	24.0	43.6	. . .	0.389
1985	3.9	9.8	16.2	24.4	45.6	17.6	0.419	4.6	10.9	16.7	23.7	44.1	. . .	0.394
1986	3.8	9.7	16.2	24.3	46.1	18.0	0.425	4.5	10.8	16.6	23.8	44.3	. . .	0.397
1987	3.8	9.6	16.1	24.3	46.2	18.2	0.426	4.4	10.8	16.7	23.8	44.4	. . .	0.399
1988	3.8	9.6	16.0	24.2	46.3	18.3	0.426	4.4	10.7	16.5	23.7	44.7	. . .	0.402
1989	3.8	9.5	15.8	24.0	46.8	18.9	0.431	4.4	10.5	16.3	23.4	45.4	. . .	0.408
1990	3.8	9.6	15.9	24.0	46.6	18.5	0.428	4.4	10.6	16.3	23.5	45.1	. . .	0.406
1991	3.8	9.6	15.9	24.2	46.5	18.1	0.428	4.3	10.6	16.5	23.7	45.0	. . .	0.406
1992	3.8	9.4	15.8	24.2	46.9	18.6	0.433	4.1	10.3	16.3	23.7	45.5	. . .	0.413
1993	3.6	9.0	15.1	23.5	48.9	21.0	0.454	3.9	9.8	15.6	23.0	47.7	. . .	0.436
1994	3.6	8.9	15.0	23.4	49.1	21.2	0.456	4.0	9.8	15.6	22.8	47.8	. . .	0.436
1995	3.7	9.1	15.2	23.3	48.7	21.0	0.450	4.1	9.9	15.6	22.8	47.6	. . .	0.433
1996	3.6	9.0	15.1	23.3	49.0	21.4	0.455	4.0	9.8	15.5	22.7	47.9	. . .	0.437
1997	3.6	8.9	15.0	23.2	49.4	21.7	0.459	4.0	9.8	15.4	22.6	48.3	. . .	0.440
1998	3.6	9.0	15.0	23.2	49.2	21.4	0.456	4.0	9.8	15.4	22.7	48.1	. . .	0.439
1999	3.6	8.9	14.9	23.2	49.4	21.5	0.458	4.0	9.7	15.3	22.6	48.4	. . .	0.441
2000	3.6	8.9	14.8	23.0	49.8	22.1	0.462	4.1	9.8	15.2	22.3	48.6	. . .	0.442
2001	3.5	8.7	14.6	23.0	50.1	22.4	0.466	4.0	9.6	15.2	22.4	48.8	. . .	0.446
2002	3.5	8.8	14.8	23.3	49.7	21.7	0.462	4.0	9.6	15.2	22.7	48.4	. . .	0.443
2003	3.4	8.7	14.8	23.4	49.8	21.4	0.464	3.9	9.5	15.2	22.8	48.6	. . .	0.445
2004	3.4	8.7	14.7	23.2	50.1	21.8	0.466	3.8	9.6	15.2	22.7	48.7	. . .	0.447
2005	3.4	8.6	14.6	23.0	50.4	22.2	0.469	3.8	9.5	15.1	22.6	49.1	. . .	0.450
2006	3.4	8.6	14.5	22.9	50.5	22.3	0.470	3.8	9.4	14.9	22.5	49.3	. . .	0.452
2007	3.4	8.7	14.8	23.4	49.7	21.2	0.463	3.8	9.5	15.3	22.9	48.5	. . .	0.444
2008	3.4	8.6	14.7	23.3	50.0	21.5	0.466	3.7	9.4	15.1	22.8	48.9	21.4	0.450
2009	3.4	8.6	14.6	23.2	50.3	21.7	0.468	3.6	9.3	15.0	22.9	49.4	21.7	0.456
2010	3.3	8.5	14.6	23.4	50.3	21.3	0.470	3.4	9.2	15.0	23.1	49.2	21.0	0.456
2011	3.2	8.4	14.3	23.0	51.1	22.3	0.477	3.4	9.0	14.8	22.8	50.0	22.1	0.463
2012	3.2	8.3	14.4	23.0	51.0	22.3	0.477	3.4	9.0	14.8	22.9	49.9	22.1	0.463
2013	3.1	8.2	14.3	23.0	51.4	22.2	0.482	3.5	8.8	14.7	22.8	50.3	22.1	0.500
2014	3.1	8.2	14.3	23.2	51.2	21.9	0.480	3.3	9.0	14.8	22.9	50.0	21.8	0.500
2015	3.1	8.2	14.3	23.2	51.1	22.1	0.479	3.4	9.0	14.8	22.9	49.8	21.8	0.500

. . . = Not available.

Table 3-4. Shares of Aggregate Income Received by Each Fifth and Top 5 Percent of Families

Year	Number of families (thousands)	Share of aggregate income (percent)						Mean family income (2014 dollars)						Gini coefficient
		Lowest fifth	Second fifth	Third fifth	Fourth fifth	Highest fifth	Top 5 percent	Lowest fifth	Second fifth	Third fifth	Fourth fifth	Highest fifth	Top 5 percent	
1947	37 237	5.0	11.9	17.0	23.1	43.0	17.5	...	...	...	...	...	...	0.376
1948	38 624	4.9	12.1	17.3	23.2	42.4	17.1	...	...	...	...	...	...	0.371
1949	39 303	4.5	11.9	17.3	23.5	42.7	16.9	...	...	...	...	...	...	0.378
1950	39 929	4.5	12.0	17.4	23.4	42.7	17.3	...	...	...	...	...	...	0.379
1951	40 578	5.0	12.4	17.6	23.4	41.6	16.8	...	...	...	...	...	...	0.363
1952	40 832	4.9	12.3	17.4	23.4	41.9	17.4	...	...	...	...	...	...	0.368
1953	41 202	4.7	12.5	18.0	23.9	40.9	15.7	...	...	...	...	...	...	0.359
1954	41 951	4.5	12.1	17.7	23.9	41.8	16.3	...	...	...	...	...	...	0.371
1955	42 889	4.8	12.3	17.8	23.7	41.3	16.4	...	...	...	...	...	...	0.363
1956	43 497	5.0	12.5	17.9	23.7	41.0	16.1	...	...	...	...	...	...	0.358
1957	43 696	5.1	12.7	18.1	23.8	40.4	15.6	...	...	...	...	...	...	0.351
1958	44 232	5.0	12.5	18.0	23.9	40.6	15.4	...	...	...	...	...	...	0.354
1959	45 111	4.9	12.3	17.9	23.8	41.1	15.9	...	...	...	...	...	...	0.361
1960	45 539	4.8	12.2	17.8	24.0	41.3	15.0	...	...	...	...	...	...	0.364
1961	46 418	4.7	11.9	17.5	23.8	42.2	16.6	...	...	...	...	...	...	0.374
1962	47 059	5.0	12.1	17.6	24.0	41.3	15.7	...	...	...	...	...	...	0.362
1963	47 540	5.0	12.1	17.7	24.0	41.2	15.8	...	...	...	...	...	...	0.362
1964	47 956	5.1	12.0	17.7	24.0	41.2	15.9	...	...	...	...	...	...	0.361
1965	48 509	5.2	12.2	17.8	23.9	40.9	15.5	...	...	...	...	...	...	0.356
1966	49 214	5.6	12.4	17.8	23.8	40.5	15.6	14 993	33 284	47 624	63 755	108 809	167 078	0.349
1967	50 111	5.4	12.2	17.5	23.5	41.4	16.4	15 226	34 048	48 940	65 636	115 896	183 367	0.358
1968	50 823	5.6	12.4	17.7	23.7	40.5	15.6	16 412	35 794	51 138	68 391	116 862	180 146	0.348
1969	51 586	5.6	12.4	17.7	23.7	40.6	15.6	16 933	37 396	53 512	71 685	122 769	188 566	0.349
1970	52 227	5.4	12.2	17.6	23.8	40.9	15.6	16 677	36 876	53 318	71 922	123 679	188 329	0.353
1971	53 296	5.5	12.0	17.6	23.8	41.1	15.7	16 691	36 334	53 161	71 995	124 004	189 074	0.355
1972	54 373	5.5	11.9	17.5	23.9	41.4	15.9	17 420	38 010	55 830	76 243	132 230	202 716	0.359
1973	55 053	5.5	11.9	17.5	24.0	41.1	15.5	17 876	38 720	56 892	77 750	133 398	201 319	0.356
1974	55 698	5.7	12.0	17.6	24.1	40.6	14.8	18 191	38 401	56 064	76 811	129 427	188 782	0.355
1975	56 245	5.6	11.9	17.7	24.2	40.7	14.9	17 478	36 949	54 940	75 223	126 765	185 955	0.357
1976	56 710	5.6	11.9	17.7	24.2	40.7	14.9	17 901	37 883	56 511	77 212	129 954	190 200	0.358
1977	57 215	5.5	11.7	17.6	24.3	40.9	14.9	17 824	38 101	57 303	79 047	133 168	194 138	0.363
1978	57 804	5.4	11.7	17.6	24.2	41.1	15.1	18 076	39 201	58 863	81 100	137 618	201 664	0.363
1979	59 550	5.4	11.6	17.5	24.1	41.4	15.3	18 251	39 460	59 509	81 929	140 526	208 011	0.365
1980	60 309	5.3	11.6	17.6	24.4	41.1	14.6	17 543	38 190	57 692	80 041	134 764	191 577	0.365
1981	61 019	5.3	11.4	17.5	24.6	41.2	14.4	16 998	36 964	56 535	79 374	133 181	186 098	0.369
1982	61 393	5.0	11.3	17.2	24.4	42.2	15.3	16 035	36 382	55 554	78 809	136 177	194 834	0.380
1983	62 015	4.9	11.2	17.2	24.5	42.4	15.3	15 800	36 354	55 933	79 716	138 220	199 286	0.382
1984	62 706	4.8	11.1	17.1	24.5	42.5	15.4	16 328	37 385	57 680	82 482	143 351	207 260	0.383
1985	63 558	4.8	11.0	16.9	24.3	43.1	16.1	16 517	37 901	58 517	83 879	149 067	222 766	0.389
1986	64 491	4.7	10.9	16.9	24.1	43.4	16.5	16 984	39 215	60 753	86 806	156 351	237 430	0.392
1987	65 204	4.6	10.7	16.8	24.0	43.8	17.2	16 965	39 708	61 659	88 246	161 272	252 462	0.393
1988	65 837	4.6	10.7	16.7	24.0	44.0	17.2	17 111	39 847	62 008	89 053	163 397	255 302	0.395
1989	66 090	4.6	10.6	16.5	23.7	44.6	17.9	17 453	40 604	63 080	90 754	170 881	273 737	0.401
1990	66 322	4.6	10.8	16.6	23.8	44.3	17.4	17 281	40 307	62 077	89 273	165 911	260 321	0.396
1991	67 173	4.5	10.7	16.6	24.1	44.2	17.1	16 507	39 181	60 795	88 174	161 996	250 662	0.397
1992	68 216	4.3	10.5	16.5	24.0	44.7	17.6	15 854	38 238	60 409	87 808	163 402	257 265	0.404
1993	68 506	4.1	9.9	15.7	23.3	47.0	20.3	15 718	37 750	59 822	88 679	179 173	309 247	0.429
1994	69 313	4.2	10.0	15.7	23.3	46.9	20.1	16 421	38 851	61 352	90 690	182 766	313 551	0.426
1995	69 597	4.4	10.1	15.8	23.2	46.5	20.0	17 390	40 067	62 732	91 785	184 402	316 251	0.421
1996	70 241	4.2	10.0	15.8	23.1	46.8	20.3	17 116	40 352	63 829	93 266	188 821	326 690	0.425
1997	70 884	4.2	9.9	15.7	23.0	47.2	20.7	17 739	41 565	65 580	96 164	197 565	345 771	0.429
1998	71 551	4.2	9.9	15.7	23.0	47.3	20.7	18 183	42 796	67 734	99 332	204 450	357 845	0.430
1999	73 206	4.3	9.9	15.6	23.0	47.2	20.3	18 915	43 968	69 399	102 431	209 934	361 964	0.429
2000	73 778	4.3	9.8	15.4	22.7	47.7	21.1	19 414	44 388	69 762	102 816	215 717	382 254	0.433
2001	74 340	4.2	9.7	15.4	22.9	47.7	21.0	18 749	43 413	68 916	102 489	213 472	374 827	0.435
2002	75 616	4.2	9.7	15.5	23.0	47.6	20.8	18 445	42 795	68 256	101 517	209 625	366 868	0.434
2003	76 232	4.1	9.6	15.5	23.2	47.6	20.5	17 855	42 344	68 242	102 606	210 227	362 303	0.436
2004	76 866	4.0	9.6	15.4	23.0	47.9	20.9	17 796	42 359	67 985	101 571	211 391	368 276	0.438
2005	77 418	4.0	9.6	15.3	22.9	48.1	21.1	17 902	42 596	68 162	101 946	213 713	374 150	0.440
2006	78 454	4.0	9.5	15.1	22.9	48.5	21.5	18 246	43 174	68 674	103 793	220 033	389 487	0.444
2007	77 908	4.1	9.7	15.6	23.3	47.3	20.1	18 347	43 737	70 158	104 912	212 984	361 523	0.432
2008	78 874	4.0	9.6	15.5	23.1	47.8	20.5	17 490	41 922	67 715	101 338	209 362	359 486	0.438
2009	78 867	3.9	9.4	15.3	23.2	48.2	20.7	16 870	40 876	66 103	100 370	209 084	358 639	0.443
2010	79 559	3.8	9.4	15.4	23.5	47.9	20.0	16 204	40 080	65 326	99 667	203 186	339 739	0.440
2011	80 529	3.8	9.3	15.1	23.0	48.9	21.3	16 087	39 534	64 246	98 142	208 356	362 675	0.450
2012	80 944	3.8	9.2	15.1	23.0	48.9	21.3	16 018	39 373	64 409	98 446	208 865	363 306	0.451
2013	82 316	3.6	9.1	15.0	22.9	49.4	21.2	16 086	40 751	66 767	101 903	220 020	377 266	0.455
2014	81 730	3.6	9.2	15.1	23.2	48.9	20.8	16 110	40 681	66 899	103 115	217 021	370 085	0.452
2015	82 199	3.7	9.2	15.2	23.2	48.6	20.9	17 367	42 700	70 500	107 517	225 279	386 829	0.448

. . . = Not available.

SECTION 3B: POVERTY

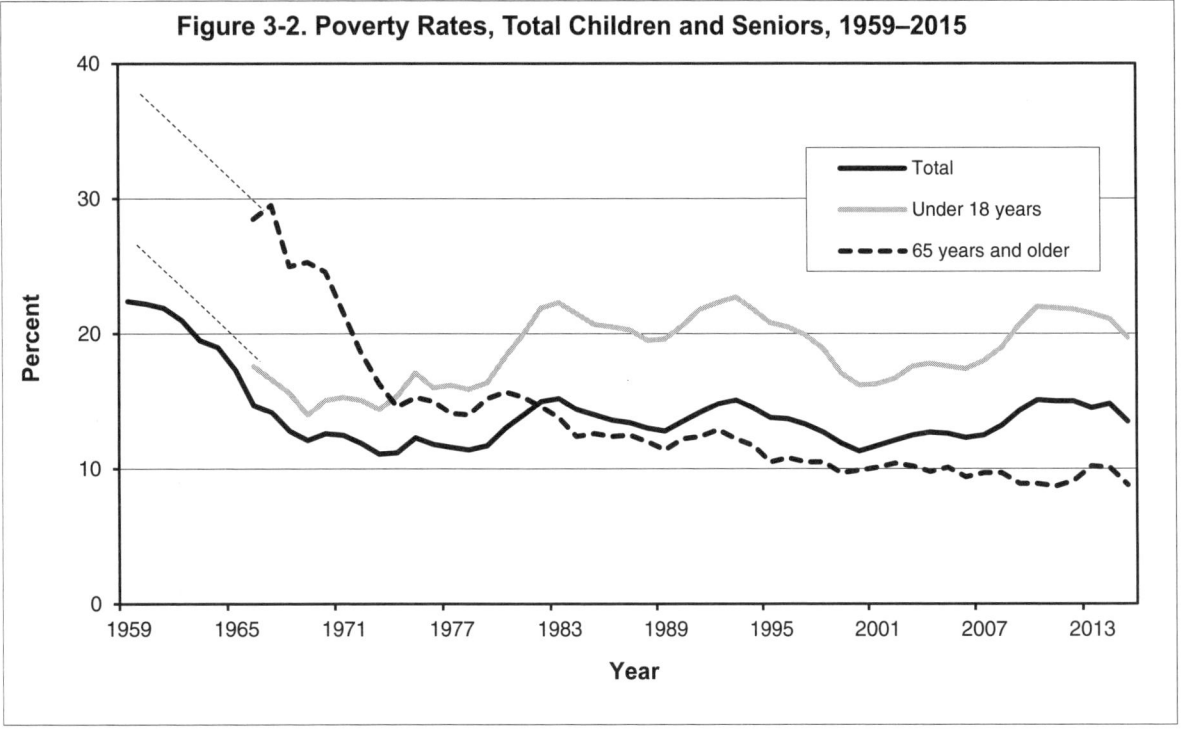

- In 2015, the official poverty rate was 13.7 percent. Children had the highest poverty rate among all age groups at 20.1 percent. (Table 3-10)

- There were 43.1 million people living in poverty in 2015—down 3.5 million from just the year before. (Table 3-6)

- Poverty thresholds vary by both family size and age. In 2015, the poverty threshold for a family of three was $18,871 while the poverty threshold for a family of six was $32,452. These levels are adjusted yearly using the Consumer Price Index for all urban consumers. (Table 3-5)

- Between 1959 and 1974, ad hoc legislative changes raised Social Security benefits by a cumulative 104 percent—exceeding the 69 percent increase in consumer prices—and since then, each year's benefits have been indexed to the rate of change in the Consumer Price Index, Urban Wage Earners and Clerical Workers (CPI-W). As a result, since the early 1980s, officially measured senior poverty has been consistently lower than the population average. (Table 3-7 and Table 3-8)

- For workers who had full-time jobs, the poverty rate fell from 2.9 percent in 2014 to 2.3 percent in 2015. (Table 3-9)

Table 3-5. Weighted Average Poverty Thresholds by Family Size

(Dollars.)

Year	Unrelated individuals			Families of 2 people			Families, all ages							CPI-U, all items (1982–1984 = 100)
	All ages	Under 65 years	65 years and older	All ages	House-holder under 65 years	House-holder 65 years and older	3 people	4 people	5 people	6 people	7 people	8 people	9 people or more	
1959	1 467	1 503	1 397	1 894	1 952	1 761	2 324	2 973	3 506	3 944	. . .	. . .	. . .	29.2
1960	1 490	1 526	1 418	1 924	1 982	1 788	2 359	3 022	3 560	4 002	. . .	. . .	. . .	29.6
1961	1 506	1 545	1 433	1 942	2 005	1 808	2 383	3 054	3 597	4 041	. . .	. . .	. . .	29.9
1962	1 519	1 562	1 451	1 962	2 027	1 828	2 412	3 089	3 639	4 088	. . .	. . .	. . .	30.3
1963	1 539	1 581	1 470	1 988	2 052	1 850	2 442	3 128	3 685	4 135	. . .	. . .	. . .	30.6
1964	1 558	1 601	1 488	2 015	2 079	1 875	2 473	3 169	3 732	4 193	. . .	. . .	. . .	31.0
1965	1 582	1 626	1 512	2 048	2 114	1 906	2 514	3 223	3 797	4 264	. . .	. . .	. . .	31.5
1966	1 628	1 674	1 556	2 107	2 175	1 961	2 588	3 317	3 908	4 388	. . .	. . .	. . .	32.5
1967	1 675	1 722	1 600	2 168	2 238	2 017	2 661	3 410	4 019	4 516	. . .	. . .	. . .	33.4
1968	1 748	1 707	1 667	2 262	2 333	2 102	2 774	3 553	4 188	4 706	. . .	. . .	. . .	34.8
1969	1 840	1 893	1 757	2 383	2 458	2 215	2 924	3 743	4 415	4 958	. . .	. . .	. . .	36.7
1970	1 954	2 010	1 861	2 525	2 604	2 348	3 099	3 968	4 680	5 260	. . .	. . .	. . .	38.8
1971	2 040	2 098	1 940	2 633	2 716	2 448	3 229	4 137	4 880	5 489	. . .	. . .	. . .	40.5
1972	2 109	2 168	2 005	2 724	2 808	2 530	3 339	4 275	5 044	5 673	. . .	. . .	. . .	41.8
1973	2 247	2 307	2 130	2 895	2 984	2 688	3 548	4 540	5 358	6 028	. . .	. . .	. . .	44.4
1974	2 495	2 562	2 364	3 211	3 312	2 982	3 936	5 038	5 950	6 699	. . .	. . .	. . .	49.3
1975	2 724	2 797	2 581	3 506	3 617	3 257	4 293	5 500	6 499	7 316	. . .	. . .	. . .	53.8
1976	2 884	2 959	2 730	3 711	3 826	3 445	4 540	5 815	6 876	7 760	. . .	. . .	. . .	56.9
1977	3 075	3 152	2 906	3 951	4 072	3 666	4 833	6 191	7 320	8 261	. . .	. . .	. . .	60.6
1978	3 311	3 392	3 127	4 249	4 383	3 944	5 201	6 662	7 880	8 891	. . .	. . .	. . .	65.2
1979	3 689	3 778	3 479	4 725	4 878	4 390	5 784	7 412	8 775	9 914	. . .	. . .	. . .	72.6
1980	4 190	4 290	3 949	5 363	5 537	4 983	6 565	8 414	9 966	11 269	12 761	14 199	16 896	82.4
1981	4 620	4 729	4 359	5 917	6 111	5 498	7 250	9 287	11 007	12 449	14 110	15 655	18 572	90.9
1982	4 901	5 019	4 626	6 281	6 487	5 836	7 693	9 862	11 684	13 207	15 036	16 719	19 698	96.5
1983	5 061	5 180	4 775	6 483	6 697	6 023	7 938	10 178	12 049	13 630	15 500	17 170	20 310	99.6
1984	5 278	5 400	4 979	6 762	6 983	6 282	8 277	10 609	12 566	14 207	16 096	17 961	21 247	103.9
1985	5 469	5 593	5 156	6 998	7 231	6 503	8 573	10 989	13 007	14 696	16 656	18 512	22 083	107.6
1986	5 572	5 701	5 255	7 138	7 372	6 630	8 737	11 203	13 259	14 986	17 049	18 791	22 497	109.6
1987	5 778	5 909	5 447	7 397	7 641	6 872	9 056	11 611	13 737	15 509	17 649	19 515	23 105	113.6
1988	6 022	6 155	5 674	7 704	7 958	7 157	9 435	12 092	14 304	16 146	18 232	20 253	24 129	118.3
1989	6 310	6 451	5 947	8 076	8 343	7 501	9 885	12 674	14 990	16 921	19 162	21 328	25 480	124.0
1990	6 652	6 800	6 268	8 509	8 794	7 905	10 419	13 359	15 792	17 839	20 241	22 582	26 848	130.7
1991	6 932	7 086	6 532	8 865	9 165	8 241	10 860	13 924	16 456	18 587	21 058	23 582	27 942	136.2
1992	7 143	7 299	6 729	9 137	9 443	8 487	11 186	14 335	16 952	19 137	21 594	24 053	28 745	140.3
1993	7 363	7 518	6 930	9 414	9 728	8 740	11 522	14 763	17 449	19 718	22 383	24 838	29 529	144.5
1994	7 547	7 710	7 108	9 661	9 976	8 967	11 821	15 141	17 900	20 235	22 923	25 427	30 300	148.2
1995	7 763	7 929	7 309	9 933	10 259	9 219	12 158	15 569	18 408	20 804	23 552	26 237	31 280	152.4
1996	7 995	8 163	7 525	10 233	10 564	9 491	12 516	16 036	18 952	21 389	24 268	27 091	31 971	156.9
1997	8 183	8 350	7 698	10 473	10 805	9 712	12 802	16 400	19 380	21 886	24 802	27 593	32 566	160.5
1998	8 316	8 480	7 818	10 634	10 972	9 862	13 003	16 660	19 680	22 228	25 257	28 166	33 339	163.0
1999	8 499	8 667	7 990	10 864	11 213	10 075	13 289	17 030	20 128	22 730	25 918	28 970	34 436	166.6
2000	8 791	8 959	8 259	11 235	11 589	10 418	13 740	17 604	20 815	23 533	26 750	29 701	35 150	172.2
2001	9 039	9 214	8 494	11 569	11 920	10 715	14 128	18 104	21 405	24 195	27 517	30 627	36 286	177.1
2002	9 183	9 359	8 628	11 756	12 110	10 885	14 348	18 392	21 744	24 576	28 001	30 907	37 062	179.9
2003	9 393	9 573	8 825	12 015	12 384	11 133	14 680	18 810	22 245	25 122	28 544	31 589	37 656	184.0
2004	9 646	9 827	9 060	12 335	12 714	11 430	15 066	19 307	22 830	25 787	29 233	32 641	39 062	188.9
2005	9 973	10 160	9 367	12 755	13 145	11 815	15 577	19 971	23 613	26 683	30 249	33 610	40 288	195.3
2006	10 294	10 488	9 669	13 167	13 569	12 201	16 079	20 614	24 382	27 560	31 205	34 774	41 499	201.6
2007	10 590	10 787	9 944	13 540	13 954	12 550	16 530	21 203	25 080	28 323	32 233	35 816	42 739	207.3
2008	10 991	11 201	10 326	14 051	14 489	13 030	17 163	22 025	26 049	29 456	33 529	37 220	44 346	215.3
2009	10 956	11 161	10 289	13 991	14 439	12 982	17 098	21 954	25 991	29 405	33 372	37 252	44 366	214.5
2010	11 137	11 344	10 458	14 216	14 676	13 194	17 373	22 315	26 442	29 904	34 019	37 953	45 224	218.1
2011	11 484	11 702	10 788	14 657	15 139	13 609	17 916	23 021	27 251	30 847	35 085	39 064	46 572	224.9
2012	11 720	11 945	11 011	14 937	15 450	13 892	18 284	23 492	27 827	31 471	35 743	39 688	47 297	229.6
2013	11 888	12 119	11 173	15 142	15 679	14 095	18 552	23 834	28 265	31 925	36 384	40 484	48 065	233.0
2014	12 071	12 316	11 354	15 379	15 934	14 326	18 850	24 230	28 695	32 473	36 927	40 968	49 021	236.7
2015	12 082	12 331	11 367	15 391	15 952	14 342	18 871	24 257	28 741	32 542	36 998	41 029	49 177	237.0

. . . = Not available.

Table 3-6. Poverty Status of People by Race and Hispanic Origin

(Thousands of people, percent of population.)

Year	Number of people, all races	Below poverty level											
		All races		White		White, not Hispanic		Black		Asian[1]		Hispanic (any race)	
		Number	Poverty rate (percent)	Number	Poverty rate (percent)	Number	Poverty rate (percent)	Number	Poverty rate (percent)	Number	Poverty rate (percent)	Number	Poverty rate (percent)
1959	176 557	39 490	22.4	28 484	18.1	...	...	9 927	55.1	...	...	...	...
1960	179 503	39 851	22.2	28 309	17.8	...	...	...	...	...	...	...	...
1961	181 277	39 628	21.9	27 890	17.4	...	...	...	...	...	...	...	...
1962	184 276	38 625	21.0	26 672	16.4	...	...	...	...	...	...	...	...
1963	187 258	36 436	19.5	25 238	15.3	...	...	...	...	...	...	...	...
1964	189 710	36 055	19.0	24 957	14.9	...	...	...	...	...	...	...	...
1965	191 413	33 185	17.3	22 496	13.3	...	...	...	...	...	...	...	...
1966	193 388	28 510	14.7	19 290	11.3	...	...	8 867	41.8	...	...	...	...
1967	195 672	27 769	14.2	18 983	11.0	...	...	8 486	39.3	...	...	...	...
1968	197 628	25 389	12.8	17 395	10.0	...	...	7 616	34.7	...	...	...	...
1969	199 517	24 147	12.1	16 659	9.5	...	...	7 095	32.2	...	...	...	...
1970	202 183	25 420	12.6	17 484	9.9	...	...	7 548	33.5	...	...	...	...
1971	204 554	25 559	12.5	17 780	9.9	...	...	7 396	32.5	...	...	...	...
1972	206 004	24 460	11.9	16 203	9.0	...	...	7 710	33.3	...	...	2 414	22.8
1973	207 621	22 973	11.1	15 142	8.4	12 864	7.5	7 388	31.4	...	...	2 366	21.9
1974	209 362	23 370	11.2	15 736	8.6	13 217	7.7	7 182	30.3	...	...	2 575	23.0
1975	210 864	25 877	12.3	17 770	9.7	14 883	8.6	7 545	31.3	...	...	2 991	26.9
1976	212 303	24 975	11.8	16 713	9.1	14 025	8.1	7 595	31.1	...	...	2 783	24.7
1977	213 867	24 720	11.6	16 416	8.9	13 802	8.0	7 726	31.3	...	...	2 700	22.4
1978	215 656	24 497	11.4	16 259	8.7	13 755	7.9	7 625	30.6	...	...	2 607	21.6
1979	222 903	26 072	11.7	17 214	9.0	14 419	8.1	8 050	31.0	...	...	2 921	21.8
1980	225 027	29 272	13.0	19 699	10.2	16 365	9.1	8 579	32.5	...	...	3 491	25.7
1981	227 157	31 822	14.0	21 553	11.1	17 987	9.9	9 173	34.2	...	...	3 713	26.5
1982	229 412	34 398	15.0	23 517	12.0	19 362	10.6	9 697	35.6	...	...	4 301	29.9
1983	231 700	35 303	15.2	23 984	12.1	19 538	10.8	9 882	35.7	...	...	4 633	28.0
1984	233 816	33 700	14.4	22 955	11.5	18 300	10.0	9 490	33.8	...	...	4 806	28.4
1985	236 594	33 064	14.0	22 860	11.4	17 839	9.7	8 926	31.3	...	...	5 236	29.0
1986	238 554	32 370	13.6	22 183	11.0	17 244	9.4	8 983	31.1	...	...	5 117	27.3
1987	240 982	32 221	13.4	21 195	10.4	16 029	8.7	9 520	32.4	1 021	16.1	5 422	28.0
1988	243 530	31 745	13.0	20 715	10.1	15 565	8.4	9 356	31.3	1 117	17.3	5 357	26.7
1989	245 992	31 528	12.8	20 785	10.0	15 599	8.3	9 302	30.7	939	14.1	5 430	26.2
1990	248 644	33 585	13.5	22 326	10.7	16 622	8.8	9 837	31.9	858	12.2	6 006	28.1
1991	251 192	35 708	14.2	23 747	11.3	17 741	9.4	10 242	32.7	996	13.8	6 339	28.7
1992	256 549	38 014	14.8	25 259	11.9	18 202	9.6	10 827	33.4	985	12.7	7 592	29.6
1993	259 278	39 265	15.1	26 226	12.2	18 882	9.9	10 877	33.1	1 134	15.3	8 126	30.6
1994	261 616	38 059	14.5	25 379	11.7	18 110	9.4	10 196	30.6	974	14.6	8 416	30.7
1995	263 733	36 425	13.8	24 423	11.2	16 267	8.5	9 872	29.3	1 411	14.6	8 574	30.3
1996	266 218	36 529	13.7	24 650	11.2	16 462	8.6	9 694	28.4	1 454	14.5	8 697	29.4
1997	268 480	35 574	13.3	24 396	11.0	16 491	8.6	9 116	26.5	1 468	14.0	8 308	27.1
1998	271 059	34 476	12.7	23 454	10.5	15 799	8.2	9 091	26.1	1 360	12.5	8 070	25.6
1999	276 208	32 791	11.9	22 169	9.8	14 735	7.7	8 441	23.6	1 285	10.7	7 876	22.7
2000	278 944	31 581	11.3	21 645	9.5	14 366	7.4	7 982	22.5	1 258	9.9	7 747	21.5
2001	281 475	32 907	11.7	22 739	9.9	15 271	7.8	8 136	22.7	1 275	10.2	7 997	21.4
2002	285 317	34 570	12.1	...	...	...	...	...	...	...	...	8 555	21.8
2003	287 699	35 861	12.5	...	...	...	...	...	...	...	...	9 051	22.5
2004	290 617	37 040	12.7	...	...	...	...	...	...	...	...	9 122	21.9
2005	293 135	36 950	12.6	...	...	...	...	...	...	...	...	9 368	21.8
2006	296 450	36 460	12.3	...	...	...	...	...	...	...	...	9 243	20.6
2007	298 699	37 276	12.5	...	...	...	...	...	...	...	...	9 890	21.5
2008	301 041	39 829	13.2	...	...	...	...	...	...	...	...	10 987	23.2
2009	303 820	43 569	14.3	...	...	...	...	...	...	...	...	12 350	25.3
2010	306 130	46 343	15.1	...	...	...	...	...	...	...	...	13 522	26.5
2011	308 456	46 247	15.0	...	...	...	...	...	...	...	...	13 244	25.3
2012	310 648	46 496	15.0	...	...	...	...	...	...	...	...	13 616	25.6
2013	312 965	45 318	14.5	...	...	...	...	...	...	...	...	12 744	23.5
2014	315 804	46 657	14.8	...	...	...	...	...	...	...	...	13 104	23.6
2015	318 454	43 123	13.5	...	...	...	...	...	...	...	...	12 133	21.4
By race													
Race alone													
2002	...	...	...	23 466	10.2	15 567	8.0	8 602	24.1	1 161	10.1	...	...
2003	...	...	...	24 272	10.5	15 902	8.2	8 781	24.4	1 401	11.8	...	...
2004	...	...	...	25 327	10.8	16 908	8.7	9 014	24.7	1 201	9.8	...	...
2005	...	...	...	24 872	10.6	16 227	8.3	9 168	24.9	1 402	11.1	...	...
2006	...	...	...	24 416	10.3	16 013	8.2	9 048	24.3	1 353	10.3	...	...
2007	...	...	...	25 120	10.5	16 032	8.2	9 237	24.5	1 349	10.2	...	...
2008	...	...	...	26 990	11.2	17 024	8.6	9 379	24.7	1 576	11.8	...	...
2009	...	...	...	29 830	12.3	18 530	9.4	9 944	25.8	1 746	12.5	...	...
2010	...	...	...	31 083	13.0	19 251	9.9	10 746	27.4	1 899	12.2	...	...
2011	...	...	...	30 849	12.8	19 171	9.8	10 929	27.6	1 973	12.3	...	...
2012	...	...	...	30 816	12.7	18 940	9.7	10 911	27.2	1 921	11.7	...	...
2013	...	...	...	29 936	12.3	18 796	9.6	11 041	27.1	1 785	10.5	...	...
2014	...	...	...	31 088	12.7	19 653	10.1	10 755	26.2	2 137	12.0	...	...
2015	...	...	...	28 566	11.6	17 786	9.1	10 020	24.1	2 078	11.4	...	...
Race alone or in combination													
2010	...	...	...	...	...	...	...	11 597	27.4	2 064	12.0	...	...
2011	...	...	...	...	...	...	...	11 730	27.5	2 189	12.3	...	...
2012	...	...	...	...	...	...	...	11 809	27.1	2 072	11.4	...	...
2013	...	...	...	...	...	...	...	11 959	27.1	1 974	10.4	...	...
2014	...	...	...	...	...	...	...	11 581	26.0	2 189	12.3	...	...
2015	...	...	...	...	...	...	...	10 797	23.9	2 234	11.2	...	...

[1] For 1987 through 2001, Asian and Pacific Islander.
. . . = Not available.

Table 3-7. Poverty Status of Families by Type of Family

(Thousands of families, percent.)

Year	Married couple families				Families with no spouse present						Unrelated individuals	
	Number of families		Poverty rate (percent)		Male householder			Female householder				
						Poverty rate (percent)			Poverty rate (percent)			
	Total	Total below poverty level	Total	With children under 18 years	Familes below poverty level	Total	With children under 18 years	Familes below poverty level	Total	With children under 18 years	Below poverty level	Poverty rate
1959	39 335	. . .	. . .	. . .	. . .	. . .	. . .	1 916	42.6	59.9	4 928	46.1
1960	39 624	. . .	. . .	. . .	. . .	. . .	. . .	1 955	42.4	56.3	4 926	45.2
1961	40 405	. . .	. . .	. . .	. . .	. . .	. . .	1 954	42.1	56.0	5 119	45.9
1962	40 923	. . .	. . .	. . .	. . .	. . .	. . .	2 034	42.9	59.7	5 002	45.4
1963	41 311	. . .	. . .	. . .	. . .	. . .	. . .	1 972	40.4	55.7	4 938	44.2
1964	41 648	. . .	. . .	. . .	. . .	. . .	. . .	1 822	36.4	49.7	5 143	42.7
1965	42 107	. . .	. . .	. . .	. . .	. . .	. . .	1 910	38.1	52.2	4 827	39.8
1966	42 553	. . .	. . .	. . .	. . .	. . .	. . .	1 721	33.1	47.1	4 701	38.3
1967	43 292	. . .	. . .	. . .	. . .	. . .	. . .	1 774	33.3	44.5	4 998	38.1
1968	43 842	. . .	. . .	. . .	. . .	. . .	. . .	1 755	32.3	44.6	4 694	34.0
1969	44 436	. . .	. . .	. . .	. . .	. . .	. . .	1 827	32.7	44.9	4 972	34.0
1970	44 739	. . .	. . .	. . .	. . .	. . .	. . .	1 952	32.5	43.8	5 090	32.9
1971	45 752	. . .	. . .	. . .	. . .	. . .	. . .	2 100	33.9	44.9	5 154	31.6
1972	46 314	. . .	. . .	. . .	. . .	. . .	. . .	2 158	32.7	44.5	4 883	29.0
1973	46 812	2 482	5.3	. . .	154	10.7	. . .	2 193	32.2	43.2	4 674	25.6
1974	47 069	2 474	5.3	6.0	125	8.9	15.4	2 324	32.1	43.7	4 553	24.1
1975	47 318	2 904	6.1	7.2	116	8.0	11.7	2 430	32.5	44.0	5 088	25.1
1976	47 497	2 606	5.5	6.4	162	10.8	15.4	2 543	33.0	44.1	5 344	24.9
1977	47 385	2 524	5.3	6.3	177	11.1	14.8	2 610	31.7	41.8	5 216	22.6
1978	47 692	2 474	5.2	5.9	152	9.2	14.7	2 654	31.4	42.2	5 435	22.1
1979	49 112	2 640	5.4	6.1	176	10.2	15.5	2 645	30.4	39.6	5 743	21.9
1980	49 294	3 032	6.2	7.7	213	11.0	18.0	2 972	32.7	42.9	6 227	22.9
1981	49 630	3 394	6.8	8.7	205	10.3	14.0	3 252	34.6	44.3	6 490	23.4
1982	49 908	3 789	7.6	9.8	290	14.4	20.6	3 434	36.3	47.8	6 458	23.1
1983	50 081	3 815	7.6	10.1	268	13.2	20.2	3 564	36.0	47.1	6 740	23.1
1984	50 350	3 488	6.9	9.4	292	13.1	18.1	3 498	34.5	45.7	6 609	21.8
1985	50 933	3 438	6.7	8.9	311	12.9	17.1	3 474	34.0	45.4	6 725	21.5
1986	51 537	3 123	6.1	8.0	287	11.4	17.8	3 613	34.6	46.0	6 846	21.6
1987	51 675	3 011	5.8	7.7	340	12.0	16.8	3 654	34.2	45.5	6 857	20.8
1988	52 100	2 897	5.6	7.2	336	11.8	18.0	3 642	33.4	44.7	7 070	20.6
1989	52 317	2 931	5.6	7.3	348	12.1	18.1	3 504	32.2	42.8	6 760	19.2
1990	52 147	2 981	5.7	7.8	349	12.0	18.8	3 768	33.4	44.5	7 446	20.7
1991	52 457	3 158	6.0	8.3	392	13.0	19.6	4 161	35.6	47.1	7 773	21.1
1992	53 090	3 385	6.4	8.6	484	15.8	22.5	4 275	35.4	46.2	8 075	21.9
1993	53 181	3 481	6.5	9.0	488	16.8	22.5	4 424	35.6	46.1	8 388	22.1
1994	53 865	3 272	6.1	8.3	549	17.0	22.6	4 232	34.6	44.0	8 287	21.5
1995	53 570	2 982	5.6	7.5	493	14.0	19.7	4 057	32.4	41.5	8 247	20.9
1996	53 604	3 010	5.6	7.5	531	13.8	20.0	4 167	32.6	41.9	8 452	20.8
1997	54 321	2 821	5.2	7.1	507	13.0	18.7	3 995	31.6	41.0	8 687	20.8
1998	54 778	2 879	5.3	6.9	476	12.0	16.6	3 831	29.9	38.7	8 478	19.9
1999	56 290	2 748	4.9	6.4	485	11.8	16.3	3 559	27.8	35.7	8 400	19.1
2000	56 598	2 637	4.7	6.0	485	11.3	15.3	3 278	25.4	33.0	8 653	19.0
2001	56 755	2 760	4.9	6.1	583	13.1	17.7	3 470	26.4	33.6	9 226	19.9
2002	57 327	3 052	5.3	6.8	564	12.1	16.6	3 613	26.5	33.7	9 618	20.4
2003	57 725	3 115	5.4	7.0	636	13.5	19.1	3 856	28.0	35.5	9 713	20.4
2004	57 983	3 216	5.5	7.0	657	13.4	17.1	3 962	28.3	35.9	9 926	20.4
2005	58 189	2 944	5.1	6.5	669	13.0	17.6	4 044	28.7	36.2	10 425	21.1
2006	58 964	2 910	4.9	6.4	671	13.2	17.9	4 087	28.3	36.5	9 977	20.0
2007	58 395	2 849	4.9	6.7	696	13.6	17.5	4 078	28.3	37.0	10 189	19.7
2008	59 137	3 261	5.5	7.5	723	13.8	17.6	4 163	28.7	37.2	10 710	20.8
2009	58 428	3 409	5.8	8.3	942	16.9	23.7	4 441	29.9	38.5	11 678	22.0
2010	58 667	3 681	6.3	9.0	892	15.8	24.1	4 827	31.7	40.9	12 449	22.9
2011	58 963	3 652	6.2	8.8	950	16.1	21.9	4 894	31.2	40.9	12 416	22.8
2012	59 224	3 705	6.3	8.9	1 023	16.4	22.6	4 793	30.9	40.9	12 558	22.4
2013	59 692	3 476	6.0	7.6	1 008	15.9	20.0	4 646	30.6	39.6	13 181	23.3
2014	60 015	3 735	6.0	8.2	969	15.7	22.0	4 646	30.6	39.8	13 374	23.1
2015	60 258	3 245	5.0	7.5	939	14.9	22.0	4 404	28.2	26.5	12 671	21.5

. . . = Not available.

Table 3-8. Poverty Status of People by Sex and Age

(Thousands of people, percent of population.)

Year	Poverty status of people by sex				Poverty status of people by age					
	Males below poverty level		Females below poverty level		Children under 18 years below poverty level		People 18 to 64 years below poverty level		People 65 years and older below poverty level	
	Number (thousands)	Poverty rate (percent)	Number (thousands)	Poverty rate (percent)	Number (thousands)	Poverty rate (percent)	Number (thousands)	Poverty rate (percent)	Number (thousands)	Poverty rate (percent)
1959	. . .	. . .	. . .	. . .	17 552	27.3	16 457	17.0	5 481	35.2
1966	12 225	13.0	16 265	16.3	12 389	17.6	11 007	10.5	5 114	28.5
1967	11 813	12.5	15 951	15.8	11 656	16.6	10 725	10.0	5 388	29.5
1968	10 793	11.3	14 578	14.3	10 954	15.6	9 803	9.0	4 632	25.0
1969	10 292	10.6	13 978	13.6	9 691	14.0	9 669	8.7	4 787	25.3
1970	10 879	11.1	14 632	14.0	10 440	15.1	10 187	9.0	4 793	24.6
1971	10 708	10.8	14 841	14.1	10 551	15.3	10 735	9.3	4 273	21.6
1972	10 190	10.2	14 258	13.4	10 284	15.1	10 438	8.8	3 738	18.6
1973	9 642	9.6	13 316	12.5	9 642	14.4	9 977	8.3	3 354	16.3
1974	9 945	9.8	13 429	12.5	10 156	15.4	10 132	8.3	3 085	14.6
1975	10 908	10.7	14 970	13.8	11 104	17.1	11 456	9.2	3 317	15.3
1976	10 373	10.1	14 603	13.4	10 273	16.0	11 389	9.0	3 313	15.0
1977	10 340	10.0	14 381	13.0	10 288	16.2	11 316	8.8	3 177	14.1
1978	10 017	9.6	14 480	13.0	9 931	15.9	11 332	8.7	3 233	14.0
1979	10 861	10.1	15 211	13.2	10 377	16.4	12 014	8.9	3 682	15.2
1980	12 207	11.2	17 065	14.7	11 543	18.3	13 858	10.1	3 871	15.7
1981	13 360	12.1	18 462	15.8	12 505	20.0	15 464	11.1	3 853	15.3
1982	14 842	13.4	19 556	16.5	13 647	21.9	17 000	12.0	3 751	14.6
1983	15 296	13.6	20 006	16.8	13 911	22.3	17 767	12.4	3 625	13.8
1984	14 537	12.8	19 163	15.9	13 420	21.5	16 952	11.7	3 330	12.4
1985	14 140	12.3	18 923	15.6	13 010	20.7	16 598	11.3	3 456	12.6
1986	13 721	11.8	18 649	15.2	12 876	20.5	16 017	10.8	3 477	12.4
1987	13 781	11.8	18 439	14.9	12 843	20.3	15 815	10.6	3 563	12.5
1988	13 599	11.5	18 146	14.5	12 455	19.5	15 809	10.5	3 481	12.0
1989	13 366	11.2	18 162	14.4	12 590	19.6	15 575	10.2	3 363	11.4
1990	14 211	11.7	19 373	15.2	13 431	20.6	16 496	10.7	3 658	12.2
1991	15 082	12.3	20 626	16.0	14 341	21.8	17 586	11.4	3 781	12.4
1992	16 222	12.9	21 792	16.6	15 294	22.3	18 793	11.9	3 928	12.9
1993	16 900	13.3	22 365	16.9	15 727	22.7	19 781	12.4	3 755	12.2
1994	16 316	12.8	21 744	16.3	15 289	21.8	19 107	11.9	3 663	11.7
1995	15 683	12.2	20 742	15.4	14 665	20.8	18 442	11.4	3 318	10.5
1996	15 611	12.0	20 918	15.4	14 463	20.5	18 638	11.4	3 428	10.8
1997	15 187	11.6	20 387	14.9	14 113	19.9	18 085	10.9	3 376	10.5
1998	14 712	11.1	19 764	14.3	13 467	18.9	17 623	10.5	3 386	10.5
1999	14 079	10.4	18 712	13.2	12 280	17.1	17 289	10.1	3 222	9.7
2000	13 536	9.9	18 045	12.6	11 587	16.2	16 671	9.6	3 323	9.9
2001	14 327	10.4	18 580	12.9	11 733	16.3	17 760	10.1	3 414	10.1
2002	15 162	10.9	19 408	13.3	12 133	16.7	18 861	10.6	3 576	10.4
2003	15 783	11.2	20 078	13.7	12 866	17.6	19 443	10.8	3 552	10.2
2004	16 399	11.5	20 641	13.9	13 041	17.8	20 545	11.3	3 453	9.8
2005	15 950	11.1	21 000	14.1	12 896	17.6	20 450	11.1	3 603	10.1
2006	16 000	11.0	20 460	13.6	12 827	17.4	20 239	10.8	3 394	9.4
2007	16 302	11.1	20 973	13.8	13 324	18.0	20 396	10.9	3 556	9.7
2008	17 698	12.0	22 131	14.4	14 068	19.0	22 105	11.7	3 656	9.7
2009	19 475	13.0	24 094	15.6	15 451	20.7	24 684	12.9	3 433	8.9
2010	20 893	14.0	25 451	16.3	16 286	22.0	26 499	13.8	3 558	8.9
2011	20 501	13.6	25 746	16.3	16 134	21.9	26 492	13.7	3 620	8.7
2012	20 656	13.6	25 840	16.3	16 073	21.8	26 497	13.7	3 926	9.1
2013	20 294	13.2	25 975	16.3	15 801	21.5	25 899	13.3	4 569	10.2
2014	20 708	13.4	25 949	16.1	15 540	21.1	26 527	13.5	4 590	10.1
2015	19 037	12.2	24 086	14.8	14 509	19.7	24 414	12.4	4 201	8.8

. . . = Not available.

Table 3-9. Working-Age Poor People by Work Experience

(Thousands of people, percent of population [poverty rate], percent of total poor people.)

Year	Total number of working-age poor people	Worked		Worked year-round, full-time			Worked less than year-round or full-time			Did not work		
		Number	Percent of total poor	Number	Poverty rate (percent)	Percent of total poor	Number	Poverty rate (percent)	Percent of total poor	Number	Poverty rate (percent)	Percent of total poor
16 Years and Over												
1978	16 914	6 599	39.0	1 309	. . .	7.7	5 290	. . .	31.3	10 315	. . .	61.0
1979	16 803	6 601	39.3	1 394	. . .	8.3	5 207	. . .	31.0	10 202	. . .	60.7
1980	18 892	7 674	40.6	1 644	. . .	8.7	6 030	. . .	31.9	11 218	. . .	59.4
1981	20 571	8 524	41.4	1 881	. . .	9.1	6 643	. . .	32.3	12 047	. . .	58.6
1982	22 100	9 013	40.8	1 999	. . .	9.0	7 014	. . .	31.7	13 087	. . .	59.2
1983	22 741	9 329	41.0	2 064	. . .	9.1	7 265	. . .	31.9	13 412	. . .	59.0
1984	21 541	8 999	41.8	2 076	. . .	9.6	6 923	. . .	32.1	12 542	. . .	58.2
1985	21 243	9 008	42.4	1 972	. . .	9.3	7 036	. . .	00.1	12 235		57.6
1986	20 688	8 743	42.3	2 007	. . .	9.7	6 736	. . .	32.6	11 945	. . .	57.7
1987	20 546	8 258	40.2	1 821	2.4	8.9	6 436	12.5	31.3	12 288	21.6	59.8
1988	20 323	8 363	41.2	1 929	2.4	9.5	6 434	12.7	31.7	11 960	21.2	58.8
1989	19 952	8 376	42.0	1 908	2.4	9.6	6 468	12.5	32.4	11 576	20.8	58.0
1990	21 242	8 716	41.0	2 076	2.6	9.8	6 639	12.6	31.3	12 526	22.1	59.0
1991	22 530	9 208	40.9	2 103	2.6	9.3	7 105	13.4	31.5	13 322	22.8	59.1
1992	23 951	9 739	40.6	2 211	2.7	9.2	7 529	14.1	31.4	14 212	23.7	59.3
1993	24 832	10 144	40.8	2 408	2.9	9.7	7 737	14.6	31.2	14 688	24.2	59.1
1994	24 108	9 829	40.8	2 520	2.9	10.5	7 309	13.9	30.3	14 279	23.6	59.2
1995	23 077	9 484	41.1	2 418	2.7	10.5	7 066	13.7	30.6	13 593	22.3	58.9
1996	23 472	9 586	40.8	2 263	2.5	9.6	7 322	14.1	31.2	13 886	22.7	59.2
1997	22 753	9 444	41.5	2 345	2.5	10.3	7 098	13.8	31.2	13 309	21.7	58.5
1998	22 256	9 133	41.0	2 804	2.9	12.6	6 330	12.7	28.4	13 123	21.1	59.0
1999	21 762	9 251	42.5	2 559	2.6	11.8	6 692	13.2	30.8	12 511	19.9	57.5
2000	21 080	8 511	40.4	2 439	2.4	11.6	6 072	12.1	28.8	12 569	19.8	59.6
2001	22 245	8 530	38.3	2 567	2.6	11.5	5 964	11.8	26.8	13 715	20.6	61.7
2002	23 601	8 954	37.9	2 635	2.6	11.2	6 318	12.4	26.8	14 647	21.0	62.1
2003	24 266	8 820	36.3	2 636	2.6	10.9	6 183	12.2	25.5	15 446	21.5	63.7
2004	25 256	9 384	37.2	2 891	2.8	11.4	6 493	12.8	25.7	15 872	21.7	62.8
2005	25 381	9 340	36.8	2 894	2.8	11.4	6 446	12.8	25.4	16 041	21.8	63.2
2006	24 896	9 181	36.9	2 906	2.7	11.7	6 275	12.6	25.2	15 715	21.1	63.1
2007	25 297	9 089	35.9	2 768	2.5	10.9	6 320	12.7	25.0	16 208	21.5	64.1
2008	27 216	10 085	37.1	2 754	2.6	10.1	7 331	13.5	26.9	17 131	22.0	62.9
2009	29 625	10 680	36.1	2 641	2.7	8.9	8 039	14.5	27.1	18 945	22.7	63.9
2010	31 731	10 742	33.9	2 640	2.7	8.3	8 102	15.0	25.5	20 989	23.9	66.1
2011	31 630	10 588	33.5	2 770	2.7	8.8	7 818	14.9	24.7	21 042	23.6	66.5
2012	31 933	10 977	34.4	2 904	2.8	9.1	8 073	15.0	25.3	20 956	23.6	65.6
2013	32 011	11 025	34.4	2 812	2.7	8.8	8 213	15.8	25.7	20 986	23.2	65.6
2014	32 508	10 469	32.2	3 142	2.9	9.7	7 327	14.3	22.5	22 039	24.2	67.8
2015	30 123	9 795	32.5	2 576	2.3	8.8	7 220	13.9	24.0	20 328	22.5	67.5

. . . = Not available.

SECTION 3C: ALTERNATIVE MEASURES OF INCOME AND POVERTY

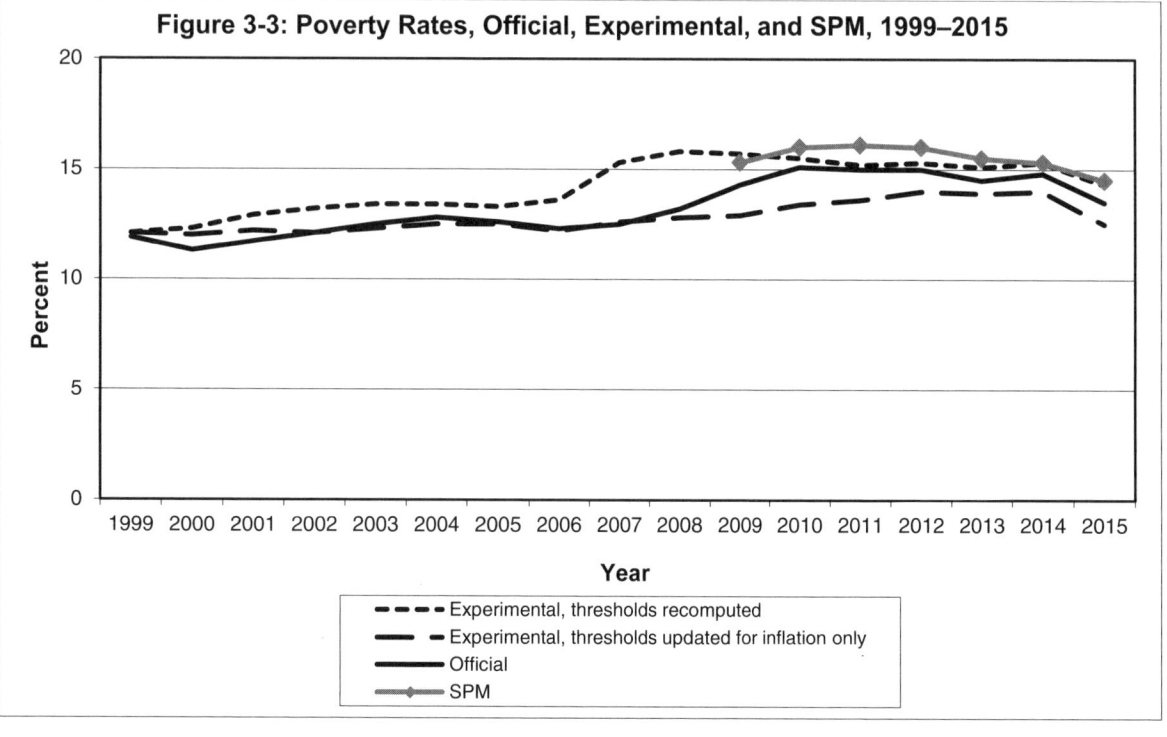

Figure 3-3: Poverty Rates, Official, Experimental, and SPM, 1999–2015

- Concerns about the adequacy of the official poverty measure which did not include government programs such as Supplemental Nutrition Assistance Program (SNAP), Medicaid, and Temporary Assistance to Needy Families (TANF) which were designed to assist low-income families and individuals.

- Since 1999, the Census Bureau has calculated several experimental poverty measures based on recommendations by a special National Academy of Sciences (NAS) panel. And for 2009 through 2015 the Bureau has released a "Supplemental Poverty Measure" (SPM), based on further refinement of these recommendations. In Figure 3-3, two of the experimental measures are shown along with the official rate and the SPM. The SPM and all of the experimental measures use broader and more realistic definitions of both needs and "resources" (income) than the official rate. Also, the SPM and the two experimental measures shown in the graph include adjustment for geographic differences in the cost of living, and adjust for differing health care needs by excluding medical out-of-pocket expenses from the resources of the measurement unit. The thresholds for the experimental measures were initially based on needs estimated for the year 1999; in that year, the two experimental measures shown in Figure 3-3 indicated a poverty rate of 14.3 percent, compared with 13.7 percent in the 2015 official rate. (Table 3-10)

- One experimental measures update the thresholds for inflation only, using the CPI-W, as is the case with the official series. This measure tracks the official series fairly closely through 2007. In the recession years, it increases less than the official measure, probably because resources are on an after-tax basis and include food aid and the Employment Tax Credit. (Table 3-11)

- Since the SPM includes many adjustments, differences do exist. For example, the poverty rate for persons 65 and older was 13.7 percent in 2015, much closer to the rate of 13.8 percent for working-age adults. The SPM rate for children, on the other hand, has always been higher than the average. In 2015, the SPM rate for children was 16.1 percent. (Table 3-10)

Table 3-10. Number and Percent of People in Poverty Using the Supplemental Poverty Measure, 2012–2015, and Comparison with Official Measures in 2015

(Numbers in thousands; percent of population.)

Characteristic	SPM 2012		SPM 2013		SPM 2014		SPM 2015		Official 2015[1]	
	Number	Percent	Number	Percent	Number	Percent	Number	Percent	Number	Percent
All People	49 730	16.0	49 427	15.3	48 390	15.3	45 651	14.3	43 538	13.7
Sex										
Male	23 278	15.3	22 973	15.0	22 497	14.5	21 385	13.7	19 233	12.3
Female	26 452	16.7	26 455	16.0	25 893	16.0	24 268	14.9	24 305	14.9
Age										
Under 18 years	13 358	18.0	13 343	18.1	12 360	16.7	11 929	16.1	14 923	20.1
18 to 64 years	29 953	15.5	29 095	14.9	29 401	15.0	27 222	13.8	24 414	12.4
65 years and older	6 419	14.8	6 990	15.5	6 629	14.4	6 500	13.7	4 201	8.8
Type of Unit										
In married-couple unit	18 703	10.0	17 235	9.2	17 878	9.4	16 920	8.9	12 120	6.4
In female householder unit	19 137	28.9	19 653	29.9	18 366	28.7	16 984	25.9	17 373	26.5
In male household unit	7 766	23.1	7 708	22.5	7 420	21.8	7 330	29.9	5 957	17.0
In new SPM unit	5 124	18.4	5 004	18.3	4 726	16.6	4 417	15.8	8 088	28.9
Race and Hispanic Origin										
White	34 002	14.0	34 349	14.1	33 346	13.6	30 852	12.8	28 835	11.7
White, not Hispanic	20 946	10.7	21 434	11.0	20 943	10.7	19 638	10.0	17 981	9.2
Black	10 363	25.8	9 922	24.4	9 662	23.4	9 575	23.0	10 099	24.2
Asian	2 737	16.7	2 692	15.6	2 999	16.8	2 921	16.0	2 086	11.4
Hispanic, any race	14 819	27.8	14 391	26.5	14 129	25.4	12 719	22.4	12 226	21.5
Nativity										
Native born	39 538	14.6	39 803	14.6	38 379	14.0	36 328	13.2	36 373	13.2
Foreign born	10 192	25.4	625	23.7	10 011	23.7	9 323	21.6	7 165	16.6
Naturalized citizen	3 361	18.5	3 333	17.3	3 467	17.6	3 347	16.7	2 258	11.2
Not a citizen	6 831	31.2	6 292	29.4	6 544	29.1	5 976	26.0	4 907	21.3
Tenure										
Owner	20 512	9.9	20 745	10.0	19 846	9.6	19 016	9.1	15 385	7.4
Owner/ mortgage	11 676	8.5	10 671	7.9	10 688	8.1	10 009	7.5	6 935	5.2
Owner/no-mortgage/rent-free	9 694	13.4	11 038	14.6	10 098	13.0	9 853	12.7	9 375	12.0
Renter	28 360	28.1	27 718	27.0	27 604	16.1	25 789	24.2	27 227	25.5
Residence										
Inside metropolitan statistical areas	43 064	16.4	42 781	16.1	41 997	15.8	39 798	14.5	36 065	13.1
Inside principal cities	21 401	21.1	20 206	20.0	20 078	20.2	18 534	17.9	17 492	16.9
Outside principal cities	21 664	13.4	22 575	13.7	21 919	13.1	21 264	12.5	18 573	10.9
Outside metropolitan statistical areas	6 666	13.9	6 647	13.9	6 393	12.8	5 853	13.2	7 473	16.8
Region										
Northeast	8 570	15.5	8 788	15.8	8 215	14.7	8 004	14.3	6 991	12.5
Midwest	8 268	12.4	8 646	12.9	7 934	11.8	7 210	10.7	7 934	11.8
South	18 939	16.3	19 002	16.2	18 509	15.6	18 552	15.4	18 464	15.4
West	13 953	19.0	12 991	17.6	13 732	18.4	11 886	15.7	10 148	13.4
Health Insurance Coverage										
With private insurance	15 273	7.7	17 244	8.6	18 143	8.7	18 350	8.6	12 462	5.8
With public, no private insurance	19 655	30.5	20 672	29.3	21 128	28.3	19 687	26.0	23 552	31.1
Not insured	14 802	30.9	11 512	27.8	9 119	27.7	7 614	26.3	7 524	26.0
Work Experience										
Total, 18 to 64 years	29 953	15.5	29 095	14.9	29 401	15.0	27 222	13.8	24 414	12.4
All workers	14 066	9.6	13 687	9.3	13 318	9.0	12 478	8.3	9 457	6.3
Full-time, year-round	5 252	5.3	5 508	5.5	5 679	5.5	4 999	4.7	2 537	2.4
Less than full-time, year-round	8 814	18.7	8 180	17.9	7 639	17.2	7 479	16.8	6 920	15.5
Did not work at least 1 week	15 887	33.2	15 407	32.5	16 083	33.1	14 744	31.4	14 957	31.8
Disability Status										
Total, 18 to 64 years	29 953	15.5	29 095	14.9	29 401	15.0	27 222	13.8	24 414	12.4
With a disability	3 979	26.5	3 633	24.1	3 997	25.9	4 042	26.5	4 358	28.5
With no disability	25 921	14.6	25 370	14.2	25 318	14.1	23 101	12.8	20 000	11.0

[1]Differs from published official rates because these figures include unrelated individuals under 15 years of age as does the SPM.

Table 3-11. Official and Experimental Poverty Rates and Supplemental Poverty Measure

(Percent of population.)

Measurement method	Capital gains included in income								
	1999	2000	2001	2002 (new tax model)	2003	2004	2005	2006	2007
Official measure	11.9	11.3	11.7	12.1	12.5	12.8	12.6	12.3	12.5
Experimental									
MSI-GA-CPI	12.1	12.0	12.2	12.1	12.3	12.5	12.5	12.2	12.6
MIT-GA-CPI	12.7	12.5	12.5	12.6	12.7	13.0	13.0	12.6	13.0
MSI-NGA-CPI	12.2	12.1	12.3	12.3	12.4	12.7	12.6	12.4	12.6
MIT-NGA-CPI	12.8	12.7	12.7	12.8	12.7	13.1	13.0	12.8	12.9
MSI-GA-CE	12.1	12.3	12.9	13.2	13.4	13.4	13.3	13.6	15.3
MIT-GA-CE	12.7	12.8	13.2	13.7	13.9	14.0	14.1	14.1	15.9
MSI-NGA-CE	12.2	12.5	13.0	13.4	13.5	13.4	13.5	13.7	15.1
MIT-NGA-CE	12.8	13.0	13.4	13.9	14.1	14.1	14.2	14.2	16.0
Supplemental poverty measure	. . .	. . .	. . .	. . .	. . .	. . .	. . .	. . .	. . .

Measurement method	Capital gains and losses excluded from income								
	2007	2008	2009	2010	2011	2012	2013	2014	2015
Official measure	12.5	13.2	14.3	15.1	15.0	15.0	14.5	14.8	13.5
Experimental									
MSI-GA-CPI	12.6	12.8	12.9	13.4	13.6	14.0	13.9	14.0	12.5
MIT-GA-CPI	13.0	13.2	13.2	13.8	13.9	14.5	14.3	14.4	12.9
MSI-NGA-CPI	12.6	12.8	12.8	13.5	13.5	14.0	13.8	14.0	12.7
MIT-NGA-CPI	13.0	13.1	13.3	14.0	13.8	14.4	14.4	14.6	13.1
MSI-GA-CE	15.3	15.8	15.7	15.5	15.2	15.3	15.1	15.3	14.3
MIT-GA-CE	15.9	16.9	17.3	17.2	16.9	16.8	16.6	16.9	16.1
MSI-NGA-CE	15.2	15.7	15.7	15.6	15.0	15.3	15.1	15.3	14.4
MIT-NGA-CE	16.1	17.1	17.3	17.3	16.9	16.9	16.6	16.9	15.9
Supplemental poverty measure	. . .	. . .	15.3	16.0	16.1	16.0	15.5	15.3	14.5

Note: The Census Bureau changed the way it modeled taxes in the experimental measures, effective with the revised 2002 estimates. Consequently, comparisons of 2002 and later data with earlier years may be affected.

MSI means "Medical out-of-pocket expenses subtracted from income."
MIT means "Medical out-of-pocket expenses in the thresholds."
GA means "Geographic adjustment (of poverty thresholds)."
NGA means "No geographic adjustment (of poverty thresholds)."
CPI means "Thresholds were adjusted since 1999 using the Consumer Price Index for All Urban Consumers."
CE means "Thresholds were recomputed since 1999 using data from the Consumer Expenditure Survey."

See notes and definitions for further explanation.
. . . = Not available.

SECTION 3D: HEALTH INSURANCE COVERAGE

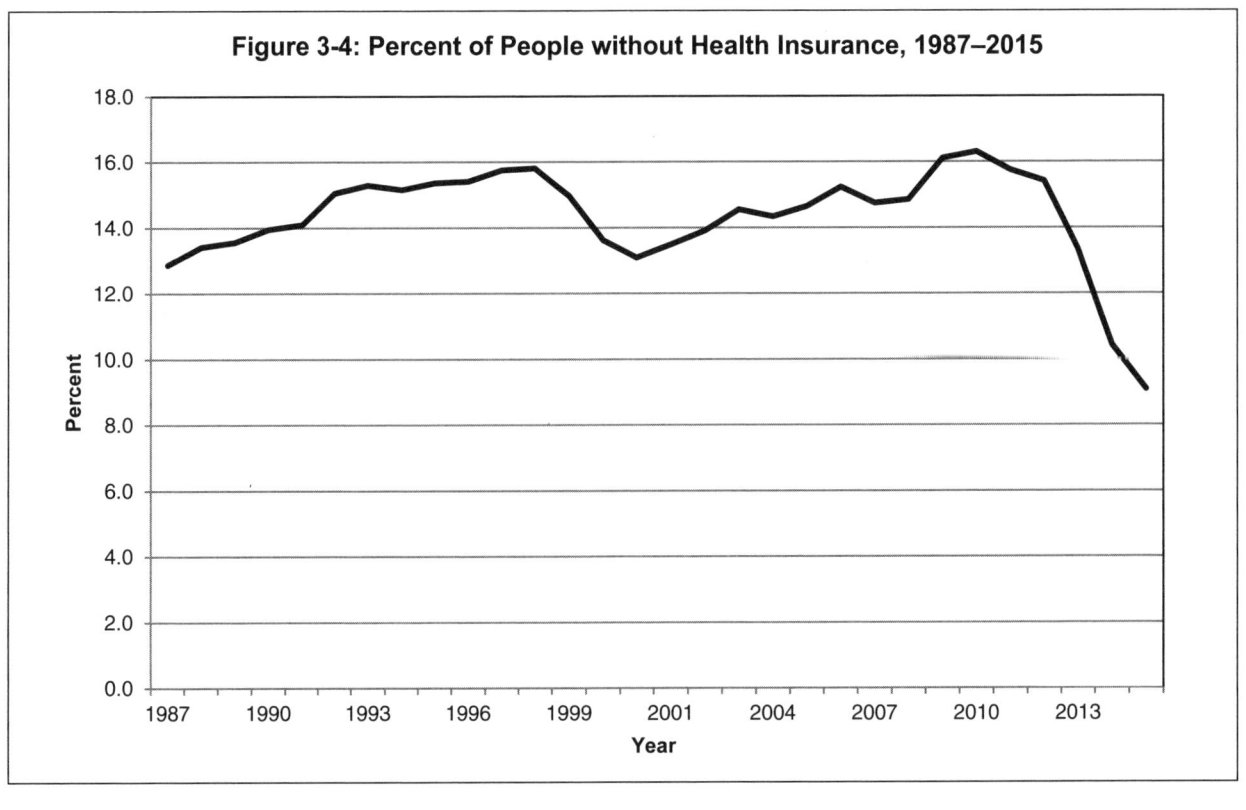

Figure 3-4: Percent of People without Health Insurance, 1987–2015

- Health insurance is a means for financing a person's health care expenses. Over time, changes in the rate of health insurance coverage and the distribution of coverage types may reflect economic trends, shifts in the demographic composition of the populace and policy changes that impact access to care. Such a policy change was the Patient Protection and Affordable Care Act (ACA) in 2010.

- In 2015, private health insurance coverage continued to be more prevalent than public coverage. Of the subtypes of health insurance, employer-based insurance covered 55.7 percent of the population for some or all of the calendar year, followed by Medicaid (19.6 percent), Medicare (16.3 percent), direct purchase (16.3 percent) and military coverage (4.7 percent). (Table 3-12)

- Immediately following the Great Recession, nearly 50 million people were without any type of health insurance coverage. Between 2010 and 2015, the non-covered rate fell, from 16.3 percent to 9.1 percent. (Table 3-12)

- In 2015, the latest data available, the percentage of uninsured children under age of 19 was 5.3 percent. This was a decrease from 7.5 percent in 2013. Also, non-Hispanic Whites had the lowest uninsured rate among race and and Hispanic origin groups, at 6.7 percent. (Table 3-13)

Table 3-12. Health Insurance Coverage

(Number in thousands. People as of March of the following year.)

Year	Total	Total covered	Private health insurance			Government health insurance				Not covered
			Total	Employment	Direct purchase	Total	Medicaid	Medicare	Military	
NUMBER										
1987	241 187	210 161	182 160	149 739	. . .	56 282	20 211	30 458	10 542	31 026
1988	243 685	211 005	182 019	150 940	. . .	56 850	20 728	30 925	10 105	32 680
1989	246 191	212 807	183 610	151 644	. . .	57 382	21 185	31 495	9 870	33 384
1990	248 886	214 167	182 135	150 215	. . .	60 965	24 261	32 260	9 922	34 719
1991	251 447	216 003	181 375	150 077	. . .	63 882	26 880	32 907	9 820	35 444
1992	256 830	218 189	181 466	148 796	. . .	66 244	29 416	33 230	9 510	38 641
1993	259 753	220 040	182 351	148 318	. . .	68 554	31 749	33 097	9 560	39 713
1994	262 105	222 387	184 318	159 634	31 349	70 163	31 645	33 901	11 165	39 718
1995	264 314	223 733	185 881	161 453	30 188	69 776	31 877	34 655	9 375	40 581
1996	266 792	225 699	188 224	164 096	28 419	69 000	31 451	35 227	8 712	41 093
1997	269 094	226 735	189 955	166 419	27 431	66 685	28 956	35 590	8 527	42 359
1998	271 743	228 800	192 507	170 105	26 165	66 087	27 854	35 887	8 747	42 943
1999	550 891	472 175	398 557	349 227	56 608	133 279	55 243	73 056	17 056	78 716
2000	279 517	242 932	205 575	181 862	28 432	68 183	28 062	37 787	8 937	36 585
2001	282 082	244 059	204 142	179 984	28 398	70 330	30 166	37 870	9 580	38 023
2002	285 933	246 157	204 163	179 563	29 287	72 825	31 934	38 359	9 892	39 776
2003	288 280	246 332	201 989	177 362	28 826	76 119	34 326	39 284	10 124	41 948
2004	291 166	249 414	203 014	177 924	29 161	79 480	38 055	39 757	10 584	41 752
2005	293 834	250 799	203 205	178 391	28 980	80 283	38 191	40 167	11 164	43 035
2006	296 824	251 610	203 942	178 880	29 033	80 343	38 370	40 336	10 543	45 214
2007	299 106	255 018	203 903	178 971	28 500	83 147	39 685	41 387	10 955	44 088
2008	301 483	256 702	202 626	177 543	28 513	87 586	42 831	43 031	11 562	44 781
2009	304 280	255 295	196 245	170 762	29 098	93 245	47 847	43 434	12 414	48 985
2010	306 553	256 603	196 147	169 372	30 347	95 525	48 533	44 906	12 927	49 950
2011	308 827	260 214	197 323	170 102	30 244	99 497	50 835	46 022	13 712	48 613
2012	311 116	263 165	198 812	170 877	30 622	101 493	50 903	48 884	13 702	47 951
2013	313 401	271 606	201 038	174 418	35 755	108 287	54 919	49 020	14 016	41 795
2014	316 168	283 200	208 600	175 027	46 165	115 470	61 650	50 546	14 143	32 968
2015	318 868	289 903	214 238	177 540	52 057	118 395	62 384	51 865	14 849	28 966

. . . = Not available.

Table 3-13. Number and Percent of People by Type of Health Insurance by Selected Demographics, 2014 and 2015

(Number in thousands. Percent. People as of March of the following year.)

Characteristic	Total		Any health insurance		Private health insurance		Government health insurance		Uninsured	
	2014	2015	2014	2015	2014	2015	2014	2015	2014	2015
TOTAL	316 168	318 868	283 200	289 903	208 600	214 236	115 470	118 395	32 968	28 966
Age										
Under 19	78 119	78 182	93.8	94.7	61.0	62.6	42.6	42.6	6.2	5.3
19-64	192 055	193 140	85.7	87.4	71.1	72.7	20.4	21.0	14.3	12.6
65 and over	45 994	47 547	98.6	98.9	52.8	52.1	93.6	93.8	1.4	1.1
Work Experience										
All workers	146 024	148 503	86.8	88.4	78.8	80.0	12.8	13.8	13.2	11.6
Full time	103 202	105 533	88.8	90.1	83.6	84.5	9.6	10.5	11.2	9.9
Part-time	42 822	42 970	81.9	84.2	67.3	69.0	20.5	21.7	18.1	15.8
Did not work	46 032	44 637	82.3	84.2	46.7	48.6	44.4	44.9	17.7	15.8
Race and Hispanic Origin										
White	244 468	245 805	89.9	91.3	68.0	69.0	35.7	36.5	10.1	8.7
White, not Hispanic	195 352	195 646	92.4	93.3	72.9	73.6	34.7	35.3	7.6	6.7
Black	41 226	41 703	88.2	88.9	54.1	55.9	44.2	44.1	11.8	11.1
Asian	17 796	18 249	90.7	92.5	72.1	75.5	28.2	27.1	9.3	7.5
Hispanic (any race)	55 614	56 873	80.1	83.8	48.7	51.6	39.5	41.2	19.9	16.2
Household Income										
Less than $25,000	55 212	51 999	46 067	44 286	16 598	16 009	36 049	34 625	9 145	7 713
$25,000 to $49,999	67 311	65 289	57 834	57 146	35 436	34 739	32 721	33 188	9 477	8 143
$50,000 to $74,999	55 664	55 131	49 707	49 813	39 295	38 802	18 297	19 074	5 957	5 318
$75,000 to $99,999	41 294	43 123	37 999	39 972	32 771	34 349	10 471	11 737	3 296	3 150
$100,000 or more	96 687	103 328	91 593	98 686	84 499	90 339	17 932	19 770	5 094	4 642
Family Status										
In families	256 308	258 121	90.5	91.7	67.3	68.3	35.9	36.6	9.5	8.3
Household	81 730	82 199	90.0	91.3	69.8	70.5	35.3	36.2	10.0	8.7
In unrelated families	1 558	1 344	85.6	87.9	51.3	52.0	47.2	47.1	14.4	12.1
Unrelated individuals	58 301	59 403	85.8	87.8	60.5	62.7	39.2	39.4	14.2	12.2

. . . = Not available.

Table 3-14. Percent of People by Type of Health Insurance by Selected Demographics, 2014 and 2015

(Numbers in thousands, percent, people as of March the following year.)

Characteristic	Total		Any health insurance			Private health insurance			Government health insurance			Uninsured		
	2014	2015	2014	2015	Change (2015 less 2014)	2014	2015	Change (2015 less 2014)	2014	2015	Change (2015 less 2014)	2014	2015	Change (2015 less 2014)
TOTAL	316 168	318 868	89.6	90.9	1.3	66.0	67.2	1.2	36.5	37.1	0.6	10.4	9.1	-1.3
Family Status														
In families	256 308	258 121	90.5	91.7	1.2	67.3	68.3	1.0	35.9	36.6	0.7	9.5	8.3	-1.2
Householder	81 730	82 199	90.0	91.3	1.3	69.8	70.5	0.7	35.3	36.2	1.0	10.0	8.7	-1.3
Related children under 18	72 383	72 558	94.0	94.8	0.8	61.0	62.7	1.7	42.7	42.7	-0.1	6.0	5.2	-0.8
Related children under 6	23 470	23 459	93.5	93.9	0.5	55.8	58.4	2.7	47.4	45.8	-1.6	6.5	6.1	-0.5
In unrelated subfamilies	1 558	1 344	85.6	87.9	2.3	51.3	52.0	0.6	47.2	47.1	-0.1	14.4	12.1	-2.3
Unrelated individuals	58 301	59 403	85.8	87.8	2.0	60.5	62.7	2.1	39.2	39.4	0.2	14.2	12.2	-2.0
Residence														
Inside metropolitan statistical areas	266 071	274 392	89.6	91.0	. . .	66.6	68.0	. . .	35.4	35.9	. . .	10.4	9.0	. . .
Inside principal cities	99 298	103 740	87.9	89.5	. . .	60.9	63.6	. . .	38.1	37.6	. . .	12.1	10.5	. . .
Outside principal cities	166 773	170 652	90.7	91.9	. . .	70.0	70.7	. . .	33.7	34.9	. . .	9.3	8.1	. . .
Outside metropolitan statistical areas	50 097	44 477	89.3	90.4	. . .	62.6	62.1	. . .	42.7	44.4	. . .	10.7	9.6	. . .
Race and Hispanic Origin														
White	244 468	245 805	89.9	91.3	1.4	68.0	69.0	1.0	35.7	36.5	0.8	10.1	8.7	-1.4
White, not Hispanic	195 352	195 646	92.4	93.3	0.9	72.9	73.6	0.6	34.7	35.3	0.6	7.6	6.7	-0.9
Black	41 226	41 703	88.2	88.9	0.7	54.1	55.9	1.9	44.2	44.1	-0.1	11.8	11.1	-0.7
Asian	17 796	18 249	90.7	92.5	1.9	72.1	75.5	3.4	28.2	27.1	-1.1	9.3	7.5	-1.9
Hispanic (any race)	55 614	56 873	80.1	83.8	3.6	48.7	51.6	3.0	39.5	41.2	1.7	19.9	16.2	-3.6
Nativity														
Native born	273 984	275 798	91.3	92.3	1.1	67.4	68.4	1.0	37.5	38.0	0.5	8.7	7.7	-1.1
Foreign born	42 184	43 070	78.6	81.9	3.2	56.7	59.4	2.8	30.4	31.8	1.3	21.4	18.1	-3.2
Naturalized citizen	19 733	20 086	89.8	91.3	1.5	65.5	66.5	1.0	35.3	36.9	1.6	10.2	8.7	-1.5
Not a citizen	22 451	22 984	68.8	73.6	4.8	48.9	53.2	4.3	26.2	27.3	1.1	31.2	26.4	-4.8

. . . = Not comparable.

NOTES AND DEFINITIONS, CHAPTER 3

TABLES 3-1 THROUGH 3-11

Income Distribution and Poverty

SOURCE: U.S. DEPARTMENT OF COMMERCE, BUREAU OF THE CENSUS

All data in this chapter are derived from the Current Population Survey (CPS), which is also the source of the data on labor force, employment, and unemployment used in Chapter 10. (See the notes and definitions for Tables 10-1 through 10-5.) In March of each year (with some data also collected in February and April), the households in this monthly survey are asked additional questions concerning earnings and other income in the previous year. This additional information, informally known as the "March Supplement," is now formally known as the Current Population Survey Annual Social and Economic Supplement (CPS-ASEC). It was previously called the Annual Demographic Supplement.

The population represented by the income and poverty survey is the civilian noninstitutional population of the United States and members of the armed forces in the United States living off post or with their families on post, but excluding all other members of the armed forces. This is slightly different from the population base for the civilian employment and unemployment data, which excludes those armed forces households. As it is a survey of households, homeless persons are not included.

Definitions: Racial classification and Hispanic origin

In 2002 and all earlier years, the CPS required respondents to report identification with only one race group. Since 2003, the CPS has allowed respondents to choose more than one race group. Income data for 2002 were collected in early 2003; thus, in the data for 2002 and all subsequent years, an individual could report identification with more than one race group. In the 2000 census, about 2.6 percent of people reported identification with more than one race.

Therefore, data from 2002 onward that are classified by race are not strictly comparable with race-classified data for 2001 and earlier years. As alternative approaches to dealing with this problem, the Census Bureau has tabulated two different race concepts for each racial category in a number of cases. In the case of Blacks, for example, this means there is one income measure for "Black alone," consisting of persons who report Black and no other race, and one for "Black alone or in combination," which includes all the "Black alone" reporters plus those who report Black in combination with any other race. The tables in this volume show both the "alone" and the "alone or in combination" values where available.

The race classifications now used in the CPS are White, Black, Asian, American Indian and Alaska Native, and Native Hawaiian and Other Pacific Islander. (Native Hawaiians and other Pacific Islanders were included in the "Asian" category in the data for 1987 through 2001.) The last two of these five racial groups are too small to provide reliable data for a single year, but in new Census Bureau tables available on the website, household income and poverty data for all five groups are presented in 2- and 3-year averages. Table 3-2 displays some of these data.

Hispanic origin is a separate question in the survey—not a racial classification—and Hispanics may be of any race. A subgroup of *White non-Hispanic* is shown in some tables. According to the Census Bureau, "Being Hispanic was reported by 14.2 percent of White householders who reported only one race, 4.6 percent of Black householders who reported only one race, and 2.6 percent of Asian householders who reported only one race. Data users should exercise caution when interpreting aggregate results for the Hispanic population or for race groups because these populations consist of many distinct groups that differ in socio-economic characteristics, culture, and recent immigration status." ("Income, Poverty, and Health Insurance Coverage in the United States: 2012," footnote 2, p. 2.)

Definitions: General

A *household* consists of all persons who occupy a housing unit. A household includes the related family members and all the unrelated persons, if any (such as lodgers, foster children, wards, or employees), who share the housing unit. A person living alone in a housing unit or a group of unrelated persons sharing a housing unit as partners is also counted as a household. The count of households excludes group quarters.

Earnings includes all income from work, including wages, salaries, armed forces pay, commissions, tips, piece-rate payments, and cash bonuses, before deductions such as taxes, bonds, pensions, and union dues. This category also includes net income from nonfarm self-employment and farm self-employment. Wage and salary supplements that are paid directly by the employer, such as the employer share of Social Security taxes and the cost of employer-provided health insurance, are not included.

Income, in the official definition used in the survey, is money income, including *earnings* from work as defined above; unemployment compensation; workers' compensation; Social Security; Supplemental Security Income; cash public assistance (welfare payments); veterans' payments; survivor benefits; disability benefits; pension or retirement income; interest income; dividends (but not capital gains); rents, royalties, and payments from estates or trusts; educational assistance, such as scholarships or grants; child support; alimony; financial assistance from outside of the household; and other cash income regularly received, such as foster child payments, military family allotments, and foreign government pensions. Receipts not counted as income include capital gains or losses, withdrawals of bank deposits, money borrowed, tax refunds, gifts, and lump-sum inheritances or insurance payments.

A *year-round, full-time worker* is a person who worked 35 or more hours per week and 50 or more weeks during the previous calendar year.

A *family* is a group of two or more persons related by birth, marriage, or adoption who reside together.

Unrelated individuals are persons 15 years old and over who are not living with any relatives. In the official poverty measure, the poverty status of unrelated individuals is determined independently of and is not affected by the incomes of other persons with whom they may share a household.

Median income is the amount of income that divides a ranked income distribution into two equal groups, with half having incomes above the median, and half having incomes below the median. The median income for persons is based on persons 15 years old and over with income. Since median income is updated annually to inflation adjusted current dollars, comparison between editions is not possible.

Mean income is the amount obtained by dividing the total aggregate income of a group by the number of units in that group. In this survey, as in most surveys of incomes, means are higher than medians because of the skewed nature of the income distribution; see the section "Whose standard of living?" in the article at the beginning of this book.

Historical income figures are shown in constant *2015 dollars.* All constant-dollar figures are converted from current-dollar values using the *CPI-U-RS* (the Consumer Price Index, All Urban, Research Series), which measures changes in prices for past periods using the methodologies of the current CPI, and is similar in concept and behavior to the deflators used in the NIPAs for consumer income and spending. See Chapter 8 for CPI-U-RS data and the corresponding notes and definitions.

Definitions: Income distribution

Income distribution is portrayed by dividing the total ranked distribution of families or households into fifths, also known as quintiles, and also by separately tabulating the top 5 percent (which is included in the highest fifth). The households or families are arrayed from those with the lowest income to those with the highest income, then divided into five groups, with each group containing one-fifth of the total number of households. Within each quintile, incomes are summed and calculated as a share of total income for all quintiles, and are averaged to show the average (mean) income within that quintile.

A statistical measure that summarizes the dispersion of income across the entire income distribution is the *Gini coefficient*

(also known as Gini ratio, Gini index, or index of income concentration), which can take values ranging from 0 to 1. A Gini value of 1 indicates "perfect" inequality; that is, one household has all the income and the rest have none. A value of 0 indicates "perfect" equality, a situation in which each household has the same income.

There are differences between the Gini coefficients for the official income measure presented in the report's main tables and those presented in Table 3-11. In the latter, the coefficients were recalculated, using a slightly different method, for comparability with the other income definitions.

A new "equivalence-adjusted" measure of household income inequality was introduced recently and is displayed in Table 3-3. For a Census-defined household, a given level of money income can have different implications for that household's well-being, depending on the size of the household and how many children, if any, are in the household. Since there have been substantial changes over past decades in the average size and composition of households, some have questioned the pertinence of standard income distribution tables. In response, the Census Bureau now also reports measures of income inequality for households using "equivalence-adjusted" income.

The equivalence adjustment is based on a three-parameter scale reflecting the size of the household and the facts that children consume less than adults; that as family size increases, expenses do not increase at the same rate; and that the increase in expenses is larger for the first child of a single-parent family than the first child of a two-adult family. The same equivalence concept is used in the poverty thresholds for the NAS-based alternative poverty estimates shown in Tables 3-11 and described later in these notes.

As can be seen in Table 3-3, the equivalence-adjusted measures generally show somewhat less inequality than the raw money income measures, but they show a greater rise in inequality over the period 1967–2015.

Definitions: Poverty

The *number of people below poverty level,* or the number of poor people, is the number of people with family or individual incomes below a specified level that is intended to measure the cost of a minimum standard of living. These minimum levels vary by size and composition of family and are known as *poverty thresholds.*

The official poverty thresholds are based on a definition developed in 1964 by Mollie Orshansky of the Social Security Administration. She calculated food budgets for families of various sizes and compositions, using an "economy food plan" developed by the U.S. Department of Agriculture (the cheapest of four plans developed). Reflecting a 1955 Department of Agriculture survey that found that families of three or more persons spent about one-third of their after-tax incomes on food,

Orshansky multiplied the costs of the food plan by 3 to arrive at a set of thresholds for poverty income for families of three or larger. For 2-person families, the multiplier was 3.7; for 1-person families, the threshold was 80 percent of the two-person threshold.

These poverty thresholds have been adjusted each year for price increases, using the percent change in the Consumer Price Index for All Urban Consumers (CPI-U).

For more information on the Orshansky thresholds (the description of which has been simplified here), see Gordon Fisher, "The Development of the Orshansky Thresholds and Their Subsequent History as the Official U.S. Poverty Measure" (May 1992), available on the Census Bureau Web site at http://www.census.gov/hhes/poverty/povmeas/papers/orshansky.html.

The *poverty rate* for a demographic group is the number of poor people or poor families in that group expressed as a percentage of the total number of people or families in the group.

Average poverty thresholds. The thresholds used to calculate the official poverty rates vary not only with the size of the family but with the number of children in the family. For example, the threshold for a three-person family in 2015 was $18,540 if there were no children in the family but $19,096 if the family consisted of 1 adult and 2 children. There are 48 different threshold values depending on size of household, number of children, and whether the householder is 65 years old or over (with <u>lower</u> thresholds for the older householders). The full matrix of thresholds is shown in the report referenced below. To give a general sense of the "poverty line," the Census Bureau also publishes the <u>average</u> threshold for each size family, based on the actual mix of family types in that year. These are the values shown in *Business Statistics* in Table 3-5 to represent the history of poverty thresholds. The preliminary <u>average</u> value for 3-person families in 2015, as shown in Table 3-5, was $18,871, a weighted average of the values actually used for the 3 different possible family compositions.

A person with *work experience* (Table 3-9) is one who, during the preceding calendar year and on a part-time or full-time basis, did any work for pay or profit or worked without pay on a family-operated farm or business at any time during the year. A *year-round* worker is one who worked for 50 weeks or more during the preceding calendar year. A person is classified as having worked *full time* if he or she worked 35 hours or more per week during a majority of the weeks worked. A *year-round, full-time worker* is a person who worked 35 or more hours per week and 50 or more weeks during the previous calendar year.

Toward better measures of income and poverty

The definition of the official poverty rate is established by the Office of Management of Budget in the Executive Office of the President and has not been substantially changed since 1969.

Criticisms of the current definition are legion. In response to these criticisms, the Census Bureau has published extensive research work illustrating the effects of various ways of modifying income definitions and poverty thresholds. Some of the results of this work are published here in Tables 3-10 and 3-11 and explained in the notes and definitions below.

Improving the income concept

One type of criticism accepted the general concept of the Orshansky threshold but recommended making the income definition more realistic by including some or all of the following: capital gains; taxes and tax credits; noncash food, housing, and health benefits provided by government and employers; and the value of homeownership. There is debate about whether it is appropriate to use income data augmented in this way in conjunction with the official thresholds. The original 1964 thresholds made no allowance for health insurance or other health expenses—in effect, they assumed that the poor would get free medical care, or at least that the poverty calculation was not required to allow for medical needs—and because of the imprecision of Orshansky's multiplier it is not clear to what extent they include housing expenses in a way that is comparable with the inclusion of a homeownership component in income. Nevertheless, the Census Bureau has calculated and published income and poverty figures based on broadened income definitions and either the official thresholds or thresholds that are closely related to the official ones. Some of these calculations are presented in Table 3-10 and 3-11 and described below.

Still accepting the validity of the basic Orshansky threshold concept, some critics have also argued that use of the CPI-U in the official measure to update the thresholds each year has overstated the price increase, and that an inflator such as the CPI-U-RS should be used instead. (See the notes and definitions for Chapter 8.) Use of the CPI-U-RS leads to lower poverty thresholds beginning in the late 1970s, when the CPI began to be distorted by housing and other biases subsequently corrected by new methods; these newer methods were not carried backward to revise the <u>official</u> CPI-U. Table 3-10 also shows poverty rates using the lower CPI-U-RS thresholds. Use of the CPI-U-RS, which does carry current methods back and thereby revises the CPI time series, eliminates a presumed upward bias in the poverty rate <u>relative to the poverty rates estimated before the bias emerged</u>. This is a bias in the behavior of the time series <u>given the concept of the Orshansky threshold</u>, not necessarily a bias in the current <u>level</u> of poverty, since all the other criticisms of the Orshansky thresholds need to be considered when assessing the general adequacy of today's poverty measurements.

Improving the concepts of income and poverty together

Another type of criticism argues that the official thresholds are also no longer relevant to today's needs, and that the concepts of income (or "resources") and of the threshold level that depicts a minimum adequate standard of living need to be rethought together. These critics cite the availability of more up-to-date and detailed information about consumer spending at various income levels. The Consumer Expenditure Survey (CEX), originally designed to provide the weights for the Consumer Price Index, is now conducted quarterly and provides extensive data on consumer spending patterns. To give just one example of the information available now that was not available to Mollie Orshansky, the CEX indicates that food now accounts for one-sixth, not one-third, of total family expenditures, even among low-income families. (For data from, and notes on, the Consumer Expenditure Survey, see Bernan Press, *Handbook of U.S. Labor Statistics*.)

A special panel of the National Academy of Sciences (NAS) undertook a study that reconsidered both resources and thresholds. The Census Bureau has calculated and published experimental poverty rates for 1999 through 2015, developed following NAS recommendations, which are presented in Table 3-10. Beginning in November 2011 the Bureau has issued "The Research Supplemental Poverty Measure" or SPM for the most recent two years, a further refinement of the NAS recommendations; SPM measures are presented in Tables 3-10.

Supplemental Poverty Measure—Tables 3-10

In March of 2010, an Interagency Technical Working Group produced suggestions for a Supplemental Poverty Measure (SPM), which were first implemented in the "Research Supplemental Poverty Measure: 2010" issued by the Census Bureau in November 2011. The SPM goes beyond the experimental measures just described, and takes advantage of new data from questions introduced in the CPS-ASEC in recent years. In the new SPM:

- The measurement unit now covers not just the family but "all related individuals who live at the same address, including any co-resident unrelated children who are cared for by the family (such as foster children) and any co-habitors and their children." This redefinition adds unrelated individuals under the age of 15 to the universe measured by the official rate. The "official" measures shown in Table 3-10 have been adjusted to include these individuals, and are therefore slightly higher than the regular published official rates shown in Tables 3-6 through 3-9.

- The SPM thresholds are calculated separately for three housing status groups: owners with mortgages, owners without mortgages, and renters. For each of these three groups the basic threshold represents the 33rd percentile of expenditures on food, clothing, shelter, and utilities (FCSU), averaged over a five-year period, by consumer units with two children, multiplied by 1.2 to allow for other needs. (Before averaging, the expenditures are converted to their dollar values in the prices of the threshold year using the CPI-U.) The consumer units selected for calculating the threshold include not only two-adult two-child families but also other types with two children, such as single-parent families. But they are adjusted to a four-person basis, using the equivalence scales, before

averaging them to determine the basic threshold appropriate to a two-adult two-child household. Then that threshold is used as the basis for calculating thresholds for other size measurement units, again using the three-parameter equivalence scales for family size and composition, and for geographic differences.

- The thresholds are updated each year, using an updated five-year moving average of FCSU at the 33rd percentile, expressed in the prices of the new threshold year. Thus the thresholds are adjusted for inflation, but in addition, the "real" (constant-dollar) purchasing power of the poverty threshold will change (gradually) over time as the real standard of FCSU spending in the 33rd percentile changes. The real value of the threshold will likely change more slowly and gradually than in the "experimental" measures described above, because of using five instead of three years in the average.

- Family resources include cash income, plus in-kind benefits that families can use to meet their FCSU needs (for example, the Supplemental Nutrition Assistance Program [SNAP] formerly known as food stamps), minus income and payroll taxes, plus tax credits, minus childcare and other work-related expenses, minus child support payments to another household, and minus out-of-pocket medical expenses.

- The SPM is not intended to replace the official poverty measure and is not to be used in calculations affecting program eligibility and funding distribution. According to the report referenced above, it is "designed to provide information on aggregate levels of economic need at a national level or within large subpopulations or areas...providing further understanding of economic conditions and trends." Census Bureau presentation of the SPM has focused on the different distribution of the poverty population indicated by the new measures, as shown in Table 3-10.

Experimental measures based on NAS recommendations—Table 3-11

Several alternative poverty rates that redefined both resources and needs were presented in "Alternative Poverty Estimates in the United States: 2003" (see below for complete reference) and have been updated through 2015 on the Census Bureau Web site at www.census.gov, under the general heading "NAS-based Experimental Poverty Estimates."

To derive these estimates, a baseline set of poverty thresholds for the year 1999, based on data from the CEX for the years 1997–1999, was developed as follows:

- A reference family type was selected: a 2-adult, 2-child family.

- The definition of necessities for the purpose of the poverty threshold was expenditures on food, clothing, shelter, and utilities (FCSU), augmented by a multiplier of between 1.15 and 1.25 to include other needs such as household and personal supplies. The definition of food includes food away from home. Expenses on shelter include interest (but not principal repayment) for homeowners and rent for renters.

- The numerical estimates were derived as follows: FCSU expenditures for reference families falling between the 30th and 35th percentile of the distribution of expenditures in the CEX, based on 1997–1999 data but expressed in 1999 dollars, were calculated and expanded by the multiplier percentages. The midpoint of these estimates was then selected as the poverty threshold; it turned out to be 96.725 percent of FCSU expenditures by the median household.

- For health care, three different treatments were developed; these treatments are described below.

- Three-parameter equivalence scale adjustments were used to convert the threshold for the reference family to thresholds for other family sizes and compositions, accounting for the differing needs of adults and children and the economies of scale of living in larger families.

- For some of the experimental measures, thresholds were adjusted geographically to reflect differences in the cost of living (in practice, difference in housing costs) in different areas.

The family incomes to be compared with these poverty thresholds were defined and measured to include the effects of all taxes, tax credits, and in-kind benefits such as food stamps, but not the value of homeownership, and to allow for expenses such as child care that are necessary to hold a job.

The eight experimental measures shown in Table 3-11 are as originally presented in Table B-3 in "Alternative Poverty Estimates in the United States: 2003," and most recently updated in the table "Official and National Academy of Sciences (NAS) Based Poverty Rates: 1999 to 2015" on the Census Bureau Web site. The following abbreviations are used to define the alternative definitions of poverty that are presented in this table.

- *MSI* indicates that in calculating the poverty rate, medical out-of-pocket expenses are subtracted from family income before comparing that income to the family's threshold.

- *MIT* indicates that poverty thresholds were increased to take the family's potential medical out-of-pocket expenses into account, using the CEX and the 1996 Medical Expenditures Panel Survey, with the amounts depending on family size, age, and health insurance coverage.

- *GA* indicates that the thresholds were adjusted for geographic differences in the cost of living. Measures labeled *NGA* were not.

- *CPI* indicates that the thresholds established for 1999 were updated to succeeding years using the percent change in the CPI-U. In effect, the thresholds for these measures have been

held constant in real (inflation-adjusted) terms since 1999, just as the official thresholds have been held constant in real terms—in intention, and in fact except for bias in the price indexes—since 1964.

- *CE* indicates that the thresholds were updated using the percent change in <u>median</u> FCSU expenditures from the latest available 12 quarters of CEX data. This means that if the actual real FCSU spending of middle-income families rises (or falls), the real standard of living represented by the poverty thresholds will rise (or fall) commensurately.

Notes on the data

The following are the principal changes that may affect year-to-year comparability of all income and poverty data from the CPS.

- Beginning in 1952, the estimates are based on 1950 census population controls. Earlier figures were based on 1940 census population controls.

- Beginning in 1962, 1960 census–based sample design and population controls are fully implemented.

- With 1971 and 1972 data, 1970 census–based sample design and population controls were introduced.

- With 1983–1985 data, 1980 census–based sample design was introduced; 1980 population controls were introduced; and these were extended back to 1979 data.

- With 1993 data, there was a major redesign of the CPS, including the introduction of computer-assisted interviewing. The limits used to "code" reported income amounts were changed, resulting in reporting of higher income values for the highest-income families and, consequently, an exaggerated year-to-year increase in income inequality. (It is possible that this jump actually reflects in one year an increase that had emerged more gradually, so that the distribution measures for 1993 and later years may be properly comparable with data for decades earlier even if they should not be directly compared with 1992.) In addition, 1990 census–based population controls were introduced, and these were extended back to the 1992 data.

- With 1995 data, the 1990 census–based sample design was implemented and the sample was reduced by 7,000 households.

- Data for 2001 implemented population controls based on the 2000 census, which were carried back to 2000 and 1999 data as well. Data from 2000 forward also incorporate results from a 28,000-household sample expansion.

- Beginning with the data for 2010 presented here, population controls based on the 2010 census were implemented. (This resulted in some revision of CPS data initially published for 2010.)

For more information on these and other changes that could affect comparability, see "Current Population Survey Technical Paper 63RV: Design and Methodology" (March 2002) and footnotes to CPS historical income tables, both available on the Census Bureau Web site at www.census.gov/hhes/income.

Data availability

Data embodying the official definitions of income and poverty are published annually in late summer or early fall by the Census Bureau, as part of a series with the general title *Current Population Reports: Consumer Income, P60*. Most of the data up to 2012 in this chapter were derived from report P60-245, "Income, Poverty, and Health Insurance Coverage in the United States: 2012" (September 2013), and from the "Historical Income Tables" and "Historical Poverty Tables" on the Census Web site (see below for the address). In 2013, the Census Bureau split the previous report in two. Health insurance coverage is now published separately from income and poverty. The historical tables can be found in the "CPS-ASEC" section under the "Data" category.

The data in Table 3-11 were first published in two reports, both issued in June 2005: P60-228, "Alternative Income Estimates in the United States: 2003," and P60-227, "Alternative Poverty Estimates in the United States: 2003." Updates available on the website are cited in the table description above. Corrections to the 2006 data on the website were obtained from Census Bureau staff.

The NAS-based experimental data used in Table 3-11 are from the Census Bureau Web site, as specified in the description above.

The SPM data in Tables 3-10 are from reports entitled "The Research Supplemental Poverty Measure." Reports for 2012, 2011, and 2010 respectively are numbered P60-247, P60-244, and P60-241, and are available on the Census Web site.

All these reports and related data, including historical tabulations, used in *Business Statistics* are available on the Census Bureau Web site at <http://www.census.gov>, under the general headings of "Income" and "Poverty."

REFERENCES

Definitions and descriptions of the concepts and data of all series are provided in the source documents listed above and in the references contained therein.

TABLES 3-12 THROUGH 3-14

Health Insurance Coverage

SOURCE: U.S. DEPARTMENT OF COMMERCE, BUREAU OF THE CENSUS

The Current Population Survey Annual Social and Economic Supplement (CPS ASEC) and the American Community Survey (ACS) is used to produce official estimates of income and poverty, and it serves as the most widely-cited source of estimates on health insurance coverage.

Due to questions of the validity of the health insurance data in previous reports, the Census Bureau implemented changes in 2014 to CPS ACS, including a complete redesign of the health insurance questions that replaced the existing questions in the CPS ASEC. Due the differences in measurement, health insurance estimates from calendar year 2013 are different from estimates in previous years.

Health insurance coverage in the CPS ASEC refers to comprehensive coverage during the calendar year. The American Community Survey (ACS) health insurance coverage status is at the time the individual is interviewed. Therefore, two uninsured measures are reported.

Since the passage of the Patient Protection and Affordable Care Act (ACA) in 2010, several provisions of the ACA have gone into effect at different times. For example, in 2010, the Young Adult Provision enabled adults under age 26 to remain as dependents on their parents' health insurance plans. In 2014 policy changes associated with the ACA provide the option for states to expand Medicaid to people whose income-to-poverty ratio full under a particular threshold. The decreases in the uninsured rates in 2013 and 2014 are consistent with what some of the provisions of the ACA intended.

Definitions

Health insurance is a means for financing a person's health care expense.

Private insurance is a plan provided through an employer or a union and coverage purchased directly by an individual from an insurance company or though an exchange.

Government health insurance includes federal programs such as Medicare, Medicaid, the Children's Health Insurance Program (CHIP), individual state health programs, TRICARE, CHAMPVA (Civilian Health and Medical Program of the Department of Veterans Affairs), as well care care provided by the Department of Veterans Affairs and the military.

Uninsured are people if, for an entire year, they were not covered by any type of health insurance. Additionally, people were considered uninsured if they only had coverage through the Indian Health Service (IHS).

Data availability

Detailed health insurance questions have been asked in the CPS since 1988 as part of a mandate to collect data on non-cash basis. However, as noted, comparing older results with newer ones is uncertain due to the changes in questions in 2013.

CHAPTER 4: CONSUMER INCOME AND SPENDING

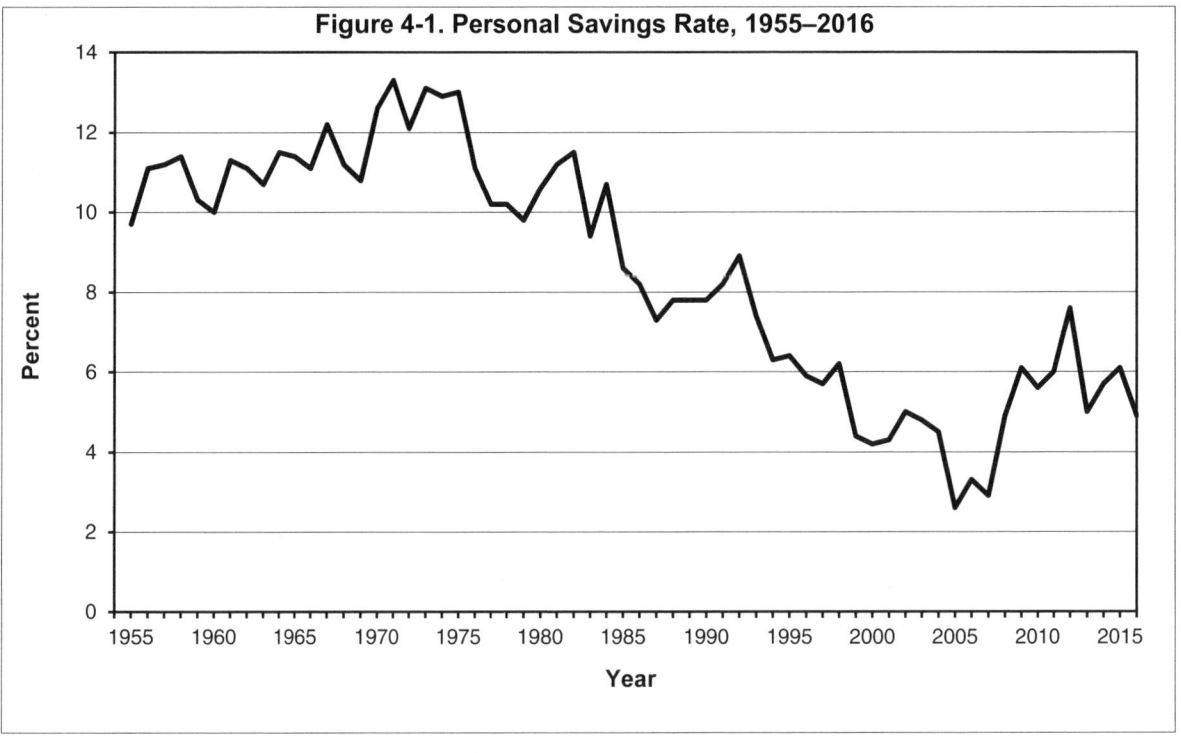

Figure 4-1. Personal Savings Rate, 1955–2016

- The personal saving rate—now defined to include saving in individual pension plans as earned benefits rather than the employer contributions—got as high as 13.3 percent in the early 1970s. (Benefits from social insurance systems such as Social Security, unlike those in private and government employee retirement plans, do not figure in personal saving; any excess of receipts over payments is counted as government saving.) Since then the personal saving rate entered a downtrend, and hit the lowest rates since the Great Depression in the real estate bubble years 2005 through 2007, 2.6, 3.3 and 2.9 respectively. Saving as a percent of disposable personal income has increased somewhat since then and reached a high 7.6 percent in 2012 but dropped to 4.9 percent in 2016. (Tables 4-1A and B)

- It should be noted that personal income does not, by definition, include any capital gains. Despite that, taxes on realized capital gains are deducted (along with all other income taxes) from personal income to get after-tax income. Capital gains, both realized and unrealized, can be a source of spending power in addition to current disposable income; during the housing price bubble they were converted into cash by asset sales, refinancing, and home equity loans, all of which were reflected in low saving rates. (Table 12-6)

- Government social benefits were 4.6 percent of personal income in 1955, rising to 14.1 percent in the high-employment year 2007. In the recession they rose further, to 18.3 percent in 2010, falling back somewhat to 17.0 percent by 2016. It should be understood that this category counts as income all spending financed by government health insurance programs such as Medicare and Medicaid, simultaneously counting that spending as personal consumption expenditures rather than direct government spending in the NIPAs. (Table 4-1)

Table 4-1A. Personal Income and Its Disposition: Recent Data

(Billions of current dollars, except as noted; quarterly data are at seasonally adjusted annual rates.)   **NIPA Table 2.1**

Year and quarter	Personal income											
					Personal income receipts on assets		Personal current transfer receipts					
								Government social benefits to persons				
	Total	Compensation of employees	Proprietors' income with IVA and CCAdj	Rental income of persons with CCAdj	Personal interest income	Personal dividend income	Total	Social Security and Medicare	Government unemployment insurance	Veterans	Medicaid	Other government benefits to persons
1955	324.6	230.9	44.3	13.4	18.9	10.5	14.8	4.9	1.6	4.4	. . .	3.9
1956	348.4	249.6	45.8	13.7	21.2	11.3	15.6	5.7	1.6	4.3	. . .	4.0
1957	368.5	263.0	47.8	14.1	23.8	11.7	18.1	7.3	1.9	4.5	. . .	4.4
1958	379.5	265.1	50.2	14.8	25.8	11.6	22.2	8.5	4.2	4.6	. . .	4.9
1959	403.2	286.3	50.3	15.6	28.0	12.6	22.9	10.2	2.9	4.5	. . .	5.4
1960	422.5	301.9	50.6	16.5	31.0	13.4	24.4	11.1	3.1	4.5	. . .	5.7
1961	441.1	311.1	53.2	17.2	33.2	13.9	28.1	12.6	4.4	4.9	. . .	6.2
1962	469.1	332.9	55.2	18.0	36.6	15.0	28.8	14.3	3.2	4.6	. . .	6.8
1963	492.8	351.2	56.4	18.7	39.8	16.2	30.3	15.2	3.1	4.8	. . .	7.3
1964	528.4	376.8	59.1	18.8	44.3	18.2	31.3	16.0	2.8	4.6	. . .	7.9
1965	570.8	406.3	63.7	19.3	48.5	20.2	33.9	18.1	2.4	4.8	. . .	8.6
1966	620.6	450.3	67.9	19.9	53.5	20.7	37.5	20.8	1.9	4.8	1.9	8.1
1967	665.7	482.9	69.5	20.3	58.3	21.5	45.8	25.8	2.2	5.5	2.7	9.4
1968	730.7	532.1	73.8	20.1	63.8	23.5	53.3	30.5	2.2	5.9	4.0	10.8
1969	800.3	586.0	77.0	20.4	74.4	24.2	59.0	33.1	2.3	6.6	4.6	12.4
1970	864.6	625.1	77.8	20.7	88.3	24.3	71.7	38.7	4.2	7.5	5.5	16.0
1971	932.1	667.0	83.9	21.9	97.3	25.0	85.4	44.6	6.2	8.4	6.7	19.4
1972	1 023.6	733.6	95.1	22.8	106.5	26.8	94.8	49.7	6.0	9.4	8.2	21.4
1973	1 138.5	815.0	112.5	23.3	120.8	29.9	108.6	60.9	4.6	10.2	9.6	23.3
1974	1 249.3	890.3	112.2	23.3	142.2	33.2	128.6	70.3	7.0	11.6	11.2	28.4
1975	1 366.9	950.2	118.2	22.5	162.4	32.9	163.1	81.5	18.1	14.0	13.9	35.7
1976	1 498.5	1 051.2	131.0	20.6	173.6	39.0	177.6	93.3	16.4	13.8	15.5	38.7
1977	1 654.6	1 169.0	144.5	16.2	198.7	44.7	189.5	105.3	13.1	13.3	16.7	40.9
1978	1 859.7	1 320.2	166.0	16.9	227.3	50.7	203.4	116.9	9.4	13.6	18.6	44.9
1979	2 078.2	1 481.0	179.4	16.6	260.9	57.4	227.3	132.5	9.7	14.2	21.1	49.9
1980	2 317.5	1 626.2	171.6	19.7	322.0	64.0	271.5	154.8	16.1	14.7	23.9	62.1
1981	2 596.5	1 795.3	179.7	25.4	399.2	73.6	307.8	182.1	15.9	15.8	27.7	66.3
1982	2 779.5	1 894.3	171.2	26.1	463.7	77.6	343.1	204.6	25.2	16.3	30.2	66.8
1983	2 970.3	2 013.9	186.3	27.5	501.0	83.3	370.5	222.2	26.4	16.4	33.9	71.5
1984	3 281.8	2 217.4	228.2	27.9	574.4	90.6	380.9	237.7	16.0	16.3	36.6	74.3
1985	3 516.3	2 389.0	241.1	29.5	615.4	97.4	403.1	253.0	15.9	16.6	39.7	78.0
1986	3 725.7	2 543.8	256.5	21.9	649.3	106.0	428.6	268.9	16.5	16.6	43.6	83.0
1987	3 955.9	2 724.3	286.5	20.2	667.7	112.2	447.9	282.6	14.6	16.5	47.8	86.4
1988	4 276.3	2 950.0	325.8	25.1	709.6	129.7	476.9	300.2	13.3	16.7	53.0	93.6
1989	4 619.9	3 142.6	341.9	24.4	794.2	157.8	521.1	325.6	14.4	17.2	60.8	103.1
1990	4 906.4	3 342.7	354.4	31.4	822.4	168.8	574.7	351.7	18.2	17.7	73.1	113.9
1991	5 073.4	3 452.0	356.0	42.0	805.3	180.2	650.5	381.7	26.8	18.1	96.9	127.0
1992	5 413.0	3 671.1	402.4	64.3	793.1	189.1	731.8	414.4	39.6	18.6	116.2	142.9
1993	5 649.0	3 820.7	430.5	93.6	783.9	204.7	778.9	444.7	34.8	19.3	130.1	150.0
1994	5 937.3	4 010.1	459.5	117.5	794.2	235.2	815.7	476.6	23.9	19.7	139.4	156.1
1995	6 281.0	4 202.6	484.5	129.2	856.0	258.0	864.7	508.9	21.7	20.5	149.6	164.0
1996	6 667.0	4 422.1	547.4	147.0	874.3	302.2	906.3	536.9	22.3	21.4	158.2	167.6
1997	7 080.7	4 714.7	587.9	152.0	920.5	337.9	935.4	563.5	20.1	22.3	163.1	166.4
1998	7 593.7	5 077.8	644.2	169.9	987.1	355.4	957.9	574.8	19.7	23.3	170.2	170.0
1999	7 988.4	5 410.3	700.4	183.1	983.3	346.4	992.2	588.6	20.5	24.1	184.6	174.4
2000	8 637.1	5 856.6	757.8	187.7	1 070.2	383.3	1 044.9	620.5	20.7	25.0	199.5	179.1
2001	8 991.6	6 046.5	836.8	207.5	1 072.2	369.2	1 145.8	667.7	31.9	26.6	227.3	192.4
2002	9 153.9	6 141.9	871.0	217.3	991.8	398.6	1 250.5	706.1	53.5	29.5	250.0	211.4
2003	9 491.1	6 364.5	900.1	238.0	988.2	432.3	1 321.1	740.2	53.2	31.8	264.5	231.3
2004	10 052.9	6 739.5	962.1	255.4	941.7	562.1	1 404.6	789.9	36.4	34.0	289.8	254.4
2005	10 614.0	7 086.8	979.0	238.4	1 088.1	578.3	1 491.0	844.9	31.8	36.4	304.4	273.6
2006	11 393.9	7 502.3	1 053.7	207.5	1 214.7	723.7	1 593.1	943.3	30.4	38.9	299.1	281.5
2007	12 000.2	7 898.3	979.2	189.4	1 350.1	816.5	1 697.5	1 004.7	32.7	41.7	324.2	294.2
2008	12 502.2	8 078.3	1 026.5	262.1	1 361.6	805.4	1 920.0	1 068.4	51.1	45.0	338.3	417.0
2009	12 094.8	7 787.0	973.0	333.7	1 264.3	553.7	2 108.8	1 159.1	131.2	51.5	369.2	397.8
2010	12 477.1	7 961.4	1 032.7	402.8	1 195.0	544.6	2 281.7	1 204.0	138.9	58.0	396.6	484.3
2011	13 254.5	8 269.0	1 143.7	485.3	1 231.6	682.2	2 310.2	1 249.3	107.2	63.3	405.7	484.9
2012	13 915.1	8 609.9	1 241.4	525.3	1 288.8	834.9	2 323.6	1 318.4	83.8	70.1	417.3	434.0
2013	14 073.7	8 842.4	1 284.7	567.1	1 261.6	794.4	2 386.9	1 374.0	62.3	79.1	439.7	431.8
2014	14 818.2	9 256.5	1 315.8	611.7	1 303.3	941.9	2 498.8	1 435.5	35.4	83.7	491.0	453.1
2015	15 553.0	9 708.3	1 318.8	662.5	1 367.3	1 019.8	2 631.2	1 505.5	32.2	89.8	536.0	467.8
2016	15 928.7	9 978.6	1 341.9	707.3	1 415.3	962.5	2 711.0	1 552.4	31.7	92.8	563.0	471.1
2014												
1st quarter	14 485.9	9 119.4	1 292.7	594.3	1 277.9	864.1	2 435.8	1 414.3	39.0	82.7	459.5	440.3
2nd quarter	14 713.5	9 175.0	1 319.3	606.7	1 297.3	930.7	2 485.8	1 429.9	35.8	82.7	481.6	455.9
3rd quarter	14 924.8	9 286.9	1 320.0	618.0	1 315.2	971.8	2 524.5	1 441.5	34.0	84.0	507.4	457.7
4th quarter	15 148.7	9 444.5	1 331.2	627.9	1 322.8	1 000.9	2 549.0	1 456.7	33.0	85.5	515.6	458.3
2015												
1st quarter	15 301.0	9 541.6	1 312.8	639.3	1 303.4	1 046.8	2 594.9	1 483.9	32.8	88.2	524.0	466.1
2nd quarter	15 516.1	9 655.9	1 313.9	658.4	1 385.0	1 021.9	2 630.3	1 500.1	31.9	89.7	538.2	470.4
3rd quarter	15 625.5	9 730.0	1 323.2	670.9	1 403.2	1 010.6	2 643.9	1 512.4	32.1	90.0	540.5	468.9
4th quarter	15 769.2	9 905.5	1 325.4	681.4	1 377.5	1 000.0	2 656.0	1 525.4	31.9	91.4	541.4	465.8
2016												
1st quarter	15 751.0	9 838.6	1 327.6	697.6	1 397.4	977.5	2 683.4	1 535.0	32.5	91.6	549.4	474.8
2nd quarter	15 910.1	9 979.6	1 339.5	704.8	1 408.4	962.9	2 703.0	1 547.5	31.9	92.7	558.0	472.8
3rd quarter	16 028.0	10 081.4	1 346.1	708.1	1 416.9	956.4	2 719.7	1 557.9	31.6	92.9	566.8	470.4
4th quarter	16 025.7	10 014.9	1 354.6	718.9	1 438.5	953.0	2 737.9	1 568.9	30.7	94.0	577.8	466.5

. . . = Not available.

Table 4-1A. Personal Income and Its Disposition: Recent Data—*Continued*

(Billions of current dollars, except as noted; quarterly data are at seasonally adjusted annual rates.)   NIPA Table 2.1

Year and quarter	Personal income—Continued: Personal current transfer receipts—Continued: From business, net	Less: Contributions for government social insurance, domestic	Less: Personal current taxes	Equals: Disposable personal income	Less: Personal outlays: Total	Personal consumption expenditures	Personal interest payments	Personal current transfer payments: Total	To government	To the rest of the world, net	Equals: Personal saving: Billions of dollars	Percent of disposable personal income	Billions of chained (2009) dollars: Percent income excluding current transfers	Disposable personal income
1955	0.9	9.1	32.9	291.7	263.5	258.7	4.0	0.9	0.4	0.4	28.2	9.7	1 955.2	1 846.5
1956	1.2	10.0	36.6	311.8	277.1	271.6	4.6	1.0	0.5	0.5	34.7	11.1	2 057.5	1 934.8
1957	1.4	11.4	38.9	329.6	292.7	286.7	4.9	1.1	0.6	0.5	36.9	11.2	2 101.5	1 984.9
1958	1.2	11.4	38.5	340.9	302.0	296.0	5.0	1.0	0.6	0.4	38.9	11.4	2 094.7	2 005.9
1959	1.3	13.8	42.3	360.9	323.8	317.5	5.5	0.8	0.3	0.5	37.1	10.3	2 196.7	2 092.1
1960	1.3	16.4	46.1	376.5	338.6	331.6	6.2	0.8	0.3	0.5	37.8	10.0	2 262.9	2 146.9
1961	1.4	17.0	47.0	390.0	349.5	342.0	6.5	1.0	0.5	0.5	41.4	11.3	2 323.1	2 222.7
1962	1.5	19.1	51.6	417.5	371.2	363.1	7.0	1.1	0.5	0.6	46.4	11.1	2 447.0	2 328.9
1963	1.9	21.7	54.6	438.3	391.6	382.5	7.9	1.2	0.5	0.7	46.7	10.7	2 539.7	2 416.5
1964	2.2	22.4	52.1	476.3	421.4	411.2	8.9	1.3	0.6	0.7	54.8	11.5	2 689.0	2 588.1
1965	2.3	23.4	57.7	513.2	454.9	443.6	9.9	1.4	0.6	0.8	58.3	11.4	2 863.9	2 748.9
1966	2.1	31.3	66.4	554.2	492.8	480.6	10.7	1.6	0.8	0.8	61.4	11.1	3 034.8	2 895.0
1967	2.3	34.9	73.0	592.8	520.6	507.4	11.1	2.0	1.0	1.0	72.2	12.2	3 147.7	3 020.6
1968	2.8	38.7	87.0	643.8	571.7	557.4	12.2	2.0	1.0	1.0	72.1	11.2	3 308.9	3 157.4
1969	3.3	44.1	104.5	695.8	620.7	604.5	14.0	2.2	1.1	1.1	75.0	10.8	3 462.5	3 264.4
1970	2.9	46.4	103.1	761.5	665.5	647.7	15.2	2.6	1.3	1.3	96.1	12.6	3 540.6	3 413.2
1971	2.7	51.2	101.7	830.4	720.3	701.0	16.6	2.8	1.5	1.4	110.1	13.3	3 628.8	3 570.4
1972	3.1	59.2	123.6	899.9	790.7	769.4	18.1	3.2	1.8	1.4	109.2	12.1	3 848.1	3 741.2
1973	3.9	75.5	132.4	1 006.1	874.3	851.1	19.8	3.4	1.8	1.6	131.8	13.1	4 046.8	3 968.6
1974	4.7	85.2	151.0	1 098.3	956.6	932.0	21.2	3.4	2.1	1.4	141.7	12.9	3 987.0	3 923.6
1975	6.8	89.3	147.6	1 219.3	1 060.3	1 032.8	23.7	3.8	2.5	1.3	159.0	13.0	3 946.3	4 020.0
1976	6.7	101.3	172.7	1 325.8	1 178.5	1 150.2	23.9	4.4	3.0	1.4	147.3	11.1	4 107.5	4 144.0
1977	5.1	113.1	197.9	1 456.7	1 308.5	1 276.7	27.0	4.8	3.5	1.4	148.2	10.2	4 284.5	4 274.8
1978	6.5	131.3	229.6	1 630.1	1 463.5	1 426.2	31.9	5.4	3.9	1.6	166.6	10.2	4 524.7	4 470.5
1979	8.2	152.7	268.9	1 809.3	1 631.7	1 589.5	36.2	6.0	4.3	1.7	177.5	9.8	4 641.9	4 557.8
1980	8.6	166.2	299.5	2 018.0	1 804.8	1 754.6	43.2	6.9	5.0	2.0	213.2	10.6	4 634.6	4 590.5
1981	11.2	195.7	345.8	2 250.7	1 998.3	1 937.5	49.2	11.5	6.0	5.6	252.5	11.2	4 761.6	4 705.6
1982	12.4	208.9	354.7	2 424.7	2 147.0	2 073.9	59.3	13.8	7.1	6.7	277.7	11.5	4 801.9	4 803.3
1983	13.8	226.0	352.9	2 617.4	2 370.4	2 286.5	68.8	15.1	8.1	7.0	247.0	9.4	4 911.4	4 971.0
1984	19.7	257.5	377.9	2 903.9	2 591.8	2 498.2	76.6	17.1	9.2	7.9	312.1	10.7	5 272.5	5 314.0
1985	22.3	281.4	417.8	3 098.5	2 833.4	2 722.7	92.0	18.8	10.4	8.3	265.1	8.6	5 462.8	5 476.2
1986	22.9	303.4	437.8	3 287.9	3 018.5	2 898.4	99.0	21.1	12.0	9.1	269.4	8.2	5 664.0	5 687.8
1987	20.2	323.1	489.6	3 466.3	3 214.2	3 092.1	98.9	23.2	13.2	10.0	252.1	7.3	5 847.0	5 811.0
1988	20.6	361.5	505.9	3 770.4	3 475.7	3 346.9	103.1	25.6	14.8	10.8	294.8	7.8	6 097.5	6 083.9
1989	23.2	385.2	567.7	4 052.1	3 735.6	3 592.8	114.8	28.0	16.5	11.6	316.5	7.8	6 305.0	6 268.7
1990	22.2	410.1	594.7	4 311.8	3 976.3	3 825.6	120.1	30.6	18.4	12.2	335.4	7.8	6 390.2	6 393.5
1991	17.6	430.2	588.9	4 484.5	4 118.6	3 960.2	121.8	36.7	22.6	14.1	365.9	8.2	6 324.7	6 438.4
1992	16.3	455.0	612.8	4 800.2	4 374.2	4 215.7	118.1	40.5	26.0	14.5	426.0	8.9	6 525.0	6 714.2
1993	14.1	477.4	648.8	5 000.2	4 632.6	4 471.0	116.0	45.6	28.6	17.1	367.6	7.4	6 626.7	6 823.6
1994	13.3	508.2	693.1	5 244.2	4 912.8	4 741.0	122.0	49.8	30.9	18.9	331.4	6.3	6 829.0	7 010.7
1995	18.7	532.8	748.4	5 532.6	5 179.6	4 984.2	142.6	52.9	32.6	20.3	352.9	6.4	7 068.9	7 245.8
1996	22.9	555.1	837.1	5 829.9	5 484.7	5 268.1	159.1	57.6	34.9	22.6	345.2	5.9	7 358.0	7 476.1
1997	19.4	587.2	931.8	6 148.8	5 796.7	5 560.7	172.1	63.9	38.2	25.7	352.2	5.7	7 722.2	7 751.3
1998	26.0	624.7	1 032.4	6 561.3	6 156.0	5 903.0	183.4	69.5	39.9	29.7	405.3	6.2	8 268.8	8 208.1
1999	34.0	661.3	1 112.1	6 876.3	6 573.0	6 307.0	190.2	75.8	44.1	31.8	303.3	4.4	8 583.7	8 477.7
2000	42.4	705.8	1 236.6	7 400.5	7 092.8	6 792.4	217.5	82.9	48.8	34.1	307.7	4.2	9 081.8	8 902.2
2001	46.8	733.2	1 239.3	7 752.3	7 417.1	7 103.1	223.2	90.8	52.9	37.9	335.2	4.3	9 203.9	9 148.7
2002	34.2	751.5	1 054.7	8 099.2	7 693.9	7 384.1	213.0	96.9	56.4	40.5	405.3	5.0	9 163.7	9 431.6
2003	26.3	779.3	1 005.3	8 485.8	8 076.2	7 765.5	209.8	100.8	60.5	40.3	409.6	4.8	9 299.5	9 690.1
2004	16.8	829.2	1 050.6	9 002.3	8 592.9	8 260.0	221.8	111.1	66.9	44.2	409.4	4.5	9 622.4	10 035.7
2005	25.7	873.3	1 213.2	9 400.8	9 157.7	8 794.1	248.8	114.8	71.6	43.2	243.1	2.6	9 860.4	10 189.4
2006	21.5	922.6	1 357.1	10 036.9	9 705.5	9 304.0	275.1	126.4	76.6	49.7	331.4	3.3	10 323.5	10 595.4
2007	30.6	961.4	1 493.2	10 507.0	10 197.2	9 750.5	305.9	140.8	81.0	59.8	309.8	2.9	10 578.7	10 820.6
2008	36.6	988.2	1 507.8	10 994.4	10 457.7	10 013.6	289.6	154.4	82.8	71.7	536.7	4.9	10 538.8	10 987.3
2009	38.7	964.4	1 152.3	10 942.5	10 275.1	9 847.0	273.9	154.2	83.5	70.7	667.4	6.1	9 947.3	10 942.5
2010	43.0	984.1	1 239.3	11 237.9	10 607.9	10 202.2	250.8	154.9	83.9	71.0	630.0	5.6	9 987.3	11 055.1
2011	50.2	917.8	1 453.2	11 801.4	11 091.2	10 689.3	241.4	160.5	85.5	75.1	710.1	6.0	10 460.1	11 331.2
2012	42.7	951.6	1 511.4	12 403.7	11 457.0	11 050.6	240.6	165.8	91.1	74.7	946.7	7.6	10 882.7	11 688.3
2013	41.1	1 104.6	1 677.8	12 395.8	11 775.7	11 361.2	243.9	170.7	93.4	77.3	620.1	5.0	10 830.0	11 527.6
2014	45.6	1 155.3	1 785.6	13 032.6	12 293.8	11 863.7	253.7	176.5	98.6	77.9	738.8	5.7	11 244.2	11 939.3
2015	53.1	1 208.0	1 937.9	13 615.0	12 786.7	12 332.3	268.7	185.7	105.4	80.2	828.4	6.1	11 754.2	12 436.0
2016	57.4	1 245.3	1 960.1	13 968.6	13 288.0	12 820.7	278.4	189.0	108.9	80.1	680.6	4.9	11 878.7	12 608.2
2014														
1st quarter	43.2	1 141.5	1 751.5	12 734.3	12 060.7	11 640.2	249.1	171.4	96.6	74.9	673.6	5.3	11 050.9	11 720.4
2nd quarter	44.6	1 145.9	1 757.8	12 955.7	12 216.2	11 791.9	250.1	174.2	98.1	76.1	739.5	5.7	11 163.6	11 871.5
3rd quarter	46.3	1 157.8	1 795.7	13 129.2	12 371.8	11 941.1	253.2	177.4	99.4	78.1	757.4	5.8	11 287.1	11 995.3
4th quarter	48.3	1 175.9	1 837.5	13 311.3	12 526.5	12 081.4	262.3	182.8	100.4	82.4	784.8	5.9	11 475.0	12 169.6
2015														
1st quarter	50.5	1 188.3	1 903.4	13 397.6	12 587.9	12 142.2	262.2	183.5	105.0	78.6	809.7	6.0	11 616.6	12 297.6
2nd quarter	52.4	1 201.7	1 934.1	13 582.0	12 737.7	12 284.2	267.6	185.9	105.4	80.4	844.4	6.2	11 729.9	12 414.2
3rd quarter	54.1	1 210.3	1 937.7	13 687.8	12 865.8	12 407.8	271.2	186.9	105.7	81.2	822.0	6.0	11 778.1	12 470.8
4th quarter	55.4	1 231.9	1 976.5	13 792.7	12 955.2	12 494.9	273.9	186.4	105.7	80.7	837.5	6.1	11 891.9	12 561.2
2016														
1st quarter	56.5	1 227.5	1 928.9	13 822.1	13 034.3	12 571.5	273.4	189.4	107.7	81.7	787.8	5.7	11 830.4	12 567.7
2nd quarter	57.3	1 245.4	1 950.7	13 959.4	13 214.2	12 755.0	276.3	183.0	108.1	74.9	745.2	5.3	11 894.9	12 627.2
3rd quarter	57.8	1 258.2	1 983.8	14 044.3	13 366.6	12 899.4	279.3	187.9	109.0	78.9	677.7	4.8	11 934.4	12 649.2
4th quarter	58.0	1 250.2	1 977.2	14 048.5	13 537.0	13 056.9	284.4	195.6	110.6	85.0	511.5	3.6	11 857.1	12 590.8

Table 4-1B. Personal Income and Its Disposition: Historical

(Billions of current dollars, except as noted; quarterly data are at seasonally adjusted annual rates.)   **NIPA Table 2.1**

| Year and quarter | Personal income | | | | | | Less: Contributions for government social insurance, domestic | Less: Personal current taxes | Equals: Disposable personal income | Less: Personal outlays | Equals: Personal saving | | Billions of chained (2009) dollars | |
	Total	Compensation of employees	Proprietors' income with IVA and CCAdj	Rental income of persons with CCAdj	Personal income receipts on assets	Personal current transfer receipts					Billions of dollars	Percent of disposable personal income	Personal income excluding current transfers	Disposable personal income
1929	85.3	51.4	14.0	6.1	12.6	1.2	0.1	1.7	83.5	79.6	3.9	4.7	848.4	843.0
1930	76.5	47.2	10.9	5.4	11.9	1.2	0.1	1.6	74.9	71.6	3.3	4.4	793.4	789.7
1931	65.6	40.1	8.3	4.4	10.5	2.3	0.1	1.0	64.6	61.8	2.8	4.3	747.0	762.9
1932	50.3	31.4	5.0	3.6	8.6	1.7	0.1	0.7	49.5	49.7	-0.1	-0.2	649.3	663.0
1933	47.2	29.8	5.3	2.9	7.6	1.7	0.1	0.8	46.4	46.8	-0.4	-0.8	631.6	643.8
1934	54.1	34.6	7.0	2.5	8.3	1.8	0.1	0.9	53.2	52.3	0.9	1.7	694.4	705.7
1935	60.8	37.7	10.1	2.6	8.5	2.0	0.1	1.1	59.8	56.8	3.0	5.1	762.5	774.3
1936	69.2	43.3	10.4	2.7	10.0	3.1	0.3	1.3	67.9	63.1	4.8	7.0	848.9	871.9
1937	74.7	48.4	12.5	3.0	10.4	2.0	1.5	1.9	72.8	67.9	4.9	6.7	900.7	901.4
1938	69.1	45.5	10.6	3.5	8.8	2.4	1.6	1.9	67.2	65.3	2.0	2.9	845.2	852.0
1939	73.6	48.6	11.1	3.7	9.4	2.5	1.8	1.5	72.1	68.2	3.9	5.4	910.0	923.2
1940	79.4	52.8	12.2	3.8	9.7	2.7	1.9	1.7	77.7	72.4	5.3	6.8	973.6	986.2
1941	97.9	66.2	16.7	4.4	10.2	2.7	2.3	2.3	95.6	82.3	13.3	13.9	1 137.6	1 141.7
1942	126.7	88.1	23.3	5.5	10.0	2.7	2.9	4.9	121.8	90.0	31.9	26.2	1 318.0	1 294.4
1943	156.2	112.8	28.2	6.0	10.4	2.5	3.8	16.7	139.4	100.8	38.6	27.7	1 495.3	1 356.7
1944	169.7	124.4	29.3	6.3	10.9	3.1	4.3	17.7	152.0	109.7	42.4	27.9	1 533.0	1 399.0
1945	175.8	126.4	30.8	6.6	11.7	5.6	5.3	19.4	156.3	121.2	35.2	22.5	1 505.2	1 383.1
1946	182.7	122.6	35.7	6.9	13.6	10.6	6.6	17.2	165.5	145.9	19.6	11.8	1 423.6	1 368.6
1947	194.6	132.5	34.6	6.9	15.4	10.8	5.6	19.8	174.8	163.8	11.0	6.3	1 380.3	1 312.9
1948	213.7	144.5	39.3	7.5	16.8	10.3	4.6	19.2	194.5	177.2	17.2	8.9	1 445.7	1 382.1
1949	211.2	144.5	34.7	7.8	17.9	11.2	4.9	16.7	194.5	180.9	13.6	7.0	1 432.9	1 393.3
1950	233.9	158.5	37.5	8.8	20.7	14.0	5.5	18.9	215.0	195.0	20.0	9.3	1 556.8	1 521.9
1951	264.5	185.9	42.6	9.7	21.4	11.4	6.6	27.1	237.4	211.5	25.9	10.9	1 677.0	1 573.3
1952	282.7	201.3	43.0	10.8	22.5	11.9	6.9	32.0	250.7	222.8	27.8	11.1	1 758.5	1 627.8
1953	299.6	215.5	42.0	12.0	24.6	12.5	7.1	33.2	266.3	237.1	29.2	11.0	1 839.7	1 706.9
1954	302.6	214.4	42.3	13.1	26.6	14.3	8.1	30.2	272.4	244.2	28.2	10.3	1 832.0	1 731.3
1955														
1st quarter	313.9	222.2	43.7	13.3	28.3	15.3	8.9	31.4	282.5	256.3	26.3	9.3	1 896.9	1 794.5
2nd quarter	321.5	228.4	44.3	13.4	28.8	15.6	9.0	32.4	289.1	261.6	27.5	9.5	1 940.7	1 834.0
3rd quarter	328.9	234.2	44.6	13.4	29.9	15.9	9.2	33.4	295.5	266.0	29.5	10.0	1 978.3	1 867.7
4th quarter	334.0	238.7	44.5	13.5	30.6	16.0	9.3	34.2	299.8	270.2	29.6	9.9	2 004.6	1 889.5
1956														
1st quarter	339.5	243.2	44.9	13.6	31.4	16.3	9.9	35.4	304.1	272.0	32.1	10.6	2 028.4	1 909.0
2nd quarter	345.3	247.9	45.3	13.6	32.0	16.6	10.0	36.2	309.1	274.8	34.3	11.1	2 049.7	1 927.1
3rd quarter	350.6	250.8	46.4	13.7	32.7	17.1	10.0	36.9	313.7	278.1	35.6	11.3	2 059.4	1 936.9
4th quarter	358.2	256.7	46.8	13.8	33.7	17.3	10.1	37.9	320.3	283.6	36.8	11.5	2 092.3	1 966.3
1957														
1st quarter	362.8	260.6	46.9	13.9	34.5	18.2	11.4	38.6	324.2	288.2	36.0	11.1	2 096.0	1 972.1
2nd quarter	367.5	262.5	47.7	14.0	35.4	19.4	11.4	39.0	328.5	290.5	38.0	11.6	2 104.0	1 986.0
3rd quarter	372.2	265.1	48.8	14.1	36.0	19.6	11.5	39.2	333.0	295.2	37.8	11.4	2 114.1	1 996.8
4th quarter	371.5	263.7	47.7	14.3	36.3	20.8	11.3	38.8	332.7	296.8	35.9	10.8	2 092.1	1 984.9
1958														
1st quarter	372.4	260.2	50.3	14.6	36.6	22.1	11.3	38.2	334.2	296.4	37.8	11.3	2 064.5	1 969.8
2nd quarter	374.8	259.9	50.3	14.8	37.2	23.9	11.3	37.7	337.1	299.2	37.8	11.2	2 064.1	1 983.0
3rd quarter	383.1	267.7	50.1	14.9	37.6	24.2	11.4	38.9	344.1	304.2	39.9	11.6	2 109.7	2 022.9
4th quarter	387.6	272.7	49.9	15.0	37.9	23.7	11.5	39.4	348.2	308.2	40.0	11.5	2 140.0	2 047.6
1959														
1st quarter	394.4	280.2	50.1	15.0	38.8	24.0	13.7	40.8	353.6	315.8	37.8	10.7	2 162.8	2 065.0
2nd quarter	402.7	286.9	50.3	15.4	40.0	23.9	13.9	42.0	360.7	322.0	38.7	10.7	2 203.0	2 098.3
3rd quarter	405.0	287.4	50.4	15.8	41.2	24.2	13.9	42.7	362.4	327.4	34.9	9.6	2 202.1	2 095.1
4th quarter	410.7	290.7	50.6	16.0	42.4	24.8	13.9	43.7	366.9	329.8	37.1	10.1	2 218.8	2 110.1
1960														
1st quarter	417.1	299.3	49.7	16.2	43.6	24.6	16.4	45.3	371.8	333.5	38.3	10.3	2 253.9	2 135.2
2nd quarter	422.1	302.3	50.7	16.4	43.9	25.3	16.5	46.0	376.1	339.6	36.5	9.7	2 267.2	2 148.6
3rd quarter	424.7	303.2	50.9	16.5	44.6	26.0	16.5	46.5	378.2	339.7	38.5	10.2	2 269.0	2 152.4
4th quarter	426.2	302.7	51.0	16.7	45.1	27.0	16.4	46.4	379.7	341.8	38.0	10.0	2 261.5	2 151.5
1961														
1st quarter	430.7	303.7	52.3	16.9	45.6	28.8	16.7	46.5	384.1	342.4	41.7	10.9	2 272.3	2 172.4
2nd quarter	436.9	308.0	52.6	17.1	46.4	29.7	16.9	46.9	390.0	347.4	42.6	10.9	2 303.1	2 205.5
3rd quarter	444.0	313.0	53.3	17.3	47.5	29.9	17.1	47.4	396.6	350.3	46.2	11.7	2 333.6	2 234.8
4th quarter	452.8	319.7	54.5	17.5	49.1	29.4	17.3	48.1	404.7	357.8	46.9	11.6	2 383.4	2 277.9
1962														
1st quarter	459.7	326.2	55.3	17.7	49.4	30.0	18.9	49.4	410.3	363.1	47.2	11.5	2 408.4	2 299.7
2nd quarter	467.0	332.1	55.0	18.0	51.1	30.0	19.1	50.9	416.1	369.0	47.2	11.3	2 440.8	2 323.9
3rd quarter	471.7	334.9	54.9	18.2	52.5	30.4	19.2	52.3	419.4	373.1	46.3	11.0	2 458.0	2 336.0
4th quarter	477.9	338.4	55.8	18.3	53.6	31.2	19.3	53.6	424.3	379.5	44.8	10.6	2 481.1	2 356.6
1963														
1st quarter	483.3	343.4	56.0	18.5	54.0	32.6	21.3	54.1	429.2	383.4	45.8	10.7	2 495.6	2 376.8
2nd quarter	488.1	348.3	55.8	18.7	55.2	31.7	21.5	54.3	433.8	387.8	46.0	10.6	2 524.0	2 398.9
3rd quarter	495.3	353.4	56.2	18.8	56.6	32.0	21.8	54.6	440.7	395.1	45.5	10.3	2 549.9	2 425.4
4th quarter	504.7	359.6	57.6	18.8	58.2	32.5	22.0	55.2	449.5	400.1	49.4	11.0	2 589.3	2 465.0

Table 4-1B. Personal Income and Its Disposition: Historical—*Continued*

(Billions of current dollars, except as noted; quarterly data are at seasonally adjusted annual rates.)   **NIPA Table 2.1**

Year and quarter	Personal income							Less: Personal current taxes	Equals: Disposable personal income	Less: Personal outlays	Equals: Personal saving		Billions of chained (2009) dollars	
	Total	Compensation of employees	Proprietors' income with IVA and CCAdj	Rental income of persons with CCAdj	Personal income receipts on assets	Personal current transfer receipts	Less: Contributions for government social insurance, domestic				Billions of dollars	Percent of disposable personal income	Personal income excluding current transfers	Disposable personal income
1964														
1st quarter	514.3	366.0	57.9	18.8	60.0	33.6	22.0	53.8	460.6	409.9	50.7	11.0	2 623.5	2 513.4
2nd quarter ...	523.7	373.5	58.8	18.8	61.7	33.2	22.3	49.7	474.0	418.2	55.8	11.8	2 670.8	2 580.9
3rd quarter	533.3	380.9	59.3	18.9	63.3	33.5	22.5	51.6	481.7	427.5	54.3	11.3	2 712.3	2 614.2
4th quarter	542.1	387.0	60.5	18.8	64.8	33.7	22.7	53.2	488.8	430.3	58.6	12.0	2 749.2	2 643.9
1965														
1st quarter	553.1	393.8	61.9	19.1	66.1	35.0	22.9	57.0	496.2	441.1	55.1	11.1	2 793.2	2 675.0
2nd quarter ...	562.7	400.8	63.2	19.3	68.0	34.6	23.2	58.4	504.3	448.5	55.8	11.1	2 832.8	2 705.3
3rd quarter	577.1	409.0	64.0	19.5	69.7	38.1	23.6	57.0	520.1	457.9	62.1	11.9	2 880.3	2 779.5
4th quarter	590.4	421.4	65.6	19.5	71.1	36.9	24.0	58.3	532.2	472.0	60.1	11.3	2 949.3	2 835.4
1966														
1st quarter	603.1	434.1	69.2	19.8	72.5	37.8	30.4	61.5	541.6	482.6	59.0	10.9	2 988.7	2 863.5
2nd quarter ...	613.0	445.4	67.2	19.8	73.6	37.9	30.8	65.6	547.5	488.0	59.5	10.9	3 016.1	2 870.9
3rd quarter	626.3	456.7	67.2	20.0	74.7	39.6	31.9	67.9	558.4	497.3	61.1	10.9	3 053.0	2 905.9
4th quarter	639.8	464.9	68.1	20.0	75.8	43.1	32.2	70.6	569.3	503.3	65.9	11.6	3 081.2	2 939.6
1967														
1st quarter	650.6	471.1	68.9	20.3	77.9	46.1	33.6	71.2	579.5	507.9	71.6	12.3	3 112.6	2 983.4
2nd quarter ...	657.7	476.8	68.5	20.4	79.4	47.2	34.6	70.9	586.7	517.6	69.1	11.8	3 128.3	3 006.8
3rd quarter	671.6	486.4	70.5	20.4	80.7	48.7	35.2	73.8	597.7	524.6	73.2	12.2	3 162.7	3 035.1
4th quarter	683.1	497.4	70.0	20.3	81.3	50.0	36.0	75.9	607.2	532.2	75.0	12.4	3 187.2	3 057.1
1968														
1st quarter	702.6	512.2	71.7	20.1	83.9	52.4	37.6	78.6	624.1	550.4	73.7	11.8	3 239.6	3 109.3
2nd quarter ...	722.6	525.3	73.2	20.1	86.5	55.9	38.4	81.7	640.9	564.6	76.4	11.9	3 288.2	3 161.2
3rd quarter	741.0	539.2	75.0	20.2	88.4	57.3	39.1	91.9	649.1	581.2	67.9	10.5	3 337.4	3 168.9
4th quarter	756.7	551.7	75.5	20.0	90.4	58.7	39.7	95.9	660.8	590.5	70.3	10.6	3 369.9	3 190.5
1969														
1st quarter	771.3	564.2	75.6	20.2	93.7	60.4	42.9	102.6	668.7	603.2	65.5	9.8	3 398.6	3 197.0
2nd quarter ...	790.4	578.2	77.1	20.3	96.9	61.5	43.7	105.7	684.8	615.3	69.5	10.1	3 440.4	3 232.2
3rd quarter	812.0	595.0	78.0	20.5	100.2	62.9	44.6	104.1	707.9	626.0	81.9	11.6	3 492.9	3 300.6
4th quarter	827.3	606.6	77.3	20.5	103.9	64.3	45.3	105.6	721.7	638.4	83.2	11.5	3 516.7	3 326.5
1970														
1st quarter	841.8	616.7	77.1	20.5	107.4	66.1	46.0	104.6	737.2	649.9	87.3	11.8	3 534.2	3 359.0
2nd quarter ...	859.6	622.0	76.7	20.3	110.8	76.1	46.3	105.5	754.1	660.2	93.9	12.5	3 531.2	3 398.5
3rd quarter	874.0	630.0	78.5	20.9	115.0	76.3	46.7	100.7	773.4	672.4	101.0	13.1	3 560.2	3 451.7
4th quarter	882.9	631.8	78.9	21.2	117.3	80.1	46.5	101.5	781.4	679.4	102.0	13.1	3 537.3	3 442.9
1971														
1st quarter	903.0	649.9	80.3	21.2	120.0	82.0	50.5	98.3	804.6	698.8	105.8	13.2	3 583.2	3 512.0
2nd quarter ...	926.4	661.8	82.8	21.8	121.4	89.6	51.0	100.7	825.7	713.3	112.4	13.6	3 611.3	3 563.2
3rd quarter	940.5	672.2	84.6	22.2	123.3	89.6	51.3	102.3	838.2	726.3	111.9	13.4	3 636.6	3 582.2
4th quarter	958.7	684.2	87.9	22.6	124.6	91.3	51.9	105.5	853.2	743.0	110.2	12.9	3 684.3	3 624.0
1972														
1st quarter	986.0	710.6	87.9	23.2	128.1	94.3	58.1	119.8	866.2	760.7	105.5	12.2	3 747.5	3 640.6
2nd quarter ...	1 003.5	724.7	91.3	20.3	131.0	94.9	58.8	123.4	880.1	779.8	100.3	11.4	3 796.8	3 677.8
3rd quarter	1 029.2	738.1	95.5	24.0	135.0	96.0	59.5	124.3	904.9	798.7	106.3	11.7	3 865.5	3 748.5
4th quarter	1 075.7	761.2	105.6	23.9	139.0	106.4	60.4	127.1	948.6	823.8	124.8	13.2	3 982.4	3 897.2
1973														
1st quarter	1 093.3	787.8	104.1	23.6	142.3	109.1	73.6	126.4	966.9	848.6	118.3	12.2	3 995.3	3 924.9
2nd quarter ...	1 122.6	805.6	109.9	23.5	146.9	111.5	74.7	129.2	993.4	864.8	128.7	13.0	4 026.8	3 956.2
3rd quarter	1 150.0	822.8	113.8	22.5	153.8	113.3	76.1	134.1	1 016.0	883.6	132.3	13.0	4 054.7	3 973.4
4th quarter	1 188.2	844.1	122.2	23.4	159.6	116.5	77.6	140.0	1 048.2	900.3	147.9	14.1	4 107.1	4 017.1
1974														
1st quarter	1 204.4	860.9	115.7	23.7	165.4	121.9	83.1	142.8	1 061.6	917.4	144.2	13.6	4 028.7	3 950.9
2nd quarter ...	1 230.4	881.1	108.6	23.1	172.4	129.9	84.7	148.9	1 081.5	946.4	135.0	12.5	3 982.8	3 914.0
3rd quarter	1 266.6	902.8	111.0	23.4	178.6	137.1	86.4	154.9	1 111.7	976.0	135.7	12.2	3 980.4	3 917.7
4th quarter	1 296.0	916.5	113.5	23.2	185.2	144.3	86.6	157.6	1 138.5	986.5	152.0	13.3	3 958.6	3 912.9
1975														
1st quarter	1 315.9	921.2	112.7	22.9	190.8	155.9	87.6	158.0	1 157.9	1 014.0	143.9	12.4	3 913.6	3 906.5
2nd quarter ...	1 347.5	934.1	114.3	22.6	192.9	171.5	88.0	121.1	1 226.5	1 043.0	183.5	15.0	3 919.6	4 087.8
3rd quarter	1 384.1	959.0	120.7	22.5	196.8	174.8	89.8	152.8	1 231.3	1 077.5	153.8	12.5	3 956.5	4 028.4
4th quarter	1 420.0	986.4	125.2	22.1	200.5	177.6	91.8	158.5	1 261.5	1 106.7	154.8	12.3	3 997.8	4 059.2
1976														
1st quarter	1 453.0	1 017.6	126.4	21.9	204.2	181.8	98.9	162.5	1 290.5	1 140.1	150.3	11.7	4 045.5	4 106.9
2nd quarter ...	1 477.4	1 038.4	128.6	20.8	210.0	180.0	100.4	169.3	1 308.1	1 159.9	148.1	11.3	4 094.4	4 128.2
3rd quarter	1 513.8	1 061.2	132.7	20.3	215.0	186.7	102.2	176.1	1 337.7	1 189.7	148.0	11.1	4 125.6	4 158.6
4th quarter	1 549.6	1 087.7	136.2	19.4	221.3	188.8	103.8	182.7	1 366.9	1 224.1	142.8	10.4	4 164.7	4 183.4
1977														
1st quarter	1 580.0	1 116.3	138.6	17.1	226.3	191.0	109.3	188.8	1 391.2	1 260.9	130.3	9.4	4 175.6	4 182.1
2nd quarter ...	1 628.3	1 153.4	140.5	16.6	238.5	191.4	112.1	195.7	1 432.6	1 289.9	142.7	10.0	4 246.8	4 234.2
3rd quarter	1 675.0	1 185.3	142.4	15.8	249.3	196.6	114.3	198.6	1 476.5	1 322.0	154.5	10.5	4 304.7	4 299.0
4th quarter	1 735.0	1 221.0	156.5	15.3	259.6	199.3	116.7	208.5	1 526.5	1 361.3	165.2	10.8	4 408.3	4 382.1

Table 4-1B. Personal Income and Its Disposition: Historical—*Continued*

(Billions of current dollars, except as noted; quarterly data are at seasonally adjusted annual rates.)

NIPA Table 2.1

| Year and quarter | Personal income | | | | | | | Less: Personal current taxes | Equals: Disposable personal income | Less: Personal outlays | Equals: Personal saving | | Billions of chained (2009) dollars | |
	Total	Compensation of employees	Proprietors' income with IVA and CCAdj	Rental income of persons with CCAdj	Personal income receipts on assets	Personal current transfer receipts	Less: Contributions for government social insurance, domestic				Billions of dollars	Percent of disposable personal income	Personal income excluding current transfers	Disposable personal income
1978														
1st quarter	1 774.9	1 255.8	158.5	16.5	266.9	203.3	126.2	212.0	1 562.9	1 392.8	170.1	10.9	4 437.5	4 413.0
2nd quarter ...	1 833.9	1 302.9	166.1	16.2	273.7	205.1	130.1	223.1	1 610.9	1 452.0	158.9	9.9	4 506.3	4 456.6
3rd quarter	1 887.3	1 339.2	168.3	17.4	281.3	213.9	132.8	236.3	1 651.0	1 484.4	166.7	10.1	4 549.7	4 488.8
4th quarter	1 942.7	1 383.0	170.9	17.6	290.1	217.2	136.0	247.2	1 695.5	1 524.9	170.7	10.1	4 604.3	4 524.2
1979														
1st quarter	1 999.4	1 427.3	180.1	17.8	300.2	222.7	148.8	253.6	1 745.7	1 561.2	184.5	10.6	4 653.2	4 572.3
2nd quarter ...	2 039.9	1 458.3	179.2	15.6	310.3	227.4	150.9	262.0	1 777.9	1 602.9	175.0	9.8	4 621.0	4 532.8
3rd quarter	2 105.4	1 498.8	180.7	15.4	321.7	243.0	154.2	274.8	1 830.5	1 658.8	171.8	9.4	4 633.5	4 554.2
4th quarter	2 168.2	1 539.7	177.8	17.6	341.2	249.1	157.1	285.2	1 883.0	1 704.1	178.9	9.5	4 661.9	4 574.3
1980														
1st quarter	2 230.8	1 579.2	167.6	20.0	367.7	259.4	163.1	284.8	1 946.0	1 756.3	189.7	9.7	4 649.7	4 589.8
2nd quarter ...	2 256.8	1 600.5	160.3	14.1	380.5	264.6	163.2	292.2	1 964.6	1 758.6	206.0	10.5	4 586.7	4 523.1
3rd quarter	2 337.2	1 631.2	173.4	17.0	385.6	296.6	166.6	302.2	2 035.0	1 816.9	218.1	10.7	4 591.0	4 578.3
4th quarter	2 445.1	1 694.0	185.0	27.8	410.1	300.0	171.8	318.9	2 126.2	1 887.3	239.0	11.2	4 709.6	4 668.1
1981														
1st quarter	2 503.9	1 745.2	188.2	26.2	429.4	306.5	191.6	330.9	2 173.0	1 947.3	225.8	10.4	4 707.9	4 655.6
2nd quarter ...	2 551.4	1 777.5	176.4	24.4	457.4	309.9	194.1	342.7	2 208.8	1 981.0	227.8	10.3	4 723.5	4 654.5
3rd quarter	2 647.8	1 815.4	182.3	24.1	495.2	328.5	197.7	356.9	2 290.9	2 023.5	267.3	11.7	4 808.7	4 749.8
4th quarter	2 682.9	1 843.0	171.8	27.0	509.5	331.1	199.4	352.7	2 330.3	2 041.2	289.0	12.4	4 803.3	4 759.1
1982														
1st quarter	2 715.1	1 866.4	165.2	27.6	526.8	336.3	207.2	352.5	2 362.6	2 083.1	279.5	11.8	4 797.5	4 764.8
2nd quarter ...	2 758.6	1 885.1	169.4	24.0	542.9	345.5	208.4	359.7	2 398.8	2 113.1	285.7	11.9	4 820.7	4 792.3
3rd quarter	2 799.8	1 905.3	170.7	25.9	545.5	362.1	209.8	350.1	2 449.6	2 163.8	285.8	11.7	4 794.4	4 818.0
4th quarter	2 844.5	1 920.4	179.5	27.0	549.9	377.9	210.2	356.6	2 487.9	2 228.2	259.7	10.4	4 798.2	4 839.7
1983														
1st quarter	2 881.8	1 949.9	183.3	27.4	560.8	380.7	220.4	350.9	2 530.9	2 270.4	260.6	10.3	4 823.7	4 881.3
2nd quarter ...	2 931.9	1 988.6	182.6	27.4	570.0	386.9	223.6	359.6	2 572.4	2 337.0	235.4	9.2	4 863.6	4 915.9
3rd quarter	2 991.1	2 031.2	183.8	27.4	593.3	382.5	227.2	345.4	2 645.6	2 409.7	235.9	8.9	4 920.2	4 990.1
4th quarter	3 076.3	2 085.9	195.3	27.7	613.0	387.0	232.6	355.7	2 720.6	2 464.5	256.1	9.4	5 038.8	5 097.6
1984														
1st quarter	3 167.4	2 147.1	221.9	26.9	628.6	393.9	251.0	361.2	2 806.3	2 512.1	294.2	10.5	5 141.1	5 201.8
2nd quarter ...	3 251.2	2 196.8	231.8	25.2	655.0	398.3	255.8	370.4	2 880.7	2 573.4	307.4	10.7	5 237.2	5 288.3
3rd quarter	3 327.0	2 242.6	232.4	27.6	683.3	401.0	259.9	384.1	2 942.9	2 614.9	328.1	11.1	5 330.0	5 360.8
4th quarter	3 381.6	2 283.1	226.9	31.9	693.4	409.4	263.1	395.9	2 985.6	2 666.8	318.8	10.7	5 380.6	5 404.9
1985														
1st quarter	3 446.4	2 327.0	240.7	30.2	703.9	420.0	275.4	432.3	3 014.1	2 749.7	264.4	8.8	5 413.9	5 392.0
2nd quarter ...	3 486.6	2 365.0	238.5	29.2	710.1	422.6	278.8	388.5	3 098.0	2 800.5	297.6	9.6	5 435.3	5 495.8
3rd quarter	3 533.8	2 406.7	240.7	30.3	710.9	427.9	282.8	421.5	3 112.2	2 877.2	235.1	7.6	5 466.1	5 477.4
4th quarter	3 598.6	2 457.1	244.3	28.4	726.3	430.9	288.4	428.9	3 169.7	2 906.3	263.4	8.3	5 536.9	5 540.3
1986														
1st quarter	3 658.5	2 493.3	245.6	24.8	749.5	443.2	297.9	426.3	3 232.2	2 952.9	279.3	8.6	5 580.0	5 609.4
2nd quarter ...	3 700.7	2 519.1	251.6	24.2	757.4	449.1	300.7	429.4	3 271.2	2 982.6	288.6	8.8	5 649.7	5 683.9
3rd quarter	3 750.6	2 557.1	264.4	20.5	757.6	456.1	305.0	439.5	3 311.2	3 050.2	260.9	7.9	5 695.4	5 724.1
4th quarter	3 793.0	2 605.9	264.2	18.1	756.9	457.8	310.1	456.0	3 336.9	3 088.4	248.6	7.4	5 731.3	5 734.4
1987														
1st quarter	3 851.1	2 651.0	275.4	18.8	759.2	463.1	316.5	450.7	3 400.4	3 118.8	281.6	8.3	5 760.5	5 781.6
2nd quarter ...	3 911.2	2 694.2	282.3	17.4	769.4	468.1	320.2	511.7	3 399.5	3 189.9	209.6	6.2	5 798.9	5 725.5
3rd quarter	3 982.7	2 741.8	289.5	21.0	785.8	469.2	324.5	489.0	3 493.7	3 256.6	237.1	6.8	5 862.6	5 829.6
4th quarter	4 078.5	2 810.3	298.6	23.7	805.0	472.2	331.2	507.0	3 571.5	3 291.5	280.0	7.8	5 965.1	5 907.5
1988														
1st quarter	4 153.8	2 861.0	319.3	23.0	812.6	489.9	352.1	502.1	3 651.7	3 374.4	277.3	7.6	6 013.6	5 993.7
2nd quarter ...	4 227.8	2 926.1	322.8	22.6	821.9	493.5	359.1	497.8	3 730.0	3 436.5	293.5	7.9	6 062.2	6 055.2
3rd quarter	4 318.9	2 978.0	334.0	23.9	847.9	499.6	364.4	506.7	3 812.3	3 507.9	304.4	8.0	6 124.9	6 113.5
4th quarter	4 404.9	3 035.1	327.3	30.9	875.1	506.8	370.3	517.2	3 887.7	3 583.8	303.8	7.8	6 189.2	6 172.6
1989														
1st quarter	4 532.7	3 084.0	348.7	26.8	921.6	531.4	379.8	552.9	3 979.8	3 644.0	335.8	8.4	6 282.5	6 248.8
2nd quarter ...	4 587.6	3 117.5	340.3	24.7	949.2	538.8	382.8	566.7	4 021.0	3 711.4	309.5	7.7	6 273.6	6 230.4
3rd quarter	4 643.0	3 157.6	338.0	22.7	963.2	547.9	386.4	571.6	4 071.5	3 769.6	301.9	7.4	6 309.4	6 272.8
4th quarter	4 716.1	3 211.2	340.7	23.4	973.9	558.8	391.9	579.8	4 136.3	3 817.5	318.8	7.7	6 355.3	6 323.2
1990														
1st quarter	4 813.2	3 278.8	346.7	25.9	986.4	579.5	404.1	582.5	4 230.7	3 902.7	328.1	7.8	6 381.0	6 376.5
2nd quarter ...	4 888.9	3 334.8	352.3	30.2	989.5	590.5	408.3	594.6	4 294.3	3 949.0	345.3	8.0	6 420.8	6 414.6
3rd quarter	4 950.6	3 373.9	360.3	34.8	995.7	600.0	414.1	600.7	4 349.9	4 015.5	334.5	7.7	6 418.1	6 417.0
4th quarter	4 972.9	3 383.2	358.4	34.6	993.1	617.5	413.9	600.9	4 372.0	4 038.1	333.9	7.6	6 341.9	6 366.2
1991														
1st quarter	4 983.8	3 395.1	349.1	36.2	986.3	641.6	424.5	580.8	4 403.0	4 046.7	356.3	8.1	6 291.5	6 379.7
2nd quarter ...	5 043.0	3 430.2	354.8	38.6	985.7	661.4	427.7	586.0	4 457.0	4 101.8	355.2	8.0	6 315.2	6 423.9
3rd quarter	5 093.7	3 469.2	355.5	43.0	987.8	670.6	432.6	590.2	4 503.4	4 148.7	354.7	7.9	6 331.9	6 447.2
4th quarter	5 173.1	3 513.5	364.5	50.2	982.0	698.8	435.9	598.6	4 574.5	4 177.2	397.3	8.7	6 360.0	6 502.3

Table 4-1B. Personal Income and Its Disposition: Historical—*Continued*

(Billions of current dollars, except as noted; quarterly data are at seasonally adjusted annual rates.)   **NIPA Table 2.1**

Year and quarter	Personal income							Less: Personal current taxes	Equals: Disposable personal income	Less: Personal outlays	Equals: Personal saving		Billions of chained (2009) dollars	
	Total	Compensation of employees	Proprietors' income with IVA and CCAdj	Rental income of persons with CCAdj	Personal income receipts on assets	Personal current transfer receipts	Less: Contributions for government social insurance, domestic				Billions of dollars	Percent of disposable personal income	Personal income excluding current transfers	Disposable personal income
1992														
1st quarter	5 290.2	3 597.6	380.8	53.9	979.5	727.0	448.7	588.8	4 701.4	4 274.3	427.1	9.1	6 446.7	6 641.9
2nd quarter ...	5 389.1	3 654.4	397.4	61.1	984.4	745.6	453.7	607.1	4 782.0	4 330.8	451.1	9.4	6 517.0	6 711.4
3rd quarter	5 449.6	3 690.7	410.1	68.0	981.0	757.6	457.8	616.1	4 833.5	4 408.3	425.1	8.8	6 543.4	6 740.7
4th quarter	5 523.3	3 741.9	421.2	74.3	983.7	762.0	459.6	639.1	4 884.2	4 483.5	400.8	8.2	6 593.7	6 763.8
1993														
1st quarter	5 557.6	3 747.9	421.3	83.2	991.0	781.6	467.5	616.8	4 940.9	4 529.3	411.5	8.3	6 574.8	6 801.7
2nd quarter ...	5 626.5	3 803.3	432.0	91.9	988.8	786.0	475.6	643.6	4 982.9	4 598.9	384.0	7.7	6 618.9	6 813.7
3rd quarter	5 666.9	3 838.0	426.0	96.3	986.7	799.9	480.1	659.2	5 007.7	4 667.0	340.6	6.8	6 626.1	6 817.7
4th quarter	5 745.0	3 893.5	442.6	103.2	907.9	801.3	486.6	675.5	5 069.5	4 735.1	334.4	6.6	6 688.1	6 862.5
1994														
1st quarter ...	5 796.7	3 917.2	452.9	112.7	994.1	818.1	498.4	673.6	5 123.1	4 805.6	317.5	6.2	6 715.7	6 910.6
2nd quarter ...	5 904.1	3 997.2	456.9	117.4	1 016.1	822.9	506.4	697.8	5 206.2	4 872.0	334.3	6.4	6 816.1	6 983.8
3rd quarter ...	5 969.9	4 035.1	459.7	120.7	1 038.1	826.9	510.6	695.4	5 274.5	4 948.2	326.3	6.2	6 850.2	7 025.3
4th quarter ...	6 078.4	4 091.0	468.5	119.0	1 069.3	848.0	517.4	705.4	5 373.0	5 025.4	347.6	6.5	6 934.0	7 123.0
1995														
1st quarter	6 174.8	4 141.3	470.5	122.2	1 092.6	874.0	525.7	724.5	5 450.3	5 065.6	384.6	7.1	6 993.7	7 190.9
2nd quarter ...	6 240.2	4 177.6	475.2	126.1	1 108.1	883.5	530.1	746.7	5 493.5	5 147.6	345.9	6.3	7 027.9	7 207.3
3rd quarter ...	6 317.0	4 223.7	487.8	130.2	1 120.4	890.4	535.3	752.2	5 564.8	5 219.4	345.5	6.2	7 091.1	7 271.7
4th quarter ...	6 391.8	4 268.0	504.4	138.3	1 135.1	886.0	540.0	770.2	5 621.6	5 286.0	335.6	6.0	7 163.0	7 313.7
1996														
1st quarter	6 508.9	4 321.4	526.8	143.9	1 145.0	916.0	544.2	801.7	5 707.2	5 363.0	344.3	6.0	7 235.8	7 383.7
2nd quarter ...	6 639.4	4 393.5	551.0	146.0	1 164.5	936.4	552.1	839.5	5 799.8	5 458.2	341.7	5.9	7 329.8	7 454.3
3rd quarter ...	6 714.6	4 455.7	551.1	148.0	1 186.7	931.8	558.7	843.6	5 871.1	5 517.8	353.3	6.0	7 400.8	7 513.7
4th quarter ...	6 805.2	4 517.9	560.6	149.9	1 209.6	932.6	565.4	863.6	5 941.6	5 600.0	341.7	5.8	7 465.1	7 552.9
1997														
1st quarter	6 929.8	4 599.5	579.4	149.0	1 227.3	950.2	575.5	902.1	6 027.7	5 684.0	343.8	5.7	7 567.8	7 628.7
2nd quarter ...	7 010.5	4 665.8	579.0	149.9	1 248.0	950.0	582.2	916.2	6 094.3	5 728.6	365.7	6.0	7 651.2	7 693.9
3rd quarter ...	7 123.8	4 745.4	592.5	152.6	1 267.4	956.2	590.2	941.1	6 182.7	5 842.5	340.2	5.5	7 766.5	7 785.5
4th quarter ...	7 258.6	4 848.1	600.6	156.8	1 291.1	963.1	601.0	967.9	6 290.7	5 931.6	359.2	5.7	7 903.1	7 897.1
1998														
1st quarter	7 420.5	4 950.4	621.4	161.5	1 324.4	974.7	611.8	996.1	6 424.4	5 988.5	435.9	6.8	8 092.2	8 065.3
2nd quarter ...	7 548.1	5 035.9	633.7	167.2	1 350.7	981.1	620.4	1 022.3	6 525.7	6 110.3	415.4	6.4	8 229.7	8 178.0
3rd quarter ...	7 655.4	5 120.9	649.0	172.6	1 357.3	984.5	629.0	1 043.2	6 612.1	6 209.6	402.6	6.1	8 334.7	8 261.4
4th quarter ...	7 750.8	5 204.2	672.7	178.1	1 337.8	995.4	637.4	1 068.0	6 682.8	6 315.4	367.4	5.5	8 419.0	8 328.5
1999														
1st quarter	7 838.1	5 298.8	686.0	180.8	1 310.4	1 014.6	652.5	1 078.1	6 760.0	6 385.7	374.4	5.5	8 482.1	8 403.1
2nd quarter ...	7 908.3	5 352.5	694.1	184.1	1 316.2	1 017.8	656.4	1 095.4	6 812.9	6 516.9	296.0	4.3	8 519.8	8 423.9
3rd quarter ...	8 015.5	5 429.7	703.8	183.9	1 329.3	1 030.9	662.2	1 120.8	6 894.7	6 626.5	268.2	3.9	8 590.9	8 480.3
4th quarter ...	8 191.7	5 560.2	717.9	183.6	1 362.8	1 041.4	674.1	1 154.2	7 037.6	6 763.0	274.6	3.9	8 743.0	8 605.1
2000														
1st quarter	8 445.3	5 759.9	724.9	184.2	1 417.0	1 056.7	697.5	1 209.0	7 236.3	6 925.8	310.5	4.3	8 959.2	8 774.6
2nd quarter ...	8 575.3	5 800.8	755.2	184.3	1 450.1	1 083.7	698.9	1 230.4	7 344.9	7 030.4	314.5	4.3	9 042.6	8 865.6
3rd quarter ...	8 724.9	5 914.0	764.7	186.9	1 472.4	1 098.0	711.2	1 247.9	7 477.0	7 154.2	322.7	4.3	9 149.0	8 969.2
4th quarter ...	8 802.8	5 951.7	786.3	195.4	1 474.5	1 110.8	715.8	1 258.9	7 543.8	7 260.9	282.9	3.8	9 176.3	8 999.5
2001														
1st quarter	8 961.2	6 059.4	816.2	201.7	1 463.7	1 155.6	735.5	1 302.1	7 659.1	7 336.1	322.9	4.2	9 249.8	9 076.2
2nd quarter ...	8 997.9	6 050.2	835.0	207.5	1 451.9	1 187.4	734.0	1 309.0	7 689.0	7 387.6	301.4	3.9	9 211.6	9 068.2
3rd quarter ...	8 000.7	6 033.7	851.5	210.1	1 434.7	1 192.2	731.5	1 114.0	7 876.7	7 419.5	457.2	5.8	9 190.5	9 282.6
4th quarter ...	9 016.5	6 042.9	844.4	210.8	1 415.0	1 235.2	731.7	1 232.2	7 704.4	7 525.2	259.2	3.3	9 164.3	9 167.8
2002														
1st quarter	9 057.7	6 074.8	861.1	215.2	1 392.0	1 259.9	745.4	1 069.5	7 988.2	7 557.6	430.6	5.4	9 167.0	9 390.8
2nd quarter ...	9 139.9	6 137.7	864.8	217.4	1 390.4	1 281.7	752.1	1 049.3	8 090.5	7 656.1	434.4	5.4	9 167.4	9 438.4
3rd quarter ...	9 173.9	6 161.4	873.9	216.8	1 383.7	1 291.6	753.5	1 053.1	8 120.8	7 745.8	375.0	4.6	9 149.5	9 426.3
4th quarter ...	9 243.9	6 193.7	884.3	219.8	1 395.5	1 305.6	755.0	1 046.7	8 197.2	7 816.2	381.0	4.6	9 172.4	9 471.6
2003														
1st quarter	9 300.4	6 226.6	880.2	226.8	1 407.5	1 323.7	764.4	1 022.4	8 278.1	7 895.2	382.9	4.6	9 152.3	9 498.0
2nd quarter ...	9 424.3	6 318.7	894.1	234.0	1 411.3	1 340.4	774.2	1 019.2	8 405.2	7 994.5	410.7	4.9	9 267.2	9 635.5
3rd quarter ...	9 550.3	6 403.8	907.2	239.9	1 421.1	1 361.6	783.4	955.2	8 595.1	8 158.2	436.9	5.1	9 330.3	9 793.4
4th quarter ...	9 689.4	6 508.7	918.7	251.3	1 442.1	1 363.6	795.0	1 024.6	8 664.8	8 257.0	407.8	4.7	9 448.4	9 833.0
2004														
1st quarter	9 807.4	6 565.7	947.2	254.6	1 451.7	1 398.7	810.4	1 013.0	8 794.5	8 398.6	395.9	4.5	9 470.2	9 904.7
2nd quarter ...	9 971.4	6 690.3	961.9	258.7	1 468.2	1 416.3	823.9	1 027.9	8 943.5	8 513.4	430.2	4.8	9 567.9	10 002.3
3rd quarter ...	10 110.5	6 823.3	962.1	254.6	1 484.6	1 424.6	838.7	1 067.5	9 042.9	8 649.7	393.2	4.3	9 658.0	10 054.9
4th quarter ...	10 322.3	6 878.9	977.1	253.8	1 610.5	1 445.8	843.7	1 094.0	9 228.2	8 809.8	418.5	4.5	9 792.6	10 180.6
2005														
1st quarter	10 359.1	6 952.6	953.3	246.1	1 577.6	1 489.3	859.8	1 172.5	9 186.6	8 912.4	274.2	3.0	9 734.8	10 082.5
2nd quarter ...	10 518.6	7 027.4	960.5	242.9	1 641.9	1 513.0	867.1	1 197.7	9 320.8	9 092.4	228.4	2.5	9 818.5	10 162.3
3rd quarter ...	10 698.1	7 142.2	991.7	231.6	1 684.2	1 527.5	879.1	1 226.6	9 471.4	9 260.4	211.1	2.2	9 890.0	10 214.4
4th quarter ...	10 880.5	7 225.0	1 010.3	233.1	1 762.1	1 537.2	887.3	1 256.1	9 624.4	9 365.6	258.8	2.7	9 997.9	10 298.7

Table 4-1B. Personal Income and Its Disposition: Historical—*Continued*

(Billions of current dollars, except as noted; quarterly data are at seasonally adjusted annual rates.)   **NIPA Table 2.1**

Year and quarter	Total	Personal income — Compensation of employees	Proprietors' income with IVA and CCAdj	Rental income of persons with CCAdj	Personal income receipts on assets	Personal current transfer receipts	Less: Contributions for government social insurance, domestic	Less: Personal current taxes	Equals: Disposable personal income	Less: Personal outlays	Equals: Personal saving — Billions of dollars	Percent of disposable personal income	Billions of chained (2009) dollars — Personal income excluding current transfers	Disposable personal income
2006														
1st quarter	11 210.5	7 406.9	1 058.7	223.2	1 847.6	1 589.4	915.4	1 320.7	9 889.8	9 513.6	376.2	3.8	10 247.7	10 534.0
2nd quarter ...	11 330.2	7 453.0	1 062.2	211.9	1 917.5	1 604.5	918.8	1 349.2	9 981.1	9 648.6	332.5	3.3	10 279.9	10 549.8
3rd quarter	11 440.1	7 508.5	1 051.1	204.3	1 969.0	1 629.1	921.9	1 358.9	10 081.2	9 782.0	299.2	3.0	10 296.3	10 579.9
4th quarter	11 595.0	7 641.0	1 042.7	190.7	2 019.5	1 635.4	934.3	1 399.5	10 195.5	9 877.8	317.8	3.1	10 470.3	10 718.4
2007														
1st quarter	11 820.6	7 832.1	992.3	177.9	2 069.2	1 706.7	957.7	1 462.6	10 358.0	10 018.5	339.5	3.3	10 534.4	10 788.7
2nd quarter ...	11 948.5	7 866.8	972.8	189.6	2 168.9	1 708.4	958.0	1 488.0	10 460.5	10 144.7	315.8	3.0	10 581.8	10 809.5
3rd quarter	12 047.4	7 902.1	966.0	192.9	2 213.4	1 732.9	959.8	1 500.1	10 547.3	10 258.8	288.6	2.7	10 598.7	10 837.9
4th quarter	12 184.2	7 992.0	985.5	197.2	2 215.1	1 764.4	970.1	1 522.0	10 662.2	10 366.8	295.4	2.8	10 600.5	10 847.0
2008														
1st quarter	12 367.0	8 077.9	1 017.7	225.3	2 228.3	1 804.1	986.5	1 535.8	10 831.2	10 433.1	398.1	3.7	10 654.6	10 925.3
2nd quarter ...	12 720.4	8 077.3	1 045.9	250.0	2 186.4	2 148.0	987.2	1 545.0	11 175.4	10 542.1	633.4	5.7	10 553.7	11 155.7
3rd quarter	12 535.5	8 094.9	1 040.9	273.4	2 173.6	1 943.3	990.7	1 505.8	11 029.7	10 572.2	457.5	4.1	10 466.9	10 899.2
4th quarter	12 386.0	8 062.8	1 001.3	299.8	2 079.8	1 930.8	988.6	1 444.6	10 941.4	10 283.5	657.8	6.0	10 481.8	10 969.2
2009														
1st quarter	12 061.8	7 762.4	944.2	310.8	1 965.9	2 039.8	961.3	1 202.8	10 858.9	10 195.1	663.9	6.1	10 104.6	10 948.5
2nd quarter ...	12 117.7	7 790.5	944.6	325.0	1 846.2	2 177.6	966.3	1 132.5	10 985.2	10 205.4	779.8	7.1	9 977.4	11 026.4
3rd quarter	12 066.8	7 774.0	976.9	344.4	1 756.6	2 178.3	963.4	1 133.8	10 933.0	10 322.6	610.4	5.6	9 863.5	10 905.4
4th quarter	12 132.9	7 821.0	1 026.3	354.6	1 703.2	2 194.4	966.6	1 139.9	10 993.0	10 377.4	615.6	5.6	9 846.3	10 891.0
2010														
1st quarter	12 234.8	7 801.7	1 017.6	380.5	1 706.0	2 301.1	972.0	1 193.4	11 041.5	10 459.1	582.4	5.3	9 808.3	10 902.0
2nd quarter ...	12 413.4	7 947.1	1 024.7	397.3	1 719.7	2 308.6	984.0	1 215.7	11 197.6	10 543.3	654.4	5.8	9 965.9	11 043.8
3rd quarter	12 543.9	8 019.1	1 029.2	408.3	1 739.4	2 336.2	988.4	1 257.2	11 286.7	10 634.5	652.1	5.8	10 037.8	11 098.8
4th quarter	12 716.4	8 077.9	1 059.3	425.0	1 793.5	2 352.9	992.0	1 290.7	11 425.7	10 794.6	631.1	5.5	10 137.2	11 176.2
2011														
1st quarter	13 077.6	8 209.7	1 103.2	460.1	1 854.2	2 304.0	913.6	1 425.4	11 652.2	10 923.8	728.4	6.3	10 401.7	11 312.9
2nd quarter ...	13 194.8	8 248.9	1 125.2	478.0	1 897.2	2 361.8	916.3	1 443.1	11 751.7	11 052.3	699.3	6.0	10 412.2	11 295.2
3rd quarter	13 347.3	8 332.0	1 161.8	491.6	1 932.2	2 353.8	924.1	1 470.7	11 876.6	11 158.0	718.6	6.1	10 510.8	11 355.1
4th quarter	13 398.4	8 285.4	1 184.5	511.6	1 971.9	2 362.3	917.2	1 473.5	11 924.9	11 230.7	694.2	5.8	10 515.2	11 362.0
2012														
1st quarter	13 662.4	8 504.0	1 213.6	517.0	2 026.0	2 343.4	941.6	1 472.4	12 190.0	11 362.0	828.0	6.8	10 722.7	11 547.8
2nd quarter ...	13 814.1	8 550.0	1 240.2	523.0	2 081.4	2 364.4	944.9	1 492.8	12 321.3	11 415.6	905.7	7.4	10 813.5	11 636.7
3rd quarter	13 867.1	8 587.6	1 245.8	527.3	2 086.0	2 368.5	948.0	1 511.7	12 355.4	11 476.9	878.5	7.1	10 824.2	11 630.8
4th quarter	14 316.9	8 798.0	1 266.0	534.0	2 301.6	2 389.1	971.8	1 568.7	12 748.1	11 573.6	1 174.6	9.2	11 168.1	11 936.1
2013														
1st quarter	13 904.2	8 705.1	1 291.5	550.6	1 280.8	759.3	1 088.7	1 644.9	12 259.3	11 668.9	590.4	4.8	10 728.1	11 437.7
2nd quarter ...	14 017.2	8 823.7	1 283.0	561.9	1 250.0	783.9	1 103.3	1 681.3	12 335.9	11 697.5	638.4	5.2	10 817.4	11 504.4
3rd quarter	14 135.3	8 880.6	1 286.7	574.4	1 252.7	811.6	1 109.2	1 681.5	12 453.8	11 792.7	661.1	5.3	10 868.3	11 571.7
4th quarter	14 238.0	8 960.4	1 277.8	581.3	1 263.0	823.0	1 117.3	1 703.6	12 534.3	11 943.8	590.6	4.7	10 906.2	11 596.6
2014														
1st quarter	14 485.9	9 119.4	1 292.7	594.3	2 142.0	2 479.0	1 141.5	1 751.5	12 734.3	12 060.7	673.6	5.3	11 050.9	11 720.4
2nd quarter ...	14 713.5	9 175.0	1 319.3	606.7	2 227.9	2 530.4	1 145.9	1 757.8	12 955.7	12 216.2	739.5	5.7	11 163.6	11 871.5
3rd quarter	14 924.8	9 286.9	1 320.0	618.0	2 286.9	2 570.8	1 157.8	1 795.7	13 129.2	12 371.8	757.4	5.8	11 287.1	11 995.3
4th quarter	15 148.7	9 444.5	1 331.2	627.9	2 323.7	2 597.3	1 175.9	1 837.5	13 311.3	12 526.5	784.8	5.9	11 475.0	12 169.6
2015														
1st quarter	15 301.0	9 541.6	1 312.8	639.3	2 350.2	2 645.4	1 188.3	1 903.4	13 397.6	12 587.9	809.7	6.0	11 616.6	12 297.6
2nd quarter ...	15 516.1	9 655.9	1 313.9	658.4	2 406.9	2 682.7	1 201.7	1 934.1	13 582.0	12 737.7	844.4	6.2	11 729.9	12 414.2
3rd quarter	15 625.5	9 730.0	1 323.2	670.9	2 413.8	2 698.0	1 210.3	1 937.7	13 687.8	12 865.8	822.0	6.0	11 778.1	12 470.8
4th quarter	15 769.2	9 905.5	1 325.4	681.4	2 377.5	2 711.4	1 231.9	1 976.5	13 792.7	12 955.2	837.5	6.1	11 891.9	12 561.2
2016														
1st quarter	15 751.0	9 838.6	1 327.6	697.6	2 374.9	2 739.9	1 227.5	1 928.9	13 822.1	13 034.3	787.8	5.7	11 830.4	12 567.7
2nd quarter ...	15 910.1	9 979.6	1 339.5	704.8	2 371.4	2 760.2	1 245.4	1 950.7	13 959.4	13 214.2	745.2	5.3	11 894.9	12 627.2
3rd quarter	16 028.0	10 081.4	1 346.1	708.1	2 373.2	2 777.4	1 258.2	1 983.8	14 044.3	13 366.6	677.7	4.8	11 934.4	12 649.2
4th quarter	16 025.7	10 014.9	1 354.6	718.9	2 391.6	2 795.9	1 250.2	1 977.2	14 048.5	13 537.0	511.5	3.6	11 857.1	12 590.8

Table 4-2. Personal Consumption Expenditures by Major Type of Product

(Billions of dollars, quarterly data are at seasonally adjusted rates.)   NIPA Table 2.3.5

Year and quarter	Personal consumption expend- itures, total	Total goods	Goods									
			Durable goods					Nondurable goods				
			Durable goods, total	Motor vehicles and parts	Furnishings and household equipment	Recreational goods and vehicles	Other durable goods	Nondurable goods, total	Food and beverages off-premises	Clothing and footwear	Gasoline and other energy goods	Other nondurable goods
1955	258.7	147.4	40.7	17.7	14.0	5.3	3.7	106.7	52.0	22.4	12.4	19.9
1956	271.6	152.2	40.2	15.7	14.8	5.7	4.0	112.0	54.2	23.4	13.3	21.1
1957	286.7	159.6	42.0	17.5	14.8	5.8	4.0	117.6	57.1	23.6	14.2	22.6
1958	296.0	161.6	39.5	15.0	14.6	5.9	4.1	122.0	59.8	23.9	14.7	23.6
1959	317.5	172.6	44.9	18.8	15.5	6.4	4.2	127.7	61.6	25.4	15.3	25.5
1960	331.6	177.0	45.6	19.6	15.4	6.4	4.3	131.4	62.6	25.9	15.8	27.1
1961	342.0	178.8	44.2	17.7	15.6	6.6	4.3	134.6	63.7	26.6	15.7	28.6
1962	363.1	189.0	49.5	21.4	16.4	6.9	4.7	139.5	64.7	27.9	16.3	30.7
1963	382.5	198.2	54.2	24.2	17.5	7.6	4.9	143.9	65.9	28.6	16.9	32.5
1964	411.2	212.3	59.6	25.8	19.5	8.8	5.5	152.7	69.5	31.1	17.7	34.5
1965	443.6	229.7	66.4	29.6	20.7	10.1	6.0	163.3	74.4	32.7	19.1	37.1
1966	480.6	249.6	71.7	29.9	22.6	12.3	6.9	177.9	80.6	35.8	20.7	40.8
1967	507.4	259.0	74.0	29.6	23.7	13.6	7.1	185.0	82.6	37.5	21.9	43.0
1968	557.4	284.6	84.8	35.4	26.1	15.3	8.0	199.8	88.8	41.3	23.2	46.5
1969	604.5	304.7	90.5	37.4	27.6	16.7	8.7	214.2	95.4	44.3	25.0	49.5
1970	647.7	318.8	90.0	34.5	28.2	17.9	9.4	228.8	103.5	45.5	26.3	53.6
1971	701.0	342.1	102.4	43.2	29.9	19.2	10.1	239.7	107.1	49.0	27.6	55.9
1972	769.4	373.8	116.4	49.4	33.5	22.6	11.0	257.4	114.5	53.5	29.4	60.0
1973	851.1	416.6	130.5	54.4	38.0	25.3	12.9	286.1	126.7	59.2	34.3	65.8
1974	932.0	451.5	130.2	48.2	40.9	26.6	14.5	321.4	143.0	62.4	43.8	72.1
1975	1 032.8	491.3	142.2	52.6	42.6	30.4	16.5	349.2	156.6	66.9	48.0	77.7
1976	1 150.2	546.3	168.6	68.2	47.2	34.2	19.1	377.7	167.3	72.2	53.0	85.2
1977	1 276.7	600.4	192.0	79.8	53.4	37.7	21.1	408.4	179.8	79.3	57.8	91.5
1978	1 426.2	663.6	213.3	89.2	59.0	41.7	23.5	450.2	196.1	89.3	61.5	103.3
1979	1 589.5	737.9	226.3	90.2	65.3	45.8	25.1	511.6	218.4	96.4	80.4	116.5
1980	1 754.6	799.8	226.4	84.4	67.8	46.5	27.6	573.4	239.2	103.0	101.9	129.3
1981	1 937.5	869.4	243.9	93.0	71.5	49.9	29.6	625.4	255.3	113.2	113.4	143.5
1982	2 073.9	899.3	253.0	100.0	71.8	51.3	29.9	646.3	267.1	116.7	108.4	154.0
1983	2 286.5	973.8	295.0	122.9	79.8	58.7	33.7	678.8	277.0	126.4	106.5	168.8
1984	2 498.2	1 063.7	342.2	147.2	88.8	67.8	38.3	721.5	291.1	137.6	108.2	184.6
1985	2 722.7	1 137.6	380.4	170.1	94.6	74.1	41.6	757.2	303.0	146.8	110.5	196.9
1986	2 898.4	1 195.6	421.4	187.5	103.5	83.0	47.5	774.2	316.4	157.2	91.2	209.4
1987	3 092.1	1 256.3	442.0	188.2	109.5	91.8	52.5	814.3	324.3	167.7	96.4	225.9
1988	3 346.9	1 337.3	475.1	202.2	115.2	99.9	57.8	862.3	342.8	178.2	99.9	241.4
1989	3 592.8	1 423.8	494.3	207.8	121.4	103.9	61.3	929.5	365.4	190.4	110.4	263.3
1990	3 825.6	1 491.4	497.1	205.1	120.9	105.6	65.5	994.2	391.2	195.2	124.2	283.6
1991	3 960.2	1 497.4	477.2	185.7	118.8	107.7	64.9	1 020.3	403.0	199.1	121.1	297.1
1992	4 215.7	1 563.3	508.1	204.8	124.3	111.0	68.0	1 055.2	404.5	211.2	125.0	314.5
1993	4 471.0	1 642.3	551.5	224.7	131.4	123.5	72.0	1 090.8	413.5	219.1	126.9	331.4
1994	4 741.0	1 746.6	607.2	249.8	140.5	140.3	76.5	1 139.4	432.1	227.4	129.2	350.6
1995	4 984.2	1 815.5	635.7	255.7	146.7	153.7	79.6	1 179.8	443.7	231.2	133.4	371.4
1996	5 268.1	1 917.7	676.3	273.5	153.5	164.9	84.3	1 241.4	461.9	239.5	144.7	395.2
1997	5 560.7	2 006.8	715.5	293.1	160.5	174.6	87.3	1 291.2	474.8	247.5	147.7	421.3
1998	5 903.0	2 108.7	779.3	320.2	173.6	191.4	94.2	1 329.4	487.4	257.8	132.4	451.8
1999	6 307.0	2 286.8	855.6	350.7	191.2	210.9	102.7	1 431.2	515.5	271.1	146.5	498.0
2000	6 792.4	2 452.9	912.6	363.2	208.1	230.9	110.4	1 540.3	540.6	280.8	184.5	534.4
2001	7 103.1	2 525.2	941.5	383.3	214.9	234.9	108.4	1 583.7	564.0	277.9	178.0	563.9
2002	7 384.1	2 598.6	985.4	401.3	225.9	244.8	113.4	1 613.2	575.1	278.8	167.9	591.4
2003	7 765.5	2 721.6	1 017.5	401.5	235.2	259.2	121.7	1 704.0	599.6	285.3	196.4	622.7
2004	8 260.0	2 900.3	1 079.8	409.3	254.3	284.1	132.1	1 820.4	632.6	297.5	232.7	657.6
2005	8 794.1	3 080.3	1 127.2	410.0	271.3	305.0	141.0	1 953.1	668.2	310.7	283.8	690.4
2000	9 304.0	3 236.8	1 156.1	395.0	283.6	324.1	153.5	2 079.7	700.3	320.2	319.7	739.6
2007	9 750.5	3 361.6	1 184.6	400.6	283.5	335.8	164.8	2 176.9	737.3	323.7	345.5	770.4
2008	10 013.6	3 375.7	1 102.3	339.6	268.7	329.3	164.6	2 273.4	772.9	319.5	389.1	791.9
2009	9 847.0	3 198.4	1 023.0	317.1	244.3	303.8	158.2	2 175.1	770.0	306.5	284.5	814.2
2010	10 202.2	3 362.8	1 070.7	342.0	250.4	312.7	165.6	2 292.1	788.9	320.6	333.4	849.2
2011	10 689.3	3 596.5	1 125.3	363.5	260.7	321.0	180.2	2 471.1	829.1	338.9	409.6	893.5
2012	11 050.6	3 739.1	1 191.9	395.8	271.4	336.6	188.1	2 547.2	848.8	354.3	416.9	927.3
2013	11 361.2	3 834.5	1 241.7	416.1	281.6	348.1	195.9	2 592.8	857.5	363.6	412.2	959.5
2014	11 863.7	3 970.5	1 296.4	441.9	294.3	357.4	202.8	2 674.1	884.4	376.0	397.8	1 015.9
2015	12 332.3	4 033.2	1 367.1	472.2	311.5	372.4	211.1	2 666.0	899.0	385.5	305.1	1 076.5
2016	12 820.7	4 121.4	1 411.0	480.8	325.2	385.5	219.6	2 710.4	915.1	393.7	273.7	1 128.0
2014												
1st quarter	11 640.2	3 904.3	1 259.0	426.0	284.8	349.2	199.1	2 645.3	873.4	366.7	421.2	983.9
2nd quarter	11 791.9	3 963.9	1 291.5	440.9	293.1	355.4	202.0	2 672.4	881.4	375.0	407.6	1 008.4
3rd quarter	11 941.1	4 000.5	1 309.6	447.2	297.6	360.7	204.0	2 690.9	888.6	377.8	396.7	1 027.8
4th quarter	12 081.4	4 013.2	1 325.5	453.4	301.6	364.2	206.2	2 687.7	894.2	384.4	365.6	1 043.6
2015												
1st quarter	12 142.2	3 975.1	1 341.8	463.4	304.0	365.7	208.7	2 633.3	897.4	382.9	300.4	1 052.6
2nd quarter	12 284.2	4 029.6	1 366.7	478.0	309.9	368.6	210.2	2 662.9	894.8	384.9	315.0	1 068.2
3rd quarter	12 407.8	4 067.2	1 376.6	476.9	314.2	373.3	212.1	2 690.6	901.1	387.1	316.0	1 086.4
4th quarter	12 494.9	4 060.7	1 383.4	470.4	317.9	381.9	213.2	2 677.3	902.5	386.9	289.2	1 098.7
2016												
1st quarter	12 571.5	4 046.9	1 382.5	465.6	321.0	380.5	215.5	2 664.3	906.4	389.9	260.6	1 107.5
2nd quarter	12 755.0	4 108.5	1 401.1	471.3	325.1	385.3	219.4	2 707.4	916.2	394.2	270.8	1 126.2
3rd quarter	12 899.4	4 134.4	1 420.2	486.3	326.3	386.9	220.6	2 714.2	915.4	395.3	269.5	1 134.0
4th quarter	13 056.9	4 195.9	1 440.2	500.0	328.2	389.2	222.8	2 755.7	922.3	395.3	294.0	1 144.1

Table 4-2. Personal Consumption Expenditures by Major Type of Product—*Continued*

(Billions of dollars, quarterly data are at seasonally adjusted rates.) NIPA Table 2.3.5

		Services											
			Household consumption expenditures for services								Nonprofit institutions serving households (NPISHs)		
Year and quarter	Services	Household services, total	Housing and utilities	Health care	Transportation services	Recreation services	Food services and accommodations	Financial services and insurance	Other services	Final consumption expenditures	Gross output	Less: receipts from sales of goods and services
1955	111.3	107.9	40.0	9.9	7.1	4.8	17.0	9.6	19.4	3.4	. . .	. . .
1956	119.4	115.6	42.9	10.9	7.6	5.2	17.7	10.4	20.9	3.8	. . .	. . .
1957	127.1	123.1	45.9	12.0	8.0	5.2	18.5	11.1	22.4	4.0	. . .	. . .
1958	134.5	130.1	49.2	13.4	8.1	5.4	18.7	11.6	23.8	4.3	. . .	. . .
1959	144.9	140.0	52.8	14.8	8.7	5.9	19.7	12.5	25.5	4.9	13.9	9.0
1960	154.6	149.5	56.7	16.0	9.2	6.5	20.5	13.6	27.1	5.1	14.8	9.8
1961	163.2	157.9	60.3	17.1	9.6	6.9	21.0	14.8	28.3	5.2	15.8	10.5
1962	174.1	168.7	64.5	19.1	10.1	7.5	22.3	15.4	29.9	5.5	16.9	11.5
1963	184.3	178.6	68.2	21.0	10.6	7.9	23.3	15.9	31.6	5.8	18.3	12.6
1964	198.9	192.5	72.1	24.2	11.4	8.5	24.9	17.7	33.8	6.4	20.3	13.8
1965	213.9	206.9	76.6	26.0	12.1	9.0	27.2	19.4	36.6	7.0	22.1	15.1
1966	231.0	223.5	81.2	28.7	13.1	9.8	29.6	21.3	39.9	7.5	24.3	16.9
1967	248.4	240.4	86.3	31.9	14.3	10.5	31.0	22.8	43.6	8.0	27.0	18.9
1968	272.8	264.0	92.7	36.6	15.9	11.7	34.6	25.8	46.8	8.8	30.3	21.6
1969	299.8	290.4	101.0	42.1	18.0	12.9	37.5	28.5	50.5	9.4	34.0	24.6
1970	328.9	318.4	109.4	47.7	20.0	14.0	41.6	31.1	54.6	10.5	38.1	27.6
1971	358.9	347.2	120.0	53.7	22.4	15.1	43.8	34.1	58.1	11.7	42.8	31.1
1972	395.6	382.8	131.2	59.8	24.5	16.3	48.9	38.3	63.7	12.8	47.4	34.5
1973	434.5	420.8	143.5	67.2	26.1	18.3	54.8	41.5	69.3	13.8	51.8	38.1
1974	480.5	465.0	158.6	76.1	28.5	20.9	60.6	45.9	74.4	15.5	58.8	43.3
1975	541.4	524.4	176.5	89.0	32.0	23.7	68.8	54.0	80.3	17.0	67.2	50.2
1976	603.9	584.9	194.7	101.8	36.2	26.5	77.8	59.3	88.6	19.0	76.3	57.3
1977	676.3	655.7	217.8	115.7	41.4	29.6	85.7	67.8	97.7	20.6	85.2	64.5
1978	762.6	739.6	244.3	131.2	45.2	32.9	97.1	80.6	108.3	23.0	96.7	73.6
1979	851.6	825.4	273.4	148.8	50.7	36.7	110.9	87.6	117.2	26.1	109.4	83.2
1980	954.8	924.8	312.5	171.7	55.4	40.8	121.7	95.6	127.1	30.0	126.1	96.1
1981	1 068.1	1 034.0	352.1	201.9	59.8	47.1	133.9	102.0	137.2	34.1	145.7	111.5
1982	1 174.6	1 136.7	387.5	225.2	61.7	52.5	142.5	116.3	150.9	38.0	163.8	125.8
1983	1 312.7	1 272.0	421.2	253.1	68.9	59.4	153.6	145.9	169.9	40.8	179.2	138.5
1984	1 434.5	1 389.1	457.5	276.5	80.0	66.1	164.9	156.6	187.5	45.4	194.4	149.0
1985	1 585.1	1 537.2	500.6	302.2	90.1	74.0	174.3	188.1	207.9	47.9	209.3	161.4
1986	1 702.8	1 650.2	537.0	330.2	95.0	80.4	186.7	199.8	221.2	52.6	227.3	174.7
1987	1 835.8	1 780.1	571.6	366.0	103.1	87.3	204.4	205.3	242.4	55.7	246.9	191.2
1988	2 009.6	1 946.3	614.4	410.1	114.2	99.2	225.8	219.8	262.8	63.3	275.5	212.2
1989	2 169.0	2 101.0	655.2	451.2	121.8	110.7	242.6	238.4	281.1	68.0	301.2	233.2
1990	2 334.3	2 258.5	696.5	506.2	126.4	121.8	262.7	247.4	297.5	75.9	334.4	258.6
1991	2 462.7	2 382.6	735.2	555.8	123.7	127.2	273.4	266.8	300.5	80.1	362.9	282.8
1992	2 652.4	2 564.5	771.1	612.8	133.6	139.8	286.3	295.1	325.7	87.9	396.4	308.5
1993	2 828.7	2 738.6	814.9	648.8	146.1	153.4	298.4	332.6	344.4	90.1	418.7	328.7
1994	2 994.5	2 896.7	863.3	680.5	161.9	164.7	308.3	346.9	371.2	97.8	440.1	342.3
1995	3 168.6	3 066.3	913.7	719.9	177.9	181.1	316.1	366.4	391.2	102.3	458.5	356.2
1996	3 350.4	3 240.4	962.4	752.1	195.0	195.6	326.6	392.3	416.4	110.0	483.1	373.1
1997	3 554.0	3 448.4	1 009.8	790.9	214.3	208.3	343.4	429.2	452.3	105.6	502.6	397.0
1998	3 794.3	3 670.5	1 065.5	832.0	227.6	220.2	361.8	467.3	496.0	123.8	542.5	418.7
1999	4 020.3	3 882.0	1 123.1	863.6	244.1	238.1	380.3	509.1	523.7	138.2	576.3	438.1
2000	4 339.5	4 181.5	1 198.6	918.4	263.5	254.4	408.8	566.3	571.5	158.0	621.6	463.6
2001	4 577.9	4 398.8	1 287.5	996.6	264.7	262.3	419.7	552.8	615.3	179.1	676.4	497.4
2002	4 785.5	4 587.1	1 333.6	1 082.9	258.2	271.4	436.3	562.6	642.2	198.3	737.1	538.7
2003	5 044.0	4 838.5	1 394.1	1 154.6	265.5	289.2	461.9	588.5	684.7	205.5	774.6	569.1
2004	5 359.8	5 153.4	1 469.1	1 240.1	276.6	312.1	496.4	635.3	723.8	206.4	819.0	612.6
2005	5 713.8	5 503.6	1 583.6	1 322.3	289.4	328.9	530.6	689.6	759.1	210.3	868.5	658.2
2006	6 068.2	5 829.0	1 682.4	1 394.2	302.1	351.9	566.3	724.2	807.9	239.2	932.2	693.0
2007	6 388.9	6 140.2	1 758.2	1 481.8	312.2	375.8	595.6	768.5	848.0	248.8	983.1	734.4
2008	6 637.9	6 355.8	1 839.1	1 556.5	311.7	384.5	612.5	771.5	880.1	282.1	1 040.9	758.8
2009	6 648.5	6 372.5	1 881.0	1 627.4	289.7	376.0	600.3	719.0	879.2	276.0	1 072.6	796.5
2010	6 839.4	6 564.0	1 909.0	1 690.7	292.9	385.1	617.7	763.2	905.4	275.4	1 105.9	830.5
2011	7 092.8	6 817.8	1 959.9	1 764.7	308.1	400.6	649.5	795.8	939.3	275.0	1 139.6	864.6
2012	7 311.5	7 018.7	1 995.4	1 835.9	319.5	419.8	685.1	789.3	973.8	292.9	1 193.0	900.1
2013	7 526.7	7 221.8	2 054.2	1 870.9	334.5	434.2	710.8	830.7	986.4	304.9	1 229.7	924.8
2014	7 893.2	7 579.6	2 143.5	1 949.9	357.5	452.5	754.1	888.4	1 033.7	313.6	1 274.6	961.0
2015	8 299.1	7 969.7	2 235.4	2 061.2	374.2	471.0	808.2	947.2	1 072.4	329.4	1 339.2	1 009.7
2016	8 699.3	8 340.4	2 331.5	2 163.7	392.5	492.6	849.2	984.7	1 126.1	358.9	1 411.3	1 052.5
2014												
1st quarter	7 735.9	7 428.7	2 127.1	1 895.6	349.0	451.0	727.2	863.5	1 015.2	307.2	1 240.9	933.7
2nd quarter	7 828.0	7 514.3	2 129.8	1 929.0	354.0	447.5	746.9	879.3	1 027.7	313.8	1 263.3	949.5
3rd quarter	7 940.7	7 626.3	2 141.1	1 970.0	361.6	453.9	761.8	899.5	1 038.6	314.4	1 284.6	970.3
4th quarter	8 068.2	7 749.2	2 175.8	2 005.1	365.2	457.7	780.5	911.5	1 053.4	319.0	1 309.7	990.7
2015												
1st quarter	8 167.0	7 852.8	2 213.1	2 031.1	367.4	462.1	788.4	927.6	1 063.0	314.3	1 321.0	1 006.8
2nd quarter	8 254.6	7 931.4	2 221.0	2 048.5	372.7	469.4	804.9	947.1	1 067.9	323.2	1 331.1	1 007.9
3rd quarter	8 340.6	8 006.9	2 246.8	2 074.6	374.7	471.3	812.2	953.7	1 073.7	333.6	1 344.1	1 010.5
4th quarter	8 434.2	8 087.5	2 260.7	2 090.7	382.2	481.3	827.1	960.5	1 085.0	346.6	1 360.5	1 013.8
2016												
1st quarter	8 524.6	8 175.1	2 284.0	2 119.0	387.3	484.3	834.3	961.8	1 104.4	349.5	1 376.5	1 027.0
2nd quarter	8 646.5	8 292.3	2 319.2	2 156.1	389.5	488.2	847.2	974.6	1 117.5	354.2	1 402.3	1 048.1
3rd quarter	8 765.0	8 400.8	2 352.9	2 171.9	394.6	496.6	854.9	995.4	1 134.4	364.2	1 420.5	1 056.3
4th quarter	8 861.0	8 493.5	2 369.9	2 208.0	398.4	501.5	860.4	1 007.1	1 148.1	367.5	1 446.1	1 078.6

. . . = Not available.

Table 4-3. Chain-Type Quantity Indexes for Personal Consumption Expenditures by Major Type of Product

(Index numbers, 2009 = 100.)

NIPA Table 2.3.3

Year and quarter	Personal consumption expenditures, total	Total goods	Goods									
			Durable goods					Nondurable goods				
			Durable goods, total	Motor vehicles and parts	Furnishings and household equipment	Recreational goods and vehicles	Other durable goods	Nondurable goods, total	Food and beverages off-premises	Clothing and footwear	Gasoline and other energy goods	Other nondurable goods
1955	16.6	17.7	8.0	20.6	12.6	0.8	8.4	26.3	41.3	14.3	44.2	15.6
1956	17.1	18.0	7.7	17.5	13.2	0.9	8.8	27.3	42.7	14.7	46.1	16.3
1957	17.5	18.3	7.8	18.3	12.9	0.9	8.9	27.8	43.7	14.6	47.3	16.9
1958	17.7	18.1	7.2	15.2	12.8	0.9	9.0	28.2	43.9	14.7	49.4	17.2
1959	18.7	19.2	8.0	18.1	13.6	1.0	9.2	29.4	45.7	15.5	50.6	18.2
1960	19.2	19.5	8.2	19.2	13.4	1.0	9.3	29.9	46.0	15.6	51.4	19.1
1961	19.6	19.7	7.9	17.3	13.5	1.0	9.5	30.5	46.7	15.9	51.1	20.1
1962	20.6	20.7	8.8	20.5	14.2	1.1	10.4	31.5	47.0	16.6	52.7	21.5
1963	21.4	21.5	9.6	23.1	15.2	1.2	10.8	32.2	47.4	16.9	54.5	22.5
1964	22.7	22.8	10.5	24.4	16.9	1.4	11.7	33.7	49.0	18.2	57.5	23.5
1965	24.1	24.4	11.8	28.2	18.0	1.6	12.9	35.4	51.4	19.0	60.2	24.9
1966	25.5	26.0	12.8	28.7	19.6	2.0	14.8	37.3	53.4	20.3	63.5	26.9
1967	26.3	26.5	13.0	28.0	20.0	2.2	14.9	38.1	54.7	20.4	65.1	27.7
1968	27.8	28.1	14.5	32.4	21.2	2.4	16.4	39.7	57.1	21.2	67.9	28.8
1969	28.8	29.0	15.0	33.5	21.7	2.5	17.0	40.8	58.6	21.6	70.8	29.6
1970	29.5	29.2	14.6	30.0	21.6	2.7	17.9	41.8	60.3	21.4	73.5	30.6
1971	30.6	30.4	16.1	35.9	22.6	2.8	18.7	42.5	61.0	22.3	76.1	30.7
1972	32.5	32.4	18.1	40.8	24.9	3.3	19.7	44.3	62.2	23.9	79.9	32.2
1973	34.1	34.1	20.0	44.8	27.6	3.6	22.4	45.5	61.1	25.6	84.5	34.4
1974	33.8	32.8	18.7	37.4	27.5	3.6	23.5	44.4	59.9	25.1	77.6	34.3
1975	34.6	33.1	18.7	37.2	26.0	3.9	24.9	44.8	61.0	25.7	79.5	33.2
1976	36.5	35.4	21.1	44.7	27.6	4.2	27.4	46.9	64.0	26.9	83.7	34.5
1977	38.0	36.9	22.9	49.4	30.2	4.5	28.9	48.0	64.9	28.4	85.2	35.1
1978	39.7	38.4	24.1	51.7	31.7	4.8	30.5	49.7	64.6	31.4	86.6	37.6
1979	40.7	39.0	24.0	48.6	33.0	5.1	30.1	51.0	65.5	33.2	84.1	39.8
1980	40.5	38.0	22.1	42.4	31.8	4.9	27.5	50.9	66.2	34.2	76.6	40.4
1981	41.1	38.5	22.3	43.3	31.2	5.0	28.0	51.6	66.0	36.4	75.7	41.4
1982	41.7	38.8	22.3	44.5	29.8	5.0	28.0	52.1	67.3	37.0	75.8	41.2
1983	44.1	41.2	25.5	53.0	32.3	5.8	30.5	53.8	69.0	39.5	77.4	42.3
1984	46.4	44.2	29.1	61.7	35.6	6.8	34.0	56.0	70.4	42.8	79.5	44.6
1985	48.9	46.5	32.0	69.7	37.5	7.6	36.5	57.7	72.4	44.7	81.1	45.8
1986	50.9	49.1	35.1	74.7	40.5	8.8	40.7	59.8	73.9	48.1	85.2	46.8
1987	52.6	50.0	35.8	71.7	42.3	9.8	42.2	60.8	73.4	49.8	86.8	48.5
1988	54.8	51.9	37.8	75.9	43.8	10.7	43.6	62.4	75.4	51.3	89.3	49.6
1989	56.4	53.2	38.6	75.7	46.0	11.2	44.1	64.1	76.3	54.0	90.7	51.3
1990	57.6	53.5	38.5	74.5	45.4	11.5	44.4	64.8	77.9	53.6	89.1	52.6
1991	57.7	52.4	36.4	65.6	44.3	11.9	42.4	64.6	77.8	53.7	88.4	52.3
1992	59.9	54.1	38.5	71.0	45.9	12.6	43.3	65.9	77.5	56.5	91.9	53.4
1993	62.0	56.3	41.4	75.0	48.2	14.5	45.5	67.6	78.1	58.9	94.2	55.3
1994	64.4	59.3	44.7	79.7	50.8	16.9	47.6	70.2	80.3	62.2	95.7	58.1
1995	66.3	61.1	46.4	78.4	53.1	19.3	48.7	71.9	80.7	64.8	97.5	60.5
1996	68.6	63.8	49.9	82.2	55.4	22.3	51.9	74.0	81.5	67.9	99.0	63.2
1997	71.2	66.9	54.0	87.8	58.0	25.8	54.5	76.2	82.2	70.2	101.0	66.6
1998	75.0	71.3	60.5	97.0	62.8	30.8	59.9	79.0	83.4	74.5	103.9	70.2
1999	79.0	76.9	68.2	105.9	70.1	37.2	67.0	83.0	86.8	79.3	106.3	74.4
2000	83.0	80.9	74.1	109.3	76.8	43.5	73.0	85.7	88.9	83.2	103.5	78.1
2001	85.1	83.4	78.0	114.9	80.8	47.5	71.4	87.2	90.1	84.0	103.4	80.6
2002	87.3	86.6	83.7	120.9	86.7	52.9	75.8	88.8	90.5	86.5	104.2	83.0
2003	90.1	90.8	89.7	124.4	92.8	59.8	82.9	91.9	92.6	90.8	104.3	87.2
2004	93.5	95.4	97.0	127.9	101.6	68.9	90.3	94.9	94.8	95.0	105.2	91.0
2005	96.8	99.3	102.3	126.2	108.4	78.2	96.9	98.0	98.4	100.1	104.7	94.1
2006	99.7	102.9	106.7	121.5	113.9	88.5	104.0	101.2	101.4	103.6	104.5	98.7
2007	102.0	105.7	111.6	123.9	114.8	98.4	108.9	103.0	102.8	105.7	104.3	101.3
2008	101.6	103.1	105.9	107.5	109.6	101.6	105.3	101.8	101.5	105.2	99.6	101.7
2009	100.0	100.0	100.0	100.0	100.0	100.0	100.0	100.0	100.0	100.0	100.0	100.0
2010	101.9	103.4	106.1	102.0	107.0	110.9	104.2	102.2	102.1	105.3	99.2	102.3
2011	104.2	106.7	112.5	105.3	113.2	121.9	110.0	104.0	103.3	109.4	96.4	106.0
2012	105.8	109.6	120.8	113.3	118.2	136.0	114.1	104.7	103.3	110.6	94.9	108.2
2013	107.3	113.0	128.3	118.5	125.2	148.8	119.1	106.5	103.3	112.5	96.8	111.6
2014	110.4	117.4	137.1	125.7	135.6	159.9	125.5	109.1	104.7	116.2	96.0	116.6
2015	114.4	122.8	147.7	134.4	146.9	174.2	134.0	112.5	105.2	120.6	100.4	122.0
2016	117.5	127.3	155.9	138.3	157.5	190.0	137.7	115.6	108.1	123.6	101.6	126.0

Table 4-3. Chain-Type Quantity Indexes for Personal Consumption Expenditures by Major Type of Product—*Continued*

(Index numbers, 2009 = 100.)   NIPA Table 2.3.3

Year and quarter	Services	Household consumption expenditures for services								Nonprofit institutions serving households (NPISHs)		
		Household services, total	Housing and utilities	Health care	Transportation services	Recreation services	Food services and accommodations	Financial services and insurance	Other services	Final consumption expenditures	Gross output	Less: receipts from sales of goods and services
1955	15.1	16.1	16.6	11.2	20.9	9.9	27.4	10.3	19.9	2.5	. . .	. . .
1956	15.8	16.8	17.5	11.9	21.4	10.4	28.2	10.9	20.7	2.7	. . .	. . .
1957	16.4	17.4	18.4	12.6	21.8	10.0	28.6	11.2	21.5	2.8	. . .	. . .
1958	16.9	18.0	19.3	13.6	21.5	10.0	28.1	11.5	22.2	2.9	. . .	. . .
1959	17.7	18.8	20.4	14.6	22.4	10.7	28.7	11.8	23.1	3.2	13.2	20.1
1960	18.4	19.5	21.5	14.8	23.1	11.3	29.0	12.2	23.9	3.6	13.7	20.1
1961	19.1	20.2	22.6	15.4	23.4	11.7	29.1	12.9	24.6	3.7	14.3	21.2
1962	20.0	21.2	23.9	16.8	24.2	12.3	30.2	12.9	25.6	3.8	15.1	22.6
1963	20.9	22.1	25.0	17.9	25.3	12.8	30.9	13.3	26.5	3.9	15.9	24.1
1964	22.1	23.4	26.2	20.0	26.7	13.3	32.5	14.3	27.7	4.3	17.2	25.6
1965	23.3	24.7	27.6	20.9	28.0	13.8	34.8	15.2	29.3	4.6	18.2	27.2
1966	24.5	25.9	28.9	22.0	29.7	14.7	36.5	15.7	31.0	4.7	19.4	29.4
1967	25.5	27.0	30.2	23.1	31.2	15.2	36.2	16.5	32.9	4.9	20.6	31.4
1968	26.8	28.4	31.7	24.8	33.2	16.1	38.4	17.4	33.8	5.2	22.0	33.7
1969	28.0	29.7	33.4	26.7	35.5	17.1	39.2	17.6	34.8	5.2	23.1	36.0
1970	29.1	30.8	34.7	28.1	36.7	17.7	40.6	18.3	35.9	5.6	24.3	37.7
1971	30.1	31.9	36.2	30.1	38.3	18.3	40.6	18.9	36.0	5.9	26.0	40.6
1972	31.9	33.7	38.1	32.2	40.4	19.3	43.7	20.0	37.6	6.2	27.5	43.0
1973	33.4	35.4	39.9	34.5	41.1	20.9	45.8	21.2	38.7	6.2	28.3	44.5
1974	34.0	36.1	41.8	35.7	41.4	22.3	45.4	21.7	37.4	6.1	28.6	45.6
1975	35.3	37.5	43.1	37.5	41.9	23.5	47.3	23.8	37.7	6.2	29.7	47.9
1976	36.8	39.1	44.4	39.2	44.0	25.1	50.2	25.1	39.2	6.6	31.3	50.3
1977	38.3	40.7	45.6	41.1	47.1	26.7	51.5	26.6	41.1	6.7	32.5	52.6
1978	40.1	42.6	47.8	43.0	48.2	28.0	53.7	28.0	43.3	7.0	34.3	55.6
1979	41.3	43.9	49.5	44.4	49.7	29.3	55.4	28.8	43.6	7.2	35.3	57.1
1980	42.0	44.6	51.2	45.7	46.8	30.3	55.4	29.2	43.4	7.6	36.4	58.4
1981	42.7	45.2	51.9	47.9	45.0	32.9	55.9	29.0	43.2	8.2	37.9	60.1
1982	43.6	45.9	52.3	48.0	44.0	34.5	56.3	31.2	44.1	9.7	39.5	60.5
1983	45.8	48.2	53.4	49.5	47.4	37.4	58.1	35.7	47.0	11.2	41.0	60.8
1984	47.6	49.8	55.2	50.3	52.9	39.9	59.8	36.1	49.3	13.0	42.4	60.7
1985	50.1	52.4	57.4	51.8	58.5	42.8	60.6	40.0	52.7	14.1	43.9	62.1
1986	51.7	54.0	58.8	53.4	61.0	44.8	62.3	41.8	53.3	16.0	46.1	63.6
1987	54.1	56.3	60.4	55.6	63.5	46.8	65.6	44.2	57.1	17.3	47.9	65.5
1988	56.5	58.7	62.5	57.8	67.2	51.3	69.5	45.1	59.4	19.8	50.5	67.3
1989	58.3	60.3	64.0	58.5	68.7	54.5	71.4	47.6	61.2	22.8	52.3	67.6
1990	60.0	61.8	65.2	60.4	68.6	56.8	73.9	48.7	62.3	27.8	55.5	68.8
1991	61.0	62.6	66.6	61.6	65.3	56.4	74.0	52.8	60.0	31.7	57.5	69.4
1992	63.5	64.8	68.0	63.5	68.7	60.1	75.9	56.5	62.4	38.3	60.6	70.4
1993	65.4	66.7	69.8	63.8	72.5	63.9	77.5	60.5	63.8	41.4	62.1	71.1
1994	67.5	68.6	72.1	64.3	79.4	67.2	78.7	61.9	66.2	45.1	63.5	71.4
1995	69.5	70.6	74.3	65.6	85.4	72.3	78.9	64.0	67.6	47.2	64.3	71.6
1996	71.5	72.6	76.0	67.0	92.4	75.6	79.3	66.3	70.0	49.9	66.0	72.8
1997	73.8	75.2	77.7	69.0	99.4	78.0	81.0	69.7	73.9	46.0	66.9	75.9
1998	77.2	78.5	80.1	71.3	103.7	80.4	83.1	75.9	79.4	50.5	70.1	78.5
1999	80.2	81.5	82.4	72.4	109.6	84.3	85.2	83.3	81.9	54.4	72.5	80.2
2000	84.2	85.5	85.1	74.9	114.9	86.7	89.1	91.7	87.7	58.9	75.3	82.0
2001	86.2	87.3	87.4	78.6	114.1	86.5	88.9	89.8	91.5	63.8	78.9	85.0
2002	87.8	88.6	87.9	83.3	110.7	87.0	90.2	89.3	92.0	70.3	83.5	88.7
2003	89.7	90.4	89.1	85.6	111.5	90.0	93.5	89.4	94.6	74.7	85.3	89.2
2004	92.6	93.4	91.3	88.6	114.4	94.6	97.3	93.0	96.8	76.2	87.5	91.8
2005	95.6	96.5	95.1	91.6	115.5	97.0	100.8	97.9	97.9	76.1	89.7	94.9
2006	98.2	98.7	96.9	93.7	115.8	100.4	104.1	100.2	100.8	85.7	93.1	95.9
2007	100.1	100.7	97.9	96.1	117.0	104.3	105.4	103.3	102.9	88.0	95.3	98.0
2008	100.9	101.0	98.9	98.2	110.9	103.5	104.3	102.6	102.6	99.1	98.4	98.1
2009	100.0	100.0	100.0	100.0	100.0	100.0	100.0	100.0	100.0	100.0	100.0	100.0
2010	101.2	101.2	101.2	101.3	99.1	101.3	101.5	102.1	100.6	100.8	101.3	101.4
2011	103.1	103.2	102.5	103.9	101.5	103.6	104.2	103.9	102.5	99.7	102.3	103.1
2012	103.9	103.8	102.6	106.1	103.3	105.7	106.9	98.3	104.1	106.6	105.3	104.8
2013	104.6	104.4	103.0	106.6	106.6	107.5	108.7	98.4	103.2	109.0	106.3	105.4
2014	107.0	107.0	104.5	109.8	112.7	110.0	112.3	100.0	106.2	107.8	107.7	107.7
2015	110.4	110.5	106.3	115.4	117.5	112.6	117.0	103.0	108.9	108.8	111.0	111.7
2016	112.9	112.8	107.7	119.8	121.9	115.0	119.9	101.4	112.6	114.7	114.6	114.6

. . . = Not available.

Table 4-3. Chain-Type Quantity Indexes for Personal Consumption Expenditures by Major Type of Product—*Continued*

(Index numbers, 2009 = 100.)   NIPA Table 2.3.3

| | | | Goods | | | | | | | | | |
| | Personal consumption expenditures, total | Total goods | Durable goods | | | | | Nondurable goods | | | | |
Year and quarter			Durable goods, total	Motor vehicles and parts	Furnishings and household equipment	Recreational goods and vehicles	Other durable goods	Nondurable goods, total	Food and beverages off-premises	Clothing and footwear	Gasoline and other energy goods	Other nondurable goods
2014												
1st quarter	108.8	115.0	132.0	121.2	129.5	153.5	122.7	107.8	104.6	113.3	96.5	113.9
2nd quarter	109.7	116.7	136.2	125.4	135.0	157.6	124.8	108.6	104.5	115.5	95.2	116.0
3rd quarter	110.8	118.0	138.7	127.1	137.5	162.3	126.0	109.4	104.7	116.5	95.2	117.7
4th quarter	112.2	119.7	141.5	129.2	140.4	166.4	128.5	110.6	104.8	119.4	97.2	118.9
2015												
1st quarter	113.2	120.9	144.2	132.0	142.6	169.1	131.2	111.3	105.1	119.4	99.2	119.7
2nd quarter	114.0	122.3	147.2	135.7	145.3	171.9	133.2	112.0	105.0	120.3	99.7	121.1
3rd quarter	114.8	123.6	149.0	135.6	148.5	175.5	134.9	113.1	105.3	121.1	101.3	123.0
4th quarter	115.6	124.4	150.5	134.2	151.4	180.4	136.6	113.7	105.5	121.8	101.4	124.1
2016												
1st quarter	116.1	125.1	150.9	133.0	153.3	182.7	135.7	114.4	106.4	122.0	103.2	124.6
2nd quarter	117.2	126.9	154.0	135.4	156.6	188.3	136.8	115.7	108.0	123.6	101.8	126.4
3rd quarter	118.0	127.9	157.5	140.2	158.9	192.0	138.5	115.8	108.5	124.1	101.0	126.1
4th quarter	118.8	129.4	161.0	144.6	161.0	197.1	139.7	116.5	109.6	124.5	100.4	126.9

(Index numbers, 2009 = 100.)   NIPA Table 2.3.3

| | | Services | | | | | | | | Nonprofit institutions serving households (NPISHs) | | |
| | Services | Household consumption expenditures for services | | | | | | | | | | |
Year and quarter		Household services, total	Housing and utilities	Health care	Transportation services	Recreation services	Food services and accommodations	Financial services and insurance	Other services	Final consumption expenditures	Gross output	Less: receipts from sales of goods and services
2014												
1st quarter	105.8	105.8	104.7	107.2	110.6	110.1	109.8	99.0	105.0	107.4	105.7	105.2
2nd quarter	106.4	106.3	104.1	108.7	111.7	108.8	111.6	99.4	105.8	108.6	107.0	106.5
3rd quarter	107.3	107.3	104.0	110.7	113.9	110.1	113.0	100.6	106.4	108.0	108.3	108.5
4th quarter	108.6	108.6	105.1	112.7	114.5	111.0	114.8	101.2	107.7	107.2	109.9	110.8
2015												
1st quarter	109.5	109.7	106.2	114.2	115.7	111.5	115.1	102.5	108.4	104.9	110.3	112.1
2nd quarter	110.1	110.2	106.0	114.8	117.0	112.4	117.0	103.5	108.8	107.0	110.4	111.6
3rd quarter	110.7	110.7	106.5	115.9	117.7	112.3	117.5	103.0	108.9	109.8	111.0	111.4
4th quarter	111.4	111.3	106.5	116.7	119.7	114.4	118.6	103.1	109.4	113.4	112.1	111.7
2016												
1st quarter	111.8	111.8	106.9	118.0	120.7	114.3	118.8	101.4	111.0	113.2	112.8	112.7
2nd quarter	112.6	112.5	107.6	119.0	120.0	111.1	120.0	100.8	112.0	113.8	114.3	114.4
3rd quarter	113.3	113.2	108.2	119.9	122.5	115.4	120.4	101.4	113.1	115.9	115.0	114.7
4th quarter	113.9	113.8	108.0	121.5	123.4	116.2	120.4	101.8	114.4	115.8	116.4	116.6

Table 4-4.   Chain-Type Price Indexes for Personal Consumption Expenditures by Major Type of Product

(Index numbers, 2009 =1000.)   NIPA Table 2.3.4

Year and quarter	Personal consumption expend-itures, total	Total goods	Goods									
			Durable goods					Nondurable goods				
			Durable goods, total	Motor vehicles and parts	Furnishings and household equipment	Recreational goods and vehicles	Other durable goods	Nondurable goods, total	Food and beverages off-premises	Clothing and footwear	Gasoline and other energy goods	Other nondurable goods
1955	15.8	26.1	49.8	27.1	45.6	208.8	28.2	18.6	16.4	51.0	9.8	15.7
1956	16.1	26.5	51.0	28.3	46.0	211.1	28.5	18.9	16.5	52.0	10.1	16.0
1957	16.6	27.3	52.9	30.1	46.8	218.6	28.6	19.4	17.0	52.7	10.6	16.5
1958	17.0	28.0	53.8	31.2	46.7	224.6	28.7	19.9	17.7	53.0	10.5	16.9
1959	17.3	28.1	54.7	32.8	46.7	218.1	28.8	19.9	17.5	53.4	10.6	17.1
1960	17.5	28.3	54.5	32.2	47.1	219.6	28.9	20.2	17.7	54.1	10.8	17.4
1961	17.7	28.4	54.6	32.4	47.3	218.4	28.8	20.3	17.7	54.5	10.8	17.5
1962	17.9	28.6	54.8	32.9	47.2	216.0	28.7	20.4	17.9	54.6	10.9	17.5
1963	18.1	28.8	55.0	33.2	47.3	215.6	28.9	20.6	18.1	55.1	10.9	17.8
1964	18.4	29.1	55.3	33.4	47.3	213.0	29.6	20.9	18.4	55.6	10.8	18.0
1965	18.7	29.4	54.8	33.1	47.0	210.0	29.4	21.2	18.8	56.1	11.2	18.3
1966	19.2	30.1	54.7	32.9	47.4	207.7	29.4	21.9	19.6	57.6	11.4	18.6
1967	19.6	30.6	55.6	33.4	48.5	209.0	30.1	22.3	19.6	60.0	11.8	19.1
1968	20.4	31.7	57.4	34.5	50.4	213.1	30.8	23.1	20.2	63.4	12.0	19.8
1969	21.3	32.9	59.0	35.2	52.2	218.0	32.3	24.1	21.1	66.8	12.4	20.6
1970	22.3	34.2	60.3	36.3	53.3	218.3	33.2	25.2	22.3	69.3	12.6	21.5
1971	23.3	35.2	62.4	38.0	54.3	226.0	34.1	25.9	22.8	71.8	12.8	22.3
1972	24.1	36.1	63.0	38.1	55.0	229.3	35.2	26.7	23.9	73.1	12.9	22.9
1973	25.4	38.2	64.0	38.3	56.3	232.8	36.3	28.9	26.9	75.5	14.3	23.5
1974	28.0	43.0	68.2	40.7	60.9	243.1	39.1	33.3	31.0	81.1	19.9	25.8
1975	30.3	46.5	74.3	44.7	67.0	259.2	42.1	35.8	33.3	84.8	21.2	28.8
1976	32.0	48.3	78.3	48.1	69.9	268.1	44.1	37.0	34.0	87.5	22.3	30.3
1977	34.1	50.9	81.8	50.9	72.4	275.8	46.1	39.1	36.0	91.2	23.9	32.0
1978	36.5	54.0	86.4	54.4	76.1	285.7	48.6	41.6	39.4	92.9	24.9	33.8
1979	39.7	59.1	92.2	58.5	80.8	298.5	52.7	46.1	43.3	94.8	33.6	36.0
1980	44.0	65.7	100.2	62.9	87.4	315.0	63.4	51.8	46.9	98.2	46.7	39.3
1981	47.9	70.6	106.8	67.7	93.9	329.2	66.0	55.0	50.3	101.5	52.7	42.6
1982	50.6	72.6	111.0	71.0	98.7	336.8	67.6	57.0	51.6	103.0	50.3	45.9
1983	52.7	73.9	113.3	73.2	101.0	332.7	69.7	58.0	52.2	104.4	48.3	49.1
1984	54.7	75.3	114.9	75.3	102.2	328.0	71.2	59.2	53.7	104.9	47.8	50.9
1985	56.7	76.5	116.2	77.0	103.3	322.3	72.0	60.3	54.3	107.2	47.9	52.9
1986	57.9	76.1	117.4	79.1	104.4	312.0	73.7	59.5	55.6	106.7	37.6	55.0
1987	59.7	78.6	120.8	82.8	106.1	308.1	78.7	61.6	57.4	109.8	39.0	57.2
1988	62.0	80.6	122.8	84.1	107.6	306.1	83.9	63.5	59.1	113.3	39.3	59.7
1989	64.6	83.7	125.0	86.5	107.9	305.3	87.8	66.7	62.2	115.0	42.8	63.0
1990	67.4	87.2	126.3	86.8	109.0	302.8	93.3	70.5	65.2	118.7	49.0	66.2
1991	69.7	89.3	128.1	89.3	109.6	299.0	96.7	72.6	67.3	121.0	48.2	69.7
1992	71.5	90.4	129.0	90.9	110.9	289.8	99.3	73.6	67.8	121.9	47.8	72.4
1993	73.3	91.2	130.3	94.5	111.5	279.4	100.1	74.2	68.7	121.3	47.3	73.6
1994	74.8	92.1	132.8	98.9	113.2	273.6	101.7	74.6	69.9	119.2	47.5	74.1
1995	76.4	92.9	133.8	102.8	113.1	262.1	103.3	75.4	71.4	116.4	48.1	75.4
1996	78.0	94.0	132.5	104.9	113.4	243.5	102.7	77.1	73.6	115.0	51.4	76.8
1997	79.3	93.9	129.6	105.3	113.2	223.1	101.3	77.9	75.0	115.1	51.4	77.6
1998	79.9	92.4	125.9	104.1	113.1	204.3	99.4	77.3	75.9	113.0	44.8	79.1
1999	81.1	92.9	122.5	104.5	111.7	186.5	96.9	79.2	77.2	111.5	48.5	82.2
2000	83.1	94.8	120.3	104.8	110.8	174.8	95.7	82.7	79.0	110.1	62.7	84.0
2001	84.7	94.7	118.0	105.3	108.9	162.9	96.0	83.5	81.3	108.0	60.5	85.9
2002	85.9	93.8	115.0	104.7	106.7	152.4	94.6	83.5	82.5	105.1	56.6	87.5
2003	87.6	93.7	110.9	101.8	103.7	142.7	92.8	85.3	84.1	102.5	66.2	87.8
2004	89.7	95.0	108.8	100.9	102.4	135.7	92.5	88.2	86.7	102.2	77.8	88.8
2005	92.3	97.0	107.7	102.5	102.4	128.4	91.9	91.6	88.2	101.3	95.2	90.1
2006	94.7	98.3	105.9	102.5	101.9	120.6	93.3	94.4	89.7	100.9	107.5	92.1
2007	97.1	99.4	103.8	102.0	101.1	112.3	95.7	97.2	93.2	99.9	116.4	93.4
2008	100.1	102.4	101.8	99.7	100.4	106.7	98.9	102.7	98.9	99.1	137.3	95.6
2009	100.0	100.0	100.0	100.0	100.0	100.0	100.0	100.0	100.0	100.0	100.0	100.0
2010	101.7	101.6	98.6	105.7	95.8	92.9	100.4	103.1	100.3	99.3	118.1	102.0
2011	104.1	105.4	97.7	108.9	94.2	86.7	103.6	109.2	104.3	101.1	149.3	103.5
2012	106.1	106.7	96.4	110.2	94.0	81.5	104.2	111.8	106.7	104.6	154.4	105.3
2013	107.5	106.1	94.6	110.8	92.1	77.0	104.0	111.9	107.8	105.4	149.6	105.6
2014	109.2	105.8	92.4	110.8	88.8	73.6	102.2	112.7	109.8	105.6	145.6	107.0
2015	109.5	102.7	90.4	110.8	86.8	70.4	99.6	109.0	111.0	104.3	106.8	108.4
2016	110.8	101.2	88.5	109.7	84.5	66.8	100.8	107.8	109.9	103.9	94.7	110.0
2014												
1st quarter	108.7	106.1	93.2	110.8	90.0	74.9	102.6	112.8	108.4	105.6	153.4	106.2
2nd quarter	109.1	106.2	92.7	110.9	88.9	74.2	102.3	113.1	109.5	105.9	150.4	106.8
3rd quarter	109.5	106.0	92.2	110.9	88.6	73.1	102.4	113.1	110.3	105.7	146.5	107.3
4th quarter	109.4	104.8	91.5	110.7	87.9	72.0	101.4	111.7	110.8	105.1	132.2	107.8
2015												
1st quarter	108.9	102.8	90.9	110.7	87.3	71.2	100.6	108.8	110.9	104.7	106.4	108.0
2nd quarter	109.4	103.1	90.7	111.1	87.3	70.6	99.8	109.3	110.6	104.4	111.0	108.4
3rd quarter	109.8	102.9	90.3	110.9	86.6	70.0	99.4	109.4	111.2	104.3	109.7	108.5
4th quarter	109.8	102.0	89.8	110.6	85.9	69.7	98.7	108.3	111.1	103.7	100.2	108.7
2016												
1st quarter	110.0	101.2	89.5	110.4	85.7	68.5	100.4	107.1	110.7	104.2	88.7	109.1
2nd quarter	110.6	101.2	88.9	109.8	84.9	67.3	101.4	107.5	110.2	104.0	93.5	109.4
3rd quarter	111.0	101.1	88.1	109.4	84.0	66.3	100.7	107.8	109.6	103.9	93.8	110.5
4th quarter	111.6	101.4	87.4	109.1	83.4	65.0	100.9	108.8	109.3	103.6	102.8	110.8

Table 4-4.   Chain-Type Price Indexes for Personal Consumption Expenditures by Major Type of Product—*Continued*

(Index numbers, 2009 =1000.)

NIPA Table 2.3.4

| Year and quarter | Services | Household consumption expenditures for services | | | | | | | | Nonprofit institutions serving households (NPISHs) | | |
		Household services, total	Housing and utilities	Health care	Transportation services	Recreation services	Food services and accommodations	Financial services and insurance	Other services	Final consumption expenditures	Gross output	Less: receipts from sales of goods and services
1955	11.1	10.6	12.8	5.4	11.8	13.1	10.3	13.2	10.9	48.3	. . .	. . .
1956	11.4	10.8	13.0	5.6	12.2	13.5	10.4	13.6	11.3	50.5	. . .	. . .
1957	11.7	11.1	13.3	5.8	12.7	14.0	10.8	14.0	11.7	52.8	. . .	. . .
1958	12.0	11.4	13.5	6.1	13.1	14.5	11.1	14.3	12.0	54.2	. . .	. . .
1959	12.3	11.7	13.7	6.2	13.4	14.9	11.5	15.1	12.3	55.2	9.8	5.7
1960	12.6	12.0	14.0	6.7	13.7	15.4	11.8	15.7	12.7	51.4	10.1	6.1
1961	12.9	12.3	14.2	6.8	14.1	15.8	12.0	16.3	12.8	52.0	10.3	6.2
1962	13.1	12.5	14.3	7.0	14.4	16.2	12.3	16.9	13.0	52.7	10.5	6.4
1963	13.3	12.7	14.5	7.2	14.5	16.6	12.6	17.0	13.3	50.0	10.7	6.6
1964	13.6	12.9	14.6	7.4	14.7	17.0	12.8	17.7	13.6	53.8	11.0	6.8
1965	13.8	13.2	14.8	7.7	14.9	17.4	13.0	18.1	14.0	55.3	11.3	7.0
1966	14.2	13.5	15.0	8.0	15.2	17.8	13.5	19.2	14.4	57.3	11.7	7.2
1967	14.7	14.0	15.2	8.5	15.8	18.5	14.3	19.7	14.8	59.2	12.2	7.6
1968	15.3	14.6	15.6	9.0	16.5	19.4	15.0	21.1	15.5	61.4	12.9	8.0
1969	16.1	15.4	16.1	9.7	17.5	20.3	15.9	23.0	16.2	65.3	13.7	8.6
1970	17.0	16.2	16.8	10.4	18.9	21.2	17.1	24.2	17.0	68.1	14.6	9.2
1971	17.9	17.1	17.6	11.0	20.2	22.1	18.0	25.6	18.0	72.0	15.3	9.6
1972	18.7	17.8	18.3	11.4	21.0	22.7	18.7	27.2	19.0	74.9	16.1	10.1
1973	19.6	18.7	19.1	12.0	21.9	23.5	19.9	27.8	20.1	79.8	17.1	10.7
1974	21.3	20.2	20.2	13.1	23.8	25.1	22.2	30.1	22.2	91.3	19.1	11.9
1975	23.1	22.0	21.8	14.6	26.4	27.0	24.2	32.3	23.8	99.7	21.1	13.2
1976	24.7	23.5	23.3	16.0	28.4	28.3	25.8	33.6	25.3	104.9	22.7	14.3
1977	26.6	25.3	25.4	17.3	30.3	29.7	27.7	36.2	26.6	112.0	24.4	15.4
1978	28.6	27.3	27.2	18.8	32.3	31.5	30.1	41.0	28.0	119.4	26.3	16.6
1979	31.0	29.5	29.4	20.6	35.2	33.5	33.4	43.2	30.1	131.1	28.9	18.3
1980	34.2	32.6	32.5	23.1	40.9	36.1	36.6	46.5	32.8	143.3	32.3	20.6
1981	37.7	36.0	36.0	25.9	45.8	38.4	39.9	50.0	36.1	150.4	35.9	23.3
1982	40.6	38.9	39.4	28.8	48.4	40.5	42.2	52.9	39.0	142.5	38.7	26.1
1983	43.2	41.5	41.9	31.5	50.2	42.2	44.0	58.0	41.2	131.8	40.8	28.6
1984	45.4	43.8	44.0	33.8	52.2	44.1	46.0	61.7	43.3	126.1	42.7	30.8
1985	47.7	46.1	46.4	35.9	53.2	46.0	47.9	66.9	44.8	123.3	44.5	32.6
1986	49.6	48.1	48.6	38.0	53.8	47.7	49.9	67.9	47.2	119.3	46.0	34.5
1987	51.1	49.6	50.3	40.4	56.0	49.6	51.9	64.7	48.3	117.0	48.0	36.7
1988	53.5	52.1	52.3	43.6	58.7	51.5	54.2	67.7	50.4	115.6	50.9	39.6
1989	56.0	54.6	54.4	47.4	61.2	54.0	56.6	69.7	52.2	108.1	53.7	43.3
1990	58.5	57.3	56.8	51.5	63.6	57.0	59.2	70.7	54.3	99.0	56.2	47.2
1991	60.7	59.8	58.7	55.4	65.3	60.0	61.6	70.3	57.0	91.5	58.8	51.1
1992	62.8	62.1	60.3	59.3	67.2	61.8	62.9	72.6	59.4	83.2	61.0	55.0
1993	65.0	64.5	62.0	62.5	69.5	63.8	64.1	76.5	61.4	78.7	62.8	58.0
1994	66.8	66.3	63.6	65.0	70.4	65.2	65.2	77.9	63.7	78.6	64.6	60.2
1995	68.6	68.2	65.4	67.4	71.9	66.6	66.8	79.6	65.8	78.5	66.5	62.4
1996	70.5	70.0	67.3	69.0	72.8	68.8	68.6	82.4	67.7	79.9	68.3	64.3
1997	72.4	72.0	69.1	70.4	74.4	71.0	70.6	85.6	69.6	83.3	70.0	65.7
1998	73.9	73.3	70.8	71.7	75.8	72.8	72.5	85.7	71.0	88.9	72.1	67.0
1999	75.4	74.8	72.4	73.3	76.9	75.1	74.4	85.0	72.8	92.1	74.1	68.6
2000	77.5	76.8	74.9	75.4	79.2	78.0	76.5	85.9	74.2	97.2	77.0	70.9
2001	79.9	79.1	78.4	77.9	80.1	80.6	78.6	85.6	76.5	101.7	80.0	73.5
2002	82.0	81.2	80.6	79.9	80.5	82.9	80.5	87.7	79.4	102.2	82.3	76.2
2003	84.5	84.0	83.2	82.9	82.2	85.5	82.2	91.5	82.4	99.6	84.7	80.1
2004	87.1	86.6	85.5	86.0	83.4	87.7	85.0	95.0	85.1	98.1	87.3	83.8
2005	89.9	89.5	88.6	88.7	86.5	90.2	87.7	97.9	88.2	100.2	90.3	87.1
2006	93.0	92.6	92.3	91.4	90.0	93.2	90.6	100.6	91.2	101.1	93.3	90.7
2007	96.0	95.7	95.5	94.8	92.1	95.9	94.2	103.5	93.7	102.4	96.2	94.0
2008	98.9	98.8	98.9	97.4	97.0	98.8	97.8	104.6	97.5	103.1	98.6	97.1
2009	100.0	100.0	100.0	100.0	100.0	100.0	100.0	100.0	100.0	100.0	100.0	100.0
2010	101.7	101.8	100.2	102.5	102.0	101.1	101.3	104.0	102.4	98.9	101.8	102.8
2011	103.5	103.7	101.7	104.4	104.8	102.8	103.9	106.5	104.2	99.9	103.9	105.2
2012	105.8	106.1	103.4	106.3	106.8	105.6	106.8	111.7	106.4	99.5	105.7	107.8
2013	108.3	108.6	106.0	107.8	108.3	107.4	108.9	117.4	108.8	101.4	107.9	110.1
2014	110.9	111.2	109.1	109.1	109.5	109.4	111.9	123.5	110.7	105.4	110.3	112.0
2015	113.1	113.2	111.8	109.7	109.9	111.2	115.0	127.9	112.0	109.7	112.5	113.5
2016	115.9	116.0	115.1	111.0	111.2	113.9	118.0	135.1	113.7	113.4	114.8	115.3
2014												
1st quarter	110.0	110.2	108.0	108.7	109.0	109.0	110.4	121.3	110.0	103.7	109.5	111.5
2nd quarter	110.7	111.0	108.8	109.0	109.4	109.4	111.5	123.1	110.5	104.7	110.1	111.9
3rd quarter	111.3	111.5	109.4	109.3	109.6	109.7	112.3	124.4	111.0	105.4	110.6	112.3
4th quarter	111.8	111.9	110.1	109.3	110.1	109.7	113.3	125.2	111.3	107.8	111.1	112.2
2015												
1st quarter	112.2	112.4	110.8	109.3	109.6	110.2	114.1	125.9	111.5	108.5	111.7	112.8
2nd quarter	112.8	112.9	111.4	109.6	109.9	111.1	114.6	127.3	111.6	109.5	112.4	113.4
3rd quarter	113.4	113.5	112.2	110.0	109.9	111.7	115.2	128.7	112.1	110.1	112.9	113.8
4th quarter	113.9	114.1	112.9	110.1	110.2	111.9	116.2	129.6	112.8	110.8	113.1	114.0
2016												
1st quarter	114.7	114.8	113.6	110.3	110.8	112.7	117.0	132.0	113.1	111.9	113.7	114.4
2nd quarter	115.5	115.6	114.6	110.8	111.2	113.8	117.6	134.5	113.5	112.8	114.4	115.0
3rd quarter	116.3	116.4	115.6	111.3	111.2	114.4	118.2	136.5	114.1	113.8	115.2	115.7
4th quarter	117.0	117.1	116.7	111.6	111.5	114.8	119.0	137.6	114.2	115.0	115.9	116.2

. . . = Not available.

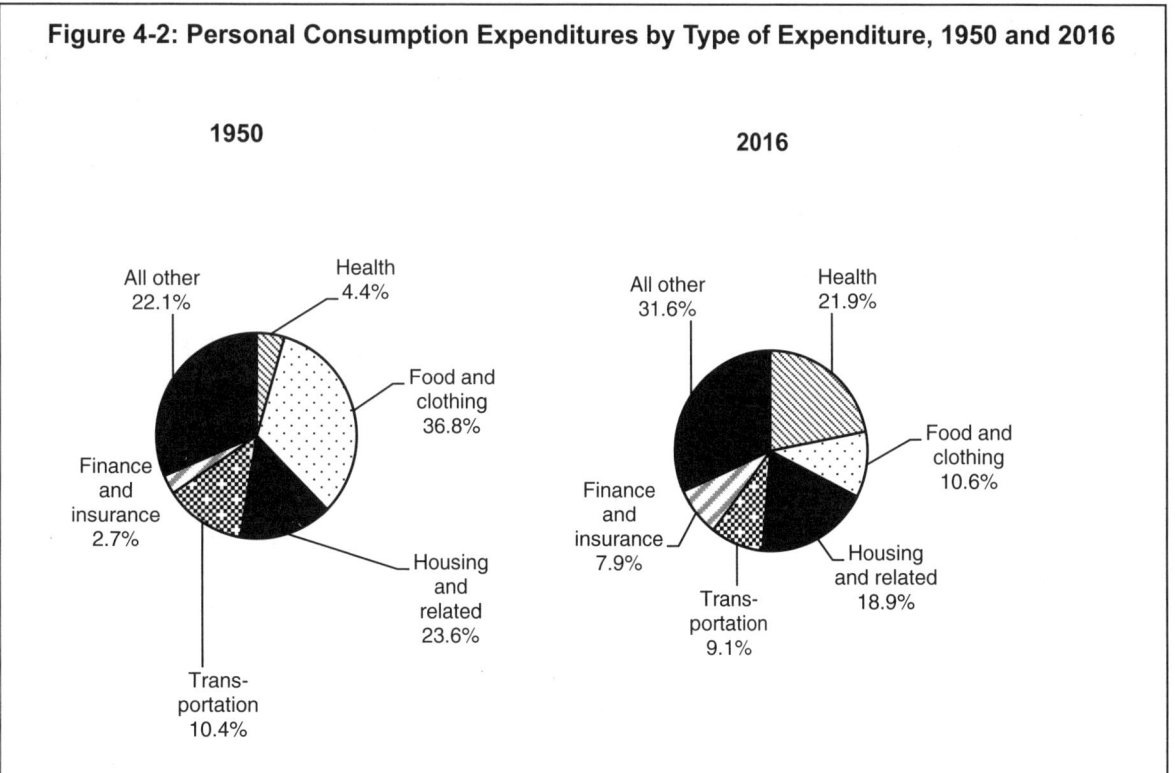

Figure 4-2: Personal Consumption Expenditures by Type of Expenditure, 1950 and 2016

- Figure 4-2 compares the composition of household consumer spending (excluding the net spending of nonprofit institutions) in 1950 and 2016, the latest available data at the time this edition of *Business Statistics* was compiled. (Table 4-5)

- Household spending on health in 2016 made up 21.9 percent of all household consumption spending—nearly five times the percentage 1950. It is important to recognize that household consumption spending, as presented in these data, includes (in health spending and in the total) medical care payments made by government and private insurance on behalf of individuals as well as out-of-pocket consumer payments. (Table 4-5)

- In 2016, a much smaller share was required for food and clothing than in 1950, as seen in Figure 4-2. The shares of housing-related spending and transportation were similar in the two years. The share of finance and insurance spending nearly tripled, and households also spent a larger share on the remaining category, here labeled "all other," which includes communication, recreation, education, food services, accommodations, and other miscellaneous goods and services. (Table 4-5)

Table 4-5. Household Consumption Expenditures by Function

(Billions of dollars.)   NIPA Table 2.5.5

Year	Household consumption expenditures, total	Food and beverages off-premises	Clothing, footwear, and related services	Housing, utilities, and fuels	Furnishings, household equipment, and maintenance	Health	Transportation	Communication	Recreation	Education	Food services and accommodations	Financial services and insurance	Other goods and services	Foreign travel and expenditures, net
1939	66.2	15.2	7.7	12.3	5.5	2.8	6.3	0.7	3.6	0.6	4.1	2.3	5.0	0.2
1940	70.2	15.9	8.1	12.8	6.0	3.0	7.0	0.7	3.9	0.6	4.4	2.4	5.3	0.1
1941	80.0	18.2	9.5	13.7	7.1	3.2	8.3	0.8	4.5	0.6	5.3	2.5	6.0	0.1
1942	87.7	21.6	11.8	14.8	7.4	3.6	5.4	1.0	4.9	0.7	6.9	2.6	6.8	0.2
1943	98.4	24.3	14.4	15.5	7.4	4.0	5.4	1.2	5.3	0.8	9.1	2.8	8.0	0.3
1944	107.0	26.0	15.7	16.2	8.0	4.5	5.7	1.3	5.8	0.9	10.9	3.0	8.5	0.6
1945	118.2	28.2	17.6	16.9	8.9	4.8	6.6	1.4	6.5	0.9	12.7	3.2	9.3	1.2
1946	142.3	34.9	19.7	18.8	12.7	5.9	12.1	1.6	9.0	1.0	12.7	3.8	10.3	-0.1
1947	159.9	40.2	20.4	21.2	15.5	6.6	15.4	1.7	9.8	1.2	12.5	4.2	11.1	0.0
1948	172.7	41.8	21.8	23.9	16.8	7.6	18.0	1.9	10.3	1.3	12.6	4.7	11.7	0.3
1949	176.1	40.4	21.1	25.6	16.3	7.9	21.2	2.1	10.6	1.4	12.4	4.9	11.8	0.6
1950	189.8	41.4	21.4	28.4	18.7	8.5	24.6	2.3	11.7	1.5	12.7	5.6	12.2	0.7
1951	205.9	46.0	23.1	31.0	19.7	9.0	21.2	2.6	12.3	1.6	15.0	6.3	13.3	0.9
1952	216.6	48.4	23.9	34.6	19.3	10.1	24.4	2.9	13.0	1.7	16.0	6.7	14.3	1.1
1953	230.0	49.3	24.2	37.9	20.0	11.0	28.0	3.2	13.8	1.8	16.5	7.8	15.0	1.5
1954	236.7	50.6	24.3	40.9	19.9	11.9	27.4	3.3	14.3	1.9	16.6	8.6	15.4	1.5
1955	255.3	52.0	25.4	43.8	22.3	12.8	33.4	3.6	15.4	2.1	17.0	9.6	16.3	1.6
1956	267.8	54.2	26.5	46.8	23.6	14.1	32.7	3.9	16.4	2.4	17.7	10.4	17.5	1.7
1957	282.7	57.1	26.8	50.0	23.9	15.5	35.7	4.3	16.8	2.6	18.5	11.1	18.8	1.7
1958	291.7	59.8	27.1	53.3	24.1	17.1	33.7	4.5	17.3	2.9	18.7	11.6	19.9	1.9
1959	312.6	61.6	28.6	56.9	25.6	18.8	38.8	4.8	18.8	3.1	19.7	12.5	21.4	2.0
1960	326.5	62.6	29.3	60.5	26.2	20.4	40.8	5.2	19.7	3.4	20.5	13.6	22.4	2.1
1961	336.7	63.7	29.9	64.0	26.8	21.8	39.3	5.6	20.5	3.6	21.0	14.8	23.7	2.0
1962	357.6	64.7	31.3	68.2	28.3	24.3	44.1	5.9	22.1	4.0	22.3	15.4	24.9	2.3
1963	376.7	65.9	32.1	72.2	29.8	26.4	47.8	6.4	23.9	4.3	23.3	15.9	26.2	2.5
1964	404.8	69.5	34.7	76.2	32.7	29.8	50.7	6.9	26.3	4.8	24.9	17.7	27.8	2.6
1965	436.6	74.4	36.5	81.0	34.7	32.0	56.5	7.5	28.9	5.5	27.2	19.4	30.2	2.9
1966	473.1	80.6	39.8	85.9	37.8	35.0	59.0	8.1	33.4	6.2	29.6	21.3	33.3	3.1
1967	499.4	82.6	41.7	91.1	39.7	38.4	61.0	8.9	35.8	6.9	31.0	22.8	35.8	3.8
1968	548.7	88.8	45.6	97.4	43.2	43.8	69.8	9.7	39.9	7.7	34.6	25.8	38.6	3.7
1969	595.0	95.4	48.8	105.5	45.4	50.0	75.9	10.7	43.7	8.7	37.5	28.5	41.0	4.0
1970	637.2	103.5	49.9	113.8	46.6	56.8	76.5	11.6	47.0	9.9	41.6	31.1	44.3	4.5
1971	689.3	107.1	53.4	124.5	48.8	63.4	88.7	12.8	50.1	10.9	43.8	34.1	47.0	4.8
1972	756.6	114.5	58.0	136.2	53.5	70.4	98.3	14.4	56.2	11.7	48.9	38.3	51.0	5.2
1973	837.4	126.7	63.7	149.7	59.9	78.7	108.6	16.1	63.0	13.0	54.8	41.5	56.9	4.7
1974	916.5	143.0	66.9	166.3	64.6	88.7	112.8	17.7	68.9	14.2	60.6	45.9	62.2	4.7
1975	1 015.7	156.6	71.4	184.8	67.8	102.7	124.4	20.0	77.1	15.9	68.8	54.0	67.8	4.4
1976	1 131.2	167.3	76.9	204.6	75.0	116.8	147.4	22.4	86.2	17.4	77.8	59.3	76.3	3.8
1977	1 256.0	179.8	84.3	228.7	84.0	131.6	168.1	24.3	94.9	18.8	85.7	67.8	83.8	4.3
1978	1 403.2	196.1	94.6	255.6	93.6	149.4	184.5	27.0	106.3	20.9	97.1	80.6	93.2	4.3
1979	1 563.4	218.4	101.9	287.5	104.3	169.9	207.1	29.4	118.9	22.9	110.9	87.6	100.4	4.1
1980	1 724.6	239.2	108.8	327.7	110.7	195.5	226.5	31.8	127.4	25.4	121.7	95.6	110.7	3.5
1981	1 903.4	255.3	119.1	367.6	118.3	228.9	250.7	36.0	141.6	28.3	133.9	102.0	121.2	0.4
1982	2 035.9	267.1	122.7	401.7	121.0	254.9	255.9	41.1	151.4	31.0	142.5	116.3	127.8	2.5
1983	2 245.8	277.0	132.9	434.6	132.3	287.1	284.9	44.8	169.3	34.3	153.6	145.9	143.4	5.4
1984	2 452.8	291.1	144.7	471.1	147.1	315.2	321.8	48.4	190.0	37.7	164.9	156.6	157.7	6.6
1985	2 674.8	303.0	154.3	513.9	156.0	345.3	357.4	53.1	207.2	41.2	174.3	188.1	173.3	7.7
1986	2 845.8	316.4	165.1	548.1	168.7	378.4	362.6	56.9	225.4	44.5	186.7	199.8	190.0	3.3
1987	3 036.4	324.3	176.4	582.6	176.9	419.9	376.6	60.0	247.0	48.8	204.4	205.3	208.2	6.1
1988	3 283.6	342.8	188.1	625.9	186.6	470.7	404.8	63.1	273.4	54.4	225.8	219.8	225.4	2.8
1989	3 524.8	365.4	201.2	666.9	197.5	519.0	428.3	67.3	295.7	60.6	242.6	238.4	245.7	-3.7
1990	3 749.8	391.2	206.5	709.3	200.6	583.7	442.9	70.1	314.7	66.0	262.7	247.4	262.3	-7.7
1991	3 880.0	403.0	210.1	747.5	199.1	638.4	418.3	73.9	326.3	70.6	273.4	266.8	268.0	-15.2
1992	4 127.7	404.5	223.0	783.3	209.4	700.4	451.3	81.1	346.8	76.4	286.3	295.1	290.1	-20.0
1993	4 380.9	413.5	231.1	827.3	221.9	741.7	485.3	85.8	378.4	81.1	298.4	332.6	304.5	-20.7
1994	4 643.3	432.1	240.1	876.1	238.6	779.9	528.2	93.3	414.0	86.4	308.3	346.9	316.9	-17.4
1995	4 881.9	443.7	244.7	926.7	251.7	826.0	554.1	98.9	449.8	92.3	316.1	366.4	332.7	-21.3
1996	5 158.0	461.9	253.5	976.7	263.7	868.3	598.9	108.3	481.5	99.6	326.6	392.3	350.8	-24.2
1997	5 455.1	474.8	262.0	1 023.1	277.3	919.9	641.8	120.1	509.5	107.1	343.4	429.2	368.4	-21.5
1998	5 779.2	487.4	273.1	1 077.0	297.1	979.7	668.6	129.5	544.3	115.2	361.8	467.3	393.7	-15.6
1999	6 168.8	515.5	287.2	1 135.5	320.2	1 033.3	729.0	142.3	589.9	123.9	380.3	509.1	429.4	-27.0
2000	6 634.4	540.6	297.5	1 214.5	343.4	1 109.6	795.4	158.3	633.7	134.3	408.8	566.3	458.5	-26.4
2001	6 924.0	564.0	294.6	1 303.0	352.4	1 209.4	810.5	164.9	647.0	143.6	419.7	552.8	477.9	-15.8
2002	7 185.7	575.1	295.2	1 347.9	365.3	1 317.1	813.1	168.9	669.3	149.5	436.3	562.6	496.8	-11.4
2003	7 560.0	599.6	301.5	1 411.6	380.4	1 411.3	846.0	174.4	704.3	159.5	461.9	588.5	526.5	-5.3
2004	8 053.6	632.6	313.5	1 488.4	407.1	1 516.2	899.3	181.1	758.7	169.0	496.4	635.3	559.1	-3.1
2005	8 583.8	668.2	326.6	1 606.0	431.2	1 614.0	960.8	187.0	804.6	180.5	530.6	689.6	589.5	-4.7
2006	9 064.8	700.3	336.3	1 706.1	449.9	1 717.3	992.9	201.2	854.1	193.1	566.3	724.2	624.5	-1.5
2007	9 501.7	737.3	339.7	1 783.8	453.7	1 826.8	1 032.7	216.4	893.8	206.0	595.6	768.5	657.6	-10.4
2008	9 731.5	772.9	335.4	1 869.9	442.0	1 914.2	1 009.7	230.7	899.6	218.4	612.5	771.5	673.0	-18.1
2009	9 571.0	770.0	321.6	1 905.3	409.8	2 000.9	867.0	230.6	861.8	229.1	600.3	719.0	672.7	-17.0
2010	9 926.8	788.9	335.8	1 935.1	417.3	2 080.4	942.1	239.6	888.3	244.9	617.7	763.2	700.6	-27.3
2011	10 414.3	829.1	354.6	1 989.0	435.2	2 176.9	1 052.0	253.7	922.9	256.3	649.5	795.8	733.1	-33.7
2012	10 757.8	848.8	370.1	2 021.8	452.4	2 266.2	1 105.7	264.6	968.2	262.5	685.1	789.3	754.9	-31.8
2013	11 056.3	857.5	380.0	2 080.8	468.6	2 323.0	1 136.2	270.9	1 003.0	269.2	710.8	830.7	774.3	-48.8
2014	11 550.1	884.4	392.9	2 171.4	490.2	2 443.4	1 169.1	288.8	1 041.9	277.9	751.1	888.4	801.6	-54.1
2015	12 002.8	899.0	402.5	2 256.6	513.3	2 595.5	1 130.4	299.6	1 085.9	286.2	808.2	947.2	837.2	-58.8
2016	12 461.8	915.1	410.9	2 350.0	533.8	2 725.1	1 128.5	309.1	1 137.6	294.6	849.2	984.7	871.7	-48.6

NOTES AND DEFINITIONS, CHAPTER 4

SOURCE: U.S. DEPARTMENT OF COMMERCE, BUREAU OF ECONOMIC ANALYSIS (BEA)

All personal income and personal consumption expenditure series are from the national income and product accounts (NIPAs). All quarterly series are shown at seasonally adjusted annual rates. Current and constant dollar values are in billions of dollars. Indexes of price and quantity are based on the average for the year 2009, which equals 100.

The 2013 NIPA comprehensive revision included a major definitional revision: accrual accounting for defined benefit pension programs. Last year this caused upward revisions to personal income receipts on assets for 1929–2012 and upward revisions to the supplements component of employee compensation for 1929–1975, 1989–2002, and 2004 forward.

Results from the 2016 Annual Update of the National Income and Products Accounts (NIPA) revised the average growth rates of GDP for 2013–2016. Other revisions were incorporated include the Census Bureau's annual retail sales, construction, manufacturing plus others.

Tables 4-1 through 4-4 cover all income and spending by the personal sector, which includes nonprofit institutions serving households (NPISHs). In a new feature introduced in the 2009 comprehensive revision of the NIPAs, Tables 4-2, 4-3, and 4-4 show the services component of personal consumption expenditures broken down into separate aggregates for "household consumption expenditures for services" and "final consumption expenditures" by NPISHs.

The last table gives further details of the separate accounts for households and NPISHs that are only available annually. Table 4-5 shows a more detailed functional breakdown of household consumption expenditures, not including NPISHs.

In several cases, the notes and definitions below will refer to *imputations* or *imputed values*. See the notes and definitions to Chapter 1 for an explanation of imputation and the role it plays in national and personal income measurement.

TABLES 4-1 THROUGH 4-4

Sources and Disposition of Personal Income; Personal Consumption Expenditures by Major Type of Product

Definitions

Personal income is the income received by persons residing in the United States from participation in production, from government and business transfer payments, and from government interest, which is treated similarly to a transfer payment rather than as income from participation in production. *Persons* denotes

the total for individuals, *nonprofit institutions that primarily serve households (NPISHs)*, private noninsured welfare funds, and private trust funds. Personal income, outlays, and saving excluding NPISHs are referred to as *household* income, outlays, and saving. All proprietors' income is treated as received by individuals. Life insurance carriers and private noninsured pension funds are not counted as persons, but their saving is credited to persons.

Income from the sale of illegal goods and services is excluded by definition from national and personal income, and the value of purchases of illegal goods and services is not included in personal consumption expenditures.

Personal income is the sum of compensation received by employees, proprietors' income with inventory valuation and capital consumption adjustments (IVA and CCAdj), rental income of persons with capital consumption adjustment, personal receipts on assets, and personal current transfer receipts, less contributions for social insurance.

Personal income differs from national income in that it includes current transfer payments and interest received by persons, regardless of source, while it excludes the following national income components: employee and employer contributions for social insurance; business transfer payments, interest payments, and other payments on assets other than to persons; taxes on production and imports less subsidies; the current surplus of government enterprises; and undistributed corporate profits with IVA and CCAdj. The relationships of GDP, gross and net national product, national income, and personal income are displayed in Table 1-11.

Compensation of employees is the sum of wages and salaries and supplements to wages and salaries, as defined in the *national* income account (see Table 1-13 and the notes and definitions to Chapter 1).

As in *national* income, the *compensation of employees* component of personal income refers to compensation received by residents of the United States, including compensation from the rest of the world, but excludes compensation from domestic industries to workers residing in the rest of the world.

Wages and salaries consists of the monetary remuneration of employees, including wages and salaries as conventionally defined; the compensation of corporate officers; corporate directors' fees paid to directors who are also employees of the corporation; the value of employee exercise of "nonqualified stock options"; commissions, tips, and bonuses; voluntary employee contributions to certain deferred-compensation plans, such as 401(k) plans; and receipts in kind that represent income. This category also now includes judicial fees to jurors and witnesses, compensation of prison inmates, and marriage fees to justices of the peace, which earlier were classified as "other labor income." As of the 2013 revision, wages and salaries are now measured on an accrual basis, that is to say when earned rather than when paid, consistent with the treatment in the gross domestic income and national income tables.

Supplements to wages and salaries consists of employer contributions to employee pension and insurance funds and to government social insurance funds. In a substantial change introduced in the 2013 revision, defined benefit pension plan transactions are now recorded on an accrual basis instead of a cash transactions basis: employees are now credited with defined pension benefits, based on actuarial estimates of pension costs, at the time they earn them. (This was already the case with defined contribution plans.)

The following two categories, *proprietors' income* and *rental income,* are both measured net of depreciation of the capital (structures, equipment, and intellectual property products) involved. BEA calculates normal depreciation, based on the estimated life of the capital, and subtracts it from the estimated value of receipts to yield net income.

Proprietors' income with inventory valuation and capital consumption adjustments is the currentproduction income (including income-in-kind) of sole proprietors and partnerships and of taxexempt cooperatives. The imputed net rental income of owneroccupants of farm dwellings is included. Dividends and monetary interest received by proprietors of nonfinancial business and rental incomes received by persons not primarily engaged in the real estate business are excluded. These incomes are included in personal income receipts on assets and rental income of persons, respectively. Fees paid to outside directors of corporations are included. The two valuation adjustments are designed to obtain income measures that exclude any element of capital gains: inventory withdrawals are valued at replacement cost, rather than historical cost, and charges for depreciation are on an economically consistent accounting basis and are valued at replacement cost.

Rental income of persons with capital consumption adjustment consists of the net currentproduction income of persons from the rental of real property (other than the incomes of persons primarily engaged in the real estate business), the imputed net rental income of owneroccupants of nonfarm dwellings, and the royalties received by persons from patents, copyrights, and rights to natural resources. The capital consumption adjustment converts charges for depreciation to an economically consistent accounting basis valued at replacement cost. Rental income is net of interest and other expenses, and hence is affected by changing indebtedness and interest payments on owner-occupied and other housing.

Personal income receipts on assets consists of personal interest income and personal dividend income.

Personal interest income is the interest income (monetary and imputed) of persons from all sources, including interest paid by

government to government employee retirement plans as well as government interest paid directly to persons.

Personal dividend income is the dividend income of persons from all sources, excluding capital gains distributions. It equals net dividends paid by corporations (dividends paid by corporations minus dividends received by corporations) less a small amount of corporate dividends received by general government. Dividends received by government employee retirement systems are included in personal dividend income.

Personal current transfer receipts is income payments to persons for which no current services are performed. It consists of government social benefits to persons and net receipts from business.

Government social benefits to persons consists of benefits from the following categories of programs:

- *Social Security and Medicare*, consisting of federal oldage, survivors, disability, and health insurance benefits distributed from the Social Security and Medicare trust funds;

- *Medicaid,* the federal-state means-tested program covering medical expenses for lower-income children and adults as well as nursing care expenses;

- *Unemployment insurance*;

- *Veterans' benefits*;

- *Other government benefits to persons*, which includes pension benefit guaranty; workers' compensation; military medical insurance; temporary disability insurance; food stamps; Black Lung benefits; supplemental security income; family assistance, which consists of aid to families with dependent children and (beginning in 1996) assistance programs operating under the Personal Responsibility and Work Opportunity Reconciliation Act of 1996; educational assistance; and the earned income credit. Government payments to nonprofit institutions, other than for work under research and development contracts, also are included. Payments from government employee retirement plans are not included.

Note that the value of Medicare and Medicaid spending, though in practice it is usually paid directly from the government to the health care provider, is treated as if it were cash income to the consumer which is then expended in personal consumption expenditures; this value is not treated in the national accounts as a government purchase of medical services but as a government benefit paid to persons, which then finances personal consumption spending.

Contributions for government social insurance, domestic, which is subtracted to arrive at personal income, includes payments by U.S. employers, employees, selfemployed, and other individuals who participate in the following programs: oldage, survivors, and disability insurance (Social Security); hospital insurance and supplementary medical insurance (Medicare); unemployment insurance; railroad retirement; veterans' life insurance; and temporary disability insurance. Contributions to government employee retirement plans are not included in this item.

In the 2009 comprehensive revision, most transactions between the U.S. government and economic agents in Guam, the U.S. Virgin Islands, American Samoa, Puerto Rico, and the Northern Mariana Islands are treated as government transactions with the rest of the world. Since the NIPAs only cover the 50 states and the District of Columbia, the *domestic* contributions to government social insurance funds are the only ones that need to be subtracted from NIPA payroll data to calculate personal income. The social insurance receipts of governments, shown in Chapter 6, will be somewhat larger than this personal income entry because they will include contributions from residents of those territories and commonwealths.

Personal current taxes is tax payments (net of refunds) by persons residing in the United States that are not chargeable to business expenses, including taxes on income, on realized net capital gains, and on personal property. As of the 1999 revisions, estate and gift taxes are classified as capital transfers and are not included in personal current taxes.

Disposable personal income is personal income minus personal current taxes. It is the income from current production that is available to persons for spending or saving. However, it is not the cash flow available, since it excludes realized capital gains. Disposable personal income in chained (2009) dollars represents the inflation-adjusted value of disposable personal income, using the implicit price deflator for personal consumption expenditures.

Personal income excluding current transfer receipts, also shown in chained (2009) dollars using the implicit price deflator for personal consumption expenditures, is an important business cycle indicator, to which particular attention is paid because it is calculated monthly as well as quarterly and annually, and thus can help establish monthly cycle turning point dates. As a pre-income-tax measure which excludes transfer payments, it is a better measure of income generated by the economy than alternative monthly income indicators such as total or disposable personal income, which are more oriented toward purchasing power.

Personal outlays is the sum of *personal consumption expenditures* (defined below), *personal interest payments,* and *personal current transfer payments.*

Personal interest payments is nonmortgage interest paid by households. As noted above in the definition of rental income, mortgage interest has been subtracted from gross rental or imputed rental receipts of persons to yield a net rental income estimate; hence, it is not included as an interest outlay in this category.

Personal current transfer payments to government includes donations, fees, and fines paid to federal, state, and local governments.

Personal current transfer payments to the rest of the world (net) is personal remittances in cash and in kind to the rest of the world less such remittances from the rest of the world.

Personal saving is derived by subtracting personal outlays from disposable personal income. It is the current net saving of individuals (including proprietors), nonprofit institutions that primarily serve individuals, life insurance carriers, retirement funds (including those of government employees), private noninsured welfare funds, and private trust funds. Conceptually, personal saving may also be viewed as the sum of the net acquisition of financial assets and the change in physical assets less the sum of net borrowing and consumption of fixed capital. In either case, it is defined to exclude both realized and unrealized capital gains.

Note that in the context of national income accounting, the term just defined is *saving,* not "savings." *Saving* refers to a <u>flow</u> of income during a particular time span (such as a year or a quarter) that is not consumed. It is therefore available to finance a commensurate <u>flow</u> of investment during that time span. Strictly defined, "savings" denotes an accumulated <u>stock</u> of monetary funds—possibly the cumulative effects of successive periods of *saving*—available to the owner in asset form, such as in a bank savings account.

Personal consumption expenditures (PCE) is goods and services purchased by persons residing in the United States. Persons are defined as individuals and nonprofit institutions that primarily serve individuals. PCE mostly consists of purchases of new goods and services by individuals from business, including purchases financed by insurance (such as both private and government medical insurance). In addition, PCE includes purchases of new goods and services by nonprofit institutions, net purchases of used goods by individuals and nonprofit institutions, and purchases abroad of goods and services by U.S. residents traveling or working in foreign countries. PCE also includes purchases for certain goods and services provided by the government, primarily tuition payments for higher education, charges for medical care, and charges for water and sanitary services. Finally, PCE includes imputed purchases that keep PCE invariant to changes in the way that certain activities are carried out. For example, to take account of the value of the services provided by owner-occupied housing, PCE includes an imputation equal to what (estimated) rent homeowners would pay if they rented their houses from themselves. (See the discussion of imputation in the notes and definitions to Chapter 1.) Actual purchases of residential structures by individuals are classified as gross private domestic investment.

In the 2009 comprehensive revision, the classification system used for breakdowns of PCE was revised, and new calculations were introduced separating the consumption spending of the household sector proper from that of nonprofit institutions serving households.

Goods is the sum of *Durable* and *Nondurable goods*.

The PCE category *Durable goods* is subdivided into *Motor vehicles and parts, Furnishings and household equipment* (which includes appliances), *Recreational goods and vehicles* (which includes video, audio, photographic, and information processing equipment and media), and *Other durable goods.*

Nondurable goods encompasses *Food and beverages off-premises, Clothing and footwear, Gasoline and other energy goods,* and *Other nondurable goods.* This food and beverages category no longer includes meals and beverages purchased for consumption on the premises, which are now included in services, since they have a high service component and since their prices are much more stable than those of off-premises food and beverages.

Services, total is subdivided into *Household services* and *Final consumption expenditures of nonprofit institutions serving households (NPISHs).* The latter is the difference between the *gross output* of NPISHs and the amounts that they receive from sales of goods and services to households—for example, payments for services of a nonprofit hospital. Such sales of goods and services appear in the appropriate category of household expenditures—for example, *Health* in the case of the hospital services.

The components of *Household services* are *Housing and utilities, Health care, Transportation services, Recreation services, Food services and accommodations* (which includes meals and beverages purchased for consumption on premises, as well as payments for hotels and similar accommodations), *Financial services and insurance,* and *Other services.*

These are the categories used in the quarterly data presented in Tables 4-2, 4-3, and 4-4. This classification system is not particularly helpful with respect to the objective of spending. For example, the *Health care* component of services does not include drugs and medicines, which are included instead in nondurable goods. For a more precise classification of consumption spending by objective, see Table 4-5, Household Consumption Expenditures by Function, described in more detail below. This classification by type of expenditure is only available on an annual basis, and later than the principal quarterly NIPA data.

Data availability

Monthly data on personal income and spending are made available in a BEA press release, usually distributed the first business day following the monthly release of the latest quarterly national income and product account (NIPA) estimates. Monthly and quarterly data are subsequently published each month in the BEA's *Survey of Current Business.* Current and historical data are available on the BEA Web site at <http://www.bea.gov>, and may also be obtained from the STAT-USA subscription Web site at <http://www.stat-usa.gov>.

REFERENCES

References can be found in the notes and definitions to Chapter 1. A discussion of monthly estimates of personal income and its disposition appears in the November 1979 edition of the *Survey of Current Business.* Additional and more recent information can be found in the articles listed in the notes and definitions for Chapter 1.

TABLE 4-5

Household Consumption Expenditures by Function

SOURCE: BUREAU OF ECONOMIC ANALYSIS (BEA)

In this table, also derived from the NIPAs, annual estimates of the current-dollar value of PCE by households—excluding the "final" consumption expenditures of nonprofit institutions serving households (NPISHs); see definition above–are presented by function.

Definitions

Food and beverages includes food and beverages (including alcoholic beverages) purchased for home consumption and food produced and consumed on farms.

Clothing, footwear, and related services includes purchases, rental, cleaning, and repair of clothing and footwear.

Housing, utilities, and fuels includes rents paid for rental housing, imputed rent of owner-occupied dwellings, and purchase of fuels and utility services.

Furnishings, household equipment, and routine household maintenance includes furniture, floor coverings, household textiles, appliances, tableware etc., tools, and other supplies and services.

Health includes drugs, other medical products and equipment, and outpatient, hospital, and nursing home services.

Transportation includes the purchase and operation of motor vehicles and public transportation services.

Communication includes telephone equipment, postal and delivery services, telecommunication services, and Internet access.

Recreation includes video and audio equipment, computers, and related services; sports vehicles and other sports goods and services; memberships and admissions; magazines, newspapers, books, and stationery; pets and related goods and services; photo goods and services; tour services; and legal gambling. (As noted earlier, purchases of goods and services that are illegal and the incomes from such purchases are outside the scope of the national income and product accounts.)

Education includes educational services and books.

Food services and accommodations includes meals and beverages purchased for consumption on the premises, food furnished to employees, and hotel and other accommodations including housing at schools.

Financial services and insurance consists of financial services and life, household, medical care, motor vehicle, and other insurance.

Other goods and services includes personal goods (such as cosmetics, jewelry, and luggage) and services, social services and religious activities, professional and other services, and tobacco.

Foreign travel and expenditures, net consists of foreign travel spending and other expenditures abroad by U.S. residents <u>minus</u> expenditures in the United States by nonresidents. A negative figure indicates that foreigners spent more here than U.S. residents spent abroad. Positive values for this foreign travel category, indicating that U.S. residents spent more abroad than foreigners spent here, appear in the 1980s when the dollar was strong against other major currencies. (The international value of the dollar is shown in Table 13-2.) Negative values in subsequent years have resulted in part from the weakening of the dollar, which discouraged U.S. residents' travel abroad and encouraged tourism by foreigners in the United States. The negative sign does not indicate a drain on GDP—these effects of a weaker dollar are in fact positive for real GDP—but rather reflects the fact that the goods and services purchased by foreigners in the United States must be subtracted from the total consumer purchases recorded in the other columns of this table in order to be added to other exports and classified in the category of exports rather than in the consumption spending of U.S. residents.

Data availability and revisions

Data are updated once a year, after the general midyear revision of the NIPAs, and are available on the BEA Web site at <http://www.bea.gov>.

CHAPTER 5: SAVING AND INVESTMENT

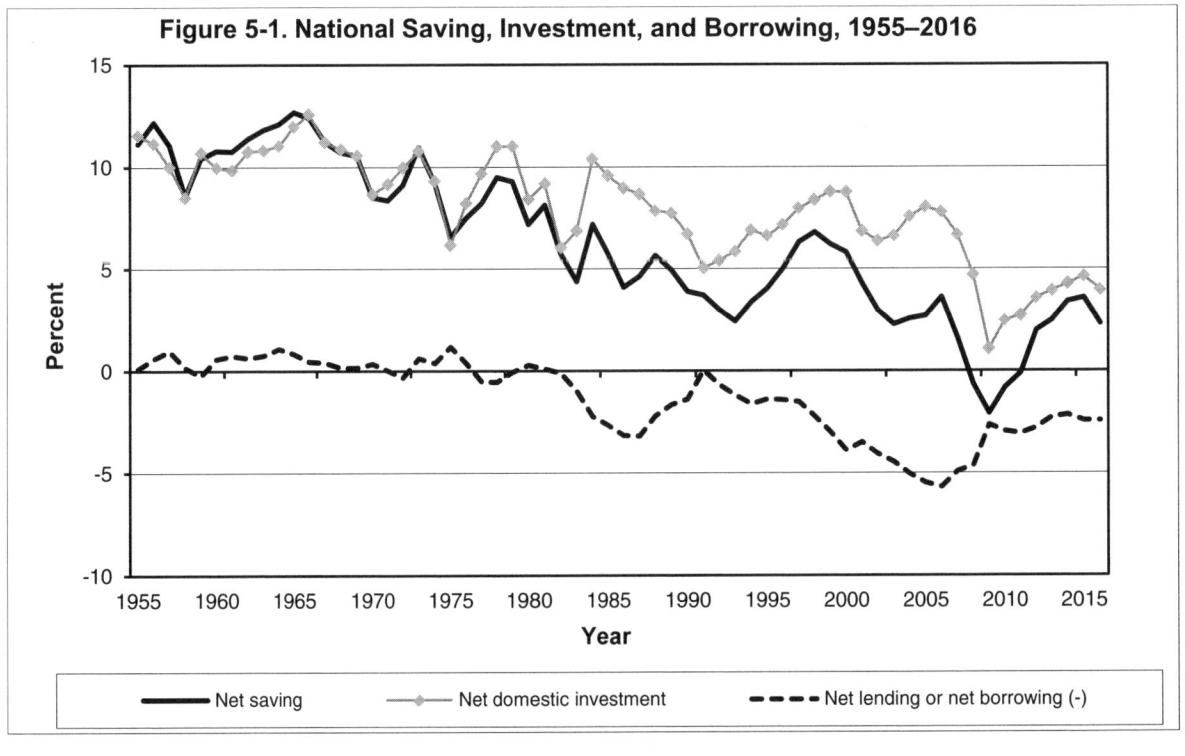

Figure 5-1. National Saving, Investment, and Borrowing, 1955–2016

- Net national saving—the middle line in Figure 5-1—averaged 4.9 percent of gross national income (GNI) in the years 1984 through 2000, which was already lower than the rates seen in the 1950s and 1960s. Net saving is gross saving by U.S. persons, businesses, and governments, <u>less</u> the consumption of fixed capital. Thus, it represents saving available for investment over and above the replacement of the existing capital stock. (Tables 5-1A and B)

- In the years 2001–2007 the net national saving rate as percent of Gross National Income (GNI) fell from 4.3 percent to 1.6 percent. Record net borrowing by the U.S. topped $718 billion in 2007, but it dropped to $384.4 in 2014. (Table 5-1A)

- In the recession that began at the end of 2007, net national saving fell into negative territory, for the first time since the depression years 1931 through 1934. Government deficits soared as the Great Recession cut deeply into tax revenues and called forth both automatic and discretionary anti-recession spending such as unemployment compensation, food stamps (Supplemental Nutrition Assistance Program (SNAP), and temporary assistance for needy families (TANF). But unlike in the Great Depression, net investment remained positive. (Tables 5-1A and B and Table 6-14B)

- By 2015, the national saving rate had recovered to 3.6 percent, as the federal deficit continued to decline. However, the savings rate fell to 2.3 percent in 2016. (Table 5-1A)

Table 5-1A. Saving and Investment: Recent Data

(Billions of dollars, except as noted; quarterly data are at seasonally adjusted annual rates.)   **NIPA Tables 1.7.5, 5.1**

Year and quarter	Gross saving Total	Net saving Total	Net saving Private Total	Private Personal saving	Private Domestic corporate business	Government Federal	Government State and local	Consumption of fixed capital Total	Private Total	Private Domestic business	Private Households and institutions	Government Federal	Government State and local
1955	96.4	47.5	45.9	28.2	17.6	-0.6	2.2	48.9	35.0	28.9	6.1	10.7	3.2
1956	109.6	55.4	51.1	34.7	16.4	1.4	3.0	54.1	38.8	32.2	6.6	11.7	3.6
1957	111.8	52.9	52.9	36.9	16.0	-2.6	2.6	58.9	42.3	35.2	7.1	12.7	3.9
1958	103.8	41.3	52.2	38.9	13.3	-12.0	1.1	62.4	44.9	37.5	7.4	13.4	4.1
1959	120.1	54.7	56.4	37.1	19.2	-3.9	2.2	65.4	46.8	39.0	7.8	14.3	4.4
1960	127.0	59.1	56.4	37.8	18.5	0.2	2.6	67.9	48.2	40.0	8.2	15.1	4.5
1961	131.7	61.1	63.5	44.4	19.2	-4.7	2.2	70.6	49.8	41.3	8.5	16.0	4.8
1962	143.5	69.4	71.3	46.4	24.9	-5.3	3.4	74.1	51.8	42.9	8.8	17.1	5.2
1963	154.2	76.2	74.6	46.7	27.9	-2.1	3.7	78.0	54.2	44.9	9.3	18.3	5.5
1964	166.0	83.6	86.2	54.8	31.4	-6.9	4.3	82.4	57.3	47.4	9.9	19.2	5.9
1965	182.9	94.9	96.3	58.3	38.0	-5.5	4.1	88.0	61.6	50.9	10.7	20.0	6.4
1966	196.4	101.1	102.9	61.4	41.6	-7.0	5.2	95.3	67.2	55.6	11.5	21.0	7.1
1967	200.4	96.9	111.7	72.2	39.5	-19.5	4.7	103.5	73.3	60.9	12.4	22.4	7.8
1968	214.5	101.2	110.7	72.1	38.6	-13.7	4.3	113.3	80.6	67.0	13.6	24.1	8.6
1969	233.1	108.2	109.2	75.0	34.2	-5.1	4.1	124.9	89.4	74.2	15.2	25.8	9.7
1970	228.2	91.4	123.2	96.1	27.2	-34.8	3.0	136.8	98.3	81.8	16.5	27.6	10.9
1971	246.2	97.3	147.5	110.1	37.5	-50.8	0.6	148.9	107.6	89.4	18.2	29.0	12.2
1972	277.7	116.8	157.2	109.2	48.0	-48.9	8.4	160.9	117.5	97.2	20.3	30.1	13.3
1973	335.3	157.2	185.3	131.8	53.5	-37.7	9.6	178.1	131.5	108.2	23.3	31.7	14.9
1974	349.3	143.1	181.4	141.7	39.7	-40.6	2.3	206.2	153.2	126.1	27.0	34.7	18.3
1975	348.2	110.7	213.3	159.0	54.3	-97.0	-5.6	237.5	178.8	147.9	30.9	37.8	21.0
1976	399.5	140.3	217.3	147.3	70.0	-79.9	2.8	259.2	196.5	162.2	34.3	40.6	22.1
1977	459.6	171.3	234.7	148.2	86.6	-71.9	8.4	288.3	221.1	181.5	39.6	43.7	23.5
1978	548.2	223.1	269.5	166.6	102.9	-59.8	13.4	325.1	252.1	205.5	46.6	47.5	25.5
1979	613.8	242.7	279.0	177.5	101.4	-44.5	8.2	371.1	290.7	236.4	54.4	51.8	28.6
1980	630.6	204.6	285.5	213.2	72.3	-86.3	5.4	426.0	335.0	272.8	62.2	57.9	33.1
1981	745.2	260.2	341.9	252.5	89.4	-85.8	4.1	485.0	381.9	313.5	68.5	65.3	37.8
1982	727.9	193.6	363.3	277.7	85.6	-164.6	-5.1	534.3	420.4	347.5	72.9	72.7	41.3
1983	719.5	158.9	362.7	247.0	115.7	-205.0	1.3	560.5	438.8	362.8	76.0	79.0	42.8
1984	884.5	290.2	461.6	312.1	149.5	-192.3	20.9	594.3	463.5	382.7	80.9	86.4	44.4
1985	884.0	247.3	422.7	265.1	157.5	-195.6	20.3	636.7	496.4	410.3	86.2	93.3	46.9
1986	867.8	185.7	377.9	269.4	108.5	-212.7	20.4	682.2	531.6	438.1	93.4	100.3	50.3
1987	952.2	224.2	375.3	252.1	123.2	-163.2	12.1	728.0	566.3	464.5	101.8	107.5	54.1
1988	1 080.1	297.7	438.1	294.8	143.3	-157.3	17.0	782.4	608.3	498.4	109.9	116.3	57.8
1989	1 113.6	277.5	426.7	316.5	110.2	-156.6	7.4	836.1	650.1	531.8	118.2	124.2	61.9
1990	1 117.6	230.7	438.1	335.4	102.7	-200.9	-6.5	886.8	689.0	563.9	125.1	131.1	66.7
1991	1 157.9	226.8	498.1	365.9	132.2	-246.2	-25.1	931.1	722.4	591.8	130.6	137.9	70.9
1992	1 152.6	192.9	563.1	426.0	137.1	-332.7	-37.5	959.7	744.2	607.9	136.3	141.4	74.1
1993	1 167.9	164.3	513.3	367.6	145.6	-311.8	-37.2	1 003.6	780.0	634.2	145.7	145.3	78.3
1994	1 299.1	243.6	524.2	331.4	192.8	-253.7	-27.0	1 055.6	824.3	669.0	155.3	148.3	82.9
1995	1 429.5	306.8	579.2	352.9	226.2	-240.8	-31.5	1 122.8	882.6	717.8	164.8	151.9	88.3
1996	1 581.3	405.3	596.3	345.2	251.1	-178.5	-12.5	1 176.0	931.0	758.4	172.7	152.4	92.6
1997	1 783.6	543.6	633.1	352.2	280.9	-91.2	1.7	1 240.0	990.1	807.9	182.1	153.0	96.9
1998	1 932.4	622.1	604.0	405.3	198.7	2.7	15.4	1 310.3	1 054.9	860.4	194.5	153.6	101.8
1999	2 003.6	602.7	526.8	303.3	223.5	66.6	9.2	1 400.9	1 135.9	925.0	210.9	156.8	108.1
2000	2 119.8	605.5	439.1	307.7	131.4	156.5	9.9	1 514.2	1 236.6	1 006.5	230.1	161.5	116.2
2001	2 068.5	464.5	515.3	335.2	180.2	14.5	-65.3	1 604.0	1 317.7	1 067.5	250.2	163.3	123.0
2002	1 990.6	328.5	719.9	405.3	314.7	-270.5	-120.9	1 662.1	1 368.0	1 101.4	266.6	165.0	129.0
2003	1 991.1	263.9	788.2	409.6	378.6	-402.9	-121.4	1 727.2	1 422.4	1 131.6	290.8	170.3	134.5
2004	2 146.7	315.0	822.6	409.4	413.2	-399.2	-108.4	1 831.7	1 509.3	1 185.9	323.4	178.6	143.8
2005	2 338.6	356.6	727.9	243.1	484.8	-304.7	-66.6	1 982.0	1 635.3	1 273.2	362.1	189.4	157.3
2006	2 648.1	512.1	778.5	331.4	447.1	-227.0	-39.4	2 136.0	1 765.0	1 368.8	396.2	200.7	170.3
2007	2 500.3	236.0	574.4	309.8	264.6	-265.7	-72.7	2 264.4	1 865.0	1 451.2	413.7	212.8	186.6
2008	2 268.4	-95.0	704.1	536.7	167.3	-634.0	-165.1	2 363.4	1 936.9	1 522.3	414.6	226.3	200.2
2009	2 067.9	-300.4	1 220.3	667.4	552.9	-1 248.8	-271.9	2 368.4	1 925.7	1 522.4	403.3	234.5	208.2
2010	2 257.5	-124.1	1 441.9	630.0	811.9	-1 328.7	-237.3	2 381.6	1 923.5	1 523.0	400.5	245.3	212.7
2011	2 434.6	-16.1	1 444.0	710.1	733.9	-1 244.1	-215.9	2 450.6	1 971.1	1 572.8	398.2	257.4	222.2
2012	2 861.2	327.0	1 637.9	946.7	691.2	-1 090.1	-220.8	2 534.2	2 038.0	1 633.4	404.6	264.3	231.9
2013	3 050.5	421.6	1 255.9	620.1	635.8	-643.8	-190.5	2 628.9	2 122.4	1 694.7	427.7	268.0	238.5
2014	3 356.7	608.6	1 387.7	738.8	648.9	-610.2	-168.9	2 748.0	2 231.2	1 775.0	456.1	271.0	245.9
2015	3 507.0	665.5	1 398.5	828.4	570.1	-586.7	-146.4	2 841.5	2 319.6	1 846.9	472.7	271.3	250.6
2016	3 353.2	436.5	1 301.1	680.6	620.6	-697.3	-167.4	2 916.7	2 390.5	1 895.3	495.3	271.3	254.9
2014													
1st quarter	3 150.1	444.0	1 214.2	673.6	540.6	-589.8	-180.4	2 706.1	2 191.8	1 742.8	449.0	270.7	243.6
2nd quarter	3 352.6	620.7	1 385.7	739.5	646.2	-607.0	-158.0	2 731.9	2 216.0	1 764.1	451.9	270.8	245.1
3rd quarter	3 426.3	663.6	1 457.0	757.4	699.6	-626.7	-166.6	2 762.6	2 244.7	1 785.7	458.9	271.1	246.9
4th quarter	3 497.7	706.2	1 494.0	784.8	709.2	-617.1	-170.7	2 791.5	2 272.1	1 807.4	464.7	271.3	248.1
2015													
1st quarter	3 509.4	697.7	1 401.3	809.7	591.7	-554.0	-149.6	2 811.7	2 291.6	1 824.5	467.2	271.5	248.6
2nd quarter	3 539.9	710.2	1 466.5	844.4	622.2	-591.0	-165.4	2 829.6	2 308.2	1 839.2	469.1	271.1	250.3
3rd quarter	3 467.9	613.5	1 424.2	822.0	602.2	-633.5	-177.1	2 854.4	2 331.3	1 856.6	474.7	271.4	251.6
4th quarter	3 510.9	640.4	1 301.9	837.5	464.4	-568.1	-93.4	2 870.5	2 347.2	1 867.3	479.9	271.3	251.9
2016													
1st quarter	3 384.8	503.8	1 372.0	787.8	584.1	-707.5	-160.6	2 880.9	2 358.1	1 875.1	482.9	270.9	252.0
2nd quarter	3 333.9	425.6	1 299.0	745.2	553.9	-688.5	-184.9	2 908.3	2 382.3	1 890.8	491.5	271.4	254.7
3rd quarter	3 401.8	474.1	1 315.4	677.7	637.7	-679.1	-162.2	2 927.6	2 400.7	1 900.9	499.8	271.3	255.6
4th quarter	3 292.2	342.3	1 218.2	511.5	706.6	-714.0	-161.9	2 950.0	2 421.2	1 914.3	506.9	271.6	257.2

Table 5-1A. Saving and Investment: Recent Data—*Continued*

(Billions of dollars, except as noted; quarterly data are at seasonally adjusted annual rates.)   **NIPA Tables 1.7.5, 5.1**

Year and quarter	Gross domestic investment, capital account transactions, and net lending, NIPAs						Statistical discrepancy	Net domestic investment	Gross national income	Gross saving as a percent of gross national income	Net saving as a percent of gross national income
	Total	Gross domestic investment			Capital account transactions, net	Net lending or net borrowing (-), NIPAs					
		Total	Private	Government							
1955	98.5	98.1	73.8	24.4	...	0.4	2.1	49.2	426.5	22.6	11.1
1956	107.5	104.8	77.7	27.1	...	2.7	-2.1	50.7	455.0	24.1	12.2
1957	111.5	106.7	76.5	30.2	...	4.7	-0.4	47.8	478.3	23.4	11.1
1958	104.4	103.6	70.9	32.6	...	0.8	0.6	41.1	484.1	21.4	8.5
1959	120.2	121.5	85.7	35.9	...	-1.3	0.1	56.1	525.1	22.9	10.4
1960	125.6	122.5	86.5	36.0	...	3.2	-1.4	54.6	547.8	23.2	10.8
1961	130.7	126.5	86.6	39.9	...	4.2	-1.0	55.9	567.8	23.2	10.8
1962	143.4	139.6	97.0	42.6	...	3.8	-0.1	65.5	609.3	23.5	11.4
1963	152.7	147.7	103.3	44.4	...	4.9	-1.5	69.7	644.6	23.9	11.8
1964	166.0	158.5	112.2	46.4	...	7.5	0.0	76.2	690.7	24.0	12.1
1965	183.7	177.5	129.6	47.9	...	6.2	0.8	89.5	748.2	24.4	12.7
1966	201.6	197.8	144.2	53.6	...	3.8	5.1	102.5	815.0	24.1	12.4
1967	203.8	200.4	142.7	57.7	...	3.5	3.4	96.8	863.7	23.2	11.2
1968	217.7	216.2	156.9	59.2	...	1.5	3.2	102.8	945.4	22.7	10.7
1969	234.7	233.1	173.6	59.5	0.0	1.6	1.6	108.2	1 024.4	22.8	10.6
1970	233.6	229.8	170.1	59.8	0.0	3.7	5.3	93.1	1 076.9	21.2	8.5
1971	255.6	255.3	196.8	58.5	0.0	0.3	9.5	106.5	1 165.9	21.1	8.3
1972	284.8	288.8	228.1	60.7	0.0	-4.1	7.1	127.9	1 283.9	21.6	9.1
1973	341.4	332.6	266.9	65.6	0.0	8.8	6.1	154.5	1 435.1	23.4	11.0
1974	356.7	350.7	274.5	76.2	0.0	5.9	7.4	144.5	1 556.9	22.4	9.2
1975	361.5	341.7	257.3	84.4	0.1	19.8	13.2	104.1	1 688.7	20.6	6.6
1976	420.0	412.9	323.2	89.6	0.1	7.0	20.5	153.7	1 874.0	21.3	7.5
1977	478.9	489.8	396.6	93.2	0.1	-11.0	19.3	201.4	2 087.0	22.0	8.2
1978	571.3	583.9	478.4	105.6	0.1	-12.7	23.2	258.9	2 355.0	23.3	9.5
1979	658.6	659.8	539.7	120.1	0.1	-1.3	44.8	288.6	2 619.3	23.4	9.3
1980	674.6	666.1	530.1	136.0	0.1	8.4	43.9	240.0	2 852.8	22.1	7.2
1981	782.0	778.6	631.2	147.3	0.1	3.3	36.7	293.5	3 207.2	23.2	8.1
1982	734.7	738.0	581.0	156.9	0.1	-3.4	6.8	203.7	3 374.7	21.6	5.7
1983	773.6	808.7	637.5	171.2	0.1	-35.2	54.2	248.1	3 621.1	19.9	4.4
1984	923.2	1 013.3	820.1	193.2	0.1	-90.2	38.7	418.9	4 038.3	21.9	7.2
1985	935.2	1 049.5	829.6	219.9	0.1	-114.4	51.3	412.9	4 320.8	20.5	5.7
1986	944.6	1 087.2	849.1	238.1	0.1	-142.8	76.7	405.1	4 530.4	19.2	4.1
1987	992.7	1 146.8	892.2	254.6	0.1	-154.2	40.6	418.9	4 847.2	19.6	4.6
1988	1 079.6	1 195.6	937.0	258.4	0.1	-115.9	-0.5	413.0	5 275.8	20.5	5.6
1989	1 177.8	1 270.1	999.7	270.4	0.3	-92.7	64.2	434.0	5 618.3	19.8	4.9
1990	1 208.9	1 283.8	993.5	290.4	7.4	-82.3	91.4	397.0	5 922.9	18.9	3.9
1991	1 246.3	1 238.4	944.3	294.1	5.3	2.6	88.4	307.3	6 117.3	18.9	3.7
1992	1 263.6	1 309.1	1 013.0	296.1	-1.3	-44.3	110.9	349.4	6 459.5	17.8	3.0
1993	1 320.2	1 398.7	1 106.8	291.9	0.9	-79.4	152.3	395.1	6 758.4	17.3	2.4
1994	1 436.0	1 550.7	1 256.5	294.2	1.3	-116.0	136.8	495.1	7 195.8	18.1	3.4
1995	1 520.1	1 625.2	1 317.5	307.7	0.4	-105.5	90.6	502.4	7 602.3	18.8	4.0
1996	1 637.9	1 752.0	1 432.1	320.0	0.2	-114.3	56.6	576.0	8 075.4	19.6	5.0
1997	1 795.8	1 925.1	1 595.6	329.5	0.5	-129.8	12.3	685.2	8 620.3	20.7	6.3
1998	1 872.2	2 076.7	1 735.3	341.4	0.2	-204.7	-60.1	766.5	9 167.6	21.1	6.8
1999	1 966.1	2 252.7	1 884.2	368.5	4.5	-291.1	-37.5	851.8	9 725.3	20.6	6.2
2000	2 020.3	2 424.0	2 033.8	390.3	0.3	-404.1	-99.5	909.8	10 421.3	20.3	5.8
2001	1 953.5	2 342.3	1 928.6	413.6	-12.9	-375.8	-115.0	738.3	10 788.6	19.2	4.3
2002	1 917.8	2 368.6	1 925.0	443.6	0.5	-451.3	-72.8	706.5	11 098.9	17.9	3.0
2003	1 977.5	2 493.2	2 027.9	465.3	2.1	-517.8	-13.6	766.0	11 591.4	17.2	2.3
2004	2 138.1	2 765.1	2 276.7	488.5	-2.8	-624.2	-8.6	933.4	12 372.6	17.4	2.5
2005	2 303.1	3 040.8	2 527.1	513.6	-12.9	-724.8	-35.5	1 058.8	13 221.8	17.7	2.7
2006	2 430.8	3 233.0	2 680.6	552.3	2.1	-804.2	-217.3	1 097.0	14 140.8	18.7	3.6
2007	2 517.8	3 236.0	2 643.7	592.2	-0.1	-718.0	17.5	971.6	14 585.7	17.1	1.6
2008	2 367.8	3 059.4	2 424.8	634.6	-5.4	-686.2	99.4	696.1	14 791.2	15.3	-0.6
2009	2 143.2	2 525.1	1 878.1	647.0	0.6	-382.5	75.3	156.8	14 494.5	14.3	-2.1
2010	2 306.7	2 752.6	2 100.8	651.8	0.7	-446.6	49.2	371.0	15 121.1	14.9	-0.8
2011	2 396.2	2 877.8	2 239.9	637.9	1.6	-483.2	-38.3	427.1	15 802.9	15.4	-0.1
2012	2 658.0	3 126.1	2 511.7	614.4	-6.5	-461.7	-203.3	591.9	16 596.1	17.2	2.0
2013	2 912.5	3 298.6	2 706.3	592.3	0.8	-386.9	-137.9	669.7	17 073.7	17.9	2.5
2014	3 126.7	3 510.8	2 916.4	594.4	0.4	-384.4	-229.9	762.7	17 892.1	18.8	3.4
2015	3 251.1	3 701.7	3 093.6	608.1	0.4	-451.0	-255.9	860.2	18 581.1	18.9	3.6
2016	3 206.0	3 666.9	3 057.2	609.7	0.4	-461.4	-147.2	750.2	18 968.7	17.7	2.3
2014											
1st quarter	2 982.3	3 363.9	2 780.7	583.2	0.5	-382.1	-167.7	657.8	17 440.3	18.1	2.5
2nd quarter	3 134.9	3 489.8	2 895.0	594.8	0.4	-355.3	-217.6	757.9	17 768.9	18.9	3.5
3rd quarter	3 220.6	3 589.0	2 992.0	597.0	0.4	-368.8	-205.7	826.4	18 073.4	19.0	3.7
4th quarter	3 169.0	3 600.2	2 997.9	602.4	0.3	-431.5	-328.7	808.7	18 285.7	19.1	3.9
2015											
1st quarter	3 236.5	3 690.6	3 094.6	596.0	0.4	-454.5	-273.0	878.9	18 364.6	19.1	3.8
2nd quarter	3 276.4	3 709.7	3 096.3	613.4	0.4	-433.8	-263.5	880.1	18 549.4	19.1	3.8
3rd quarter	3 248.3	3 731.1	3 115.7	615.5	0.4	-483.1	-219.6	876.8	18 638.9	18.6	3.3
4th quarter	3 243.2	3 675.4	3 067.7	607.6	0.4	-432.5	-267.6	804.9	18 771.7	18.7	3.4
2016											
1st quarter	3 158.6	3 650.1	3 031.6	618.5	0.6	-492.1	-226.1	769.2	18 727.4	18.1	2.7
2nd quarter	3 201.0	3 632.8	3 023.1	609.7	0.4	-432.1	-132.9	724.4	18 865.9	17.7	2.3
3rd quarter	3 206.5	3 649.9	3 048.0	602.0	0.4	-443.8	-195.2	722.3	19 112.7	17.8	2.5
4th quarter	3 257.8	3 734.9	3 126.2	608.7	0.4	-477.4	-34.4	784.9	19 168.9	17.2	1.8

. . . = Not available.

Table 5-1B. Saving and Investment: Historical Data

(Billions of dollars, except as noted; quarterly data are at seasonally adjusted annual rates.)   **NIPA Tables 1.7.5, 5.1**

Year and quarter	Gross saving									Gross domestic investment and net lending, NIPAs				Net domestic invest-ment	Gross national income	Net saving as a percent-age of gross national income
	Total	Net saving			Consumption of fixed capital				Gross domestic investment			Net lending or net borrow-ing (-), NIPAs			
		Private	Government		Total	Private	Government		Total	Private	Govern-ment				
			Federal	State and local			Federal	State and local							
1929	20.1	7.6	0.8	1.3	10.4	9.4	0.2	0.8	20.1	17.2	2.9	0.8	9.7	104.6	9.3
1930	15.8	4.5	0.0	1.1	10.2	9.2	0.2	0.8	14.7	11.4	3.3	0.7	4.5	93.3	6.0
1931	9.1	1.2	-2.3	0.8	9.5	8.6	0.2	0.7	9.6	6.5	3.1	0.2	0.1	77.2	-0.5
1932	4.0	-3.2	-1.6	0.5	8.3	7.5	0.2	0.7	4.1	1.8	2.3	0.2	-4.2	59.6	-7.3
1933	3.9	-3.1	-1.2	0.2	8.0	7.0	0.2	0.7	4.3	2.3	2.0	0.2	-3.7	57.0	-7.1
1934	7.0	0.1	-2.6	1.1	8.4	7.3	0.3	0.9	7.0	4.3	2.7	0.4	-1.4	66.7	-2.1
1935	10.4	3.2	-2.3	1.0	8.5	7.3	0.3	0.8	10.2	7.4	2.9	-0.1	1.8	74.8	2.6
1936	12.3	5.1	-3.6	2.1	8.8	7.5	0.3	0.9	13.6	9.4	4.2	-0.1	4.8	83.9	4.2
1937	17.1	5.8	-0.2	1.8	9.7	8.4	0.4	1.0	16.9	13.0	3.9	0.2	7.1	93.4	7.9
1938	12.7	2.8	-1.8	1.7	10.0	8.6	0.4	1.0	12.2	7.9	4.3	1.2	2.2	87.1	3.1
1939	14.6	5.3	-2.5	1.7	10.1	8.6	0.4	1.1	14.8	10.2	4.6	1.0	4.7	92.6	4.8
1940	19.5	8.3	-1.0	1.6	10.6	9.0	0.5	1.1	19.0	14.6	4.4	1.5	8.4	102.2	8.7
1941	31.1	16.9	0.6	1.6	12.1	10.0	0.9	1.2	30.2	19.4	10.8	1.3	18.1	129.5	14.7
1942	41.6	37.0	-11.4	1.1	14.9	11.2	2.2	1.4	40.7	11.8	29.0	-0.1	25.9	167.3	16.0
1943	47.0	45.0	-17.1	1.1	18.0	11.5	5.0	1.5	47.3	7.4	39.9	-2.1	29.3	205.3	14.1
1944	42.8	49.8	-29.5	1.1	21.4	12.0	7.9	1.5	47.3	9.2	38.1	-2.0	25.9	222.4	9.7
1945	32.6	40.3	-32.1	1.1	23.2	12.5	9.3	1.4	37.7	12.4	25.3	-1.3	14.5	224.6	4.2
1946	41.5	23.1	-8.2	0.8	25.8	14.2	10.0	1.6	37.8	33.1	4.7	4.9	12.1	227.2	6.9
1947	49.3	17.6	2.4	0.1	29.2	17.7	9.6	1.9	42.8	37.1	5.7	9.3	13.6	248.2	8.1
1948	61.5	29.2	0.9	0.1	31.4	20.8	8.4	2.1	58.8	50.3	8.5	2.4	27.4	276.5	10.9
1949	49.6	25.3	-8.5	0.5	32.3	22.6	7.6	2.2	50.4	39.1	11.3	0.9	18.1	272.4	6.3
1950	64.9	29.3	1.8	0.3	33.4	24.3	6.9	2.2	68.0	56.5	11.5	-1.8	34.6	300.4	10.5
1951	79.8	36.0	4.5	1.5	37.8	27.7	7.4	2.6	82.3	62.8	19.6	0.9	44.6	345.8	12.2
1952	79.9	39.5	-2.1	1.9	40.6	29.5	8.3	2.8	81.9	57.3	24.6	0.6	41.3	367.1	10.7
1953	82.0	40.4	-4.2	2.3	43.5	31.3	9.2	2.9	87.1	60.4	26.7	-1.3	43.6	387.9	9.9
1954	80.8	40.7	-8.0	2.0	46.0	33.0	10.1	3.0	83.5	58.1	25.4	0.2	37.5	390.4	8.9
1947															
1st quarter	47.5	16.8	2.8	0.1	27.7	16.3	9.7	1.8	40.8	35.9	5.0	9.4	13.1	241.3	8.2
2nd quarter	46.8	15.7	2.1	0.2	28.8	17.3	9.6	1.8	39.6	34.5	5.1	9.9	10.9	244.6	7.4
3rd quarter	48.9	19.8	-0.7	0.0	29.8	18.2	9.7	1.9	41.0	34.9	6.1	10.1	11.2	249.1	7.7
4th quarter	53.8	18.1	5.3	-0.1	30.5	19.1	9.4	2.0	49.8	43.2	6.6	7.8	19.3	257.7	9.0
1948															
1st quarter	59.0	23.6	5.0	-0.3	30.8	19.9	8.9	2.0	54.7	47.2	7.5	6.5	24.0	266.9	10.6
2nd quarter	62.7	29.0	2.5	0.1	31.2	20.6	8.5	2.1	58.6	50.3	8.3	4.5	27.4	275.5	11.5
3rd quarter	62.0	31.4	-1.1	0.0	31.7	21.2	8.3	2.2	61.3	52.5	8.8	4.3	29.6	280.8	10.8
4th quarter	62.4	32.7	-2.7	0.4	32.0	21.7	8.1	2.2	60.7	51.3	9.4	3.9	28.7	283.0	10.7
1949															
1st quarter	54.7	27.9	-6.0	0.6	32.3	22.1	8.0	2.2	53.4	43.1	10.2	5.9	21.1	275.9	8.1
2nd quarter	48.6	25.0	-9.2	0.4	32.3	22.4	7.7	2.2	47.5	36.2	11.3	5.8	15.2	272.4	6.0
3rd quarter	50.1	26.6	-9.5	0.6	32.3	22.8	7.4	2.2	51.5	39.5	11.9	4.7	19.1	272.5	6.5
4th quarter	44.8	21.6	-9.5	0.3	32.4	23.1	7.2	2.2	49.2	37.5	11.8	2.5	16.8	268.7	4.6
1950															
1st quarter	53.2	32.3	-11.6	0.0	32.5	23.4	7.0	2.1	57.4	46.7	10.7	1.7	25.0	279.1	7.4
2nd quarter	61.7	29.8	-0.6	-0.3	32.8	23.9	6.8	2.1	63.4	52.3	11.1	1.2	30.6	291.6	9.9
3rd quarter	67.1	23.1	9.6	0.8	33.6	24.6	6.8	2.2	70.4	58.6	11.7	-1.2	36.8	309.5	10.8
4th quarter	77.6	32.0	10.0	0.8	34.9	25.5	7.0	2.3	80.8	68.4	12.3	-0.6	45.9	321.3	13.3
1951															
1st quarter	74.3	23.7	12.7	1.7	36.3	26.6	7.2	2.5	79.5	64.6	14.9	-0.2	43.2	334.5	11.4
2nd quarter	82.5	38.6	5.0	1.5	37.4	27.5	7.3	2.6	85.6	67.4	18.2	1.6	48.2	342.9	13.2
3rd quarter	80.8	41.7	-0.6	1.3	38.3	28.2	7.4	2.7	83.1	62.0	21.1	3.4	44.8	349.2	12.2
4th quarter	81.6	40.1	0.7	1.6	39.1	28.7	7.7	2.7	81.2	57.1	24.1	3.8	42.1	356.4	11.9
1952															
1st quarter	82.0	39.5	1.2	1.8	39.6	29.0	7.9	2.7	82.2	58.1	24.1	3.3	42.7	358.5	11.8
2nd quarter	76.0	37.0	-2.4	1.3	40.2	29.3	8.1	2.8	77.3	53.0	24.3	1.6	37.1	361.1	9.9
3rd quarter	79.3	41.0	-4.8	2.1	41.0	29.7	8.4	2.9	82.1	57.2	24.8	-0.4	41.1	368.4	10.4
4th quarter	82.3	40.8	-2.5	2.3	41.7	30.2	8.7	2.8	86.0	60.7	25.3	-1.4	44.3	380.6	10.7
1953															
1st quarter	84.0	41.3	-1.5	1.7	42.5	30.7	8.9	2.9	88.2	61.7	26.5	-1.1	45.7	387.5	10.7
2nd quarter	84.2	41.5	-3.3	2.8	43.2	31.1	9.2	2.9	89.3	62.1	27.1	-1.7	46.0	391.1	10.5
3rd quarter	83.7	40.2	-2.6	2.3	43.8	31.6	9.3	2.9	88.4	61.4	27.0	-1.0	44.6	390.0	10.2
4th quarter	76.0	38.5	-9.3	2.4	44.4	32.0	9.5	2.9	82.4	56.4	25.9	-0.8	38.0	382.9	8.3
1954															
1st quarter	78.9	41.3	-9.8	2.4	45.0	32.4	9.8	2.8	82.1	55.7	26.4	-0.7	37.2	385.2	8.8
2nd quarter	79.3	39.8	-8.4	2.1	45.7	32.8	10.0	3.0	81.4	55.4	25.9	-0.2	35.7	386.2	8.7
3rd quarter	80.2	39.7	-7.6	1.8	46.3	33.2	10.2	3.0	83.7	59.0	24.7	-0.1	37.4	390.2	8.7
4th quarter	84.7	42.1	-6.3	1.9	47.0	33.5	10.4	3.0	86.6	62.1	24.5	0.7	39.7	399.8	9.4
1955															
1st quarter	89.9	43.7	-2.9	1.7	47.5	33.9	10.5	3.0	92.9	68.7	24.1	0.7	45.4	412.8	10.3
2nd quarter	95.4	45.8	-0.6	2.0	48.2	34.5	10.6	3.1	97.4	72.7	24.8	-0.6	49.2	422.9	11.2
3rd quarter	97.9	46.8	-0.7	2.5	49.3	35.3	10.8	3.2	99.0	74.7	24.3	0.3	49.7	431.4	11.2
4th quarter	102.3	47.2	1.9	2.6	50.6	36.2	11.0	3.3	103.2	78.9	24.3	-0.2	52.6	439.0	11.8
1956															
1st quarter	105.7	48.3	2.3	2.9	52.1	37.3	11.4	3.5	103.9	78.3	25.6	-0.1	51.7	444.2	12.1
2nd quarter	107.6	50.3	0.7	3.1	53.5	38.4	11.6	3.6	103.6	77.0	26.6	1.4	50.1	451.4	12.0
3rd quarter	111.6	52.6	1.2	3.1	54.8	39.3	11.8	3.7	106.0	78.3	27.7	2.1	51.2	457.5	12.4
4th quarter	113.4	53.1	1.4	2.9	56.0	40.2	12.0	3.8	105.8	77.1	28.6	4.0	49.8	466.9	12.3

Table 5-1B. Saving and Investment: Historical Data—*Continued*

(Billions of dollars, except as noted; quarterly data are at seasonally adjusted annual rates.)   **NIPA Tables 1.7.5, 5.1**

Year and quarter	Gross saving								Gross domestic investment and net lending, NIPAs				Net domestic invest-ment	Gross national income	Net saving as a percent-age of gross national income
	Total	Net saving			Consumption of fixed capital				Gross domestic investment			Net lending or net borrow-ing (-), NIPAs			
		Private	Government		Total	Private	Government		Total	Private	Govern-ment				
			Federal	State and local			Federal	State and local							
1957															
1st quarter	114.3	53.2	0.4	3.4	57.3	41.1	12.4	3.8	107.5	77.7	29.8	4.3	50.2	474.9	12.0
2nd quarter	114.3	54.6	-1.5	2.8	58.4	41.9	12.6	3.9	107.6	77.9	29.7	3.6	49.2	478.1	11.7
3rd quarter	114.2	53.8	-1.6	2.5	59.5	42.7	12.8	4.0	109.9	79.3	30.6	3.5	50.4	482.9	11.3
4th quarter	104.6	49.9	-7.7	1.9	60.4	43.4	13.1	4.0	101.9	71.0	30.8	2.9	41.4	477.3	9.2
1958															
1st quarter	100.7	48.8	-10.2	1.0	61.1	44.0	13.1	4.0	98.0	66.7	31.3	0.6	36.9	472.2	8.4
2nd quarter	97.3	49.5	-15.0	0.8	62.0	44.7	13.2	4.1	97.0	65.1	32.0	0.0	35.1	475.0	7.4
3rd quarter	104.9	53.6	-12.5	0.9	62.9	45.2	13.5	4.2	104.9	72.0	32.9	0.5	42.0	488.2	8.6
4th quarter	112.1	56.9	-10.6	1.9	63.8	45.7	13.8	4.2	114.3	80.0	34.3	-0.7	50.6	500.9	9.6
1959															
1st quarter	117.8	56.5	-4.5	1.4	64.5	46.2	14.0	4.3	119.4	83.2	36.2	-4.1	54.9	513.6	10.4
2nd quarter	124.9	59.6	-1.8	2.0	65.1	46.6	14.2	4.3	125.5	89.4	36.1	-4.7	60.4	528.3	11.3
3rd quarter	117.3	53.2	-4.2	2.6	65.8	47.0	14.4	4.4	119.7	83.6	36.1	-3.4	54.0	526.2	9.8
4th quarter	120.4	56.1	-4.9	2.8	66.4	47.4	14.6	4.4	121.5	86.5	34.9	-3.9	55.1	532.1	10.1
1960															
1st quarter	133.1	58.7	4.7	2.7	67.0	47.7	14.8	4.5	131.6	96.5	35.1	-1.2	64.6	546.0	12.1
2nd quarter	126.4	55.0	1.3	2.5	67.6	48.0	15.0	4.5	122.3	87.1	35.2	-0.5	54.7	547.3	10.8
3rd quarter	127.1	56.7	-0.4	2.5	68.2	48.4	15.2	4.6	123.2	86.4	36.8	0.5	55.0	549.4	10.7
4th quarter	121.5	55.0	-4.9	2.5	68.8	48.7	15.5	4.6	112.8	76.0	36.9	1.4	44.0	548.3	9.6
1961															
1st quarter	124.7	57.8	-4.7	2.1	69.5	49.1	15.7	4.7	118.0	78.4	39.6	1.8	48.5	550.9	10.0
2nd quarter	127.1	61.4	-6.4	1.9	70.2	49.5	15.9	4.8	122.6	84.1	38.5	0.6	52.4	561.3	10.1
3rd quarter	134.6	66.1	-4.9	2.4	70.9	50.0	16.1	4.8	130.8	90.9	39.9	0.3	59.8	571.8	11.1
4th quarter	140.3	68.8	-2.9	2.6	71.8	50.5	16.4	4.9	134.5	92.9	41.6	0.1	62.8	587.2	11.7
1962															
1st quarter	141.6	71.3	-5.4	3.0	72.7	51.0	16.7	5.0	140.0	98.1	42.0	-0.6	67.3	597.3	11.5
2nd quarter	142.1	71.0	-5.6	3.2	73.5	51.5	16.9	5.1	138.6	96.7	41.9	0.8	65.0	605.3	11.3
3rd quarter	144.5	71.0	-4.9	3.8	74.6	52.1	17.3	5.2	141.3	98.2	43.1	0.1	66.7	612.7	11.4
4th quarter	145.6	71.8	-5.5	3.7	75.6	52.6	17.7	5.3	138.4	95.0	43.5	-1.5	62.8	621.8	11.3
1963															
1st quarter	149.2	72.7	-3.4	3.4	76.5	53.2	17.9	5.4	142.9	99.7	43.3	-0.6	66.4	629.5	11.5
2nd quarter	153.9	73.9	-1.1	3.6	77.5	53.8	18.2	5.5	145.2	101.6	43.6	1.0	67.7	639.6	11.9
3rd quarter	154.7	73.8	-1.6	4.0	78.5	54.5	18.4	5.6	150.4	104.6	45.8	0.2	72.0	649.0	11.7
4th quarter	159.0	78.0	-2.3	3.8	79.5	55.2	18.7	5.7	152.3	107.2	45.1	1.3	72.8	660.2	12.0
1964															
1st quarter	161.9	82.4	-5.5	4.5	80.6	55.9	18.9	5.8	156.2	110.5	45.8	3.2	75.6	673.6	12.1
2nd quarter	163.0	87.2	-10.2	4.3	81.8	56.8	19.1	5.9	157.0	110.5	46.5	1.9	75.3	684.9	11.9
3rd quarter	166.4	85.7	-6.7	4.4	83.0	57.7	19.3	6.0	159.2	112.6	46.6	2.5	76.2	697.5	12.0
4th quarter	172.8	89.5	-5.1	4.1	84.2	58.7	19.5	6.1	161.7	115.0	46.7	2.6	77.5	706.9	12.5
1965															
1st quarter	180.7	92.2	-0.9	3.9	85.6	59.7	19.6	6.2	172.7	126.5	46.2	0.3	87.2	726.9	13.1
2nd quarter	182.7	93.5	-2.0	4.1	87.1	60.9	19.8	6.4	173.9	127.0	46.9	1.4	86.8	739.7	12.9
3rd quarter	183.2	99.8	-9.4	4.1	88.8	62.1	20.1	6.5	180.1	131.2	48.9	0.7	91.3	752.6	12.6
4th quarter	184.9	99.8	-9.6	4.2	90.5	63.5	20.3	6.7	183.2	133.8	49.5	1.1	92.8	773.7	12.2
1966															
1st quarter	194.3	100.9	-4.1	5.2	92.3	65.0	20.5	6.8	196.1	144.2	51.9	-0.3	103.8	795.8	12.8
2nd quarter	194.8	100.7	-5.6	5.4	94.3	66.4	20.9	7.0	195.4	143.5	51.9	-1.1	101.1	807.7	12.4
3rd quarter	195.3	101.5	-7.8	5.4	96.3	67.9	21.2	7.2	197.4	143.2	54.2	-2.2	101.1	821.0	12.1
4th quarter	201.3	108.6	-10.3	4.8	98.3	69.4	21.5	7.4	202.1	145.9	56.2	-1.3	103.8	835.5	12.3
1967															
1st quarter	197.6	111.3	-19.3	5.2	100.2	70.9	21.8	7.5	200.7	142.8	57.9	-0.8	100.5	843.8	11.5
2nd quarter	194.0	107.4	-20.5	4.7	102.3	72.5	22.2	7.7	194.0	137.5	56.6	-1.5	91.7	852.5	10.7
3rd quarter	201.8	111.8	-18.8	4.2	104.6	74.1	22.6	7.9	200.8	142.8	57.9	-2.5	96.2	870.2	11.2
4th quarter	208.4	116.1	-19.4	4.8	106.9	75.8	23.1	8.1	205.9	147.7	58.3	-2.8	99.0	888.4	11.4
1968															
1st quarter	207.2	110.5	-16.9	4.3	109.4	77.6	23.5	8.3	210.6	152.3	58.4	-4.2	101.2	911.9	10.7
2nd quarter	214.0	115.6	-18.6	5.1	111.9	79.5	23.9	8.5	218.5	158.9	59.5	-3.8	106.5	935.6	10.9
3rd quarter	215.4	106.9	-10.1	4.0	114.5	81.6	24.3	8.6	215.2	155.7	59.5	-4.8	100.7	957.3	10.5
4th quarter	221.4	109.6	-9.3	3.6	117.4	83.7	24.7	8.9	220.3	160.8	59.5	-5.5	102.9	976.7	10.6
1969															
1st quarter	229.9	103.6	2.2	3.7	120.5	86.1	25.2	9.2	233.9	172.4	61.5	-4.7	113.4	996.2	11.0
2nd quarter	231.1	105.3	-1.5	3.9	123.5	88.3	25.6	9.5	232.4	172.7	59.7	-5.5	109.0	1 015.6	10.6
3rd quarter	238.1	115.9	-8.6	4.6	126.3	90.6	26.0	9.8	237.5	177.6	59.9	-4.5	111.2	1 037.1	10.8
4th quarter	233.2	112.2	-12.5	4.3	129.2	92.8	26.4	10.1	228.6	171.6	57.0	-3.3	99.4	1 048.6	9.9
1970															
1st quarter	227.2	113.0	-22.2	4.3	132.2	94.9	26.9	10.4	227.1	168.1	59.0	-2.5	94.9	1 056.1	9.0
2nd quarter	229.8	123.5	-32.6	3.7	135.2	97.1	27.4	10.8	230.3	171.5	58.8	-1.4	95.1	1 071.0	8.8
3rd quarter	231.1	129.4	-39.5	3.0	138.3	99.4	27.8	11.1	234.1	173.9	60.2	-3.1	95.8	1 088.6	8.5
4th quarter	224.7	127.1	-44.7	0.9	141.4	101.7	28.2	11.5	227.8	166.8	61.1	-3.7	86.4	1 092.0	7.6
1971															
1st quarter	238.6	139.6	-45.5	0.0	144.6	104.1	28.6	11.8	247.5	189.5	58.0	-3.1	103.0	1 132.0	8.3
2nd quarter	243.2	147.6	-52.4	0.5	147.5	106.5	28.9	12.1	255.7	197.3	58.3	-7.9	108.1	1 154.8	8.3
3rd quarter	249.1	150.3	-51.7	0.2	150.3	108.8	29.1	12.3	261.2	202.1	59.2	-7.6	110.9	1 175.8	8.4
4th quarter	253.7	152.7	-53.7	1.7	153.1	111.1	29.3	12.7	256.9	198.4	58.5	-10.6	103.8	1 201.0	8.4

Table 5-1B. Saving and Investment: Historical Data—*Continued*

(Billions of dollars, except as noted; quarterly data are at seasonally adjusted annual rates.)   NIPA Tables 1.7.5, 5.1

Year and quarter	Gross saving Total	Net saving Private	Net saving Government Federal	Net saving Government State and local	Consumption of fixed capital Total	Consumption of fixed capital Private	Consumption of fixed capital Government Federal	Consumption of fixed capital Government State and local	Gross domestic investment Total	Gross domestic investment Private	Gross domestic investment Government	Net lending or net borrowing (-), NIPAs	Net domestic investment	Gross national income	Net saving as a percentage of gross national income
1972															
1st quarter	263.3	150.5	-45.7	2.4	156.1	113.4	29.8	12.9	273.0	213.0	60.0	-13.2	116.9	1 237.4	8.7
2nd quarter	265.5	146.6	-51.4	11.2	159.0	116.0	29.9	13.1	287.8	226.8	61.0	-12.9	128.7	1 260.7	8.4
3rd quarter	279.7	155.4	-40.7	2.6	162.4	118.8	30.2	13.4	292.2	233.1	59.1	-12.6	129.8	1 293.8	9.1
4th quarter	302.2	176.4	-57.8	17.5	166.0	121.8	30.4	13.8	302.3	239.7	62.6	-11.8	136.3	1 343.7	10.1
1973															
1st quarter	316.3	173.6	-40.0	12.4	170.2	125.2	30.9	14.2	320.5	254.3	66.2	-8.5	150.3	1 384.9	10.5
2nd quarter	324.5	180.4	-40.8	9.7	175.1	129.0	31.4	14.6	333.8	268.2	65.6	-6.3	158.7	1 414.5	10.6
3rd quarter	338.9	186.4	-36.6	8.7	180.4	133.4	32.0	15.0	328.9	264.3	64.6	-1.4	148.5	1 448.3	10.9
4th quarter	361.7	200.8	-33.4	7.7	186.6	138.3	32.6	15.6	347.1	280.9	66.2	1.0	160.5	1 492.6	11.7
1974															
1st quarter	355.9	192.2	-35.3	5.4	193.6	143.8	33.3	16.5	339.3	268.4	71.0	-0.6	145.7	1 511.8	10.7
2nd quarter	346.1	178.5	-37.9	3.8	201.6	149.7	34.1	17.8	353.5	277.4	76.1	-13.8	151.9	1 540.5	9.4
3rd quarter	346.1	169.1	-36.2	2.8	210.3	156.1	35.2	19.1	349.1	271.0	78.1	-15.0	138.8	1 575.3	8.6
4th quarter	349.0	185.9	-53.3	-2.7	219.1	163.0	36.1	20.0	360.8	281.3	79.5	-9.0	141.7	1 600.2	8.1
1975															
1st quarter	330.0	185.0	-75.1	-7.5	227.7	170.3	36.8	20.6	327.4	244.3	83.1	6.4	99.7	1 615.7	6.3
2nd quarter	329.6	233.0	-132.4	-5.9	235.0	176.6	37.5	20.8	322.5	243.3	79.2	9.7	87.5	1 653.8	5.7
3rd quarter	360.3	213.5	-89.7	-4.6	241.1	182.0	38.1	21.1	350.6	265.2	85.4	5.3	109.5	1 718.1	6.9
4th quarter	373.1	221.6	-90.7	-4.3	246.4	186.3	38.8	21.4	366.1	276.2	89.9	5.6	119.7	1 767.3	7.2
1976															
1st quarter	392.5	222.7	-80.8	-0.1	250.8	189.6	39.5	21.7	397.6	304.6	92.9	-2.7	146.8	1 822.1	7.8
2nd quarter	399.4	218.0	-76.2	1.8	255.8	193.7	40.1	22.0	411.3	322.3	89.0	-7.7	155.5	1 852.7	7.8
3rd quarter	402.5	217.9	-79.5	2.3	261.7	198.6	41.0	22.2	417.0	328.3	88.7	-14.8	155.3	1 890.7	7.4
4th quarter	403.5	210.8	-83.0	7.2	268.5	204.2	41.9	22.4	425.6	337.6	87.9	-14.1	157.0	1 930.4	7.0
1977															
1st quarter	412.2	202.9	-72.2	5.3	276.2	210.7	42.6	22.9	451.8	360.3	91.5	-28.8	175.6	1 981.7	6.9
2nd quarter	454.2	229.3	-66.3	7.2	284.1	217.5	43.4	23.3	483.9	389.7	94.2	-29.7	199.8	2 060.1	8.3
3rd quarter	481.6	251.7	-73.1	10.8	292.2	224.5	44.0	23.7	507.8	414.1	93.6	-28.8	215.6	2 125.0	8.9
4th quarter	490.3	255.0	-76.0	10.4	300.9	231.8	45.0	24.1	515.6	422.3	93.3	-37.8	214.7	2 181.2	8.7
1978															
1st quarter	502.9	259.2	-78.2	11.9	309.9	239.4	46.0	24.6	528.4	434.8	93.6	-47.2	218.5	2 230.3	8.7
2nd quarter	541.4	262.5	-58.9	18.1	319.7	247.5	47.0	25.2	575.6	470.6	105.0	-31.7	255.9	2 334.0	9.5
3rd quarter	561.2	273.7	-53.1	10.7	330.0	256.2	48.0	25.8	602.1	492.4	109.7	-32.4	272.1	2 390.3	9.7
4th quarter	587.1	282.5	-49.2	13.1	340.7	265.4	48.8	26.4	629.7	515.8	113.9	-25.9	289.0	2 465.4	10.0
1979															
1st quarter	609.9	288.7	-39.6	8.7	352.2	275.2	49.8	27.2	635.6	525.8	109.8	-27.6	283.4	2 533.3	10.2
2nd quarter	612.3	279.2	-39.2	7.8	364.5	285.3	51.0	28.1	656.3	539.3	117.0	-32.3	291.8	2 584.0	9.6
3rd quarter	615.0	273.2	-44.8	9.3	377.3	295.8	52.4	29.1	671.0	545.6	125.4	-33.8	293.6	2 648.1	9.0
4th quarter	618.0	274.8	-54.4	7.1	390.5	306.6	53.8	30.2	676.1	547.9	128.2	-39.2	285.6	2 711.7	8.4
1980															
1st quarter	615.9	268.4	-63.5	6.9	404.2	317.7	55.3	31.3	690.3	554.6	135.8	-48.8	286.1	2 770.8	7.6
2nd quarter	604.6	271.6	-87.4	2.0	418.5	329.0	57.0	32.5	654.0	519.3	134.7	-26.1	235.6	2 776.5	6.7
3rd quarter	622.0	284.9	-100.3	4.3	433.2	340.7	58.7	33.8	629.4	495.1	134.4	-6.4	196.2	2 858.8	6.6
4th quarter	680.0	317.2	-93.7	8.4	448.2	352.5	60.6	35.0	690.4	551.5	138.9	-22.0	242.2	3 004.9	7.7
1981															
1st quarter	710.2	310.3	-71.8	8.4	463.3	364.7	62.4	36.3	765.8	619.4	146.4	-29.9	302.5	3 105.9	7.9
2nd quarter	720.6	313.3	-75.6	4.6	478.3	376.4	64.4	37.4	755.2	609.8	145.4	-30.0	276.9	3 162.5	7.7
3rd quarter	777.2	363.1	-82.6	4.3	492.4	387.8	66.2	38.4	798.0	652.3	145.7	-25.7	305.6	3 266.0	8.7
4th quarter	773.0	380.8	-113.3	-0.7	506.2	398.8	68.1	39.3	795.3	643.4	151.9	-33.2	289.0	3 294.3	8.1
1982															
1st quarter	740.8	358.0	-133.2	-3.5	519.6	409.4	70.0	40.2	738.5	588.3	150.2	-35.5	219.0	3 311.5	6.7
2nd quarter	764.6	377.0	-139.3	-4.1	531.1	418.0	72.0	41.0	750.2	593.6	156.6	-23.6	219.1	3 369.1	6.9
3rd quarter	732.3	373.7	-175.8	-5.6	540.0	424.7	73.6	41.7	750.5	593.0	157.5	-49.2	210.5	3 398.0	5.7
4th quarter	674.0	344.7	-210.2	-7.2	546.7	429.5	75.1	42.1	712.8	549.2	163.6	-51.5	166.1	3 420.4	3.7
1983															
1st quarter	693.5	359.9	-207.0	-10.8	551.3	432.3	76.6	42.4	730.1	565.5	164.5	-42.1	178.8	3 485.7	4.1
2nd quarter	703.8	348.8	-200.8	-0.8	556.6	436.0	78.0	42.6	781.1	613.8	167.3	-64.5	224.5	3 570.9	4.1
3rd quarter	706.8	354.6	-217.3	6.2	563.4	440.6	79.8	42.9	826.9	652.3	174.7	-85.9	263.5	3 657.9	3.9
4th quarter	773.8	387.4	-194.9	10.4	570.9	446.2	81.5	43.2	896.7	718.5	178.2	-96.5	325.8	3 769.7	5.4
1984															
1st quarter	857.7	438.3	-179.8	19.1	580.0	452.6	83.8	43.6	974.7	790.9	183.8	-115.7	394.7	3 911.4	7.1
2nd quarter	875.8	451.8	-189.0	23.7	589.3	459.5	85.6	44.2	1 008.7	818.9	189.8	-125.6	419.4	4 007.6	7.1
3rd quarter	901.4	479.5	-195.4	18.3	599.0	467.0	87.3	44.7	1 032.9	838.9	194.1	-127.9	433.9	4 083.6	7.4
4th quarter	903.4	476.9	-205.2	22.7	609.1	474.9	89.0	45.2	1 036.8	831.7	205.1	-136.8	427.7	4 150.9	7.1
1985															
1st quarter	893.1	418.2	-167.8	22.6	620.1	483.4	90.8	45.9	1 017.7	809.9	207.9	-115.2	397.6	4 227.5	6.5
2nd quarter	890.7	455.2	-217.1	21.8	630.9	492.0	92.4	46.5	1 045.7	827.0	218.7	-139.2	414.8	4 286.3	6.1
3rd quarter	868.9	403.3	-196.1	19.5	642.1	500.7	94.2	47.2	1 048.9	822.2	226.7	-143.9	406.8	4 358.3	5.2
4th quarter	883.1	413.9	-201.5	17.1	653.5	509.6	95.9	48.0	1 085.8	859.5	226.2	-160.9	432.3	4 411.2	5.2
1986															
1st quarter	899.3	410.2	-201.5	25.6	665.0	518.6	97.6	48.8	1 092.0	863.5	228.6	-128.4	427.1	4 474.0	5.2
2nd quarter	874.3	402.5	-224.2	19.4	676.6	527.4	99.4	49.8	1 089.9	855.2	234.7	-142.0	413.3	4 497.0	4.4
3rd quarter	841.8	361.7	-229.9	22.3	687.8	536.0	101.1	50.7	1 082.1	835.8	246.3	-150.3	394.3	4 547.7	3.4
4th quarter	855.8	337.2	-195.1	14.5	699.3	544.3	103.2	51.8	1 084.8	842.1	242.8	-150.4	385.5	4 602.7	3.4

Table 5-1B. Saving and Investment: Historical Data—*Continued*

(Billions of dollars, except as noted; quarterly data are at seasonally adjusted annual rates.)   **NIPA Tables 1.7.5, 5.1**

Year and quarter	Gross saving Total	Net saving Private	Government Federal	Government State and local	Consumption of fixed capital Total	Private	Government Federal	Government State and local	Gross domestic investment Total	Private	Government	Net lending or net borrowing (-), NIPAs	Net domestic investment	Gross national income	Net saving as a percentage of gross national income
1987															
1st quarter	902.1	379.9	-194.7	7.1	709.8	552.3	104.8	52.7	1 118.6	871.2	247.4	-151.1	408.8	4 685.0	4.1
2nd quarter	929.0	329.8	-141.6	19.5	721.2	561.2	106.4	53.7	1 128.3	874.6	253.7	-154.5	407.1	4 794.7	4.3
3rd quarter	964.1	372.3	-153.3	11.5	733.7	570.7	108.4	54.6	1 135.5	876.5	259.0	-154.2	401.8	4 901.0	4.7
4th quarter	1 013.5	419.2	-163.1	10.2	747.1	581.0	110.6	55.4	1 204.9	946.5	258.4	-157.2	457.8	5 008.0	5.3
1988															
1st quarter	1 032.9	420.7	-163.8	14.4	761.6	592.1	113.1	56.4	1 162.1	908.6	253.5	-127.0	400.5	5 113.2	5.3
2nd quarter	1 072.7	439.5	-155.8	13.3	775.6	603.0	115.4	57.3	1 193.0	934.5	258.5	-110.1	417.4	5 220.1	5.7
3rd quarter	1 100.1	440.7	-151.2	21.2	789.4	613.8	117.4	58.3	1 200.7	942.0	258.7	-106.6	411.4	5 325.4	5.8
4th quarter	1 114.8	451.4	-158.6	19.0	803.0	624.4	119.4	59.2	1 225.6	962.8	262.8	-119.7	422.6	5 444.2	5.7
1989															
1st quarter	1 152.0	453.4	-136.3	18.5	816.4	634.9	121.4	60.2	1 268.8	1 005.4	263.4	-106.8	452.4	5 539.6	6.1
2nd quarter	1 109.8	424.7	-158.2	13.6	829.7	645.1	123.3	61.3	1 268.5	1 001.0	267.5	-93.7	438.8	5 585.0	5.0
3rd quarter	1 103.4	416.9	-163.5	7.2	842.8	655.2	125.1	62.4	1 271.5	996.5	275.0	-81.8	428.7	5 649.3	4.6
4th quarter	1 089.3	411.9	-168.5	-9.7	855.5	665.1	126.8	63.6	1 271.7	995.9	275.8	-88.5	416.2	5 699.3	4.1
1990															
1st quarter	1 107.5	432.1	-195.3	2.5	868.2	674.8	128.7	64.8	1 297.5	1 010.8	286.6	-90.9	429.2	5 820.5	4.1
2nd quarter	1 139.6	463.9	-201.7	-3.4	880.8	684.4	130.3	66.1	1 303.2	1 014.8	288.4	-73.0	422.4	5 915.5	4.4
3rd quarter	1 110.4	421.7	-196.7	-7.9	893.3	693.8	132.0	67.5	1 291.4	1 000.7	290.7	-82.5	398.1	5 958.0	3.6
4th quarter	1 112.8	434.7	-209.9	-17.0	905.0	703.0	133.6	68.5	1 243.2	947.6	295.7	-82.7	338.2	5 997.7	3.5
1991															
1st quarter	1 205.7	493.5	-184.1	-20.9	917.2	712.1	135.7	69.4	1 215.4	924.6	290.7	42.1	298.1	6 038.1	4.8
2nd quarter	1 148.4	489.7	-244.1	-25.0	927.8	719.9	137.4	70.5	1 221.7	926.6	295.1	14.2	293.9	6 084.1	3.6
3rd quarter	1 127.8	483.5	-269.3	-23.0	936.6	726.2	139.0	71.4	1 243.0	947.5	295.6	-29.0	306.4	6 141.3	3.1
4th quarter	1 149.8	525.7	-287.4	-31.4	942.9	731.2	139.6	72.1	1 273.7	978.8	294.9	-17.0	330.8	6 205.4	3.3
1992															
1st quarter	1 161.5	570.2	-324.7	-31.4	947.4	734.8	139.9	72.7	1 257.1	956.8	300.3	-22.0	309.7	6 339.8	3.4
2nd quarter	1 178.2	591.1	-331.4	-36.0	954.6	740.0	140.9	73.7	1 310.8	1 013.1	297.7	-39.8	356.2	6 431.2	3.5
3rd quarter	1 129.3	553.3	-343.9	-43.1	963.0	746.7	141.7	74.6	1 318.5	1 024.2	294.3	-46.8	355.5	6 479.2	2.6
4th quarter	1 141.6	537.8	-330.6	-39.5	973.9	755.1	143.2	75.6	1 350.2	1 058.0	292.2	-68.6	376.3	6 587.7	2.5
1993															
1st quarter	1 135.3	538.1	-340.6	-48.0	985.8	765.0	144.0	76.8	1 372.3	1 083.9	288.4	-59.2	386.6	6 605.7	2.3
2nd quarter	1 173.5	522.2	-306.0	-40.5	997.7	774.9	144.9	78.0	1 387.8	1 094.5	293.3	-73.9	390.1	6 720.4	2.6
3rd quarter	1 147.4	494.5	-317.2	-39.2	1 009.3	784.9	145.6	78.8	1 387.4	1 095.9	291.4	-77.0	378.1	6 777.8	2.0
4th quarter	1 215.3	498.3	-283.4	-21.2	1 021.6	795.0	146.7	79.8	1 447.3	1 153.0	294.3	-107.6	425.8	6 929.6	2.8
1994															
1st quarter	1 236.1	498.9	-266.5	-29.5	1 033.2	805.1	146.9	81.1	1 485.3	1 202.1	283.3	-92.2	452.2	7 007.3	2.9
2nd quarter	1 301.7	521.4	-236.8	-29.6	1 046.8	816.9	147.7	82.2	1 555.4	1 265.1	290.3	-111.9	508.7	7 148.2	3.6
3rd quarter	1 311.3	523.7	-254.6	-20.3	1 062.4	830.2	148.7	83.6	1 553.9	1 251.6	302.4	-121.9	491.5	7 252.6	3.4
4th quarter	1 347.5	552.8	-256.9	-28.4	1 079.9	845.1	150.0	84.9	1 607.9	1 307.2	300.7	-137.9	528.0	7 375.1	3.6
1995															
1st quarter	1 400.0	584.0	-254.1	-29.4	1 099.5	861.7	151.5	86.4	1 632.8	1 327.3	305.5	-118.6	533.3	7 461.6	4.0
2nd quarter	1 397.1	567.2	-241.8	-44.3	1 116.1	876.6	151.7	87.7	1 613.9	1 303.8	310.1	-118.3	497.8	7 540.2	3.7
3rd quarter	1 439.3	585.2	-245.2	-31.9	1 131.3	890.1	152.3	88.9	1 609.9	1 303.2	306.7	-101.0	478.6	7 654.6	4.0
4th quarter	1 481.7	580.3	-222.3	-20.5	1 144.3	902.0	152.2	90.1	1 644.1	1 335.6	308.4	-84.0	499.8	7 752.7	4.4
1996															
1st quarter	1 522.5	605.4	-223.1	-15.8	1 156.0	912.3	152.5	91.2	1 670.0	1 355.2	314.7	-102.2	514.0	7 885.8	4.6
2nd quarter	1 562.5	590.9	-179.9	-16.9	1 168.3	923.9	152.4	92.0	1 736.5	1 418.6	317.9	-108.6	568.1	8 025.9	4.9
3rd quarter	1 598.6	596.2	-169.6	-10.3	1 182.3	936.9	152.4	93.1	1 796.1	1 474.4	321.7	-132.8	613.8	8 120.9	5.1
4th quarter	1 641.7	592.6	-141.4	-6.8	1 197.4	951.1	152.2	94.1	1 805.5	1 480.0	325.5	-113.6	608.1	8 269.0	5.4
1997															
1st quarter	1 701.9	613.1	-120.7	-4.8	1 214.2	966.6	152.5	95.2	1 852.3	1 522.0	330.4	-131.4	638.1	8 406.7	5.8
2nd quarter	1 771.3	644.7	-102.5	-2.6	1 231.7	982.2	153.1	96.3	1 919.9	1 589.9	330.0	-101.7	688.2	8 535.9	6.3
3rd quarter	1 820.4	634.2	-68.7	6.5	1 248.5	997.9	153.3	97.3	1 956.6	1 625.3	331.3	-122.7	708.2	8 701.4	6.6
4th quarter	1 840.6	640.3	-72.8	7.7	1 265.5	1 013.6	153.1	98.7	1 971.8	1 645.3	326.5	-163.3	706.3	8 837.3	6.5
1998															
1st quarter	1 912.0	638.8	-22.6	13.9	1 281.9	1 029.5	152.7	99.7	2 036.9	1 712.3	324.6	-164.3	754.9	8 955.1	7.0
2nd quarter	1 917.5	615.2	-8.8	11.0	1 300.1	1 046.0	153.3	100.8	2 031.7	1 694.8	336.9	-195.4	731.5	9 099.2	6.8
3rd quarter	1 960.4	605.2	21.7	14.2	1 319.3	1 063.2	153.7	102.5	2 091.5	1 739.8	351.8	-224.1	772.2	9 249.5	6.9
4th quarter	1 939.6	556.9	20.6	22.5	1 339.7	1 081.0	154.6	104.0	2 146.8	1 794.4	352.4	-235.2	807.1	9 366.4	6.4
1999															
1st quarter	2 035.6	615.8	47.5	12.2	1 360.2	1 099.5	155.2	105.5	2 206.9	1 850.6	356.3	-241.2	846.7	9 538.8	7.1
2nd quarter	1 987.5	535.7	62.8	3.9	1 385.1	1 121.5	156.3	107.3	2 210.0	1 845.8	364.2	-273.7	824.9	9 635.2	6.3
3rd quarter	1 974.7	481.7	71.5	8.7	1 412.8	1 146.9	157.0	108.9	2 261.5	1 890.9	370.6	-306.6	848.7	9 756.3	5.8
4th quarter	2 016.5	474.2	84.8	12.1	1 445.4	1 175.8	158.6	111.0	2 332.2	1 949.4	382.8	-342.9	886.8	9 970.8	5.7
2000															
1st quarter	2 143.1	463.7	176.2	22.0	1 481.2	1 208.2	160.0	112.9	2 333.6	1 945.9	387.7	-376.5	852.5	10 247.4	6.5
2nd quarter	2 124.8	447.3	146.4	22.2	1 508.9	1 232.5	161.0	115.4	2 457.7	2 071.8	386.0	-386.4	948.8	10 365.2	5.9
3rd quarter	2 142.0	453.7	153.7	6.5	1 528.1	1 248.7	162.1	117.3	2 447.4	2 055.8	391.6	-424.0	919.2	10 505.0	5.8
4th quarter	2 069.1	391.7	149.8	-11.2	1 538.7	1 256.8	162.8	119.1	2 457.3	2 061.6	395.7	-429.4	918.6	10 567.4	5.0
2001															
1st quarter	2 143.9	467.8	130.0	-24.7	1 570.8	1 287.0	162.9	120.9	2 369.2	1 967.5	401.7	-419.2	798.4	10 742.3	5.3
2nd quarter	2 128.5	490.5	92.8	-53.5	1 598.7	1 313.2	163.3	122.3	2 388.7	1 967.0	421.7	-379.9	790.0	10 807.5	4.9
3rd quarter	2 046.6	637.4	-130.2	-76.5	1 616.0	1 328.9	163.4	123.6	2 344.0	1 937.3	406.7	-360.0	728.1	10 781.5	4.0
4th quarter	1 954.9	465.7	-34.7	-106.4	1 630.4	1 341.6	163.6	125.2	2 267.1	1 842.7	424.4	-344.2	636.7	10 823.2	3.0

Table 5-1B. Saving and Investment: Historical Data—*Continued*

(Billions of dollars, except as noted; quarterly data are at seasonally adjusted annual rates.)   **NIPA Tables 1.7.5, 5.1**

Year and quarter	Gross saving Total	Net saving Private	Net saving Government Federal	Net saving Government State and local	Consumption of fixed capital Total	Consumption of fixed capital Private	Consumption of fixed capital Government Federal	Consumption of fixed capital Government State and local	Gross domestic investment Total	Gross domestic investment Private	Gross domestic investment Government	Net lending or net borrowing (-), NIPAs	Net domestic investment	Gross national income	Net saving as a percentage of gross national income
2002															
1st quarter	2 010.1	715.2	-228.0	-117.3	1 640.2	1 349.3	164.1	126.8	2 344.4	1 910.0	434.4	-406.9	704.2	10 957.8	3.4
2nd quarter	1 993.4	730.7	-266.5	-123.3	1 652.5	1 359.6	164.5	128.4	2 365.0	1 925.6	439.4	-451.7	712.5	11 047.0	3.1
3rd quarter	1 964.0	687.7	-276.9	-116.1	1 669.3	1 374.1	165.4	129.8	2 375.8	1 927.9	448.0	-453.3	706.6	11 124.7	2.6
4th quarter	1 994.9	746.1	-310.6	-126.9	1 686.3	1 389.0	166.2	131.1	2 389.0	1 936.5	452.5	-493.1	702.7	11 266.1	2.7
2003															
1st quarter	1 941.7	728.0	-333.4	-154.9	1 702.0	1 401.6	167.7	132.7	2 415.5	1 960.2	455.3	-533.4	713.6	11 339.2	2.1
2nd quarter	1 977.3	799.8	-401.8	-136.7	1 716.5	1 413.2	169.4	133.9	2 431.6	1 970.5	461.0	-519.2	715.1	11 494.5	2.3
3rd quarter	1 985.2	829.7	-472.5	-107.0	1 735.0	1 428.6	171.3	135.1	2 520.5	2 048.3	472.2	-516.5	785.5	11 668.0	2.1
4th quarter	2 059.9	795.3	-403.8	-87.0	1 755.4	1 446.0	173.0	136.4	2 605.2	2 132.8	472.4	-502.2	849.8	11 864.0	2.6
2004															
1st quarter	2 068.5	841.5	-441.0	-115.2	1 783.3	1 470.1	175.0	138.1	2 630.4	2 155.2	475.3	-540.6	847.2	12 075.6	2.4
2nd quarter	2 144.0	855.6	-402.2	-122.6	1 813.2	1 494.4	177.4	141.3	2 747.1	2 259.5	487.6	-617.7	933.9	12 279.7	2.7
3rd quarter	2 213.2	849.4	-373.1	-109.1	1 846.1	1 520.7	179.7	145.8	2 805.7	2 311.3	494.4	-623.0	959.6	12 505.4	2.9
4th quarter	2 161.0	743.8	-380.5	-86.6	1 884.3	1 552.0	182.4	149.9	2 877.4	2 380.8	496.6	-715.6	993.1	12 630.0	2.2
2005															
1st quarter	2 282.7	740.2	-312.9	-66.6	1 922.0	1 584.9	185.2	151.9	2 973.3	2 475.2	498.2	-686.5	1 051.3	12 903.7	2.8
2nd quarter	2 286.0	707.3	-310.0	-70.7	1 959.3	1 616.0	187.9	155.4	2 979.1	2 469.5	509.6	-705.8	1 019.8	13 077.9	2.5
3rd quarter	2 328.7	705.5	-307.9	-69.9	2 000.9	1 650.8	190.6	159.5	3 046.6	2 527.2	519.4	-674.3	1 045.7	13 325.3	2.5
4th quarter	2 456.8	758.7	-288.1	-59.3	2 045.5	1 689.5	193.7	162.4	3 163.9	2 636.5	527.4	-832.7	1 118.4	13 580.2	3.0
2006															
1st quarter	2 668.7	855.5	-242.5	-26.5	2 082.2	1 721.4	196.6	164.2	3 233.9	2 699.7	534.3	-792.5	1 151.7	13 946.4	4.2
2nd quarter	2 641.6	788.2	-244.3	-21.3	2 119.1	1 751.1	199.4	168.6	3 250.7	2 697.0	553.7	-815.2	1 131.6	14 074.1	3.7
3rd quarter	2 630.2	761.1	-234.0	-49.7	2 152.8	1 779.0	202.0	171.8	3 240.2	2 684.4	555.8	-859.0	1 087.4	14 214.3	3.4
4th quarter	2 652.0	709.4	-187.3	-60.1	2 190.0	1 808.6	204.8	176.6	3 207.2	2 641.6	565.7	-750.2	1 017.2	14 328.3	3.2
2007															
1st quarter	2 561.9	614.3	-213.8	-66.0	2 227.4	1 837.5	208.2	181.7	3 209.8	2 634.2	575.6	-799.5	982.3	14 453.2	2.3
2nd quarter	2 568.3	622.0	-251.9	-55.4	2 253.7	1 857.5	211.3	185.0	3 262.6	2 671.9	590.7	-756.3	1 009.0	14 576.5	2.2
3rd quarter	2 456.7	542.0	-286.9	-74.9	2 276.5	1 874.0	214.4	188.1	3 255.5	2 658.2	597.2	-686.0	979.0	14 604.5	1.2
4th quarter	2 414.3	519.1	-309.9	-94.6	2 299.8	1 891.0	217.3	191.6	3 215.9	2 610.6	605.3	-630.3	916.1	14 708.6	0.8
2008															
1st quarter	2 359.9	558.4	-409.0	-117.3	2 327.7	1 911.7	221.2	194.9	3 138.4	2 527.0	611.4	-732.3	810.6	14 802.2	0.2
2nd quarter	2 278.7	827.0	-780.5	-120.9	2 353.0	1 930.3	224.8	197.9	3 126.0	2 493.3	632.8	-718.2	773.0	14 867.9	-0.5
3rd quarter	2 248.9	716.1	-663.6	-183.2	2 379.7	1 949.6	228.4	201.6	3 081.6	2 435.9	645.8	-684.6	701.9	14 920.9	-0.9
4th quarter	2 186.1	714.7	-682.8	-238.9	2 393.0	1 955.9	231.0	206.2	2 891.7	2 243.1	648.6	-609.8	498.7	14 573.8	-1.4
2009															
1st quarter	2 104.8	1 026.4	-1 040.1	-267.1	2 385.6	1 944.4	232.7	208.5	2 614.9	1 972.1	642.7	-393.1	229.3	14 395.0	-2.0
2nd quarter	2 020.4	1 254.9	-1 334.7	-266.7	2 367.0	1 924.8	234.0	208.1	2 477.8	1 825.9	651.9	-361.4	110.8	14 368.9	-2.4
3rd quarter	1 990.2	1 261.6	-1 340.9	-285.6	2 355.2	1 912.6	234.8	207.7	2 437.8	1 786.4	651.4	-373.5	82.6	14 489.4	-2.5
4th quarter	2 154.9	1 337.0	-1 279.6	-268.3	2 365.8	1 920.7	236.6	208.4	2 570.1	1 928.0	642.1	-401.9	204.3	14 724.5	-1.4
2010															
1st quarter	2 128.7	1 371.1	-1 351.9	-260.3	2 369.8	1 919.7	240.2	210.0	2 624.9	1 989.5	635.4	-435.8	255.1	14 826.8	-1.6
2nd quarter	2 194.5	1 420.9	-1 338.4	-262.9	2 374.9	1 918.9	244.1	211.9	2 748.0	2 092.7	655.3	-450.4	373.1	14 995.7	-1.2
3rd quarter	2 337.3	1 495.6	-1 319.2	-221.6	2 382.5	1 921.9	246.9	213.6	2 825.1	2 164.6	660.5	-475.8	442.6	15 251.3	-0.3
4th quarter	2 346.0	1 456.6	-1 305.3	-204.4	2 399.1	1 933.6	250.1	215.4	2 812.5	2 156.5	656.0	-424.4	413.4	15 410.7	-0.3
2011															
1st quarter	2 318.2	1 350.3	-1 236.4	-215.1	2 419.4	1 947.8	253.9	217.7	2 761.1	2 123.5	637.7	-487.6	341.8	15 510.6	-0.7
2nd quarter	2 353.4	1 424.1	-1 313.2	-200.5	2 442.9	1 965.5	256.7	220.7	2 851.8	2 212.7	639.1	-509.0	408.9	15 698.8	-0.6
3rd quarter	2 479.7	1 475.2	-1 231.2	-226.9	2 462.6	1 979.8	258.9	223.8	2 865.7	2 228.2	637.5	-462.3	403.1	15 917.3	0.1
4th quarter	2 587.0	1 526.3	-1 195.8	-221.2	2 477.7	1 991.1	260.1	226.5	3 032.5	2 395.2	637.3	-473.6	554.7	16 084.9	0.7
2012															
1st quarter	2 791.1	1 621.6	-1 107.1	-224.7	2 501.2	2 010.2	262.2	228.8	3 084.4	2 460.8	623.6	-512.6	583.1	16 443.8	1.8
2nd quarter	2 830.4	1 638.4	-1 102.0	-230.4	2 524.4	2 029.1	264.0	231.3	3 157.6	2 534.8	622.8	-496.9	633.2	16 521.6	1.9
3rd quarter	2 850.5	1 605.9	-1 079.5	-222.3	2 546.5	2 047.9	265.4	233.2	3 142.8	2 529.9	612.9	-438.4	596.3	16 608.8	1.8
4th quarter	2 973.0	1 685.6	-1 071.6	-205.6	2 564.7	2 064.7	265.8	234.3	3 119.7	2 521.3	598.4	-398.7	555.0	16 810.2	2.4
2013															
1st quarter	2 943.5	1 333.0	-791.8	-184.1	2 586.4	2 084.8	265.9	235.7	3 209.0	2 617.6	-0.6	-426.5	622.6	16 862.6	2.1
2nd quarter	3 047.2	1 142.0	-530.9	-178.8	2 615.0	2 110.1	267.4	237.4	3 248.4	2 658.1	-5.8	-413.7	633.4	16 997.3	2.5
3rd quarter	3 078.8	1 347.8	-709.7	-200.1	2 640.7	2 133.0	268.4	239.3	3 345.7	2 750.8	-10.1	-386.4	705.0	17 120.1	2.6
4th quarter	3 132.4	1 200.9	-542.9	-199.0	2 673.5	2 161.7	270.2	241.5	3 391.4	2 798.6	-10.9	-321.2	718.0	17 315.0	2.7
2014															
1st quarter	3 150.1	1 214.2	-589.8	-180.4	2 706.1	2 191.8	270.7	243.6	3 363.9	2 780.7	583.2	-382.1	657.8	17 440.3	2.5
2nd quarter	3 352.6	1 385.7	-607.0	-158.0	2 731.9	2 216.0	270.8	245.1	3 489.8	2 895.0	594.8	-355.3	757.9	17 768.9	3.5
3rd quarter	3 426.3	1 457.0	-626.7	-166.6	2 762.6	2 244.7	271.1	246.9	3 589.0	2 992.0	597.0	-368.8	826.4	18 073.4	3.7
4th quarter	3 497.7	1 494.0	-617.1	-170.7	2 791.5	2 272.1	271.3	248.1	3 600.2	2 997.9	602.4	-431.5	808.7	18 285.7	3.9
2015															
1st quarter	3 509.4	1 401.3	-554.0	-149.6	2 811.7	2 291.6	271.5	248.6	3 690.6	3 094.6	596.0	-454.5	878.9	18 364.6	3.8
2nd quarter	3 539.9	1 466.5	-591.0	-165.4	2 829.6	2 308.2	271.1	250.3	3 709.7	3 096.3	613.4	-433.8	880.1	18 549.4	3.8
3rd quarter	3 467.9	1 424.2	-633.5	-177.1	2 854.4	2 331.3	271.4	251.6	3 731.1	3 115.7	615.5	-483.1	876.8	18 638.9	3.3
4th quarter	3 510.9	1 301.9	-568.1	-93.4	2 870.5	2 347.2	271.3	251.9	3 675.4	3 067.7	607.6	-432.5	804.9	18 771.7	3.4
2016															
1st quarter	3 384.8	1 372.0	-707.5	-160.6	2 880.9	2 358.1	270.9	252.0	3 650.1	3 031.6	618.5	-492.1	769.2	18 727.4	2.7
2nd quarter	3 333.9	1 299.0	-688.5	-184.9	2 908.3	2 382.3	271.4	254.7	3 632.8	3 023.1	609.7	-432.1	724.4	18 865.9	2.3
3rd quarter	3 401.8	1 315.4	-679.1	-162.2	2 927.6	2 400.7	271.3	255.6	3 649.9	3 048.0	602.0	-443.8	722.3	19 112.7	2.5
4th quarter	3 292.2	1 218.2	-714.0	-161.9	2 950.0	2 421.2	271.6	257.2	3 734.9	3 126.2	608.7	-477.4	784.9	19 168.9	1.8

Table 5-2. Gross Private Fixed Investment by Type

(Billions of dollars, quarterly data are at seasonally adjusted annual rates.)

NIPA Table 5.3.5

Year and quarter	Total gross private fixed investment	Nonresidential Total	Structures Total	Commercial and health care	Manufacturing	Power and communication	Mining exploration, shafts, and wells	Other nonresidential structures	Equipment Total	Information processing equipment Total	Computers and peripheral equipment	Other information processing	Industrial equipment
1955	68.8	43.4	15.2	3.4	2.3	3.3	2.5	3.7	23.9	2.8	...	2.8	7.3
1956	73.7	49.7	18.2	4.2	3.2	4.1	2.7	4.0	26.3	3.4	...	3.4	8.8
1957	75.7	53.1	19.0	4.1	3.6	4.5	2.6	4.1	28.6	4.0	...	4.0	9.6
1958	71.3	48.5	17.6	4.2	2.4	4.4	2.4	4.2	24.9	3.6	...	3.6	8.2
1959	81.7	53.1	18.1	4.6	2.1	4.3	2.5	4.7	28.3	4.0	0.0	4.0	8.5
1960	83.2	56.4	19.6	4.8	2.9	4.4	2.3	5.2	29.7	4.7	0.2	4.6	9.4
1961	83.6	56.6	19.7	5.5	2.8	4.1	2.3	5.0	28.9	5.1	0.3	4.8	8.8
1962	90.9	61.2	20.8	6.2	2.8	4.1	2.5	5.2	32.1	5.5	0.3	5.1	9.3
1963	97.7	64.8	21.2	6.1	2.9	4.4	2.3	5.6	34.4	6.1	0.7	5.4	10.0
1964	107.3	72.2	23.7	6.8	3.6	4.8	2.4	6.2	38.7	6.8	0.9	5.9	11.4
1965	120.4	85.2	28.3	8.2	5.1	5.4	2.4	7.2	45.8	7.8	1.2	6.7	13.7
1966	130.6	97.2	31.3	8.3	6.6	6.3	2.5	7.8	53.0	9.7	1.7	8.0	16.2
1967	132.8	99.2	31.5	8.2	6.0	7.1	2.4	7.8	53.7	10.1	1.9	8.2	16.9
1968	147.9	107.7	33.6	9.4	6.0	8.3	2.6	7.3	58.5	10.6	1.9	8.7	17.3
1969	164.4	120.0	37.7	11.7	6.8	8.7	2.8	7.8	65.2	12.8	2.4	10.4	19.1
1970	168.0	124.6	40.3	12.5	7.0	10.2	2.8	7.8	66.4	14.3	2.7	11.6	20.3
1971	188.6	130.4	42.7	14.9	6.3	11.0	2.7	7.9	69.1	14.9	2.8	12.2	19.5
1972	219.0	146.6	47.2	17.6	5.9	12.1	3.1	8.6	78.9	16.7	3.5	13.2	21.4
1973	251.1	172.7	55.0	19.8	7.9	13.8	3.5	9.9	95.1	19.9	3.5	16.3	26.0
1974	260.5	191.1	61.2	20.6	10.0	15.1	5.2	10.3	104.3	23.1	3.9	19.2	30.7
1975	263.5	196.8	61.4	17.7	10.6	15.7	7.4	10.1	107.6	23.8	3.6	20.2	31.3
1976	306.1	219.3	65.9	18.1	10.1	18.2	8.6	11.0	121.2	27.5	4.4	23.1	34.1
1977	374.3	259.1	74.6	20.3	11.1	19.3	11.5	12.5	148.7	33.7	5.7	28.0	39.4
1978	452.6	314.6	93.6	25.3	16.2	21.4	15.4	15.2	180.6	42.3	7.6	34.8	47.7
1979	521.7	373.8	117.7	33.5	22.0	24.6	19.0	18.5	208.1	50.4	10.2	40.2	56.2
1980	536.4	406.9	136.2	41.0	20.5	27.3	27.4	20.0	216.4	58.9	12.5	46.4	60.7
1981	601.4	472.9	167.3	48.3	25.4	30.0	42.5	21.2	240.9	69.6	17.1	52.5	65.5
1982	595.9	485.1	177.6	55.8	26.1	29.6	44.8	21.3	234.9	74.2	18.9	55.3	62.7
1983	643.3	482.2	154.3	55.8	19.5	25.8	30.0	23.3	246.5	83.7	23.9	59.8	58.9
1984	754.7	564.3	177.4	70.6	20.9	26.5	31.3	28.1	291.9	101.2	31.6	69.6	68.1
1985	807.8	607.7	194.5	84.1	24.1	26.5	27.9	31.8	307.9	106.6	33.7	72.9	72.5
1986	842.6	607.8	176.5	80.9	21.0	28.3	15.7	30.7	317.7	111.1	33.4	77.7	75.4
1987	865.0	615.2	174.2	80.8	21.2	25.4	13.1	33.7	320.9	112.2	35.8	76.4	76.7
1988	918.5	662.3	182.8	86.3	23.2	25.0	15.7	32.5	346.8	120.8	38.0	82.8	84.2
1989	972.0	716.0	193.7	88.3	28.8	27.5	14.9	34.3	372.2	130.7	43.1	87.6	93.3
1990	978.9	739.2	202.9	87.5	33.6	26.3	17.9	37.6	371.9	129.6	38.6	90.9	92.1
1991	944.7	723.6	183.6	68.9	31.4	31.6	18.5	33.2	360.8	129.2	37.7	91.5	89.3
1992	996.7	741.9	172.6	64.5	29.0	33.9	14.2	31.0	381.7	142.1	44.0	98.1	93.0
1993	1 086.0	799.2	177.2	69.4	23.6	33.2	16.6	34.5	425.1	153.3	47.9	105.4	102.2
1994	1 192.7	868.9	186.8	75.4	28.9	31.2	16.4	34.9	476.4	167.0	52.4	114.6	113.6
1995	1 286.3	962.2	207.3	83.1	35.5	33.1	15.0	40.6	528.1	188.4	66.1	122.3	129.0
1996	1 401.3	1 043.2	224.6	91.5	38.2	29.2	16.8	48.9	565.3	204.7	72.8	131.9	136.5
1997	1 524.7	1 149.1	250.3	104.3	37.6	28.8	22.4	57.2	610.9	222.8	81.4	141.4	140.4
1998	1 671.6	1 252.8	275.1	116.0	40.5	34.2	22.3	62.2	660.0	240.1	87.9	152.2	147.4
1999	1 823.4	1 361.6	283.9	125.4	35.1	40.4	18.3	64.7	713.6	259.8	97.2	162.5	149.1
2000	1 979.2	1 493.8	318.1	139.3	37.6	48.1	23.7	69.4	766.1	293.8	103.2	190.6	162.9
2001	1 966.9	1 453.9	329.7	137.3	37.8	51.1	34.6	68.9	711.5	265.9	87.6	178.4	151.9
2002	1 906.5	1 348.9	282.9	119.4	22.7	51.0	30.2	59.5	659.6	236.7	79.7	157.0	141.7
2003	2 008.7	1 371.7	281.8	115.0	21.4	48.1	38.5	58.8	669.0	241.0	78.3	162.8	143.4
2004	2 212.8	1 463.1	301.8	125.3	23.2	43.1	47.3	62.9	719.2	253.1	81.5	171.6	144.2
2005	2 467.5	1 611.5	345.6	135.9	28.4	48.1	69.4	63.9	790.7	262.8	80.0	182.8	162.4
2006	2 613.7	1 776.3	415.6	156.3	32.3	55.8	96.0	75.1	856.1	282.3	86.4	195.9	181.6
2007	2 609.3	1 920.6	496.9	181.8	40.2	81.6	102.2	91.1	885.8	303.2	87.7	215.5	194.1
2008	2 456.8	1 941.0	552.4	181.8	52.8	95.6	117.0	105.2	825.1	291.2	83.8	207.5	192.9
2009	2 025.7	1 633.4	438.2	126.7	56.3	95.8	75.0	84.5	644.3	256.1	76.8	179.3	152.1
2010	2 039.3	1 658.2	362.0	92.0	39.8	83.8	86.2	60.3	731.8	276.7	81.3	195.4	152.9
2011	2 198.1	1 812.1	381.6	93.2	39.0	61.8	112.3	55.4	838.2	277.7	76.4	201.3	190.5
2012	2 449.9	2 007.7	448.0	103.7	45.8	102.4	134.1	62.0	937.9	288.6	79.7	208.9	211.4
2013	2 613.9	2 094.4	463.6	109.8	48.8	98.9	139.4	66.7	982.8	297.2	79.1	218.2	209.0
2014	2 838.4	2 268.3	537.5	127.3	57.0	115.3	163.1	74.8	1 046.5	299.5	80.5	219.0	219.1
2015	2 981.6	2 336.2	537.5	143.3	77.7	113.0	118.4	85.1	1 081.9	302.8	77.1	225.8	220.8
2016	3 022.1	2 316.3	516.2	166.6	73.1	118.6	63.4	94.5	1 043.9	303.9	73.1	230.8	225.0
2014													
1st quarter	2 736.9	2 194.7	515.5	118.2	50.7	130.9	145.7	70.0	1 010.3	293.3	77.3	216.0	212.4
2nd quarter	2 812.3	2 251.5	537.1	125.3	52.3	122.7	163.5	73.3	1 038.5	303.7	81.7	222.0	220.1
3rd quarter	2 893.4	2 316.0	542.3	130.2	57.1	111.3	168.9	74.9	1 085.0	298.9	81.0	217.9	226.9
4th quarter	2 911.1	2 310.9	555.1	135.7	67.7	96.3	174.5	80.9	1 052.0	302.2	82.1	220.2	217.1
2015													
1st quarter	2 946.0	2 328.6	552.7	136.6	76.0	105.5	154.4	80.2	1 073.4	298.3	77.1	221.2	216.8
2nd quarter	2 978.2	2 343.2	556.8	145.7	80.7	121.5	122.7	86.1	1 073.6	299.1	77.4	221.7	221.9
3rd quarter	3 010.0	2 353.5	536.2	144.6	78.6	118.0	106.6	88.5	1 097.3	306.7	79.3	227.5	220.7
4th quarter	2 992.3	2 319.7	504.3	146.4	75.3	107.1	89.9	85.7	1 083.5	307.1	74.4	232.7	224.0
2016													
1st quarter	2 989.4	2 291.2	504.6	155.0	74.8	111.3	74.6	89.0	1 046.2	299.1	73.2	225.9	220.6
2nd quarter	3 010.9	2 311.2	508.7	161.7	74.0	117.9	60.2	95.0	1 044.3	302.6	73.9	228.7	224.4
3rd quarter	3 031.5	2 329.1	525.6	172.4	74.5	123.0	59.5	96.2	1 040.9	306.8	73.4	233.4	226.0
4th quarter	3 056.7	2 333.7	525.8	177.3	69.2	122.3	59.1	97.8	1 044.3	307.1	72.1	235.0	229.0

. . . = Not available.

Table 5-2. Gross Private Fixed Investment by Type—*Continued*

(Billions of dollars, quarterly data are at seasonally adjusted annual rates.)   NIPA Table 5.3.5

Year and quarter	Nonresidential—*Continued*						Residential						
	Equipment—*Continued*		Intellectual property					Residential structures					Residential equipment
							Total	Total		Permanent site			Other residential structures	
	Transportation equipment	Other nonresidential equipment	Total	Software [1]	Research and development [2]	Entertainment, literary, and artistic originals			Total	Total	Single family	Multifamily		
1955	7.5	6.3	4.3	...	2.7	1.6	25.4	25.0	18.6	...	...	6.4	0.4
1956	7.4	6.7	5.2	...	3.6	1.7	24.0	23.5	16.5	...	...	7.0	0.5
1957	8.3	6.7	5.6	...	3.7	1.9	22.6	22.2	15.1	...	...	7.1	0.5
1958	6.1	6.9	6.0	...	4.0	2.0	22.8	22.3	15.4	13.1	2.3	6.9	0.5
1959	8.3	7.6	6.6	0.0	4.4	2.2	28.6	28.1	19.7	16.7	3.0	8.4	0.6
1960	8.5	7.1	7.1	0.1	4.9	2.2	26.9	26.3	17.5	14.9	2.6	8.8	0.5
1961	8.0	7.0	8.0	0.2	5.2	2.7	27.0	26.5	17.4	14.1	3.3	9.1	0.5
1962	9.8	7.5	8.4	0.2	5.6	2.6	29.6	29.1	19.9	15.1	4.8	9.2	0.5
1963	9.4	8.8	9.2	0.4	6.0	2.8	32.9	32.3	22.4	16.0	6.4	9.8	0.6
1964	10.6	9.9	9.8	0.5	6.5	2.8	35.1	34.5	24.1	17.6	6.4	10.4	0.6
1965	13.2	11.0	11.1	0.7	7.2	3.2	35.2	34.5	23.8	17.8	6.0	10.6	0.7
1966	14.5	12.7	12.8	1.0	8.1	3.7	33.4	32.7	21.8	16.6	5.2	10.9	0.7
1967	14.3	12.4	14.0	1.2	9.0	3.8	33.6	32.9	21.5	16.8	4.7	11.4	0.7
1968	17.6	13.0	15.6	1.3	9.9	4.3	40.2	39.3	26.7	19.5	7.2	12.6	0.9
1969	18.9	14.4	17.2	1.8	11.0	4.4	44.4	43.4	29.2	19.7	9.5	14.1	1.0
1970	16.2	15.6	17.9	2.3	11.5	4.1	43.4	42.3	27.1	17.5	9.5	15.2	1.1
1971	18.4	16.3	18.7	2.4	11.9	4.4	58.2	56.9	38.7	25.8	12.9	18.2	1.3
1972	21.8	19.0	20.6	2.8	12.9	4.9	72.4	70.9	50.1	32.8	17.2	20.8	1.5
1973	26.6	22.6	22.7	3.2	14.6	4.9	78.3	76.6	54.6	35.2	19.4	22.0	1.7
1974	26.3	24.3	25.5	3.9	16.4	5.2	69.5	67.6	43.4	29.7	13.7	24.2	1.9
1975	25.2	27.4	27.8	4.8	17.5	5.5	66.7	64.8	36.3	29.6	6.7	28.5	1.9
1976	30.0	29.6	32.2	5.2	19.6	7.4	86.8	84.6	50.8	43.9	6.9	33.9	2.1
1977	39.3	36.3	35.8	5.5	21.8	8.6	115.2	112.8	72.2	62.2	10.0	40.6	2.4
1978	47.3	43.2	40.4	6.3	24.9	9.1	138.0	135.3	85.6	72.8	12.8	49.7	2.7
1979	53.6	47.9	48.1	8.1	29.1	10.9	147.8	144.7	89.3	72.3	17.0	55.4	3.2
1980	48.4	48.3	54.4	9.8	34.2	10.3	129.5	126.1	69.6	52.9	16.7	56.5	3.4
1981	50.6	55.2	64.8	11.8	39.7	13.2	128.5	124.9	69.4	52.0	17.5	55.4	3.6
1982	46.8	51.2	72.7	14.0	44.8	13.9	110.8	107.2	57.0	41.5	15.5	50.2	3.7
1983	53.5	50.4	81.3	16.4	49.6	15.3	161.1	156.9	95.0	72.5	22.4	61.9	4.2
1984	64.4	58.1	95.1	20.4	56.9	17.8	190.4	185.6	114.6	86.4	28.2	71.0	4.7
1985	69.0	59.9	105.3	23.8	63.0	18.6	200.1	195.0	115.9	87.4	28.5	79.1	5.1
1986	70.5	60.7	113.5	25.6	66.5	21.4	234.8	229.3	135.2	104.1	31.0	94.1	5.5
1987	68.1	63.9	120.1	29.0	69.2	21.9	249.8	244.0	142.7	117.2	25.5	101.3	5.8
1988	72.9	69.0	132.7	34.2	75.5	23.0	256.2	250.1	142.4	120.1	22.3	107.7	6.1
1989	67.9	80.2	150.1	41.9	82.8	25.4	256.0	249.9	143.2	120.9	22.3	106.6	6.1
1990	70.0	80.2	164.4	47.6	89.3	27.5	239.7	233.7	132.1	112.9	19.3	101.5	6.0
1991	71.5	70.8	179.1	53.7	96.0	29.4	221.2	215.4	114.6	99.4	15.1	100.8	5.7
1992	74.7	72.0	187.7	57.9	98.6	31.2	254.7	248.8	135.1	122.0	13.1	113.8	5.9
1993	89.4	80.2	196.9	64.3	99.2	33.4	286.8	280.7	150.9	140.1	10.8	129.8	6.1
1994	107.7	88.1	205.7	68.3	101.3	36.1	323.8	317.6	176.4	162.3	14.1	141.2	6.2
1995	116.1	94.7	226.8	74.6	112.0	40.2	324.1	317.7	171.4	153.5	17.9	146.3	6.3
1996	123.2	101.0	253.3	85.5	123.6	44.3	358.1	351.7	191.1	170.8	20.3	160.6	6.3
1997	135.5	112.1	288.0	107.5	134.4	46.1	375.6	369.3	198.1	175.2	22.9	171.3	6.3
1998	147.1	125.4	317.7	126.0	143.3	48.3	418.8	412.1	224.0	199.4	24.6	188.2	6.7
1999	174.4	130.4	364.0	157.3	155.7	51.0	461.8	454.5	251.3	223.8	27.4	203.2	7.3
2000	170.8	138.6	409.5	184.5	169.5	55.6	485.4	477.7	265.0	236.8	28.3	212.7	7.7
2001	154.2	139.5	412.6	186.6	171.3	54.7	513.0	505.2	279.4	249.1	30.3	225.8	7.8
2002	141.6	139.6	406.4	183.0	165.7	57.6	557.6	549.6	298.8	265.9	33.0	250.7	8.0
2003	134.1	150.5	420.9	191.0	167.2	62.7	636.9	628.7	345.7	310.6	35.1	283.0	8.3
2004	159.2	162.7	442.1	205.1	173.0	64.1	749.7	740.7	417.5	377.6	39.9	323.2	9.0
2005	179.6	186.0	475.1	217.2	188.1	69.8	856.1	846.4	480.8	433.5	47.3	365.6	9.6
2006	194.3	198.0	504.6	228.9	204.5	71.2	837.4	827.4	468.8	416.0	52.8	358.6	10.0
2007	188.8	199.6	537.9	244.2	223.3	70.4	688.7	678.8	354.1	305.2	49.0	324.7	9.9
2008	146.2	194.9	563.4	258.5	237.7	67.2	515.9	506.5	230.1	185.8	44.3	276.4	9.3
2009	70.6	165.6	550.9	256.8	229.0	65.1	392.2	383.9	133.9	105.3	28.5	250.1	8.3
2010	127.5	174.7	564.3	252.0	240.2	72.2	381.1	372.7	127.3	112.6	14.7	245.5	8.3
2011	173.9	196.2	592.2	269.8	250.0	72.4	386.0	377.5	123.2	108.2	15.0	254.2	8.6
2012	213.1	224.8	621.7	284.3	263.0	74.5	442.2	433.4	154.5	132.0	22.5	278.9	8.9
2013	240.6	235.9	647.9	294.6	278.5	74.9	519.5	510.3	202.3	170.8	31.5	308.0	9.2
2014	272.3	255.5	684.3	317.1	292.3	74.9	570.2	560.6	235.2	193.6	41.6	325.5	9.5
2015	305.6	252.7	716.8	332.5	304.5	79.8	645.4	635.5	273.7	221.1	52.5	361.9	9.9
2016	286.7	228.3	756.2	352.8	320.8	82.6	705.9	695.7	303.0	242.5	60.5	392.7	10.1
2014													
1st quarter	257.1	247.5	668.9	306.5	288.0	74.4	542.2	532.9	221.6	184.6	37.0	311.3	9.3
2nd quarter	267.9	246.9	675.8	314.7	286.7	74.4	560.8	551.3	229.7	188.9	40.8	321.6	9.5
3rd quarter	286.4	272.8	688.8	322.7	291.2	74.9	577.4	567.8	236.1	193.1	42.9	331.7	9.6
4th quarter	277.9	254.8	703.7	324.7	303.2	75.9	600.2	590.5	253.2	207.8	45.5	337.3	9.7
2015													
1st quarter	301.4	256.8	702.5	328.6	296.1	77.8	617.4	607.7	262.0	213.8	48.2	345.7	9.7
2nd quarter	298.9	253.7	712.9	330.5	302.9	79.5	635.0	625.1	266.0	215.5	50.5	359.1	9.9
3rd quarter	316.3	253.6	719.9	333.2	306.1	80.6	656.5	646.6	278.8	224.4	54.4	367.9	9.9
4th quarter	305.7	246.7	731.9	337.8	312.8	81.3	672.6	662.6	287.8	230.9	57.0	374.8	10.0
2016													
1st quarter	290.4	236.0	740.4	344.4	314.3	81.7	698.3	688.2	300.7	240.9	59.7	387.5	10.1
2nd quarter	291.8	225.5	758.2	351.6	324.6	82.1	699.7	689.6	301.1	241.3	59.8	388.6	10.1
3rd quarter	283.3	224.9	762.5	356.1	323.6	82.9	702.4	692.3	298.5	237.7	60.8	393.8	10.1
4th quarter	281.3	226.9	763.7	359.1	320.8	83.7	723.0	712.8	311.7	250.0	61.8	401.1	10.2

[1]Excludes software "embedded," or bundled, in computers and other equipment. Includes software development expenditures.
[2]Excludes software development.
. . . = Not available.

Table 5-3. Real Gross Private Fixed Investment by Type

(Billions of chained [2009] dollars, quarterly data are at seasonally adjusted annual rates.)   NIPA Table 5.3.6

Year and quarter	Total gross private fixed investment	Nonresidential											
		Total	Structures						Equipment				
			Total	Commer-cial and health care	Manufac-turing	Power and communi-cation	Mining explor-ation, shafts, and wells	Other non-residential structures	Total	Information processing equipment			Industrial equipment
										Total	Computers and peripheral equipment[1]	Other information processing	
1999	2 165.9	1 510.1	494.9	199.0	53.9	62.8	64.5	94.7	662.4	149.5	29.2	127.3	182.8
2000	2 316.2	1 647.7	533.5	212.3	55.6	72.5	80.5	97.5	726.9	180.4	35.4	153.2	198.5
2001	2 280.0	1 608.4	525.4	202.0	54.1	74.7	94.9	93.0	695.7	178.2	36.3	148.5	183.9
2002	2 201.1	1 498.0	432.5	171.1	31.6	72.9	69.4	78.6	658.0	169.9	38.0	135.0	171.6
2003	2 289.5	1 526.1	415.8	160.3	29.2	67.2	79.3	75.6	679.0	185.8	41.7	147.3	172.2
2004	2 443.9	1 605.4	414.1	164.2	30.1	56.1	84.2	76.7	731.2	204.5	46.8	160.7	169.1
2005	2 611.0	1 717.4	421.2	162.8	34.2	58.1	92.1	72.7	801.6	222.2	52.1	172.6	183.6
2006	2 662.5	1 839.6	451.5	172.6	36.5	61.7	99.5	79.7	870.8	250.9	64.3	187.5	199.1
2007	2 609.6	1 948.4	509.0	189.9	43.1	85.9	97.9	91.8	898.3	279.9	72.7	207.9	205.3
2008	2 432.6	1 934.4	540.2	182.8	53.8	94.5	105.0	103.4	836.1	281.0	77.1	204.2	195.5
2009	2 025.7	1 633.4	438.2	126.7	56.3	95.8	75.0	84.5	644.3	256.1	76.8	179.3	152.1
2010	2 056.2	1 673.8	366.3	95.2	40.8	80.4	87.8	62.0	746.7	281.4	84.7	196.8	151.3
2011	2 186.7	1 802.3	374.7	94.7	39.1	74.1	110.9	56.2	847.9	285.9	83.0	202.8	183.3
2012	2 400.4	1 964.1	423.1	102.8	44.9	89.7	123.8	61.5	939.2	303.1	88.4	214.5	199.8
2013	2 521.4	2 032.9	428.8	106.4	46.7	85.7	126.0	64.1	982.3	317.7	88.5	228.9	196.7
2014	2 677.3	2 172.7	474.0	120.2	52.8	98.5	134.2	68.7	1 047.4	329.6	90.2	238.9	205.0
2015	2 782.7	2 223.5	465.4	132.9	70.7	95.2	95.9	75.9	1 084.5	343.9	87.1	256.2	207.3
2016	2 803.4	2 210.4	446.4	152.3	66.2	99.6	54.5	81.5	1 047.8	350.2	84.0	265.6	212.1
2007													
1st quarter	2 618.2	1 897.2	474.8	183.8	37.3	72.6	97.7	82.4	886.1	270.6	71.1	200.0	197.7
2nd quarter	2 624.9	1 934.4	500.6	189.7	39.4	82.3	98.3	90.2	896.2	272.7	69.8	203.8	210.6
3rd quarter	2 609.0	1 964.4	524.0	192.8	46.2	90.6	98.6	95.5	900.9	279.5	72.6	207.7	211.7
4th quarter	2 586.3	1 997.6	536.8	193.2	49.7	98.2	96.9	98.9	910.0	296.7	77.5	220.0	201.2
2008													
1st quarter	2 539.1	1 998.1	539.0	191.3	50.0	100.2	96.5	101.0	899.4	294.6	81.1	213.8	201.0
2nd quarter	2 503.4	1 986.6	547.7	188.9	53.8	95.4	103.4	105.6	876.6	294.1	81.9	212.4	199.4
3rd quarter	2 424.1	1 933.0	543.7	183.3	55.1	90.0	108.7	105.7	831.6	281.2	76.3	205.2	195.6
4th quarter	2 263.8	1 820.1	530.3	167.8	56.3	92.2	111.4	101.4	736.8	254.1	68.9	185.4	186.0
2009													
1st quarter	2 089.3	1 688.3	490.5	146.2	61.5	93.8	96.7	92.0	653.9	245.6	69.9	175.8	161.0
2nd quarter	2 011.0	1 634.0	453.3	133.1	60.1	96.3	73.6	90.3	631.6	246.4	73.2	173.1	152.5
3rd quarter	2 008.4	1 613.1	422.6	120.1	55.1	100.9	63.9	82.6	639.9	261.4	77.5	183.9	148.5
4th quarter	1 994.1	1 598.4	386.5	107.4	48.5	92.0	65.7	73.1	651.9	270.9	86.5	184.5	146.3
2010													
1st quarter	1 997.9	1 615.0	359.7	99.7	46.2	72.7	76.5	65.0	697.7	276.0	87.6	188.5	143.0
2nd quarter	2 062.8	1 659.3	369.8	95.6	44.2	80.4	86.8	62.9	735.2	277.8	86.4	191.5	151.1
3rd quarter	2 060.8	1 692.8	364.4	93.1	38.8	78.3	93.1	60.9	766.2	282.5	83.0	199.5	152.8
4th quarter	2 103.1	1 728.1	371.2	92.4	34.1	90.0	94.7	59.0	787.8	289.5	81.6	207.7	158.3
2011													
1st quarter	2 098.4	1 724.1	343.0	89.5	33.1	67.9	99.6	53.2	810.6	279.8	76.9	202.5	171.8
2nd quarter	2 140.2	1 761.0	366.7	93.9	37.6	73.3	105.9	56.2	819.3	286.6	83.5	203.0	174.1
3rd quarter	2 227.5	1 840.8	388.2	97.1	42.0	77.7	114.5	56.9	871.0	288.9	86.7	202.2	188.2
4th quarter	2 280.6	1 883.1	400.9	98.2	43.8	77.3	123.6	58.3	890.8	288.2	84.7	203.4	198.9
2012													
1st quarter	2 360.4	1 938.1	419.5	100.7	42.8	89.4	126.8	59.1	924.4	304.6	91.0	213.6	197.0
2nd quarter	2 399.8	1 973.7	429.9	103.0	44.7	91.8	128.1	61.6	944.0	302.2	89.0	213.1	203.0
3rd quarter	2 400.4	1 963.4	425.5	104.3	45.5	90.4	122.3	62.7	936.0	297.3	83.1	213.8	197.5
4th quarter	2 441.0	1 981.4	417.5	103.2	46.6	87.1	118.1	62.5	952.6	308.2	90.7	217.4	201.7
2013													
1st quarter	2 482.7	2 006.7	412.0	105.0	46.1	75.1	124.2	62.4	972.7	317.5	91.4	225.9	200.1
2nd quarter	2 508.8	2 019.0	422.3	103.0	44.4	81.5	129.1	64.6	979.6	319.6	85.7	233.3	195.8
3rd quarter	2 526.7	2 029.6	439.3	105.9	48.6	89.4	130.0	65.3	966.6	317.8	86.6	230.7	197.7
4th quarter	2 567.2	2 076.3	441.6	111.7	47.9	96.6	120.9	64.3	1 010.5	316.1	90.2	225.6	193.2
2014													
1st quarter	2 599.4	2 112.6	463.5	112.4	47.3	112.9	125.0	65.2	1 012.6	320.3	87.0	232.7	199.2
2nd quarter	2 663.0	2 160.6	477.0	118.6	48.7	105.1	136.5	67.9	1 039.1	332.5	91.5	240.6	205.9
3rd quarter	2 722.5	2 215.1	474.9	122.5	52.8	94.7	137.0	68.5	1 085.8	329.4	90.6	238.3	212.0
4th quarter	2 724.2	2 202.4	480.5	127.2	62.5	81.3	138.2	73.1	1 052.3	336.3	91.9	243.9	202.9
2015													
1st quarter	2 751.5	2 214.7	477.9	127.3	69.6	88.6	123.3	72.1	1 073.2	334.9	86.5	247.8	203.0
2nd quarter	2 783.4	2 230.7	483.3	135.9	73.7	102.2	99.4	77.2	1 075.3	338.5	87.3	250.6	208.1
3rd quarter	2 806.6	2 238.8	463.8	133.9	71.3	99.4	86.4	78.7	1 101.3	350.1	89.8	259.6	207.2
4th quarter	2 789.4	2 209.9	436.7	134.5	68.1	90.5	74.5	75.6	1 088.3	352.2	84.7	266.8	210.8
2016													
1st quarter	2 787.8	2 187.5	439.1	142.8	67.8	94.1	63.6	78.0	1 050.7	343.7	83.7	259.3	208.1
2nd quarter	2 797.5	2 205.3	439.7	147.4	66.7	99.3	51.4	82.3	1 049.0	347.9	84.4	262.8	211.7
3rd quarter	2 808.2	2 224.0	454.6	157.8	67.7	103.0	51.4	82.6	1 043.4	353.4	84.2	268.5	212.9
4th quarter	2 820.3	2 224.9	452.1	161.2	62.5	101.8	51.5	83.0	1 048.0	355.9	83.6	271.7	215.8

[1]See notes and definitions.

Table 5-3. Real Gross Private Fixed Investment by Type—*Continued*

(Billions of chained [2009] dollars, quarterly data are at seasonally adjusted annual rates.)

NIPA Table 5.3.6

Year and quarter	Nonresidential—*Continued*						Residential						
	Equipment—*Continued*		Intellectual property					Residential structures					
									Permanent site				
	Transportation equipment	Other nonresidential equipment	Total	Software [2]	Research and development [3]	Entertainment, literary, and artistic originals	Total	Total	Total	Single family	Multifamily	Other residential structures	Residential equipment
1999	208.4	161.4	391.1	154.5	183.9	55.9	633.8	626.5	357.7	311.2	43.6	269.4	7.2
2000	204.1	170.5	426.1	175.9	193.0	59.3	637.9	630.1	360.6	314.6	42.8	270.1	7.6
2001	184.9	169.2	428.0	177.1	195.6	57.5	643.7	635.7	362.7	315.1	44.7	273.5	7.8
2002	167.2	167.9	425.9	176.9	190.5	60.3	682.7	674.5	377.3	327.3	47.1	297.2	8.0
2003	154.8	179.3	442.2	189.0	189.1	64.8	744.5	735.9	414.2	362.2	48.3	321.9	8.5
2004	176.5	192.4	464.9	207.9	191.0	65.8	818.9	809.2	462.2	405.7	52.0	347.6	9.5
2005	197.9	210.9	495.0	221.2	202.3	71.3	872.6	862.5	494.8	433.0	57.2	368.3	9.9
2006	212.6	219.6	517.5	230.3	215.0	72.1	806.6	796.3	451.6	390.7	57.6	345.2	10.1
2007	203.6	217.0	542.4	244.2	227.9	70.3	654.8	644.9	336.1	283.7	51.0	309.3	9.8
2008	156.9	206.5	558.8	256.2	235.5	67.1	497.7	488.4	223.1	178.2	44.9	265.6	9.3
2009	70.6	165.6	550.9	256.8	229.0	65.1	392.2	383.9	133.9	105.3	28.5	250.1	8.3
2010	136.9	179.8	561.3	254.2	234.4	72.7	382.4	373.6	128.5	114.4	14.3	245.1	8.8
2011	183.0	199.3	581.3	271.8	236.7	73.1	384.5	375.3	123.9	109.2	15.0	251.3	9.2
2012	218.9	221.7	603.8	286.6	242.9	74.8	436.5	427.1	153.8	132.1	21.9	273.4	9.4
2013	243.0	230.4	624.5	295.5	254.1	75.2	488.3	478.1	191.5	161.9	29.8	287.0	10.1
2014	271.3	246.9	653.1	318.8	260.5	74.6	505.2	494.3	208.3	170.9	37.8	286.5	10.9
2015	299.5	240.4	677.8	336.7	264.2	78.7	556.9	545.1	233.0	190.5	42.9	312.7	11.8
2016	277.6	216.9	720.4	360.4	281.5	80.4	587.4	574.8	246.3	199.9	46.8	329.1	12.6
2007													
1st quarter	212.8	213.2	537.0	241.5	224.7	70.8	711.2	701.1	371.9	313.7	56.6	329.7	9.9
2nd quarter	201.8	219.5	538.9	242.2	226.2	70.5	682.7	672.8	355.2	301.4	52.0	318.1	9.8
3rd quarter	199.2	217.9	541.1	244.7	225.9	70.5	639.2	629.4	328.0	277.7	48.8	301.8	9.7
4th quarter	200.5	217.4	552.4	248.3	234.7	69.4	586.1	576.4	289.4	241.8	46.7	287.5	9.7
2008													
1st quarter	198.5	211.1	561.2	256.0	236.6	68.6	540.0	530.5	255.7	209.4	46.0	275.2	9.5
2nd quarter	175.8	211.8	563.3	257.0	238.6	67.7	516.3	506.7	239.5	193.0	46.4	267.6	9.6
3rd quarter	147.7	210.6	558.2	257.7	234.2	66.3	490.9	481.7	213.5	168.2	45.3	268.4	9.2
4th quarter	105.5	192.7	552.5	254.2	232.7	65.6	443.6	434.9	183.9	142.2	41.8	251.0	8.6
2009													
1st quarter	68.6	178.8	543.6	252.8	226.2	64.6	401.0	392.6	147.0	109.5	37.6	245.6	8.4
2nd quarter	67.2	165.5	549.4	255.2	229.1	65.1	377.0	368.8	124.5	93.1	31.4	244.4	8.1
3rd quarter	70.0	159.9	550.9	257.7	228.4	64.7	395.4	387.1	132.1	106.8	25.3	255.0	8.3
4th quarter	76.5	158.2	559.8	261.4	232.3	66.1	395.7	387.2	131.9	112.0	20.0	255.3	8.4
2010													
1st quarter	109.7	170.7	557.6	256.0	232.7	68.9	383.0	374.4	131.3	115.7	15.8	243.1	8.6
2nd quarter	130.9	177.8	554.7	250.9	231.5	72.3	403.5	394.6	135.5	121.7	14.1	259.1	8.9
3rd quarter	152.0	182.2	563.0	253.3	235.6	74.0	368.1	359.3	126.0	112.6	13.7	233.3	8.8
4th quarter	155.1	188.3	570.0	256.7	237.8	75.4	375.1	366.2	121.2	107.7	13.8	245.0	8.9
2011													
1st quarter	168.1	194.4	571.9	262.2	236.5	73.2	374.4	365.4	121.6	108.2	13.6	243.7	9.1
2nd quarter	167.1	194.9	576.3	268.4	235.7	72.4	379.3	370.2	121.1	107.2	14.1	249.0	9.2
3rd quarter	188.5	209.0	583.5	275.2	235.9	72.8	386.8	377.5	124.9	109.5	15.6	252.6	9.3
4th quarter	208.5	199.0	593.3	281.2	238.6	74.0	397.6	388.2	128.1	111.8	16.5	260.1	9.4
2012													
1st quarter	213.9	213.4	596.1	282.3	239.6	74.7	422.5	413.1	138.7	120.6	18.3	274.4	9.4
2nd quarter	220.7	222.2	601.7	286.4	241.1	74.8	426.3	417.1	146.9	126.3	20.9	270.2	9.2
3rd quarter	217.6	227.4	603.7	286.4	243.1	74.7	437.3	427.9	157.4	134.5	23.0	270.7	9.3
4th quarter	223.5	223.8	613.8	291.5	247.7	75.1	459.8	450.2	172.3	147.0	25.5	278.2	9.5
2013													
1st quarter	228.8	231.4	625.2	295.9	254.2	75.4	475.9	466.0	183.5	156.3	27.4	282.9	9.9
2nd quarter	244.6	225.4	620.1	290.3	254.3	75.5	489.5	479.4	191.6	163.2	28.6	288.3	10.0
3rd quarter	238.9	217.8	625.5	296.2	254.6	74.9	496.8	486.4	195.2	165.4	30.0	291.7	10.3
4th quarter	259.5	247.1	627.2	299.5	253.2	75.0	491.1	480.7	195.8	162.9	33.1	285.3	10.4
2014													
1st quarter	258.2	240.3	637.9	307.2	256.9	74.3	487.6	477.2	200.1	165.8	34.6	277.6	10.4
2nd quarter	267.6	239.0	645.8	316.4	256.3	74.1	503.0	492.1	207.5	170.1	37.7	285.2	10.9
3rd quarter	285.2	263.4	657.8	324.7	259.9	74.4	508.5	497.5	207.7	169.2	38.9	290.4	11.0
4th quarter	274.4	244.9	670.9	326.9	269.0	75.8	521.8	510.5	218.1	178.5	40.0	292.9	11.3
2015													
1st quarter	296.0	245.1	666.1	331.7	259.1	77.2	536.1	524.6	224.2	183.6	41.0	300.9	11.5
2nd quarter	293.3	241.4	674.1	335.0	262.6	78.3	551.1	539.4	228.2	186.9	41.6	311.8	11.7
3rd quarter	309.7	241.4	678.9	337.1	264.2	79.5	565.2	553.2	237.2	193.7	43.8	316.6	11.9
4th quarter	299.1	233.9	692.2	342.8	271.1	79.9	575.3	563.1	242.4	197.6	45.1	321.4	12.1
2016													
1st quarter	282.8	224.1	702.8	350.6	274.3	79.8	593.7	581.2	250.5	204.2	46.7	331.4	12.4
2nd quarter	283.4	214.7	721.5	359.3	284.5	79.3	586.5	574.0	247.0	201.0	46.3	327.6	12.5
3rd quarter	273.3	213.6	729.0	364.9	285.2	80.8	579.8	567.1	240.5	193.9	46.7	327.3	12.7
4th quarter	270.8	215.3	728.3	366.8	282.2	81.6	589.8	576.9	247.5	200.4	47.4	330.0	13.0

[2] Excludes software "embedded," or bundled, in computers and other equipment.
[3] Excludes software development.

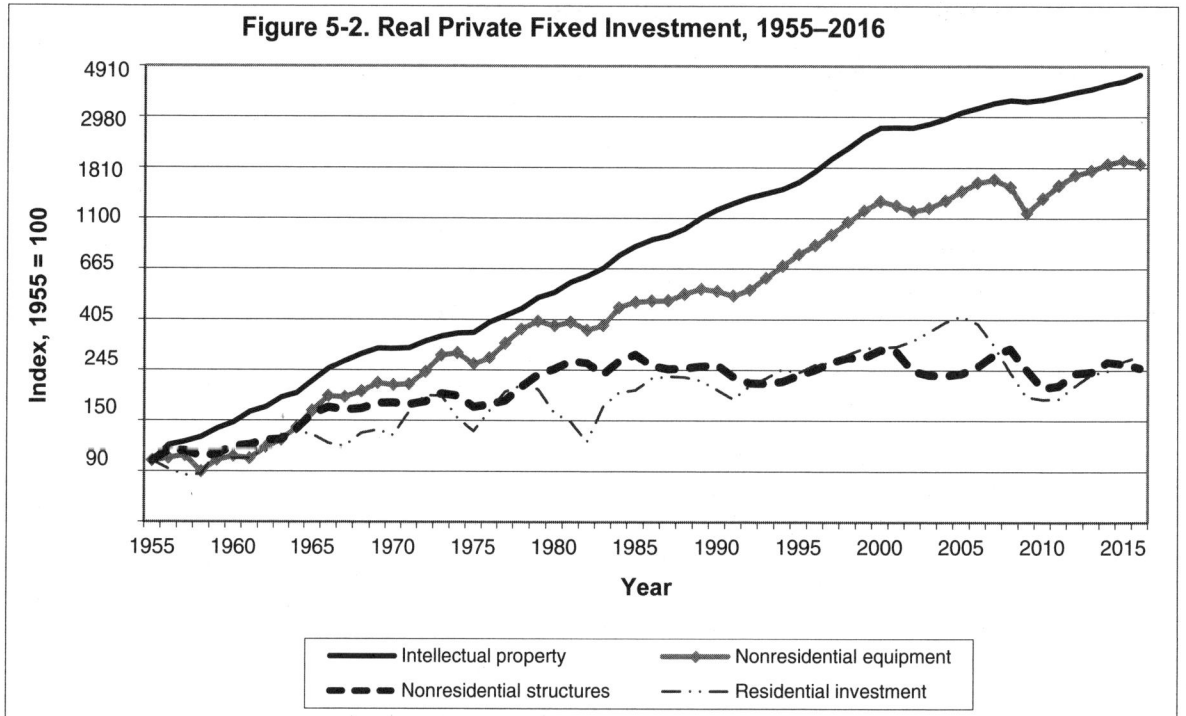

Figure 5-2. Real Private Fixed Investment, 1955–2016

- Between 1955 and 2006, which was the recent high point for total real (constant-dollar) investment, the quantity of real gross private fixed investment increased eightfold, with an average annual growth rate of 4.2 percent. Every major type of investment grew in real terms between those two years, but as Figure 5-2 indicates, by far the fastest-growing major category has been "intellectual property products." Computer software is the main driver of growth in this category, but it also includes research and development and "entertainment, literary, and artistic originals." (Table 5-3)

- Between 2006 and 2009, overall gross investment fell 23.9 percent in real terms—a collapse unprecedented in the postwar period. By 2016, gross investment surpassed 2006 level by 5.3 percent, achieving the all time high. (Table 5-4)

- Intellectual property investment barely hesitated in 2009 and went on to new record peaks in each following year. Equipment purchases regained their previous high in 2012 and went on to a new record in 2015 before declining in 2016. Meanwhile, residential investment dropped significantly after 2006. By 2016, even though residential investment increased steadily from 2011, investment was still below the 2006 totals. (Table 5-4)

Table 5-4. Chain-Type Quantity Indexes for Private Fixed Investment by Type

(Index numbers, 2009 = 100, quarterly data are seasonally adjusted.) NIPA Table 5.3.3

Year and quarter	Total gross private fixed investment	Nonresidential Total	Structures Total	Structures Commercial and health care	Structures Manufacturing	Structures Power and communication	Structures Mining exploration, shafts, and wells	Structures Other non-residential structures	Equipment Total	Information processing equipment Total	Computers and peripheral equipment[1]	Other information processing	Industrial equipment
1955	16.4	10.4	40.7	29.5	42.7	29.9	84.6	43.9	8.7	0.2	. . .	2.8	37.0
1956	16.6	11.1	45.0	33.3	56.1	35.0	81.8	43.4	8.9	0.3	. . .	3.2	40.8
1957	16.5	11.3	45.0	31.6	59.5	36.3	77.2	43.4	9.1	0.3	. . .	3.7	41.3
1958	15.5	10.3	42.5	33.3	41.0	34.9	72.2	45.4	7.8	0.3	. . .	3.3	34.4
1959	17.6	11.1	43.5	36.1	36.6	33.5	74.1	50.2	8.7	0.3	0.0	3.6	35.0
1960	17.8	11.7	47.0	38.4	49.6	33.8	69.6	55.7	9.1	0.4	0.0	4.1	37.7
1961	17.9	11.8	47.6	43.8	48.5	31.6	70.9	54.4	8.9	0.4	0.0	4.4	35.7
1962	19.4	12.7	49.8	48.9	49.0	31.8	74.3	55.6	9.9	0.5	0.0	4.6	37.5
1963	20.9	13.5	50.4	47.3	49.2	34.0	69.8	58.8	10.7	0.5	0.0	4.8	40.5
1964	22.8	14.9	55.6	51.4	59.1	37.0	74.8	64.4	12.0	0.6	0.0	5.3	45.8
1965	25.2	17.4	64.5	60.3	81.7	40.9	73.8	72.5	14.2	0.7	0.0	6.0	54.0
1966	26.8	19.6	68.9	58.9	101.6	46.7	70.0	75.2	16.4	0.9	0.0	7.0	62.1
1967	26.5	19.5	67.2	56.6	89.4	51.1	66.9	73.6	16.2	1.0	0.0	7.0	62.4
1968	28.4	20.4	68.1	61.9	86.0	56.7	67.3	65.0	17.2	1.0	0.0	7.2	61.1
1969	30.0	21.8	71.8	71.5	90.5	56.7	70.1	64.5	18.6	1.2	0.0	8.4	65.2
1970	29.4	21.7	72.0	72.4	87.4	62.1	66.0	60.6	18.3	1.4	0.0	9.0	66.1
1971	31.4	21.6	70.8	79.1	72.1	62.6	61.1	56.8	18.4	1.4	0.0	9.1	60.7
1972	35.0	23.5	73.0	86.4	63.0	65.3	65.5	57.5	20.8	1.6	0.0	9.7	65.5
1973	38.0	26.6	79.0	90.3	78.1	69.4	69.9	61.9	24.6	2.0	0.0	11.7	77.4
1974	35.9	26.9	77.3	84.7	89.0	65.0	83.1	56.6	25.2	2.2	0.0	13.0	83.3
1975	32.4	24.4	69.2	66.0	85.3	59.9	97.1	49.9	22.5	2.2	0.0	12.5	70.7
1976	35.6	25.8	70.8	65.1	78.8	65.3	104.8	52.4	23.9	2.5	0.0	13.7	71.0
1977	40.4	28.6	73.7	68.5	80.9	64.3	118.3	55.3	27.6	3.1	0.1	16.4	75.3
1978	45.1	32.6	84.4	78.1	107.9	67.4	134.9	62.8	31.8	4.0	0.1	19.6	83.7
1979	47.7	35.8	95.1	93.1	132.6	70.0	143.7	69.0	34.4	4.9	0.2	22.0	89.7
1980	44.9	35.8	100.7	102.4	110.9	70.6	201.9	67.0	32.9	5.7	0.3	23.7	85.9
1981	46.1	38.0	108.7	110.8	125.9	72.4	234.7	64.9	34.1	6.6	0.4	25.0	84.5
1982	43.0	36.6	106.9	120.7	121.6	68.4	217.0	61.2	31.5	6.6	0.4	25.2	77.2
1983	46.2	36.5	95.4	117.1	87.9	58.8	179.6	64.6	33.0	7.7	0.6	26.5	71.1
1984	53.7	42.6	108.7	142.6	91.0	60.1	204.2	75.7	39.4	9.8	1.0	30.1	81.3
1985	56.6	45.4	116.4	164.6	101.8	59.4	182.0	83.3	41.5	10.7	1.2	31.1	85.1
1986	57.7	44.6	103.7	152.9	85.5	63.4	106.6	78.3	42.0	11.5	1.4	32.4	84.7
1987	58.0	44.6	100.7	147.4	83.3	56.4	104.2	82.9	42.1	12.0	1.8	31.1	82.6
1988	59.9	46.9	101.3	151.8	87.9	53.2	114.3	77.3	44.9	13.1	2.0	33.2	86.7
1989	61.8	49.5	103.3	149.8	105.4	55.3	103.4	78.9	47.3	14.4	2.5	34.7	92.8
1990	61.0	50.1	104.9	143.9	119.3	51.4	119.5	83.8	46.3	14.6	2.5	35.6	87.4
1991	57.8	48.1	93.2	111.8	109.9	61.1	116.8	72.7	44.2	14.9	2.7	35.4	81.8
1992	61.0	49.5	87.6	103.9	100.9	64.7	96.7	67.4	46.8	17.0	3.7	37.5	83.3
1993	65.7	53.2	87.3	108.1	79.3	61.7	112.4	72.7	52.8	19.4	4.7	40.4	90.4
1994	71.0	57.4	88.9	113.1	93.8	56.0	109.2	71.1	59.2	22.0	5.8	44.2	98.4
1995	75.4	63.0	94.6	119.8	110.6	57.1	92.7	79.6	66.4	26.5	8.8	47.5	108.0
1996	82.1	68.7	100.0	129.1	116.3	49.1	98.8	93.6	72.7	32.1	12.7	52.1	112.0
1997	89.1	76.1	107.3	142.6	111.1	47.4	116.2	106.2	80.8	38.7	18.4	56.6	114.5
1998	98.2	84.3	112.8	151.5	114.8	55.6	101.6	112.0	91.4	47.8	26.7	63.7	119.4
1999	106.9	92.4	112.9	157.0	95.8	65.6	86.0	112.1	102.8	58.4	38.0	71.0	120.2
2000	114.3	100.9	121.7	167.6	98.8	75.7	107.4	115.4	112.8	70.4	46.1	85.4	130.6
2001	112.6	98.5	119.9	159.4	96.0	78.0	126.6	110.1	108.0	69.6	47.2	82.8	120.9
2002	108.7	91.7	98.7	135.0	56.1	76.1	92.6	93.0	102.1	66.3	49.5	75.3	112.8
2003	113.0	93.4	94.9	126.5	51.9	70.1	105.8	89.5	105.4	72.5	54.4	82.2	113.3
2004	120.6	98.3	94.5	129.6	53.5	58.6	112.3	90.8	113.5	79.9	61.0	89.7	111.2
2005	128.9	105.1	96.1	128.5	60.8	60.7	122.9	86.0	124.4	86.8	67.9	96.3	120.7
2006	131.4	112.6	103.0	136.3	64.8	64.4	132.7	94.3	135.2	98.0	83.8	104.6	130.9
2007	128.8	119.3	116.2	149.9	76.6	89.7	130.6	108.6	139.4	109.3	94.7	115.9	135.0
2008	120.1	118.4	123.3	144.3	95.6	98.6	140.1	122.4	129.8	109.7	100.4	113.9	128.5
2009	100.0	100.0	100.0	100.0	100.0	100.0	100.0	100.0	100.0	100.0	100.0	100.0	100.0
2010	101.5	102.5	83.6	75.1	72.5	83.9	117.1	73.3	115.9	109.9	110.3	109.8	99.5
2011	107.9	110.3	85.5	74.7	69.5	77.3	147.9	66.5	131.6	111.6	108.1	113.1	120.5
2012	118.5	120.2	96.6	81.1	79.7	93.6	165.2	72.8	145.8	118.3	115.2	119.6	131.4
2013	124.5	124.5	97.9	84.0	83.0	89.4	168.1	75.9	152.5	124.1	115.2	127.6	129.3
2014	132.2	133.0	108.2	94.8	93.8	102.8	179.0	81.3	162.6	128.7	117.5	133.2	134.8
2015	137.4	136.1	106.2	104.9	125.6	99.4	127.9	89.8	168.3	134.3	113.4	142.9	136.3
2016	138.4	135.3	101.9	120.2	117.5	103.9	72.7	96.5	162.6	136.8	109.4	148.1	139.5
2014													
1st quarter	128.3	129.3	105.8	88.7	84.1	117.9	166.8	77.2	157.2	125.1	113.3	129.8	131.0
2nd quarter	131.5	132.3	108.9	93.6	86.5	109.8	182.0	80.4	161.3	129.9	119.1	134.2	135.4
3rd quarter	134.4	135.6	108.4	96.7	93.7	98.9	182.8	81.0	168.5	128.6	118.0	132.9	139.4
4th quarter	134.5	134.8	109.6	100.4	111.0	84.9	184.3	86.6	163.3	131.3	119.7	136.0	133.5
2015													
1st quarter	135.8	135.6	109.1	100.5	123.7	92.5	164.4	85.4	166.6	130.8	112.7	138.2	133.5
2nd quarter	137.4	136.6	110.3	107.3	131.0	106.7	132.7	91.4	166.9	132.2	113.7	139.8	136.9
3rd quarter	138.6	137.1	105.8	105.7	126.6	103.8	115.2	93.1	170.9	136.7	117.0	144.8	136.2
4th quarter	137.7	135.3	99.6	106.1	121.0	94.5	99.4	89.5	168.9	137.5	110.3	148.8	138.6
2016													
1st quarter	137.6	133.9	100.2	112.7	120.4	98.3	84.8	92.3	163.1	134.2	109.0	144.6	136.8
2nd quarter	138.1	135.0	100.3	116.4	118.4	103.7	68.6	97.4	162.8	135.8	110.0	146.6	139.2
3rd quarter	138.6	136.2	103.7	124.5	120.2	107.5	68.6	97.8	161.9	138.0	109.7	149.8	140.0
4th quarter	139.2	136.2	103.2	127.2	111.1	106.3	68.7	98.3	162.6	139.0	108.8	151.5	141.9

[1]See notes and definitions.
. . . = Not available.

Table 5-4. Chain-Type Quantity Indexes for Private Fixed Investment by Type—*Continued*

(Index numbers, 2009 = 100, quarterly data are seasonally adjusted.)

NIPA Table 5.3.3

Year and quarter	Equipment—*Continued*		Intellectual property				Residential							Residential equipment
	Transportation equipment	Other nonresidential equipment	Total	Software[2]	Research and development[3]	Entertainment, literary, and artistic originals	Total	Residential structures					Other residential structures	
								Total	Permanent site				
									Total	Single family	Multifamily		
1955	54.1	26.3	2.9	...	6.2	17.1	53.1	55.0	123.1	...	...	20.2	8.9
1956	48.6	27.1	3.4	...	7.9	16.8	48.9	50.5	106.6	...	...	21.6	9.9
1957	52.0	25.7	3.5	...	8.0	18.0	46.0	47.4	96.9	...	...	21.9	9.9
1958	37.9	26.0	3.6	...	8.5	18.4	46.5	47.9	99.4	103.2	77.8	21.4	10.5
1959	50.2	28.0	4.0	0.0	9.2	20.3	58.1	60.0	126.6	131.3	100.0	25.8	12.1
1960	51.8	25.7	4.2	0.0	10.1	18.9	54.2	55.9	111.8	116.1	88.0	26.9	11.3
1961	48.9	25.4	4.7	0.0	10.7	22.8	54.4	56.1	111.2	110.0	110.9	27.5	11.4
1962	60.3	27.1	4.9	0.1	11.6	21.9	59.6	61.5	126.8	117.3	161.3	27.9	12.0
1963	58.4	31.5	5.4	0.1	12.5	23.5	66.6	68.8	143.9	125.3	216.5	30.1	13.4
1964	66.1	34.9	5.6	0.2	13.4	22.3	70.6	72.9	153.6	137.4	215.0	31.4	14.4
1965	82.8	38.8	6.3	0.2	15.0	24.8	68.8	70.8	146.9	134.3	193.3	31.6	16.1
1966	91.0	43.6	7.2	0.3	16.8	27.0	63.0	64.7	128.9	119.6	162.0	31.5	16.5
1967	88.0	41.2	7.7	0.4	18.5	26.8	61.4	63.0	122.8	117.2	140.7	31.9	16.9
1968	105.8	41.7	8.3	0.4	20.0	28.1	69.7	71.4	144.3	128.9	203.3	33.7	20.1
1969	110.0	44.5	8.8	0.6	21.3	26.5	71.9	73.5	148.5	122.3	252.9	34.7	22.9
1970	90.3	46.5	8.8	0.7	21.4	23.2	68.1	69.4	134.3	106.3	247.6	35.6	25.0
1971	97.5	46.3	8.8	0.7	21.4	22.9	86.2	88.2	181.0	147.6	315.1	40.3	28.0
1972	113.3	52.5	9.4	0.9	22.4	24.6	101.2	103.4	219.0	175.4	394.5	44.1	33.6
1973	136.2	61.3	9.9	1.0	23.9	23.6	100.6	102.5	218.0	171.6	405.6	43.2	37.8
1974	123.3	60.6	10.2	1.2	24.0	23.9	80.8	81.9	157.7	131.7	261.1	42.6	38.5
1975	106.2	56.1	10.2	1.4	23.6	23.1	71.1	71.9	120.7	120.2	116.5	46.0	35.8
1976	118.1	56.5	11.4	1.5	25.1	29.4	86.8	88.1	158.7	167.4	112.8	51.2	37.7
1977	143.6	63.6	12.1	1.5	26.4	32.8	104.6	106.4	204.8	215.1	149.6	55.5	41.3
1978	158.7	70.1	13.0	1.8	28.5	32.2	111.6	113.5	214.2	222.2	168.5	61.3	44.9
1979	165.6	71.4	14.5	2.3	30.6	37.0	107.4	108.9	200.4	196.9	205.8	61.4	49.2
1980	135.2	64.2	15.2	2.7	32.7	33.5	84.9	85.7	140.8	129.4	184.3	56.5	49.2
1981	131.5	65.9	16.9	3.1	34.8	40.5	77.9	78.4	129.9	117.8	177.2	51.3	49.2
1982	116.5	57.0	17.9	3.6	36.6	40.8	63.8	63.9	101.2	90.3	144.5	44.1	47.2
1983	131.2	55.0	19.3	4.3	38.6	43.0	90.6	91.4	165.4	156.8	197.8	52.8	52.7
1984	156.3	62.3	22.0	5.4	42.6	47.9	104.0	105.0	194.3	181.9	241.7	58.6	58.5
1985	162.4	62.8	23.9	6.4	46.3	47.7	106.4	107.2	191.8	180.4	235.5	63.1	63.1
1986	156.2	61.7	25.6	7.2	48.2	52.7	119.6	120.6	214.1	206.5	242.5	71.8	68.2
1987	148.5	63.4	26.6	8.2	49.1	51.8	121.9	123.0	217.0	223.1	191.3	73.7	71.0
1988	157.2	66.5	28.5	9.7	51.1	52.3	120.8	121.7	209.2	220.4	163.2	75.7	73.4
1989	141.8	74.2	31.8	12.5	54.4	54.7	116.9	117.7	204.0	214.0	162.8	72.4	73.8
1990	139.9	71.4	34.5	14.8	57.3	56.6	107.0	107.5	184.3	194.5	142.1	67.1	71.6
1991	136.0	61.0	36.7	16.7	59.9	57.2	97.5	97.8	158.6	170.5	109.5	65.3	68.8
1992	139.1	60.7	38.9	19.7	60.0	60.0	110.9	111.6	185.0	207.0	93.0	72.6	70.9
1993	165.8	66.5	40.6	22.0	59.7	63.3	120.0	120.9	197.5	226.7	75.0	80.0	72.3
1994	194.3	71.8	42.2	24.2	59.7	66.6	130.7	131.9	221.1	250.9	96.9	84.7	72.8
1995	209.0	75.7	45.3	26.6	62.7	72.1	126.3	127.3	206.5	227.8	120.1	85.1	73.8
1996	215.9	78.6	50.4	31.2	68.2	77.3	136.6	138.0	225.9	248.8	132.8	91.1	73.4
1997	231.5	86.2	57.0	40.4	72.1	79.6	139.9	141.4	227.1	248.0	143.1	95.5	72.8
1998	250.3	95.0	63.1	48.8	75.7	83.4	152.0	153.6	248.7	275.1	141.5	102.8	77.9
1999	295.3	97.5	71.0	60.2	80.3	85.9	161.6	163.2	267.2	295.4	152.7	107.7	86.1
2000	289.3	102.9	77.3	68.5	84.3	91.0	162.6	164.1	269.3	298.7	150.1	108.0	91.6
2001	262.1	102.2	77.7	69.0	85.4	88.2	164.1	165.6	270.9	299.1	156.6	109.4	93.3
2002	237.0	101.4	77.3	68.9	83.2	92.6	174.0	175.7	281.8	310.7	164.9	118.9	96.1
2003	219.4	108.3	80.3	73.6	82.6	99.6	189.8	191.7	309.4	343.8	169.2	128.7	102.0
2004	250.1	116.2	84.4	81.0	83.4	101.1	208.8	210.8	345.2	385.1	182.4	139.0	113.7
2005	280.5	127.4	89.8	86.1	88.3	109.5	222.5	224.7	369.6	411.1	200.6	147.3	118.7
2006	301.3	132.6	93.9	89.7	93.9	110.7	205.6	207.4	337.3	370.9	201.9	138.1	121.0
2007	288.5	131.0	98.4	95.1	99.5	108.0	166.9	168.0	251.1	269.3	178.8	123.7	117.5
2008	222.3	124.7	101.4	99.8	102.8	103.0	126.9	127.2	166.7	169.2	157.2	106.2	111.3
2009	100.0	100.0	100.0	100.0	100.0	100.0	100.0	100.0	100.0	100.0	100.0	100.0	100.0
2010	194.0	108.6	101.9	99.0	102.4	111.6	97.5	97.3	96.0	108.6	50.2	98.0	106.0
2011	259.4	120.4	105.5	105.8	103.3	112.3	98.0	97.8	92.6	103.6	52.4	100.5	111.0
2012	310.2	133.9	109.6	111.6	106.0	114.9	111.3	111.2	114.9	125.4	76.9	109.3	112.6
2013	344.3	139.2	113.4	115.1	110.9	115.4	124.5	124.5	143.1	153.7	104.4	114.8	121.7
2014	384.5	149.1	118.5	124.1	113.8	114.6	128.8	128.7	155.6	162.2	132.4	114.6	131.4
2015	424.5	145.2	123.0	131.1	115.4	120.9	142.0	142.0	174.1	180.8	150.3	125.0	141.8
2016	393.3	131.0	130.8	140.4	122.9	123.4	149.8	149.7	184.0	189.8	163.8	131.6	151.9
2014													
1st quarter	365.9	145.1	115.8	119.6	112.2	114.1	124.3	124.3	149.5	157.4	121.1	111.0	125.3
2nd quarter	379.2	144.3	117.2	123.2	111.9	113.7	128.2	128.2	155.0	161.5	132.1	114.0	131.2
3rd quarter	404.1	159.0	119.4	126.4	113.5	114.3	129.6	129.6	155.1	160.6	136.1	116.1	132.9
4th quarter	388.9	147.9	121.8	127.3	117.5	116.4	133.0	133.0	162.9	169.5	140.2	117.1	136.4
2015													
1st quarter	419.5	148.0	120.9	129.2	113.1	118.5	136.7	136.6	167.5	174.3	143.6	120.3	138.2
2nd quarter	415.6	145.8	122.4	130.5	114.7	120.2	140.5	140.5	170.5	177.5	145.9	124.7	140.9
3rd quarter	438.9	145.8	123.2	131.3	115.4	122.0	144.1	144.1	177.2	183.9	153.6	126.6	142.9
4th quarter	423.9	141.3	125.6	133.5	118.4	122.7	146.7	146.7	181.0	187.6	158.0	128.5	145.3
2016													
1st quarter	400.7	135.3	127.6	136.5	119.8	122.5	151.4	151.4	187.1	193.8	163.5	132.5	148.8
2nd quarter	401.6	129.7	131.0	139.9	124.2	121.7	149.5	149.5	184.5	190.8	162.1	131.0	150.0
3rd quarter	387.2	129.0	132.3	142.1	124.5	124.1	147.8	147.7	179.6	184.1	163.8	130.9	152.8
4th quarter	383.8	130.0	132.2	142.9	123.2	125.4	150.4	150.3	184.9	190.2	165.9	132.0	156.0

[2]Excludes software "embedded," or bundled, in computers and other equipment.
[3]Excludes software development.
. . . = Not available.

Table 5-5A. Current-Cost Net Stock of Fixed Assets: Recent Data

(Billions of dollars, year-end estimates.)

Year	Total	Private						Government							
		Total	Nonresidential				Residential	Total	Nonresidential				Residential	Federal	State and local
			Total	Equipment	Structures	Intellectual property products			Total	Equipment	Structures	Intellectual property products			
1950	871.9	655.2	335.4	98.8	223.7	12.8	319.9	216.7	210.4	39.1	163.5	7.7	6.4	107.5	109.2
1951	957.7	713.3	365.7	109.1	243.0	13.6	347.6	244.4	236.5	43.0	184.8	8.8	7.9	120.0	122.9
1952	1 012.5	751.3	385.8	114.9	256.3	14.6	365.6	261.2	253.8	49.4	194.7	9.6	7.4	127.0	130.2
1953	1 051.6	782.7	403.2	124.4	262.6	16.2	379.5	268.9	261.0	56.3	194.2	10.5	7.8	135.1	128.8
1954	1 099.4	814.7	414.5	128.2	268.6	17.7	400.2	284.8	274.3	62.9	199.7	11.6	10.5	138.7	134.5
1955	1 196.3	888.2	456.6	141.2	295.8	19.6	431.7	308.1	300.5	68.3	218.9	13.3	7.6	148.1	149.4
1956	1 301.0	957.9	505.0	158.6	324.4	22.1	452.9	343.1	334.2	72.4	245.9	15.9	8.9	159.1	169.4
1957	1 368.6	1 008.3	540.1	172.9	342.8	24.4	468.2	360.3	350.9	74.7	257.2	19.0	9.4	168.5	177.6
1958	1 414.8	1 033.4	550.9	178.0	346.4	26.4	482.6	381.4	371.2	76.2	272.9	22.1	10.2	172.6	189.7
1959	1 471.3	1 077.5	573.5	186.6	357.9	29.0	504.0	393.8	382.7	80.5	277.2	24.9	11.1	180.2	196.0
1960	1 521.4	1 110.5	586.4	192.7	362.6	31.2	524.0	410.9	399.2	83.5	287.6	28.1	11.7	185.4	205.5
1961	1 581.3	1 147.1	603.9	196.1	374.1	33.7	543.3	434.2	421.6	87.5	302.6	31.5	12.5	188.4	217.9
1962	1 653.5	1 189.9	626.3	203.7	386.8	35.9	563.5	463.6	450.2	94.5	320.4	35.3	13.4	194.7	233.3
1963	1 717.0	1 228.2	650.2	212.3	399.0	38.9	578.1	488.7	475.0	96.6	337.8	40.6	13.7	204.8	248.7
1964	1 829.9	1 313.4	688.9	224.9	422.1	41.9	624.6	516.5	501.9	98.7	356.9	46.3	14.6	215.4	265.4
1965	1 953.8	1 402.4	738.4	242.5	450.1	45.8	664.0	551.4	536.1	100.4	383.6	52.2	15.3	227.9	288.9
1966	2 119.4	1 521.6	803.8	270.0	483.3	50.5	717.7	597.8	581.4	104.1	418.2	59.1	16.4	249.5	319.2
1967	2 284.0	1 636.0	870.7	296.2	518.2	56.3	765.3	648.0	630.7	109.9	454.3	66.6	17.3	271.9	348.8
1968	2 510.4	1 804.2	957.4	326.5	568.1	62.8	846.8	706.2	686.8	113.8	498.0	75.1	19.4	302.1	387.3
1969	2 742.0	1 962.3	1 055.3	360.1	624.7	70.5	907.0	779.7	758.1	117.4	555.9	84.8	21.6	329.7	437.4
1970	2 988.6	2 120.4	1 161.1	394.7	688.8	77.5	959.3	868.3	845.2	123.0	627.6	94.6	23.0	354.3	499.0
1971	3 293.2	2 352.1	1 274.6	422.5	769.6	82.5	1 077.5	941.1	915.3	124.0	688.7	102.6	25.8	377.9	550.1
1972	3 619.0	2 593.3	1 385.1	455.1	841.3	88.7	1 208.1	1 025.7	996.8	126.4	759.6	110.8	28.9	409.5	603.3
1973	4 102.1	2 946.4	1 560.1	507.1	954.6	98.4	1 386.3	1 155.7	1 123.0	130.5	868.9	123.6	32.7	454.0	692.2
1974	4 876.0	3 467.8	1 893.4	625.5	1 156.0	111.9	1 574.4	1 408.1	1 371.6	143.7	1 089.2	138.7	36.6	525.7	876.5
1975	5 267.8	3 785.6	2 083.1	716.2	1 245.4	121.5	1 702.5	1 482.3	1 442.2	157.4	1 135.4	149.5	40.1	578.0	918.2
1976	5 738.0	4 168.4	2 279.9	792.5	1 354.4	132.9	1 888.6	1 569.5	1 524.8	170.9	1 193.3	160.6	44.7	635.5	959.4
1977	6 408.3	4 735.4	2 532.4	891.6	1 494.9	145.8	2 203.0	1 672.9	1 621.5	188.2	1 259.4	173.8	51.5	705.1	1 026.0
1978	7 241.3	5 412.2	2 869.9	1 018.0	1 688.7	163.2	2 542.3	1 829.1	1 769.6	200.6	1 378.7	190.3	59.5	795.1	1 129.3
1979	8 343.6	6 264.0	3 313.6	1 181.9	1 944.9	186.8	2 950.3	2 079.7	2 008.9	216.5	1 579.4	213.0	70.8	895.7	1 299.2
1980	9 494.9	7 117.3	3 799.9	1 369.9	2 216.2	213.8	3 317.4	2 377.6	2 299.9	241.7	1 817.7	240.5	77.7	990.9	1 508.0
1981	10 476.9	7 859.9	4 299.9	1 528.4	2 526.5	244.9	3 560.0	2 617.0	2 531.9	271.0	1 991.3	269.6	85.1	1 060.8	1 671.8
1982	11 065.2	8 296.6	4 588.8	1 619.9	2 694.8	274.1	3 707.8	2 768.6	2 678.4	294.0	2 091.3	293.1	90.2	1 102.4	1 764.8
1983	11 448.5	8 599.0	4 744.4	1 670.5	2 769.8	304.1	3 854.6	2 849.6	2 748.8	322.1	2 110.4	316.4	100.7	1 175.0	1 788.5
1984	12 081.7	9 111.9	5 040.7	1 758.8	2 943.4	338.5	4 071.2	2 969.8	2 865.3	343.2	2 182.1	340.1	104.4	1 269.6	1 850.4
1985	12 723.9	9 618.4	5 332.1	1 858.0	3 101.5	372.6	4 286.3	3 105.5	2 999.9	362.3	2 273.9	363.6	105.6	1 377.0	1 935.4
1986	13 524.6	10 230.1	5 603.4	1 964.7	3 232.2	406.4	4 626.7	3 294.6	3 185.0	388.6	2 412.1	384.3	109.5	1 522.3	2 063.4
1987	14 320.6	10 842.8	5 918.7	2 055.3	3 414.7	448.7	4 924.0	3 477.8	3 358.4	410.7	2 532.9	414.8	119.4	1 652.7	2 185.0
1988	15 201.4	11 535.3	6 310.7	2 178.0	3 641.4	491.3	5 224.6	3 666.1	3 531.1	442.2	2 642.1	446.7	135.0	1 800.3	2 289.8
1989	16 067.4	12 201.9	6 699.1	2 300.6	3 858.4	540.1	5 502.9	3 865.4	3 721.3	476.3	2 772.8	472.2	144.2	1 925.7	2 415.0
1990	16 828.8	12 772.0	7 070.0	2 423.7	4 055.0	591.4	5 702.0	4 056.8	3 907.9	514.1	2 897.4	496.4	148.9	2 039.1	2 541.3
1991	17 252.2	13 056.3	7 240.3	2 482.2	4 116.3	641.7	5 816.0	4 195.9	4 046.0	545.4	2 985.0	515.6	150.0	2 117.4	2 621.0
1992	17 978.9	13 607.2	7 485.7	2 544.4	4 253.0	688.3	6 121.5	4 371.7	4 212.9	571.1	3 110.0	531.8	158.8	2 193.4	2 738.9
1993	18 883.3	14 319.9	7 836.6	2 642.4	4 462.6	731.5	6 483.3	4 563.4	4 393.3	594.2	3 254.9	544.3	170.0	2 302.2	2 879.2
1994	20 010.7	15 198.9	8 269.5	2 785.0	4 701.0	783.6	6 929.4	4 811.8	4 630.4	622.2	3 445.5	562.6	181.5	2 424.1	3 060.5
1995	20 980.1	15 945.2	8 717.6	2 959.2	4 917.2	841.2	7 227.6	5 034.9	4 846.8	630.0	3 639.8	577.0	188.1	2 529.3	3 240.8
1996	21 976.9	16 758.6	9 143.6	3 104.0	5 139.3	900.2	7 615.0	5 218.3	5 021.9	629.7	3 808.0	584.1	196.4	2 627.9	3 394.8
1997	23 119.4	17 692.7	9 664.1	3 235.2	5 449.2	979.7	8 028.6	5 426.7	5 229.9	622.1	4 011.7	596.1	196.8	2 718.0	3 576.6
1998	24 411.0	18 761.2	10 213.0	3 384.7	5 762.9	1 065.4	8 548.2	5 649.9	5 443.0	626.3	4 206.6	610.1	206.8	2 833.8	3 766.5
1999	25 974.3	20 010.2	10 833.0	3 578.7	6 067.1	1 187.2	9 177.2	5 964.1	5 744.2	644.1	4 468.6	631.4	219.9	2 991.1	4 020.3
2000	27 695.3	21 397.7	11 588.0	3 805.5	6 471.4	1 311.1	9 809.7	6 297.7	6 066.0	645.5	4 767.3	653.2	231.7	3 201.8	4 309.9
2001	29 244.4	22 679.7	12 163.2	3 912.3	6 884.4	1 366.5	10 516.5	6 564.7	6 318.2	642.0	5 011.0	665.2	246.5	3 364.3	4 553.5
2002	30 682.8	23 824.8	12 603.0	3 968.7	7 220.0	1 414.3	11 221.9	6 857.9	6 597.8	655.1	5 257.3	685.4	260.1	3 527.5	4 798.5
2003	32 367.4	25 212.6	13 052.3	4 040.8	7 522.7	1 488.7	12 160.3	7 154.8	6 876.2	671.5	5 480.9	723.8	278.6	3 679.2	5 024.4
2004	35 681.5	27 741.6	14 158.6	4 257.2	8 343.9	1 557.5	13 583.1	7 939.9	7 633.8	701.6	6 170.2	762.0	306.1	3 899.5	5 662.8
2005	39 294.7	30 609.2	15 461.0	4 481.8	9 320.4	1 658.8	15 148.3	8 685.5	8 350.4	727.7	6 818.2	804.5	335.1	4 107.8	6 259.0
2006	42 506.5	32 918.8	16 729.9	4 784.0	10 187.1	1 758.8	16 188.9	9 587.8	9 238.9	763.4	7 632.9	842.6	348.9	4 300.5	7 008.0
2007	44 400.8	34 066.4	17 667.0	5 020.9	10 770.8	1 875.3	16 399.4	10 334.4	9 988.5	798.1	8 294.2	896.2	345.9	4 476.0	7 623.1
2008	45 856.4	34 833.9	18 748.7	5 267.6	11 511.8	1 969.4	16 085.2	11 022.5	10 686.6	852.6	8 897.2	936.8	335.9	4 578.6	8 193.3
2009	44 944.9	33 859.9	18 151.4	5 182.7	10 943.7	2 025.0	15 708.5	11 085.1	10 756.6	890.6	8 901.2	964.8	328.5	4 588.1	8 243.0
2010	45 859.5	34 344.5	18 561.6	5 268.0	11 188.6	2 105.0	15 782.9	11 515.0	11 182.9	926.3	9 228.0	1 028.5	332.1	4 586.7	8 557.5
2011	47 313.6	35 178.1	19 287.1	5 478.3	11 606.4	2 202.3	15 891.1	12 135.4	11 798.2	957.5	9 781.6	1 059.1	337.2	4 723.3	9 068.6
2012	48 806.0	36 284.0	19 920.5	5 670.6	11 952.4	2 297.4	16 363.6	12 521.9	12 173.9	973.3	10 114.7	1 085.9	348.0	4 848.9	9 384.7
2013	51 154.2	38 226.8	20 693.4	5 895.7	12 376.0	2 421.8	17 533.3	12 927.4	12 553.9	982.1	10 449.5	1 122.4	373.5	4 941.2	9 710.3
2014	53 152.1	39 913.7	21 418.1	6 137.8	12 752.1	2 528.2	18 495.6	13 238.4	12 843.4	995.2	10 711.1	1 137.2	394.9	5 052.9	9 969.0
2015	54 082.8	40 679.1	21 879.4	6 352.1	12 879.2	2 648.0	18 799.8	13 403.6	13 004.3	992.8	10 864.6	1 146.8	399.3	5 236.8	10 135.7

Table 5-5B. Current-Cost Net Stock of Fixed Assets: Historical Data

(Billions of dollars, year-end estimates.)

Year	Total	Private						Government							
		Total	Nonresidential				Resi-dential	Total	Nonresidential				Resi-dential	Federal	State and local
			Total	Equip-ment	Struc-tures	Intellect-ual property products			Total	Equip-ment	Struc-tures	Intellect-ual property products			
1925	260.9	222.9	126.5	31.1	93.5	1.9	96.4	38.1	38.1	2.9	35.1	0.1	0.0	9.2	28.9
1926	270.0	231.1	131.0	32.8	96.2	2.0	100.0	39.0	39.0	2.8	36.0	0.1	0.0	9.0	30.0
1927	276.2	236.4	133.7	33.5	98.1	2.1	102.7	39.8	39.8	2.8	36.9	0.1	0.0	8.7	31.1
1928	288.6	248.1	137.3	34.2	100.9	2.3	110.8	40.5	40.5	2.6	37.7	0.1	0.0	8.3	32.2
1929	291.9	251.2	136.6	34.3	99.9	2.5	114.6	40.7	40.7	2.4	38.1	0.2	0.0	7.9	32.8
1930	278.6	239.0	129.8	32.7	94.7	2.5	109.2	39.6	39.6	2.3	37.1	0.2	0.0	7.5	32.1
1931	241.2	205.1	115.9	29.7	83.7	2.5	89.2	36.1	36.1	2.3	33.6	0.2	0.0	7.0	29.2
1932	223.1	187.3	107.4	26.7	78.3	2.4	79.9	35.8	35.8	2.3	33.2	0.3	0.0	6.9	28.9
1933	238.1	196.1	109.0	26.4	80.2	2.4	87.2	41.9	41.9	2.3	39.2	0.4	0.0	7.8	34.1
1934	244.2	198.3	110.3	26.5	81.3	2.6	87.9	46.0	45.9	2.5	43.0	0.4	0.0	8.8	37.1
1935	248.0	199.2	110.0	25.9	81.3	2.8	89.2	48.8	48.8	2.7	45.6	0.4	0.0	10.0	38.8
1936	274.4	220.1	121.0	27.8	90.1	3.1	99.0	54.3	54.2	2.9	50.8	0.5	0.1	11.6	42.7
1937	288.8	231.4	126.2	29.9	92.8	3.4	105.2	57.4	57.2	3.1	53.6	0.5	0.2	12.8	44.6
1938	291.1	231.6	124.9	29.9	91.3	3.7	106.8	59.4	59.2	3.3	55.4	0.5	0.2	13.5	45.9
1939	297.1	235.3	125.2	30.5	90.7	4.0	110.1	61.8	61.5	3.5	57.5	0.6	0.3	14.2	47.6
1940	321.9	254.1	133.3	32.8	96.1	4.3	120.8	67.8	67.3	3.8	62.8	0.6	0.5	16.0	51.8
1941	367.1	282.4	150.6	37.6	107.8	5.1	131.8	84.6	83.6	7.2	75.5	0.9	1.0	24.5	60.1
1942	419.5	302.0	160.2	38.5	115.6	6.0	141.8	117.6	115.9	20.4	94.2	1.3	1.7	50.2	67.4
1943	467.3	316.7	163.0	38.9	117.2	6.8	153.7	150.6	148.1	44.8	101.0	2.2	2.6	82.1	68.5
1944	501.3	328.9	164.9	38.8	118.6	7.5	164.1	172.3	169.5	64.7	101.3	3.4	2.8	105.5	66.9
1945	543.9	352.6	179.8	44.2	127.6	8.1	172.8	191.3	188.3	74.7	109.3	4.3	3.0	121.8	69.5
1946	637.2	433.5	220.5	53.3	158.1	9.1	212.9	203.7	199.7	69.4	125.2	5.0	4.0	125.9	77.8
1947	734.2	516.1	265.2	65.5	189.1	10.6	250.9	218.1	212.5	60.6	146.4	5.5	5.6	124.9	93.3
1948	780.2	561.6	291.0	80.3	199.4	11.3	270.5	218.7	213.7	50.9	156.7	6.1	5.0	117.2	101.5
1949	785.9	580.6	296.2	84.6	199.9	11.7	284.4	205.4	200.2	43.0	150.4	6.8	5.2	108.4	96.9

Table 5-6A. Chain-Type Quantity Indexes for Net Stock of Fixed Assets: Recent Data

(Index numbers, 2009 = 100.)

Year	Total	Private						Government							
		Total	Nonresidential				Resi-dential	Total	Nonresidential				Resi-dential	Federal	State and local
			Total	Equip-ment	Struc-tures	Intellect-ual property products			Total	Equip-ment	Struc-tures	Intellect-ual property products			
1950	17.8	16.9	15.4	9.3	24.2	3.6	18.9	20.9	21.0	24.6	23.1	4.9	17.1	34.0	15.1
1951	18.5	17.5	15.9	9.9	24.8	3.7	19.7	21.7	21.8	26.4	23.8	5.2	18.4	35.5	15.6
1952	19.2	18.1	16.4	10.3	25.4	3.9	20.4	22.9	23.0	29.6	24.7	5.6	19.9	38.0	16.2
1953	20.0	18.8	17.0	10.8	26.0	4.3	21.2	24.1	24.2	33.0	25.6	6.1	21.2	40.7	16.9
1954	20.7	19.4	17.5	11.2	26.7	4.6	22.0	25.2	25.3	34.8	26.7	6.7	21.8	42.4	17.7
1955	21.6	20.2	18.1	11.7	27.5	4.9	23.0	26.2	26.3	35.5	27.7	7.4	22.2	43.4	18.6
1956	22.4	21.0	18.8	12.2	28.4	5.3	23.8	27.2	27.3	35.9	28.8	8.6	22.8	44.5	19.5
1957	23.2	21.7	19.5	12.8	29.2	5.7	24.6	28.2	28.3	36.4	29.8	10.0	23.9	45.8	20.5
1958	23.9	22.3	20.0	12.9	29.9	6.1	25.4	29.4	29.5	37.0	31.1	11.3	25.9	47.1	21.6
1959	24.8	23.0	20.5	13.2	30.7	6.5	26.4	30.7	30.8	38.6	32.3	12.6	28.0	49.0	22.7
1960	25.6	23.7	21.1	13.6	31.5	6.9	27.3	32.0	32.0	39.7	33.5	14.0	29.6	50.6	23.8
1961	26.5	24.5	21.7	13.9	32.4	7.4	28.2	33.4	33.5	41.4	34.8	15.7	31.6	52.7	25.1
1962	27.5	25.3	22.4	14.4	33.3	7.8	29.2	35.0	35.0	43.2	36.1	17.5	33.8	54.9	26.3
1963	28.5	26.2	23.1	15.0	34.2	8.3	30.4	36.5	36.6	44.2	37.6	20.0	34.9	56.9	27.7
1964	29.7	27.3	24.0	15.7	35.3	8.8	31.6	38.1	38.1	44.9	39.1	22.7	36.1	58.8	29.1
1965	31.0	28.5	25.2	16.9	36.6	9.4	32.8	39.7	39.7	44.9	40.8	25.5	37.4	60.4	30.7
1966	32.4	29.7	26.7	18.3	38.1	10.2	33.8	41.4	41.5	45.5	42.5	28.7	38.8	62.3	32.4
1967	33.6	30.8	27.9	19.5	39.4	10.9	34.7	43.3	43.3	46.5	44.2	31.8	40.4	64.3	34.2
1968	35.0	32.1	29.2	20.7	40.7	11.7	35.8	45.0	45.0	46.5	46.0	34.8	42.0	65.6	36.1
1969	36.3	33.3	30.6	22.1	42.2	12.4	36.9	46.4	46.4	46.1	47.6	37.5	43.9	66.5	37.8
1970	37.4	34.5	31.9	23.2	43.6	13.0	37.9	47.6	47.6	45.5	48.9	39.4	46.0	66.9	39.3
1971	38.6	35.7	32.9	24.2	44.9	13.4	39.4	48.4	48.4	43.6	50.2	40.9	47.9	66.5	40.8
1972	39.9	37.2	34.2	25.4	46.3	13.9	41.1	49.3	49.2	42.0	51.3	42.4	49.5	66.3	42.1
1973	41.3	38.8	35.8	27.3	47.8	14.4	42.8	50.1	50.1	40.8	52.5	43.8	51.1	66.2	43.3
1974	42.5	40.1	37.2	29.0	49.1	14.9	43.9	51.0	51.0	40.6	53.6	44.7	52.5	66.3	44.6
1975	43.4	41.0	38.1	29.9	50.2	15.3	44.8	51.9	51.8	40.6	54.6	45.4	54.3	66.5	45.8
1976	44.5	42.1	39.2	31.0	51.3	15.9	46.0	52.8	52.7	40.8	55.6	46.4	55.7	66.9	46.9
1977	45.8	43.6	40.5	32.6	52.4	16.6	47.7	53.6	53.5	41.1	56.4	47.5	56.9	67.3	47.9
1978	47.4	45.3	42.2	34.6	53.8	17.5	49.5	54.5	54.5	41.4	57.5	48.9	58.0	67.9	49.0
1979	49.0	47.1	44.1	36.9	55.6	18.6	51.1	55.7	55.6	42.1	58.5	50.4	59.1	68.7	50.2
1980	50.4	48.5	45.8	38.5	57.5	19.6	52.1	56.8	56.7	43.1	59.6	51.9	60.4	69.6	51.4
1981	51.7	49.9	47.7	40.0	59.7	21.0	52.9	57.8	57.6	44.3	60.4	53.5	62.0	70.7	52.4
1982	52.7	50.9	49.1	40.8	61.7	22.3	53.3	58.7	58.5	45.8	61.1	55.1	63.4	72.0	53.1
1983	53.8	52.1	50.4	41.6	63.2	23.8	54.5	59.7	59.5	47.9	61.8	56.9	65.2	73.6	53.9
1984	55.4	53.8	52.3	43.3	65.3	25.7	55.9	61.0	60.8	50.8	62.6	59.0	66.6	75.5	54.9
1985	57.2	55.6	54.3	44.9	67.6	27.8	57.3	62.6	62.4	54.5	63.6	61.8	68.5	78.1	56.1
1986	58.9	57.3	56.0	46.2	69.4	29.8	59.1	64.3	64.1	58.7	64.7	64.5	70.4	80.8	57.4
1987	60.5	58.9	57.5	47.2	71.1	31.7	60.9	66.1	65.9	62.9	65.8	67.4	72.4	83.7	58.7
1988	62.1	60.6	59.1	48.4	72.8	33.6	62.5	67.7	67.5	66.1	67.0	69.7	74.2	85.6	60.1
1989	63.7	62.1	60.7	49.8	74.4	36.0	64.0	69.2	68.9	69.4	68.1	71.5	75.8	87.2	61.6
1990	65.2	63.6	62.3	50.7	76.2	38.4	65.3	70.8	70.6	72.8	69.4	73.1	77.6	88.8	63.2
1991	66.3	64.6	63.4	51.3	77.4	40.8	66.2	72.3	72.0	75.3	70.7	74.1	79.1	89.8	64.9
1992	67.4	65.7	64.4	52.0	78.2	43.2	67.4	73.6	73.4	77.3	72.1	74.7	80.8	90.6	66.5
1993	68.8	67.1	65.8	53.5	79.2	45.4	68.8	74.7	74.5	78.1	73.3	75.0	82.2	90.8	68.0
1994	70.2	68.7	67.3	55.6	80.0	47.4	70.5	75.7	75.4	78.3	74.6	75.2	83.4	90.6	69.5
1995	71.8	70.4	69.2	58.2	81.2	49.6	72.0	76.8	76.5	78.4	75.9	75.2	84.8	90.5	71.1
1996	73.7	72.5	71.5	61.2	82.6	52.6	73.8	78.0	77.7	78.5	77.5	75.3	86.3	90.7	72.7
1997	75.7	74.7	74.1	64.6	84.2	56.4	75.6	79.2	78.9	78.1	79.1	75.6	87.8	90.3	74.6
1998	78.0	77.3	77.1	68.6	85.9	60.5	77.7	80.4	80.1	78.2	80.6	76.1	89.1	90.0	76.5
1999	80.4	80.0	80.2	73.1	87.6	65.4	79.9	81.8	81.5	78.8	82.3	76.7	90.4	89.8	78.6
2000	83.0	82.9	83.7	77.9	89.6	70.4	82.1	83.3	83.0	79.1	84.1	77.6	91.5	89.5	80.9
2001	85.1	85.2	86.2	81.1	91.4	74.1	84.2	85.0	84.7	79.6	85.9	78.9	92.7	89.5	83.2
2002	87.1	87.2	87.8	83.1	92.4	76.8	86.6	86.9	86.6	80.9	88.0	80.8	94.0	90.1	85.6
2003	89.1	89.2	89.3	85.1	93.3	79.5	89.2	88.9	88.7	82.3	90.0	83.3	95.3	91.2	88.0
2004	91.3	91.4	90.9	87.7	94.0	82.5	92.1	90.9	90.7	84.3	91.9	86.2	96.4	92.5	90.3
2005	93.4	93.7	92.7	91.1	94.7	85.9	94.9	92.6	92.4	86.5	93.4	89.1	97.4	93.8	92.1
2006	95.8	96.2	95.0	95.2	95.8	89.6	97.6	94.4	94.3	89.4	95.1	92.0	97.8	95.1	94.2
2007	97.8	98.3	97.5	99.2	97.4	93.6	99.3	96.3	96.2	92.5	96.7	94.8	98.5	96.6	96.2
2008	99.4	99.8	99.6	101.4	99.2	97.4	99.9	98.2	98.1	96.6	98.4	97.5	99.2	98.3	98.1
2009	100.0	100.0	100.0	100.0	100.0	100.0	100.0	100.0	100.0	100.0	100.0	100.0	100.0	100.0	100.0
2010	100.7	100.3	100.6	100.5	100.2	102.7	100.0	101.7	101.7	103.2	101.5	102.4	101.6	101.9	101.7
2011	101.5	101.0	101.7	102.6	100.5	105.8	100.1	103.1	103.1	105.0	102.8	104.5	102.6	103.2	103.0
2012	102.5	102.0	103.4	105.8	101.2	109.2	100.3	104.0	104.0	106.3	103.6	105.8	102.9	103.9	104.1
2013	103.6	103.3	105.2	109.3	101.9	112.7	101.1	104.7	104.8	106.7	104.4	106.7	103.0	103.9	105.0
2014	104.9	104.8	107.3	113.0	103.1	116.4	101.8	105.3	105.4	106.8	105.1	107.0	102.8	103.6	105.9
2015	106.4	106.5	109.5	117.1	104.1	120.5	103.0	106.0	106.1	106.8	105.9	107.2	103.0	103.2	107.0

Table 5-6B. Chain-Type Quantity Indexes for Net Stock of Fixed Assets: Historical Data

(Index numbers, 2009 = 100.)

Year	Total	Private						Government							
		Total	Nonresidential				Resi-dential	Total	Nonresidential				Resi-dential	Federal	State and local
			Total	Equip-ment	Struc-tures	Intellect-ual property products			Total	Equip-ment	Struc-tures	Intellect-ual property products			
1925	10.4	12.0	11.2	5.4	19.9	0.8	13.2	5.8	6.0	2.1	8.6	0.10	0.00	4.3	6.7
1926	10.8	12.5	11.5	5.6	20.5	0.8	13.8	6.0	6.2	2.1	9.0	0.12	0.00	4.2	7.1
1927	11.2	12.9	11.8	5.7	21.2	0.9	14.3	6.3	6.5	2.1	9.4	0.13	0.00	4.1	7.5
1928	11.5	13.3	12.2	5.8	21.7	1.0	14.8	6.6	6.8	2.1	9.9	0.14	0.00	4.1	8.0
1929	11.9	13.6	12.6	6.0	22.4	1.1	15.0	7.1	7.3	2.2	10.6	0.15	0.03	4.1	8.7
1930	12.1	13.8	12.8	6.0	22.9	1.2	15.1	7.5	7.7	2.2	11.2	0.20	0.06	4.1	9.3
1931	12.2	13.8	12.7	5.8	23.0	1.2	15.1	7.9	8.1	2.2	11.9	0.26	0.08	4.2	9.9
1932	12.1	13.6	12.5	5.5	22.8	1.3	15.0	8.2	8.5	2.2	12.4	0.33	0.11	4.4	10.4
1933	12.0	13.4	12.2	5.2	22.6	1.3	14.9	8.5	8.7	2.2	12.8	0.39	0.13	4.7	10.6
1934	12.0	13.3	12.1	5.0	22.4	1.4	14.8	8.8	9.0	2.2	13.2	0.42	0.15	5.0	10.0
1935	12.0	13.2	12.0	5.0	22.2	1.5	14.8	9.1	9.4	2.4	13.7	0.45	0.23	5.6	11.1
1936	12.2	13.3	12.1	5.1	22.2	1.6	14.9	9.6	9.9	2.5	14.4	0.49	0.65	6.1	11.6
1937	12.4	13.4	12.2	5.3	22.2	1.8	15.0	10.1	10.3	2.6	15.1	0.52	1.22	6.5	12.0
1938	12.6	13.4	12.2	5.3	22.2	1.9	15.0	10.6	10.8	2.8	15.8	0.56	1.45	7.0	12.6
1939	12.8	13.5	12.3	5.3	22.2	2.0	15.2	11.1	11.4	2.9	16.6	0.60	1.88	7.3	13.2
1940	13.1	13.7	12.4	5.6	22.3	2.2	15.5	11.6	11.9	3.0	17.3	0.65	3.15	7.9	13.7
1941	13.6	14.0	12.7	5.8	22.4	2.4	15.7	13.0	13.2	5.6	18.5	0.88	5.71	11.5	14.0
1942	14.5	14.0	12.6	5.8	22.2	2.6	15.8	16.7	16.9	17.1	20.8	1.21	8.53	22.9	14.0
1943	15.4	13.9	12.5	5.6	22.0	2.6	15.7	21.1	21.4	39.4	21.7	2.13	12.13	37.6	13.9
1944	16.2	13.8	12.5	5.7	21.8	2.7	15.6	24.8	25.2	60.8	21.9	2.51	12.99	50.0	13.7
1945	16.6	13.9	12.7	6.0	21.8	2.8	15.5	26.1	26.5	68.1	22.0	3.12	13.19	54.6	13.6
1946	16.6	14.4	13.2	6.6	22.3	3.0	16.0	24.3	24.6	55.6	21.9	3.54	14.64	48.5	13.6
1947	16.7	15.0	13.8	7.4	22.7	3.2	16.6	22.6	22.9	44.0	21.9	3.82	15.09	42.8	13.8
1948	17.0	15.6	14.4	8.3	23.2	3.4	17.3	21.5	21.7	34.5	22.1	4.16	15.37	38.4	14.1
1949	17.3	16.2	14.8	8.8	23.7	3.5	18.0	21.1	21.3	29.5	22.6	4.51	16.30	36.2	14.5

Table 5-7. Capital Expenditures

(Millions of dollars, except totals are shown in billions.)

Capital expenditures	All companies												
	2003	2004	2005	2006	2007	2008	2009	2010	2011	2012	2013	2014	2015
TOTAL (billions)	975.0	1 042.1	1 144.8	1 309.9	1 354.7	1 374.2	1 090.7	1 105.7	1 243.0	1 424.2	1 491.3	1 597.9	1 638.6
Structures	344 641	368 707	401 653	488 701	525 273	562 381	449 545	428 713	471 779	570 489	581 836	643 590	645 704
New	305 291	324 680	365 938	448 861	480 839	522 999	422 780	394 517	442 745	534 696	549 359	606 980	592 332
Used	39 350	44 028	35 715	39 840	44 434	39 382	26 765	34 196	29 034	35 793	32 477	36 610	53 373
Equipment	630 373	673 353	743 130	821 238	829 455	811 779	641 149	676 989	771 177	853 661	909 477	954 261	992 888
New	579 414	628 591	701 247	777 059	790 407	765 279	606 576	639 214	730 033	800 519	856 012	898 581	934 758
Used	50 960	44 762	41 884	44 179	39 048	46 501	34 572	37 775	41 144	53 142	53 466	55 680	58 130
Not distributed as structures or equipment	0	0	0	0	0	0	0	0	. . .	0	0	0	0
CAPITALIZED COMPUTER SOFTWARE [1]	. . .	. . .	. . .	. . .	. . .	. . .	. . .	. . .	. . .	. . .	. . .	. . .	. . .
Prepackaged	. . .	. . .	. . .	. . .	. . .	. . .	. . .	. . .	. . .	. . .	. . .	. . .	. . .
Vendor-customized	. . .	. . .	. . .	. . .	. . .	. . .	. . .	. . .	. . .	. . .	. . .	. . .	. . .
Internally-developed	. . .	. . .	. . .	. . .	. . .	. . .	. . .	. . .	. . .	. . .	. . .	. . .	. . .
CAPITAL LEASE AND CAPITALIZED INTEREST EXPENSES [1]													
Capital leases	15 641	17 996	18 103	24 442	20 210	20 169	17 410	15 780	20 509	26 087	26 252	31 114	35 362

Capital expenditures	Companies with employees												
	2003	2004	2005	2006	2007	2008	2009	2010	2011	2012	2013	2014	2015
TOTAL (billions)	886.9	953.2	1 062.6	1 217.1	1 270.5	1 294.5	1 015.3	1 036.2	1 169.6	1 334.9	1 400.9	1 506.6	1 544.7
Structures	314 021	335 405	368 791	453 893	490 779	529 393	414 051	395 531	440 893	533 115	546 056	608 698	603 611
New	281 892	300 371	341 223	420 090	457 233	500 474	395 022	366 853	414 958	501 420	518 430	577 743	560 284
Used	32 128	35 034	27 568	33 802	33 546	28 919	19 030	28 678	25 935	31 695	27 625	30 955	43 327
Equipment	572 825	617 766	693 745	763 215	779 744	765 098	601 270	640 631	728 710	801 820	854 827	897 885	941 057
New	540 611	588 110	664 648	734 160	750 353	728 322	577 051	612 441	697 766	759 632	813 972	853 888	893 980
Used	32 214	29 656	29 096	29 055	29 391	36 776	24 219	28 190	30 944	42 189	40 855	43 996	47 077
Not distributed as structures or equipment	0	0	0	0	0	0	. . .	0	0	0	0	0	0
CAPITALIZED COMPUTER SOFTWARE [1]	49 869	49 868	49 149	58 522	63 116	72 241	. . .	63 780	71 068	87 474	89 893	90 023	94 054
Prepackaged	17 307	17 306	17 630	21 181	21 777	26 260	. . .	21 749	23 242	27 868	28 986	27 901	26 904
Vendor-customized	15 554	15 553	13 876	16 912	17 990	19 259	. . .	17 264	20 346	23 507	24 207	23 638	25 531
Internally-developed	17 008	17 008	17 643	20 433	23 350	26 723	. . .	24 768	27 480	36 099	36 701	38 484	41 619
CAPITAL LEASE AND CAPITALIZED INTEREST EXPENSES [1]													
Capital leases	15 137	17 526	17 640	23 923	19 432	19 422	. . .	15 212	20 145	25 301	25 550	30 400	34 581

Capital expenditures	Companies without employees												
	2003	2004	2005	2006	2007	2008	2009	2010	2011	2012	2013	2014	2015
TOTAL (billions)	88.2	88.9	82.2	92.8	84.2	79.7	75.4	69.5	73.4	89.2	90.4	91.3	93.9
Structures	30 621	33 302	32 862	34 809	34 494	32 988	35 493	33 182	30 886	37 374	35 780	34 892	42 093
New	23 399	24 309	24 715	28 771	23 606	22 525	27 758	27 664	27 787	33 276	30 929	29 237	32 048
Used	7 222	8 993	8 146	6 038	10 888	10 463	7 735	5 518	3 099	4 098	4 851	5 655	10 045
Equipment	57 549	55 587	49 386	58 023	49 711	46 681	39 878	36 357	42 467	51 840	54 650	56 376	51 831
New	38 803	40 481	36 598	42 899	40 054	36 957	29 525	26 773	32 267	40 887	42 040	44 693	40 778
Used	18 746	15 106	12 787	15 124	9 657	9 724	10 353	9 585	10 200	10 953	12 610	11 684	11 053
Not distributed as structures or equipment	0	0	0	0	0	0	0	0	0	0	0	0	0
CAPITALIZED COMPUTER SOFTWARE [1]	. . .	. . .	. . .	. . .	. . .	. . .	. . .	. . .	. . .	. . .	. . .	. . .	. . .
Prepackaged	. . .	. . .	. . .	. . .	. . .	. . .	. . .	. . .	. . .	. . .	. . .	. . .	. . .
Vendor-customized	. . .	. . .	. . .	. . .	. . .	. . .	. . .	. . .	. . .	. . .	. . .	. . .	. . .
Internally-developed	. . .	. . .	. . .	. . .	. . .	. . .	. . .	. . .	. . .	. . .	. . .	. . .	. . .
CAPITAL LEASE AND CAPITALIZED INTEREST EXPENSES [1]													
Capital leases	504	469	463	519	778	747	577	568	365	786	702	714	781

[1]Included in structures and equipment data shown above.
. . . = Not available.

Table 5-8. Capital Expenditures for Structures and Equipment for Companies with Employees by Major Industry Sector

(Millions of dollars.)

Year and type of expenditure	Total	Forestry, fishing, and agricultural services (113–115)	Mining (21)	Utilities (22)	Construction (23)	Manufacturing (31–33) Total	Durable goods industries (321, 327, 33)	Nondurable goods industries (31, 322–326)	Wholesale trade (42)	Retail trade (44–45)	Transportation and warehousing (48–49)	Information (51)
1998												
Total expenditures	896 452	854	40 424	36 010	26 867	203 587	117 901	85 685	29 169	57 276	51 287	96 487
Structures, total	300 283	206	26 503	18 574	7 062	39 028	19 406	19 622	7 480	25 105	13 036	24 721
New	260 008	158	24 714	17 771	4 749	37 122	18 449	18 673	6 738	23 104	12 365	24 218
Used	40 275	49	1 789	804	2 313	1 906	957	949	742	2 001	671	503
Equipment, total	596 169	648	13 921	17 436	19 805	164 559	98 496	66 063	21 690	32 171	38 251	71 766
New	570 397	603	12 625	17 266	15 346	159 363	95 571	63 792	20 470	30 359	33 409	70 827
Used	25 773	46	1 296	170	4 458	5 196	2 925	2 271	1 220	1 812	4 842	939
1999												
Total expenditures	974 631	1 716	30 586	42 802	23 110	196 399	117 005	79 394	32 442	64 063	57 299	122 827
Structures, total	293 787	344	17 626	21 241	1 753	33 985	17 020	16 065	7 264	29 494	14 122	34 924
New	276 094	331	17 039	20 784	1 505	32 814	16 581	16 233	6 508	28 670	13 859	33 733
Used	17 693	13	587	457	248	1 171	739	432	756	824	263	1 191
Equipment, total	680 843	1 371	12 960	21 561	21 356	162 414	99 685	62 729	25 179	34 569	43 178	87 903
New	656 344	1 190	12 167	20 545	18 600	157 715	96 434	61 281	23 714	33 567	40 425	85 310
Used	24 499	182	793	1 016	2 756	4 699	3 251	1 448	1 465	1 002	2 752	2 593
2000												
Total expenditures	1 089 862	1 488	42 522	61 302	25 049	214 827	133 786	81 041	33 579	69 791	59 851	160 177
Structures, total	338 120	139	28 620	29 472	2 803	39 434	21 228	18 207	8 923	32 037	13 457	41 502
New	309 541	134	25 500	29 258	2 583	36 643	19 748	16 895	8 364	30 413	13 190	40 062
Used	28 579	5	3 120	214	220	2 791	1 480	1 312	559	1 624	267	1 440
Equipment, total	751 742	1 350	13 902	31 830	22 245	175 393	112 558	62 835	24 656	37 754	46 394	118 675
New	718 227	1 086	12 854	27 937	17 788	169 454	108 703	60 751	23 610	36 428	43 455	117 835
Used	33 515	264	1 048	3 893	4 458	5 939	3 856	2 083	1 046	1 326	2 938	841
2001												
Total expenditures	1 052 344	1 532	51 278	82 823	24 802	192 835	118 875	73 959	29 981	66 917	57 756	144 793
Structures, total	346 221	226	32 678	38 093	3 859	39 815	22 032	17 784	6 932	30 010	16 594	41 742
New	323 871	149	31 825	36 504	3 389	38 001	20 701	17 301	5 357	29 118	14 479	41 384
Used	22 349	77	853	1 588	470	1 814	1 331	483	1 575	892	2 116	358
Equipment, total	706 123	1 306	18 600	44 731	20 943	153 019	96 844	56 176	23 049	36 906	41 161	103 051
New	679 090	1 091	17 567	42 939	17 432	148 397	94 251	54 145	20 757	35 074	38 521	102 410
Used	27 033	215	1 033	1 792	3 511	4 623	2 592	2 030	2 292	1 833	2 640	641
2002												
Total expenditures	917 490	1 910	42 467	65 502	24 773	157 243	84 062	73 181	26 789	59 316	47 124	88 156
Structures, total	325 168	184	30 685	29 893	1 890	32 643	15 133	17 510	5 885	26 286	14 498	33 607
New	299 941	118	29 775	29 008	1 254	31 022	14 396	16 626	5 447	25 051	13 870	33 472
Used	25 227	66	910	886	456	1 622	737	885	438	1 234	628	135
Equipment, total	592 321	1 726	11 783	35 609	23 063	124 600	68 929	55 671	20 904	33 030	32 626	54 550
New	564 218	1 319	10 262	34 816	19 257	118 621	66 112	52 510	18 562	31 157	29 178	54 247
Used	28 103	407	1 520	793	3 806	5 978	2 817	3 161	2 342	1 873	3 447	303
2003												
Total expenditures	886 846	1 894	50 548	54 569	23 159	149 065	80 226	68 839	26 014	65 868	44 460	80 524
Structures, total	314 021	202	36 617	24 841	1 676	31 108	13 330	17 778	5 615	29 675	13 005	30 765
New	281 892	177	35 897	24 580	1 424	29 315	12 631	16 685	4 921	27 393	11 779	30 406
Used	32 128	25	720	261	251	1 793	700	1 093	694	2 282	1 226	358
Equipment, total	572 825	1 692	13 931	29 729	21 484	117 956	66 895	51 061	20 399	36 193	31 454	49 759
New	540 611	1 267	12 135	29 044	16 170	112 102	62 810	49 292	19 457	32 162	26 786	47 857
Used	32 214	425	1 796	685	5 313	5 855	4 086	1 769	942	4 031	4 668	1 902
2004												
Total expenditures	953 171	2 081	51 253	50 409	28 627	156 651	85 119	71 532	32 314	72 170	46 054	83 488
Structures, total	335 405	324	34 564	24 398	4 511	31 823	13 606	18 217	7 133	33 308	13 992	28 636
New	300 371	309	33 583	23 626	4 167	30 016	12 818	17 198	6 555	31 486	13 018	26 253
Used	35 034	15	982	772	345	1 807	788	1 019	578	1 822	975	2 384
Equipment, total	617 766	1 757	16 689	26 011	24 115	124 828	71 513	53 315	25 181	38 862	32 062	54 852
New	588 110	1 507	15 415	25 724	18 939	120 481	68 904	51 576	21 888	36 965	28 472	53 120
Used	29 656	250	1 274	286	5 176	4 347	2 609	1 738	3 293	1 897	3 590	1 732
2005												
Total expenditures	1 062 536	2 702	66 746	58 032	30 072	165 634	92 180	73 455	40 578	73 531	56 926	91 373
Structures, total	368 791	344	46 433	24 186	2 544	34 132	14 735	19 397	9 184	34 119	17 855	31 977
New	341 223	283	45 655	23 485	2 247	32 564	14 033	18 531	8 830	33 360	16 954	31 716
Used	27 568	61	777	701	297	1 569	703	866	355	759	901	262
Equipment, total	693 745	2 358	20 313	33 847	27 528	131 502	77 444	54 058	31 394	39 412	39 072	59 396
New	664 648	2 016	18 495	33 083	22 082	126 387	73 889	52 498	28 224	38 301	34 953	59 071
Used	29 096	341	1 818	764	5 446	5 115	3 555	1 560	3 169	1 111	4 119	325
2006												
Total expenditures	1 217 107	2 672	99 309	69 757	30 257	192 364	106 843	85 521	36 600	86 735	68 021	104 373
Structures, total	453 893	391	68 662	30 587	2 556	41 617	17 515	24 103	10 375	43 188	20 852	31 947
New	420 090	316	67 322	29 294	2 217	39 419	16 243	23 176	9 956	41 985	19 765	31 621
Used	33 802	75	1 340	1 293	338	2 198	1 272	926	419	1 203	1 087	326
Equipment, total	763 215	2 281	30 647	39 170	27 701	150 747	89 328	61 419	26 226	43 547	47 168	72 425
New	734 160	1 846	28 813	37 617	23 276	146 551	86 637	59 914	24 366	41 943	41 258	71 830
Used	29 055	435	1 833	1 553	4 425	4 196	2 692	1 504	1 860	1 604	5 911	595

Table 5-8. Capital Expenditures for Structures and Equipment for Companies with Employees by Major Industry Sector—*Continued*

(Millions of dollars.)

Year and type of expenditure	Finance and insurance (52)	Real estate and rental and leasing (53)	Professional, scientific, and technical services (54)	Management of companies and enterprises (55)	Administrative and support and waste management (56)	Educational services (61)	Health care and social assistance (62)	Arts, entertainment, and recreation (71)	Accommodation and food services (72)	Other services, except public administration (81)	Structure and equipment expenditures serving multiple industries
1998											
Total expenditures	118 173	85 184	22 277	1 821	13 110	12 983	47 109	8 994	20 822	20 627	3 392
Structures, total	27 221	36 775	4 886	753	4 288	9 109	23 971	5 045	12 045	13 737	738
New	16 858	24 109	4 572	502	3 745	8 734	21 328	4 838	10 402	13 280	699
Used	10 362	12 666	314	251	543	374	2 643	206	1 643	457	39
Equipment, total	90 952	48 409	17 390	1 068	8 822	3 874	23 138	3 949	8 777	6 890	2 654
New	90 058	46 877	16 868	1 030	8 346	3 825	22 465	3 752	8 005	6 296	2 609
Used	894	1 532	522	38	476	49	672	197	772	594	46
1999											
Total expenditures	130 101	100 629	29 546	6 065	16 227	13 532	51 342	13 355	23 328	16 902	2 359
Structures, total	20 080	33 903	6 780	1 668	2 875	9 767	25 922	8 119	13 431	9 975	516
New	17 918	30 295	6 168	1 509	2 773	9 140	24 159	7 971	11 391	9 033	495
Used	2 162	3 608	613	159	102	627	1 763	148	2 040	941	21
Equipment, total	110 021	66 726	22 766	4 397	13 353	3 766	25 420	5 236	9 897	6 928	1 843
New	109 577	63 555	22 153	4 319	12 323	3 668	24 945	5 125	9 324	6 370	1 752
Used	444	3 171	613	78	1 029	97	475	111	573	558	91
2000											
Total expenditures	133 684	92 456	34 055	5 054	17 506	18 223	52 166	19 125	26 307	21 125	1 572
Structures, total	23 010	24 815	8 141	1 570	4 032	13 699	26 868	12 245	13 873	13 274	206
New	20 298	17 793	7 470	955	3 504	12 965	23 999	11 627	12 879	11 705	200
Used	2 712	7 022	671	615	528	735	2 869	618	993	1 569	6
Equipment, total	110 675	67 641	25 914	3 484	13 475	4 523	25 299	6 880	12 434	7 852	1 366
New	109 678	62 175	24 847	3 403	12 723	4 338	24 407	6 161	11 501	7 192	1 357
Used	997	5 466	1 067	81	752	186	892	719	933	659	10
2001											
Total expenditures	131 105	82 674	30 464	3 035	15 785	17 377	52 932	14 974	21 365	29 006	911
Structures, total	22 744	20 489	7 258	933	3 527	12 852	27 030	8 998	12 248	20 031	163
New	19 571	17 325	6 793	869	3 367	11 860	25 241	8 157	11 402	18 918	162
Used	3 173	3 164	465	64	160	991	1 789	841	846	1 112	0
Equipment, total	108 361	62 185	23 206	2 102	12 258	4 525	25 902	5 976	9 117	8 976	749
New	107 268	60 295	22 330	2 019	11 644	4 238	24 573	5 590	7 921	8 300	725
Used	1 093	1 891	876	83	613	287	1 329	386	1 196	676	24
2002											
Total expenditures	128 444	94 529	25 864	3 430	14 719	19 532	59 311	13 169	22 409	21 269	1 532
Structures, total	24 308	35 579	7 129	933	3 276	14 655	30 291	7 758	12 157	13 261	250
New	19 748	30 227	6 424	913	2 948	13 601	27 273	7 332	10 848	11 363	248
Used	4 739	5 352	706	21	328	1 055	3 018	425	1 309	1 899	2
Equipment, total	103 956	58 949	18 735	2 497	11 443	4 876	29 021	5 412	10 252	8 007	1 282
New	103 421	56 847	18 021	2 481	10 585	4 690	28 196	5 132	9 290	6 858	1 276
Used	535	2 102	714	16	857	186	825	280	962	1 149	6
2003											
Total expenditures	120 787	87 952	24 703	3 298	16 612	16 667	61 151	11 029	21 036	26 035	1 476
Structures, total	26 200	25 028	5 314	925	3 976	11 984	30 996	6 800	10 568	18 518	209
New	17 908	16 446	4 671	869	3 213	11 569	28 885	6 532	9 417	16 288	202
Used	8 292	8 583	643	56	763	415	2 111	268	1 151	2 230	7
Equipment, total	94 587	62 923	19 389	2 373	12 636	4 683	30 155	4 229	10 468	7 517	1 267
New	94 205	61 253	18 675	2 368	11 374	4 569	29 497	4 038	9 684	6 706	1 263
Used	383	1 671	714	5	1 262	114	658	192	783	811	4
2004											
Total expenditures	153 629	91 606	26 688	2 825	17 455	18 919	64 561	12 165	20 641	19 701	1 572
Structures, total	43 919	27 277	6 007	860	2 567	13 728	32 608	7 360	9 860	12 278	321
New	30 216	21 610	5 714	798	2 309	12 781	30 668	7 196	9 126	10 867	307
Used	13 703	5 667	293	62	259	947	1 939	164	734	1 411	13
Equipment, total	109 710	64 329	20 681	1 965	14 888	5 190	31 953	4 804	10 781	7 423	1 252
New	109 244	61 947	20 081	1 931	12 692	4 965	31 280	4 677	10 373	6 788	1 248
Used	466	2 382	600	34	2 196	225	673	128	408	635	3
2005											
Total expenditures	161 389	103 022	33 066	2 809	18 194	17 484	73 825	14 165	30 718	20 105	2 163
Structures, total	39 383	24 791	8 717	857	3 051	12 711	39 089	9 242	17 679	12 036	460
New	31 023	17 341	7 633	795	2 759	11 913	37 493	8 805	16 567	11 350	452
Used	8 360	7 450	1 084	62	292	798	1 597	436	1 112	686	8
Equipment, total	122 005	78 231	24 350	1 951	15 143	4 773	34 736	4 924	13 039	8 069	1 703
New	121 511	76 894	23 887	1 917	13 523	4 597	34 110	4 757	11 950	7 209	1 681
Used	494	1 337	463	34	1 620	176	626	166	1 089	861	22
2006											
Total expenditures	163 069	132 073	30 284	3 306	19 231	22 615	75 296	17 156	36 217	25 959	1 813
Structures, total	41 326	40 794	6 971	875	3 613	17 537	41 197	11 733	22 585	16 621	467
New	34 028	30 240	6 375	799	3 485	16 203	37 765	11 326	21 774	15 754	446
Used	7 298	10 554	596	76	128	1 334	3 433	406	811	866	21
Equipment, total	121 743	91 280	23 313	2 432	15 618	5 078	34 099	5 424	13 632	9 339	1 346
New	121 157	88 957	22 867	2 188	14 932	4 983	33 508	5 121	13 161	8 463	1 322
Used	586	2 323	446	244	686	95	591	303	472	875	24

Table 5-8. Capital Expenditures for Structures and Equipment for Companies with Employees by Major Industry Sector—*Continued*

(Millions of dollars.)

Year and type of expenditure	Total	Forestry, fishing, and agricultural services (113–115)	Mining (21)	Utilities (22)	Construction (23)	Manufacturing (31–33) Total	Durable goods industries (321, 327, 33)	Nondurable goods industries (31, 322–326)	Wholesale trade (42)	Retail trade (44–45)	Transportation and warehousing (48–49)	Information (51)
2007												
Total expenditures	1 270 522	2 149	120 681	85 354	36 692	197 298	107 664	89 633	30 776	82 511	67 351	106 084
Structures, total	490 779	469	85 242	40 178	3 529	42 458	17 879	24 579	7 526	41 527	23 712	29 081
New	457 233	320	83 206	37 647	2 704	41 247	17 431	23 816	7 091	40 471	22 808	28 304
Used	33 546	149	2 036	2 531	824	1 211	447	763	436	1 056	904	777
Equipment, total	779 744	1 681	35 440	45 176	33 164	154 840	89 786	65 054	23 250	40 983	43 639	77 003
New	750 353	1 368	33 095	44 107	27 325	150 333	87 020	63 313	21 690	39 668	39 238	76 143
Used	29 391	313	2 344	1 069	5 838	4 507	2 766	1 741	1 560	1 316	4 400	861
2008												
Total expenditures	1 294 491	2 337	149 272	98 668	40 838	213 117	103 022	110 095	32 370	73 234	79 617	103 327
Structures, total	529 393	421	109 683	43 515	11 129	49 346	18 896	30 450	8 387	36 147	30 078	27 376
New	500 474	417	105 064	41 746	10 525	48 184	18 168	30 015	7 958	35 342	29 214	27 080
Used	28 919	4	4 618	1 769	603	1 162	728	434	430	805	863	296
Equipment, total	765 098	1 917	39 590	55 154	29 709	163 771	84 125	79 645	23 982	37 087	49 539	75 951
New	728 322	1 610	35 928	53 486	22 404	158 104	80 690	77 414	22 554	36 328	41 877	75 342
Used	36 776	307	3 662	1 668	7 305	5 667	3 435	2 232	1 429	759	7 662	609
2009												
Total expenditures	1 015 322	2 168	100 564	103 024	19 751	155 153	76 039	79 114	25 252	58 428	55 702	88 373
Structures, total	414 051	460	72 255	45 973	4 556	35 735	13 054	22 680	5 485	28 205	22 088	21 764
New	395 022	453	69 942	45 168	4 215	34 537	12 273	22 264	5 131	27 220	21 128	21 410
Used	19 030	7	2 313	805	341	1 198	782	416	354	985	961	354
Equipment, total	601 270	1 708	28 308	57 051	15 195	119 418	62 985	56 434	19 767	30 223	33 614	66 609
New	577 051	1 428	26 790	54 848	11 815	115 470	60 699	54 772	18 512	29 063	30 182	65 879
Used	24 219	279	1 518	2 204	3 380	3 948	2 286	1 662	1 255	1 160	3 432	731
2010												
Total expenditures	1 036 153	3 255	115 749	94 462	17 856	160 798	86 570	74 227	31 075	65 252	58 952	97 150
Structures, total	396 398	679	85 221	43 896	2 633	31 166	14 099	17 068	6 879	29 169	23 401	21 771
New	367 759	671	82 147	42 853	2 361	30 069	13 492	16 576	5 709	27 608	22 622	20 696
Used	28 639	8	3 074	1 044	272	1 098	606	491	1 170	1 561	778	1 074
Equipment, total	639 755	2 576	30 528	50 566	15 223	129 631	72 472	57 160	24 196	36 084	35 551	75 379
New	611 573	1 979	28 820	48 675	11 377	125 911	70 692	55 219	21 756	34 457	29 912	74 657
Used	28 182	597	1 708	1 891	3 846	3 720	1 780	1 940	2 440	1 626	5 639	723
2011												
Total expenditures	1 169 604	3 063	165 693	98 047	21 778	192 441	110 151	82 290	35 745	68 131	72 722	100 057
Structures, total	440 893	529	124 508	46 729	2 867	36 339	17 394	18 946	7 988	27 332	29 026	20 152
New	414 958	518	120 421	45 882	2 590	34 737	16 655	18 081	7 512	26 419	28 148	19 734
Used	25 935	11	4 086	847	277	1 602	738	864	476	912	878	418
Equipment, total	728 710	2 534	41 185	51 319	18 910	156 102	92 758	63 344	27 757	40 799	43 696	79 905
New	697 766	2 050	39 373	48 843	13 895	151 094	89 389	61 705	26 699	39 575	37 612	79 686
Used	30 944	484	1 813	2 476	5 015	5 009	3 369	1 639	1 058	1 224	6 084	219
2012												
Total expenditures	1 334 421	3 149	196 653	124 958	23 555	203 119	113 299	89 820	40 852	77 567	81 792	106 537
Structures, total	533 042	496	150 653	70 940	1 975	43 080	20 181	22 900	9 367	33 443	32 397	23 263
New	501 764	452	146 020	69 578	1 821	41 765	19 563	22 202	8 324	30 978	31 393	22 844
Used	31 279	44	4 633	1 362	154	1 316	618	697	1 043	2 464	1 003	419
Equipment, total	801 378	2 653	46 000	54 017	21 580	160 039	93 118	66 921	31 485	44 124	49 395	83 274
New	759 355	2 266	43 985	50 358	16 446	153 572	89 830	63 742	29 297	42 466	42 663	82 762
Used	42 023	387	2 015	3 660	5 134	6 467	3 288	3 179	2 187	1 658	6 732	512
2013												
Total expenditures	1 400 883	2 965	202 213	111 310	27 562	221 345	121 494	99 850	37 505	77 520	92 616	123 881
Structures, total	546 056	492	152 441	58 051	2 545	46 594	20 303	26 291	9 659	33 865	37 645	33 297
New	518 430	474	148 917	56 353	2 102	44 100	19 536	24 564	9 223	33 160	36 454	32 663
Used	27 625	18	3 523	1 698	442	2 494	767	1 727	435	705	1 191	634
Equipment, total	854 827	2 473	49 773	53 260	25 018	174 751	101 191	73 560	27 846	43 655	54 971	90 584
New	813 972	2 124	47 372	49 935	20 641	169 310	98 239	71 071	26 704	42 561	47 951	90 180
Used	40 855	349	2 401	3 324	4 377	5 441	2 952	2 489	1 142	1 094	7 020	404
2014												
Total expenditures	1 506 582	3 985	230 776	118 895	30 277	231 089	124 797	106 292	44 758	82 402	111 010	132 049
Structures, total	608 698	952	187 348	63 844	3 815	50 481	19 520	30 962	12 288	35 564	40 557	33 315
New	577 743	792	183 822	61 741	2 873	49 175	18 898	30 276	10 679	34 099	39 136	32 785
Used	30 955	160	3 526	2 103	942	1 307	621	685	1 609	1 466	1 421	530
Equipment, total	897 885	3 033	43 428	55 052	26 462	180 608	105 277	75 331	32 470	46 838	70 453	98 734
New	853 888	2 488	39 552	51 676	19 642	174 845	101 761	73 084	31 021	45 233	62 902	98 307
Used	43 996	545	3 876	3 375	6 820	5 763	3 516	2 247	1 449	1 605	7 551	426
2015												
Total expenditures	1 544 668	3 377	174 710	130 232	33 480	239 588	122 961	116 627	42 844	85 832	116 678	135 550
Structures, total	603 611	641	140 090	71 254	2 658	52 290	20 889	31 402	12 561	36 879	42 516	32 984
New	560 284	570	138 441	68 587	2 262	51 341	20 522	30 819	12 430	34 446	41 350	32 751
Used	43 327	71	1 649	2 667	396	950	367	583	131	2 432	1 167	233
Equipment, total	941 057	2 735	34 621	58 978	30 821	187 298	102 073	85 225	30 283	48 954	74 161	102 566
New	893 980	2 392	31 972	55 339	24 468	181 624	98 985	82 639	28 452	47 576	65 269	101 652
Used	47 077	343	2 649	3 639	6 353	5 674	3 088	2 586	1 831	1 378	8 892	915

Table 5-8. Capital Expenditures for Structures and Equipment for Companies with Employees by Major Industry Sector—*Continued*

(Millions of dollars.)

Year and type of expenditure	Finance and insurance (52)	Real estate and rental and leasing (53)	Professional, scientific, and technical services (54)	Manage-ment of companies and enterprises (55)	Adminis-trative and support and waste manage-ment (56)	Educational services (61)	Health care and social assistance (62)	Arts, entertain-ment, and recreation (71)	Accom-modation and food services (72)	Other services, except public admin-istration (81)	Structure and equipment expenditures serving multiple industries
2007											
Total expenditures	172 894	117 969	31 804	4 542	18 167	23 238	84 160	18 769	38 021	29 680	2 380
Structures, total	45 159	41 222	7 453	1 472	3 859	17 910	45 361	12 589	22 211	19 165	656
New	36 507	34 026	6 944	1 404	3 677	17 322	43 522	11 894	21 226	16 264	650
Used	8 652	7 196	509	69	182	588	1 839	695	984	2 901	6
Equipment, total	127 735	76 747	24 351	3 070	14 308	5 328	38 799	6 180	15 810	10 515	1 725
New	126 763	74 735	23 931	2 943	13 599	5 253	38 258	5 916	14 671	9 593	1 724
Used	972	2 012	420	127	709	75	541	264	1 139	922	1
2008											
Total expenditures	132 913	106 910	32 980	4 567	16 552	27 426	90 248	17 109	40 519	28 312	4 175
Structures, total	25 058	45 929	8 836	1 304	4 133	21 698	50 105	11 594	24 947	18 673	1 035
New	22 640	36 532	8 481	1 241	3 789	20 632	47 205	11 224	24 271	17 899	1 030
Used	2 418	9 397	355	63	344	1 065	2 900	370	675	775	6
Equipment, total	107 855	60 981	24 144	3 264	12 420	5 728	40 143	5 515	15 572	9 638	3 139
New	107 108	59 117	23 349	3 146	11 687	5 672	39 161	5 340	14 012	8 974	3 124
Used	747	1 864	794	117	733	56	981	175	1 560	664	15
2009											
Total expenditures	99 466	72 902	28 163	4 719	19 234	28 018	79 370	16 265	26 439	29 296	3 034
Structures, total	21 825	26 564	6 669	1 371	5 876	22 388	44 375	11 035	14 735	22 054	641
New	20 419	22 350	5 975	1 334	5 361	21 577	42 188	10 804	13 607	21 564	639
Used	1 406	4 214	694	36	515	810	2 187	231	1 128	490	2
Equipment, total	77 641	46 339	21 494	3 349	13 359	5 630	34 994	5 230	11 704	7 243	2 393
New	77 169	44 594	20 980	3 311	12 471	5 403	34 271	5 073	10 858	6 545	2 389
Used	473	1 745	514	38	888	227	723	157	846	698	4
2010											
Total expenditures	103 093	81 282	28 203	4 946	16 873	23 368	78 381	12 121	19 915	20 951	2 471
Structures, total	16 209	32 375	5 706	1 567	3 552	17 673	42 861	7 709	9 765	13 605	562
New	13 653	23 085	5 365	1 517	3 466	16 678	40 113	7 551	9 051	11 987	558
Used	2 556	9 290	341	50	86	995	2 748	158	714	1 618	4
Equipment, total	86 884	48 908	22 497	3 379	13 321	5 695	35 520	4 412	10 151	7 346	1 909
New	86 401	47 593	21 889	3 359	12 626	5 553	34 808	4 164	8 856	6 879	1 902
Used	483	1 315	608	20	695	142	713	248	1 294	467	7
2011											
Total expenditures	109 229	91 124	28 109	5 449	18 423	21 019	83 114	11 430	24 833	16 064	3 133
Structures, total	14 405	33 540	6 733	1 368	3 536	15 037	42 910	6 589	12 021	8 675	608
New	12 238	24 764	6 340	1 308	3 422	14 444	40 534	. . .	11 352	7 867	. . .
Used	2 167	8 776	393	60	114	593	2 376	. . .	669	807	. . .
Equipment, total	94 823	57 583	21 376	4 081	14 887	5 982	40 204	4 841	12 811	7 389	2 524
New	94 551	55 163	20 822	4 020	14 340	5 910	39 342	. . .	10 892	7 031	. . .
Used	272	2 420	554	61	546	72	862	. . .	1 920	358	. . .
2012											
Total expenditures	130 168	115 652	31 605	6 916	18 811	21 629	88 860	13 296	28 802	16 789	3 711
Structures, total	17 749	42 034	7 536	2 555	3 578	15 721	45 981	8 055	14 154	9 078	988
New	14 141	31 344	7 098	2 429	3 452	15 449	43 773	8 031	13 359	8 537	977
Used	3 608	10 690	438	126	126	272	2 208	24	794	541	12
Equipment, total	112 419	73 618	24 069	4 361	15 233	5 908	42 879	5 241	14 649	7 711	2 722
New	107 539	70 375	23 183	4 290	14 059	5 806	41 973	5 052	13 471	7 110	2 683
Used	4 880	3 243	886	71	1 174	102	905	189	1 178	601	40
2013											
Total expenditures	137 824	114 181	35 655	6 147	21 760	22 619	94 181	14 981	34 532	18 615	3 472
Structures, total	15 458	39 359	8 571	1 577	4 123	16 583	49 364	8 263	16 304	10 999	868
New	13 167	31 813	8 346	1 523	3 995	15 417	47 088	7 969	14 303	10 505	860
Used	2 291	7 547	225	54	129	1 166	2 276	294	2 000	494	8
Equipment, total	122 366	74 821	27 084	4 570	17 637	6 036	44 817	6 718	18 228	7 616	2 604
New	117 827	69 780	26 419	4 526	16 709	5 891	43 564	6 221	16 509	7 166	2 582
Used	4 539	5 041	665	44	927	145	1 253	497	1 719	450	22
2014											
Total expenditures	153 260	121 919	30 383	5 366	22 568	25 823	89 011	19 550	29 836	20 304	3 321
Structures, total	17 843	44 677	7 228	1 237	4 112	19 710	47 481	12 153	14 181	11 075	837
New	16 127	33 225	6 603	1 214	3 984	18 871	45 661	11 987	13 568	10 574	828
Used	1 716	11 452	625	24	128	839	1 819	167	614	500	8
Equipment, total	135 417	77 241	23 156	4 128	18 456	6 114	41 531	7 397	15 654	9 230	2 484
New	130 479	74 946	22 303	4 093	17 451	5 863	40 180	7 007	14 760	8 681	2 461
Used	4 938	2 296	853	36	1 005	251	1 351	390	895	549	23
2015											
Total expenditures	164 520	152 331	33 614	5 163	26 414	31 391	93 587	16 151	32 642	23 149	3 415
Structures, total	19 879	62 419	8 395	1 045	6 534	24 287	49 114	8 822	16 964	13 221	1 057
New	18 194	37 637	8 163	1 042	5 145	23 733	46 298	8 760	16 123	11 955	1 055
Used	1 685	24 782	232	2	1 388	554	2 816	62	841	1 266	3
Equipment, total	144 641	89 912	25 219	4 118	19 880	7 104	44 473	7 330	15 678	9 928	2 357
New	138 838	86 874	24 024	4 102	18 003	6 975	43 296	7 164	14 351	9 271	2 338
Used	5 802	3 038	1 195	16	1 878	129	1 177	165	1 327	657	19

. . . = Not available.

NOTES AND DEFINITIONS, CHAPTER 5

TABLES 5-1 THROUGH 5-4

Gross Saving and Investment Accounts

SOURCE: U.S. DEPARTMENT OF COMMERCE, BUREAU OF ECONOMIC ANALYSIS (BEA)

All of the data in these tables are from the July 28, 2017 National Income and Product Accounts (NIPA), publication. Explanation of NIPA data are described in the Notes and Definitions to Chapter 1. All quarterly series are shown at seasonally adjusted annual rates. Current and constant dollar values are in billions of dollars. Constant dollar values are in 2009 dollars. Indexes of quantity are based on the average for the year 2009, set to equal 100.

The 2013 revision included a major expansion of the investment accounts. Expenditures for research and development are now recognized as fixed investment. Before 2013, they were treated as if they were costs of producing this year's output. R&D spending by business, government, and nonprofit institutions serving households (NPISHs) is now counted as fixed investment. It is depreciated (with the estimated depreciation added to capital consumption allowances), so that there can be either positive or negative net investment in R&D. A similar treatment is now given to expenditures by private enterprises for the creation of entertainment, literary, and artistic originals. Finally, an expanded set of ownership transfer costs for residential fixed assets is recognized as fixed investment.

Results from the 2017 Annual Update of NIPA slightly revised the average growth rates of GDP between 2013 and 2016. Other revisions were incorporated include the Census Bureau's annual retail sales, construction, manufacturing plus others.

Definitions: Table 5-1

Gross saving is saving before the deduction of allowances for the consumption of fixed capital. It represents the amount of saving available to finance gross investment. *Net saving* is gross saving less allowances for fixed capital consumption. It represents the amount of saving available for financing expansion of the capital stock, and comprises net private saving (the sum of personal saving, undistributed corporate profits, and wage accruals less disbursements) and the net saving of federal, state, and local governments.

Personal saving is derived by subtracting personal outlays from disposable personal income. (See Chapter 4 for more information.) It is the current net saving of individuals (including proprietors of unincorporated businesses), nonprofit institutions that primarily serve individuals, life insurance carriers, retirement funds, private noninsured welfare funds, and private trust funds. Conceptually, personal saving may also be viewed as the sum for all persons (including institutions as previously defined) of

the net acquisition of financial assets and the change in physical assets, less the sum of net borrowing and consumption of fixed capital. In either case, it is defined to exclude capital gains. That is, it excludes profits on the increase in the value of homes, securities, and other property—whether realized or unrealized—and therefore includes the noncorporate inventory valuation adjustment and the capital consumption adjustment (IVA and CCAdj, respectively). (See notes and definitions to Chapter 1.)

The net saving of *Domestic corporate business* is corporate profits after tax less dividends plus the corporate IVA and corporate CCAdj. (See notes and definitions for Chapter 1.)

Government net saving was formerly called "current surplus or deficit (–) of general government." (See Chapter 6 for further detail from the government accounts.) Where current receipts of government exceed current expenditures, government has a current surplus (indicated by a positive value) and saving is made available to finance investment by government or other sectors—for example, by the repayment of debt, which can free up funds for private investment. Where current expenditures exceed current receipts, there is a government deficit (indicated by a negative value) and government must borrow, drawing on funds that would otherwise be available for private investment. In these accounts, current expenditures are defined to include a charge for the consumption of fixed capital.

Consumption of fixed capital is an accounting charge for the using-up of private and government fixed capital, including software, located in the United States. It is based on studies of prices of used equipment and structures in resale markets. As of the 2013 revision, it also includes estimated charges for the using-up of the research and development and other intellectual property capital now defined as investment spending.

For general government and nonprofit institutions that primarily serve individuals, consumption of fixed capital is recorded in government consumption expenditures and in personal consumption expenditures (PCE), respectively, and taken to be the value of the current services of the fixed capital assets owned and used by these entities and the estimated using-up of R&D and other intellectual property.

Private consumption of fixed capital consists of tax-return-based depreciation charges for corporations and nonfarm proprietorships and historical-cost depreciation (calculated by the Bureau of Economic Analysis [BEA] using a geometric pattern of price declines) for farm proprietorships, rental income of persons, and nonprofit institutions, minus the capital consumption adjustments. (In other words, in the NIPA treatment of saving, the amount of the CCAdj is taken out of book depreciation and added to income and profits—a reallocation from one form of gross saving to another.) It also includes the charges for the using-up of private R&D and other intellectual property, as described above.

Gross private domestic investment consists of gross private fixed investment and change in private inventories. (See the notes and definitions for Chapter 1.)

Gross government investment consists of federal, state, and local general government and government enterprise expenditures for fixed assets (structures, equipment, and intellectual property). Government inventory investment is included in government consumption expenditures. For further detail, see Chapter 6.

Capital account transactions, net are the net cash or in-kind transfers between the United States and the rest of the world that are linked to the acquisition or disposition of assets rather than the purchase or sale of currently-produced goods and services. When positive, it represents a net transfer from the United States to the rest of the world; when negative, it represents a net transfer to the United States from the rest of the world. This is a definitional category that was introduced in the 1999 revision of the NIPAs. Estimates are available only from 1982 forward. With the new treatment of disaster losses and disaster insurance introduced in the 2009 revision, this line will include disaster-related insurance payouts to the rest of the world less what is received from the rest of the world.

Net lending or net borrowing (–), NIPAs is equal to the international balance on current account as measured in the NIPAs (see Chapter 7) less capital account transactions, net. When positive, this represents net investment by the United States in the rest of the world; when negative, it represents net borrowing by the United States from the rest of the world. For data before 1982, net lending or net borrowing equals the NIPA balance on current account, because estimates of capital account transactions are not available.

By definition, gross national saving must equal the sum of gross domestic investment, capital account transactions, and net international lending (where net international borrowing appears as negative lending). In practice, due to differences in measurement, these two aggregates differ by the *statistical discrepancy* calculated in the product and income accounts. (See Chapter 1.) Gross saving is therefore equal to the sum of gross domestic investment, capital account transactions, and net international lending minus the statistical discrepancy. Where the statistical discrepancy is negative, it means that the sum of measured investment, capital transactions, and net international lending has fallen short of measured saving.

Net domestic investment is gross domestic investment minus consumption of fixed capital, calculated by the editors from the data shown in the table.

Gross national income is national income plus the consumption of fixed capital. (See Chapter 1 for further information.) This is

a new concept introduced in the 2003 revision. It is conceptually equal to gross national product, but differs by the statistical discrepancy. Gross national income is an appropriate denominator for the national saving ratios. Saving was previously shown as a percentage of gross national product; in the revision, it is instead shown as a percentage of the income-side equivalent of gross national product. Since saving is measured as a residual from income, it is appropriate to involve consistent measurements—and consistent imperfections in those measurements—in both the numerator and the denominator of the fraction.

Definitions: Tables 5-2 through 5-4

Gross private fixed investment comprises both nonresidential and residential fixed investment. It consists of purchases of fixed assets, which are commodities that will be used in a production process for more than one year, including replacements and additions to the capital stock, and intellectual property, including software, research and development, and entertainment, literary, and artistic originals. It is "gross" in the sense that it is measured before a deduction for consumption of fixed capital. It covers investment by private businesses and nonprofit institutions in the United States, regardless of whether the investment is owned by U.S. residents. It does not include purchases of the same types of equipment, structures, or intellectual property by government agencies, which are included in government gross investment. It also does not include investment by U.S. residents in other countries.

Gross nonresidential fixed investment consists of structures, equipment, and intellectual property that are not related to personal residences.

Nonresidential structures consists of new construction, brokers' commissions on sales of structures, and net purchases (purchases less sales) of used structures by private business and by nonprofit institutions from government agencies. New construction includes hotels, motels, and mining exploration, shafts, and wells.

Other nonresidential structures consists primarily of religious, educational, vocational, lodging, railroads, farm, and amusement and recreational structures, net purchases of used structures, and brokers' commissions on the sale of structures.

Nonresidential equipment consists of private business purchases—on capital account—of new machinery, equipment, and vehicles; dealers' margins on sales of used equipment; and net purchases (purchases less sales) of used equipment from government agencies, persons, and the rest of the world. (However, it does not include the personal-use portion of equipment purchased for both business and personal use. This is included in PCE.)

Computers have displayed phenomenal growth in numbers and power not easily represented by index numbers or constant-dollar estimates at the scale shown in these tables. Zero entries shown in the quantity indexes for early years actually represent very small quantities. Because of rapid growth in computing power and declines in its price, constant-dollar measures are deemed not meaningful and are not calculated by BEA.

Other information processing includes communication equipment, nonmedical instruments, medical equipment and instruments, photocopy and related equipment, and office and accounting equipment.

Other nonresidential equipment consists primarily of furniture and fixtures, agricultural machinery, construction machinery, mining and oilfield machinery, service industry machinery, and electrical equipment not elsewhere classified.

Intellectual property comprises information processing software, research and development, and entertainment, literary, and artistic originals.

Software excludes the value of software "embedded," or bundled, in computers and other equipment, which is instead included in the value of that equipment.

Research and development consists of expenditures for both purchased and own-account R&D by businesses, NPISHs, and general governments. Government R&D expenditures are treated as investment regardless of whether the R&D is protected or made freely available to the public. Investment is measured as the sum of production costs.

Entertainment, literary, and other artistic originals include theatrical movies, long-lived television programs, books, music, and other miscellaneous entertainment.

Residential private fixed investment consists of both *structures* and residential producers' durable *equipment*—that is, equipment owned by landlords and rented to tenants. Investment in *structures* consists of new units, improvements to existing units, manufactured homes, brokers' commissions and other ownership transfer costs on the sale of residential property, and net purchases (purchases less sales) of used structures from government agencies.

Other residential structures consists primarily of manufactured homes, improvements, dormitories, net purchases of used structures, and brokers' commissions on the sale of residential structures.

Real gross private investment (Table 5-3) and *chain-type quantity indexes for private fixed investment* (Table 5-4) are defined and explained in the notes and definitions to Chapter 1. The chained-dollar (2009) estimates in Table 5-3 are constructed by applying the changes in the chain-type quantity indexes, as shown in Table 5-4, to the 2009 current-dollar values. Thus, they do not contain any information about time trends that is not already present in the quantity indexes.

In Table 5-4, the user may wish to distinguish between the use of the "not available" symbol (...) and the publication of zero values (0.0). The "not available" values shown for computers and software mean that BEA has no separate estimates of their values; they are included in total "information processing equipment and software." The zeroes indicate quantities so small relative to the 2009 base that they round to zero, but they do exist and are included in the higher-level aggregates.

As the quantity indexes are chain-weighted at the basic level of aggregation, chained constant-dollar components generally do not add to the chained constant-dollar totals. For this reason, BEA only makes available year-2009-dollar estimates back to 1999 (except for the very highest levels of aggregation of gross domestic product [GDP]), since the addition problem is less severe for years close to the base year. However, the addition problem is so severe for computers that BEA does not even publish recent year-2009-dollar values for this component. BEA notes that "The quantity index for computers can be used to accurately measure the real growth rate of this component. However, because computers exhibit rapid changes in prices relative to other prices in the economy, the chained-dollar estimates should not be used to measure the component's relative importance or its contribution to the growth rate of more aggregate series." (Footnote to BEA Table 5.3.6, *Survey of Current Business*, available on the BEA Web site at <http://www.bea.gov>.) Accurate estimates of these contributions are shown in BEA Table 5.3.2, which is published in the *Survey of Current Business* and can be found on the BEA Web site.

Data availability, revisions, and references

See the information on the NIPAs at the end of the notes and definitions to Chapter 1. All current and historical data are available on the BEA Web site at <http://www.bea.gov> or the STAT-USA subscription Web site at <http://www.stat-usa.gov>.

TABLES 5-5 AND 5-6

Current-Cost Net Stock of Fixed Assets; Chain-Type Quantity Indexes for Net Stock of Fixed Assets

SOURCE: U.S. DEPARTMENT OF COMMERCE, BUREAU OF ECONOMIC ANALYSIS (BEA)

The Bureau of Economic Analysis (BEA) calculates annual, end-of-year measurements, integrated with the national income and product accounts (NIPAs), of the level of the stock of fixed assets in the U.S. economy, or what is commonly called the "capital stock." (The fixed investment component of the GDP is a flow, or the increment of new capital goods into the capital stock.) Data on consumer stocks of durable goods are also included in the accounts, but are not shown here. Historical data are available back to 1901, with detailed estimates of net stocks, depreciation, and investment by type and by NAICS (North American Industry Classification System) industry. From this data system,

Business Statistics presents time series data on the net stock of fixed assets valued in current dollars and also as constant-dollar quantity indexes.

The expanded definition of investment introduced in the 2013 comprehensive revision of the NIPAs, explained at the beginning of the Notes and Definitions to this chapter, was not incorporated in the fixed assets accounts until October 2013, so this edition of *Business Statistics* now publishes for the first time fixed assets data including the new NIPA categories.

Definitions and methods

The definitions of capital stock categories are now the same as the fixed investment categories listed earlier in these Notes and Definitions.

The values of fixed capital and depreciation typically reported by businesses are inadequate for economic analysis and are not typically used in these measures. In business reports, capital is generally valued at historical costs—each year's capital acquisition in the prices of the year acquired—and the totals thus represent a mixture of pricing bases. Reported depreciation is generally based on historical cost and on depreciation rates allowable by federal income tax law, rather than on a realistic rate of economic depreciation.

In these data, the *net stock of fixed assets* is measured by a perpetual inventory method. In other words, net stock at any given time is the cumulative value of past gross investment less the cumulative value of past depreciation (measured by "consumption of fixed capital," the component of the NIPAs that is subtracted from GDP in order to yield net domestic product) and also less damages from disasters and war losses that exceed normal depreciation (such as Hurricane Katrina and the terrorist attacks of September 11, 2001).

The initial calculations using this perpetual inventory method are performed in real terms for each type of asset. They are then aggregated to higher levels using an annual-weighted Fisher-type index. (See the definition of *real or chained-dollar estimates* in the notes and definitions for Chapter 1.) This provides the *chain-type quantity indexes* shown in Table 5-6. Growth rates in these indexes measure real growth in the capital stock.

The real values are then converted to a *current-cost* basis to yield the values shown in Table 5-5. They are converted by multiplying the real values by the appropriate price index for the period under consideration. A major use of the current-cost net stock figures is comparison with the value of output in that year; for example, the current-cost net stock of fixed assets for the total economy divided by the current-dollar value of GDP yields a capital-output ratio for the entire economy. Growth rates in current-cost values will reflect both the real growth measured by the quantity indexes and the increase in the value at current prices of the existing stock.

DATA AVAILABILITY AND REFERENCES

The 2017 Capital Spending Report: U.S.: Capital Spending Patterns, 2006–2015 was released on May 3, 2017. Full historical data are available on the BEA website at www.bea.gov.

TABLES 5-7 AND 5-8

Annual Capital Expenditures

SOURCE: U.S. DEPARTMENT OF COMMERCE, CENSUS BUREAU

These data are from the Census Bureau's Annual Capital Expenditures Survey (ACES). The survey provides detailed information on capital investment in new and used structures and equipment by nonfarm businesses.

The survey is based on a stratified random sample of approximately 45,000 companies with employees and 30,000 nonemployer businesses (businesses with an owner but no employees). For companies with employees, the Census Bureau reports data for 132 separate industry categories from the North American Industry Classification System (NAICS). Major exclusions are foreign operations of U.S. businesses, businesses in U.S. territories, government operations (including the U.S. Postal Service, agricultural production companies and private households.

Table 5-8 shows these data for the major NAICS sectors. Total capital expenditures, with no industry detail, are reported for the nonemployer businesses and are shown in Table 5-7, where they can be compared with the totals for companies with employees. The 1999 ACES was the first to use NAICS, providing data for the years 1998 forward on that basis.

Definitions

Capital expenditures include all capitalized costs during the year for both new and used structures and equipment, including software, that were chargeable to fixed asset accounts for which depreciation or amortization accounts are ordinarily maintained. For projects lasting longer than one year, this definition includes gross additions to construction-in-progress accounts, even if the asset was not in use and not yet depreciated. For *capital leases*, the company using the asset (lessee) is asked to include the cost or present value of the leased assets in the year in which the lease was entered. Also included in capital expenditures are capitalized leasehold improvements and capitalized interest charges on loans used to finance capital projects.

Structures consist of the capitalized costs of buildings and other structures and all necessary expenditures to acquire, construct, and prepare the structures. The costs of any machinery and equipment that is integral to or built-in features of the structures are classified as structures. Also included are major additions and alterations to existing structures and capitalized repairs and improvements to buildings.

New structures include new buildings and other structures not previously owned, as well as buildings and other structures that have been previously owned but not used or occupied.

Used structures are buildings and other structures that have been previously owned and occupied.

Equipment includes machinery, furniture and fixtures, computers, and vehicles used in the production and distribution of goods and services. Expenditures for machinery and equipment that is housed in structures and can be removed or replaced without significantly altering the structure are classified as equipment.

New equipment consists of machinery and equipment purchased new, as well as equipment produced in the company for the company's own use.

Used equipment is secondhand machinery and equipment.

Capital leases consist of new assets acquired under capital lease arrangements entered into during the year. Capital leases are defined by the criteria in the Financial Accounting Standards (FASB) Number 13.

Capitalized computer software consists of costs of materials and services directly related to the development or acquisition of software; payroll and payroll-related costs for employees directly associated with software development; and interest cost incurred while developing the software. Capitalized computer software is defined by the criteria in Statement of Position 98-1, Accounting for the Costs of Computer Software Developed or Obtained for Internal Use.

Prepackaged software is purchased off-the-shelf through retailers or other mass-market outlets for internal use by the company and includes the cost of licensing fees and service/maintenance agreements.

Vendor-customized software is externally developed by vendors and customized for the company's use.

Internally-developed software is developed by the company's employees for internal use and includes loaded payroll (salaries, wages, benefits, and bonuses related to all software development activities).

DATA AVAILABILITY AND REFERENCES

Current and historical data and references are available on the Census Bureau Web site at https://www.census.gov/programs-surveys/aces.html.

CHAPTER 6: GOVERNMENT

SECTION 6A: FEDERAL GOVERNMENT IN THE NATIONAL INCOME AND PRODUCT ACCOUNTS

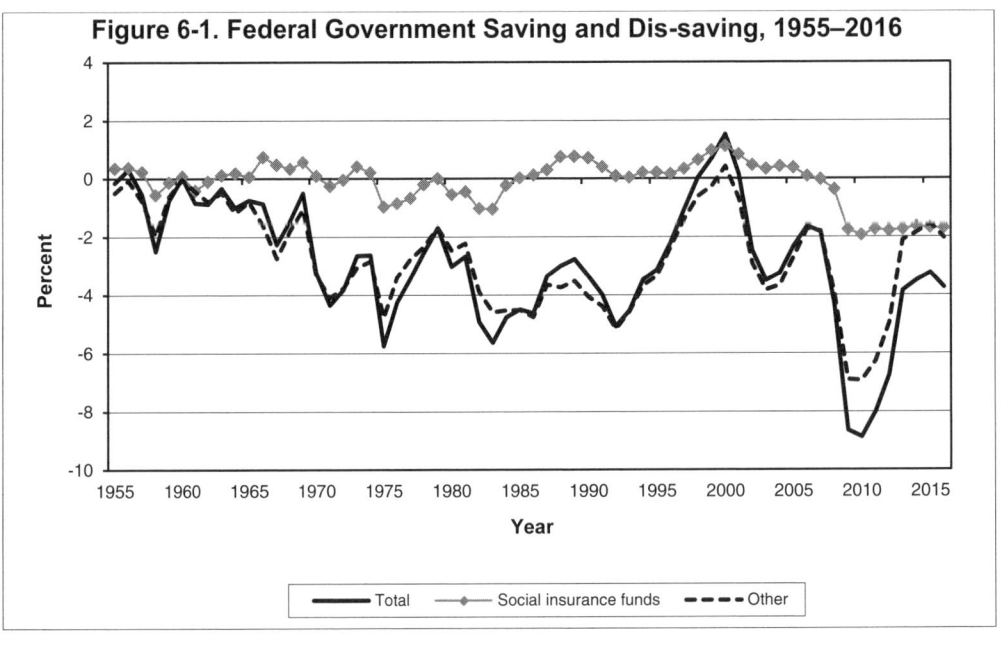

Figure 6-1. Federal Government Saving and Dis-saving, 1955–2016

- In the recovery and economic expansion of the 2000s, the federal budget never got back to a surplus such as those achieved in 1999 and 2000. With the onset of the most severe recession of the postwar period beginning in December 2007, deficits grew rapidly, due both to the "automatic stabilizers"; such as unemployment insurance, built into the budget structure and to anti-recession programs, such as the American Recovery and Reinvestment Act of 2009. (Table 6-1)

- In 2009, the NIPA budget deficit peaked at 10.8 percent of GDP. This was not as great as World War II deficits but exceeded in scale the deficits of the 1930s. By 2015, the deficit shrank to 2.6 percent of GDP, the smallest since 2007. However, in 2016 the deficit rose by 0.8 percentage points to 3.4 percent of GDP. (Tables 6-1, 1-1, and 6-14B)

- The main contributors to the rise in the deficit from 2007 to 2010 were increasing social benefits to persons, such as Social Security and unemployment insurance, and a drop in non-social-insurance tax receipts. Federal consumption spending and grants to state and local governments also rose. The deficit shrinkage from 2010 to 2016 was powered mainly by a resurgence in non-social-insurance tax receipts. (Table 6-1)

- The deficit in the social insurance funds failed to improve. The payroll-based taxes that fund Social Security and Medicare reflect the sluggishness in wage growth and do not benefit from increases in profits or higher-income compensation. In fact, median household income recorded its first significant increase in several years in 2016. (Table 6-1)

- Total federal government current expenditures have increased from 17.2 percent of gross domestic product (GDP) in 1960 to 24.2 percent in 2009, falling back somewhat to 22.3 percent in 2016. The composition of current expenditures changed significantly over the last 60+ years. "Consumption" spending on defense and nondefense programs fell significantly while benefits to persons, such as Social Security and Medicare, increased significantly. (Tables 6-1, 1-1 and 6-3)

Table 6-1. Federal Government Current Receipts and Expenditures

(National income and product accounts, calendar years, billions of dollars, quarterly data are at seasonally adjusted annual rates.)

NIPA Table 3.2

Year and quarter	Total current receipts	Current tax receipts								Contributions for government social insurance	Income receipts on assets			Current transfer receipts	Current surplus of government enterprises
		Total tax receipts [1]	Personal current taxes	Taxes on production and imports		Taxes on corporate income		Taxes from the rest of the world			Interest receipts	Dividends	Rents and royalties		
				Excise taxes	Customs duties	Federal Reserve banks	Other corporate taxes								
1960	93.6	76.5	41.8	12.0	1.1	0.9	20.6	0.1	16.0	1.3	...	0.2	0.3	-0.7
1961	95.1	77.5	42.7	12.1	1.0	0.7	20.8	0.1	16.6	1.4	...	0.2	0.4	-0.9
1962	103.2	83.3	46.5	12.9	1.2	0.8	21.7	0.1	18.6	1.6	...	0.2	0.4	-0.9
1963	111.3	88.6	49.1	13.5	1.2	0.9	23.7	0.2	21.1	1.7	...	0.2	0.5	-0.7
1964	111.3	87.7	46.0	14.1	1.3	1.6	24.6	0.2	21.8	1.7	...	0.2	0.6	-0.8
1965	120.4	95.6	51.1	13.8	1.6	1.3	27.6	0.2	22.7	1.8	...	0.2	0.9	-0.9
1966	137.4	104.7	58.6	12.6	1.9	1.6	29.8	0.2	30.6	2.0	...	0.2	1.0	-1.2
1967	146.3	109.8	64.4	13.3	1.9	1.9	28.1	0.2	34.1	2.3	...	0.3	1.0	-1.3
1968	170.6	129.7	76.4	14.6	2.3	2.5	33.6	0.3	37.9	2.7	...	0.3	1.0	-1.0
1969	191.8	146.0	91.7	15.4	2.4	3.0	33.0	0.4	43.3	2.5	...	0.3	1.0	-1.3
1970	185.1	137.9	88.9	15.6	2.5	3.5	27.1	0.4	45.5	2.8	...	0.4	1.0	-2.5
1971	190.7	138.6	85.8	15.9	3.1	3.4	30.1	0.4	50.3	3.1	...	0.5	0.9	-2.8
1972	219.0	158.2	102.8	15.5	3.0	3.2	33.4	0.4	58.3	3.3	...	0.5	1.1	-2.4
1973	249.2	173.0	109.6	16.5	3.3	4.3	38.9	0.4	74.5	3.4	...	0.7	1.0	-3.4
1974	278.5	192.1	126.5	16.4	3.7	5.6	39.6	0.4	84.1	3.6	...	0.9	1.1	-3.3
1975	276.8	186.8	120.7	16.2	5.9	5.4	38.2	0.5	88.1	4.3	...	1.0	1.1	-4.4
1976	322.6	218.3	141.6	16.8	4.6	5.9	48.7	0.7	99.8	5.2	...	1.1	1.2	-2.9
1977	363.9	247.6	162.5	17.3	5.4	5.9	55.7	0.7	111.1	5.8	...	1.3	1.6	-3.4
1978	423.8	286.8	189.2	18.2	7.1	7.0	64.4	1.0	128.7	7.4	...	1.5	2.2	-2.9
1979	487.0	326.1	224.9	18.2	7.5	9.3	65.1	1.1	149.8	9.2	...	2.1	2.5	-2.7
1980	533.7	356.2	250.6	26.5	7.2	11.7	58.6	1.6	163.6	11.3	...	3.0	3.1	-3.6
1981	621.1	408.3	291.2	41.3	8.6	14.0	51.7	1.5	193.0	14.8	...	4.4	3.1	-2.6
1982	618.7	387.0	295.6	32.3	8.6	15.2	33.8	1.4	206.0	18.3	...	5.1	4.4	-2.1
1983	644.8	393.7	286.8	35.3	9.1	14.2	47.1	1.2	223.1	20.4	...	4.3	5.2	-1.9
1984	711.2	425.7	301.9	35.4	11.9	16.1	59.2	1.3	254.1	22.8	...	4.9	6.3	-2.7
1985	775.7	460.7	336.5	33.9	12.2	17.8	58.5	1.9	277.9	25.6	...	4.6	8.6	-1.6
1986	817.9	479.8	350.6	30.0	13.7	17.8	66.0	1.7	298.9	28.8	...	3.3	7.6	-0.6
1987	899.5	544.2	393.0	30.4	15.5	17.7	85.4	2.0	317.4	25.1	...	3.1	10.2	-0.5
1988	962.4	567.2	403.8	33.4	16.4	17.4	93.8	2.4	354.8	27.4	...	2.8	9.6	0.7
1989	1 042.5	622.8	453.1	32.3	17.5	21.6	95.6	2.7	378.0	25.9	...	3.0	11.8	1.1
1990	1 087.6	644.2	472.1	33.4	17.5	23.6	94.5	3.0	402.0	26.9	...	3.5	13.3	-2.3
1991	1 107.8	637.9	463.6	44.9	16.8	20.8	89.2	2.6	420.6	26.2	...	3.8	17.2	2.1
1992	1 154.4	662.2	477.5	45.0	18.3	16.8	102.0	2.6	444.0	22.2	...	3.5	18.4	4.1
1993	1 231.0	715.3	507.7	46.5	19.8	16.0	122.5	2.7	465.5	22.8	...	3.8	20.2	3.5
1994	1 329.3	783.9	545.1	57.5	21.4	20.5	136.3	3.1	496.2	20.0	...	3.6	21.6	4.0
1995	1 417.4	849.1	590.3	55.7	19.8	23.4	155.9	3.9	521.9	20.8	...	3.0	17.5	5.0
1996	1 536.3	937.0	668.4	53.6	19.2	20.1	170.5	5.2	545.4	22.5	...	4.1	22.7	4.5
1997	1 667.3	1 035.8	749.8	58.2	19.6	20.7	182.3	5.1	579.4	21.0	...	4.5	20.1	6.6
1998	1 789.8	1 121.8	831.2	61.1	19.6	26.6	177.7	5.7	617.4	17.3	...	4.2	21.5	7.6
1999	1 905.4	1 199.9	897.6	64.3	19.2	25.4	187.6	5.9	654.8	17.1	...	4.0	22.4	7.2
2000	2 068.2	1 313.9	999.8	66.1	21.1	25.3	194.1	7.3	698.6	19.3	...	6.3	24.8	5.3
2001	2 031.8	1 253.9	996.3	64.6	20.6	27.1	137.6	7.7	723.3	18.0	...	8.4	25.5	2.8
2002	1 870.6	1 077.7	832.8	66.9	19.9	24.5	126.0	7.6	739.4	15.3	...	6.5	24.9	6.9
2003	1 895.1	1 075.5	778.5	68.7	21.4	22.0	175.8	9.0	763.2	16.5	...	7.0	26.2	6.7
2004	2 027.4	1 158.7	803.2	72.0	23.3	18.1	232.2	10.0	808.9	16.6	0.1	8.7	29.6	4.9
2005	2 303.5	1 389.3	936.8	74.1	25.3	21.5	319.5	12.1	853.4	17.3	0.2	9.7	32.7	0.9
2006	2 537.7	1 563.4	1 054.6	72.6	26.7	29.1	366.0	14.6	905.7	18.8	0.3	9.9	37.9	1.8
2007	2 667.2	1 642.4	1 169.7	65.8	28.8	34.6	328.2	15.3	947.2	22.1	0.2	11.1	42.0	2.0
2008	2 579.5	1 520.7	1 174.3	64.7	29.2	31.7	202.0	18.8	974.4	19.5	0.6	13.8	49.7	0.8
2009	2 238.4	1 171.1	864.5	68.3	23.1	47.4	153.0	14.8	950.8	22.8	18.7	7.0	67.2	0.8
2010	2 443.3	1 352.7	941.6	68.2	28.6	79.3	219.4	15.7	970.9	29.5	17.0	8.0	68.1	-3.1
2011	2 574.1	1 553.8	1 129.1	76.7	31.9	75.4	224.0	16.7	904.0	27.7	18.8	9.9	67.1	-7.1
2012	2 699.1	1 661.1	1 164.7	81.7	33.5	88.4	274.7	18.2	938.1	21.3	21.1	10.2	56.1	-8.9
2013	3 138.4	1 824.3	1 302.0	89.4	35.5	79.6	298.4	19.4	1 091.3	22.8	131.3	9.2	70.7	-11.1
2014	3 291.2	1 995.4	1 403.0	98.0	37.4	96.9	339.6	20.5	1 140.9	23.8	40.7	10.6	87.8	-8.0
2015	3 441.4	2 126.9	1 528.5	102.1	38.1	110.4	326.7	21.0	1 193.4	26.4	16.0	6.6	77.0	-4.7
2016	3 452.1	2 100.2	1 540.5	99.5	37.5	91.5	309.8	21.4	1 230.2	27.3	14.8	4.7	78.3	-3.5
2014														
1st quarter	3 258.2	1 962.4	1 369.1	98.0	36.6	101.8	335.3	21.7	1 127.4	22.9	71.1	10.1	72.8	-8.4
2nd quarter	3 291.8	2 002.9	1 387.6	98.2	36.9	101.9	358.2	20.1	1 131.5	23.3	41.4	10.8	90.2	-8.3
3rd quarter	3 307.0	1 998.2	1 412.1	98.6	37.3	92.6	337.3	20.3	1 143.3	23.8	23.0	11.5	115.0	-7.8
4th quarter	3 307.9	2 018.3	1 443.2	97.4	38.7	91.4	327.8	19.9	1 161.5	24.9	27.4	10.1	73.3	-7.5
2015														
1st quarter	3 399.8	2 113.5	1 502.5	101.4	37.5	86.4	365.0	20.8	1 173.8	25.8	11.2	7.5	73.4	-5.5
2nd quarter	3 440.4	2 131.0	1 521.8	101.9	41.1	91.5	354.0	20.7	1 187.1	26.4	10.4	6.5	84.0	-5.0
3rd quarter	3 430.6	2 106.0	1 531.1	102.2	35.4	94.2	321.1	22.1	1 195.5	27.1	33.3	6.7	66.6	-4.5
4th quarter	3 494.7	2 157.1	1 558.7	102.9	38.6	169.8	266.7	20.5	1 217.0	26.1	9.0	5.6	84.0	-4.0
2016														
1st quarter	3 400.9	2 060.1	1 514.4	98.8	38.7	101.0	285.2	22.1	1 212.4	25.9	18.6	4.3	82.6	-2.8
2nd quarter	3 441.7	2 096.3	1 537.9	98.4	37.0	101.0	300.8	21.0	1 230.2	26.4	3.9	4.9	84.0	-4.0
3rd quarter	3 486.3	2 131.6	1 557.9	99.4	37.3	90.8	325.3	20.9	1 243.1	27.4	15.4	4.8	67.8	-3.8
4th quarter	3 479.4	2 113.0	1 552.0	101.4	37.1	73.1	327.7	21.8	1 235.1	29.6	21.4	5.0	78.9	-3.5

[1] Does not include "contributions for government social insurance" (the taxes that fund Social Security, Medicare, and unemployment insurance), which are shown separately in column 9.
. . . = Not available.

Table 6-1. Federal Government Current Receipts and Expenditures—*Continued*

(National income and product accounts, calendar years, billions of dollars, quarterly data are at seasonally adjusted annual rates.)

NIPA Table 3.2

Year and quarter	Current expenditures										Net federal government saving, NIPA (surplus + / deficit -)		
	Total current expenditures	Consumption expenditures	Government social benefits		Other current transfer payments		Interest payments			Subsidies	Total	Social insurance funds	Other
			Benefits to persons	Benefits to the rest of the world	Grants-in-aid to state and local governments	Payments to the rest of the world (net)	Total	To persons and business	To the rest of the world				
1960	93.4	50.9	19.9	0.2	3.8	3.5	13.9	13.5	0.3	1.1	0.2	0.4	-0.2
1961	99.8	52.7	23.1	0.3	4.3	3.5	13.9	13.6	0.3	2.0	-4.7	-2.3	-2.4
1962	108.5	59.0	23.5	0.3	4.7	3.6	15.1	14.8	0.3	2.3	-5.3	-0.6	-4.8
1963	113.5	61.2	24.6	0.3	5.2	3.6	16.3	15.9	0.4	2.2	-2.1	0.8	-3.0
1964	118.2	63.1	25.2	0.3	6.0	3.4	17.5	17.0	0.5	2.7	-6.9	1.3	-8.1
1965	125.9	66.5	27.3	0.5	6.6	3.6	18.6	18.1	0.5	3.0	-5.5	0.4	-5.9
1966	144.3	76.5	29.9	0.5	9.4	4.0	20.3	19.7	0.5	3.9	-7.0	6.0	-13.0
1967	165.7	88.0	36.5	0.6	10.9	4.0	21.9	21.3	0.6	3.8	-19.5	4.1	-23.6
1968	181.3	06.8	41.0	0.6	11.0	4.5	£4.C	£0.9	0.7	4.1	-13.7	3.2	-10.9
1969	196.9	100.4	45.8	0.6	13.7	4.5	27.5	26.7	0.8	4.5	-5.1	5.7	-10.8
1970	219.9	102.3	55.6	0.7	18.3	4.8	33.3	32.4	0.9	4.8	-34.8	1.0	-35.7
1971	241.5	106.6	66.1	0.8	22.1	6.0	35.2	33.5	1.8	4.6	-50.8	-3.0	-47.8
1972	267.9	112.2	72.9	1.0	30.5	7.2	37.6	35.1	2.6	6.6	-48.9	-0.6	-48.2
1973	286.9	113.9	84.5	1.2	33.5	5.4	43.3	39.6	3.7	5.1	-37.7	5.9	-43.6
1974	319.1	122.5	103.3	1.3	34.9	6.0	48.0	43.9	4.0	3.2	-40.6	3.2	-43.9
1975	373.8	132.9	132.3	2.0	43.6	6.1	52.5	48.1	4.3	4.3	-97.0	-16.3	-80.7
1976	402.4	139.0	143.5	2.5	49.1	4.5	58.9	54.6	4.3	4.9	-79.9	-16.0	-63.8
1977	435.8	149.6	152.4	2.6	54.8	4.2	65.3	60.0	5.2	6.9	-71.9	-14.1	-57.8
1978	483.7	162.0	162.7	2.7	63.5	5.0	79.1	70.9	8.2	8.7	-59.8	-4.7	-55.1
1979	531.5	176.0	183.0	3.0	64.0	5.8	91.5	80.9	10.6	8.2	-44.5	0.0	-44.5
1980	619.9	202.1	220.3	3.5	69.7	7.3	107.5	95.7	11.9	9.4	-86.3	-15.8	-70.5
1981	706.9	231.3	250.7	4.3	69.4	6.7	133.4	117.2	16.3	11.1	-85.8	-14.3	-71.5
1982	783.3	255.7	281.9	4.1	66.3	8.1	152.7	134.7	18.0	14.6	-164.6	-34.4	-130.3
1983	849.8	277.9	303.6	3.6	67.9	8.9	167.0	148.9	18.1	20.9	-205.0	-37.9	-167.2
1984	903.5	292.0	309.7	3.7	72.3	11.2	193.8	173.7	20.2	20.7	-192.3	-9.4	-183.0
1985	971.3	316.8	325.9	4.0	76.2	13.8	213.7	191.6	22.2	21.0	-195.6	0.9	-196.5
1986	1 030.6	336.5	344.3	4.4	82.4	14.2	224.2	200.9	23.3	24.6	-212.7	5.7	-218.3
1987	1 062.7	347.8	357.2	4.3	78.4	12.7	232.3	208.2	24.1	30.0	-163.2	14.5	-177.6
1988	1 119.8	360.8	378.4	4.6	85.7	13.2	247.9	219.2	28.8	29.2	-157.3	39.1	-196.4
1989	1 199.1	380.2	411.7	5.1	91.8	13.5	269.7	235.1	34.5	27.1	-156.6	42.6	-199.3
1990	1 288.5	401.8	447.0	6.2	104.4	13.5	289.0	253.0	36.1	26.6	-200.9	42.4	-243.3
1991	1 354.0	423.9	494.0	6.3	124.0	-25.6	304.4	268.3	36.1	27.1	-246.2	24.7	-270.9
1992	1 487.0	430.2	551.8	6.2	141.7	20.6	306.9	272.6	34.3	29.7	-332.7	5.4	-338.0
1993	1 542.8	427.7	583.7	6.2	155.7	21.7	311.4	277.3	34.2	36.3	-311.8	2.8	-314.6
1994	1 583.0	427.3	609.0	6.8	166.8	19.9	320.8	284.5	36.4	32.2	-253.7	15.4	-269.0
1995	1 658.2	427.7	647.1	6.8	174.5	15.4	352.3	305.2	47.1	34.5	-240.8	15.6	-256.5
1996	1 714.8	428.4	682.1	7.6	181.5	20.4	360.0	303.2	56.8	34.9	-178.5	12.9	-191.4
1997	1 758.5	438.7	707.9	7.9	188.1	17.0	365.6	295.9	69.7	33.4	-91.2	28.9	-120.1
1998	1 787.0	436.4	722.1	8.2	200.8	18.0	365.6	293.5	72.1	35.9	2.7	58.3	-55.6
1999	1 838.8	455.6	739.9	8.5	219.2	18.7	352.2	285.4	66.7	44.8	66.6	92.5	-25.9
2000	1 911.7	475.1	773.4	8.7	233.1	22.4	353.7	289.3	64.4	45.3	156.5	114.3	42.2
2001	2 017.4	505.4	840.8	9.4	261.3	18.3	331.2	274.1	57.1	51.1	14.5	88.1	-73.7
2002	2 141.1	560.3	917.5	9.7	287.2	23.3	302.7	253.4	49.3	40.5	-270.5	49.7	-320.2
2003	2 297.9	628.5	967.5	10.1	321.7	28.6	292.6	245.2	47.4	49.0	-402.9	37.8	-440.7
2004	2 426.6	681.4	1 019.5	10.7	332.2	30.8	306.1	251.3	54.8	46.0	-399.2	51.2	-450.4
2005	2 608.2	723.4	1 084.4	11.2	343.4	40.9	344.4	276.4	68.0	60.5	-304.7	48.4	-353.2
2006	2 764.8	763.9	1 189.2	12.4	340.8	35.0	372.3	286.5	85.9	51.1	-227.0	11.8	-238.8
2007	2 932.8	798.4	1 264.2	13.3	359.0	42.3	408.2	309.2	99.0	47.5	-265.7	-4.1	-261.6
2008	3 213.5	879.8	1 464.6	15.5	371.0	45.0	388.0	290.9	97.1	49.6	-634.0	-54.9	-579.1
2009	3 487.2	933.7	1 616.2	16.0	458.1	52.7	353.6	264.8	88.8	56.9	-1 248.8	-253.1	-995.7
2010	3 772.0	1 003.9	1 757.9	16.5	505.3	53.5	380.6	288.0	92.6	54.3	-1 328.7	-290.9	-1 037.8
2011	3 818.3	1 006.1	1 779.9	17.1	472.5	57.6	425.7	328.2	97.5	59.5	-1 244.1	-271.0	-973.2
2012	3 789.1	1 007.8	1 783.6	18.0	444.0	55.3	422.9	327.0	95.9	57.6	-1 090.1	-289.1	-800.9
2013	3 782.2	961.0	1 823.5	18.9	450.0	53.8	416.2	319.7	96.5	58.8	-643.8	-291.0	-352.8
2014	3 901.4	954.5	1 881.9	19.3	494.8	52.8	440.6	346.9	93.7	57.6	-610.2	-287.1	-323.0
2015	4 028.0	960.0	1 967.2	20.2	532.1	53.3	438.4	344.6	93.9	56.7	-586.7	-306.4	-280.3
2016	4 149.4	964.5	2 018.4	20.9	555.5	53.6	475.1	378.5	96.6	61.3	-697.3	-318.1	-379.1
2014													
1st quarter	3 848.1	956.0	1 851.4	18.9	467.4	53.2	443.3	349.9	93.5	57.9	-589.8	-279.9	-310.0
2nd quarter	3 898.8	950.7	1 878.6	19.2	492.1	50.9	449.3	356.6	92.7	57.9	-607.0	-290.4	-316.6
3rd quarter	3 933.6	964.2	1 890.9	19.7	511.5	52.1	437.3	343.3	94.0	57.8	-626.7	-290.7	-336.0
4th quarter	3 925.0	946.9	1 906.6	19.4	508.0	55.0	432.3	337.8	94.5	56.7	-617.1	-287.5	-329.6
2015													
1st quarter	3 953.8	957.3	1 943.7	19.8	524.9	59.6	392.8	298.3	94.5	55.7	-554.0	-303.8	-250.2
2nd quarter	4 031.4	960.2	1 964.2	20.1	527.0	48.7	455.1	361.1	94.0	56.0	-591.0	-306.8	-284.1
3rd quarter	4 064.2	959.1	1 975.0	20.5	531.7	57.3	463.4	370.3	93.0	57.2	-633.5	-311.7	-321.9
4th quarter	4 062.8	963.6	1 986.0	20.4	544.7	47.7	442.5	348.6	93.9	58.1	-568.1	-303.2	-264.9
2016													
1st quarter	4 108.5	961.5	2 005.2	20.6	540.8	60.3	460.2	366.1	94.1	59.9	-707.5	-318.3	-389.3
2nd quarter	4 130.3	962.5	2 015.9	20.8	549.4	48.1	472.1	375.6	96.5	61.5	-688.5	-313.0	-375.5
3rd quarter	4 165.3	968.2	2 022.6	21.3	565.7	53.9	471.1	374.2	97.0	62.5	-679.1	-311.2	-367.8
4th quarter	4 193.3	965.9	2 029.8	21.0	566.3	52.2	497.0	398.0	99.0	61.1	-714.0	-330.1	-383.9

Table 6-2. Federal Government Consumption Expenditures and Gross Investment

(National income and product accounts, calendar years, billions of dollars, quarterly data are at seasonally adjusted annual rates.)

NIPA Tables 3.9.5, 3.10.5

Year and quarter	Total	Consumption expenditures					Gross investment						
		Total	Compensation of general government employees	Consumption of general government fixed capital	Intermediate goods and services purchased ¹	Less: Own-account investment and sales to other sectors	Total	National defense			Nondefense		
								Structures	Equipment	Intellectual property	Structures	Equipment	Intellectual property
1955	61.0	46.8	22.9	10.7	15.5	2.2	14.2	2.1	7.8	3.0	0.6	0.2	0.4
1956	63.1	47.4	23.5	11.6	14.1	1.8	15.8	2.1	7.8	4.1	0.9	0.2	0.6
1957	68.4	50.9	24.3	12.6	16.4	2.4	17.6	2.3	8.2	4.9	1.1	0.2	0.9
1958	71.5	52.6	25.3	13.3	16.5	2.6	18.9	2.6	8.5	5.2	1.4	0.2	1.1
1959	73.5	51.8	25.8	14.2	14.5	2.7	21.8	2.5	10.7	5.7	1.5	0.2	1.1
1960	72.8	50.9	26.6	15.0	12.0	2.7	21.9	2.2	10.1	5.9	1.7	0.3	1.7
1961	77.4	52.7	27.7	15.9	11.9	2.8	24.6	2.4	11.5	6.5	1.9	0.3	2.1
1962	85.5	59.0	29.5	17.0	15.6	3.1	26.5	2.0	12.5	6.7	2.1	0.3	2.9
1963	87.8	61.2	30.8	18.1	15.6	3.4	26.7	1.6	10.9	6.9	2.3	0.4	4.5
1964	90.2	63.1	33.0	19.0	14.9	3.8	27.1	1.3	10.1	6.9	2.5	0.6	5.7
1965	93.1	66.5	34.8	19.8	16.0	4.2	26.7	1.1	8.9	6.7	2.8	0.5	6.8
1966	106.5	76.5	39.8	20.8	20.6	4.7	30.1	1.3	10.4	7.0	2.8	0.6	7.9
1967	120.0	88.0	43.8	22.2	26.5	4.5	31.9	1.2	12.2	7.9	2.2	0.6	7.8
1968	127.9	96.8	48.3	23.8	29.3	4.6	31.1	1.2	10.8	7.9	2.1	0.5	8.6
1969	131.1	100.4	51.4	25.5	28.7	5.1	30.7	1.5	9.7	8.2	1.9	0.6	8.8
1970	132.7	102.3	55.2	27.2	25.3	5.4	30.5	1.3	9.5	8.1	2.1	0.7	8.8
1971	134.4	106.6	58.8	28.6	25.0	5.8	27.8	1.8	5.5	8.4	2.5	0.8	8.9
1972	141.5	112.2	62.6	29.6	26.9	6.9	29.3	1.8	5.3	9.2	2.7	1.1	9.2
1973	145.6	113.9	64.6	31.2	25.8	7.7	31.7	2.1	6.0	9.7	3.1	1.1	9.6
1974	158.1	122.5	67.8	34.0	29.2	8.6	35.7	2.2	8.2	10.0	3.4	1.5	10.4
1975	172.8	132.9	72.5	37.0	31.8	8.4	39.8	2.3	9.9	10.5	4.1	1.6	11.5
1976	183.8	139.0	76.5	39.8	31.3	8.5	44.7	2.1	12.1	11.3	4.6	1.8	12.7
1977	198.8	149.6	80.9	42.8	35.6	9.7	49.2	2.4	13.3	12.3	5.0	2.3	14.0
1978	216.7	162.0	87.1	46.4	39.3	10.8	54.7	2.5	14.3	13.3	6.1	2.7	15.9
1979	237.7	176.0	92.0	50.6	45.8	12.4	61.7	2.5	17.4	14.9	6.3	2.7	17.9
1980	272.4	202.1	100.8	56.6	58.4	13.6	70.3	3.2	19.8	17.2	7.1	3.2	19.8
1981	311.7	231.3	112.2	63.8	69.6	14.3	80.4	3.2	24.1	20.9	7.7	3.3	21.2
1982	345.6	255.7	122.0	71.0	77.6	14.9	90.0	4.0	29.1	25.2	6.8	3.9	21.1
1983	380.2	277.9	127.7	77.2	88.8	15.9	102.3	4.8	35.2	29.8	6.7	4.3	21.6
1984	407.6	292.0	136.5	84.6	88.3	17.4	115.6	4.9	41.1	35.0	7.0	4.7	22.8
1985	449.3	316.8	145.0	91.4	99.1	18.7	132.5	6.2	47.9	41.3	7.3	5.1	24.6
1986	478.4	336.5	149.1	98.2	108.8	19.6	141.9	6.8	52.7	43.9	8.0	4.8	25.7
1987	500.2	347.8	153.1	105.4	110.2	20.9	152.4	7.7	55.0	48.1	9.0	5.2	27.4
1988	508.8	360.8	161.9	114.0	107.4	22.5	148.0	7.4	49.6	48.5	6.8	6.1	29.6
1989	531.4	380.2	168.5	121.6	114.0	23.9	151.2	6.4	51.5	47.3	6.9	7.2	31.9
1990	560.0	401.8	176.0	128.3	123.1	25.6	158.2	6.1	54.6	46.6	8.0	8.1	34.8
1991	580.7	423.9	186.5	134.8	129.4	26.8	156.8	4.6	53.4	43.3	9.2	8.9	37.4
1992	586.6	430.2	189.6	138.1	129.4	26.9	156.4	5.2	50.7	41.3	10.3	10.0	38.9
1993	578.4	427.7	188.1	141.7	125.1	27.2	150.7	5.3	44.7	39.2	11.2	9.9	40.4
1994	572.7	427.3	186.1	144.5	126.1	29.3	145.4	5.8	41.9	38.1	10.2	7.5	41.9
1995	575.4	427.7	183.3	148.0	123.5	27.3	147.7	6.7	39.8	38.4	10.8	8.6	43.4
1996	578.2	428.4	182.2	148.3	125.5	27.6	149.8	6.3	39.9	38.9	11.3	9.7	43.8
1997	582.4	438.7	183.5	148.9	131.9	25.6	143.7	6.1	33.6	39.2	9.9	10.0	44.9
1998	584.1	436.4	185.8	149.2	128.1	26.6	147.7	5.8	34.0	39.4	10.8	10.2	47.5
1999	610.4	455.6	191.7	152.0	137.4	25.6	154.9	5.4	36.8	39.3	10.7	11.9	50.7
2000	632.4	475.1	202.4	156.3	144.6	28.2	157.4	5.4	37.8	40.2	8.4	10.8	54.8
2001	669.2	505.4	211.2	158.0	165.8	29.6	163.8	5.3	39.9	42.5	8.1	10.0	58.1
2002	740.6	560.3	236.4	159.8	195.6	31.5	180.3	6.1	45.6	47.0	10.0	12.0	59.6
2003	824.8	628.5	266.9	165.1	229.9	33.5	196.4	7.1	50.2	53.7	10.3	12.4	62.7
2004	892.4	681.4	284.2	173.3	258.5	34.6	211.0	6.9	56.7	59.8	9.6	13.4	64.6
2005	946.3	723.4	303.7	183.8	275.2	39.2	222.9	7.2	60.7	64.5	8.1	15.2	67.3
2006	1 002.0	763.9	314.8	194.8	294.4	40.0	238.0	7.8	66.8	67.5	9.4	17.4	69.2
2007	1 049.8	798.4	329.6	206.7	302.3	40.2	251.4	10.0	70.8	71.9	11.4	16.1	71.3
2008	1 155.6	879.8	350.2	220.1	352.3	42.8	275.8	13.7	83.8	73.8	11.4	17.6	75.5
2009	1 217.5	933.7	375.5	228.1	374.4	44.3	284.0	17.1	86.0	71.8	12.0	17.7	79.3
2010	1 303.9	1 003.9	404.8	238.8	406.6	46.3	300.0	16.7	90.3	72.6	16.0	19.1	85.3
2011	1 303.5	1 006.1	413.6	250.5	392.6	50.6	297.4	13.3	87.5	73.8	16.7	18.3	87.7
2012	1 292.5	1 007.8	411.6	257.2	385.9	47.0	284.7	8.1	85.2	70.6	14.5	18.8	87.5
2013	1 229.5	961.0	402.4	260.7	344.8	46.9	268.4	6.5	78.7	68.0	11.7	16.0	87.5
2014	1 218.1	954.5	405.8	263.6	334.0	48.9	263.7	5.3	74.8	65.6	12.0	17.3	88.7
2015	1 224.0	960.0	412.5	263.9	332.1	48.4	264.0	4.3	72.6	66.5	12.6	18.9	89.1
2016	1 231.5	964.5	422.2	263.7	328.7	50.2	267.0	3.4	72.3	68.1	13.1	19.1	91.1
2014													
1st quarter	1 216.6	956.0	405.0	263.4	335.1	47.5	260.6	5.7	72.3	66.1	11.8	16.7	88.1
2nd quarter	1 215.5	950.7	405.5	263.5	331.7	50.0	264.7	5.2	76.6	65.5	11.7	17.2	88.5
3rd quarter	1 228.3	964.2	406.3	263.7	343.1	48.8	264.1	5.4	75.1	65.4	11.8	17.4	89.0
4th quarter	1 212.2	946.9	406.5	263.9	326.0	49.6	265.4	4.8	75.1	65.5	12.9	18.1	89.1
2015													
1st quarter	1 218.7	957.3	410.1	264.1	331.6	48.6	261.4	4.5	70.6	66.1	12.6	18.6	89.0
2nd quarter	1 224.9	960.2	411.6	263.7	334.9	50.1	264.7	4.4	73.1	66.5	12.7	19.0	89.0
3rd quarter	1 222.6	959.1	413.5	263.9	329.3	47.6	263.5	3.8	72.0	66.7	12.6	19.3	89.0
4th quarter	1 229.9	963.6	414.6	263.8	332.5	47.4	266.3	4.4	74.7	66.7	12.5	18.8	89.2
2016													
1st quarter	1 227.9	961.5	419.7	263.4	327.5	49.0	266.4	3.7	74.2	66.7	12.9	18.8	89.9
2nd quarter	1 228.2	962.5	421.5	263.8	326.9	49.8	265.8	3.3	72.5	67.3	13.1	19.0	90.7
3rd quarter	1 234.6	968.2	423.5	263.7	332.6	51.5	266.3	3.2	71.4	68.4	12.9	19.1	91.5
4th quarter	1 235.4	965.9	424.1	264.0	328.0	50.2	269.5	3.3	71.0	70.0	13.5	19.5	92.2

¹Includes general government intermediate inputs for goods and services sold to other sectors and for own-account investment.

Table 6-3. Federal Government Defense and Nondefense Consumption Expenditures by Type

(National income and product accounts, calendar years, billions of dollars, quarterly data are at seasonally adjusted annual rates.)

NIPA Table 3.10.5

Year and quarter	Defense consumption expenditures [1]						Nondefense consumption expenditures [1]					
	Total	Compensation of general government employees	Consumption of general government fixed capital	Intermediate goods and services purchased [2]			Total	Compensation of general government employees	Consumption of general government fixed capital	Intermediate goods and services purchased [2]		
				Durable goods	Nondurable goods	Services				Durable goods	Nondurable goods	Services
1955	39.4	19.3	9.8	6.0	1.7	3.9	7.4	3.7	0.8	0.0	2.4	1.5
1956	40.9	19.6	10.7	5.9	1.7	4.2	6.4	3.9	0.9	0.1	0.5	1.7
1957	44.6	20.1	11.7	6.7	2.0	5.6	6.3	4.2	0.9	0.1	0.3	1.8
1958	46.0	20.6	12.3	7.0	2.0	5.8	6.6	4.8	1.0	0.0	0.5	1.2
1959	42.0	20.7	13.0	5.0	1.8	3.2	9.8	5.1	1.1	0.1	2.4	2.1
1960	42.6	21.1	13.8	4.4	1.7	3.5	8.3	5.6	1.2	0.0	0.5	1.9
1961	44.2	21.7	14.5	3.6	2.2	4.0	8.5	6.1	1.4	0.1	-0.3	2.3
1962	48.6	22.9	15.4	4.6	2.8	4.7	10.4	6.5	1.6	0.1	1.1	2.4
1963	50.5	23.6	16.3	4.7	2.5	5.2	10.7	7.2	1.9	0.1	0.6	2.6
1964	51.4	25.2	16.7	4.0	2.8	4.7	11.7	7.8	2.3	0.1	0.3	3.0
1965	53.9	26.4	17.1	4.2	3.2	5.1	12.5	8.3	2.7	0.1	0.4	3.1
1966	63.8	30.8	17.5	6.2	4.7	7.0	12.7	9.0	3.3	0.1	-0.7	3.3
1967	73.7	34.2	18.4	6.2	7.3	9.7	14.3	9.7	3.8	0.1	0.1	3.1
1968	81.4	37.6	19.4	7.5	8.4	10.5	15.4	10.7	4.4	0.1	0.8	2.0
1969	82.6	40.0	20.3	6.5	7.6	10.5	17.8	11.5	5.1	0.1	1.4	2.6
1970	81.8	41.9	21.3	6.1	5.4	9.6	20.5	13.3	5.9	0.1	0.5	3.6
1971	82.3	43.4	21.9	4.6	4.4	10.6	24.3	15.5	6.7	0.1	0.9	4.4
1972	84.4	45.6	22.3	5.5	4.7	9.5	27.8	17.0	7.3	0.2	1.2	5.8
1973	84.3	46.1	23.0	5.3	4.3	9.3	29.6	18.4	8.2	0.2	1.0	5.8
1974	88.8	47.7	24.6	5.0	5.2	10.7	33.6	20.1	9.4	0.2	1.4	6.7
1975	94.3	50.2	26.3	5.8	5.1	10.9	38.6	22.3	10.7	0.3	2.1	7.6
1976	98.2	51.8	28.1	5.7	4.4	11.7	40.8	24.7	11.7	0.3	2.1	7.1
1977	104.9	53.9	30.0	7.6	4.5	12.7	44.7	27.0	12.8	0.4	2.5	7.8
1978	113.0	57.6	32.2	9.0	4.9	13.3	49.0	29.5	14.2	0.5	3.2	8.4
1979	122.9	60.9	34.5	10.8	6.2	14.9	53.0	31.1	16.1	0.6	3.3	10.0
1980	140.8	66.7	38.1	12.3	10.0	18.7	61.3	34.0	18.4	0.8	5.5	11.2
1981	162.9	76.3	42.8	15.7	11.8	22.0	68.4	35.9	21.0	0.8	8.7	10.5
1982	184.6	84.8	47.8	19.1	11.5	28.1	71.1	37.2	23.2	0.8	7.5	10.7
1983	199.6	89.3	52.5	24.6	11.3	28.9	78.3	38.4	24.7	0.8	10.1	13.1
1984	213.6	95.9	58.2	26.6	10.4	30.7	78.4	40.7	26.3	0.9	5.8	13.9
1985	230.5	102.4	63.7	29.0	9.9	34.7	86.2	42.6	27.7	0.9	8.9	15.7
1986	245.8	106.2	69.4	31.7	10.2	38.3	90.7	42.9	28.8	0.9	11.7	16.1
1987	259.2	109.5	75.3	33.6	10.2	40.9	88.6	43.6	30.1	1.0	6.2	18.3
1988	274.2	113.8	81.9	33.4	10.6	45.4	86.7	48.1	32.1	1.1	-0.8	17.7
1989	283.5	117.9	87.5	32.0	10.8	46.5	96.7	50.6	34.1	1.2	5.1	18.2
1990	295.4	121.2	92.2	31.6	11.0	51.8	106.4	54.8	36.1	1.4	5.0	22.2
1991	310.6	126.8	96.4	31.0	10.7	58.1	113.3	59.7	38.4	1.5	5.9	22.3
1992	307.5	126.8	98.1	28.4	9.4	57.6	122.7	62.8	40.1	1.6	6.5	25.9
1993	300.8	121.0	99.7	26.4	8.5	58.1	126.9	67.1	42.0	1.6	7.6	22.9
1994	294.5	117.4	100.8	22.9	7.6	60.3	132.8	68.7	43.7	1.5	6.1	27.7
1995	291.1	114.1	101.8	20.9	6.3	60.1	136.6	69.2	46.2	1.4	7.5	27.3
1996	291.5	112.0	100.6	20.8	7.6	62.9	136.9	70.2	47.7	1.5	6.6	26.0
1997	292.5	111.4	99.5	20.9	7.6	65.0	146.2	72.0	49.4	1.6	8.5	28.4
1998	288.5	110.8	98.2	20.9	7.0	63.0	148.0	75.1	51.0	1.5	9.4	26.2
1999	301.2	112.7	98.4	22.2	8.2	71.3	154.3	79.0	53.6	1.7	7.2	26.9
2000	308.3	116.9	99.4	22.1	10.4	71.8	166.8	85.5	56.9	1.8	9.3	29.0
2001	325.1	123.2	99.0	22.3	10.3	84.6	180.3	88.0	59.0	1.9	12.2	34.6
2002	358.1	139.4	99.0	23.2	11.5	101.1	202.2	97.0	60.8	2.2	12.7	44.8
2003	408.9	160.5	101.9	25.7	13.4	124.4	219.5	106.4	63.2	2.3	15.6	48.5
2004	446.8	172.2	107.3	28.8	17.1	138.8	234.6	112.1	66.0	2.5	17.2	54.0
2005	475.9	186.1	114.4	29.6	20.9	144.1	247.5	117.6	69.4	2.7	19.1	58.8
2006	500.3	192.9	121.8	33.0	22.3	151.6	263.6	121.9	73.0	3.0	20.2	64.3
2007	526.1	201.5	129.9	36.3	23.8	156.5	272.3	128.1	76.9	3.0	20.0	62.7
2008	582.8	214.4	139.1	42.9	30.5	179.1	297.0	135.9	81.0	3.3	23.7	72.9
2009	613.3	228.8	144.6	45.8	24.4	192.8	320.4	146.7	83.5	3.5	26.4	81.4
2010	653.2	245.0	151.1	47.0	26.8	206.8	350.7	159.7	87.7	3.9	28.4	93.7
2011	662.3	251.3	158.3	45.0	33.1	200.6	343.8	162.3	92.3	3.6	24.5	85.7
2012	653.9	248.7	161.7	45.3	31.9	192.2	353.9	163.0	95.5	3.7	24.0	88.8
2013	613.7	240.5	162.3	39.8	27.6	169.6	347.3	161.9	98.4	3.4	22.1	82.3
2014	600.0	239.5	162.4	36.9	26.0	161.8	354.5	166.3	101.2	3.6	21.8	83.9
2015	588.2	239.1	160.9	35.6	20.8	158.2	371.8	173.4	103.0	3.8	23.3	90.3
2016	585.2	242.1	159.0	35.3	20.9	154.6	379.4	180.1	104.7	3.9	23.1	90.8
2014												
1st quarter	604.7	240.2	162.9	37.4	27.0	163.9	351.3	164.8	100.5	3.5	21.4	82.0
2nd quarter	600.1	240.1	162.5	37.1	26.7	160.4	350.6	165.5	101.0	3.5	21.0	83.0
3rd quarter	607.7	239.4	162.2	35.2	26.0	171.5	356.6	167.0	101.5	3.6	22.4	84.3
4th quarter	587.4	238.4	162.1	37.8	24.3	151.5	359.4	168.1	101.8	3.7	22.3	86.4
2015												
1st quarter	590.6	238.8	161.8	34.7	21.9	159.9	366.7	171.3	102.3	3.7	23.0	88.4
2nd quarter	591.0	238.7	161.0	34.9	21.0	161.9	369.2	173.0	102.7	3.8	23.2	90.1
3rd quarter	584.2	239.5	160.7	34.9	20.3	155.3	374.8	174.0	103.3	3.9	23.7	91.2
4th quarter	587.1	239.5	160.2	38.0	20.0	155.9	376.5	175.2	103.6	3.9	23.3	91.5
2016												
1st quarter	584.2	241.6	159.3	34.9	20.0	155.0	377.3	178.2	104.0	3.9	23.1	90.7
2nd quarter	583.9	241.7	159.2	34.2	20.8	154.6	378.6	179.8	104.6	3.9	23.0	90.5
3rd quarter	589.3	242.6	158.8	35.7	21.3	157.7	378.9	180.9	104.9	3.9	23.1	90.8
4th quarter	583.2	242.5	158.5	36.6	21.6	151.3	382.7	181.6	105.4	3.9	23.2	91.3

[1]Excludes government sales to other sectors and government own-account investment (construction and software).
[2]Includes general government intermediate inputs for goods and services sold to other sectors and for own-account investment.

Table 6-4. National Defense Consumption Expenditures and Gross Investment: Selected Detail

(National income and product accounts, calendar years, billions of dollars, quarterly data are at seasonally adjusted annual rates.)

NIPA Table 3.11.5

Year and quarter	Defense consumption expenditures								Defense gross investment				
	Compensation of general government employees		Intermediate goods and services purchased [1]						Aircraft	Missiles	Ships	Software	Research and develop-ment
			Durable goods	Nondurable goods		Services							
	Military	Civilian	Aircraft	Petroleum products	Ammu-nition	Installation support	Weapons support	Personnel support					
1972	32.0	18.2	2.1	2.9	1.1	4.8	1.7	1.6	3.6	1.3	2.2	0.5	10.0
1976	32.6	19.2	2.0	2.5	0.6	5.3	1.9	1.7	3.4	1.4	2.4	0.5	10.8
1977	33.7	20.2	3.3	2.4	0.8	5.8	1.9	1.9	3.7	1.2	3.1	0.6	11.7
1978	35.4	22.2	3.5	2.5	1.0	5.9	2.1	2.1	3.7	1.1	3.9	0.7	12.6
1979	37.4	23.5	4.8	3.6	1.2	6.6	2.7	2.1	4.8	1.8	4.3	0.8	14.0
1980	41.5	25.2	5.6	6.8	1.4	8.3	3.9	2.3	6.1	2.3	4.1	1.0	16.2
1981	48.8	27.6	7.8	7.7	1.6	9.6	4.8	2.9	7.5	2.8	5.1	1.3	19.6
1982	54.9	29.9	10.2	6.8	2.1	12.6	6.3	3.6	8.4	3.4	6.2	1.4	23.7
1983	57.8	31.5	13.6	6.4	2.5	12.4	7.0	3.9	10.1	4.6	7.1	1.7	28.1
1984	62.0	33.9	14.0	5.9	2.2	13.8	7.2	3.7	10.9	5.7	8.0	2.2	32.8
1985	66.2	36.1	15.4	5.8	1.3	15.1	8.4	5.0	13.4	6.6	9.0	2.7	38.6
1986	69.4	36.8	17.2	3.6	3.6	16.0	9.4	6.2	17.9	7.9	8.9	3.2	40.7
1987	72.2	37.3	18.2	3.9	2.8	17.7	9.2	6.8	17.6	8.7	8.8	3.6	44.5
1988	74.8	39.0	17.9	3.5	3.5	18.3	10.3	9.5	13.5	7.8	8.6	4.3	44.3
1989	76.5	41.4	16.4	4.2	3.1	18.0	10.5	10.2	12.2	8.8	10.0	4.8	42.5
1990	78.5	42.7	14.8	5.3	2.8	21.4	11.6	10.1	12.0	11.2	10.8	5.2	41.4
1991	82.4	44.4	13.6	4.7	2.7	22.9	10.0	9.5	9.2	10.8	10.2	5.4	37.9
1992	80.9	45.9	12.2	3.5	2.6	23.1	9.4	13.7	8.3	10.6	10.1	5.6	35.6
1993	75.1	45.9	10.7	3.2	2.5	25.2	8.8	14.7	9.3	7.9	8.7	5.4	33.7
1994	71.7	45.7	9.2	3.0	1.8	26.2	9.4	16.3	10.5	5.7	8.1	5.3	32.8
1995	69.5	44.6	8.9	2.8	1.2	25.2	9.5	17.0	9.0	4.7	8.0	5.3	33.1
1996	67.7	44.3	8.8	3.4	1.4	26.0	9.0	19.3	9.2	4.1	6.8	5.5	33.4
1997	67.8	43.6	9.4	2.9	1.7	25.1	10.5	21.3	5.8	2.9	6.1	5.6	33.6
1998	68.0	42.8	9.9	2.1	1.9	23.9	10.0	20.6	5.8	3.3	6.4	5.9	33.5
1999	69.8	42.9	10.5	2.6	1.9	25.0	11.3	26.0	7.0	2.9	6.8	5.9	33.3
2000	72.9	44.1	9.8	4.1	1.8	25.1	11.7	26.1	7.8	2.7	6.6	6.0	34.2
2001	78.4	44.8	9.8	4.2	2.1	27.4	14.8	32.4	8.5	3.3	7.2	5.8	36.7
2002	89.7	49.7	9.8	4.6	2.5	30.7	18.2	42.1	9.4	3.3	8.7	5.6	41.4
2003	107.4	53.1	11.3	5.3	2.6	35.7	22.5	49.5	9.4	3.5	9.5	5.4	48.2
2004	113.9	58.3	12.0	7.0	3.6	36.6	23.5	61.9	11.1	4.0	10.0	5.7	54.1
2005	123.3	62.7	10.7	10.1	4.0	35.8	26.1	66.3	13.5	4.0	9.8	5.9	58.5
2006	127.8	65.1	11.1	11.4	4.2	38.2	27.5	71.0	13.6	4.5	10.5	6.2	61.3
2007	133.2	68.3	11.5	12.2	4.1	38.2	28.6	70.0	12.9	4.3	10.3	6.5	65.4
2008	142.8	71.6	12.8	17.6	4.5	41.4	30.9	86.1	13.7	4.3	11.0	6.9	67.0
2009	152.0	76.8	14.7	10.5	4.2	44.1	32.6	93.6	13.5	5.1	11.1	6.8	65.0
2010	159.6	85.5	16.1	13.7	4.2	46.2	36.8	99.1	16.9	5.6	11.8	7.3	65.3
2011	160.6	90.7	18.0	19.2	4.3	44.2	35.0	96.8	20.7	5.1	11.7	7.7	66.2
2012	158.7	90.0	19.4	18.3	4.3	41.8	33.4	98.1	20.1	6.9	12.0	7.7	62.9
2013	153.2	87.2	17.9	14.4	3.6	34.8	27.9	91.9	21.6	6.4	12.5	7.7	60.3
2014	150.0	89.5	16.4	13.3	3.1	37.2	28.3	81.9	19.2	6.6	13.3	7.9	57.7
2015	147.3	91.8	15.6	8.2	2.8	34.5	29.8	80.7	17.6	6.6	13.5	8.0	58.5
2016	147.9	94.2	15.5	6.9	3.2	35.7	30.7	75.0	16.5	5.2	14.3	8.4	59.7
2010													
1st quarter	160.1	82.6	13.8	13.1	4.2	44.9	33.6	97.4	15.0	5.6	10.7	7.2	65.1
2nd quarter	160.1	84.4	15.4	14.0	4.5	46.0	36.2	98.6	17.0	5.7	11.3	7.2	65.2
3rd quarter	159.3	86.6	16.3	13.4	3.9	48.3	40.6	103.4	16.0	5.4	11.9	7.4	65.4
4th quarter	158.8	88.2	19.0	14.2	4.2	45.7	36.8	97.2	19.6	5.5	13.2	7.5	65.5
2011													
1st quarter	160.3	89.0	15.6	17.8	4.1	43.8	32.9	94.3	19.3	5.2	10.6	7.6	65.7
2nd quarter	160.7	90.0	17.6	19.5	4.1	45.2	36.5	100.9	21.1	5.7	11.5	7.7	65.9
3rd quarter	161.0	91.4	18.9	19.8	4.3	45.7	38.0	103.6	21.6	5.1	11.4	7.7	66.3
4th quarter	160.3	92.5	19.9	19.4	4.6	42.2	32.6	88.6	20.7	4.6	13.1	7.8	66.8
2012													
1st quarter	160.5	90.5	18.5	20.2	4.4	42.9	34.8	95.1	19.3	6.8	12.1	7.7	64.5
2nd quarter	159.4	90.1	18.6	18.4	4.4	41.9	33.7	94.9	20.2	7.0	12.2	7.8	63.3
3rd quarter	158.4	89.9	19.8	17.4	4.3	42.3	34.0	101.7	22.5	6.6	11.6	7.7	62.3
4th quarter	156.5	89.3	20.5	17.0	4.1	40.3	31.2	100.7	18.6	7.0	11.9	7.7	61.6
2013													
1st quarter	154.4	88.9	17.1	15.3	3.8	35.7	28.4	98.4	22.2	5.2	11.6	7.8	61.0
2nd quarter	153.7	88.4	17.7	14.3	3.7	34.6	27.7	94.9	18.8	6.5	12.5	7.6	60.7
3rd quarter	152.9	82.8	18.4	13.7	3.5	34.1	27.2	90.0	21.3	7.9	12.8	7.7	60.2
4th quarter	151.8	88.9	18.3	14.3	3.4	34.9	28.2	84.3	24.2	6.2	13.0	7.7	59.4
2014													
1st quarter	151.5	88.7	16.5	14.1	3.3	36.6	28.3	84.2	17.2	6.1	12.7	7.8	58.3
2nd quarter	150.8	89.3	16.5	13.9	3.2	37.5	28.1	80.0	20.6	6.4	13.7	7.8	57.6
3rd quarter	149.7	89.6	15.3	13.3	3.0	38.4	29.3	89.5	19.4	6.6	13.6	8.0	57.4
4th quarter	148.1	90.3	17.1	11.8	2.9	36.2	27.4	73.9	19.5	7.4	13.0	7.9	57.5
2015													
1st quarter	147.8	91.0	14.9	9.4	2.8	35.2	28.6	82.6	15.5	6.5	14.1	8.0	58.1
2nd quarter	147.3	91.4	14.9	8.5	2.8	35.1	30.8	82.9	19.2	6.3	12.9	8.0	58.5
3rd quarter	147.3	92.2	15.6	7.7	2.8	33.7	29.5	79.1	18.1	5.8	13.5	8.0	58.7
4th quarter	146.9	92.6	16.9	7.1	2.8	34.1	30.5	78.1	17.6	7.8	13.7	8.0	58.7
2016													
1st quarter	147.9	93.7	15.3	6.7	2.9	34.7	30.5	76.1	18.6	5.1	14.5	8.2	58.5
2nd quarter	147.7	94.0	14.3	7.0	3.1	35.6	30.8	74.6	16.7	5.8	13.7	8.3	58.9
3rd quarter	148.2	94.5	15.6	7.1	3.3	36.2	31.3	77.1	15.2	5.6	14.3	8.4	59.9
4th quarter	147.8	94.7	16.9	7.0	3.7	36.4	30.2	72.4	15.6	4.3	14.6	8.4	61.6

[1]Includes general government intermediate inputs for goods and services sold to other sectors and for own-account investment.

Table 6-5. Federal Government Output, Lending and Borrowing, and Net Investment

(National income and product accounts, calendar years, billions of dollars, quarterly data are at seasonally adjusted annual rates.)

NIPA Tables 3.2, 3.10.5

Year and quarter	Output						Net lending (net borrowing -)							Net investment
	Gross		Value added		Intermediate goods and services purchased ¹		Net saving, current (surplus +, deficit -)	Plus: capital transfer receipts	Minus			Plus: Consumption of fixed capital	Equals: Net lending (borrowing -)	
	Defense	Non-defense	Defense	Non-defense	Defense	Non-defense			Gross investment	Capital transfer payments	Net purchases of non-produced assets			
1960	44.4	9.2	34.8	6.8	9.6	2.4	0.2	1.8	21.9	2.6	0.5	15.1	-7.9	6.8
1961	46.0	9.6	36.2	7.4	9.8	2.1	-4.7	2.0	24.6	2.9	0.5	16.0	-14.7	8.6
1962	50.4	11.6	38.4	8.1	12.1	3.5	-5.3	2.1	26.5	3.1	0.6	17.1	-16.3	9.4
1963	52.3	12.3	39.9	9.1	12.4	3.2	-2.1	2.2	26.7	3.6	0.5	18.3	-12.3	8.4
1964	53.3	13.6	41.9	10.1	11.4	3.5	-6.9	2.6	27.1	4.1	0.6	19.2	-16.9	7.9
1965	55.9	14.7	43.5	11.1	12.4	3.6	-5.5	2.8	26.7	4.0	0.5	20.0	-13.9	6.7
1966	66.1	15.0	48.3	12.3	17.9	2.7	-7.0	3.0	30.1	4.4	0.6	21.0	-18.0	9.1
1967	75.7	16.8	52.5	13.5	23.2	3.3	-19.5	3.1	31.9	4.3	-0.2	22.4	-30.0	9.5
1968	80.4	10.0	57.0	15.1	26.4	2.0	13.7	3.1	31.1	6.0	-0.9	24.1	-22.7	7.0
1969	84.9	20.7	60.3	16.6	24.6	4.1	-5.1	3.6	30.7	5.9	0.1	25.8	-12.5	4.9
1970	84.2	23.5	63.2	19.2	21.0	4.3	-34.8	3.7	30.5	5.3	-0.3	27.6	-38.9	2.9
1971	84.9	27.5	65.3	22.1	19.6	5.4	-50.8	4.6	27.8	5.9	-0.4	29.0	-50.5	-1.2
1972	87.6	31.5	67.9	24.4	19.7	7.2	-48.9	5.4	29.3	6.1	-0.7	30.1	-48.1	-0.8
1973	88.0	33.6	69.2	26.6	18.9	6.9	-37.7	5.1	31.7	6.0	-3.2	31.7	-35.3	0.0
1974	93.2	37.8	72.3	29.5	20.9	8.3	-40.6	4.8	35.7	7.9	-5.7	34.7	-39.1	1.0
1975	98.4	43.0	76.6	33.0	21.8	10.0	-97.0	4.9	39.8	9.7	-0.4	37.8	-103.4	2.0
1976	101.7	45.9	79.9	36.3	21.8	9.5	-79.9	5.6	44.7	10.6	-2.4	40.6	-86.6	4.1
1977	108.7	50.5	83.9	39.8	24.9	10.8	-71.9	7.2	49.2	11.2	-1.4	43.7	-80.0	5.5
1978	117.0	55.8	89.8	43.7	27.2	12.1	-59.8	5.2	54.7	12.0	-0.6	47.5	-73.2	7.2
1979	127.3	61.1	95.4	47.1	31.9	13.9	-44.5	5.5	61.7	14.5	-2.8	51.8	-60.7	9.9
1980	145.8	69.9	104.9	52.5	40.9	17.4	-86.3	6.5	70.3	16.7	-4.1	57.9	-104.8	12.4
1981	168.7	76.9	119.1	56.9	49.6	20.1	-85.8	6.9	80.4	15.7	-5.5	65.3	-104.3	15.1
1982	191.3	79.4	132.6	60.4	58.7	19.0	-164.6	7.5	90.0	14.7	-3.7	72.7	-185.4	17.3
1983	206.5	87.2	141.7	63.2	64.8	24.0	-205.0	5.8	102.3	15.6	-4.9	79.0	-233.2	23.3
1984	221.8	87.6	154.1	67.0	67.7	20.5	-192.3	6.0	115.6	17.8	-4.0	86.4	-229.4	29.2
1985	239.7	95.7	166.1	70.3	73.7	25.4	-195.6	6.4	132.5	19.6	-1.2	93.3	-246.8	39.2
1986	255.7	100.3	175.6	71.7	80.1	28.6	-212.7	7.0	141.9	20.1	-3.0	100.3	-264.3	41.6
1987	269.5	99.2	184.8	73.7	84.8	25.5	-163.2	7.2	152.4	19.1	-0.4	107.5	-219.5	44.9
1988	285.1	98.2	195.7	80.2	89.4	18.0	-157.3	7.6	148.0	19.8	-0.2	116.3	-201.0	31.7
1989	294.8	109.2	205.4	84.7	89.4	24.5	-156.6	8.9	151.2	20.2	-0.7	124.2	-194.3	27.0
1990	307.9	119.5	213.4	90.9	94.5	28.6	-200.9	11.6	158.2	28.2	-0.8	131.1	-243.8	27.1
1991	322.9	127.9	223.1	98.2	99.7	29.7	-246.2	11.0	156.8	26.5	0.1	137.9	-280.8	18.9
1992	320.2	136.9	224.8	102.9	95.4	34.0	-332.7	11.3	156.4	22.6	0.2	141.4	-359.1	15.0
1993	313.7	141.1	220.7	109.0	93.0	32.1	-311.8	12.9	150.7	24.3	0.2	145.3	-328.8	5.4
1994	309.0	147.7	218.2	112.5	90.8	35.3	-253.7	15.1	145.4	26.0	0.1	148.3	-261.7	-2.9
1995	303.3	151.6	215.9	115.4	87.4	36.2	-240.8	14.9	147.7	27.9	-7.9	151.9	-241.6	-4.2
1996	304.0	152.0	212.6	117.9	91.4	34.1	-178.5	17.5	149.8	28.4	-4.8	152.4	-182.0	-2.6
1997	304.3	159.9	210.9	121.4	93.5	38.5	-91.2	20.6	143.7	29.2	-8.8	153.0	-81.7	-9.3
1998	299.9	163.2	208.9	126.1	91.0	37.1	2.7	25.2	147.7	28.9	-6.0	153.6	10.9	-5.9
1999	312.7	168.4	211.0	132.7	101.7	35.7	66.6	28.8	154.9	36.6	-1.2	156.8	62.0	-1.9
2000	320.7	182.6	216.3	142.4	104.4	40.2	156.5	28.1	157.4	37.0	-0.6	161.5	152.3	-4.1
2001	339.4	195.6	222.2	147.0	117.2	48.7	14.5	28.0	163.8	42.5	-1.5	163.3	0.8	0.5
2002	374.2	217.6	238.3	157.8	135.8	59.8	-270.5	25.3	180.3	49.7	-0.3	165.0	-309.9	15.3
2003	426.0	235.9	262.5	169.6	163.6	66.3	-402.9	22.0	196.4	63.1	-0.9	170.3	-469.1	26.1
2004	464.2	251.8	279.5	178.1	184.7	73.8	-399.2	24.6	211.0	64.0	-0.8	178.6	-470.1	32.4
2005	495.1	267.5	300.5	187.0	194.6	80.5	-304.7	25.0	222.9	85.3	-2.0	189.4	-396.6	33.5
2006	521.6	282.4	314.7	194.9	206.9	87.5	-227.0	27.8	238.0	71.0	-14.4	200.7	-293.2	37.3
2007	548.0	290.6	331.4	204.9	216.6	85.7	-265.7	26.5	251.4	79.4	-3.3	212.8	-353.9	38.6
2008	605.9	316.7	353.4	216.9	252.4	99.9	-634.0	28.3	275.8	145.9	-20.4	226.3	-780.6	49.5
2009	636.5	341.5	373.5	230.2	263.1	111.3	-1 248.8	20.6	284.0	206.9	-8.9	234.5	-1 475.7	49.5
2010	676.8	373.4	396.1	247.5	280.6	126.0	-1 328.7	15.1	300.0	141.4	-1.0	245.3	-1 508.7	54.7
2011	688.3	368.4	409.6	254.5	278.7	113.9	-1 244.1	9.6	297.4	123.5	-0.9	257.4	-1 397.1	40.0
2012	679.7	375.0	410.4	258.5	269.4	116.5	-1 090.1	14.1	284.7	99.0	-2.0	264.3	-1 193.4	20.4
2013	639.9	368.1	402.8	260.4	237.1	107.7	-643.8	20.9	268.4	79.0	-2.4	268.0	-700.0	0.4
2014	626.6	376.8	401.9	267.5	224.7	109.3	-610.2	18.8	263.7	77.2	-2.6	271.0	-658.6	-7.3
2015	614.7	393.7	400.0	276.3	214.7	117.4	-586.7	20.2	264.0	71.6	-30.7	271.3	-600.0	-7.3
2016	612.0	402.7	401.1	284.9	210.9	117.9	-697.3	20.0	267.0	73.7	-8.6	271.3	-738.0	-4.3
2014														
1st quarter	631.3	372.2	403.1	265.4	228.3	106.8	-589.8	19.9	260.6	77.5	-1.2	270.7	-636.1	-10.1
2nd quarter	626.8	374.0	402.6	266.5	224.2	107.5	-607.0	18.8	264.7	78.7	-1.8	270.8	-659.1	-6.1
3rd quarter	634.3	378.7	401.6	268.4	232.8	110.3	-626.7	18.1	264.1	78.9	-6.5	271.1	-674.0	-7.0
4th quarter	614.1	382.4	400.5	269.9	213.6	112.5	-617.1	18.4	265.4	73.6	-1.1	271.3	-665.2	-5.9
2015														
1st quarter	617.1	388.7	400.6	273.6	216.5	115.1	-554.0	19.6	261.4	70.5	-0.6	271.5	-594.2	-10.1
2nd quarter	617.5	392.7	399.7	275.6	217.9	117.1	-591.0	20.2	264.7	71.4	-121.4	271.1	-514.3	-6.4
3rd quarter	610.7	396.0	400.2	277.2	210.5	118.8	-633.5	20.4	263.5	75.3	-0.7	271.4	-679.8	-7.9
4th quarter	613.5	397.5	399.6	278.8	213.8	118.7	-568.1	20.5	266.3	69.0	-0.2	271.3	-611.5	-5.0
2016														
1st quarter	610.6	399.9	400.9	282.2	209.8	117.7	-707.5	19.8	266.4	72.9	0.0	270.9	-756.1	-4.5
2nd quarter	610.5	401.8	400.9	284.4	209.5	117.4	-688.5	20.1	265.8	72.4	-32.6	271.4	-702.6	-5.6
3rd quarter	616.2	403.6	401.5	285.8	214.7	117.9	-679.1	19.9	266.3	74.1	-1.5	271.3	-726.8	-5.0
4th quarter	610.6	405.5	401.1	287.0	209.5	118.5	-714.0	20.4	269.5	75.2	-0.2	271.6	-766.5	-2.1

¹Includes general government intermediate inputs for goods and services sold to other sectors and for own-account investment.

Table 6-6. Chain-Type Quantity Indexes for Federal Government Defense and Nondefense Consumption Expenditures and Gross Investment

(Seasonally adjusted, 2009 = 100.)   NIPA Tables 3.9.3, 3.10.3

| Year and quarter | Defense consumption expenditures [1] | | | | | | | Nondefense consumption expenditures [1] | | | | | | |
| | Total | Compensation of general government employees | Consumption of general government fixed capital | Intermediate goods and services purchased [2] | | | Defense gross investment | Total | Compensation of general government employees | Consumption of general government fixed capital | Intermediate goods and services purchased [2] | | | Nondefense gross investment |
				Durable goods	Non-durable goods	Services					Durable goods	Non-durable goods excluding CCC inventory change	Services	
1960	57.5	121.2	45.2	36.9	61.5	17.5	41.2	21.3	50.1	6.9	2.0	5.5	15.6	13.9
1961	59.0	123.8	47.2	30.3	78.3	19.4	45.5	21.0	51.4	7.7	2.7	8.5	18.6	16.3
1962	64.0	129.1	49.5	37.4	102.6	22.2	46.7	24.9	54.1	8.6	3.3	12.7	18.5	20.1
1963	64.3	126.8	51.5	37.7	91.6	23.2	42.8	24.8	57.2	10.2	3.7	12.7	19.4	26.8
1964	63.0	126.8	52.8	31.9	104.3	19.1	40.1	25.8	58.6	12.1	4.7	12.9	22.0	32.2
1965	63.9	127.0	53.5	33.1	117.8	19.6	36.4	26.7	59.7	14.3	4.9	13.6	21.6	36.8
1966	72.6	139.9	54.1	48.2	168.0	25.1	40.4	25.9	62.1	17.0	5.2	13.7	22.3	41.2
1967	81.7	152.3	55.7	47.5	257.7	32.0	45.4	28.6	65.1	19.5	5.1	15.4	20.3	37.9
1968	85.4	154.3	57.1	55.1	295.9	33.2	41.4	28.9	66.6	22.0	3.4	10.2	12.5	38.6
1969	82.5	154.5	57.6	46.0	262.6	31.0	38.6	31.6	67.2	24.3	3.5	10.6	15.2	37.2
1970	75.8	143.3	57.3	41.2	182.8	28.7	35.3	32.9	68.1	26.3	4.0	13.4	20.8	35.8
1971	70.1	132.4	55.8	29.6	149.5	29.2	27.6	35.8	70.4	28.0	5.1	16.5	24.2	35.7
1972	65.7	122.4	54.0	36.8	152.3	24.6	24.8	39.0	72.4	29.5	8.1	20.1	31.8	36.9
1973	61.2	116.1	52.6	33.6	113.2	22.7	25.9	39.0	72.6	31.0	7.4	19.2	30.1	37.0
1974	59.5	114.4	51.5	29.1	97.8	23.8	27.8	41.6	76.2	32.3	8.0	20.3	31.2	37.2
1975	58.3	112.8	50.8	30.7	81.0	21.9	28.9	43.4	77.6	33.7	8.6	18.4	31.6	38.2
1976	57.0	110.6	50.6	27.8	65.0	21.9	30.7	43.3	81.4	35.1	9.0	18.3	26.5	40.5
1977	57.4	109.6	50.6	34.8	61.4	21.9	31.4	45.0	83.2	36.7	11.7	18.0	28.8	43.0
1978	57.8	110.4	50.7	38.3	62.2	21.0	31.7	46.7	85.4	38.7	13.3	26.6	29.6	47.5
1979	58.3	109.5	51.1	41.7	64.1	21.6	34.7	47.6	85.3	40.8	15.6	26.1	32.3	48.1
1980	60.0	110.1	51.9	44.0	70.1	24.0	37.3	50.8	87.6	42.9	17.5	25.4	33.0	49.3
1981	63.0	113.5	53.3	51.6	74.1	26.0	41.2	52.1	85.0	44.8	16.5	47.5	28.0	48.4
1982	66.5	116.1	55.4	56.8	73.8	31.3	46.5	51.1	83.4	46.3	15.1	35.5	26.5	44.8
1983	69.5	117.9	58.5	67.9	77.3	31.4	53.9	54.6	84.6	47.7	16.3	44.3	32.0	44.7
1984	71.3	119.6	62.6	69.0	73.1	32.7	61.0	52.9	84.7	49.0	17.6	46.2	32.9	46.1
1985	75.1	121.8	67.9	74.7	71.3	36.3	72.0	55.9	84.8	50.4	18.2	40.1	35.7	48.6
1986	79.1	122.3	73.9	80.2	90.4	38.8	79.8	57.8	83.6	51.9	17.9	34.2	35.5	49.9
1987	81.9	123.4	79.8	85.3	88.5	39.7	86.7	56.3	85.1	53.3	20.3	39.7	39.9	53.3
1988	83.8	121.9	84.7	87.9	85.8	42.0	81.2	53.1	87.2	54.9	21.5	39.5	37.6	52.6
1989	84.3	121.9	88.1	84.5	83.0	42.0	79.2	57.5	87.7	56.5	24.2	35.3	37.3	55.2
1990	84.7	121.1	90.6	81.5	74.1	44.3	79.1	61.6	92.1	58.3	27.7	37.5	44.2	59.4
1991	86.0	120.7	91.8	77.7	75.5	47.8	72.8	62.0	91.8	60.3	29.2	32.9	43.8	63.2
1992	82.4	113.7	91.9	69.9	69.8	46.5	68.9	65.6	93.5	62.1	31.8	40.9	49.4	67.0
1993	79.6	108.9	90.9	63.6	64.0	45.8	61.7	65.0	93.4	63.8	31.0	44.5	41.8	68.3
1994	76.1	103.3	89.1	54.5	58.3	46.3	57.8	65.6	90.8	65.3	29.2	37.4	49.2	65.1
1995	73.1	97.6	87.1	49.7	47.7	44.7	55.4	65.0	87.2	66.8	28.6	42.2	47.4	66.6
1996	71.8	93.5	85.2	49.3	52.7	45.8	55.0	63.7	84.8	68.6	32.5	36.4	44.7	68.5
1997	70.8	90.1	83.4	49.5	53.1	46.5	51.1	66.4	84.3	70.1	35.1	44.4	47.5	68.2
1998	68.9	87.2	81.6	49.9	54.8	44.2	51.2	66.0	85.3	72.1	35.1	48.3	43.5	72.0
1999	70.0	85.1	80.2	53.0	61.3	49.2	51.7	66.8	85.4	74.6	39.4	36.0	44.1	76.4
2000	69.0	84.4	79.0	52.5	64.3	48.1	52.3	69.5	88.1	77.2	43.5	40.9	46.2	75.4
2001	71.0	85.0	78.3	52.9	66.1	54.7	55.3	73.5	88.0	79.4	46.6	54.3	53.0	77.2
2002	74.8	87.2	78.1	55.0	75.5	63.6	62.5	79.0	89.7	81.6	57.2	59.5	67.0	82.6
2003	80.7	90.2	79.5	60.5	81.8	75.5	69.5	82.4	91.9	83.8	59.0	73.3	70.7	85.6
2004	84.8	91.9	81.9	66.9	93.0	81.6	76.1	84.4	91.1	85.9	65.2	81.9	76.3	86.4
2005	85.7	92.2	85.1	67.4	93.6	82.4	80.0	85.5	90.9	88.4	71.3	82.3	80.3	87.5
2006	86.6	90.8	88.5	73.4	91.5	83.8	84.5	88.2	90.9	91.3	79.9	80.1	85.0	91.4
2007	88.0	90.5	92.1	80.6	92.6	84.1	89.2	88.1	91.5	94.2	81.6	78.0	80.1	92.5
2008	94.0	93.9	96.1	94.2	95.6	93.1	97.9	93.6	94.9	97.1	92.6	88.1	90.0	95.8
2009	100.0	100.0	100.0	100.0	100.0	100.0	100.0	100.0	100.0	100.0	100.0	100.0	100.0	100.0
2010	103.7	103.2	103.1	102.5	96.4	105.4	101.4	105.9	104.3	102.8	110.6	105.6	111.9	108.2
2011	102.1	104.3	105.4	97.4	98.8	99.1	96.4	100.9	103.1	106.2	102.8	86.3	98.8	108.3
2012	99.7	102.2	106.2	97.2	94.4	93.7	89.5	103.1	103.6	109.0	104.2	82.0	100.7	105.5
2013	92.9	98.6	105.6	84.9	81.9	81.6	83.3	99.4	100.6	110.9	96.6	73.7	92.3	99.4
2014	89.6	96.6	104.2	78.3	79.3	76.7	78.3	99.4	100.5	112.2	101.3	72.9	92.8	100.3
2015	87.6	94.3	102.4	75.2	79.5	74.8	76.8	103.1	101.8	113.7	108.0	79.4	100.2	102.2
2016	86.7	94.2	101.2	74.8	85.8	72.5	77.2	104.1	103.6	115.2	110.2	80.0	100.4	104.1
2014														
1st quarter	90.7	97.6	104.8	79.5	79.6	78.0	77.4	99.2	100.7	111.7	98.8	71.2	91.2	99.2
2nd quarter	89.7	97.1	104.4	78.9	79.4	76.0	79.2	98.5	100.4	112.0	100.4	70.9	91.7	99.9
3rd quarter	90.6	96.3	104.0	74.7	79.3	81.0	78.5	99.7	100.5	112.4	101.9	74.3	92.8	100.3
4th quarter	87.5	95.3	103.5	80.1	78.9	71.6	78.1	100.2	100.4	112.7	103.9	75.1	95.3	101.9
2015														
1st quarter	87.9	94.5	103.0	73.4	78.5	75.8	75.6	102.0	101.3	113.1	105.3	78.1	98.2	101.9
2nd quarter	88.0	94.1	102.6	73.8	79.1	76.5	77.4	102.3	101.6	113.5	107.7	78.5	99.9	102.4
3rd quarter	87.0	94.3	102.2	73.7	79.8	73.4	76.3	103.7	101.9	113.9	109.2	80.5	101.1	102.3
4th quarter	87.5	94.2	101.9	80.1	80.8	73.7	78.1	104.1	102.2	114.3	109.9	80.4	101.6	102.0
2016														
1st quarter	86.8	94.1	101.6	73.8	82.7	73.1	77.8	103.9	102.8	114.7	109.5	80.8	100.8	102.2
2nd quarter	86.5	94.1	101.3	72.3	85.2	72.6	76.8	103.9	103.5	115.1	109.9	79.5	100.2	103.7
3rd quarter	87.2	94.4	101.0	75.5	86.9	73.8	76.8	103.8	103.9	115.4	110.3	79.7	100.2	104.2
4th quarter	86.1	94.1	100.7	77.5	88.4	70.5	77.5	104.7	104.3	115.8	111.0	79.8	100.2	105.5

[1]Excludes government sales to other sectors and government own-account investment (construction and software).
[2]Includes general government intermediate inputs for goods and services sold to other sectors and for own-account investment.

Table 6-7. Chain-Type Quantity Indexes for National Defense Consumption Expenditures and Gross Investment: Selected Detail

(Seasonally adjusted, 2009 = 100.)   NIPA Table 3.11.3

Year and quarter	Defense consumption expenditures								Defense gross investment				
	Compensation of general government employees		Intermediate goods and services purchased [1]						Aircraft	Missiles	Ships	Software	Research and development
			Durable goods	Nondurable goods		Services							
	Military	Civilian	Aircraft	Petroleum products	Ammunition	Installation support	Weapons support	Personnel support					
1975	107.4	122.4	36.5	149.7	70.5	39.7	18.6	9.9	34.3	25.7	68.7	9.7	46.0
1976	104.8	120.9	30.6	124.1	35.4	40.8	19.8	9.5	32.1	21.9	70.4	10.2	47.4
1977	103.9	119.8	46.7	105.6	48.4	40.5	18.8	9.7	33.5	17.1	82.2	10.5	48.8
1978	102.9	124.0	47.7	105.0	55.9	37.9	18.5	9.5	31.7	14.1	92.5	12.3	49.4
1979	101.3	124.6	59.4	106.8	62.1	39.8	22.4	8.4	39.7	28.4	95.2	14.7	51.3
1980	102.3	124.4	64.5	118.2	62.3	45.1	29.0	8.3	47.5	41.0	83.7	16.8	54.0
1981	105.6	127.9	83.1	116.1	70.4	48.9	31.9	9.3	54.9	47.6	95.4	20.0	60.0
1982	107.5	132.1	97.2	109.3	86.7	59.8	39.6	11.1	55.2	61.4	111.2	22.0	67.6
1983	109.4	133.7	118.3	117.0	101.7	56.6	41.6	12.2	62.7	77.8	123.6	25.5	76.7
1984	110.7	135.9	111.8	116.7	86.1	61.2	41.7	11.3	67.4	93.5	130.9	33.7	85.8
1985	112.3	139.6	120.1	118.7	51.3	65.3	47.4	14.7	92.0	100.0	143.0	41.1	98.8
1986	113.3	138.8	132.9	118.6	138.2	65.7	52.4	17.3	140.3	135.1	138.9	48.9	102.6
1987	114.7	139.2	142.3	121.8	104.9	69.9	50.6	17.6	161.0	153.7	135.1	54.6	110.4
1988	113.9	136.2	147.3	102.6	121.0	69.6	55.0	20.9	132.3	139.9	128.0	63.3	105.1
1989	113.3	137.5	138.9	112.6	101.2	67.8	53.9	21.3	121.0	160.2	142.1	72.5	97.8
1990	113.6	134.3	122.0	111.7	91.3	76.2	57.5	19.6	111.6	208.1	149.9	78.6	93.1
1991	115.0	130.1	109.2	110.3	86.1	80.7	47.2	17.4	80.3	209.2	134.5	80.8	82.6
1992	105.2	129.4	95.2	92.3	81.8	80.0	42.5	24.0	70.3	206.9	130.0	87.2	75.9
1993	99.8	125.8	82.5	88.7	81.2	86.3	38.3	25.0	75.7	150.2	109.7	83.2	70.5
1994	95.0	118.6	70.1	91.3	55.9	87.4	39.9	26.8	75.6	110.3	98.7	81.9	67.0
1995	90.1	111.6	66.8	82.9	35.8	81.1	39.5	26.9	61.1	92.9	92.9	80.4	64.8
1996	86.8	105.8	66.2	83.8	41.9	82.6	36.6	29.6	59.3	82.7	78.5	84.5	64.4
1997	84.5	100.3	70.8	75.2	51.5	79.4	41.6	32.0	41.2	61.2	69.6	86.9	63.3
1998	82.6	95.7	75.1	73.4	58.3	74.7	39.2	30.2	41.5	68.9	73.6	92.7	62.2
1999	81.1	92.3	79.3	81.2	59.3	76.9	43.7	36.9	43.2	62.4	78.0	92.4	60.7
2000	81.8	89.2	73.8	74.9	56.4	76.3	43.8	35.5	50.4	58.8	74.2	91.2	60.4
2001	83.5	87.7	72.8	87.6	64.4	81.0	54.4	42.5	58.9	73.8	81.3	86.4	64.6
2002	86.6	88.4	73.1	100.9	78.3	88.3	65.8	53.4	67.9	73.8	97.3	84.5	72.7
2003	91.3	88.2	82.4	97.9	81.1	98.2	79.7	60.9	68.3	76.0	104.7	82.6	83.2
2004	92.3	91.0	85.9	103.2	106.3	96.3	81.1	74.3	82.0	86.3	106.2	86.4	91.4
2005	91.8	93.1	75.8	100.5	110.6	90.1	87.6	77.8	102.8	83.7	101.2	89.5	96.6
2006	89.6	93.3	76.3	99.4	108.7	92.5	90.0	81.0	104.7	93.0	105.2	92.4	99.2
2007	88.9	93.8	79.2	98.4	101.8	89.0	91.7	77.2	99.8	88.6	98.3	96.4	103.1
2008	92.9	96.1	88.0	99.3	104.2	93.1	96.6	93.4	102.2	86.0	101.2	100.6	102.7
2009	100.0	100.0	100.0	100.0	100.0	100.0	100.0	100.0	100.0	100.0	100.0	100.0	100.0
2010	101.6	106.5	109.9	101.4	99.2	101.8	111.3	104.7	124.2	108.1	103.4	107.4	98.1
2011	101.2	110.3	122.2	104.6	95.3	93.1	103.2	100.5	148.2	95.5	97.7	112.5	96.4
2012	98.5	109.5	130.4	99.3	95.1	87.6	96.6	100.5	147.9	125.6	98.9	113.2	90.0
2013	96.1	103.7	119.5	79.5	79.2	71.8	79.5	92.9	163.1	116.9	102.7	112.5	85.3
2014	93.0	103.5	108.8	78.2	67.9	75.5	79.1	81.6	144.0	122.7	107.6	114.8	80.2
2015	89.6	103.2	103.3	79.2	61.1	71.5	82.5	79.5	137.6	122.8	109.7	117.4	80.2
2016	89.1	103.8	102.9	80.6	72.6	73.4	83.8	72.9	129.6	98.1	115.7	123.1	82.2
2010													
1st quarter	101.9	104.3	94.1	102.1	100.3	99.6	102.3	103.4	111.8	110.2	94.9	105.8	98.8
2nd quarter	101.9	105.3	104.7	104.1	105.2	101.3	109.8	104.3	126.4	111.9	98.8	105.5	98.1
3rd quarter	101.5	107.2	111.1	100.0	93.1	106.6	122.7	108.9	117.9	105.8	104.3	108.4	98.3
4th quarter	101.1	109.0	129.6	99.3	98.0	99.7	110.4	102.0	140.7	104.5	115.6	109.8	97.2
2011													
1st quarter	101.1	109.4	106.6	105.8	92.2	93.9	98.1	98.4	134.1	98.7	89.9	110.8	96.3
2nd quarter	101.3	109.7	119.5	100.1	91.2	94.5	107.9	104.8	151.7	104.9	96.9	112.1	96.0
3rd quarter	101.3	110.4	128.1	104.2	95.7	95.3	111.6	107.2	155.3	94.2	94.8	113.1	96.2
4th quarter	101.2	111.7	134.8	108.3	102.1	88.9	95.3	91.6	151.6	84.3	109.1	114.1	96.9
2012													
1st quarter	99.7	110.2	124.8	107.5	97.5	90.0	101.0	97.9	140.7	120.4	100.7	112.8	92.8
2nd quarter	98.8	109.6	125.3	101.8	97.2	87.6	97.6	97.4	146.9	129.7	101.0	113.8	90.6
3rd quarter	98.3	109.4	133.5	97.2	95.3	88.5	97.9	103.9	164.4	122.9	95.3	112.6	88.7
4th quarter	97.4	108.7	138.1	90.7	90.5	84.2	90.0	102.7	139.4	129.4	98.8	113.5	87.9
2013													
1st quarter	96.5	108.1	114.8	80.5	84.0	74.0	81.4	100.0	167.6	96.4	96.2	114.2	87.2
2nd quarter	96.4	106.8	118.4	82.1	80.4	71.4	79.1	96.0	142.4	117.0	103.4	111.3	86.3
3rd quarter	96.1	99.2	123.0	76.1	77.2	70.0	77.5	90.8	161.7	141.9	105.3	112.3	85.0
4th quarter	95.3	100.6	121.9	79.1	75.2	71.7	80.0	84.9	180.5	112.4	106.0	112.2	82.8
2014													
1st quarter	94.4	103.7	110.1	77.2	71.8	74.5	79.6	84.4	127.5	112.1	103.5	113.0	81.1
2nd quarter	93.8	103.7	109.6	78.1	69.4	76.0	78.9	79.9	154.2	118.5	110.7	113.9	80.2
3rd quarter	92.7	103.3	101.9	78.4	66.4	77.7	81.7	89.0	146.0	122.6	110.4	116.3	79.8
4th quarter	91.1	103.3	113.6	78.9	64.2	73.9	76.4	73.3	148.3	137.6	105.7	116.2	79.8
2015													
1st quarter	90.1	103.1	98.9	78.0	62.1	73.0	79.2	81.8	118.3	120.2	114.5	117.1	80.0
2nd quarter	89.6	102.9	98.7	79.5	60.6	72.7	85.1	81.8	151.3	116.9	104.5	118.0	80.1
3rd quarter	89.6	103.4	103.5	80.1	60.5	69.6	81.4	77.8	141.7	109.0	109.0	117.1	80.2
4th quarter	89.3	103.5	112.2	79.3	61.0	70.7	84.2	76.7	139.3	145.1	110.9	117.5	80.3
2016													
1st quarter	89.2	103.5	101.5	79.6	63.8	72.1	83.7	74.4	146.5	97.3	117.4	120.8	80.3
2nd quarter	89.1	103.6	94.6	80.9	68.6	73.4	84.1	72.5	131.9	107.3	111.0	122.5	81.0
3rd quarter	89.3	104.0	103.4	81.2	74.9	74.3	85.2	74.6	118.2	105.1	116.0	124.4	82.6
4th quarter	88.8	104.2	111.9	80.7	83.2	73.9	82.2	70.0	121.8	82.7	118.5	124.5	84.7

[1] Includes general government intermediate inputs for goods and services sold to other sectors and for own-account investment.

SECTION 6B: STATE AND LOCAL GOVERNMENT IN THE NATIONAL INCOME AND PRODUCT ACCOUNTS

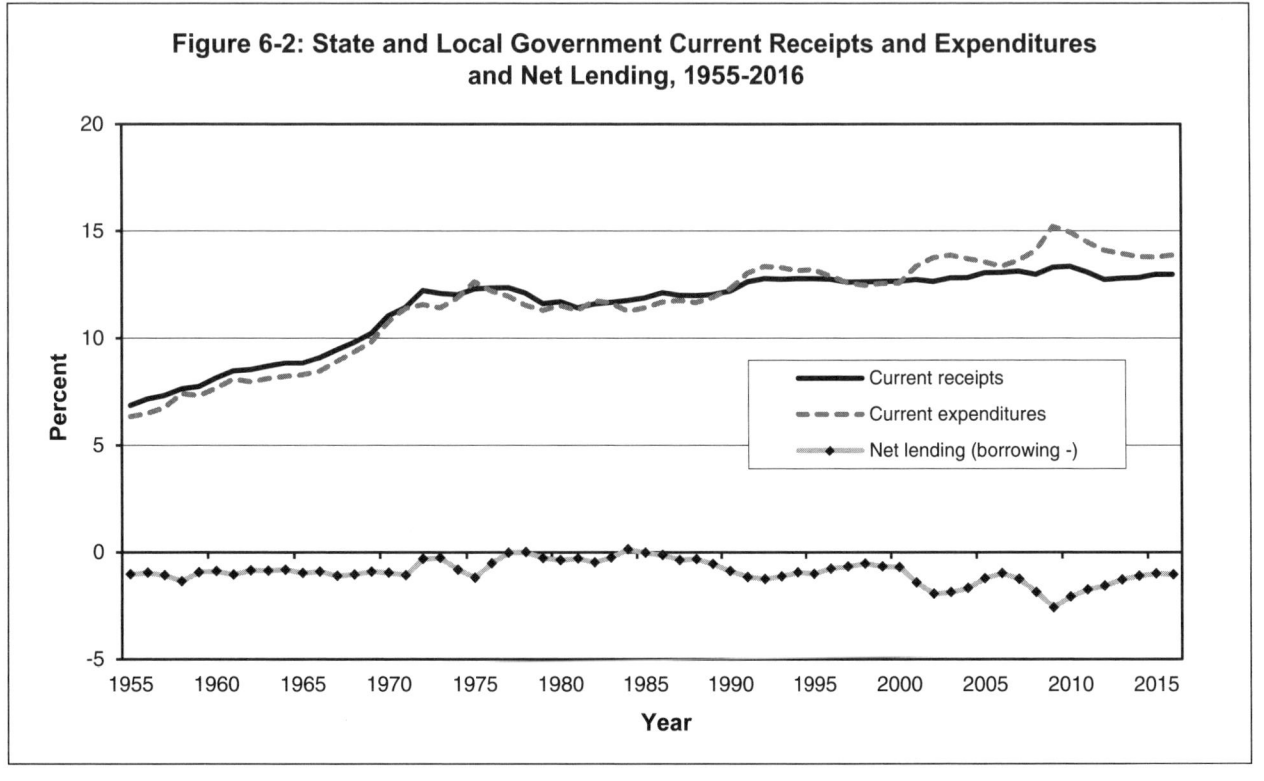

- Both current receipts and current spending of state and local governments have increased as a share of gross domestic product (GDP) over the postwar period, but the growth slowed markedly after the early 1970s. (Tables 6-8 and 1-1)

- State and local governments have consistently been net borrowers in capital markets, as can be seen by the negative values in Figure 6-2. Although they are usually constrained to balance their statutory budgets, they have consistently made net investments and been able to borrow for that purpose. In addition, as revealed by the accrual accounting adopted in the NIPA accounts last year, they have often incurred hidden deficits by failing to fund commitments for public employee retirement benefits. (Table 6-10)

- A larger gap between current expenditures and current receipts appeared during the slow-growth years 2001–2003, and a still-greater one during the Great Recession beginning in late 2007. Generally, in both of those periods of rising deficits, receipts barely kept pace with the economy, while general ("consumption") expenditures, social benefits, and interest payments all fueled higher spending. (Table 6-8)

- After 2009, aggregate state and local spending and borrowing declined as the economy continued to struggle after the Great Recession. (Table 6-8)

Table 6-8. State and Local Government Current Receipts and Expenditures

(National income and product accounts, calendar years, billions of dollars, quarterly data are at seasonally adjusted annual rates.)

NIPA Table 3.3

Year and quarter	Total current receipts	Current receipts										
		Current tax receipts						Taxes on corporate income	Contributions for government social insurance	Income receipts on assets		
		Total tax receipts	Personal current taxes		Taxes on production and imports							
			Income taxes	Other personal taxes	Sales taxes	Property taxes	Other taxes on prod. and imports			Interest receipts	Dividends	Rents and royalties
1955	29.2	24.4	1.3	1.0	7.1	10.4	3.5	1.0	0.3	0.6	. . .	0.3
1956	32.2	27.0	1.6	1.1	8.0	11.5	3.8	1.0	0.4	0.7	. . .	0.3
1957	34.8	29.0	1.7	1.2	8.6	12.6	3.9	1.0	0.4	0.7	. . .	0.3
1958	36.8	30.6	1.8	1.2	10.0	13.8	2.8	1.0	0.4	0.8	. . .	0.4
1959	40.4	33.8	2.2	1.6	11.1	14.8	2.9	1.2	0.4	0.9	. . .	0.3
1960	44.2	37.0	2.5	1.7	12.2	16.2	3.1	1.2	0.5	1.0	. . .	0.3
1961	47.7	39.7	2.8	1.8	13.0	17.6	3.2	1.3	0.5	1.1	. . .	0.4
1962	51.6	42.8	3.2	1.8	14.0	19.0	3.3	1.5	0.5	1.1	. . .	0.4
1963	55.5	45.8	3.4	2.0	15.0	20.2	3.5	1.7	0.6	1.2	. . .	0.4
1964	60.6	49.8	4.0	2.1	16.5	21.7	3.7	1.8	0.7	1.5	. . .	0.4
1965	65.8	53.9	4.4	2.2	18.2	23.2	3.9	2.0	0.8	1.8	. . .	0.4
1966	74.1	58.8	5.4	2.4	20.0	24.5	4.3	2.2	0.8	2.1	. . .	0.5
1967	81.6	64.0	6.1	2.5	21.4	27.0	4.4	2.6	0.9	2.4	. . .	0.6
1968	92.5	73.4	7.8	2.7	25.1	29.9	4.6	3.3	0.9	2.8	. . .	0.7
1969	104.3	82.5	9.8	3.0	28.6	32.8	4.7	3.6	1.0	3.6	. . .	0.8
1970	118.9	91.3	10.9	3.3	31.6	36.7	5.0	3.7	1.1	4.3	. . .	0.8
1971	133.6	101.7	12.4	3.5	35.4	40.4	5.7	4.3	1.2	4.6	. . .	0.9
1972	156.9	115.6	17.2	3.7	39.8	43.2	6.4	5.3	1.3	4.9	. . .	1.0
1973	172.8	126.3	18.9	4.0	44.1	46.4	7.0	6.0	1.5	6.6	0.0	1.1
1974	186.4	136.0	20.4	4.2	48.2	49.0	7.7	6.7	1.7	8.9	0.0	1.3
1975	207.7	147.4	22.5	4.4	51.7	53.4	8.1	7.3	1.8	9.8	0.0	1.3
1976	231.9	165.7	26.3	4.8	57.8	58.2	9.0	9.6	2.2	9.0	0.0	1.3
1977	257.9	183.7	30.4	5.0	64.0	63.2	9.7	11.4	2.8	10.4	0.0	1.3
1978	285.3	198.2	35.0	5.5	71.0	63.7	10.9	12.1	3.4	13.3	0.1	1.3
1979	305.8	212.0	38.2	5.8	77.3	64.4	12.7	13.6	3.9	18.1	0.1	1.9
1980	335.3	230.0	42.6	6.3	82.9	68.8	15.0	14.5	3.6	23.1	0.1	3.1
1981	367.0	255.8	47.9	6.7	90.7	77.1	17.9	15.4	3.9	28.5	0.1	3.3
1982	388.1	273.2	51.9	7.3	96.2	85.3	18.5	14.0	4.0	33.1	0.2	3.5
1983	424.8	300.9	58.3	7.8	107.7	91.9	19.4	15.9	4.1	37.0	0.2	4.3
1984	475.6	337.3	67.5	8.6	121.0	99.7	21.8	18.8	4.7	42.6	0.2	4.9
1985	516.9	363.7	72.1	9.2	131.1	107.5	23.5	20.2	4.9	50.1	0.2	5.4
1986	556.8	389.5	77.4	9.8	139.9	116.2	23.7	22.7	6.0	52.6	0.2	6.2
1987	585.0	422.1	86.0	10.6	150.3	126.4	24.9	23.9	7.2	53.0	0.2	5.3
1988	629.9	452.8	90.6	11.5	162.4	136.5	25.7	26.0	8.4	56.6	0.2	4.4
1989	680.8	488.0	102.3	12.4	172.3	149.9	26.9	24.2	9.0	62.3	0.2	4.1
1990	729.6	519.1	109.6	13.0	184.3	161.5	28.3	22.5	10.0	64.1	0.2	4.2
1991	779.5	544.3	111.7	13.6	190.7	176.1	28.6	23.6	11.6	62.4	0.3	4.5
1992	835.6	579.8	120.4	14.9	204.3	184.7	31.1	24.4	13.1	58.8	0.5	4.8
1993	877.1	604.7	126.2	14.8	216.4	187.3	33.1	26.9	14.1	56.0	0.6	4.5
1994	934.1	644.2	132.2	15.7	231.4	199.4	35.5	30.0	14.5	58.2	0.8	4.5
1995	979.8	672.1	141.7	16.4	242.7	202.6	37.0	31.7	13.6	63.6	1.0	4.5
1996	1 032.6	709.6	152.3	16.3	256.2	212.4	39.4	33.0	12.5	67.7	1.4	4.6
1997	1 085.8	749.9	164.7	17.3	268.7	223.5	41.6	34.1	10.8	71.8	1.5	4.8
1998	1 148.7	794.9	183.0	18.2	283.9	231.0	43.9	34.9	10.4	75.0	1.6	4.6
1999	1 221.8	840.4	195.5	19.0	301.6	242.8	45.8	35.8	9.8	78.6	1.5	5.1
2000	1 303.1	893.2	217.4	19.4	316.8	254.7	49.8	35.2	10.8	86.3	1.4	6.3
2001	1 352.6	914.3	223.3	19.7	321.8	268.0	52.6	28.9	13.7	81.3	1.4	6.5
2002	1 388.4	928.5	201.3	20.5	331.1	289.3	55.4	30.9	15.8	70.5	1.6	6.6
2003	1 474.6	978.6	204.7	22.1	348.9	307.0	62.0	34.0	19.9	64.5	1.7	7.6
2004	1 575.1	1 057.8	223.6	23.8	371.1	326.2	71.5	41.7	24.7	66.4	2.0	8.5
2005	1 708.8	1 166.5	251.5	24.9	402.5	351.3	81.4	54.9	24.6	76.8	2.0	9.8
2006	1 810.9	1 254.5	276.2	26.3	431.8	375.0	85.9	59.2	21.5	94.7	2.1	10.4
2007	1 900.6	1 321.3	296.4	27.1	448.9	403.8	87.2	57.9	18.9	104.2	2.2	11.5
2008	1 909.1	1 328.9	307.0	26.5	444.8	413.8	89.4	47.4	18.7	91.0	2.6	12.1
2009	1 919.2	1 268.1	259.5	28.3	423.9	435.1	75.8	45.6	18.6	74.4	2.1	11.2
2010	1 998.5	1 305.6	267.1	30.5	446.0	435.0	79.4	47.7	18.1	69.1	2.3	11.2
2011	2 030.5	1 368.3	292.9	31.2	466.7	439.2	88.1	50.2	18.2	64.8	2.6	11.7
2012	2 057.2	1 416.1	314.3	32.4	482.8	442.2	92.0	52.5	18.0	59.8	3.3	12.3
2013	2 136.8	1 481.4	342.8	33.0	505.1	448.8	96.2	55.5	18.5	58.9	3.6	12.9
2014	2 236.7	1 526.7	348.5	34.1	523.4	465.1	97.8	57.8	19.6	58.6	3.8	12.9
2015	2 350.7	1 584.1	374.1	35.4	542.9	479.4	93.3	59.2	19.8	59.4	4.2	12.7
2016	2 416.3	1 628.7	383.2	36.4	556.8	499.8	94.3	58.1	20.3	60.3	4.6	13.3
2014												
1st quarter	2 178.7	1 505.5	349.0	33.4	512.1	457.7	95.9	57.4	19.2	58.7	3.7	13.1
2nd quarter	2 231.4	1 510.4	336.0	34.2	521.7	463.3	98.9	56.3	19.6	58.6	3.8	13.0
3rd quarter	2 261.4	1 535.2	349.1	34.5	526.6	467.8	99.0	58.2	19.8	58.6	3.7	12.9
4th quarter	2 275.2	1 555.7	359.8	34.5	533.1	471.3	97.5	59.4	19.8	58.7	3.8	12.7
2015												
1st quarter	2 302.1	1 563.7	366.0	34.9	534.6	473.7	94.6	59.9	19.8	59.0	4.0	12.6
2nd quarter	2 326.9	1 582.4	377.1	35.1	539.8	476.9	93.4	60.1	19.8	59.3	4.1	12.6
3rd quarter	2 335.6	1 586.0	371.0	35.6	547.1	481.0	92.5	58.8	19.8	59.6	4.3	12.7
4th quarter	2 438.0	1 604.4	382.1	35.8	550.1	485.9	92.7	57.9	19.9	59.8	4.3	12.9
2016												
1st quarter	2 379.3	1 610.9	378.5	36.1	552.3	491.7	93.5	58.9	20.1	59.9	4.6	13.1
2nd quarter	2 388.9	1 612.0	376.7	36.1	550.4	497.2	93.3	58.3	20.2	60.2	4.5	13.3
3rd quarter	2 438.7	1 644.2	389.5	36.4	561.9	502.6	95.3	58.9	20.3	60.5	4.5	13.4
4th quarter	2 458.2	1 647.3	388.2	37.0	562.6	507.8	95.2	56.5	20.4	60.7	4.7	13.5

. . . = Not available.

Table 6-8. State and Local Government Current Receipts and Expenditures—*Continued*

(National income and product accounts, calendar years, billions of dollars, quarterly data are at seasonally adjusted annual rates.)

NIPA Table 3.3

Year and quarter	Current receipts—*Continued*					Current expenditures					Net state and local government saving, NIPA (surplus + / deficit -)		
	Current transfer receipts				Current surplus of government enterprises	Total	Consumption expenditures	Government social benefits to persons	Interest payments	Subsidies	Total	Social insurance funds	Other
	Total	Federal grants-in-aid	From business, net	From persons									
1955	2.9	2.3	0.2	0.4	0.7	27.0	22.1	3.3	1.6	. . .	2.2	0.1	2.1
1956	3.0	2.4	0.2	0.4	0.8	29.2	24.0	3.3	1.9	. . .	3.0	0.1	2.9
1957	3.5	2.8	0.2	0.5	0.8	32.1	26.4	3.6	2.1	. . .	2.6	0.1	2.5
1958	4.0	3.2	0.2	0.5	0.8	35.7	29.4	4.0	2.3	. . .	1.1	0.0	1.1
1959	4.0	3.6	0.1	0.3	1.0	38.2	31.2	4.3	2.7	0.0	2.2	0.0	2.2
1960	4.3	3.8	0.2	0.3	1.2	41.6	34.1	4.6	3.0	0.0	2.6	0.0	2.5
1961	4.9	4.3	0.2	0.4	1.2	45.5	37.2	5.0	3.3	0.0	2.2	0.0	2.2
1962	5.5	4.7	0.2	0.5	1.3	48.2	39.3	5.3	3.5	0.0	3.4	0.0	3.4
1963	6.0	5.2	0.3	0.5	1.5	51.8	42.3	5.7	3.8	0.0	3.7	0.0	3.7
1964	6.8	6.0	0.3	0.5	1.5	56.3	46.0	6.2	4.1	0.0	4.3	0.0	4.3
1965	7.4	6.6	0.3	0.5	1.6	61.7	50.6	6.7	4.5	0.0	4.1	0.1	4.0
1966	10.4	9.4	0.3	0.7	1.5	68.9	56.4	7.6	4.9	0.0	5.2	0.1	5.1
1967	12.3	10.9	0.5	0.9	1.4	76.9	62.4	9.2	5.2	0.0	4.7	0.1	4.6
1968	13.3	11.8	0.5	1.0	1.3	88.2	70.7	11.4	6.0	0.0	4.3	0.1	4.1
1969	15.3	13.7	0.5	1.1	1.3	100.2	80.4	13.2	6.6	0.0	4.1	0.2	3.9
1970	20.1	18.3	0.6	1.2	1.3	115.9	92.1	16.1	7.7	0.0	3.0	0.2	2.8
1971	24.1	22.1	0.6	1.4	1.1	133.0	104.2	19.3	9.4	0.0	0.6	0.2	0.4
1972	32.8	30.5	0.7	1.7	1.2	148.5	115.4	22.0	11.1	0.1	8.4	0.3	8.2
1973	36.1	33.5	0.9	1.7	1.2	163.1	126.8	24.1	12.2	0.1	9.6	0.3	9.3
1974	37.9	34.9	1.1	2.0	0.6	184.1	144.5	25.3	14.2	0.1	2.3	0.4	1.9
1975	47.2	43.6	1.2	2.4	0.1	213.3	165.6	30.8	16.7	0.2	-5.6	0.5	-6.0
1976	53.3	49.1	1.4	2.9	0.2	229.1	177.2	34.1	17.6	0.2	2.8	0.6	2.2
1977	59.6	54.8	1.6	3.3	0.1	249.5	193.0	37.0	19.2	0.2	8.4	1.0	7.5
1978	69.0	63.5	1.9	3.7	0.0	271.9	209.9	40.8	21.0	0.2	13.4	1.5	12.0
1979	70.3	64.0	2.2	4.1	-0.5	297.6	229.4	44.3	23.5	0.3	8.2	1.8	6.4
1980	76.9	69.7	2.5	4.7	-1.4	329.9	252.8	51.2	25.6	0.4	5.4	1.3	4.1
1981	78.0	69.4	2.9	5.7	-2.6	362.9	276.1	57.1	29.3	0.4	4.1	1.3	2.8
1982	75.9	66.3	3.2	6.4	-1.7	393.2	297.4	61.2	34.2	0.5	-5.1	1.2	-0.3
1983	78.7	67.9	3.6	7.2	-0.4	423.6	316.7	66.9	39.5	0.4	1.3	1.2	0.1
1984	84.7	72.3	4.2	8.1	1.3	454.7	340.0	71.2	43.2	0.4	20.9	1.4	19.5
1985	89.8	76.2	4.4	9.2	2.9	496.7	371.8	77.3	47.3	0.3	20.3	1.3	18.9
1986	99.8	82.4	6.7	10.6	2.6	536.4	399.9	84.3	51.8	0.3	20.4	1.9	18.6
1987	94.4	78.4	4.9	11.2	2.7	572.9	428.3	90.7	53.5	0.3	12.1	2.2	9.9
1988	103.1	85.7	5.4	12.0	4.4	612.9	458.9	98.5	55.1	0.4	17.0	2.5	14.5
1989	111.6	91.8	6.4	13.4	5.6	673.4	501.3	109.3	62.3	0.4	7.4	2.3	5.1
1990	126.4	104.4	7.1	14.9	5.6	736.0	546.2	127.7	61.8	0.4	-6.5	2.0	-8.4
1991	150.7	124.0	7.9	18.7	5.7	804.6	580.1	156.5	67.6	0.4	-25.1	2.4	-27.5
1992	172.8	141.7	9.2	21.9	5.8	873.1	619.0	180.0	73.6	0.4	-37.5	3.1	-40.7
1993	189.8	155.7	10.5	23.5	7.3	914.3	646.5	195.2	72.2	0.4	-37.2	4.2	-41.4
1994	204.1	166.8	12.0	25.2	7.8	961.0	682.2	206.7	71.8	0.3	-27.0	4.6	-31.6
1995	214.4	174.5	13.5	26.5	10.6	1 011.4	716.8	217.6	76.6	0.3	-31.5	4.0	-35.6
1996	224.4	181.5	15.2	27.8	12.4	1 045.0	748.1	224.3	72.4	0.3	-12.5	2.8	-15.3
1997	236.1	188.1	17.7	30.3	10.9	1 084.1	785.9	227.6	70.2	0.4	1.7	1.2	0.5
1998	253.5	200.8	21.6	31.1	8.7	1 133.3	835.7	235.8	61.4	0.4	15.4	1.7	13.7
1999	277.4	219.2	24.0	34.2	9.0	1 212.6	902.0	252.3	57.8	0.4	9.2	1.7	7.5
2000	299.7	233.1	28.6	38.0	5.4	1 293.2	969.1	271.4	52.1	0.5	9.9	2.0	7.9
2001	333.1	261.3	29.8	42.0	2.4	1 417.9	1 039.7	305.1	65.4	7.7	-65.3	2.6	-67.9
2002	365.4	287.2	32.6	45.6	0.1	1 509.4	1 091.0	333.0	84.4	0.9	-120.9	1.4	-122.3
2003	405.0	321.7	33.8	49.5	-2.8	1 596.0	1 127.1	353.6	115.2	0.1	-121.4	3.2	-124.7
2004	422.4	332.2	36.5	53.7	-6.7	1 683.4	1 187.6	385.0	110.5	0.4	-108.4	7.3	-115.7
2005	436.4	343.4	36.5	56.5	-7.3	1 775.4	1 256.6	406.6	111.8	0.4	-66.6	7.2	-73.8
2006	438.9	340.8	38.8	59.3	-11.1	1 850.3	1 325.9	403.9	120.1	0.4	-39.4	4.6	-44.0
2007	460.9	359.0	40.5	61.4	-18.5	1 973.3	1 411.4	433.3	121.5	7.1	-72.7	2.7	-75.4
2008	477.8	371.0	43.6	63.3	-22.0	2 074.1	1 488.7	455.4	127.0	3.0	-165.1	1.7	-166.8
2009	566.1	458.1	44.0	64.0	-21.4	2 191.2	1 508.4	492.6	188.8	1.4	-271.9	2.2	-274.1
2010	612.0	505.3	43.4	63.2	-19.8	2 235.8	1 518.3	523.8	192.1	1.6	-237.3	3.2	-240.5
2011	582.1	472.5	44.2	65.4	-17.4	2 246.4	1 524.8	530.4	190.7	0.5	-215.9	4.4	-220.4
2012	558.0	444.0	44.0	70.1	-10.4	2 277.9	1 536.3	540.0	201.2	0.5	-220.8	4.2	-225.0
2013	571.3	450.0	49.5	71.7	-9.8	2 327.3	1 562.7	563.4	200.7	0.5	-190.5	4.3	-194.8
2014	625.0	494.8	50.0	75.0	-9.9	2 405.6	1 608.2	616.9	180.0	0.5	-168.9	5.1	-174.0
2015	680.0	532.1	68.3	79.1	-9.6	2 497.0	1 650.8	664.0	181.7	0.5	-146.4	5.3	-151.7
2016	695.6	555.5	58.5	81.6	-6.6	2 583.7	1 693.6	692.6	197.0	0.5	-167.4	5.4	-172.8
2014													
1st quarter	588.6	467.4	47.9	73.4	-10.2	2 359.1	1 587.6	584.4	186.5	0.5	-180.4	4.8	-185.2
2nd quarter	635.8	492.1	48.5	74.4	-9.8	2 389.4	1 601.1	607.2	180.6	0.5	-158.0	5.0	-163.0
3rd quarter	641.0	511.5	54.0	75.5	-9.7	2 428.1	1 617.0	633.6	177.0	0.5	-166.6	5.2	-171.9
4th quarter	634.4	508.0	49.7	76.6	-9.9	2 445.9	1 627.2	642.4	175.8	0.5	-170.7	5.3	-176.0
2015													
1st quarter	653.1	524.9	50.4	77.8	-10.2	2 451.7	1 622.9	651.2	177.1	0.5	-149.6	5.3	-154.9
2nd quarter	658.9	527.0	51.0	78.8	-10.1	2 492.2	1 646.2	666.0	179.5	0.5	-165.4	5.3	-170.7
3rd quarter	662.8	531.7	51.5	79.6	-9.6	2 512.8	1 660.5	668.8	182.9	0.5	-177.1	5.3	-182.5
4th quarter	745.1	544.7	120.2	80.2	-8.4	2 531.4	1 673.5	670.0	187.4	0.5	-93.4	5.4	-98.8
2016													
1st quarter	677.6	540.8	56.2	80.6	-6.9	2 539.9	1 668.3	678.2	192.9	0.5	-160.6	5.4	-166.0
2nd quarter	685.0	549.4	54.4	81.2	-6.4	2 573.8	1 689.4	687.1	196.8	0.5	-184.9	5.4	-190.3
3rd quarter	701.5	565.7	54.0	81.9	-6.3	2 600.9	1 704.4	697.1	198.9	0.5	-162.2	5.4	-167.6
4th quarter	718.4	566.3	69.5	82.7	-6.7	2 620.1	1 712.2	708.1	199.3	0.5	-161.9	5.4	-167.3

. . . = Not available.

Table 6-9. State and Local Government Consumption Expenditures and Gross Investment

(National income and product accounts, calendar years, billions of dollars, quarterly data are at seasonally adjusted annual rates.)

NIPA Tables 3.9.5, 3.10.5

Year and quarter	Total	State and local government consumption expenditures and gross investment											
		Consumption expenditures [1]								Gross investment			
		Total	Compensation of general government employees	Consumption of general government fixed capital	Intermediate goods and services purchased [2]	Less				Total	Structures	Equipment	Intellectual property
						Own-account investment	Sales to other sectors						
							Total [3]	Tuition and related educational charges	Health and hospital charges				
1960	48.2	34.1	26.4	3.6	8.9	0.9	3.9	0.4	1.0	14.1	12.7	1.2	0.2
1961	52.5	37.2	29.1	3.8	9.6	1.0	4.3	0.5	1.0	15.3	13.8	1.2	0.2
1962	55.4	39.3	31.2	4.1	10.1	1.1	4.9	0.6	1.3	16.1	14.5	1.3	0.2
1963	60.0	42.3	33.9	4.4	10.8	1.3	5.6	0.7	1.3	17.8	16.0	1.5	0.3
1964	65.3	46.0	37.0	4.7	11.9	1.3	6.3	0.8	1.5	19.3	17.2	1.7	0.3
1965	71.7	50.0	40.7	5.1	13.4	1.4	7.2	1.0	1.8	21.2	19.0	1.8	0.4
1966	79.8	56.4	45.5	5.7	14.9	1.5	8.2	1.2	2.1	23.5	21.0	2.0	0.4
1967	88.1	62.4	50.6	6.2	16.4	1.6	9.3	1.4	2.5	25.7	23.0	2.2	0.5
1968	98.8	70.7	57.6	6.9	18.6	1.8	10.7	1.6	3.1	28.1	25.2	2.3	0.6
1969	109.3	80.4	64.6	7.8	21.8	1.9	11.8	1.9	3.5	28.8	25.6	2.6	0.7
1970	121.4	92.1	73.2	8.8	25.3	2.1	13.1	2.4	3.8	29.3	25.8	2.8	0.8
1971	134.9	104.2	82.4	9.9	29.1	2.2	14.9	2.9	4.6	30.7	27.0	2.9	0.8
1972	146.7	115.4	91.7	10.7	32.0	2.3	16.7	3.2	5.6	31.3	27.1	3.3	0.9
1973	160.8	126.8	100.7	11.9	35.3	2.4	18.7	3.7	6.6	34.0	29.1	3.8	1.0
1974	185.0	144.5	110.5	14.7	42.6	2.8	20.5	4.0	7.4	40.5	34.7	4.6	1.2
1975	210.2	165.6	124.0	16.7	50.5	3.0	22.6	4.3	8.5	44.6	38.1	5.1	1.3
1976	222.1	177.2	133.3	17.4	55.0	3.0	25.6	4.7	9.9	44.9	38.1	5.3	1.5
1977	237.0	193.0	145.1	18.4	60.8	3.1	28.3	5.2	10.9	44.0	36.9	5.4	1.6
1978	260.7	209.9	158.9	19.9	66.6	3.5	32.0	5.8	12.7	50.8	42.8	6.1	1.9
1979	287.8	229.4	174.2	22.2	73.9	4.3	36.6	6.4	15.2	58.4	49.0	7.1	2.2
1980	318.5	252.8	191.6	25.7	81.6	4.9	41.2	7.2	17.3	65.7	55.1	8.1	2.6
1981	343.0	276.1	208.5	29.4	91.1	5.3	47.6	8.3	21.0	66.9	55.4	8.5	3.0
1982	364.4	297.4	224.8	32.1	100.0	5.7	53.8	9.4	24.5	67.0	54.2	9.4	3.4
1983	385.6	316.7	240.9	33.1	109.0	6.1	60.1	10.6	27.8	68.8	54.2	10.8	3.8
1984	417.5	340.0	259.2	34.1	118.4	7.0	64.7	11.7	29.4	77.6	60.5	12.7	4.4
1985	459.2	371.8	283.2	35.9	131.4	7.9	70.8	12.7	32.0	87.3	67.6	14.8	5.0
1986	496.1	399.9	305.8	38.6	141.7	8.8	77.4	13.8	34.8	96.2	74.2	16.4	5.6
1987	530.5	428.3	329.6	41.6	150.0	9.5	83.4	15.0	37.0	102.2	78.8	17.2	6.2
1988	569.3	458.9	356.3	44.5	159.8	10.4	91.2	16.6	40.3	110.4	84.8	18.6	7.0
1989	620.5	501.3	391.1	47.7	175.8	11.9	101.4	18.4	45.0	119.2	88.7	21.9	8.6
1990	678.3	546.2	428.7	51.6	190.5	13.1	111.6	20.3	50.0	132.2	98.5	23.9	9.7
1991	717.4	580.1	458.5	55.1	204.7	14.1	124.1	22.6	57.0	137.3	103.2	23.5	10.6
1992	758.8	619.0	495.3	57.6	218.9	14.4	138.4	25.4	65.3	139.7	104.2	24.0	11.4
1993	787.7	646.5	519.2	60.8	233.8	14.8	152.5	27.4	73.1	141.2	104.5	24.9	11.9
1994	831.1	682.2	545.5	64.3	251.3	15.4	163.5	29.3	78.8	148.8	108.7	28.1	12.0
1995	876.8	716.8	569.6	68.6	270.3	16.1	175.6	31.1	85.0	160.0	117.3	30.5	12.3
1996	918.2	748.1	591.4	72.0	285.5	16.8	184.0	32.9	86.6	170.2	126.8	30.5	12.8
1997	971.8	785.9	619.0	75.7	304.1	18.5	194.3	35.4	89.9	185.8	139.5	32.0	14.3
1998	1 029.4	835.7	652.5	79.8	326.4	19.3	203.7	37.9	93.4	193.7	143.6	34.7	15.5
1999	1 115.6	902.0	695.1	84.9	357.1	20.7	214.4	40.5	96.7	213.6	159.7	37.4	16.5
2000	1 202.0	969.1	740.4	91.4	391.9	22.8	231.8	43.6	104.0	232.9	176.0	38.8	18.1
2001	1 289.5	1 039.7	794.4	96.9	425.0	25.2	251.4	46.1	116.2	249.8	192.3	38.4	19.1
2002	1 354.3	1 091.0	836.4	101.4	444.0	26.1	264.6	49.3	120.7	263.3	205.8	38.0	19.4
2003	1 396.0	1 127.1	876.5	105.2	450.8	26.6	278.8	53.4	124.8	268.9	211.1	37.6	20.2
2004	1 465.0	1 187.6	926.3	111.6	472.2	27.8	294.7	56.7	130.9	277.5	219.1	37.2	21.2
2005	1 547.4	1 256.6	965.0	121.8	507.3	29.6	308.0	60.9	132.3	290.8	231.5	37.1	22.1
2006	1 640.2	1 325.9	1 011.4	131.7	542.2	31.6	327.5	65.7	141.3	314.3	251.2	39.1	24.0
2007	1 752.2	1 411.4	1 065.5	144.7	577.8	33.6	343.0	69.6	149.8	340.8	271.2	43.9	25.8
2008	1 847.6	1 488.7	1 117.7	155.5	606.6	35.8	355.2	73.8	157.6	358.8	285.3	45.7	27.8
2009	1 871.4	1 508.4	1 141.9	162.1	609.9	36.2	369.4	79.2	167.0	363.0	289.8	44.5	28.7
2010	1 870.2	1 518.3	1 167.4	164.9	610.0	35.2	388.8	85.2	175.3	351.9	280.5	41.8	29.5
2011	1 865.3	1 524.8	1 171.4	171.6	618.8	35.5	401.5	88.7	181.6	340.5	271.1	39.3	30.1
2012	1 866.1	1 536.3	1 180.9	178.9	622.2	35.2	410.5	91.3	186.0	329.7	259.8	38.9	31.0
2013	1 886.6	1 562.7	1 206.1	183.8	630.4	35.4	422.1	94.1	193.2	323.9	251.2	39.6	33.0
2014	1 938.9	1 608.2	1 239.8	189.4	653.7	36.0	438.8	96.5	203.3	330.7	256.5	39.9	34.2
2015	1 994.9	1 650.8	1 282.0	192.9	668.5	37.5	455.0	98.9	213.5	344.1	267.8	40.8	35.5
2016	2 036.3	1 693.6	1 318.0	196.1	686.9	37.7	469.7	100.8	223.2	342.7	264.4	42.0	36.3
2014													
1st quarter	1 910.3	1 587.6	1 224.5	187.7	643.6	36.0	432.2	95.7	199.2	322.7	249.8	39.1	33.7
2nd quarter	1 931.2	1 601.1	1 233.7	188.9	651.3	35.7	437.2	96.3	202.2	330.1	256.4	39.7	34.0
3rd quarter	1 949.6	1 617.0	1 244.6	190.1	659.3	35.8	441.2	96.9	204.8	332.9	258.7	39.9	34.4
4th quarter	1 964.2	1 627.2	1 256.5	190.9	660.7	36.3	444.6	97.2	206.9	337.0	261.3	41.1	34.6
2015													
1st quarter	1 957.5	1 622.9	1 263.0	191.2	655.0	37.6	448.7	97.9	209.4	334.6	259.4	40.0	35.2
2nd quarter	1 994.8	1 646.2	1 276.1	192.6	668.0	37.2	453.3	98.7	212.3	348.6	273.3	39.9	35.5
3rd quarter	2 012.5	1 660.5	1 286.4	193.7	675.2	37.3	457.5	99.2	214.9	352.0	275.0	41.3	35.7
4th quarter	2 014.8	1 673.5	1 302.6	194.0	675.7	38.0	460.7	99.7	217.3	341.3	263.6	41.9	35.9
2016													
1st quarter	2 020.4	1 668.3	1 303.0	194.0	673.0	37.2	464.5	100.1	220.0	352.1	273.9	42.2	36.0
2nd quarter	2 033.3	1 689.4	1 314.7	196.1	684.5	37.7	468.2	100.6	222.5	343.9	265.2	42.5	36.2
3rd quarter	2 040.0	1 704.4	1 325.5	196.6	691.8	38.1	471.5	101.1	224.3	335.6	257.3	42.0	36.4
4th quarter	2 051.4	1 712.2	1 328.9	197.6	698.2	37.8	474.7	101.6	225.8	339.2	261.5	41.2	36.5

[1] Excludes government sales to other sectors and government own-account investment (construction and software).
[2] Includes general government intermediate inputs for goods and services sold to other sectors and for own-account investment.
[3] Includes components not shown separately.

Table 6-10. State and Local Government Output, Lending and Borrowing, and Net Investment

(National income and product accounts, calendar years, billions of dollars, quarterly data are at seasonally adjusted annual rates.)

NIPA Tables 3.3, 3.10.5

Year and quarter	Output			Net lending (net borrowing -)							Net investment
	Gross	Value added	Intermediate goods and services purchased [1]	Net saving, current (surplus +, deficit -)	Plus: Capital transfer receipts	Minus			Plus: consumption of fixed capital	Equals: Net lending (borrowing -)	
						Gross investment	Capital transfer payments	Net purchases of nonproduced assets			
1955	25.1	19.1	6.0	2.2	1.0	10.1	...		0.6	3.2	-4.4	6.9
1956	27.2	21.3	5.9	3.0	1.1	11.4	...		0.7	3.6	-4.3	7.8
1957	30.0	23.6	6.4	2.6	1.6	12.7	...		0.7	3.9	-5.1	8.8
1958	33.4	25.9	7.5	1.1	2.7	13.7	...		0.8	4.1	-6.5	9.6
1959	35.8	27.4	8.3	2.2	3.5	14.1	...		0.8	4.4	-4.9	9.7
1960	38.9	30.0	8.9	2.6	3.0	14.1	...		0.9	4.5	-4.8	9.6
1961	42.6	32.9	9.6	2.2	3.3	15.3	...		1.0	4.8	-5.9	10.5
1962	45.4	35.3	10.1	3.4	3.5	16.1	...		1.1	5.2	-5.1	10.9
1963	49.1	38.3	10.8	3.7	4.1	17.8	...		1.2	5.5	-5.5	12.3
1964	53.6	41.7	11.9	4.3	4.7	19.3	...		1.3	5.9	-5.6	13.4
1965	59.2	45.8	13.4	4.1	4.7	21.2	...		1.3	6.4	-7.2	14.8
1966	66.1	51.2	14.9	5.2	5.1	23.5	...		1.4	7.1	-7.4	16.4
1967	73.3	56.9	16.4	4.7	5.1	25.7	...		1.4	7.8	-9.5	17.9
1968	83.2	64.5	18.6	4.3	6.8	28.1	...		1.4	8.6	-9.8	19.5
1969	94.2	72.4	21.8	4.1	6.8	28.8	...		1.0	9.7	-9.2	19.1
1970	107.3	82.0	25.3	3.0	6.2	29.3	...		1.1	10.9	-10.3	18.4
1971	121.4	92.2	29.1	0.6	7.0	30.7	...		1.6	12.2	-12.5	18.5
1972	134.4	102.4	32.0	8.4	7.3	31.3	...		1.7	13.3	-4.0	18.0
1973	147.9	112.6	35.3	9.6	7.3	34.0	...		1.7	14.9	-3.9	19.1
1974	167.8	125.2	42.6	2.3	9.2	40.5	...		1.9	18.3	-12.6	22.2
1975	191.2	140.7	50.5	-5.6	11.0	44.6	...		1.9	21.0	-20.1	23.6
1976	205.7	150.8	55.0	2.8	12.0	44.9	...		1.7	22.1	-9.7	22.8
1977	224.4	163.5	60.8	8.4	13.1	44.0	...		1.6	23.5	-0.5	20.5
1978	245.4	178.8	66.6	13.4	13.7	50.8	...		1.8	25.5	0.0	25.3
1979	270.3	196.4	73.9	8.2	16.2	58.4	...		2.0	28.6	-7.3	29.8
1980	298.9	217.3	81.6	5.4	18.6	65.7	...		2.2	33.1	-10.8	32.6
1981	329.0	237.8	91.1	4.1	17.8	66.9	...		2.2	37.8	-9.4	29.1
1982	356.9	256.9	100.0	-5.1	16.9	67.0	...		2.2	41.3	-16.1	25.7
1983	382.9	273.9	109.0	1.3	18.0	68.8	...		2.2	42.8	-9.0	26.0
1984	411.7	293.3	118.4	20.9	20.1	77.6	...		2.6	44.4	5.3	33.2
1985	450.5	319.1	131.4	20.3	22.0	87.3	...		3.1	46.9	-1.3	40.4
1986	486.1	344.4	141.7	20.4	23.0	96.2	...		3.7	50.3	-6.1	45.9
1987	521.3	371.2	150.0	12.1	22.3	102.2	...		4.2	54.1	-17.9	48.1
1988	560.5	400.8	159.8	17.0	23.1	110.4	...		4.3	57.8	-16.9	52.6
1989	614.6	438.8	175.8	7.4	23.4	119.2	0.0		4.9	61.9	-31.4	57.3
1990	670.8	480.3	190.5	-6.5	25.0	132.2	0.0		5.7	66.7	-52.7	65.5
1991	718.3	513.7	204.7	-25.1	25.8	137.3	0.0		5.8	70.9	-71.6	66.4
1992	771.9	553.0	218.9	-37.5	26.9	139.7	0.0		5.9	74.1	-82.0	65.6
1993	813.8	580.0	233.8	-37.2	28.2	141.2	0.0		5.9	78.3	-77.8	62.9
1994	861.1	609.9	251.3	-27.0	29.9	148.8	0.0		6.2	82.9	-69.1	65.9
1995	908.6	638.2	270.3	-31.5	32.4	160.0	0.0		6.6	88.3	-77.5	71.7
1996	948.9	663.4	285.5	-12.5	33.8	170.2	0.0		6.0	92.6	-62.2	77.6
1997	998.7	694.7	304.1	1.7	35.2	185.8	0.0		5.8	96.9	-57.9	88.9
1998	1 058.7	732.3	326.4	15.4	35.9	193.7	0.0		7.6	101.8	-48.3	91.9
1999	1 137.1	780.0	357.1	9.2	40.0	213.6	0.0		8.6	108.1	-64.8	105.5
2000	1 223.7	831.8	391.9	9.9	44.2	232.9	0.0		8.6	116.2	-71.2	116.7
2001	1 316.3	891.3	425.0	-65.3	51.7	249.8	0.0		10.1	123.0	-150.5	126.8
2002	1 381.8	937.8	444.0	-120.9	52.9	263.3	0.0		11.2	129.0	-213.5	134.3
2003	1 432.5	981.7	450.8	-121.4	52.0	268.9	0.0		11.4	134.5	-215.2	134.4
2004	1 510.1	1 037.9	472.2	-108.4	52.4	277.5	4.5		11.3	143.8	-205.4	133.7
2005	1 594.1	1 086.8	507.3	-66.6	56.8	290.8	6.4		10.0	157.3	-159.7	133.5
2006	1 685.0	1 142.8	542.2	-39.4	57.8	314.3	0.0		11.0	170.3	-136.6	144.0
2007	1 788.0	1 210.2	577.8	-72.7	59.3	340.8	0.0		13.6	186.6	-181.2	154.2
2008	1 879.7	1 273.2	606.6	-165.1	63.2	358.8	0.0		13.8	200.2	-274.3	158.6
2009	1 913.9	1 304.0	609.9	-271.9	67.7	363.0	0.0		12.3	208.2	-371.4	154.8
2010	1 942.3	1 332.3	610.0	-237.3	76.7	351.9	0.0		10.6	212.7	-310.3	139.2
2011	1 961.8	1 343.0	618.8	-215.9	73.8	340.5	0.0		9.2	222.2	-269.6	118.3
2012	1 982.0	1 359.8	622.2	-220.8	74.2	329.7	0.0		9.1	231.9	-253.6	97.8
2013	2 020.3	1 389.9	630.4	-190.5	71.6	323.9	0.0		9.0	238.5	-213.3	85.4
2014	2 083.0	1 429.2	653.7	-168.9	70.7	330.7	0.0		9.5	245.9	-192.5	84.8
2015	2 143.4	1 474.9	668.5	-146.4	69.0	344.1	0.0		10.2	250.6	-181.2	93.5
2016	2 201.0	1 514.1	686.9	-167.4	72.4	342.7	0.0		10.5	254.9	-193.4	87.8
2014												
1st quarter	2 055.8	1 412.3	643.6	-180.4	70.3	322.7	0.0		9.2	243.6	-198.3	79.1
2nd quarter	2 073.9	1 422.6	651.3	-158.0	71.9	330.1	0.0		9.4	245.1	-180.4	85.0
3rd quarter	2 094.0	1 434.7	659.3	-166.6	74.7	332.9	0.0		9.6	246.9	-187.6	86.0
4th quarter	2 108.1	1 447.3	660.7	-170.7	65.8	337.0	0.0		9.8	248.1	-203.6	88.9
2015												
1st quarter	2 109.2	1 454.2	655.0	-149.6	67.9	334.6	0.0		10.0	248.6	-177.8	86.0
2nd quarter	2 136.7	1 468.7	668.0	-165.4	67.4	348.6	0.0		10.2	250.3	-206.5	98.3
3rd quarter	2 155.3	1 480.0	675.2	-177.1	72.2	352.0	0.0		10.3	251.6	-215.6	100.4
4th quarter	2 172.2	1 496.6	675.7	-93.4	68.4	341.3	0.0		10.4	251.9	-124.8	89.4
2016												
1st quarter	2 170.0	1 497.0	673.0	-160.6	72.4	352.1	0.0		10.4	252.0	-198.8	100.1
2nd quarter	2 195.3	1 510.9	684.5	-184.9	72.2	343.9	0.0		10.5	254.7	-212.4	89.2
3rd quarter	2 213.9	1 522.1	691.8	-162.2	73.9	335.6	0.0		10.5	255.6	-178.8	80.0
4th quarter	2 224.7	1 526.5	698.2	-161.9	71.1	339.2	0.0		10.6	257.2	-183.4	82.0

[1] Includes general government intermediate inputs for goods and services sold to other sectors and for own-account investment.
. . . = Not available.

Table 6-11. Chain-Type Quantity Indexes for State and Local Government Consumption Expenditures and Gross Investment

(Seasonally adjusted, 2009 = 100.)   NIPA Tables 3.9.3, 3.10.3

Year and quarter	State and local government consumption expenditures and gross investment												
	Consumption expenditures [1]									Gross investment			
						Less							
							Sales to other sectors						
	Total	Total	Compensation of general government employees	Consumption of general government fixed capital	Intermediate goods and services purchased [2]	Own-account investment	Total [3]	Tuition and related educational charges	Health and hospital charges	Total	Structures	Equipment	Intellectual property
1960	25.6	24.3	32.6	14.5	10.5	20.3	13.8	14.0	10.6	29.2	44.0	5.4	2.4
1961	27.1	25.6	34.3	15.3	11.2	21.4	14.9	15.3	10.9	31.5	47.7	5.5	2.7
1962	27.9	26.3	35.5	16.1	11.7	23.0	16.6	17.3	12.7	32.7	49.2	5.9	3.0
1963	29.6	27.5	37.3	17.1	12.4	25.8	18.5	19.7	13.2	35.6	53.3	6.7	3.6
1964	31.6	29.3	39.5	18.2	13.6	26.1	20.4	23.1	14.2	38.2	56.8	7.6	4.0
1965	33.7	31.1	41.9	19.4	15.0	27.2	22.8	26.8	16.3	40.9	60.8	8.1	4.5
1966	35.8	33.0	44.3	20.6	16.2	29.0	24.9	30.4	18.6	43.6	64.7	8.8	5.2
1967	37.5	34.5	46.1	22.0	17.5	29.3	27.4	33.9	21.1	46.4	68.8	9.2	5.9
1968	39.8	36.8	48.8	23.3	19.3	30.9	29.9	38.1	24.6	48.5	71.0	9.6	6.3
1969	41.2	39.1	51.0	24.7	21.4	31.4	31.0	41.9	25.5	46.5	68.1	10.2	7.0
1970	42.4	41.5	53.3	25.9	23.6	32.2	32.3	48.8	25.9	43.7	63.1	10.6	7.7
1971	43.7	43.6	55.4	27.0	25.8	32.6	35.1	55.0	30.2	42.6	61.0	10.7	8.0
1972	44.7	45.2	57.3	28.0	27.4	32.3	37.6	58.4	34.6	41.2	58.0	12.0	8.4
1973	45.9	46.8	59.3	29.1	28.2	32.2	39.1	63.0	38.4	41.5	57.5	13.4	8.9
1974	47.6	48.9	61.5	30.1	29.5	33.8	39.0	62.8	39.6	41.9	57.4	14.6	9.2
1975	49.3	51.3	63.3	31.1	31.9	32.7	39.5	62.8	40.7	41.5	56.9	14.1	9.9
1976	49.7	52.0	64.1	32.1	32.9	30.6	41.8	64.9	43.2	40.9	55.9	13.8	10.5
1977	49.9	53.0	65.0	32.8	34.0	29.3	43.2	67.5	44.0	38.5	52.2	13.4	11.0
1978	51.6	54.1	66.5	33.6	35.0	31.6	45.4	71.2	47.1	41.9	57.1	14.0	12.2
1979	52.3	54.4	67.6	34.5	35.0	35.3	47.6	73.2	51.1	44.0	59.6	15.2	13.4
1980	52.2	54.2	68.5	35.4	33.7	36.8	48.4	75.7	51.5	44.3	59.3	16.1	14.2
1981	51.2	54.0	68.2	36.2	33.9	36.2	50.2	77.3	54.8	40.6	53.5	15.8	15.1
1982	51.2	54.8	68.6	36.9	35.4	36.8	51.5	77.2	56.4	38.2	49.1	16.6	16.2
1983	51.9	55.5	68.1	37.7	37.8	37.2	53.3	79.5	57.9	38.8	48.6	18.9	17.5
1984	53.9	56.7	68.3	38.7	39.8	40.5	53.4	79.3	56.5	43.4	53.9	22.1	19.4
1985	56.9	59.2	70.2	40.1	43.1	43.9	55.3	79.3	57.8	48.1	59.1	25.5	21.8
1986	59.8	61.9	72.2	41.8	46.7	48.0	57.3	79.9	59.3	51.5	62.8	28.0	24.2
1987	61.1	63.2	73.4	43.5	47.7	49.9	58.5	80.5	59.3	52.9	64.2	29.2	25.9
1988	63.4	65.4	75.8	45.3	49.2	52.3	59.7	82.9	59.4	55.7	67.0	31.1	28.8
1989	66.0	67.8	78.0	47.6	51.6	56.9	61.4	85.5	59.8	58.7	68.4	35.9	34.2
1990	68.7	70.0	80.1	50.2	53.3	59.7	62.6	87.4	60.5	63.3	73.5	38.6	38.0
1991	70.2	71.5	80.8	52.7	56.0	62.1	64.7	88.8	63.0	64.8	76.0	37.2	40.9
1992	71.6	73.1	82.0	55.0	58.7	61.5	67.6	90.4	66.7	65.6	76.3	38.0	44.4
1993	72.5	74.4	82.8	57.1	61.3	61.4	70.7	89.3	70.6	65.0	74.5	39.3	45.4
1994	74.5	76.4	84.1	59.2	64.7	62.2	73.1	89.4	73.4	66.9	75.1	44.2	45.9
1995	76.5	78.2	85.6	61.3	67.3	63.0	75.7	89.7	76.7	69.7	77.7	48.4	45.7
1996	78.3	79.7	86.7	63.6	69.1	64.7	77.1	90.0	76.4	72.9	81.6	49.7	48.0
1997	81.1	81.8	88.2	66.2	72.6	70.2	79.7	92.1	78.2	78.4	87.1	54.3	53.8
1998	84.3	85.1	89.8	69.3	78.3	72.1	82.1	94.6	80.5	80.7	86.9	61.8	58.9
1999	87.8	88.0	90.9	72.7	83.7	75.4	84.3	97.4	81.9	87.1	93.1	69.3	62.4
2000	90.3	89.9	92.6	76.1	87.0	79.8	88.5	100.8	85.9	92.0	98.2	73.2	66.7
2001	93.6	92.9	94.5	79.5	93.2	86.1	93.3	101.4	93.1	96.6	103.8	74.8	69.7
2002	96.3	95.4	96.2	82.5	96.8	88.0	95.2	101.4	93.5	100.1	108.1	76.3	71.2
2003	95.9	94.8	96.5	84.9	94.3	87.5	95.7	101.4	91.9	100.8	108.3	77.0	74.5
2004	95.8	94.9	96.6	87.4	94.3	88.4	96.6	98.2	92.2	99.6	106.3	76.9	78.0
2005	95.8	95.5	97.0	89.7	94.7	90.9	97.0	98.2	90.1	97.0	102.2	78.1	81.1
2006	96.7	96.2	97.6	92.1	96.2	94.6	99.1	99.2	92.6	98.7	102.3	84.9	87.0
2007	98.1	97.7	98.8	94.8	97.6	97.5	99.7	99.1	95.0	99.7	101.0	97.2	91.9
2008	98.5	97.9	99.9	97.6	95.2	99.9	98.9	98.9	97.1	100.6	100.7	102.1	96.9
2009	100.0	100.0	100.0	100.0	100.0	100.0	100.0	100.0	100.0	100.0	100.0	100.0	100.0
2010	97.3	97.4	99.0	101.9	96.2	95.7	102.2	102.3	102.2	96.7	96.4	94.7	102.1
2011	94.1	94.8	97.5	103.4	92.3	94.1	102.6	101.5	103.8	91.0	90.0	89.7	102.6
2012	92.3	94.0	96.7	104.6	90.9	91.4	102.2	99.7	103.9	85.3	83.1	87.9	104.3
2013	91.6	93.8	96.5	105.7	90.7	90.5	102.4	98.5	105.9	82.3	78.7	89.7	109.8
2014	92.1	94.4	96.6	106.8	92.7	89.9	104.3	97.5	110.0	82.3	78.4	89.6	112.4
2015	94.2	96.4	97.2	108.1	98.0	93.8	106.7	96.5	114.5	84.9	80.9	91.0	117.4
2016	95.3	98.0	98.2	109.3	101.0	93.3	108.6	95.9	118.2	83.9	79.0	94.0	119.8
2014													
1st quarter	91.3	93.7	96.4	106.4	91.2	90.6	103.3	97.8	108.1	80.8	76.9	88.1	110.8
2nd quarter	91.9	94.2	96.6	106.7	92.0	89.2	104.0	97.6	109.4	82.3	78.5	89.1	111.8
3rd quarter	92.3	94.5	96.6	107.0	93.1	89.4	104.6	97.5	110.4	82.6	78.8	89.2	113.0
4th quarter	92.8	95.0	96.8	107.3	94.5	90.5	105.2	97.1	111.9	83.5	79.3	91.9	114.0
2015													
1st quarter	93.2	95.6	96.9	107.6	96.2	94.3	105.9	96.8	112.9	82.9	78.8	89.3	116.0
2nd quarter	94.2	96.1	97.0	107.9	97.5	93.1	106.5	96.7	113.9	86.0	82.5	89.0	117.3
3rd quarter	94.8	96.8	97.4	108.2	98.7	93.1	107.0	96.5	115.0	86.5	82.7	92.0	117.8
4th quarter	94.6	97.0	97.4	108.5	99.6	94.7	107.6	96.1	116.2	84.0	79.4	93.7	118.5
2016													
1st quarter	95.5	97.5	97.7	108.8	100.3	92.7	108.1	96.0	117.4	86.8	82.7	94.6	119.0
2nd quarter	95.2	97.9	98.0	109.1	100.9	93.5	108.5	95.8	118.1	84.1	79.2	95.0	119.6
3rd quarter	95.2	98.3	98.5	109.4	101.3	94.0	108.8	96.0	118.5	82.0	76.7	94.0	120.2
4th quarter	95.3	98.3	98.5	109.7	101.5	93.0	109.1	95.8	118.9	82.5	77.6	92.4	120.3

[1]Excludes government sales to other sectors and government own-account investment (construction and software).
[2]Includes general government intermediate inputs for goods and services sold to other sectors and for own-account investment.
[3]Includes components not shown separately.

Table 6-12. State Government Current Receipts and Expenditures

(National income and product accounts, calendar years, billions of dollars.)　　　　　　　　　**NIPA Table 3.20**

Year	Current receipts												
		Current tax receipts								Contribu-tions for govern-ment social insurance	Income receipts on assets		
	Total [1]	Total	Personal current taxes		Taxes on production and imports				Taxes on corporate income		Total [1]	Interest receipts	Rents and royalties
			Total [1]	Income taxes	Total	Sales taxes	Property taxes	Other					
1959	21.6	16.7	3.1	2.0	12.5	10.0	0.5	2.0	1.1	0.4	0.5	0.3	0.2
1960	23.3	18.1	3.4	2.3	13.5	10.8	0.5	2.2	1.2	0.5	0.5	0.4	0.2
1961	25.0	19.3	3.7	2.5	14.4	11.6	0.5	2.3	1.3	0.5	0.6	0.4	0.2
1962	27.1	21.0	4.0	2.8	15.4	12.6	0.6	2.3	1.5	0.5	0.6	0.4	0.2
1963	29.1	22.4	4.3	3.1	16.4	13.4	0.6	2.4	1.6	0.6	0.6	0.4	0.2
1964	31.8	24.5	4.9	3.6	17.7	14.5	0.6	2.6	1.8	0.7	0.7	0.4	0.2
1965	35.1	26.9	5.4	3.9	19.6	16.1	0.7	2.8	1.9	0.8	0.8	0.5	0.3
1966	41.5	30.2	6.4	4.8	21.7	18.0	0.7	3.0	2.2	0.8	0.9	0.6	0.3
1967	45.6	32.7	7.0	5.3	23.3	19.4	0.7	3.1	2.5	0.9	1.1	0.8	0.3
1968	53.8	38.6	8.8	6.9	26.7	22.8	0.8	3.2	3.1	0.9	1.7	1.4	0.3
1969	61.6	44.0	10.8	8.6	29.9	25.7	0.9	3.3	3.4	1.0	2.1	1.8	0.3
1970	69.1	48.1	12.0	9.6	32.7	28.2	0.9	3.6	3.5	1.1	2.5	2.2	0.3
1971	78.2	53.8	13.4	11.0	36.3	31.4	1.0	3.9	4.0	1.2	2.7	2.3	0.4
1972	95.0	63.5	17.9	15.2	40.7	35.2	1.1	4.4	5.0	1.3	2.9	2.5	0.4
1973	103.1	70.2	19.8	16.8	44.7	38.8	1.2	4.7	5.7	1.5	3.9	3.3	0.5
1974	112.1	75.9	21.1	18.0	48.4	42.0	1.1	5.3	6.3	1.7	5.0	4.4	0.6
1975	125.8	81.9	23.2	19.9	51.8	44.7	1.4	5.6	6.9	1.8	5.6	5.0	0.6
1976	141.7	93.8	27.0	23.4	57.7	49.9	1.5	6.3	9.1	2.2	5.3	4.7	0.6
1977	158.1	105.1	30.9	27.2	63.4	55.0	1.5	6.9	10.8	2.8	6.1	5.4	0.6
1978	177.2	117.4	35.6	31.6	70.3	60.8	1.9	7.6	11.5	3.4	7.4	6.7	0.6
1979	194.8	128.9	38.9	34.6	77.1	65.7	2.3	9.0	12.9	3.9	10.3	9.2	1.1
1980	216.0	140.9	43.7	39.1	83.4	70.0	2.6	10.8	13.7	3.6	13.4	11.2	2.0
1981	236.4	155.6	48.5	43.6	92.7	76.5	2.7	13.6	14.5	3.9	15.6	13.2	2.2
1982	244.7	162.3	52.3	47.0	97.0	80.3	2.8	13.9	13.1	4.0	17.5	15.3	2.1
1983	269.3	180.5	58.9	53.2	106.8	90.0	3.0	13.8	14.9	4.1	19.5	17.2	2.2
1984	303.7	205.4	68.2	61.9	119.7	100.9	3.4	15.5	17.4	4.7	22.4	19.8	2.5
1985	328.6	220.9	73.2	66.1	129.0	109.0	3.5	16.5	18.7	4.9	26.1	23.4	2.6
1986	354.0	234.0	78.3	70.7	134.9	115.8	3.6	15.6	20.7	6.0	27.5	24.6	2.7
1987	375.0	253.7	87.5	79.1	144.3	124.6	3.7	16.0	21.8	7.2	28.4	25.6	2.6
1988	403.1	269.4	90.4	81.5	155.2	135.1	3.8	16.3	23.8	8.4	30.8	28.0	2.7
1989	435.2	288.4	102.4	92.9	163.5	142.3	4.3	17.0	22.4	9.0	32.8	30.2	2.4
1990	469.2	305.6	109.6	99.6	175.4	152.5	4.6	18.3	20.5	10.0	33.9	31.4	2.3
1991	504.1	314.2	111.8	101.4	180.8	157.5	4.9	18.3	21.6	11.6	34.1	31.2	2.6
1992	551.4	338.8	120.6	109.0	195.9	169.7	6.1	20.1	22.2	13.1	33.6	30.4	2.7
1993	584.8	357.1	126.3	114.9	206.3	179.4	5.9	21.0	24.5	14.1	32.4	29.4	2.5
1994	621.6	380.4	132.1	120.2	220.8	191.7	7.0	22.1	27.5	14.5	33.9	30.6	2.5
1995	653.2	401.5	140.9	128.4	231.3	200.5	7.2	23.6	29.2	13.6	36.9	33.4	2.6
1996	686.2	425.9	150.9	138.6	245.0	211.8	8.2	25.0	29.9	12.5	39.4	35.3	2.7
1997	719.6	449.1	162.7	149.7	255.4	221.3	8.1	26.0	31.0	10.8	41.8	37.5	2.7
1998	764.1	480.7	180.4	166.8	268.8	233.3	8.5	27.0	31.6	10.4	43.3	39.2	2.4
1999	812.5	507.9	192.6	178.4	283.0	245.9	9.1	27.9	32.3	9.8	46.6	42.5	2.6
2000	867.7	540.1	213.5	199.2	294.8	255.5	7.8	31.6	31.7	10.8	49.3	44.3	3.6
2001	904.5	546.8	220.1	205.7	300.8	259.9	8.1	32.8	25.9	13.7	46.5	41.4	3.7
2002	917.8	533.7	199.1	184.3	309.6	268.0	7.7	33.9	25.0	15.8	42.4	37.2	3.7
2003	970.5	558.8	202.4	186.4	328.9	282.0	9.1	37.8	27.5	19.9	42.0	35.9	4.4
2004	1 048.7	606.4	220.3	203.4	352.3	300.5	8.3	43.5	33.8	24.7	44.4	37.4	5.1
2005	1 136.5	676.3	246.5	229.0	385.3	325.6	9.1	50.6	44.5	24.6	50.6	42.7	6.0
2006	1 193.9	728.1	271.0	252.5	409.1	346.6	9.7	52.7	48.0	21.5	59.2	50.7	6.5
2007	1 247.9	759.7	288.9	269.8	424.0	359.0	9.8	55.2	46.9	18.9	65.0	55.3	7.5
2008	1 264.0	763.6	299.8	280.9	425.4	354.3	9.7	61.3	38.4	18.7	60.1	49.6	7.9
2009	1 267.1	688.2	256.6	236.3	393.2	335.6	10.4	47.2	38.4	18.6	52.2	43.0	7.0
2010	1 336.1	720.0	264.7	242.2	415.5	354.7	10.7	50.1	39.8	18.1	51.3	42.4	6.6
2011	1 357.8	773.2	293.2	270.5	437.6	369.9	9.8	57.9	42.4	18.3	50.7	41.8	6.7
2012	1 372.3	804.9	313.8	290.4	448.3	379.2	9.7	59.3	42.9	17.5	50.1	40.8	6.9

[1] Includes components not shown separately.

Table 6-12. State Government Current Receipts and Expenditures—*Continued*

(National income and product accounts, calendar years, billions of dollars.)   **NIPA Table 3.20**

Year	Current receipts—*Continued*					Current expenditures					Net state government saving, NIPA (surplus + / deficit -)		
	Current transfer receipts					Total [1]	Consumption expenditures	Government social benefits to persons	Grants-in-aid to local governments	Interest payments	Total	Social insurance funds	Other
	Total	Federal grants-in-aid	Local grants-in-aid	From business, net	From persons								
1959	3.6	3.2	0.2	0.0	0.1	20.9	8.2	3.6	7.8	1.2	0.7	0.0	0.7
1960	3.7	3.3	0.2	0.0	0.1	22.9	8.9	3.8	8.8	1.3	0.4	0.0	0.4
1961	4.2	3.7	0.3	0.0	0.1	25.0	9.6	4.1	9.8	1.5	0.0	0.0	0.0
1962	4.6	4.1	0.3	0.1	0.2	27.0	10.2	4.4	10.8	1.6	0.1	0.0	0.1
1963	5.0	4.5	0.3	0.1	0.2	29.4	11.0	4.7	11.9	1.7	-0.3	0.0	-0.3
1964	5.5	4.9	0.3	0.1	0.2	31.9	11.8	5.1	13.0	1.8	-0.1	0.0	-0.1
1965	6.1	5.5	0.3	0.1	0.3	35.6	13.0	5.5	15.0	2.0	-0.4	0.1	-0.5
1966	8.9	8.2	0.4	0.1	0.3	40.7	14.6	6.4	17.4	2.2	0.8	0.1	0.6
1967	10.3	9.4	0.5	0.1	0.3	46.8	16.7	7.7	19.9	2.3	-1.2	0.1	-1.3
1968	11.8	10.7	0.6	0.1	0.3	54.6	19.2	9.5	23.0	2.7	-0.8	0.1	-1.0
1969	13.7	12.4	0.8	0.1	0.4	62.8	22.4	10.8	26.4	2.9	-1.2	0.2	-1.3
1970	16.6	15.2	0.9	0.1	0.4	72.8	25.8	12.9	30.4	3.4	-3.7	0.2	-3.9
1971	19.9	18.4	1.0	0.1	0.4	82.9	28.8	15.3	34.3	4.2	-4.7	0.2	-5.0
1972	26.4	24.6	1.1	0.2	0.5	92.9	31.5	17.5	38.5	5.0	2.2	0.3	1.9
1973	26.6	24.5	1.2	0.2	0.7	103.3	35.3	19.4	42.6	5.4	-0.1	0.3	-0.4
1974	28.6	26.3	1.3	0.2	0.8	116.5	42.1	19.9	47.3	6.4	-4.4	0.4	-4.8
1975	35.4	32.4	1.7	0.2	1.0	134.8	49.1	24.2	52.8	7.5	-9.0	0.5	-9.5
1976	39.1	35.4	2.3	0.3	1.2	145.6	52.8	26.9	57.0	7.7	-4.0	0.6	-4.6
1977	42.8	38.8	2.4	0.3	1.4	158.0	57.5	29.1	61.6	8.5	0.1	1.0	-0.9
1978	47.4	43.1	2.5	0.3	1.5	174.2	63.1	32.0	68.2	9.3	3.0	1.5	1.5
1979	50.1	45.9	2.2	0.4	1.6	193.8	70.0	35.4	76.3	10.3	1.0	1.8	-0.8
1980	56.5	52.1	2.3	0.4	1.7	217.8	78.8	41.3	84.6	11.1	-1.8	1.3	-3.2
1981	59.7	54.6	2.7	0.5	2.0	239.8	86.9	46.7	91.3	12.6	-3.4	1.3	-4.7
1982	58.7	52.7	3.1	0.6	2.3	257.0	93.7	51.0	95.3	14.6	-12.4	1.2	-13.6
1983	62.4	55.0	4.2	0.6	2.6	274.7	99.5	55.9	99.9	16.7	-5.5	1.2	-6.7
1984	67.7	59.0	5.0	0.8	3.0	297.5	106.9	59.8	109.8	17.9	6.2	1.4	4.8
1985	72.2	62.6	5.2	0.9	3.6	327.9	117.4	65.2	121.2	20.8	0.6	1.3	-0.7
1986	81.5	69.3	5.3	2.8	4.1	352.3	124.9	71.4	130.1	22.2	1.7	1.9	-0.1
1987	80.3	69.4	5.5	0.9	4.5	374.8	132.7	77.4	139.5	20.9	0.2	2.2	-2.0
1988	88.0	76.2	5.6	1.1	5.2	402.7	142.4	84.4	149.8	21.2	0.4	2.5	-2.1
1989	98.1	85.1	5.8	1.3	5.9	440.8	153.9	94.4	162.6	24.7	-5.6	2.3	-7.9
1990	112.4	97.6	6.2	1.6	6.9	480.7	167.2	111.0	173.1	23.8	-11.5	2.0	-13.4
1991	136.7	117.1	7.6	2.0	10.0	532.2	175.4	137.6	186.1	27.3	-28.1	2.4	-30.5
1992	158.0	134.3	9.0	2.6	12.1	580.8	183.9	159.5	201.0	30.4	-29.4	3.1	-32.6
1993	172.7	147.6	10.1	2.9	12.1	614.6	193.1	173.6	212.9	29.1	-29.8	4.2	-34.0
1994	183.7	156.9	11.0	3.4	12.4	649.8	204.5	184.4	226.2	28.4	-28.1	4.6	-32.8
1995	191.3	164.0	11.1	4.1	12.2	685.0	213.6	194.8	239.0	30.8	-31.8	4.0	-35.8
1996	197.9	168.9	12.0	5.0	12.0	708.1	219.7	202.5	250.3	27.9	-21.8	2.8	-24.7
1997	207.2	174.1	13.5	6.6	13.0	735.5	231.4	206.8	263.0	25.7	-15.9	1.2	-17.1
1998	219.3	182.9	13.3	9.8	13.2	774.0	248.3	214.6	282.4	19.8	-9.9	1.7	-11.6
1999	238.2	199.1	12.9	11.4	14.9	836.1	272.6	230.3	306.6	17.1	-23.6	1.7	-25.3
2000	258.8	212.6	14.0	15.0	17.2	896.0	292.8	248.4	331.0	13.5	-28.4	2.0	-30.3
2001	289.7	238.9	14.9	16.1	19.8	984.0	314.4	281.0	350.7	20.2	-79.5	2.6	-82.1
2002	317.7	263.5	15.5	17.2	21.5	1 037.5	320.3	307.2	367.5	31.5	-119.7	1.4	-121.1
2003	340.5	285.1	16.4	16.6	22.3	1 086.6	319.2	326.2	383.5	47.5	-116.1	3.2	-119.4
2004	363.4	303.4	17.6	17.7	24.6	1 139.7	327.1	355.8	401.6	44.5	-91.0	7.3	-98.3
2005	374.1	312.2	16.6	18.4	26.9	1 195.2	347.4	375.2	413.9	46.8	-58.7	7.2	-65.9
2006	375.4	314.2	15.6	18.2	28.0	1 239.7	361.2	371.3	441.7	52.3	-45.8	4.6	-50.5
2007	397.4	332.2	17.7	19.0	29.0	1 324.9	384.6	398.5	469.2	51.8	-77.0	2.7	-79.7
2008	415.6	346.6	17.7	21.1	30.7	1 383.9	407.7	418.6	486.1	54.1	-119.9	1.7	-121.6
2009	501.2	432.8	16.5	21.7	30.7	1 455.0	411.7	453.0	486.3	87.3	-187.9	2.2	-190.1
2010	539.5	473.3	16.6	20.1	30.1	1 487.1	411.2	481.5	488.8	88.4	-151.0	3.2	-154.2
2011	507.6	441.0	16.6	19.7	31.3	1 515.1	425.5	489.9	494.6	88.4	-157.2	4.2	-161.4
2012	491.2	424.0	16.8	18.8	32.4	1 579.2	459.7	501.9	502.8	97.8	-206.9	3.9	-210.9

[1]Includes components not shown separately.

Table 6-13. Local Government Current Receipts and Expenditures

(National income and product accounts, calendar years, billions of dollars.)   **NIPA Table 3.21**

Year	Current receipts Total [1]	Current tax receipts Total	Personal current taxes Total [1]	Personal current taxes Income taxes	Taxes on production and imports Total	Taxes on production and imports Sales taxes	Taxes on production and imports Property taxes	Taxes on production and imports Other	Taxes on corporate income	Contributions for government social insurance	Income receipts on assets Total [1]	Income receipts on assets Interest receipts	Income receipts on assets Rents and royalties
1959	27.0	17.1	0.8	0.2	16.4	1.2	14.3	0.9	0.0	. . .	0.7	0.5	0.1
1960	30.0	18.8	0.8	0.3	18.0	1.3	15.7	0.9	0.0	. . .	0.8	0.7	0.1
1961	32.9	20.3	0.9	0.3	19.4	1.4	17.0	1.0	0.0	. . .	0.9	0.7	0.2
1962	35.6	21.8	1.0	0.3	20.8	1.5	18.4	1.0	0.0	. . .	1.0	0.8	0.2
1963	38.7	23.4	1.1	0.4	22.3	1.6	19.7	1.0	0.0	. . .	1.0	0.9	0.2
1964	42.3	25.3	1.2	0.5	24.1	1.9	21.1	1.1	0.0	. . .	1.3	1.1	0.2
1965	46.1	27.0	1.2	0.5	25.7	2.1	22.5	1.1	0.0	. . .	1.4	1.2	0.2
1966	50.5	28.5	1.4	0.6	27.1	2.0	23.8	1.3	0.0	. . .	1.7	1.4	0.3
1967	56.5	31.3	1.6	0.8	29.5	1.9	26.2	1.3	0.2	. . .	2.0	1.6	0.3
1968	62.6	34.8	1.7	0.9	32.8	2.3	29.1	1.4	0.3	. . .	1.7	1.4	0.4
1969	70.1	38.4	2.0	1.1	36.1	2.9	31.9	1.4	0.3	. . .	2.2	1.8	0.4
1970	81.4	43.2	2.3	1.3	40.6	3.5	35.7	1.5	0.2	. . .	2.6	2.2	0.5
1971	90.9	47.9	2.5	1.5	45.2	4.0	39.5	1.8	0.3	. . .	2.8	2.3	0.5
1972	101.9	52.0	3.0	2.0	48.8	4.6	42.2	2.0	0.3	. . .	3.0	2.4	0.6
1973	114.0	56.1	3.0	2.0	52.7	5.2	45.2	2.3	0.3	. . .	3.9	3.3	0.6
1974	123.8	60.2	3.4	2.3	56.4	6.1	47.9	2.4	0.3	. . .	5.2	4.5	0.7
1975	137.7	65.5	3.7	2.5	61.4	7.0	51.9	2.5	0.4	. . .	5.6	4.9	0.7
1976	150.8	71.9	4.1	2.8	67.3	7.9	56.7	2.7	0.5	. . .	5.1	4.4	0.7
1977	165.3	78.6	4.5	3.2	73.6	9.0	61.7	2.9	0.6	. . .	5.6	4.9	0.7
1978	180.5	80.8	4.9	3.4	75.3	10.2	61.8	3.3	0.6	. . .	7.2	6.5	0.7
1979	191.3	83.1	5.1	3.6	77.3	11.5	62.1	3.7	0.6	. . .	9.8	8.9	0.9
1980	208.3	89.1	5.1	3.5	83.3	12.8	66.2	4.2	0.7	. . .	12.9	11.8	1.1
1981	226.9	100.2	6.2	4.3	93.0	14.3	74.4	4.3	1.0	. . .	16.4	15.3	1.1
1982	244.4	110.8	6.9	4.9	103.0	15.9	82.5	4.6	1.0	. . .	19.2	17.8	1.4
1983	262.5	120.4	7.2	5.1	112.1	17.7	88.9	5.5	1.0	. . .	21.9	19.8	2.1
1984	289.9	131.9	7.8	5.6	122.7	20.1	96.3	6.3	1.4	. . .	25.2	22.8	2.4
1985	318.4	142.8	8.2	6.0	133.1	22.1	104.0	7.0	1.5	. . .	29.5	26.7	2.7
1986	342.5	155.6	8.9	6.8	144.7	24.1	112.6	8.1	2.0	. . .	31.4	27.9	3.5
1987	360.1	168.5	9.1	6.8	157.3	25.7	122.7	8.9	2.1	. . .	30.1	27.4	2.7
1988	387.9	183.3	11.7	9.1	169.4	27.2	132.7	9.4	2.3	. . .	30.4	28.6	1.7
1989	420.0	199.6	12.3	9.4	185.6	30.1	145.6	10.0	1.8	. . .	33.8	32.1	1.7
1990	446.2	213.6	12.9	10.0	198.7	31.8	157.0	9.9	2.0	. . .	34.5	32.7	1.8
1991	475.9	230.1	13.5	10.3	214.5	33.2	171.1	10.2	2.1	. . .	33.2	31.2	1.9
1992	501.1	241.0	14.7	11.4	224.2	34.6	178.6	11.0	2.1	. . .	30.4	28.4	2.0
1993	522.2	247.7	14.8	11.3	230.5	37.0	181.3	12.1	2.4	. . .	28.7	26.6	2.1
1994	556.9	263.8	15.9	12.0	245.4	39.7	192.4	13.3	2.5	. . .	29.6	27.6	2.0
1995	584.6	270.7	17.2	13.3	251.0	42.2	195.3	13.4	2.5	. . .	32.2	30.3	2.0
1996	617.4	283.7	17.8	13.7	262.9	44.4	204.2	14.4	3.1	. . .	34.3	32.4	2.0
1997	652.4	300.8	19.3	14.9	278.4	47.4	215.5	15.6	3.1	. . .	36.3	34.3	2.1
1998	690.4	314.2	20.9	16.2	290.0	50.6	222.5	16.9	3.4	. . .	38.0	35.8	2.2
1999	739.5	332.5	21.9	17.1	307.1	55.6	233.7	17.8	3.5	. . .	38.6	36.1	2.5
2000	791.8	353.1	23.2	18.1	326.5	61.3	246.9	18.3	3.5	. . .	44.6	42.0	2.7
2001	825.4	367.5	22.9	17.6	341.6	61.9	260.0	19.8	3.0	. . .	42.6	39.8	2.8
2002	865.1	394.8	22.7	17.1	366.2	63.1	281.6	21.5	5.9	. . .	36.2	33.2	2.9
2003	915.7	419.8	24.4	18.3	389.0	66.8	297.9	24.2	6.5	. . .	31.9	28.6	3.2
2004	957.8	451.5	27.1	20.3	416.4	70.5	317.9	28.0	7.9	. . .	32.4	29.0	3.4
2005	1 016.4	490.2	30.0	22.5	449.8	76.8	342.3	30.7	10.4	. . .	38.0	34.2	3.8
2006	1 089.2	526.4	31.5	23.6	483.6	85.2	365.3	33.1	11.3	. . .	48.0	44.0	3.9
2007	1 154.8	561.6	34.6	26.5	516.0	90.0	394.1	32.0	11.0	. . .	52.9	48.9	4.0
2008	1 164.4	565.3	33.8	26.1	522.6	90.4	404.0	28.1	9.0	. . .	45.6	41.4	4.2
2009	1 171.2	580.0	31.2	23.3	541.6	88.3	424.7	28.6	7.2	. . .	35.7	31.4	4.2
2010	1 184.5	585.7	33.0	25.0	544.9	91.2	424.4	29.3	7.8	. . .	31.3	26.7	4.6
2011	1 200.4	593.1	33.8	25.7	550.9	93.8	427.1	30.1	8.4	. . .	29.3	24.5	4.8
2012	1 204.4	600.3	35.1	26.9	556.7	95.7	430.3	30.7	8.5	. . .	28.4	23.4	5.0

[1] Includes components not shown separately.
. . . = Not available.

Table 6-13. Local Government Current Receipts and Expenditures—*Continued*

(National income and product accounts, calendar years, billions of dollars.)   **NIPA Table 3.21**

Year	Current receipts—*Continued*					Current expenditures					Net local government saving, NIPA (surplus + / deficit -)		
	Current transfer receipts												
	Total	Federal grants-in-aid	State grants-in-aid	From business, net	From persons	Total [1]	Consumption expenditures	Government social benefits to persons	Grants-in-aid to state governments	Interest payments	Total	Social insurance funds	Other
1959	8.4	0.4	7.8	0.1	0.1	25.5	23.0	0.7	0.2	1.5	1.5	. . .	1.5
1960	9.6	0.5	8.8	0.1	0.2	27.9	25.2	0.8	0.2	1.7	2.2	. . .	2.2
1961	10.8	0.6	9.8	0.2	0.3	30.7	27.7	0.9	0.3	1.8	2.2	. . .	2.2
1962	11.9	0.6	10.8	0.2	0.3	32.3	29.1	0.9	0.3	1.9	3.3	. . .	3.3
1963	13.1	0.8	11.9	0.2	0.3	34.7	31.3	1.0	0.3	2.1	4.0	. . .	4.0
1964	14.6	1.1	13.0	0.2	0.3	37.9	34.2	1.0	0.3	2.3	4.4	. . .	4.4
1965	16.6	1.1	15.0	0.3	0.3	41.6	37.6	1.1	0.3	2.5	4.5	. . .	4.5
1966	19.3	1.2	17.4	0.2	0.4	46.1	41.7	1.3	0.4	2.7	4.4	. . .	4.4
1967	22.4	1.5	19.9	0.4	0.6	50.6	45.6	1.6	0.5	2.9	5.9	. . .	5.9
1968	25.2	1.1	23.0	0.4	0.7	57.5	51.5	2.0	0.6	3.3	5.1	. . .	5.1
1969	28.8	1.3	26.4	0.4	0.7	64.9	58.1	2.4	0.8	3.6	5.3	. . .	5.3
1970	34.8	3.2	30.4	0.4	0.8	74.7	66.3	3.2	0.9	4.3	6.7	. . .	6.7
1971	39.5	3.8	34.3	0.5	0.9	85.6	75.4	4.0	1.0	5.2	5.3	. . .	5.3
1972	46.0	5.9	38.5	0.5	1.1	95.6	83.9	4.5	1.1	6.1	6.3	. . .	6.3
1973	53.2	8.9	42.6	0.7	1.0	104.3	91.5	4.7	1.2	6.8	9.8	. . .	9.8
1974	57.9	8.7	47.3	0.9	1.1	117.0	102.4	5.4	1.3	7.9	6.8	. . .	6.8
1975	66.4	11.2	52.8	1.0	1.4	134.3	116.5	6.6	1.7	9.2	3.5	. . .	3.5
1976	73.5	13.6	57.0	1.1	1.7	144.0	124.4	7.3	2.3	9.8	6.8	. . .	6.8
1977	80.9	16.0	61.6	1.3	1.9	156.9	135.5	8.0	2.4	10.7	8.4	. . .	8.4
1978	92.3	20.4	68.2	1.5	2.2	170.1	146.8	8.7	2.5	11.7	10.4	. . .	10.4
1979	98.8	18.1	76.3	1.8	2.6	184.0	159.4	8.9	2.2	13.2	7.2	. . .	7.2
1980	107.3	17.6	84.6	2.0	3.0	201.1	174.0	9.9	2.3	14.5	7.2	. . .	7.2
1981	112.2	14.8	91.3	2.4	3.7	219.4	189.2	10.4	2.7	16.7	7.5	. . .	7.5
1982	115.6	13.5	95.3	2.7	4.1	237.1	203.7	10.2	3.1	19.6	7.3	. . .	7.3
1983	120.4	13.0	99.9	3.0	4.5	255.8	217.2	11.0	4.2	22.8	6.7	. . .	6.7
1984	131.7	13.3	109.8	3.4	5.2	275.2	233.0	11.4	5.0	25.3	14.7	. . .	14.7
1985	144.0	13.6	121.2	3.5	5.7	298.8	254.4	12.1	5.2	26.4	19.6	. . .	19.6
1986	153.7	13.2	130.1	3.9	6.5	323.8	275.0	12.9	5.3	29.6	18.7	. . .	18.7
1987	159.2	9.0	139.5	4.0	6.7	348.3	295.6	13.4	5.5	32.6	11.9	. . .	11.9
1988	170.5	9.5	149.8	4.3	6.9	371.3	316.5	14.1	5.6	33.8	16.6	. . .	16.6
1989	181.9	6.8	162.6	5.1	7.5	407.0	347.4	15.0	5.8	37.6	13.0	. . .	13.0
1990	193.4	6.7	173.1	5.5	8.0	441.2	379.0	16.6	6.2	38.0	5.0	. . .	5.0
1991	207.7	7.0	186.1	5.9	8.7	472.9	404.7	18.9	7.6	40.3	3.0	. . .	3.0
1992	224.8	7.4	201.0	6.7	9.8	509.2	435.2	20.5	9.0	43.2	-8.1	. . .	-8.1
1993	240.0	8.1	212.9	7.7	11.4	529.6	453.4	21.6	10.1	43.1	-7.4	. . .	-7.4
1994	257.6	9.9	226.2	8.6	12.9	555.8	477.7	22.4	11.0	43.3	1.2	. . .	1.2
1995	273.2	10.5	239.0	9.4	14.3	584.3	503.2	22.9	11.1	45.8	0.3	. . .	0.3
1996	288.7	12.6	250.3	10.2	15.7	608.0	528.4	21.8	12.0	44.5	9.4	. . .	9.4
1997	305.4	14.0	263.0	11.1	17.3	634.8	554.5	20.8	13.5	44.5	17.6	. . .	17.6
1998	330.0	17.9	282.4	11.8	17.9	665.1	587.4	21.1	13.3	41.7	25.3	. . .	25.3
1999	358.7	20.1	306.6	12.7	19.3	706.6	629.4	22.1	12.9	40.7	32.9	. . .	32.9
2000	385.8	20.5	331.0	13.5	20.8	753.6	676.3	23.0	14.0	38.6	38.3	. . .	38.3
2001	409.1	22.4	350.7	13.7	22.3	811.2	725.4	24.0	14.9	45.3	14.2	. . .	14.2
2002	430.7	23.7	367.5	15.4	24.1	866.4	770.8	25.8	15.5	52.8	-1.2	. . .	-1.2
2003	464.4	36.6	383.5	17.2	27.1	921.0	808.0	27.3	16.4	67.7	-5.3	. . .	-5.3
2004	478.3	28.8	401.6	18.8	29.1	975.2	860.5	29.2	17.6	65.9	-17.4	. . .	-17.4
2005	492.8	31.1	413.9	18.1	29.6	1 024.3	909.2	31.4	16.6	65.0	-7.9	. . .	-7.9
2006	520.8	26.6	441.7	20.6	31.3	1 082.8	964.8	32.6	15.6	67.8	6.4	. . .	6.4
2007	550.4	26.8	469.2	21.5	32.5	1 150.6	1 026.8	34.8	17.7	69.7	4.3	. . .	4.3
2008	566.0	24.4	486.1	22.4	32.6	1 209.6	1 081.0	36.8	17.7	73.0	-45.2	. . .	-45.2
2009	567.7	25.3	486.3	22.3	33.3	1 255.2	1 096.7	39.6	16.5	101.4	-84.0	. . .	-84.0
2010	577.8	31.9	488.8	23.3	33.1	1 270.8	1 107.1	42.3	16.6	103.7	-86.3	. . .	-86.3
2011	585.4	31.4	494.6	24.4	33.9	1 256.2	1 092.0	42.1	16.6	104.5	-55.9	. . .	-55.9
2012	581.0	19.2	502.8	23.1	35.1	1 250.2	1 076.7	42.4	16.8	113.2	-45.8	. . .	-45.8

[1]Includes components not shown separately.
. . . = Not available.

SECTION 6C: FEDERAL GOVERNMENT BUDGET ACCOUNTS

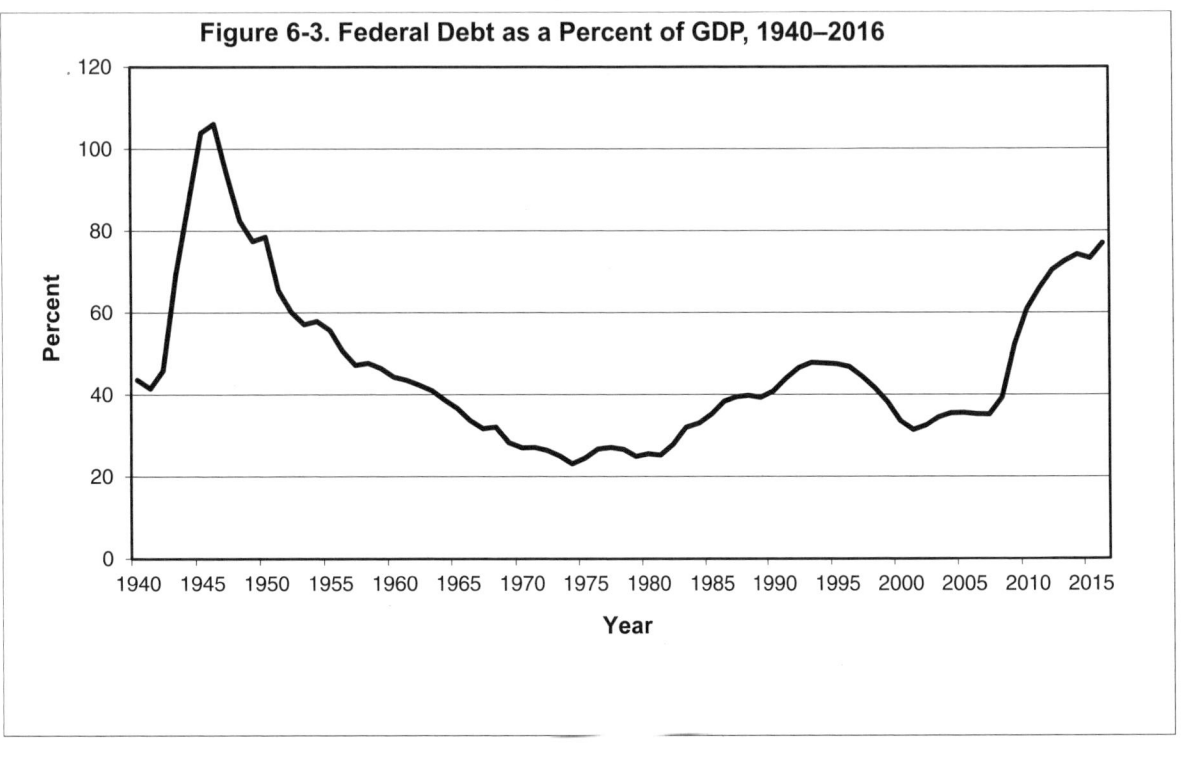

Figure 6-3. Federal Debt as a Percent of GDP, 1940–2016

- The "debt held by the public" is generally thought to be a more significant measure of the burden of the federal debt on credit markets than the gross debt, because it nets out the intragovernmental debt of the Social Security and other U.S. government trust funds. The ratio of debt held by the public to GDP was reduced in the late 1990s, began to creep back upward after 2001, and then rose rapidly beginning in 2008, as the recession reduced revenues and increased spending, and taxes were reduced further. The spending increases were a result of both automatic stabilizer programs, such as unemployment insurance, and an unprecedented level of spending for stimulus and financial rescue programs. At the end of fiscal year 2016, the debt held by the public was 77.0 percent of GDP, the highest since 1950. (Tables 6-14 and 6-15)

- At the end of 2016, foreign residents—including central banks—held $6.2 trillion of Treasury debt, 43.4 percent of the $14.2 trillion total debt held by the public. (Table 6-15)

Table 6-14A. Federal Government Receipts and Outlays by Fiscal Year [1]

(Budget accounts, millions of dollars.)

Year	Total receipts, net	Total outlays, net	Budget surplus or deficit (-)			Sources of financing, total		Individual income taxes	Corporate income taxes	Social insurance taxes and contributions		
			Total	On-budget	Off-budget	Borrowing from the public	Other financing			Employment taxes and contributions	Unemployment insurance	Other retirement contributions
1940	6 548	9 468	-2 920	-3 484	564	. . .	. . .	892	1 197	725	1 015	45
1941	8 712	13 653	-4 941	-5 594	653	5 451	-510	1 314	2 124	827	1 056	57
1942	14 634	35 137	-20 503	-21 333	830	19 530	973	3 263	4 719	1 064	1 299	89
1943	24 001	78 555	-54 554	-55 595	1 041	60 013	-5 459	6 505	9 557	1 338	1 477	229
1944	43 747	91 304	-47 557	-48 735	1 178	57 030	-9 473	19 705	14 838	1 557	1 644	272
1945	45 159	92 712	-47 553	-48 720	1 167	50 386	-2 833	18 372	15 988	1 592	1 568	291
1946	39 296	55 232	-15 936	-16 964	1 028	6 679	9 257	16 098	11 883	1 517	1 316	282
1947	38 514	34 496	4 018	2 861	1 157	-17 522	13 504	17 935	8 615	1 835	1 329	259
1948	41 560	29 764	11 796	10 548	1 248	-8 069	-3 727	19 315	9 678	2 168	1 343	239
1949	39 415	38 835	580	-684	1 263	-1 948	1 368	15 552	11 192	2 246	1 205	330
1950	39 443	42 562	-3 119	-4 702	1 583	4 701	-1 582	15 755	10 449	2 648	1 332	358
1951	51 616	45 514	6 102	4 259	1 843	-4 697	-1 405	21 616	14 101	3 688	1 609	377
1952	66 167	67 000	1 519	-3 383	1 864	432	1 087	27 934	21 226	4 315	1 712	418
1953	69 608	76 101	-6 493	-8 259	1 766	3 625	2 000	29 816	21 238	4 722	1 675	423
1954	69 701	70 855	-1 154	-2 831	1 677	6 116	-4 962	29 542	21 101	5 192	1 561	455
1955	65 451	68 444	-2 993	-4 091	1 098	2 117	876	28 747	17 861	5 981	1 449	431
1956	74 587	70 640	3 947	2 494	1 452	-4 460	513	32 188	20 880	7 059	1 690	571
1957	79 990	76 578	3 412	2 639	773	-2 836	-576	35 620	21 167	7 405	1 950	642
1958	79 636	82 405	-2 769	-3 315	546	7 016	-4 247	34 724	20 074	8 624	1 933	682
1959	79 249	92 098	-12 849	-12 149	-700	8 365	4 484	36 719	17 309	8 821	2 131	770
1960	92 492	92 191	301	510	-209	2 139	-2 440	40 715	21 494	11 248	2 667	768
1961	94 388	97 723	-3 335	-3 766	431	1 517	1 818	41 338	20 954	12 679	2 903	857
1962	99 676	106 821	-7 146	-5 881	-1 265	9 653	-2 507	45 571	20 523	12 835	3 337	875
1963	106 560	111 316	-4 756	-3 966	-789	5 968	-1 212	47 588	21 579	14 746	4 112	946
1964	112 613	118 528	-5 915	-6 546	632	2 871	3 044	48 697	23 493	16 959	3 997	1 007
1965	116 817	118 228	-1 411	-1 605	194	3 929	-2 518	48 792	25 461	17 358	3 803	1 081
1966	130 835	134 532	-3 698	-3 068	-630	2 936	762	55 446	30 073	20 662	3 755	1 129
1967	148 822	157 464	-8 643	-12 620	3 978	2 912	5 731	61 526	33 971	27 823	3 575	1 221
1968	152 973	178 134	-25 161	-27 742	2 581	22 919	2 242	68 726	28 665	29 224	3 346	1 354
1969	186 882	183 640	3 242	-507	3 749	-11 437	8 195	87 249	36 678	34 236	3 328	1 451
1970	192 807	195 649	-2 842	-8 694	5 852	5 090	-2 248	90 412	32 829	39 133	3 464	1 765
1971	187 139	210 172	-23 033	-26 052	3 019	19 839	3 194	86 230	26 785	41 699	3 674	1 952
1972	207 309	230 681	-23 373	-26 068	2 695	19 340	4 033	94 737	32 166	46 120	4 357	2 097
1973	230 799	245 707	-14 908	-15 246	338	18 533	-3 625	103 246	36 153	54 876	6 051	2 187
1974	263 224	269 359	-6 135	-7 198	1 063	2 789	3 346	118 952	38 620	65 888	6 837	2 347
1975	279 090	332 332	-53 242	-54 148	906	51 001	2 241	122 386	40 621	75 199	6 771	2 565
1976	298 060	371 792	-73 732	-69 427	-4 306	82 704	-8 972	131 603	41 409	79 901	8 054	2 814
TQ	81 232	95 975	-14 744	-14 065	-679	18 105	-3 361	38 801	8 460	21 801	2 698	720
1977	355 559	409 218	-53 659	-49 933	-3 726	53 595	64	157 626	54 892	92 199	11 312	2 974
1978	399 561	458 746	-59 185	-55 416	-3 770	58 022	1 163	180 988	59 952	10 388	13 850	3 237
1979	463 302	504 028	-40 726	-39 633	-1 093	33 180	7 546	217 841	65 677	12 005	15 387	3 494
1980	517 112	590 941	-73 830	-73 141	-689	71 617	2 213	244 069	64 600	13 874	15 336	3 719
1981	599 272	678 241	-78 968	-73 859	-5 109	77 487	1 481	285 917	61 137	16 297	15 763	3 984
1982	617 766	745 743	-127 977	-120 593	-7 384	135 165	-7 188	297 744	49 207	18 068	16 600	4 212
1983	600 562	808 364	-207 802	-207 692	-110	212 693	-4 891	288 938	37 022	18 576	18 799	4 429
1984	666 438	851 805	-185 367	-185 269	-98	169 707	15 660	298 415	56 893	20 965	25 138	4 580
1985	734 037	946 344	-212 308	-221 529	9 222	200 285	12 023	334 531	61 331	23 464	25 758	4 759
1986	769 155	990 382	-221 227	-237 915	16 688	233 363	-12 136	348 959	63 143	25 506	24 098	4 742
1987	854 287	1 004 017	-149 730	-168 357	18 627	149 130	600	392 557	83 926	27 302	25 575	4 715
1988	909 238	1 064 416	-155 178	-192 265	37 087	161 863	-6 685	401 181	94 508	30 509	24 584	4 658
1989	991 104	1 143 743	-152 639	-205 393	52 754	139 100	13 539	445 690	10 329	33 285	22 011	4 546
1990	1 031 958	1 252 993	-221 036	-277 626	56 590	220 842	194	466 884	93 507	35 389	21 635	4 522
1991	1 054 988	1 324 226	-269 238	-321 435	52 198	277 441	-8 203	467 827	98 086	37 052	20 922	4 568
1992	1 091 208	1 381 529	-290 321	-340 408	50 087	310 738	-20 417	475 964	10 027	38 549	23 410	4 788
1993	1 154 334	1 409 386	-255 051	-300 398	45 347	248 659	6 392	509 680	11 752	39 693	26 556	4 805
1994	1 258 566	1 461 752	-203 186	-258 840	55 654	184 669	18 517	543 055	14 038	42 881	28 004	4 661
1995	1 351 790	1 515 742	-163 952	-226 367	62 415	171 313	-7 361	590 244	15 700	45 104	28 878	4 550
1996	1 453 053	1 560 484	-107 431	-174 019	66 588	129 695	-22 264	656 417	17 182	47 636	28 584	4 469
1997	1 579 232	1 601 116	-21 884	-103 248	81 364	38 271	-16 387	737 466	18 229	50 675	28 202	4 418
1998	1 721 728	1 652 458	69 270	-29 925	99 195	-51 245	-18 025	828 586	18 867	54 001	27 484	4 333
1999	1 827 452	1 701 842	125 610	1 920	123 690	-88 736	-36 874	879 480	18 468	58 088	26 480	4 473
2000	2 025 191	1 788 950	236 241	86 422	149 819	-222 559	-13 682	100 446	20 728	62 045	27 640	4 761
2001	1 991 082	1 862 846	128 236	-32 445	160 681	-90 189	-38 047	994 339	15 107	66 144	27 812	4 713
2002	1 853 136	2 010 894	-157 758	-317 417	159 659	220 812	-63 054	858 345	14 804	66 854	27 619	4 594
2003	1 782 314	2 159 899	-377 585	-538 418	160 833	373 016	4 569	793 699	131 778	674 981	33 366	4 631
2004	1 880 114	2 292 841	-412 727	-567 961	155 234	382 101	30 626	808 959	189 371	689 360	39 453	4 594
2005	2 153 611	2 471 957	-318 346	-493 611	175 265	296 668	21 678	927 222	278 282	747 664	42 002	4 459
2006	2 406 869	2 655 050	-248 181	-434 494	186 313	236 760	11 421	1 043 908	353 915	790 043	43 420	4 358
2007	2 567 985	2 728 686	-160 701	-342 153	181 452	206 157	-45 456	1 163 472	370 243	824 258	41 091	4 258
2008	2 523 991	2 982 544	-458 553	-641 848	183 295	767 921	-309 368	1 145 747	304 346	856 459	39 527	4 169
2009	2 104 989	3 517 677	-1 412 688	-1 549 681	136 993	1 741 657	-328 969	915 308	138 229	848 885	37 889	4 143
2010	2 162 706	3 457 079	-1 294 373	-1 371 378	77 005	1 474 175	-179 802	898 549	191 437	815 894	44 823	4 097
2011	2 303 466	3 603 065	-1 299 599	-1 366 781	67 182	1 109 305	190 294	1 091 473	181 085	758 516	56 241	4 035
2012	2 449 990	3 536 946	-1 086 955	-1 148 868	61 913	1 152 944	-65 989	1 132 206	242 289	774 927	66 647	3 740
2013	2 775 105	3 454 647	-679 542	-719 005	39 463	701 582	-22 040	1 316 405	273 506	887 445	56 811	3 564
2014	3 021 491	3 506 091	-484 600	-514 112	29 512	797 186	-312 586	1 394 568	320 731	965 029	54 957	3 472
2015	3 249 887	3 688 383	-438 496	-465 791	27 295	336 793	101 703	1 540 802	343 797	101 042	51 178	3 652
2016	3 267 961	3 852 612	-584 651	-620 158	35 507	1 051 033	-466 382	1 546 075	299 571	106 230	48 856	3 904

[1]Fiscal years through 1976 are from July 1 through June 30. Beginning with October 1976 (fiscal year 1977), fiscal years are from October 1 through September 30. The period from July 1 through September 30, 1976, is a separate fiscal period known as the transition quarter (TQ) and is not included in any fiscal year.
. . . = Not available.

Table 6-14A. Federal Government Receipts and Outlays by Fiscal Year [1]—Continued

(Budget accounts, millions of dollars.)

Year	Receipts by source—Continued					Outlays by function						
				Miscellaneous receipts								
	Excise taxes	Estate and gift taxes	Customs duties and fees	Federal reserve deposits	All other	National defense	International affairs	General science, space, and technology	Energy	Natural resources and environment	Agriculture	Commerce and housing credit
1940	1 977	353	331	...	14	1 660	51	...	88	997	369	550
1941	2 552	403	365	...	14	6 435	145	...	91	817	339	398
1942	3 399	420	369	...	11	25 658	968	4	156	819	344	1 521
1943	4 096	441	308	...	50	66 699	1 286	1	116	726	343	2 151
1944	4 759	507	417	...	48	79 143	1 449	48	65	642	1 275	624
1945	6 265	637	341	...	105	82 965	1 913	111	25	455	1 635	-2 630
1946	6 998	668	424	...	109	42 681	1 935	34	41	482	610	-1 857
1947	7 211	771	477	15	69	12 808	5 791	5	18	700	814	-923
1948	7 356	890	403	100	68	9 105	4 566	1	292	780	69	306
1949	7 502	780	367	187	54	13 150	6 052	48	341	1 080	1 924	800
1950	7 550	698	407	192	55	13 724	4 673	55	327	1 308	2 049	1 035
1951	8 648	708	609	189	72	23 566	3 647	51	383	1 310	-323	1 228
1952	8 852	818	533	278	81	46 089	2 691	49	474	1 233	176	1 278
1953	9 877	881	596	298	81	52 802	2 119	49	425	1 289	2 253	910
1954	9 945	934	542	341	88	49 266	1 596	46	432	1 007	1 817	-184
1955	9 131	924	585	251	90	42 729	2 223	74	325	940	3 514	92
1956	9 929	1 161	682	287	140	42 523	2 414	79	174	870	3 486	506
1957	9 055	1 365	735	434	139	45 430	3 147	122	240	1 098	2 288	1 424
1958	8 612	1 393	782	664	123	46 815	3 364	141	348	1 407	2 411	930
1959	8 504	1 333	925	491	171	49 015	3 144	294	382	1 632	4 509	1 933
1960	9 137	1 606	1 105	1 093	119	48 130	2 988	599	464	1 559	2 623	1 618
1961	9 063	1 896	982	788	130	49 601	3 184	1 042	510	1 779	2 641	1 203
1962	9 585	2 016	1 142	718	125	52 345	5 639	1 723	604	2 044	3 562	1 424
1963	9 915	2 167	1 205	828	194	53 400	5 308	3 051	530	2 251	4 384	62
1964	10 211	2 394	1 252	947	139	54 757	4 945	4 897	572	2 364	4 609	418
1965	10 911	2 716	1 442	1 372	222	50 620	5 273	5 823	699	2 531	3 954	1 157
1966	9 145	3 066	1 767	1 713	163	58 111	5 580	6 717	612	2 719	2 447	3 245
1967	9 278	2 978	1 901	1 805	302	71 417	5 566	6 233	782	2 869	2 990	3 979
1968	9 700	3 051	2 038	2 091	400	81 926	5 301	5 524	1 037	2 988	4 544	4 280
1969	10 585	3 491	2 319	2 662	247	82 497	4 600	5 020	1 010	2 900	5 826	-119
1970	10 352	3 644	2 430	3 266	158	81 692	4 330	4 511	997	3 065	5 166	2 112
1971	10 510	3 735	2 591	3 533	325	78 872	4 159	4 182	1 035	3 915	4 290	2 366
1972	9 506	5 436	3 287	3 252	380	79 174	4 781	4 175	1 296	4 241	5 227	2 222
1973	9 836	4 917	3 188	3 495	425	76 681	4 149	4 032	1 237	4 775	4 821	931
1974	9 743	5 035	3 334	4 845	523	79 347	5 710	3 980	1 303	5 697	2 194	4 705
1975	9 400	4 611	3 676	5 777	935	86 509	7 097	3 991	2 916	7 346	2 997	9 947
1976	10 612	5 216	4 074	5 451	2 576	89 619	6 433	4 373	4 204	8 184	3 109	7 619
TQ	2 520	1 455	1 212	1 500	111	22 269	2 458	1 162	1 129	2 524	972	931
1977	9 648	7 327	5 150	5 908	623	97 241	6 353	4 736	5 770	10 032	6 734	3 093
1978	10 054	5 285	6 573	6 641	778	10 449	7 482	4 926	7 991	10 983	11 301	6 254
1979	9 808	5 411	7 439	8 327	925	11 634	7 459	5 234	9 179	12 135	11 176	4 686
1980	15 563	6 389	7 174	11 767	981	13 399	12 714	5 831	10 156	13 858	8 774	9 390
1981	34 128	6 787	8 083	12 834	956	15 751	13 104	6 468	15 166	13 568	11 241	8 206
1982	28 670	7 991	8 854	15 186	975	18 530	12 300	7 199	13 527	12 998	15 866	6 256
1983	24 086	6 053	8 655	14 492	1 108	20 990	11 848	7 934	9 353	12 672	22 807	6 681
1984	22 279	6 010	11 370	15 684	1 328	22 741	15 869	8 311	7 073	12 586	13 477	6 959
1985	19 097	6 422	12 079	17 059	1 460	25 274	16 169	8 622	5 608	13 345	25 427	4 337
1986	16 053	6 958	13 327	18 374	1 574	27 337	14 146	8 962	4 690	13 628	31 319	5 058
1987	14 844	7 493	15 085	16 817	2 635	28 199	11 645	9 200	4 072	13 355	26 466	6 434
1988	16 185	7 594	16 198	17 163	3 031	29 036	10 466	10 820	2 296	14 601	17 088	19 163
1989	13 147	8 745	16 334	19 604	3 639	30 355	9 583	12 821	2 705	16 169	16 698	29 709
1990	15 591	11 500	16 707	24 319	3 647	29 932	13 758	14 426	3 341	17 055	11 637	67 599
1991	18 275	11 138	15 949	19 158	4 412	27 328	15 846	16 092	2 436	18 544	14 886	76 270
1992	21 836	11 143	17 359	22 920	4 293	29 834	16 090	16 389	4 499	20 001	14 922	10 918
1993	24 522	12 577	18 802	14 908	4 491	29 108	17 218	17 006	4 319	20 224	20 081	-2 185
1994	31 226	15 225	20 099	18 023	5 081	28 164	17 067	16 189	5 218	21 000	14 795	-4 228
1995	26 941	14 763	19 301	23 378	5 143	27 206	16 429	16 692	4 936	21 889	9 671	-1 780
1996	25 447	17 189	18 670	20 477	5 048	26 574	13 487	16 684	2 839	21 503	9 035	-1 047
1997	27 831	19 845	17 928	19 636	5 769	27 050	15 173	17 136	1 475	21 201	8 889	-1 464
1998	21 665	24 076	18 297	24 540	8 048	26 819	13 054	18 172	1 270	22 278	12 077	1 007
1999	19 293	27 782	18 336	25 917	9 010	27 476	15 239	18 084	911	23 943	22 879	2 641
2000	22 692	29 010	19 914	32 293	10 506	29 436	17 213	18 594	-761	25 003	36 458	3 207
2001	24 286	28 400	19 369	26 124	11 576	30 473	16 485	19 753	9	25 532	26 252	5 731
2002	24 017	26 507	18 602	23 683	10 206	34 845	22 315	20 734	475	29 426	21 965	-407
2003	23 804	21 959	19 862	21 878	12 636	40 473	21 199	20 831	-725	29 667	22 496	727
2004	24 566	24 831	21 083	19 652	12 956	45 581	26 870	23 029	-147	30 694	15 439	5 265
2005	22 547	24 764	23 379	19 297	13 448	495 294	34 565	23 597	440	27 983	26 565	7 566
2006	22 460	27 877	24 810	29 945	14 632	521 820	29 499	23 584	785	33 025	25 969	6 187
2007	11 076	26 044	26 010	32 043	15 497	551 258	28 482	24 407	-852	31 721	17 662	487
2008	15 726	28 844	27 568	33 598	16 399	616 066	28 857	26 773	631	31 820	18 387	27 870
2009	13 854	23 482	22 453	34 318	17 799	661 012	37 529	28 417	4 755	35 573	22 237	291 535
2010	18 256	18 885	25 298	75 845	20 969	693 485	45 195	30 100	11 618	43 667	21 356	-82 316
2011	18 904	7 399	29 519	82 546	20 271	705 554	45 685	29 466	12 174	45 473	20 662	-12 564
2012	20 359	13 973	30 307	81 957	24 883	677 852	47 184	29 060	14 858	41 631	17 791	40 647
2013	28 330	18 912	31 815	75 767	26 873	633 446	46 231	28 908	11 042	38 145	29 678	-83 199
2014	34 240	19 300	33 926	99 235	36 905	603 457	46 686	28 570	5 270	36 171	24 386	-94 861
2015	37 759	19 232	35 041	96 468	51 011	589 659	48 576	29 412	6 838	36 034	18 500	-37 905
2016	33 991	21 354	34 838	115 672	40 360	593 372	45 306	30 174	3 719	39 534	18 342	-34 077

[1]Fiscal years through 1976 are from July 1 through June 30. Beginning with October 1976 (fiscal year 1977), fiscal years are from October 1 through September 30. The period from July 1 through September 30, 1976, is a separate fiscal period known as the transition quarter (TQ) and is not included in any fiscal year.
. . . = Not available.

Table 6-14A. Federal Government Receipts and Outlays by Fiscal Year [1]—*Continued*

(Budget accounts, millions of dollars.)

Year	Transportation	Community and regional development	Education, employment, and social services	Health	Medicare	Income security	Social Security	Veterans benefits and services	Administration of justice	General government	Net interest
1940	392	285	1 972	55	0	1 514	28	570	81	274	899
1941	353	123	1 592	60	0	1 855	91	560	92	306	943
1942	1 283	113	1 062	71	0	1 828	137	501	117	397	1 052
1943	3 220	219	375	92	0	1 739	177	276	154	673	1 529
1944	3 901	238	160	174	0	1 503	217	-126	192	900	2 219
1945	3 654	243	134	211	0	1 137	267	110	178	581	3 112
1946	1 970	200	85	201	0	2 384	358	2 465	176	825	4 111
1947	1 130	302	102	177	0	2 820	466	6 344	176	1 114	4 204
1948	787	78	191	162	0	2 499	558	6 457	170	1 045	4 341
1949	916	-33	178	197	0	3 174	657	6 599	184	824	4 523
1950	967	30	241	268	0	4 097	781	8 834	193	986	4 812
1951	956	47	235	323	0	3 352	1 565	5 526	218	1 097	4 665
1952	1 124	73	339	347	0	3 655	2 063	5 341	267	1 163	4 701
1953	1 264	117	441	336	0	3 823	2 717	4 510	243	1 209	5 156
1954	1 229	100	370	307	0	4 434	3 352	4 613	257	799	4 811
1955	1 246	129	445	291	0	5 071	4 427	4 675	256	651	4 850
1956	1 450	92	591	359	0	4 734	5 478	4 891	302	1 201	5 079
1957	1 662	135	590	479	0	5 427	6 661	5 005	303	1 360	5 354
1958	2 334	169	643	541	0	7 535	8 219	5 350	325	655	5 604
1959	3 655	211	789	685	0	8 239	9 737	5 443	356	926	5 762
1960	4 126	224	968	795	0	7 378	11 602	5 441	366	1 184	6 947
1961	3 987	275	1 063	913	0	9 683	12 474	5 705	400	1 354	6 716
1962	4 290	469	1 241	1 198	0	9 207	14 365	5 619	429	1 049	6 889
1963	4 596	574	1 458	1 451	0	9 311	15 788	5 514	465	1 230	7 740
1964	5 242	933	1 555	1 788	0	9 657	16 620	5 675	489	1 518	8 199
1965	5 763	1 114	2 140	1 791	0	9 469	17 460	5 716	536	1 499	8 591
1966	5 730	1 105	4 363	2 543	64	9 678	20 694	5 916	564	1 603	9 386
1967	5 936	1 108	6 453	3 351	2 748	10 261	21 725	6 735	618	1 719	10 268
1968	6 316	1 382	7 634	4 390	4 649	11 816	23 854	7 032	659	1 757	11 090
1969	6 526	1 552	7 548	5 162	5 695	13 076	27 298	7 631	766	1 939	12 699
1970	7 008	2 392	8 634	5 907	6 213	15 655	30 270	8 669	959	2 320	14 380
1971	8 052	2 917	9 849	6 843	6 622	22 946	35 872	9 768	1 307	2 442	14 841
1972	8 392	3 423	12 529	8 674	7 479	27 650	40 157	10 720	1 684	2 960	15 478
1973	9 066	4 605	12 744	9 356	8 052	28 278	49 090	12 003	2 174	9 774	17 349
1974	9 172	4 229	12 455	10 733	9 639	33 714	55 867	13 374	2 505	10 032	21 449
1975	10 918	4 322	16 022	12 930	12 875	50 176	64 658	16 584	3 028	10 374	23 244
1976	13 739	5 442	18 910	15 734	15 834	60 799	73 899	18 419	3 430	9 706	26 727
TQ	3 358	1 569	5 169	3 924	4 264	14 985	19 763	3 960	918	3 878	6 949
1977	14 829	7 021	21 104	17 302	19 345	61 060	85 061	18 022	3 701	12 791	29 901
1978	15 521	11 841	26 706	18 524	22 768	61 509	93 861	18 961	3 923	11 961	35 458
1979	18 079	10 480	30 218	20 494	26 495	66 382	10 407	19 914	4 286	12 241	42 633
1980	21 329	11 252	31 835	23 169	32 090	86 565	11 854	21 169	4 702	12 975	52 533
1981	23 379	10 568	33 146	26 866	39 149	10 030	13 958	22 973	4 908	11 373	68 766
1982	20 625	8 347	26 609	27 445	46 567	10 815	15 596	23 938	4 842	10 861	85 032
1983	21 334	7 564	26 194	28 641	52 588	12 304	17 072	24 824	5 246	11 181	89 808
1984	23 669	7 673	26 916	30 417	57 540	11 340	17 822	25 575	5 811	11 746	11 110
1985	25 838	7 676	28 589	33 541	65 822	12 903	18 862	26 251	6 426	11 515	12 947
1986	28 113	7 233	29 773	35 933	70 164	12 068	19 875	26 314	6 735	12 491	13 601
1987	26 222	5 049	28 818	39 964	75 120	12 413	20 735	26 729	7 715	7 487	13 861
1988	27 272	5 293	30 928	44 483	78 878	13 043	21 934	29 367	9 397	9 399	15 180
1989	27 608	5 362	35 325	48 380	84 964	13 758	23 254	30 003	9 644	9 317	16 898
1990	29 485	8 531	37 167	57 699	98 102	14 883	24 862	29 034	10 185	10 462	18 434
1991	31 099	6 810	41 231	71 168	10 448	17 263	26 901	31 275	12 486	11 568	19 444
1992	33 332	6 836	42 735	89 486	11 902	19 973	28 758	34 037	14 650	12 883	19 934
1993	35 004	9 146	47 374	99 401	13 055	21 013	30 458	35 642	15 193	12 944	19 871
1994	38 066	10 620	43 281	10 710	14 474	21 729	31 956	37 559	15 516	11 159	20 293
1995	39 350	10 746	51 020	11 539	15 985	22 380	33 584	37 862	16 508	13 799	23 213
1996	39 565	10 741	48 311	11 936	17 422	22 974	34 967	36 956	17 898	11 755	24 105
1997	40 767	11 049	48 972	12 383	19 001	23 503	36 525	39 283	20 617	12 547	24 398
1998	40 343	9 771	50 512	13 142	19 282	23 775	37 921	41 741	23 359	15 544	24 111
1999	42 532	11 865	50 605	14 104	19 044	24 247	39 003	43 155	26 536	15 363	22 975
2000	46 853	10 623	53 764	15 450	19 711	25 372	40 942	46 989	28 499	13 013	22 294
2001	54 447	11 773	57 094	17 223	21 738	26 977	43 295	44 974	30 201	14 358	20 616
2002	61 833	12 981	70 566	19 649	23 085	31 272	45 598	50 929	35 061	16 951	17 094
2003	67 069	18 850	82 587	219 433	249 433	334 632	474 680	56 984	35 340	23 164	153 073
2004	64 627	15 820	87 974	240 122	269 360	333 059	495 548	59 746	45 576	22 338	160 245
2005	67 894	26 262	97 555	250 548	298 638	345 847	523 305	70 120	40 019	16 997	183 986
2006	70 244	54 465	118 482	252 739	329 868	352 477	548 549	69 811	41 016	18 177	226 603
2007	72 905	29 567	91 656	266 382	375 407	365 975	586 153	72 818	42 362	17 425	237 109
2008	77 616	23 952	91 287	280 599	390 758	431 313	617 027	84 653	48 097	20 323	252 757
2009	84 289	27 676	79 749	334 335	430 093	533 224	682 963	95 429	52 581	22 017	186 902
2010	91 972	23 894	128 598	369 068	451 636	622 210	706 737	108 384	54 383	23 014	196 194
2011	92 966	23 883	101 233	372 504	485 653	597 349	730 811	127 189	56 056	27 476	229 962
2012	93 019	25 132	90 823	346 742	471 793	541 344	773 290	124 595	56 277	28 035	220 408
2013	91 673	32 336	72 808	358 315	497 826	536 511	813 551	138 938	52 601	27 737	220 885
2014	91 915	20 670	90 615	409 449	511 688	513 644	850 533	149 616	50 457	26 913	228 956
2015	89 533	20 669	122 061	482 230	546 202	508 843	887 753	159 738	51 906	20 956	223 181
2016	92 566	20 140	109 737	511 317	594 536	514 139	916 067	174 516	55 768	22 674	240 033

[1]Fiscal years through 1976 are from July 1 through June 30. Beginning with October 1976 (fiscal year 1977), fiscal years are from October 1 through September 30. The period from July 1 through September 30, 1976, is a separate fiscal period known as the transition quarter (TQ) and is not included in any fiscal year.
. . . = Not available.

Table 6-14B. The Federal Budget and GDP

(Billions of dollars; percent.)

Year	Fiscal year GDP	Billions of dollars						Percent of GDP					
		Receipts			Outlays		Total budget surplus or deficit	Receipts			Outlays		Total budget surplus or deficit
		Total	Individual income taxes	Corporate income taxes	Total	National defense		Total	Individual income taxes	Corporate income taxes	Total	National defense	
1929	. . .	3.9	. . .	. . .	3.1	. . .	0.7	. . .	. . .	. . .	. . .	. . .	. . .
1930	98.4	4.1	. . .	. . .	3.3	. . .	0.7	4.1	. . .	. . .	3.4	. . .	0.8
1931	84.8	3.1	. . .	. . .	3.6	. . .	-0.5	3.7	. . .	. . .	4.2	. . .	-0.5
1932	68.5	1.9	. . .	. . .	4.7	. . .	-2.7	2.8	. . .	. . .	6.8	. . .	-4.0
1933	58.3	2.0	. . .	. . .	4.6	. . .	-2.6	3.4	. . .	. . .	7.9	. . .	-4.5
1934	62.0	3.0	0.4	0.4	6.5	. . .	-3.6	4.8	0.7	0.6	10.6	. . .	-5.8
1935	70.5	3.6	0.5	0.5	6.4	. . .	-2.8	5.1	0.7	0.8	9.1	. . .	-4.0
1936	79.6	3.9	0.7	0.7	8.2	. . .	-4.3	4.9	0.8	0.9	10.3	. . .	-5.4
1937	88.9	5.4	1.1	1.0	7.6	. . .	-2.5	6.1	1.2	1.2	8.5	. . .	-2.8
1938	90.2	6.8	1.3	1.3	6.8	. . .	-0.5	7.5	1.4	1.4	7.6	. . .	-0.5
1939	90.4	6.3	1.0	1.1	9.1	. . .	-3.4	7.0	1.1	1.2	10.1	. . .	-3.7
1940	98.2	6.5	0.9	1.2	9.5	1.7	-3.5	6.7	0.9	1.2	9.6	1.7	-3.5
1941	116.2	8.7	1.3	2.1	13.7	6.4	-5.6	7.5	1.1	1.8	11.7	5.5	-4.8
1942	147.7	14.6	3.3	4.7	35.1	25.7	-21.3	9.9	2.2	3.2	23.8	17.4	-14.4
1943	184.6	24.0	6.5	9.6	78.6	66.7	-55.6	13.0	3.5	5.2	42.6	36.1	-30.1
1944	213.8	43.7	19.7	14.8	91.3	79.1	-48.7	20.5	9.2	6.9	42.7	37.0	-22.8
1945	226.4	45.2	18.4	16.0	92.7	83.0	-48.7	19.9	8.1	7.1	41.0	36.6	-21.5
1946	228.0	39.3	16.1	11.9	55.2	42.7	-17.0	17.2	7.1	5.2	24.2	18.7	-7.4
1947	238.9	38.5	17.9	8.6	34.5	12.8	2.9	16.1	7.5	3.6	14.4	5.4	1.2
1948	262.4	41.6	19.3	9.7	29.8	9.1	10.5	15.8	7.4	3.7	11.3	3.5	4.0
1949	276.8	39.4	15.6	11.2	38.8	13.2	-0.7	14.2	5.6	4.0	14.0	4.8	-0.2
1950	279.0	39.4	15.8	10.4	42.6	13.7	-4.7	14.1	5.6	3.7	15.3	4.9	-1.7
1951	327.4	51.6	21.6	14.1	45.5	23.6	4.3	15.8	6.6	4.3	13.9	7.2	1.3
1952	357.5	66.2	27.9	21.2	67.7	46.1	-3.4	18.5	7.8	5.9	18.9	12.9	-0.9
1953	382.5	69.6	29.8	21.2	76.1	52.8	-8.3	18.2	7.8	5.6	19.9	13.8	-2.2
1954	387.7	69.7	29.5	21.1	70.9	49.3	-2.8	18.0	7.6	5.4	18.3	12.7	-0.7
1955	407.0	65.5	28.7	17.9	68.4	42.7	-4.1	16.1	7.1	4.4	16.8	10.5	-1.0
1956	439.0	74.6	32.2	20.9	70.6	42.5	2.5	17.0	7.3	4.8	16.1	9.7	0.6
1957	464.2	80.0	35.6	21.2	76.6	45.4	2.6	17.2	7.7	4.6	16.5	9.8	0.6
1958	474.3	79.6	34.7	20.1	82.4	46.8	-3.3	16.8	7.3	4.2	17.4	9.9	-0.7
1959	505.6	79.2	36.7	17.3	92.1	49.0	-12.1	15.7	7.3	3.4	18.2	9.7	-2.4
1960	535.1	92.5	40.7	21.5	92.2	48.1	0.5	17.3	7.6	4.0	17.2	9.0	0.1
1961	547.6	94.4	41.3	21.0	97.7	49.6	-3.8	17.2	7.5	3.8	17.8	9.1	-0.7
1962	586.9	99.7	45.6	20.5	106.8	52.3	-5.9	17.0	7.8	3.5	18.2	8.9	-1.0
1963	619.3	106.6	47.6	21.6	111.3	53.4	-4.0	17.2	7.7	3.5	18.0	8.6	-0.6
1964	662.9	112.6	48.7	23.5	118.5	54.8	-6.5	17.0	7.3	3.5	17.9	8.3	-1.0
1965	710.7	116.8	48.8	25.5	118.2	50.6	-1.6	16.4	6.9	3.6	16.6	7.1	-0.2
1966	781.9	130.8	55.4	30.1	134.5	58.1	-3.1	16.7	7.1	3.8	17.2	7.4	-0.4
1967	838.2	148.8	61.5	34.0	157.5	71.4	-12.6	17.8	7.3	4.1	18.8	8.5	-1.5
1968	899.3	153.0	68.7	28.7	178.1	81.9	-27.7	17.0	7.6	3.2	19.8	9.1	-3.1
1969	982.3	186.9	87.2	36.7	183.6	82.5	-0.5	19.0	8.9	3.7	18.7	8.4	-0.1
1970	1 049.1	192.8	90.4	32.8	195.6	81.7	-8.7	18.4	8.6	3.1	18.6	7.8	-0.8
1971	1 119.3	187.1	86.2	26.8	210.2	78.9	-26.1	16.7	7.7	2.4	18.8	7.0	-2.3
1972	1 219.5	207.3	94.7	32.2	230.7	79.2	-26.1	17.0	7.8	2.6	18.9	6.5	-2.1
1973	1 356.0	230.8	103.2	36.2	245.7	76.7	-15.2	17.0	7.6	2.7	18.1	5.7	-1.1
1974	1 486.2	263.2	119.0	38.6	269.4	79.3	-7.2	17.7	8.0	2.6	18.1	5.3	-0.5
1975	1 610.6	279.1	122.4	40.6	332.3	86.5	-54.1	17.3	7.6	2.5	20.6	5.4	-3.4
1976	1 790.3	298.1	131.6	41.4	371.8	89.6	-69.4	16.6	7.4	2.3	20.8	5.0	-3.9
1977	2 028.4	355.6	157.6	54.9	409.2	97.2	-49.9	17.5	7.8	2.7	20.2	4.8	-2.5
1978	2 278.2	399.6	181.0	60.0	458.7	104.5	-55.4	17.5	7.9	2.6	20.1	4.6	-2.4
1979	2 570.0	463.3	217.8	65.7	504.0	116.3	-39.6	18.0	8.5	2.6	19.6	4.5	-1.5
1980	2 796.8	517.1	244.1	64.6	590.9	134.0	-73.1	18.5	8.7	2.3	21.1	4.8	-2.6
1981	3 138.4	599.3	285.9	61.1	678.2	157.5	-73.9	19.1	9.1	1.9	21.6	5.0	-2.4
1982	3 313.9	617.8	297.7	49.2	745.7	185.3	-120.6	18.6	9.0	1.5	22.5	5.6	-3.6
1983	3 541.1	600.6	288.9	37.0	808.4	209.9	-207.7	17.0	8.2	1.0	22.8	5.9	-5.9
1984	3 952.8	666.4	298.4	56.9	851.8	227.4	-185.3	16.9	7.5	1.4	21.5	5.8	-4.7
1985	4 270.4	734.0	334.5	61.3	946.3	252.7	-221.5	17.2	7.8	1.4	22.2	5.9	-5.2
1986	4 536.1	769.2	349.0	63.1	990.4	273.4	-237.9	17.0	7.7	1.4	21.8	6.0	-5.2
1987	4 781.9	854.3	392.6	83.9	1 004.0	282.0	-168.4	17.9	8.2	1.8	21.0	5.9	-3.5
1988	5 155.1	909.2	401.2	94.5	1 064.4	290.4	-192.3	17.6	7.8	1.8	20.6	5.6	-3.7
1989	5 570.0	991.1	445.7	103.3	1 143.7	303.6	-205.4	17.8	8.0	1.9	20.5	5.4	-3.7
1990	5 914.6	1 032.0	466.9	93.5	1 253.0	299.3	-277.6	17.4	7.9	1.6	21.2	5.1	-4.7
1991	6 110.1	1 055.0	467.8	98.1	1 324.2	273.3	-321.4	17.3	7.7	1.6	21.7	4.5	-5.3
1992	6 434.7	1 091.2	476.0	100.3	1 381.5	298.3	-340.4	17.0	7.4	1.6	21.5	4.6	-5.3
1993	6 794.9	1 154.3	509.7	117.5	1 409.4	291.1	-300.4	17.0	7.5	1.7	20.7	4.3	-4.4
1994	7 197.8	1 258.6	543.1	140.4	1 461.8	281.6	-258.8	17.5	7.5	2.0	20.3	3.9	-3.6

. . . = Not available.

Table 6-14B. The Federal Budget and GDP—*Continued*

(Billions of dollars; percent.)

Year	Fiscal year GDP	Billions of dollars						Percent of GDP					
		Receipts			Outlays		Total budget surplus or deficit	Receipts			Outlays		Total budget surplus or deficit
		Total	Individual income taxes	Corporate income taxes	Total	National defense		Total	Individual income taxes	Corporate income taxes	Total	National defense	
1995	7 583.4	1 351.8	590.2	157.0	1 515.7	272.1	-226.4	17.8	7.8	2.1	20.0	3.6	-3.0
1996	7 978.3	1 453.1	656.4	171.8	1 560.5	265.7	-174.0	18.2	8.2	2.2	19.6	3.3	-2.2
1997	8 483.2	1 579.2	737.5	182.3	1 601.1	270.5	-103.2	18.6	8.7	2.1	18.9	3.2	-1.2
1998	8 954.8	1 721.7	828.6	188.7	1 652.5	268.2	-29.9	19.2	9.3	2.1	18.5	3.0	-0.3
1999	9 510.5	1 827.5	879.5	184.7	1 701.8	274.8	1.9	19.2	9.2	1.9	17.9	2.9	. . .
2000	10 148.2	2 025.2	1 004.5	207.3	1 789.0	294.4	86.4	20.0	9.9	2.0	17.6	2.9	0.9
2001	10 564.6	1 991.1	994.3	151.1	1 862.8	304.7	-32.4	18.8	9.4	1.4	17.6	2.9	-0.3
2002	10 876.9	1 853.1	858.3	148.0	2 010.9	348.5	-317.4	17.0	7.9	1.4	18.5	3.2	-2.9
2003	11 332.4	1 782.3	793.7	131.8	2 159.9	404.7	-538.4	15.7	7.0	1.2	19.1	3.6	-4.8
2004	12 088.6	1 880.1	809.0	189.4	2 292.8	455.8	-568.0	15.6	6.7	1.6	19.0	3.8	-4.7
2005	12 888.9	2 153.6	927.2	278.3	2 472.0	406.3	-493.6	16.7	7.2	2.2	19.2	3.8	-3.8
2006	13 684.7	2 406.9	1 043.9	353.9	2 655.1	521.8	-434.5	17.6	7.6	2.6	19.4	3.8	-3.2
2007	14 322.9	2 568.0	1 163.5	370.2	2 728.7	551.3	-342.2	17.9	8.1	2.6	19.1	3.8	-2.4
2008	14 752.4	2 524.0	1 145.7	304.3	2 982.5	616.1	-641.8	17.1	7.8	2.1	20.2	4.2	-4.4
2009	14 414.6	2 105.0	915.3	138.2	3 517.7	661.0	-1 549.7	14.6	6.3	1.0	24.4	4.6	-10.8
2010	14 798.5	2 162.7	898.5	191.4	3 457.1	693.5	-1 371.4	14.6	6.1	1.3	23.4	4.7	-9.3
2011	15 379.2	2 303.5	1 091.5	181.1	3 603.1	705.6	-1 366.8	15.0	7.1	1.2	23.4	4.6	-8.9
2012	16 027.2	2 450.0	1 132.2	242.3	3 536.9	677.9	-1 148.9	15.3	7.1	1.5	22.1	4.2	-7.2
2013	16 515.9	2 775.1	1 316.4	273.5	3 454.6	633.4	-719.0	16.8	8.0	1.7	20.9	3.8	-4.4
2014	17 220.0	3 021.5	1 394.6	320.7	3 506.1	603.5	-514.1	17.5	8.1	1.9	20.4	3.5	-3.0
2015	17 904.0	3 249.9	1 540.8	343.8	3 688.4	589.7	-465.8	18.2	8.6	1.9	20.6	3.3	-2.6
2016	18 407.4	3 268.0	1 546.1	299.6	3 852.6	593.4	-620.2	17.8	8.4	1.6	20.9	3.2	-3.4

. . . = Not available.

Table 6-15. Federal Government Debt by Fiscal Year

(Billions of dollars, except as noted.)

| Year | Federal government debt held by the public at end of fiscal year | | Gross federal debt at end of fiscal year held by: | | | | | | |
| | Debt held by the public | Debt/GDP ratio (percent) | Total | Social Security funds [1] | Other U.S. government accounts | Federal Reserve System | Private investors | | |
							Total	Foreign residents	Domestic investors
1940	43	43.6	51	2	6	2	40	. . .	. . .
1941	48	41.5	58	2	7	2	46	. . .	. . .
1942	68	45.9	79	3	8	3	65	. . .	. . .
1943	128	69.2	143	4	11	7	121	. . .	. . .
1944	185	86.4	204	5	14	15	170	. . .	. . .
1945	235	103.9	260	7	18	22	213	. . .	. . .
1946	242	106.1	271	8	21	24	218	. . .	. . .
1947	224	93.9	257	9	24	22	202	. . .	. . .
1948	216	82.4	252	10	26	21	195	. . .	. . .
1949	214	77.4	253	11	27	19	195	. . .	. . .
1950	219	78.5	257	13	25	18	201	. . .	. . .
1951	214	65.5	255	15	26	23	191	. . .	. . .
1952	215	60.1	259	17	28	23	192	. . .	. . .
1953	218	57.1	266	18	29	25	194	. . .	. . .
1954	224	57.9	271	20	26	25	199	. . .	. . .
1955	227	55.7	274	21	27	24	203	. . .	. . .
1956	222	50.6	273	23	28	24	198	. . .	. . .
1957	219	47.2	272	23	30	23	196	. . .	. . .
1958	226	47.7	280	24	29	25	201	. . .	. . .
1959	235	46.4	287	23	30	26	209	. . .	. . .
1960	237	44.3	291	23	31	27	210	. . .	. . .
1961	238	43.5	293	23	31	27	211	. . .	. . .
1962	248	42.3	303	22	33	30	218	. . .	. . .
1963	254	41.0	310	21	35	32	222	. . .	. . .
1964	257	38.7	316	22	37	35	222	. . .	. . .
1965	261	36.7	322	22	39	39	222	12	210
1966	264	33.7	328	22	43	42	222	12	211
1967	267	31.8	340	26	48	47	220	11	209
1968	290	32.2	369	28	51	52	237	11	227
1969	278	28.3	366	32	56	54	224	10	210
1970	283	27.0	381	38	60	58	225	14	193
1971	303	27.1	408	41	64	66	238	32	189
1972	322	26.4	436	44	70	71	251	49	192
1973	341	25.1	466	44	81	75	266	59	209
1974	344	23.1	484	46	94	81	263	57	197
1975	395	24.5	542	48	99	85	310	66	240
1976	477	26.7	629	45	107	95	383	70	287
1977	549	27.1	706	40	118	105	444	96	323
1978	607	26.6	777	35	134	115	492	121	372
1979	640	24.9	829	33	156	116	525	120	403
1980	712	25.5	909	32	165	121	591	122	460
1981	789	25.2	995	27	178	124	665	131	524
1982	925	27.9	1 137	19	193	134	790	141	630
1983	1 137	32.1	1 372	32	202	156	982	160	806
1984	1 307	33.1	1 565	32	225	155	1 152	176	929
1985	1 507	35.3	1 817	40	270	170	1 337	223	1 071
1986	1 741	38.4	2 121	46	334	191	1 550	266	1 270
1987	1 890	39.5	2 346	65	391	212	1 678	280	1 332
1988	2 052	39.8	2 601	104	445	229	1 822	346	1 427
1989	2 191	39.3	2 868	157	520	220	1 971	395	1 507
1990	2 412	40.8	3 206	215	580	234	2 177	464	1 671
1991	2 689	44.0	3 598	268	641	259	2 430	506	1 867
1992	3 000	46.6	4 002	319	683	296	2 703	563	2 084
1993	3 248	47.8	4 351	366	737	326	2 923	619	2 241
1994	3 433	47.7	4 643	423	788	355	3 078	682	2 258
1995	3 604	47.5	4 921	483	833	374	3 230	820	2 237
1996	3 734	46.8	5 181	550	898	391	3 343	993	2 112
1997	3 772	44.5	5 369	631	966	425	3 348	1 231	2 124
1998	3 721	41.6	5 478	730	1 027	458	3 263	1 224	1 982
1999	3 632	38.2	5 606	855	1 118	497	3 136	1 281	2 097
2000	3 410	33.6	5 629	1 007	1 212	511	2 898	1 039	1 892
2001	3 320	31.4	5 770	1 170	1 280	534	2 785	1 006	1 584
2002	3 540	32.5	6 198	1 329	1 329	604	2 936	1 201	1 482
2003	3 913	34.5	6 760	1 485	1 362	656	3 257	1 454	1 458
2004	4 296	35.5	7 355	1 635	1 424	700	3 595	1 799	1 665
2005	4 592	35.6	7 905	1 809	1 504	736	3 856	1 930	1 831
2006	4 829	35.3	8 451	1 994	1 628	769	4 060	2 025	1 825
2007	5 035	35.2	8 951	2 181	1 735	780	4 255	2 235	1 453
2008	5 803	39.3	9 986	2 366	1 817	491	5 312	2 802	1 741
2009	7 545	52.3	11 876	2 504	1 827	769	6 776	3 571	2 451
2010	9 019	60.9	13 529	2 585	1 924	812	8 207	4 324	3 295
2011	10 128	65.9	14 764	2 653	1 983	1 665	8 464	4 912	2 988
2012	11 281	70.4	16 051	2 718	2 052	1 645	9 636	5 476	3 984
2013	11 983	72.6	16 719	2 756	1 981	2 072	9 910	5 652	3 841
2014	12 780	74.2	17 794	2 783	2 232	2 452	10 328	6 069	4 222
2015	13 117	73.3	18 120	2 808	2 195	2 462	10 655	6 106	4 500
2016	14 168	77.0	19 539	2 842	2 529	2 463	11 704	6 155	11 704

[1]Sum of old age and survivors insurance fund and disability insurance trust fund.
. . . = Not available.

SECTION 6D: GOVERNMENT OUTPUT AND EMPLOYMENT

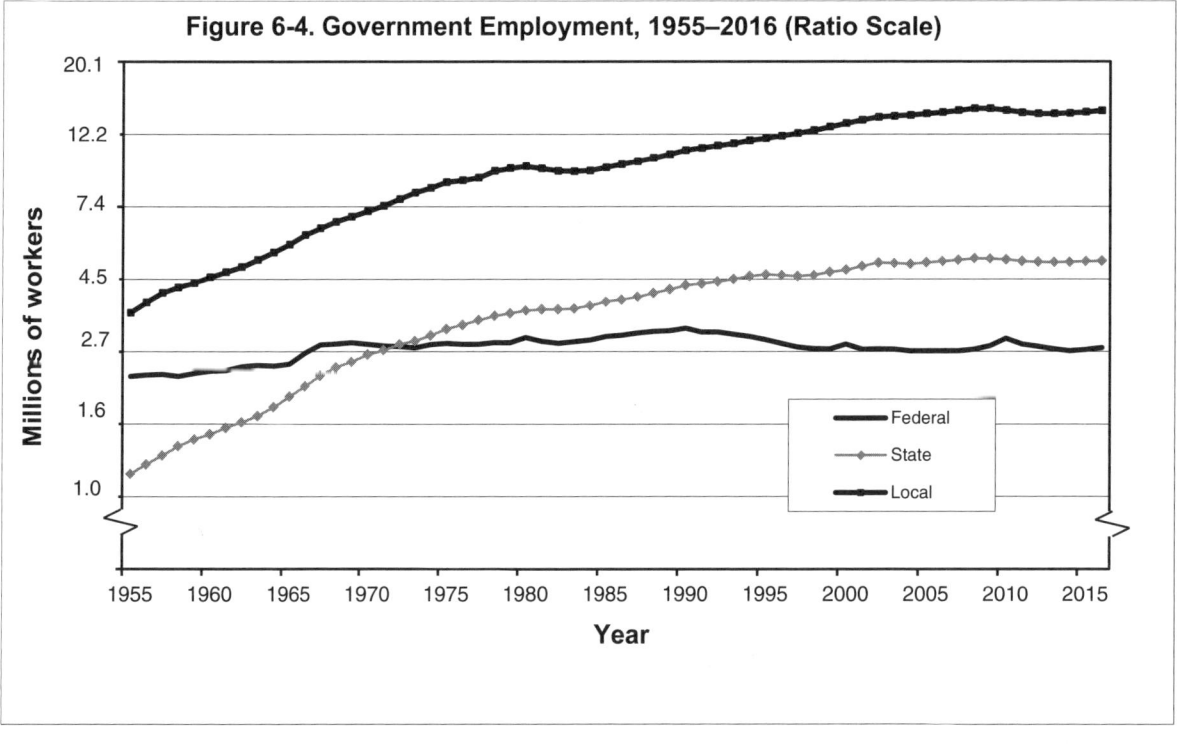

Figure 6-4. Government Employment, 1955–2016 (Ratio Scale)

- From 1955 to 2016, total reported employment of civilians by all levels of government has increased 216.5 percent. Federal employment rose 21.8 percent; state government employment rose 335 percent, with 53.7 percent of this increase due to education; and local government rose 303 percent, with 57.2 percent of this increase due to education. However, budget cuts hit all levels of government employment. For example, the Defense Department lost 29 percent of its employees between 1955 and 2016. (Tables 6-17 and 10-8B)

- Contracting and outsourcing of federal government spending can be seen in comparisons between government purchases and government value added. From 1955 to 2016, the volume (measured by the quantity index) of "intermediate" goods and services purchased for nondefense purposes rose 493.8 percent, compared with the 373 percent rise in real nondefense value added by government itself in such activities. (Real value added comprises the input of government employees and government-owned capital, valued in constant dollars). For defense, government value added rose 17 percent over that period, while purchases of goods and services rose 122 percent in real terms. (Table 6-16)

- A similar process has occurred at state and local governments, where real value added increased 336 percent while goods and services purchased rose 1,147 percent. (Table 6-16)

Table 6-16. Chain-Type Quantity Indexes for Government Output

(Seasonally adjusted, 2009 = 100.)   NIPA Table 3.10.3

Year and quarter	Federal government									State and local government		
	Gross output of general government			Value added			Intermediate goods and services purchased [1]			Gross output of general government	Value added	Intermediate goods and services purchased [1]
	Total	Defense	Nondefense	Total	Defense	Nondefense	Total	Defense	Nondefense			
1955	46.5	60.3	22.5	59.9	83.0	22.8	27.4	33.4	16.1	17.3	22.8	8.1
1956	44.8	59.7	18.8	59.7	82.4	23.3	24.4	32.9	9.7	18.0	24.3	7.8
1957	46.5	62.4	18.6	60.2	82.7	24.1	27.1	37.9	8.8	18.9	25.6	8.2
1958	46.0	61.8	18.0	59.2	80.7	25.0	27.0	38.8	7.0	20.5	27.2	9.4
1959	45.1	56.4	25.3	59.3	80.6	25.4	25.1	27.5	19.2	21.4	28.3	10.0
1960	44.0	56.8	21.6	61.0	82.1	27.4	21.0	26.7	10.4	22.5	29.8	10.5
1961	44.9	58.2	21.5	62.9	84.6	28.5	20.5	26.9	9.0	23.8	31.3	11.2
1962	49.4	63.0	25.5	66.0	88.4	30.4	26.4	32.6	14.5	24.6	32.5	11.7
1963	49.8	63.1	26.3	67.2	88.9	32.8	25.8	32.5	13.2	26.0	34.2	12.4
1964	49.6	62.1	27.5	68.5	89.8	34.7	23.7	29.0	13.5	27.8	36.2	13.6
1965	50.7	63.1	28.8	69.6	90.3	36.7	24.8	30.6	13.7	29.7	38.4	15.0
1966	56.0	71.7	28.4	74.4	96.4	39.4	30.5	42.1	9.8	31.6	40.7	16.2
1967	62.3	79.9	31.2	79.4	102.8	42.4	37.7	52.4	11.8	33.2	42.4	17.5
1968	64.6	83.4	31.5	81.4	104.6	44.6	40.3	57.9	9.8	35.5	45.0	19.3
1969	63.9	80.8	34.2	82.3	105.0	46.3	37.8	51.6	13.1	37.6	47.0	21.4
1970	60.2	74.4	35.2	79.7	99.8	47.8	32.9	43.7	13.4	39.8	49.1	23.6
1971	57.7	68.9	37.9	76.8	93.8	49.9	31.0	38.6	16.5	41.9	51.1	25.8
1972	56.7	65.2	41.4	73.9	88.0	51.7	32.4	37.5	21.8	43.7	52.9	27.4
1973	54.0	61.1	41.2	71.9	84.2	52.6	28.8	32.7	20.3	45.2	54.8	28.2
1974	54.0	59.7	43.7	72.0	82.8	55.1	28.6	31.2	22.5	46.9	56.8	29.5
1975	53.6	58.1	45.4	71.9	81.7	56.5	27.8	29.0	24.3	48.9	58.5	31.9
1976	52.6	56.5	45.5	72.1	80.5	59.2	25.3	27.0	21.0	49.8	59.3	32.9
1977	53.6	56.9	47.5	72.5	80.1	60.9	26.9	28.4	23.0	50.8	60.2	34.0
1978	54.6	57.3	49.6	73.6	80.5	63.1	27.8	28.8	24.7	52.1	61.6	35.0
1979	55.4	57.9	50.9	73.9	80.3	64.1	29.2	30.2	26.2	52.8	62.8	35.0
1980	57.5	59.6	53.6	75.2	81.0	66.4	32.0	32.9	29.1	52.8	63.6	33.7
1981	59.6	62.6	54.3	76.6	83.4	66.1	34.9	36.2	30.9	52.8	63.6	33.9
1982	61.5	66.1	53.0	78.1	85.8	66.2	37.1	40.7	28.0	53.8	64.0	35.4
1983	64.6	69.0	56.5	80.2	88.4	67.5	41.1	43.8	34.0	54.6	63.8	37.8
1984	65.4	71.0	54.9	82.4	91.5	68.3	40.1	44.5	29.3	55.7	64.2	39.8
1985	69.0	74.9	57.9	85.3	95.5	69.2	44.3	47.9	35.0	58.1	66.0	43.1
1986	72.3	78.9	59.9	87.5	98.9	69.3	48.9	52.5	39.4	60.7	68.0	46.7
1987	73.8	81.7	58.9	90.3	102.5	70.8	48.6	54.2	34.9	62.0	69.3	47.7
1988	74.1	83.6	56.2	92.1	104.3	72.7	47.0	56.2	25.6	64.0	71.7	49.2
1989	75.9	84.1	60.6	93.6	106.1	73.8	49.2	55.2	35.0	66.3	73.9	51.6
1990	77.6	84.7	64.4	95.4	107.0	77.0	50.7	55.3	39.7	68.4	76.1	53.3
1991	78.6	85.7	65.3	96.0	107.4	77.9	52.1	57.0	40.6	70.0	77.1	56.0
1992	77.4	82.3	68.3	94.4	103.9	79.6	51.4	53.8	45.6	71.8	78.4	58.7
1993	75.2	79.5	67.3	92.9	100.9	80.4	48.5	51.4	41.5	73.4	79.5	61.3
1994	73.5	76.5	68.0	90.3	97.2	79.8	48.0	49.4	44.7	75.5	80.9	64.7
1995	71.0	73.0	67.3	87.5	93.3	78.5	45.9	46.4	44.8	77.4	82.5	67.3
1996	69.7	71.8	65.9	85.4	90.2	78.1	45.7	47.4	41.8	78.9	83.8	69.1
1997	69.5	70.6	67.7	84.0	87.6	78.5	47.4	48.0	46.0	81.2	85.4	72.6
1998	68.4	68.6	68.0	83.1	85.2	79.9	45.9	46.5	44.2	84.3	87.2	78.3
1999	69.1	69.7	68.1	82.5	83.4	81.1	48.5	51.2	42.0	87.0	88.7	83.7
2000	69.6	68.9	71.0	83.0	82.5	83.8	49.1	50.6	45.7	89.4	90.5	87.0
2001	72.3	71.1	74.5	83.3	82.5	84.7	55.1	55.6	53.9	92.8	92.7	93.2
2002	76.6	75.0	79.5	84.8	83.6	86.6	63.8	63.3	65.0	95.3	94.5	96.8
2003	81.5	80.8	82.9	87.0	85.9	88.8	72.8	73.6	70.7	94.9	95.1	94.3
2004	84.7	84.7	84.8	88.4	87.9	89.1	79.0	80.2	76.1	95.1	95.5	94.3
2005	86.1	85.8	86.6	89.6	89.4	89.9	80.6	80.9	79.8	95.7	96.1	94.7
2006	87.5	87.0	88.5	90.3	89.9	91.1	83.0	82.8	83.4	96.7	96.9	96.2
2007	88.3	88.3	88.2	91.6	91.1	92.5	82.9	84.4	79.5	98.1	98.3	97.6
2008	94.0	94.3	93.6	95.1	94.8	95.7	92.3	93.6	89.4	98.2	99.6	95.2
2009	100.0	100.0	100.0	100.0	100.0	100.0	100.0	100.0	100.0	100.0	100.0	100.0
2010	104.3	103.5	105.8	103.4	103.2	103.8	105.8	104.0	110.1	98.3	99.3	96.2
2011	102.0	102.3	101.5	104.5	104.7	104.2	97.9	98.9	95.8	96.3	98.2	92.3
2012	100.8	99.9	102.5	104.4	103.7	105.5	95.0	94.4	96.2	95.5	97.7	90.9
2013	95.3	93.3	98.9	102.4	101.3	104.2	84.0	82.3	88.0	95.4	97.6	90.7
2014	93.4	90.2	99.2	101.5	99.5	104.7	80.5	77.3	88.1	96.2	97.8	92.7
2015	93.3	88.2	102.5	100.7	97.4	106.0	81.4	75.5	95.4	98.3	98.5	98.0
2016	93.2	87.4	103.8	101.1	96.9	107.8	80.6	74.2	95.6	100.0	99.5	101.0
2014												
1st quarter	93.8	91.2	98.6	102.0	100.4	104.6	80.9	78.5	86.5	95.5	97.6	91.2
2nd quarter	93.2	90.3	98.7	101.7	99.9	104.5	79.8	76.9	86.6	96.0	97.8	92.0
3rd quarter	94.0	91.1	99.4	101.3	99.2	104.7	82.5	79.9	88.6	96.4	97.9	93.1
4th quarter	92.4	88.2	100.1	100.9	98.5	104.8	78.9	73.9	90.6	96.9	98.1	94.5
2015												
1st quarter	93.1	88.6	101.6	100.8	97.8	105.5	81.1	75.8	93.5	97.6	98.2	96.2
2nd quarter	93.4	88.6	102.2	100.7	97.4	105.8	82.0	76.5	94.9	98.1	98.4	97.5
3rd quarter	93.1	87.7	102.9	100.8	97.4	106.2	80.8	74.1	96.4	98.7	98.7	98.7
4th quarter	93.5	88.1	103.2	100.8	97.2	106.5	81.9	75.6	96.6	99.0	98.8	99.6
2016												
1st quarter	93.1	87.5	103.4	100.9	97.0	107.0	80.8	74.2	96.1	99.5	99.1	100.3
2nd quarter	93.0	87.2	103.6	101.0	96.9	107.6	80.3	73.8	95.4	99.8	99.4	100.9
3rd quarter	93.5	87.9	103.9	101.2	96.9	108.0	81.4	75.4	95.4	100.2	99.8	101.3
4th quarter	93.0	86.9	104.1	101.2	96.6	108.4	80.0	73.4	95.4	100.3	99.8	101.5

[1] Includes general government intermediate inputs for goods and services sold to other sectors and for own-account investment.

Table 6-17. Government Employment

(Calendar years, payroll employment in thousands.)

Year and month	Total government employment	Federal			State			Local		
		Total	Department of Defense	Postal Service	Total	Education	State government hospitals	Total	Education	Local government hospitals
1950	6 120	2 023	533	516	...	...	...	...	...	...
1951	6 502	2 415	797	521	...	...	...	...	...	...
1952	6 727	2 539	868	542	...	...	...	...	...	...
1953	6 758	2 418	818	530	...	...	...	...	...	...
1954	6 858	2 295	744	533	...	...	...	...	...	...
1955	7 021	2 295	744	534	1 168	308	...	3 558	1 751	...
1956	7 386	2 318	749	539	1 249	334	...	3 819	1 884	...
1957	7 724	2 326	729	555	1 328	363	...	4 071	2 026	...
1958	7 946	2 298	695	567	1 415	389	...	4 232	2 115	...
1959	8 192	2 342	699	578	1 484	420	...	4 366	2 198	...
1960	8 464	2 381	681	591	1 536	448	...	4 547	2 314	...
1961	8 706	2 391	683	601	1 607	474	...	4 708	2 411	...
1962	9 004	2 455	607	601	1 669	511	...	4 881	2 522	...
1963	9 341	2 473	687	603	1 747	557	...	5 121	2 674	...
1964	9 711	2 463	676	604	1 856	609	...	5 392	2 839	...
1965	10 191	2 495	679	619	1 996	679	...	5 700	3 031	...
1966	10 910	2 690	741	686	2 141	775	...	6 080	3 297	...
1967	11 525	2 852	802	719	2 302	873	...	6 371	3 490	...
1968	11 972	2 871	801	729	2 442	958	...	6 660	3 649	...
1969	12 330	2 893	815	737	2 533	1 042	...	6 904	3 785	...
1970	12 687	2 865	756	741	2 664	1 104	...	7 158	3 912	...
1971	13 012	2 828	731	731	2 747	1 149	...	7 437	4 091	...
1972	13 465	2 815	720	703	2 859	1 188	459	7 790	4 262	467
1973	13 862	2 794	696	698	2 923	1 205	472	8 146	4 433	477
1974	14 303	2 858	698	710	3 039	1 267	483	8 407	4 584	483
1975	14 820	2 882	704	699	3 179	1 323	503	8 758	4 722	489
1976	15 001	2 863	693	676	3 273	1 371	518	8 865	4 786	492
1977	15 258	2 859	676	657	3 377	1 385	538	9 023	4 859	494
1978	15 812	2 893	661	660	3 474	1 367	541	9 446	4 958	535
1979	16 068	2 894	649	673	3 541	1 378	538	9 633	4 989	571
1980	16 375	3 000	645	673	3 610	1 398	530	9 765	5 090	604
1981	16 180	2 922	655	675	3 640	1 420	515	9 619	5 095	622
1982	15 982	2 884	690	684	3 640	1 433	494	9 458	5 049	635
1983	16 011	2 915	699	685	3 662	1 450	471	9 434	5 020	644
1984	16 159	2 943	716	706	3 734	1 488	459	9 482	5 076	623
1985	16 533	3 014	738	750	3 832	1 540	449	9 687	5 221	608
1986	16 838	3 044	736	792	3 893	1 561	438	9 901	5 358	601
1987	17 156	3 089	736	815	3 967	1 586	439	10 100	5 469	606
1988	17 540	3 124	719	835	4 076	1 621	446	10 339	5 590	619
1989	17 927	3 136	735	838	4 182	1 668	442	10 609	5 740	632
1990	18 415	3 196	722	825	4 305	1 730	426	10 914	5 902	646
1991	18 545	3 110	702	813	4 355	1 768	417	11 081	5 994	653
1992	18 787	3 111	702	800	4 408	1 799	419	11 267	6 076	665
1993	18 989	3 063	670	793	4 488	1 834	414	11 438	6 206	673
1994	19 275	3 018	657	821	4 576	1 882	407	11 682	6 329	673
1995	19 432	2 949	627	850	4 635	1 919	395	11 849	6 453	669
1996	19 539	2 877	597	867	4 606	1 911	376	12 056	6 592	648
1997	19 664	2 806	588	866	4 582	1 904	360	12 276	6 759	632
1998	19 909	2 772	550	881	4 612	1 922	346	12 525	6 921	630
1999	20 307	2 769	525	890	4 709	1 983	344	12 829	7 120	626
2000	20 790	2 865	510	880	4 786	2 031	343	13 139	7 294	622
2001	21 118	2 764	504	873	4 905	2 113	345	13 449	7 479	628
2002	21 513	2 766	499	842	5 029	2 243	349	13 718	7 654	642
2003	21 583	2 761	486	809	5 002	2 255	348	13 820	7 709	651
2004	21 621	2 730	473	782	4 982	2 238	348	13 909	7 765	656
2005	21 804	2 732	488	774	5 032	2 260	350	14 041	7 856	655
2006	21 974	2 732	493	770	5 075	2 293	357	14 167	7 913	647
2007	22 218	2 734	491	769	5 122	2 318	360	14 362	7 987	654
2008	22 509	2 762	496	747	5 177	2 354	361	14 571	8 084	659
2009	22 555	2 832	519	703	5 169	2 360	359	14 554	8 079	661
2010	22 490	2 977	545	659	5 137	2 373	354	14 376	8 013	650
2011	22 086	2 859	559	631	5 078	2 374	348	14 150	7 873	648
2012	21 920	2 820	552	611	5 055	2 389	349	14 045	7 778	647
2013	21 853	2 769	537	595	5 046	2 393	350	14 037	7 777	646
2014	21 882	2 733	524	593	5 050	2 389	347	14 098	7 815	642
2015	22 029	2 757	526	597	5 077	2 401	354	14 195	7 871	648
2016	22 223	2 795	529	609	5 089	2 412	367	14 339	7 920	661

. . . = Not available.

NOTES AND DEFINITIONS, CHAPTER 6

TABLES 6-1 THROUGH 6-11 AND 6-16

Federal, State, and Local Government in the National Income and Product Accounts

SOURCE: U.S. DEPARTMENT OF COMMERCE, BUREAU OF ECONOMIC ANALYSIS (BEA)

These data are from the national income and product accounts (NIPAs), as redefined in the 2013 comprehensive NIPA revision and updated in the 2017 annual revision. For general information about the NIPAs and the 2013 revision, see the notes and definitions for Chapter 1.

Changes in definitions made in the 2013 revision had significant effects on some components of the government accounts. Recognition of research and development spending, whether undertaken by private industry and organizations or by government, as fixed, depreciable capital investment increased the amount of investment and capital consumption charges. The change to accrual accounting for defined benefit plans, which increased personal income and saving by recognizing benefits of such plans when earned instead of when paid, generally increased employee compensation spending and government deficits. (An exception occurs in the Federal accounts in some years when the Federal government has made large cash contributions to its pension funds as "catch up" payments, which under the previous cash accounting was registered as personal income and compensation at the time instead of when accrued. In those years, the redefinition makes employee compensation smaller.)

The framework for the government accounts

In an earlier major revision in 2003, a new framework was introduced for government consumption expenditures—federal, state, and local—that explicitly recognizes the services produced by general government. Governments serve several functions in the economy. Three of these functions are recognized in the NIPAs: the production of nonmarket services; the consumption of these services, as the value of services provided to the general public is treated as government consumption expenditures; and the provision of transfer payments. These functions are financed through taxation, through contributions to social insurance funds, and by borrowing in the world's capital markets.

In this framework, the value of the government services produced and consumed (most of which are not sold in the market) is measured as the sum of the costs of the three major inputs: compensation of government employees, consumption of fixed capital (CFC), and intermediate goods and services purchased. The purchase from the private sector of goods and services by government, classified as final sales to government before the 2003 revision, was reclassified as intermediate purchases.

The value of government final purchases of consumption expenditures and gross investment, which constitutes the contribution of government demand to the gross domestic product (GDP), was not changed by this reclassification, since the previous definition of that contribution was the sum of compensation, CFC, and goods and services purchased. However, the distribution of GDP by type of product was changed—final sales of goods were reduced by the amount of goods purchased by government, and final sales of services were increased by the same amount.

In addition to this change in the conceptual framework, a number of the categories of government receipts and expenditures were redefined to make more precise distinctions. For example, items that used to be called "nontax payments" and included with taxes are now classified as transfer or fee payments and not included in taxes.

Finally, the concept previously known as "current surplus or deficit (–), national income and product accounts" was renamed "net government saving." This recognizes, in part, the role of government in the capital markets. When government runs a current surplus, net government saving is positive and funds are made available (for example, by retiring outstanding government debt) to finance investment—both private-sector capital spending and government investment. By the same token, when government runs a current deficit, or "dis-saves," it must borrow funds that would otherwise be available to finance investment.

However, this definition of net government saving does not give a complete picture of governments' role in capital markets, because it is based on current receipts and expenditures alone and does not include government investment activity.

In the NIPAs, the capital spending of all levels of government is treated the same way as the accounts treat private investment spending. A depreciation, or more precisely "consumption of fixed capital" (CFC), entry for existing capital is calculated, using estimated replacement costs and realistic depreciation rates. In the government accounts this CFC value is entered as one element of current expenditures and output. Capital spending is excluded from government current expenditures but appears in the account for "net lending or borrowing (-)."

The basic concept expressed in the net lending section of the NIPAs is that when CFC exceeds actual investment expenditures, governments have a positive net cash flow and can lend (or repay debt); if gross investment exceeds CFC, government must borrow to finance the difference, indicating negative net cash flow and requiring borrowing. (As will be seen below in the definitions, capital transfer and purchase accounts also enter into the calculation of net lending.)

The federal *budget* accounts (see Tables 6-1 and 6-2) do not draw a distinction between current and capital spending. The budget accounts of individual state and local governments typically separate capital from current spending and allow capital spending to be financed by borrowing—even when deficit financing of current spending is constitutionally forbidden. However, neither federal nor state and local government budget accounts typically show depreciation as a current expense in the way that is standard to private-sector accounting or in the way adopted in the NIPAs.

Notes on the data

Government receipts and expenditures data are derived from the U.S. government accounts and from Census Bureau censuses and surveys of the finances of state and local governments. However, BEA makes a number of adjustments to the data to convert them from fiscal year to calendar year and quarter bases and to agree with the concepts of national income accounting. Data are converted from the cash basis usually found in financial statements to the timing bases required for the NIPAs. In the NIPAs, receipts from businesses are generally on an accrual basis, purchases of goods and services are recorded when delivered, and receipts from and transfer payments to persons are on a cash basis. The federal receipts and expenditure data from the NIPAs in Table 6-1 therefore differ from the federal receipts and outlay data in Table 6-14. Among other differences, the latter are by fiscal year and are on a modified cash basis.

The NIPA data on government receipts and expenditures record transactions of governments (federal, state, and local) with other U.S. residents and foreigners. Each entry in the government receipts and expenditures account has a corresponding entry elsewhere in the NIPAs. Thus, for example, the sum of personal current taxes received by federal and state and local governments (Tables 6-1 and 6-8) is equal to personal current taxes paid, as shown in personal income (Table 4-1).

Definitions: general

In the 2003 revision of the NIPAs, several items appear separately that were previously treated as "negative expenditures" and netted against other items on the expenditures side. This grossing-up of the accounts raises both receipts and outlays and has no effect on net saving. Grossing-up has been applied to taxes from the rest of the world, interest receipts (back to 1960 for the federal government and back to 1946 for state and local governments), dividends, and subsidies and the current surplus of government enterprises (back to 1959).

Definitions: current receipts

Current tax receipts includes personal current taxes, taxes on production and imports, taxes on corporate income and (for the federal government only) taxes from the rest of the world. The category *total tax receipts* does not include *contributions*

for government social insurance, which are the taxes levied to finance Social Security, unemployment insurance, and Medicare, and are included in *receipts* in the budget accounts (Table 6-14). Analysts using NIPA data to analyze tax burdens as they are usually understood should add *contributions for government social insurance* to *tax receipts* for this purpose.

Personal current taxes is personal tax payments from residents of the United States that are not chargeable to business expense. Personal taxes consist of taxes on income, including on realized net capital gains, and on personal property. Personal contributions for social insurance are not included in this category. As of the 1999 revisions, estate and gift taxes are classified as capital transfers and are no longer included in personal current taxes. However, estate and gift taxes continue to be included in federal government receipts in Table 6-14.

Taxes on production and imports in the case of the federal government consists of *excise taxes* and *customs duties*. In the case of state and local governments, these taxes include *sales taxes*, *property taxes* (including residential real estate taxes), and *Other* taxes such as motor vehicle licenses, severance taxes, and special assessments. Before the 2003 revision, all of these taxes were components of "indirect business tax and nontax liabilities."

Taxes on corporate income covers federal, state, and local government taxes on all corporate income subject to taxes. This taxable income includes capital gains and other income excluded from NIPA profits. The taxes are measured on an accrual basis, net of applicable tax credits. Federal corporate income tax receipts in the NIPAs include, but show separately, receipts from *Federal Reserve Banks* that represent the return of the surplus earnings of the Federal Reserve system. (In the budget accounts in Table 6-14, these are classified not as corporate taxes but as the major component of "Miscellaneous receipts.")

Contributions for social insurance includes employer and personal contributions for Social Security, Medicare, unemployment insurance, and other government social insurance programs. As of the 1999 revisions, contributions to government employee retirement plans are no longer included in this category; these plans are now treated the same as private pension plans.

Income receipts on assets consists of *interest*, *dividends* and *rents and royalties.*

Interest receipts (1960 to the present for federal government; 1946 to the present for state and local governments) consists of monetary and imputed interest received on loans and investments. In the NIPAs, this no longer includes interest received by government employee retirement plans, which is now credited to personal income. However, such interest received is still deducted from interest paid in the budget accounts that are shown in Table 6-14. Before the indicated years, receipts are deducted from aggregate interest payments in the NIPAs. Hence, they are not shown as receipts, and net interest is presented on the expenditure side. In the federal budget accounts in Table 6-14, net interest (total interest expenditures minus interest receipts) is the interest "expenditure" concept used throughout the period covered.

Current transfer receipts include receipts in categories other than those specified above from persons and business. In the case of state and local government accounts (Table 6-8), it also includes *federal grants-in-aid,* a component of federal expenditures. Receipts from *business* and *persons* were previously included with income taxes in "tax and nontax payments." They consist of federal deposit insurance premiums and other nontaxes (largely fines and regulatory and inspection fees), state and local fines and other nontaxes (largely donations and tobacco settlements), and net insurance settlements paid to governments as policyholders.

The *current surplus of government enterprises* is the current operating revenue and subsidies received from other levels of government by such enterprises less their current expenses. No deduction is made for depreciation charges or net interest paid. Before 1959, this category of receipts is treated as a deduction from subsidies. In the federal NIPA accounts before 1959, there is no entry shown for the current surplus on the receipts side, and on the expenditure side, there is an entry for subsidies, which is net of the current surplus. (Subsidies are usually a larger amount than the enterprise surplus in the federal accounts.) In the state and local NIPA accounts before 1959, there is an entry for the surplus on the receipts side, which is net of subsidies. (Subsidies are typically smaller than the enterprise surplus in state and local finance.)

Definitions: consumption expenditures, saving, and gross investment

Government consumption expenditures is expenditures by governments (federal or state and local) on services for current consumption. It includes *compensation of general government employees* (including employer contributions to government employee retirement plans, as of the 1999 revision); an allowance for *consumption of general government fixed capital (CFC),* including R&D and software (depreciation); and *intermediate goods and services purchased.* (See the general discussion above for an explanation.) The estimated value of *own-account investment*—investment goods, including R&D and software, produced by government resources and purchased inputs—is subtracted here, and added to *government gross investment. Sales to other sectors*—primarily tuition payments received from individuals for higher education and charges for medical care to individuals—are also deducted, since these are counted elsewhere in the accounts, as (for example) personal consumption expenditures for those categories.

Government social benefits consists of payments to individuals for which the individuals do not render current services. Examples are Social Security benefits, Medicare, Medicaid, unemployment benefits, and public assistance. Retirement payments to retired

government employees from their pension plans are no longer included in this category.

Government social benefits to persons consists of payments to persons residing in the United States (with a corresponding entry of an equal amount in the personal income receipts accounts). Government social benefits to the *rest of the world* appear only in the federal government account, and are transfers, mainly retirement benefits, to former residents of the United States.

Other current transfer payments (federal account only) includes *grants-in-aid to state and local governments* and *grants to the rest of the world*—military and nonmilitary grants to foreign governments.

Federal grants-in-aid comprises net payments from federal to state and local governments that are made to help finance programs such as health (Medicaid), public assistance (the old Aid to Families with Dependent Children and the new Temporary Assistance for Needy Families), and education. Investment grants to state and local governments for highways, transit, air transportation, and water treatment plants are now classified as capital transfers and are no longer included in this category. However, such investment grants continue to be included as federal government outlays in Table 6-14.

Interest payments is monetary interest paid to U.S. and foreign persons and businesses and to foreign governments for public debt and other financial obligations. As noted above, from 1960 forward for the federal government and from 1946 forward for state and local governments, this represents gross total (not net) interest payments. Before those dates in the NIPAs, and throughout the federal budget accounts presented in Table 6-14, net instead of aggregate interest is shown; that is, gross total interest paid less interest received.

Subsidies are monetary grants paid by government to business, including to government enterprises at another level of government. Subsidies no longer include federal maritime construction subsidies, which are now classified as a capital transfer. For years prior to 1959, subsidies continue to be presented net of the *current surplus of government enterprises,* because detailed data to separate the series are not available for this period. See the entry for *current surplus of government enterprises,* described above, for explanation of the pre-1959 treatment of this item in the federal accounts in *Business Statistics,* which differs from the treatment in the state and local accounts.

Net saving, NIPA (surplus+/deficit-), is the sum of current receipts less the sum of current expenditures. This is shown separately for *social insurance funds* (which, in the case of the federal government, include Social Security and other trust funds) and *other* (all other government).

Gross government investment consists of general government and government enterprise expenditures for fixed assets—*structures, equipment*, and *intellectual property* (R&D and software). The expenditures include the compensation of government employees producing the assets and the purchase of goods and services as intermediate inputs to be incorporated in the assets. Government inventory investment is included in government consumption expenditures.

Capital consumption. Consumption of fixed capital (CFC; economic depreciation) is included in government consumption expenditures as a partial measure of the value of the services of general government fixed assets, including structures, equipment, R&D, and software.

Definitions: output, lending and borrowing, and net investment

In Tables 6-5 and 6-10, current-dollar values of gross output and value added of government are presented, as described in the general discussion above. *Gross output* of government is the sum of the *intermediate goods and services purchased* by government and the value added by government as a producing industry. *Value added* consists of compensation of general government employees and consumption of general government fixed capital. Since this depreciation allowance is the only entry on the product side of the accounts measuring the output associated with such capital, a zero <u>net</u> return on these assets is implicitly assumed.

Gross output minus own-account investment and sales to other sectors (see the previous description) yields *government consumption expenditures*, which represents the contribution of government consumption spending to final demands in GDP.

Net lending (net borrowing -) consists of current *net saving* as defined above, plus the *consumption of fixed capital* (CFC, from the current expenditure account), minus *gross investment*, plus *capital transfer receipts*, and minus *capital transfer payments* and *net purchases of non-produced assets*. (If this definition sounds somehow counter-intuitive, it should be remembered that "subtraction" in this context means "increasing the deficit [negative value] which must be financed.)

Capital transfer receipts and *payments* include grants between levels of government, or between government and the private sector, associated with acquisition or disposal of assets rather than with current consumption expenditures. Examples are federal grants to state and local government for highways, transit, air transportation, and water treatment plants; federal shipbuilding subsidies and other subsidies to businesses; and lump-sum payments to amortize the unfunded liability of the Uniformed Services Retiree Health Care Fund. Government capital transfer receipts include estate and gift taxes, which are no longer included in personal tax receipts. (Federal estate and gift taxes are shown in Table 6-14, where they are reported on a fiscal year basis, and are similar in order of magnitude to the calendar year values for federal capital transfer receipts in Table 6-5.)

Non-produced assets are land and radio spectrum. Unusually large negative entries for net purchases of non-produced assets in some recent years result from the negative purchase–that is, the sale–of spectrum.

The values of *net investment* shown in these tables are calculated by the editor, as gross investment minus the consumption of fixed capital.

Definitions: chain-type quantity indexes

Chain-type quantity indexes represent changes over time in real values, removing the effects of inflation. Indexes for key categories in the government expenditure accounts, as well as for government gross output, value added, and intermediate goods and services purchased, use the chain formula described in the notes and definitions for Chapter 1 and are expressed as index numbers, with the average for the year 2009 equal to 100.

Data availability

The most recent data are published each month in the *Survey of Current Business*. Current and historical data may be obtained from the BEA Web site at <http://www.bea.gov> and the STAT-USA subscription Web site at <http://www.stat-usa.gov>.

REFERENCES

See the references regarding the 2013 comprehensive revision of the NIPAs in the notes and definitions for Chapter 1. NIPA concepts and their differences from the budget estimates are discussed in "NIPA Estimates of the Federal Sector and the Federal Budget Estimates," *Survey of Current Business,* March 2007, p. 11.

For information about the classification of government expenditures into current consumption and gross investment, first undertaken in the 1996 comprehensive revisions, see the *Survey of Current Business* article, "Preview of the Comprehensive Revision of the National Income and Product Accounts: Recognition of Government Investment and Incorporation of a New Methodology for Calculating Depreciation" September 1995. Other sources of information about the NIPAs are listed in the notes and definitions for Chapter 1.

TABLES 6-12 AND 6-13

State Government Current Receipts and Expenditures; Local Government Current Receipts and Expenditures

SOURCE: BUREAU OF ECONOMIC ANALYSIS (BEA)

In the standard presentation of the state and local sector of the national income and product accounts (NIPAs) such as in Tables 6-8 through 6-11 above, state and local governments are combined. Annual measures for aggregate state governments and aggregate local governments are also available on the BEA Web site. These measures are shown in Tables 6-12 and 6-13. The definitions are the same as in the other NIPA tables described above.

The data shown here now reflect the 2013 comprehensive revision, affecting some concepts, that has been incorporated in the quarterly and annual data elsewhere in this chapter and this volume.

Two categories not shown in Table 6-8 appear in each table, detailing inter-governmental flows that are consolidated in Table 6-8. State government receipts include not only *federal grants-in-aid* but also *local grants-in-aid*, and state government expenditures include *grants-in-aid to local governments*. Local government receipts include not only *federal grants-in-aid* but also *state grants-in-aid*, and local government expenditures include *grants-in-aid to state governments*. To make room for these columns, the components *current surplus of government enterprises* and *subsidies* are not shown, though they are included in total current receipts and total current expenditures respectively.

These measures are described in "Receipts and Expenditures of State Governments and of Local Governments," *Survey of Current Business*, October 2005. Data back to 1959 are available on the BEA Web site at <http://www.bea.gov>.

Tables 6-14A and 6-14B

Federal Government Receipts and Outlays by Fiscal Year; The Federal Budget and GDP

SOURCE: U.S. OFFICE OF MANAGEMENT AND BUDGET

These data on federal government receipts and outlays are on a modified cash basis and are from the *Budget of the United States Government: Historical Tables*. The data are by federal fiscal years, which are defined as July 1 through June 30 through 1976 and October 1 through September 30 for 1977 and subsequent years. They are identified by the year of the final fiscal quarter—i.e., the year from July 1, 1975, through June 30, 1976, is identified as Fiscal 1976, and the year from October 1, 1976, through June 30, 1977, is identified as Fiscal Year 1977. The period July 1 through September 30, 1976, is a separate fiscal period known as the transition quarter (TQ) and is not included in any fiscal year.

There are numerous differences in both timing and definition between these estimates and the NIPA estimates in Tables 6-1 through 6-7. See the notes and definitions for those tables for the definitional differences that were introduced with the 1999 comprehensive revision of the NIPAs.

Definitions

The definitions for these tables are not affected by the 2013, 2003, or 1999 changes in the government sectors of the NIPAs.

Table references will be given indicating the source of each item in the *Historical Tables*; for example, "HT Table 1.1."

Receipts consist of gifts and of taxes or other compulsory payments to the government. Other types of payments to the government are netted against outlays. (HT Table 1.1)

Outlays occur when the federal government liquidates an obligation through a cash payment or when interest accrues on public debt issues. Beginning with the data for 1992, outlays include the subsidy cost of direct and guaranteed loans made. Before 1992, the costs and repayments associated with such loans are recorded on a cash basis. As noted previously, various types of nontax receipts are netted against cash outlays. These accounts do not distinguish between investment outlays and current consumption and do not include allowances for depreciation. (HT Table 1.1)

The *total budget surplus (deficit-)* is receipts minus outlays. It is sometimes presented, including in Table 6-14, as composed of two components, *on-budget and off-budget*. By law, two government programs that are included in the federal receipts and outlays totals are "off-budget"—old-age, survivors, and disability insurance (Social Security) and the Postal Service. The former accounts for nearly all of the off-budget activity. The *surplus (deficit-)* not accounted for by these two programs is the on-budget surplus or deficit. The *on-budget deficit* is based on an arbitrary distinction and is not customarily referred to as the *budget deficit,* a term reserved in customary use for the total deficit. (HT Table 1.1)

Sources of financing is the means by which the total deficit is financed or the surplus is distributed. By definition, sources of financing sum to the total deficit or surplus with the sign reversed. The principal source is *borrowing from the public*, shown as a positive number, that is, the increase in the debt held by the public. (This entry is calculated by the editors as the change in the debt held by the public as shown in HT Table 7.1.) When there is a budget surplus, as in fiscal years 1998 to 2001, this provides resources for debt reduction, which is indicated by a minus sign in this column. *Other financing* includes drawdown (or buildup, shown here with a minus sign) in Treasury cash balances, seigniorage on coins, direct and guaranteed loan account cash transactions, and miscellaneous other transactions. Large negative "other financing" in 2008 through 2010 resulted from direct loans and asset purchases under TARP and other emergency financial procedures; in other words, the government borrowed from the public to undertake these loans and asset purchases, but they are not included in budget expenditures or the budget deficit. *Other financing* is calculated by the editors, by reversing the sign of the surplus/deficit—so that the deficit becomes a positive number—and subtracting the value of borrowing from the public.

Some of the categories of *receipts by source* are self-explanatory. *Employment taxes and contributions* includes taxes for old-age, survivors, and disability insurance (Social Security), hospital insurance (Medicare), and railroad retirement funds. *Other retirement contributions* includes the employee share of payments for retirement pensions, mainly those for federal employees. *Excise taxes* includes federal taxes on alcohol, tobacco, telephone service, and transportation fuels, as well as taxes funding smaller programs such as black lung disability and vaccine injury compensation. *Miscellaneous receipts* includes deposits of earnings by the Federal Reserve system and all other receipts. (HT Tables 2.1, 2.4, and 2.5)

Outlays by function presents outlays according to the major purpose of the spending. Functional classifications cut across departmental and agency lines. Most categories of offsetting receipts are netted against cash outlays in the appropriate function, which explains how recorded outlays in *energy* and *commerce and housing credit* (which, as its name suggests, includes loan programs) can be negative. There is also a category of "undistributed offsetting receipts" (not shown), always with a negative sign, that includes proceeds from the sale or lease of assets and payments from federal agencies to federal retirement funds and to the Social Security and Medicare trust funds. Note that *Social Security* is recorded separately from other *income security* outlays, and *Medicare* separately from other *health* outlays. (HT Table 3.1) For further explanation, consult the *Budget of the United States Government.*

In order to provide authoritative comparisons of these budget values with the overall size of the economy, a special calculation of gross domestic product by fiscal year is supplied to the Office of Management and Budget by the BEA, and is shown in Table 6-14B. That table also displays selected budget aggregates in dollar values and as a percent of GDP. (HT Tables 1.2, 1.3, 2.3, and 3.1)

DATA AVAILABILITY AND REFERENCES

Definitions, budget concepts, and historical data are from *Budget of the United States Government for Fiscal Year 2015: Historical Tables*, available on the Office of Management and Budget Web site at <http://www.whitehouse.gov/omb/Budget/historicals>.

Similarly defined data for the latest month, the year-ago month, and the current and year-ago fiscal year to date are published in the *Monthly Treasury Statement* prepared by the Financial Management Service, U.S. Department of the Treasury. For those who need up-to-date budget information, this publication is available on the Financial Management Service Web site at <http://www.fms.treas.gov>. As these monthly figures are never revised to agree with the final annual data, they are not published in this volume.

TABLE 6-15

Federal Government Debt by Fiscal Year

SOURCE: U.S. OFFICE OF MANAGEMENT AND BUDGET

Debt outstanding at the end of each fiscal year is from the *Budget of the United States Government.* Most securities are recorded at sales price plus amortized discount or less amortized premium.

Definitions

Federal government debt held by the public consists of all federal debt held outside the federal government accounts—by individuals, financial institutions (including the Federal Reserve Banks), and foreign individuals, businesses, and central banks. It does not include federal debt held by federal government trust funds such as the Social Security trust fund. The level and change of the ratio of this debt to the value of gross domestic product (GDP) provide proportional measures of the impact of federal borrowing on credit markets. (HT Table 7.1) This measure of debt held by the public is very similar in concept and scope to the total federal government credit market debt outstanding in the flow-of-funds accounts.

Gross federal debt—total. This is the total debt owed by the U.S. Treasury. It includes a small amount of matured debt. (HT Table 7.1)

Debt held by Social Security funds is the sum of the end-year trust fund balances for old age and survivors insurance and disability insurance. The separate disability trust fund begins in 1957. (HT Table 13.1)

Debt held by other U.S. government accounts is calculated by the editors by subtracting the Social Security debt holdings from the total debt held by federal government accounts, which is shown in HT Table 7.1. It includes the balances in all the other trust funds, including the Medicare funds, federal employee retirement funds, and the highway trust fund.

Debt held by the Federal Reserve System is the total value of Treasury securities held by the 12 Federal Reserve Banks, which are acquired in open market operations that carry out monetary policy. (HT Table 7.1)

Debt held by private investors is calculated by subtracting the Federal Reserve debt from the total debt held by the public, and is shown as "Debt Held by the Public: Other" in HT Table 7.1.

Debt held by foreign residents is based on surveys by the Treasury Department. (Table 5-7, *Budget of the United States for Fiscal Year 2015: Analytical Perspectives*)

Debt held by domestic investors is calculated by the editors by subtracting the foreign-held debt from the total debt held by private investors.

The "debt subject to statutory limitation," not shown here, is close to the gross federal debt in concept and size, but there are some relatively minor definitional differences specified by law. The debt limit can only be changed by an Act of Congress. For information about the debt subject to limit and other debt subjects, see the latest *Budget of the United States Government: Historical Statistics* and *Analytical Perspectives*.

DATA AVAILABILITY AND REFERENCES

For the end-of-fiscal-year data, see Historical Tables and Analytical Perspectives in the Budget of the United States Government, which is available on the OMB Web site at <http://www.whitehouse.gov/omb/Budget>. In the Analytical Perspectives, debt analysis and data are included in the "Economic and Budget Analysis" section.

Recent quarterly data, measured on a somewhat different basis, are found in the *Treasury Bulletin* in the chapter on "Ownership of Federal Securities (OFS)," in Tables OFS-1 and OFS-2. The *Treasury Bulletin* can be accessed on the Internet at <http://www.fms.treas.gov/bulletin>. Holdings by Social Security funds are also available in the *Bulletin* in the chapter on "Federal Debt,"

Table FD-3. The Disability Fund is listed separately from the Old-Age and Survivors Fund.

TABLE 6-17

Government Employment

SOURCE: U.S. DEPARTMENT OF LABOR, BUREAU OF LABOR STATISTICS (SEE NOTES AND DEFINITIONS FOR TABLE 10-8)

Government payroll employment includes federal, state, and local activities such as legislative, executive, and judicial functions, as well as all government-owned and government-operated business enterprises, establishments, and institutions (arsenals, navy yards, hospitals, etc.), and government force account construction. The figures relate to civilian employment only. The Bureau of Labor Statistics (BLS) considers regular fulltime teachers (private and governmental) to be employed during the summer vacation period, regardless of whether they are specifically paid in those months.

Employment in federal government establishments reflects employee counts as of the pay period containing the 12th of the month. Federal government employment excludes employees of the Central Intelligence Agency and the National Security Agency.

CHAPTER 7: U.S. FOREIGN TRADE AND FINANCE

SECTION 7A: FOREIGN TRANSACTIONS IN THE NATIONAL INCOME AND PRODUCT ACCOUNTS

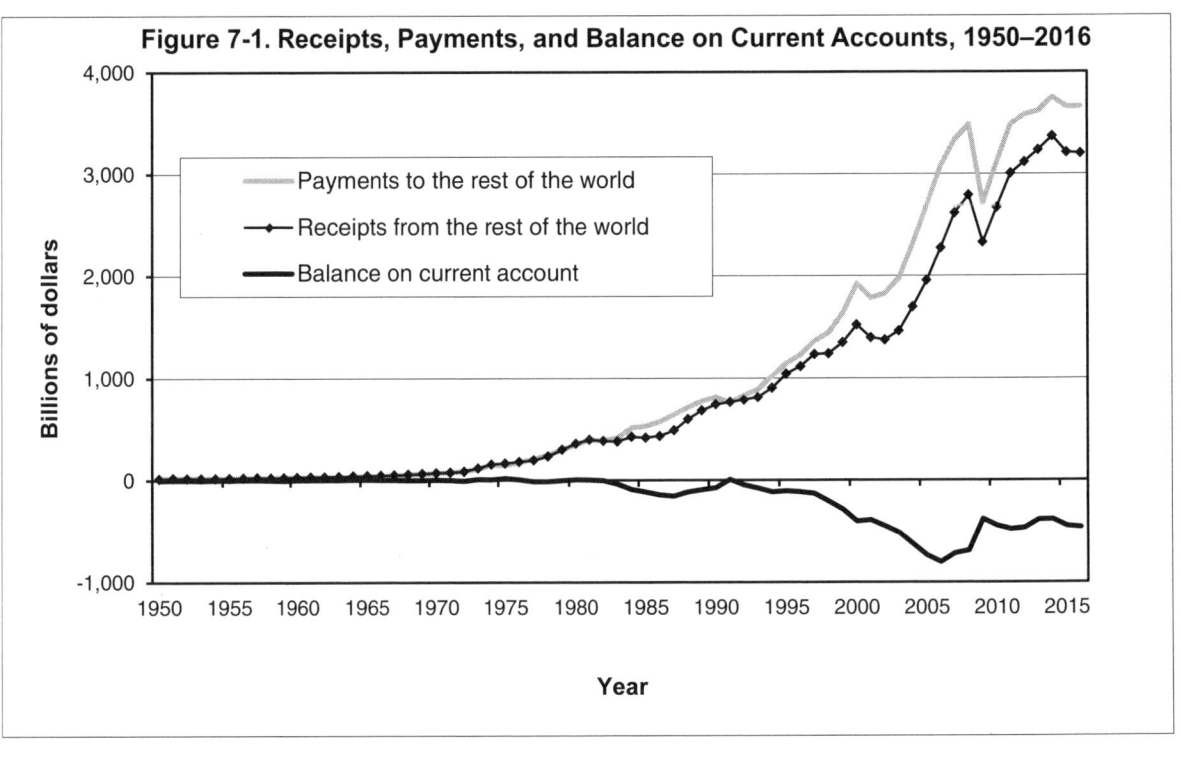

Figure 7-1. Receipts, Payments, and Balance on Current Accounts, 1950–2016

- Beginning in 1983, chronic current-account deficits in U.S. transactions with the rest of the world have emerged and increased, requiring increasing net capital inflows from abroad to finance them. The only current-account surplus since then occurred in 1991, when payments from other countries financed most of the cost of the first Gulf War. In 2006, the NIPA deficit reached a record $804 billion, 5.8 percent of GDP. From 2007 through 2014, the current account deficit declined by half until 2014. However, it increased 17.3 percent in 2015 and 2.3 percent in 2016. (Tables 7-1 and 1-1A)

- The NIPA current-account deficit of $461.4 billion in 2016 included a deficit of $778.2 billion on goods, a surplus of $256.9 billion on services, a surplus of $197.1 in net receipts and a deficit of $136.8 billion in taxes and transfers. (Table 7-1)

- Looking at quarterly data on the real volume of flows of goods and services in U.S. trade, the quantity index for exports of goods and services was 107.6 in the first quarter of 2010 but rebounded to 133.8 in the fourth quarter of 2016. Imports of goods and services, also in real terms, followed the same trend as exports. The quantity index for imports was 106.7 in the first quarter of 2010 but increased to 138.9 by the fourth quarter of 2016. (Table 7-2)

Table 7-1. Foreign Transactions in the National Income and Product Accounts

(Billions of dollars, quarterly data are at seasonally adjusted annual rates.)   NIPA Table 4.1

Year and quarter	Current receipts from the rest of the world					Current payments to the rest of the world						Balance on current account, NIPAs	Net lending or net borrowing (-), NIPAs
	Total	Exports of goods and services			Income receipts	Total	Imports of goods and services			Income payments	Current taxes and transfer payments, net		
		Goods 1		Services 1			Goods 1		Services 1				
		Durable	Nondurable				Durable	Nondurable					
1955	21.2	8.2	6.2	3.3	3.5	20.8	4.5	7.1	5.7	1.1	2.6	0.4	0.4
1956	25.2	9.8	7.8	3.7	3.9	22.5	5.2	7.6	6.1	1.1	2.5	2.7	2.7
1957	28.3	10.9	8.6	4.5	4.3	23.6	5.3	8.0	6.7	1.2	2.4	4.7	4.7
1958	24.4	9.0	7.4	4.1	3.9	23.6	5.0	8.0	7.1	1.2	2.4	0.8	0.8
1959	27.0	8.9	7.5	6.3	4.3	28.3	6.6	8.7	7.0	1.5	4.4	-1.3	-1.3
1960	31.9	11.3	9.2	6.6	4.9	28.8	6.4	8.9	7.6	1.8	4.1	3.2	3.2
1961	32.9	11.5	9.4	6.7	5.3	28.7	6.0	9.0	7.6	1.8	4.2	4.2	4.2
1962	35.0	12.0	9.7	7.4	5.9	31.2	6.9	9.9	8.1	1.8	4.4	3.8	3.8
1963	37.6	12.7	10.7	7.7	6.5	32.7	7.4	10.3	8.4	2.1	4.5	4.9	4.9
1964	42.3	14.7	12.1	8.3	7.2	34.8	8.4	11.0	8.7	2.3	4.4	7.5	7.5
1965	45.0	15.8	12.1	9.2	7.9	38.9	10.4	11.8	9.3	2.6	4.7	6.2	6.2
1966	49.0	17.7	13.4	9.8	8.1	45.2	13.3	13.1	10.7	3.0	5.1	3.8	3.8
1967	52.1	18.6	13.9	10.9	8.7	48.7	14.5	13.2	12.2	3.3	5.5	3.5	3.5
1968	58.0	21.2	14.5	12.2	10.1	56.5	18.8	15.1	12.6	4.0	5.9	1.5	1.5
1969	63.7	23.9	14.8	13.2	11.8	62.1	20.8	16.1	13.7	5.7	5.9	1.6	1.6
1970	72.5	27.4	17.7	14.7	12.8	68.8	22.8	18.1	14.9	6.4	6.6	3.7	3.7
1971	77.0	27.9	18.3	16.8	14.0	76.7	26.6	19.9	15.8	6.4	7.9	0.3	0.3
1972	87.1	31.4	21.2	18.3	16.3	91.2	33.3	23.6	17.3	7.7	9.2	-4.0	-4.1
1973	118.8	42.3	33.5	19.5	23.5	109.9	40.8	31.0	19.3	10.9	7.9	8.9	8.8
1974	156.5	57.7	45.8	23.2	29.8	150.5	50.3	54.2	22.9	14.3	8.7	6.0	5.9
1975	166.7	65.2	47.3	26.2	28.0	146.9	45.6	53.4	23.7	15.0	9.1	19.8	19.8
1976	181.9	70.9	50.6	28.0	32.4	174.8	56.8	67.8	26.5	15.5	8.1	7.1	7.0
1977	196.6	74.4	54.0	30.9	37.2	207.5	69.2	83.4	29.8	16.9	8.1	-10.9	-11.0
1978	233.1	87.5	62.4	37.0	46.3	245.8	89.0	88.4	34.8	24.7	8.8	-12.6	-12.7
1979	298.5	109.6	77.6	42.9	68.3	299.6	100.4	112.3	39.9	36.4	10.6	-1.2	-1.3
1980	359.9	135.7	94.8	50.3	79.1	351.4	111.9	136.6	45.3	44.9	12.6	8.5	8.4
1981	397.3	143.2	102.0	60.0	92.0	393.9	126.0	141.8	49.9	59.1	17.0	3.4	3.3
1982	384.2	128.5	94.1	60.7	101.0	387.5	125.1	125.4	52.6	64.5	19.8	-3.3	-3.4
1983	378.9	123.8	90.3	62.9	101.9	413.9	147.3	125.4	56.0	64.8	20.5	-35.1	-35.2
1984	424.2	135.2	96.1	71.1	121.9	514.3	192.4	143.9	68.8	85.6	23.6	-90.1	-90.2
1985	415.9	139.9	87.6	75.7	112.7	530.2	204.2	139.1	73.9	87.3	25.7	-114.3	-114.4
1986	432.3	145.3	86.1	89.6	111.3	575.0	238.8	131.2	82.9	94.4	27.8	-142.7	-142.8
1987	487.2	166.9	98.6	98.4	123.3	641.3	264.2	150.6	93.9	105.8	26.8	-154.1	-154.2
1988	596.7	211.9	120.1	112.5	152.1	712.4	294.8	157.3	101.9	129.5	29.0	-115.7	-115.9
1989	682.0	242.5	132.2	129.5	177.7	774.3	310.3	174.5	106.2	152.9	30.4	-92.4	-92.7
1990	740.7	265.3	138.0	148.6	188.8	815.6	314.5	193.5	121.7	154.2	31.7	-74.9	-82.3
1991	763.3	285.6	144.6	164.8	168.4	755.4	315.5	185.2	122.8	136.8	-4.9	7.9	2.6
1992	785.1	304.2	151.1	177.7	152.1	830.7	346.7	198.2	122.9	121.0	41.9	-45.6	-44.3
1993	810.4	317.9	149.9	187.1	155.6	888.9	386.4	206.4	127.2	123.6	45.4	-78.5	-79.4
1994	905.5	353.8	164.6	202.6	184.5	1 020.2	454.0	222.8	136.6	160.7	46.1	-114.7	-116.0
1995	1 042.6	398.6	193.8	220.4	229.8	1 147.7	510.8	246.7	145.1	201.1	44.1	-105.1	-105.5
1996	1 114.0	426.4	202.4	238.8	246.4	1 228.1	533.4	274.1	156.5	214.6	49.5	-114.1	-114.3
1997	1 233.9	488.4	211.5	253.9	280.1	1 363.2	588.5	297.1	170.1	256.0	51.4	-129.3	-129.8
1998	1 239.4	492.4	200.2	260.4	286.8	1 444.3	637.7	293.0	184.9	268.5	60.0	-204.5	-204.7
1999	1 350.0	508.7	203.0	280.3	321.4	1 636.6	715.8	335.4	197.4	294.3	93.7	-286.6	-291.1
2000	1 520.4	573.4	223.9	299.6	382.7	1 924.1	822.9	428.6	221.2	345.7	105.8	-403.7	-404.1
2001	1 396.8	525.3	218.6	282.9	325.3	1 785.6	757.7	419.0	218.7	273.5	116.7	-388.8	-375.8
2002	1 374.6	492.8	220.4	289.3	315.8	1 825.4	774.2	425.1	229.6	267.2	129.2	-450.8	-451.3
2003	1 462.2	501.8	239.6	298.9	356.1	1 977.9	806.3	489.9	247.7	289.0	144.9	-515.7	-517.8
2004	1 697.2	565.7	268.7	347.1	451.4	2 324.2	936.5	575.0	289.1	362.3	161.3	-627.0	-624.2
2005	1 954.3	629.8	296.8	382.3	575.8	2 692.0	1 025.7	693.7	310.7	483.2	178.7	-737.7	-724.8
2006	2 276.3	715.0	334.6	426.7	724.2	3 078.5	1 131.2	768.5	347.6	656.6	174.6	-802.2	-804.2
2007	2 616.3	782.9	383.5	498.2	875.7	3 334.4	1 176.2	827.5	379.4	750.1	201.2	-718.1	-718.0
2008	2 790.3	829.2	469.6	543.1	856.9	3 482.0	1 163.0	986.4	415.6	684.9	232.0	-691.6	-686.2
2009	2 330.1	671.6	393.5	522.6	648.9	2 712.0	893.8	696.5	392.9	497.8	231.0	-381.9	-382.5
2010	2 669.6	801.4	478.2	572.7	720.0	3 115.5	1 106.9	842.9	415.2	514.1	236.4	-445.9	-446.6
2011	3 004.2	894.0	572.9	639.5	792.6	3 485.8	1 238.7	1 006.0	441.6	546.0	253.4	-481.5	-483.2
2012	3 113.9	939.9	586.1	672.2	801.5	3 582.1	1 328.5	977.3	458.0	563.9	254.3	-468.2	-461.7
2013	3 234.0	957.1	605.5	713.9	825.5	3 620.1	1 360.2	941.3	467.1	581.3	270.2	-386.1	-386.9
2014	3 366.1	994.5	623.4	755.7	847.2	3 750.2	1 452.5	943.5	487.1	612.6	254.4	-384.0	-384.4
2015	3 209.1	955.3	541.9	767.7	812.9	3 659.7	1 489.6	800.9	498.5	608.4	262.3	-450.6	-451.0
2016	3 199.1	926.3	519.8	768.5	844.3	3 660.1	1 466.4	757.9	511.6	647.2	277.1	-460.9	-461.1
2014													
1st quarter	3 321.8	972.1	625.5	742.4	840.4	3 703.4	1 396.9	980.9	478.6	599.2	247.8	-381.6	-382.1
2nd quarter	3 412.9	994.5	638.9	757.8	843.0	3 767.8	1 455.6	961.2	487.2	612.6	251.3	-354.9	-355.3
3rd quarter	3 377.5	1 006.6	625.3	757.0	858.1	3 745.9	1 460.0	930.7	487.4	612.6	255.2	-368.4	-368.8
4th quarter	3 352.4	1 004.7	604.0	765.7	847.2	3 783.6	1 497.6	901.3	495.3	626.1	263.3	-431.2	-431.5
2015													
1st quarter	3 234.8	968.3	552.7	768.1	814.6	3 688.9	1 500.7	834.7	491.9	597.6	264.1	-454.1	-454.5
2nd quarter	3 263.8	965.8	567.0	771.1	823.1	3 697.2	1 491.4	822.1	497.5	630.4	255.7	-433.4	-433.8
3rd quarter	3 204.7	951.5	538.4	766.7	822.0	3 687.4	1 489.2	795.8	502.4	630.4	269.6	-482.8	-483.1
4th quarter	3 133.0	935.5	509.7	764.9	791.9	3 565.1	1 477.2	750.9	502.1	575.1	259.9	-432.1	-432.5
2016													
1st quarter	3 104.6	919.8	488.1	758.6	802.8	3 596.1	1 451.8	737.5	503.5	626.7	276.6	-491.5	-492.1
2nd quarter	3 186.2	922.7	513.4	765.7	843.8	3 617.9	1 448.0	749.4	506.0	648.8	265.8	-431.7	-432.1
3rd quarter	3 237.2	928.7	544.3	775.5	848.4	3 680.6	1 466.9	758.3	516.1	660.1	279.3	-443.4	-443.8
4th quarter	3 268.6	933.9	533.3	774.3	882.1	3 745.6	1 498.7	786.3	520.7	653.1	286.7	-477.0	-477.4

1Exports and imports of certain goods, primarily military equipment purchased and sold by the federal government, are included in services. Beginning with 1986, repairs and alterations of equipment are reclassified from goods to services.

Table 7-2. Chain-Type Quantity Indexes for Exports and Imports of Goods and Services

(Index numbers, 2009 = 100; quarterly indexes are seasonally adjusted.)   NIPA Table 4.2.3

Year and quarter	Exports of goods and services					Imports of goods and services				
	Total	Goods [1]			Services [1]	Total	Goods [1]			Services [1]
		Total	Durable	Nondurable			Total	Durable	Nondurable	
1970	11.78	11.31	8.61	19.00	13.35	12.79	11.29	6.68	22.57	20.40
1971	11.99	11.30	8.57	19.09	14.32	13.47	12.24	7.36	23.96	19.82
1972	12.92	12.52	9.47	21.26	14.26	14.99	13.90	8.46	26.76	20.66
1973	15.35	15.59	11.93	26.06	14.51	15.68	14.89	9.01	28.87	19.97
1974	16.57	16.92	13.82	26.04	15.30	15.33	14.47	9.04	27.07	19.94
1975	16.46	16.57	13.56	25.42	16.21	13.62	12.65	7.39	25.11	19.08
1976	17.18	17.42	13.81	27.95	16.38	16.29	15.51	9.05	30.81	20.40
1977	17.60	17.76	13.85	29.11	17.12	18.07	17.40	10.25	34.32	21.41
1978	19.45	19.60	15.35	31.97	19.04	19.63	18.96	11.84	35.44	22.94
1979	21.38	21.68	17.30	34.42	20.39	19.96	19.28	12.11	35.85	23.25
1980	23.68	24.34	19.35	38.86	21.24	18.63	17.85	12.21	30.86	22.74
1981	23.97	24.18	18.74	40.05	23.32	19.12	18.22	13.23	29.94	24.07
1982	22.14	22.14	16.30	30.04	22.00	18.88	17.76	13.38	28.19	25.35
1983	21.57	21.42	16.00	37.33	22.26	21.27	20.17	16.12	30.02	27.39
1984	23.33	22.94	17.60	38.50	24.88	26.44	25.06	21.45	34.19	34.26
1985	24.11	23.74	18.98	37.49	25.58	28.16	26.62	23.60	34.61	36.87
1986	25.96	25.02	20.12	39.12	29.25	30.56	29.35	25.79	38.69	37.28
1987	28.79	28.07	23.14	42.08	31.46	32.37	30.71	26.93	40.64	41.68
1988	33.46	33.06	28.48	45.93	35.21	33.64	31.96	28.05	42.19	43.09
1989	37.33	36.84	32.37	49.38	39.43	35.13	33.33	29.29	43.91	45.18
1990	40.62	39.99	35.86	51.61	43.19	36.38	34.30	30.07	45.39	48.13
1991	43.31	42.68	38.47	54.49	45.93	36.33	34.46	30.23	45.52	46.88
1992	46.31	45.89	41.55	58.09	48.40	38.88	37.71	33.40	49.00	45.61
1993	47.83	47.38	43.70	57.73	50.02	42.24	41.48	37.36	52.30	46.83
1994	52.06	51.93	48.93	60.40	53.52	47.27	47.02	43.53	56.18	49.32
1995	57.41	57.97	55.86	64.31	57.14	51.06	51.25	48.52	58.49	50.81
1996	62.10	63.13	62.31	66.63	60.73	55.50	56.06	53.72	62.40	53.46
1997	69.50	72.27	73.60	71.20	63.92	62.97	64.14	62.58	68.89	58.11
1998	71.13	73.85	75.94	71.07	65.69	70.33	71.74	70.83	75.19	64.43
1999	73.01	76.93	79.48	73.19	64.79	77.46	80.92	81.05	82.24	62.47
2000	79.26	84.71	89.22	76.73	67.80	87.55	91.52	93.35	89.65	70.35
2001	74.63	79.49	81.82	76.27	64.40	85.06	88.56	87.51	92.04	69.90
2002	73.34	76.78	77.23	77.69	66.15	88.18	91.88	91.22	94.66	72.18
2003	74.64	78.22	78.61	79.29	67.13	92.12	96.40	95.14	100.34	73.71
2004	81.91	84.92	87.25	82.18	75.66	102.63	107.16	108.45	107.06	83.08
2005	87.04	91.12	95.44	84.67	78.51	109.13	114.31	117.66	111.25	86.82
2006	94.90	99.71	105.72	90.26	84.86	116.03	121.07	128.13	113.09	94.30
2007	103.69	107.17	114.76	95.03	96.46	118.95	123.30	131.40	114.03	100.16
2008	109.64	113.75	120.63	102.73	101.08	115.91	118.71	126.32	109.99	103.91
2009	100.00	100.00	100.00	100.00	100.00	100.00	100.00	100.00	100.00	100.00
2010	111.90	114.38	116.85	110.31	106.77	112.72	114.87	122.54	105.64	103.79
2011	119.56	121.82	126.86	113.90	114.92	118.88	121.50	134.02	107.09	107.98
2012	123.65	126.20	132.63	116.29	118.39	121.53	124.01	143.59	102.68	111.25
2013	127.95	130.10	135.69	121.34	123.56	122.86	125.47	149.04	100.23	111.96
2014	133.42	136.03	141.42	127.53	128.06	128.38	131.62	160.56	101.04	114.84
2015	133.97	135.49	138.19	131.16	130.73	134.75	138.41	169.85	105.21	119.44
2016	133.53	135.90	136.19	135.71	128.74	136.46	139.60	170.77	106.73	123.20
2010										
1st quarter	107.58	110.20	110.91	108.97	102.21	106.75	108.12	112.58	102.57	101.10
2nd quarter	110.10	113.05	116.36	107.64	104.01	111.83	114.08	120.97	105.72	102.51
3rd quarter	113.21	115.48	118.44	110.61	108.54	115.77	118.24	126.79	107.98	105.52
4th quarter	116.68	118.80	121.70	114.02	112.32	116.52	119.04	129.81	106.30	106.03
2011										
1st quarter	117.29	119.62	123.39	113.51	112.50	117.41	120.59	131.76	107.48	104.02
2nd quarter	119.08	121.07	126.48	112.62	115.03	118.29	120.81	131.52	108.21	107.78
3rd quarter	120.33	122.10	127.93	113.05	116.78	119.25	121.48	135.00	106.13	110.06
4th quarter	121.54	124.51	129.63	116.43	115.37	120.58	123.11	137.80	106.56	110.05
2012										
1st quarter	122.35	125.07	133.26	112.69	116.73	121.29	123.87	143.32	102.70	110.49
2nd quarter	123.72	126.52	132.55	117.18	117.93	121.88	124.39	143.89	103.11	111.46
3rd quarter	124.33	127.22	132.63	118.74	118.37	122.07	124.58	143.57	103.79	111.65
4th quarter	124.19	125.99	132.10	116.53	120.52	120.91	123.21	143.57	101.09	111.41
2013										
1st quarter	125.41	126.80	133.13	117.02	122.60	121.30	123.75	145.66	100.14	111.11
2nd quarter	126.94	128.84	136.47	117.21	123.05	122.86	125.52	148.41	100.92	111.81
3rd quarter	127.92	129.96	135.22	121.66	123.73	123.39	126.06	150.00	100.44	112.29
4th quarter	131.54	134.79	137.92	129.49	124.86	123.87	126.57	152.09	99.40	112.64
2014										
1st quarter	130.74	132.71	138.13	124.19	126.67	125.39	128.36	154.08	100.96	112.98
2nd quarter	133.64	136.14	141.14	128.17	128.50	128.48	131.75	160.57	101.31	114.77
3rd quarter	133.85	136.88	143.04	127.26	127.64	128.17	131.40	161.23	99.98	114.62
4th quarter	135.46	138.41	143.39	130.51	129.44	131.49	134.95	166.34	101.89	117.00
2015										
1st quarter	133.93	135.34	138.91	129.64	130.89	133.65	137.54	168.71	104.68	117.42
2nd quarter	135.15	137.13	139.29	133.69	131.05	134.73	138.58	169.40	106.09	118.69
3rd quarter	133.78	135.40	138.01	131.20	130.37	135.31	138.83	170.64	105.18	120.58
4th quarter	133.02	134.09	136.54	130.11	130.61	135.31	138.70	170.64	104.89	121.07
2016										
1st quarter	132.14	134.18	135.18	132.75	127.98	135.25	138.54	168.96	106.56	121.42
2nd quarter	133.05	135.11	135.53	134.68	128.83	135.38	138.63	168.56	107.23	121.71
3rd quarter	135.12	137.75	136.61	140.08	129.84	136.28	139.06	170.76	105.53	124.35
4th quarter	133.80	136.56	137.46	135.32	128.31	138.94	142.16	174.81	107.60	125.33

[1]Exports and imports of certain goods, primarily military equipment purchased and sold by the federal government, are included in services. Beginning with 1986, repairs and alterations of equipment are reclassified from goods to services.

Table 7-3. Chain-Type Price Indexes for Exports and Imports of Goods and Services

(Index numbers, 2009 = 100; quarterly indexes are seasonally adjusted.) **NIPA Table 4.2.4**

Year and quarter	Exports of goods and services					Imports of goods and services				
	Total	Goods [1]			Services [1]	Total	Goods [1]			Services [1]
		Total	Durable	Nondurable			Total	Durable	Nondurable	
1970	32.62	37.40	18.89	19.63	22.76	22.20	22.75	18.30	7.24	19.80
1971	33.81	38.40	19.20	19.95	24.23	23.57	23.92	18.65	7.56	21.59
1972	35.30	39.42	19.90	20.53	26.50	25.22	25.75	20.07	7.99	22.66
1973	39.94	45.62	22.90	23.75	27.82	29.60	30.35	24.05	9.81	26.22
1974	49.21	57.43	33.50	35.00	31.33	42.35	45.42	34.85	23.93	31.18
1975	54.23	63.74	37.76	39.23	33.49	45.87	49.22	36.11	24.72	33.71
1976	56.01	65.46	37.71	39.18	35.43	47.26	50.54	35.70	25.81	35.23
1977	58.29	67.89	39.27	40.80	37.42	51.42	55.17	38.98	27.97	37.73
1978	61.85	71.81	41.07	42.70	40.22	55.05	58.85	41.93	28.47	41.16
1979	69.29	81.11	49.79	51.71	43.52	64.46	69.39	50.02	38.35	46.48
1980	76.32	88.88	55.95	58.09	49.07	80.29	87.56	60.40	58.41	53.94
1981	81.97	95.19	58.01	60.24	53.35	84.61	92.44	61.18	64.20	56.29
1982	82.35	94.39	56.24	58.42	56.37	81.76	88.70	58.86	59.68	56.34
1983	82.68	93.83	54.66	56.75	58.61	78.70	85.00	55.72	54.48	55.41
1984	83.44	94.67	56.36	58.52	59.22	78.02	84.41	55.12	54.18	54.46
1985	80.97	89.96	54.10	55.66	61.35	75.45	81.09	52.28	50.87	54.39
1986	79.60	86.84	55.00	51.53	63.45	75.45	79.27	53.76	34.92	60.28
1987	81.38	88.82	59.95	57.99	64.81	80.02	84.93	58.22	39.53	61.14
1988	85.55	94.30	67.35	63.80	66.25	83.85	88.97	69.07	37.51	64.12
1989	86.97	95.51	69.11	64.74	68.09	85.68	91.46	72.99	42.04	63.78
1990	87.46	94.67	68.77	65.83	71.31	88.14	93.14	69.90	47.01	68.56
1991	88.44	94.62	68.16	63.69	74.36	87.40	91.38	67.86	42.25	71.07
1992	88.00	93.15	69.27	60.43	76.11	87.47	90.88	67.95	40.82	73.06
1993	88.14	92.68	73.55	58.92	77.51	86.80	89.87	68.01	38.54	73.68
1994	89.16	93.73	76.25	63.80	78.45	87.62	90.52	70.42	37.63	75.13
1995	91.15	95.95	81.67	74.52	79.92	90.02	92.93	75.86	41.61	77.48
1996	89.94	93.51	78.85	70.62	81.50	88.45	90.58	74.79	45.32	79.41
1997	88.35	90.92	78.14	70.52	82.32	85.38	86.84	76.13	43.61	79.41
1998	86.26	88.05	74.93	66.26	82.15	80.78	81.59	72.55	34.85	77.85
1999	85.58	86.86	72.98	65.84	82.77	81.28	81.69	72.69	39.41	80.43
2000	87.16	88.37	74.77	73.21	84.54	84.82	85.99	76.74	55.95	80.01
2001	86.65	87.85	73.53	70.62	84.05	82.72	83.55	74.16	51.02	79.64
2002	86.09	87.21	73.72	68.52	83.70	81.71	82.09	71.46	49.60	80.97
2003	87.79	88.99	76.97	74.38	85.19	84.51	84.55	73.28	58.51	85.55
2004	90.85	92.25	86.83	82.53	87.79	88.47	88.70	86.14	69.24	88.58
2005	94.72	95.47	94.74	93.74	93.18	93.80	94.58	90.96	88.96	91.09
2006	97.98	98.83	106.60	101.47	96.22	97.66	98.67	99.59	102.41	93.83
2007	101.11	102.19	113.49	109.79	98.82	101.02	102.19	107.16	112.14	96.42
2008	105.81	107.20	115.94	126.04	102.81	111.59	113.85	118.21	152.93	101.81
2009	100.00	100.00	100.00	100.00	100.00	100.00	100.00	100.00	100.00	100.00
2010	104.26	105.03	111.43	116.00	102.64	105.80	106.74	114.08	124.59	101.82
2011	110.96	113.05	123.35	139.53	106.48	113.94	116.18	126.06	158.30	104.11
2012	111.97	113.53	120.64	136.37	108.64	114.67	116.92	120.20	160.42	104.79
2013	112.06	112.77	116.96	134.12	110.56	113.63	115.34	117.59	155.79	106.20
2014	112.05	111.66	115.22	131.59	112.91	113.24	114.48	116.99	151.22	107.96
2015	106.48	103.75	108.26	104.72	112.37	104.36	104.06	106.66	98.53	106.22
2016	104.46	99.90	104.15	93.13	114.23	101.09	100.19	101.78	81.93	105.69
2010										
1st quarter	102.68	103.03	108.14	109.97	101.96	105.93	106.95	111.39	127.06	101.56
2nd quarter	103.82	104.40	111.04	115.28	102.60	105.39	106.31	114.89	122.66	101.46
3rd quarter	104.06	104.77	110.98	115.41	102.59	104.74	105.51	112.31	119.55	101.48
4th quarter	106.49	107.93	115.57	123.35	103.41	107.14	108.17	117.73	129.08	102.76
2011										
1st quarter	109.20	111.16	120.57	133.83	105.01	111.49	113.29	124.71	148.60	103.60
2nd quarter	111.52	113.82	123.89	143.32	106.58	114.90	117.21	127.57	162.52	104.75
3rd quarter	112.16	114.40	126.27	143.02	107.35	114.83	117.18	128.34	160.81	104.46
4th quarter	110.95	112.81	122.67	137.93	106.97	114.55	117.04	123.61	161.27	103.62
2012										
1st quarter	111.69	113.44	121.88	139.56	107.93	115.76	118.35	121.85	167.52	104.33
2nd quarter	111.99	113.53	121.31	137.51	108.68	115.05	117.42	120.93	162.38	104.60
3rd quarter	111.92	113.48	119.22	134.24	108.58	113.37	115.31	118.33	152.79	104.84
4th quarter	112.29	113.66	120.13	134.17	109.37	114.51	116.59	119.71	158.97	105.38
2013										
1st quarter	112.61	113.84	119.14	135.66	110.00	114.81	116.87	120.60	161.46	105.75
2nd quarter	111.79	112.56	117.12	132.65	110.15	113.59	115.39	117.72	155.26	105.74
3rd quarter	111.97	112.59	115.36	134.29	110.65	113.07	114.69	115.54	153.86	106.04
4th quarter	111.89	112.11	116.21	133.86	111.45	113.07	114.42	116.51	152.58	107.26
2014										
1st quarter	112.72	113.00	116.02	138.13	112.14	114.85	116.46	116.67	163.47	107.82
2nd quarter	112.69	112.63	115.68	133.74	112.85	113.95	115.32	116.59	156.09	108.04
3rd quarter	112.41	111.92	115.63	132.29	113.49	113.21	114.38	118.25	150.04	108.24
4th quarter	110.39	109.11	113.56	122.22	113.18	110.96	111.75	116.46	135.29	107.74
2015										
1st quarter	107.65	105.51	111.30	108.18	112.28	106.65	106.76	112.63	109.16	106.62
2nd quarter	107.38	104.96	109.81	109.73	112.59	105.19	104.97	108.19	102.62	106.68
3rd quarter	106.25	103.32	107.10	104.19	112.53	103.87	103.50	104.32	97.22	106.04
4th quarter	104.65	101.20	104.84	96.77	112.06	101.74	101.01	101.52	85.12	105.54
2016										
1st quarter	103.27	98.52	102.89	87.11	113.43	100.39	99.37	99.20	77.23	105.54
2nd quarter	104.23	99.80	103.80	91.86	113.73	100.69	99.68	101.01	79.53	105.81
3rd quarter	104.81	100.40	104.42	94.84	114.28	101.44	100.63	103.31	83.84	105.63
4th quarter	105.52	100.88	105.48	98.69	115.48	101.84	101.09	103.61	87.11	105.76

[1] Exports and imports of certain goods, primarily military equipment purchased and sold by the federal government, are included in services. Beginning with 1986, repairs and alterations of equipment are reclassified from goods to services.

Table 7-4. Exports and Imports of Selected NIPA Types of Product

(Billions of dollars, quarterly data are at seasonally adjusted annual rates.)   NIPA Table 4.2.5

Year and quarter	Exports							Imports							
	Goods					Services		Goods						Services	
	Foods, feeds, and beverages	Industrial supplies and materials	Capital goods, except auto-motive	Auto-motive vehicles, engines, and parts	Consumer goods, except food and auto-motive	Travel	Other business services	Foods, feeds, and beverages	Industrial supplies and materials, except petroleum and products	Petroleum and products	Capital goods, except auto-motive	Auto-motive vehicles, engines, and parts	Consumer goods, except food and auto-motive	Travel	Other business services
1970	5.9	13.8	14.7	3.9	2.8	2.3	1.0	6.1	15.2	2.9	4.0	5.7	7.4	4.0	0.6
1971	6.1	12.6	15.4	4.7	2.9	2.5	1.3	6.4	17.2	3.7	4.3	7.6	8.4	4.4	0.7
1972	7.5	13.9	16.9	5.5	3.6	2.8	1.5	7.3	20.6	4.7	5.9	9.0	11.1	5.0	0.8
1973	15.2	19.7	22.0	7.0	4.8	3.4	1.7	9.1	27.6	8.4	8.3	10.7	12.9	5.5	0.9
1974	18.6	29.9	30.9	8.8	6.4	4.0	3.0	10.6	53.6	26.6	9.8	12.4	14.4	6.0	1.9
1975	19.2	29.3	36.6	10.8	6.6	4.7	3.7	9.6	50.6	27.0	10.2	12.1	13.2	6.4	2.3
1976	19.8	31.6	39.1	12.2	8.0	5.7	4.5	11.5	63.1	34.6	12.3	16.8	17.2	6.9	3.0
1977	19.7	33.2	39.8	13.5	8.9	6.2	4.9	14.0	78.4	45.0	14.0	19.4	21.8	7.5	3.2
1978	25.7	38.4	47.5	15.2	11.4	7.2	6.2	15.8	81.9	42.6	19.3	25.0	29.4	8.5	3.9
1979	30.5	53.3	60.2	17.9	14.0	8.4	7.3	18.0	105.4	60.4	24.6	26.6	31.3	9.4	4.6
1980	36.3	68.0	76.3	17.4	17.8	10.6	8.6	18.6	126.9	79.5	31.6	28.3	34.3	10.4	5.1
1981	38.8	65.7	84.2	19.7	17.7	15.6	10.5	18.6	130.4	78.4	37.1	31.0	38.4	11.8	6.0
1982	32.2	61.8	76.5	17.2	16.1	15.5	13.8	17.5	107.3	62.0	38.4	34.3	39.7	12.8	7.0
1983	32.1	57.1	71.7	18.5	14.9	14.5	14.1	18.8	106.2	55.1	43.7	43.0	47.3	13.6	6.8
1984	32.2	61.9	77.0	22.4	15.1	21.3	14.5	21.9	120.7	58.1	60.4	56.5	61.1	23.4	7.7
1985	24.6	59.4	79.3	24.9	14.6	22.4	14.8	21.8	110.6	51.4	61.3	64.9	66.3	25.1	8.8
1986	23.5	59.0	82.8	25.1	16.7	25.5	23.3	24.4	96.7	34.3	72.0	78.1	79.4	26.5	13.3
1987	25.2	67.4	92.7	27.6	20.3	29.0	24.2	24.8	109.0	42.9	85.1	85.2	88.8	29.9	16.7
1988	33.8	84.2	119.1	33.4	27.0	35.2	25.7	24.9	116.3	39.6	102.2	87.9	96.4	32.8	17.8
1989	36.3	95.4	136.9	35.1	35.9	43.0	30.3	24.9	129.7	50.9	112.3	87.4	103.6	34.2	19.2
1990	35.1	101.9	153.0	36.2	43.5	50.9	32.7	26.4	140.5	62.3	116.4	88.2	105.0	38.2	22.4
1991	35.7	106.2	166.6	39.9	46.6	56.7	39.9	26.2	127.4	51.7	121.1	85.5	107.7	36.2	25.9
1992	40.3	105.2	176.4	46.9	51.2	64.0	41.1	27.6	134.0	51.6	134.8	91.5	122.4	39.6	24.3
1993	40.5	102.9	182.7	51.6	54.5	67.9	43.5	27.9	140.2	51.5	153.2	102.1	133.7	41.9	26.6
1994	42.4	115.4	205.7	57.5	59.7	69.4	49.9	31.0	156.2	51.3	185.0	118.1	145.9	45.1	30.3
1995	50.8	141.0	234.4	61.4	64.2	74.9	53.6	33.2	175.6	56.0	222.1	123.7	159.7	46.4	33.7
1996	56.0	141.3	254.0	64.4	69.3	81.8	61.3	35.7	197.3	72.7	228.4	128.7	172.5	49.7	38.1
1997	52.0	153.0	295.8	73.4	77.0	86.2	71.2	39.7	206.5	71.8	253.6	139.4	195.2	53.8	41.4
1998	46.8	143.3	299.8	72.5	79.4	85.1	78.1	41.3	193.1	50.9	269.8	148.6	218.5	58.5	45.6
1999	46.0	145.7	311.2	75.3	80.9	92.3	79.6	44.1	221.9	72.1	296.1	178.2	243.7	59.6	56.2
2000	47.9	171.1	357.0	80.4	89.3	100.2	83.1	46.5	301.3	126.1	347.7	195.0	284.6	65.8	61.6
2001	49.4	159.5	321.7	75.4	88.3	86.7	87.9	47.2	276.8	109.4	299.2	188.7	287.1	60.7	66.9
2002	49.6	157.3	290.4	78.9	84.3	81.9	95.1	50.3	270.7	109.3	284.9	202.8	311.3	59.9	74.1
2003	55.0	173.3	293.7	80.6	89.9	80.3	102.1	56.5	317.8	140.4	297.6	209.2	338.4	61.9	79.6
2004	56.6	206.3	327.5	89.2	103.2	92.4	118.4	63.0	418.1	189.9	346.1	227.3	378.1	74.0	89.9
2005	59.0	236.8	358.4	98.4	115.2	101.5	128.5	69.1	531.1	263.2	382.8	238.7	412.7	80.0	95.8
2006	66.0	279.1	404.0	107.3	129.0	105.1	150.8	76.1	610.2	316.7	422.6	256.0	447.6	84.2	126.6
2007	84.3	316.3	433.0	121.3	145.9	119.0	183.9	83.0	644.6	346.7	449.1	258.5	479.8	89.2	149.3
2008	108.3	386.9	457.7	121.5	161.2	133.8	202.3	90.4	794.9	476.1	458.7	233.2	485.7	92.5	174.0
2009	93.9	293.5	391.5	81.7	149.3	119.9	210.9	82.9	464.4	267.7	374.1	159.2	429.9	81.4	178.5
2010	107.7	388.6	447.8	112.0	164.9	137.0	226.7	92.5	603.1	353.6	450.4	225.6	485.1	86.6	183.6
2011	126.2	485.3	494.2	133.0	174.7	150.9	249.4	108.3	754.9	462.1	513.4	255.2	515.9	89.7	197.3
2012	133.0	483.2	527.5	146.2	181.0	161.6	263.6	111.1	723.2	434.3	551.8	298.5	518.8	100.3	200.2
2013	136.2	492.4	534.8	152.7	188.1	177.5	286.3	116.0	679.0	387.8	559.0	309.6	532.9	98.1	208.1
2014	143.7	500.7	551.8	159.8	198.4	191.9	309.0	126.8	669.9	353.6	598.8	329.5	558.7	105.7	214.7
2015	127.7	417.4	539.8	151.9	197.4	205.4	314.5	128.8	487.7	197.2	606.8	350.0	596.6	114.7	218.5
2016	130.6	386.8	519.8	150.3	193.4	205.9	318.8	131.0	436.8	159.6	593.9	351.1	585.4	123.6	218.3
2011															
1st quarter	127.6	461.4	473.3	127.7	169.3	144.7	241.4	103.0	723.6	441.7	492.3	251.8	510.0	85.2	186.2
2nd quarter	127.6	489.8	493.5	128.9	175.4	153.6	248.7	108.8	778.1	480.8	508.1	232.5	519.4	91.1	200.0
3rd quarter	125.9	495.8	499.7	136.6	176.1	152.4	255.9	108.1	761.7	459.8	520.8	262.6	515.6	90.4	204.3
4th quarter	123.9	494.0	510.3	139.0	178.1	152.7	251.6	113.2	756.1	466.2	532.5	274.1	518.5	92.1	198.8
2012															
1st quarter	117.9	488.2	526.5	147.8	177.5	155.9	259.4	112.2	754.1	466.6	552.8	296.4	513.4	99.1	198.0
2nd quarter	132.4	490.8	525.0	148.1	180.8	161.6	262.1	109.9	734.5	446.6	556.9	296.9	517.9	100.0	200.1
3rd quarter	150.9	475.3	531.1	144.2	182.1	164.4	261.3	110.4	699.1	407.9	550.0	300.0	521.4	100.8	200.5
4th quarter	130.9	478.6	527.2	144.5	183.5	164.6	271.5	112.0	704.9	416.2	547.4	300.7	522.6	101.6	202.2
2013															
1st quarter	136.0	482.7	526.3	151.1	182.6	174.0	280.0	115.1	699.0	404.1	553.4	296.4	529.6	97.7	203.8
2nd quarter	125.7	478.6	539.1	154.3	193.4	175.4	283.1	116.5	677.1	384.6	551.3	308.0	533.6	96.5	207.4
3rd quarter	134.1	493.0	534.5	151.8	187.0	177.9	287.4	115.3	676.6	389.2	561.5	315.6	530.7	97.9	210.0
4th quarter	148.9	515.4	539.2	153.4	189.4	182.6	295.0	117.2	663.6	373.1	569.7	318.3	537.6	100.4	211.3
2014															
1st quarter	150.2	498.4	542.5	153.6	194.0	187.0	302.6	120.8	707.9	399.5	577.2	314.4	547.3	102.0	212.9
2nd quarter	148.0	510.8	550.1	160.3	199.8	190.6	312.7	129.1	683.8	366.5	596.3	332.6	562.1	106.8	214.6
3rd quarter	134.9	513.2	556.2	165.1	199.4	193.8	307.0	128.3	658.6	341.2	607.8	334.9	551.5	106.3	212.7
4th quarter	141.7	480.2	558.2	160.2	200.4	196.4	313.9	129.1	629.1	307.3	613.8	336.2	573.9	107.6	218.6
2015															
1st quarter	133.5	431.4	546.4	150.6	202.4	199.5	321.7	129.2	537.1	228.8	615.4	337.5	593.9	110.7	216.0
2nd quarter	132.6	442.0	545.6	152.0	194.9	207.7	313.1	130.9	502.5	208.5	611.2	353.1	597.3	114.9	217.9
3rd quarter	125.2	414.0	535.9	154.5	196.0	207.3	308.6	128.7	480.1	193.9	601.6	355.9	600.3	115.4	221.2
4th quarter	119.5	382.4	531.2	150.6	196.3	207.2	314.7	126.3	431.1	157.8	598.9	353.7	594.7	117.9	219.0
2016															
1st quarter	116.0	366.0	519.6	150.4	193.5	205.6	311.3	130.3	406.6	141.9	583.4	352.6	589.6	120.6	217.9
2nd quarter	123.1	385.8	519.4	151.3	189.9	204.5	315.0	129.2	424.0	152.8	595.0	345.8	580.4	122.1	216.6
3rd quarter	153.2	392.9	516.2	151.8	195.6	206.1	323.9	130.5	449.3	166.9	594.7	350.1	578.1	124.9	217.8
4th quarter	130.0	402.4	524.2	147.7	194.7	207.7	325.2	134.1	467.4	176.8	602.6	355.7	593.4	126.9	220.9

Table 7-5. Chain-Type Quantity Indexes for Exports and Imports of Selected NIPA Types of Product

(Index numbers, 2009 = 100; quarterly indexes are seasonally adjusted.)   NIPA Table 4.2.3

Year and quarter	Exports							Imports							
	Goods					Services		Goods						Services	
	Foods, feeds, and beverages	Industrial supplies and materials	Capital goods, except automotive	Automotive vehicles, engines, and parts	Consumer goods, except food and automotive	Travel	Other business services	Foods, feeds, and beverages	Industrial supplies and materials, except petroleum and products	Petroleum and products	Capital goods, except automotive	Automotive vehicles, engines, and parts	Consumer goods, except food and automotive	Travel	Other business services
1970	25.60	24.03	4.38	23.93	6.21	12.22	1.67	30.90	33.25	25.80	0.88	21.91	6.43	22.46	1.05
1971	24.92	21.72	4.58	27.13	6.23	12.76	1.93	31.90	36.59	29.51	0.87	26.72	6.76	22.43	1.16
1972	29.42	23.14	5.01	30.44	7.28	13.70	2.16	33.96	41.10	36.04	1.12	28.95	8.24	24.26	1.19
1973	38.08	28.47	6.36	35.75	8.88	15.74	2.35	34.83	45.30	51.20	1.38	29.88	8.46	22.89	1.34
1974	34.13	29.29	7.95	39.87	11.05	17.13	3.84	32.22	43.93	49.29	1.47	31.73	7.61	20.55	2.69
1975	36.10	25.63	8.07	41.98	10.18	18.52	4.45	28.50	40.08	48.47	1.40	25.18	5.90	19.82	3.04
1976	40.97	27.68	7.96	43.89	11.48	21.10	5.15	32.44	48.54	58.45	1.69	33.37	7.62	21.08	3.65
1977	40.93	27.91	7.83	44.21	12.42	21.14	5.31	32.11	55.61	70.32	1.81	35.35	9.20	21.72	3.82
1978	50.57	30.84	8.94	45.39	14.34	22.71	6.29	36.05	56.19	66.48	2.33	38.25	11.30	22.44	4.47
1979	53.65	35.32	10.73	45.68	15.08	24.35	7.01	37.01	55.53	67.25	2.85	36.99	11.39	21.89	5.06
1980	60.48	40.09	12.53	38.47	18.27	27.20	7.49	32.21	46.26	54.31	3.36	36.64	11.47	21.86	5.17
1981	61.74	37.39	12.58	38.03	17.52	36.19	8.60	33.51	44.03	47.59	3.96	35.46	12.56	23.83	5.79
1982	58.01	36.26	11.12	31.16	15.77	33.40	10.65	34.16	38.70	40.93	4.31	37.96	13.13	28.27	6.53
1983	55.45	34.50	10.72	32.24	14.42	29.67	10.35	37.08	41.59	40.50	5.21	46.46	15.80	32.02	6.06
1984	53.96	36.26	11.88	38.04	14.35	41.21	10.32	42.00	47.60	42.78	7.79	59.69	19.95	57.88	6.77
1985	46.69	36.47	13.05	41.40	13.92	41.25	10.16	43.82	46.34	40.17	8.78	66.89	21.77	63.86	7.56
1986	48.17	38.10	14.24	40.71	15.40	45.51	15.53	44.85	52.14	49.67	9.96	72.41	24.12	59.42	11.01
1987	51.56	39.05	16.44	43.89	18.12	49.37	15.54	45.97	52.67	51.88	11.38	74.30	24.90	70.34	12.62
1988	56.66	44.02	20.91	52.09	23.14	57.58	16.46	44.15	55.02	57.38	13.11	72.43	25.27	72.36	13.46
1989	58.94	48.95	24.25	53.55	29.67	68.03	19.20	45.14	55.81	62.05	14.83	70.59	26.45	74.63	15.75
1990	60.80	51.84	28.05	53.62	34.81	76.37	19.99	46.87	56.57	62.71	16.02	70.69	25.98	79.73	17.09
1991	61.96	55.36	30.70	57.51	36.07	79.96	23.50	44.75	55.87	62.48	17.23	65.91	26.43	72.41	19.07
1992	70.23	56.40	33.63	66.29	38.85	88.02	23.75	47.24	60.20	65.31	19.96	69.30	29.18	74.68	17.76
1993	69.88	54.90	35.83	72.27	40.82	92.10	24.84	47.80	65.56	71.54	23.28	76.15	31.60	78.39	18.82
1994	70.61	57.75	41.35	79.89	44.60	93.22	28.29	48.89	73.42	76.38	28.55	85.39	34.24	81.25	21.26
1995	78.00	62.30	49.27	84.20	47.27	99.07	29.86	50.12	75.29	75.00	35.15	86.87	36.93	82.13	23.40
1996	76.75	65.46	57.10	87.31	50.42	105.49	33.64	55.13	80.28	81.32	41.30	89.81	39.76	85.40	25.66
1997	77.23	71.17	69.99	98.83	55.61	108.51	38.70	60.71	85.71	84.69	51.83	97.07	45.55	92.82	27.50
1998	76.45	70.38	72.97	97.49	57.30	105.55	42.72	65.16	94.08	90.53	59.61	103.35	51.69	105.02	30.67
1999	78.68	72.60	77.01	100.56	58.58	111.46	35.12	71.99	100.06	97.29	68.42	123.08	58.05	105.16	29.27
2000	82.62	79.02	88.59	106.20	64.43	115.58	37.89	76.69	105.52	100.84	82.20	133.14	68.35	118.66	33.82
2001	84.84	75.82	79.80	99.25	63.92	98.98	41.80	80.13	104.48	103.81	72.86	128.78	69.46	110.29	38.06
2002	83.09	76.19	72.87	103.34	61.37	93.27	46.55	84.40	105.38	101.39	71.74	137.92	76.14	104.97	41.61
2003	84.53	78.33	74.59	104.81	65.04	89.00	50.88	90.90	109.21	108.16	75.94	141.51	82.95	99.92	45.37
2004	79.37	83.58	83.51	115.18	73.98	98.26	59.18	96.41	121.65	115.31	89.47	151.45	92.22	112.87	52.69
2005	83.67	85.65	91.13	125.49	81.69	93.93	63.45	99.77	126.93	117.63	99.63	157.13	99.74	115.17	57.56
2006	90.30	91.99	102.00	135.12	90.33	92.96	72.91	105.93	128.37	115.42	110.93	167.81	107.76	115.34	73.69
2007	98.17	96.91	110.29	151.02	100.00	101.36	88.16	107.24	124.40	112.68	118.39	167.81	113.97	112.91	87.56
2008	104.78	107.53	116.90	149.67	108.19	108.70	94.61	106.02	117.98	108.81	120.33	147.91	112.59	109.91	99.12
2009	100.00	100.00	100.00	100.00	100.00	100.00	100.00	100.00	100.00	100.00	100.00	100.00	100.00	100.00	100.00
2010	110.34	115.61	113.70	136.42	109.28	110.82	106.38	102.28	106.16	100.49	121.33	140.87	112.92	104.14	103.22
2011	109.98	123.16	124.45	159.27	114.24	116.11	114.39	104.21	107.59	98.59	138.00	154.42	118.04	104.96	110.88
2012	108.86	125.46	131.83	171.90	116.61	121.11	119.32	108.22	102.97	90.46	147.88	177.28	117.00	116.28	112.03
2013	111.16	130.52	133.43	178.57	122.52	131.52	126.10	112.46	99.41	84.17	152.61	184.59	120.40	112.50	114.90
2014	120.00	135.10	138.10	185.87	130.93	139.25	132.86	118.29	100.43	80.90	165.50	197.64	125.79	119.85	117.28
2015	122.35	134.86	136.19	176.88	133.08	150.31	134.13	123.01	101.86	81.89	172.31	214.25	135.49	135.26	119.25
2016	129.17	137.17	132.70	176.39	133.37	149.45	131.90	124.83	104.74	86.28	173.34	216.50	133.48	148.44	117.24
2011															
1st quarter	113.05	121.43	119.74	154.54	111.25	113.40	111.43	101.73	108.70	101.37	132.24	155.32	118.30	100.22	104.37
2nd quarter	110.50	121.84	124.31	155.03	114.79	118.29	113.52	102.65	108.29	99.19	136.34	140.19	119.37	105.70	112.07
3rd quarter	107.50	122.78	125.54	162.92	114.63	116.32	116.75	103.15	106.78	96.83	139.92	157.66	117.41	105.32	114.95
4th quarter	108.88	126.58	128.22	164.58	116.30	116.45	115.87	109.33	106.56	96.97	143.50	164.49	117.08	108.60	112.12
2012															
1st quarter	102.87	124.31	131.80	174.45	114.95	117.56	118.39	107.95	103.43	91.32	147.84	177.42	115.73	114.72	111.26
2nd quarter	111.86	124.67	131.11	173.86	116.50	121.26	118.68	106.00	103.45	91.57	149.19	176.24	116.69	116.39	112.07
3rd quarter	118.26	125.21	132.83	169.32	117.17	123.14	118.37	108.22	103.81	90.73	147.47	177.84	117.84	117.20	112.29
4th quarter	102.44	125.85	131.58	169.97	117.81	122.46	121.84	110.71	101.19	88.21	147.00	177.62	117.75	116.80	112.50
2013															
1st quarter	107.57	126.24	130.79	176.84	118.15	129.11	124.77	113.12	98.96	84.25	149.99	175.11	119.36	112.32	112.96
2nd quarter	101.54	127.82	134.57	180.61	126.00	130.68	125.18	113.07	99.35	84.93	150.35	183.15	120.34	110.92	115.03
3rd quarter	109.93	131.03	133.25	177.65	122.18	131.49	126.25	111.16	100.39	84.91	153.58	189.24	120.14	112.50	115.83
4th quarter	125.61	137.01	135.09	179.19	123.76	134.82	128.19	112.49	98.92	82.58	156.55	190.86	121.75	114.26	115.76
2014															
1st quarter	125.00	129.52	135.91	179.15	127.77	136.81	130.62	113.78	100.04	83.43	159.06	188.03	123.32	115.68	116.34
2nd quarter	118.40	135.98	137.47	186.51	131.89	137.91	135.12	120.96	100.15	80.20	164.58	198.61	126.39	120.40	117.66
3rd quarter	112.47	137.76	139.21	191.78	131.20	139.91	131.44	119.52	99.04	78.31	167.96	201.35	123.97	120.27	115.98
4th quarter	124.14	137.15	139.81	186.03	132.87	142.38	134.24	118.92	102.50	81.64	170.40	202.59	129.48	123.04	119.15
2015															
1st quarter	121.78	135.09	136.96	175.15	135.81	146.56	137.77	120.94	102.79	82.11	172.47	205.55	134.58	129.57	118.00
2nd quarter	127.11	137.68	137.50	176.84	131.27	152.02	132.85	124.47	101.66	81.65	172.73	216.09	135.58	135.12	118.45
3rd quarter	121.72	138.74	138.50	179.88	132.19	151.35	131.10	123.28	102.00	82.22	171.66	218.01	136.50	136.35	120.84
4th quarter	118.80	131.91	134.80	175.66	133.05	151.32	134.83	123.37	100.98	81.60	172.39	217.33	135.29	140.01	119.69
2016															
1st quarter	116.75	136.47	132.33	176.01	133.33	150.23	130.11	127.61	102.28	84.61	169.08	217.80	133.89	144.43	117.48
2nd quarter	120.64	138.26	132.30	177.48	130.91	148.98	130.76	126.57	103.98	85.68	173.27	212.98	132.24	145.55	116.37
3rd quarter	149.76	137.45	131.93	178.44	134.35	149.79	133.29	121.28	105.63	87.83	173.90	216.12	132.09	149.89	116.71
4th quarter	129.54	136.50	134.23	173.64	134.90	148.81	133.46	123.85	107.05	87.00	177.12	219.10	135.68	153.89	118.41

SECTION 7B: U.S. INTERNATIONAL TRANSACTIONS ACCOUNTS

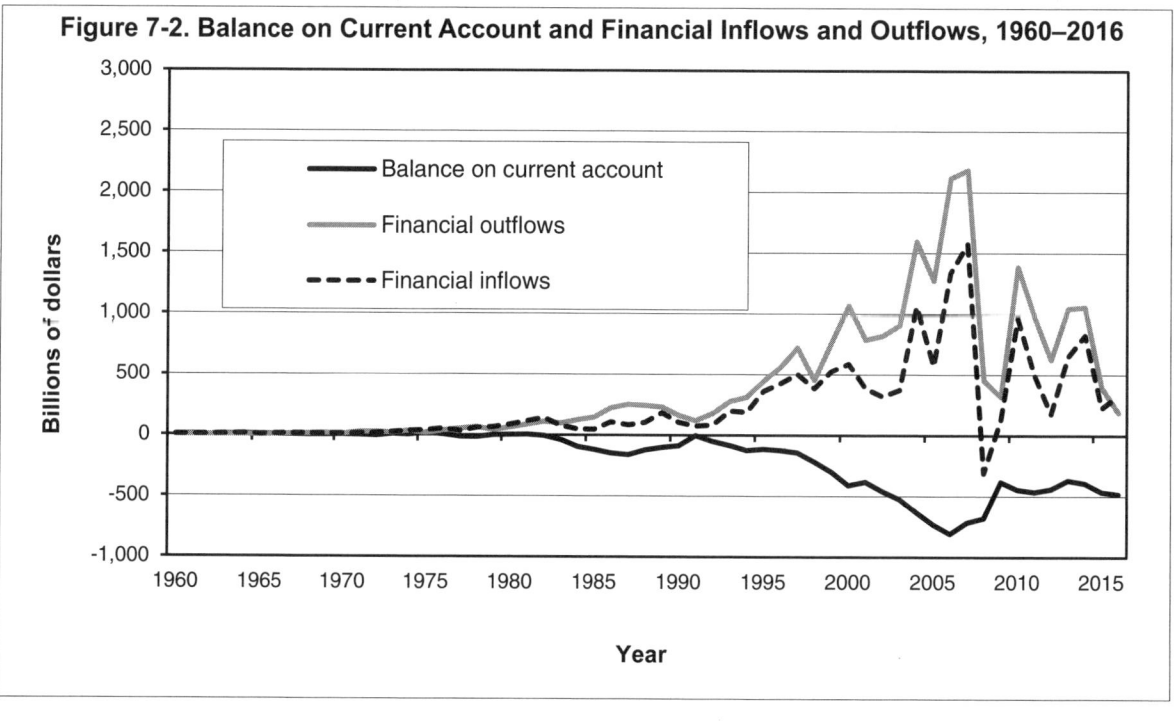

Figure 7-2. Balance on Current Account and Financial Inflows and Outflows, 1960–2016

- The U.S. current-account international balance is also recorded in the International Transactions Accounts (ITAs). The definitional differences between this balance and the balance in the NIPAs are minor, and the trends in the two measures are similar. The ITAs measure the current account surplus or deficit (commonly known as the "balance of payments") and directly measure the financial flows required to finance it. (Table 7-6A and B)

- Figure 7-2 above shows the current-account balance since 1960, culminating in a $481 billion deficit in 2016, and the corresponding estimated financial flows. U.S. acquisition of financial assets abroad contributed a further outflow, amounting to $331 billion, in 2016. Financing the sum of these was borrowing ("incurrence of liabilities") estimated at $759 billion. The net of the estimated financial flows does not exactly equal the current-account balance because of capital transactions, derivatives, and the ITA statistical discrepancy. (Table 7-6A)

- Large quarterly and annual variations in 2008 and subsequent years in many types of financial flows, including those involving official assets, are evidence of an extreme amount of international financial turbulence and official intervention. (Table 7-6A and B)

- Through the early 1980s, the United States was still a net creditor with respect to the rest of the world, meaning that the value of the stock of U.S.-owned assets abroad exceeded the value of U.S. liabilities to the rest of the world. Since then, persistent borrowing to finance current-account deficits has cumulated, resulting in a growing net debtor status, with the value of U.S. liabilities exceeding the value of its assets by $8.1 trillion as of the end of 2016. (Table 7-8)

Table 7-6A. U.S. International Transactions: Recent Data

(Millions of dollars, seasonally adjusted.)

	Current account — Exports of goods and services and income receipts (credits)											Secondary income (current transfer) receipts
	Exports of goods and services				Primary income receipts							
Year and quarter	Total goods and services and income receipts	Total goods and services exports	Goods exports	Services exports	Total primary income receipts	Investment income receipts					Compensation of employees receipts	
						Total investment income receipts	Direct investment income receipts	Portfolio investment income receipts	Other investment income receipts	Reserve asset income receipts		
1960	30 555	25 939	19 650	6 289	4 616	4 616	...	...	...	...	...	...
1961	31 403	26 403	20 108	6 295	5 000	5 000	...	...	...	...	...	...
1962	33 340	27 722	20 781	6 941	5 618	5 618	...	...	...	...	...	...
1963	35 776	29 620	22 272	7 348	6 156	6 156	...	...	...	...	...	...
1964	40 164	33 340	25 501	7 839	6 824	6 824	...	...	...	...	...	...
1965	42 722	35 285	26 461	8 824	7 437	7 437	...	...	...	...	...	...
1966	46 454	38 926	29 310	9 616	7 528	7 528	...	...	...	...	...	...
1967	49 354	41 333	30 666	10 667	8 021	8 021	...	...	...	...	...	...
1968	54 912	45 544	33 626	11 918	9 368	9 368	...	...	...	...	...	...
1969	60 133	49 220	36 414	12 806	10 913	10 913	...	...	...	...	...	...
1970	68 388	56 640	42 469	14 171	11 748	11 748	...	...	...	...	...	...
1971	72 383	59 677	43 319	16 358	12 706	12 706	...	...	...	...	...	...
1972	81 987	67 223	49 381	17 842	14 764	14 764	...	...	...	...	...	...
1973	113 051	91 242	71 410	19 832	21 809	21 809	...	...	...	...	...	...
1974	148 484	120 897	98 306	22 591	27 587	27 587	...	...	...	...	...	...
1975	157 936	132 585	107 088	25 497	25 351	25 351	...	...	...	...	...	...
1976	172 090	142 716	114 745	27 971	29 374	29 374	...	...	...	...	...	...
1977	184 657	152 302	120 816	31 486	32 355	32 355	...	...	...	...	...	...
1978	220 515	178 428	142 075	36 353	42 087	42 087	...	...	...	...	...	...
1979	287 967	224 132	184 439	39 693	63 835	63 835	...	...	...	...	...	...
1980	344 440	271 835	224 250	47 585	72 605	72 605	...	...	...	...	...	...
1981	380 928	294 399	237 044	57 355	86 529	86 529	...	...	...	...	...	...
1982	371 757	275 235	211 157	64 078	96 522	96 522	...	...	...	...	...	...
1983	362 137	266 106	201 799	64 307	96 031	96 031	...	...	...	...	...	...
1984	406 733	291 094	219 926	71 168	115 639	115 639	...	...	...	...	...	...
1985	394 117	289 071	215 915	73 156	105 046	105 046	...	...	...	...	...	...
1986	412 832	310 034	223 344	86 690	102 798	101 890	...	...	...	...	908	...
1987	462 472	348 869	250 208	98 661	113 603	112 609	...	...	...	...	994	...
1988	572 816	431 150	320 230	110 920	141 666	140 671	...	...	...	...	995	...
1989	653 387	487 003	359 916	127 087	166 384	165 367	...	...	...	...	1 017	...
1990	712 128	535 234	387 401	147 833	176 894	175 722	...	...	...	...	1 172	...
1991	733 670	578 343	414 083	164 260	155 327	154 037	...	...	...	...	1 290	...
1992	755 964	616 882	439 631	177 251	139 082	137 286	...	...	...	...	1 796	...
1993	784 469	642 863	456 943	185 920	141 606	139 786	...	...	...	...	1 820	...
1994	872 701	703 254	502 859	200 395	169 447	167 504	...	...	...	...	1 943	...
1995	1 008 048	794 387	575 204	219 183	213 661	211 482	...	...	...	...	2 179	...
1996	1 081 132	851 602	612 113	239 489	229 530	227 349	...	...	...	...	2 181	...
1997	1 195 810	934 453	678 366	256 087	261 357	259 087	...	...	...	...	2 270	...
1998	1 199 418	933 174	670 416	262 758	266 244	263 807	...	...	...	...	2 437	...
1999	1 304 557	969 867	698 524	271 343	300 300	296 054	136 502	72 171	86 145	1 236	4 246	34 390
2000	1 471 532	1 075 321	784 940	290 381	358 822	354 427	158 182	78 401	116 573	1 270	4 395	37 390
2001	1 345 165	1 005 654	731 331	274 323	298 203	293 691	134 437	73 914	84 029	1 311	4 512	41 308
2002	1 318 790	978 706	698 036	280 670	287 505	282 936	150 395	81 923	49 568	1 050	4 570	52 580
2003	1 409 053	1 020 418	730 446	289 972	326 698	322 026	190 704	90 652	39 587	1 083	4 671	61 938
2004	1 642 291	1 161 549	823 584	337 966	420 590	415 856	255 405	108 647	50 637	1 165	4 734	60 152
2005	1 895 983	1 286 022	913 016	373 006	543 982	539 186	301 184	129 691	107 126	1 185	4 796	65 980
2006	2 222 124	1 457 642	1 040 905	416 738	693 089	688 020	333 235	166 146	187 414	1 226	5 069	71 393
2007	2 569 492	1 653 548	1 165 151	488 396	844 033	838 814	380 844	221 610	234 910	1 449	5 219	71 912
2008	2 751 949	1 841 612	1 308 795	532 817	823 707	818 342	423 365	241 329	152 076	1 572	5 364	86 630
2009	2 285 922	1 583 053	1 070 331	512 722	614 379	608 639	370 301	184 417	53 140	781	5 740	88 491
2010	2 630 799	1 853 606	1 290 273	563 333	684 915	678 984	447 773	194 852	35 660	699	5 931	92 278
2011	2 987 571	2 127 021	1 499 240	627 781	759 727	753 622	477 415	237 343	38 018	846	6 105	100 822
2012	3 097 063	2 218 989	1 562 578	656 411	768 956	762 653	465 796	260 429	35 954	474	6 302	109 119
2013	3 214 804	2 293 457	1 592 002	701 455	794 658	788 045	478 051	278 441	31 179	374	6 613	126 688
2014	3 338 757	2 376 577	1 633 320	743 257	821 807	815 123	478 381	304 984	31 457	302	6 684	140 373
2015	3 172 693	2 261 163	1 510 303	750 860	782 915	775 846	432 498	311 619	31 515	214	7 069	128 614
2016	3 142 175	2 212 079	1 459 667	752 412	801 923	794 723	428 434	326 342	39 842	105	7 200	128 172
2013												
1st quarter	793 621	567 448	394 717	172 731	195 307	193 679	118 172	67 288	8 090	129	1 627	30 867
2nd quarter	798 065	569 122	395 114	174 008	198 969	197 313	119 921	69 391	7 898	103	1 656	29 975
3rd quarter	802 689	572 124	396 192	175 933	198 893	197 223	119 417	70 084	7 645	78	1 670	31 671
4th quarter	820 428	584 763	405 980	178 784	201 490	199 829	120 541	71 678	7 547	64	1 660	34 176
2014												
1st quarter	822 994	586 586	403 365	183 220	202 351	200 687	118 723	74 085	7 783	96	1 664	34 058
2nd quarter	843 566	595 912	409 701	186 211	204 485	202 825	118 262	76 462	8 027	74	1 660	43 169
3rd quarter	838 941	597 822	412 087	185 735	209 622	207 950	121 900	78 174	7 805	70	1 672	31 497
4th quarter	833 257	596 258	408 167	188 091	205 349	203 661	119 496	76 263	7 841	61	1 688	31 650
2015												
1st quarter	799 184	572 268	383 936	188 332	194 716	192 977	109 908	75 721	7 308	40	1 738	32 200
2nd quarter	805 411	572 383	383 935	188 448	199 359	197 596	111 269	78 387	7 880	59	1 764	33 669
3rd quarter	791 880	564 276	377 157	187 118	196 752	194 969	106 676	80 014	8 227	53	1 782	30 852
4th quarter	776 218	552 236	365 275	186 962	192 089	190 304	104 645	77 497	8 101	61	1 785	31 893
2016												
1st quarter	757 974	538 104	353 355	184 748	188 282	186 485	95 756	81 617	9 083	28	1 797	31 588
2nd quarter	780 154	545 590	359 440	186 149	202 250	200 451	109 282	81 031	10 117	21	1 799	32 315
3rd quarter	800 035	564 980	375 146	189 834	203 478	201 673	110 509	80 967	10 204	-6	1 805	31 577
4th quarter	804 012	563 406	371 725	191 680	207 914	206 114	112 887	82 728	10 438	62	1 800	32 692

. . . = Not available.

Table 7-6A. U.S. International Transactions: Recent Data—*Continued*

(Millions of dollars, seasonally adjusted.)

Year and quarter	Total goods and services and income receipts	Imports of goods and services and income payments (debits)									
		Imports of goods and services			Primary income payments						Secondary income (current transfer) payments
		Total goods and services imports	Goods	Services	Total primary income payments	Investment income payments				Compensation of employees payments	
						Total investment income payments	Direct investment income payments	Portfolio investment income payments	Other investment income payments		
1960	27 732	22 433	14 758	7 675	1 238	1 238	. . .	. . .	. . .	. . .	4 061
1961	27 581	22 208	14 537	7 671	1 245	1 245	. . .	. . .	. . .	. . .	4 128
1962	29 953	24 352	16 260	8 092	1 324	1 324	. . .	. . .	. . .	. . .	4 277
1963	31 365	25 411	17 048	8 363	1 561	1 561	. . .	. . .	. . .	. . .	4 393
1964	33 342	27 319	18 700	8 619	1 783	1 783	. . .	. . .	. . .	. . .	4 240
1965	37 293	30 621	21 510	9 111	2 088	2 088	. . .	. . .	. . .	. . .	4 584
1966	43 425	35 987	25 493	10 494	2 482	2 482	. . .	. . .	. . .	. . .	4 956
1967	40 770	38 720	26 866	11 863	2 747	2 747	. . .	. . .	. . .	. . .	5 294
1968	54 299	45 292	32 991	12 301	3 378	3 378	. . .	. . .	. . .	. . .	5 629
1969	59 734	49 130	35 807	13 323	4 869	4 869	. . .	. . .	. . .	. . .	5 735
1970	66 055	54 385	39 866	14 519	5 514	5 514	. . .	. . .	. . .	. . .	6 156
1971	73 818	60 980	45 579	15 401	5 436	5 436	. . .	. . .	. . .	. . .	7 402
1972	87 780	72 664	55 797	16 867	6 572	6 572	. . .	. . .	. . .	. . .	8 544
1973	105 912	89 342	70 499	18 843	9 656	9 656	. . .	. . .	. . .	. . .	6 914
1974	146 521	125 189	103 811	21 378	12 084	12 084	. . .	. . .	. . .	. . .	9 248
1975	139 822	120 181	98 185	21 996	12 565	12 565	. . .	. . .	. . .	. . .	7 076
1976	167 796	148 798	124 228	24 570	13 312	13 312	. . .	. . .	. . .	. . .	5 686
1977	198 992	179 547	151 907	27 640	14 218	14 218	. . .	. . .	. . .	. . .	5 227
1978	235 659	208 191	176 002	32 189	21 680	21 680	. . .	. . .	. . .	. . .	5 788
1979	288 250	248 696	212 007	36 689	32 961	32 961	. . .	. . .	. . .	. . .	6 593
1980	342 124	291 242	249 750	41 492	42 533	42 533	. . .	. . .	. . .	. . .	8 349
1981	375 898	310 570	265 067	45 503	53 626	53 626	. . .	. . .	. . .	. . .	11 702
1982	377 296	299 392	247 642	51 750	61 359	61 359	. . .	. . .	. . .	. . .	16 545
1983	400 828	323 874	268 901	54 973	59 643	59 643	. . .	. . .	. . .	. . .	17 311
1984	501 074	400 166	332 418	67 748	80 574	80 574	. . .	. . .	. . .	. . .	20 334
1985	512 274	410 951	338 088	72 863	79 324	79 324	. . .	. . .	. . .	. . .	21 999
1986	560 007	448 572	368 425	80 147	87 304	84 626	. . .	. . .	. . .	2 678	24 131
1987	623 127	500 553	409 765	90 788	99 309	96 971	. . .	. . .	. . .	2 338	23 265
1988	693 969	545 714	447 189	98 525	122 981	121 134	. . .	. . .	. . .	1 847	25 274
1989	752 874	580 145	477 665	102 480	146 560	144 274	. . .	. . .	. . .	2 286	26 169
1990	791 097	616 098	498 438	117 660	148 345	144 881	. . .	. . .	. . .	3 464	26 654
1991	730 773	609 479	491 020	118 459	131 198	127 172	. . .	. . .	. . .	4 026	-9 904
1992	807 574	656 094	536 528	119 566	114 845	110 093	. . .	. . .	. . .	4 752	36 635
1993	869 272	713 174	589 394	123 780	116 287	111 155	. . .	. . .	. . .	5 132	39 811
1994	994 314	801 747	668 690	133 057	152 302	146 350	. . .	. . .	. . .	5 952	40 265
1995	1 121 616	890 771	749 374	141 397	192 771	186 508	. . .	. . .	. . .	6 263	38 074
1996	1 205 896	955 667	803 113	152 554	207 212	200 912	. . .	. . .	. . .	6 300	43 017
1997	1 336 538	1 042 726	876 794	165 932	248 750	242 084	. . .	. . .	. . .	6 666	45 062
1998	1 414 479	1 099 314	918 637	180 677	261 978	254 984	. . .	. . .	. . .	6 994	53 187
1999	1 600 087	1 228 485	1 035 592	192 893	288 366	276 957	58 313	145 305	73 339	11 410	83 236
2000	1 882 288	1 447 837	1 231 722	216 115	339 643	328 688	63 253	164 757	100 678	10 955	94 808
2001	1 740 493	1 367 165	1 153 701	213 465	268 474	256 761	18 555	162 458	75 748	11 713	104 853
2002	1 776 877	1 397 660	1 173 281	224 379	262 331	249 969	48 049	159 827	42 093	12 362	116 886
2003	1 930 395	1 514 308	1 272 089	242 219	283 938	271 030	78 037	163 525	29 467	12 908	132 150
2004	2 276 059	1 771 433	1 488 349	283 083	356 463	342 490	104 554	195 794	42 142	13 973	148 164
2005	2 641 418	2 000 267	1 695 820	304 448	476 349	460 441	127 979	238 558	93 904	15 909	164 801
2006	3 028 851	2 219 358	1 878 194	341 165	649 752	633 326	159 189	304 934	169 203	16 426	159 740
2007	3 288 135	2 358 922	1 986 347	372 575	743 429	727 707	136 261	381 788	209 658	15 722	185 784
2008	3 438 590	2 550 339	2 141 287	409 052	677 561	660 500	139 073	400 032	121 395	17 061	210 691
2009	2 666 714	1 966 827	1 580 025	386 801	490 794	476 376	112 610	332 495	31 271	14 418	209 093
2010	3 074 729	2 348 263	1 938 950	409 313	507 254	493 292	159 757	313 527	20 008	13 962	219 212
2011	3 447 924	2 675 646	2 239 886	435 761	538 766	524 582	178 862	324 944	20 776	14 184	233 512
2012	3 543 591	2 755 762	2 303 749	452 013	553 163	538 218	171 985	345 249	20 984	14 946	234 665
2013	3 581 225	2 755 334	2 294 247	461 087	575 689	559 662	181 777	361 750	16 135	16 026	250 203
2014	3 730 817	2 866 754	2 385 489	481 264	597 802	580 871	189 375	377 521	13 974	16 931	266 261
2015	3 635 658	2 761 525	2 272 868	488 657	600 531	582 466	167 103	400 396	14 967	18 065	273 602
2016	3 623 381	2 712 639	2 209 592	503 047	621 333	602 974	160 873	416 022	26 080	18 358	289 409
2013											
1st quarter	892 601	687 058	573 154	113 904	145 068	141 176	45 934	90 834	4 408	3 892	60 476
2nd quarter	892 899	686 853	572 239	114 614	144 187	140 174	45 722	90 365	4 087	4 013	61 859
3rd quarter	895 414	689 194	573 762	115 432	142 132	138 069	44 174	90 058	3 837	4 063	64 087
4th quarter	900 312	692 229	575 092	117 137	144 302	140 243	45 949	90 492	3 803	4 059	63 781
2014											
1st quarter	917 648	707 099	589 078	118 022	145 604	141 513	44 032	94 040	3 441	4 092	64 944
2nd quarter	937 626	721 746	601 537	120 209	149 862	145 614	48 622	93 372	3 619	4 248	66 018
3rd quarter	934 560	717 237	596 763	120 474	150 297	145 981	47 642	94 863	3 475	4 316	67 026
4th quarter	940 983	720 671	598 111	122 560	152 039	147 764	49 080	95 245	3 439	4 275	68 273
2015											
1st quarter	913 733	698 782	577 452	121 329	146 365	142 013	39 798	98 849	3 366	4 352	68 587
2nd quarter	917 315	696 411	574 812	121 599	154 288	149 835	45 754	100 471	3 611	4 453	66 616
3rd quarter	914 985	689 887	566 925	122 961	154 903	150 301	45 387	101 101	3 813	4 602	70 195
4th quarter	889 625	676 445	553 678	122 767	144 974	140 316	36 165	99 975	4 177	4 658	68 205
2016											
1st quarter	891 045	664 307	540 698	123 609	154 523	149 994	41 116	103 113	5 765	4 529	72 215
2nd quarter	899 899	671 396	547 229	124 167	158 459	153 837	45 651	101 973	6 213	4 621	70 044
3rd quarter	916 041	681 210	553 798	127 412	161 894	157 297	47 016	103 519	6 762	4 596	72 938
4th quarter	916 395	695 726	567 867	127 859	146 458	141 846	27 089	107 417	7 340	4 612	74 211

. . . = Not available.

Table 7-6A. U.S. International Transactions: Recent Data—*Continued*

(Millions of dollars, seasonally adjusted.)

Year and quarter	Capital account		Financial account							
			Net U.S. acquisition of financial assets excluding financial derivatives (net increase in assets/financial outflows+)							
	Capital transfer receipts and other credits	Capital transfer payments and other debits	Total net acquisition of assets	Direct investment assets			Portfolio investment assets			
				Total direct investment assets	Direct equity assets	Direct debt instruments assets	Total portfolio investment assets	Equity and investment fund shares assets	Short-term debt securities assets	Long-term debt securities assets
1960	...	...	4 099	2 940	...	...	...	...	...	...
1961	...	...	5 538	2 654	...	...	...	...	...	...
1962	...	...	4 174	2 851	...	...	...	...	...	...
1963	...	...	7 270	3 483	...	...	...	...	...	...
1964	...	...	9 560	3 759	...	...	...	...	...	...
1965	...	...	5 715	5 011	...	...	...	...	...	...
1966	...	...	7 321	5 419	...	...	...	...	...	...
1967	...	...	9 757	4 806	...	...	...	...	...	...
1968	...	...	10 977	5 294	...	...	...	...	...	...
1969	...	...	11 584	5 960	...	...	...	...	...	...
1970	...	...	9 336	7 590	...	...	...	...	...	...
1971	...	...	12 474	7 618	...	...	...	...	...	...
1972	...	...	14 497	7 747	...	...	...	...	...	...
1973	...	...	22 874	11 353	...	...	...	...	...	...
1974	...	...	34 745	9 052	...	...	...	...	...	...
1975	...	...	39 703	14 244	...	...	...	...	...	...
1976	...	...	51 269	11 949	...	...	...	...	...	...
1977	...	...	34 785	11 891	...	...	...	...	...	...
1978	...	...	61 130	16 057	...	...	...	...	...	...
1979	...	...	66 053	25 223	...	...	...	...	...	...
1980	...	...	86 968	19 222	...	...	...	...	...	...
1981	...	...	114 147	9 624	...	...	...	...	...	...
1982	...	...	142 722	19 397	...	...	...	...	...	...
1983	...	...	74 690	20 844	...	...	...	...	...	...
1984	...	...	50 740	26 770	...	...	...	...	...	...
1985	...	...	47 064	21 241	...	...	...	...	...	...
1986	...	...	107 252	19 524	...	...	...	...	...	...
1987	...	...	84 058	39 795	...	...	...	...	...	...
1988	...	...	105 747	21 701	...	...	...	...	...	...
1989	...	...	182 908	50 973	...	...	...	...	...	...
1990	...	...	103 985	59 934	...	...	...	...	...	...
1991	...	...	75 753	49 253	...	...	...	...	...	...
1992	...	...	84 899	58 755	...	...	...	...	...	...
1993	...	...	199 399	82 799	...	...	...	...	...	...
1994	...	...	188 758	89 988	...	...	...	...	...	...
1995	...	...	363 555	110 041	...	...	...	...	...	...
1996	...	...	424 548	103 024	...	...	...	...	...	...
1997	...	...	502 024	121 352	...	...	...	...	...	...
1998	...	...	385 936	174 751	...	...	...	...	...	...
1999	36	4 212	527 407	248 279	163 178	85 101	141 007	114 311	18 771	7 925
2000	35	36	589 315	188 004	171 644	16 360	159 713	106 714	31 805	21 194
2001	13 228	30	387 067	146 800	130 725	16 076	106 919	109 119	16 275	-18 475
2002	52	193	319 742	179 556	127 976	51 579	79 532	16 954	30 964	31 614
2003	80	1 900	373 016	197 160	156 173	40 987	133 059	118 003	-12 910	27 967
2004	3 754	705	1 062 783	378 134	296 184	81 951	191 956	84 753	20 523	86 679
2005	15 462	2 346	572 317	61 925	51 621	10 304	267 290	186 684	18 822	61 784
2006	0	1 788	1 336 866	296 059	266 312	29 748	493 366	137 331	115 742	240 293
2007	494	110	1 572 509	532 939	431 378	101 561	380 807	147 782	15 190	217 835
2008	6 170	159	-309 468	351 724	360 130	-8 406	-284 269	-38 550	-82 645	-163 075
2009	0	140	132 204	313 726	262 058	51 669	375 883	63 696	136 127	176 059
2010	0	157	963 449	354 575	343 040	11 535	199 620	79 150	62 279	58 190
2011	0	1 186	496 320	440 405	401 533	38 872	85 365	6 950	-51 256	129 671
2012	7 668	764	177 747	378 222	322 211	56 011	248 760	103 974	-8 599	153 385
2013	0	412	651 427	394 635	336 545	58 090	481 298	287 432	48 761	145 105
2014	0	45	823 343	343 441	340 942	2 499	582 688	431 625	11 389	139 674
2015	0	42	225 398	348 646	316 346	32 300	153 968	202 574	42 484	-91 090
2016	0	59	330 956	347 528	332 858	14 670	20 682	-24 835	-20 605	66 123
2013										
1st quarter	0	40	212 235	73 254	79 931	-6 677	152 224	70 800	18 153	63 271
2nd quarter	0	227	216 264	135 436	83 181	52 255	168 818	149 707	21 592	-2 480
3rd quarter	0	146	24 312	97 519	97 738	-219	14 954	-28 990	22 784	21 160
4th quarter	0	*	198 615	88 426	75 696	12 730	145 302	95 916	-13 768	63 154
2014										
1st quarter	0	43	153 627	54 287	49 304	4 983	102 090	86 491	-11 822	27 421
2nd quarter	0	2	229 606	69 849	85 003	-15 154	204 484	91 727	46 282	66 475
3rd quarter	0	1	330 098	101 811	92 152	9 659	128 515	109 483	-5 157	24 190
4th quarter	0	*	110 012	117 494	114 484	3 010	147 598	143 925	-17 915	21 588
2015										
1st quarter	0	22	357 562	86 576	81 311	5 265	233 068	197 183	27 562	8 323
2nd quarter	0	20	104 122	114 779	81 904	32 875	140 675	113 691	22 795	4 188
3rd quarter	0	1	-83 824	51 322	79 509	-28 186	-97 468	-54 115	12 690	-56 044
4th quarter	0	0	-152 461	95 969	73 622	22 347	-122 306	-54 186	-20 563	-47 558
2016										
1st quarter	0	58	59 062	66 612	76 840	-10 228	-57 326	-60 527	45 866	-42 666
2nd quarter	0	0	322 678	105 525	89 419	16 106	146 397	155 767	-24 286	14 916
3rd quarter	0	1	28 343	94 663	81 080	13 583	-35 268	-25 653	-45 992	36 378
4th quarter	0	...	-79 128	80 728	85 518	-4 790	-33 121	-94 422	3 807	57 494

... = Not available.
* = Between zero and +/- $500,000.

Table 7-6A. U.S. International Transactions: Recent Data—*Continued*

(Millions of dollars, seasonally adjusted.)

Year and quarter	Financial account—*Continued*										
	Net U.S. acquisition of financial assets excluding financial derivatives (net increase in assets/financial outflows +)—*Continued*										
	Other investment assets				Reserve assets						
									Other reserve assets		
	Total other investment assets[1]	Currency and deposits assets	Loan assets	Trade credit and advances assets	Total reserve assets	Monetary gold	Special drawing rights assets	Reserve positions in the IMF	Total other reserve assets[2]	Currency and deposits reserve assets	Securities reserve assets
1960	2 641	. . .	. . .	. . .	. . .	. . .	. . .	. . .	-2 145	. . .	. . .
1961	2 729	. . .	. . .	. . .	. . .	. . .	. . .	. . .	-607	. . .	. . .
1962	1 889	. . .	. . .	. . .	. . .	. . .	. . .	. . .	-1 535	. . .	. . .
1963	3 060	. . .	. . .	. . .	. . .	. . .	. . .	. . .	-378	. . .	. . .
1964	5 294	. . .	. . .	. . .	. . .	. . .	. . .	. . .	-171	. . .	. . .
1965	1 170	. . .	. . .	. . .	. . .	. . .	. . .	. . .	-1 225	. . .	. . .
1966	1 752	. . .	. . .	. . .	. . .	. . .	. . .	. . .	-570	. . .	. . .
1967	3 696	. . .	. . .	. . .	. . .	. . .	. . .	. . .	-53	. . .	. . .
1968	3 244	. . .	. . .	. . .	. . .	. . .	. . .	. . .	870	. . .	. . .
1969	2 896	. . .	. . .	. . .	. . .	. . .	. . .	. . .	1 179	. . .	. . .
1970	3 151	. . .	. . .	. . .	. . .	. . .	. . .	. . .	-2 481	. . .	. . .
1971	6 092	. . .	. . .	. . .	. . .	. . .	. . .	. . .	-2 349	. . .	. . .
1972	6 127	. . .	. . .	. . .	. . .	. . .	. . .	. . .	4	. . .	. . .
1973	11 007	. . .	. . .	. . .	. . .	. . .	. . .	. . .	-158	. . .	. . .
1974	22 373	. . .	. . .	. . .	. . .	. . .	. . .	. . .	1 467	. . .	. . .
1975	18 363	. . .	. . .	. . .	. . .	. . .	. . .	. . .	849	. . .	. . .
1976	27 877	. . .	. . .	. . .	. . .	. . .	. . .	. . .	2 558	. . .	. . .
1977	17 060	. . .	. . .	. . .	. . .	. . .	. . .	. . .	375	. . .	. . .
1978	42 179	. . .	. . .	. . .	. . .	. . .	. . .	. . .	-732	. . .	. . .
1979	27 267	. . .	. . .	. . .	. . .	. . .	. . .	. . .	1 133	. . .	. . .
1980	53 550	. . .	. . .	. . .	. . .	. . .	. . .	. . .	8 154	. . .	. . .
1981	83 697	. . .	. . .	. . .	. . .	. . .	. . .	. . .	5 176	. . .	. . .
1982	105 965	. . .	. . .	. . .	. . .	. . .	. . .	. . .	4 965	. . .	. . .
1983	50 588	. . .	. . .	. . .	. . .	. . .	. . .	. . .	1 195	. . .	. . .
1984	17 340	. . .	. . .	. . .	. . .	. . .	. . .	. . .	3 132	. . .	. . .
1985	18 957	. . .	. . .	. . .	. . .	. . .	. . .	. . .	3 858	. . .	. . .
1986	79 057	. . .	. . .	. . .	. . .	. . .	. . .	. . .	-313	. . .	. . .
1987	45 508	. . .	. . .	. . .	. . .	. . .	. . .	. . .	-9 148	. . .	. . .
1988	75 544	. . .	. . .	. . .	. . .	. . .	. . .	. . .	3 913	. . .	. . .
1989	75 476	. . .	. . .	. . .	. . .	. . .	. . .	. . .	25 293	. . .	. . .
1990	11 336	. . .	. . .	. . .	. . .	. . .	. . .	. . .	2 158	. . .	. . .
1991	210	. . .	. . .	. . .	. . .	. . .	. . .	. . .	-5 763	. . .	. . .
1992	-20 639	. . .	. . .	. . .	. . .	. . .	. . .	. . .	-3 901	. . .	. . .
1993	-22 696	. . .	. . .	. . .	. . .	. . .	. . .	. . .	1 379	. . .	. . .
1994	50 028	. . .	. . .	. . .	. . .	. . .	. . .	. . .	-5 346	. . .	. . .
1995	100 266	. . .	. . .	. . .	. . .	. . .	. . .	. . .	9 742	. . .	. . .
1996	168 013	. . .	. . .	. . .	. . .	. . .	. . .	. . .	-6 668	. . .	. . .
1997	258 626	. . .	. . .	. . .	. . .	. . .	. . .	. . .	1 010	. . .	. . .
1998	72 216	. . .	. . .	. . .	. . .	. . .	. . .	. . .	6 783	. . .	. . .
1999	146 868	. . .	. . .	5 227	-8 747	0	-10	-5 484	-3 253	. . .	. . .
2000	241 308	. . .	. . .	680	290	0	722	-2 308	1 876	. . .	. . .
2001	128 437	. . .	. . .	-5 267	4 911	0	630	3 600	681	. . .	. . .
2002	56 973	. . .	. . .	-633	3 681	0	475	2 632	574	. . .	. . .
2003	44 321	51 302	-9 261	2 280	-1 524	0	-601	-1 494	571	293	191
2004	495 498	240 360	256 244	-1 106	-2 806	0	398	-3 826	623	242	298
2005	257 196	82 879	173 031	1 286	-14 094	0	-4 511	-10 200	617	224	309
2006	549 814	154 026	392 255	3 534	-2 373	0	223	-3 331	735	309	308
2007	658 641	375 146	272 812	10 683	122	0	154	-1 021	989	517	288
2008	-381 770	123 493	-501 550	-3 712	4 848	0	106	3 473	1 269	587	443
2009	-609 662	-394 461	-215 735	535	52 256	0	48 230	3 357	669	138	480
2010	407 420	150 249	251 128	6 043	1 835	0	31	1 293	511	55	439
2011	-45 327	-89 161	39 821	4 013	15 877	0	-1 752	18 079	-450	110	-598
2012	-453 695	-521 922	67 538	689	4 460	0	37	4 032	391	24	365
2013	-221 408	-126 959	-104 254	9 805	-3 099	0	22	-3 438	317	3	313
2014	-99 203	-160 433	67 055	-5 824	-3 583	0	23	-3 849	243	5	234
2015	-270 924	-194 429	-74 774	-1 721	-6 292	0	9	-6 485	185	-20	205
2016	-39 344	-100 673	60 543	786	2 090	0	684	1 348	58	-56	114
2013											
1st quarter	-14 118	-57 886	44 343	-576	875	0	5	755	115	1	115
2nd quarter	-87 799	-17 678	-74 348	4 228	-191	0	6	-287	90	1	89
3rd quarter	-87 160	-52 371	-36 382	1 593	-1 001	0	5	-1 071	65	1	64
4th quarter	-32 331	976	-37 867	4 560	-2 782	0	6	-2 835	47	1	45
2014											
1st quarter	-1 794	-38 668	43 318	-6 445	-956	0	8	-1 040	76	2	72
2nd quarter	-45 500	-21 306	-26 969	2 774	773	0	8	710	55	2	51
3rd quarter	100 661	31 893	70 435	-1 667	-889	0	4	-951	59	1	58
4th quarter	-152 569	-132 353	-19 730	-486	-2 511	0	3	-2 568	54	1	53
2015											
1st quarter	42 077	-7 436	50 580	-1 066	-4 159	0	3	-4 195	33	*	33
2nd quarter	-150 455	-70 144	-79 588	-723	-877	0	2	-930	52	-4	56
3rd quarter	-37 412	-66 480	28 173	895	-266	0	2	-314	46	-7	53
4th quarter	-125 134	-50 368	-73 938	-828	-990	0	2	-1 046	54	-8	63
2016											
1st quarter	50 968	72 116	-24 242	3 094	-1 191	0	2	-1 214	21	-10	31
2nd quarter	70 566	-25 267	98 186	-2 353	189	0	*	175	14	-14	28
3rd quarter	-32 694	-88 661	53 959	2 008	1 642	0	2	1 654	-14	-18	4
4th quarter	-128 184	-58 861	-67 360	-1 963	1 450	0	680	732	37	-14	51

[1]Includes insurance technical reserves, not shown separately.
[2]Includes financial derivatives and other claims, not shown seperately.
. . . = Not available.

Table 7-6A. U.S. International Transactions: Recent Data—*Continued*

(Millions of dollars, seasonally adjusted.)

		Financial account—*Continued*											
		Net U.S. incurrence of liabilities excluding financial derivatives (net increase in liabilities/financial inflow+)											
		Direct investment liabilities			Portfolio investment liabilities				Other investment liabilities				
Year and quarter	Total net incurrence of liabilities	Total direct investment liabilities	Direct equity liabilities	Direct debt instruments liabilities	Total portfolio liabilities	Equity and investment fund shares liabilities	Short-term debt securities liabilities	Long-term debt securities liabilities	Total other investment liabilities[1]	Currency and deposits liabilities	Loan liabilities	Trade credit and advances liabilities	Special drawing rights allocations
1960	2 294	315	...	...	...	...	...	...	1 406	...	...	...	...
1961	2 705	311	...	...	...	...	...	...	1 685	...	...	...	...
1962	1 912	346	...	...	...	...	...	...	88	...	...	...	...
1963	3 217	231	...	...	...	...	...	...	2 033	...	...	...	...
1964	3 643	322	...	...	...	...	...	...	3 120	...	...	...	...
1965	741	414	...	...	...	...	...	...	957	...	...	...	...
1966	3 661	426	...	...	...	...	...	...	4 212	...	...	...	...
1967	7 379	698	...	...	...	...	...	...	3 537	...	...	...	...
1968	9 928	808	...	...	...	...	...	...	5 340	...	...	...	...
1969	12 702	1 263	...	...	...	...	...	...	10 720	...	...	...	...
1970	7 226	1 464	...	...	...	...	...	...	-5 948	...	...	...	...
1971	23 687	368	...	...	...	...	...	...	-5 516	...	...	...	...
1972	22 171	948	...	...	...	...	...	...	8 100	...	...	...	...
1973	18 388	2 800	...	...	...	...	...	...	10 798	...	...	...	...
1974	35 228	4 761	...	...	...	...	...	...	24 967	...	...	...	...
1975	16 870	2 603	...	...	...	...	...	...	1 506	...	...	...	...
1976	37 840	4 347	...	...	...	...	...	...	17 328	...	...	...	...
1977	52 770	3 728	...	...	...	...	...	...	11 427	...	...	...	...
1978	66 275	7 896	...	...	...	...	...	...	28 296	...	...	...	...
1979	40 693	11 876	...	...	...	...	...	...	42 319	...	...	...	...
1980	62 036	16 918	...	...	...	...	...	...	21 293	...	...	...	...
1981	85 684	25 196	...	...	...	...	...	...	42 979	...	...	...	...
1982	109 897	27 475	...	...	...	...	...	...	62 727	...	...	...	...
1983	95 715	18 688	...	...	...	...	...	...	58 645	...	...	...	...
1984	126 413	34 832	...	...	...	...	...	...	52 886	...	...	...	...
1985	146 544	22 057	...	...	...	...	...	...	56 483	...	...	...	...
1986	223 854	30 946	...	...	...	...	...	...	88 411	...	...	...	...
1987	251 863	63 232	...	...	...	...	...	...	109 000	...	...	...	...
1988	244 008	56 910	...	...	...	...	...	...	100 312	...	...	...	...
1989	230 302	75 801	...	...	...	...	...	...	79 649	...	...	...	...
1990	162 109	71 247	...	...	...	...	...	...	65 095	...	...	...	...
1991	119 586	34 535	...	...	...	...	...	...	12 489	...	...	...	...
1992	178 842	30 315	...	...	...	...	...	...	56 328	...	...	...	...
1993	278 607	50 211	...	...	...	...	...	...	54 009	...	...	...	...
1994	312 995	55 942	...	...	...	...	...	...	125 204	...	...	...	...
1995	446 393	69 067	...	...	...	...	...	...	122 895	...	...	...	...
1996	559 027	97 644	...	...	...	...	...	...	69 276	...	...	...	...
1997	720 999	122 150	...	...	...	...	...	...	287 744	...	...	...	...
1998	452 901	211 152	...	...	...	...	...	...	15 871	...	...	...	...
1999	765 555	312 789	225 690	87 099	278 697	112 289	-6 900	173 308	174 069	...	...	-4 526	0
2000	1 067 016	350 066	259 380	90 686	441 966	193 600	5 393	242 973	274 984	...	...	10 375	0
2001	787 321	171 472	107 051	64 420	431 492	121 464	3 149	306 879	184 357	...	...	5 156	0
2002	820 257	109 468	106 927	2 541	504 155	54 067	76 547	373 541	206 634	...	...	15 754	0
2003	905 899	111 346	107 707	3 638	550 163	33 981	31 099	485 083	244 390	30 846	214 539	-995	0
2004	1 595 116	207 878	142 434	65 444	867 340	61 786	99 851	705 703	519 899	131 503	386 418	1 979	0
2005	1 273 038	138 328	112 459	25 869	832 037	89 258	-45 310	788 088	302 673	-124 782	415 824	11 632	0
2006	2 116 304	294 289	184 143	110 146	1 126 735	145 481	22 756	958 498	695 280	224 386	465 221	5 673	0
2007	2 183 538	340 066	190 418	149 648	1 156 612	275 617	158 983	722 012	686 860	239 302	426 981	20 576	0
2008	454 051	332 734	294 861	37 874	523 683	126 804	287 226	109 652	-402 367	74 441	-483 554	6 746	0
2009	318 350	153 787	148 465	5 322	357 352	219 302	-124 007	262 056	-192 789	-74 225	-172 464	6 301	47 598
2010	1 386 345	259 345	203 148	56 197	820 434	178 952	-53 031	694 513	306 566	115 678	172 256	18 632	0
2011	977 073	257 411	185 051	72 361	311 626	123 357	-86 722	274 991	408 036	475 678	-84 789	17 147	0
2012	625 352	243 010	204 085	38 925	747 017	239 065	16 331	491 622	-364 675	-246 001	-130 307	11 633	0
2013	1 044 635	276 978	200 616	76 362	511 987	-62 642	45 675	528 954	255 670	202 838	41 333	11 499	0
2014	1 056 374	207 368	112 000	95 368	701 861	154 311	22 329	525 221	147 145	59 579	73 581	13 985	0
2015	395 234	379 435	301 108	78 327	250 936	-178 266	45 783	383 419	-235 137	33 406	-282 713	14 169	0
2016	759 370	425 256	340 752	84 504	270 924	-130 184	-12 828	413 936	63 190	24 912	28 691	9 588	0
2013													
1st quarter	252 808	32 891	32 041	850	150 986	-19 840	69 256	101 570	68 931	895	64 630	3 406	0
2nd quarter	245 645	96 409	60 765	35 644	-8 446	-30 609	-32 556	54 719	157 682	104 763	47 877	5 042	0
3rd quarter	171 639	76 142	56 008	20 133	200 041	70 037	-53 025	183 029	-104 544	-28 781	-77 656	1 893	0
4th quarter	374 543	71 536	51 802	19 734	169 406	-82 230	62 000	189 636	133 601	125 960	6 482	1 158	0
2014													
1st quarter	289 054	-86 791	-90 207	3 416	248 214	104 032	12 986	131 196	127 631	-5 550	120 319	12 862	0
2nd quarter	293 401	69 348	65 278	4 070	99 475	15 451	-24 942	108 967	124 578	110 727	8 935	4 916	0
3rd quarter	371 787	118 119	56 580	61 539	230 476	71 219	-8 171	167 428	23 192	39 967	-12 170	-4 605	0
4th quarter	102 132	106 691	80 348	26 343	123 696	-36 390	42 456	117 630	-128 255	-85 565	-43 503	813	0
2015													
1st quarter	348 004	194 067	160 334	33 733	102 922	31 104	37 005	34 814	51 015	559	46 254	4 202	0
2nd quarter	205 435	108 005	59 370	48 635	256 154	-22 605	-5 818	284 577	-158 723	-1 720	-162 179	5 175	0
3rd quarter	-39 884	50 590	40 520	10 069	-126 250	-33 301	-51 361	-41 588	35 775	10 946	19 479	5 351	0
4th quarter	-118 322	26 773	40 884	-14 111	18 109	-153 464	65 957	105 616	-163 204	23 621	-186 267	-559	0
2016													
1st quarter	119 117	92 245	90 547	1 698	-21 197	-95 660	-10 464	84 927	48 069	-40 969	84 376	4 662	0
2nd quarter	368 588	175 271	123 070	52 201	11 934	-48 482	-27 272	87 688	181 383	96 940	79 639	4 805	0
3rd quarter	259 245	124 741	89 755	34 986	218 594	121 599	30 237	66 758	-84 090	-42 389	-39 784	-1 917	0
4th quarter	12 420	33 000	37 380	-4 381	61 593	-107 641	-5 330	174 564	-82 173	11 330	-95 541	2 038	0

[1]Includes insurance technical resreves, not shown separately.
. . . = Not available.

Table 7-6A. U.S. International Transactions: Recent Data—*Continued*

(Millions of dollars, seasonally adjusted.)

Year and quarter	Financial account— *Continued* Financial derivatives other than reserves, net	Statistical discrepancy Total	Seasonal adjustment discrepancy	Balances — Current account Total balance on current account	Balances on goods and services Total balance on goods and services	Balance on goods	Balance on services	Balance on primary income	Balance on secondary income	Balance on capital account	Net lending (+) or net borrowing (-) Based on current and capital account transactions	Based on financial account transactions
1960	...	-1 019	0	2 825	3 508	4 892	-1 385	3 378	-4 061	0	2 825	1 805
1961	...	-989	0	3 821	4 194	5 571	-1 377	3 755	-4 128	0	3 821	2 833
1962	...	-1 123	0	3 387	3 371	4 521	-1 151	4 294	-4 277	0	3 387	2 262
1963	...	-361	0	4 414	4 210	5 224	-1 014	4 595	-4 393	0	4 414	4 053
1964	...	-907	0	6 823	6 022	6 801	-780	5 041	-4 240	0	6 823	5 917
1965	...	-457	0	5 430	4 664	4 951	-287	5 349	-4 584	0	5 430	4 974
1966	...	629	0	3 031	2 939	3 817	-878	5 046	-4 956	0	3 031	3 660
1967	...	-205	0	2 584	2 604	3 800	-1 196	5 274	-5 294	0	2 584	2 378
1968	...	438	0	611	250	635	-385	5 990	-5 629	0	611	1 049
1969	...	-1 517	0	399	90	607	-517	6 044	-5 735	0	399	-1 118
1970	...	-219	0	2 331	2 255	2 603	-348	6 234	-6 156	0	2 331	2 110
1971	...	-9 779	0	-1 433	-1 301	-2 260	959	7 270	-7 402	0	-1 433	-11 213
1972	...	-1 879	0	-5 796	-5 443	-6 416	973	8 192	-8 544	0	-5 796	-7 674
1973	...	-2 654	0	7 140	1 900	911	989	12 153	-6 914	0	7 140	4 486
1974	...	-2 444	0	1 961	-4 293	-5 505	1 212	15 503	-9 248	0	1 961	-483
1975	...	4 717	0	18 117	12 403	8 903	3 500	12 786	-7 076	0	18 117	22 833
1976	...	9 134	0	4 296	-6 082	-9 483	3 402	16 062	-5 686	0	4 296	13 429
1977	...	-3 651	0	-14 336	-27 247	-31 091	3 845	18 137	-5 227	0	-14 336	-17 985
1978	...	9 997	0	-15 143	-29 763	-33 927	4 164	20 407	-5 788	0	-15 143	-5 145
1979	...	25 647	0	-285	-24 566	-27 568	3 003	30 874	-6 593	0	-285	25 360
1980	...	22 614	0	2 318	-19 407	-25 500	6 093	30 072	-8 349	0	2 318	24 932
1981	...	23 433	0	5 029	-16 172	-28 023	11 851	32 903	-11 702	0	5 029	28 463
1982	...	38 362	0	-5 537	-24 156	-36 485	12 330	35 163	-16 545	0	-5 537	32 825
1983	...	17 666	0	-38 691	-57 767	-67 102	9 335	36 388	-17 311	0	-38 691	-21 025
1984	...	18 673	0	-94 344	-109 074	-112 492	3 418	35 065	-20 334	0	-94 344	-75 673
1985	...	18 677	0	-118 155	-121 879	-122 173	294	25 722	-21 999	0	-118 155	-99 480
1986	...	30 570	0	-147 176	-138 539	-145 081	6 543	15 494	-24 131	0	-147 176	-116 602
1987	...	-7 149	0	-160 655	-151 683	-159 557	7 874	14 294	-23 265	0	-160 655	-167 805
1988	...	-17 108	0	-121 153	-114 566	-126 959	12 394	18 685	-25 274	0	-121 153	-138 261
1989	...	52 299	0	-99 487	-93 142	-117 749	24 607	19 824	-26 169	-207	-99 694	-47 394
1990	...	28 066	0	-78 969	-80 865	-111 037	30 173	28 549	-26 654	-7 221	-86 190	-58 124
1991	...	-41 601	0	2 897	-31 136	-76 937	45 802	24 129	9 904	-5 129	-2 232	-43 833
1992	...	-43 776	0	-51 613	-39 212	-96 897	57 685	24 237	-36 635	1 449	-50 164	-93 943
1993	...	6 313	0	-84 805	-70 311	-132 451	62 141	25 319	-39 811	-714	-85 519	-79 208
1994	...	-1 514	0	-121 612	-98 493	-165 831	67 338	17 145	-40 265	-1 112	-122 724	-124 237
1995	...	30 951	0	-113 567	-96 384	-174 170	77 786	20 890	-38 074	-221	-113 788	-82 838
1996	...	-9 706	0	-124 764	-104 065	-191 000	86 935	22 318	-43 017	-8	-124 772	-134 479
1997	...	-77 995	0	-140 726	-108 273	-198 428	90 155	12 607	-45 062	-256	-140 982	-218 975
1998	...	148 106	0	-215 062	-166 140	-248 221	82 081	4 266	-53 187	-7	-215 069	-66 965
1999	...	61 558	0	-295 530	-258 617	-337 068	78 450	11 933	-48 846	-4 176	-299 706	-238 148
2000	...	-66 944	0	-410 756	-372 517	-446 783	74 266	19 178	-57 418	-1	-410 757	-477 701
2001	...	-18 124	0	-395 328	-361 511	-422 370	60 858	29 729	-63 545	13 198	-382 130	-400 254
2002	...	-42 287	0	-458 087	-418 955	-475 245	56 290	25 174	-64 307	-141	-458 228	-500 515
2003	...	-9 721	0	-521 342	-493 890	-541 643	47 754	42 760	-70 212	-1 821	-523 162	-532 883
2004	...	98 385	0	-633 768	-609 883	-664 766	54 882	64 127	-88 012	3 049	-630 719	-532 334
2005	...	31 597	0	-745 434	-714 245	-782 804	68 558	67 632	-98 822	13 116	-732 319	-700 721
2006	-29 710	-634	0	-806 726	-761 716	-837 289	75 573	43 337	-88 347	-1 788	-808 514	-809 148
2007	-6 222	101 008	0	-718 643	-705 375	-821 196	115 821	100 604	-113 872	384	-718 260	-617 251
2008	32 947	-49 941	0	-686 641	-708 726	-832 492	123 765	146 146	-124 061	6 010	-680 631	-730 572
2009	-44 816	149 970	0	-380 792	-383 774	-509 694	125 920	123 584	-120 602	-140	-380 932	-230 962
2010	-14 076	7 116	0	-443 930	-494 658	-648 678	154 020	177 661	-126 934	-157	-444 087	-436 972
2011	-35 006	-54 219	0	-460 354	-548 625	-740 646	192 020	220 961	-132 690	-1 186	-461 540	-515 759
2012	7 064	-917	0	-446 527	-536 773	-741 171	204 398	215 792	-125 547	6 904	-439 623	-440 540
2013	2 222	-24 153	0	-366 422	-461 876	-702 244	240 368	218 970	-123 515	-412	-366 833	-390 987
2014	-54 347	104 727	0	-392 060	-490 176	-752 169	261 993	224 005	-125 888	-45	-392 105	-287 378
2015	-25 392	267 780	0	-462 965	-500 361	-762 565	262 203	182 385	-144 988	-42	-463 007	-195 227
2016	21 951	74 802	0	-481 206	-500 560	-749 926	249 365	180 591	-161 237	-59	-481 265	-406 463
2013												
1st quarter	-3 948	54 499	13 228	-98 980	-119 610	-178 437	58 827	50 239	-29 609	-40	-99 020	-44 521
2nd quarter	-3 302	62 377	-13 771	-94 833	-117 731	-177 126	59 394	54 783	-31 885	-227	-95 060	-32 683
3rd quarter	6 569	-47 888	-27 448	-92 725	-117 070	-177 570	60 500	56 761	-32 416	-146	-92 870	-140 758
4th quarter	2 903	-93 141	27 991	-79 883	-107 466	-169 112	61 647	57 187	-29 605	...	-79 883	-173 025
2014												
1st quarter	6 105	-34 625	14 505	-94 654	-120 514	-185 712	65 199	56 746	-30 887	-43	-94 697	-129 322
2nd quarter	-4 423	25 843	-8 978	-94 060	-125 834	-191 836	66 002	54 623	-22 849	-2	-94 062	-68 218
3rd quarter	-24 304	29 627	-28 654	-95 619	-119 415	-184 677	65 262	59 325	-35 529	-1	-95 620	-65 993
4th quarter	-31 725	83 881	23 127	-107 726	-124 414	-189 944	65 531	53 310	-36 623	...	-107 726	-23 845
2015												
1st quarter	-40 199	83 929	16 120	-114 549	-126 514	-193 517	67 003	48 351	-36 386	-22	-114 571	-30 642
2nd quarter	1 708	12 318	-9 621	-111 904	-124 028	-190 876	66 848	45 071	-32 947	*	-111 924	-99 605
3rd quarter	746	79 913	-24 223	-123 106	-125 611	-189 768	64 157	41 848	-39 343	-1	-123 106	-43 194
4th quarter	12 353	91 620	17 725	-113 406	-124 209	-188 404	64 195	47 115	-36 312	0	-113 406	-21 786
2016												
1st quarter	12 994	86 069	15 240	-133 072	-126 204	-187 343	61 139	33 759	-40 627	-58	-133 130	-47 061
2nd quarter	2 904	76 739	-10 305	-119 745	-125 806	-187 789	61 983	43 791	-37 730	*	-119 745	-43 006
3rd quarter	6 500	-108 394	-29 312	-116 007	-116 230	-178 652	62 422	41 585	-41 361	-1	-116 008	-224 402
4th quarter	-447	20 387	24 377	-112 382	-132 320	-196 142	63 822	61 457	-41 519	0	-112 382	-91 995

. . . = Not available.
* = Between zero and +/-$500,000

Table 7-6B. U.S. International Transactions: Historical Quarterly

(Millions of dollars, seasonally adjusted.)

	Current account											
	Exports of goods and services and income receipts (credits)											Secondary income (current transfer) receipts
	Total goods and services and income receipts	Exports of goods and services			Primary income receipts							
		Total goods and services exports	Goods exports	Services exports	Total primary income receipts	Investment income receipts					Compensation of employees receipts	
Year and quarter						Total investment income receipts	Direct investment income receipts	Portfolio investment income receipts	Other investment income receipts	Reserve asset income receipts		
2002												
1st quarter	317 160	237 401	168 795	68 607	67 918	66 779	35 080	19 215	12 222	262	1 140	11 840
2nd quarter	330 213	246 016	175 834	70 181	71 444	70 303	37 174	20 092	12 800	237	1 141	12 753
3rd quarter	338 319	249 202	178 451	70 751	75 471	74 327	39 713	21 656	12 678	280	1 144	13 646
4th quarter	333 101	246 085	174 956	71 129	72 676	71 531	38 432	20 961	11 867	271	1 145	14 340
2003												
1st quarter	337 839	247 468	177 549	69 919	76 297	75 134	42 908	22 306	9 613	307	1 164	14 074
2nd quarter	343 382	248 233	178 539	69 694	79 062	77 896	45 297	21 875	10 446	278	1 167	16 086
3rd quarter	353 826	255 843	182 340	73 503	81 975	80 805	47 712	23 102	9 737	254	1 169	16 008
4th quarter	374 001	268 873	192 018	76 855	89 359	88 187	54 785	23 370	9 787	245	1 172	15 770
2004												
1st quarter	393 020	280 458	198 160	82 298	97 696	96 513	61 265	25 462	9 499	287	1 183	14 866
2nd quarter	403 930	287 866	204 315	83 551	101 654	100 474	62 918	26 699	10 602	255	1 180	14 410
3rd quarter	413 288	291 660	207 629	84 031	107 020	105 835	64 547	27 609	13 395	285	1 184	14 609
4th quarter	432 053	301 565	213 480	88 086	114 220	113 033	66 676	28 877	17 142	338	1 187	16 268
2005												
1st quarter	457 649	311 731	219 595	92 135	126 709	125 512	73 077	31 156	20 973	305	1 197	19 209
2nd quarter	464 003	319 410	227 952	91 458	130 577	129 380	73 141	31 720	24 244	275	1 197	14 017
3rd quarter	476 236	321 561	228 416	93 145	138 300	137 100	75 602	32 467	28 729	302	1 200	16 375
4th quarter	498 094	333 321	237 053	96 268	148 394	147 193	79 364	34 348	33 179	302	1 201	16 378
2006												
1st quarter	525 635	348 984	249 672	99 312	157 652	156 392	79 449	36 773	39 897	274	1 259	18 999
2nd quarter	550 892	361 325	258 172	103 152	172 108	170 843	83 795	40 449	46 326	273	1 264	17 459
3rd quarter	560 339	365 686	262 364	103 322	178 404	177 134	84 203	43 154	49 436	341	1 270	16 249
4th quarter	585 258	381 648	270 696	110 952	184 925	183 651	85 788	45 770	51 755	338	1 275	18 685
2007												
1st quarter	599 916	391 610	276 803	114 807	192 957	191 660	87 357	49 395	54 547	361	1 297	15 349
2nd quarter	630 323	404 234	285 920	118 314	209 426	208 125	93 837	53 570	60 372	347	1 301	16 662
3rd quarter	658 173	419 325	295 651	123 674	219 999	218 692	97 526	58 726	62 075	364	1 308	18 848
4th quarter	681 081	438 378	306 777	131 601	221 651	220 337	102 124	59 919	57 917	377	1 313	21 052
2008												
1st quarter	691 838	454 689	323 714	130 975	218 387	217 051	110 051	62 413	44 139	448	1 336	18 763
2nd quarter	716 264	479 164	342 964	136 200	216 645	215 304	115 089	61 940	37 905	371	1 341	20 454
3rd quarter	713 731	481 623	347 210	134 413	210 713	209 367	110 630	60 156	38 091	491	1 346	21 394
4th quarter	630 118	426 136	294 907	131 229	177 963	176 621	87 595	56 821	31 943	263	1 341	26 018
2009												
1st quarter	552 102	378 634	254 211	124 423	150 426	149 005	81 622	48 899	18 246	237	1 421	23 042
2nd quarter	549 098	379 502	254 057	125 445	147 059	145 627	86 869	44 090	14 512	156	1 432	22 538
3rd quarter	574 553	398 428	270 281	128 147	155 049	153 606	97 135	45 390	10 851	231	1 443	21 076
4th quarter	610 170	426 489	291 783	134 707	161 845	160 401	104 675	46 038	9 532	157	1 444	21 835
2010												
1st quarter	624 806	438 333	304 463	133 870	165 373	163 897	108 450	46 725	8 498	223	1 476	21 100
2nd quarter	644 991	452 371	315 242	137 129	169 200	167 716	110 740	47 748	9 106	122	1 484	23 419
3rd quarter	662 831	468 345	325 220	143 125	171 337	169 851	111 924	48 667	9 077	182	1 486	23 149
4th quarter	698 170	494 555	345 348	149 208	179 006	177 521	116 659	51 712	8 979	172	1 484	24 609
2011												
1st quarter	719 078	511 743	360 151	151 592	182 773	181 249	118 012	53 915	9 103	219	1 523	24 562
2nd quarter	745 539	530 519	373 260	157 259	189 491	187 964	119 612	58 495	9 632	225	1 527	25 529
3rd quarter	763 083	542 974	382 183	160 791	194 717	193 185	121 324	62 415	9 215	232	1 531	25 392
4th quarter	759 871	541 785	383 646	158 139	192 746	191 224	118 467	62 518	10 069	170	1 523	25 340
2012												
1st quarter	768 599	549 028	388 086	160 942	194 976	193 453	120 265	63 067	9 952	170	1 523	24 594
2nd quarter	770 282	555 386	391 877	163 509	189 164	187 611	112 599	65 950	8 937	126	1 553	25 732
3rd quarter	777 002	556 248	392 367	163 881	192 380	190 796	116 837	65 030	8 832	97	1 585	28 373
4th quarter	781 181	558 326	390 248	168 078	192 435	190 793	116 095	66 383	8 233	82	1 642	30 419
2013												
1st quarter	793 621	567 448	394 717	172 731	195 307	193 679	118 172	67 288	8 090	129	1 627	30 867
2nd quarter	798 065	569 122	395 114	174 008	198 969	197 313	119 921	69 391	7 898	103	1 656	29 975
3rd quarter	802 689	572 124	396 192	175 933	198 893	197 223	119 417	70 084	7 645	78	1 670	31 671
4th quarter	820 428	584 763	405 980	178 784	201 490	199 829	120 541	71 678	7 547	64	1 660	34 176
2014												
1st quarter	822 994	586 586	403 365	183 220	202 351	200 687	118 723	74 085	7 783	96	1 664	34 058
2nd quarter	843 566	595 912	409 701	186 211	204 485	202 825	118 262	76 462	8 027	74	1 660	43 169
3rd quarter	838 941	597 822	412 087	185 735	209 622	207 950	121 900	78 174	7 805	70	1 672	31 497
4th quarter	833 257	596 258	408 167	188 091	205 349	203 661	119 496	76 263	7 841	61	1 688	31 650
2015												
1st quarter	799 184	572 268	383 936	188 332	194 716	192 977	109 908	75 721	7 308	40	1 738	32 200
2nd quarter	805 411	572 383	383 935	188 448	199 359	197 596	111 269	78 387	7 880	59	1 764	33 669
3rd quarter	791 880	564 276	377 157	187 118	196 752	194 969	106 676	80 014	8 227	53	1 782	30 852
4th quarter	776 218	552 236	365 275	186 962	192 089	190 304	104 645	77 497	8 101	61	1 785	31 893
2016												
1st quarter	757 974	538 104	353 355	184 748	188 282	186 485	95 756	81 617	9 083	28	1 797	31 588
2nd quarter	780 154	545 590	359 440	186 149	202 250	200 451	109 282	81 031	10 117	21	1 799	32 315
3rd quarter	800 035	564 980	375 146	189 834	203 478	201 673	110 509	80 967	10 204	-6	1 805	31 577
4th quarter	804 012	563 406	371 725	191 680	207 914	206 114	112 887	82 728	10 438	62	1 800	32 692

Table 7-6B. U.S. International Transactions: Historical Quarterly—*Continued*

(Millions of dollars, seasonally adjusted.)

Year and quarter	Total goods and services and income receipts	Imports of goods and services and income payments (debits)										
		Imports of goods and services			Primary income payments					Compensation of employees payments	Secondary income (current transfer) payments
		Total goods and services imports	Goods	Services	Total primary income payments	Investment income payments					
						Total investment income payments	Direct investment income payments	Portfolio investment income payments	Other investment income payments		
2002											
1st quarter	421 151	329 867	274 921	54 946	60 966	57 907	8 886	39 029	9 992	3 059	30 318
2nd quarter	445 226	348 503	293 371	55 132	69 139	66 004	14 455	40 006	11 543	3 135	27 584
3rd quarter	453 188	355 116	299 455	55 660	69 630	66 607	15 321	40 531	10 754	3 023	28 443
4th quarter	457 310	364 175	305 534	58 641	62 595	59 449	9 385	40 260	9 804	3 146	30 540
2003											
1st quarter	472 826	370 927	312 769	58 158	69 728	66 500	18 645	40 102	7 753	3 229	32 171
2nd quarter	472 651	370 618	313 208	57 409	69 134	65 958	18 247	39 920	7 791	3 176	32 899
3rd quarter	484 200	378 715	316 504	62 211	72 119	68 887	20 418	41 475	6 994	3 232	33 366
4th quarter	500 721	394 048	329 607	64 441	72 958	69 686	20 728	42 028	6 930	3 272	33 715
2004											
1st quarter	530 605	415 616	347 597	68 019	76 716	73 333	21 996	43 880	7 457	3 383	38 274
2nd quarter	560 746	438 214	367 997	70 217	86 955	83 433	28 164	46 908	8 361	3 522	35 576
3rd quarter	572 832	447 757	376 563	71 194	89 606	86 149	26 120	48 629	11 399	3 458	35 469
4th quarter	611 878	469 846	396 192	73 654	103 186	99 575	28 274	56 377	14 925	3 610	38 846
2005											
1st quarter	627 457	477 364	403 172	74 192	107 251	103 357	30 522	54 982	17 852	3 894	42 841
2nd quarter	643 484	491 049	415 859	75 190	113 911	109 936	31 016	57 750	21 170	3 976	38 524
3rd quarter	662 563	502 936	426 218	76 718	118 945	114 926	28 663	60 826	25 437	4 019	40 681
4th quarter	707 913	528 917	450 570	78 347	136 242	132 222	37 778	64 999	29 445	4 020	42 755
2006											
1st quarter	723 694	541 090	458 054	83 036	144 842	140 792	35 970	69 043	35 779	4 050	37 762
2nd quarter	753 264	552 494	467 891	84 603	160 543	156 416	39 989	74 466	41 961	4 127	40 227
3rd quarter	776 402	564 969	480 544	84 425	170 207	166 124	43 418	78 208	44 498	4 083	41 226
4th quarter	775 491	560 805	471 705	89 100	174 161	169 994	39 812	83 216	46 966	4 166	40 525
2007											
1st quarter	799 009	569 542	479 603	89 939	181 944	178 100	39 676	88 701	49 723	3 844	47 523
2nd quarter	819 439	583 556	491 220	92 336	193 043	189 030	39 632	95 364	54 034	4 013	42 841
3rd quarter	829 126	594 038	499 623	94 415	189 166	185 285	32 398	97 775	55 112	3 881	45 922
4th quarter	840 562	611 787	515 902	95 885	179 276	175 293	24 555	99 948	50 789	3 984	49 499
2008											
1st quarter	873 469	640 240	540 391	99 850	179 716	175 246	37 384	99 561	38 301	4 470	53 512
2nd quarter	893 477	665 513	563 433	102 081	176 911	172 703	41 284	101 116	30 303	4 208	51 052
3rd quarter	890 064	671 072	566 834	104 238	166 672	162 508	31 226	101 394	29 887	4 164	52 320
4th quarter	781 582	573 513	470 629	102 883	154 261	150 042	29 178	97 960	22 904	4 219	53 808
2009											
1st quarter	648 884	473 405	377 709	95 696	125 107	121 293	18 325	91 869	11 099	3 814	50 372
2nd quarter	637 138	460 946	366 041	94 905	122 693	119 035	28 377	81 812	8 846	3 658	53 499
3rd quarter	667 930	496 976	400 231	96 745	117 126	113 612	27 967	79 425	6 221	3 514	53 829
4th quarter	712 764	535 501	436 044	99 456	125 868	122 436	37 941	79 389	5 106	3 433	51 395
2010											
1st quarter	733 779	556 287	456 924	99 363	121 588	118 249	35 332	78 336	4 582	3 339	55 903
2nd quarter	759 541	581 125	480 442	100 683	124 968	121 474	38 291	77 907	5 276	3 494	53 447
3rd quarter	781 206	597 721	494 007	103 715	128 508	124 908	42 088	77 587	5 234	3 600	54 977
4th quarter	800 204	613 130	507 578	105 552	132 190	128 660	44 046	79 697	4 917	3 529	54 884
2011											
1st quarter	837 317	646 061	541 686	104 375	132 471	129 038	44 119	80 014	4 904	3 434	58 785
2nd quarter	866 570	669 398	559 978	109 421	138 272	134 753	48 817	80 778	5 158	3 519	58 900
3rd quarter	871 492	676 936	565 490	111 446	137 104	133 525	46 040	82 474	5 011	3 579	57 452
4th quarter	872 546	683 251	572 732	110 519	130 919	127 266	39 886	81 677	5 703	3 653	58 377
2012											
1st quarter	888 892	693 799	582 062	111 737	137 014	133 395	44 212	83 428	5 755	3 619	58 079
2nd quarter	887 090	692 071	579 060	113 011	136 399	132 580	41 737	85 441	5 402	3 819	58 620
3rd quarter	882 426	683 789	570 324	113 465	139 427	135 610	44 691	85 756	5 163	3 817	59 210
4th quarter	885 183	686 103	572 303	113 800	140 324	136 634	41 345	90 624	4 664	3 690	58 757
2013											
1st quarter	892 601	687 058	573 154	113 904	145 068	141 176	45 934	90 834	4 408	3 892	60 476
2nd quarter	892 899	686 853	572 239	114 614	144 187	140 174	45 722	90 365	4 087	4 013	61 859
3rd quarter	895 414	689 194	573 762	115 432	142 132	138 069	44 174	90 058	3 837	4 063	64 087
4th quarter	900 312	692 229	575 092	117 137	144 302	140 243	45 949	90 492	3 803	4 059	63 781
2014											
1st quarter	917 648	707 099	589 078	118 022	145 604	141 513	44 032	94 040	3 441	4 092	64 944
2nd quarter	937 626	721 746	601 537	120 209	149 862	145 614	48 622	93 372	3 619	4 248	66 018
3rd quarter	934 560	717 237	596 763	120 474	150 297	145 981	47 642	94 863	3 475	4 316	67 026
4th quarter	940 983	720 671	598 111	122 560	152 039	147 764	49 080	95 245	3 439	4 275	68 273
2015											
1st quarter	913 733	698 782	577 452	121 329	146 365	142 013	39 798	98 849	3 366	4 352	68 587
2nd quarter	917 315	696 411	574 812	121 599	154 288	149 835	45 754	100 471	3 611	4 453	66 616
3rd quarter	914 985	689 887	566 925	122 961	154 903	150 301	45 387	101 101	3 813	4 602	70 195
4th quarter	889 625	676 445	553 678	122 767	144 974	140 316	36 165	99 975	4 177	4 658	68 205
2016											
1st quarter	891 045	664 307	540 698	123 609	154 523	149 994	41 116	103 113	5 765	4 529	72 215
2nd quarter	899 899	671 396	547 229	124 167	158 459	153 837	45 651	101 973	6 213	4 621	70 044
3rd quarter	916 041	681 210	553 798	127 412	161 894	157 297	47 016	103 519	6 762	4 596	72 938
4th quarter	916 395	695 726	567 867	127 859	146 458	141 846	27 089	107 417	7 340	4 612	74 211

Table 7-6B. U.S. International Transactions: Historical Quarterly—*Continued*

(Millions of dollars, seasonally adjusted.)

Year and quarter	Capital account		Financial account							
			Net U.S. acquisition of financial assets excluding financial derivatives (net increase in assets/financial outflows+)							
				Direct investment assets			Portfolio investment assets			
	Capital transfer receipts and other credits	Capital transfer payments and other debits	Total net acquisition of assets	Total direct investment assets	Direct equity assets	Direct debt instruments assets	Total portfolio investment assets	Equity and investment fund shares assets	Short-term debt securities assets	Long-term debt securities assets
2002										
1st quarter	12	5	89 344	52 658	39 543	13 115	14 587	-1 999	5 575	11 011
2nd quarter	13	15	158 367	54 818	26 636	28 182	42 115	19 007	21 380	1 728
3rd quarter	13	82	4 431	38 488	33 304	5 184	-9 506	-12 825	-4 622	7 941
4th quarter	14	91	67 602	33 594	28 497	5 097	32 336	12 771	8 631	10 934
2003										
1st quarter	18	100	91 398	31 741	32 586	-845	11 012	33 519	-20 656	-1 852
2nd quarter	19	1 271	162 163	51 249	36 244	15 005	42 216	18 705	9 437	14 073
3rd quarter	21	513	9 494	49 338	36 829	12 509	13 261	38 797	-15 010	-10 527
4th quarter	22	16	109 958	64 829	50 511	14 318	66 571	26 981	13 318	26 272
2004										
1st quarter	14	71	371 068	94 373	70 219	24 154	44 589	16 883	9 204	18 502
2nd quarter	15	15	181 437	86 313	67 917	18 396	53 688	40 251	5 605	7 831
3rd quarter	3 707	535	185 655	68 192	48 773	19 420	46 656	17 914	-4 567	33 309
4th quarter	17	85	324 622	129 255	109 275	19 980	47 023	9 705	10 281	27 038
2005										
1st quarter	19	2 179	129 547	59 175	57 489	1 685	60 613	46 089	1 499	13 024
2nd quarter	20	103	238 470	57 621	45 043	12 578	61 965	30 023	4 713	27 229
3rd quarter	15 401	40	207 876	-8 649	-22 309	13 660	58 471	51 420	-4 842	11 893
4th quarter	22	25	-3 576	-46 222	-28 603	-17 619	86 242	59 152	17 453	9 637
2006										
1st quarter	0	1 220	425 750	96 862	72 181	24 681	100 461	42 452	24 403	33 606
2nd quarter	0	487	244 758	55 963	43 652	12 311	109 822	21 858	26 206	61 758
3rd quarter	0	2	298 490	75 251	71 246	4 006	145 027	9 052	67 335	68 640
4th quarter	0	79	367 869	67 983	79 233	-11 250	138 056	63 969	-2 203	76 289
2007										
1st quarter	0	0	548 472	162 170	120 837	41 333	97 818	51 222	-21 214	67 810
2nd quarter	494	51	577 929	103 145	102 037	1 108	173 884	34 154	61 495	78 235
3rd quarter	0	57	214 487	101 921	79 745	22 176	131 122	64 311	13 834	52 977
4th quarter	0	2	231 621	165 703	128 759	36 944	-22 018	-1 906	-38 924	18 812
2008										
1st quarter	0	8	251 987	105 855	89 761	16 094	26 446	18 023	9 007	-583
2nd quarter	0	18	-162 285	110 839	90 634	20 205	-6 532	12 510	-7 559	-11 484
3rd quarter	6 170	126	-95 456	84 700	92 874	-8 174	-139 775	-23 639	-24 284	-91 853
4th quarter	0	7	-303 714	50 330	86 861	-36 531	-164 407	-45 444	-59 809	-59 155
2009										
1st quarter	0	20	-120 969	77 013	50 774	26 240	71 200	-640	28 244	43 596
2nd quarter	0	29	-26 790	87 319	53 244	34 075	138 043	35 252	34 830	67 960
3rd quarter	0	36	315 013	92 331	76 769	15 562	144 273	26 223	77 021	41 028
4th quarter	0	56	-35 051	57 063	81 271	-24 208	22 368	2 861	-3 969	23 475
2010										
1st quarter	0	3	254 955	98 741	114 335	-15 595	78 773	11 291	31 918	35 564
2nd quarter	0	2	161 680	69 595	82 187	-12 592	-1 863	22 259	-16 057	-8 064
3rd quarter	0	146	305 667	103 639	88 347	15 292	49 064	16 899	9 994	22 171
4th quarter	0	7	241 147	82 600	58 170	24 430	73 645	28 701	36 424	8 519
2011										
1st quarter	0	29	389 189	130 051	91 591	38 460	115 962	27 881	27 876	60 205
2nd quarter	0	854	-334	142 096	121 388	20 708	69 344	6 401	17 964	44 979
3rd quarter	0	300	81 134	67 344	84 865	-17 521	-43 647	2 052	-79 058	33 360
4th quarter	0	3	26 331	100 915	103 689	-2 774	-56 295	-29 384	-18 037	-8 873
2012										
1st quarter	0	53	-77 076	110 706	80 453	30 253	2 218	17 906	-17 386	1 697
2nd quarter	0	241	-176 029	87 895	80 653	7 242	54 810	53 636	6 365	-5 191
3rd quarter	0	470	289 383	79 857	78 750	1 107	131 686	35 614	35 468	60 604
4th quarter	7 668	*	141 470	99 765	82 355	17 410	60 047	-3 182	-33 047	96 275
2013										
1st quarter	0	40	212 235	73 254	79 931	-6 677	152 224	70 800	18 153	63 271
2nd quarter	0	227	216 264	135 436	83 181	52 255	168 818	149 707	21 592	-2 480
3rd quarter	0	146	24 312	97 519	97 738	-219	14 954	-28 990	22 784	21 160
4th quarter	0	*	198 615	88 426	75 696	12 730	145 302	95 916	-13 768	63 154
2014										
1st quarter	0	43	153 627	54 287	49 304	4 983	102 090	86 491	-11 822	27 421
2nd quarter	0	2	229 606	69 849	85 003	-15 154	204 484	91 727	46 282	66 475
3rd quarter	0	1	330 098	101 811	92 152	9 659	128 515	109 483	-5 157	24 190
4th quarter	0	*	110 012	117 494	114 484	3 010	147 598	143 925	-17 915	21 588
2015										
1st quarter	0	22	357 562	86 576	81 311	5 265	233 068	197 183	27 562	8 323
2nd quarter	0	20	104 122	114 779	81 904	32 875	140 675	113 691	22 795	4 188
3rd quarter	0	1	-83 824	51 322	79 509	-28 186	-97 468	-54 115	12 690	-56 044
4th quarter	0	0	-152 461	95 969	73 622	22 347	-122 306	-54 186	-20 563	-47 558
2016										
1st quarter	0	58	59 062	66 612	76 840	-10 228	-57 326	-60 527	45 866	-42 666
2nd quarter	0	0	322 678	105 525	89 419	16 106	146 397	155 767	-24 286	14 916
3rd quarter	0	1	28 343	94 663	81 080	13 583	-35 268	-25 653	-45 992	36 378
4th quarter	0	0	-79 128	80 728	85 518	-4 790	-33 121	-94 422	3 807	57 494

* = Between zero and +/- $500,000 .

Table 7-6B. U.S. International Transactions: Historical Quarterly—*Continued*

(Millions of dollars, seasonally adjusted.)

Year and quarter	Financial account—*Continued*											
	Net U.S. acquisition of financial assets excluding financial derivatives (net increase in assets/financial outflows+)—*Continued*											
	Other investment assets				Reserve assets								
										Other reserve assets		
	Total other investment assets[1]	Currency and deposits assets	Loan assets	Trade credit and advances assets	Total reserve assets	Monetary gold	Special drawing rights assets	Reserve positions in the IMF	Total other reserve assets[2]	Currency and deposits reserve assets	Securities reserve assets
---	---	---	---	---	---	---	---	---	---	---	---
2002											
1st quarter	22 489	. . .	. . .	-1 488	-390	0	109	-652	153	. . .	. . .
2nd quarter	59 591	. . .	. . .	-1 562	1 843	0	107	1 607	129	. . .	. . .
3rd quarter	-25 967	. . .	. . .	-760	1 416	0	132	1 136	148	. . .	. . .
4th quarter	860	. . .	. . .	3 177	812	0	127	541	144	. . .	. . .
2003											
1st quarter	48 728	14 629	35 084	-986	-83	0	-897	644	170	80	66
2nd quarter	60 629	62 656	3 600	2 373	170	0	102	-86	154	79	52
3rd quarter	-53 715	-41 378	-11 305	-1 032	611	0	97	383	131	70	41
4th quarter	-19 221	15 394	-36 541	1 926	-2 221	0	97	-2 435	117	64	32
2004											
1st quarter	232 663	84 764	147 635	264	-557	0	100	-815	158	65	72
2nd quarter	42 558	41 318	519	721	-1 122	0	90	-1 345	133	59	54
3rd quarter	71 235	-365	74 283	-2 683	-429	0	98	-676	149	55	74
4th quarter	149 041	114 643	33 807	591	-697	0	110	-990	183	63	99
2005											
1st quarter	15 091	93 898	-78 615	-192	-5 331	0	-1 713	-3 763	145	60	64
2nd quarter	118 087	8 743	108 816	528	797	0	97	564	136	56	59
3rd quarter	162 818	31 213	133 148	-1 543	-4 765	0	-2 976	-1 951	162	55	87
4th quarter	-38 799	-50 974	9 681	2 493	-4 796	0	81	-5 050	174	54	100
2006											
1st quarter	228 939	151 125	75 714	2 099	-513	0	67	-729	149	60	66
2nd quarter	78 412	18 484	58 896	1 033	560	0	51	351	158	70	62
3rd quarter	79 218	-51 720	131 893	-955	-1 006	0	54	-1 275	215	83	101
4th quarter	163 245	36 137	125 751	1 357	-1 415	0	51	-1 678	212	96	79
2007											
1st quarter	288 412	127 453	160 213	746	72	0	43	-212	241	110	91
2nd quarter	300 926	105 985	189 735	5 205	-26	0	39	-294	229	125	60
3rd quarter	-18 611	5 831	-24 549	107	54	0	37	-230	247	135	64
4th quarter	87 914	135 876	-52 587	4 625	22	0	35	-285	272	147	73
2008											
1st quarter	119 409	-65 984	186 877	-1 484	276	0	29	-112	359	155	148
2nd quarter	-267 858	-74 301	-197 882	4 326	1 267	0	22	955	290	161	70
3rd quarter	-40 559	25 875	-64 059	-2 374	179	0	30	-256	405	167	165
4th quarter	-192 762	237 904	-426 485	-4 180	3 126	0	25	2 886	215	104	59
2009											
1st quarter	-270 164	-195 260	-77 750	2 846	982	0	15	754	213	45	142
2nd quarter	-255 783	-129 850	-122 709	-3 224	3 632	0	8	3 485	139	40	84
3rd quarter	29 388	-52 726	82 994	-881	49 021	0	47 720	1 098	203	34	164
4th quarter	-113 102	-16 625	-98 270	1 793	-1 379	0	487	-1 980	114	20	90
2010											
1st quarter	76 668	21 615	56 223	-1 171	773	0	7	581	185	14	168
2nd quarter	93 783	15 594	75 057	3 131	165	0	6	77	82	14	66
3rd quarter	151 867	58 505	93 881	-519	1 096	0	8	956	132	12	115
4th quarter	85 102	54 535	25 966	4 601	-200	0	10	-321	111	15	90
2011											
1st quarter	139 558	107 550	36 980	-4 972	3 619	0	-1 961	6 428	-848	17	-873
2nd quarter	-218 041	-208 168	-9 558	-315	6 267	0	159	5 974	134	28	93
3rd quarter	53 358	64 551	-19 675	8 482	4 079	0	27	3 909	143	33	99
4th quarter	-20 201	-53 094	32 073	819	1 912	0	23	1 768	121	32	82
2012											
1st quarter	-191 232	-194 802	6 273	-2 703	1 233	0	11	1 078	144	15	127
2nd quarter	-322 023	-329 146	5 527	1 596	3 289	0	10	3 179	100	5	94
3rd quarter	77 007	23 404	53 783	-180	833	0	10	744	79	2	77
4th quarter	-17 447	-21 377	1 955	1 976	-895	0	6	-969	68	2	67
2013											
1st quarter	-14 118	-57 886	44 343	-576	875	0	5	755	115	1	115
2nd quarter	-87 799	-17 678	-74 348	4 228	-191	0	6	-287	90	1	89
3rd quarter	-87 160	-52 371	-36 382	1 593	-1 001	0	5	-1 071	65	1	64
4th quarter	-32 331	976	-37 867	4 560	-2 782	0	6	-2 835	47	1	45
2014											
1st quarter	-1 794	-38 668	43 318	-6 445	-956	0	8	-1 040	76	2	72
2nd quarter	-45 500	-21 306	-26 969	2 774	773	0	8	710	55	2	51
3rd quarter	100 661	31 893	70 435	-1 667	-889	0	4	-951	59	1	58
4th quarter	-152 569	-132 353	-19 730	-486	-2 511	0	3	-2 568	54	1	53
2015											
1st quarter	42 077	-7 436	50 580	-1 066	-4 159	0	3	-4 195	33	*	33
2nd quarter	-150 455	-70 144	-79 588	-723	-877	0	2	-930	52	-4	56
3rd quarter	-37 412	-66 480	28 173	895	-266	0	2	-314	46	-7	53
4th quarter	-125 134	-50 368	-73 938	-828	-990	0	2	-1 046	54	-8	63
2016											
1st quarter	50 968	72 116	-24 242	3 094	-1 191	0	2	-1 214	21	-10	31
2nd quarter	70 566	-25 267	98 186	-2 353	189	0	*	175	14	-14	28
3rd quarter	-32 694	-88 661	53 959	2 008	1 642	0	2	1 654	-14	-18	4
4th quarter	-128 184	-58 861	-67 360	-1 963	1 450	0	680	732	37	-14	51

[1]Includes insurance technical reserves, not shown separately.
[2]Includes financial derivatives and other claims, not shown seperately.
. . . = Not available.

Table 7-6B. U.S. International Transactions: Historical Quarterly—*Continued*

(Millions of dollars, seasonally adjusted.)

Year and quarter	Financial account—*Continued*												
	Net U.S. incurrence of liabilities excluding financial derivatives (net increase in liabilities/financial inflows+)												
	Total net incurrence of liabilities	Direct investment liabilities			Portfolio investment liabilities				Other investment liabilities				Special drawing rights allocations
		Total direct investment liabilities	Direct equity liabilities	Direct debt instruments liabilities	Total portfolio liabilities	Equity and investment fund shares liabilities	Short-term debt securities liabilities	Long-term debt securities liabilities	Total other investment liabilities[1]	Currency and deposits liabilities	Loan liabilities	Trade credit and advances liabilities	
2002													
1st quarter	177 728	28 988	18 625	10 363	105 962	23 561	15 154	67 247	42 778	. . .	. . .	4 950	0
2nd quarter	249 980	25 849	30 662	-4 813	159 177	10 735	38 426	110 016	64 954	. . .	. . .	6 506	0
3rd quarter	165 658	19 252	28 773	-9 521	118 453	7 157	14 722	96 574	27 953	. . .	. . .	4 211	0
4th quarter	226 890	35 378	28 866	6 512	120 563	12 614	8 245	99 704	70 949	. . .	. . .	87	0
2003													
1st quarter	249 994	46 254	46 711	-457	98 883	-2 736	10 511	91 109	104 857	2 301	103 326	-769	0
2nd quarter	222 468	-723	-1 001	278	192 011	19 656	16 300	156 055	31 180	43 382	-10 319	-1 884	0
3rd quarter	137 917	7 167	16 487	-9 320	82 599	-4 760	-11 509	98 868	48 151	-42 634	91 901	-1 116	0
4th quarter	295 521	58 649	45 512	13 137	176 670	21 822	15 797	139 051	60 202	27 797	29 630	2 775	0
2004													
1st quarter	476 574	43 090	17 471	25 619	220 812	5 266	41 581	173 965	212 671	14 690	194 030	3 951	0
2nd quarter	342 567	43 594	41 148	2 446	223 468	8 562	5 802	209 104	75 505	17 638	58 631	-764	0
3rd quarter	290 343	50 308	34 518	15 789	162 890	982	24 547	137 362	77 145	35 721	41 605	-181	0
4th quarter	485 633	70 886	49 297	21 589	260 169	46 977	27 921	185 272	154 578	63 454	92 151	-1 027	0
2005													
1st quarter	234 558	39 247	36 487	2 760	185 008	19 272	-23 527	189 263	10 303	-74 180	81 122	3 361	0
2nd quarter	320 955	7 069	17 169	-10 100	160 648	12 282	-9 470	157 836	153 238	116 413	30 253	6 571	0
3rd quarter	428 918	41 530	18 534	22 997	215 051	31 743	-28 550	211 858	172 337	62 474	110 276	-412	0
4th quarter	288 608	50 481	40 269	10 212	271 331	25 961	16 238	229 132	-33 204	-229 490	194 173	2 112	0
2006													
1st quarter	583 709	82 419	48 634	33 784	246 292	64 241	-4 928	186 980	254 998	70 161	180 702	4 135	0
2nd quarter	428 454	86 414	46 414	39 999	264 826	23 008	34 501	207 318	77 215	42 382	30 675	4 157	0
3rd quarter	528 542	58 597	38 580	20 017	304 112	35 406	-10 951	279 656	165 833	-13 928	180 819	-1 058	0
4th quarter	575 599	66 859	50 515	16 345	311 505	22 826	4 134	284 545	197 234	125 771	73 025	-1 561	0
2007													
1st quarter	787 854	110 946	54 979	55 967	376 689	42 505	43 203	290 980	300 219	35 832	261 858	2 529	0
2nd quarter	732 101	79 920	53 374	26 546	393 364	104 760	-30 338	318 942	258 817	67 839	179 843	11 135	0
3rd quarter	294 397	110 805	68 654	42 151	73 339	20 534	60 335	-7 530	110 252	49 516	55 977	4 759	0
4th quarter	369 187	38 395	13 411	24 984	313 221	107 818	85 783	119 620	17 571	86 115	-70 697	2 153	0
2008													
1st quarter	469 902	102 201	71 215	30 986	234 853	69 376	55 597	109 881	132 848	-58 884	180 810	10 921	0
2nd quarter	-4 165	82 335	44 641	37 694	222 919	38 344	-1 713	186 288	-309 419	-82 602	-232 727	5 910	0
3rd quarter	90 107	80 728	72 147	8 581	25 970	11 297	75 421	-60 748	-16 590	16 253	-34 877	2 035	0
4th quarter	-101 793	67 471	106 858	-39 387	39 941	7 788	157 922	-125 769	-209 205	199 673	-396 759	-12 119	0
2009													
1st quarter	-114 662	1 786	7 758	-5 972	95 940	15 113	69 628	11 199	-212 388	-157 224	-53 540	-1 624	0
2nd quarter	-16 403	51 646	27 323	24 323	71 704	49 891	-30 798	52 612	-139 753	-109 843	-33 328	3 418	0
3rd quarter	341 399	60 730	41 250	19 480	72 049	85 700	-32 105	18 454	208 621	107 086	45 526	8 410	47 598
4th quarter	108 016	39 625	72 134	-32 509	117 659	68 599	-130 731	179 791	-49 268	85 756	-131 121	-3 903	0
2010													
1st quarter	315 593	40 376	30 030	10 346	187 308	65 165	-27 618	149 761	87 909	24 164	55 567	8 178	0
2nd quarter	184 104	34 099	31 115	2 984	131 528	34 570	5 822	91 136	18 477	22 112	-10 010	6 376	0
3rd quarter	553 513	102 800	76 185	26 615	328 881	40 716	24 538	263 628	121 832	37 366	84 797	-331	0
4th quarter	333 134	82 070	65 818	16 251	172 716	38 502	-55 774	189 988	78 348	32 036	41 903	4 409	0
2011													
1st quarter	592 847	69 714	38 586	31 128	149 211	38 993	-33 158	143 377	373 921	150 002	222 517	1 403	0
2nd quarter	125 789	74 432	56 468	17 964	105 650	34 442	-14 924	86 133	-54 293	78 386	-135 202	2 523	0
3rd quarter	245 696	57 328	47 078	10 250	77 147	18 955	-23 362	81 554	111 221	222 985	-124 494	12 730	0
4th quarter	12 742	55 937	42 919	13 019	-20 383	30 967	-15 277	-36 072	-22 813	24 306	-47 609	490	0
2012													
1st quarter	188 045	46 209	35 421	10 788	249 786	64 095	-11 110	196 802	-107 951	-126 802	14 939	3 913	0
2nd quarter	-127 089	90 100	65 608	24 493	7 887	30 709	-12 226	-10 595	-225 076	-180 248	-46 983	2 154	0
3rd quarter	293 673	40 539	33 645	6 893	222 636	30 869	49 629	142 138	30 498	79 901	-55 911	6 508	0
4th quarter	270 723	66 161	69 411	-3 250	266 708	113 393	-9 962	163 277	-62 146	-18 852	-42 353	-942	0
2013													
1st quarter	252 808	32 891	32 041	850	150 986	-19 840	69 256	101 570	68 931	895	64 630	3 406	0
2nd quarter	245 645	96 409	60 765	35 644	-8 446	-30 609	-32 556	54 719	157 682	104 763	47 877	5 042	0
3rd quarter	171 639	76 142	56 008	20 133	200 041	70 037	-53 025	183 029	-104 544	-28 781	-77 656	1 893	0
4th quarter	374 543	71 536	51 802	19 734	169 406	-82 230	62 000	189 636	133 601	125 960	6 482	1 158	0
2014													
1st quarter	289 054	-86 791	-90 207	3 416	248 214	104 032	12 986	131 196	127 631	-5 550	120 319	12 862	0
2nd quarter	293 401	69 348	65 278	4 070	99 475	15 451	-24 942	108 967	124 578	110 727	8 935	4 916	0
3rd quarter	371 787	118 119	56 580	61 539	230 476	71 219	-8 171	167 428	23 192	39 967	-12 170	-4 605	0
4th quarter	102 132	106 691	80 348	26 343	123 696	-36 390	42 456	117 630	-128 255	-85 565	-43 503	813	0
2015													
1st quarter	348 004	194 067	160 334	33 733	102 922	31 104	37 005	34 814	51 015	559	46 254	4 202	0
2nd quarter	205 435	108 005	59 370	48 635	256 154	-22 605	-5 818	284 577	-158 723	-1 720	-162 179	5 175	0
3rd quarter	-39 884	50 590	40 520	10 069	-126 250	-33 301	-51 361	-41 588	35 775	10 946	19 479	5 351	0
4th quarter	-118 322	26 773	40 884	-14 111	18 109	-153 464	65 957	105 616	-163 204	23 621	-186 267	-559	0
2016													
1st quarter	119 117	92 245	90 547	1 698	-21 197	-95 660	-10 464	84 927	48 069	-40 969	84 376	4 662	0
2nd quarter	368 588	175 271	123 070	52 201	11 934	-48 482	-27 272	87 688	181 383	96 940	79 639	4 805	0
3rd quarter	259 245	124 741	89 755	34 986	218 594	121 599	30 237	66 758	-84 090	-42 389	-39 784	-1 917	0
4th quarter	12 420	33 000	37 380	-4 381	61 593	-107 641	-5 330	174 564	-82 173	11 330	-95 541	2 038	0

[1]Includes financial derivatives and other claims, not shown seperately.
. . . = Not available.

Table 7-6B. U.S. International Transactions: Historical Quarterly—*Continued*

(Millions of dollars, seasonally adjusted.)

Year and quarter	Financial account—Continued: Financial derivatives other than reserves, net	Statistical discrepancy: Total	Seasonal adjustment discrepancy	Balances: Current account: Total balance on current account	Balances on goods and services: Total balance on goods and services	Balance on goods	Balance on services	Balance on primary income	Balance on secondary income	Balance on capital account	Net lending (+) or net borrowing (-): Based on current and capital account transactions	Based on financial account transactions
2002												
1st quarter	. . .	15 601	10 097	-103 992	-92 466	-106 126	13 661	6 953	-18 479	7	-103 985	-88 384
2nd quarter	. . .	23 402	-2 395	-115 013	-102 488	-117 537	15 049	2 305	-14 831	-2	-115 015	-91 613
3rd quarter	. . .	-46 289	-14 507	-114 869	-105 913	-121 004	15 091	5 842	-14 797	-69	-114 938	-161 227
4th quarter	. . .	-35 002	6 804	-124 209	-118 090	-130 578	12 488	10 081	-16 200	-77	-124 286	-159 288
2003												
1st quarter	. . .	-23 528	8 593	-134 986	-123 459	-135 220	11 762	6 569	-18 097	-82	-135 068	-158 597
2nd quarter	. . .	70 216	-1 101	-129 269	-122 384	-134 670	12 285	9 928	-16 813	-1 252	-130 521	-60 305
3rd quarter	. . .	2 440	13 166	-130 374	-122 872	-134 164	11 292	9 855	-17 358	-492	-130 866	-128 423
4th quarter	. . .	-58 849	5 678	-126 719	-125 175	-137 590	12 414	16 401	-17 945	5	+120 714	105 563
2004												
1st quarter	. . .	32 137	7 506	-137 586	-135 158	-149 437	14 279	20 980	-23 408	-56	-137 642	-105 505
2nd quarter	. . .	-4 314	-1 661	-156 815	-150 348	-163 682	13 334	14 699	-21 166	*	-156 815	-161 130
3rd quarter	. . .	51 683	-17 132	-159 544	-156 097	-168 934	12 837	17 413	-20 860	3 173	-156 371	-104 688
4th quarter	. . .	18 882	11 289	-179 825	-168 281	-182 712	14 431	11 034	-22 578	-68	-179 893	-161 011
2005												
1st quarter	. . .	66 956	12 116	-169 807	-165 634	-183 577	17 943	19 458	-23 632	-2 160	-171 967	-105 011
2nd quarter	. . .	97 078	-711	-179 480	-171 639	-187 907	16 268	16 666	-24 507	-83	-179 563	-82 485
3rd quarter	. . .	-50 077	-22 777	-186 327	-181 376	-197 802	16 427	19 355	-24 306	15 362	-170 965	-221 042
4th quarter	. . .	-82 361	11 372	-209 820	-195 596	-213 518	17 922	12 153	-26 376	-3	-209 822	-292 184
2006												
1st quarter	-1 633	39 686	9 207	-198 058	-192 106	-208 382	16 276	12 810	-18 763	-1 220	-199 278	-159 592
2nd quarter	-14 090	5 072	-2 993	-202 372	-191 169	-209 719	18 550	11 565	-22 768	-487	-202 859	-197 787
3rd quarter	-15 134	-29 121	-19 887	-216 063	-199 284	-218 180	18 896	8 197	-24 976	-2	-216 065	-245 186
4th quarter	1 147	-16 271	13 673	-190 233	-179 157	-201 009	21 851	10 765	-21 840	-79	-190 312	-206 583
2007												
1st quarter	-14 795	-55 083	10 249	-199 093	-177 931	-202 800	24 868	11 013	-32 175	0	-199 093	-254 176
2nd quarter	1 007	35 509	-1 542	-189 117	-179 322	-205 300	25 978	16 384	-26 179	443	-188 674	-153 165
3rd quarter	-5 942	85 159	-24 306	-170 954	-174 713	-203 972	29 259	30 833	-27 074	-57	-171 011	-85 852
4th quarter	13 508	35 425	15 601	-159 481	-173 409	-209 124	35 716	42 374	-28 447	-2	-159 483	-124 058
2008												
1st quarter	7 966	-28 312	7 721	-181 630	-185 551	-216 677	31 126	38 670	-34 749	-8	-183 095	-209 950
2nd quarter	2 355	21 466	-5 107	-177 213	-186 349	-220 469	34 120	39 734	-30 598	-18	-178 261	-155 765
3rd quarter	4 886	-10 387	-30 220	-176 334	-189 449	-219 624	30 175	44 041	-30 926	6 043	-170 869	-180 677
4th quarter	17 740	-32 708	27 607	-151 465	-147 376	-175 722	28 346	23 701	-27 790	-7	-152 555	-184 180
2009												
1st quarter	-7 146	83 349	10 808	-96 782	-94 771	-123 499	28 728	25 319	-27 330	-20	-98 252	-13 453
2nd quarter	-7 561	70 120	-7 354	-88 040	-81 444	-111 984	30 540	24 366	-30 962	-29	-89 060	-17 948
3rd quarter	-10 645	56 382	-23 012	-93 378	-98 547	-129 950	31 403	37 922	-32 753	-36	-94 167	-37 032
4th quarter	-19 464	-59 880	19 560	-102 595	-109 012	-144 262	35 250	35 977	-29 560	-56	-102 686	-162 530
2010												
1st quarter	-16 152	32 185	12 928	-108 972	-117 954	-152 461	34 507	43 785	-34 803	-3	-108 215	-76 790
2nd quarter	-9 980	82 148	-11 474	-114 550	-128 754	-165 200	36 446	44 232	-30 028	-2	-114 038	-32 404
3rd quarter	11 893	-117 432	-21 882	-118 375	-129 376	-168 786	39 411	42 828	-31 828	-146	-117 990	-235 953
4th quarter	163	10 216	20 429	-102 033	-118 575	-162 230	43 656	46 816	-30 275	-7	-101 876	-91 825
2011												
1st quarter	-2 952	-88 341	14 289	-118 240	-134 319	-181 536	47 217	50 302	-34 223	-29	-118 268	-206 609
2nd quarter	-9 806	-14 044	-13 659	-121 031	-138 879	-186 717	47 838	51 219	-33 371	-854	-121 885	-135 929
3rd quarter	1 617	-54 236	-28 322	-108 409	-133 962	-183 307	49 345	57 613	-32 060	-300	-108 709	-162 945
4th quarter	-23 865	102 402	27 693	-112 675	-141 466	-189 086	47 620	61 827	-33 036	-3	-112 678	-10 276
2012												
1st quarter	7 339	-137 435	12 187	-120 294	-144 771	-193 976	49 205	57 962	-33 485	-53	-120 346	-257 781
2nd quarter	-2 419	65 689	-15 932	-116 808	-136 685	-187 183	50 498	52 765	-32 888	-241	-117 049	-51 360
3rd quarter	5 129	106 732	-30 129	-105 423	-127 540	-177 957	50 416	52 954	-30 836	-470	-105 893	839
4th quarter	-2 985	-35 903	33 875	-104 003	-127 777	-182 055	54 278	52 112	-28 338	7 668	-96 335	-132 238
2013												
1st quarter	-3 948	54 499	13 228	-98 980	-119 610	-178 437	58 827	50 239	-29 609	-40	-99 020	-44 521
2nd quarter	-3 302	62 377	-13 771	-94 833	-117 731	-177 126	59 394	54 783	-31 885	-227	-95 060	-32 683
3rd quarter	6 569	-47 888	-27 448	-92 725	-117 070	-177 570	60 500	56 761	-32 416	-146	-92 870	-140 758
4th quarter	2 903	-93 141	27 991	-79 883	-107 466	-169 112	61 647	57 187	-29 605	*	-79 883	-173 025
2014												
1st quarter	6 105	-34 625	14 505	-94 654	-120 514	-185 712	65 199	56 746	-30 887	-43	-94 697	-129 322
2nd quarter	-4 423	25 843	-8 978	-94 060	-125 834	-191 836	66 002	54 623	-22 849	-2	-94 062	-68 218
3rd quarter	-24 304	29 627	-28 654	-95 619	-119 415	-184 677	65 262	59 325	-35 529	-1	-95 620	-65 993
4th quarter	-31 725	83 881	23 127	-107 726	-124 414	-189 944	65 531	53 310	-36 623	*	-107 726	-23 845
2015												
1st quarter	-40 199	83 929	16 120	-114 549	-126 514	-193 517	67 003	48 351	-36 386	-22	-114 571	-30 642
2nd quarter	1 708	12 318	-9 621	-111 904	-124 028	-190 876	66 848	45 071	-32 947	-20	-111 924	-99 605
3rd quarter	746	79 913	-24 223	-123 106	-125 611	-189 768	64 157	41 848	-39 343	-1	-123 106	-43 194
4th quarter	12 353	91 620	17 725	-113 406	-124 209	-188 404	64 195	47 115	-36 312	0	-113 406	-21 786
2016												
1st quarter	12 994	86 069	15 240	-133 072	-126 204	-187 343	61 139	33 759	-40 627	-58	-133 130	-47 061
2nd quarter	2 904	76 739	-10 305	-119 745	-125 806	-187 789	61 983	43 791	-37 730	0	-119 745	-43 006
3rd quarter	6 500	-108 394	-29 312	-116 007	-116 230	-178 652	62 422	41 585	-41 361	-1	-116 008	-224 402
4th quarter	-447	20 387	24 377	-112 382	-132 320	-196 142	63 822	61 457	-41 519	0	-112 382	-91 995

. . . = Not available.
* = Less than $500,000 (+/-).

Table 7-7. Foreigners' Transactions in Long-Term Securities with U.S. Residents

(Billions of dollars, not seasonally adjusted.)

Year and month	Gross purchases from U.S. residents	Gross sales to U.S. residents	Transactions in U.S. domestic securities between foreigners and U.S. residents							
			Net purchases							
			Total	Private					Official	
				Total	Treasury bonds and notes	Government agency bonds	Corporate bonds	Equities	Total	Treasury bonds and notes
1980	106.9	91.1	15.8	6.6	1.0	0.4	0.9	4.3	9.2	3.9
1981	126.5	100.5	26.0	10.2	3.3	0.3	1.9	4.8	15.6	11.7
1982	159.5	136.8	22.7	9.2	2.8	0.3	2.5	3.6	13.5	14.6
1983	223.4	211.7	11.7	13.2	4.6	0.5	1.7	6.4	-1.5	0.8
1984	335.5	304.0	31.5	33.8	21.0	1.2	12.5	-0.9	-2.4	0.5
1985	667.2	588.9	78.3	71.9	21.1	4.6	41.4	4.8	6.3	8.1
1986	1 355.4	1 266.9	88.5	76.4	5.2	8.2	45.1	18.0	12.1	14.2
1987	1 692.1	1 623.0	69.1	37.5	-5.5	3.5	22.7	16.8	31.7	31.1
1988	1 827.9	1 753.1	74.8	49.4	22.2	5.4	21.3	0.4	25.4	26.6
1989	2 431.7	2 335.2	96.5	66.5	27.4	13.7	17.5	7.9	30.0	26.8
1990	2 111.2	2 092.4	18.8	-3.6	-5.3	5.6	9.8	-13.7	22.5	23.3
1991	2 382.1	2 324.0	58.1	54.3	18.7	8.9	16.5	10.1	3.8	1.2
1992	2 677.8	2 604.6	73.2	63.1	32.4	14.3	20.0	-3.7	10.1	6.9
1993	3 212.5	3 101.4	111.1	103.2	22.2	31.4	29.9	19.6	7.9	1.3
1994	3 351.1	3 210.7	140.4	94.9	37.0	15.6	38.0	4.3	45.4	41.8
1995	3 737.6	3 505.7	231.9	185.3	94.5	25.0	57.6	8.2	46.5	39.6
1996	4 667.6	4 297.4	370.2	278.1	146.4	36.7	82.2	12.7	92.1	85.8
1997	6 573.3	6 185.3	388.0	339.7	140.2	45.3	82.8	71.3	48.3	44.0
1998	7 633.5	7 355.7	277.8	270.8	44.9	50.5	121.7	53.7	6.9	4.1
1999	7 483.5	7 133.3	350.2	338.8	-0.1	71.9	158.8	108.2	11.4	-9.9
2000	8 684.1	8 226.3	457.8	420.1	-47.7	111.9	182.1	173.8	37.7	-6.3
2001	10 261.8	9 740.9	520.8	494.2	15.0	146.6	218.2	114.4	26.7	3.5
2002	13 022.9	12 475.4	547.6	508.3	112.8	166.6	176.7	52.2	39.3	7.1
2003	13 526.0	12 806.1	719.9	585.0	159.7	129.9	260.3	35.0	134.9	103.8
2004	15 178.9	14 262.4	916.5	680.9	150.9	205.7	298.0	26.2	235.6	201.1
2005	17 157.5	16 145.9	1 011.6	891.1	269.4	187.6	353.1	81.0	120.4	68.7
2006	21 077.1	19 933.9	1 143.2	946.6	125.9	193.8	482.2	144.6	196.6	69.6
2007	29 730.6	28 724.8	1 005.8	818.1	195.0	99.9	342.8	180.4	187.8	3.0
2008	30 724.9	30 310.0	414.9	311.9	238.7	-7.4	59.2	21.4	103.0	76.2
2009	20 479.7	19 840.9	638.9	511.0	377.0	31.4	-38.4	141.1	127.9	161.4
2010	25 017.0	24 108.7	908.3	776.1	531.6	146.2	-14.0	112.3	132.2	172.1
2011	27 818.8	27 325.5	493.4	322.6	288.4	57.6	-44.0	20.6	170.7	144.2
2012	24 593.4	23 959.2	634.1	408.2	206.6	134.2	-31.0	98.4	225.9	209.9
2013	27 769.9	27 690.5	79.4	0.7	49.3	-3.7	-5.8	-39.1	78.8	-8.4
2014	27 867.8	27 618.5	249.3	171.0	120.6	43.2	18.4	-11.2	78.3	44.9
2015	29 904.8	29 749.2	155.6	368.0	205.6	123.2	137.9	-98.7	-212.4	-225.9
2016	29 603.8	29 552.5	513.3	340.3	392.1	225.3	130.1	-190.8	-289.0	-329.8
2014										
January	2 350.9	2 369.3	-18.4	-1.9	12.1	-3.8	-4.9	-5.3	-16.5	-16.7
February	2 226.7	2 137.7	89.0	70.5	73.9	-0.9	-1.5	-0.8	18.5	16.6
March	2 541.4	2 529.1	12.4	6.0	17.8	-7.2	5.5	-10.1	6.4	12.1
April	2 444.9	2 454.9	-10.0	-28.0	-29.4	-2.4	-8.2	12.0	18.0	18.8
May	2 299.9	2 263.3	36.6	12.2	8.3	2.8	-9.0	10.0	24.4	19.7
June	2 237.7	2 256.1	-18.4	-44.6	-40.8	-1.6	-3.3	1.1	26.3	20.0
July	1 972.3	1 976.3	-3.9	1.9	5.2	7.2	-8.5	-2.0	-5.8	-6.0
August	2 062.7	2 036.2	26.5	20.7	22.1	11.3	-8.6	-4.2	5.9	3.6
September	2 399.1	2 304.8	94.2	79.7	44.2	11.7	19.4	4.4	14.6	3.9
October	2 807.9	2 822.8	-15.0	-15.4	3.1	2.2	6.3	-27.1	0.5	-2.5
November	2 076.1	2 016.9	59.2	53.0	2.7	18.7	25.5	6.0	6.2	-7.5
December	2 448.2	2 451.2	-3.0	17.0	1.4	5.3	5.6	4.6	-19.9	-17.0
2015										
January	2 392.6	2 416.2	-23.6	-11.6	-42.6	6.2	6.6	18.2	-12.0	-12.4
February	2 527.7	2 514.7	13.0	23.2	5.0	8.0	10.1	0.1	-10.2	-11.2
March	2 753.0	2 743.0	10.0	27.8	31.7	13.3	9.2	-26.4	-17.8	-23.7
April	2 267.4	2 222.0	45.4	62.6	26.5	23.8	4.7	7.6	-17.1	-20.1
May	2 420.8	2 338.8	82.0	78.3	58.0	10.0	20.7	-10.4	3.7	-4.6
June	2 724.7	2 635.4	89.3	94.7	82.9	18.0	16.0	-22.2	-5.4	-10.9
July	2 706.3	2 699.2	7.1	24.5	-8.4	7.8	18.5	6.6	-17.5	-20.3
August	2 611.6	2 639.7	-28.1	13.5	6.2	11.5	9.6	-13.9	-41.5	-41.1
September	2 522.8	2 517.3	5.4	30.8	34.6	4.4	18.3	-26.5	-25.3	-17.2
October	2 419.3	2 465.1	-45.8	-28.2	-38.0	9.4	12.8	-12.3	-17.6	-17.1
November	2 370.5	2 326.3	44.3	44.4	37.5	10.2	6.9	-10.1	-0.2	0.9
December	2 188.1	2 231.5	-43.4	8.0	12.2	0.7	4.5	-9.5	-51.3	-48.1
2016										
January	2 316.0	2 350.5	-34.5	21 808.0	67.8	45.8	46.2	5.8	-5.6	-57.2
February	2 741.7	2 714.8	26.9	67 066.0	57.6	12.2	12.7	-15.4	-4.0	-47.2
March	2 539.2	2 473.9	65.3	83 533.0	42.8	28.4	26.0	-13.6	-1.8	-16.3
April	2 211.7	2 257.5	-45.8	-37 543.0	-62.8	25.1	2.3	-2.1	-8.2	-11.1
May	2 497.9	2 481.6	163.4	37 240.0	33.3	26.3	18.9	-1.1	-2.1	-23.2
June	2 538.3	2 539.9	-16.4	27 240.0	69.2	21.8	7.6	-9.1	-2.9	-33.7
July	2 272.4	2 208.7	63.7	81 595.0	15.4	26.9	17.4	2.2	-1.8	-28.2
August	2 551.1	2 528.4	22.8	62 581.0	19.3	22.5	18.5	2.3	-4.0	-42.1
September	2 413.0	2 465.6	-52.7	-13 816.0	-32.1	19.2	1.8	-2.7	-3.9	-42.2
October	2 385.7	2 397.8	-12.2	26 644.0	-13.3	14.2	6.2	2.0	-38.8	-46.4
November	2 798.4	2 780.0	18.4	17 305.0	12.1	12.7	8.3	-4.9	1.1	-0.9
December	2 338.5	2 353.8	-15.3	-33 363.0	-41.1	11.5	5.7	-9.5	18.1	18.6

Table 7-7. Foreigners' Transactions in Long-Term Securities with U.S. Residents—*Continued*

(Billions of dollars, not seasonally adjusted.)

Year and month	Transactions in U.S. domestic securities between foreigners and U.S. residents—Continued			Transactions in foreign securities between foreigners and U.S. residents					Net long-term securities transactions	Other acquisitions of long-term securities, net	Net foreign acquisition of long-term securities
	Net purchases—Continued			Gross purchases from U.S. residents	Gross sales to U.S. residents	Net purchases [1]					
	Official—Continued										
	Government agency bonds	Corporate bonds	Equities			Total	Bonds	Equities			
1980	2.2	2.0	1.1	25.0	28.1	-3.1	-1.0	-2.1	12.7	-1.6	11.0
1981	1.3	1.6	1.0	26.9	32.6	-5.7	-5.5	-0.2	20.3	-5.2	15.0
1982	-0.7	-0.7	0.3	34.3	42.3	-8.0	-6.6	-1.3	14.7	-5.4	9.3
1983	-0.5	-0.8	-1.0	49.6	56.6	-7.0	-3.2	-3.8	4.7	-3.2	1.5
1984	0.0	-0.8	-2.1	70.8	75.9	-5.1	-3.9	-1.1	26.4	-1.5	24.9
1985	-0.3	-1.6	0.1	102.1	110.0	-7.9	-4.0	-3.9	70.4	-2.3	68.1
1986	-1.2	-1.6	0.7	216.1	221.7	-5.6	-3.7	-1.9	82.9	-2.3	80.8
1987	1.6	-0.4	-0.0	294.5	301.4	-6.9	-8.0	1.1	62.2	-1.0	61.3
1988	1.3	-0.1	-2.4	293.9	303.3	-9.4	-7.4	-2.0	65.4	0.2	65.6
1989	1.4	-0.2	2.0	344.6	363.2	-18.6	-5.5	-13.1	77.9	0.0	78.0
1990	0.7	-0.1	-1.4	437.7	468.9	-31.2	-21.9	-9.2	-12.4	3.9	-8.5
1991	1.3	0.4	0.9	450.9	497.7	-46.8	-14.8	-32.0	11.3	0.4	11.7
1992	3.9	0.8	-1.5	663.6	711.5	-47.9	-15.6	-32.3	25.3	-0.3	25.0
1993	4.0	0.6	2.0	991.4	1 134.5	-143.1	-80.4	-62.7	-32.0	1.1	-30.8
1994	6.1	0.0	-2.5	1 234.5	1 291.8	-57.3	-9.2	-48.1	83.1	0.5	83.5
1995	3.7	0.2	3.0	1 235.1	1 333.8	-98.7	-48.4	-50.3	133.2	0.4	133.6
1996	5.0	1.5	-0.2	1 564.4	1 675.0	-110.6	-51.4	-59.3	259.6	-0.5	259.1
1997	4.5	1.5	-1.7	2 207.7	2 296.8	-89.1	-48.1	-40.9	298.9	0.0	298.9
1998	6.3	0.2	-3.7	2 257.8	2 269.0	-11.2	-17.3	6.2	266.6	0.1	266.7
1999	20.4	1.5	-0.6	1 975.6	1 965.6	10.0	-5.7	15.6	360.2	0.0	360.2
2000	40.9	2.0	1.1	2 761.1	2 778.3	-17.1	-4.1	-13.1	440.7	-59.8	380.8
2001	17.4	3.8	2.0	2 557.8	2 577.4	-19.6	30.5	-50.1	501.2	-41.5	459.8
2002	28.6	5.6	-2.0	2 640.0	2 613.0	27.0	28.5	-1.5	574.6	-39.3	535.2
2003	25.9	5.4	-0.3	2 761.8	2 818.4	-56.5	32.0	-88.6	663.3	-138.9	524.5
2004	20.8	11.5	2.2	3 123.1	3 276.0	-152.8	-67.9	-85.0	763.6	-38.8	724.8
2005	31.6	19.1	1.0	3 700.0	3 872.4	-172.4	-45.1	-127.3	839.2	-143.0	696.2
2006	92.6	28.6	5.8	5 515.9	5 766.8	-250.9	-144.5	-106.5	892.3	-174.6	717.7
2007	119.1	50.6	15.1	8 189.1	8 418.3	-229.2	-133.9	-95.3	776.6	-235.2	541.4
2008	-31.3	34.7	23.4	7 714.9	7 640.7	74.2	53.9	20.2	489.1	-197.9	291.2
2009	-42.9	-2.3	11.7	5 121.4	5 308.3	-186.8	-127.5	-59.4	452.0	-205.1	246.9
2010	-38.2	0.8	-2.5	7 323.8	7 439.1	-115.3	-54.6	-60.6	793.0	-234.7	558.3
2011	23.3	-1.2	4.5	7 499.3	7 623.6	-124.3	-52.6	-71.7	369.0	-174.2	194.8
2012	-1.3	7.0	10.3	7 385.4	7 406.7	-21.2	19.9	-41.1	612.9	-244.0	369.0
2013	75.2	16.2	-4.1	8 157.1	8 378.1	-221.0	-46.8	-174.2	-141.5	-230.6	-372.2
2014	31.4	7.0	-4.9	9 145.0	9 119.0	25.9	131.7	-105.7	275.3	-84.0	191.2
2015	33.5	-3.8	-16.2	10 726.6	10 564.9	161.7	276.1	-114.4	317.3	-285.4	31.9
2016	40.7	-5.3	54.3	10 105.4	9 918.0	187.5	258.7	-712.7	238.8	-273.1	-34.3
2014											
January	0.5	0.0	-0.4	774.0	751.8	22.2	33.5	-11.4	3.7	-9.7	-6.0
February	2.5	-0.5	0.0	691.2	691.9	-0.7	0.8	-1.5	88.3	-10.4	77.9
March	-1.4	1.0	-5.2	813.9	870.0	-56.1	1.4	-57.5	-43.7	53.2	9.5
April	0.3	-0.3	-0.9	778.9	807.1	-28.2	-0.2	-28.0	-38.2	-9.9	-48.2
May	3.7	1.2	-0.2	778.0	795.2	-17.2	-1.0	-16.2	19.4	-10.5	8.9
June	5.0	-0.3	1.5	809.8	810.8	-1.1	-13.9	12.8	-19.4	-11.1	-30.5
July	0.3	1.4	-1.5	703.1	717.8	-14.7	-6.1	-8.6	-18.6	-29.5	-48.1
August	-1.0	1.3	2.0	652.7	627.2	25.5	8.1	17.5	52.1	-17.2	34.9
September	9.3	1.3	0.0	853.0	786.9	66.1	40.1	26.0	160.4	-11.2	149.1
October	1.6	1.6	-0.2	856.9	843.3	13.6	27.6	-14.0	-1.4	-13.1	-14.5
November	14.6	-0.5	-0.3	680.1	705.8	-25.7	3.6	-29.3	33.5	-12.4	21.2
December	-4.0	0.9	0.3	753.3	711.1	42.2	37.9	4.3	39.2	-2.2	37.0
2015											
January	2.9	-0.9	-1.7	840.4	827.8	12.7	25.9	-13.2	-10.9	-87.2	-98.1
February	0.9	-0.8	0.8	793.4	786.6	6.7	14.1	-7.3	19.7	-14.2	5.5
March	4.2	2.3	-0.6	965.0	970.1	-5.1	7.2	-12.4	4.9	-50.0	-45.1
April	6.5	-0.4	-3.1	972.2	959.5	12.6	33.4	-20.7	58.1	-17.9	40.1
May	4.9	2.8	0.5	948.0	934.4	13.7	24.9	-11.3	95.6	-15.8	79.8
June	7.6	-2.2	0.0	1 032.6	1 016.6	16.0	29.4	-13.4	105.3	-16.3	89.0
July	2.6	0.6	-0.2	1 015.9	1 012.5	3.4	20.4	-17.1	10.4	-15.6	-5.2
August	-1.8	-0.1	1.5	824.0	782.1	41.9	42.0	-0.1	13.8	-14.0	-0.1
September	0.2	-2.7	-5.6	846.9	822.7	24.2	34.8	-10.6	29.6	-14.9	14.8
October	0.7	-0.7	-0.5	938.9	907.6	31.3	36.1	-4.8	-14.5	-12.9	-27.4
November	3.7	-1.8	-2.9	803.2	812.9	-9.6	-11.3	1.7	34.6	-14.4	20.3
December	1.0	0.1	-4.3	746.2	732.2	14.0	19.1	-5.1	-29.4	-12.2	-41.6
2016											
January	1.8	0.4	-1.2	755.7	734.7	21.0	27.7	-6.7	-13.5	-34.4	-47.9
February	6.3	-0.5	1.2	798.3	756.1	42.2	43.9	-1.7	69.1	-10.9	58.2
March	1.1	-0.5	-2.6	922.1	909.2	12.8	23.1	-10.3	78.1	-13.3	64.8
April	3.2	-1.6	1.3	898.7	912.4	-13.7	3.8	-17.5	-59.5	-24.0	-83.5
May	0.5	0.6	1.1	793.7	764.2	29.4	27.2	2.2	45.8	-23.5	22.2
June	3.1	0.5	1.2	813.1	821.1	-8.0	1.7	-9.7	-9.6	-37.7	-47.3
July	6.5	-1.1	4.8	817.8	786.3	31.4	32.1	-0.7	95.1	-16.5	78.6
August	1.5	1.2	-0.5	788.2	770.4	17.8	20.1	-2.2	40.6	-18.7	21.9
September	4.7	-1.0	-0.4	901.7	881.2	20.4	22.4	-1.9	-32.2	-36.5	-68.7
October	7.8	-1.1	0.9	856.6	841.2	15.4	20.6	-5.2	3.3	-22.4	-19.2
November	3.0	-1.1	0.1	928.3	910.8	17.5	17.0	0.4	35.8	-18.7	17.2
December	1.1	-1.1	-0.5	831.4	830.2	1.1	19.3	-18.2	-14.1	-16.6	-30.7

[1] (-) indicates net U.S. acquisitions of foreign securities.

Table 7-8. International Investment Position of the United States

(End of period, millions of dollars.)

Year	U.S. net international investment position			U.S. assets							
						By functional category					
	Total	Total, excluding financial derivatives	Financial derivatives other than reserves, net	Total assets	Assets excluding financial derivatives	Direct investment at market value	Portfolio investment			Gross positive fair value, financial derivatives other than reserves	Other investment
							Total[1]	Equity and investment fund shares	Long-term debt securities		
1980	296 862	296 862	. . .	839 083	839 083	297 349	78 028	18 930	43 524	. . .	292 294
1981	226 992	226 992	. . .	832 943	832 943	239 080	88 494	16 467	45 675	. . .	380 801
1982	238 366	238 366	. . .	1 030 358	1 030 358	295 981	104 809	17 442	56 604	. . .	486 123
1983	261 494	261 494	. . .	1 206 656	1 206 656	351 325	110 787	26 154	58 569	. . .	621 434
1984	140 140	140 140	. . .	1 214 478	1 214 478	357 920	112 609	25 994	62 810	. . .	638 909
1985	104 281	104 281	. . .	1 392 053	1 392 053	475 693	138 735	44 383	75 020	. . .	659 695
1986	109 232	109 232	. . .	1 679 716	1 679 716	615 138	182 167	72 399	85 724	. . .	742 536
1987	59 616	59 616	. . .	1 850 216	1 850 216	681 751	215 285	94 700	93 889	. . .	790 810
1988	21 479	21 479	. . .	2 098 851	2 098 851	782 947	305 186	128 662	104 187	. . .	866 539
1989	-33 713	-33 713	. . .	2 447 740	2 447 740	929 965	395 727	197 345	116 949	. . .	953 334
1990	-149 523	-149 523	. . .	2 415 654	2 415 654	853 331	425 538	197 596	144 717	. . .	962 121
1991	-243 314	-243 314	. . .	2 605 674	2 605 674	962 582	525 355	278 976	176 774	. . .	958 514
1992	-432 129	-432 129	. . .	2 611 230	2 611 230	943 364	586 206	314 266	200 817	. . .	934 225
1993	-121 772	-121 772	. . .	3 234 733	3 234 733	1 204 611	916 315	543 862	309 666	. . .	948 862
1994	-110 311	-110 311	. . .	3 434 637	3 434 637	1 234 084	990 838	626 762	310 391	. . .	1 046 321
1995	-277 567	-277 567	. . .	4 094 375	4 094 375	1 493 609	1 278 722	790 615	413 310	. . .	1 145 983
1996	-328 306	-328 306	. . .	4 791 796	4 791 796	1 749 299	1 573 208	1 006 135	481 411	. . .	1 308 550
1997	-788 225	-788 225	. . .	5 536 514	5 536 514	2 036 671	1 841 029	1 207 787	543 396	. . .	1 523 978
1998	-1 033 775	-1 033 775	. . .	6 368 620	6 368 620	2 469 095	2 149 431	1 474 983	594 400	. . .	1 604 088
1999	-1 002 268	-1 002 268	. . .	7 611 443	7 611 443	3 051 404	2 650 768	2 003 716	548 233	. . .	1 772 853
2000	-1 536 826	-1 536 826	. . .	7 641 748	7 641 748	2 934 570	2 556 158	1 852 842	572 692	. . .	2 022 620
2001	-2 295 050	-2 295 050	. . .	7 170 013	7 170 013	2 554 463	2 316 634	1 612 673	557 062	. . .	2 168 955
2002	-2 410 951	-2 410 951	. . .	7 065 177	7 065 177	2 283 141	2 276 589	1 373 980	716 249	. . .	2 346 845
2003	-2 293 013	-2 293 013	. . .	8 620 934	8 620 934	3 037 312	3 176 287	2 079 422	880 963	. . .	2 223 758
2004	-2 363 392	-2 363 392	. . .	10 589 003	10 589 003	3 746 863	3 828 305	2 560 418	1 003 420	. . .	2 824 244
2005	-1 857 865	-1 915 780	57 915	13 357 001	12 166 972	4 047 170	4 628 978	3 317 705	1 037 271	1 190 029	3 302 781
2006	-1 808 474	-1 868 310	59 836	16 409 857	15 170 862	4 929 892	6 017 080	4 328 960	1 299 281	1 238 995	4 004 037
2007	-1 279 493	-1 350 965	71 472	20 704 503	18 145 171	5 857 923	7 262 045	5 247 990	1 630 165	2 559 332	4 747 993
2008	-3 995 303	-4 154 938	159 635	19 423 416	13 295 966	3 707 211	4 320 819	2 748 428	1 258 288	6 127 450	4 974 204
2009	-2 627 626	-2 753 961	126 335	19 426 459	15 936 680	4 945 292	6 058 554	3 995 295	1 625 768	3 489 779	4 529 030
2010	-2 511 788	-2 622 170	110 382	21 767 827	18 115 514	5 486 391	7 160 366	4 900 246	1 787 310	3 652 313	4 980 084
2011	-4 454 997	-4 541 036	86 039	22 208 896	17 492 318	5 214 826	6 871 732	4 501 438	1 953 663	4 716 578	4 868 723
2012	-4 518 300	-4 576 076	57 776	22 562 162	18 942 401	5 969 502	7 983 961	5 321 857	2 247 195	3 619 761	4 416 570
2013	-5 372 654	-5 450 211	77 557	24 144 775	21 127 675	9 206 105	6 472 877	2 283 544	3 017 100	4 352 549
2014	-7 046 149	-7 131 655	85 506	24 717 536	21 503 427	7 133 132	9 704 259	6 770 629	2 486 440	3 214 109	4 231 785
2015	-7 280 637	-7 337 870	57 233	23 340 771	20 945 418	6 978 349	9 606 176	6 828 231	2 291 702	2 395 353	3 977 292
2016	-8 109 652	-8 170 958	61 306	23 916 652	21 707 672	7 411 794	9 922 346	7 066 312	2 394 910	2 208 980	3 966 310
2011											
1st quarter	-2 638 599	-2 743 797	105 198	22 149 169	18 954 866	7 497 835	5 159 980	1 853 998	3 194 303	5 142 596	503 346
2nd quarter	-2 785 715	-2 883 910	98 195	22 447 716	18 439 472	7 644 691	5 204 875	1 929 578	3 473 224	4 945 067	529 062
3rd quarter	-4 133 952	-4 239 860	105 908	22 300 371	17 086 773	6 672 316	4 287 221	1 955 276	5 213 598	4 898 673	559 845
4th quarter	-4 454 997	-4 541 036	86 039	22 208 896	17 492 318	6 871 732	4 501 438	1 953 663	4 716 578	4 868 723	537 037
2012											
1st quarter	-4 547 907	-4 624 193	76 286	22 274 610	18 324 371	7 402 530	5 005 403	1 995 931	3 950 239	4 673 268	572 578
2nd quarter	-5 222 050	-5 289 639	67 589	21 545 834	17 390 014	7 084 752	4 673 015	2 002 974	4 155 820	4 334 824	556 620
3rd quarter	-4 953 117	-5 005 610	52 493	22 360 331	18 434 725	7 628 749	5 048 350	2 132 183	3 925 606	4 420 072	606 277
4th quarter	-4 518 300	-4 576 076	57 776	22 562 162	18 942 401	7 983 961	5 321 857	2 247 195	3 619 761	4 416 570	572 368
2013											
1st quarter	-5 042 555	-5 082 580	40 025	22 725 944	19 477 567	8 256 721	5 546 349	2 278 886	3 248 377	4 424 961	553 058
2nd quarter	-5 467 480	-5 526 832	59 352	22 006 114	19 181 047	8 181 737	5 541 381	2 188 415	2 825 067	4 332 855	446 207
3rd quarter	-4 933 500	-4 981 463	47 963	23 048 676	20 287 260	8 785 811	6 084 914	2 225 257	2 761 416	4 256 415	483 426
4th quarter	-5 372 654	-5 450 211	77 557	24 144 775	21 127 675	9 206 105	6 472 877	2 283 544	3 017 100	4 352 549	448 333
2014											
1st quarter	-5 513 216	-5 582 844	69 628	24 112 181	21 459 271	9 433 307	6 647 696	2 354 553	2 652 910	4 355 006	470 884
2nd quarter	-5 493 772	-5 559 155	65 383	25 035 748	22 339 469	10 065 636	7 101 816	2 486 709	2 696 279	4 311 313	477 865
3rd quarter	-6 232 077	-6 313 143	81 066	24 628 378	21 841 556	9 759 712	6 828 948	2 462 159	2 786 822	4 398 222	443 987
4th quarter	-7 046 149	-7 131 655	85 506	24 717 536	21 503 427	9 704 259	6 770 629	2 486 440	3 214 109	4 231 785	434 251
2015											
1st quarter	-6 838 027	-6 926 714	88 687	25 494 530	22 130 812	10 137 830	7 188 489	2.476 828	3 363 718	4 242 685	418 485
2nd quarter	-6 701 444	-6 750 187	48 743	24 695 796	22 240 077	10 282 380	7 353 305	2 433 710	2 455 719	4 158 184	415 377
3rd quarter	-7 239 731	-7 296 530	56 799	23 477 891	20 759 182	9 461 342	6 605 553	2 348 647	2 718 709	4 112 466	400 352
4th quarter	-7 280 637	-7 337 870	57 233	23 340 771	20 945 418	9 606 176	6 828 231	2 291 702	2 395 353	3 977 292	383 601
2016											
1st quarter	-7 581 977	-7 620 975	38 998	24 061 810	21 079 471	9 607 115	6 738 823	2 333 688	2 982 339	4 047 296	432 011
2nd quarter	-8 026 906	-8 084 986	58 080	24 514 946	21 291 208	9 706 800	6 796 776	2 397 921	3 223 738	4 150 272	454 415
3rd quarter	-7 807 346	-7 862 547	55 201	24 871 435	22 096 378	10 137 121	7 218 045	2 452 114	2 775 057	4 137 356	457 105
4th quarter	-8 109 652	-8 170 958	61 306	23 916 652	21 707 672	9 922 346	7 066 312	2 394 910	2 208 980	3 966 310	407 223

[1]Includes components not shown separately.
. . . = Not available.

Table 7-8. International Investment Position of the United States—*Continued*

(End of period, millions of dollars.)

Year	U.S. assets — By functional category — Reserve assets — Total¹	Reserve assets — Monetary gold	Total	Liabilities excluding financial derivatives	U.S. liabilities — Direct investment at market value	Portfolio investment — Total¹	Equity and investment fund shares	Long-term debt securities — Treasury bonds and notes	Long-term debt securities — Other long-term securities
1980	171 412	155 816	542 221	542 221	99 867	242 620	74 586	69 855	20 506
1981	124 568	105 644	605 951	605 951	109 292	253 037	74 683	80 195	24 057
1982	143 445	120 635	791 992	791 992	199 771	289 863	88 324	95 059	30 216
1983	123 110	100 484	945 162	945 162	230 300	319 827	109 555	94 894	29 243
1984	105 040	81 202	1 074 338	1 074 338	259 723	367 974	104 852	123 920	44 086
1985	117 930	85 834	1 287 772	1 287 772	309 338	473 731	136 791	157 259	92 584
1986	139 875	102 428	1 570 484	1 570 484	350 000	616 611	183 172	178 990	148 634
1987	162 370	127 648	1 790 600	1 790 600	407 706	676 649	189 006	194 558	174 566
1988	144 179	107 434	2 077 372	2 077 372	482 015	784 911	213 813	238 782	200 833
1989	168 714	105 164	2 481 453	2 481 453	632 239	958 808	276 100	332 642	239 440
1990	174 664	102 406	2 565 177	2 565 177	661 170	946 844	243 789	341 567	247 114
1991	159 223	92 561	2 848 988	2 848 988	804 182	1 076 499	298 957	365 555	282 589
1992	147 435	87 168	3 043 359	3 043 359	840 912	1 180 655	328 988	392 695	309 354
1993	164 945	102 556	3 356 505	3 356 505	911 710	1 371 827	373 521	417 812	367 466
1994	163 394	100 110	3 544 948	3 544 948	877 354	1 456 081	397 720	469 633	383 251
1995	176 061	101 279	4 371 942	4 371 942	1 135 542	1 900 950	549 513	619 592	482 290
1996	160 739	96 698	5 120 102	5 120 102	1 370 076	2 356 160	672 397	803 456	571 422
1997	134 836	75 929	6 324 739	6 324 739	1 794 795	2 861 123	952 893	959 973	661 376
1998	146 006	75 291	7 402 395	7 402 395	2 368 530	3 340 370	1 250 342	982 750	782 085
1999	136 418	75 950	8 613 711	8 613 711	3 009 958	3 715 693	1 611 534	872 690	913 177
2000	128 400	71 799	9 178 574	9 178 574	3 023 792	4 008 473	1 643 205	843 580	1 198 002
2001	129 961	72 328	9 465 063	9 465 063	2 799 823	4 324 590	1 572 681	876 971	1 485 952
2002	158 602	90 806	9 476 128	9 476 128	2 282 370	4 571 348	1 335 792	1 016 580	1 720 841
2003	183 577	108 866	10 913 947	10 913 947	2 763 061	5 546 317	1 839 509	1 222 605	1 953 987
2004	189 591	113 947	12 952 395	12 952 395	3 101 450	6 621 226	2 123 259	1 489 885	2 365 314
2005	188 043	134 175	15 214 866	14 082 752	3 227 144	7 337 835	2 304 013	1 719 663	2 725 265
2006	219 853	165 267	18 218 331	17 039 172	3 752 602	8 843 523	2 791 893	1 872 847	3 557 374
2007	277 211	218 025	21 983 996	19 496 136	4 134 239	10 326 974	3 231 651	2 073 744	4 221 532
2008	293 732	227 439	23 418 718	17 450 903	3 091 240	9 475 873	2 132 433	2 494 964	3 748 688
2009	403 804	284 380	22 054 085	18 690 641	3 618 630	10 463 234	2 917 681	2 920 160	3 647 956
2010	488 673	367 537	24 279 615	20 737 684	4 099 097	11 869 262	3 545 769	3 748 544	3 655 679
2011	537 037	400 355	26 663 893	22 033 354	4 199 225	12 647 243	3 841 901	4 356 681	3 617 936
2012	572 368	433 434	27 080 461	23 518 476	4 662 434	13 978 865	4 545 361	4 909 828	3 678 933
2013	448 333	314 975	29 517 429	26 577 886	5 814 935	15 541 251	5 864 600	5 107 089	3 677 916
2014	434 251	315 368	31 763 685	28 635 082	6 350 052	16 919 795	6 642 507	5 484 398	3 881 099
2015	383 601	277 189	30 621 408	28 283 288	6 543 809	16 676 993	6 218 865	5 423 369	4 079 593
2016	407 223	301 090	32 026 304	29 878 630	7 419 335	17 352 869	6 541 578	5 333 904	4 535 707
2011									
1st quarter	376 297	24 787 768	21 698 663	3 089 105	12 215 888	3 793 751	8 422 137	3 659 899	3 875 948
2nd quarter	393 687	25 233 431	21 858 402	3 375 029	12 432 716	3 829 897	8 602 819	3 682 190	4 049 180
3rd quarter	423 628	26 434 323	21 326 633	5 107 690	12 212 692	3 366 482	8 846 210	3 660 084	4 339 272
4th quarter	400 355	26 663 893	22 033 354	4 630 539	12 647 243	3 841 901	8 805 342	3 617 936	4 356 681
2012									
1st quarter	434 742	26 822 517	22 948 564	3 873 953	13 323 328	4 355 167	8 968 161	3 640 438	4 510 887
2nd quarter	418 006	26 767 883	22 679 652	4 088 231	13 297 524	4 261 853	9 035 671	3 551 049	4 680 774
3rd quarter	464 422	27 313 448	23 440 335	3 873 113	13 814 026	4 508 580	9 305 446	3 657 579	4 793 665
4th quarter	433 434	27 080 461	23 518 476	3 561 985	13 978 865	4 545 361	9 433 504	3 678 933	4 909 828
2013									
1st quarter	417 941	27 768 499	24 560 147	3 208 352	14 569 596	5 000 428	9 569 168	3 653 589	5 001 076
2nd quarter	311 707	27 473 595	24 707 880	2 765 715	14 433 052	5 076 822	9 356 230	3 554 128	4 919 650
3rd quarter	346 878	27 982 176	25 268 723	2 713 453	14 893 588	5 406 318	9 487 270	3 649 847	5 007 789
4th quarter	314 975	29 517 429	26 577 886	2 939 543	15 541 251	5 864 600	9 676 651	3 677 916	5 107 089
2014									
1st quarter	337 791	29 625 398	27 042 116	2 583 282	15 936 280	6 051 072	9 885 208	3 721 651	5 258 984
2nd quarter	343 871	30 529 520	27 898 624	2 630 896	16 421 470	6 352 073	10 069 397	3 798 693	5 391 081
3rd quarter	318 113	30 860 455	28 154 699	2 705 756	16 568 406	6 436 702	10 131 704	3 806 222	5 455 085
4th quarter	315 368	31 763 685	28 635 082	3 128 603	16 919 795	6 642 507	10 277 288	3 881 099	5 484 398
2015									
1st quarter	310 399	32 332 557	29 057 526	3 275 031	17 135 059	6 728 462	10 406 597	3 989 171	5 470 341
2nd quarter	306 215	31 397 240	28 990 264	2 406 976	17 164 537	6 659 703	10 504 834	4 101 448	5 461 863
3rd quarter	291 310	30 717 622	28 055 712	2 661 910	16 546 372	6 099 365	10 447 007	4 118 294	5 439 175
4th quarter	277 189	30 621 408	28 283 288	2 338 120	16 676 993	6 218 865	10 458 128	4 079 593	5 423 369
2016									
1st quarter	323 474	31 643 787	28 700 446	2 943 341	16 916 888	6 136 562	10 780 326	4 272 810	5 562 077
2nd quarter	345 375	32 541 852	29 376 194	3 165 658	17 139 105	6 166 543	10 972 562	4 459 546	5 594 893
3rd quarter	345 832	32 678 781	29 958 925	2 719 856	17 498 102	6 467 026	11 031 076	4 623 282	5 459 328
4th quarter	301 090	32 026 304	29 878 630	2 147 674	17 352 869	6 541 578	10 811 291	4 535 707	5 333 904

¹Includes components not shown separately.

SECTION 7C: EXPORTS AND IMPORTS

- U.S. imports of goods and services exceeded exports by a record $762 billion in 2006. This negative "trade balance" (to differentiate it from the more comprehensive "current account deficit" including income payments and receipts that is shown in earlier pages) diminished to $384 billion in 2009 but was back at $505 billion in 2016. (Table 7-9)

- Canada and Mexico are the principal trading partners of the United States, with relations governed by the North American Free Trade Agreement (NAFTA). In 2016, U.S. goods exports to those two countries brought in $496 billion, compared with $270 billion in exports to the European Union and $179 billion in exports to China and Japan. (With the June 3, 2016 Annual Revision for 2015, the area grouping "Newly Industrialized Countries has been removed from all exhibits and Hong Kong, South Korea, Singapore, and Taiwan are presented separately." (Table 7-13)

- U.S. goods imports from Canada and Mexico in 2016 amounted to $572 billion, more than the $416 billion imported from the European Union but less than the $595 billion from China and Japan. (Table 7-14)

- The value of imports from China, which grew by an average of 23 percent per year from 2001 to 2006, slowed drastically between 2006 and 2016. (Table 7-14)

- The continual and growing U.S. surplus on services is in contrast with the goods deficit, though it offsets only about a third of it. Revised categories permit a more detailed look at the composition of the total services surplus, which was $248 billion in 2016. The largest component, $82 billion, was "travel for all purposes including education," which includes the spending of foreigners here for tourism and education The next highest category was $80 billion for "Charges for the use of intellectual property" (formerly known as "royalties and license fees"). The U.S. runs a deficit on insurance services but a $72 billion surplus on financial services. (Tables 7-15A and 7-16A)

Table 7-9. U.S. Exports and Imports of Goods and Services

(Balance of payments basis; millions of dollars, seasonally adjusted.)

Year and month	Goods and services			Goods			Services		
	Exports	Imports	Balance	Exports	Imports	Balance	Exports	Imports	Balance
1970	56 640	54 386	2 254	42 469	39 866	2 603	14 171	14 520	-349
1971	59 677	60 979	-1 302	43 319	45 579	-2 260	16 358	15 400	958
1972	67 222	72 665	-5 443	49 381	55 797	-6 416	17 841	16 868	973
1973	91 242	89 342	1 900	71 410	70 499	911	19 832	18 843	989
1974	120 897	125 190	-4 293	98 306	103 811	-5 505	22 591	21 379	1 212
1975	132 585	120 181	12 404	107 088	98 185	8 903	25 497	21 996	3 501
1976	142 716	148 798	-6 082	114 745	124 228	-9 483	27 971	24 570	3 401
1977	152 301	179 547	-27 246	120 816	151 907	-31 091	31 485	27 640	3 845
1978	178 428	208 191	-29 763	142 075	176 002	-33 927	36 353	32 189	4 164
1979	224 131	248 696	-24 565	184 439	212 007	-27 568	39 692	36 689	3 003
1980	271 834	291 241	-19 407	224 250	249 750	-25 500	47 584	41 491	6 093
1981	294 398	310 570	-16 172	237 044	265 067	-28 023	57 354	45 503	11 851
1982	275 236	299 391	-24 156	211 157	247 642	-36 485	64 079	51 740	12 339
1983	266 106	323 874	-57 767	201 799	268 901	-67 102	64 307	54 973	9 335
1984	291 094	400 166	-109 072	219 926	332 418	-112 492	71 168	67 748	3 420
1985	289 070	410 950	-121 880	215 915	338 088	-122 173	73 155	72 862	294
1986	310 033	448 572	-138 538	223 344	368 425	-145 081	86 689	80 147	6 543
1987	348 869	500 552	-151 684	250 208	409 765	-159 557	98 661	90 787	7 874
1988	431 149	545 715	-114 566	320 230	447 189	-126 959	110 919	98 526	12 393
1989	487 003	580 144	-93 141	359 916	477 665	-117 749	127 087	102 479	24 607
1990	535 233	616 097	-80 864	387 401	498 438	-111 037	147 832	117 659	30 173
1991	578 344	609 479	-31 135	414 083	491 020	-76 937	164 261	118 459	45 802
1992	616 882	656 094	-39 212	439 631	536 528	-96 897	177 251	119 566	57 685
1993	642 863	713 174	-70 311	456 943	589 394	-132 451	185 920	123 780	62 141
1994	703 254	801 747	-98 493	502 859	668 690	-165 831	200 395	133 057	67 338
1995	794 387	890 771	-96 384	575 204	749 374	-174 170	219 183	141 397	77 786
1996	851 602	955 667	-104 065	612 113	803 113	-191 000	239 489	152 554	86 935
1997	934 453	1 042 726	-108 273	678 366	876 794	-198 428	256 087	165 932	90 155
1998	933 174	1 099 314	-166 140	670 416	918 637	-248 221	262 758	180 677	82 081
1999	969 867	1 228 485	-258 617	698 524	1 035 592	-337 068	271 343	192 893	78 450
2000	1 075 321	1 447 837	-372 517	784 940	1 231 722	-446 783	290 381	216 115	74 266
2001	1 005 654	1 367 165	-361 511	731 331	1 153 701	-422 370	274 323	213 465	60 858
2002	978 706	1 397 660	-418 955	698 036	1 173 281	-475 245	280 670	224 379	56 290
2003	1 020 418	1 514 308	-493 890	730 446	1 272 089	-541 643	289 972	242 219	47 754
2004	1 161 549	1 771 433	-609 883	823 584	1 488 349	-664 766	337 966	283 083	54 882
2005	1 286 022	2 000 267	-714 245	913 016	1 695 820	-782 804	373 006	304 448	68 558
2006	1 457 642	2 219 358	-761 716	1 040 905	1 878 194	-837 289	416 738	341 165	75 573
2007	1 653 548	2 358 922	-705 375	1 165 151	1 986 347	-821 196	488 396	372 575	115 821
2008	1 841 612	2 550 339	-708 726	1 308 795	2 141 287	-832 492	532 817	409 052	123 765
2009	1 583 053	1 966 827	-383 774	1 070 331	1 580 025	-509 694	512 722	386 801	125 920
2010	1 853 606	2 348 263	-494 658	1 290 273	1 938 950	-648 678	563 333	409 313	154 020
2011	2 127 021	2 675 646	-548 625	1 499 240	2 239 886	-740 646	627 781	435 761	192 020
2012	2 218 989	2 755 762	-536 773	1 562 578	2 303 749	-741 171	656 411	452 013	204 398
2013	2 293 457	2 755 334	-461 876	1 592 002	2 294 247	-702 244	701 455	461 087	240 368
2014	2 375 905	2 866 241	-490 336	1 633 986	2 385 480	-751 494	741 919	480 761	261 157
2015	2 263 907	2 764 352	-500 445	1 510 757	2 272 612	-761 855	753 150	491 740	261 410
2016	2 208 072	2 712 866	-504 794	1 455 704	2 208 211	-752 507	752 368	504 654	247 714
2015									
January	191 774	233 593	-41 819	128 988	193 141	-64 154	62 786	40 452	22 334
February	190 110	226 309	-36 199	127 400	186 196	-58 795	62 709	40 114	22 596
March	191 051	240 092	-49 041	128 146	199 337	-71 191	62 906	40 755	22 151
April	192 593	233 317	-40 724	129 722	192 541	-62 819	62 870	40 775	22 095
May	190 972	230 731	-39 759	127 976	189 812	-61 836	62 995	40 919	22 076
June	190 685	233 181	-42 496	127 391	192 171	-64 780	63 294	41 010	22 284
July	190 262	230 706	-40 444	127 445	189 480	-62 034	62 817	41 226	21 590
August	186 924	231 174	-44 250	124 120	189 866	-65 746	62 804	41 309	21 495
September	187 263	229 325	-42 062	124 847	187 956	-63 109	62 416	41 369	21 047
October	185 501	227 098	-41 597	122 943	185 816	-62 873	62 558	41 282	21 276
November	183 854	224 781	-40 927	121 418	183 467	-62 049	62 436	41 314	21 122
December	182 919	224 044	-41 125	120 360	182 829	-62 469	62 559	41 215	21 344
2016									
January	178 660	222 070	-43 410	116 655	180 750	-64 096	62 005	41 319	20 686
February	180 892	226 182	-45 290	119 138	184 648	-65 509	61 754	41 534	20 220
March	179 897	217 277	-37 380	117 977	175 979	-58 003	61 921	41 298	20 623
April	181 895	220 317	-38 422	119 815	178 709	-58 893	62 080	41 609	20 471
May	182 166	223 686	-41 520	119 760	182 106	-62 347	62 407	41 580	20 827
June	183 770	227 605	-43 835	120 824	186 030	-65 206	62 946	41 575	21 372
July	185 330	226 624	-41 294	122 227	184 951	-62 724	63 102	41 673	21 430
August	187 385	228 514	-41 129	124 075	185 311	-61 236	63 310	43 203	20 106
September	188 123	226 588	-38 465	124 741	184 175	-59 435	63 382	42 413	20 969
October	185 599	228 668	-43 069	122 514	185 913	-63 399	63 084	42 754	20 330
November	184 848	231 221	-46 373	121 653	188 483	-66 830	63 196	42 738	20 458
December	189 507	234 114	-44 607	126 326	191 155	-64 829	63 181	42 959	20 222

Table 7-10. U.S. Exports of Goods by End-Use and Advanced Technology Categories

(Census basis, except as noted; billions of dollars; seasonally adjusted, except as noted.)

Year and month	Total exports of goods			Principal end-use category							Advanced technology products [1]
	Total, balance of payments basis	Net adjustments	Total, Census basis	Foods, feeds, and beverages	Industrial supplies and materials		Capital goods, except automotive	Automotive vehicles, engines, and parts	Consumer goods, except automotive	Other goods	
					Total	Petroleum and products					
1980	224.25	3.55	220.70	36.28	72.09	3.57	76.28	17.44	17.75	. . .	. . .
1981	237.04	3.31	233.74	38.84	70.19	4.56	84.17	19.69	17.70	. . .	. . .
1982	211.16	-1.12	212.28	32.20	64.05	6.87	76.50	17.23	16.13	. . .	. . .
1983	201.80	0.09	201.71	32.09	58.94	5.59	71.66	18.46	14.93	. . .	. . .
1984	219.93	1.18	218.74	32.20	64.12	5.43	77.01	22.42	15.09	. . .	. . .
1985	215.92	3.29	212.62	24.57	61.16	5.71	79.32	24.95	14.59	. . .	. . .
1986	223.34	-3.13	226.47	23.52	64.72	4.43	82.82	25.10	16.73	. . .	. . .
1987	250.21	-3.70	253.90	25.23	70.05	4.63	92.71	27.58	20.31	. . .	. . .
1988	320.23	-3.11	323.34	33.77	90.02	4.48	119.10	33.40	26.98	. . .	. . .
1989	359.92	-3.08	363.00	36.34	98.36	6.46	136.94	35.05	36.01	. . .	. . .
1990	387.40	-5.57	392.97	35.18	105.55	8.36	153.07	36.07	43.60	20.73	. . .
1991	414.08	-7.77	421.85	35.79	109.69	8.40	166.72	39.72	46.65	23.66	. . .
1992	439.63	-8.54	448.17	40.34	109.59	7.62	176.50	46.71	51.31	24.39	. . .
1993	456.94	-7.92	464.86	40.59	111.89	7.49	182.85	51.35	54.56	23.89	. . .
1994	502.86	-9.77	512.63	41.96	121.55	6.97	205.82	57.31	59.86	26.50	. . .
1995	575.20	-9.54	584.74	50.47	146.37	8.10	234.46	61.26	64.31	28.72	. . .
1996	612.11	-12.96	625.08	55.53	147.98	9.63	253.99	64.24	70.11	33.85	. . .
1997	678.37	-10.82	689.18	51.51	158.32	10.42	295.87	73.30	77.96	33.51	. . .
1998	670.42	-11.72	682.14	46.40	148.31	8.08	299.87	72.39	80.29	35.44	. . .
1999	683.97	-11.83	695.80	45.98	147.52	8.62	310.79	75.26	80.92	35.32	200.28
2000	771.99	-9.92	781.92	47.87	172.62	12.01	356.93	80.36	89.38	34.77	227.40
2001	718.71	-10.39	729.10	49.41	160.10	10.64	321.71	75.44	88.33	34.11	199.63
2002	682.42	-10.68	693.10	49.62	156.81	10.34	290.44	78.94	84.36	32.94	178.57
2003	713.42	-11.36	724.77	55.03	173.04	12.69	293.67	80.63	89.91	32.49	180.21
2004	807.52	-11.26	818.78	56.57	203.96	17.08	331.56	89.21	103.08	34.40	201.56
2005	894.63	-11.35	905.98	58.96	233.05	22.66	363.32	98.41	115.29	36.96	216.82
2006	1 015.81	-10.16	1 025.97	65.96	276.05	31.57	404.03	107.26	129.08	43.59	247.07
2007	1 138.38	-9.82	1 148.20	84.26	316.38	37.76	433.02	121.26	145.98	47.30	264.88
2008	1 307.50	20.06	1 287.44	108.35	388.03	67.18	457.66	121.45	161.28	50.67	270.13
2009	1 069.73	13.69	1 056.04	93.91	296.51	49.18	391.24	81.72	149.46	43.22	244.71
2010	1 288.80	10.30	1 278.50	107.72	391.66	70.83	447.54	112.01	165.23	54.34	273.31
2011	1 495.85	15.56	1 480.29	126.25	501.08	113.71	493.96	133.04	175.30	52.89	287.72
2012	1 562.58	16.76	1 545.82	133.05	483.23	142.02	527.46	146.16	180.99	53.85	304.98
2013	1 592.00	13.48	1 578.52	136.16	492.42	137.42	534.76	152.66	188.09	53.56	319.73
2014	1 633.99	12.11	1 621.87	143.72	505.81	145.24	551.49	159.81	1 990.03	62.04	338.48
2015	1 510.76	7.66	1 503.10	127.74	426.32	97.94	539.50	151.92	197.84	59.79	343.13
2016	1 455.70	4.69	1 451.01	130.56	396.44	88.66	519.58	1 503.13	193.84	60.29	345.52
2014											
January	134.14	1.63	132.51	12.44	43.25	12.03	44.63	12.29	15.68	4.23	25.32
February	132.81	0.67	132.14	12.32	40.85	11.37	44.92	12.72	16.42	4.91	24.45
March	137.50	1.27	136.24	12.80	42.45	12.21	46.01	13.38	16.58	5.02	29.34
April	136.05	1.13	134.92	12.54	42.28	12.12	45.54	12.97	16.54	5.06	27.07
May	137.66	1.25	136.41	12.47	42.19	12.90	45.89	13.49	16.86	5.52	27.66
June	137.09	1.12	135.96	12.00	42.56	13.07	46.03	13.63	16.72	5.02	28.48
July	137.68	1.22	136.45	11.50	42.90	13.52	46.11	14.54	16.43	4.97	27.15
August	138.11	0.75	137.36	10.77	43.89	13.57	47.00	13.30	17.05	5.35	28.88
September	135.35	0.72	134.64	11.47	42.12	12.20	45.88	13.44	16.50	5.23	28.32
October	137.66	0.91	136.75	11.78	42.13	11.15	47.42	13.41	16.95	5.06	30.47
November	135.75	1.00	134.75	11.70	41.89	11.14	45.80	13.09	16.64	5.63	28.22
December	134.19	0.44	133.74	11.94	39.29	9.96	46.27	13.56	16.64	6.04	31.12
2015											
January	128.99	0.86	128.13	11.10	37.15	8.50	45.82	12.87	16.76	4.43	27.12
February	127.40	0.73	126.67	11.03	36.31	8.33	45.18	12.13	17.53	4.48	25.62
March	128.15	0.98	127.16	11.26	36.52	7.69	45.54	12.65	16.43	4.77	29.80
April	129.72	0.75	128.97	11.36	37.44	9.07	46.81	12.51	16.12	4.74	28.83
May	127.98	0.50	127.48	11.15	37.71	9.45	44.86	12.65	16.10	5.02	27.47
June	127.39	0.60	126.79	10.66	36.70	8.98	44.66	12.84	16.60	5.34	29.86
July	127.45	0.61	126.84	10.61	37.02	8.97	44.34	13.06	16.33	5.49	27.97
August	124.12	0.53	123.60	10.42	34.95	7.84	44.60	12.73	15.94	4.95	28.21
September	124.85	0.35	124.50	10.28	34.55	7.81	44.95	12.84	16.86	5.02	29.40
October	122.94	0.74	122.20	9.95	33.25	7.23	44.16	12.64	16.48	5.72	31.03
November	121.42	0.48	120.94	10.06	32.60	7.19	44.70	12.72	15.97	4.89	28.11
December	120.36	0.52	119.84	9.88	32.13	6.89	43.88	12.28	16.73	4.94	29.71
2016											
January	116.66	0.45	116.21	9.50	31.24	6.26	42.97	12.34	16.07	4.09	25.47
February	119.14	0.45	118.69	9.95	31.03	6.02	43.27	12.99	16.72	4.74	25.55
March	117.98	0.37	117.60	9.55	31.02	6.67	43.60	12.27	15.70	5.46	31.51
April	119.82	0.64	119.18	9.92	32.41	7.12	43.41	12.86	15.78	4.81	28.48
May	119.76	0.29	119.47	10.09	32.69	8.22	43.01	12.65	15.73	5.29	27.88
June	120.82	0.43	120.39	10.77	32.64	8.12	43.37	12.33	16.07	5.22	31.08
July	122.23	0.22	122.01	13.10	32.57	7.48	43.06	12.53	16.03	4.72	27.98
August	124.08	0.54	123.54	13.36	34.04	7.35	42.34	12.91	16.16	4.73	27.76
September	124.74	0.46	124.28	11.83	34.66	7.74	43.58	12.52	16.79	4.89	29.56
October	122.51	0.15	122.36	10.89	33.60	7.55	43.76	12.46	15.99	5.66	30.51
November	121.65	0.45	121.21	10.79	34.80	7.94	42.15	12.16	16.37	4.94	27.56
December	126.33	0.26	126.07	10.82	35.74	8.21	45.07	12.30	16.43	5.72	32.18

[1]Not seasonally adjusted.
. . . = Not available.

Table 7-11. U.S. Imports of Goods by End-Use and Advanced Technology Categories

(Census basis, except as noted; billions of dollars; seasonally adjusted, except as noted.)

Year and month	Total imports of goods			Principal end-use category							Advanced technology products [1]
	Total, balance of payments basis	Net adjustments	Total, Census basis	Foods, feeds, and beverages	Industrial supplies and materials		Capital goods, except automotive	Automotive vehicles, engines, and parts	Consumer goods, except automotive	Other goods	
					Total	Petroleum and products					
1980	249.75	4.23	245.52	18.55	124.96	. . .	30.72	28.13	34.22	. . .	. . .
1981	265.07	3.76	261.31	18.53	131.10	. . .	36.86	30.80	38.30	. . .	. . .
1982	247.64	3.70	243.94	17.47	107.82	. . .	38.22	34.26	39.66	. . .	. . .
1983	268.90	7.18	261.72	18.56	105.63	. . .	42.61	42.04	46.59	. . .	. . .
1984	332.42	1.91	330.51	21.92	122.72	. . .	60.15	56.77	61.19	. . .	. . .
1985	338.09	1.71	336.38	21.89	112.48	. . .	60.81	65.21	66.43	. . .	. . .
1986	368.43	2.75	365.67	24.40	101.37	. . .	71.86	78.25	79.43	. . .	. . .
1987	409.77	3.48	406.28	24.81	110.67	. . .	84.77	85.17	88.82	. . .	. . .
1988	447.19	5.26	441.93	24.93	118.06	. . .	101.79	87.95	96.42	. . .	. . .
1989	477.37	3.72	473.65	25.08	132.40	. . .	112.45	87.38	102.26	. . .	. . .
1990	498.34	2.36	495.98	26.65	140.41	62.16	116.04	87.69	105.29	16.09	. . .
1991	490.98	2.53	488.45	26.21	131.38	51.78	120.80	84.94	107.78	15.94	. . .
1992	536.58	3.92	532.67	27.61	138.64	51.60	134.25	91.79	122.66	17.71	71.87
1993	589.44	8.78	580.66	27.87	145.61	51.50	152.37	102.42	134.02	18.39	81.23
1994	668.70	5.44	663.26	30.96	162.11	51.28	184.37	118.27	146.27	21.27	98.12
1995	749.37	5.83	743.54	33.18	181.85	56.16	221.43	123.80	159.90	23.39	124.79
1996	803.11	7.92	795.19	35.71	204.48	72.75	228.07	128.94	172.00	26.10	130.36
1997	876.40	6.70	869.70	39.69	213.77	71.77	253.28	139.81	193.81	29.34	147.28
1998	917.64	5.74	911.90	41.24	200.14	50.90	269.45	148.68	217.00	35.39	156.75
1999	1 035.60	10.98	1 024.62	43.60	221.39	67.81	295.72	178.96	241.91	43.04	181.18
2000	1 231.72	13.70	1 218.02	45.98	298.98	120.28	347.03	195.88	281.83	48.33	222.08
2001	1 153.70	12.70	1 141.00	46.64	273.87	103.59	297.99	189.78	284.29	48.42	195.18
2002	1 173.28	11.91	1 161.37	49.69	267.69	103.51	283.32	203.74	307.84	49.08	195.15
2003	1 272.10	14.98	1 257.12	55.83	313.82	133.10	295.87	210.14	333.88	47.59	207.03
2004	1 488.35	18.65	1 469.70	62.14	412.77	180.46	343.58	228.20	372.94	50.11	238.28
2005	1 695.82	22.36	1 673.46	68.09	523.77	251.86	379.33	239.45	407.24	55.57	259.74
2006	1 878.19	24.25	1 853.94	74.94	601.99	302.43	418.26	256.63	442.64	59.49	290.76
2007	1 986.35	29.39	1 956.96	81.68	634.75	330.98	444.51	256.67	474.55	64.81	326.81
2008	2 141.29	37.65	2 103.64	89.00	779.48	453.28	453.74	231.24	481.64	68.54	331.15
2009	1 580.03	20.40	1 559.63	81.62	462.38	253.69	370.48	157.65	427.33	60.17	300.89
2010	1 938.95	25.09	1 913.86	91.75	603.10	336.11	449.39	225.10	483.23	61.30	354.25
2011	2 239.89	31.93	2 207.95	107.48	755.78	439.34	510.80	254.62	514.11	65.17	386.44
2012	2 303.75	27.45	2 276.30	110.27	730.64	415.17	548.71	297.78	516.93	71.95	396.23
2013	2 294.25	26.26	2 267.99	115.15	681.53	369.68	555.65	308.80	531.67	75.20	401.14
2014	2 385.48	29.12	2 356.36	125 878.00	667 024.00	334.00	594.14	328.64	557.09	83.59	422.13
2015	2 272.61	24.43	2 248.18	127.80	485.74	181.98	602.06	349.15	594.32	89.12	434.92
2016	2 208.21	20.41	2 187.81	130 049.00	443.31	146.63	589.97	350.12	583.56	90.80	429.19
2014											
January	193.71	233.54	41.35	192.19	9.71	57.67	194.55	47.91	25.48	45.14	6.28
February	193.06	235.44	42.12	193.31	9.65	58.86	195.78	47.24	26.25	44.94	6.38
March	198.97	240.40	42.00	198.40	10.57	59.70	200.96	48.16	26.67	46.34	6.97
April	199.88	242.24	42.22	200.03	10.64	58.52	202.37	48.68	27.19	47.60	7.39
May	199.40	240.72	42.49	198.24	10.58	56.39	200.68	49.71	27.98	46.77	6.82
June	197.98	238.92	42.81	196.11	10.81	55.24	198.63	49.63	27.75	45.76	6.93
July	198.58	239.24	42.50	196.73	10.74	55.16	199.20	49.66	28.39	45.40	7.38
August	198.98	238.07	42.42	195.65	10.49	54.97	198.07	50.52	27.64	45.23	6.79
September	198.45	239.49	42.62	196.87	10.67	54.15	199.26	50.56	27.46	46.83	7.22
October	200.02	240.77	43.11	197.66	10.90	54.10	200.10	50.82	28.14	46.57	7.13
November	195.80	237.61	43.00	194.61	10.50	50.49	196.95	50.72	27.54	48.45	6.91
December	199.26	239.81	43.25	196.57	10.64	51.77	198.95	50.54	28.14	48.07	7.40
2015											
January	193.54	233.59	42.68	190.91	10.63	47.09	193.14	50.93	27.76	47.34	7.16
February	185.96	226.31	42.21	184.10	10.42	43.32	186.20	49.18	26.98	46.81	7.39
March	197.95	240.09	42.74	197.36	10.99	43.07	199.34	52.54	29.41	53.90	7.45
April	192.13	233.32	43.05	190.26	10.81	42.31	192.54	51.61	28.87	49.61	7.05
May	189.95	230.73	42.89	187.84	10.49	41.19	189.81	50.56	29.19	49.05	7.37
June	192.73	233.18	43.16	190.02	11.17	41.74	192.17	49.41	29.99	50.09	7.63
July	189.10	230.71	43.29	187.42	10.61	42.01	189.48	49.76	30.04	47.79	7.21
August	190.25	231.17	43.39	187.78	10.62	39.45	189.87	49.88	29.73	50.52	7.59
September	187.57	229.33	43.28	186.05	10.76	38.09	187.96	49.62	28.98	51.20	7.41
October	186.15	227.10	43.32	183.77	10.32	36.12	185.82	49.96	29.16	50.57	7.65
November	183.77	224.78	43.20	181.58	10.44	35.66	183.47	49.34	29.23	49.13	7.78
December	183.76	224.04	42.95	181.10	10.56	35.70	182.83	49.27	29.82	48.31	7.44
2016											
January	193.54	222.07	42.95	179.12	10.66	34.66	180.75	48.26	29.97	48.39	7.18
February	185.96	226.18	43.22	182.97	11.08	34.33	184.65	49.14	29.34	51.83	7.26
March	197.95	217.28	43.02	174.26	10.54	33.25	175.98	47.52	28.61	46.61	7.73
April	192.13	220.32	43.29	177.03	10.72	33.99	178.71	49.40	28.63	46.86	7.43
May	189.95	223.69	43.42	180.26	10.74	36.34	182.11	48.68	28.98	48.08	7.43
June	192.73	227.61	43.51	184.10	10.58	38.14	186.03	49.57	28.61	49.68	7.52
July	189.10	226.62	43.50	183.13	10.68	38.91	184.95	48.99	28.58	48.58	7.39
August	190.25	228.51	44.94	183.57	10.88	38.00	185.31	49.93	28.89	48.06	7.81
September	187.57	226.59	43.95	182.64	10.88	38.04	184.18	48.78	29.81	47.44	7.69
October	186.15	228.67	44.32	184.35	10.90	37.62	185.91	49.63	29.14	49.26	7.80
November	183.77	231.22	44.34	186.88	11.16	39.75	188.48	49.70	29.16	49.27	7.85
December	183.76	234.11	44.61	189.51	11.25	40.28	191.16	50.38	30.39	49.50	7.71

[1]Not seasonally adjusted.
. . . = Not available.

Table 7-12. U.S. Exports and Imports of Goods by Principal End-Use Category in Constant Dollars

(Census basis; billions of 2009 chain-weighted dollars, except as noted; seasonally adjusted.)

Year and month	Exports							Imports						
	Total	Foods, feeds, and beverages	Industrial supplies and materials	Capital goods, except automotive	Automotive vehicles, engines, and parts	Consumer goods, except automotive	Other goods	Total	Foods, feeds, and beverages	Industrial supplies and materials	Capital goods, except automotive	Automotive vehicles, engines, and parts	Consumer goods, except automotive	Other goods
1990 I	393.60	35.10	104.40	152.70	37.40	39.22	18.70	495.30	26.60	146.20	116.40	87.30	105.70	14.46
1991 I	421.70	35.70	109.70	166.70	40.00	40.42	21.11	488.50	26.50	131.60	120.70	85.70	108.00	14.15
1992 I	448.20	40.30	109.10	175.90	47.00	43.60	21.71	532.70	27.60	138.60	134.30	91.80	122.70	15.46
1993 I	471.17	40.19	111.08	190.02	51.93	54.03	23.91	591.45	28.03	151.26	160.16	100.73	132.92	18.35
1994 I	522.29	40.43	114.17	225.76	56.54	58.97	26.41	675.05	29.52	168.80	199.56	112.13	144.22	20.82
1994	550.74	70.21	177.34	158.53	64.72	68.86	34.59	718.78	40.30	351.05	104.93	134.94	149.71	24.36
1995	607.14	77.48	189.34	184.12	68.50	72.85	35.52	780.92	41.33	361.34	126.52	137.25	161.15	25.72
1996	671.49	75.01	200.96	218.55	71.29	78.19	41.47	862.39	45.76	383.36	152.61	141.93	172.59	28.71
1997	761.13	74.80	217.46	267.75	80.44	85.87	41.19	982.15	50.15	409.79	191.10	153.44	196.50	32.48
1998	779.10	74.33	216.64	279.58	78.51	89.22	44.60	1 097.87	53.96	449.16	219.20	163.03	222.76	40.02
1999	804.15	76.88	218.21	294.71	81.30	89.85	44.57	1 230.04	58.93	456.33	251.42	194.72	250.12	48.84
2000	892.79	81.16	240.09	341.04	85.97	98.62	42.90	1 393.19	62.76	484.79	301.69	211.69	294.21	54.02
2001	837.60	83.31	229.28	307.59	80.38	97.52	42.14	1 347.00	65.19	482.40	266.29	205.19	299.06	54.53
2002	799.01	81.43	225.53	280.73	83.78	93.44	40.58	1 395.87	69.49	484.45	261.65	219.65	326.76	56.27
2003	822.70	82.79	235.44	288.75	85.14	98.54	39.09	1 472.99	75.91	503.93	279.49	225.32	354.90	53.72
2004	894.61	76.45	251.33	324.20	93.52	112.18	39.64	1 646.37	80.59	566.27	329.08	240.95	393.62	54.98
2005	957.75	79.97	258.79	353.83	102.09	123.61	40.79	1 762.48	83.57	595.14	365.98	250.30	425.74	58.94
2006	1 054.35	85.72	278.59	398.12	110.10	135.92	46.00	1 867.72	88.43	597.42	408.89	267.07	459.94	61.62
2007	1 138.01	91.11	297.50	428.78	123.19	149.94	47.50	1 904.34	89.18	579.33	435.52	264.43	485.82	65.33
2008	1 219.45	96.38	333.48	455.75	122.03	162.16	48.10	1 848.83	87.20	552.02	445.24	232.70	480.18	65.65
2009	1 056.04	93.91	296.51	391.24	81.72	149.46	43.22	1 559.63	81.62	462.38	370.48	157.65	427.33	60.17
2010	1 213.96	103.02	339.99	447.21	111.51	161.64	51.24	1 790.74	84.71	488.95	453.76	223.75	482.77	59.53
2011	1 307.42	101.01	370.11	494.78	130.44	168.23	45.82	1 900.89	87.25	497.19	514.57	246.10	505.47	60.39
2012	1 359.25	101.09	374.73	528.63	141.12	172.51	48.73	1 948.07	90.10	479.32	554.63	282.46	500.85	66.46
2013	1 399.71	100.84	391.20	536.96	146.63	181.14	50.57	1 974.11	93.14	463.62	573.90	293.82	516.04	70.18
2014	1 452.14	107.73	398.80	554.25	152.65	193.71	54.39	2 062.53	97.55	463.87	618.65	314.32	538.38	77.82
2015	1 443.46	110.12	397.19	545.54	145.26	196.90	56.35	2 159.82	100.92	465.57	641.61	340.38	578.83	85.53
2016	1 443.82	119.63	397.22	532.79	144.85	196.90	58.73	2 178.37	102.32	483.19	645.80	343.98	570.47	88.55
2013														
January	113.90	8.34	31.27	44.42	11.92	14.96	3.77	162.84	7.82	39.24	47.02	22.74	42.94	5.64
February	115.17	8.38	32.36	43.97	12.38	14.30	4.29	164.69	8.02	38.12	48.20	23.76	44.56	5.39
March	113.54	7.80	32.03	43.49	11.99	14.34	4.49	158.55	7.67	37.95	45.96	23.24	40.42	5.89
April	115.58	7.75	31.83	44.34	12.47	16.14	3.98	162.27	7.79	37.86	46.88	24.05	42.73	6.04
May	115.39	7.62	31.94	45.07	12.44	14.99	4.26	166.59	7.90	39.56	47.01	24.42	43.82	6.67
June	117.74	7.82	32.86	45.86	12.16	15.45	4.44	163.52	7.75	38.48	47.55	24.43	42.54	5.76
July	116.69	8.16	33.62	44.59	11.58	15.14	4.08	164.76	7.69	39.11	47.38	24.45	43.05	5.95
August	116.97	8.10	33.14	44.70	12.38	15.05	4.21	164.79	7.68	38.89	48.24	24.96	42.18	5.87
September	116.06	8.66	31.77	44.89	12.51	15.02	3.98	167.13	7.64	39.02	48.75	25.87	43.36	5.74
October	120.03	9.35	33.82	45.02	12.32	15.63	4.26	167.31	7.74	39.39	48.56	25.00	43.57	6.14
November	120.36	9.47	33.35	45.65	12.47	15.24	4.65	166.45	7.75	38.25	49.01	25.88	43.39	5.45
December	118.27	9.40	33.22	44.96	12.00	14.88	4.17	165.20	7.71	37.78	49.13	25.04	43.46	5.65
2014														
January	117.76	9.42	33.10	45.00	11.77	15.20	3.68	166.94	7.70	38.84	49.82	24.31	43.74	5.86
February	117.09	9.23	31.01	45.29	12.19	16.02	4.26	166.57	7.65	38.57	49.25	25.04	43.52	5.93
March	120.14	9.30	32.05	46.36	12.83	16.19	4.33	170.49	8.08	39.09	50.23	25.42	44.80	6.44
April	119.70	8.97	32.75	45.84	12.40	16.13	4.39	172.82	8.18	39.03	50.75	25.90	45.97	6.86
May	121.00	8.88	32.78	46.09	12.89	16.44	4.79	172.59	8.23	38.64	51.67	26.65	45.15	6.34
June	121.13	8.70	33.39	46.20	13.01	16.30	4.38	170.98	8.54	37.96	51.54	26.42	44.15	6.45
July	121.40	8.43	33.48	46.33	13.86	15.91	4.32	171.36	8.38	37.75	51.62	27.21	43.79	6.86
August	122.73	8.11	34.46	47.21	12.70	16.49	4.68	171.43	8.09	38.50	52.55	26.49	43.60	6.32
September	120.77	8.75	33.36	46.04	12.82	16.01	4.59	172.84	8.22	38.11	52.65	26.34	45.16	6.72
October	123.84	9.29	34.03	47.54	12.79	16.52	4.48	174.74	8.33	39.00	52.93	27.04	45.03	6.65
November	123.07	9.19	34.71	45.95	12.48	16.27	5.03	173.64	8.05	37.58	52.89	26.46	46.87	6.46
December	123.50	9.45	33.68	46.42	12.92	16.23	5.47	178.13	8.10	40.81	52.76	27.04	46.59	6.92
2015														
January	120.70	8.90	33.70	45.96	12.28	16.51	4.10	176.64	8.29	39.50	53.41	26.88	46.08	6.76
February	119.44	9.08	32.65	45.35	11.60	17.38	4.15	172.51	8.01	38.21	51.77	26.19	45.53	6.99
March	120.17	9.37	32.88	45.80	12.08	16.31	4.42	186.98	8.56	39.57	55.46	28.60	52.40	7.09
April	122.78	9.60	34.21	47.20	11.97	16.05	4.42	181.30	8.48	39.49	54.66	28.14	48.31	6.74
May	120.71	9.54	33.71	45.29	12.08	16.01	4.66	179.14	8.22	38.50	53.69	28.44	47.76	7.04
June	120.49	9.32	32.98	45.16	12.26	16.44	4.97	180.94	8.80	38.57	52.54	29.26	48.78	7.30
July	121.00	9.04	33.82	44.90	12.49	16.22	5.13	178.91	8.36	39.02	53.12	29.27	46.59	6.93
August	119.67	9.15	33.14	45.24	12.17	15.90	4.70	181.55	8.37	38.64	53.39	29.02	49.26	7.31
September	121.41	9.19	33.35	45.61	12.27	16.84	4.80	181.68	8.55	39.02	53.22	28.29	49.86	7.15
October	119.34	8.87	32.19	44.87	12.10	16.48	5.48	180.90	8.35	38.04	53.77	28.50	49.27	7.41
November	118.81	9.09	32.05	45.46	12.19	15.96	4.72	179.12	8.42	37.81	53.25	28.60	47.86	7.56
December	118.93	8.99	32.51	44.70	11.77	16.81	4.81	180.15	8.52	39.20	53.33	29.20	47.13	7.26
2016														
January	116.63	8.75	32.51	43.86	11.84	16.33	4.03	179.17	8.54	38.93	52.41	29.49	47.17	7.01
February	119.79	9.11	32.89	44.22	12.48	17.03	4.70	184.08	8.95	39.74	53.40	28.86	50.40	7.10
March	118.78	8.91	32.72	44.60	11.81	15.99	5.41	175.77	8.63	38.55	51.75	28.13	45.46	7.59
April	119.84	9.20	33.73	44.39	12.38	16.06	4.74	178.24	8.66	38.95	53.94	28.13	45.82	7.28
May	118.87	9.11	33.05	44.01	12.19	15.97	5.16	180.43	8.69	40.58	53.17	28.41	46.94	7.27
June	118.66	9.46	32.18	44.40	11.87	16.35	5.04	183.54	8.67	41.38	54.25	28.06	48.58	7.37
July	120.18	11.51	32.08	44.17	12.05	16.19	4.55	181.54	8.35	41.51	53.71	28.11	47.50	7.19
August	122.93	12.32	33.92	43.50	12.49	16.36	4.61	181.86	8.25	40.60	54.78	28.44	47.08	7.58
September	123.33	11.04	34.06	44.81	12.10	16.97	4.75	180.66	8.22	40.41	53.52	29.31	46.50	7.46
October	121.04	10.17	32.56	45.06	12.04	16.21	5.47	182.21	8.32	39.75	54.57	28.58	48.17	7.59
November	119.81	10.02	33.63	43.42	11.73	16.64	4.78	184.34	8.39	41.53	54.80	28.61	48.27	7.62
December	123.96	10.05	33.90	46.36	11.88	16.80	5.49	186.53	8.67	41.28	55.51	29.84	48.59	7.50

IData on the 2009 chain-weighted dollar basis are only available from 1994 forward. To provide more historical range, values in 1992 dollars are shown for the years 1986–1994.

Table 7-13. U.S. Exports of Goods by Selected Regions and Countries

(Census f.a.s. basis; millions of dollars, not seasonally adjusted.)

Year and month	Total, all countries	Selected regions [1]				Selected countries				
		European Union, 15 countries	European Union	Asian NICS [2]	OPEC	Brazil	Canada	China	Japan	Mexico
1980	. . .	53 679	. . .	. . .	17 759	4 344	40 331	3 755	20 790	15 145
1981	. . .	52 363	. . .	. . .	21 533	3 798	44 602	3 603	21 823	17 789
1982	. . .	47 932	. . .	. . .	22 863	3 423	37 887	2 912	20 966	11 817
1983	201 708	44 311	. . .	. . .	16 905	2 557	43 345	2 173	21 894	9 082
1984	218 743	46 976	. . .	. . .	14 387	2 640	51 777	3 004	23 575	11 992
1985	212 621	48 994	. . .	16 918	12 478	3 140	47 251	3 856	22 631	13 635
1986	226 471	53 154	. . .	18 290	10 844	3 885	45 333	3 106	26 882	12 392
1987	254 122	60 575	. . .	23 547	11 057	4 040	59 814	3 497	28 249	14 582
1988	322 426	75 755	. . .	34 816	13 994	4 266	71 622	5 022	37 725	20 629
1989	363 812	86 331	. . .	38 429	13 196	4 804	78 809	5 755	44 494	24 982
1990	393 592	98 027	. . .	40 734	13 703	5 048	83 674	4 806	48 580	28 279
1991	421 730	103 123	. . .	45 020	10 061	6 148	85 150	6 278	48 125	33 277
1992	448 165	102 958	. . .	48 592	21 960	5 751	90 594	7 419	47 813	40 592
1993	465 090	96 973	. . .	52 501	19 500	6 058	100 444	8 763	47 892	41 581
1994	512 625	102 818	. . .	59 595	17 868	8 102	114 439	9 282	53 488	50 844
1995	584 740	123 671	. . .	74 234	19 533	11 439	127 226	11 754	64 343	46 292
1996	625 073	127 710	. . .	75 768	22 275	12 718	134 210	11 993	67 607	56 792
1997	689 180	140 773	. . .	78 225	25 525	15 915	151 767	12 862	65 549	71 389
1998	682 139	149 035	. . .	63 269	25 154	15 142	156 604	14 241	57 831	78 773
1999	695 797	151 814	. . .	70 989	20 166	13 203	166 600	13 111	57 466	86 909
2000	781 918	165 065	. . .	84 624	19 078	15 321	178 941	16 185	64 924	111 349
2001	729 101	158 768	. . .	71 981	20 052	15 879	163 424	19 182	57 452	101 297
2002	693 101	143 691	. . .	69 770	18 812	12 376	160 923	22 128	51 449	97 470
2003	724 771	151 731	. . .	71 601	17 279	11 211	169 924	28 368	52 004	97 412
2004	814 875	168 572	171 733	82 997	22 550	13 870	190 042	34 833	53 458	110 837
2005	901 082	. . .	188 164	86 003	31 781	15 343	212 340	41 874	54 817	120 444
2006	1 025 967	. . .	215 643	96 496	39 265	19 008	231 346	54 813	59 276	133 998
2007	1 148 199	. . .	248 868	105 751	48 766	24 303	249 819	64 313	62 798	136 167
2008	1 287 442	. . .	277 137	108 947	65 392	32 435	262 282	71 346	67 130	151 610
2009	1 056 043	. . .	225 282	90 380	50 402	26 097	205 457	70 636	52 943	129 214
2010	1 278 495	. . .	242 795	120 450	54 401	35 345	250 283	93 059	61 444	163 723
2011	1 482 508	. . .	273 712	137 075	65 225	42 895	282 678	105 445	67 251	198 622
2012	1 545 703	. . .	269 548	134 599	80 778	43 550	294 156	111 855	71 565	216 394
2013	1 579 593	. . .	265 610	140 201	83 139	44 061	302 118	122 852	66 559	226 647
2014	1 621 172	. . .	279 188	142 237	81 600	42 415	313 872	124 692	68 060	240 804
2015	1 503 102	. . .	271 896	. . .	72 883	31 641	280 855	115 932	62 393	236 204
2016	1 451 011	. . .	269 617	. . .	71 056	30 107	266 797	115 602	63 236	229 702
2014										
January	132 420	. . .	22 573	13 063	70 803	3 936	24 536	11 013	5 715	19 438
February	132 113	. . .	22 098	11 646	71 767	3 691	25 505	10 357	5 660	19 965
March	135 327	. . .	22 949	11 720	69 718	3 760	25 694	10 476	5 635	19 722
April	134 475	. . .	23 051	11 774	76 640	3 452	25 965	9 801	5 526	19 699
May	136 244	. . .	23 349	11 657	82 791	3 659	26 128	10 015	5 308	20 691
June	135 447	. . .	24 060	11 739	72 737	3 413	26 545	9 966	5 576	20 191
July	136 694	. . .	24 350	10 902	76 077	3 570	26 998	9 928	5 611	20 314
August	137 512	. . .	23 800	11 595	80 817	3 424	26 669	10 240	6 003	20 330
September	135 167	. . .	22 017	12 163	78 656	3 449	26 365	9 942	5 474	20 044
October	136 654	. . .	22 867	12 853	76 993	3 578	26 538	10 693	5 443	20 054
November	135 173	. . .	22 405	11 639	75 113	3 324	26 092	10 555	5 042	20 180
December	133 946	. . .	22 689	11 485	74 775	3 179	25 781	10 635	5 884	19 705
2015										
January	128 128	. . .	23 042	. . .	63 066	3 101	24 057	10 096	5 307	19 905
February	126 665	. . .	23 261	. . .	64 565	3 169	23 973	9 391	5 385	19 651
March	127 162	. . .	22 648	. . .	59 376	2 724	24 001	9 652	5 482	19 114
April	128 971	. . .	23 375	. . .	61 380	3 071	23 774	10 019	5 779	19 893
May	127 476	. . .	22 827	. . .	59 827	2 830	24 285	9 550	5 327	19 955
June	126 790	. . .	22 076	. . .	63 649	2 872	23 213	10 292	5 223	19 967
July	126 837	. . .	22 377	. . .	66 575	2 351	23 480	10 146	5 244	20 653
August	123 595	. . .	22 032	. . .	56 871	2 290	22 993	9 704	5 211	19 605
September	124 501	. . .	22 393	. . .	65 871	2 459	22 612	9 942	4 604	19 569
October	122 200	. . .	22 831	. . .	52 888	2 109	22 554	9 380	4 984	19 624
November	120 941	. . .	22 815	. . .	64 124	2 241	22 640	9 021	4 985	18 933
December	119 836	. . .	22 203	. . .	52 675	2 425	22 473	8 740	4 863	19 335
2016										
January	116 210	. . .	21 509	. . .	50 071	2 311	22 490	8 830	4 958	19 279
February	118 692	. . .	22 977	. . .	68 733	2 234	22 242	8 756	5 106	18 807
March	117 604	. . .	22 690	. . .	60 098	2 274	21 991	8 840	5 070	18 842
April	119 179	. . .	22 477	. . .	54 433	2 327	22 624	9 411	4 809	18 905
May	119 467	. . .	22 148	. . .	52 517	2 539	22 274	9 437	5 375	18 742
June	120 392	. . .	22 943	. . .	50 607	2 394	22 707	9 515	5 067	18 912
July	122 011	. . .	22 527	. . .	52 620	2 545	22 293	9 851	5 212	18 872
August	123 538	. . .	22 756	. . .	55 062	2 710	22 397	9 999	5 296	18 926
September	124 282	. . .	22 935	. . .	50 521	2 534	22 270	10 097	5 567	19 721
October	122 361	. . .	22 247	. . .	44 795	2 557	21 990	10 378	5 630	19 209
November	121 205	. . .	21 143	. . .	50 956	3 082	21 438	10 301	5 493	19 083
December	126 070	. . .	23 265	. . .	59 904	2 600	22 082	10 187	5 652	20 404

[1]See notes and definitions for definitions of regions.
[2]With the June 3, 2016 Annual Revision for 2015, the area grouping "Newly Industrialized Countries" has been revised.
. . . = Not available.

Table 7-14. U.S. Imports of Goods by Selected Regions and Countries

(Census Customs basis; millions of dollars, not seasonally adjusted.)

Year and month	Total, all countries	Selected regions [1]				Selected countries				
		European Union, 15 countries	European Union	Asian NICS [2]	OPEC	Brazil	Canada	China	Japan	Mexico
1980	. . .	35 958	. . .	. . .	. . .	3 715	41 455	. . .	30 701	12 520
1981	. . .	41 624	. . .	. . .	. . .	4 475	46 414	. . .	37 612	13 765
1982	. . .	42 509	. . .	. . .	. . .	4 285	46 477	. . .	37 744	15 566
1983	261 723	43 892	. . .	. . .	. . .	4 946	52 130	. . .	41 183	16 776
1984	330 510	57 360	. . .	. . .	. . .	7 621	66 478	. . .	57 135	18 020
1985	336 383	67 822	. . .	39 066	22 801	7 526	69 006	3 862	68 783	19 132
1986	365 672	75 736	. . .	46 136	19 751	6 813	68 253	4 771	81 911	17 302
1987	406 241	81 188	. . .	57 663	23 952	7 865	71 085	6 294	84 575	20 271
1988	440 952	84 939	. . .	63 030	22 962	9 294	81 398	8 511	89 519	23 260
1989	473 211	85 153	. . .	62 774	30 611	8 410	87 953	11 990	93 553	27 162
1990	495 311	91 868	. . .	60 573	38 052	7 898	91 380	15 237	89 684	30 157
1991	488 453	86 481	. . .	59 276	32 644	6 717	91 064	18 969	91 511	31 130
1992	532 662	93 993	. . .	62 384	33 200	7 609	98 630	25 728	97 414	35 211
1993	580 656	97 941	. . .	64 572	31 739	7 479	111 216	31 540	107 246	39 918
1994	663 252	110 875	. . .	71 388	31 685	8 683	128 406	38 787	119 156	49 494
1995	743 545	131 871	. . .	82 008	35 606	8 833	144 370	45 543	123 479	62 100
1996	795 287	142 947	. . .	82 770	44 285	8 773	155 893	51 513	115 187	74 297
1997	869 703	157 528	. . .	86 164	44 025	9 625	167 234	62 558	121 663	85 938
1998	911 897	176 380	. . .	85 960	33 925	10 102	173 256	71 169	121 845	94 629
1999	1 024 616	195 227	. . .	95 103	41 977	11 314	198 711	81 788	130 864	109 721
2000	1 218 023	220 019	. . .	111 438	67 090	13 853	230 838	100 018	146 479	135 926
2001	1 140 998	220 057	. . .	93 202	59 754	14 466	216 268	102 278	126 473	131 338
2002	1 161 366	225 771	. . .	91 850	53 245	15 781	209 088	125 193	121 429	134 616
2003	1 257 121	244 826	. . .	92 818	68 344	17 910	221 595	152 436	118 037	138 060
2004	1 469 705	272 439	281 959	105 476	92 099	21 160	256 360	196 682	129 805	155 902
2005	1 673 454	298 879	309 628	102 609	127 169	24 436	290 384	243 470	138 004	170 109
2006	1 853 938	319 590	330 482	109 730	150 758	26 367	302 438	287 774	148 181	198 253
2007	1 956 961	. . .	354 409	111 260	165 651	25 644	317 057	321 443	145 463	210 714
2008	2 103 641	. . .	367 617	106 763	242 579	30 453	339 491	337 773	139 262	215 942
2009	1 559 625	. . .	281 801	86 854	111 602	20 070	226 248	296 374	95 804	176 654
2010	1 913 857	. . .	319 264	106 446	149 893	23 958	277 637	364 953	120 552	229 986
2011	2 207 954	. . .	368 464	121 592	191 470	31 737	315 325	399 371	128 928	262 874
2012	2 276 302	. . .	381 753	123 450	180 752	32 123	324 264	425 626	146 438	277 594
2013	2 267 987	. . .	392 520	123 854	153 921	27 130	338 332	441 616	141 313	286 732
2014	2 385 489	. . .	425 498	132 395	133 492	29 586	355 863	469 669	137 321	303 068
2015	2 272 868	. . .	427 537	. . .	66 233	27 441	296 231	483 189	131 383	296 401
2016	2 187 805	. . .	416 377	. . .	77 558	26 054	277 756	462 618	132 046	294 056
2014										
January	192 218	. . .	33 217	10 295	14 589	2 469	26 566	40 491	11 644	24 403
February	192 666	. . .	33 289	9 959	15 305	2 374	25 443	37 472	9 884	24 541
March	196 795	. . .	34 799	11 434	14 318	2 380	24 646	49 249	11 793	24 433
April	199 284	. . .	35 768	11 278	13 709	2 368	24 544	38 795	12 401	24 578
May	198 347	. . .	35 961	11 202	12 860	2 142	24 753	39 827	11 460	24 486
June	196 618	. . .	35 816	11 206	11 921	2 312	26 130	39 703	10 385	25 653
July	196 511	. . .	35 089	10 791	13 100	2 154	25 188	39 654	10 593	24 790
August	196 013	. . .	36 192	11 200	11 866	2 446	24 882	41 668	10 457	24 668
September	196 979	. . .	34 859	11 153	11 734	2 215	24 211	40 105	10 276	24 821
October	197 981	. . .	34 430	11 094	11 277	2 151	22 842	39 363	10 513	25 578
November	195 090	. . .	35 461	11 499	10 189	2 201	23 493	38 972	10 713	24 228
December	197 863	. . .	35 711	11 284	10 891	2 256	23 637	37 944	11 245	24 230
2015										
January	190 914	. . .	35 909	. . .	7 013	2 476	26 438	39 625	11 621	24 211
February	184 096	. . .	35 623	. . .	6 346	2 386	25 503	36 652	9 991	24 563
March	197 355	. . .	34 159	. . .	5 392	2 382	24 912	50 567	11 728	24 440
April	190 264	. . .	35 753	. . .	5 774	2 416	24 705	39 115	12 478	24 623
May	187 840	. . .	36 282	. . .	5 792	2 179	24 607	40 025	11 724	24 486
June	190 021	. . .	35 988	. . .	5 792	2 351	26 144	39 988	10 318	25 823
July	187 418	. . .	35 448	. . .	5 958	2 174	25 198	39 608	10 522	24 856
August	187 781	. . .	35 882	. . .	4 666	2 376	24 849	41 362	10 456	24 721
September	186 049	. . .	35 754	. . .	4 892	2 243	24 314	40 514	10 379	24 758
October	183 774	. . .	36 092	. . .	4 660	2 123	22 719	39 222	10 458	25 441
November	181 577	. . .	35 477	. . .	5 046	2 151	23 301	38 923	10 789	24 324
December	181 095	. . .	35 168	. . .	5 241	2 184	23 541	37 588	10 919	24 156
2016										
January	179 117	. . .	33 870	. . .	4 304	1 800	23 348	38 863	10 380	25 181
February	182 967	. . .	34 526	. . .	4 131	1 879	23 100	40 581	10 544	24 140
March	174 256	. . .	34 155	. . .	4 427	2 363	22 174	36 622	10 840	24 242
April	177 026	. . .	34 575	. . .	4 095	1 989	22 824	36 615	10 796	24 160
May	180 263	. . .	34 193	. . .	4 591	2 085	22 950	37 977	10 632	24 289
June	184 097	. . .	35 584	. . .	5 177	2 050	23 113	37 939	10 895	23 958
July	183 125	. . .	34 309	. . .	5 072	2 015	22 940	39 115	11 167	24 186
August	193 573	. . .	34 735	. . .	4 986	2 555	23 182	38 956	10 965	24 413
September	182 638	. . .	34 880	. . .	4 978	2 330	22 862	37 777	11 060	24 670
October	184 350	. . .	34 967	. . .	5 246	2 345	23 414	39 285	11 394	24 884
November	186 884	. . .	34 696	. . .	5 600	2 264	24 306	39 082	11 312	24 825
December	189 508	. . .	35 886	. . .	5 756	2 379	23 544	39 807	12 062	25 108

[1]See notes and definitions for definitions of regions.
[2]With the June 3, 2016 Annual Revision for 2015, the area grouping "Newly Industrialized Countries" has been revised.
. . . = Not available.

Table 7-15A. U.S. Exports of Services: Recent Data

(Balance of payments basis, millions of dollars, seasonally adjusted.)

Year and month	Total services	Maintenance and repair services, n.i.e.	Transport	Travel for all purposes including education	Insurance services	Financial services	Charges for the use of intellectual property n.i.e	Telecommun- ications, computer and information services	Other business services	Government goods and services, n.i.e.
1999	271 343	3 812	43 218	92 338	3 052	19 433	47 731	12 287	40 976	8 495
2000	290 381	4 686	45 758	100 187	3 631	22 117	51 808	12 215	40 497	9 481
2001	274 323	5 575	41 716	86 733	3 424	21 899	49 489	12 829	44 146	8 514
2002	280 670	5 769	41 912	81 869	4 415	24 496	53 859	12 451	47 996	7 903
2003	289 972	5 458	41 446	80 332	5 974	27 840	56 813	14 061	48 775	9 274
2004	337 966	5 342	47 723	92 387	7 314	36 389	67 094	14 962	54 398	12 357
2005	373 006	7 218	52 622	101 470	7 566	39 878	74 448	15 515	58 302	15 989
2006	416 738	7 673	57 462	105 140	9 445	47 882	83 549	17 184	68 619	19 783
2007	488 396	9 062	65 824	119 037	10 841	61 376	97 803	20 192	82 382	21 879
2008	532 817	10 019	74 973	133 761	13 403	63 027	102 125	23 119	92 700	10 652
2009	512 722	12 077	62 189	119 902	14 586	64 437	98 406	23 816	95 984	21 324
2010	563 333	13 860	71 656	137 010	14 397	72 348	107 521	25 038	101 029	20 474
2011	627 781	14 279	79 830	150 867	15 114	78 271	123 333	29 171	112 568	24 348
2012	654 850	15 115	83 592	161 249	16 534	76 605	125 492	32 103	119 892	24 267
2013	701 455	18 568	86 776	177 484	16 696	95 131	128 034	34 419	121 530	22 816
2014	743 257	22 132	90 701	191 325	17 312	107 712	129 890	35 044	128 817	20 325
2015	753 150	23 406	87 609	205 418	16 229	102 595	124 442	35 664	136 622	21 165
2016	752 368	25 628	84 318	205 940	16 348	98 180	124 453	36 455	142 231	18 814
2014										
January	60 732	1 715	7 348	15 583	1 402	8 544	10 803	2 853	10 527	1 957
February	61 067	1 750	7 299	15 711	1 393	8 633	10 864	2 847	10 601	1 970
March	61 421	1 838	7 294	15 565	1 411	9 014	10 914	2 886	10 602	1 897
April	61 861	1 867	7 486	15 525	1 458	9 354	10 952	2 972	10 529	1 718
May	62 258	1 899	7 618	15 763	1 479	9 426	10 948	3 006	10 491	1 629
June	62 091	1 891	7 512	15 853	1 475	9 358	10 902	2 987	10 488	1 625
July	61 839	1 857	7 584	15 996	1 445	9 003	10 812	2 917	10 519	1 706
August	61 823	1 877	7 729	16 079	1 433	8 720	10 764	2 883	10 621	1 715
September	62 073	1 817	7 715	16 233	1 438	8 778	10 757	2 885	10 796	1 654
October	62 651	1 858	7 690	16 272	1 460	9 061	10 791	2 923	11 043	1 553
November	62 394	1 870	7 569	16 324	1 465	8 770	10 750	2 943	11 233	1 469
December	63 046	1 893	7 856	16 420	1 454	9 049	10 633	2 944	11 367	1 432
2015										
January	62 786	1 722	7 339	16 584	1 412	9 199	10 401	2 914	11 485	1 730
February	62 709	1 787	7 237	16 570	1 384	9 208	10 270	2 936	11 525	1 793
March	62 906	1 838	7 255	16 718	1 365	9 185	10 270	2 940	11 518	1 817
April	62 870	1 852	7 295	17 003	1 356	8 784	10 400	2 926	11 464	1 792
May	62 995	1 849	7 412	17 278	1 347	8 509	10 487	2 925	11 381	1 807
June	63 294	1 882	7 397	17 632	1 339	8 466	10 528	2 937	11 269	1 842
July	62 817	1 882	7 362	17 323	1 332	8 381	10 526	2 962	11 129	1 920
August	62 804	1 925	7 372	17 329	1 331	8 362	10 476	2 987	11 097	1 927
September	62 416	1 985	7 243	17 179	1 337	8 253	10 377	3 010	11 172	1 859
October	62 558	2 170	7 372	17 186	1 350	8 234	10 230	3 033	11 356	1 627
November	62 436	2 255	7 212	17 234	1 347	8 055	10 198	3 045	11 530	1 559
December	62 559	2 260	7 113	17 382	1 328	7 959	10 281	3 048	11 694	1 493
2016										
January	62 005	2 025	7 117	17 167	1 292	7 792	10 291	3 042	11 849	1 431
February	61 754	2 002	6 882	17 115	1 275	7 714	10 399	3 035	11 902	1 430
March	61 921	2 003	6 998	17 109	1 278	7 741	10 421	3 027	11 856	1 487
April	62 080	2 044	6 988	17 010	1 301	7 862	10 543	3 020	11 709	1 602
May	62 407	2 116	7 003	17 048	1 327	8 032	10 492	3 013	11 692	1 685
June	62 946	2 232	7 069	17 057	1 356	8 230	10 458	3 005	11 804	1 734
July	63 102	2 213	6 959	17 170	1 387	8 138	10 441	2 997	12 047	1 751
August	63 310	2 171	7 055	17 130	1 410	8 287	10 402	3 006	12 131	1 718
September	63 382	2 250	7 002	17 218	1 423	8 423	10 341	3 031	12 057	1 637
October	63 084	2 227	6 968	17 274	1 426	8 524	10 260	3 073	11 824	1 508
November	63 196	2 148	7 092	17 315	1 432	8 774	10 211	3 099	11 695	1 429
December	63 181	2 196	7 184	17 328	1 440	8 661	10 195	3 109	11 667	1 401

n.i.e = Not included elsewhere.

Table 7-15B. U.S. Exports of Services: Historical

(Balance of payments basis, millions of dollars, seasonally adjusted.)

Year	Total	Travel	Passenger fares	Other transportation	Royalties and license fees	Other private services (financial, professional, etc.)	Transfers under U.S. military sales contracts 1	U.S. government miscellaneous services
1960	6 290	919	175	1 607	837	570	2 030	153
1961	6 295	947	183	1 620	906	607	1 867	164
1962	6 941	957	191	1 764	1 056	585	2 193	195
1963	7 348	1 015	205	1 898	1 162	613	2 219	236
1964	7 840	1 207	241	2 076	1 314	651	2 086	265
1965	8 824	1 380	271	2 175	1 534	714	2 465	285
1966	9 616	1 590	317	2 333	1 516	814	2 721	326
1967	10 667	1 646	371	2 426	1 747	951	3 191	336
1968	11 917	1 775	411	2 548	1 867	1 024	3 939	353
1969	12 806	2 043	450	2 652	2 019	1 160	4 138	343
1970	14 171	2 331	544	3 125	2 331	1 294	4 214	332
1971	16 358	2 534	615	3 299	2 545	1 546	5 472	347
1972	17 841	2 817	699	3 579	2 770	1 764	5 856	357
1973	19 832	3 412	975	4 465	3 225	1 985	5 369	401
1974	22 591	4 032	1 104	5 697	3 821	2 321	5 197	419
1975	25 497	4 697	1 039	5 840	4 300	2 920	6 256	446
1976	27 971	5 742	1 229	6 747	4 353	3 584	5 826	489
1977	31 485	6 150	1 366	7 090	4 920	3 848	7 554	557
1978	36 353	7 183	1 603	8 136	5 885	4 717	8 209	620
1979	39 692	8 441	2 156	9 971	6 184	5 439	6 981	520
1980	47 584	10 588	2 591	11 618	7 085	6 276	9 029	398
1981	57 354	12 913	3 111	12 560	7 284	10 250	10 720	517
1982	64 079	12 393	3 174	12 317	5 603	17 444	12 572	576
1983	64 307	10 947	3 610	12 590	5 778	18 192	12 524	666
1984	71 168	17 177	4 067	13 809	6 177	19 255	9 969	714
1985	73 155	17 762	4 411	14 674	6 678	20 035	8 718	878
1986	86 689	20 385	5 582	15 438	8 113	28 027	8 549	595
1987	98 661	23 563	7 003	17 027	10 174	29 263	11 106	526
1988	110 919	29 434	8 976	19 311	12 139	31 111	9 284	664
1989	127 087	36 205	10 657	20 526	13 818	36 729	8 564	587
1990	147 832	43 007	15 298	22 042	16 634	40 251	9 932	668
1991	164 261	48 385	15 854	22 631	17 819	47 748	11 135	690
1992	177 252	54 742	16 618	21 531	20 841	50 292	12 387	841
1993	185 920	57 875	16 528	21 958	21 695	53 510	13 471	883
1994	200 395	58 417	16 997	23 754	26 712	60 841	12 787	887
1995	219 183	63 395	18 909	26 081	30 289	65 048	14 643	818
1996	239 489	69 809	20 422	26 074	32 470	73 340	16 446	928
1997	256 087	73 426	20 868	27 006	33 228	83 929	16 675	955
1998	262 758	71 325	20 098	25 604	35 626	91 774	17 405	926
1999	268 790	75 161	19 425	23 792	47 731	96 812	5 211	657

Note: The category "Royalties and license fees" is the earlier terminology for the category called "Charges for the use of intellectual property n.i.e" in the revised and updated data shown in Tables 7-15A/7-16A. Other categories differ in both title and content; see the Notes and Definitions.

1Contains goods that cannot be separately identified.

Table 7-16A. U.S. Imports of Services: Recent Data

(Balance of payments basis, millions of dollars, seasonally adjusted.)

Year and month	Total services	Maintenance and repair services, n.i.e.	Transport	Travel for all purposes including education	Insurance services	Financial services	Charges for the use of intellectual property n.i.e	Telecommun- ications, computer and information services	Other business services	Government goods and services, n.i.e.
1999	192 893	1 278	49 620	59 592	9 389	8 280	13 302	13 332	23 887	14 212
2000	216 115	2 569	57 606	65 787	11 284	10 936	16 606	12 397	24 414	14 516
2001	213 465	1 999	53 840	60 730	16 706	10 157	16 661	12 421	25 629	15 322
2002	224 379	2 217	51 491	59 942	21 927	8 963	19 493	11 721	29 274	19 353
2003	242 219	2 246	57 863	61 884	25 233	8 948	19 259	13 063	30 103	23 619
2004	283 083	2 395	69 158	74 024	29 089	11 156	23 691	14 210	33 065	26 296
2005	304 448	3 015	75 643	79 988	28 710	12 126	25 577	15 975	35 960	27 454
2006	341 165	4 583	77 962	84 206	39 382	14 733	25 038	19 776	48 130	27 353
2007	372 575	5 209	79 326	89 235	47 517	19 197	26 479	22 384	54 968	28 260
2008	409 052	5 742	83 988	92 545	58 913	17 218	29 623	24 655	67 400	20 000
2009	386 801	5 938	64 133	81 421	63 801	14 415	31 297	25 784	68 553	31 460
2010	409 313	6 909	74 628	86 623	61 478	15 502	32 551	29 015	70 646	31 960
2011	435 761	8 236	81 377	89 700	55 654	17 368	36 087	32 756	83 289	31 293
2012	450 360	7 970	85 029	100 317	53 203	16 975	39 502	32 156	87 347	27 861
2013	461 087	7 420	90 634	98 120	53 420	21 545	38 860	35 034	90 714	25 341
2014	481 264	7 521	94 160	105 529	51 824	24 906	42 208	36 313	94 568	24 236
2015	491 740	9 010	97 061	114 723	47 822	25 740	39 858	36 270	99 665	21 592
2016	504 654	8 810	96 827	123 618	48 077	25 629	44 392	36 851	98 922	21 528
2014										
January	38 635	568	7 623	8 706	4 154	1 574	3 277	2 783	7 933	2 018
February	39 270	587	7 642	8 742	4 107	1 510	3 987	2 781	7 903	2 010
March	38 908	607	7 827	8 860	4 119	1 562	3 232	2 777	7 912	2 012
April	39 417	627	7 783	9 127	4 189	1 602	3 336	2 770	7 958	2 025
May	39 934	627	7 877	9 396	4 222	1 638	3 411	2 768	7 959	2 035
June	39 968	623	7 756	9 377	4 217	1 673	3 589	2 774	7 917	2 043
July	39 734	625	7 725	9 320	4 174	1 663	3 562	2 785	7 831	2 048
August	39 599	606	7 783	9 246	4 157	1 652	3 491	2 789	7 833	2 041
September	39 793	623	7 869	9 200	4 165	1 688	3 518	2 785	7 924	2 021
October	40 489	636	7 992	9 567	4 198	1 680	3 550	2 773	8 103	1 990
November	40 417	657	7 947	9 455	4 206	1 628	3 576	2 766	8 216	1 967
December	41 264	681	8 395	9 792	4 188	1 634	3 595	2 763	8 262	1 953
2015										
January	40 452	693	8 023	9 216	4 055	2 049	3 295	3 015	8 247	1 859
February	40 114	696	7 961	9 196	3 980	2 048	3 192	2 993	8 231	1 818
March	40 755	716	8 511	9 257	3 943	2 129	3 180	2 992	8 224	1 803
April	40 775	708	8 098	9 545	3 945	2 170	3 260	3 012	8 224	1 814
May	40 919	709	8 096	9 588	3 957	2 180	3 302	3 031	8 237	1 820
June	41 010	772	7 996	9 595	3 980	2 231	3 306	3 049	8 262	1 820
July	41 226	813	8 142	9 561	4 014	2 245	3 271	3 066	8 299	1 814
August	41 309	820	8 185	9 595	4 026	2 196	3 282	3 063	8 338	1 803
September	41 369	814	8 151	9 686	4 016	2 159	3 339	3 040	8 379	1 786
October	41 282	783	7 943	9 794	3 984	2 156	3 442	2 996	8 421	1 764
November	41 314	754	8 016	9 828	3 965	2 096	3 493	2 990	8 422	1 749
December	41 215	732	7 940	9 862	3 958	2 080	3 494	3 024	8 382	1 742
2016										
January	41 319	711	7 970	10 012	3 964	2 076	3 445	3 097	8 302	1 743
February	41 534	714	8 140	10 058	3 957	2 097	3 423	3 118	8 273	1 753
March	41 298	712	7 856	10 088	3 935	2 118	3 430	3 089	8 298	1 771
April	41 609	696	8 082	10 189	3 900	2 095	3 464	3 008	8 375	1 799
May	41 580	689	8 078	10 175	3 898	2 071	3 502	2 975	8 379	1 814
June	41 575	716	8 006	10 151	3 930	2 119	3 541	2 988	8 309	1 815
July	41 673	721	7 977	10 247	3 995	2 132	3 583	3 048	8 167	1 803
August	43 203	751	8 006	10 393	4 044	2 160	4 865	3 088	8 098	1 797
September	42 413	774	8 092	10 577	4 077	2 189	3 696	3 108	8 102	1 799
October	42 754	759	8 236	10 634	4 094	2 173	3 766	3 108	8 179	1 807
November	42 738	782	8 148	10 517	4 122	2 208	3 820	3 110	8 219	1 813
December	42 959	784	8 237	10 578	4 161	2 191	3 858	3 113	8 221	1 815

n.i.e = Not included elsewhere.

Table 7-16B. U.S. Imports of Services: Historical

(Balance of payments basis, millions of dollars, seasonally adjusted.)

Year	Total	Travel	Passenger fares	Other transportation	Royalties and license fees	Other private services (financial, professional, etc.)	Direct defense expenditures [1]	U.S. government miscellaneous services
1960	7 674	1 750	513	1 402	74	593	3 087	254
1961	7 671	1 785	506	1 437	89	588	2 998	268
1962	8 092	1 939	567	1 558	100	528	3 105	296
1963	8 362	2 114	612	1 701	112	493	2 961	370
1964	8 619	2 211	642	1 817	127	527	2 880	415
1965	9 111	2 438	717	1 951	135	461	2 952	457
1966	10 494	2 657	753	2 161	140	506	3 764	513
1967	11 863	3 207	829	2 157	166	565	4 378	561
1968	12 302	3 030	885	2 367	186	668	4 535	631
1969	13 322	3 373	1 080	2 455	221	751	4 856	586
1970	14 520	3 980	1 215	2 843	224	827	4 855	576
1971	15 400	4 373	1 290	3 130	241	956	4 819	592
1972	16 868	5 042	1 596	3 520	294	1 043	4 784	589
1973	18 843	5 526	1 790	4 694	385	1 180	4 629	640
1974	21 379	5 980	2 095	5 942	346	1 262	5 032	722
1975	21 996	6 417	2 263	5 708	472	1 551	4 795	789
1976	24 570	6 856	2 568	6 852	482	2 006	4 895	911
1977	27 640	7 451	2 748	7 972	504	2 190	5 823	951
1978	32 189	8 475	2 896	9 124	671	2 573	7 352	1 099
1979	36 689	9 413	3 184	10 906	831	2 822	8 294	1 239
1980	41 491	10 397	3 607	11 790	724	2 909	10 851	1 214
1981	45 503	11 479	4 487	12 474	650	3 562	11 564	1 287
1982	51 749	12 394	4 772	11 710	795	8 159	12 460	1 460
1983	54 973	13 149	6 003	12 222	943	8 001	13 087	1 568
1984	67 748	22 913	5 735	14 843	1 168	9 040	12 516	1 534
1985	72 862	24 558	6 444	15 643	1 170	10 203	13 108	1 735
1986	80 147	25 913	6 505	17 766	1 401	13 146	13 730	1 686
1987	90 787	29 310	7 283	19 010	1 857	16 485	14 950	1 893
1988	98 526	32 114	7 729	20 891	2 601	17 667	15 604	1 921
1989	102 479	33 416	8 249	22 172	2 528	18 930	15 313	1 871
1990	117 659	37 349	10 531	24 966	3 135	22 229	17 531	1 919
1991	118 459	35 322	10 012	24 975	4 035	25 590	16 409	2 116
1992	119 566	38 552	10 603	23 767	5 161	25 386	13 835	2 263
1993	123 779	40 713	11 410	24 524	5 032	27 760	12 086	2 255
1994	133 057	43 782	13 062	26 019	5 852	31 565	10 217	2 560
1995	141 397	44 916	14 663	27 034	6 919	35 199	10 043	2 623
1996	152 554	48 078	15 809	27 403	7 837	39 679	11 061	2 687
1997	165 932	52 051	18 138	28 959	9 161	43 154	11 707	2 762
1998	180 677	56 483	19 971	30 363	11 235	47 591	12 185	2 849
1999	195 172	59 332	20 946	31 494	13 302	55 885	11 849	2 364

Note: The category "Royalties and license fees" is the earlier terminology for the category called "Charges for the use of intellectual property n.i.e" in the revised and updated data shown in Tables 7-15A/7-16A. Other categories differ in both title and content; see the Notes and Definitions.

[1]Contains goods that cannot be separately identified.

Table 7-17. U.S. Export and Import Price Indexes by End-Use Category

(2000 = 100, not seasonally adjusted.)

Year and month	Exports			Imports		
	All commodities	Agricultural	Nonagricultural	All commodities	Petroleum [1]	Nonpetroleum
1990	95.5	105.1	94.4	94.0	75.5	97.1
1991	96.3	103.4	95.4	94.2	67.3	98.7
1992	96.3	102.5	95.7	94.9	62.9	100.0
1993	96.9	104.4	96.2	94.6	57.7	100.6
1994	98.9	109.4	98.0	96.2	54.3	103.2
1995	103.9	119.0	102.5	100.6	59.8	107.2
1996	104.5	132.6	101.6	101.6	71.1	106.4
1997	103.1	120.6	101.3	99.1	66.0	104.1
1998	99.7	108.8	98.8	93.1	44.8	100.4
1999	98.4	101.1	98.2	93.9	60.1	99.0
2000	100.0	100.0	100.0	100.0	100.0	100.0
2001	99.2	101.2	99.0	96.5	82.8	98.5
2002	98.2	103.2	97.8	94.1	85.3	96.2
2000	99.7	112.3	98.8	96.9	103.2	97.3
2004	103.6	123.4	102.1	102.3	134.6	99.8
2005	106.9	121.0	105.9	110.0	185.1	102.5
2006	110.7	125.8	109.6	115.4	223.3	104.2
2007	116.1	150.9	113.6	120.2	249.1	107.0
2008	123.1	183.5	118.8	134.1	343.2	112.7
2009	117.4	160.0	114.3	118.6	219.9	108.0
2010	123.1	172.6	119.6	126.8	282.2	111.0
2011	133.0	211.0	127.5	140.6	385.1	115.9
2012	133.5	216.1	127.6	141.0	384.0	116.3
2013	133.0	219.7	126.7	139.5	374.2	115.6
2014	132.3	213.8	126.3	138.0	353.2	115.7
2015	123.9	185.4	119.3	123.9	190.8	112.7
2016	119.9	175.5	115.7	119.8	153.1	110.8
2013						
January	134.1	224.6	127.5	140.1	371.2	116.6
February	135.1	229.1	128.3	141.3	385.7	116.6
March	134.4	224.9	127.9	141.2	385.6	116.5
April	133.6	220.1	127.3	140.2	374.2	116.5
May	132.9	222.5	126.4	139.4	367.4	116.1
June	132.8	224.2	126.2	138.8	364.9	115.7
July	132.6	223.5	126.0	138.9	374.4	115.0
August	131.9	214.2	126.0	139.4	385.2	114.8
September	132.4	215.4	126.4	139.8	389.6	114.8
October	131.6	212.6	125.8	138.9	375.6	114.9
November	131.8	212.1	125.9	137.7	358.4	115.0
December	132.3	212.8	126.4	137.8	357.7	115.2
2014						
January	132.7	212.7	126.9	138.3	358.0	115.7
February	133.7	215.6	127.7	139.8	376.7	116.0
March	134.9	221.7	128.6	140.5	378.8	116.5
April	133.5	225.0	127.0	139.7	374.5	116.1
May	133.7	225.6	127.0	140.1	381.5	116.0
June	133.0	221.4	126.6	140.5	387.9	115.8
July	133.1	217.5	126.9	140.1	382.2	115.8
August	132.4	210.8	126.6	139.0	368.6	115.7
September	131.9	207.5	126.3	137.9	354.9	115.6
October	130.7	202.9	125.4	136.0	329.4	115.4
November	129.5	203.2	124.1	133.5	297.6	115.1
December	128.3	201.8	122.9	130.1	248.7	115.1
2015						
January	126.1	199.0	120.7	126.0	196.0	114.3
February	125.9	194.6	120.9	125.5	193.3	114.0
March	125.9	191.4	121.1	125.3	197.6	113.5
April	125.1	189.7	120.3	125.1	202.4	113.0
May	125.7	187.3	121.0	126.5	226.1	112.9
June	125.3	184.3	120.9	126.6	229.7	112.8
July	124.8	186.1	120.2	125.4	215.3	112.5
August	123.0	181.5	118.6	123.2	186.2	112.1
September	122.3	178.9	118.0	121.9	168.7	111.9
October	122.0	179.0	117.7	121.5	168.3	111.5
November	121.1	177.3	116.9	120.8	161.5	111.2
December	119.8	175.7	115.6	119.3	144.6	110.8
2016						
January	118.7	173.5	114.6	117.8	119.8	110.7
February	118.2	174.7	113.9	117.2	111.2	110.5
March	118.1	171.0	114.1	117.7	123.2	110.4
April	118.7	172.4	114.6	118.5	136.4	110.4
May	120.0	177.5	115.7	119.9	155.4	110.8
June	120.9	181.9	116.3	120.7	173.1	110.5
July	121.1	181.3	116.6	120.8	167.8	111.0
August	120.1	175.1	115.9	120.5	160.9	111.1
September	120.5	173.3	116.5	120.6	162.3	111.2
October	120.7	174.2	116.7	121.2	174.4	111.1
November	120.8	175.4	116.7	121.1	171.5	111.1
December	121.3	175.1	117.2	121.6	181.6	111.1

[1]Petroleum and petroleum products.

NOTES AND DEFINITIONS, CHAPTER 7

CHAPTER 7: U.S. FOREIGN TRADE AND FINANCE

This chapter presents data from two different data systems on international flows of goods, services, income payments, and financial transactions as they affect the U.S. economy. Tables 7-1 through 7-5 present data on the value, quantities, and prices of foreign transactions in the national income and product accounts (NIPAs). Tables 7-6 through 7-8 show foreign transactions and investment positions in current-dollar values as depicted in the U.S. international transactions accounts (ITAs). Both sets of accounts are prepared by the Bureau of Economic Analysis (BEA) and draw on the same original source data. The Census Bureau source data for exports and imports of goods and services are presented in greater detail in Tables 7-9 through 7-16. Table 7-17 shows selected summary values for export and import price indexes compiled by the Bureau of Labor Statistics (BLS).

Due to a few differences in concept, scope, and definitions, the aggregate values of international transactions in the NIPAs (shown in Tables 7-1 and 7-4) are not exactly equal to the values for similar concepts in the ITAs or the Census values that serve as their sources, shown in Tables 7-6 through 7-16. The principal sources of differences are as follows:

- The NIPAs cover only the 50 states and the District of Columbia. The ITAs include the U.S. territories and Puerto Rico as part of the U.S. economy.

- Gold is treated differently.

- Services without payment by financial intermediaries except life insurance carriers (imputed interest) is treated differently.

A reconciliation of the two sets of international accounts is published from time to time in the *Survey of Current Business*.

The conventions of presentation no longer differ between the two sets of international accounts. In all the tables that follow, as in their source documents, values of imports of goods and services and of all other transactions that result in a payment to the rest of the world—income payments to foreigners, net transfers to foreigners, and net acquisition of assets from abroad—are presented normally as positive. Where a minus sign does appear, it means that the usual direction of flow is reversed—for example, in the columns of the financial account in Table 7-6 labeled as "Net U.S. acquisition of financial assets," a minus sign would indicate net sales of such assets.

TABLES 7-1 AND 7-4

Foreign Transactions in the National Income and Product Accounts

SOURCE: U.S. DEPARTMENT OF COMMERCE, BUREAU OF ECONOMIC ANALYSIS

See the notes and definitions to Chapter 1 for an overview of the national income and product accounts (NIPAs).

In the 2003 comprehensive revision, the NIPA foreign transactions account was split into two accounts—the current account and the capital account. (This change had already been made in the ITAs.) Most international transactions fall into the current account, but occasionally there are substantial flows in the capital account when major already-existing assets are transferred. An example of this is the U.S. government's transfer of the Panama Canal to the Republic of Panama in 1999.

Results from the 2017 Annual Update of the National Income and Products Accounts (NIPAs) slightly revised gross domestic product for 2013 to 2016. Other revisions were incorporated include the Census Bureau's annual retail sales, construction, manufacturing plus others.

Definitions

In accordance with the split between current and capital account, there are now two NIPA measures of the balance of international transactions.

The *balance on current account, national income and product accounts* is *current receipts from the rest of the world* minus *current payments to the rest of the world*. A negative value indicates that current payments exceed current receipts.

Net lending or net borrowing (-), national income and product accounts is equal to the balance on current account less capital account transactions with the rest of the world (net). Capital account transactions with the rest of the world (net) is not shown separately in Table 7-1 (for space reasons) but can be calculated from that table as the difference between net lending/borrowing and the current account balance. (A similar measure, a component of the ITAs, is shown explicitly in Table 7-6.) Capital account transactions with the rest of the world are cash or in-kind transfers linked to the acquisition or disposition of an existing, nonproduced, nonfinancial asset. In contrast, the current account is limited to flows associated with current production of goods and services.

Net lending or net borrowing provides an indirect measure of the net acquisition of foreign assets by U.S. residents less the net acquisition of U.S. assets by foreign residents. These asset flows are measured directly in the ITAs. See Table 7-6 and its notes and definitions for a more extensive discussion of the relationship between the balances on current and capital account and international asset flows.

Current receipts from the rest of the world is *exports of goods and services* plus *income receipts.*

Current payments to the rest of the world is *imports of goods and services* plus *income payments* plus *current taxes and transfer payments (net).*

Exports and imports of goods and services. Goods, in general, are products that can be stored or inventoried. *Services,* in general, are products that cannot be stored and are consumed at the place and time of their purchase. Goods imports include expenditures abroad by U.S. residents, except for travel. Services include foreign travel by U.S. residents, expenditures in the United States by foreign travelers, and exports and imports of certain goods—primarily military equipment purchased and sold by the federal government. See the following paragraph for the definition of *travel.*

Table 7-4 shows values for selected components of total goods and services; the components shown will not add to the total because of omitted items. In the case of goods, a miscellaneous "other" category is not shown. In the case of services, only two components are shown in this table. One is *travel* (for all purposes including education), which does not include passenger fares but includes as exports spending by foreign tourists and students in the United States, and includes as imports all other spending abroad by tourists and students from the United States. The other component shown here is a category called *other business services,* which includes the professional and financial services (for example, computer services) that have accounted for a large part of the long-term growth in the service category. The remaining components of total services are transport (of both persons and goods), charges for the use of intellectual property not elsewhere classified, government goods and services not elsewhere classified, and a miscellaneous, smaller *other* category. They are shown separately in Tables 7-15 and 7-16.

Income receipts and payments. Income receipts—receipts from abroad of factor (labor or capital) income by U.S. residents—are analogous to exports and are combined with them to yield total *current receipts from the rest of the world. Income payments* by U.S. entities of factor income to entities abroad are analogous to imports.

Current taxes and transfer payments (net) consists of net payments between the United States and abroad that do not involve payment for the services of the labor or capital factors of production, purchase of currently-produced goods and services, or transfer of an existing asset. It includes net flows from persons, government, and business. The types of payments included are personal remittances from U.S. residents to the rest of the world, net of remittances from foreigners to U.S. residents; government grants; and transfer payments from businesses. Only the net payment to the rest of the world is shown. It usually appears in these accounts as a positive value, with transfers from the United States to abroad exceeding the reverse flow. An exception came in 1991, when U.S. allies in the Gulf War reimbursed the United States for the cost of the war, causing the only current-account surplus since 1981. This resulted in net payments to the United States from the rest of the world and appears as a negative entry in the net transfer payments column of the NIPA accounts.

TABLES 7-2, 7-3 AND 7-5

Chain-Type Quantity and Price Indexes for NIPA Foreign Transactions

These indexes represent the separation of the current-dollar values in Tables 7-1 and 7-4 into their real quantity and price trends components. (See the notes and definitions to Chapter 1 for a general explanation of chained-dollar estimates of real output and prices.) As those notes explain, quantity indexes are shown instead of constant-dollar estimates, because BEA no longer publishes its real output estimates before 1999 in any detail in the constant-dollar form. Therefore, quantity indexes are the only comprehensive source of information about longer-term trends in real volumes.

TABLE 7-6A AND B

U.S. International Transactions: Recent Data

SOURCE: U.S. DEPARTMENT OF COMMERCE, BUREAU OF ECONOMIC ANALYSIS

The U.S. international transactions accounts (ITAs), or "balance of payments accounts," provide a comprehensive view of economic and financial transactions between the United States and foreign countries, measured in current dollars only–unlike the NIPAs, in which price and quantity trends are also estimated. Direct measurement of financial asset and liability flows further distinguishes this set of accounts from the NIPAs.

As was mentioned briefly in the introduction to these Notes and Definitions, the ITAs have been revised and updated, and in addition are now presented in an entirely different manner.

There is no change in the underlying concept: the U.S. balance on current account is still the sum of exports and income receipts, minus the sum of imports and income payments. When it is positive, it necessarily implies net acquisition of assets abroad, and when it is negative, it necessarily implies incurrence of liabilities abroad.

The old, pre-2014 system, which was shown in previous editions of *Business Statistics,* classified all current and financial transactions into debit and credit entries and presented all debits with a negative sign, so that the whole system in theory summed to zero. This method of presentation was not in agreement with other reporting systems, such as the NIPAs and the trade accounts published by the Census Bureau; and while it was internally consistent and logical, it was difficult to interpret and explain. The new system is more straightforward, much easier to explain, and brings the statistics into closer alignment with other statistical systems and international guidelines. Because the debit flows are now presented as normally positive values, balances must be defined as subtractions rather than algebraic sums, probably making them easier to grasp.

The data set now presents as positive values exports, imports, income receipts, income payments, transfers made, transfers received, acquisitions of assets, and incurrences of liabilities. Negative signs are only uses to specify negative income (losses), net sales of assets, net repayment of liabilities, and balances. Current-account and capital-account balances indicate the difference between underlying gross credit and debit flows (for example, exports less imports) and can be positive or negative. For the financial account, net borrowing is calculated as the difference between the net acquisition of financial assets excluding financial derivatives and the net incurrence of liabilities excluding financial derivatives, plus net transactions in financial derivatives.

Definitions

Exports and imports of goods and services. See Tables 7-9 through 7-16 for composition and definitions of goods and services.

Primary income payments and receipts comprise *investment income* and *compensation of employees.*

Investment income includes *direct investment income receipts* (income from direct international ownership of businesses), *portfolio investment income* (dividends and interest from international holdings of stocks and bonds), *other investment income receipts,* and in the case of the United States, *reserve asset income receipts* from official ownership of international reserve assets.

Secondary income includes foreign aid, remittances, U.S. government pensions, and other current international receipts and payments that are not compensation or investment income.

The *capital account* includes capital transfers and the acquisition and disposal of non-produced nonfinancial assets. The major type of *capital transfers* is debt forgiveness. As of the 2010 comprehensive revision, and beginning with the data for 1982, migrants' transfers—the net worth of individuals who immigrate or emigrate during a period—are excluded from the capital account, as they do not generate transactions between a resident and a nonresident. This change is in accordance with international guidelines. Migrants' investments in their country of origin will continue to be recorded in the international investment position accounts (shown in Table 7-8) when migration changes the status of these investments from domestic to international, but they will enter the position as "other changes in value." Non-produced nonfinancial assets include rights to natural resources, patents, copyrights, trademarks, franchises, and leases. In the July 2009 revision, insurance payments for extraordinary disaster losses such as those caused by major hurricanes and the 2001 terror attack were shifted to the capital account from the current unilateral transfers account.

The *financial account* comprises *net U.S. acquisition of financial assets excluding financial derivatives,* which when positive represent a financial outflow, or U.S. investment abroad; *net U.S. incurrence of liabilities excluding financial derivatives,* which when positive represents a financial inflow, or U.S. borrowing abroad; and *financial derivatives other than reserves, net.*

Financial assets include *direct investment assets,* which in turn comprise *direct equity assets* and *direct debt instruments assets; portfolio investment assets,* which in turn comprise *equity and investment fund shares assets, short-term debt securities assets,* and *long term debt securities assets; other investment assets,* which include *currency and deposits, loans, trade credit and advances,* and insurance technical reserves; and U.S. *reserve assets.* (For the definition of *direct investment,* see the Notes and Definitions for Table 7-8.)

Net U.S. incurrence of liabilities excluding financial derivatives, i.e. U.S. borrowing, is reported in categories comparable to those in the asset accounts.

Financial derivatives other than reserves are reported on a net basis.

The *total balance on current account,* the featured measure of U.S. transactions with the rest of the world, is the sum of the *balance on goods and services, balance on primary income,* and *balance on secondary income.* It is sometimes just referred to as the "balance of payments."

The *balance on goods* is the excess of exports of goods over imports of goods. A minus sign indicates an excess of imports over exports. A similar concept, which appears in monthly trade reports, is called the "merchandise trade balance."

The *balance on services* is the excess of service exports over service imports. A minus sign indicates an excess of imports over exports.

The *balance on goods and services* is the sum of the balance on goods and the balance on services. This concept is accurately described as the "balance of trade."

The *balance on capital account* is *capital transfer receipts and other credits* minus *capital transfer payments and other debits*.

By definition, the sum of the current and capital account balances should be the amount of *net lending (+) or net borrowing (−)* required, and it is shown at the end of Table 7-6A, in the column headed *Based on current and capital account transactions*. Also shown is the actual estimate of net lending or net borrowing *Based on financial account transactions*, which is *Total net acquisition of assets* minus *Total net incurrence of liabilities* plus *Financial derivatives other than reserves, net.* This sum is usually not equal to the sum of the current and capital accounts, which are measured from different sources. The difference between the two estimates of lending/borrowing is the *statistical discrepancy.* (Note that there is also a statistical discrepancy in the NIPAs, which also arises from measurement differences, but is not the same as the discrepancy in the ITAs.) In the quarterly accounts, a part of this discrepancy, the *seasonal adjustment discrepancy*, results from separate seasonal adjustments of the components of the accounts.

Data availability

Quarterly estimates are reported in a press release around the middle of the third month of each quarter, available on the BEA Web site at <http://www.bea.gov>. The data published here were released on June 2, 2017, and provide revised and restructured information in detail back to the first quarter of 1999. Data for earlier years have not been revised, but key aggregates and components for those years are presented in a format consistent with the new structure. Complete historical data are available on the BEA Web site at <http://www.bea.gov/>.

REFERENCES

Articles in the March 2014 and June 2014 *Survey of Current Business* describe the 2014 restructuring and revision of the U.S. International Transactions Accounts (ITAs). The *SCB* is available on the BEA Web site. Further information is provided in "U.S. International Economic Accounts: Concepts and Methods," also available on the BEA website.

TABLE 7-7

Foreigners' Transactions in Long-Term Securities with U.S. Residents

SOURCE: U.S. DEPARTMENT OF THE TREASURY

Some of the transactions that go into the ITA financial account are collected monthly. Since December 2003, these transactions have been reported by the Treasury Department in a monthly press release. They are presented in Table 7-7.

These data cover transactions in long-term securities, measured at market value plus or minus commissions and fees, between foreigners and U.S. residents. They have more reporting gaps than the more comprehensive quarterly current account data in Table 7-6. These monthly data do not include direct investment, currency flows, changes in bank accounts, or transactions in short-term securities. They may be distorted by inappropriate reporting of repurchases and securities lending transactions. The data are more timely but less detailed than other information sources and are not reliable for country-by-country detail. They are based on a reporting panel of some 250 banks, securities dealers, and other enterprises with cross-border transactions of at least $50 million. This survey was designed to provide timely information for the balance of payments accounts, and its use for other applications—particularly those involving country detail—is less appropriate.

Definitions and notes on the data

U.S. residents includes any individual, corporation, or organization located in the United States (including branches, subsidiaries, and affiliates of foreign entities located in the United States) and any corporation incorporated in the United States, even if it has no physical presence in the country.

Gross purchases minus *gross sales* equals *net purchases*. Positive values for net purchases of U.S. securities by foreigners indicate capital inflows from foreigners to U.S. residents (and increased liabilities to foreigners on the part of the U.S. residents). Negative values for net purchases of foreign securities from U.S. residents indicate a capital outflow from U.S. residents to foreigners (and increased liabilities to U.S. residents on the part of foreigners). The algebraic sum of the two net purchases components gives *net long-term securities transactions.* When positive, this indicates that the net capital inflows on U.S. securities exceed the net U.S. acquisitions of foreign securities.

Other acquisitions of long-term securities, net consists of estimated foreign acquisitions of U.S. equity through stock swaps, plus the increase in nonmarketable treasury bonds and notes issued to official institutions and other residents of foreign countries, minus estimated unrecorded principal payments to foreigners on domestic corporate and agency asset-backed securities, minus estimated U.S. acquisitions of foreign equity through stock swaps.

Net foreign acquisition of long-term securities is the sum of *net long-term securities transactions* and *other acquisitions of long-term securities.*

Revisions

The monthly and annual data are revised frequently, when quarterly and annual benchmark data become available. The June release usually includes the final results from an annual survey of foreign holding of U.S. securities.

262 BUSINESS STATISTICS OF THE UNITED STATES

DATA AVAILABILITY AND REFERENCES

Data for the latest month and recent historical data are published in a press release available around the middle of the second following month. The press release, supporting descriptions, references, and other relevant information concerning the Treasury International Capital System (TIC) can be found online at <http://www.treas.gov/tic>.

TABLE 7-8

International Investment Position of the United States

SOURCE: U.S. DEPARTMENT OF COMMERCE, BUREAU OF ECONOMIC ANALYSIS

The data presented in Tables 7-1 through 7-7 all represent flows of goods, services, and money over the designated time periods. Table 7-8, in contrast, is a measure of stocks, or total holdings of money and other claims. The data on the international investment position of the United States measure the extent to which the United States and its residents hold claims of ownership on foreigners or are creditors of foreigners; the extent to which foreigners, including foreign governments, hold claims of ownership on assets located in the United States or are creditors of U.S. residents and entities; and the net difference between the two amounts. This difference measures the amount by which the United States is a net creditor of the rest of the world or a net debtor to the rest of the world. A position of net U.S. indebtedness is represented by a minus sign in the net international investment position.

These accounts were revised in June 2014 consistent with the 2014 comprehensive revision of the International Transaction Accounts (ITAs) described in the Notes and Definitions to Table 7-6, above. The principal difference from earlier presentations is that direct investment is now valued at market value. (Previously, the featured measure was based on estimates of current replacement costs.) Quarterly estimates of the position are now available for the first time.

Changes in the net investment position can arise in two principal ways.

The first way is through inflows or outflows of capital. A net inflow of capital increases U.S. indebtedness to foreigners, while a net outflow increases foreigners' indebtedness to the United States. A deficit in the U.S. international current account requires an equivalent inflow of foreign capital, while a surplus would require an equivalent outflow of U.S. capital; see the notes for Table 7-6 for further explanation.

The second way is through valuation adjustments, which are of several kinds: changes in market prices of assets; changes in exchange rates, which can cause revaluation of foreign-currency-denominated assets; and miscellaneous other adjustments due to changes in coverage, statistical discrepancies, and the like. Valuation adjustments are shown separately from financial flows in the *Survey of Current Business* articles accompanying each annual update (see below for reference). They were particularly sharp in 2008 and 2009, far exceeding the actual net volume of financial flows in both years.

For the years 2005 forward, assets and the net position include financial derivatives, which introduces a break in the series. The values for financial derivatives are shown separately so that the user can eliminate them from the calculation if desired.

Definitions: direct investment, current cost, and market value

Direct investment occurs when an individual or business in one country (the parent) obtains a lasting interest in, and a degree of influence over the management of, a business enterprise in another country (the affiliate). The U.S. data define this degree of interest to be ownership of at least 10 percent of the voting securities of an incorporated business enterprise or the equivalent interest in an unincorporated business enterprise.

When direct investment positions are valued at the historical costs carried on the books of the affiliated companies, much of the investment will reflect the price levels of earlier time periods. Restating it at *market value* revalues the owners' equity portion of the direct investment positions using indexes of stock market prices. Stock price changes reflect changes not only in the value of tangible assets, but also in the value of intangible assets and in the outlook for a country or industry.

Definitions: net international investment position

U.S. net international investment position is defined as the value of *U.S. assets* minus the value of *U.S. liabilities.*

U.S. assets is the sum of *direct investment at market value, portfolio investment, gross positive fair value of financial derivatives other than reserves, other investment,* and *U.S. reserve assets.*

As a component of U.S. assets, the *financial derivatives* category is the sum of derivatives positions with a positive "fair value" to U.S. residents. The fair value of a derivatives contract is the amount for which the contract could be exchanged between willing parties. A derivatives contract between a U.S. and a foreign resident with a positive fair value represents the amount that the foreign resident would have to pay to the U.S. resident if the contract was terminated.

Reserve assets includes gold, valued at the current market price; special drawing rights; the U.S. reserve position in the International Monetary Fund; and official holdings of foreign currencies.

U.S. liabilities is the sum of foreign *direct investment* in the United States *at market value, portfolio investment, long-term*

debt securities, gross negative fair value of financial derivatives other than reserves, and *other investment,* which includes *currency and deposits* and *loans.*

As a component of foreign-owned assets in the United States, the *financial derivatives* entry consists of derivatives positions with a negative "fair value" to U.S. residents. A contract with a negative fair value represents the amount that the U.S. resident would have to pay to the foreign resident if the contract was terminated.

Data availability

Data on the U.S. International Investment Position (IIP) are now released quarterly, around the end of the succeeding quarter. The estimates shown here reflect the annual revisions released June 30, 2015. All the data are available on the BEA Web site at <http://www.bea.gov>.

REFERENCES

A detailed discussion of the IIP statistics and the comprehensive revision is scheduled for publication in the July 2014 issue of the *Survey of Current Business.* Also see the references for Table 7-6.

TABLES 7-9 THROUGH 7-16

Exports and Imports of Goods and Services

SOURCES: U.S. DEPARTMENT OF COMMERCE, CENSUS BUREAU AND BUREAU OF ECONOMIC ANALYSIS

These tables present the source data used to build up the aggregate measures of goods and services flows shown in Tables 7-1 through 7-6. These data are compiled and published monthly, making trends evident before the publication of the quarterly aggregate estimates. They also provide more detail than the quarterly aggregates.

Monthly and annual data on exports and imports of *goods* are compiled by the Census Bureau from documents collected by the U.S. Customs Service. The Bureau of Economic Analysis (BEA) makes certain adjustments to these data (as described below) to place the estimates on a *balance of payments* basis—a basis consistent with the national and international accounts.

Data on exports and imports of *services* are prepared by BEA from a variety of sources. Monthly data on services are available from January 1992. Annual and quarterly data for earlier years are available as part of the international transactions accounts. Current data on goods and services are available each month in a joint Census Bureau-BEA press release.

In the case of some of the detailed breakdowns of exports and imports, such as by end-use categories, monthly data may not sum exactly to annual totals. This is due to later revisions, which are made only to annual data and are not allocated to monthly data.

Also, the constant-dollar figures expressed in 2009 dollars are now calculated using chain weights. Therefore, the 2009-dollar detail will not add to the 2009-dollar totals.

In addition, monthly and annual data on exports and imports of goods for individual countries and various country groupings do not reflect subsequent revisions of annual total data. These country data are compiled by the Census Bureau for all countries, although this volume includes only a selection of the most significant countries and areas. The full set of data can be accessed on the Census Web site at <http://www.census.gov>.

Definitions: Goods

Goods: Census basis. The Census basis goods data are compiled from documents collected by the U.S. Customs Service. They reflect the movement of goods between foreign countries and the 50 states, the District of Columbia, Puerto Rico, the U.S. Virgin Islands, and U.S. Foreign Trade Zones. They include government and nongovernment shipments of goods, and exclude shipments between the United States and its territories and possessions; transactions with U.S. military, diplomatic, and consular installations abroad; U.S. goods returned to the United States by its armed forces; personal and household effects of travelers; and intransit shipments. The general import values reflect the total arrival of merchandise from foreign countries that immediately enters consumption channels, warehouses, or Foreign Trade Zones.

For *imports,* the value reported is the U.S. Customs Service appraised value of merchandise (generally, the price paid for merchandise for export to the United States). Import duties, freight, insurance, and other charges incurred in bringing merchandise to the United States are excluded.

Exports are valued at the f.a.s. (free alongside ship) value of merchandise at the U.S. port of export, based on the transaction price including inland freight, insurance, and other charges incurred in placing the merchandise alongside the carrier at the U.S. port of exportation.

Goods: balance of payments (BOP) basis. Goods on a Census basis are adjusted by BEA to goods on a BOP basis to bring the data in line with the concepts and definitions used to prepare the international and national accounts. In general, the adjustments include changes in ownership that occur without goods passing into or out of the customs territory of the United States. These adjustments are necessary to supplement coverage of the Census basis data, to eliminate duplication of transactions recorded elsewhere in the international accounts, and to value transactions according to a standard definition. With the June 4, 2013 release, improved BOP adjustments involving U.S. military transactions were introduced for data beginning with 1999.

The *export* adjustments include the following: (1) The deduction of *U.S. military sales contracts.* The Census Bureau has included these contracts in the goods data, but BEA includes them in the service category "Transfers Under U.S. Military Sales Contracts." BEA's source material for these contracts is more comprehensive but does not distinguish between goods and services. (2) The addition of *private gift parcels* mailed to foreigners by individuals through the U.S. Postal Service. Only commercial shipments are covered in Census goods exports. (3) The addition to *nonmonetary gold exports* of gold purchased by foreign official agencies from private dealers in the United States and held at the Federal Reserve Bank of New York. The Census data include only gold that leaves the customs territory. (4) *Smaller adjustments* includes deductions for repairs of goods, exposed motion picture film, and military grant aid, and additions for sales of fish in U.S. territorial waters, exports of electricity to Mexico, and vessels and oil rigs that change ownership without export documents being filed.

The *import* adjustments include the following: (1) On *inland freight in Canada*, the customs value for imports for certain Canadian goods is the point of origin in Canada. BEA makes an addition for the inland freight charges of transporting these Canadian goods to the U.S. border. (2) An addition is made to *nonmonetary gold imports* for gold sold by foreign official agencies to private purchasers out of stock held at the Federal Reserve Bank of New York. The Census Bureau data include only gold that enters the customs territory. (3) A deduction is made for *imports by U.S. military agencies*. The Census Bureau has included these contracts in the goods data, but BEA includes them in the service category "Direct Defense Expenditures." BEA's source material is more comprehensive but does not distinguish between goods and services. (4) *Smaller adjustments* includes deductions for repairs of goods and for exposed motion picture film and additions for imported electricity from Mexico, conversion of vessels for commercial use, and repairs to U.S. vessels abroad.

Definitions: Services

These statistics are estimates of service transactions between foreign countries and the 50 states, the District of Columbia, Puerto Rico, the U.S. Virgin Islands, and other U.S. territories and possessions. Transactions with U.S. military, diplomatic, and consular installations abroad are excluded because they are considered to be part of the U.S. economy.

In the 2014 comprehensive revision of the ITAs, new categories have been introduced in the services reports, beginning with January 1999. The 9 new categories, shown in Tables 7-15A and 7-16A, are as follows:

Maintenance and repair services n.i.e. (not included elsewhere) were previously included in "other private services."

Transport includes the previous categories of "passenger fares" and "other transportation."

Travel for all purposes including education is broader than the previous "travel" category and now includes business travel,

expenditures by border, seasonal, and other short-term workers, and personal travel including that related to health and education. As before, it consists of expenditures for food, lodging, recreation, gifts, and other items incidental to a foreign visit but not the actual transportation expenses.

Insurance services and *financial services* were previously included in other private services.

Charges for the use of intellectual property n.i.e. was previously named "royalties and license fees."

Telecommunications, computer, and information services and *other business services* were previously included in "other private services."

Government goods and services n.i.e. replaces the government categories in the previous system.

Earlier services definitions

In Tables 7-15B and 7-16B, showing data before 1999, services are classified in the broad categories described below. For six of these categories, the definitions are the same for imports and exports. For the seventh, the export category is "Transfers under U.S. Military Sales Contracts," while for imports, the category is "Direct Defense Expenditures."

Travel includes purchases of services and goods by U.S. travelers abroad and by foreign visitors to the United States. A traveler is defined as a person who stays for a period of less than one year in a country where the person is not a resident. Included are expenditures for food, lodging, recreation, gifts, and other items incidental to a foreign visit. Not included are the international costs of the travel itself, which are covered in *passenger fares* (see below).

Passenger fares consists of fares paid by residents of one country to residents in other countries. Receipts consist of fares received by U.S. carriers from foreign residents for travel between the United States and foreign countries and between two foreign points. Payments consist of fares paid by U.S. residents to foreign carriers for travel between the United States and foreign countries.

Other transportation includes charges for the transportation of goods by ocean, air, waterway, pipeline, and rail carriers to and from the United States. Included are freight charges, operating expenses that transportation companies incur in foreign ports, and payments for vessel charter and aircraft and freight car rentals.

Royalties and license fees consists of transactions with foreign residents involving intangible assets and proprietary rights, such as the use of patents, techniques, processes, formulas, designs, knowhow, trademarks, copyrights, franchises, and manufacturing rights. The term *royalties* generally refers to payments for the utilization of copyrights or trademarks, and the term *license fees* generally refers to payments for the use of patents or industrial processes.

Other private services includes transactions with "affiliated" foreigners for which no identification by type is available and transactions with unaffiliated foreigners.

The term "affiliated" refers to a direct investment relationship, which exists when a U.S. person has ownership or control (directly or indirectly) of 10 percent or more of a foreign business enterprise, or when a foreign person has a similar interest in a U.S. enterprise.

Transactions with "unaffiliated" foreigners in this "other private services" category consist of education services, financial services, insurance services, telecommunications services, and business, professional, and technical services. Included in the last group are advertising services; computer and data processing services; database and other information services; research, development, and testing services; management, consulting, and public relations services; legal services; construction, engineering, architectural, and mining services; industrial engineering services; installation, maintenance, and repair of equipment; and other services, including medical services and film and tape rental.

The insurance component of "other private services" was measured before the July 2003 revision as premiums less actual losses paid or recovered. Furthermore, catastrophic losses were entered immediately when the loss occurred, rather than when the insurance claim was actually paid out. This led to sharp swings for any month in which catastrophic losses occurred, such as Hurricane Katrina in August 2005 or the September 11, 2001, terror attacks. In the accounts as revised in July 2003 and presented here, insurance services are now measured as premiums less "normal" losses. Normal losses consist of a measure of expected regularly occurring losses based on six years of past experience plus an additional allowance for catastrophic loss. Catastrophic losses, when they occur, are added in equal increments to the estimate of regularly occurring losses over the 20 years following the occurrence. As adoption of this methodology introduces a difference between actual and normal losses, an amount equal to the difference is entered in the international accounts as a capital account transaction.

Transfers under U.S. military sales contracts (exports only) includes exports in which U.S. government military agencies participate. This category has included both goods, such as equipment, and services, such as repair services and training, that could not be separately identified. In the 2010 and 2013 annual revisions, more precise breakdowns between goods and services in this category were introduced and incorporated as revised estimates of services and of the BOP goods adjustment, beginning

with the data for 2007. Transfers of goods and services under U.S. military grant programs are included.

Direct defense expenditures (imports only) consists of expenditures incurred by U.S. military agencies abroad, including expenditures by U.S. personnel, payments of wages to foreign residents, construction expenditures, payments for foreign contractual services, and procurement of foreign goods. Improved breakdowns between goods and services are now incorporated beginning with statistics for 1999.

U.S. government miscellaneous services includes transactions of U.S. government nonmilitary agencies with foreign residents. Most of these transactions involve the provision of services to, or purchases of services from, foreigners. Transfers of some goods are also included.

Services estimates are based on quarterly, annual, and benchmark surveys and partial information generated from monthly reports. Service transactions are estimated at market prices. Estimates are seasonally adjusted when statistically significant seasonal patterns are present.

Definitions: Area groupings

The Census trade statistics for groups of countries present "groups as they were at the time of reporting," which means that as multinational organizations such as the European Union expand, the statistics for trade with that group include the added country only beginning with the year it entered the group. The European Union was expanded from 15 to 28 nations as of July 1, 2013, and data for that year are available for both the new and the old group; to provide historical perspective, they are both shown here, along with the historical data back to 1974 for the original group.

The *European Union* now includes 28 countries: Austria, Belgium, Bulgaria, Croatia, Cyprus, Czech Republic, Denmark, Estonia, Finland, France, Germany, Greece, Hungary, Ireland, Italy, Latvia, Lithuania, Luxembourg, Malta, Netherlands, Poland, Portugal, Romania, Slovakia, Slovenia, Spain, Sweden, and the United Kingdom. The last country to join was Croatia in July 2013.

The *Euro area* now includes Austria, Belgium, Cyprus, Estonia, Finland, France, Germany, Greece, Ireland, Italy, Luxembourg, Malta, the Netherlands, Portugal, Slovakia, Slovenia, and Spain. See the notes and definitions in Table 13-2 for further information about the euro.

With the June 3, 2016 International Trade and Services Annual Revision for 2015, the area grouping *Asian Newly Industrialized Countries (NICS)* has been removed from all relevant exhibits and publications and are listed separately as Hong Kong, South Korea, Singapore, and Taiwan. This group was initially called the *Four Asian Tigers*.

The *Organization of Petroleum Exporting Countries (OPEC)* currently consists of Algeria, Angola, Ecuador, Equatorial Guinea, Iran, Iraq, Kuwait, Libya, Nigeria, Qatar, Saudi Arabia, the United Arab Emirates, and Venezuela.

Notes on the data

U.S./Canada data exchange and substitution. The data for U.S. exports to Canada are derived from import data compiled by Canada. The use of Canada's import data to produce U.S. export data requires several alignments in order to compare the two series.

- *Coverage*: Canadian imports are based on country of origin. U.S. goods shipped from a third country are included, but U.S. exports exclude these foreign shipments. U.S. export coverage also excludes certain Canadian postal shipments.

- *Valuation*: Canadian imports are valued at their point of origin in the United States. However, U.S. exports are valued at the port of exit in the United States and include inland freight charges, making the U.S. export value slightly larger. Canada requires inland freight to be reported.

- *Re-exports*: U.S. exports include re-exports of foreign goods. Again, the aggregate U.S. export figure is slightly larger.

- *Exchange Rate*: Average monthly exchange rates are applied to convert the published data to U.S. currency.

End-use categories and seasonal adjustment of trade in goods. Goods are initially classified under the Harmonized System, which describes and measures the characteristics of goods traded. Combining trade into approximately 140 export and 140 import enduse categories makes it possible to examine goods according to their principal uses. These categories are used as the basis for computing the seasonal and working-day adjusted data. Adjusted data are then summed to the six end-use aggregates for publication.

The seasonal adjustment procedure is based on a model that estimates the monthly movements as percentages above or below the general level of each end-use commodity series (unlike other methods that redistribute the actual series values over the calendar year). Imports of petroleum and petroleum products are adjusted for the length of the month.

Data availability

Data are released monthly in a joint Census Bureau-BEA press release (FT-900), which is published about six weeks after the end of the month to which the data pertain. The release and historical data are available on the Census Bureau Web site at <https://www.census.gov/foreign-trade/index.html>.

Revisions

Data for recent years are normally revised annually. In some cases, revisions to annual totals are not distributed to monthly data; therefore, monthly data may not sum to the revised total shown. Data on trade in services may be subject to extensive revision as part of BEA's annual revision of the international transactions accounts (ITAs), usually released in July.

REFERENCES

See the references for Table 7-6.

TABLE 7-17

Export and Import Price Indexes

SOURCE: U.S. DEPARTMENT OF LABOR, BUREAU OF LABOR STATISTICS

The International Price Program of the Bureau of Labor Statistics (BLS) collects price data for nonmilitary goods traded between the United States and the rest of the world and for selected transportation services in international markets. BLS aggregates the goods price data into export and import price indexes. Summary values of these price indexes for goods are presented in *Business Statistics*. For product and locality detail on international prices for both goods and services, see the *Handbook of U.S. Labor Statistics,* also published by Bernan Press.

Definitions

The *export* price index provides a measure of price change for all goods sold by U.S. residents (businesses and individuals located within the geographic boundaries of the United States, whether or not owned by U.S. citizens) to foreign buyers.

The *import* price index provides a measure of price change for goods purchased from other countries by U.S. residents.

Notes on the data

Published index series use a base year of 2000 = 100 whenever possible.

The product universe for both the import and export indexes includes raw materials, agricultural products, and manufactures. Price data are primarily collected by mail questionnaire, and directly from the exporter or importer in all but a few cases.

To the greatest extent possible, the data refer to prices at the U.S. border for exports and at either the foreign border or the U.S. border for imports. For nearly all products, the prices refer to transactions completed during the first week of the month and represent the actual price for which the product was bought or sold, including discounts, allowances, and rebates.

For the export price indexes, the preferred pricing basis is f.a.s. (free alongside ship) U.S. port of exportation. Where necessary, adjustments are made to reported prices to place them on this basis. An attempt is made to collect two prices for imports: f.o.b. (free on board) at the port of exportation and c.i.f. (cost, insurance, and freight) at the U.S. port of importation. Adjustments are made to account for changes in product characteristics in order to obtain a pure measure of price change.

The indexes are weighted indexes of the Laspeyres type. (See "General Notes" at the beginning of this volume for further explanation.) The values assigned to each weight category are based on trade value figures compiled by the Census Bureau. They are reweighted annually, with a two-year lag (as concurrent value data are not available) in revisions.

The merchandise price indexes are published using three different classification systems: the Harmonized System, the Bureau of Economic Analysis End-Use System, and the Standard International Trade Classification (SITC) system. The aggregate indexes shown here are from the End-Use System.

Data availability

Indexes are published monthly in a press release and a more detailed report. Indexes are published for detailed product categories, as well as for all commodities. Aggregate import indexes by country or region of origin also are available, as are indexes for selected categories of internationally traded services. Additional information is available from the Division of International Prices in the Bureau of Labor Statistics. Complete historical data are available on the BLS Web site at <http://www.bls.gov>.

REFERENCES

The indexes are described in "BLS to Produce Monthly Indexes of Export and Import Prices," *Monthly Labor Review* (December 1988), and Chapter 15, "International Price Indexes," *BLS Handbook of Methods* Bulletin 2490 (April 1997).

CHAPTER 8: PRICES

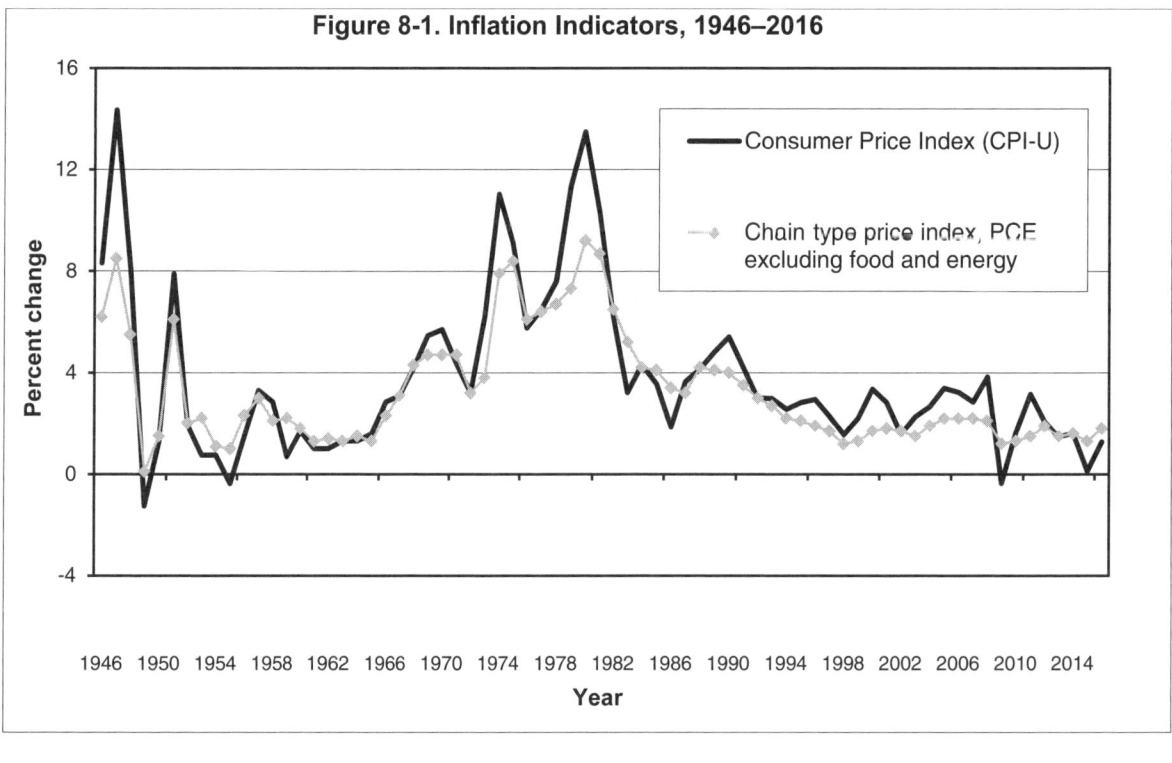

Figure 8-1. Inflation Indicators, 1946–2016

- Figure 8-1 shows annual rates of change in the Consumer Price Index for All Urban Consumers (CPI-U), the most widely used measure of the general price level. It also shows changes in the chain-type price index for personal consumption expenditures (PCE) excluding food and energy, which provides one widely used measure of the "core" or underlying rate of inflation. (Tables 8-1, 8-4, and 1-6)

- Sharp swings in energy prices caused the all-items CPI to drop 0.4 percent in 2009—the first year-to-year deflation registered since 1955—and swing back up to 3.2 percent inflation in 2011. Inflation measured by CPI-U dropped back to 0.1 percent in 2015 then grew by only 1.3 percent in 2016. (Table 8-4)

- The Producer Price Index (PPI) measures prices at the point of production, rather than at the consumer level. For most of its history, the PPI has measured goods only. The Finished Goods PPI continued to decline in 2016 after reaching a record high in 2014. The PPI for "unprocessed nonfood materials less energy," also known (in the old goods-only system) as "crude nonfood materials less energy") is a sensitive leading indicator, not of aggregate prices, but of general business conditions. (Tables 8-1A and B)

Table 8-1A. Summary Consumer and Producer Price Indexes: Recent Data

(Seasonally adjusted.)

Year and month	Urban wage earners and clerical workers (CPI-W), all items	All items	Food	Energy	All items less food and energy	Commodities	Services	Finished goods Total	Finished goods Less energy	Processed goods Total	Processed materials less food and energy	Unprocessed Total	Unprocessed nonfood materials less energy
1965	31.7	31.5	32.2	22.9	32.7	35.2	26.6	34.1	...	31.2	...	31.1	...
1966	32.6	32.4	33.8	23.3	33.5	36.1	27.6	35.2	...	32.0	...	33.1	...
1967	33.6	33.4	34.1	23.8	34.7	36.8	28.8	35.6	...	32.2	...	31.3	...
1968	35.0	34.8	35.3	24.2	36.3	38.1	30.3	36.6	...	33.0	...	31.8	...
1969	36.9	36.7	37.1	24.8	38.4	39.9	32.4	38.0	...	34.1	...	33.9	...
1970	39.0	38.8	39.2	25.5	40.8	41.7	35.0	39.3	...	35.4	...	35.2	...
1971	40.7	40.5	40.4	26.5	42.7	43.2	37.0	40.5	...	36.8	...	36.0	...
1972	42.1	41.8	42.1	27.2	44.0	44.5	38.4	41.8	...	38.2	...	39.9	...
1973	44.7	44.4	48.2	29.4	45.6	47.8	40.1	45.6	...	42.4	44.3	54.5	70.8
1974	49.6	49.3	55.1	38.1	49.4	53.5	43.8	52.6	...	52.5	54.0	61.4	83.3
1975	54.1	53.8	59.8	42.1	53.9	58.2	48.0	58.2	62.4	58.0	60.2	61.6	69.3
1976	57.2	56.9	61.6	45.1	57.4	60.7	52.0	60.8	64.8	60.9	63.8	63.4	80.2
1977	60.9	60.6	65.5	49.4	61.0	64.2	56.0	64.7	68.6	64.9	67.6	65.5	79.8
1978	65.6	65.2	72.0	52.5	65.5	68.8	60.8	69.8	74.0	69.5	72.5	73.4	87.8
1979	73.1	72.6	79.9	65.7	71.9	76.6	67.5	77.6	80.7	78.4	80.7	85.9	106.2
1980	82.9	82.4	86.8	86.0	80.8	86.0	77.9	88.0	88.4	90.3	90.3	95.3	113.1
1981	91.4	90.9	93.6	97.7	89.2	93.2	88.1	96.1	95.4	98.6	97.7	103.0	111.7
1982	96.9	96.5	97.4	99.2	95.8	97.0	96.0	100.0	100.0	100.0	100.0	100.0	100.0
1983	99.8	99.6	99.4	99.9	99.6	99.8	99.4	101.6	102.5	100.6	101.6	101.3	105.3
1984	103.3	103.9	103.2	100.9	104.6	103.2	104.6	103.7	105.5	103.1	104.7	103.5	111.7
1985	106.9	107.6	105.6	101.6	109.1	105.4	109.9	104.7	107.2	102.7	105.2	95.8	104.9
1986	108.6	109.6	109.0	88.2	113.5	104.4	115.4	103.2	109.7	99.1	104.9	87.7	103.1
1987	112.5	113.6	113.5	88.6	118.2	107.7	120.2	105.4	112.3	101.5	107.8	93.7	115.7
1988	117.0	118.3	118.2	89.3	123.4	111.5	125.7	108.0	115.8	107.1	115.2	96.0	133.0
1989	122.6	124.0	125.1	94.3	129.0	116.7	131.9	113.6	121.2	112.0	120.2	103.1	137.9
1990	129.0	130.7	132.4	102.1	135.5	122.8	139.2	119.2	126.0	114.5	120.9	108.9	136.3
1991	134.3	136.2	136.3	102.5	142.1	126.6	146.3	121.7	129.1	114.4	121.4	101.2	128.2
1992	138.2	140.3	137.9	103.0	147.3	129.1	152.0	123.2	131.1	114.7	122.0	100.4	128.4
1993	142.1	144.5	140.9	104.2	152.2	131.5	157.9	124.7	132.9	116.2	123.8	102.4	140.2
1994	145.6	148.2	144.3	104.6	156.5	133.8	163.1	125.5	134.2	118.5	127.1	101.8	156.2
1995	149.8	152.4	148.4	105.2	161.2	136.4	168.7	127.9	136.9	124.9	135.2	102.7	173.6
1996	154.1	156.9	153.3	110.1	165.6	139.9	174.1	131.3	139.6	125.7	134.0	113.8	155.8
1997	157.6	160.5	157.3	111.5	169.5	141.8	179.4	131.8	140.2	125.6	134.2	111.1	156.5
1998	159.7	163.0	160.7	102.9	173.4	141.9	184.2	130.7	141.1	123.0	133.5	96.8	142.1
1999	163.2	166.6	164.1	106.6	177.0	144.4	188.8	133.0	143.0	123.2	133.1	98.2	135.2
2000	168.9	172.2	167.8	124.6	181.3	149.2	195.3	138.0	144.9	129.2	136.6	120.6	145.2
2001	173.5	177.1	173.1	129.3	186.1	150.7	203.4	140.7	147.6	129.7	136.4	121.0	130.7
2002	175.9	179.9	176.2	121.7	190.5	149.7	209.8	138.9	147.3	127.8	135.8	108.1	135.7
2003	179.8	184.0	180.0	136.5	193.2	151.2	216.5	143.3	149.0	133.7	138.5	135.3	152.5
2004	184.5	188.9	186.2	151.4	196.6	154.7	222.8	148.5	152.4	142.6	146.5	159.0	193.0
2005	191.0	195.3	190.7	177.1	200.9	160.2	230.1	155.7	155.9	154.0	154.6	182.2	202.4
2006	197.1	201.6	195.2	196.9	205.9	164.0	238.9	160.4	157.9	164.0	163.8	184.8	244.5
2007	202.8	207.3	202.9	207.7	210.7	167.5	246.8	166.6	162.8	170.7	168.4	207.1	282.6
2008	211.1	215.3	214.1	236.7	215.6	174.8	255.5	177.1	169.8	188.3	180.9	251.8	324.4
2009	209.6	214.5	218.0	193.1	219.2	169.7	259.2	172.5	172.3	172.5	173.4	175.2	248.4
2010	214.0	218.1	219.6	211.4	221.3	174.6	261.3	179.8	175.5	183.4	180.8	212.2	329.1
2011	221.6	224.9	227.8	243.9	225.0	183.9	265.8	190.7	181.4	199.9	192.0	249.4	390.4
2012	226.2	229.6	233.8	246.1	229.8	187.6	271.4	194.3	186.1	200.7	192.6	241.4	369.6
2013	229.3	233.0	237.0	244.4	233.8	187.7	277.9	196.7	189.2	200.8	193.8	246.7	351.2
2014	232.8	236.7	242.7	243.6	237.9	187.9	285.1	200.4	194.0	201.9	195.2	249.3	345.7
2015	231.8	237.0	247.2	202.9	242.2	181.7	291.7	193.9	196.2	188.0	189.4	189.1	296.0
2016	234.1	240.0	247.9	189.5	247.6	179.2	299.9	191.9	197.3	182.2	186.9	173.4	288.0
2015													
January	229.7	234.9	246.1	201.0	239.9	180.6	288.6	193.2	196.0	190.9	191.8	200.8	325.5
February	230.4	235.5	246.4	204.3	240.2	181.3	289.0	193.7	195.7	190.3	191.2	194.5	308.6
March	230.9	236.0	246.1	205.6	240.8	181.9	289.5	193.9	195.6	189.7	190.6	192.6	304.2
April	231.1	236.2	246.1	203.0	241.4	181.5	290.2	193.1	195.3	188.4	190.2	193.8	304.3
May	231.8	236.9	246.3	207.9	241.7	182.6	290.6	195.5	196.1	189.7	190.2	199.5	303.5
June	232.4	237.4	247.0	209.6	242.0	182.9	291.3	196.4	197.0	190.4	190.1	200.8	304.2
July	232.8	237.9	247.2	210.5	242.5	183.2	291.9	195.8	196.6	189.9	189.9	194.8	303.3
August	232.7	237.8	247.7	206.6	242.8	182.6	292.4	195.3	196.9	188.4	189.1	187.8	290.0
September	232.1	237.5	248.5	197.5	243.2	181.2	293.1	192.8	196.9	185.8	188.0	183.5	289.1
October	232.4	237.8	248.7	196.8	243.7	181.0	293.9	192.2	196.3	185.1	187.6	181.3	281.2
November	232.7	238.2	248.5	196.9	244.2	181.0	294.6	192.6	196.4	184.3	187.1	172.6	270.5
December	232.3	237.8	248.1	191.0	244.6	179.8	295.1	190.9	196.1	182.3	186.5	166.0	267.8
2016													
January	232.4	238.1	248.2	188.3	245.2	179.6	295.8	190.8	197.1	180.7	185.8	166.0	266.5
February	231.8	237.8	248.4	179.2	245.8	178.2	296.6	189.6	197.2	179.3	185.3	163.1	268.3
March	232.2	238.1	248.1	180.8	246.1	178.2	297.2	189.6	196.8	179.2	185.3	165.3	275.4
April	233.1	238.9	248.4	185.7	246.5	179.1	298.0	190.4	196.9	179.9	185.8	168.9	285.3
May	233.4	239.4	248.0	187.1	247.0	179.0	298.9	191.4	197.1	181.3	186.3	173.8	294.9
June	233.9	239.8	247.9	189.6	247.4	179.3	299.6	192.5	197.6	182.7	186.6	178.2	294.4
July	233.9	239.9	247.8	187.6	247.7	178.7	300.3	192.2	197.4	183.0	186.8	179.6	296.1
August	234.3	240.4	247.8	187.5	248.4	178.7	301.3	191.8	197.1	182.9	187.4	175.8	297.1
September	235.0	241.0	247.8	192.0	248.6	179.3	301.9	192.7	197.7	183.5	187.6	174.8	291.2
October	235.7	241.7	247.7	196.8	249.0	180.1	302.5	193.5	197.3	184.1	187.9	173.5	287.3
November	236.2	242.2	247.6	198.7	249.5	180.2	303.3	193.4	197.2	184.5	188.7	174.6	294.4
December	236.9	242.8	247.5	201.1	250.0	180.6	304.1	194.6	197.9	185.6	189.4	187.4	304.5

. . . = Not available.

Table 8-1B. Summary Consumer and Producer Price Indexes: Historical Data, 1946 to Date

(Seasonally adjusted.)

Year and month	Urban wage earners and clerical workers (CPI-W), all items	Consumer Price Index, 1982–1984 = 100						Producer Price Index for goods, 1982 = 100					
		All urban consumers (CPI-U)						Finished goods		Processed goods for intermediate demand		Unprocessed goods for intermediate demand	
		All items	Food	Energy	All items less food and energy	Commodities	Services	Total	Less food and energy	Total	Processed materials less foods and energy	Total	Unprocessed nonfood materials less energy
1946	19.6	19.5	19.8	. . .	. . .	22.9	14.1	. . .	. . .	. . .	. . .	. . .	. . .
1947	22.5	22.3	24.1	. . .	. . .	27.6	14.7	26.4	. . .	23.3	. . .	31.7	. . .
1948	24.2	24.1	26.1	. . .	. . .	29.6	15.6	28.5	. . .	25.2	. . .	34.7	. . .
1949	24.0	23.8	25.0	. . .	. . .	28.8	16.4	27.7	. . .	24.2	. . .	30.1	. . .
1950	24.2	24.1	25.4	. . .	. . .	29.0	16.9	28.2	. . .	25.3	. . .	32.7	. . .
1951	26.1	26.0	28.2	. . .	. . .	31.6	17.8	30.8	. . .	28.4	. . .	37.6	. . .
1952	26.7	26.5	28.7	. . .	. . .	32.0	18.6	30.6	. . .	27.5	. . .	34.5	. . .
1953	26.9	26.7	28.3	. . .	. . .	31.9	19.4	30.3	. . .	27.7	. . .	31.9	. . .
1954	27.0	26.9	28.2	. . .	. . .	31.6	20.0	30.4	. . .	27.9	. . .	31.6	. . .
1955	26.9	26.8	27.8	. . .	. . .	31.3	20.4	30.5	. . .	28.4	. . .	30.4	. . .
1956	27.3	27.2	28.0	. . .	. . .	31.6	20.9	31.3	. . .	29.6	. . .	30.6	. . .
1957	28.3	28.1	28.9	21.5	28.9	32.6	21.8	32.5	. . .	30.3	. . .	31.2	. . .
1958	29.1	28.9	30.2	21.5	29.6	33.3	22.6	33.2	. . .	30.4	. . .	31.9	. . .
1959	29.3	29.1	29.7	21.9	30.2	33.3	23.3	33.1	. . .	30.8	. . .	31.1	. . .
1960	29.8	29.6	30.0	22.4	30.6	33.6	24.1	33.4	. . .	30.8	. . .	30.4	. . .
1961	30.1	29.9	30.4	22.5	31.0	33.8	24.5	33.4	. . .	30.6	. . .	30.2	. . .
1962	30.4	30.2	30.6	22.6	31.4	34.1	25.0	33.5	. . .	30.6	. . .	30.5	. . .
1963	30.8	30.6	31.1	22.6	31.8	34.4	25.5	33.4	. . .	30.7	. . .	29.9	. . .
1964	31.2	31.0	31.5	22.5	32.3	34.8	26.0	33.5	. . .	30.8	. . .	29.6	. . .
1947													
January	21.6	21.5	22.8	. . .	. . .	. . .	. . .	. . .	. . .	. . .	. . .	. . .	. . .
February	21.7	21.6	23.1	. . .	. . .	. . .	. . .	. . .	. . .	. . .	. . .	. . .	. . .
March	22.1	22.0	23.8	. . .	. . .	. . .	. . .	. . .	. . .	. . .	. . .	. . .	. . .
April	22.1	22.0	23.5	. . .	. . .	. . .	. . .	26.0	. . .	23.1	. . .	30.7	. . .
May	22.1	22.0	23.4	. . .	. . .	. . .	. . .	26.1	. . .	23.0	. . .	30.4	. . .
June	22.2	22.1	23.5	. . .	. . .	. . .	. . .	26.2	. . .	23.2	. . .	30.6	. . .
July	22.4	22.2	23.8	. . .	. . .	. . .	. . .	26.2	. . .	23.2	. . .	31.0	. . .
August	22.5	22.4	24.1	. . .	. . .	. . .	. . .	26.3	. . .	23.3	. . .	31.6	. . .
September	23.0	22.8	24.8	. . .	. . .	. . .	. . .	26.7	. . .	23.7	. . .	32.4	. . .
October	23.0	22.9	24.9	. . .	. . .	. . .	. . .	26.8	. . .	24.0	. . .	33.7	. . .
November	23.2	23.1	25.2	. . .	. . .	. . .	. . .	27.1	. . .	24.3	. . .	33.9	. . .
December	23.5	23.4	25.7	. . .	. . .	. . .	. . .	27.7	. . .	24.5	. . .	35.3	. . .
1948													
January	23.8	23.7	26.1	. . .	. . .	. . .	. . .	28.1	. . .	25.0	. . .	36.2	. . .
February	23.8	23.7	25.9	. . .	. . .	. . .	. . .	27.9	. . .	24.7	. . .	34.4	. . .
March	23.6	23.5	25.3	. . .	. . .	. . .	. . .	28.0	. . .	24.8	. . .	33.5	. . .
April	24.0	23.8	26.0	. . .	. . .	. . .	. . .	28.1	. . .	25.1	. . .	34.2	. . .
May	24.1	24.0	26.3	. . .	. . .	. . .	. . .	28.4	. . .	25.1	. . .	35.3	. . .
June	24.3	24.2	26.5	. . .	. . .	. . .	. . .	28.6	. . .	25.4	. . .	36.2	. . .
July	24.5	24.4	26.7	. . .	. . .	. . .	. . .	28.8	. . .	25.4	. . .	36.1	. . .
August	24.6	24.4	26.5	. . .	. . .	. . .	. . .	28.9	. . .	25.5	. . .	35.5	. . .
September	24.5	24.4	26.3	. . .	. . .	. . .	. . .	28.8	. . .	25.5	. . .	34.9	. . .
October	24.4	24.3	26.1	. . .	. . .	. . .	. . .	28.7	. . .	25.5	. . .	33.8	. . .
November	24.3	24.2	25.7	. . .	. . .	. . .	. . .	28.5	. . .	25.4	. . .	33.5	. . .
December	24.2	24.1	25.5	. . .	. . .	. . .	. . .	28.5	. . .	25.2	. . .	33.0	. . .
1949													
January	24.2	24.0	25.4	. . .	. . .	. . .	. . .	28.3	. . .	25.2	. . .	32.0	. . .
February	24.1	23.9	25.3	. . .	. . .	. . .	. . .	28.0	. . .	24.8	. . .	30.9	. . .
March	24.0	23.9	25.3	. . .	. . .	. . .	. . .	28.0	. . .	24.7	. . .	30.8	. . .
April	24.1	23.9	25.3	. . .	. . .	. . .	. . .	27.9	. . .	24.5	. . .	30.2	. . .
May	24.0	23.9	25.2	. . .	. . .	. . .	. . .	27.8	. . .	24.3	. . .	30.1	. . .
June	24.1	23.9	25.3	. . .	. . .	. . .	. . .	27.7	. . .	24.1	. . .	29.7	. . .
July	23.8	23.7	24.8	. . .	. . .	. . .	. . .	27.5	. . .	24.1	. . .	29.2	. . .
August	23.8	23.7	24.8	. . .	. . .	. . .	. . .	27.4	. . .	23.9	. . .	29.2	. . .
September	23.9	23.8	25.0	. . .	. . .	. . .	. . .	27.4	. . .	23.9	. . .	29.5	. . .
October	23.8	23.7	24.8	. . .	. . .	. . .	. . .	27.3	. . .	23.8	. . .	29.5	. . .
November	23.8	23.7	24.8	. . .	. . .	. . .	. . .	27.2	. . .	23.7	. . .	29.6	. . .
December	23.8	23.6	24.5	. . .	. . .	. . .	. . .	27.2	. . .	23.8	. . .	29.6	. . .
1950													
January	23.6	23.5	24.3	. . .	. . .	. . .	. . .	27.2	. . .	23.8	. . .	29.6	. . .
February	23.7	23.6	24.7	. . .	. . .	. . .	. . .	27.2	. . .	23.9	. . .	30.5	. . .
March	23.8	23.6	24.6	. . .	. . .	. . .	. . .	27.3	. . .	24.1	. . .	30.3	. . .
April	23.8	23.7	24.6	. . .	. . .	. . .	. . .	27.3	. . .	24.2	. . .	30.5	. . .
May	23.9	23.8	24.8	. . .	. . .	. . .	. . .	27.5	. . .	24.6	. . .	31.6	. . .
June	24.0	23.9	25.1	. . .	. . .	. . .	. . .	27.6	. . .	24.7	. . .	32.1	. . .
July	24.2	24.1	25.6	. . .	. . .	. . .	. . .	28.0	. . .	25.3	. . .	33.3	. . .
August	24.3	24.2	25.8	. . .	. . .	. . .	. . .	28.6	. . .	25.6	. . .	34.0	. . .
September	24.5	24.3	25.8	. . .	. . .	. . .	. . .	28.9	. . .	26.2	. . .	34.5	. . .
October	24.6	24.5	26.0	. . .	. . .	. . .	. . .	29.0	. . .	26.7	. . .	34.5	. . .
November	24.7	24.6	26.1	. . .	. . .	. . .	. . .	29.4	. . .	26.9	. . .	35.4	. . .
December	25.1	25.0	26.9	. . .	. . .	. . .	. . .	30.0	. . .	27.8	. . .	36.7	. . .

. . . = Not available.

Table 8-1B. Summary Consumer and Producer Price Indexes: Historical Data, 1946 to Date—*Continued*

(Seasonally adjusted.)

Year and month	Urban wage earners and clerical workers (CPI-W), all items	Consumer Price Index, 1982–1984 = 100						Producer Price Index for goods, 1982 = 100					
		All urban consumers (CPI-U)						Finished goods		Processed goods for intermediate demand		Unprocessed goods for intermediate demand	
		All items	Food	Energy	All items less food and energy	Commod-ities	Services	Total	Less food and energy	Total	Processed materials less foods and energy	Total	Unproces-sed nonfood materials less energy
1951													
January	25.5	25.4	27.6	. . .	. . .	. . .	. . .	30.5	. . .	28.5	. . .	38.2	. . .
February	26.0	25.8	28.5	. . .	. . .	. . .	. . .	30.8	. . .	28.7	. . .	39.6	. . .
March	26.0	25.9	28.4	. . .	. . .	. . .	. . .	30.9	. . .	28.8	. . .	39.1	. . .
April	26.1	25.9	28.2	. . .	. . .	. . .	. . .	30.9	. . .	28.8	. . .	39.1	. . .
May	26.1	26.0	28.3	. . .	. . .	. . .	. . .	31.1	. . .	28.8	. . .	38.4	. . .
June	26.1	25.9	28.0	. . .	. . .	. . .	. . .	31.0	. . .	28.7	. . .	38.1	. . .
July	26.1	25.9	27.9	. . .	. . .	. . .	. . .	30.8	. . .	28.4	. . .	36.8	. . .
August	26.0	25.9	27.8	. . .	. . .	. . .	. . .	30.7	. . .	28.0	. . .	36.2	. . .
September	26.2	26.0	27.9	. . .	. . .	. . .	. . .	30.6	. . .	28.0	. . .	35.9	. . .
October	26.3	26.2	28.4	. . .	. . .	. . .	. . .	30.8	. . .	27.9	. . .	36.7	. . .
November	26.5	26.3	28.6	. . .	. . .	. . .	. . .	30.9	. . .	27.9	. . .	36.4	. . .
December	26.6	26.5	28.9	. . .	. . .	. . .	. . .	30.9	. . .	27.8	. . .	36.6	. . .
1952													
January	26.6	26.5	28.9	. . .	. . .	. . .	. . .	30.8	. . .	27.8	. . .	35.8	. . .
February	26.6	26.4	28.6	. . .	. . .	. . .	. . .	30.7	. . .	27.7	. . .	35.5	. . .
March	26.5	26.4	28.5	. . .	. . .	. . .	. . .	30.9	. . .	27.6	. . .	35.0	. . .
April	26.6	26.5	28.7	. . .	. . .	. . .	. . .	30.7	. . .	27.5	. . .	34.9	. . .
May	26.6	26.5	28.7	. . .	. . .	. . .	. . .	30.7	. . .	27.5	. . .	34.8	. . .
June	26.7	26.5	28.6	. . .	. . .	. . .	. . .	30.7	. . .	27.6	. . .	34.6	. . .
July	26.8	26.7	28.9	. . .	. . .	. . .	. . .	30.8	. . .	27.5	. . .	34.6	. . .
August	26.8	26.7	28.9	. . .	. . .	. . .	. . .	30.7	. . .	27.6	. . .	34.7	. . .
September	26.8	26.6	28.7	. . .	. . .	. . .	. . .	30.6	. . .	27.6	. . .	33.8	. . .
October	26.8	26.7	28.8	. . .	. . .	. . .	. . .	30.5	. . .	27.5	. . .	33.8	. . .
November	26.8	26.7	28.8	. . .	. . .	. . .	. . .	30.4	. . .	27.4	. . .	33.7	. . .
December	26.9	26.7	28.6	. . .	. . .	. . .	. . .	30.2	. . .	27.3	. . .	32.9	. . .
1953													
January	26.8	26.6	28.4	. . .	. . .	. . .	. . .	30.3	. . .	27.4	. . .	32.5	. . .
February	26.7	26.6	28.3	. . .	. . .	. . .	. . .	30.2	. . .	27.4	. . .	32.4	. . .
March	26.8	26.6	28.3	. . .	. . .	. . .	. . .	30.3	. . .	27.5	. . .	32.4	. . .
April	26.8	26.7	28.1	. . .	. . .	. . .	. . .	30.2	. . .	27.5	. . .	31.6	. . .
May	26.9	26.7	28.2	. . .	. . .	. . .	. . .	30.3	. . .	27.6	. . .	31.8	. . .
June	26.9	26.8	28.4	. . .	. . .	. . .	. . .	30.4	. . .	27.7	. . .	31.4	. . .
July	26.9	26.8	28.2	. . .	. . .	. . .	. . .	30.5	. . .	28.0	. . .	32.3	. . .
August	27.0	26.9	28.3	. . .	. . .	. . .	. . .	30.4	. . .	27.9	. . .	31.8	. . .
September	27.0	26.9	28.4	. . .	. . .	. . .	. . .	30.4	. . .	27.9	. . .	32.0	. . .
October	27.1	27.0	28.4	. . .	. . .	. . .	. . .	30.4	. . .	27.9	. . .	31.4	. . .
November	27.0	26.9	28.1	. . .	. . .	. . .	. . .	30.3	. . .	27.8	. . .	31.2	. . .
December	27.0	26.9	28.3	. . .	. . .	. . .	. . .	30.4	. . .	27.8	. . .	31.7	. . .
1954													
January	27.1	26.9	28.5	. . .	. . .	. . .	. . .	30.5	. . .	27.9	. . .	32.0	. . .
February	27.1	27.0	28.5	. . .	. . .	. . .	. . .	30.4	. . .	27.9	. . .	32.0	. . .
March	27.1	26.9	28.4	. . .	. . .	. . .	. . .	30.4	. . .	27.9	. . .	32.1	. . .
April	27.0	26.9	28.4	. . .	. . .	. . .	. . .	30.6	. . .	27.9	. . .	32.2	. . .
May	27.1	26.9	28.4	. . .	. . .	. . .	. . .	30.6	. . .	27.9	. . .	32.1	. . .
June	27.1	26.9	28.4	. . .	. . .	. . .	. . .	30.4	. . .	27.8	. . .	31.5	. . .
July	27.0	26.9	28.4	. . .	. . .	. . .	. . .	30.5	. . .	27.9	. . .	31.4	. . .
August	27.0	26.9	28.3	. . .	. . .	. . .	. . .	30.4	. . .	27.9	. . .	31.3	. . .
September	27.0	26.8	28.0	. . .	. . .	. . .	. . .	30.3	. . .	27.8	. . .	31.5	. . .
October	26.9	26.7	27.9	. . .	. . .	. . .	. . .	30.2	. . .	27.8	. . .	31.2	. . .
November	26.9	26.8	27.9	. . .	. . .	. . .	. . .	30.3	. . .	27.9	. . .	31.4	. . .
December	26.9	26.8	27.8	. . .	. . .	. . .	. . .	30.3	. . .	27.9	. . .	30.8	. . .
1955													
January	26.9	26.8	27.8	. . .	. . .	. . .	. . .	30.4	. . .	27.9	. . .	31.1	. . .
February	27.0	26.8	28.0	. . .	. . .	. . .	. . .	30.5	. . .	28.0	. . .	31.0	. . .
March	26.9	26.8	28.0	. . .	. . .	. . .	. . .	30.3	. . .	28.0	. . .	30.7	. . .
April	26.9	26.8	28.0	. . .	. . .	. . .	. . .	30.4	. . .	28.1	. . .	31.0	. . .
May	26.9	26.8	27.9	. . .	. . .	. . .	. . .	30.4	. . .	28.1	. . .	30.2	. . .
June	26.9	26.7	27.7	. . .	. . .	. . .	. . .	30.5	. . .	28.2	. . .	30.7	. . .
July	26.9	26.8	27.7	. . .	. . .	. . .	. . .	30.4	. . .	28.4	. . .	30.4	. . .
August	26.9	26.7	27.6	. . .	. . .	. . .	. . .	30.4	. . .	28.5	. . .	30.1	. . .
September	27.0	26.9	27.8	. . .	. . .	. . .	. . .	30.5	. . .	28.8	. . .	30.4	. . .
October	27.0	26.8	27.7	. . .	. . .	. . .	. . .	30.6	. . .	28.9	. . .	30.4	. . .
November	27.0	26.9	27.6	. . .	. . .	. . .	. . .	30.6	. . .	28.9	. . .	29.4	. . .
December	27.0	26.9	27.6	. . .	. . .	. . .	. . .	30.7	. . .	29.0	. . .	29.5	. . .
1956													
January	27.0	26.8	27.5	. . .	. . .	31.2	20.7	30.7	. . .	29.1	. . .	29.4	. . .
February	27.0	26.9	27.5	. . .	. . .	31.1	20.7	30.8	. . .	29.2	. . .	29.9	. . .
March	27.1	26.9	27.5	. . .	. . .	31.2	20.7	30.9	. . .	29.4	. . .	29.8	. . .
April	27.1	26.9	27.6	. . .	. . .	31.3	20.8	31.0	. . .	29.5	. . .	30.3	. . .
May	27.2	27.0	27.8	. . .	. . .	31.4	20.8	31.2	. . .	29.6	. . .	30.7	. . .
June	27.3	27.2	28.1	. . .	. . .	31.5	20.9	31.4	. . .	29.6	. . .	30.5	. . .
July	27.4	27.3	28.4	. . .	. . .	31.8	20.9	31.3	. . .	29.4	. . .	30.5	. . .
August	27.5	27.3	28.2	. . .	. . .	31.7	21.0	31.4	. . .	29.7	. . .	31.0	. . .
September	27.5	27.4	28.2	. . .	. . .	31.8	21.1	31.6	. . .	29.8	. . .	31.0	. . .
October	27.7	27.5	28.3	. . .	. . .	32.0	21.1	31.8	. . .	30.0	. . .	31.0	. . .
November	27.7	27.5	28.4	. . .	. . .	32.0	21.2	31.9	. . .	30.0	. . .	31.1	. . .
December	27.8	27.6	28.5	. . .	. . .	32.1	21.3	31.9	. . .	30.1	. . .	31.7	. . .

. . . = Not available.

Table 8-1B. Summary Consumer and Producer Price Indexes: Historical Data, 1946 to Date—*Continued*

(Seasonally adjusted.)

Year and month	Urban wage earners and clerical workers (CPI-W), all items	Consumer Price Index, 1982–1984 = 100						Producer Price Index for goods, 1982 = 100					
		All urban consumers (CPI-U)						Finished goods		Processed goods for intermediate demand		Unprocessed goods for intermediate demand	
		All items	Food	Energy	All items less food and energy	Commodities	Services	Total	Less food and energy	Total	Processed materials less foods and energy	Total	Unprocessed nonfood materials less energy
1957													
January	27.8	27.7	28.4	21.3	28.5	32.1	21.4	32.1	. . .	30.3	. . .	31.3	. . .
February	28.0	27.8	28.7	21.4	28.6	32.3	21.4	32.2	. . .	30.3	. . .	31.0	. . .
March	28.0	27.9	28.6	21.5	28.7	32.3	21.6	32.1	. . .	30.3	. . .	30.9	. . .
April	28.1	27.9	28.6	21.6	28.8	32.4	21.6	32.3	. . .	30.2	. . .	30.8	. . .
May	28.2	28.0	28.7	21.6	28.8	32.4	21.7	32.3	. . .	30.2	. . .	30.7	. . .
June	28.3	28.1	28.9	21.6	28.9	32.5	21.8	32.5	. . .	30.3	. . .	31.5	. . .
July	28.4	28.2	29.1	21.5	29.0	32.6	21.8	32.6	. . .	30.3	. . .	32.0	. . .
August	20.4	00.3	29.4	21.4	29.0	32.8	21.9	32.6	. . .	30.4	. . .	32.0	. . .
September	28.5	28.3	29.2	21.4	29.1	32.8	22.0	32.6	. . .	30.4	. . .	31.2	. . .
October	28.5	28.3	29.2	21.4	29.2	32.7	22.1	32.7	. . .	30.3	. . .	31.0	. . .
November	28.6	28.4	29.2	21.5	29.3	32.8	22.2	32.9	. . .	30.4	. . .	31.1	. . .
December	28.6	28.5	29.2	21.5	29.3	32.9	22.2	33.0	. . .	30.4	. . .	31.5	. . .
1958													
January	28.8	28.6	29.8	21.6	29.3	33.1	22.3	33.2	. . .	30.4	. . .	31.4	. . .
February	28.9	28.7	29.9	21.3	29.4	33.2	22.4	33.2	. . .	30.3	. . .	31.9	. . .
March	29.0	28.9	30.5	21.4	29.5	33.4	22.4	33.4	. . .	30.3	. . .	32.3	. . .
April	29.1	28.9	30.6	21.4	29.5	33.5	22.5	33.2	. . .	30.2	. . .	31.8	. . .
May	29.1	28.9	30.5	21.5	29.5	33.5	22.6	33.2	. . .	30.3	. . .	32.4	. . .
June	29.1	28.9	30.3	21.5	29.6	33.4	22.6	33.3	. . .	30.3	. . .	32.0	. . .
July	29.1	28.9	30.2	21.6	29.6	33.3	22.7	33.2	. . .	30.3	. . .	32.1	. . .
August	29.1	28.9	30.1	21.7	29.6	33.3	22.7	33.2	. . .	30.4	. . .	31.9	. . .
September	29.1	28.9	30.0	21.7	29.7	33.3	22.8	33.2	. . .	30.4	. . .	31.6	. . .
October	29.1	28.9	30.0	21.7	29.7	33.2	22.8	33.2	. . .	30.4	. . .	31.9	. . .
November	29.1	29.0	30.0	21.4	29.8	33.3	22.8	33.2	. . .	30.5	. . .	32.1	. . .
December	29.1	29.0	29.9	21.4	29.9	33.3	22.8	33.1	. . .	30.6	. . .	31.6	. . .
1959													
January	29.2	29.0	30.0	21.4	29.9	33.3	22.9	33.1	. . .	30.6	. . .	31.6	. . .
February	29.2	29.0	29.8	21.6	29.9	33.3	23.0	33.2	. . .	30.7	. . .	31.4	. . .
March	29.1	29.0	29.7	21.7	30.0	33.2	23.0	33.2	. . .	30.7	. . .	31.5	. . .
April	29.1	29.0	29.5	21.8	30.0	33.2	23.1	33.2	. . .	30.7	. . .	31.7	. . .
May	29.2	29.0	29.5	21.8	30.1	33.3	23.2	33.3	. . .	30.9	. . .	31.5	. . .
June	29.3	29.1	29.7	21.9	30.2	33.3	23.2	33.2	. . .	30.9	. . .	31.3	. . .
July	29.3	29.2	29.6	21.8	30.2	33.3	23.3	33.1	. . .	30.8	. . .	31.0	. . .
August	29.3	29.2	29.6	21.9	30.2	33.4	23.4	33.0	. . .	30.8	. . .	30.7	. . .
September	29.4	29.3	29.7	21.9	30.3	33.5	23.5	33.4	. . .	30.8	. . .	30.9	. . .
October	29.5	29.4	29.7	22.2	30.4	33.5	23.6	33.1	. . .	30.8	. . .	30.7	. . .
November	29.5	29.4	29.7	22.2	30.4	33.5	23.6	33.0	. . .	30.9	. . .	30.5	. . .
December	29.6	29.4	29.6	22.3	30.5	33.5	23.7	33.0	. . .	30.9	. . .	30.3	. . .
1960													
January	29.5	29.4	29.6	22.3	30.5	33.5	23.7	33.1	. . .	30.8	. . .	30.4	. . .
February	29.6	29.4	29.5	22.2	30.6	33.4	23.8	33.1	. . .	30.9	. . .	30.4	. . .
March	29.6	29.4	29.6	22.3	30.6	33.5	23.9	33.4	. . .	30.9	. . .	30.7	. . .
April	29.7	29.5	30.0	22.4	30.6	33.6	23.9	33.4	. . .	30.8	. . .	30.8	. . .
May	29.7	29.6	30.0	22.3	30.6	33.6	24.0	33.4	. . .	30.8	. . .	30.8	. . .
June	29.8	29.6	30.0	22.4	30.7	33.6	24.0	33.4	. . .	30.9	. . .	30.4	. . .
July	29.7	29.6	29.9	22.5	30.6	33.5	24.1	33.5	. . .	30.8	. . .	30.4	. . .
August	29.8	29.6	30.0	22.5	30.6	33.6	24.1	33.4	. . .	30.8	. . .	29.8	. . .
September	29.8	29.6	30.1	22.6	30.6	33.6	24.2	33.4	. . .	30.8	. . .	30.0	. . .
October	29.9	29.8	30.3	22.5	30.8	33.7	24.2	33.7	. . .	30.8	. . .	30.2	. . .
November	30.0	29.8	30.5	22.7	30.8	33.8	24.3	33.7	. . .	30.7	. . .	30.2	. . .
December	30.0	29.8	30.5	22.6	30.7	33.9	24.3	33.6	. . .	30.7	. . .	30.3	. . .
1961													
January	30.0	29.8	30.5	22.7	30.8	33.8	24.4	33.6	. . .	30.6	. . .	30.4	. . .
February	30.0	29.8	30.5	22.6	30.8	33.8	24.4	33.7	. . .	30.7	. . .	30.5	. . .
March	30.0	29.8	30.5	22.6	30.9	33.8	24.4	33.6	. . .	30.8	. . .	30.3	. . .
April	30.0	29.8	30.4	22.2	30.9	33.8	24.5	33.4	. . .	30.7	. . .	30.2	. . .
May	30.0	29.8	30.3	22.4	30.9	33.8	24.5	33.3	. . .	30.6	. . .	29.9	. . .
June	30.0	29.8	30.2	22.5	31.0	33.8	24.5	33.3	. . .	30.5	. . .	29.5	. . .
July	30.1	29.9	30.3	22.5	31.0	33.9	24.5	33.3	. . .	30.5	. . .	29.7	. . .
August	30.1	29.9	30.3	22.5	31.1	33.9	24.6	33.4	. . .	30.5	. . .	30.5	. . .
September	30.2	30.0	30.3	22.6	31.1	33.9	24.6	33.3	. . .	30.5	. . .	30.3	. . .
October	30.2	30.0	30.3	22.4	31.1	33.9	24.7	33.3	. . .	30.4	. . .	30.3	. . .
November	30.2	30.0	30.3	22.5	31.2	33.8	24.7	33.4	. . .	30.5	. . .	30.2	. . .
December	30.2	30.0	30.3	22.4	31.2	33.9	24.8	33.4	. . .	30.6	. . .	30.6	. . .
1962													
January	30.2	30.0	30.4	22.4	31.2	33.9	24.8	33.5	. . .	30.5	. . .	30.6	. . .
February	30.3	30.1	30.5	22.6	31.2	34.0	24.8	33.6	. . .	30.6	. . .	30.5	. . .
March	30.4	30.2	30.6	22.4	31.3	34.0	24.9	33.5	. . .	30.6	. . .	30.5	. . .
April	30.4	30.2	30.7	22.7	31.3	34.1	24.9	33.5	. . .	30.6	. . .	30.1	. . .
May	30.4	30.2	30.6	22.7	31.4	34.1	25.0	33.4	. . .	30.6	. . .	30.1	. . .
June	30.4	30.2	30.5	22.5	31.4	34.1	25.0	33.4	. . .	30.6	. . .	29.9	. . .
July	30.4	30.2	30.4	22.3	31.4	34.0	25.1	33.4	. . .	30.6	. . .	30.2	. . .
August	30.5	30.3	30.6	22.4	31.5	34.1	25.1	33.5	. . .	30.6	. . .	30.5	. . .
September	30.6	30.4	30.9	22.8	31.5	34.3	25.1	33.8	. . .	30.6	. . .	31.2	. . .
October	30.6	30.4	30.8	22.7	31.5	34.2	25.1	33.6	. . .	30.5	. . .	30.8	. . .
November	30.6	30.4	30.9	22.7	31.5	34.3	25.2	33.6	. . .	30.5	. . .	31.0	. . .
December	30.6	30.4	30.7	22.8	31.6	34.2	25.2	33.5	. . .	30.5	. . .	30.6	. . .

. . . = Not available.

Table 8-1B. Summary Consumer and Producer Price Indexes: Historical Data, 1946 to Date—*Continued*

(Seasonally adjusted.)

Year and month	Consumer Price Index, 1982–1984 = 100							Producer Price Index for goods, 1982 = 100					
	Urban wage earners and clerical workers (CPI-W), all items	All urban consumers (CPI-U)						Finished goods		Processed goods for intermediate demand		Unprocessed goods for intermediate demand	
		All items	Food	Energy	All items less food and energy	Commodities	Services	Total	Less food and energy	Total	Processed materials less foods and energy	Total	Unprocessed nonfood materials less energy
1963													
January	30.6	30.4	31.0	22.8	31.5	34.3	25.3	33.4	...	30.5	...	30.3	...
February	30.7	30.5	31.1	22.7	31.6	34.3	25.3	33.4	...	30.5	...	30.0	...
March	30.7	30.5	31.0	22.7	31.7	34.3	25.3	33.3	...	30.5	...	29.6	...
April	30.7	30.5	30.9	22.6	31.7	34.3	25.4	33.3	...	30.5	...	29.8	...
May	30.7	30.5	30.9	22.6	31.7	34.3	25.4	33.4	...	30.7	...	29.6	...
June	30.8	30.6	31.0	22.5	31.8	34.4	25.5	33.5	...	30.7	...	29.9	...
July	30.9	30.7	31.2	22.7	31.8	34.5	25.5	33.4	...	30.7	...	30.0	...
August	30.9	30.8	31.2	22.6	31.9	34.6	25.6	33.4	...	30.7	...	29.9	...
September	30.9	30.7	31.1	22.5	31.9	34.5	25.6	33.4	...	30.7	...	29.8	...
October	30.9	30.8	31.0	22.7	32.0	34.5	25.6	33.5	...	30.8	...	29.9	...
November	31.0	30.8	31.2	22.6	32.0	34.6	25.7	33.5	...	30.8	...	30.2	...
December	31.1	30.9	31.3	22.6	32.1	34.7	25.8	33.4	...	30.8	...	29.4	...
1964													
January	31.1	30.9	31.4	22.8	32.2	34.7	25.8	33.5	...	30.8	...	29.8	...
February	31.1	30.9	31.4	22.2	32.2	34.7	25.8	33.5	...	30.8	...	29.4	...
March	31.1	30.9	31.4	22.6	32.2	34.7	25.8	33.4	...	30.8	...	29.5	...
April	31.1	31.0	31.4	22.5	32.2	34.7	25.9	33.5	...	30.8	...	29.5	...
May	31.2	31.0	31.4	22.5	32.2	34.7	25.9	33.5	...	30.7	...	29.4	...
June	31.2	31.0	31.4	22.6	32.3	34.7	26.0	33.5	...	30.6	...	29.0	...
July	31.2	31.0	31.5	22.5	32.3	34.7	26.0	33.5	...	30.7	...	29.2	...
August	31.2	31.1	31.4	22.6	32.3	34.7	26.0	33.6	...	30.6	...	29.4	...
September	31.3	31.1	31.6	22.5	32.3	34.8	26.0	33.6	...	30.7	...	30.1	...
October	31.3	31.1	31.6	22.5	32.4	34.8	26.1	33.6	...	30.8	...	29.8	...
November	31.4	31.2	31.7	22.5	32.5	34.9	26.2	33.6	...	30.8	...	29.9	...
December	31.4	31.3	31.7	22.6	32.5	35.0	26.2	33.6	...	30.9	...	29.8	...
1965													
January	31.5	31.3	31.6	22.8	32.6	35.0	26.3	33.6	...	30.9	...	29.5	...
February	31.5	31.3	31.5	22.7	32.6	34.9	26.4	33.7	...	30.9	...	29.9	...
March	31.5	31.3	31.7	22.6	32.6	35.0	26.4	33.7	...	31.0	...	30.0	...
April	31.6	31.4	31.8	22.9	32.7	35.0	26.5	34.0	...	31.1	...	30.4	...
May	31.7	31.5	32.1	23.0	32.7	35.1	26.5	34.1	...	31.1	...	30.8	...
June	31.8	31.6	32.6	23.1	32.7	35.3	26.5	34.2	...	31.2	...	31.6	...
July	31.8	31.6	32.5	23.0	32.7	35.3	26.6	34.1	...	31.2	...	31.2	...
August	31.7	31.6	32.4	23.0	32.7	35.2	26.6	34.2	...	31.3	...	31.5	...
September	31.8	31.6	32.3	23.1	32.8	35.2	26.7	34.3	...	31.3	...	31.4	...
October	31.8	31.7	32.5	23.0	32.8	35.3	26.8	34.4	...	31.3	...	31.8	...
November	31.9	31.8	32.6	23.1	32.9	35.4	26.9	34.5	...	31.4	...	32.1	...
December	32.0	31.9	32.8	23.1	33.0	35.5	26.9	34.7	...	31.4	...	32.7	...
1966													
January	32.1	31.9	33.0	23.1	33.0	35.6	27.0	34.7	...	31.4	...	33.1	...
February	32.3	32.1	33.5	23.2	33.1	35.8	27.0	35.0	...	31.6	...	33.7	...
March	32.4	32.2	33.8	23.2	33.1	35.9	27.1	35.0	...	31.7	...	33.5	...
April	32.5	32.3	33.8	23.2	33.3	36.0	27.3	35.1	...	31.8	...	33.3	...
May	32.5	32.4	33.7	23.2	33.4	36.0	27.4	35.1	...	32.0	...	33.0	...
June	32.6	32.4	33.7	23.3	33.5	36.0	27.5	34.9	...	32.0	...	33.0	...
July	32.6	32.5	33.5	23.4	33.6	36.1	27.7	35.1	...	32.2	...	33.4	...
August	32.8	32.7	34.0	23.3	33.7	36.2	27.7	35.4	...	32.3	...	33.5	...
September	32.9	32.8	34.1	23.4	33.8	36.4	27.9	35.6	...	32.2	...	33.4	...
October	33.0	32.9	34.2	23.4	34.0	36.4	28.0	35.5	...	32.1	...	32.9	...
November	33.1	32.9	34.1	23.5	34.0	36.4	28.2	35.5	...	32.2	...	32.3	...
December	33.1	32.9	34.0	23.5	34.1	36.4	28.2	35.4	...	32.2	...	32.1	...
1967													
January	33.1	32.9	33.9	23.6	34.2	36.4	28.3	35.4	...	32.2	...	32.2	...
February	33.2	33.0	33.8	23.7	34.2	36.4	28.4	35.3	...	32.1	...	31.5	...
March	33.2	33.0	33.8	23.6	34.3	36.4	28.5	35.3	...	32.1	...	31.1	...
April	33.3	33.1	33.7	23.9	34.4	36.4	28.6	35.3	...	32.1	...	30.7	...
May	33.3	33.1	33.7	23.9	34.5	36.5	28.6	35.4	...	32.1	...	31.1	...
June	33.5	33.3	34.0	23.8	34.6	36.6	28.8	35.7	...	32.2	...	31.4	...
July	33.6	33.4	34.1	23.8	34.7	36.8	28.8	35.7	...	32.2	...	31.3	...
August	33.7	33.5	34.3	23.9	34.9	37.0	28.9	35.8	...	32.2	...	31.3	...
September	33.8	33.6	34.3	24.0	35.0	37.0	29.0	35.8	...	32.3	...	31.2	...
October	33.9	33.7	34.4	23.9	35.1	37.1	29.2	35.9	...	32.3	...	31.3	...
November	34.0	33.9	34.5	24.0	35.2	37.2	29.2	35.9	...	32.4	...	31.1	...
December	34.1	34.0	34.6	23.9	35.4	37.4	29.4	36.0	...	32.6	...	31.5	...
1968													
January	34.3	34.1	34.6	24.0	35.5	37.5	29.5	36.1	...	32.6	...	31.4	...
February	34.4	34.2	34.8	24.1	35.7	37.6	29.6	36.2	...	32.7	...	31.5	...
March	34.5	34.3	34.9	24.1	35.8	37.7	29.8	36.3	...	32.8	...	31.6	...
April	34.6	34.4	35.0	24.0	35.9	37.8	29.9	36.5	...	32.8	...	31.7	...
May	34.7	34.5	35.1	24.1	36.0	37.8	30.0	36.5	...	32.8	...	31.5	...
June	34.9	34.7	35.2	24.2	36.2	38.0	30.2	36.6	...	32.9	...	31.3	...
July	35.0	34.9	35.3	24.2	36.4	38.1	30.4	36.7	...	33.0	...	31.6	...
August	35.2	35.0	35.4	24.3	36.5	38.3	30.6	36.8	...	33.0	...	31.7	...
September	35.3	35.1	35.6	24.3	36.7	38.4	30.7	37.0	...	33.1	...	31.9	...
October	35.5	35.3	35.9	24.3	36.9	38.6	30.9	37.0	...	33.2	...	32.1	...
November	35.6	35.4	35.9	24.4	37.1	38.7	31.0	37.1	...	33.2	...	32.8	...
December	35.8	35.6	36.0	24.3	37.2	38.8	31.2	37.1	...	33.4	...	32.4	...

. . . = Not available.

Table 8-1B. Summary Consumer and Producer Price Indexes: Historical Data, 1946 to Date—*Continued*

(Seasonally adjusted.)

| Year and month | Urban wage earners and clerical workers (CPI-W), all items | Consumer Price Index, 1982–1984 = 100 | | | | | | Producer Price Index for goods, 1982 = 100 | | | | | |
| | | All urban consumers (CPI-U) | | | | | | Finished goods | | Processed goods for intermediate demand | | Unprocessed goods for intermediate demand | |
		All items	Food	Energy	All items less food and energy	Commodities	Services	Total	Less food and energy	Total	Processed materials less foods and energy	Total	Unprocessed nonfood materials less energy
1969													
January	35.9	35.7	36.1	24.4	37.3	38.9	31.4	37.2	...	33.6	...	32.6	...
February	36.0	35.8	36.1	24.4	37.6	39.0	31.5	37.2	...	33.7	...	32.3	...
March	36.3	36.1	36.2	24.7	37.8	39.3	31.8	37.4	...	33.9	...	32.7	...
April	36.5	36.3	36.4	24.9	38.1	39.4	32.0	37.6	...	33.8	...	33.1	...
May	36.6	36.4	36.6	24.8	38.1	39.5	32.2	37.8	...	33.9	...	34.0	...
June	36.8	36.6	37.0	25.0	38.3	39.8	32.3	38.0	...	34.0	...	34.5	...
July	37.0	36.8	37.3	24.9	38.5	39.9	32.5	38.1	...	34.0	...	34.1	...
August	37.1	36.0	37.6	24.9	38.7	40.1	32.7	38.2	...	34.2	...	34.4	...
September	37.3	37.1	37.7	25.0	38.9	40.2	33.0	38.3	...	34.2	...	34.4	...
October	37.5	37.3	37.8	25.0	39.1	40.4	33.1	38.5	...	34.4	...	34.8	...
November	37.7	37.5	38.2	25.0	39.2	40.6	33.3	38.8	...	34.6	...	35.2	...
December	37.9	37.7	38.6	25.1	39.4	40.8	33.5	38.9	...	34.7	...	35.1	...
1970													
January	38.1	37.9	38.7	25.1	39.6	41.0	33.8	39.1	...	35.0	...	35.1	...
February	38.3	38.1	38.9	25.1	39.8	41.2	34.0	39.0	...	35.0	...	35.2	...
March	38.5	38.3	38.9	25.0	40.1	41.2	34.4	39.1	...	34.9	...	35.6	...
April	38.7	38.5	39.0	25.5	40.4	41.4	34.6	39.1	...	35.1	...	35.5	...
May	38.8	38.6	39.2	25.4	40.5	41.5	34.8	39.1	...	35.2	...	35.0	...
June	39.0	38.8	39.2	25.3	40.8	41.6	35.0	39.2	...	35.3	...	35.0	...
July	39.1	38.9	39.2	25.5	40.9	41.7	35.2	39.2	...	35.5	...	35.1	...
August	39.2	39.0	39.2	25.4	41.1	41.8	35.4	39.2	...	35.5	...	34.7	...
September	39.4	39.2	39.4	25.6	41.3	42.0	35.6	39.6	...	35.6	...	35.5	...
October	39.6	39.4	39.5	25.9	41.5	42.2	35.8	39.6	...	35.8	...	35.5	...
November	39.8	39.6	39.5	26.0	41.8	42.3	36.0	39.8	...	35.9	...	35.1	...
December	40.0	39.8	39.5	26.2	42.0	42.5	36.2	39.8	...	35.9	...	34.5	...
1971													
January	40.1	39.9	39.4	26.3	42.1	42.5	36.4	39.9	...	36.0	...	34.8	...
February	40.2	39.9	39.5	26.2	42.2	42.6	36.5	40.1	...	36.1	...	35.9	...
March	40.2	40.0	39.8	26.2	42.2	42.7	36.5	40.2	...	36.3	...	35.4	...
April	40.4	40.1	40.1	26.1	42.4	42.9	36.6	40.3	...	36.3	...	36.0	...
May	40.5	40.3	40.3	26.2	42.6	43.1	36.7	40.5	...	36.5	...	36.0	...
June	40.7	40.5	40.5	26.3	42.8	43.2	37.0	40.6	...	36.7	...	36.2	...
July	40.9	40.6	40.6	26.3	42.9	43.3	37.1	40.4	...	36.9	...	35.9	...
August	41.0	40.7	40.6	26.8	43.0	43.4	37.3	40.7	...	37.2	...	35.8	...
September	41.0	40.8	40.6	26.9	43.0	43.4	37.4	40.7	...	37.2	...	35.7	...
October	41.1	40.9	40.7	27.0	43.1	43.5	37.5	40.7	...	37.1	...	36.4	...
November	41.2	41.0	40.9	26.9	43.2	43.5	37.6	40.8	...	37.2	...	37.0	...
December	41.4	41.1	41.3	27.0	43.3	43.8	37.7	41.1	...	37.4	...	37.2	...
1972													
January	41.5	41.2	41.1	27.0	43.5	43.8	37.9	41.0	...	37.5	...	37.8	...
February	41.6	41.4	41.7	26.8	43.6	44.0	38.0	41.3	...	37.7	...	38.1	...
March	41.7	41.4	41.6	26.9	43.6	44.0	38.1	41.3	...	37.8	...	38.1	...
April	41.7	41.5	41.6	26.9	43.8	44.1	38.2	41.3	...	37.9	...	38.7	...
May	41.8	41.6	41.7	27.0	43.9	44.2	38.3	41.5	...	38.0	...	39.3	...
June	41.9	41.7	41.9	27.0	44.0	44.3	38.4	41.7	...	38.0	...	39.4	...
July	42.1	41.8	42.1	27.1	44.1	44.5	38.5	41.8	...	38.1	...	40.0	...
August	42.2	41.9	42.2	27.3	44.3	44.5	38.6	42.0	...	38.2	...	40.3	...
September	42.3	42.1	42.5	27.6	44.3	44.8	38.7	42.2	...	38.5	...	40.5	...
October	42.5	42.2	42.8	27.7	44.4	44.9	38.8	42.0	...	38.7	...	40.9	...
November	42.6	42.4	43.0	27.9	44.4	45.1	38.9	42.3	...	39.0	...	42.0	...
December	42.8	42.5	43.2	27.8	44.6	45.2	39.0	42.7	...	39.6	...	43.8	...
1973													
January	43.0	42.7	44.0	27.9	44.6	45.5	39.1	43.0	...	39.8	...	45.0	...
February	43.2	43.0	44.6	28.2	44.8	45.9	39.2	43.5	...	40.4	...	47.1	...
March	43.6	43.4	45.8	28.3	45.0	46.4	39.4	44.4	...	41.1	...	49.3	...
April	43.9	43.7	46.5	28.6	45.1	46.8	39.5	44.7	...	41.3	...	50.1	...
May	44.2	43.9	47.1	28.8	45.3	47.2	39.6	45.0	...	42.2	...	52.5	...
June	44.4	44.2	47.6	29.2	45.4	47.5	39.8	45.5	...	43.0	...	55.0	...
July	44.5	44.2	47.7	29.2	45.5	47.5	39.9	45.4	...	42.3	...	52.5	...
August	45.3	45.0	50.5	29.4	45.7	48.7	40.2	47.0	...	43.5	...	64.1	...
September	45.4	45.2	50.4	29.4	46.0	48.7	40.5	46.9	...	43.0	...	60.9	...
October	45.8	45.6	50.7	30.3	46.3	49.0	41.0	46.8	...	43.4	...	58.5	...
November	46.2	45.9	51.4	31.5	46.5	49.5	41.3	47.2	...	43.8	...	59.0	...
December	46.5	46.3	51.9	32.5	46.7	49.9	41.5	47.6	...	44.8	...	59.1	...
1974													
January	47.0	46.8	52.5	34.1	46.9	50.5	41.8	48.8	49.7	45.9	47.5	63.3	86.3
February	47.6	47.3	53.6	35.4	47.2	51.3	42.0	49.7	50.0	46.8	48.1	64.3	86.5
March	48.1	47.8	54.2	36.9	47.6	51.9	42.4	50.2	50.5	48.1	49.5	62.3	88.3
April	48.3	48.1	54.1	37.6	47.9	52.1	42.6	50.7	51.1	49.0	50.9	60.6	89.7
May	48.8	48.6	54.5	38.3	48.5	52.7	43.1	51.3	52.2	50.6	52.5	58.3	83.8
June	49.2	49.0	54.5	38.6	49.0	53.1	43.5	51.3	53.1	51.5	53.7	55.4	82.9
July	49.6	49.3	54.3	38.9	49.5	53.3	44.0	52.7	54.0	53.4	55.2	59.8	84.2
August	50.2	49.9	55.1	39.2	50.2	54.1	44.5	53.7	55.0	55.8	57.0	62.9	85.5
September	50.9	50.6	56.2	39.3	50.7	54.8	45.0	54.3	55.7	55.9	57.6	60.9	82.5
October	51.3	51.0	56.8	39.2	51.2	55.3	45.4	55.3	56.7	57.2	58.2	63.2	80.6
November	51.8	51.5	57.5	39.4	51.6	55.8	45.8	56.4	57.4	57.8	58.8	64.2	77.6
December	52.2	51.9	58.2	39.6	52.0	56.3	46.2	56.4	57.9	57.8	59.1	61.5	71.6

. . . = Not available.

Table 8-1B. Summary Consumer and Producer Price Indexes: Historical Data, 1946 to Date—*Continued*

(Seasonally adjusted.)

Year and month	Urban wage earners and clerical workers (CPI-W), all items	Consumer Price Index, 1982–1984 = 100						Producer Price Index for goods, 1982 = 100					
		All urban consumers (CPI-U)						Finished goods		Processed goods for intermediate demand		Unprocessed goods for intermediate demand	
		All items	Food	Energy	All items less food and energy	Commod-ities	Services	Total	Less food and energy	Total	Processed materials less foods and energy	Total	Unproces-sed nonfood materials less energy
1975													
January	52.6	52.3	58.4	40.0	52.3	56.7	46.5	56.7	58.3	58.0	59.6	59.6	69.8
February	52.9	52.6	58.5	40.3	52.8	56.9	46.9	56.6	58.7	57.8	59.8	57.9	69.2
March	53.1	52.8	58.4	40.6	53.0	57.1	47.0	56.6	59.0	57.4	59.7	57.1	68.2
April	53.3	53.0	58.3	41.0	53.3	57.2	47.3	57.1	59.2	57.5	59.7	59.5	67.7
May	53.4	53.1	58.6	41.3	53.5	57.5	47.5	57.4	59.3	57.3	59.7	61.2	68.8
June	53.8	53.5	59.2	41.7	53.8	57.9	47.8	57.9	59.5	57.3	59.8	61.5	66.5
July	54.3	54.0	60.3	42.5	54.0	58.6	48.0	58.4	59.8	57.5	59.9	62.4	66.5
August	54.5	54.2	60.3	42.8	54.2	58.7	48.3	58.9	59.9	58.0	60.1	63.0	67.7
September	54.9	54.6	60.7	43.2	54.5	59.0	48.7	59.3	60.2	58.2	60.3	64.5	71.2
October	55.2	54.9	61.3	43.5	54.8	59.4	49.0	59.8	60.6	58.8	61.0	65.1	71.5
November	55.6	55.3	61.7	43.9	55.2	59.7	49.6	60.0	61.0	59.0	61.4	64.4	71.9
December	55.9	55.6	62.1	44.1	55.5	59.9	49.9	60.1	61.4	59.2	61.8	64.0	73.1
1976													
January	56.2	55.8	61.9	44.5	55.9	60.0	50.5	60.0	61.7	59.4	62.1	63.0	72.4
February	56.2	55.9	61.3	44.4	56.2	59.9	50.8	59.9	61.9	59.6	62.3	62.1	73.8
March	56.3	56.0	60.9	44.1	56.5	59.8	51.1	60.0	62.2	59.8	62.6	61.5	74.5
April	56.5	56.1	60.9	43.9	56.7	59.9	51.3	60.3	62.3	60.0	62.8	63.9	78.1
May	56.7	56.4	61.1	44.1	57.0	60.2	51.4	60.4	62.4	60.3	63.2	63.6	80.6
June	57.0	56.7	61.3	44.4	57.2	60.4	51.7	60.5	62.8	60.8	63.6	65.2	82.8
July	57.3	57.0	61.6	44.8	57.6	60.7	52.1	60.7	63.1	61.1	63.9	64.8	87.3
August	57.6	57.3	61.8	45.2	57.9	61.0	52.4	60.9	63.5	61.3	64.3	63.6	84.1
September	57.9	57.6	62.1	45.7	58.2	61.3	52.8	61.1	63.9	61.9	64.7	63.4	84.4
October	58.2	57.9	62.4	46.1	58.5	61.6	53.1	61.4	64.1	62.0	65.0	63.0	82.2
November	58.4	58.1	62.3	46.8	58.7	61.7	53.4	61.9	64.6	62.4	65.3	63.4	81.8
December	58.7	58.4	62.5	47.5	58.9	62.0	53.7	62.4	64.9	62.8	65.6	64.5	81.1
1977													
January	59.1	58.7	62.7	48.1	59.3	62.3	54.1	62.5	65.1	63.0	65.8	64.3	78.7
February	59.6	59.3	63.9	48.1	59.7	63.0	54.4	63.2	65.4	63.3	65.9	65.7	79.7
March	59.9	59.6	64.2	48.4	60.0	63.2	54.8	63.7	65.7	63.9	66.4	66.6	81.5
April	60.3	60.0	65.0	48.6	60.3	63.7	55.2	64.0	65.9	64.4	66.7	68.3	82.1
May	60.6	60.2	65.3	48.9	60.6	63.9	55.4	64.4	66.1	64.9	67.1	67.6	82.5
June	60.9	60.5	65.7	48.9	61.0	64.2	55.8	64.6	66.5	64.9	67.4	65.5	79.7
July	61.2	60.8	65.9	49.1	61.2	64.4	56.3	64.8	66.8	65.1	67.9	64.7	78.8
August	61.4	61.1	66.2	49.5	61.5	64.6	56.6	65.2	67.3	65.4	68.2	63.9	79.2
September	61.7	61.3	66.4	49.8	61.8	64.8	56.9	65.5	67.8	65.7	68.7	63.7	79.2
October	61.9	61.6	66.6	50.5	62.0	65.0	57.2	65.9	68.2	65.8	68.8	64.0	78.5
November	62.3	62.0	67.1	51.3	62.3	65.5	57.6	66.4	68.8	66.3	69.1	65.4	78.4
December	62.6	62.3	67.4	51.6	62.7	65.7	57.9	66.7	69.0	66.6	69.4	66.4	80.1
1978													
January	63.0	62.7	67.9	51.1	63.1	66.1	58.3	67.0	69.2	66.9	69.8	67.3	80.3
February	63.3	63.0	68.6	50.6	63.4	66.4	58.7	67.5	69.5	67.4	70.3	68.4	80.6
March	63.8	63.4	69.5	51.0	63.8	66.8	59.1	67.8	69.9	67.8	70.6	69.8	80.3
April	64.2	63.9	70.6	51.4	64.3	67.4	59.6	68.6	70.6	68.1	71.1	72.1	82.2
May	64.8	64.5	71.6	51.7	64.7	68.0	60.0	69.1	71.1	68.7	71.6	72.8	84.6
June	65.3	65.0	72.7	51.9	65.2	68.6	60.5	69.7	71.7	69.2	72.2	74.6	87.4
July	65.8	65.5	73.0	52.1	65.6	69.1	61.0	70.3	72.3	69.4	72.5	74.2	89.6
August	66.2	65.9	73.3	52.6	66.1	69.4	61.5	70.4	72.8	69.9	73.2	73.7	90.4
September	66.7	66.5	73.6	53.2	66.7	70.0	62.1	71.1	73.5	70.5	73.7	75.1	92.3
October	67.4	67.1	74.2	54.1	67.2	70.6	62.6	71.4	73.4	71.3	74.5	77.0	94.7
November	67.8	67.5	74.7	54.9	67.6	71.1	63.1	72.0	74.1	71.9	75.2	77.4	96.3
December	68.3	67.9	75.1	55.9	68.0	71.6	63.3	72.8	74.7	72.4	75.6	78.0	96.8
1979													
January	68.8	68.5	76.4	55.8	68.5	72.2	63.8	73.7	75.3	73.1	76.3	80.1	96.4
February	69.6	69.2	77.7	55.9	69.2	72.9	64.4	74.4	75.9	73.7	77.0	82.1	99.6
March	70.3	69.9	78.4	57.4	69.8	73.8	64.9	75.0	76.4	74.6	77.8	83.8	104.2
April	71.1	70.6	79.0	59.5	70.3	74.7	65.5	75.8	77.0	75.7	78.9	84.4	105.1
May	71.9	71.4	79.7	62.0	70.8	75.6	66.2	76.2	77.4	76.6	79.6	84.7	106.7
June	72.7	72.2	80.0	64.7	71.3	76.4	66.8	76.6	78.0	77.5	80.1	85.6	111.6
July	73.5	73.0	80.5	67.3	71.9	77.2	67.6	77.4	78.5	78.7	81.1	86.5	109.4
August	74.2	73.7	80.4	69.7	72.7	77.9	68.5	78.2	78.8	79.8	81.8	85.5	106.4
September	75.0	74.4	80.9	71.9	73.3	78.6	69.2	79.5	79.7	81.1	82.7	87.9	106.5
October	75.7	75.2	81.5	73.5	74.0	79.3	70.1	80.4	80.4	82.4	83.9	88.8	108.9
November	76.5	76.0	82.0	74.8	74.8	80.0	71.1	81.4	81.0	83.2	84.5	90.0	111.3
December	77.3	76.9	82.8	76.8	75.7	80.8	72.0	82.2	81.7	84.0	85.2	91.2	111.3
1980													
January	78.5	78.0	83.3	79.1	76.7	82.0	73.1	83.4	83.3	86.0	87.2	90.9	112.6
February	79.4	79.0	83.4	81.9	77.5	82.8	74.1	84.6	84.2	87.6	88.2	92.6	115.3
March	80.6	80.1	84.1	84.5	78.6	83.9	75.4	85.5	84.7	88.2	88.6	90.8	111.7
April	81.4	80.9	84.7	85.4	79.5	84.4	76.6	86.2	85.5	88.5	88.8	88.3	109.9
May	82.2	81.7	85.2	86.4	80.1	84.9	77.6	86.6	85.7	89.0	89.1	89.5	107.2
June	83.0	82.5	85.7	86.5	81.0	85.3	79.0	87.3	86.6	89.8	89.8	90.1	106.1
July	83.1	82.6	86.6	86.7	80.8	85.9	78.5	88.7	87.7	90.5	90.3	94.6	109.6
August	83.7	83.2	88.0	87.2	81.3	86.9	78.5	89.7	88.4	91.5	91.1	99.0	112.4
September	84.4	83.9	89.1	87.5	82.1	87.8	79.0	90.1	88.8	91.9	91.4	100.4	116.2
October	85.3	84.7	89.8	88.0	83.0	88.5	80.0	90.8	89.6	92.8	92.1	102.2	118.2
November	86.2	85.6	90.8	88.8	83.9	89.2	81.1	91.4	90.1	93.5	92.6	103.5	119.8
December	87.0	86.4	91.3	90.7	84.9	89.7	82.2	91.8	90.4	94.4	93.7	102.7	119.3

Table 8-1B. Summary Consumer and Producer Price Indexes: Historical Data, 1946 to Date—*Continued*

(Seasonally adjusted.)

Year and month	Urban wage earners and clerical workers (CPI-W), all items	Consumer Price Index, 1982–1984 = 100						Producer Price Index for goods, 1982 = 100					
		All urban consumers (CPI-U)						Finished goods		Processed goods for intermediate demand		Unprocessed goods for intermediate demand	
		All items	Food	Energy	All items less food and energy	Commodities	Services	Total	Less food and energy	Total	Processed materials less foods and energy	Total	Unprocessed nonfood materials less energy
1981													
January	87.7	87.2	91.6	92.1	85.4	90.4	83.0	92.8	91.4	95.6	94.7	103.4	113.3
February	88.6	88.0	92.1	95.2	85.9	91.4	83.7	93.6	92.0	96.1	94.9	104.2	106.2
March	89.1	88.6	92.6	97.4	86.4	91.9	84.4	94.7	92.6	97.1	95.6	103.8	108.9
April	89.6	89.1	92.8	97.6	87.0	92.0	85.3	95.7	93.5	98.3	96.6	104.2	111.9
May	90.2	89.7	92.8	97.9	87.8	92.4	86.4	96.0	94.0	98.7	97.1	103.8	113.7
June	90.9	90.5	93.2	97.3	88.6	92.9	87.5	96.5	94.6	99.0	97.7	104.9	115.5
July	92.0	91.5	93.9	97.3	89.8	93.6	88.9	96.7	94.8	99.2	98.4	105.0	116.4
August	92.7	92.2	94.4	97.8	90.7	94.0	89.9	96.8	95.3	99.7	98.9	104.0	115.5
September	93.5	93.1	94.8	98.6	91.8	94.6	91.2	97.2	96.0	99.7	99.3	102.7	112.6
October	93.8	93.4	95.0	99.2	92.1	94.7	91.7	97.6	96.5	99.8	99.5	101.2	110.8
November	94.2	93.8	95.1	100.5	92.5	94.9	92.5	97.9	97.0	99.9	99.7	99.7	107.5
December	94.5	94.1	95.3	101.5	93.0	95.1	93.0	98.3	97.6	100.0	99.8	98.8	106.0
1982													
January	94.8	94.4	95.6	100.6	93.3	95.2	93.5	98.9	98.1	100.4	99.9	99.7	101.2
February	95.1	94.7	96.3	98.0	93.8	95.4	93.9	98.8	98.1	100.3	100.0	100.0	100.7
March	95.0	94.7	96.2	96.6	93.9	95.3	94.0	98.8	98.7	99.9	99.9	99.7	100.0
April	95.3	95.0	96.4	94.2	94.7	95.1	94.9	99.0	99.0	99.7	99.8	100.2	101.1
May	96.1	95.9	97.2	95.7	95.4	96.0	95.7	99.0	99.4	99.7	100.1	101.9	102.2
June	97.3	97.0	98.1	98.4	96.1	97.4	96.5	99.8	99.9	99.8	100.0	101.8	101.0
July	97.8	97.5	98.2	99.3	96.7	97.9	97.0	100.2	100.1	100.0	99.8	100.7	101.4
August	98.1	97.7	98.0	99.8	97.1	97.9	97.6	100.6	100.6	99.9	99.7	99.8	100.0
September	98.1	97.7	98.2	100.3	97.2	97.8	97.6	100.7	100.8	100.0	100.2	99.2	98.9
October	98.5	98.1	98.2	101.7	97.5	98.2	97.9	101.0	101.3	99.9	100.2	98.7	97.7
November	98.4	98.0	98.2	102.5	97.3	98.3	97.7	101.4	101.6	100.1	100.2	99.2	96.3
December	98.1	97.7	98.2	102.8	97.2	98.3	96.9	101.8	102.2	100.1	100.3	98.8	95.9
1983													
January	98.2	97.9	98.1	99.6	97.6	98.3	97.5	101.0	101.8	99.8	100.3	98.8	97.3
February	98.2	98.0	98.2	97.7	98.0	98.1	97.9	101.1	102.2	100.0	100.8	100.0	99.8
March	98.5	98.1	98.8	96.8	98.2	98.2	98.1	101.0	102.5	99.7	100.8	100.5	102.2
April	99.1	98.8	99.2	98.9	98.6	98.9	98.7	101.1	102.4	99.5	100.9	101.2	102.1
May	99.5	99.2	99.5	100.4	98.9	99.5	98.9	101.4	102.6	99.8	101.0	100.9	103.4
June	99.7	99.4	99.6	100.6	99.2	99.8	99.2	101.6	102.8	100.2	101.3	100.5	104.8
July	100.0	99.8	99.6	100.9	99.8	100.2	99.6	101.6	103.1	100.5	101.8	99.5	106.2
August	100.5	100.1	99.7	101.2	100.1	100.5	99.8	101.9	103.5	100.9	102.0	100.2	108.4
September	100.7	100.4	100.0	101.0	100.5	100.7	100.2	102.2	103.5	101.6	102.3	103.3	109.0
October	101.0	100.8	100.3	100.8	101.0	101.0	100.7	102.2	103.6	101.7	102.5	103.2	109.1
November	101.2	101.1	100.3	100.5	101.5	101.1	101.3	102.0	103.8	101.8	102.8	102.3	109.9
December	101.3	101.4	100.6	100.0	101.8	101.2	101.6	102.3	104.1	101.9	103.1	103.5	111.2
1984													
January	101.8	102.1	102.0	100.2	102.5	101.9	102.1	103.0	104.5	102.1	103.4	104.6	111.5
February	102.0	102.6	102.7	101.4	102.8	102.4	102.6	103.4	104.7	102.5	103.8	103.8	113.8
March	102.0	102.9	102.9	101.4	103.2	102.6	103.0	103.8	105.2	103.0	104.4	105.7	114.8
April	102.2	103.3	102.9	101.7	103.7	102.9	103.5	103.9	105.3	103.2	104.5	105.2	115.1
May	102.5	103.5	102.7	101.6	104.1	103.0	103.9	103.8	105.3	103.4	104.6	104.5	115.7
June	102.7	103.7	103.1	100.8	104.5	103.1	104.2	103.8	105.5	103.6	104.8	103.3	114.1
July	103.2	104.1	103.3	100.5	105.0	103.2	104.9	104.0	105.7	103.4	104.9	104.0	112.0
August	104.1	104.4	103.9	100.1	105.4	103.4	105.4	103.8	105.9	103.2	105.1	103.3	109.6
September	104.5	104.7	103.8	100.6	105.8	103.6	105.9	103.8	106.2	103.1	105.0	102.8	110.5
October	104.7	105.1	104.0	101.1	106.2	103.9	106.3	103.6	105.9	103.2	105.1	101.5	108.5
November	104.8	105.3	104.1	100.8	106.4	103.9	106.7	104.0	106.2	103.3	105.3	101.9	107.7
December	104.9	105.5	104.5	100.1	106.8	103.9	107.1	104.0	106.3	103.2	105.3	101.4	107.3
1985													
January	105.2	105.7	104.7	100.3	107.1	104.1	107.4	104.0	106.9	103.1	105.3	99.9	107.4
February	105.7	106.3	105.2	100.3	107.7	104.7	107.9	104.1	107.3	102.8	105.3	99.4	107.2
March	106.1	106.8	105.5	101.3	108.1	105.1	108.4	104.1	107.6	102.7	105.2	97.6	107.0
April	106.4	107.0	105.4	102.3	108.4	105.4	108.7	104.6	107.6	102.9	105.2	96.7	107.4
May	106.6	107.2	105.2	102.2	108.8	105.2	109.4	104.9	107.8	103.2	105.3	95.8	105.3
June	106.9	107.5	105.5	102.2	109.1	105.3	109.8	104.6	108.2	102.6	105.5	95.2	103.6
July	107.0	107.7	105.5	102.2	109.4	105.3	110.3	104.7	108.4	102.3	105.3	94.9	104.3
August	107.1	107.9	105.6	101.2	109.8	105.2	110.7	104.5	108.5	102.3	105.3	92.9	103.6
September	107.3	108.1	105.8	101.2	110.0	105.4	111.0	103.8	107.9	102.2	105.2	91.8	103.3
October	107.7	108.5	105.8	101.2	110.5	105.6	111.5	104.9	108.9	102.3	105.1	94.1	103.7
November	108.2	109.0	106.5	101.8	111.1	106.1	112.1	105.5	109.1	102.5	105.1	95.7	103.0
December	108.7	109.5	107.3	102.4	111.4	106.6	112.5	106.0	109.1	102.9	105.1	95.5	102.4
1986													
January	109.1	109.9	107.5	102.6	111.9	106.9	113.1	105.5	109.3	102.4	105.0	94.2	103.6
February	108.8	109.7	107.3	99.5	112.2	106.0	113.5	104.1	109.5	101.2	104.9	90.5	103.5
March	108.1	109.1	107.5	92.6	112.5	104.5	114.1	102.8	109.6	99.9	105.0	88.2	103.8
April	107.7	108.7	107.7	87.2	112.9	103.3	114.6	102.3	110.1	98.9	104.7	85.6	103.9
May	107.8	109.0	108.2	87.2	113.1	103.5	114.8	102.8	110.2	98.7	104.6	86.5	104.1
June	108.3	109.4	108.3	88.8	113.4	103.8	115.5	103.1	110.5	98.6	104.7	86.2	104.7
July	108.3	109.5	109.1	85.6	113.8	103.7	115.7	102.3	110.7	98.0	104.8	86.4	105.3
August	108.4	109.6	110.1	83.6	114.2	103.6	116.1	102.7	110.8	98.0	104.9	86.7	99.7
September	108.8	110.0	110.2	84.4	114.6	104.0	116.5	102.9	110.7	98.5	105.1	86.6	100.3
October	108.9	110.2	110.5	82.8	115.0	104.0	116.9	103.5	111.8	98.3	105.1	87.4	102.0
November	109.2	110.4	111.1	82.1	115.3	104.2	117.2	103.4	112.0	98.3	105.2	87.6	102.8
December	109.5	110.8	111.4	82.5	115.6	104.5	117.5	103.6	112.1	98.5	105.3	86.9	104.1

Table 8-1B. Summary Consumer and Producer Price Indexes: Historical Data, 1946 to Date—*Continued*

(Seasonally adjusted.)

Year and month	Urban wage earners and clerical workers (CPI-W), all items	Consumer Price Index, 1982–1984 = 100						Producer Price Index for goods, 1982 = 100					
		All urban consumers (CPI-U)						Finished goods		Processed goods for intermediate demand		Unprocessed goods for intermediate demand	
		All items	Food	Energy	All items less food and energy	Commod-ities	Services	Total	Less food and energy	Total	Processed materials less foods and energy	Total	Unproces-sed nonfood materials less energy
1987													
January	110.2	111.4	111.8	85.4	115.9	105.5	117.9	104.1	112.5	99.0	105.6	89.3	105.4
February	110.7	111.8	112.2	87.4	116.2	106.1	118.3	104.4	112.3	99.8	105.9	90.2	106.2
March	111.1	112.2	112.4	87.6	116.6	106.5	118.6	104.5	112.4	99.9	106.2	90.5	106.5
April	111.6	112.7	112.6	87.6	117.3	106.9	119.2	105.1	112.9	100.3	106.5	92.5	107.5
May	111.9	113.0	113.2	87.1	117.7	107.2	119.6	105.2	113.0	100.8	107.0	93.8	110.0
June	112.4	113.5	113.9	88.5	117.9	107.7	120.0	105.5	113.1	101.4	107.5	94.5	113.2
July	112.7	113.8	113.7	89.2	118.3	108.0	120.3	105.7	113.3	101.9	107.9	95.6	115.9
August	113.2	114.3	113.9	90.5	118.7	108.5	120.9	105.9	113.6	102.4	108.3	96.5	119.1
September	113.6	114.7	114.3	90.3	119.2	108.8	121.4	106.2	113.9	102.6	108.9	96.0	122.8
October	113.9	115.0	114.5	89.6	119.8	109.0	121.8	106.0	114.0	103.1	109.6	95.8	126.6
November	114.2	115.4	114.5	90.0	120.1	109.3	122.2	106.0	114.2	103.5	110.1	95.1	127.5
December	114.4	115.6	115.1	89.5	120.4	109.3	122.6	105.8	114.3	103.8	110.7	94.9	127.9
1988													
January	114.7	116.0	115.6	88.8	120.9	109.5	123.0	106.4	115.0	104.1	111.8	94.2	129.4
February	114.9	116.2	115.6	88.7	121.2	109.5	123.5	106.3	115.3	104.4	112.2	95.2	131.7
March	115.2	116.5	115.8	88.4	121.7	109.8	123.9	106.6	115.6	104.8	112.8	94.1	133.0
April	115.8	117.2	116.4	88.8	122.3	110.5	124.4	107.0	115.9	105.5	113.6	95.4	132.1
May	116.2	117.5	116.9	88.5	122.7	110.7	124.8	107.2	116.2	106.2	114.3	95.8	130.7
June	116.6	118.0	117.6	88.9	123.2	111.2	125.4	107.5	116.6	107.4	114.9	97.0	131.1
July	117.3	118.5	118.8	89.4	123.6	111.9	125.8	108.4	117.2	108.3	115.8	96.7	133.2
August	117.7	119.0	119.4	90.1	124.0	112.2	126.4	108.8	117.7	108.5	116.3	97.0	134.3
September	118.2	119.5	120.1	89.8	124.7	112.8	126.9	109.0	118.1	108.7	116.8	97.0	133.3
October	118.6	119.9	120.3	89.8	125.2	113.0	127.5	109.2	118.4	108.6	117.3	96.6	133.6
November	118.9	120.3	120.5	89.8	125.6	113.3	127.9	109.6	118.7	108.8	118.0	95.2	136.0
December	119.3	120.7	121.1	89.6	126.0	113.5	128.4	110.0	119.2	109.4	118.6	98.1	137.6
1989													
January	119.9	121.2	121.6	90.3	126.5	114.1	128.9	111.1	119.9	110.8	119.5	102.0	140.6
February	120.3	121.6	122.5	90.8	126.9	114.5	129.4	111.9	120.5	111.3	119.9	101.7	140.3
March	120.9	122.2	123.2	91.8	127.4	115.1	130.0	112.3	120.7	111.9	120.2	102.9	140.6
April	121.9	123.1	123.9	96.6	127.8	116.5	130.5	113.1	120.8	112.5	120.5	104.1	140.3
May	122.5	123.7	124.7	97.4	128.3	117.1	131.1	114.0	121.6	112.6	120.6	104.5	139.8
June	122.8	124.1	125.1	96.9	128.8	117.2	131.6	114.0	122.2	112.5	120.6	103.2	137.9
July	123.2	124.5	125.6	96.7	129.2	117.3	132.3	113.8	122.1	112.2	120.3	103.5	135.9
August	123.2	124.5	125.9	94.9	129.5	117.0	132.8	113.4	122.7	111.8	120.2	101.2	136.8
September	123.4	124.8	126.3	93.8	129.9	117.2	133.1	114.0	123.1	112.1	120.2	102.5	137.5
October	123.9	125.4	126.8	94.4	130.6	117.8	133.7	114.6	123.5	112.2	120.3	102.7	137.9
November	124.4	125.9	127.4	93.9	131.1	118.1	134.3	114.8	123.9	112.0	120.0	103.5	134.9
December	124.9	126.3	127.8	94.2	131.6	118.4	134.9	115.5	124.2	112.2	119.8	105.1	132.8
1990													
January	126.1	127.5	129.7	98.9	132.1	120.2	135.4	117.7	124.5	113.7	120.0	106.7	132.7
February	126.6	128.0	130.8	98.2	132.7	120.7	136.0	117.6	124.9	112.8	119.9	106.8	131.6
March	127.0	128.6	131.0	97.6	133.5	120.9	136.8	117.5	125.3	112.9	120.2	105.1	133.9
April	127.3	128.9	130.8	97.5	134.0	121.0	137.4	117.4	125.5	113.1	120.5	102.7	137.0
May	127.5	129.1	131.1	96.7	134.4	121.0	137.9	117.5	126.0	113.1	120.6	103.1	138.0
June	128.2	129.9	132.1	97.3	135.1	121.6	138.8	117.6	126.4	112.9	120.4	100.6	137.3
July	128.8	130.5	132.8	97.1	135.8	122.0	139.6	117.9	126.6	112.8	120.6	101.0	138.0
August	129.9	131.6	133.2	101.6	136.6	123.2	140.6	119.2	127.1	114.0	120.8	110.5	140.1
September	130.9	132.5	133.6	106.5	137.1	124.5	141.1	120.7	127.7	115.8	121.5	115.8	139.9
October	131.7	133.4	134.1	110.8	137.6	125.8	141.6	121.9	128.0	117.4	122.1	125.8	138.4
November	132.1	133.7	134.5	111.2	138.0	126.0	142.2	122.6	128.4	117.7	122.3	117.8	135.7
December	132.5	134.2	134.6	111.0	138.6	126.3	142.7	122.0	128.6	116.9	122.1	110.8	133.8
1991													
January	132.9	134.7	135.0	108.5	139.5	126.3	143.7	122.6	129.5	116.9	122.4	113.3	134.2
February	132.9	134.8	135.1	104.5	140.2	125.9	144.4	121.8	129.8	115.9	122.1	104.1	133.7
March	133.0	134.8	135.3	101.9	140.5	125.5	144.7	121.3	130.1	114.7	121.7	100.5	131.8
April	133.3	135.1	136.1	101.2	140.9	126.0	144.9	121.3	130.4	114.2	121.5	100.2	131.7
May	133.8	135.6	136.6	102.1	141.3	126.4	145.4	121.6	130.6	114.1	121.3	100.9	130.4
June	134.1	136.0	137.4	101.1	141.8	126.7	145.9	121.4	130.7	113.9	121.3	99.2	126.1
July	134.3	136.2	136.7	100.7	142.3	126.6	146.5	121.1	131.0	113.6	121.1	99.4	125.4
August	134.6	136.6	136.2	101.1	142.9	126.8	146.9	121.3	131.3	113.8	121.0	99.1	125.8
September	135.0	137.0	136.4	101.5	143.4	127.0	147.6	121.5	131.8	114.0	121.0	98.4	125.7
October	135.2	137.2	136.2	101.6	143.7	127.0	148.0	121.9	132.3	114.0	121.1	100.8	125.4
November	135.8	137.8	136.7	102.4	144.2	127.6	148.5	122.4	132.5	114.1	121.1	100.7	124.4
December	136.2	138.2	137.0	103.1	144.7	127.9	149.2	122.3	132.6	114.0	121.1	98.2	123.4
1992													
January	136.2	138.3	136.6	101.5	145.1	127.6	149.6	122.0	133.0	113.4	121.0	97.2	123.4
February	136.5	138.6	137.1	101.2	145.4	127.8	149.9	122.3	133.1	113.8	121.3	98.6	125.2
March	136.9	139.1	137.6	101.2	145.9	128.2	150.4	122.4	133.4	113.9	121.5	97.1	127.7
April	137.2	139.4	137.5	101.4	146.3	128.3	150.9	122.5	133.8	114.1	121.7	98.1	128.4
May	137.5	139.7	137.2	102.0	146.8	128.6	151.3	122.9	134.3	114.5	121.8	100.3	129.1
June	138.0	140.1	137.6	103.3	147.1	129.1	151.7	123.4	134.1	115.1	122.0	101.6	128.8
July	138.4	140.5	137.4	103.7	147.6	129.3	152.2	123.3	134.3	115.2	122.1	101.6	129.6
August	138.7	140.8	138.4	103.5	147.9	129.6	152.6	123.4	134.3	115.1	122.3	100.7	130.4
September	139.0	141.1	138.9	103.6	148.1	129.9	152.9	123.7	134.6	115.3	122.4	102.8	130.4
October	139.5	141.7	138.9	104.3	148.8	130.2	153.7	124.2	134.9	115.3	122.4	102.8	128.9
November	139.8	142.1	138.7	105.1	149.2	130.3	154.3	124.1	135.1	115.1	122.4	102.5	128.2
December	140.1	142.3	138.8	105.3	149.6	130.5	154.7	124.2	135.2	115.1	122.5	101.3	130.5

Table 8-1B. Summary Consumer and Producer Price Indexes: Historical Data, 1946 to Date—*Continued*

(Seasonally adjusted.)

Year and month	Urban wage earners and clerical workers (CPI-W), all items	Consumer Price Index, 1982–1984 = 100						Producer Price Index for goods, 1982 = 100					
		All urban consumers (CPI-U)						Finished goods		Processed goods for intermediate demand		Unprocessed goods for intermediate demand	
		All items	Food	Energy	All items less food and energy	Commod-ities	Services	Total	Less food and energy	Total	Processed materials less foods and energy	Total	Unprocessed nonfood materials less energy
1993													
January	140.5	142.8	139.1	105.0	150.1	130.7	155.3	124.4	135.6	115.4	122.9	101.7	135.0
February	140.8	143.1	139.6	104.3	150.6	131.1	155.6	124.7	135.9	115.9	123.5	101.2	136.8
March	141.0	143.3	139.6	104.9	150.8	131.1	156.0	125.0	136.1	116.3	123.8	101.7	137.0
April	141.4	143.8	140.0	104.9	151.4	131.4	156.7	125.7	136.5	116.6	124.0	103.2	138.4
May	141.8	144.2	141.0	104.3	151.8	131.6	157.3	125.7	136.6	116.3	123.7	105.6	140.3
June	142.0	144.3	140.6	103.9	152.1	131.3	157.8	125.2	136.4	116.3	123.7	103.8	140.3
July	142.1	144.5	140.6	103.4	152.3	131.3	158.1	125.1	136.6	116.3	123.7	101.6	142.1
August	142.4	144.8	141.1	103.4	152.0	131.0	158.6	123.0	134.9	116.2	123.9	100.8	140.4
September	142.5	145.0	141.4	103.0	152.9	131.3	159.0	124.1	134.9	116.3	124.0	101.2	140.7
October	143.2	145.6	142.0	105.3	153.4	132.2	159.4	124.2	135.0	116.4	124.0	103.7	142.6
November	143.4	146.0	142.3	104.4	153.9	132.4	159.9	124.4	135.3	116.5	124.3	103.0	144.1
December	143.7	146.3	142.8	103.7	154.3	132.4	160.5	124.4	135.7	116.2	124.5	101.7	145.3
1994													
January	143.8	146.3	142.9	102.8	154.5	132.3	160.8	124.8	136.3	116.5	124.7	103.8	148.3
February	144.0	146.7	142.7	104.1	154.8	132.4	161.4	125.0	136.3	116.9	124.9	102.1	151.0
March	144.3	147.1	142.7	104.3	155.3	132.5	162.0	125.1	136.4	117.1	125.1	103.8	151.5
April	144.5	147.2	143.0	103.7	155.5	132.6	162.2	125.1	136.6	117.1	125.3	103.8	150.7
May	144.8	147.5	143.3	102.8	155.9	132.9	162.4	125.1	137.0	117.2	125.6	102.2	149.7
June	145.3	147.9	143.8	103.1	156.4	133.5	162.8	125.2	137.2	117.8	126.3	102.7	151.2
July	145.9	148.4	144.6	104.5	156.7	134.1	163.1	125.7	137.3	118.3	126.7	101.7	155.5
August	146.5	149.0	145.1	106.7	157.1	134.7	163.8	126.2	137.6	119.1	127.4	101.6	158.8
September	146.8	149.3	145.3	106.1	157.5	134.8	164.1	125.9	137.7	119.6	128.4	99.7	160.5
October	146.9	149.4	145.3	105.7	157.8	134.8	164.5	125.5	137.4	120.1	129.3	98.6	161.3
November	147.3	149.8	145.6	106.1	158.2	135.0	165.0	126.1	137.6	121.0	130.3	99.8	166.6
December	147.6	150.1	146.8	105.9	158.3	135.4	165.2	126.6	137.9	121.5	131.0	101.1	169.9
1995													
January	148.0	150.5	146.7	105.7	159.0	135.4	166.0	126.9	138.4	122.8	132.6	102.1	174.5
February	148.4	150.9	147.3	105.8	159.4	135.6	166.5	127.2	138.7	123.7	133.7	102.9	176.5
March	148.6	151.2	147.1	105.5	159.9	135.6	167.1	127.4	139.0	124.3	134.3	102.3	177.8
April	149.2	151.8	148.1	105.6	160.4	136.2	167.7	127.7	139.3	125.0	135.2	103.7	180.2
May	149.5	152.1	148.2	105.8	160.7	136.4	168.1	127.8	139.7	125.2	135.5	102.4	179.6
June	149.8	152.4	148.3	106.7	161.1	136.6	168.5	127.8	139.8	125.5	135.7	103.0	179.5
July	149.9	152.6	148.5	105.8	161.4	136.6	168.9	128.0	140.2	125.6	136.1	101.6	176.4
August	150.2	152.9	148.6	105.6	161.8	136.8	169.3	127.9	140.2	125.6	136.1	99.7	173.4
September	150.4	153.1	149.1	104.1	162.2	136.8	169.7	128.1	140.2	125.5	136.2	102.0	170.9
October	150.8	153.5	149.5	104.4	162.7	137.1	170.3	128.4	141.0	125.4	135.8	101.9	166.6
November	150.9	153.7	149.6	103.4	163.0	137.0	170.7	128.7	141.3	125.2	135.5	104.1	163.6
December	151.3	153.9	149.9	104.4	163.1	137.3	170.9	129.3	141.5	125.4	135.2	106.5	162.3
1996													
January	152.0	154.7	150.4	106.9	163.7	138.2	171.5	129.7	141.5	125.5	134.8	109.8	162.6
February	152.3	155.0	150.8	107.1	164.0	138.3	172.0	129.7	141.6	125.0	134.4	111.6	162.1
March	152.9	155.5	151.4	108.3	164.4	139.0	172.4	130.5	141.6	125.3	134.1	109.8	158.2
April	153.4	156.1	152.0	111.2	164.6	139.6	172.8	130.9	141.6	125.7	133.8	114.2	156.7
May	153.8	156.4	151.9	112.0	165.0	139.7	173.4	130.9	142.0	126.2	134.0	114.6	157.6
June	154.0	156.7	152.9	110.3	165.4	139.8	173.8	131.3	142.2	125.8	133.9	112.2	154.6
July	154.3	157.0	153.4	110.1	165.7	139.8	174.4	131.2	142.2	125.5	133.6	114.6	152.2
August	154.5	157.2	153.9	109.7	166.0	139.8	174.9	131.6	142.3	125.6	133.6	115.3	152.5
September	154.9	157.7	154.6	109.8	166.5	140.3	175.4	131.7	142.2	126.1	134.0	112.7	153.5
October	155.4	158.2	155.5	110.5	166.8	140.8	175.8	132.4	142.3	126.0	133.7	111.9	153.3
November	155.9	158.7	156.1	111.8	167.2	141.4	176.3	132.5	142.1	125.8	133.7	115.7	153.0
December	156.3	159.1	156.3	113.9	167.4	141.7	176.7	132.9	142.3	126.4	133.9	122.5	153.6
1997													
January	156.6	159.4	155.9	115.2	167.8	141.8	177.3	133.0	142.5	126.6	134.1	127.5	156.2
February	156.9	159.7	156.5	115.0	168.1	142.1	177.6	132.7	142.4	126.5	134.1	116.6	157.6
March	156.9	159.8	156.6	113.0	168.4	141.8	178.0	132.6	142.6	126.1	134.2	107.5	158.7
April	157.0	159.9	156.5	111.0	168.9	141.6	178.4	131.8	142.6	125.6	134.1	107.8	155.8
May	157.0	159.9	156.6	108.8	169.2	141.4	178.7	131.5	142.4	125.4	134.2	109.1	157.0
June	157.3	160.2	156.9	110.0	169.4	141.5	179.2	131.3	142.4	125.4	134.2	106.2	156.9
July	157.4	160.4	157.2	109.1	169.7	141.4	179.7	130.9	142.2	125.1	134.2	106.2	155.7
August	157.8	160.8	157.7	110.9	169.8	141.9	179.9	131.4	142.3	125.3	134.3	106.8	156.8
September	158.2	161.2	158.0	112.4	170.2	142.2	180.4	131.6	142.6	125.5	134.3	108.4	155.8
October	158.4	161.5	158.3	111.8	170.6	142.2	180.9	131.9	142.6	125.4	134.3	113.4	156.7
November	158.6	161.7	158.6	111.4	170.8	142.1	181.4	131.6	142.4	125.6	134.4	115.8	156.5
December	158.6	161.8	158.7	109.8	171.2	142.1	181.7	131.4	142.3	125.4	134.4	108.8	154.2
1998													
January	158.8	162.0	159.5	107.5	171.6	142.0	182.1	130.7	142.4	124.6	134.3	102.8	150.4
February	158.7	162.0	159.4	105.1	171.9	141.8	182.3	130.6	142.6	124.2	134.2	100.8	150.1
March	158.7	162.0	159.7	103.3	172.2	141.4	182.8	130.5	143.3	123.7	134.1	99.5	148.7
April	158.8	162.2	159.7	102.4	172.5	141.3	183.3	130.7	143.4	123.6	134.0	100.6	147.3
May	159.3	162.6	160.3	103.2	172.9	141.7	183.7	130.5	143.5	123.5	133.9	99.6	146.2
June	159.5	162.8	160.2	103.6	173.2	141.8	184.0	130.4	143.5	123.1	133.6	97.1	145.9
July	159.8	163.2	160.6	103.3	173.5	142.1	184.3	130.7	143.8	123.0	133.5	97.4	143.4
August	160.0	163.4	161.0	102.1	174.0	142.2	184.7	130.4	143.8	122.7	133.4	93.6	139.4
September	160.1	163.5	161.1	101.3	174.2	142.0	185.1	130.4	144.0	122.3	133.1	91.4	137.6
October	160.5	163.9	162.0	101.5	174.4	142.3	185.5	130.9	144.2	122.2	132.7	93.9	134.0
November	160.7	164.1	162.2	101.1	174.8	142.2	186.0	130.8	144.3	122.0	132.5	93.6	131.6
December	161.1	164.4	162.4	100.1	175.4	142.5	186.4	131.3	145.8	121.3	132.2	90.2	129.4

Table 8-1B. Summary Consumer and Producer Price Indexes: Historical Data, 1946 to Date—*Continued*

(Seasonally adjusted.)

Year and month	Urban wage earners and clerical workers (CPI-W), all items	Consumer Price Index, 1982–1984 = 100						Producer Price Index for goods, 1982 = 100					
		All urban consumers (CPI-U)						Finished goods		Processed goods for intermediate demand		Unprocessed goods for intermediate demand	
		All items	Food	Energy	All items less food and energy	Commod-ities	Services	Total	Less food and energy	Total	Processed materials less foods and energy	Total	Unprocessed nonfood materials less energy
1999													
January	161.4	164.7	163.0	99.7	175.6	142.8	186.6	131.7	145.6	121.2	132.0	91.0	128.7
February	161.3	164.7	163.3	99.2	175.6	142.4	186.9	131.2	145.7	120.8	131.8	89.0	130.5
March	161.4	164.8	163.3	100.4	175.7	142.4	187.4	131.5	145.7	121.1	131.9	89.6	129.6
April	162.4	165.9	163.5	105.5	176.3	144.0	187.9	132.1	145.7	121.9	132.0	91.3	128.7
May	162.6	166.0	163.8	104.9	176.5	143.9	188.1	132.3	145.7	122.2	132.4	96.8	130.5
June	162.6	166.0	163.7	104.5	176.6	143.8	188.3	132.4	145.8	122.6	132.8	97.0	131.6
July	163.3	166.7	163.9	106.7	177.1	144.5	188.9	132.7	145.8	123.4	133.3	97.3	133.6
August	163.8	167.1	164.2	109.5	177.3	145.0	189.3	133.5	145.7	124.1	133.6	102.4	136.3
September	164.6	167.8	164.6	111.8	177.8	145.9	189.8	134.5	146.5	124.6	133.9	106.4	138.8
October	164.9	168.1	165.0	112.0	178.1	146.1	190.2	134.4	146.9	124.9	134.3	103.8	142.5
November	165.1	168.4	165.3	111.5	178.4	145.9	190.9	134.9	146.9	125.4	134.5	109.7	144.4
December	165.6	168.8	165.5	113.8	178.7	146.5	191.2	135.2	147.0	125.8	134.7	104.4	147.6
2000													
January	166.0	169.3	165.6	115.0	179.3	146.7	192.0	135.2	146.8	126.4	135.1	106.8	150.5
February	166.7	170.0	166.2	118.8	179.4	147.6	192.5	136.6	147.3	127.5	135.5	111.0	151.3
March	167.8	171.0	166.5	124.3	180.0	149.1	193.1	137.3	147.4	128.4	136.0	113.2	150.5
April	167.6	170.9	166.7	120.9	180.3	148.5	193.5	136.9	147.4	128.3	136.5	111.3	148.8
May	167.9	171.2	167.3	120.0	180.7	148.5	194.0	137.0	147.8	128.2	136.6	115.1	147.8
June	169.0	172.2	167.4	126.8	181.1	149.6	194.9	138.1	147.8	129.3	136.9	124.8	145.1
July	169.5	172.7	168.3	127.3	181.5	149.8	195.7	138.2	148.1	129.6	137.1	122.1	142.8
August	169.3	172.7	168.7	123.8	181.9	149.2	196.3	137.9	148.2	129.3	136.9	117.6	141.2
September	170.3	173.6	168.9	129.2	182.3	150.4	196.9	139.0	148.6	130.3	137.0	125.6	142.9
October	170.5	173.9	169.0	129.6	182.6	150.1	197.7	139.5	148.5	130.7	137.1	130.2	142.1
November	170.8	174.2	169.2	129.2	183.1	150.3	198.1	140.2	148.7	130.7	136.9	129.1	139.6
December	171.2	174.6	170.0	130.1	183.3	150.4	198.8	140.5	148.9	131.3	136.9	141.1	139.5
2001													
January	172.2	175.6	170.3	135.0	183.9	150.6	200.6	141.7	149.5	132.1	137.1	165.6	138.7
February	172.5	176.0	171.2	134.1	184.4	150.8	201.2	141.9	149.2	131.8	137.3	141.7	136.5
March	172.6	176.1	171.7	131.7	184.7	150.5	201.6	141.2	149.5	131.0	137.4	132.4	135.0
April	173.0	176.4	172.1	132.3	185.1	150.9	202.0	142.0	149.8	130.9	137.3	133.0	131.3
May	174.0	177.3	172.4	138.4	185.3	151.9	202.7	142.3	150.1	131.1	137.3	130.5	130.9
June	174.2	177.7	173.1	136.9	186.0	151.9	203.5	141.8	150.2	130.9	137.1	119.9	129.7
July	173.8	177.4	173.6	129.6	186.4	150.9	203.8	140.1	150.5	129.4	136.4	113.3	130.6
August	173.8	177.4	174.0	127.3	186.7	150.4	204.4	140.7	150.5	129.1	135.9	112.3	128.4
September	174.7	178.1	174.2	130.9	187.1	151.6	204.5	141.3	150.7	129.3	135.9	107.2	128.8
October	173.9	177.6	174.8	122.9	187.4	150.3	204.8	139.0	149.8	127.6	135.4	97.4	126.5
November	173.7	177.5	174.9	116.9	188.1	149.2	205.6	138.5	150.2	127.0	135.1	102.7	126.2
December	173.4	177.4	174.7	113.9	188.4	148.3	206.1	138.0	150.4	126.1	134.8	95.5	125.7
2002													
January	173.7	177.7	175.3	114.2	188.7	148.3	206.8	137.7	150.0	125.7	134.7	99.8	126.2
February	173.9	178.0	175.7	113.5	189.1	148.3	207.5	138.0	150.1	125.5	134.6	98.4	127.5
March	174.5	178.5	176.1	117.6	189.2	149.0	207.9	138.8	150.0	126.4	135.0	103.8	128.1
April	175.4	179.3	176.4	121.5	189.7	150.0	208.5	138.7	150.3	127.2	135.3	108.1	130.8
May	175.5	179.5	175.8	121.9	190.0	149.7	209.0	138.4	150.2	127.1	135.3	109.0	134.2
June	175.7	179.6	175.9	121.6	190.2	149.7	209.3	138.8	150.5	127.3	135.6	105.1	138.2
July	176.1	180.0	176.1	122.4	190.5	149.9	209.9	138.6	150.0	127.7	136.0	106.5	140.8
August	176.6	180.5	176.1	123.1	191.1	150.2	210.6	138.7	149.9	128.0	136.2	108.3	140.0
September	176.8	180.8	176.5	123.7	191.3	150.2	211.1	139.2	150.3	128.9	136.5	110.8	140.2
October	177.2	181.2	176.4	126.9	191.5	150.5	211.7	140.0	150.5	129.8	136.7	112.6	140.0
November	177.5	181.5	176.9	126.7	191.9	150.5	212.4	140.0	150.3	129.9	136.8	116.6	141.0
December	177.7	181.8	177.1	127.1	192.1	150.3	213.0	139.7	149.5	130.0	136.7	118.9	141.3
2003													
January	178.6	182.6	177.1	133.5	192.4	151.3	213.7	141.1	149.8	131.4	137.2	128.0	143.3
February	179.7	183.6	178.1	140.8	192.5	152.7	214.2	142.7	149.9	133.8	138.1	134.3	148.1
March	180.1	183.9	178.4	143.9	192.5	152.6	215.0	144.0	150.7	136.3	138.6	152.2	147.5
April	179.2	183.2	178.5	136.5	192.5	151.1	215.1	142.2	149.9	133.1	138.3	128.2	145.9
May	178.7	182.9	178.8	129.4	192.9	149.4	216.0	141.9	150.1	132.4	138.4	129.9	146.0
June	178.9	183.1	179.7	129.8	193.0	149.7	216.2	142.7	150.1	133.1	138.4	135.5	145.7
July	179.4	183.7	179.8	132.2	193.4	150.3	216.8	142.8	150.3	133.3	138.2	131.9	148.5
August	180.3	184.5	180.5	137.8	193.6	151.4	217.2	143.7	150.5	133.9	138.4	130.8	152.1
September	180.9	185.1	180.9	142.9	193.7	152.1	217.8	144.0	150.4	133.8	138.8	134.4	156.2
October	180.6	184.9	181.6	137.8	194.0	151.1	218.4	144.8	151.1	134.2	139.1	138.2	160.2
November	180.6	185.0	182.6	136.9	194.0	151.1	218.6	144.6	151.0	134.2	139.3	137.9	165.6
December	181.0	185.5	183.5	138.8	194.2	151.6	219.0	145.1	151.0	135.0	139.6	142.4	171.0
2004													
January	181.9	186.3	183.4	143.9	194.6	152.5	219.7	145.9	151.4	136.6	140.5	148.7	179.7
February	182.4	186.7	183.9	145.8	194.9	153.1	220.1	145.8	151.3	137.8	141.8	150.8	190.0
March	182.7	187.1	184.2	145.1	195.5	153.3	220.8	146.2	151.8	138.4	142.9	153.2	195.0
April	182.8	187.4	184.6	143.4	195.9	153.0	221.4	147.2	151.9	140.1	144.6	156.2	187.1
May	183.8	188.2	186.1	147.6	196.2	154.2	221.9	148.4	152.3	141.7	145.7	160.6	177.6
June	184.4	188.9	186.4	151.5	196.6	154.9	222.7	148.4	152.8	142.2	146.2	161.5	176.3
July	184.6	189.1	186.8	151.1	196.8	154.6	223.2	148.2	152.5	142.9	146.9	161.3	195.7
August	184.7	189.2	187.0	151.5	196.9	154.4	223.7	148.6	152.9	144.4	148.4	161.7	201.6
September	185.3	189.8	186.9	152.9	197.5	154.9	224.2	148.8	153.2	144.8	149.6	154.0	198.3
October	186.4	190.8	187.8	158.6	197.9	156.7	224.6	151.2	153.7	146.6	150.2	161.0	204.6
November	187.4	191.7	188.4	163.8	198.3	157.8	225.4	152.1	154.1	147.9	150.7	172.7	208.9
December	187.4	191.7	188.4	162.3	198.6	157.4	225.8	151.4	154.5	147.7	151.3	167.2	206.0

Table 8-1B. Summary Consumer and Producer Price Indexes: Historical Data, 1946 to Date—*Continued*

(Seasonally adjusted.)

| Year and month | Consumer Price Index, 1982–1984 = 100 | | | | | | | Producer Price Index for goods, 1982 = 100 | | | | | |
| | Urban wage earners and clerical workers (CPI-W), all items | All urban consumers (CPI-U) | | | | | | Finished goods | | Processed goods for intermediate demand | | Unprocessed goods for intermediate demand | |
		All items	Food	Energy	All items less food and energy	Commod-ities	Services	Total	Less food and energy	Total	Processed materials less foods and energy	Total	Unprocessed nonfood materials less energy
2005													
January	187.2	191.6	188.7	157.2	199.0	156.8	226.2	151.9	155.4	148.5	152.4	164.2	203.7
February	188.0	192.4	188.6	161.8	199.4	157.5	226.9	152.7	155.3	149.5	153.2	162.9	200.2
March	188.6	193.1	189.1	163.5	200.1	157.9	228.0	153.7	155.6	150.7	153.8	170.5	199.6
April	189.3	193.7	190.4	166.7	200.2	158.6	228.5	154.2	156.0	151.3	153.9	175.0	203.5
May	189.1	193.6	190.6	163.3	200.5	158.1	228.9	153.9	156.4	150.6	153.5	169.1	196.6
June	189.3	193.7	190.5	163.7	200.6	158.0	229.1	153.9	156.2	151.1	153.3	165.5	188.9
July	190.6	194.9	190.9	172.8	200.9	159.6	229.9	155.0	156.8	152.3	153.5	174.4	190.5
August	192.0	196.1	191.1	183.5	201.1	161.5	230.9	156.3	156.9	153.2	153.4	181.5	200.9
September	195.1	198.8	191.5	208.2	201.3	166.0	231.4	158.8	157.1	157.2	155.0	200.3	211.3
October	195.2	199.1	192.0	205.9	202.0	164.8	233.1	160.5	156.8	162.3	157.2	212.7	207.7
November	193.7	198.1	192.6	191.0	202.5	161.8	234.2	158.7	156.8	160.3	157.9	209.9	214.0
December	193.7	198.1	192.9	187.6	202.8	161.5	234.4	159.6	156.8	160.2	158.5	202.0	216.7
2006													
January	195.1	199.3	193.6	196.6	203.2	162.9	235.5	160.5	157.5	162.4	159.9	203.2	216.7
February	195.0	199.4	193.7	194.1	203.6	162.5	235.9	158.7	158.0	161.6	160.4	186.6	224.0
March	195.3	199.7	194.0	192.0	204.3	162.6	236.5	159.3	158.4	161.5	161.1	179.6	227.1
April	196.4	200.7	193.8	198.5	204.8	164.1	237.1	160.6	158.5	163.0	162.0	182.9	238.2
May	197.0	201.3	194.1	199.8	205.4	164.6	237.8	160.6	158.9	164.4	163.7	184.4	259.1
June	197.4	201.8	194.7	199.8	205.9	164.8	238.5	161.4	159.0	165.2	164.7	178.5	255.3
July	198.6	202.9	195.2	207.9	206.3	166.4	239.2	161.0	158.1	165.5	165.6	180.5	259.5
August	199.5	203.8	195.7	211.9	206.8	167.2	239.9	162.1	158.7	166.5	166.3	187.0	251.7
September	198.3	202.8	196.3	198.1	207.2	164.6	240.7	160.2	159.2	164.7	166.2	182.7	255.2
October	197.1	201.9	196.9	184.1	207.6	162.5	241.0	158.7	158.5	163.0	166.2	168.6	249.7
November	197.2	202.0	197.0	184.1	207.8	162.0	241.7	160.0	159.9	163.8	165.5	189.4	249.8
December	198.4	203.1	197.1	192.7	208.1	163.4	242.4	161.1	160.0	164.7	165.6	195.4	253.7
2007													
January	198.6	203.4	198.4	190.3	208.6	163.3	243.2	160.9	160.2	164.1	165.6	184.9	257.2
February	199.4	204.2	199.7	192.3	209.1	164.1	244.1	162.7	160.9	165.3	165.6	201.6	265.9
March	200.7	205.3	200.4	200.2	209.4	165.6	244.7	164.1	160.9	166.7	166.3	203.6	282.7
April	201.3	205.9	201.0	203.3	209.7	166.2	245.3	165.3	161.0	168.3	167.7	204.0	285.1
May	202.3	206.8	201.7	208.6	210.1	167.3	245.9	166.0	161.4	169.7	168.6	204.8	280.3
June	202.7	207.2	202.6	209.8	210.4	167.5	246.6	166.1	161.7	170.4	169.0	205.9	280.7
July	203.0	207.6	203.2	209.6	210.8	167.8	247.1	167.2	162.1	171.8	169.6	203.7	283.0
August	203.0	207.7	204.0	206.4	211.1	167.5	247.5	166.0	162.3	170.1	168.9	198.6	284.2
September	204.0	208.5	205.0	210.7	211.6	168.5	248.2	167.6	162.3	171.4	169.0	203.2	290.8
October	204.7	209.2	205.7	212.4	212.1	169.0	249.1	169.3	162.9	172.7	169.7	214.4	295.0
November	206.5	210.8	206.5	223.8	212.7	171.5	249.8	172.4	163.4	176.7	171.0	229.5	293.4
December	207.1	211.4	206.9	225.6	213.2	172.0	250.5	171.7	163.4	176.9	171.2	235.6	294.7
2008													
January	207.9	212.2	208.1	226.8	213.8	172.7	251.3	173.3	164.1	179.2	172.7	243.3	309.4
February	208.4	212.6	208.9	229.7	213.9	173.0	251.8	173.9	164.8	180.8	173.8	253.3	319.5
March	209.2	213.4	209.3	233.3	214.4	173.7	252.9	175.4	165.1	184.6	175.9	264.2	329.6
April	209.8	214.0	211.1	234.8	214.6	174.1	253.6	175.9	165.8	186.4	178.3	272.8	362.2
May	211.1	215.2	212.0	243.9	214.9	175.5	254.7	178.4	166.3	191.1	181.1	287.3	368.9
June	213.7	217.5	213.3	262.1	215.4	178.8	255.8	181.2	166.6	195.3	183.7	294.2	372.2
July	215.5	219.1	215.4	271.1	216.0	180.7	257.1	183.4	167.4	200.6	187.4	303.4	384.8
August	215.0	218.7	216.5	262.6	216.4	179.6	257.6	182.0	168.1	198.1	188.6	270.3	373.5
September	215.1	218.9	217.8	260.1	216.7	179.8	257.6	182.7	168.9	198.0	188.8	255.2	338.4
October	212.7	217.0	218.7	238.1	216.8	175.8	257.7	178.3	170.5	189.4	184.9	215.9	278.6
November	207.9	213.1	219.1	195.2	216.9	168.0	257.8	172.9	170.4	179.7	180.4	187.3	226.9
December	205.9	211.4	219.1	176.6	216.9	164.5	258.0	169.7	170.8	172.3	176.2	176.7	223.0
2009													
January	206.5	212.0	219.2	178.8	217.3	165.3	258.4	170.8	170.8	172.4	174.8	173.1	226.0
February	207.4	212.8	219.0	184.9	217.8	166.8	258.7	170.6	170.9	170.9	173.5	163.4	224.5
March	207.1	212.6	218.5	178.8	218.3	166.2	258.7	169.1	171.2	168.3	172.7	160.1	221.3
April	207.4	212.7	218.2	177.1	218.7	166.5	258.7	170.0	171.3	168.4	171.8	162.4	222.1
May	207.8	213.0	217.8	179.7	218.9	167.2	258.6	170.3	171.2	169.4	171.8	167.5	232.2
June	209.9	214.7	217.8	196.9	219.2	170.7	258.7	173.5	171.8	171.7	171.8	175.0	240.5
July	210.0	214.7	217.4	195.6	219.3	170.5	258.7	171.5	171.4	171.1	172.2	168.0	246.6
August	210.9	215.5	217.4	201.5	219.5	171.3	259.3	173.9	171.8	173.8	173.2	176.1	263.8
September	211.3	215.9	217.3	202.8	219.9	171.9	259.6	173.5	171.6	174.3	174.2	174.1	268.8
October	211.9	216.5	217.5	204.6	220.5	172.7	260.0	174.3	171.5	175.0	174.5	186.9	273.8
November	212.7	217.1	217.6	210.3	220.6	173.8	260.2	176.6	172.1	176.9	174.9	195.3	274.4
December	213.0	217.3	217.9	210.3	220.8	174.2	260.3	177.1	172.1	177.8	175.9	200.8	288.3
2010													
January	213.4	217.5	218.5	212.8	220.6	174.9	259.8	178.9	172.5	180.8	177.0	214.0	305.2
February	213.3	217.3	218.6	209.6	220.7	174.3	260.0	177.7	172.6	180.4	178.4	208.8	306.1
March	213.3	217.4	219.0	209.3	220.8	174.1	260.3	178.9	172.9	181.3	179.6	212.1	322.3
April	213.2	217.4	219.2	209.2	220.8	173.9	260.7	178.9	172.9	182.8	181.4	210.6	332.9
May	212.9	217.3	219.3	206.6	221.0	173.4	260.9	178.9	173.4	183.4	181.8	206.2	328.1
June	212.9	217.2	219.3	203.8	221.2	172.9	261.2	178.3	173.6	182.4	180.9	201.5	315.4
July	213.5	217.6	219.2	206.9	221.4	173.4	261.5	178.5	173.7	181.9	180.2	207.1	312.8
August	213.9	217.9	219.5	208.8	221.5	173.8	261.7	179.4	173.9	182.8	180.5	211.4	324.5
September	214.3	218.3	220.2	209.8	221.7	174.4	261.9	180.1	174.3	183.5	180.9	209.7	335.1
October	215.1	219.0	220.5	216.7	221.8	175.7	262.1	181.6	174.3	185.8	182.0	216.9	346.1
November	2,155.0	219.6	220.9	219.5	222.1	176.5	262.4	182.4	174.3	187.3	183.1	219.5	355.5
December	216.9	220.5	221.2	227.1	222.3	177.9	262.7	183.9	174.6	189.3	184.1	229.7	367.6

Table 8-1B. Summary Consumer and Producer Price Indexes: Historical Data, 1946 to Date—*Continued*

(Seasonally adjusted.)

Year and month	Urban wage earners and clerical workers (CPI-W), all items	Consumer Price Index, 1982–1984 = 100						Producer Price Index for goods, 1982 = 100					
		All urban consumers (CPI-U)						Finished goods		Processed goods for intermediate demand		Unprocessed goods for intermediate demand	
		All items	Food	Energy	All items less food and energy	Commod-ities	Services	Total	Less food and energy	Total	Processed materials less foods and energy	Total	Unprocessed nonfood materials less energy
2011													
January	217.5	221.2	222.5	229.3	222.8	178.9	263.2	185.4	177.9	192.0	186.6	237.4	382.5
February	218.2	221.9	223.5	232.1	223.2	179.8	263.7	187.4	179.8	194.8	188.8	243.4	391.7
March	219.5	223.0	225.2	240.1	223.5	181.8	264.1	188.8	180.1	197.6	190.2	247.8	386.9
April	220.8	224.1	226.1	248.0	223.7	183.5	264.5	190.5	180.5	200.2	192.4	260.3	397.0
May	221.6	224.8	226.9	250.7	224.2	184.5	264.9	191.5	180.3	202.0	193.5	253.1	391.6
June	221.5	224.8	227.5	245.5	224.7	184.1	265.3	190.8	180.9	202.2	193.7	253.8	396.7
July	222.1	225.4	228.5	246.2	225.2	184.6	266.0	191.6	181.7	203.1	194.2	254.5	399.2
August	222.8	226.1	229.6	246.9	225.9	185.3	266.7	191.1	182.3	201.6	194.2	250.7	402.4
September	223.4	226.6	230.7	248.6	226.1	185.8	267.1	192.8	182.9	202.6	194.2	251.4	401.6
October	223.5	226.8	230.9	246.7	226.5	185.7	267.5	192.4	183.1	200.7	193.0	244.4	383.4
November	224.0	227.2	231.1	247.6	226.9	186.2	267.8	192.9	183.6	200.9	192.3	251.2	376.5
December	223.9	227.2	231.6	243.4	227.4	185.7	268.5	192.7	183.7	200.2	191.3	244.9	375.4
2012													
January	224.5	227.8	232.2	244.9	227.9	186.5	268.9	193.4	184.4	200.4	192.0	246.8	383.5
February	225.1	228.3	232.1	248.9	228.0	187.4	269.0	193.9	184.6	201.1	193.2	245.4	382.8
March	225.7	228.8	232.6	249.7	228.5	187.9	269.6	194.1	185.1	203.4	194.5	247.0	386.2
April	226.0	229.2	233.0	249.7	228.9	188.1	270.1	194.0	185.2	202.3	194.7	239.7	380.6
May	225.4	228.7	233.2	241.8	229.2	186.8	270.4	192.9	185.4	200.5	194.1	232.4	372.5
June	225.0	228.5	233.7	235.9	229.6	185.8	271.0	192.1	185.7	198.5	191.9	225.0	355.8
July	224.9	228.6	233.8	233.6	230.0	185.5	271.4	192.4	186.3	197.7	191.2	232.5	354.8
August	226.4	229.9	234.2	245.0	230.2	187.5	272.1	194.7	186.8	199.7	191.3	243.1	362.6
September	227.7	231.0	234.4	253.0	230.7	189.1	272.7	196.5	187.0	201.7	192.0	246.1	366.7
October	228.4	231.6	234.8	256.0	231.0	189.8	273.2	196.7	187.2	202.1	192.2	244.7	359.1
November	227.8	231.2	235.3	248.8	231.3	188.5	273.8	195.7	187.9	200.6	192.1	246.5	364.3
December	227.7	231.2	235.7	244.7	231.7	187.7	274.4	195.3	187.8	200.7	192.6	248.3	368.4
2013													
January	228.0	231.6	235.9	244.3	232.2	187.9	275.1	196.2	188.4	201.7	193.8	248.6	364.4
February	229.7	233.0	236.0	256.0	232.6	190.0	275.7	197.5	188.2	203.9	194.7	246.8	362.2
March	228.8	232.3	236.2	246.7	232.8	188.2	276.2	196.5	188.9	201.7	194.4	246.9	365.2
April	228.1	231.8	236.7	240.3	232.8	186.8	276.5	195.4	188.6	200.4	193.9	246.9	356.1
May	228.2	231.9	236.5	240.1	233.1	186.5	277.0	196.2	189.0	200.2	193.6	249.6	349.2
June	228.7	232.4	237.0	241.9	233.4	187.0	277.5	196.3	189.1	200.1	193.5	248.4	346.6
July	229.2	232.9	237.2	243.0	233.9	187.3	278.1	196.1	189.2	200.1	193.2	252.0	347.5
August	229.6	233.3	237.5	243.6	234.3	187.6	278.8	196.9	189.6	200.4	193.6	247.5	346.8
September	229.9	233.6	237.5	244.0	234.7	187.5	279.4	196.7	189.3	200.4	193.6	247.3	343.5
October	230.0	233.7	237.7	242.7	234.9	187.3	279.8	197.0	189.7	200.2	193.6	243.2	340.6
November	230.4	234.1	237.9	243.2	235.3	187.6	280.3	197.4	190.1	199.9	193.6	238.4	343.5
December	231.0	234.7	238.1	246.0	235.7	188.2	280.9	198.0	190.5	200.8	194.0	243.0	347.1
2014													
January	231.8	235.4	238.4	251.0	236.0	188.7	281.7	199.6	191.6	202.6	194.7	247.2	354.2
February	232.0	235.7	239.3	251.1	236.2	188.6	282.4	200.2	192.0	203.6	195.3	259.9	350.6
March	232.2	236.0	240.4	249.4	236.6	188.1	283.5	200.4	192.6	203.3	194.8	261.0	349.2
April	232.8	236.5	241.3	249.7	237.1	188.8	283.8	201.7	193.7	203.7	195.2	264.0	354.1
May	233.0	236.8	242.4	247.8	237.6	188.5	284.8	201.2	193.7	203.0	195.1	260.1	352.6
June	233.2	237.0	242.6	247.5	237.8	188.6	285.1	201.6	194.1	202.9	195.1	257.6	347.5
July	233.5	237.4	243.3	247.8	238.2	188.7	285.7	201.5	194.6	203.1	195.8	253.9	349.2
August	233.2	237.3	243.9	243.5	238.4	188.1	286.0	201.3	194.6	203.1	196.3	246.0	346.7
September	233.5	237.5	244.6	242.1	238.7	188.2	286.3	200.9	194.8	202.6	196.3	246.9	346.9
October	233.4	237.5	244.9	238.3	239.1	187.7	286.9	200.2	195.6	200.6	195.7	238.2	336.9
November	232.8	237.1	245.4	231.2	239.4	186.4	287.3	199.4	195.5	198.8	194.8	234.9	331.5
December	231.6	236.3	246.2	219.3	239.6	184.1	288.0	196.4	195.5	195.5	193.9	222.0	328.6
2015													
January	229.7	234.9	246.1	201.0	239.9	180.6	288.6	193.2	196.0	190.9	191.8	200.8	325.5
February	230.4	235.5	246.4	204.3	240.2	181.3	289.0	193.7	195.7	190.3	191.2	194.5	308.6
March	230.9	236.0	246.1	205.6	240.8	181.9	289.5	193.9	195.6	189.7	190.6	192.6	304.2
April	231.1	236.2	246.1	203.0	241.4	181.5	290.2	193.1	195.3	188.4	190.2	193.8	304.3
May	231.8	236.9	246.3	207.9	241.7	182.6	290.6	195.5	196.1	189.7	190.2	199.5	303.5
June	232.4	237.4	247.0	209.6	242.0	182.9	291.3	196.4	197.0	190.4	190.1	200.8	304.2
July	232.8	237.9	247.2	210.5	242.5	183.2	291.9	195.8	196.6	189.9	189.9	194.8	303.3
August	232.7	237.8	247.7	206.6	242.8	182.6	292.4	195.3	196.9	188.4	189.1	187.8	290.0
September	232.1	237.5	248.5	197.5	243.2	181.2	293.1	192.8	196.9	185.8	188.0	183.5	289.1
October	232.4	237.8	248.7	196.8	243.7	181.0	293.9	192.2	196.3	185.1	187.6	181.3	281.2
November	232.7	238.2	248.5	196.9	244.2	181.0	294.6	192.6	196.4	184.3	187.1	172.6	270.5
December	232.3	237.8	248.1	191.0	244.6	179.8	295.1	190.9	196.1	182.3	186.5	166.0	267.8
2016													
January	232.4	238.1	248.2	188.3	245.2	179.6	295.8	190.8	197.1	180.7	185.8	166.0	266.5
February	231.8	237.8	248.4	179.2	245.8	178.2	296.6	189.6	197.2	179.3	185.3	163.1	268.3
March	232.2	238.1	248.1	180.8	246.1	178.2	297.2	189.6	196.8	179.2	185.3	165.3	275.4
April	233.1	238.9	248.4	185.7	246.5	179.1	298.0	190.4	196.9	179.9	185.8	168.9	285.3
May	233.4	239.4	248.0	187.1	247.0	179.0	298.9	191.4	197.1	181.3	186.3	173.8	294.9
June	233.9	239.8	247.9	189.6	247.4	179.3	299.6	192.5	197.6	182.7	186.6	178.2	294.4
July	233.9	239.9	247.8	187.6	247.7	178.7	300.3	192.2	197.4	183.0	186.8	179.6	296.1
August	234.3	240.4	247.8	187.5	248.4	178.7	301.3	191.8	197.1	182.9	187.4	175.8	297.1
September	235.0	241.0	247.8	192.0	248.6	179.3	301.9	192.7	197.7	183.5	187.6	174.8	291.2
October	235.7	241.7	247.7	196.8	249.0	180.1	302.5	193.5	197.3	184.1	187.9	173.5	287.3
November	236.2	242.2	247.6	198.7	249.5	180.2	303.3	193.4	197.2	184.5	188.7	174.6	294.4
December	236.9	242.8	247.5	201.1	250.0	180.6	304.1	194.6	197.9	185.6	189.4	187.4	304.5

Table 8-1C. Consumer and Producer Price Indexes: Historical Data, 1913–1949

(Not seasonally adjusted.)

Year and month	Consumer price indexes, 1982–1984 =100				Producer Price Indexes for goods, 1982 = 100			
	All urban consumers (CPI-U)		Urban wage earners and clerical workers (CPI-W)		All commodities		Farm products	Industrial commodities
	Index	Percent change	Index	Percent change	Index	Percent change		
1913	9.9	. . .	10.0	. . .	12.0	. . .	18.0	11.9
1914	10.0	1.0	10.1	1.0	11.8	-1.7	17.9	11.3
1915	10.1	1.0	10.2	1.0	12.0	1.7	18.0	11.6
1916	10.9	7.9	11.0	7.8	14.7	22.5	21.3	15.0
1917	12.8	17.4	12.9	17.3	20.2	37.4	32.6	19.5
1918	15.1	18.0	15.1	17.1	22.6	11.9	37.4	21.1
1919	17.3	14.6	17.4	15.2	23.9	5.8	39.8	22.0
1920	20.0	15.6	20.1	15.5	26.6	11.3	38.0	27.4
1921	17.9	-10.5	18.0	-10.4	16.8	-36.8	22.3	17.8
1922	16.8	-6.1	16.9	-6.1	16.7	-0.6	23.7	17.4
1923	17.1	1.8	17.2	1.8	17.3	3.6	24.9	17.8
1924	17.1	0.0	17.2	0.0	16.9	-2.3	25.2	17.0
1925	17.5	2.3	17.6	2.3	17.8	5.3	27.7	17.5
1926	17.7	1.1	17.8	1.1	17.2	-3.4	25.3	17.0
1927	17.4	-1.7	17.5	-1.7	16.5	-4.1	25.1	16.0
1928	17.1	-1.7	17.2	-1.7	16.7	1.2	26.7	15.8
1929	17.1	0.0	17.2	0.0	16.4	-1.8	26.4	15.6
1930	16.7	-2.3	16.8	-2.3	14.9	-9.1	22.4	14.5
1931	15.2	-9.0	15.3	-8.9	12.6	-15.4	16.4	12.8
1932	13.7	-9.9	13.7	-10.5	11.2	-11.1	12.2	11.9
1933	13.0	-5.1	13.0	-5.1	11.4	1.8	13.0	12.1
1934	13.4	3.1	13.5	3.8	12.9	13.2	16.5	13.3
1935	13.7	2.2	13.8	2.2	13.8	7.0	19.8	13.3
1936	13.9	1.5	13.9	0.7	13.9	0.7	20.4	13.5
1937	14.4	3.6	14.4	3.6	14.9	7.2	21.8	14.5
1938	14.1	-2.1	14.2	-1.4	13.5	-9.4	17.3	13.9
1939	13.9	-1.4	14.0	-1.4	13.3	-1.5	16.5	13.9
1940	14.0	0.7	14.1	0.7	13.5	1.5	17.1	14.1
1941	14.7	5.0	14.8	5.0	15.1	11.9	20.8	15.1
1942	16.3	10.9	16.4	10.8	17.0	12.6	26.7	16.2
1943	17.3	6.1	17.4	6.1	17.8	4.7	30.9	16.5
1944	17.6	1.7	17.7	1.7	17.9	0.6	31.2	16.7
1945	18.0	2.3	18.1	2.3	18.2	1.7	32.4	17.0
1946	19.5	8.3	19.6	8.3	20.8	14.3	37.5	18.6
1947	22.3	14.4	22.5	14.8	25.6	23.1	45.1	22.7
1948	24.1	8.1	24.2	7.6	27.7	8.2	48.5	24.6
1949	23.8	-1.2	24.0	-0.8	26.3	-5.1	41.9	24.1
1913								
January	9.8	. . .	9.9	. . .	12.1	. . .	17.6	12.3
February	9.8	0.0	9.8	-1.0	12.0	-0.8	17.5	12.2
March	9.8	0.0	9.8	0.0	12.0	0.0	17.6	12.1
April	9.8	0.0	9.9	1.0	12.0	0.0	17.5	12.0
May	9.7	-1.0	9.8	-1.0	11.9	-0.8	17.4	11.9
June	9.8	1.0	9.8	0.0	11.9	0.0	17.6	11.8
July	9.9	1.0	9.9	1.0	12.0	0.8	18.1	11.8
August	9.9	0.0	10.0	1.0	12.0	0.0	18.2	11.7
September	10.0	1.0	10.0	0.0	12.2	1.7	18.8	11.8
October	10.0	0.0	10.1	1.0	12.2	0.0	18.8	11.8
November	10.1	1.0	10.1	0.0	12.1	-0.8	18.9	11.7
December	10.0	-1.0	10.1	0.0	11.9	-1.7	18.5	11.6
1914								
January	10.0	0.0	10.1	0.0	11.8	-0.8	18.4	11.5
February	9.9	-1.0	10.0	-1.0	11.8	0.0	18.3	11.5
March	9.9	0.0	10.0	0.0	11.7	-0.8	18.2	11.5
April	9.8	-1.0	9.9	-1.0	11.7	0.0	18.0	11.5
May	9.9	1.0	9.9	0.0	11.6	-0.9	18.0	11.4
June	9.9	0.0	10.0	1.0	11.6	0.0	18.1	11.3
July	10.0	1.0	10.1	1.0	11.6	0.0	18.0	11.2
August	10.2	2.0	10.2	1.0	12.0	3.4	18.3	11.2
September	10.2	0.0	10.3	1.0	12.1	0.8	17.9	11.3
October	10.1	-1.0	10.2	-1.0	11.7	-3.3	17.2	11.0
November	10.2	1.0	10.2	0.0	11.7	0.0	17.6	11.0
December	10.1	-1.0	10.2	0.0	11.6	-0.9	17.4	11.0
1915								
January	10.1	0.0	10.2	0.0	11.8	1.7	18.1	11.1
February	10.0	-1.0	10.1	-1.0	11.8	0.0	18.4	11.0
March	9.9	-1.0	10.0	-1.0	11.8	0.0	17.9	11.0
April	10.0	1.0	10.1	1.0	11.8	0.0	18.2	11.1
May	10.1	1.0	10.1	0.0	11.9	0.8	18.2	11.2
June	10.1	0.0	10.2	1.0	11.8	-0.8	17.7	11.4
July	10.1	0.0	10.2	0.0	11.9	0.8	18.1	11.5
August	10.1	0.0	10.2	0.0	11.8	-0.8	17.9	11.5
September	10.1	0.0	10.2	0.0	11.8	0.0	17.5	11.7
October	10.2	1.0	10.3	1.0	12.1	2.5	18.1	11.9
November	10.3	1.0	10.4	1.0	12.3	1.7	18.0	12.3
December	10.3	0.0	10.4	0.0	12.8	4.1	18.4	12.9

. . . = Not available.

Table 8-1C. Consumer and Producer Price Indexes: Historical Data, 1913–1949—*Continued*

(Not seasonally adjusted.)

| Year and month | Consumer price indexes, 1982–1984 =100 | | | | Producer Price Indexes for goods, 1982 = 100 | | | |
| | All urban consumers (CPI-U) | | Urban wage earners and clerical workers (CPI-W) | | All commodities | | Farm products | Industrial commodities |
	Index	Percent change	Index	Percent change	Index	Percent change		
1916								
January	10.4	1.0	10.5	1.0	13.3	3.9	19.4	13.6
February	10.4	0.0	10.5	0.0	13.5	1.5	19.4	14.0
March	10.5	1.0	10.6	1.0	13.9	3.0	19.4	14.4
April	10.6	1.0	10.7	0.9	14.1	1.4	19.6	14.6
May	10.7	0.9	10.7	0.0	14.2	0.7	19.8	14.7
June	10.8	0.9	10.9	1.9	14.3	0.7	19.7	14.8
July	10.8	0.0	10.9	0.0	14.4	0.7	20.3	14.6
August	10.9	0.9	11.0	0.9	14.7	2.1	21.7	14.6
September	11.1	1.8	11.2	1.8	15.0	2.0	22.6	14.8
October	11.3	1.8	11.3	0.9	15.7	4.7	23.7	15.5
November	11.5	1.8	11.5	1.8	16.8	7.0	25.3	16.8
December	11.6	0.9	11.6	0.9	17.1	1.8	25.0	17.7
1917								
January	11.7	0.9	11.8	1.7	17.6	2.9	26.2	18.3
February	12.0	2.6	12.0	1.7	18.0	2.3	27.2	18.6
March	12.0	0.0	12.1	0.8	18.5	2.8	28.6	18.8
April	12.6	5.0	12.6	4.1	19.7	6.5	31.6	19.0
May	12.8	1.6	12.9	2.4	20.8	5.6	33.6	19.8
June	13.0	1.6	13.0	0.8	21.0	1.0	33.8	20.4
July	12.8	-1.5	12.9	-0.8	21.2	1.0	34.0	20.7
August	13.0	1.6	13.1	1.6	21.5	1.4	34.6	20.7
September	13.3	2.3	13.3	1.5	21.3	-0.9	34.3	20.1
October	13.5	1.5	13.6	2.3	21.1	-0.9	35.2	19.1
November	13.5	0.0	13.6	0.0	21.2	0.5	36.0	19.2
December	13.7	1.5	13.8	1.5	21.2	0.0	35.6	19.5
1918								
January	14.0	2.2	14.0	1.4	21.6	1.9	37.0	19.9
February	14.1	0.7	14.2	1.4	21.1	-2.3	37.1	19.0
March	14.0	-0.7	14.1	-0.7	21.8	3.3	37.3	20.2
April	14.2	1.4	14.3	1.4	22.1	1.4	36.6	20.7
May	14.5	2.1	14.5	1.4	22.1	0.0	35.4	21.0
June	14.7	1.4	14.8	2.1	22.2	0.5	35.4	21.3
July	15.1	2.7	15.2	2.7	22.7	2.3	37.0	21.5
August	15.4	2.0	15.4	1.3	23.2	2.2	38.6	21.7
September	15.7	1.9	15.8	2.6	23.7	2.2	39.6	22.1
October	16.0	1.9	16.1	1.9	23.5	-0.8	38.2	22.1
November	16.3	1.9	16.3	1.2	23.5	0.0	38.0	22.1
December	16.5	1.2	16.6	1.8	23.5	0.0	38.1	21.8
1919								
January	16.5	0.0	16.6	0.0	23.2	-1.3	38.9	21.1
February	16.2	-1.8	16.2	-2.4	22.4	-3.4	37.5	20.6
March	16.4	1.2	16.5	1.9	22.6	0.9	38.5	20.1
April	16.7	1.8	16.8	1.8	22.9	1.3	40.0	20.0
May	16.9	1.2	17.0	1.2	23.3	1.7	40.9	20.2
June	16.9	0.0	17.0	0.0	23.4	0.4	39.6	21.1
July	17.4	3.0	17.5	2.9	24.3	3.8	41.5	22.1
August	17.7	1.7	17.8	1.7	24.9	2.5	41.3	23.1
September	17.8	0.6	17.9	0.6	24.3	-2.4	38.7	23.2
October	18.1	1.7	18.2	1.7	24.4	0.4	38.5	23.5
November	18.5	2.2	18.6	2.2	24.9	2.0	40.3	23.8
December	18.9	2.2	19.0	2.2	26.0	4.4	41.8	24.7
1920								
January	19.3	2.1	19.4	2.1	27.2	4.6	43.0	26.1
February	19.5	1.0	19.6	1.0	27.1	-0.4	41.2	27.1
March	19.7	1.0	19.8	1.0	27.3	0.7	41.5	27.7
April	20.3	3.0	20.4	3.0	28.5	4.4	42.5	28.7
May	20.6	1.5	20.7	1.5	28.8	1.1	42.8	29.0
June	20.9	1.5	21.0	1.4	28.7	-0.3	42.3	29.0
July	20.8	-0.5	20.9	-0.5	28.6	-0.3	40.5	29.5
August	20.3	-2.4	20.4	-2.4	27.8	-2.8	37.8	29.7
September	20.0	-1.5	20.1	-1.5	26.8	-3.6	36.4	28.5
October	19.9	-0.5	20.0	-0.5	24.9	-7.1	32.2	26.9
November	19.8	-0.5	19.9	-0.5	23.0	-7.6	30.0	24.5
December	19.4	-2.0	19.5	-2.0	20.8	-9.6	26.4	22.7
1921								
January	19.0	-2.1	19.1	-2.1	19.6	-5.8	25.6	21.1
February	18.4	-3.2	18.5	-3.1	18.1	-7.7	23.4	19.4
March	18.3	-0.5	18.4	-0.5	17.7	-2.2	22.7	18.7
April	18.1	-1.1	18.2	-1.1	17.0	-4.0	20.9	18.4
May	17.7	-2.2	17.8	-2.2	16.6	-2.4	21.0	17.9
June	17.6	-0.6	17.7	-0.6	16.1	-3.0	20.3	17.4
July	17.7	0.6	17.8	0.6	16.1	0.0	21.8	16.9
August	17.7	0.0	17.8	0.0	16.1	0.0	22.5	16.5
September	17.5	-1.1	17.6	-1.1	16.1	0.0	22.7	16.5
October	17.5	0.0	17.6	0.0	16.2	0.6	22.7	17.0
November	17.4	-0.6	17.5	-0.6	16.2	0.0	22.1	17.3
December	17.3	-0.6	17.4	-0.6	16.0	-1.2	22.2	17.0

Table 8-1C. Consumer and Producer Price Indexes: Historical Data, 1913–1949—*Continued*

(Not seasonally adjusted.)

Year and month	Consumer price indexes, 1982–1984 =100				Producer Price Indexes for goods, 1982 = 100			
	All urban consumers (CPI-U)		Urban wage earners and clerical workers (CPI-W)		All commodities		Farm products	Industrial commodities
	Index	Percent change	Index	Percent change	Index	Percent change		
1922								
January	16.9	-2.3	17.0	-2.3	15.7	-1.9	22.2	16.7
February	16.9	0.0	17.0	0.0	16.0	1.9	24.0	16.6
March	16.7	-1.2	16.8	-1.2	16.0	0.0	23.6	16.5
April	16.7	0.0	16.8	0.0	16.1	0.6	23.4	16.6
May	16.7	0.0	16.8	0.0	16.6	3.1	23.8	17.4
June	16.7	0.0	16.8	0.0	16.6	0.0	23.4	17.4
July	16.8	0.6	16.9	0.6	17.1	3.0	24.1	18.1
August	16.6	-1.2	16.7	-1.2	17.0	-0.6	23.0	18.2
September	16.6	0.0	16.7	0.0	17.1	0.6	23.3	18.2
October	16.7	0.6	16.8	0.6	17.2	0.6	23.8	17.9
November	16.8	0.6	16.9	0.6	17.3	0.6	24.7	17.7
December	16.9	0.6	17.0	0.6	17.3	0.0	25.0	17.7
1923								
January	16.8	-0.6	16.9	-0.6	17.6	1.7	25.1	18.2
February	16.8	0.0	16.9	0.0	17.8	1.1	25.3	18.6
March	16.8	0.0	16.9	0.0	18.0	1.1	25.3	18.8
April	16.9	0.6	17.0	0.6	17.9	-0.6	24.8	18.7
May	16.9	0.0	17.0	0.0	17.5	-2.2	24.4	18.3
June	17.0	0.6	17.1	0.6	17.3	-1.1	24.2	17.9
July	17.2	1.2	17.3	1.2	17.0	-1.7	23.7	17.6
August	17.1	-0.6	17.2	-0.6	16.9	-0.6	24.2	17.4
September	17.2	0.6	17.3	0.6	17.2	1.8	25.3	17.3
October	17.3	0.6	17.4	0.6	17.1	-0.6	25.4	17.1
November	17.3	0.0	17.4	0.0	17.0	-0.6	25.7	16.9
December	17.3	0.0	17.4	0.0	16.9	-0.6	25.5	16.9
1924								
January	17.3	0.0	17.4	0.0	17.2	1.8	25.6	17.4
February	17.2	-0.6	17.3	-0.6	17.2	0.0	25.0	17.6
March	17.1	-0.6	17.2	-0.6	17.0	-1.2	24.2	17.5
April	17.0	-0.6	17.1	-0.6	16.7	-1.8	24.6	17.3
May	17.0	0.0	17.1	0.0	16.5	-1.2	24.0	17.0
June	17.0	0.0	17.1	0.0	16.4	-0.6	23.8	16.7
July	17.1	0.6	17.2	0.6	16.5	0.6	24.9	16.6
August	17.0	-0.6	17.1	-0.6	16.7	1.2	25.7	16.6
September	17.1	0.6	17.2	0.6	16.7	0.0	25.3	16.6
October	17.2	0.6	17.3	0.6	16.9	1.2	26.0	16.6
November	17.2	0.0	17.3	0.0	17.1	1.2	26.2	16.8
December	17.3	0.6	17.4	0.6	17.5	2.3	27.3	17.1
1925								
January	17.3	0.0	17.4	0.0	17.7	1.1	28.7	17.3
February	17.2	-0.6	17.3	-0.6	17.9	1.1	28.4	17.7
March	17.3	0.6	17.4	0.6	17.9	0.0	28.5	17.5
April	17.2	-0.6	17.3	-0.6	17.5	-2.2	27.1	17.2
May	17.3	0.6	17.4	0.6	17.5	0.0	27.1	17.3
June	17.5	1.2	17.6	1.1	17.7	1.1	27.6	17.5
July	17.7	1.1	17.8	1.1	18.0	1.7	28.3	17.6
August	17.7	0.0	17.8	0.0	17.9	-0.6	28.1	17.4
September	17.7	0.0	17.8	0.0	17.8	-0.6	27.7	17.4
October	17.7	0.0	17.8	0.0	17.8	0.0	27.0	17.5
November	18.0	1.7	18.1	1.7	18.0	1.1	27.3	17.6
December	17.9	-0.6	18.0	-0.6	17.8	-1.1	26.6	17.6
1926								
January	17.9	0.0	18.0	0.0	17.8	0.0	27.1	17.5
February	17.9	0.0	18.0	0.0	17.6	-1.1	26.5	17.3
March	17.8	-0.6	17.9	-0.6	17.3	-1.7	25.7	17.1
April	17.9	0.6	18.0	0.6	17.3	0.0	26.0	17.0
May	17.8	-0.6	17.9	-0.6	17.3	0.0	25.8	17.0
June	17.7	-0.6	17.8	-0.6	17.3	0.0	25.5	17.0
July	17.5	-1.1	17.6	-1.1	17.1	-1.2	24.9	16.9
August	17.4	-0.6	17.5	-0.6	17.1	0.0	24.6	16.9
September	17.5	0.6	17.6	0.6	17.2	0.6	25.1	16.9
October	17.6	0.6	17.7	0.6	17.1	-0.6	24.7	16.9
November	17.7	0.6	17.8	0.6	17.0	-0.6	23.9	16.9
December	17.7	0.0	17.8	0.0	16.9	-0.6	24.0	16.7
1927								
January	17.5	-1.1	17.6	-1.1	16.4	-3.0	24.3	16.4
February	17.4	-0.6	17.5	-0.6	16.6	1.2	24.1	16.3
March	17.3	-0.6	17.4	-0.6	16.5	-0.6	23.8	16.1
April	17.3	0.0	17.4	0.0	16.3	-1.2	23.8	15.9
May	17.4	0.6	17.5	0.6	16.2	-0.6	24.3	15.9
June	17.6	1.1	17.7	1.1	16.2	0.0	24.3	15.9
July	17.3	-1.7	17.4	-1.7	16.2	0.0	24.6	15.9
August	17.2	-0.6	17.3	-0.6	16.4	1.2	25.8	15.9
September	17.3	0.6	17.4	0.6	16.6	1.2	26.7	16.0
October	17.4	0.6	17.5	0.6	16.7	0.6	26.5	15.9
November	17.3	-0.6	17.4	-0.6	16.6	-0.6	26.3	15.8
December	17.3	0.0	17.4	0.0	16.6	0.0	26.3	15.9

Table 8-1C. Consumer and Producer Price Indexes: Historical Data, 1913–1949—*Continued*

(Not seasonally adjusted.)

| Year and month | Consumer price indexes, 1982–1984 =100 | | | | Producer Price Indexes for goods, 1982 = 100 | | | | |
| | All urban consumers (CPI-U) | | Urban wage earners and clerical workers (CPI-W) | | All commodities | | Farm products | Industrial commodities |
	Index	Percent change	Index	Percent change	Index	Percent change		
1928								
January	17.3	0.0	17.4	0.0	16.6	0.0	26.8	15.8
February	17.1	-1.2	17.2	-1.1	16.5	-0.6	26.4	15.8
March	17.1	0.0	17.2	0.0	16.5	0.0	26.1	15.8
April	17.1	0.0	17.2	0.0	16.7	1.2	27.1	15.8
May	17.2	0.6	17.3	0.6	16.8	0.6	27.7	15.8
June	17.1	-0.6	17.2	-0.6	16.7	-0.6	26.9	15.8
July	17.1	0.0	17.2	0.0	16.8	0.6	27.4	15.8
August	17.1	0.0	17.2	0.0	16.8	0.0	27.0	15.8
September	17.3	1.2	17.4	1.2	17.0	1.2	27.5	15.8
October	17.2	-0.6	17.3	-0.6	16.7	-1.8	26.1	15.8
November	17.2	0.0	17.3	0.0	16.5	-1.2	25.7	15.8
December	17.1	-0.6	17.2	-0.6	16.5	0.0	26.2	15.8
1929								
January	17.1	0.0	17.2	0.0	16.5	0.0	26.7	15.7
February	17.1	0.0	17.2	0.0	16.4	-0.6	26.6	15.6
March	17.0	-0.6	17.1	-0.6	16.6	1.2	27.1	15.7
April	16.9	-0.6	17.0	-0.6	16.5	-0.6	26.5	15.6
May	17.0	0.6	17.1	0.6	16.3	-1.2	25.8	15.6
June	17.1	0.6	17.2	0.6	16.4	0.6	26.1	15.6
July	17.3	1.2	17.4	1.2	16.6	1.2	27.1	15.6
August	17.3	0.0	17.4	0.0	16.6	0.0	27.1	15.5
September	17.3	0.0	17.4	0.0	16.6	0.0	26.9	15.6
October	17.3	0.0	17.4	0.0	16.4	-1.2	26.2	15.6
November	17.3	0.0	17.4	0.0	16.1	-1.8	25.5	15.5
December	17.2	-0.6	17.3	-0.6	16.1	0.0	25.7	15.4
1930								
January	17.1	-0.6	17.2	-0.6	15.9	-1.2	25.5	15.2
February	17.0	-0.6	17.1	-0.6	15.7	-1.3	24.7	15.1
March	16.9	-0.6	17.0	-0.6	15.5	-1.3	23.9	15.0
April	17.0	0.6	17.1	0.6	15.5	0.0	24.2	15.0
May	16.9	-0.6	17.0	-0.6	15.3	-1.3	23.5	14.9
June	16.8	-0.6	16.9	-0.6	15.0	-2.0	22.5	14.6
July	16.6	-1.2	16.7	-1.2	14.5	-3.3	21.0	14.4
August	16.5	-0.6	16.6	-0.6	14.5	0.0	21.4	14.2
September	16.6	0.6	16.7	0.6	14.5	0.0	21.5	14.2
October	16.5	-0.6	16.6	-0.6	14.3	-1.4	20.8	14.0
November	16.4	-0.6	16.5	-0.6	14.0	-2.1	20.0	13.8
December	16.1	-1.8	16.2	-1.8	13.7	-2.1	19.0	13.6
1931								
January	15.9	-1.2	16.0	-1.2	13.5	-1.5	18.4	13.4
February	15.7	-1.3	15.7	-1.9	13.2	-2.2	17.7	13.3
March	15.6	-0.6	15.6	-0.6	13.1	-0.8	17.8	13.1
April	15.5	-0.6	15.5	-0.6	12.9	-1.5	17.7	12.9
May	15.3	-1.3	15.4	-0.6	12.6	-2.3	16.9	12.8
June	15.1	-1.3	15.2	-1.3	12.4	-1.6	16.5	12.6
July	15.1	0.0	15.2	0.0	12.4	0.0	16.4	12.6
August	15.1	0.0	15.1	-0.7	12.4	0.0	16.1	12.6
September	15.0	-0.7	15.1	0.0	12.3	-0.8	15.3	12.6
October	14.9	-0.7	15.0	-0.7	12.1	-1.6	14.8	12.4
November	14.7	-1.3	14.8	-1.3	12.1	0.0	14.8	12.5
December	14.6	-0.7	14.7	-0.7	11.8	-2.5	14.1	12.3
1932								
January	14.3	-2.1	14.4	-2.0	11.6	-1.7	13.3	12.2
February	14.1	-1.4	14.2	-1.4	11.4	-1.7	12.8	12.1
March	14.0	-0.7	14.1	-0.7	11.4	0.0	12.7	12.0
April	13.9	-0.7	14.0	-0.7	11.3	-0.9	12.4	12.0
May	13.7	-1.4	13.8	-1.4	11.1	-1.8	11.8	11.9
June	13.6	-0.7	13.7	-0.7	11.0	-0.9	11.6	11.9
July	13.6	0.0	13.7	0.0	11.1	0.9	12.1	11.8
August	13.5	-0.7	13.5	-1.5	11.2	0.9	12.4	11.9
September	13.4	-0.7	13.5	0.0	11.3	0.9	12.4	11.9
October	13.3	-0.7	13.4	-0.7	11.1	-1.8	11.8	11.9
November	13.2	-0.8	13.3	-0.7	11.0	-0.9	11.8	11.9
December	13.1	-0.8	13.2	-0.8	10.8	-1.8	11.1	11.7
1933								
January	12.9	-1.5	13.0	-1.5	10.5	-2.8	10.8	11.4
February	12.7	-1.6	12.8	-1.5	10.3	-1.9	10.3	11.2
March	12.6	-0.8	12.7	-0.8	10.4	1.0	10.8	11.2
April	12.6	0.0	12.6	-0.8	10.4	0.0	11.2	11.1
May	12.6	0.0	12.7	0.8	10.8	3.8	12.7	11.3
June	12.7	0.8	12.8	0.8	11.2	3.7	13.4	11.7
July	13.1	3.1	13.2	3.1	11.9	6.3	15.2	12.3
August	13.2	0.8	13.3	0.8	12.0	0.8	14.6	12.6
September	13.2	0.0	13.3	0.0	12.2	1.7	14.4	13.0
October	13.2	0.0	13.3	0.0	12.3	0.8	14.1	13.1
November	13.2	0.0	13.3	0.0	12.3	0.0	14.3	13.1
December	13.2	0.0	13.2	-0.8	12.2	-0.8	14.0	13.2

Table 8-1C. Consumer and Producer Price Indexes: Historical Data, 1913–1949—*Continued*

(Not seasonally adjusted.)

Year and month	Consumer price indexes, 1982–1984 =100				Producer Price Indexes for goods, 1982 = 100			
	All urban consumers (CPI-U)		Urban wage earners and clerical workers (CPI-W)		All commodities		Farm products	Industrial commodities
	Index	Percent change	Index	Percent change	Index	Percent change		
1934								
January	13.2	0.0	13.3	0.8	12.4	1.6	14.8	13.3
February	13.3	0.8	13.4	0.8	12.7	2.4	15.5	13.4
March	13.3	0.0	13.4	0.0	12.7	0.0	15.5	13.4
April	13.3	0.0	13.4	0.0	12.7	0.0	15.1	13.4
May	13.3	0.0	13.4	0.0	12.7	0.0	15.1	13.4
June	13.4	0.8	13.4	0.0	12.9	1.6	16.0	13.3
July	13.4	0.0	13.4	0.0	12.9	0.0	16.3	13.3
August	13.4	0.0	13.5	0.7	13.2	2.3	17.6	13.3
September	13.6	1.5	13.7	1.5	13.4	1.5	18.5	13.3
October	13.5	-0.7	13.6	-0.7	13.2	-1.5	17.8	13.3
November	13.5	0.0	13.5	-0.7	13.2	0.0	17.8	13.3
December	13.4	-0.7	13.5	0.0	10.0	0.8	18.2	13.3
1935								
January	13.6	1.5	13.7	1.5	13.6	2.3	19.6	13.2
February	13.7	0.7	13.8	0.7	13.7	0.7	20.0	13.2
March	13.7	0.0	13.8	0.0	13.7	0.0	19.7	13.2
April	13.8	0.7	13.9	0.7	13.8	0.7	20.3	13.1
May	13.8	0.0	13.8	-0.7	13.8	0.0	20.3	13.2
June	13.7	-0.7	13.8	0.0	13.8	0.0	19.8	13.3
July	13.7	0.0	13.7	-0.7	13.7	-0.7	19.5	13.3
August	13.7	0.0	13.7	0.0	13.9	1.5	20.0	13.3
September	13.7	0.0	13.8	0.7	13.9	0.0	20.1	13.2
October	13.7	0.0	13.8	0.0	13.9	0.0	19.7	13.3
November	13.8	0.7	13.9	0.7	13.9	0.0	19.6	13.4
December	13.8	0.0	13.9	0.0	14.0	0.7	19.8	13.4
1936								
January	13.8	0.0	13.9	0.0	13.9	-0.7	19.7	13.4
February	13.8	0.0	13.8	-0.7	13.9	0.0	20.1	13.4
March	13.7	-0.7	13.8	0.0	13.7	-1.4	19.3	13.4
April	13.7	0.0	13.8	0.0	13.7	0.0	19.4	13.4
May	13.7	0.0	13.8	0.0	13.5	-1.5	19.0	13.4
June	13.8	0.7	13.9	0.7	13.7	1.5	19.7	13.4
July	13.9	0.7	14.0	0.7	13.9	1.5	20.5	13.5
August	14.0	0.7	14.1	0.7	14.0	0.7	21.2	13.5
September	14.0	0.0	14.1	0.0	14.0	0.0	21.2	13.5
October	14.0	0.0	14.1	0.0	14.0	0.0	21.2	13.6
November	14.0	0.0	14.1	0.0	14.2	1.4	21.5	13.8
December	14.0	0.0	14.1	0.0	14.5	2.1	22.4	14.0
1937								
January	14.1	0.7	14.2	0.7	14.8	2.1	23.1	14.2
February	14.1	0.0	14.2	0.0	14.9	0.7	23.1	14.3
March	14.2	0.7	14.3	0.7	15.1	1.3	23.8	14.5
April	14.3	0.7	14.4	0.7	15.2	0.7	23.3	14.7
May	14.4	0.7	14.4	0.0	15.1	-0.7	22.7	14.7
June	14.4	0.0	14.5	0.7	15.0	-0.7	22.3	14.6
July	14.5	0.7	14.5	0.0	15.2	1.3	22.6	14.7
August	14.5	0.0	14.6	0.7	15.1	-0.7	21.8	14.6
September	14.6	0.7	14.7	0.7	15.1	0.0	21.7	14.6
October	14.6	0.0	14.6	-0.7	14.7	-2.6	20.3	14.5
November	14.5	-0.7	14.5	-0.7	14.4	-2.0	19.1	14.3
December	14.4	-0.7	14.5	0.0	14.1	-2.1	18.4	14.2
1938								
January	14.2	-1.4	14.3	-1.4	14.0	-0.7	18.1	14.2
February	14.1	-0.7	14.2	-0.7	13.8	-1.4	17.6	14.1
March	14.1	0.0	14.2	0.0	13.7	-0.7	17.7	14.1
April	14.2	0.7	14.2	0.0	13.5	-1.5	17.2	14.0
May	14.1	-0.7	14.2	0.0	13.5	0.0	17.0	13.9
June	14.1	0.0	14.2	0.0	13.5	0.0	17.3	13.8
July	14.1	0.0	14.2	0.0	13.6	0.7	17.5	13.9
August	14.1	0.0	14.2	0.0	13.4	-1.5	17.0	13.9
September	14.1	0.0	14.2	0.0	13.5	0.7	17.2	13.9
October	14.0	-0.7	14.1	-0.7	13.4	-0.7	16.8	13.8
November	14.0	0.0	14.1	0.0	13.4	0.0	17.1	13.7
December	14.0	0.0	14.1	0.0	13.3	-0.7	17.0	13.6
1939								
January	14.0	0.0	14.0	-0.7	13.3	0.0	17.0	13.6
February	13.9	-0.7	14.0	0.0	13.3	0.0	16.9	13.6
March	13.9	0.0	13.9	-0.7	13.2	-0.8	16.6	13.7
April	13.8	-0.7	13.9	0.0	13.1	-0.8	16.1	13.7
May	13.8	0.0	13.9	0.0	13.1	0.0	16.1	13.7
June	13.8	0.0	13.9	0.0	13.0	-0.8	15.7	13.6
July	13.8	0.0	13.9	0.0	13.0	0.0	15.8	13.6
August	13.8	0.0	13.9	0.0	12.9	-0.8	15.4	13.6
September	14.1	2.2	14.2	2.2	13.6	5.4	17.3	14.0
October	14.0	-0.7	14.1	-0.7	13.7	0.7	16.9	14.2
November	14.0	0.0	14.1	0.0	13.6	-0.7	17.0	14.3
December	14.0	0.0	14.0	-0.7	13.7	0.7	17.1	14.3

Table 8-1C. Consumer and Producer Price Indexes: Historical Data, 1913–1949—*Continued*

(Not seasonally adjusted.)

Year and month	Consumer price indexes, 1982–1984 =100				Producer Price Indexes for goods, 1982 = 100			
	All urban consumers (CPI-U)		Urban wage earners and clerical workers (CPI-W)		All commodities		Farm products	Industrial commodities
	Index	Percent change	Index	Percent change	Index	Percent change		
1940								
January	13.9	-0.7	14.0	0.0	13.7	0.0	17.4	14.3
February	14.0	0.7	14.1	0.7	13.6	-0.7	17.3	14.2
March	14.0	0.0	14.1	0.0	13.5	-0.7	17.1	14.1
April	14.0	0.0	14.1	0.0	13.5	0.0	17.5	14.0
May	14.0	0.0	14.1	0.0	13.5	0.0	17.1	14.0
June	14.1	0.7	14.1	0.0	13.4	-0.7	16.7	14.0
July	14.0	-0.7	14.1	0.0	13.4	0.0	16.8	14.0
August	14.0	0.0	14.1	0.0	13.4	0.0	16.5	14.0
September	14.0	0.0	14.1	0.0	13.4	0.0	16.7	14.0
October	14.0	0.0	14.1	0.0	13.6	1.5	16.8	14.2
November	14.0	0.0	14.1	0.0	13.7	0.7	17.2	14.3
December	14.1	0.7	14.2	0.7	13.8	0.7	17.6	14.3
1941								
January	14.1	0.0	14.2	0.0	13.9	0.7	18.1	14.3
February	14.1	0.0	14.2	0.0	13.9	0.0	17.7	14.3
March	14.2	0.7	14.2	0.0	14.0	0.7	18.1	14.4
April	14.3	0.7	14.4	1.4	14.4	2.9	18.8	14.6
May	14.4	0.7	14.5	0.7	14.6	1.4	19.3	14.9
June	14.7	2.1	14.7	1.4	15.0	2.7	20.7	15.1
July	14.7	0.0	14.8	0.7	15.3	2.0	21.7	15.2
August	14.9	1.4	14.9	0.7	15.6	2.0	22.1	15.5
September	15.1	1.3	15.2	2.0	15.8	1.3	23.0	15.6
October	15.3	1.3	15.4	1.3	15.9	0.6	22.7	15.9
November	15.4	0.7	15.5	0.6	15.9	0.0	22.9	15.9
December	15.5	0.6	15.5	0.0	16.2	1.9	23.9	15.9
1942								
January	15.7	1.3	15.7	1.3	16.5	1.9	25.5	16.1
February	15.8	0.6	15.9	1.3	16.7	1.2	25.6	16.1
March	16.0	1.3	16.1	1.3	16.8	0.6	26.0	16.2
April	16.1	0.6	16.2	0.6	17.0	1.2	26.4	16.2
May	16.3	1.2	16.3	0.6	17.0	0.0	26.3	16.3
June	16.3	0.0	16.4	0.6	17.0	0.0	26.3	16.3
July	16.4	0.6	16.5	0.6	17.0	0.0	26.6	16.3
August	16.5	0.6	16.6	0.6	17.1	0.6	26.8	16.2
September	16.5	0.0	16.6	0.0	17.2	0.6	27.2	16.2
October	16.7	1.2	16.8	1.2	17.2	0.0	27.5	16.2
November	16.8	0.6	16.9	0.6	17.3	0.6	27.9	16.3
December	16.9	0.6	17.0	0.6	17.4	0.6	28.7	16.3
1943								
January	16.9	0.0	17.0	0.0	17.5	0.6	29.5	16.4
February	16.9	0.0	17.0	0.0	17.7	1.1	30.0	16.4
March	17.2	1.8	17.3	1.8	17.8	0.6	31.0	16.4
April	17.4	1.2	17.5	1.2	17.9	0.6	31.2	16.5
May	17.5	0.6	17.6	0.6	17.9	0.0	31.7	16.5
June	17.5	0.0	17.6	0.0	17.9	0.0	31.9	16.5
July	17.4	-0.6	17.5	-0.6	17.8	-0.6	31.5	16.5
August	17.3	-0.6	17.4	-0.6	17.8	0.0	31.2	16.5
September	17.4	0.6	17.5	0.6	17.8	0.0	31.0	16.5
October	17.4	0.0	17.5	0.0	17.8	0.0	30.9	16.5
November	17.4	0.0	17.5	0.0	17.7	-0.6	30.6	16.6
December	17.4	0.0	17.5	0.0	17.8	0.6	30.7	16.6
1944								
January	17.4	0.0	17.5	0.0	17.8	0.0	30.7	16.6
February	17.4	0.0	17.5	0.0	17.8	0.0	30.9	16.7
March	17.4	0.0	17.5	0.0	17.9	0.6	31.2	16.7
April	17.5	0.6	17.6	0.6	17.9	0.0	31.1	16.7
May	17.5	0.0	17.6	0.0	17.9	0.0	31.0	16.7
June	17.6	0.6	17.7	0.6	18.0	0.6	31.5	16.7
July	17.7	0.6	17.8	0.6	17.9	-0.6	31.3	16.7
August	17.7	0.0	17.8	0.0	17.9	0.0	30.9	16.8
September	17.7	0.0	17.8	0.0	17.9	0.0	31.0	16.8
October	17.7	0.0	17.8	0.0	17.9	0.0	31.2	16.8
November	17.7	0.0	17.8	0.0	18.0	0.6	31.4	16.8
December	17.8	0.6	17.9	0.6	18.0	0.0	31.6	16.8
1945								
January	17.8	0.0	17.9	0.0	18.1	0.6	31.9	16.8
February	17.8	0.0	17.9	0.0	18.1	0.0	32.1	16.9
March	17.8	0.0	17.9	0.0	18.1	0.0	32.1	16.9
April	17.8	0.0	17.9	0.0	18.2	0.6	32.5	16.9
May	17.9	0.6	18.0	0.6	18.3	0.5	32.8	16.9
June	18.1	1.1	18.2	1.1	18.3	0.0	32.9	16.9
July	18.1	0.0	18.2	0.0	18.3	0.0	32.5	17.0
August	18.1	0.0	18.2	0.0	18.2	-0.5	32.0	17.0
September	18.1	0.0	18.2	0.0	18.1	-0.5	31.4	17.0
October	18.1	0.0	18.2	0.0	18.2	0.6	32.1	17.0
November	18.1	0.0	18.2	0.0	18.4	1.1	33.1	17.0
December	18.2	0.6	18.3	0.5	18.4	0.0	33.2	17.1

Table 8-1C. Consumer and Producer Price Indexes: Historical Data, 1913–1949—*Continued*

(Not seasonally adjusted.)

| Year and month | Consumer price indexes, 1982–1984 =100 | | | | Producer Price Indexes for goods, 1982 = 100 | | | |
| | All urban consumers (CPI-U) | | Urban wage earners and clerical workers (CPI-W) | | All commodities | | Farm products | Industrial commodities |
	Index	Percent change	Index	Percent change	Index	Percent change		
1946								
January	18.2	0.0	18.3	0.0	18.4	0.0	32.7	17.1
February	18.1	-0.5	18.2	-0.5	18.5	0.5	33.0	17.2
March	18.3	1.1	18.4	1.1	18.8	1.6	33.6	17.4
April	18.4	0.5	18.5	0.5	19.0	1.1	34.1	17.5
May	18.5	0.5	18.6	0.5	19.1	0.5	34.7	17.7
June	18.7	1.1	18.8	1.1	19.4	1.6	35.4	18.0
July	19.8	5.9	19.9	5.9	21.5	10.8	39.6	18.6
August	20.2	2.0	20.3	2.0	22.2	3.3	40.6	19.0
September	20.4	1.0	20.5	1.0	21.4	-3.6	39.0	19.1
October	20.8	2.0	20.9	2.0	23.1	7.9	41.7	19.7
November	21.3	2.4	21.5	2.9	24.1	4.3	42.8	20.6
December	21.5	0.9	21.6	0.5	24.3	0.8	42.4	21.2
1947								
January	21.5	0.0	21.6	0.0	24.5	0.8	41.6	21.8
February	21.5	0.0	21.6	0.0	24.7	0.8	42.6	22.0
March	21.9	1.9	22.1	2.3	25.3	2.4	45.5	22.3
April	21.9	0.0	22.1	0.0	25.1	-0.8	44.0	22.4
May	21.9	0.0	22.0	-0.5	25.0	-0.4	43.6	22.3
June	22.0	0.5	22.2	0.9	25.0	0.0	43.8	22.4
July	22.2	0.9	22.4	0.9	25.3	1.2	44.3	22.5
August	22.5	1.4	22.6	0.9	25.6	1.2	44.8	22.8
September	23.0	2.2	23.1	2.2	26.1	2.0	46.6	23.1
October	23.0	0.0	23.1	0.0	26.4	1.1	47.4	23.3
November	23.1	0.4	23.3	0.9	26.7	1.1	47.7	23.6
December	23.4	1.3	23.6	1.3	27.2	1.9	50.1	23.9
1948								
January	23.7	1.3	23.8	0.8	27.7	1.8	51.2	24.3
February	23.5	-0.8	23.6	-0.8	27.2	-1.8	47.7	24.1
March	23.4	-0.4	23.6	0.0	27.2	0.0	47.6	24.1
April	23.8	1.7	23.9	1.3	27.4	0.7	48.3	24.3
May	23.9	0.4	24.1	0.8	27.5	0.4	49.4	24.3
June	24.1	0.8	24.2	0.4	27.7	0.7	50.4	24.4
July	24.4	1.2	24.5	1.2	28.0	1.1	50.2	24.6
August	24.5	0.4	24.6	0.4	28.2	0.7	49.6	24.9
September	24.5	0.0	24.6	0.0	28.1	-0.4	48.8	25.0
October	24.4	-0.4	24.5	-0.4	27.8	-1.1	46.9	25.0
November	24.2	-0.8	24.4	-0.4	27.8	0.0	46.3	25.1
December	24.1	-0.4	24.2	-0.8	27.6	-0.7	45.2	25.1
1949								
January	24.0	-0.4	24.2	0.0	27.3	-1.1	43.8	24.9
February	23.8	-0.8	23.9	-1.2	26.8	-1.8	42.0	24.7
March	23.8	0.0	24.0	0.4	26.8	0.0	42.7	24.6
April	23.9	0.4	24.0	0.0	26.5	-1.1	42.7	24.3
May	23.8	-0.4	24.0	0.0	26.3	-0.8	42.7	24.0
June	23.9	0.4	24.0	0.0	26.0	-1.1	41.8	23.8
July	23.7	-0.8	23.8	-0.8	26.0	0.0	41.7	23.7
August	23.8	0.4	23.9	0.4	26.0	0.0	41.7	23.8
September	23.9	0.4	24.0	0.4	26.1	0.4	41.8	23.8
October	23.7	-0.8	23.9	-0.4	26.0	-0.4	41.0	23.8
November	23.8	0.4	23.9	0.0	26.0	0.0	40.9	23.8
December	23.6	-0.8	23.8	-0.4	25.9	-0.4	40.3	23.8

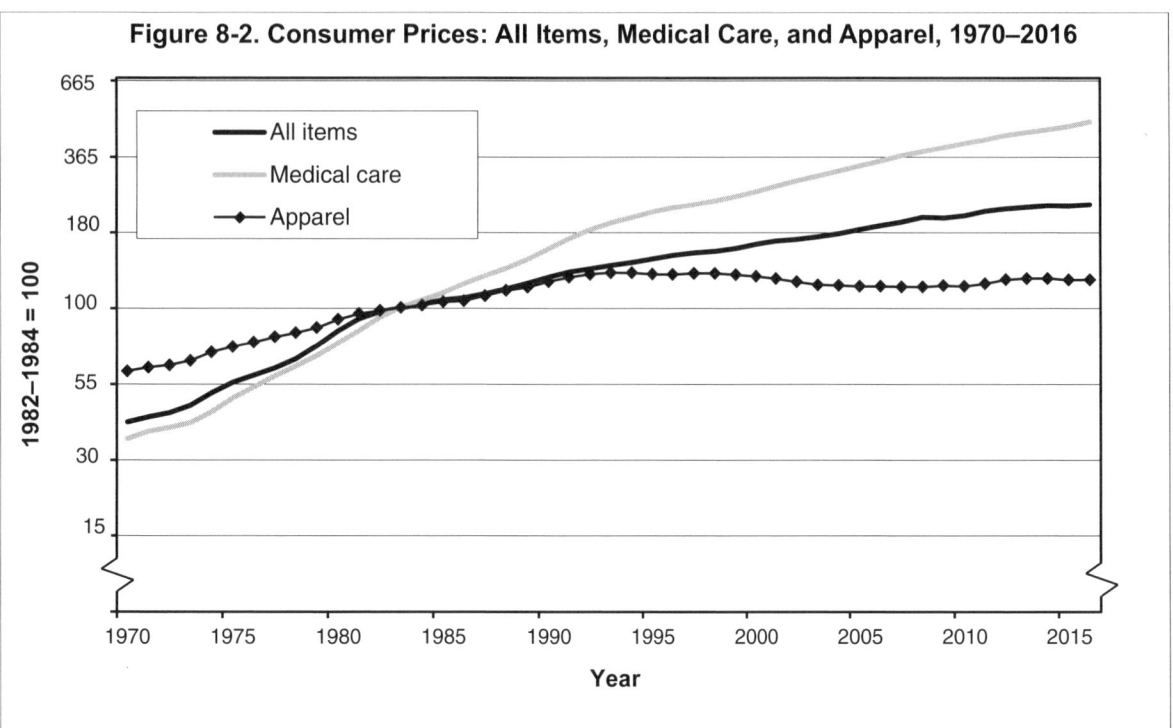

Figure 8-2. Consumer Prices: All Items, Medical Care, and Apparel, 1970–2016

- Figure 8-2 charts two components of the Consumer Price Index for All Urban Consumers (CPI-U) along with the all-items total. Since all three indexes have the base years 1982–1984, they converge around 100 in those years. However, over the entire postwar period, the trends of the two components are very different. (Table 8-2)

- Apparel has been one of the areas most subject to international competition, and the apparel index shows far less growth than the overall average of prices.

- Medical care, on the other hand, has little price competition from producers in other countries. It is often paid for by third-party insurers, both government and private, rather than directly by consumers. Furthermore, it is characterized by trend growth in demand, due to rising income and expectations and to technological progress. All of these economic factors cause medical care prices to rise faster than the general price level.

- Medical care has arguably been overstated in the CPI due to the difficulties of making quality adjustments. Quality adjustments in the indexes have been much improved in recent years, although such improvements are not retroactively introduced into the official CPIs. But even since 1997, when a major improvement was introduced into the hospital cost component of the CPI, measured medical care prices have increased at a much higher rate than the CPI-U for all items. (Table 8-2)

- A broader system of PPIs including services and construction as well as goods was introduced in 2014, featuring a more detailed representation by stages of production as well. These new measures only go back to November 2009—not enough time yet to determine what kind of signals about future inflation they will contain. (Tables 8-5 and 8-6)

Table 8-2. Consumer Price Indexes and Purchasing Power of the Dollar

(1982–1984 = 100, seasonally adjusted, except as noted.)

Year and month	CPI-U, All items			CPI-U, Food and beverages										
	Not seasonally adjusted	Seasonally adjusted		Total	Total food	Food at home							Food away from home¹	Alcoholic beverages
		Index	Percent change from previous period			Total	Cereals and bakery products	Meats, poultry, fish, and eggs	Dairy and related products¹	Fruits and vegetables	Non-alcoholic beverages	Other food at home		
1970	38.8	38.8	5.7	40.1	39.2	39.9	37.1	44.6	44.7	37.8	27.1	32.9	37.5	52.1
1971	40.5	40.5	4.4	41.4	40.4	40.9	38.8	44.1	46.1	39.7	28.1	34.3	39.4	54.2
1972	41.8	41.8	3.2	43.1	42.1	42.7	39.0	48.0	46.8	41.6	28.0	34.6	41.0	55.4
1973	44.4	44.4	6.2	48.8	48.2	49.7	43.5	60.9	51.2	47.4	30.1	36.7	44.2	56.8
1974	49.3	49.3	11.0	55.5	55.1	57.1	56.5	62.2	60.7	55.2	35.9	47.8	49.8	61.1
1975	53.8	53.8	9.1	60.2	59.8	61.8	62.9	67.0	62.6	56.9	41.3	55.4	54.5	65.9
1976	56.9	56.9	5.8	62.1	61.6	63.1	61.5	68.0	67.7	58.4	49.4	56.4	58.2	68.1
1977	60.6	60.6	6.5	65.8	65.5	66.8	62.5	67.4	69.5	63.8	74.4	68.4	62.6	70.0
1978	65.2	65.2	7.6	72.2	72.0	73.8	68.1	77.6	74.2	70.9	78.7	73.6	68.3	74.1
1979	72.6	72.6	11.3	79.9	79.9	81.8	74.9	89.0	82.8	70.0	82.0	70.0	76.0	79.9
1980	82.4	82.4	13.5	86.7	86.8	88.4	83.9	92.0	90.9	82.1	91.4	88.4	83.4	86.4
1981	90.9	90.9	10.3	93.5	93.6	94.8	92.3	96.0	97.4	92.0	95.3	94.9	90.9	92.5
1982	96.5	96.5	6.2	97.3	97.4	98.1	96.5	99.6	98.8	97.0	97.9	97.3	95.8	96.7
1983	99.6	99.6	3.2	99.5	99.4	99.1	99.6	99.2	100.0	97.3	99.8	99.5	100.0	100.4
1984	103.9	103.9	4.3	103.2	103.2	102.8	103.9	101.3	101.3	105.7	102.3	103.1	104.2	103.0
1985	107.6	107.6	3.6	105.6	105.6	104.3	107.9	100.1	103.2	108.4	104.3	105.7	108.3	106.4
1986	109.6	109.6	1.9	109.1	109.0	107.3	110.9	104.5	103.3	109.4	110.4	109.4	112.5	111.1
1987	113.6	113.6	3.6	113.5	113.5	111.9	114.8	110.5	105.9	119.1	107.5	110.5	117.0	114.1
1988	118.3	118.3	4.1	118.2	118.2	116.6	122.1	114.3	108.4	128.1	107.5	113.1	121.8	118.6
1989	124.0	124.0	4.8	124.9	125.1	124.2	132.4	121.3	115.6	138.0	111.3	119.1	127.4	123.5
1990	130.7	130.7	5.4	132.1	132.4	132.3	140.0	130.0	126.5	149.0	113.5	123.4	133.4	129.3
1991	136.2	136.2	4.2	136.8	136.3	135.8	145.8	132.6	125.1	155.8	114.1	127.3	137.9	142.8
1992	140.3	140.3	3.0	138.7	137.9	136.8	151.5	130.9	128.5	155.4	114.3	128.8	140.7	147.3
1993	144.5	144.5	3.0	141.6	140.9	140.1	156.6	135.5	129.4	159.0	114.6	130.5	143.2	149.6
1994	148.2	148.2	2.6	144.9	144.3	144.1	163.0	137.2	131.7	165.0	123.2	135.6	145.7	151.5
1995	152.4	152.4	2.8	148.9	148.4	148.8	167.5	138.8	132.8	177.7	131.7	140.8	149.0	153.9
1996	156.9	156.9	3.0	153.7	153.3	154.3	174.0	144.8	142.1	183.9	128.6	142.9	152.7	158.5
1997	160.5	160.5	2.3	157.7	157.3	158.1	177.6	148.5	145.5	187.5	133.4	147.3	157.0	162.8
1998	163.0	163.0	1.6	161.1	160.7	161.1	181.1	147.3	150.8	198.2	133.0	150.8	161.1	165.7
1999	166.6	166.6	2.2	164.6	164.1	164.2	185.0	147.9	159.6	203.1	134.3	153.5	165.1	169.7
2000	172.2	172.2	3.4	168.4	167.8	167.9	188.3	154.5	160.7	204.6	137.8	155.6	169.0	174.7
2001	177.1	177.1	2.8	173.6	173.1	173.4	193.8	161.3	167.1	212.2	139.2	159.6	173.9	179.3
2002	179.9	179.9	1.6	176.8	176.2	175.6	198.0	162.1	168.1	220.9	139.2	160.8	178.3	183.6
2003	184.0	184.0	2.3	180.5	180.0	179.4	202.8	169.3	167.9	225.9	139.8	162.6	182.1	187.2
2004	188.9	188.9	2.7	186.6	186.2	186.2	206.0	181.7	180.2	232.7	140.4	164.9	187.5	192.1
2005	195.3	195.3	3.4	191.2	190.7	189.8	209.0	184.7	182.4	241.4	144.4	167.0	193.4	195.9
2006	201.6	201.6	3.2	195.7	195.2	193.1	212.8	186.6	181.4	252.9	147.4	169.6	199.4	200.7
2007	207.3	207.3	2.8	203.3	202.9	201.2	222.1	195.6	194.8	262.6	153.4	173.3	206.7	207.0
2008	215.3	215.3	3.8	214.2	214.1	214.1	244.9	204.7	210.4	278.9	160.0	184.2	215.8	214.5
2009	214.5	214.5	-0.4	218.2	218.0	215.1	252.6	203.8	197.0	272.9	163.0	191.2	223.3	220.8
2010	218.1	218.1	1.6	220.0	219.6	215.8	250.4	207.7	199.2	273.5	161.6	191.1	226.1	223.3
2011	224.9	224.9	3.2	227.9	227.8	226.2	260.3	223.2	212.7	284.7	166.8	197.4	231.4	226.7
2012	229.6	229.6	2.1	233.7	233.8	231.8	267.7	231.0	217.3	282.8	168.6	204.8	238.0	230.8
2013	233.0	233.0	1.5	237.0	237.0	233.9	270.4	236.0	217.6	290.0	166.9	204.8	243.1	234.6
2014	236.7	236.7	1.6	242.4	242.7	239.5	271.1	253.0	225.3	294.4	166.0	206.2	249.0	237.3
2015	237.0	237.0	0.1	246.8	247.2	242.3	274.1	260.3	222.4	293.8	167.9	209.3	256.1	239.5
2016	240.0	240.0	1.3	247.7	247.9	239.1	273.1	247.7	217.3	296.3	167.3	209.5	262.7	242.5
2015														
January	233.7	234.9	-0.2	245.7	246.1	242.4	273.2	262.3	225.9	293.6	167.3	207.9	253.0	238.5
February	234.7	235.5	-0.1	245.9	246.4	242.4	272.7	262.1	224.0	292.3	167.8	208.7	253.7	238.7
March	236.1	236.0	0.0	245.7	246.1	241.7	273.9	260.8	224.3	290.0	167.3	208.5	254.1	239.0
April	236.6	236.2	-0.1	245.7	246.1	241.3	273.0	259.2	222.9	291.5	167.6	208.4	254.7	239.0
May	237.8	236.9	0.0	245.9	246.3	241.2	273.3	257.6	222.6	292.1	167.7	208.9	255.3	239.5
June	238.6	237.4	0.2	246.6	247.0	242.1	274.1	261.3	222.1	291.1	167.9	209.3	255.8	239.2
July	238.7	237.9	0.2	246.8	247.2	242.4	274.7	261.3	223.4	291.2	168.2	209.3	255.9	239.4
August	238.3	237.8	0.2	247.3	247.7	242.9	274.5	262.6	221.5	294.4	168.3	209.4	256.4	239.6
September	237.9	237.5	0.0	248.0	248.5	243.2	274.1	261.6	221.9	296.2	168.3	210.6	257.8	239.7
October	237.8	237.8	0.1	248.2	248.7	243.2	276.0	260.5	220.3	296.4	168.7	210.8	258.4	240.0
November	237.3	238.2	0.4	248.0	248.5	242.5	274.7	258.7	219.7	298.1	167.9	210.3	258.8	240.7
December	236.5	237.8	0.7	247.6	248.1	241.7	274.5	255.5	219.3	298.6	167.8	209.8	259.1	240.4
2016														
January	236.9	238.1	1.4	247.8	248.2	241.2	274.1	252.9	219.1	301.2	167.5	209.6	260.0	241.2
February	237.1	237.8	1.0	248.0	248.4	241.4	274.5	252.4	219.0	303.0	168.1	209.2	260.3	241.8
March	238.1	238.1	0.9	248.1	248.4	240.5	273.2	251.6	218.1	298.5	167.9	209.8	260.9	241.8
April	239.3	238.9	1.1	248.1	248.4	240.7	273.6	251.2	218.5	297.7	168.0	210.7	261.5	242.2
May	240.2	239.4	1.0	247.7	248.0	239.6	272.9	249.7	217.7	295.3	167.9	209.9	262.1	242.1
June	241.0	239.8	1.0	247.6	247.9	239.1	273.0	248.1	217.3	295.4	167.1	209.9	262.5	242.4
July	240.6	239.9	0.9	247.5	247.8	238.6	272.6	246.5	216.5	295.8	167.4	209.5	263.1	242.4
August	240.8	240.4	1.1	247.5	247.8	238.3	272.6	245.5	216.4	295.3	167.3	209.3	263.6	242.3
September	241.4	241.0	1.5	247.6	247.8	237.9	272.7	245.0	216.3	294.1	166.8	209.3	264.1	243.1
October	241.7	241.7	1.6	247.5	247.7	237.5	272.7	243.8	216.5	293.9	166.4	209.1	264.5	243.7
November	241.4	242.2	1.7	247.4	247.6	237.2	272.8	243.3	216.0	293.3	166.6	208.7	264.7	243.5
December	241.4	242.8	2.1	247.3	247.5	236.8	272.6	242.1	216.3	291.4	166.4	209.2	265.1	243.8

¹Not seasonally adjusted.

Table 8-2. Consumer Price Indexes and Purchasing Power of the Dollar—Continued

(1982–1984 = 100, seasonally adjusted, except as noted.)

Year and month	CPI-U, Housing												
	Total	Shelter						Fuels and utilities				Household furnishings and operations	
		Total	Rent of shelter[2]	Rent of primary residence	Lodging away from home[3]	Owners' equivalent rent of primary residence[2]	Tenants' and household insurance[1,3]	Total	Fuels		Water and sewer and trash collection services[3]	Total	Household operations[1,3]
									Fuel oil and other fuels	Energy services			
1970	36.4	35.5	...	46.5	...	...	...	29.1	17.0	25.4	...	46.8	...
1971	38.0	37.0	...	48.7	...	...	...	31.1	18.2	27.1	...	48.6	...
1972	39.4	38.7	...	50.4	...	...	...	32.5	18.3	28.5	...	49.7	...
1973	41.2	40.5	...	52.5	...	...	...	34.3	21.1	29.9	...	51.1	...
1974	45.8	44.4	...	55.2	...	...	...	40.7	33.2	34.5	...	56.8	...
1975	50.7	48.8	...	58.0	...	...	...	45.4	36.4	40.1	...	63.4	...
1976	53.8	51.5	...	61.1	...	...	...	49.4	38.8	44.7	...	67.3	...
1977	57.4	54.9	...	64.8	...	...	...	54.7	43.9	50.5	...	70.4	...
1978	62.4	60.5	...	69.3	...	...	...	58.5	46.2	55.0	...	74.7	...
1979	70.1	68.9	...	74.3	...	...	...	64.8	62.4	61.0	...	79.9	...
1980	81.1	81.0	...	80.9	...	...	...	75.4	86.1	71.4	...	86.3	...
1981	90.4	90.5	...	87.9	...	...	...	86.4	104.6	81.9	...	93.0	...
1982	96.9	96.9	...	94.6	...	...	...	94.9	103.4	93.2	...	98.0	...
1983	99.5	99.1	102.7	100.1	...	102.5	...	100.2	97.2	101.5	...	100.2	...
1984	103.6	104.0	107.7	105.3	...	107.3	...	104.8	99.4	105.4	...	101.9	...
1985	107.7	109.8	113.9	111.8	...	113.2	...	106.5	95.9	107.1	...	103.8	...
1986	110.9	115.8	120.2	118.3	...	119.4	...	104.1	77.6	105.7	...	105.2	...
1987	114.2	121.3	125.9	123.1	...	124.8	...	103.0	77.9	103.8	...	107.1	...
1988	118.5	127.1	132.0	127.8	...	131.1	...	104.4	78.1	104.6	...	109.4	...
1989	123.0	132.8	138.0	132.8	...	137.4	...	107.8	81.7	107.5	...	111.2	...
1990	128.5	140.0	145.5	138.4	...	144.8	...	111.6	99.3	109.3	...	113.3	...
1991	133.6	146.3	152.1	143.3	...	150.4	...	115.3	94.6	112.6	...	116.0	...
1992	137.5	151.2	157.3	146.9	...	155.5	...	117.8	90.7	114.8	...	118.0	...
1993	141.2	155.7	162.0	150.3	...	160.5	...	121.3	90.3	118.5	...	119.3	...
1994	144.8	160.5	167.0	154.0	...	165.8	...	122.8	88.8	119.2	...	121.0	...
1995	148.5	165.7	172.4	157.8	...	171.3	...	123.7	88.1	119.2	...	123.0	...
1996	152.8	171.0	178.0	162.0	...	176.8	...	127.5	99.2	122.1	...	124.7	...
1997	156.8	176.3	183.4	166.7	...	181.9	...	130.8	99.8	125.1	...	125.4	...
1998	160.4	182.1	189.6	172.1	109.0	187.8	99.8	128.5	90.0	121.2	101.6	126.6	101.5
1999	163.9	187.3	195.0	177.5	112.3	192.9	101.3	128.8	91.4	120.9	104.0	126.7	104.5
2000	169.6	193.4	201.3	183.9	117.5	198.7	103.7	137.9	129.7	128.0	106.5	128.2	110.5
2001	176.4	200.6	208.9	192.1	118.6	206.3	106.2	150.2	129.3	142.4	109.6	129.1	115.6
2002	180.3	208.1	216.7	199.7	118.3	214.7	108.7	143.6	115.5	134.4	113.0	128.3	119.0
2003	184.8	213.1	221.9	205.5	119.3	219.9	114.8	154.5	139.5	145.0	117.2	126.1	121.8
2004	189.5	218.8	227.9	211.0	125.9	224.9	116.2	161.9	160.5	150.6	124.0	125.5	125.0
2005	195.7	224.4	233.7	217.3	130.3	230.2	117.6	179.0	208.6	166.5	130.3	126.1	130.3
2006	203.2	232.1	241.9	225.1	136.0	238.2	116.5	194.7	234.9	182.1	136.8	127.0	136.6
2007	209.6	240.6	250.8	234.7	142.8	246.2	117.0	200.6	251.5	186.3	143.7	126.9	140.6
2008	216.3	246.7	257.2	243.3	143.7	252.4	118.8	220.0	334.4	202.2	152.1	127.8	147.5
2009	217.1	249.4	259.9	248.8	134.2	256.6	121.5	210.7	239.8	193.6	161.1	128.7	150.3
2010	216.3	248.4	258.8	249.4	133.7	256.6	125.7	214.2	275.1	192.9	170.9	125.5	150.3
2011	219.1	251.6	262.2	253.6	137.4	259.6	127.4	220.4	337.1	194.4	179.6	124.9	151.8
2012	222.7	257.1	267.8	260.4	140.5	264.8	131.3	219.0	335.9	189.7	189.3	125.7	155.2
2013	227.4	263.1	274.0	267.7	142.4	270.7	135.4	225.2	332.0	194.8	197.6	124.8	157.6
2014	233.2	270.5	281.8	276.2	148.5	277.8	141.9	234.6	338.9	203.4	204.9	123.1	161.6
2015	238.1	278.8	290.4	286.0	153.0	285.9	146.4	230.1	256.2	198.7	214.0	122.6	166.9
2016	244.0	288.2	300.3	296.8	158.1	295.3	147.7	228.9	226.3	196.1	221.7	121.6	171.6
2015													
January	235.8	274.8	286.1	281.2	152.9	281.8	145.9	233.8	274.3	203.5	210.2	122.4	164.1
February	236.3	275.5	286.9	282.1	152.5	282.5	145.9	233.9	272.7	203.4	211.0	122.4	164.6
March	236.6	276.2	287.7	283.0	153.7	283.2	145.8	231.9	273.1	200.9	211.5	122.6	164.8
April	237.2	277.1	288.5	283.8	154.5	284.0	146.3	231.3	267.5	200.2	212.0	123.3	166.2
May	237.3	277.6	289.0	284.6	152.2	284.7	146.4	230.1	265.2	198.6	212.7	122.9	166.5
June	237.8	278.3	289.9	285.5	148.8	285.6	146.0	230.4	263.3	198.9	213.4	122.8	167.5
July	238.2	279.2	290.9	286.5	153.2	286.4	146.3	229.0	255.4	197.4	214.0	122.6	167.5
August	238.6	279.9	291.5	287.4	152.4	287.1	146.3	229.2	246.4	197.5	215.4	122.4	168.2
September	239.1	280.7	292.4	288.4	153.2	287.8	146.5	228.4	241.5	196.7	216.0	122.6	168.1
October	239.5	281.4	293.1	289.2	153.7	288.5	146.6	228.3	241.1	196.4	216.4	122.4	168.2
November	240.0	282.1	293.9	290.0	155.3	289.1	147.0	228.2	242.4	196.1	217.1	122.4	168.4
December	240.3	282.8	294.6	290.7	154.6	289.9	147.8	226.9	228.2	194.9	217.8	122.5	169.3
2016													
January	240.8	283.7	295.5	291.6	157.5	290.7	147.9	226.0	219.4	194.0	218.3	122.3	169.3
February	241.3	284.6	296.3	292.5	159.1	291.5	148.3	226.0	213.8	194.1	218.7	122.3	170.1
March	241.6	285.1	297.0	293.4	156.9	292.1	147.9	226.1	206.8	194.3	219.4	122.2	170.3
April	242.2	285.9	297.8	294.4	156.4	293.0	147.5	226.6	216.2	194.2	220.4	121.8	169.9
May	242.9	286.9	298.9	295.4	157.5	294.0	147.7	227.6	222.2	194.8	221.5	121.6	170.4
June	243.5	287.8	300.0	296.4	158.0	294.9	147.7	227.4	229.4	194.1	221.9	121.4	171.9
July	244.0	288.4	300.5	297.2	154.9	295.7	147.8	228.6	228.4	195.7	221.6	121.5	172.5
August	244.8	289.4	301.5	298.2	157.6	296.6	147.7	229.7	227.4	196.9	222.1	121.4	172.4
September	245.6	290.3	302.5	299.1	158.9	297.5	147.6	231.0	230.7	198.0	223.0	121.3	172.3
October	246.4	291.3	303.5	300.2	160.6	298.4	147.4	232.0	236.6	198.8	223.5	121.4	172.8
November	246.9	292.2	304.4	301.2	159.6	299.4	147.7	232.4	239.7	198.8	224.5	121.1	173.0
December	247.6	293.1	305.4	302.2	160.9	300.3	147.8	232.8	246.3	198.9	225.1	121.1	174.3

[1]Not seasonally adjusted.
[2]December 1982 = 100.
[3]December 1997 = 100.
. . . = Not available.

Table 8-2. Consumer Price Indexes and Purchasing Power of the Dollar—*Continued*

(1982–1984 = 100, seasonally adjusted, except as noted.)

Year and month	CPI-U, Apparel					CPI-U, Transportation								
							Private transportation						Motor vehicle parts and equipment	Motor vehicle mainte-nance and repair [1]
								New and used motor vehicles			Motor fuel			
	Total	Men's and boys' apparel	Women's and girls' apparel	Infants' and toddlers' apparel	Footwear	Total	Total	Total [3]	New vehicles	Used cars and trucks	Total	Gasoline (all types)		
1970	59.2	62.2	71.8	39.2	56.8	37.5	37.5	. . .	53.1	31.2	27.9	27.9	. . .	36.6
1971	61.1	63.9	74.4	40.0	58.6	39.5	39.4	. . .	55.3	33.0	28.1	28.1	. . .	39.3
1972	62.3	64.7	76.2	41.1	60.3	39.9	39.7	. . .	54.8	33.1	28.4	28.4	. . .	41.1
1973	64.6	67.1	78.8	42.5	62.8	41.2	41.0	. . .	54.8	35.2	31.2	31.2	. . .	43.2
1974	69.4	72.4	83.5	54.2	66.6	45.8	46.2	. . .	58.0	36.7	42.2	42.2	. . .	47.6
1975	72.5	75.5	85.5	64.5	69.6	50.1	50.6	. . .	63.0	43.8	45.1	45.1	. . .	53.7
1976	75.2	78.1	87.9	68.0	72.3	55.1	55.6	. . .	67.0	50.3	47.0	47.0	. . .	57.6
1977	78.6	81.7	90.6	74.6	75.7	59.0	59.7	. . .	70.5	54.7	49.7	49.7	. . .	61.9
1078	81.4	83.6	92.4	77.4	79.0	61.7	62.5	. . .	75.9	55.8	51.8	51.8	77.6	67.0
1979	84.9	85.4	94.0	79.0	85.3	70.5	71.7	. . .	81.9	60.2	70.1	70.2	85.1	73.7
1980	90.9	89.4	96.0	85.5	91.8	83.1	84.2	. . .	88.5	62.3	97.4	97.5	95.3	81.5
1981	95.3	94.2	97.5	92.9	96.7	93.2	93.8	. . .	93.9	76.9	108.5	108.5	101.0	89.2
1982	97.8	97.6	98.5	96.3	99.1	97.0	97.1	. . .	97.5	88.8	102.8	102.8	103.6	96.0
1983	100.2	100.3	100.2	101.1	99.8	99.3	99.3	. . .	99.9	98.7	99.4	99.4	100.7	100.3
1984	102.1	102.1	101.3	102.6	101.1	103.7	103.6	. . .	102.6	112.5	97.9	97.8	95.6	103.8
1985	105.0	105.0	104.9	107.2	102.3	106.4	106.2	. . .	106.1	113.7	98.7	98.6	95.9	106.8
1986	105.9	106.2	104.0	111.8	101.9	102.3	101.2	. . .	110.6	108.8	77.1	77.0	95.4	110.3
1987	110.6	109.1	110.4	112.1	105.1	105.4	104.2	. . .	114.4	113.1	80.2	80.1	96.1	114.8
1988	115.4	113.4	114.9	116.4	109.9	108.7	107.6	. . .	116.5	118.0	80.9	80.8	97.9	119.7
1989	118.6	117.0	116.4	119.1	114.4	114.1	112.9	. . .	119.2	120.4	88.5	88.5	100.2	124.9
1990	124.1	120.4	122.6	125.8	117.4	120.5	118.8	. . .	121.4	117.6	101.2	101.0	100.9	130.1
1991	128.7	124.2	127.6	128.9	120.9	123.8	121.9	. . .	126.0	118.1	99.4	99.2	102.2	136.0
1992	131.9	126.5	130.4	129.3	125.0	126.5	124.6	. . .	129.2	123.2	99.0	99.0	103.1	141.3
1993	133.7	127.5	132.6	127.1	125.9	130.4	127.5	91.8	132.7	133.9	98.0	97.7	101.6	145.9
1994	133.4	126.4	130.9	128.1	126.0	134.3	131.4	95.5	137.6	141.7	98.5	98.2	101.4	150.2
1995	132.0	126.2	126.9	127.2	125.4	139.1	136.3	99.4	141.0	156.5	100.0	99.8	102.1	154.0
1996	131.7	127.7	124.7	129.7	126.6	143.0	140.0	101.0	143.7	157.0	106.3	105.9	102.2	158.4
1997	132.9	130.1	126.1	129.0	127.6	144.3	141.0	100.5	144.3	151.1	106.2	105.8	101.9	162.7
1998	133.0	131.8	126.0	126.1	128.0	141.6	137.9	100.1	143.4	150.6	92.2	91.6	101.1	167.1
1999	131.3	131.1	123.3	129.0	125.7	144.4	140.5	100.1	142.9	152.0	100.7	100.1	100.5	171.9
2000	129.6	129.7	121.5	130.6	123.8	153.3	149.1	100.8	142.8	155.8	129.3	128.6	101.5	177.3
2001	127.3	125.7	119.3	129.2	123.0	154.3	150.0	101.3	142.1	158.7	124.7	124.0	104.8	183.5
2002	124.0	121.7	115.8	126.4	121.4	152.9	148.8	99.2	140.0	152.0	116.6	116.0	106.9	190.2
2003	120.9	118.0	113.1	122.1	119.6	157.6	153.6	96.5	137.9	142.9	135.8	135.1	107.8	195.6
2004	120.4	117.5	113.0	118.5	119.3	163.1	159.4	94.2	137.1	133.3	160.4	159.7	108.7	200.2
2005	119.5	116.1	110.8	116.7	122.6	173.9	170.2	95.6	137.9	139.4	195.7	194.7	111.9	206.9
2006	119.5	114.1	110.7	116.5	123.5	180.9	177.0	95.6	137.6	140.0	221.0	219.9	117.3	215.6
2007	119.0	112.4	110.3	113.9	122.4	184.7	180.8	94.3	136.3	135.7	239.1	238.0	121.6	223.0
2008	118.9	113.0	107.5	113.8	124.2	195.5	191.0	93.3	134.2	134.0	279.7	277.5	128.7	233.9
2009	120.1	113.6	108.1	114.5	126.9	179.3	174.8	93.5	135.6	127.0	202.0	201.6	134.1	243.3
2010	119.5	111.9	107.1	114.2	128.0	193.4	188.7	97.1	138.0	143.1	239.2	238.6	137.0	248.0
2011	122.1	114.7	109.2	113.6	128.5	212.4	207.6	99.8	141.9	149.0	302.6	301.7	143.9	253.1
2012	126.3	119.5	113.0	119.7	131.8	217.3	212.8	100.6	144.2	150.3	312.7	311.5	148.6	257.6
2013	127.4	121.6	113.3	116.5	135.0	217.4	212.4	100.9	145.8	149.9	303.9	302.6	146.4	261.6
2014	127.5	120.6	114.4	117.6	135.5	215.9	211.0	100.8	146.3	149.1	292.4	290.9	144.8	266.0
2015	125.9	119.6	111.2	119.7	136.8	199.1	193.7	100.8	147.1	147.1	213.1	212.0	144.2	270.7
2016	126.0	118.8	111.2	115.9	137.3	194.9	189.5	100.2	147.4	143.5	188.4	187.6	143.6	275.4
2015														
January	126.3	118.8	112.7	117.6	136.7	195.5	189.9	100.3	147.7	146.6	203.7	202.1	145.8	271.7
February	126.2	120.4	111.8	116.6	136.3	197.6	192.2	100.5	147.9	147.1	211.3	209.9	146.1	271.9
March	126.8	121.8	111.8	118.1	137.1	199.2	193.9	100.8	148.1	148.6	216.7	215.4	145.4	271.7
April	126.6	120.2	112.2	119.0	137.1	198.2	193.0	101.0	148.3	149.9	212.0	210.8	145.2	272.8
May	125.9	119.8	111.3	118.5	136.8	201.6	196.2	101.0	148.5	148.8	224.5	223.5	145.5	273.6
June	125.6	119.4	110.7	119.5	136.9	202.6	197.2	101.1	148.8	148.8	227.9	227.0	144.9	273.8
July	125.9	118.4	111.5	119.5	137.3	203.5	198.3	100.9	148.6	148.6	232.0	231.2	144.7	274.0
August	126.2	118.5	111.8	122.9	137.9	201.6	196.4	100.8	148.6	148.3	223.8	223.1	144.8	273.6
September	125.9	119.6	110.9	123.5	136.8	197.3	192.0	100.8	148.6	148.0	204.9	204.2	145.5	274.0
October	125.2	118.8	110.2	121.4	136.2	197.0	191.5	100.6	148.3	147.9	204.0	203.4	144.2	274.6
November	125.2	119.4	110.0	122.5	136.4	197.6	192.1	100.7	148.5	147.8	204.5	203.9	144.9	274.8
December	125.3	120.2	110.0	117.5	136.0	195.2	189.7	100.7	148.4	147.9	193.5	193.0	145.1	275.7
2016														
January	125.7	119.7	110.4	117.1	137.2	194.6	189.0	100.9	148.8	147.8	188.9	188.3	145.7	275.8
February	127.2	119.8	111.7	120.6	138.7	190.6	184.8	101.1	149.0	147.5	168.6	167.9	145.5	275.9
March	126.0	117.9	111.7	117.9	137.7	191.4	185.7	100.9	149.0	147.6	172.7	172.0	145.0	276.7
April	125.8	118.3	111.1	115.9	137.9	193.7	188.1	100.6	148.5	147.5	183.2	182.5	145.5	277.6
May	126.6	119.2	111.6	116.2	137.5	194.3	188.7	100.4	148.5	145.0	185.4	184.6	144.6	278.3
June	126.1	118.7	112.3	113.3	135.8	195.4	190.0	100.2	148.3	144.1	191.5	190.8	144.7	278.6
July	126.1	119.3	111.9	115.7	135.6	194.0	188.6	100.1	148.4	143.2	185.2	184.4	143.8	279.1
August	126.4	120.5	110.9	115.8	137.1	193.7	188.3	99.8	148.5	142.6	183.8	183.0	144.6	278.8
September	125.8	119.1	110.9	115.1	136.9	195.3	190.0	99.6	148.5	142.2	192.3	191.5	143.5	278.4
October	126.1	119.0	111.0	114.3	137.9	197.3	192.2	99.6	148.8	142.2	201.7	201.1	143.9	278.7
November	125.7	117.8	111.1	114.2	137.6	198.5	193.6	99.6	148.7	142.4	205.6	205.1	142.8	280.2
December	125.2	116.7	110.6	114.6	137.9	200.0	195.1	99.7	149.0	142.8	210.6	210.1	144.0	281.0

[1]Not seasonally adjusted.
[3]December 1997 = 100.
. . . = Not available.

Table 8-2. Consumer Price Indexes and Purchasing Power of the Dollar—*Continued*

(1982–1984 = 100, seasonally adjusted, except as noted.)

Year and month	CPI-U, Transportation—*Continued*		CPI-U, Medical care					CPI-U, Recreation		CPI-U, Education and communication			
					Medical care services						Education		
	Public transportation	Transportation services	Medical care, total	Medical care commodities	Total	Professional services	Hospital and related services	Total [3]	Video and audio [3]	Total [3]	Total [3]	Educational books and supplies	Tuition, other school fees, and childcare
1970	35.2	40.2	34.0	46.5	32.3	37.0	...	...	...	...	...	38.8	...
1971	37.8	43.4	36.1	47.3	34.7	39.4	...	...	...	...	...	41.4	...
1972	39.3	44.4	37.3	47.4	35.9	40.8	...	...	...	...	...	44.2	...
1973	39.7	44.7	38.8	47.5	37.5	42.2	...	...	...	...	...	45.6	...
1974	40.6	46.3	42.4	49.2	41.4	45.8	...	...	...	...	...	47.2	...
1975	43.5	49.8	47.5	53.3	46.6	50.8	...	...	...	...	...	50.3	...
1976	47.8	56.9	52.0	56.5	51.3	55.5	...	...	...	...	...	53.7	...
1977	50.0	61.5	57.0	60.2	56.4	60.0	...	...	...	...	...	56.9	...
1978	51.5	64.4	61.8	64.4	61.2	64.5	55.1	...	...	...	...	61.6	59.8
1979	54.9	69.5	67.5	69.0	67.2	70.1	61.0	...	...	...	...	65.7	64.7
1980	69.0	79.2	74.9	75.4	74.8	77.9	69.2	...	...	...	...	71.4	71.2
1981	85.6	88.6	82.9	83.7	82.8	85.9	79.1	...	...	...	...	80.3	79.9
1982	94.9	96.1	92.5	92.3	92.6	93.2	90.3	...	...	...	...	91.0	90.5
1983	99.5	99.1	100.6	100.2	100.7	99.8	100.5	...	...	...	...	100.3	99.7
1984	105.7	104.8	106.8	107.5	106.7	107.0	109.2	...	...	...	...	108.7	109.8
1985	110.5	110.0	113.5	115.2	113.2	113.5	116.1	...	...	...	...	118.2	119.7
1986	117.0	116.3	122.0	122.8	121.9	120.8	123.1	...	...	...	...	128.1	129.6
1987	121.1	121.9	130.1	131.0	130.0	128.8	131.6	...	...	...	...	138.1	140.0
1988	123.3	128.0	138.6	139.9	138.3	137.5	143.9	...	...	...	...	148.1	151.0
1989	129.5	135.6	149.3	150.8	148.9	146.4	160.5	...	...	...	...	158.0	162.7
1990	142.6	144.2	162.8	163.4	162.7	156.1	178.0	...	...	...	...	171.3	175.7
1991	148.9	151.2	177.0	176.8	177.1	165.7	196.1	...	...	...	...	180.3	191.4
1992	151.4	155.7	190.1	188.1	190.5	175.8	214.0	...	...	...	...	190.3	208.5
1993	167.0	162.9	201.4	195.0	202.9	184.7	231.9	90.7	96.5	85.5	78.4	197.6	225.3
1994	172.0	168.6	211.0	200.7	213.4	192.5	245.6	92.7	95.4	88.8	83.3	205.5	239.8
1995	175.9	175.9	220.5	204.5	224.2	201.0	257.8	94.5	95.1	92.2	88.0	214.4	253.8
1996	181.9	180.5	228.2	210.4	232.4	208.3	269.5	97.4	96.6	95.3	92.7	226.9	267.1
1997	186.7	185.0	234.6	215.3	239.1	215.4	278.4	99.6	99.4	98.4	97.3	238.4	280.4
1998	190.3	187.9	242.1	221.8	246.8	222.2	287.5	101.1	101.1	100.3	102.1	250.8	294.2
1999	197.7	190.7	250.6	230.7	255.1	229.2	299.5	102.0	100.7	101.2	107.0	261.7	308.4
2000	209.6	196.1	260.8	238.1	266.0	237.7	317.3	103.3	101.0	102.5	112.5	279.9	324.0
2001	210.6	201.9	272.8	247.6	278.8	246.5	338.3	104.9	101.5	105.2	118.5	295.9	341.1
2002	207.4	209.1	285.6	256.4	292.9	253.9	367.8	106.2	102.8	107.9	126.0	317.6	362.1
2003	209.3	216.3	297.1	262.8	306.0	261.2	394.8	107.5	103.6	109.8	134.4	335.4	386.7
2004	209.1	220.6	310.1	269.3	321.3	271.5	417.9	108.6	104.2	111.6	143.7	351.0	414.3
2005	217.3	225.7	323.2	276.0	336.7	281.7	439.9	109.4	104.2	113.7	152.7	365.6	440.9
2006	226.6	230.8	336.2	285.9	350.6	289.3	468.1	110.9	104.6	116.8	162.1	388.9	468.1
2007	230.0	233.7	351.1	290.0	369.3	300.8	498.9	111.4	102.9	119.6	171.4	420.4	494.1
2008	250.5	244.1	364.1	296.0	384.9	311.0	534.0	113.3	102.6	123.6	181.3	450.2	522.1
2009	236.3	251.0	375.6	305.1	397.3	319.4	567.9	114.3	101.3	127.4	190.9	482.1	549.0
2010	251.4	259.8	388.4	314.7	411.2	328.2	607.7	113.3	99.1	129.9	199.3	505.6	573.2
2011	269.4	268.0	400.3	324.1	423.8	335.7	641.5	113.4	98.4	131.5	207.8	529.5	597.2
2012	271.4	272.9	414.9	333.6	440.3	342.0	672.1	114.7	99.4	133.8	216.3	562.6	621.0
2013	278.9	280.0	425.1	335.1	454.0	349.5	701.3	115.3	99.7	135.9	224.5	594.7	643.7
2014	276.4	285.3	435.3	343.4	464.8	355.2	733.8	115.5	99.8	137.5	231.9	615.4	664.8
2015	268.7	291.0	446.8	354.6	476.2	361.5	761.9	115.9	99.6	138.2	240.5	648.2	688.8
2016	265.4	299.4	463.7	366.8	494.8	371.5	795.1	117.0	100.9	139.1	247.5	678.8	708.1
2015													
January	269.8	292.0	444.2	341.5	475.5	361.6	757.1	111.6	100.9	129.2	232.6	644.2	650.3
February	270.7	293.3	443.8	342.7	474.4	361.1	755.5	111.6	101.0	129.1	233.2	646.7	651.7
March	268.3	293.8	445.6	343.6	476.5	362.3	760.3	111.7	100.7	129.0	234.4	651.2	655.1
April	268.1	294.2	448.5	344.1	480.3	363.3	771.0	111.7	100.7	129.2	235.8	652.5	659.2
May	274.8	295.6	449.0	345.4	480.5	363.5	773.1	111.8	100.6	128.9	236.2	653.5	660.4
June	277.0	296.4	448.9	345.4	480.4	364.3	769.1	111.9	100.6	129.0	236.8	651.6	662.4
July	271.3	296.9	449.7	345.5	481.4	365.2	770.9	111.8	100.6	129.1	237.5	655.2	664.2
August	268.5	296.8	449.5	345.7	481.0	365.0	771.4	111.8	100.7	129.4	237.9	656.9	665.2
September	266.9	297.4	450.2	345.1	482.3	365.8	772.7	112.0	100.9	129.8	238.7	658.4	667.6
October	271.6	298.0	454.0	346.1	487.0	366.3	788.7	112.1	101.2	130.0	239.2	661.2	668.8
November	274.5	300.3	455.6	347.4	488.8	368.4	786.7	112.1	101.3	130.4	239.9	663.7	670.7
December	271.2	300.7	456.2	347.7	489.5	368.8	787.4	112.0	101.4	130.4	240.3	668.1	671.6
2016													
January	271.7	301.9	458.3	348.9	492.0	369.8	792.0	112.1	101.2	130.5	240.8	668.3	672.9
February	271.6	302.5	460.2	350.2	494.0	370.9	795.1	112.3	101.7	130.1	241.4	670.0	674.6
March	271.2	303.4	461.3	351.7	494.9	371.5	795.3	112.6	102.3	130.2	241.8	671.2	675.7
April	271.7	305.2	462.8	352.9	496.6	372.4	797.4	112.8	102.3	130.2	242.4	677.1	677.0
May	271.8	306.7	464.3	352.0	498.9	374.6	801.2	112.9	102.5	130.0	242.8	679.0	678.3
June	271.2	307.4	466.1	354.7	500.4	374.9	803.5	112.9	102.9	130.0	243.6	691.3	679.8
July	267.3	307.6	468.5	356.5	503.0	376.4	807.8	112.7	102.9	129.9	244.1	693.5	681.2
August	266.9	308.0	472.9	360.6	507.4	378.0	820.1	112.7	102.6	130.0	244.4	695.6	681.9
September	266.8	308.1	473.8	362.8	507.8	378.4	819.8	112.7	102.2	129.4	245.0	699.1	683.3
October	265.5	308.1	474.3	363.1	508.3	378.8	821.8	112.5	102.1	129.1	245.8	700.3	685.6
November	265.5	310.2	474.5	361.8	509.1	379.9	821.4	112.7	102.9	129.3	246.4	705.3	687.1
December	266.8	311.8	475.6	363.5	509.9	380.5	823.2	112.7	103.1	129.4	247.2	705.7	689.6

[3]December 1997 = 100.
. . . = Not available.

Table 8-2. Consumer Price Indexes and Purchasing Power of the Dollar—*Continued*

(1982–1984 = 100, seasonally adjusted except as noted.)

Year and month	CPI-U, Education and communication—*Continued* (Communication)					CPI-U, Other goods and services					CPI-W, All items, not seasonally adjusted	Purchasing power of the dollar, CPI-U, 1982–1984 = $1.00, not seasonally adjusted
	Total 3	Information and information processing				Total	Tobacco and smoking products 1	Personal care				
		Total 3	Telephone services 1,3	Information technology, hardware, and services				Total	Personal care products 1	Personal care services 1		
				Total 1,4	Personal computers and peripheral equipment 1,5							
1970	. . .	. . .	. . .	. . .	. . .	40.9	43.1	43.5	42.7	44.2	39.0	2.574
1971	. . .	. . .	. . .	. . .	. . .	42.9	44.9	44.9	44.0	45.7	40.7	2.466
1972	. . .	. . .	. . .	. . .	. . .	44.7	47.4	46.0	45.2	46.8	42.1	2.391
1973	. . .	. . .	. . .	. . .	. . .	46.4	48.7	48.1	46.4	49.7	44.7	2.251
1974	. . .	. . .	. . .	. . .	. . .	49.8	51.1	52.8	51.5	53.9	49.6	2.029
1975	. . .	. . .	. . .	. . .	. . .	53.9	54.7	57.9	.58.0	57.7	54.1	1.859
1976	. . .	. . .	. . .	. . .	. . .	57.0	57.0	61.7	61.3	61.9	57.2	1.757
1977	. . .	. . .	. . .	. . .	. . .	60.4	59.8	65.7	64.7	66.4	60.9	1.649
1978	. . .	. . .	. . .	. . .	. . .	64.3	63.0	69.9	68.2	71.3	65.6	1.532
1979	. . .	. . .	. . .	. . .	. . .	68.9	66.8	75.2	72.9	77.2	73.1	1.380
1980	. . .	. . .	. . .	. . .	. . .	75.2	72.0	81.9	79.6	83.7	82.9	1.215
1981	. . .	. . .	. . .	. . .	. . .	82.6	77.8	89.1	87.8	90.2	91.4	1.098
1982	. . .	. . .	. . .	. . .	. . .	91.1	86.5	95.4	95.1	95.7	96.9	1.035
1983	. . .	. . .	. . .	. . .	. . .	101.1	103.4	100.3	100.7	100.0	99.8	1.003
1984	. . .	. . .	. . .	. . .	. . .	107.9	110.1	104.3	104.2	104.4	103.3	0.961
1985	. . .	. . .	. . .	. . .	. . .	114.5	116.7	108.3	107.6	108.9	106.9	0.928
1986	. . .	. . .	. . .	. . .	. . .	121.4	124.7	111.9	111.3	112.5	108.6	0.913
1987	. . .	. . .	. . .	. . .	. . .	128.5	133.6	115.1	113.9	116.2	112.5	0.880
1988	. . .	. . .	. . .	. . .	. . .	137.0	145.8	119.4	118.1	120.7	117.0	0.846
1989	. . .	. . .	. . .	96.3	. . .	147.7	164.4	125.0	123.2	126.8	122.6	0.807
1990	. . .	. . .	. . .	93.5	. . .	159.0	181.5	130.4	128.2	132.8	129.0	0.766
1991	. . .	. . .	. . .	88.6	. . .	171.6	202.7	134.9	132.8	137.0	134.3	0.734
1992	. . .	. . .	. . .	83.7	. . .	183.3	219.8	138.3	136.5	140.0	138.2	0.713
1993	96.7	97.7	. . .	78.8	. . .	192.9	228.4	141.5	139.0	144.0	142.1	0.692
1994	97.6	98.6	. . .	72.0	. . .	198.5	220.0	144.6	141.5	147.9	145.6	0.675
1995	98.8	98.7	. . .	63.8	. . .	206.9	225.7	147.1	143.1	151.5	149.8	0.656
1996	99.6	99.5	. . .	57.2	. . .	215.4	232.8	150.1	144.3	156.6	154.1	0.638
1997	100.3	100.4	. . .	50.1	. . .	224.8	243.7	152.7	144.2	162.4	157.6	0.623
1998	98.7	98.5	100.7	39.9	875.1	237.7	274.8	156.7	148.3	166.0	159.7	0.614
1999	96.0	95.5	100.1	30.5	598.7	258.3	355.8	161.1	151.8	171.4	163.2	0.600
2000	93.6	92.8	98.5	25.9	459.9	271.1	394.9	165.6	153.7	178.1	168.9	0.581
2001	93.3	92.3	99.3	21.3	330.1	282.6	425.2	170.5	155.1	184.3	173.5	0.565
2002	92.3	90.8	99.7	18.3	248.4	293.2	461.5	174.7	154.7	188.4	175.9	0.556
2003	89.7	87.8	98.3	16.1	196.9	298.7	469.0	178.0	153.5	193.2	179.8	0.544
2004	86.7	84.6	95.8	14.8	171.2	304.7	478.0	181.7	153.9	197.6	184.5	0.530
2005	84.7	82.6	94.9	13.6	143.2	313.4	502.8	185.6	154.4	203.9	191.0	0.512
2006	84.1	81.7	95.8	12.5	120.9	321.7	519.9	190.2	155.8	209.7	197.1	0.496
2007	83.4	80.7	98.2	10.6	108.4	333.3	554.2	195.6	158.3	216.6	202.8	0.482
2008	84.2	81.4	100.5	10.1	94.9	345.4	588.7	201.3	159.3	223.7	211.1	0.465
2009	85.0	81.9	102.4	9.7	82.3	368.6	730.3	204.6	162.6	227.6	209.6	0.466
2010	84.7	81.5	102.4	9.4	76.4	381.3	807.3	206.6	161.1	229.6	214.0	0.459
2011	83.3	80.0	101.2	9.0	68.9	387.2	834.8	208.6	160.5	230.8	221.6	0.445
2012	83.1	79.5	101.7	8.7	62.3	394.4	853.5	212.1	162.2	234.2	226.2	0.436
2013	82.6	78.9	101.6	8.5	56.8	401.0	876.8	215.0	161.8	238.8	229.3	0.429
2014	82.1	78.2	101.1	8.4	52.6	408.1	903.3	218.0	163.4	242.0	232.8	0.422
2015	80.2	76.4	99.3	8.1	47.9	414.9	930.8	220.8	163.3	247.2	231.8	0.422
2016	79.2	75.4	98.8	7.8	44.4	423.1	963.4	224.3	163.1	252.9	234.1	0.417
2015												
January	82.9	80.2	98.0	8.8	49.0	446.0	922.1	217.7	165.1	244.8	229.7	0.438
February	82.7	80.0	97.8	8.8	48.8	445.8	925.9	217.1	164.9	243.3	230.4	0.436
March	82.3	79.7	97.4	8.7	48.4	446.4	928.8	217.2	164.7	244.8	230.9	0.433
April	82.3	79.6	97.3	8.7	48.4	446.6	930.2	217.2	164.0	245.0	231.1	0.432
May	81.9	79.2	96.8	8.7	48.2	447.9	934.9	217.6	163.6	245.7	231.8	0.429
June	81.8	79.2	96.9	8.6	47.7	449.7	938.8	218.4	163.0	249.2	232.4	0.428
July	81.8	79.2	97.1	8.6	47.5	449.8	941.5	218.2	162.7	249.6	232.8	0.428
August	82.0	79.3	97.8	8.5	47.1	450.1	944.6	218.1	162.1	249.4	232.7	0.429
September	82.2	79.6	98.1	8.5	47.2	451.0	945.5	218.6	162.7	250.1	232.1	0.430
October	82.4	79.7	98.3	8.6	46.9	452.6	948.3	219.5	163.8	250.3	232.4	0.430
November	82.6	79.9	98.7	8.5	46.6	453.6	953.0	219.6	163.6	251.5	232.7	0.432
December	82.5	79.8	98.7	8.5	46.0	453.8	955.5	219.5	163.4	251.0	232.3	0.433
2016												
January	82.5	79.9	98.7	8.5	45.4	454.5	957.9	219.7	163.6	251.8	232.4	0.433
February	82.0	79.4	98.1	8.5	44.7	455.4	960.2	220.1	164.1	252.1	231.8	0.433
March	82.0	79.4	98.1	8.5	44.7	456.2	963.7	220.3	164.0	252.6	232.2	0.431
April	81.9	79.3	98.1	8.4	44.5	457.2	966.4	220.7	163.8	253.0	233.1	0.428
May	81.6	79.0	97.6	8.4	44.2	458.5	968.9	221.4	163.3	253.7	233.4	0.427
June	81.5	78.8	97.5	8.4	44.0	459.2	971.9	221.6	162.4	253.7	233.9	0.425
July	81.3	78.7	97.3	8.4	43.7	459.2	968.3	221.9	162.9	253.7	233.9	0.426
August	81.4	78.7	97.3	8.4	43.7	460.5	974.6	222.2	163.5	254.4	234.3	0.426
September	80.7	78.1	96.2	8.4	43.5	462.2	978.5	223.0	163.2	254.7	235.0	0.425
October	80.3	77.6	95.8	8.3	43.3	462.3	982.4	222.7	162.7	254.9	235.7	0.424
November	80.3	77.7	95.6	8.4	43.1	463.4	986.3	223.0	162.4	255.8	236.2	0.425
December	80.3	77.6	95.6	8.3	43.2	464.9	990.2	223.7	162.8	256.1	236.9	0.425

[1]Not seasonally adjusted.
[3]December 1997 = 100.
[4]December 1988 = 100.
[5]December 2007 = 100.
. . . = Not available.

Table 8-3. Alternative Measures of Total and Core Consumer Prices: Index Levels

(Various bases; monthly data seasonally adjusted, except as noted.)

Year and month	CPIs, all items					CPIs, all items less food and energy		
	CPI-U, 1982–1984 = 100	CPI-W, 1982–1984 = 100	CPI-U-X1, 1982–1984 = 100	CPI-U-RS, Dec. 1977 = 100, not seasonally adjusted	C-CPI-U, Dec. 1999 = 100, not seasonally adjusted	CPI-U, 1982–1984 = 100	CPI-U-RS, Dec. 1977 = 100, not seasonally adjusted	C-CPI-U, Dec. 1999 = 100, not seasonally adjusted
1975	53.8	54.1	56.2	. . .	. . .	53.9	. . .	. . .
1976	56.9	57.2	59.4	. . .	. . .	57.4	. . .	. . .
1977	60.6	60.9	63.2	. . .	. . .	61.0	. . .	. . .
1978	65.2	65.6	67.5	104.4	. . .	65.5	103.5	. . .
1979	72.6	73.1	74.0	114.3	. . .	71.9	111.0	. . .
1980	82.4	82.9	82.3	127.1	. . .	80.8	120.9	. . .
1981	90.9	91.4	90.1	139.1	. . .	89.2	132.2	. . .
1982	96.5	96.9	95.6	147.5	. . .	95.8	142.4	. . .
1983	99.6	99.8	99.6	153.8	. . .	99.6	150.4	. . .
1984	103.9	103.3	103.9	160.2	. . .	104.6	158.1	. . .
1985	107.6	106.9	107.6	165.7	. . .	109.1	165.0	. . .
1986	109.6	108.6	109.6	168.6	. . .	113.5	171.7	. . .
1987	113.6	112.5	113.6	174.4	. . .	118.2	178.1	. . .
1988	118.3	117.0	118.3	180.7	. . .	123.4	185.2	. . .
1989	124.0	122.6	124.0	188.6	. . .	129.0	192.6	. . .
1990	130.7	129.0	130.7	197.9	. . .	135.5	201.4	. . .
1991	136.2	134.3	136.2	205.1	. . .	142.1	209.9	. . .
1992	140.3	138.2	140.3	210.2	. . .	147.3	216.4	. . .
1993	144.5	142.1	144.5	215.5	. . .	152.2	222.5	. . .
1994	148.2	145.6	148.2	220.0	. . .	156.5	227.7	. . .
1995	152.4	149.8	152.4	225.3	. . .	161.2	233.4	. . .
1996	156.9	154.1	156.9	231.3	. . .	165.6	239.1	. . .
1997	160.5	157.6	160.5	236.3	. . .	169.5	244.4	. . .
1998	163.0	159.7	163.0	239.5	. . .	173.4	249.6	. . .
1999	166.6	163.2	166.6	244.6	. . .	177.0	254.6	. . .
2000	172.2	168.9	172.2	252.9	102.0	181.3	260.9	101.4
2001	177.1	173.5	177.1	260.1	104.3	186.1	267.9	103.5
2002	179.9	175.9	179.9	264.2	105.6	190.5	274.1	105.4
2003	184.0	179.8	184.0	270.2	107.8	193.2	278.1	106.6
2004	188.9	184.5	188.9	277.5	110.5	196.6	283.1	108.4
2005	195.3	191.0	195.3	286.9	113.7	200.9	289.2	110.4
2006	201.6	197.1	201.6	296.2	117.0	205.9	296.4	112.9
2007	207.3	202.8	207.3	304.6	120.0	210.7	303.4	115.0
2008	215.3	211.1	215.3	316.3	124.4	215.6	310.3	117.3
2009	214.5	209.6	214.5	315.2	123.9	219.2	315.6	119.1
2010	218.1	214.0	218.1	320.3	125.6	221.3	318.6	120.0
2011	224.9	221.6	224.9	330.5	129.5	225.0	323.9	121.9
2012	229.6	226.2	229.6	337.3	132.0	229.8	330.8	124.3
2013	233.0	229.3	233.0	342.2	. . .	233.8	336.6	. . .
2014	236.7	232.8	236.7	347.8	. . .	237.9	342.5	. . .
2015	237.0	231.8	237.0	348.2	. . .	242.2	348.8	. . .
2016	240.0	234.1	240.0	352.6	. . .	247.6	356.5	. . .
2015								
January	234.9	229.7	234.9	345.1	133.5	232.5	345.4	128.4
February	235.5	230.4	235.5	346.0	134.1	232.9	345.9	128.8
March	236.0	230.9	236.0	346.7	135.0	233.5	346.7	129.4
April	236.2	231.1	236.2	347.0	135.2	234.1	347.5	129.8
May	236.9	231.8	236.9	348.0	136.0	234.3	347.9	130.0
June	237.4	232.4	237.4	348.8	136.4	234.6	348.5	130.1
July	237.9	232.8	237.9	349.5	136.4	235.0	349.1	130.2
August	237.8	232.7	237.8	349.4	136.1	235.3	349.5	130.2
September	237.5	232.1	237.5	348.9	135.8	235.8	350.2	130.4
October	237.8	232.4	237.8	349.4	135.7	236.2	350.9	130.7
November	238.2	232.7	238.2	349.9	135.4	236.7	351.6	130.7
December	237.8	232.3	237.8	349.5	134.8	237.1	352.2	130.4
2016								
January	238.1	232.4	238.1	349.8	135.0	237.7	353.1	130.8
February	237.8	231.8	237.8	349.4	135.0	238.2	354.0	131.3
March	238.1	232.2	238.1	349.8	135.7	238.5	354.3	131.7
April	238.9	233.1	238.9	351.0	136.3	239.0	354.9	132.1
May	239.4	233.4	239.4	351.7	136.9	239.3	355.7	132.4
June	239.8	233.9	239.8	352.4	137.3	[1]239.6	356.2	132.5
July	239.9	233.9	239.9	352.5	137.0	[1]239.9	356.7	132.4
August	240.4	234.3	240.4	353.2	137.0	[1]240.5	357.6	132.5
September	241.0	235.0	241.0	354.1	137.3	[1]240.7	358.0	132.7
October	241.7	235.7	241.7	355.1	137.5	[1]241.1	358.5	133.0
November	242.2	236.2	242.2	355.9	137.2	[1]241.5	359.2	133.0
December	242.8	236.9	242.8	356.8	137.3	242.1	360.0	132.9

[1]Interim values.
. . . = Not available.

Table 8-4. Alternative Measures of Total and Core Consumer Prices: Inflation Rates

(Percent changes from year earlier, except as noted; monthly data seasonally adjusted, except as noted.)

Year and month	CPIs, all items					CPIs, all items less food and energy		
	CPI-U, 1982–1984 = 100	CPI-W, 1982–1984 = 100	CPI-U-X1, 1982–1984 = 100	CPI-U-RS, Dec. 1977 = 100, not seasonally adjusted	C-CPI-U, Dec. 1999 = 100, not seasonally adjusted	CPI-U, 1982–1984 = 100	CPI-U-RS, Dec. 1977 = 100, not seasonally adjusted	C-CPI-U, Dec. 1999 = 100, not seasonally adjusted
1960	1.7	1.7	1.9	. . .	. . .	1.3	. . .	. . .
1961	1.0	1.0	0.9	. . .	. . .	1.3	. . .	. . .
1962	1.0	1.0	0.9	. . .	. . .	1.3	. . .	. . .
1963	1.3	1.3	1.5	. . .	. . .	1.3	. . .	. . .
1964	1.3	1.3	1.2	. . .	. . .	1.6	. . .	. . .
1965	1.6	1.6	1.5	. . .	. . .	1.2	. . .	. . .
1966	2.9	2.8	2.9	. . .	. . .	2.4	. . .	. . .
1967	3.1	3.1	3.1	. . .	. . .	3.6	. . .	. . .
1968	4.2	4.2	3.9	. . .	. . .	4.6	. . .	. . .
1969	5.5	5.4	4.5	. . .	. . .	5.8	. . .	. . .
1970	5.7	5.7	4.8	. . .	. . .	6.3	. . .	. . .
1971	4.4	4.4	4.4	. . .	. . .	4.7	. . .	. . .
1972	3.2	3.4	3.0	. . .	. . .	3.0	. . .	. . .
1973	6.2	6.2	6.3	. . .	. . .	3.6	. . .	. . .
1974	11.0	11.0	10.0	. . .	. . .	8.3	. . .	. . .
1975	9.1	9.1	8.3	. . .	. . .	9.1	. . .	. . .
1976	5.8	5.7	5.7	. . .	. . .	6.5	. . .	. . .
1977	6.5	6.5	6.4	. . .	. . .	6.3	. . .	. . .
1978	7.6	7.7	6.8	. . .	. . .	7.4	. . .	. . .
1979	11.3	11.4	9.6	9.5	. . .	9.8	7.2	. . .
1980	13.5	13.4	11.2	11.1	. . .	12.4	8.9	. . .
1981	10.3	10.3	9.5	9.6	. . .	10.4	9.3	. . .
1982	6.2	6.0	6.1	6.0	. . .	7.4	7.7	. . .
1983	3.2	3.0	4.2	4.2	. . .	4.0	5.6	. . .
1984	4.3	3.5	4.3	4.2	. . .	5.0	5.1	. . .
1985	3.6	3.5	3.6	3.4	. . .	4.3	4.4	. . .
1986	1.9	1.6	1.9	1.9	. . .	4.0	4.1	. . .
1987	3.6	3.6	3.6	3.3	. . .	4.1	3.7	. . .
1988	4.1	4.0	4.1	3.7	. . .	4.4	4.0	. . .
1989	4.8	4.8	4.8	4.3	. . .	4.5	4.0	. . .
1990	5.4	5.2	5.4	4.9	. . .	5.0	4.6	. . .
1991	4.2	4.1	4.2	3.6	. . .	4.9	4.2	. . .
1992	3.0	2.9	3.0	2.5	. . .	3.7	3.1	. . .
1993	3.0	2.8	3.0	2.5	. . .	3.3	2.8	. . .
1994	2.6	2.5	2.6	2.1	. . .	2.8	2.3	. . .
1995	2.8	2.9	2.8	2.4	. . .	3.0	2.5	. . .
1996	3.0	2.9	3.0	2.7	. . .	2.7	2.4	. . .
1997	2.3	2.3	2.3	2.2	. . .	2.4	2.2	. . .
1998	1.6	1.3	1.6	1.4	. . .	2.3	2.1	. . .
1999	2.2	2.2	2.2	2.1	. . .	2.1	2.0	. . .
2000	3.4	3.5	3.4	3.4	. . .	2.4	2.5	. . .
2001	2.8	2.7	2.8	2.8	2.3	2.6	2.7	2.1
2002	1.6	1.4	1.6	1.6	1.2	2.4	2.3	1.8
2003	2.3	2.2	2.3	2.3	2.1	1.4	1.5	1.1
2004	2.7	2.6	2.7	2.7	2.5	1.8	1.8	1.7
2005	3.4	3.5	3.4	3.4	2.9	2.2	2.2	1.8
2006	3.2	3.2	3.2	3.2	2.9	2.5	2.5	2.3
2007	2.8	2.9	2.8	2.9	2.5	2.3	2.4	1.8
2008	3.8	4.1	3.8	3.8	3.7	2.3	2.3	2.0
2009	-0.4	-0.7	-0.4	-0.3	-0.5	1.7	1.7	1.5
2010	1.6	2.1	1.6	1.6	1.4	1.0	1.0	0.7
2011	3.2	3.6	3.2	3.1	3.1	1.7	1.7	1.6
2012	2.1	2.1	2.1	2.1	1.9	2.1	2.1	2.0
2013	1.5	1.4	1.5	1.5	. . .	[1]1.8	1.8	. . .
2014	1.6	1.5	1.6	1.6	. . .	[1]1.7	1.8	. . .
2015	0.1	-0.4	0.1	0.1	. . .	[1]1.8	1.8	. . .
2016	1.3	1.0	1.3	1.3	. . .	[1]2.2	2.2	. . .
2016								
January	1.4	1.2	1.4	1.4	1.1	[1]2.2	2.2	1.8
February	1.0	0.6	1.0	1.0	0.7	[1]2.3	2.3	2.0
March	0.9	0.5	0.9	0.9	0.5	[1]2.2	2.2	1.8
April	1.1	0.9	1.1	1.1	0.8	[1]2.1	2.1	1.8
May	1.0	0.7	1.0	1.0	0.7	[1]2.2	2.2	1.8
June	1.0	0.7	1.0	1.0	0.7	[1]2.1	2.2	1.8
July	0.9	0.5	0.9	0.9	0.5	[1]2.1	2.2	1.7
August	1.1	0.7	1.1	1.1	0.7	[1]2.2	2.3	1.8
September	1.5	1.2	1.5	1.5	1.1	[1]2.1	2.2	1.8
October	1.6	1.4	1.6	1.7	1.3	[1]2.1	2.2	1.7
November	1.7	1.5	1.7	1.7	1.4	[1]2.0	2.2	1.7
December	2.1	2.0	2.1	2.1	1.9	[1]2.1	2.2	1.9

[1]Interim values.
. . . = Not available.

Table 8-5. Producer Price Indexes for Goods and Services: Final Demand

(November 2009 =100, except as noted.)

Year and month	Final demand	Final demand goods			Final demand goods less food and energy			Final demand services				Final demand construction	Final demand less food and energy (April 2010 =100)
		Final demand goods	Final demand foods	Final demand energy goods	Total	Finished goods less foods and energy (1982 =100)		Final demand services	Final demand trade services	Final demand transportation and warehousing services	Final demand services less trade, transportation, and warehousing		
						Total	Private capital equipment						
NOT SEASONALLY ADJUSTED													
2010	101.8	102.8	103.7	107.2	101.4	173.6	157.3	101.3	101.7	103.2	100.9	100.3	. . .
2011	105.7	109.9	112.5	126.2	104.9	177.8	159.7	103.4	104.0	110.0	102.5	102.5	102.7
2012	107.7	111.7	115.9	126.3	106.8	182.4	162.8	105.4	106.7	114.2	103.9	105.5	104.7
2013	109.1	112.6	117.8	125.3	107.9	185.1	164.2	107.1	108.2	115.3	105.8	107.5	106.2
2014	110.9	114.0	121.6	124.2	109.5	188.6	166.4	109.0	110.2	117.7	107.5	110.6	108.1
2015	109.9	109.1	118.4	98.6	109.9	192.3	168.5	110.0	111.6	115.3	108.7	112.7	108.9
2016	110.4	107.6	115.1	90.4	110.7	195.3	169.3	111.5	113.1	113.5	110.6	114.0	110.2
2013													
January	108.3	111.9	118.4	121.9	107.6	184.5	163.8	106.2	107.2	114.9	104.8	106.4	105.5
February	108.8	112.8	117.3	127.2	107.9	184.7	163.9	106.5	107.4	115.0	105.1	106.4	105.7
March	109.1	112.9	118.6	126.2	107.9	184.7	163.8	106.9	108.3	116.0	105.3	106.4	106.1
April	109.0	112.4	117.0	125.1	107.9	184.7	163.9	107.0	108.6	115.0	105.4	106.8	106.1
May	108.8	112.8	118.3	126.3	107.8	184.7	163.9	106.5	107.0	114.4	105.4	106.9	105.7
June	109.2	112.9	118.6	126.8	107.8	184.7	163.8	107.0	107.8	115.7	105.7	106.9	106.1
July	109.5	113.0	118.7	126.9	107.9	184.9	163.8	107.4	108.6	116.0	105.9	107.4	106.4
August	109.5	113.1	118.0	128.3	107.8	184.9	163.7	107.4	108.3	116.2	106.1	107.5	106.4
September	109.4	112.9	117.6	127.7	107.7	184.6	163.9	107.4	108.6	114.4	106.1	107.7	106.4
October	109.7	112.5	117.3	124.3	108.2	185.9	165.2	108.0	109.5	115.3	106.4	109.0	106.9
November	109.4	112.0	117.2	121.1	108.2	186.1	165.4	107.8	109.1	114.6	106.5	109.1	106.8
December	109.3	112.2	117.0	121.7	108.6	186.8	165.6	107.5	107.6	116.6	106.4	109.2	106.6
2014													
January	109.7	113.1	117.6	123.2	109.3	188.1	166.2	107.6	107.4	116.1	106.9	109.8	107.0
February	110.1	113.5	118.1	124.7	109.4	188.2	166.3	108.2	108.7	115.8	107.1	109.9	107.4
March	110.8	114.3	120.0	127.9	109.2	187.9	166.1	108.8	109.9	117.4	107.4	110.0	107.8
April	111.0	115.2	123.0	129.8	109.4	187.9	166.1	108.7	109.4	118.1	107.3	110.3	107.7
May	111.1	115.0	122.6	129.4	109.3	188.0	166.1	108.8	110.2	118.1	107.2	110.3	107.9
June	111.2	115.4	123.1	130.7	109.4	188.2	166.1	108.8	109.3	119.0	107.4	110.4	107.8
July	111.6	115.3	123.0	129.9	109.6	188.4	166.2	109.5	111.1	119.0	107.6	110.8	108.4
August	111.6	115.0	122.5	128.9	109.5	188.4	166.1	109.5	110.5	119.3	108.0	110.9	108.4
September	111.1	114.6	122.2	127.0	109.5	188.4	166.1	109.1	109.8	117.4	107.8	110.9	108.1
October	111.4	113.6	122.4	119.6	110.0	189.9	167.5	110.0	112.6	117.4	107.9	111.4	108.9
November	110.8	112.5	122.3	113.9	109.8	189.9	167.4	109.7	111.6	117.2	107.9	111.4	108.6
December	110.3	110.9	122.1	105.6	109.8	190.0	167.2	109.8	111.9	117.5	107.9	111.6	108.7
2015													
January	109.7	109.0	120.6	95.7	110.1	191.3	168.0	109.8	111.9	116.8	108.0	112.0	108.8
February	109.5	108.9	118.8	96.8	110.0	191.8	168.5	109.5	110.8	115.8	108.2	112.1	108.5
March	109.8	109.2	118.1	99.7	109.9	191.8	168.5	109.8	111.4	116.4	108.3	112.1	108.7
April	109.8	108.9	117.5	98.6	109.8	191.6	168.4	110.0	111.4	115.9	108.6	112.1	108.8
May	110.2	110.4	118.9	104.8	109.9	191.7	168.4	109.7	111.1	115.7	108.5	112.2	108.7
June	110.6	111.1	119.8	106.9	110.2	192.5	168.3	110.0	111.2	116.5	108.8	112.2	109.0
July	110.8	110.9	119.0	106.6	110.2	192.7	168.5	110.4	112.0	116.4	109.0	112.8	109.3
August	110.5	110.1	119.3	103.2	109.9	192.4	168.3	110.3	111.6	115.3	109.2	112.9	109.1
September	109.9	108.7	118.5	97.0	109.7	192.4	168.2	110.1	112.0	113.7	108.9	112.9	108.9
October	109.8	108.1	117.3	94.0	109.9	193.3	169.0	110.3	112.4	114.0	108.9	113.9	109.1
November	109.4	107.5	117.0	92.0	109.7	193.2	169.0	110.1	112.0	114.0	108.7	113.8	108.9
December	109.1	106.7	115.8	88.3	109.7	193.4	169.0	110.0	111.9	113.4	108.8	113.9	108.9
2016													
January	109.7	106.4	116.4	85.1	110.1	194.5	169.1	111.1	113.1	114.1	109.8	113.4	109.7
February	109.6	105.9	116.4	81.9	110.2	194.7	169.2	111.2	113.4	113.5	110.0	113.4	109.9
March	109.7	106.1	115.1	84.3	110.2	194.6	169.1	111.2	113.0	114.2	110.2	113.3	109.9
April	110.0	106.7	115.0	86.5	110.5	194.7	169.1	111.3	113.2	113.7	110.3	114.4	110.0
May	110.2	107.6	115.9	90.2	110.6	194.7	169.2	111.2	113.2	112.8	110.1	114.4	110.0
June	110.8	108.7	116.9	94.5	110.8	195.3	169.3	111.6	113.7	113.6	110.5	114.4	110.3
July	110.8	108.5	115.9	94.5	110.8	195.1	169.0	111.6	112.7	114.2	110.9	113.6	110.3
August	110.5	108.0	114.4	92.9	110.8	195.1	168.8	111.4	111.9	113.7	111.1	113.7	110.2
September	110.6	108.3	114.8	94.2	110.7	195.1	168.7	111.6	112.9	111.7	111.0	113.7	110.2
October	111.0	108.5	113.5	94.5	111.2	196.3	169.7	112.1	113.9	113.0	111.2	114.6	110.7
November	110.8	108.0	112.9	92.2	111.3	196.3	169.7	112.0	113.6	113.5	111.1	114.6	110.7
December	111.0	108.7	113.9	93.9	111.6	196.7	170.1	111.8	113.0	114.7	111.0	114.5	110.7

. . . = Not available.

Table 8-5. Producer Price Indexes for Goods and Services: Final Demand—*Continued*

(November 2009 =100, except as noted.)

Year and month	Final demand	Final demand goods						Final demand services				Final demand con-struction	Final demand less food and energy (April 2010 =100)
		Final demand goods	Final demand foods	Final demand energy goods	Final demand goods less food and energy			Final demand services	Final demand trade services	Final demand transpor-tation and ware-housing services	Final demand services less trade, transpor-tation, and ware-housing		
					Total	Finished goods less foods and energy (1982 =100)							
						Total	Private capital equip-ment						
SEASONALLY ADJUSTED													
2013													
January	108.7	112.7	118.9	126.5	107.4	183.9	163.4	106.4	108.0	114.9	104.7	106.4	105.6
February	108.9	113.4	117.8	130.9	107.7	184.2	163.5	106.4	107.4	115.0	105.0	106.4	105.6
March	108.9	112.8	118.9	125.8	107.8	184.4	163.7	106.7	107.8	115.4	105.2	106.3	105.8
April	108.7	112.0	117.0	123.3	107.8	184.6	163.8	106.8	108.2	114.5	105.3	106.8	106.0
May	108.6	112.3	118.3	123.8	107.8	184.8	164.0	106.5	106.9	114.4	105.5	106.9	105.7
June	109.0	112.3	118.1	123.8	107.9	185.0	164.1	107.1	108.0	115.0	105.7	106.9	106.2
July	109.2	112.4	118.3	123.5	107.9	185.2	164.1	107.4	108.9	115.4	105.9	107.4	106.4
August	109.3	112.6	117.6	125.0	108.0	185.4	164.2	107.4	108.3	115.7	106.0	107.5	106.4
September	109.4	112.5	117.3	125.0	108.0	185.4	164.6	107.5	108.6	115.5	106.1	107.7	106.5
October	109.5	112.6	117.4	124.9	108.1	185.5	164.7	107.7	108.8	115.7	106.3	109.0	106.7
November	109.7	112.6	117.3	124.8	108.2	186.0	165.1	107.9	109.1	115.2	106.6	109.1	106.9
December	109.7	113.1	117.0	126.1	108.6	186.8	165.4	107.7	107.9	117.2	106.6	109.2	106.9
2014													
January	110.1	113.9	118.2	128.1	109.1	187.5	165.8	107.9	108.2	116.1	106.8	109.8	107.1
February	110.4	114.2	118.8	128.8	109.2	187.7	166.0	108.1	108.7	115.9	107.0	109.9	107.3
March	110.7	114.3	120.5	128.2	109.1	187.7	165.9	108.6	109.5	116.8	107.3	109.9	107.6
April	110.8	114.9	123.2	128.6	109.3	187.8	166.0	108.5	108.9	117.8	107.3	110.3	107.6
May	111.0	114.6	122.6	127.1	109.3	188.2	166.2	108.9	110.2	118.2	107.2	110.3	107.9
June	111.0	114.7	122.6	127.1	109.4	188.5	166.4	108.8	109.5	118.3	107.4	110.4	107.9
July	111.3	114.5	122.3	125.9	109.6	188.7	166.5	109.4	111.4	118.3	107.5	110.8	108.4
August	111.3	114.5	121.9	125.4	109.7	188.9	166.6	109.4	110.6	118.8	107.8	110.9	108.4
September	111.1	114.2	121.7	123.9	109.9	189.2	166.8	109.2	109.8	118.4	107.9	110.9	108.2
October	111.3	113.6	122.4	119.8	109.9	189.6	167.1	109.8	111.9	117.8	107.9	111.5	108.7
November	111.1	113.1	122.4	117.3	109.8	189.8	167.1	109.8	111.6	117.8	108.1	111.4	108.7
December	110.7	111.5	121.9	108.8	109.8	189.9	166.9	110.0	112.1	118.1	108.2	111.6	108.9
2015													
January	110.1	109.6	121.4	98.8	109.9	190.7	167.6	110.1	112.7	116.7	108.0	112.0	108.9
February	109.7	109.4	119.4	99.9	109.8	191.3	168.1	109.5	110.8	115.9	108.1	112.1	108.5
March	109.7	109.4	118.6	100.5	109.8	191.5	168.3	109.6	111.0	115.9	108.2	112.1	108.5
April	109.7	108.9	117.6	98.4	109.8	191.5	168.3	109.8	110.9	115.7	108.6	112.1	108.7
May	110.1	110.0	118.8	103.2	109.9	191.8	168.5	109.8	111.1	115.9	108.5	112.2	108.7
June	110.4	110.4	119.3	103.6	110.3	192.7	168.5	110.0	111.4	115.9	108.7	112.2	109.0
July	110.5	110.2	118.4	102.9	110.3	193.0	168.8	110.4	112.3	115.8	108.9	112.8	109.2
August	110.3	109.7	118.8	100.5	110.1	193.0	168.8	110.3	111.7	114.8	109.1	112.9	109.1
September	109.8	108.5	118.2	94.7	110.1	193.3	168.9	110.2	112.0	114.5	108.9	112.9	109.1
October	109.6	108.1	117.5	94.1	109.8	193.0	168.7	110.0	111.7	114.3	108.8	113.9	108.9
November	109.7	108.0	117.0	94.5	109.7	193.2	168.7	110.2	111.9	114.5	108.9	113.8	109.0
December	109.5	107.2	115.8	90.7	109.8	193.4	168.8	110.3	112.1	113.8	109.2	113.9	109.1
2016													
January	110.0	106.9	117.1	87.8	109.9	193.8	168.7	111.3	114.0	114.0	109.8	113.4	109.9
February	109.8	106.3	117.0	84.4	110.0	194.1	168.8	111.3	113.5	113.7	110.0	113.4	109.8
March	109.6	106.3	115.6	85.2	110.1	194.3	168.9	111.0	112.6	113.7	110.0	113.3	109.7
April	109.9	106.7	115.1	86.7	110.4	194.6	169.0	111.2	112.8	113.6	110.3	114.4	109.9
May	110.1	107.4	115.6	89.2	110.6	194.9	169.2	111.2	113.0	113.0	110.2	114.4	110.0
June	110.6	108.1	116.1	91.6	110.8	195.5	169.5	111.6	113.8	113.1	110.4	114.4	110.3
July	110.5	107.9	115.3	91.3	110.8	195.4	169.3	111.6	112.9	113.5	110.8	113.6	110.3
August	110.3	107.6	114.0	90.5	111.0	195.6	169.3	111.4	112.1	112.9	110.9	113.7	110.2
September	110.6	108.1	114.6	91.9	111.1	196.0	169.5	111.7	112.9	112.4	111.1	113.7	110.4
October	110.9	108.4	113.7	94.4	111.1	196.0	169.3	111.8	113.3	113.3	111.1	114.6	110.5
November	111.1	108.5	113.0	94.6	111.4	196.3	169.5	112.1	113.5	113.8	111.3	114.6	110.8
December	111.3	109.2	113.9	96.4	111.7	196.8	169.9	112.1	113.1	115.1	111.4	114.6	110.9

Table 8-6. Producer Price Indexes for Goods and Services: Intermediate Demand

(November 2009 = 100, except as noted.)

Year and month	Intermediate demand by commodity type						Intermediate demand by production flow (Prices of inputs to indicated stage of production)			
	Processed goods (1982=100)	Unprocessed goods (1982=100)	Services	Construction	Processed materials less foods and energy (1982=100)	Unprocessed nonfood materials less energy (1982 =100)	Stage 4 intermediate demand	Stage 3 intermediate demand	Stage 2 intermediate demand	Stage 1 intermediate demand
NOT SEASONALLY ADJUSTED										
2010	183.4	212.2	101.1	101.1	180.8	329.1	102.0	104.2	103.5	106.2
2011	199.9	249.4	103.2	102.3	192.0	390.4	106.9	111.7	112.9	115.7
2012	200.7	241.4	105.3	103.8	192.6	369.6	108.6	112.7	110.7	114.7
2013	200.8	246.7	107.2	105.7	193.8	351.2	109.9	114.1	112.8	114.8
2014	201.9	249.3	108.9	108.0	195.2	345.7	111.2	116.9	112.2	116.1
2015	188.0	189.1	110.2	110.1	189.4	296.0	109.9	110.5	98.9	106.8
2016	182.2	173.4	112.1	111.7	186.9	288.0	109.8	107.3	98.3	104.2
2013										
January	200.0	247.3	106.8	104.9	193.5	364.2	109.4	113.5	112.3	114.2
February	202.5	246.1	106.7	105.3	194.7	363.0	109.8	114.3	112.5	115.4
March	201.5	248.7	106.9	105.7	194.6	367.1	109.7	114.1	112.6	115.3
April	200.8	249.2	107.4	105.6	194.2	358.3	109.9	114.3	113.4	114.6
May	201.0	252.5	106.9	105.6	193.9	351.3	109.8	114.5	113.3	114.5
June	201.3	251.3	107.2	105.6	193.8	349.0	110.0	114.6	113.4	114.9
July	201.3	252.9	107.2	105.6	193.4	347.0	110.1	114.0	114.4	115.3
August	201.6	247.2	107.4	105.8	193.6	345.7	110.3	114.1	113.6	115.7
September	201.5	246.2	107.4	106.1	193.5	342.0	110.2	114.0	113.8	115.3
October	200.1	241.2	107.6	106.1	193.4	338.7	110.1	113.8	112.0	114.4
November	198.8	236.7	107.8	106.1	193.3	341.7	109.8	113.7	110.3	114.0
December	199.3	240.7	107.5	106.0	193.5	346.1	109.8	113.6	111.4	114.4
2014										
January	200.9	246.0	108.0	107.0	194.4	354.2	110.3	115.1	112.3	116.1
February	202.1	258.6	108.2	107.2	195.2	351.3	110.5	115.9	116.5	116.4
March	203.0	262.0	108.7	107.3	195.0	350.7	111.2	117.5	115.3	116.6
April	203.8	265.4	108.5	107.6	195.5	356.3	111.4	118.0	115.4	116.6
May	203.8	263.0	108.5	107.6	195.4	354.4	111.4	117.7	115.1	116.5
June	204.3	260.5	108.6	107.8	195.4	349.1	111.6	117.7	115.0	117.1
July	204.5	255.3	109.2	108.1	196.0	348.7	111.9	118.1	113.9	118.2
August	204.4	245.9	109.2	108.2	196.4	345.6	111.9	117.6	112.0	118.2
September	203.8	245.6	109.0	108.4	196.2	345.4	111.8	117.8	111.3	117.4
October	200.5	236.2	109.5	108.7	195.5	335.2	111.3	117.0	108.5	115.5
November	197.7	232.9	109.4	108.9	194.6	329.9	110.8	116.3	107.0	113.2
December	194.2	219.7	109.4	108.9	193.4	327.9	110.3	113.8	104.3	111.6
2015										
January	189.7	199.7	109.8	109.2	191.6	325.5	110.0	111.1	100.1	108.8
February	189.2	193.4	109.6	109.2	191.1	309.5	109.8	110.1	99.8	107.7
March	189.3	193.9	110.0	109.4	190.6	306.0	110.0	111.1	99.6	107.8
April	188.3	195.5	110.6	109.5	190.4	306.3	110.1	111.0	99.8	107.6
May	190.2	202.5	110.4	110.0	190.5	305.6	110.5	112.8	100.7	108.3
June	191.6	203.3	110.5	110.3	190.5	306.3	110.8	113.1	101.0	109.1
July	191.2	196.1	110.7	110.4	190.1	303.0	110.8	112.5	100.3	109.0
August	189.6	187.6	110.9	110.4	189.2	288.3	110.6	111.8	99.0	107.7
September	186.8	182.4	110.2	110.5	188.0	286.8	109.9	109.6	97.9	105.8
October	185.1	179.5	109.7	110.6	187.4	278.8	109.3	108.5	97.5	104.6
November	183.4	171.3	109.8	110.7	186.8	268.6	109.0	107.6	96.1	103.4
December	181.3	164.1	109.9	110.7	186.1	267.2	108.6	106.2	95.6	102.0
2016										
January	179.6	164.7	111.5	110.8	185.6	266.6	109.0	106.7	95.6	102.0
February	178.3	161.7	111.7	110.9	185.1	269.2	108.9	106.0	95.1	101.6
March	178.8	166.0	111.8	110.9	185.3	276.9	109.0	106.5	95.6	102.2
April	179.7	170.1	111.8	111.0	185.9	287.1	109.2	106.7	96.5	103.2
May	181.6	176.6	111.6	111.3	186.5	297.0	109.5	107.4	97.8	104.3
June	183.8	181.3	112.1	111.3	186.9	296.8	110.2	108.5	99.1	105.6
July	184.2	181.2	112.6	111.4	187.0	295.8	110.4	108.6	99.9	105.6
August	183.9	175.4	112.3	112.1	187.5	295.4	110.2	107.7	99.2	105.0
September	184.4	173.5	112.2	112.4	187.5	289.1	110.2	107.4	99.3	105.0
October	184.0	171.6	112.3	112.5	187.8	285.2	110.0	106.6	100.2	104.7
November	183.6	173.0	112.7	112.8	188.4	292.6	110.1	107.4	99.7	105.2
December	184.6	185.4	112.8	113.2	189.0	303.9	110.4	108.3	101.7	106.5

Table 8-6. Producer Price Indexes for Goods and Services: Intermediate Demand—*Continued*

(November 2009 = 100, except as noted.)

Year and month	Intermediate demand by commodity type						Intermediate demand by production flow (Prices of inputs to indicated stage of production)			
	Processed goods (1982=100)	Unprocessed goods (1982=100)	Services	Construction	Processed materials less foods and energy (1982=100)	Unprocessed nonfood materials less energy (1982 =100)	Stage 4 intermediate demand	Stage 3 intermediate demand	Stage 2 intermediate demand	Stage 1 intermediate demand
SEASONALLY ADJUSTED										
2013										
January	201.7	248.6	106.8	104.8	193.8	364.4	109.8	114.1	112.7	115.1
February	203.9	246.8	106.7	105.2	194.7	362.2	110.1	114.7	112.8	116.1
March	201.7	246.9	106.8	105.6	194.4	365.2	109.7	113.9	112.6	115.5
April	200.4	246.9	107.3	105.6	193.9	356.1	109.7	113.9	113.2	114.7
May	200.2	249.6	106.8	105.5	193.6	349.2	109.5	113.9	113.0	114.2
June	200.1	240.4	107.1	105.6	193.6	346.6	109.6	114.0	112.9	114.1
July	200.1	252.0	107.1	105.6	193.2	347.5	109.8	113.6	114.2	114.3
August	200.4	247.5	107.3	105.9	193.6	346.8	109.9	113.8	113.5	114.7
September	200.4	247.3	107.5	106.2	193.6	343.5	110.0	113.8	113.7	114.5
October	200.2	243.2	107.6	106.2	193.6	340.6	110.1	114.0	112.1	114.5
November	199.9	238.4	107.9	106.2	193.6	343.5	110.2	114.2	110.6	114.9
December	200.8	243.0	107.7	106.1	194.0	347.1	110.3	114.5	111.8	115.3
2014										
January	202.6	247.2	108.1	106.9	194.7	354.2	110.7	115.8	112.7	117.0
February	203.6	259.9	108.2	107.1	195.3	350.6	110.9	116.5	116.8	117.2
March	203.3	261.0	108.6	107.2	194.8	349.2	111.2	117.5	115.3	116.9
April	203.7	264.0	108.5	107.6	195.2	354.4	111.3	117.8	115.2	116.8
May	203.0	260.1	108.4	107.5	195.1	352.6	111.1	117.2	114.8	116.3
June	202.9	257.6	108.5	107.8	195.1	347.5	111.2	117.0	114.6	116.2
July	203.1	253.9	109.1	108.1	195.8	349.2	111.5	117.5	113.7	117.1
August	203.1	246.0	109.1	108.3	196.3	346.7	111.5	117.2	111.9	117.1
September	202.6	246.9	109.1	108.4	196.3	346.9	111.5	117.5	111.3	116.6
October	200.6	238.2	109.4	108.8	195.7	336.9	111.4	117.2	108.6	115.5
November	198.8	234.9	109.5	109.1	194.8	331.5	111.2	116.9	107.2	114.1
December	195.5	222.0	109.7	109.0	193.9	328.6	110.8	114.7	104.7	112.4
2015										
January	190.9	200.8	109.8	109.1	191.8	325.5	110.2	111.9	100.2	109.5
February	190.3	194.5	109.6	109.1	191.2	308.6	110.0	110.9	99.9	108.2
March	189.7	192.6	109.9	109.4	190.6	304.2	110.0	111.1	99.4	107.9
April	188.4	193.8	110.5	109.5	190.2	304.3	110.1	110.7	99.7	107.5
May	189.7	199.5	110.3	109.9	190.2	303.5	110.4	112.0	100.5	108.1
June	190.4	200.8	110.4	110.3	190.1	304.2	110.5	112.3	100.7	108.5
July	189.9	194.8	110.7	110.4	189.9	303.3	110.5	111.8	100.0	108.4
August	188.4	187.8	110.9	110.4	189.1	290.0	110.3	111.3	98.9	107.3
September	185.8	183.5	110.3	110.5	188.0	289.1	109.7	109.4	98.1	105.6
October	185.1	181.3	109.8	110.6	187.6	281.2	109.4	108.6	97.6	104.6
November	184.3	172.6	109.9	110.8	187.1	270.5	109.3	108.2	96.4	103.8
December	182.3	166.0	110.1	110.8	186.5	267.8	108.9	107.1	95.9	102.5
2016										
January	180.7	166.0	111.5	110.7	185.8	266.5	109.2	107.3	95.8	102.5
February	179.3	163.1	111.7	110.8	185.3	268.3	109.1	106.6	95.2	102.0
March	179.2	165.3	111.7	110.9	185.3	275.4	109.0	106.6	95.6	102.3
April	179.9	168.9	111.7	111.1	185.8	285.3	109.2	106.6	96.4	103.2
May	181.3	173.8	111.6	111.3	186.3	294.9	109.4	106.8	97.6	104.1
June	182.7	178.2	112.1	111.3	186.6	294.4	109.9	107.7	98.7	105.0
July	183.0	179.6	112.5	111.4	186.8	296.1	110.1	107.9	99.6	105.1
August	182.9	175.8	112.3	112.1	187.4	297.1	109.9	107.3	99.1	104.6
September	183.5	174.8	112.2	112.4	187.6	291.2	110.0	107.2	99.4	104.7
October	184.1	173.5	112.3	112.5	187.9	287.3	110.1	106.7	100.4	104.7
November	184.5	174.6	112.8	112.8	188.7	294.4	110.3	107.9	100.0	105.5
December	185.6	187.4	113.0	113.3	189.4	304.5	110.7	109.2	102.0	107.0

Table 8-7. Producer Price Indexes by Major Commodity Groups

(1982 = 100.)

Year and month	All commodities	Farm products	Processed foods and feeds	Industrial commodities													
				Total	Textile products and apparel	Hides, leather, and related products	Fuels and related products and power	Chemicals and allied products	Rubber and plastics products	Lumber and wood products	Pulp, paper, and allied products	Metals and metal products	Machinery and equipment	Furniture and household durables	Nonmetallic mineral products	Transportation equipment	Miscellaneous products
1950	27.3	44.0	33.2	25.0	50.2	32.9	12.6	30.4	35.6	31.4	25.7	22.0	22.6	40.9	23.5	. . .	28.6
1951	30.4	51.2	36.9	27.6	56.0	37.7	13.0	34.8	43.7	34.1	30.5	24.5	25.3	44.4	25.0	. . .	30.3
1952	29.6	48.4	36.4	26.9	50.5	30.5	13.0	33.0	39.6	33.2	29.7	24.5	25.3	43.5	25.0	. . .	30.2
1953	29.2	43.8	34.8	27.2	49.3	31.0	13.4	33.4	36.9	33.1	29.6	25.3	25.9	44.4	26.0	. . .	31.0
1954	29.3	43.2	35.4	27.2	48.2	29.5	13.2	33.8	37.5	32.5	29.6	25.5	26.3	44.9	26.6	. . .	31.3
1955	29.3	40.5	33.8	27.8	48.2	29.4	13.2	33.7	42.4	34.1	30.4	27.2	27.2	45.1	27.3	. . .	31.3
1956	30.3	40.0	33.8	29.1	48.2	31.2	13.6	33.9	43.0	34.6	32.4	29.6	29.3	46.3	28.5	. . .	31.7
1957	31.2	41.1	34.8	29.9	48.3	31.2	14.3	34.6	42.8	32.8	33.0	30.2	31.4	47.5	29.6	. . .	32.6
1958	31.6	42.9	36.5	30.0	47.4	31.6	13.7	34.9	42.8	32.5	33.4	30.0	32.1	47.9	29.9	. . .	33.3
1959	31.7	40.2	35.6	30.5	48.1	35.9	13.7	34.8	42.6	34.7	33.7	30.6	32.8	48.0	30.3	. . .	33.4
1960	31.7	40.1	35.6	30.5	48.6	34.6	13.9	34.8	42.7	33.5	34.0	30.6	33.0	47.8	30.4	. . .	33.6
1961	31.6	39.7	36.2	30.4	47.8	34.9	14.0	34.5	41.1	32.0	33.0	30.5	33.0	47.5	30.5	. . .	33.7
1962	31.7	40.4	36.5	30.4	48.2	35.3	14.0	33.9	39.9	32.2	33.4	30.2	33.0	47.2	30.5	. . .	33.9
1963	31.6	39.6	36.8	30.3	48.2	34.3	13.9	33.5	40.1	32.8	33.1	30.3	33.1	46.9	30.3	. . .	34.2
1964	31.6	39.0	36.7	30.5	48.5	34.4	13.5	33.6	39.6	33.5	33.0	31.1	33.3	47.1	30.4	. . .	34.4
1965	32.3	40.7	38.0	30.9	48.8	35.9	13.8	33.9	39.7	33.7	33.3	32.0	33.7	46.8	30.4	. . .	34.7
1966	33.3	43.7	40.2	31.5	48.9	39.4	14.1	34.0	40.5	35.2	34.2	32.8	34.7	47.4	30.7	. . .	35.3
1967	33.4	41.3	39.8	32.0	48.9	38.1	14.4	34.2	41.4	35.1	34.6	33.2	35.9	48.3	31.2	. . .	36.2
1968	34.2	42.3	40.6	32.8	50.7	39.3	14.3	34.1	42.8	39.8	35.0	34.0	37.0	49.7	32.4	. . .	37.0
1969	35.6	45.0	42.7	33.9	51.8	41.5	14.6	34.2	43.6	44.0	36.0	36.0	38.2	50.7	33.6	40.4	38.1
1970	36.9	45.8	44.6	35.2	52.4	42.0	15.3	35.0	44.9	39.9	37.5	38.7	40.0	51.9	35.3	41.9	39.8
1971	38.1	46.6	45.5	36.5	53.3	43.4	16.6	35.6	45.2	44.7	38.1	39.4	41.4	53.1	38.2	44.2	40.8
1972	39.8	51.6	48.0	37.8	55.5	50.0	17.1	35.6	45.3	50.7	39.3	40.9	42.3	53.8	39.4	45.5	41.5
1973	45.0	72.7	58.9	40.3	60.5	54.5	19.4	37.6	46.6	62.2	42.3	44.0	43.7	55.7	40.7	46.1	43.3
1974	53.5	77.4	68.0	49.2	68.0	55.2	30.1	50.2	56.4	64.5	52.5	57.0	50.0	61.8	47.8	50.3	48.1
1975	58.4	77.0	72.6	54.9	67.4	56.5	35.4	62.0	62.2	62.1	59.0	61.5	57.9	67.5	54.4	56.7	53.4
1976	61.1	78.8	70.8	58.4	72.4	63.9	38.3	64.0	66.0	72.2	62.1	65.0	61.3	70.3	58.2	60.5	55.6
1977	64.9	79.4	74.0	62.5	75.3	68.3	43.6	65.9	69.4	83.0	64.6	69.3	65.2	73.2	62.6	64.6	59.4
1978	69.9	87.7	80.6	67.0	78.1	76.1	46.5	68.0	72.4	96.9	67.7	75.3	70.3	77.5	69.6	69.5	66.7
1979	78.7	99.6	88.5	75.7	82.5	96.1	58.9	76.0	80.5	105.5	75.9	86.0	76.7	82.8	77.6	75.3	75.5
1980	89.8	102.9	95.9	88.0	89.7	94.7	82.8	89.0	90.1	101.5	86.3	95.0	86.0	90.7	88.4	82.9	93.6
1981	98.0	105.2	98.9	97.4	97.6	99.3	100.2	98.4	96.4	102.8	94.8	99.6	94.4	95.9	96.7	94.3	96.1
1982	100.0	100.0	100.0	100.0	100.0	100.0	100.0	100.0	100.0	100.0	100.0	100.0	100.0	100.0	100.0	100.0	100.0
1983	101.3	102.4	101.8	101.1	100.3	103.2	95.9	100.3	100.8	107.9	103.3	101.8	102.7	103.4	101.6	102.8	104.8
1984	103.7	105.5	105.4	103.3	102.7	109.0	94.8	102.9	102.3	108.0	110.3	104.8	105.1	105.7	105.4	105.2	107.0
1985	103.2	95.1	103.5	103.7	102.9	108.9	91.4	103.7	101.9	106.6	113.3	104.4	107.2	107.1	108.6	107.9	109.4
1986	100.2	92.9	105.4	100.0	103.2	113.0	69.8	102.6	101.9	107.2	116.1	103.2	108.8	108.2	110.0	110.5	111.6
1987	102.8	95.5	107.9	102.6	105.1	120.4	70.2	106.4	103.0	112.8	121.8	107.1	110.4	109.9	110.0	112.5	114.9
1988	106.9	104.9	112.7	106.3	109.2	131.4	66.7	116.3	109.3	118.9	130.4	118.7	113.2	113.1	111.2	114.3	120.2
1989	112.2	110.9	117.8	111.6	112.3	136.3	72.9	123.0	112.6	126.7	137.8	124.1	117.4	116.9	112.6	117.7	126.5
1990	116.3	112.2	121.9	115.8	115.0	141.7	82.3	123.6	113.6	129.7	141.2	122.9	120.7	119.2	114.7	121.5	134.2
1991	116.5	105.7	121.9	116.5	116.3	138.9	81.2	125.6	115.1	132.1	142.9	120.2	123.0	121.2	117.2	126.4	140.8
1992	117.2	103.6	122.1	117.4	117.8	140.4	80.4	125.9	115.1	146.6	145.2	119.2	123.4	122.2	117.3	130.4	145.3
1993	118.9	107.1	124.0	119.0	118.0	143.7	80.0	128.2	116.0	174.0	147.3	119.2	124.0	123.7	120.0	133.7	145.4
1994	120.4	106.3	125.5	120.7	118.3	148.5	77.8	132.1	117.6	180.0	152.5	124.8	125.1	126.1	124.2	137.2	141.9
1995	124.7	107.4	127.0	125.5	120.8	153.7	78.0	142.5	124.3	178.1	172.2	134.5	126.6	128.2	129.0	139.7	145.4
1996	127.7	122.4	133.3	127.3	122.4	150.5	85.8	142.1	123.8	176.1	168.7	131.0	126.5	130.0	131.0	141.7	147.7
1997	127.6	112.9	134.0	127.7	122.6	154.2	86.1	143.6	123.2	183.8	167.9	131.8	125.9	130.8	133.2	141.6	150.9
1998	124.4	104.6	131.6	124.8	122.9	148.0	75.3	143.9	122.6	179.1	171.7	127.8	124.9	131.3	135.4	141.2	156.0
1999	125.5	98.4	131.1	126.5	121.1	146.0	80.5	144.2	122.5	183.6	174.1	124.6	124.3	131.7	138.9	141.8	166.6
2000	132.7	99.5	133.1	134.8	121.4	151.5	103.5	151.0	125.5	178.2	183.7	128.1	124.0	132.6	142.5	143.8	170.8
2001	134.2	103.8	137.3	135.7	121.3	158.4	105.3	151.8	127.2	174.4	184.8	125.4	123.7	133.2	144.3	145.2	181.3
2002	131.1	99.0	136.2	132.4	119.9	157.6	93.2	151.9	126.8	173.3	185.9	125.9	122.9	133.5	146.2	144.6	182.4
2003	138.1	111.5	143.4	139.1	119.8	162.3	112.9	161.8	130.1	177.4	190.0	129.2	121.9	133.8	148.2	145.7	179.6
2004	146.7	123.3	151.2	147.6	121.0	164.5	126.9	174.4	133.8	195.6	195.7	149.6	122.1	135.1	153.2	148.6	183.2
2005	157.4	118.5	153.1	160.2	122.8	165.4	156.4	192.0	143.8	196.5	202.6	160.8	123.7	139.4	164.2	151.0	195.1
2006	164.7	117.0	153.8	168.8	124.5	168.4	166.7	205.8	153.8	194.4	209.8	181.6	126.2	142.6	179.9	152.6	205.6
2007	172.6	143.4	165.1	175.1	125.8	173.6	177.6	214.8	155.0	192.4	216.9	193.5	127.3	144.7	186.2	155.0	210.3
2008	189.6	161.3	180.5	192.3	128.9	173.1	214.6	245.5	165.9	191.3	226.8	213.0	129.7	148.9	197.1	158.6	216.6
2009	172.9	134.6	176.2	174.8	129.5	157.0	158.7	229.4	165.2	182.8	225.6	186.8	131.3	153.1	202.4	162.2	217.5
2010	184.7	151.0	182.3	187.0	131.7	181.4	185.8	246.6	170.7	192.7	236.9	207.6	131.1	153.2	201.8	163.4	221.5
2011	201.0	186.7	197.5	202.0	141.7	199.9	215.9	275.1	182.7	194.7	245.1	225.9	132.7	156.4	205.0	166.1	229.2
2012	202.2	192.5	205.2	202.1	142.2	202.3	212.1	276.6	186.9	201.6	244.2	219.9	134.2	160.6	211.0	169.8	235.6
2013	203.4	195.3	208.3	203.0	143.4	217.9	211.8	279.2	189.0	214.9	248.8	213.5	135.2	161.1	216.9	171.8	239.5
2014	205.3	197.4	216.5	204.1	145.5	229.1	209.8	280.9	190.2	224.2	250.5	215.0	136.2	163.2	223.7	174.1	243.0
2015	190.4	173.8	209.1	188.8	144.1	210.4	160.5	266.0	187.0	221.9	248.8	200.3	136.9	164.7	228.9	176.5	247.4
2016	185.4	157.0	203.5	184.6	143.3	195.1	145.9	265.1	184.6	222.7	247.7	194.3	136.9	165.1	233.3	177.4	252.1

. . . = Not available.

NOTES AND DEFINITIONS, CHAPTER 8

This chapter presents price indexes (Consumer and Producer) from two major price collection systems, both conducted by the U.S. Bureau of Labor Statistics. Effective on February 26, 2015, the Bureau of Labor Statistics began utilizing a new estimation system for the Consumer Price Index. The new estimation system, the first major improvement to the existing system in over 25 years. This system is redesigned, state-of-the-art with improved flexibility and review capabilities.

In 2014, the Producer Price Index system was expanded to include services and construction as well as goods. A new index for "Final Demand" for goods, services and construction, with more than double the scope, is now presented alongside the familiar Finished Goods index. The expanded system is only available beginning in November 2009, and the historical Producer Price Indexes for goods—with data going back to 1913—are also maintained and carried forward. See the Notes and Definitions for Tables 8-5 through 8-7, below, for further information.

TABLES 8-1 THROUGH 8-4

Consumer Price Indexes

SOURCES: U.S. DEPARTMENT OF LABOR, BUREAU OF LABOR STATISTICS (BLS) AND U.S. DEPARTMENT OF COMMERCE, BUREAU OF ECONOMIC ANALYSIS (BEA)

The Consumer Price Index (CPI), which is compiled by the Bureau of Labor Statistics (BLS), was originally conceived as a statistical measure of the average change in the cost to consumers of a market basket of goods and services purchased by urban wage earners and clerical workers. In 1978, its scope was broadened to also provide a measure of the change in the cost of the average market basket for all urban consumers. There was still a demand for a wage-earner index, so both versions have been calculated and published since then. The most commonly cited measure in this system is the Consumer Price Index for All Urban Consumers (CPI-U). The wage-earner alternative, used according to law for calculating cost of living adjustments in many government programs, including Social Security, and also used by choice of the contracting parties in wage agreements, is called the Consumer Price Index for Urban Wage Earners and Clerical Workers (CPI-W). Both are presented by the BLS back to 1913, and reproduced in *Business Statistics*; however, the movements (percent changes) in the two indexes before 1978 are identical and are based on the wage-earner market basket. (The pre-1978 levels of the two indexes differ because of differences between 1978 and the reference base period.)

These CPIs have typically been called "cost-of-living" indexes, even though the original fixed market basket concept does not correspond to economists' definition of a cost-of-living index, which is the cost of maintaining a constant standard of living

or level of satisfaction. In recent years, the concept measured in practice in the CPI has developed into something intended to be closer to the theoretical definition of a cost-of-living index. In addition, a new variation of the CPI—the Chained Consumer Price Index for All Urban Consumers (C-CPI-U)—is intended to provide an even closer approximation.

The reference base for the total BLS Consumer Price Index and most of its components is currently 1982–1984 = 100. However, new products that have been introduced into the index since January 1982 are shown on later reference bases, as is the entire C-CPI-U.

Price indexes for personal consumption expenditures (PCE) are calculated and published by the Bureau of Economic Analysis (BEA) as a part of the national income and product accounts (NIPAs). (See Chapters 1 and 4 and their notes and definitions.) Monthly, quarterly, and annual values are all available. The reference base for these indexes is the average in the NIPA base year, 2009. These indexes differ in a number of other respects from the CPIs, and are often emphasized by the Federal Reserve in its analyses of the nation's economy. The Federal Reserve is mandated to maximize employment (see Chapter 10) and maintain price stability as measured by the Consumer Price Index (CPI). The target inflation rate is 2 percent. Four important NIPA aggregate price indexes are shown in Tables 8-3 and 8-4 for convenient comparison with the CPIs. See the definitions for those tables for more information.

The CPI-U and the CPI-W

The *CPI-U*, which is displayed in Tables 8-1 through 8-4 and also provides all of the component category sub-indexes shown in Table 8-2, uses the consumption patterns for all urban consumers, who currently comprise about 89 percent of the population.

A slightly different index that is widely used for adjusting wages and government benefits is the *CPI-W*, of which the all-items total is shown in each of Tables 8-1 through 8-4. It represents the buying habits of only urban wage earners and clerical workers, who currently comprise about 28 percent of the population. The weights are derived from the same Consumer Expenditure Surveys (CES) used for the CPI-U weights, and are changed on the same schedule. However, they include only consumers from the specified categories instead of all urban consumers.

Beginning with February 2016, the weights in both indexes are based on consumer expenditures in the 2014-2015 period. In January 2012, the weights in both indexes are based on consumer expenditures in the 2009–2010 period. From January 2010 to December 2011, 2007–2008 weights were used; from January 2008 to December 2009, 2005–2006 weights; from January 2006 to December 2007, 2003–2004 weights; from January 2004 to December 2005, 2001–2002 weights; from January 2002 to December 2003, 1999–2000 weights; and from January 1998 to December 2001, 1993–1995 weights. The weights will continue to be updated at two-year intervals, with new weights introduced in the January indexes of each even-numbered year. Previously, new weights were introduced only at the time of a major revision, which translated into a lag of a decade or more.

Specifically, the CPI weights for 1964 through 1977 were derived from reported expenditures of a sample of wageearner and clericalworker families and individuals in 1960–1961 and adjusted for price changes between the survey dates and 1963. Weights for the 1978–1986 period were derived from a survey undertaken during the 1972–1974 period and adjusted for price change between the survey dates and December 1977. For 1987 through 1997, the spending patterns reflected in the CPI were derived from a survey undertaken during the 1982–1984 period. The reported expenditures were adjusted for price change between the survey dates and December 1986.

The CPI was overhauled and updated in the latest major revision, which took effect in January 1998. In addition, new products and improved methods are regularly introduced into the index, usually in January.

The latest change in methods was the introduction of a geometric mean formula for calculating many of the basic components of the index. Beginning with the index for January 1999, this formula is used for categories comprising approximately 61 percent of total consumer spending. The new formula allows for the possibility that some consumers may react to changing relative prices within a category by substituting items whose relative prices have declined for products whose relative prices have risen, while maintaining their overall level of satisfaction. The geometric mean formula is not used for a few categories in which consumer substitution in the short term is not feasible, currently housing rent and utilities.

The CPI-U was introduced in 1978. Before that time, only CPI-W data were available. The movements of the CPI-U before 1978 are therefore based on the changes in the CPI-W. However, the index levels are different because the two indexes differed in the 1982–1984 base period.

Because the official CPI-U and CPI-W are so widely used in "escalation"—the calculation of cost-of-living adjustments for wages and other private contracts, and for government payments and tax parameters—these price indexes are not retrospectively revised to incorporate new information and methods. (An exception is occasionally made for outright error, which happened in September 2000 and affected the data for January through August of that year.) Instead, the new information and methods of calculation are introduced in the current index and affect future index changes only. In Tables 8-3 and 8-4, PCE indexes, which are subject to routine revision, and special CPI indexes that have been retrospectively revised are presented. These indexes can be used by researchers to provide more consistent historical information.

Notes on the CPI data

The CPI is based on prices of food, clothing, shelter, fuel, utilities, transportation, medical care, and other goods and services that people buy for daytoday living. The quantity and quality of these priced items are kept essentially constant between revisions to ensure that only price changes will be measured. All taxes directly associated with the purchase and use of these items, such as sales and property taxes, are included in the index; the effects of income and payroll tax changes are not included.

Data are collected on about 83,400 individually defined goods and services from about 27,000 retail and service establishments in 87 urban areas across the country. Data on rents are collected from about 50,000 landlords or tenants. These data are used to develop the U.S. city average.

Periodic major revisions of the indexes update the content and weights of the market basket of goods and services; update the statistical sample of urban areas, outlets, and unique items used in calculating the CPI; and improve the statistical methods used. In addition, retail outlets and items are resampled on a rotating 5-year basis. Adjustments for changing quality are made at times of major product changes, such as the annual auto model changeover. Other methodological changes are introduced from time to time.

The Consumer Expenditure Survey (CES) provides the weights—that is, the relative importance—used to combine the individual price changes into subtotals and totals. This survey is composed of two separate surveys: an interview survey and a diary survey, both of which are conducted by the Census Bureau for BLS. Each expenditure reported in the two surveys is classified into a series of detailed categories, which are then combined into expenditure classes and ultimately into major expenditure groups. CPI data as of 1998 are grouped into eight such categories: (1) food and beverages, (2) housing, (3) apparel, (4) transportation, (5) medical care, (6) recreation, (7) education and communication, and (8) other goods and services.

Seasonally adjusted national CPI indexes are published for selected series for which there is a significant seasonal pattern of price change. The factors currently in use were derived by the X-13-ARIMA-SEATS seasonal adjustment method. Some series with extreme or sharp movements are seasonally adjusted using Intervention Analysis Seasonal Adjustment. Seasonally adjusted indexes and seasonal factors for the preceding five years are updated annually based on data through the previous December. Due to these revisions, BLS advises against the use of seasonally adjusted data for escalation. Detailed descriptions of seasonal adjustment procedures are available upon request from BLS.

BLS estimates the "standard error"—the error due to collecting data from a sample instead of the universe—of the one-month percent change in the not-seasonally-adjusted U.S. all-items index in 2013 was 0.03 percentage point. This means that for the 2013 median 0.12 percent change in the All Items CPI-U, BLS is 95 percent confident that the actual percent change based on all retail prices would fall between 0.06 and 0.18 percent. Monthly percent changes in the seasonally adjusted indexes, in contrast, may be revised by 0.1 percentage point when reviewed at the end of the year, and occasionally by even more.

CPI Definitions

Definitions of the major CPI groupings were modified beginning with the data for January 1998. These modifications were carried back to 1993. The following definitions are the current definitions currently used for the CPI components.

The *food and beverage index* includes both food at home and food away from home (restaurant meals and other food bought and eaten away from home).

The *housing index* measures changes in rental costs and expenses connected with the acquisition and operation of a home. The CPIU, beginning with data for January 1983, and the CPIW, beginning with data for January 1985, reflect a change in the methodology used to compute the homeownership component. A rental equivalence measure replaced an assetprice approach, which included purchase prices and interest costs. The intent of the change was to separate shelter costs from the investment component of homeownership, so that the index would only reflect the cost of the shelter services provided by owner-occupied homes. In addition to measures of the cost of shelter, the housing category includes insurance, fuel, utilities, and household furnishings and operations.

The *apparel index* includes the purchase of apparel and footwear.

The *private transportation index* includes prices paid by urban consumers for such items as new and used automobiles and other vehicles, gasoline, motor oil, tires, repairs and maintenance, insurance, registration fees, driver's licenses, parking fees, and the like. Auto finance charges, like mortgage interest payments, are considered to be a cost of asset acquisition, not of current consumption. Therefore, they are no longer included in the CPI. City bus, streetcar, subway, taxicab, intercity bus, airplane, and railroad coach fares are some of the components of the *public transportation index*.

The *medical care index* includes prices for professional medical services, hospital and related services, prescription and nonprescription drugs, and other medical care commodities. The weight for the portion of health insurance premiums that is used to cover the costs of these medical goods and services is distributed among the items; the weight for the portion of health insurance costs attributable to administrative expenses and profits of insurance providers constitutes a separate health insurance item. Effective with the January 1997 data, the method of calculating the hospital cost component was changed from the pricing of individual commodities and services to a more comprehensive cost-of-treatment approach.

Recreation includes components formerly listed in housing, apparel, entertainment, and "other goods and services."

Education and communication is a new group including components formerly categorized in housing and "other goods and services," such as college tuition and books, telephone and internet services, and computers.

Other goods and services now includes tobacco, personal care, and miscellaneous.

TABLE 8-2

Purchasing Power of the Dollar

SOURCE: U.S. DEPARTMENT OF LABOR, BUREAU OF LABOR STATISTICS (BLS)

The purchasing power of the dollar measures changes in the quantity of goods and services a dollar will buy at a particular date compared with a selected base date. It must be defined in terms of the following: (1) the specific commodities and services that are to be purchased with the dollar; (2) the market level (producer, retail, etc.) at which they are purchased; and (3) the dates for which the comparison is to be made. Thus, the purchasing power of the dollar for a selected period, compared with another period, may be measured in terms of a single commodity or a large group of commodities such as all goods and services purchased by consumers at retail.

The purchasing power of the dollar is computed by dividing the price index number for the base period by the price index number for the comparison date and expressing the result in dollars and cents. The base period is the period in which the price index equals 100; the average purchasing power in that base period—1982–1984 in the case of the measure shown here—is therefore $1.00.

Purchasing power estimates in terms of both the CPI-U and the CPI-W are calculated by BLS, based on indexes not adjusted for seasonal variation, and published in the CPI press release. The CPI-U version is shown here.

Alternative price measures in Tables 8-3 and 8-4

Table 8-3 shows the all-items CPI-U and CPI-W, along with a number of other indexes that various analysts of price trends have preferred as measures of the price level. Table 8-4 shows the inflation rates (percent changes in price levels) implied by each of the indexes in Table 8-3.

As food and energy prices are volatile and frequently determined by forces separate from monetary aggregate demand pressures, many analysts prefer an index of prices excluding those components. Indexes *excluding food and energy* are known as *core* indexes, and inflation rates calculated from them are known as *core inflation rates.*

The *CPI-U-X1* is a special experimental version of the CPI that researchers have used to provide a more historically consistent series. As explained above, the official CPI-U treated homeownership on an asset-price basis until January 1983. It then changed to a rental equivalence method. The CPI-U-X1 incorporates a rental equivalence approach to homeowners' costs for the years 1967–1982 as well. It is rebased to the December 1982 value of the CPI-U (1982–1984 = 100); thus, it is identical to the CPI-U in December 1982 and all subsequent periods, as can be seen in Table 8-3. For this reason, it is not updated or published in the CPI news release or on the BLS Web site. We continue to present it here because it provides the only available data before 1978 on changes in an improved and more consistent CPI.

The *CPI-E* is an experimental re-weighting of components of the CPI-U to represent price change for the goods and services purchased by Americans age 62 years and over, who accounted for 16.5 percent of the total number of urban consumer units in the 2001–2002 CES.

BLS does not consider the CPI-E to be an ideal measure of price change for older Americans. Because the sample is small, the sampling error in the weights is greater than the error in the all-urban index. The products and outlets sampled are those characteristic of the general urban population rather than older residents. In addition, senior discounts are not included in the prices collected. Such discounts are included—appropriately—in the weights, which are based on the expenditures reported by the older consumers' households. Therefore, such discounts are only a problem if they do not move proportionately to general prices.

The *CPI-U-RS* is a "research series" CPI that retroactively incorporates estimates of the effects of most of the methodological changes implemented since 1978, including the rental equivalence method, new or improved quality adjustments, and improvement of formulas to eliminate bias and allow for some consumer substitution within categories. This index is calculated from 1977 onward. Its reference base is December 1977 = 100. Thus, although it generally shows less <u>increase</u> than the official index, its current <u>levels</u> are considerably higher because the earlier reference base period had lower prices. Unlike the official CPIs and the CPI-U-X1, its historical values will be revised each time a significant change is made in the calculation of the current index. This index is not seasonally adjusted and is not included in the CPI news release. It is available on the BLS Web site, along with an explanation and background material. The CPI-U-RS is used by BLS in the calculation of historical trends in real compensation per hour in its Productivity and Costs system; see Table 9-3 and its notes and definitions. It is also now used by the Census Bureau to convert household incomes into constant dollars, as seen in Chapter 3. And it is used by the editor in some analytical calculations in this volume.

The *C-CPI-U* (Chained Consumer Price Index for All Urban Consumers) is a new, supplemental index that has been published in the monthly CPI news release since August 2002. It is available only from December 1999 to date and is calculated with the base December 1999 = 100; it is not seasonally adjusted. It is designed to be a still-closer approximation to a true cost-of-living index than the CPI-U and the CPI-W, in that it assumes that consumers substitute between as well as within categories as relative prices change, in order to maintain a fixed basket of "consumer satisfaction."

The C-CPI-U is technically a "superlative" index, using a method known as the "Tornqvist formula" to incorporate the composition of consumer spending in the current period as well as in the earlier base period. (All of the other Consumer Price Indexes use a "Laspeyres" formula; see the General Notes at the beginning of this volume.) As it requires consumer expenditure data for the current as well as the earlier period, its final version can only be calculated after the expenditure data become available—about two years later—and is approximated in more recent periods by making more extensive use of the geometric mean formula (see above). With the release of January 2014 data, the indexes for 2012 were revised to their final form, and the initial indexes for 2013 were revised to "interim" levels, shown in Tables 8-3 and 8-4.

Personal consumption expenditure (PCE) chain-type price indexes are calculated by the Bureau of Economic Analysis (BEA) in the framework of the national income and product accounts (NIPAs). (See the notes and definitions for Chapters 1 and 4.) The scope of NIPA PCE is broader than the scope of the CPI. PCE includes the rural as well as the urban population and also covers the consumption spending of nonprofit entities. The CPI includes only consumer out-of-pocket cash spending, whereas PCE includes some imputed servi and includes expenditures financed by government and private insurance, particularly in the medical care area. For this reason, there is a large difference between the relatively small weight of medical care spending in the CPI and the markedly greater percentage of PCE that is accounted for by total medical care spending. Housing, on the other hand, has a somewhat smaller weight in PCE while all non-housing components have a higher weight. The reason for this is that the CES—the survey on which the CPI weights are based—tends to report housing expenditures accurately and somewhat underestimate other spending. This suggests that the weight of housing relative to all other products may be overestimated in the CPI but measured more correctly in the PCE price index.

PCE chain-type indexes use the expenditure weights of both the earlier and the later period to determine the aggregate price change between the two periods. (See the notes and definitions for Chapter 1, as well as the General Notes on index number formulas.) Thus, they are subject to revision as improved data on the composition of consumption spending become available, and in this respect resemble the C-CPI-U.

For a large share of PCE, the price movements for basic individual spending categories are determined by CPI components. Hence, the differences between the rates of change in the aggregate CPI and PCE indexes are largely the result of the different weights, but also reflect some alternative methodologies and the previously mentioned differences in scope.

Market-based PCE indexes are based on household expenditures for which there are observable price measures. They exclude most implicit prices (for example, the services furnished without payment by financial intermediaries) and they exclude items not deflated by a detailed component of either the Consumer Price Index (CPI) or the Producer Price Index (PPI). This means that the price observations that make up these new aggregate measures are all based on observed market transactions, making them "market-based price indexes." The imputed rent for owner-occupied housing is included in the market-based price index, since it is based on observed rentals of comparable homes. Household insurance premiums are also included in the market-based index, since they are deflated by the CPI for tenants' and household insurance. Excluded are services furnished without payment by financial intermediaries, most insurance purchases, expenses of NPISHs (nonprofit institutions serving households), legal gambling (illegal gambling is excluded from all measures), margins on used light motor vehicles, and expenditures by U.S. residents working and traveling abroad. Also excluded are medical, hospitalization, and income loss insurance; expense of handling life insurance; motor vehicle insurance; and workers' compensation.

The *inflation rates* shown in Table 8-4 are percent changes in the price indexes introduced in Table 8-3. For annual indexes, the rate is the percent change from the previous year. For monthly indexes, the rate is the percent change from the same month a year earlier. To give an indication of the longer-run implications of these different price indicators, comparisons of compound annual inflation rates, calculated by the editor, are also shown for the 1978–2013, 1983–2013, 2000–2013 and 2013–2015 periods, using the growth rate formula presented in the article at the beginning of this volume.

DATA AVAILABILITY AND REFERENCES

The CPI-U, CPI-W, and C-CPI-U are initially issued in a press release two to three weeks after the end of the month for which the data were collected. This release and detailed and complete current and historical data on the CPI and its variants and components, along with extensive documentation, are available on the BLS Web site at <http://www.bls.gov/cpi>. Seasonal factors and seasonally adjusted indexes are revised once a year with the issuance of the January index.

Information available on the BLS Web site includes "Common Misconceptions about the Consumer Price Index: Questions and Answers"; another fact sheet on frequently asked questions; a fact sheet on seasonal adjustment; Chapter 17 of the *BLS Handbook of Methods*, entitled "The Consumer Price Index"; a section entitled "Note on Chained Consumer Price Index for All Urban Consumers"; and a number of explanatory CPI fact sheets on specific subjects.

As previously indicated, the CPI-U-X1 is not currently published because its recent values are identical to the CPI-U. The CPI-E is presented in articles in the CPI section of the BLS Web site, the most recent of which is "Experimental Consumer Price Index for Americans 62 Years of Age and Older, 1998-2005"; recent values are available by request from BLS. The CPI-U-RS is updated each month in a report entitled "CPI Research Series Using Current Methods" on the site. In both cases, the reports describe the indexes and provide references.

The monthly PCE indexes are included in the personal income report issued by BEA, which is published near the end of the following month. These indexes are revised month-by-month to reflect new information and annually to reflect the annual and quinquennial benchmarking of the NIPAs. The complete historical record can be found on the BEA Web site at <http://www.bea.gov> in the Personal Income and Outlays section of the NIPA tables, in tables entitled "Price Indexes for Personal Consumption Expenditures by Major Type of Product."

Two special editions of the *Monthly Labor Review* were devoted to CPI issues. The December 1996 issue describes the subsequently implemented 1997 and 1998 revisions in a series of articles, and the December 1993 issue, entitled *The Anatomy of Price Change*, includes the following articles: "The Consumer Price Index: Underlying Concepts and Caveats"; "Basic Components of the CPI: Estimation of Price Changes"; "The Commodity Substitution Effect in CPI Data, 1982–1991"; and "Quality Adjustment of Price Indexes."

The new formula for calculating basic components is described in "Incorporating a Geometric Mean Formula into the CPI," *Monthly Labor Review* (October 1998). For a detailed discussion of the treatment of homeownership, see "Changing the Homeownership Component of the Consumer Price Index to Rental Equivalence," *CPI Detailed Report* (January 1983).

For a comprehensive professional review of CPI concepts and methodology, see Charles Schultze and Christopher Mackie, ed., *At What Price? Conceptualizing and Measuring Cost-of-Living and Price Indexes* (Washington, DC: National Academy Press, 2001). Earlier references include: "Using Survey Data to Assess Bias in the Consumer Price Index," *Monthly Labor Review* (April 1998); Joel Popkin, "Improving the CPI: The Record and Suggested Next Steps," *Business Economics*, Vol. XXXII, No. 3 (July 1997), pages 42–47; *Measurement Issues in the Consumer*

Price Index (Bureau of Labor Statistics, U.S. Department of Labor, June 1997); *Toward a More Accurate Measure of the Cost of Living* (Final Report to the Senate Finance Committee from the Advisory Commission to Study the Consumer Price Index, December 4, 1996)—also known as the "Boskin Commission" report; and *Government Price Statistics* (U.S. Congress Joint Economic Committee, 87th Congress, 1st Session, January 24, 1961)—also known as the "Stigler Committee" report.

For an explanation of the differences between the CPI-U and the PCE index, see Clinton P. McCully, Brian C. Moyer, and Kenneth J. Stewart, "Comparing the Consumer Price Index and the Personal Consumption Expenditures Price Index," *Survey of Current Business,* November 2007, pp. 26-33.

TABLES 8-1 AND 8-5 THROUGH 8-7

Producer Price Indexes

SOURCE: U.S. DEPARTMENT OF LABOR, BUREAU OF LABOR STATISTICS (BLS)

The Bureau of Labor Statistics first compiled and published a "Wholesale Price Index," measuring prices of various goods from the perspective of the seller, in 1902; it covered the years 1890-1901. Over the years this index was broadened and refined. In a major revamping in 1978, it was structured into an input-output format, differentiated between stages of processing, and renamed the Producer Price Index. The index for "Finished Goods," from the stage-of-processing system, became the featured "headline" number. Still, this index only covered goods.

New FD-ID system (Tables 8-5 and 8-6)

Over subsequent years the Bureau instituted collection of an increasing number of prices for services as well. All prices are collected within an industry input-output structure, with one of the most important purposes being to measure real output quantities by deflating industry outputs and inputs. In the new aggregation system introduced in February 2014, prices for goods, services, and construction have been integrated into a set of Final Demand-Intermediate Demand (FD-ID) indexes, organized by class of buyer, degree of fabrication, and stage of production. Its principal components are calculated beginning in November 2009 with that month as the reference base (i.e. November 2009 = 100). Components of the previous goods PPI system continue to be calculated on the base 1982 = 100 as well.

In the new FD-ID system, all products, including services and construction, are referred to as "commodities." In the old PPI system and in the CPI system, the term "commodities" refers to goods only; note, for example, how the CPI components are aggregated into summary measures of "commodities" [goods] and services, displaying different trends and behaviors. Unless and until these terminologies are reconciled, users need to be mindful of which system they are operating in.

More that 100,000 producer price quotations from over 25,000 establishment are collected each month; more than 10,000 indexes for individual products and groups of products are released each month. The prices are organized into three sets of PPIs: the FD-ID indexes; commodity indexes; and indexes for the net output of industries and their products.

Final demand. The final demand portion of the FD-ID structure measures price change for commodities sold for personal consumption, capital investment, government, and export. *Final demand trade services* measures changes in margins received by wholesalers and retailers. The other main components are *final demand goods, final demand transportation and warehousing services, other final demand services,* and *final demand construction.* The total index for final demand is now featured by BLS in its press release as its "headline number," replacing the previously featured Finished Goods index.

Intermediate demand. This portion of the system tracks price changes for goods, services, and construction products sold to businesses as inputs to production and not as capital investment. There are two parallel treatments.

The first treatment organizes intermediate demand commodities by type, including the distinction between *processed goods* and *unprocessed goods,* which is carried over from the older PPI goods system.

The second system organizes intermediate demand commodities into production stages, with the explicit goal of developing a forward-flow model of production and price change. For each production stage, the intermediate demand index measures the prices of inputs to the included industries. Many commodities, for example energy products, are sold to both final demand and various intermediate stages of production; their weight is allocated proportionately to all the consuming stages of production and their price movements are proportionately represented in each stage.

Industries assigned to *Stage 4* primarily produce final demand commodities. The intermediate demand index for Stage 4 measures inputs to those industries, such as motor vehicle parts, beef and veal, and long distance motor carrying.

Industries assigned to *Stage 3* produce the output sold to Stage 4, and therefore include motor vehicle parts and slaughtering. Examples of inputs to Stage 3 included in their intermediate demand index include slaughter steers and heifers, industrial electric power, steel plates, and temporary help services.

Industries assigned to *Stage 2* include petroleum refining, electricity, and insurance agencies. The goods and services that they purchase and that are included in their intermediate demand index include crude oil and business loans.

Industries assigned to *Stage 1* include oil and gas extraction, paper mills, and advertising services. Inputs to those industries include electric power and solid waste collection. According to BLS, "It should be noted that all inputs purchased by stage 1 industries are by definition produced either within stage 1 or by later stages of processing, leaving stage 1 less useful for price transmission analysis."

Commodity indexes

Aggregation by *commodity* organizes the price measures by similarity of product or end use, disregarding industry of origin. For the original Wholesale Price Index (goods only), this was the principal means of aggregation; in Table 8-1C, producer price indexes are shown for *farm products, industrial commodities*, and "*all commodities*" back to the year 1913. Table 8-7 shows 16 goods commodity groups from 1950 to date. Whatever their imperfections, these measures provide the longest historical perspective for producer prices.

The major goods commodity groups—particularly the totals for all commodities and industrial commodities—came under criticism in the energy price crisis of the early 1970s, for aggregating successive stages of processing of the same product (e.g. crude oil) and thus exaggerating price trends. As a result, the stage-of-processing grouping was introduced in 1978, and the finished goods components, in total and minus food and energy, became the headline Producer Price Indexes.

Stage of processing indexes

In the PPI for goods as reconstructed in 1978 and shown in Table 8-1B, the three major indexes are: (1) *finished goods*, or goods that will not undergo further processing and are ready for sale to the ultimate user (such as automobiles, meats, apparel, and machine tools, and also unprocessed foods such as eggs and fresh vegetables, that are ready for the consumer); (2) *processed goods for intermediate demand* (formerly *intermediate materials, supplies, and components)*, or goods that have been processed but require further processing before they become finished goods (such as steel mill products, cotton yarns, lumber, and flour), as well as physically complete goods that are purchased by business firms as inputs for their operations (such as diesel fuel and paper boxes); and (3) *unprocessed goods for intermediate demand (formerly crude materials for further processing)*, or goods entering the market for the first time that have not been manufactured or fabricated and are not sold directly to consumers (such as ores, scrap metals, crude petroleum, raw cotton, and livestock).

Notes on the data

The probability sample used for calculating the PPI provides more than 100,000 price quotations per month. To the greatest extent possible, prices used in calculating the PPI represent prices received by domestic producers in the first important commercial transaction for each commodity. These indexes attempt to measure only price changes (changes in receipts per unit of

measurement not influenced by changes in quality, quantity sold, terms of sale, or level of distribution). Transaction prices are sought instead of list or book prices. Price data are collected monthly via Internet, mail, and fax. Prices are obtained directly from producing companies on a voluntary and confidential basis. Prices are generally reported for the Tuesday of the week containing the 13th day of the month. Samples are updated regularly.

The BLS revises the PPI weighting structure when data from economic censuses become available. Beginning with data for January 2012, the weights used to construct the PPI reflect 2007 shipments values as measured by the 2007 Economic Censuses. Data for January 2007 through December 2011 used 2002 values; 2002 through 2006, 1997 shipments values; 1996 through 2001, 1992 values; 1992 through 1995, 1987 values; 1987 through 1991, 1982 values; 1976 through 1986, 1972 values; and 1967 through 1975, 1963 values.

Price indexes are available in unadjusted form and are also adjusted for seasonal variation using the X-12-ARIMA method. Since January 1988, BLS has also used X-12-ARIMA Intervention Analysis Seasonal Adjustment for a small number of series to remove unusual values that might distort seasonal patterns before calculating the seasonal adjustment factors. Seasonal factors for the PPI are revised annually to take into account the most recent 12 months of data. Seasonally adjusted data for the previous 5 years are subject to these annual revisions.

The newer FD-ID indexes are only available beginning in November 2009. Hence, they only regard, so far, the recovery and expansion phase of a particularly severe business cycle; the editor suggests that up to now, both seasonal adjustments and broader inferences about relative price behavior are necessarily based on a short and possibly unrepresentative time period. Partly for that reason, we present both unadjusted and seasonally adjusted indexes in Tables 8-5 and 8-6.

DATA AVAILABILITY AND REFERENCES

The indexes are initially issued in a press release two to three weeks after the end of the month for which the data were collected. Data are subsequently published in greater detail in a monthly BLS publication, *PPI Detailed Report*. Each month, data for the fourth previous month (both unadjusted and seasonally adjusted) are revised to reflect late reports and corrections.

The press release, the *PPI Detailed Report*, detailed and complete current and historical data, and extensive documentation are available at <http://www.bls.gov/ppi>. The items available on this Web site include Chapter 14 of the *BLS Handbook of Methods*, "Producer Price Indexes"; a selection of *Monthly Labor Review* articles on the PPI; and fact sheets on a number of issues and index components.

CHAPTER 9: EMPLOYMENT COSTS, PRODUCTIVITY, AND PROFITS

SECTION 9A: EMPLOYMENT COST INDEXES

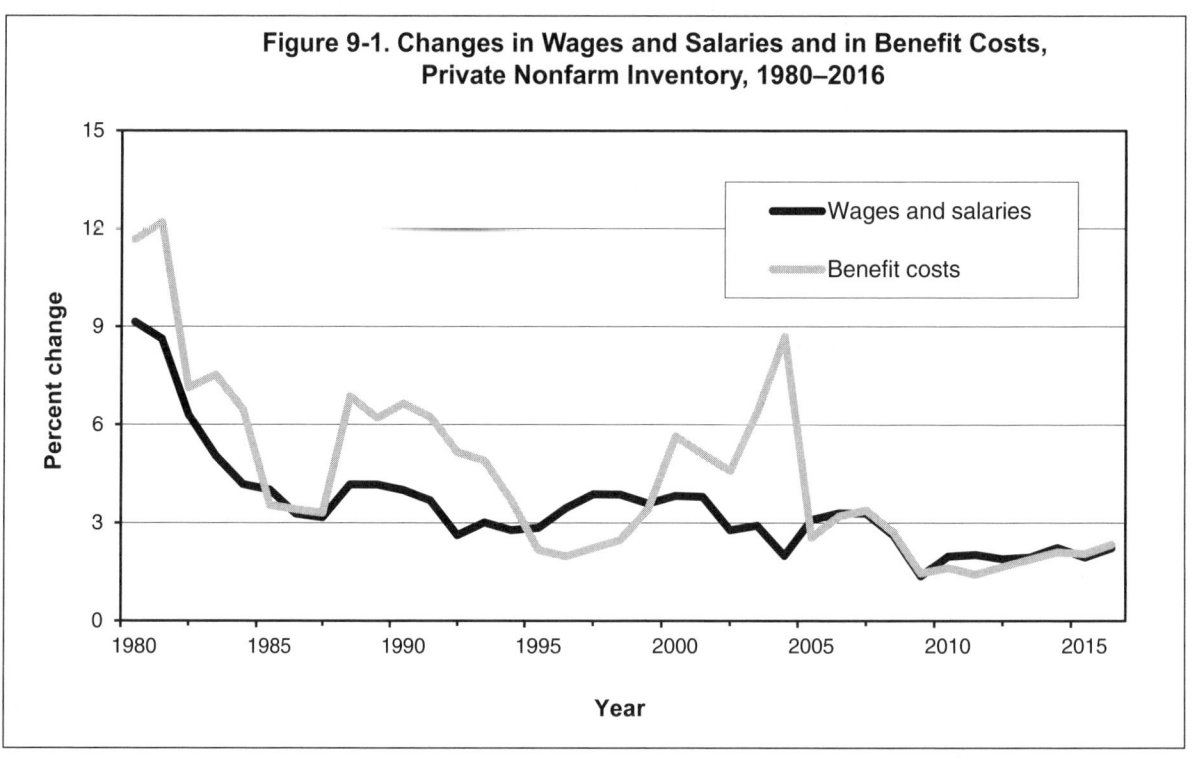

Figure 9-1. Changes in Wages and Salaries and in Benefit Costs, Private Nonfarm Inventory, 1980–2016

- The Employment Cost Index measures average increases in the dollar value of hourly compensation for nonfarm wage and salary workers, holding the composition of employment constant so as to reflect only the aggregate of changes affecting individual defined jobs. (The analogy is to the Consumer Price Index, which holds the market basket constant in any individual time period so as to reflect only an aggregate of price changes affecting individual defined products.) This makes the ECI the most accurate indicator of changes in price for a typical unit of labor.

- From 2007 to 2016, average annual compensation for all civilian workers rose 19.9 percent. Compensation includes wages, salaries, and benefits, but not stock options. Benefits rose even more, at 22.8 percent. Much of rise in benefits was due to medical care costs. (Tables 9-1, 9-2, and 8-2)

- The ECI reports separately the rates of increase for wages and salaries and for benefits such as health insurance, as shown in Figure 9-1. (Tables 9-1 and 9-2)

Table 9-1. Employment Cost Indexes, NAICS Basis

(December 2005 [not seasonally adjusted] = 100; annual values are for December, not seasonally adjusted; quarterly values, seasonally adjusted, except as noted.)

Year and month	All civilian workers [1]	State and local government workers	All private industry workers	Management, professional, and related	Sales and office	Natural resources, construction, and maintenance	Production, transportation, and material moving	Service occupations	Goods-producing industries Total	Manufacturing	Service-providing	Union [2]	Non-union [2]
TOTAL COMPENSATION													
2004	97.0	96.1	97.2	97.1	96.8	97.0	97.8	97.7	96.9	96.9	97.3	97.3	97.2
2005	100.0	100.0	100.0	100.0	100.0	100.0	100.0	100.0	100.0	100.0	100.0	100.0	100.0
2006	103.3	104.1	103.2	103.5	103.0	103.6	102.3	103.1	102.5	101.8	103.4	103.0	103.2
2007	106.7	108.4	106.3	106.8	106.4	106.8	104.5	107.0	105.0	103.8	106.7	105.1	106.5
2008	109.5	111.6	108.9	109.9	108.3	109.8	106.9	109.8	107.5	105.9	109.4	108.0	109.1
2009	111.0	114.2	110.2	110.7	109.7	111.5	108.9	111.8	108.6	107.0	110.8	111.1	110.1
2010	113.2	116.2	112.5	113.0	112.1	113.6	111.5	113.5	111.1	110.0	113.0	114.8	112.1
2011	115.5	117.7	115.0	115.4	114.6	116.1	114.2	115.4	113.8	113.1	115.3	117.9	114.5
2012	117.7	119.9	117.1	117.7	116.7	118.1	116.0	117.4	115.6	114.9	117.6	120.5	116.6
2013	120.0	122.2	119.4	120.2	119.4	120.4	118.0	119.0	117.7	117.0	120.0	122.6	119.0
2014	122.7	124.7	122.2	123.0	122.3	123.5	120.6	121.1	120.3	119.8	122.8	126.7	121.5
2015	125.1	127.8	124.5	125.3	124.4	125.4	123.7	123.2	123.2	122.8	124.9	128.7	123.8
2016	127.9	130.9	127.2	127.4	127.4	128.1	127.0	127.2	125.8	125.5	127.7	130.6	126.6
2005													
March	98.0	97.0	98.2	98.4	97.9	98.0	98.5	98.4	98.0	98.2	98.3	97.9	98.3
June	98.6	97.8	98.8	99.0	98.4	98.7	99.0	99.0	98.9	99.0	98.8	98.8	98.9
September	99.3	98.7	99.5	99.6	99.2	99.4	99.6	99.6	99.7	99.7	99.4	99.6	99.5
December	100.1	99.8	100.2	100.3	100.1	100.2	100.1	100.1	100.2	100.2	100.2	100.0	100.0
2006													
March	100.7	100.5	100.8	101.0	100.6	100.9	100.4	100.8	100.3	99.9	100.9	100.5	100.9
June	101.6	101.5	101.6	101.8	101.5	102.0	101.0	101.5	101.2	100.9	101.8	101.8	101.7
September	102.6	102.8	102.5	102.9	102.2	102.9	101.7	102.2	101.9	101.4	102.7	102.4	102.6
December	103.4	103.9	103.3	103.8	103.0	103.7	102.4	103.2	102.7	102.0	103.5	103.0	103.2
2007													
March	104.2	105.1	103.9	104.5	103.8	104.1	102.5	104.4	102.9	101.9	104.3	102.7	104.2
June	105.1	106.2	104.8	105.5	104.5	104.9	103.3	105.2	103.8	102.8	105.2	103.9	105.1
September	105.9	107.2	105.6	106.3	105.2	105.8	103.9	106.3	104.4	103.2	106.0	104.4	105.9
December	106.8	108.3	106.5	107.1	106.2	106.8	104.7	107.2	105.2	104.0	106.9	105.1	106.5
2008													
March	107.6	109.0	107.2	108.0	106.8	107.7	105.5	107.8	106.0	104.6	107.6	105.9	107.5
June	108.3	109.8	108.0	108.8	107.4	108.2	106.0	108.7	106.7	105.0	108.4	106.7	108.3
September	109.1	110.9	108.6	109.6	107.8	108.9	106.5	109.4	107.2	105.6	109.1	107.4	108.9
December	109.6	111.6	109.1	110.2	108.0	109.7	107.0	109.9	107.7	106.1	109.5	108.0	109.1
2008													
March	109.9	112.4	109.3	110.2	108.1	109.9	107.7	110.6	107.9	106.4	109.8	109.1	109.4
June	110.2	113.2	109.5	110.4	108.2	110.3	108.1	111.0	108.1	106.6	110.0	109.8	109.6
September	110.7	113.5	109.9	110.6	108.8	110.7	108.6	111.6	108.3	106.8	110.5	110.5	109.9
December	111.1	114.1	110.4	111.0	109.3	111.3	109.0	112.0	108.8	107.3	110.9	111.1	110.1
2010													
March	111.8	114.5	111.1	111.7	109.9	112.3	109.9	112.3	109.7	108.4	111.5	112.8	110.9
June	112.3	115.1	111.6	112.1	110.6	112.6	110.4	112.6	110.2	109.0	112.1	113.7	111.4
September	112.8	115.5	112.1	112.7	111.1	112.9	111.2	113.3	110.9	109.9	112.5	114.6	111.8
December	113.3	116.1	112.6	113.3	111.7	113.4	111.6	113.6	111.2	110.2	113.1	114.8	112.1
2011													
March	114.0	116.7	113.3	114.0	112.2	113.9	112.2	114.5	112.0	111.3	113.8	115.6	113.0
June	114.7	117.0	114.2	114.7	113.2	114.8	113.5	114.7	113.2	112.6	114.5	117.1	113.8
September	115.1	117.3	114.6	115.1	113.7	115.4	113.7	115.0	113.3	112.8	115.0	117.4	114.2
December	115.6	117.7	115.1	115.7	114.3	115.9	114.3	115.5	113.9	113.3	115.5	117.9	114.5
2012													
March	116.3	118.3	115.7	116.3	115.1	116.4	114.5	116.0	114.1	113.4	116.3	118.3	115.3
June	116.8	118.9	116.3	117.0	115.7	116.9	115.0	116.5	114.6	113.9	116.9	119.3	116.0
September	117.3	119.5	116.8	117.3	116.2	117.5	115.6	116.8	115.2	114.6	117.3	120.2	116.3
December	117.8	119.9	117.2	118.0	116.5	118.0	116.1	117.4	115.7	115.1	117.7	120.5	116.6
2013													
March	118.4	120.5	117.9	118.5	117.3	118.7	116.7	117.8	116.4	115.7	118.4	121.5	117.3
June	119.0	121.0	118.5	119.3	117.7	119.0	117.1	118.3	116.9	116.2	119.0	122.1	118.0
September	119.5	121.4	119.0	119.9	118.4	119.7	117.5	118.4	117.4	116.7	119.5	122.5	118.5
December	120.1	122.2	119.6	120.4	119.2	120.3	118.1	119.0	117.8	117.2	120.1	122.6	119.0
2014													
March	120.5	122.8	119.9	120.7	119.4	120.9	118.8	119.1	118.6	118.0	120.4	123.5	119.4
June	121.4	123.4	120.9	121.8	120.3	121.9	119.4	119.6	119.1	118.6	121.5	125.0	120.4
September	122.2	124.0	121.7	122.6	121.1	122.6	120.2	120.5	119.8	119.3	122.3	125.8	121.1
December	122.8	124.7	122.3	123.1	122.1	123.4	120.8	121.1	120.4	120.0	122.9	126.7	121.5
2015													
March	123.6	125.4	123.2	123.8	123.4	123.6	121.7	121.9	121.1	120.8	123.8	127.4	122.5
June	123.8	126.2	123.2	124.1	122.5	124.0	122.4	122.1	121.8	121.5	123.7	127.5	122.7
September	124.5	126.9	124.0	124.8	123.5	124.5	123.0	122.6	122.4	122.1	124.5	128.0	123.4
December	125.2	127.8	124.6	125.4	124.2	125.1	123.8	123.3	123.2	123.0	125.1	128.7	123.8
2016													
March	126.0	128.5	125.4	126.0	125.2	125.8	124.7	124.3	123.9	123.7	125.9	129.6	124.7
June	126.7	129.2	126.1	126.4	126.4	126.5	125.5	125.5	124.6	124.4	126.6	130.0	125.7
September	127.4	130.2	126.7	127.0	126.7	127.0	126.3	126.4	125.1	125.1	127.3	130.4	126.3
December	128.0	131.0	127.3	127.6	127.1	127.8	127.2	127.3	125.8	125.7	127.8	130.6	126.6

[1]Excludes farm workers, private household workers, and federal government employees.
[2]Not seasonally adjusted.

Table 9-1. Employment Cost Indexes, NAICS Basis—*Continued*

(December 2005 [not seasonally adjusted] = 100; annual values are for December, not seasonally adjusted; quarterly values, seasonally adjusted, except as noted.)

Year and month	All civilian workers [1]	State and local government workers	All private industry workers	Management, professional, and related	Sales and office	Natural resources, construction, and maintenance	Production, transportation, and material moving	Service occupations	Goods-producing industries Total	Manufacturing	Service-providing	Union [2]	Non-union [2]
WAGES AND SALARIES													
2004	97.5	97.0	97.6	97.8	97.2	97.5	97.8	97.9	97.2	97.4	97.7	98.0	97.7
2005	100.0	100.0	100.0	100.0	100.0	100.0	100.0	100.0	100.0	100.0	100.0	100.0	100.0
2006	103.2	103.5	103.2	103.6	103.0	103.4	102.4	102.9	102.9	102.3	103.3	102.2	103.4
2007	106.7	107.1	106.6	107.2	106.2	107.1	105.0	107.1	106.0	104.9	106.8	104.9	107.0
2008	109.6	110.4	109.4	110.5	108.0	110.5	107.8	110.1	109.0	107.7	109.6	108.3	109.7
2009	111.2	112.5	110.8	111.5	109.4	112.0	109.6	112.3	110.0	108.9	111.1	111.6	111.0
2010	113.0	113.8	112.8	113.7	111.5	113.3	111.3	113.5	111.6	110.7	113.1	114.2	113.0
2011	114.6	114.9	114.6	115.5	113.6	115.4	112.8	115.1	113.5	112.7	114.9	116.3	114.8
2012	116.5	116.2	116.6	117.7	115.8	116.7	115.1	116.8	115.4	114.8	117.0	119.1	116.8
2013	118.7	117.5	119.0	120.2	118.4	118.8	117.2	118.3	117.6	117.2	119.4	121.8	119.2
2014	121.2	119.4	121.6	122.8	121.3	121.4	119.9	120.7	120.1	119.8	122.1	125.6	121.7
2015	123.7	121.6	124.2	125.6	123.5	123.5	122.8	122.8	123.2	123.0	124.5	128.0	124.2
2016	126.6	124.1	127.1	128.1	126.2	126.7	126.6	127.1	126.2	126.2	127.4	129.4	127.3
2005													
March	98.2	97.7	98.3	98.6	98.0	98.0	98.4	. . .	97.9	98.2	98.4	97.9	98.3
June	98.7	98.3	98.8	99.1	98.4	98.6	98.9	. . .	98.6	98.8	98.9	98.7	98.9
September	99.3	98.8	99.4	99.5	99.2	99.3	99.5	. . .	99.4	99.6	99.4	99.5	99.5
December	100.1	99.8	100.1	100.2	100.1	100.1	100.1	. . .	100.2	100.2	100.1	100.0	100.0
2006													
March	98.2	100.4	100.8	101.0	100.6	100.8	100.6	100.6	100.7	100.6	100.8	100.3	100.8
June	98.7	101.2	101.6	101.9	101.5	101.8	101.1	101.3	101.7	101.6	101.6	101.2	101.8
September	99.3	102.4	102.5	102.9	102.2	102.7	101.7	101.9	102.2	101.8	102.6	101.7	102.7
December	100.1	103.4	103.3	103.8	103.0	103.4	102.5	103.0	103.0	102.5	103.4	102.3	103.3
2007													
March	104.3	104.2	104.3	104.9	104.0	104.3	103.2	104.6	103.9	103.2	104.4	102.8	104.5
June	105.1	105.0	105.1	105.7	104.7	105.1	103.8	105.4	104.6	103.8	105.2	103.7	105.3
September	105.9	106.0	105.9	106.6	105.2	106.1	104.4	106.4	105.4	104.4	106.1	104.4	106.2
December	106.8	107.0	106.7	107.4	106.2	107.1	105.0	107.2	106.1	105.1	106.9	104.7	106.9
2008													
March	107.6	107.8	107.6	108.4	106.9	108.2	106.0	107.8	107.1	105.9	107.7	105.5	107.9
June	108.5	108.6	108.4	109.2	107.5	108.9	106.8	108.9	107.9	106.7	108.6	106.7	108.7
September	109.2	109.7	109.0	110.1	107.9	109.7	107.4	109.6	108.5	107.3	109.2	107.4	109.4
December	109.7	110.3	109.5	110.7	108.0	110.5	107.9	110.2	109.1	107.9	109.7	108.1	109.6
2009													
March	110.0	111.0	109.8	110.9	108.1	110.7	108.3	110.9	109.2	108.0	110.0	108.8	110.0
June	110.4	111.7	110.1	111.1	108.2	111.1	108.8	111.3	109.4	108.3	110.2	109.6	110.2
September	110.8	111.9	110.5	111.3	108.9	111.5	109.3	112.0	109.7	108.6	110.7	110.2	110.6
December	111.2	112.4	111.0	111.8	109.5	112.1	109.7	112.4	110.2	109.1	111.2	110.9	110.9
2010													
March	111.7	112.8	111.4	112.3	109.8	112.6	109.9	112.5	110.5	109.3	111.7	111.5	111.4
June	112.1	113.2	111.9	112.8	110.5	112.8	110.3	112.8	110.9	109.9	112.2	112.1	111.9
September	112.5	113.3	112.3	113.4	110.8	113.0	111.0	113.2	111.4	110.5	112.6	112.7	112.4
December	113.0	113.8	112.9	113.9	111.5	113.3	111.3	113.5	111.7	110.9	113.2	112.9	112.7
2011													
March	113.4	114.1	113.2	114.4	111.8	113.8	111.6	114.2	112.2	111.5	113.6	113.6	113.2
June	113.9	114.4	113.7	114.8	112.5	114.5	112.0	114.3	112.7	111.9	114.1	114.0	113.8
September	114.3	114.6	114.2	115.2	113.1	115.0	112.4	114.6	113.1	112.5	114.6	114.6	114.3
December	114.7	114.8	114.7	115.7	113.7	115.4	112.9	115.1	113.0	113.0	115.0	114.9	114.6
2012													
March	115.3	115.2	115.3	116.3	114.5	115.7	113.7	115.4	114.0	113.5	115.7	115.6	115.2
June	115.8	115.6	115.8	116.9	115.0	116.0	114.0	115.9	114.4	113.9	116.2	116.2	115.9
September	116.2	115.8	116.3	117.2	115.7	116.4	114.6	116.2	115.0	114.5	116.7	116.9	116.3
December	116.6	116.1	116.7	117.8	115.9	116.8	115.2	116.8	115.5	115.0	117.1	117.4	116.5
2013													
March	117.2	116.4	117.4	118.5	116.7	117.3	115.8	117.2	116.1	115.6	117.7	118.4	117.2
June	117.7	116.7	118.0	119.3	117.1	117.6	116.2	117.7	116.7	116.3	118.3	119.0	117.9
September	118.2	116.9	118.4	119.7	117.7	118.4	116.6	117.6	117.2	116.8	118.8	119.6	118.4
December	118.8	117.4	119.1	120.3	118.6	118.9	117.3	118.3	117.7	117.4	119.5	119.8	118.9
2014													
March	119.1	117.8	119.4	120.6	118.7	119.4	118.0	118.5	118.2	118.0	119.7	120.5	119.2
June	119.9	118.3	120.2	121.6	119.4	120.0	118.7	119.0	118.9	118.8	120.6	121.2	120.2
September	120.6	118.8	121.1	122.4	120.3	120.7	119.6	120.1	119.5	119.3	121.5	122.1	121.0
December	121.3	119.4	121.7	122.9	121.5	121.4	120.0	120.7	120.2	120.0	122.2	123.1	121.5
2015													
March	122.1	120.0	122.6	123.5	123.3	121.8	120.7	121.6	120.9	120.8	123.1	123.7	122.4
June	122.4	120.6	122.8	124.2	122.0	122.6	121.5	121.6	121.7	121.6	123.2	124.5	122.7
September	123.1	121.0	123.6	125.0	123.1	123.1	122.1	122.1	122.4	122.3	124.0	124.8	123.6
December	123.8	121.5	124.3	125.7	123.7	123.6	123.0	122.8	123.3	123.2	124.6	125.5	124.0
2016													
March	124.6	122.1	125.1	126.5	124.6	124.5	123.9	124.0	124.0	124.0	125.5	126.4	125.0
June	125.4	122.7	126.0	126.9	125.9	125.4	124.9	125.2	124.8	124.8	126.3	126.8	126.0
September	126.0	123.4	126.6	127.5	126.1	125.8	125.8	126.3	125.4	125.6	127.0	127.2	126.6
December	126.6	124.0	127.2	128.2	126.5	126.8	126.8	127.2	126.2	126.4	127.6	127.3	127.1

[1]Excludes farm workers, private household workers, and federal government employees.
[2]Not seasonally adjusted.
. . . = Not available.

Table 9-1. Employment Cost Indexes, NAICS Basis—*Continued*

(December 2005 [not seasonally adjusted] = 100; annual values are for December, not seasonally adjusted; quarterly values, seasonally adjusted, except as noted.)

Year and month	All civilian workers [1]	State and local government workers	All private industry workers	Management, professional, and related	Sales and office	Natural resources, construction, and maintenance	Production, transportation, and material moving	Service occupations	Goods-producing industries Total	Manufacturing	Service-providing	Union [2]	Non-union [2]
TOTAL BENEFITS													
2004	95.7	94.1	96.2	95.4	95.8	96.4	97.7	97.0	96.3	96.0	96.1	96.8	96.0
2005	100.0	100.0	100.0	100.0	100.0	100.0	100.0	100.0	100.0	100.0	100.0	100.0	100.0
2006	103.6	105.2	103.1	103.4	102.9	104.0	102.0	103.6	101.7	100.8	103.7	104.2	102.9
2007	106.8	111.0	105.6	106.0	106.0	105.9	103.7	106.7	103.2	101.7	106.6	105.8	105.6
2008	109.1	114.2	107.7	108.5	107.8	107.7	105.1	108.8	104.7	102.5	108.9	107.8	107.6
2009	110.7	117.7	108.7	108.8	108.7	109.5	107.4	110.5	105.8	103.6	109.9	111.4	108.2
2010	113.9	121.1	111.9	111.2	111.8	113.2	112.0	113.5	110.1	108.8	112.6	117.9	110.6
2011	117.5	123.6	115.9	115.2	115.5	116.8	117.0	116.4	114.4	113.9	116.4	122.8	114.4
2012	120.3	127.8	118.2	117.9	117.6	120.2	118.0	119.2	116.0	115.0	119.1	125.6	116.7
2013	123.0	132.0	120.5	120.2	120.5	122.9	119.5	121.0	118.0	116.6	121.5	127.3	119.1
2014	126.2	135.8	123.5	123.4	123.4	127.1	122.1	122.2	120.7	119.8	124.6	132.6	121.7
2015	128.4	140.6	125.1	124.5	125.0	127.9	125.4	124.3	123.1	122.5	125.9	133.9	123.3
2016	131.1	145.0	127.3	126.0	128.4	129.9	127.9	127.1	124.9	124.3	128.3	136.1	125.5
2005													
March	97.5	95.6	98.0	97.9	97.5	98.0	98.7	98.0	98.3	98.2	97.9	98.0	98.2
June	98.4	96.8	98.8	98.8	98.4	98.9	99.2	98.8	99.5	99.4	98.6	98.9	99.0
September	99.4	98.4	99.7	99.8	99.3	99.7	99.9	99.5	100.3	100.1	99.4	99.8	99.6
December	100.2	99.9	100.3	100.4	100.2	100.4	100.1	100.3	100.2	100.1	100.3	100.0	100.0
2006													
March	100.8	100.8	100.8	101.0	100.7	101.1	100.0	101.3	99.4	98.6	101.3	100.8	101.0
June	101.7	102.0	101.6	101.7	101.5	102.4	100.8	102.1	100.3	99.6	102.2	102.7	101.5
September	102.7	103.5	102.5	102.8	102.1	103.4	101.6	103.0	101.3	100.7	103.0	103.4	102.3
December	103.7	105.1	103.4	103.8	103.0	104.4	102.3	103.9	102.0	101.1	104.0	104.2	102.9
2007													
March	104.0	107.1	103.1	103.5	103.3	103.5	101.1	104.0	100.9	99.4	104.0	102.4	103.4
June	105.2	108.7	104.2	104.8	104.2	104.5	102.3	105.0	102.1	100.8	105.1	104.1	104.3
September	106.0	109.7	105.0	105.5	105.2	105.2	102.7	106.0	102.4	100.9	106.0	104.3	105.1
December	107.0	110.9	105.9	106.4	106.1	106.3	103.9	107.0	103.4	101.9	106.9	105.8	105.6
2008													
March	107.5	111.4	106.4	107.1	106.5	106.6	104.4	107.4	104.0	102.2	107.4	106.6	106.5
June	108.1	112.4	106.9	107.8	106.9	106.7	104.4	108.3	104.3	102.0	108.0	106.6	107.1
September	108.8	113.3	107.5	108.5	107.6	107.4	104.8	108.7	104.6	102.4	108.7	107.2	107.6
December	109.3	114.1	107.9	109.0	108.0	108.0	105.3	109.2	105.0	102.8	109.1	107.8	107.6
2009													
March	109.6	115.3	108.1	108.5	108.0	108.3	106.4	109.5	105.4	103.4	109.2	109.5	107.9
June	109.9	116.2	108.2	108.7	108.0	108.5	106.7	109.8	105.5	103.4	109.3	110.3	108.0
September	110.4	116.8	108.6	108.9	108.6	109.1	107.1	110.4	105.6	103.4	109.9	110.9	108.2
December	110.9	117.7	109.1	109.2	108.9	109.8	107.5	110.9	106.2	104.0	110.2	111.4	108.2
2010													
March	112.0	118.1	110.3	110.0	110.1	111.6	109.9	111.5	108.4	106.6	111.1	114.8	109.5
June	112.7	119.1	110.9	110.3	110.9	112.1	110.7	112.3	108.9	107.4	111.7	116.2	110.0
September	113.5	120.2	111.6	110.9	111.6	112.8	111.7	113.3	110.0	108.7	112.3	117.6	110.4
December	114.1	121.2	112.1	111.7	112.1	113.5	112.2	113.8	110.2	108.9	112.9	117.9	110.6
2011													
March	115.4	122.0	113.6	113.2	113.3	114.2	113.5	115.2	111.7	111.0	114.4	119.0	112.6
June	116.8	122.5	115.2	114.6	114.9	115.6	116.4	115.9	114.1	113.9	115.7	122.3	113.9
September	117.1	123.2	115.4	114.7	115.3	116.1	116.3	116.0	113.8	113.4	116.0	122.0	114.0
December	117.7	123.7	116.1	115.6	115.8	117.1	117.1	116.7	114.5	114.0	116.7	122.8	114.4
2012													
March	118.5	124.7	116.8	116.6	116.6	117.9	116.1	117.8	114.2	113.2	117.8	122.9	115.6
June	119.3	125.8	117.5	117.1	117.4	118.8	117.0	118.2	114.8	113.9	118.5	124.3	116.2
September	119.9	127.1	117.9	117.7	117.4	119.9	117.6	118.8	115.7	114.7	118.8	125.5	116.4
December	120.5	127.9	118.5	118.3	117.9	120.6	118.1	119.4	116.1	115.1	119.4	125.6	116.7
2013													
March	121.3	129.1	119.1	118.5	118.9	121.5	118.7	119.8	117.0	115.7	120.0	126.6	117.7
June	121.9	129.9	119.7	119.3	119.4	122.0	119.0	120.3	117.3	116.1	120.6	127.3	118.3
September	122.6	130.9	120.3	120.2	120.1	122.6	119.1	120.8	117.6	116.4	121.4	127.1	118.9
December	123.2	132.1	120.8	120.6	120.7	123.2	119.7	121.2	118.1	116.7	121.8	127.3	119.1
2014													
March	123.8	133.0	121.3	120.9	121.2	123.9	120.5	120.9	119.2	118.1	122.2	128.5	119.9
September	125.1	134.2	122.6	122.4	122.6	126.0	120.9	121.1	119.4	118.2	123.8	131.3	120.9
December	125.7	134.8	123.2	123.1	123.0	126.7	121.6	121.7	120.3	119.3	124.3	131.9	121.4
December	126.4	135.8	123.8	123.8	123.6	127.4	122.3	122.4	120.8	119.9	125.0	132.6	121.7
2015													
March	127.1	136.7	124.5	124.6	123.7	127.6	123.5	122.9	121.4	120.8	125.7	133.4	122.7
June	127.2	137.8	124.2	123.9	124.0	126.9	124.2	123.3	122.0	121.5	125.2	132.3	122.7
September	127.8	138.9	124.8	124.3	124.7	127.6	124.9	123.9	122.3	121.6	125.8	133.2	123.0
December	128.6	140.6	125.3	124.8	125.3	128.2	125.5	124.5	123.2	122.6	126.2	133.9	123.3
2016													
March	129.3	141.5	125.9	124.9	126.7	128.5	126.3	125.2	123.6	123.1	126.9	135.0	124.2
June	129.9	142.4	126.4	125.3	127.5	128.9	126.7	126.0	124.1	123.6	127.3	135.3	124.7
September	130.7	143.9	127.0	125.8	128.3	129.4	127.4	126.7	124.5	124.1	128.1	135.6	125.3
December	131.3	144.9	127.5	126.3	128.6	130.1	128.1	127.3	124.9	124.4	128.5	136.1	125.5

[1] Excludes farm workers, private household workers, and federal government employees.
[2] Not seasonally adjusted.

Table 9-2. Employment Cost Indexes, SIC Basis

(Not seasonally adjusted, December 2005 = 100; annual values are for December.)

Year	All civilian workers [1,2]	State and local government workers [2]	Private industry workers — All private industry workers [2]	Private industry workers excluding sales occupations	By occupational group — Production and nonsupervisory occupations	White-collar occupations	Blue-collar occupations	Service occupations [2]	Goods-producing industries — Total [2]	Construction [2]	Manufacturing [2]	Service-providing industries — Total [2]	Transportation and utilities	Wholesale trade	Retail trade	Finance, insurance, and real estate [2]	Services
TOTAL COMPENSATION																	
1979	...	...	32.8	32.5	...	31.2	35.0	33.9	33.7	...	33.1	32.0	...	...	...	...	...
1980	...	...	36.0	36.0	...	34.2	38.5	37.1	37.0	...	36.4	35.1	...	...	...	...	...
1981	39.0	36.8	39.5	39.4	40.1	37.6	42.2	40.5	40.7	...	40.0	38.6	...	...	...	...	...
1982	41.5	39.4	42.0	42.0	42.8	40.3	44.7	43.9	43.2	...	42.4	41.1	...	...	...	...	...
1983	43.9	41.8	44.4	44.4	45.2	42.7	47.0	46.3	45.3	...	44.6	43.8	...	...	...	...	...
1984	46.2	44.6	46.6	46.7	47.3	44.8	49.0	49.4	47.4	...	46.9	46.0	...	...	...	...	...
1985	48.2	47.1	48.4	48.3	49.1	47.0	50.5	50.9	49.0	50.8	48.4	48.1	50.6	...	52.4	44.7	46.1
1986	49.9	49.6	49.9	49.9	50.5	48.6	51.9	52.4	50.5	52.3	50.0	49.6	51.8	48.5	53.5	46.1	48.1
1987	51.7	51.8	51.6	51.7	52.2	50.4	53.5	53.7	52.1	54.2	51.5	51.4	53.3	50.4	54.8	47.0	50.5
1988	54.2	54.7	54.1	54.1	54.8	52.9	55.9	56.5	54.4	56.5	53.8	54.0	54.9	52.5	58.0	50.0	53.5
1989	56.9	58.1	56.7	56.5	57.6	55.7	58.2	59.0	56.7	59.0	56.3	56.8	56.9	57.1	59.9	52.7	56.4
1990	59.7	61.5	59.3	59.3	60.1	58.4	60.7	61.8	59.4	60.9	59.1	59.4	59.1	58.2	62.5	54.9	59.9
1991	62.3	63.7	61.9	62.0	62.7	61.0	63.4	64.7	62.1	63.3	61.9	61.9	61.7	60.7	65.2	57.2	62.5
1992	64.4	66.0	64.1	64.2	64.9	63.1	65.6	66.7	64.5	65.6	64.3	63.9	63.9	62.5	66.9	57.9	65.2
1993	66.7	67.9	66.4	66.6	67.3	65.4	68.1	68.8	67.0	67.1	66.9	66.2	66.1	64.8	68.9	60.5	67.5
1994	68.7	69.9	68.5	68.6	69.2	67.5	70.0	70.8	69.0	69.6	69.0	68.1	68.7	66.4	70.8	61.8	69.4
1995	70.6	72.0	70.2	70.4	71.0	69.4	71.7	72.1	70.7	71.1	70.8	70.0	71.2	69.4	72.3	64.0	70.9
1996	72.6	73.9	72.4	72.4	73.1	71.7	73.6	74.2	72.7	72.9	72.9	72.3	73.4	71.5	75.1	65.5	73.1
1997	75.0	75.6	74.9	74.9	75.4	74.4	75.5	77.2	74.5	74.8	74.6	75.1	75.5	73.8	77.7	69.9	75.9
1998	77.6	77.8	77.5	77.2	78.1	77.3	77.6	79.4	76.5	77.4	76.6	78.0	78.4	78.0	80.0	74.1	78.2
1999	80.2	80.5	80.2	80.0	80.4	79.9	80.2	82.1	79.1	79.9	79.2	80.6	80.1	81.1	83.0	77.1	80.9
2000	83.6	82.9	83.6	83.6	84.0	83.6	83.6	85.3	82.6	84.6	82.3	84.2	83.5	84.4	86.4	81.0	84.5
2001	87.0	86.4	87.1	87.0	87.4	87.1	86.7	89.1	85.7	88.2	85.3	87.8	87.5	87.2	90.3	83.9	88.3
2002	90.0	89.9	90.0	89.9	90.2	89.9	89.8	92.0	88.9	91.0	88.5	90.5	91.0	91.1	91.9	87.6	90.7
2003	93.5	92.9	93.6	93.6	93.6	93.6	93.4	94.9	92.4	94.1	92.2	94.2	94.0	94.0	94.9	94.1	94.0
2004	96.9	96.1	97.1	97.2	97.2	96.9	97.5	97.7	96.8	96.4	96.7	97.3	97.6	96.5	97.1	96.7	97.5
2005	100.0	100.0	100.0	100.0	100.0	100.0	100.0	100.0	100.0	100.0	100.0	100.0	100.0	100.0	100.0	100.0	100.0
WAGES AND SALARIES																	
1979	...	...	36.1	36.1	36.8	34.1	39.4	37.9	38.2	41.4	37.5	34.9	39.1	33.7	39.7	32.8	31.7
1980	...	...	39.4	39.3	40.3	37.1	43.1	41.0	41.8	45.0	41.0	38.0	43.5	37.1	42.5	35.2	34.5
1981	42.3	40.1	42.8	42.9	43.9	40.4	46.8	44.4	45.4	49.0	44.5	41.4	47.1	40.0	45.6	38.8	38.1
1982	45.0	42.7	45.5	45.6	46.7	43.1	49.4	48.2	48.0	51.5	47.0	44.2	50.5	42.5	47.5	41.3	41.2
1983	47.3	45.0	47.8	47.9	48.9	45.7	51.3	50.4	49.9	53.0	49.0	46.7	53.0	45.1	49.5	44.3	43.9
1984	49.4	47.7	49.8	50.1	50.8	47.6	53.1	53.5	51.8	53.7	51.2	48.7	54.8	47.6	52.0	43.9	46.7
1985	51.5	50.3	51.8	51.9	52.9	50.0	55.0	54.8	53.6	55.3	53.0	51.0	56.9	49.7	54.5	47.9	48.4
1986	53.3	53.0	53.5	53.6	54.3	51.7	56.4	56.2	55.3	56.7	54.8	52.5	57.9	51.5	55.7	49.2	50.3
1987	55.2	55.2	55.2	55.5	56.0	53.6	58.1	57.6	57.1	58.6	56.6	54.3	59.1	53.6	57.2	49.8	53.0
1988	57.5	57.9	57.5	57.5	58.4	56.1	59.9	60.1	58.9	60.7	58.3	56.9	60.6	55.6	60.1	52.9	55.6
1989	60.1	61.0	59.9	59.8	61.0	58.7	62.0	62.3	61.2	62.8	60.6	59.5	62.2	60.7	62.0	55.7	58.3
1990	62.6	64.2	62.3	62.4	63.2	61.2	64.2	64.8	63.4	64.1	63.1	61.8	64.3	61.2	64.2	57.6	61.6
1991	64.9	66.4	64.6	64.7	65.4	63.5	66.4	67.4	65.8	66.0	65.6	64.1	66.6	63.6	66.6	59.6	63.8
1992	66.6	68.4	66.3	66.5	67.2	65.2	68.1	68.8	67.6	67.3	67.6	65.7	68.7	65.5	68.2	59.5	66.0
1993	68.7	70.2	68.3	68.5	69.2	67.4	70.0	70.3	69.6	68.6	69.7	67.8	70.9	67.1	70.2	62.1	68.0
1994	70.6	72.4	70.2	70.5	71.1	69.3	72.0	72.4	71.7	70.8	71.8	69.6	73.5	69.1	71.9	62.8	70.0
1995	72.7	74.7	72.2	72.5	73.0	71.3	74.1	74.0	73.7	72.5	73.9	71.7	76.0	72.4	73.6	65.1	71.7
1996	75.1	76.8	74.7	74.9	75.5	73.8	76.3	76.6	76.0	74.6	76.3	74.2	78.1	74.7	76.8	67.2	74.2
1997	77.9	78.9	77.6	77.7	78.3	77.0	78.8	79.9	78.3	77.1	78.6	77.4	80.7	77.0	79.7	71.8	77.5
1998	80.8	81.3	80.6	80.4	81.4	80.3	81.3	82.4	81.1	79.9	81.3	80.5	83.0	81.5	82.2	76.9	80.1
1999	83.6	84.2	83.5	83.4	83.8	83.1	84.0	85.1	83.8	82.5	84.1	83.4	84.8	84.5	85.2	79.8	83.0
2000	86.7	87.0	86.7	86.7	87.1	86.4	87.1	88.3	87.1	86.9	87.1	86.6	87.5	87.4	88.6	83.4	86.3
2001	90.0	90.2	90.0	90.0	90.4	89.6	90.5	91.8	90.2	90.4	90.2	89.9	91.7	89.3	91.9	85.8	90.0
2002	92.6	93.1	92.4	92.5	92.6	92.0	93.0	94.1	92.9	92.8	93.0	92.3	94.7	92.8	93.2	89.4	92.0
2003	95.2	95.0	95.2	95.4	95.1	95.2	95.2	96.2	95.1	95.1	95.2	95.3	96.2	95.3	95.5	95.9	94.8
2004	97.5	97.0	97.5	97.8	97.5	97.5	97.6	97.9	97.4	97.0	97.5	97.7	98.6	96.6	97.2	97.7	97.8
2005	100.0	100.0	100.0	100.0	100.0	100.0	100.0	100.0	100.0	100.0	100.0	100.0	100.0	100.0	100.0	100.0	100.0

[1]Excludes farm workers, private household workers, and federal government employees.
[2]Roughly continuous and comparable with new NAICS-based series. See notes and definitions for more information.
... = Not available.

Table 9-2. Employment Cost Indexes, SIC Basis—*Continued*

(Not seasonally adjusted, December 2005 = 100; annual values are for December.)

| Year | All civilian workers [1,2] | State and local government workers [2] | All private industry workers [2] | Private industry workers excluding sales occupations | By occupational group | | | | By industry division | | | | | | | | |
| | | | | | Production and nonsupervisory occupations | White-collar occupations | Blue-collar occupations | Service occupations [2] | Goods-producing industries | | | Service-providing industries | | | | | |
									Total [2]	Construction [2]	Manufacturing [2]	Total [2]	Transportation and utilities	Wholesale trade	Retail trade	Finance, insurance, and real estate [2]	Services
TOTAL BENEFITS																	
1979	. . .	. . .	25.7	. . .	. . .	24.7	27.4	. . .	26.0	. . .	25.8	25.4	. . .	. . .	. . .	. . .	. . .
1980	. . .	. . .	28.7	. . .	. . .	27.7	30.4	. . .	28.8	. . .	28.5	28.6	. . .	. . .	. . .	. . .	. . .
1981	31.8	. . .	32.2	. . .	. . .	31.1	34.0	. . .	32.4	. . .	32.1	31.9	. . .	. . .	. . .	. . .	. . .
1982	34.2	. . .	34.5	. . .	. . .	33.3	36.5	. . .	34.8	. . .	34.4	34.1	. . .	. . .	. . .	. . .	. . .
1983	36.8	. . .	37.1	. . .	. . .	35.8	39.1	. . .	37.2	. . .	36.9	36.8	. . .	. . .	. . .	. . .	. . .
1984	39.3	. . .	39.5	. . .	. . .	38.3	41.4	. . .	39.6	. . .	39.3	39.4	. . .	. . .	. . .	. . .	. . .
1985	40.8	. . .	40.9	. . .	. . .	40.0	42.5	41.2	40.8	. . .	40.4	40.9	. . .	. . .	. . .	. . .	. . .
1986	42.4	. . .	42.3	. . .	. . .	41.4	43.8	42.9	42.0	. . .	41.6	42.5	. . .	. . .	. . .	. . .	. . .
1987	44.0	. . .	43.7	. . .	. . .	42.9	45.3	43.9	43.2	. . .	42.7	44.2	. . .	. . .	. . .	. . .	. . .
1988	47.0	. . .	46.7	. . .	. . .	45.6	48.6	47.4	46.3	. . .	46.0	47.1	. . .	. . .	. . .	. . .	. . .
1989	50.1	52.2	49.6	. . .	. . .	48.6	51.2	50.5	48.8	. . .	48.7	50.2	. . .	. . .	. . .	. . .	. . .
1990	53.5	55.8	52.9	. . .	. . .	52.0	54.4	53.8	52.3	. . .	52.1	53.4	. . .	. . .	. . .	. . .	. . .
1991	56.5	58.0	56.2	. . .	. . .	55.2	57.8	57.7	55.5	. . .	55.2	56.7	. . .	. . .	. . .	. . .	. . .
1992	59.5	61.1	59.1	. . .	. . .	57.8	61.0	61.0	58.7	. . .	58.3	59.4	. . .	. . .	. . .	. . .	. . .
1993	62.2	62.9	62.0	. . .	. . .	60.5	64.4	64.4	62.0	. . .	61.8	62.0	. . .	. . .	. . .	. . .	. . .
1994	64.4	64.6	64.3	. . .	. . .	63.2	66.2	66.0	64.1	. . .	63.9	64.4	. . .	. . .	. . .	. . .	. . .
1995	65.8	66.3	65.7	. . .	. . .	64.8	67.2	66.6	65.2	. . .	65.0	66.0	. . .	. . .	. . .	. . .	. . .
1996	67.1	67.8	67.0	. . .	. . .	66.2	68.4	67.3	66.4	. . .	66.5	67.3	. . .	. . .	. . .	. . .	. . .
1997	68.5	68.6	68.5	. . .	. . .	68.0	69.4	69.6	67.3	. . .	67.4	69.2	. . .	. . .	. . .	. . .	. . .
1998	70.3	70.7	70.2	. . .	. . .	69.9	70.7	70.9	68.1	. . .	67.9	71.4	. . .	. . .	. . .	. . .	. . .
1999	72.6	72.7	72.6	. . .	. . .	72.3	73.0	73.4	70.5	. . .	70.3	73.8	. . .	. . .	. . .	. . .	. . .
2000	76.2	74.4	76.7	. . .	. . .	76.5	76.9	76.6	74.3	. . .	73.6	78.1	. . .	. . .	. . .	. . .	. . .
2001	80.2	78.5	80.6	. . .	. . .	81.1	79.5	81.3	77.3	. . .	76.3	82.5	. . .	. . .	. . .	. . .	. . .
2002	84.2	83.3	84.4	. . .	. . .	84.6	83.8	85.7	81.3	. . .	80.4	86.1	. . .	. . .	. . .	. . .	. . .
2003	89.5	88.4	89.8	. . .	. . .	89.7	89.8	91.3	87.4	. . .	86.7	91.2	. . .	. . .	. . .	. . .	. . .
2004	95.7	94.3	96.0	. . .	. . .	95.3	97.3	97.1	95.7	. . .	95.3	96.2	. . .	. . .	. . .	. . .	. . .
2005	100.0	100.0	100.0	. . .	. . .	100.0	100.0	100.0	100.0	. . .	100.0	100.0	. . .	. . .	. . .	. . .	. . .

[1]Excludes farm workers, private household workers, and federal government employees.
[2]Roughly continuous and comparable with new NAICS-based series. See notes and definitions for more information.
. . . = Not available.

SECTION 9B: PRODUCTIVITY AND RELATED DATA

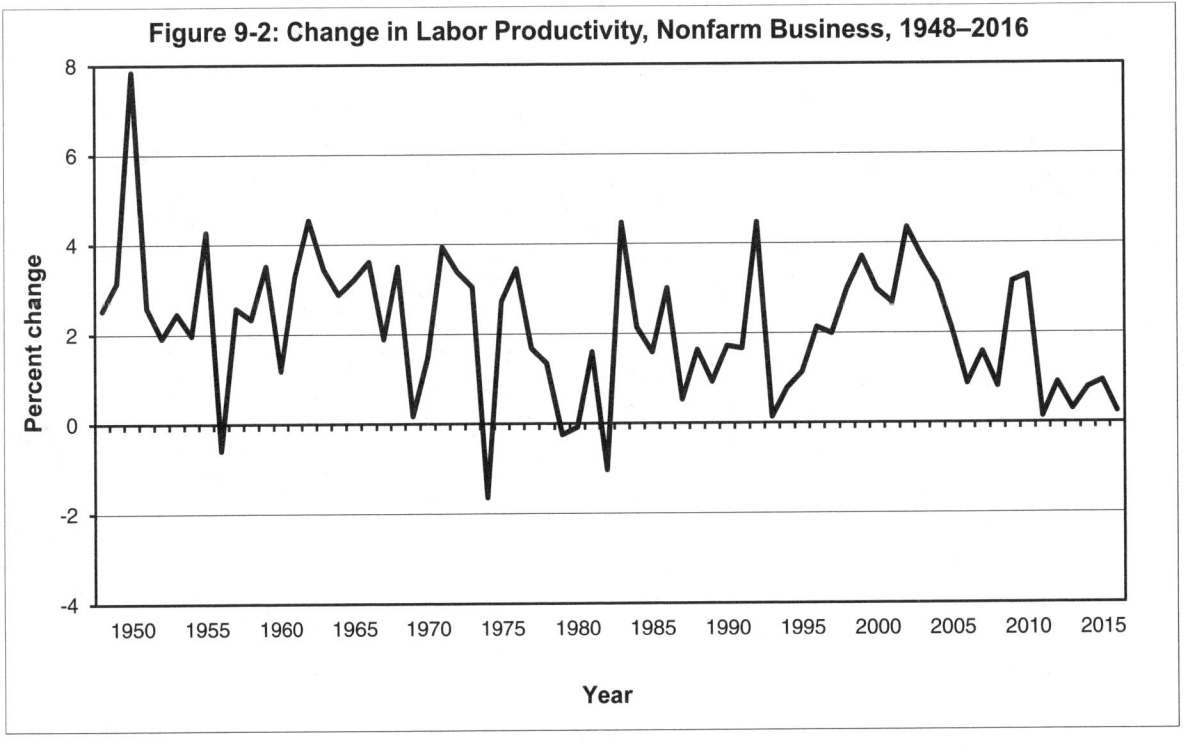

Figure 9-2: Change in Labor Productivity, Nonfarm Business, 1948–2016

- As Figure 9-2 demonstrates, the rate of change in U.S. nonfarm labor productivity has often been quite variable from year to year. Up through the 1980s, productivity tended to decline (growth rates were less than zero) in recession years but rebound sharply in recovery. One explanation of this was that firms expected that declines in demand would be temporary, and therefore held on to their experienced workers in order to be prepared for the recovery. (Tables 9-3A and B)

- In the 1990s and 2000s, productivity growth rates were still variable, but output per hour no longer declined even in a severe recession. This suggests a somewhat greater tendency to regard negative demand trends as lasting. (Table 9-3A)

- On average, measuring between cyclically high growth years, nonfarm productivity grew at a 2.8 percent annual rate from 1948 to 1973. Productivity growth slowed between 1973 and 1989, averaging just 1.4 percent. From 1989 to 2016, however, productivity in the business sector increased each year from 1989 through 2016, except between 2010 and 2011, when it remained stable. (Tables 9-3A and B)

Table 9-3A. Productivity and Related Data: Recent Data

(2009 = 100, seasonally adjusted.)

Year and quarter	Output per hour of all persons	Output	Hours of all persons	Employ-ment	Average weekly hours	Unit labor costs	Compen-sation per hour	Real hourly compen-sation	Labor share	Unit nonlabor payments	Implicit price deflator	Current dollar output	Compen-sation	Nonlabor payments	Output per job
1950	24.9	14.0	56.3	48.2	116.9	18.2	4.5	36.8	108.5	14.8	16.8	2.4	2.6	2.1	29.1
1951	25.7	14.9	58.1	49.5	117.5	19.4	5.0	37.4	107.1	16.3	18.1	2.7	2.9	2.4	30.2
1952	26.4	15.4	58.3	49.7	117.2	20.0	5.3	39.0	109.1	16.0	18.3	2.8	3.1	2.5	31.0
1953	27.4	16.2	59.0	50.4	117.1	20.5	5.6	41.1	111.0	15.6	18.4	3.0	3.3	2.5	32.1
1954	28.0	16.0	57.0	49.2	116.0	20.7	5.8	42.2	111.5	15.6	18.5	3.0	3.3	2.5	32.5
1955	29.2	17.3	59.1	50.6	116.9	20.3	5.9	43.4	108.3	16.6	18.8	3.2	3.5	2.9	34.2
1956	29.3	17.6	60.0	51.6	116.3	21.6	6.3	45.6	111.5	16.3	19.4	3.4	3.8	2.9	34.1
1957	30.2	17.9	59.2	51.5	114.9	22.3	6.7	47.0	111.5	16.8	20.0	3.6	4.0	3.0	34.7
1958	31.1	17.6	56.5	49.6	114.1	22.6	7.0	47.7	111.2	17.2	20.4	3.6	4.0	3.0	35.5
1959	32.2	19.0	58.9	51.1	115.2	22.7	7.3	49.3	110.5	17.6	20.6	3.9	4.3	3.3	37.1
1960	32.8	19.3	59.0	51.4	114.8	23.3	7.6	50.5	111.9	17.4	20.8	4.0	4.5	3.4	37.6
1961	34.0	19.7	58.1	50.8	114.3	23.3	7.9	51.9	111.3	17.7	21.0	4.1	4.6	3.5	38.8
1962	35.5	21.0	59.1	51.5	114.9	23.3	8.3	53.7	110.1	18.2	21.2	4.4	4.9	3.8	40.8
1963	36.9	22.0	59.5	51.8	115.0	23.2	8.6	54.9	109.1	18.6	21.3	4.7	5.1	4.1	42.5
1964	38.1	23.4	61.3	52.7	116.2	23.3	8.9	56.2	108.3	19.1	21.5	5.0	5.5	4.5	44.3
1965	39.5	25.0	63.3	54.3	116.8	23.4	9.2	57.4	106.8	19.8	21.9	5.5	5.8	5.0	46.2
1966	41.2	26.7	65.0	55.9	116.4	23.9	9.9	59.5	106.8	20.3	22.4	6.0	6.4	5.4	47.9
1967	42.1	27.3	64.8	56.6	114.5	24.7	10.4	61.0	107.5	20.6	23.0	6.3	6.7	5.6	48.2
1968	43.6	28.7	65.8	57.7	113.9	25.7	11.2	63.1	107.7	21.4	23.9	6.9	7.4	6.1	49.7
1969	43.8	29.6	67.5	59.5	113.3	27.4	12.0	64.1	109.7	21.7	25.0	7.4	8.1	6.4	49.6
1970	44.7	29.5	66.1	59.4	111.4	28.9	12.9	65.1	110.8	22.2	26.1	7.7	8.5	6.5	49.8
1971	46.5	30.7	65.9	59.5	110.9	29.4	13.7	66.2	108.4	24.0	27.2	8.3	9.0	7.4	51.5
1972	48.0	32.7	68.0	61.2	111.1	30.3	14.5	68.1	107.7	25.1	28.1	9.2	9.9	8.2	53.3
1973	49.4	34.9	70.6	63.9	110.6	31.7	15.7	69.2	107.3	26.6	29.6	10.3	11.1	9.3	54.7
1974	48.6	34.4	70.7	64.8	109.1	35.3	17.2	68.2	108.7	28.6	32.5	11.2	12.1	9.8	53.0
1975	50.3	34.0	67.7	62.9	107.6	37.8	19.0	69.1	106.0	32.7	35.6	12.1	12.9	11.1	54.1
1976	52.0	36.3	69.9	64.8	107.8	39.5	20.5	70.6	105.2	34.8	37.5	13.6	14.3	12.6	56.0
1977	52.9	38.4	72.6	67.7	107.3	41.9	22.2	71.6	105.4	36.8	39.7	15.3	16.1	14.1	56.8
1978	53.5	40.8	76.3	71.4	106.9	44.9	24.0	72.5	105.6	39.2	42.5	17.4	18.3	16.0	57.2
1979	53.6	42.3	78.9	74.2	106.4	49.2	26.4	72.7	106.7	41.8	46.1	19.5	20.8	17.7	57.0
1980	53.5	41.9	78.2	74.3	105.2	54.5	29.2	72.4	108.6	44.2	50.2	21.0	22.8	18.5	56.3
1981	54.7	43.1	78.7	75.1	104.9	58.4	31.9	72.4	106.5	49.9	54.8	23.6	25.2	21.5	57.4
1982	54.3	41.8	77.0	73.9	104.2	63.1	34.3	73.3	108.9	50.9	58.0	24.2	26.4	21.3	56.6
1983	56.3	44.1	78.3	74.5	105.1	63.7	35.8	73.4	106.1	54.9	60.0	26.5	28.1	24.2	59.2
1984	57.9	48.0	82.9	78.3	105.9	64.7	37.4	73.6	104.7	57.7	61.7	29.6	31.0	27.7	61.3
1985	59.2	50.2	84.8	80.2	105.8	66.5	39.3	74.8	104.7	59.3	63.5	31.9	33.4	29.8	62.6
1986	60.8	52.0	85.5	81.5	104.9	68.3	41.5	77.7	106.1	58.9	64.3	33.5	35.5	30.6	63.8
1987	61.2	53.9	88.1	83.8	105.1	70.5	43.1	77.9	107.4	58.8	65.6	35.3	38.0	31.7	64.3
1988	62.1	56.2	90.5	86.3	104.8	73.1	45.4	79.2	108.0	60.1	67.7	38.0	41.1	33.8	65.1
1989	62.8	58.3	92.9	88.2	105.3	74.5	46.8	78.2	106.1	64.2	70.2	40.9	43.4	37.4	66.1
1990	64.1	59.3	92.5	88.8	104.2	77.6	49.7	79.1	107.0	65.4	72.5	43.0	46.0	38.8	66.8
1991	65.1	58.9	90.5	87.4	103.6	79.9	52.0	79.9	107.1	67.2	74.5	43.9	47.1	39.6	67.4
1992	68.1	61.4	90.2	86.9	103.7	81.0	55.2	82.7	106.9	68.4	75.7	46.5	49.8	42.0	70.7
1993	68.2	63.2	92.6	88.8	104.4	82.1	56.0	81.9	106.0	71.1	77.5	49.0	51.9	44.9	71.2
1994	68.6	66.2	96.5	91.8	105.1	82.2	56.4	80.8	104.2	74.2	78.9	52.2	54.5	49.2	72.2
1995	69.2	68.3	98.8	94.4	104.7	83.6	57.8	80.9	104.1	75.6	80.2	54.8	57.1	51.7	72.4
1996	70.9	71.5	100.9	96.5	104.6	84.5	59.9	81.6	103.6	77.4	81.5	58.3	60.4	55.3	74.1
1997	72.5	75.3	103.9	99.1	104.9	85.9	62.3	83.1	103.9	78.1	82.7	62.3	64.7	58.8	76.0
1998	74.7	79.2	106.0	101.1	104.8	88.3	65.9	86.8	106.2	75.9	83.1	65.8	69.9	60.1	78.3
1999	77.6	83.6	107.7	102.8	104.8	89.1	69.1	89.1	106.4	76.3	83.7	70.0	74.5	63.7	81.3
2000	80.0	87.3	109.2	104.5	104.5	92.5	73.9	92.1	108.4	75.3	85.3	74.5	80.7	65.8	83.5
2001	82.1	87.9	107.0	103.8	103.1	94.1	77.3	93.6	108.4	76.7	86.8	76.3	82.7	67.4	84.7
2002	85.7	89.5	104.4	101.5	102.9	92.2	79.0	94.2	105.5	80.7	87.4	78.2	82.5	72.2	88.1
2003	89.0	92.3	103.8	101.3	102.4	92.1	82.0	95.6	104.0	83.7	88.6	81.8	85.1	77.3	91.1
2004	91.8	96.5	105.1	102.7	102.3	93.4	85.8	97.5	103.1	86.8	90.7	87.5	90.1	83.7	94.0
2005	93.8	100.1	106.8	104.6	102.1	94.8	88.9	97.7	101.4	91.6	93.5	93.6	94.9	91.8	95.8
2006	94.7	103.3	109.1	106.6	102.4	97.6	92.4	98.3	101.6	93.9	96.0	99.2	100.8	97.0	96.9
2007	96.0	105.5	109.8	107.5	102.2	100.4	96.4	99.8	102.2	95.3	98.2	103.6	105.9	100.5	98.1
2008	96.8	104.2	107.6	106.0	101.6	102.2	99.0	98.7	102.5	96.3	99.8	104.0	106.6	100.4	98.4
2009	100.0	100.0	100.0	100.0	100.0	100.0	100.0	100.0	100.0	100.0	100.0	100.0	100.0	100.0	100.0
2010	103.3	103.2	99.9	98.8	101.1	98.6	101.8	100.2	97.5	104.7	101.1	104.4	101.7	108.0	104.4
2011	103.3	105.3	102.0	100.4	101.5	100.7	104.0	99.2	97.4	107.0	103.3	108.9	106.1	112.7	104.9
2012	104.0	108.4	104.2	102.4	101.8	102.7	106.8	99.8	97.5	108.9	105.3	114.2	111.4	118.0	105.9
2013	104.8	110.8	105.8	104.1	101.7	103.4	108.3	99.7	96.7	111.8	106.9	118.5	114.6	123.9	106.5
2014	105.4	114.1	108.3	106.3	101.9	105.4	111.1	100.7	97.1	112.9	108.5	123.9	120.3	128.8	107.4
2015	106.2	117.6	110.7	108.7	101.8	107.5	114.2	103.4	98.4	111.7	109.3	128.6	126.5	131.4	108.2
2016	106.6	119.8	112.4	110.7	101.6	109.8	117.0	104.6	99.5	111.1	110.4	132.2	131.5	133.1	108.2
2014															
1st quarter	104.8	112.0	106.9	105.3	101.5	105.8	101.0	101.0	98.1	110.8	107.9	120.9	118.5	124.1	106.4
2nd quarter	105.2	113.4	107.8	105.8	101.9	104.9	99.9	99.9	96.6	113.6	108.5	123.0	118.9	128.8	107.1
3rd quarter	106.0	115.1	108.6	106.5	102.0	104.8	100.5	100.5	96.3	114.5	108.9	125.4	120.7	131.8	108.1
4th quarter	105.6	115.9	109.8	107.5	102.1	106.1	101.5	101.5	97.5	112.6	108.9	126.2	123.1	130.6	107.9
2015															
1st quarter	105.8	116.6	110.2	108.0	102.0	106.4	102.6	102.6	97.8	112.0	108.7	126.8	124.0	130.6	108.0
2nd quarter	106.2	117.5	110.7	108.7	101.8	107.3	103.2	103.2	98.2	112.0	109.3	128.4	126.1	131.6	108.1
3rd quarter	106.7	118.1	110.6	108.7	101.7	107.5	103.5	103.5	98.1	112.4	109.5	129.4	126.9	132.8	108.6
4th quarter	106.2	118.3	111.5	109.6	101.7	108.9	104.3	104.3	99.4	110.5	109.6	129.7	128.9	130.7	108.0
2016															
1st quarter	106.0	118.6	111.9	110.1	101.6	108.8	104.0	104.0	99.2	110.8	109.7	130.1	129.1	131.4	107.7
2nd quarter	105.9	119.1	112.4	110.6	101.7	110.4	104.8	104.8	100.2	110.0	110.3	131.3	131.5	131.0	107.6
3rd quarter	106.9	120.3	112.6	110.8	101.6	110.6	105.5	105.5	100.1	110.3	110.5	132.9	133.1	132.8	108.6
4th quarter	107.5	121.1	112.7	111.2	101.3	109.4	104.1	104.1	98.6	113.2	111.0	134.4	132.5	137.1	108.9

Table 9-3A. Productivity and Related Data: Recent Data—*Continued*

(2009 = 100, seasonally adjusted.)

Year and quarter	Output per hour of all persons	Output	Hours of all persons	Employ-ment	Average weekly hours	Unit labor costs	Compen-sation per hour	Real hourly compen-sation	Labor share	Unit nonlabor payments	Implicit price deflator	Current dollar output	Compen-sation	Nonlabor payments	Output per job
1950	28.2	13.7	48.8	41.2	118.5	17.3	4.9	39.7	108.3	14.2	16.0	2.2	2.4	1.9	33.4
1951	28.9	14.8	51.1	43.0	118.7	18.4	5.3	40.0	107.7	15.2	17.1	2.5	2.7	2.2	34.3
1952	29.5	15.2	51.6	43.5	118.6	19.0	5.6	41.4	109.3	15.2	17.4	2.6	2.9	2.3	34.9
1953	30.2	16.0	52.9	44.8	118.1	19.6	5.9	43.4	110.5	15.2	17.8	2.8	3.1	2.4	35.6
1954	30.8	15.7	51.1	43.6	117.2	19.8	6.1	44.4	110.8	15.2	17.9	2.8	3.1	2.4	36.1
1955	32.1	17.1	53.2	44.9	118.4	19.7	6.3	46.2	108.2	16.1	18.2	3.1	3.4	2.8	38.0
1956	31.9	17.4	54.5	46.2	117.9	21.1	6.7	48.3	111.5	15.8	18.9	3.3	3.7	2.8	37.6
1957	32.7	17.7	54.2	46.5	116.6	21.7	7.1	49.5	111.5	16.4	19.5	3.5	3.9	2.9	38.1
1958	33.5	17.4	51.9	44.8	115.8	22.1	7.4	50.0	111.6	16.5	19.8	3.4	3.8	2.9	38.8
1959	34.7	18.8	54.3	46.5	116.9	22.1	7.7	51.6	110.2	17.2	20.1	3.8	4.2	3.2	40.5
1960	35.1	19.2	54.6	47.0	116.4	22.8	8.0	52.9	112.3	16.8	20.3	3.9	4.4	3.2	40.8
1961	36.2	19.0	54.1	46.6	116.0	22.8	8.3	54.1	111.5	17.2	20.5	4.0	4.5	3.4	42.0
1962	37.9	20.9	55.2	47.5	116.4	22.7	8.6	55.7	110.0	17.8	20.7	4.3	4.8	3.7	44.1
1963	39.2	21.9	55.9	48.0	116.4	22.7	8.9	56.9	109.1	18.2	20.8	4.6	5.0	4.0	45.6
1964	40.3	23.3	57.9	49.2	117.8	22.8	9.2	57.9	108.0	18.7	21.1	4.9	5.3	4.4	47.5
1965	41.6	25.0	60.2	50.9	118.2	22.8	9.5	58.9	106.7	19.4	21.4	5.3	5.7	4.8	49.1
1966	43.1	26.8	62.2	52.9	117.6	23.3	10.0	60.6	106.6	19.8	21.8	5.9	6.2	5.3	50.7
1967	43.9	27.3	62.2	53.8	115.7	24.2	10.6	62.3	107.4	20.2	22.5	6.2	6.6	5.5	50.8
1968	45.4	28.8	63.3	55.1	115.0	25.1	11.4	64.3	107.5	21.0	23.4	6.7	7.2	6.0	52.3
1969	45.5	29.7	65.1	57.0	114.2	26.8	12.2	65.1	109.7	21.1	24.4	7.2	8.0	6.3	52.0
1970	46.2	29.6	64.1	57.1	112.3	28.3	13.1	65.9	110.7	21.7	25.5	7.6	8.4	6.4	51.9
1971	48.0	30.7	64.0	57.2	111.8	28.9	13.9	67.0	108.4	23.5	26.6	8.2	8.9	7.2	53.7
1972	49.6	32.8	66.1	59.0	112.0	29.7	14.7	69.1	108.3	24.3	27.4	9.0	9.7	8.0	55.6
1973	51.1	35.2	68.7	61.6	111.6	31.0	15.9	70.0	109.2	24.8	28.4	10.0	10.9	8.7	57.1
1974	50.3	34.6	68.8	62.6	110.0	34.5	17.4	69.0	110.1	27.0	31.4	10.9	12.0	9.3	55.3
1975	51.7	34.1	65.9	60.8	108.4	37.2	19.2	69.9	107.0	31.3	34.7	11.8	12.7	10.7	56.0
1976	53.5	36.5	68.2	62.9	108.6	38.7	20.7	71.2	105.7	33.7	36.6	13.4	14.1	12.3	58.0
1977	54.3	38.6	70.9	65.7	107.9	41.2	22.4	72.3	105.8	35.7	38.9	15.0	15.9	13.8	58.7
1978	55.1	41.1	74.6	69.4	107.6	44.1	24.3	73.4	106.3	37.8	41.5	17.1	18.1	15.5	59.2
1979	54.9	42.5	77.3	72.3	106.9	48.5	26.6	73.4	107.7	40.1	45.0	19.1	20.6	17.1	58.7
1980	54.9	42.1	76.7	72.6	105.7	53.7	29.5	73.1	109.0	43.1	49.3	20.7	22.6	18.1	58.0
1981	55.8	43.1	77.2	73.4	105.3	58.0	32.3	73.3	107.4	48.4	54.0	23.2	25.0	20.8	58.7
1982	55.2	41.7	75.5	72.2	104.6	62.8	34.7	74.1	109.5	49.8	57.4	23.9	26.2	20.8	57.8
1983	57.7	44.4	77.0	72.9	105.6	62.9	36.3	74.3	106.2	54.1	59.2	26.3	27.9	24.0	60.9
1984	58.9	48.1	81.7	76.8	106.3	64.2	37.8	74.4	105.4	56.3	60.9	29.3	30.9	27.1	62.6
1985	59.8	50.2	83.9	79.0	106.1	66.3	39.6	75.4	105.3	58.3	62.9	31.6	33.2	29.2	63.5
1986	61.6	52.1	84.5	80.4	105.1	68.0	41.9	78.4	106.6	58.0	63.8	33.2	35.4	30.2	64.8
1987	62.0	54.0	87.1	82.7	105.3	70.3	43.5	78.7	107.9	57.9	65.1	35.1	37.9	31.2	65.3
1988	63.0	56.4	89.6	85.3	105.0	72.7	45.8	79.8	108.3	59.3	67.1	37.8	41.0	33.4	66.1
1989	63.6	58.5	92.0	87.2	105.5	74.1	47.1	78.7	106.6	63.1	69.5	40.6	43.3	36.9	67.0
1990	64.6	59.4	91.9	87.9	104.5	77.2	49.9	79.5	107.4	64.4	71.8	42.7	45.8	38.2	67.6
1991	65.7	59.0	89.8	86.4	103.9	79.6	52.3	80.4	107.4	66.4	74.1	43.7	47.0	39.2	68.3
1992	68.7	61.4	89.5	86.0	104.1	80.9	55.5	83.3	107.4	67.5	75.3	46.2	49.7	41.5	71.4
1993	68.8	63.3	92.1	88.0	104.7	81.8	56.2	82.2	106.1	70.4	77.0	48.8	51.8	44.6	72.0
1994	69.3	66.3	95.6	90.9	105.2	82.0	56.8	81.4	104.5	73.5	78.5	52.0	54.3	48.7	72.9
1995	70.1	68.6	97.9	93.5	104.7	83.1	58.2	81.4	104.1	75.3	79.8	54.7	57.0	51.6	73.3
1996	71.6	71.7	100.1	95.7	104.6	84.1	60.2	82.1	104.0	76.4	80.9	58.0	60.3	54.8	74.9
1997	73.0	75.4	103.3	98.4	105.0	85.7	62.6	83.5	104.1	77.5	82.3	62.1	64.6	58.5	76.6
1998	75.2	79.4	105.6	100.6	104.9	88.0	66.2	87.1	106.3	75.5	82.8	65.7	69.8	60.0	78.9
1999	78.0	83.8	107.5	102.5	104.9	88.8	69.2	89.2	106.3	76.2	83.6	70.0	74.4	63.9	81.8
2000	80.3	87.5	109.0	104.3	104.5	92.3	74.1	92.4	108.3	75.3	85.2	74.5	80.7	65.8	83.9
2001	82.4	88.1	106.9	103.7	103.1	93.8	77.3	93.7	108.3	76.6	86.6	76.3	82.6	67.5	85.0
2002	86.0	89.7	104.3	101.3	102.9	91.9	79.1	94.3	105.3	80.9	87.3	78.3	82.4	72.5	88.5
2003	89.2	92.5	103.7	101.3	102.4	92.0	82.0	95.7	104.0	83.5	88.5	81.8	85.1	77.2	91.3
2004	92.0	96.6	105.1	102.7	102.3	93.3	85.8	97.4	103.3	86.2	90.3	87.2	90.1	83.2	94.1
2005	93.9	100.2	106.8	104.5	102.1	94.7	88.9	97.7	101.5	91.5	93.4	93.6	95.0	91.7	95.9
2006	94.7	103.4	109.2	106.6	102.5	97.5	92.3	98.3	101.6	93.9	96.0	99.3	100.9	97.1	97.0
2007	96.2	105.8	110.0	107.6	102.3	100.1	96.3	99.6	102.2	94.9	97.9	103.6	105.9	100.4	98.4
2008	97.0	104.4	107.7	106.0	101.6	102.1	99.0	98.6	102.6	95.8	99.4	103.9	106.6	100.0	98.5
2009	100.0	100.0	100.0	100.0	100.0	100.0	100.0	100.0	100.0	100.0	100.0	100.0	100.0	100.0	100.0
2010	103.3	103.2	99.9	98.8	101.1	98.7	101.9	100.3	97.7	104.2	101.0	104.2	101.8	107.5	104.4
2011	103.4	105.5	102.0	100.4	101.6	100.7	104.2	99.3	98.0	105.7	102.8	108.4	106.2	111.5	105.1
2012	104.3	108.8	104.2	102.4	101.8	102.5	106.9	99.9	97.8	107.9	104.7	113.9	111.4	117.4	106.2
2013	104.7	110.9	106.0	104.2	101.7	103.3	108.2	99.6	97.2	110.5	106.3	117.9	114.6	122.5	106.4
2014	105.5	114.3	108.4	106.3	101.9	105.4	111.2	100.8	97.5	111.9	108.1	123.6	120.5	127.9	107.5
2015	106.4	117.8	110.7	108.7	101.8	107.5	114.5	103.6	98.5	111.5	109.2	128.6	126.7	131.3	108.4
2016	106.7	119.8	112.3	110.6	101.5	109.9	117.3	104.8	99.5	111.3	110.5	132.4	131.7	133.3	108.3
2014															
1st quarter	104.7	112.1	107.1	105.4	101.6	105.9	110.8	100.9	98.5	109.8	107.5	120.5	120.7	123.1	106.4
2nd quarter	105.1	113.5	108.0	105.9	101.9	104.9	110.2	99.9	97.1	112.4	108.0	122.6	121.3	127.6	107.2
3rd quarter	106.2	115.3	108.6	106.5	102.0	104.8	111.3	100.6	96.6	113.7	108.5	125.1	122.8	131.1	108.3
4th quarter	105.8	116.1	109.7	107.5	102.1	106.1	112.3	101.7	97.8	111.8	108.5	126.0	124.3	129.8	108.1
2015															
1st quarter	106.1	116.8	110.1	107.9	102.0	106.3	112.9	102.8	97.9	111.8	108.6	126.9	126.5	130.6	108.3
2nd quarter	106.4	117.7	110.6	108.6	101.8	107.3	114.1	103.4	98.3	111.8	109.1	128.0	128.0	131.5	108.4
3rd quarter	106.9	118.2	110.6	108.8	101.7	107.5	114.9	103.7	98.3	112.1	109.4	129.3	129.1	132.5	108.7
4th quarter	106.3	118.5	111.4	109.5	101.7	109.0	115.9	104.5	99.5	110.3	109.5	129.8	130.9	130.6	108.2
2016															
1st quarter	106.2	118.7	110.1	110.0	101.6	108.9	115.6	104.2	99.3	110.9	109.7	130.2	130.4	131.6	107.9
2nd quarter	106.1	119.1	110.6	110.5	101.6	110.6	117.3	105.2	100.2	110.1	110.3	131.5	132.7	131.1	107.9
3rd quarter	107.0	120.4	110.6	110.7	101.6	110.8	118.5	105.7	100.1	110.5	110.6	133.2	134.7	133.0	108.7
4th quarter	107.5	121.2	111.4	111.3	101.3	109.4	117.6	104.2	98.4	113.6	111.2	134.7	134.1	137.7	108.9

Table 9-3B. Productivity and Related Data: Historical Data

(2009 = 100, seasonally adjusted.)

Year and quarter	Business sector								Nonfarm business sector							
	Output per hour of all persons	Output	Hours of all persons	Compensation per hour	Real compensation per hour	Unit labor costs	Unit nonlabor payments	Implicit price deflator	Output per hour of all persons	Output	Hours of all persons	Compensation per hour	Real compensation per hour	Unit labor costs	Unit nonlabor payments	Implicit price deflator
1947	21.5	12.3	57.1	3.8	33.7	17.9	12.9	15.8	24.9	12.1	48.5	4.1	36.1	16.5	12.2	14.7
1948	22.5	12.9	57.5	4.2	33.9	18.6	14.3	16.8	25.6	12.6	49.2	4.5	36.3	17.5	13.2	15.7
1949	23.0	12.8	55.7	4.2	34.8	18.4	14.1	16.6	26.4	12.5	47.3	4.6	37.8	17.5	13.6	15.8
1947																
1st quarter	21.5	12.2	56.7	3.7	33.4	17.2	12.7	15.3	24.6	11.9	48.3	4.0	35.7	16.1	11.7	14.3
2nd quarter	21.6	12.2	56.6	3.8	33.8	17.6	12.6	15.5	25.2	12.2	48.3	4.1	36.0	16.1	12.2	14.5
3rd quarter	21.4	12.2	57.1	3.9	33.6	18.1	12.9	15.9	24.4	11.8	48.4	4.2	36.3	17.1	12.4	15.1
4th quarter	21.7	12.5	57.5	4.0	33.9	18.5	13.4	16.4	25.5	12.4	48.9	4.3	36.1	16.8	12.6	15.1
1948																
1st quarter	22.2	12.7	57.2	4.1	33.6	18.3	13.9	16.5	25.6	12.6	49.2	4.4	36.2	17.1	12.8	15.3
2nd quarter	22.7	13.0	57.2	4.1	33.5	18.2	14.5	16.6	25.5	12.5	49.2	4.4	36.1	17.4	13.0	15.6
3rd quarter	22.6	13.0	57.8	4.2	33.8	18.7	14.4	16.9	25.5	12.6	49.5	4.5	36.3	17.7	13.3	15.9
4th quarter	22.7	13.0	57.4	4.3	34.8	19.0	14.1	17.0	25.6	12.6	49.1	4.6	37.0	17.8	13.7	16.1
1949																
1st quarter	22.6	12.8	56.6	4.2	34.5	18.7	14.2	16.8	25.9	12.5	48.2	4.6	37.5	17.8	13.5	16.0
2nd quarter	22.7	12.7	56.1	4.2	34.2	18.5	14.0	16.6	26.2	12.4	47.4	4.6	37.7	17.6	13.4	15.8
3rd quarter	23.3	12.9	55.2	4.2	35.0	18.2	14.2	16.5	26.8	12.6	46.9	4.6	38.1	17.2	13.8	15.8
4th quarter	23.4	12.7	54.5	4.3	35.4	18.3	13.9	16.5	26.6	12.5	46.8	4.6	38.0	17.3	13.6	15.7
1950																
1st quarter	24.5	13.4	54.6	4.4	36.7	18.1	14.1	16.4	27.6	13.0	47.1	4.7	39.1	17.1	13.9	15.8
2nd quarter	24.7	13.8	55.8	4.5	36.9	18.2	14.2	16.5	27.9	13.5	48.3	4.8	39.7	17.3	13.8	15.9
3rd quarter	25.1	14.4	57.3	4.6	36.8	18.2	15.1	16.9	28.5	14.2	49.8	4.9	39.7	17.3	14.3	16.0
4th quarter	25.2	14.5	57.6	4.6	36.8	18.4	15.7	17.3	28.5	14.3	50.3	5.0	39.9	17.7	14.5	16.4
1951																
1st quarter	25.2	14.7	58.2	4.8	36.6	19.1	16.3	17.9	28.6	14.6	51.1	5.2	39.3	18.1	15.1	16.8
2nd quarter	25.3	14.8	58.5	4.9	37.3	19.5	16.0	18.1	28.5	14.7	51.5	5.3	39.8	18.5	15.0	17.0
3rd quarter	26.1	15.1	57.8	5.0	37.8	19.3	16.4	18.1	29.1	14.9	51.0	5.3	40.2	18.3	15.5	17.1
4th quarter	26.0	15.1	58.0	5.1	37.8	19.6	16.4	18.3	29.2	14.9	51.0	5.4	40.4	18.6	15.4	17.3
1952																
1st quarter	26.1	15.2	58.3	5.1	37.9	19.6	16.2	18.2	29.3	15.1	51.4	5.5	40.7	18.7	15.3	17.3
2nd quarter	26.3	15.2	57.7	5.2	38.5	19.8	15.9	18.2	29.3	15.0	51.1	5.5	40.9	18.9	15.1	17.3
3rd quarter	26.4	15.3	57.9	5.3	38.9	20.1	16.0	18.4	29.2	15.0	51.5	5.6	41.1	19.2	15.1	17.5
4th quarter	26.8	15.9	59.3	5.4	39.7	20.3	15.8	18.4	29.8	15.7	52.9	5.7	42.1	19.3	15.3	17.6
1953																
1st quarter	27.2	16.2	59.6	5.5	40.6	20.3	15.7	18.4	30.0	16.0	53.4	5.8	42.7	19.4	15.2	17.6
2nd quarter	27.5	16.4	59.5	5.6	40.8	20.3	15.7	18.4	30.1	16.1	53.5	5.9	43.0	19.5	15.3	17.7
3rd quarter	27.5	16.2	59.0	5.7	41.2	20.6	15.5	18.5	30.2	16.0	53.0	5.9	43.3	19.6	15.2	17.8
4th quarter	27.4	15.9	58.0	5.7	41.1	20.7	15.5	18.5	30.1	15.7	52.2	6.0	43.6	19.9	14.9	17.8
1954																
1st quarter	27.4	15.8	57.6	5.7	41.3	20.8	15.4	18.6	30.2	15.5	51.5	6.0	43.9	20.0	14.9	17.9
2nd quarter	27.8	15.8	56.8	5.8	42.0	20.8	15.3	18.5	30.4	15.5	51.1	6.1	44.0	19.9	15.1	17.9
3rd quarter	28.2	16.0	56.6	5.8	42.2	20.5	15.7	18.5	30.9	15.7	50.9	6.1	44.5	19.7	15.3	17.9
4th quarter	28.7	16.3	57.0	5.9	42.9	20.5	15.8	18.5	31.3	16.1	51.5	6.2	45.1	19.7	15.6	18.0
1955																
1st quarter	29.1	16.9	58.1	5.8	42.7	20.1	16.6	18.6	31.9	16.7	52.3	6.2	45.3	19.4	16.1	18.1
2nd quarter	29.3	17.2	58.7	5.9	43.2	20.2	16.5	18.7	32.0	17.0	53.0	6.3	45.8	19.6	16.1	18.1
3rd quarter	29.3	17.5	59.6	5.9	43.5	20.3	16.7	18.8	32.1	17.2	53.6	6.4	46.5	19.8	16.2	18.3
4th quarter	29.1	17.5	60.2	6.0	43.7	20.6	16.7	19.0	32.0	17.4	54.2	6.4	46.8	20.1	16.2	18.5
1956																
1st quarter	29.0	17.4	60.1	6.2	44.8	21.3	16.3	19.2	31.6	17.3	54.6	6.5	47.5	20.6	15.9	18.6
2nd quarter	29.2	17.6	60.2	6.3	45.4	21.6	16.1	19.3	31.8	17.4	54.7	6.7	48.1	20.9	15.7	18.8
3rd quarter	29.2	17.5	60.0	6.3	45.4	21.8	16.4	19.5	31.8	17.3	54.5	6.8	48.4	21.2	15.8	19.0
4th quarter	29.8	17.8	59.8	6.5	46.1	21.8	16.5	19.6	32.1	17.6	54.8	6.9	48.8	21.4	15.9	19.1
1957																
1st quarter	30.0	17.9	59.8	6.6	46.6	22.1	16.7	19.9	32.5	17.8	54.8	7.0	49.1	21.4	16.4	19.3
2nd quarter	30.0	17.8	59.5	6.7	46.7	22.3	16.7	20.0	32.4	17.7	54.7	7.0	49.1	21.7	16.2	19.4
3rd quarter	30.3	18.0	59.4	6.7	46.7	22.3	17.0	20.1	32.8	17.9	54.4	7.1	49.4	21.7	16.5	19.5
4th quarter	30.6	17.8	58.0	6.9	47.3	22.5	16.7	20.1	32.9	17.6	53.3	7.2	49.8	21.9	16.3	19.6
1958																
1st quarter	30.4	17.2	56.5	6.9	47.1	22.8	16.8	20.3	32.5	16.9	52.1	7.2	49.2	22.3	16.1	19.7
2nd quarter	30.8	17.3	56.0	6.9	46.9	22.5	17.1	20.3	33.1	17.0	51.3	7.3	49.3	22.0	16.4	19.7
3rd quarter	31.4	17.7	56.4	7.1	48.2	22.7	17.2	20.4	33.7	17.5	52.0	7.5	50.5	22.1	16.5	19.8
4th quarter	31.8	18.2	57.3	7.1	48.3	22.5	17.7	20.5	34.3	18.1	52.7	7.5	50.6	21.8	17.1	19.9
1959																
1st quarter	32.0	18.6	58.1	7.2	48.9	22.7	17.5	20.5	34.3	18.5	53.8	7.6	51.1	22.0	17.1	20.0
2nd quarter	32.2	19.1	59.5	7.2	48.8	22.5	17.7	20.5	34.7	19.0	54.8	7.6	51.4	22.0	17.3	20.0
3rd quarter	32.3	19.0	59.0	7.3	49.1	22.7	17.6	20.6	34.7	18.9	54.6	7.7	51.4	22.1	17.3	20.1
4th quarter	32.4	19.1	58.9	7.4	49.5	23.0	17.5	20.7	34.6	18.9	54.6	7.7	51.6	22.4	17.1	20.2
1960																
1st quarter	33.3	19.6	58.8	7.6	50.8	23.0	17.7	20.7	35.4	19.5	55.0	7.9	52.7	22.3	17.3	20.2
2nd quarter	32.6	19.4	59.3	7.6	50.2	23.3	17.3	20.8	34.9	19.2	55.1	8.0	52.7	22.8	16.7	20.3
3rd quarter	32.7	19.4	59.3	7.6	50.2	23.2	17.5	20.8	35.0	19.2	54.8	8.0	53.0	22.9	16.8	20.3
4th quarter	32.5	19.0	58.6	7.7	50.3	23.6	17.0	20.9	34.6	18.8	54.2	8.0	52.9	23.3	16.4	20.4

Table 9-3B. Productivity and Related Data: Historical Data—*Continued*

(2009 = 100, seasonally adjusted.)

Year and quarter	Business sector								Nonfarm business sector							
	Output per hour of all persons	Output	Hours of all persons	Compensation per hour	Real compensation per hour	Unit labor costs	Unit nonlabor payments	Implicit price deflator	Output per hour of all persons	Output	Hours of all persons	Compensation per hour	Real compensation per hour	Unit labor costs	Unit nonlabor payments	Implicit price deflator
1961																
1st quarter	32.9	19.1	58.3	7.7	50.7	23.6	17.2	20.9	35.0	18.9	53.9	8.1	53.2	23.2	16.6	20.4
2nd quarter	34.0	19.6	57.6	7.9	51.8	23.3	17.6	20.9	36.1	19.4	53.8	8.2	54.0	22.8	17.2	20.5
3rd quarter	34.4	19.9	58.0	8.0	52.0	23.2	17.9	21.0	36.5	19.8	54.1	8.3	54.2	22.7	17.4	20.5
4th quarter	34.7	20.3	58.6	8.1	52.5	23.2	18.0	21.0	36.9	20.2	54.8	8.4	54.5	22.6	17.5	20.5
1962																
1st quarter	35.0	20.7	59.2	8.1	52.8	23.2	18.2	21.1	37.5	20.6	55.0	8.5	55.1	22.6	17.7	20.6
2nd quarter	35.2	21.0	59.5	8.2	53.3	23.4	18.1	21.2	37.4	20.8	55.7	8.5	55.3	22.8	17.7	20.7
3rd quarter	35.8	21.2	59.2	8.3	53.5	23.2	18.3	21.2	37.9	21.1	55.6	8.6	55.5	22.7	17.9	20.7
4th quarter	36.1	21.2	58.8	8.4	54.1	23.3	18.2	21.2	38.3	21.1	55.2	8.7	55.9	22.7	17.8	20.7
1963																
1st quarter	36.3	21.5	59.2	8.4	54.2	23.3	18.4	21.2	38.4	21.3	55.5	8.8	56.3	22.8	17.9	20.8
2nd quarter	36.6	21.8	59.6	8.5	54.3	23.2	18.5	21.3	38.8	21.7	55.9	8.8	56.5	22.7	18.1	20.8
3rd quarter	37.4	22.3	59.5	8.6	54.8	23.1	18.8	21.3	39.6	22.2	56.0	8.9	56.7	22.5	18.4	20.8
4th quarter	37.4	22.4	59.9	8.7	55.2	23.3	18.8	21.4	39.6	22.4	56.5	9.0	57.2	22.7	18.3	20.9
1964																
1st quarter	37.9	23.0	60.6	8.8	55.4	23.1	19.1	21.5	39.9	23.0	57.5	9.0	56.9	22.5	18.8	21.0
2nd quarter	38.0	23.2	61.1	8.8	55.7	23.2	19.1	21.5	40.2	23.2	57.8	9.1	57.5	22.6	18.8	21.0
3rd quarter	38.4	23.6	61.5	8.9	56.3	23.3	19.1	21.6	40.5	23.6	58.1	9.2	58.1	22.7	18.9	21.1
4th quarter	38.2	23.6	61.9	9.0	56.5	23.6	18.9	21.7	40.2	23.6	58.7	9.3	58.2	23.1	18.5	21.2
1965																
1st quarter	38.9	24.4	62.6	9.1	56.8	23.4	19.4	21.8	40.8	24.3	59.6	9.3	58.3	22.9	19.0	21.3
2nd quarter	38.9	24.7	63.4	9.1	56.8	23.5	19.5	21.8	41.0	24.7	60.2	9.4	58.3	22.9	19.1	21.3
3rd quarter	39.8	25.2	63.3	9.3	57.3	23.3	20.0	21.9	41.7	25.2	60.4	9.5	58.8	22.7	19.5	21.4
4th quarter	40.5	25.9	64.0	9.4	57.7	23.2	20.4	22.0	42.5	25.9	60.9	9.6	59.3	22.7	19.8	21.5
1966																
1st quarter	41.2	26.6	64.6	9.6	58.5	23.3	20.5	22.1	43.1	26.6	61.8	9.8	59.8	22.7	19.9	21.5
2nd quarter	41.0	26.7	65.1	9.8	59.0	23.8	20.1	22.3	42.8	26.7	62.4	9.9	60.2	23.2	19.7	21.8
3rd quarter	41.0	26.8	65.2	9.9	59.4	24.2	20.2	22.5	42.9	26.9	62.7	10.1	60.5	23.5	19.7	21.9
4th quarter	41.4	26.9	65.1	10.1	59.9	24.4	20.4	22.7	43.2	27.0	62.5	10.2	60.8	23.7	20.1	22.2
1967																
1st quarter	41.8	27.2	65.0	10.2	60.3	24.4	20.6	22.8	43.5	27.2	62.5	10.4	61.5	23.8	20.2	22.3
2nd quarter	42.2	27.1	64.4	10.3	61.0	24.6	20.5	22.9	43.7	27.1	62.1	10.5	62.1	24.1	20.0	22.4
3rd quarter	42.2	27.3	64.8	10.5	61.1	24.8	20.6	23.1	43.9	27.3	62.3	10.7	62.3	24.3	20.2	22.6
4th quarter	42.3	27.5	65.1	10.6	61.1	25.1	20.8	23.3	44.1	27.6	62.6	10.8	62.5	24.6	20.4	22.8
1968																
1st quarter	43.2	28.2	65.1	10.9	62.3	25.2	21.2	23.5	45.0	28.2	62.7	11.1	63.6	24.7	20.8	23.0
2nd quarter	43.7	28.7	65.6	11.1	62.8	25.4	21.5	23.8	45.5	28.8	63.3	11.3	64.0	24.8	21.2	23.3
3rd quarter	43.7	28.9	66.0	11.3	63.1	25.9	21.3	24.0	45.5	29.0	63.7	11.5	64.2	25.2	20.9	23.5
4th quarter	43.7	29.0	66.4	11.5	63.6	26.4	21.4	24.3	45.4	29.1	64.1	11.7	64.6	25.8	21.0	23.8
1969																
1st quarter	43.8	29.5	67.3	11.6	63.1	26.5	21.9	24.6	45.7	29.6	64.7	11.9	64.7	25.9	21.4	24.1
2nd quarter	43.8	29.5	67.5	11.9	63.7	27.2	21.7	24.9	45.4	29.6	65.3	12.1	64.7	26.6	21.2	24.3
3rd quarter	43.9	29.7	67.7	12.1	64.2	27.7	21.6	25.1	45.4	29.8	65.6	12.3	65.0	27.0	21.1	24.6
4th quarter	43.8	29.5	67.3	12.4	64.6	28.3	21.4	25.4	45.2	29.6	65.4	12.5	65.3	27.7	20.8	24.8
1970																
1st quarter	44.0	29.5	67.0	12.6	64.8	28.7	21.4	25.7	45.3	29.5	65.2	12.7	65.4	28.1	20.9	25.1
2nd quarter	44.5	29.5	66.3	12.8	64.7	28.8	22.2	26.0	46.0	29.6	64.3	12.9	65.5	28.1	21.7	25.5
3rd quarter	45.3	29.8	65.9	13.0	65.1	28.8	22.5	26.2	46.7	29.9	64.0	13.2	65.9	28.2	22.0	25.6
4th quarter	45.0	29.4	65.3	13.2	65.0	29.3	22.6	26.5	46.3	29.4	63.5	13.3	65.6	28.7	22.2	26.0
1971																
1st quarter	46.3	30.3	65.6	13.4	65.7	29.0	23.7	26.8	47.7	30.4	63.8	13.6	66.4	28.4	23.1	26.2
2nd quarter	46.3	30.6	66.0	13.6	65.8	29.3	24.0	27.1	47.8	30.6	64.0	13.8	66.8	28.8	23.5	26.5
3rd quarter	46.9	30.8	65.8	13.8	66.3	29.5	24.4	27.3	48.2	30.9	64.0	13.9	67.0	28.9	23.8	26.8
4th quarter	46.5	30.9	66.5	13.9	66.3	29.9	24.1	27.5	47.9	31.0	64.7	14.0	67.0	29.3	23.5	26.9
1972																
1st quarter	47.0	31.6	67.3	14.2	67.4	30.4	24.2	27.8	48.5	31.8	65.5	14.4	68.2	29.7	23.8	27.2
2nd quarter	48.1	32.6	67.7	14.4	67.7	30.0	25.1	27.9	49.5	32.7	66.0	14.6	68.6	29.4	24.4	27.3
3rd quarter	48.2	32.9	68.2	14.6	67.9	30.2	25.4	28.2	49.8	33.0	66.3	14.8	69.0	29.7	24.5	27.5
4th quarter	48.7	33.5	68.8	14.9	68.6	30.5	25.7	28.5	50.2	33.6	67.0	15.1	69.5	30.0	24.4	27.7
1973																
1st quarter	49.6	34.6	69.7	15.3	69.5	30.8	25.9	28.8	51.3	34.9	68.0	15.5	70.3	30.1	24.7	27.8
2nd quarter	49.8	35.1	70.5	15.5	69.0	31.2	26.5	29.2	51.4	35.3	68.7	15.7	69.8	30.5	24.9	28.1
3rd quarter	49.1	34.8	70.9	15.8	68.9	32.2	26.5	29.8	50.9	35.2	69.2	15.9	69.6	31.3	24.6	28.5
4th quarter	49.3	35.1	71.3	16.1	68.5	32.7	27.4	30.5	50.6	35.2	69.6	16.3	69.3	32.2	25.0	29.2
1974																
1st quarter	48.6	34.6	71.3	16.4	67.7	33.8	27.5	31.1	50.4	34.9	69.3	16.6	68.8	33.0	25.5	29.8
2nd quarter	48.8	34.7	71.2	16.9	68.0	34.7	28.1	31.9	50.3	34.9	69.4	17.1	68.8	33.9	26.8	30.9
3rd quarter	48.3	34.2	70.8	17.4	68.3	36.1	28.6	33.0	49.8	34.4	69.2	17.6	68.9	35.3	27.1	31.9
4th quarter	48.7	34.0	69.7	17.9	67.9	36.7	30.2	34.0	50.2	34.2	68.0	18.1	68.7	36.0	28.5	32.9
1975																
1st quarter	49.4	33.3	67.5	18.4	68.6	37.4	31.2	34.8	50.6	33.4	65.9	18.6	69.3	36.8	30.0	33.9
2nd quarter	50.2	33.6	67.0	18.8	69.2	37.6	32.1	35.3	51.5	33.6	65.3	19.0	69.9	36.9	31.0	34.4
3rd quarter	50.7	34.3	67.6	19.1	68.8	37.7	33.5	35.9	52.0	34.3	65.9	19.3	69.7	37.2	32.0	35.0
4th quarter	50.9	34.9	68.6	19.5	68.9	38.3	33.9	36.5	52.1	34.9	67.0	19.7	69.6	37.7	32.4	35.5

Table 9-3B. Productivity and Related Data: Historical Data—*Continued*

(2009 = 100, seasonally adjusted.)

Year and quarter	Business sector								Nonfarm business sector							
	Output per hour of all persons	Output	Hours of all persons	Compensation per hour	Real compensation per hour	Unit labor costs	Unit nonlabor payments	Implicit price deflator	Output per hour of all persons	Output	Hours of all persons	Compensation per hour	Real compensation per hour	Unit labor costs	Unit nonlabor payments	Implicit price deflator
1976																
1st quarter	51.6	35.9	69.6	19.9	69.6	38.6	34.3	36.8	52.9	36.0	68.1	20.0	70.1	37.9	33.1	35.9
2nd quarter	52.0	36.2	69.8	20.2	70.2	39.0	34.6	37.2	53.4	36.4	68.2	20.4	70.8	38.2	33.6	36.3
3rd quarter	52.0	36.4	70.1	20.6	70.4	39.7	34.8	37.7	53.5	36.6	68.4	20.8	71.2	39.0	33.8	36.8
4th quarter	52.3	36.8	70.2	21.1	71.1	40.4	35.4	38.3	53.6	36.9	68.8	21.3	71.6	39.7	34.4	37.5
1977																
1st quarter	52.6	37.3	70.9	21.5	71.1	41.0	36.1	38.9	54.0	37.5	69.5	21.7	71.7	40.2	35.0	38.0
2nd quarter	52.7	38.2	72.5	21.9	71.0	41.6	36.5	39.4	54.2	38.4	70.9	22.1	71.9	40.8	35.6	38.6
3rd quarter	53.4	39.0	73.1	22.3	71.5	41.9	37.0	39.9	54.7	39.2	71.6	22.6	72.3	41.2	36.3	39.1
4th quarter	52.8	39.0	73.8	22.7	71.7	43.1	37.4	40.7	54.0	39.1	72.3	22.9	72.5	42.5	36.2	39.8
1978																
1st quarter	52.6	39.1	74.2	23.4	72.9	44.6	37.0	41.4	54.1	39.3	72.7	23.7	73.8	43.9	35.7	40.5
2nd quarter	53.6	40.9	76.3	23.7	72.1	44.2	39.1	42.1	55.1	41.2	74.8	24.0	73.0	43.5	37.7	41.1
3rd quarter	53.8	41.4	77.0	24.1	71.9	44.8	39.9	42.8	55.1	41.6	75.4	24.3	72.8	44.2	38.5	41.8
4th quarter	54.0	42.0	77.8	24.6	72.2	45.8	40.8	43.7	55.5	42.3	76.3	24.9	73.0	44.9	39.4	42.6
1979																
1st quarter	53.7	42.0	78.3	25.4	72.8	47.4	40.4	44.5	55.0	42.3	76.9	25.7	73.5	46.7	38.7	43.3
2nd quarter	53.6	42.1	78.6	26.0	72.5	48.6	41.7	45.7	54.8	42.3	77.2	26.2	73.2	47.8	40.1	44.6
3rd quarter	53.6	42.4	79.2	26.6	72.3	49.7	42.4	46.7	54.8	42.6	77.8	26.8	73.0	49.0	40.8	45.6
4th quarter	53.4	42.5	79.5	27.2	72.2	51.0	42.7	47.5	54.7	42.7	78.0	27.5	73.0	50.3	41.1	46.5
1980																
1st quarter	53.8	42.6	79.1	28.0	72.1	52.2	43.4	48.5	55.0	42.8	77.8	28.3	72.8	51.5	42.2	47.6
2nd quarter	53.2	41.4	77.8	28.8	72.2	54.2	43.3	49.6	54.4	41.6	76.4	29.0	72.9	53.4	42.8	49.0
3rd quarter	53.2	41.2	77.5	29.4	72.2	55.4	44.2	50.7	54.6	41.5	76.1	29.8	72.9	54.5	43.1	49.7
4th quarter	53.8	42.2	78.5	30.2	72.3	56.3	46.1	52.0	55.2	42.5	77.0	30.6	73.2	55.4	44.4	50.8
1981																
1st quarter	54.9	43.3	78.9	31.0	72.1	56.6	48.9	53.3	56.1	43.5	77.5	31.4	73.1	55.9	47.4	52.4
2nd quarter	54.4	42.9	78.8	31.6	72.2	58.1	49.2	54.4	55.4	42.9	77.5	31.9	73.0	57.6	47.6	53.4
3rd quarter	55.1	43.4	78.8	32.2	72.2	58.6	50.9	55.3	55.9	43.3	77.5	32.6	73.1	58.4	49.2	54.6
4th quarter	54.4	42.7	78.5	32.7	72.1	60.3	50.6	56.3	55.2	42.6	77.2	33.1	73.0	60.0	49.4	55.6
1982																
1st quarter	54.0	41.7	77.2	33.6	73.1	62.3	49.6	57.0	54.8	41.6	75.9	34.0	73.9	62.0	48.5	56.4
2nd quarter	54.2	42.0	77.4	33.9	73.1	62.7	50.6	57.7	54.9	41.9	76.2	34.3	73.8	62.4	49.6	57.1
3rd quarter	54.2	41.7	76.9	34.4	72.9	63.6	51.3	58.4	55.0	41.6	75.7	34.8	73.7	63.3	50.1	57.8
4th quarter	54.7	41.7	76.2	34.9	73.1	63.9	52.1	58.9	55.5	41.6	75.0	35.3	73.9	63.6	51.0	58.4
1983																
1st quarter	55.3	42.4	76.7	35.3	73.3	63.9	53.1	59.4	56.3	42.5	75.4	35.7	74.3	63.4	51.9	58.6
2nd quarter	56.3	43.6	77.4	35.6	73.3	63.4	54.5	59.7	57.6	43.9	76.3	36.1	74.2	62.6	53.5	58.8
3rd quarter	56.5	44.6	79.0	35.8	72.9	63.5	55.8	60.3	58.0	45.1	77.8	36.3	73.9	62.5	55.4	59.5
4th quarter	57.0	45.7	80.2	36.3	73.2	63.8	56.3	60.6	58.3	46.2	79.2	36.7	74.0	62.9	55.7	59.9
1984																
1st quarter	57.3	46.9	81.8	36.7	73.1	64.2	56.8	61.1	58.4	47.1	80.7	37.1	73.9	63.6	55.4	60.2
2nd quarter	57.8	47.9	82.8	37.1	73.1	64.3	57.8	61.6	58.7	48.1	81.8	37.5	73.9	63.8	56.4	60.7
3rd quarter	58.1	48.4	83.2	37.6	73.6	64.8	58.0	62.0	59.0	48.5	82.2	38.0	74.4	64.4	56.7	61.2
4th quarter	58.2	48.7	83.7	37.9	73.6	65.3	58.2	62.3	59.0	48.8	82.7	38.3	74.3	64.9	56.9	61.5
1985																
1st quarter	58.4	49.3	84.4	38.4	73.9	65.9	59.0	63.0	59.1	49.3	83.4	38.8	74.6	65.6	57.8	62.4
2nd quarter	58.7	49.8	84.8	38.8	74.0	66.3	59.3	63.4	59.3	49.8	83.9	39.2	74.7	66.0	58.2	62.8
3rd quarter	59.6	50.6	84.9	39.5	74.7	66.3	59.9	63.6	60.1	50.6	84.2	39.8	75.3	66.2	59.1	63.2
4th quarter	59.9	51.0	85.2	40.2	75.5	67.3	59.1	63.9	60.3	51.0	84.6	40.5	76.0	67.1	58.1	63.4
1986																
1st quarter	60.4	51.5	85.3	40.7	76.1	67.6	59.3	64.1	61.0	51.6	84.5	41.1	76.7	67.3	58.6	63.7
2nd quarter	60.8	51.7	85.1	41.2	77.3	67.9	59.2	64.2	61.5	51.8	84.3	41.6	78.0	67.6	58.4	63.7
3rd quarter	61.1	52.3	85.5	41.7	77.7	68.3	59.0	64.4	61.8	52.3	84.7	42.1	78.5	68.1	57.9	63.8
4th quarter	61.0	52.5	86.2	42.2	78.3	69.4	58.1	64.6	61.7	52.6	85.3	42.6	79.0	69.1	57.0	64.1
1987																
1st quarter	60.7	52.9	87.2	42.4	77.8	70.0	58.1	65.0	61.4	53.0	86.3	42.8	78.5	69.8	57.1	64.5
2nd quarter	61.1	53.6	87.7	42.7	77.5	70.1	58.8	65.4	61.8	53.7	86.8	43.1	78.3	69.8	57.9	64.9
3rd quarter	61.2	54.0	88.2	43.2	77.6	70.7	59.1	65.9	61.8	54.1	87.4	43.6	78.3	70.5	58.2	65.4
4th quarter	61.7	55.0	89.1	43.7	77.9	71.1	59.4	66.2	62.3	55.1	88.4	44.1	78.6	70.8	58.5	65.6
1988																
1st quarter	61.9	55.2	89.2	44.5	78.8	72.1	59.3	66.7	62.6	55.3	88.4	44.9	79.5	71.8	58.2	66.1
2nd quarter	62.0	56.0	90.4	45.1	78.9	72.9	59.5	67.3	62.7	56.3	89.7	45.4	79.5	72.4	58.6	66.7
3rd quarter	62.2	56.3	90.6	45.6	79.1	73.6	60.5	68.1	62.9	56.6	89.9	46.0	79.6	73.1	59.5	67.4
4th quarter	62.3	57.1	91.7	45.9	78.8	73.9	61.3	68.6	63.2	57.4	90.9	46.3	79.5	73.3	60.7	68.1
1989																
1st quarter	62.4	57.7	92.5	46.1	78.4	74.1	62.7	69.3	63.1	57.9	91.8	46.5	79.0	73.7	61.4	68.6
2nd quarter	62.7	58.2	92.8	46.4	77.6	74.1	64.4	70.0	63.3	58.4	92.2	46.7	78.1	73.7	63.3	69.4
3rd quarter	63.0	58.6	93.1	46.7	77.7	74.4	65.0	70.4	63.6	58.8	92.4	47.1	78.2	74.0	64.1	69.8
4th quarter	63.0	58.7	93.1	47.4	78.1	75.3	64.6	70.8	63.7	58.8	92.4	47.7	78.6	75.0	63.5	70.2
1990																
1st quarter	63.7	59.4	93.2	48.5	78.6	76.2	65.2	71.6	64.2	59.5	92.6	48.7	79.0	75.8	64.0	70.9
2nd quarter	64.2	59.6	92.8	49.5	79.6	77.1	65.4	72.2	64.8	59.7	92.1	49.7	79.9	76.7	64.3	71.6
3rd quarter	64.5	59.5	92.2	50.2	79.4	77.8	65.8	72.8	65.1	59.6	91.5	50.4	79.7	77.5	64.7	72.2
4th quarter	63.9	58.7	91.9	50.6	78.8	79.1	65.2	73.3	64.5	58.8	91.1	50.8	79.1	78.8	64.4	72.8

Table 9-3B. Productivity and Related Data: Historical Data—*Continued*

(2009 = 100, seasonally adjusted.)

Year and quarter	Business sector								Nonfarm business sector							
	Output per hour of all persons	Output	Hours of all persons	Compensation per hour	Real compensation per hour	Unit labor costs	Unit nonlabor payments	Implicit price deflator	Output per hour of all persons	Output	Hours of all persons	Compensation per hour	Real compensation per hour	Unit labor costs	Unit nonlabor payments	Implicit price deflator
1991																
1st quarter	64.0	58.3	91.0	51.0	78.9	79.4	66.2	73.9	64.7	58.3	90.1	51.2	79.3	79.1	65.5	73.4
2nd quarter	65.0	58.8	90.5	51.9	80.0	79.6	67.0	74.3	65.8	58.9	89.6	52.2	80.4	79.3	66.1	73.8
3rd quarter	65.5	59.2	90.4	52.5	80.4	80.0	67.7	74.8	66.3	59.3	89.5	52.8	80.9	79.7	67.0	74.4
4th quarter	65.9	59.4	90.2	53.1	80.8	80.5	67.6	75.1	66.6	59.5	89.4	53.4	81.3	80.2	66.7	74.6
1992																
1st quarter	67.3	60.3	89.6	54.5	82.4	80.9	67.3	75.2	67.9	60.3	88.9	54.8	82.9	80.7	66.4	74.7
2nd quarter	67.8	61.1	90.1	54.9	82.5	80.8	68.1	75.5	68.4	61.1	89.3	55.3	83.1	80.8	67.1	75.1
3rd quarter	68.5	61.8	90.2	55.5	82.9	81.1	68.6	75.9	69.0	61.7	89.5	55.9	83.5	81.0	67.6	75.4
4th quarter	68.9	62.5	90.8	55.9	82.9	81.2	69.6	76.4	69.4	62.5	90.1	56.3	83.4	81.1	68.8	75.9
1993																
1st quarter	68.3	62.5	91.4	55.5	81.8	81.2	70.6	76.8	68.9	62.6	90.9	55.8	82.2	80.9	70.1	70.4
2nd quarter	68.0	62.9	92.4	56.0	82.0	82.3	70.3	77.3	68.5	63.0	91.9	56.2	82.3	82.0	69.6	76.8
3rd quarter	68.0	63.2	92.9	56.1	81.7	82.4	71.2	77.7	68.7	63.4	92.4	56.3	82.0	81.9	70.7	77.3
4th quarter	68.5	64.2	93.8	56.5	81.9	82.4	72.0	78.1	69.1	64.4	93.2	56.8	82.2	82.2	71.2	77.6
1994																
1st quarter	68.7	65.0	94.7	56.2	81.2	81.6	73.7	78.3	69.5	65.0	93.5	56.5	81.7	81.4	72.9	77.8
2nd quarter	68.6	66.1	96.3	56.6	81.3	82.2	73.6	78.6	69.5	66.1	95.1	57.0	81.9	82.0	72.9	78.2
3rd quarter	68.3	66.5	97.4	56.6	80.6	82.6	74.0	79.0	69.0	66.5	96.3	56.9	81.2	82.5	73.5	78.7
4th quarter	68.9	67.4	97.8	56.8	80.7	82.4	75.2	79.4	69.7	67.5	96.8	57.3	81.3	82.1	74.7	79.0
1995																
1st quarter	68.8	67.6	98.3	57.1	80.5	83.1	75.1	79.7	69.6	67.8	97.5	57.5	81.1	82.6	74.9	79.4
2nd quarter	69.0	67.8	98.3	57.4	80.3	83.4	75.5	80.1	69.8	68.1	97.5	57.8	81.0	82.8	75.4	79.7
3rd quarter	69.1	68.6	99.2	57.8	80.5	83.8	75.7	80.4	69.8	68.9	98.6	58.2	81.0	83.3	75.4	80.0
4th quarter	69.6	69.2	99.4	58.4	81.0	83.9	76.2	80.7	70.4	69.5	98.7	58.8	81.5	83.5	75.6	80.2
1996																
1st quarter	70.1	69.8	99.6	59.2	81.5	84.3	76.5	81.0	71.0	70.0	98.5	59.6	82.1	84.0	75.5	80.5
2nd quarter	70.9	71.2	100.5	59.9	81.7	84.2	77.6	81.4	71.9	71.4	99.3	60.3	82.3	83.9	76.4	80.8
3rd quarter	71.2	72.0	101.2	60.5	82.1	84.6	77.3	81.6	72.2	72.2	100.1	60.8	82.5	84.2	76.6	81.0
4th quarter	71.3	73.0	102.3	60.7	81.8	84.9	77.8	81.9	72.2	73.1	101.4	61.0	82.2	84.6	77.0	81.4
1997																
1st quarter	71.3	73.6	103.3	61.2	82.0	85.8	77.6	82.4	72.0	73.7	102.4	61.6	82.5	85.6	76.7	81.9
2nd quarter	72.2	74.9	103.7	61.7	82.5	85.4	78.5	82.5	72.8	75.0	103.1	62.1	83.0	85.2	78.0	82.2
3rd quarter	72.9	76.0	104.2	62.4	83.0	85.6	78.9	82.8	73.4	76.1	103.7	62.7	83.4	85.4	78.3	82.4
4th quarter	73.3	76.7	104.6	63.6	84.2	86.8	77.6	83.0	73.7	76.8	104.2	63.8	84.4	86.6	77.2	82.6
1998																
1st quarter	73.7	77.5	105.2	64.7	85.6	87.8	76.3	83.0	74.2	77.7	104.8	64.9	85.8	87.5	75.8	82.7
2nd quarter	74.0	78.4	105.8	65.6	86.4	88.5	75.5	83.0	74.7	78.6	105.2	65.8	86.7	88.1	75.2	82.7
3rd quarter	75.1	79.6	105.9	66.6	87.3	88.6	75.7	83.2	75.7	79.8	105.4	66.8	87.7	88.3	75.4	82.9
4th quarter	75.8	81.2	107.2	66.9	87.4	88.3	76.2	83.2	76.2	81.4	106.9	67.1	87.6	88.0	75.7	82.9
1999																
1st quarter	76.7	82.0	106.8	68.1	88.6	89.0	75.9	83.5	76.9	82.2	106.9	68.2	88.7	88.6	75.5	83.2
2nd quarter	77.0	82.7	107.4	68.2	88.2	89.0	76.0	83.6	77.0	82.9	107.7	68.3	88.3	88.7	76.0	83.4
3rd quarter	77.7	83.9	108.1	68.8	88.2	89.0	76.6	83.8	77.7	84.2	108.4	68.9	88.3	88.7	76.6	83.7
4th quarter	78.8	85.6	108.6	70.1	89.3	89.3	76.8	84.1	79.0	85.9	108.7	70.3	89.5	89.1	76.9	84.0
2000																
1st quarter	78.5	85.8	109.2	72.9	92.0	92.8	73.1	84.6	78.9	85.9	108.9	73.2	92.3	92.7	73.1	84.5
2nd quarter	80.2	87.7	109.3	73.1	91.6	91.2	76.5	85.1	80.5	87.8	109.1	73.3	91.8	91.1	76.4	85.0
3rd quarter	80.1	87.7	109.4	74.6	92.5	93.1	75.1	85.5	80.5	87.8	109.1	74.8	92.7	92.9	75.1	85.5
4th quarter	81.0	88.2	108.8	75.1	92.5	92.7	76.6	85.9	81.3	88.3	108.7	75.2	92.6	92.5	76.5	85.8
2001																
1st quarter	80.7	87.7	108.7	76.8	93.8	95.2	74.0	86.3	80.9	87.9	108.6	76.9	93.8	95.0	73.9	86.2
2nd quarter	82.0	88.2	107.6	77.1	93.4	94.1	76.8	86.9	82.3	88.5	107.5	77.1	93.4	93.7	76.8	86.7
3rd quarter	82.4	87.7	106.4	77.2	93.3	93.7	77.5	86.9	82.7	88.0	106.3	77.2	93.3	93.3	77.4	86.7
4th quarter	83.5	87.9	105.3	77.9	94.2	93.2	78.3	87.0	83.8	88.1	105.1	77.9	94.2	93.0	78.4	86.9
2002																
1st quarter	85.1	88.9	104.4	78.2	94.3	91.9	80.2	87.0	85.7	89.2	104.2	78.3	94.4	91.4	80.3	86.8
2nd quarter	85.4	89.3	104.6	78.9	94.4	92.4	80.0	87.2	85.7	89.6	104.5	79.0	94.5	92.2	80.4	87.2
3rd quarter	86.2	89.8	104.2	79.3	94.4	92.1	81.2	87.5	86.4	90.0	104.1	79.4	94.4	91.9	81.3	87.5
4th quarter	86.0	89.8	104.4	79.5	94.0	92.5	81.5	87.9	86.2	89.9	104.3	79.6	94.1	92.3	81.6	87.8
2003																
1st quarter	86.9	90.2	103.8	80.0	93.7	92.1	82.9	88.2	87.1	90.3	103.7	80.1	93.8	91.9	82.9	88.2
2nd quarter	88.3	91.3	103.3	81.6	95.6	92.4	82.8	88.4	88.3	91.3	103.4	81.5	95.5	92.3	82.7	88.3
3rd quarter	90.0	93.3	103.6	82.6	96.2	91.9	84.5	88.8	90.2	93.4	103.5	82.7	96.2	91.7	84.3	88.6
4th quarter	90.7	94.5	104.2	83.7	97.0	92.3	84.6	89.1	91.1	94.8	104.1	83.8	97.2	92.0	84.1	88.7
2004																
1st quarter	91.0	95.1	104.5	83.7	96.2	92.0	86.6	89.7	91.1	95.2	104.5	83.7	96.2	91.9	85.8	89.4
2nd quarter	91.6	95.9	104.7	85.3	97.3	93.1	86.8	90.4	91.9	96.2	104.6	85.3	97.3	92.8	85.9	89.9
3rd quarter	92.0	96.9	105.4	86.8	98.3	94.3	86.1	90.9	92.3	97.1	105.3	86.8	98.4	94.1	85.6	90.6
4th quarter	92.7	97.9	105.6	87.4	98.0	94.3	87.8	91.6	92.6	97.9	105.8	87.2	97.7	94.2	87.3	91.3
2005																
1st quarter	93.5	99.1	105.9	88.0	98.1	94.0	90.0	92.3	93.6	99.2	106.0	87.9	98.0	93.9	89.8	92.2
2nd quarter	93.3	99.6	106.8	88.2	97.8	94.6	90.8	93.0	93.5	99.7	106.7	88.3	97.9	94.5	90.6	92.9
3rd quarter	94.1	100.6	106.9	89.4	97.6	95.0	92.4	93.9	94.2	100.7	106.9	89.4	97.6	95.0	92.3	93.8
4th quarter	94.2	101.3	107.5	90.0	97.3	95.6	93.3	94.6	94.2	101.4	107.6	90.0	97.3	95.5	93.2	94.6

Table 9-3B. Productivity and Related Data: Historical Data—*Continued*

(2009 = 100, seasonally adjusted.)

Year and quarter	Business sector								Nonfarm business sector							
	Output per hour of all persons	Output	Hours of all persons	Compensation per hour	Real compensation per hour	Unit labor costs	Unit nonlabor payments	Implicit price deflator	Output per hour of all persons	Output	Hours of all persons	Compensation per hour	Real compensation per hour	Unit labor costs	Unit nonlabor payments	Implicit price deflator
2006																
1st quarter	94.8	102.8	108.4	92.0	98.9	97.0	92.7	95.2	94.8	102.9	108.6	91.9	98.8	96.9	92.6	95.1
2nd quarter	94.8	103.1	108.8	91.9	97.9	97.0	94.4	95.9	94.7	103.1	108.9	91.9	97.9	97.0	94.4	95.9
3rd quarter	94.3	103.1	109.4	92.0	97.2	97.6	94.9	96.5	94.3	103.3	109.5	92.0	97.2	97.6	94.9	96.5
4th quarter	94.8	104.2	109.9	93.5	99.2	98.7	93.8	96.6	95.0	104.4	109.9	93.6	99.2	98.6	93.6	96.5
2007																
1st quarter	94.8	104.3	109.9	95.8	100.6	101.0	92.8	97.6	95.1	104.5	109.9	95.9	100.7	100.9	92.5	97.4
2nd quarter	95.6	105.3	110.1	96.0	99.7	100.5	95.0	98.2	95.6	105.6	110.4	95.8	99.5	100.2	94.8	97.9
3rd quarter	96.7	106.1	109.7	96.5	99.5	99.8	96.6	98.4	96.8	106.5	110.0	96.2	99.3	99.4	96.3	98.1
4th quarter	97.0	106.3	109.6	97.3	99.2	100.3	96.5	98.8	97.2	106.7	109.7	97.2	99.1	100.0	96.0	98.4
2008																
1st quarter	96.2	105.1	109.3	98.3	99.1	102.2	94.9	99.1	96.3	105.3	109.4	98.2	99.0	102.0	94.2	98.7
2nd quarter	97.1	105.6	108.7	98.4	98.0	101.3	97.1	99.6	97.2	105.8	108.9	98.3	97.9	101.1	96.5	99.2
3rd quarter	97.3	104.7	107.5	99.2	97.3	102.0	97.9	100.3	97.5	105.0	107.7	99.2	97.2	101.7	97.4	99.9
4th quarter	96.8	101.6	105.0	100.2	100.5	103.5	95.3	100.1	96.9	101.7	105.0	100.2	100.6	103.5	95.0	100.0
2009																
1st quarter	97.5	99.7	102.3	97.7	98.7	100.2	100.4	100.3	97.6	99.8	102.2	97.7	98.7	100.1	100.5	100.3
2nd quarter	99.4	99.4	100.1	100.1	100.6	100.7	98.7	99.9	99.5	99.5	100.0	100.1	100.6	100.7	98.8	99.9
3rd quarter	101.0	99.8	98.9	100.8	100.5	99.9	99.7	99.8	100.9	99.7	98.8	100.8	100.4	99.9	99.8	99.9
4th quarter	102.2	101.0	98.8	101.4	100.3	99.2	101.2	100.1	102.1	101.0	98.9	101.4	100.3	99.3	100.9	100.0
2010																
1st quarter	102.6	101.5	98.9	100.6	99.3	98.1	103.8	100.5	102.6	101.5	98.9	100.7	99.4	98.1	103.6	100.4
2nd quarter	103.0	102.8	99.8	101.7	100.5	98.8	103.7	100.9	103.0	102.7	99.7	101.9	100.6	98.9	103.4	100.8
3rd quarter	103.6	103.8	100.2	102.3	100.7	98.7	104.9	101.3	103.5	103.8	100.2	102.3	100.7	98.8	104.4	101.2
4th quarter	103.9	104.7	100.7	102.7	100.3	98.8	106.2	101.9	103.9	104.7	100.8	102.8	100.4	98.9	105.5	101.6
2011																
1st quarter	103.0	104.1	101.0	104.4	100.9	101.4	103.7	102.3	103.1	104.1	101.0	104.6	101.1	101.5	102.4	101.9
2nd quarter	103.3	105.1	101.7	103.9	99.3	100.6	106.6	103.1	103.4	105.2	101.7	104.0	99.4	100.6	105.3	102.6
3rd quarter	103.1	105.3	102.2	104.5	99.2	101.4	107.2	103.8	103.2	105.5	102.2	104.7	99.4	101.4	105.7	103.2
4th quarter	103.8	106.9	103.0	103.2	97.5	99.4	110.5	104.0	103.9	107.0	103.0	103.3	97.6	99.4	109.3	103.5
2012																
1st quarter	103.8	107.8	103.8	105.6	99.2	101.7	108.4	104.5	104.1	108.1	103.8	105.7	99.3	101.5	107.4	104.0
2nd quarter	104.4	108.5	103.9	106.2	99.6	101.7	109.6	105.0	104.7	108.8	103.9	106.3	99.7	101.5	108.8	104.5
3rd quarter	104.1	108.6	104.3	106.3	99.3	102.1	110.6	105.7	104.5	109.1	104.3	106.4	99.3	101.8	109.7	105.1
4th quarter	103.7	108.7	104.8	109.3	101.3	105.3	107.0	106.0	104.1	109.1	104.9	109.2	101.3	105.0	105.9	105.3
2013																
1st quarter	104.3	109.7	105.2	106.9	98.7	102.5	111.9	106.4	104.3	109.9	105.4	106.7	98.5	102.3	110.3	105.6
2nd quarter	104.3	110.0	105.5	108.4	100.3	104.0	110.2	106.6	104.1	110.1	105.7	108.2	100.1	103.9	108.7	105.9
3rd quarter	104.7	111.1	106.1	108.6	99.9	103.7	111.6	107.1	104.5	111.1	106.3	108.5	99.8	103.8	110.3	106.5
4th quarter	105.7	112.6	106.4	109.2	100.1	103.3	113.4	107.5	105.7	112.6	106.6	109.2	100.0	103.3	112.5	107.1
2014																
1st quarter	104.8	112.0	106.9	110.9	101.0	105.8	110.8	107.9	104.7	112.1	107.1	110.8	100.9	105.9	109.8	107.5
2nd quarter	105.2	113.4	107.8	110.3	99.9	104.9	113.6	108.5	105.1	113.5	108.0	110.2	99.9	104.9	112.4	108.0
3rd quarter	106.0	115.1	108.6	111.2	100.5	104.8	114.5	108.9	106.2	115.3	108.6	111.3	100.6	104.8	113.7	108.5
4th quarter	105.6	115.9	109.8	112.1	101.5	106.1	112.6	108.9	105.8	116.1	109.7	112.3	101.7	106.1	111.8	108.5
2015																
1st quarter	105.8	116.6	110.2	112.6	102.6	106.4	112.0	108.7	106.1	116.8	110.1	112.9	102.8	106.3	111.8	108.6
2nd quarter	106.2	117.5	110.7	113.9	103.2	107.3	112.0	109.3	106.4	117.7	110.6	114.1	103.4	107.3	111.8	109.1
3rd quarter	106.7	118.1	110.6	114.7	103.5	107.5	112.4	109.5	106.9	118.2	110.6	114.9	103.7	107.5	112.1	109.4
4th quarter	106.2	118.3	111.5	115.7	104.3	108.9	110.5	109.6	106.3	118.5	111.4	115.9	104.5	109.0	110.3	109.5
2016																
1st quarter	106.0	118.6	111.9	115.3	104.0	108.8	110.8	109.7	106.2	118.7	111.8	115.6	104.2	108.9	110.9	109.7
2nd quarter	105.9	119.1	112.4	116.9	104.8	110.4	110.0	110.3	106.1	119.1	112.2	117.3	105.2	110.6	110.1	110.3
3rd quarter	106.9	120.3	112.6	118.2	105.5	110.6	110.3	110.5	107.0	120.4	112.5	118.5	105.7	110.8	110.5	110.6
4th quarter	107.5	121.1	112.7	117.6	104.1	109.4	113.2	111.0	107.5	121.2	112.7	117.6	104.2	109.4	113.6	111.2

Table 9-4. Corporate Profits with Inventory Valuation Adjustment by Industry Group, NAICS Basis

(Billions of dollars, quarterly data are at seasonally adjusted annual rates.)   **NIPA Table 6.16D**

Year and quarter	Total	Domestic industries											
		Financial			Nonfinancial								
		Total	Federal Reserve banks	Other financial	Total	Utilities	Manufacturing						
							Total	Durable goods					
								Fabricated metal products	Machinery	Computer and electronic products	Electrical equipment, appliances, and components	Motor vehicles, bodies and trailers, and parts	Other durable goods
1999	762.2	640.2	26.7	127.9	485.6	34.4	184.5	16.4	12.7	6.6	10.2	13.8	37.4
2000	730.3	584.1	31.2	118.5	434.4	24.3	175.6	15.6	9.4	20.5	6.9	4.0	25.8
2001	698.7	528.3	28.9	166.1	333.3	22.5	75.1	9.2	2.2	-29.1	1.1	-6.8	14.0
2002	795.1	636.3	23.5	247.2	365.6	11.1	75.1	8.7	3.2	-24.3	-2.1	-3.0	20.6
2003	959.9	793.3	20.1	286.5	486.7	13.5	125.3	8.6	3.2	-6.3	1.5	7.9	17.8
2004	1 215.2	1 010.1	20.0	329.4	660.7	20.5	182.7	12.3	8.5	1.2	-0.2	-5.0	33.8
2005	1 621.2	1 382.1	26.6	383.1	972.4	30.8	277.7	18.2	18.0	15.7	1.8	0.3	56.8
2006	1 815.7	1 559.6	33.8	381.3	1 144.4	55.1	349.7	18.4	23.2	29.0	10.7	-5.3	68.0
2007	1 708.9	1 355.5	36.0	265.5	1 054.0	49.5	321.9	21.0	25.0	24.7	-1.5	-15.7	65.2
2008	1 345.5	938.8	35.1	60.4	843.4	30.1	240.6	16.5	18.8	26.1	4.4	-39.6	38.1
2009	1 479.2	1 122.0	47.3	315.5	759.2	23.8	171.4	11.7	9.4	26.4	8.9	-54.3	32.3
2010	1 799.7	1 404.5	71.6	334.8	998.2	30.3	287.6	15.3	17.4	46.9	10.2	-9.7	48.0
2011	1 738.5	1 316.6	75.9	300.0	940.7	9.8	298.1	16.1	24.3	32.7	4.8	-0.3	54.8
2012	2 116.6	1 706.3	71.7	407.3	1 227.2	12.5	395.7	23.4	32.1	47.4	11.6	21.9	64.9
2013	2 159.4	1 747.6	79.6	349.8	1 318.2	26.9	429.6	23.7	34.2	51.6	19.2	21.3	68.8
2014	2 253.2	1 855.6	103.5	380.5	1 371.7	31.5	452.0	23.9	34.6	53.2	14.2	30.7	73.5
2015	2 210.9	1 826.0	100.7	397.1	1 328.1	21.8	417.1	23.6	24.2	53.9	19.6	26.3	70.7
2016	2 161.6	1 766.9	92.0	409.9	1 265.1	19.3	392.6	20.1	17.8	49.9	23.7	26.4	74.3
2015													
1st quarter	2 275.7	1 886.6	97.4	418.7	1 370.5	35.7	466.0	24.9	31.2	55.8	17.0	23.8	69.7
2nd quarter	2 270.4	1 897.8	101.2	439.4	1 357.2	27.4	449.0	23.7	26.0	54.2	18.8	30.9	77.3
3rd quarter	2 228.7	1 852.2	104.4	369.8	1 378.0	20.1	450.5	22.6	20.7	55.3	20.3	28.5	72.5
4th quarter	2 068.8	1 667.2	100.0	360.6	1 206.7	4.0	303.1	23.4	18.8	50.3	22.4	22.2	63.3
2016													
1st quarter	2 132.7	1 766.9	97.3	334.9	1 334.6	22.8	424.3	22.9	18.5	55.3	21.0	30.2	72.1
2nd quarter	2 087.5	1 698.5	93.0	380.5	1 225.0	17.1	374.0	16.9	16.8	46.5	22.7	32.4	62.9
3rd quarter	2 187.0	1 798.6	89.5	447.3	1 261.8	16.1	385.4	19.6	17.6	48.6	24.7	23.1	72.8
4th quarter	2 239.4	1 803.7	88.1	476.7	1 238.9	21.2	386.8	20.9	18.1	49.3	26.5	20.1	89.3

Year and quarter	Domestic industries—Continued										Rest of the world, net
	Nonfinancial—Continued										
	Manufacturing—Continued					Wholesale trade	Retail trade	Transportation and warehousing	Information	Other nonfinancial	
	Nondurable goods										
	Total	Food and beverage and tobacco products	Petroleum and coal products	Chemical products	Other nondurable goods						
1999	87.5	31.7	2.4	31.8	21.7	55.6	59.5	7.2	20.8	123.5	122.0
2000	93.3	25.8	25.9	25.1	16.6	59.5	51.3	9.5	-11.9	126.1	146.2
2001	84.5	28.5	27.5	22.0	6.6	51.1	71.3	-0.7	-26.4	140.2	170.4
2002	72.0	26.9	3.8	29.9	11.4	55.8	83.7	-6.0	-3.1	149.0	158.8
2003	92.6	25.9	26.0	32.2	8.5	59.3	90.5	4.8	16.3	177.1	166.6
2004	132.1	26.8	50.1	39.2	16.0	74.7	93.2	12.0	52.7	224.9	205.0
2005	170.5	29.5	79.9	41.2	19.9	96.2	121.7	27.7	91.3	327.2	239.1
2006	205.7	35.0	73.5	70.0	27.1	109.5	132.5	41.2	107.0	353.1	256.2
2007	203.0	31.7	78.7	69.3	23.3	103.2	119.0	23.9	108.4	328.2	353.4
2008	176.3	31.0	89.9	50.1	5.4	90.6	80.3	28.8	92.2	280.8	406.7
2009	137.0	46.4	13.7	58.6	18.2	89.3	108.7	22.4	81.2	262.3	357.2
2010	159.5	46.1	24.8	64.7	23.9	102.4	118.6	44.7	95.1	319.5	395.2
2011	165.6	40.6	45.8	58.2	20.9	94.4	114.3	30.4	83.8	309.9	421.9
2012	194.5	44.3	50.2	69.6	30.4	135.3	154.1	53.8	100.6	375.2	410.3
2013	210.7	54.4	47.9	76.0	32.4	142.7	154.5	50.6	125.4	388.5	411.8
2014	222.0	58.9	58.5	75.6	29.1	149.8	159.8	60.4	114.8	403.5	397.5
2015	198.7	71.7	17.3	73.7	36.0	147.6	171.8	61.2	137.2	371.3	385.0
2016	180.4	76.0	-2.2	68.9	37.7	125.4	179.1	56.1	137.6	355.0	394.7
2015											
1st quarter	243.5	75.7	51.8	80.8	35.2	145.3	181.0	62.2	126.9	353.4	389.1
2nd quarter	218.1	66.6	46.1	71.3	34.1	140.4	168.7	59.3	138.3	374.1	372.7
3rd quarter	230.6	73.1	46.2	76.4	34.8	146.2	169.6	63.2	141.9	386.5	376.5
4th quarter	102.7	71.4	-74.9	66.2	40.0	158.6	168.1	60.1	141.7	371.1	401.6
2016											
1st quarter	204.3	73.7	7.9	82.2	40.5	144.3	176.1	63.3	140.6	363.2	365.9
2nd quarter	175.8	78.5	-2.1	64.8	34.5	116.9	171.4	57.3	135.7	352.5	389.0
3rd quarter	179.0	77.4	-2.4	67.1	36.9	141.9	185.1	54.1	132.3	346.9	388.4
4th quarter	162.5	74.4	-12.2	61.3	38.9	98.3	183.8	49.7	141.9	357.3	435.6

NOTES AND DEFINITIONS, CHAPTER 9

GENERAL NOTE ON DATA ON COMPENSATION PER HOUR

This chapter includes two data series with similar names—the Employment Cost Index for total compensation and the index of compensation per hour—that often display different behavior. Both are compiled and published by the Bureau of Labor Statistics (BLS), but the definitions, sources, and methods of compilation are different. Users should be aware of these differences and of the consequent differences in the appropriate uses and interpretations for each of the two series.

The *Employment Cost Index (ECI)* (Tables 9-1 and 9-2) measures changes in hourly compensation for "all civilian workers," which is not quite as broad as it sounds, as it excludes federal government workers, farm workers, and private household workers. Indexes are also published for subgroups including state and local workers, "all private industry" (again excluding farm and private household workers), and a number of industry and occupational subgroups.

The ECI is calculated and published separately for *total compensation* and for the two components of hourly compensation, *wages and salaries* and the employer cost of employee *benefits*. It is constructed by analogy with the Consumer Price Index (CPI); that is, it holds the composition of employment constant in order to isolate hourly compensation trends that take place for individual occupations, which are then aggregated, using fixed relative importance weights. The ECI is based on a sample survey and may be revised from time to time, due to updated classification, weighting, and seasonal adjustments. However, it is not subject to major benchmark revision of the underlying wage, salary, and benefit rate observations. By design, it excludes any representation of employee stock options. As it is based on a sample survey, the ECI is measured "from the bottom up," aggregating from individual employers' reports to higher levels. The ECI is frequently and appropriately used as the best available measure of the general trend of wages and of the extent of inflationary pressure exerted on prices by labor costs.

The *compensation per hour* component of the report on "Productivity and Costs" (Table 9-3) is calculated and published for total compensation in total business, nonfarm business, nonfinancial corporations, and manufacturing. The nonfarm business category is similar in scope to the "all private industry" category in the ECI. The measures in Table 9-3, however, are compiled "from the top down," starting with aggregate estimates of compensation and hours, then dividing the former by the latter. Compensation per hour is affected by changes in the composition of employment. If the composition of employment shifts toward a larger proportion of higher-paid employees and/or industries, compensation per hour will rise even if there is no increase in hourly compensation for any individual worker.

In addition, *compensation per hour* includes the value of exercised stock options as expensed by companies. Also included are other transitory payments, many of which may be of little relevance to the typical worker or to ongoing production costs. These values are not reported immediately. Instead, they are incorporated when later, more comprehensive reports are received. This process can lead to dramatic revisions in compensation per hour and in the unit labor costs index, which is based on compensation. For example, the fourth-quarter 2004 increase in compensation per hour in nonfarm business was initially reported at an annual rate of 3.1 percent. Four months later, the reported rate for the same time period was 10.2 percent. The rate of increase from a year earlier was revised from 3.6 to 5.9 percent. According to then-Federal Reserve Chairman Alan Greenspan, in testimony before the Joint Economic Committee on June 9, 2005, this reflected "a large but apparently transitory surge in bonuses and the proceeds of stock option exercises," not a potentially inflationary acceleration in the rate of labor compensation increase. More recently, it was reported in August 2009 that "first-quarter unit labor costs were revised to negative 2.7% from positive 3%." (*Wall Street Journal*, August 12, 2009, p. A2.)

These characteristics suggest that *compensation per hour* should not be considered a reliable or appropriate indicator of wage or compensation trends for typical workers. It is useful in conjunction with the productivity series, because aggregate productivity is subject to the same composition shifts—higher-productivity industries also tend to have higher-paid employees. Hence, the measure of *unit labor costs* (derived by dividing compensation per hour by output per hour in this system) is not distorted when the composition of output shifts toward higher-productivity industries. The shift affects the numerator and denominator of the ratio similarly. However, both compensation and unit labor costs can still be distorted by transitory payments, such as those discussed above.

There are other, probably less important differences between the two measures. Compensation per hour refers to the entire quarter, while the ECI is observed in the terminal month of each quarter. Tips and other forms of compensation not provided by employers are included in hourly compensation but not in the ECI. The ECI excludes persons working for token wages, business owners and others who set their own wage, and family workers who do not earn a market wage; all of these workers are included in the productivity and cost accounts. Hourly compensation excludes employees of nonprofit institutions serving individuals—about 10 percent of private workers (mostly in education and medical care) who are within the scope of the ECI. Hourly compensation measures include an estimate for the unincorporated self-employed, who are assumed to earn the same hourly compensation as other employees in the sector. Implicitly, unpaid family workers also are included in the hourly compensation measures with the assumption that their hourly compensation is zero. Both of these groups are also excluded from the ECI.

TABLES 9-1 AND 9-2

Employment Cost Indexes

SOURCE: U.S. DEPARTMENT OF LABOR, BUREAU OF LABOR STATISTICS (BLS)

The Employment Cost Index (ECI) is a quarterly measure of the change in the cost of labor, independent of the influence of employment shifts among occupations and industries. It uses a fixed market basket of labor—similar in concept to the Consumer Price Index's fixed market basket of goods and services—to measure changes over time in employer costs of employing labor. Data are quarterly in all cases and are reported for the final month of each quarter. These measures are expressed as indexes, with the not-seasonally-adjusted value for December 2005 set at 100.

Care should be used in comparing the ECI with other data sets. The "all private industry" category in the ECI excludes farm and household workers (it is sometimes, and more precisely, called "private nonfarm industry"), and the "all civilian workers" category excludes federal government, farm, and household workers.

The data for 1979 through 2016, which are presented in Table 9-2 and are the official ECI measures for that time period, were based on the 1987 Standard Industrial Classification (SIC) and 2010 Occupational Classification System (OCS).

Currently the ECI is compiled based on the 2012 North American Industry Classification System (NAICS) and the 2010 Standard Occupational Classification Manual (SOC). These data, along with comparable data for 2004 through 2016, are shown in Table 9-1.

For certain broad categories shown in this volume—indicated by footnote 2 in Table 9-2—the old SIC categories are roughly comparable and continuous with the data for 2006 and subsequent years. (However, they differ slightly on overlap dates, and should be "linked" if a continuous time series is desired; see the article at the beginning of this volume.) Many of the new industry and occupational categories are not continuous with the old series shown here, and some of the old categories are not being continued because BLS finds them obsolete and no longer meaningful.

Definitions

Total compensation comprises wages, salaries, and the employer's costs for employee benefits. Excluded from wages and salaries and employee benefits are the value of stock option exercises and items such as payment-in-kind, free room and board, and tips.

Wages and salaries consists of straight-time earnings per hour before payroll deductions, including production bonuses, incentive earnings, commissions, and cost-of-living adjustments. These wage rates exclude premium pay for overtime and for work on weekends and holidays, shift differentials, and nonproduction bonuses such as lump-sum payments provided in lieu of

wage increases. According to BLS, wages and salaries are about 70 percent of total compensation.

Benefits includes the cost to employers for paid leave—vacations, holidays, sick leave, and other leave; for supplemental pay—premium pay for work in addition to the regular work schedule (such as overtime, weekends, and holidays), shift differentials, and nonproduction bonuses (such as referral bonuses and lump-sum payments provided in lieu of wage increases); for insurance benefits—life, health, short-term disability, and long-term disability; for retirement and savings benefits—defined benefit and defined contribution plans; and for legally required benefits—Social Security, Medicare, federal and state unemployment insurance, and workers' compensation. Severance pay and supplemental unemployment benefit (SUB) plans are included in the data through December 2005 but were dropped beginning with the March 2006 data. The combined cost of these two benefits accounted for less than one-tenth of one percent of compensation, and according to BLS, dropping these benefits has had virtually no impact on the index. According to BLS, benefit costs are about 30 percent of total compensation.

Civilian workers are private industry workers, as defined below, and workers in state and local government. Federal workers are not included.

Private industry workers are paid workers in private industry excluding farms and private households. To be included in the ECI, employees in occupations must receive cash payments from the establishment for services performed and the establishment must pay the employer's portion of Medicare taxes on that individual's wages. Major exclusions from the survey are the self-employed, individuals who set their own pay (for example, proprietors, owners, major stockholders, and partners in unincorporated firms), volunteers, unpaid workers, family members being paid token wages, individuals receiving long-term disability compensation, and U.S. citizens working overseas.

Private industry workers excluding incentive paid occupations is a new category introduced in the 2006 revision to eliminate the quarter-to-quarter variability related to the way workers (for example, salespersons working on commission) are paid. (The category *private industry workers excluding sales occupations* was intended to serve a similar purpose in the previous SIC-based classification system, but was much less accurate in separately identifying workers with highly variable compensation.)

Goods-producing industries include mining, construction, and manufacturing.

Service-providing industries include the following NAICS industries: wholesale trade; retail trade; transportation and warehousing; utilities; information; finance and insurance; real estate and rental and leasing; professional, scientific, and technical services; management of companies and enterprises; administrative and support and waste management and remediation services; education services; health care and social assistance; arts, entertainment, and recreation; accommodation and food services; and other services, except public administration.

Notes on the data

Employee benefit costs are calculated as cents per hour worked.

The June 2017 data were collected from probability samples of approximately 27,700 occupational observations in about 6,700 sample establishments in private industry, and approximately 8,100 occupations within about 1,400 establishments in state and local governments. The private industry sample is rotated over approximately five years. The state and local government sample is replaced less frequently; the latest sample was introduced in September 2007.

Currently, the sample establishments are classified in industry categories based on the NAICS. Within an establishment, specific job categories are selected and classified into approximately 800 occupational classifications according to the SOC. Similar procedures were followed under the previous classification systems. Data are collected each quarter for the pay periods including the 12th day of March, June, September, and December.

Aggregate indexes are calculated using fixed employment weights. Beginning with December 2013, estimates are based on 2012 employment weight, using Occupational Employment counts. From March 2006 through June 2017, ECI weights were based on fixed employment counts for 2012 from the BLS Occupational Employment Statistics survey. Employment data from the 2012 Survey were introduced in December 2013. ECI measures were based on 1990 employment counts from March 1995 through December 2005 and 1980 census employment counts from June 1986 through December 1994. Prior to June 1986, they were based on 1970 census employment counts.

Use of fixed weights ensures that changes in the indexes reflect only changes in hourly compensation, not employment shifts among industries or occupations with different levels of wages and compensation. This feature distinguishes the ECI from other compensation series such as average hourly earnings (see Chapter 10 and its notes and definitions) and the compensation per hour component of the productivity series (see Table 9-3 and its notes and definitions, and the general note above), each of which is affected by such employment shifts.

Data availability

Data for wages and salaries for the private nonfarm economy are available beginning with the data for 1975; data for compensation begin with the 1980 data. The series for state and local government and for the civilian nonfarm economy begin with the 1981 data. All series are available on the BLS Web site at <http://www.bls.gov>.

Wage and salary change and compensation cost change data also are available by major occupational and industry groups, as well as by region and collective bargaining status. Information on wage and salary change is available from 1975 to the present for most of these series. Compensation cost change data are available from 1980 to the present for most series. For 10 occupational and industry series, benefit cost change data are available from the early 1980s to the present. For state and local governments and the civilian economy (state and local governments plus private industry), wage and salary change and compensation cost change data are available for major occupational and industry series. BLS provides data for all these series from June 1981 to the present.

Updates are available about four weeks after the end of the reference quarter. Reference quarters end in March, June, September, and December. Seasonal adjustment factors and seasonally adjusted indexes are released in late April.

REFERENCES

Explanatory notes, including references, are included in a Technical Note in each quarter's ECI news release, and can be found on the BLS Web site, in the PDF version of the release.

More detailed information on the ECI is available from Chapter 8, "National compensation measures," (www.bls.gov/opub/hom/pdf/homch8.pdf) from the *BLS Handbook of Methods*, and several articles published in the Monthly Labor Review and Compensation and Working Conditions. The articles and other descriptive pieces are available at www.bls.gov/ect/#publications, by calling (202) 691-6199, or sending e-mail to NCSinfo@bls.gov.

Table 9-3A and 9-3B

Productivity and Related Data

The indexes of productivity and costs for the entire postwar period, 1947 through 2016, have been revised to reflect the 2013 and 2014 comprehensive revisions of the National Income and Product Accounts (NIPAs).

Productivity measures relate real physical output to real input. They encompass a family of measures that includes single-factor input measures, such as output per unit of labor input or output per unit of capital input, as well as measures of multifactor productivity—that is, output per unit of combined labor and capital inputs. The indexes published in this book are indexes of labor productivity expressed in terms of output per hour of labor input. (A larger group of BLS productivity measures can be found in Bernan Press's *Handbook of U.S. Labor Statistics*.) All data are presented as indexes with a base of 2009 = 100.

Definitions

Current dollar output is the current-dollar value of the goods and services produced in the specified sector. *Output* is the constant-dollar value of the same goods and services, derived as current-dollar output divided by the sector *implicit price deflator.* All these data are derived from components of the NIPAs; see Notes on the data below, and for general information on the NIPAs, see the Notes and Definitions to Chapter 1.

Output per hour of all persons (labor productivity) is the value of goods and services in constant dollars produced per hour of labor input. By definition, nonfinancial corporations include no self-employed persons. Productivity in this sector is expressed as *output per hour of all employees. Output per person* is output divided by the index for employment instead of by the index for hours of all persons.

Compensation is the total value of the wages and salaries of employees, plus employers' contributions for social insurance and private benefit plans, plus wages, salaries, and supplementary payments for the self-employed. *Compensation per hour* is compensation divided by *hours of all persons.* Included in compensation is the value of exercised stock options that companies report as a charge against earnings. Stock option values are reported with a delay; consequently, recent values are estimated based on extrapolation. They are revised to actual values when the data become available; sometimes the revisions are very large. The labor compensation of proprietors cannot be explicitly identified and must be estimated. This is done by assuming that proprietors have the same hourly compensation as employees in the same sector. The quarterly labor productivity and cost measures do not contain estimates of compensation for unpaid family workers.

Real compensation per hour is compensation per hour deflated by the Consumer Price Index Research Series (CPI-U-RS) for the period 1978 through 2016 (For current quarters, before the CPI-U-RS becomes available, changes in the CPI-U are used.) Changes in the Consumer Price Index for Urban Wage Earners and Clerical Workers (CPI-W) are used for data before 1978, as there was no CPI-U (or CPIU-RS) for that period. See the Notes and Definitions to Chapter 8 for explanation of the CPI-U, the CPI-W, and the CPI-U-RS.

Unit labor costs are the current-dollar labor costs expended in the production of a unit of output. They are derived by dividing compensation by output.

Unit nonlabor payments include profits, depreciation, interest, rental income of persons, and indirect taxes per unit of output. They are computed by subtracting current-dollar compensation of all persons from current-dollar value of output, providing the data for the index of total *nonlabor payments,* which is then divided by output.

Unit nonlabor costs are available for nonfinancial corporations only. They contain all the components of unit nonlabor payments except unit profits (and rental income of persons, which is zero by definition for nonfinancial corporations).

Unit profits, the other component of unit nonlabor payments, are also only available for nonfinancial corporations.

Hours of all persons (labor input) consists of the total hours at work (*employment* multiplied by *average weekly hours*) of payroll workers, self-employed persons, and unpaid family workers. For the nonfinancial corporations data, there are no self-employed persons; the data represent *employee hours.*

Labor share is the total dollar amount of labor compensation divided by the total current-dollar value of output.

Notes on the data

Output for the business sector is equal to constant-dollar gross domestic product minus: the rental value of owner-occupied dwellings, the output of nonprofit institutions, the output of paid employees of private households, and general government output. The measures are derived from national income and product account (NIPA) data supplied by the U.S. Department of Commerce's Bureau of Economic Analysis (BEA). For manufacturing, BLS produces annual estimates of sectoral output. Quarterly manufacturing output indexes derived from the Federal Reserve Board of Governors' monthly indexes of industrial production (see Chapter 2) are adjusted to these annual measures by the BLS, and are also used to project the quarterly values in the current period.

Nonfinancial corporate output consists of business output minus unincorporated businesses and those corporations classified as offices of bank holding companies, offices of other holding companies, or offices in the finance and insurance sector.. Unit profits and unit nonlabor costs can be calculated separately for this sector and are shown in this table.

Compensation and hours data are developed from BLS and BEA data. The primary source for hours and employment is BLS's Current Employment Statistics (CES) program (see the notes and definitions for Chapter 10). Other data sources are the Current Population Survey (CPS) and the National Compensation Survey (NCS). Weekly paid hours are adjusted to hours at work using the NCS. For paid employees, hours at work differ from hours paid, in that they exclude paid vacation and holidays, paid sick leave, and other paid personal or administrative leave.

Although the labor productivity measures relate output to labor input, they do not measure the contribution of labor or any other specific factor of production. Instead, they reflect the joint effect of many influences, including changes in technology; capital investment; level of output; utilization of capacity, energy, and materials; the organization of production; managerial skill; and the characteristics and efforts of the work force.

Revisions

Data for recent years are revised frequently to take account of revisions in the output and labor input measures that underlie the estimates. Customarily, all revisions to source data are reflected in the release following the source data revision. Data in this volume were released July 28, 2017, and reflect the midyear 2016 revisions to the NIPAs and all revisions in labor input and compensation available up to that release date, including the annual benchmark revision of the CES and updated seasonal factors.

Data availability

Series are available quarterly and annually. Quarterly measures are based entirely on seasonally adjusted data. For some detailed manufacturing series (not shown here), only annual averages are available. Productivity indexes are published early in the second and third months of each quarter, reflecting new data for preceding quarters. Complete historical data are available on the BLS Web site at <http://www.bls.gov>.

BLS also publishes productivity estimates for a number of individual industries. A release entitled "Productivity and Costs by Industry" is available on the BLS Web site at <http://www.bls.gov>.

REFERENCES

Further information is available in the Technical Notes and footnotes on the most current monthly release, available on the Web site, and from the following sources: Chapter 10, "Productivity Measures: Business Sector and Major Subsectors," *BLS Handbook of Methods*—Bulletin 2490 (April 1997) and the following *Monthly Labor Review* articles: "Alternative Measures of Supervisory Employee Hours and Productivity Growth" (April 2004); "Possible Measurement Bias in Aggregate Productivity Growth" (February 1999); "Improvements to the Quarterly Productivity Measures" (October 1995); "Hours of Work: A New Base for BLS Productivity Statistics" (February 1990); and "New Sector Definitions for Productivity Series" (October 1976).

Table 9-4

Corporate Profits with Inventory Valuation Adjustment by Industry Group

SOURCE: U.S. DEPARTMENT OF COMMERCE, BUREAU OF ECONOMIC ANALYSIS

These profits measures are derived from the NIPAs and classified according to the NAICS. See the notes and definitions to Chapter 1 for definitions, data availability, and references. Note that this industry breakdown of profits incorporates the inventory valuation adjustment (IVA), which eliminates any capital gain element in profits arising from changes in the prices at which inventories are valued, but does <u>not</u> incorporate the capital consumption adjustment (CCAdj), which adjusts historical costs of fixed capital to replacement costs and uses actual rather than tax-based service lives. This is because the CCAdj is calculated by BEA at an aggregate level, whereas the IVA is calculated at an industry level.

CHAPTER 10: EMPLOYMENT, HOURS, AND EARNINGS

SECTION 10A: LABOR FORCE, EMPLOYMENT, AND UNEMPLOYMENT

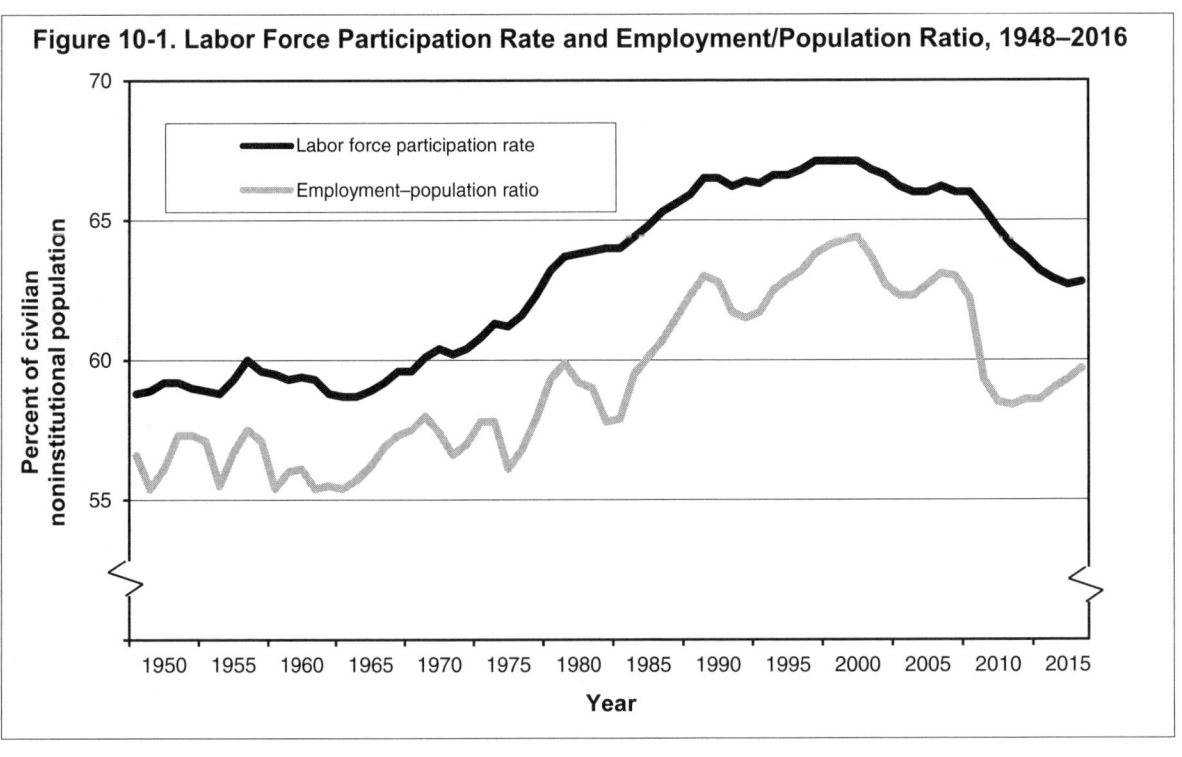

Figure 10-1. Labor Force Participation Rate and Employment/Population Ratio, 1948–2016

- From a high point in January 2008 to a low in December 2009, 8.1 million Americans lost jobs, based on total civilian employment smoothed for population adjustments. (Table 10-6) The employment/population ratio, charted in Figure 10-1 above, registered the steepest plunge of the postwar period. (Tables 10-1A and B) However, this 5.5 percent employment decline during 2008 and 2009 was nowhere near the length and scale of job loss in the Great Depression, when jobs dropped 22 percent from 1929 to 1932. (Table 10-21)

- By December 2016, there were 14.1 million more persons employed than in December 2009. The employment/population ratio, which got as low as 58.4 percent in 2011 but rose to 59.7 percent in 2016. (Tables 10-1A and B, 10-6, and recent data)

- Beginning in 2001, the number of people who either had jobs or were unemployed and looking for a job began to decline relative to the size of the total working-age population. This drop in labor force participation, unprecedented in the period since 1948 during which these data have been collected, accelerated in 2009 through 2011—even as the recovery was beginning. The labor force participation rate increased slightly in 2016 after declining or remaining the same each year from 2006 to 2015. (Tables 10-1A and B)

Table 10-1A. Summary Labor Force, Employment, and Unemployment: Recent Data

(Thousands of persons, percent, seasonally adjusted, except as noted.)

Year and month	Civilian noninsti-tutional population [1]	Civilian labor force		Employment, thousands of persons						Employ-ment-popul-ation ratio, percent	Unemployment		
		Thous-ands of persons	Participa-tion rate (percent)	Total	By age and sex			By industry			Thousands of persons		Rate (percent)
					Men, 20 years and over	Women, 20 years and over	Both sexes, 16 to 19 years	Agri-cultural	Nonagri-cultural		Total	Unem-ployed 15 weeks and over	
1965	126 513	74 455	58.9	71 088	43 422	22 630	5 037	4 361	66 726	56.2	3 366	755	4.5
1966	128 058	75 770	59.2	72 895	43 668	23 510	5 721	3 979	68 915	56.9	2 875	526	3.8
1967	129 874	77 347	59.6	74 372	44 294	24 397	5 681	3 844	70 527	57.3	2 975	448	3.8
1968	132 028	78 737	59.6	75 920	44 859	25 281	5 780	3 817	72 103	57.5	2 817	412	3.6
1969	134 335	80 734	60.1	77 902	45 388	26 397	6 117	3 606	74 296	58.0	2 832	375	3.5
1970	137 085	82 771	60.4	78 678	45 581	26 952	6 144	3 463	75 215	57.4	4 093	663	4.9
1971	140 216	84 382	60.2	79 367	45 912	27 246	6 209	3 394	75 972	56.6	5 016	1 187	5.9
1972	144 126	87 034	60.4	82 153	47 130	28 276	6 746	3 484	78 669	57.0	4 882	1 167	5.6
1973	147 096	89 429	60.8	85 064	48 310	29 484	7 271	3 470	81 594	57.8	4 365	826	4.9
1974	150 120	91 949	61.3	86 794	48 922	30 424	7 448	3 515	83 279	57.8	5 156	955	5.6
1975	153 153	93 775	61.2	85 846	48 018	30 726	7 103	3 408	82 438	56.1	7 929	2 505	8.5
1976	156 150	96 158	61.6	88 752	49 190	32 226	7 336	3 331	85 421	56.8	7 406	2 366	7.7
1977	159 033	99 009	62.3	92 017	50 555	33 775	7 688	3 283	88 734	57.9	6 991	1 942	7.1
1978	161 910	102 251	63.2	96 048	52 143	35 836	8 070	3 387	92 661	59.3	6 202	1 414	6.1
1979	164 863	104 962	63.7	98 824	53 308	37 434	8 083	3 347	95 477	59.9	6 137	1 241	5.8
1980	167 745	106 940	63.8	99 303	53 101	38 492	7 710	3 364	95 938	59.2	7 637	1 871	7.1
1981	170 130	108 670	63.9	100 397	53 582	39 590	7 225	3 368	97 030	59.0	8 273	2 285	7.6
1982	172 271	110 204	64.0	99 526	52 891	40 086	6 549	3 401	96 125	57.8	10 678	3 485	9.7
1983	174 215	111 550	64.0	100 834	53 487	41 004	6 342	3 383	97 450	57.9	10 717	4 210	9.6
1984	176 383	113 544	64.4	105 005	55 769	42 793	6 444	3 321	101 685	59.5	8 539	2 737	7.5
1985	178 206	115 461	64.8	107 150	56 562	44 154	6 434	3 179	103 971	60.1	8 312	2 305	7.2
1986	180 587	117 834	65.3	109 597	57 569	45 556	6 472	3 163	106 434	60.7	8 237	2 232	7.0
1987	182 753	119 865	65.6	112 440	58 726	47 074	6 641	3 208	109 232	61.5	7 425	1 983	6.2
1988	184 613	121 669	65.9	114 968	59 781	48 383	6 805	3 169	111 800	62.3	6 701	1 610	5.5
1989	186 393	123 869	66.5	117 342	60 837	49 745	6 750	3 199	114 142	63.0	6 528	1 375	5.3
1990	189 164	125 840	66.5	118 793	61 678	50 535	6 610	3 223	115 570	62.8	7 047	1 525	5.6
1991	190 925	126 346	66.2	117 718	61 178	50 634	5 906	3 269	114 449	61.7	8 628	2 357	6.8
1992	192 805	128 105	66.4	118 492	61 496	51 328	5 669	3 247	115 245	61.5	9 613	3 408	7.5
1993	194 838	129 200	66.3	120 259	62 355	52 099	6 035	3 115	117 144	61.7	8 940	3 094	6.9
1994	196 814	131 056	66.6	123 060	63 294	53 606	6 162	3 409	119 651	62.5	7 996	2 860	6.1
1995	198 584	132 304	66.6	124 900	64 085	54 396	6 419	3 440	121 460	62.9	7 404	2 363	5.6
1996	200 591	133 943	66.8	126 708	64 897	55 311	6 500	3 443	123 264	63.2	7 236	2 316	5.4
1997	203 133	136 297	67.1	129 558	66 284	56 613	6 661	3 399	126 159	63.8	6 739	2 062	4.9
1998	205 220	137 673	67.1	131 463	67 135	57 278	7 051	3 378	128 085	64.1	6 210	1 637	4.5
1999	207 753	139 368	67.1	133 488	67 761	58 555	7 172	3 281	130 207	64.3	5 880	1 480	4.2
2000	212 577	142 583	67.1	136 891	69 634	60 067	7 190	2 464	134 427	64.4	5 692	1 318	4.0
2001	215 092	143 734	66.8	136 933	69 776	60 417	6 740	2 299	134 635	63.7	6 801	1 752	4.7
2002	217 570	144 863	66.6	136 485	69 734	60 420	6 332	2 311	134 174	62.7	8 378	2 904	5.8
2003	221 168	146 510	66.2	137 736	70 415	61 402	5 919	2 275	135 461	62.3	8 774	3 378	6.0
2004	223 357	147 401	66.0	139 252	71 572	61 773	5 907	2 232	137 020	62.3	8 149	3 072	5.5
2005	226 082	149 320	66.0	141 730	73 050	62 702	5 978	2 197	139 532	62.7	7 591	2 619	5.1
2006	228 815	151 428	66.2	144 427	74 431	63 834	6 163	2 206	142 221	63.1	7 001	2 266	4.6
2007	231 867	153 124	66.0	146 047	75 337	64 799	5 911	2 095	143 952	63.0	7 078	2 303	4.6
2008	233 788	154 287	66.0	145 362	74 750	65 039	5 573	2 168	143 194	62.2	8 924	3 188	5.8
2009	235 801	154 142	65.4	139 877	71 341	63 699	4 837	2 103	137 775	59.3	14 265	7 272	9.3
2010	237 830	153 889	64.7	139 064	71 230	63 456	4 378	2 206	136 858	58.5	14 825	8 786	9.6
2011	239 618	153 617	64.1	139 869	72 182	63 360	4 327	2 254	137 615	58.4	13 747	8 077	8.9
2012	243 284	154 975	63.7	142 469	73 403	64 640	4 426	2 186	140 283	58.6	12 506	6 996	8.1
2013	245 679	155 389	63.2	143 929	74 176	65 295	4 458	2 130	141 799	58.6	11 460	6 117	7.4
2014	247 947	155 922	62.9	146 305	75 471	66 287	4 548	2 237	144 068	59.0	9 617	4 714	6.2
2015	250 801	157 130	62.7	148 834	76 776	67 323	4 737	2 422	146 411	59.3	8 296	3 595	5.3
2016	253 538	159 187	62.8	151 436	78 084	66 387	4 965	2 460	148 976	59.7	7 751	3 163	4.9
2015													
January	249 723	157 022	62.9	148 061	75 364	66 894	4 294	2 234	144 317	59.3	8 962	4 250	5.7
February	249 899	156 771	62.7	148 108	75 671	67 058	4 389	2 234	144 884	59.3	8 663	4 248	5.5
March	250 080	156 781	62.7	148 244	76 122	67 022	4 491	2 405	145 230	59.3	8 538	4 064	5.4
April	250 266	157 043	62.8	148 522	76 749	67 303	4 536	2 294	146 293	59.3	8 521	3 802	5.4
May	250 455	157 447	62.9	148 792	77 137	67 493	4 718	2 431	146 918	59.4	8 655	3 851	5.5
June	250 663	156 993	62.6	148 742	77 315	67 003	5 327	2 703	146 942	59.3	8 251	3 369	5.3
July	250 876	157 125	62.6	148 890	77 541	66 485	5 696	2 601	147 121	59.3	8 235	3 245	5.2
August	251 096	157 109	62.6	149 092	77 311	66 874	5 042	2 539	146 689	59.4	8 017	3 318	5.1
September	251 325	156 809	62.4	148 932	77 110	67 394	4 476	2 471	146 509	59.3	7 877	3 207	5.0
October	251 541	157 123	62.5	149 255	77 258	67 885	4 574	2 518	147 198	59.3	7 869	3 301	5.0
November	251 747	157 358	62.5	149 419	76 911	68 335	4 520	2 363	147 404	59.4	7 939	3 256	5.0
December	251 936	157 957	62.7	150 030	76 827	68 131	4 745	2 273	147 430	59.6	7 927	3 231	5.0
2016													
January	252 397	158 362	62.7	150 533	76 644	67 904	4 490	2 200	146 838	59.6	7 829	3 297	4.9
February	252 577	158 888	62.9	151 043	77 148	68 305	4 608	2 274	147 787	59.8	7 845	3 525	4.9
March	252 768	159 278	63.0	151 301	77 639	68 451	4 648	2 491	148 247	59.9	7 977	3 651	5.0
April	252 969	158 938	62.8	151 028	78 028	68 346	4 701	2 478	148 597	59.7	7 910	3 499	5.0
May	253 174	158 510	62.6	151 058	78 241	68 496	4 857	2 620	148 974	59.7	7 451	3 113	4.7
June	253 397	158 889	62.7	151 090	78 673	67 769	5 548	2 661	149 329	59.6	7 799	2 970	4.9
July	253 620	159 295	62.8	151 546	78 695	67 702	6 040	2 597	149 840	59.8	7 749	3 060	4.9
August	253 854	159 508	62.8	151 655	78 562	67 776	5 466	2 718	149 086	59.7	7 853	2 942	4.9
September	254 091	159 830	62.9	151 926	78 459	68 709	4 810	2 526	149 451	59.8	7 904	3 004	4.9
October	254 321	159 643	62.8	151 902	78 538	68 997	4 800	2 408	149 927	59.7	7 740	3 087	4.8
November	254 540	159 456	62.6	152 048	78 405	69 203	4 778	2 366	150 020	59.7	7 409	2 859	4.6
December	254 742	159 640	62.7	152 111	77 984	68 984	4 831	2 180	149 617	59.7	7 529	2 945	4.7

[1] Not seasonally adjusted.

Table 10-1B. Summary Labor Force, Employment, and Unemployment: Historical

(Thousands of persons, percent, seasonally adjusted, except as noted.)

Year and month	Civilian noninstitutional population [1]	Civilian labor force		Employment, thousands of persons						Employment-population ratio, percent	Unemployment		
		Thousands of persons	Participation rate (percent)	Total	By age and sex			By industry			Thousands of persons		Rate (percent) [2]
					Men, 20 years and over	Women, 20 years and over	Both sexes, 16 to 19 years	Agricultural	Nonagricultural		Total	Unemployed 15 weeks and over	
14 Years and Over													
1929	...	49 180	...	47 630	...	...	...	10 450	37 180	...	1 550	...	3.2
1930	...	49 820	...	45 480	...	...	...	10 340	35 140	...	4 340	...	8.7
1931	...	50 420	...	42 400	...	...	...	10 290	32 110	...	8 020	...	15.9 (15.3)
1932	...	51 000	...	38 940	...	...	...	10 170	28 770	...	12 060	...	23.6 (22.5)
1933	...	51 590	...	38 760	...	...	...	10 090	28 670	...	12 830	...	24.9 (20.6)
1934	...	52 230	...	40 890	...	...	...	9 900	30 990	...	11 340	...	21.7 (16.0)
1935	...	52 870	...	42 260	...	...	...	10 110	32 150	...	10 610	...	20.1 (14.2)
1936	...	53 440	...	44 410	...	...	...	10 000	34 410	...	9 030	...	16.9 (9.9)
1937	...	54 000	...	46 300	...	...	...	9 820	36 480	...	7 700	...	14.3 (9.1)
1938	...	54 610	...	44 220	...	...	...	9 690	34 530	...	10 390	...	19.0 (12.5)
1939	...	55 230	...	45 750	...	...	...	9 610	36 140	...	9 480	...	17.2 (11.3)
1940	99 840	55 640	55.7	47 520	...	...	...	9 540	37 980	47.6	8 120	...	14.6 (9.5)
1941	99 900	55 910	56.0	50 350	...	...	...	9 100	41 250	50.4	5 560	...	9.9 (6.0)
1942	98 640	56 410	57.2	53 750	...	...	...	9 250	44 500	54.5	2 660	...	4.7 (3.1)
1943	94 640	55 540	58.7	54 470	...	...	...	9 080	45 390	57.6	1 070	...	1.9 (1.8)
1944	93 220	54 630	58.6	53 960	...	...	...	8 950	45 010	57.9	670	...	1.2
1945	94 090	53 860	57.2	52 820	...	...	...	8 580	44 240	56.1	1 040	...	1.9
1946	103 070	57 520	55.8	55 250	...	...	...	8 320	46 930	53.6	2 270	...	3.9
1947	106 018	60 168	56.8	57 812	...	...	...	8 256	49 557	54.5	2 356	...	3.9
16 Years and Over													
1947	101 827	59 350	58.3	57 038	...	...	...	7 890	49 148	56.0	2 311	...	3.9
1948	103 068	60 621	58.8	58 343	39 382	14 936	4 026	7 629	50 714	56.6	2 276	309	3.8
1949	103 994	61 286	58.9	57 651	38 803	15 137	3 712	7 658	49 993	55.4	3 637	684	5.9
1950	104 995	62 208	59.2	58 918	39 394	15 824	3 703	7 160	51 758	56.1	3 288	782	5.3
1951	104 621	62 017	59.2	59 961	39 626	16 570	3 767	6 726	53 235	57.3	2 055	303	3.3
1952	105 231	62 138	59.0	60 250	39 578	16 958	3 719	6 500	53 749	57.3	1 883	232	3.0
1953	107 056	63 015	58.9	61 179	40 296	17 164	3 720	6 260	54 919	57.1	1 834	210	2.9
1954	108 321	63 643	58.8	60 109	39 634	17 000	3 475	6 205	53 904	55.5	3 532	812	5.5
1955	109 683	65 023	59.3	62 170	40 526	18 002	3 642	6 450	55 722	56.7	2 852	702	4.4
1956	110 954	66 552	60.0	63 799	41 216	18 767	3 818	6 283	57 514	57.5	2 750	533	4.1
1957	112 265	66 929	59.6	64 071	41 239	19 052	3 778	5 947	58 123	57.1	2 859	560	4.3
1958	113 727	67 639	59.5	63 036	40 411	19 043	3 582	5 586	57 450	55.4	4 602	1 452	6.8
1959	115 329	68 369	59.3	64 630	41 267	19 524	3 838	5 565	59 065	56.0	3 740	1 040	5.5
1960	117 245	69 628	59.4	65 778	41 543	20 105	4 129	5 458	60 318	56.1	3 852	957	5.5
1961	118 771	70 459	59.3	65 746	41 342	20 296	4 108	5 200	60 546	55.4	4 714	1 532	6.7
1962	120 153	70 614	58.8	66 702	41 815	20 693	4 195	4 944	61 759	55.5	3 911	1 119	5.5
1963	122 416	71 833	58.7	67 762	42 251	21 257	4 255	4 687	63 076	55.4	4 070	1 088	5.7
1964	124 485	73 091	58.7	69 305	42 886	21 903	4 516	4 523	64 782	55.7	3 786	973	5.2
1948													
January	102 603	60 095	58.6	58 061	39 386	14 556	4 119	8 077	49 984	56.6	2 034	311	3.4
February	102 698	60 524	58.9	58 196	39 480	14 621	4 095	7 696	50 500	56.7	2 328	283	3.8
March	102 771	60 070	58.5	57 671	39 098	14 481	4 092	7 333	50 338	56.1	2 399	292	4.0
April	102 831	60 677	59.0	58 291	39 157	15 001	4 133	7 557	50 734	56.7	2 386	324	3.9
May	102 923	59 972	58.3	57 854	39 139	14 712	4 003	7 141	50 713	56.2	2 118	329	3.5
June	102 992	60 957	59.2	58 743	39 392	15 213	4 138	7 591	51 152	57.0	2 214	322	3.6
July	103 216	61 181	59.3	58 968	39 607	15 348	4 013	7 602	51 366	57.1	2 213	295	3.6
August	103 240	60 806	58.9	58 456	39 510	14 994	3 952	7 562	50 894	56.6	2 350	332	3.9
September	103 291	60 815	58.9	58 513	39 324	15 207	3 982	7 865	50 648	56.6	2 302	298	3.8
October	103 361	60 646	58.7	58 387	39 522	14 956	3 909	7 626	50 761	56.5	2 259	324	3.7
November	103 424	60 702	58.7	58 417	39 459	15 054	3 904	7 624	50 793	56.5	2 285	282	3.8
December	103 468	61 169	59.1	58 740	39 539	15 137	4 064	7 984	50 756	56.8	2 429	305	4.0
1949													
January	103 529	60 771	58.7	58 175	39 233	14 991	3 951	7 790	50 385	56.2	2 596	315	4.3
February	103 559	61 057	59.0	58 208	39 117	15 117	3 974	8 022	50 186	56.2	2 849	374	4.7
March	103 665	61 073	58.9	58 043	39 015	15 069	3 959	8 008	50 035	56.0	3 030	414	5.0
April	103 739	61 007	58.8	57 747	38 993	14 978	3 776	7 911	49 836	55.7	3 260	483	5.3
May	103 845	61 259	59.0	57 552	38 701	15 066	3 785	8 067	49 485	55.4	3 707	602	6.1
June	103 930	60 948	58.6	57 172	38 632	15 003	3 537	7 802	49 370	55.0	3 776	705	6.2
July	104 042	61 301	58.9	57 190	38 405	15 244	3 541	8 021	49 169	55.0	4 111	848	6.7
August	104 121	61 590	59.2	57 397	38 610	15 181	3 606	7 604	49 793	55.1	4 193	917	6.8
September	104 219	61 633	59.1	57 584	38 744	15 129	3 711	7 297	50 287	55.3	4 049	973	6.6
October	104 338	62 185	59.6	57 269	38 394	15 260	3 615	6 814	50 455	54.9	4 916	1 000	7.9
November	104 421	62 005	59.4	58 009	38 860	15 422	3 727	7 497	50 512	55.6	3 996	1 056	6.4
December	104 524	61 908	59.2	57 845	38 908	15 300	3 637	7 379	50 466	55.3	4 063	961	6.6

[1] Not seasonally adjusted.
[2] In 1930 through 1943, the official BLS data count persons on work relief as unemployed. The unemployment rates for those years shown in parentheses count persons on work relief as employed, which is more consistent with the postwar practice. See notes and definitions.
. . . = Not available.

Table 10-1B. Summary Labor Force, Employment, and Unemployment: Historical—*Continued*

(Thousands of persons, percent, seasonally adjusted, except as noted.)

Year and month	Civilian noninstitutional population [1]	Civilian labor force		Employment, thousands of persons						Employment-population ratio, percent	Unemployment		
					By age and sex			By industry			Thousands of persons		Rate (percent) [2]
		Thousands of persons	Participation rate (percent)	Total	Men, 20 years and over	Women, 20 years and over	Both sexes, 16 to 19 years	Agricultural	Nonagricultural		Total	Unemployed 15 weeks and over	
1950													
January	104 619	61 661	58.9	57 635	38 780	15 255	3 600	7 065	50 570	55.1	4 026	947	6.5
February	104 737	61 687	58.9	57 751	38 818	15 339	3 594	7 057	50 694	55.1	3 936	947	6.4
March	104 844	61 604	58.8	57 728	38 851	15 366	3 511	7 116	50 612	55.1	3 876	912	6.3
April	104 943	62 158	59.2	58 583	39 100	15 831	3 652	7 264	51 319	55.8	3 575	920	5.8
May	105 014	62 083	59.1	58 649	39 416	15 628	3 605	7 277	51 372	55.8	3 434	890	5.5
June	105 104	62 419	59.4	59 052	39 476	15 953	3 623	7 285	51 767	56.2	3 367	868	5.4
July	105 194	62 121	59.1	59 001	39 517	15 793	3 691	7 126	51 875	56.1	3 120	769	5.0
August	105 282	62 596	59.5	59 797	39 879	16 124	3 794	7 248	52 549	56.8	2 799	633	4.5
September	105 269	62 349	59.2	59 575	39 865	15 902	3 808	6 992	52 583	56.6	2 774	648	4.4
October	105 096	62 428	59.4	59 803	39 737	16 175	3 891	7 371	52 432	56.9	2 625	545	4.2
November	104 979	62 286	59.3	59 697	39 668	16 195	3 834	7 163	52 534	56.9	2 589	507	4.2
December	104 872	62 068	59.2	59 429	39 536	16 149	3 744	6 760	52 669	56.7	2 639	482	4.3
1951													
January	104 844	61 941	59.1	59 636	39 595	16 279	3 762	6 828	52 808	56.9	2 305	438	3.7
February	104 604	61 778	59.1	59 661	39 695	16 257	3 709	6 738	52 923	57.0	2 117	386	3.4
March	104 629	62 526	59.8	60 401	40 013	16 557	3 831	6 858	53 543	57.7	2 125	355	3.4
April	104 541	61 808	59.1	59 889	39 804	16 426	3 659	6 722	53 167	57.3	1 919	294	3.1
May	104 491	62 044	59.4	60 188	39 752	16 581	3 855	6 752	53 436	57.6	1 856	269	3.0
June	104 488	61 615	59.0	59 620	39 538	16 368	3 714	6 529	53 091	57.1	1 995	258	3.2
July	104 504	62 106	59.4	60 156	39 483	16 898	3 775	6 601	53 555	57.6	1 950	260	3.1
August	104 536	61 927	59.2	59 994	39 508	16 665	3 821	6 790	53 204	57.4	1 933	249	3.1
September	104 588	61 780	59.1	59 713	39 416	16 504	3 793	6 558	53 155	57.1	2 067	223	3.3
October	104 690	62 204	59.4	60 010	39 555	16 674	3 781	6 636	53 374	57.3	2 194	269	3.5
November	104 740	62 014	59.2	59 836	39 504	16 669	3 663	6 699	53 137	57.1	2 178	316	3.5
December	104 810	62 457	59.6	60 497	39 691	16 946	3 860	7 065	53 432	57.7	1 960	269	3.1
1952													
January	104 862	62 432	59.5	60 460	39 714	17 001	3 745	7 148	53 312	57.7	1 972	282	3.2
February	104 868	62 419	59.5	60 462	39 772	16 935	3 755	7 020	53 442	57.7	1 957	248	3.1
March	104 860	61 721	58.9	59 908	39 580	16 627	3 701	6 468	53 440	57.1	1 813	234	2.9
April	104 906	61 720	58.8	59 909	39 542	16 659	3 708	6 525	53 384	57.1	1 811	242	2.9
May	104 996	62 058	59.1	60 195	39 588	16 844	3 763	6 334	53 861	57.3	1 863	219	3.0
June	105 118	62 103	59.1	60 219	39 558	16 837	3 824	6 529	53 690	57.3	1 884	210	3.0
July	105 246	61 962	58.9	59 971	39 496	16 778	3 697	6 334	53 637	57.0	1 991	194	3.2
August	105 346	61 877	58.7	59 790	39 289	16 867	3 634	6 174	53 616	56.8	2 087	211	3.4
September	105 436	62 457	59.2	60 521	39 386	17 477	3 658	6 537	53 984	57.4	1 936	249	3.1
October	105 591	61 971	58.7	60 132	39 451	17 032	3 649	6 363	53 769	56.9	1 839	230	3.0
November	105 706	62 491	59.1	60 748	39 549	17 450	3 749	6 509	54 239	57.5	1 743	216	2.8
December	105 812	62 621	59.2	60 954	40 011	17 181	3 762	6 361	54 593	57.6	1 667	238	2.7
1953													
January	106 594	63 439	59.5	61 600	40 256	17 482	3 862	6 642	54 958	57.8	1 839	268	2.9
February	106 678	63 520	59.5	61 884	40 546	17 321	4 017	6 463	55 421	58.0	1 636	208	2.6
March	106 744	63 657	59.6	62 010	40 648	17 397	3 965	6 420	55 590	58.1	1 647	213	2.6
April	106 826	63 167	59.1	61 444	40 346	17 242	3 856	6 362	55 082	57.5	1 723	180	2.7
May	106 910	62 615	58.6	61 019	40 323	16 983	3 713	5 937	55 082	57.1	1 596	176	2.5
June	106 978	63 063	58.9	61 456	40 358	17 301	3 797	6 361	55 095	57.4	1 607	213	2.5
July	107 034	63 057	58.9	61 397	40 378	17 341	3 678	6 267	55 130	57.4	1 660	168	2.6
August	107 132	62 816	58.6	61 151	40 352	17 108	3 691	6 319	54 832	57.1	1 665	177	2.7
September	107 253	62 727	58.5	60 906	40 192	17 063	3 651	6 198	54 708	56.8	1 821	178	2.9
October	107 383	62 867	58.5	60 893	40 155	17 236	3 502	6 096	54 797	56.7	1 974	190	3.1
November	107 504	62 949	58.6	60 738	40 163	16 974	3 601	6 345	54 393	56.5	2 211	259	3.5
December	107 623	62 795	58.3	59 977	39 885	16 599	3 493	5 929	54 048	55.7	2 818	309	4.5
1954													
January	107 763	63 101	58.6	60 024	39 834	16 574	3 616	6 073	53 951	55.7	3 077	372	4.9
February	107 880	63 994	59.3	60 663	39 899	17 162	3 602	6 590	54 073	56.2	3 331	532	5.2
March	107 987	63 793	59.1	60 186	39 497	17 022	3 667	6 395	53 791	55.7	3 607	765	5.7
April	108 080	63 934	59.2	60 185	39 613	17 015	3 557	6 142	54 043	55.7	3 749	774	5.9
May	108 184	63 675	58.9	59 908	39 467	16 975	3 466	6 210	53 698	55.4	3 767	879	5.9
June	108 267	63 343	58.5	59 792	39 476	16 894	3 422	6 162	53 630	55.2	3 551	880	5.6
July	108 344	63 302	58.4	59 643	39 467	16 777	3 399	6 222	53 421	55.0	3 659	932	5.8
August	108 440	63 707	58.7	59 853	39 582	16 868	3 403	6 087	53 766	55.2	3 854	1 002	6.0
September	108 546	64 209	59.2	60 282	39 702	17 133	3 447	6 453	53 829	55.5	3 927	1 017	6.1
October	108 668	63 936	58.8	60 270	39 618	17 209	3 443	6 242	54 028	55.5	3 666	1 009	5.7
November	108 798	63 759	58.6	60 357	39 745	17 213	3 399	5 934	54 423	55.5	3 402	975	5.3
December	108 892	63 312	58.1	60 116	39 763	17 121	3 232	5 848	54 268	55.2	3 196	827	5.0

[1] Not seasonally adjusted.
[2] In 1930 through 1943, the official BLS data count persons on work relief as unemployed. The unemployment rates for those years shown in parentheses count persons on work relief as employed, which is more consistent with the postwar practice. See notes and definitions.

Table 10-1B. Summary Labor Force, Employment, and Unemployment: Historical—*Continued*

(Thousands of persons, percent, seasonally adjusted, except as noted.)

Year and month	Civilian noninstitutional population [1]	Civilian labor force		Employment, thousands of persons						Employment-population ratio, percent	Unemployment		
					By age and sex			By industry			Thousands of persons		Rate (percent) [2]
		Thousands of persons	Participation rate (percent)	Total	Men, 20 years and over	Women, 20 years and over	Both sexes, 16 to 19 years	Agricultural	Nonagricultural		Total	Unemployed 15 weeks and over	
1955													
January	109 059	63 910	58.6	60 753	39 937	17 375	3 441	6 113	54 640	55.7	3 157	882	4.9
February	109 078	63 696	58.4	60 727	39 964	17 413	3 350	5 854	54 873	55.7	2 969	826	4.7
March	109 254	63 882	58.5	60 964	40 111	17 415	3 438	6 242	54 722	55.8	2 918	816	4.6
April	109 377	64 564	59.0	61 515	40 120	17 867	3 528	6 363	55 152	56.2	3 049	811	4.7
May	109 544	64 381	58.8	61 634	40 410	17 665	3 559	6 327	55 307	56.3	2 747	734	4.3
June	109 680	64 482	58.8	61 781	40 444	17 837	3 500	6 243	55 538	56.3	2 701	668	4.2
July	109 792	65 145	59.3	62 513	40 751	18 123	3 639	6 438	56 075	56.9	2 632	640	4.0
August	109 882	65 581	59.7	62 797	40 747	18 377	3 673	6 575	56 222	57.1	2 784	535	4.2
September	109 977	65 628	59.7	62 950	40 920	18 285	3 745	6 819	56 131	57.2	2 678	558	4.1
October	110 085	65 821	59.8	62 991	40 858	18 327	3 806	6 728	56 263	57.2	2 830	572	4.3
November	110 177	66 037	59.9	63 257	40 936	18 422	3 899	6 655	56 602	57.4	2 780	564	4.2
December	110 296	66 445	60.2	63 684	41 063	18 630	3 991	6 653	57 031	57.7	2 761	581	4.2
1956													
January	110 390	66 419	60.2	63 753	41 203	18 691	3 859	6 590	57 163	57.8	2 666	561	4.0
February	110 478	66 124	59.9	63 518	41 175	18 582	3 761	6 457	57 061	57.5	2 606	545	3.9
March	110 582	66 175	59.8	63 411	41 199	18 496	3 716	6 221	57 190	57.3	2 764	521	4.2
April	110 650	66 264	59.9	63 614	41 289	18 629	3 696	6 460	57 154	57.5	2 650	476	4.0
May	110 810	66 722	60.2	63 861	41 166	18 844	3 851	6 375	57 486	57.6	2 861	506	4.3
June	110 903	66 702	60.1	63 820	41 196	18 748	3 876	6 335	57 485	57.5	2 882	516	4.3
July	111 019	66 752	60.1	63 800	41 216	18 718	3 866	6 320	57 480	57.5	2 952	523	4.4
August	111 099	66 673	60.0	63 972	41 265	18 864	3 843	6 280	57 692	57.6	2 701	543	4.1
September	111 222	66 714	60.0	64 079	41 221	19 019	3 839	6 375	57 704	57.6	2 635	577	3.9
October	111 335	66 546	59.8	63 975	41 261	18 928	3 786	6 137	57 838	57.5	2 571	530	3.9
November	111 432	66 657	59.8	63 796	41 208	18 846	3 742	5 997	57 799	57.3	2 861	575	4.3
December	111 526	66 700	59.8	63 910	41 192	18 859	3 859	5 806	58 104	57.3	2 790	567	4.2
1957													
January	111 626	66 428	59.5	63 632	41 168	18 740	3 724	5 790	57 842	57.0	2 796	509	4.2
February	111 711	66 879	59.9	64 257	41 341	19 115	3 801	6 125	58 132	57.5	2 622	530	3.9
March	111 824	66 913	59.8	64 404	41 500	19 066	3 838	5 963	58 441	57.6	2 509	514	3.7
April	111 933	66 647	59.5	64 047	41 345	18 937	3 765	5 836	58 211	57.2	2 600	516	3.9
May	112 031	66 695	59.5	63 985	41 334	18 897	3 754	5 999	57 986	57.1	2 710	538	4.1
June	112 172	67 052	59.8	64 196	41 411	18 973	3 812	6 002	58 194	57.2	2 856	526	4.3
July	112 317	67 336	60.0	64 540	41 472	19 262	3 806	6 401	58 139	57.5	2 796	535	4.2
August	112 421	66 706	59.3	63 959	41 243	19 020	3 696	5 898	58 061	56.9	2 747	542	4.1
September	112 554	67 064	59.6	64 121	41 213	19 116	3 792	5 728	58 393	57.0	2 943	559	4.4
October	112 710	67 066	59.5	64 046	41 069	19 160	3 817	5 875	58 171	56.8	3 020	650	4.5
November	112 874	67 123	59.5	63 669	40 853	19 082	3 734	5 686	57 983	56.4	3 454	674	5.1
December	113 013	67 398	59.6	63 922	40 884	19 285	3 753	6 037	57 885	56.6	3 476	731	5.2
1958													
January	113 138	67 095	59.3	63 220	40 617	19 035	3 568	5 831	57 389	55.9	3 875	879	5.8
February	113 234	67 201	59.3	62 898	40 336	18 951	3 611	5 654	57 244	55.5	4 303	1 005	6.4
March	113 337	67 223	59.3	62 731	40 180	18 968	3 583	5 561	57 170	55.3	4 492	1 128	6.7
April	113 415	67 647	59.6	62 631	40 129	18 969	3 533	5 602	57 029	55.2	5 016	1 387	7.4
May	113 534	67 895	59.8	62 874	40 253	18 978	3 643	5 647	57 227	55.4	5 021	1 493	7.4
June	113 647	67 674	59.5	62 730	40 208	19 008	3 514	5 510	57 220	55.2	4 944	1 677	7.3
July	113 727	67 824	59.6	62 745	40 270	19 039	3 436	5 525	57 220	55.2	5 079	1 796	7.5
August	113 835	68 037	59.8	63 012	40 343	19 103	3 566	5 673	57 339	55.4	5 025	1 888	7.4
September	113 977	68 002	59.7	63 181	40 564	19 033	3 584	5 453	57 728	55.4	4 821	1 795	7.1
October	114 138	68 045	59.6	63 475	40 699	19 091	3 685	5 563	57 912	55.6	4 570	1 708	6.7
November	114 283	67 658	59.2	63 470	40 684	19 157	3 629	5 571	57 899	55.5	4 188	1 570	6.2
December	114 429	67 740	59.2	63 549	40 666	19 170	3 713	5 521	58 028	55.5	4 191	1 490	6.2
1959													
January	114 582	67 936	59.3	63 868	40 769	19 292	3 807	5 481	58 387	55.7	4 068	1 396	6.0
February	114 712	67 649	59.0	63 684	40 699	19 167	3 818	5 429	58 255	55.5	3 965	1 277	5.9
March	114 849	68 068	59.3	64 267	41 079	19 379	3 809	5 677	58 590	56.0	3 801	1 210	5.6
April	114 986	68 339	59.4	64 768	41 419	19 498	3 851	5 893	58 875	56.3	3 571	1 039	5.2
May	115 144	68 178	59.2	64 699	41 355	19 565	3 779	5 792	58 907	56.2	3 479	965	5.1
June	115 287	68 278	59.2	64 849	41 387	19 658	3 804	5 712	59 137	56.3	3 429	963	5.0
July	115 429	68 539	59.4	65 011	41 596	19 595	3 820	5 564	59 447	56.3	3 528	889	5.1
August	115 555	68 432	59.2	64 844	41 485	19 568	3 791	5 442	59 402	56.1	3 588	889	5.2
September	115 668	68 545	59.3	64 770	41 351	19 531	3 888	5 447	59 323	56.0	3 775	895	5.5
October	115 798	68 821	59.4	64 911	41 362	19 702	3 847	5 355	59 556	56.1	3 910	883	5.7
November	115 916	68 533	59.1	64 530	41 062	19 594	3 874	5 480	59 050	55.7	4 003	982	5.8
December	116 040	68 994	59.5	65 341	41 651	19 717	3 973	5 458	59 883	56.3	3 653	920	5.3

[1] Not seasonally adjusted.
[2] In 1930 through 1943, the official BLS data count persons on work relief as unemployed. The unemployment rates for those years shown in parentheses count persons on work relief as employed, which is more consistent with the postwar practice. See notes and definitions.

Table 10-1B. Summary Labor Force, Employment, and Unemployment: Historical—*Continued*

(Thousands of persons, percent, seasonally adjusted, except as noted.)

Year and month	Civilian noninstitutional population [1]	Civilian labor force		Employment, thousands of persons						Employment-population ratio, percent	Unemployment		
		Thousands of persons	Participation rate (percent)	Total	By age and sex			By industry			Thousands of persons		Rate (percent) [2]
					Men, 20 years and over	Women, 20 years and over	Both sexes, 16 to 19 years	Agricultural	Nonagricultural		Total	Unemployed 15 weeks and over	
1960													
January	116 594	68 962	59.1	65 347	41 637	19 686	4 024	5 458	59 889	56.0	3 615	915	5.2
February	116 702	68 949	59.1	65 620	41 729	19 765	4 126	5 443	60 177	56.2	3 329	841	4.8
March	116 827	68 399	58.5	64 673	41 320	19 388	3 965	4 959	59 714	55.4	3 726	959	5.4
April	116 910	69 579	59.5	65 959	41 641	20 110	4 208	5 471	60 488	56.4	3 620	896	5.2
May	117 033	69 626	59.5	66 057	41 668	20 186	4 203	5 359	60 698	56.4	3 569	797	5.1
June	117 167	69 934	59.7	66 168	41 553	20 290	4 325	5 416	60 752	56.5	3 766	854	5.4
July	117 281	69 745	59.5	65 909	41 490	20 257	4 162	5 542	60 367	56.2	3 836	921	5.5
August	117 431	69 841	59.5	65 895	41 503	20 316	4 076	5 520	60 375	56.1	3 946	927	5.6
September	117 521	70 151	59.7	66 267	41 604	20 493	4 170	5 755	60 512	56.4	3 884	982	5.5
October	117 643	69 884	59.4	65 632	41 464	20 076	4 092	5 436	60 196	55.8	4 252	1 189	6.1
November	117 829	70 439	59.8	66 109	41 543	20 384	4 182	5 513	60 596	56.1	4 330	1 223	6.1
December	118 001	70 395	59.7	65 778	41 416	20 332	4 030	5 622	60 156	55.7	4 617	1 142	6.6
1961													
January	118 155	70 447	59.6	65 776	41 363	20 325	4 088	5 422	60 354	55.7	4 671	1 328	6.6
February	118 250	70 420	59.6	65 588	41 177	20 392	4 019	5 472	60 116	55.5	4 832	1 416	6.9
March	118 358	70 703	59.7	65 850	41 273	20 459	4 118	5 406	60 444	55.6	4 853	1 463	6.9
April	118 503	70 267	59.3	65 374	41 206	20 145	4 023	5 037	60 337	55.2	4 893	1 598	7.0
May	118 638	70 452	59.4	65 449	41 139	20 261	4 049	5 099	60 350	55.2	5 003	1 686	7.1
June	118 767	70 878	59.7	65 993	41 349	20 446	4 198	5 220	60 773	55.6	4 885	1 651	6.9
July	118 889	70 536	59.3	65 608	41 245	20 252	4 111	5 153	60 455	55.2	4 928	1 830	7.0
August	119 006	70 534	59.3	65 852	41 362	20 279	4 211	5 366	60 486	55.3	4 682	1 649	6.6
September	119 107	70 217	59.0	65 541	41 400	20 112	4 029	5 021	60 520	55.0	4 676	1 531	6.7
October	119 202	70 492	59.1	65 919	41 509	20 338	4 072	5 203	60 716	55.3	4 573	1 481	6.5
November	119 153	70 376	59.1	66 081	41 556	20 330	4 195	5 090	60 991	55.5	4 295	1 388	6.1
December	119 214	70 077	58.8	65 900	41 534	20 287	4 079	4 992	60 908	55.3	4 177	1 361	6.0
1962													
January	119 300	70 189	58.8	66 108	41 547	20 501	4 060	5 094	61 014	55.4	4 081	1 235	5.8
February	119 360	70 409	59.0	66 538	41 745	20 693	4 100	5 289	61 249	55.7	3 871	1 244	5.5
March	119 476	70 414	58.9	66 493	41 696	20 567	4 230	5 157	61 336	55.7	3 921	1 162	5.6
April	119 702	70 278	58.7	66 372	41 647	20 567	4 158	5 009	61 363	55.4	3 906	1 122	5.6
May	119 813	70 551	58.9	66 688	41 847	20 558	4 283	4 964	61 724	55.7	3 863	1 134	5.5
June	119 943	70 514	58.8	66 670	41 761	20 547	4 362	4 943	61 727	55.6	3 844	1 079	5.5
July	120 128	70 302	58.5	66 483	41 671	20 592	4 220	4 840	61 643	55.3	3 819	1 049	5.4
August	120 323	70 981	59.0	66 968	41 900	20 841	4 227	4 866	62 102	55.7	4 013	1 081	5.7
September	120 653	71 153	59.0	67 192	42 020	20 982	4 190	4 867	62 325	55.7	3 961	1 096	5.6
October	120 856	70 917	58.7	67 114	42 086	20 856	4 172	4 816	62 298	55.5	3 803	1 022	5.4
November	121 045	70 871	58.5	66 847	41 985	20 794	4 068	4 831	62 016	55.2	4 024	1 051	5.7
December	121 236	70 854	58.4	66 947	41 934	20 831	4 182	4 647	62 300	55.2	3 907	1 068	5.5
1963													
January	121 463	71 146	58.6	67 072	41 938	20 933	4 201	4 882	62 190	55.2	4 074	1 122	5.7
February	121 633	71 262	58.6	67 024	41 876	21 046	4 102	4 652	62 372	55.1	4 238	1 137	5.9
March	121 824	71 423	58.6	67 351	42 047	21 162	4 142	4 696	62 655	55.3	4 072	1 087	5.7
April	121 986	71 697	58.8	67 642	42 131	21 281	4 230	4 670	62 972	55.5	4 055	1 071	5.7
May	122 162	71 832	58.8	67 615	42 145	21 225	4 245	4 729	62 886	55.3	4 217	1 157	5.9
June	122 352	71 626	58.5	67 649	42 268	21 185	4 196	4 642	63 007	55.3	3 977	1 067	5.6
July	122 521	71 956	58.7	67 905	42 427	21 268	4 210	4 694	63 211	55.4	4 051	1 070	5.6
August	122 667	71 786	58.5	67 908	42 400	21 185	4 323	4 604	63 304	55.4	3 878	1 114	5.4
September	122 821	72 131	58.7	68 174	42 500	21 317	4 357	4 650	63 524	55.5	3 957	1 069	5.5
October	123 014	72 281	58.8	68 294	42 437	21 456	4 401	4 702	63 592	55.5	3 987	1 071	5.5
November	123 192	72 418	58.8	68 267	42 415	21 553	4 299	4 694	63 573	55.4	4 151	1 054	5.7
December	123 360	72 188	58.5	68 213	42 427	21 481	4 305	4 629	63 584	55.3	3 975	1 007	5.5
1964													
January	123 560	72 356	58.6	68 327	42 510	21 462	4 355	4 603	63 724	55.3	4 029	1 057	5.6
February	123 707	72 683	58.8	68 751	42 579	21 652	4 520	4 563	64 188	55.6	3 932	1 015	5.4
March	123 857	72 713	58.7	68 763	42 600	21 685	4 478	4 366	64 397	55.5	3 950	1 039	5.4
April	124 019	73 274	59.1	69 356	42 885	22 110	4 361	4 414	64 942	55.9	3 918	934	5.3
May	124 204	73 395	59.1	69 631	43 025	22 103	4 503	4 603	65 028	56.1	3 764	975	5.1
June	124 386	73 032	58.7	69 218	42 760	21 995	4 463	4 556	64 662	55.6	3 814	1 047	5.2
July	124 567	73 007	58.6	69 399	42 998	21 846	4 555	4 591	64 808	55.7	3 608	1 002	4.9
August	124 731	73 118	58.6	69 463	42 963	22 002	4 498	4 573	64 890	55.7	3 655	934	5.0
September	124 920	73 290	58.7	69 578	43 009	21 863	4 706	4 619	64 959	55.7	3 712	917	5.1
October	125 108	73 308	58.6	69 582	43 023	21 984	4 575	4 550	65 032	55.6	3 726	903	5.1
November	125 291	73 286	58.5	69 735	43 171	21 954	4 610	4 496	65 239	55.7	3 551	922	4.8
December	125 468	73 465	58.6	69 814	43 109	22 136	4 569	4 322	65 492	55.6	3 651	873	5.0

[1] Not seasonally adjusted.
[2] In 1930 through 1943, the official BLS data count persons on work relief as unemployed. The unemployment rates for those years shown in parentheses count persons on work relief as employed, which is more consistent with the postwar practice. See notes and definitions.

Table 10-1B. Summary Labor Force, Employment, and Unemployment: Historical—Continued

(Thousands of persons, percent, seasonally adjusted, except as noted.)

Year and month	Civilian noninstitutional population [1]	Civilian labor force — Thousands of persons	Civilian labor force — Participation rate (percent)	Employment — Total	By age and sex — Men, 20 years and over	By age and sex — Women, 20 years and over	By age and sex — Both sexes, 16 to 19 years	By industry — Agricultural	By industry — Nonagricultural	Employment-population ratio, percent	Unemployment — Total	Unemployment — Unemployed 15 weeks and over	Unemployment Rate (percent) [2]
1965													
January	125 647	73 569	58.6	69 997	43 237	22 282	4 478	4 271	65 726	55.7	3 572	793	4.9
February	125 810	73 857	58.7	70 127	43 279	22 276	4 572	4 322	65 805	55.7	3 730	919	5.1
March	125 985	73 949	58.7	70 439	43 370	22 373	4 696	4 318	66 121	55.9	3 510	796	4.7
April	126 155	74 228	58.8	70 633	43 397	22 416	4 820	4 424	66 209	56.0	3 595	796	4.8
May	126 320	74 466	59.0	71 034	43 579	22 494	4 961	4 724	66 310	56.2	3 432	736	4.6
June	126 499	74 412	58.8	71 025	43 487	22 759	4 779	4 444	66 581	56.1	3 387	786	4.6
July	126 573	74 761	59.1	71 460	43 489	22 841	5 130	4 390	67 070	56.5	3 301	683	4.4
August	126 756	74 616	58.9	71 362	43 447	22 783	5 132	4 355	67 007	56.3	3 254	733	4.4
September	126 906	74 502	58.7	71 286	43 371	22 684	5 231	4 271	67 015	56.2	3 216	732	4.3
October	127 043	74 838	58.9	71 695	43 461	22 819	5 415	4 118	67 277	56.4	3 140	672	4.2
November	127 171	74 797	58.8	71 724	43 447	22 829	5 448	4 093	67 631	56.4	3 073	645	4.1
December	127 294	75 093	59.0	72 062	43 513	22 983	5 566	4 159	67 903	56.6	3 031	659	4.0
1966													
January	127 394	75 186	59.0	72 198	43 495	23 098	5 605	4 077	68 121	56.7	2 988	623	4.0
February	127 514	74 954	58.8	72 134	43 528	23 089	5 517	4 078	68 056	56.6	2 820	594	3.8
March	127 626	75 075	58.8	72 188	43 576	23 109	5 503	4 069	68 119	56.6	2 887	583	3.8
April	127 744	75 338	59.0	72 510	43 679	23 227	5 604	4 108	68 402	56.8	2 828	575	3.8
May	127 879	75 447	59.0	72 497	43 710	23 282	5 505	3 930	68 567	56.7	2 950	534	3.9
June	127 983	75 647	59.1	72 775	43 662	23 359	5 754	3 967	68 808	56.9	2 872	475	3.8
July	128 102	75 736	59.1	72 860	43 574	23 422	5 864	3 920	68 940	56.9	2 876	427	3.8
August	128 240	76 046	59.3	73 146	43 636	23 605	5 905	3 921	69 225	57.0	2 900	464	3.8
September	128 359	76 056	59.3	73 258	43 718	23 881	5 659	3 952	69 306	57.1	2 798	488	3.7
October	128 494	76 199	59.3	73 401	43 776	23 881	5 744	3 912	69 489	57.1	2 798	494	3.7
November	128 627	76 610	59.6	73 840	43 804	24 130	5 906	3 945	69 895	57.4	2 770	464	3.6
December	128 730	76 641	59.5	73 729	43 820	24 025	5 884	3 906	69 823	57.3	2 912	488	3.8
1967													
January	128 909	76 639	59.5	73 671	44 029	23 872	5 770	3 890	69 781	57.1	2 968	489	3.9
February	129 032	76 521	59.3	73 606	43 997	23 919	5 690	3 723	69 883	57.0	2 915	459	3.8
March	129 190	76 328	59.1	73 439	43 922	23 832	5 685	3 757	69 682	56.8	2 889	436	3.8
April	129 344	76 777	59.4	73 882	44 061	24 161	5 660	3 748	70 134	57.1	2 895	428	3.8
May	129 515	76 773	59.3	73 844	44 100	24 172	5 572	3 658	70 186	57.0	2 929	417	3.8
June	129 722	77 270	59.6	74 278	44 230	24 303	5 745	3 689	70 589	57.3	2 992	422	3.9
July	129 918	77 464	59.6	74 520	44 364	24 416	5 740	3 833	70 687	57.4	2 944	412	3.8
August	130 187	77 712	59.7	74 767	44 410	24 600	5 757	3 963	70 804	57.4	2 945	441	3.8
September	130 392	77 812	59.7	74 854	44 535	24 683	5 636	3 851	71 003	57.4	2 958	448	3.8
October	130 582	78 194	59.9	75 051	44 610	24 802	5 639	4 008	71 043	57.5	3 143	472	4.0
November	130 754	78 191	59.8	75 125	44 625	24 914	5 586	3 933	71 192	57.5	3 066	490	3.9
December	130 936	78 491	59.9	75 473	44 719	25 104	5 650	4 076	71 397	57.6	3 018	485	3.8
1968													
January	131 112	77 578	59.2	74 700	44 606	24 581	5 513	3 908	70 792	57.0	2 878	503	3.7
February	131 277	78 230	59.6	75 229	44 659	24 881	5 689	3 959	71 270	57.3	3 001	468	3.8
March	131 412	78 256	59.6	75 379	44 663	25 019	5 697	3 904	71 475	57.4	2 877	447	3.7
April	131 553	78 270	59.5	75 561	44 753	25 072	5 736	3 875	71 686	57.4	2 709	393	3.5
May	131 712	78 847	59.9	76 107	44 841	25 513	5 753	3 814	72 293	57.8	2 740	395	3.5
June	131 872	79 120	60.0	76 182	44 914	25 466	5 802	3 806	72 376	57.8	2 938	405	3.7
July	132 053	78 970	59.8	76 087	44 935	25 347	5 805	3 820	72 267	57.6	2 883	426	3.7
August	132 251	78 811	59.6	76 043	44 897	25 201	5 945	3 736	72 307	57.5	2 768	393	3.5
September	132 446	78 858	59.5	76 172	44 893	25 445	5 834	3 758	72 414	57.5	2 686	375	3.4
October	132 617	78 913	59.5	76 224	44 884	25 475	5 865	3 741	72 483	57.5	2 689	386	3.4
November	132 903	79 209	59.6	76 494	44 996	25 674	5 824	3 758	72 736	57.6	2 715	357	3.4
December	133 120	79 463	59.7	76 778	45 262	25 712	5 804	3 746	73 032	57.7	2 685	351	3.4
1969													
January	133 324	79 523	59.6	76 805	45 154	25 777	5 874	3 704	73 101	57.6	2 718	339	3.4
February	133 465	80 019	60.0	77 327	45 339	26 092	5 896	3 770	73 557	57.9	2 692	358	3.4
March	133 639	80 079	59.9	77 367	45 305	26 115	5 947	3 668	73 699	57.9	2 712	353	3.4
April	133 821	80 281	60.0	77 523	45 262	26 233	6 028	3 629	73 894	57.9	2 758	386	3.4
May	134 027	80 125	59.8	77 412	45 278	26 283	5 851	3 706	73 706	57.8	2 713	387	3.4
June	134 213	80 696	60.1	77 880	45 313	26 429	6 138	3 663	74 217	58.0	2 816	368	3.5
July	134 414	80 827	60.1	77 959	45 305	26 516	6 138	3 548	74 411	58.0	2 868	377	3.5
August	134 597	81 106	60.3	78 250	45 513	26 556	6 181	3 613	74 637	58.1	2 856	373	3.5
September	134 774	81 290	60.3	78 250	45 447	26 572	6 231	3 551	74 699	58.1	3 040	391	3.7
October	135 012	81 494	60.4	78 445	45 488	26 658	6 299	3 517	74 928	58.1	3 049	374	3.7
November	135 239	81 397	60.2	78 541	45 505	26 652	6 384	3 477	75 064	58.1	2 856	392	3.5
December	135 489	81 624	60.2	78 740	45 577	26 832	6 331	3 409	75 331	58.1	2 884	413	3.5

[1]Not seasonally adjusted.
[2]In 1930 through 1943, the official BLS data count persons on work relief as unemployed. The unemployment rates for those years shown in parentheses count persons on work relief as employed, which is more consistent with the postwar practice. See notes and definitions.

Table 10-1B. Summary Labor Force, Employment, and Unemployment: Historical—*Continued*

(Thousands of persons, percent, seasonally adjusted, except as noted.)

Year and month	Civilian noninstitutional population [1]	Civilian labor force		Employment, thousands of persons						Employment-population ratio, percent	Unemployment		
		Thousands of persons	Participation rate (percent)	Total	By age and sex			By industry			Thousands of persons		Rate (percent) [2]
					Men, 20 years and over	Women, 20 years and over	Both sexes, 16 to 19 years	Agricultural	Nonagricultural		Total	Unemployed 15 weeks and over	
1970													
January	135 713	81 981	60.4	78 780	45 654	26 908	6 218	3 422	75 358	58.0	3 201	431	3.9
February	135 957	82 151	60.4	78 698	45 627	26 828	6 243	3 439	75 259	57.9	3 453	470	4.2
March	136 179	82 498	60.6	78 863	45 668	26 933	6 262	3 499	75 364	57.9	3 635	534	4.4
April	136 416	82 727	60.6	78 930	45 679	27 114	6 137	3 568	75 362	57.9	3 797	602	4.6
May	136 686	82 483	60.3	78 564	45 666	26 739	6 159	3 547	75 017	57.5	3 919	591	4.8
June	136 928	82 484	60.2	78 413	45 554	26 904	5 955	3 555	74 858	57.3	4 071	657	4.9
July	137 196	82 901	60.4	78 726	45 516	27 083	6 127	3 517	75 209	57.4	4 175	662	5.0
August	137 455	82 880	60.3	78 624	45 495	27 011	6 118	3 418	75 206	57.2	4 256	705	5.1
September	137 717	82 954	60.2	78 498	45 535	26 784	6 179	3 451	75 047	57.0	4 456	788	5.4
October	137 988	83 276	60.4	78 685	45 508	27 058	6 119	3 337	75 348	57.0	4 591	771	5.5
November	138 264	83 548	60.4	78 650	45 540	27 020	6 090	3 372	75 278	56.9	4 898	871	5.9
December	138 529	83 670	60.4	78 594	45 466	27 038	6 090	3 380	75 214	56.7	5 076	1 102	6.1
1971													
January	138 795	83 850	60.4	78 864	45 527	27 173	6 164	3 393	75 471	56.8	4 986	1 113	5.9
February	139 021	83 603	60.1	78 700	45 455	27 040	6 205	3 288	75 412	56.6	4 903	1 068	5.9
March	139 285	83 575	60.0	78 588	45 520	26 967	6 101	3 356	75 232	56.4	4 987	1 098	6.0
April	139 566	83 946	60.1	78 987	45 789	26 984	6 214	3 574	75 413	56.6	4 959	1 149	5.9
May	139 826	84 135	60.2	79 139	45 917	27 056	6 166	3 449	75 690	56.6	4 996	1 173	5.9
June	140 090	83 706	59.8	78 757	45 879	27 013	5 865	3 334	75 423	56.2	4 949	1 167	5.9
July	140 343	84 340	60.1	79 305	46 000	27 054	6 251	3 386	75 919	56.5	5 035	1 251	6.0
August	140 596	84 673	60.2	79 539	46 041	27 171	6 327	3 395	76 144	56.6	5 134	1 261	6.1
September	140 869	84 731	60.1	79 689	46 090	27 390	6 209	3 367	76 322	56.6	5 042	1 239	6.0
October	141 146	84 872	60.1	79 918	46 132	27 538	6 248	3 405	76 513	56.6	4 954	1 268	5.8
November	141 393	85 458	60.4	80 297	46 209	27 721	6 367	3 410	76 887	56.8	5 161	1 277	6.0
December	141 666	85 625	60.4	80 471	46 280	27 791	6 400	3 371	77 100	56.8	5 154	1 283	6.0
1972													
January	142 736	85 978	60.2	80 959	46 471	27 956	6 532	3 366	77 593	56.7	5 019	1 257	5.8
February	143 017	86 036	60.2	81 108	46 600	28 016	6 492	3 358	77 750	56.7	4 928	1 292	5.7
March	143 263	86 611	60.5	81 573	46 821	28 126	6 626	3 438	78 135	56.9	5 038	1 232	5.8
April	143 483	86 614	60.4	81 655	46 863	28 114	6 678	3 382	78 273	56.9	4 959	1 203	5.7
May	143 760	86 809	60.4	81 887	46 950	28 184	6 753	3 412	78 475	57.0	4 922	1 168	5.7
June	144 033	87 006	60.4	82 083	47 147	28 175	6 761	3 402	78 681	57.0	4 923	1 141	5.7
July	144 285	87 143	60.4	82 230	47 244	28 225	6 761	3 461	78 769	57.0	4 913	1 154	5.6
August	144 522	87 517	60.6	82 578	47 321	28 382	6 875	3 603	78 975	57.1	4 939	1 156	5.6
September	144 761	87 392	60.4	82 543	47 394	28 417	6 732	3 568	78 975	57.0	4 849	1 131	5.5
October	144 988	87 491	60.3	82 616	47 354	28 438	6 824	3 634	78 982	57.0	4 875	1 123	5.6
November	145 211	87 592	60.3	82 990	47 529	28 567	6 894	3 517	79 473	57.2	4 602	1 040	5.3
December	145 446	87 943	60.5	83 400	47 747	28 698	6 955	3 596	79 804	57.3	4 543	1 006	5.2
1973													
January	145 720	87 487	60.0	83 161	47 701	28 596	6 864	3 456	79 705	57.1	4 326	947	4.9
February	145 943	88 364	60.5	83 912	47 884	28 995	7 033	3 415	80 497	57.5	4 452	894	5.0
March	146 230	88 846	60.8	84 452	48 111	29 110	7 225	3 469	80 983	57.8	4 394	889	4.9
April	146 459	89 018	60.8	84 559	48 098	29 304	7 157	3 407	81 152	57.7	4 459	809	5.0
May	146 719	88 977	60.6	84 648	48 068	29 432	7 148	3 376	81 272	57.7	4 329	816	4.9
June	146 981	89 548	60.9	85 185	48 244	29 505	7 436	3 509	81 676	58.0	4 363	779	4.9
July	147 233	89 604	60.9	85 299	48 452	29 592	7 255	3 540	81 759	57.9	4 305	756	4.8
August	147 471	89 509	60.7	85 204	48 353	29 578	7 273	3 425	81 779	57.8	4 305	788	4.8
September	147 731	89 838	60.8	85 488	48 408	29 710	7 370	3 342	82 146	57.9	4 350	785	4.8
October	147 980	90 131	60.9	85 987	48 631	29 885	7 471	3 424	82 563	58.1	4 144	793	4.6
November	148 219	90 716	61.2	86 320	48 764	30 071	7 485	3 593	82 727	58.2	4 396	832	4.8
December	148 479	90 890	61.2	86 401	48 902	29 991	7 508	3 658	82 743	58.2	4 489	767	4.9
1974													
January	148 753	91 199	61.3	86 555	49 107	29 893	7 555	3 756	82 799	58.2	4 644	799	5.1
February	148 982	91 485	61.4	86 754	49 057	30 146	7 551	3 824	82 930	58.2	4 731	829	5.2
March	149 225	91 453	61.3	86 819	48 986	30 293	7 540	3 726	83 093	58.2	4 634	849	5.1
April	149 478	91 287	61.1	86 669	48 853	30 376	7 440	3 582	83 087	58.0	4 618	889	5.1
May	149 750	91 596	61.2	86 891	49 039	30 424	7 428	3 529	83 362	58.0	4 705	880	5.1
June	150 012	91 868	61.2	86 941	48 946	30 512	7 483	3 386	83 555	58.0	4 927	926	5.4
July	150 248	92 212	61.4	87 149	48 883	30 869	7 397	3 436	83 713	58.0	5 063	924	5.5
August	150 493	92 059	61.2	87 037	48 950	30 662	7 425	3 429	83 608	57.8	5 022	960	5.5
September	150 753	92 488	61.4	87 051	48 978	30 569	7 504	3 460	83 591	57.7	5 437	1 021	5.9
October	151 009	92 518	61.3	86 995	48 959	30 570	7 466	3 431	83 564	57.6	5 523	1 072	6.0
November	151 256	92 766	61.3	86 626	48 833	30 424	7 369	3 405	83 221	57.3	6 140	1 128	6.6
December	151 494	92 780	61.2	86 144	48 458	30 431	7 255	3 361	82 783	56.9	6 636	1 326	7.2

[1] Not seasonally adjusted.
[2] In 1930 through 1943, the official BLS data count persons on work relief as unemployed. The unemployment rates for those years shown in parentheses count persons on work relief as employed, which is more consistent with the postwar practice. See notes and definitions.

Table 10-1B. Summary Labor Force, Employment, and Unemployment: Historical—*Continued*

(Thousands of persons, percent, seasonally adjusted, except as noted.)

| Year and month | Civilian noninsti-tutional popu-lation [1] | Civilian labor force | | Employment, thousands of persons | | | | | | Employ-ment-population ratio, percent | Unemployment | | |
| | | Thousands of persons | Participa-tion rate (percent) | Total | Men, 20 years and over | Women, 20 years and over | Both sexes, 16 to 19 years | Agri-cultural | Nonagri-cultural | | Thousands of persons | | Rate (percent) [2] |
											Total	Unem-ployed 15 weeks and over	
1975													
January	151 755	93 128	61.4	85 627	48 086	30 343	7 198	3 401	82 226	56.4	7 501	1 555	8.1
February	151 990	92 776	61.0	85 256	47 927	30 215	7 114	3 361	81 895	56.1	7 520	1 841	8.1
March	152 217	93 165	61.2	85 187	47 776	30 334	7 077	3 358	81 829	56.0	7 978	2 074	8.6
April	152 443	93 399	61.3	85 189	47 759	30 410	7 020	3 315	81 874	55.9	8 210	2 442	8.8
May	152 704	93 884	61.5	85 451	47 835	30 483	7 133	3 560	81 891	56.0	8 433	2 643	9.0
June	152 976	93 575	61.2	85 355	47 754	30 618	6 983	3 368	81 987	55.8	8 220	2 843	8.8
July	153 309	94 021	61.3	85 894	48 050	30 794	7 050	3 457	82 437	56.0	8 127	2 943	8.6
August	153 580	94 162	61.3	86 234	48 239	30 966	7 029	3 429	82 805	56.1	7 928	2 862	8.4
September	153 848	94 202	61.2	86 279	48 126	30 979	7 174	3 508	82 771	56.1	7 923	2 906	8.4
October	154 082	94 267	61.2	86 370	48 165	31 121	7 084	3 397	82 973	56.1	7 897	2 680	8.1
November	154 338	94 250	61.1	86 456	48 203	31 135	7 118	3 331	83 125	56.0	7 794	2 789	8.3
December	154 589	94 409	61.1	86 665	48 266	31 268	7 131	3 259	83 406	56.1	7 744	2 868	8.2
1976													
January	154 853	94 934	61.3	87 400	48 592	31 595	8 967	3 387	84 013	56.4	7 534	2 713	7.9
February	155 066	94 998	61.3	87 672	48 721	31 680	8 981	3 304	84 368	56.5	7 326	2 519	7.7
March	155 306	95 215	61.3	87 985	48 836	31 842	9 007	3 296	84 689	56.7	7 230	2 441	7.6
April	155 529	95 746	61.6	88 416	49 097	31 951	9 151	3 438	84 978	56.8	7 330	2 210	7.7
May	155 765	95 847	61.5	88 794	49 193	32 147	9 155	3 367	85 427	57.0	7 053	2 115	7.4
June	156 026	95 885	61.5	88 563	49 010	32 267	8 943	3 310	85 253	56.8	7 322	2 332	7.6
July	156 276	96 583	61.8	89 093	49 236	32 334	9 204	3 358	85 735	57.0	7 490	2 316	7.8
August	156 525	96 741	61.8	89 223	49 417	32 437	9 168	3 380	85 843	57.0	7 518	2 378	7.8
September	156 779	96 553	61.6	89 173	49 485	32 390	8 968	3 278	85 895	56.9	7 380	2 296	7.6
October	156 993	96 704	61.6	89 274	49 524	32 412	9 054	3 316	85 958	56.9	7 430	2 292	7.7
November	157 235	97 254	61.9	89 634	49 561	32 753	9 055	3 263	86 371	57.0	7 620	2 354	7.8
December	157 438	97 348	61.8	89 803	49 599	32 914	9 011	3 251	86 552	57.0	7 545	2 375	7.8
1977													
January	157 688	97 208	61.6	89 928	49 738	32 872	9 025	3 185	86 743	57.0	7 280	2 200	7.5
February	157 913	97 785	61.9	90 342	49 838	32 997	9 198	3 222	87 120	57.2	7 443	2 174	7.6
March	158 131	98 115	62.0	90 808	50 031	33 246	9 257	3 212	87 596	57.4	7 307	2 057	7.4
April	158 371	98 330	62.1	91 271	50 185	33 470	9 289	3 313	87 958	57.6	7 059	1 936	7.2
May	158 657	98 665	62.2	91 754	50 280	33 851	9 279	3 432	88 322	57.8	6 911	1 928	7.0
June	158 928	99 093	62.4	91 959	50 544	33 678	9 525	3 340	88 619	57.9	7 134	1 918	7.2
July	159 185	98 913	62.1	92 084	50 597	33 749	9 377	3 247	88 837	57.8	6 829	1 907	6.9
August	159 430	99 366	62.3	92 441	50 745	33 809	9 550	3 260	89 181	58.0	6 925	1 836	7.0
September	159 674	99 453	62.3	92 702	50 825	34 218	9 340	3 201	89 501	58.1	6 751	1 853	6.8
October	159 915	99 815	62.4	93 052	51 046	34 187	9 441	3 272	89 780	58.2	6 763	1 789	6.8
November	160 129	100 576	62.8	93 761	51 316	34 536	9 551	3 375	90 386	58.6	6 815	1 804	6.8
December	160 376	100 491	62.7	94 105	51 492	34 668	9 406	3 320	90 785	58.7	6 386	1 717	6.4
1978													
January	160 617	100 873	62.8	94 384	51 542	34 948	9 473	3 434	90 950	58.8	6 489	1 643	6.4
February	160 831	100 837	62.7	94 519	51 578	35 118	9 448	3 320	91 199	58.8	6 318	1 584	6.3
March	161 038	101 092	62.8	94 755	51 635	35 310	9 441	3 351	91 404	58.8	6 337	1 531	6.3
April	161 263	101 574	63.0	95 394	51 912	35 546	9 518	3 349	92 045	59.2	6 180	1 502	6.1
May	161 518	101 896	63.1	95 769	52 050	35 597	9 668	3 325	92 444	59.3	6 127	1 420	6.0
June	161 794	102 371	63.3	96 343	52 240	35 828	9 781	3 483	92 860	59.5	6 028	1 352	5.9
July	162 034	102 399	63.2	96 090	52 190	35 764	9 749	3 441	92 649	59.3	6 309	1 373	6.2
August	162 259	102 511	63.2	96 431	52 228	35 856	9 903	3 401	93 030	59.4	6 080	1 242	5.9
September	162 502	102 795	63.3	96 670	52 284	36 274	9 700	3 400	93 270	59.5	6 125	1 308	6.0
October	162 783	103 080	63.3	97 133	52 448	36 525	9 727	3 409	93 724	59.7	5 947	1 319	5.8
November	163 017	103 562	63.5	97 485	52 802	36 559	9 704	3 284	94 201	59.8	6 077	1 242	5.9
December	163 272	103 809	63.6	97 581	52 807	36 686	9 708	3 396	94 185	59.8	6 228	1 269	6.0
1979													
January	163 516	104 057	63.6	97 948	53 072	36 697	9 749	3 305	94 643	59.9	6 109	1 250	5.9
February	163 726	104 502	63.8	98 329	53 233	36 904	9 762	3 373	94 956	60.1	6 173	1 297	5.9
March	164 027	104 589	63.8	98 480	53 120	37 159	9 751	3 368	95 112	60.0	6 109	1 365	5.8
April	164 162	104 172	63.5	98 103	53 085	36 944	9 652	3 291	94 812	59.8	6 069	1 272	5.8
May	164 459	104 171	63.3	98 331	53 178	37 134	9 553	3 272	95 059	59.8	5 840	1 239	5.6
June	164 720	104 638	63.5	98 679	53 309	37 221	9 664	3 331	95 348	59.9	5 959	1 171	5.7
July	164 970	105 002	63.6	99 006	53 384	37 514	9 606	3 335	95 671	60.0	5 996	1 123	5.7
August	165 198	105 096	63.6	98 776	53 336	37 548	9 456	3 374	95 402	59.8	6 320	1 203	6.0
September	165 431	105 530	63.8	99 340	53 510	37 798	9 623	3 371	95 969	60.0	6 190	1 172	5.9
October	165 813	105 700	63.7	99 404	53 478	37 931	9 574	3 325	96 079	59.9	6 296	1 219	6.0
November	166 051	105 812	63.7	99 574	53 435	38 065	9 599	3 436	96 138	60.0	6 238	1 239	5.9
December	166 300	106 258	63.9	99 933	53 555	38 259	9 690	3 400	96 533	60.1	6 325	1 277	6.0

[1] Not seasonally adjusted.
[2] In 1930 through 1943, the official BLS data count persons on work relief as unemployed. The unemployment rates for those years shown in parentheses count persons on work relief as employed, which is more consistent with the postwar practice. See notes and definitions.

Table 10-1B. Summary Labor Force, Employment, and Unemployment: Historical—*Continued*

(Thousands of persons, percent, seasonally adjusted, except as noted.)

Year and month	Civilian noninsti-tutional popu-lation [1]	Civilian labor force		Employment, thousands of persons						Employ-ment-population ratio, percent	Unemployment		
					By age and sex			By industry			Thousands of persons		Rate (percent) [2]
		Thousands of persons	Participa-tion rate (percent)	Total	Men, 20 years and over	Women, 20 years and over	Both sexes, 16 to 19 years	Agri-cultural	Nonagri-cultural		Total	Unem-ployed 15 weeks and over	
1980													
January	166 544	106 562	64.0	99 879	53 501	38 367	9 590	3 316	96 563	60.0	6 683	1 353	6.3
February	166 759	106 697	64.0	99 995	53 686	38 389	9 501	3 397	96 598	60.0	6 702	1 358	6.3
March	166 984	106 442	63.7	99 713	53 353	38 406	9 500	3 418	96 295	59.7	6 729	1 457	6.3
April	167 197	106 591	63.8	99 233	53 035	38 427	9 272	3 326	95 907	59.4	7 358	1 694	6.9
May	167 407	106 929	63.9	98 945	52 915	38 335	9 457	3 382	95 563	59.1	7 984	1 740	7.5
June	167 643	106 780	63.7	98 682	52 712	38 312	9 438	3 296	95 386	58.9	8 098	1 760	7.6
July	167 932	107 159	63.8	98 796	52 733	38 374	9 499	3 319	95 477	58.8	8 363	1 995	7.8
August	168 103	107 105	63.7	98 824	52 815	38 511	9 247	3 234	95 590	58.8	8 281	2 162	7.7
September	168 297	107 098	63.6	99 077	52 866	38 595	9 289	3 443	95 634	58.9	8 021	2 309	7.5
October	168 503	107 405	63.7	99 317	53 094	38 620	9 319	3 372	95 945	58.9	8 088	2 306	7.5
November	168 695	107 568	63.8	99 545	53 210	38 795	9 246	3 396	96 149	59.0	8 023	2 329	7.5
December	168 883	107 352	63.6	99 634	53 333	38 737	9 175	3 492	96 142	59.0	7 718	2 406	7.2
1981													
January	169 104	108 026	63.9	99 955	53 392	39 042	9 300	3 429	96 526	59.1	8 071	2 389	7.5
February	169 280	108 242	63.9	100 191	53 445	39 280	9 257	3 345	96 846	59.2	8 051	2 344	7.4
March	169 453	108 553	64.1	100 571	53 662	39 464	9 212	3 365	97 206	59.4	7 982	2 276	7.4
April	169 641	108 925	64.2	101 056	53 886	39 628	9 289	3 529	97 527	59.6	7 869	2 231	7.2
May	169 829	109 222	64.3	101 048	53 879	39 759	9 160	3 369	97 679	59.5	8 174	2 221	7.5
June	170 042	108 396	63.7	100 298	53 576	39 682	8 780	3 334	96 964	59.0	8 098	2 250	7.5
July	170 246	108 556	63.8	100 693	53 814	39 683	8 839	3 296	97 397	59.1	7 863	2 166	7.2
August	170 399	108 725	63.8	100 689	53 718	39 723	8 931	3 379	97 310	59.1	8 036	2 241	7.4
September	170 593	108 294	63.5	100 064	53 625	39 342	8 835	3 361	96 703	58.7	8 230	2 261	7.6
October	170 809	109 024	63.8	100 378	53 482	39 843	8 851	3 412	96 966	58.8	8 646	2 303	7.9
November	170 996	109 236	63.9	100 207	53 335	39 908	8 852	3 415	96 792	58.6	9 029	2 345	8.3
December	171 166	108 912	63.6	99 645	53 149	39 708	8 602	3 227	96 418	58.2	9 267	2 374	8.5
1982													
January	171 335	109 089	63.7	99 692	53 103	39 821	8 676	3 393	96 299	58.2	9 397	2 409	8.6
February	171 489	109 467	63.8	99 762	53 172	39 859	8 697	3 375	96 387	58.2	9 705	2 758	8.9
March	171 667	109 567	63.8	99 672	53 054	39 936	8 550	3 372	96 300	58.1	9 895	2 965	9.0
April	171 844	109 820	63.9	99 576	53 081	39 848	8 605	3 351	96 225	57.9	10 244	3 086	9.3
May	172 026	110 451	64.2	100 116	53 234	40 121	8 753	3 434	96 682	58.2	10 335	3 276	9.4
June	172 190	110 081	63.9	99 543	52 933	40 219	8 293	3 331	96 212	57.8	10 538	3 451	9.6
July	172 364	110 342	64.0	99 493	52 896	40 228	8 380	3 402	96 091	57.7	10 849	3 555	9.8
August	172 511	110 514	64.1	99 633	52 797	40 336	8 514	3 408	96 225	57.8	10 881	3 696	9.8
September	172 690	110 721	64.1	99 504	52 760	40 275	8 469	3 385	96 119	57.6	11 217	3 889	10.1
October	172 881	110 744	64.1	99 215	52 624	40 105	8 499	3 489	95 726	57.4	11 529	4 185	10.4
November	173 058	111 050	64.2	99 112	52 537	40 111	8 520	3 510	95 602	57.3	11 938	4 485	10.8
December	173 199	111 083	64.1	99 032	52 497	40 164	8 397	3 414	95 618	57.2	12 051	4 662	10.8
1983													
January	173 354	110 695	63.9	99 161	52 487	40 268	8 335	3 439	95 722	57.2	11 534	4 668	10.4
February	173 505	110 634	63.8	99 089	52 453	40 336	8 159	3 382	95 707	57.1	11 545	4 641	10.4
March	173 656	110 587	63.7	99 179	52 615	40 368	8 098	3 360	95 819	57.1	11 408	4 612	10.3
April	173 794	110 828	63.8	99 560	52 814	40 542	8 094	3 341	96 219	57.3	11 268	4 370	10.2
May	173 953	110 796	63.7	99 642	52 922	40 538	8 006	3 328	96 314	57.3	11 154	4 538	10.1
June	174 125	111 879	64.3	100 633	53 515	40 695	8 448	3 462	97 171	57.8	11 246	4 470	10.1
July	174 306	111 756	64.1	101 208	53 835	41 041	8 207	3 481	97 727	58.1	10 548	4 329	9.4
August	174 440	112 231	64.3	101 608	53 837	41 314	8 379	3 502	98 106	58.2	10 623	4 070	9.5
September	174 602	112 298	64.3	102 016	53 983	41 650	8 147	3 347	98 669	58.4	10 282	3 854	9.2
October	174 779	111 926	64.0	102 039	54 146	41 597	8 010	3 303	98 736	58.4	9 887	3 648	8.8
November	174 951	112 228	64.1	102 729	54 499	41 788	8 075	3 291	99 438	58.7	9 499	3 535	8.5
December	175 121	112 327	64.1	102 996	54 662	41 852	8 089	3 332	99 664	58.8	9 331	3 379	8.3
1984													
January	175 533	112 209	63.9	103 201	54 975	41 812	7 965	3 293	99 908	58.8	9 008	3 254	8.0
February	175 679	112 615	64.1	103 824	55 213	42 196	7 958	3 353	100 471	59.1	8 791	2 991	7.8
March	175 824	112 713	64.1	103 967	55 281	42 328	7 926	3 233	100 734	59.1	8 746	2 881	7.8
April	175 969	113 098	64.3	104 336	55 373	42 512	7 988	3 291	101 045	59.3	8 762	2 858	7.7
May	176 123	113 649	64.5	105 193	55 661	43 071	7 944	3 343	101 850	59.7	8 456	2 884	7.4
June	176 284	113 817	64.6	105 591	55 996	42 944	8 131	3 383	102 208	59.9	8 226	2 612	7.2
July	176 440	113 972	64.6	105 435	55 921	42 979	8 045	3 344	102 091	59.8	8 537	2 638	7.5
August	176 583	113 682	64.4	105 163	55 930	42 885	7 809	3 286	101 877	59.6	8 519	2 604	7.5
September	176 763	113 857	64.4	105 490	56 095	42 967	7 951	3 393	102 097	59.7	8 367	2 538	7.3
October	176 956	114 019	64.4	105 638	56 183	43 052	7 862	3 194	102 444	59.7	8 381	2 526	7.4
November	177 135	114 170	64.5	105 972	56 274	43 244	7 844	3 394	102 578	59.8	8 198	2 438	7.2
December	177 306	114 581	64.6	106 223	56 313	43 472	7 933	3 385	102 838	59.9	8 358	2 401	7.3

[1] Not seasonally adjusted.
[2] In 1930 through 1943, the official BLS data count persons on work relief as unemployed. The unemployment rates for those years shown in parentheses count persons on work relief as employed, which is more consistent with the postwar practice. See notes and definitions.

Table 10-1B. Summary Labor Force, Employment, and Unemployment: Historical—*Continued*

(Thousands of persons, percent, seasonally adjusted, except as noted.)

Year and month	Civilian noninsti- tutional popu- lation [1]	Civilian labor force		Employment, thousands of persons						Employ- ment- population ratio, percent	Unemployment		
		Thousands of persons	Participa- tion rate (percent)	Total	By age and sex			By industry			Thousands of persons		Rate (percent) [2]
					Men, 20 years and over	Women, 20 years and over	Both sexes, 16 to 19 years	Agri- cultural	Nonagri- cultural		Total	Unem- ployed 15 weeks and over	
1985													
January	177 384	114 725	64.7	106 302	56 184	43 589	8 036	3 317	102 985	59.9	8 423	2 284	7.3
February	177 516	114 876	64.7	106 555	56 216	43 787	8 020	3 317	103 238	60.0	8 321	2 389	7.2
March	177 667	115 328	64.9	106 989	56 356	44 035	8 062	3 250	103 739	60.2	8 339	2 394	7.2
April	177 799	115 331	64.9	106 936	56 374	44 000	7 958	3 306	103 630	60.1	8 395	2 393	7.3
May	177 944	115 234	64.8	106 932	56 531	43 905	7 966	3 280	103 652	60.1	8 302	2 292	7.2
June	178 096	114 965	64.6	106 505	56 288	43 958	7 680	3 161	103 344	59.8	8 460	2 310	7.4
July	178 263	115 320	64.7	106 807	56 435	43 975	8 013	3 143	103 664	59.9	8 513	2 329	7.4
August	178 405	115 291	64.6	107 095	56 655	44 103	7 714	3 121	103 974	60.0	8 196	2 258	7.1
September	178 572	115 905	64.9	107 657	56 845	44 395	7 818	3 064	104 593	60.3	8 248	2 242	7.1
October	178 770	116 145	65.0	107 947	56 969	44 566	7 890	3 061	104 706	60.3	8 208	2 206	7.1
November	178 940	116 135	64.9	108 007	56 972	44 617	7 852	3 062	104 945	60.4	8 128	2 207	7.0
December	179 112	116 354	65.0	108 216	56 995	44 889	7 826	3 141	105 075	60.4	8 138	2 208	7.0
1986													
January	179 670	116 682	64.9	108 887	57 637	44 944	7 704	3 287	105 600	60.6	7 795	2 089	6.7
February	179 821	116 882	65.0	108 480	57 269	44 804	7 895	3 083	105 397	60.3	8 402	2 308	7.2
March	179 985	117 220	65.1	108 837	57 353	44 960	7 977	3 200	105 637	60.5	8 383	2 261	7.2
April	180 148	117 316	65.1	108 952	57 358	45 081	8 058	3 153	105 799	60.5	8 364	2 162	7.1
May	180 311	117 528	65.2	109 089	57 287	45 289	7 997	3 150	105 939	60.5	8 439	2 232	7.2
June	180 503	118 084	65.4	109 576	57 471	45 621	8 024	3 193	106 383	60.7	8 508	2 320	7.2
July	180 682	118 129	65.4	109 810	57 514	45 837	7 914	3 141	106 669	60.8	8 319	2 269	7.0
August	180 828	118 150	65.3	110 015	57 597	45 926	7 920	3 082	106 933	60.8	8 135	2 276	6.9
September	180 997	118 395	65.4	110 085	57 630	45 972	7 945	3 171	106 914	60.8	8 310	2 318	7.0
October	181 186	118 516	65.4	110 273	57 660	46 046	7 977	3 128	107 145	60.9	8 243	2 188	7.0
November	181 363	118 634	65.4	110 475	57 941	46 070	7 891	3 220	107 255	60.9	8 159	2 202	6.9
December	181 547	118 611	65.3	110 728	58 185	46 132	7 769	3 148	107 580	61.0	7 883	2 161	6.6
1987													
January	181 827	118 845	65.4	110 953	58 264	46 219	7 861	3 143	107 810	61.0	7 892	2 168	6.6
February	181 998	119 122	65.5	111 257	58 279	46 444	7 969	3 208	108 049	61.1	7 865	2 117	6.6
March	182 179	119 270	65.5	111 408	58 362	46 549	7 913	3 214	108 194	61.2	7 862	2 070	6.6
April	182 344	119 336	65.4	111 794	58 503	46 746	7 916	3 246	108 548	61.3	7 542	2 091	6.3
May	182 533	120 008	65.7	112 434	58 713	47 052	8 075	3 345	109 089	61.6	7 574	2 104	6.3
June	182 703	119 644	65.5	112 246	58 581	47 102	7 857	3 216	109 030	61.4	7 398	2 087	6.2
July	182 885	119 902	65.6	112 634	58 740	47 229	7 911	3 235	109 399	61.6	7 268	1 921	6.1
August	183 002	120 318	65.7	113 057	58 810	47 322	8 232	3 112	109 945	61.8	7 261	1 878	6.0
September	183 161	120 011	65.5	112 909	58 964	47 285	7 945	3 189	109 720	61.6	7 102	1 866	5.9
October	183 311	120 509	65.7	113 282	59 073	47 533	8 074	3 219	110 063	61.8	7 227	1 794	6.0
November	183 470	120 540	65.7	113 505	59 210	47 622	8 002	3 145	110 360	61.9	7 035	1 797	5.8
December	183 620	120 729	65.7	113 793	59 217	47 781	8 092	3 213	110 580	62.0	6 936	1 767	5.7
1988													
January	183 822	120 969	65.8	114 016	59 346	47 862	8 110	3 247	110 769	62.0	6 953	1 714	5.7
February	183 969	121 156	65.9	114 227	59 535	47 919	8 025	3 201	111 026	62.1	6 929	1 738	5.7
March	184 111	120 913	65.7	114 037	59 393	48 090	7 854	3 169	110 868	61.9	6 876	1 744	5.7
April	184 232	121 251	65.8	114 650	59 832	48 147	7 937	3 224	111 426	62.2	6 601	1 563	5.4
May	184 374	121 071	65.7	114 292	59 644	47 946	7 912	3 121	111 171	62.0	6 779	1 647	5.6
June	184 562	121 473	65.8	114 927	59 751	48 146	8 193	3 111	111 816	62.3	6 546	1 531	5.4
July	184 729	121 665	65.9	115 060	59 888	48 186	8 198	3 060	112 000	62.3	6 605	1 601	5.4
August	184 830	122 125	66.1	115 282	59 877	48 467	8 201	3 119	112 163	62.4	6 843	1 639	5.6
September	184 962	121 960	65.9	115 356	59 980	48 511	8 124	3 165	112 191	62.4	6 604	1 569	5.4
October	185 114	122 206	66.0	115 638	60 023	48 859	7 961	3 231	112 407	62.5	6 568	1 562	5.4
November	185 244	122 637	66.2	116 100	60 042	49 254	7 904	3 241	112 859	62.7	6 537	1 468	5.3
December	185 402	122 622	66.1	116 104	60 059	49 257	7 966	3 194	112 910	62.6	6 518	1 490	5.3
1989													
January	185 641	123 390	66.5	116 708	60 477	49 529	8 019	3 287	113 421	62.0	6 682	1 480	5.4
February	185 777	123 135	66.3	116 776	60 588	49 497	7 871	3 234	113 542	62.9	6 359	1 304	5.2
March	185 897	123 227	66.3	117 022	60 795	49 503	7 809	3 198	113 824	62.9	6 205	1 353	5.0
April	186 024	123 565	66.4	117 097	60 764	49 565	7 929	3 162	113 935	62.9	6 468	1 397	5.2
May	186 181	123 474	66.3	117 099	60 795	49 583	7 890	3 125	113 974	62.9	6 375	1 348	5.2
June	186 329	123 995	66.5	117 418	61 054	49 542	8 094	3 068	114 350	63.0	6 577	1 300	5.3
July	186 483	123 967	66.5	117 472	60 947	49 693	7 961	3 227	114 245	63.0	6 495	1 435	5.2
August	186 598	124 166	66.5	117 655	60 915	49 804	8 126	3 284	114 371	63.1	6 511	1 302	5.2
September	186 726	123 944	66.4	117 354	60 668	50 015	7 870	3 219	114 135	62.8	6 590	1 360	5.3
October	186 871	124 211	66.5	117 581	60 958	49 871	7 940	3 215	114 366	62.9	6 630	1 392	5.3
November	187 017	124 637	66.6	117 912	60 958	50 221	7 964	3 132	114 780	63.0	6 725	1 418	5.4
December	187 165	124 497	66.5	117 830	61 068	50 116	7 851	3 188	114 642	63.0	6 667	1 375	5.4

[1]Not seasonally adjusted.
[2]In 1930 through 1943, the official BLS data count persons on work relief as unemployed. The unemployment rates for those years shown in parentheses count persons on work relief as employed, which is more consistent with the postwar practice. See notes and definitions.

Table 10-1B. Summary Labor Force, Employment, and Unemployment: Historical—*Continued*

(Thousands of persons, percent, seasonally adjusted, except as noted.)

Year and month	Civilian noninstitutional population [1]	Civilian labor force		Employment, thousands of persons						Employment-population ratio, percent	Unemployment		Rate (percent) [2]
					By age and sex			By industry			Thousands of persons		
		Thousands of persons	Participation rate (percent)	Total	Men, 20 years and over	Women, 20 years and over	Both sexes, 16 to 19 years	Agricultural	Nonagricultural		Total	Unemployed 15 weeks and over	
1990													
January	188 413	125 833	66.8	119 081	61 742	50 436	8 103	3 210	115 871	63.2	6 752	1 412	5.4
February	188 516	125 710	66.7	119 059	61 805	50 438	8 015	3 188	115 871	63.2	6 651	1 350	5.3
March	188 630	125 801	66.7	119 203	61 832	50 463	8 061	3 260	115 943	63.2	6 598	1 331	5.2
April	188 778	125 649	66.6	118 852	61 579	50 457	7 987	3 231	115 621	63.0	6 797	1 376	5.4
May	188 913	125 893	66.6	119 151	61 778	50 646	7 911	3 266	115 885	63.1	6 742	1 415	5.4
June	189 058	125 573	66.4	118 983	61 762	50 550	7 783	3 245	115 738	62.9	6 590	1 436	5.2
July	189 188	125 732	66.5	118 810	61 683	50 514	7 777	3 192	115 618	62.8	6 922	1 534	5.5
August	189 342	125 990	66.5	118 802	61 715	50 635	7 708	3 197	115 605	62.7	7 188	1 607	5.7
September	189 528	125 892	66.4	118 524	61 608	50 587	7 575	3 206	115 318	62.5	7 368	1 695	5.9
October	189 710	125 995	66.4	118 536	61 606	50 616	7 565	3 270	115 266	62.5	7 459	1 689	5.9
November	189 872	126 070	66.4	118 306	61 545	50 541	7 506	3 189	115 117	62.3	7 764	1 831	6.2
December	190 017	126 142	66.4	118 241	61 506	50 530	7 516	3 245	114 996	62.2	7 901	1 804	6.3
1991													
January	190 163	125 955	66.2	117 940	61 383	50 472	7 478	3 208	114 732	62.0	8 015	1 866	6.4
February	190 271	126 020	66.2	117 755	61 117	50 523	7 405	3 270	114 485	61.9	8 265	1 955	6.6
March	190 381	126 238	66.3	117 652	61 144	50 422	7 447	3 177	114 475	61.8	8 586	2 137	6.8
April	190 517	126 548	66.4	118 109	61 280	50 760	7 381	3 241	114 868	62.0	8 439	2 206	6.7
May	190 650	126 176	66.2	117 440	61 052	50 457	7 303	3 275	114 165	61.6	8 736	2 252	6.9
June	190 800	126 331	66.2	117 639	61 147	50 585	7 248	3 300	114 339	61.7	8 692	2 533	6.9
July	190 946	126 154	66.1	117 568	61 179	50 636	7 138	3 319	114 249	61.6	8 586	2 388	6.8
August	191 116	126 150	66.0	117 484	61 122	50 601	7 105	3 313	114 171	61.5	8 666	2 460	6.9
September	191 302	126 650	66.2	117 928	61 279	50 864	7 123	3 319	114 609	61.6	8 722	2 497	6.9
October	191 497	126 642	66.1	117 800	61 174	50 811	7 185	3 289	114 511	61.5	8 842	2 638	7.0
November	191 657	126 701	66.1	117 770	61 201	50 759	7 169	3 296	114 474	61.4	8 931	2 718	7.0
December	191 798	126 664	66.0	117 466	61 074	50 728	7 104	3 146	114 320	61.2	9 198	2 892	7.3
1992													
January	191 953	127 261	66.3	117 978	61 116	51 095	7 138	3 155	114 823	61.5	9 283	3 060	7.3
February	192 067	127 207	66.2	117 753	61 062	51 033	7 083	3 239	114 514	61.3	9 454	3 182	7.4
March	192 204	127 604	66.4	118 144	61 363	51 204	6 998	3 236	114 908	61.5	9 460	3 196	7.4
April	192 354	127 841	66.5	118 426	61 468	51 323	6 910	3 245	115 181	61.6	9 415	3 130	7.4
May	192 503	128 119	66.6	118 375	61 513	51 245	7 028	3 213	115 162	61.5	9 744	3 444	7.6
June	192 663	128 459	66.7	118 419	61 537	51 383	7 137	3 297	115 122	61.5	10 040	3 758	7.8
July	192 826	128 563	66.7	118 713	61 641	51 458	7 087	3 285	115 428	61.6	9 850	3 614	7.7
August	193 018	128 613	66.6	118 826	61 681	51 386	7 194	3 279	115 547	61.6	9 787	3 579	7.6
September	193 229	128 501	66.5	118 720	61 663	51 359	7 216	3 274	115 446	61.4	9 781	3 504	7.6
October	193 442	128 026	66.2	118 628	61 550	51 373	6 985	3 254	115 374	61.3	9 398	3 505	7.3
November	193 621	128 441	66.3	118 876	61 644	51 535	7 164	3 207	115 669	61.4	9 565	3 397	7.4
December	193 784	128 554	66.3	118 997	61 721	51 524	7 174	3 259	115 738	61.4	9 557	3 651	7.4
1993													
January	193 962	128 400	66.2	119 075	61 895	51 505	7 089	3 222	115 853	61.4	9 325	3 346	7.3
February	194 108	128 458	66.2	119 275	61 963	51 573	7 144	3 125	116 150	61.4	9 183	3 190	7.1
March	194 248	128 598	66.2	119 542	62 007	51 808	7 132	3 119	116 423	61.5	9 056	3 115	7.0
April	194 398	128 584	66.1	119 474	62 032	51 732	7 091	3 074	116 400	61.5	9 110	3 014	7.1
May	194 549	129 264	66.4	120 115	62 309	51 996	7 244	3 100	117 015	61.7	9 149	3 101	7.1
June	194 719	129 411	66.5	120 290	62 409	52 183	7 114	3 108	117 182	61.8	9 121	3 141	7.0
July	194 882	129 397	66.4	120 467	62 497	52 088	7 205	3 126	117 341	61.8	8 930	3 046	6.9
August	195 063	129 619	66.4	120 856	62 634	52 294	7 264	3 026	117 830	62.0	8 763	3 026	6.8
September	195 259	129 268	66.2	120 554	62 437	52 241	7 180	3 174	117 380	61.7	8 714	3 042	6.7
October	195 444	129 573	66.3	120 823	62 614	52 379	7 171	3 084	117 739	61.8	8 750	3 029	6.8
November	195 625	129 711	66.3	121 169	62 732	52 531	7 248	3 157	118 012	61.9	8 542	2 986	6.6
December	195 794	129 941	66.4	121 464	62 760	52 813	7 178	3 116	118 348	62.0	8 477	2 968	6.5
1994													
January	195 953	130 596	66.6	121 966	62 798	53 052	7 486	3 302	118 664	62.2	8 630	3 060	6.6
February	196 090	130 669	66.6	122 086	62 708	53 266	7 457	3 339	118 747	62.3	8 583	3 118	6.6
March	196 213	130 400	66.5	121 930	62 780	53 099	7 381	3 354	118 576	62.1	8 470	3 055	6.5
April	196 363	130 621	66.5	122 290	62 906	53 274	7 551	3 428	118 862	62.3	8 331	2 921	6.4
May	196 510	130 779	66.6	122 864	63 116	53 624	7 466	3 409	119 455	62.5	7 915	2 836	6.1
June	196 693	130 561	66.4	122 634	63 041	53 393	7 527	3 299	119 335	62.3	7 927	2 735	6.1
July	196 859	130 652	66.4	122 706	63 034	53 531	7 453	3 333	119 373	62.3	7 946	2 822	6.1
August	197 043	131 275	66.6	123 342	63 294	53 744	7 619	3 451	119 891	62.6	7 933	2 750	6.0
September	197 248	131 421	66.6	123 687	63 631	53 991	7 352	3 430	120 257	62.7	7 734	2 746	5.9
October	197 430	131 744	66.7	124 112	63 818	54 071	7 543	3 490	120 622	62.9	7 632	2 955	5.8
November	197 607	131 891	66.7	124 516	64 080	54 168	7 423	3 574	120 942	63.0	7 375	2 666	5.6
December	197 765	131 951	66.7	124 721	64 359	54 054	7 599	3 577	121 144	63.1	7 230	2 488	5.5

[1] Not seasonally adjusted.
[2] In 1930 through 1943, the official BLS data count persons on work relief as unemployed. The unemployment rates for those years shown in parentheses count persons on work relief as employed, which is more consistent with the postwar practice. See notes and definitions.

Table 10-1B. Summary Labor Force, Employment, and Unemployment: Historical—*Continued*

(Thousands of persons, percent, seasonally adjusted, except as noted.)

Year and month	Civilian noninsti- tutional popu- lation [1]	Civilian labor force		Employment, thousands of persons						Employ- ment- population ratio, percent	Unemployment		
		Thousands of persons	Participa- tion rate (percent)	Total	By age and sex			By industry			Thousands of persons		Rate (percent) [2]
					Men, 20 years and over	Women, 20 years and over	Both sexes, 16 to 19 years	Agri- cultural	Nonagri- cultural		Total	Unem- ployed 15 weeks and over	
1995													
January	197 753	132 038	66.8	124 663	64 185	54 087	7 650	3 519	121 144	63.0	7 375	2 396	5.6
February	197 886	132 115	66.8	124 928	64 378	54 226	7 659	3 620	121 308	63.1	7 187	2 345	5.4
March	198 007	132 108	66.7	124 955	64 321	54 141	7 742	3 634	121 321	63.1	7 153	2 287	5.4
April	198 148	132 590	66.9	124 945	64 165	54 366	7 774	3 566	121 379	63.1	7 645	2 473	5.8
May	198 286	131 851	66.5	124 421	63 829	54 272	7 664	3 349	121 072	62.7	7 430	2 577	5.6
June	198 452	131 949	66.5	124 522	63 992	54 020	7 850	3 461	121 061	62.7	7 427	2 266	5.6
July	198 615	132 343	66.6	124 816	63 962	54 476	7 798	3 379	121 437	62.8	7 527	2 311	5.7
August	198 801	132 336	66.6	124 852	63 875	54 434	7 910	3 374	121 478	62.8	7 484	2 391	5.7
September	199 005	132 611	66.6	125 133	64 179	54 507	7 825	3 285	121 848	62.9	7 478	2 306	5.6
October	199 192	132 716	66.6	125 388	64 272	54 692	7 774	3 438	121 950	62.9	7 328	2 272	5.5
November	199 355	132 614	66.5	125 188	63 931	54 850	7 765	3 338	121 850	62.8	7 426	2 339	5.6
December	199 508	132 511	66.4	125 088	64 041	54 674	7 768	3 352	121 736	62.7	7 423	2 331	5.6
1996													
January	199 634	132 616	66.4	125 125	64 180	54 580	7 733	3 483	121 642	62.7	7 491	2 371	5.6
February	199 772	132 952	66.6	125 639	64 398	54 844	7 688	3 547	122 092	62.9	7 313	2 307	5.5
March	199 921	133 180	66.6	125 862	64 506	54 994	7 673	3 489	122 373	63.0	7 318	2 454	5.5
April	200 101	133 409	66.7	125 994	64 481	55 067	7 774	3 406	122 588	63.0	7 415	2 455	5.6
May	200 278	133 667	66.7	126 244	64 683	55 034	7 841	3 473	122 771	63.0	7 423	2 403	5.6
June	200 459	133 697	66.7	126 602	64 940	55 177	7 739	3 424	123 178	63.2	7 095	2 355	5.3
July	200 641	134 284	66.9	126 947	65 068	55 362	7 859	3 433	123 514	63.3	7 337	2 297	5.5
August	200 847	134 054	66.7	127 172	65 216	55 525	7 731	3 395	123 777	63.3	6 882	2 267	5.1
September	201 060	134 515	66.9	127 169	65 169	55 669	7 935	3 448	124 088	63.4	6 979	2 220	5.2
October	201 273	134 921	67.0	127 890	65 460	55 750	7 980	3 463	124 427	63.5	7 031	2 268	5.2
November	201 463	135 007	67.0	127 771	65 320	55 896	7 875	3 356	124 415	63.4	7 236	2 159	5.4
December	201 636	135 113	67.0	127 860	65 435	55 849	7 883	3 445	124 415	63.4	7 253	2 124	5.4
1997													
January	202 285	135 456	67.0	128 298	65 679	56 024	7 930	3 449	124 849	63.4	7 158	2 162	5.3
February	202 388	135 400	66.9	128 298	65 758	55 955	7 948	3 353	124 945	63.4	7 102	2 140	5.2
March	202 513	135 891	67.1	128 891	65 974	56 270	7 951	3 419	125 472	63.6	7 000	2 110	5.2
April	202 674	136 016	67.1	129 143	66 092	56 347	7 974	3 462	125 681	63.7	6 873	2 176	5.1
May	202 832	136 119	67.1	129 464	66 328	56 446	7 964	3 437	126 027	63.8	6 655	2 121	4.9
June	203 000	136 211	67.1	129 412	66 308	56 573	7 849	3 409	126 003	63.7	6 799	2 085	5.0
July	203 166	136 477	67.2	129 822	66 422	56 785	7 975	3 422	126 400	63.9	6 655	2 119	4.9
August	203 364	136 618	67.2	130 010	66 508	56 852	7 922	3 359	126 651	63.9	6 608	2 004	4.8
September	203 570	136 675	67.1	130 019	66 483	56 931	7 873	3 392	126 627	63.9	6 656	2 074	4.9
October	203 767	136 633	67.1	130 179	66 511	56 982	7 876	3 312	126 867	63.9	6 454	1 950	4.7
November	203 941	136 961	67.2	130 653	66 765	57 039	8 042	3 386	127 267	64.1	6 308	1 817	4.6
December	204 098	137 155	67.2	130 679	66 643	57 219	7 923	3 405	127 274	64.0	6 476	1 901	4.7
1998													
January	204 238	137 095	67.1	130 726	66 750	56 941	8 171	3 299	127 389	64.0	6 368	1 833	4.6
February	204 400	137 112	67.1	130 807	66 856	56 992	8 137	3 284	127 522	64.0	6 306	1 809	4.6
March	204 546	137 236	67.1	130 814	66 721	57 080	8 235	3 146	127 650	64.0	6 422	1 772	4.7
April	204 731	137 150	67.0	131 209	67 151	57 074	8 071	3 334	127 852	64.1	5 941	1 476	4.3
May	204 899	137 372	67.0	131 325	67 164	57 155	8 228	3 360	127 959	64.1	6 047	1 490	4.4
June	205 085	137 455	67.0	131 244	67 054	57 156	8 268	3 380	127 874	64.0	6 212	1 613	4.5
July	205 270	137 588	67.0	131 329	67 119	57 192	8 221	3 455	127 913	64.0	6 259	1 577	4.5
August	205 479	137 570	67.0	131 390	66 985	57 332	8 289	3 509	127 970	63.9	6 179	1 626	4.5
September	205 699	138 286	67.2	131 986	67 254	57 520	8 489	3 500	128 399	64.2	6 300	1 688	4.6
October	205 919	138 279	67.2	131 999	67 433	57 529	8 347	3 593	128 389	64.1	6 280	1 582	4.5
November	206 104	138 381	67.1	132 280	67 591	57 638	8 269	3 375	128 897	64.2	6 100	1 590	4.4
December	206 270	138 634	67.2	132 602	67 548	57 840	8 340	3 246	129 320	64.3	6 032	1 559	4.4
1999													
January	206 719	139 003	67.2	133 027	67 679	58 256	8 367	3 233	129 802	64.4	5 976	1 490	4.3
February	206 873	138 967	67.2	132 856	67 498	58 129	8 399	3 246	129 647	64.2	6 111	1 551	4.4
March	207 036	138 730	67.0	132 947	67 660	58 132	8 343	3 238	129 656	64.2	5 783	1 472	4.2
April	207 236	138 959	67.1	132 955	67 542	58 260	8 334	3 336	129 615	64.2	6 004	1 480	4.3
May	207 427	139 107	67.1	133 311	67 539	58 440	8 454	3 335	129 937	64.3	5 796	1 505	4.2
June	207 632	139 329	67.1	133 378	67 700	58 641	8 175	3 386	129 982	64.2	5 951	1 624	4.3
July	207 828	139 439	67.1	133 414	67 731	58 490	8 306	3 346	130 146	64.2	6 025	1 513	4.3
August	208 038	139 430	67.0	133 591	67 768	58 707	8 208	3 234	130 366	64.2	5 838	1 455	4.2
September	208 265	139 622	67.0	133 707	67 882	58 735	8 323	3 173	130 434	64.2	5 915	1 449	4.2
October	208 483	139 771	67.0	133 993	67 840	58 921	8 394	3 229	130 758	64.3	5 778	1 438	4.1
November	208 666	140 025	67.1	134 309	68 094	59 018	8 358	3 343	130 989	64.4	5 716	1 378	4.1
December	208 832	140 177	67.1	134 523	68 217	59 056	8 370	3 260	131 257	64.4	5 653	1 375	4.0

[1]Not seasonally adjusted.
[2]In 1930 through 1943, the official BLS data count persons on work relief as unemployed. The unemployment rates for those years shown in parentheses count persons on work relief as employed, which is more consistent with the postwar practice. See notes and definitions.

Table 10-1B. Summary Labor Force, Employment, and Unemployment: Historical—*Continued*

(Thousands of persons, percent, seasonally adjusted, except as noted.)

Year and month	Civilian noninsti-tutional popu-lation [1]	Civilian labor force		Employment, thousands of persons						Employ-ment-population ratio, percent	Unemployment		
					By age and sex			By industry			Thousands of persons		Rate (percent) [2]
		Thousands of persons	Participa-tion rate (percent)	Total	Men, 20 years and over	Women, 20 years and over	Both sexes, 16 to 19 years	Agri-cultural	Nonagri-cultural		Total	Unem-ployed 15 weeks and over	
2000													
January	211 410	142 267	67.3	136 559	69 419	59 842	8 360	2 613	133 863	64.6	5 708	1 380	4.0
February	211 576	142 456	67.3	136 598	69 505	59 887	8 359	2 731	133 912	64.6	5 858	1 300	4.1
March	211 772	142 434	67.3	136 701	69 482	59 977	8 355	2 579	134 022	64.6	5 733	1 312	4.0
April	212 018	142 751	67.3	137 270	69 519	60 358	8 458	2 505	134 806	64.7	5 481	1 261	3.8
May	212 242	142 388	67.1	136 630	69 399	59 951	8 344	2 480	134 144	64.4	5 758	1 325	4.0
June	212 466	142 591	67.1	136 940	69 629	60 027	8 308	2 445	134 528	64.5	5 651	1 242	4.0
July	212 677	142 278	66.9	136 531	69 525	60 011	8 078	2 408	134 196	64.2	5 747	1 343	4.0
August	212 916	142 514	66.9	136 662	69 823	59 719	8 280	2 433	134 311	64.2	5 853	1 394	4.1
September	213 163	142 518	66.9	136 893	69 700	60 083	8 176	2 384	134 489	64.2	5 625	1 290	3.9
October	213 405	142 622	66.8	137 088	69 762	60 238	8 124	2 319	134 808	64.2	5 534	1 337	3.9
November	213 540	142 962	66.9	137 322	69 910	60 269	8 211	2 330	134 921	64.3	5 639	1 315	3.9
December	213 736	143 248	67.0	137 614	69 939	60 503	8 258	2 389	135 194	64.4	5 634	1 329	3.9
2001													
January	213 888	143 800	67.2	137 778	70 064	60 609	8 243	2 360	135 304	64.4	6 023	1 372	4.2
February	214 110	143 701	67.1	137 612	69 959	60 615	8 154	2 370	135 291	64.3	6 089	1 491	4.2
March	214 305	143 924	67.2	137 783	69 881	60 902	8 120	2 350	135 372	64.3	6 141	1 521	4.3
April	214 525	143 569	66.9	137 299	69 916	60 523	7 970	2 336	135 036	64.0	6 271	1 499	4.4
May	214 732	143 318	66.7	137 092	69 865	60 509	7 760	2 353	134 735	63.8	6 226	1 502	4.3
June	214 950	143 357	66.7	136 873	69 690	60 371	7 942	2 082	134 755	63.7	6 484	1 532	4.5
July	215 180	143 654	66.8	137 071	69 808	60 480	7 929	2 295	134 858	63.7	6 583	1 653	4.6
August	215 420	143 284	66.5	136 241	69 585	60 301	7 531	2 305	133 944	63.2	7 042	1 861	4.9
September	215 665	143 989	66.8	136 846	69 933	60 265	7 836	2 322	134 558	63.5	7 142	1 950	5.0
October	215 903	144 086	66.7	136 392	69 621	60 168	7 858	2 327	134 098	63.2	7 694	2 082	5.3
November	216 117	144 240	66.7	136 238	69 444	60 174	7 873	2 203	133 955	63.0	8 003	2 318	5.5
December	216 315	144 305	66.7	136 047	69 551	60 095	7 712	2 293	133 751	62.9	8 258	2 444	5.7
2002													
January	216 506	143 883	66.5	135 701	69 308	60 032	7 619	2 385	133 233	62.7	8 182	2 578	5.7
February	216 663	144 653	66.8	136 438	69 534	60 479	7 650	2 397	134 127	63.0	8 215	2 608	5.7
March	216 823	144 481	66.6	136 177	69 480	60 190	7 802	2 368	133 816	62.8	8 304	2 719	5.7
April	217 006	144 725	66.7	136 126	69 554	60 204	7 621	2 371	133 833	62.7	8 599	2 852	5.9
May	217 198	144 938	66.7	136 539	69 981	60 226	7 588	2 260	134 278	62.9	8 399	2 967	5.8
June	217 407	144 808	66.6	136 415	69 769	60 297	7 617	2 161	134 135	62.7	8 393	3 023	5.8
July	217 630	144 803	66.5	136 413	69 806	60 290	7 591	2 324	134 107	62.7	8 390	2 966	5.8
August	217 866	145 009	66.6	136 705	69 937	60 560	7 477	2 127	134 593	62.7	8 304	2 887	5.7
September	218 107	145 552	66.7	137 302	70 207	60 679	7 667	2 285	135 102	63.0	8 251	2 971	5.7
October	218 340	145 314	66.6	137 008	69 948	60 663	7 537	2 471	134 580	62.7	8 307	3 042	5.7
November	218 548	145 041	66.4	136 521	69 615	60 697	7 487	2 261	134 171	62.5	8 520	3 062	5.9
December	218 741	145 066	66.3	136 426	69 620	60 667	7 385	2 352	134 071	62.4	8 640	3 271	6.0
2003													
January	219 897	145 937	66.4	137 417	69 919	61 406	7 358	2 337	135 045	62.5	8 520	3 166	5.8
February	220 114	146 100	66.4	137 482	70 262	61 159	7 322	2 234	135 306	62.5	8 618	3 161	5.9
March	220 317	146 022	66.3	137 434	70 243	61 317	7 143	2 263	135 232	62.4	8 588	3 161	5.9
April	220 540	146 474	66.4	137 633	70 311	61 374	7 223	2 150	135 561	62.4	8 842	3 348	6.0
May	220 768	146 500	66.4	137 544	70 215	61 393	7 228	2 183	135 370	62.3	8 957	3 318	6.1
June	221 014	147 056	66.5	137 790	70 159	61 747	7 268	2 185	135 419	62.3	9 266	3 552	6.3
July	221 252	146 485	66.2	137 474	70 190	61 437	7 150	2 187	135 242	62.1	9 011	3 633	6.2
August	221 507	146 445	66.1	137 549	70 237	61 442	7 035	2 313	135 200	62.1	8 896	3 557	6.1
September	221 779	146 530	66.1	137 609	70 631	61 119	7 112	2 349	135 355	62.0	8 921	3 486	6.1
October	222 039	146 716	66.1	137 984	70 685	61 451	7 060	2 479	135 571	62.1	8 732	3 451	6.0
November	222 279	147 000	66.1	138 424	70 935	61 494	7 112	2 373	136 003	62.3	8 576	3 420	5.8
December	222 509	146 729	65.9	138 411	71 170	61 396	6 978	2 243	136 145	62.2	8 317	3 366	5.7
2004													
January	222 161	146 842	66.1	138 472	71 318	61 183	7 194	2 196	136 228	62.3	8 370	3 364	5.7
February	222 357	146 709	66.0	138 542	71 122	61 514	7 077	2 210	136 362	62.3	8 167	3 248	5.6
March	222 550	146 944	66.0	138 453	71 155	61 534	6 930	2 180	136 302	62.2	8 491	3 314	5.8
April	222 757	146 850	65.9	138 680	71 121	61 647	7 093	2 241	136 474	62.3	8 170	2 971	5.6
May	222 967	147 065	66.0	138 852	71 180	61 762	7 126	2 300	136 556	62.3	8 212	3 103	5.6
June	223 196	147 460	66.1	139 174	71 562	61 793	7 007	2 237	136 748	62.4	8 286	3 130	5.6
July	223 422	147 692	66.1	139 556	71 780	61 884	7 166	2 222	137 354	62.5	8 136	2 918	5.5
August	223 677	147 564	66.0	139 573	71 808	61 836	7 123	2 333	137 230	62.4	7 990	2 846	5.4
September	223 941	147 415	65.8	139 487	71 744	61 859	7 056	2 251	137 323	62.3	7 927	2 910	5.4
October	224 192	147 793	65.9	139 732	71 860	61 942	7 180	2 216	137 598	62.3	8 061	3 041	5.5
November	224 422	148 162	66.0	140 231	72 110	62 088	7 216	2 206	137 978	62.5	7 932	2 960	5.4
December	224 640	148 059	65.9	140 125	72 058	62 136	7 202	2 171	137 947	62.4	7 934	2 927	5.4

[1]Not seasonally adjusted.
[2]In 1930 through 1943, the official BLS data count persons on work relief as unemployed. The unemployment rates for those years shown in parentheses count persons on work relief as employed, which is more consistent with the postwar practice. See notes and definitions.

Table 10-1B. Summary Labor Force, Employment, and Unemployment: Historical—*Continued*

(Thousands of persons, percent, seasonally adjusted, except as noted.)

Year and month	Civilian noninstitutional population [1]	Civilian labor force		Employment, thousands of persons						Employment-population ratio, percent	Unemployment		
		Thousands of persons	Participation rate (percent)	Total	By age and sex			By industry			Thousands of persons		Rate (percent) [2]
					Men, 20 years and over	Women, 20 years and over	Both sexes, 16 to 19 years	Agricultural	Nonagricultural		Total	Unemployed 15 weeks and over	
2005													
January	224 837	148 029	65.8	140 245	72 063	62 260	7 071	2 112	138 111	62.4	7 784	2 851	5.3
February	225 041	148 364	65.9	140 385	72 299	62 253	7 073	2 129	138 267	62.4	7 980	2 896	5.4
March	225 236	148 391	65.9	140 654	72 478	62 222	7 185	2 180	138 462	62.4	7 737	2 817	5.2
April	225 441	148 926	66.1	141 254	72 860	62 483	7 190	2 248	138 992	62.7	7 672	2 678	5.2
May	225 670	149 261	66.1	141 609	73 133	62 557	7 201	2 225	139 379	62.8	7 651	2 683	5.1
June	225 911	149 238	66.1	141 714	73 223	62 516	7 140	2 302	139 276	62.7	7 524	2 405	5.0
July	226 153	149 432	66.1	142 026	73 337	62 691	7 150	2 308	139 789	62.8	7 406	2 449	5.0
August	226 421	149 779	66.2	142 434	73 513	62 844	7 240	2 183	140 277	62.9	7 345	2 569	4.9
September	226 693	149 954	66.1	142 401	73 333	63 035	7 141	2 181	140 276	62.8	7 553	2 537	5.0
October	226 959	150 001	66.1	142 548	73 445	63 127	7 124	2 191	140 405	62.8	7 450	2 402	5.0
November	227 204	150 065	66.0	142 499	73 341	63 127	7 265	2 174	140 299	62.7	7 566	2 486	5.0
December	227 425	150 030	66.0	142 752	73 467	63 209	7 139	2 094	140 635	62.8	7 279	2 429	4.9
2006													
January	227 553	150 214	66.0	143 150	73 892	63 151	7 197	2 164	140 933	62.9	7 064	2 270	4.7
February	227 763	150 641	66.1	143 457	73 972	63 304	7 298	2 178	141 254	63.0	7 184	2 546	4.8
March	227 975	150 813	66.2	143 741	74 228	63 353	7 342	2 153	141 604	63.1	7 072	2 373	4.7
April	228 199	150 881	66.1	143 761	74 204	63 413	7 198	2 249	141 388	63.0	7 120	2 353	4.7
May	228 428	151 069	66.1	144 089	74 229	63 656	7 215	2 194	141 859	63.1	6 980	2 303	4.6
June	228 671	151 354	66.2	144 353	74 261	63 866	7 393	2 256	142 019	63.1	7 001	2 127	4.6
July	228 912	151 377	66.1	144 202	74 011	64 030	7 324	2 278	142 066	63.0	7 175	2 289	4.7
August	229 167	151 716	66.2	144 625	74 384	64 139	7 266	2 240	142 440	63.1	7 091	2 293	4.7
September	229 420	151 662	66.1	144 815	74 866	63 922	7 196	2 182	142 661	63.1	6 847	2 231	4.5
October	229 675	152 041	66.2	145 314	74 833	64 298	7 289	2 183	143 222	63.3	6 727	2 062	4.4
November	229 905	152 406	66.3	145 534	74 962	64 328	7 331	2 164	143 350	63.3	6 872	2 159	4.5
December	230 108	152 732	66.4	145 970	75 232	64 518	7 287	2 233	143 716	63.4	6 762	2 083	4.4
2007													
January	230 650	153 144	66.4	146 028	75 238	64 621	7 240	2 214	143 785	63.3	7 116	2 156	4.6
February	230 834	152 983	66.3	146 057	75 239	64 750	7 133	2 295	143 741	63.3	6 927	2 211	4.5
March	231 034	153 051	66.2	146 320	75 386	64 928	7 061	2 178	144 153	63.3	6 731	2 255	4.4
April	231 253	152 435	65.9	145 586	75 342	64 366	6 985	2 069	143 385	63.0	6 850	2 281	4.5
May	231 480	152 670	66.0	145 903	75 386	64 724	6 888	2 081	143 773	63.0	6 766	2 231	4.4
June	231 713	153 041	66.0	146 063	75 327	64 788	7 109	1 946	144 112	63.0	6 979	2 281	4.6
July	231 958	153 054	66.0	145 905	75 247	64 766	6 953	2 016	144 041	62.9	7 149	2 364	4.7
August	232 211	152 749	65.8	145 682	75 195	64 838	6 714	1 863	143 865	62.7	7 067	2 333	4.6
September	232 461	153 414	66.0	146 244	75 273	65 086	7 001	2 095	144 148	62.9	7 170	2 355	4.7
October	232 715	153 183	65.8	145 946	75 146	64 842	7 039	2 121	143 926	62.7	7 237	2 300	4.7
November	232 939	153 835	66.0	146 595	75 683	64 985	7 071	2 148	144 413	62.9	7 240	2 366	4.7
December	233 156	153 918	66.0	146 273	75 510	64 910	7 032	2 219	144 018	62.7	7 645	2 501	5.0
2008													
January	232 616	154 063	66.2	146 378	75 551	65 058	7 015	2 205	144 168	62.9	7 685	2 540	5.0
February	232 809	153 653	66.0	146 156	75 450	65 021	6 820	2 190	143 943	62.8	7 497	2 446	4.9
March	232 995	153 908	66.1	146 086	75 294	65 074	6 813	2 172	143 871	62.7	7 822	2 491	5.1
April	233 198	153 769	65.9	146 132	75 182	65 107	6 947	2 115	143 874	62.7	7 637	2 687	5.0
May	233 405	154 303	66.1	145 908	74 953	65 137	7 182	2 113	143 737	62.5	8 395	2 780	5.4
June	233 627	154 313	66.1	145 737	74 975	65 169	6 925	2 127	143 629	62.4	8 575	2 913	5.6
July	233 864	154 469	66.1	145 532	74 950	65 103	6 909	2 134	143 519	62.2	8 937	3 114	5.8
August	234 107	154 641	66.1	145 203	74 658	65 008	6 801	2 148	143 086	62.0	9 438	3 420	6.1
September	234 360	154 570	66.0	145 076	74 456	65 078	6 850	2 231	142 796	61.9	9 494	3 626	6.1
October	234 612	154 876	66.0	144 802	74 263	65 103	6 793	2 199	142 689	61.7	10 074	3 990	6.5
November	234 828	154 639	65.9	144 100	73 943	64 885	6 612	2 207	141 962	61.4	10 538	3 923	6.8
December	235 035	154 655	65.8	143 369	73 311	64 813	6 601	2 209	141 139	61.0	11 286	4 547	7.3
2009													
January	234 739	154 210	65.7	142 152	72 724	64 209	5 218	2 147	140 029	60.6	12 058	4 764	7.8
February	234 913	154 538	65.8	141 640	72 260	64 195	5 185	2 130	139 493	60.3	12 898	5 455	8.3
March	235 086	154 133	65.6	140 707	71 629	64 027	5 051	2 031	138 664	59.9	13 426	5 886	8.7
April	235 271	154 509	65.7	140 656	71 599	64 021	5 036	2 146	138 437	59.8	13 853	6 385	9.0
May	235 452	154 747	65.7	140 248	71 410	63 807	5 031	2 145	138 036	59.6	14 499	7 022	9.4
June	235 655	154 716	65.7	140 009	71 326	63 747	4 937	2 165	137 841	59.4	14 707	7 837	9.5
July	235 870	154 502	65.5	139 901	71 273	63 761	4 867	2 126	137 819	59.3	14 601	7 839	9.5
August	236 087	154 307	65.4	139 492	71 111	63 633	4 749	2 088	137 371	59.1	14 814	7 828	9.6
September	236 322	153 827	65.1	138 818	70 844	63 324	4 649	2 033	136 734	58.7	15 009	8 402	9.8
October	236 550	153 784	65.0	138 432	70 713	63 275	4 445	2 039	136 483	58.5	15 352	8 648	10.0
November	236 743	153 878	65.0	138 659	70 774	63 422	4 463	2 098	136 640	58.6	15 219	8 755	9.9
December	236 924	153 111	64.6	138 013	70 479	63 086	4 449	2 087	135 904	58.3	15 098	8 835	9.9
2010													
January	236 832	153 404	64.8	138 451	70 506	63 515	4 430	2 131	136 390	58.5	14 953	8 903	9.7
February	236 998	153 720	64.9	138 599	70 601	63 505	4 493	2 307	136 333	58.5	15 121	8 933	9.8
March	237 159	153 964	64.9	138 752	70 876	63 378	4 498	2 211	136 588	58.5	15 212	9 096	9.9
April	237 329	154 642	65.2	139 309	71 356	63 416	4 537	2 288	136 966	58.7	15 333	9 133	9.9
May	237 499	154 106	64.9	139 247	71 378	63 436	4 433	2 197	136 998	58.6	14 858	8 892	9.6
June	237 690	153 631	64.6	139 148	71 353	63 555	4 240	2 140	136 975	58.5	14 483	8 898	9.4
July	237 890	153 706	64.6	139 179	71 457	63 415	4 307	2 172	136 934	58.5	14 527	8 704	9.5
August	238 099	154 087	64.7	139 427	71 607	63 420	4 400	2 163	137 187	58.6	14 660	8 405	9.5
September	238 322	153 971	64.6	139 393	71 592	63 533	4 268	2 161	137 209	58.5	14 578	8 444	9.5
October	238 530	153 631	64.4	139 111	71 432	63 382	4 297	2 338	136 891	58.3	14 520	8 617	9.5
November	238 715	154 127	64.6	139 030	71 140	63 494	4 396	2 191	136 872	58.2	15 097	8 697	9.8
December	238 889	153 639	64.3	139 266	71 470	63 493	4 302	2 186	137 072	58.3	14 373	8 549	9.4

[1] Not seasonally adjusted.
[2] In 1930 through 1943, the official BLS data count persons on work relief as unemployed. The unemployment rates for those years shown in parentheses count persons on work relief as employed, which is more consistent with the postwar practice. See notes and definitions.

Table 10-1B. Summary Labor Force, Employment, and Unemployment: Historical—*Continued*

(Thousands of persons, percent, seasonally adjusted, except as noted.)

Year and month	Civilian noninstitutional population [1]	Civilian labor force — Thousands of persons	Participation rate (percent)	Employment Total	Men, 20 years and over	Women, 20 years and over	Both sexes, 16 to 19 years	Agricultural	Nonagricultural	Employment-population ratio, percent	Unemployment Total	Unemployed 15 weeks and over	Rate (percent) [2]
2011													
January	238 704	153 198	64.2	139 287	71 544	63 413	4 330	2 270	137 036	58.4	13 910	8 430	9.1
February	238 851	153 280	64.2	139 422	71 819	63 281	4 322	2 266	137 182	58.4	13 858	8 213	9.0
March	239 000	153 403	64.2	139 655	71 834	63 461	4 360	2 260	137 471	58.4	13 748	8 184	9.0
April	239 146	153 566	64.2	139 622	71 946	63 373	4 302	2 143	137 438	58.4	13 944	8 007	9.1
May	239 313	153 526	64.2	139 653	72 120	63 267	4 266	2 230	137 395	58.4	13 873	8 189	9.0
June	239 489	153 379	64.0	139 409	71 999	63 134	4 276	2 253	137 136	58.2	13 971	8 107	9.1
July	239 671	153 309	64.0	139 524	72 008	63 293	4 223	2 225	137 215	58.2	13 785	8 151	9.0
August	239 871	153 724	64.1	139 904	72 217	63 339	4 348	2 344	137 470	58.3	13 820	8 214	9.0
September	240 071	154 059	64.2	140 154	72 409	63 372	4 372	2 232	137 904	58.4	13 905	8 282	9.0
October	240 269	153 940	64.1	140 335	72 415	63 540	4 381	2 211	138 283	58.4	13 604	7 808	8.8
November	240 441	154 072	64.1	140 747	72 861	63 489	4 396	2 251	138 500	58.5	13 326	7 713	8.6
December	240 584	153 927	64.0	140 836	73 039	63 406	4 390	2 362	138 454	58.5	13 090	7 555	8.5
2012													
January	242 269	154 328	63.7	141 677	73 083	64 219	4 375	2 211	139 437	58.5	12 650	7 467	8.2
February	242 435	154 826	63.9	141 943	73 103	64 436	4 403	2 193	139 782	58.5	12 883	7 373	8.3
March	242 604	154 811	63.8	142 079	73 181	64 521	4 377	2 246	139 888	58.6	12 732	7 216	8.2
April	242 784	154 565	63.7	141 963	73 131	64 456	4 376	2 203	139 712	58.5	12 603	7 056	8.2
May	242 966	154 946	63.8	142 257	73 245	64 600	4 412	2 278	139 980	58.6	12 689	7 069	8.2
June	243 155	155 134	63.8	142 432	73 294	64 629	4 509	2 221	140 246	58.6	12 702	7 170	8.2
July	243 354	154 970	63.7	142 272	73 301	64 456	4 515	2 212	140 020	58.5	12 698	6 946	8.2
August	243 566	154 669	63.5	142 204	73 197	64 644	4 364	2 106	140 017	58.4	12 464	6 848	8.1
September	243 772	155 018	63.6	142 947	73 677	64 857	4 414	2 178	140 773	58.6	12 070	6 728	7.8
October	243 983	155 507	63.7	143 369	73 923	64 980	4 466	2 176	141 379	58.8	12 138	6 795	7.8
November	244 174	155 279	63.6	143 233	73 807	64 962	4 465	2 126	141 110	58.7	12 045	6 563	7.8
December	244 350	155 485	63.6	143 212	73 924	64 901	4 387	2 066	141 121	58.6	12 273	6 634	7.9
2013													
January	244 663	155 699	63.6	143 384	74 084	64 790	4 510	2 057	141 234	58.6	12 315	6 573	7.9
February	244 828	155 511	63.5	143 464	74 183	64 911	4 370	2 070	141 393	58.6	12 047	6 485	7.7
March	244 995	155 099	63.3	143 393	74 190	64 838	4 365	2 020	141 350	58.5	11 706	6 355	7.5
April	245 175	155 359	63.4	143 676	74 161	65 148	4 368	2 048	141 604	58.6	11 683	6 329	7.5
May	245 363	155 609	63.4	143 919	74 137	65 323	4 459	2 081	141 860	58.7	11 690	6 287	7.5
June	245 552	155 822	63.5	144 075	74 265	65 340	4 470	2 091	142 021	58.7	11 747	6 218	7.5
July	245 756	155 693	63.4	144 285	74 301	65 514	4 470	2 171	142 081	58.7	11 408	6 031	7.3
August	245 959	155 435	63.2	144 179	74 015	65 743	4 421	2 205	141 918	58.6	11 256	5 973	7.2
September	246 168	155 473	63.2	144 270	74 151	65 539	4 580	2 208	142 058	58.6	11 203	5 927	7.2
October	246 381	154 625	62.8	143 485	73 808	65 229	4 448	2 208	141 449	58.2	11 140	5 824	7.2
November	246 567	155 284	63.0	144 443	74 373	65 547	4 523	2 139	142 317	58.6	10 841	5 786	7.0
December	246 745	154 937	62.8	144 586	74 467	65 617	4 502	2 229	142 337	58.6	10 351	5 530	6.7
2014													
January	230 244	149 943	65.1	140 818	74 905	65 913	4 388	1 999	141 527	58.1	10 280	5 392	6.6
February	230 421	150 207	65.2	140 989	74 820	66 168	4 312	1 973	142 160	58.3	10 387	5 657	6.7
March	230 600	150 488	65.3	141 293	75 284	66 009	4 504	2 008	143 082	58.7	10 384	5 708	6.6
April	230 787	149 878	64.9	141 239	75 163	66 076	4 485	2 048	143 718	58.9	9 696	5 139	6.2
May	230 978	150 006	64.9	141 323	75 159	66 164	4 545	2 101	144 297	59.1	9 761	4 898	6.3
June	231 178	150 059	64.9	141 771	75 504	66 267	4 476	2 288	144 815	59.4	9 453	4 448	6.1
July	231 394	150 396	65.0	141 881	75 631	66 250	4 520	2 403	144 862	59.4	9 648	4 452	6.2
August	231 607	150 441	65.0	141 956	75 668	66 289	4 495	2 472	144 175	59.1	9 568	4 321	6.1
September	231 831	150 200	64.8	142 081	75 889	66 192	4 527	2 482	144 459	59.1	9 237	4 242	5.9
October	232 049	150 377	64.8	142 488	75 928	66 560	4 772	2 517	145 419	59.5	8 983	4 251	5.7
November	232 243	150 627	64.9	142 569	75 675	66 894	4 762	2 332	145 335	59.3	9 071	4 144	5.8
December	232 432	150 383	64.7	142 658	76 026	66 632	4 784	2 220	144 970	59.1	8 688	3 922	5.6
2015													
January	249 723	157 022	62.9	148 061	75 364	66 894	4 294	2 234	144 317	59.3	8 962	4 250	5.7
February	249 899	156 771	62.7	148 108	75 671	67 058	4 389	2 234	144 884	59.3	8 663	4 248	5.5
March	250 080	156 781	62.7	148 244	76 122	67 022	4 491	2 405	145 230	59.3	8 538	4 064	5.4
April	250 266	157 043	62.8	148 522	76 749	67 303	4 536	2 294	146 293	59.3	8 521	3 802	5.4
May	250 455	157 447	62.9	148 792	77 137	67 493	4 718	2 431	146 918	59.4	8 655	3 851	5.5
June	250 663	156 993	62.6	148 742	77 315	67 003	5 327	2 703	146 942	59.3	8 251	3 369	5.3
July	250 876	157 125	62.6	148 890	77 541	66 485	5 696	2 601	147 121	59.3	8 235	3 245	5.2
August	251 096	157 109	62.6	149 092	77 311	66 874	5 042	2 539	146 689	59.4	8 017	3 318	5.1
September	251 325	156 809	62.4	148 932	77 110	67 394	4 476	2 471	146 509	59.3	7 877	3 207	5.0
October	251 541	157 123	62.5	149 255	77 258	67 885	4 574	2 518	147 198	59.3	7 869	3 301	5.0
November	251 747	157 358	62.5	149 419	76 911	68 335	4 520	2 363	147 404	59.4	7 939	3 256	5.0
December	251 936	157 957	62.7	150 030	76 827	68 131	4 745	2 273	147 430	59.6	7 927	3 231	5.0
2016													
January	252 397	158 362	62.7	150 533	76 644	67 904	4 490	2 200	146 838	59.6	7 829	3 297	4.9
February	252 577	158 888	62.9	151 043	77 148	68 305	4 608	2 274	147 787	59.8	7 845	3 525	4.9
March	252 768	159 278	63.0	151 301	77 639	68 451	4 648	2 491	148 247	59.9	7 977	3 651	5.0
April	252 969	158 938	62.8	151 028	78 028	68 346	4 701	2 478	148 597	59.7	7 910	3 499	5.0
May	253 174	158 510	62.6	151 058	78 241	68 496	4 857	2 620	148 974	59.7	7 451	3 113	4.7
June	253 397	158 889	62.7	151 090	78 673	67 769	5 548	2 661	149 329	59.6	7 799	2 970	4.9
July	253 620	159 295	62.8	151 546	78 695	67 702	6 040	2 597	149 840	59.8	7 749	3 060	4.9
August	253 854	159 508	62.8	151 655	78 562	67 776	5 466	2 718	149 086	59.7	7 853	2 942	4.9
September	254 091	159 830	62.9	151 926	78 459	68 709	4 810	2 526	149 451	59.8	7 904	3 004	4.9
October	254 321	159 643	62.8	151 902	78 538	68 997	4 800	2 408	149 597	59.7	7 740	3 087	4.8
November	254 540	159 456	62.6	152 048	78 405	69 203	4 778	2 366	150 020	59.7	7 409	2 859	4.6
December	254 742	159 640	62.7	152 111	77 984	68 984	4 831	2 180	149 617	59.7	7 529	2 945	4.7

[1] Not seasonally adjusted.
[2] In 1930 through 1943, the official BLS data count persons on work relief as unemployed. The unemployment rates for those years shown in parentheses count persons on work relief as employed, which is more consistent with the postwar practice. See notes and definitions.

Table 10-2. Labor Force and Employment by Major Age and Sex Groups

(Thousands of persons, percent, seasonally adjusted.)

Year and month	Civilian labor force (thousands)			Participation rate (percent)			Employment (thousands)			Employment-population ratio, percent		
	Men, 20 years and over	Women, 20 years and over	Both sexes, 16 to 19 years	Men, 20 years and over	Women, 20 years and over	Both sexes, 16 to 19 years	Men, 20 years and over	Women, 20 years and over	Both sexes, 16 to 19 years	Men, 20 years and over	Women, 20 years and over	Both sexes, 16 to 19 years
1965	44 857	23 686	5 910	83.9	39.4	45.7	43 422	22 630	5 036	81.2	39.4	38.9
1966	44 788	24 431	6 558	83.6	40.1	48.2	43 668	23 510	5 721	81.5	40.1	42.1
1967	45 354	25 475	6 521	83.4	41.1	48.4	44 294	24 397	5 682	81.5	41.1	42.2
1968	45 852	26 266	6 619	83.1	41.6	48.3	44 859	25 281	5 781	81.3	41.6	42.2
1969	46 351	27 413	6 970	82.8	42.7	49.4	45 388	26 397	6 117	81.1	42.7	43.4
1970	47 220	28 301	7 249	82.6	43.3	49.9	45 581	26 952	6 144	79.7	43.3	42.3
1971	48 009	28 904	7 470	82.1	43.3	49.7	45 912	27 246	6 208	78.5	43.3	41.3
1972	49 079	29 901	8 054	81.6	43.7	51.9	47 130	28 276	6 746	78.4	43.7	43.5
1973	49 932	30 991	8 507	81.3	44.4	53.7	48 310	29 484	7 271	78.6	44.4	45.9
1974	50 879	32 201	8 871	81.0	45.3	54.8	48 922	30 424	7 448	77.9	45.3	46.0
1975	51 494	33 410	8 870	80.3	46.0	54.0	48 018	30 726	7 104	74.8	46.0	43.3
1976	52 288	34 814	9 056	79.8	47.0	54.5	49 190	32 226	7 336	75.1	47.0	44.2
1977	53 348	36 310	9 351	79.7	48.1	56.0	50 555	33 775	7 688	75.6	48.1	46.1
1978	54 471	38 128	9 652	79.8	49.6	57.8	52 143	35 836	8 070	76.4	49.6	48.3
1979	55 615	39 708	9 638	79.8	50.6	57.9	53 308	37 434	8 083	76.5	50.6	48.5
1980	56 455	41 106	9 378	79.4	51.3	56.7	53 101	38 492	7 710	74.6	51.3	46.6
1981	57 197	42 485	8 988	79.0	52.1	55.4	53 582	39 590	7 225	74.0	52.1	44.6
1982	57 980	43 699	8 526	78.7	52.7	54.1	52 891	40 086	6 549	71.8	52.7	41.5
1983	58 744	44 636	8 171	78.5	53.1	53.5	53 487	41 004	6 342	71.4	53.1	41.5
1984	59 701	45 900	7 943	78.3	53.7	53.9	55 769	42 793	6 444	73.2	53.7	43.7
1985	60 277	47 283	7 901	78.1	54.7	54.5	56 562	44 154	6 434	73.3	54.7	44.4
1986	61 320	48 589	7 926	78.1	55.5	54.7	57 569	45 556	6 472	73.3	55.5	44.6
1987	62 095	49 783	7 988	78.0	56.2	54.7	58 726	47 074	6 640	73.8	56.2	45.5
1988	62 768	50 870	8 031	77.9	56.8	55.3	59 781	48 383	6 805	74.2	56.8	46.8
1989	63 704	52 212	7 954	78.1	57.7	55.9	60 837	49 745	6 759	74.5	57.7	47.5
1990	64 916	53 131	7 792	78.2	58.0	53.7	61 678	50 535	6 581	74.3	58.0	45.3
1991	65 374	53 708	7 265	77.7	57.9	51.6	61 178	50 634	5 906	72.7	57.9	42.0
1992	66 213	54 796	7 096	77.7	58.5	51.3	61 496	51 328	5 669	72.1	58.5	41.0
1993	66 642	55 388	7 170	77.3	58.5	51.5	62 355	52 099	5 805	72.3	58.5	41.7
1994	66 921	56 655	7 481	76.8	59.3	52.7	63 294	53 606	6 161	72.6	59.3	43.4
1995	67 324	57 215	7 765	76.7	59.4	53.5	64 085	54 396	6 419	73.0	59.4	44.2
1996	68 044	58 094	7 806	76.8	59.9	52.3	64 897	55 311	6 500	73.2	59.9	43.5
1997	69 166	59 198	7 932	77.0	60.5	51.6	66 284	56 613	6 661	73.7	60.5	43.4
1998	69 715	59 702	8 256	76.8	60.4	52.8	67 135	57 278	7 051	73.9	60.4	45.1
1999	70 194	60 840	8 333	76.7	60.7	52.0	67 761	58 555	7 172	74.0	60.7	44.7
2000	72 010	62 301	8 271	76.7	60.6	52.0	69 634	60 067	7 189	74.2	60.6	45.2
2001	72 816	63 016	7 902	76.5	60.6	49.6	69 776	60 417	6 740	73.3	60.6	42.3
2002	73 630	63 648	7 585	76.3	60.5	47.4	69 734	60 420	6 332	72.3	60.5	39.6
2003	74 623	64 716	7 170	75.9	60.6	44.5	70 415	61 402	5 919	71.7	60.6	36.8
2004	75 364	64 923	7 114	75.8	60.3	43.9	71 572	61 773	5 907	71.9	60.3	36.4
2005	76 443	65 714	7 164	75.8	60.4	43.7	73 050	62 702	5 978	72.4	60.4	36.5
2006	77 562	66 585	7 281	75.9	60.5	43.7	74 431	63 834	6 162	72.9	60.5	36.9
2007	78 596	67 516	7 012	75.9	60.6	41.3	75 337	64 799	5 911	72.8	60.6	34.8
2008	79 047	68 382	6 858	75.7	60.9	40.2	74 750	65 039	5 573	71.6	60.9	32.6
2009	78 897	68 856	6 390	74.8	60.8	37.5	71 341	63 699	4 837	67.6	60.8	28.4
2010	78 994	68 990	5 906	74.1	60.3	34.9	71 230	63 456	4 378	66.8	60.3	25.9
2011	79 080	68 810	5 727	73.4	59.8	34.1	72 182	63 360	4 327	67.0	59.8	25.8
2012	79 387	69 765	5 823	73.0	59.3	34.3	73 403	64 640	4 426	67.5	59.3	26.1
2013	79 744	69 860	5 785	72.5	58.8	34.5	74 176	65 295	4 458	67.4	58.8	26.6
2014	80 056	70 212	5 654	71.9	58.5	34.0	75 471	66 287	4 548	67.8	55.2	27.3
2015	80 735	70 695	5 700	71.7	58.2	34.3	76 776	67 323	4 734	68.1	55.4	28.5
2016	81 759	71 538	5 889	71.7	58.3	35.2	78 074	68 387	4 965	68.5	55.7	29.7
2015												
January	80 179	70 554	4 294	71.5	58.3	32.0	75 364	66 894	4 294	67.2	55.3	25.8
February	80 394	70 526	4 389	71.6	58.3	31.8	75 671	67 058	4 389	67.4	55.4	26.4
March	80 533	70 374	4 491	71.7	58.1	32.5	76 122	67 022	4 491	67.8	55.3	27.0
April	80 670	70 509	4 536	71.8	58.2	32.3	76 749	67 303	4 536	68.3	55.5	27.3
May	81 102	70 874	4 718	72.1	58.4	34.6	77 137	67 493	4 718	68.6	55.6	28.4
June	81 074	70 436	5 327	72.0	58.0	40.8	77 315	67 003	5 327	68.7	55.2	32.1
July	81 320	70 339	5 696	72.1	57.9	41.3	77 541	66 485	5 696	68.8	54.7	34.3
August	80 892	70 460	5 042	71.7	57.9	36.4	77 311	66 874	5 042	68.5	55.0	30.4
September	80 633	70 633	4 476	71.4	58.0	32.1	77 110	67 394	4 476	68.3	55.3	26.9
October	80 817	71 093	4 574	71.5	58.3	32.5	77 258	67 885	4 574	68.3	55.7	27.5
November	80 548	71 482	4 520	71.2	58.6	32.0	76 911	68 335	4 520	68.0	56.0	27.2
December	80 663	71 055	4 745	71.2	58.2	33.2	76 827	68 131	4 745	67.8	55.8	28.5
2016												
January	80 731	71 242	4 490	71.1	58.3	32.3	76 644	67 904	4 490	67.5	55.5	27.0
February	81 306	71 518	4 608	71.6	58.5	32.7	77 148	68 305	4 608	67.9	55.8	27.6
March	81 659	71 700	4 648	71.8	58.6	32.9	77 639	68 451	4 648	68.3	55.9	27.9
April	81 655	71 329	4 701	71.8	58.2	33.0	78 028	68 346	4 701	68.6	55.8	28.2
May	81 637	71 366	4 857	71.7	58.2	34.7	78 241	68 496	4 857	68.7	55.9	29.1
June	82 209	71 057	5 548	72.1	57.9	41.1	78 673	67 769	5 548	69.0	55.2	33.2
July	82 393	71 092	6 040	72.2	57.9	43.2	78 695	67 702	6 040	69.0	55.1	36.1
August	82 048	71 290	5 466	71.9	58.0	38.6	78 562	67 776	5 466	68.8	55.1	32.7
September	82 020	71 902	4 810	71.8	58.4	34.1	78 459	68 709	4 810	68.6	55.8	28.7
October	82 065	72 061	4 800	71.7	58.5	33.8	78 538	68 997	4 800	68.7	56.0	28.7
November	81 751	72 109	4 778	71.4	58.5	33.4	78 405	69 203	4 778	68.5	56.1	28.5
December	81 640	71 794	4 831	71.2	58.2	33.0	77 984	68 984	4 831	68.0	55.9	28.8

Table 10-3. Employment by Type of Job

(Thousands of persons, seasonally adjusted, except as noted.)

Year and month	By class of worker									Multiple jobholders		Employed and at work part-time	
	Agricultural	Nonagricultural industries								Total (thousands)	Percent of total employed	Economic reasons	Non-economic reasons
		Total	Wage and salary				Self-employed (unincor-porated)	Unpaid family workers [1]					
			Total	Government	Private industries								
					Private house-holds [1]	Other private industries							
1965	4 361	66 726	60 031	9 608	...	...	6 097	600	...	...	2 209	8 466
1966	3 979	68 915	62 362	10 323	...	...	5 991	564	...	...	1 960	8 112
1967	3 844	70 527	64 848	11 146	...	...	5 174	505	...	...	2 163	8 701
1968	3 817	72 103	66 519	11 590	...	...	5 102	485	...	...	1 970	9 075
1969	3 606	74 296	68 528	12 025	...	...	5 252	517	...	...	2 056	9 652
1970	3 463	75 215	69 491	12 431	...	...	5 221	502	...	...	2 446	9 999
1971	3 394	75 972	70 120	12 799	...	...	5 327	522	...	...	2 688	10 152
1972	3 484	78 669	72 785	13 393	...	...	5 365	519	...	...	2 648	10 612
1973	3 470	81 594	75 580	13 655	...	...	5 474	540	...	...	2 554	10 972
1974	3 515	83 279	77 094	14 124	...	...	5 697	489	...	...	2 988	11 153
1975	3 408	82 438	76 249	14 675	...	...	5 705	483	...	...	3 804	11 228
1976	3 331	85 421	79 175	15 132	...	...	5 783	464	...	...	3 607	11 607
1977	3 283	88 734	82 121	15 361	...	...	6 114	498	...	...	3 608	12 120
1978	3 387	92 661	85 753	15 525	...	...	6 429	479	...	...	3 516	12 650
1979	3 347	95 477	88 222	15 635	...	...	6 791	463	...	...	3 577	12 893
1980	3 364	95 938	88 525	15 912	...	...	7 000	413	...	...	4 321	13 067
1981	3 368	97 030	89 543	15 689	...	...	7 097	390	...	...	4 768	13 025
1982	3 401	96 125	88 462	15 516	...	...	7 262	401	...	...	6 170	12 953
1983	3 383	97 450	89 500	15 537	...	...	7 575	376	...	...	6 266	12 911
1984	3 321	101 685	93 565	15 770	...	...	7 785	335	...	...	5 744	13 169
1985	3 179	103 971	95 871	16 031	...	...	7 811	289	...	...	5 590	13 489
1986	3 163	106 434	98 299	16 342	...	...	7 881	255	...	...	5 588	13 935
1987	3 208	109 232	100 771	16 800	...	...	8 201	260	...	...	5 401	14 395
1988	3 169	111 800	103 021	17 114	...	...	8 519	260	...	...	5 206	14 963
1989	3 199	114 142	105 259	17 469	...	...	8 605	279	...	...	4 894	15 393
1990	3 223	115 570	106 598	17 769	...	...	8 719	253	...	...	5 204	15 341
1991	3 269	114 449	105 373	17 934	...	...	8 851	226	...	...	6 161	15 172
1992	3 247	115 245	106 437	18 136	...	...	8 575	233	...	...	6 520	14 918
1993	3 115	117 144	107 966	18 579	...	...	8 959	218	...	...	6 481	15 240
1994	3 409	119 651	110 517	18 293	...	...	9 003	131	7 260	5.9	4 625	17 638
1995	3 440	121 460	112 448	18 362	...	...	8 902	110	7 693	6.2	4 473	17 734
1996	3 443	123 264	114 171	18 217	...	...	8 971	122	7 832	6.2	4 315	17 770
1997	3 399	126 159	116 983	18 131	...	...	9 056	120	7 955	6.1	4 068	18 149
1998	3 378	128 085	119 019	18 383	...	...	8 962	103	7 926	6.0	3 665	18 530
1999	3 281	130 207	121 323	18 903	...	...	8 790	95	7 802	5.8	3 357	18 758
2000	2 464	134 427	125 114	19 248	718	105 148	9 205	108	7 604	5.6	3 227	18 814
2001	2 299	134 635	125 407	19 335	694	105 378	9 121	107	7 357	5.4	3 715	18 790
2002	2 311	134 174	125 156	19 636	757	104 764	8 923	95	7 291	5.3	4 213	18 843
2003	2 275	135 461	126 015	19 634	764	105 616	9 344	101	7 315	5.3	4 701	19 014
2004	2 232	137 020	127 463	19 983	779	106 701	9 467	90	7 473	5.4	4 567	19 380
2005	2 197	139 532	129 931	20 357	812	108 761	9 509	93	7 546	5.3	4 350	19 491
2006	2 206	142 221	132 449	20 337	803	111 309	9 685	87	7 576	5.2	4 162	19 591
2007	2 095	143 952	134 283	21 003	813	112 467	9 557	112	7 655	5.2	4 401	19 756
2008	2 168	143 194	133 882	21 258	805	111 819	9 219	93	7 620	5.2	5 875	19 343
2009	2 103	137 775	128 713	21 178	783	106 752	8 995	66	7 271	5.2	8 913	18 710
2010	2 206	136 858	127 914	21 003	667	106 244	8 860	84	6 878	4.9	8 874	18 251
2011	2 254	137 615	128 934	20 536	722	107 676	8 603	78	6 880	4.9	8 560	18 334
2012	2 186	140 283	131 452	20 360	738	110 355	8 749	81	6 943	4.9	8 122	18 806
2013	2 130	141 799	133 111	20 247	723	112 141	8 619	70	7 002	4.9	7 935	18 903
2014	2 237	144 068	135 402	20 135	820	114 456	8 602	64	7 146	4.9	7 213	19 489
2015	2 422	146 411	137 678	20 601	798	116 279	8 665	68	7 262	4.9	6 371	20 018
2016	2 460	148 975	140 161	20 630	724	118 807	8 715	65	7 531	5.0	5 843	20 680
2015												
January	2 234	144 317	135 748	20 555	937	114 257	8 512	57	7 289	5.0	7 269	20 033
February	2 234	144 884	136 577	20 893	817	114 866	8 238	69	7 221	4.9	6 772	20 437
March	2 405	145 230	136 563	20 729	798	115 037	8 588	79	7 264	4.9	6 672	20 159
April	2 294	146 293	137 371	20 840	793	115 738	8 837	84	7 000	4.7	6 356	20 992
May	2 431	146 918	137 648	20 902	770	115 976	9 207	63	7 081	4.7	6 363	20 192
June	2 703	146 942	138 083	20 416	854	116 813	8 780	80	7 025	4.7	6 776	19 649
July	2 601	147 121	138 143	19 720	792	117 632	8 879	99	6 997	4.7	6 511	18 273
August	2 539	146 689	137 890	19 994	825	117 072	8 747	52	6 901	4.6	6 361	17 933
September	2 471	146 509	138 008	20 446	733	116 829	8 452	49	7 297	4.9	5 693	20 109
October	2 518	147 198	138 477	20 667	791	117 019	8 660	61	7 620	5.1	5 536	20 754
November	2 363	147 404	138 642	21 140	736	116 766	8 692	70	7 596	5.1	5 967	21 094
December	2 273	147 430	138 989	20 905	735	117 348	8 386	55	7 855	5.2	6 179	20 585
2016												
January	2 200	146 838	138 298	20 956	714	116 628	8 500	39	7 314	4.9	6 406	20 554
February	2 274	147 787	139 112	21 104	685	117 322	8 606	69	7 454	5.0	6 106	21 347
March	2 491	148 247	139 398	20 911	629	117 858	8 791	58	7 592	5.0	6 138	20 824
April	2 478	148 597	139 607	20 615	747	118 245	8 941	50	7 383	4.9	5 771	21 460
May	2 620	148 974	139 978	20 889	732	118 357	8 914	82	7 472	4.9	6 238	20 888
June	2 661	149 329	140 363	19 821	790	119 751	8 909	58	7 059	4.6	6 119	19 659
July	2 597	149 840	140 983	19 605	756	120 621	8 777	80	7 190	4.7	6 157	19 088
August	2 718	149 086	140 323	20 065	763	119 495	8 661	101	7 234	4.8	5 963	18 495
September	2 526	149 451	140 780	20 708	715	119 358	8 607	64	7 846	5.2	5 550	20 782
October	2 408	149 927	141 123	20 746	757	119 620	8 748	57	8 050	5.3	5 648	21 265
November	2 366	150 020	141 210	21 114	717	119 380	8 757	53	8 107	5.3	5 518	22 084
December	2 180	149 617	140 753	21 029	680	119 044	8 800	64	7 675	5.1	5 707	21 711

[1]Not seasonally adjusted.
... = Not available.

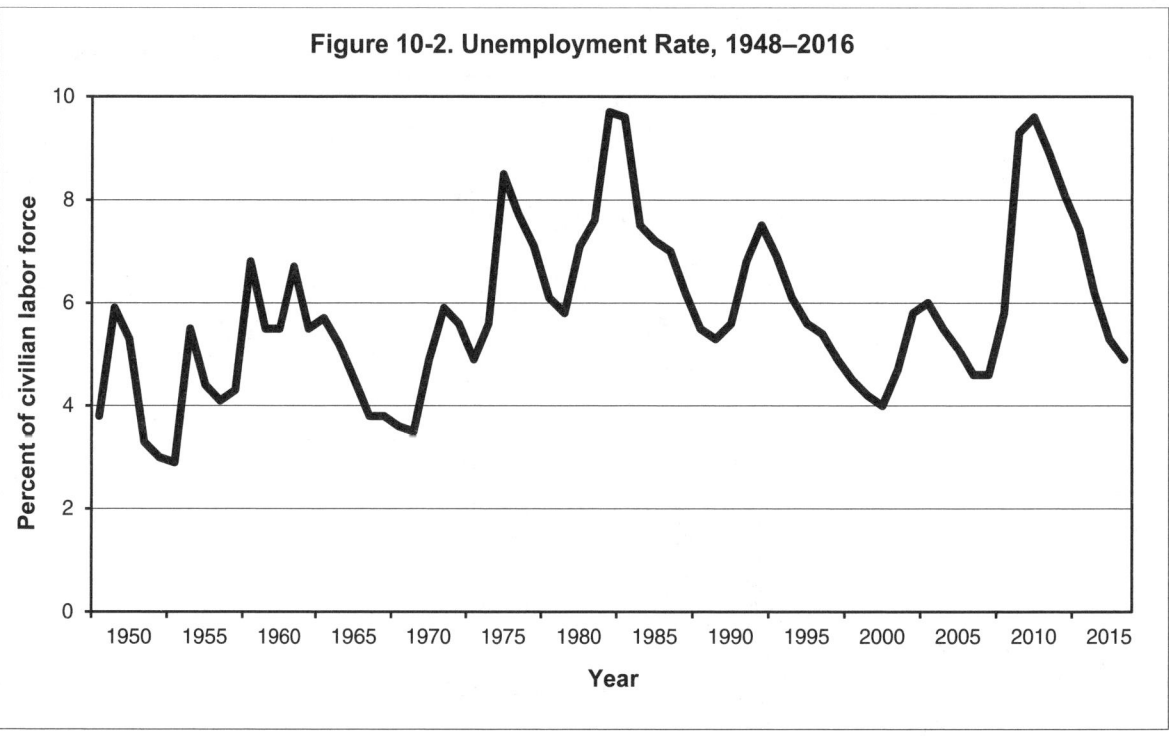

Figure 10-2. Unemployment Rate, 1948–2016

- The unemployment rate peaked at 10.0 percent in October 2009 (lagging, as it usually does, the business cycle trough, which was in June 2009). This was not quite as high as the postwar record of 10.8 percent, set in November and December 1982. Yet the employment losses of 2008–2009 were proportionately greater than the 2 percent drop in 1981–1982. The discrepancy is in labor force behavior. Recently, workers responded to job losses by dropping out of the labor force. However, in 1982, in contrast, labor force participation rates actually increased slightly. (Tables 10-1A and B)

- Unemployment hovered near 10 percent through early 2010, but has declined significantly since then to 4.7 percent in December 2016 reflecting continued employment growth with little or no labor force expansion. (Tables 10-1A and B and recent data)

- In 2010 and 2011, the median unemployed worker had been out of work for a median of 21.4 weeks, but duration then declined rapidly to 10.6 weeks in 2016. Still, this was in excess of the 10.1 weeks of the recession years 1983 and 2003. Median duration is more representative of the typical job-seeker than "average duration," which is distorted by the presence of a few extremely long-term unemployed and recently by a technical statistical problem. Even by this better measure, the rise in long-term unemployment has been large—and even understates the problem, since it does not include discouraged workers. (Table 10-5)

- Adding discouraged workers, workers marginally attached to the labor force, and persons on involuntary part time to get a comprehensive measure of the work gap, BLS calculates the "U-6" rate of combined unemployment and underutilization, which rose from 8.3 percent in the high-employment year 2007 to 16.7 percent in 2010. U-6 has since declined to 9.6 percent in 2017. (Table 10-5 and recent data)

Table 10-4. Unemployment by Demographic Group

(Unemployment in thousands of persons and as a percent of the civilian labor force in group, seasonally adjusted, except as noted.)

Year and month	Unemployment (thousands of persons)				Unemployment rate (percent)							
						By age and sex			By race			
	Total	Men, 20 years and over	Women, 20 years and over	Both sexes, 16 to 19 years	All civilian workers	Men, 20 years and over	Women, 20 years and over	Both sexes, 16 to 19 years	White	Black or African American	Asian [1]	Hispanic or Latino ethnicity
1970	4 093	1 638	1 349	1 106	4.9	3.5	4.8	15.3	4.5	...	...	...
1971	5 016	2 097	1 658	1 262	5.9	4.4	5.7	16.9	5.4	...	...	...
1972	4 882	1 948	1 625	1 308	5.6	4.0	5.4	16.2	5.1	10.4	...	...
1973	4 365	1 624	1 507	1 235	4.9	3.3	4.9	14.5	4.3	9.4	...	7.5
1974	5 156	1 957	1 777	1 422	5.6	3.8	5.5	16.0	5.0	10.5	...	8.1
1975	7 929	3 476	2 684	1 767	8.5	6.8	8.0	19.9	7.8	14.8	...	12.2
1976	7 406	3 098	2 588	1 719	7.7	5.9	7.4	19.0	7.0	14.0	...	11.5
1977	6 991	2 794	2 535	1 663	7.1	5.2	7.0	17.8	6.2	14.0	...	10.1
1978	6 202	2 328	2 292	1 583	6.1	4.3	6.0	16.4	5.2	12.8	...	9.1
1979	6 137	2 308	2 276	1 555	5.8	4.2	5.7	16.1	5.1	12.3	...	8.3
1980	7 637	3 353	2 615	1 669	7.1	5.9	6.4	17.8	6.3	14.3	...	10.1
1981	8 273	3 615	2 895	1 763	7.6	6.3	6.8	19.6	6.7	15.6	...	10.4
1982	10 678	5 089	3 613	1 977	9.7	8.8	8.3	23.2	8.6	18.9	...	13.8
1983	10 717	5 257	3 632	1 829	9.6	8.9	8.1	22.4	8.4	19.5	...	13.7
1984	8 539	3 932	3 107	1 499	7.5	6.6	6.8	18.9	6.5	15.9	...	10.7
1985	8 312	3 715	3 129	1 468	7.2	6.2	6.6	18.6	6.2	15.1	...	10.5
1986	8 237	3 751	3 032	1 454	7.0	6.1	6.2	18.3	6.0	14.5	...	10.6
1987	7 425	3 369	2 709	1 347	6.2	5.4	5.4	16.9	5.3	13.0	...	8.8
1988	6 701	2 987	2 487	1 226	5.5	4.8	4.9	15.3	4.7	11.7	...	8.2
1989	6 528	2 867	2 467	1 194	5.3	4.5	4.7	15.0	4.5	11.4	...	8.0
1990	7 047	3 239	2 596	1 212	5.6	5.0	4.9	15.5	4.8	11.4	...	8.2
1991	8 628	4 195	3 074	1 359	6.8	6.4	5.7	18.7	6.1	12.5	...	10.0
1992	9 613	4 717	3 469	1 427	7.5	7.1	6.3	20.1	6.6	14.2	...	11.6
1993	8 940	4 287	3 288	1 365	6.9	6.4	5.9	19.0	6.1	13.0	...	10.8
1994	7 996	3 627	3 049	1 320	6.1	5.4	5.4	17.6	5.3	11.5	...	9.9
1995	7 404	3 239	2 819	1 346	5.6	4.8	4.9	17.3	4.9	10.4	...	9.3
1996	7 236	3 146	2 783	1 306	5.4	4.6	4.8	16.7	4.7	10.5	...	8.9
1997	6 739	2 882	2 585	1 271	4.9	4.2	4.4	16.0	4.2	10.0	...	7.7
1998	6 210	2 580	2 424	1 205	4.5	3.7	4.1	14.6	3.9	8.9	...	7.2
1999	5 880	2 433	2 285	1 162	4.2	3.5	3.8	13.9	3.7	8.0	...	6.4
2000	5 692	2 376	2 235	1 081	4.0	3.3	3.6	13.1	3.5	7.6	3.6	5.7
2001	6 801	3 040	2 599	1 162	4.7	4.2	4.1	14.7	4.2	8.6	4.5	6.6
2002	8 378	3 896	3 228	1 253	5.8	5.3	5.1	16.5	5.1	10.2	5.9	7.5
2003	8 774	4 209	3 314	1 251	6.0	5.6	5.1	17.5	5.2	10.8	6.0	7.7
2004	8 149	3 791	3 150	1 208	5.5	5.0	4.9	17.0	4.8	10.4	4.4	7.0
2005	7 591	3 392	3 013	1 186	5.1	4.4	4.6	16.6	4.4	10.0	4.0	6.0
2006	7 001	3 131	2 751	1 119	4.6	4.0	4.1	15.4	4.0	8.9	3.0	5.2
2007	7 078	3 259	2 718	1 101	4.6	4.1	4.0	15.7	4.1	8.3	3.2	5.6
2008	8 924	4 297	3 342	1 285	5.8	5.4	4.9	18.7	5.2	10.1	4.0	7.6
2009	14 265	7 555	5 157	1 552	9.3	9.6	7.5	24.3	8.5	14.8	7.3	12.1
2010	14 825	7 763	5 534	1 528	9.6	9.8	8.0	25.9	8.7	16.0	7.5	12.5
2011	13 747	6 898	5 450	1 400	8.9	8.7	7.9	24.4	7.9	15.8	7.0	11.5
2012	12 506	5 984	5 125	1 397	8.1	7.5	7.3	24.0	7.2	13.8	5.9	10.3
2013	11 460	5 568	4 565	1 327	7.4	7.0	6.5	22.9	6.5	13.1	5.2	9.1
2014	9 617	4 585	3 926	1 106	6.2	5.7	5.6	19.6	5.3	11.3	5.0	7.4
2015	8 296	3 959	3 371	966	5.3	4.9	4.8	16.9	4.6	9.6	3.8	6.6
2016	7 751	3 675	3 151	925	4.9	4.5	5.5	15.7	4.3	8.4	3.6	5.8
2015												
January	9 498	4 815	3 660	1 023	6.1	6.0	5.2	19.2	5.3	10.7	4.1	7.5
February	9 095	4 723	3 468	904	5.8	5.9	4.9	17.1	5.1	10.4	4.1	7.3
March	8 682	4 411	3 352	920	5.6	5.5	4.8	17.0	4.9	10.0	3.1	7.0
April	7 966	3 921	3 206	840	5.1	4.9	4.5	15.6	4.4	8.9	4.2	6.3
May	8 370	3 965	3 381	1 025	5.3	4.9	4.8	17.8	4.5	10.0	3.9	6.3
June	8 638	3 759	3 433	1 446	5.5	4.6	4.9	21.4	4.8	9.8	4.1	6.8
July	8 805	3 779	3 854	1 172	5.6	4.6	5.5	17.1	4.9	9.7	4.2	7.0
August	8 162	3 581	3 585	996	5.2	4.4	5.1	16.5	4.5	9.9	3.4	6.6
September	7 628	3 523	3 239	865	4.9	4.4	4.6	16.2	4.2	9.1	3.5	5.9
October	7 597	3 559	3 209	830	4.8	4.4	4.5	15.4	4.1	9.1	3.5	6.0
November	7 573	3 637	3 147	790	4.8	4.5	4.4	14.9	4.1	9.1	3.9	6.3
December	7 542	3 836	2 924	782	4.8	4.8	4.1	14.2	4.2	8.1	4.0	6.2
2016												
January	8 309	4 087	3 338	885	5.3	5.1	4.7	16.5	4.7	9.1	3.7	6.6
February	8 219	4 158	3 213	848	5.2	5.1	4.5	15.5	4.6	8.9	3.9	5.9
March	8 116	4 020	3 248	848	5.1	4.9	4.5	15.4	4.4	9.0	3.9	5.7
April	7 413	3 628	2 983	802	4.7	4.4	4.2	14.6	4.1	8.2	3.6	5.6
May	7 207	3 396	2 870	940	4.5	4.2	4.0	16.2	3.9	8.0	3.9	5.2
June	8 144	3 536	3 288	1 320	5.1	4.3	4.6	19.2	4.5	8.8	3.7	6.0
July	8 267	3 698	3 389	1 179	5.1	4.5	4.8	16.3	4.5	8.9	4.1	5.6
August	7 996	3 487	3 514	996	5.0	4.2	4.9	15.4	4.4	8.4	4.2	5.6
September	7 658	3 561	3 193	904	4.8	4.3	4.4	15.8	4.2	8.2	3.8	6.1
October	7 447	3 527	3 064	856	4.7	4.3	4.3	15.1	4.1	8.4	3.3	5.5
November	7 066	3 347	2 906	814	4.4	4.1	4.0	14.6	3.9	7.8	3.0	5.6
December	7 170	3 656	2 810	704	4.5	4.5	3.9	12.7	4.1	7.4	2.6	5.9

[1] Not seasonally adjusted.
... = Not available.

Table 10-5. Unemployment Rates and Related Data

(Seasonally adjusted, except as noted.)

Year and month	Unemployment rates by marital status (percent of labor force in group)			Unemployment rates by reason for unemployment (percent of total civilian labor force in group.)					Duration of unemployment		Alternative measures of labor under-utilization (percent)		
	Married men, spouse present	Married women, spouse present	Women who maintain families[1]	Total	Job losers and persons who completed temporary jobs	Job leavers	Reentrants	New entrants	Average (mean) weeks unemployed	Median weeks unemployed	Including discouraged workers (U-4)	Including all marginally attached workers (U-5)	Including marginally attached and under-employed (U-6)
1970	2.6	4.9	5.4	4.9	2.2	0.7	1.5	0.6	8.6	4.9	. . .	. . .	. . .
1971	3.2	5.7	7.3	5.9	2.8	0.7	1.7	0.7	11.3	6.3	. . .	. . .	. . .
1972	2.8	5.4	7.2	5.6	2.4	0.7	1.7	0.8	12.0	6.2	. . .	. . .	. . .
1973	2.3	4.7	7.1	4.9	1.9	0.8	1.5	0.7	10.0	5.2	. . .	. . .	. . .
1974	2.7	5.3	7.0	5.6	2.4	0.8	1.6	0.7	9.8	5.2	. . .	. . .	. . .
1975	5.1	7.9	10.0	8.5	4.7	0.9	2.0	0.9	14.2	8.4	. . .	. . .	. . .
1976	4.2	7.1	10.1	7.7	3.8	0.9	2.0	0.9	15.8	8.2	. . .	. . .	. . .
1977	3.6	6.5	9.4	7.1	3.2	0.9	2.0	1.0	14.3	7.0	. . .	. . .	. . .
1978	2.8	5.5	8.5	6.1	2.5	0.9	1.8	0.9	11.9	5.9	. . .	. . .	. . .
1979	2.8	5.1	8.3	5.8	2.5	0.8	1.7	0.8	10.8	5.4	. . .	. . .	. . .
1980	4.2	5.8	9.2	7.1	3.7	0.8	1.8	0.8	11.9	6.5	. . .	. . .	. . .
1981	4.3	6.0	10.4	7.6	3.9	0.8	1.9	0.9	13.7	6.9	. . .	. . .	. . .
1982	6.5	7.4	11.7	9.7	5.7	0.8	2.2	1.1	15.6	8.7	. . .	. . .	. . .
1983	6.5	7.0	12.2	9.6	5.6	0.7	2.2	1.1	20.0	10.1	. . .	. . .	. . .
1984	4.6	5.7	10.3	7.5	3.9	0.7	1.9	1.0	18.2	7.9	. . .	. . .	. . .
1985	4.3	5.6	10.4	7.2	3.6	0.8	2.0	0.9	15.6	6.8	. . .	. . .	. . .
1986	4.4	5.2	9.8	7.0	3.4	0.9	1.8	0.9	15.0	6.9	. . .	. . .	. . .
1987	3.9	4.3	9.2	6.2	3.0	0.8	1.6	0.8	14.5	6.5	. . .	. . .	. . .
1988	3.3	3.9	8.1	5.5	2.5	0.8	1.5	0.7	13.5	5.9	. . .	. . .	. . .
1989	3.0	3.7	8.1	5.3	2.4	0.8	1.5	0.5	11.9	4.8	. . .	. . .	. . .
1990	3.4	3.8	8.3	5.6	2.7	0.8	1.5	0.5	12.0	5.3	. . .	. . .	. . .
1991	4.4	4.5	9.3	6.8	3.7	0.8	1.7	0.6	13.7	6.8	. . .	. . .	. . .
1992	5.1	5.0	10.0	7.5	4.2	0.8	1.8	0.7	17.7	8.7	. . .	. . .	. . .
1993	4.4	4.6	9.7	6.9	3.8	0.8	1.7	0.7	18.0	8.3	. . .	. . .	. . .
1994	3.7	4.1	8.9	6.1	2.9	0.6	2.1	0.5	18.8	9.2	6.5	7.4	10.9
1995	3.3	3.9	8.0	5.6	2.6	0.6	1.9	0.4	16.6	8.3	5.9	6.7	10.1
1996	3.0	3.6	8.2	5.4	2.5	0.6	1.9	0.4	16.7	8.3	5.7	6.5	9.7
1997	2.7	3.1	8.1	4.9	2.2	0.6	1.7	0.4	15.8	8.0	5.2	5.9	8.9
1998	2.4	2.9	7.2	4.5	2.1	0.5	1.5	0.4	14.5	6.7	4.7	5.4	8.0
1999	2.2	2.7	6.4	4.2	1.9	0.6	1.4	0.3	13.4	6.4	4.4	5.0	7.4
2000	2.0	2.7	5.9	4.0	1.8	0.5	1.4	0.3	12.6	5.9	4.2	4.8	7.0
2001	2.7	3.1	6.6	4.7	2.4	0.6	1.4	0.3	13.1	6.8	4.9	5.6	8.1
2002	3.6	3.7	8.0	5.8	3.2	0.6	1.6	0.4	16.6	9.1	6.0	6.7	9.6
2003	3.8	3.7	8.5	6.0	3.3	0.6	1.7	0.4	19.2	10.1	6.3	7.0	10.1
2004	3.1	3.5	8.0	5.5	2.8	0.6	1.6	0.5	19.6	9.8	5.8	6.5	9.6
2005	2.8	3.3	7.8	5.1	2.5	0.6	1.6	0.4	18.4	8.9	5.4	6.1	8.9
2006	2.4	2.9	7.1	4.6	2.2	0.5	1.5	0.4	16.8	8.3	4.9	5.5	8.2
2007	2.5	2.8	6.5	4.6	2.3	0.5	1.4	0.4	16.8	8.5	4.9	5.5	8.3
2008	3.4	3.6	8.0	5.8	3.1	0.6	1.6	0.5	17.9	9.4	6.1	6.8	10.5
2009	6.6	5.5	11.5	9.3	5.9	0.6	2.1	0.7	24.4	15.1	9.7	10.5	16.2
2010	6.8	5.9	12.3	9.6	6.0	0.6	2.3	0.8	33.0	21.4	10.3	11.1	16.7
2011	5.8	5.6	12.4	8.9	5.3	0.6	2.2	0.8	39.3	21.4	9.5	10.4	15.9
2012	4.9	5.3	11.4	8.1	4.4	0.6	2.2	0.8	39.4	19.3	8.6	9.5	14.7
2013	4.3	4.6	10.2	7.4	3.9	0.6	2.1	0.8	36.5	17.0	7.9	8.8	13.8
2014	3.4	3.8	6.6	6.2	3.1	0.5	1.8	0.7	33.7	14.0	6.6	7.5	12.0
2015	2.8	3.2	7.4	5.3	2.6	0.5	1.6	0.6	29.2	11.6	5.7	6.5	10.4
2016	2.7	3.0	6.8	4.9	2.3	0.5	1.5	0.5	27.5	10.6	5.2	5.9	9.6
2015													
January	3.0	3.4	8.1	5.7	3.1	0.6	1.8	0.6	30.3	12.3	6.1	7.0	11.3
February	3.0	3.3	7.7	5.5	3.0	0.6	1.7	0.5	31.1	13.1	6.0	6.8	11.0
March	2.8	3.0	8.1	5.4	2.9	0.5	1.7	0.5	31.3	13.2	5.9	6.7	10.9
April	3.0	3.3	7.0	5.4	2.5	0.5	1.6	0.5	32.8	13.5	5.9	6.7	10.8
May	2.9	3.3	6.8	5.5	2.5	0.5	1.7	0.6	31.9	12.6	5.8	6.6	10.7
June	2.8	3.1	7.8	5.3	2.5	0.5	1.7	0.8	26.2	9.4	5.6	6.4	10.5
July	2.8	3.2	8.0	5.2	2.7	0.6	1.6	0.7	26.5	9.4	5.6	6.4	10.3
August	2.8	3.1	8.1	5.1	2.5	0.5	1.5	0.6	27.6	11.0	5.5	6.2	10.2
September	2.7	3.0	7.1	5.0	2.2	0.5	1.6	0.5	26.2	11.4	5.4	6.2	10.0
October	2.7	3.0	7.5	5.0	2.3	0.5	1.6	0.5	28.9	11.7	5.4	6.2	9.8
November	2.7	3.1	6.9	5.0	2.3	0.5	1.5	0.5	29.1	11.4	5.4	6.1	9.9
December	2.7	3.0	5.8	5.0	2.4	0.5	1.4	0.5	27.6	10.9	5.4	6.1	9.9
2016													
January	2.6	3.0	7.1	4.9	2.7	0.5	1.6	0.5	27.6	10.5	5.3	6.2	9.9
February	2.5	3.0	7.0	4.9	2.7	0.5	1.6	0.5	29.0	11.7	5.3	6.0	9.8
March	2.9	3.1	6.8	5.0	2.6	0.5	1.5	0.4	29.1	12.7	5.4	6.0	9.8
April	2.7	3.1	6.7	5.0	2.3	0.5	1.4	0.5	29.8	13.2	5.3	6.0	9.7
May	2.6	2.9	6.6	4.7	2.1	0.5	1.5	0.5	27.8	11.4	5.0	5.7	9.7
June	2.7	3.2	7.3	4.9	2.3	0.5	1.5	0.8	25.7	8.3	5.2	6.0	9.6
July	2.6	3.0	7.2	4.9	2.4	0.5	1.5	0.7	26.3	9.6	5.2	6.0	9.7
August	2.7	3.0	7.9	4.9	2.4	0.6	1.4	0.6	26.7	10.3	5.3	5.9	9.7
September	2.9	3.0	6.4	4.9	2.2	0.6	1.5	0.5	27.2	10.2	5.3	6.0	9.7
October	2.8	3.0	6.1	4.8	2.1	0.6	1.5	0.5	27.9	10.5	5.1	5.9	9.5
November	2.7	2.7	6.2	4.6	2.1	0.6	1.4	0.4	27.1	10.5	5.0	5.8	9.3
December	2.7	2.9	5.8	4.7	2.3	0.5	1.3	0.4	25.8	10.5	5.0	5.7	9.2

[1]Not seasonally adjusted.
. . . = Not available.

Table 10-6. Labor Force and Employment Estimates Smoothed for Population Adjustments (Unofficial)

(Thousands of persons, seasonally adjusted.)

Year	January	February	March	April	May	June	July	August	September	October	November	December
CIVILIAN LABOR FORCE												
1990	125 845	125 734	125 837	125 697	125 953	125 645	125 816	126 087	126 001	126 116	126 203	126 287
1991	126 112	126 189	126 742	126 742	126 382	126 549	126 384	126 392	126 905	126 909	126 981	126 956
1992	127 566	127 524	127 934	128 184	128 475	128 829	128 945	129 008	128 908	128 444	128 872	128 998
1993	128 856	128 926	129 079	129 077	129 772	129 932	129 931	130 166	129 826	130 145	130 296	130 539
1994	131 210	131 296	131 038	131 272	131 444	131 237	131 341	131 980	132 139	132 477	132 637	132 710
1995	132 811	132 901	132 906	133 404	132 673	132 784	133 193	133 199	133 489	133 607	133 517	133 426
1996	133 545	133 896	134 138	134 381	134 654	134 697	135 302	135 083	135 560	135 982	136 082	136 202
1997	136 560	136 517	137 025	137 164	137 281	137 387	137 668	137 824	137 894	137 865	138 209	138 418
1998	138 370	138 401	138 539	138 465	138 703	138 800	138 947	138 942	139 679	139 685	139 801	140 070
1999	140 456	140 433	140 207	140 452	140 615	140 852	140 977	140 981	141 189	141 353	141 623	141 790
2000	142 260	142 443	142 414	142 724	142 355	142 551	142 232	142 461	142 458	142 556	142 889	143 168
2001	143 713	143 607	143 823	143 462	143 204	143 237	143 527	143 150	143 848	143 938	144 085	144 143
2002	143 715	144 477	144 299	144 536	144 742	144 605	144 593	144 792	145 327	145 083	144 803	144 822
2003	145 054	145 193	145 091	145 517	145 519	146 047	146 047	145 392	145 453	145 614	145 871	145 579
2004	146 111	145 963	146 182	146 074	146 273	146 651	146 867	146 724	146 561	146 922	147 274	147 156
2005	147 161	147 480	147 493	148 010	148 329	148 292	148 470	148 800	148 960	148 992	149 041	148 992
2006	149 292	149 704	149 862	149 917	150 091	150 361	150 371	150 695	150 629	150 993	151 342	151 653
2007	151 885	151 711	151 764	151 138	151 356	151 709	151 708	151 390	152 035	151 791	152 422	152 490
2008	153 260	152 844	153 090	152 943	153 466	153 468	153 614	153 777	153 698	153 994	153 750	153 758
2009	153 759	154 082	153 674	154 044	154 277	154 242	154 025	153 826	153 344	153 297	153 386	152 618
2010	153 161	153 478	153 724	154 402	153 869	153 396	153 473	153 855	153 741	153 403	153 900	153 414
2011	153 485	153 572	153 701	153 870	153 835	153 694	153 629	154 051	154 392	154 278	154 416	154 276
2012	154 422	154 924	154 913	154 671	155 056	155 248	155 087	154 790	155 143	155 636	155 412	155 622
2013	156 059	155 635	155 271	155 653	155 820	156 026	155 903	155 806	155 832	154 903	155 600	155 348
2014	155 771	155 979	156 478	155 722	155 937	156 014	156 369	156 345	156 177	156 582	156 747	156 479
2015	156 842	156 588	156 595	156 854	157 254	156 798	156 927	156 908	156 606	156 916	157 148	157 743
2016	157 922	158 440	158 823	158 479	158 045	158 418	158 816	159 022	159 338	159 145	158 953	159 130
CIVILIAN EMPLOYMENT, TOTAL												
1990	119 093	119 082	119 238	118 898	119 209	119 052	118 891	118 894	118 628	118 651	118 432	118 379
1991	118 089	117 915	117 823	118 293	117 634	117 845	117 785	117 712	118 169	118 052	118 033	117 740
1992	118 265	118 050	118 454	118 748	118 709	118 764	119 071	119 195	119 101	119 020	119 280	119 413
1993	119 503	119 715	119 995	119 938	120 594	120 781	120 970	121 373	121 081	121 363	121 722	122 031
1994	122 547	122 679	122 534	122 908	123 497	123 277	123 362	124 013	124 372	124 811	125 230	125 448
1995	125 402	125 681	125 720	125 722	125 207	125 321	125 629	125 677	125 972	126 241	126 052	125 963
1996	126 013	126 542	126 779	126 924	127 189	127 562	127 922	128 161	128 540	128 909	128 801	128 904
1997	129 358	129 370	129 981	130 247	130 584	130 544	130 970	131 172	131 194	131 368	131 859	131 898
1998	131 958	132 053	132 072	132 484	132 614	132 545	132 643	132 718	133 333	133 359	133 655	133 994
1999	134 436	134 276	134 381	134 402	134 775	134 855	134 905	135 097	135 227	135 529	135 862	136 092
2000	136 552	136 585	136 681	137 243	136 597	136 900	136 485	136 609	136 833	137 022	137 249	137 534
2001	137 691	137 519	137 683	137 193	136 979	136 754	136 945	136 109	136 707	136 246	136 086	135 889
2002	135 536	136 266	135 998	135 941	136 347	136 216	136 207	136 492	137 082	136 781	136 289	136 187
2003	136 580	136 622	136 552	136 727	136 616	136 838	136 501	136 553	136 590	136 940	137 354	137 318
2004	137 771	137 827	137 724	137 935	138 092	138 398	138 763	138 766	138 666	138 895	139 377	139 257
2005	139 407	139 533	139 786	140 369	140 708	140 798	141 094	141 486	141 439	141 571	141 508	141 746
2006	142 251	142 544	142 814	142 821	143 135	143 385	143 222	143 630	143 806	144 289	144 495	144 915
2007	144 807	144 821	145 068	144 326	144 626	144 770	144 599	144 364	144 907	144 597	145 226	144 892
2008	145 583	145 354	145 276	145 314	145 083	144 905	144 693	144 358	144 223	143 943	143 237	142 502
2009	141 691	141 176	140 242	140 187	139 776	139 534	139 422	139 010	138 334	137 946	138 168	137 520
2010	138 202	138 351	138 505	139 062	139 002	138 904	138 937	139 186	139 153	138 873	138 793	139 030
2011	139 529	139 669	139 908	139 880	139 916	139 676	139 796	140 182	140 437	140 624	141 042	141 136
2012	141 764	142 034	142 174	142 061	142 359	142 537	142 381	142 316	143 063	143 489	143 357	143 339
2013	143 539	143 646	143 597	143 894	144 125	144 266	144 522	144 541	144 556	143 716	144 761	144 948
2014	145 467	145 568	146 069	146 002	146 152	146 537	146 696	146 752	146 914	147 573	147 650	147 767
2015	147 888	147 933	148 065	148 340	148 607	148 554	148 699	148 898	148 735	149 055	149 216	149 823
2016	150 114	150 616	150 867	150 590	150 614	150 640	151 088	151 192	151 456	151 426	151 566	151 623

Table 10-7. Insured Unemployment

(Averages of weekly data; thousands of persons, except as noted.)

Year and month	State programs, seasonally adjusted		
	Initial claims	Insured unemployment	Insured unemployment rate (percent) [1]
1976	383	2 978	4.5
1977	374	2 644	3.9
1978	341	2 337	3.3
1979	383	2 428	3.0
1980	488	3 365	3.9
1981	451	3 032	3.5
1982	586	4 094	4.7
1983	441	3 337	3.9
1984	374	2 452	2.8
1985	392	2 584	2.9
1986	378	2 632	2.8
1987	325	2 273	2.4
1988	309	2 075	2.1
1989	330	2 174	2.1
1990	385	2 539	2.4
1991	447	3 338	3.2
1992	409	3 208	3.1
1993	344	2 768	2.6
1994	340	2 667	2.5
1995	359	2 590	2.4
1996	352	2 552	2.3
1997	322	2 300	2.0
1998	317	2 213	1.9
1999	298	2 186	1.8
2000	299	2 112	1.7
2001	406	3 016	2.4
2002	404	3 570	2.8
2003	402	3 532	2.8
2004	342	2 930	2.3
2005	331	2 660	2.1
2006	312	2 456	1.9
2007	321	2 548	1.9
2008	418	3 337	2.5
2009	574	5 808	4.4
2010	459	4 544	3.6
2011	409	3 744	3.0
2012	374	3 319	2.6
2013	343	2 978	2.3
2014	308	2 599	2.0
2015	278	2 267	1.7
2016	263	2 136	1.6
2014			
January	327	2 893	2.2
February	336	2 867	2.2
March	323	2 790	2.1
April	324	2 724	2.1
May	314	2 652	2.0
June	314	2 584	2.0
July	302	2 536	1.9
August	301	2 504	1.9
September	298	2 441	1.9
October	287	2 413	1.8
November	293	2 407	1.8
December	285	2 388	1.8
2015			
January	288	2 373	1.8
February	301	2 366	1.8
March	286	2 343	1.8
April	287	2 283	1.7
May	274	2 241	1.7
June	275	2 266	1.7
July	277	2 245	1.7
August	274	2 253	1.7
September	272	2 231	1.7
October	265	2 192	1.6
November	270	2 205	1.6
December	272	2 216	1.6
2016			
January	280	2 233	1.6
February	268	2 221	1.6
March	268	2 187	1.6
April	265	2 153	1.6
May	275	2 151	1.6
June	267	2 145	1.6
July	260	2 143	1.6
August	261	2 145	1.6
September	255	2 097	1.5
October	254	2 055	1.5
November	250	2 041	1.5
December	253	2 071	1.5

[1] Insured unemployed as a percent of employment covered by state programs.

SECTION 10B: PAYROLL EMPLOYMENT, HOURS, AND EARNINGS

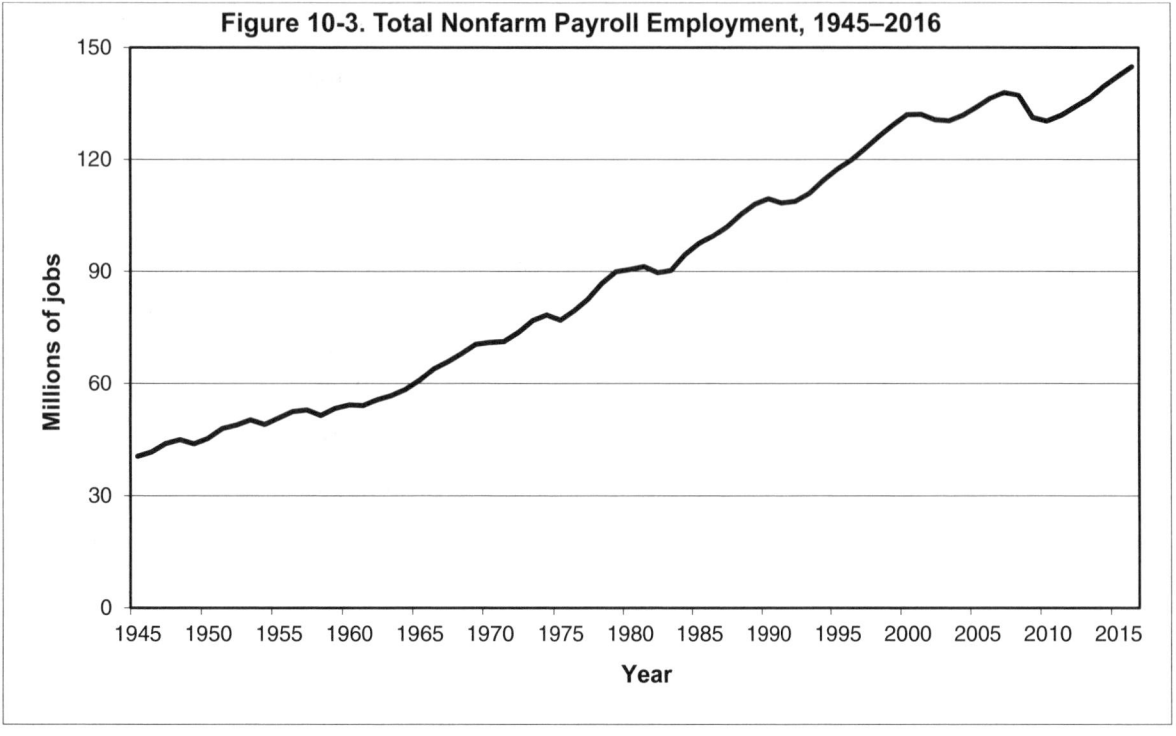

Figure 10-3. Total Nonfarm Payroll Employment, 1945–2016

- Nonfarm payroll employment peaked in January 2008 and plunged 6.3 percent, a postwar record, between then and its lowest point in February 2010. The total number of jobs lost by this measure was 8.7 million. (Table 10-9)

- Data for December 2016 indicate a nonfarm payroll job gain of nearly 16 million since the February 2010 low, comparable to the recent gains in the household survey featured in the previous section. Differences in concepts and measurement practice between these two employment surveys are discussed in the Notes and Definitions to this chapter. (Table 10-9)

- The diffusion index indicates the percentage of private industries in which employment is higher than six months earlier. Diffusion indexes measure the extent to which expansion or contraction have spread throughout the economy; indexes below 50 percent indicate recession. This index reached a low of 12.2 percent in April 2009—lower than the lowest points reached in any of the previous four recessions (1980, 1981–1982, 1990–1991, and 2001), and thus indicating the most widespread and pervasive decline in 30 years or more. Gains have been widespread during the recovery, with 75 percent of industries showing increases in early 2012. However, the August 2016 rate fell to 58.6. By December 2016, the diffusion index rose to 60.2 percent. (Table 10-8)

Table 10-8. Nonfarm Payroll Employment by NAICS Supersector: Recent Data

(Thousands; seasonally adjusted, except as noted.)

Year and month	Total	Private Total	Goods-producing Total	Mining and logging	Construction	Manufacturing Total	Durable	Nondurable	Service-providing Total	Private Total	Trade, transportation, and utilities Total	Wholesale trade	Retail trade
2005	134 005	112 201	22 190	628	7 336	14 227	8 956	5 271	111 814	90 010	25 959	5 764	15 280
2006	136 398	114 424	22 530	684	7 691	14 155	8 981	5 174	113 867	91 894	26 276	5 905	15 353
2007	137 936	115 718	22 233	724	7 630	13 879	8 808	5 071	115 703	93 485	26 630	6 015	15 520
2008	137 170	114 661	21 335	767	7 162	13 406	8 463	4 943	115 835	93 326	26 293	5 943	15 283
2009	131 233	108 678	18 558	694	6 016	11 847	7 284	4 564	112 675	90 121	24 906	5 587	14 522
2010	130 275	107 785	17 751	705	5 518	11 528	7 064	4 464	112 524	90 034	24 636	5 452	14 440
2011	131 842	109 756	18 047	788	5 533	11 726	7 273	4 453	113 795	91 708	25 065	5 543	14 668
2012	134 104	112 184	18 420	848	5 646	11 927	7 470	4 457	115 683	93 763	25 476	5 667	14 841
2013	136 368	114 504	18 700	868	5 827	12 006	7 543	4 463	117 668	95 804	25 870	5 747	15 077
2014	130 678	117 670	19 260	904	6 231	12 225	7 708	4 517	120 218	98 310	26 490	5 824	15 414
2015	142 253	120 196	19 614	778	6 490	12 346	7 769	4 577	122 639	100 582	26 938	5 843	15 631
2016	144 882	122 566	19 718	661	6 727	12 330	7 693	4 637	125 164	102 848	27 322	5 878	15 887
2012													
January	133 188	111 246	18 304	840	5 627	11 837	7 395	4 442	114 884	92 942	25 355	5 621	14 818
February	133 414	111 474	18 327	846	5 622	11 859	7 419	4 440	115 087	93 147	25 368	5 632	14 803
March	133 657	111 720	18 377	849	5 627	11 901	7 447	4 454	115 280	93 343	25 396	5 642	14 808
April	133 753	111 822	18 396	850	5 630	11 916	7 460	4 456	115 357	93 426	25 417	5 656	14 833
May	133 863	111 953	18 394	853	5 613	11 928	7 470	4 458	115 469	93 559	25 457	5 666	14 827
June	133 951	112 028	18 411	852	5 620	11 939	7 480	4 459	115 540	93 617	25 447	5 673	14 814
July	134 111	112 200	18 465	851	5 635	11 979	7 518	4 461	115 646	93 735	25 451	5 680	14 802
August	134 261	112 336	18 452	849	5 647	11 956	7 492	4 464	115 809	93 884	25 470	5 683	14 802
September	134 422	112 495	18 436	846	5 648	11 942	7 477	4 465	115 986	94 059	25 495	5 673	14 834
October	134 647	112 750	18 452	839	5 666	11 947	7 481	4 466	116 195	94 298	25 545	5 688	14 861
November	134 850	112 961	18 484	846	5 687	11 951	7 493	4 458	116 366	94 477	25 618	5 693	14 915
December	135 064	113 176	18 536	851	5 720	11 965	7 505	4 460	116 528	94 640	25 638	5 698	14 917
2013													
January	135 261	113 395	18 579	854	5 743	11 982	7 514	4 468	116 682	94 816	25 691	5 714	14 944
February	135 541	113 658	18 651	858	5 789	12 004	7 527	4 477	116 890	95 007	25 691	5 717	14 953
March	135 682	113 822	18 680	860	5 813	12 007	7 533	4 474	117 002	95 142	25 683	5 718	14 944
April	135 885	114 010	18 669	857	5 811	12 001	7 533	4 468	117 216	95 341	25 718	5 724	14 967
May	136 084	114 232	18 671	861	5 816	11 994	7 531	4 463	117 413	95 561	25 760	5 732	15 002
June	136 285	114 433	18 684	864	5 829	11 991	7 532	4 459	117 601	95 749	25 811	5 737	15 040
July	136 434	114 603	18 679	867	5 830	11 982	7 526	4 456	117 755	95 924	25 862	5 749	15 089
August	136 636	114 783	18 696	870	5 836	11 990	7 540	4 450	117 940	96 087	25 911	5 760	15 118
September	136 800	114 936	18 718	876	5 849	11 993	7 549	4 444	118 082	96 218	25 973	5 771	15 146
October	137 037	115 183	18 756	881	5 864	12 011	7 562	4 449	118 281	96 427	26 017	5 769	15 187
November	137 311	115 455	18 824	882	5 896	12 046	7 581	4 465	118 487	96 631	26 090	5 786	15 210
December	137 395	115 541	18 811	882	5 876	12 053	7 581	4 472	118 584	96 730	26 156	5 797	15 262
2014													
January	137 564	115 759	18 947	870	5 989	12 088	7 586	4 502	118 617	96 812	26 150	5 776	15 255
February	137 715	115 898	18 994	874	6 010	12 110	7 607	4 503	118 721	96 904	26 134	5 783	15 233
March	137 987	116 159	19 052	880	6 047	12 125	7 624	4 501	118 935	97 107	26 167	5 787	15 244
April	138 316	116 458	19 114	886	6 086	12 142	7 635	4 507	119 202	97 344	26 243	5 803	15 292
May	138 562	116 710	19 150	888	6 112	12 150	7 650	4 500	119 412	97 560	26 293	5 807	15 310
June	138 866	116 969	19 196	893	6 132	12 171	7 669	4 502	119 670	97 773	26 365	5 818	15 348
July	139 068	117 195	19 256	898	6 174	12 184	7 684	4 500	119 812	97 939	26 415	5 824	15 370
August	139 298	117 433	19 311	899	6 204	12 208	7 698	4 510	119 987	98 122	26 439	5 825	15 379
September	139 578	117 670	19 360	904	6 231	12 225	7 708	4 517	120 218	98 310	26 490	5 824	15 414
October	139 805	117 884	19 402	899	6 251	12 252	7 727	4 525	120 403	98 482	26 545	5 833	15 435
November	140 117	118 186	19 442	898	6 269	12 275	7 741	4 534	120 675	98 744	26 627	5 836	15 486
December	140 372	118 426	19 477	894	6 292	12 291	7 752	4 539	120 895	98 949	26 664	5 847	15 491
2015													
January	140 606	118 653	19 521	886	6 336	12 299	7 756	4 543	121 085	99 132	26 705	5 849	15 508
February	140 844	118 875	19 542	874	6 362	12 306	7 763	4 543	121 302	99 333	26 738	5 858	15 525
March	140 930	118 972	19 530	860	6 351	12 319	7 769	4 550	121 400	99 442	26 765	5 859	15 538
April	141 192	119 207	19 560	844	6 395	12 321	7 765	4 556	121 632	99 647	26 783	5 856	15 550
May	141 536	119 531	19 591	822	6 432	12 337	7 775	4 562	121 945	99 940	26 846	5 859	15 590
June	141 742	119 726	19 603	819	6 446	12 338	7 775	4 563	122 139	100 123	26 888	5 857	15 611
July	141 996	119 965	19 627	808	6 467	12 352	7 774	4 578	122 369	100 338	26 935	5 857	15 634
August	142 153	120 080	19 624	795	6 482	12 347	7 774	4 573	122 529	100 456	26 935	5 855	15 628
September	142 253	120 196	19 614	778	6 490	12 346	7 769	4 577	122 639	100 582	26 938	5 843	15 631
October	142 574	120 510	19 656	769	6 534	12 353	7 765	4 588	122 918	100 854	26 963	5 850	15 651
November	142 846	120 770	19 688	753	6 589	12 346	7 748	4 598	123 158	101 082	27 041	5 852	15 690
December	143 085	120 987	19 730	743	6 628	12 359	7 748	4 611	123 355	101 257	27 043	5 853	15 678
2016													
January	143 211	121 097	19 754	728	6 639	12 387	7 766	4 621	123 457	101 343	27 072	5 856	15 718
February	143 448	121 318	19 747	710	6 662	12 375	7 753	4 622	123 701	101 571	27 123	5 854	15 767
March	143 673	121 507	19 752	692	6 705	12 355	7 736	4 619	123 921	101 755	27 167	5 856	15 797
April	143 826	121 665	19 743	683	6 704	12 356	7 735	4 621	124 083	101 922	27 177	5 861	15 792
May	143 869	121 682	19 699	674	6 690	12 335	7 712	4 623	124 170	101 983	27 187	5 857	15 800
June	144 166	121 951	19 705	668	6 690	12 347	7 714	4 633	124 461	102 246	27 209	5 858	15 825
July	144 457	122 200	19 731	664	6 708	12 359	7 723	4 636	124 726	102 469	27 245	5 861	15 843
August	144 633	122 343	19 707	661	6 704	12 342	7 703	4 639	124 926	102 636	27 282	5 864	15 860
September	144 882	122 566	19 718	661	6 727	12 330	7 693	4 637	125 164	102 848	27 322	5 878	15 887
October	145 006	122 698	19 727	659	6 743	12 325	7 692	4 633	125 279	102 971	27 331	5 881	15 881
November	145 170	122 876	19 762	666	6 771	12 325	7 695	4 630	125 408	103 114	27 346	5 887	15 868
December	145 325	123 026	19 794	668	6 783	12 343	7 708	4 635	125 531	103 232	27 374	5 888	15 881

Table 10-8. Nonfarm Payroll Employment by NAICS Supersector: Recent Data—*Continued*

(Thousands; seasonally adjusted, except as noted.)

Year and month	Information	Financial activities	Professional and business services	Education and health services	Leisure and hospitality	Other services	Government Total	Federal Total	Federal Department of Defense 1	State Total	State Education	Local Total	Local Education	Diffusion index, 6-month span, private nonfarm 2
2005	3 061	8 197	16 954	17 630	12 816	5 395	21 804	2 732	488	5 032	2 260	14 041	7 856	63.2
2006	3 038	8 367	17 566	18 099	13 110	5 438	21 974	2 732	493	5 075	2 293	14 167	7 913	59.6
2007	3 032	8 348	17 942	18 613	13 427	5 494	22 218	2 734	491	5 122	2 318	14 362	7 987	57.1
2008	2 984	8 206	17 735	19 156	13 436	5 515	22 509	2 762	496	5 177	2 354	14 571	8 084	27.4
2009	2 804	7 838	16 579	19 550	13 077	5 367	22 555	2 832	519	5 169	2 360	14 554	8 079	19.2
2010	2 707	7 695	16 728	19 889	13 049	5 331	22 490	2 977	545	5 137	2 373	14 376	8 013	61.3
2011	2 674	7 697	17 332	20 228	13 353	5 360	22 086	2 859	559	5 078	2 374	14 150	7 873	73.8
2012	2 676	7 784	17 932	20 698	13 768	5 430	21 920	2 820	552	5 055	2 389	14 045	7 778	62.6
2013	2 685	7 880	18 560	21 102	14 242	5 464	21 864	2 766	537	5 048	2 393	14 050	7 783	64.4
2014	2 734	8 006	19 189	21 541	14 775	5 575	21 908	2 736	524	5 043	2 379	14 129	7 847	78.0
2015	2 764	8 149	19 705	22 140	15 266	5 620	22 057	2 761	526	5 086	2 407	14 210	7 865	64.6
2016	2 786	8 324	20 279	22 745	15 684	5 708	22 316	2 811	529	5 101	2 423	14 404	7 968	63.6
2012														
January	2 673	7 733	17 694	20 479	13 594	5 414	21 942	2 833	557	5 048	2 373	14 061	7 793	72.4
February	2 673	7 741	17 752	20 563	13 638	5 412	21 940	2 827	555	5 049	2 376	14 064	7 796	75.1
March	2 675	7 765	17 790	20 593	13 703	5 421	21 937	2 826	552	5 053	2 379	14 058	7 788	74.3
April	2 677	7 766	17 835	20 613	13 700	5 418	21 931	2 826	554	5 058	2 383	14 047	7 781	74.7
May	2 680	7 778	17 864	20 656	13 705	5 419	21 910	2 825	553	5 049	2 379	14 036	7 770	75.1
June	2 675	7 781	17 912	20 666	13 711	5 425	21 923	2 824	553	5 056	2 387	14 043	7 772	70.5
July	2 679	7 781	17 964	20 689	13 739	5 432	21 911	2 814	552	5 053	2 388	14 044	7 774	67.0
August	2 680	7 789	17 998	20 706	13 810	5 431	21 925	2 819	551	5 058	2 397	14 048	7 781	63.2
September	2 673	7 803	18 014	20 765	13 868	5 441	21 927	2 819	550	5 074	2 411	14 034	7 772	62.6
October	2 672	7 812	18 078	20 858	13 889	5 444	21 897	2 821	551	5 052	2 395	14 024	7 762	63.8
November	2 681	7 816	18 132	20 862	13 921	5 447	21 889	2 816	547	5 052	2 395	14 021	7 760	64.2
December	2 674	7 827	18 165	20 904	13 981	5 451	21 888	2 814	547	5 050	2 393	14 024	7 763	67.4
2013														
January	2 673	7 835	18 210	20 921	14 028	5 458	21 866	2 809	547	5 034	2 371	14 023	7 763	66.7
February	2 692	7 847	18 295	20 948	14 078	5 456	21 883	2 810	546	5 049	2 392	14 024	7 764	67.0
March	2 694	7 853	18 362	20 989	14 112	5 449	21 860	2 789	545	5 056	2 400	14 015	7 764	68.8
April	2 688	7 863	18 434	21 040	14 145	5 453	21 875	2 791	543	5 053	2 400	14 031	7 768	68.0
May	2 686	7 872	18 511	21 069	14 198	5 465	21 852	2 768	540	5 047	2 394	14 037	7 769	68.4
June	2 685	7 885	18 570	21 084	14 249	5 465	21 852	2 767	538	5 034	2 383	14 051	7 770	67.6
July	2 697	7 901	18 621	21 108	14 272	5 463	21 831	2 756	535	5 025	2 372	14 050	7 779	65.9
August	2 669	7 897	18 663	21 172	14 306	5 469	21 853	2 749	533	5 039	2 386	14 065	7 795	62.6
September	2 682	7 896	18 700	21 181	14 315	5 471	21 864	2 744	531	5 051	2 397	14 069	7 798	64.4
October	2 688	7 903	18 753	21 212	14 380	5 474	21 854	2 732	530	5 057	2 400	14 065	7 794	68.2
November	2 689	7 899	18 826	21 237	14 417	5 473	21 856	2 739	528	5 060	2 405	14 057	7 781	69.9
December	2 674	7 901	18 842	21 242	14 435	5 480	21 854	2 736	527	5 064	2 410	14 054	7 773	71.3
2014														
January	2 724	7 915	18 772	21 226	14 492	5 533	21 805	2 733	525	5 047	2 394	14 025	7 762	74.1
February	2 718	7 932	18 841	21 247	14 499	5 533	21 817	2 729	524	5 058	2 403	14 030	7 767	73.4
March	2 723	7 935	18 884	21 286	14 560	5 552	21 828	2 728	524	5 055	2 403	14 045	7 775	74.9
April	2 721	7 943	18 946	21 312	14 615	5 564	21 858	2 725	523	5 058	2 404	14 075	7 803	74.7
May	2 717	7 952	18 986	21 370	14 675	5 567	21 852	2 726	524	5 056	2 398	14 070	7 786	73.8
June	2 722	7 965	19 047	21 409	14 701	5 564	21 897	2 728	523	5 063	2 403	14 106	7 815	75.3
July	2 726	7 979	19 090	21 453	14 710	5 566	21 873	2 731	524	5 028	2 365	14 114	7 824	76.2
August	2 735	7 991	19 145	21 503	14 728	5 581	21 865	2 735	525	5 021	2 360	14 109	7 816	78.5
September	2 734	8 006	19 189	21 541	14 775	5 575	21 908	2 736	525	5 043	2 379	14 129	7 847	78.0
October	2 728	8 014	19 216	21 581	14 818	5 580	21 921	2 737	525	5 050	2 383	14 134	7 839	78.0
November	2 737	8 032	19 272	21 628	14 856	5 592	21 931	2 741	525	5 051	2 384	14 139	7 841	79.3
December	2 737	8 042	19 344	21 674	14 896	5 592	21 946	2 742	525	5 058	2 387	14 146	7 847	78.2
2015														
January	2 739	8 062	19 371	21 739	14 918	5 598	21 953	2 744	524	5 062	2 390	14 147	7 853	74.7
February	2 740	8 072	19 424	21 789	14 966	5 604	21 969	2 746	526	5 071	2 397	14 152	7 862	74.5
March	2 733	8 085	19 447	21 824	14 983	5 605	21 958	2 747	526	5 064	2 390	14 147	7 849	72.2
April	2 740	8 088	19 502	21 901	15 021	5 612	21 985	2 749	526	5 067	2 394	14 169	7 861	70.5
May	2 748	8 097	19 576	21 950	15 100	5 623	22 005	2 752	526	5 072	2 395	14 181	7 867	68.8
June	2 747	8 113	19 634	21 996	15 126	5 619	22 016	2 751	525	5 073	2 397	14 192	7 871	66.1
July	2 756	8 131	19 672	22 047	15 167	5 630	22 031	2 756	526	5 069	2 391	14 206	7 880	67.4
August	2 755	8 144	19 703	22 100	15 199	5 620	22 073	2 760	526	5 082	2 404	14 231	7 898	65.3
September	2 764	8 149	19 705	22 140	15 266	5 620	22 057	2 761	527	5 086	2 407	14 210	7 865	64.6
October	2 768	8 162	19 785	22 223	15 323	5 630	22 064	2 759	526	5 088	2 409	14 217	7 866	66.7
November	2 756	8 178	19 826	22 266	15 376	5 639	22 076	2 766	527	5 089	2 410	14 221	7 869	64.8
December	2 762	8 188	19 882	22 318	15 413	5 651	22 098	2 774	528	5 089	2 411	14 235	7 875	65.1
2016														
January	2 763	8 207	19 877	22 334	15 443	5 647	22 114	2 771	528	5 088	2 412	14 255	7 883	65.1
February	2 773	8 213	19 902	22 408	15 488	5 664	22 130	2 777	528	5 084	2 408	14 269	7 887	65.5
March	2 779	8 231	19 928	22 443	15 537	5 670	22 166	2 781	528	5 091	2 411	14 294	7 901	70.1
April	2 781	8 249	19 994	22 495	15 552	5 674	22 161	2 769	528	5 089	2 410	14 303	7 904	64.9
May	2 739	8 263	20 022	22 544	15 561	5 667	22 187	2 791	528	5 079	2 404	14 317	7 914	61.3
June	2 780	8 280	20 081	22 603	15 610	5 683	22 215	2 798	529	5 089	2 412	14 328	7 917	59.0
July	2 778	8 300	20 165	22 644	15 652	5 685	22 257	2 802	530	5 093	2 417	14 362	7 942	62.1
August	2 778	8 315	20 196	22 697	15 673	5 695	22 290	2 805	530	5 094	2 413	14 391	7 961	58.6
September	2 786	8 324	20 279	22 745	15 684	5 708	22 316	2 811	530	5 101	2 423	14 404	7 968	63.6
October	2 780	8 330	20 334	22 790	15 695	5 711	22 308	2 817	531	5 092	2 414	14 399	7 953	64.8
November	2 768	8 342	20 380	22 821	15 739	5 718	22 294	2 811	527	5 088	2 410	14 395	7 934	65.7
December	2 762	8 364	20 416	22 871	15 744	5 701	22 299	2 819	530	5 085	2 414	14 395	7 945	60.2

1Not seasonally adjusted.
2See notes and definitions for explanation. September value used to represent year.

Table 10-9. Employment, Hours, and Earnings, Total Nonfarm and Manufacturing, Historical Annual and Monthly

(Wage and salary workers on nonfarm payrolls, seasonally adjusted.)

Year and month	All wage and salary workers (thousands)					Production and nonsupervisory workers on private payrolls							
	Total	Private			Service-providing	Number (thousands)		Average hours per week		Average hourly earnings, dollars		Average weekly earnings, dollars	
		Total	Goods-producing			Total private	Manufacturing	Total private	Manufacturing	Total private	Manufacturing	Total private	Manufacturing
			Total	Manufacturing									
1939	30 645	26 606	11 511	9 450	19 134	. . .	8 163	. . .	37.7	. . .	0.49	. . .	18.47
1940	32 407	28 156	12 378	10 099	20 029	. . .	8 737	. . .	38.2	. . .	0.53	. . .	20.25
1941	36 600	31 874	14 940	12 121	21 660	. . .	10 641	. . .	40.7	. . .	0.61	. . .	24.83
1942	40 213	34 621	17 275	14 030	22 938	. . .	12 447	. . .	43.2	. . .	0.74	. . .	31.97
1943	42 574	36 353	18 738	16 153	23 837	. . .	14 407	. . .	45.1	. . .	0.86	. . .	38.79
1944	42 006	35 819	17 981	15 903	24 026	. . .	14 031	. . .	45.4	. . .	0.91	. . .	41.31
1945	40 510	34 428	16 308	14 255	24 203	. . .	12 445	. . .	43.6	. . .	0.90	. . .	39.24
1946	41 759	36 054	16 122	13 513	25 637	. . .	11 781	. . .	40.4	. . .	0.95	. . .	38.38
1947	43 945	38 379	17 314	14 287	26 631	. . .	12 453	. . .	40.5	. . .	1.10	. . .	44.55
1948	44 954	39 213	17 579	14 324	27 376	. . .	12 383	. . .	40.1	. . .	1.20	. . .	48.12
1949	43 843	37 893	16 464	13 281	27 379	. . .	11 355	. . .	39.2	. . .	1.25	. . .	49.00
1950	45 287	39 167	17 343	14 013	27 945	. . .	12 032	. . .	40.6	. . .	1.32	. . .	53.59
1951	47 930	41 427	18 703	15 070	29 227	. . .	12 808	. . .	40.7	. . .	1.45	. . .	59.02
1952	48 909	42 182	18 928	15 291	29 981	. . .	12 797	. . .	40.8	. . .	1.53	. . .	62.42
1953	50 310	43 552	19 733	16 131	30 577	. . .	13 437	. . .	40.6	. . .	1.63	. . .	66.18
1954	49 093	42 235	18 515	15 002	30 578	. . .	12 300	. . .	39.7	. . .	1.66	. . .	65.90
1955	50 744	43 722	19 234	15 524	31 510	. . .	12 735	. . .	40.8	. . .	1.74	. . .	70.99
1956	52 473	45 087	19 799	15 858	32 674	. . .	12 869	. . .	40.5	. . .	1.84	. . .	74.52
1957	52 959	45 235	19 669	15 798	33 290	. . .	12 640	. . .	39.9	. . .	1.93	. . .	77.01
1958	51 426	43 480	18 319	14 656	33 107	. . .	11 532	. . .	39.2	. . .	1.99	. . .	78.01
1959	53 374	45 182	19 163	15 325	34 211	. . .	12 089	. . .	40.3	. . .	2.08	. . .	83.82
1960	54 296	45 832	19 182	15 438	35 114	. . .	12 074	. . .	39.8	. . .	2.15	. . .	85.57
1961	54 105	45 399	18 647	15 011	35 458	. . .	11 612	. . .	39.9	. . .	2.20	. . .	87.78
1962	55 659	46 655	19 203	15 498	36 455	. . .	11 986	. . .	40.5	. . .	2.27	. . .	91.94
1963	56 764	47 423	19 385	15 631	37 379	. . .	12 051	. . .	40.6	. . .	2.34	. . .	95.00
1964	58 391	48 680	19 733	15 888	38 658	40 575	12 298	38.5	40.8	2.53	2.41	97.41	98.33
1947													
January	43 539	37 920	17 213	14 328	26 326	. . .	12 445	. . .	40.5	. . .	1.03	. . .	41.72
February	43 563	37 957	17 200	14 278	26 363	. . .	12 487	. . .	40.4	. . .	1.04	. . .	42.02
March	43 606	38 018	17 196	14 259	26 410	. . .	12 518	. . .	40.3	. . .	1.06	. . .	42.72
April	43 492	37 934	17 178	14 240	26 314	. . .	12 531	. . .	40.5	. . .	1.06	. . .	42.93
May	43 638	38 087	17 176	14 189	26 462	. . .	12 449	. . .	40.4	. . .	1.08	. . .	43.63
June	43 808	38 284	17 253	14 200	26 555	. . .	12 389	. . .	40.4	. . .	1.10	. . .	44.44
July	43 743	38 219	17 106	14 076	26 637	. . .	12 265	. . .	40.4	. . .	1.10	. . .	44.44
August	43 959	38 440	17 280	14 200	26 679	. . .	12 370	. . .	40.0	. . .	1.11	. . .	44.40
September	44 201	38 662	17 398	14 315	26 803	. . .	12 430	. . .	40.5	. . .	1.11	. . .	44.96
October	44 415	38 849	17 499	14 393	26 916	. . .	12 464	. . .	40.5	. . .	1.13	. . .	45.77
November	44 487	38 902	17 517	14 414	26 970	. . .	12 494	. . .	40.5	. . .	1.14	. . .	46.17
December	44 579	38 974	17 563	14 428	27 016	. . .	12 526	. . .	40.8	. . .	1.16	. . .	47.33
1948													
January	44 682	39 058	17 625	14 438	27 057	. . .	12 520	. . .	40.5	. . .	1.16	. . .	46.98
February	44 537	38 922	17 447	14 339	27 090	. . .	12 437	. . .	40.2	. . .	1.16	. . .	46.63
March	44 681	39 058	17 544	14 364	27 137	. . .	12 489	. . .	40.4	. . .	1.16	. . .	46.86
April	44 370	38 727	17 302	14 183	27 068	. . .	12 304	. . .	40.1	. . .	1.17	. . .	46.92
May	44 795	39 114	17 508	14 235	27 287	. . .	12 344	. . .	40.2	. . .	1.18	. . .	47.44
June	45 033	39 297	17 633	14 318	27 400	. . .	12 402	. . .	40.3	. . .	1.19	. . .	47.96
July	45 160	39 386	17 649	14 359	27 511	. . .	12 417	. . .	40.2	. . .	1.21	. . .	48.64
August	45 176	39 385	17 655	14 353	27 521	. . .	12 397	. . .	40.2	. . .	1.23	. . .	49.45
September	45 295	39 490	17 741	14 441	27 554	. . .	12 450	. . .	40.1	. . .	1.24	. . .	49.72
October	45 251	39 422	17 683	14 390	27 568	. . .	12 364	. . .	39.8	. . .	1.25	. . .	49.75
November	45 194	39 325	17 599	14 292	27 595	. . .	12 302	. . .	39.8	. . .	1.26	. . .	50.15
December	45 029	39 141	17 417	14 086	27 612	. . .	12 127	. . .	39.6	. . .	1.26	. . .	49.90
1949													
January	44 671	38 777	17 170	13 867	27 501	. . .	11 905	. . .	39.4	. . .	1.26	. . .	49.64
February	44 500	38 607	17 019	13 734	27 481	. . .	11 792	. . .	39.4	. . .	1.26	. . .	49.64
March	44 238	38 323	16 848	13 581	27 390	. . .	11 654	. . .	39.1	. . .	1.26	. . .	49.27
April	44 230	38 282	16 685	13 439	27 545	. . .	11 517	. . .	38.8	. . .	1.25	. . .	48.50
May	43 982	38 020	16 492	13 269	27 490	. . .	11 352	. . .	38.9	. . .	1.25	. . .	48.63
June	43 739	37 783	16 351	13 178	27 388	. . .	11 266	. . .	39.0	. . .	1.26	. . .	49.14
July	43 529	37 567	16 222	13 067	27 307	. . .	11 168	. . .	39.2	. . .	1.26	. . .	49.39
August	43 622	37 637	16 327	13 158	27 295	. . .	11 251	. . .	39.2	. . .	1.25	. . .	49.00
September	43 784	37 794	16 403	13 225	27 381	. . .	11 284	. . .	39.4	. . .	1.25	. . .	49.25
October	42 950	36 980	15 739	12 891	27 211	. . .	10 940	. . .	39.6	. . .	1.24	. . .	49.10
November	43 245	37 295	16 040	12 882	27 205	. . .	10 964	. . .	39.1	. . .	1.24	. . .	48.48
December	43 517	37 565	16 217	13 062	27 300	. . .	11 173	. . .	39.4	. . .	1.25	. . .	49.25
1950													
January	43 528	37 594	16 255	13 161	27 273	. . .	11 258	. . .	39.6	. . .	1.27	. . .	50.29
February	43 298	37 372	16 035	13 169	27 263	. . .	11 262	. . .	39.7	. . .	1.26	. . .	50.02
March	43 952	37 874	16 482	13 290	27 470	. . .	11 362	. . .	39.7	. . .	1.28	. . .	50.82
April	44 376	38 282	16 718	13 471	27 658	. . .	11 528	. . .	40.3	. . .	1.29	. . .	51.99
May	44 718	38 675	17 080	13 780	27 638	. . .	11 855	. . .	40.3	. . .	1.30	. . .	52.39
June	45 084	39 062	17 288	13 923	27 796	. . .	11 979	. . .	40.6	. . .	1.30	. . .	52.78
July	45 454	39 364	17 464	14 072	27 990	. . .	12 107	. . .	40.9	. . .	1.31	. . .	53.58
August	46 188	40 001	17 917	14 461	28 271	. . .	12 476	. . .	41.3	. . .	1.33	. . .	54.93
September	46 442	40 214	18 040	14 561	28 402	. . .	12 519	. . .	40.8	. . .	1.33	. . .	54.26
October	46 712	40 463	18 249	14 737	28 463	. . .	12 659	. . .	41.1	. . .	1.36	. . .	55.90
November	46 778	40 516	18 288	14 762	28 490	. . .	12 682	. . .	41.0	. . .	1.37	. . .	56.17
December	46 855	40 541	18 283	14 782	28 572	. . .	12 710	. . .	40.9	. . .	1.39	. . .	56.85

. . . = Not available.

Table 10-9. Employment, Hours, and Earnings, Total Nonfarm and Manufacturing, Historical Annual and Monthly—*Continued*

(Wage and salary workers on nonfarm payrolls, seasonally adjusted.)

Year and month	All wage and salary workers (thousands)					Production and nonsupervisory workers on private payrolls								
	Total	Private			Service-providing	Number (thousands)		Average hours per week		Average hourly earnings, dollars		Average weekly earnings, dollars	
		Total	Goods-producing			Total private	Manufac-turing	Total private	Manufac-turing	Total private	Manufac-turing	Total private	Manufac-turing
			Total	Manufac-turing									
1951													
January	47 288	40 936	18 518	14 950	28 770	...	12 816	...	41.0	...	1.40	...	57.40
February	47 577	41 195	18 666	15 076	28 911	...	12 929	...	40.9	...	1.41	...	57.67
March	47 871	41 461	18 754	15 125	29 117	...	12 936	...	41.0	...	1.42	...	58.22
April	47 856	41 405	18 810	15 166	29 046	...	12 960	...	41.0	...	1.43	...	58.63
May	47 953	41 536	18 829	15 164	29 124	...	12 941	...	41.0	...	1.44	...	59.04
June	48 068	41 569	18 826	15 176	29 242	...	12 934	...	40.9	...	1.45	...	59.31
July	48 062	41 524	18 747	15 110	29 315	...	12 848	...	40.6	...	1.45	...	58.87
August	48 009	41 490	18 709	15 061	29 300	...	12 772	...	40.4	...	1.46	...	58.98
September	47 955	41 403	18 622	14 996	29 333	...	12 659	...	40.4	...	1.46	...	58.98
October	48 009	41 432	18 630	14 973	29 379	...	12 615	...	40.3	...	1.47	...	59.24
November	48 148	41 522	18 617	14 999	29 531	...	12 628	...	40.4	...	1.48	...	59.79
December	48 309	41 621	18 698	15 045	29 611	...	12 667	...	40.7	...	1.49	...	60.64
1952													
January	48 298	41 709	18 719	15 067	29 579	...	12 675	...	40.8	...	1.49	...	60.79
February	48 522	41 872	18 813	15 105	29 709	...	12 689	...	40.8	...	1.49	...	60.79
March	48 504	41 842	18 775	15 127	29 729	...	12 695	...	40.6	...	1.51	...	61.31
April	48 616	41 954	18 806	15 162	29 810	...	12 713	...	40.3	...	1.51	...	60.85
May	48 645	41 951	18 784	15 143	29 861	...	12 676	...	40.5	...	1.51	...	61.16
June	48 286	41 574	18 419	14 828	29 867	...	12 353	...	40.6	...	1.51	...	61.31
July	48 144	41 407	18 268	14 707	29 876	...	12 233	...	40.2	...	1.50	...	60.30
August	48 923	42 205	18 928	15 279	29 995	...	12 764	...	40.7	...	1.53	...	62.27
September	49 319	42 585	19 206	15 553	30 113	...	13 007	...	41.1	...	1.55	...	63.71
October	49 598	42 782	19 312	15 690	30 286	...	13 122	...	41.2	...	1.56	...	64.27
November	49 816	43 015	19 473	15 843	30 343	...	13 262	...	41.2	...	1.58	...	65.10
December	50 164	43 229	19 610	15 973	30 554	...	13 375	...	41.2	...	1.58	...	65.10
1953													
January	50 145	43 351	19 721	16 067	30 424	...	13 447	...	41.1	...	1.59	...	65.35
February	50 339	43 542	19 841	16 158	30 498	...	13 529	...	41.0	...	1.61	...	66.01
March	50 475	43 691	19 909	16 270	30 566	...	13 620	...	41.2	...	1.61	...	66.33
April	50 432	43 662	19 908	16 293	30 524	...	13 629	...	40.9	...	1.62	...	66.26
May	50 491	43 774	19 930	16 341	30 561	...	13 645	...	41.0	...	1.62	...	66.42
June	50 522	43 788	19 909	16 343	30 613	...	13 636	...	40.9	...	1.63	...	66.67
July	50 536	43 813	19 910	16 353	30 626	...	13 653	...	40.7	...	1.64	...	66.75
August	50 487	43 733	19 834	16 278	30 653	...	13 564	...	40.7	...	1.64	...	66.75
September	50 365	43 616	19 726	16 151	30 639	...	13 419	...	40.1	...	1.65	...	66.17
October	50 242	43 478	19 578	15 981	30 664	...	13 244	...	40.1	...	1.65	...	66.17
November	49 907	43 158	19 315	15 728	30 592	...	12 990	...	40.0	...	1.65	...	66.00
December	49 702	42 959	19 173	15 581	30 529	...	12 847	...	39.7	...	1.65	...	65.51
1954													
January	49 468	42 708	18 963	15 440	30 505	...	12 706	...	39.5	...	1.65	...	65.18
February	49 382	42 599	18 880	15 307	30 502	...	12 593	...	39.7	...	1.65	...	65.51
March	49 158	42 362	18 748	15 197	30 410	...	12 493	...	39.6	...	1.65	...	65.34
April	49 178	42 372	18 602	15 065	30 576	...	12 361	...	39.7	...	1.65	...	65.51
May	48 965	42 136	18 476	14 974	30 489	...	12 282	...	39.7	...	1.67	...	66.30
June	48 896	42 050	18 400	14 910	30 496	...	12 220	...	39.7	...	1.67	...	66.30
July	48 835	41 967	18 280	14 799	30 555	...	12 121	...	39.7	...	1.66	...	65.90
August	48 825	41 933	18 251	14 772	30 574	...	12 089	...	39.8	...	1.66	...	66.07
September	48 882	41 988	18 261	14 805	30 621	...	12 104	...	39.9	...	1.66	...	66.23
October	48 944	42 044	18 321	14 841	30 623	...	12 142	...	39.7	...	1.67	...	66.30
November	49 178	42 214	18 438	14 913	30 740	...	12 206	...	40.1	...	1.68	...	67.37
December	49 331	42 374	18 508	14 967	30 823	...	12 254	...	40.1	...	1.68	...	67.37
1955													
January	49 497	42 544	18 609	15 034	30 888	...	12 309	...	40.4	...	1.69	...	68.28
February	49 644	42 721	18 726	15 138	30 918	...	12 408	...	40.6	...	1.70	...	69.02
March	49 963	43 025	18 910	15 258	31 053	...	12 524	...	40.7	...	1.71	...	69.60
April	50 247	43 288	19 067	15 375	31 180	...	12 626	...	40.8	...	1.71	...	69.77
May	50 512	43 521	19 223	15 493	31 289	...	12 731	...	41.1	...	1.73	...	71.10
June	50 790	43 770	19 331	15 585	31 459	...	12 810	...	40.8	...	1.73	...	70.58
July	50 985	43 936	19 376	15 614	31 609	...	12 818	...	40.7	...	1.75	...	71.23
August	51 111	44 088	19 432	15 679	31 679	...	12 866	...	40.7	...	1.76	...	71.63
September	51 262	44 195	19 427	15 668	31 835	...	12 830	...	40.7	...	1.77	...	72.04
October	51 431	44 313	19 482	15 740	31 949	...	12 896	...	41.0	...	1.77	...	72.57
November	51 592	44 509	19 554	15 813	32 038	...	12 967	...	41.1	...	1.78	...	73.16
December	51 805	44 673	19 608	15 859	32 197	...	13 009	...	40.9	...	1.78	...	72.80
1956													
January	51 975	44 808	19 665	15 882	32 310	...	13 011	...	40.8	...	1.78	...	72.62
February	52 167	44 955	19 731	15 889	32 436	...	12 986	...	40.7	...	1.79	...	72.85
March	52 295	45 043	19 691	15 829	32 604	...	12 905	...	40.6	...	1.80	...	73.08
April	52 375	45 099	19 811	15 909	32 564	...	12 970	...	40.5	...	1.82	...	73.71
May	52 506	45 139	19 825	15 893	32 681	...	12 925	...	40.4	...	1.83	...	73.93
June	52 584	45 217	19 905	15 835	32 679	...	12 836	...	40.3	...	1.83	...	73.75
July	51 954	44 549	19 390	15 468	32 564	...	12 435	...	40.3	...	1.82	...	73.35
August	52 630	45 179	19 922	15 893	32 708	...	12 860	...	40.3	...	1.85	...	74.56
September	52 601	45 120	19 860	15 863	32 741	...	12 822	...	40.5	...	1.87	...	75.74
October	52 781	45 262	19 918	15 937	32 863	...	12 908	...	40.6	...	1.88	...	76.33
November	52 822	45 269	19 886	15 916	32 936	...	12 864	...	40.4	...	1.88	...	75.95
December	52 930	45 346	19 926	15 957	33 004	...	12 882	...	40.6	...	1.91	...	77.55

. . . = Not available.

Table 10-9. Employment, Hours, and Earnings, Total Nonfarm and Manufacturing, Historical Annual and Monthly—*Continued*

(Wage and salary workers on nonfarm payrolls, seasonally adjusted.)

Year and month	All wage and salary workers (thousands)					Production and nonsupervisory workers on private payrolls							
	Total	Private			Service-providing	Number (thousands)		Average hours per week		Average hourly earnings, dollars		Average weekly earnings, dollars	
		Total	Goods-producing			Total private	Manufac-turing	Total private	Manufac-turing	Total private	Manufac-turing	Total private	Manufac-turing
			Total	Manufac-turing									
1957													
January	52 888	45 268	19 833	15 970	33 055	...	12 881	...	40.4	...	1.90	...	76.76
February	53 097	45 451	19 933	15 998	33 164	...	12 885	...	40.5	...	1.91	...	77.36
March	53 157	45 485	19 936	15 994	33 221	...	12 855	...	40.4	...	1.92	...	77.57
April	53 238	45 537	19 887	15 970	33 351	...	12 811	...	40.0	...	1.91	...	76.40
May	53 149	45 436	19 834	15 931	33 315	...	12 762	...	40.0	...	1.92	...	76.80
June	53 066	45 364	19 777	15 873	33 289	...	12 697	...	40.0	...	1.92	...	76.80
July	53 123	45 369	19 735	15 854	33 388	...	12 669	...	40.0	...	1.93	...	77.20
August	53 126	45 369	19 728	15 867	33 398	...	12 673	...	40.0	...	1.94	...	77.60
September	52 932	45 183	19 545	15 710	33 387	...	12 528	...	39.7	...	1.95	...	77.42
October	52 765	44 997	19 421	15 599	33 344	...	12 437	...	39.4	...	1.96	...	77.22
November	52 559	44 790	19 260	15 466	33 299	...	12 301	...	39.2	...	1.96	...	76.83
December	52 385	44 539	19 111	15 332	33 274	...	12 170	...	39.1	...	1.95	...	76.25
1958													
January	52 077	44 256	18 902	15 130	33 175	...	11 969	...	38.9	...	1.95	...	75.86
February	51 576	43 744	18 529	14 908	33 047	...	11 757	...	38.7	...	1.95	...	75.47
March	51 300	43 452	18 335	14 670	32 965	...	11 532	...	38.8	...	1.96	...	76.05
April	51 027	43 159	18 120	14 506	32 907	...	11 373	...	38.9	...	1.96	...	76.24
May	50 913	43 019	18 008	14 414	32 905	...	11 294	...	38.9	...	1.97	...	76.63
June	50 912	42 986	17 984	14 408	32 928	...	11 300	...	39.1	...	1.98	...	77.42
July	51 037	43 065	18 038	14 450	32 999	...	11 349	...	39.3	...	1.98	...	77.81
August	51 231	43 219	18 147	14 524	33 084	...	11 412	...	39.5	...	2.01	...	79.40
September	51 506	43 490	18 331	14 658	33 175	...	11 556	...	39.5	...	2.00	...	79.00
October	51 486	43 455	18 218	14 503	33 268	...	11 394	...	39.6	...	2.00	...	79.20
November	51 944	43 916	18 610	14 827	33 334	...	11 702	...	39.9	...	2.03	...	81.00
December	52 088	43 988	18 592	14 877	33 496	...	11 743	...	39.9	...	2.04	...	81.40
1959													
January	52 480	44 375	18 796	14 998	33 684	...	11 849	...	40.2	...	2.04	...	82.01
February	52 687	44 571	18 890	15 115	33 797	...	11 950	...	40.3	...	2.05	...	82.62
March	53 016	44 884	19 069	15 259	33 947	...	12 078	...	40.4	...	2.07	...	83.63
April	53 320	45 178	19 269	15 385	34 051	...	12 185	...	40.5	...	2.08	...	84.24
May	53 549	45 396	19 378	15 487	34 171	...	12 277	...	40.7	...	2.08	...	84.66
June	53 679	45 536	19 462	15 554	34 217	...	12 330	...	40.6	...	2.09	...	84.85
July	53 803	45 630	19 529	15 623	34 274	...	12 366	...	40.3	...	2.09	...	84.23
August	53 334	45 153	19 049	15 202	34 285	...	11 936	...	40.4	...	2.07	...	83.63
September	53 429	45 190	19 052	15 254	34 377	...	11 984	...	40.4	...	2.08	...	84.03
October	53 359	45 094	18 925	15 158	34 434	...	11 864	...	40.1	...	2.07	...	83.01
November	53 635	45 351	19 108	15 300	34 527	...	11 991	...	39.9	...	2.07	...	82.59
December	54 175	45 807	19 425	15 573	34 750	...	12 254	...	40.3	...	2.11	...	85.03
1960													
January	54 274	45 967	19 491	15 687	34 783	...	12 362	...	40.6	...	2.13	...	86.48
February	54 513	46 187	19 605	15 765	34 908	...	12 434	...	40.3	...	2.14	...	86.24
March	54 458	45 933	19 373	15 707	35 085	...	12 362	...	40.0	...	2.14	...	85.60
April	54 812	46 278	19 446	15 654	35 366	...	12 299	...	40.0	...	2.14	...	85.60
May	54 473	46 041	19 374	15 575	35 099	...	12 218	...	40.1	...	2.14	...	85.81
June	54 347	45 915	19 240	15 466	35 107	...	12 102	...	39.9	...	2.14	...	85.39
July	54 304	45 862	19 170	15 413	35 134	...	12 047	...	39.9	...	2.14	...	85.39
August	54 271	45 799	19 105	15 360	35 166	...	11 986	...	39.7	...	2.15	...	85.36
September	54 228	45 734	19 057	15 330	35 171	...	11 956	...	39.4	...	2.16	...	85.10
October	54 144	45 642	18 952	15 231	35 192	...	11 846	...	39.7	...	2.16	...	85.75
November	53 962	45 446	18 799	15 112	35 163	...	11 726	...	39.3	...	2.15	...	84.50
December	53 744	45 147	18 548	14 947	35 196	...	11 556	...	38.4	...	2.16	...	82.94
1961													
January	53 683	45 119	18 508	14 863	35 175	...	11 473	...	39.3	...	2.16	...	84.89
February	53 556	44 969	18 418	14 801	35 138	...	11 414	...	39.4	...	2.16	...	85.10
March	53 662	45 051	18 438	14 802	35 224	...	11 410	...	39.5	...	2.16	...	85.32
April	53 626	44 997	18 432	14 825	35 194	...	11 444	...	39.5	...	2.18	...	86.11
May	53 785	45 121	18 523	14 932	35 262	...	11 544	...	39.7	...	2.19	...	86.94
June	53 977	45 289	18 618	14 981	35 359	...	11 593	...	40.0	...	2.20	...	88.00
July	54 123	45 399	18 640	15 029	35 483	...	11 639	...	40.0	...	2.21	...	88.40
August	54 298	45 534	18 725	15 093	35 573	...	11 701	...	40.1	...	2.22	...	89.02
September	54 388	45 592	18 730	15 080	35 658	...	11 679	...	39.5	...	2.20	...	86.90
October	54 522	45 717	18 805	15 143	35 717	...	11 731	...	40.3	...	2.23	...	89.87
November	54 743	45 931	18 927	15 259	35 816	...	11 842	...	40.7	...	2.23	...	90.76
December	54 871	46 035	18 981	15 309	35 890	...	11 872	...	40.4	...	2.24	...	90.50
1962													
January	54 891	46 040	18 936	15 322	35 955	...	11 865	...	40.0	...	2.25	...	90.00
February	55 187	46 309	19 109	15 411	36 078	...	11 950	...	40.4	...	2.26	...	91.30
March	55 276	46 375	19 109	15 451	36 167	...	11 970	...	40.6	...	2.26	...	91.76
April	55 602	46 680	19 258	15 524	36 344	...	12 034	...	40.6	...	2.26	...	91.76
May	55 627	46 669	19 253	15 513	36 374	...	12 011	...	40.6	...	2.27	...	92.16
June	55 644	46 644	19 186	15 518	36 458	...	12 006	...	40.5	...	2.26	...	91.53
July	55 746	46 720	19 248	15 522	36 498	...	12 004	...	40.5	...	2.27	...	91.94
August	55 838	46 775	19 251	15 517	36 587	...	11 990	...	40.5	...	2.28	...	92.34
September	55 977	46 888	19 305	15 568	36 672	...	12 033	...	40.5	...	2.28	...	92.34
October	56 041	46 927	19 301	15 569	36 740	...	12 034	...	40.3	...	2.29	...	92.29
November	56 056	46 911	19 260	15 530	36 796	...	11 977	...	40.5	...	2.29	...	92.75
December	56 028	46 902	19 219	15 520	36 809	...	11 961	...	40.3	...	2.29	...	92.29

. . . = Not available.

Table 10-9. Employment, Hours, and Earnings, Total Nonfarm and Manufacturing, Historical Annual and Monthly—Continued

(Wage and salary workers on nonfarm payrolls, seasonally adjusted.)

Year and month	All wage and salary workers (thousands)					Production and nonsupervisory workers on private payrolls							
	Total	Private				Number (thousands)		Average hours per week		Average hourly earnings, dollars		Average weekly earnings, dollars	
		Total	Goods-producing		Service-providing	Total private	Manufac-turing	Total private	Manufac-turing	Total private	Manufac-turing	Total private	Manufac-turing
			Total	Manufac-turing									
1963													
January	56 116	46 912	19 257	15 545	36 859	...	11 974	...	40.5	...	2.30	...	93.15
February	56 230	46 999	19 228	15 542	37 002	...	11 965	...	40.5	...	2.31	...	93.56
March	56 322	47 077	19 233	15 564	37 089	...	11 990	...	40.5	...	2.32	...	93.96
April	56 580	47 316	19 343	15 602	37 237	...	12 029	...	40.5	...	2.32	...	93.96
May	56 616	47 328	19 399	15 641	37 217	...	12 066	...	40.5	...	2.33	...	94.37
June	56 658	47 356	19 371	15 624	37 287	...	12 050	...	40.7	...	2.34	...	95.24
July	56 794	47 460	19 423	15 646	37 371	...	12 080	...	40.6	...	2.35	...	95.41
August	56 910	47 542	19 437	15 644	37 473	...	12 060	...	40.6	...	2.34	...	95.00
September	57 077	47 660	19 483	15 674	37 594	...	12 088	...	40.6	...	2.36	...	95.82
October	57 284	47 805	19 517	15 714	37 767	...	12 131	...	40.7	...	2.36	...	96.05
November	57 255	47 771	19 456	15 675	37 799	...	12 072	...	40.7	...	2.37	...	96.46
December	57 360	47 863	19 493	15 712	37 867	...	12 108	...	40.6	...	2.38	...	96.63
1964													
January	57 487	47 925	19 406	15 715	38 081	39 913	12 132	38.2	40.1	2.50	2.38	95.50	95.44
February	57 751	48 170	19 570	15 742	38 181	40 123	12 165	38.5	40.7	2.50	2.38	96.25	96.87
March	57 898	48 287	19 587	15 770	38 311	40 171	12 190	38.5	40.6	2.50	2.38	96.25	96.63
April	57 922	48 278	19 593	15 785	38 329	40 209	12 211	38.6	40.7	2.52	2.40	97.27	97.68
May	58 089	48 419	19 630	15 812	38 459	40 332	12 231	38.6	40.8	2.52	2.40	97.27	97.92
June	58 221	48 552	19 682	15 839	38 539	40 448	12 255	38.6	40.8	2.53	2.41	97.66	98.33
July	58 413	48 736	19 740	15 887	38 673	40 624	12 309	38.5	40.8	2.53	2.41	97.41	98.33
August	58 619	48 887	19 810	15 948	38 809	40 771	12 354	38.5	40.9	2.55	2.42	98.18	98.98
September	58 903	49 117	19 943	16 073	38 960	41 026	12 479	38.5	40.9	2.55	2.44	98.18	99.80
October	58 794	48 949	19 723	15 821	39 071	40 828	12 224	38.5	40.7	2.55	2.40	98.18	97.68
November	59 217	49 338	20 026	16 096	39 191	41 157	12 477	38.6	41.0	2.56	2.42	98.82	99.22
December	59 421	49 524	20 111	16 176	39 310	41 307	12 551	38.7	41.2	2.58	2.44	99.85	100.53
1965													
January	59 583	49 646	20 173	16 245	39 410	41 453	12 603	38.7	41.3	2.58	2.45	99.85	101.19
February	59 800	49 826	20 216	16 291	39 584	41 583	12 644	38.7	41.3	2.59	2.46	100.23	101.60
March	60 003	49 993	20 292	16 353	39 711	41 674	12 701	38.7	41.3	2.60	2.47	100.62	102.01
April	60 259	50 208	20 317	16 418	39 942	41 885	12 752	38.7	41.2	2.60	2.47	100.62	101.76
May	60 492	50 398	20 444	16 477	40 048	42 044	12 792	38.8	41.3	2.62	2.49	101.66	102.84
June	60 690	50 562	20 522	16 554	40 168	42 183	12 854	38.6	41.2	2.62	2.49	101.13	102.59
July	60 963	50 762	20 611	16 669	40 352	42 364	12 962	38.6	41.2	2.63	2.49	101.52	102.59
August	61 228	50 957	20 726	16 732	40 502	42 537	12 994	38.5	41.1	2.64	2.50	101.64	102.75
September	61 490	51 152	20 808	16 802	40 682	42 726	13 046	38.6	41.1	2.65	2.51	102.29	103.16
October	61 718	51 340	20 895	16 864	40 823	42 871	13 100	38.5	41.2	2.66	2.52	102.41	103.82
November	61 997	51 561	21 021	16 962	40 976	43 045	13 175	38.6	41.3	2.67	2.52	103.06	104.08
December	62 321	51 822	21 151	17 051	41 170	43 270	13 243	38.6	41.3	2.68	2.53	103.45	104.49
1966													
January	62 528	51 987	21 214	17 143	41 314	43 401	13 301	38.6	41.5	2.68	2.54	103.45	105.41
February	62 796	52 185	21 315	17 288	41 481	43 552	13 426	38.7	41.7	2.69	2.56	104.10	106.75
March	63 192	52 500	21 515	17 400	41 677	43 801	13 508	38.7	41.6	2.70	2.56	104.49	106.50
April	63 436	52 677	21 568	17 517	41 868	43 959	13 598	38.7	41.8	2.71	2.58	104.88	107.84
May	63 711	52 890	21 675	17 625	42 036	44 138	13 678	38.5	41.5	2.72	2.58	104.72	107.07
June	64 110	53 208	21 846	17 733	42 264	44 390	13 753	38.5	41.4	2.72	2.58	104.72	106.81
July	64 301	53 327	21 872	17 760	42 429	44 484	13 758	38.4	41.2	2.74	2.60	105.22	107.12
August	64 507	53 501	21 972	17 882	42 535	44 596	13 843	38.4	41.4	2.75	2.61	105.60	108.05
September	64 644	53 581	21 948	17 886	42 696	44 659	13 841	38.3	41.2	2.76	2.63	105.71	108.36
October	64 854	53 727	21 991	17 956	42 863	44 789	13 906	38.4	41.3	2.77	2.64	106.37	109.03
November	65 019	53 816	21 988	17 981	43 031	44 834	13 918	38.3	41.2	2.78	2.65	106.47	109.18
December	65 200	53 944	22 008	17 998	43 192	44 916	13 906	38.2	40.9	2.78	2.64	106.20	107.98
1967													
January	65 407	54 092	22 057	18 033	43 350	45 051	13 925	38.3	41.1	2.79	2.65	106.86	108.92
February	65 428	54 075	21 987	17 978	43 441	44 967	13 853	37.9	40.4	2.81	2.67	106.50	107.87
March	65 530	54 133	21 919	17 940	43 611	44 991	13 797	37.9	40.5	2.81	2.67	106.50	108.14
April	65 467	54 032	21 842	17 878	43 625	44 871	13 712	37.8	40.4	2.82	2.68	106.60	108.27
May	65 619	54 145	21 779	17 832	43 840	44 961	13 664	37.8	40.4	2.83	2.69	106.97	108.68
June	65 750	54 216	21 761	17 812	43 989	45 004	13 632	37.8	40.4	2.84	2.69	107.35	108.68
July	65 887	54 343	21 772	17 784	44 115	45 105	13 602	37.8	40.5	2.86	2.71	108.11	109.76
August	66 142	54 552	21 887	17 905	44 255	45 267	13 681	37.8	40.6	2.87	2.73	108.49	110.84
September	66 164	54 541	21 775	17 794	44 389	45 236	13 559	37.8	40.6	2.88	2.73	108.86	110.84
October	66 225	54 583	21 779	17 800	44 446	45 278	13 587	37.8	40.6	2.89	2.74	109.24	111.24
November	66 703	55 008	21 996	17 985	44 707	45 701	13 777	37.9	40.6	2.91	2.75	110.29	111.65
December	66 900	55 165	22 037	18 025	44 863	45 800	13 782	37.7	40.7	2.92	2.77	110.08	112.74
1968													
January	66 805	55 011	21 917	18 040	44 888	45 655	13 798	37.6	40.4	2.94	2.81	110.54	113.52
February	67 215	55 396	22 117	18 054	45 098	45 980	13 793	37.8	40.8	2.95	2.82	111.51	115.06
March	67 295	55 453	22 119	18 067	45 176	46 041	13 803	37.7	40.8	2.97	2.84	111.97	115.87
April	67 555	55 677	22 207	18 131	45 348	46 239	13 858	37.6	40.3	2.98	2.85	112.05	114.86
May	67 653	55 748	22 255	18 190	45 398	46 267	13 900	37.7	40.9	3.00	2.87	113.10	117.38
June	67 904	55 917	22 264	18 228	45 640	46 402	13 921	37.8	40.9	3.01	2.88	113.78	117.79
July	68 125	56 107	22 329	18 265	45 796	46 563	13 953	37.7	40.8	3.03	2.89	114.23	117.91
August	68 328	56 286	22 350	18 254	45 978	46 670	13 903	37.7	40.7	3.03	2.89	114.23	117.62
September	68 487	56 420	22 390	18 252	46 097	46 792	13 914	37.7	40.9	3.06	2.92	115.36	119.43
October	68 720	56 619	22 419	18 293	46 301	46 990	13 974	37.7	41.0	3.07	2.94	115.74	120.54
November	68 985	56 878	22 512	18 346	46 473	47 244	14 028	37.5	40.9	3.09	2.96	115.88	121.06
December	69 246	57 101	22 617	18 410	46 629	47 385	14 044	37.5	40.7	3.11	2.97	116.63	120.88

. . . = Not available.

Table 10-9. Employment, Hours, and Earnings, Total Nonfarm and Manufacturing, Historical Annual and Monthly—*Continued*

(Wage and salary workers on nonfarm payrolls, seasonally adjusted.)

Year and month	All wage and salary workers (thousands)					Production and nonsupervisory workers on private payrolls							
	Total	Private			Service-providing	Number (thousands)		Average hours per week		Average hourly earnings, dollars		Average weekly earnings, dollars	
		Total	Goods-producing			Total private	Manufacturing	Total private	Manufacturing	Total private	Manufacturing	Total private	Manufacturing
			Total	Manufacturing									
1969													
January	69 438	57 229	22 644	18 432	46 794	47 529	14 086	37.7	40.8	3.12	2.99	117.62	121.99
February	69 700	57 476	22 755	18 502	46 945	47 696	14 134	37.5	40.4	3.14	3.00	117.75	121.20
March	69 905	57 676	22 813	18 558	47 092	47 852	14 169	37.6	40.8	3.15	3.01	118.44	122.81
April	70 072	57 827	22 815	18 554	47 257	47 959	14 144	37.7	41.0	3.17	3.03	119.51	124.23
May	70 328	58 044	22 899	18 588	47 429	48 122	14 161	37.6	40.7	3.19	3.04	119.94	123.73
June	70 636	58 277	22 981	18 640	47 655	48 329	14 206	37.5	40.7	3.20	3.05	120.00	124.14
July	70 729	58 389	22 990	18 642	47 739	48 435	14 194	37.5	40.6	3.22	3.08	120.75	125.05
August	71 006	58 533	23 111	18 767	47 895	48 010	14 207	37.5	40.0	3.24	3.10	121.50	126.86
September	70 917	58 538	22 988	18 620	47 929	48 524	14 159	37.5	40.6	3.26	3.12	122.25	126.67
October	71 120	58 690	22 976	18 613	48 144	48 669	14 174	37.4	40.5	3.28	3.13	122.67	126.77
November	71 087	58 639	22 840	18 467	48 247	48 589	14 035	37.5	40.5	3.29	3.14	123.38	127.17
December	71 240	58 763	22 884	18 485	48 356	48 638	14 013	37.5	40.6	3.30	3.15	123.75	127.89
1970													
January	71 176	58 680	22 726	18 424	48 450	48 564	13 964	37.3	40.4	3.31	3.16	123.46	127.66
February	71 304	58 786	22 747	18 361	48 557	48 600	13 897	37.3	40.2	3.33	3.17	124.21	127.43
March	71 452	58 849	22 738	18 360	48 714	48 690	13 917	37.2	40.1	3.35	3.19	124.62	127.92
April	71 348	58 643	22 552	18 207	48 796	48 480	13 785	37.0	39.8	3.36	3.19	124.32	126.96
May	71 123	58 455	22 336	18 029	48 787	48 287	13 616	37.0	39.8	3.38	3.22	125.06	128.16
June	71 029	58 362	22 241	17 930	48 788	48 225	13 554	36.9	39.8	3.39	3.24	125.09	128.95
July	71 053	58 356	22 195	17 877	48 858	48 243	13 527	37.0	40.0	3.41	3.25	126.17	130.00
August	70 933	58 222	22 105	17 779	48 828	48 088	13 449	37.0	39.8	3.43	3.26	126.91	129.75
September	70 948	58 207	21 988	17 692	48 960	48 101	13 401	36.8	39.6	3.45	3.29	126.96	130.28
October	70 519	57 726	21 477	17 173	49 042	47 619	12 905	36.8	39.5	3.46	3.26	127.33	128.77
November	70 409	57 579	21 345	17 024	49 064	47 466	12 781	36.7	39.5	3.47	3.26	127.35	128.77
December	70 790	57 945	21 673	17 309	49 117	47 778	13 062	36.8	39.5	3.50	3.32	128.80	131.14
1971													
January	70 866	57 988	21 594	17 280	49 272	47 859	13 069	36.8	39.9	3.52	3.36	129.54	134.06
February	70 806	57 929	21 514	17 216	49 292	47 779	13 033	36.7	39.7	3.54	3.39	129.92	134.58
March	70 859	57 951	21 491	17 154	49 368	47 819	12 984	36.7	39.8	3.56	3.39	130.65	134.92
April	71 037	58 092	21 552	17 149	49 485	47 966	12 993	36.8	39.9	3.57	3.41	131.38	136.06
May	71 247	58 277	21 645	17 225	49 602	48 153	13 081	36.7	40.0	3.60	3.43	132.12	137.20
June	71 253	58 245	21 568	17 139	49 685	48 108	13 012	36.8	39.9	3.62	3.45	133.22	137.66
July	71 315	58 304	21 564	17 126	49 751	48 169	13 001	36.7	40.0	3.63	3.46	133.22	138.40
August	71 370	58 329	21 570	17 115	49 800	48 164	12 993	36.7	39.8	3.66	3.48	134.32	138.50
September	71 617	58 549	21 650	17 154	49 967	48 363	13 038	36.7	39.7	3.67	3.48	134.69	138.16
October	71 642	58 527	21 604	17 126	50 038	48 305	13 027	36.8	39.9	3.68	3.50	135.42	139.65
November	71 846	58 698	21 684	17 166	50 162	48 441	13 064	36.9	40.0	3.69	3.49	136.16	139.60
December	72 108	58 918	21 741	17 202	50 367	48 613	13 078	36.9	40.2	3.73	3.55	137.64	142.71
1972													
January	72 445	59 179	21 865	17 283	50 580	49 035	13 173	36.9	40.2	3.80	3.57	140.22	143.51
February	72 652	59 354	21 915	17 361	50 737	49 143	13 235	36.9	40.4	3.82	3.61	140.96	145.84
March	72 945	59 616	22 036	17 447	50 909	49 437	13 316	36.9	40.4	3.84	3.63	141.70	146.65
April	73 163	59 805	22 099	17 508	51 064	49 562	13 373	36.9	40.5	3.86	3.65	142.43	147.83
May	73 467	60 051	22 222	17 602	51 245	49 745	13 451	36.8	40.5	3.87	3.67	142.42	148.64
June	73 760	60 355	22 282	17 641	51 478	49 995	13 475	36.9	40.6	3.88	3.68	143.17	149.41
July	73 708	60 226	22 162	17 556	51 546	49 844	13 387	36.8	40.5	3.90	3.69	143.52	149.45
August	74 138	60 608	22 400	17 741	51 738	50 155	13 562	36.8	40.6	3.92	3.73	144.26	151.44
September	74 263	60 688	22 456	17 774	51 807	50 226	13 572	36.8	40.6	3.94	3.75	145.39	152.25
October	74 673	61 067	22 613	17 893	52 060	50 552	13 681	37.0	40.7	3.97	3.78	146.89	153.85
November	74 967	61 324	22 688	18 005	52 279	50 789	13 783	36.9	40.7	3.98	3.79	146.86	154.25
December	75 270	61 586	22 772	18 158	52 498	51 054	13 902	36.8	40.6	4.01	3.83	147.57	155.50
1973													
January	75 621	61 931	22 955	18 276	52 666	51 349	14 006	36.8	40.4	4.03	3.86	148.30	155.94
February	76 017	62 306	23 160	18 410	52 857	51 685	14 127	36.9	40.9	4.04	3.87	149.08	158.28
March	76 285	62 540	23 262	18 493	53 023	51 901	14 181	37.0	40.9	4.06	3.88	150.22	158.69
April	76 455	62 678	23 316	18 530	53 139	51 983	14 192	36.9	40.8	4.08	3.91	150.55	159.53
May	76 646	62 829	23 382	18 564	53 264	52 082	14 217	36.9	40.7	4.10	3.93	151.29	159.95
June	76 887	63 015	23 485	18 606	53 402	52 233	14 253	36.9	40.7	4.12	3.95	152.03	160.77
July	76 911	63 046	23 522	18 598	53 389	52 240	14 232	36.9	40.7	4.15	3.98	153.14	161.99
August	77 166	63 262	23 559	18 629	53 607	52 394	14 251	36.9	40.6	4.16	4.00	153.50	162.40
September	77 276	63 384	23 548	18 609	53 728	52 410	14 213	36.8	40.7	4.19	4.03	154.19	164.02
October	77 606	63 629	23 641	18 702	53 965	52 655	14 289	36.7	40.6	4.21	4.05	154.51	164.43
November	77 912	63 877	23 719	18 773	54 193	52 845	14 342	36.9	40.6	4.23	4.07	156.09	165.24
December	78 035	63 965	23 779	18 820	54 256	52 954	14 386	36.7	40.6	4.25	4.09	155.98	166.05
1974													
January	78 104	64 014	23 709	18 788	54 395	52 896	14 340	36.6	40.5	4.26	4.10	155.92	166.05
February	78 254	64 119	23 718	18 727	54 536	52 970	14 269	36.6	40.4	4.29	4.13	157.01	166.85
March	78 296	64 144	23 687	18 700	54 609	52 951	14 223	36.6	40.4	4.31	4.15	157.75	167.66
April	78 382	64 191	23 670	18 702	54 712	53 006	14 225	36.4	39.5	4.34	4.16	157.98	164.32
May	78 547	64 326	23 635	18 688	54 912	53 094	14 199	36.5	40.3	4.39	4.25	160.24	171.28
June	78 602	64 363	23 591	18 690	55 011	53 106	14 197	36.5	40.2	4.43	4.30	161.70	172.86
July	78 635	64 347	23 462	18 656	55 173	53 046	14 152	36.5	40.1	4.45	4.33	162.43	173.63
August	78 619	64 291	23 396	18 570	55 223	53 026	14 089	36.5	40.2	4.49	4.38	163.89	176.08
September	78 611	64 189	23 274	18 492	55 337	52 915	14 025	36.4	40.0	4.53	4.42	164.89	176.80
October	78 629	64 145	23 118	18 364	55 511	52 835	13 884	36.3	40.0	4.56	4.48	165.53	179.20
November	78 261	63 729	22 773	18 077	55 488	52 411	13 607	36.1	39.5	4.57	4.49	164.98	177.36
December	77 657	63 098	22 303	17 693	55 354	51 856	13 259	36.1	39.3	4.61	4.52	166.42	177.64

Table 10-9. Employment, Hours, and Earnings, Total Nonfarm and Manufacturing, Historical Annual and Monthly—*Continued*

(Wage and salary workers on nonfarm payrolls, seasonally adjusted.)

Year and month		All wage and salary workers (thousands)				Production and nonsupervisory workers on private payrolls							
	Total	Private			Service-providing	Number (thousands)		Average hours per week		Average hourly earnings, dollars		Average weekly earnings, dollars	
		Total	Goods-producing			Total private	Manufac-turing	Total private	Manufac-turing	Total private	Manufac-turing	Total private	Manufac-turing
			Total	Manufac-turing									
1975													
January	77 297	62 673	21 974	17 344	55 323	51 438	12 933	36.1	39.2	4.61	4.54	166.42	177.97
February	76 919	62 172	21 512	17 004	55 407	50 934	12 622	35.9	38.9	4.63	4.58	166.22	178.16
March	76 649	61 895	21 274	16 853	55 375	50 665	12 483	35.7	38.8	4.66	4.63	166.36	179.64
April	76 461	61 666	21 109	16 759	55 352	50 442	12 407	35.8	39.0	4.66	4.63	166.83	180.57
May	76 623	61 796	21 097	16 746	55 526	50 557	12 406	35.9	39.0	4.68	4.65	168.01	181.35
June	76 520	61 736	21 018	16 690	55 502	50 537	12 371	35.9	39.2	4.72	4.68	169.45	183.46
July	76 769	61 908	20 981	16 678	55 788	50 729	12 374	35.9	39.4	4.73	4.71	169.81	185.57
August	77 155	62 285	21 176	16 824	55 979	51 070	12 538	36.1	39.7	4.77	4.75	172.20	188.58
September	77 230	62 406	21 284	16 904	55 946	51 182	12 617	36.1	39.8	4.79	4.78	172.92	190.24
October	77 535	62 635	21 384	16 984	56 151	51 375	12 687	36.1	39.9	4.81	4.80	173.64	191.52
November	77 680	62 777	21 442	17 025	56 238	51 456	12 700	36.1	39.9	4.85	4.83	175.09	192.72
December	78 018	63 072	21 602	17 140	56 416	51 759	12 811	36.2	40.2	4.87	4.86	176.29	195.37
1976													
January	78 506	63 537	21 799	17 287	56 707	52 182	12 945	36.3	40.3	4.90	4.90	177.87	197.47
February	78 817	63 836	21 893	17 384	56 924	52 430	13 030	36.3	40.4	4.94	4.94	179.32	199.58
March	79 049	64 062	21 980	17 470	57 069	52 615	13 092	36.0	40.2	4.96	4.98	178.56	200.20
April	79 292	64 307	22 050	17 541	57 242	52 812	13 160	36.0	39.6	4.98	4.98	179.28	197.21
May	79 311	64 340	21 988	17 513	57 323	52 802	13 130	36.1	40.3	5.02	5.04	181.22	203.11
June	79 376	64 413	21 982	17 521	57 394	52 830	13 121	36.1	40.2	5.04	5.07	181.94	203.81
July	79 547	64 554	21 988	17 524	57 559	52 975	13 124	36.1	40.3	5.07	5.11	183.03	205.93
August	79 704	64 697	22 038	17 596	57 666	53 072	13 195	36.0	40.2	5.12	5.16	184.32	207.43
September	79 892	64 921	22 142	17 665	57 750	53 268	13 253	36.0	40.2	5.15	5.20	185.40	209.04
October	79 905	64 877	22 037	17 548	57 868	53 164	13 109	35.9	40.0	5.17	5.19	185.60	207.60
November	80 237	65 164	22 207	17 682	58 030	53 362	13 199	35.9	40.1	5.21	5.25	187.04	210.53
December	80 448	65 373	22 261	17 719	58 187	53 542	13 230	35.9	39.9	5.23	5.29	187.76	211.07
1977													
January	80 692	65 636	22 320	17 803	58 372	53 755	13 305	35.6	39.4	5.26	5.35	187.26	210.79
February	80 988	65 932	22 478	17 843	58 510	54 016	13 331	36.0	40.2	5.30	5.36	190.80	215.47
March	81 391	66 341	22 672	17 941	58 719	54 389	13 424	35.9	40.3	5.33	5.40	191.35	217.62
April	81 729	66 654	22 807	18 024	58 922	54 672	13 490	36.0	40.4	5.37	5.45	193.32	220.18
May	82 089	66 957	22 919	18 107	59 170	54 940	13 567	36.0	40.5	5.40	5.49	194.40	222.35
June	82 488	67 281	23 046	18 192	59 442	55 194	13 622	36.0	40.5	5.43	5.54	195.48	224.37
July	82 836	67 537	23 106	18 259	59 730	55 396	13 670	35.9	40.4	5.46	5.58	196.01	225.43
August	83 074	67 746	23 124	18 276	59 950	55 543	13 679	35.9	40.4	5.48	5.61	196.73	226.64
September	83 532	68 129	23 244	18 334	60 288	55 858	13 714	35.9	40.4	5.51	5.65	197.81	228.26
October	83 794	68 331	23 279	18 356	60 515	56 003	13 722	36.0	40.6	5.56	5.69	200.16	231.01
November	84 173	68 658	23 371	18 419	60 802	56 281	13 771	35.9	40.5	5.59	5.72	200.68	231.66
December	84 408	68 870	23 371	18 531	61 037	56 465	13 861	35.8	40.4	5.61	5.75	200.84	232.30
1978													
January	84 595	68 984	23 374	18 593	61 221	56 547	13 917	35.3	39.5	5.66	5.83	199.80	230.29
February	84 948	69 277	23 453	18 639	61 495	56 768	13 950	35.6	39.9	5.69	5.86	202.56	233.81
March	85 461	69 730	23 649	18 699	61 812	57 176	13 992	35.8	40.5	5.73	5.88	205.13	238.14
April	86 163	70 366	24 008	18 772	62 155	57 711	14 037	35.8	40.4	5.79	5.93	207.28	239.57
May	86 509	70 675	24 082	18 848	62 427	57 941	14 096	35.8	40.4	5.82	5.96	208.36	240.78
June	86 951	71 099	24 238	18 919	62 713	58 262	14 129	35.9	40.6	5.87	6.01	210.73	244.01
July	87 205	71 304	24 300	18 951	62 905	58 422	14 152	35.9	40.6	5.90	6.06	211.81	246.04
August	87 481	71 590	24 374	19 006	63 107	58 626	14 187	35.8	40.5	5.93	6.09	212.29	246.65
September	87 618	71 799	24 444	19 068	63 174	58 819	14 241	35.8	40.5	5.97	6.15	213.73	249.08
October	87 954	72 096	24 548	19 142	63 406	59 017	14 291	35.8	40.5	6.03	6.20	215.87	251.10
November	88 391	72 497	24 678	19 257	63 713	59 377	14 388	35.7	40.6	6.06	6.26	216.34	254.16
December	88 673	72 762	24 758	19 334	63 915	59 599	14 459	35.7	40.5	6.10	6.31	217.77	255.56
1979													
January	88 810	72 873	24 740	19 388	64 070	59 659	14 497	35.6	40.4	6.14	6.36	218.58	256.94
February	89 054	73 107	24 784	19 409	64 270	59 840	14 501	35.7	40.5	6.18	6.40	220.63	259.20
March	89 480	73 524	24 998	19 453	64 482	60 216	14 526	35.8	40.6	6.22	6.45	222.68	261.87
April	89 418	73 441	24 958	19 450	64 460	60 069	14 515	35.3	39.3	6.22	6.43	219.57	252.70
May	89 791	73 801	25 071	19 509	64 720	60 369	14 551	35.6	40.2	6.28	6.52	223.57	262.10
June	90 109	74 064	25 161	19 553	64 948	60 583	14 566	35.6	40.2	6.32	6.56	224.99	263.71
July	90 215	74 065	25 163	19 531	65 052	60 559	14 536	35.6	40.2	6.36	6.59	226.42	264.92
August	90 297	74 068	25 059	19 406	65 238	60 517	14 397	35.6	40.1	6.40	6.63	227.84	265.86
September	90 325	74 197	25 088	19 442	65 237	60 631	14 440	35.6	40.1	6.45	6.67	229.62	267.47
October	90 482	74 346	25 038	19 390	65 444	60 748	14 384	35.6	40.2	6.47	6.71	230.33	269.74
November	90 576	74 403	24 947	19 299	65 629	60 781	14 295	35.6	40.1	6.51	6.74	231.76	270.27
December	90 673	74 493	24 970	19 301	65 703	60 863	14 300	35.5	40.1	6.57	6.80	233.24	272.68
1980													
January	90 802	74 601	24 949	19 282	65 853	60 899	14 241	35.4	40.0	6.57	6.82	232.58	272.80
February	90 882	74 656	24 874	19 219	66 008	60 966	14 170	35.4	40.1	6.63	6.88	234.70	275.89
March	90 994	74 698	24 818	19 217	66 176	60 990	14 165	35.3	39.9	6.70	6.95	236.51	277.31
April	90 850	74 267	24 507	18 973	66 343	60 544	13 914	35.2	39.8	6.72	6.97	236.54	277.41
May	90 419	73 965	24 234	18 726	66 185	60 198	13 632	35.1	39.3	6.76	7.02	237.28	275.89
June	90 099	73 658	23 968	18 490	66 131	59 895	13 405	35.0	39.2	6.82	7.10	238.70	278.32
July	89 837	73 419	23 698	18 276	66 139	59 698	13 227	34.9	39.1	6.86	7.16	239.41	279.96
August	90 097	73 687	23 860	18 414	66 237	59 913	13 349	35.1	39.5	6.91	7.24	242.54	285.98
September	90 210	73 880	23 931	18 445	66 279	60 079	13 396	35.1	39.6	6.95	7.30	243.95	289.08
October	90 491	74 105	24 012	18 506	66 479	60 244	13 437	35.2	39.8	7.02	7.38	247.10	293.72
November	90 748	74 357	24 123	18 601	66 625	60 455	13 528	35.3	39.9	7.09	7.47	250.28	298.05
December	90 943	74 570	24 182	18 640	66 761	60 611	13 550	35.3	40.1	7.13	7.52	251.69	301.55

Table 10-9. Employment, Hours, and Earnings, Total Nonfarm and Manufacturing, Historical Annual and Monthly—*Continued*

(Wage and salary workers on nonfarm payrolls, seasonally adjusted.)

Year and month	All wage and salary workers (thousands)					Production and nonsupervisory workers on private payrolls							
	Total	Private			Service-providing	Number (thousands)		Average hours per week		Average hourly earnings, dollars		Average weekly earnings, dollars	
		Total	Goods-producing			Total private	Manufac-turing	Total private	Manufac-turing	Total private	Manufac-turing	Total private	Manufac-turing
			Total	Manufac-turing									
1981													
January	91 037	74 677	24 152	18 639	66 885	60 715	13 545	35.4	40.1	7.19	7.58	254.53	303.96
February	91 105	74 759	24 118	18 613	66 987	60 742	13 518	35.2	39.8	7.23	7.62	254.50	303.28
March	91 210	74 918	24 203	18 647	67 007	60 881	13 550	35.3	40.0	7.29	7.68	257.34	307.20
April	91 283	75 023	24 151	18 711	67 132	60 979	13 594	35.3	40.1	7.33	7.76	258.75	311.18
May	91 293	75 095	24 148	18 766	67 145	60 981	13 633	35.3	40.2	7.37	7.81	260.16	313.96
June	91 490	75 331	24 290	18 789	67 200	61 141	13 632	35.2	40.0	7.42	7.85	261.18	314.00
July	91 602	75 427	24 302	18 785	67 300	61 228	13 629	35.2	39.9	7.46	7.89	262.59	314.81
August	91 566	75 456	24 258	18 748	67 308	61 223	13 573	35.2	40.0	7.53	7.97	265.06	318.80
September	91 479	75 448	24 210	18 712	67 269	61 241	13 565	35.0	39.6	7.57	8.03	264.95	317.99
October	91 380	75 311	24 051	18 566	67 329	61 074	13 399	35.1	39.6	7.59	8.06	266.41	319.18
November	91 171	75 093	23 875	18 409	67 296	60 825	13 235	35.1	39.4	7.64	8.08	268.16	318.35
December	90 893	74 820	23 656	18 223	67 237	60 520	13 033	34.9	39.2	7.64	8.09	266.64	317.13
1982													
January	90 567	74 526	23 362	18 047	67 205	60 218	12 874	34.1	37.3	7.72	8.26	263.25	308.10
February	90 562	74 551	23 361	17 981	67 201	60 285	12 831	35.1	39.6	7.73	8.21	271.32	325.12
March	90 432	74 408	23 214	17 857	67 218	60 150	12 727	34.9	39.1	7.76	8.24	270.82	322.18
April	90 152	74 142	22 996	17 683	67 156	59 877	12 566	34.8	39.1	7.77	8.28	270.40	323.75
May	90 107	74 104	22 884	17 588	67 223	59 851	12 506	34.8	39.1	7.83	8.33	272.48	325.70
June	89 864	73 848	22 643	17 430	67 221	59 599	12 365	34.8	39.2	7.85	8.37	273.18	328.10
July	89 522	73 632	22 434	17 278	67 088	59 422	12 261	34.8	39.2	7.89	8.40	274.57	329.28
August	89 364	73 434	22 268	17 160	67 096	59 213	12 153	34.7	39.0	7.94	8.43	275.52	328.77
September	89 183	73 260	22 146	17 074	67 037	59 078	12 104	34.8	39.0	7.94	8.45	276.31	329.55
October	88 906	72 950	21 879	16 853	67 027	58 761	11 880	34.6	38.9	7.96	8.44	275.42	328.32
November	88 783	72 806	21 736	16 722	67 047	58 625	11 766	34.6	39.0	7.98	8.46	276.11	329.94
December	88 769	72 788	21 688	16 690	67 081	58 599	11 746	34.7	39.0	8.02	8.49	278.29	331.11
1983													
January	88 993	72 970	21 757	16 705	67 236	58 828	11 783	34.8	39.3	8.06	8.52	280.49	334.84
February	88 918	72 914	21 676	16 706	67 242	58 803	11 794	34.5	39.3	8.10	8.59	279.45	337.59
March	89 090	73 085	21 649	16 711	67 441	58 971	11 817	34.7	39.6	8.10	8.59	281.07	340.16
April	89 366	73 376	21 729	16 794	67 637	59 214	11 894	34.8	39.7	8.13	8.61	282.92	341.82
May	89 643	73 638	21 829	16 885	67 814	59 458	11 987	34.9	40.0	8.17	8.64	285.13	345.60
June	90 022	74 002	21 949	16 960	68 073	59 819	12 054	34.9	40.1	8.19	8.66	285.83	347.27
July	90 440	74 429	22 103	17 059	68 337	60 203	12 155	34.9	40.3	8.23	8.71	287.23	351.01
August	90 132	74 116	22 207	17 118	67 925	59 834	12 200	34.9	40.3	8.20	8.71	286.18	351.01
September	91 247	75 205	22 381	17 255	68 866	60 859	12 318	35.0	40.6	8.26	8.76	289.10	355.66
October	91 518	75 532	22 546	17 367	68 972	61 108	12 408	35.2	40.6	8.31	8.80	292.51	357.28
November	91 871	75 874	22 698	17 479	69 173	61 392	12 503	35.1	40.6	8.32	8.84	292.03	358.90
December	92 227	76 219	22 803	17 551	69 424	61 680	12 553	35.1	40.5	8.33	8.87	292.38	359.24
1984													
January	92 673	76 663	22 942	17 630	69 731	61 925	12 617	35.1	40.6	8.06	8.91	294.14	361.75
February	93 154	77 129	23 146	17 728	70 008	62 342	12 703	35.3	41.1	8.10	8.92	295.46	366.61
March	93 429	77 399	23 209	17 806	70 220	62 531	12 768	35.1	40.7	8.10	8.96	295.19	364.67
April	93 792	77 717	23 305	17 872	70 487	62 817	12 814	35.2	40.8	8.13	8.98	297.44	366.38
May	94 100	77 997	23 389	17 916	70 711	63 029	12 840	35.1	40.7	8.17	8.99	296.24	365.89
June	94 479	78 352	23 497	17 967	70 982	63 313	12 871	35.1	40.6	8.19	9.03	297.65	366.62
July	94 792	78 620	23 571	18 013	71 221	63 532	12 901	35.1	40.6	8.23	9.05	299.05	367.43
August	95 034	78 810	23 608	18 034	71 426	63 670	12 906	35.0	40.5	8.20	9.09	298.20	368.15
September	95 344	79 089	23 617	18 019	71 727	63 889	12 880	35.1	40.5	8.26	9.12	300.46	369.36
October	95 630	79 356	23 626	18 024	72 004	64 100	12 868	34.9	40.5	8.31	9.15	298.40	370.58
November	95 979	79 668	23 639	18 016	72 340	64 343	12 846	35.0	40.4	8.32	9.19	299.95	371.28
December	96 107	79 825	23 673	18 023	72 434	64 460	12 848	35.1	40.5	8.33	9.22	302.21	373.41
1985													
January	96 373	80 037	23 672	18 009	72 701	64 678	12 833	34.9	40.3	8.61	9.27	300.49	373.58
February	96 497	80 148	23 621	17 966	72 876	64 775	12 784	34.8	40.1	8.64	9.29	300.67	372.53
March	96 843	80 448	23 661	17 939	73 182	65 026	12 758	34.9	40.4	8.67	9.32	302.58	376.53
April	97 039	80 609	23 644	17 886	73 395	65 133	12 701	34.9	40.5	8.69	9.35	303.28	378.68
May	97 313	80 839	23 632	17 855	73 681	65 328	12 673	34.9	40.4	8.70	9.37	303.63	378.55
June	97 459	80 961	23 592	17 819	73 867	65 403	12 635	34.9	40.5	8.74	9.39	305.03	380.30
July	97 649	81 029	23 549	17 776	74 100	65 450	12 596	34.8	40.4	8.74	9.42	304.15	380.57
August	97 842	81 223	23 546	17 756	74 296	65 633	12 593	34.8	40.6	8.77	9.43	305.20	382.86
September	98 045	81 407	23 528	17 718	74 517	65 769	12 556	34.8	40.6	8.80	9.44	306.24	383.26
October	98 233	81 579	23 529	17 708	74 704	65 939	12 556	34.8	40.7	8.79	9.46	305.89	385.02
November	98 442	81 768	23 520	17 697	74 922	66 089	12 545	34.8	40.7	8.82	9.49	306.94	386.24
December	98 609	81 915	23 518	17 693	75 091	66 219	12 550	34.9	40.9	8.87	9.55	309.56	390.60
1986													
January	98 734	82 019	23 530	17 686	75 204	66 316	12 546	35.0	40.7	8.85	9.53	309.75	387.87
February	98 841	82 082	23 485	17 663	75 356	66 387	12 530	34.8	40.7	8.88	9.56	309.02	389.09
March	98 935	82 180	23 428	17 624	75 507	66 425	12 498	34.8	40.7	8.89	9.58	309.37	389.91
April	99 122	82 357	23 427	17 616	75 695	66 554	12 495	34.7	40.5	8.89	9.56	308.48	387.18
May	99 249	82 459	23 349	17 593	75 900	66 635	12 474	34.8	40.7	8.90	9.59	309.72	390.31
June	99 155	82 376	23 263	17 530	75 892	66 558	12 424	34.7	40.7	8.91	9.58	309.18	389.91
July	99 473	82 694	23 235	17 497	76 238	66 829	12 389	34.6	40.6	8.92	9.60	308.63	389.76
August	99 587	82 787	23 225	17 489	76 362	66 927	12 399	34.7	40.7	8.94	9.61	310.22	391.13
September	99 934	83 024	23 216	17 498	76 718	67 133	12 411	34.6	40.7	8.94	9.60	309.32	390.72
October	100 120	83 151	23 208	17 477	76 912	67 230	12 396	34.6	40.6	8.96	9.62	310.02	390.57
November	100 306	83 301	23 204	17 472	77 102	67 368	12 407	34.7	40.7	9.00	9.64	312.30	392.35
December	100 511	83 490	23 237	17 478	77 274	67 517	12 425	34.6	40.8	9.01	9.66	311.75	394.13

Table 10-9. Employment, Hours, and Earnings, Total Nonfarm and Manufacturing, Historical Annual and Monthly—Continued

(Wage and salary workers on nonfarm payrolls, seasonally adjusted.)

Year and month	All wage and salary workers (thousands)					Production and nonsupervisory workers on private payrolls							
	Total	Private			Service-providing	Number (thousands)		Average hours per week		Average hourly earnings, dollars		Average weekly earnings, dollars	
		Total	Goods-producing			Total private	Manufac-turing	Total private	Manufac-turing	Total private	Manufac-turing	Total private	Manufac-turing
			Total	Manufac-turing									
1987													
January	100 683	83 638	23 232	17 465	77 451	67 638	12 405	34.7	40.8	9.02	9.67	312.99	394.54
February	100 915	83 879	23 296	17 499	77 619	67 869	12 438	34.9	41.2	9.05	9.69	315.85	399.23
March	101 164	84 100	23 307	17 507	77 857	68 015	12 446	34.7	41.0	9.07	9.71	314.73	398.11
April	101 502	84 393	23 342	17 525	78 160	68 261	12 465	34.7	40.8	9.08	9.71	315.08	396.17
May	101 728	84 616	23 390	17 542	78 338	68 467	12 481	34.8	41.0	9.11	9.73	317.03	398.93
June	101 900	84 776	23 390	17 537	78 510	68 579	12 482	34.7	40.9	9.11	9.74	316.12	398.37
July	102 247	85 087	23 455	17 593	78 792	68 819	12 521	34.7	41.0	9.12	9.74	316.46	399.34
August	102 418	85 246	23 506	17 630	78 912	68 941	12 560	34.9	40.9	9.18	9.80	320.38	400.82
September	102 646	85 511	23 566	17 691	79 080	69 164	12 614	34.7	40.8	9.19	9.85	318.89	401.88
October	103 138	85 869	23 655	17 729	79 483	69 442	12 637	34.8	41.1	9.22	9.84	320.86	404.42
November	103 370	86 071	23 711	17 775	79 659	69 621	12 678	34.8	41.0	9.27	9.87	322.60	404.67
December	103 664	86 317	23 772	17 809	79 892	69 852	12 707	34.6	41.0	9.28	9.89	321.09	405.49
1988													
January	103 758	86 393	23 668	17 790	80 090	69 859	12 684	34.6	41.1	9.29	9.91	321.43	407.30
February	104 211	86 822	23 769	17 823	80 442	70 255	12 706	34.7	41.1	9.29	9.92	322.36	407.71
March	104 487	87 040	23 824	17 844	80 663	70 397	12 712	34.5	40.9	9.31	9.94	321.20	406.55
April	104 732	87 280	23 880	17 874	80 852	70 604	12 733	34.6	41.0	9.36	9.99	323.86	409.59
May	104 961	87 480	23 896	17 892	81 065	70 749	12 747	34.6	41.0	9.41	10.02	325.59	410.82
June	105 324	87 809	23 951	17 916	81 373	71 031	12 767	34.6	41.1	9.42	10.04	325.93	412.64
July	105 546	88 052	23 966	17 926	81 580	71 235	12 774	34.7	41.1	9.45	10.05	327.92	413.06
August	105 670	88 126	23 926	17 891	81 744	71 287	12 752	34.5	40.9	9.46	10.07	326.37	411.86
September	106 009	88 375	23 942	17 914	82 067	71 487	12 764	34.5	41.0	9.51	10.12	328.10	414.92
October	106 277	88 607	23 987	17 966	82 290	71 680	12 812	34.7	41.1	9.56	10.16	331.73	417.58
November	106 616	88 870	24 030	18 003	82 586	71 902	12 851	34.5	41.1	9.58	10.19	330.51	418.81
December	106 906	89 170	24 054	18 025	82 852	72 175	12 864	34.6	40.9	9.60	10.20	332.16	417.18
1989													
January	107 168	89 394	24 097	18 057	83 071	72 393	12 882	34.7	41.1	9.65	10.23	334.86	420.45
February	107 426	89 614	24 080	18 055	83 346	72 577	12 880	34.5	41.2	9.68	10.26	333.96	422.71
March	107 619	89 797	24 069	18 060	83 550	72 695	12 878	34.5	41.1	9.70	10.29	334.65	422.92
April	107 792	89 952	24 100	18 055	83 692	72 819	12 867	34.6	41.1	9.75	10.28	337.35	422.51
May	107 910	90 034	24 089	18 040	83 821	72 889	12 852	34.4	41.0	9.73	10.30	334.71	422.30
June	108 026	90 114	24 052	18 013	83 974	72 941	12 822	34.4	40.9	9.77	10.33	336.09	422.50
July	108 066	90 161	24 027	17 980	84 039	72 972	12 790	34.5	40.9	9.82	10.36	338.79	423.72
August	108 115	90 126	24 048	17 964	84 067	72 940	12 790	34.5	40.9	9.83	10.39	339.14	424.95
September	108 365	90 338	24 000	17 922	84 365	73 114	12 745	34.4	40.8	9.87	10.41	339.53	424.73
October	108 476	90 443	23 997	17 895	84 479	73 211	12 723	34.6	40.8	9.93	10.43	343.58	425.54
November	108 753	90 696	24 009	17 886	84 744	73 427	12 713	34.4	40.7	9.93	10.44	341.59	424.91
December	108 849	90 774	23 949	17 881	84 900	73 504	12 705	34.3	40.5	9.98	10.49	342.31	424.85
1990													
January	109 183	91 032	23 981	17 796	85 202	73 738	12 738	34.5	40.5	10.02	10.52	345.69	426.06
February	109 432	91 255	24 071	17 893	85 361	73 935	12 848	34.4	40.6	10.07	10.64	346.41	431.98
March	109 647	91 353	24 023	17 868	85 624	73 995	12 821	34.4	40.7	10.11	10.70	347.78	435.49
April	109 688	91 311	23 967	17 846	85 721	73 961	12 804	34.3	40.5	10.12	10.68	347.46	432.54
May	109 838	91 239	23 887	17 796	85 951	73 873	12 755	34.3	40.6	10.16	10.74	348.49	436.04
June	109 863	91 307	23 850	17 777	86 013	73 867	12 739	34.4	40.7	10.20	10.78	351.22	438.75
July	109 833	91 273	23 745	17 703	86 088	73 807	12 673	34.2	40.6	10.22	10.80	349.52	438.48
August	109 613	91 156	23 648	17 649	85 965	73 744	12 624	34.2	40.5	10.24	10.81	350.21	437.81
September	109 525	91 088	23 571	17 609	85 954	73 636	12 596	34.2	40.5	10.28	10.86	351.58	439.83
October	109 366	90 923	23 473	17 577	85 893	73 504	12 577	34.1	40.4	10.30	10.92	351.23	441.17
November	109 216	90 766	23 283	17 428	85 933	73 351	12 439	34.2	40.2	10.32	10.89	352.94	437.78
December	109 160	90 692	23 203	17 395	85 957	73 285	12 415	34.2	40.3	10.35	10.93	353.97	440.48
1991													
January	109 039	90 565	23 060	17 329	85 979	73 143	12 351	34.1	40.2	10.38	10.98	353.96	441.40
February	108 735	90 253	22 900	17 211	85 835	72 855	12 242	34.1	40.1	10.39	10.97	354.30	439.90
March	108 577	90 089	22 779	17 140	85 798	72 704	12 191	34.0	40.0	10.41	11.00	353.94	440.00
April	108 367	89 882	22 688	17 094	85 679	72 535	12 157	34.0	40.1	10.46	11.05	355.64	443.11
May	108 240	89 742	22 617	17 069	85 623	72 438	12 148	34.0	40.1	10.49	11.09	356.66	444.71
June	108 338	89 777	22 571	17 044	85 767	72 459	12 135	34.1	40.5	10.51	11.13	358.73	450.77
July	108 302	89 704	22 507	17 015	85 795	72 427	12 130	34.1	40.5	10.54	11.17	359.41	452.39
August	108 308	89 741	22 493	17 025	85 815	72 484	12 153	34.1	40.6	10.56	11.18	360.10	453.91
September	108 340	89 797	22 466	17 010	85 874	72 501	12 140	34.1	40.6	10.58	11.22	360.78	455.53
October	108 356	89 763	22 418	16 999	85 938	72 476	12 138	34.2	40.6	10.59	11.25	362.18	456.75
November	108 299	89 672	22 316	16 961	85 983	72 405	12 102	34.1	40.7	10.61	11.26	361.80	458.28
December	108 324	89 683	22 274	16 916	86 050	72 448	12 075	34.1	40.7	10.64	11.27	362.82	458.69
1992													
January	108 378	89 690	22 214	16 840	86 164	72 490	12 013	34.1	40.6	10.65	11.24	363.17	456.34
February	108 313	89 624	22 141	16 828	86 172	72 467	12 015	34.1	40.7	10.67	11.30	363.85	459.91
March	108 368	89 653	22 127	16 805	86 241	72 484	12 006	34.1	40.7	10.70	11.32	364.87	460.72
April	108 527	89 788	22 132	16 831	86 395	72 637	12 029	34.3	41.0	10.72	11.36	367.70	464.62
May	108 654	89 901	22 135	16 835	86 519	72 752	12 046	34.3	40.9	10.74	11.39	368.38	465.85
June	108 721	89 959	22 097	16 826	86 624	72 788	12 042	34.2	40.8	10.77	11.41	368.33	465.53
July	108 790	89 973	22 075	16 820	86 715	72 809	12 049	34.2	40.8	10.79	11.43	369.02	466.34
August	108 930	90 047	22 045	16 783	86 885	72 886	12 020	34.2	40.8	10.82	11.46	370.04	467.57
September	108 966	90 137	22 020	16 761	86 946	72 988	12 002	34.3	40.7	10.82	11.45	371.13	466.02
October	109 145	90 317	22 028	16 750	87 117	73 143	11 999	34.2	40.8	10.85	11.47	371.41	467.98
November	109 284	90 443	22 042	16 758	87 242	73 294	12 012	34.2	40.9	10.87	11.49	371.75	469.94
December	109 494	90 616	22 075	16 768	87 419	73 478	12 031	34.2	40.9	10.89	11.51	372.78	470.76

Table 10-9. Employment, Hours, and Earnings, Total Nonfarm and Manufacturing, Historical Annual and Monthly—Continued

(Wage and salary workers on nonfarm payrolls, seasonally adjusted.)

Year and month	All wage and salary workers (thousands)					Production and nonsupervisory workers on private payrolls							
	Total	Private			Service-providing	Number (thousands)		Average hours per week		Average hourly earnings, dollars		Average weekly earnings, dollars	
		Total	Goods-producing			Total private	Manufac-turing	Total private	Manufac-turing	Total private	Manufac-turing	Total private	Manufac-turing
			Total	Manufac-turing									
1993													
January	109 805	90 904	22 133	16 791	87 672	73 754	12 060	34.3	41.1	10.93	11.55	375.24	474.71
February	110 047	91 145	22 188	16 805	87 859	74 011	12 072	34.3	41.1	10.94	11.57	375.59	475.53
March	109 998	91 091	22 142	16 795	87 856	73 928	12 074	34.1	40.8	10.99	11.59	374.76	472.87
April	110 306	91 368	22 131	16 772	88 175	74 153	12 056	34.4	41.5	10.99	11.64	378.40	483.06
May	110 573	91 622	22 189	16 766	88 384	74 410	12 056	34.3	41.1	11.02	11.66	377.99	479.23
June	110 754	91 785	22 165	16 742	88 589	74 511	12 039	34.3	40.9	11.03	11.67	378.67	477.30
July	111 053	91 993	22 184	16 740	88 869	74 706	12 043	34.4	41.1	11.05	11.69	380.46	480.46
August	111 212	92 104	22 203	16 741	89 000	74 881	12 060	34.3	41.1	11.08	11.72	380.01	481.60
September	111 451	92 410	22 252	16 769	89 199	75 072	12 080	34.4	41.3	11.10	11.76	381.84	485.69
October	111 737	92 695	22 306	16 778	89 431	75 318	12 092	34.4	41.3	11.13	11.79	382.87	486.93
November	111 999	92 931	22 347	16 800	89 652	75 537	12 119	34.4	41.3	11.15	11.83	383.56	488.58
December	112 311	93 202	22 413	16 815	89 898	75 762	12 140	34.4	41.4	11.18	11.88	384.59	491.83
1994													
January	112 583	93 436	22 465	16 855	90 118	75 967	12 181	34.4	41.4	11.21	11.89	385.62	492.25
February	112 783	93 633	22 451	16 862	90 332	76 174	12 198	34.2	40.9	11.25	11.97	384.75	489.57
March	113 248	94 058	22 550	16 897	90 698	76 536	12 234	34.5	41.7	11.25	11.95	388.13	498.32
April	113 597	94 374	22 641	16 933	90 956	76 833	12 276	34.5	41.8	11.27	11.96	388.82	498.73
May	113 931	94 667	22 704	16 962	91 227	77 112	12 304	34.5	41.8	11.29	11.98	389.85	500.76
June	114 247	94 973	22 764	17 010	91 483	77 363	12 351	34.5	41.8	11.31	12.01	390.54	502.02
July	114 624	95 323	22 806	17 025	91 818	77 658	12 367	34.6	41.8	11.34	12.02	392.36	502.44
August	114 902	95 596	22 876	17 081	92 026	77 901	12 428	34.5	41.7	11.36	12.05	391.92	502.49
September	115 253	95 916	22 947	17 114	92 306	78 166	12 459	34.5	41.6	11.39	12.09	392.96	502.94
October	115 468	96 124	22 975	17 145	92 493	78 349	12 489	34.5	41.8	11.42	12.11	394.34	506.20
November	115 887	96 520	23 050	17 186	92 837	78 697	12 529	34.5	41.7	11.45	12.15	395.03	507.87
December	116 162	96 774	23 095	17 217	93 067	78 942	12 558	34.5	41.8	11.47	12.17	396.06	508.71
1995													
January	116 487	97 090	23 146	17 261	93 341	79 181	12 593	34.5	41.8	11.49	12.19	396.41	509.54
February	116 691	97 284	23 103	17 265	93 588	79 338	12 602	34.4	41.7	11.52	12.24	396.63	510.41
March	116 913	97 486	23 151	17 263	93 762	79 518	12 600	34.3	41.5	11.55	12.25	396.17	508.38
April	117 075	97 641	23 174	17 278	93 901	79 651	12 608	34.3	41.1	11.56	12.25	396.85	503.48
May	117 059	97 641	23 120	17 259	93 939	79 673	12 590	34.2	41.2	11.60	12.28	396.72	505.94
June	117 294	97 849	23 137	17 247	94 157	79 842	12 574	34.3	41.2	11.63	12.31	398.91	507.17
July	117 395	97 958	23 118	17 217	94 277	79 909	12 538	34.3	41.1	11.67	12.38	400.28	508.82
August	117 644	98 215	23 164	17 240	94 480	80 159	12 566	34.3	41.2	11.69	12.39	401.31	510.47
September	117 885	98 455	23 207	17 246	94 678	80 356	12 567	34.3	41.2	11.73	12.41	402.34	511.29
October	118 041	98 577	23 207	17 217	94 834	80 477	12 535	34.3	41.2	11.75	12.43	403.37	512.12
November	118 189	98 726	23 200	17 209	94 989	80 551	12 515	34.3	41.3	11.78	12.45	404.05	514.19
December	118 321	98 855	23 208	17 230	95 113	80 702	12 551	34.2	40.9	11.81	12.49	403.90	510.84
1996													
January	118 303	98 853	23 196	17 208	95 107	80 627	12 517	33.8	39.7	11.87	12.60	401.21	500.22
February	118 735	99 250	23 281	17 230	95 454	81 019	12 533	34.3	41.3	11.87	12.55	407.14	518.32
March	119 001	99 469	23 276	17 193	95 725	81 197	12 488	34.3	41.1	11.89	12.50	407.83	513.75
April	119 165	99 650	23 316	17 204	95 849	81 364	12 505	34.2	41.1	11.96	12.69	409.03	521.56
May	119 485	99 956	23 357	17 221	96 128	81 625	12 518	34.3	41.4	11.97	12.71	410.91	526.19
June	119 774	100 246	23 399	17 226	96 375	81 838	12 522	34.4	41.5	12.03	12.76	414.18	529.54
July	120 029	100 482	23 417	17 222	96 612	82 037	12 517	34.3	41.4	12.06	12.79	413.66	529.51
August	120 202	100 698	23 479	17 255	96 723	82 234	12 546	34.4	41.5	12.09	12.83	416.24	532.45
September	120 427	100 860	23 497	17 252	96 930	82 358	12 544	34.4	41.6	12.14	12.85	417.62	534.56
October	120 677	101 123	23 546	17 268	97 131	82 606	12 559	34.4	41.4	12.16	12.83	418.30	531.16
November	120 976	101 411	23 585	17 278	97 391	82 791	12 560	34.4	41.5	12.21	12.88	420.02	534.52
December	121 146	101 575	23 598	17 284	97 548	82 960	12 571	34.4	41.7	12.25	12.95	421.40	540.02
1997													
January	121 382	101 789	23 619	17 298	97 763	83 106	12 579	34.3	41.4	12.29	12.99	421.89	537.79
February	121 684	102 086	23 686	17 316	97 998	83 387	12 592	34.4	41.6	12.32	13.00	423.81	540.80
March	122 000	102 392	23 739	17 340	98 261	83 617	12 613	34.5	41.8	12.37	13.04	426.77	545.07
April	122 293	102 690	23 766	17 350	98 527	83 868	12 618	34.6	41.8	12.39	13.03	428.69	544.65
May	122 551	102 950	23 809	17 362	98 742	84 093	12 633	34.6	41.7	12.43	13.07	430.08	545.02
June	122 818	103 158	23 834	17 387	98 984	84 232	12 647	34.3	41.5	12.46	13.09	427.72	543.24
July	123 131	103 445	23 862	17 389	99 269	84 480	12 645	34.5	41.6	12.50	13.09	431.25	544.54
August	123 092	103 475	23 952	17 452	99 140	84 427	12 699	34.6	41.7	12.57	13.17	434.92	549.19
September	123 604	103 925	23 996	17 465	99 608	84 822	12 711	34.6	41.7	12.60	13.17	436.31	549.19
October	123 945	104 207	24 053	17 513	99 892	85 032	12 746	34.6	41.8	12.67	13.29	438.38	555.52
November	124 251	104 490	24 112	17 556	100 139	85 226	12 777	34.5	41.8	12.72	13.32	440.11	556.78
December	124 554	104 788	24 184	17 588	100 370	85 459	12 800	34.6	41.9	12.75	13.35	441.50	559.37
1998													
January	124 830	105 060	24 262	17 619	100 568	85 621	12 818	34.6	41.9	12.79	13.35	442.88	559.37
February	125 026	105 240	24 283	17 627	100 743	85 790	12 828	34.5	41.7	12.84	13.39	444.61	558.36
March	125 177	105 385	24 264	17 637	100 913	85 820	12 822	34.5	41.6	12.88	13.43	444.71	558.69
April	125 456	105 640	24 340	17 637	101 116	86 040	12 814	34.4	41.3	12.92	13.40	444.79	553.42
May	125 862	105 987	24 361	17 624	101 501	86 320	12 790	34.5	41.5	12.97	13.45	448.76	558.18
June	126 080	106 201	24 387	17 608	101 693	86 470	12 769	34.4	41.4	12.99	13.43	447.20	556.00
July	126 204	106 274	24 238	17 422	101 966	86 488	12 558	34.5	41.4	13.01	13.34	448.85	552.28
August	126 551	106 592	24 420	17 563	102 131	86 774	12 702	34.5	41.4	13.08	13.46	451.61	557.24
September	126 775	106 790	24 420	17 558	102 355	86 935	12 715	34.4	41.3	13.11	13.52	451.33	558.38
October	126 971	106 970	24 405	17 511	102 566	87 085	12 673	34.5	41.4	13.15	13.53	453.68	560.14
November	127 254	107 210	24 394	17 465	102 860	87 251	12 634	34.4	41.4	13.17	13.54	453.39	560.56
December	127 601	107 522	24 454	17 449	103 147	87 517	12 625	34.5	41.5	13.22	13.56	456.09	562.74

Table 10-9. Employment, Hours, and Earnings, Total Nonfarm and Manufacturing, Historical Annual and Monthly—Continued

(Wage and salary workers on nonfarm payrolls, seasonally adjusted.)

	All wage and salary workers (thousands)					Production and nonsupervisory workers on private payrolls							
		Private				Number (thousands)		Average hours per week		Average hourly earnings, dollars		Average weekly earnings, dollars	
Year and month	Total	Total	Goods-producing		Service-providing	Total private	Manufac-turing	Total private	Manufac-turing	Total private	Manufac-turing	Total private	Manufac-turing
			Total	Manufac-turing									
1999													
January	127 726	107 642	24 401	17 427	103 325	87 577	12 605	34.4	41.3	13.27	13.59	456.83	561.27
February	128 137	107 993	24 434	17 395	103 703	87 891	12 575	34.4	41.3	13.30	13.63	457.52	564.28
March	128 244	108 076	24 378	17 368	103 866	87 954	12 562	34.3	41.3	13.33	13.69	457.56	565.40
April	128 619	108 382	24 424	17 343	104 195	88 183	12 540	34.4	41.4	13.38	13.73	460.62	567.05
May	128 831	108 602	24 445	17 333	104 386	88 368	12 534	34.3	41.4	13.43	13.80	460.65	571.32
June	129 092	108 820	24 434	17 295	104 658	88 543	12 503	34.4	41.3	13.47	13.86	463.71	572.42
July	129 411	109 072	24 474	17 308	104 937	88 751	12 525	34.4	41.4	13.52	13.92	465.09	576.29
August	129 578	109 203	24 468	17 288	105 110	88 862	12 502	34.4	41.5	13.54	13.93	466.12	578.10
September	129 791	109 387	24 485	17 281	105 306	89 003	12 495	34.3	41.5	13.61	13.99	467.17	580.59
October	130 192	109 735	24 506	17 273	105 686	89 307	12 484	34.4	41.4	13.64	13.99	469.22	579.19
November	130 483	109 987	24 561	17 282	105 922	89 526	12 488	34.4	41.4	13.66	14.01	469.90	580.01
December	130 778	110 238	24 582	17 280	106 196	89 745	12 490	34.4	41.4	13.70	14.06	471.62	582.08
2000													
January	131 008	110 437	24 627	17 283	106 381	89 897	12 491	34.4	41.5	13.75	14.13	473.34	586.40
February	131 138	110 539	24 608	17 284	106 530	89 977	12 481	34.4	41.5	13.80	14.15	474.72	587.23
March	131 606	110 873	24 705	17 302	106 901	90 244	12 490	34.4	41.4	13.84	14.18	476.44	587.05
April	131 893	111 091	24 688	17 298	107 205	90 468	12 477	34.4	41.6	13.90	14.23	478.50	591.97
May	132 119	110 972	24 647	17 279	107 472	90 375	12 464	34.3	41.3	13.94	14.23	478.14	587.70
June	132 074	111 187	24 674	17 298	107 400	90 544	12 468	34.3	41.3	13.98	14.30	479.86	590.59
July	132 251	111 384	24 717	17 322	107 534	90 674	12 474	34.3	41.5	14.03	14.32	481.23	594.28
August	132 237	111 400	24 684	17 288	107 553	90 698	12 431	34.2	41.0	14.07	14.36	481.19	588.76
September	132 371	111 636	24 642	17 230	107 729	90 847	12 382	34.3	41.1	14.13	14.40	484.66	591.84
October	132 357	111 614	24 639	17 218	107 718	90 835	12 357	34.3	41.1	14.18	14.49	486.37	595.54
November	132 582	111 822	24 624	17 203	107 958	90 966	12 336	34.2	41.1	14.24	14.52	487.01	596.77
December	132 724	111 920	24 576	17 182	108 148	91 015	12 307	34.0	40.4	14.29	14.50	485.86	585.80
2001													
January	132 694	111 859	24 531	17 102	108 163	90 965	12 229	34.2	40.6	14.29	14.48	489.06	587.89
February	132 766	111 860	24 473	17 027	108 293	90 923	12 155	34.0	40.5	14.37	14.55	490.02	589.28
March	132 741	111 796	24 408	16 937	108 333	90 876	12 085	34.1	40.5	14.42	14.58	492.06	590.49
April	132 460	111 468	24 254	16 802	108 206	90 640	11 982	34.0	40.5	14.45	14.64	491.64	592.92
May	132 422	111 393	24 119	16 661	108 303	90 565	11 859	34.0	40.4	14.50	14.69	493.00	593.48
June	132 293	111 156	23 967	16 517	108 326	90 369	11 739	34.0	40.3	14.55	14.74	494.70	594.02
July	132 178	110 993	23 836	16 381	108 342	90 253	11 632	34.0	40.6	14.55	14.82	495.04	601.69
August	132 020	110 802	23 668	16 233	108 352	90 100	11 495	33.9	40.3	14.60	14.85	494.94	598.46
September	131 778	110 536	23 537	16 117	108 241	89 837	11 400	33.8	40.2	14.64	14.89	495.17	598.58
October	131 454	110 179	23 379	15 973	108 075	89 552	11 286	33.7	40.1	14.66	14.90	494.38	597.49
November	131 160	109 834	23 210	15 826	107 950	89 232	11 175	33.8	40.1	14.72	14.96	497.87	599.90
December	130 989	109 634	23 095	15 712	107 894	89 142	11 081	33.9	40.2	14.75	15.01	500.36	603.40
2002													
January	130 847	109 470	22 959	15 585	107 888	89 083	10 993	33.8	40.1	14.76	15.05	499.23	603.51
February	130 714	109 324	22 875	15 514	107 839	89 048	10 951	33.8	40.3	14.78	15.11	499.90	608.93
March	130 695	109 264	22 786	15 443	107 909	89 006	10 901	33.9	40.6	14.82	15.15	502.74	615.09
April	130 615	109 172	22 689	15 392	107 926	88 851	10 859	33.9	40.6	14.84	15.17	503.08	615.90
May	130 607	109 093	22 604	15 337	108 003	88 711	10 824	33.9	40.6	14.88	15.24	504.77	618.74
June	130 664	109 115	22 579	15 299	108 085	88 636	10 797	34.0	40.7	14.94	15.27	506.81	621.49
July	130 579	109 035	22 521	15 256	108 058	88 487	10 764	33.8	40.4	14.98	15.29	506.66	617.72
August	130 564	108 975	22 450	15 172	108 114	88 414	10 697	33.9	40.5	15.02	15.34	509.52	621.27
September	130 504	108 958	22 398	15 120	108 106	88 395	10 668	33.9	40.5	15.07	15.38	511.21	622.89
October	130 629	109 070	22 326	15 061	108 303	88 469	10 631	33.8	40.3	15.12	15.46	511.39	623.04
November	130 639	109 058	22 283	14 993	108 356	88 432	10 583	33.8	40.4	15.15	15.48	512.41	625.39
December	130 481	108 893	22 189	14 912	108 292	88 246	10 523	33.8	40.5	15.21	15.53	514.44	628.97
2003													
January	130 575	108 949	22 149	14 869	108 426	88 294	10 484	33.8	40.3	15.22	15.59	514.77	628.28
February	130 422	108 798	22 024	14 782	108 398	88 148	10 416	33.7	40.3	15.29	15.63	515.61	629.89
March	130 212	108 602	21 946	14 722	108 266	87 860	10 357	33.8	40.4	15.29	15.64	517.14	631.86
April	130 167	108 572	21 864	14 609	108 303	87 815	10 256	33.6	40.1	15.27	15.62	513.74	626.36
May	130 156	108 589	21 831	14 556	108 325	87 775	10 218	33.7	40.2	15.33	15.69	516.96	630.74
June	130 166	108 560	21 788	14 493	108 378	87 764	10 165	33.7	40.3	15.36	15.72	517.97	633.52
July	130 189	108 556	21 707	14 401	108 482	87 740	10 093	33.6	40.1	15.40	15.76	517.78	631.98
August	130 148	108 592	21 707	14 377	108 441	87 806	10 084	33.7	40.2	15.42	15.79	519.99	634.76
September	130 250	108 746	21 700	14 347	108 550	87 924	10 059	33.6	40.5	15.42	15.84	518.45	641.52
October	130 446	108 888	21 691	14 334	108 755	88 022	10 054	33.7	40.6	15.43	15.82	520.33	642.29
November	130 462	108 927	21 687	14 315	108 775	88 061	10 039	33.8	40.9	15.47	15.89	523.22	649.90
December	130 586	109 040	21 703	14 300	108 883	88 130	10 031	33.6	40.7	15.47	15.91	520.13	647.54
2004													
January	130 747	109 209	21 716	14 291	109 031	88 236	10 027	33.7	40.9	15.50	15.94	522.69	651.95
February	130 791	109 241	21 692	14 278	109 099	88 250	10 012	33.8	41.0	15.54	15.98	525.59	655.18
March	131 123	109 535	21 758	14 287	109 365	88 506	10 025	33.7	40.9	15.56	16.01	524.71	654.81
April	131 372	109 758	21 803	14 316	109 569	88 752	10 060	33.7	40.7	15.59	16.06	525.72	653.64
May	131 679	110 065	21 881	14 342	109 798	89 062	10 091	33.8	41.0	15.64	16.07	528.97	660.48
June	131 753	110 152	21 885	14 332	109 868	89 200	10 087	33.6	40.7	15.67	16.11	526.85	655.68
July	131 785	110 179	21 899	14 329	109 886	89 304	10 095	33.7	40.8	15.70	16.14	529.43	658.51
August	131 917	110 291	21 943	14 344	109 974	89 440	10 115	33.8	40.8	15.74	16.20	532.35	660.96
September	132 079	110 444	21 956	14 330	110 123	89 625	10 104	33.8	40.8	15.78	16.30	533.70	665.04
October	132 425	110 769	22 004	14 332	110 421	89 940	10 103	33.8	40.5	15.81	16.27	535.05	660.56
November	132 490	110 798	21 998	14 308	110 492	89 973	10 078	33.7	40.5	15.84	16.30	534.15	660.15
December	132 619	110 926	22 006	14 288	110 613	90 116	10 063	33.7	40.6	15.87	16.34	536.74	663.40

Table 10-9. Employment, Hours, and Earnings, Total Nonfarm and Manufacturing, Historical Annual and Monthly—*Continued*

(Wage and salary workers on nonfarm payrolls, seasonally adjusted.)

Year and month	All wage and salary workers (thousands)					Production and nonsupervisory workers on private payrolls							
	Total	Private			Service-providing	Number (thousands)		Average hours per week		Average hourly earnings, dollars		Average weekly earnings, dollars	
		Total	Goods-producing			Total private	Manufac-turing	Total private	Manufac-turing	Total private	Manufac-turing	Total private	Manufac-turing
			Total	Manufac-turing									
2005													
January	132 753	111 018	21 959	14 258	110 794	90 228	10 045	33.7	40.6	15.91	16.38	536.50	665.03
February	132 992	111 248	22 037	14 274	110 955	90 456	10 052	33.8	40.6	15.93	16.43	538.77	667.06
March	133 126	111 386	22 066	14 269	111 060	90 633	10 056	33.7	40.4	15.97	16.44	538.53	664.18
April	133 489	111 735	22 136	14 250	111 353	90 972	10 048	33.8	40.4	16.01	16.46	541.48	664.98
May	133 664	111 883	22 171	14 255	111 493	91 098	10 061	33.7	40.4	16.04	16.53	540.89	667.81
June	133 909	112 146	22 186	14 228	111 723	91 350	10 047	33.7	40.4	16.08	16.54	542.23	668.22
July	134 282	112 425	22 204	14 225	112 078	91 587	10 039	33.7	40.5	16.15	16.58	544.93	671.49
August	134 478	112 615	22 227	14 202	112 251	91 773	10 043	33.7	40.6	16.17	16.63	545.27	673.52
September	134 545	112 700	22 226	14 175	112 319	91 866	10 046	33.8	40.7	16.19	16.59	547.90	675.21
October	134 629	112 800	22 292	14 192	112 337	91 967	10 073	33.8	41.0	16.29	16.69	550.94	685.96
November	134 966	113 107	22 357	14 187	112 609	92 318	10 093	33.8	40.9	16.31	16.67	551.62	681.80
December	135 125	113 246	22 377	14 194	112 748	92 471	10 112	33.7	40.8	16.36	16.67	551.67	680.14
2006													
January	135 402	113 555	22 468	14 211	112 934	92 825	10 153	33.9	41.0	16.42	16.69	557.32	684.29
February	135 717	113 839	22 536	14 210	113 181	93 092	10 164	33.8	41.0	16.48	16.69	557.36	684.29
March	135 997	114 094	22 572	14 214	113 425	93 389	10 174	33.8	41.1	16.54	16.71	559.39	686.78
April	136 179	114 260	22 631	14 226	113 548	93 568	10 190	33.9	41.3	16.64	16.75	564.44	691.78
May	136 202	114 276	22 596	14 202	113 606	93 631	10 179	33.8	41.1	16.65	16.77	563.11	689.25
June	136 279	114 357	22 597	14 212	113 682	93 695	10 190	33.9	41.2	16.72	16.79	567.49	691.75
July	136 486	114 513	22 590	14 188	113 896	93 836	10 177	33.9	41.4	16.78	16.80	569.52	695.52
August	136 670	114 659	22 571	14 158	114 099	93 978	10 158	33.9	41.2	16.83	16.83	570.88	693.40
September	136 827	114 745	22 537	14 125	114 290	94 019	10 120	33.8	41.0	16.87	16.83	570.54	691.71
October	136 829	114 761	22 455	14 074	114 374	94 039	10 071	33.9	41.1	16.94	16.90	574.61	696.28
November	137 039	114 956	22 408	14 041	114 631	94 269	10 047	33.8	41.0	16.98	16.91	574.26	693.31
December	137 210	115 122	22 404	14 014	114 806	94 447	10 041	33.9	41.1	17.05	16.97	578.33	695.77
2007													
January	137 448	115 353	22 439	14 008	115 009	94 676	10 036	33.8	41.0	17.09	17.02	577.98	697.82
February	137 536	115 405	22 334	13 997	115 202	94 706	10 035	33.7	40.9	17.16	17.06	578.63	699.46
March	137 724	115 575	22 391	13 970	115 333	94 917	10 011	33.9	41.3	17.22	17.10	584.44	706.23
April	137 802	115 627	22 350	13 945	115 452	95 003	10 006	33.9	41.3	17.28	17.21	586.47	710.77
May	137 946	115 753	22 322	13 928	115 624	95 152	10 007	33.8	41.1	17.34	17.23	586.43	709.88
June	138 017	115 810	22 322	13 910	115 695	95 265	9 996	33.9	41.3	17.41	17.28	590.88	715.39
July	137 984	115 813	22 277	13 889	115 707	95 350	9 990	33.8	41.3	17.46	17.29	590.82	714.08
August	137 968	115 742	22 166	13 829	115 802	95 304	9 944	33.8	41.3	17.51	17.35	592.18	716.56
September	138 053	115 774	22 093	13 790	115 960	95 381	9 933	33.8	41.3	17.57	17.37	594.20	717.38
October	138 135	115 838	22 055	13 763	116 080	95 486	9 911	33.8	41.2	17.58	17.35	594.54	714.82
November	138 253	115 919	22 015	13 757	116 238	95 589	9 920	33.8	41.3	17.64	17.43	596.91	719.86
December	138 350	115 974	21 976	13 746	116 374	95 679	9 924	33.8	41.1	17.70	17.44	598.60	716.78
2008													
January	138 365	115 977	21 947	13 725	116 418	95 688	9 914	33.7	41.1	17.75	17.50	598.51	719.25
February	138 279	115 862	21 898	13 697	116 381	95 592	9 888	33.8	41.2	17.80	17.57	602.32	723.88
March	138 199	115 756	21 820	13 659	116 379	95 539	9 866	33.8	41.3	17.87	17.63	604.68	728.12
April	137 985	115 535	21 680	13 598	116 305	95 359	9 810	33.7	41.1	17.92	17.62	606.37	724.18
May	137 803	115 320	21 599	13 564	116 204	95 192	9 779	33.7	41.1	17.98	17.69	606.60	727.06
June	137 631	115 114	21 483	13 504	116 148	95 008	9 721	33.7	41.0	18.04	17.75	608.62	729.53
July	137 421	114 853	21 360	13 430	116 061	94 805	9 655	33.6	41.0	18.11	17.80	609.17	729.80
August	137 162	114 595	21 250	13 358	115 912	94 590	9 586	33.7	40.9	18.18	17.80	613.34	728.02
September	136 710	114 173	21 101	13 275	115 609	94 222	9 504	33.6	40.5	18.21	17.83	612.53	722.12
October	136 236	113 687	20 897	13 149	115 339	93 822	9 384	33.5	40.5	18.27	17.91	614.21	725.36
November	135 471	112 911	20 625	13 036	114 846	93 199	9 290	33.4	40.2	18.32	17.95	612.56	719.80
December	134 774	112 218	20 323	12 851	114 451	92 532	9 137	33.3	39.8	18.38	18.00	612.72	716.40
2009													
January	133 976	111 397	19 888	12 560	114 088	91 792	8 889	33.3	39.7	18.41	18.01	613.72	715.00
February	133 275	110 699	19 576	12 381	113 699	91 235	8 741	33.2	39.6	18.45	18.08	613.20	715.97
March	132 449	109 889	19 226	12 207	113 223	90 546	8 592	33.1	39.3	18.50	18.13	613.01	712.51
April	131 765	109 088	18 893	12 029	112 872	89 846	8 453	33.1	39.6	18.51	18.17	613.67	717.32
May	131 411	108 794	18 655	11 862	112 756	89 635	8 311	33.1	39.3	18.53	18.13	614.01	712.51
June	130 944	108 368	18 422	11 726	112 522	89 262	8 203	33.0	39.6	18.57	18.18	613.14	719.93
July	130 617	108 096	18 276	11 666	112 341	89 055	8 172	33.1	39.9	18.60	18.28	616.65	730.17
August	130 401	107 864	18 150	11 625	112 251	88 869	8 148	33.1	40.0	18.66	18.33	618.31	733.60
September	130 174	107 723	18 042	11 590	112 132	88 757	8 133	33.1	40.0	18.71	18.43	619.96	736.80
October	129 976	107 452	17 917	11 540	112 059	88 525	8 100	33.0	40.2	18.75	18.39	619.41	738.88
November	129 970	107 437	17 871	11 511	112 099	88 538	8 079	33.2	40.5	18.81	18.42	624.82	745.61
December	129 687	107 205	17 794	11 477	111 893	88 401	8 050	33.2	40.6	18.84	18.41	626.15	747.85
2010													
January	129 705	107 225	17 716	11 462	111 989	88 410	8 040	33.3	40.8	18.89	18.43	629.04	751.94
February	129 655	107 187	17 635	11 453	112 020	88 365	8 032	33.1	40.4	18.91	18.46	625.92	745.78
March	129 811	107 300	17 676	11 458	112 135	88 501	8 030	33.3	41.0	18.92	18.47	630.04	757.27
April	130 062	107 492	17 735	11 493	112 327	88 646	8 053	33.4	41.2	18.96	18.51	633.26	762.61
May	130 578	107 586	17 747	11 527	112 831	88 704	8 080	33.4	41.4	19.01	18.59	634.93	769.63
June	130 456	107 696	17 756	11 543	112 700	88 816	8 101	33.4	41.0	19.03	18.58	635.60	761.78
July	130 395	107 816	17 781	11 551	112 614	88 895	8 115	33.4	41.2	19.06	18.62	636.60	767.14
August	130 353	107 933	17 792	11 550	112 561	88 971	8 093	33.5	41.2	19.11	18.65	640.19	768.38
September	130 296	108 040	17 783	11 557	112 513	89 060	8 092	33.5	41.3	19.13	18.72	640.86	773.14
October	130 537	108 239	17 795	11 557	112 742	89 240	8 090	33.5	41.3	19.22	18.72	643.87	773.14
November	130 674	108 388	17 822	11 581	112 852	89 356	8 101	33.5	41.3	19.22	18.76	643.87	774.79
December	130 745	108 482	17 788	11 592	112 957	89 464	8 110	33.5	41.3	19.22	18.78	643.87	775.61

Table 10-9. Employment, Hours, and Earnings, Total Nonfarm and Manufacturing, Historical Annual and Monthly—*Continued*

(Wage and salary workers on nonfarm payrolls, seasonally adjusted.)

Year and month	All wage and salary workers (thousands)					Production and nonsupervisory workers on private payrolls							
	Total	Private			Service-providing	Number (thousands)		Average hours per week		Average hourly earnings, dollars		Average weekly earnings, dollars	
		Total	Goods-producing			Total private	Manufac-turing	Total private	Manufac-turing	Total private	Manufac-turing	Total private	Manufac-turing
			Total	Manufac-turing									
2011													
January	130 815	108 554	17 788	11 620	113 027	89 487	8 133	33.4	41.0	19.31	18.89	644.95	774.49
February	130 983	108 777	17 855	11 653	113 128	89 657	8 160	33.5	41.3	19.31	18.90	646.89	780.57
March	131 195	109 008	17 904	11 675	113 291	89 901	8 186	33.6	41.4	19.32	18.90	649.15	782.46
April	131 517	109 328	17 967	11 704	113 550	90 166	8 213	33.6	41.4	19.36	18.91	650.50	782.87
May	131 619	109 494	18 008	11 711	113 611	90 295	8 218	33.6	41.5	19.41	18.93	652.18	785.60
June	131 836	109 680	18 036	11 723	113 800	90 461	8 224	33.6	41.3	19.42	18.91	652.51	780.98
July	131 942	109 899	18 106	11 755	113 836	90 652	8 251	33.7	41.4	19.49	18.94	656.81	784.12
August	132 064	110 024	18 122	11 763	113 942	90 751	8 256	33.6	41.4	19.49	18.90	654.86	782.46
September	132 285	110 292	18 171	11 766	114 114	90 997	8 261	33.6	41.4	19.51	18.91	655.54	782.87
October	132 468	110 469	18 177	11 773	114 291	91 151	8 269	33.7	41.6	19.55	18.99	658.84	789.98
November	132 632	110 660	18 181	11 771	114 451	91 341	8 267	33.7	41.5	19.57	18.96	659.51	786.84
December	132 828	110 882	18 236	11 798	114 592	91 564	8 293	33.7	41.6	19.57	18.99	659.51	789.98
2012													
January	133 188	111 246	18 304	11 837	114 884	91 909	8 323	33.8	41.8	19.58	19.02	661.80	795.04
February	133 414	111 474	18 327	11 859	115 087	92 152	8 352	33.7	41.8	19.60	19.01	660.52	794.62
March	133 657	111 720	18 377	11 901	115 280	92 344	8 392	33.7	41.6	19.65	19.02	662.21	791.23
April	133 753	111 822	18 396	11 916	115 357	92 444	8 400	33.7	41.6	19.70	19.09	663.89	794.14
May	133 863	111 953	18 394	11 928	115 469	92 531	8 412	33.6	41.5	19.69	19.02	661.58	789.33
June	133 951	112 028	18 411	11 939	115 540	92 579	8 414	33.7	41.6	19.72	19.08	664.56	793.73
July	134 111	112 200	18 465	11 979	115 646	92 721	8 453	33.7	41.7	19.76	19.11	665.91	796.89
August	134 261	112 336	18 452	11 956	115 809	92 847	8 426	33.6	41.5	19.75	19.06	663.60	790.99
September	134 422	112 495	18 436	11 942	115 986	92 995	8 406	33.6	41.5	19.78	19.07	664.61	791.41
October	134 647	112 750	18 452	11 947	116 195	93 220	8 411	33.6	41.5	19.80	19.10	665.28	792.65
November	134 850	112 961	18 484	11 951	116 366	93 371	8 414	33.7	41.6	19.85	19.15	668.95	796.64
December	135 064	113 176	18 536	11 965	116 528	93 543	8 416	33.7	41.7	19.89	19.14	670.29	798.14
2013													
January	135 261	113 395	18 579	11 982	116 682	93 686	8 423	33.6	41.6	19.95	19.15	670.32	796.64
February	135 541	113 658	18 651	12 004	116 890	93 903	8 429	33.8	41.9	20.00	19.22	676.00	805.32
March	135 682	113 822	18 680	12 007	117 002	94 016	8 420	33.8	41.9	20.02	19.22	676.68	805.32
April	135 885	114 010	18 669	12 001	117 216	94 175	8 414	33.7	41.8	20.04	19.21	675.35	802.98
May	136 084	114 232	18 671	11 994	117 413	94 352	8 397	33.7	41.8	20.06	19.25	676.02	804.65
June	136 285	114 433	18 684	11 991	117 601	94 505	8 391	33.7	41.9	20.12	19.28	678.04	807.83
July	136 434	114 603	18 679	11 982	117 755	94 660	8 383	33.5	41.7	20.15	19.27	675.03	803.56
August	136 636	114 783	18 696	11 990	117 940	94 815	8 390	33.7	41.9	20.17	19.33	679.73	809.93
September	136 800	114 936	18 718	11 993	118 082	94 932	8 394	33.6	41.9	20.21	19.35	679.06	810.77
October	137 037	115 183	18 756	12 011	118 281	95 172	8 410	33.6	41.9	20.25	19.37	680.40	811.60
November	137 311	115 455	18 824	12 046	118 487	95 397	8 442	33.7	42.0	20.30	19.42	684.11	815.64
December	137 395	115 541	18 811	12 053	118 584	95 471	8 444	33.5	41.9	20.35	19.45	681.73	814.96
2014													
January	137 642	115 831	18 984	12 102	117 060	95 644	8 486	33.5	41.6	20.40	19.47	683.40	809.95
February	137 830	116 006	19 031	12 122	117 766	95 860	8 512	33.5	41.6	20.48	19.49	684.37	810.78
March	138 055	116 229	19 073	12 131	118 539	96 056	8 524	33.7	42.0	20.50	19.53	690.18	820.26
April	138 385	116 542	19 131	12 142	119 454	96 322	8 534	33.7	41.9	20.52	19.48	691.19	818.16
May	138 621	116 780	19 156	12 154	120 122	96 516	8 539	33.7	42.2	20.55	19.53	692.54	824.17
June	138 866	117 052	19 190	12 177	120 426	96 772	8 561	33.7	42.1	20.59	19.54	693.88	822.63
July	139 156	117 295	19 243	12 191	119 238	96 953	8 573	33.7	42.0	20.63	19.58	694.89	822.36
August	139 369	117 504	19 277	12 205	119 551	97 118	8 588	33.7	42.0	20.68	19.59	698.65	822.78
September	139 619	117 739	19 315	12 214	120 289	97 266	8 588	33.7	42.1	20.68	19.59	696.92	826.70
October	139 840	117 957	19 349	12 237	121 362	97 388	8 601	33.7	42.1	20.72	19.64	697.93	826.84
November	140 263	118 371	19 425	12 282	121 933	97 671	8 640	33.8	42.2	20.77	19.67	702.03	830.07
December	140 592	118 690	19 489	12 301	122 095	97 923	8 663	33.8	42.1	20.72	19.64	700.67	826.84
2015													
January	140 606	118 653	19 521	12 299	121 085	97 893	8 656	33.7	42.0	20.81	19.65	701.30	825.30
February	140 844	118 875	19 542	12 306	121 302	98 087	8 661	33.7	41.9	20.82	19.73	701.63	826.69
March	140 930	118 972	19 530	12 319	121 400	98 147	8 668	33.7	41.8	20.89	19.77	703.99	826.39
April	141 192	119 207	19 560	12 321	121 632	98 292	8 665	33.6	41.8	20.92	19.80	702.91	827.64
May	141 536	119 531	19 591	12 337	121 945	98 566	8 688	33.6	41.8	20.99	19.86	705.26	830.15
June	141 742	119 726	19 603	12 338	122 139	98 720	8 691	33.7	41.8	21.00	19.88	707.70	830.98
July	141 996	119 965	19 627	12 352	122 369	98 842	8 695	33.7	41.8	21.04	19.95	709.05	833.91
August	142 153	120 080	19 624	12 347	122 529	98 957	8 688	33.7	41.8	21.10	20.01	711.07	836.42
September	142 253	120 196	19 614	12 346	122 639	99 055	8 685	33.7	41.7	21.12	20.06	711.74	836.50
October	142 574	120 510	19 656	12 353	122 918	99 308	8 698	33.7	41.7	21.19	20.05	714.10	836.09
November	142 846	120 770	19 688	12 346	123 158	99 484	8 690	33.7	41.8	21.21	20.08	714.78	839.34
December	143 085	120 987	19 730	12 359	123 355	99 715	8 698	33.8	41.7	21.26	20.13	718.59	839.42
2016													
January	143 211	121 097	19 754	12 387	123 457	99 833	8 716	33.7	41.9	21.32	20.16	718.48	844.70
February	143 448	121 318	19 747	12 375	123 701	99 989	8 703	33.6	41.8	21.33	20.20	716.69	844.36
March	143 673	121 507	19 752	12 355	123 921	100 111	8 689	33.6	41.7	21.40	20.27	719.04	845.26
April	143 826	121 665	19 743	12 356	124 083	100 179	8 679	33.6	41.9	21.46	20.39	721.06	852.30
May	143 869	121 682	19 699	12 335	124 170	100 140	8 655	33.6	41.9	21.48	20.41	721.73	855.18
June	144 166	121 951	19 705	12 347	124 461	100 376	8 668	33.6	41.8	21.53	20.42	723.41	853.56
July	144 457	122 200	19 731	12 359	124 726	100 603	8 673	33.7	42.0	21.59	20.47	727.58	859.74
August	144 633	122 343	19 707	12 342	124 926	100 690	8 653	33.6	41.8	21.62	20.56	726.43	859.41
September	144 882	122 566	19 718	12 330	125 164	100 854	8 640	33.6	41.8	21.68	20.55	728.45	858.99
October	145 006	122 698	19 727	12 325	125 279	100 987	8 634	33.6	42.0	21.72	20.61	729.79	865.62
November	145 170	122 876	19 762	12 325	125 408	101 164	8 639	33.6	41.8	21.74	20.60	730.46	861.08
December	145 325	123 026	19 794	12 343	125 531	101 372	8 656	33.6	41.9	21.80	20.63	732.48	864.40

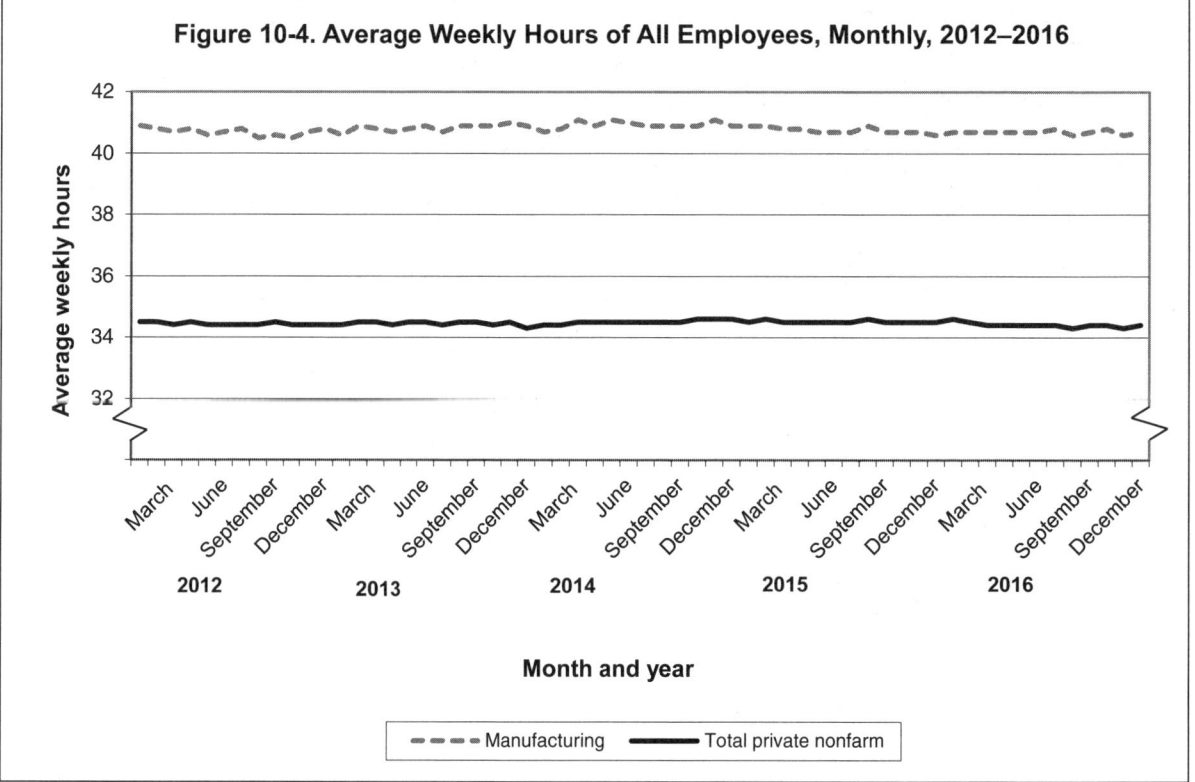

Figure 10-4. Average Weekly Hours of All Employees, Monthly, 2012–2016

- The payroll survey includes hours and earnings data for all nonfarm jobs, as well as the hours and earnings for production and nonsupervisory worker jobs that have been collected for many years. The newer, more comprehensive series are available beginning with March 2006. The new monthly data on the workweek for all nonfarm jobs and for manufacturing are shown in Figure 10-4. (Table 10-10)

- Firms experiencing increases in demand are likely to meet that demand, at first, by having their existing employees work longer hours. If the demand increase is sustained, they become more likely to hire more people. This is the basis for the long-time reputation of the workweek as a leading indicator for employment. As Figure 10-4 demonstrates, the all-employee workweek in manufacturing—the most cyclical sector—has been trending upward, though irregularly, since a low point of 39.0 hours in 2009. In November 2014, it reached 41.1 hours. The workweek for all private nonfarm industry reached a low point of 33.9 hours in 2009. It has increased little since then and has hovered around 34.5 hours through 2016. (Table 10-10)

- It is important to note that the "average" all-employee workweek of less than 34 1/2 hours reported in the payroll survey is not necessarily an accurate representation of how many hours per week a typical American worker works. This is because it is based on a count of <u>jobs</u>, as reported by <u>employers</u>. Suppose a full-time worker takes a second, "moonlighting" part-time job, newly created in another industry. This <u>reduces</u> the average workweek reported by the payroll survey, even though the individual is working <u>longer</u> hours than before. If a new labor force entrant takes a half-time job, it reduces the average workweek even if no other workers are working less. For measures of the workweek as reported by persons in the Current Population Survey, see Table 10-19, Figure 10-5, and the discussions of each.

Table 10-10. Average Weekly Hours of All Employees on Private Nonfarm Payrolls by NAICS Supersector

(Hours per week, seasonally adjusted.)

Year and month	Total private	Mining and logging	Construction	Manufacturing		Trade, transportation, and utilities			Information	Financial activities	Professional and business services	Education and health services	Leisure and hospitality	Other services
				Average weekly hours	Overtime hours	Total	Wholesale trade	Retail trade						
2008	34.4	43.7	37.8	39.8	3.0	34.4	38.4	31.4	36.5	36.5	35.2	33.6	25.9	32.9
2009	33.9	42.1	37.1	39.0	2.3	34.1	37.9	31.3	36.5	36.6	35.0	32.9	25.6	31.6
2010	34.1	43.4	37.8	40.2	3.0	34.2	38.1	31.3	36.5	36.9	35.4	32.7	25.7	31.6
2011	34.4	44.5	38.3	40.5	3.2	34.6	38.6	31.6	36.6	37.3	35.7	32.7	25.9	31.7
2012	34.5	44.0	38.7	40.7	3.3	34.6	38.7	31.7	36.6	37.4	36.0	32.8	26.1	31.6
2013	34.4	43.9	39.0	40.8	3.4	34.5	38.7	31.4	36.7	37.1	36.1	32.7	26.0	31.7
2014	34.5	34.5	39.0	41.0	3.5	34.5	38.9	31.3	36.8	37.3	36.3	32.7	26.2	31.8
2015	34.5	44.0	39.2	40.8	3.3	34.6	38.9	31.4	36.2	37.6	36.2	32.8	26.3	31.9
2016	34.4	43.4	39.0	40.7	3.3	34.3	38.9	31.0	36.0	37.5	36.1	32.9	26.1	31.9
2012														
January	34.5	45.5	38.6	40.9	3.4	34.7	38.8	31.8	36.8	37.3	35.8	32.7	26.2	31.7
February	34.5	44.7	38.7	40.8	3.3	34.7	38.8	31.9	36.8	37.3	35.9	32.8	26.0	31.7
March	34.4	44.1	38.6	40.7	3.3	34.6	38.7	31.8	36.7	37.3	35.8	32.8	26.1	31.7
April	34.5	44.1	38.8	40.8	3.3	34.6	38.7	31.7	36.6	37.2	35.9	32.8	26.1	31.7
May	34.4	43.6	38.5	40.6	3.3	34.5	38.6	31.6	36.6	37.0	35.9	32.8	26.1	31.6
June	34.4	43.9	38.6	40.7	3.2	34.5	38.6	31.6	36.6	37.1	35.9	32.8	26.1	31.6
July	34.4	44.0	38.5	40.8	3.2	34.5	38.5	31.5	36.5	37.1	36.0	32.8	26.0	31.6
August	34.4	43.5	38.6	40.5	3.2	34.5	38.6	31.5	36.4	37.2	36.0	32.8	26.0	31.5
September	34.5	43.3	38.9	40.6	3.2	34.6	38.9	31.6	36.5	37.3	36.1	32.8	26.0	31.6
October	34.4	43.4	38.8	40.5	3.2	34.5	38.5	31.5	36.3	37.2	35.8	32.8	26.0	31.6
November	34.4	43.2	39.0	40.7	3.3	34.6	38.5	31.6	36.4	37.3	36.0	32.7	26.0	31.5
December	34.4	43.5	39.2	40.8	3.3	34.5	38.6	31.5	36.6	37.2	36.0	32.7	26.1	31.6
2013														
January	34.4	42.7	38.9	40.6	3.3	34.4	38.5	31.4	36.4	37.0	36.0	32.7	26.1	31.6
February	34.5	43.4	39.2	40.9	3.3	34.6	38.7	31.6	36.4	37.2	36.1	32.8	26.1	31.7
March	34.5	43.3	39.1	40.8	3.4	34.7	38.8	31.7	36.5	37.2	36.1	32.8	26.2	31.9
April	34.4	43.2	39.0	40.7	3.4	34.5	38.5	31.4	36.6	37.2	36.0	32.7	26.1	31.8
May	34.5	43.8	39.2	40.8	3.3	34.6	38.8	31.6	36.7	37.2	36.1	32.8	26.0	31.9
June	34.5	44.2	39.0	40.9	3.4	34.5	38.8	31.4	37.0	37.3	36.1	32.8	26.0	31.8
July	34.4	44.0	38.9	40.7	3.2	34.6	38.7	31.5	36.8	37.0	36.0	32.7	25.9	31.7
August	34.5	44.1	39.1	40.9	3.4	34.6	38.9	31.5	36.8	37.3	36.1	32.7	26.0	31.8
September	34.5	44.3	39.2	40.9	3.4	34.6	38.8	31.4	36.8	37.1	36.1	32.7	26.0	31.7
October	34.4	44.1	38.8	40.9	3.4	34.5	38.9	31.3	36.8	37.1	36.0	32.7	25.9	31.7
November	34.5	44.6	39.2	41.0	3.4	34.4	38.9	31.2	36.8	37.2	36.2	32.7	26.0	31.7
December	34.3	44.8	38.7	40.9	3.5	34.4	38.6	31.3	36.9	37.0	36.0	32.6	25.7	31.6
2014														
January	34.4	44.1	38.6	40.7	3.5	34.4	38.8	31.1	36.6	37.1	36.1	32.7	26.1	31.7
February	34.4	45.1	38.5	40.8	3.4	34.3	38.7	31.1	36.8	37.2	36.1	32.7	26.1	31.7
March	34.5	45.7	39.1	41.1	3.5	34.4	38.9	31.2	36.9	37.3	36.3	32.7	26.2	31.8
April	34.5	44.6	39.1	40.9	3.5	34.5	38.8	31.4	36.8	37.1	36.2	32.7	26.2	31.8
May	34.5	44.5	39.0	41.1	3.5	34.5	38.9	31.3	36.8	37.3	36.3	32.7	26.1	31.8
June	34.5	44.9	39.1	41.0	3.5	34.4	38.9	31.2	36.6	37.2	36.2	32.7	26.1	31.7
July	34.5	44.5	39.2	40.9	3.5	34.5	38.9	31.3	36.7	37.2	36.2	32.7	26.2	31.7
August	34.5	44.9	39.2	40.9	3.4	34.5	38.9	31.3	36.6	37.2	36.2	32.8	26.2	31.8
September	34.5	44.5	39.0	40.9	3.5	34.5	38.9	31.3	36.7	37.3	36.2	32.8	26.2	31.8
October	34.6	45.0	39.1	40.9	3.4	34.6	38.9	31.4	36.7	37.4	36.3	32.8	26.2	31.8
November	34.6	44.9	39.0	41.1	3.5	34.6	38.9	31.4	36.7	37.3	36.3	32.8	26.2	31.8
December	-34.6	44.9	39.2	40.9	3.6	34.6	38.9	31.4	36.3	37.4	36.3	32.7	26.3	31.8
2015														
January	34.5	44.7	39.0	40.9	3.5	34.5	38.9	31.3	36.4	37.4	36.2	32.8	26.3	31.8
February	34.6	44.2	39.3	40.9	3.4	34.6	38.9	31.4	36.4	37.4	36.2	32.8	26.4	31.9
March	34.5	43.9	39.0	40.8	3.3	34.6	38.7	31.4	36.4	37.5	36.2	32.8	26.3	31.9
April	34.5	43.8	38.9	40.8	3.4	34.5	38.8	31.3	36.3	37.6	36.0	32.8	26.2	31.8
May	34.5	43.8	39.0	40.7	3.4	34.7	38.9	31.5	36.3	37.6	36.2	32.8	26.2	31.8
June	34.5	43.7	39.2	40.7	3.4	34.6	38.8	31.4	36.3	37.7	36.2	32.8	26.3	31.8
July	34.5	43.9	39.0	40.7	3.4	34.6	38.9	31.4	36.3	37.6	36.2	32.8	26.2	31.9
August	34.6	43.8	39.2	40.9	3.3	34.7	38.8	31.5	36.3	37.6	36.2	32.9	26.2	31.9
September	34.5	43.9	38.8	40.7	3.2	34.8	38.8	31.7	36.0	37.7	36.1	32.8	26.3	31.8
October	34.5	43.8	39.6	40.7	3.3	34.6	38.9	31.4	36.0	37.7	36.2	32.8	26.3	31.9
November	34.5	43.9	39.1	40.7	3.2	34.6	38.9	31.4	36.0	37.6	36.1	32.8	26.2	31.9
December	34.5	44.3	39.7	40.6	3.3	34.6	38.9	31.3	36.0	37.7	36.2	32.8	26.2	31.9
2016														
January	34.6	43.5	39.3	40.7	3.3	34.6	38.9	31.3	36.2	37.7	36.3	32.9	26.2	31.9
February	34.5	43.1	39.2	40.7	3.3	34.5	38.9	31.2	36.0	37.7	36.1	32.8	26.2	31.9
March	34.4	42.8	38.7	40.7	3.3	34.3	38.8	31.0	36.0	37.6	36.1	32.8	26.1	31.9
April	34.4	43.0	39.1	40.7	3.3	34.4	38.9	31.1	36.0	37.6	36.1	32.8	26.1	31.9
May	34.4	43.1	39.1	40.7	3.3	34.3	38.8	31.0	36.0	37.4	36.1	32.8	26.1	31.9
June	34.4	43.0	39.1	40.7	3.2	34.3	38.8	31.0	36.0	37.5	36.0	32.9	26.1	32.0
July	34.4	43.3	39.2	40.8	3.3	34.4	38.9	31.1	36.1	37.6	36.1	32.9	26.1	32.0
August	34.3	43.6	38.8	40.6	3.3	34.2	38.9	30.8	35.9	37.5	36.0	32.9	26.0	31.9
September	34.4	43.7	38.8	40.7	3.3	34.2	38.9	30.8	35.8	37.5	36.1	32.9	26.1	31.9
October	34.4	43.9	39.2	40.8	3.3	34.2	38.9	30.8	35.9	37.3	36.1	32.9	26.0	32.0
November	34.3	43.6	39.1	40.6	3.2	34.2	38.9	30.8	36.0	37.5	36.0	32.9	26.1	31.9
December	34.4	43.7	38.9	40.7	3.3	34.4	38.9	31.1	36.1	37.4	36.0	32.9	26.0	31.9

Table 10-11. Indexes of Aggregate Weekly Hours of All Employees on Private Nonfarm Payrolls by NAICS Supersector

(2007 =100, seasonally adjusted.)

| Year and month | Total private | Mining and logging | Construc-tion | Manu-facturing | Trade, transportation, and utilities | | | Information | Financial activities | Profes-sional and business services | Education and health services | Leisure and hospitality | Other services |
					Total	Wholesale trade	Retail trade						
2008	98.7	105.2	93.3	96.0	98.5	99.6	97.6	99.6	98.2	98.2	103.4	99.1	100.4
2009	92.4	92.1	77.2	83.2	92.5	92.4	92.2	93.3	94.0	91.3	104.9	95.4	97.0
2010	92.4	96.3	72.0	83.4	91.9	90.8	92.1	90.5	93.3	93.2	106.7	95.9	97.3
2011	94.7	110.2	72.9	85.3	94.3	93.5	94.1	89.6	93.9	97.4	108.7	98.8	98.1
2012	97.0	116.6	75.2	87.3	95.9	95.6	95.4	89.3	94.9	101.4	111.1	102.4	98.9
2013	99.0	119.2	78.6	88.2	97.1	96.9	96.2	90.6	95.9	105.0	112.6	105.7	100.5
2014	101.4	125.3	82.6	89.8	98.9	98.5	97.6	91.4	97.3	108.6	114.5	109.7	102.1
2015	103.8	112.3	87.2	90.4	101.2	99.2	99.6	91.0	100.0	111.7	118.0	113.5	103.3
2016	105.4	92.4	90.3	90.4	101.7	99.5	99.7	91.2	101.8	114.3	121.4	116.2	104.7
2012													
January	96.4	118.0	74.9	86.9	92.8	95.1	96.0	89.5	94.8	99.9	110.2	101.7	99.0
February	96.6	118.4	74.7	87.1	93.1	95.3	95.9	89.9	94.6	100.2	110.6	101.2	99.0
March	96.8	117.7	75.0	87.1	93.7	95.2	95.6	89.8	94.9	100.2	110.8	102.1	99.1
April	96.9	116.7	74.9	87.5	94.4	95.4	95.8	89.6	94.7	100.7	110.9	102.1	99.0
May	96.5	118.2	74.4	87.1	93.9	95.4	94.9	89.7	94.3	100.9	110.8	101.7	98.4
June	96.8	119.1	74.6	87.4	94.4	95.8	95.4	89.3	94.5	101.2	111.1	102.0	98.8
July	96.9	117.1	74.6	87.8	94.6	95.6	95.0	89.3	94.5	101.7	110.9	102.3	98.7
August	97.1	116.1	75.0	87.4	94.3	95.5	94.8	89.1	94.6	101.9	111.4	102.4	98.6
September	97.2	114.8	75.7	87.3	95.0	96.1	95.3	89.0	95.3	102.1	111.3	103.3	99.2
October	97.4	114.1	75.9	87.4	94.9	95.6	95.1	88.7	95.1	101.8	111.8	103.0	99.2
November	97.5	114.4	76.0	87.3	95.0	95.6	95.8	88.9	95.5	102.6	111.5	103.2	99.0
December	98.0	115.1	77.1	87.6	95.1	96.3	95.4	89.2	95.6	103.1	112.1	104.1	99.3
2013													
January	97.9	114.3	77.0	87.5	95.7	96.0	95.3	88.5	95.0	103.1	112.2	104.1	99.4
February	98.4	116.9	77.9	88.3	95.7	96.4	95.6	89.7	95.7	103.9	112.3	104.8	99.8
March	98.6	117.3	78.1	88.1	95.8	96.7	96.2	90.0	95.7	104.3	112.5	105.5	100.2
April	98.5	118.0	77.7	87.9	95.9	96.3	95.4	89.9	95.9	104.3	112.4	105.0	99.7
May	98.7	119.7	78.6	87.9	95.5	96.8	96.0	90.9	95.8	105.0	112.5	105.4	100.3
June	99.1	120.1	78.5	88.1	95.8	96.9	95.9	90.7	96.3	104.8	112.8	105.8	100.5
July	98.9	120.1	78.4	87.7	95.8	96.8	96.5	91.1	95.8	105.2	112.2	105.6	100.2
August	99.4	120.0	79.0	88.4	95.6	97.2	96.8	90.7	96.3	105.6	112.9	106.3	100.8
September	99.3	120.6	79.4	88.5	96.0	97.1	96.7	90.8	96.0	105.5	112.8	106.0	100.9
October	99.5	120.4	79.3	88.7	95.9	97.3	96.6	91.4	96.1	105.7	113.0	106.8	100.7
November	100.0	122.1	80.3	88.9	96.4	97.7	96.1	91.5	96.7	106.6	113.2	107.1	101.0
December	99.5	121.0	78.9	88.9	96.5	97.1	96.8	91.6	95.9	105.9	112.8	105.6	101.0
2014													
January	99.9	121.1	79.9	88.5	96.1	97.5	96.4	91.1	96.2	106.6	113.3	107.5	101.1
February	99.8	122.8	78.9	88.7	96.7	97.6	95.9	91.3	96.6	107.0	113.1	107.6	101.1
March	100.9	124.4	81.5	89.4	96.9	98.0	96.9	91.8	96.9	108.1	113.7	109.3	102.4
April	100.8	125.3	82.0	89.3	96.5	98.2	97.5	91.4	96.5	107.9	113.8	109.3	102.0
May	101.1	124.5	82.2	89.8	96.9	98.6	97.0	91.1	96.9	108.4	114.1	109.3	102.1
June	101.3	126.6	82.4	89.8	96.8	98.8	97.6	91.0	97.0	108.4	114.3	109.5	101.7
July	101.5	126.1	83.4	89.7	97.2	98.8	97.7	91.1	96.9	108.7	114.2	109.5	101.7
August	101.7	127.1	83.8	90.0	97.5	98.9	97.8	91.7	97.4	109.0	115.2	110.5	102.3
September	101.9	127.3	84.0	90.2	97.5	99.1	98.0	91.6	97.8	109.3	115.0	110.5	102.2
October	102.1	126.3	84.0	90.2	97.6	98.7	98.4	91.4	97.9	109.4	115.6	110.8	102.3
November	102.6	125.9	84.5	90.8	97.5	99.3	98.8	91.5	98.4	110.0	115.8	111.5	102.5
December	102.8	126.7	85.0	90.7	97.8	99.0	99.1	91.2	98.5	110.4	116.1	111.4	102.5
2015													
January	102.7	124.4	85.2	90.5	97.6	99.3	98.6	91.1	98.7	110.3	116.4	111.9	102.6
February	103.2	121.4	86.2	90.5	97.5	99.4	99.0	91.1	98.9	110.6	116.7	112.7	103.1
March	103.0	118.6	85.4	90.4	98.2	98.9	99.1	90.9	99.3	110.7	116.9	112.4	103.1
April	103.2	116.2	85.8	90.4	98.5	99.1	98.9	90.8	99.6	110.4	117.3	112.3	102.9
May	103.5	113.1	86.5	90.3	98.4	99.4	99.8	91.1	99.7	111.5	117.6	112.9	103.1
June	103.7	112.5	87.1	90.3	98.9	99.2	99.6	91.1	100.2	111.8	117.8	113.5	103.0
July	103.9	111.5	86.9	90.4	99.1	99.4	99.7	91.4	100.1	112.0	118.1	113.4	103.6
August	104.3	109.4	87.6	90.8	99.2	99.1	100.0	91.3	100.3	112.2	118.7	113.6	103.4
September	104.1	107.3	86.8	90.4	99.4	98.9	100.6	90.9	100.6	111.9	118.6	114.6	103.0
October	104.4	105.8	89.2	90.4	99.9	99.3	99.8	91.0	100.8	112.6	119.0	115.0	103.6
November	104.6	103.9	88.8	90.4	100.2	99.3	100.1	90.6	100.7	112.6	119.3	114.9	103.7
December	104.8	103.4	90.7	90.3	100.3	99.3	99.7	90.8	101.1	113.2	119.5	115.2	103.9
2016													
January	105.2	99.5	89.9	90.7	100.2	99.4	99.9	91.3	101.3	113.5	120.0	115.4	103.9
February	105.1	96.2	90.0	90.6	100.6	99.4	99.9	91.2	101.4	113.0	120.0	115.8	104.2
March	104.9	93.1	89.4	90.5	100.7	99.1	99.5	91.4	101.4	113.1	120.2	115.7	104.3
April	105.0	92.3	90.4	90.5	100.5	99.5	99.8	91.4	101.6	113.5	120.5	115.8	104.4
May	105.1	91.3	90.2	90.3	101.3	99.2	99.5	90.1	101.2	113.7	120.7	115.9	104.2
June	105.3	90.3	90.2	90.4	101.2	99.2	99.6	91.4	101.7	113.7	121.4	116.2	104.9
July	105.5	90.3	90.6	90.7	101.4	99.5	100.1	91.6	102.2	114.5	121.6	116.6	104.9
August	105.3	90.6	89.7	90.1	101.7	99.5	99.2	91.1	102.1	114.4	121.9	116.3	104.7
September	105.8	90.8	90.0	90.3	102.0	99.8	99.4	91.1	102.2	115.1	122.2	116.8	105.0
October	105.9	90.9	91.1	90.5	101.5	99.8	99.4	91.1	101.8	115.5	122.4	116.4	105.4
November	105.8	91.2	91.3	90.0	101.8	99.9	99.3	91.0	102.5	115.4	122.6	117.2	105.2
December	106.2	91.7	91.0	90.4	101.8	99.9	100.3	91.1	102.4	115.6	122.9	116.8	104.9

Table 10-12. Average Hourly Earnings of All Employees on Private Nonfarm Payrolls by NAICS Supersector

(Dollars, seasonally adjusted.)

Year and month	Total private	Mining and logging	Construction	Manu-facturing	Trade, transportation, and utilities			Information	Financial activities	Profes-sional and business services	Education and health services	Leisure and hospitality	Other services
					Total	Wholesale trade	Retail trade						
2009	22.17	27.29	24.83	23.04	19.32	25.41	15.39	29.40	26.53	27.03	22.12	12.97	19.68
2010	22.56	27.39	25.19	23.31	19.65	26.13	15.56	30.53	27.21	27.24	22.76	13.08	20.16
2011	23.03	28.10	25.41	23.69	20.04	26.38	15.86	31.59	27.91	27.76	23.42	13.23	20.50
2012	23.49	28.76	25.73	23.92	20.50	26.89	16.30	31.83	29.26	28.13	24.01	13.37	20.85
2013	23.96	29.72	26.12	24.35	20.96	27.64	16.63	32.91	30.15	28.55	24.42	13.50	21.40
2014	24.47	30.79	26.69	24.81	21.39	28.09	17.00	34.07	30.76	29.29	24.72	13.91	21.97
2015	25.02	31.15	27.37	25.25	21.83	28.65	17.52	35.14	31.52	30.08	25.24	14.32	22.48
2016	25.65	32.09	28.11	25.99	22.33	29.50	17.87	36.65	32.29	30.80	25.75	14.86	23.05
2012													
January	23.26	28.05	25.50	23.87	20.23	26.55	16.05	31.62	28.60	27.92	23.82	13.34	20.62
February	23.28	28.63	25.55	23.84	20.25	26.57	16.09	31.61	28.74	27.91	23.80	13.34	20.64
March	23.36	28.69	25.66	23.87	20.29	26.64	16.10	31.62	28.91	28.01	23.96	13.35	20.70
April	23.40	28.86	25.65	23.95	20.36	26.65	16.18	31.70	29.06	27.99	23.94	13.37	20.72
May	23.39	28.46	25.69	23.80	20.40	26.72	16.20	31.83	29.16	28.02	23.87	13.33	20.79
June	23.46	28.78	25.71	23.91	20.50	26.79	16.34	31.80	29.12	28.06	24.00	13.39	20.81
July	23.50	29.02	25.75	23.95	20.55	26.87	16.34	31.88	29.22	28.08	24.01	13.40	20.86
August	23.49	28.73	25.77	23.90	20.54	26.89	16.34	31.70	29.27	28.04	24.00	13.38	20.92
September	23.57	28.93	25.86	23.95	20.58	26.92	16.41	31.81	29.44	28.19	24.11	13.40	20.96
October	23.56	28.57	25.84	23.91	20.60	27.06	16.42	31.85	29.53	28.20	24.07	13.37	20.99
November	23.64	28.88	25.95	23.99	20.64	27.18	16.36	31.82	29.67	28.24	24.18	13.41	21.01
December	23.72	29.20	25.95	24.09	20.76	27.40	16.50	32.19	29.77	28.32	24.26	13.39	21.08
2013													
January	23.74	29.06	25.99	24.03	20.79	27.30	16.54	32.50	29.92	28.39	24.21	13.39	21.12
February	23.79	28.88	26.03	24.13	20.80	27.36	16.55	32.46	29.98	28.42	24.27	13.40	21.21
March	23.80	29.09	25.98	24.14	20.85	27.49	16.59	32.62	29.90	28.46	24.29	13.43	21.20
April	23.86	29.19	26.01	24.21	20.90	27.57	16.59	32.75	30.02	28.48	24.33	13.44	21.29
May	23.89	29.44	26.03	24.31	20.90	27.56	16.58	32.72	30.05	28.47	24.34	13.45	21.33
June	23.97	29.78	26.09	24.38	20.99	27.72	16.63	32.95	30.14	28.53	24.44	13.48	21.38
July	23.98	29.63	26.17	24.36	20.98	27.71	16.62	32.85	30.28	28.55	24.45	13.50	21.42
August	24.02	29.88	26.20	24.41	21.05	27.69	16.71	32.94	30.29	28.58	24.49	13.53	21.45
September	24.06	30.02	26.17	24.50	21.05	27.78	16.66	33.17	30.27	28.63	24.53	13.57	21.53
October	24.09	30.24	26.21	24.48	21.10	27.83	16.70	33.33	30.33	28.70	24.52	13.57	21.61
November	24.16	30.56	26.25	24.57	21.15	27.93	16.71	33.37	30.33	28.80	24.55	13.60	21.65
December	24.19	30.64	26.37	24.63	21.12	27.87	16.68	33.44	30.36	28.85	24.58	13.67	21.69
2014													
January	24.22	30.61	26.39	24.65	21.20	27.94	16.77	33.41	30.36	28.92	24.58	13.69	21.77
February	24.32	30.76	26.75	24.73	21.27	27.95	16.83	33.40	30.44	29.05	24.61	13.77	21.78
March	24.31	30.76	26.46	24.74	21.31	27.99	16.90	33.69	30.56	29.04	24.58	13.75	21.71
April	24.34	30.74	26.55	24.69	21.36	28.06	16.96	33.88	30.55	29.09	24.60	13.76	21.87
May	24.40	30.92	26.59	24.73	21.40	28.05	16.99	33.94	30.58	29.20	24.65	13.82	21.88
June	24.45	31.02	26.67	24.84	21.38	27.97	17.02	34.08	30.74	29.26	24.68	13.90	21.95
July	24.48	30.84	26.67	24.85	21.39	27.97	17.06	34.29	30.75	29.33	24.71	13.92	21.99
August	24.55	30.89	26.73	24.88	21.47	28.23	17.07	34.37	30.87	29.40	24.78	13.98	22.05
September	24.55	30.90	26.82	24.83	21.44	28.12	17.07	34.45	30.90	29.39	24.78	14.03	22.07
October	24.58	30.87	26.85	24.91	21.44	28.10	17.10	34.31	30.95	29.44	24.83	14.08	22.10
November	24.65	30.74	26.90	24.93	21.52	28.25	17.18	34.41	31.10	29.52	24.92	14.12	22.18
December	24.64	30.74	26.86	24.89	21.46	28.29	17.06	34.44	31.08	29.59	24.90	14.10	22.18
2015													
January	24.75	30.64	27.05	24.98	21.63	28.32	17.35	34.54	31.12	29.74	24.99	14.16	22.21
February	24.79	30.88	27.10	25.04	21.67	28.38	17.35	34.58	31.20	29.74	25.04	14.22	22.27
March	24.85	31.08	27.23	25.10	21.66	28.37	17.30	34.69	31.26	29.85	25.11	14.23	22.32
April	24.89	30.79	27.27	25.12	21.71	28.45	17.37	34.75	31.35	29.96	25.09	14.26	22.34
May	24.96	30.96	27.32	25.12	21.78	28.70	17.42	34.88	31.55	30.01	25.18	14.29	22.43
June	24.96	30.92	27.34	25.10	21.75	28.67	17.42	34.98	31.52	30.00	25.22	14.27	22.50
July	25.02	31.28	27.37	25.24	21.83	28.65	17.52	35.05	31.48	30.09	25.27	14.32	22.44
August	25.10	31.53	27.45	25.39	21.86	28.71	17.57	35.39	31.53	30.17	25.34	14.37	22.56
September	25.12	31.57	27.37	25.41	21.91	28.78	17.67	35.40	31.66	30.26	25.31	14.37	22.60
October	25.21	31.49	27.51	25.45	22.03	28.93	17.72	35.55	31.72	30.31	25.41	14.43	22.64
November	25.24	31.79	27.64	25.49	22.01	28.83	17.70	35.78	31.78	30.36	25.46	14.45	22.67
December	25.26	31.41	27.61	25.51	22.05	28.88	17.75	35.88	31.86	30.32	25.47	14.49	22.71
2016													
January	25.37	30.64	27.63	25.61	22.09	29.02	17.75	36.04	32.08	30.52	25.54	14.60	22.82
February	25.38	30.88	27.74	25.62	22.10	29.10	17.76	36.19	32.01	30.51	25.56	14.61	22.83
March	25.46	31.08	27.87	25.72	22.20	29.31	17.82	36.05	32.13	30.59	25.60	14.68	22.90
April	25.54	30.79	27.96	25.87	22.23	29.40	17.81	36.28	32.15	30.68	25.67	14.76	22.93
May	25.59	30.96	28.06	25.99	22.26	29.46	17.85	36.56	32.15	30.75	25.70	14.81	22.96
June	25.62	30.92	28.13	25.97	22.35	29.50	17.91	36.56	32.12	30.81	25.69	14.84	22.97
July	25.71	31.28	28.22	26.03	22.39	29.69	17.89	36.65	32.39	30.91	25.75	14.90	23.05
August	25.74	31.53	28.21	26.07	22.44	29.70	17.93	36.82	32.47	30.91	25.76	14.94	23.11
September	25.81	31.57	28.33	26.16	22.45	29.73	17.91	36.98	32.55	30.97	25.87	15.01	23.17
October	25.90	31.49	28.42	26.35	22.52	29.78	17.95	37.20	32.49	31.04	25.96	15.05	23.22
November	25.91	31.79	28.34	26.22	22.57	29.79	18.07	37.31	32.58	31.14	25.91	15.06	23.34
December	25.98	31.41	28.40	26.33	22.54	29.91	17.97	37.45	32.71	31.23	26.02	15.12	23.39

Table 10-13. Average Weekly Earnings of All Employees on Private Nonfarm Payrolls by NAICS Supersector

(Dollars, seasonally adjusted.)

| Year and month | Total private | Mining and logging | Construc- tion | Manu- facturing | Trade, transportation, and utilities | | | Information | Financial activities | Profes- sional and business services | Education and health services | Leisure and hospitality | Other services |
					Total	Wholesale trade	Retail trade						
2009	749.98	1 150.12	922.54	898.44	659.78	963.44	481.18	1 073.27	971.73	947.10	723.82	331.64	618.33
2010	769.63	1 189.32	952.78	937.34	672.58	994.71	487.66	1 114.65	1 004.14	963.57	743.41	336.83	637.65
2011	791.05	1 250.91	973.85	958.84	692.51	1 019.05	500.75	1 156.56	1 039.70	991.87	766.88	342.67	649.87
2012	809.57	1 263.98	997.01	973.96	709.33	1 041.41	515.81	1 166.45	1 093.00	1 013.76	787.43	349.12	659.49
2013	825.02	1 306.16	1 018.01	994.33	723.31	1 070.25	522.26	1 206.05	1 119.71	1 030.55	798.73	350.95	679.43
2014	844.91	1 380.77	1 040.85	1 016.42	738.22	1 092.30	532.57	1 252.44	1 146.22	1 062.48	809.11	364.07	698.41
2015	864.21	1 371.13	1 070.93	1 029.68	756.37	1 114.41	550.31	1 274.99	1 185.77	1 088.53	828.36	376.20	716.17
2016	881.55	1 389.27	1 100.51	1 057.73	766.83	1 144.62	553.98	1 315.24	1 207.97	1 109.64	845.30	387.19	735.14
2012													
January	802.47	1 263.84	984.30	973.00	701.08	1 030.11	512.00	1 163.62	1 060.64	1 002.33	781.30	340.51	653.65
February	803.16	1 276.90	983.68	972.67	702.68	1 030.92	513.27	1 163.25	1 072.00	1 001.97	780.64	346.84	654.29
March	805.92	1 265.23	993.04	971.51	704.06	1 030.97	511.98	1 160.45	1 078.34	1 002.76	785.89	348.44	656.19
April	807.30	1 261.18	992.66	977.16	706.49	1 031.36	514.52	1 160.22	1 081.03	1 004.84	785.23	348.96	656.82
May	802.28	1 252.24	989.07	966.28	703.80	1 031.39	510.30	1 164.98	1 078.92	1 005.92	780.55	346.58	654.89
June	807.02	1 277.83	989.84	973.14	709.30	1 036.77	517.98	1 163.88	1 080.35	1 007.35	787.20	349.48	657.60
July	808.40	1 271.08	988.80	977.16	711.03	1 037.18	516.34	1 163.62	1 084.06	1 010.88	785.13	349.74	657.09
August	808.06	1 246.88	992.15	970.34	708.63	1 035.27	514.71	1 157.05	1 085.92	1 009.44	787.20	347.88	658.98
September	810.81	1 249.78	1 003.37	972.37	712.07	1 044.50	518.56	1 161.07	1 098.11	1 014.84	788.40	349.74	662.34
October	810.46	1 239.94	1 002.59	970.75	710.70	1 041.81	517.23	1 159.34	1 098.52	1 009.56	789.50	347.62	663.28
November	813.22	1 247.62	1 006.86	973.99	714.14	1 046.43	516.98	1 158.25	1 106.69	1 016.64	790.69	348.66	661.82
December	818.34	1 261.44	1 014.65	980.46	718.30	1 060.38	519.75	1 174.94	1 110.42	1 022.35	795.73	349.48	666.13
2013													
January	816.66	1 240.86	1 011.01	975.62	715.18	1 051.05	519.36	1 183.00	1 107.04	1 022.04	794.09	348.14	667.39
February	820.76	1 253.39	1 015.17	986.92	719.68	1 058.83	521.33	1 181.54	1 115.26	1 025.96	796.06	349.74	672.36
March	821.10	1 262.51	1 013.22	984.91	723.50	1 066.61	525.90	1 190.63	1 112.28	1 027.41	796.71	351.87	676.28
April	820.78	1 278.52	1 011.79	985.35	721.05	1 064.20	520.93	1 195.38	1 116.74	1 025.28	795.59	349.44	674.89
May	821.82	1 301.25	1 017.77	989.42	723.14	1 069.33	522.27	1 200.82	1 114.86	1 027.77	795.92	349.70	678.29
June	826.97	1 316.28	1 014.90	994.70	724.16	1 075.54	522.18	1 209.27	1 124.22	1 027.08	801.63	350.48	679.88
July	824.91	1 312.61	1 015.40	991.45	725.91	1 072.38	523.53	1 205.60	1 120.36	1 027.80	797.07	349.65	679.01
August	828.69	1 317.71	1 021.80	998.37	728.33	1 074.37	526.37	1 215.49	1 126.79	1 031.74	800.82	351.78	682.11
September	827.66	1 326.88	1 020.63	1 002.05	726.23	1 075.09	523.12	1 217.34	1 123.02	1 030.68	802.13	351.46	684.65
October	828.70	1 333.58	1 016.95	1 001.23	727.95	1 079.80	522.71	1 226.54	1 125.24	1 033.20	801.80	352.82	685.04
November	833.52	1 369.09	1 026.38	1 004.91	727.56	1 086.48	519.68	1 224.68	1 131.31	1 042.56	802.79	353.60	688.47
December	829.72	1 363.48	1 017.88	1 007.37	726.53	1 075.78	520.42	1 230.59	1 123.32	1 038.60	801.31	349.95	687.57
2014													
January	833.17	1 356.02	1 011.01	1 003.26	727.16	1 081.28	521.55	1 222.81	1 126.36	1 044.01	803.77	355.94	690.11
February	834.18	1 374.97	1 015.17	1 006.51	729.56	1 081.67	521.73	1 229.12	1 132.37	1 048.71	802.29	358.02	690.43
March	841.13	1 384.20	1 013.22	1 014.34	735.20	1 086.01	528.97	1 243.16	1 139.89	1 057.06	803.77	361.63	694.72
April	839.73	1 383.30	1 011.79	1 009.82	736.92	1 088.73	532.54	1 246.78	1 133.41	1 053.06	804.42	360.51	695.47
May	841.80	1 379.03	1 017.77	1 016.40	736.16	1 091.15	530.09	1 245.60	1 137.58	1 059.96	806.06	360.70	695.78
June	843.53	1 399.00	1 014.90	1 018.44	737.61	1 088.03	532.73	1 247.33	1 143.53	1 059.21	807.04	362.79	695.82
July	844.56	1 378.55	1 015.40	1 016.37	737.96	1 088.03	533.98	1 255.01	1 140.83	1 061.75	805.55	363.31	697.08
August	846.98	1 390.05	1 021.80	1 020.08	740.72	1 098.15	534.29	1 261.38	1 148.36	1 064.28	812.78	367.67	701.19
September	846.98	1 384.32	1 020.63	1 018.03	739.68	1 096.68	534.29	1 264.32	1 152.57	1 063.92	810.31	367.59	701.83
October	848.01	1 379.89	1 016.95	1 018.82	741.82	1 090.28	536.94	1 259.18	1 154.44	1 065.73	814.42	368.90	702.78
November	852.89	1 371.00	1 026.38	1 024.62	744.59	1 101.75	539.45	1 259.41	1 163.14	1 071.58	817.38	371.36	705.32
December	852.54	1 386.37	1 017.88	1 020.49	742.52	1 097.65	537.39	1 257.06	1 162.39	1 074.12	816.72	369.42	705.32
2015													
January	853.88	1 369.61	1 054.95	1 021.68	746.24	1 101.65	543.06	1 257.26	1 163.89	1 076.59	819.67	372.41	706.28
February	857.73	1 364.90	1 065.03	1 024.14	749.78	1 103.98	544.79	1 258.71	1 166.88	1 076.59	821.31	375.41	710.41
March	857.33	1 364.41	1 061.97	1 024.08	749.44	1 097.92	543.22	1 262.72	1 172.25	1 080.57	823.61	374.25	712.01
April	858.71	1 348.60	1 060.80	1 024.90	749.00	1 103.86	543.68	1 261.43	1 178.76	1 078.56	822.95	373.61	710.41
May	861.12	1 356.05	1 065.48	1 022.38	755.77	1 116.43	548.73	1 266.14	1 186.28	1 086.36	825.90	374.40	713.27
June	861.12	1 351.20	1 071.73	1 021.57	752.55	1 112.40	546.99	1 269.77	1 188.30	1 086.00	827.22	375.30	715.50
July	863.19	1 373.19	1 067.43	1 027.27	755.32	1 114.49	550.13	1 272.32	1 183.65	1 089.26	828.86	375.18	715.84
August	868.46	1 381.01	1 076.04	1 038.45	758.54	1 113.95	553.46	1 284.66	1 185.53	1 092.15	830.49	376.49	719.66
September	866.64	1 385.92	1 061.96	1 034.19	762.47	1 116.66	560.14	1 274.40	1 193.58	1 092.39	830.17	377.93	718.68
October	869.75	1 379.26	1 089.40	1 035.82	762.24	1 125.38	556.41	1 279.80	1 195.84	1 097.22	833.45	379.51	722.22
November	870.78	1 395.58	1 080.72	1 037.44	761.55	1 121.49	555.78	1 288.08	1 194.93	1 096.00	835.09	378.59	723.17
December	871.47	1 391.46	1 096.12	1 035.71	762.93	1 123.43	555.58	1 291.68	1 201.12	1 097.58	835.42	379.64	724.45
2016													
January	877.80	1 388.96	1 085.86	1 042.33	764.31	1 128.88	555.58	1 304.65	1 209.42	1 107.88	840.27	382.52	727.96
February	875.61	1 363.68	1 087.41	1 042.73	762.45	1 131.99	554.11	1 302.84	1 206.78	1 101.41	838.37	382.78	728.28
March	875.82	1 366.18	1 078.57	1 046.80	761.46	1 137.23	552.42	1 297.80	1 208.09	1 104.30	839.68	383.15	730.51
April	878.58	1 381.16	1 093.24	1 052.91	764.71	1 143.66	553.89	1 306.08	1 208.84	1 107.55	841.98	385.24	731.47
May	880.30	1 393.42	1 097.15	1 057.79	763.52	1 143.05	553.35	1 316.16	1 202.41	1 110.08	842.96	386.54	732.42
June	881.33	1 382.02	1 099.88	1 056.98	766.61	1 144.60	555.21	1 316.16	1 204.50	1 109.16	845.20	387.32	735.04
July	884.42	1 389.93	1 106.22	1 062.02	770.22	1 154.94	556.38	1 323.07	1 217.86	1 115.85	847.18	388.89	737.60
August	882.88	1 386.48	1 094.55	1 058.44	767.45	1 155.33	552.24	1 321.84	1 217.63	1 112.76	847.50	388.44	737.21
September	887.86	1 403.64	1 099.20	1 064.71	767.79	1 156.50	551.63	1 323.88	1 220.63	1 118.02	851.12	391.76	739.12
October	890.96	1 424.56	1 114.06	1 075.08	770.18	1 158.44	552.86	1 335.48	1 211.88	1 120.54	854.08	391.30	743.04
November	888.71	1 399.12	1 108.09	1 064.53	771.89	1 158.83	556.56	1 343.16	1 221.75	1 121.04	852.44	393.07	744.55
December	893.71	1 419.38	1 104.76	1 071.63	775.38	1 163.50	558.87	1 351.95	1 223.35	1 124.28	856.06	393.12	746.14

Table 10-14. Production and Nonsupervisory Workers on Private Nonfarm Payrolls by NAICS Supersector

(Thousands, seasonally adjusted.)

Year and month	Total private	Mining and logging	Construction	Manufacturing	Trade, transportation, and utilities			Information	Financial activities	Professional and business services	Education and health services	Leisure and hospitality	Other services
					Total	Wholesale trade	Retail trade						
1965	42 302	523	2 906	12 905	10 702	. . .	. . .	1 268	2 434	3 515	3 443	3 443	1 161
1966	44 292	517	2 977	13 703	11 095	. . .	. . .	1 334	2 492	3 715	3 623	3 607	1 230
1967	45 185	501	2 903	13 714	11 369	. . .	. . .	1 365	2 585	3 890	3 818	3 734	1 306
1968	46 519	491	2 986	13 908	11 688	. . .	. . .	1 394	2 700	4 067	4 008	3 898	1 379
1969	48 246	501	3 177	14 147	12 152	. . .	. . .	1 438	2 841	4 252	4 196	4 089	1 452
1970	48 180	496	3 158	13 490	12 388	. . .	. . .	1 422	2 922	4 321	4 305	4 185	1 494
1971	48 151	474	3 238	13 034	12 502	. . .	. . .	1 392	2 978	4 354	4 372	4 286	1 521
1972	49 971	494	3 425	13 497	12 954	2 920	7 257	1 437	3 066	4 518	4 531	4 467	1 583
1973	52 235	502	3 576	14 227	13 437	3 041	7 551	1 504	3 164	4 748	4 747	4 664	1 666
1974	52 846	550	3 469	14 040	13 700	3 148	7 673	1 516	3 217	4 907	4 941	4 766	1 740
1975	51 010	581	2 990	12 576	13 578	3 121	7 714	1 416	3 227	4 939	5 088	4 821	1 795
1976	52 916	606	2 999	13 127	14 038	3 212	8 048	1 459	3 300	5 153	5 309	5 046	1 880
1977	55 207	636	3 209	13 591	14 579	3 323	8 396	1 514	3 452	5 404	5 561	5 284	1 978
1978	58 188	658	3 544	14 150	15 329	3 509	8 861	1 586	3 645	5 717	5 874	5 588	2 099
1979	60 404	737	3 760	14 458	15 843	3 667	9 113	1 650	3 825	5 993	6 158	5 772	2 209
1980	60 377	785	3 623	13 667	15 907	3 708	9 158	1 626	3 957	6 197	6 447	5 850	2 318
1981	60 967	861	3 469	13 492	16 004	3 753	9 238	1 633	4 052	6 396	6 700	5 944	2 414
1982	59 475	834	3 208	12 315	15 821	3 662	9 254	1 564	4 055	6 421	6 822	5 976	2 458
1983	60 018	698	3 240	12 121	15 999	3 639	9 494	1 502	4 128	6 581	7 045	6 161	2 542
1984	63 333	714	3 614	12 821	16 797	3 821	9 964	1 631	4 289	6 918	7 385	6 491	2 672
1985	65 456	686	3 868	12 648	17 427	3 935	10 399	1 660	4 476	7 258	7 789	6 817	2 827
1986	66 825	577	3 984	12 449	17 769	3 941	10 704	1 663	4 698	7 532	8 130	7 066	2 957
1987	68 725	541	4 088	12 537	18 196	3 989	10 986	1 717	4 861	7 859	8 513	7 310	3 104
1988	71 059	545	4 199	12 765	18 771	4 132	11 306	1 775	4 894	8 256	8 985	7 587	3 280
1989	72 960	526	4 257	12 805	19 230	4 235	11 565	1 807	4 931	8 648	9 465	7 833	3 459
1990	73 721	538	4 115	12 669	19 032	4 198	11 308	1 866	4 973	8 889	9 784	8 299	3 555
1991	72 567	515	3 674	12 164	18 640	4 122	11 008	1 871	4 914	8 748	10 257	8 247	3 539
1992	72 854	478	3 546	12 020	18 506	4 071	10 931	1 871	4 924	8 971	10 607	8 406	3 526
1993	74 671	462	3 704	12 070	18 752	4 072	11 114	1 896	5 084	9 451	10 961	8 667	3 623
1994	77 478	461	3 973	12 361	19 392	4 196	11 502	1 928	5 220	10 078	11 397	8 979	3 689
1995	79 943	458	4 113	12 567	19 984	4 361	11 841	2 007	5 199	10 645	11 829	9 330	3 812
1996	81 888	461	4 325	12 532	20 325	4 423	12 057	2 096	5 322	11 161	12 195	9 565	3 907
1997	84 313	479	4 546	12 673	20 698	4 523	12 274	2 181	5 482	11 896	12 566	9 780	4 013
1998	86 516	473	4 807	12 729	21 059	4 605	12 440	2 217	5 692	12 566	12 903	9 947	4 124
1999	88 647	438	5 105	12 524	21 576	4 673	12 772	2 351	5 818	13 184	13 217	10 216	4 219
2000	90 547	446	5 295	12 428	21 965	4 686	13 040	2 502	5 819	13 790	13 491	10 516	4 296
2001	90 214	457	5 332	11 677	21 709	4 555	12 952	2 531	5 888	13 588	13 998	10 662	4 373
2002	88 664	436	5 196	10 768	21 337	4 474	12 774	2 398	5 964	13 049	14 491	10 576	4 449
2003	87 965	420	5 123	10 189	21 078	4 396	12 655	2 347	6 052	12 911	14 753	10 666	4 426
2004	89 246	440	5 309	10 072	21 319	4 444	12 788	2 371	6 052	13 287	15 018	10 955	4 425
2005	91 443	473	5 611	10 060	21 830	4 584	13 030	2 386	6 127	13 854	15 401	11 263	4 438
2006	93 776	519	5 903	10 137	22 166	4 724	13 110	2 399	6 312	14 446	15 832	11 568	4 494
2007	95 260	547	5 883	9 975	22 546	4 851	13 317	2 403	6 365	14 784	16 318	11 861	4 578
2008	94 675	574	5 521	9 629	22 337	4 822	13 134	2 388	6 320	14 585	16 842	11 873	4 606
2009	89 629	510	4 567	8 322	21 116	4 506	12 472	2 240	6 066	13 520	17 240	11 560	4 488
2010	88 954	525	4 172	8 077	20 874	4 378	12 425	2 170	5 942	13 699	17 531	11 507	4 458
2011	90 619	594	4 184	8 228	21 234	4 443	12 647	2 148	5 900	14 251	17 818	11 772	4 491
2012	92 780	641	4 246	8 400	21 617	4 562	12 793	2 164	5 986	14 802	18 230	12 154	4 541
2013	94 589	636	4 423	8 422	21 875	4 621	12 923	2 194	6 068	15 305	18 505	12 589	4 573
2014	96 701	653	4 640	8 565	22 280	4 696	13 107	2 209	6 155	15 766	18 827	12 969	4 637
2015	98 782	592	4 866	8 683	22 629	4 702	13 264	2 226	6 278	16 133	19 337	13 360	4 678
2016	100 531	476	5 062	8 666	22 882	4 696	13 424	2 235	6 429	16 479	19 839	13 749	4 715
2015													
January	97 893	648	4 771	8 656	22 498	4 712	13 191	2 219	6 223	15 973	19 081	13 162	4 662
February	98 087	640	4 803	8 661	22 535	4 722	13 211	2 217	6 231	16 004	19 125	13 207	4 664
March	98 147	630	4 786	8 668	22 559	4 713	13 233	2 211	6 242	16 013	19 157	13 213	4 668
April	98 292	618	4 812	8 665	22 568	4 706	13 240	2 218	6 249	16 033	19 224	13 236	4 669
May	98 566	604	4 837	8 688	22 598	4 702	13 257	2 224	6 250	16 110	19 265	13 305	4 685
June	98 720	599	4 844	8 691	22 634	4 700	13 273	2 224	6 273	16 136	19 315	13 326	4 678
July	98 842	589	4 854	8 695	22 654	4 699	13 276	2 230	6 281	16 155	19 356	13 353	4 675
August	98 957	581	4 870	8 688	22 671	4 696	13 282	2 233	6 291	16 170	19 398	13 383	4 672
September	99 055	560	4 874	8 685	22 667	4 693	13 275	2 239	6 301	16 167	19 441	13 445	4 676
October	99 308	557	4 911	8 698	22 673	4 694	13 289	2 245	6 316	16 224	19 505	13 496	4 683
November	99 484	544	4 957	8 690	22 719	4 691	13 314	2 230	6 332	16 247	19 534	13 541	4 690
December	99 715	539	5 020	8 698	22 739	4 690	13 310	2 232	6 336	16 301	19 580	13 570	4 700
2016													
January	99 833	525	5 028	8 716	22 764	4 691	13 351	2 228	6 351	16 312	19 603	13 611	4 695
February	99 989	508	5 054	8 703	22 807	4 688	13 395	2 239	6 361	16 303	19 657	13 649	4 708
March	100 111	492	5 085	8 689	22 853	4 684	13 435	2 245	6 378	16 312	19 674	13 683	4 700
April	100 179	482	5 068	8 679	22 853	4 686	13 425	2 243	6 391	16 357	19 721	13 679	4 706
May	100 140	474	5 051	8 655	22 843	4 685	13 415	2 204	6 405	16 370	19 763	13 675	4 700
June	100 376	468	5 035	8 668	22 859	4 687	13 426	2 240	6 422	16 421	19 832	13 721	4 710
July	100 603	464	5 038	8 673	22 883	4 691	13 438	2 236	6 444	16 502	19 878	13 771	4 714
August	100 690	461	5 033	8 653	22 910	4 694	13 449	2 237	6 456	16 516	19 920	13 785	4 719
September	100 854	457	5 052	8 640	22 943	4 705	13 464	2 240	6 460	16 589	19 952	13 784	4 737
October	100 987	455	5 061	8 634	22 963	4 712	13 465	2 243	6 470	16 632	19 989	13 812	4 728
November	101 164	466	5 095	8 639	22 971	4 713	13 451	2 232	6 481	16 667	20 016	13 860	4 737
December	101 372	468	5 123	8 656	23 009	4 712	13 462	2 227	6 512	16 697	20 069	13 886	4 725

. . . = Not available.

Table 10-15. Average Weekly Hours of Production and Nonsupervisory Workers on Private Nonfarm Payrolls by NAICS Supersector

(Hours per week, seasonally adjusted.)

Year and month	Total private	Mining and logging	Construc-tion	Manufacturing Average weekly hours	Overtime hours	Trade, transportation, and utilities Total	Wholesale trade	Retail trade	Informa-tion	Financial activities	Profes-sional and business services	Education and health services	Leisure and hospitality	Other services
1965	38.6	43.7	37.9	41.2	3.6	39.6	...	...	38.3	37.1	37.3	35.2	32.5	36.1
1966	38.5	44.1	38.1	41.4	3.9	39.1	...	...	38.3	37.2	37.0	34.9	31.9	35.8
1967	37.9	43.9	38.1	40.6	3.3	38.5	...	...	37.6	36.9	36.6	34.5	31.3	35.4
1968	37.7	44.0	37.8	40.7	3.6	38.2	...	...	37.6	36.8	36.3	34.1	30.8	35.0
1969	37.5	44.3	38.4	40.6	3.6	37.9	...	...	37.6	36.9	36.3	34.1	30.4	35.0
1970	37.0	43.9	37.8	39.8	2.9	37.6	...	...	37.2	36.6	35.9	33.8	30.0	34.7
1971	36.7	43.7	37.6	39.9	2.9	37.4	...	...	37.0	36.4	35.5	33.3	29.9	34.2
1972	36.9	44.1	37.0	40.6	3.4	37.4	39.8	35.1	37.3	36.4	35.5	33.3	29.7	34.2
1973	36.9	43.8	37.2	40.7	3.8	37.2	39.6	34.8	37.3	36.4	35.5	33.3	29.4	34.1
1974	36.4	43.7	37.1	40.0	3.2	36.8	39.2	34.3	37.0	36.3	35.3	33.1	29.1	33.9
1975	36.0	43.7	36.9	39.5	2.6	36.4	39.1	34.0	36.6	36.2	35.1	33.0	28.9	33.9
1976	36.1	44.2	37.3	40.1	3.1	36.3	39.1	33.8	36.7	36.2	34.9	32.7	28.5	33.6
1977	35.9	44.7	37.0	40.3	3.4	36.0	39.2	33.3	36.8	36.2	34.7	32.5	28.1	33.4
1978	35.8	44.9	37.3	40.4	3.6	35.6	39.2	32.7	36.8	36.1	34.6	32.3	27.7	33.2
1979	35.6	44.7	37.5	40.2	3.3	35.4	39.2	32.4	36.6	35.9	34.4	32.2	27.4	33.0
1980	35.2	44.9	37.5	39.6	2.8	35.0	38.8	31.9	36.4	36.0	34.3	32.1	27.0	33.0
1981	35.2	45.1	37.4	39.8	2.8	35.0	38.9	31.9	36.3	36.0	34.3	32.1	26.9	33.0
1982	34.7	44.1	37.2	38.9	2.3	34.6	38.7	31.7	35.8	36.0	34.2	32.1	26.8	33.0
1983	34.9	43.9	37.6	40.1	2.9	34.6	38.8	31.6	36.2	35.9	34.4	32.1	26.8	33.0
1984	35.1	44.6	38.2	40.6	3.4	34.7	38.9	31.6	36.6	36.2	34.3	32.0	26.7	32.9
1985	34.9	44.6	38.2	40.5	3.3	34.4	38.8	31.2	36.5	36.1	34.2	31.9	26.4	32.8
1986	34.7	43.6	37.9	40.7	3.4	34.1	38.7	31.0	36.4	36.1	34.3	32.0	26.2	32.9
1987	34.7	43.5	38.2	40.9	3.7	34.1	38.5	31.0	36.5	36.0	34.3	32.0	26.3	32.8
1988	34.6	43.3	38.2	41.0	3.8	33.8	38.5	30.9	36.1	35.6	34.2	32.0	26.3	32.9
1989	34.5	44.1	38.3	40.9	3.8	33.8	38.4	30.7	36.1	35.6	34.2	32.0	26.1	32.9
1990	34.3	45.0	38.3	40.5	3.9	33.7	38.4	30.6	35.8	35.5	34.2	31.9	26.0	32.8
1991	34.1	45.3	38.1	40.4	3.8	33.6	38.4	30.4	35.6	35.4	34.0	31.9	25.6	32.7
1992	34.2	44.6	38.0	40.7	4.0	33.8	38.5	30.7	35.8	35.6	34.0	32.0	25.7	32.6
1993	34.3	44.9	38.4	41.1	4.4	34.1	38.5	30.7	36.0	35.5	34.0	32.0	25.9	32.6
1994	34.5	45.3	38.8	41.7	5.0	34.3	38.8	30.9	36.0	35.5	34.1	32.0	26.0	32.7
1995	34.3	45.3	38.8	41.3	4.7	34.1	38.6	30.8	36.0	35.5	34.0	32.0	25.9	32.6
1996	34.3	46.0	38.9	41.3	4.8	34.1	38.6	30.7	36.3	35.5	34.1	31.9	25.9	32.5
1997	34.5	46.2	38.9	41.7	5.1	34.3	38.8	30.9	36.3	35.8	34.3	32.2	26.1	32.7
1998	34.5	44.9	38.8	41.4	4.8	34.2	38.6	30.9	36.6	36.0	34.3	32.2	26.2	32.6
1999	34.3	44.2	39.0	41.4	4.9	33.9	38.6	30.8	36.7	35.8	34.4	32.1	26.1	32.5
2000	34.3	44.4	39.2	41.3	4.7	33.8	38.8	30.7	36.8	35.9	34.5	32.2	26.1	32.5
2001	33.9	44.6	38.7	40.3	4.0	33.5	38.4	30.7	36.9	35.8	34.2	32.3	25.8	32.3
2002	33.9	43.2	38.4	40.5	4.2	33.6	38.0	30.9	36.5	35.6	34.2	32.4	25.8	32.1
2003	33.7	43.6	38.4	40.4	4.2	33.6	37.9	30.9	36.2	35.6	34.1	32.3	25.6	31.4
2004	33.7	44.5	38.3	40.8	4.6	33.5	37.8	30.7	36.3	35.6	34.2	32.4	25.7	31.0
2005	33.8	45.6	38.6	40.7	4.6	33.4	37.7	30.6	36.5	36.0	34.2	32.6	25.7	30.9
2006	33.9	45.6	39.0	41.1	4.4	33.4	38.0	30.5	36.6	35.8	34.6	32.5	25.7	30.9
2007	33.8	45.9	39.0	41.2	4.2	33.3	38.2	30.2	36.5	35.9	34.8	32.5	25.5	30.9
2008	33.6	45.1	38.5	40.8	3.7	33.2	38.2	30.0	36.7	35.9	34.8	32.4	25.2	30.8
2009	33.1	43.2	37.6	39.8	2.9	32.9	37.6	29.9	36.6	36.1	34.7	32.2	24.8	30.5
2010	33.4	44.6	38.4	41.1	3.8	33.3	37.9	30.2	36.3	36.2	35.1	32.0	24.8	30.7
2011	33.6	46.7	39.0	41.4	4.1	33.7	38.5	30.5	36.2	36.4	35.2	32.2	24.8	30.8
2012	33.7	46.6	39.3	41.7	4.2	33.8	38.7	30.6	36.0	36.8	35.3	32.3	25.0	30.7
2013	33.7	45.9	39.6	41.8	4.3	33.7	38.7	30.2	35.9	36.7	35.4	32.1	25.0	30.8
2014	33.7	47.3	39.6	42.0	4.5	33.6	38.6	30.0	35.9	36.7	35.6	32.0	25.1	30.7
2015	33.7	45.8	39.6	41.8	4.3	33.7	38.6	30.1	35.7	37.1	35.5	32.1	25.1	30.7
2016	33.6	45.3	39.7	41.9	4.3	33.5	38.6	29.7	35.6	36.9	35.4	32.2	24.9	30.8
2015														
January	33.7	46.8	39.7	42.0	4.4	33.6	38.6	30.0	35.9	36.7	35.5	32.1	25.2	30.8
February	33.7	46.1	39.7	41.9	4.4	33.6	38.6	30.0	35.9	36.9	35.5	32.0	25.3	30.7
March	33.7	45.7	39.4	41.8	4.3	33.7	38.6	30.0	35.9	37.0	35.4	32.0	25.1	30.7
April	33.6	45.8	39.3	41.8	4.3	33.6	38.6	30.0	35.9	37.0	35.2	32.1	25.0	30.6
May	33.6	45.7	39.4	41.8	4.3	33.7	38.5	30.1	35.8	37.1	35.3	32.0	25.0	30.6
June	33.7	45.4	39.8	41.8	4.4	33.6	38.5	30.0	35.6	37.0	35.4	32.1	25.1	30.6
July	33.7	46.2	39.5	41.8	4.3	33.7	38.6	30.0	35.7	37.1	35.5	32.1	25.1	30.7
August	33.7	45.4	39.8	41.8	4.4	33.7	38.5	30.1	35.7	37.1	35.5	32.1	25.0	30.8
September	33.7	45.3	39.6	41.7	4.2	33.8	38.5	30.2	35.5	37.1	35.3	32.1	25.0	30.7
October	33.7	45.5	40.0	41.7	4.2	33.7	38.5	30.0	35.5	37.2	35.5	32.1	25.0	30.8
November	33.7	45.4	39.7	41.8	4.2	33.7	38.5	30.1	35.6	37.1	35.5	32.1	25.0	30.7
December	33.8	46.1	40.2	41.7	4.2	33.7	38.6	30.0	35.5	37.2	35.6	32.2	25.0	30.8
2016														
January	33.7	46.1	39.8	41.9	4.3	33.7	38.5	30.0	35.8	37.1	35.6	32.2	24.9	30.7
February	33.6	44.9	39.6	41.8	4.3	33.6	38.6	29.9	35.6	37.0	35.4	32.2	24.9	30.7
March	33.6	44.5	39.4	41.7	4.3	33.5	38.5	29.7	35.4	37.0	35.5	32.2	24.9	30.7
April	33.6	44.9	39.5	41.8	4.3	33.5	38.6	29.8	35.6	37.1	35.5	32.2	24.9	30.9
May	33.6	45.0	39.6	41.9	4.2	33.5	38.5	29.7	35.6	36.9	35.4	32.2	24.9	30.8
June	33.6	44.9	39.7	41.8	4.3	33.6	38.6	29.8	35.7	37.0	35.4	32.2	24.9	30.9
July	33.7	45.4	39.7	42.0	4.3	33.6	38.7	29.8	35.7	37.0	35.5	32.2	24.9	31.0
August	33.6	45.4	39.4	41.8	4.3	33.5	38.6	29.7	35.7	36.8	35.4	32.2	24.8	30.8
September	33.6	45.6	39.6	41.8	4.3	33.5	38.7	29.6	35.7	36.9	35.4	32.2	24.9	30.8
October	33.6	45.5	39.6	42.0	4.4	33.5	38.8	29.6	35.7	36.9	35.4	32.1	24.8	30.8
November	33.6	45.5	39.8	41.8	4.3	33.5	38.8	29.7	35.4	36.9	35.3	32.2	25.1	30.8
December	33.6	45.5	39.2	41.9	4.3	33.6	38.8	29.8	35.8	37.0	35.2	32.2	24.8	30.9

. . . = Not available.

Table 10-16. Indexes of Aggregate Weekly Hours of Production and Nonsupervisory Workers on Private Nonfarm Payrolls by NAICS Supersector

(2002 = 100, seasonally adjusted.)

Year and month	Total private	Mining and logging	Construc-tion	Manu-facturing	Trade, transportation, and utilities			Information	Financial activities	Profes-sional and business services	Education and health services	Leisure and hospitality	Other services
					Total	Wholesale trade	Retail trade						
1965	54.4	121.6	55.2	122.1	59.0	...	...	55.5	42.6	29.4	25.9	41.0	29.4
1966	56.8	121.1	56.8	130.2	60.5	...	...	58.3	43.6	30.8	27.0	42.2	30.9
1967	57.0	117.0	55.4	127.8	61.1	...	...	58.6	44.9	31.9	28.1	42.9	32.4
1968	58.4	114.9	56.5	130.1	62.2	...	...	59.9	46.8	33.1	29.1	44.0	33.9
1969	60.3	118.1	61.0	131.9	64.3	...	...	61.8	49.4	34.6	30.5	45.6	35.6
1970	59.3	115.7	59.8	123.3	64.9	...	...	60.4	50.3	34.7	31.0	46.1	36.3
1971	58.9	109.9	61.0	119.3	65.1	...	...	58.7	51.1	34.7	31.1	46.9	36.5
1972	61.4	115.6	63.4	125.7	67.5	68.4	64.4	61.1	52.5	36.0	32.2	48.5	37.9
1973	64.2	117.0	66.7	132.9	69.6	71.0	66.4	64.1	54.2	37.8	33.7	50.3	39.9
1974	64.2	127.7	64.5	129.0	70.2	72.7	66.7	64.0	54.9	38.8	34.9	50.8	41.4
1975	61.1	134.9	55.2	113.9	68.9	71.8	66.4	59.1	55.0	38.9	35.8	50.9	42.6
1976	63.6	142.4	56.0	120.8	70.9	73.9	68.8	61.2	56.2	40.3	37.0	52.8	44.3
1977	66.1	151.1	59.4	125.8	73.1	76.7	70.7	63.5	58.8	42.1	38.5	54.4	46.3
1978	69.3	156.9	66.2	131.3	76.1	81.0	73.4	66.6	62.0	44.3	40.4	56.6	48.8
1979	71.6	175.2	70.6	133.3	78.3	84.6	74.7	69.0	64.7	46.3	42.2	57.9	51.2
1980	70.8	187.2	68.0	124.4	77.6	84.8	74.0	67.5	67.0	47.7	44.1	57.8	53.6
1981	71.4	206.2	64.9	123.1	78.0	86.0	74.5	67.7	68.6	49.2	45.8	58.7	55.8
1982	68.8	195.5	59.7	109.9	76.4	83.4	74.2	64.0	68.6	49.2	46.7	58.7	56.8
1983	69.8	162.8	61.0	111.6	77.2	83.3	76.0	62.1	69.8	50.7	48.3	60.4	58.9
1984	74.1	169.3	69.1	119.6	81.2	87.5	79.8	68.0	73.0	53.2	50.4	63.6	61.7
1985	76.0	162.7	73.9	117.5	83.5	89.9	82.2	69.1	76.1	55.6	53.0	66.0	65.0
1986	77.3	133.5	75.5	116.3	84.5	89.8	83.9	69.1	79.9	57.8	55.4	67.9	68.1
1987	79.5	125.2	78.1	117.8	86.5	90.5	86.3	71.5	82.3	60.3	58.0	70.5	71.5
1988	81.9	125.6	80.4	120.3	88.6	93.6	88.5	73.1	82.0	63.3	61.3	73.0	75.6
1989	83.9	123.2	81.7	120.3	90.5	95.9	90.0	74.4	82.6	66.3	64.6	74.9	79.7
1990	84.2	128.6	78.8	117.7	89.5	94.9	87.5	76.2	83.1	68.1	66.6	78.9	81.8
1991	82.4	123.8	70.1	112.8	87.4	93.3	84.8	76.1	82.0	66.7	69.7	77.3	81.1
1992	83.0	113.3	67.5	112.4	87.3	92.4	85.1	76.5	82.4	68.4	72.4	79.2	80.6
1993	85.3	110.3	71.3	113.9	89.1	92.4	86.3	78.0	84.9	71.9	74.8	82.1	82.8
1994	89.1	111.0	77.3	118.3	92.7	95.8	89.8	79.2	87.2	77.0	77.8	85.5	84.5
1995	91.4	110.3	79.9	119.0	95.1	99.2	92.3	82.5	86.9	81.2	80.6	88.5	87.0
1996	93.6	112.7	84.3	118.8	96.6	100.7	93.7	86.9	89.1	85.2	82.9	90.7	89.1
1997	97.0	117.6	88.6	121.4	98.9	103.4	95.9	90.4	92.3	91.5	86.2	93.4	91.9
1998	99.4	112.8	93.4	121.1	100.3	104.8	97.2	92.6	96.4	96.7	88.6	95.5	94.3
1999	101.4	102.9	99.7	119.0	101.9	106.2	99.5	98.5	98.1	101.7	90.4	97.8	96.2
2000	103.5	105.1	104.0	117.8	103.5	107.0	101.3	105.0	98.4	106.6	92.6	100.5	97.8
2001	102.0	108.3	103.2	108.1	101.5	102.9	100.5	106.7	99.3	104.0	96.5	100.6	99.0
2002	100.0	100.0	100.0	100.0	100.0	100.0	100.0	100.0	100.0	100.0	100.0	100.0	100.0
2003	98.7	97.4	98.4	94.5	98.6	98.0	98.9	97.0	101.3	98.7	101.7	100.0	97.4
2004	100.3	104.0	101.7	94.3	99.6	98.8	99.4	98.2	101.4	101.8	103.8	103.0	96.1
2005	102.8	114.7	108.3	93.9	101.6	101.8	100.8	99.4	103.7	106.3	107.0	106.2	96.2
2006	105.8	125.8	115.4	95.6	103.3	105.7	101.1	100.2	106.3	112.1	109.6	108.8	97.4
2007	107.4	133.5	114.7	94.4	104.8	109.2	101.8	100.1	107.6	115.3	113.2	110.8	99.3
2008	106.1	137.6	106.5	90.2	103.3	108.6	99.8	100.0	106.8	113.9	116.5	109.7	99.5
2009	98.8	117.2	85.9	76.1	96.8	99.9	94.3	93.5	103.1	105.2	118.3	105.1	96.0
2010	99.0	124.5	80.2	76.2	96.8	97.7	95.0	90.0	101.3	107.6	119.8	104.6	96.0
2011	101.4	147.4	81.7	78.3	99.7	100.7	97.7	88.9	101.2	112.4	122.3	106.9	96.8
2012	104.3	158.7	83.6	80.3	101.8	104.0	98.9	88.9	103.7	117.2	125.4	111.3	97.7
2013	106.1	155.0	87.7	80.9	102.7	105.3	98.7	89.8	104.7	121.3	126.6	115.2	98.7
2014	108.6	164.3	92.0	82.6	104.4	106.8	99.5	90.5	106.5	125.8	128.5	119.3	99.9
2015	110.9	144.1	96.5	83.3	106.3	106.8	100.9	90.8	109.6	128.2	132.3	122.7	100.7
2016	112.5	114.4	100.6	83.3	107.0	106.7	101.1	90.7	111.6	130.6	136.0	125.2	101.7
2015													
January	109.9	161.2	94.8	83.5	105.4	107.1	100.2	90.9	107.5	127.1	130.6	121.5	100.7
February	110.1	156.8	95.5	83.3	105.6	107.3	100.3	90.8	108.2	127.3	130.5	122.4	100.4
March	110.2	153.0	94.4	83.2	106.0	107.1	100.5	90.6	108.7	127.0	130.7	121.5	100.5
April	110.0	150.4	94.7	83.1	105.7	107.0	100.5	90.9	108.8	126.5	131.6	121.2	100.2
May	110.3	146.7	95.4	83.4	106.2	106.6	101.0	90.9	109.2	127.5	131.4	121.8	100.5
June	110.8	144.5	96.5	83.4	106.0	106.6	100.8	90.4	109.3	128.0	132.2	122.5	100.4
July	111.0	144.6	96.0	83.4	106.4	106.8	100.8	90.9	109.7	128.5	132.5	122.8	100.7
August	111.1	140.2	97.0	83.4	106.5	106.5	101.2	91.0	109.9	128.7	132.8	122.6	100.9
September	111.2	134.8	96.6	83.1	106.8	106.4	101.5	90.7	110.0	127.9	133.1	123.1	100.7
October	111.5	134.7	98.4	83.3	106.5	106.4	100.9	91.0	110.6	129.1	133.5	123.6	101.2
November	111.7	131.2	98.5	83.4	106.7	106.4	101.4	90.6	110.6	129.3	133.7	124.0	101.0
December	112.3	132.0	101.0	83.3	106.8	106.6	101.1	90.4	111.0	130.1	134.4	124.3	101.5
2016													
January	112.1	128.6	100.2	83.8	106.9	106.3	101.4	91.0	110.9	130.1	134.6	124.1	101.1
February	111.9	121.2	100.2	83.5	106.8	106.6	101.4	91.0	110.8	129.3	135.0	124.5	101.4
March	112.1	116.3	100.3	83.2	106.7	106.2	101.0	90.7	111.1	129.8	135.1	124.8	101.2
April	112.1	115.0	100.2	83.3	106.7	106.5	101.3	91.1	111.6	130.1	135.4	124.8	102.0
May	112.1	113.3	100.1	83.2	106.7	106.2	100.9	89.6	111.3	129.9	135.7	124.7	101.5
June	112.4	111.7	100.1	83.2	107.1	106.5	101.3	91.3	111.9	130.3	136.2	125.1	102.1
July	113.0	111.9	100.1	83.6	107.2	106.9	101.4	91.1	112.2	131.3	136.5	125.6	102.5
August	112.7	111.2	99.3	83.0	107.0	106.7	101.1	91.1	111.8	131.0	136.8	125.2	101.9
September	112.9	110.7	100.2	82.9	107.1	107.2	100.9	91.3	112.2	131.6	137.0	125.7	102.3
October	113.1	110.0	100.3	83.2	107.2	107.7	100.9	91.4	112.4	132.0	136.8	125.5	102.1
November	113.2	112.7	101.5	82.9	107.3	107.7	101.1	90.2	112.6	131.9	137.4	127.4	102.3
December	113.5	113.2	100.6	83.3	107.8	107.7	101.5	91.0	113.4	131.7	137.8	126.1	102.4

. . . = Not available.

Table 10-17. Average Hourly Earnings of Production and Nonsupervisory Workers on Private Nonfarm Payrolls by NAICS Supersector

(Dollars, seasonally adjusted.)

Year and month	Total private	Mining and logging	Construc-tion	Manu-facturing	Trade, transportation, and utilities			Information	Financial activities	Profes-sional and business services	Education and health services	Leisure and hospitality	Other services
					Total	Wholesale trade	Retail trade						
1965	2.63	2.87	3.23	2.49	2.94	. . .	. . .	4.47	2.38	3.28	2.12	1.17	1.25
1966	2.73	3.00	3.41	2.60	3.04	. . .	. . .	4.56	2.47	3.39	2.23	1.26	1.37
1967	2.85	3.14	3.63	2.71	3.15	. . .	. . .	4.68	2.58	3.51	2.36	1.37	1.49
1968	3.02	3.30	3.92	2.89	3.32	. . .	. . .	4.85	2.75	3.65	2.49	1.53	1.62
1969	3.22	3.54	4.30	3.07	3.48	. . .	. . .	5.05	2.92	3.84	2.68	1.69	1.81
1970	3.40	3.77	4.74	3.24	3.65	. . .	. . .	5.25	3.07	4.04	2.88	1.82	2.01
1971	3.63	3.99	5.17	3.45	3.86	. . .	. . .	5.53	3.23	4.26	3.11	1.95	2.24
1972	3.90	4.28	5.55	3.70	4.23	4.58	3.52	5.87	3.37	4.50	3.33	2.08	2.46
1973	4.14	4.59	5.89	3.97	4.46	4.80	3.69	6.17	3.55	4.72	3.54	2.20	2.67
1974	4.43	5.09	6.29	4.31	4.74	5.11	3.92	6.52	3.80	5.01	3.82	2.40	2.95
1975	4.73	5.68	6.78	4.71	5.01	5.45	4.14	6.92	4.08	5.29	4.09	2.58	3.21
1976	5.06	6.19	7.17	5.10	5.31	5.75	4.36	7.37	4.30	5.60	4.39	2.78	3.51
1977	5.44	6.70	7.56	5.55	5.67	6.12	4.65	7.84	4.50	5.95	4.72	3.03	3.84
1978	5.88	7.44	8.11	6.05	6.11	6.61	5.00	8.34	4.93	6.32	5.07	3.33	4.19
1979	6.34	8.20	8.71	6.57	6.56	7.12	5.34	8.86	5.31	6.71	5.44	3.63	4.56
1980	6.85	8.97	9.37	7.15	7.04	7.68	5.71	9.47	5.82	7.22	5.93	3.98	5.05
1981	7.44	9.89	10.24	7.87	7.55	8.28	6.09	10.21	6.34	7.80	6.49	4.36	5.61
1982	7.87	10.64	11.04	8.36	7.91	8.81	6.34	10.76	6.82	8.30	7.00	4.63	6.11
1983	8.20	11.14	11.36	8.70	8.23	9.27	6.60	11.18	7.32	8.70	7.39	4.89	6.51
1984	8.49	11.54	11.56	9.05	8.45	9.61	6.73	11.50	7.65	8.98	7.66	4.99	6.79
1985	8.74	11.87	11.75	9.40	8.60	9.88	6.83	11.81	7.97	9.28	7.97	5.10	7.10
1986	8.93	12.14	11.92	9.60	8.74	10.07	6.93	12.08	8.37	9.55	8.24	5.20	7.38
1987	9.14	12.17	12.15	9.77	8.92	10.32	7.02	12.36	8.73	9.85	8.56	5.30	7.69
1988	9.44	12.45	12.52	10.05	9.15	10.71	7.23	12.63	9.07	10.22	8.95	5.50	8.08
1989	9.80	12.90	12.98	10.35	9.46	11.12	7.46	12.99	9.54	10.69	9.45	5.76	8.58
1990	10.20	13.40	13.42	10.78	9.83	11.58	7.71	13.40	9.98	11.14	9.98	6.02	9.08
1991	10.51	13.82	13.65	11.13	10.08	11.95	7.89	13.90	10.43	11.50	10.48	6.22	9.39
1992	10.77	14.09	13.81	11.40	10.30	12.21	8.12	14.29	10.86	11.78	10.86	6.36	9.66
1993	11.05	14.12	14.04	11.70	10.55	12.57	8.36	14.86	11.38	11.96	11.20	6.48	9.90
1994	11.34	14.41	14.38	12.04	10.80	12.93	8.61	15.32	11.84	12.15	11.48	6.62	10.18
1995	11.65	14.78	14.73	12.34	11.10	13.34	8.85	15.68	12.31	12.53	11.78	6.79	10.51
1996	12.04	15.09	15.11	12.75	11.46	13.80	9.21	16.30	12.75	13.00	12.15	6.99	10.85
1997	12.51	15.57	15.67	13.14	11.90	14.41	9.59	17.14	13.28	13.57	12.53	7.32	11.29
1998	13.01	16.20	16.23	13.45	12.40	15.07	10.05	17.67	14.00	14.27	12.96	7.67	11.79
1999	13.49	16.33	16.80	13.85	12.82	15.62	10.45	18.40	14.55	14.85	13.40	7.96	12.26
2000	14.02	16.55	17.48	14.32	13.31	16.28	10.87	19.07	15.04	15.52	13.91	8.32	12.73
2001	14.54	17.00	18.00	14.76	13.70	16.77	11.29	19.80	15.65	16.33	14.58	8.57	13.27
2002	14.96	17.19	18.52	15.29	14.02	16.98	11.67	20.20	16.25	16.80	15.15	8.81	13.72
2003	15.37	17.56	18.95	15.74	14.34	17.36	11.90	21.01	17.21	17.21	15.56	9.00	13.84
2004	15.68	18.07	19.23	16.14	14.58	17.65	12.08	21.40	17.58	17.48	16.07	9.15	13.98
2005	16.12	18.72	19.46	16.56	14.92	18.16	12.36	22.06	17.98	18.08	16.62	9.38	14.34
2006	16.75	19.90	20.02	16.81	15.39	18.91	12.57	23.23	18.83	19.13	17.28	9.75	14.77
2007	17.42	20.97	20.95	17.26	15.78	19.59	12.75	23.96	19.67	20.15	17.99	10.41	15.42
2008	18.06	22.50	21.87	17.75	16.16	20.13	12.87	24.78	20.32	21.18	18.73	10.84	16.09
2009	18.61	23.29	22.66	18.24	16.48	20.84	13.01	25.45	20.90	22.35	19.34	11.12	16.59
2010	19.05	23.82	23.22	18.61	16.82	21.54	13.25	25.87	21.55	22.78	19.95	11.31	17.06
2011	19.44	24.50	23.65	18.93	17.15	21.97	13.51	26.62	21.93	23.12	20.60	11.45	17.32
2012	19.74	25.79	23.97	19.08	17.43	22.24	13.82	27.04	22.82	23.29	20.91	11.62	17.59
2013	20.13	26.80	24.22	19.30	17.74	22.62	14.02	27.98	23.87	23.72	21.29	11.78	18.00
2014	20.61	26.84	24.67	19.56	18.27	23.24	14.40	28.70	24.71	24.29	21.64	12.09	18.51
2015	21.03	26.48	25.20	19.91	18.67	23.63	14.82	29.05	25.34	24.79	22.09	12.41	19.01
2016	21.54	27.05	25.97	20.43	18.99	24.18	15.05	30.04	26.11	25.42	22.53	12.85	19.36
2015													
January	20.81	26.53	24.99	19.65	18.50	23.40	14.68	28.69	25.05	24.44	21.89	12.30	18.78
February	20.82	26.49	24.77	19.73	18.51	23.41	14.65	28.71	25.08	24.49	21.91	12.33	18.85
March	20.89	26.49	25.09	19.77	18.56	23.51	14.63	28.70	25.12	24.58	21.97	12.34	18.90
April	20.92	26.30	25.17	19.80	18.56	23.53	14.68	28.90	25.15	24.63	21.96	12.37	18.90
May	20.99	26.37	25.19	19.86	18.61	23.65	14.73	29.05	25.24	24.75	22.06	12.39	18.97
June	21.00	26.28	25.26	19.88	18.60	23.54	14.81	28.95	25.30	24.72	22.10	12.34	19.03
July	21.04	26.40	25.14	19.95	18.67	23.60	14.83	29.04	25.37	24.77	22.10	12.40	19.02
August	21.10	26.54	25.19	20.01	18.72	23.72	14.90	29.12	25.40	24.84	22.16	12.45	19.08
September	21.12	26.79	25.01	20.06	18.75	23.69	15.01	28.92	25.48	24.96	22.18	12.45	19.12
October	21.19	26.65	25.34	20.05	18.82	23.80	15.02	29.20	25.52	24.99	22.24	12.51	19.13
November	21.21	26.63	25.44	20.08	18.79	23.76	14.96	29.52	25.56	25.02	22.24	12.54	19.14
December	21.26	26.59	25.44	20.13	18.83	23.85	14.98	29.62	25.65	25.06	22.29	12.57	19.18
2016													
January	21.32	26.84	25.41	20.16	18.88	23.97	14.98	29.61	25.85	25.13	22.32	12.66	19.19
February	21.33	26.86	25.41	20.20	18.86	23.96	14.98	29.77	25.88	25.13	22.39	12.68	19.21
March	21.40	26.90	25.69	20.27	18.92	24.06	15.03	29.69	25.97	25.20	22.41	12.73	19.27
April	21.46	27.13	25.72	20.39	18.94	24.11	15.03	29.84	26.11	25.27	22.47	12.78	19.28
May	21.48	27.12	25.86	20.41	18.95	24.19	15.03	29.91	26.04	25.34	22.45	12.80	19.31
June	21.53	27.16	26.05	20.42	18.98	24.18	14.99	30.03	26.11	25.43	22.44	12.83	19.32
July	21.59	27.07	26.12	20.47	19.01	24.27	15.03	30.14	26.15	25.50	22.54	12.90	19.37
August	21.62	27.08	26.07	20.56	18.98	24.23	15.01	30.23	26.31	25.53	22.58	12.92	19.39
September	21.68	27.09	26.21	20.55	19.06	24.35	15.03	30.33	26.33	25.62	22.62	12.96	19.43
October	21.72	27.20	26.28	20.61	19.09	24.39	15.02	30.30	26.38	25.64	22.66	12.97	19.50
November	21.74	27.07	26.24	20.60	19.13	24.36	15.18	30.31	26.28	25.72	22.73	13.01	19.55
December	21.80	27.36	26.23	20.63	19.19	24.45	15.28	30.44	26.32	25.81	22.77	13.04	19.57

. . . = Not available.

Table 10-18. Average Weekly Earnings of Production and Nonsupervisory Workers on Private Nonfarm Payrolls by NAICS Supersector

(Dollars, seasonally adjusted.)

Year and month	Total private	Mining and logging	Construction	Manu-facturing	Trade, transportation, and utilities			Information	Financial activities	Profes-sional and business services	Education and health services	Leisure and hospitality	Other services
					Total	Wholesale trade	Retail trade						
1965	101.51	125.48	122.35	102.69	116.36	...	...	171.24	88.50	122.30	74.84	38.06	45.30
1966	105.23	132.50	130.11	107.47	118.78	...	...	174.52	91.83	125.53	78.04	40.34	48.94
1967	108.07	137.76	138.55	109.85	121.57	...	...	176.09	95.35	128.34	81.34	43.06	52.69
1968	113.82	145.26	148.22	117.73	126.69	...	...	182.65	101.18	132.47	85.02	47.07	56.81
1969	120.70	157.11	164.88	124.74	132.13	...	...	190.18	107.91	139.37	91.46	51.29	63.44
1970	125.79	165.82	179.11	128.84	137.15	...	...	195.24	112.32	144.76	97.23	54.57	69.67
1971	133.22	174.18	194.70	137.59	144.11	...	...	204.50	117.60	151.51	103.57	58.39	76.58
1972	143.87	188.76	205.04	150.23	158.09	181.98	123.57	218.72	122.86	159.88	111.12	61.78	84.14
1973	152.59	201.43	219.32	161.59	165.61	190.33	128.16	230.48	129.32	167.40	117.85	64.92	91.06
1974	161.61	222.24	233.24	172.37	174.18	200.53	134.39	241.07	137.71	176.47	126.50	69.90	99.98
1975	170.29	248.38	249.70	185.69	182.61	212.85	140.99	253.21	147.75	185.81	134.83	74.49	108.67
1976	182.65	273.69	267.00	204.41	192.62	224.66	147.21	270.80	155.54	195.61	143.47	79.47	117.85
1977	195.58	299.46	279.61	224.01	203.87	239.57	154.51	288.29	165.47	206.78	153.38	85.20	128.12
1978	210.29	334.27	302.27	244.49	217.53	258.75	163.74	306.71	177.96	218.42	163.48	92.16	138.74
1979	225.69	366.58	326.55	263.99	232.36	278.74	173.18	324.51	190.72	231.16	174.80	99.47	150.47
1980	241.07	402.51	351.49	283.35	246.60	298.24	182.25	344.38	209.21	247.64	190.16	107.52	166.32
1981	261.53	446.10	382.75	312.74	263.93	322.08	193.97	370.36	228.21	267.46	208.06	117.49	184.77
1982	273.10	469.10	410.39	325.07	274.09	340.84	200.74	385.82	245.16	284.11	224.53	124.14	201.49
1983	286.43	488.89	427.00	348.89	284.76	359.98	208.81	404.89	262.83	298.74	237.40	130.82	214.87
1984	298.26	514.77	441.28	367.77	292.99	373.78	212.82	420.45	276.50	308.24	245.16	133.49	223.33
1985	304.62	529.62	448.35	380.60	295.81	383.22	213.38	430.86	287.66	317.41	254.19	134.71	232.81
1986	309.78	529.20	451.22	390.46	298.07	389.73	214.52	439.84	302.32	327.30	263.41	136.34	242.33
1987	317.39	529.72	463.78	400.00	304.10	397.39	218.05	450.77	314.01	337.57	273.49	139.45	252.58
1988	326.48	539.63	478.74	412.62	309.58	411.71	223.67	455.59	322.87	349.89	286.57	144.51	265.83
1989	338.34	568.55	497.43	423.58	319.40	427.40	229.14	468.77	339.46	365.93	302.70	150.29	282.09
1990	349.63	602.43	513.43	436.13	331.55	444.48	235.56	479.50	354.60	380.61	318.90	156.32	297.88
1991	358.46	625.46	520.41	449.74	339.10	459.17	240.13	495.14	369.57	391.06	334.10	159.20	306.75
1992	368.20	628.94	525.13	464.43	348.60	470.41	249.66	511.95	386.31	400.64	347.64	163.70	315.08
1993	378.80	634.77	539.81	480.89	359.51	484.46	256.89	535.19	403.68	406.20	358.34	167.54	322.69
1994	391.17	653.13	558.53	501.95	370.38	501.14	265.74	551.21	420.18	414.16	367.50	172.27	332.44
1995	400.04	670.40	571.57	509.26	378.79	515.14	272.63	564.92	437.26	426.54	376.77	175.74	342.36
1996	413.25	695.04	588.48	526.55	390.67	533.36	282.74	592.45	453.05	442.81	387.45	181.02	352.68
1997	431.86	720.07	609.48	548.26	407.63	559.39	295.94	622.37	475.03	465.51	403.42	190.66	368.63
1998	448.59	727.19	629.75	557.24	423.33	582.21	310.23	646.52	503.94	490.13	417.47	200.82	384.25
1999	463.15	721.77	655.11	573.29	434.31	602.77	321.71	675.47	520.74	510.99	429.76	208.05	398.77
2000	480.99	734.88	685.78	591.04	449.96	631.24	333.41	700.92	540.39	535.07	447.80	217.20	413.30
2001	493.61	757.96	695.86	595.15	459.53	643.45	346.16	731.18	560.46	557.84	471.33	220.73	428.64
2002	506.54	741.97	711.82	618.62	471.27	644.38	360.84	737.94	578.94	574.60	490.38	227.31	439.87
2003	517.76	765.94	727.00	636.03	481.14	657.29	367.18	760.84	611.82	587.02	503.05	230.49	434.41
2004	528.84	804.01	735.55	658.49	488.51	666.79	371.13	776.72	625.53	597.54	521.06	234.86	433.04
2005	544.00	853.87	750.37	673.34	498.46	685.00	377.58	805.11	646.48	618.71	541.40	241.36	443.40
2006	567.22	907.95	781.59	690.88	514.37	718.50	383.12	850.64	673.63	662.27	561.02	250.34	456.50
2007	589.18	962.63	816.23	711.50	525.91	748.94	385.00	874.45	706.52	700.82	585.44	265.54	477.06
2008	607.42	1 014.69	842.61	724.46	536.11	769.62	386.21	908.78	729.64	737.90	607.82	273.39	495.57
2009	615.96	1 006.67	851.76	726.12	541.88	784.49	388.57	931.08	754.90	775.81	622.30	275.95	506.26
2010	636.19	1 063.11	891.83	765.18	559.63	816.50	400.07	939.85	780.19	798.54	639.37	280.87	523.70
2011	652.89	1 144.64	921.84	784.29	577.71	845.44	412.09	964.85	798.68	813.37	663.04	283.82	532.63
2012	665.65	1 201.69	942.14	794.63	588.86	860.70	422.10	973.52	840.04	822.58	674.48	290.54	539.46
2013	677.70	1 229.70	958.72	807.37	597.40	875.79	423.07	1 003.65	875.04	838.67	683.24	294.31	553.77
2014	694.85	1 270.91	977.11	822.03	613.95	897.73	431.82	1 030.17	907.98	864.45	692.56	303.81	568.92
2015	708.90	1 211.91	998.02	832.05	628.76	911.41	445.52	1 038.10	939.46	878.71	709.25	311.32	583.54
2016	723.69	1 224.33	1 031.16	855.69	636.64	933.16	447.62	1 068.25	962.73	898.76	724.40	319.52	595.73
2015													
January	701.30	1 241.60	992.10	825.30	621.60	903.24	440.40	1 029.97	919.34	867.62	702.67	309.96	578.42
February	701.63	1 221.19	983.37	826.69	621.94	903.63	439.50	1 030.69	925.45	869.40	701.12	311.95	578.70
March	703.99	1 210.59	988.55	826.39	625.47	907.49	438.90	1 030.33	929.44	870.13	703.04	309.73	580.23
April	702.91	1 204.54	989.18	827.64	623.62	908.26	440.40	1 037.51	930.55	866.98	704.92	309.25	578.34
May	705.26	1 205.11	992.49	830.15	627.16	910.53	443.37	1 039.99	936.40	873.68	705.92	309.75	580.48
June	707.70	1 193.11	1 005.35	830.98	624.96	906.29	444.30	1 030.62	936.10	875.09	709.41	309.73	582.32
July	709.05	1 219.68	993.03	833.91	629.18	910.96	444.90	1 036.73	941.23	879.34	709.41	311.24	583.91
August	711.07	1 204.92	1 002.56	836.42	630.86	913.22	448.49	1 039.58	942.34	881.82	711.34	311.25	587.66
September	711.74	1 213.59	990.40	836.50	633.75	912.07	453.30	1 026.66	945.31	881.09	711.98	311.25	586.98
October	714.10	1 212.58	1 013.60	836.09	634.23	916.30	450.60	1 036.60	949.34	887.15	713.90	312.75	589.20
November	714.78	1 209.00	1 009.97	839.34	633.22	914.76	450.30	1 050.91	948.28	888.21	713.90	313.50	587.60
December	718.59	1 225.80	1 022.69	839.42	634.57	920.61	449.40	1 051.51	954.18	892.14	717.74	314.25	590.74
2016													
January	718.48	1 237.32	1 011.32	844.70	636.26	922.85	449.40	1 060.04	959.04	894.63	718.70	315.23	589.13
February	716.69	1 206.01	1 006.24	844.36	633.70	924.86	447.90	1 059.81	957.56	889.60	720.96	315.73	589.75
March	719.04	1 197.05	1 012.19	845.26	633.82	926.31	446.39	1 051.03	960.89	894.60	721.60	316.98	591.59
April	721.06	1 218.14	1 015.94	852.30	634.49	930.65	447.89	1 062.30	968.68	897.09	723.53	318.22	595.75
May	721.73	1 220.40	1 024.06	855.18	634.83	931.32	446.39	1 064.80	960.88	897.04	722.89	318.72	594.75
June	723.41	1 219.48	1 034.19	853.56	637.73	933.35	446.70	1 072.07	966.07	900.22	722.57	319.47	596.99
July	727.58	1 228.98	1 036.96	859.74	638.74	939.25	447.89	1 076.00	967.55	905.25	725.79	321.21	600.47
August	726.43	1 229.43	1 027.16	859.41	635.83	935.28	445.80	1 079.21	966.33	903.76	727.08	320.42	597.21
September	728.45	1 235.30	1 037.92	858.99	638.51	942.35	444.89	1 082.78	971.58	906.95	728.36	322.70	598.44
October	729.79	1 237.60	1 040.69	865.62	639.52	946.33	444.59	1 081.71	973.42	907.66	727.39	321.66	600.60
November	730.46	1 231.69	1 044.35	861.08	640.86	945.17	450.85	1 072.97	969.73	907.92	731.91	326.55	602.14
December	732.48	1 244.88	1 028.22	864.40	644.78	948.66	455.34	1 089.75	973.84	908.51	733.19	323.39	604.71

. . . = Not available.

SECTION 10C: OTHER SIGNIFICANT LABOR MARKET DATA

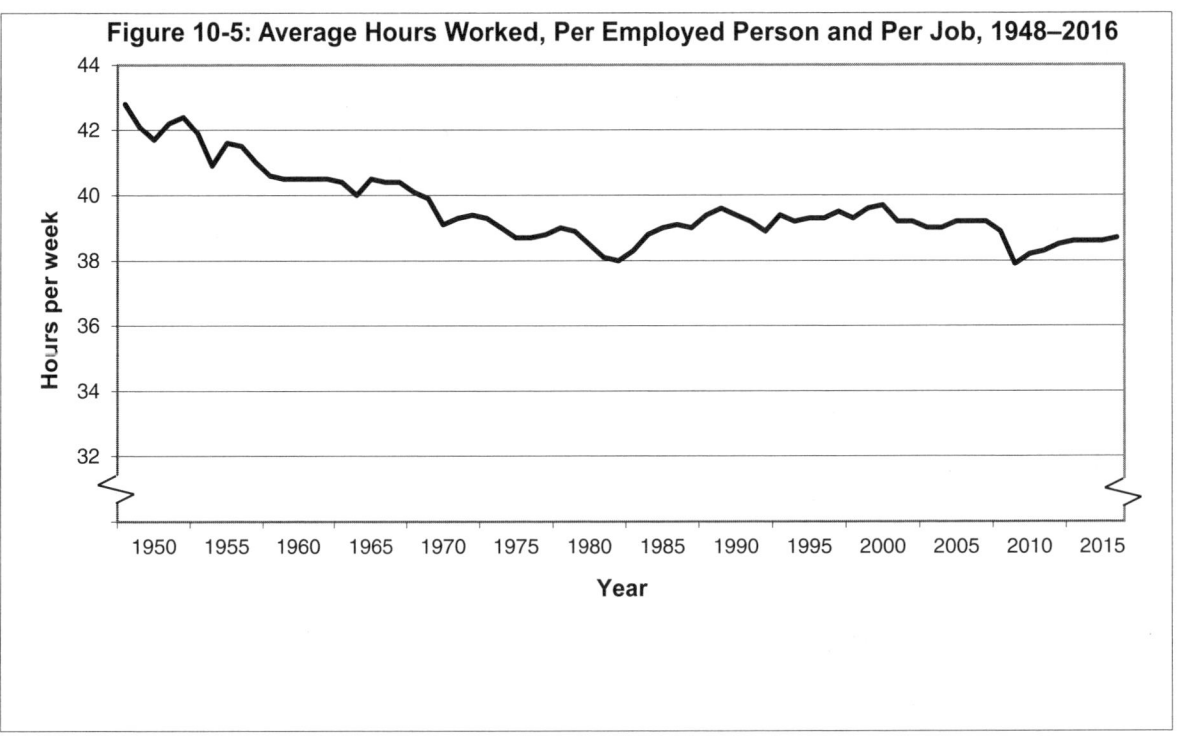

- This section of *Business Statistics* includes indicators of hours and earnings from the Current Population Statistics (household) survey that are, for some purposes, more appropriate than similarly-named indicators produced by the payroll survey and shown in the previous section. It also includes annual employment data from the Bureau of Economic Analysis, produced as part of the National Income and Product Accounts (NIPA), that provide a consistent historical record of U.S. employment from 1929 through 2000.

- Figure 10-5 above shows annual averages of hours worked per week reported by all persons in the household survey employed in nonagricultural industries. Along with the recession dips expected in any measure of the average workweek, it displays a clear downward trend through the early 1970s, but no trend since then. The recession low in 2009 was actually slightly higher than the recession low in 1982. The 2000 peak is equal to the 1969 level. In 2016, hours per person increased slightly to 38.7 hours after remaining at 38.6 hours the previous three years. (Table 10-19)

- For comparison, average weekly hours for nonfarm production and nonsupervisory workers are also graphed in Figure 10-5. These are the workweeks reported by employers in the Current Employment Statistics (payroll) survey and they pertain to jobs, not to workers. (Table 10-15) This CES measure of "hours per job" represents many of the same workers as those in the "hours per employed person" measure shown in the graph, and was selected for the graph because it has the longest available history. But it is increasingly pulled downward by the increasing prevalence of part-time jobs. It is not a good indicator of either the level or the trend of the amount of work being done each week by the typical American worker. (Table 10-19)

- A look at some of the other categories in Table 10-19 confirms the absence of any significant downtrend in the workers' workweek in recent years. Note, for example, that men reported working an average of 41.7 hours at the pre-recession peak in 2007—just 18 minutes less than the 1979 peak of 42.0—while women actually reported working 1 1/2 hours longer—36.1 hours in 2007 against 34.5 hours in 1979. (Table 10-19)

Table 10-19. Hours at Work, Current Population Survey

(Hours per week.)

Year and month	Hours per person, all industries				Hours per person, nonagricultural industries	
	Total	Men	Women	Persons who usually work full-time	All workers	
					Total	Usually work full-time
1948	42.8	. . .	. . .	. . .	41.6	. . .
1949	42.1	. . .	. . .	. . .	40.9	. . .
1950	41.7	. . .	. . .	. . .	40.7	. . .
1951	42.2	. . .	. . .	. . .	41.3	. . .
1952	42.4	. . .	. . .	. . .	41.6	. . .
1953	41.9	. . .	. . .	. . .	41.1	. . .
1954	40.9	. . .	. . .	. . .	40.0	. . .
1955	41.6	. . .	. . .	. . .	40.9	. . .
1956	41.5	43.8	36.5	. . .	40.9	. . .
1957	41.0	43.4	36.1	. . .	40.5	. . .
1958	40.6	42.9	35.8	. . .	40.1	. . .
1959	40.5	42.8	35.6	. . .	40.0	. . .
1960	40.5	43.0	35.4	. . .	40.0	. . .
1961	40.5	43.0	35.3	. . .	40.1	. . .
1962	40.5	43.2	35.2	. . .	40.1	. . .
1963	40.4	43.2	35.1	. . .	40.1	. . .
1964	40.0	42.8	34.7	. . .	39.7	. . .
1965	40.5	43.3	35.1	. . .	40.2	. . .
1966	40.4	43.2	35.2	. . .	40.1	. . .
1967	40.4	43.3	35.2	. . .	40.0	. . .
1968	40.1	43.0	34.9	. . .	39.7	. . .
1969	39.9	42.9	34.9	. . .	39.5	. . .
1970	39.1	42.0	34.2	. . .	38.7	. . .
1971	39.3	42.2	34.3	. . .	38.9	. . .
1972	39.4	42.3	34.5	. . .	39.0	. . .
1973	39.3	42.4	34.4	. . .	39.0	. . .
1974	39.0	42.0	34.3	. . .	38.7	. . .
1975	38.7	41.6	34.1	. . .	38.4	. . .
1976	38.7	41.7	34.1	. . .	38.4	. . .
1977	38.8	41.9	34.2	. . .	38.5	. . .
1978	39.0	42.1	34.5	. . .	38.7	. . .
1979	38.9	42.0	34.5	. . .	38.6	. . .
1980	38.5	41.5	34.5	. . .	38.3	. . .
1981	38.1	41.1	34.1	. . .	37.9	. . .
1982	38.0	40.9	34.1	. . .	37.7	. . .
1983	38.3	41.2	34.5	. . .	38.1	. . .
1984	38.8	41.8	34.9	. . .	38.6	. . .
1985	39.0	42.0	35.2	. . .	38.9	. . .
1986	39.1	42.1	35.4	. . .	38.9	. . .
1987	39.0	42.0	35.3	. . .	38.8	. . .
1988	39.4	42.4	35.7	. . .	39.3	. . .
1989	39.6	42.6	35.8	. . .	39.4	. . .
1990	39.4	42.3	35.8	. . .	39.3	. . .
1991	39.2	42.0	35.8	. . .	39.1	. . .
1992	38.9	41.7	35.6	. . .	38.8	. . .
1993	39.4	42.2	36.0	. . .	39.3	. . .
1994	39.2	42.2	35.5	43.4	39.1	43.3
1995	39.3	42.3	35.6	43.4	39.2	43.2
1996	39.3	42.3	35.7	43.3	39.2	43.2
1997	39.5	42.4	36.0	43.4	39.4	43.3
1998	39.3	42.2	35.8	43.2	39.2	43.1
1999	39.6	42.4	36.2	43.4	39.5	43.3
2000	39.7	42.5	36.4	43.4	39.6	43.3
2001	39.2	41.9	36.1	42.9	39.2	42.8
2002	39.2	41.8	36.0	42.9	39.1	42.8
2003	39.0	41.7	35.9	42.9	39.0	42.7
2004	39.0	41.7	35.9	42.9	39.0	42.8
2005	39.2	41.8	36.1	42.9	39.1	42.8
2006	39.2	41.8	36.2	42.9	39.2	42.8
2007	39.2	41.7	36.1	42.8	39.1	42.7
2008	38.9	41.3	36.1	42.6	38.8	42.5
2009	37.9	40.2	35.3	41.9	37.8	41.8
2010	38.2	40.5	35.5	42.2	38.1	42.2
2011	38.3	40.6	35.6	42.4	38.2	42.3
2012	38.5	40.8	35.8	42.5	38.4	42.4
2013	38.6	40.9	36.0	42.6	38.5	42.5
2014	38.6	40.9	35.9	42.5	38.6	42.5
2015	38.6	40.9	35.9	42.4	38.5	42.3
2016	38.7	40.9	36.2	42.5	38.7	42.4

. . . = Not available.

Table 10-20. Median Usual Weekly Earnings of Full-Time Wage and Salary Workers

(Current dollars, except as noted; not seasonally adjusted.)

Year and quarter	Total, 16 years and over	Sex and age								Race and ethnicity			
		Men, 16 years and over				Women, 16 years and over				White	Black or African American	Asian	Hispanic or Latino ethnicity
		Total	16 to 24 years	25 to 54 years	55 years and over	Total	16 to 24 years	25 to 54 years	55 years and over				
1979	241	292	196	. . .	. . .	182	154	. . .	. . .	248	199	. . .	194
1980	262	313	208	. . .	. . .	201	167	. . .	. . .	269	212	. . .	209
1981	284	340	218	. . .	. . .	219	180	. . .	. . .	291	235	. . .	223
1982	302	364	225	. . .	. . .	239	192	. . .	. . .	310	245	. . .	240
1983	313	379	223	. . .	. . .	252	198	. . .	. . .	320	261	. . .	250
1984	326	392	231	. . .	. . .	265	203	. . .	. . .	336	269	. . .	259
1985	344	407	241	. . .	. . .	277	211	. . .	. . .	356	277	. . .	270
1986	359	419	246	. . .	. . .	291	219	. . .	. . .	371	291	. . .	277
1987	374	434	257	. . .	. . .	303	227	. . .	. . .	384	301	. . .	285
1988	385	449	262	. . .	. . .	315	235	. . .	. . .	395	314	. . .	290
1989	399	468	271	. . .	. . .	328	246	. . .	. . .	409	319	. . .	298
1990	412	481	282	. . .	. . .	346	254	. . .	. . .	424	329	. . .	304
1991	426	493	285	. . .	. . .	366	266	. . .	. . .	442	348	. . .	312
1992	440	501	284	. . .	. . .	380	267	. . .	. . .	458	357	. . .	321
1993	459	510	288	. . .	. . .	393	273	. . .	. . .	475	369	. . .	331
1994	467	522	294	. . .	. . .	399	276	. . .	. . .	484	371	. . .	324
1995	479	538	303	. . .	. . .	406	275	. . .	. . .	494	383	. . .	329
1996	490	557	307	. . .	. . .	418	284	. . .	. . .	506	387	. . .	339
1997	503	579	317	. . .	. . .	431	292	. . .	. . .	519	400	. . .	351
1998	523	598	334	. . .	. . .	456	305	. . .	. . .	545	426	. . .	370
1999	549	618	356	. . .	. . .	473	324	. . .	. . .	573	445	. . .	385
2000	576	641	375	690	714	493	344	519	497	590	474	615	399
2001	596	670	391	717	742	512	353	547	519	610	491	639	417
2002	608	679	391	727	773	529	367	571	556	623	498	658	424
2003	620	695	398	736	797	552	371	584	584	636	514	693	440
2004	638	713	400	755	819	573	375	599	601	657	525	708	456
2005	651	722	409	763	829	585	381	610	619	672	520	753	471
2006	671	743	418	784	870	600	395	624	641	690	554	784	486
2007	695	766	443	809	902	614	409	644	657	716	569	830	503
2008	722	798	461	843	920	638	420	666	687	742	589	861	529
2009	739	819	458	857	944	657	424	683	706	757	601	880	541
2010	747	824	443	854	961	669	422	700	716	765	611	855	535
2011	756	832	455	864	976	684	421	713	738	775	615	866	549
2012	768	854	468	890	987	691	416	719	752	792	621	920	568
2013	776	860	479	891	999	706	423	733	766	802	629	942	578
2014	791	871	493	899	1 007	719	451	746	773	816	639	953	594
2015	809	895	510	921	1 054	726	450	757	774	835	641	993	604
2016	832	915	512	943	1 082	749	486	778	801	862	678	1 021	624
2009													
1st quarter	738	823	461	865	942	649	448	672	707	758	577	869	545
2nd quarter	734	815	450	854	945	652	413	674	703	754	592	909	547
3rd quarter	738	812	448	849	957	657	415	691	693	753	607	877	527
4th quarter	748	825	476	860	930	670	436	695	726	763	629	877	547
2010													
1st quarter	754	844	473	869	964	665	422	698	701	772	610	859	554
2nd quarter	740	810	442	843	937	672	417	701	712	756	607	873	529
3rd quarter	740	813	424	848	967	662	419	696	725	759	611	854	522
4th quarter	752	830	449	858	980	679	436	705	723	772	614	828	539
2011													
1st quarter	755	829	470	856	970	683	426	709	741	774	604	831	549
2nd quarter	753	825	446	863	965	689	417	714	744	770	623	872	565
3rd quarter	753	827	440	869	964	673	422	707	737	772	616	869	545
4th quarter	764	843	466	869	1 005	688	420	721	730	786	621	880	537
2012													
1st quarter	769	848	469	882	980	697	421	723	761	793	635	918	567
2nd quarter	771	865	460	902	991	689	409	722	748	792	637	930	576
3rd quarter	758	828	459	873	960	685	414	715	755	780	606	915	556
4th quarter	775	875	480	902	1 016	692	422	717	746	802	615	910	571
2013													
1st quarter	773	867	487	902	969	704	419	729	754	802	622	951	575
2nd quarter	776	860	479	890	1 018	707	422	735	769	799	634	973	572
3rd quarter	771	847	452	885	984	698	414	729	765	794	630	922	587
4th quarter	786	869	492	888	1 036	713	449	739	776	813	632	916	576
2014													
1st quarter	796	872	480	905	979	722	434	750	767	819	646	955	593
2nd quarter	780	857	481	892	993	716	449	744	768	802	649	954	583
3rd quarter	790	870	498	894	1 034	715	448	743	778	816	638	945	598
4th quarter	799	882	508	905	1 019	724	469	749	784	823	621	959	600
2015													
1st quarter	808	895	491	922	1 029	730	461	757	768	835	650	966	590
2nd quarter	801	886	497	918	1 032	726	444	753	782	829	647	965	601
3rd quarter	803	889	517	916	1 069	721	442	757	781	829	624	974	602
4th quarter	825	907	543	926	1 092	729	453	764	768	847	643	1 091	624
2016													
1st quarter	830	912	511	935	1 102	750	488	771	821	857	673	1 032	612
2nd quarter	824	909	505	944	1 049	744	470	774	785	854	677	1 021	618
3rd quarter	827	911	510	943	1 095	745	480	782	793	854	685	1 010	632
4th quarter	849	927	522	953	1 084	758	506	788	810	881	675	1 022	646

. . . = Not available.

NOTES AND DEFINITIONS, CHAPTER 10

GENERAL NOTE ON MONTHLY EMPLOYMENT DATA

This chapter presents data from two different data sets that measure employment monthly. Both are compiled and published by the Bureau of Labor Statistics (BLS), but each set has different characteristics. Users should be aware of these dissimilarities and the consequent differences in the appropriate uses and interpretations of data from the two systems.

One set of monthly employment estimates comes from the Current Population Survey (CPS), a large sample survey of approximately 60,000 U.S. households. The numbers in the sample are expanded to match the latest estimates of the total U.S. population. These are the most comprehensive estimates in their scope—that is, in the universe that they are designed to measure. These estimates represent all civilian workers, including the following groups that are excluded by definition from the other set of estimates: all farm workers; household workers (domestic servants); nonagricultural, nonincorporated self-employed workers; and nonagricultural unpaid family workers.

However, official CPS data are characterized by periodic discontinuities, which occur when new benchmarks for Census measures of the total population are introduced. These updates take place in a single month—usually January—and the official data for previous months are typically <u>not</u> modified to provide a smooth transition. Therefore, shorter-term comparisons (for a year or two or for a business cycle phase) will be misleading if such a discontinuity is included in the period. A recent example will illustrate. Beginning with January 2016, the estimates for civilian noninstitutional population, civilian labor force, and employment were all adjusted upward by about 265,000 persons. The reported seasonally adjusted change in employment from December 2009 to January 2010 was an increase of 541,000. If there had been no population control adjustment, the increase in employment would have been 784,000. Such discontinuities occur throughout the history of the series.

> For users who would like to examine monthly CPS data in which these discontinuities have been smoothed, BLS now provides unofficial smoothed estimates of total labor force and total employment from January 1990 through December 2012 on its Web site, <http://www.bls.gov>. These two series are shown in Table 10-6.

The CPS is a count of persons employed, rather than a count of jobs. A person is counted as employed in this data set only once, no matter how many jobs he or she may hold. The CPS count is limited to persons 16 years of age and over.

The second set of employment estimates—the payroll survey—comes from a very large sample survey of about 147,000 business and government employers at approximately 634,000 worksites, the Current Employment Statistics (CES) survey. It is benchmarked annually to a survey of all employers. Benchmark data are introduced with a smooth adjustment back to the previous benchmark, thus preserving the continuity of the series and making it more appropriate for measurement of employment change over a year or two, a business cycle, or other short- to medium-length periods. This sample is much larger than the CPS sample, including about one-third of all nonfarm payroll employees, and consequently the threshold of statistical significance for changes is lower. The minimum size of the over-the-month change required to be statistically significant is about 90,000 jobs in the payroll survey, versus about 400,000 persons in the household survey.

Over recent years, benchmark revisions to payroll survey employment have ranged in magnitude from an upward revision of 0.6 percent, in 2006, to the March 2009 benchmark, which reduced the seasonally adjusted level of payroll employment in that month by 902,000 persons, or 0.7 percent. The most recent revision decreased the level of employment in March 2016 by 81,000, or -0.1 percent. In absolute terms (that is, disregarding the sign), revisions have ranged from 0.1 to 0.7 percentage points over the latest 11 years and averaged 0.24 percentage points. Within that range, relatively large upward revisions have been seen for strong economies, and relatively large downward revisions for weak ones.

The scope of the CES survey is smaller than that of the CPS survey, as it is limited to wage and salary workers on nonfarm payrolls. There is also a significant definitional difference, because the CES survey is a count of jobs. Thus, a person with more than one nonfarm wage or salary job is counted as employed in each job. In addition, workers are not classified by age; as a result, there may be some workers younger than 16 years old in the job count.

Persons with a job but not at work (absent due to bad weather, work stoppages, personal reasons, and the like) are included in the household survey. However, they are excluded from the payroll survey if on leave without pay for the entire payroll period.

In addition to the differences in definitions and scope between the two series, there are also differences in sample design, collection methodology, and the sampling variability inherent in the surveys.

The payroll survey provides the most reliable and detailed information on employment by industry (for example, the data shown in Table 15-1). In addition, it provides data on weekly hours per job and hourly and weekly earnings per job.

The CPS employment estimates provide information not collected in the CES on employment by demographic characteristics, such as age, race, and Hispanic ethnicity; by education levels; and by occupation. A few of these tabulations are shown in *Business Statistics*. Many more breakdowns, in richer detail, can be found in the *Handbook of U.S. Labor Statistics*, also published by Bernan Press.

The differences between the two employment measurement systems are discussed in an article on the BLS Web site, "Employment from the BLS household and payroll surveys: summary of recent trends," which is updated monthly along with the release of the monthly data, and can be found under "Publications" on the CPS homepage at http://www.bls.gov. This article also includes references to further relevant studies.

Additional annual employment data

In addition to the CPS and CES monthly and annual data series, a third set of historical, annual-only estimates of employment is presented at the end of this chapter. These estimates of "full-time and part-time employees" by industry are compiled by the U.S. Department of Commerce, Bureau of Economic Analysis, as part of the National Income and Product Accounts (NIPAs). These estimates provide the most comprehensive and consistent employment estimates for the years before 1948.

Further detail on the historical and other characteristics of all of these employment series is presented below in the notes associated with specific data tables.

TABLES 10-1 THROUGH 10-5

Labor Force, Employment, and Unemployment

SOURCE: U.S. DEPARTMENT OF LABOR, BUREAU OF LABOR STATISTICS (BLS)

Labor force, employment, and unemployment data are derived from the Current Population Survey (CPS), a sample survey of households conducted each month by the Census Bureau for the Bureau of Labor Statistics (BLS). The data pertain to the U.S. civilian noninstitutional population age 16 years and over.

Due to changes in questionnaire design and survey methodology, data for 1994 and subsequent years are not fully comparable with data for 1993 and earlier years. Additionally, discontinuities in the reported number of persons in the population, and consequently in the estimated numbers of employed and unemployed persons and the number of persons in the labor force, are introduced whenever periodic updates are made to U.S. population estimates.

For example, population controls based on Census 2000 were introduced beginning with the data for January 2000. These data are therefore not comparable with data for December 1999 and

earlier. Data for 1990 through 1999 incorporate 1990 census-based population controls and are not comparable with the preceding years. An additional large population adjustment was introduced in January 2004, making the data from that time forward not comparable with data for December 2003 and earlier; further adjustments have been made in each subsequent January and other discontinuities have been introduced in various earlier years, usually with January data. See "Notes on the Data," below, for information on adjustments in other years, including the incorporation of the 2010 Census count beginning in January 2012.

For the most part, these population adjustments distort comparisons involving the <u>numbers of persons</u> in the population, labor force, and employment. They generally have negligible effects on the <u>percentages</u> that comprise the most important features of the CPS: the unemployment rates, the labor force participation rates, and the employment-population ratios.

BLS now makes available unofficial smoothed data for the total number of persons in the civilian labor force and the number of persons employed for 1990 through 2012, which introduce the population adjustments gradually within the period shown. These data are shown in Table 10-6.

Beginning with the data for January 2000, data classified by industry and occupation use the North American Industry Classification System (NAICS) and the 2000 Standard Occupational Classification System. This creates breaks in the time series between December 1999 and January 2000 for occupational and industry data at all levels of aggregation. Since the recent history is so short, most CPS industry and occupation data have been dropped from *Business Statistics* in favor of other important and economically meaningful data for which a longer consistent history can be supplied. However, detailed employment data by occupation and industry can be found in Bernan Press's *Handbook of U.S. Labor Statistics*.

Pre-1948 data

The Census Bureau began the survey of households that provides labor force data in 1942, and the Census of Population supplied data for 1940. For the years before that, annual data for labor force, employment, and unemployment are retrospective estimates. The 1929-1947 estimates were made by BLS. The 1890-1929 estimates shown in Table 10-1B were made by Stanley Lebergott. Both of those used trend interpolation of labor force participation between Census years, and the Census and Lebergott estimates are identical in 1929.

From 1929 to 1947, the data collected pertained to persons 14 years of age and over. From 1947 to the present the survey pertains to persons 16 years of age and over. Table 10-1C shows summary data for both age definitions in the overlap year, 1947. In that year, the unemployment rates are the same (3.9 percent) for both age definitions. However, the labor force participation rate and the employment/population ratio are higher when the 14- and 15-year-olds are excluded. Naturally, the raw numbers for population, labor force, and employment are smaller when the 14- and 15-year-olds are excluded.

The 1940 Census and the BLS data for 1931 through 1942 did not treat government work relief employment as employment; persons engaged in such work were counted as unemployed. In the labor force survey used today, anyone who worked for pay or profit is counted as employed (see the definitions below). Therefore, today's survey would count work relief as employment and not unemployment, and the BLS figures for the period before 1942 are not consistent with today's unemployment rates. Michael Darby calculated an alternative unemployment rate in which such workers are counted as employed, and this rate is shown in parentheses in Table 10-1C. Work relief employment is included in the BEA total employment figures in Table 10-21.

Race and ethnic origin

Data for two broad racial categories were made available beginning in 1954: *White* and *Black and other.* The latter included Asians and all other "nonwhite" races, and was discontinued after 2002. Data for *Blacks* only are available beginning with 1972; this category is now called *Black or African American.* Data for *Asians* are shown beginning with 2000. Persons in the remaining race categories—American Indian or Alaska Native, Native Hawaiian or Other Pacific Islanders, and persons who selected more than one race category when that became possible, beginning in 2003 (see below)—are included in the estimates of total employment and unemployment, but are not shown separately because their numbers are too small to yield quality estimates.

Hispanic or Latino ethnicity, previously labeled *Hispanic origin*, is not a racial category and is established in a survey question separate from the question about race. Persons of Hispanic or Latino ethnicity may be of any race.

In January 2003, changes that affected classification by race and Hispanic ethnicity were introduced. These changes caused discontinuities in race and ethnic group data between December 2002 and January 2003.

• Individuals in the sample are now asked whether they are of Hispanic ethnicity before being asked about their race. Prior to 2003, individuals were asked their ethnic origin after they were asked about their race. Furthermore, respondents are now asked directly if they are Spanish, Hispanic, or Latino. Previously, they were identified based on their or their ancestors' country of origin.

• Individuals in the sample are now allowed to choose more than one race category. Before 2003, they were required to select a single primary race. This change had no impact on the size of the overall civilian noninstitutional population and labor force. It did reduce the population and labor force levels of Whites and Blacks beginning in January 2003, as individuals who reported more than one race are now excluded from those groups.

BLS has estimated, based on a special survey, that these changes reduced the population and labor force levels for Whites by about 950,000 and 730,000 persons, respectively, and for Blacks by about 320,000 and 240,000 persons, respectively, while having little or no impact on either of their unemployment rates. The changes did not affect the size of the Hispanic population or labor force, but they did cause an increase of about half a percentage point in the Hispanic unemployment rate.

Definitions

The employment status of the civilian population is surveyed each month with respect to a specific week in mid-month—not for the entire month. This is known as the "reference week." For a precise definition and explanation of the reference week, see Notes on the Data, which follows these definitions.

The *civilian noninstitutional population* comprises all civilians 16 years of age and over who are not inmates of penal or mental institutions, sanitariums, or homes for the aged, infirm, or needy.

Civilian employment includes those civilians who (1) worked for pay or profit at any time during the Sunday-through-Saturday week that includes the 12th day of the month (the reference week), or who worked for 15 hours or more as an unpaid worker in a family-operated enterprise; or (2) were temporarily absent from regular jobs because of vacation, illness, industrial dispute, bad weather, or similar reasons. Each employed person is counted only once; those who hold more than one job are counted as being in the job at which they worked the greatest number of hours during the reference week.

Unemployed persons are all civilians who were not employed (according to the above definition) during the reference week, but who were available for work—except for temporary illness—and who had made specific efforts to find employment sometime during the previous four weeks. Persons who did not look for work because they were on layoff are also counted as unemployed.

The *civilian labor force* comprises all civilians classified as employed or unemployed.

Civilians 16 years of age and over in the noninstitutional population who are not classified as employed or unemployed are defined as *not in the labor force*. This group includes those engaged in own-home housework; in school; unable to work because of longterm illness, retirement, or age; seasonal workers for whom the reference week fell in an "off" season (if not qualifying as unemployed by looking for a job); persons who became discouraged and gave up the search for work; and the voluntarily idle. Also included are those doing only incidental work (less than 15 hours) in a family-operated business during the reference week.

The civilian *labor force participation rate* represents the percentage of the civilian noninstitutional population (age 16 years and over) that is in the civilian labor force.

The *employment-population ratio* represents the percentage of the civilian noninstitutional population (age 16 years and over) that is employed. This is traditionally called a "ratio," although it is also traditionally expressed as a percent and therefore would be more appropriately called a "rate," as is the case with the labor force participation rate.

Employment is shown by *class of worker,* including a breakdown of total employment into *agricultural* and *nonagricultural* industries. Employment in *nonagricultural industries* includes *wage and salary workers*, the *self-employed*, and *unpaid family workers*.

Wage and salary workers receive wages, salaries, commissions, tips, and/or pay-in-kind. This category includes owners of self-owned incorporated businesses.

Self-employed workers are those who work for profit or for fees in their own business, profession, trade, or farm. This category includes only the unincorporated; a person whose business is incorporated is considered to be a wage and salary worker since he or she is a paid employee of a corporation, even if he or she is the corporation's president and sole employee. These categories are now labeled "Self-employed workers, unincorporated" to clarify this definition.

Wage and salary employment comprises *government* and *private industry* wage and salary workers. Domestic workers and other employees of *private households*, who are not included in the payroll employment series, are shown separately from *all other private industries*. The series for *government* and *other private industries* wage and salary workers are the closest in scope to similar categories in the payroll employment series.

Multiple jobholders are employed persons who, during the reference week, either had two or more jobs as a wage and salary worker, were self-employed and also held a wage and salary job, or worked as an unpaid family worker and also held a wage and salary job. This category does not include self-employed persons with multiple businesses or persons with multiple jobs as unpaid family workers. For purposes of industry and occupational classification, multiple jobholders are counted as being in the job at which they worked the greatest number of hours during the reference week.

Employed and at work part time does not include employed persons who were absent from their jobs during the entire reference week for reasons such as vacation, illness, or industrial dispute.

At work part time for economic reasons ("involuntary" part time) refers to individuals who worked 1 to 34 hours during the reference week because of slack work, unfavorable business conditions, an inability to find full-time work, or seasonal declines in demand. To be included in this category, workers must also indicate that they want and are available for full-time work.

At work part time for noneconomic reasons ("voluntary" part time) refers to persons who usually work part time and were at work for 1 to 34 hours during the reference week for reasons such as illness, other medical limitations, family obligations, education, retirement, Social Security limits on earnings, or working in an industry where the workweek is less than 35 hours. It also includes respondents who gave an economic reason but were not available for, or did not want, full-time work. At work part time for noneconomic reasons excludes persons who usually work full time, but who worked only 1 to 34 hours during the reference week for reasons such as holidays, illnesses, and bad weather.

The *long-term unemployed* are persons currently unemployed (searching or on layoff) who have been unemployed for 15 consecutive weeks or longer. If a person ceases to look for work for two weeks or more, or becomes temporarily employed, the continuity of longterm unemployment is broken. If he or she starts searching for work or is laid off again, the monthly CPS will record the length of his or her unemployment from the time the search recommenced or since the latest layoff.

The civilian *unemployment rate* is the number of unemployed as a percentage of the civilian labor force. The unemployment rates for groups within the civilian population (such as males age 20 years and over) are the number of unemployed in a group as a percent of that group's labor force.

Unemployment rates by reason provides a breakdown of the total unemployment rate. Each unemployed person is classified into one of four groups.

Job losers and persons who completed temporary jobs includes persons on temporary layoff, permanent job losers, and persons who completed temporary jobs and began looking for work after those jobs ended. These three categories are shown separately without seasonal adjustment in the BLS's "Employment Situation" news release and on its Web site. They are combined, under the title shown here, for the purpose of seasonal adjustment. This is the category of unemployment that responds most strongly to the business cycle.

Job leavers terminated their employment voluntarily and immediately began looking for work.

Reentrants are persons who previously worked, but were out of the labor force prior to beginning their current job search.

New entrants are persons searching for a first job who have never worked.

Each of these categories is expressed as a proportion of the entire civilian labor force, so that the sum of the four rates equals the unemployment rate for all civilian workers, except for possible discrepancies due to rounding or separate seasonal adjustment.

Median and average weeks unemployed are summary measures of the length of time that persons classified as unemployed have been looking for work. For persons on layoff, the duration represents the number of full weeks of the layoff. The *average (mean)* number of weeks is computed by aggregating all the weeks of unemployment experienced by all unemployed persons during their current spell of unemployment and dividing by the number of unemployed. The average can be distorted by what is called "top coding" because the length of unemployment is reported in ranges, including a top range of "over __ weeks," rather than exact numbers. See the paragraph below for further explanation. The *median* number of weeks unemployed is the number of weeks of unemployment experienced by the person at the midpoint of the distribution of all unemployed persons, as ranked by duration of unemployment, and is not distorted by top coding. Like medians in other economic time series, it is likely to be a better measure of typical experience.

Beginning with the data for January 2011 and phasing in through April 2011, respondents could report unemployment durations of up to 5 years; before that time, the "top code" was up to 2 years. This change causes a sharp increase in January 2011 and continued rises through April for *average weeks unemployed.* It did not affect total unemployment, total long-term unemployment, or the *median weeks unemployed.* Comparisons of the average weeks statistics on the old and new basis are available on the BLS Web site.

Alternative measures of labor underutilization are calculated by BLS and published in the monthly Employment Situation release. They measure alternative concepts of unused working capacity, and are numbered "U-1" through "U-6" in order of increasing breadth of the definition of underutilization.

"U-1" is persons unemployed 15 weeks or longer, as a percent of the civilian labor force. It is not shown in *Business Statistics.*

"U-2" is job losers and persons who completed temporary jobs, as a percent of the civilian labor force; it is shown in *Business Statistics* in the fifth column of Table 10-5.

"U-3" is the official rate, described above and shown in the final columns of Tables 10-1, the fifth column of Table 10-4, and the fourth column of Table 10-5.

"U-4" through "U-6" are shown in the last three columns of Table 10-5. They are based on additional labor force status questions, now included in the CPS survey, that were introduced beginning in 1994. U-4 and U-5 are increasingly broader rates of unemployment, while U-6 can be described as an "unemployment and underemployment rate."

"U-4" adds discouraged workers to unemployment and the labor force. Discouraged workers are persons not in the officially defined labor force who have given a job-market-related reason for not looking currently for a job—for example, they have not looked for a job because they believed that no jobs were available.

"U-5" adds both discouraged workers and all other "marginally attached" workers to unemployment and the labor force. "Marginally attached" workers are all persons who currently are neither working nor looking for work but indicate that they want and are available for a job and have looked for work some time in the recent past.

"U-6" adds persons employed part time for economic reasons, as shown in Table 10-3, to the number of persons counted as unemployed in "U-5," with the same labor force definition as in "U-5." This statistic, which measures a combination of unemployment and underemployment, is often cited in media reports on the employment situation.

For more information, see "BLS introduced new range of alternative unemployment measures" in the October 1995 issue of the *Monthly Labor Review.*

Notes on the data

The CPS data are collected by trained interviewers from about 60,000 sample households selected to represent the U.S. civilian noninstitutional population. The sample size has fluctuated between 50,000 and 60,000 households In January 1996, the size was reduced to 50,00 due to budgetary reasons. The sample size was increased back to 60,000 households, beginning with the data for July 2001, as part of a plan to meet the requirements of the State Children's Health Insurance Program legislation. The CPS provides data for other data series in addition to the BLS employment status data, such as household income and poverty and health insurance (see Chapter 3).

The employment status data are based on the activity or status reported for the calendar week, Sunday through Saturday, that includes the 12th day of the month (the reference week). This specification is chosen so as to avoid weeks that contain major holidays. Households are interviewed in the week following the reference week. Sample households are phased in and out of the sample on a rotating basis. Consequently, three-fourths of the sample is the same for any two consecutive months. One-half of the sample is the same as the sample in the same month a year earlier.

Data relating to 1994 and subsequent years are not strictly comparable with data for 1993 and earlier years because of the major 1994 redesign of the survey questionnaire and collection methodology. The redesign included new and revised questions for the classification of individuals as employed or unemployed, the collection of new data on multiple jobholding, a change in the definition of discouraged workers, and the implementation of a more completely automated data collection.

The 1994 redesign of the CPS was the most extensive since 1967. However, there are many other significant periods of year-to-year noncomparability in the labor force data. These typically result from the introduction of new decennial census data into the CPS estimation procedures, expansions of the sample, or other improvements made to increase the reliability of the estimates. Each change introduces a new discontinuity, usually between December of the previous year and January of the newly altered year. The discontinuities are usually minor or negligible with respect to figures expressed as nationwide percentages (such as the unemployment rate or the labor force participation rate), but can be significant with respect to levels (such as labor force and employment in thousands of persons). A list of the dates of the major discontinuities follows, with BLS estimates of their quantitative impact on the national totals. (There are likely to be larger impacts on population subgroups.) The discontinuities occur in January unless otherwise indicated. Note that some of the changes caused adjustments that were carried back to an earlier year.

- 1953: 1950 census data introduced. Labor force and employment were raised by about 350,000.

- 1960: Alaska and Hawaii included. The labor force was increased by about 300,000, mainly in nonagricultural employment.

- 1962: 1960 census data introduced. Labor force and employment were reduced by about 200,000.

- 1972: 1970 census data introduced. Labor force and employment were raised by about 300,000.

- March 1973: Further 1970 census data were introduced, reducing White labor force and employment by about 150,000 and raising Black and other labor force and employment by approximately 210,000.

- July 1975: Adjustment for Vietnamese refugee inflow, raising total and Black and other population by 76,000.

- 1978: Sample expansion and revised estimation procedures increased labor force and employment by about 250,000.

- 1982: Change in estimation procedures introduced. To avoid major breaks, many series were reestimated back to 1970. This did not smooth the breaks occurring between 1972 and 1979.

- 1986, with revisions carried back to 1980: Adjustment for better estimates of immigration, raising labor force by nearly 400,000 and employment by 350,000, mainly among Hispanics.

- 1994: 1990 census data introduced and carried back to 1990, when employment was increased by about 880,000 and the unemployment rate was raised by about 0.1 percentage point.

- 1997: New estimates of immigration and emigration, raising labor force and employment by about 300,000, again mainly among Hispanics.

- 1998: New population estimates and estimation procedures, reducing labor force and employment by around 250,000.

- 1999: New information on immigration, raising labor force and employment by around 60,000, but lowering Hispanic employment by about 200,000.

- 2000: Census 2000 data introduced, using the 2002 NAICS and the 2000 Standard Occupational Classification System. The labor force was increased by about 1.6 million in January 2000, growing to around 2.5 million by December 2002.

- 2003: Further population estimates introduced (based on an annual population update and therefore not carried back to 2000), raising the labor force by 614,000.

- 2004: Population controls updated to reflect revised migration estimates, reducing labor force and employment by around 400,000, mostly among Hispanics.

- 2005: Updated migration and vital statistics data decreased labor force and employment by around 45,000.

- 2006: Updated migration and vital statistics data decreased labor force and employment by about 125,000.

- 2007: Updated migration and vital statistics data increased labor force and employment by about 150,000.

- 2008: Updated migration and vital statistics data decreased labor force by 637,000 and employment by 598,000.

- 2009: Updated migration adjustments, new vital statistics data, and methodological changes decreased labor force by 449,000 and employment by 407,000.

- 2010: Updated information on migration, vital statistics, and other data and methodological changes decreased labor force by 249,000 and employment by 243,000.

- 2011: Updated estimates reduced the labor force by 504,000, employment by 472,000, and unemployment by 32,000; raised the number of persons not in the labor force by 157,000; and had no effect on the unemployment rate.

- 2012: Reflecting the 2010 Census, the civilian noninstitutional population was increased by 1,510,000; the civilian labor force by 258,000; employment by 216,000; and unemployment by 42,000. BLS states, "Although the total unemployment rate was unaffected, the labor force participation rate and the employment-population ratio were each reduced by 0.3 percentage point. This was because the population increase was primarily among persons 55 and older and, to a lesser degree, persons 16 to 24 years of age. Both these age groups have lower levels of labor force participation than the general population."

• 2013: Updated population estimates increased the population by 138,000, the labor force by 136,000, and employment by 127,000. The rates and ratios were not affected.

• 2014: the smallest population control adjustment on record increased labor force by 24,000 and employment by 22,000, with no effect on rates or ratios.

For further information on these changes, see "Publications and Other Documentation" at http://www.bls.gov/cps.

The monthly labor force, employment, and unemployment data are seasonally adjusted by the X-12-ARIMA method. All seasonally adjusted civilian labor force and unemployment rate statistics, as well as major employment and unemployment estimates, are computed by aggregating independently adjusted series. For example, the seasonally adjusted level of total unemployment is the sum of the seasonally adjusted levels of unemployment for the four age/sex groups (men and women age 16 to 19 years, and men and women age 20 years and over). Seasonally adjusted employment is the sum of the seasonally adjusted levels of employment for the same four groups. The seasonally adjusted civilian labor force is the sum of all eight components. Finally, the seasonally adjusted civilian worker unemployment rate is calculated by taking total seasonally adjusted unemployment as a percent of the total seasonally adjusted civilian labor force.

To minimize subsequent revisions, BLS uses a concurrent technique that estimates factors for the latest month using the most recent data. Then, seasonal adjustment factors are fully revised at the end of each year to reflect recent experience. The revisions also affect the preceding four years. An article describing the seasonal adjustment methodology for the household survey data is available at http://www.bls.gov/cps/cpsrs2010.pdf.

Breakdowns other than the basic age/sex classification described above—such as the employment data by class of worker in Table 10-3—will not necessarily add to totals because of independent seasonal adjustment.

Data availability

Data for each month are usually released on the first Friday of the following month in the "Employment Situation" press release, which also includes data from the establishment survey (Tables 10-8 through 10-18 and Chapter 15). (The release date actually is determined by the timing of the survey week.) The press release and data are available on the BLS Web site at <http://www.bls.gov>. The *Monthly Labor Review*, also available online at the BLS Web site, features frequent articles analyzing developments in the labor force, employment, and unemployment.

Monthly and annual data on the current basis are available beginning with 1948. Historical unadjusted data are published in *Labor Force Statistics Derived from the Current Population Survey* (BLS Bulletin 2307). Historical seasonally adjusted data are available from BLS upon request. Complete historical data are available on the BLS Web site at <http://www.bls.gov/cps>.

Seasonal adjustment factors are revised each year for the five previous years, with the release of December data in early January. New population controls are introduced with the release of January data in early February.

BLS annual data for 1940 through 1947 are published on their Web site at <http://www.bls.gov>. The data for 1929 through 1939 were published in *Employment and Earnings,* May 1972, and in U.S. Commerce Department, Bureau of Economic Analysis, *Long-Term Economic Growth, 1860–1970,* June 1973, p. 163. The Lebergott estimates are also found in the latter volume.

The Darby alternative unemployment rate is found in Michael Darby, "Three-and-a-Half Million U.S. Employees Have Been Mislaid," *Journal of Political Economy,* February 1976, v. 84, no. 1. It is also displayed and discussed in Robert A. Margo, "Employment and Unemployment in the 1930s," *Journal of Economic Perspectives,* v. 7, no. 2, Spring 1993.

REFERENCES

Comprehensive descriptive material can be found at <http://www.bls.gov/cps> under the "Publications and Other Documentation" section. Historical background on the CPS, as well as a description of the 1994 redesign, can be found in three articles from the September 1993 edition of *Monthly Labor Review*: "Why Is It Necessary to Change?"; "Redesigning the Questionnaire"; and "Evaluating Changes in the Estimates." The redesign is also described in the February 1994 issue of *Employment and Earnings.* See also Chapter 1, "Labor Force Data Derived from the Current Population Survey," *BLS Handbook of Methods*, Bulletin 2490 (April 1997).

TABLE 10-6

Labor Force and Employment Estimates Smoothed for Population Adjustments

SOURCE: U.S. DEPARTMENT OF LABOR, BUREAU OF LABOR STATISTICS

This table presents seasonally adjusted monthly estimates of total civilian labor force and total civilian employment in which discontinuities caused by the introduction of new population controls in the official series—as described above—have been smoothed (see box above). The method of smoothing is described in Marisa L. Di Natale, "Creating Comparability in CPS Employment Series," on the BLS Web site at <http://www.bls.gov/cps/cpscomp.pdf>. BLS notes that these series do not match the official estimates in BLS publications, which are also the data shown in all other tables in this volume.

Because the January 2014 population control adjustment was negligible in size (see above), no smoothing of the 2013 data was required. Hence, Table 10-6 was calculated only through the end of 2012, which can be considered continuous with the official data for 2013 and 2014.

TABLE 10-7

Insured Unemployment

SOURCE: U.S. DEPARTMENT OF LABOR, EMPLOYMENT AND TRAINING ADMINISTRATION

Definitions

State programs of unemployment insurance cover operations of regular programs under state unemployment insurance laws. In 1976, the law was amended to extend coverage to include virtually all state and local government employees, as well as many agricultural and domestic workers. (This took effect on January 1, 1978.) Benefits under state programs are financed by taxes levied by the states on employers.

An *initial claim* is the first claim in a benefit year filed by a worker after losing his or her job, or the first claim filed at the beginning of a subsequent period of unemployment in the same benefit year. The initial claim establishes the starting date for any insured unemployment that may result if the claimant is unemployed for one week or longer. Transitional claims (filed by claimants as they start a new benefit year in a continuing spell of unemployment) are excluded; therefore, these data more closely represent instances of new unemployment and are widely followed as a leading indicator of job market conditions.

Insured unemployment and *persons claiming benefits* both describe the average number of persons receiving benefits in the indicated month or year.

The *insured unemployment rate* for state programs is the level of insured unemployment as a percentage of employment covered by state programs.

Monthly averages in this book are averages, calculated by the editor, of the weekly data published by the Employment and Training Administration. Annual data are averages of the monthly data.

Data availability

Data are published in weekly press releases from the Employment and Training Administration. These releases are available on their Web site at <http://www.doleta.gov> under "Labor Market Data," as are historical data, under the category "UI/Program Statistics."

TABLES 10-8, 10-9, 10-14, 15-1, AND 15-2

Nonfarm Payroll Employment

SOURCE: U.S. DEPARTMENT OF LABOR, BUREAU OF LABOR STATISTICS (BLS)

These nonfarm employment data, as well as the hours and earnings data in Tables 10-9 through 10-13, 10-15 through 10-18, and 15-3 through 15-6, are compiled from payroll records. Information is reported monthly on a voluntary basis to BLS and its cooperating state agencies by a large sample of establishments, representing all industries except farming. These data, formally known as the Current Employment Statistics (CES) survey, are often referred to as the "establishment data" or the "payroll data." They are also known as the BLS-790 survey.

The survey, originally based on a stratified quota sample, has been replaced on a phased-in basis by a stratified probability sample. The new sampling procedure went into effect for wholesale trade in June 2000; for mining, construction, and manufacturing in June 2001; and for retail trade, transportation and public utilities, and finance, insurance, and real estate in June 2002. The phase-in was completed in June 2003, upon its extension to the service industries. The phase-in schedule was slightly different for the state and area series.

The sample has always been very large. Currently, it includes approximately 147,000 businesses and government agencies covering about 634,000 individual worksites, which account for about one-third of total benchmark employment of payroll workers. The sample is drawn from a sampling frame of over 9.7 million unemployment insurance tax accounts.

Data are classified according to the North American Industry Classification System. BLS has reconstructed historical time series to conform with NAICS, to ensure that all published series have a NAICS-based history extending back to at least January 1990. NAICS-based history extends back to January 1939 for total nonfarm and other high-level aggregates. For more detailed series, the starting date for NAICS data varies depending on the extent of the definitional changes between the old Standard Industrial Classification (SIC) and NAICS.

Definitions

An *establishment* is an economic unit, such as a factory, store, or professional office, that produces goods or services at a single location and is engaged in one type of economic activity.

Employment comprises all persons who received pay (including holiday and sick pay) for any part of the payroll period that includes the 12th day of the month. The definition of the payroll period for each reporting respondent is that used by the employer; it could be weekly, biweekly, monthly, or other. Included are all fulltime and parttime workers in nonfarm establishments, including salaried officers of corporations. Persons holding more than one job are counted in each establishment that reports them. Not covered are proprietors, the self-employed, unpaid volunteer and family workers, farm workers, domestic workers in households, and military personnel. Employees of the Central Intelligence Agency, the Defense Intelligence Agency, the National Geospatial-Intelligence Agency, and the National Security Agency are not included.

Persons on an establishment payroll who are on paid sick leave (when pay is received directly from the employer), on paid holiday or vacation, or who work during a portion of the pay period despite being unemployed or on strike during the rest of the period, are counted as employed. Not counted as employed are persons who are laid off, on leave without pay, on strike for the entire period, or hired but not paid during the period.

Intermittent workers are counted if they performed any service during the month. BLS considers regular full-time teachers (private and government) to be employed during the summer vacation period, regardless of whether they are specifically paid during those months.

The *government* division includes federal, state, and local activities such as legislative, executive, and judicial functions, as well as the U.S. Postal Service and all government-owned and government-operated business enterprises, establishments, and institutions (arsenals, navy yards, hospitals, state-owned utilities, etc.), and government force account construction. However, as indicated earlier, members of the armed forces and employees of certain national-security-related agencies are not included.

The monthly *diffusion index of employment change*, currently based on 271 private nonfarm NAICS industries, represents the percentage of those industries in which the seasonally adjusted level of employment in that month was higher than six months earlier, plus one-half of the percentage of industries with unchanged employment. Therefore, the diffusion index reported for September represents the change from March to September. *Business Statistics* uses the September value to represent the year as a whole, since it spans the year's midpoint. Diffusion indexes measure the dispersion of economic gains and losses, with values below 50 percent associated with recessions. The current NAICS-based series begins with January 1991. For October 1976 through December 1990, an earlier series is available based on 347 SIC industries (there are more industries using the older classification system because in SIC manufacturing industries were represented in greater detail). September values from this series are used here to represent the years 1977 through 1990.

Production and nonsupervisory workers include all *production and related workers* in mining and manufacturing; *construction workers* in construction; and *nonsupervisory workers* in transportation, communication, electric, gas, and sanitary services; wholesale and retail trade; finance, insurance, and real estate; and services. These groups account for about four-fifths of the total

employment on private nonagricultural payrolls. Previously, this category was called "production or nonsupervisory workers." The definitions have not changed.

Production and related workers include working supervisors and all nonsupervisory workers (including group leaders and trainees) engaged in fabricating, processing, assembling, inspecting, receiving, storing, handling, packing, warehousing, shipping, trucking, hauling, maintenance, repair, janitorial, guard services, product development, auxiliary production for plant's own use (such as a power plant), record keeping, and other services closely associated with these production operations.

Construction workers include the following employees in the construction division of the NAICS: working supervisors, qualified craft workers, mechanics, apprentices, laborers, and the like, who are engaged in new work, alterations, demolition, repair, maintenance, and other tasks, whether working at the site of construction or working in shops or yards at jobs (such as pre-cutting and preassembling) ordinarily performed by members of the construction trades.

Nonsupervisory employees include employees (not above the working supervisory level) such as office and clerical workers, repairers, salespersons, operators, drivers, physicians, lawyers, accountants, nurses, social workers, research aides, teachers, drafters, photographers, beauticians, musicians, restaurant workers, custodial workers, attendants, line installers and repairers, laborers, janitors, guards, and other employees at similar occupational levels whose services are closely associated with those of the employees listed.

Notes on the data

Benchmark adjustments. The establishment survey data are adjusted annually to comprehensive counts of employment, called "benchmarks." Benchmark information on employment by industry is compiled by state agencies from reports of establishments covered under state unemployment insurance laws; these form an annual compilation of administrative data known as the ES-202. These tabulations cover about 97 percent of all employees on nonfarm payrolls. Benchmark data for the residual are obtained from alternate sources, primarily from Railroad Retirement Board records and the Census Bureau's *County Business Patterns*. The latest benchmark adjustment, which is incorporated into the data in this volume, increased the employment level in the benchmark month March 2017 by 8,100 jobs, which was -0.1 percent.

The estimates for the benchmark month are compared with new benchmark levels for each industry. If revisions are necessary, the monthly series of estimates between benchmark periods are adjusted by graduated amounts between the new benchmark and the preceding one ("wedged back"), and the new benchmark level for each industry is then carried forward month by month based on the sample.

More specifically, the month-to-month changes for each estimation cell are based on changes in a matched sample for that cell, plus an estimate of net business births and deaths. The matched sample for each pair of months consists of establishments that have reported data for both months (which automatically excludes establishments that have gone out of business by the second month). Since new businesses are not immediately incorporated into the sample, a model-based estimate of net business births and deaths in that estimating cell is added. The birth/death adjustment factors are re-estimated quarterly based on the Quarterly Census of Employment and Wages.

Not-seasonally-adjusted data for all months since the last benchmark date are subject to revision

Beginning in 1959, the data include Alaska and Hawaii. This inclusion resulted in an increase of 212,000 (0.4 percent) in total nonfarm employment for the March 1959 benchmark month.

Seasonal adjustment. The seasonal movements that recur periodically—such as warm and cold weather, holidays, and vacations—are generally the largest single component of month-to-month changes in employment. After adjusting the data to remove such seasonal variation, basic trends become more evident. BLS uses X-12-ARIMA software to produce seasonal factors and perform concurrent seasonal adjustment, using the most recent 10 years of data. New factors are developed each month adding the most current data.

For most series, a special procedure called REGARIMA (regression with autocorrelated errors) is used before calculating the seasonal factors; this adjusts for the length of the interval (which can be either four or five weeks) between the survey weeks. REGARIMA has also been used to isolate extreme weather effects that distort the measurement of seasonal patterns in the construction industry, and to identify variations in local government employment due to the presence or absence of election poll workers.

Seasonal adjustment factors are directly applied to the component levels. Seasonally adjusted totals for employment series are then obtained by aggregating the seasonally adjusted components directly, while hours and earnings series represent weighted averages of the seasonally adjusted component series. Seasonally adjusted data are not published for a small number of series characterized by small seasonal components relative to their trend and/or irregular components. However, these series are used in aggregating to broader seasonally adjusted levels.

Revisions of the seasonally adjusted data, usually for the most recent five-year period, are made once a year coincident with the benchmark revisions. This means that these revisions typically extend back farther than the benchmark revisions.

Data availability

Employment data by industry division are available beginning with 1919. Data for each month usually are released on the first Friday of the following month in a press release that also contains data from the household survey (Tables 10-1 through 10-5). (The release date actually is determined by the timing of the survey week.) The *Monthly Labor Review* frequently contains articles analyzing developments in the labor force, employment, and unemployment. The *Monthly Labor Review*, press releases, and complete historical data are available on the BLS Web site at <http://www.bls.gov>.

Benchmark revisions and revised seasonally adjusted data for recent years are made each year with the release of January data in early February. Before 2004, the benchmark revisions were not made until June; the acceleration is due to earlier availability of the benchmark UI (ES-202) data.

REFERENCES

References can be found at <http://www.bls.gov/ces> under the headings "Special Notices," "Benchmark Information," and "Technical Notes." Extensive changes incorporated in June 2003 are described in "Recent Changes in the National Current Employment Statistics Survey," *Monthly Labor Review*, June 2003. The latest benchmark revision is discussed in an article available on the Website. See also Chapter 2, "Employment, Hours, and Earnings from the Establishment Survey," *BLS Handbook of Methods*, Bulletin 2490 (April 1997).

TABLES 10-9 THROUGH 10-11, 10-15, 10-16, 15-3 AND 15-6

Average Hours Per Week; Aggregate Employee Hours

SOURCE: U.S. DEPARTMENT OF LABOR, BUREAU OF LABOR STATISTICS (BLS)

See the notes and definitions to Tables 10-8 and related tables for an overall description of the "establishment" or "payroll" survey that is the source of these earnings data.

Hours and earnings have been reported for production and non-supervisory workers, as defined above, since the inception of the CES. Beginning with data for March 2006, such data have also been collected for all payroll employees. With sufficient history for calculation of seasonal adjustment factors, BLS began publishing all-employee hours and earnings in February 2010, and these new data are presented in *Business Statistics* Tables 10-10 through 10-13.

Definitions

Average weekly hours represents the average hours paid per worker during the pay period that includes the 12th of the month.

Included are hours paid for holidays and vacations, as well as those paid for sick leave when pay is received directly from the firm.

Average weekly hours are different from standard or scheduled hours. Factors such as unpaid absenteeism, labor turnover, part-time work, and work stoppages can cause average weekly hours to be lower than scheduled hours of work for an establishment.

An important characteristic of these data is that average weekly hours pertain to jobs, not to persons; thus, a person with half-time jobs in two different establishments is represented in this series as two jobs that have 20-hour workweeks, not as one person with a 40-hour workweek.

Overtime hours represent the portion of average weekly hours worked in excess of regular hours, for which overtime premiums were paid. Weekend and holiday hours are included only if overtime premiums were paid. Hours for which only shift differential, hazard, incentive, or other similar types of premiums were paid are excluded.

Aggregate hours provide measures of changes over time in labor input to the industry, in index-number form. The indexes are obtained by multiplying seasonally adjusted employment by seasonally adjusted average weekly hours, dividing the resulting series by their monthly averages for a base period, and multiplying the results by 100, so that the annual average for the base period equals 100. For total private, goods-producing, service-providing, and major industry divisions, the indexes are obtained by summing the seasonally adjusted aggregate weekly employee hours for the component industries, dividing by the monthly average for the base period, and multiplying by 100. For the series covering production and nonsupervisory workers, the base period is 2002; for the all-employee series, the base period is 2007.

Notes on the data

Benchmark adjustments. Independent benchmarks are not available for the hours and earnings series. However, at the time of the annual adjustment of the employment series to new benchmarks, the levels of hours and earnings may be affected by the revised employment weights (which are used in computing the industry averages for hours and earnings), as well as by the changes in seasonal adjustment factors introduced with the benchmark revision.

Method of computing industry series. "Average weekly hours" for individual industries are computed by dividing worker hours (reported by establishments classified in each industry) by the number of workers reported for the same establishments. Estimates for divisions and major industry groups are averages (weighted by employment) of the figures for component industries.

Seasonal adjustment. Hours and earnings series are seasonally adjusted by applying factors directly to the corresponding unadjusted series. Data for some industries are not seasonally adjusted because the seasonal component is small relative to the trendcycle and/or irregular components. Consequently, they cannot be separated with sufficient precision.

Special adjustments are made to average weekly hours to account for the presence or absence of religious holidays in the April survey reference period and the occasional occurrence of Labor Day in the September reference period. In addition, REGARIMA modeling is used prior to seasonal adjustment to correct for reporting and processing errors associated with the number of weekdays in a month (rather than to correct for the 4- and 5-week effect, which is less significant for hours than it is for employment). This is of particular importance for average weekly hours in the service-providing industries other than retail trade. For this reason, BLS advises that calculations of over-the-year changes (for example, the change for the current month from a year earlier) should use seasonally adjusted data, since the actual not-seasonally-adjusted monthly data may be distorted.

Data availability

See data availability for Tables 10-8 and related, above.

REFERENCES
See references for Tables 10-8 and related, above.

TABLES 10-9, 10-12, 10-13, 10-17, 10-18, 15-4, AND 15-5

Hourly and Weekly Earnings

SOURCE: U.S. DEPARTMENT OF LABOR, BUREAU OF LABOR STATISTICS (BLS)

See the notes and definitions to Tables 10-8 and related for an overall description of the "establishment" or "payroll" survey that is the source of these earnings data.

Hours and earnings have been reported for production and nonsupervisory workers, as defined above, since the inception of the CES. Beginning with data for March 2006, such data have also been collected for all payroll employees. With sufficient history for calculation of seasonal adjustment factors, BLS began publishing all-employee hours and earnings in February 2010, and these data are presented in new *Business Statistics* Tables 10-10 through 10-13.

Definitions

Earnings are the payments that workers receive during the survey period (before deductions for taxes and other items), including premium pay for overtime or late-shift work but excluding irregular bonuses and other special payments. After being previously excluded, tips were asked to be reported beginning in September 2005. This made little difference in most industries, and BLS asserts that many respondents had already been including tips. In two industries, full-service restaurants and cafeterias, there was a substantial difference, and the historical earnings data for those industries have been reconstructed to reflect the new higher level of earnings.

Notes on the data

The hours and earnings series are based on reports of gross payroll and corresponding paid hours for full and parttime workers who received pay for any part of the pay period that included the 12th of the month.

Total payrolls are before deductions, such as for the employee share of oldage and unemployment insurance, group insurance, withholding taxes, bonds, and union dues. The payroll figures also include pay for overtime, holidays, vacations, and sick leave (paid directly by the employer for the period reported). Excluded from the payroll figures are fringe benefits (health and other types of insurance and contributions to retirement, paid by the employer, and the employer share of payroll taxes), bonuses (unless earned and paid regularly each pay period), other pay not earned in the pay period reported (retroactive pay), and the value of free rent, fuel, meals, or other payment-in-kind.

Average hourly earnings data reflect not only changes in basic hourly and incentive wage rates, but also such variable factors as premium pay for overtime and lateshift work and changes in output of workers paid on an incentive basis. Shifts in the volume of employment between relatively highpaid and lowpaid work also affect the general average of hourly earnings.

Averages of hourly earnings should not be confused with wage rates, which represent the rates stipulated for a given unit of work or time, while earnings refer to the actual return to the worker for a stated period of time. The earnings series do not represent total labor cost to the employer because of the inclusion of tips and the exclusion of irregular bonuses, retroactive items, the cost of employer-provided benefits, and payroll taxes paid by employers.

Average weekly earnings are not the amounts available to workers for spending, since they do not reflect deductions such as income taxes and Social Security taxes. It is also important to understand that average weekly earnings represent earnings per job, not per worker (since a worker may have more than one job) and not per family (since a family may have more than one worker). A person with two half-time jobs will be reflected as two earners with low weekly earnings rather than as one person with the total earnings from his or her two jobs.

Method of computing industry series. Average hourly earnings are obtained by dividing the reported total worker payroll by total worker hours. Estimates for both hours and hourly earnings for nonfarm divisions and major industry groups are employment-weighted averages of the figures for component industries.

Average weekly earnings are computed by multiplying average hourly earnings by average weekly hours. In addition to the factors mentioned above, which exert varying influences upon average hourly earnings, average weekly earnings are affected by changes in the length of the workweek, parttime work, work stoppages, labor turnover, and absenteeism. Persistent long-term uptrends in the proportion of parttime workers in retail trade and many of the service industries have reduced average workweeks (as measured here), and have similarly affected the average weekly earnings series.

Benchmark adjustments. Independent benchmarks are not available for the hours and earnings series. At the time of the annual adjustment of the employment series to new benchmarks, the levels of hours and earnings may be affected by the revised employment weights (which are used in computing the industry averages for hours and earnings), as well as by the changes in seasonal adjustment factors that were also introduced with the benchmark revision.

Seasonal adjustment. Hours and earnings series are seasonally adjusted by applying factors directly to the corresponding unadjusted series; seasonally adjusted average weekly earnings are the product of seasonally adjusted hourly earnings and weekly hours.

REGARIMA modeling is used to correct for reporting and processing errors associated with variations in the number of weekdays in a month (rather than for the 4- and 5-week effect, which is less significant for earnings than for employment). This is of particular importance for average hourly earnings in wholesale trade, financial activities, professional and business services, and other services. For this reason, BLS advises that calculations of over-the-year changes, for example the change for the current month from a year earlier, should use seasonally adjusted data, since the actual not seasonally adjusted monthly data may be distorted.

Data availability

See data availability for Tables 10-8 and related, above.

REFERENCES

See references for Tables 10-8 and related, above.

TABLE 10-19

Hours at Work, Current Population Survey

This table presents annual average measures of hours worked per week reported by workers in the Current Population Survey, in response to questions asking for the hours worked in the survey week by each worker in the household on all his or her jobs combined. These measures are not published in regular BLS reports but are available on request. *Business Statistics* obtained these numbers from BLS staff and presents them here in annual average form.

Do CPS respondents overestimate the number of hours they work? One study made that claim, but a careful re-examination of the data by Harley Frazis and Jay Stewart in the June 2014 *Monthly Labor Review* indicates that respondents slightly underreport the hours that they actually worked during the reference week. (On the other hand, the authors also note that the reference week overestimates the average for the entire month because of the absence of holidays.) (*Monthly Labor Review* is available online at www.bls.gov.) In any event, the CPS data give a more accurate picture of trends in the workweeks of typical American workers than does the establishment (CES) survey.

Table 10-20

Median Usual Weekly Earnings of Full-Time Wage and Salary Workers

SOURCE: U.S. DEPARTMENT OF LABOR, BUREAU OF LABOR STATISTICS

These data are from the Current Population Survey, which was described in the notes to Tables 10-1 through 10-6. Because they are earnings per worker, not per job, and are limited to full-time workers, the data are not distorted by the increasing proportion of part-time workers, as the CES earnings data are.

Definitions

Full-time wage and salary workers are those workers reported as "employed" in the CPS who receive wages, salaries, commissions, tips, pay in kind, or piece rates, and usually work 35 hours or more per week at their sole or principal job. Both private-sector and public-sector employees are included.

All self-employed persons are excluded (even those whose businesses are incorporated). The number of full-time wage and salary workers was 98.1 million in the first quarter of 2010. By first quarter of 2017, there were 111.9 million full-time workers, seasonally adjusted, for an increase of 14.0 percent.

Usual weekly earnings are earnings before taxes and other deductions and include any overtime pay, commissions, or tips usually received. In the case of multiple jobholders they refer to the main job. The wording of the question was changed in January 1994 to better deal with persons who found it easier to report earnings on other than a weekly basis. Such reports are then converted to the weekly equivalent. According to BLS, "the term 'usual' is as perceived by the respondent. If the respondent asks for a definition of usual, interviewers are instructed to define the term as more than half the weeks worked during the past 4 or 5 months."

The *median* is the amount that divides a given earnings distribution into two equal groups, one having earnings above the median and the other having earnings below the median.

Race and ethnicity. See the notes to Tables 10-1 through 10-6 for the definitions of these categories.

Data availability

These data become available about 3 weeks after the end of each quarter in the "Usual Weekly Earnings of Wage and Salary Workers" press release, available on the BLS Web site at <http://www.bls.gov/cps>. Recent data are available at that location. Also available are greater detail by demographic and age groups, by occupation, by union status, and by education; distributional data, by deciles and quartiles; and earnings for part-time workers. Also available are earnings in 1982 dollars using the CPI-U. (In the opinion of the editor, these give a less accurate depiction of longer-term trends, which is why *Business Statistics* provides the CPI-U-RS data explained above.) Historical data are available upon request from BLS by telephone at (202) 691-6555.

CHAPTER 11: ENERGY

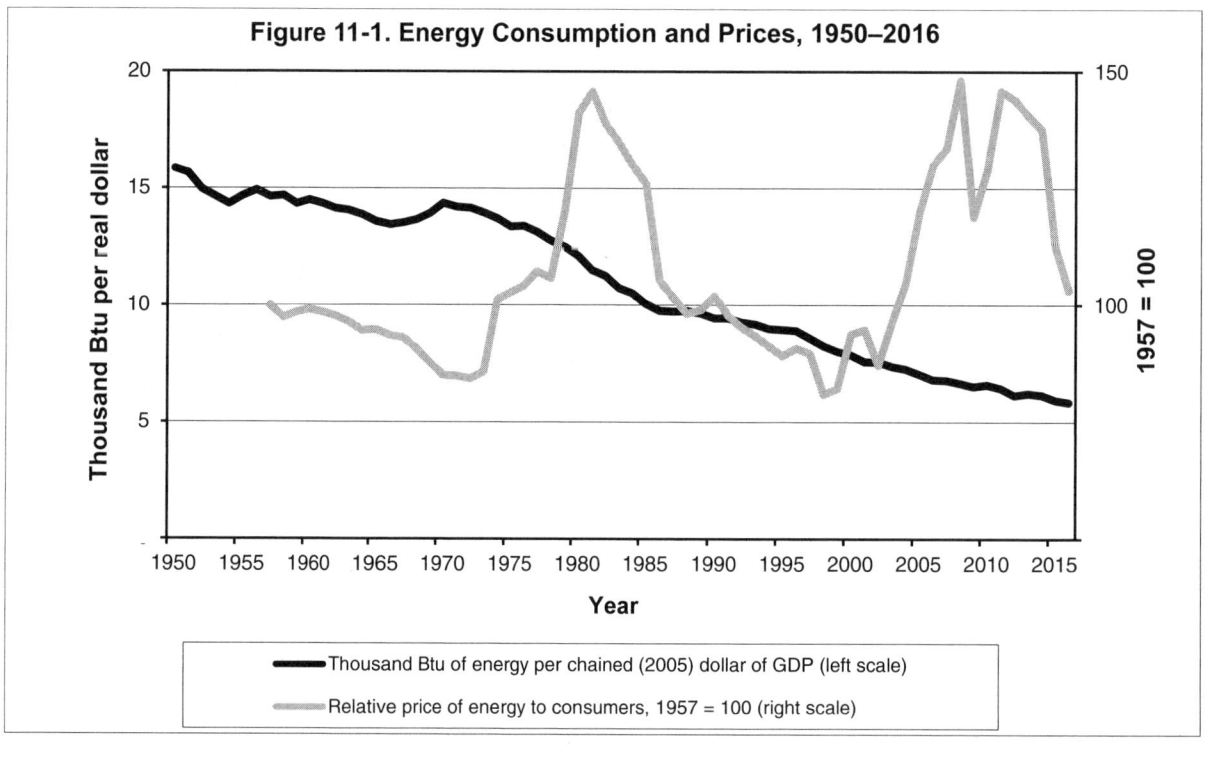

Figure 11-1. Energy Consumption and Prices, 1950–2016

Legend:
- Thousand Btu of energy per chained (2005) dollar of GDP (left scale)
- Relative price of energy to consumers, 1957 = 100 (right scale)

- Coal production dropped to 14.58 quadrillion (Q) Btu's in 2016, a 28 percent tumble from 2014. This low production was the lowest since 1974 at 14.07 Q Btu. However, natural gas production and renewable energy production attained its highest levels in 2016. (Table 11-1)

- Energy consumption by end use is split relatively even with residential and commercial at 33 percent, industrial at 32 percent and transportation at 29 percent. (Table 11-1)

- Net imports of petroleum and products peaked in 2005 at 12.55 million barrels. By 2016, net imports were 2.48 million barrels, a decline of over 80 percent. As production of energy increased, imports fell. (Table 11-3)

- After reaching a high of $101, per barrel for crude oil in 2012, the price plummeted to $36 in 2016. Factors influencing this decline include an oversupply of petroleum worldwide. Some of this oversupply is due to the United States increasing its production. Demand for petroleum also declined with China's economic growth slowing and the continued sluggish economies of the European Union. (Table 11-3)

Table 11-1. Energy Supply and Consumption

(Quadrillion Btu.)

Year and month	Imports	Exports	Production, by source								Consumption, by end-use sector			
			Total	Fossil fuels					Nuclear electric power	Renewable energy, total	Total	Residential and commercial	Industrial	Transportation
				Total	Coal	Natural gas	Crude oil	Natural gas plant liquids						
1965	5.892	1.829	50.674	47.235	13.055	15.775	16.521	1.883	0.043	3.396	54.015	16.485	25.098	12.432
1966	6.146	1.829	53.532	50.035	13.468	17.011	17.561	1.996	0.064	3.432	57.014	17.493	26.422	13.100
1967	6.159	2.115	56.376	52.597	13.825	17.943	18.651	2.177	0.088	3.690	58.905	18.538	26.614	13.752
1968	6.905	1.998	58.220	54.306	13.609	19.068	19.308	2.321	0.142	3.773	62.415	19.665	27.883	14.866
1969	7.676	2.126	60.534	56.286	13.863	20.446	19.556	2.420	0.154	4.095	65.614	21.002	29.105	15.507
1970	8.342	2.632	63.495	59.186	14.607	21.666	20.401	2.512	0.239	4.070	67.838	22.112	29.628	16.098
1971	9.535	2.151	62.717	58.042	13.186	22.280	20.033	2.544	0.413	4.262	69.283	22.967	29.586	16.730
1972	11.387	2.118	63.904	58.938	14.092	22.208	20.041	2.598	0.584	4.382	72.688	24.040	30.930	17.717
1973	14.613	2.033	63.563	58.241	13.992	22.187	19.493	2.569	0.910	4.411	75.684	24.440	32.623	18.613
1974	14.304	2.203	62.345	56.331	14.074	21.210	18.575	2.471	1.272	4.742	73.962	24.048	31.787	18.120
1975	14.032	2.323	61.320	54.733	14.989	19.640	17.729	2.374	1.900	4.687	71.965	24.306	29.413	18.245
1976	16.760	2.172	61.561	54.723	15.654	19.480	17.262	2.327	2.111	4.727	75.975	25.474	31.393	19.101
1977	19.948	2.052	62.012	55.101	15.755	19.565	17.454	2.327	2.702	4.209	77.961	25.869	32.263	19.822
1978	19.106	1.920	63.104	55.074	14.910	19.485	18.434	2.245	3.024	5.005	79.950	26.644	32.688	20.617
1979	19.460	2.855	65.904	58.006	17.540	20.076	18.104	2.286	2.776	5.123	80.859	26.461	33.925	20.472
1980	15.796	3.695	67.175	59.008	18.598	19.908	18.249	2.254	2.739	5.428	78.067	26.332	32.039	19.697
1981	13.719	4.307	66.951	58.529	18.377	19.699	18.146	2.307	3.008	5.414	76.106	25.877	30.712	19.514
1982	11.861	4.608	66.569	57.458	18.639	18.319	18.309	2.191	3.131	5.980	73.099	26.391	27.614	19.089
1983	11.752	3.693	64.114	54.416	17.247	16.593	18.392	2.184	3.203	6.496	72.971	26.363	27.428	19.177
1984	12.471	3.786	68.840	58.849	19.719	18.008	18.848	2.274	3.553	6.438	76.632	27.403	29.570	19.656
1985	11.781	4.196	67.698	57.539	19.325	16.980	18.992	2.241	4.076	6.084	76.392	27.493	28.816	20.088
1986	14.151	4.021	67.066	56.575	19.509	16.541	18.376	2.149	4.380	6.111	76.647	27.581	28.274	20.789
1987	15.398	3.812	67.542	57.167	20.141	17.136	17.675	2.215	4.754	5.622	79.054	28.209	29.379	21.469
1988	17.296	4.366	68.919	57.875	20.738	17.599	17.279	2.260	5.587	5.457	82.709	29.711	30.677	22.318
1989	18.766	4.661	69.320	57.483	21.360	17.847	16.117	2.158	5.602	6.235	84.786	30.979	31.320	22.478
1990	18.817	4.752	70.705	58.560	22.488	18.326	15.571	2.175	6.104	6.041	84.485	30.265	31.810	22.420
1991	18.335	5.141	70.362	57.872	21.636	18.229	15.701	2.306	6.422	6.069	84.438	30.920	31.399	22.118
1992	19.372	4.937	69.956	57.655	21.694	18.375	15.223	2.363	6.479	5.821	85.783	30.797	32.571	22.415
1993	21.218	4.227	68.315	55.822	20.336	18.584	14.494	2.408	6.410	6.083	87.366	32.037	32.628	22.712
1994	22.307	4.035	70.726	58.044	22.202	19.348	14.103	2.391	6.694	5.988	89.088	32.209	33.520	23.365
1995	22.180	4.496	71.174	57.540	22.130	19.082	13.887	2.442	7.075	6.558	91.032	33.208	33.970	23.851
1996	23.633	4.613	72.486	58.387	22.790	19.344	13.723	2.530	7.087	7.012	94.022	34.675	34.903	24.439
1997	25.119	4.493	72.472	58.857	23.310	19.394	13.658	2.495	6.597	7.018	94.602	34.645	35.199	24.751
1998	26.473	4.237	72.876	59.314	24.045	19.613	13.235	2.420	7.068	6.494	95.019	34.921	34.841	25.260
1999	27.152	3.669	71.742	57.614	23.295	19.341	12.451	2.528	7.610	6.517	96.650	35.932	34.763	25.949
2000	28.865	3.962	71.332	57.366	22.735	19.662	12.358	2.611	7.862	6.104	98.819	37.599	34.662	26.555
2001	30.052	3.731	71.735	58.541	23.547	20.166	12.282	2.547	8.029	5.164	96.172	37.177	32.719	26.282
2002	29.331	3.608	70.713	56.834	22.732	19.382	12.160	2.559	8.145	5.734	97.647	38.135	32.661	26.846
2003	31.007	4.013	69.938	56.033	22.094	19.633	11.960	2.346	7.960	5.946	97.921	38.469	32.553	26.900
2004	33.492	4.351	70.232	55.942	22.852	19.074	11.550	2.466	8.223	6.067	100.090	38.741	33.515	27.843
2005	34.659	4.462	69.431	55.044	23.185	18.556	10.969	2.334	8.161	6.226	100.190	39.472	32.441	28.280
2006	34.649	4.727	70.746	55.938	23.790	19.022	10.771	2.356	8.215	6.594	99.492	38.386	32.390	28.717
2007	34.679	5.338	71.415	56.436	23.493	19.786	10.748	2.409	8.459	6.520	101.020	39.783	32.385	28.859
2008	32.970	6.949	73.220	57.587	23.851	20.703	10.613	2.419	8.426	7.206	98.906	40.086	31.333	27.486
2009	29.690	6.920	72.658	56.662	21.624	21.139	11.325	2.574	8.355	7.641	94.138	38.986	28.464	26.687
2010	29.866	8.176	74.777	58.230	22.038	21.806	11.605	2.781	8.434	8.112	97.480	32.719	30.526	27.059
2011	28.748	10.373	77.972	60.548	22.221	23.406	11.950	2.970	8.269	9.155	96.902	32.661	30.843	26.712
2012	27.068	11.267	79.199	62.324	20.677	24.610	13.791	3.246	8.062	8.813	94.416	32.553	30.915	26.219
2013	24.626	11.787	81.894	64.319	20.001	24.991	15.795	3.532	8.244	9.330	97.157	33.515	31.409	26.750
2014	23.241	12.270	87.597	69.368	20.286	26.718	18.552	4.096	8.338	9.607	98.329	32.441	31.643	26.996
2015	23.794	12.902	88.045	70.221	17.946	20.061	19.647	4.567	8.335	9.487	97.365	32.390	31.327	27.355
2016	25.423	13.934	83.953	65.310	14.578	27.412	18.586	4.753	8.422	10.220	97.397	32.385	30.841	27.925
2015														
January	2.066	1.102	7.686	6.070	1.730	2.335	1.659	0.346	0.777	0.839	9.611	4.350	2.725	2.232
February	1.838	1.014	6.850	5.406	1.445	2.123	1.516	0.325	0.664	0.777	8.441	4.055	2.512	2.023
March	2.070	1.040	7.593	6.078	1.628	2.367	1.713	0.369	0.675	0.840	8.536	3.513	2.590	2.333
April	1.913	1.106	7.291	5.837	1.495	2.304	1.666	0.372	0.625	0.829	7.562	2.704	2.506	2.249
May	1.998	1.114	7.328	5.818	1.400	2.357	1.683	0.377	0.689	0.821	7.653	2.694	2.589	2.356
June	1.956	1.034	7.095	5.596	1.331	2.297	1.601	0.366	0.717	0.782	7.785	2.939	2.606	2.337
July	2.024	. . .	7.532	5.974	1.533	2.385	1.675	0.381	0.747	0.811	8.238	3.285	2.690	2.457
August	2.068	1.063	7.648	6.108	1.655	2.397	1.671	0.385	0.757	0.783	8.220	3.216	2.666	2.449
September	1.924	1.082	7.319	5.889	1.558	2.332	1.625	0.376	0.695	0.734	7.660	2.869	2.506	2.313
October	1.897	1.072	7.358	5.951	1.515	2.373	1.666	0.398	0.634	0.774	7.770	2.743	2.539	2.362
November	1.897	1.047	7.111	5.658	1.374	2.295	1.603	0.386	0.630	0.823	8.213	2.976	2.501	2.251
December	2.076	1.156	7.264	5.673	1.262	2.380	1.635	0.397	0.728	0.862	9.075	3.455	2.610	2.297
2016														
January	2.111	1.080	7.202	5.582	1.214	2.357	1.631	0.381	0.758	0.861	9.058	4.185	2.683	2.189
February	2.022	1.038	6.805	5.267	1.148	2.242	1.518	0.359	0.686	0.852	8.206	3.561	2.526	2.122
March	2.139	1.151	7.110	5.495	1.107	2.356	1.627	0.405	0.692	0.924	7.968	3.051	2.562	2.361
April	2.031	1.113	6.684	5.157	0.963	2.267	1.536	0.391	0.652	0.875	7.439	2.711	2.453	2.279
May	2.169	1.225	6.965	5.382	1.061	2.331	1.576	0.414	0.696	0.887	7.573	2.696	2.513	2.367
June	2.078	1.153	6.861	5.314	1.189	2.225	1.495	0.404	0.703	0.845	7.939	3.026	2.522	2.388
July	2.252	1.124	7.076	5.484	1.238	2.292	1.542	0.412	0.736	0.856	8.471	3.414	2.595	2.455
August	2.211	1.185	7.187	5.635	1.367	2.322	1.554	0.392	0.748	0.804	8.523	3.373	2.680	2.463
September	2.101	1.151	6.844	5.387	1.302	2.233	1.471	0.382	0.684	0.773	7.771	2.933	2.513	2.321
October	2.063	1.115	7.066	5.612	1.374	2.271	1.558	0.408	0.635	0.819	7.650	2.749	2.561	2.339
November	2.111	1.253	6.996	5.497	1.344	2.230	1.521	0.402	0.682	0.817	7.726	2.908	2.538	2.282
December	2.134	1.348	7.157	5.499	1.271	2.285	1.557	0.386	0.749	0.908	9.075	2.713	2.691	2.358

. . . = Not available.

Table 11-2. Energy Consumption Per Dollar of Real Gross Domestic Product

Year	Primary energy consumption (quadrillion Btu)			Gross domestic product (billions of chained [2009] dollars)	Energy consumption per real dollar of GDP (thousand Btu per chained [2005] dollar)		
	Total	Petroleum and natural gas	Other energy		Total	Petroleum and natural gas	Other energy
1950	34.616	19.284	15.332	2 184.0	15.85	8.83	7.02
1951	36.974	21.477	15.497	2 360.0	15.67	9.10	6.57
1952	36.748	22.505	14.243	2 456.1	14.96	9.16	5.80
1953	37.664	23.462	14.202	2 571.4	14.65	9.12	5.52
1954	36.639	24.169	12.470	2 556.9	14.33	9.45	4.88
1955	40.208	26.253	13.955	2 739.0	14.68	9.58	5.09
1956	41.754	27.551	14.203	2 797.4	14.93	9.85	5.08
1957	41.787	28.122	13.665	2 856.3	14.63	9.85	4.78
1958	41.645	29.190	12.455	2 835.3	14.69	10.30	4.39
1959	43.466	31.040	12.426	3 031.0	14.34	10.24	4.10
1960	45.086	32.305	12.782	3 108.7	14.50	10.39	4.11
1961	45.738	33.143	12.595	3 188.1	14.35	10.40	3.95
1962	47.826	34.780	13.047	3 383.1	14.14	10.28	3.86
1963	49.644	36.104	13.540	3 530.4	14.06	10.23	3.84
1964	51.815	37.589	14.226	3 734.0	13.88	10.07	3.81
1965	54.015	39.014	15.001	3 976.7	13.58	9.81	3.77
1966	57.014	41.396	15.618	4 238.9	13.45	9.77	3.68
1967	58.905	43.228	15.676	4 355.2	13.53	9.93	3.60
1968	62.415	46.189	16.225	4 569.0	13.66	10.11	3.55
1969	65.614	49.016	16.598	4 712.5	13.92	10.40	3.52
1970	67.838	51.315	16.523	4 722.0	14.37	10.87	3.50
1971	69.283	53.030	16.253	4 877.6	14.20	10.87	3.33
1972	72.688	55.645	17.043	5 134.3	14.16	10.84	3.32
1973	75.684	57.350	18.334	5 424.1	13.95	10.57	3.38
1974	73.962	55.186	18.776	5 396.0	13.71	10.23	3.48
1975	71.965	52.680	19.284	5 385.4	13.36	9.78	3.58
1976	75.975	55.523	20.452	5 675.4	13.39	9.78	3.60
1977	77.961	57.054	20.907	5 937.0	13.13	9.61	3.52
1978	79.950	57.963	21.987	6 267.2	12.76	9.25	3.51
1979	80.859	57.788	23.070	6 466.2	12.50	8.94	3.57
1980	78.067	54.440	23.627	6 450.4	12.10	8.44	3.66
1981	76.106	51.680	24.426	6 617.7	11.50	7.81	3.69
1982	73.099	48.588	24.511	6 491.3	11.26	7.49	3.78
1983	72.971	47.273	25.698	6 792.0	10.74	6.96	3.78
1984	76.632	49.447	27.185	7 285.0	10.52	6.79	3.73
1985	76.392	48.628	27.764	7 593.8	10.06	6.40	3.66
1986	76.647	48.790	27.857	7 860.5	9.75	6.21	3.54
1987	79.054	50.504	28.551	8 132.6	9.72	6.21	3.51
1988	82.709	52.671	30.038	8 474.5	9.76	6.22	3.54
1989	84.785	53.811	30.974	8 786.4	9.65	6.12	3.53
1990	84.484	53.155	31.330	8 955.0	9.43	5.94	3.50
1991	84.437	52.879	31.558	8 948.4	9.44	5.91	3.53
1992	85.782	54.239	31.544	9 266.6	9.26	5.85	3.40
1993	87.365	54.916	32.449	9 521.0	9.18	5.77	3.41
1994	89.087	56.286	32.802	9 905.4	8.99	5.68	3.31
1995	91.031	57.112	33.918	10 174.8	8.95	5.61	3.33
1996	94.021	58.760	35.261	10 561.0	8.90	5.56	3.34
1997	94.600	59.381	35.219	11 034.9	8.57	5.38	3.19
1998	95.018	59.648	35.370	11 525.9	8.24	5.18	3.07
1999	96.648	60.745	35.903	12 065.9	8.01	5.03	2.98
2000	98.817	62.090	36.727	12 559.7	7.87	4.94	2.92
2001	96.170	60.962	35.207	12 682.2	7.58	4.81	2.78
2002	97.643	61.736	35.908	12 908.8	7.56	4.78	2.78
2003	97.918	61.620	36.297	13 271.1	7.38	4.64	2.74
2004	100.090	63.150	36.940	13 773.5	7.27	4.58	2.68
2005	100.188	62.868	37.320	14 234.2	7.04	4.42	2.62
2006	99.485	62.062	37.422	14 613.8	6.81	4.25	2.56
2007	101.015	63.152	37.863	14 873.7	6.79	4.25	2.55
2008	98.891	60.750	38.141	14 830.4	6.67	4.10	2.57
2009	94.118	58.375	35.743	14 418.7	6.53	4.05	2.48
2010	97.445	60.064	37.381	14 783.8	6.59	4.06	2.53
2011	96.842	59.778	37.064	15 020.6	6.45	3.98	2.47
2012	94.416	60.105	34.312	15 354.6	6.15	3.91	2.23
2013	97.157	61.418	35.739	15 612.2	6.22	3.93	2.29
2014	98.329	62.264	36.065	15 982.3	6.15	3.90	2.26
2015	97.365	63.799	33.566	16 397.2	5.94	3.89	2.05
2016	97.397	64.366	33.030	16 662.1	5.85	3.86	1.98

Table 11-3. Petroleum and Petroleum Products—Prices, Imports, Domestic Production, and Stocks

(Not seasonally adjusted.)

Year and month	Crude oil futures price (dollars per barrel)		Imports				Supply (thousands of barrels per day)					Stocks (end of period, millions of barrels)		
			Total energy-related petroleum products (thousands of barrels)	Crude petroleum			Petroleum and products			Domestic production			Crude petroleum	
				Thousands of barrels		Unit price (dollars per barrel)						Crude oil and petroleum products		
	Current dollars	2009 dollars		Total	Average per day		Exports	Imports	Net imports	Crude oil	Natural gas plant liquids		Non-SPR	Strategic petroleum reserve
1983	30.66	69.52	. . .	1 293 819	3 545	30.00	739	5 051	4 312	6 974	1 559	1 454	723	379
1984	29.44	63.41	. . .	1 319 683	3 616	28.00	722	5 437	4 715	7 157	1 630	1 556	796	451
1985	27.89	57.07	. . .	1 260 856	3 454	26.00	781	5 067	4 286	7 146	1 609	1 519	814	493
1986	15.05	29.56	. . .	1 634 567	4 478	14.00	785	6 224	5 439	6 814	1 551	1 593	843	512
1987	19.15	36.38	. . .	1 744 977	4 781	17.00	764	6 678	5 914	6 387	1 595	1 607	890	541
1988	15.96	29.10	. . .	1 887 860	5 172	14.00	815	7 402	6 587	6 123	1 625	1 597	890	560
1989	19.58	34.69	. . .	2 146 552	5 881	16.00	859	8 061	7 202	5 739	1 546	1 581	921	580
1990	24.50	42.53	. . .	2 216 604	6 073	20.00	857	8 018	7 161	5 582	1 559	1 621	908	586
1991	21.50	37.24	2 828 953	2 146 064	5 880	17.00	1 001	7 627	6 626	5 618	1 659	1 617	893	569
1992	20.58	34.37	2 947 582	2 294 570	6 269	17.00	950	7 888	6 938	5 457	1 697	1 592	893	575
1993	18.48	29.82	3 257 008	2 543 374	6 968	15.00	1 003	8 620	7 618	5 264	1 736	1 647	922	587
1994	17.19	26.71	3 416 045	2 704 196	7 409	14.00	942	8 996	8 054	5 103	1 727	1 653	929	592
1995	18.40	27.76	3 361 882	2 767 312	7 582	16.00	949	8 835	7 886	5 076	1 762	1 563	895	592
1996	22.03	32.11	3 622 385	2 893 647	7 906	19.00	981	9 478	8 498	5 071	1 830	1 507	850	566
1997	20.61	28.95	3 802 574	3 069 430	8 409	18.00	1 003	10 162	9 158	5 156	1 817	1 560	868	563
1998	14.40	19.20	4 088 027	3 242 711	8 884	11.00	945	10 708	9 764	5 077	1 759	1 647	895	571
1999	19.30	24.44	4 081 181	3 228 092	8 844	16.00	940	10 852	9 912	4 832	1 850	1 493	852	567
2000	30.26	36.47	4 314 825	3 399 239	9 288	26.00	1 040	11 459	10 419	4 851	1 911	1 468	826	541
2001	25.95	30.48	4 475 026	3 471 067	9 510	21.00	971	11 871	10 900	4 839	1 868	1 586	862	550
2002	26.15	29.95	4 337 075	3 418 022	9 364	23.00	984	11 530	10 546	4 759	1 880	1 548	877	599
2003	30.99	34.41	4 654 638	3 676 005	10 071	27.00	1 027	12 264	11 238	4 675	1 719	1 568	907	638
2004	41.47	44.35	4 917 591	3 820 979	10 440	34.00	1 048	13 145	12 097	4 533	1 809	1 645	961	676
2005	56.70	58.57	5 004 339	3 754 671	10 287	47.00	1 165	13 714	12 549	4 320	1 717	1 698	992	685
2006	66.25	66.42	4 880 734	3 734 226	10 231	58.00	1 317	13 707	12 390	4 345	1 739	1 720	984	689
2007	72.41	71.01	4 807 811	3 690 568	10 111	64.00	1 433	13 468	12 036	4 355	1 783	1 665	965	697
2008	99.75	98.15	4 613 444	3 590 628	9 810	95.00	1 802	12 915	11 114	4 317	1 784	1 737	1 010	702
2009	62.09	62.09	4 266 007	3 314 787	9 082	57.00	2 024	11 691	9 667	4 708	1 910	1 776	1 034	727
2010	79.61	78.11	4 279 611	3 377 077	9 252	75.00	2 353	11 793	9 441	4 875	2 074	1 794	1 039	727
2011	95.11	91.25	4 164 117	3 321 918	9 101	100.00	2 986	11 436	8 450	5 085	2 216	1 750	1 004	696
2012	94.15	89.03	3 847 545	3 097 407	8 463	101.00	3 205	10 598	7 393	5 961	2 408	1 808	1 033	695
2013	98.05	91.17	3 549 945	2 813 770	7 709	97.00	3 621	9 859	6 237	6 953	2 606	1 761	1 023	696
2014	92.91	84.12	3 381 460	2 700 939	7 400	91.00	4 175	9 240	5 065	8 267	3 015	1 856	1 052	691
2015	48.79	44.54	3 384 807	2 661 968	7 293	47.00	4 751	9 401	4 650	8 932	3 342	2 015	1 144	695
2016	43.32	39.20	3 576 378	2 806 413	7 689	36.00	5 188	7 668	2 480	8 385	3 478	2 031	1 179	695
2015														
January	47.33	42.06	294 942	224 349	615	59.00	4 575	9 461	4 825	9 341	2 980	1 850	1 080	691
February	50.73	45.03	252 877	193 397	530	50.00	4 640	9 272	4 544	9 451	3 100	1 850	1 106	691
March	47.85	42.32	282 629	223 451	612	46.00	4 092	9 619	5 432	9 648	3 181	1 883	1 134	691
April	54.63	48.25	294 994	235 855	646	47.00	4 938	9 374	4 364	9 694	3 313	1 909	1 144	691
May	59.37	52.22	266 545	201 887	553	51.00	4 853	9 502	4 596	9 479	3 249	1 931	1 141	692
June	59.83	52.61	286 560	223 381	612	54.00	4 657	9 605	4 884	9 315	3 259	1 941	1 133	694
July	50.93	44.66	299 744	236 579	648	54.00	4 960	9 571	4 544	9 432	3 284	1 939	1 120	695
August	42.89	37.53	279 672	219 476	601	49.00	4 507	9 858	5 205	9 407	3 319	1 962	1 121	695
September	45.47	39.67	293 359	231 374	634	43.00	4 851	9 358	4 451	9 453	3 343	1 971	1 124	695
October	46.25	40.34	262 992	206 782	567	40.00	4 617	8 842	4 172	9 379	3 428	1 979	1 150	695
November	42.92	37.35	263 623	212 819	583	39.19	4 903	9 151	4 308	9 329	3 436	1 992	1 151	695
December	37.33	32.38	308 428	252 618	692	36.63	5 266	9 742	4 451	9 246	3 375	1 985	1 144	695
2016														
January	31.78	28.90	291 438	226 663	621	32.05	4 878	9 734	4 857	9 194	3 303	2 009	1 164	695
February	30.62	27.87	275 539	214 905	589	27.49	4 948	10 020	5 072	9 147	3 329	2 013	1 184	695
March	37.96	34.51	302 334	243 940	668	27.67	5 002	10 002	5 000	9 174	3 509	2 021	1 197	695
April	41.13	37.42	291 510	228 862	627	29.53	5 154	9 829	4 674	8 947	3 504	2 032	1 201	695
May	46.80	42.55	286 181	223 398	612	34.19	5 658	10 183	4 525	8 882	3 593	2 048	1 204	695
June	48.84	44.26	314 612	244 772	671	39.38	5 240	10 076	4 836	8 711	3 618	2 047	1 193	695
July	44.80	40.53	294 855	225 593	618	41.02	5 209	10 507	5 298	8 691	3 573	2 062	1 185	695
August	44.80	40.48	329 428	256 644	703	39.38	5 114	10 311	5 196	8 759	3 399	2 063	1 179	695
September	45.23	40.85	301 713	238 506	653	39.01	5 250	10 194	4 944	8 567	3 420	2 048	1 164	695
October	49.87	44.97	285 911	224 658	616	40.03	4 942	9 723	4 781	8 785	3 541	2 050	1 184	695
November	45.87	41.27	305 703	240 407	659	40.81	5 392	10 312	4 921	8 863	3 598	2 054	1 184	695
December	52.17	46.85	297 154	238 064	652	41.40	5 460	9 814	4 355	8 780	3 344	2 031	1 179	695

. . . = Not available.

NOTES AND DEFINITIONS, CHAPTER 11

TABLES 11-1 AND 11-2

Energy Supply and Consumption

SOURCES: U.S. DEPARTMENT OF ENERGY, ENERGY INFORMATION ADMINISTRATION; U.S. DEPARTMENT OF COMMERCE, BUREAU OF ECONOMIC ANALYSIS

Definitions

The *British thermal unit (Btu)* is a measure used to combine data for different energy sources into a consistent aggregate. It is the amount of energy required to raise the temperature of 1 pound of water 1 degree Fahrenheit when the water is near a temperature of 39.2 degrees Fahrenheit. To illustrate one of the factors used to convert volumes to Btu, conventional motor gasoline has a heat content of 5.253 million Btu per barrel. For further information, see the Energy Information Administration's *Monthly Energy Review*, Appendix A.

Production: Crude oil includes lease condensates.

Renewable energy, total includes conventional hydroelectric power, geothermal, solar thermal and photovoltaic, wind, and biomass. Hydroelectric power includes conventional electrical utility and industrial generation. Biomass includes wood, waste, and alcohol fuels (ethanol blended into motor gasoline).

The sum of domestic energy *production* and net imports of energy (*imports* minus *exports*) does not exactly equal domestic energy *consumption*. The difference is attributed to inventory changes; losses and gains in conversion, transportation, and distribution; the addition of blending compounds; shipments of anthracite to U.S. armed forces in Europe; and adjustments to account for discrepancies between reporting systems.

Consumption by end-use sector is based on total, not net, consumption—that is, each sector's consumption includes its electricity purchases as well as its own energy production. Electric utilities are not treated as a separate end-use sector. However, they are counted as primary producers in the production accounts, which measure only primary production. As a result, total national supply and consumption are in rough balance, though components may not add to exact totals, not only because of the miscellaneous adjustments described above, but also because of different sector-specific conversion factors.

REFERENCES AND NOTES ON THE DATA

All of these data are published each month in Tables 1.1, 1.2, 1.7, and 2.1 in the *Monthly Energy Review*. Annual data before 1973 are published in the *Annual Energy Review*. These two publications are no longer published in printed form but are available, along with all current and historical data, on the EIA Web site at <http://www.eia.doe.gov>.

The real gross domestic product (GDP) data used to calculate energy consumption per dollar of real GDP are from the Bureau of Economic Analysis; see Table 1-2 and the applicable notes and definitions in this volume of *Business Statistics*. The GDP numbers shown in this table reflect the comprehensive revision of July 2013, which increased the overall level of GDP by including as investment research, development, and creation of intellectual property. This changed the average level of the energy-to-GDP ratio but had little effect on its downward trend. The GDP estimate shown here also reflects subsequent revisions and updates made through June 2016.

TABLE 11-3

Petroleum and Petroleum Products—Prices, Imports, Domestic Production, and Stocks

SOURCES: FUTURES PRICES—U.S. DEPARTMENT OF ENERGY, ENERGY INFORMATION ADMINISTRATION (EIA), AND U.S. DEPARTMENT OF COMMERCE, BUREAU OF ECONOMIC ANALYSIS; IMPORTS—U.S. DEPARTMENT OF COMMERCE, CENSUS BUREAU (SEE NOTES AND DEFINITIONS FOR TABLES 7-9 THROUGH 7-14); SUPPLY (NET IMPORTS AND DOMESTIC PRODUCTION) AND STOCKS—EIA

Definitions and notes on the data

The *crude oil futures price* in *current dollars per barrel* is the price for next-month delivery in Cushing, Oklahoma (a pipeline hub), of light, sweet crude oil, as determined by trading on the New York Mercantile Exchange (NYMEX). Official daily closing prices are reported each day at 2:30 p.m., and are tabulated weekly in Table 13 of *EIA's Weekly Petroleum Status Report*. The monthly averages shown in this volume are the average prices for the nearest future from each trading day of the month. For example, for most days in January, the futures contract priced will be for February; for the last few days in January, the February contract will have expired and the March contract will be quoted. The annual averages are averages of the monthly averages.

The *crude oil futures price* in *2009 dollars* is calculated by the editors, by dividing each month's current-dollar price by that month's chain price index for total personal consumption expenditures (PCE), with the price index average for the year 2009 set at 1.0000. The PCE chain price index is compiled by the Bureau of Economic Analysis (BEA). It is described in the notes and definitions for Chapter 1 and is also presented in Chapter 8, Table 8-2, and discussed in its notes and definitions.

The import data in Columns 3 through 6 of this table are those published as Exhibit 17, "Imports of Energy-related Petroleum

Products, including Crude Petroleum," in the monthly Census-BEA foreign trade press release, FT900. *Total energy-related petroleum products* includes the following Standard International Trade Classification (SITC) commodity groupings: crude oil, petroleum preparations, and liquefied propane and butane gas.

The data in Columns 7 through 11, on exports, imports, and net imports (imports minus exports) of petroleum and products and domestic production of crude oil and natural gas plant liquids (all expressed as thousands of barrels per day), and in Columns 12 through 14, depicting stocks of crude oil in millions of barrels, are derived from the Department of Energy's weekly petroleum supply reporting system. They are published in EIA's *Monthly Energy Review*, Tables 3.1 and 3.4, which can be reached by searching the Web site. Stock totals are as of the end of the period. Geographic coverage includes the 50 states and the District of Columbia.

Data availability

Data on futures prices, petroleum supply and stocks are available from the EIA Web site at <http://www.eia.doe.gov>, under the categories "Publications and Reports/Monthly Energy Review" and "Petroleum/Weekly Petroleum Status Report." The *Monthly Energy Review* is no longer published in printed form.

The import data are available in the FT900 report from the Census Bureau at www.census.gov. See the notes and definitions for Tables 7-9 through 7-14 for further information.

CHAPTER 12: MONEY, INTEREST, ASSETS, LIABILITIES, AND ASSET PRICES

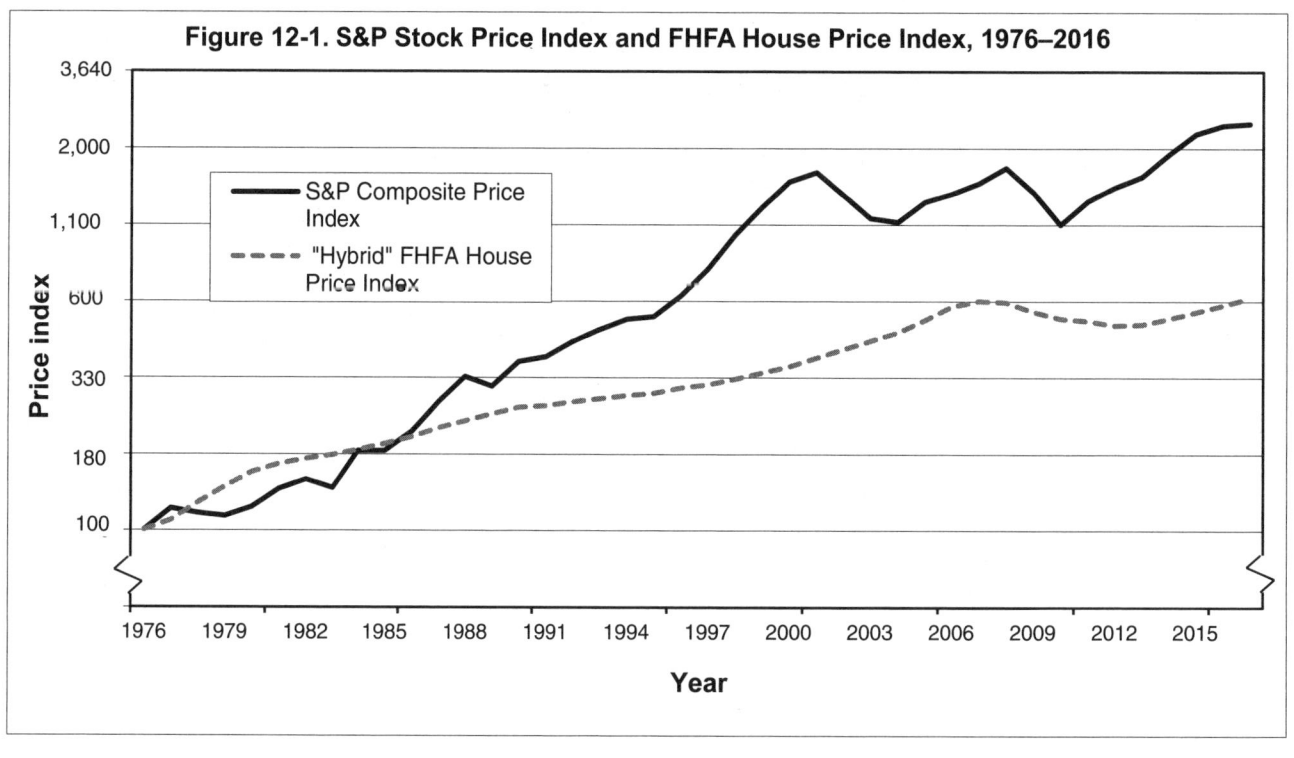

Figure 12-1. S&P Stock Price Index and FHFA House Price Index, 1976–2016

- During the Great Recession, the Federal Reserve began a program called Quantitative Easing. The Federal Reserve added $1.3 trillion to its balance sheet during 2008 and another $1.8 trillion by the end of 2013. In October 2014, the Federal Reserve Board stopped buying bonds. Over the six years of the quantitative easing program, the Fed bought $4.5 trillion in bonds. (Tables 12-1 and 12-3)

- U.S. net worth is a concept that measures the total nonfinancial wealth, including land, machines and patent rights, of the U.S. as a whole. Household net worth increased from $49,426 billion in 2003 to $92,805 billion in 2016. (Table 12-4)

- The long-term gains in national average housing prices as estimated here have been no for no match for those in the prices of common stocks, as measured by the S&P 500-stock index, averaged for the year and also rebased to 1975 = 100. The housing price index increased each year from 1975 to 2006 then decreased from 2007 to 2011 before increasing again each year from 2012 to 2016. (Table 12-6)

Table 12-1A. Money Stock Measures and Components of M1: Recent Data

(Billions of dollars, monthly data are averages of daily figures, annual data are for December.)

Year and month	Not seasonally adjusted		Seasonally adjusted					Other checkable deposits		
	M1	M2	M1	M2	Currency	Traveler's checks	Demand deposits	At commercial banks	At thrift institutions	Total
1960	144.5	315.3	140.7	312.4	28.7	0.3	111.6	0.0	0.0	0.0
1961	149.2	338.5	145.2	335.5	29.3	0.4	115.5	0.0	0.0	0.0
1962	151.9	365.8	147.8	362.7	30.3	0.4	117.1	0.0	0.0	0.0
1963	157.5	396.4	153.3	393.2	32.2	0.4	120.6	0.0	0.1	0.1
1964	164.9	428.3	160.3	424.7	33.9	0.5	125.8	0.0	0.1	0.1
1965	172.6	463.1	167.8	459.2	36.0	0.5	131.3	0.0	0.1	0.1
1966	176.9	483.7	172.0	480.2	38.0	0.6	133.4	0.0	0.1	0.1
1967	188.4	528.0	183.3	524.8	40.0	0.6	142.5	0.0	0.1	0.1
1968	202.8	569.7	197.4	566.8	43.0	0.7	153.6	0.0	0.1	0.1
1969	209.3	590.1	203.9	587.9	45.7	0.8	157.3	0.0	0.1	0.1
1970	220.1	627.8	214.4	626.5	48.6	0.9	164.7	0.0	0.1	0.1
1971	234.5	711.2	228.3	710.3	52.0	1.0	175.1	0.0	0.2	0.2
1972	256.1	803.1	249.2	802.3	56.2	1.2	191.6	0.0	0.2	0.2
1973	270.2	856.5	262.9	855.5	60.8	1.4	200.3	0.0	0.3	0.3
1974	281.8	903.5	274.2	902.1	67.0	1.7	205.1	0.2	0.4	0.4
1975	295.3	1 017.8	287.1	1 016.2	72.8	2.1	211.3	0.4	0.5	0.9
1976	314.5	1 153.5	306.2	1 152.0	79.5	2.6	221.5	1.3	1.4	2.7
1977	340.0	1 273.0	330.9	1 270.3	87.4	2.9	236.4	1.8	2.3	4.2
1978	367.9	1 370.8	357.3	1 366.0	96.0	3.3	249.5	5.3	3.1	8.5
1979	393.2	1 479.0	381.8	1 473.7	104.8	3.5	256.6	12.7	4.2	16.8
1980	419.5	1 604.8	408.5	1 599.8	115.3	3.9	261.2	20.8	7.3	28.1
1981	447.0	1 760.3	436.7	1 755.5	122.5	4.1	231.4	63.0	15.6	78.7
1982	485.8	1 913.8	474.8	1 905.9	132.5	4.1	234.1	80.5	23.6	104.1
1983	533.3	2 134.0	521.4	2 123.5	146.2	4.7	238.5	97.3	34.8	132.1
1984	564.6	2 318.5	551.6	2 306.4	156.1	5.0	243.4	104.7	42.4	147.1
1985	633.3	2 504.1	619.8	2 492.1	167.7	5.6	266.9	124.7	54.9	179.5
1986	739.8	2 740.7	724.7	2 728.0	180.4	6.1	302.9	161.0	74.2	235.2
1987	765.4	2 838.3	750.2	2 826.4	196.7	6.6	287.7	178.2	81.0	259.2
1988	803.1	3 000.6	786.7	2 988.2	212.0	7.0	287.1	192.5	88.1	280.6
1989	810.6	3 165.4	792.9	3 152.3	222.3	6.9	278.6	197.4	87.7	285.1
1990	842.7	3 284.0	824.7	3 270.7	246.5	7.7	276.8	208.7	85.0	293.7
1991	915.6	3 384.2	897.0	3 370.0	267.1	7.7	289.6	241.6	90.9	332.5
1992	1 045.6	3 438.5	1 024.9	3 421.9	292.1	8.2	340.0	280.8	103.8	384.6
1993	1 153.3	3 491.9	1 129.6	3 471.3	321.6	8.0	385.4	302.6	112.0	414.6
1994	1 174.5	3 502.8	1 150.7	3 481.3	354.5	8.6	383.6	297.4	106.6	404.0
1995	1 152.7	3 646.5	1 127.5	3 622.7	372.8	9.0	389.0	249.0	107.6	356.6
1996	1 105.8	3 823.3	1 081.3	3 802.1	394.6	8.8	402.1	172.1	103.6	275.8
1997	1 097.5	4 036.0	1 072.3	4 013.8	425.3	8.4	393.5	148.4	96.7	245.1
1998	1 121.2	4 377.7	1 095.0	4 353.3	460.4	8.5	376.3	143.9	105.9	249.8
1999	1 148.2	4 639.8	1 122.2	4 613.3	517.9	8.6	352.5	139.7	103.6	243.3
2000	1 111.7	4 926.7	1 088.5	4 898.7	531.3	8.3	310.4	133.3	105.3	238.5
2001	1 208.5	5 431.2	1 183.2	5 400.0	581.2	8.0	336.3	142.2	115.5	257.7
2002	1 245.5	5 768.3	1 220.2	5 736.2	626.2	7.8	306.9	154.4	124.9	279.3
2003	1 332.2	6 062.8	1 306.0	6 031.4	662.5	7.7	326.0	175.3	134.5	309.8
2004	1 401.2	6 412.9	1 375.9	6 383.6	697.8	7.5	343.1	187.0	140.4	327.4
2005	1 396.9	6 674.0	1 374.8	6 646.9	724.6	7.2	324.8	180.6	137.5	318.1
2006	1 387.3	7 064.0	1 367.4	7 035.3	750.2	6.7	305.7	176.2	128.5	304.7
2007	1 394.5	7 468.8	1 374.7	7 435.9	760.6	6.3	303.0	171.8	133.0	304.7
2008	1 631.9	8 196.5	1 603.6	8 156.8	816.2	5.5	472.0	176.9	132.9	309.8
2009	1 724.0	8 508.7	1 694.1	8 460.6	863.7	5.1	447.8	228.8	148.7	377.5
2010	1 870.9	8 822.5	1 837.5	8 766.8	918.8	4.7	518.2	233.1	162.8	395.8
2011	2 207.7	9 696.3	2 164.6	9 630.0	1 001.5	4.3	752.2	231.5	175.1	406.6
2012	2 509.3	10 498.9	2 460.7	10 426.0	1 090.6	3.8	927.0	243.6	195.7	439.2
2013	2 713.2	11 069.7	2 660.7	10 993.9	1 160.5	3.5	1 031.1	256.2	209.4	465.6
2014	2 988.7	11 726.7	2 932.9	11 647.8	1 252.7	2.9	1 193.2	265.5	218.6	484.1
2015	3 137.4	12 396.3	3 083.4	12 311.2	1 338.6	2.5	1 228.4	277.0	236.9	513.9
2016	3 378.6	13 273.0	3 326.7	13 180.8	1 419.7	2.2	1 353.3	293.8	257.7	551.5
2015										
January	2 937.7	11 725.7	2 941.9	11 713.5	1 266.2	2.9	1 185.4	265.2	222.2	487.4
February	2 976.3	11 814.3	2 999.8	11 831.2	1 272.5	2.9	1 228.2	268.8	227.4	496.2
March	3 020.4	11 924.2	3 001.4	11 853.1	1 279.3	2.8	1 220.4	272.7	226.2	498.9
April	3 032.0	11 972.4	2 998.4	11 898.2	1 284.9	2.8	1 210.8	271.7	228.2	499.9
May	2 972.4	11 876.0	2 988.0	11 932.8	1 289.4	2.7	1 196.2	270.3	229.4	499.7
June	3 017.2	11 930.5	3 017.4	11 977.4	1 295.0	2.7	1 215.2	275.6	228.9	504.6
July	3 034.8	11 981.4	3 032.4	12 031.1	1 301.6	2.7	1 222.3	275.9	229.9	505.8
August	3 018.7	12 039.1	3 030.3	12 082.0	1 309.7	2.6	1 214.1	272.3	231.6	503.9
September	3 012.7	12 106.9	3 038.4	12 135.0	1 318.5	2.6	1 209.3	276.3	231.8	508.1
October	3 008.2	12 139.7	3 011.7	12 148.3	1 325.2	2.6	1 176.2	275.0	232.6	507.7
November	3 052.5	12 266.2	3 074.1	12 250.9	1 333.0	2.5	1 228.9	276.3	233.3	509.6
December	3 137.4	12 396.3	3 083.4	12 311.2	1 338.6	2.5	1 228.4	277.0	236.9	513.9
2016										
January	3 091.0	12 448.0	3 103.5	12 441.5	1 345.8	2.5	1 240.9	276.0	238.4	514.4
February	3 094.2	12 488.0	3 119.9	12 509.8	1 351.4	2.4	1 249.0	279.3	237.8	517.1
March	3 178.2	12 656.7	3 158.4	12 582.7	1 359.5	2.4	1 277.2	279.4	239.9	519.3
April	3 233.7	12 751.2	3 200.2	12 668.3	1 366.4	2.4	1 311.9	278.2	241.3	519.5
May	3 234.3	12 681.2	3 245.8	12 742.2	1 375.4	2.4	1 342.8	282.7	242.6	525.3
June	3 247.4	12 762.1	3 246.5	12 811.3	1 382.6	2.3	1 332.2	283.9	245.5	529.4
July	3 244.2	12 820.7	3 242.6	12 872.3	1 388.9	2.3	1 320.4	283.7	247.3	531.0
August	3 316.6	12 914.4	3 319.9	12 955.2	1 395.8	2.3	1 380.4	290.9	250.5	541.5
September	3 295.7	12 988.6	3 322.5	13 014.3	1 401.7	2.2	1 373.1	292.2	253.2	545.5
October	3 326.7	13 055.9	3 332.8	13 068.0	1 407.6	2.2	1 373.6	292.6	256.9	549.4
November	3 322.9	13 163.8	3 341.7	13 144.8	1 414.2	2.2	1 372.4	294.3	258.6	552.9
December	3 378.6	13 273.0	3 326.7	13 180.8	1 419.7	2.2	1 353.3	293.8	257.7	551.5

Table 12-1B. Money Stock, Historical: 1892–1924

(Not seasonally adjusted, millions of dollars.)

Classification	1892	1893	1894	1895	1896	1897	1898	1899	1900	1901	1902
June 30											
Currency outside banks	1 015	1 081	972	971	974	1 013	1 150	1 181	1 331	1 395	1 431
Demand deposits adjusted	2 880	2 766	2 807	2 960	2 839	2 871	3 432	4 162	4 420	5 204	5 719
M1	3 895	3 847	3 779	3 931	3 813	3 884	4 582	5 343	5 751	6 599	7 150
Time deposits	1 929	2 007	1 994	2 088	2 220	2 305	2 397	2 617	3 015	3 315	3 565
M2	5 824	5 854	5 773	6 019	6 033	6 189	6 979	7 960	8 766	9 914	10 715
December 31											
Currency outside banks	. . .	. . .	. . .	. . .	. . .	. . .	. . .	. . .	. . .	. . .	. . .
Demand deposits adjusted	. . .	. . .	. . .	. . .	. . .	. . .	. . .	. . .	. . .	. . .	. . .
M1	. . .	. . .	. . .	. . .	. . .	. . .	. . .	. . .	. . .	. . .	. . .
Time deposits	. . .	. . .	. . .	. . .	. . .	. . .	. . .	. . .	. . .	. . .	. . .
M2	. . .	. . .	. . .	. . .	. . .	. . .	. . .	. . .	. . .	. . .	. . .

Classification	1903	1904	1905	1906	1907	1908	1909	1910	1911	1912	1913
June 30											
Currency outside banks	1 543	1 562	1 629	1 759	1 700	1 711	1 691	1 725	1 709	1 762	1 858
Demand deposits adjusted	5 962	6 256	7 069	7 504	7 872	7 384	7 768	8 254	8 668	9 156	9 140
M1	7 505	7 818	8 698	9 263	9 572	9 095	9 459	9 979	10 377	10 918	10 998
Time deposits	3 800	4 045	4 464	4 769	5 350	5 493	6 265	6 944	7 337	7 889	8 356
M2	11 305	11 863	13 162	14 032	14 922	14 588	15 724	16 923	17 714	18 807	19 354
December 31											
Currency outside banks	. . .	. . .	. . .	. . .	. . .	. . .	. . .	. . .	. . .	. . .	. . .
Demand deposits adjusted	. . .	. . .	. . .	. . .	. . .	. . .	. . .	. . .	. . .	. . .	. . .
M1	. . .	. . .	. . .	. . .	. . .	. . .	. . .	. . .	. . .	. . .	. . .
Time deposits	. . .	. . .	. . .	. . .	. . .	. . .	. . .	. . .	. . .	. . .	. . .
M2	. . .	. . .	. . .	. . .	. . .	. . .	. . .	. . .	. . .	. . .	. . .

Classification	1914	1915	1916	1917	1918	1919	1920	1921	1922	1923	1924
June 30											
Currency outside banks	1 533	1 575	1 876	2 276	3 298	3 593	4 105	3 677	3 346	3 739	3 650
Demand deposits adjusted	10 082	9 828	11 973	13 501	14 843	17 624	19 616	17 113	18 045	18 958	19 412
M1	11 615	11 403	13 849	15 777	18 141	21 217	23 721	20 790	21 391	22 697	23 062
Time deposits	8 350	9 231	10 313	11 543	11 717	13 423	15 834	16 583	17 437	19 722	21 259
M2	19 965	20 634	24 162	27 320	29 858	34 640	39 555	37 373	48 828	42 419	44 321
December 31											
Currency outside banks	. . .	. . .	. . .	. . .	. . .	. . .	. . .	. . .	. . .	3 726	3 696
Demand deposits adjusted	. . .	. . .	. . .	. . .	. . .	. . .	. . .	. . .	. . .	19 144	20 898
M1	. . .	. . .	. . .	. . .	. . .	. . .	. . .	. . .	. . .	22 870	24 594
Time deposits	. . .	. . .	. . .	. . .	. . .	. . .	. . .	. . .	. . .	20 379	22 232
M2	. . .	. . .	. . .	. . .	. . .	. . .	. . .	. . .	. . .	43 249	46 826

. . . = Not available.

Table 12-1C. Money Stock, Historical: January 1947–January 1959

(Averages of daily figures; seasonally adjusted, billions of dollars.)

Year and month	Money stock (M1)			Time deposits adjusted	M2 (M1 plus time deposits)
	Total	Currency component	Demand deposit component		
1947					
January	109.5	26.7	82.8	33.3	142.8
February	109.7	26.7	83.0	33.5	143.2
March	110.3	26.7	83.7	33.6	143.9
April	111.1	26.6	84.5	33.7	144.8
May	111.7	26.6	85.1	33.8	145.5
June	112.1	26.6	85.5	33.9	146.0
July	112.2	26.5	85.7	34.0	146.2
August	112.6	26.5	86.1	34.4	147.0
September	113.0	26.7	86.3	34.7	147.7
October	112.9	26.5	86.4	35.0	147.9
November	113.3	26.5	86.8	35.2	148.5
December	113.1	26.4	86.7	35.4	148.5
1948					
January	113.4	26.4	87.0	35.5	148.9
February	113.2	26.3	86.8	35.7	148.9
March	112.6	26.2	86.4	35.7	148.3
April	112.3	26.1	86.3	35.7	148.0
May	112.1	26.0	86.0	35.7	147.8
June	112.0	26.0	86.0	35.8	147.8
July	112.2	26.0	86.2	35.8	148.0
August	112.3	26.0	86.2	35.9	148.2
September	112.2	26.0	86.2	35.9	148.1
October	112.1	26.0	86.1	35.9	148.0
November	111.8	26.0	85.9	36.0	147.8
December	111.5	25.8	85.8	36.0	147.5
1949					
January	111.2	25.7	85.5	36.1	147.3
February	111.2	25.7	85.5	36.1	147.3
March	111.2	25.7	85.6	36.1	147.3
April	113.3	25.7	85.6	36.2	149.5
May	111.5	25.7	85.8	36.3	147.8
June	111.3	25.6	85.7	36.4	147.7
July	111.2	25.5	85.7	36.4	147.6
August	111.0	25.5	85.6	36.4	147.4
September	110.9	25.3	85.6	36.4	147.3
October	110.9	25.3	85.6	36.4	147.3
November	111.0	25.2	85.8	36.4	147.4
December	111.2	25.1	86.0	36.4	147.6
1950					
January	111.5	25.1	86.4	36.4	147.9
February	112.1	25.1	86.9	36.6	148.7
March	112.5	25.2	87.3	36.6	149.1
April	113.2	25.3	88.0	36.7	149.9
May	113.7	25.2	88.5	36.9	150.6
June	114.1	25.1	89.0	36.9	151.0
July	114.6	25.0	89.6	36.8	151.4
August	115.0	24.9	90.1	36.7	151.7
September	115.2	24.9	90.3	36.6	151.8
October	115.7	24.9	90.8	36.5	152.2
November	115.9	24.9	90.9	36.6	152.5
December	116.2	25.0	91.2	36.7	152.9
1951					
January	116.7	25.0	91.7	36.7	153.4
February	117.1	25.1	92.0	36.6	153.7
March	117.6	25.2	92.4	36.6	154.2
April	117.8	25.2	92.6	36.7	154.5
May	118.2	25.3	92.8	36.8	155.0
June	118.6	25.4	93.2	36.9	155.5
July	119.1	25.6	93.4	37.2	156.3
August	119.6	25.7	93.8	37.4	157.0
September	120.4	25.8	94.5	37.7	158.1
October	121.0	26.0	95.1	37.8	158.8
November	122.0	26.0	96.0	38.0	160.0
December	122.7	26.1	96.5	38.2	160.9
1952					
January	123.1	26.2	96.9	38.4	161.5
February	123.6	26.3	97.3	38.7	162.3
March	123.8	26.4	97.5	38.9	162.7
April	124.1	26.4	97.6	39.1	163.2
May	124.5	26.5	98.0	39.3	163.8
June	125.0	26.7	98.4	39.5	164.5
July	125.3	26.7	98.6	39.7	165.0
August	125.7	26.8	98.9	40.0	165.7
September	126.4	26.9	99.4	40.3	166.7
October	126.7	27.0	99.7	40.5	167.2
November	127.1	27.2	99.9	40.9	168.0
December	127.4	27.3	100.1	41.1	168.5

Table 12-1C. Money Stock, Historical: January 1947–January 1959—*Continued*

(Averages of daily figures; seasonally adjusted, billions of dollars.)

Year and month	Money stock (M1)			Time deposits adjusted	M2 (M1 plus time deposits)
	Total	Currency component	Demand deposit component		
1953					
January	127.3	27.4	99.9	41.4	168.7
February	127.4	27.5	99.9	41.6	169.0
March	128.0	27.6	100.4	41.9	169.9
April	128.3	27.7	100.7	42.1	170.4
May	128.5	27.7	100.7	42.4	170.9
June	128.5	27.7	100.7	42.6	171.1
July	128.6	27.8	100.8	42.9	171.5
August	128.7	27.8	100.9	43.2	171.9
September	128.6	27.8	100.8	43.5	172.1
October	128.7	27.8	100.9	43.9	172.6
November	128.7	27.8	100.9	44.2	172.9
December	128.8	27.7	101.1	44.5	173.3
1954					
January	129.0	27.7	101.3	44.8	173.8
February	129.1	27.7	101.5	45.2	174.3
March	129.2	27.6	101.6	45.6	174.8
April	128.6	27.6	101.0	46.1	174.7
May	129.7	27.6	102.1	46.5	176.2
June	129.9	27.5	102.3	46.8	176.7
July	130.3	27.5	102.8	47.3	177.6
August	130.7	27.5	103.2	47.8	178.5
September	130.9	27.4	103.5	47.9	178.8
October	131.5	27.4	104.1	48.1	179.6
November	132.1	27.4	104.7	48.2	180.3
December	132.3	27.4	104.9	48.3	180.6
1955					
January	133.0	27.4	105.6	48.5	181.5
February	133.9	27.5	106.4	48.7	182.6
March	133.6	27.5	106.0	48.8	182.4
April	133.9	27.5	106.3	49.0	182.9
May	134.6	27.6	107.0	49.0	183.6
June	134.4	27.6	106.8	49.2	183.6
July	134.8	27.7	107.2	49.3	184.1
August	134.8	27.7	107.0	49.3	184.1
September	135.0	27.7	107.3	49.6	184.6
October	135.2	27.8	107.4	49.7	184.9
November	134.9	27.8	107.1	49.9	184.8
December	135.2	27.8	107.4	50.0	185.2
1956					
January	135.5	27.9	107.7	49.9	185.4
February	135.5	27.9	107.7	49.9	185.4
March	135.7	27.9	107.8	50.1	185.8
April	136.0	27.9	108.1	50.3	186.3
May	135.8	27.9	107.9	50.4	186.2
June	136.0	27.9	108.1	50.7	186.7
July	136.0	28.0	108.0	50.9	186.9
August	135.7	28.0	107.8	51.2	186.9
September	136.2	28.0	108.2	51.5	187.7
October	136.3	28.0	108.2	51.6	187.9
November	136.6	28.1	108.4	51.8	188.4
December	136.9	28.2	108.7	51.9	188.8
1957					
January	136.9	28.2	108.6	52.6	189.5
February	136.8	28.2	108.6	53.1	189.9
March	136.9	28.2	108.7	53.7	190.6
April	136.9	28.2	108.7	54.0	190.9
May	137.0	28.2	108.8	54.5	191.5
June	136.9	28.3	108.6	54.8	191.7
July	137.0	28.3	108.7	55.3	192.3
August	137.1	28.3	108.8	55.7	192.8
September	136.8	28.3	108.4	56.1	192.9
October	136.5	28.3	108.2	56.6	193.1
November	136.3	28.3	108.0	57.0	193.3
December	135.9	28.3	107.6	57.4	193.3
1958					
January	135.5	28.3	107.2	57.6	193.1
February	136.2	28.2	107.9	59.2	195.4
March	136.5	28.2	108.3	60.5	197.0
April	137.0	28.2	108.7	61.5	198.5
May	137.5	28.3	109.2	62.3	199.8
June	138.4	28.3	110.1	63.2	201.6
July	138.4	28.4	110.0	64.0	202.4
August	139.1	28.4	110.7	64.6	203.7
September	139.5	28.5	111.1	64.8	204.3
October	140.1	28.5	111.6	64.9	205.0
November	140.9	28.5	112.4	65.2	206.1
December	141.1	28.6	112.6	65.4	206.5
1959					
January	142.2	28.7	113.5	66.3	208.5

Table 12-2. Components of Non-M1 M2

(Billions of dollars, seasonally adjusted; monthly data are averages of daily figures, annual data are for December.)

Year and month	Savings deposits			Small-denomination time deposits			Retail money funds	Total non-M1 M2
	At commercial banks	At thrift institutions	Total	At commercial banks	At thrift institutions	Total		
1960	58.3	100.8	159.1	9.7	2.8	12.5	. . .	171.7
1961	64.2	111.3	175.5	11.1	3.7	14.8	. . .	190.3
1962	71.3	123.4	194.8	15.5	4.6	20.1	. . .	214.9
1963	76.8	137.6	214.4	19.9	5.7	25.5	. . .	240.0
1964	82.9	152.4	235.2	22.4	6.8	29.2	. . .	264.4
1965	92.4	164.5	256.9	26.7	7.8	34.5	. . .	291.3
1966	89.9	163.3	253.1	38.7	16.3	55.0	. . .	308.1
1967	94.1	169.6	263.7	50.7	27.1	77.8	. . .	341.5
1968	96.1	172.8	268.9	63.5	37.1	100.5	. . .	369.4
1969	93.8	169.8	263.7	71.6	48.8	120.4	. . .	384.0
1970	98.6	162.3	261.0	79.3	71.9	151.2	. . .	412.1
1971	112.8	179.4	292.2	94.7	95.1	189.7	. . .	481.9
1972	124.8	196.6	321.4	108.2	123.5	231.6	. . .	553.0
1973	128.0	198.7	326.8	116.8	149.0	265.8	0.1	592.6
1974	136.8	201.8	338.6	123.1	164.8	287.9	1.4	627.9
1975	161.2	227.6	388.9	142.3	195.5	337.9	2.4	729.1
1976	201.8	251.4	453.2	155.5	235.2	390.7	1.8	845.8
1977	218.8	273.4	492.2	167.5	278.0	445.5	1.8	939.4
1978	216.5	265.4	481.9	185.1	335.8	521.0	5.8	1 008.7
1979	195.0	228.8	423.8	235.5	398.7	634.3	33.9	1 092.0
1980	185.7	214.5	400.3	286.2	442.3	728.5	62.5	1 191.3
1981	159.0	184.9	343.9	347.7	475.4	823.1	151.7	1 318.8
1982	190.1	210.0	400.1	379.9	471.0	850.9	180.1	1 431.1
1983	363.2	321.7	684.9	350.9	433.1	784.1	133.1	1 602.1
1984	389.3	315.4	704.7	387.9	500.9	888.8	161.4	1 754.8
1985	456.6	358.6	815.3	386.4	499.3	885.7	171.3	1 872.3
1986	533.5	407.4	940.9	369.4	489.0	858.4	204.1	2 003.3
1987	534.8	402.6	937.4	391.7	529.3	921.0	217.7	2 076.2
1988	542.4	383.9	926.4	451.2	585.9	1 037.1	238.0	2 201.5
1989	541.1	352.6	893.7	533.8	617.6	1 151.3	314.3	2 359.4
1990	581.3	341.6	922.9	610.7	562.6	1 173.3	349.8	2 445.9
1991	664.8	379.6	1 044.5	602.2	463.1	1 065.3	363.2	2 473.0
1992	754.2	433.1	1 187.2	508.1	359.7	867.7	342.0	2 396.9
1993	785.3	434.0	1 219.3	467.9	313.5	781.4	341.0	2 341.6
1994	752.8	398.5	1 151.3	503.6	313.9	817.5	361.9	2 330.6
1995	774.8	361.0	1 135.9	575.8	356.5	932.3	427.0	2 495.2
1996	906.0	368.7	1 274.8	594.2	353.7	947.9	498.1	2 720.8
1997	1 022.5	378.7	1 401.2	625.5	342.2	967.6	572.7	2 941.5
1998	1 187.4	416.1	1 603.6	626.4	324.9	951.3	703.4	3 258.3
1999	1 288.9	451.2	1 740.2	636.9	318.3	955.2	795.7	3 491.1
2000	1 425.3	454.3	1 879.6	700.8	345.3	1 046.1	884.5	3 810.2
2001	1 740.3	571.2	2 311.6	636.0	338.5	974.6	930.7	4 216.8
2002	2 057.9	713.1	2 771.0	591.3	303.5	894.7	850.3	4 516.0
2003	2 335.1	823.9	3 159.0	541.9	276.2	818.1	748.3	4 725.4
2004	2 633.6	873.0	3 506.6	552.3	276.1	828.4	672.7	5 007.7
2005	2 776.4	825.2	3 601.6	647.2	346.5	993.7	676.8	5 272.1
2006	2 911.9	779.9	3 691.9	781.4	424.6	1 206.0	769.9	5 667.9
2007	3 041.0	823.4	3 864.4	859.5	416.5	1 276.0	920.8	6 061.2
2008	3 320.7	765.2	4 085.9	1 079.6	378.0	1 457.6	1 009.7	6 553.2
2009	3 977.0	833.0	4 810.0	868.9	319.0	1 187.8	768.6	6 766.4
2010	4 411.2	919.4	5 330.7	662.3	270.4	932.7	665.9	6 929.3
2011	5 037.4	996.4	6 033.8	546.8	228.5	775.3	656.2	7 465.4
2012	5 728.7	956.5	6 685.2	466.8	176.7	643.5	636.5	7 965.3
2013	6 110.8	1 021.1	7 131.9	423.1	144.2	567.3	634.0	8 333.1
2014	6 501.4	1 078.7	7 580.1	387.5	131.5	519.1	615.7	8 714.9
2015	7 034.7	1 145.2	8 179.9	298.6	109.9	408.5	639.4	9 227.8
2016	7 567.2	1 260.0	8 827.1	246.7	100.2	346.9	680.0	9 854.1
2015								
January	6 557.8	1 086.4	7 644.2	383.7	130.2	513.9	613.5	8 771.6
February	6 616.6	1 094.4	7 710.9	382.4	127.9	510.3	610.2	8 831.4
March	6 647.5	1 095.3	7 742.9	374.4	125.9	500.3	608.6	8 851.8
April	6 696.9	1 103.7	7 800.6	365.7	125.3	491.1	608.2	8 899.8
May	6 742.7	1 117.9	7 860.6	357.1	124.3	481.4	602.8	8 944.8
June	6 760.1	1 121.2	7 881.3	349.8	123.3	473.2	605.5	8 960.0
July	6 811.0	1 119.9	7 931.0	337.7	122.0	459.8	607.9	8 998.7
August	6 870.8	1 122.1	7 992.9	324.5	121.9	446.4	612.4	9 051.7
September	6 919.7	1 125.6	8 045.3	308.3	121.1	429.4	621.9	9 096.6
October	6 959.2	1 135.8	8 095.0	301.5	119.8	421.2	620.4	9 136.6
November	7 004.6	1 133.5	8 138.1	303.3	111.9	415.1	623.6	9 176.8
December	7 034.7	1 145.2	8 179.9	298.6	109.9	408.5	639.4	9 227.8
2016								
January	7 059.5	1 158.5	8 218.0	294.9	109.0	403.9	716.0	9 337.9
February	7 089.9	1 172.8	8 262.7	291.3	108.5	399.8	727.3	9 389.9
March	7 131.6	1 183.9	8 315.5	285.4	108.5	393.9	714.8	9 424.2
April	7 176.8	1 194.9	8 371.7	281.0	108.4	389.4	707.0	9 468.1
May	7 195.6	1 210.4	8 405.9	278.2	107.5	385.7	704.8	9 496.4
June	7 273.0	1 215.5	8 488.5	275.9	106.8	382.7	693.6	9 564.8
July	7 342.4	1 223.3	8 565.6	272.2	106.4	378.7	685.3	9 629.7
August	7 365.6	1 228.5	8 594.1	265.4	106.4	371.8	669.4	9 635.3
September	7 440.9	1 232.3	8 673.2	260.6	105.7	366.3	652.2	9 691.8
October	7 471.1	1 243.8	8 714.9	256.1	104.4	360.5	659.7	9 735.2
November	7 518.4	1 249.6	8 768.0	251.5	102.4	353.9	681.2	9 803.1
December	7 567.2	1 260.0	8 827.1	246.7	100.2	346.9	680.0	9 854.1

. . . = Not available.

Table 12-3. Aggregate Reserves, Monetary Base, and FR Balance Sheet

(Millions of dollars; through May 2013, total, nonborrowed, and required reserves and monetary base adjusted for seasonality and changes in reserve requirements; annual data are for December.)

Year and month	Reserves					Monetary base	Federal Reserve balance sheet: total assets
	Total	Nonborrowed	Nonborrowed plus extended credit [1]	Required	Excess reserves		
1965	12 316	11 872	11 872	11 892	423	49 620	. . .
1966	12 223	11 690	11 690	11 884	339	51 565	. . .
1967	13 180	12 952	12 952	12 805	375	54 579	. . .
1968	13 767	13 021	13 021	13 341	426	58 357	. . .
1969	14 168	13 049	13 049	13 882	286	61 569	. . .
1970	14 558	14 225	14 225	14 309	249	65 013	. . .
1971	15 230	15 104	15 104	15 049	182	69 108	. . .
1972	16 645	15 595	15 595	16 361	284	75 167	. . .
1973	17 021	15 723	15 723	16 717	304	81 073	. . .
1974	17 550	16 823	16 970	17 292	258	87 535	. . .
1975	17 822	17 692	17 704	17 556	266	93 887	. . .
1976	18 388	18 335	18 335	18 115	274	101 515	. . .
1977	18 990	18 420	18 420	10 000	190	110 324	. . .
1978	19 753	18 885	18 885	19 521	232	120 445	. . .
1979	20 720	19 248	19 248	20 279	442	131 143	. . .
1980	22 015	20 325	20 328	21 501	514	142 004	. . .
1981	22 443	21 807	21 956	22 124	319	149 021	. . .
1982	23 600	22 966	23 152	23 100	500	160 127	. . .
1983	25 367	24 593	24 595	24 806	561	175 467	. . .
1984	26 913	23 727	26 331	26 078	835	187 253	. . .
1985	31 569	30 251	30 749	30 505	1 064	203 556	. . .
1986	38 841	38 014	38 317	37 667	1 174	223 417	. . .
1987	38 913	38 136	38 618	37 893	1 020	239 830	. . .
1988	40 454	38 738	39 982	39 392	1 062	256 897	. . .
1989	40 487	40 222	40 241	39 545	942	267 761	. . .
1990	41 767	41 441	41 463	40 101	1 665	293 339	. . .
1991	45 516	45 324	45 325	44 526	990	317 523	. . .
1992	54 422	54 298	54 298	53 267	1 155	350 885	. . .
1993	60 567	60 485	60 484	59 497	1 070	386 720	. . .
1994	59 466	59 257	59 257	58 295	1 171	418 474	. . .
1995	56 484	56 226	56 226	55 193	1 291	434 645	. . .
1996	50 185	50 030	50 030	48 766	1 419	451 935	. . .
1997	46 876	46 551	46 551	45 189	1 687	479 798	. . .
1998	45 174	45 058	45 053	43 662	1 513	513 821	. . .
1999	42 149	41 829	41 787	40 855	1 295	593 383	. . .
2000	38 685	38 475	38 465	37 359	1 326	584 928	. . .
2001	41 384	41 317	41 338	39 740	1 643	635 575	. . .
2002	40 275	40 195	40 207	38 267	2 008	681 486	. . .
2003	42 542	42 496	. . .	41 495	1 047	720 115	. . .
2004	46 425	46 362	. . .	44 517	1 908	759 085	. . .
2005	44 963	44 795	. . .	43 063	1 900	787 369	. . .
2006	43 124	42 933	. . .	41 261	1 863	812 367	. . .
2007	43 133	27 702	. . .	41 348	1 785	824 809	890 662
2008	820 187	166 621	. . .	52 868	767 318	1 654 974	2 239 457
2009	1 138 682	968 755	. . .	63 483	1 075 199	2 019 228	2 234 067
2010	1 077 359	1 031 871	. . .	70 723	1 006 636	2 011 078	2 420 570
2011	1 597 100	1 587 574	. . .	94 894	1 502 206	2 612 081	2 926 095
2012	1 569 017	1 568 221	. . .	110 266	1 458 751	2 672 578	2 907 300
2012							
January	1 614 301	1 605 687	. . .	94 850	1 519 451	2 638 114	2 919 545
February	1 657 931	1 649 998	. . .	97 811	1 560 121	2 690 184	2 925 722
March	1 607 819	1 600 490	. . .	98 226	1 509 593	2 648 070	2 878 137
April	1 584 770	1 577 905	. . .	98 593	1 486 176	2 631 478	2 866 561
May	1 556 689	1 550 503	. . .	99 230	1 457 460	2 609 131	2 842 654
June	1 557 175	1 551 961	. . .	99 699	1 457 475	2 615 664	2 863 547
July	1 584 049	1 579 791	. . .	101 000	1 483 049	2 649 396	2 846 757
August	1 582 288	1 579 017	. . .	104 538	1 477 750	2 654 458	2 812 806
September	1 515 888	1 513 923	. . .	106 447	1 409 441	2 597 251	2 804 457
October	1 525 145	1 523 679	. . .	106 870	1 418 275	2 615 620	2 823 137
November	1 546 809	1 545 758	. . .	111 505	1 435 304	2 643 297	2 851 362
December	1 569 017	1 568 221	. . .	110 266	1 458 751	2 672 578	2 907 300
2013							
January	1 630 872	1 630 307	. . .	111 413	1 519 460	2 740 902	3 008 704
February	1 731 409	1 730 944	. . .	114 621	1 616 788	2 843 658	3 090 600
March	1 813 069	1 812 675	. . .	114 915	1 698 154	2 929 464	3 202 256
April	1 882 385	1 881 984	. . .	113 551	1 768 834	3 004 480	3 318 649
May	1 980 436	1 980 025	. . .	117 090	1 863 346	3 109 893	3 385 128
BREAK IN SERIES: FOLLOWING DATA NOT SEASONALLY ADJUSTED. SEE NOTES AND DEFINITIONS							
May	1 930 723	1 981 574	. . .	67 375	1 863 348	3 116 932	3 385 128
June	2 010 604	2 062 555	. . .	63 667	1 946 937	3 201 472	3 478 672
July	2 094 225	2 147 346	. . .	63 296	2 030 929	3 290 898	3 571 797
August	2 199 056	2 252 314	. . .	65 189	2 133 867	3 398 930	3 644 456
September	2 281 080	2 333 577	. . .	67 208	2 213 872	3 486 917	3 734 018
October	2 374 958	2 427 559	. . .	66 713	2 308 245	3 589 503	3 843 396
November	2 463 012	2 516 872	. . .	70 483	2 392 529	3 684 554	3 925 876
December	2 485 248	2 540 848	. . .	69 029	2 416 219	3 717 466	4 032 575

[1]Extended credit program discontinued January 9, 2003. See notes and definitions for more information.
. . . = Not available.

Table 12-4. Derivation of U.S. Net Wealth

(Billions of dollars, amounts outstanding at end of period, not seasonally adjusted.)

Year and month	Household Net Worth[1]	Growth of nonfinacial debt[2]				State and local governments
		Total	Households	Business	Federal	
2003	49 426	8.0	11.8	2.2	10.9	8.3
2004	56 581	9.3	11.1	6.8	9.0	11.4
2005	61 789	8.6	10.6	8.1	6.6	5.8
2006	66 184	8.4	10.5	9.8	3.9	4.4
2007	66 499	8.1	7.2	12.4	4.7	6.0
2008	56 191	5.8	0.1	5.9	21.4	1.2
2009	57 953	3.6	0.4	-4.0	20.4	4.4
2010	62 100	4.4	-0.4	-0.7	18.5	2.4
2011	63 390	3.5	-0.4	2.7	10.8	-1.5
2012	69 240	5.0	2.0	4.6	10.1	-0.2
2013	78 904	3.8	1.8	4.6	6.7	-1.8
2014	83 884	4.3	3.0	6.1	5.4	-1.1
2015	87 287	4.4	2.8	6.8	5.9	0.3
2016	92 805	4.7	4.6	5.7	5.6	1.0
2014						
1st Quarter	80 623	4.2	2.1	6.4	5.7	-1.7
2nd Quarter	82 218	4.3	5.2	5.3	3.5	0.1
3rd Quarter	82 513	4.5	3.0	6.1	6.0	-1.7
4th Quarter	84 201	4.4	2.2	6.1	5.9	1.5
2015						
1st Quarter	85 798	2.7	2.0	7.4	-0.3	1.6
2nd Quarter	86 434	4.4	3.8	8.0	2.1	0.2
3rd Quarter	85 249	2.7	1.3	5.5	2.1	0.2
4th Quarter	87 287	7.8	3.8	5.6	15.4	-1.2
2016						
1st Quarter	87 889	5.3	2.3	9.4	5.6	0.7
2nd Quarter	88 708	4.3	4.3	4.0	5.0	2.2
3rd Quarter	90 762	5.8	3.9	6.3	8.2	0.7
4th Quarter	92 805	2.9	3.8	2.6	2.9	0.2

[1]Amounts outstanding at the end of the period, not seasonally adjusted.
[2]Percentage changes calculated as seasonally adjusted flow divided by previous quarter's seasonally adjusted level, shown as an annual rate.

Table 12-5. Consumer Credit

(Outstanding at end of period, billions of dollars.)

Year and month	Seasonally adjusted			Not seasonally adjusted						
	Total	By major credit type		Total 1	By major holder					
		Revolving	Non-revolving		Depository institutions	Finance companies 2	Credit unions	Federal government 2	Nonfinancial businesses	Securitized pools 3
1965	96.0	...	96.0	97.5	49.1	23.9	6.5	0.0	18.1	0.0
1966	101.8	...	101.8	103.4	52.2	24.8	7.5	0.0	19.0	0.0
1967	106.8	...	106.8	108.6	55.8	24.6	8.3	0.0	19.9	0.0
1968	117.4	2.0	115.4	119.3	62.7	26.1	9.7	0.0	20.8	0.0
1969	127.2	3.6	123.6	129.2	67.8	27.8	11.7	0.0	21.9	0.0
1970	131.6	5.0	126.6	133.7	70.1	27.6	13.0	0.0	23.0	0.0
1971	146.9	8.2	138.7	149.2	79.0	29.2	14.8	0.0	26.2	0.0
1972	166.2	9.4	156.8	168.8	92.1	31.9	17.0	0.0	27.8	0.0
1973	190.1	11.3	178.7	193.0	108.1	35.4	19.6	0.0	29.8	0.0
1974	198.9	13.2	185.7	201.9	112.1	36.1	21.9	0.0	31.8	0.0
1975	204.0	14.5	189.5	207.0	116.2	32.6	25.7	0.0	32.6	0.0
1976	225.7	16.5	209.2	229.0	128.9	33.7	31.2	0.0	35.2	0.0
1977	260.0	37.4	223.1	264.9	152.1	37.3	37.6	0.5	37.4	0.0
1978	306.1	45.7	260.4	311.3	179.6	44.4	45.2	0.9	41.2	0.0
1979	348.6	53.6	295.0	354.6	205.7	55.4	47.4	1.5	44.6	0.0
1980	351.9	55.0	297.0	358.0	202.9	62.2	44.1	2.6	46.2	0.0
1981	371.3	60.9	310.4	377.9	208.2	70.1	46.7	4.8	48.1	0.0
1982	389.8	66.3	323.5	396.7	217.5	75.3	48.8	6.4	48.7	0.0
1983	437.1	79.0	358.0	444.9	245.2	83.3	56.1	4.6	55.7	0.0
1984	517.3	100.4	416.9	526.6	303.1	89.9	67.9	5.6	60.2	0.0
1985	599.7	124.5	475.2	610.6	354.8	111.7	74.0	6.8	63.3	0.0
1986	654.8	141.1	513.7	666.4	383.1	134.0	77.1	8.2	64.0	0.0
1987	686.3	160.9	525.5	698.6	399.4	140.0	81.0	10.0	68.1	0.0
1988	731.9	184.6	547.3	745.2	427.6	144.7	88.3	13.2	71.4	0.0
1989	794.6	211.2	583.4	809.3	445.8	138.9	91.7	16.0	69.6	47.3
1990	808.2	238.6	569.6	824.4	431.6	133.4	91.6	19.2	71.9	76.7
1991	798.0	263.8	534.3	815.6	412.3	121.6	90.3	21.1	67.3	103.0
1992	806.1	278.4	527.7	824.8	400.3	118.1	91.7	24.2	70.3	120.3
1993	865.7	309.9	555.7	886.2	433.6	116.1	101.6	27.2	77.2	130.5
1994	997.3	365.6	631.7	1 021.2	497.2	134.4	119.6	37.2	86.6	146.1
1995	1 140.7	443.9	696.8	1 168.2	542.4	152.1	131.9	43.5	85.1	213.1
1996	1 253.4	507.5	745.9	1 273.9	572.2	154.9	144.1	51.4	77.7	273.5
1997	1 324.8	540.0	784.8	1 344.2	562.2	167.5	152.4	57.2	84.4	320.5
1998	1 421.0	581.4	839.6	1 441.3	564.4	183.3	155.4	64.9	79.3	393.9
1999	1 531.1	610.7	920.4	1 553.6	569.5	201.6	167.9	81.8	76.1	456.7
2000	1 717.0	682.6	1 034.3	1 741.3	615.8	234.4	184.4	96.7	81.5	528.4
2001	1 867.9	714.8	1 153.0	1 891.8	639.5	280.0	189.6	111.9	73.1	597.8
2002	1 972.1	750.9	1 221.2	1 997.0	671.3	307.5	195.7	117.3	74.8	630.4
2003	2 077.4	768.3	1 309.1	2 102.9	747.3	393.0	205.9	102.9	59.1	594.8
2004	2 192.2	799.6	1 392.7	2 220.1	795.6	492.3	215.4	86.1	59.2	571.5
2005	2 290.9	829.5	1 461.4	2 320.6	816.1	516.5	228.6	89.8	59.6	609.9
2006	2 456.7	923.9	1 532.8	2 456.7	836.7	534.9	236.1	108.7	48.3	617.2
2007	2 609.5	1 001.6	1 607.9	2 609.5	894.9	577.9	236.6	115.7	49.4	652.5
2008	2 643.8	1 004.0	1 639.8	2 643.8	965.0	561.4	236.2	135.2	46.9	610.2
2009	2 555.0	916.1	1 638.9	2 555.0	906.3	480.8	237.1	232.6	43.2	572.5
2010	2 646.8	839.1	1 807.7	2 646.8	1 185.5	705.0	226.5	363.8	44.4	50.3
2011	2 757.8	841.1	1 916.7	2 757.8	1 192.6	687.6	223.0	494.8	46.6	46.2
2012	2 919.7	845.2	2 074.5	2 919.7	1 218.6	679.8	243.6	622.2	47.4	50.0
2013	3 095.6	857.1	2 238.5	3 095.6	1 271.6	679.1	265.6	735.5	42.8	49.1
2014	3 317.4	891.1	2 426.4	3 317.4	1 343.1	684.1	302.8	846.2	43.8	49.8
2015	3 537.5	938.8	2 598.7	3 537.5	1 428.3	681.7	342.3	949.7	44.6	46.0
2016	3 765.8	998.7	2 767.1	3 765.8	1 532.1	668.4	380.3	1 049.3	43.8	50.0
2015										
January	3 331.5	891.5	2 440.0	3 326.9	1 327.6	680.2	304.5	874.8	43.6	48.9
February	3 350.5	892.3	2 458.2	3 315.5	1 310.0	677.6	307.8	881.7	43.1	48.2
March	3 373.2	898.4	2 474.8	3 322.7	1 312.1	677.5	307.7	887.3	43.0	48.2
April	3 394.0	904.6	2 489.4	3 346.7	1 328.1	678.3	312.3	890.0	43.2	48.3
May	3 412.1	906.9	2 505.2	3 369.4	1 338.6	680.1	315.7	895.4	44.9	48.5
June	3 436.8	912.8	2 524.0	3 398.1	1 349.6	682.1	322.7	901.4	45.0	51.2
July	3 455.0	916.3	2 538.7	3 415.2	1 359.5	683.2	327.2	904.2	45.2	50.0
August	3 468.3	919.3	2 549.0	3 451.5	1 373.3	684.9	330.2	923.0	45.6	48.6
September	3 495.8	925.5	2 570.3	3 482.0	1 383.6	689.3	333.4	936.5	45.7	48.0
October	3 511.4	927.6	2 583.8	3 492.9	1 390.4	687.9	335.5	942.8	43.6	47.4
November	3 530.4	933.6	2 596.7	3 509.8	1 407.9	684.6	337.1	944.5	43.9	46.7
December	3 537.5	938.8	2 598.7	3 537.5	1 428.3	681.7	342.3	949.7	44.6	46.0
2016										
January	3 554.4	940.9	2 613.5	3 549.3	1 413.6	677.9	345.9	977.9	43.7	45.5
February	3 568.2	942.2	2 625.9	3 532.4	1 398.2	670.6	347.5	983.5	43.1	44.9
March	3 592.5	953.2	2 639.4	3 541.5	1 405.8	669.4	345.1	989.7	42.6	44.4
April	3 612.2	955.9	2 656.4	3 564.9	1 417.4	667.7	353.9	993.3	42.7	45.7
May	3 633.1	960.3	2 672.8	3 590.4	1 432.0	667.1	360.6	996.8	42.8	47.1
June	3 647.8	968.1	2 679.7	3 609.5	1 446.6	666.8	359.6	1 001.1	42.9	48.7
July	3 664.8	971.2	2 693.6	3 625.6	1 455.8	665.8	362.8	1 005.1	42.9	49.5
August	3 689.9	976.8	2 713.1	3 673.5	1 473.1	670.9	369.6	1 023.2	43.2	50.2
September	3 708.0	980.7	2 727.3	3 695.0	1 475.7	673.4	372.2	1 036.7	43.1	50.8
October	3 729.2	984.2	2 745.0	3 711.2	1 481.5	671.5	378.8	1 042.9	43.1	50.6
November	3 754.4	997.0	2 757.4	3 735.8	1 505.2	670.3	380.3	1 044.2	43.2	50.2
December	3 765.8	998.7	2 767.1	3 765.8	1 532.1	668.4	380.3	1 049.3	43.8	50.0

1Includes nonprofit and educational institutions, not shown.
2Student Loan Marketing Association (Sallie Mae) included in federal government sector until end of 2004, and in finance companies since then.
3Outstanding balances of pools upon which securities have been issued; these balances are no longer carried on the balance sheets of the loan originators.
. . . = Not available.

Table 12-6. Selected Stock and Housing Market Data

Year and month	Stock price indexes			FHFA House Price Indexes			
				House Price Index (purchases and refinance)		Purchase-Only Index	
	Dow Jones industrials (30 stocks)	Standard and Poor's composite (500 stocks) (1941–1943 = 10)	Nasdaq composite (Feb. 5, 1971 = 100)	Level at end of period (1980:I = 100)	Appreciation from same quarter one year earlier (percent)	Level at end of period (1991:I = 100)	Appreciation from same quarter one year earlier (percent)
1965	910.88	88.17	. . .	. . .	. . .	. . .	. . .
1966	873.60	85.26	. . .	. . .	. . .	. . .	. . .
1967	879.12	91.93	. . .	. . .	. . .	. . .	. . .
1968	906.00	98.70	. . .	. . .	. . .	. . .	. . .
1969	876.72	97.84	. . .	. . .	. . .	. . .	. . .
1970	753.19	83.22	. . .	. . .	. . .	. . .	. . .
1971	884.76	98.29	107.44	. . .	. . .	. . .	. . .
1972	950.71	109.20	128.52	. . .	. . .	. . .	. . .
1973	923.88	107.43	109.90	. . .	. . .	. . .	. . .
1974	759.37	82.85	76.29	. . .	. . .	. . .	. . .
1975	802.49	86.16	77.20	62.35	. . .	. . .	. . .
1976	974.92	102.01	89.90	67.26	7.87	. . .	. . .
1977	894.63	98.20	98.71	77.20	14.78	. . .	. . .
1978	820.23	96.02	117.53	87.45	13.28	. . .	. . .
1979	844.40	103.01	136.57	98.23	12.33	. . .	. . .
1980	891.41	118.78	168.61	104.74	6.63	. . .	. . .
1981	932.92	128.05	203.18	109.12	4.18	. . .	. . .
1982	884.36	119.71	188.97	112.23	2.85	. . .	. . .
1983	1 190.34	160.41	285.43	117.02	4.27	. . .	. . .
1984	1 178.48	160.46	248.88	122.47	4.66	. . .	. . .
1985	1 328.23	186.84	290.19	129.47	5.72	. . .	. . .
1986	1 792.76	236.34	366.96	138.86	7.25	. . .	. . .
1987	2 275.99	286.83	402.57	146.36	5.40	. . .	. . .
1988	2 060.82	265.79	374.43	154.59	5.62	. . .	. . .
1989	2 508.91	322.84	437.81	163.24	5.60	. . .	. . .
1990	2 678.94	334.59	409.17	165.18	1.19	. . .	. . .
1991	2 929.33	376.18	491.69	170.33	3.12	101.47	. . .
1992	3 284.29	415.74	599.26	174.45	2.42	104.24	2.73
1993	3 522.06	451.41	715.16	179.07	2.65	107.09	2.73
1994	3 793.77	460.42	751.65	181.90	1.58	110.15	2.86
1995	4 493.76	541.72	925.19	190.19	4.56	113.08	2.66
1996	5 742.89	670.50	1 164.96	195.03	2.54	116.24	2.79
1997	7 441.15	873.43	1 469.49	203.65	4.42	120.08	3.30
1998	8 625.52	1 085.50	1 794.91	213.96	5.06	126.92	5.70
1999	10 464.88	1 327.33	2 728.15	224.51	4.93	134.78	6.19
2000	10 734.90	1 427.22	3 783.67	240.41	7.08	144.20	6.99
2001	10 189.13	1 194.18	2 035.00	257.50	7.11	153.92	6.74
2002	9 226.43	993.94	1 539.73	274.75	6.70	165.72	7.67
2003	8 993.59	965.23	1 647.17	293.87	6.96	178.72	7.84
2004	10 317.39	1 130.65	1 986.53	324.15	10.30	196.82	10.13
2005	10 547.67	1 207.06	2 099.03	360.51	11.22	216.86	10.18
2006	11 408.67	1 310.67	2 265.17	376.85	4.53	223.27	2.96
2007	13 169.98	1 476.66	2 577.12	372.65	-1.11	217.50	-2.58
2008	11 252.61	1 220.89	2 162.46	346.29	-7.07	195.66	-10.04
2009	8 876.15	946.73	1 841.03	328.20	-5.22	190.92	-2.42
2010	10 662.80	1 139.31	2 347.70	322.08	-1.86	183.25	-4.02
2011	11 966.36	1 268.89	2 680.42	311.59	-3.26	178.92	-2.36
2012	12 967.08	1 379.56	2 965.77	313.62	0.65	187.99	5.07
2013	14 999.67	1 642.51	3 537.69	328.35	4.70	201.56	7.22
2014	16 773.99	1 930.67	4 374.31	345.65	5.27	211.32	4.84
2015	17 590.61	2 061.20	4 943.49	364.75	5.53	223.77	5.89
2016	17 908.08	2 092.39	4 982.49	385.67	5.74	237.73	6.24
2015							
January	17 542.26	2 028.18	4 673.70	. . .	. . .	. . .	. . .
February	17 945.41	2 082.20	4 854.26	. . .	. . .	. . .	. . .
March	17 931.75	2 079.99	4 938.01	349.12	5.37	213.01	5.14
April	17 970.51	2 094.86	4 985.95	. . .	. . .	. . .	. . .
May	18 124.71	2 111.94	5 029.43	. . .	. . .	. . .	. . .
June	17 927.22	2 099.28	5 073.04	355.55	5.26	220.59	5.56
July	17 795.02	2 094.14	5 082.81	. . .	. . .	. . .	. . .
August	17 061.59	2 039.87	4 934.62	. . .	. . .	. . .	. . .
September	16 339.95	1 944.40	4 748.00	361.35	5.42	223.38	5.60
October	17 182.28	2 024.81	4 879.04	. . .	. . .	. . .	. . .
November	17 723.77	2 080.62	5 082.51	. . .	. . .	. . .	. . .
December	17 542.86	2 054.08	5 040.54	364.75	5.53	223.77	5.89
2016							
January	16 305.25	1 918.60	4 610.71	. . .	. . .	. . .	. . .
February	16 299.90	1 904.42	4 463.21	. . .	. . .	. . .	. . .
March	17 302.14	2 021.95	4 754.48	368.39	5.52	225.93	6.07
April	17 844.37	2 075.54	4 892.17	. . .	. . .	. . .	. . .
May	17 692.32	2 065.55	4 788.24	. . .	. . .	. . .	. . .
June	17 754.87	2 083.89	4 856.23	375.81	5.70	233.62	5.91
July	18 341.18	2 148.90	5 023.99	. . .	. . .	. . .	. . .
August	18 495.19	2 177.48	5 217.04	. . .	. . .	. . .	. . .
September	18 267.40	2 157.69	5 254.15	382.36	5.81	237.32	6.24
October	18 184.55	2 143.02	5 255.99	. . .	. . .	. . .	. . .
November	18 697.33	2 164.99	5 260.57	. . .	. . .	. . .	. . .
December	19 712.42	2 246.63	5 413.12	385.67	5.74	237.73	6.24

. . . = Not available.

NOTES AND DEFINITIONS, CHAPTER 12

Most of the data in this chapter are found on the Federal Reserve Board Web site, <http://www.federalreserve.gov>. Current releases and most historical data are found at that site by selecting Economic Research & Data/Statistical Releases and Historical Data and then selecting the appropriate report. This is the location for all data not otherwise specified.

Historical data not found online are taken from two printed volumes of statistical data that were published by the Board of Governors of the Federal Reserve System: *Banking and Monetary Statistics*, 1943, and *Banking and Monetary Statistics, 1941-1970*, 1976. These will be referred to as *B&MS* 1943 and *B&MS* 1976.

Tables 12-1 and 12-2

Money Stock Measures and Components

SOURCE: BOARD OF GOVERNORS OF THE FEDERAL RESERVE SYSTEM

Estimates of two monetary aggregates (M1 and M2) and the components of these measures are published weekly. The monthly data are averages of daily figures.

The Federal Reserve Board ceased publication of the M3 aggregate on March 23, 2006. Weekly publication was also discontinued for the following components of M3: large-denomination time deposits, repurchase agreements (RPs), and Eurodollars. The Board continues to publish institutional money market mutual funds as a memorandum item in this release. Measures of large-denomination time deposits continue to be published in the Financial Accounts (Z.1 release) and in the H.8 release weekly for commercial banks.

The Board stated that "M3 does not appear to convey any additional information about economic activity that is not already embodied in M2 and has not played a role in the monetary policy process for many years. Consequently, the Board judged that the costs of collecting the underlying data and publishing M3 outweigh the benefits." ("Discontinuance of M3," H.6, Money Stock Measures [November 10, 2005, revised March 9, 2006]. [Accessed November 6, 2006.])

Definitions

M1 consists of (1) currency, (2) traveler's checks of nonbank issuers, (3) demand deposits, and (4) other checkable deposits.

M2 consists of M1 plus savings deposits (including money market deposit accounts), small denomination time deposits, and balances in retail money market mutual funds.

Currency consists of currency outside the U.S. Treasury, the Federal Reserve Banks, and the vaults of depository institutions.

Traveler's checks is the outstanding amount of U.S. dollar-denominated traveler's checks of nonbank issuers. Traveler's checks issued by depository institutions are included in demand deposits.

Demand deposits consists of demand deposits at domestically chartered commercial banks, U.S. branches and agencies of foreign banks, and Edge Act corporations (excluding those amounts held by depository institutions, the U.S. government, and foreign banks and official institutions) less cash items in the process of collection and Federal Reserve float. A "demand deposit" is a deposit that the depositor has a right to withdraw at any time without prior notice to the depository institution—most commonly, a checking account. "Federal Reserve float" is Federal Reserve credit that appears on the books of the depository institution of both the check writer and the check receiver while a check is being processed. This amount and cash items in the process of collection are subtracted to avoid double counting of deposits, so that they will not be counted both at the bank in which the check is deposited and at the bank on which the check is drawn.

Other checkable deposits at commercial banks consists of negotiable order of withdrawal (NOW) and automatic transfer service (ATS) balances at domestically chartered commercial banks, U.S. branches and agencies of foreign banks, and Edge Act corporations.

Other checkable deposits at thrift institutions consists of NOW and ATS balances at thrift institutions, credit union share draft balances, and demand deposits at thrift institutions.

Savings deposits includes money market deposit accounts and other savings deposits at *commercial banks* and *thrift institutions*.

Small time deposits are deposits issued at *commercial banks* and *thrift institutions* in amounts less than $100,000. All Individual Retirement Account (IRA) and Keogh account balances at commercial banks and thrift institutions are subtracted from small time deposits.

Retail money funds exclude IRA and Keogh account balances at money market mutual funds.

Institutional money funds are included in the money stock report for informational purposes only. They are not part of M1 or M2.

Notes on the data

Seasonal adjustment. Seasonally adjusted M1 is calculated by summing currency, traveler's checks, demand deposits, and other checkable deposits (each seasonally adjusted separately). Seasonally adjusted M2 is computed by adjusting each of its non-M1 components and then adding this result to seasonally adjusted M1.

Revisions. Money stock measures are revised frequently and have a benchmark and seasonal factor review in the middle of the year; this review typically extends back a number of years. The monetary aggregates were redefined in major revisions introduced in 1980.

Historical: January 1947–January 1959. These data are not currently maintained online and are found in *B&MS* 1976. They are not continuous with the current data series; for that reason the values for January 1959 are shown so that users can link to the current data. The *demand deposit component* includes demand deposits held in commercial banks by individuals, partnerships, and corporations both domestic and foreign, and demand deposits held by nonbank financial institutions and foreign banks. Note that this includes demand deposit liabilities to foreign governments, central banks, and international institutions—said to be "relatively small" in the source document. *Time deposits adjusted* is time and savings deposits at commercial banks, other than large negotiable certificates of deposit (CDs), and excluding all deposits due to the U.S. government and domestic commercial banks. The editor has added this to the *Money stock (M1)* to approximate *M2*, which is not shown as such in the source document, over this period.

Historical: 1892–1946. These data are from *B&MS* 1943 and *B&MS* 1976. They pertain only to the last day of June and, after 1922, the last day of December, the "call dates" on which banks reported to the federal government. For more data and analysis concerning monetary developments in this period, including monthly money supply estimates, see Milton Friedman and Anna Jacobson Schwartz, *A Monetary History of the United States, 1867–1960,* Princeton, Princeton University Press, 1963. In Table 12-1B, *Demand deposits adjusted* refers to the elimination of interbank and U.S. government deposits and cash items in process of collection, not to seasonal adjustment, which is not applicable to call report data because they are only reported once or twice a year. The editor has retitled as *M1* the "Total" money stock shown in the source document, and has added time deposits to it in order to approximate *M2*, which is not shown in the source document.

Data availability

Estimates are released weekly in Federal Reserve Statistical Release H.6, "Money Stock Measures." Current and historical data are available on the Federal Reserve Web site.

REFERENCES

Board of Governors of the Federal Reserve System, *The Federal Reserve System: Purposes and Functions,* available online at <http://www.federalreserve.gov> in the category "About the Fed/Features," includes a chapter discussing monetary policy and the monetary aggregates and a glossary of terms as an appendix.

An explanation of the 1980 redefinition of the monetary aggregates is found in the *Federal Reserve Bulletin* for February 1980.

TABLES 12-3

Aggregate Reserves, Monetary Base, and FR Balance Sheet

SOURCE: BOARD OF GOVERNORS OF THE FEDERAL RESERVE SYSTEM

New reporting basis, May 2013

In July 2013 the Federal Reserve Board issued a substantially revised format for reporting reserves of depository institutions and the monetary base. The revisions were made in response to the substantial growth in reserves undertaken beginning in 2008 to mitigate the effects of the financial crisis, and to recent changes in the administration of bank reserves. The concepts and procedures incorporated in the data through May 2013 in this volume and described below will not apply to the data that the Fed will be showing in the H.3 release going forward, which are shown in Table 12-3 for May through December 2013. Seasonally adjusted data—no longer relevant in a situation of vastly expanded reserves—are no longer published. Several new aggregates and interest rates are published to "give the public insight into how depository institutions collectively manage their reserves within the current framework for the implementation of monetary policy."

The new format enables calculations of concepts similar to "excess reserves," and a new simplified monetary base is nearly identical with the historical time series of that name; both are without seasonal adjustment, and are shown in Table 12-3.

Definitions for the data from May 2013 forward:

Values are shown in millions of dollars. Monthly data are prorated averages of biweekly averages.

Reserves, total equals total reserve balances maintained plus vault cash used to satisfy required reserves.

Nonborrowed reserves equals total reserves less total borrowings from the Federal Reserve.

Required reserves. Under the new reserve determination system, this is a data series now reported in the H.3 which represents the midpoint of a penalty-free band.

Excess reserves. This is no longer officially reported by the Federal Reserve because it "no longer aligns with the remuneration structure," and is no longer helpful in determining how depository institutions collectively manage their reserves; see "simplification of reserves administration," via links from "Frequently asked questions," in the H.3 portion of the Fed website. Excess reserves is calculated by the editors as total reserves minus required reserves.

Monetary base is defined as total balances maintained plus currency in circulation.

The series *Federal Reserve balance sheet: total assets* was introduced in the 14th edition of *Business Statistics*. It demonstrates the extent to which the Federal Reserve has, beginning in 2007, undertaken "quantitative easing"—direct purchases of financial assets—in addition to conventional easing, which has consisted of reducing short-term interest rates to near zero and supporting that rate level with purchases and sales of short-term securities on the open market. The balance sheet data are accessed on a different part of the Federal Reserve Web site—"Monetary Policy" instead of "Economic Research and Data"—which features an extensive explanation and discussion of the meaning and importance of this indicator. The balance sheet is reported in millions of dollars for each Wednesday, and is shown here with the last Wednesday of the month representing the month and the last Wednesday of December representing the year. These values are not adjusted for seasonal variation.

Federal Reserve balance sheet: total assets is total assets from the Consolidated Statement of Condition of All Federal Reserve Banks, which is reported each Wednesday. The last Wednesday of the month is used to represent the month, and the last Wednesday in December is used to represent the year. Currently, the principal components of total assets are Treasury, federal agency, and mortgage-backed securities. Other types of assets representing Federal Reserve credit extension, some of which have varied during the course of the crisis, have been repurchase agreements; term auction credit; portfolio holdings of various limited liability companies (LLCs) set up to manage assets taken over from other institutions; liquidity swaps with foreign central banks; and other loans, including traditional loans to member commercial banks made at the discount rate (see the definitions for Table 12-9). Total assets are equal to the sum of Federal Reserve liabilities and capital. The principal components of liabilities are Federal Reserve notes and the deposits of member banks representing their reserves.

For further information, see "Aggregate Reserves of Depository Institutions and the Monetary Base - H.3" at <www.federalreserve. gov> under Economic Research & Data/Statistical Releases and Historical Data.

Definitions for data for May 2013 and earlier

The data on reserves and the monetary base presented here are in millions of dollars, seasonally adjusted (with one exception), and adjusted for changes in reserve requirements ("break-adjusted") in order to provide a consistent gauge of the effect of Federal Reserve open-market operations. Break adjustment is required because an observed increase in reserves will not represent an easing in monetary conditions if it is simply equal to the increase in reserves required by the Federal Reserve. Therefore, the mandated increases and decreases are deducted to provide the break-adjusted series. Monthly data are averages of daily figures. Annual data are for December.

Total reserves consist of reserve balances with the Federal Reserve Banks plus vault cash used to satisfy reserve requirements. Seasonally adjusted, break-adjusted total reserves equal seasonally adjusted, break-adjusted required reserves plus unadjusted excess reserves.

Seasonally adjusted, break-adjusted *non-borrowed reserves* equal seasonally adjusted, break-adjusted total reserves less unadjusted total borrowings of depository institutions from the Federal Reserve.

Extended credit consisted of borrowing at the discount window under the terms and conditions established for the extended credit program to help depository institutions deal with sustained liquidity pressures. Since there was not the same need to repay such borrowing promptly as there was with traditional short-term adjustment credit, the money market impact of extended credit was similar to that of non-borrowed reserves. The extended credit program was significant in the 1980s but used infrequently in subsequent years. It ended with the 2002 revision of the discount window program, effective January 9, 2003.

To adjust *required reserves* for discontinuities due to regulatory changes in reserve requirements, a multiplicative procedure is used to estimate what required reserves would have been in past periods, had current reserve requirements been in effect. Break-adjusted required reserves include required reserves against transactions deposits and personal time and savings deposits (but not reservable nondeposit liabilities).

Excess reserves, not seasonally adjusted equals unadjusted total reserves less unadjusted required reserves.

The seasonally adjusted, break-adjusted *monetary base* consists of (1) seasonally adjusted, break-adjusted total reserves; plus (2) the seasonally adjusted currency component of the money stock; plus (3) the seasonally adjusted, break-adjusted difference between current vault cash and the amount applied to satisfy current reserve requirements for all quarterly reporters on the "Report of Transaction Accounts, Other Deposits and Vault Cash" and for all weekly reporters whose vault cash exceeds their required reserves.

Federal Reserve balance sheet: total assets is as defined above—it has not been changed by the new reserve calculating and reporting system.

Data availability

Reserve and monetary base data are released weekly in Federal Reserve Release H.3, "Aggregate Reserves of Depository Institutions and the Monetary Base." Current and historical data are available on the Federal Reserve Web site.

The Federal Reserve balance sheet appears each week in the H.4.1 release, Factors Affecting Reserve Balances, released each Thursday at 4:30 p.m., and available on the Federal Reserve Web site under Economic Research and Data/Statistical Releases and Historical Data. However, to obtain the full historical data for total assets, the user must go to Monetary policy/Credit and liquidity programs and the balance sheet/Recent balance sheet trends/Total assets/View as table/All/Copy data. Other explanatory material, including a monthly report on changes in these programs, is available at the Monetary policy location.

TABLE 12-4

Household Net Worth and Growth of Domestic Nonfinancial Debt

SOURCE: BOARD OF GOVERNORS OF THE FEDERAL RESERVE SYSTEM

The Z.1 "Financial Accounts of the United States" (FA), published by the Federal Reserve, are the U.S. national accounts and provides information on macro-financial flows and aggregate balance sheets for major sectors of the economy, including households, financial institutions, nonfinancial businesses, governments and the international sector. The basic framework of the FA allows understanding of the economic relationships underlying the major sections of the economy, as well as for monitoring the effects of macro-financial developments in the United States and globally.

The Federal Reserve Board announced on August 1, 2014 the Enhanced Financial Accounts (EFA) initiative which is an ambitious and long-term effort to enhance the "Financial Accounts" (FA) by providing additional detail and disaggregation, higher-frequency data, and additional documentation and analysis of financial data, in order to improve the picture of financial intermediation and activity in the United States. These large-scale and fundamental improvements will expand the detail, dimensionality, and scope of the FA in order to improve the overall picture of financial intermediation and activity in the United States.

Definitions and notes on the data

Researchers and analysts have used the FA to investigates the causes and consequences of the financial crisis and to create and analyze indicators of financial stability. However, they were not originally designed to be a comprehensive source of data for all the complex financial relationships and transactions whose importance to the macro-economy were made clear during the financial crisis of 2007–2009.

A new table on the derivation on U.S. net wealth has been added to the summary section of the "Financial Accounts." The calculation of U.S. net wealth (table 12.4), Household Net Worth and Growth of Domestic Nonfinancial Debt, includes the value of nonfinancial assets (real estate, equipment, intellectual property products, consumer durables and inventories) held by households and nonprofit organizations and noncorporate businesses. The measure of U.S. net wealth includes the market value of domestic nonfinancial and financial corporations and is adjusted to reflect U.S. financial claims on the rest of the world.

Taking all this together, we define net U.S wealth as the value of tangible assets controlled by households and nonprofits, noncorporate business, and government sectors of the U.S. economy, plus the market value of domestic nonfinancial and financial corporations, net of U.S. financial obligations to the rest of the world.

The concept of *U.S. net wealth* ignores all domestic financial intermediation and just counts the value of the land, machines, houses, cars, etc., plus intangible wealth but does not include financial wealth.

Household net worth is the value of net worth for the household and nonprofit organizations sector, as reported on table B.101 in the *Financial Accounts*. Net worth is calculated as the difference between a sector's total assets, including both financial and nonfinancial assets, and liabilities (debts owed to other sectors) and does include financial wealth.

*Noncorporate business*es includes both sole proprietorships and partnerships, including noncorporate farms.

Debt equates to the sum of debt securities and loans.

Domestic Nonfinancial entities include households, corporations, nonfarm noncorporate businesses, farm business, federal, state and local governments.

Domestic Nonfinancial assets include housing, property, automobiles, equipment, business equity, intellectual properties such as patents, copyrights and trademarks.

Firms are designated as *nonfinancial* if their 4-digit Standard Industry Classification (SIC) code is below 6000 or at or above 7000. This system identifies establishments by the principal activity in which they are engaged.

For corporate *businesses,* wealth is the market value of their outstanding equity shares and is used to better capture the value of intangible assets, such as intellectual property.

A *corporation* is formed under state law by the filing of articles of incorporation with the state.

Federal Government consists of all federal government agencies and funds included in the unified budget. However, the

District of Columbia government is included in the state and local sector.

State and Local Governments assets are measured by the value of their holdings at replacement (current) cost as reported by the Bureau of Economic Analysis (BEA). These nonfinancial assets include structures, equipment and intellectual property products.

Nonprofits includes private foundations and organizations that are tax-exempt under Sections 501(c)(3) through 501(c)(9) of the Internal Revenue Code. Does not include religious organizations or organizations with less than $25,000 in gross annual receipts.

Revision

Data shown for the most recent quarters are based on preliminary and potentially incomplete information. Nonetheless, when source data are revised or estimation methods are improved, all data are subject to revision. There is no specific revision schedule; rather, data are revised on an ongoing basis.

Data availability

The "Financial Accounts" are published online and in print four times per year, about 10 weeks following the end of each calendar quarter. The publication with series mnemonics and the guide are available online: www.federalreserve.gov/releases/Z1.

Table 12-5

Consumer Credit

SOURCE: BOARD OF GOVERNORS OF THE FEDERAL RESERVE SYSTEM

The consumer credit series cover most-short and intermedia-teterm credit extended to individuals through regular business channels, excluding loans secured by real estate (such as first and second mortgages and home equity credit). In October 2003, the scope of this survey was expanded to incorporate student loans extended by the federal government and by SLM Holding Corporation (SLM), the parent company of Sallie Mae (Student Loan Marketing Association). The historical data have been revised back to 1977 to reflect this inclusion.

Consumer credit is categorized by major types of credit and by major holders.

Definitions and notes on the data

The major types of consumer credit are *revolving* and *nonrevolving*.

Revolving credit includes credit arising from purchases on credit card plans of retail stores and banks, cash advances and check credit plans of banks, and some overdraft credit arrangements.

Nonrevolving credit includes automobile loans, mobile home loans, and all other loans not included in revolving credit, such as loans for education, boats, trailers, or vacations. These loans may be secured or unsecured.

Debt secured by real estate (including first liens, junior liens, and home equity loans) is excluded. Credit extended to governmental agencies and nonprofit or charitable organizations, as well as credit extended to business or to individuals exclusively for business purposes, is excluded.

Categories of *holders* include *U.S.-chartered depository institutions* (comprising commercial banks and savings institutions), *finance companies, credit unions, federal government, nonprofit and educational institutions, nonfinancial businesses*, and *pools of securitized assets*. The Student Loan Marketing Association (Sallie Mae) is included in "Federal government" until the end of 2004, at which time it became fully privatized. Beginning with the end of 2004, Sallie Mae is included in "Finance companies." Retailers and gasoline companies are included in the nonfinancial businesses category.

Federal government includes student loans originated by the Department of Education under the Federal Direct Loan Program and the Perkins Loan Program, as well as Federal Family Education Loan Program loans that the government purchased under the Ensuring Continued Access to Student Loans Act.

Nonprofit and educational institutions includes student loans originated under the Federal Family Education Loan Program and held by educational institutions and nonprofit organizations that are affiliated with state governments.

Pools of securitized assets comprises the outstanding balances of pools upon which securities have been issued; these balances are no longer carried on the balance sheets of the loan originators.

The consumer credit series are benchmarked to comprehensive data that periodically become available. Current monthly estimates are brought forward from the latest benchmarks in accordance with weighted changes indicated by sample data. Classifications are made on a "holder" basis. Thus, installment paper sold by retail outlets is included in the figures for the banks and finance companies that purchased the paper.

The amount of outstanding credit represents the sum of the balances in the installment receivable accounts of financial institutions and retail outlets at the end of each month.

The estimates of the amount of credit outstanding include any finance and insurance charges included as part of the installment contract. Unearned income on loans is included in some cases when lenders cannot separate the components.

The seasonally-adjusted data are adjusted for differences in the number of trading days and for seasonal influences.

Data availability

Current data are available monthly in the Federal Reserve Statistical Release G.19, "Consumer Credit," available along with all current and historical data on the Federal Reserve Web site. In the autumn of each year there is a revision of several years of past data reflecting benchmarking and seasonal factor review.

TABLES 12-6

Stock Prices and Housing Market Data

MOODY'S INVESTORS SERVICE; THE BOND BUYER; DOW JONES, INC.; STANDARD AND POOR'S CORPORATION; NEW YORK STOCK EXCHANGE; FEDERAL HOUSING FINANCE AGENCY (FHFA), PREVIOUSLY OFHEO (OFFICE OF FEDERAL HOUSING ENTERPRISE OVERSIGHT)

Definitions and notes on the data

Stock price indexes and yields. The *Dow Jones industrial* average is an average price of 30 stocks compiled by Dow Jones, Inc. The *Standard and Poor's composite* is an index of the prices of 500 stocks that are weighted by the volume of shares outstanding, accounting for about 90 percent of New York Stock Exchange value, with a base of 1941–1943 = 10, compiled by Standard and Poor's Corporation. (Before February 1957, these data are based on a conversion of an earlier 90-stock index, and are obtained from *B&MS* 1943 and 1976.) The *dividend-price ratio* is compiled by Standard and Poor's, covering the 500 stocks in the S&P index. It represents aggregate cash dividends (based on the latest known annual rate) divided by aggregate market value based on Wednesday closing prices. The *earnings/price ratio* measures earnings (after taxes) for four quarters, ending with the indicated quarter, as a ratio to stock prices for the last day of that quarter. Monthly data are averages of weekly figures; annual data are averages of monthly or quarterly figures. The *Nasdaq composite index* is an average price of over 5,000 stocks traded on the Nasdaq exchange.

The *fixed-rate first mortgage rates* are primary market contract interest rates on commitments for fixed-rate conventional 30-year mortgages. The rates are obtained by the Federal Reserve from the Federal Home Loan Mortgage Corporation (FHLMC or Freddie Mac).

FHFA (formerly OFHEO) House Price Indexes. The value of single-family owner-occupied houses was an increasingly important element in the latest household wealth and credit expansion and subsequent collapse. The Federal Housing Finance Agency (FHFA), a government agency charged with regulation of the government-sponsored mortgage finance institutions Fannie Mae and Freddie Mac and the 12 Federal Home Loan Banks, uses data from those institutions to compile quarterly House Price Indexes of the value of existing single-family homes. Not included are condominiums, cooperatives, multi-unit properties, and planned unit developments. These indexes were developed by the predecessor agency, the Office of Federal Housing

Enterprise Oversight (OFHEO), and have been published since the fourth quarter of 1995.

Fannie Mae and Freddie Mac are restricted by law to purchasing single-family mortgages with origination balances below a specific amount, known as the "conforming loan limit." Loans above this limit are known as jumbo loans.

The national conforming loan limit for mortgages that finance single-family one-unit properties increased from $33,000 in the early 1970s to $417,000 for 2006–2008, with limits 50 percent higher for four statutorily-designated high cost areas: Alaska, Hawaii, Guam, and the U.S. Virgin Islands. Since 2008, various legislative acts increased the loan limits in certain high-cost areas in the United States. While some of the legislative initiatives established temporary limits for loans originated in select time periods, a permanent formula was established under the Housing and Economic Recovery Act of 2008 (HERA). Loan limits in some high-cost areas are nearly $1.0 million.

The data come from all properties for which a conventional, "conforming" mortgage has been purchased or guaranteed by Fannie Mae or Freddie Mac since January 1975. Conventional mortgages are those not insured or guaranteed by the FHA, VA, or other federal government entities. A conforming mortgage is one no larger than the maximum that the insuring institution will insure. The limit has increased over time and has been $417,000 since the beginning of 2006. Loan limits for mortgages originated in the latter half of 2007 through Dec. 31, 2008, were raised to as much as nearly $1 million in high-cost areas in the continental United States. Legislation generally extended those limits for 2009-originated mortgages, and the limits for 2010 originations were further extended for certain places. Every new mortgage transaction that can be matched against a previous transaction for that property yields a rate of price change over the period between the two transactions, which enters into the calculation of the index. This data set is very large, with about 32 million repeat transactions over the 32-year span. The index is computed using a modified version of the Case-Shiller geometric weighted repeat-sales procedure.

Due to the size of this data set, indexes so defined can be calculated, and are published, not only for the United States as a whole but also for regions, states, metropolitan statistical areas (MSAs) and metropolitan divisions (subdivisions of MSAs). Obviously, the national average price trend shown here is not representative of price behavior in some "hot" local markets.

In addition, FHFA now publishes Purchase-Only Indexes for the house purchase subgroup of new mortgage transactions, excluding refinancing transactions. Nation-wide, this index is based on 4.7 million transactions over the latest 16 years. While this is still a very large statistical base, it is subject to somewhat greater revision and is less reliable for smaller geographical areas.

The FHFA price indexes are subject to revision for preceding quarters and years, because each new transaction, when reported, affects the rate of price change for all periods since the last time that the property involved in the new transaction changed hands or was refinanced. Indeed, these indexes originally indicated that prices peaked in 2007, but more recent data show a 2006 peak.

Seasonally adjusted data are also available for the purchase-only indexes. Seasonal price patterns appear to have some significance, especially for regional indexes. The seasonally adjusted indexes are not shown here because the year-over-change, calculated from not-seasonally-adjusted data, is the main focus of attention.

The FHFA indexes do not come from a random sample of house prices, and users need to consider possible sources of bias. Expensive houses are under-represented in general because the transactions are limited to conforming mortgages. This is important if the price trends for expensive houses are different.

It has also been suspected that prices of houses that are refinanced may behave differently from the prices of houses sold. However, data for the period since 1991 in which both series are available provide little support for this view. Between the end of 1991 and the peak at the end of 2006, the total House Price Index rose 121 percent, identical with the Purchase-Only Index. Since then the total index has declined 12 percent and the prices of purchased homes, 9 percent.

In addition to these government-supplied measures, new privately-developed house price indexes—not available for publication in *Business Statistics*—are now receiving regular media attention, and even provide the basis for a futures contract trading on the Chicago Mercantile Exchange. Standard & Poor's now issues S&P/Case-Shiller® Home Price Indexes each month. They cover resales only for houses at all price ranges, based on information obtained from county assessor and recorder offices. They are value-weighted, meaning that price trends for more expensive homes have greater influence on changes in the index. (The FHFA index weights price trends equally for all properties.) S&P/Case-Shiller data are only collected for 20 major metropolitan statistical areas. Series description and data can be found at <http://www.homeprice.standardandpoors.com>.

Data availability and references

Stock market data are published monthly in *Economic Indicators*, and until 2014 annually in *Economic Report of the President*, both available online at <http://www.gpo.gov>. Some historical interest rate data that are not available on the Federal Reserve Web site were also taken from past *Economic Reports of the President*.

The FHFA house price indexes for the United States as a whole, regions, states, and metropolitan and sub-metropolitan groups are published every 3 months, approximately 2 months after the end of the previous quarter. The release and supporting data and explanatory material are available at <http://www.fhfa.gov>.

The OFHEO (now FHFA) and other price indexes for houses are discussed and compared in Jordan Rappaport, "Comparing Aggregate Housing Price Measures," *Business Economics*, October 2007, pp. 55–65.

CHAPTER 13: INTERNATIONAL COMPARISONS

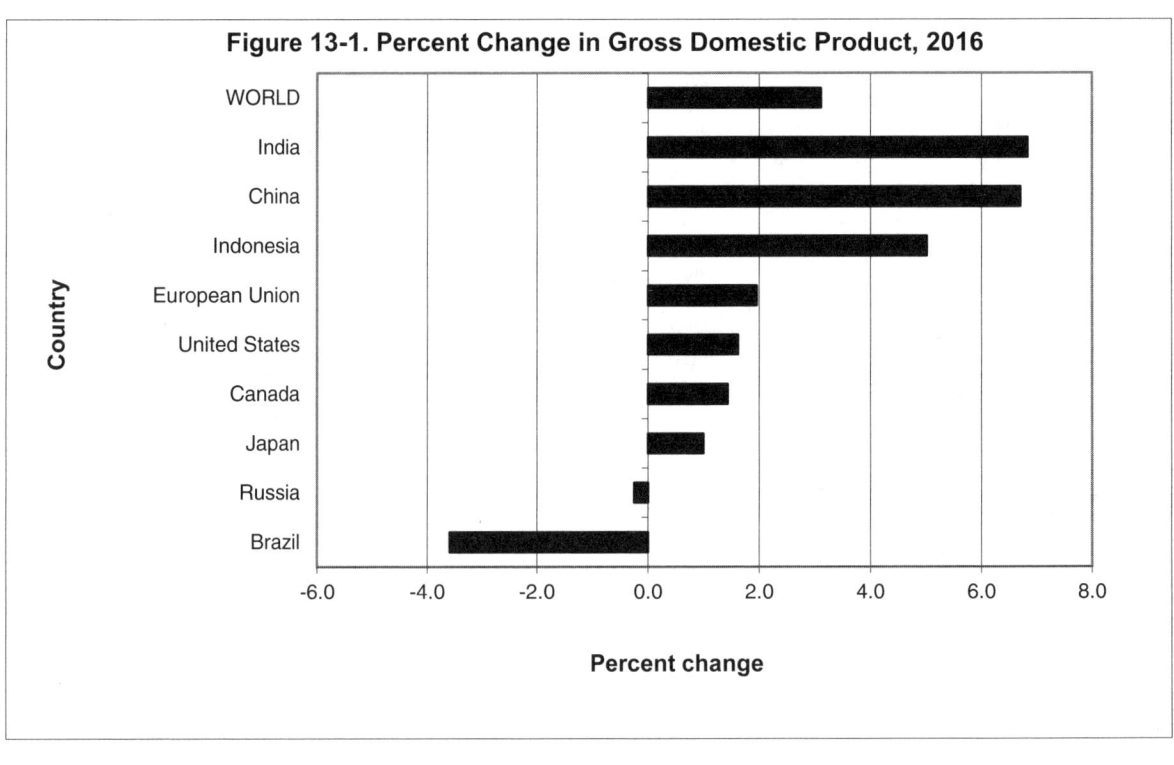

Figure 13-1. Percent Change in Gross Domestic Product, 2016

- Global economic growth, as measured by the changes in GDP, was 3.1 percent in 2016. The United States' growth rate was nearly half that at 1.6 percent. The best performing economies were China, India, and Indonesia at 6.7 percent, 6.8 percent and 5.0 percent respectively. (Table 13-1)

- Forecasts by the International Monetary Fund (IMF) put U.S. growth at 2.5 in 2020, with China, India, and Indonesia continuing to thrive. World economic growth is projected to be 3.6 percent. (Table 13-1)

- Unemployment in Brazil was double-digit in 2016 at 11.3 percent. Unemployment in the United States has declined from 8.1 percent in 2012 to 4.9 percent in 2016. Inflation has been relatively quiet for America's top trading partners. (Table 13-1)

- Listed in table 13-2 are six 'major' currencies, the euro, the British pound, the Canadian dollar, the Japanese yen, and the Swiss franc. These are all major industrial countries whose currencies are freely traded on world markets. All of these measures are defined as the foreign currency price of the U.S dollar.

- The other currency listed is the Chinese yuan, which is not freely traded. China is able to control the international values of their currencies (through, for example, direct capital controls) and keep their currencies from appreciating relative to the dollar to maintain their competitiveness in the U.S. market. Chinese have allowed some yuan appreciation, as can be seen in the lower yuan value of the dollar in Table 13-2, and inflation in China has also affected its real exchange rate.

Table 13-1 Gross Domestic Product Based on Purchasing Power Parity (PPP) Valuation of Country GDP

(Number in billions, percent.)

Country	Gross domestic product, percent change[1]			Unemployment rate[2]			Inflation, end of period consumer prices			Current account balances[3]		
	2012	2016	2020[4]	2012	2016	2020	2012	2016	2020	2012	2016	2020[4]
WORLD	3.5	3.1	3.6	. . .	. . .	. . .	4.0	2.9	3.1	. . .	. . .	. . .
European Union	-0.4	1.7	1.6	11.4	10.9	9.4	0.2	0.2	1.5	1.3	3.4	3.0
Germany	0.7	1.8	1.5	5.4	4.2	4.2	0.4	0.4	1.7	7.0	8.5	8.0
United Kingdom	1.3	1.8	1.5	8.0	4.9	5.1	0.6	0.9	2.6	-3.7	-4.4	-2.9
Brazil	1.9	-3.6	1.7	7.4	11.3	10.3	5.8	8.7	4.3	-3.0	-1.3	-1.7
Canada	1.7	1.4	2.0	7.3	7.0	7.0	1.0	1.4	2.1	-3.6	-3.3	-2.7
China	7.9	6.7	6.2	4.1	4.0	4.0	2.5	2.0	2.3	2.5	1.8	1.2
India	5.5	6.8	7.7	. . .	. . .	. . .	9.9	4.9	5.1	-4.8	-0.9	-1.5
Indonesia	6.0	5.0	5.3	6.1	5.6	5.6	3.7	3.5	4.5	-2.7	-1.8	-1.9
Japan	1.5	1.0	0.6	4.3	3.6	3.1	-0.2	-0.1	0.6	1.0	4.6	4.3
Russia	3.5	-0.2	1.4	5.5	5.5	5.5	6.6	7.0	4.2	3.3	1.7	3.5
United States	2.2	1.6	2.5	8.1	4.9	4.6	1.8	1.3	2.4	-2.8	-2.6	-3.3

[1]Gross domestic product corresponding to fiscal year is the country's GDP based on the same period during the year as their fiscal data. In the case of countries whose fiscal data are based on a fiscal calendar (e.g., July to June), this series would be the country's GDP over that same period. For countries whose fiscal data are based on a calendar year (i.e., January to December), this series will be the same as their GDP in current prices.

[2]Unemployment rate can be defined by either the national definition, the ILO harmonized definition, or the OECD harmonized definition. The OECD harmonized unemployment rate gives the number of unemployed persons as a percentage of the labor force (the total number of people employed plus unemployed). [OECD Main Economic Indicators, OECD, monthly] As defined by the International Labour Organization, unemployed workers are those who are currently not working but are willing and able to work for pay, currently available to work, and have actively searched for work.

[3]Current account is all transactions other than those in financial and capital items. The major classifications are goods and services, income and current transfers. The focus of the BOP is on transactions (between an economy and the rest of the world) in goods, services, and income.

[4]Projected by the International Monetary Fund (IMF).

. . . = Not available.

Table 13-2. Foreign Exchange Rates

(Not seasonally adjusted.)

Year and month	Foreign currency per U.S. dollar					
	Canadian dollar	Chinese yuan	European currency unit	Japananese yen	Switzerland franc	British pound
1971	1.0099	. . .	. . .	348.05	4.1158	0.4091
1972	0.9908	. . .	. . .	303.11	3.8181	0.3995
1973	1.0002	. . .	. . .	271.40	3.1698	0.4077
1974	0.9781	. . .	. . .	291.94	2.9791	0.4273
1975	1.0173	. . .	. . .	296.77	2.5834	0.4501
1976	0.9861	. . .	. . .	296.48	2.5003	0.5541
1977	1.0635	. . .	. . .	268.38	2.4038	0.5731
1978	1.1408	. . .	. . .	210.46	1.7899	0.5213
1979	1.1716	. . .	. . .	219.21	1.6635	0.4712
1980	1.1694	. . .	. . .	226.58	1.6776	0.4302
1981	1.1989	1.7090	. . .	220.45	1.9647	0.4940
1982	1.2339	1.8973	. . .	249.05	2.0318	0.5721
1983	1.2326	1.9809	. . .	237.45	2.1004	0.6597
1984	1.2952	2.3346	. . .	237.59	2.3517	0.7481
1985	1.3659	2.0440	. . .	238.47	2.4576	0.7708
1986	1.3898	3.4610	. . .	168.50	1.7988	0.6813
1987	1.3262	3.7314	. . .	144.62	1.4916	0.6098
1988	1.2309	3.7314	. . .	128.14	1.4633	0.5614
1989	1.1841	3.7690	. . .	137.99	1.6354	0.6104
1990	1.1670	4.7955	. . .	144.82	1.3898	0.5605
1991	1.1460	5.3348	. . .	134.51	1.4338	0.5658
1992	1.2088	5.5266	. . .	126.75	1.4069	0.5662
1993	1.2902	5.7767	. . .	111.23	1.4780	0.6660
1994	1.3659	8.6401	. . .	102.20	1.3668	0.6528
1995	1.3727	8.3709	. . .	94.11	1.1822	0.6335
1996	1.3637	8.3387	. . .	108.80	1.2364	0.6407
1997	1.3849	8.3193	. . .	121.09	1.4508	0.6106
1998	1.4836	8.3006	. . .	130.82	1.4497	0.6034
1999	1.4858	8.2783	0.9375	113.71	1.5027	0.6184
2000	1.4855	8.2784	1.0830	107.82	1.6899	0.6598
2001	1.5490	8.2770	1.1167	121.52	1.6880	0.6946
2002	1.5706	8.2771	1.0579	125.27	1.5571	0.6656
2003	1.4012	8.2772	0.8836	115.92	1.3452	0.6117
2004	1.3016	8.2768	0.8039	108.16	1.2428	0.5456
2005	1.2115	8.1940	0.8034	110.14	1.2462	0.5493
2006	1.1344	7.9720	0.7962	116.35	1.2535	0.5425
2007	1.0742	7.6059	0.7294	117.77	1.1999	0.4995
2008	1.0668	6.9482	0.6801	103.38	1.0829	0.5392
2009	1.1414	6.8307	0.7177	93.60	1.0861	0.6389
2010	1.0301	6.7690	0.7532	87.75	1.0426	0.6466
2011	0.9890	6.4633	0.7184	79.71	0.8876	0.6236
2012	0.9994	6.3085	0.7774	79.81	0.9374	0.6307
2013	1.0300	6.1480	0.7527	97.56	0.9300	0.6391
2014	1.1043	6.1620	0.7520	105.74	0.9100	0.6066
2015	1.2791	6.2827	0.9012	121.05	0.9600	0.6540
2016	1.4208	6.5726	0.9212	118.23	1.0100	0.6950
2015						
January	1.2122	6.2181	0.8610	118.25	0.9443	0.6604
February	1.2499	6.2518	0.8811	118.76	0.9361	0.6524
March	1.2618	6.2386	0.9243	120.39	0.9798	0.6685
April	1.2337	6.2010	0.9240	119.51	0.9595	0.6681
May	1.2176	6.2035	0.8955	120.80	0.9316	0.6470
June	1.2365	6.2052	0.8908	123.72	0.9321	0.6420
July	1.2863	6.2085	0.9093	123.31	0.9547	0.6427
August	1.3147	6.3383	0.8980	123.00	0.9685	0.6419
September	1.3266	6.3676	0.8906	120.15	0.9725	0.6520
October	1.3072	6.3505	0.8906	120.05	0.9687	0.6518
November	1.3279	6.3640	0.9322	122.64	1.0098	0.6582
December	1.3713	6.4491	0.9184	121.64	0.9951	0.6675
2016						
January	1.4208	6.5726	0.9212	118.23	1.0082	0.6948
February	1.3797	6.5501	0.9016	114.62	0.9920	0.6998
March	1.3226	6.5027	0.8981	112.93	0.9811	0.7018
April	1.2818	6.4754	0.8814	109.55	0.9634	0.6984
May	1.2945	6.5259	0.8840	108.85	0.9777	0.6885
June	1.2894	6.5892	0.8903	105.35	0.9695	0.7044
July	1.3052	6.6771	0.9046	104.19	0.9830	0.7614
August	1.2998	6.6466	0.8923	101.24	0.9711	0.7633
September	1.3108	6.6702	0.8914	101.78	0.9732	0.7610
October	1.3251	6.7303	0.9079	103.91	0.9876	0.8110
November	1.3434	6.8402	0.9266	108.44	0.9963	0.8044
December	1.3339	6.9198	0.9483	116.00	1.0194	0.8011

. . . = Not available.

NOTES AND DEFINITIONS, CHAPTER 13

Table 13-1

International Comparisons: Gross Domestic Product Growth, Unemployment Rates, Inflation and Current Account Balances

Chapter 7, Table 13, identifies the major trading partners of the United States. Table 13-1 provides international comparisons of the major economic indicators of real gross domestic product (GDP), employment rates, inflation, and current account balances as percent of GDP by country for years 2012, 2016, and the International Monetary Fund projections.

SOURCE: THE CENTRAL INTELLIGENCE AGENCY, THE *WORLDBOOK FACTBOOK*, AND THE APRIL 2017 WORLD ECONOMIC OUTLOOK *(WEO)*, INTERNATIONAL MONETARY FUND

Definitions and notes on the data

The basic measure of the overall health of an economy is the *gross domestic product* (GDP). It is the market value of all goods and services produced by labor and property located in the United States. *Real GDP* is an inflation-adjusted measure that reflects the value of all goods and services produced by an economy in a given year, expressed in base-year prices. See chapter 1 for in depth and historical data, notes and definitions.

The *unemployment rate* represents the number unemployed as a percent of the labor force. See Chapter 10.

The *Consumer Price Index* (CPI) measures the change in prices paid by consumers for goods and services. *Inflation/deflation* is the change over time of the CPI. Japan experienced deflation in 2012 and 2016 while Brazil's inflation rate reached nearly 9 percent in 2016. See Chapter 8 for more information on the CPI and inflation.

The *current account* of the balance of payment consists of transactions between U.S. residents and nonresidents in goods, services, investment income and net transfers such as international aid. Table 13-1 presents the current account balance as a percent of GDP. This measure provides an indication on the level of international competitiveness of a country. Usually, countries recording a strong current account surplus have an economy heavily dependent on exports revenues, with high savings rates but weak domestic demand. On the other hand, countries recording a current account deficit have strong imports, a low saving rates and high personal consumption rates as a percentage of disposable incomes. See Chapter 7.

REFERENCES AND NOTES ON THE DATA

This data is published by the International Monetary Fund (IMF) on an annual basis.

Table 13-2

Foreign Exchange Rates

SOURCE: BOARD OF GOVERNORS OF THE FEDERAL RESERVE SYSTEM

Definitions and notes on the data

The price of a nation's currency in terms of another currency. An *exchange rate* thus has two components, the domestic currency and a foreign currency, and can be quoted either directly or indirectly. In a direct quotation, the price of a unit of foreign currency is expressed in terms of the domestic currency. In an indirect quotation, the price of a unit of domestic currency is expressed in terms of the foreign currency.

This table shows the U.S. dollar relative to the currencies of some important individual countries and also relative to average values for major groups of countries. In *Business Statistics,* all of these measures are defined as the foreign currency price of the U.S. dollar. When the measure is relatively high, the dollar is relatively strong—but less competitive (in the sense of price competition)—and the other currency or group of currencies named in the measure is relatively weak and more competitive.

For consistency, this definition is used in *Business Statistics* even in the case of currencies that are commonly quoted in the financial press and elsewhere as dollars per foreign currency unit instead of foreign currency units per dollar. Notably, this is the case for the euro and for the British pound. Where *Business Statistics* shows the average 2016 value of the dollar as 0.9212 euros, the more usual statement—and the one found on the Federal Reserve release used as a source for this information—is that in 2016, the euro was worth on average $1.0855. (The value shown in the table is 1 divided by 1.0855, with slight rounding differences.) Where *Business Statistics* shows the 2016 value of the dollar as 0.6950 British pounds, the more usual statement is that the pound was worth $1.4392. The Canadian dollar is also sometimes quoted relative to the U.S. dollar, rather than as shown here.

The definition of the dollar's value used in *Business Statistics* is the most useful for economic analysis from the U.S. point of view and for foreign tourists in the United States. For American tourists overseas, it is easier to use the inverse of this measure, the value of the other currency; for example, the traveler in Paris can more easily translate prices into dollars by multiplying the dollar value of the euro than by dividing by the euro value of the dollar.

The foreign exchange rates shown are averages of the daily noon buying rates for cable transfers in New York City certified for customs purposes by the Federal Reserve Bank of New York.

The introduction of the euro was in January 1999 as the common currency for 11 European countries and marked a major change in the international currency system. Over time, the Eurozone has increased to 19 countries: Austria, Belgium, Cyprus, Estonia, Finland, France, Germany, Greece, Ireland, Italy, Latvia, Lithuania, Luxembourg, Malta, Netherlands, Portugal, Slovakia, Slovenia and Spain. In addition, the euro is also the national currency in Monaco, the Vatican City and San Marino, and is the de facto currency in Andorra, Kosovo, and Montenegro. The values of the currencies of these countries no longer fluctuate relative to each other, but the value of the euro still fluctuates relative to the dollar and to currencies for countries outside the EMU. The currency and coins of the individual countries continued to circulate from 1999 through the end of 2001, but in January 2002, new euro currency and coins were introduced, replacing the currency and coins of the individual countries. Once a country has entered the monetary union, its values relative to the <u>dollar</u> will continue to fluctuate—but only due to fluctuations in the value of the euro relative to the dollar.

There is no fully satisfactory historical equivalent to the euro. For comparisons over time, the Federal Reserve Board uses a "restated German mark," derived simply by dividing each historical value of the mark by the euro conversion factor, 1.95583. The G-10 dollar index described below includes five of the currencies that later merged into the euro, but also includes the currencies of Canada, Japan, the United Kingdom, Switzerland, and Sweden.

DATA AVAILABILITY AND REFERENCES

Current press releases, historical data, and information on weights and methods for exchange rates and exchange rate indexes are available on the Federal Reserve Web site at <http://www.federalreserve.gov/>; go to Data, then "Foreign Exchange Rates H10/G5," and select DDP, the new Data Download Program. The dollar value indexes are described in the article "Indexes of the Foreign Exchange Value of the Dollar," *Federal Reserve Bulletin* (Winter 2005), also available on the Federal Reserve Web site.

Additional information on exchange rates can be found on the Federal Reserve Bank of St. Louis Web site at <http://www.stls.frb.org/fred/data/exchange.html>.

PART B: INDUSTRY PROFILES

CHAPTER 14: PRODUCT AND INCOME BY INDUSTRY

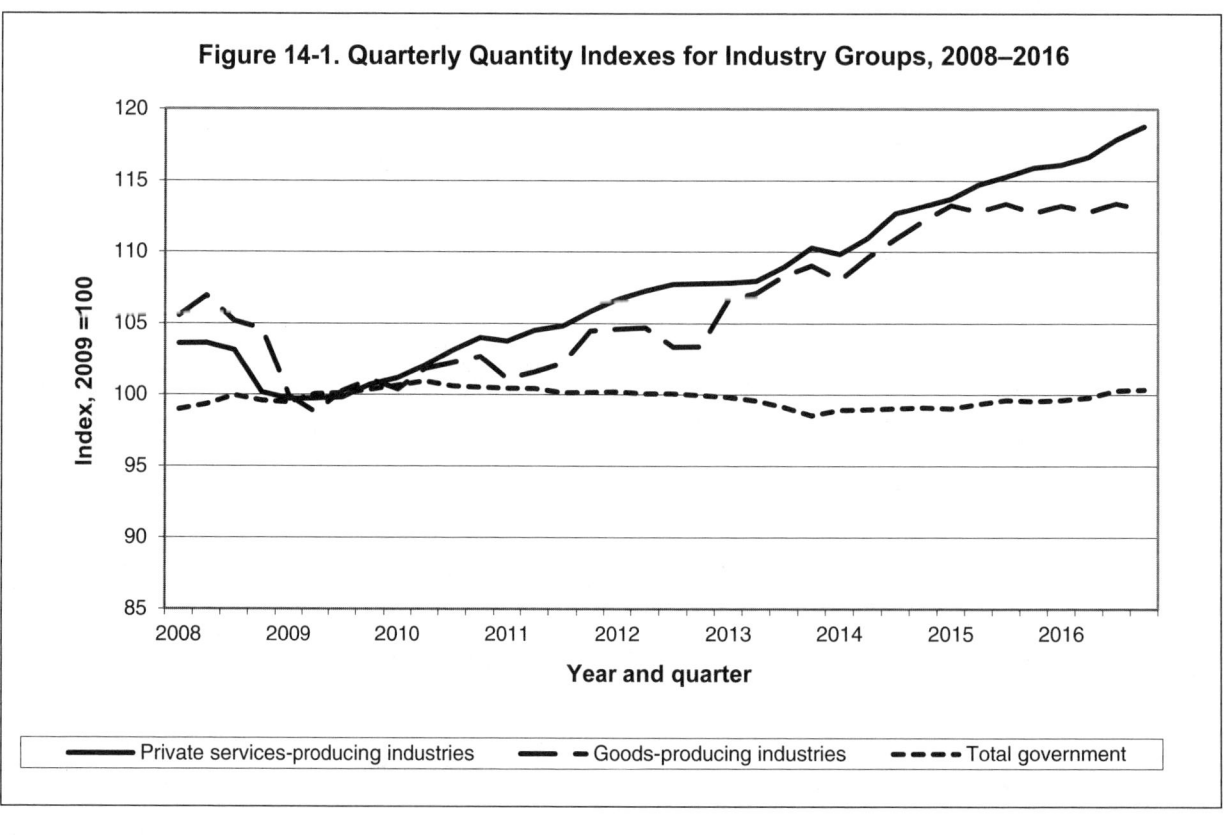

Figure 14-1. Quarterly Quantity Indexes for Industry Groups, 2008–2016

Index, 2009 =100

Year and quarter

——— Private services-producing industries ——— Goods-producing industries ———— Total government

- BEA now publishes quarterly measures of GDP by industrial origin, in both current-dollar and real (quantity) terms. Industry output, sometimes referred to as "gross product originating in the industry," is here termed "value added." Figure 14-1 shows quantity indexes for real value added in the three major industry groupings of GDP. The quantity indexes, as well as the price indexes, all have, for statistical convenience, a base year of 2009, which happens to be the low point of the 2007–2009 Great Recession.

- Private services-producing industries, which accounted for 68.9 percent of total GDP in 2016, display less cyclical swing and more real growth than the goods sector, which was 18.2 percent of the total. Government production—the other 12.9 percent of total GDP—was comparatively stable, but this is an incomplete measurement of the counter-cyclical impact of government, as it does not include the effects of changes in tax receipts and payments. (Tables 14-1 and 14-2)

- Table 14-3 can be used to assess the share of each industry group in total gross domestic factor income and the shares paid to employees and accruing to land and capital in each industry. For these purposes factor income is a better measure than the BEA definition of value added because value added includes, but factor income excludes, taxes on production and imports.

Table 14-1. Gross Domestic Product (Value Added) by Industry

(Billions of dollars.)

Year	Total gross domestic product	Private industries Total	Agriculture, forestry, fishing, and hunting	Mining	Utilities	Construction	Manufacturing Durable goods	Manufacturing Nondurable goods	Wholesale trade	Retail trade	Transportation and warehousing	Information	Finance and insurance	Real estate and rental and leasing
1997	8 608.5	7 459.4	108.8	95.1	172.1	340.7	827.3	562.7	530.2	588.4	256.1	395.7	578.6	1 044.5
1998	9 089.2	7 894.0	99.9	81.4	163.9	380.5	852.7	582.4	565.5	635.8	278.2	435.5	639.8	1 083.2
1999	9 660.6	8 403.2	92.8	84.3	180.1	418.4	876.9	616.8	585.9	661.7	288.3	486.1	679.5	1 173.5
2000	10 284.8	8 956.0	98.5	110.5	180.2	462.3	927.0	628.4	625.0	695.6	305.6	472.2	750.4	1 241.9
2001	10 621.8	9 223.5	100.0	125.2	184.0	488.0	835.1	643.4	617.9	713.5	307.8	501.2	817.5	1 339.2
2002	10 977.5	9 499.5	95.8	113.4	180.1	494.9	834.7	638.0	617.2	738.3	305.3	549.5	835.2	1 411.2
2003	11 510.7	9 951.0	116.1	140.1	187.1	527.1	865.9	665.2	647.1	775.8	320.9	564.0	866.8	1 464.9
2004	12 274.9	10 628.0	142.7	167.6	202.7	587.5	908.5	710.7	703.5	802.7	351.1	620.8	890.3	1 534.0
2005	13 093.7	11 366.3	128.6	226.6	201.4	654.1	959.5	744.7	759.4	848.8	375.1	641.6	991.8	1 649.2
2006	13 855.9	12 045.4	128.3	273.4	230.0	698.2	1 005.4	798.9	815.7	878.1	407.6	649.0	1 048.8	1 721.9
2007	14 477.6	12 572.4	142.0	314.0	235.1	715.0	1 030.0	824.3	860.8	877.6	409.6	702.4	1 040.5	1 836.6
2008	14 718.6	12 716.2	154.5	401.5	237.5	653.0	994.4	819.7	877.8	856.1	422.4	730.5	907.2	1 897.3
2009	14 418.7	12 353.0	137.7	290.3	250.8	577.3	874.3	852.4	822.8	842.1	398.8	705.3	969.3	1 904.8
2010	14 964.4	12 826.5	160.2	331.7	267.0	541.6	956.6	874.0	868.5	868.8	425.1	730.2	1 005.8	1 945.7
2011	15 517.9	13 348.4	197.2	398.6	272.0	546.6	1 003.8	903.5	907.3	891.7	446.9	728.4	1 038.0	2 014.4
2012	16 155.3	13 957.5	185.8	410.9	262.9	583.6	1 053.3	930.4	962.5	932.6	467.4	737.5	1 142.7	2 086.3
2013	16 691.5	14 468.5	221.8	450.9	269.2	620.8	1 086.0	949.2	1 001.6	968.6	487.2	791.5	1 136.4	2 157.4
2014	17 393.1	15 115.8	203.2	482.7	283.1	672.1	1 129.2	970.2	1 047.9	1 003.6	510.2	793.2	1 251.2	2 244.8
2015	18 036.6	15 698.7	175.2	327.8	284.3	732.1	1 176.4	993.9	1 093.2	1 056.8	542.5	839.9	1 293.1	2 363.3
2016	18 569.1	16 177.5	159.9	264.6	288.1	784.0	1 184.7	990.5	1 098.0	1 087.1	562.9	886.0	1 355.5	2 461.8
2008														
1st quarter	14 668.4	12 698.2	165.1	362.9	222.1	670.5	1 009.2	805.3	870.6	850.8	413.0	726.1	1 010.8	1 886.4
2nd quarter	14 813.0	12 822.4	158.6	436.9	237.4	655.7	1 006.4	826.1	882.4	858.5	418.4	744.0	953.1	1 895.5
3rd quarter	14 843.0	12 827.9	149.5	443.4	246.4	645.3	998.7	846.2	887.0	863.7	423.7	743.8	889.7	1 897.3
4th quarter	14 549.9	12 516.2	144.9	362.6	244.1	640.4	963.5	801.1	871.3	851.5	434.4	708.0	775.3	1 909.9
2009														
1st quarter	14 383.9	12 337.3	130.3	301.5	256.5	606.3	891.7	819.4	828.8	837.1	405.6	703.1	909.7	1 914.6
2nd quarter	14 340.4	12 277.7	132.2	275.9	246.3	580.8	861.7	837.8	811.8	837.7	393.1	699.7	980.6	1 902.4
3rd quarter	14 384.1	12 312.7	138.0	280.0	243.9	570.5	858.9	865.8	814.0	836.3	393.4	698.6	990.2	1 903.8
4th quarter	14 566.5	12 484.3	150.1	304.0	256.4	551.5	884.9	886.8	836.7	857.4	403.2	719.9	996.5	1 898.4
2010														
1st quarter	14 681.1	12 568.1	149.3	329.6	267.4	533.3	903.0	881.2	844.4	854.6	407.1	714.7	995.7	1 919.3
2nd quarter	14 888.6	12 747.0	156.3	319.5	263.2	543.3	947.3	866.9	861.5	871.7	420.5	721.8	1 008.0	1 942.6
3rd quarter	15 057.7	12 911.6	164.0	326.6	267.8	544.8	980.7	867.6	884.3	871.8	433.4	742.5	996.2	1 948.0
4th quarter	15 230.2	13 079.4	171.2	351.3	269.6	545.1	995.4	880.2	883.6	877.1	439.5	741.7	1 023.4	1 973.0
2011														
1st quarter	15 238.4	13 080.0	197.9	368.1	260.6	528.7	990.7	874.0	886.4	878.7	439.8	724.5	1 029.3	1 961.2
2nd quarter	15 460.9	13 289.1	192.3	402.3	273.7	542.6	991.0	908.0	904.6	885.1	445.7	731.5	1 020.1	2 003.1
3rd quarter	15 587.1	13 410.9	200.4	402.6	274.0	552.8	1 000.6	913.8	906.7	893.8	446.2	726.3	1 047.0	2 024.5
4th quarter	15 785.3	13 613.7	198.3	421.5	279.9	562.4	1 033.1	918.0	931.4	909.2	455.8	731.4	1 055.7	2 068.8
2012														
1st quarter	15 973.9	13 783.4	189.0	418.0	256.2	575.3	1 039.8	925.8	946.1	925.2	460.5	729.2	1 107.9	2 062.8
2nd quarter	16 121.9	13 928.4	184.4	403.5	265.0	582.5	1 059.3	932.1	958.0	930.2	470.8	748.7	1 132.7	2 081.3
3rd quarter	16 227.9	14 028.6	180.2	403.9	266.5	584.6	1 058.1	944.5	969.5	936.2	470.4	743.0	1 162.0	2 101.9
4th quarter	16 297.3	14 089.8	189.6	418.4	263.7	592.2	1 056.0	919.0	976.5	938.8	467.9	728.9	1 168.0	2 099.1
2013														
1st quarter	16 475.4	14 261.1	230.4	430.9	271.4	605.4	1 076.0	952.1	984.9	963.4	481.8	782.6	1 088.4	2 127.5
2nd quarter	16 541.4	14 322.2	226.4	446.7	269.5	611.2	1 073.8	930.0	987.9	959.7	480.6	787.1	1 116.5	2 130.4
3rd quarter	16 749.3	14 527.6	225.7	468.3	265.2	626.6	1 087.7	935.7	1 008.4	972.1	486.0	786.7	1 140.3	2 173.2
4th quarter	16 999.9	14 763.0	204.8	457.6	270.6	639.9	1 105.4	978.9	1 025.2	979.1	500.4	809.6	1 200.4	2 198.5
2014														
1st quarter	17 025.2	14 770.4	202.0	474.8	285.7	653.4	1 099.1	954.6	1 017.6	975.8	493.3	791.9	1 209.0	2 198.1
2nd quarter	17 285.6	15 016.9	215.6	496.5	279.9	663.1	1 115.2	970.5	1 035.3	995.9	505.2	791.3	1 252.5	2 226.6
3rd quarter	17 569.4	15 284.1	198.1	499.1	282.7	676.8	1 148.8	982.0	1 063.6	1 013.7	517.6	793.6	1 266.2	2 265.7
4th quarter	17 692.2	15 392.0	197.0	460.5	284.1	694.9	1 153.6	973.9	1 075.0	1 029.1	524.8	795.9	1 276.9	2 289.0
2015														
1st quarter	17 783.6	15 468.5	170.8	358.2	285.8	704.1	1 167.5	980.4	1 083.6	1 032.3	535.2	816.2	1 299.4	2 325.1
2nd quarter	17 998.3	15 665.1	173.7	359.3	282.7	725.3	1 174.9	993.6	1 097.0	1 051.3	537.8	833.7	1 296.8	2 351.1
3rd quarter	18 141.9	15 795.4	183.1	317.3	286.9	741.9	1 177.2	1 010.6	1 093.7	1 067.5	545.5	844.4	1 298.4	2 377.4
4th quarter	18 222.8	15 865.6	173.2	276.3	282.0	757.3	1 186.0	990.8	1 098.6	1 076.0	551.7	865.4	1 277.8	2 399.5
2016														
1st quarter	18 281.6	15 913.8	165.0	235.1	282.2	774.1	1 177.1	977.5	1 088.9	1 081.6	552.4	880.1	1 311.2	2 425.1
2nd quarter	18 450.1	16 069.1	162.1	258.3	283.9	779.0	1 177.9	993.8	1 088.3	1 081.1	561.1	877.6	1 330.6	2 451.9
3rd quarter	18 675.3	16 273.1	160.1	271.6	293.9	784.9	1 188.1	992.8	1 101.5	1 089.2	565.9	892.4	1 374.8	2 469.5
4th quarter	18 869.4	16 454.1	152.5	293.3	292.5	798.1	1 195.9	997.8	1 113.2	1 096.4	572.1	893.7	1 405.6	2 500.9

Table 14-1. Gross Domestic Product (Value Added) by Industry—*Continued*

(Billions of dollars.)

Year	Professional, scientific, and technical services	Management of companies and enterprises	Administrative and waste management services	Educational services	Health care and social assistance	Arts, entertainment, and recreation	Accommodation and food services	Other services except government	Total government	Federal	State and local	Private goods-producing industries	Private services-producing industries	Information-communications-technology-producing industries[1]
1997	503.3	126.7	215.5	71.8	509.4	301.6	221.3	230.8	1 149.1	389.4	759.7	1 934.7	5 524.7	507.6
1998	546.8	141.0	231.6	74.5	531.2	321.3	238.5	248.8	1 195.2	394.6	800.6	1 996.9	5 897.1	540.5
1999	600.2	150.3	252.5	80.4	561.4	353.3	262.9	260.9	1 257.5	404.6	852.8	2 089.2	6 314.0	571.6
2000	656.0	173.2	281.9	86.1	595.4	385.8	286.8	279.9	1 328.8	421.9	906.9	2 226.7	6 729.3	624.0
2001	691.6	174.4	295.5	91.7	642.0	389.3	292.7	266.5	1 398.3	429.3	969.0	2 191.7	7 031.9	605.2
2002	718.2	176.6	300.7	98.6	692.7	413.2	309.4	285.9	1 478.0	460.8	1 017.2	2 176.8	7 322.7	623.1
2003	739.5	187.5	321.3	106.5	738.0	432.2	321.1	284.9	1 559.7	496.2	1 063.5	2 314.4	7 636.6	659.3
2004	787.4	206.7	346.5	116.7	788.8	461.4	343.5	298.5	1 646.9	523.7	1 123.3	2 516.9	8 111.0	713.0
2005	842.8	219.3	380.5	121.0	828.9	481.3	359.0	311.7	1 727.4	550.4	1 177.1	2 713.5	8 652.8	762.4
2006	903.7	238.5	399.4	129.9	883.0	510.0	379.7	325.7	1 810.4	575.2	1 235.2	2 904.2	9 141.2	800.3
2007	967.3	259.5	430.4	138.7	925.9	532.1	394.5	330.5	1 905.2	602.4	1 302.9	3 025.3	9 547.1	851.7
2008	1 053.3	261.5	438.2	149.3	996.0	535.1	394.9	330.8	2 002.4	633.3	1 369.2	3 023.1	9 693.1	884.0
2009	1 000.4	247.1	413.6	163.0	1 051.0	522.3	383.5	329.5	2 065.8	664.0	1 401.8	2 732.0	9 621.0	852.4
2010	1 022.0	268.2	439.5	169.3	1 079.2	540.7	396.2	332.4	2 137.9	701.1	1 436.7	2 864.1	9 962.4	876.3
2011	1 074.1	281.0	457.5	175.5	1 111.6	561.4	413.9	338.9	2 169.5	716.3	1 453.2	3 049.8	10 298.6	894.1
2012	1 128.8	304.3	479.6	183.0	1 153.8	596.9	439.9	355.4	2 197.7	718.6	1 479.1	3 164.0	10 793.5	915.6
2013	1 148.3	322.4	494.6	185.6	1 186.8	626.8	462.6	363.5	2 223.1	708.5	1 514.6	3 328.6	11 139.8	983.6
2014	1 204.5	338.0	522.4	195.1	1 223.2	660.1	486.7	381.2	2 277.3	719.8	1 557.4	3 457.4	11 658.5	1 002.3
2015	1 292.8	356.2	558.3	202.3	1 298.9	710.0	524.2	401.7	2 338.0	729.4	1 608.6	3 405.4	12 293.2	. . .
2016	1 355.7	367.8	585.1	207.3	1 368.7	749.3	551.5	420.4	2 391.6	740.0	1 651.6	3 383.7	12 793.8	. . .
2008														
1st quarter	1 028.9	259.1	438.9	144.9	970.4	138.8	395.2	329.2	1 970.2	622.9	1 347.3	3 013.1	9 685.1	. . .
2nd quarter	1 052.3	260.9	438.9	147.3	985.8	139.5	395.7	329.2	1 990.5	630.2	1 360.3	3 083.6	9 738.8	. . .
3rd quarter	1 068.7	263.6	439.1	151.1	1 003.1	140.1	396.5	330.8	2 015.1	637.8	1 377.4	3 083.1	9 744.7	. . .
4th quarter	1 063.6	262.5	436.0	153.9	1 024.8	142.1	392.2	334.1	2 033.8	642.1	1 391.6	2 912.5	9 603.7	. . .
2009														
1st quarter	1 025.0	239.6	418.5	161.1	1 035.6	139.2	383.2	330.4	2 046.7	655.6	1 391.1	2 749.1	9 588.1	. . .
2nd quarter	999.6	245.5	411.0	162.6	1 048.7	137.9	382.5	329.7	2 062.7	662.4	1 400.3	2 688.5	9 589.3	. . .
3rd quarter	991.0	250.8	409.0	163.4	1 053.9	139.3	383.6	328.4	2 071.5	666.5	1 405.0	2 713.1	9 599.6	. . .
4th quarter	985.8	252.7	416.0	164.9	1 066.0	138.9	384.5	329.6	2 082.2	671.4	1 410.8	2 777.4	9 706.9	. . .
2010														
1st quarter	997.8	260.1	427.2	166.8	1 061.2	141.3	387.3	326.6	2 113.0	690.8	1 422.2	2 796.5	9 771.6	. . .
2nd quarter	1 010.9	264.3	436.2	168.8	1 074.6	144.1	394.6	330.9	2 141.6	704.1	1 437.5	2 833.3	9 913.7	. . .
3rd quarter	1 032.4	269.8	444.0	170.3	1 087.1	145.1	399.9	335.4	2 146.1	703.7	1 442.3	2 883.7	10 027.9	. . .
4th quarter	1 046.9	278.7	450.6	171.1	1 093.9	147.4	403.1	336.8	2 150.8	705.9	1 444.9	2 943.1	10 136.3	. . .
2011														
1st quarter	1 053.0	281.2	450.4	173.7	1 095.7	146.1	405.4	334.6	2 158.3	711.6	1 446.8	2 959.5	10 120.5	. . .
2nd quarter	1 072.3	281.6	455.3	174.9	1 108.3	147.5	412.0	337.4	2 171.8	716.0	1 455.8	3 036.2	10 252.9	. . .
3rd quarter	1 082.1	279.7	460.5	176.6	1 117.5	149.9	416.0	340.1	2 176.2	718.4	1 457.8	3 070.1	10 340.9	. . .
4th quarter	1 088.9	281.7	463.8	176.7	1 124.8	146.5	422.3	343.4	2 171.7	719.2	1 452.4	3 133.3	10 480.3	. . .
2012														
1st quarter	1 113.2	293.8	476.1	181.6	1 144.6	153.8	434.4	350.0	2 190.5	721.0	1 469.4	3 147.9	10 635.5	. . .
2nd quarter	1 127.3	295.7	477.8	182.7	1 148.0	155.9	438.0	354.6	2 193.4	720.1	1 473.3	3 161.7	10 766.7	. . .
3rd quarter	1 126.6	305.1	481.6	183.3	1 155.0	157.8	440.5	357.7	2 199.4	718.4	1 480.9	3 171.3	10 857.3	. . .
4th quarter	1 148.0	322.5	482.7	184.5	1 167.5	160.6	446.7	359.2	2 207.5	714.8	1 492.7	3 175.2	10 914.6	. . .
2013														
1st quarter	1 125.3	310.4	486.5	182.9	1 182.1	161.7	456.4	360.9	2 214.4	711.2	1 503.2	3 294.8	10 966.2	. . .
2nd quarter	1 139.7	322.3	490.2	184.9	1 182.8	162.5	458.8	361.2	2 219.2	709.3	1 509.9	3 288.2	11 033.9	. . .
3rd quarter	1 157.2	327.0	498.3	186.3	1 188.8	164.6	465.0	363.4	2 221.7	703.5	1 518.2	3 345.0	11 182.6	. . .
4th quarter	1 171.0	330.1	503.5	188.4	1 193.5	167.9	470.1	368.3	2 236.9	709.9	1 527.0	3 386.5	11 376.5	. . .
2014														
1st quarter	1 172.2	331.6	508.2	192.1	1 198.5	169.8	472.0	371.0	2 254.8	717.0	1 537.8	3 383.9	11 386.5	. . .
2nd quarter	1 185.4	331.3	517.0	194.4	1 210.6	171.5	481.6	377.5	2 268.7	719.0	1 549.7	3 460.9	11 556.0	. . .
3rd quarter	1 222.7	341.3	527.7	196.5	1 234.1	175.1	492.7	386.2	2 285.4	720.9	1 564.4	3 504.8	11 779.3	. . .
4th quarter	1 237.7	348.0	536.6	197.6	1 249.4	177.3	500.6	390.0	2 300.1	722.4	1 577.7	3 479.9	11 912.1	. . .
2015														
1st quarter	1 266.9	352.6	544.5	199.0	1 263.5	180.4	509.8	393.2	2 315.1	728.9	1 586.2	3 381.1	12 087.4	. . .
2nd quarter	1 286.9	355.9	554.1	200.9	1 286.0	184.8	519.7	399.8	2 333.1	729.8	1 603.4	3 426.8	12 238.4	. . .
3rd quarter	1 301.8	356.2	562.5	203.1	1 309.2	187.1	528.0	403.4	2 346.6	730.2	1 616.4	3 430.2	12 365.2	. . .
4th quarter	1 315.5	360.3	572.0	206.0	1 336.9	190.9	539.3	410.2	2 357.1	728.8	1 628.4	3 383.6	12 482.0	. . .
2016														
1st quarter	1 333.3	357.7	574.8	205.7	1 341.0	192.9	543.2	414.9	2 367.8	734.8	1 633.0	3 328.8	12 585.0	. . .
2nd quarter	1 348.7	367.9	580.3	205.5	1 361.1	195.3	547.4	417.5	2 381.0	736.9	1 644.1	3 371.1	12 698.0	. . .
3rd quarter	1 363.6	372.9	588.3	207.8	1 378.1	200.1	555.3	422.3	2 402.2	742.1	1 660.1	3 397.5	12 875.6	. . .
4th quarter	1 377.3	372.8	597.0	210.3	1 394.6	203.3	560.0	427.0	2 415.3	746.3	1 669.0	3 437.6	13 016.5	. . .

[1]Consists of computer and electronic products manufacturing; publishing, including software; information and data processing services; and computer systems design and related services.
. . . = Not available.

Table 14-2. Chain-Type Quantity Indexes for Value Added by Industry

(New Series, 2009 = 100.)

Year	Total gross domestic product	Private industries												
		Total	Agriculture, forestry, fishing, and hunting	Mining	Utilities	Construction	Manufacturing		Wholesale trade	Retail trade	Transportation and warehousing	Information	Finance and insurance	Real estate and rental and leasing
							Durable goods	Nondurable goods						
1997	76.5	76.3	66.1	81.5	106.4	119.0	71.5	92.5	75.4	79.8	89.6	53.0	60.1	74.2
1998	79.9	79.9	63.6	85.6	101.5	123.9	77.4	92.5	81.7	87.3	92.9	58.0	67.0	75.0
1999	83.7	84.1	66.9	81.8	118.8	128.4	82.8	95.5	84.8	90.2	93.7	64.5	73.5	78.9
2000	87.1	87.6	76.8	72.6	121.2	133.2	92.2	94.7	90.0	92.9	95.3	63.1	80.8	80.8
2001	88.0	88.5	72.9	84.9	102.7	130.8	86.3	94.0	91.7	95.6	88.9	66.6	89.0	84.2
2002	89.5	90.0	75.7	83.4	104.7	126.7	88.0	93.8	92.0	99.2	86.1	73.1	89.4	85.7
2003	92.0	92.5	83.0	74.4	101.7	129.0	93.9	96.6	97.5	104.8	89.6	75.1	90.0	86.9
2004	95.5	96.2	88.2	73.7	106.6	133.5	100.0	102.7	102.8	106.3	98.4	83.4	89.8	89.2
2005	98.7	99.7	92.4	73.3	99.9	133.9	106.4	99.8	108.1	109.8	103.9	88.0	97.8	93.8
2006	101.4	102.6	96.2	81.2	105.3	130.5	113.8	102.3	112.2	110.4	110.3	90.1	102.0	95.4
2007	103.2	104.2	83.0	86.6	106.6	125.6	118.6	104.2	116.0	107.4	108.9	98.9	99.3	99.7
2008	102.9	103.3	88.6	87.6	107.5	114.7	117.3	99.0	114.7	102.9	108.8	103.8	86.4	101.4
2009	100.0	100.0	100.0	100.0	100.0	100.0	100.0	100.0	100.0	100.0	100.0	100.0	100.0	100.0
2010	102.5	102.4	101.9	93.9	109.4	95.6	111.6	99.0	103.1	102.4	105.7	104.2	99.9	102.7
2011	104.2	104.2	97.3	99.9	110.8	95.0	118.7	93.1	105.2	103.0	109.4	104.4	100.9	105.5
2012	106.5	106.6	89.3	110.3	110.4	98.6	122.3	90.6	108.3	104.9	110.3	105.6	106.1	107.1
2013	108.3	108.5	104.5	117.8	109.5	101.3	123.8	93.2	111.7	108.0	111.5	112.4	101.3	108.7
2014	110.8	111.3	103.8	129.6	107.1	103.0	125.8	93.3	116.0	111.0	112.9	112.7	106.4	110.9
2015	113.7	114.5	106.4	135.0	105.4	108.1	126.9	95.5	119.5	115.1	111.8	121.2	106.0	113.7
2016	115.6	116.4	114.8	120.2	110.6	111.8	127.0	95.2	120.4	117.5	114.0	128.9	107.5	114.9
2008														
1st quarter	103.3	104.0	90.2	80.5	107.2	117.7	119.3	97.7	117.4	105.0	111.6	103.1	94.7	101.3
2nd quarter ..	103.8	104.4	86.1	79.5	113.3	116.5	119.7	104.9	116.9	104.0	110.2	105.7	89.3	101.6
3rd quarter ...	103.3	103.6	83.7	84.9	112.7	115.5	118.6	97.8	114.8	102.8	110.2	106.1	85.1	101.2
4th quarter ...	101.1	101.2	94.5	105.2	96.8	109.2	111.4	95.8	109.6	99.8	103.2	100.3	76.4	101.3
2009														
1st quarter	99.7	99.8	95.4	110.0	95.5	101.3	101.3	94.7	102.1	99.7	97.0	98.8	94.0	100.8
2nd quarter ..	99.6	99.5	95.7	99.6	97.8	99.9	98.2	98.7	98.5	99.5	99.7	98.9	101.4	99.7
3rd quarter ...	99.9	99.9	107.0	96.6	100.6	101.3	98.6	101.6	98.1	99.4	100.6	99.3	103.1	99.7
4th quarter ...	100.9	100.8	101.9	93.8	106.1	97.5	102.0	105.0	101.3	101.4	102.6	102.9	101.5	99.8
2010														
1st quarter	101.3	101.0	98.6	92.3	111.7	94.5	105.0	102.9	100.3	101.0	102.7	102.3	100.7	101.2
2nd quarter ..	102.3	102.0	104.6	93.5	107.8	96.4	110.0	99.8	102.3	101.8	103.4	103.0	100.2	102.6
3rd quarter ...	103.0	102.9	104.2	93.7	108.9	95.7	114.3	97.4	105.0	103.5	107.0	106.3	98.2	102.9
4th quarter ...	103.6	103.7	100.0	96.2	109.2	95.5	117.3	95.9	104.9	103.2	109.5	105.3	100.6	104.2
2011														
1st quarter	103.2	103.2	100.9	94.7	105.0	93.1	117.1	93.2	105.0	103.1	108.9	103.5	101.6	103.4
2nd quarter ..	104.0	103.9	94.2	97.0	111.5	95.1	117.5	93.7	104.1	102.6	110.0	104.3	99.6	105.3
3rd quarter ...	104.2	104.2	94.7	101.1	110.7	95.6	118.6	92.4	103.7	102.9	108.8	105.0	101.0	105.8
4th quarter ...	105.4	105.5	99.5	106.9	116.0	96.4	121.6	93.0	108.3	103.4	110.0	104.7	101.3	107.5
2012														
1st quarter	106.1	106.2	94.1	106.4	107.1	98.2	121.8	93.5	106.7	105.2	111.0	104.8	104.6	106.7
2nd quarter ..	106.5	106.7	92.5	110.1	112.3	98.4	123.0	91.5	108.8	102.9	110.6	107.4	105.9	107.2
3rd quarter ...	106.7	106.7	85.8	110.8	112.1	98.1	122.0	89.6	108.9	106.4	109.9	105.8	107.4	107.7
4th quarter ...	106.7	106.8	84.8	114.0	110.2	99.7	122.2	87.8	108.8	105.1	109.6	104.2	106.6	106.9
2013														
1st quarter	107.4	107.6	96.4	114.9	113.3	100.9	123.9	92.7	109.7	107.9	112.1	111.0	99.1	107.9
2nd quarter ..	107.6	107.8	103.7	116.8	111.1	100.7	122.8	92.8	110.4	107.0	110.3	111.5	100.3	107.8
3rd quarter ...	108.5	108.8	110.0	118.0	107.8	102.0	123.8	93.1	112.7	108.0	110.6	111.9	101.1	109.2
4th quarter ...	109.5	110.0	107.8	121.3	105.7	101.7	124.5	94.1	114.2	109.1	113.2	115.3	104.6	109.9
2014														
1st quarter	109.2	109.4	103.4	120.1	106.4	102.1	123.2	93.1	112.5	109.0	111.9	111.9	104.3	109.7
2nd quarter ..	110.3	110.7	104.2	124.7	105.2	102.9	124.8	94.1	114.5	111.1	112.2	112.4	106.8	110.3
3rd quarter ...	111.6	112.3	102.7	132.2	108.3	102.9	127.8	93.0	118.3	112.2	114.2	112.7	107.0	111.6
4th quarter ...	112.3	113.0	105.0	141.4	108.4	104.2	127.5	93.1	118.8	111.8	113.1	113.7	107.5	112.1
2015														
1st quarter	112.8	113.6	103.5	143.2	101.3	104.6	127.1	96.5	118.8	112.3	110.3	117.5	108.2	113.2
2nd quarter ..	113.6	114.3	102.9	136.3	106.1	107.8	127.1	95.2	119.9	114.8	111.5	120.3	106.5	113.5
3rd quarter ...	114.1	114.9	109.0	133.9	107.6	109.3	126.5	96.0	119.4	115.7	112.9	121.6	105.7	114.0
4th quarter ...	114.4	115.2	110.0	126.8	106.7	110.6	126.9	94.4	120.1	117.6	112.4	125.2	103.7	114.0
2016														
1st quarter	114.6	115.5	111.7	125.5	107.5	112.5	126.1	95.4	118.8	117.4	110.4	127.5	106.0	114.5
2nd quarter ..	115.0	115.8	114.0	118.6	109.4	111.4	126.1	95.7	119.1	116.6	114.1	127.5	106.0	114.9
3rd quarter ...	116.0	116.9	118.1	117.5	113.1	111.6	127.7	95.6	121.5	117.3	115.1	130.2	108.3	114.9
4th quarter ...	116.6	117.5	115.6	119.0	112.5	111.9	127.9	93.9	122.2	118.9	116.5	130.4	109.9	115.2

Table 14-2. Chain-Type Quantity Indexes for Value Added by Industry—*Continued*

(New Series, 2009 = 100.)

Year	Private industries—*Continued*								Government			Private goods-producing industries	Private services-producing industries	Information-communications-technology-producing industries[1]
	Professional, scientific, and technical services	Management of companies and enterprises	Administrative and waste management services	Educational services	Health care and social assistance	Arts, entertainment, and recreation	Accommodation and food services	Other services except government	Total government	Federal	State and local			
1997	70.7	101.1	67.4	73.0	71.4	86.3	88.0	114.4	87.0	88.2	86.4	84.1	74.0	31.1
1998	74.4	104.5	69.7	71.9	72.2	86.2	90.8	118.9	88.0	88.0	88.0	87.7	77.6	37.0
1999	78.2	105.0	73.7	74.0	74.1	89.2	96.3	119.8	89.1	87.5	89.9	91.8	81.8	42.8
2000	81.8	110.4	79.4	76.4	75.9	93.2	102.2	122.4	90.8	88.5	92.0	96.6	85.0	50.7
2001	84.1	113.6	80.9	79.0	77.8	87.8	99.8	110.3	91.6	87.4	93.7	94.1	86.8	53.1
2002	86.2	112.8	81.1	80.3	81.2	92.0	101.7	113.3	93.3	89.1	95.4	94.2	88.8	56.8
2003	86.8	116.6	87.0	83.9	83.8	95.6	104.5	109.8	94.4	90.8	96.2	97.5	91.1	62.5
2004	90.0	110.9	91.1	88.1	87.0	99.0	109.6	111.5	95.3	92.5	96.6	102.6	94.3	70.6
2005	92.7	111.7	99.4	87.8	88.8	99.3	110.0	111.9	96.1	93.2	97.5	104.4	98.3	78.9
2006	96.0	112.7	101.7	89.9	92.4	102.3	112.2	112.3	96.7	93.7	98.1	108.1	101.0	86.2
2007	99.0	109.8	106.2	91.8	93.1	103.9	111.8	109.5	97.7	94.5	99.2	109.2	102.7	95.4
2008	106.5	109.2	107.0	95.4	98.2	103.5	108.2	105.4	99.5	97.1	100.6	105.6	102.6	102.3
2009	100.0	100.0	100.0	100.0	100.0	100.0	100.0	100.0	100.0	100.0	100.0	100.0	100.0	100.0
2010	100.9	107.7	107.1	101.1	100.4	104.4	103.4	98.3	100.7	102.5	99.8	101.8	102.6	104.6
2011	104.6	112.4	111.1	101.9	102.2	106.5	108.1	97.9	100.3	102.7	99.1	102.3	104.7	108.3
2012	108.1	120.8	115.2	102.8	104.3	110.0	110.5	100.0	100.1	102.2	99.1	104.0	107.4	111.8
2013	108.2	127.2	117.0	100.7	106.1	113.3	112.9	99.2	99.3	99.7	99.0	107.8	108.8	119.6
2014	111.8	136.8	121.1	102.8	108.1	117.3	115.7	101.4	99.0	98.9	99.0	110.2	111.7	122.5
2015	117.5	140.1	125.4	103.1	113.0	121.4	118.6	103.1	99.4	98.3	99.9	113.1	114.9	. . .
2016	121.4	141.8	127.7	102.2	116.3	124.5	119.4	104.9	100.0	98.4	100.7	113.1	117.4	. . .
2008														
1st quarter	105.5	107.6	107.1	93.6	96.3	103.6	109.9	106.7	99.0	95.9	100.5	105.5	103.6	. . .
2nd quarter	107.4	109.6	107.8	94.7	97.6	103.5	109.6	105.6	99.3	96.6	100.6	106.9	103.6	. . .
3rd quarter	108.4	110.7	107.9	96.7	99.0	103.2	108.1	105.1	99.9	97.7	101.0	105.2	103.1	. . .
4th quarter	106.8	109.2	105.1	96.8	100.0	103.8	105.2	104.4	99.6	98.2	100.2	104.6	100.2	. . .
2009														
1st quarter	101.6	97.5	100.8	100.3	99.8	100.4	101.2	101.7	99.5	98.6	99.9	99.9	99.7	. . .
2nd quarter	99.7	99.0	99.3	99.8	100.1	100.2	99.8	100.6	100.1	100.0	100.1	98.8	99.7	. . .
3rd quarter	99.4	101.4	99.2	99.7	99.8	99.5	99.0	99.1	100.1	100.4	100.0	100.3	99.8	. . .
4th quarter	99.3	102.1	100.7	100.2	100.4	99.9	100.0	98.6	100.4	100.9	100.1	101.0	100.7	. . .
2010														
1st quarter	101.3	104.5	104.8	100.7	99.6	102.5	101.2	97.3	100.6	101.8	100.1	100.4	101.2	. . .
2nd quarter	102.5	106.6	106.4	101.2	100.3	103.8	102.9	98.0	100.9	103.0	100.0	101.8	102.0	. . .
3rd quarter	104.2	108.0	107.9	101.1	100.8	104.2	104.0	99.0	100.6	102.5	99.7	102.2	103.1	. . .
4th quarter	105.6	111.4	109.2	101.5	101.2	107.0	105.4	99.0	100.5	102.6	99.5	102.7	104.0	. . .
2011														
1st quarter	105.9	112.4	109.3	102.5	101.3	105.6	106.6	97.9	100.4	102.7	99.4	101.1	103.8	. . .
2nd quarter	107.6	113.4	110.8	102.4	102.1	106.5	108.4	97.9	100.4	102.8	99.3	101.6	104.5	. . .
3rd quarter	107.7	111.3	111.8	101.9	102.5	108.4	108.9	97.9	100.1	102.6	99.0	102.2	104.8	. . .
4th quarter	108.2	112.3	112.2	100.9	102.7	105.4	108.7	98.0	100.1	102.7	98.9	104.5	105.8	. . .
2012														
1st quarter	110.6	117.1	115.1	103.0	104.1	109.0	110.6	99.4	100.2	102.6	99.0	104.6	106.7	. . .
2nd quarter	111.3	118.1	114.9	103.0	103.8	109.5	110.1	99.9	100.1	102.3	99.0	104.7	107.3	. . .
3rd quarter	111.4	120.4	115.4	102.8	104.1	109.8	109.9	100.4	100.1	102.1	99.1	103.4	107.8	. . .
4th quarter	113.6	127.7	115.5	102.6	105.1	111.0	111.3	100.4	100.0	101.7	99.1	103.4	107.8	. . .
2013														
1st quarter	110.9	119.9	115.6	100.4	106.1	112.5	113.4	99.7	99.8	101.1	99.2	106.7	107.8	. . .
2nd quarter	112.2	125.1	116.2	100.7	106.0	112.7	112.3	98.9	99.6	100.5	99.1	107.1	108.0	. . .
3rd quarter	114.2	130.2	117.6	100.7	106.2	113.0	112.5	98.9	99.1	99.3	99.0	108.3	108.9	. . .
4th quarter	115.4	133.4	118.5	100.9	106.3	114.8	113.5	99.5	98.5	97.9	98.8	109.1	110.3	. . .
2014														
1st quarter	115.3	133.8	119.3	102.4	106.6	115.4	113.9	99.7	98.9	99.4	98.7	108.0	109.9	. . .
2nd quarter	116.3	134.2	120.3	102.6	107.2	116.1	115.0	100.7	99.0	99.1	98.9	109.6	111.0	. . .
3rd quarter	119.2	139.3	121.8	103.4	108.9	118.0	116.6	102.4	99.0	98.8	99.1	110.9	112.7	. . .
4th quarter	120.2	139.8	123.2	102.9	109.9	119.8	117.2	102.5	99.1	98.5	99.4	112.2	113.2	. . .
2015														
1st quarter	121.3	139.4	123.8	103.0	110.9	119.8	117.2	102.3	99.0	98.6	99.3	113.3	113.8	. . .
2nd quarter	122.3	139.3	124.7	102.7	112.3	120.7	118.4	103.0	99.3	98.4	99.8	112.8	114.7	. . .
3rd quarter	123.3	140.6	126.1	103.1	113.5	121.4	119.0	103.0	99.6	98.3	100.2	113.4	115.3	. . .
4th quarter	124.2	141.1	126.9	103.5	115.2	123.7	120.1	103.9	99.6	98.1	100.2	112.7	115.9	. . .
2016														
1st quarter	124.3	138.9	126.2	102.4	114.7	123.0	118.8	104.1	99.6	98.0	100.3	113.3	116.1	. . .
2nd quarter	125.4	141.4	126.6	101.6	116.0	123.0	118.9	104.3	99.8	98.3	100.5	112.8	116.7	. . .
3rd quarter	126.6	143.1	128.4	102.2	116.8	124.5	119.4	105.2	100.3	98.7	101.0	113.4	117.9	. . .
4th quarter	127.7	144.1	129.7	102.7	117.7	127.5	120.3	105.9	100.4	98.8	101.1	112.9	118.8	. . .

[1]Consists of computer and electronic products manufacturing; publishing, including software; information and data processing services; and computer systems design and related services.
. . . = Not available.

Table 14-3. Gross Domestic Factor Income by Industry

(Billions of current dollars.)

NAICS industry	2003	2004	2005	2006	2007	2008	2009	2010	2011	2012	2013	2014	2015
Gross domestic factor income, total	10 751.7	11 457.4	12 220.1	12 915.4	13 497.7	13 729.3	13 451.0	13 963.1	14 475.4	15 081.2	15 575.9	16 239.6	16 855.7
Compensation of employees	6 372.7	6 748.8	7 097.9	7 513.7	7 908.8	8 090.0	7 795.7	7 969.5	8 277.1	8 618.5	8 851.9	9 263.7	9 704.1
Gross operating surplus	4 379.0	4 708.6	5 122.2	5 401.7	5 588.9	5 639.3	5 655.3	5 993.6	6 198.3	6 462.7	6 724.0	6 975.9	7 151.6
Private industries	9 176.5	9 793.9	10 475.7	11 087.5	11 573.8	11 706.5	11 362.7	11 804.5	12 283.2	12 861.0	13 328.7	13 938.5	14 493.4
Compensation of employees	5 106.2	5 405.9	5 693.8	6 047.5	6 367.8	6 472.5	6 129.5	6 246.0	6 540.0	6 875.3	7 090.3	7 459.8	7 845.6
Gross operating surplus	4 070.3	4 388.0	4 781.9	5 040.0	5 206.0	5 234.0	5 233.2	5 558.5	5 743.2	5 985.7	6 238.4	6 478.7	6 647.8
Agriculture, forestry, fishing, and hunting	124.2	147.6	143.1	134.8	144.5	156.7	140.1	162.5	197.2	185.6	221.4	200.2	172.4
Compensation of employees	31.7	35.0	34.7	38.0	41.5	42.2	42.2	41.4	41.0	47.9	48.3	50.3	52.8
Gross operating surplus	92.5	112.6	108.4	96.8	103.0	114.5	97.9	121.1	156.2	137.7	173.1	149.9	119.6
Mining	122.8	147.8	201.2	244.3	280.4	358.7	260.6	298.2	358.9	371.2	408.5	440.9	289.1
Compensation of employees	37.1	41.5	47.1	57.0	62.7	72.8	64.7	69.1	80.3	90.5	93.4	99.7	91.1
Gross operating surplus	85.7	106.3	154.1	187.3	217.7	285.9	195.9	229.1	278.6	280.7	315.1	341.2	198.0
Utilities	146.4	159.7	155.3	179.4	180.5	184.8	196.6	211.2	214.8	204.7	211.2	225.2	226.1
Compensation of employees	52.9	55.6	56.1	60.9	63.1	66.3	66.8	67.6	71.2	69.8	72.3	74.5	76.9
Gross operating surplus	93.5	104.1	99.2	118.5	117.4	118.5	129.8	143.6	143.6	134.9	138.9	150.7	149.2
Construction	521.0	580.8	646.8	690.4	707.1	645.4	570.0	534.6	539.4	576.4	613.3	664.3	724.0
Compensation of employees	335.7	357.9	387.5	421.4	439.8	433.3	369.1	344.9	348.9	366.6	388.0	420.4	453.1
Gross operating surplus	185.3	222.9	259.3	269.0	267.3	212.1	200.9	189.7	190.5	209.8	225.3	243.9	270.9
Durable goods manufacturing	846.4	888.5	938.3	983.4	1 006.6	969.3	848.1	931.5	978.4	1 027.1	1 057.3	1 100.3	1 147.1
Compensation of employees	550.0	573.4	590.5	615.6	628.2	616.2	540.1	547.0	579.7	605.3	610.6	637.2	660.0
Gross operating surplus	296.4	315.1	347.8	367.8	378.4	353.1	308.0	384.5	398.7	421.8	446.7	463.1	487.1
Nondurable goods manufacturing	633.8	678.0	710.1	763.1	787.5	778.8	800.8	820.6	847.6	874.1	892.7	914.5	939.5
Compensation of employees	297.5	300.6	305.3	309.1	316.2	316.4	295.9	300.9	303.8	312.6	318.9	333.3	342.6
Gross operating surplus	336.3	377.4	404.8	454.0	471.3	462.4	504.9	519.7	543.8	561.5	573.8	581.2	596.9
Wholesale trade	501.9	548.9	595.4	641.4	685.5	705.0	664.2	699.0	723.3	770.9	800.7	841.7	881.3
Compensation of employees	337.0	357.1	379.3	404.7	429.2	435.5	405.3	412.5	436.7	457.9	467.8	491.3	511.1
Gross operating surplus	164.9	191.8	216.1	236.7	256.3	269.5	258.9	286.5	286.6	313.0	332.9	350.4	370.2
Retail trade	628.3	645.1	678.0	696.8	693.3	676.9	674.2	690.3	705.2	740.5	765.8	793.3	838.3
Compensation of employees	444.7	459.2	477.5	492.3	506.1	500.5	474.5	479.5	496.6	510.6	527.0	546.6	572.8
Gross operating surplus	183.6	185.9	200.5	204.5	187.2	176.4	199.7	210.8	208.6	229.9	238.8	246.7	265.5
Transportation and warehousing	304.4	330.8	352.5	385.3	384.9	398.3	375.5	402.5	420.7	441.2	457.2	479.7	510.9
Compensation of employees	209.6	221.9	231.5	241.1	255.8	255.5	241.3	245.7	260.0	274.7	282.7	294.3	315.5
Gross operating surplus	94.8	108.9	121.0	144.2	129.1	142.8	134.2	156.8	160.7	166.5	174.5	185.4	195.4
Information	523.3	578.9	597.9	605.3	659.2	686.5	662.0	686.6	683.8	693.0	746.4	746.8	792.5
Compensation of employees	230.4	237.9	241.4	248.8	260.4	257.8	251.6	248.6	260.2	271.6	286.1	304.2	317.9
Gross operating surplus	292.9	341.0	356.5	356.5	398.8	428.7	410.4	438.0	423.6	421.4	460.3	442.6	474.6
Finance and insurance	833.0	853.2	952.1	1 007.1	996.0	860.9	921.2	957.7	988.0	1 094.3	1 086.1	1 190.4	1 226.5
Compensation of employees	460.5	498.5	535.4	579.8	618.2	612.9	549.0	574.3	606.8	630.2	640.3	681.1	714.2
Gross operating surplus	372.5	354.7	416.7	427.3	377.8	248.0	372.2	383.4	381.2	464.1	445.8	509.3	512.3
Real estate and rental and leasing	1 304.8	1 363.8	1 471.4	1 527.3	1 633.2	1 686.5	1 684.1	1 725.2	1 791.8	1 855.8	1 923.7	2 006.7	2 124.2
Compensation of employees	87.4	94.9	101.4	107.9	111.8	109.9	103.4	103.7	106.8	114.4	119.1	127.1	136.8
Gross operating surplus	1 217.4	1 268.9	1 370.0	1 419.4	1 521.4	1 576.6	1 580.7	1 621.5	1 685.0	1 741.4	1 804.6	1 879.6	1 987.4
Professional, scientific, and technical services	1 211.5	1 298.6	1 393.1	1 491.3	1 607.4	1 707.3	1 619.7	1 687.4	1 767.5	1 865.3	1 914.8	2 012.6	2 152.3
Compensation of employees	872.0	934.0	1 012.2	1 099.3	1 183.3	1 226.6	1 165.6	1 215.9	1 287.5	1 376.8	1 430.6	1 514.4	1 611.0
Gross operating surplus	339.5	364.6	380.9	392.0	424.1	480.7	454.1	471.5	480.0	488.5	484.2	498.2	541.3
Management of companies and enterprises	180.7	199.3	211.3	229.8	250.1	251.8	238.1	259.2	271.8	295.4	313.6	329.0	347.1
Compensation of employees	159.5	175.4	185.1	200.4	219.4	220.5	207.6	227.0	237.9	259.1	275.2	288.7	303.2
Gross operating surplus	21.2	23.9	26.2	29.4	30.7	31.3	30.5	32.2	33.9	36.3	38.4	40.3	43.9
Administrative and waste management services	314.4	339.0	372.6	390.9	421.3	429.3	404.7	430.2	447.7	469.2	483.8	511.2	546.8
Compensation of employees	235.4	253.0	274.6	292.4	310.0	313.9	289.2	306.6	322.3	341.5	353.9	377.4	398.2
Gross operating surplus	79.0	86.0	98.0	98.5	111.3	115.4	115.5	123.6	125.4	127.7	129.9	133.8	148.6
Educational services	101.7	111.5	115.2	123.6	132.0	142.4	155.4	161.6	167.5	175.0	177.3	186.8	193.8
Compensation of employees	94.2	101.9	105.5	112.8	120.7	129.1	139.5	145.2	152.4	161.0	164.5	173.9	180.0
Gross operating surplus	7.5	9.6	9.7	10.8	11.3	13.3	15.9	16.4	15.1	14.0	12.8	12.9	13.8
Health care and social assistance	720.1	769.4	807.2	859.6	900.6	972.3	1 026.0	1 054.1	1 090.0	1 129.1	1 162.0	1 197.4	1 271.0
Compensation of employees	606.4	650.2	687.5	733.3	775.1	824.6	863.0	889.2	923.0	964.4	996.9	1 028.6	1 085.9
Gross operating surplus	113.7	119.2	119.7	126.3	125.5	147.7	163.0	164.9	167.0	164.7	165.1	168.8	185.1
Arts, entertainment, and recreation ...	381.5	407.2	421.9	445.5	461.7	463.6	452.3	467.0	488.6	520.2	546.8	577.0	624.0
Compensation of employees	262.9	280.2	291.4	306.5	324.7	332.9	321.5	328.0	344.4	369.0	385.5	409.7	438.0
Gross operating surplus	118.6	127.0	130.5	139.0	137.0	130.7	130.8	139.0	144.2	151.2	161.3	167.3	186.0
Accommodation and food services	280.4	300.2	311.5	328.2	339.3	338.8	328.5	338.4	357.1	380.7	400.1	421.8	456.8
Compensation of employees	198.7	213.0	222.8	233.4	247.7	252.3	242.9	248.5	262.7	282.8	295.7	314.6	337.7
Gross operating surplus	81.7	87.2	88.7	94.8	91.6	86.5	85.6	89.9	94.4	97.9	104.4	107.2	119.1
Other services, except government ...	271.4	284.1	296.2	309.0	313.2	313.3	311.8	314.7	320.5	336.5	343.7	360.7	380.6
Compensation of employees	196.3	206.1	209.5	219.0	231.1	240.0	235.9	232.7	240.6	251.9	258.4	273.3	286.0
Gross operating surplus	75.1	78.0	86.7	90.0	82.1	73.3	75.9	82.0	79.9	84.6	85.3	87.4	94.6
Government	1 575.2	1 663.5	1 744.4	1 827.9	1 923.9	2 022.8	2 088.3	2 158.7	2 192.2	2 220.2	2 247.2	2 301.1	2 362.2
Compensation of employees	1 266.5	1 342.9	1 404.1	1 466.2	1 541.0	1 617.5	1 666.2	1 723.5	1 737.1	1 743.3	1 761.6	1 803.9	1 858.5
Gross operating surplus	308.7	320.6	340.3	361.7	382.9	405.3	422.1	435.2	455.1	476.9	485.6	497.2	503.7
Addenda:													
Private goods-producing industries ..	2 248.1	2 442.7	2 639.5	2 815.9	2 926.1	2 908.8	2 619.7	2 747.3	2 921.4	3 034.4	3 193.1	3 320.2	3 272.0
Compensation of employees	1 251.9	1 308.4	1 365.1	1 441.1	1 488.3	1 480.9	1 312.1	1 303.2	1 353.7	1 422.9	1 459.2	1 540.9	1 599.6
Gross operating surplus	996.2	1 134.3	1 274.4	1 374.8	1 437.8	1 427.9	1 307.6	1 444.1	1 567.7	1 611.5	1 733.9	1 779.3	1 672.4
Private services-producing industries	6 928.4	7 351.2	7 836.3	8 271.5	8 647.6	8 797.7	8 743.0	9 057.2	9 361.7	9 826.6	10 135.6	10 618.3	11 221.4
Compensation of employees	3 854.3	4 097.5	4 328.7	4 606.3	4 879.5	4 991.6	4 817.4	4 942.8	5 186.3	5 452.3	5 631.1	5 918.9	6 246.0
Gross operating surplus	3 074.1	3 253.7	3 507.6	3 665.2	3 768.1	3 806.1	3 925.6	4 114.4	4 175.4	4 374.3	4 504.5	4 699.4	4 975.4
Information-communications-technology-producing industries [1]	616.2	669.7	716.2	753.8	805.4	839.4	808.8	832.3	848.5	870.3	937.2	954.7	1 013.1
Compensation of employees	342.4	356.5	373.5	398.7	419.7	422.5	408.2	414.4	442.2	468.0	489.6	520.2	551.3
Gross operating surplus	273.8	313.2	342.7	355.1	385.7	416.9	400.6	417.9	406.3	402.3	447.6	434.5	461.8

[1] Consists of computer and electronic products manufacturing; publishing, including software; information and data processing services; and computer systems design and related services.

NOTES AND DEFINITIONS, CHAPTER 14

TABLES 14-1 THROUGH 14-3

Gross Domestic Product (VALUE ADDED) and Gross Factor Income by Industry

SOURCE: U.S. DEPARTMENT OF COMMERCE, BUREAU OF ECONOMIC ANALYSIS (BEA)

In the introduction to the notes and definitions for Chapter 1, it was observed that gross domestic product (GDP), while primarily measured as the sum of final demands for goods and services, is also the sum of the values created by each industry in the economy. In this chapter, selected data are presented from the industry accounts in the national income and product accounts (NIPAs). The industry accounts measure the contribution of each major industry to GDP.

Quarterly estimates of current- and constant-dollar GDP by industry were new in the 20th edition of *Business Statistics*. These measures have been computed starting with the first quarter of 2005 and extending through a preliminary estimate for the first quarter of 2015; they are displayed for 2005-2014 in Tables 14-1A and 14-2A. They provide a complete accounting of the industrial origin of GDP, and measure the output of major industries on a more up-to-date basis than the annual measures previously available—within 120 days after the end of the reference quarter.

In recent years, estimates of GDP by industry have been prepared using a methodology integrated with annual input-output accounts in order to produce estimates of gross industry output, industry input, and the difference between the two—industry value added—with greater consistency and timeliness than was previously possible. The current integrated industry accounts also include a wealth of related information too extensive for inclusion here, such as quantity and price indexes for gross output and intermediate inputs, cost per unit of real value added allocated to the three components of value added, and components of domestic supply (domestic output, imports, exports, and inventory change).

The most precise estimates of GDP by NAICS industry begin with 1997, but the annual series were extended back to 1947, using approximations of current methods in earlier years when the source data were less comprehensive and were initially compiled on the older SIC classifications. Table 14-1B presents this "old series" current-dollar GDP for NAICS industry groups from 1947 through 2009; Table 14-2B presents "old series" indexes of real value added for each industry group.

The new figures for 1997 forward, unlike the "old series" data from last year's edition, reflect the conceptual and data changes made in the 2013 comprehensive revision of the NIPAs.

In Table 14-3, the editor presents a measure derived from the components of current-dollar value added as published by BEA. This measure, "gross domestic factor income," enables users to obtain a clearer picture of the quantitative impact of each industry on the economy's factors of production and of the shares of capital and labor in each industry.

The 2004 revision incorporated a change in terminology. An industry's contribution to total GDP, formerly referred to as "gross product originating" (GPO) or "gross product by industry," is now called "value added." This is consistent with the use of the term "value added" in most economic writing. However, it should not be confused with a concept known as "Census value added," which is used in U.S. censuses and surveys of manufactures. Census value added is calculated at the individual establishment level and, for that reason, does not exclude purchased business services. This means that census value added, while still an important gauge of relative importance, is not a true measure of economic value added.

Definitions and notes on the data

An industry's *gross domestic product (value added)*, formerly *GPO*, is equal to the market value of its gross output (which consists of the value, including taxes, of sales or receipts and other operating income plus the value of inventory change) minus the value of its intermediate inputs (energy, raw materials, semifinished goods, and services that are purchased from domestic industries or from foreign sources).

In concept, this is also equal to the sum of *compensation of employees, taxes on production and imports less subsidies,* and *gross operating surplus.* (See Chapter 1 and its notes and definitions for more information.)

The GDP data from 1997 forward are not comparable with the "old series" data for earlier years presented in Tables 14-1B and 14-2B, the major reason being that they do not reflect the conceptual revisions introduced in the comprehensive 2013 revision of the NIPAs (see the Notes and Definitions to Chapter 1). In particular, the new data include, while the old data exclude, the capitalized values of research and development, intellectual property, and all real estate transfer costs. This does not change labor compensation values—the associated workers were always included; it was just that their costs were taken to be written off in the first year. But it does increase across the board the non-labor share of the total value of output, by the amount of capital consumption and net investment. This is seen in labor compensation shares derived from Table 14-3, compared with those that would have been calculated on the old basis last year.

Compensation of employees consists of wage and salary accruals and supplements to wages and salaries. This approximates the labor share of production, subject to the note below about proprietors' income.

Taxes on production and imports less subsidies. Although this is shown in BEA source data as a single net line item, it represents two separate components.

Taxes on production and imports are included in the market value of the goods and services sold to final consumers and therefore in the consumer valuation of those goods. Since they are not part of the payments to the labor and capital inputs in the producing industries, they must be <u>added</u> to the sum of the returns to those inputs in order to account for the total value to consumers. Taxes that fall into this classification include property taxes, sales and excise taxes, and Customs duties.

BEA allocates these taxes to the industry level at which they are assessed by law. Most sales taxes are considered by BEA to be part of the value added by retail trade. Some sales taxes, most fuel taxes, and all customs duties are allocated by BEA to wholesale trade. Residential real property taxes, including those on owner-occupied dwellings, are allocated by BEA to the real estate industry.

Subsidies to business by government are included in the labor and/or capital payments made by that industry. Since they are payments to the industry in addition to the market values paid by consumers, they are *subtracted* from the values of the labor and capital inputs to make them consistent with the market values as defined in value added. The role of subsidies is obvious in the source data for the agricultural sector, where the net "taxes on production and imports less subsidies" has a negative sign: farm subsidies more than offset this industry's taxes on production and imports, which mainly consist of property taxes, since sales, excise, and import taxes are not levied on farms.

For private sector businesses, *gross operating surplus* consists of business income (corporate profits before tax, proprietors' income, and rental income of persons), net interest and miscellaneous payments, business current transfer payments (net), and capital consumption allowances. For government, households, and institutions, it consists of consumption of fixed capital and (for government) government enterprises' current surplus. This approximates the share of the value of production ascribable to capital and land as measured in the NIPAs accounts; however, as BEA notes, "an unknown portion [of proprietors' income] reflects the labor contribution of proprietors." (*Survey of Current Business*, June 2004, p. 27, footnote 7.) Another aspect to be noted is that gross operating surplus includes the return to owner-occupied housing in the real estate sector. Because there is in the NIPAs no employee compensation attributed to owner-occupied housing, the capital share in that industry as measured by gross operating surplus is very large.

Quantity indexes for value added. Measures of the constant-dollar change in each industry's gross output minus its intermediate input use are calculated by BEA, using a Fisher index-number formula which incorporates weights from two adjacent years. The changes for successive years are chained together in indexes, with the value for the year 2009 set at 100. The indexes are multiplied by 2009 current-dollar value added to provide estimates of value added in "chained 2009 dollars," but because the actual weights used change from year to year, components in chained 2009 dollars typically do not add up to total GDP in 2009 dollars—and do not contain any information not already summarized in the indexes. For that reason, only the indexes are published here.

Gross domestic factor income (not a category published as such in the NIPAs) is calculated by the editor as the sum of "compensation of employees" and "gross operating surplus," which the same as value added minus "taxes on production and imports less subsidies." The effect of this procedure is to take out the specified taxes, and to leave in the subsidies embedded in the employee compensation and gross operating surplus components. The editor believes that this provides a valuable alternative basis for assessing the importance of different industries in the economy, by measuring the value paid for by its labor and capital inputs, and for calculating the shares of labor and capital in each industry's output. The components shown in this table are found on the BEA website in a table entitled "Components of Value Added by Industry."

The editor's reasoning is based on the facts that more than half of these taxes are sales, excise, and import taxes, and the assignment of these taxes to industries is economically arbitrary. BEA assigns them to the industry with the legal liability to pay, not to the entity bearing the major incidence of the tax. Yet economists have demonstrated that most of the burdens of sales and excise taxes and import duties are not borne by the factors in the legally liable industry; instead, they are passed on to consumers. In addition, because the wholesale and retail trade industries are classified as "services-producing," BEA's allocation of those taxes has a very peculiar result: taxes on goods are represented as paid by "service" industries. The process adopted instead by the editor in Table 14-3, which excludes these taxes and focuses on "gross domestic factor income," has the effect (for example) of keeping the wholesale trade industry from appearing to be both larger and more heavily taxed than it really is.

Private goods-producing industries consists of agriculture, forestry, fishing, and hunting; mining; construction; and manufacturing.

Private services-producing industries consists of utilities; wholesale trade; retail trade; transportation and warehousing; information; finance, insurance, real estate, rental, and leasing; professional and business services; educational services, health care, and social assistance; arts, entertainment, recreation, accommodation, and food services; and other services, except government.

Information-communications-technology-producing industries is a category that cuts across the goods and services framework, consisting of computer and electronic products manufacturing; publishing industries (which includes software) from the information sector; information and data processing services; and computer systems design and related services.

DATA AVAILABILITY AND REFERENCES

The comprehensive revision of the industry accounts from 1997 forward and the new quarterly statistics are described in "Industry Economic Accounts: Results of the Comprehensive Revision, Revised Statistics for 1997-2012" (*Survey of Current Business,* February 2014); "New Quarterly Statistics Detail Industries' Economic Performance," BEA news release, April 25, 2014; and

"Prototype Quarterly Statistics on U.S. GDP by Industry, 2007-2011," June 2012, a "BEA Briefing." All are available on the BEA website, http://www.bea.gov. To access the historical data at <http://www.bea.gov>, click on "Annual Industry Accounts" and click on "Interactive Tables" under "Gross Domestic Product (GDP) by Industry."

"Old basis" annual GDP by industry data shown here were recalculated back to 1947 consistent with the 2009 comprehensive revision of the NIPAs. They were most recently presented and described in "Annual Industry Statistics: Revised Statistics for 2009-2011," *Survey of Current Business,* December 2012.

CHAPTER 15: EMPLOYMENT, HOURS, AND EARNINGS BY NAICS INDUSTRY

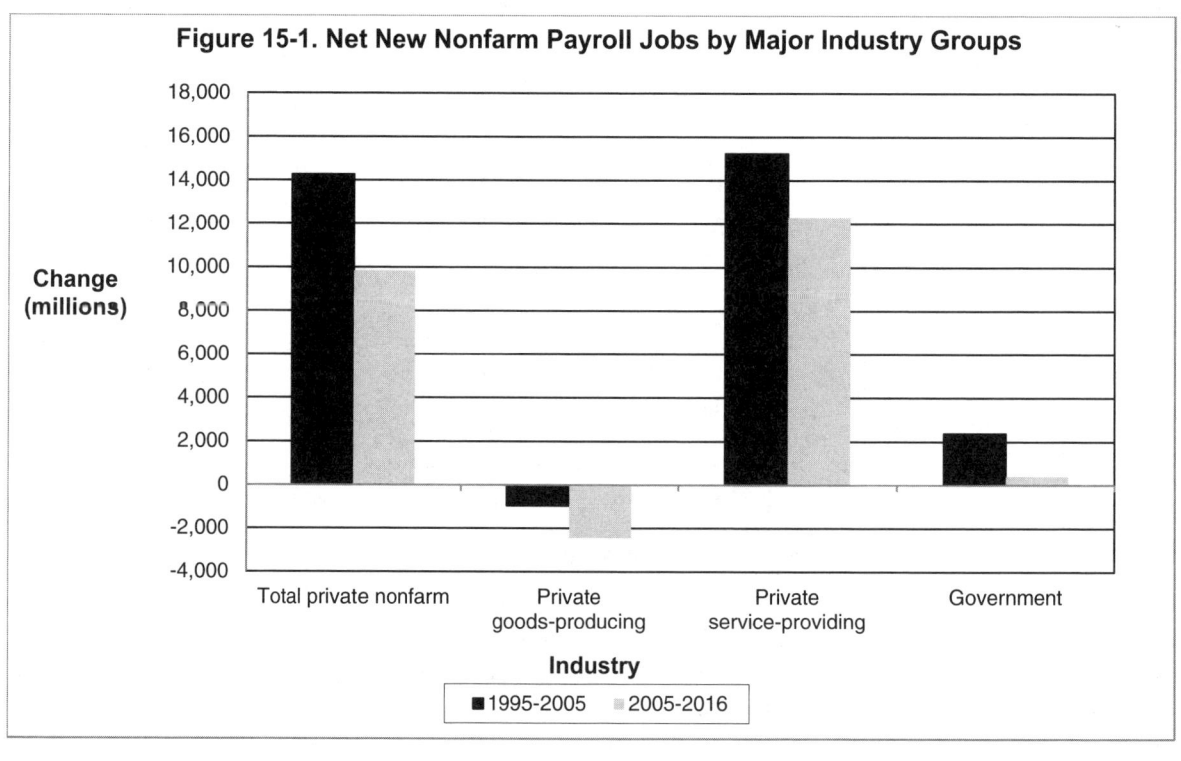

Figure 15-1. Net New Nonfarm Payroll Jobs by Major Industry Groups

- Employment began to decline in February 2008 and didn't begin to increase until February 2010, eight months after the end of recession, which the National Bureau of Economic Research Business Cycle Dating Committee places at June 2009. ("Business Cycle Perspectives" at the beginning of this volume, Table 10-1 and Table 15-1)

- Employment increased for the sixth consecutive year in 2016 after decreasing from 2008 to 2010. (Table 15-1)

- However, the U.S. economy continues to shed goods-producing and government jobs. For example, construction jobs declined 919,000 between 2007 and 2016. On the other hand, service-providing industries added over 8.8 millions jobs between 2007 and 2016, up 7.6 percent. Knowledge-based employment, such as in internet publishing and computer systems design companies, continues to grow. (Table 15-1)

- The average workweek for production and nonsupervisory workers is up since 2009 in most industries and industry groups. Goods-producing workers averaged 41.2 hours per week while service-providing workers averaged 32.3 hours a week in 2016. (Table 15-3)

- Average hourly earnings for production and nonsupervisory workers in 2016 ranged from a low of $12.85 in the leisure and hospitality sector to $38.84 in petroleum and coal products manufacturing. (Table 15-4)

Table 15-1. Nonfarm Employment by Sector and Industry

(Wage and salary workers on nonfarm payrolls, thousands.)

Industry	1995	1996	1997	1998	1999	2000	2001	2002	2003	2004	2005
TOTAL NONFARM	117 407	119 836	122 951	126 157	129 240	132 024	132 087	130 649	130 347	131 787	134 051
Total Private	97 975	100 297	103 287	106 248	108 933	111 235	110 969	109 136	108 764	110 166	112 247
Goods-Producing	23 156	23 409	23 886	24 354	24 465	24 649	23 873	22 557	21 816	21 882	22 190
Mining and logging	641	637	654	645	598	599	606	583	572	591	628
Logging	82.5	80.7	82.1	80.0	80.8	79.0	73.5	70.4	69.4	67.6	65.2
Mining	558.1	556.4	571.3	564.7	517.4	520.2	532.5	512.2	502.7	523.0	562.2
Oil and gas extraction	151.7	146.9	144.1	140.8	131.2	124.9	123.7	121.9	120.2	123.4	125.7
Mining, except oil and gas [1]	252.4	249.4	249.5	243.1	234.5	224.8	218.7	210.6	202.7	205.1	212.8
Coal mining	96.7	90.5	89.4	85.3	78.6	72.2	74.3	74.4	70.0	70.6	73.9
Support activities for mining	154.0	160.1	177.7	180.8	151.7	170.6	190.1	179.8	179.8	194.6	223.7
Construction	5 274	5 536	5 813	6 149	6 545	6 787	6 826	6 716	6 735	6 976	7 336
Construction of buildings	1 325.4	1 380.2	1 435.4	1 508.8	1 586.3	1 632.5	1 588.9	1 574.8	1 575.8	1 630.0	1 711.9
Heavy and civil engineering	774.7	800.1	824.9	865.3	908.7	937.0	953.0	930.6	903.1	907.4	951.2
Specialty trade contractors	3 174.1	3 355.1	3 552.6	3 775.1	4 049.6	4 217.0	4 283.9	4 210.4	4 255.7	4 438.6	4 673.1
Manufacturing	17 241	17 237	17 419	17 560	17 322	17 263	16 441	15 259	14 509	14 315	14 227
Durable goods	10 373	10 486	10 705	10 911	10 831	10 877	10 336	9 485	8 964	8 925	8 956
Wood products	576.1	585.2	597.8	611.6	622.7	615.4	576.3	557.0	539.5	551.6	561.0
Nonmetallic mineral products	513.1	517.3	525.7	535.3	540.8	554.2	544.5	516.0	494.2	505.5	505.3
Primary metals	641.7	639.3	638.8	641.5	625.0	621.8	570.9	509.4	477.4	466.8	466.0
Fabricated metal products	1 623.4	1 647.5	1 695.8	1 739.5	1 728.4	1 752.6	1 676.4	1 548.5	1 478.9	1 497.1	1 522.0
Machinery	1 442.3	1 468.9	1 495.9	1 514.1	1 468.3	1 457.0	1 370.6	1 231.8	1 151.6	1 145.2	1 165.5
Computer and electronic products [1]	1 688.4	1 746.6	1 803.3	1 830.9	1 780.5	1 820.0	1 748.8	1 507.2	1 355.2	1 322.8	1 316.4
Computer and peripheral equipment	295.6	304.6	316.7	322.1	310.1	301.9	286.2	250.0	224.0	210.0	205.1
Communications equipment	224.3	228.9	235.0	237.4	228.7	238.6	225.4	179.0	149.2	143.0	141.4
Semiconductors and electronic components	571.0	606.6	639.8	649.8	630.5	676.3	645.4	524.5	461.1	454.1	452.0
Electronic instruments	490.5	497.8	502.8	509.2	498.3	487.7	483.6	456.8	435.4	436.9	441.0
Electrical equipment and appliances	592.8	591.0	586.3	591.6	588.0	590.9	556.9	496.5	459.6	445.1	433.5
Transportation equipment [1]	1 978.5	1 975.1	2 027.6	2 078.4	2 088.6	2 057.1	1 939.1	1 830.0	1 775.1	1 766.7	1 772.3
Motor vehicles and parts	1 241.5	1 240.3	1 253.9	1 271.5	1 312.5	1 313.6	1 212.9	1 151.2	1 125.3	1 112.8	1 096.7
Furniture and related products	607.0	604.2	615.5	641.6	665.2	680.1	642.9	604.7	573.7	574.1	566.3
Miscellaneous manufacturing	709.7	710.7	718.2	726.8	724.0	728.0	709.5	683.3	658.3	650.6	647.2
Nondurable goods [1]	6 868	6 751	6 714	6 649	6 491	6 386	6 105	5 774	5 546	5 390	5 271
Food manufacturing	1 560.0	1 562.0	1 557.9	1 554.9	1 549.8	1 553.1	1 551.2	1 525.7	1 517.5	1 493.7	1 477.6
Textile mills	468.5	443.2	436.2	424.5	397.1	378.2	332.9	290.9	261.3	236.9	217.6
Textile product mills	242.1	237.1	236.4	234.7	232.4	229.6	217.0	204.2	187.7	183.2	176.4
Apparel	791.1	722.3	680.8	621.4	540.5	483.5	415.2	350.0	303.9	278.0	250.5
Paper and paper products	639.5	631.4	630.6	624.9	615.6	604.7	577.6	546.6	516.2	495.5	484.2
Printing and related support activities	817.3	815.8	821.1	827.9	814.6	806.8	768.3	706.6	680.4	662.6	646.3
Petroleum and coal products	140.4	137.3	136.0	134.5	127.8	123.2	121.1	118.1	114.3	111.7	112.1
Chemicals	987.9	984.5	986.8	992.6	982.5	980.4	959.0	927.5	906.1	887.0	872.1
Plastics and rubber products	913.7	918.7	932.7	941.4	947.0	950.9	896.2	846.8	814.3	804.7	802.3
Service-Providing	94 251	96 427	99 065	101 803	104 775	107 375	108 214	108 092	108 531	109 905	111 861
Private Service-Providing	74 819	76 888	79 401	81 894	84 468	86 585	87 096	86 579	86 948	88 284	90 057
Trade, transportation, and utilities	23 834	24 239	24 700	25 186	25 771	26 225	25 983	25 497	25 287	25 533	25 959
Wholesale trade	5 433.1	5 522.0	5 663.9	5 795.2	5 892.5	5 933.2	5 772.7	5 652.3	5 607.5	5 662.9	5 764.4
Durable goods	2 908.8	2 977.8	3 071.9	3 162.4	3 219.6	3 250.7	3 130.4	3 007.9	2 940.6	2 950.5	2 999.2
Nondurable goods	1 969.3	1 977.5	2 007.9	2 032.7	2 061.1	2 064.8	2 031.3	2 015.0	2 004.6	2 010.0	2 022.4
Electronic markets, agents, and brokers	555.0	566.7	584.1	600.1	611.8	617.7	611.1	629.4	662.2	702.4	742.8
Retail trade	13 896.7	14 142.5	14 388.9	14 609.3	14 970.1	15 279.8	15 238.6	15 025.1	14 917.3	15 058.2	15 279.6
Motor vehicle and parts dealers [1]	1 627.1	1 685.6	1 723.4	1 740.9	1 796.6	1 846.9	1 854.6	1 879.4	1 882.9	1 902.3	1 918.6
Automobile dealers	1 071.6	1 113.0	1 134.5	1 142.0	1 179.7	1 216.5	1 225.1	1 252.8	1 254.4	1 257.3	1 261.4
Furniture and home furnishings stores	461.2	474.2	484.7	499.1	524.4	543.5	541.2	538.7	547.3	563.4	576.1
Electronics and appliance stores	534.7	555.5	575.2	590.6	623.8	647.3	632.6	594.8	573.9	571.5	585.0
Building material and garden supply stores	981.8	1 007.2	1 043.1	1 062.3	1 101.0	1 142.1	1 151.8	1 176.5	1 185.0	1 227.1	1 276.1
Food and beverage stores	2 879.8	2 927.8	2 956.9	2 965.7	2 984.5	2 993.0	2 950.5	2 881.6	2 838.4	2 821.6	2 817.8
Health and personal care stores	811.9	826.4	853.3	876.0	898.2	927.6	951.5	938.8	938.1	941.1	953.7
Gasoline stations	922.3	946.4	956.2	961.3	943.5	935.7	925.3	895.9	882.0	875.6	871.1
Clothing and clothing accessories stores	1 246.3	1 220.6	1 235.9	1 268.6	1 306.6	1 321.6	1 321.1	1 312.5	1 304.5	1 364.3	1 414.6
Sporting goods, hobby, book, and music stores	519.8	528.8	545.1	555.1	582.7	602.7	601.1	591.8	584.7	585.9	597.9
General merchandise stores [1]	2 635.4	2 657.3	2 657.6	2 686.5	2 751.8	2 819.8	2 842.2	2 812.0	2 812.0	2 863.1	2 934.3
Department stores	1 493.9	1 440.8	1 445.2	1 486.8	1 560.4	1 629.8	1 645.0	1 653.5	1 679.2	1 709.2	1 755.0
Miscellaneous store retailers	841.1	874.3	913.2	950.3	985.5	1 007.1	993.3	959.5	930.7	913.5	899.9
Nonstore retailers	435.4	438.5	444.5	453.0	471.6	492.4	473.5	443.7	427.3	428.8	434.6

[1] Includes other industries, not shown separately.

Table 15-1. Nonfarm Employment by Sector and Industry—*Continued*

(Wage and salary workers on nonfarm payrolls, thousands.)

Industry	2006	2007	2008	2009	2010	2011	2012	2013	2014	2015	2016
TOTAL NONFARM	136 453	137 999	137 242	131 313	130 361	131 932	134 175	136 381	138 958	141 843	144 306
Total Private	114 479	115 781	114 732	108 758	107 871	109 845	112 255	114 529	117 076	119 814	122 083
Goods-Producing	22 530	22 233	21 335	18 558	17 751	18 047	18 420	18 738	19 226	19 610	19 736
Mining and logging	684	724	767	694	705	788	848	863	891	813	677
Logging	64.4	60.1	56.6	50.4	49.7	48.7	50.8	51.8	52.0	52.4	51.2
Mining	619.7	663.8	709.8	643.3	654.8	739.2	797.2	811.0	838.5	760.4	626.1
Oil and gas extraction	134.5	146.2	160.5	159.8	158.7	172.0	187.4	193.5	197.7	193.4	180.0
Mining, except oil and gas [1]	220.3	223.4	226.0	208.3	204.5	218.4	218.7	209.6	207.2	197.8	181.0
Coal mining	78.0	77.2	81.2	81.5	80.8	87.3	84.7	78.1	73.2	64.2	50.5
Support activities for mining	264.9	294.3	323.4	275.2	291.6	348.8	391.1	407.9	433.6	369.2	265.0
Construction	7 691	7 630	7 162	6 016	5 518	5 533	5 646	5 856	6 151	6 461	6 711
Construction of buildings	1 804.9	1 774.2	1 641.7	1 357.2	1 229.7	1 222.1	1 240.2	1 285.9	1 358.0	1 423.7	1 490.3
Heavy and civil engineering	985.1	1 005.4	964.5	851.3	825.1	800.0	808.3	885.0	912.3	937.6	944.2
Specialty trade contractors	4 901.1	4 850.2	4 555.8	3 807.9	3 463.4	3 474.4	3 537.1	3 684.4	3 880.6	4 099.7	4 276.6
Manufacturing	14 155	13 879	13 406	11 847	11 528	11 726	11 927	12 020	12 185	12 336	12 348
Durable goods	8 981	8 808	8 463	7 284	7 064	7 273	7 470	7 548	7 674	7 765	7 719
Wood products	560.6	517.1	457.7	360.2	342.1	337.1	339.1	353.2	371.6	382.5	392.2
Nonmetallic mineral products	509.6	500.5	465.0	394.3	370.9	366.6	365.3	373.4	384.1	398.0	407.5
Primary metals	464.0	455.8	442.0	362.1	362.3	388.3	402.0	395.3	398.7	394.0	377.9
Fabricated metal products	1 553.1	1 562.8	1 527.5	1 311.6	1 281.7	1 347.3	1 409.8	1 432.3	1 454.2	1 457.8	1 424.8
Machinery	1 183.2	1 187.1	1 187.6	1 028.6	996.1	1 055.8	1 098.5	1 104.5	1 127.3	1 120.8	1 080.3
Computer and electronic products [1]	1 307.5	1 272.5	1 244.2	1 136.9	1 094.6	1 103.5	1 089.0	1 065.6	1 048.7	1 052.8	1 048.0
Computer and peripheral equipment	196.2	186.2	183.2	166.4	157.6	157.4	157.4	157.5	159.8	160.3	164.1
Communications equipment	136.2	128.1	127.3	120.5	117.4	115.3	108.2	101.1	93.2	88.4	85.6
Semiconductors and electronic components	457.9	447.5	431.8	378.1	369.4	383.4	383.1	374.9	367.4	369.5	367.0
Electronic instruments	444.5	443.2	441.0	421.6	406.4	404.2	399.7	393.7	390.8	398.9	396.1
Electrical equipment and appliances	432.7	429.4	424.3	373.6	359.5	366.1	373.2	374.1	377.8	383.7	383.4
Transportation equipment [1]	1 768.9	1 711.9	1 608.0	1 347.9	1 333.1	1 381.5	1 461.1	1 508.8	1 559.0	1 604.9	1 624.9
Motor vehicles and parts	1 070.0	994.2	875.5	664.1	678.5	717.7	777.3	824.8	872.1	913.7	940.1
Furniture and related products	558.3	529.4	478.0	384.3	357.2	353.1	351.4	359.9	370.3	381.0	389.1
Miscellaneous manufacturing	643.7	641.7	628.9	584.4	566.8	573.7	580.1	580.5	581.9	589.9	590.9
Nondurable goods [1]	5 174	5 071	4 943	4 564	4 464	4 453	4 457	4 472	4 512	4 571	4 629
Food manufacturing	1 479.4	1 484.1	1 480.9	1 456.4	1 450.6	1 458.8	1 468.8	1 473.7	1 484.4	1 511.8	1 554.1
Textile mills	195.0	169.7	151.2	124.4	119.0	120.1	118.7	117.2	117.0	116.6	113.9
Textile product mills	166.7	157.7	147.2	125.7	119.0	117.6	116.3	114.4	115.0	116.1	115.0
Apparel	232.4	214.6	199.0	167.5	156.6	151.7	148.0	144.7	140.1	136.5	131.3
Paper and paper products	470.5	458.2	444.9	407.0	394.7	387.4	379.8	378.0	373.3	372.7	370.8
Printing and related support activities	634.4	622.0	594.1	521.9	487.6	471.8	461.8	452.0	453.7	450.3	446.7
Petroleum and coal products	113.2	114.5	117.4	115.3	113.9	111.8	112.1	110.4	111.6	112.9	111.6
Chemicals	865.9	860.9	847.1	804.1	786.5	783.6	783.3	792.7	803.0	807.3	811.1
Plastics and rubber products	785.5	757.2	729.4	624.9	624.8	635.2	645.1	659.2	674.3	689.4	698.8
Service-Providing	113 922	115 767	115 907	112 755	112 610	113 884	115 755	117 643	119 732	122 233	124 569
Private Service-Providing	91 949	93 548	93 398	90 201	90 120	91 798	93 834	95 791	97 850	100 204	102 346
Trade, transportation, and utilities	26 276	26 630	26 293	24 906	24 636	25 065	25 476	25 862	26 383	26 887	27 233
Wholesale trade	5 904.5	6 015.2	5 942.7	5 586.6	5 452.1	5 543.1	5 666.6	5 732.9	5 813.4	5 854.8	5 866.8
Durable goods	3 074.8	3 121.5	3 052.0	2 809.9	2 713.5	2 765.2	2 832.3	2 864.2	2 905.4	2 928.6	2 929.7
Nondurable goods	2 041.3	2 062.2	2 047.7	1 966.1	1 928.1	1 939.0	1 965.3	1 984.5	2 012.0	2 027.8	2 041.0
Electronic markets, agents, and brokers	788.5	831.5	842.9	810.7	810.5	839.0	869.1	884.3	896.0	898.4	896.2
Retail trade	15 353.3	15 520.0	15 283.0	14 522.3	14 440.4	14 667.8	14 840.8	15 078.8	15 357.3	15 604.7	15 820.2
Motor vehicle and parts dealers [1]	1 909.7	1 908.3	1 831.2	1 637.5	1 629.2	1 691.2	1 737.0	1 793.1	1 862.2	1 929.0	1 981.8
Automobile dealers	1 246.7	1 242.2	1 176.7	1 018.2	1 011.5	1 056.9	1 095.5	1 138.4	1 187.9	1 238.7	1 281.6
Furniture and home furnishings stores	586.9	574.6	531.1	449.2	437.9	438.9	439.4	445.8	455.9	466.8	473.5
Electronics and appliance stores	580.5	582.5	569.6	515.7	522.3	527.4	507.4	496.7	497.2	522.3	521.9
Building material and garden supply stores	1 324.1	1 309.3	1 248.0	1 155.6	1 131.8	1 145.7	1 174.2	1 207.7	1 228.1	1 234.4	1 271.9
Food and beverage stores	2 821.1	2 843.6	2 862.0	2 830.0	2 808.2	2 822.8	2 861.3	2 929.7	3 004.0	3 062.3	3 088.9
Health and personal care stores	961.1	993.1	1 002.8	986.0	980.5	980.9	997.9	1 015.8	1 022.5	1 033.7	1 049.8
Gasoline stations	864.1	861.5	842.4	825.5	819.3	831.0	843.5	866.3	881.3	905.3	925.7
Clothing and clothing accessories stores	1 450.9	1 500.0	1 468.0	1 363.9	1 352.5	1 360.9	1 391.4	1 390.9	1 370.4	1 353.7	1 346.4
Sporting goods, hobby, book, and music stores	606.0	623.3	621.9	589.2	579.1	577.9	582.2	602.5	618.8	623.2	620.7
General merchandise stores [1]	2 935.0	3 020.6	3 025.6	2 966.2	2 997.7	3 085.2	3 065.4	3 060.4	3 102.1	3 131.4	3 170.9
Department stores	1 768.3	1 684.0	1 620.6	1 605.3	1 595.1	1 557.2	1 591.5	1 540.5	1 472.9	1 501.6	1 538.6
Miscellaneous store retailers	881.0	865.4	842.5	782.4	761.5	772.4	794.0	802.5	818.3	828.0	832.6
Nonstore retailers	432.8	437.9	438.0	421.1	420.6	433.5	447.1	467.4	496.6	514.7	536.1

[1]Includes other industries, not shown separately.

Table 15-1. Nonfarm Employment by Sector and Industry—*Continued*

(Wage and salary workers on nonfarm payrolls, thousands.)

Industry	1995	1996	1997	1998	1999	2000	2001	2002	2003	2004	2005
Transportation and warehousing	3 837.8	3 935.3	4 026.5	4 168.0	4 300.3	4 410.3	4 372.0	4 223.6	4 185.4	4 248.6	4 360.9
Air transportation	510.9	525.7	542.0	562.7	586.3	614.4	615.3	563.5	528.3	514.5	500.8
Rail transportation	232.5	225.2	221.0	225.0	228.8	231.7	226.7	217.8	217.7	225.7	227.8
Water transportation	50.8	51.0	50.7	50.5	51.7	56.0	54.0	52.6	54.5	56.4	60.6
Truck transportation	1 249.1	1 282.4	1 308.2	1 354.4	1 391.5	1 405.8	1 386.8	1 339.3	1 325.6	1 351.7	1 397.6
Transit and ground passenger transportation	327.9	339.1	349.6	362.7	371.0	372.1	374.8	380.8	382.2	384.9	389.2
Pipeline transportation	53.6	51.4	49.7	48.1	46.9	46.0	45.4	41.7	40.2	38.4	37.8
Scenic and sightseeing transportation	22.0	23.2	24.5	25.4	26.1	27.5	29.1	25.6	26.6	27.2	28.8
Support activities for transportation	430.4	445.8	473.4	496.8	518.1	537.4	539.2	524.7	520.3	535.1	552.2
Couriers and messengers	516.8	539.9	546.0	568.2	585.9	605.0	587.0	560.9	561.7	556.6	571.4
Warehousing and storage	443.8	451.8	461.5	474.2	494.1	514.4	513.8	516.7	528.3	558.1	594.7
Utilities	666	640	621	613	608	601	599	596	577	564	554
Information	2 843	2 940	3 084	3 218	3 419	3 630	3 629	3 395	3 188	3 118	3 061
Publishing industries, except Internet	910.7	927.2	955.5	982.3	1 004.8	1 035.0	1 020.7	964.1	924.8	909.1	904.1
Motion picture and sound recording industries	311.1	334.7	353.0	369.5	384.4	382.6	376.8	387.9	376.2	385.0	377.5
Broadcasting, except Internet	298.1	309.1	313.0	321.2	329.4	343.5	344.6	334.1	324.3	325.0	327.7
Telecommunications	1 009.3	1 038.1	1 108.0	1 167.4	1 270.8	1 396.6	1 423.9	1 280.9	1 166.8	1 115.1	1 071.3
Data processing, hosting, and related services	242.6	252.0	268.4	282.8	307.1	315.7	316.8	303.9	280.0	267.1	262.5
Other information services [1]	71.8	79.0	85.5	95.3	121.9	157.1	146.5	123.6	115.9	116.9	117.7
Internet publishing and broadcasting	33.7	39.6	45.4	53.9	78.1	110.8	100.4	76.3	67.2	66.1	67.2
Financial activities	6 866	7 018	7 255	7 565	7 753	7 783	7 900	7 956	8 078	8 105	8 197
Finance and insurance	5 107.5	5 200.6	5 378.9	5 631.7	5 770.2	5 772.8	5 862.0	5 922.2	6 020.5	6 019.4	6 062.9
Monetary authorities–central bank	23.0	22.8	22.1	21.7	22.6	22.8	23.0	23.4	22.6	21.8	20.8
Credit intermediation and related activities [1]	2 314.4	2 368.2	2 433.6	2 531.9	2 591.0	2 547.8	2 597.7	2 686.0	2 792.4	2 817.0	2 869.0
Depository credit intermediation [1]	1 700.2	1 691.4	1 696.6	1 708.9	1 709.7	1 681.2	1 701.2	1 733.0	1 748.5	1 751.5	1 769.2
Commercial banking	1 281.7	1 275.1	1 277.9	1 286.0	1 281.2	1 250.5	1 258.4	1 278.1	1 280.1	1 280.8	1 296.0
Securities, commodity contracts, investments, and funds and trusts	597.4	625.7	674.5	734.5	782.2	851.1	879.0	836.4	803.9	813.1	834.2
Insurance carriers and related activities	2 172.7	2 183.9	2 248.8	2 343.7	2 374.5	2 351.1	2 362.3	2 376.4	2 401.5	2 367.5	2 338.9
Real estate and rental and leasing	1 758.1	1 817.1	1 875.9	1 933.7	1 982.5	2 010.6	2 038.4	2 033.3	2 057.5	2 085.5	2 133.5
Real estate	1 181.7	1 208.6	1 243.8	1 277.7	1 302.6	1 316.0	1 343.4	1 356.6	1 387.1	1 418.7	1 460.8
Rental and leasing services	557.4	587.7	609.5	630.8	653.1	666.8	666.3	649.1	643.1	641.1	645.8
Lessors of nonfinancial intangible assets	19.0	20.8	22.6	25.3	26.8	27.8	28.7	27.6	27.3	25.7	26.9
Professional and business services	12 844	13 462	14 335	15 147	15 957	16 666	16 476	15 976	15 987	16 394	16 954
Professional and technical services [1]	5 078.4	5 312.7	5 628.8	5 992.3	6 345.4	6 701.7	6 871.1	6 648.8	6 602.7	6 747.1	7 024.6
Legal services	959.2	968.4	987.5	1 021.1	1 051.4	1 065.7	1 091.3	1 115.3	1 142.1	1 163.1	1 168.0
Accounting and bookkeeping services	706.3	729.8	761.2	802.0	837.6	866.4	872.2	837.3	815.3	805.9	849.3
Architectural and engineering services	997.1	1 024.5	1 063.4	1 114.8	1 168.1	1 237.9	1 274.7	1 246.1	1 226.9	1 258.2	1 310.9
Computer systems design and related services	611.2	701.4	826.7	974.9	1 132.9	1 254.3	1 297.8	1 152.8	1 116.6	1 148.6	1 195.2
Management and technical consulting services	451.8	492.7	541.7	590.4	619.0	672.7	715.1	707.7	718.0	763.0	824.2
Management of companies and enterprises	1 685.8	1 702.7	1 729.7	1 756.1	1 773.8	1 796.0	1 779.0	1 705.4	1 687.2	1 724.4	1 758.9
Administrative and waste services	6 079.7	6 446.5	6 976.6	7 398.0	7 837.5	8 168.3	7 826.0	7 621.9	7 696.8	7 922.9	8 170.2
Administrative and support services [1]	5 806.4	6 164.5	6 686.0	7 098.7	7 527.0	7 855.4	7 508.7	7 303.6	7 374.7	7 594.4	7 832.5
Employment services [1]	2 448.1	2 625.3	2 953.9	3 245.8	3 581.6	3 849.3	3 468.2	3 273.2	3 326.4	3 455.5	3 606.9
Temporary help services	1 743.8	1 849.0	2 059.7	2 245.2	2 469.6	2 635.6	2 337.7	2 193.7	2 224.2	2 387.2	2 549.4
Business support services	629.8	678.3	733.9	772.2	780.5	786.7	779.7	756.6	749.7	757.8	766.4
Services to buildings and dwellings	1 302.4	1 361.5	1 424.1	1 460.0	1 534.7	1 570.5	1 606.2	1 606.1	1 636.1	1 693.7	1 737.5
Waste management and remediation services	273.3	282.0	290.5	299.3	310.5	312.9	317.3	318.3	322.1	328.6	337.6
Education and health services	13 360	13 761	14 185	14 570	14 939	15 252	15 814	16 398	16 835	17 230	17 676
Educational services	2 010.0	2 078.0	2 155.0	2 233.0	2 320.0	2 390.0	2 511.0	2 643.0	2 695.0	2 763.0	2 836.0
Health care and social assistance	11 349.0	11 683.8	12 029.5	12 336.9	12 618.3	12 861.1	13 302.9	13 755.2	14 139.6	14 467.8	14 840.4
Health care	9 809.0	10 092.6	10 358.0	10 540.9	10 690.9	10 857.8	11 188.1	11 536.0	11 817.1	12 055.3	12 313.9
Ambulatory health care services [1]	3 768.0	3 939.9	4 093.0	4 161.2	4 226.6	4 320.3	4 461.5	4 633.2	4 786.4	4 952.3	5 113.5
Offices of physicians	1 508.0	1 570.0	1 625.4	1 687.2	1 748.9	1 801.1	1 870.9	1 926.3	1 960.3	2 004.6	2 049.4
Outpatient care centers	361.0	374.0	387.2	399.6	413.1	425.2	440.0	454.5	469.0	493.7	517.3
Home health care services	622.0	667.2	702.8	659.5	629.6	633.3	638.6	679.8	732.6	776.6	821.0
Hospitals	3 734.0	3 772.8	3 821.6	3 892.4	3 935.5	3 954.3	4 050.9	4 159.6	4 244.6	4 284.7	4 345.4
Nursing and residential care facilities [1]	2 308.0	2 379.9	2 443.4	2 487.3	2 528.8	2 583.2	2 675.8	2 743.3	2 786.2	2 818.4	2 855.0
Nursing care facilities	1 413.0	1 448.4	1 474.6	1 489.3	1 501.0	1 513.6	1 546.8	1 573.2	1 579.8	1 576.9	1 577.4
Social assistance [1]	1 540.0	1 591.2	1 671.5	1 796.0	1 927.5	2 003.3	2 114.7	2 219.2	2 322.5	2 412.5	2 526.5
Child day care services	557.0	559.2	570.4	615.1	673.7	695.8	714.6	744.1	755.3	764.7	789.7

[1]Includes other industries, not shown separately.

Table 15-1. Nonfarm Employment by Sector and Industry—*Continued*

(Wage and salary workers on nonfarm payrolls, thousands.)

Industry	2006	2007	2008	2009	2010	2011	2012	2013	2014	2015	2016
Transportation and warehousing	4 469.6	4 540.9	4 508.3	4 236.4	4 190.7	4 301.6	4 415.8	4 498.0	4 660.9	4 871.2	4 989.4
Air transportation	487.0	491.8	490.7	462.8	458.3	456.9	459.2	444.3	444.2	458.6	475.9
Rail transportation	227.5	233.7	231.0	218.2	216.4	228.1	230.6	231.2	236.1	240.9	214.7
Water transportation	62.7	65.5	67.1	63.4	62.3	61.3	63.9	65.3	67.3	65.8	65.5
Truck transportation	1 435.8	1 439.2	1 389.0	1 268.2	1 250.4	1 300.5	1 349.4	1 382.1	1 417.2	1 452.2	1 453.6
Transit and ground passenger transportation	399.3	412.1	423.3	421.7	429.7	439.9	440.3	448.5	466.5	477.5	478.4
Pipeline transportation	38.7	39.9	41.7	42.6	42.3	42.9	43.6	44.5	47.0	49.7	49.5
Scenic and sightseeing transportation	27.5	28.6	28.0	27.6	27.3	27.5	28.0	29.1	30.6	32.9	34.6
Support activities for transportation	570.6	584.2	592.0	548.5	542.5	562.2	579.9	598.3	625.8	651.8	660.1
Couriers and messengers	582.4	580.7	573.4	546.3	528.1	529.2	534.1	543.9	576.5	612.8	641.9
Warehousing and storage	638.1	665.2	672.1	637.1	633.4	653.1	686.9	710.9	749.6	829.0	915.1
Utilities	548	553	559	560	553	553	553	552	552	556	556
Information	3 038	3 032	2 984	2 804	2 707	2 674	2 676	2 706	2 726	2 750	2 772
Publishing industries, except Internet	902.4	901.2	880.4	796.4	759.0	748.6	739.5	732.7	726.9	726.5	729.9
Motion picture and sound recording industries	375.7	380.6	371.3	357.6	370.2	362.1	362.3	370.5	379.3	397.9	419.6
Broadcasting, except Internet	328.3	325.2	318.7	300.5	290.3	283.2	285.1	283.7	282.8	276.7	269.1
Telecommunications	1 047.6	1 030.6	1 019.4	965.7	902.9	873.6	856.8	853.2	838.5	810.9	794.7
Data processing, hosting, and related services	263.2	267.8	260.3	248.5	243.0	245.8	254.9	269.6	279.5	296.2	299.6
Other information services [1]	120.8	126.3	133.5	135.0	141.7	160.0	177.2	196.2	219.0	241.4	259.3
Internet publishing and broadcasting	69.1	72.9	80.6	83.3	92.0	109.6	125.2	142.3	163.3	184.3	200.7
Financial activities	8 367	8 348	8 206	7 838	7 695	7 697	7 784	7 886	7 977	8 123	8 285
Finance and insurance	6 194.0	6 179.1	6 076.3	5 843.9	5 761.0	5 769.0	5 828.4	5 886.1	5 930.9	6 034.9	6 142.1
Monetary authorities–central bank	21.2	21.6	22.4	21.0	20.0	18.3	17.5	18.0	18.2	18.0	18.5
Credit intermediation and related activities [1]	2 924.9	2 866.3	2 732.7	2 590.2	2 550.0	2 554.1	2 583.3	2 614.1	2 564.0	2 570.7	2 612.1
Depository credit intermediation [1]	1 802.0	1 823.5	1 815.2	1 753.8	1 728.8	1 735.1	1 738.7	1 733.6	1 702.9	1 683.8	1 698.7
Commercial banking	1 322.9	1 351.4	1 357.5	1 316.9	1 305.9	1 314.5	1 320.6	1 313.9	1 292.8	1 284.7	1 307.0
Securities, commodity contracts, investments, and funds and trusts	868.9	899.6	916.2	862.1	850.4	860.1	859.3	865.0	882.9	907.8	928.4
Insurance carriers and related activities	2 379.1	2 391.6	2 405.1	2 370.6	2 340.6	2 336.4	2 368.3	2 388.9	2 465.8	2 538.3	2 583.1
Real estate and rental and leasing	2 172.5	2 169.1	2 129.6	1 994.0	1 933.8	1 927.4	1 955.2	2 000.2	2 045.7	2 088.4	2 142.6
Real estate	1 499.0	1 500.4	1 485.0	1 420.2	1 395.7	1 400.8	1 420.0	1 458.7	1 487.1	1 517.1	1 559.4
Rental and leasing services	645.5	640.3	616.9	547.3	513.5	502.2	511.0	517.7	535.0	547.5	559.7
Lessors of nonfinancial intangible assets	28.1	28.4	27.7	26.5	24.6	24.4	24.2	23.7	23.7	23.8	23.5
Professional and business services	17 566	17 942	17 735	16 579	16 728	17 332	17 932	18 515	19 062	19 633	20 136
Professional and technical services [1]	7 356.7	7 659.5	7 799.4	7 508.5	7 441.3	7 666.2	7 892.3	8 120.9	8 335.6	8 608.2	8 876.7
Legal services	1 173.2	1 175.4	1 161.5	1 124.9	1 114.2	1 115.7	1 124.0	1 128.5	1 119.0	1 118.6	1 121.1
Accounting and bookkeeping services	889.0	935.9	951.0	914.2	886.5	898.9	908.9	931.5	948.5	968.5	985.7
Architectural and engineering services	1 385.7	1 432.2	1 439.4	1 324.7	1 275.4	1 293.5	1 322.5	1 345.6	1 375.2	1 400.6	1 410.8
Computer systems design and related services	1 284.6	1 372.1	1 439.6	1 422.6	1 449.0	1 535.9	1 621.4	1 702.3	1 790.6	1 908.5	1 990.7
Management and technical consulting services	886.4	952.7	1 002.0	994.9	999.4	1 065.2	1 118.1	1 180.3	1 232.2	1 282.4	1 372.5
Management of companies and enterprises	1 810.9	1 866.4	1 904.5	1 866.9	1 872.3	1 933.6	2 023.3	2 102.9	2 168.4	2 207.4	2 240.7
Administrative and waste services	8 398.3	8 416.3	8 031.5	7 203.3	7 414.0	7 731.9	8 016.2	8 290.8	8 558.1	8 817.5	9 018.2
Administrative and support services [1]	8 050.2	8 061.3	7 674.7	6 851.6	7 056.7	7 366.7	7 644.3	7 913.3	8 172.1	8 420.9	8 613.4
Employment services [1]	3 680.9	3 545.9	3 133.0	2 480.8	2 722.5	2 942.1	3 134.1	3 268.5	3 406.9	3 527.2	3 566.5
Temporary help services	2 637.4	2 597.4	2 348.4	1 823.3	2 093.6	2 313.0	2 495.3	2 616.8	2 760.1	2 876.9	2 916.3
Business support services	792.9	817.4	832.3	820.0	808.6	814.5	828.5	856.1	877.3	893.6	912.1
Services to buildings and dwellings	1 801.4	1 849.5	1 839.8	1 753.3	1 745.0	1 788.6	1 830.0	1 884.7	1 943.9	2 006.6	2 070.2
Waste management and remediation services	348.1	355.0	356.8	351.7	357.3	365.3	371.9	377.5	386.1	396.5	404.8
Education and health services	18 154	18 676	19 228	19 630	19 975	20 318	20 769	21 086	21 439	22 029	22 616
Educational services	2 901.0	2 941.0	3 040.0	3 090.0	3 155.0	3 250.0	3 341.0	3 354.0	3 417.0	3 472.0	3 560.0
Health care and social assistance	15 253.2	15 734.5	16 188.2	16 539.9	16 820.0	17 068.6	17 428.1	17 731.1	18 022.2	18 557.4	19 056.3
Health care	12 601.8	12 946.8	13 289.9	13 543.0	13 776.9	14 025.9	14 281.6	14 491.5	14 676.5	15 042.3	15 420.4
Ambulatory health care services [1]	5 285.8	5 473.5	5 646.6	5 793.4	5 974.7	6 136.2	6 306.5	6 476.5	6 631.5	6 855.5	7 081.8
Offices of physicians	2 102.5	2 155.1	2 205.0	2 231.0	2 263.9	2 294.6	2 339.8	2 378.0	2 411.2	2 471.0	2 527.7
Outpatient care centers	537.9	558.4	580.8	605.6	648.7	670.2	699.0	731.1	763.7	805.7	856.3
Home health care services	865.6	913.8	961.4	1 027.1	1 084.6	1 140.3	1 185.0	1 230.3	1 262.4	1 314.7	1 362.0
Hospitals	4 423.4	4 515.0	4 627.3	4 667.4	4 678.5	4 721.7	4 779.0	4 785.8	4 786.8	4 895.8	5 024.9
Nursing and residential care facilities [1]	2 892.5	2 958.3	3 016.1	3 082.2	3 123.7	3 168.1	3 196.2	3 229.2	3 258.2	3 290.9	3 313.7
Nursing care facilities	1 581.4	1 602.6	1 618.7	1 644.9	1 657.1	1 669.6	1 662.8	1 653.8	1 650.3	1 648.3	1 644.0
Social assistance [1]	2 651.4	2 787.7	2 898.3	2 996.9	3 043.1	3 042.6	3 146.5	3 239.6	3 345.6	3 515.1	3 635.9
Child day care services	818.3	850.4	859.4	852.8	848.0	849.4	851.3	843.3	854.0	878.0	906.1

[1] Includes other industries, not shown separately.

Table 15-1. Nonfarm Employment by Sector and Industry—*Continued*

(Wage and salary workers on nonfarm payrolls, thousands.)

Industry	1995	1996	1997	1998	1999	2000	2001	2002	2003	2004	2005
Leisure and hospitality	10 501	10 777	11 018	11 232	11 543	11 862	12 036	11 986	12 173	12 493	12 816
Arts, entertainment, and recreation	1 459.4	1 522.1	1 599.9	1 645.2	1 709.1	1 787.9	1 824.4	1 782.6	1 812.9	1 849.6	1 892.3
Performing arts and spectator sports	307.7	328.6	349.6	350.0	361.1	381.8	382.3	363.7	371.7	367.5	376.3
Museums, historical sites, zoos, and parks	83.9	88.9	93.8	97.4	103.1	110.4	115.0	114.0	114.7	118.3	120.7
Amusements, gambling, and recreation	1 067.8	1 104.5	1 156.5	1 197.9	1 244.9	1 295.7	1 327.1	1 305.0	1 326.5	1 363.8	1 395.3
Accommodation and food services	9 041.6	9 254.3	9 417.9	9 586.2	9 833.7	10 073.5	10 211.3	10 203.2	10 359.8	10 643.2	10 923.0
Accommodation	1 652.5	1 698.9	1 729.5	1 773.5	1 831.7	1 884.4	1 852.2	1 778.6	1 775.4	1 789.5	1 818.6
Food services and drinking places	7 389.1	7 555.4	7 688.5	7 812.7	8 002.0	8 189.1	8 359.1	8 424.6	8 584.4	8 853.7	9 104.4
Other services	4 572	4 690	4 825	4 976	5 087	5 168	5 258	5 372	5 401	5 409	5 395
Repair and maintenance	1 078.9	1 135.5	1 169.3	1 189.2	1 222.0	1 241.5	1 256.5	1 246.9	1 233.6	1 228.8	1 236.0
Personal and laundry services	1 143.9	1 165.7	1 180.4	1 205.6	1 220.3	1 242.9	1 255.0	1 257.2	1 263.5	1 272.9	1 276.6
Membership associations and organizations	2 348.9	2 389.1	2 474.9	2 581.3	2 644.4	2 683.3	2 746.4	2 867.8	2 903.6	2 907.5	2 882.2
Government	19 432	19 539	19 664	19 909	20 307	20 790	21 118	21 513	21 583	21 621	21 804
Federal	2 949.0	2 877.0	2 806.0	2 772.0	2 769.0	2 865.0	2 764.0	2 766.0	2 761.0	2 730.0	2 732.0
Federal, except U.S. Postal Service	2 098.8	2 009.8	1 940.2	1 891.3	1 879.5	1 984.8	1 891.0	1 923.8	1 952.4	1 947.5	1 957.3
U.S. Postal Service	849.9	867.2	866.0	880.5	889.7	879.7	873.0	842.4	808.6	782.1	774.2
State government	4 635.0	4 606.0	4 582.0	4 612.0	4 709.0	4 786.0	4 905.0	5 029.0	5 002.0	4 982.0	5 032.0
State government education	1 919.0	1 910.7	1 904.0	1 922.2	1 983.2	2 030.6	2 112.9	2 242.8	2 254.7	2 238.1	2 259.9
State government, excluding education	2 715.5	2 695.1	2 677.9	2 690.2	2 725.6	2 755.9	2 791.8	2 786.3	2 747.6	2 743.9	2 771.6
Local government	11 849.0	12 056.0	12 276.0	12 525.0	12 829.0	13 139.0	13 449.0	13 718.0	13 820.0	13 909.0	14 041.0
Local government education	6 453.1	6 592.3	6 758.5	6 920.9	7 120.4	7 293.9	7 479.3	7 654.4	7 709.4	7 765.2	7 856.1
Local government, excluding education	5 396.0	5 464.1	5 516.9	5 603.9	5 708.6	5 844.6	5 970.0	6 063.2	6 110.2	6 144.1	6 184.6

Industry	2006	2007	2008	2009	2010	2011	2012	2013	2014	2015	2016
Leisure and hospitality	13 110	13 427	13 436	13 077	13 049	13 353	13 768	14 254	14 696	15 160	15 620
Arts, entertainment, and recreation	1 928.5	1 969.2	1 970.1	1 915.5	1 913.3	1 919.1	1 968.6	2 029.7	2 103.1	2 166.4	2 234.8
Performing arts and spectator sports	398.5	405.0	405.7	396.8	406.2	394.2	402.4	419.2	443.3	450.4	455.8
Museums, historical sites, zoos, and parks	123.8	130.3	131.6	129.4	127.7	132.7	136.1	140.3	146.9	153.0	159.7
Amusements, gambling, and recreation	1 406.3	1 433.9	1 432.8	1 389.2	1 379.4	1 392.2	1 430.1	1 470.2	1 512.9	1 563.1	1 619.3
Accommodation and food services	11 181.1	11 457.4	11 466.3	11 161.9	11 135.4	11 433.6	11 799.7	12 224.2	12 592.9	12 993.8	13 385.6
Accommodation	1 832.1	1 866.9	1 868.7	1 763.0	1 759.6	1 800.5	1 825.1	1 864.9	1 894.5	1 923.0	1 946.9
Food services and drinking places	9 349.0	9 590.4	9 597.5	9 398.9	9 375.8	9 633.1	9 974.6	10 359.2	10 698.3	11 070.8	11 438.7
Other services	5 438	5 494	5 515	5 367	5 331	5 360	5 430	5 483	5 567	5 622	5 685
Repair and maintenance	1 248.5	1 253.4	1 227.0	1 150.4	1 138.8	1 168.7	1 194.0	1 216.6	1 242.1	1 277.2	1 289.4
Personal and laundry services	1 288.4	1 309.7	1 322.6	1 280.6	1 265.3	1 288.6	1 313.6	1 341.7	1 371.2	1 405.0	1 445.3
Membership associations and organizations	2 901.2	2 931.1	2 965.7	2 936.0	2 926.4	2 903.0	2 922.4	2 924.6	2 953.6	2 939.5	2 950.1
Government	21 974	22 218	22 509	22 555	22 490	22 086	21 920	21 853	21 882	22 029	22 223
Federal	2 732.0	2 734.0	2 762.0	2 832.0	2 977.0	2 859.0	2 820.0	2 769.0	2 733.0	2 757.0	2 795.0
Federal, except U.S. Postal Service	1 962.6	1 964.7	2 014.4	2 128.5	2 318.1	2 227.6	2 209.2	2 174.5	2 140.4	2 160.0	2 186.4
U.S. Postal Service	769.7	769.1	747.4	703.4	658.5	630.9	611.2	594.9	593.0	596.9	608.9
State government	5 075.0	5 122.0	5 177.0	5 169.0	5 137.0	5 078.0	5 055.0	5 046.0	5 050.0	5 077.0	5 089.0
State government education	2 292.5	2 317.5	2 354.4	2 360.2	2 373.1	2 374.0	2 388.5	2 393.3	2 389.3	2 401.4	2 411.8
State government, excluding education	2 782.0	2 804.3	2 822.5	2 808.8	2 764.1	2 703.7	2 666.4	2 652.8	2 660.5	2 675.6	2 677.2
Local government	14 167.0	14 362.0	14 571.0	14 554.0	14 376.0	14 150.0	14 045.0	14 037.0	14 098.0	14 195.0	14 339.0
Local government education	7 913.0	7 986.8	8 083.9	8 078.8	8 013.4	7 872.5	7 777.9	7 776.7	7 814.9	7 870.9	7 920.0
Local government, excluding education	6 253.8	6 375.5	6 486.5	6 474.9	6 362.9	6 277.7	6 266.8	6 260.1	6 283.4	6 324.0	6 418.8

¹Includes other industries, not shown separately.

Table 15-2. Production and Nonsupervisory Workers on Private Nonfarm Payrolls by Industry

(Wage and salary workers on nonfarm payrolls, thousands.)

Industry	1995	1996	1997	1998	1999	2000	2001	2002	2003	2004	2005
Total Private	79 943	81 888	84 313	86 516	88 647	90 547	90 214	88 664	87 965	89 246	91 443
Goods-Producing	17 137	17 318	17 698	18 008	18 067	18 169	17 466	16 400	15 732	15 821	16 145
Mining and logging	458	461	479	473	438	446	457	436	420	440	473
Construction	4 113	4 325	4 546	4 807	5 105	5 295	5 332	5 196	5 123	5 309	5 611
Manufacturing	12 567	12 532	12 673	12 729	12 524	12 428	11 677	10 768	10 189	10 072	10 060
Durable goods	7 352	7 426	7 599	7 721	7 651	7 659	7 164	6 530	6 152	6 140	6 220
Wood products	479	487	498	510	516	507	470	450	434	445	454
Nonmetallic mineral products	400	405	412	421	426	440	427	399	375	388	387
Primary metals	500	500	502	505	492	490	447	396	370	364	363
Fabricated metal products	1 223	1 242	1 285	1 320	1 305	1 326	1 261	1 147	1 092	1 109	1 129
Machinery	970	984	1 007	1 016	978	961	891	787	732	730	749
Computer and electronic products	890	915	951	965	933	949	876	744	673	656	700
Electrical equipment and appliances	438	434	428	432	433	433	402	352	320	307	300
Transportation equipment [1]	1 472	1 481	1 522	1 530	1 526	1 498	1 399	1 310	1 269	1 265	1 277
Motor vehicles and parts	1 049	1 052	1 062	1 050	1 076	1 073	987	931	906	903	894
Furniture and related products	480	478	490	512	532	544	509	475	444	444	436
Miscellaneous manufacturing	499	500	503	511	509	510	490	469	442	432	424
Nondurable goods [1]	5 214	5 106	5 075	5 008	4 872	4 769	4 513	4 238	4 037	3 932	3 841
Food manufacturing	1 221	1 228	1 228	1 228	1 229	1 228	1 221	1 202	1 192	1 178	1 170
Textile mills	393	372	367	357	334	315	276	242	217	194	174
Textile product mills	198	192	193	190	187	183	174	162	148	147	143
Apparel	698	631	594	534	458	404	341	286	242	219	193
Paper and paper products	494	488	489	484	474	468	446	421	393	374	365
Printing and related support activities	599	594	597	598	585	576	544	493	471	460	447
Petroleum and coal products	89	87	88	87	85	83	81	78	74	77	75
Chemicals	598	595	593	601	595	588	562	532	525	520	510
Plastics and rubber products	719	720	732	739	746	753	704	662	633	626	620
Private Service-Providing	62 806	64 570	66 615	68 508	70 580	72 378	72 748	72 264	72 233	73 426	75 298
Trade, transportation, and utilities	19 984	20 325	20 698	21 059	21 576	21 965	21 709	21 337	21 078	21 319	21 830
Wholesale trade	4 361	4 423	4 523	4 605	4 673	4 686	4 555	4 474	4 396	4 444	4 584
Retail trade	11 841	12 057	12 274	12 440	12 772	13 040	12 952	12 774	12 655	12 788	13 030
Transportation and warehousing	3 260	3 339	3 407	3 522	3 642	3 753	3 718	3 611	3 563	3 637	3 774
Utilities	522	506	494	492	489	485	483	478	464	450	443
Information	2 007	2 096	2 181	2 217	2 351	2 502	2 531	2 398	2 347	2 371	2 386
Financial activities	5 199	5 322	5 482	5 692	5 818	5 819	5 888	5 964	6 052	6 052	6 127
Professional and business services	10 645	11 161	11 896	12 566	13 184	13 790	13 588	13 049	12 911	13 287	13 854
Education and health services	11 829	12 195	12 566	12 903	13 217	13 491	13 998	14 491	14 753	15 018	15 401
Leisure and hospitality	9 330	9 565	9 780	9 947	10 216	10 516	10 662	10 576	10 666	10 955	11 263
Other services	3 812	3 907	4 013	4 124	4 219	4 296	4 373	4 449	4 426	4 425	4 438

[1]Includes other industries, not shown separately.

Table 15-2. Production and Nonsupervisory Workers on Private Nonfarm Payrolls by Industry
—Continued

(Wage and salary workers on nonfarm payrolls, thousands.)

Industry	2006	2007	2008	2009	2010	2011	2012	2013	2014	2015	2016
Total Private	93 776	95 260	94 675	89 629	88 954	90 619	92 780	94 589	96 701	98 782	100 531
Goods-Producing	16 559	16 405	15 724	13 399	12 774	13 005	13 287	13 481	13 858	14 141	14 204
Mining and logging	519	547	574	510	525	594	641	636	653	592	476
Construction	5 903	5 883	5 521	4 567	4 172	4 184	4 246	4 423	4 640	4 866	5 062
Manufacturing	10 137	9 975	9 629	8 322	8 077	8 228	8 400	8 422	8 565	8 683	8 666
Durable goods	6 355	6 250	5 975	4 990	4 829	4 986	5 152	5 185	5 282	5 350	5 307
Wood products	451	407	358	278	269	269	272	283	298	306	309
Nonmetallic mineral products	391	384	363	303	284	278	273	275	280	297	307
Primary metals	363	358	348	272	275	301	317	306	310	307	296
Fabricated metal products	1 162	1 171	1 143	960	935	994	1 050	1 063	1 071	1 069	1 038
Machinery	770	774	772	641	616	662	700	699	716	711	688
Computer and electronic products	756	744	730	654	629	630	628	610	589	594	596
Electrical equipment and appliances	303	305	305	266	251	248	249	245	248	258	259
Transportation equipment [1]	1 304	1 274	1 177	948	937	972	1 024	1 053	1 103	1 139	1 147
Motor vehicles and parts	873	804	696	510	525	556	598	642	690	718	736
Furniture and related products	433	409	364	284	263	260	259	266	276	284	286
Miscellaneous manufacturing	423	425	416	382	370	373	380	386	390	384	382
Nondurable goods [1]	3 782	3 725	3 653	3 332	3 248	3 241	3 248	3 237	3 283	3 333	3 359
Food manufacturing	1 172	1 184	1 184	1 161	1 152	1 158	1 169	1 169	1 176	1 189	1 211
Textile mills	158	137	122	99	96	98	96	92	91	90	90
Textile product mills	135	123	115	98	92	89	85	83	86	88	88
Apparel	182	173	163	132	120	112	109	106	103	104	99
Paper and paper products	357	350	344	313	302	295	288	279	277	277	275
Printing and related support activities	447	443	424	369	342	327	316	310	312	310	311
Petroleum and coal products	72	73	77	70	70	70	72	70	72	74	76
Chemicals	508	504	512	479	474	480	491	490	497	507	516
Plastics and rubber products	608	592	572	476	472	482	487	497	518	532	534
Private Service-Providing	77 217	78 855	78 951	76 230	76 180	77 614	79 493	81 109	82 843	84 642	86 326
Trade, transportation, and utilities	22 166	22 546	22 337	21 116	20 874	21 234	21 617	21 875	22 280	22 629	22 882
Wholesale trade	4 724	4 851	4 822	4 506	4 378	4 443	4 562	4 621	4 696	4 702	4 696
Retail trade	13 110	13 317	13 134	12 472	12 425	12 647	12 793	12 923	13 107	13 264	13 424
Transportation and warehousing	3 889	3 935	3 931	3 688	3 627	3 703	3 820	3 886	4 032	4 217	4 316
Utilities	443	444	450	451	444	441	441	445	446	447	446
Information	2 399	2 403	2 388	2 240	2 170	2 148	2 164	2 194	2 209	2 226	2 235
Financial activities	6 312	6 365	6 320	6 066	5 942	5 900	5 986	6 068	6 155	6 278	6 429
Professional and business services	14 446	14 784	14 585	13 520	13 699	14 251	14 802	15 305	15 766	16 133	16 479
Education and health services	15 832	16 318	16 842	17 240	17 531	17 818	18 230	18 505	18 827	19 337	19 839
Leisure and hospitality	11 568	11 861	11 873	11 560	11 507	11 772	12 154	12 589	12 969	13 360	13 749
Other services	4 494	4 578	4 606	4 488	4 458	4 491	4 541	4 573	4 637	4 678	4 715

[1]Includes other industries, not shown separately.

Table 15-3. Average Weekly Hours of Production and Nonsupervisory Workers on Private Nonfarm Payrolls by Industry

(Hours.)

Industry	1995	1996	1997	1998	1999	2000	2001	2002	2003	2004	2005
Total Private	34.3	34.3	34.5	34.5	34.3	34.3	33.9	33.9	33.7	33.7	33.8
Goods-Producing	40.8	40.8	41.1	40.8	40.8	40.7	39.9	39.9	39.8	40.0	40.1
Mining and logging	45.3	46.0	46.2	44.9	44.2	44.4	44.6	43.2	43.6	44.5	45.6
Construction	38.8	38.9	38.9	38.8	39.0	39.2	38.7	38.4	38.4	38.3	38.6
Manufacturing	41.3	41.3	41.7	41.4	41.4	41.3	40.3	40.5	40.4	40.8	40.7
Overtime hours	4.7	4.8	5.1	4.8	4.9	4.7	4.0	4.2	4.2	4.6	4.6
Durable goods	42.1	42.1	42.6	42.1	41.9	41.8	40.6	40.7	40.8	41.3	41.1
Overtime hours	5.0	5.0	5.4	5.0	5.0	4.8	3.9	4.2	4.3	4.7	4.6
Wood products	41.0	41.2	41.4	41.4	41.3	41.0	40.2	39.9	40.4	40.7	40.0
Nonmetallic mineral products	41.8	42.0	41.9	42.2	42.1	41.6	41.6	42.0	42.2	42.4	42.2
Primary metals	43.4	43.6	44.3	43.5	43.8	44.2	42.4	42.4	42.3	43.1	43.1
Fabricated metal products	41.9	41.9	42.3	41.9	41.7	41.9	40.7	40.6	40.7	41.1	41.0
Machinery	43.5	43.3	44.0	43.1	42.3	42.3	40.9	40.5	40.8	42.0	42.1
Computer and electronic products	42.2	41.9	42.5	41.9	41.5	41.4	39.8	39.7	40.4	40.4	40.0
Electrical equipment and appliances	41.9	42.1	42.1	41.8	41.8	41.6	39.8	40.1	40.6	40.7	40.6
Transportation equipment [1]	43.7	43.8	44.2	43.3	43.6	43.3	41.9	42.5	41.9	42.5	42.4
Motor vehicles and parts	43.8	43.8	43.9	42.6	43.8	43.4	41.6	42.6	42.0	42.6	42.3
Furniture and related products	38.5	38.2	39.1	39.4	39.3	39.2	38.3	39.1	38.9	39.5	39.2
Miscellaneous manufacturing	39.2	39.1	39.7	39.2	39.3	39.0	38.8	38.7	38.4	38.5	38.7
Nondurable goods [1]	40.1	40.1	40.5	40.5	40.5	40.3	39.9	40.0	39.8	40.0	39.9
Overtime hours	4.3	4.4	4.6	4.6	4.6	4.5	4.1	4.2	4.1	4.4	4.4
Food manufacturing	39.6	39.5	39.8	40.1	40.2	40.1	39.6	39.6	39.3	39.3	39.0
Textile mills	40.9	40.8	41.6	41.0	41.0	41.4	40.0	40.6	39.1	40.1	40.3
Textile product mills	38.6	38.8	39.2	39.2	39.1	38.7	38.4	39.0	39.4	38.7	38.9
Apparel	35.3	35.2	35.6	35.5	35.4	35.7	36.0	36.7	35.6	36.1	35.8
Paper and paper products	43.4	43.5	43.9	43.6	43.6	42.8	42.1	41.8	41.5	42.1	42.5
Printing and related support activities	39.1	39.1	39.5	39.3	39.1	39.2	38.7	38.4	38.2	38.4	38.4
Petroleum and coal products	43.7	43.7	43.1	43.6	42.6	42.7	43.8	43.0	44.5	44.9	45.5
Chemicals	43.4	43.3	43.4	43.2	42.8	42.2	41.9	42.3	42.4	42.8	42.3
Plastics and rubber products	41.1	41.0	41.4	41.3	41.3	40.8	40.0	40.6	40.4	40.4	40.0
Private Service-Providing	32.6	32.6	32.8	32.8	32.7	32.7	32.5	32.5	32.4	32.3	32.4
Trade, transportation, and utilities	34.1	34.1	34.3	34.2	33.9	33.8	33.5	33.6	33.6	33.5	33.4
Wholesale trade	38.6	38.6	38.8	38.6	38.6	38.8	38.4	38.0	37.9	37.8	37.7
Retail trade	30.8	30.7	30.9	30.9	30.8	30.7	30.7	30.9	30.9	30.7	30.6
Transportation and warehousing	38.9	39.1	39.4	38.7	37.6	37.4	36.7	36.8	36.8	37.2	37.0
Utilities	42.3	42.0	42.0	42.0	42.0	42.0	41.4	40.9	41.1	40.9	41.1
Information	36.0	36.3	36.3	36.6	36.7	36.8	36.9	36.5	36.2	36.3	36.5
Financial activities	35.5	35.5	35.8	36.0	35.8	35.9	35.8	35.6	35.6	35.6	36.0
Professional and business services	34.0	34.1	34.3	34.3	34.4	34.5	34.2	34.2	34.1	34.2	34.2
Education and health services	32.0	31.9	32.2	32.2	32.1	32.2	32.3	32.4	32.3	32.4	32.6
Leisure and hospitality	25.9	25.9	26.1	26.2	26.1	26.1	25.8	25.8	25.6	25.7	25.7
Other services	32.6	32.5	32.7	32.6	32.5	32.5	32.3	32.1	31.4	31.0	30.9

[1]Includes other industries, not shown separately.

Table 15-3. Average Weekly Hours of Production and Nonsupervisory Workers on Private Nonfarm Payrolls by Industry—*Continued*

(Hours.)

Industry	2006	2007	2008	2009	2010	2011	2012	2013	2014	2015	2016
Total Private	33.9	33.8	33.6	33.1	33.4	33.6	33.7	33.7	33.7	33.7	33.6
Goods-Producing	40.5	40.6	40.2	39.2	40.4	40.9	41.1	41.3	41.5	41.2	41.2
Mining and logging	45.6	45.9	45.1	43.2	44.6	46.7	46.6	45.9	47.3	45.8	45.3
Construction	39.0	39.0	38.5	37.6	38.4	39.0	39.3	39.6	39.6	39.6	39.7
Manufacturing	41.1	41.2	40.8	39.8	41.1	41.4	41.7	41.8	42.0	41.8	41.9
Overtime hours	4.4	4.2	3.7	2.9	3.8	4.1	4.2	4.3	4.5	4.3	4.3
Durable goods	41.4	41.5	41.1	39.8	41.4	41.9	42.0	42.2	42.5	42.1	42.3
Overtime hours	4.4	4.2	3.7	2.7	3.8	4.2	4.3	4.4	4.6	4.3	4.4
Wood products	39.8	39.4	38.6	37.4	39.1	39.7	41.1	42.7	42.0	41.3	41.8
Nonmetallic mineral products	43.0	42.3	42.1	40.8	41.7	42.3	42.2	42.5	43.3	42.4	42.0
Primary metals	43.6	42.9	42.2	40.7	43.7	44.6	43.8	43.8	44.2	43.8	43.4
Fabricated metal products	41.4	41.6	41.3	39.4	41.4	42.0	42.1	42.2	42.6	42.3	42.1
Machinery	42.4	42.6	42.3	40.1	42.1	43.1	42.8	42.9	43.0	41.9	42.1
Computer and electronic products	40.5	40.6	41.0	40.4	40.9	40.5	40.4	40.5	40.8	40.9	41.2
Electrical equipment and appliances	41.0	41.2	40.9	39.3	41.1	40.8	41.6	41.8	41.7	42.2	42.9
Transportation equipment [1]	42.7	42.8	42.0	41.2	42.9	43.2	43.8	43.6	43.6	43.7	44.1
Motor vehicles and parts	42.2	42.3	41.4	40.1	43.4	43.4	44.2	43.7	43.8	44.1	44.7
Furniture and related products	38.8	39.2	38.1	37.7	38.5	39.9	40.0	40.3	40.9	39.8	40.0
Miscellaneous manufacturing	38.7	38.9	38.9	38.5	38.7	38.9	39.2	40.1	40.2	40.1	40.8
Nondurable goods [1]	40.6	40.8	40.4	39.8	40.8	40.8	41.1	41.2	41.3	41.4	41.2
Overtime hours	4.4	4.2	3.7	3.3	3.8	4.0	4.1	4.3	4.3	4.3	4.1
Food manufacturing	40.1	40.7	40.5	40.0	40.7	40.2	40.6	40.8	40.8	41.0	41.4
Textile mills	40.6	40.3	38.7	37.7	41.2	41.7	42.6	41.5	41.5	42.5	41.2
Textile product mills	39.8	39.7	38.6	37.9	39.0	39.1	39.7	38.4	38.0	37.0	37.7
Apparel	36.5	37.2	36.4	36.0	36.6	38.2	37.1	38.1	38.5	38.2	36.4
Paper and paper products	42.9	43.1	42.9	41.8	42.9	42.9	42.9	43.1	43.7	43.0	42.7
Printing and related support activities	39.2	39.1	38.3	38.0	38.2	38.0	38.5	38.6	39.0	39.8	39.2
Petroleum and coal products	45.0	44.1	44.6	43.4	43.0	43.8	47.1	46.4	46.1	45.2	44.2
Chemicals	42.5	41.9	41.5	41.4	42.2	42.5	42.4	42.9	42.7	42.6	41.8
Plastics and rubber products	40.6	41.3	41.0	40.2	41.9	42.0	41.8	41.8	42.2	42.4	42.4
Private Service-Providing	32.4	32.4	32.3	32.1	32.2	32.4	32.5	32.4	32.4	32.4	32.3
Trade, transportation, and utilities	33.4	33.3	33.2	32.9	33.3	33.7	33.8	33.7	33.6	33.7	33.5
Wholesale trade	38.0	38.2	38.2	37.6	37.9	38.5	38.7	38.7	38.6	38.6	38.6
Retail trade	30.5	30.2	30.0	29.9	30.2	30.5	30.6	30.2	30.0	30.1	29.7
Transportation and warehousing	36.9	37.0	36.4	36.0	37.1	37.8	38.0	38.5	38.4	38.8	38.8
Utilities	41.4	42.4	42.7	42.0	42.0	42.1	41.1	41.7	42.3	42.4	42.5
Information	36.6	36.5	36.7	36.6	36.3	36.2	36.0	35.9	35.9	35.7	35.6
Financial activities	35.8	35.9	35.9	36.1	36.2	36.4	36.8	36.7	36.7	37.1	36.9
Professional and business services	34.6	34.8	34.8	34.7	35.1	35.2	35.3	35.4	35.6	35.5	35.4
Education and health services	32.5	32.5	32.4	32.2	32.0	32.2	32.3	32.1	32.0	32.1	32.2
Leisure and hospitality	25.7	25.5	25.2	24.8	24.8	24.8	25.0	25.0	25.1	25.1	24.9
Other services	30.9	30.9	30.8	30.5	30.7	30.8	30.7	30.8	30.7	30.7	30.8

[1]Includes other industries, not shown separately.

Table 15-4. Average Hourly Earnings of Production and Nonsupervisory Workers on Private Nonfarm Payrolls by Industry

(Dollars.)

Industry	1995	1996	1997	1998	1999	2000	2001	2002	2003	2004	2005
Total Private	11.65	12.04	12.51	13.01	13.49	14.02	14.54	14.96	15.37	15.68	16.12
Goods-Producing	12.96	13.38	13.82	14.23	14.71	15.27	15.78	16.33	16.80	17.19	17.60
Mining and logging	14.78	15.09	15.57	16.20	16.33	16.55	17.00	17.19	17.56	18.07	18.72
Construction	14.73	15.11	15.67	16.23	16.80	17.48	18.00	18.52	18.95	19.23	19.46
Manufacturing	12.34	12.75	13.14	13.45	13.85	14.32	14.76	15.29	15.74	16.14	16.56
Excluding overtime [1]	11.68	12.05	12.38	12.71	13.08	13.55	14.06	14.54	14.96	15.29	15.68
Durable goods	13.05	13.45	13.83	14.07	14.46	14.93	15.38	16.02	16.45	16.82	17.33
Wood products	9.92	10.24	10.52	10.85	11.18	11.63	11.99	12.33	12.71	13.03	13.16
Nonmetallic mineral products	12.39	12.80	13.17	13.60	10.97	14.53	14.86	15.39	15.76	16.25	16.61
Primary metals	14.75	15.12	15.39	15.66	16.00	16.64	17.06	17.68	18.13	18.57	18.94
Fabricated metal products	11.91	12.26	12.64	12.97	13.34	13.77	14.19	14.68	15.01	15.31	15.80
Machinery	13.13	13.49	13.94	14.23	14.77	15.21	15.48	15.92	16.29	16.67	17.02
Computer and electronic products	12.29	12.75	13.24	13.85	14.37	14.73	15.42	16.20	16.68	17.27	18.39
Electrical equipment and appliances	11.25	11.80	12.24	12.51	12.90	13.23	13.78	13.98	14.36	14.90	15.24
Transportation equipment [2]	17.21	17.66	17.99	17.91	18.24	18.89	19.47	20.63	21.22	21.48	22.09
Motor vehicles and parts	17.72	18.14	18.43	18.21	18.49	19.11	19.66	21.09	21.68	21.71	22.26
Furniture and related products	9.76	10.09	10.50	10.89	11.28	11.73	12.14	12.62	12.99	13.16	13.45
Miscellaneous manufacturing	10.23	10.59	10.89	11.18	11.55	11.93	12.45	12.91	13.30	13.84	14.07
Nondurable goods [2]	11.30	11.68	12.04	12.45	12.85	13.31	13.75	14.15	14.63	15.05	15.26
Food manufacturing	10.27	10.50	10.77	11.09	11.40	11.77	12.18	12.55	12.80	12.98	13.04
Textile mills	9.63	9.88	10.22	10.58	10.90	11.23	11.40	11.73	11.99	12.13	12.38
Textile product mills	8.60	8.95	9.30	9.61	10.04	10.31	10.49	10.85	11.15	11.31	11.61
Apparel	7.22	7.45	7.76	8.05	8.35	8.61	8.83	9.11	9.58	9.77	10.26
Paper and paper products	13.94	14.38	14.76	15.20	15.58	15.91	16.38	16.85	17.33	17.91	17.99
Printing and related support activities	12.08	12.41	12.78	13.20	13.67	14.09	14.48	14.93	15.37	15.71	15.74
Petroleum and coal products	20.24	20.18	21.10	21.75	22.22	22.80	22.90	23.04	23.63	24.39	24.47
Chemicals	14.86	15.37	15.78	16.23	16.40	17.09	17.57	17.97	18.50	19.17	19.67
Plastics and rubber products	10.86	11.17	11.48	11.79	12.25	12.70	13.21	13.55	14.18	14.59	14.80
Private Service-Providing	11.21	11.59	12.07	12.61	13.09	13.62	14.18	14.58	14.98	15.28	15.72
Trade, transportation, and utilities	11.10	11.46	11.90	12.40	12.82	13.31	13.70	14.02	14.34	14.58	14.92
Wholesale trade	13.34	13.80	14.41	15.07	15.62	16.28	16.77	16.98	17.36	17.65	18.16
Retail trade	8.85	9.21	9.59	10.05	10.45	10.87	11.29	11.67	11.90	12.08	12.36
Transportation and warehousing	13.18	13.45	13.78	14.12	14.56	15.05	15.33	15.76	16.25	16.52	16.70
Utilities	19.19	19.78	20.59	21.48	22.03	22.75	23.58	23.96	24.77	25.61	26.68
Information	15.68	16.30	17.14	17.67	18.40	19.07	19.80	20.20	21.01	21.40	22.06
Financial activities	12.31	12.75	13.28	14.00	14.55	15.04	15.65	16.25	17.21	17.58	17.98
Professional and business services	12.53	13.00	13.57	14.27	14.85	15.52	16.33	16.80	17.21	17.48	18.08
Education and health services	11.78	12.15	12.53	12.96	13.40	13.91	14.58	15.15	15.56	16.07	16.62
Leisure and hospitality	6.79	6.99	7.32	7.67	7.96	8.32	8.57	8.81	9.00	9.15	9.38
Other services	10.51	10.85	11.29	11.79	12.26	12.73	13.27	13.72	13.84	13.98	14.34

[1]Derived by assuming that overtime hours are paid at the rate of time and one-half.
[2]Includes other industries, not shown separately.

Table 15-4. Average Hourly Earnings of Production and Nonsupervisory Workers on Private Nonfarm Payrolls by Industry—*Continued*

(Dollars.)

Industry	2006	2007	2008	2009	2010	2011	2012	2013	2014	2015	2016
Total Private	16.75	17.42	18.06	18.61	19.05	19.44	19.74	20.13	20.61	21.03	21.54
Goods-Producing	18.02	18.67	19.33	19.90	20.28	20.67	20.94	21.24	21.59	21.96	22.58
Mining and logging	19.90	20.97	22.50	23.29	23.82	24.50	25.79	26.80	26.84	26.48	27.05
Construction	20.02	20.95	21.87	22.66	23.22	23.65	23.97	24.22	24.67	25.20	25.97
Manufacturing	16.81	17.26	17.75	18.24	18.61	18.93	19.08	19.30	19.56	19.91	20.43
Excluding overtime [1]	15.96	16.43	16.97	17.59	17.78	18.03	18.16	18.34	18.57	18.93	19.43
Durable goods	17.68	18.20	18.70	19.36	19.80	20.11	20.18	20.35	20.66	20.97	21.48
Wood products	13.39	13.68	14.19	14.92	14.85	14.81	14.99	15.47	15.57	16.16	16.81
Nonmetallic mineral products	16.59	16.93	16.90	17.28	17.48	18.16	18.15	18.40	19.16	19.92	20.30
Primary metals	19.36	19.66	20.19	20.10	20.13	19.94	20.70	21.94	22.41	22.47	23.11
Fabricated metal products	16.17	16.53	16.99	17.48	17.94	18.13	18.26	18.35	18.68	19.02	19.67
Machinery	17.20	17.72	17.97	18.39	18.96	19.54	20.17	20.58	21.00	21.34	21.81
Computer and electronic products	18.94	19.94	21.04	21.87	22.78	23.32	23.34	23.41	23.36	23.30	24.27
Electrical equipment and appliances	15.53	15.93	15.78	16.27	16.87	17.96	18.03	18.04	18.28	18.85	19.29
Transportation equipment [2]	22.41	23.03	23.85	24.98	25.23	25.34	24.57	24.57	24.96	25.05	25.05
Motor vehicles and parts	22.14	22.00	22.21	21.86	22.02	21.93	21.27	21.08	21.38	21.49	21.56
Furniture and related products	13.80	14.32	14.54	15.04	15.06	15.24	15.46	15.59	15.67	16.09	16.82
Miscellaneous manufacturing	14.36	14.66	15.20	16.13	16.56	16.82	17.05	17.03	17.31	17.72	18.44
Nondurable goods [2]	15.33	15.67	16.15	16.56	16.80	17.06	17.29	17.57	17.75	18.16	18.74
Food manufacturing	13.13	13.55	14.00	14.39	14.41	14.63	15.02	15.44	15.55	15.90	16.51
Textile mills	12.55	13.00	13.58	13.71	13.56	13.79	13.51	13.90	14.15	14.72	15.71
Textile product mills	11.86	11.78	11.73	11.44	11.79	12.21	12.77	12.88	13.35	13.31	13.64
Apparel	10.65	11.05	11.40	11.37	11.43	11.96	12.89	13.21	13.51	13.65	13.73
Paper and paper products	18.01	18.44	18.89	19.29	20.04	20.28	20.42	20.32	20.35	21.46	21.71
Printing and related support activities	15.80	16.15	16.75	16.75	16.91	17.28	17.28	17.77	18.01	18.31	18.59
Petroleum and coal products	24.11	25.21	27.41	29.61	31.31	31.75	32.15	34.58	35.39	37.32	38.84
Chemicals	19.60	19.55	19.50	20.30	21.07	21.45	21.45	21.40	21.49	21.76	22.71
Plastics and rubber products	14.97	15.39	15.85	16.01	15.71	15.95	16.05	16.20	16.51	16.82	17.17
Private Service-Providing	16.40	17.09	17.75	18.33	18.78	19.18	19.48	19.90	20.40	20.84	21.33
Trade, transportation, and utilities	15.39	15.78	16.16	16.48	16.82	17.15	17.43	17.74	18.27	18.67	18.99
Wholesale trade	18.91	19.59	20.13	20.84	21.54	21.97	22.24	22.62	23.24	23.63	24.18
Retail trade	12.57	12.75	12.87	13.01	13.25	13.51	13.82	14.02	14.40	14.82	15.05
Transportation and warehousing	17.27	17.72	18.41	18.81	19.16	19.49	19.54	19.81	20.51	20.75	20.92
Utilities	27.40	27.88	28.83	29.48	30.04	30.82	31.61	32.27	32.86	34.02	35.31
Information	23.23	23.96	24.78	25.45	25.87	26.62	27.04	27.98	28.70	29.05	30.04
Financial activities	18.83	19.67	20.32	20.90	21.55	21.93	22.82	23.87	24.71	25.34	26.11
Professional and business services	19.13	20.15	21.18	22.35	22.78	23.12	23.29	23.72	24.29	24.79	*25.42
Education and health services	17.28	17.99	18.73	19.34	19.95	20.60	20.91	21.29	21.64	22.09	22.53
Leisure and hospitality	9.75	10.41	10.84	11.12	11.31	11.45	11.62	11.78	12.09	12.41	12.85
Other services	14.77	15.42	16.09	16.59	17.06	17.32	17.59	18.00	18.51	19.01	19.36

[1]Derived by assuming that overtime hours are paid at the rate of time and one-half.
[2]Includes other industries, not shown separately.

Table 15-5. Average Weekly Earnings of Production and Nonsupervisory Workers on Private Nonfarm Payrolls by Industry

(Dollars.)

Industry	1995	1996	1997	1998	1999	2000	2001	2002	2003	2004	2005
Total Private	400.04	413.25	431.86	448.59	463.15	480.99	493.61	506.54	517.76	528.84	544.00
Goods-Producing	528.55	546.44	568.43	580.99	599.99	621.86	629.88	651.64	669.13	688.17	705.28
Mining and logging	670.40	695.04	720.07	727.19	721.77	734.88	757.96	741.97	765.94	804.01	853.87
Construction	571.57	588.48	609.48	629.75	655.11	685.78	695.86	711.82	727.00	735.55	750.37
Manufacturing	509.26	526.55	548.26	557.24	573.29	591.04	595.15	618.62	636.03	658.49	673.34
Durable goods	549.45	566.53	589.06	591.80	606.55	624.38	624.51	652.70	671.35	694.06	712.85
Wood products	406.53	422.30	435.66	449.77	461.46	476.97	481.33	492.07	514.06	530.15	526.65
Nonmetallic mineral products	517.75	538.10	551.65	573.04	587.42	604.76	618.91	647.00	664.96	688.33	700.63
Primary metals	639.82	658.73	681.64	681.47	700.80	704.03	723.86	749.17	767.15	799.69	815.90
Fabricated metal products	498.48	513.47	534.38	543.24	555.86	576.71	576.71	596.42	610.44	628.83	647.21
Machinery	571.15	584.62	613.19	613.73	625.07	643.94	632.68	645.38	664.48	699.45	716.27
Computer and electronic products	518.19	534.39	562.68	579.85	596.37	609.97	613.18	642.77	674.69	697.97	735.59
Electrical equipment and appliances	471.72	496.69	515.77	522.54	538.98	550.48	548.03	560.33	583.27	607.00	618.88
Transportation equipment [1]	751.59	773.73	795.75	774.77	795.57	817.56	816.74	877.50	889.42	912.56	937.72
Motor vehicles and parts	776.41	794.09	808.28	775.56	809.31	828.73	818.68	898.54	910.02	924.72	940.64
Furniture and related products	375.18	385.82	410.48	428.67	443.68	459.95	464.87	493.95	505.26	519.61	527.49
Miscellaneous manufacturing	400.88	413.94	431.72	437.95	454.14	464.80	483.07	499.01	510.54	533.27	545.01
Nondurable goods [1]	452.77	467.91	487.04	504.02	520.02	536.85	548.30	566.72	582.61	602.56	609.04
Food manufacturing	406.75	414.74	428.58	444.72	458.73	472.09	481.81	497.25	502.92	509.55	508.55
Textile mills	394.17	403.08	425.53	434.15	447.38	464.51	456.64	476.52	469.33	486.68	498.47
Textile product mills	332.12	347.05	364.12	376.37	392.46	398.93	402.53	423.05	438.67	437.89	451.36
Apparel	254.91	261.99	276.01	286.17	295.62	307.51	317.63	334.24	340.73	352.04	366.93
Paper and paper products	604.66	625.38	647.64	662.27	679.05	681.38	689.76	705.20	719.55	754.17	764.15
Printing and related support activities	472.37	484.99	504.46	518.32	534.15	552.15	560.89	573.05	587.58	603.97	604.73
Petroleum and coal products	883.68	881.24	908.50	949.28	947.60	973.53	1 003.34	990.88	1 052.32	1 095.00	1 114.51
Chemicals	644.46	666.28	685.43	700.53	701.06	721.41	735.57	759.56	784.26	819.93	831.79
Plastics and rubber products	446.01	458.29	475.04	487.04	505.45	517.56	528.62	550.14	572.53	589.99	591.59
Private Service-Providing	364.80	377.37	395.57	413.65	427.98	445.74	461.02	473.84	484.76	494.03	509.23
Trade, transportation, and utilities	378.79	390.67	407.63	423.33	434.31	449.96	459.53	471.27	481.14	488.51	498.46
Wholesale trade	515.14	533.36	559.39	582.21	602.77	631.24	643.45	644.38	657.29	666.79	685.00
Retail trade	272.63	282.74	295.94	310.33	321.71	333.41	346.16	360.84	367.18	371.13	377.58
Transportation and warehousing	513.40	525.72	542.51	546.89	548.00	562.56	562.57	579.91	598.41	614.89	618.55
Utilities	811.72	831.24	865.02	902.44	924.40	955.09	977.25	979.26	1 017.44	1 048.01	1 095.91
Information	564.92	592.45	622.37	646.52	675.47	700.92	731.18	737.94	760.84	776.72	805.11
Financial activities	437.26	453.05	475.03	503.94	520.74	540.39	560.46	578.94	611.82	625.53	646.48
Professional and business services	426.54	442.81	465.51	490.13	510.99	535.07	557.84	574.60	587.02	597.54	618.71
Education and health services	376.77	387.45	403.42	417.47	429.76	447.80	471.33	490.38	503.05	521.06	541.40
Leisure and hospitality	175.74	181.02	190.66	200.82	208.05	217.20	220.73	227.31	230.49	234.86	241.36
Other services	342.36	352.68	368.63	384.25	398.77	413.30	428.64	439.87	434.41	433.04	443.40

[1]Includes other industries, not shown separately.

Table 15-5. Average Weekly Earnings of Production and Nonsupervisory Workers on Private Nonfarm Payrolls by Industry—*Continued*

(Dollars.)

Industry	2006	2007	2008	2009	2010	2011	2012	2013	2014	2015	2016
Total Private	567.22	589.18	607.42	615.96	636.19	652.89	665.65	677.70	694.85	708.90	723.69
Goods-Producing	730.16	757.50	776.63	779.68	818.96	844.89	861.39	877.09	895.09	905.43	930.33
Mining and logging	907.95	962.63	1 014.69	1 006.67	1 063.11	1 144.64	1 201.69	1 229.70	1 270.91	1 211.91	1 224.33
Construction	781.59	816.23	842.61	851.76	891.83	921.84	942.14	958.72	977.11	998.02	1 031.16
Manufacturing	690.88	711.50	724.46	726.12	765.18	784.29	794.63	807.37	822.03	832.05	855.69
Durable goods	731.97	754.61	767.92	771.24	819.02	841.89	848.35	859.69	877.31	882.88	909.02
Wood products	533.12	539.41	547.53	557.65	580.74	587.77	615.76	661.10	653.87	666.82	703.35
Nonmetallic mineral products	712.67	716.78	711.11	705.54	728.22	768.35	766.16	782.69	829.79	844.77	852.53
Primary metals	843.79	843.42	851.12	817.70	880.46	889.34	907.23	960.61	991.13	984.77	1 004.23
Fabricated metal products	668.94	687.16	701.57	689.22	742.76	762.14	767.83	775.35	795.77	804.67	827.81
Machinery	728.84	754.34	760.09	737.97	797.62	842.96	864.16	883.06	903.42	894.65	918.15
Computer and electronic products	766.75	809.10	861.58	883.02	932.26	943.88	944.02	948.79	952.82	953.04	999.76
Electrical equipment and appliances	637.04	656.46	645.60	639.34	693.49	732.16	749.91	753.07	763.08	794.79	827.24
Transportation equipment [1]	957.47	986.75	1 000.87	1 028.51	1 081.60	1 094.46	1 075.00	1 070.88	1 088.27	1 094.01	1 105.10
Motor vehicles and parts	934.41	930.51	920.57	876.45	956.36	952.12	940.00	920.56	936.90	948.30	963.33
Furniture and related products	535.90	561.08	553.90	566.75	579.66	608.00	617.74	628.36	641.27	640.01	672.23
Miscellaneous manufacturing	555.87	570.12	591.95	620.74	640.85	654.90	668.95	682.97	695.67	709.56	751.87
Nondurable goods [1]	622.00	639.99	652.22	658.54	685.07	696.03	710.13	723.57	733.64	751.05	771.31
Food manufacturing	526.02	551.21	566.88	575.40	586.52	588.19	609.69	629.70	634.95	652.26	683.51
Textile mills	509.39	524.40	525.00	516.86	559.13	574.61	575.75	577.18	586.40	625.84	647.60
Textile product mills	472.10	467.80	453.06	433.09	459.46	477.49	507.00	494.76	507.19	493.03	513.81
Apparel	389.05	411.57	415.10	408.86	418.28	456.97	478.33	503.01	520.57	520.73	499.80
Paper and paper products	772.57	795.58	809.57	806.19	858.65	870.53	877.14	874.85	888.07	923.13	926.04
Printing and related support activities	618.92	632.02	642.50	635.68	646.11	655.81	665.45	685.33	701.55	729.57	728.40
Petroleum and coal products	1 085.50	1 112.73	1 222.07	1 284.44	1 345.72	1 390.80	1 513.36	1 605.02	1 630.84	1 685.27	1 718.26
Chemicals	833.84	819.51	809.29	841.18	888.25	910.88	910.02	918.69	917.96	927.83	949.98
Plastics and rubber products	608.37	635.63	649.02	643.91	658.55	669.54	671.28	677.72	697.67	713.74	727.97
Private Service-Providing	532.19	554.18	573.29	587.56	605.07	620.97	633.06	644.98	661.59	676.05	689.70
Trade, transportation, and utilities	514.37	525.91	536.11	541.88	559.63	577.71	588.86	597.40	613.95	628.76	636.64
Wholesale trade	718.50	748.94	769.62	784.49	816.50	845.44	860.70	875.79	897.73	911.41	933.16
Retail trade	383.12	385.00	386.21	388.57	400.07	412.09	422.10	423.07	431.82	445.52	447.62
Transportation and warehousing	636.80	654.95	670.22	677.56	710.85	737.00	742.23	762.06	788.77	804.49	811.02
Utilities	1 135.57	1 182.65	1 230.65	1 239.34	1 262.89	1 296.92	1 298.23	1 344.70	1 388.91	1 444.03	1 501.50
Information	850.64	874.45	908.78	931.08	939.85	964.85	973.52	1 003.65	1 030.17	1 038.10	1 068.25
Financial activities	673.63	706.52	729.64	754.90	780.19	798.68	840.04	875.04	907.98	939.46	962.73
Professional and business services	662.27	700.82	737.90	775.81	798.54	813.37	822.58	838.67	864.45	878.71	898.76
Education and health services	561.02	585.44	607.82	622.30	639.37	663.04	674.48	683.24	692.56	709.25	724.40
Leisure and hospitality	250.34	265.54	273.39	275.95	280.87	283.82	290.54	294.31	303.81	311.32	319.52
Other services	456.50	477.06	495.57	506.26	523.70	532.63	539.46	553.77	568.92	583.54	595.73

[1] Includes other industries, not shown separately.

Table 15-6. Indexes of Aggregate Weekly Hours of Production and Nonsupervisory Workers on Private Nonfarm Payrolls by Industry

(2002 = 100.)

Industry	1995	1996	1997	1998	1999	2000	2001	2002	2003	2004	2005
Total Private	91.4	93.6	97.0	99.4	101.4	103.5	102.0	100.0	98.7	100.3	102.8
Goods-Producing	106.8	108.1	111.2	112.3	112.6	113.1	106.5	100.0	95.7	96.8	98.9
Mining and logging	110.3	112.7	117.6	112.8	102.9	105.1	108.3	100.0	97.4	104.0	114.7
Construction	79.9	84.3	88.6	93.4	99.7	104.0	103.2	100.0	98.4	101.7	108.3
Manufacturing	119.0	118.8	121.4	121.1	119.0	117.8	108.1	100.0	94.5	94.3	93.9
Durable goods	116.4	117.6	121.6	122.0	120.6	120.4	109.4	100.0	94.4	95.2	96.2
Wood products	109.3	111.6	114.8	117.5	118.5	115.8	105.0	100.0	97.8	100.8	101.2
Nonmetallic mineral products	99.7	101.5	103.1	105.8	106.9	109.1	106.1	100.0	94.3	98.0	97.4
Primary metals	129.3	129.9	132.4	131.1	128.4	129.9	110.0	100.0	93.4	93.3	93.1
Fabricated metal products	109.9	111.6	116.6	118.6	116.7	119.1	109.3	100.0	95.3	97.7	99.2
Machinery	132.2	133.7	138.9	137.4	129.8	127.6	114.1	100.0	93.6	96.0	98.8
Computer and electronic products	127.1	130.0	136.8	136.7	131.1	133.1	117.9	100.0	92.1	89.8	94.8
Electrical equipment and appliances	130.3	129.4	127.7	127.8	128.3	127.7	113.4	100.0	92.0	88.7	86.4
Transportation equipment [1]	115.4	116.5	120.8	118.8	119.5	116.3	105.3	100.0	95.5	96.5	97.3
Motor vehicles and parts	115.9	116.1	117.5	112.8	118.7	117.3	103.6	100.0	95.9	97.0	95.2
Furniture and related products	99.2	98.3	102.9	108.4	112.6	114.7	104.8	100.0	93.0	94.3	91.9
Miscellaneous manufacturing	107.8	107.7	110.1	110.4	110.3	109.5	104.7	100.0	93.6	91.8	90.6
Nondurable goods [1]	123.1	120.5	120.9	119.4	116.1	113.3	106.0	100.0	94.7	92.7	90.3
Food manufacturing	101.6	101.8	102.6	103.3	103.7	103.4	101.4	100.0	98.4	97.1	95.8
Textile mills	163.5	154.1	155.2	148.9	139.1	132.4	112.2	100.0	86.3	79.0	71.3
Textile product mills	121.0	118.1	119.4	117.7	115.6	112.3	105.5	100.0	92.4	90.2	88.0
Apparel	234.8	211.6	201.3	180.9	154.6	137.5	117.1	100.0	81.9	75.1	65.7
Paper and paper products	121.5	120.2	121.6	119.6	117.2	113.5	106.6	100.0	92.5	89.2	88.0
Printing and related support activities	123.9	122.8	124.6	124.3	120.9	119.4	111.5	100.0	95.3	93.4	90.9
Petroleum and coal products	115.5	113.5	112.7	113.4	107.6	105.8	105.6	100.0	98.7	102.6	102.4
Chemicals	115.4	114.8	114.7	115.4	113.2	110.4	104.7	100.0	99.0	99.0	95.9
Plastics and rubber products	109.8	110.0	112.7	113.7	114.6	114.2	104.9	100.0	95.2	94.2	92.3
Private Service-Providing	87.1	89.5	93.0	95.7	98.3	100.8	100.7	100.0	99.5	101.1	103.8
Trade, transportation, and utilities	95.1	96.6	98.9	100.3	101.9	103.5	101.5	100.0	98.6	99.6	101.6
Wholesale trade	99.2	100.7	103.4	104.8	106.2	107.0	102.9	100.0	98.0	98.8	101.8
Retail trade	92.3	93.7	95.9	97.2	99.5	101.3	100.5	100.0	98.9	99.4	100.8
Transportation and warehousing	95.6	98.3	101.0	102.6	103.2	105.6	102.7	100.0	98.8	101.9	105.2
Utilities	112.9	108.6	106.1	105.7	105.0	104.1	102.3	100.0	97.4	94.2	93.1
Information	82.5	86.9	90.4	92.6	98.5	105.0	106.7	100.0	97.0	98.2	99.4
Financial activities	86.9	89.1	92.3	96.4	98.1	98.4	99.3	100.0	101.3	101.4	103.7
Professional and business services	81.2	85.2	91.5	96.7	101.7	106.6	104.0	100.0	98.7	101.8	106.3
Education and health services	80.6	82.9	86.2	88.6	90.4	92.6	96.5	100.0	101.7	103.8	107.0
Leisure and hospitality	88.5	90.7	93.4	95.5	97.8	100.5	100.6	100.0	100.0	103.0	106.2
Other services	87.0	89.1	91.9	94.3	96.2	97.8	99.0	100.0	97.4	96.1	96.2

[1]Includes other industries, not shown separately.

Table 15-6. Indexes of Aggregate Weekly Hours of Production and Nonsupervisory Workers on Private Nonfarm Payrolls by Industry—*Continued*

(2002 = 100.)

Industry	2006	2007	2008	2009	2010	2011	2012	2013	2014	2015	2016
Total Private	105.8	107.4	106.1	98.8	99.0	101.4	104.3	106.1	108.6	110.9	112.5
Goods-Producing	102.5	101.7	96.5	80.2	78.8	81.2	83.5	85.1	87.8	89.1	89.4
Mining and logging	125.8	133.5	137.6	117.2	124.5	147.4	158.7	155.0	164.3	144.1	114.4
Construction	115.4	114.7	106.5	85.9	80.2	81.7	83.6	87.7	92.0	96.5	100.6
Manufacturing	95.6	94.4	90.2	76.1	76.2	78.3	80.3	80.9	82.6	83.3	83.3
Durable goods	98.9	97.4	92.2	74.7	75.1	78.4	81.4	82.3	84.3	84.6	84.4
Wood products	99.9	89.3	76.7	57.8	58.5	59.3	62.1	67.3	69.6	70.2	71.9
Nonmetallic mineral products	100.3	96.9	91.2	73.8	70.5	70.1	68.9	69.7	72.4	75.0	76.9
Primary metals	94.2	91.4	87.4	66.1	71.7	80.1	82.7	79.8	81.7	80.1	76.5
Fabricated metal products	103.1	104.5	101.3	81.3	83.1	89.6	94.8	96.3	97.9	97.0	93.8
Machinery	102.2	103.3	102.3	80.6	81.2	89.6	94.0	94.0	96.6	93.4	90.9
Computer and electronic products	103.6	102.2	101.2	89.4	87.2	86.4	86.0	83.7	81.4	82.3	83.1
Electrical equipment and appliances	88.0	89.1	88.5	74.1	73.2	71.6	73.4	72.4	73.5	77.2	78.7
Transportation equipment [1]	99.9	98.0	88.6	70.1	72.1	75.3	80.4	82.4	86.3	89.3	90.8
Motor vehicles and parts	92.9	85.8	72.7	51.6	57.5	60.9	66.6	70.7	76.2	79.8	82.9
Furniture and related products	90.4	86.1	74.6	57.6	54.4	55.8	55.6	57.6	60.7	60.8	61.5
Miscellaneous manufacturing	90.4	91.0	89.2	81.1	79.0	80.0	82.2	85.3	86.3	84.9	85.8
Nondurable goods [1]	90.4	89.6	86.9	78.1	78.0	77.9	78.6	78.6	80.0	81.2	81.5
Food manufacturing	98.6	101.1	100.6	97.5	98.5	97.7	99.6	100.1	100.8	102.4	105.2
Textile mills	65.1	56.3	47.9	37.8	40.2	41.6	41.7	39.0	38.4	39.1	37.6
Textile product mills	85.0	77.5	70.5	58.5	56.5	55.2	53.3	50.5	51.5	51.5	52.7
Apparel	63.4	61.5	56.7	45.4	42.0	40.7	38.4	38.5	38.0	37.8	34.4
Paper and paper products	86.9	85.8	83.5	74.2	73.5	71.9	70.0	68.2	68.5	67.5	66.6
Printing and related support activities	92.5	91.6	86.1	74.1	69.0	65.6	64.3	63.2	64.2	65.2	64.5
Petroleum and coal products	96.9	95.6	102.4	90.2	89.1	91.2	101.6	96.8	98.5	100.1	99.8
Chemicals	96.1	94.1	94.6	88.3	88.9	90.6	92.6	93.6	94.4	96.1	96.0
Plastics and rubber products	91.9	91.1	87.1	71.3	73.6	75.3	75.8	77.3	81.4	84.0	84.2
Private Service-Providing	106.7	108.9	108.6	104.0	104.5	107.0	110.0	112.0	114.4	116.9	118.9
Trade, transportation, and utilities	103.3	104.8	103.3	96.8	96.8	99.7	101.8	102.7	104.4	106.3	107.0
Wholesale trade	105.7	109.2	108.6	99.9	97.7	100.7	104.0	105.3	106.8	106.8	106.7
Retail trade	101.1	101.8	99.8	94.3	95.0	97.7	98.9	98.7	99.5	100.9	101.1
Transportation and warehousing	107.9	109.4	107.7	100.0	101.3	105.4	109.2	112.5	116.7	123.1	125.9
Utilities	93.8	96.2	98.3	97.0	95.4	94.9	92.6	94.9	96.3	97.0	97.0
Information	100.2	100.1	100.0	93.5	90.0	88.9	88.9	89.8	90.5	90.8	90.7
Financial activities	106.3	107.6	106.8	103.1	101.3	101.2	103.7	104.7	106.5	109.6	111.6
Professional and business services	112.1	115.3	113.9	105.2	107.6	112.4	117.2	121.3	125.8	128.2	130.6
Education and health services	109.6	113.2	116.5	118.3	119.8	122.3	125.4	126.6	128.5	132.3	136.0
Leisure and hospitality	108.8	110.8	109.7	105.1	104.6	106.9	111.3	115.2	119.3	122.7	125.2
Other services	97.4	99.3	99.5	96.0	96.0	96.8	97.7	98.7	99.9	100.7	101.7

[1]Includes other industries, not shown separately.

NOTES AND DEFINITIONS, CHAPTER 15

TABLES 15-1 THROUGH 15-6

Employment, Hours, and Earnings by NAICS Industry

SOURCE: U.S. DEPARTMENT OF LABOR, BUREAU OF LABOR STATISTICS

See the notes and definitions for Tables 10-8 through 10-18 regarding definitions of *employment, production and nonsupervisory workers,* *average weekly hours, overtime hours, average hourly earnings,* *average weekly earnings,* and the *indexes of aggregate weekly hours.* Availability and reference information is also provided in those notes and definitions.

CHAPTER 16: KEY SECTOR STATISTICS

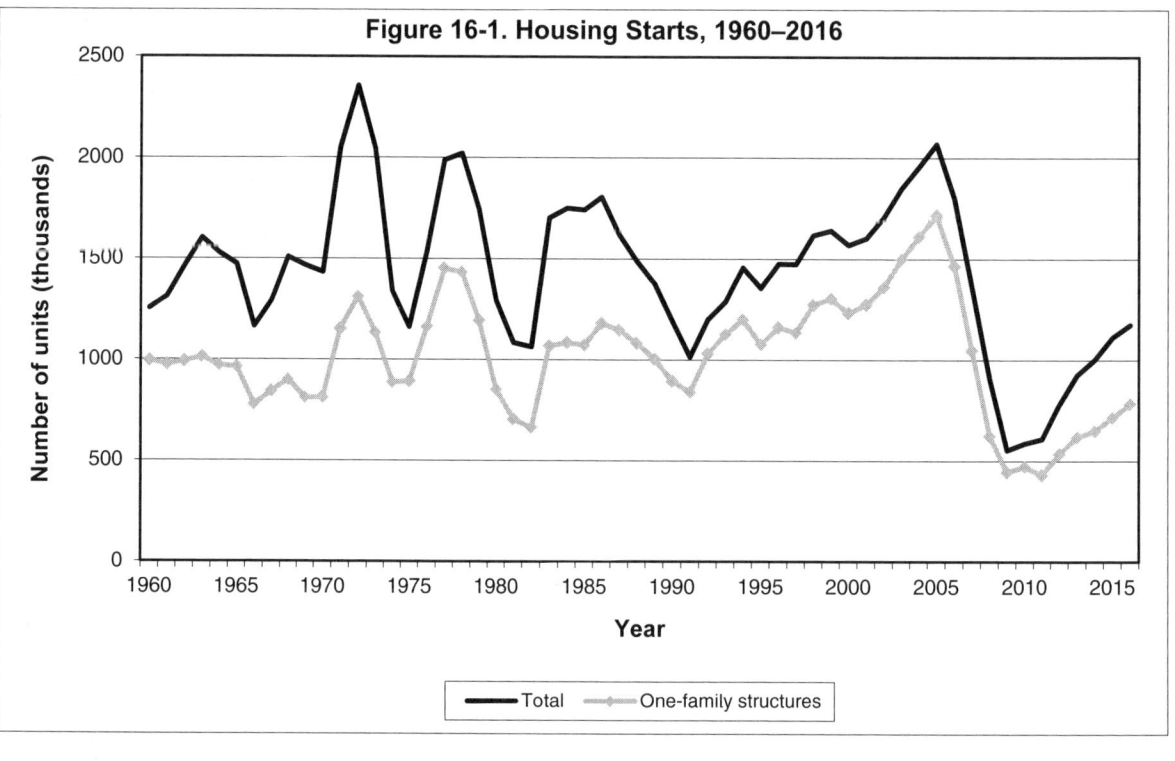

Figure 16-1. Housing Starts, 1960–2016

- The housing sector and associated financial excesses had the leading role in the boom and bust cycle of 2001–2009. In 2005, as shown in Figure 16-1, 2.1 million housing units were started, the highest since 1972. Of those, 1.7 million were one-family homes, an all-time record. By 2009, both total and single-family starts had plunged to the lowest levels of their 50-year history. With very modest recovery since then, starts remain at levels once viewed as recessionary. However, in 2016, 1.2 million housing units were started. (Table 16-2)

- New orders for nondefense capital goods at U.S. manufacturing firms is a widely followed advance indicator for production of investment goods. The value of such orders fell 38.7 percent from 2007 to 2009. The value of new orders in 2014 surpassed the peak in 2007 but fell 11.4 percent in 2015 and 6.8 percent in 2016. (Table 16-5)

- Sales of cars and light trucks fell to 10.4 million in 2009, down 6.5 million from their recent high in 2005. From 2009 to 2015, sales increased each year but declined 11.3 percent in 2016. (Table 16-7)

- E-commerce grew from 1.6 percent of total retail sales at the end of 2003 to 8.2 percent (seasonally adjusted) at the end of 2016. (Table 16-9)

Table 16-1. New Construction Put in Place

(Billions of dollars, monthly data are at seasonally adjusted annual rates.)

Year and month	Total	Private											
		Total ¹	Residential	Office	Commercial		Health care	Educational	Amusement and recreation	Transportation	Communication	Power	Manufacturing
					Total ¹	Multi-retail							
1975	152.6	109.3	51.6	...	...	...	...	...	...	...	...	...	...
1976	172.1	128.2	68.3	...	...	...	...	...	...	...	...	...	...
1977	200.5	157.4	92.0	...	...	...	...	...	...	...	...	...	...
1978	239.9	189.7	109.8	...	...	...	...	...	...	...	...	...	...
1979	272.9	216.2	116.4	...	...	...	...	...	...	...	...	...	...
1980	273.9	210.3	100.4	...	...	...	...	...	...	...	...	...	...
1981	289.1	224.4	99.2	...	...	...	...	...	...	...	...	...	...
1982	279.3	216.3	84.7	...	...	...	...	...	...	...	...	...	...
1983	311.9	248.4	125.8	...	...	...	...	...	...	...	...	...	...
1984	370.2	300.0	155.0	...	...	...	...	...	...	...	...	...	...
1985	403.4	325.6	160.5	...	...	...	...	...	...	...	...	...	...
1986	433.5	348.9	190.7	...	...	...	...	...	...	...	...	...	...
1987	446.6	356.0	199.7	...	...	...	...	...	...	...	...	...	...
1988	462.0	367.3	204.5	...	...	...	...	...	...	...	...	...	...
1989	477.5	379.3	204.3	...	...	...	...	...	...	...	...	...	...
1990	476.8	369.3	191.1	...	...	...	...	...	...	...	...	...	...
1991	432.6	322.5	166.3	...	...	...	...	...	...	...	...	...	...
1992	463.7	347.8	199.4	...	...	...	...	...	...	...	...	...	...
1993	485.5	358.2	208.2	20.0	34.4	11.5	14.9	4.8	4.6	4.7	9.8	23.6	23.4
1994	531.9	401.5	241.0	20.4	39.6	12.2	15.4	5.0	5.1	4.7	10.1	21.0	28.8
1995	548.7	408.7	228.1	23.0	44.1	12.0	15.3	5.7	5.9	4.8	11.1	22.0	35.4
1996	599.7	453.0	257.5	26.5	49.4	13.3	15.4	7.0	7.0	5.8	11.8	17.4	38.1
1997	631.9	478.4	264.7	32.8	53.1	12.2	17.4	8.8	8.5	6.2	12.5	16.4	37.6
1998	688.5	533.7	296.3	40.4	55.7	13.3	17.7	9.8	8.6	7.3	12.5	21.7	40.5
1999	744.6	575.5	326.3	45.1	59.4	15.2	18.4	9.8	9.6	6.5	18.4	22.0	35.1
2000	802.8	621.4	346.1	52.4	64.1	14.9	19.5	11.7	8.8	6.9	18.8	29.3	37.6
2001	840.2	638.3	364.4	49.7	63.6	16.4	19.5	12.8	7.8	7.1	19.6	31.5	37.8
2002	847.9	634.4	402.0	44.3	62.5	15.6	27.1	73.9	17.3	25.8	18.5	36.8	22.9
2003	891.5	675.4	451.3	39.4	61.5	15.4	29.3	74.3	16.8	24.7	14.6	41.5	21.5
2004	991.4	771.2	538.4	42.4	67.1	18.8	32.2	74.3	16.7	25.1	15.5	35.6	23.4
2005	1 116.8	882.7	624.6	37.3	66.6	22.8	28.5	12.8	7.5	7.1	18.8	29.2	28.4
2006	1 161.3	905.9	607.8	45.7	73.4	29.2	32.0	13.8	9.3	8.7	22.2	33.7	32.3
2007	1 148.0	858.9	488.8	53.8	85.9	34.8	35.6	16.7	10.2	9.0	27.5	54.1	40.2
2008	1 077.4	768.6	359.2	55.5	82.7	32.0	38.4	18.6	10.5	9.9	26.3	69.2	53.6
2009	906.5	591.6	247.5	37.3	51.1	18.4	35.3	16.9	8.4	9.1	19.7	76.1	57.4
2010	809.3	505.3	242.0	24.4	37.2	12.5	29.6	13.4	6.5	9.9	17.7	66.1	40.6
2011	788.3	501.9	244.1	23.7	39.2	13.4	28.9	14.1	6.7	9.5	17.5	64.3	39.8
2012	850.5	571.1	269.8	27.4	44.3	14.9	31.4	16.6	6.2	10.9	16.0	86.4	46.8
2013	906.4	635.7	323.4	30.1	50.9	16.7	29.7	16.9	6.9	11.0	17.6	81.3	49.9
2014	1 005.6	729.5	369.8	38.9	60.9	19.5	28.9	16.6	7.7	12.2	17.1	98.2	58.1
2015	1 112.4	823.5	433.7	47.2	64.3	19.6	32.2	16.9	9.6	13.5	20.3	81.9	77.5
2016	1 164.5	879.0	457.8	61.2	71.3	20.7	32.8	18.9	11.8	12.2	19.6	87.4	74.4
2014													
January	977.1	711.8	361.4	35.9	53.3	18.5	28.6	16.3	7.1	10.8	18.0	107.4	53.4
February	984.7	721.4	361.8	35.8	55.4	19.6	28.6	15.6	7.0	11.4	18.9	115.5	51.6
March	993.3	726.2	367.4	35.3	56.5	19.7	28.2	16.5	7.1	11.5	18.3	116.0	50.0
April	1 003.0	729.5	369.3	38.7	56.9	18.5	28.6	17.0	7.4	12.2	17.4	110.7	51.7
May	1 004.8	727.2	368.2	38.4	58.5	19.0	29.1	16.8	7.3	12.5	17.3	107.9	51.6
June	1 003.9	726.9	364.0	39.4	59.6	19.0	28.4	17.4	7.8	12.3	16.7	104.7	56.3
July	1 004.2	722.3	361.9	39.1	60.9	19.2	28.8	16.7	7.8	11.6	16.4	102.0	55.9
August	1 001.0	722.4	361.3	39.1	62.7	20.0	28.6	16.7	7.5	11.2	16.7	99.2	58.1
September	1 004.6	728.7	369.5	40.5	65.2	21.0	28.6	15.8	7.8	11.8	16.5	90.6	60.2
October	1 029.3	741.9	374.8	41.1	66.3	20.6	29.4	16.7	8.3	12.8	16.4	84.5	68.4
November	1 029.7	753.6	386.6	40.6	65.8	19.9	29.5	16.9	8.4	13.4	16.8	81.5	70.6
December	1 042.5	761.8	397.6	41.6	66.5	19.3	30.1	16.6	8.8	13.7	16.6	78.8	67.9
2015													
January	1 038.1	765.9	404.1	41.3	63.1	18.9	30.5	16.0	8.1	13.8	17.9	75.9	72.0
February	1 047.1	773.5	409.9	42.1	60.3	18.3	30.3	16.1	8.7	13.6	18.1	76.1	75.1
March	1 062.4	783.0	414.2	43.3	62.0	19.1	30.4	16.0	8.3	13.7	18.2	77.4	75.7
April	1 094.3	805.9	422.2	45.2	64.7	20.1	30.4	16.3	9.2	13.0	19.9	82.9	77.0
May	1 112.2	820.7	428.7	46.0	66.0	21.0	30.6	16.8	9.4	12.9	20.9	84.4	78.6
June	1 130.5	829.9	434.5	47.5	62.7	18.5	33.5	17.4	10.5	13.0	19.9	84.0	78.8
July	1 135.9	838.3	437.3	49.2	63.5	19.6	33.8	17.5	10.1	13.5	20.8	86.0	79.3
August	1 145.2	848.6	443.0	49.5	64.6	19.4	34.3	17.5	10.1	13.6	21.3	86.1	80.4
September	1 152.1	858.9	449.7	49.6	64.9	20.0	35.5	17.3	10.2	14.0	21.1	85.6	82.1
October	1 134.4	845.7	445.4	48.8	66.6	20.1	31.9	17.1	10.5	13.7	21.9	82.3	80.0
November	1 135.5	853.7	449.5	52.0	65.0	19.3	34.0	17.3	10.3	14.0	21.5	84.0	79.0
December	1 133.7	844.1	450.1	50.2	67.3	20.0	30.6	17.3	10.2	13.5	21.0	84.8	72.4
2016													
January	1 144.9	849.7	450.0	50.7	68.9	19.9	30.6	17.7	10.3	12.6	21.9	84.9	74.5
February	1 157.7	858.1	455.7	54.6	68.3	20.3	31.5	18.3	11.0	12.0	19.6	84.3	74.0
March	1 176.4	879.0	468.4	55.8	68.8	19.3	33.1	17.9	11.2	12.5	18.2	86.3	76.4
April	1 142.5	854.6	445.5	56.4	68.0	19.4	31.6	17.8	11.0	12.9	18.6	87.5	74.1
May	1 143.8	860.3	444.4	56.6	69.4	20.1	33.0	17.9	11.4	12.7	18.8	88.9	74.9
June	1 154.1	867.9	448.1	61.2	68.5	19.7	33.2	18.1	12.3	12.8	18.7	89.8	72.8
July	1 160.4	884.9	456.6	62.7	70.1	20.4	32.4	19.0	12.0	13.1	18.9	90.2	78.0
August	1 166.5	888.4	456.2	64.0	71.4	20.5	33.6	19.2	12.4	11.6	18.9	90.0	78.4
September	1 164.4	883.6	451.0	66.5	71.4	20.7	34.1	20.4	12.4	11.9	18.5	88.7	75.6
October	1 173.7	886.2	459.5	66.5	73.3	21.8	33.2	19.8	12.3	12.4	19.9	85.6	72.6
November	1 191.5	904.7	470.8	67.0	76.0	22.6	32.7	20.8	12.6	11.5	20.5	86.8	72.9
December	1 188.9	909.7	475.2	68.1	78.5	23.0	32.7	20.4	12.6	11.4	21.5	89.1	67.9

¹Includes categories not shown separately.
. . . = Not available.

Table 16-1. New Construction Put in Place—*Continued*

(Billions of dollars, monthly data are at seasonally adjusted annual rates.)

Year and month	Total	Public												Federal
		State and local												
		Total [1]	Residential	Office	Health care	Educa-tional	Public safety	Amuse-ment and recreation	Transpor-tation	Power	Highway and street	Sewage and waste disposal	Water supply	
1975	43.3	37.2	. . .	. . .	. . .	. . .	. . .	. . .	. . .	. . .	. . .	. . .	. . .	6.1
1976	44.0	37.2	. . .	. . .	. . .	. . .	. . .	. . .	. . .	. . .	. . .	. . .	. . .	6.8
1977	43.1	36.0	. . .	. . .	. . .	. . .	. . .	. . .	. . .	. . .	. . .	. . .	. . .	7.1
1978	50.1	42.0	. . .	. . .	. . .	. . .	. . .	. . .	. . .	. . .	. . .	. . .	. . .	8.1
1979	56.6	48.1	. . .	. . .	. . .	. . .	. . .	. . .	. . .	. . .	. . .	. . .	. . .	8.6
1980	63.6	54.0	. . .	. . .	. . .	. . .	. . .	. . .	. . .	. . .	. . .	. . .	. . .	9.6
1981	64.7	54.3	. . .	. . .	. . .	. . .	. . .	. . .	. . .	. . .	. . .	. . .	. . .	10.4
1982	63.1	53.1	. . .	. . .	. . .	. . .	. . .	. . .	. . .	. . .	. . .	. . .	. . .	10.0
1983	63.5	52.9	. . .	. . .	. . .	. . .	. . .	. . .	. . .	. . .	. . .	. . .	. . .	10.6
1984	70.2	59.0	. . .	. . .	. . .	. . .	. . .	. . .	. . .	. . .	. . .	. . .	. . .	11.2
1985	77.8	65.8	. . .	. . .	. . .	. . .	. . .	. . .	. . .	. . .	. . .	. . .	. . .	12.0
1986	84.6	72.2	. . .	. . .	. . .	. . .	. . .	. . .	. . .	. . .	. . .	. . .	. . .	12.4
1987	90.6	76.6	. . .	. . .	. . .	. . .	. . .	. . .	. . .	. . .	. . .	. . .	. . .	14.1
1988	94.7	82.5	. . .	. . .	. . .	. . .	. . .	. . .	. . .	. . .	. . .	. . .	. . .	12.3
1989	98.2	86.0	. . .	. . .	. . .	. . .	. . .	. . .	. . .	. . .	. . .	. . .	. . .	12.2
1990	107.5	95.4	. . .	. . .	. . .	. . .	. . .	. . .	. . .	. . .	. . .	. . .	. . .	12.1
1991	110.1	97.3	. . .	. . .	. . .	. . .	. . .	. . .	. . .	. . .	. . .	. . .	. . .	12.8
1992	115.8	101.5	. . .	. . .	. . .	. . .	. . .	. . .	. . .	. . .	. . .	. . .	. . .	14.4
1993	127.4	112.9	3.4	2.8	2.3	24.2	4.6	4.3	9.8	7.4	34.5	11.2	6.4	14.4
1994	130.4	116.0	4.2	3.0	2.4	25.3	4.5	4.7	9.2	5.1	37.3	12.0	6.4	14.4
1995	140.0	124.3	4.5	3.3	2.6	27.5	5.0	5.1	9.6	5.7	38.6	13.0	7.3	15.8
1996	146.7	131.4	3.7	3.6	2.8	31.0	5.5	5.0	10.4	4.8	40.6	13.6	7.7	15.3
1997	153.4	139.4	3.3	3.8	2.9	34.3	5.6	5.7	10.3	4.4	44.4	13.1	8.1	14.1
1998	154.8	140.5	3.2	3.7	2.3	35.1	6.1	6.2	10.5	2.8	45.4	13.2	8.9	14.3
1999	169.1	155.1	3.2	3.6	2.5	39.8	6.2	7.2	11.4	2.9	51.0	14.5	9.6	14.0
2000	181.3	167.2	3.0	4.5	2.8	46.8	5.9	7.6	13.0	5.5	51.6	14.0	9.5	14.2
2001	201.9	186.8	3.5	5.6	2.9	52.8	6.1	9.1	15.9	5.3	56.4	14.2	11.4	15.1
2002	213.4	196.9	3.8	6.3	3.5	59.5	6.0	9.2	17.3	3.8	56.7	15.3	11.7	16.6
2003	216.1	198.2	3.7	6.1	4.0	59.3	5.8	8.4	16.5	6.8	56.3	15.6	11.7	17.9
2004	220.2	201.8	4.1	6.0	5.0	59.7	5.5	7.8	16.4	7.0	57.4	17.1	12.0	18.3
2005	234.2	216.9	4.0	5.2	5.1	65.8	6.0	7.3	16.3	8.3	63.2	18.3	13.5	17.3
2006	255.4	237.8	4.3	5.6	5.6	69.8	6.6	9.4	17.7	7.8	71.0	21.5	14.3	17.6
2007	289.1	268.5	5.1	7.2	7.0	78.4	8.4	10.7	21.1	11.4	75.5	23.3	15.0	20.6
2008	308.7	285.0	4.9	8.5	7.0	84.5	9.7	10.9	23.2	11.0	80.4	24.1	16.0	23.7
2009	314.9	286.5	5.8	9.2	6.8	83.7	9.4	10.6	25.5	11.8	81.3	23.5	14.8	28.4
2010	304.0	272.8	7.6	8.3	6.2	71.9	7.6	9.7	26.5	10.8	81.3	24.6	14.4	31.1
2011	286.4	254.8	6.0	7.4	7.0	68.0	7.2	8.5	23.3	9.5	78.4	21.2	13.4	31.7
2012	279.3	252.4	4.7	6.1	7.0	65.6	7.6	8.9	24.8	9.8	79.7	20.9	12.7	26.9
2013	270.7	247.0	4.5	5.2	6.9	60.0	6.6	8.1	25.9	11.0	80.6	21.0	12.9	23.7
2014	276.1	253.7	4.1	5.4	6.2	61.2	6.4	8.7	27.8	10.7	84.0	21.9	12.7	22.4
2015	288.9	266.3	5.6	5.8	5.4	64.8	6.0	9.8	29.8	9.2	88.9	23.1	12.5	22.6
2016	285.5	263.0	5.7	5.5	5.3	68.2	5.8	9.6	28.0	7.2	89.7	21.1	11.7	22.5
2014														
January	265.2	242.8	3.8	5.3	6.5	58.3	6.6	7.9	26.0	12.9	81.2	19.4	11.2	22.4
February	263.4	240.1	3.8	5.7	6.1	57.9	6.4	7.5	26.9	11.2	80.5	19.3	11.0	23.2
March	267.0	245.0	3.9	5.8	5.9	57.7	6.5	8.2	27.3	11.1	83.0	19.6	12.0	22.4
April	273.5	250.9	3.9	5.5	6.1	61.5	6.6	8.3	26.1	11.1	84.5	20.4	12.7	22.5
May	277.6	257.1	3.9	5.5	6.2	62.1	6.8	9.2	29.0	9.9	85.2	21.1	13.6	20.5
June	277.1	254.3	4.1	5.4	6.3	63.6	6.2	9.0	28.6	10.5	80.3	22.8	12.8	22.8
July	281.8	258.9	4.0	5.3	6.5	62.4	6.7	9.0	27.9	13.2	83.3	22.5	13.1	23.0
August	278.6	256.9	4.3	5.3	6.3	63.1	6.2	9.0	27.8	10.1	84.2	22.5	13.0	21.7
September	275.9	255.2	4.5	5.4	6.3	61.3	6.5	8.9	27.8	9.2	84.1	22.5	13.3	20.7
October	287.4	263.0	4.2	5.3	6.5	62.2	6.6	8.9	28.5	11.3	88.0	23.2	13.2	24.4
November	276.1	253.2	4.4	5.3	5.8	60.1	5.9	9.0	28.4	8.2	85.2	23.2	13.2	22.9
December	280.8	258.1	4.7	5.5	5.6	61.9	5.9	8.9	27.7	10.5	85.3	24.4	13.1	22.7
2015														
January	272.2	251.2	5.0	5.6	5.2	59.7	5.8	9.1	28.5	9.3	82.2	23.1	13.0	21.0
February	274.2	251.4	5.0	5.7	5.2	60.0	5.7	9.4	28.4	9.6	82.7	23.5	11.3	22.8
March	279.5	257.1	5.5	5.7	5.5	61.4	5.9	9.7	29.9	9.9	83.1	23.3	12.1	22.3
April	288.3	266.6	5.8	6.1	5.5	65.0	5.7	10.0	30.4	9.5	87.7	23.6	12.4	21.7
May	291.5	268.6	5.7	6.2	5.9	65.4	5.7	10.1	30.4	8.8	89.4	23.3	12.7	22.9
June	300.6	278.3	5.6	5.9	5.8	68.9	6.0	10.7	30.0	8.9	92.8	24.2	14.0	22.3
July	297.6	275.1	5.8	6.0	5.3	67.8	6.4	10.2	30.1	10.0	90.4	23.8	13.0	22.5
August	296.7	274.0	5.8	5.8	5.0	65.7	6.4	9.9	30.5	11.4	91.6	22.8	12.7	22.7
September	293.2	270.8	5.9	5.8	5.3	65.1	6.2	10.0	30.6	10.1	89.9	23.1	12.7	22.4
October	288.7	264.0	5.7	5.9	5.3	62.8	6.1	9.5	29.9	7.5	90.4	22.8	12.7	24.7
November	281.8	258.6	5.6	5.6	5.3	65.6	5.9	9.0	29.7	8.2	85.0	21.8	11.9	23.2
December	289.6	267.6	5.7	5.4	5.8	67.2	6.0	9.6	29.1	7.7	92.2	22.5	11.5	22.1
2016														
January	295.2	272.5	5.7	5.4	5.4	66.2	5.8	9.5	28.9	8.9	95.6	24.8	11.6	22.7
February	299.6	275.6	5.9	5.4	5.3	69.6	6.0	9.6	29.5	8.8	92.6	25.1	12.1	24.0
March	297.4	274.8	5.9	5.5	5.6	70.5	5.4	9.7	30.2	7.2	92.9	23.8	12.1	22.6
April	287.9	266.4	5.4	5.4	5.5	69.2	5.8	10.4	26.7	8.1	88.5	23.3	11.8	21.5
May	283.5	260.4	5.5	5.4	5.1	65.5	5.8	10.0	28.4	8.2	88.3	20.9	11.9	23.0
June	286.2	263.9	5.4	5.5	5.3	70.4	5.8	9.8	27.9	9.1	87.6	20.4	12.0	22.3
July	275.6	254.4	5.4	5.4	5.0	66.1	5.8	9.4	28.6	6.0	87.2	19.9	11.1	21.2
August	278.1	255.8	6.0	5.6	5.3	67.7	5.7	9.1	26.6	6.2	86.7	20.5	11.4	22.3
September	280.8	258.8	5.6	5.6	5.2	67.1	5.8	9.0	27.2	5.9	90.9	19.9	11.5	22.0
October	287.6	265.1	6.3	5.4	5.4	68.0	5.9	9.7	27.8	6.2	93.5	20.0	11.8	22.5
November	286.8	264.1	5.9	6.1	5.2	70.3	5.8	9.6	27.9	6.0	91.1	19.7	11.5	22.7
December	279.3	255.5	5.8	5.6	5.1	68.5	6.0	9.4	28.3	6.0	86.3	18.3	11.8	23.8

[1]Includes categories not shown separately.
. . . = Not available.

Table 16-2. Housing Starts and Building Permits; New House Sales and Prices

Year and month	Housing starts and building permits										New house sales and prices			
	New private housing units (thousands)									Shipments of manufactured homes (thousands, seasonally adjusted annual rate)	Seasonally adjusted		Median sales price (dollars)	Price index (2005 = 100)
	Started (not seasonally adjusted)			Seasonally adjusted annual rate										
				Started			Authorized by building permits							
	Total [1]	One-family structures	Five units or more	Total [1]	One-family structures	Five units or more	Total [1]	One-family structures	Five units or more		Sold (thousands, annual rate)	For sale, end-of-period (thousands)		
1975	1 160	892	204	1 160	892	204	939	675	200	213	549	316	39 300	22.1
1976	1 538	1 162	289	1 538	1 162	289	1 296	894	309	246	646	358	44 200	24.0
1977	1 987	1 451	414	1 987	1 451	414	1 690	1 126	443	266	819	408	48 800	27.0
1978	2 020	1 433	462	2 020	1 433	462	1 801	1 183	487	276	817	419	55 700	30.9
1979	1 745	1 194	429	1 745	1 194	429	1 552	982	445	277	709	402	62 900	35.3
1980	1 292	852	331	1 292	852	331	1 191	710	366	222	545	342	64 600	38.9
1981	1 084	705	288	1 084	705	288	986	564	319	241	436	278	68 900	42.0
1982	1 062	663	320	1 062	663	320	1 000	546	366	240	412	255	69 300	43.0
1983	1 703	1 068	522	1 703	1 068	522	1 605	901	570	296	623	304	75 300	43.9
1984	1 750	1 084	544	1 750	1 084	544	1 682	922	617	295	639	358	79 900	45.7
1985	1 742	1 072	576	1 742	1 072	576	1 733	957	657	284	688	350	84 300	46.2
1986	1 805	1 179	542	1 805	1 179	542	1 769	1 078	583	244	750	361	92 000	48.0
1987	1 621	1 146	409	1 621	1 146	409	1 535	1 024	421	233	671	370	104 500	50.6
1988	1 488	1 081	348	1 488	1 081	348	1 456	994	386	218	676	371	112 500	52.5
1989	1 376	1 003	318	1 376	1 003	318	1 338	932	340	198	650	366	120 000	54.6
1990	1 193	895	260	1 193	895	260	1 111	794	263	188	534	321	122 900	55.7
1991	1 014	840	138	1 014	840	138	949	754	152	171	509	284	120 000	56.4
1992	1 200	1 030	139	1 200	1 030	139	1 095	911	138	211	610	267	121 500	57.2
1993	1 288	1 126	133	1 288	1 126	133	1 199	987	160	254	666	295	126 500	59.4
1994	1 457	1 198	224	1 457	1 198	224	1 372	1 069	241	304	670	340	130 000	62.9
1995	1 354	1 076	244	1 354	1 076	244	1 333	997	272	340	667	374	133 900	64.3
1996	1 477	1 161	271	1 477	1 161	271	1 426	1 070	290	363	757	326	140 000	66.0
1997	1 474	1 134	296	1 474	1 134	296	1 441	1 062	310	354	804	287	146 000	67.5
1998	1 617	1 271	303	1 617	1 271	303	1 612	1 188	355	373	886	300	152 500	69.2
1999	1 641	1 302	307	1 641	1 302	307	1 664	1 247	351	348	880	315	161 000	72.8
2000	1 569	1 231	299	1 569	1 231	299	1 592	1 198	329	250	877	301	169 000	75.6
2001	1 603	1 273	293	1 603	1 273	293	1 637	1 236	335	193	908	310	175 200	77.9
2002	1 705	1 359	308	1 705	1 359	308	1 748	1 333	341	169	973	344	187 600	81.4
2003	1 848	1 499	315	1 848	1 499	315	1 889	1 461	346	131	1 086	377	195 000	86.0
2004	1 956	1 611	303	1 956	1 611	303	2 070	1 613	366	131	1 203	431	221 000	92.8
2005	2 068	1 716	311	2 068	1 716	311	2 155	1 682	389	147	1 283	515	240 900	100.0
2006	1 801	1 465	293	1 801	1 465	293	1 839	1 378	384	117	1 051	537	246 500	104.7
2007	1 355	1 046	277	1 355	1 046	277	1 398	980	359	96	776	496	247 900	104.9
2008	906	622	266	906	622	266	905	576	295	82	485	352	232 100	99.5
2009	554	445	97	554	445	97	583	441	121	50	375	232	216 700	95.1
2010	587	471	104	587	471	104	605	447	135	50	323	188	221 800	95.0
2011	609	431	167	609	431	167	624	418	184	52	306	150	227 200	94.3
2012	781	535	234	781	535	234	830	519	285	55	368	148	245 200	97.6
2013	925	618	294	925	618	294	991	621	341	60	429	186	268 900	104.7
2014	1 003	648	342	1 003	648	342	1 052	640	382	64	437	212	282 800	112.3
2015	1 112	715	386	1 112	715	386	1 183	696	455	71	501	235	296 400	113.6
2016	1 174	782	381	1 174	782	381	1 207	751	421	81	561	257	316 200	122.6
2014														
January	61	39	22	902	579	315	1 001	621	350	58	447	190	69 800	. . .
February	65	41	24	948	596	341	1 032	614	391	61	423	188	268 400	. . .
March	80	55	25	973	653	306	1 078	622	426	63	410	192	282 300	106.8
April	95	61	33	1 038	646	383	1 080	622	431	63	401	191	274 500	. . .
May	93	61	31	987	638	340	1 007	625	351	64	452	193	285 600	. . .
June	87	61	25	928	600	305	1 015	648	328	63	416	198	287 000	112.7
July	101	61	38	1 085	651	418	1 053	643	382	66	402	203	280 400	. . .
August	86	58	27	984	639	327	1 045	644	366	66	449	206	291 700	. . .
September	94	58	35	999	659	329	1 062	655	382	66	466	207	261 500	114.5
October	92	58	32	1 094	715	362	1 123	651	440	66	474	209	299 400	. . .
November	76	47	28	994	661	324	1 073	661	383	66	446	211	302 700	. . .
December	73	48	24	1 081	722	339	1 070	680	365	67	492	211	302 000	119.2
2015														
January	73	46	26	1 101	708	387	1 069	667	375	68	523	207	292 000	. . .
February	62	41	21	887	587	292	1 127	635	463	66	549	204	293 900	. . .
March	80	53	25	974	624	329	1 079	657	395	68	481	205	293 400	112.8
April	109	70	37	1 200	745	436	1 178	675	471	68	500	206	292 700	. . .
May	100	67	32	1 066	696	361	1 255	692	528	69	504	210	287 400	. . .
June	112	69	42	1 201	694	493	1 363	701	626	67	476	216	289 200	111.5
July	107	72	35	1 140	763	367	1 134	698	405	74	498	216	296 000	. . .
August	99	66	32	1 134	737	390	1 159	712	416	72	513	217	300 200	. . .
September	112	65	46	1 209	744	454	1 125	711	376	69	461	223	307 600	112.8
October	91	59	31	1 059	704	343	1 166	724	406	73	482	225	298 700	. . .
November	90	57	33	1 176	781	389	1 267	736	503	75	508	229	317 000	. . .
December	78	50	27	1 138	764	358	1 218	734	450	78	536	234	299 000	116.7
2016														
January	74	50	23	1 123	771	334	1 193	733	424	84	520	237	291 100	. . .
February	84	58	25	1 209	841	356	1 195	737	423	81	525	240	311 300	. . .
March	91	62	28	1 128	748	370	1 115	731	348	80	533	243	311 400	120.4
April	106	73	33	1 164	767	384	1 163	743	387	80	566	241	321 300	. . .
May	105	70	34	1 119	732	382	1 178	735	412	79	560	241	296 000	. . .
June	112	75	35	1 190	770	402	1 193	743	419	78	559	243	321 600	120.7
July	115	73	42	1 223	772	443	1 175	718	427	72	627	237	295 000	. . .
August	103	66	35	1 164	727	420	1 200	743	421	76	567	241	302 400	. . .
September	95	67	26	1 062	783	265	1 270	749	482	80	570	242	323 700	124.7
October	114	73	40	1 328	871	447	1 285	779	474	80	577	248	302 000	. . .
November	88	61	27	1 149	823	323	1 255	786	428	83	579	248	318 300	. . .
December	86	53	33	1 268	808	449	1 266	830	397	102	548	256	332 700	125.1

[1] Includes structures with 2 to 4 units, not shown separately.
. . . = Not available.

Table 16-3. Manufacturers' Shipments

(Millions of dollars, seasonally adjusted.)

Year and month	Total	Total durable goods [1]	Total nondurable goods[1]	Construction materials and supplies	Information technology industries	Capital goods Total	Nondefense Total	Nondefense Excluding aircraft and parts	Defense	Consumer goods Total	Consumer goods Durable	Consumer goods Nondurable
1992	2 904 024	1 518 862	1 385 162	281 232	236 015	566 268	471 485	435 696	94 783	1 098 480	253 111	845 369
1993	3 020 497	1 604 544	1 415 953	303 391	241 680	580 859	493 875	463 753	86 984	1 127 629	274 813	852 816
1994	3 238 112	1 764 061	1 474 051	332 734	264 092	616 435	538 203	512 327	78 232	1 192 098	314 931	877 167
1995	3 479 677	1 902 815	1 576 862	353 198	291 885	666 167	590 578	565 729	75 589	1 256 611	324 036	932 575
1996	3 597 188	1 978 597	1 618 591	371 401	311 028	704 635	630 932	605 295	73 703	1 292 955	328 402	964 553
1997	3 834 699	2 147 384	1 687 315	399 880	349 846	779 232	702 971	665 074	76 261	1 358 516	360 193	998 323
1998	3 899 813	2 231 588	1 668 225	418 756	362 564	821 736	747 046	695 717	74 690	1 351 812	373 404	978 408
1999	4 031 887	2 326 736	1 705 151	434 138	374 384	839 754	768 799	713 042	70 955	1 424 828	412 646	1 012 182
2000	4 208 584	2 373 688	1 834 896	444 812	399 751	875 396	808 345	757 617	67 051	1 500 532	391 463	1 109 069
2001	3 970 499	2 174 406	1 796 093	424 517	353 237	801 999	728 495	678 288	73 504	1 480 496	367 522	1 112 973
2002	3 014 720	2 123 021	1 791 102	424 008	284 799	728 585	652 342	609 595	76 243	1 494 575	395 953	1 098 622
2003	4 015 388	2 142 589	1 872 799	429 183	274 829	719 602	634 273	600 616	85 329	1 584 329	418 821	1 165 508
2004	4 308 970	2 264 667	2 044 303	463 148	287 837	752 905	661 740	629 146	91 165	1 700 835	419 182	1 281 653
2005	4 742 077	2 424 844	2 317 233	509 865	295 447	821 906	730 368	686 939	91 538	1 895 119	422 555	1 472 564
2006	5 015 552	2 562 194	2 453 358	546 866	319 890	884 199	794 638	744 282	89 561	1 980 031	421 860	1 558 171
2007	5 319 457	2 687 028	2 632 429	560 208	322 846	936 404	836 426	768 662	99 978	2 106 081	421 822	1 684 259
2008	5 468 994	2 616 667	2 852 327	543 819	319 032	955 412	840 250	774 775	115 162	2 254 007	357 546	1 896 461
2009	4 423 779	2 056 829	2 366 950	426 663	271 678	820 521	697 469	642 555	123 052	1 849 113	268 036	1 581 077
2010	4 911 277	2 280 712	2 630 565	443 880	270 118	858 123	727 818	674 747	130 305	2 058 913	323 432	1 735 481
2011	5 491 894	2 479 086	3 012 808	471 598	274 110	923 876	803 248	740 848	120 628	2 373 512	344 299	2 029 213
2012	5 696 728	2 627 582	3 069 146	500 848	272 578	884 994	799 591	115 591	115 591	2 437 147	373 352	2 063 795
2013	5 809 745	2 695 807	3 113 938	523 707	271 444	1 007 645	891 684	799 052	115 961	2 496 085	402 805	2 093 280
2014	5 887 559	2 796 927	3 090 632	547 183	262 545	1 017 011	905 668	803 674	111 343	2 507 589	435 589	2 072 000
2015	5 546 997	2 778 970	2 768 027	554 286	259 449	995 174	884 018	779 997	111 156	2 267 770	462 028	1 805 742
2016	5 446 982	2 741 945	2 705 037	570 146	259 233	943 511	828 683	734 805	114 828	2 206 224	455 601	1 750 623
2013												
January	481 006	219 389	261 617	43 473	22 497	82 468	73 217	66 446	9 251	207 166	32 180	174 986
February	490 399	223 649	266 750	43 786	23 099	83 896	74 141	67 889	9 755	214 233	33 325	180 908
March	482 127	223 868	258 259	42 633	23 010	85 296	75 671	68 053	9 625	206 805	32 760	174 045
April	477 061	222 035	255 026	43 516	22 332	81 627	72 147	65 982	9 480	203 510	33 243	170 267
May	483 116	225 378	257 738	43 521	22 887	86 208	76 589	67 560	9 619	204 813	32 906	171 907
June	480 182	225 667	254 515	43 404	22 901	84 968	75 223	66 751	9 745	203 039	33 373	169 666
July	480 887	220 242	260 645	43 392	22 282	82 509	73 308	65 417	9 201	208 483	32 475	176 008
August	484 625	224 685	259 940	43 777	22 270	83 707	73 691	65 756	10 016	208 788	33 484	175 304
September	484 851	225 754	259 097	44 166	22 821	82 946	73 208	65 532	9 738	208 449	33 967	174 482
October	484 991	225 946	259 045	44 273	22 525	82 341	72 906	65 086	9 435	208 930	34 885	174 045
November	493 869	233 377	260 492	44 566	22 324	85 996	75 680	67 751	10 316	211 999	36 452	175 547
December	488 713	226 032	262 681	43 503	22 185	85 264	75 752	67 445	9 512	211 861	33 862	177 999
2014												
January	486 712	224 021	262 691	43 728	22 326	82 524	73 134	65 550	9 390	211 337	32 991	178 346
February	494 060	229 453	264 607	43 960	22 163	84 282	74 939	66 693	9 343	215 111	35 406	179 705
March	493 585	231 443	262 142	44 903	22 176	85 055	75 887	67 311	9 168	212 896	35 651	177 245
April	492 760	229 265	263 495	45 095	22 121	83 283	73 793	65 875	9 490	214 225	34 968	179 257
May	492 283	231 332	260 951	45 461	21 942	83 144	73 900	66 474	9 244	212 248	36 549	175 699
June	493 475	232 839	260 636	46 006	22 451	84 744	75 693	66 853	9 051	211 199	35 614	175 585
July	496 791	238 538	258 253	46 027	21 818	84 358	75 328	66 678	9 030	211 122	38 484	172 638
August	496 861	238 211	258 650	46 258	21 971	87 778	78 488	69 490	9 290	209 924	36 785	173 139
September	493 878	237 300	256 578	46 503	21 623	88 123	78 967	69 757	9 156	208 093	36 630	171 463
October	487 819	235 086	252 733	46 195	21 195	84 001	74 851	66 149	9 150	205 414	37 436	167 978
November	481 883	232 743	249 140	46 135	21 343	83 546	74 307	65 873	9 239	201 637	37 145	164 492
December	478 005	237 044	240 961	46 702	21 595	85 580	75 657	67 053	9 923	195 650	38 450	157 200
2015												
January	463 374	230 528	232 846	46 072	21 181	83 610	75 215	65 707	8 395	186 344	35 754	150 590
February	464 465	229 221	235 244	45 630	21 097	82 861	74 784	65 223	8 077	190 184	36 115	154 069
March	468 914	234 667	234 247	45 602	21 810	84 041	74 952	65 808	9 089	193 007	39 123	153 884
April	466 537	231 526	235 011	45 786	21 599	83 594	74 568	65 068	9 026	192 075	38 053	154 022
May	465 909	231 448	234 461	45 489	21 263	82 444	73 624	64 774	8 820	193 007	38 919	154 088
June	469 393	234 307	235 086	47 397	21 726	83 638	73 959	65 102	9 679	193 838	39 241	154 597
July	466 759	233 997	232 762	46 191	21 830	83 519	73 683	65 658	9 836	192 240	39 963	152 277
August	462 480	233 596	228 884	46 130	21 658	84 538	75 013	65 083	9 525	188 105	39 180	148 925
September	460 469	233 361	227 108	46 487	21 881	83 617	73 851	65 253	9 766	187 518	39 840	147 678
October	457 160	230 546	226 614	46 442	21 769	83 037	72 978	64 845	10 059	185 720	38 188	147 532
November	456 228	231 961	224 267	46 506	21 632	83 290	74 095	63 846	9 195	184 491	39 076	145 415
December	447 412	225 908	221 504	46 534	21 606	78 689	69 247	63 704	9 442	181 123	38 493	142 630
2016												
January	447 646	229 491	218 155	46 949	21 426	79 969	71 045	62 581	8 924	178 736	38 902	139 834
February	444 060	227 657	216 403	46 875	21 024	78 230	68 912	61 333	9 318	177 005	39 120	137 885
March	447 446	225 933	221 513	47 266	20 979	77 909	68 606	61 301	9 303	179 954	37 606	142 348
April	449 628	226 709	222 919	47 374	21 476	78 291	69 424	61 499	8 867	181 859	38 386	143 473
May	449 673	225 829	223 844	47 076	21 455	78 799	69 699	60 783	9 100	181 591	36 824	144 767
June	453 067	226 370	226 697	47 156	21 384	77 968	68 485	60 598	9 483	184 406	37 278	147 128
July	452 034	227 592	224 442	47 102	22 109	78 665	68 840	60 437	9 825	182 792	37 548	145 244
August	451 885	227 081	224 804	47 438	21 861	77 123	67 565	60 475	9 558	183 299	37 824	145 475
September	456 079	229 071	227 008	47 246	21 597	78 873	69 224	60 903	9 649	184 699	37 583	147 116
October	457 862	229 215	228 647	47 791	21 932	78 592	68 628	60 768	9 964	186 478	37 823	148 655
November	457 850	229 176	228 674	48 281	21 778	78 048	67 789	61 011	10 259	186 187	37 377	148 810
December	469 319	233 300	236 019	49 002	21 903	79 636	69 551	61 878	10 085	194 082	38 162	155 920

[1]Includes categories not shown separately.

Table 16-4. Manufacturers' Inventories

(Current cost basis, end of period; seasonally adjusted, millions of dollars.)

Year and month	Total	Total durable goods	Durables total by stage of fabrication			Total nondurable goods	Nondurables total by stage of fabrication		
			Materials and supplies	Work in process	Finished goods		Materials and supplies	Work in process	Finished goods
1992	378 609	237 854	69 621	104 132	64 101	140 755	53 149	23 383	64 223
1993	379 806	238 719	72 633	101 948	64 138	141 087	54 233	23 394	63 460
1994	399 934	253 095	78 482	106 521	68 092	146 839	57 113	24 444	65 282
1995	424 802	267 437	85 545	106 634	75 258	157 365	60 778	25 776	70 811
1996	430 366	272 428	86 265	110 527	75 636	157 938	59 157	26 485	72 296
1997	443 227	280 730	92 253	109 714	78 763	162 497	60 175	28 523	73 799
1998	448 373	290 071	93 406	114 928	81 737	158 302	58 156	27 049	73 097
1999	463 004	296 009	97 722	113 805	84 482	166 995	60 975	28 791	77 229
2000	480 748	306 002	105 848	110 909	89 245	174 746	61 465	30 090	83 191
2001	427 353	267 409	91 168	93 768	82 473	159 944	55 671	27 157	77 116
2002	423 005	260 469	88 538	92 376	79 555	162 536	56 617	28 016	77 903
2003	408 303	246 898	82 419	88 596	75 883	161 405	56 833	27 223	77 349
2004	440 838	264 943	92 300	90 893	81 750	175 895	61 797	30 115	83 983
2005	473 653	283 609	98 601	98 420	86 588	190 044	66 708	33 032	90 304
2006	522 212	317 359	111 723	106 311	99 325	204 853	70 183	37 190	97 480
2007	560 725	334 537	116 603	117 326	100 608	226 188	74 814	44 943	106 431
2008	542 238	329 802	117 778	110 881	101 143	212 436	72 379	41 248	98 809
2009	503 659	294 660	100 612	106 162	87 886	208 999	71 526	41 974	95 499
2010	552 863	321 456	107 039	122 161	92 256	231 407	76 522	45 769	109 116
2011	605 858	352 766	119 397	133 220	100 149	253 092	81 772	50 662	120 658
2012	624 256	367 491	125 146	138 749	103 596	256 765	83 071	51 137	122 557
2013	629 768	370 441	125 252	141 749	103 440	259 327	84 733	52 254	122 340
2014	639 933	387 776	132 691	147 121	107 964	252 157	83 588	51 277	117 292
2015	639 527	394 158	130 577	153 438	110 143	245 369	84 968	46 004	114 397
2016	644 446	391 248	130 645	149 855	110 748	253 198	86 762	49 708	116 728
2013									
January	627 026	367 700	125 011	139 245	103 444	259 326	83 950	51 418	123 958
February	628 016	368 224	125 175	140 242	102 807	259 792	83 098	52 491	124 203
March	628 126	366 566	124 353	140 192	102 021	261 560	83 986	52 839	124 735
April	627 847	367 325	123 898	141 595	101 832	260 522	82 775	53 453	124 294
May	625 293	366 114	124 200	140 402	101 512	259 179	83 017	52 146	124 016
June	623 241	365 862	123 125	140 648	102 089	257 379	81 590	51 732	124 057
July	625 935	366 438	123 495	141 172	101 771	259 497	82 436	52 284	124 777
August	627 912	366 179	124 671	139 651	101 857	261 733	84 179	52 434	125 120
September	629 038	368 228	124 800	141 018	102 410	260 810	83 875	52 591	124 344
October	628 905	368 937	124 748	141 515	102 674	259 968	83 757	52 221	123 990
November	627 617	369 506	124 884	141 420	103 202	258 111	83 832	51 917	122 362
December	629 768	370 441	125 252	141 749	103 440	259 327	84 733	52 254	122 340
2014									
January	632 272	371 754	126 539	141 911	103 304	260 518	85 377	52 997	122 144
February	636 942	374 762	127 940	142 296	104 526	262 180	85 514	54 696	121 970
March	637 761	375 741	128 108	142 217	105 416	262 020	84 933	55 644	121 443
April	639 182	376 127	128 725	142 052	105 350	263 055	85 242	55 839	121 974
May	643 564	379 724	130 212	143 902	105 610	263 840	85 966	56 052	121 822
June	642 140	380 419	130 591	144 422	105 406	261 721	85 275	55 637	120 809
July	643 427	381 937	131 944	144 309	105 684	261 490	85 052	55 686	120 752
August	644 521	383 273	132 139	144 924	106 210	261 248	84 777	56 339	120 132
September	645 672	384 750	131 391	145 671	107 688	260 922	84 952	56 215	119 755
October	644 991	386 182	131 640	146 808	107 734	258 809	84 709	54 705	119 395
November	644 417	387 649	132 082	147 543	108 024	256 768	84 322	53 754	118 692
December	639 933	387 776	132 691	147 121	107 964	252 157	83 588	51 277	117 292
2015									
January	639 508	390 846	133 230	148 511	109 105	248 662	82 667	49 869	116 126
February	640 036	391 886	133 244	149 274	109 368	248 150	82 990	49 974	115 186
March	641 082	392 637	133 285	149 731	109 621	248 445	82 720	49 320	116 405
April	642 277	393 516	133 473	150 308	109 735	248 761	83 262	49 180	116 319
May	642 895	393 438	132 987	150 997	109 454	249 457	83 441	49 369	116 647
June	647 898	397 760	134 688	153 403	109 669	250 138	84 088	49 765	116 285
July	646 740	396 378	132 283	153 764	110 331	250 362	84 493	49 589	116 280
August	644 156	395 704	132 151	154 032	109 521	248 452	83 931	48 908	115 613
September	642 370	394 037	131 019	153 538	109 480	248 333	84 678	47 715	115 940
October	641 960	393 289	130 846	152 884	109 559	248 671	85 087	48 012	115 572
November	640 128	392 391	130 170	152 205	110 016	247 737	85 528	47 052	115 157
December	639 527	394 158	130 577	153 438	110 143	245 369	84 968	46 004	114 397
2016									
January	636 691	393 189	130 414	153 269	109 506	243 502	84 774	44 669	114 059
February	634 031	391 265	129 752	152 308	109 205	242 766	84 835	44 948	112 983
March	634 659	390 754	129 628	152 528	108 598	243 905	85 301	44 831	113 773
April	634 554	389 910	129 337	151 915	108 658	244 644	85 454	45 918	113 272
May	634 967	389 038	129 274	152 298	107 466	245 929	86 044	47 020	112 865
June	635 108	388 210	129 529	149 689	108 992	246 898	86 153	47 381	113 364
July	636 357	389 623	131 986	148 529	109 108	246 734	86 120	46 834	113 780
August	638 066	390 210	131 522	149 127	109 561	247 856	85 823	47 489	114 544
September	637 983	390 574	131 513	149 568	109 493	247 409	85 548	47 460	114 401
October	637 557	389 979	131 090	149 089	109 800	247 578	86 186	47 053	114 339
November	641 142	391 244	130 904	149 922	110 418	249 898	87 109	47 425	115 364
December	644 446	391 248	130 645	149 855	110 748	253 198	86 762	49 708	116 728

Table 16-4. Manufacturers' Inventories—*Continued*

(Current cost basis, end of period; seasonally adjusted, millions of dollars.)

Year and month	Construction materials and supplies	Information technology industries	Capital goods				Consumer goods		
			Total	Nondefense		Defense	Total	Durable	Nondurable
				Total	Excluding aircraft and parts				
1992	36 730	40 177	120 501	97 319	78 883	23 182	103 310	20 805	82 505
1993	38 307	39 176	118 460	97 118	79 585	21 342	104 873	21 820	83 053
1994	40 879	41 538	123 368	103 320	85 717	20 048	109 536	23 948	85 588
1995	43 420	46 936	129 709	111 563	94 673	18 146	116 404	25 316	91 088
1996	44 124	43 556	132 746	115 211	93 441	17 535	116 351	24 752	91 599
1997	45 725	48 094	137 556	122 598	98 870	14 958	119 660	24 905	94 755
1998	46 500	45 333	145 048	127 108	97 362	17 940	117 343	24 895	92 448
1999	48 541	46 174	146 244	126 278	99 610	19 966	124 220	26 097	98 123
2000	50 518	52 719	148 992	131 655	110 122	17 337	130 823	27 295	103 528
2001	46 341	42 967	128 670	114 908	93 305	13 762	121 377	25 410	95 967
2002	46 571	39 085	122 526	108 092	88 644	14 434	124 821	25 752	99 069
2003	45 328	35 274	115 029	99 195	81 816	15 834	126 055	25 050	100 002
2004	51 180	33 157	117 767	99 002	83 830	18 765	133 984	26 242	107 742
2005	55 055	39 123	127 143	110 614	92 942	16 529	144 663	28 111	116 552
2006	60 894	39 879	139 464	122 466	101 853	16 998	153 172	27 757	125 415
2007	62 600	38 746	150 219	131 422	104 773	18 797	170 514	27 629	142 885
2008	61 469	38 061	150 724	134 390	107 751	16 334	154 447	24 097	130 350
2009	50 958	36 574	145 479	125 809	97 594	19 670	157 953	21 121	136 832
2010	53 331	37 565	160 099	139 661	103 746	20 438	174 041	21 903	152 138
2011	57 619	39 503	174 434	154 523	113 823	19 911	187 535	22 828	164 707
2012	60 114	39 380	184 328	164 059	118 427	20 269	190 854	24 982	165 872
2013	61 140	37 929	185 387	165 560	116 786	19 827	193 745	26 161	167 584
2014	65 000	36 645	192 418	172 742	120 829	19 676	187 050	27 581	159 469
2015	64 638	37 662	199 360	178 593	120 641	20 767	186 635	29 182	157 453
2016	64 915	37 835	198 112	176 831	120 445	21 281	193 872	29 061	164 811
2013									
January	60 108	39 786	185 699	165 277	118 711	20 422	192 401	24 494	167 907
February	60 186	39 663	186 589	165 730	118 319	20 859	192 217	24 488	167 729
March	60 218	39 116	185 677	165 340	117 977	20 337	193 004	24 237	168 767
April	60 414	38 895	186 209	165 735	117 490	20 474	191 897	24 440	167 457
May	60 262	38 915	185 153	164 812	117 078	20 341	191 230	24 460	166 770
June	60 008	39 111	184 984	164 368	116 684	20 616	188 528	24 252	164 276
July	60 075	38 873	184 659	164 087	116 493	20 572	190 982	24 375	166 607
August	60 156	38 145	183 888	164 432	116 257	19 456	193 320	24 798	168 522
September	60 034	38 135	184 801	164 698	116 449	20 103	193 264	25 584	167 680
October	60 304	37 749	185 183	165 273	116 797	19 910	193 109	25 748	167 361
November	60 824	37 915	184 867	165 376	116 606	19 491	192 754	25 951	166 803
December	61 140	37 929	185 387	165 560	116 786	19 827	193 745	26 161	167 584
2014									
January	61 459	37 701	185 497	165 839	116 578	19 658	195 699	26 728	168 971
February	61 734	37 619	187 437	167 158	117 706	20 279	197 218	27 109	170 109
March	61 935	37 476	187 676	167 331	117 900	20 345	196 940	27 348	169 592
April	62 271	37 138	187 635	167 759	118 394	19 876	197 896	27 314	170 582
May	62 638	37 112	190 105	170 291	119 044	19 814	197 538	27 139	170 399
June	62 869	36 680	189 832	169 720	118 931	20 112	196 380	27 380	169 000
July	63 190	37 013	191 155	171 215	119 814	19 940	195 970	27 452	168 518
August	63 505	37 197	191 400	171 492	120 355	19 908	195 421	27 452	167 969
September	63 557	36 886	191 923	172 286	120 906	19 637	195 348	27 597	167 751
October	63 916	36 757	192 734	172 973	121 348	19 761	192 448	27 404	165 044
November	64 456	36 791	193 337	173 507	121 321	19 830	190 464	27 448	163 016
December	65 000	36 645	192 418	172 742	120 829	19 676	187 050	27 581	159 469
2015									
January	65 132	36 754	193 829	174 126	121 661	19 703	184 480	27 910	156 579
February	65 311	37 111	194 488	174 215	121 537	20 273	184 644	27 939	156 705
March	65 946	37 198	194 512	174 426	121 614	20 086	186 253	28 633	157 620
April	65 913	37 632	196 013	175 272	122 121	20 741	186 679	28 754	157 925
May	65 385	37 718	196 312	175 205	121 894	21 107	188 102	28 833	159 269
June	67 101	38 002	198 802	176 693	121 860	22 109	188 912	28 958	159 954
July	65 202	38 001	200 144	177 976	122 273	22 168	189 059	28 629	160 430
August	64 768	37 897	200 344	177 524	121 656	22 820	187 543	28 666	158 877
September	64 903	37 500	199 476	177 348	121 153	22 128	187 702	28 535	159 167
October	64 622	37 513	198 729	177 402	120 312	21 327	189 325	29 064	160 261
November	64 571	37 663	198 154	177 247	120 329	20 907	188 580	28 957	159 623
December	64 638	37 662	199 360	178 593	120 641	20 767	186 635	29 182	157 453
2016									
January	64 367	37 393	199 736	177 932	119 714	21 804	185 230	29 560	155 670
February	64 092	37 234	198 678	177 422	119 284	21 256	184 194	29 380	154 814
March	63 981	37 298	198 355	177 452	119 349	20 903	185 739	29 158	156 581
April	63 869	37 324	198 070	176 965	118 841	21 105	186 734	29 093	157 641
May	64 043	37 323	197 516	176 276	118 260	21 240	187 162	28 690	158 472
June	64 085	37 354	195 917	175 158	118 631	20 759	189 115	29 685	159 430
July	64 261	37 597	196 945	175 173	119 007	21 772	188 507	29 345	159 162
August	64 617	37 442	196 985	175 603	119 213	21 382	189 597	29 255	160 342
September	64 903	37 520	197 342	176 016	119 337	21 326	188 878	29 103	159 775
October	64 927	37 495	197 088	175 409	119 110	21 679	188 299	28 962	159 337
November	64 975	37 524	197 594	176 195	119 636	21 399	190 513	29 032	161 481
December	64 915	37 835	198 112	176 831	120 445	21 281	193 872	29 061	164 811

Table 16-5. Manufacturers' New Orders

(Net, millions of dollars, seasonally adjusted.)

Year and month	Total [1]	Total durable goods [1]	Construction materials and supplies	Information technology industries	Capital goods — Total	Capital goods — Nondefense — Total	Capital goods — Nondefense — Excluding aircraft and parts	Capital goods — Defense	Consumer goods — Total	Consumer goods — Durable	Consumer goods — Nondurable
1993	2 960 015	1 544 062	304 264	239 387	561 097	488 166	466 433	72 931	1 128 447	275 631	852 816
1994	3 199 686	1 725 635	335 962	265 010	616 252	542 094	523 461	74 158	1 192 584	315 417	877 167
1995	3 426 503	1 849 641	355 161	297 605	680 857	612 132	576 769	68 725	1 256 721	324 146	932 575
1996	3 567 384	1 948 793	373 536	310 074	737 268	648 797	607 174	88 471	1 293 537	328 984	964 553
1997	3 779 835	2 092 520	403 860	352 700	792 859	728 362	676 119	64 497	1 360 010	361 687	998 323
1998	3 808 143	2 139 918	419 330	365 723	809 727	745 600	698 279	64 127	1 352 708	374 300	978 408
1999	3 957 242	2 252 091	435 034	389 160	840 603	772 703	728 089	67 900	1 425 617	413 435	1 012 182
2000	4 161 472	2 326 576	446 792	409 500	910 933	831 335	767 754	79 598	1 501 810	392 741	1 109 069
2001	3 868 855	2 072 762	420 817	336 935	775 315	691 552	656 944	83 763	1 477 201	364 228	1 112 973
2002	3 823 145	2 032 043	423 561	273 788	698 865	622 403	589 148	76 462	1 494 406	395 484	1 098 622
2003	3 975 812	2 103 013	431 569	282 289	737 032	636 821	608 175	100 211	1 585 029	419 521	1 165 508
2004	4 289 001	2 244 698	468 746	293 836	787 748	688 813	643 997	98 935	1 701 565	419 912	1 281 653
2005	4 764 032	2 446 799	516 797	300 367	896 672	814 286	703 796	82 386	1 894 021	421 457	1 472 564
2006	5 089 646	2 636 288	549 467	332 649	992 499	889 370	775 156	103 129	1 979 165	420 994	1 558 171
2007	5 397 027	2 764 598	564 717	324 248	1 061 415	957 485	786 665	103 930	2 105 784	421 525	1 684 259
2008	5 452 124	2 599 797	543 218	318 571	1 006 627	879 429	781 810	127 198	2 252 724	356 263	1 896 461
2009	4 205 737	1 838 787	413 497	265 602	690 674	587 116	608 664	103 558	1 848 693	267 616	1 581 077
2010	4 895 899	2 265 334	450 921	272 817	885 135	747 708	685 492	137 427	2 058 565	323 084	1 735 481
2011	5 511 660	2 498 852	471 284	286 080	994 126	861 040	765 584	133 086	2 373 717	344 504	2 029 213
2012	5 709 710	2 640 564	500 617	274 254	1 051 261	932 086	803 477	119 175	2 437 479	373 684	2 063 795
2013	5 827 326	2 713 388	524 490	256 182	1 061 823	970 129	803 660	91 694	2 496 383	403 103	2 093 280
2014	5 931 254	2 840 622	548 105	258 999	1 087 361	979 793	807 542	107 568	2 507 842	435 842	2 072 000
2015	5 476 253	2 708 226	554 355	258 368	974 126	867 652	772 287	106 474	2 267 925	462 183	1 805 742
2016	5 373 935	2 668 898	570 364	266 634	927 416	808 436	737 706	118 980	2 206 452	455 829	1 750 623
2013											
January	478 536	216 919	42 984	21 272	82 736	76 883	69 370	5 853	207 092	32 106	174 986
February	495 952	229 202	44 014	21 259	91 885	83 745	66 031	8 140	214 212	33 304	180 908
March	470 016	211 757	42 443	19 931	78 389	73 688	66 516	4 701	206 743	32 698	174 045
April	475 312	220 286	43 127	21 910	83 116	76 732	67 098	6 384	203 553	33 286	170 267
May	488 931	231 193	43 730	22 759	93 933	85 128	68 745	8 805	204 925	33 018	171 907
June	495 410	240 895	43 259	22 179	102 347	92 266	68 375	10 081	203 142	33 476	169 666
July	476 097	215 452	43 547	21 217	81 918	74 104	66 082	7 814	208 541	32 533	176 008
August	481 689	221 749	44 039	20 605	83 916	75 727	66 120	8 189	208 934	33 630	175 304
September	490 492	231 395	44 391	21 866	91 336	82 061	66 683	9 275	208 344	33 862	174 482
October	483 650	224 605	44 493	21 463	83 485	75 938	64 261	7 547	208 879	34 834	174 045
November	498 787	238 295	44 728	21 354	94 922	87 157	68 288	7 765	212 067	36 520	175 547
December	493 416	230 735	44 122	20 621	92 216	85 691	67 166	6 525	211 949	33 950	177 999
2014											
January	484 589	221 898	43 924	21 901	84 642	77 289	67 727	7 353	211 246	32 900	178 346
February	494 429	229 822	44 147	21 490	83 295	74 964	66 722	8 331	214 933	35 228	179 705
March	495 892	233 750	44 736	21 847	88 658	78 881	68 452	9 777	212 940	35 695	177 245
April	499 785	236 290	45 470	22 449	93 262	76 860	66 311	16 402	214 246	34 989	179 257
May	493 616	232 665	45 957	20 956	86 083	77 104	65 488	8 979	212 272	36 573	175 699
June	498 760	238 124	46 072	22 415	89 936	80 332	69 685	9 604	211 421	35 836	175 585
July	548 962	290 709	45 938	21 187	138 271	130 741	67 719	7 530	210 993	38 355	172 638
August	497 386	238 736	46 523	22 155	91 488	83 382	69 242	8 106	209 857	36 718	173 139
September	492 225	235 647	46 250	21 514	87 792	80 389	70 343	7 403	208 220	36 757	171 463
October	483 258	230 525	46 820	21 410	81 868	72 276	64 998	9 592	205 450	37 472	167 978
November	477 556	228 416	46 135	20 980	82 704	74 989	64 626	7 715	201 642	37 150	164 492
December	464 702	223 741	45 963	20 896	77 477	70 514	65 982	6 963	195 825	38 625	157 200
2015											
January	459 652	226 806	46 089	20 934	83 765	75 881	66 334	7 884	186 231	35 641	150 590
February	454 548	219 304	45 467	20 960	80 609	72 647	64 584	7 962	190 080	36 011	154 069
March	464 584	230 337	45 558	22 560	84 810	75 911	65 210	8 899	193 156	39 272	153 884
April	461 971	226 960	45 745	21 468	83 167	75 232	64 385	7 935	192 242	38 220	154 022
May	455 140	220 679	45 266	21 186	77 361	68 725	63 791	8 636	192 982	38 894	154 088
June	468 188	233 102	47 933	21 476	86 555	76 598	64 038	9 957	193 857	39 260	154 597
July	464 274	231 512	46 235	21 613	86 072	74 960	65 233	11 112	192 141	39 864	152 277
August	456 094	227 210	46 057	21 792	83 063	75 241	64 456	7 822	188 149	39 224	148 925
September	448 250	221 142	46 642	21 678	72 775	67 553	64 756	5 222	187 478	39 800	147 678
October	453 724	227 110	46 036	21 488	84 239	75 671	64 640	8 568	185 821	38 289	147 532
November	450 194	225 927	46 347	21 503	83 372	70 308	63 843	13 064	184 587	39 172	145 415
December	442 424	220 920	47 051	21 388	70 605	61 519	60 997	9 086	181 133	38 503	142 630
2016											
January	444 735	226 580	47 120	22 231	81 905	73 169	62 895	8 736	178 848	39 014	139 834
February	432 289	215 886	47 022	21 770	71 449	65 424	61 187	6 025	176 965	39 080	137 885
March	440 146	218 633	46 972	21 437	75 806	63 136	61 262	12 670	179 977	37 629	142 348
April	451 940	229 021	47 603	22 270	84 215	72 282	61 086	11 933	181 793	38 320	143 473
May	446 003	222 159	47 118	22 235	78 732	70 567	59 866	8 165	181 631	36 864	144 767
June	438 150	211 453	47 205	21 704	67 183	61 131	60 054	6 052	184 417	37 289	147 128
July	444 481	220 039	47 021	22 686	75 391	67 983	61 655	7 408	182 853	37 609	145 244
August	446 229	221 425	47 211	22 261	76 118	65 625	62 503	10 493	183 404	37 929	145 475
September	447 341	220 333	46 986	22 022	76 241	65 315	61 186	10 926	184 785	37 669	147 116
October	462 386	233 739	47 955	22 358	88 740	78 150	61 186	10 590	186 507	37 852	148 655
November	451 753	223 079	48 905	22 772	75 183	61 494	62 128	13 689	186 110	37 300	148 810
December	459 700	223 681	48 718	22 919	76 412	64 526	61 918	11 886	194 043	38 123	155 920

[1]Includes categories not shown separately.

Table 16-6. Manufacturers' Unfilled Orders, Durable Goods Industries

(End of period, millions of dollars, seasonally adjusted.)

Year and month	Total [1]	Transportation equipment		Construction materials and supplies	Information technology industries	By topical categories				Consumer durable goods
		Nondefense aircraft and parts	Defense aircraft and parts			Capital goods				
						Total	Nondefense		Defense	
							Total	Excluding aircraft and parts		
1993	425 607	110 927	46 545	21 760	77 976	299 265	173 881	95 287	125 384	4 611
1994	434 899	101 157	44 651	25 090	79 071	299 296	178 007	106 779	121 289	5 121
1995	447 510	109 506	42 360	27 155	84 919	313 963	199 613	118 006	114 350	5 282
1996	489 147	130 580	45 203	29 436	84 227	346 596	217 605	120 276	128 991	5 821
1997	513 317	143 183	40 842	33 584	87 704	360 636	243 413	132 076	117 223	7 330
1998	496 363	137 228	37 711	34 268	90 930	348 398	241 565	134 417	106 833	8 262
1999	505 667	126 256	35 616	35 246	105 883	349 497	245 603	149 679	103 894	9 035
2000	549 507	138 159	42 421	37 405	115 679	384 834	268 323	159 844	116 511	10 349
2001	509 910	124 656	52 002	33 580	98 908	357 539	230 560	137 637	126 979	6 988
2002	479 541	114 507	57 347	33 148	88 051	327 826	200 834	117 404	126 992	6 577
2003	506 254	109 805	63 702	35 594	95 633	345 115	203 320	125 001	141 795	7 295
2004	558 872	123 094	57 409	41 385	101 429	379 885	229 995	139 879	149 890	8 215
2005	654 556	188 373	55 234	48 518	106 544	453 234	312 489	156 886	140 745	7 258
2006	797 897	265 572	59 790	51 090	119 250	560 378	405 898	187 886	154 480	6 421
2007	946 612	376 899	63 340	55 571	120 264	683 914	525 098	205 853	158 816	6 132
2008	995 050	417 110	72 414	54 864	119 951	735 800	564 703	213 247	171 097	4 614
2009	825 970	342 494	61 651	41 341	113 716	607 284	455 735	178 847	151 549	4 174
2010	871 268	349 225	62 239	48 526	116 338	634 991	476 141	190 139	158 850	3 741
2011	954 423	389 112	65 366	48 268	128 469	705 427	534 085	215 711	171 342	3 915
2012	1 014 371	442 356	76 002	48 001	129 932	754 971	579 925	219 411	175 046	4 199
2013	1 075 872	525 914	70 713	48 868	115 235	807 944	657 512	224 478	150 432	4 504
2014	1 164 968	607 101	69 355	49 830	111 711	877 002	730 289	228 017	146 713	4 693
2015	1 142 191	602 684	66 852	49 990	110 705	856 517	714 566	220 213	141 951	4 898
2016	1 122 589	576 855	71 565	50 270	118 446	841 789	695 600	223 572	146 189	5 143
2013										
January	1 015 188	443 938	17 851	47 512	128 707	755 239	583 591	222 335	171 648	4 125
February	1 024 328	455 779	18 112	47 740	126 867	763 228	593 195	220 477	170 033	4 104
March	1 016 244	455 678	18 249	47 550	123 788	756 321	591 212	218 940	165 109	4 042
April	1 018 193	460 038	18 200	47 161	123 366	757 810	595 797	220 056	162 013	4 085
May	1 027 718	468 611	18 271	47 370	123 238	765 535	604 336	221 241	161 199	4 197
June	1 047 018	486 558	18 319	47 225	122 516	782 914	621 379	222 865	161 535	4 300
July	1 046 040	485 944	18 198	47 380	121 451	782 323	622 175	223 530	160 148	4 358
August	1 046 816	488 762	18 134	47 642	119 786	782 532	624 211	223 894	158 321	4 504
September	1 056 346	497 891	17 939	47 867	118 831	790 922	633 064	225 045	157 858	4 399
October	1 058 538	502 916	17 773	48 087	117 769	792 066	636 096	224 220	155 970	4 348
November	1 067 315	514 791	17 662	48 249	116 799	800 992	647 573	224 757	153 419	4 416
December	1 075 872	525 914	17 780	48 868	115 235	807 944	657 512	224 478	150 432	4 504
2014										
January	1 077 534	527 762	18 026	49 064	114 810	810 062	661 667	226 655	148 395	4 413
February	1 081 654	532 559	18 136	49 251	114 137	809 075	661 692	226 684	147 383	4 235
March	1 087 885	535 640	18 547	49 084	113 808	812 678	664 686	227 825	147 992	4 279
April	1 098 820	538 729	18 835	49 459	114 136	822 657	667 753	228 261	154 904	4 300
May	1 103 643	542 992	19 154	49 955	113 150	825 596	670 957	227 275	154 639	4 324
June	1 112 633	545 948	19 673	50 021	113 114	830 788	675 596	230 107	155 192	4 546
July	1 169 322	603 221	19 885	49 932	112 483	884 701	731 009	231 148	153 692	4 417
August	1 173 745	608 943	20 416	50 197	112 667	888 411	735 903	230 900	152 508	4 350
September	1 175 861	611 309	20 976	49 944	112 558	888 080	737 325	231 486	150 755	4 477
October	1 175 151	610 343	21 247	50 569	112 773	885 947	734 750	230 335	151 197	4 513
November	1 174 487	611 986	21 667	50 569	112 410	885 105	735 432	229 088	149 673	4 518
December	1 164 968	607 101	22 100	49 830	111 711	877 002	730 289	228 017	146 713	4 693
2015										
January	1 164 762	606 476	22 568	49 847	111 464	877 157	730 955	228 644	146 202	4 580
February	1 158 912	604 112	22 886	49 684	111 327	874 905	728 818	228 005	146 087	4 476
March	1 158 481	605 602	22 712	49 640	112 077	875 674	729 777	227 407	145 897	4 625
April	1 157 664	606 611	22 958	49 599	111 946	875 247	730 441	226 724	144 806	4 792
May	1 151 095	601 966	23 014	49 376	111 869	870 164	725 542	225 741	144 622	4 767
June	1 154 037	605 868	23 183	49 912	111 619	873 081	728 181	224 677	144 900	4 786
July	1 155 292	607 131	23 284	49 956	111 402	875 634	729 458	224 252	146 176	4 687
August	1 152 993	607 875	23 226	49 883	111 536	874 159	729 686	223 625	144 473	4 731
September	1 144 882	603 395	23 290	50 038	111 333	863 317	723 388	223 128	139 929	4 691
October	1 145 285	604 672	23 683	49 632	111 052	864 519	726 081	222 923	138 438	4 792
November	1 143 295	600 273	24 178	49 473	110 923	864 601	722 294	222 920	142 307	4 888
December	1 142 191	602 684	24 071	49 990	110 705	856 517	714 566	220 213	141 951	4 898
2016										
January	1 143 181	604 151	23 517	50 161	111 510	858 453	716 690	220 527	141 763	5 010
February	1 135 415	600 324	23 320	50 308	112 256	851 672	713 202	220 381	138 470	4 970
March	1 132 582	594 415	23 227	50 014	112 714	849 569	707 732	220 342	141 837	4 993
April	1 138 442	597 773	23 001	50 243	113 508	855 493	710 590	219 929	144 903	4 927
May	1 138 898	600 162	23 079	50 285	114 288	855 426	711 458	219 012	143 968	4 967
June	1 128 148	592 810	22 863	50 334	114 608	844 641	704 104	218 468	140 537	4 978
July	1 124 740	589 989	22 873	50 253	115 185	841 367	703 247	219 686	138 120	5 039
August	1 123 567	585 984	23 244	50 026	115 585	840 362	701 307	221 714	139 055	5 144
September	1 119 324	581 423	23 115	49 766	116 010	837 730	697 398	221 997	140 332	5 230
October	1 128 435	589 897	22 769	49 930	116 436	847 878	706 920	222 415	140 958	5 259
November	1 127 271	583 121	22 624	50 554	117 430	845 013	700 625	223 532	144 388	5 182
December	1 122 589	576 855	22 687	50 270	118 446	841 789	695 600	223 572	146 189	5 143

[1]Includes categories not shown separately.

Table 16-7. Motor Vehicle Sales and Inventories

(Units.)

Year and month	Retail sales of new passenger cars						Retail inventories of new domestic passenger cars (thousands of units, end of period)		
	Thousands of units, not seasonally adjusted			Millions of units, seasonally adjusted annual rate					
	Total	Domestic	Foreign	Total	Domestic	Foreign	Not seasonally adjusted	Seasonally adjusted	Inventory to sales ratio
1975	8 537.9	6 950.9	1 586.9	8.538	6.951	1.587	1 419.0	1 468.0	2.200
1976	9 994.0	8 492.0	1 502.0	9.994	8.492	1.502	1 465.0	1 494.0	1.900
1977	11 046.0	8 971.2	2 074.8	11.046	8.971	2.075	1 731.0	1 743.0	2.300
1978	11 164.0	9 163.9	2 000.1	11.164	9.164	2.000	1 729.0	1 731.0	2.300
1979	10 558.8	8 230.1	2 328.7	10.559	8.230	2.329	1 691.0	1 667.0	2.400
1980	8 981.8	6 581.4	2 400.4	8.982	6.581	2.401	1 448.0	1 440.0	2.600
1981	8 534.3	6 208.8	2 325.5	8.535	6.209	2.326	1 471.0	1 495.0	3.600
1982	7 979.4	5 758.2	2 221.2	7.979	5.758	2.221	1 126.0	1 127.0	2.200
1983	9 178.6	6 793.0	2 385.6	9.179	6.793	2.386	1 352.0	1 350.0	2.000
1984	10 390.2	7 951.7	2 438.5	10.391	7.952	2.439	1 415.0	1 411.0	2.100
1985	10 978.4	8 204.7	2 773.7	10.979	8.205	2.774	1 630.0	1 619.0	2.500
1986	10 418.3	8 215.0	3 190.7	11.406	8.215	3.191	1 499.0	1 515.0	2.000
1987	10 170.9	7 080.9	3 090.0	10.171	7.081	3.090	1 680.0	1 716.0	2.800
1988	10 545.6	7 539.4	3 006.2	10.545	7.539	3.006	1 601.0	1 601.0	2.300
1989	9 776.8	7 078.1	2 698.7	9.777	7.078	2.699	1 669.0	1 687.0	3.100
1990	9 300.2	6 896.9	2 403.3	9.300	6.897	2.403	1 408.0	1 418.0	2.600
1991	8 175.0	6 136.9	2 038.1	8.175	6.137	2.038	1 283.0	1 296.0	2.600
1992	8 214.4	6 276.6	1 937.8	8.215	6.277	1.938	1 276.0	1 288.0	2.300
1993	8 517.7	6 734.0	1 783.7	8.518	6.734	1.784	1 364.9	1 377.3	2.359
1994	8 990.4	7 255.2	1 735.2	8.990	7.255	1.735	1 436.6	1 445.3	2.319
1995	8 620.4	7 114.1	1 506.3	8.620	7.114	1.506	1 618.5	1 629.8	2.565
1996	8 478.6	7 206.3	1 272.3	8.478	7.206	1.272	1 363.4	1 367.0	2.478
1997	8 217.7	6 862.3	1 355.4	8.218	6.862	1.356	1 329.9	1 339.6	2.368
1998	8 084.9	6 705.1	1 379.8	8.085	6.705	1.380	1 324.4	1 309.4	2.222
1999	8 637.7	6 918.8	1 718.9	8.638	6.919	1.719	1 367.6	1 346.5	2.369
2000	8 777.7	6 761.6	2 016.1	8.778	6.762	2.016	1 377.0	1 334.9	2.810
2001	8 352.1	6 254.4	2 097.7	8.352	6.254	2.098	955.7	919.8	2.267
2002	8 042.1	5 816.5	2 225.6	8.043	5.817	2.226	1 132.0	1 170.1	2.539
2003	7 555.6	5 472.6	2 083.0	7.556	5.473	2.083	1 115.8	1 162.1	2.722
2004	7 482.5	5 333.6	2 148.9	7.482	5.333	2.149	1 034.2	1 077.7	2.415
2005	7 660.4	5 473.6	2 186.8	7.661	5.474	2.187	930.6	965.9	2.345
2006	7 761.3	5 416.7	2 344.6	7.762	5.417	2.345	1 031.7	1 048.8	2.532
2007	7 562.1	5 197.1	2 365.0	7.562	5.197	2.365	906.8	917.1	2.291
2008	6 769.2	4 491.0	2 278.2	6.769	4.491	2.278	1 144.2	1 160.7	4.185
2009	5 401.5	3 558.4	1 843.1	5.401	3.558	1.843	686.4	702.1	2.293
2010	5 635.7	3 791.5	1 844.2	5.636	3.792	1.844	759.1	762.3	2.526
2011	6 089.7	4 142.8	1 946.9	6.090	4.143	1.947	813.0	777.5	2.392
2012	7 244.4	5 119.1	2 125.3	7.245	5.119	2.125	1 069.5	1 037.6	2.447
2013	7 585.3	5 432.7	2 152.6	7.586	5.434	2.153	1 259.3	1 216.9	2.931
2014	7 687.6	5 589.4	2 098.2	7.688	5.589	2.098	1 250.0	1 269.1	2.633
2015	7 526.3	5 604.3	1 922.0	7.507	5.591	1.916	1 179.9	1 223.2	2.701
2016	523.2	383.9	139.3	7.750	5.636	2.114	1 131.1	1 116.3	2.377
2014									
January	601.1	443.3	157.9	7.785	5.594	2.191	1 144.1	1 114.7	2.391
February	739.2	544.0	195.2	7.504	5.505	1.999	1 123.1	1 141.0	2.487
March	639.0	466.6	172.4	7.436	5.400	2.036	1 129.6	1 163.0	2.584
April	708.1	517.2	190.9	7.386	5.318	2.068	1 109.8	1 188.6	2.682
May	689.3	501.9	187.5	7.559	5.452	2.107	1 109.9	1 210.6	2.665
June	639.6	448.5	191.1	7.651	5.483	2.168	982.2	1 151.5	2.520
July	733.3	516.1	217.2	7.630	5.402	2.228	986.3	1 182.2	2.626
August	553.2	386.8	166.4	7.597	5.346	2.251	1 064.3	1 210.2	2.717
September	563.8	397.9	165.8	7.460	5.311	2.149	1 217.0	1 235.8	2.792
October	581.5	403.4	178.2	7.796	5.503	2.293	1 301.3	1 248.6	2.723
November	614.0	423.2	190.8	7.469	5.242	2.227	1 259.3	1 280.5	2.931
December	476.8	341.1	135.7	7.202	5.104	2.098	1 322.5	1 291.3	3.036
2015									
January	563.9	411.4	152.5	7.302	5.185	2.117	1 366.6	1 324.4	3.065
February	740.9	533.8	207.0	7.650	5.484	2.166	1 329.5	1 323.0	2.895
March	657.3	470.8	186.5	7.513	5.347	2.166	1 287.3	1 308.5	2.937
April	773.7	563.6	210.2	7.827	5.609	2.218	1 201.0	1 291.5	2.763
May	684.2	498.9	185.3	7.936	5.733	2.203	1 196.6	1 295.4	2.712
June	670.4	479.3	191.1	7.756	5.656	2.100	1 135.4	1 320.7	2.802
July	747.2	551.7	195.5	8.071	5.983	2.088	1 075.7	1 294.9	2.597
August	563.0	412.0	151.0	7.558	5.559	1.999	1 130.8	1 289.7	2.784
September	577.4	427.4	150.0	7.725	5.758	1.967	1 234.8	1 265.3	2.637
October	576.7	426.3	150.4	7.863	5.888	1.975	1 288.6	1 273.3	2.595
November	656.0	473.1	182.8	7.850	5.767	2.083	1 250.0	1 269.1	2.633
December	515.5	386.7	128.8	7.458	5.533	1.925	1 263.8	1 269.8	2.753
2016									
January	557.6	419.6	138.0	7.189	5.284	1.905	1 297.3	1 293.6	2.934
February	713.4	521.7	191.7	7.575	5.524	2.051	1 282.1	1 298.9	2.818
March	648.6	480.2	168.3	7.339	5.406	1.933	1 271.4	1 324.3	2.936
April	745.9	562.2	183.7	7.823	5.816	2.007	1 218.9	1 339.9	2.761
May	659.9	491.1	168.8	7.424	5.477	1.947	1 210.3	1 331.7	2.915
June	652.9	487.6	165.3	7.622	5.803	1.819	1 125.2	1 327.9	2.744
July	670.8	497.9	172.9	7.540	5.610	1.930	1 099.9	1 328.7	2.838
August	599.2	447.9	151.3	7.659	5.759	1.900	1 134.9	1 305.8	2.716
September	601.2	450.4	150.8	7.761	5.844	1.917	1 178.0	1 241.8	2.544
October	527.2	386.1	141.0	7.538	5.602	1.936	1 223.0	1 223.0	2.615
November	634.1	472.8	161.3	7.158	5.434	1.724	1 179.9	1 223.2	2.701
December	. . .	. . .	. . .	. . .	. . .	. . .	. . .	. . .	. . .

. . . = Not available.

Table 16-7. Motor Vehicle Sales and Inventories—*Continued*

(Units.)

Year and month	Retail sales of new trucks and buses								Unit sales of cars and light trucks (millions of units, seasonally adjusted annual rate)		
	Thousands of units, not seasonally adjusted				Millions of units, seasonally adjusted annual rate						
	Total	0–14,000 pounds		14,001 pounds and over	Total	0–14,000 pounds		14,001 pounds and over	Total	Domestic	Foreign
		Domestic	Foreign			Domestic	Foreign				
1975	. . .	2 052.6	. . .	298.3	. . .	2.055	. . .	0.298	. . .	9.006	. . .
1976	3 300.5	2 738.3	237.5	324.7	3.296	2.733	0.239	0.324	12.966	11.225	1.741
1977	3 813.0	3 112.8	323.1	377.1	3.818	3.116	0.324	0.378	14.486	12.087	2.399
1978	4 256.8	3 481.1	335.9	439.8	4.249	3.469	0.340	0.440	14.973	12.633	2.340
1979	3 589.7	2 730.2	469.4	390.1	3.599	2.740	0.469	0.390	13.768	10.970	2.798
1980	2 487.4	1 731.1	484.6	271.7	2.482	1.731	0.480	0.271	11.193	8.312	2.881
1981	2 255.6	1 581.7	447.6	226.3	2.255	1.585	0.444	0.226	10.564	7.794	2.770
1982	2 562.8	1 967.5	410.4	184.9	2.569	1.971	0.413	0.185	10.363	7.729	2.634
1983	3 117.3	2 465.2	463.3	188.8	3.130	2.480	0.461	0.189	12.120	9.273	2.847
1984	4 093.1	3 207.2	607.7	278.2	4.086	3.199	0.609	0.278	14.199	11.151	3.048
1985	4 741.7	3 618.4	828.3	295.0	4.760	3.634	0.831	0.295	15.444	11.839	3.605
1986	4 912.1	3 671.4	967.2	273.5	4.918	3.676	0.969	0.273	16.051	11.891	4.160
1987	4 991.5	3 792.0	912.2	287.3	4.978	3.783	0.907	0.288	14.861	10.864	3.997
1988	5 231.9	4 199.7	097.9	004.0	5.225	4.104	0.697	0.334	15 436	11 733	3.703
1989	5 055.9	4 113.6	630.3	312.0	5.065	4.123	0.629	0.313	14.529	11.201	3.328
1990	4 837.0	3 956.8	602.7	277.5	4.840	3.960	0.602	0.278	13.862	10.857	3.005
1991	4 355.4	3 605.6	528.8	221.0	4.361	3.612	0.528	0.221	12.315	9.749	2.566
1992	4 892.2	4 247.0	395.9	249.3	4.893	4.247	0.398	0.248	12.860	10.524	2.336
1993	5 667.8	5 000.5	364.5	302.8	5.658	4.991	0.365	0.302	13.874	11.725	2.149
1994	6 407.3	5 658.2	396.3	352.8	6.408	5.659	0.395	0.354	15.044	12.914	2.130
1995	6 496.4	5 705.9	402.1	388.4	6.498	5.706	0.402	0.390	14.728	12.820	1.908
1996	6 977.6	6 179.8	438.7	359.1	6.976	6.180	0.439	0.357	15.097	13.386	1.711
1997	7 280.4	6 324.7	579.5	376.2	7.280	6.325	0.579	0.376	15.122	13.187	1.935
1998	7 882.4	6 802.0	656.1	424.3	7.883	6.802	0.656	0.425	15.543	13.507	2.036
1999	8 777.3	7 480.7	775.3	521.3	8.777	7.481	0.775	0.521	16.894	14.400	2.494
2000	9 033.9	7 719.7	852.3	461.9	9.033	7.720	0.852	0.461	17.350	14.482	2.868
2001	9 120.4	7 789.0	981.3	350.1	9.120	7.789	0.981	0.350	17.122	14.043	3.079
2002	9 096.5	7 707.8	1 066.3	322.4	9.096	7.708	1.066	0.322	16.817	13.525	3.292
2003	9 411.9	7 856.3	1 227.2	328.4	9.411	7.856	1.227	0.328	16.639	13.329	3.310
2004	9 815.8	8 138.0	1 246.2	431.6	9.813	8.138	1.246	0.429	16.866	13.471	3.395
2005	9 784.4	8 072.4	1 215.5	496.5	9.784	8.072	1.215	0.497	16.948	13.546	3.402
2006	9 287.0	7 396.0	1 346.6	544.4	9.288	7.396	1.347	0.545	16.505	12.813	3.692
2007	8 897.9	7 138.7	1 388.1	371.1	8.900	7.139	1.388	0.373	16.089	12.336	3.753
2008	15 408.6	5 329.2	9 780.9	298.5	6.724	5.329	1.097	0.298	13.195	9.820	3.375
2009	5 200.5	4 116.5	884.2	199.8	5.200	4.117	0.884	0.199	10.402	7.675	2.727
2010	6 136.6	5 020.3	898.7	217.6	6.137	5.021	0.899	0.218	11.555	8.812	2.743
2011	6 951.2	5 662.6	982.5	306.1	6.950	5.663	0.983	0.305	12.735	9.805	2.929
2012	7 544.1	6 137.5	1 060.8	345.8	7.545	6.138	1.061	0.346	14.443	11.257	3.186
2013	8 297.9	6 707.1	1 239.1	351.7	8.297	6.707	1.239	0.351	15.533	12.141	3.392
2014	9 154.4	7 387.7	1 359.9	406.7	9.153	7.388	1.360	0.405	16.435	12.977	3.458
2015	10 310.3	8 080.6	1 780.3	449.5	10.274	8.055	1.769	0.450	17.332	13.646	3.686
2016	542.1	438.1	79.1	24.9	7.952	6.519	1.098	0.335	15.367	12.155	3.212
2014											
January	613.6	501.2	87.6	24.8	8.090	6.595	1.149	0.346	15.529	12.189	3.340
February	736.3	599.1	111.5	25.7	8.158	6.692	1.162	0.304	15.358	12.197	3.161
March	672.9	551.4	91.1	30.5	8.310	6.795	1.156	0.359	15.387	12.195	3.192
April	760.9	623.0	107.6	30.2	8.344	6.772	1.225	0.347	15.383	12.090	3.293
May	740.0	602.6	106.5	30.9	8.481	6.821	1.286	0.374	15.666	12.273	3.393
June	699.8	559.8	110.0	29.9	8.399	6.745	1.306	0.348	15.702	12.228	3.474
July	793.1	640.5	123.8	28.8	8.400	6.800	1.261	0.339	15.691	12.202	3.489
August	609.0	487.9	92.5	28.6	8.153	6.531	1.267	0.355	15.395	11.877	3.518
September	670.7	533.0	103.8	33.8	8.273	6.588	1.320	0.365	15.368	11.899	3.469
October	684.4	547.4	109.3	27.7	8.683	6.977	1.338	0.368	16.111	12.480	3.631
November	775.3	623.1	116.3	35.9	8.325	6.649	1.302	0.374	15.420	11.891	3.529
December	557.2	444.5	86.4	26.3	8.443	6.878	1.206	0.359	15.286	11.982	3.304
2015											
January	650.7	523.4	100.8	26.5	8.582	6.891	1.320	0.371	15.513	12.076	3.437
February	822.3	656.0	134.3	32.0	9.189	7.363	1.447	0.379	16.460	12.847	3.613
March	759.2	617.8	106.1	35.3	9.109	7.382	1.314	0.413	16.209	12.729	3.480
April	860.9	706.4	121.3	33.2	9.201	7.475	1.336	0.390	16.638	13.084	3.554
May	764.6	622.2	108.6	33.8	9.197	7.412	1.387	0.398	16.735	13.145	3.590
June	794.1	638.3	119.9	36.0	9.111	7.326	1.367	0.418	16.449	12.982	3.467
July	866.2	692.6	138.3	35.3	9.584	7.683	1.470	0.431	17.224	13.666	3.558
August	712.5	566.6	108.8	37.1	9.298	7.427	1.437	0.434	16.422	12.986	3.436
September	734.8	588.8	106.6	39.3	9.164	7.383	1.355	0.426	16.463	13.141	3.322
October	747.6	609.4	108.2	30.0	9.576	7.784	1.374	0.418	17.021	13.672	3.349
November	884.3	721.6	120.6	42.1	9.373	7.647	1.306	0.420	16.803	13.414	3.389
December	662.2	531.5	100.0	30.7	9.607	7.811	1.364	0.432	16.632	13.344	3.288
2016											
January	725.6	583.6	111.0	30.9	9.562	7.678	1.450	0.434	16.317	12.962	3.355
February	864.8	682.5	144.0	38.3	9.933	7.910	1.580	0.444	17.064	13.434	3.630
March	836.3	667.2	132.9	36.2	9.782	7.733	1.626	0.424	16.698	13.139	3.559
April	919.0	731.6	150.1	37.2	10.269	8.097	1.712	0.459	17.633	13.914	3.719
May	853.5	666.9	144.1	42.5	10.006	7.761	1.769	0.476	16.954	13.238	3.716
June	892.1	695.2	156.6	40.3	10.321	8.077	1.774	0.470	17.473	13.880	3.594
July	938.5	725.0	174.1	39.4	10.666	8.210	1.978	0.478	17.729	13.820	3.908
August	874.1	691.6	144.4	38.1	10.857	8.621	1.790	0.445	18.070	14.380	3.690
September	883.8	677.6	167.9	38.4	10.789	8.301	2.062	0.427	18.124	14.145	3.980
October	819.9	626.3	157.4	36.1	11.012	8.415	2.106	0.491	18.059	14.017	4.042
November	1 040.8	801.6	197.7	41.5	10.486	8.049	2.021	0.416	17.228	13.482	3.746
December	. . .	. . .	. . .	. . .	. . .	. . .	. . .	. . .	. . .	. . .	. . .

. . . = Not available.

Table 16-8. Retail and Food Services Sales

(All retail establishments and food services; millions of dollars; not seasonally adjusted.)

Year and month	Retail and food services, total [1]	GAFO (department store type goods), total [2]	Motor vehicles and parts	Furniture and home furnishings	Electronics and appliances	Building materials and garden	Food and beverages	Health and personal care	Gasoline	Clothing and accessories	General merchandise	Nonstore retailers	Food services and drinking places
1992	2 014 102	533 388	418 393	52 336	42 631	130 989	370 513	89 699	156 324	120 103	247 876	78 501	202 865
1993	2 153 095	570 782	472 916	55 456	48 614	140 964	374 516	92 589	162 376	124 749	265 996	85 811	215 467
1994	2 330 235	616 347	541 141	60 416	57 266	157 228	384 340	96 359	171 222	129 083	285 190	96 280	225 000
1995	2 450 628	650 040	579 715	63 470	64 770	164 561	390 386	101 632	181 113	131 333	300 498	103 516	233 012
1996	2 603 794	682 613	627 507	67 707	68 363	176 683	401 073	109 554	194 425	136 581	315 305	117 761	242 245
1997	2 726 131	713 387	653 817	72 715	70 061	191 063	409 373	118 670	199 700	140 293	331 363	126 190	257 364
1998	2 852 956	757 936	688 415	77 412	74 527	202 423	416 525	129 582	191 727	149 151	351 081	133 904	271 194
1999	3 086 990	815 665	764 204	84 294	78 977	218 290	433 699	142 697	212 524	159 751	380 179	151 797	283 900
2000	3 287 537	862 739	796 210	91 170	82 206	228 994	444 764	155 233	249 816	167 674	404 228	180 453	304 261
2001	3 378 906	882 700	815 579	91 484	80 240	239 379	462 429	166 532	251 383	167 287	427 468	180 563	316 638
2002	3 459 077	912 707	818 811	94 438	83 740	248 539	464 856	179 983	250 619	172 304	446 520	189 279	330 525
2003	3 612 457	946 114	841 588	96 736	86 442	263 463	474 385	275 187	178 694	178 694	468 771	206 359	349 726
2004	3 846 605	1 003 891	866 372	103 757	93 896	295 274	490 380	324 006	324 006	190 253	497 382	228 977	373 557
2005	4 085 746	1 059 599	888 307	109 120	100 461	320 802	508 484	378 923	378 923	200 969	528 385	255 579	396 463
2006	4 294 359	1 110 155	899 997	112 795	105 477	334 130	525 232	421 976	421 976	213 189	554 256	284 343	422 786
2007	4 439 733	1 143 426	910 139	111 144	106 599	320 854	547 837	451 822	451 822	221 205	578 582	308 767	444 551
2008	4 391 580	1 136 376	785 865	98 720	105 317	301 833	569 276	246 573	503 639	215 583	595 041	319 152	456 265
2009	4 064 476	1 088 197	671 772	84 749	95 364	261 637	568 418	252 794	391 234	204 475	588 918	311 152	452 005
2010	4 284 968	1 114 374	742 913	85 205	97 396	260 566	580 530	260 435	448 349	213 286	603 757	340 957	466 920
2011	4 598 302	1 155 666	812 938	87 586	99 928	269 480	609 137	271 612	533 457	228 606	624 766	376 344	495 350
2012	4 826 390	1 191 843	886 494	91 542	102 060	281 533	628 205	274 000	555 419	239 493	642 313	408 171	524 161
2013	5 001 763	1 212 493	959 294	95 349	102 998	301 797	640 847	281 840	549 613	244 722	651 874	433 126	543 313
2014	5 215 656	1 238 694	1 020 851	99 718	103 518	318 352	669 165	299 263	538 790	250 409	667 163	470 867	576 216
2015	5 350 508	1 258 529	1 095 412	106 779	102 108	331 644	685 568	315 257	443 817	255 831	674 928	509 267	623 081
2016	5 522 929	1 261 673	1 140 142	110 509	97 600	350 511	701 552	329 207	418 727	258 411	675 802	565 951	660 076
2014													
January	383 396	86 162	70 375	7 203	7 885	19 934	54 048	24 171	42 139	15 177	47 311	37 955	42 932
February	380 267	89 390	74 939	7 227	7 865	19 032	49 913	22 781	40 168	17 504	48 878	35 289	42 890
March	432 879	99 188	90 507	8 105	8 190	24 408	54 314	24 633	45 802	20 070	53 966	38 060	49 410
April	431 569	96 915	87 984	7 791	7 256	30 528	54 180	24 430	46 741	20 321	52 798	36 464	47 708
May	459 028	103 721	93 250	8 385	7 745	33 851	57 765	25 168	49 974	21 569	56 917	36 457	51 054
June	433 358	97 375	86 710	7 881	7 654	30 496	55 248	24 424	48 014	18 949	53 892	35 815	47 895
July	443 331	99 190	91 278	8 403	7 937	29 074	57 377	24 815	49 143	19 826	53 669	36 512	48 690
August	451 369	107 462	92 619	8 735	8 220	26 864	57 269	24 850	48 673	21 992	57 077	36 496	50 086
September	421 367	95 491	83 350	8 371	8 254	26 632	54 264	24 816	45 487	18 644	50 698	37 222	47 070
October	438 376	101 000	84 325	8 440	8 162	27 793	56 799	25 719	45 438	20 219	54 672	39 542	50 135
November	438 675	115 490	78 958	8 949	10 794	25 255	56 851	24 286	40 214	23 493	61 904	43 177	47 614
December	502 041	147 310	86 556	10 228	13 556	24 485	61 137	29 170	36 997	32 645	75 381	57 878	50 732
2015													
January	398 163	90 178	78 469	7 974	8 079	21 140	56 545	25 689	32 440	15 774	49 497	39 534	47 935
February	388 155	90 362	79 596	7 537	7 782	19 888	51 951	24 108	31 573	17 994	49 169	37 856	46 562
March	446 027	101 213	96 542	8 647	7 976	26 471	56 513	26 843	36 758	20 775	54 769	41 629	53 068
April	439 653	97 260	93 763	8 298	7 236	31 433	55 484	25 623	37 051	20 411	52 525	39 774	52 229
May	464 454	105 713	97 597	8 934	7 756	31 380	59 083	25 560	41 230	22 170	57 562	38 689	55 343
June	449 893	99 905	94 779	8 613	8 099	31 590	56 635	25 787	41 797	19 687	54 245	39 360	51 980
July	459 646	102 234	97 889	9 147	8 027	30 562	59 114	25 957	42 852	20 577	54 938	40 097	53 086
August	457 996	107 523	98 014	9 174	8 218	27 787	57 796	25 882	40 913	22 315	56 780	39 405	53 129
September	432 978	97 610	90 906	8 983	8 163	27 564	55 651	26 285	36 614	19 146	51 699	40 376	50 736
October	446 815	102 772	90 432	9 110	8 006	28 386	57 594	26 813	37 007	20 617	55 672	42 046	54 029
November	446 500	114 471	84 106	9 471	10 171	26 744	57 029	25 963	33 004	23 058	61 534	47 793	50 288
December	520 228	149 288	93 319	10 891	12 595	26 899	62 173	30 747	32 578	33 307	76 538	62 708	54 696
2016													
January	402 645	89 294	80 013	8 166	7 465	21 975	56 978	26 174	29 986	15 627	49 168	41 628	50 279
February	416 044	94 376	89 217	8 363	7 711	23 157	54 204	26 842	27 961	18 834	51 196	41 789	51 782
March	461 954	103 723	100 052	9 233	7 833	29 874	58 170	28 427	31 350	21 350	55 829	45 476	56 193
April	452 609	98 468	96 610	8 632	6 965	32 342	56 375	27 063	33 975	20 311	53 481	43 288	56 726
May	471 434	103 642	97 804	8 964	7 466	34 608	59 344	27 598	37 337	21 494	56 308	44 970	57 466
June	465 901	101 449	97 437	9 067	7 623	34 196	58 603	27 452	38 499	19 977	55 016	44 714	55 038
July	463 245	102 144	98 760	9 124	7 655	30 194	59 897	26 564	38 162	20 487	55 263	43 107	56 392
August	473 169	106 629	103 208	9 513	8 122	30 078	58 607	27 922	37 157	22 248	55 753	46 147	55 467
September	449 948	97 783	94 771	9 483	7 708	29 046	57 354	27 141	36 316	19 649	51 432	44 910	54 452
October	454 601	100 902	92 180	9 031	7 387	28 834	58 550	26 607	37 284	20 385	55 038	45 867	55 793
November	469 324	114 530	89 676	9 967	9 677	28 896	58 887	26 725	34 212	23 529	61 190	55 144	53 193
December	542 055	148 733	100 414	10 966	11 988	27 311	64 583	30 692	35 465	34 520	76 128	68 911	57 295

[1] Includes store categories not shown separately.
[2] Includes furniture, home furnishings, electronics, appliances, clothing, sporting goods, hobby, book, music, general merchandise, office supplies, stationery, and gifts.

Table 16-8. Retail and Food Services Sales—*Continued*

(All retail establishments and food services; millions of dollars; seasonally adjusted.)

Year and month	Total	Retail and food services										
		Retail (NAICS industry categories)										
		Total	GAFO (department store type goods) [2]	Motor vehicles and parts	Furniture and home furnishings	Electronics and appliances	Building materials and garden	Food and beverages			Health and personal care	Gasoline
								Total [1]	Groceries	Beer, wine, and liquor		
1992	2 014 102	1 811 231	533 388	418 393	52 336	42 631	130 989	370 513	337 370	21 687	89 699	156 324
1993	2 153 095	1 937 623	570 782	472 916	55 456	48 614	140 964	374 516	341 318	21 538	92 589	162 376
1994	2 330 235	2 105 231	616 347	541 141	60 416	57 266	157 228	384 340	350 523	22 101	96 359	171 222
1995	2 450 628	2 217 613	650 040	579 715	63 470	64 770	164 561	390 386	356 409	22 007	101 632	181 113
1996	2 603 794	2 361 546	682 613	627 507	67 707	68 363	176 683	401 073	365 547	23 157	109 554	194 425
1997	2 726 131	2 468 765	713 387	653 817	72 715	70 061	191 063	409 373	372 570	24 081	118 670	199 700
1998	2 852 956	2 581 761	757 936	688 415	77 412	74 527	202 423	416 525	378 188	25 382	129 582	191 727
1999	3 086 990	2 803 088	815 665	764 204	84 294	78 977	218 290	433 699	394 250	26 476	142 697	212 524
2000	3 287 537	2 983 275	862 739	796 210	91 170	82 206	228 994	444 764	402 515	28 507	155 233	249 816
2001	3 378 906	3 062 267	882 700	815 579	91 484	80 240	239 379	462 429	418 127	29 621	166 532	251 383
2002	3 459 077	3 128 552	912 707	818 811	94 438	83 740	248 539	461 956	410 813	20 804	170 000	250 019
2003	3 612 457	3 262 731	946 114	841 588	96 736	86 442	263 463	474 385	427 987	30 469	275 187	178 694
2004	3 846 605	3 473 048	1 003 891	866 372	103 757	93 896	295 274	490 380	441 136	32 189	324 006	324 006
2005	4 085 746	3 689 283	1 059 599	888 307	109 120	100 461	320 802	508 484	457 667	33 567	378 923	378 923
2006	4 294 359	3 871 573	1 110 155	899 997	112 795	105 477	334 130	525 232	471 699	36 016	421 976	421 976
2007	4 439 733	3 995 182	1 143 426	910 139	111 144	106 599	320 854	547 837	491 360	38 128	451 822	451 822
2008	4 391 580	3 935 315	105 317	785 865	98 720	105 317	301 833	569 276	511 222	39 504	246 573	503 639
2009	4 064 476	3 612 471	95 364	671 772	84 749	95 364	261 637	568 418	510 033	40 245	252 794	391 234
2010	4 284 968	3 818 048	97 396	742 913	85 205	97 396	260 566	580 530	520 750	41 401	260 435	448 349
2011	4 598 302	4 102 952	99 928	812 938	87 586	99 928	269 480	609 137	547 476	42 392	271 612	533 457
2012	4 826 390	4 302 229	102 060	886 494	91 542	102 060	281 533	628 205	563 645	44 365	274 000	555 419
2013	5 001 763	4 458 450	102 998	959 294	95 349	102 998	301 797	640 847	574 547	46 076	281 840	549 613
2014	5 215 656	4 639 440	103 518	1 020 851	99 718	103 518	318 352	669 165	599 603	48 286	299 263	538 790
2015	5 350 508	4 727 427	102 108	1 095 412	106 779	102 108	331 644	685 568	613 225	50 658	315 257	443 817
2016	5 522 929	4 862 853	97 600	1 140 142	110 509	97 600	350 511	701 552	626 981	52 633	329 207	418 727
2014												
January	418 800	373 079	100 157	78 791	7 770	8 472	25 234	54 758	49 067	3 959	24 003	46 614
February	424 117	377 749	101 712	80 752	8 039	8 527	25 163	54 730	49 099	3 917	24 107	46 870
March	429 720	382 663	102 224	84 014	8 195	8 607	25 481	54 864	49 182	3 935	24 293	46 218
April	433 675	386 533	103 375	85 264	8 279	8 557	26 557	55 197	49 469	3 994	24 553	46 648
May	434 334	386 798	102 792	85 517	8 302	8 469	26 722	55 315	49 595	3 967	24 894	46 101
June	435 094	387 342	102 812	85 493	8 313	8 407	26 944	55 815	49 959	4 085	25 076	45 084
July	435 688	387 623	103 332	85 775	8 303	8 467	26 525	55 944	50 121	4 048	25 116	44 839
August	439 554	391 162	104 185	86 833	8 440	8 507	27 047	56 173	50 342	4 049	25 280	45 026
September	438 687	389 808	103 810	86 027	8 379	8 733	26 954	56 349	50 545	4 045	25 245	44 815
October	440 396	390 708	104 224	86 418	8 432	8 699	26 997	56 617	50 740	4 094	25 389	43 817
November	442 106	392 405	105 047	87 479	8 507	8 968	27 190	56 606	50 742	4 054	25 511	42 918
December	439 323	388 894	104 563	87 287	8 639	8 829	26 905	56 934	50 946	4 109	25 633	39 825
2015												
January	435 929	385 630	103 986	88 204	8 602	8 689	27 015	56 979	51 014	4 139	25 844	35 885
February	434 153	383 816	103 442	86 190	8 421	8 546	26 191	56 978	51 030	4 148	25 565	36 971
March	442 225	391 247	104 559	90 389	8 734	8 450	26 869	57 029	51 024	4 225	26 188	37 508
April	442 183	390 624	104 187	90 591	8 828	8 565	27 301	56 914	50 885	4 191	25 830	36 977
May	446 238	394 564	105 410	91 876	9 043	8 569	27 330	56 953	50 940	4 220	25 792	38 282
June	446 238	394 465	104 945	91 658	8 852	8 759	27 123	57 113	51 063	4 228	25 943	38 881
July	449 403	397 256	105 355	91 542	9 003	8 547	28 030	57 211	51 145	4 246	26 193	38 850
August	449 592	397 197	105 277	92 090	8 985	8 477	28 005	57 321	51 226	4 263	26 303	37 953
September	449 496	397 083	105 560	93 030	8 938	8 549	28 005	57 334	51 255	4 238	26 767	36 108
October	448 616	395 853	104 996	92 615	9 056	8 493	28 136	57 159	51 150	4 222	26 733	35 584
November	450 509	397 463	105 276	93 323	9 037	8 437	28 369	57 499	51 460	4 261	26 877	35 148
December	452 756	398 762	105 895	93 249	9 144	8 283	29 179	57 395	51 329	4 264	27 090	34 768
2016												
January	448 171	395 246	103 796	92 341	9 033	8 135	25 140	57 788	51 772	4 233	26 900	33 467
February	451 209	396 930	105 118	93 641	9 080	8 267	25 357	57 740	51 590	4 317	27 362	31 666
March	451 274	397 086	104 971	92 140	9 043	8 235	25 673	57 406	51 310	4 301	27 281	33 034
April	454 231	399 739	104 905	92 967	9 105	8 137	24 971	58 015	51 925	4 308	27 475	33 873
May	456 384	401 550	105 196	93 197	9 147	8 236	24 668	58 280	52 090	4 370	27 515	34 764
June	459 431	404 503	105 446	93 180	9 271	8 176	25 529	58 366	52 172	4 384	27 701	35 614
July	459 520	404 717	104 972	94 874	9 170	8 177	25 448	58 043	51 830	4 397	27 556	34 819
August	459 222	404 031	104 731	94 862	9 130	8 196	25 274	58 308	52 101	4 390	27 536	34 309
September	463 728	408 165	104 700	96 431	9 352	8 018	25 583	58 658	52 368	4 456	27 471	35 534
October	466 393	411 043	104 861	97 117	9 282	7 976	25 902	59 072	52 740	4 470	27 067	36 446
November	466 974	410 981	104 754	96 894	9 254	7 957	26 150	58 989	52 589	4 532	27 270	36 280
December	470 996	415 639	104 428	99 902	9 169	7 921	26 334	58 769	52 688	4 235	27 209	37 450

[1] Includes store categories not shown separately.
[2] Includes furniture, home furnishings, electronics, appliances, clothing, sporting goods, hobby, book, music, general merchandise, office supplies, stationery, and gifts.

Table 16-9. Quarterly U.S. Retail Sales: Total and E-Commerce

Year and quarter	Retail sales (millions of dollars)		E-commerce as a percent of total sales	Percent change from prior quarter		Percent change from same quarter a year ago	
	Total	E-commerce		Total sales	E-commerce sales	Total sales	E-commerce sales
NOT SEASONALLY ADJUSTED							
2015							
1st quarter	1 084 780	74 572	6.9	-11.9	-20.8	2.2	13.7
2nd quarter	1 194 448	78 212	6.5	10.1	4.9	1.5	13.7
3rd quarter	1 193 669	80 198	6.7	-0.1	2.5	2.0	14.3
4th quarter	1 254 530	107 433	8.6	5.1	34.0	1.9	14.1
2016							
1st quarter	1 122 389	85 431	7.6	-10.5	-20.5	3.5	14.6
2nd quarter	1 220 714	90 397	7.4	8.8	5.8	2.2	15.6
3rd quarter	1 220 051	92 644	7.6	-0.1	2.5	2.2	15.5
4th quarter	1 299 699	122 515	9.4	6.5	32.2	3.6	14.0
SEASONALLY ADJUSTED							
2003							
1st quarter	798 317	12 796	1.6	0.9	4.7	3.5	28.0
2nd quarter	805 019	13 779	1.7	0.8	7.7	3.4	28.1
3rd quarter	827 707	14 787	1.8	2.8	7.3	5.0	28.8
4th quarter	830 668	15 585	1.9	0.4	5.4	5.0	27.5
2004							
1st quarter	846 082	16 719	2.0	1.9	7.3	6.0	30.7
2nd quarter	855 367	17 510	2.0	1.1	4.7	6.3	27.1
3rd quarter	868 427	18 494	2.1	1.5	5.6	4.9	25.1
4th quarter	890 999	19 644	2.2	2.6	6.2	7.3	26.0
2005							
1st quarter	898 488	20 816	2.3	0.8	6.0	6.2	24.5
2nd quarter	916 834	22 231	2.4	2.0	6.8	7.2	27.0
3rd quarter	933 865	23 642	2.5	1.9	6.3	7.5	27.8
4th quarter	937 482	24 360	2.6	0.4	3.0	5.2	24.0
2006							
1st quarter	963 611	26 420	2.7	2.8	8.5	7.2	26.9
2nd quarter	967 411	27 378	2.8	0.4	3.6	5.5	23.2
3rd quarter	972 479	28 850	3.0	0.5	5.4	4.1	22.0
4th quarter	973 184	30 137	3.1	0.1	4.5	3.8	23.7
2007							
1st quarter	986 001	31 731	3.2	1.3	5.3	2.3	20.1
2nd quarter	994 790	33 493	3.4	0.9	5.6	2.8	22.3
3rd quarter	1 001 567	34 823	3.5	0.7	4.0	3.0	20.7
4th quarter	1 015 174	35 792	3.5	1.4	2.8	4.3	18.8
2008							
1st quarter	1 007 165	36 025	3.6	-0.8	0.7	2.1	13.5
2nd quarter	1 011 353	36 513	3.6	0.4	1.4	1.7	9.0
3rd quarter	998 437	36 282	3.6	-1.3	-0.6	-0.3	4.2
4rd quarter	910 527	33 045	3.6	-8.8	-8.9	-10.3	-7.7
2009							
1st quarter	889 045	34 145	3.8	-2.4	3.3	-11.7	-5.2
2nd quarter	891 993	35 279	4.0	0.3	3.3	-11.8	-3.4
3rd quarter	912 479	37 391	4.1	2.3	6.0	-8.6	3.1
4th quarter	919 395	38 106	4.1	0.8	1.9	1.0	15.3
2010							
1st quarter	933 469	39 291	4.2	1.5	3.1	5.0	15.1
2nd quarter	949 018	41 308	4.4	1.7	5.1	6.4	17.1
3rd quarter	952 428	43 507	4.6	0.4	5.3	4.4	16.4
4th quarter	981 545	45 064	4.6	3.1	3.6	6.8	18.3
2011							
1st quarter	1 004 961	46 908	4.7	2.4	4.1	7.7	19.4
2nd quarter	1 021 096	48 696	4.8	1.6	3.8	7.6	17.9
3rd quarter	1 028 864	49 985	4.9	0.8	2.6	8.0	14.9
4rd quarter	1 047 272	52 984	5.1	1.8	6.0	6.7	17.6
2012							
1st quarter	1 068 607	54 896	5.1	2.0	3.6	6.3	17.0
2nd quarter	1 064 966	56 067	5.3	-0.3	2.1	4.3	15.1
3rd quarter	1 073 438	58 157	5.4	0.8	3.7	4.3	16.3
4rd quarter	1 089 625	60 439	5.5	1.5	3.9	4.0	14.1
2013							
1st quarter	1 107 777	62 025	5.6	1.7	2.6	3.7	13.0
2nd quarter	1 108 338	63 949	5.8	0.1	3.1	4.1	14.1
3rd quarter	1 117 793	65 804	5.9	0.9	2.9	4.1	13.1
4rd quarter	1 124 565	68 179	6.1	0.6	3.6	3.2	12.8
2014							
1st quarter	1 133 491	70 492	6.2	0.8	3.4	2.3	13.7
2nd quarter	1 160 673	73 480	6.3	2.4	4.2	4.7	14.9
3rd quarter	1 168 593	75 883	6.5	0.7	3.3	4.5	15.3
4rd quarter	1 172 007	77 755	6.6	0.3	2.5	4.2	14.0
2015							
1st quarter	1 160 693	80 344	6.9	-1.0	3.3	2.4	14.0
2nd quarter	1 179 653	83 370	7.1	1.6	3.8	1.6	13.5
3rd quarter	1 191 536	86 569	7.3	1.0	3.8	2.0	14.1
4th quarter	1 192 078	88 968	7.5	0.0	2.8	1.7	14.4
2016							
1st quarter	1 189 262	92 182	7.8	-0.2	3.6	2.5	14.7
2nd quarter	1 205 936	96 283	8.0	1.4	4.4	2.2	15.5
3rd quarter	1 216 913	99 870	8.2	0.9	3.7	2.1	15.4
4rd quarter	1 237 663	101 606	8.2	1.7	1.7	3.8	14.2

Table 16-10. Retail Inventories

(All retail stores; end of period, millions of dollars.)

Year and month	Not seasonally adjusted			Seasonally adjusted							General merchandise	
	Total	Excluding motor vehicles and parts	Motor vehicles and parts	Total	Excluding motor vehicles and parts	Motor vehicles and parts	Furniture, home furnishings, electronics, and appliances	Building materials and garden	Food and beverages	Clothing and accessories	Total	Department stores [1]
1992	256 167	184 701	71 466	260 277	191 119	69 158	16 183	21 099	27 408	27 390	49 306	37 878
1993	274 072	196 419	77 653	278 445	203 311	75 134	18 113	22 621	27 498	28 080	53 283	40 458
1994	299 812	211 223	88 589	304 519	218 757	85 762	20 397	24 857	28 112	29 518	56 581	41 908
1995	317 304	220 921	96 383	322 216	228 842	93 374	21 817	26 337	28 718	29 298	59 530	43 455
1996	328 160	227 888	100 272	333 255	236 015	97 240	22 253	27 447	29 658	29 778	60 591	44 124
1997	338 790	234 270	104 520	343 825	242 518	101 307	22 109	28 897	29 891	31 079	60 715	44 309
1998	351 255	245 400	105 855	356 518	253 888	102 630	22 665	30 921	30 837	32 308	61 542	43 438
1999	378 813	259 879	118 934	384 078	268 567	115 511	24 096	33 005	32 635	33 735	64 297	43 835
2000	400 394	268 982	131 412	405 931	277 829	128 102	25 622	34 269	32 108	36 753	64 929	42 667
2001	387 859	266 370	121 489	393 638	274 796	118 842	24 497	34 235	33 165	35 627	64 790	40 464
2002	409 314	271 757	137 557	415 174	280 277	134 897	25 853	36 123	32 907	37 401	66 006	38 750
2003	425 748	277 471	148 277	431 199	285 668	145 531	27 152	37 398	32 504	38 503	66 655	36 823
2004	454 848	297 561	157 287	460 335	305 941	154 394	30 043	41 593	33 433	41 417	70 969	37 230
2005	465 791	310 227	155 564	471 616	318 849	152 767	30 550	45 072	33 784	43 003	74 179	38 030
2006	480 338	324 005	156 333	486 403	332 972	153 431	30 807	47 010	34 700	47 272	75 592	37 133
2007	494 372	334 566	159 806	500 489	343 476	157 013	31 356	49 074	36 484	47 381	75 820	36 428
2008	471 330	323 360	147 970	477 148	331 531	145 617	27 772	46 496	37 273	45 958	72 777	33 090
2009	423 380	114 772	114 772	429 159	315 870	113 289	25 710	42 707	37 254	40 811	69 575	30 817
2010	448 771	320 456	128 315	454 511	327 872	126 639	27 356	42 926	38 607	41 931	73 214	30 900
2011	464 428	330 868	133 560	470 493	338 752	131 741	26 209	43 510	40 166	44 239	76 485	31 165
2012	499 015	340 840	158 175	504 818	348 948	155 870	27 183	44 964	41 080	46 689	77 858	30 040
2013	536 246	356 779	179 467	542 324	365 851	176 473	27 455	48 067	42 646	49 690	80 599	29 829
2014	552 767	366 136	186 631	558 570	375 211	183 359	27 579	49 445	44 130	50 886	80 952	28 261
2015	581 931	380 982	200 949	584 802	389 335	195 467	27 662	51 497	45 606	52 337	82 507	28 277
2016	600 495	387 154	213 341	606 741	396 174	210 567	27 112	54 068	46 953	52 934	81 081	26 829
2013												
January	504 641	343 421	161 220	512 612	353 569	159 043	27 289	45 902	41 433	47 106	79 542	30 113
February	508 560	346 085	162 475	514 208	354 446	159 762	27 794	46 037	41 610	47 323	79 151	30 199
March	510 754	348 141	162 613	512 066	352 465	159 601	27 043	46 200	41 516	46 992	78 811	30 052
April	514 708	350 583	164 125	514 967	354 765	160 202	26 800	46 459	41 871	47 732	79 266	30 135
May	513 135	349 831	163 304	518 411	355 886	162 525	26 706	46 810	42 202	47 669	79 221	30 026
June	510 750	347 916	162 834	518 978	355 869	163 109	26 317	46 917	42 243	47 772	79 069	29 893
July	508 405	350 729	157 676	521 699	358 093	163 606	26 366	47 170	42 323	48 080	79 526	29 961
August	512 536	355 773	156 763	523 625	359 390	164 235	26 360	47 418	42 251	48 447	79 330	29 796
September	530 438	369 327	161 111	527 810	360 947	166 863	26 766	47 671	42 296	48 669	79 784	29 773
October	558 807	386 906	171 901	532 924	361 760	171 164	27 030	47 632	42 492	48 756	80 162	29 820
November	570 788	392 310	178 478	539 508	364 633	174 875	26 956	47 993	42 743	49 248	80 645	29 775
December	536 216	357 044	179 172	542 324	365 851	176 473	27 455	48 067	42 646	49 690	80 599	29 829
2014												
January	537 132	358 033	179 099	544 748	368 094	176 654	26 806	48 398	42 484	50 455	81 245	29 911
February	538 690	360 482	178 208	544 415	368 749	175 666	27 447	48 425	42 696	49 986	80 877	29 675
March	543 093	365 313	177 780	544 653	369 718	174 935	27 133	48 675	43 014	49 915	81 533	29 698
April	546 114	365 300	180 814	546 156	369 829	176 327	27 431	48 656	43 458	49 596	80 775	29 118
May	541 768	363 422	178 346	547 892	370 220	177 672	27 503	48 270	43 359	49 899	80 767	29 071
June	541 049	362 508	178 541	549 595	370 911	178 684	27 647	48 474	43 274	49 946	80 759	28 948
July	541 241	365 051	176 190	554 949	372 609	182 340	27 648	48 691	43 457	49 936	81 070	28 789
August	541 874	368 895	172 979	554 000	372 708	181 292	27 665	48 712	43 625	49 777	81 167	28 866
September	557 016	382 018	174 998	554 180	373 238	180 942	27 315	49 234	43 740	50 067	81 220	28 731
October	583 656	400 626	183 030	557 026	374 762	182 264	27 158	49 420	43 994	50 502	80 953	28 581
November	586 596	402 516	184 080	554 993	374 302	180 691	27 339	49 177	43 886	50 437	80 858	28 569
December	552 427	366 238	186 189	558 570	375 211	183 359	27 579	49 445	44 130	50 886	80 952	28 261
2015												
January	550 395	365 169	185 226	558 092	375 094	182 998	27 542	49 060	44 280	51 012	81 002	28 398
February	554 712	369 115	185 597	560 342	377 213	183 129	27 622	49 596	44 236	50 929	81 515	28 480
March	559 637	372 860	186 777	560 970	377 166	183 804	27 546	49 586	44 852	51 339	80 629	28 221
April	566 280	375 640	190 640	566 155	380 412	185 743	27 376	50 007	44 453	51 680	82 689	28 735
May	557 621	371 631	185 990	564 192	378 906	185 286	27 211	50 033	44 473	51 140	81 898	28 659
June	560 448	372 831	187 617	568 808	381 379	187 429	27 436	50 672	44 729	51 311	82 405	28 710
July	559 053	374 566	184 487	572 993	382 423	190 570	27 467	50 741	44 927	51 142	82 137	28 381
August	562 316	380 302	182 014	574 826	384 209	190 617	27 532	50 988	45 104	51 891	82 341	28 495
September	583 444	395 848	187 596	580 110	386 478	193 632	27 756	51 125	45 339	52 075	82 768	28 947
October	609 122	414 589	194 533	581 833	387 939	193 894	27 775	51 589	45 516	52 137	82 789	28 736
November	614 761	417 658	197 103	582 486	388 666	193 820	28 322	51 704	45 597	52 129	82 574	28 471
December	578 560	380 188	198 372	584 802	389 335	195 467	27 662	51 497	45 606	52 337	82 507	28 277
2016												
January	578 538	379 636	198 902	586 612	389 787	196 825	27 471	51 728	45 671	52 653	82 604	28 000
February	583 773	382 132	201 641	589 681	390 544	199 137	27 386	52 006	46 046	52 857	82 487	28 020
March	595 230	387 513	207 717	595 856	391 840	204 016	27 430	52 195	45 742	52 790	82 545	27 889
April	595 916	386 423	209 493	595 148	391 278	203 870	27 341	52 038	46 025	52 950	82 004	27 654
May	591 231	385 148	206 083	598 018	392 718	205 300	27 448	52 474	46 042	53 091	82 279	27 434
June	592 553	385 006	207 547	600 835	393 683	207 152	27 418	52 381	46 388	53 003	82 038	27 306
July	584 274	383 971	200 303	598 910	392 147	206 763	27 401	52 690	46 315	52 890	81 415	27 377
August	589 468	389 368	200 100	602 713	393 258	209 455	27 502	53 052	46 450	52 114	81 876	27 050
September	607 923	403 482	204 441	604 804	393 915	210 889	27 381	53 094	46 507	52 562	81 626	26 872
October	628 059	418 771	209 288	601 300	392 506	208 794	27 104	53 316	46 403	52 399	81 131	26 797
November	638 900	423 170	215 730	606 974	394 476	212 498	27 141	53 912	46 538	52 770	81 037	26 783
December	600 495	387 154	213 341	606 741	396 174	210 567	27 112	54 068	46 953	52 934	81 081	26 829

[1]Excluding leased departments.

Table 16-11. Merchant Wholesalers—Sales and Inventories

(Millions of dollars.)

Year and month	Not seasonally adjusted						Seasonally adjusted					
	Sales			Inventories (current cost, end of period)			Sales			Inventories (current cost, end of period)		
	Total	Durable goods establishments	Nondurable goods establishments	Total	Durable goods establishments	Nondurable goods establishments	Total	Durable goods establishments	Nondurable goods establishments	Total	Durable goods establishments	Nondurable goods establishments
1992	1 767 130	861 182	905 948	197 793	121 809	75 984	1 767 130	861 182	905 948	196 914	123 435	73 479
1993	1 848 215	939 945	908 270	205 815	127 094	78 721	1 848 215	939 945	908 270	204 842	128 851	75 991
1994	1 974 899	1 037 638	937 261	222 826	139 941	82 885	1 974 899	1 037 638	937 261	221 978	141 975	80 003
1995	2 158 980	1 141 701	1 017 279	239 275	151 709	87 566	2 158 980	1 141 701	1 017 279	238 392	154 089	84 303
1996	2 284 343	1 190 342	1 094 001	241 396	154 207	87 189	2 284 343	1 190 342	1 094 001	241 058	156 683	84 375
1997	2 377 845	1 256 384	1 121 461	258 900	165 371	93 529	2 377 845	1 256 384	1 121 461	258 454	168 089	90 365
1998	2 427 120	1 306 545	1 120 575	272 575	175 994	96 581	2 427 120	1 306 545	1 120 575	272 297	178 918	93 379
1999	2 599 159	1 406 371	1 192 788	290 382	187 738	102 644	2 599 159	1 406 371	1 192 788	290 182	190 899	99 283
2000	2 814 554	1 486 673	1 327 881	309 710	198 525	111 185	2 814 554	1 486 673	1 327 881	309 191	201 797	107 394
2001	2 785 152	1 422 195	1 362 957	298 577	182 521	116 056	2 785 152	1 422 195	1 362 957	297 536	185 517	112 019
2002	2 835 528	1 421 503	1 414 025	302 715	182 150	120 565	2 835 528	1 421 503	1 414 025	301 281	185 048	116 233
2003	2 978 282	1 466 158	1 512 124	310 115	186 435	123 680	2 978 282	1 466 158	1 512 124	308 305	189 372	118 933
2004	3 330 011	1 689 588	1 640 423	341 642	213 590	128 052	3 330 011	1 689 588	1 640 423	340 100	216 684	123 416
2005	3 638 496	1 830 347	1 808 149	369 380	233 199	136 181	3 638 496	1 830 347	1 808 149	367 951	236 438	131 513
2006	3 941 257	2 005 139	1 936 118	400 297	256 731	143 566	3 941 257	2 005 139	1 936 118	398 917	260 115	138 802
2007	4 223 473	2 101 969	2 121 504	426 254	263 195	163 059	4 223 473	2 101 969	2 121 504	424 428	266 704	157 724
2008	4 524 357	2 126 715	2 397 642	445 447	280 262	165 185	4 524 357	2 126 715	2 397 642	444 849	284 002	160 847
2009	3 829 378	1 745 557	2 083 821	398 006	233 583	164 423	3 829 378	1 745 557	2 083 821	396 388	237 018	159 370
2010	4 337 359	1 999 247	2 338 112	442 631	256 702	185 929	4 337 359	1 999 247	2 338 112	440 159	260 695	179 464
2011	4 885 076	2 229 683	2 655 393	487 018	285 924	201 094	4 885 076	2 229 683	2 655 393	485 044	290 437	194 607
2012	5 208 023	2 389 576	2 818 447	522 427	311 050	211 377	5 208 023	2 389 576	2 818 447	520 338	316 223	204 115
2013	5 370 550	2 461 025	2 909 525	541 811	326 263	215 548	5 370 550	2 461 025	2 909 525	540 671	332 068	208 603
2014	5 564 180	2 556 641	3 007 539	573 325	348 770	224 555	5 564 180	2 556 641	3 007 539	572 083	355 111	216 972
2015	5 292 436	2 520 142	2 772 294	579 486	349 553	229 933	5 292 436	2 520 142	2 772 294	578 774	356 114	222 660
2016	5 272 515	2 527 211	2 745 304	594 466	352 852	241 614	5 272 515	2 527 211	2 745 304	592 996	359 259	233 737
2013												
January	429 108	193 942	235 166	530 729	317 105	213 624	443 725	203 825	239 900	524 442	318 916	205 526
February	401 898	179 935	221 963	528 055	318 608	209 447	448 224	204 428	243 796	523 029	318 983	204 046
March	446 167	205 794	240 373	529 102	318 970	210 132	441 023	203 483	237 540	523 406	320 307	203 099
April	451 272	207 497	243 775	526 985	322 444	204 541	439 541	204 116	235 425	524 404	321 766	202 638
May	469 783	209 797	259 986	516 913	319 209	197 704	445 373	204 002	241 371	520 833	319 221	201 612
June	440 359	204 572	235 787	514 501	319 907	194 594	445 247	205 088	240 159	521 376	319 730	201 646
July	449 748	203 689	246 059	517 748	324 412	193 336	441 985	201 782	240 203	522 129	321 885	200 244
August	455 313	210 447	244 866	517 399	324 093	193 306	447 106	204 504	242 602	526 109	323 496	202 613
September	441 668	209 560	232 108	524 916	326 129	198 787	448 828	207 234	241 594	528 371	324 312	204 059
October	483 556	225 339	258 217	540 697	328 713	211 984	452 222	207 647	244 575	534 301	325 866	208 435
November	443 507	201 144	242 363	543 308	327 946	215 362	455 360	206 382	248 978	538 588	327 634	210 954
December	458 171	209 309	248 862	541 811	326 263	215 548	457 577	206 434	251 143	540 671	332 068	208 603
2014												
January	433 126	193 673	239 453	549 069	331 366	217 703	450 392	204 239	246 153	543 620	333 259	210 361
February	406 377	180 609	225 768	551 708	335 663	216 045	454 094	205 690	248 404	547 175	335 988	211 187
March	465 454	210 362	255 092	557 792	336 768	221 024	462 987	208 804	254 183	551 817	338 001	213 816
April	475 627	213 257	262 370	559 245	341 238	218 007	464 738	210 873	253 865	556 022	340 133	215 889
May	480 405	211 687	268 718	552 952	343 120	209 832	467 047	211 720	255 327	556 680	342 694	213 986
June	474 266	220 445	253 821	551 076	345 279	205 797	466 139	214 256	251 883	557 679	345 018	212 661
July	478 901	217 304	261 597	553 975	348 738	205 237	469 331	214 775	254 556	558 486	346 055	212 431
August	463 516	215 354	248 162	553 211	348 537	204 674	468 562	216 582	251 980	562 575	347 623	214 952
September	475 821	226 455	249 366	559 541	353 005	206 536	466 819	215 850	250 969	563 113	351 334	211 779
October	496 816	234 918	261 898	572 424	353 395	219 029	464 624	216 729	247 895	566 104	351 017	215 087
November	440 165	204 875	235 290	576 445	354 141	222 304	464 866	216 651	248 215	571 181	353 986	217 195
December	473 706	227 702	246 004	573 325	348 770	224 555	458 161	217 680	240 481	572 083	355 111	216 972
2015												
January	414 455	197 764	216 691	577 861	354 944	222 917	443 543	214 626	228 917	572 656	356 979	215 677
February	391 787	182 229	209 558	579 201	358 366	220 835	439 827	208 324	231 503	575 840	358 751	217 089
March	452 232	217 955	234 277	581 610	359 021	222 589	438 025	209 784	228 241	576 683	360 283	216 400
April	452 556	213 020	239 536	579 692	360 503	219 189	443 374	211 216	232 158	576 861	359 141	217 720
May	442 350	203 618	238 732	576 342	361 742	214 600	445 148	210 958	234 190	579 498	361 067	218 431
June	468 618	222 716	245 902	576 994	361 510	215 484	445 060	208 541	236 519	583 174	361 132	222 042
July	451 610	212 633	238 977	577 278	363 466	213 812	444 444	210 348	234 096	582 277	360 447	221 830
August	434 412	207 164	227 248	573 570	361 765	211 805	439 801	208 680	231 121	583 545	360 946	222 599
September	451 068	219 858	231 210	581 042	360 903	220 139	441 452	210 214	231 238	585 270	359 441	225 829
October	461 100	220 410	240 690	589 163	361 070	228 093	440 425	208 612	231 813	582 979	359 068	223 911
November	423 729	203 458	220 271	584 946	357 907	227 039	435 007	208 379	226 628	579 909	357 527	222 382
December	448 519	219 317	229 202	579 486	349 553	229 933	431 433	208 308	223 125	578 774	356 114	222 660
2016												
January	382 714	181 427	201 287	584 387	352 548	231 839	424 509	204 275	220 234	579 126	354 710	224 416
February	392 290	188 610	203 680	577 813	352 803	225 010	422 933	206 879	216 054	575 784	353 318	222 466
March	453 421	221 135	232 286	581 350	351 787	229 563	426 743	206 877	219 866	577 081	352 712	224 369
April	426 877	202 893	223 984	583 346	354 336	229 010	430 909	207 052	223 857	581 533	353 222	228 311
May	442 313	207 268	235 045	577 787	354 838	222 949	432 917	208 142	224 775	581 287	354 085	227 202
June	464 213	225 104	239 109	577 155	353 660	223 495	441 502	211 360	230 142	583 030	353 127	229 903
July	420 959	201 104	219 855	577 480	356 874	220 606	438 859	210 983	227 876	582 967	353 858	229 109
August	462 575	221 740	240 835	571 984	355 553	216 431	441 959	210 091	231 868	582 338	354 660	227 678
September	453 484	221 028	232 456	579 261	354 435	224 826	443 150	210 669	232 501	583 135	353 048	230 087
October	455 304	216 850	238 454	587 934	354 385	233 549	448 362	212 383	235 979	582 183	352 652	229 531
November	452 257	215 089	237 168	594 397	357 189	237 208	450 064	213 473	236 591	588 360	356 779	231 581
December	466 108	224 963	241 145	594 466	352 852	241 614	460 860	219 461	241 399	592 996	359 259	233 737

. . . = Not available.

Table 16-12. Manufacturing and Trade Sales and Inventories

Year and month	Sales, billions of dollars					Inventories, billions of dollars, end of period, seasonally adjusted				Ratios, inventories to sales, seasonally adjusted [1]			
	Not seasonally adjusted, total	Seasonally adjusted				Total	Manufac-turing	Retail trade	Merchant wholesalers	Total	Manufac-turing	Retail trade	Merchant wholesalers
		Total	Manufac-turing	Retail trade	Merchant wholesalers								
1995	7 856.3	7 865.3	3 481.4	2 220.3	2 163.7	985.4	424.8	322.2	238.4	1.48	1.44	1.72	1.29
1996	8 243.1	8 217.6	3 586.0	2 355.6	2 276.0	1 004.7	430.4	333.3	241.1	1.45	1.44	1.67	1.27
1997	8 681.3	8 684.0	3 836.1	2 470.8	2 377.1	1 045.5	443.2	343.8	258.5	1.42	1.37	1.64	1.26
1998	8 908.7	8 906.4	3 897.4	2 582.6	2 426.3	1 077.2	448.4	356.5	272.3	1.44	1.39	1.62	1.32
1999	9 434.1	9 431.6	4 033.3	2 801.4	2 597.0	1 137.3	463.0	384.1	290.2	1.40	1.35	1.59	1.30
2000	10 006.4	9 999.0	4 202.4	2 979.3	2 817.3	1 195.9	480.7	405.9	309.2	1.41	1.35	1.59	1.29
2001	9 817.9	9 819.4	3 971.2	3 062.3	2 785.9	1 118.5	427.4	393.6	297.5	1.42	1.38	1.58	1.32
2002	9 878.8	9 880.8	3 916.7	3 129.7	2 834.5	1 139.5	423.0	415.2	301.3	1.36	1.29	1.55	1.26
2003	10 256.4	10 255.6	4 016.5	3 261.7	2 977.4	1 147.8	408.3	431.2	308.3	1.34	1.24	1.56	1.22
2004	11 112.0	11 069.5	4 293.2	3 460.9	3 315.4	1 241.3	440.8	460.3	340.1	1.30	1.19	1.56	1.17
2005	12 069.9	12 073.3	4 743.2	3 686.7	3 643.4	1 313.2	473.7	471.6	368.0	1.27	1.17	1.51	1.17
2006	12 828.4	12 840.6	5 017.3	3 876.7	3 946.6	1 407.5	522.2	486.4	398.9	1.28	1.20	1.50	1.17
2007	13 538.1	13 538.9	5 320.3	3 997.5	4 221.1	1 485.6	560.7	500.5	424.4	1.28	1.22	1.49	1.17
2008	13 928.7	13 879.9	5 446.1	3 927.5	4 506.3	1 464.2	542.2	477.1	444.8	1.31	1.26	1.52	1.20
2009	11 865.6	11 869.1	4 427.1	3 612.9	3 829.0	1 329.2	503.7	429.2	396.4	1.38	1.39	1.47	1.28
2010	13 066.7	13 064.2	4 915.2	3 816.5	4 332.6	1 447.5	552.9	454.5	440.2	1.27	1.28	1.39	1.14
2011	14 479.9	14 490.6	5 196.6	4 102.2	4 001.9	1 501.4	605.9	470.5	485.0	1.26	1.29	1.35	1.14
2012	15 207.0	15 185.1	5 688.7	4 296.6	5 199.8	1 649.4	624.3	504.8	520.3	1.27	1.30	1.38	1.17
2013	15 638.7	15 635.5	5 811.8	4 458.5	5 366.2	1 712.8	629.8	542.3	540.7	1.29	1.30	1.41	1.18
2014	16 091.2	16 080.6	5 888.1	4 634.8	5 557.8	1 770.6	639.9	558.6	572.1	1.31	1.31	1.43	1.21
2015	15 566.9	15 560.6	5 549.1	4 724.0	5 287.5	1 803.1	639.5	584.8	578.8	1.38	1.39	1.45	1.32
2016	15 582.4	15 548.9	5 436.5	4 849.6	5 262.8	1 844.2	644.4	606.7	593.0	1.40	1.41	1.48	1.33
2012													
January	1 151.6	1 251.5	472.1	352.6	426.8	1 568.4	608.9	473.4	486.1	1.25	1.29	1.34	1.14
February	1 188.4	1 261.6	473.6	357.0	430.9	1 582.0	611.5	477.4	493.1	1.25	1.29	1.34	1.14
March	1 324.6	1 268.1	476.5	358.9	432.7	1 588.8	612.8	481.3	494.7	1.25	1.29	1.34	1.14
April	1 259.7	1 270.3	474.2	356.7	439.4	1 595.6	613.1	484.3	498.2	1.26	1.29	1.36	1.13
May	1 322.3	1 261.5	474.1	356.1	431.3	1 602.0	612.6	489.8	499.5	1.27	1.29	1.38	1.16
June	1 277.5	1 244.6	466.6	352.2	425.8	1 606.8	612.1	492.4	502.3	1.29	1.31	1.40	1.18
July	1 226.6	1 247.4	467.7	353.7	426.1	1 618.8	614.7	496.5	507.5	1.30	1.31	1.40	1.19
August	1 316.2	1 259.6	471.3	358.1	430.2	1 628.2	618.6	499.7	509.9	1.29	1.31	1.40	1.19
September	1 245.8	1 278.2	476.6	361.6	440.0	1 638.1	622.1	499.6	516.4	1.28	1.31	1.38	1.17
October	1 309.5	1 271.7	476.3	362.1	433.3	1 640.7	622.7	502.2	515.8	1.29	1.31	1.39	1.19
November	1 277.7	1 284.0	479.3	363.0	441.7	1 646.4	623.0	503.5	519.9	1.28	1.30	1.39	1.18
December	1 307.2	1 286.6	480.4	364.6	441.6	1 649.4	624.3	504.8	520.3	1.28	1.30	1.38	1.18
2013													
January	1 210.8	1 292.0	481.0	367.2	443.7	1 664.1	627.0	512.6	524.4	1.29	1.30	1.40	1.18
February	1 188.0	1 310.4	490.4	371.7	448.2	1 665.3	628.0	514.2	523.0	1.27	1.28	1.38	1.17
March	1 321.9	1 292.0	482.1	368.8	441.0	1 663.6	628.1	512.1	523.4	1.29	1.30	1.39	1.19
April	1 296.1	1 284.5	477.1	367.9	439.5	1 667.2	627.8	515.0	524.4	1.30	1.32	1.40	1.19
May	1 361.4	1 297.8	483.1	369.3	445.4	1 664.5	625.3	518.4	520.8	1.28	1.29	1.40	1.17
June	1 306.4	1 296.5	480.2	371.1	445.2	1 663.6	623.2	519.0	521.4	1.28	1.30	1.40	1.17
July	1 299.3	1 296.1	480.9	373.2	442.0	1 669.8	625.9	521.7	522.1	1.29	1.30	1.40	1.18
August	1 345.8	1 304.1	484.6	372.4	447.1	1 677.6	627.9	523.6	526.1	1.29	1.30	1.41	1.18
September	1 291.4	1 305.9	484.9	372.2	448.8	1 685.2	629.0	527.8	528.4	1.29	1.30	1.42	1.18
October	1 355.5	1 310.9	485.0	373.7	452.2	1 696.1	628.9	532.9	534.3	1.29	1.30	1.43	1.18
November	1 297.1	1 323.3	493.9	374.1	455.4	1 705.7	627.6	539.5	538.6	1.29	1.27	1.44	1.18
December	1 365.2	1 323.1	488.7	376.8	457.6	1 712.8	629.8	542.3	540.7	1.29	1.29	1.44	1.18
2014													
January	1 225.2	1 310.2	486.7	373.1	450.4	1 720.6	632.3	544.7	543.6	1.31	1.30	1.46	1.21
February	1 201.0	1 325.9	494.1	377.7	454.1	1 728.5	636.9	544.4	547.2	1.30	1.29	1.44	1.20
March	1 362.5	1 339.2	493.6	382.7	463.0	1 734.2	637.8	544.7	551.8	1.29	1.29	1.42	1.19
April	1 355.8	1 344.0	492.8	386.5	464.7	1 741.4	639.2	546.2	556.0	1.30	1.30	1.41	1.20
May	1 394.8	1 346.1	492.3	386.8	467.0	1 748.1	643.6	547.9	556.7	1.30	1.31	1.42	1.19
June	1 376.5	1 347.0	493.5	387.3	466.1	1 749.4	642.1	549.6	557.7	1.30	1.30	1.42	1.20
July	1 361.4	1 353.7	496.8	387.6	469.3	1 756.9	643.4	554.9	558.5	1.30	1.30	1.43	1.19
August	1 371.7	1 356.6	496.9	391.2	468.6	1 761.1	644.5	554.0	562.6	1.30	1.30	1.42	1.20
September	1 363.6	1 350.5	493.9	389.8	466.8	1 763.0	645.7	554.2	563.1	1.31	1.31	1.42	1.21
October	1 390.5	1 343.2	487.8	390.7	464.6	1 768.1	645.0	557.0	566.1	1.32	1.32	1.43	1.22
November	1 290.3	1 339.2	481.9	392.4	464.9	1 770.6	644.4	555.0	571.2	1.32	1.34	1.41	1.23
December	1 397.9	1 325.1	478.0	388.9	458.2	1 770.6	639.9	558.6	572.1	1.34	1.34	1.44	1.25
2015													
January	1 189.1	1 292.5	463.4	385.6	443.5	1 770.3	639.5	558.1	572.7	1.37	1.38	1.45	1.29
February	1 164.1	1 288.1	464.5	383.8	439.8	1 776.2	640.0	560.3	575.8	1.38	1.38	1.46	1.31
March	1 338.7	1 298.2	468.9	391.2	438.0	1 778.7	641.1	561.0	576.7	1.37	1.37	1.43	1.32
April	1 310.1	1 300.5	466.5	390.6	443.4	1 785.3	642.3	566.2	576.9	1.37	1.38	1.45	1.30
May	1 321.5	1 305.6	465.9	394.6	445.1	1 786.6	642.9	564.2	579.5	1.37	1.38	1.43	1.30
June	1 365.5	1 308.9	469.4	394.5	445.1	1 799.9	647.9	568.8	583.2	1.38	1.38	1.44	1.31
July	1 314.1	1 308.5	466.8	397.3	444.4	1 802.0	646.7	573.0	582.3	1.38	1.39	1.44	1.31
August	1 310.9	1 299.5	462.5	397.2	439.8	1 802.5	644.2	574.8	583.5	1.39	1.39	1.45	1.33
September	1 313.8	1 299.0	460.5	397.1	441.5	1 807.8	642.4	580.1	585.3	1.39	1.40	1.46	1.33
October	1 322.4	1 293.4	457.2	395.9	440.4	1 806.8	642.0	581.8	583.0	1.40	1.40	1.47	1.32
November	1 259.4	1 288.7	456.2	397.5	435.0	1 802.5	640.1	582.5	579.9	1.40	1.40	1.47	1.33
December	1 357.3	1 277.6	447.4	398.8	431.4	1 803.1	639.5	584.8	578.8	1.41	1.43	1.47	1.34
2016													
January	1 138.2	1 267.4	447.6	395.2	424.5	1 802.4	636.7	586.6	579.1	1.42	1.42	1.48	1.36
February	1 185.9	1 263.9	444.1	396.9	422.9	1 799.5	634.0	589.7	575.8	1.42	1.43	1.49	1.36
March	1 337.7	1 271.3	447.4	397.1	426.7	1 807.4	634.7	595.6	577.1	1.42	1.42	1.50	1.35
April	1 269.4	1 280.3	449.6	399.7	430.9	1 811.9	634.6	595.8	581.5	1.42	1.41	1.49	1.35
May	1 315.0	1 284.1	449.7	401.6	432.9	1 814.3	635.0	598.0	581.3	1.41	1.41	1.49	1.34
June	1 357.4	1 299.1	453.1	404.5	441.5	1 819.0	635.1	600.8	583.0	1.40	1.40	1.49	1.32
July	1 257.2	1 295.6	452.0	404.7	438.9	1 818.2	636.4	598.9	583.0	1.40	1.41	1.48	1.33
August	1 353.7	1 297.9	451.9	404.0	442.0	1 823.1	638.1	602.7	582.3	1.40	1.41	1.49	1.32
September	1 325.6	1 307.4	456.1	408.2	443.2	1 825.9	640.4	604.8	583.1	1.40	1.40	1.48	1.32
October	1 316.2	1 317.3	457.9	411.0	448.4	1 821.0	637.6	601.3	582.2	1.38	1.39	1.46	1.30
November	1 315.5	1 318.9	457.9	411.0	450.1	1 836.5	641.1	607.0	588.4	1.39	1.40	1.48	1.31
December	1 410.5	1 345.8	469.3	415.6	460.9	1 844.2	644.4	606.7	593.0	1.37	1.37	1.46	1.29

[1] Annual data are averages of monthly ratios.

Table 16-13. Real Manufacturing and Trade Sales and Inventories

(Billions of chained [2009] dollars, ratios; seasonally adjusted; annual sales figures are averages of seasonally adjusted monthly data.)

NIPA Tables 1BU, 2BU, 3BU

Year and month	Sales, monthly average				Inventories, end of period				Ratios, end-of-period inventories to monthly average sales			
	Total	Manufac- turing	Retail trade	Merchant wholesalers	Total	Manufac- turing	Retail trade	Merchant wholesalers	Total	Manufac- turing	Retail trade	Merchant wholesalers
1999	956.8	427.0	270.6	262.8	1 345.4	582.8	414.1	354.8	1.41	1.37	1.53	1.35
2000	986.2	432.1	280.7	276.5	1 395.1	591.6	435.9	373.0	1.42	1.37	1.55	1.35
2001	973.0	408.2	288.0	278.3	1 345.5	562.3	424.6	363.1	1.38	1.38	1.47	1.31
2002	987.8	406.0	296.1	286.6	1 375.7	561.2	452.3	364.2	1.39	1.38	1.53	1.27
2003	1 006.7	406.8	307.5	292.5	1 390.1	552.3	471.4	366.6	1.38	1.36	1.53	1.25
2004	1 045.1	415.3	319.9	309.8	1 444.4	558.7	496.6	388.6	1.38	1.35	1.55	1.25
2005	1 090.8	434.0	332.0	324.8	1 493.6	581.6	501.8	410.4	1.37	1.34	1.51	1.26
2006	1 120.5	439.4	342.8	338.2	1 540.1	600.6	511.5	428.3	1.37	1.37	1.49	1.27
2007	1 144.1	450.1	347.5	346.4	1 574.3	618.1	518.1	438.2	1.38	1.37	1.49	1.27
2008	1 098.0	426.4	332.7	338.7	1 532.3	600.3	487.9	444.1	1.40	1.41	1.47	1.31
2009	991.5	368.8	314.4	308.3	1 410.3	574.0	438.2	398.0	1.42	1.56	1.39	1.29
2010	1 036.8	388.2	324.9	323.6	1 471.4	596.1	456.6	418.6	1.42	1.54	1.41	1.29
2011	1 072.0	402.5	335.1	334.2	1 504.7	617.3	455.5	431.1	1.40	1.53	1.36	1.29
2012	1 105.1	412.6	345.8	346.6	1 562.8	628.4	481.3	452.7	1.41	1.52	1.39	1.31
2013	1 138.6	419.6	360.6	358.5	1 634.4	641.6	511.0	481.7	1.44	1.53	1.42	1.34
2014	1 169.6	421.8	375.7	372.7	1 691.8	658.2	522.9	510.4	1.45	1.56	1.39	1.37
2015	1 196.3	419.8	396.1	381.9	1 766.8	691.2	547.4	527.9	1.48	1.65	1.38	1.38
2016	1 224.5	420.9	415.3	390.2	1 798.8	700.8	561.0	536.6	1.47	1.67	1.35	1.38
2012												
January	1 095.4	413.6	341.6	340.1	1 509.1	619.8	457.9	430.7	1.38	1.50	1.34	1.27
February	1 098.7	412.2	344.8	341.8	1 516.1	620.8	460.2	434.5	1.38	1.51	1.34	1.27
March	1 097.7	410.3	345.5	342.0	1 518.8	620.8	463.5	434.0	1.38	1.51	1.34	1.27
April	1 100.9	408.8	343.1	348.8	1 523.1	621.2	465.4	436.0	1.38	1.52	1.36	1.25
May	1 106.0	412.3	344.3	349.2	1 528.5	621.3	469.3	437.4	1.38	1.51	1.36	1.25
June	1 099.2	408.4	342.1	348.5	1 534.9	622.9	471.4	440.2	1.40	1.53	1.38	1.26
July	1 104.9	412.6	344.5	347.6	1 545.6	625.0	474.9	445.2	1.40	1.52	1.38	1.28
August	1 102.0	410.2	345.9	345.8	1 551.7	628.0	477.4	445.9	1.41	1.53	1.38	1.29
September	1 107.5	411.2	348.2	348.1	1 557.0	629.9	476.6	450.0	1.41	1.53	1.37	1.29
October	1 100.6	411.9	346.3	342.5	1 555.3	628.5	478.2	448.3	1.41	1.53	1.38	1.31
November	1 121.4	419.3	349.8	352.1	1 559.0	627.7	479.0	451.8	1.39	1.50	1.37	1.28
December	1 126.6	420.5	353.1	352.9	1 562.8	628.4	481.3	452.7	1.39	1.49	1.36	1.28
2013												
January	1 129.8	421.0	355.1	353.8	1 575.4	630.9	487.3	457.0	1.39	1.50	1.37	1.29
February	1 133.6	422.7	357.0	354.0	1 576.7	630.8	489.3	456.6	1.39	1.49	1.37	1.29
March	1 122.6	415.9	355.1	351.7	1 577.5	630.9	487.9	458.5	1.41	1.52	1.37	1.30
April	1 126.1	413.4	358.5	354.6	1 583.6	631.8	490.2	461.4	1.41	1.53	1.37	1.30
May	1 138.1	419.5	360.2	358.5	1 583.7	630.8	493.0	459.9	1.39	1.50	1.37	1.28
June	1 134.1	415.5	361.7	357.2	1 586.5	630.8	494.4	461.3	1.40	1.52	1.37	1.29
July	1 132.8	416.4	363.1	353.8	1 593.1	633.6	496.5	463.0	1.41	1.52	1.37	1.31
August	1 137.5	418.3	361.8	357.7	1 601.8	636.4	497.8	467.4	1.41	1.52	1.38	1.31
September	1 142.2	419.3	361.9	361.1	1 609.6	637.0	501.9	470.6	1.41	1.52	1.39	1.30
October	1 148.4	420.3	363.5	364.7	1 618.7	638.4	504.0	476.2	1.41	1.52	1.39	1.31
November	1 160.1	428.9	363.8	367.3	1 627.7	638.0	509.3	480.3	1.40	1.49	1.40	1.31
December	1 158.1	424.6	365.8	367.8	1 634.4	641.6	511.0	481.7	1.41	1.51	1.40	1.31
2014												
January	1 144.1	421.4	361.2	361.6	1 639.3	642.9	512.9	483.4	1.43	1.53	1.42	1.34
February	1 153.9	425.4	365.6	363.0	1 644.5	645.3	513.8	485.3	1.43	1.52	1.41	1.34
March	1 165.0	423.1	371.1	371.1	1 646.4	644.8	513.3	488.1	1.41	1.52	1.38	1.32
April	1 163.9	420.0	374.0	370.4	1 651.4	646.4	514.1	490.8	1.42	1.54	1.37	1.33
May	1 166.6	419.9	375.0	372.3	1 657.3	650.8	515.1	491.1	1.42	1.55	1.37	1.32
June	1 166.5	421.1	375.5	370.5	1 659.7	650.6	516.0	492.8	1.42	1.55	1.37	1.33
July	1 173.1	423.7	375.6	374.3	1 668.1	652.9	520.2	494.8	1.42	1.54	1.39	1.32
August	1 177.3	423.1	380.0	374.9	1 673.9	654.7	519.3	499.7	1.42	1.55	1.37	1.33
September	1 175.8	421.6	378.8	376.0	1 676.8	656.4	518.8	501.3	1.43	1.56	1.37	1.33
October	1 177.6	419.9	380.7	377.7	1 683.3	657.2	521.4	504.5	1.43	1.57	1.37	1.34
November	1 182.1	419.0	385.1	379.0	1 688.6	658.8	520.2	509.2	1.43	1.57	1.35	1.34
December	1 189.6	422.9	385.7	381.8	1 691.8	658.2	522.9	510.4	1.42	1.56	1.36	1.34
2015												
January	1 188.5	419.2	389.0	381.4	1 697.6	661.2	524.1	512.0	1.43	1.58	1.35	1.34
February	1 184.3	420.6	385.6	379.0	1 708.2	665.1	526.8	515.9	1.44	1.58	1.37	1.36
March	1 192.2	423.0	392.0	378.5	1 714.6	668.9	528.1	517.3	1.44	1.58	1.35	1.37
April	1 197.9	422.5	392.4	384.1	1 722.2	671.9	532.2	517.8	1.44	1.59	1.36	1.35
May	1 190.4	417.6	394.5	379.8	1 724.8	673.9	530.6	519.9	1.45	1.61	1.35	1.37
June	1 191.2	420.0	394.2	378.2	1 736.5	679.7	533.6	522.9	1.46	1.62	1.35	1.38
July	1 192.9	418.5	396.5	379.3	1 740.2	681.0	536.4	522.5	1.46	1.63	1.35	1.38
August	1 195.1	418.2	398.1	380.3	1 746.2	682.1	538.8	525.0	1.46	1.63	1.35	1.38
September	1 208.6	421.5	400.8	387.7	1 756.4	684.3	543.2	528.4	1.45	1.62	1.36	1.36
October	1 204.9	419.4	400.3	386.7	1 760.8	687.2	545.2	528.2	1.46	1.64	1.36	1.37
November	1 204.3	420.6	402.4	382.9	1 761.2	688.4	545.4	527.1	1.46	1.64	1.36	1.38
December	1 205.8	416.5	406.9	384.3	1 766.8	691.2	547.4	527.9	1.47	1.66	1.35	1.37
2016												
January	1 204.3	419.9	403.9	382.2	1 770.3	691.7	548.9	529.5	1.47	1.65	1.36	1.39
February	1 210.4	419.1	409.1	384.1	1 769.5	691.6	550.1	527.6	1.46	1.65	1.35	1.37
March	1 216.5	421.5	409.5	387.3	1 776.2	693.1	553.7	529.1	1.46	1.64	1.35	1.37
April	1 217.3	420.6	410.4	388.2	1 779.6	693.0	554.0	532.2	1.46	1.65	1.35	1.37
May	1 213.0	418.2	412.6	384.2	1 778.9	692.6	555.7	530.2	1.47	1.66	1.35	1.38
June	1 218.4	417.7	415.3	387.5	1 778.8	691.7	556.8	529.9	1.46	1.66	1.34	1.37
July	1 219.5	417.1	417.0	387.6	1 777.1	692.7	554.7	529.4	1.46	1.66	1.33	1.37
August	1 226.4	418.8	416.5	393.2	1 781.9	694.7	557.2	529.7	1.45	1.66	1.34	1.35
September	1 233.6	421.7	419.6	394.4	1 786.3	695.5	559.7	530.8	1.45	1.65	1.33	1.35
October	1 237.1	421.8	421.4	396.1	1 782.4	695.7	556.9	529.5	1.44	1.65	1.32	1.34
November	1 239.4	423.1	422.2	396.3	1 792.9	698.7	559.5	534.3	1.45	1.65	1.33	1.35
December	1 257.6	431.8	426.2	401.7	1 798.8	700.8	561.0	536.6	1.43	1.62	1.32	1.34

Table 16-14. Selected Services—Quarterly Estimated Revenue for Employer Firms

(Millions of dollars.)

2007 NAICS code	Kind of business	4th quarter 2015	1st quarter 2016	2rd quarter 2016	3rd quarter 2016	4th quarter 2016	1st quarter 2017
SEASONALLY ADJUSTED							
51	**Information**	359 079	363 729	364 652	370 715	373 490	378 954
5112	Software publishers	49 869	50 619	50 053	50 922	51 690	53 100
512	Motion picture and sound recording industries	25 350	27 538	25 013	26 117	25 221	27 211
54	**Professional, Scientific, and Technical Services**	414 732	428 465	431 333	435 087	440 552	444 024
5411	Legal services	69 247	72 030	71 913	71 100	74 765	74 133
5412	Accounting, tax preparation, bookkeeping, and payroll services	41 013	42 002	42 427	43 264	44 068	45 532
56 pt	**Administrative and Support and Waste Management and Remediation Services**	207 107	209 214	215 247	220 104	224 611	231 094
5613	Employment services	81 420	82 146	85 670	87 850	90 511	95 295
5615	Travel arrangement and reservation services	. . .	10 629	10 517	11 279	11 182	11 261
562	Waste management and remediation services	22 390	22 586	22 451	22 764	23 186	23 384
622	**Hospitals**	252 511	257 961	265 764	266 555	272 413	273 060
NOT SEASONALLY ADJUSTED							
51	**Information**	375 238	357 909	361 735	363 301	389 924	372 891
511	Publishing industries (except Internet)	78 989	70 972	73 220	71 572	79 811	72 908
51111	Newspaper publishers	7 115	6 078	6 391	6 235	6 653	5 847
51112	Periodical publishers	7 210	6 341	7 093	6 806	7 185	6 325
5111 pt	Book, directory and mailing list, and other publishers	10 207	8 744	10 083	11 072	9 579	8 379
5112	Software publishers	54 457	49 809	49 653	47 459	56 394	52 357
512	Motion picture and sound recording industries	27 631	27 125	24 338	24 863	27 466	26 884
515	Broadcasting (except Internet)	40 391	37 721	38 482	38 872	43 006	39 573
5151	Radio and television broadcasting	19 618	17 463	17 518	18 285	20 975	18 147
5152	Cable and other subscription programming	20 773	20 258	20 964	20 587	22 031	21 426
517	Telecommunications [1]	154 821	151 514	152 341	153 287	157 207	151 689
5171	Wired telecommunications carriers	79 008	78 621	79 019	78 824	80 145	79 169
5172	Wireless telecommunications carriers (except satellite)	65 216	62 447	62 749	63 870	66 339	61 904
54	**Professional, Scientific, and Technical Services** [1]	423 027	418 182	435 215	432 912	448 922	434 255
5411	Legal services	77 280	63 891	71 122	71 527	83 438	65 978
5412	Accounting, tax preparation, bookkeeping, and payroll services	35 599	49 100	45 185	38 894	38 163	53 273
5413	Architectural, engineering, and related services	74 391	73 210	75 053	77 228	77 970	75 192
5415	Computer systems design and related services	88 040	88 409	90 879	92 245	92 253	91 174
5416	Management, scientific, and technical consulting services	62 157	60 792	63 865	64 391	65 470	63 587
5417	Scientific research and development services	35 010	33 125	36 137	35 461	37 109	33 328
5418	Advertising and related services	25 855	24 762	25 822	26 117	27 007	25 788
56	**Administrative and Support and Waste Management and Remediation Services** [1]	208 865	204 278	216 293	222 186	226 392	225 867
561	Administrative and support services	186 587	182 957	193 191	198 739	203 276	203 769
5613	Employment services	84 677	82 392	83 357	86 444	93 950	95 581
5615	Travel arrangement and reservation services	. . .	10 278	10 906	11 629	10 791	10 878
562	Waste management and remediation services	22 278	21 321	23 102	23 447	23 116	22 098
622	**Hospitals**	253 010	259 509	260 422	261 757	272 058	274 426
623	**Nursing and Residential Care Facilities**	57 212	56 541	58 733	59 123	60 580	59 092

. . . = Not available.
[1] Includes components not shown separately.

NOTES AND DEFINITIONS, CHAPTER 16

TABLE 16-1

Construction Put in Place

SOURCE: U.S. DEPARTMENT OF COMMERCE, CENSUS BUREAU

The Census Bureau's estimates of the value of new construction put in place are intended to provide monthly estimates of the total dollar value of construction work done in the United States.

Definitions and notes on the data

The estimates cover all construction work done each month on new private residential and nonresidential buildings and structures, public construction, and improvements to existing buildings and structures. Included are the cost of labor, materials, and equipment rental; cost of architectural and engineering work; overhead costs assigned to the project; interest and taxes paid during construction; and contractor's profits.

The total value put in place for a given period is the sum of the value of work done on all projects underway during this period, regardless of when work on each individual project was started or when payment was made to the contractors. For some categories, estimates are derived by distributing the total construction cost of the project by means of historic construction progress patterns. Published estimates represent payments made during a period for some categories.

The statistics on the value of construction put in place result from direct measurement and indirect estimation. A series results from direct measurement when it is based on reports of the actual value of construction progress or construction expenditures obtained in a complete census or a sample survey. All other series are developed by indirect estimation using related construction statistics. On an annual basis, estimates for series directly measured monthly, quarterly, or annually accounted for about 71 percent of total construction in 1998 (private multifamily residential, private residential improvements, private nonresidential buildings, farm nonresidential construction, public utility construction, all other private construction, and virtually all of public construction). On a monthly basis, directly measured data are available for about 55 percent of the value in place estimates.

Beginning in 1993, the Construction Expenditures Branch of the Census Bureau's Manufacturing and Construction Division began collecting these data using a new classification system, which bases project types on their end usage instead of on building/nonbuilding types. Data collection on this system for federal construction began in January 2002.

With the changes in project classifications, data presented in these tables for 1993 to date are not directly comparable with data for previous years, except at aggregate levels. For that reason, *Business Statistics* shows earlier historical data only at these aggregate levels. Although some categories, such as lodging, office, education, and religion, have the same names as categories in previously published data, there have been changes within the classifications that make these values noncomparable. For example, private medical office buildings were classified as "office" buildings previously, but are categorized as "health care" under the new classification.

The seasonally adjusted data are obtained by removing normal seasonal movement from the unadjusted data to bring out underlying trends and business cycles, which is accomplished by using the Census X-12-ARIMA method. Seasonal adjustment accounts for month-to-month variations resulting from normal or average changes in any phenomena affecting the data, such as weather conditions, the differing lengths of months, and the varying number of holidays, weekdays, and weekends within each month. It does not adjust for abnormal conditions within each month or for year-to-year variations in weather. The seasonally adjusted annual rate is the seasonally adjusted monthly rate multiplied by 12.

Residential consists of new houses, town houses, apartments, and condominiums for sale or rent; these dwellings are built by the owner or for the owner on contract. It includes improvements inside and outside residential structures, such as remodeling, additions, major replacements, and additions of swimming pools and garages. Manufactured housing, houseboats, and maintenance and repair work are not included.

Office includes general office buildings, administration buildings, professional buildings, and financial institution buildings. Office buildings at manufacturing sites are classified as *manufacturing,* but office buildings owned by manufacturing companies but not at such a site are included in the *office* category. In the state and local government category, *office* includes capitols, city halls, courthouses, and similar buildings.

Commercial includes buildings and structures used by the retail, wholesale, farm, and selected service industries. One of the subgroups of this category is *multi-retail,* which consists of department and variety stores, shopping centers and malls, and warehouse-type retail stores.

Health care includes hospitals, medical buildings, nursing homes, adult day-care centers, and similar institutions.

Educational includes schools at all levels, higher education facilities, trade schools, libraries, museums, and similar institutions.

Amusement and recreation includes theme and amusement parks, sports structures not located at educational institutions, fitness centers and health clubs, neighborhood centers, camps, movie theaters, and similar establishments.

Transportation includes airport facilities; rail facilities, track, and bridges; bus, rail, maritime, and air terminals; and docks, marinas, and similar structures.

Communication includes telephone, television, and radio distribution and maintenance structures.

Power includes electricity production and distribution and gas and crude oil transmission, storage, and distribution.

Manufacturing includes all buildings and structures at manufacturing sites but not the installation of production machinery or special-purpose equipment.

Included in *total private construction*, but not shown separately in these pages, are lodging facilities (hotels and motels), religious structures, and private public safety, sewage and waste disposal, water supply, highway and street, and conservation and development spending.

Included in *total state and local construction,* but not shown separately in these pages, are state and local construction of commercial buildings, conservation and development (dams, levees, jetties, and dredging), lodging, religious facilities, and communication structures.

Public safety includes correctional facilities, police and sheriffs' stations, fire stations, and similar establishments.

Highway and street includes pavement, lighting, retaining walls, bridges, tunnels, toll facilities, and maintenance and rest facilities.

Sewage and waste disposal includes sewage systems, solid waste disposal, and recycling.

Water supply includes water supply, transmission, and storage facilities.

Among the data sources for construction expenditures are the Census Bureau's Survey of Construction, Building Permits Survey, Consumer Expenditure Survey (conducted for the Bureau of Labor Statistics), Annual Capital Expenditures Survey, and Construction Progress Reporting Survey; also included are data from the F.W. Dodge Division of the McGraw-Hill Information Systems Company, the U.S. Department of Agriculture, and utility regulatory agencies.

Data availability

Each month's "Construction Spending" press release is released on the last workday of the following month. The release, more detailed data, and a discussion of methodologies can be found on the Census Bureau's Web site at <http://www.census.gov/ constructionspending>. Current data at this site may reflect benchmarking since Table 16-1 was compiled.

TABLE 16-2

Housing Starts and Building Permits; New House Sales and Prices

SOURCES: U.S. DEPARTMENT OF COMMERCE, CENSUS BUREAU

These data are mainly found in two major Census Bureau reports, "New Residential Construction" and "New Residential Sales." They cover new housing units intended for occupancy and maintained by the occupants, excluding hotels, motels, and group residential structures. Manufactured home units are reported in a separate survey.

Definitions

A *housing unit* is a house, an apartment, or a group of rooms or single room intended for occupancy as separate living quarters. Occupants must live separately from other individuals in the building and have direct access to the housing unit from the outside of the building or through a common hall. Each apartment unit in an apartment building is counted as one housing unit. As of January 2000, a previous requirement for residents to have the capability to eat separately has been eliminated. (Based on the old definition, some senior housing projects were excluded from the multifamily housing statistics because individual units did not have their own eating facilities.) Housing starts exclude group quarters such as dormitories or rooming houses, transient accommodations such as motels, and manufactured homes. Publicly owned housing units are excluded, but units in structures built by private developers with subsidies or for sale to local public housing authorities are both classified as private housing.

The *start* of construction of a privately owned housing unit is when excavation begins for the footings or foundation of a building primarily intended as a housekeeping residential structure and designed for nontransient occupancy. All housing units in a multifamily building are defined as being started when excavation for the building begins.

One-family structures includes fully detached, semi-detached, row houses, and townhouses. In the case of attached units, each must be separated from the adjacent unit by a ground-to-roof wall to be classified as a one-unit structure and must not share facilities such as heating or water supply. Units built one on top of another and those built side-by-side without a ground-to-roof wall and/or with common facilities are classified by the number of units in the structure.

Apartment buildings are defined as buildings containing *five units or more*. The type of ownership is not the criterion—a condominium apartment building is not classified as one-family structures but as a multifamily structure.

A *manufactured* home is a moveable dwelling, 8 feet or more wide and 40 feet or more long, designed to be towed on its own chassis with transportation gear integral to the unit when it leaves the factory, and without need of a permanent foundation. Multiwides and expandable manufactured homes are included. Excluded are travel trailers, motor homes, and modular housing. The shipments figures are based on reports submitted by manufacturers on the number of homes actually shipped during the survey month. Shipments to dealers may not necessarily be placed for residential use in the same month as they are shipped. The number of manufactured "homes" used for nonresidential purposes (for example, those used for offices) is not known.

Units authorized by building permits represents the approximately 97 percent of housing in permit-requiring areas.

The *start* occurs when excavation begins for the footing or foundation. Starts are estimated for all areas, regardless of whether permits are required.

New house *sales* are reported only for new single-family residential structures. The sales transaction must intend to include both house and land. Excluded are houses built for rent, houses built by the owner, and houses built by a contractor on the owner's land. A sale is reported when a deposit is taken or a sales agreement is signed; this can occur prior to a permit being issued.

Once the sale is reported, the sold housing unit drops out of the survey. Consequently, the Census Bureau does not find out if the sales contract is cancelled or if the house is ever resold. As a result, if conditions are worsening and cancellations are high, sales are temporarily overestimated. When conditions improve and the cancelled sales materialize as actual sales, the Census sales estimates are then underestimated because the case did not re-enter the survey. In the long run, cancellations do not cause the survey to overestimate or underestimate sales; but in the short run, cancellations and ultimate resales are not reflected in this survey, and fluctuations can appear less severe than in reality.

A house is *for sale* when a permit to build has been issued (or work begun in non-permit areas) and a sales contract has not been signed nor a deposit accepted.

The *sales price* used in this survey is the price agreed upon between the purchaser and the seller at the time the first sales contract is signed or deposit made. It includes the price of the improved lot. The *median sales price* is the sales price of the house that falls on the middle point of a distribution by price of the total number of houses sold. Half of the houses sold have a price lower than the median; half have a price higher than the median. Changes in the *sales price* data reflect changes in the distribution of houses by region, size, and the like, as well as changes in the prices of houses with identical characteristics.

The *price index* measures the change in price of a new single-family house of constant physical characteristics, using the characteristics of houses built in 2005. Characteristics held constant include floor area, whether inside or outside a metropolitan area, number of bedrooms, number of bathrooms, number of fireplaces, type of parking facility, type of foundation, presence of a deck, construction method, exterior wall material, type of heating, and presence of air-conditioning. The indexes are calculated separately for attached and detached houses and combined with base period weights. The price measured includes the value of the lot.

Notes on the data

Monthly permit authorizations are based on data collected by a mail survey from a sample of about 9,000 permit-issuing places, selected from and representing a universe of 20,000 such places in the United States. The remaining places are surveyed annually. Data for 1994 through 2003 represented 19,000 places; data for 1984 through 1993 represented 17,000 places; data for 1978 through 1983 represented 16,000 places; data for 1972 through 1977 represented 14,000 places; data for 1967 through 1971 represented 13,000 places; data for 1963 through 1966 represented 12,000 places; and data for 1959 through 1962 represented 10,000 places.

Housing starts and sales data are obtained from the Survey of Construction, for which Census Bureau field representatives sample both permit-issuing and non-permit-issuing places.

Effective with the January 2005 data release, the Survey of Construction implemented a new sample of building permit offices, replacing a previous sample selected in 1985. As a result, writes the Census Bureau, "Data users should use caution when analyzing year over year changes in housing prices and characteristics between 2004 and 2005." In the newer sample, land may be more abundant, lot sizes larger, and sales prices lower.

For 2004, the permit data were compiled for both the new 20,000 place universe and the old 19,000 place universe. Ratios of the new estimates to the old were calculated by state for total housing units, structures by number of units, and valuation. For the United States as a whole, the new estimate was 100.9 percent of the old estimate.

Effective with the data for April 2001, the Census Bureau made changes to the methodology used for new house sales, including discontinuing an adjustment for construction in areas in which building permits are required without a permit being issued. It was believed that such unauthorized construction has virtually ceased. The upward adjustment was not phased out but dropped completely in revised estimates as of January 1999. The total effect of these changes was to lower the number of sales by about 2.9 percent relative to those published for earlier years.

The data used in the price index are collected in the Survey of Construction, through monthly interviews with the builders or owners. The size of the sample is currently about 20,000 observations per year.

DATA AVAILABILITY AND REFERENCES

Housing starts and building permit data have been collected monthly by the Bureau of the Census since 1959.

The monthly report for "New Residential Construction" (permits, starts, and completions) is issued in the middle of the following month. The monthly report and associated descriptions and historical data can be found at <http://www.census.gov/construction/nrc>.

The monthly report for "New Residential Sales" (sales, houses for sale, and prices) is issued toward the end of the following month. The monthly report and associated descriptions and historical data can be found at <http://www.census.gov/construction/nrs>.

The manufactured housing data (not seasonally adjusted) and background information can be found at <http://www. manufacturedhousing.org/statistics>. Data with and without seasonal adjustment can be found at <http://www.census.gov/ construction/mhs>.

Data and background on the price index for new one-family houses can be found at <http://www.census/gov>, in the alphabetical index under the category "Construction price indexes."

Tables 16-3 through 16-6

Manufacturers' Shipments, Inventories, and Orders

SOURCE: U.S. DEPARTMENT OF COMMERCE, CENSUS BUREAU

These data are from the Census Bureau's monthly M3 survey, a sample-based survey that provides measures of changes in the value of domestic manufacturing activity and indications of future production commitments. The sample is not a probability sample. It includes approximately 4,300 reporting units, including companies with $500 million or more in annual shipments and a selection of smaller companies. Currently, reported monthly data represent approximately 60 percent of shipments at the total manufacturing level.

One important technology industry, semiconductors, is represented in the shipments and inventories data in this report but not in new or unfilled orders. This affects the new and unfilled orders totals for computers and electronic products, durable goods industries, and total manufacturing. Based on shipments data, semiconductors accounted for about 15 percent of computers and electronic products, 3 percent of durable goods industries, and 1.5 percent of total manufacturing. Since semiconductors are intermediate materials and components rather than finished final products, the absence of these data does not distort new and unfilled orders data for important final demand categories, such as capital goods and information technology.

Definitions and notes on the data

Shipments. The value of shipments data represent net selling values, f.o.b. (free on board) plant, after discounts and allowances and excluding freight charges and excise taxes. For multi-establishment companies, the M3 reports are typically company- or division-level reports that encompass groups of plants or products. The data reported are usually net sales and receipts from customers and do not include the value of inter-plant transfers. The reported sales are used to calculate month-to-month changes that bring forward the estimates for the entire industry (that is, estimates of the statistical "universe") that have been developed from the Annual Survey of Manufactures (ASM). The value of products made elsewhere under contract from materials owned by the plant is also included in shipments, along with receipts for contract work performed for others, resales, miscellaneous activities such as the sale of scrap and refuse, and installation and repair work performed by employees of the plant.

Inventories. Inventories in the M3 survey are collected on a current cost or pre-LIFO (last in, first out) basis. As different inventory valuation methods are reflected in the reported data, the estimates differ slightly from replacement cost estimates. Companies using the LIFO method for valuing inventories report their pre-LIFO value; the adjustment to their base-period prices is excluded. In the ASM, inventories are collected according to this same definition.

Inventory data are requested from respondents by three stages of fabrication: finished goods, work in process, and raw materials and supplies. Response to the stage of fabrication inquiries is lower than for total inventories; not all companies keep their monthly data at this level of detail. It should be noted that a product considered to be a finished good in one industry, such as steel mill shapes, may be reported as a raw material in another industry, such as stamping plants. For some purposes, this difference in definitions is an advantage. When a factory accumulates inventory that it considers to be raw materials, it can be expected that that accumulation is intentional. But when a factory—whether a materials-making or a final-product producer—has a buildup of finished goods inventories, it may indicate involuntary accumulation as a result of sales falling short of expectations. Hence, the two types of accumulation can have different economic interpretations, even if they represent identical types of goods.

Like total inventories, stage of fabrication inventories are benchmarked to the ASM data. Stage of fabrication data are benchmarked at the major group level, as opposed to the level of total inventories, which is benchmarked at the individual industry level.

New orders (durable goods), as reported in the monthly survey, are net of order cancellations and include orders received and filled during the month as well as orders received for future delivery. They also include the value of contract changes that increase or decrease the value of the unfilled orders to which they relate. Orders are defined to include those supported by binding legal documents such as signed contracts, letters of award, or letters of intent, although this definition may not be strictly applicable in some industries.

New orders (nondurable goods) are equal to shipments, as order backlogs are not reported for these industries.

Unfilled orders (durable goods) includes new orders (as defined above) that have not been reflected as shipments. Generally, unfilled orders at the end of the reporting period are equal to unfilled orders at the beginning of the period plus net new orders received less net shipments.

Series are adjusted for seasonal variation and variation in the number of trading days in the month using the X-12-ARIMA version of the Census Bureau's seasonal adjustment program.

Benchmarking and revisions

The data shown in the volume have been benchmarked to the 2007 Economic Census and to ASMs through 2011. In each benchmark revision, new and unfilled orders are adjusted to be consistent with the benchmarked shipments and inventory data, seasonal adjustment factors are revised and updated, and other corrections are made.

DATA AVAILABILITY AND REFERENCES

Data have been collected monthly since 1958.

The "Advance Report on Durable Goods Manufacturers' Shipments, Inventories and Orders" is available as a press release about 18 working days after the end of each month. It includes seasonally adjusted and not seasonally adjusted estimates of shipments, new orders, unfilled orders, and inventories for durable goods industries.

The monthly "Manufacturers' Shipments, Inventories, and Orders" report is released on the 23rd working day after the end of the month. Content includes revisions to the advance durable goods data, estimates for nondurable goods industries, tabulations by market category, and ratios of shipments to inventories and to unfilled orders. Revisions may affect selected data for the two previous months.

Press releases, historical data, descriptions of the survey, and documentation are available on the Census Bureau Web site at <http://www.census.gov>, under the category "Manufacturing" in the alphabetic listing there.

TABLE 16-7

Motor Vehicle Sales and Inventories

SOURCE: U.S. DEPARTMENT OF COMMERCE, BUREAU OF ECONOMIC ANALYSIS

Retail sales and *inventories of cars, trucks, and buses.* These estimates are prepared by the Bureau of Economic Analysis (BEA), based on data from the American Automobile Manufacturers Association, Ward's Automotive Reports, and other sources. Seasonal adjustments are recalculated annually. Data are available on the BEA Web site at <http://www.bea.gov> as a part of the national income and product accounts data set; they are found under the "Supplemental Estimates" heading. They are also available on the STAT-USA subscription Web site at <http://www.stat-usa.gov>.

TABLES 16-8 AND 16-10

Retail and Food Services Sales; Retail Inventories

SOURCE: U.S. DEPARTMENT OF COMMERCE, CENSUS BUREAU

Every month, the Census Bureau prepares estimates of retail sales and inventories by kind of business, based on a mail-out/mail-back survey of about 12,000 retail businesses with paid employees.

Retail sales and inventories are now compiled using the new NAICS classification system, which replaced the old SIC system. Historical data have been restated on the NAICS basis back to January 1992. In NAICS, Eating and drinking places and Mobile food services have been reclassified out of retail trade and into sector 72, Accommodation and food services, which also includes hotels. The retail sales survey still collects and publishes sales data for food services and drinking places. It no longer includes them in the retail total, but they are included in a new retail and food services total.

Subtotals of durable and nondurable goods are no longer published. They were always imprecise for retail sales, since general merchandise stores (including department stores) were included in nondurable goods, yet obviously sold substantial quantities of durable goods.

Definitions

Sales is the value of merchandise sold for cash or credit at retail or wholesale. Services that are incidental to the sale of merchandise, and excise taxes that are paid by the manufacturer or wholesaler and passed along to the retailer, are also included. Sales are net, after deductions for refunds and merchandise returns. They exclude sales taxes collected directly from customers and paid directly to a local, state, or federal tax agency. The sales estimates include only sales by establishments primarily engaged in retail trade, and are not intended to measure the total sales for a given commodity or merchandise line.

Inventories is the value of stocks of goods held for sale through retail stores, valued at cost, as of the last day of the report period. Stocks may be held either at the store or at warehouses that maintain supplies primarily intended for distribution to retail stores within the organization.

Leased departments consists of the operations of one company conducted within the establishment of another company, such as jewelry counters or optical centers within department stores. The values for sales and inventories at department stores in Tables 16-9 and 16-10 exclude sales of leased departments.

GAFO (department store type goods) is a special aggregate grouping of sales at general merchandise stores and at other stores that sell merchandise normally sold in department stores—clothing and accessories, furniture and home furnishings, electronics, appliances, sporting goods, hobby, book, music, office supplies, stationery, and gifts.

Notes on the data

The data published here have been benchmarked to the 2007, 2002, 1997, and 1992 Economic Censuses and the Annual Retail Trade Surveys for 2012 and previous years. Each year, the monthly series are benchmarked to the latest annual survey and new factors are incorporated to adjust for seasonal, trading-day, and holiday variations, using the Census Bureau's X-12-ARIMA program.

The survey sample is stratified by kind of business and estimated sales. All firms with sales above applicable size cutoffs are included. Firms are selected randomly from the remaining strata. The sample used for the end-of-month inventory estimates is a sub-sample of the monthly sales sample, about one-third of the size of the whole sample.

New samples, designed to produce NAICS estimates, were introduced with the 1999 Annual Retail Trade Survey and the March 2001 Monthly Retail Trade Survey. On November 30, 2006, another new sample was introduced, affecting the data for September 2006 and the following months. The sample is updated quarterly to take account of business births and deaths.

DATA AVAILABILITY AND REFERENCES

An "Advance Monthly Retail Sales" report is released about nine working days after the close of the reference month, based on responses from a sub-sample of the complete retail sample.

The revised and more complete monthly "Retail Trade, Sales, and Inventories" reports are released six weeks after the close

of the reference month. They contain preliminary figures for the current month and final figures for the prior 12 months. Statistics include retail sales, inventories, and ratios of inventories to sales. Data are both seasonally adjusted and unadjusted.

The "Annual Benchmark Report for Retail Trade" is released each spring. It includes updated seasonal adjustment factors; revised and benchmarked monthly estimates of sales and inventories; monthly data for the most recent 10 or more years; detailed annual estimates and ratios for the United States by kind of business; and comparable prior-year statistics and year-to-year changes.

All data are available on the Census Bureau Web site at <http://www.census.gov/retail>.

TABLE 16-9

Quarterly Retail Sales: Total and E-Commerce

SOURCE: U.S. DEPARTMENT OF COMMERCE, CENSUS BUREAU

Beginning with the fourth quarter of 1999, the Census Bureau has conducted a quarterly survey of retail e-commerce sales from the Monthly Retail Trade Survey sample. (The monthly survey does not report electronic shopping separately; it is combined with mail order.) E-commerce sales are the sales of goods and services in which an order is placed by the buyer or the price and terms of sale are negotiated over the Internet or an extranet, Electronic Data Interchange (EDI) network, electronic mail, or other online system. Payment may or may not be made online. The quarterly release is issued around the 20th of February, May, August, and November, and is available along with full historical data on the Census Bureau Web site at <http://www.census.gov>. It can be located under the heading "Retail" in the alphabetical Web site index, under "E" for "Economic data and information."

These estimates reflect the NAICS definition of retail sales, which excludes food service. Online travel services, financial brokers and dealers, and ticket sales agencies are not classified as retail and are not included in these estimates; they are, however, included in the annual survey of selected services.

TABLE 16-11

Merchant Wholesalers—Sales and Inventories

SOURCE: U.S. DEPARTMENT OF COMMERCE, CENSUS BUREAU

These data are based on a monthly mail-out/mail-back sample survey conducted by the Census Bureau. The sample consists of about 4,900 establishments, with a response rate of about 60 percent; missing reports are imputed based on reports of similar reporters.

These data are now based on the new NAICS classification system, which replaced the old SIC system. Historical data have been restated on the NAICS basis back to January 1992.

Classification changes in NAICS

NAICS shifts a significant number of businesses from the Wholesale to the Retail sector. An important new criterion for classification concerns whether or not the establishment is intended to solicit walk-in traffic. If it is, and if it uses mass-media advertising, it is now classified as Retail, even if it also serves business and institutional clients.

Definitions

Merchant wholesalers includes merchant wholesalers that take title of the goods they sell, as well as jobbers, industrial distributors, exporters, and importers. The survey does not cover marketing sales offices and branches of manufacturing, refining, and mining firms, nor does it include NAICS 4251: Wholesale Electronic Markets and Agents and Brokers.

Notes on the data

Inventories are valued using methods other than LIFO (last in, first out) in order to better reflect the current costs of goods held as inventory.

A survey has been conducted monthly since 1946. New samples are drawn every 5 years, most recently in 2009. The samples are updated every quarter to add new businesses and to drop companies that are no longer active.

DATA AVAILABILITY AND REFERENCES

"Monthly Wholesale Trade, Sales and Inventories" reports are released six weeks after the close of the reference month. They contain preliminary current-month figures and final figures for the previous month. Statistics include sales, inventories, and stock/sale ratios, along with standard errors. Data are both seasonally adjusted and unadjusted.

The "Annual Benchmark Report for Wholesale Trade" is released each spring. It contains estimated annual sales, monthly and yearend inventories, inventory/sales ratios, purchases, gross margins, and gross margin/sales ratios by kind of business. Annual estimates are benchmarked to annual surveys and the most recent census of wholesale trade. Monthly sales and inventories estimates are revised consistent with the annual data, seasonal adjustment factors are updated, and revised data for both seasonally adjusted and unadjusted values are published.

Data and documentation are available on the Census Bureau Web site at <http://www.census.gov>, under "Economic Indicators" and in the alphabetic index under "E" for economic data.

TABLES 16-12 AND 16-13

Manufacturing and Trade Sales and Inventories

SOURCES: U.S. DEPARTMENT OF COMMERCE, CENSUS BUREAU (CURRENT-DOLLAR SERIES) AND U.S. DEPARTMENT OF COMMERCE, BUREAU OF ECONOMIC ANALYSIS (BEA; CONSTANT-DOLLAR SERIES)

The current-dollar data on which these tables are based bring together summary data from the separate series on manufacturers' shipments, inventories, and orders; merchant wholesalers' sales and inventories; and retail sales and inventories, all of which are included in this chapter. Generally, current-dollar inventories are collected on a current cost (or pre-LIFO [last in, first out]) basis. See the notes and definitions for Tables 16-3, 16-4, 16-8 16-10, and 16-11 for further information about these data.

Based on these current-dollar values and relevant price data, BEA makes estimates of real sales, inventories, and inventory-sales ratios. Note, however, that annual figures for sales are shown as annual <u>totals</u> in Table 16-12 but as <u>averages</u> of the monthly data in Table 16-13, reflecting the practices of the respective source agencies. Also note that constant-dollar detail may not add to constant-dollar totals because of the chain-weighting formula; see the discussion of chain-weighted measures in the notes and definitions for Chapter 1. The constant-dollar estimates shown in this volume of *Business Statistics* are stated in 2009 dollars.

Inventory values are as of the end of the month or year. In Table 16-13, annual values for monthly current-dollar inventory-sales ratios are averages of seasonally adjusted monthly ratios. However, for the real ratios in Table 16-14, annual figures for inventory-sales ratios are calculated by BEA as year-end (December) inventories divided by the monthly average of sales for the entire year; this means that the annual ratios will not be equivalent to averages of month ratios. In all cases, the ratios in these two tables (like those in Table 1-8) represent the number of months' sales on hand as inventory at the end of the reporting period.

Data availability

Sales, inventories, and inventory-sales ratios for manufacturers, merchant wholesalers, and retailers are published monthly by the Census Bureau in a press release entitled "Manufacturing and Trade Inventories and Sales." Recent and historical data are available on the Census Bureau Web site at <http://www.census.gov/mtis/www/mtis.html>. They can also be found by going to the general Census website, <http://www.census.gov>, going to the alphabetical index, finding "Economic Data and Information" under "E" and then finding "Manufacturing and trade" under "Manufacturing" or "Sales."

Sales and inventories in constant dollars are available on the BEA Web site at <http://www.bea.gov>. To locate these data on that site, click on "National Economic Accounts." Scroll down to "Supplemental Estimates," click "Underlying Detail Tables," and then click on "List of Underlying Detail Tables." For the most recent data, if there is more than one table with the same title, select the last table listed.

Table 16-14

Selected Services, Quarterly: Estimated Revenue for Employer Firms

SOURCE: U.S. DEPARTMENT OF COMMERCE, CENSUS BUREAU

Census data on quarterly revenue for selected service industries are based on information collected from a probability sample that has been expanded over recent years to approximately 19,000 employer firms (firms with employees), chosen from the sample for the larger Service Annual Survey and expanded to represent totals—for employer firms only—for the selected industries. The sample is updated quarterly to account for business births, deaths, and other changes. Industries are defined according to the 2007 NAICS.

The scope of the survey and the size of the sample have increased several times since the inception of this survey in 2004. More industries are now available than are shown here in Table 16-15, which focuses on industries with a longer statistical history.

Definitions and notes on the data

These data are collected in current dollars only. See the Producer Price Indexes in Chapter 8 for indicators of price trends in various sectors.

Both taxable and tax-exempt firms are covered unless otherwise specified.

Generally, government enterprises are not within the scope (that is, the industries it is designed to cover) of the survey. *Utilities* excludes government-owned utilities and *Transportation and warehousing* excludes the U.S. Postal Service.

Private industries that are not within the scope of the survey are NAICS 482, rail transportation; 525, funds, trusts, and other financial vehicles; 51112, offices of notaries; 6111, 6112, and 6113, elementary, secondary, and post-secondary schools; 8131, religious organizations; 81393 (labor unions and similar), 81394 (political organizations, and 814 (private households).

Totals shown for sectors and subsectors may include data for kinds of business that are in the scope of the survey but are not shown separately in the detail beneath.

Data for selected industry groups are adjusted for seasonal variation using the Census Bureau's X-13 ARIMA-SEATS program.

DATA AVAILABILITY AND REFERENCES

The quarterly release "U.S. Government Estimates of Quarterly Revenue for Selected Services" is available on the Census Web site at <http://www.census.gov/>, as "Quarterly Services Survey" listed under Q in the alphabetic index; historical, technical, and background information, including sampling errors, is also available there.

The revised and updated data through the first quarter of 2017 shown in this volume, benchmarked to Service Annual Surveys through 2012, were released on August 18, 2017.